A Biographical Guide to the Great Jazz and Pop Singers

A Biographical Guide to the Great Jazz and Pop Singers

WILL FRIEDWALD

Pantheon Books   New York

All rights reserved. Published in the United States by Pantheon Books, a division of
Random House, Inc., New York, and in Canada by Random House of Canada Limited, Toronto.

Pantheon Books and colophon are registered trademarks of Random House, Inc.

Library of Congress Cataloging-in-Publication Data
Friedwald, Will, [date]
A biographical guide to the great jazz and pop singers / Will Friedwald.
p. cm.
ISBN 978-0-375-42149-5
1. Jazz singers—Biography—Dictionaries.   2. Jazz—Bio-bibliography—Dictionaries.
3. Singers—Biography—Dictionaries.   4. Popular music—Bio-bibliography—Dictionaries.
I. Title.
ML102.J3F75 2010
782.42164092'273—dc22
[B]   2009044405

www.pantheonbooks.com
Printed in the United States of America
First Edition
2 4 6 8 9 7 5 3 1

To Rosemary, who was there at the beginning

And to Pamela, who was there at the end

It doesn't matter what you think about me, but it matters a whole lot what I think about you.

—Louis Jordan, "Beans and Cornbread"

Contents

This table of contents includes an alphabetical list of all the artists featured in the dictionary: individual artists, the five "extras" (iconic singers in other genres), and those included in multiple artist entries. These multiple artist groupings, which are in more or less chronological order, are also listed below for your reference.

Multiple Artists

Introduction

Jazz singing and popular singing are two extremely broad fields that have a great deal of territory in common—there's a considerable amount of pop in a jazz singer like Ella Fitzgerald and a great deal of jazz in a pop singer like Steve Lawrence. Indeed, the two genres are frequently so close that it's difficult, and often pointless, to distinguish between them. By and large, both kinds of singers collaborate with the same musicians, and, more importantly, they both rely upon what has come to be known as the Great American Songbook as their basic source of material.

Traditionally, those of us who write about jazz vocalists devote a lot of verbiage to discussing what does and what doesn't constitute jazz singing, and who is and who isn't. Although there is a degree of consensus, in the main it's a highly subjective call, and one that, after years of literature debating the subject, seems tired. Perhaps too much time has been spent arguing who is and who isn't a jazz singer; better to spend time worrying about who is and who isn't a good singer.

This book is about singers—make no mistake. However, like my previous work (*Stardust Melodies*, which was also suggested and edited by Robert Gottlieb), this current work is driven, to a degree, by songs. Songs were the essential criteria by which artists were or were not included. Of the thousands of artists of the last hundred years or so who could be described as either jazz or pop singers, my first consideration was to focus on those who primarily sang the American songbook, and, even more so, to concentrate on those artists who made a vital contribution to the way the songbook is sung. All kinds of people have sung the songbook, particularly in recent decades, from opera divas (like Renée Fleming) to rock stars (like Rod Stewart, who is, in fact, covered in a special section). But, for this book, the idea was to focus on those artists for whom the songbook was bread-and-butter, or, as Eliza Doolittle would put it, mother's milk.

Obviously, there's a lot of gray area: Joe Williams and Jimmy Rushing can comfortably be described as blues singers, yet the majority of their output is based in the songbook. Other singers are more problematic: In the case of Ray Charles, Bobby Darin, and Nina Simone, it seemed that they had all made a substantial contribution to the art of singing this music, and therefore my essays on these artists focus on this one aspect of their careers, and are not intended as comprehensive coverage of their entire canon.

To a degree, this book still has a jazz bias; I have tried to include all the major jazz singers and as many pop singers as there was room for. Most of the singers I've picked, even from the pop side—Vic Damone, Steve and Eydie, Jack Jones—have some

sort of jazz credentials and they almost all swing (whenever they need to, at least), even if they don't necessarily scat up a storm.

Obviously, the great singers of Broadway are part of this picture. I have given due attention, I hope, to four of the major leading ladies of musical comedy (Ethel Merman, Mary Martin, Julie Andrews, Barbara Cook) as well as to half a dozen or so of the most important, name-above-the-title baritones and leading men. My criterion was to look for those Broadway leads who also had substantial careers as recording artists (beyond original cast albums)—and there were surprisingly few. I have also included an essay on four major leading ladies from the great movie musicals of the thirties and forties ("Hollywood Divas"), whose recording careers were generally scattershot, but were very interesting, to say the least.

So who isn't here? Obviously not blues singers who sing the blues exclusively, as well as Brazilian singers who include jazz elements in their music or occasionally sing "Skylark." We have also left out concert singers and opera singers, such as the imposing figure of Paul Robeson; they sang standards occasionally but weren't focused on them. More recently, there's been a trend for rock and pop stars—mainly, by some unexplained coincidence, those who were popular in the seventies—to do whole albums of standards, and these are discussed in an essay of their own.

There also is something of a generational bias, in that I focus on the middle of the twentieth century. There are many earlier artists and some more recent ones, but on the whole, it seems the golden years for singing the American songbook came a generation or so after the songs themselves were written, in the immediate postwar era. More major singers seem to have been actively working and recording in the fifties than in any other decade. In this high-growth period, the new medium of the long-playing disc led to a commercial boom in record sales; virtually everyone who had the least bit of celebrity or could remotely carry a tune (sometimes not even that) was given the chance to make records, and the major stars of the medium, your Fitzgeralds, Vaughans, and Sinatras, were constantly in the studio, their productivity not limited by the market but by their own stamina. (Nat King Cole recorded seven full albums in 1958 alone, although not all of them were issued in that year.)

The main perspective of this book is historical; it should not be taken as a survey of the current scene (as of 2010). You will find only a handful of contemporary and younger artists who sing the songbook, all of whom already have a proven track record. There is just a smattering here of artists born after 1950 (Cassandra Wilson, Dianne Reeves, Dee Dee

Bridgewater) and even fewer born after 1970. When I began this undertaking, there were only three artists I planned to include who were under forty (that description then applied to myself as well): Diana Krall, Kurt Elling, and Audra McDonald. By the time you read this, all four of us have traveled past the forty-year mark. At the very last minute, I decided to add an essay on Harry Connick Jr.—I figured that after doing twenty-four albums over a twenty-year period he deserved a little attention—and I also added a few briefer comments about other boy crooners of a similar disposition.

The focus is on the middle, not so much the contemporary, and equally less so the beginning. The process known as acoustic recording was the only game in town for the first thirty-five or so years of the life of the new industry and entertainment medium called the record business—which is a long time. (By comparison, the age of the long-playing vinyl record lasted only thirty years, from 1955 to 1985.) I haven't devoted any essays to artists who spent the entirety of their careers in this prehistoric period, which ended in 1925 with the introduction of the electrical microphone. However, I do give space to many singers who started in the teens and early twenties and then just kept going, hitting their stride in the electrical era: Al Jolson, Sophie Tucker, Eddie Cantor, Cliff Edwards, Nick Lucas, Gene Austin, and Marion Harris. (Harris may be the exception: She kept recording until 1934, but did the bulk of her best work before 1925.)

Within the parameters of those considerations, the artists included in this book were not chosen by consensus or committee, but entirely by myself and Bob Gottlieb. By necessity, I'm sure that I've left out some significant artists; as it was, the book kept growing and growing—every time we turned around, either Bob or myself had thought of someone else who deserved some kind of coverage. After I had finished a first draft of the essential 150 or so "core" essays, Bob suggested that I write five essays about the iconic American vocal stylists who worked in areas outside of the songbook: Bessie Smith (blues), Mahalia Jackson (gospel), Hank Williams (country and western), Elvis Presley (rock 'n' roll), and Bob Dylan (and I admit that it isn't quite so easy to identify Dylan by a strict musical genre and put it between a pair of parentheses). Since the emphasis is on songbook-centric artists, these artists are primarily meant to be representative of their fields.

But even once decisions were made about the artists to be profiled here, space still remained an issue: There simply wasn't room to write everything that needed to be said about every performer worth talking about. When we started this project in early 2001, we were using David Thomson's *A Biographical Dictionary of Film* as a model and originally intended our entries to be as short and to-the-point as Mr. Thomson's. However, as I started writing it became clear to me that brevity was not going to serve our purposes well—thus the pieces kept getting longer and longer, eventually taking the form of full essays rather than condensed encyclopedia entries. Even given the overall length of the present work, it was impossible to write as much as I wanted, particularly on bigger figures like Sarah Vaughan and Carmen McRae. On the other hand, I'm very happy that some artists with smaller but important careers—Joe Mooney and Jeri Southern, for instance—were given more attention than I believe they're ever received before in any previous book. (I am also delighted to report that my opinions and appreciation of such neglected figures as Nellie Lutches and Johnny Desmond have gone way up since covering them for this book.)

As with my previous books, so many individuals have contributed to both the form and content of this one that their names could easily be on the front cover. Being too selfish to allow that, I will restrict myself to thanking them here. I am especially grateful to the "specialists," those individuals who have spent copious amounts of time researching one artist or group of artists and who have shared their information, opinions, recordings, and other materials with me—people like Tony Sachs (Buddy Greco), Jonathan Cohen (Jon Hendricks and Lambert, Hendricks & Ross), David Torreson and Ivan Santiago (Peggy Lee), Bob Conrad and Tom Bumbera (Buddy Clark), Chris Bamberger (Fred Astaire), Barbara Rosene (Ruth Etting, Annette Hanshaw), James Coffrey (Sheila Jordan), Dr. Ruth Prigozy (Dick Haymes), Ken Crossland (Perry Como), Tim Brooks (the entire acoustic era), Rob Waldman, James Kaplan, and Michael Kraus (Frank Sinatra). The gentlemen (and lady) of the Toast of New York collective—John Leifert, Peter Doyle, Steve Ashley, Steven Abrams, Henry Schmidt, Paul Lindemeyer, Dan Levinson, Merle Sprinzen, David Garrick, David Lennick, Dave Dawes, Dave Dixon—deserve special credit for helping provide sound files and factoids regarding virtually every vocalist of the twenties and thirties. Special thanks also to Gordon Anderson of Collectors' Choice Music (www.ccmusic.com) for providing me with a box of CDs to listen to.

Thanks also to Shannon McCarty and Rob Vrabel for editorial help. Rob and Chris Bamberger, Randy Skretved, and David J. Weiner deserve special credit for going through stacks of manuscript (thank you, Google Docs) and helping me eliminate mistakes. At the last minute, Dan Langan and Bob Porter—experts, respectively, on Broadway and the blues—volunteered to go through sections pertaining to those genres and sent me much-appreciated reams of feedback. Ken Bloom and Larry Maslon were also a big help on theatrically oriented artists.

About those mistakes: The history of jazz and popular music remains rife with conventional wisdoms, received myths, and tales that have taken on the guise of credibility—as well as half-truths that have often taken the place of the real thing. I've made every effort not to perpetuate canards and assorted herrings (red or otherwise), but have probably added plenty of mistakes of my own. (A note on song titles: as Bob learned when he compiled his highly recommended anthology *Reading Lyrics*, it's often impossible to get a definitive version of a song title—particularly if question marks, commas, or exclamation points are involved. Often the same song will be spelled or punctuated differently from one performance to the next, or the sheet music cover will differ from the recording, and just as often the title of the same performance will be spelled differently on the 78 rpm, LP, and CD release. Yes, I do have a CD somewhere in which Richard Tauber does a song from an operetta identified as "White Whores Inn.")

The person Bob and I most need to thank is his assistant, Sarah Rothbard; her impressive organizational skills—and angelic patience—were exactly what were needed to get the manuscript to the finish line. I repeatedly make a point of telling her that we couldn't have finished the book without her. Sarah always answers back that any reasonably well organized person could have done as well. But, just this once, she is wrong.

Around the time I started work on this project, I had lunch with one of my oldest friends, the jazz trumpeter and critic Richard Sudhalter. His now classic history *Lost Chords* had only recently been published, and I remember chiding him about how it couldn't possibly have taken ten years to write a book—even a magnum opus like *Lost Chords*. God has obviously punished me for this offhand remark; karmic balance has been restored, because it has taken me a full ten years to see this book through from start to finish. I began work on this project in 2001, after *Stardust Melodies* went into editing. In 2002, shortly after work on this book began, I started writing for *The New York Sun*, and, over the seven years of that newspaper's existence, I did roughly seven hundred columns on jazz and cabaret. This book was written, for the most part, while I was doing two columns a week for the paper. At the end of 2008, the *Sun* set (as pundits punned at the time), and I was lucky enough to find a new home at *The Wall Street Journal*, which has been keeping me off the streets ever since. (God bless Rupert Murdoch.) Throughout 2009 and through the summer of 2010, Bob and I spent many, many long days editing and revising, trimming and expanding the manuscript

and, in particular, updating the essays on living artists. At one point, we considered restricting this book to "historical" artists, which generally meant those no longer living (or, if still alive, were no longer active) or born before a certain year (say, 1950). That, however, would give the false impression that this is a dead art form, rather than a living, breathing, vital music actively performed by thousands of contemporary artists. Accordingly, we have included a smaller number of younger and currently active artists, even though the downside was that their essays had to be constantly updated—some of the sections on younger performers have been revised four or five times.

I hope that the book in your hands is only the first of many editions. It's a dream of mine to revisit and update it every six or seven years—whatever the traffic will allow—and that, like the wonderful Thomson work, it can be something of a perennial. I hope to keep revising it, to update the sections on those artists who are still alive and active and to rediscover vintage performers who may have fallen through the cracks the first time around. As big as this book is, at a certain point we just ran out of room. Sometime after the last minute, I was planning to do an essay on the brilliant and chronically neglected Marilyn Maye when Altie Karper (the equally brilliant and much-appreciated managing editor of Pantheon) firmly put her foot down and told us we had neither the time nor the space to add anyone else. (So don't complain to me—talk to Altie!) Apologies to the fans of David Allyn, Ernie Andrews, Shirley Bassey, Eva Cassidy, Alan Dale, Francis Faye, Earl Grant, Gogi Grant (no, they weren't related), Rebecca Kilgore, Nancy Lamott, Julius LaRosa, Maude Maggart, Tony Martin, John Pizzarelli, Sue Raney, Catherine Russell, K. T. Sullivan (and Mark Nadler), Kay Thompson, Paula West, and possibly even others.

I also hope that new reissues of recordings and the discovery of previously undocumented ones will allow me to reevaluate many historical performers (about two years after I had written the Dick Haymes essay, a member of the Haymes Society sent me the singer's entire singles output on a homemade series of CDRs). I look forward to the day when the important works of every artist in this book are all available on compact disc, at least somewhere in the world, or as digital downloads.

Better yet, I hope that subsequent editions of this book will require me to write new essays discussing new singers who have yet to make their first record, and that you will be here to read it.

Individual Artists

Ernestine Anderson (1928–)

"I'd like to have a little boy someday," Miles Davis once said, "with red hair, green eyes, and a black face, who plays piano like Ahmad Jamal." If Miles had a daughter, she'd sing like Ernestine Anderson. Like the trumpeter, Anderson heads straight for the melodic core of a song, in a way that makes Tin Pan Alley an extension of the blues and vice versa. She playfully reshuffles each tune into a series of phrases: some smooth, some jagged, some staccato, others legato, all swinging. She seductively lags behind the beat on a ballad and races in front of it on an up-tempo and isn't afraid to tap into her reserve of gospel melisma when the spirit moves her.

Quincy Jones, who figures in her career at several intersections, once described her sound as "honey at dusk." While that metaphor may be a little on the obscure side, we still know what he means: Honey is sweeter than gin or coffee, and dusk is a more relaxed, ruminative time of the day than noon. Anderson mines a vein of genuine emotion that shows no sign of running out.

Ernestine Anderson is one of the greatest spiritual descendants of Ethel Waters and Dinah Washington. Waters (1896–1977) and Washington (1924–63) were the foremothers of a whole new strain of (almost always) African American and (generally) female artist who combined blues, jazz, and mainstream pop into a seamless whole. Like many major developments in mid-twentieth-century pop, the outstanding blues-jazz divas were generally found attached to big bands—usually that of vibraphonist Lionel Hampton. Just as Hampton launched Dinah Washington, Joe Williams, Little Jimmy Scott, and Ernestine Anderson—who all crossed the line between blues and jazz—so, too, did the R&B-oriented big bands of Buddy Johnson and Johnny Otis.

Anderson, however, does not strictly fit the career patterns of some of these other individuals. Washington, Williams, and Scott were all well known within the world of "race" (read "black") music long before they became popular in the larger world of mainstream (read "white") show business. Anderson, in contrast, was known to no one but a few jazz fans before her late fifties breakthrough, and was also famous in Europe long before she was able to play the top rooms in the United States.

The most significant difference between her and most of these other vocalists is that they generally tended to come out of the blues and into the popular song mainstream. Anderson had been born and raised in the heart of the Southwest blues country, in Houston, Texas, yet her breakthrough albums (particularly *Hot Cargo*, 1956–58, and *Ernestine Anderson: The Toast of the Nation's Critics*, 1958) present her as more of a jazz–supper club chanteuse. Indeed,

her 1958 "Star Dust" has more in common with Sarah Vaughan or Jo Stafford than Ma Rainey. It was only later in her career, in the seventies and eighties (particularly in the fine series of albums that she cut for the Concord Jazz label), that she let her blues-and-roots influence become dominant.

In both phases, though, Anderson could be described as a perfect balance between the two poles of jazz and the blues. She doesn't soar as fancifully into the stratosphere as Vaughan, nor does she sear as intensely as Washington, but rather finds the sweet spot somewhere in between them: more flexible in a traditionally jazzy way than Washington, more intense in a traditionally bluesy way than Vaughan.

Ernestine Anderson was born on November 11, 1928. Her family was musical and she grew up immersed in gospel and the blues. When she was twelve, her grandmother entered her in a talent contest at the El Dorado Ballroom. She started to sing "On the Sunny Side of the Street," which was one of only two songs that she knew "all the way through," as she later told Calvin Ahlgren of the *San Francisco Chronicle*. "Well, the piano player asked me what key I sang in, and I didn't know, so I said 'C' and was wrong. But my grandma had told me, 'To be professional, when you start singing, don't stop. Nine times out of ten, people won't know the difference,' so I was shaking in my boots, but I kept singing. The key was wrong, so I went all around the melody. And when I finished, one of the musicians told me I was a jazz singer."

Anderson would sing lots of jazz and blues over the next fifteen or so years. In Houston she worked with a local but major band led by trumpeter Russell Jacquet; even at age fourteen or fifteen, Anderson was already in the big leagues. In 1944 Russell Jacquet left Houston to join his more famous younger brother, Illinois Jacquet, and Anderson moved with her family to Seattle. At eighteen, she left home to tour with one of the early editions of the Johnny Otis Orchestra; although the band was one of the mainstays of the R&B circuit, Otis, like Hampton, always played a great deal of jazz. In 1947—still only eighteen—she recorded for the first time, for the Black & White label of Los Angeles: "K.C. Lover" and "Good Lovin' Man," a coupling that historian Jim Gavin describes as being in a distinctly Dinah Washington–style vein. (Washington was only four years older than Anderson and had herself only recorded for the first time a few seasons earlier.)

She also toured with pianist Eddie "Begin the Beguine" Heywood, and in 1953 she recorded again, this time for the Network label in New York, with vibraphone star Milt Jackson on piano and two ringers in the trumpet section: old friend from

Houston Russell Jacquet and new friend from Seattle Quincy Jones. By this time, both she and Jones were regular members of Lionel Hampton's orchestra. Unfortunately, Hampton was without a recording contract over most of the two years she stayed with the band. "This was the band with Jimmy Cleveland, Gigi Gryce and all the young players," Anderson told *Melody Maker* in 1960. "I should have made the trip to Europe but I got left behind." For whatever reason, Anderson didn't get to come along on Hampton's well-known overseas tour of fall 1953 (Annie Ross signed on as Hamp's female vocalist), but Europe would come calling soon enough.

The Hampton association paid off in another way: In 1955, fellow ex-Hamptonite Gryce assembled a big band session for Signal Records, and recruited Anderson to sing on two titles. She had the good fortune to introduce the altoist-composer's most famous song, "Social Call" (lyric by Jon Hendricks), and to be marvelously showcased in an all-star band that also included Art Farmer (yet another Hamptonian), Eddie Bert, Julius Watkins, Cecil Payne, Horace Silver, Oscar Pettiford, and Art Blakey. There's a bit of the blues in her singing here, but not much more than a hint: She's a distinctly jazz singer with a light and airy, swinging sound.

At least someone was paying attention: The two Signal sides, which were eventually absorbed into the enormous Savoy catalogue, attracted the notice of Swedish trumpet star Rolf Ericson. This time she made it to Europe: Ericson was putting together an all-star band, mostly of Americans, to tour Scandinavia in the summer of 1956, and Anderson got the call to come along as vocalist. She was so well liked by the Swedes (who called her "Stene," a nickname that she had earlier used on her 1953 session) that she went on working in Scandinavia for three months after the tour was over.

Anderson began work on her first full-length album in Stockholm in the fall of 1956. "I went out and bought all these artists' albums that I admired, and brought 'em back to my hotel room," she recalled in 1982. "I listened to 'em for about a week; I didn't want to sound like 'em, but I never made [an album] before and I wanted to see what they did. I noticed that Ella, no matter what, was always on target. Sarah's complete control came across and [her] phrasing. I think she's incredible. I started listening to Carmen McRae later. I listened to Ella for intonation, Sarah for control, and Anita [O'Day] for speed. She can sing faster than any jazz singer I know and will still make sense." (She also told critic Ralph Gleason that "I listen to all singers and I like a lot of them: Mary Ann McAll gasses me no end, Billie Holiday, Ella, Earl Coleman—remember 'Dark Shadows'?—Frank Sinatra and this will surprise you, Babs Gonsales.")

Anderson claimed she forged her mature sound during this week of intense study. However, as "Social Call" proved, she already was well on the way to sounding like Ernestine Anderson months before the Swedish episode. The album, produced by Metronome Records, one of the world's important jazz labels, was impressive enough for Bob Shad of Mercury Records to license and release it in the United States as *Hot Cargo*, the title referring to the import status of the recordings.

Anderson began to be known back in the States in 1957 and 1958, especially after an appearance in San Francisco that drew rave notices from Gleason. She finally reached the payoff in Los Angeles in August 1958, when *Time* printed what amounted to a lengthy love letter (the magazine could actually make careers back then). According to Gleason, she was living on credit the week the story appeared, but as soon as it did, she was sought after by bookers, agents, and producers from all over the place. Over the next three years, she taped four albums for Bobby Shad and Mercury, including *Ernestine Anderson: The Toast of the Nation's Critics* (1958), *Fascinating Ernestine* (1959), and *Moanin'! Moanin'! Moanin'!* (1960). The company also had her record a few singles, including the doo-woppy "A Lover's Question," which has the earmarks of those popmeisters Clyde Otis and Belford Hendricks all over it.

The best and most generally heard of these is the first, despite its unwieldy and rather immodest title. The mood throughout is light and swinging, a condition guaranteed by the presence of arranger Pete Rugolo, who keeps the proceedings in a more traditionally rhythmic vein than his somewhat more off-beat orchestrations for June Christy. Anderson and Rugolo romp throughout, a mood instilled by the presence of several players associated with the West Coast cool school (including altoist Bud Shank and drummer Shelly Manne), especially on such apostrophe-oriented arias as the opener, "Runnin' Wild," and "Sleepin' Bee."

The big dramatic numbers are "Star Dust," done very straight-as-written with lots of strings (sounding similar to Sarah Vaughan's and Carmen McRae's "pop" projects from this period), and "Interlude," a haunting original by Rugolo with a Bob Russell lyric (also recorded by Christy). What's remarkable in the light of her earlier and later work is the utter absence of any blues-oriented material: The closest she comes is Wild Bill Davis's "Azure Te (Paris Blues)" and "Welcome to the Club," a torch song by Mel Tormé that she recorded two years before its composer got around to it.

After a promising start, the sixties was not the greatest of decades for Anderson. She seems to have cut only two albums in the whole period: *The New Sound of Ernestine Anderson*, for the independent Sue label in 1963, in which the material ranged from Bobby Blue Bland's "I Pity the Fool" to Frank Loesser's "I Believe in You"; many tracks, like "You're Not the Guy for Me," were exceedingly poppy. The rarest album of her career, *Miss Ernestine Anderson*, was taped in London circa 1966, and so far has been released only on a long-out-of-print English Columbia LP.

The end of the decade was an even leaner period. She said later, "In about 1969, I was very depressed because my work situation was bad. I had been living in London for two years and moved back to Los Angeles, where, as a singer, I had to start over. I just felt like one more singer down there, so I just decided to stop singing altogether. I just walked off, left my music, my wardrobe, everything. I knew that if I took the stuff with me, it wouldn't be a clean break." She wound up working in a Hollywood hotel as a telephone-switchboard operator, and found herself fielding calls from celebrities and old friends such as Johnny Mercer, Cannonball Adderley, and Lorne (*Bonanza*) Greene. The good news was that, during this period, she discovered Buddhism, which she felt helped to center her spiritually.

Around 1975, Anderson was rescued by two old friends, Benny Carter and Ray Brown. The alto saxophonist–trumpeter–composer–arranger giant recruited her to sing on an album he was making, and even though it was never released, it helped get her into a music-making frame of mind again. The virtuoso bassist also encouraged her to start singing again and, apparently, helped bring her to the attention of Carl Jefferson of Concord Jazz Records. Between 1976 and 1990, she would appear on roughly twenty Concord releases, most of which were her own projects, although she also made guest appearances on several all-star concert albums. Along with Rosemary Clooney, Mel Tormé, and Carol Sloane, Anderson became one of those major artists who enjoyed a very fruitful second career thanks to Jefferson and Concord. By far the major portion of her recorded output is on the Northern California–based imprint.

Not surprisingly, Anderson's voice is ten years darker and deeper than it had been in the sixties. She still has that honey-at-dusk sound that Quincy Jones described, only now it's honeyer and duskier. The most striking aspect of her work in the seventies and eighties is a renewed interest in the blues. If this element is overlooked in the earlier albums, it more than comes to the fore in her sessions from 1976 onward. In 1984, she recorded *When the Sun Goes Down*, a whole album of blues (such as the titular "In the Evening" and "Down Home Blues") and blues-inspired (such as Ellington's "Just a Lucky So and So" and Peggy Lee's "I Love Being Here with You," which she infuses with blue energy) material. She also varies between such traditional blues as "Goin' to Chicago," from the repertory of Basie and Jimmy Rushing, and the more contemporary, somewhat funkish "Steppin' In," which could have been sung by Clarence Carter. There's a distinctly blue growl inherent in her voice, not just here on the blues album but throughout the post-1976 recordings.

Anderson's chief aides-de-camp on her blues project are two specialists in the field, howling tenorist Ron Holloway and thunderous pianist Gene Harris. Throughout the Concord years, her sessions were graced by the presence of the best musicians around, starting with Ray Brown, whose bass work is at the center of most of these releases. Piano legend Hank Jones lends his class to *Live from Concord to London* (1976), *Hello Like Before* (1967), and *Big City* (1983), as does the equally classy Benny Carter on *Be Mine Tonight* (1983, which contains a number called "Sack Full of Dreams," which more singers ought to do), while the versatile Monty Alexander makes his presence felt on *Sunshine* (1979) and *Never Make Your Move Too Soon* (1980). *A Perfect Match* (1988), which teams Anderson with George Shearing, is a well-named project, even in comparison with the pianist's history of outstanding vocal collaborations (Nat King Cole, Teddy King, Dakota Staton, Nancy Wilson, Mel Tormé, Michael Feinstein, John Pizzarelli, etc.). Although most of the album features Shearing's trio, the highlight of *A Perfect Match* is a masterful voice-and-piano duet on "Body and Soul," which is dark, deep, and soulful without overdoing anything.

Many basically jazz singers who use the blues for coloration often, in fact, tend to overdo it—they exaggerate the external manifestations of the form, the growls and yells, without yielding up enough of the raw feeling that should be behind it. Not so Anderson, who is never less than subtle, whether belting the blues or tearing up a torch tune. The Concord albums are notable for the seamless juxtaposition of hard-core blues material—from classics dating back to the Bessie Smith era to more contemporary items by onetime Jazz Crusader Stix Hooper to Cole Porter and George Gershwin.

The title track is the centerpiece of *Never Make Your Move Too Soon* (1980)—an extended funk piece by Hooper, with a clever, witty, and very adult lyric (in several senses of the word), which has become a bluesy showstopper for Anderson. It has served as the climax of nearly every show she's done over the last twenty-five years; on *Live at the 1990 Concord Jazz Festival, Third Set*, Anderson refers to it as "The Anthem." Yet the rest of the album is all venerable standards out of the Great American Songbook, Arlen's "My Shining Hour" and "As Long as I Live," the Bing Crosby–associated "Just One More Chance," Willard Robison's rambling and rustic "Old Folks"—somewhat funkified by electric piano—and, best of all, a stunning duet on "Why Did I Choose You?" by Anderson and Monty Alexander.

The Concord years are also distinguished by several outstanding live recordings, such as her first Concord project, *Live from Concord to London*, *Live at the 1979 Concord Jazz Festival*, and *Live at the 1990 Concord Jazz Festival, Third Set*. The first features a treatment of "Am I Blue" that declares her stylistic allegiance to the great Ethel Waters, both in terms of material and style (her performance is in the classic Waters mold: first chorus straight, second chorus jazzy), as well as five outstanding Ellington songs. The second has her doing "Please Send Me Somebody to Love" so well she makes me forget how tired I am of that Percy Mayfield hit, which has been done to death in recent years (since Nancy Wilson and Cannonball Adderley). The 1990 live album, one of her last for Concord, climaxes in a completely captivating treatment of the now anthemic "Never Make Your Move Too Soon."

While the great bulk of the Concords used trios and quartets, her last studio album for the label was *Boogie Down,* a 1989 project that backs her with the full John Clayton–Jeff Hamilton big band, which, among other highlights, contains superlative readings of Marvin Fisher's "Nothing Ever Changes My Love for You" and Benny Carter's "Only Trust Your Heart." Even while still under contract to Concord, Anderson made an album for release initially only in Holland entitled *Isn't It Romantic,* which posited her in front of the Metropole Orchestra—a full-blooded ensemble complete with largish string section. (Originally cut in 1987 and 1988, the disc wasn't released in the United States until ten years later.) After leaving Concord, she briefly moved a notch or two up the food chain by reuniting with old friend Quincy Jones, who greenlighted two high-profile projects, *Now and Then* (1992) and *Blues, Dues and Love News* (1994), both produced and arranged by Stix Hooper, for Qwest Records.

If the best thing about the Concord series is the way Anderson integrates blues and standards, the key strength of the post-Concord projects is the way she segregates the two genres. *Isn't It Romantic* consists entirely of very familiar standards (no interesting obscurities like "Sack Full of Dreams"), mostly done in ballad time, but with a pronounced jazz feeling. The concept is similar to "Star Dust" and her other early ballads, but the feeling in her voice—deep and intense—dates this as mature Anderson. She's completely convincing throughout, never more so than on "My Ship," almost a textbook example of how to be jazzy and lyrically true at the same time, repeating the word "never" for emphasis at the end of the first chorus.

The two records for Qwest seem to be aimed not at fans of jazz or standards but to middle-aged purchasers of black pop and Chitlin Circuit soul, in roughly the same vein as Millie Jackson or Betty Wright. When *Blues, Dues and Love News* (done live at B. B. King's in Universal City) was first released, I was initially disappointed that it didn't contain more standards, of either the blues or the nonblues variety. Yet upon relistening to these two CDs ten years later, I found that both albums hold up as well-crafted exercises in acoustic funk. The studio album, *Now and Then,* contains an overproduced version of "Night in Tunisia" that incorporates other Dizzy Gillespie melodies, as well as several elaborate "Never Make Your Move Too Soon" constructs that mix in funk and rap elements, "When It All Comes Down" and "Ain't No Easy Way." *Blues, Dues and Love News* reaches a peak with her treatment of B. B. King's own biggest hit, "The Thrill Is Gone." Along the way, she refers to jazz icons like Miles Davis ("All Blues," although the booklet doesn't credit lyricist Oscar Brown Jr.) and Teddy Edwards ("Don't Touch Me"), the Motown mantra "Reach Out," and pop stars like Sting ("Sister Moon") and Willie Nelson ("You Were Always on My Mind"), and another fine reading of Benny Carter's "Only Trust Your Heart." In retrospect, it's an eminently satisfying package.

It would be difficult to claim Ernestine Anderson as a Mount Rushmore–level talent—a Carmen McRae or a Dinah Washington—yet over the course of her fifty-five-year career she's made the most of those assets she does have and has been extremely productive and consistently excellent. It was highly gratifying to see her back in New York for several stints at Dizzy's beginning in 2005, and there was a new album, *Love Makes the Changes,* for HighNote in 2003, and more recently, *A Song for You,* in 2008. Ernestine Anderson has enjoyed a remarkable career: Few singers, either more or less talented, can claim to have done as well.

The Andrews Sisters
LaVerne Sofia Andrews: born July 6, 1911; died May 8, 1967
Maxene Angelyn Andrews: born January 3, 1916; died October 21, 1995
Patty (Patricia) Marie Andrews: born February 16, 1918

Artie Shaw should know. He was driven out of the music business, as he told me (and anyone else who would listen), because of the conflict between the kind of music he wanted to make and that which he felt his audiences wanted. Having had time to give considerable thought to the matter, Mr. Shaw waxed most eloquent on the subject of the differences between "artists" and "entertainers." He especially admired musicians who could be both at the same time—Louis Armstrong, Bing Crosby, Frank Sinatra, Fats Waller. (He's somewhat less effusive about his fellow bandleaders in this regard, especially competitors like Benny Goodman and Glenn Miller.) The problem with Shaw's own career, to extrapolate from what he told me (and not just me), is that he could never come up with a balance between the two, the way Armstrong and Duke Ellington did, in that they made music that was ultimately satisfying both to themselves and to their audiences.

This is a useful way to think about the difference between the Boswell Sisters and the Andrews Sisters. The Boswells were musical innovators, the Andrewses were mere entertainers. Yet this is just indulging the snob in me—there's significant value, cultural and otherwise, in entertainment at the level that the Andrews girls created it.

For too many years I held it against the Andrewses as that they weren't the Boswells—much the same way I was prejudiced against Gene Austin, Rudy Vallee, and Russ Columbo for not being Bing Crosby. They weren't as hip or as breathtakingly original as the Boswells, and rather than being timeless, they were tied umbilically to a specific era. As British screenwriter and ideologue Dennis Potter said to me, "Nostalgia is portable." People who have experienced the forties vicariously, through Abbott & Costello movies or PBS documentaries, can feel a sentimental attachment for the era even if it was over well before they were born. The Boswell music is primarily art, the Andrews music is firstly nostalgia, yet they will be remembered and celebrated (and re-created and re-re-created) long after the World War II generation is gone.

Much as I love the Boswells, they could not have gotten us through the war the way that Patty, Maxene, and LaVerne did. The Boswells were musicians, who all possessed instrumental skills enough for them to have been able to play in bands; the Andrewses were comedians who could deliver punchlines in radio comedy sketches. Patty Andrews, who was usually the dominant voice of the trio and the only one to enjoy anything like a solo career, was a musical comedian to compete with Betty Hutton and Martha Raye. The Andrews Sisters' songs and music had less depth and dimension than the Boswells', and were more jingoistic—delivering the kind of affirmative message that was necessary for a nation at war. (If you want to call it "propaganda," so be it.) But the Andrews Sisters were also much more upbeat in tempo and message and everything else—in fact, they were irresistibly cheerful. The fun of the Andrewses was that you didn't have to take them seriously—how seriously could you take a group that sings "(I'm Getting) Corns for My Country?" One of the reasons they enjoyed such an inspired collaboration with Crosby was that he always seemed to be having such a ball when he worked with them, and that joy was easily communicated to the audience. As Patty Andrews said in an interview with historian William Ruhlmann, "Doesn't [Bing] sound like he's having fun?" No one will deny it.

The Andrews Sisters were unquestionably the most popular vocal ensemble of the mid-twentieth century (perhaps even up to the Beatles), and probably second only to Crosby and Sinatra as the biggest-selling vocal act of any kind of the forties. With the exception of the Mills Brothers, no other group of the period—the Pied Pipers, the Modernaires, the Merry Macs, the Smoothies, the Mel-Tones, the Cats and the Fiddle—comes remotely close. The three Andrews sisters sold a total number of discs that has been given in various reference books as anywhere from 30 to 90 million. And it wasn't only on records

that the girls were omnipresent: Between 1940 and 1948 they appeared in eighteen Hollywood feature films and were constantly on the radio.

If I've overindulged in comparing the Andrewses to the Boswells, it's partly because the Andrews girls themselves frequently cited Connie, Vet, and Martha as their primary role models. In her 1993 *Over Here, Over There*, Maxene writes, "We loved them and their music and began imitating their singing style around the house. LaVerne had a wonderful ear for music. She'd listen to a song by the Boswell Sisters and work it out for our three-part harmony."

As it happened, the eldest Andrews (LaVerne) was born in 1911, the same year as the youngest Boswell (Vet). All three Andrews sisters were born and raised in Minneapolis. While the Boswells were Italian, the Andrewses were of Greek and Norwegian parentage. Yet the Andrews girls were already working professionally around the Midwest when the Boswells broke through to the big time in 1931–32. By that point, Patty, Maxene, and LaVerne were part of a massive fifty-five-member troupe of entertainers helmed by one Larry Rich.

By 1936, the sisters had hooked up with Leon Belasco, a B-level sweet bandleader touring the Midwest (the joint that they were playing in Kansas City burned to the ground) who introduced them to arranger Vic Schoen. In March 1937, the band made it to New York, where Belasco, who had last made twelve sides for Vocalion in 1933, now made four sides for Brunswick. Of the four titles, two featured the Andrews Sisters ("Wake Up and Live" and "Jammin'") and the remaining two ("There's a Lull in My Life" and "Turn Off the Moon") spotlighted Patty, who had already established herself as the dominant voice of the threesome.

While in New York, they also auditioned for Fred Waring, the bandleader–glee club leader who hosted a top-rated variety show. Charlie Ryan, who then sang on the Waring show with a trio of the period called the Smoothies, told me that Waring was set to hire the threesome until he got a look at them and decided that they were too homely even for radio. It was cruel and sexist, and only partly accurate: Patty was rather cute and Maxene was quite the glamour-puss. Only LaVerne was decidedly horse-faced; photographers seem to have had an impossible time trying to make her look like something other than one of the Ritz Brothers in drag.

Schoen then hooked them up with an even more obscure bandleader named Billy Swanson, then leading the orchestra at the ballroom of the Hotel Edison (today known as the Supper Club). The timing was everything: The Edison had a wire, and Dave Kapp of Decca Records happened to tune in to the Swanson-Andrews broadcast combination in a cab. And Kapp and Decca happened to be in the market for a new sisters act, since the Boswells had broken up only a short time earlier. Family groups were a Decca specialty: The brothers Jack and Dave Kapp would be prime movers in the careers of the Boswell Sisters, the Mills Brothers, Tommy and Jimmy Dorsey, and Bob and Bing Crosby, in addition to the Andrews Sisters.

Their fortunate timing continued: This was at the exact moment when the then aspiring song-writer Sammy Cahn had come up with a surefire hit, a contagiously infectious Yiddish song entitled "Bei Mir Bist Du Schoen." (By another coincidence, the song had the same name as their musical director, Vic Schoen, which means "beautiful" in German and Yiddish.) The way Sammy told the story, he and his partners and roommates Saul Chaplin (composer) and Lou Levy (publisher) heard the song at the Apollo Theater in Harlem. The black crowd, most of whom, it was fair to say, were not conversant in Yiddish, were digging it like crazy. Cahn in particular knew it was going to be big, and went around push-ing it to various performers: Tommy Dorsey said no, but Patty Andrews said yes; in fact, she liked "Bei Mir" so much that she wanted to record it even before there was an English lyric. It was Dave Kapp, as Cahn later told me, who had the idea of com-missioning an English version from Cahn and Chaplin—which Sammy said had never occurred to him. (Yeah, right!) Soon "Bei Mir Bist Du Schoen" by the Andrews Sisters was a mammoth hit, one of the most successful songs of the early swing era. A controversy developed in which it was alleged that Cahn, Chaplin, and Levy had swiped the song from the original Yiddish-language composer-lyricist Sholom Secunda. However, to the day he died, Sammy insisted that Secunda received his fair piece of the action. At the time, Cahn and Chaplin even went on the Rudy Vallee radio show to tell the world that they had not taken advantage of their less assimilated landsman.

They followed "Bei Mir Bist Du Schoen" with "Joseph, Joseph," another Yiddish song, in which the three shiksas from Minnesota became a collective yenta, whining for the man in question to "name the day." Appropriately enough, in real life Patty married Marty Melcher and Maxene married Lou Levy, a pair of alliterative Jewish music businessmen (the first an agent who would later marry Doris Day, the second a publisher). "Bei Mir Bist Du Schoen" and "Joseph" put the Andrews Sisters on the map—by the time they hit the jukeboxes, any previous sister act was strictly yesterday's ice cubes—and set the formula for the group's subsequent hits. But whereas every Boswell record was different, the Andrewses were more likely to rely on a set formula—a less rigid one, perhaps, than that of the Ink Spots (fellow Decca contractees), but a formula just the same.

The Andrews Sisters' sound was distinguished from other vocal groups of the thirties and forties by an idiosyncratic use of rhythm. But although they flourished in the age of the great big bands, they usually didn't employ the familiar four-four swing time that Benny Goodman had made de rigueur for 99 percent of the swing bands. Rather, the Andrews Sisters had a beat all their own, a swing-Dixieland hybrid that relied heavily on a two-beat sound, which also incorporated elements, as we shall see, of the dance form known as the schottische and, soon, the Slavic polka.

As developed by musical director Vic Schoen, the Andrews two-beat wasn't quite as flexible as that of the Bob Crosby or Jimmie Lunceford bands, but it served to distinguish the trio—not just from other vocal acts but from anyone else making records at the time. In 1939, Jack Kapp insisted that they do a song called "Beer Barrel Polka," which led to a break-through as significant as "Bei Mir Bist Du Schoen," as it provided the final element of their rhythmic equation. Maxene and Patty, as they later told anno-tator William Ruhlmann, protested, "My God, we're not going to sing a polka!" because "that's all we heard when we were kids!" Kapp threatened to drop them from the label if they didn't sing it. Vic Schoen, however, had a few ideas of his own. "I hated 'Beer Barrel Polka,'" the arranger told critic George Simon, "so I arranged it as badly as I could, but it turned out to be their biggest hit. So I gave up trying to do anything musically worthwhile."

In retrospect, it does seem rather repetitive—where the Boswells experimented with rumbas and all manner of tempi, the Andrewses just stick to this two-beat thing: Even when they do a South Ameri-can number like "Aurora," it still sounds more like South Minneapolis. In 1940, they recorded "Rhum-boogie" and "Beat Me Daddy Eight to the Bar," two "boogie-woogie" numbers associated with the Will Bradley–Ray McKinley Orchestra. They quickly became one of the chief proponents and populariz-ers of the boogie-woogie fad. Yet these discs have only a very faint echo of the eight-to-the-bar great-ness of the real boogie-woogie piano giants like Albert Ammons or Meade Lux Lewis. For the most part, the Andrews Sisters sing songs with boogie-woogie allusions in the same basic Dixie-polka beat that they do everything else. In fact, one of the rea-sons the trio faded in the LP era is that even fans would have had a hard time listening to too many of their records in a row. This is, I realize, completely irrelevant to their career, in that when the sisters were at their height, people only rarely listened to more than one or two songs in a row by any single artist.

The big swing bands utilized essentially a combi-nation of African American and mainstream Ameri-can influences (i.e., songs from Broadway shows and Hollywood musicals), with singers who dared not even have ethnic names. The major exception was Lawrence Welk, who appealed to older, more con-servative middle Americans, many of whom had spent their first few decades dancing to polkas, mazurkas, and waltzes; *Metronome*'s Barry Ulanov, in a remarkable fit of charity, once described Welk's "Champagne Music" as the swing era equivalent of a Northern European musette orchestra. The Andrewses appealed to the same core audience as Welk—and a great many more listeners as well. They were demonstrably ethnic—and yet they were not. As we have seen, the Greek-Norwegian sisters followed "Bei Mir Bist Du Schoen" with another Sammy Cahn Yiddish hit, "Joseph, Joseph," based on "Yossels, Yossels." ("Joseph" is virtually the only worthwhile Andrews Sisters record that was, mysteriously, omitted from the recommended two-CD anthology, *The Andrews Sisters—Their All-Time Greatest Hits,* on MCA.)

Although they were somewhat musically limited, the sisters' repertoire was genuinely ethnically diverse. In fact they were literally all over the map. The following is a by no means complete sampling of the sisters' musical journeys, taken mostly from their first few years at the top:

South of the Border:
"Ti-Pi-Tin" (by the Mexican composer María Grever)
"Begin the Beguine"
"Love Is Where You Find It" (tango)
"Chico's Love Song" (which details the exploits of one "Chico from Puerto Rico")
"South American Way"
"Say Si Si (Para Vigo Me Voy)"
"Rhumboogie"
"I Want My Mama (Mama Yo Quiero)"
"Aurora"
"I Yi, Yi, Yi, Yi (I Like You Very Much)"

Various Islands:
"The Cockeyed Mayor of Kaunakakai" (later there would be a whole album of Hawaiian novelty songs)
"Rum and Coca-Cola"
"Christmas Island" (part of an album of Christmas songs that teamed them with Guy Lombardo's Royal Canadians)

Sunny Italy:

"Oh Ma-Ma!"
"Ciribiribin"
"Ferry Boat Serenade (La Piccinana)"

Swiss Misses:
"Toolie Oolie Doolie (The Yodel Polka)"
"Yodelin' Jive"
"The Yodeling Ghost"

Assorted Euro Nonsense:
"Tu-Li-Tulip Time" (Dutch)
"Pross-Tchai" (Russian)
"Sweet Molly Malone" (Irish)

The Yiddish Are Coming! The Yiddish Are Coming!:
"I Love You Much Too Much"
"Yes, My Darling Daughter"

"Bei Mir Bist Du Schoen"
"Joseph, Joseph"
"At Sonya's Cafe (Shikker Izzer Trinkan Mizzer)" (that's Yiddish for getting drunk, or "umbriago," as the Italians say)

Songs for Swingin' Slavs:
"The Beer Barrel Polka"
"The Pennsylvania Polka"

Although posterity has been kinder to the Boswells than to the Andrewses, the Andrewses stayed together much longer, and, as we've seen, sold many times more records than the Boswells could imagine in their wildest dreams. Like Bing Crosby, they were the embodiment of Jack Kapp's machinations—Crosby was the ultimate musical Everyman, and the Andrewes were everybody's favorite group. The Boswells were too hip, too cerebral, too soulful to fit into Kapp's plans; the Boswells liked to mess around, even with good songs. Yet while the Andrewses certainly have a sense of humor, they are entirely unfamiliar with the concept of irony. They take all those polka-dancing, ghost-yodeling, ferryboat-serenadin' Chicos at absolute face value. Where Crosby's records in the years surrounding the war sometimes have a touch of blandness about them, the Andrews Sisters take the blandness and even the mediocrity and wear them proudly, like a badge of honor. They don't do anything halfway. When a song is bad, they don't try to salvage it by rewriting it, but rather they accept it and love it—warts and all, for better or for worse.

Kapp also teamed them up with his major swing bands, Jimmy Dorsey, Bob Crosby, and Woody Herman (a session as yet unissued). The most listenable Andrews Sisters music comes out of their many team-ups, not with any of the Decca bands, but with Glenn Miller and His Orchestra. The widely popular threesome teamed with the widely popular trombonist-arranger-bandleader for thirteen weeks in 1939–40 in a series of radio broadcasts sponsored by a cigarette company. Much like the Miller band itself, which could sound sterile in the studio but soulful on live broadcasts, the Andrews Sisters have a pizzazz on the *Chesterfield* series (luckily two discs of excerpts were issued by BMG as *The Chesterfield Broadcasts*) unlike almost anything they cut for Kapp. The best result of the Miller teaming is that the rhythms behind the group sound for once more like regular swing band stuff; there's almost none of that overfamiliar Andrews Sisters Dixie-polka two-beat thing. Here is where they make good on Maxene's boast, "The thing that I always wanted us to sound like were three trumpets," as she told Ruhlmann. "You get with an orchestra and you listen to three great trumpets playing." The Miller broadcasts represent the only time that the Andrews Sisters almost kick ass.

In terms of actual commercial recordings, though, there's no question that the greatest of the sisters' sessions were done with Bing Crosby. Decca obviously agreed: After the first waxing together went over so well (two Euro-items: Harry James's Italianate theme "Ciribiribin" and the ersatz Swiss "Yodelin' Jive"), they would record nearly fifty songs as a four-voice combination. Crosby worked a lot with the Boswell Sisters in the mid-thirties, but as far as can be determined, he never actually sang with them. A Crosby-Boswell combination would have been redundant: Connie, Vet, and Martha were perfect without him. Whereas Patty, Maxene, and LaVerne need Crosby; he elevates their work from mere nostalgia to great pop music. They give him energy, and he gives them both class and sex.

Though there were some yodelers and pistol-packin' mamas in the mix, the Crosby-Andrews sides also featured some of the classiest compositions the trio ever recorded, including hits by the likes of Harold Arlen and Johnny Mercer (the classic "Acc-Cent-Tchu-Ate the Positive") and even Cole Porter (his biggest hit of the war years, "Don't Fence Me In"). (MCA has collated all forty-six masters and six alternates onto an indispensable two-CD set, *Bing Crosby and the Andrews Sisters: Their Complete Recordings Together;* the only thing it lacks are the marvelous Crosby–Patty Andrews *mano a femme* duets.) The sisters also backed up Dick Haymes (the hit "Teresa"), Danny Kaye (the somewhat less high-minded hit "Woody Woodpecker"), and fat folkie Burl Ives ("The Blue Tail Fly"), while the only woman they accompanied was Brazilian bombshell Carmen Miranda ("Cuanto la Gusta"). But none of these teamings had the magic of their encounters with Der Bingle.

The war years were golden ones for the Andrews Sisters: No entertainers were more beloved by American troops. The sisters were way up there with Crosby, Sinatra, Major Glenn Miller, Bob Hope, and Kay Kyser; like those other great Americans, they gave of themselves tirelessly and completely selflessly to performing for the troops. By the end of the war, they were firmly entrenched in the national consciousness as hit makers, and they kept on making hits for a time. When the general quality of pop songs began to go south, the Andrews Sisters, unlike Sinatra, were hardly going to protest. As cheesy as some of their early forties hits were, the late forties songs are still worse. The sisters were key players in the novelty song stakes of the era, although it's hard to believe even they could sing "Toolie-Oolie-Doolie (The Yodel Polka)," and Allie Wrubel's "The Lady from 29 Palms" with a straight face. These are about as far away from Cole Porter—even "Don't Fence Me In"—as can be imagined.

But there was some good news as well; after the war, their ability to sing ballads and slow love songs grew considerably. Early on, their only successful love song was a revival of the World War I "I'll be with You in Apple Blossom Time" (later the inspiration for Danny Kaye's immortal "When It's Apple Blossom Time in Orange, New Jersey, We'll Make a Peach of a Pair"). "Apple Blossom" introduced a favorite bit, in which Patty sings a solo passage more or less straight, while the other two chide her in harmony from the sidelines. The sisters reprise the routine in "Jealous," this time with a mostly male choir doing the sidelines chiding.

To do a ballad completely seriously, Patty more or less had to go solo, with the other two merely supplying background. By 1949, they had at last created a worthy ballad in the hit "I Can Dream, Can't I," the second Sammy Fain–Irving Kahal song from the 1937 flop show *Walk This Way* to catch on years after the fact (the first was "I'll Be Seeing You"). It's a beautiful job of balladeering, even if it's not an Andrews Sisters record; it's Patty with Gordon Jenkins's orchestra at its most melancholy, with Maxene and LaVerne somewhere in the choral mix.

Meanwhile, the partnership with Crosby continued to produce magic. They recorded together even more frequently between 1945 and 1952, and the relationship reached a climax when the trio appeared with Crosby onscreen in *The Road to Rio* (1947). The foursome cut cowboy songs and Hawaiian songs and everything else, from Harry Warren and Leo Robin's witty and urbane "I'll See-See Ya in Bahaia" (which he sang unfortunately Andrewsless in *Just for You*) to utter trash like "Wedding Day." Their last session together yielded two superior titles, one being a vocal version of brother Bob Crosby's big band Dixieland hit "South Rampart Street Parade" (lyrics by Steve Allen) that anticipates Lambert, Hendricks & Ross. The other was their answer to the Sons of the Pioneers' epic of the barren waste, "Cool Water," rendered with the sisters providing a ghostly voice. The use of an echo chamber here suggests Mitch Miller, an indication that the era of forties icons like the Andrews Sisters was at an end.

Even at their height, the Andrews gals were infamous for not getting along. It has seemed to some that they weren't merely a family who squabbled a lot but loved one another just the same; in the opinion of some, Patty and Maxene really hated each other, but fortunately LaVerne was around to keep the peace. Larry Bruff, announcer on the Glenn Miller–Andrews Sisters *Chesterfield* show, told George Simon that during the thirteen-week run of the series, "The girls weren't even talking to each other, so we were having a helluva time trying to figure out what they were going to sing." Vet Boswell often said that she couldn't understand that—that the Boswells loved one another dearly, and she couldn't relate to sisters who couldn't stand one another. The comment is somewhat facetious, in that it was the Andrewses who kept working for decades, while the Boswells broke up when Vet was barely twenty-five. According to Billy Daugherty, a singer and friend of the late Maxene Andrews, the cause of their dispute was Patty's inability to accept her older sister's homosexuality.

By the early fifties the bloom was off the sisters'

career. Their Decca contract expired in 1953 (four years after Jack Kapp's death), and the trio stopped working for a while. Patty struck out as a solo; though still in her mid-thirties she just seemed like old news. Perhaps at that point she realized why the Boswells broke up and Connie went out as a single at the height of that trio's popularity, rather than waiting for the cheering to die down. Still, Patty as a single was a good idea, she was potentially a singer-comedian to rival the best of them, and it's a shame she never caught on.

The Andrews Sisters, like many big names of the forties, reunited for a few years in 1956 with a new contract at Capitol Records. But where bandleaders like Harry James and Les Brown kept on making great new music—in addition to hi-fi remakes of their big hits—the Andrewses never came up with anything new of note after their original incarnation. When LaVerne died of cancer in 1967 (age fifty-six), the bond between Maxene and Patty was permanently severed. The only major instance when they worked together after that was for the successful 1974 Broadway musical *Over Here* (John Travolta was also in the cast), which re-created the wartime era with clever facsimile songs by Richard M. and Robert B. Sherman.

In 1985, Maxene recorded a solo album for DRG, *Maxene: An Andrews Sister*, with smooth jazz trumpeter Chuck Mangione (of all unlikely people) as a guest soloist. In 1993 she wrote a book—not a full-dress autobiography of the sisters' entire lives and career, but a very readable, very personal memoir of their World War II experiences. In 1995, the middle Andrews replaced author and "leading lady" dragster Charles Busch in the off-Broadway hit *Swingtime Canteen*. For Maxene, this was self-parody, as the show was an affectionate send-up of the wartime culture that the Andrews Sisters symbolized. She died shortly after she left the production that October. According to Bill Daugherty, she and Patty hadn't spoken for years. Maxene was never happy with the way Patty dominated the group and took most of the bows—and Patty never reconciled herself to Maxene's lifestyle. The last I heard of Patty, who turned ninety in 2008, it was rumored that she, too, was considering writing an autobiography.

The Andrews Sisters were still potent icons in the seventies, when kitsch queen Bette Midler made Andrews Sisters re-creations—most important, the "Boogie-Woogie Bugle Boy of Company B"—a recurring part of her act; there was even a disco trio called Company B (it's difficult to say which was more heavily processed, the girls' hair or their voices). The most meaningful representation of the Andrewses' career was not a CD reissue (although there was a fine, forty-seven-track package issued by MCA titled *Their All-Time Greatest Hits*) but a superb 1991 dance piece by choreographer Paul Taylor. Also called *Company B*, it proved, among other things, that it's possible to listen to a bunch of the Andrews Sisters' records in a row.

Yet by the time Midler evoked their memory again in *For the Boys*, her 1991 tearjerker about USO and World War II life, something had changed. When Bill Clinton was about to take office in early 1993, *The New York Times Sunday Magazine* ran a special issue centered around the idea that the end of the George H. W. Bush presidency meant the end of the World War II generation as the dominant force in American politics. Around that time, Johnny Carson retired from his post at *The Tonight Show*, offering further proof that the "Greatest Generation" had stepped down. The impact of the war on pop culture had long since faded, but the image of three perky sisters, not in glamorous gowns but regulation WAC and WAVE outfits—down-to-earth gals making down-to-earth music for regular Joes in uniform—is not likely to be stricken from the American consciousness anytime soon.

Louis Armstrong (1901–1971)

Billy Eckstine once called attention to the irony of Louis Armstrong's position as the single most important figure in jazz and popular singing. The juxtaposition is an extreme one: Eckstine possessed what might have been the smoothest, most mellifluous voice in popular music, and Armstrong had the roughest, most rasping sound imaginable. In fact, it was a sound that no one prior to the twentieth century would have described as beautiful or musical, much less one that would inspire hundreds of other singers. The story that Eckstine told was that at one time he was stricken with a case of strep throat and was surprised to receive a call from Armstrong: "This is me, Pops, I heard you had trouble with your throat." Armstrong proceeded to recommend one of his quasi-homemade medical solutions, and added, "I took this and I been clear ever since." Eckstine couldn't help laughing. "Here's this guy, singing like he's in a gravel pit, and he's gonna help me clear my throat!" Armstrong frequently told similar stories on himself: He went through four weddings and three divorces in his life, the last of which was the only instance he actually had to make an appearance in marital court. "When I was up in the box and the judge heard my sawmill voice, he said, 'Have you got a cold, Mr. Armstrong?' I said, 'No, Your Honor, that's my ordinary voice.' The judge rocked for about five minutes and then said, 'Divorce granted.'"

Armstrong's voice was indeed rough and gravelly, but it was the sweetest sound American music has ever known. It was a voice that sounded as if it had been made abrasive by the jagged edges of pure emotion. To a certain extent, the innovations that Armstrong introduced into jazz were made relevant for popular singing by his number-one fan, Bing Crosby, who added considerable contributions of his own in the process. Yet it's also true that Armstrong didn't need anyone to pass the word along for him—or to translate his instrumental achievements into vocal style—since he himself was one of the greatest singers music has ever known.

In the twenties and early thirties, Armstrong's singing would have sounded all but unintelligible to the average mainstream listener, raised on Gene Austin and Rudy Vallee (who were, if nothing else, certainly precise in their diction). In fact, when he was scat singing—an art form that he perfected—he probably would have seemed only slightly less incomprehensible. As the decades wore on, Armstrong's voice came to sound smoother even as his articulation became ever more precise—like a blurry image gradually coming into focus. In the fifties, Armstrong was a double whammy as far as that same average listener was concerned: Like the similarly gravel-voiced Jimmy Durante, he was a cuddly entertainer and family favorite; at the same time, like such acolytes as Crosby and Sinatra, he was an established hit maker and a consistent presence on the *Billboard* charts.

Duke Ellington opened his first *Concert of Sacred Music*, in 1965, with a witty slice of theology entitled "In the Beginning God," a contemplation of existence at the beginning of creation. In order to help us fathom His miracles, Ellington asked to consider a world without them: "No night, no day / No bills to pay." We can begin to access the contribution of Louis Armstrong in much the same way: Without Armstrong there would have been no Benny Goodman and no swing era, no Charlie Parker, Dizzy Gillespie, and modern jazz; no jazz divas like Billie Holiday, Ella Fitzgerald, or Sarah Vaughan; no hip pop singers like Bing Crosby, Frank Sinatra, or Tony Bennett; no Miles Davis or John Coltrane, no Louis Jordan or Prima, no Hoagy Carmichael and no Harold Arlen, no Ray Charles and no Aretha Franklin, no Beatles and no Rolling Stones. Even Hank Williams and Elvis Presley would have sounded vastly different had Louis Armstrong never existed. In fact, the face of American and even world music would be so unrecognizable that it would be pointless to speculate on what it would sound like without Armstrong.

It's also hardly a coincidence that "West End Blues," the record that is generally named as Armstrong's masterpiece, features the Great Man on vocals as well as trumpet. Thus, the entire art of jazz singing and American pop singing, as well as the art of the instrumental jazz solo, can point to "West End Blues" as a milestone point of origin.

In Ellington's famous one-sentence summary of Armstrong's career—"He was born poor, died rich, and never hurt anyone along the way"—he stresses the extreme contrasts of the man's life. Contrast was indeed one of Armstrong's most useful tools. On trumpet Armstrong was forever soaring for high notes and levitating to heights undreamed of even by the accompanying ensembles that surrounded him, and depicting the sky above. Yet his singing voice, so thick and juicy and completely direct in its emotional appeal, is the sound of the earth below.

Like many another iconic figure, Armstrong even shaped his own mythology in the details he chose to give about his own life, most notably his date of birth. Remarkably, it wasn't until nearly twenty years after Armstrong's death that the world, courtesy of jazz-rabbi Gary Giddins, learned that the trumpeter was actually born on August 4, 1901. Until then, the world believed what the man himself had told us, that he had emerged into the world on July 4, 1900—a date now fixed as a commemorative birthday for the man who would establish the next hundred years as the American century in music.

Ellington understates the circumstances of Armstrong's childhood: He was actually born poorer than poor. In an age when social services such as welfare were unknown, Armstrong and his mother and sister lived barely a step above what would today be considered homelessness. Louis Armstrong and jazz itself were born in the same place—New Orleans—at roughly the same time, and grew up together. As a Crescent City youngster, Armstrong was immersed from the beginning in the burgeoning jazz and blues movement. He was also exposed to other kinds of music as well: Italian opera played a key part in his musical upbringing, as did the traditional Jewish music he heard courtesy of the Karnovskys, a local family that provided him with his first employment and sense of family structure.

The mere fact of the young Armstrong having the opportunity to study music to begin with was a matter of a curious quirk of fate: as a twelve-year-old, Armstrong found a pistol belonging to his stepfather and innocently fired it in the air. He was taken into police custody and sent to a local home for boys. Luckily, the Waifs' Home had a music teacher who recognized the young man's ability. Armstrong received cornet lessons and later learned how to sight read music, and quickly became the star of the institution's marching band.

Which set into motion a pattern that encompassed much of his subsequent career: Graduating from the boys band as a young man, Armstrong, whose chief inspiration was New Orleans trumpet patriarch Joseph "King" Oliver, eventually became a local hero, the star cornetist of a town filled with music and musicians. His next move was to follow Joe Oliver to Chicago, where he quickly established himself as the number-one trumpeter in Chicago, the city that had now replaced New Orleans as the epicenter of the jazz world. From Chicago, it was on to New York, then as now the hub of the music business. By the time Armstrong toured Europe (where he would return after the war, launching several decades of international globe-trotting for the man later known as "Ambassador Satch") in the mid-thirties, he was widely regarded as the single most important performer—not merely trumpeter or even instrumentalist—in all of jazz.

The different ensembles he worked with, and the recordings they made, kept pace with his artistic evolution. King Oliver's Creole Jazz Band, which held forth at Chicago's Lincoln Garden, in fact boasted two kings on cornet, given Papa Joe and his precocious protégé, and had few challengers to its position as the greatest band in the history of the New Orleans idiom. When Armstrong left Oliver to join Fletcher Henderson's orchestra in New York, the bandleader and his chief arranger, Don Redman, were already on their way to forming the first great jazz orchestra, and Armstrong's stellar cornet work galvanized the band and inspired them to finish the task. When Armstrong returned to Chicago in the mid-twenties, he worked as a featured soloist in a number of theater orchestras. But it was his recording work, with a series of ensembles known as the Hot Fives and Hot Sevens, that amazed first the jazz community and then the world. In these sessions, Armstrong all but single-handedly created both the concept and the basic vocabulary of the jazz soloist—small wonder that generation after generation of trumpeters and singers came along trying to sound as much like Armstrong as they could.

As I've suggested, with his 1928 "West End Blues," Armstrong created what is generally regarded—by musicians and musicologists alike—as the most perfect and powerful jazz solo of all time. The concept of solo improvisation had existed in jazz before Armstrong, but he perfected the art of the jazz solo so overwhelmingly that it became, forevermore, the focal point of the music. So, too, the rhythmic ideal that came to be known as "swing" (as he defined it, in four-four rhythm, with a strong use of triplets, three notes played in the space of two) had also existed before Armstrong, but after him, swinging became the fundamental goal of all jazz. Armstrong also helped create a new intimacy, a dynamic personal relationship between performer and audience. Well before he had turned thirty, Armstrong had completely changed the face of music.

In terms of Armstrong's contribution to (or rather, creation of) the jazz vocal style, 1926's "Heebie Jeebies" is perhaps even more of a breakthrough than "West End Blues" two years later. Scat singing was still another element of jazz performance that Armstrong did not invent: Cliff Edwards and others had done it quite effectively to the point where it was fairly common by the time electrical recording was introduced in 1925; Paul Whiteman's "Charleston" from that year contains a fully formed, not to mention wild and crazy, scat vocal that's heard throughout the side. As with the instrumental solo, Armstrong refined and perfected the art of the wordless vocal improvisation. "Squeeze Me" and "Basin Street" have Pops scatting melodic variations atop a humming background provided by several members of the band—as if to indicate that no matter how far out the wordless episode may get, Armstrong is still essentially singing a song.

Other early Armstrong records, out of the eighty or so sides cut between 1925 and 1929, present other aspects of his vocal art as works in progress. "Gully Low Blues" shows that Armstrong is as powerful a blues shouter as any produced in the Mississippi Delta. Likewise, "That's When I'll Come Back to You" and "Big Butter and Egg Man" reveal that Armstrong is as great a comedian as any then performing in vaudeville. These elements—scat, the blues, and humor—would be intermingled in his singing for the rest of his life.

As great as the Hot Fives (1925–29) are, Armstrong the singer is even more powerfully spotlighted in his early big band years, 1929–34. His genius for phrasing, rhythm, and melodic invention comes to the fore most notably on a long series of tunes that he transformed into instant jazz standards. These were primarily by black songwriters, most notably Fats Waller and Andy Razaf ("I Hate to Leave You Now," "Squeeze Me," "Black and Blue," "Ain't Misbehavin'," "Keepin' Out of Mischief Now," "Blue Turnin' Grey over You," "Sweet Savannah Sue," "That Rhythm Man," "Dusky Stevedore") and Eubie Blake and Noble Sissle ("You're Lucky to Me," "Memories of You") but also by writers with proclivities toward jazz, such as Hoagy Carmichael ("Rockin' Chair," "Lazy River," "Georgia on My Mind," "Star Dust," "Snow Ball") and Johnny Green ("Body and Soul," "I Cover the Waterfront"). He also helped Jimmy McHugh and Dorothy Fields ("Blue Again," "I Can't Give You Anything but Love," "On the Sunny Side of the Street," "Exactly Like You"), Harold Arlen ("I've Got the World on a String", "I Gotta Right to Sing the Blues"), and the Gershwin brothers ("I Got Rhythm") establish themselves as writers whose music could simultaneously serve the needs of both the jazz and Broadway communities.

Armstrong's musical innovations were the primary inspiration for what became the swing era, and it was only fitting that for most of the thirties and forties, the trumpeter would tour accompanied by big bands of his own. It was in 1935, following his return from Europe and Benny Goodman's swing band breakthrough, that Armstrong came into his own as the leader of a full-sized jazz orchestra. He sings on the majority of selections that he recorded with his orchestra, and with a few exceptions, most of the masterpiece selections from this period feature his presence vocally as well as on the horn: Few singers can match the jubilance Armstrong displays on such bravura performances as "Jubilee" and "Swing That Music," while there also are astonishingly moving ballads (like "Eventide").

Some of Armstrong's best singing from the swing era (1935–45) comes in the form of surprises: Who would have thought, for instance, that he would have taken the trouble to mix scat and Spanish on "La Cucaracha"? On a similarly international note, and in a clear-cut example of Armstrong being influenced by his own "pupil," in 1936, shortly after Bing Crosby began recording Hawaiian songs with Hawaiian backing, Armstrong began doing the same. Armstrong's crooning is particularly effective in this setting, as on "On a Coconut Island." Somebody once described the singing of Ray Charles as "a mixture of gravel and honey"; that's precisely what Armstrong achieves here. He sings especially sweetly on a wonderful series of eight sides done with the Mills Brothers, with whom he indulged in such inspired ideas as treatments of quasi-folk songs from out of the black experience ("My Darling Nellie Grey") and highly original interpretations of swing era hits for other artists (like Tommy Dorsey's "Marie").

As we've seen, in the early thirties, the Armstrong sides that attract the most attention are those written by black songwriters (Waller, Blake, Handy), or those composers with either strong affiliations to jazz and/or the Cotton Club (Arlen, Carmichael, McHugh). By the late thirties, Armstrong is recording material from all over the map, geographically as well as stylistically—including lots of excellent show and movie tunes such as "Got a Brand New Suit." There also continue to be a large number of Jimmy McHugh songs: "I'm in the Mood for Love," his first recording for Decca, a new "Sunny Side of the Street" from one of his earliest surviving airchecks, "Thanks a Million," "I've Got My Fingers Crossed," and "I'm Shooting High" from 1935 alone. His most recorded songwriter, however, would be Carmichael—some label should attempt a retrospective collection entitled "Satch Sings Hoagy."

In the late thirties, Armstrong also laid down exemplary performances of many daily-bread-and-butter pop songs, including several written for Bing Crosby. Fittingly, it was Crosby, Armstrong's greatest fan and supporter, who was largely responsible for Armstrong's crossing over into Hollywood feature films, which was to be a major facet of the Armstrong career. The big band era was, generally speaking, the period when musicians and leaders, like Benny Goodman and Harry James, were most likely to achieve celebrity status. Yet though Armstrong could still claim legions of fans in these years, he did not attain the very uppermost heights of showbiz nirvana until some years later.

Traditional jazz lovers were ecstatic when Armstrong announced the formation of his "All-Stars" in 1947, a new band in what was accepted as the classic New Orleans mold of three horns and three rhythm. The hot cognoscenti considered big bands to be commercially tainted and small groups free from sin; how surprised they would be to discover that this would be the most commercially lucrative period of Armstrong's entire career. In the twenties and the thirties Armstrong was primarily known to musicians, the black audience, and jazz fans; by the fifties, thanks to film and television work as much as recording, he would be known to everybody.

Previously, he had played mainly dance and movie theater dates in this country; now he would concentrate almost exclusively on concerts and nightclubs. The All-Stars were also an international experience: When Armstrong returned to Europe for the first time since the early thirties, his popularity transcended geographical and political boundaries, and he was probably the first American musical star to devote so much of his career to touring the four corners of the globe. (His status as goodwill ambassador and champion of the American way abroad also gave him further right to speak his mind against those who threatened freedom back home, as when, in 1957, he startled the world by outspokenly attacking the pro-segregation policies of Governor Orval Faubus of Arkansas and supporting the decision of President Dwight Eisenhower and the Supreme Court to abolish the ancient Jim Crow laws in schools.)

Although Armstrong would continue to tour with the All-Stars lineup for the remainder of his life, he would frequently team up with full-size studio orchestras and an assortment of guest stars in the recording studio. In the fifties and sixties, Armstrong enjoyed a spectacular journey through the Hit Parade, in which he created classics such as "Blueberry Hill" and "Mack the Knife." It was a crucial era in his long career: Just as he was the single most significant figure of jazz, his emergence in the twenties and thirties also coincides with the beginning of what we now know as modern pop music. He immediately exerted a crucial influence on such master stylists as Billie Holiday, Bing Crosby, and—both through them as well as directly—Frank Sinatra. Finally, in the fifties, Armstrong's own singing was at last appreciated for itself by the mass-market audience. They didn't need to know that he was a pioneer and a musical innovator, they only knew that his rough-voiced singing and exuberant trumpet touched their hearts.

Armstrong's greatest years as a singer were his—and the century's—fifties and sixties. There continued to be exceptional singles, generally with orchestras directed by Sy Oliver (collected recently on a much expanded edition of the old album *Satchmo Serenades*) and Gordon Jenkins (ditto for these on *Satchmo in Style*). The 1951 remake of his theme, "Sleepytime Down South," with Jenkins's distinctive string scoring, is an all-time classic, particularly in the way Armstrong drops into the basso profundo register for the repeats of the title phrase.

The Oliver-Jenkins dichotomy extends through two albums in which Pops is touched by an angel: the secular *Louis and the Angels* (1957) and the sacred *Louis and the Good Book* (1958, both also reissued). Oliver was clearly the perfect choice for the latter, which combined the All-Stars with a gospel choir. The standout vocal here is the most rhythmic, namely "Shadrach": The Gospel that inspired this traditional hymn may have been apocryphal, but the heart and soul that Armstrong invests in it is the real thing.

The *Angels* album seems, in retrospect, more of a

natural for Jenkins, who throughout his career showed an insatiable appetite for angelic choirs and seraphic strings. However, Jenkins was no longer contractually available, so it fell upon Oliver to orchestrate *Angels* in what seems like a distinctly Jenkinsian fashion, employing strings and choirs to the hilt. The two instrumental features, "Angela Mia" and "And the Angels Sing," are rare examples of the most famous horn in jazz being heard in a strictly pop setting, with choir and strings decorating his trumpet solos.

A fair amount of Armstrong's best work from this period comes in the form of collaborations: with Ella Fitzgerald (eight singles from 1946 to 1951 with orchestral backing, two full-length albums accompanied by Oscar Peterson's quartet from 1956 to 1957, and the magnificent *Porgy and Bess* from 1957), Bing Crosby, Duke Ellington, Oscar Peterson, and an underappreciated retro New Orleans band called the Dukes of Dixieland. Then there were the two triumphant songbook albums, featuring the All-Stars and produced by George Avakian for Columbia, *Louis Armstrong Plays W. C. Handy* and *Satch Plays Fats*, which, if not true collaborations, still had Pops sharing his cover billing. The two albums with Ellington (playing piano with Armstrong's All-Stars) amount to a third songbook project, since all the tunes on this 1961 project are the Duke's.

In 1957, Armstrong made two primarily vocal albums with orchestrator Russ Garcia, *I've Got the World on a String* and *Louis Under the Stars.* These afford the Great Man the opportunity to revisit some old favorites he helped put on the map ("Body and Soul") as well as some nice things he missed the first time around ("East of the Sun"). "Stormy Weather," a song that incorporates blues-based repeats of the sort that composer Harold Arlen probably learned directly from Armstrong, is an obvious highlight. Like Bing Crosby's 1956 *Bing Sings Whilst Bregman Swings*, the idea was to allow one of the founding figures of pop singing the chance to make a solo album with a hip, contemporary orchestra in the style of such disciples as Fitzgerald and Sinatra.

However, it wasn't until the sixties that Armstrong enjoyed his most successful chart hits, "Hello, Dolly!" and "What a Wonderful World." The latter spoke to some of the more admirable values of that era, the civil rights movement and the campaign to end the Vietnam War. In one of the more remarkable tales of American pop, "What a Wonderful World" became a still bigger hit and a standard twenty years later when it was reintroduced in the hit Robin Williams movie *Good Morning, Vietnam.* No one but Armstrong could have created such a posthumous achievement. The man himself had died in July 1971 after a protracted illness.

His last major album was a frequently inspired collection of Disney material (*Disney Songs the Satchmo Way*), which features a long, transcendental reading of "Chim-Chim-Cheree"—it almost seems inspired by John Coltrane. There was still another album done after Armstrong could no longer play, yet even considering the lack of trumpet and the basic premise of the record, entitled *Louis "Country and Western" Armstrong*, that last album, from 1970, still possessed a few classic cuts.

A few years earlier, Armstrong reminisced for an interviewer about a particular concert, during which the crowd demanded that he repeat certain key tunes again and again, and in general seemed to be deeply moved—even more than usual—by Armstrong's performance. "Most touching thing I ever saw," he said. "I almost cried then and there. We really hit something inside each person there." If anything, Armstrong is underestimating his own talent, because he "really hit something inside" everybody who was ever fortunate enough to listen to him.

Armstrong transcended the decades of the twentieth century just as his music will surely transcend the decades and centuries of the third millennium. When asked, Armstrong gave all credit for his successes to his audience. As he put it, "They know I'm in there—in the cause of happiness."

Fred Astaire (1899–1987)

Were it not for Fred Astaire, would the body of work that we think of as the Great American Songbook even exist?

Tony Bennett—a lifelong Astaire buff—feels strongly that the American songbook has been created by performers as much as by composers. Had it not been for Judy Garland, for instance, "Over the Rainbow" would have been a completely different song, and probably not the masterpiece it is. This is admittedly an extreme case, but it's fair to say that Garland not only made the song a permanent part of the canon of American pop and jazz, but that her performance has influenced all subsequent interpretations, vocal and instrumental, in whatever medium—the way Garland sang it is as much a determining factor as the notes that Harold Arlen put down.

In the 1960s, pop singers began writing their own material (inspired by the examples of Bob Dylan and Lennon and McCartney). Bennett feels that, in a peculiar way, this development had the unintended effect of demeaning all the previous generations of noncomposing singers. "[Columbia Records president] Clive Davis really started minimizing performers. You know, he started saying, 'If you don't write songs, if you just perform, then you're just one-dimensional.' And to this day, the performers are the only ones who don't get paid royalties from their performances on television or radio. The publisher gets paid, the composers get paid. Everybody gets paid except the performer."

Bennett's response to the issue was to initiate a

series of songbook albums organized by performers rather than by composers, starting with Frank Sinatra (*Perfectly Frank*) and Fred Astaire (*Steppin' Out*). He more than makes his point with the Astaire album alone. It's not merely that so many entries in the Great American Songbook were written with Astaire in mind, but that Astaire's style helped to shape the songs and influence the way they would sound before they were even written. Consider three of the classic songs of the Astaire canon—Berlin's "Top Hat," Gershwin's "Slap That Bass," and Kern's "Pick Yourself Up." It could be argued that these three songs by three different composers sound more like one another than they do other works by the same authors. There's a certain rhythmic urgency that one finds in songs written for Astaire that makes them singular, so that the idea of an "Astaire songbook" is not merely a commercial conceit but as valid as that of a Berlin or Gershwin songbook.

Think of those syncopated interjections that the Gershwins plug into "Fascinating Rhythm" ("Start a-hoppin'/Never stoppin'") and "I've Got Beginner's Luck" ("Gosh I'm fortunate"). Would they even be part of the song were not the brothers writing with Astaire in mind? Likewise, the verse to "Nice Work if You Can Get It": Every time I hear another singer—even hipster Mel Tormé—tackle the line "A life that isn't *necessarily* sunny," I always think how awkward; why five beats when two would seem to fit; why not "a life that isn't *always* sunny"? The answer lies in the way Astaire sings it: He makes the syncopation *sing* like no one else I've ever heard. Other singers, as a general rule, are better off avoiding this verse altogether. Or consider those odd breakups of the lyric in "Flying Down to Rio"—"Looking down on Rio from a Hea—/—ven of blue" or "My Rio/everything will be o—/—kay!" Surely Vincent Youmans (a Gershwin acolyte), Kahn, and Eliscu wrote that knowing Astaire would make sense of it.

Perhaps the reason that ASCAP doesn't share the wealth with performers is because they would go broke if they had to pony up what they owe to Fred Astaire. Is it possible to go to a jazz club or cabaret and hear a set, whether vocal or instrumental, that doesn't contain at least one song introduced by him? The distance by which Astaire leads the pack—by far the most standards introduced by a single performer (only Ethel Merman can compete)—is astonishing; Bing Crosby and Frank Sinatra, two dominant voices of twentieth-century pop, don't come close.

Astaire was still more than that. He was also, after Armstrong and Crosby, the most important conduit for the concept of jazz and syncopation into the American mainstream. In a sense, syncopation was a necessity for the dancer: He didn't have the operatic chops to hold every note for as long as it was written, so he broke notes up, and the rhythm along with them. And the way he broke up those notes—or as Sinatra would say, his phrasing—was a big part of what made his singing so special.

Sammy Davis Jr., in his capacity as an impressionist, delivered the only accurate impression of Astaire singing. On "One for My Baby (and One More for the Road)," he illustrates how Astaire's rhythmic creativity involves clinging to the beat—other singers may lag behind to deliberately increase pathos or whatever, but Astaire stays just where he is, and makes it work even so. Even though he lacks Crosby's remarkable melodic range, his voice has the same warm, human baritone quality, the same naturalness. People who think Astaire was a big star because he was so sophisticated and elegant are missing the point: Astaire was a great artist because he was so down-to-earth and human.

He did more with less chops than most full-time singers did with bigger and more fully trained voices. To paraphrase Artie Shaw's famous comment about Lester Young, Fred Astaire was a better singer than most guys who were better singers.

No arguments please: Fred Astaire was the single most significant figure in the entire Broadway and Hollywood musical experience.

It's difficult to imagine who could challenge him. No other star, no composer, no choreographer, no singer or dancer, no producer or director so personified everything that was great about musical comedy, both on stage and on the screen, and in Tin Pan Alley, as Astaire. He was the embodiment of all that was wonderful about the intertwined arts of song and dance. Indeed, no artist ennobled so many productions over so many years—eleven major Broadway shows and thirty classic films—and, as we've established, had so many all-time standard songs written expressly for him. As Jeffrey Cordova (Jack Buchanan) describes Tony Hunter in *The Band Wagon*, Astaire was the original Mr. Show Business. Not for nothing did Astaire's trademarks—the top hat, the white gloves, the cane, even a song he introduced—become representative icons of the entire movie musical genre.

The key word that describes Astaire in action is "magic." Although he played an amateur magician in *Three Little Words*, his kind of magic has nothing to do with rabbits and hats, and some of his more imaginative numbers in *Royal Wedding* and *The Belle of New York* aside, it rarely depends on camera tricks or special effects. Magic is Astaire dancing with Ginger Rogers. Magic is Astaire dancing with a chorus line. Magic is Astaire dancing by himself. Magic is Astaire dancing with a cane, a coat rack, a set of drums. Magic is Astaire dancing. Magic is Astaire. Long before costumed superheroes, Astaire made us believe that a man could fly.

Astaire and his longtime first partner, his older sister Adele, were born in Omaha, Nebraska (he on May 10, 1899); the family was of Austrian origin (the actual name was Austerlitz). Their mother brought them to New York in 1904 to enroll them in a dancing school, and less than eighteen months later, they were hoofing professionally in vaudeville. Over the next dozen years, the brother-and-sister team gradually worked its way up from minor to major league vaudeville houses to Broadway—then known as the "legitimate" theater (which implies, obviously, that vaudeville was not)—where they landed with the 1917 revue *Over the Top*. Ironically, the title of that show described everything that Astaire was not.

Not every production was a hit, but the Astaires were well-enough received by audiences and critics even in flop shows so that the quality and status level of their productions got better and better. By the time the siblings were in their mid-twenties, they were regarded as regular fixtures both on Broadway and in London's West End. A decade before he became Hollywood's preeminent song-and-dance man, the young Astaire was already a theatrical icon. Even though we have no cinematic document of his eleven New York and four British productions, two elements of these early efforts became essential to Astaire's later film work. First, he was a Jazz Age hero, no less so than Paul Whiteman, Al Jolson, or any other celebrity musician—primarily, for the sheer rhythmic power of his performances.

In fact, Astaire's sorcery is of a very particular nature: It's almost exclusively fueled by rhythm. He didn't have a virtuoso's voice, but his gift of rhythm empowered him to do more with a song than any ten crooners with gorgeous baritones and super-wide ranges. Astaire begrudgingly became the archetypical top-hat-and-tails song-and-dance man, but he wasn't the first—that honor more properly belongs to the British entertainer Jack Buchanan (who later co-starred with Astaire in the film *The Band Wagon*). It seems clear, to me at least, that Astaire regarded himself as more of a rhythmic and jazz guy than he did as a romantic and elegant guy, as most of his fans seem to have perceived him. Even more than romance, rhythm was his thing.

In the words of Irving Berlin, who supplied more songs (six complete film scores) for Astaire than any other composer, "his heart was in a song before his feet took over." But leave us not forget that the heart is as much an instrument of rhythm as the feet. As Astaire described it in *Swing Time's* "Never Gonna Dance," his heart is forever "beating out weird tattoos / Of the 'St. Louis Blues.'" With Astaire, heart and feet are inseparable. Rhythm is power, the only tool necessary for vanquishing a foe or scoring a romantic conquest.

As the Astaires sing in "I'd Rather Charleston," "There's no sensation / Like syncopation!" Rhythm is so powerful that Astaire repeatedly employs it as a weapon in any number of dance sequences: "Don't Monkey with Broadway," which opens *Broadway Melody of 1940*, is one of his great mano a mano comedy dances. The premise has Astaire and George Murphy hoofing together in a lyric that begins with the two beefing about (and warning against) possible changes to old New York ("put bathrooms in the zoo," "put Brooklyn anywhere!" but "don't mon-

key with Broadway"); at first they're in cahoots, nice and chummy with each other, but within a few choruses of sour gripes, they're at each other's throats. Previously, in the title number of the 1935 *Top Hat*, Astaire transformed his cane into a machine gun and bumped off a line of anonymous chorus boys. On "Don't Monkey" the canes become swords, and the duet becomes a duel. Rhythm is a weapon.

Yet Astaire also had an astute appreciation for melody. More than other performers of his era, he had the brains and the taste to know who the best songwriters were and the wherewithal to make a point of regularly working with them. The Astaire siblings and the Gershwin brothers both made a major impact with the 1924 show *Lady, Be Good*, which they repeated with the 1927 *Funny Face*, and Astaire likewise helped Cole Porter earn his reputation as one of Broadway's essential composer-lyricists with the 1932 *Gay Divorce*. By 1931, when Arthur Schwartz and Howard Dietz wrote *The Band Wagon* for the team, being commissioned to compose a score for Fred Astaire was just about the highest accolade a songwriter could achieve. In Hollywood, Irving Berlin, Johnny Mercer, Harry Warren, Jerome Kern, Dorothy Fields, and Harold Arlen would join that short list. (The only canonical songwriters of the era who never wrote a vehicle for Astaire were Richard Rodgers and Lorenz Hart, and it's said that they actually did compose the *On Your Toes* score with him in mind.)

The years 1932 and 1933 brought the biggest sea changes in Astaire's career: When his sister retired from the stage to marry an English nobleman, Fred switched from half of a team to a solo act and, soon enough, from a stage to a movie performer. *Gay Divorce*, in which he introduced Porter's über-classic "Night and Day," was the vehicle that allowed him to make both transitions, even though its adaptation as *The Gay Divorcee* wasn't his first film.

Astaire's movie career roughly divides into three distinct periods. In his first classic era, he would make ten essential films for RKO Pictures, beginning with *Flying Down to Rio* (1933) and concluding with *The Story of Vernon and Irene Castle* (1939). All but one of these would co-star Ginger Rogers, the most famous partner of his career. Then, for almost ten years, Astaire enters into a wild and wonderful "experimental" period, in which he tries out all kinds of different formats—films with no plot (*Ziegfeld Follies*), overt fantasies (*Yolanda and the Thief*), films with two leading men (*Holiday Inn, Blue Skies*)—for all the major studios. Then, between *Easter Parade* in 1948 and *Silk Stockings* in 1957, Astaire experiences a second classical era, in which he turned out a masterpiece a year, most of which were produced at MGM.

There's a concert in the 1980s at which Frank Sinatra makes a surprisingly uncharitable remark about Fred Astaire's singing: How could a guy who wasn't even primarily a vocalist introduce so many great songs? Sinatra genuinely sounds jealous that the Gershwins and Jerome Kern weren't writing directly for him. I think Ol' Blue Eyes was just being perverse; deep down, like Mel Tormé and Tony Bennett and so many other colleagues, Sinatra knew that Fred Astaire was a great singer. Yet Astaire himself seemed to go along with Sinatra's grouse. Denigrating his vocal abilities was an essential part of Astaire's persona, which was generally modest. Part of his own charm was that he didn't take himself too seriously: He took great pains to control his image as a dancing virtuoso, and he was even less inclined to present himself as a great singer. But it followed that there was a price to pay, for us if not for him. Because he professed not to be much impressed with his own vocal talents, he didn't put nearly enough effort into his recording career, unless it was to suppress it. True, he would never be a vocal Everyman— Ralph Gleason once famously said that he would like to hear every song he ever liked being sung by Sinatra, and I think that's a phenomenon which is even more applicable to Crosby and to Ella Fitzgerald. No, I don't think I'd want to hear Astaire sing every song ever written, no more than I would Billie Holiday. But I do wish Astaire had made a lot more recordings.

Fittingly, Astaire first discovered his voice, recording-wise, as it were, in London (the English labels had a long history of recording American stars earlier and more extensively than their stateside counterparts). Astaire's first commercial recordings—the earliest surviving documents of his performances—were done in London in 1923. He was not yet a superstar or an icon, just the lead in a hit show (*Stop Flirting*, which had been titled *For Goodness Sake* during its earlier, less successful run on Broadway) and the British were much more inclined than Americans to make original cast recordings. Even so, he had the chance to record comparatively few of the song successes he introduced in the twenties, whether in London or New York.

The first pairing, "The Whichness of the Whatness" and "Oh Gee! Oh Gosh!" has Adele sounding both kittenish and squirrelish, to mix my animal metaphors. She sounds thoroughly a product of the times, a flapper, a vamp, a sweet young thing, as well as the product of the acoustic recording technology. But from the beginning, even at twenty-four, Fred has a warm baritone voice—no feminized tenor, he. Although the Gershwins contributed a few numbers to the *For Goodness Sake/Stop Flirting* score, "The Whichness of the Whatness" and "Oh Gee! Oh Gosh!" were the work of the otherwise unknown William Daly and Paul Lannin. "Whichness" is, however, the kind of literary nonsense of which Ira Gershwin would have approved.

George and Ira take over for the 1924 *Lady, Be Good,* a venture that was a major hit for both family acts involved, the Gershwins and the Astaires; the combined run on Broadway and in London lasted more than two years, and Fred and Adele did not return to Broadway with a new vehicle until 1927. *Lady, Be Good* also represented the most notable Broadway success for veteran entertainer and jazz pioneer Cliff Edwards, who introduced *Lady, Be Good*'s other major standard, "Fascinating Rhythm," in tandem with the Astaires. Both Fred and Adele, in England, and Edwards, earlier in New York, recorded "Fascinating Rhythm," yet one longs for a true original cast recording, to get an idea of how the two acts would have performed it together.

The follow-up vehicle, the 1927 *Funny Face,* followed the same general trajectory—again Fred and Adele and George and Ira, again a long run in New York (1927) and then in London (1928). Shortly after these shows opened in London, the Astaires recorded highlights from the scores for the English Columbia label. Apart from the obvious virtue of having Gershwin's own accompaniments on most of the *Lady, Be Good* recordings, the major virtue of the two Fred and Adele–George and Ira vehicles is the sense they offer of the chemistry between the famous brother-and-sister team.

Listening to Astaire's tracks with his older sister, some of the reasons why he constantly put down his own singing became plain—as charming as Adele must have been on stage, her appeal does not come through on records. Astaire must have been conscious of how some great stars just don't translate to the purely audio, living room medium (most of the recordings by Adele's contemporary, megastar and Gershwin diva Gertrude Lawrence, leave me equally cold), and was concerned that the same fate would befall his own singing. Even in the new electric recording process, Adele sounds like the product of another time—as indeed she was. As for himself, Fred needn't have worried. Even in his earliest recordings, he speaks to us with the same warmth and familiarity that he would on the screen a few years later. Adele also recorded two duets with her *Funny Face* leading man, Bernard Clifton, and these are merely period pieces, heavy on the quaintness. But the two duets with Fred—"Funny Face" and "The Babbit and the Bromide"—are much more, and seem more like artifacts of the future rather than the past.

Astaire's two *Funny Face* solos, "My One and Only" and "High Hat," are even more than that: Astaire is all projection, energy, and syncopation. He seems to have another trait in common with Crosby: Because he's not comfortable with excessive sentiment or emotion, the feelings that he does show—of yearning, of amorous energy, of exhilaration—seem incredibly genuine. "My One and Only" begins with the central chorus, followed by the verse (putting the verse in the center would be a tradition for both Astaire and Crosby) and a remarkable tap-dancing sequence, in which he exchanges phrases with a pair of pianists. It's one of the most compelling song-and-dance numbers ever documented, and it almost doesn't matter that you can't see it—Astaire communicates so much with his voice and his tapping feet that you get a sense of movement even without a visual element. The voice is a remarkable exponent of melody, and he makes the two melodies of "My One and Only" seem equally important, as if neither is secondary—indeed, the verse to "My One and Only" is more tuneful than the main refrain of most other songs.

In *The Bunch and Judy,* Fred and Adele play boyfriend and girlfriend (as they had in *For Goodness Sake* and *Stop Flirting*), whereas in their two most celebrated book shows, *Lady, Be Good* and *Funny Face,* they're just pals, strictly platonic. Perhaps the reason *Bunch* ran only sixty-five performances, in spite of the Kern score, was that audiences found the Astaires' relationship a bit too incestuous. "I'd Rather Charleston" (from the London production of *Lady, Be Good*) is the most successful document of their chemistry, and it autobiographically illuminates what we know about their professional relationship.

He: Take a lesson from me . . .
She: I'd rather Charleston!

He's embodying the hard work side of show business; she's the spirit of fun and spontaneity. In one respect, the Fred and Adele relationship anticipates not Fred and Ginger but Astaire and his greatest platonic partner, Bing Crosby, and those two movies (*Holiday Inn* and especially *Blue Skies*) where Astaire is Mr. Ambition and Crosby is Mr. Lie-Back-and-Take-It-Easy. In another sense, the two poles of personality as embodied by Fred and Adele would combine into the mature Fred Astaire screen persona, whose strength is that he is at once studied and spontaneous. The *Swing Time* version of "Pick Yourself Up," for instance, shows Fred leaping into what the plot would have us believe is a completely improvised dance routine with Ginger, whereas on the record we hear a radio-style scenario in which Astaire is depicted as carefully polishing a dance routine and trying to get it exactly right.

There are only a handful of recorded duets between Adele and the younger brother she dubbed "Moaning Minnie" for his incessant perfectionism; Adele was not to be a major figure in Fred's recording career. But in the early days, he seems to have had a keen interest in recording; in fact, not coincidentally, the pre-Hollywood period contains some of his most exciting work on disc. After 1935, when *Top Hat* established him as a major film star, he takes less of an interest in the recording process, possibly because the soundstage and motion picture camera were much more interesting toys for him to play with.

A goodly portion of Astaire's 1929–35 sessions were done in London, starting with four very jazzy sides with two of the hotter British dance bands of the day, Al Starita and Van Phillips. The four sides represent a thoroughly Anglo-American alliance: Starita, like many "British" bandleaders, had grown up in the States, while Phillips, in 1930, was playing host to a number of American stars.

The songs are all American. "Louisiana," which opens in a haunting minor key, is a jazz classic by African American tunesmiths Andy Razaf and J. C. Johnson, while the 1930 titles are both equally jazz- and dance-oriented: "Puttin' on the Ritz" and "Crazy Feet." Astaire is exuberant throughout, swinging, syncopated, thoroughly in the jazz idiom. "Louisiana," replete with loving Jolsonisms, was also recorded at the time by the Crosby-Whiteman combination, reminding us that Crosby was probably the only other white man then in showbiz who was as swinging and soulful.

"Ritz" and "Crazy Feet" feature actual Astaire dancing. Irving Berlin wrote "Ritz" for Harry Richman, a second-string Jolson of the early sound era, but between this 1930 recording and his 1946 film *Blue Skies,* Astaire claimed it as his rightful property; "Ritz" is even more playful than "My One and Only"—he's playing with the time like mad, rushing ahead of the beat and also ritarding all over, often in unexpected places. "Ritz" also has a couple of endearingly inept Englishmen doing blackface accents, mimicking the Two Black Crows (Moran and Mack) as they comment upon the craziness of Astaire's feet.

From 1931 to 1933, Astaire enjoyed the first of only a few relatively long-term relationships with a record company, in this case RCA Victor, which captured him in the very final stages of his relationship with Adele and the very beginning of his solo career. The center of the Victor association is the commercial recordings for that last Adele show, *The Band Wagon* (1931), and that first sisterless effort, *Gay Divorce* (1932). There are twelve RCA sides altogether, all of which feature the orchestra of Leo Reisman. (Although as far as I know, RCA never issued them together on a 12" LP, they are all available with a few extras on an out of print BMG CD, *Fred Astaire Rarities.*) In those days before the American labels had committed themselves to actual original cast recordings, the idea of having Broadway stars making dance band recordings of their big numbers was a happy compromise. Usually it was Reisman's band—thanks to the leader's close Broadway affiliations—that got the assignment.

A listen to the Astaire-Reisman sides reveals that, even as Astaire was ahead of the curve in 1929, in 1931–33 he still is one of the great, hot jazz singers of this or any era—his deprecation of his vocal skills has never seemed so patently absurd. He has, in fact, a great voice and terrific time. Even on the sides that are more Broadway-oriented, including the comedy-rhythm numbers, Astaire is supremely hip and swinging (and for that matter, it's pleasant to hear Adele one last time before she runs off to become Lady Cavendish). Astaire was in the vanguard in another sense in that he participated in one of the first experimental long-playing recordings, *Gems from The Band Wagon,* a two-sided medley that amounts to twenty minutes of pure delight.

The last recorded duet with Adele is "Hoops," a rather savage send-up of French culture with the siblings in Gallic kiddie drag. "Hoops" is one of Astaire's funniest and most scathing attacks on Euroculture. Since just before the start of the Depression, the team of composer Arthur Schwartz and lyricist-librettist Howard Dietz had been responsible for some of the era's most acclaimed shows, smart and intimate revues that were both more cost-effective and more intellectually satisfying than the Ziegfeld spectacles of the height of the twenties boom years just a season or two earlier. It seemed perfectly fitting that Schwartz and Dietz would cross paths with the Astaires, even if it was for that team's final venture.

There are four sides by Astaire and Reisman that are especially notable in that Astaire was recruited exclusively for his singing, doing songs other than those he had done in a film or show. Two songs were British and thereby could be said to represent Astaire's past: "A Heart of Stone" (by the same team who wrote "You're Blasé") and "My Temptation" (which had been known as "Mona Lisa" in England, with no relation to Nat King Cole). But the other two represent connections with Astaire's future. "Maybe It's Because I Love You Too Much" marks Astaire's second reading of a Berlin ballad. "The Gold Diggers' Song," coincidentally, was introduced by Ginger Rogers (in *Gold Diggers of 1933*), the performer who would be most closely associated with Astaire. He sings it with an astute knowledge of rhythm, employing behind-the-beat phrasing inspired by Armstrong and Crosby.

For *Gay Divorce,* Astaire made four tracks of three songs: In November 1932 he did one pairing (with Reisman) for American Victor of the earth-shattering hit "Night and Day" and the sprightly, peppy "I've Got You on My Mind"; six months later, he did two tracks for the British market, including a repeat version of "Night and Day," backed with "After You, Who?" Importantly, the 1932 American Victor version of "Night and Dry" is a dance record with Astaire singing a vocal refrain while the band gets most of the play; the 1933 English Columbia recording of the same song is a vocal record, with the band being subservient to the singer (and not even identified). Both versions, however, are for dancing. Astaire sings "Night and Day" at a proper dance tempo—the age when singers like Sinatra would slow down love songs to a painfully emotional crawl tempo was far in the future.

And yet the balance between rhythm and emotion was clearly tipped in Astaire's favor. He famously recounted how, on hearing "Night and Day," he was shocked that Cole Porter expected him to sing a song with such a wide range. Yet the first words of the verse are "Like the beat-beat-beat of the tom-toms." Obviously, tom-toms aren't the only thing that beat-beat-beat. Porter knew what he was doing when he wrote it for Astaire; the song is all rhythm and emotion—the two are carriers of each other. Astaire's time is fantastic, and his ability to convey a multilayered, profound emotional message is even more so. The rhythm keeps the drama from being too overbaked and the extreme romantic mood keeps the thing from being a mere counting exercise. Over the years, "Night and Day" would be sung by nearly every pop vocalist of note, including many versions by Sinatra, but no one sang it better than Astaire.

In between the Broadway and RKO versions of *Gay Divorce,* Astaire participated in his first two Hollywood ventures, a single number in *Dancing Lady* and a supporting character (who pretty much steals the show) in *Flying Down to Rio.* While it would be marvelous to have him doing a pairing of songs from *Dancing Lady*—say, "Let's Go Bavarian" backed with "My Dancing Lady" or "Everything I Have Is Yours"—Astaire's next recording, and last of the early period, was a pairing of *Flying Down to Rio* songs by Vincent Youmans, the title number and "Music Makes Me." Both were done for British Columbia; Astaire's voice is once again powerful testimony to the irresistible attraction of the beat, and his tap dance solo really drives the point home. Like Bill Bojangles Robinson's in his few recordings, Astaire's feet are an instrument, and as vocalist-instrumentalists, Robinson and Astaire are both in a class with Armstrong.

"Music Makes Me" is one of Astaire's most potent paeans to the power of rhythm and melody—a recurring theme in the dancer's art. The lyrics, by Gus Kahn and Edward Eliscu, much like Ira Gershwin's text to "Fascinating Rhythm," equate music with temptation—just a time step away from delirium, vice, substances, and sex: "Music makes me do the things I never should do." In both songs, Astaire sings of the seductive energy of music, and at this stage he is its victim. Before long, he would be its master, using its power in all of the first nine Fred-and-Ginger epics to turn his leading lady's mood from annoyance to intrigue to infatuation. In his last two major musicals, *Funny Face* and *Silk Stockings,* music is his secret weapon in transforming Audrey Hepburn and Cyd Charisse from heartless, artless, frigid, sterile creatures into high-glam women of passion. Music is the tool by which he seduces sexless women and brings out their latent femininity.

As must be clear, the relationship of Astaire's records to his film and stage vehicles was at this point somewhat haphazard. It was often delightfully so, but not in the case of his next film. After *The Gay Divorcee,* Astaire and Rogers were in *Roberta* (in which they play more or less the second-banana couple), and he made absolutely no commercial 78s of any of those classic Jerome Kern songs. The 1935 *Top Hat* changed the equation: It was the first original screenplay written for Astaire and the first of six Astaire classics with scores by Irving Berlin.

In 1935 Astaire signed a long-term deal with Brunswick records. For *Top Hat* and the rest of his six remaining RKO films (including five more with Rogers) of 1936–39, he would record roughly four songs per picture, for a total of thirty tracks. This number includes one instrumental, "Waltz from Swing Time," by Johnny Green's Orchestra, which is generally considered part of the Astaire-Brunswick canon. (There's also a faster alternate take of "A Fine Romance," in which Astaire sings the verse, not used on the originally issued version, and an alternate of the "Waltz from Swing Time," in which he is heard tap-dancing throughout.)

The bands that Astaire employed on the 1935–39 sessions are less hot and swinging than those on the earlier sessions, but are still sublimely musical. Still, the Brunswicks are ace, most of the commercial 78 accompaniments being the work of two remarkable composer-arranger-conductors: Johnny Green (who would graduate to working with Astaire on his films in the forties) and Ray Noble (who would appear with Astaire as actor and musician in *A Damsel in Distress*). Many of these titles continue to blur the line between dance records (meaning records to dance to, not recordings of dancers) and what they used to call "personality" records (which is a prewar way of saying vocal records). "Top Hat, White Tie and Tails" and "The Piccolino" open with an instrumental chorus before Astaire sings, the first commencing with a full serving of Green's virtuoso Broadway/society-style piano. ("The Piccolino" also proves that Berlin shares Astaire's penchant for ridiculing the pretentious upper crust of society—which generally meant Europeans—by revealing that a classic Italian song was composed by a gondolier in Brooklyn.)

On the one hand, one wishes Astaire had had enough faith in his vocalizing to make regular vocal records—and more of them—but then, his dissatisfaction led to his constantly experimenting with the recording medium itself. As noted, the Brunswick version of "Pick Yourself Up" is a complete routine unto itself, an entirely independent entity from the RKO number with Rogers. Throughout the routine, he presents himself as, to use Mel Tormé's phrase, "a total neophyte," trying to cure himself of terminal two-left-feet, and repeatedly returns to the theme—expressed through spoken lines and dialogue chanted between himself and the gentlemen of Johnny Green's band, who answer him back like a Greek chorus.

None of the Brunswicks is more winning than "I Can't Be Bothered Now": There's an arresting intro in which the bandsmen (like a collective pageboy) chant "Telegram for Mr. Astaire! Paging Mr. Astaire. Telephone for Mr. Astaire." He responds with both voice and taps to let them—and us—know that he's dancing and he can't be bothered now. Along with

"Who Cares?" which Astaire recorded for Columbia in 1940, this is the Gershwin brothers' greatest Depression-era song. Astaire verbally and terpsichoreally delineates the difference between dancing "up among the clouds" and his "bonds and shares" that "fall downstairs." Thanks to Ray Noble's expert orchestration, the dance routine and the interchange between Astaire's taps and the band are his richest on record, as is the way he dives for a low note at the end of the bridge on "throwing off the bars that held me *down*."

Fortunately, Noble returned to supply more brilliant background work behind the dancer on the equally great Berlin score to *Carefree*. The songwriter came up with a new dance for Astaire titled "The Yam," and both he and Astaire were so sold on it that Astaire and Noble, who was then establishing himself as a radio comic in addition to his achievements as composer-arranger-bandleader, recorded something titled "The Yam Step Explained" as the B-side of the original single. Even a "Yamateur" could do it, they tell us, but failed to explain why the "Yam" never caught on as a national craze (possibly "The Big Apple" had cornered the market on dancing fruit). Sadly, Astaire's arrangement with Brunswick Records didn't continue long enough for him to record any of the fine songs, old and new, in his last classic RKO picture, *The Story of Vernon and Irene Castle*. The major new tune is "Only When You're in My Arms." This is a first-rate song by Bert Talmar and Harry Ruby (who, coincidentally, would be the subject of Astaire's only other biopic, 1950's *Three Little Words*).

Astaire is also at his best on six tunes done for Columbia Records in 1940, four from his film *Second Chorus* but none, unfortunately, from the brilliant Cole Porter score to *Broadway Melody of 1940*. (Ironically, the two best songs in the picture are "Begin the Beguine" and "I Concentrate on You," and Astaire doesn't sing either one of them.) *Second Chorus* was his first venture (other than a song that they wrote together) with Johnny Mercer, who would compete with Berlin for the honor of writing the most film scores for Astaire.

Astaire later said that the only reason he agreed to do *Second Chorus*, among the most egregious turkeys of his entire career, was because of the chance it offered him to work with a first-rate swing band, Artie Shaw and His Orchestra. His delight in working with jazz musicians goes back to the beginning of his career, to the 1922 *The Bunch and Judy*, which featured the pioneering saxophone ensemble the Six Brown Brothers as a specialty act. Astaire never recorded with Shaw, though Shaw spent much of his own career helping to preserve many of the songs that Astaire introduced, much as Sinatra would do a few years later.

The first two of Astaire's 1940 titles pair him with Shaw's rival as the clarinet King of Swing, the one and only Benny Goodman. The Gershwins' "Who

Cares?" (from *Of Thee I Sing*, 1931) and the dancer's own "Just Like Taking Candy from a Baby" are among his finest efforts on wax, thanks to the remarkable synergy he achieves with the Goodman-ites. "Candy" is particularly sweet in that it features an interlude in which the full Goodman big band lays out and Astaire taps along with the legendary Goodman Sextet featuring Charlie Christian and Lionel Hampton.

Astaire made his last sides of the 78 era for Decca, nineteen songs from five films of the period: two Columbia Pictures vehicles with Rita Hayworth, *You'll Never Get Rich* (Porter) and *You Were Never Lovelier* (Kern and Mercer); the two buddy epics with Crosby for Paramount, *Holiday Inn* and *Blue Skies* (both with masterful scores by Berlin); and *Ziegfeld Follies*, a spectacular revue that was intended to showcase the entire MGM musical roster but became mostly Astaire's show over the course of the two years it took to produce.

The two Columbia-Hayworth pictures are traditionally underrated episodes in Astaire's output; in fact, they're second only to the best of the Fred-and-Ginger RKOs in the overall pecking order of his career. Fortunately, Astaire recorded a full nine songs from these two excellent scores. Cole Porter's "The Wedding Cake Walk" has him getting more low-down and funky than we expect of the ultimate Broadway sophisticate; asked to come up with a hip swing-era dance number, Porter instead turns out what's almost a parody of a jive number, a slightly tongue-in-cheek attempt to jitterbug to a turn-of-the-century cakewalk. The tune ends with a knowing self-reference to the first Astaire-Porter classic, "Night and Day." "Dream Dancing" represents the Porter-Astaire collaboration at its apogee, perhaps even more so than "Night and Day." The composer-lyricist has come up with a melody and a text (unfortunately not used in the film, in which the song is done strictly as a dance) that perfectly depict Astaire's poetry in motion.

Even though Kern had written the score for *Swing Time*, he's not generally regarded as a composer sympathetic to the swing era; it might have been counterintuitive for Columbia to pair him with Johnny Mercer, the hippest and most jazz-oriented lyricist in Hollywood. The pairing, which lasted only for this project, was a fortuitous one: On "The Shorty George" and "On the Beam," Mercer pushes Kern into topical swing band–World War II ephemera, quite a ways removed from "Yesterdays" or "Smoke Gets in Your Eyes." "You Were Never Lovelier" and "I'm Old Fashioned" have Mercer writing a more traditional lyric—"the kind they classify as quaint"—that suggests, particularly in the verse, such previous Kern partners as Oscar Hammerstein and Otto Harbach (although lines like "the starry song that April sings" are quintessential Mercer).

Unfortunately, as late as 2010, there is still no definitive American edition of the nineteen Astaire Decca titles, although there is a Japanese release (with the uncomely title of *Fred Astaire on Decca—Universal Legends*) that is well worth tracking down. One would also like to see Ginger Rogers's nine Decca titles reissued somewhere. The thirty-six titles owned by Sony (the Brunswicks and American Columbias) could also stand being repackaged in a new edition (which would improve over the older two-CD *Starring Fred Astaire*), or perhaps even being combined with the eighteen or so titles in the BMG (RCA) catalogue. Right now, the best way to hear most of the Astaire 78s is a three-disc set issued in France in 1995 entitled *Fred Astaire: Ses Films et Ses Chansons, Songs and Pictures, 1928–1944* (EPM Musique). Naxos has thus far released three excellent, comprehensive volumes of a series titled *Fred Astaire Complete Recordings*, which, when finished, should cover his entire 78-era output. Rhino/Turner has also released two double-disc sets of Astaire sound tracks, both of which are highly listenable: *Fred Astaire and Ginger Rogers at RKO* and *Fred Astaire at MGM*. In the late forties MGM Records released a number of Astaire singles, which weren't true commercial recordings but rather edited versions of his sound track vocals. (Today, these sound just fine on the Rhino/Turner double.)

One of the most tantalizing slices of Astaireiana may never be heard by his fans. In 1936 and 1937, Astaire's most notable radio venture was *The Packard Hour*, an hourly broadcast for which he served as singing host for thirty-six weeks, with Charles Butterworth for comic relief and Johnny Green as conductor. Fortunately, Green kept a set of acetate airchecks from the show, which have circulated to a very limited degree among collectors. (The Astaire estate probably also has copies.) The great thing about this series is the abundant number of songs sung here by Mr. A that he never performed elsewhere: "Johnny One-Note" (a rare instance of Astaire doing a song by Richard Rodgers), "He Ain't Got Rhythm," and "I've Got You Under My Skin," to name just a couple by Berlin and Porter. There are also lots of very worthy swing-era trifles, like "Mama Don't Allow," "The Organ Grinder's Swing," "Christopher Columbus," "Sing Me a Swing Song (and Let Me Dance)," "With Plenty of Money and You," and even two Crosby movie songs, the nursery rhyme hit "One, Two, Button Your Shoe" and the Halloweeny "Skeleton in the Closet." Photos of Astaire in the broadcast studio show a large board on the floor, indicating that many of these rhythm tunes were probably tap dance features. If anyone could make tap-dancing work on radio, it was he.

In 1952, Fred Astaire made a dramatic break-through into the long-playing format with *The Astaire Story*, and here he galvanized that medium the same way he did the talking picture twenty years earlier, helping still another nascent art form reach an early pinnacle. On *The Astaire Story*, the singer-dancer looks, Januslike, at once backward and forward, in a project that breaks new ground and yet can be considered a last hurrah. When he introduces "Night and Day," he comments that *Gay Divorce* was the only one of his stage shows to be filmed by Hollywood, which shows that his career was far from over, in that there would be two more films that utilized the titles and scores of his Broadway successes, *The Band Wagon* and *Funny Face.*

The album, released as four 10" LPs or three 12"-ers and more recently as a double CD, was a retrospective of the major additions to the Great American Songbook that Astaire had introduced over the years, focusing on his films. In fact, it was generally only the most familiar of these. He begins with *The Band Wagon,* and, curiously, there's only one song ("Fascinating Rhythm") from *Lady, Be Good* and *Funny Face.*

There are a couple of rarities. We finally get to hear him sing several numbers he never did in his films, including "I Concentrate on You" and "The Continental" (which won the first Academy Award for best song, even though Astaire didn't get to sing it), as well as one or two he hadn't previously recorded, such as "I've Got My Eyes on You" (a very nice, laid-back reading with the verse). The songs are terrific, but it's Astaire's interaction with the accompaniment that makes this such a special project; in fact, the opportunity to work with musicians like Oscar Peterson, Charlie Shavers, and Flip Phillips is what enticed Astaire to consent to the project to begin with. Peterson is at the center, with a rhythm section of Barney Kessel (guitar), Ray Brown (bass), and Alvin Stoller (drums), plus horns Shavers (trumpet) and Phillips (tenor sax). "I'm grateful for the opportunity to have made this album," Astaire writes at the end of the notes, "and for becoming a sort of new addition to the Jazz at the Philharmonic group."

In the notes, Astaire also observes that the difference between himself and his sister Adele was that she hated to rehearse whereas he, "Moaning Minnie," was obsessive about reviewing every little detail over and over. Yet, as he also tells us, *The Astaire Story* was done almost completely off-the-cuff. He showed up at the studio, the musicians knew the songs, Astaire had apparently not forgotten them, and so off to the races they went. (He's so off-the-cuff that in his spoken intro to "I Love Louisa," he states that *The Band Wagon* was produced in 1929, two years before it actually made it to Broadway.)

The whole point of the project was that it was going to be a jazz album, and indeed it is, with lots of solos throughout for the instrumentalists (Charlie Shavers is particularly juicy playing muted on "Fascinating Rhythm"): Still, most of the tracks are in medium or slow tempos. Which doesn't make them any less swinging, as Sinatra would demonstrate several years later on *In the Wee Small Hours* or, indeed, Billie Holiday had demonstrated through the many slow and very slow numbers of her career. Astaire is incessantly swinging throughout, no matter what the tempo; this isn't the wildly exuberant, over-the-top stuff he was doing in the 1929 "Not My Girl." This new treatment opens with Astaire himself playing his own song on the piano, but swinging nonetheless, in a mature, considered, and no less irresistible fashion. (This performance of "Not My Girl" is apparently the only commercial recording of Astaire's piano-playing.)

The Astaire Story is the climax, but not the end, of the Astaire story on records. There are a handful of singles (from Verve and Victor and his own Ava label, named for his daughter) and sound track albums, including that of his 1957 Paramount movie version of *Funny Face,* as well as ones for his three *Evening with Fred Astaire* TV specials. In 1975, the British producer Ken Barnes was responsible for the two final documents of Astaire's music, *Attitude Dancing* and *Bing Crosby and Fred Astaire: A Couple of Song and Dance Men.* On the first (solo) set, some of the song choices are suspect (he sounds uncomfortable singing "My eyes adored you / though I never laid a hand on you") and some of Pete Moore's arrangements have dated badly. Yet the good moments are very good indeed, particularly the opener, Lew Spence's "That Face"; likewise, Charles Aznavour's "The Old-Fashioned Way" is an inspired choice. One is tempted to grouse that there are too many of the song-and-dance man's not always brilliant original songs, but his two very best later efforts are both here: "City of the Angels" and "Life Is Beautiful," both of which would soon be adopted by Tony Bennett.

The set of duets with Crosby is a premise so inspired that it can't miss—and indeed it doesn't. As Barnes has related, when these two masters of self-deprecation were paired together, the hardest part was that each gentleman insisted on deferring to the other in terms of top billing—so much so that Barnes and Moore wound up composing an original song about the matter. The songs are, overall, much better than those on *Attitude Dancing.* It's a highly agreeable mix of good contemporary tunes (the catchy "Roxie" from *Chicago* and "How Lucky Can You Get?" from *Funny Lady,* both by John Kander and Fred Ebb), duets from each other's past ("In the Cool, Cool, Cool of the Evening," originally done by Crosby and Jane Wyman, and the Fred-and-Ginger classic "Pick Yourself Up"), and the brilliant stroke of having each do a solo song associated with the other, Astaire doing "It's Easy to Remember" and Crosby, "Change Partners." Tops in their fields, Mr. A and Mr. C were the all-time masters of the art of interplay, which comes to the fore in Johnny Mercer's "Spring, Spring, Spring" from *Seven Brides for Seven Brothers* and Cole Porter's veddy droll "I've a Shooting Box in Scotland" from 1916.

Astaire lived until 1987, twelve years after his last album and nearly twenty years after his final musical film, *Finian's Rainbow* (although he sings and to a lesser degree dances in the 1976 *That's Entertainment, Part II*). The two seventies albums may not reveal the great song-and-dance man at his absolute peak (although he sounds remarkably robust for his age), but they are a very fitting way for us to say goodbye to an old friend.

Gene Austin (1900–1972)

Rarely has an artist been so defined by circumstance as Gene Austin. There were three major male popular singers who emerged in the mid- to late twenties—the dawn of electrical recordings: in reverse order, Bing Crosby, Rudy Vallee, and Gene Austin. Crosby is remembered as the force that completely altered the face of American culture—indeed it's impossible to imagine pop music without his presence. Vallee, who regarded himself as more of a bandleader than a singer and as a radio star more than a recording artist, is considerably less known than Crosby, but at least pop music scholars remember him as an artist who flourished briefly and then was eclipsed by Crosby. (Even so, Vallee later enjoyed such career triumphs—and self-parodies—as *The Palm Beach Story* and Frank Loesser's Pulitzer Prize–winning musical *How to Succeed in Business Without Really Trying*, and so is at least remembered by somebody for something.)

But Austin—except for a few extreme antique phonography buffs—is almost completely forgotten. Which is ironic considering that he was by far the most popular recording artist of the immediate pre-Depression era, selling, it was at one point claimed, a total of 86 million discs, 7 million of which were of a single title, "My Blue Heaven." He gained a popularity in the recorded medium (this being before radio was any kind of a major force in the industry) that Al Jolson undoubtedly envied, and at a time when Crosby was still anonymous. But Austin might have preferred being forgotten to the way he's remembered in such texts as my own *Jazz Singing* and Gary Giddins's *A Pocketful of Dreams*, in which we take him to task both for not being a jazz singer and for being inferior to Bing. Both charges are true, but both miss the point—and the beauty—of Austin's music.

In some accounts Austin is rightfully given credit for being the first really popular singer to use the technique of electrical recording; in other tellings, sole credit is given to Crosby. More important, Austin was probably the first superstar to base a career primarily on phonograph recordings, though that's a highly qualifiable statement. There were many popular recording artists for decades before Austin made his first disc at the tail end of the acoustic era in 1924—the best known of whom was Billy Murray, whose total output probably exceeded the works of Crosby, Sinatra, Fitzgerald, and Austin combined. However, one gets the impression that in the earliest years of phonography, records were a generic product, somewhat like sheet music. Folks would just show up at a music store and ask for a recording of a specific song. They might specify whether they wanted a vocalist or a band, but by and large one tenor was as good as another. Billy Murray did make many specialty records, including a long series of duets with soprano Aileen Stanley, but for all the discs he turned out, he was never a headliner—any more than the anonymous actors in the earliest narrative films were movie stars. Gene Austin, however, was every inch a singing star—in many ways, like Jolson, a prototype for the many pop singers who came after him.

He was born Eugene Lucas on June 24, 1900, in Gainesville, Texas. According to his daughter, actress Charlotte Austin, there was at least some Native American blood in the family; her father told her that they were descended from Sacajawea, the Indian guide who had led the way for Lewis and Clark on their famous expedition. Not long after Austin was born, his mother moved to Louisiana and remarried, giving her son the surname of his stepfather.

According to some accounts, he ran away from home as a boy to join the circus. It is certain that at sixteen, he enlisted in the army, where he served under Black Jack Pershing in the manhunt for Mexican revolutionary Pancho Villa; when his mother and stepfather realized where he was and what he was doing, they successfully petitioned for his release. However, on the very day the United States declared war on Germany, Austin reenlisted, and served in France as a bugler during the European war. Returning stateside after the Armistice, he settled in Baltimore, where he studied both law and dentistry.

But by 1924 he was already set on a musical career, and had achieved some success as both a singer and a songwriter. That year, his first really big song, "When My Sugar Walks Down the Street," co-written with Jimmy McHugh, was published; it would later be something of a perennial, and there were notable recordings by great teams: Ivie Anderson with Duke Ellington, Nat King Cole with Billy May, and Peggy Lee with Nelson Riddle, all going "tweet-tweet-tweet." Austin would write several other notable tunes, including two songs for Mae West in her 1936 *Klondike Annie*, "Occidental Woman" and "Mister Deep Blue Sea," the latter with music by James P. Johnson, and a less famous song recorded memorably by Crosby, "Ridin' Around in the Rain."

His most famous works, however, were "The Lonesome Road" (quoted by Bob Dylan in "Sugar Baby"), and the 1924 "How Come You Do Me Like You Do?" Both would become jazz standards. "How Come" became a staple of early jazz and then of the Dixieland revival, with more than 150 known recordings. "Lonesome Road" is so entrenched in the jazz repertoire (cut hysterically by Louis Armstrong in 1931 and swingingly by Sinatra in 1956) that listeners tend to assume that it's a genuine spiritual rather than a Tin Pan Alley concoction. (All told, the accumulated royalties on his three standards should have been more than enough to support his many wives as well as his daughter Charlotte, who is best known as the leading lady in the Ed Wood–scripted killer-gorilla epic *The Bride and the Beast*, aka *Queen of the Gorillas*, 1958.)

In the early twenties, Austin, then playing piano and occasionally singing, led his own bands and crossed the country in a vaudeville act with fellow singer Roy Bergere, his collaborator on "How Come You Do Me Like You Do?" Around this time he also began appearing on early radio broadcasts. In 1924 he started recording, and from the beginning took to the format as if it were his native language, participating in dozens of sides in his first year of working in the medium. The early sides are a mixture of vaudeville, pop songs, and hillbilly material, solos as well as duets with Roy Bergere, and a considerable number of sides with guitarist George Reneau, who was billed as "The Blind Musician of the Smoky Mountains."

In spring 1925, Austin began a long-standing, exclusive arrangement with the Victor Recording Corp., which would result in around 150 songs recorded between then and 1931. Between April and November 1925, he stayed out of the studios, apparently preferring to wait out the transition from acoustic to electrical recording. He knew what he was doing: From the end of 1925 onward, Austin's career skyrocketed. He soon became the single biggest star the recorded medium had known or, indeed, would know until Crosby's breakthrough in the early thirties.

He reached his pinnacle in 1927, the year he latched on to a three-year-old song called "My Blue Heaven." This most sentimental of odes to the virtues of family life was written by then confirmed bachelor Walter Donaldson. According to showbiz lore, Donaldson wrote it not in front of familial hearth and fireplace but while sitting on a pool table. The lyric was supplied not by Donaldson's usual partner, Richard Whiting (who was a family man), as is sometimes assumed, but by a more obscure and apparently unrelated Whiting named George. George Whiting and Irving Berlin had co-written "My Wife's Gone to the Country (Hooray Hooray)" a generation earlier, but apparently he had recanted this hedonistic, anti-family attitude by the time he was ready to sing the praises of Molly and me and the baby who makes three.

"My Blue Heaven" first began to catch on when another early radio singer, Tommy Lyman, included the song in his act. When Austin recorded "My Blue Heaven" on September 13, 1927, the floodgates burst open. The twenties were the first boom years of the phonograph industry, and Austin and "My Blue Heaven" provided the hit that most exemplified the era. The Jazz Age—the years of boom and bust—

exciting as they were, would be forever identified with this extremely sentimental song that sounded retro even then.

Austin's popularity throughout the late twenties is not really a point of debate. However, we still haven't broached the key questions:

Is Gene Austin's singing any good? and
Has it dated by the standards of the post-Crosby, post-Sinatra, post-Elvis, and post-Beatles world?

Austin had a light, high sweet voice—he could either be described as a high baritone or a low tenor. It's my assumption that most people reading this will be more familiar with his somewhat more comprehensively reissued contemporary Cliff "Ukelele Ike" Edwards. One might then say that Austin sounds something like Edwards when he's singing a ballad—that is, like Ukelele Ike when he's not scatting or swinging.

Singers of the pre-Crosby period are often described as overwrought, in the manner of Jolson and other vaudeville-Broadway types at their most flamboyant. Not Austin. He was cool and subtle, again anticipating Crosby. There's something very appealing about his voice, yet at the same time it's very plain-vanilla—although these two qualities are not necessarily mutually exclusive. The bulk of his catalogue somewhat anticipates the blandness of Crosby's bread-and-butter work of the early forties. Austin was a pop singer of his era even as Jack Jones and Steve Lawrence were (and indeed still are) pop singers of *their* era. Yet Jones and Lawrence come much closer to a jazz sensibility, and are more predisposed to employ a swinging rhythmic foundation, making them more inclined to personalize or reinterpret their material in the manner perfected by Armstrong, as filtered to them through Crosby and Sinatra.

Austin is nothing like that; he sings every tune more or less straight and exactly as written, at least in his 1925–31 Victor period. Only very rarely does he personalize a song in the way that a modern jazz or even pop singer would: His recording, for instance, of his friend Fats Waller's future standard "Ain't Misbehavin' " isn't singing so much as what might be regarded as "interpretation" in the modern sense of the word. But we shouldn't judge him by applying the standards of something he is not.

What does apply is what you hear: He sings in a clear, straightforward fashion. Unlike Crosby and Sinatra, his singing isn't driven by rhythm, and unlike Jolson and Garland it isn't motivated by emotion. However, if you want to hear a "pure," exactly-as-written version of one of the great twenties standards, this is the place to go. Perhaps the fact of his being a songwriter himself had something to do with it, but he was exceptionally well served by his material. Whether he himself was picking the songs or whether it was Nat Shilkret or some other Victor executive, Austin had an extraordinarily high batting average in terms of the quality of the songs he recorded: "Five Foot Two, Eyes of Blue," "Sleepy Time Gal," "Bye Bye Blackbird," "Ain't She Sweet?," "Someday Sweetheart," "Muddy Water," "Ramona," "Just Like a Melody Out of the Sky," "Jeannine I Dream of Lilac Time," "I Can't Give You Anything but Love," "Wedding Bells (Are Breaking Up That Old Gang of Mine)," "A Garden in the Rain," "After You've Gone," "You're Driving Me Crazy," "When Your Lover Has Gone," "Nobody's Sweetheart Now," and "Love Letters in the Sand," to name just a few. Even the otherwise forgotten songs that he recorded in the Victor series often turn out to be quite good; rare, indeed, is the song that he can't help (like the sentimental waltz "I Wish I Had Died in My Cradle").

With his subtle, understated style, clear voice, and unsentimental approach, and his excellent taste in material (and accompaniments), Austin makes his Victor series one of the terrific listening experiences of the era. (Only a smattering of his sides have been reissued on compact disc, although the entire run of Austin Victor electrics has been preserved on a series of six homemade CDRs by several zealous Austin fans who put their enthusiasm to productive use. While there is no full-dress biography of him, there is a comprehensive discography.)

Austin, it turns out, was the best straight-ahead male pop singer of his era—and, as we've seen, he also had roots in hillbilly music, as evidenced by his recording of the traditional square dance number "Cindy" for Victor (under the pseudonym Bill Collins) in 1927. In fact, there were a lot of traditional, almost irritatingly straight tenors who were still recording in the early electric era (guys like Charles Harrison and Charles Hart), and compared to them Austin sounds refreshingly modern. He was nothing if not subtle, a rare commodity in twenties pop.

Once we've progressed to the point where we don't have to castigate Austin for not being a jazz singer, an ironic point emerges, namely that it turns out he did have a considerable connection to the world of jazz and black music. He emerges as a benefactor of Fats Waller, having rescued Fats from prison on several occasions, and having recorded with him on four sessions, twice in 1929 (in which he recorded Waller's "I've Got a Feeling I'm Falling" and "My Fate Is in Your Hands"), and in 1931 and 1939. He also recorded a considerable number of songs by black composers and even a few blues, such as "St. Louis Blues," "St. James Infirmary," James P. Johnson's "If I Could Be with You (One Hour Tonight)," and Duke Ellington's "Mood Indigo."

"Mood Indigo," recorded in 1931, would be one of Austin's final discs for Victor. He continued recording off and on for a number of years, doing some fine sides for ARC in 1931–33, but by the early thirties he was clearly old news, supplanted by the Crosby–Ross Columbo–Vallee triumvirate. He worked a number of sessions in his familiar twenties style—the standard tenor-with-orchestra format—for several labels (including Decca and Victor again), but his genteel style seemed incongruous with the harsh realities of the Depression.

Although in the thirties Austin showed that he could sing in a more vigorous, even jazzy style, his star had already waned. He launched a series of small-group sessions built around his vocals and piano and two comedian-musicians, guitarist Otto "Coco" Heimel and bassist Candy Candido, the basso profundo comic responsible for one of radio's most endearing catchphrases, "I'm feelin' mighty low!" Austin sings with considerably more jazz lilt on the Candy and Coco sessions (done on both commercial sessions and transcriptions), which include such notable items as the best vocal version ever of the jazz standard "China Boy."

He still had miles to go. He would be married five times and he appeared in several feature films in the thirties, including Joan Crawford's *Sadie McKee*. He went on working in radio even in periods when he wasn't recording. He also toured the country—primarily the South—in a tent show promoted by Colonel Tom Parker, who was then making a transition from carny and dogcatcher to becoming the most successful personal manager in entertainment history. It's tempting to speculate what influence Austin might have had on Elvis Presley, Parker's most famous client, who went considerably further in his mixing of pop, hillbilly, and race music. (It's been claimed Austin passed the 1927 song "Are You Lonesome Tonight?"—which he never recorded—to Presley via Colonel and Mrs. Parker, although I personally believe that Elvis learned it from Jolson's 1950 recording.)

The low point of his career would seem to be the war and immediate postwar years. Then, in 1957, interest in Austin was revived when the *Goodyear TV Playhouse* mounted a one-hour TV drama entitled *The Gene Austin Story*, with George Grizzard playing Austin onscreen and the subject himself supplying his own vocals, à la Larry Parks and Al Jolson. The real Austin himself appeared on the screen at the end of the program and plugged a newly recorded LP of new versions of his most famous songs. He also says, "My, the things you won't do when you're young . . . My, my!"

On New Year's Eve 1971, the singer appeared at Jack London's in Palm Springs, California. Three weeks later, at the age of seventy-one, Gene Austin died. Quickly, RCA rushed out what must be the shortest two-LP package in history, containing a meager sixteen tracks altogether—but at least well-selected ones. TV producer Paul Henning (responsible for *The George Burns and Gracie Allen Show, The Beverly Hillbillies,* and *Green Acres*), a longtime Austin fan, gave the eulogy, reprinted in the RCA liner notes. "Gene was a millionaire several times over before the crash. He made it . . . He spent it . . . He gave it away . . . He enjoyed it . . . He had no regrets. He never looked back. He didn't reminisce about his glorious, affluent past. He lived for now.

He was always doing new things." As his daughter Charlotte (born in 1933 in the town of that name in North Carolina) later said, "Daddy knew what soul was long before it became a popular word."

B

Mildred Bailey (1903–1951)

Tony Bennett and Rosemary Clooney first met each other around 1948, when both future stars were still unknowns. When Clooney heard Bennett sing for the first time, she asked him, "You've been listening a lot to Mildred Bailey, haven't you?" Bennett answered in the affirmative, as Bailey was indeed one of his all-time favorites. He then complimented Clooney on her perception: certainly fifty years ago he didn't sound any more like Mildred Bailey than he does today. Yet the influence was there—and indeed, still is.

What did Clooney hear in Bennett's singing that she recognized as Bailey's influence? Bailey had a small but extremely firm voice, not particularly high or low, which allowed her to have it both ways—to be demure and innocent when the material called for it and then to be hot and funky. Mildred Bailey is one of the primary colors of American jazz and pop singing. Thanks to her impact on Bing Crosby alone, we can say that many of the subsequent developments in jazz and pop were influenced by her.

The essential appeal behind Bailey's art is the same that's to be found in that of Louis Armstrong (earlier), Bing Crosby (concurrently), and Billie Holiday and Sinatra (later). They all understood that by swinging a number, a vocalist doesn't necessarily have to strip the lyric of its meaning; that a good jazz singer can put a text over conceptually and dramatically while at the same time making it move. Armstrong had shown that jazz is essentially an art of spontaneity—or at least the appearance of spontaneity—and intimacy is a direct outgrowth of that. In jazz, the idea is to make it seem as if everything is happening right now, for the first time, on the spot. That ideal applies both to a trumpet solo that's being improvised or a love lyric that the singer is making the audience feel she's singing as if the words and the thoughts were occurring to her right then and there. This idea probably couldn't have occurred without Armstrong, but it's worth noting that even before the Great Man had recorded much as a singer, Crosby and Bailey were already helping perfect what Armstrong had begun.

As pianist Bill Miller put it, Bailey "knew how to ad-lib, I mean, she never quite sang anything the same way more than once. Maybe she wasn't quite a jazz singer, but I wouldn't know how else to describe her."

In "I've Got My Love to Keep Me Warm," for instance, hear how she puts the stress on the word "off," which occurs twice in the bridge, as in "*off* with my overcoat / *off* with my gloves." By accenting those two utterances of that key word, she gives each line an extra push, as if she's kicking off into the water from the side of the pool. The rest of the line now has all the momentum it needs. She makes the lyric come alive. It's a subtle thing, perhaps not even worth noticing among the dozens of interesting things that Bailey does with the words and music of the hundreds of songs she recorded in her career. Every record she made is loaded with masterful moments like that.

When, in August 1938, *Down Beat* asked Bailey to explain her style, she responded, "I don't know exactly and I've tried to dope it out several times. The only answer I get is this: Sheet music was hard to get in my home town and a tune had to be learned [from] a recording or traveling band. It had to be memorized. I could never get the exact notes of a song, so I used to sit down and try to scheme out the best way to sing it smoothly. Sometimes I would think how a tune might have been improved if the composer had changed certain parts of the melody, and I would try singing it my own way. It sort of stuck this way through the years and before I could straighten myself out—I got to thinking I was traveling down the wrong trail—I found out that they were calling this 'swing' [quotations mine] and liking it!"

Bing Crosby later gave Bailey credit for giving him his start. Her relationship with him was crucial: When Crosby and Bailey's kid brother, Al Rinker, came down to Los Angeles and camped on her doorstep, Bailey was then an established singer there. She helped the boys find work (actually, she and Crosby were the same age) and they succeeded wildly, so much so that a few years later "the boys" were able to do something for her. When in turn they helped her join the Whiteman band, it was the start of a lifetime of Crosby doing what he could for her. As popular as she was in the 1930s, neither she nor anyone else came anywhere near him. One can only imagine how Bailey, whose self-esteem issues went hand in hand with her weight problems, must have felt when, for instance, the latest Bing Crosby movie would come out and the best she could do was to sing songs from the score. When she was sick and broke at the end, Crosby helped defray her hospital expenses and gave her a guest spot on his radio show, which turned out to be one of her final performances.

But from the evidence on hand, we can only surmise that if Bailey could have hooked up with a major band or begun recording in 1926 instead of 1929, what we know of the development of pop and jazz singing might be quite different. Many of the innovations rightfully credited to Crosby—his intimate, direct way with a lyric, his incorporation of jazz techniques into the love song, his cultivation of the microphone and the mass media to create a newer, more immediate relationship between performer and audience—must also have been deployed by Bailey during the mid-twenties. We can assume that she was, as Crosby himself averred, a direct influence on him, as opposed to the hundreds of subsequent singers who learned these things from him. (Speculating from the opposite point of view, if either Bailey or the equally corpulent Kate Smith had come along twenty years later, in the age of TV rather than radio, it's unlikely that either one of them would have made it at all.)

In her own time, Bailey didn't need any "might-have-been" mentality. In the thirties, when Bennett and Clooney were kids first discovering the great bands and singers via the medium of radio, Mildred Bailey was one of the biggest stars on the air. By the late forties, through, her moment had long since passed. The postwar years were the period in which pop singers came to dominate the musical marketplace (chief among them being Clooney and Bennett, who both became recording icons thanks largely to Bailey's onetime associate Mitch Miller). But Bailey had been a national name, especially in the early years of the swing era, first as vocalist with the biggest band of the Jazz Age (led by Paul Whiteman, a leader even more physically imposing than she was) and then as co-leader and featured star with one of the great ensembles of the swing era. Paradoxically, when her fellow singers, many directly inspired by her, began usurping mass-market popularity from the bands after the war, Bailey's star began falling rather than rising.

By the time Clooney and Bennett hooked up, Bailey had already assumed the position she would maintain in death. Although she was no longer a force in the pop industry, her work was nonetheless cherished by the cognoscenti: the jazz press, lovers of the Great American Songbook, followers of the great jazz and pop stylists, musicians, and, most of all, other singers. Nearly all of them cited her, particularly Sinatra, who was not only deeply moved by Bailey's singing itself but was also inspired by the way she was backed in the dozens of sides she cut with her husband Red Norvo's orchestra. Yet except by these insiders, Bailey was almost completely forgotten at the end of her own lifetime.

Bailey's glory years were the thirties, and her richest period is those years with the Norvo orchestra, from 1936 to 1939. Her output in this brief period is as large as the lady herself, and though collectors had to wait a long time, her complete catalogue is currently available on CD, which is fortunate in that virtually every record she made—

especially in these years—is worth owning. A list of some of the other talent involved reveals the high regard in which Bailey was held by her colleagues, starting with producers Jack Kapp, John Hammond, and Morty Palitz, and extending on to the biggest names of that era, starting with Benny Goodman, Coleman Hawkins, the Dorsey brothers, and Artie Shaw. Indeed, it's hard to think of a major figure or jazz faction of the era who is not represented here on some level. Even though Duke Ellington and Count Basie didn't personally record with Bailey, major sidemen from their orchestras appear on her sessions, which should be taken as a sign of Ducal and Countal approval.

With the possible exception of Billie Holiday (who could to a degree even be considered Bailey's own discovery), Bailey was the most consistent and prolific female jazz singer of the thirties, and the competition was formidable. For starters, there was the prodigiously gifted Lee Wiley (who only recorded sporadically in these early years; her own great work was to come later), Connee Boswell (the early thirties work both with and without the Boswell Sisters is the most outstanding; the later solos aren't always as consistent), and Ella Fitzgerald (a contender certainly, but not yet what she would become). Apart from Holiday, none of them could match Bailey's amazing output for either quantity or quality. No understanding of pop and jazz singing can be considered complete without factoring in Mildred Bailey.

"As far back as I can remember, I sang," Bailey herself wrote in a brief autobiographical article in the early forties, "sang at school, at church socials, sang every place and every time I got a chance." She was born Mildred Rinker in either 1901 or 1903—a date also given as 1907—the first of four children (including Alton "Al" Rinker) who grew up on a farm in Tekoa, Washington. Her father was of Swiss-American stock and her mother was part Coeur d'Alene Indian (giving her something in common with Lee Wiley, Kay Starr, and Keely Smith, who all had Native American blood in them). As Richard Sudhalter has observed, Coeur d'Alene traditions enabled Bailey to move between the head voice and the chest voice with far more ease than most vocalists. She studied piano and then voice at school, but left home early to escape an evil stepmother.

"As soon as I was old enough, it seemed only natural to go to work singing and playing the piano at Eiler's music store in downtown Spokane," continued Bailey, who also worked in the music department of her local Woolworth's. "Eiler's music store had a record department, and that's where I first heard jazz bands. I'll never forget the kick I got when I first heard 'Tin Roof Blues' by some unremembered orchestra, or the thrill when Bessie Smith arrived in a batch of race records. From then on, I couldn't get enough of Bessie Smith and Mamie Smith, and I still can't. They didn't have sheet music for that kind of song at Eiler's, but I wrote away to Clarence Williams and other music publishers in New York and got my own copies of songs like 'A Good Man Is Hard to Find' and 'After You've Gone.'"

After working in the music stores, Bailey began to get work singing in Seattle nightclubs, which after the coming of Prohibition in 1920 became speakeasies. Local bandleader "Tiny Burtnett heard me and hired me to sing with his Butler Hotel band," Bailey recalled in 1932. "I set out for San Francisco, where I was working in Marquand's Cafe on the beach." Before leaving Washington, she had met and married—and then un-married—a Spokane merchant named Ted Bailey, keeping his moniker as her showbiz name. Her second husband was one Benny Stafford, another enterprising soul, who managed to keep the healing waters flowing even though the stuff was now prohibited. Before long, she was firmly established in joints up and down the West Coast. At one point she played through her hometown, Spokane. Her little brother Al was too young to get in (apparently even speakeasies had a sense of propriety), but his new, older friend, Spokanite Bing Crosby, did attend and was mightily impressed.

In fact, inspired by Bailey's success along "the circuit," Al and Bing, already singing professionally around town, decided to try to make the big time in Los Angeles. First they bunked with Bailey, who helped them get started, and within a year or so they attained the upper echelon of showbiz when they were hired to sing with Paul Whiteman's orchestra, the leading pop music aggregation of the entire era. Eventually, as we've seen, they were able to return the favor by encouraging Whiteman to hire her—making her the first full-time female band singer.

Bailey worked for three years with Whiteman, but their collaboration was hardly as magical or triumphant as Crosby's relationship with the bandleader. Perhaps because female band singers were such an anomaly, it took Whiteman forever to finally get around to letting her sing on his record dates. Even then, the Whiteman-Bailey sides contain no masterpieces on the level of the best Whiteman-Crosby sides. Bailey and Whiteman ultimately parted company on unfriendly terms, and, unfortunately, the music industry seems to have taken Whiteman's side in the professional fracas—the split didn't do anything for her reputation.

She made her first record in October 1929, with a group of Whitemanites under the leadership of guitarist Eddie Lang. It's a wonderful, ebonically driven Hoagy Carmichael aria (featuring Hoagland on piano) called "What Kind o' Man Is You," and that this recording is virtually its only hearing somehow makes it even more special. Rather than just running through a chorus, Bailey is given a full verse to sing in addition to the refrain, itself a rarity on a twenties dance disc. There are a couple of places where she lets notes ring like an old-fashioned, twenties-style singer, yet it's also a harbinger of things to come at the end when she utters her final declaration of the title phrase, "What kind o' man is you?" She presents it in a declarative fashion that goes outside the melody, just steps right out of the song in order to emphasize it—it's a quite remarkable move that anticipates the future, and not just of Bailey's own work.

Her's first "solo" session, done in 1931 with the Casa Loma Orchestra, also shows her at an early pinnacle; Benny Carter's "Blues in My Heart" reveals that, if one is seeking an amazing combination of blues and Tin Pan Alley aspirations, the singer to beat is Mildred Bailey. The sides with Whiteman, which actually came after the Casa Loma session, have some interesting moments, but there's nothing as exciting as the consistently exciting sides she cut in 1933–34 with the Dorsey Brothers' band and Benny Goodman. Both she and Crosby at this time were assigned a disproportionate number of songs concerning themselves with African American and/or Southern life and/or religion. Writers like Willard Robison were trying to be more sympathetic to black people at the time, though to later generations their work doesn't seem any less politically unfortunate than the old-time mammy songs of Al Jolson's era. Bailey, however, makes such texts as "Harlem Lullaby," "Is That Religion," "Cabin in the Pines," "Emaline," and "Ol' Pappy" ring completely true. (All of her early, pre-1935 recordings have been gathered on two compact discs on the TOM label, *Sweet Beginnings* and *Band Vocalist*.)

By the mid-thirties Bailey was an established radio star—never on the level of Crosby or Kate Smith, but still popular. In 1935 and 1936, she began the most prolific period of her career, working in two distinct formats, which are best characterized as collaborations with two very different musical visionaries: producer John Hammond and her personal-professional partner, Red Norvo. Virtually all of her classic sessions were done for the ARC and Columbia labels, and are included on the essential ten-CD set *The Complete Columbia Recordings of Mildred Bailey*, released in 2000 by Mosaic Records. (If Mosaic had waited five years, they could have included the Whiteman sessions, too, which are now controlled by the Sony-BMG conglomerate.) Mosaic presented all the material chronologically, which makes sense, but they could just as easily have divided it up and put all the Bailey-Hammond sessions together and the Bailey-Norvo sessions somewhere else, even though there's a fair amount of crossover between the two groups of recordings.

John Hammond spotlighted Bailey in a series of sessions similar to those he was overseeing simultaneously with Billie Holiday: loose, informal small-group sessions with lots of great soloists and something of an intimate feel. Over the years, soloists like Roy Eldridge regularly turn up on her dates, while there are also special sessions with a bunch of Count Basie–ites (including Buck Clayton and

Herschel Evans) and various Benny Good–men. Pianist Teddy Wilson, who was also a regular (and frequent leader) on the Holiday series, was Bailey's favorite accompanist.

There's an especially wonderful session from November 1936, with Ziggy Elman, Ben Webster, Teddy Wilson, and Artie Shaw, which yielded another marvelous sample of ebonics, "'Long About Midnight," one exceptional new song, "It's Love I'm After," and a terrific reading of "More Than You Know," already a standard with jazz credentials (Goodman had cut it a few months earlier). In January 1938, Bailey did a session that's remarkable even by her very high standards, co-starring Chu Berry, drummer Davey Tough, and Wilson. She establishes Schwartz and Dietz's brand-new "I See Your Face Before Me" as a future jazz standard and finds even more pathos than Bob Hope does in "Thanks for the Memory." Most remarkable is what she does with two longhair items, "From the Land of the Sky Blue Waters" and "Lover, Come Back to Me." The first comes from the tradition of "serious" concert music, the second from operetta. Bailey was the first heavyweight jazz singer to invade either field, and while she inaugurated only a brief vogue for swinging "Sky Blue Waters," she turned "Lover Come Back" into a perennial for jazz singers and players.

In 1932, Bailey had married xylophonist and composer Red Norvo, the first major jazz virtuoso on his instrument, and at the time a star soloist in the Whiteman organization. Between 1933, when they jointly left Whiteman, and 1936, Norvo gradually worked out a style and a sound for his own dance orchestra. The band's slogan was "soft, subtle swing," meaning that even though it swung like crazy, the Norvo band wasn't screaming in your face like the average post–Benny Goodman big band. Sometimes the two were billed jointly as co-leaders—appropriately as "Mr. and Mrs. Swing"—but even when they weren't, Bailey's name was prominently bannered as the band's star attraction. She sang on the vast majority of the Norvo band's recordings, some of which were released under her name.

Norvo and Bailey complemented each other beautifully—they were one of the best partnerships in jazz, like Reinhardt and Grappelli, Beiderbecke and Trumbauer, Holiday and Young. She had a light, mid-range sound, and his jazz ensemble depended for excitement neither on exaggerated dynamics nor a particularly wide harmonic range. Together, Mr. and Mrs. Norvo were potentially the great power couple of jazz, and the music business held high hopes for the success of their band, hopes that were realized artistically, though not, in the long run, commercially.

The third contributor to the overall excellence of the band was the brilliant, far-sighted arranger Eddie Sauter, who further ensured that the Bailey-Norvo combination would never sound like anything else in jazz. The very first session by the newly established Norvo-Bailey band includes "Smoke Dreams," an average pop song that Sauter and Bailey elevate to Olympian proportions. His orchestration is a complex grab bag of twentieth-century classical music, including polytonality and various approaches to dissonance. For her part, Bailey makes the song work by swinging it as simply and sincerely as possible and singing it so vividly that you, too, begin to see hallucinations in a campfire.

The sides released under Bailey's name originally appeared on Brunswick, whereas the sides with Norvo top-billed were first issued on Vocalion. The division was quite random: Two of Bailey's very finest and funniest features, "Weekend of a Private Secretary" and "Arthur Murray Taught Me Dancing in a Hurry," were both released under Norvo's name. She sings all the way through—she's not confined to a 32-bar vocal refrain—and each number amounts to a fairly sophisticated yet swinging comedy monologue by Johnny Mercer. As I've mentioned, the Hammond-produced sessions and the Norvocentric dates were not rigidly segregated: Norvo and his sidemen often appear on the Hammond "jam session" dates, along with members of the bands of Basie, Goodman, and even Ellington.

After the Mr. and Mrs. Swing band broke up in 1939, Bailey herself was still popular enough to keep recording for the ARC corporation as it evolved into the newly reactivated Columbia Records. With Hammond and other producers, she continued to find new and interesting formats to work in: There are twenty or so titles she sings with the remarkable John Kirby Sextet, and another, equally productive, series of sessions in which she's accompanied by an ensemble inspired by Alec Wilder's chamber octet. Sauter continued to serve as her musical director on both of these projects—the first featuring predominantly black musicians (but also showcasing Norvo), the second primarily white players (as well as Roy Eldridge and the beloved Teddy Wilson)—and both utilized orchestrations that, as was Sauter's wont, combined jazz and classical elements. Around the same time, however, Bailey joined forces with Mary Lou Williams and a group of sidemen from Andy Kirk's Clouds of Joy for a session that consisted entirely of songs based in the blues, as if she wanted to prove that she hadn't lost touch with the music's roots. She and Norvo reunited occasionally on records as late as 1945, even though by then they were no longer Mr. and Mrs. anything.

Bailey's great years as a recording artist were the thirties, the period right before, during, and immediately after the glory days of the Norvo band. In the early forties, the combination of the ASCAP ban against radio stations (1941), the American Federation of Musicians strike against the record labels (1942–44), and the war upset everybody's apple cart, not just Bailey's. In fact, she was still quite visible—or audible—on the radio for the duration. There are ten first-class sides done for Decca in 1941–42, some of which, like her Sauter-Wilder-Chamber sessions of 1939–40, use a black gospel vocal group for backing. (These sides are gathered, along with some earlier and later items under MCA's jurisdiction, on *The Rockin' Chair Lady*.) One positive outcome of the war situation was a 1943 duet date with Teddy Wilson waxed for the army V-Disc program, which includes a tremendous "Sunday, Monday or Always" and perhaps her tenderest reading ever of her theme song, "Rockin' Chair."

From June 1944 to February 1945, Bailey headlined in a weekly radio program called both *Mildred Bailey and Company* and *Music Till Midnight*. The thirty-four programs featured not only the singer with an all-star, interracial orchestra (practically a first for radio) but—between guest stars and regulars—many of the finest and biggest-name instrumental stars of the swing era. CBS presented the shows live on civilian radio, but the show was also planned as a source of material for V-Discs and the Armed Forces Radio Service. It was certainly Bailey's finest hour, radio-wise. (The shows were rebroadcast on NPR in the seventies and early eighties, and occasionally one hears a rumor that a label like George Buck's Audiophile will issue the series complete on CD, which would certainly be a major mitzvah.)

Which makes it all the more surprising that Bailey was not given a contract with a major label when the war was over. Instead, she cut her last date with Norvo in 1945, the same year they were officially divorced, for the tiny Crown label (John Kirby and Sarah Vaughan were recording for that company around the same time). Old friend John Hammond was then running the jazz and pop division for the equally diminutive Majestic Records, and made about sixteen sides with her, many conducted and arranged by Eddie Sauter, her most consistent and prolific recordings outside the Columbia/Mosaic package. The Majestics include some of her most poignant ballads, "You Started Something" and "I'll Close My Eyes"; her funniest novelties, "A Woman's Prerogative" (from *St. Louis Woman*), "All That Glitters" (a rather scathing calypso); and her two all-time greatest show tunes, "Almost Like Being in Love" and "The Heather on the Hill" from *Brigadoon*. (The most recent issue of the Majestic material is a Denon CD entitled *Me and the Blues*, an import well worth seeking out.)

Bailey was clearly still close to the peak of her powers in 1946–47, as also evidenced by a rare single on RCA, Nat Cole's "That Ain't Right," and her last Willard Robison song, "I Don't Want to Miss Mississippi." During this period, pianist Ellis Larkins—who would eventually prove himself with Ella Fitzgerald and Lee Wiley, among others, as one of the finest accompanists of all time—serves as a worthy replacement for Teddy Wilson.

Though she was singing as well as ever in the mid- to late forties, her health was beginning to fade.

After the demise of the Norvo band, she was never quite strong enough to tour so extensively again. Her health hadn't been good throughout her whole adult life, and the rigors of the road had been especially rough on her during the years she was trying to help make her husband's big band a success. Encyclopedist Roger Kinkle reports that she was seriously injured in a car accident sometime in the mid-thirties, but even if that isn't true, her health seems to have been in a downward spiral throughout the forties.

She did, however, land some major gigs in New York: the Bon Soir (around 1946) and Cafe Society (June 1948). At that point, *Time* magazine gave her a huge rave review: "Not a pound underweight (at 190), in a shroud-like black gown, her swarthy features and shoe-button eyes gleaming in the spotlight." But that was about it. Gradually she was less and less able to work, and began spending more time at her farm in Poughkeepsie, New York. (As jazz scholar Phil Schaap has revealed, she kept up with the new music—even as Norvo did. At a March 1949 broadcast by the Charlie Parker Quintet, emcee Symphony Sid spots her in the Royal Roost and announces her to the crowd.)

After one particularly rough bout with illness, she appeared on the *Philco Radio Time* program (with Bing Crosby, who refers to her being on "the sick list") and *Refreshment Time* with Morton Downey, like Crosby a friend from the Whiteman days. "I really got a big lift out of doing that radio show with Bing," she said in *Down Beat* (June 1950, probably her last mention in that magazine during her lifetime). "That man makes everybody feel good who works with him." She also added, "Now that I'm beginning to feel good again, I'm looking forward to some really happy sessions under my new contract with Decca." Unfortunately, that contract would only lead to one session, her last, on April 25, 1950 ("Cry Baby Cry" and "Blue Prelude") in which she ominously and presciently anticipates her "last go-round."

Bailey had long since stopped supporting herself: Frank Sinatra, whom she had never met, and Bing Crosby paid her hospital bills, and Crosby paid off her mortgage. She died on December 12, 1951, at home in Poughkeepsie, not long after collapsing during an engagement in Detroit.

"One time I was doing a jazz concert and they asked me to sing 'Rockin' Chair,' " Lee Wiley reminisced shortly before her own death in 1975. "Well, I did sing it, and right in the middle I started crying, because it reminded me too much of Mildred. When she died, I wrote a card with the orchids I sent and I said, 'To the greatest of them all.' I think that sums up what I thought of her."

Pearl Bailey (1918–1990)

There's a little bit of Pearlie Mae in all of us, and there's a lot more to this Pearlie Mae gal than immediately meets the eye. She wants the same trappings of wealth and luxury that the rich folks and the high-class folks have, those fancy cars and apartments, furs and jewelry, power and security, yet at the same time, the allure of respectability and a life of luxury may not be enough to entice her to give up what we might call those baser pleasures—high-living, raising the devil, and just plain old jelly roll. Pearlie Mae must continually balance her lust for social climbing against her more deeply rooted lust for lust.

As created and performed by Pearl Bailey, Pearlie Mae is a deep and complex character, drawn in both intricate, subtle lines and bold, dramatic brush-strokes. Like the best ethnic performers of any era, she spoke both to and for the rest of her group. She not only communicated the feelings of her own people in the postwar era, and women in particular—and did so in a way that they could laugh at—but articulated those concerns so that the larger public beyond could understand them, too.

"St. Louis Blues," which she recorded several times, is a traditional air of woman's suffering, but she makes W. C. Handy's tune jump in the double-time Louis Jordan–Tympany Five manner so effectively that she divests it of its usual self-pity. When singing "Tired"—the number most associated with her in the early days—in her first film, *Variety Girl* (1947), she could easily have been dressed in a maid's uniform while she sang, like practically every other black woman in Hollywood history up to that point. But she and Paramount did their own little bit for human rights when they made Pearlie Mae a housewife, singing with an ironic twist about the same frustrations and yearnings that all women were (and still are) feeling.

From a broader perspective, it's remarkable that Bailey, who is rarely given credit for being the exceptional singer she was, was actually able to create a consistent character in song—something that few popular or jazz singers were able to do. "Tired" contains a spoken interlude in the middle, in which Pearl refers to a psychiatrist as "one of them rich people's doctors," and such observations were essential elements of Bailey's art. "When I'm called a great 'singer,' I always disagree," she wrote. "I think of myself as telling stories in tune to music. The words become very important, and that I love. And it doesn't hurt if you've lived a bit, too."

As with the best popular art, there's a timelessness to her very timeliness. Bailey's spiels not only anticipate the entire current rap movement, they exceed it. "Legalize My Name" resounds as a more substantial "Justify My Love" of the forties. "Legalize" is Arlen and Mercer's answer to the traditional spiritual "Scandalize My Name," which Louis Armstrong had already updated in his 1941 "Do You Call That a Buddy?" When Pearlie Mae insists that her errant swain bring her before a justice of the peace, she makes sure he spells it "peace" and not "piece." (If you know what I mean, child. Have mercy!)

A gifted singer and a fine actress, Pearlie Mae Bailey put it all together in a manner reminiscent of shamanism. A storyteller who tapped into a tradition as ancient as campfire folklore and as up-to-date as bebop, Bailey put over a series of narratives through a combination of music and speech; as with her close friend Nat King Cole (with whom she co-starred in the film *St. Louis Blues*), both the message itself and the methods of its expression were equally remarkable. From the beginning of her career—the dozens of excellent sides she cut for Columbia and Harmony Records in the postwar era—Bailey artfully turns monologue into music and back again. The best aspects of both conventions are clay in her hands, waiting to be forged into 100 percent genuine pearls by the force of her charisma, overpowered by her personality even when she's characteristically relaxing.

Bailey sold her music short when she said, "My hands are my words." I never saw her work live in concert, and I imagine she must have been wonderful, but she mastered the recording medium fairly early, and enjoyed a consistently excellent album and singles career. Pearlie Mae uses inflections and asides (such as "Have mercy!") like no one else, with the possible exception of her onetime mentor, Fats Waller. At times she exaggerates an idea as outrageously as a cartoon character (or even as Fats Waller), and yet she also is the master of understatement (as when, on "Tired," she compares her looks, after a day of washing, to Hedy Lamarr), rambling, and what they used to call rabulating—not to mention signifying, shucking and jiving, putting us on—to get her message across.

As was true of Ethel Waters, her diction and articulation are generally razor-sharp and impossible to misunderstand, but then, like Marlon Brando, she is also the master of the mumble. Nobody else—with the possible exception of Bob Hope—can make a punch line seem more funny by burying it under his breath. No one else can score equally well with the most rudimentary blues and with the most sophisticated—or faux-sophisticated—lyric by Cole Porter or Lorenz Hart. Other people have sung Porter's "Josephine" from *Silk Stockings* (Janis Paige in the movie version, for one), but only Pearlie Mae makes it sound completely natural that Napoleon's future bride "Tripped away to Paris France / In her ye olde Creole fancy pants."

When she wants to play it cute, as on the classic Burke and Van Heusen *Road* movie song "Personality," the title word gets sung rather than spoken directly because Ol' Pearl wants you to think twice about what it means (and how it also reflects back on the singer: "The madam has the cutest [pause] personality"). On "Legalize My Name" and "A Woman's Prerogative," her two showstoppers from *St. Louis Woman*, she plays the game of half-understanding and half-mispronouncing all those humongous twenty-dollar Noah Webster gems, trying to find some legal and social justification—or as she says, "precedent"—to have it both ways. She can make her man march to the altar when she says "Forward!" Conversely, when some possessive male tries to tighten the screws on her, she's always got an exit strategy.

Pearl Bailey was born in Newport News, Virginia, on March 29, 1918 (slightly less than a year after that city's other major contribution to world culture, Ella Fitzgerald); she grew up in Washington and Philadelphia. Bailey began singing for audiences in Washington's Jewish neighborhood in the very early thirties, and had her first taste of a career because of inner-family reverse psychology. Her brother, Bill Bailey, was a rising dance star (according to one old showbiz story when he got into trouble with the law later on, a judge very somberly pronounced, "Bill Bailey, you ain't goin' home!") who ordered his little sister to stop following him around backstage. Just to get back at him, she entered an amateur contest being held at the theater where her brother was working, and won.

For the next decade the young Pearl scuffled across the country, working as both a dancer and a singer. "Singers should learn to dance," she said later; "then their phrasing would be smoother and their body movements would synchronize with the phrasing." She gained valuable experience in the chorus line of Noble Sissle's *Shuffle Along* (the most popular all-black show of the interwar era, productions of which stayed on the road deep into the thirties). She also entered into and summarily exited from a quickly forgotten first marriage while hoofing in the Pennsylvania coal circuit. She worked as a band vocalist with Harlem-based Edgar Hayes and just missed a chance to work with Count Basie (her brother, Bill, headlined with Basie at the Orpheum in Los Angeles in 1943, and she appears with the band on a 1945 aircheck).

In late 1943 and early 1944, she worked with former Ellingtonian and Goodmanite trumpeter Cootie Williams, then leading his own orchestra. This was a band full of future stars, nearly all with nicknames (perhaps inspired by the leader), Earl "Bud" Powell, Eddie "Lockjaw" Davis, Eddie "Cleanhead" Vinson, and Bailey. There was a recording ban going on, but by a fortuitous set of circumstances, at the time Williams was recording for Eli Oberstein's Hit Records, and that enterprising entrepreneur wasn't about to let a little thing like a labor union stop him. Hit released two Bailey-Williams titles, "Now I Know" and "Tess's Torch Song," both written by Harold Arlen for Dinah Shore (who couldn't record them herself because of the ban) in Danny Kaye's first film, *Up in Arms*. "Tess's Torch Song" was actually better suited to Bailey than Shore, both for its blues undercurrent and the way its narrative suited her half-singing, half-spieling style. Bailey helped make "Tess's Torch Song" into a hit, even though the Hit Records label was not widely distributed. While tour-

ing with Williams she also met the brilliant arranger Don Redman, one of the founding fathers of the entire swing era and her future musical director.

"Oh, ambition was mine when I was young," she later said. After Cootie Williams, Bailey joined a USO tour, and recorded several tunes for V-Disc in late 1944, backed by jazz stars Herman Chittison (piano) and Charlie Shavers (trumpet). "The Quicker I Gets to Where I'm Going" illustrates Bailey's evolving earthy narrative style, underscored both by a bluesy feeling and wartime patriotic sentiment. As a single, she also sang in an L.A. club operated by former Ellington vocalist Herb Jeffries, and in 1944 she had a guest shot with violinist Stuff Smith on an obscure independent label. She had already begun to catch on with the smart set at New York's Village Vanguard and Blue Angel when she finally got her big break with the public at large in 1945.

Cab Calloway and His Orchestra were headlining at the Strand Theatre in Times Square, and Sister Rosetta Tharpe was set as the featured female vocalist. When the good Sister took sick, Bailey got the call to fill in. She strutted out and treated the customers to "Fifteen Years," "Straighten Up and Fly Right," her specialty, "Tired," and, for an encore, "St. Louis Blues." "I heard something perhaps I'd never heard [before]," Bailey later remembered. "It was applause, real. Thunder and lightning, and all the elements spoke at once. The next thing I knew, I was walking to the far corner backstage and someone said, 'Where are you going?' and I said, 'Over to that corner—to pray.'" She remained with Calloway's troupe for a spell at the posh Zanzibar Club on Broadway (two decades later she and "The Mighty Calloway," as she called him, would headline together again in *Hello, Dolly!*—also on Broadway).

Following her success with Calloway, Bailey went national and then international with the Broadway show *St. Louis Woman*. The show itself was far from a hit: The Harold Arlen–Johnny Mercer score was absolutely tops, but the NAACP and a lot of other people objected to the outdated portrayal of blacks in the script, and *Annie Get Your Gun* was a blockbuster hit that blasted away all the competition that season. Yet *St. Louis Woman* was a triumph for Bailey herself: "Lucky duck me had the two showstoppers, 'Legalize My Name' and 'A Woman's Prerogative,'" she remembered. In fact "Any Place I Hang My Hat Is Home" and especially "Come Rain or Come Shine" have both become standards, recorded by dozens of other artists, but precious few other female singers have had the nerve to try to compete with Bailey on those first two songs. (The only one who comes even close to out-Baileying Bailey is the older Mildred Bailey on "A Woman's Prerogative.")

Around the time of Bailey's Broadway debut, Manie Sachs signed her to Columbia Records. By this time, she was connected to the worlds of jazz, Broadway, and pop, and her Columbia sides of

1945–50 utilize a succession of perfectly chosen small groups, all consisting of inspired soloists and studio men who had cut their teeth in the swing-band era.

But—as Bailey would sing just a little later on in her career—it really took two to tango. The best of Pearlie Mae's early sides are her duets, which allow her to more fully balance speech and song and just plain carryin' on. Columbia combined her with its number-one male artist, Frank Sinatra, for the two-sided 78 "A Little Learnin' Is a Dangerous Thing," believed to be the first interracial duet ever recorded (even preceding Louis Armstrong and Bing Crosby's commercial collaborations), which unfortunately led to its obscurity, as it had to be specially ordered even in shops that normally carried all of Bailey's and Sinatra's latest Columbia waxings. There were several titles with the much loved black comedienne Jackie "Moms" Mabley, most notably on Louis Jordan's "Saturday Night Fish Fry." Mabley was never to make much of an impression as a vocalist, but in back-and-forthing with Pearlie Mae here, she more than justifies Bailey's description of her as "the funniest woman alive—no script but her own." In the early seventies, Bailey would assume Louis Armstrong's role on the famous Bing Crosby–Louis Armstrong duet on "Gone Fishin'." (YouTube makes available a lot of amazing TV duets between Bailey and Carol Channing, Dinah Shore, and others.)

Bailey was so nimble-footed and quick-tongued she inevitably ended up outshining her co-stars, and the records boosted her career but not theirs. Her most formidable partner and adversary was the outstanding trumpeter and vocalist Hot Lips Page, who duetted with her on one of the best of all boy-girl recordings, "Baby, It's Cold Outside"—a strong contender for the title of history's all-time jive duet classic. This was despite steep competition: Frank Loesser wrote the words and music as a party piece for himself and his wife, and it was also recorded commercially by the teams of Margaret Whiting and Johnny Mercer, Louis Armstrong and Velma Middleton, Sammy Davis Jr. and Carmen McRae, and Ray Charles and Betty Carter. In the MGM movie *Dangerous When Wet*, it was sung by two teams: romantic leads Esther Williams and Ricardo Montalban, and comedy couple Red Skelton and Betty Garrett, who (even though Garrett was the only one of the four who could actually sing) were enough to earn "Baby" the 1949 Academy Award for Best Song.

Columbia's A&R staff liked the song so much that they cut it twice, once on the main Columbia label with Buddy Clark and Dinah Shore and then again in the definitive rendition, by Pearlie Mae and Hot Lips. Their Oxford gray version was issued on Columbia's subsidiary label, Harmony Records, which explains why, when Hot Lips pleads "(Let me) put some records on while I pour," she inquires, "Harmony records?"

Bailey was so successful in terms of rhythm and comedy that Columbia downplayed her ballad singing: Two of her best straight-ahead love songs (with no spieling or humor), "They Didn't Believe Me" and "Here You Come with Love" were not issued until the CD era. It will no doubt come as a surprise to those who know Pearlie Mae only as a spieler and homespun philosopher that she could also turn on the tender—and so effectively.

Bailey's parting gift to Columbia Records was helping to discover Tony Bennett, whom she installed in a Greenwich Village revue (she was the headliner and mistress of ceremonies) and introduced to Bob Hope—to this day Bennett gives her credit as the mother of his career. In 1950, she switched from Columbia's Harmony subsidiary to Decca's relatively new Coral subsidiary. Her backing bands got bigger, less jazzish, and more poppish, but with astute arrangements by Don Redman. She landed a hit in "Two to Tango," which she followed up with other quasi–South American items (including another tango, "I Love My Argentine," and "Sing Something Special," not to mention "Perandez from the Andes"). She also acquired a husband who would stick with her for the rest of her life, the star drummer Louis Bellson. The superb percussionist was at the time with Duke Ellington, and he would spend the next forty years alternating between leading his own groups and serving as his wife's musical director. In 1954 she would reteam with Harold Arlen for another unsuccessful show with a great score, *A House of Flowers*. Redman served as orchestrator here, too, and Bailey, by the evidence of the original cast album, stopped the show with Arlen's beautiful "Don't Like Goodbyes."

At around the same time, Bailey recorded two albums for Mercury, *The One and Only Pearl Bailey* (which was subtitled ". . . For Adult Listening") and *The Intoxicating Pearl Bailey,* but she would come into her own as an album artist at Roulette Records. She seems to be the first of many great African American entertainers who worked on Roulette (Count Basie, Sarah Vaughan, Billy Eckstine, and Dinah Washington came later), and the label's strategy regarding her was unique: Roulette seems to have taken the low road and the high road at the same time with her. Much of her output was, as on *The One and Only*, ". . . For Adult Listening." It's not as if they were trying to sell her as a low-rent purveyor of "party records" (like Rusty Warren, who sang about knockers and dingies, and whose records were generally buried deep in closets where kids inevitably found them). Mostly everything on Bailey's "adult" records is perfectly clean; the lure for adolescent listeners may well have been the mere implication that something here may not be suitable in the Tipper Gore household. *The One and Only* even framed her picture on the album cover with the giant shape of a keyhole.

Other albums that dwell on this theme (all on Roulette) include *Pearl Bailey a Broad* (a set of travel-related songs), *For Adults Only, More for Adults Only, Songs of the Bad Old Days, Naughty but Nice* (which includes something titled "Since I Became a Hussy"), *All About Good Little Girls, The Risque World of Pearl Bailey,* and *For Women Only,* among others. Compared to the rampant salaciousness of later generations (not to mention the explicit blues numbers of the twenties and thirties) these records are fairly tame in terms of satisfying those who would buy them for a cheap thrill. But they are decidedly "adult" in that they feature intelligent, often classic pop numbers sung intelligibly for a grown-up sensibility. There's nothing for kiddies here; in fact, she disses the entire teen idiom in a very funny (albeit untrue) specialty number titled "I Can't Rock and Roll to Save My Soul."

While the "adult" albums had a specific audience, Roulette also promoted Pearl Bailey as their approximate equivalent of Ella Fitzgerald in a series of songbook albums that numbered at least four: *Pearl Bailey Sings Porgy and Bess and Other Gershwin Favorites, Pearl Bailey Sings Songs She Loves by Her Favorite Composer Harold Arlen, St. Louis Blues* (the songs of W. C. Handy), and *The Songs of Academy Award Winner James Van Heusen.* For her Cole Porter album, she combined the high and low strains of her talent by concentrating on Porter's saucier material, a very wide subgenre of his work. The Arlen album was an outgrowth of the two Broadway shows she had done with the songwriter, while the Handy and Gershwin projects were tie-ins with two of her movies, *St. Louis Blues* and *Porgy and Bess.*

Mysteriously, none of this material is on American CD reissues (although there is a recommended three-disc package from France, *Pearl Bailey: The Best of the Roulette Years,* which totals fifty-four first-rate tracks). Yet the delights of the Mercury and especially the Roulette LPs are manifold. The *Arlen* set includes virtually the entire scores of *St. Louis Woman* and *House of Flowers,* including all the songs that Bailey didn't do in those Broadway productions. The Porter package is highlighted by his parody "Josephine" and his ode to undies, "Satin and Silk," both from *Silk Stockings.* Bailey is especially effective on Porter's tale of those two social-climbing so-and-sos, "Mister and Missus Fitch"; only Pearlie Mae can get so high-toned and so gully-low all at the same time. She shows us what a "sophisticated" song, like one of Cole Porter's, and a low-down blues number, like one of W. C. Handy's, have in common.

The W. C. Handy collection has her sounding more like a genuine Delta blues singer than anywhere else in her career. In the film *St. Louis Blues,* Nat Cole sings a new Mack David song called "Morning Star" that was supposedly inspired by Handy, but on *her* Handy album, Bailey sings the actual Handy piece, "Shine Like the Morning Star," a comparatively rough-hewn blues-gospel hybrid. The new version of "A Woman's Prerogative" on the

Arlen album is even better than the original, with Bailey literally growling and blasting out the text.

The Gershwin *Porgy and Bess* album is also very satisfying; the only disappointment is that Bailey doesn't do "I Can't Sit Down" here—this was her big number as Serena in the 1959 Otto Preminger film of the Gershwin opera (although she did sing it on the original sound track LP). The *James Van Heusen* album (which consists mostly of songs associated with either Crosby or Sinatra) uses a large and lavish string orchestra; contrastingly—and unusually—the Gershwin collection finds her accompanied by merely a rhythm section (sometimes just a piano) and a full, gospelly choir, billed as "The Voices of the Ambassadors." The overall effect is to instill in the Gershwin canon a very down-home, churchy feeling, especially in "Oh, Lady, Be Good" in which the Ambassadors are reminiscent of the Charioteers, who had backed Bailey a decade earlier. The Roulette albums are a great body of work by a seminal entertainer, and they deserve to be more thoroughly explored in the digital era.

Bailey seems to have lasted longer with Roulette than any other artist, going up to the mid-sixties. She was more visible than ever in 1968. In that year she headlined on Broadway as Dolly Levi in *Hello, Dolly!,* in which her onetime boss Cab Calloway co-starred as leading man Horace Vandergelder, and she also published *The Raw Pearl,* her first of two books. She cut two new albums, one titled *The Real Pearl,* for Enoch Light's Project 3 Records, for which she teamed up with arranger-conductor Marty Paich. Some of the tracks are a little too deep into the sixties idiom (like Burt Bacharach's "A Tower of Strength"), but most are more tasteful than you might imagine they could get away with in 1968. The standout is one of the top "talking songs" of all time, Bert Williams's "Nobody." There are also two songs by Ervin Drake (the inspirational "I Believe" and the nostalgic "Ukelele Talk"), the only version of the Mercer-Rowles "Baby Don't You Quit Now" that challenges Tony Bennett's, and a very exciting, decidedly post-Sinatra reading of "That's Life" (very Vegas, as you can well imagine). In 1971, she released an album called *Pearl's Pearls* on RCA, with more good songs and an all-star team of arrangers (Benny Carter, Bill Holman et al.), whose charts were played by Louis Bellson's big band.

Bailey never faded. She was more of a constant presence in the seventies than in any other decade, thanks to a TV series. She had always had a tendency for dispensing advice, and was a natural talker in a formal interview setting as well as in a song. While she was alive, Dick Ables, who worked as Louis Bellson's New York band contractor and librarian, consistently described her as "the kind of woman that likes to run everybody's life," although he painted a considerably more genteel picture of the lady after she died in 1990.

In her fifty years of performing professionally,

Bailey triumphed as one of the world's best-loved jazz-influenced popular entertainers—a singer who was also a brilliant comedian and a comedian who was also a brilliant singer.

Chet Baker (1929–1988)

For most musicians, art is what you make on the bandstand and life is dealing with things like rent and relationships. Chet Baker had it the other way around: When he ambled up to the microphone, what came out of his trumpet or his mouth was life. His music was so natural and direct, it wasn't even a reflection of his soul, but his soul itself. Nearly every portrait or profile of Baker describes him as a cipher, neutral, devoid of any personality but what came through in his music. His playing and singing were all that he was.

Baker had to work no harder to sound the way he did than he did to talk or look the way he did. So what did he do when he wanted to create art? He got lost. He went to Europe, got high for three weeks, disappeared on a boat somewhere, found a new girl, went flying off balconies, or all of the above. Getting "lost" was the only way Baker could achieve distance, a concept that was critical in his life and work. He could settle down with one lady love after another and yet not really be there at all. He could spill his guts out in a song and calmly pack his trumpet away at the end of a gig and call a cab.

He also seems to have had little appetite for looking at himself, his own pictures, listening to his records, or reflecting philosophically on the meaning of his existence. If so, he was the only one. Bruce Weber's 1989 film *Let's Get Lost*, produced with Baker's participation but not released until after his death, is less about Baker himself than it is about the act of listening to him. The filmmakers spend much time with record producer Dick Bock (of Pacific Jazz) and photographer William Claxton. Later in the film, Weber takes his place in the celluloid cat-fight competition among the parade of Baker's significant others that marches by. All who come into contact with Chet want to (1) save him from drugs and from himself and, failing that, (2) explain him to the world. Baker himself remained supremely uninterested in either goal.

All stories must have an ending—in a sense, Weber could not complete and release his film until Baker provided him with a finish. Ex–dope fiends, like other reformed sinners, from Saint Augustine and Jelly Roll Morton onward, can't stop confessing. Art Pepper filled an excellent documentary and autobiography with loving nostalgia for his years as a junkie and criminal, as if talking about heroin served as a substitute for shooting it. Baker was still using the stuff, practically to the day he died, and thus had no need to talk about it.

Some critics seemed almost to resent his success—perhaps because he became a star in the big, mainstream world beyond jazz even before the jazz community had given him its seal of approval. Early writings about Baker try to impose a sense of guilt upon him, claiming that his "flaw was tragic in the classical sense" or that he was "fighting a losing battle with heroin." It wouldn't do to portray Baker for what he really was: a relatively happy, guilt-free junkie, one who, in terms of the quality and quantity (at least two hundred albums) of his recorded work, could hardly have been more productive. Nor did his art ever become complacent or stagnant: Baker was always eager to try new ideas, new combinations, and new compositions.

Playing or singing, Baker was a font of melody—he had more of it in him than virtually any other jazz instrumentalist or singer you could name—and he was more generous with it than most. Tunes of all sorts poured forth from his lips like water from a faucet. Improvising, Baker could simultaneously spin songlike lines that seem as fully developed as a Cole Porter song; singing or playing the written melody, Baker could put it over as movingly as Billie Holiday. His improvisations were so eminently singable that Susannah McCorkle even once put lyrics to his solo on "Look for the Silver Lining." Baker just stood back and let it flow out of him, with what seemed like precious little forethought or even practice. Never was a musician's passiveness such a positive component: It required no conscious effort either to create breathtaking solos or to maintain his identity in diverse contexts, whether as spare as the pianoless Gerry Mulligan Quartet or as overwhelming as a full symphony orchestra.

In a 1978 interview with Gudrun Endress of *Jazz Podium* magazine, Baker was asked how he was able to not think about all the "trouble" in his life when he was up on the bandstand trying to create beauty. "I just kind of had it in my head to try to put that part of me in a sort of unreachable place, you know?" Apparently, he never ran out of storage space in that unreachable place. Yet by all indications, his term for it was something of a misnomer—to Baker, the unreachable place was so easily within his grasp that he never once seemed to be reaching for it. Creativity and inspiration were almost always there and almost never failed him.

Baker didn't so much make records as permit others to make records of him. And records and records and records, from his first recorded appearance (with Charlie Parker) and his breakthrough to international acclaim (with Gerry Mulligan) to a March 1988 performance claiming to be *The Last Great Concert*. Just in the eighteen months between his death in Amsterdam (May 13, 1988) and the end of the eighties, dozens of Baker packages were released, a number that twenty years later continues to mushroom.

Where does Chet Baker's singing fit within his canon? It's a tricky question. When he first established himself as a singer, he was anointed the most outstanding instrumentalist-vocalist since Nat King

Cole and Louis Armstrong (presumably that includes Jack Teagarden and Fats Waller). As with Cole and Armstrong, there were ultimately two different audiences for his playing and his singing. And there's no predictable response to his music: Jazz critic Nat Hentoff, hardly a specialist in songs and singers, pooh-poohs Baker's vocalizing, whereas Rex Reed, who writes mainly about cabaret and musical theater (when he covers music rather than film), feels that Baker is one of the all-time great jazz singers. You would think their opinions would be exactly the reverse.

Baker's singing found favor especially among Brazilian instrumentalist-composers like João Gilberto and Antonio Carlos Jobim, who discovered in him a role model in the craft of singing without a trained voice, and in how to get so much music and emotion from an inversely proportioned vocal instrument. Much of his audience wanted to hear him sing as much as they came to hear him play, yet he made surprisingly few vocal albums, especially in the later period, when someone was recording him almost weekly.

He was widely perceived as a creature of pure feeling and of pure instinct rather than of musical technique, and indeed he was not a schooled musician. As Dexter Gordon observed, Baker didn't know the first thing about what key he was supposed to be playing in, "but when he started playing, it was so natural and so beautiful." Drummer Larry Bunker once told Ted Gioia how Baker would struggle with trying to read one of collaborator Gerry Mulligan's orchestrations. "'I don't know the chord changes,' he'd say, but Gerry would correct him, 'You know the changes, you just don't know their names.'"

To begin with, there's the very matter of being able to play the trumpet at all. This is surely the most demanding of instruments—there are no garage brass bands—and properly improvising a jazz trumpet solo takes considerably more training than learning how to walk a tightrope. Yet Baker's fans preferred to see him as an untutored philosopher. To a certain degree, this was in accord with Baker's own manipulation of his image and sound; the way he played and the way he lived were embodiments of pure passion. "I play every set as if it were the final one," he once said. "I don't have too much time left, and it's important to show the musicians I'm playing with—more than anybody else—that I give everything I've got in me."

Chesney Henry Baker was born in the Oklahoma Dust Bowl on the eve of the Depression (in fact, shortly after the Wall Street crash), on December 23, 1929. At the start of the war, his family relocated to Glendale, California, where his father worked in the Lockheed plant, allowing Baker to grow up in the jazz scene of Los Angeles. His father was a semiprofessional musician, his mom was a classic stage mother who encouraged him to sing, which he did, starting around the age of eleven or twelve. "She'd drag me around to amateur contests that they had in L.A. I had to compete with girls playing accordion or tap-dancing. I never won. Even at that time I was singing the current ballads." His father (who had played guitar in hillbilly bands back in Oklahoma) was a jazz fan who encouraged him to play the trombone in the manner of his idol, Jack Teagarden. His arms, however, weren't long enough to reach all the positions, so little Chettie had to settle for the trumpet.

Between the ages of thirteen and sixteen, Baker learned his horn. By 1946, when he reached sixteen, he was playing so well that when he joined the service and was shipped to occupied Berlin, he was proficient enough to join the post band. Upon returning home, Baker, who was still only eighteen, attended El Camino College in Los Angeles courtesy of the GI Bill. He stayed for only two years, which included the only formal musical training he ever had, and then officially flunked. (The lack of compositional training partially explains why, virtually alone among major modern jazzmen, Baker composed next to nothing.)

He reenlisted in 1950, and by now was playing at a level where he could join a more prestigious army orchestra based in San Francisco. He was also by now comfortable enough with his playing to sit in at several local clubs. According to discographer Thorbjorn Sjogren, in the second year of his second hitch (1951–52), Baker was transferred to a post in the middle of the Arizona desert. Since there were no clubs for him to play in after hours there, he contrived to get out of the army on a psychiatric discharge, and he returned to Los Angeles a professional jazz musician.

His first important job upon coming home was with Charlie Parker (he later paid homage to Bird by recording Parker's intro to "All the Things You Are"). The legendary Bird had apparently run out of trumpet players and was actually holding auditions among West Coast brassmen; after Baker played (a story Baker himself told and which Jim Gavin questions in his recent biography, *Deep in a Dream*), Parker stopped the audition and hired him on the spot. The gig with Parker's quintet was brief, but the two were documented playing together in a privately recorded jam session in spring 1952.

However, a few weeks later—in July—Baker began appearing with the group that would make him into a jazz celebrity, the legendary Gerry Mulligan pianoless quartet. Within a short while, the combination of Mulligan (baritone sax), Baker (trumpet), and bass and drums was the hottest new thing in jazz. This was the most striking jazz ensemble almost since the beginning of the music not to use a piano or guitar or other conventional chordal instrument, and its absence seemed to make the interplay between Mulligan's baritone saxophone and Baker's trumpet even more intense. As marvelous a soloist as Mulligan was, he was primarily a composer and bandleader, whereas Baker was purely a player and improviser. Even as soloists, they were perfectly balanced. Mulligan was a creature of intellect, a thinking man's jazz musician, studied and articulate. Baker, by contrast, was nature's wild child.

The original Mulligan quartet with Baker enjoyed, essentially, one very good year, from July 1952 to June 1953, in which they recorded prolifically, the high point being an inspired series of sessions in which the quartet became a quintet thanks to the addition of the brilliant Lee Konitz. Yet even at the height of the group's unprecedented success there were signs it wasn't going to last forever. As archivist James Harrod has established, Baker first recorded with his own quartet as early as the end of 1952; yet when Mulligan was incarcerated for drug use (Baker was later to follow his example), the initial idea was to keep the quartet going with tenor colossus Stan Getz in Mulligan's place (a fascinating series of live recordings that were finally issued in the late nineties). However, probably even before the Baker-Getz date, the trumpeter had recorded again with his own group, and the Baker quartet with Russ Freeman made its official concert debut in August.

The emergence of the Baker quartet is important to his singing career, because it's only when Baker began to be featured as the leader of his own groups that he began singing—on records at least. Between October 27, 1953, and July 1956, Baker recorded the essential twenty vocal tracks of his career, all with his original quartet featuring pianist Russ Freeman. If Baker had never opened his mouth again, he still would be regarded as one of the best of all jazz singers.

These vocal cuts, all collected on the early CD *Let's Get Lost: The Best of Chet Baker Sings* (released within a year of Baker's death), have been issued and reissued in various forms and the collection remains the definitive compilation of Baker's singing. There are a few additional vocal items, including two more World Pacific (now Blue Note) discs, that go up and down in ensemble size. *Grey December* contains four 1954 tracks of Baker singing with strings, and *Embraceable You*, a 1957 date not released until 1995, has Baker playing and singing with very spare bass and guitar accompaniment. There are also two exceptional post-Pacific albums of his singing: *Chet Baker Sings It Could Happen to You* (Riverside, 1958) and *Baker's Holiday: Chet Baker Plays and Sings Billie Holiday* (Limelight, 1965).

Baker's trumpet playing spills over with virtuosity. It's been pointed out that he doesn't have the amazing range of Dizzy Gillespie or the raw power of Clifford Brown, but he can improvise deftly on all kinds of chord changes from blues to standards, he can read off a complicated piece of music like the four compositions by Bob Zieff he recorded in 1957, he can hit a million notes in a bar, and he can play a tricky tongue-twister like Russ Freeman's "Maid in Mexico," which requires him to zip through one fast

run after another in a swinging, Latin tempo. Baker is without question a great modern jazz trumpeter, worthy of being mentioned in the same breath with Miles Davis and Art Farmer.

In contrast, as a singer he seems to have no technique whatsoever, and yet this state of being completely natural is something he had to carefully cultivate. Baker's singing has also been described as sexually ambiguous; like Jimmy Scott's, his voice could either be high male or low female, somewhere between tenor and contralto, and there's never an attempt to sound cocky or masculine. He sounds so passive, so vulnerable—even more so than the young Sinatra; one imagines that women must primarily have wanted to mother him. And it had to have helped that unlike Jimmy Scott, and perhaps even more than Sinatra, he had poster-boy looks. As with Julie London, one wonders if he would have made it in the 78 rpm singles era. Surely those very appealing pictures of Chettie by Bill Claxton on all those big 12" LP jackets really helped move product. For men, Baker is an object of identification—I listen to these records and part of my brain thinks "If only I could be that talented, that irresistible, that unspeakably cool." For women, Baker is an object of desire, both romantic and maternal.

Baker is essentially a modern jazz musician: His solos are bebop solos that use bebop harmonies and bebop rhythm, his drummers use the cymbals more than the bass drum. Yet at the same time there's something fundamentally traditional about him, starting with, as we have seen, the whole idea of the horn-playing leader as singing entertainer, like Satchmo. His repertoire as a singer is fundamentally songs that were at least a decade old—the newest song on *Let's Get Lost* is "I've Never Been in Love Before," from the 1950 *Guys and Dolls*. More important, though Baker and the quartet may be playing bebop time, they've kept everything more than danceable.

There's a funny moment on the group's 1954 concert at Ann Arbor, Michigan, in which Baker, apparently in answer to a genuine request, informs the crowd, "We don't play 'In the Mood.'" But what they play is no less appealing to dancers and listeners who may not be hard-core jazz concertgoers. "But Not for Me" is a fast dance, "The Thrill Is Gone" is a slow dance, but there's nothing here that a clinging couple couldn't keep time to. "That Old Feeling" and "But Not for Me" even start out with the verses, played instrumentally and in swinging dance time. "But Not for Me," even more than "My Funny Valentine," may be the quintessentially perfect Baker vocal record. Starting with the verse in swing time, there's a pause before he enters singing the chorus. Both the vocal and the trumpet passages restore to the song the comic irony that was originally its birthright. The intentions of Baker and the composers, the Gershwin brothers, are surprisingly in step. George and Ira wrote it as a torch song with a comic underbelly; that's how Ginger Rogers performed it in the original 1930 *Girl Crazy*, and how underaged impressionist Mitzi Green belted it, doing a wry parody of Bing Crosby, in the only memorable moment in the dreadful 1932 film of that show. By the time Judy Garland sang it in the superior 1943 adaptation, despite Miss Garland's own verdant wit, "But Not for Me" was primarily a torch song, and even its many funny lines were meant to sound disconsolate.

Yet Baker reinfuses "But Not for Me" with self-deprecating humor. The message of both the playing and singing would seem to be: Even if your heart is breaking, don't take yourself too seriously. The trumpet solo, while intricate and boppy, is also as relentlessly cheerful as any Pollyanna. The two 16-bar halves of the chorus solo (as opposed to the verse solo that opens the disc) are separated by what could be called a "false modulation," in which Baker brightens his tone in a way that suggests raising a half-step without actually going there. Pianist Russ Freeman, not just Baker's accompanist but also his musical director and even co-leader, catches the mood perfectly with Erroll Garner–like ebullience, propelled by Bob Nell's Shelly Mannely brushwork before Baker reenters right at that precisely perfect part of the beat in the middle of a stop time break for the "out" half-chorus. It's surely one of the most rewarding ways to spend 180 seconds that I can think of.

The music is not only danceable but lyrical as well. The two aren't always the same thing—both Count Basie and Bill Evans (who only crossed paths once with Baker, on the 1958 album *Chet*) represent one but not necessarily the other. In a 1959 interview conducted in Florence, Baker pooh-poohed the nascent strain of modern jazz that was then beginning to be known as hard bop. According to Baker (who would certainly cut some fairly hard music himself in the company of Johnny Griffin and George Coleman), this new stuff "could only be appreciated by a very few people" and he thought that people would continue to like Chet Baker–style music "because it is more lyrical." In his view, his own music came more directly out of Charlie Parker and the original bop of the forties: "The old bop was profoundly lyrical. And also it was like a fountain springing continuously, an uninterrupted musical flood, easy to follow."

Baker's singing is, from the first note, utterly disarming. Yes, you can qualify a word like "disarming"—it may be true that either it is or it isn't, but some things are more disarming than others, and Baker's singing is one of them. He seems so devoid of pretense, so direct in his emotion (or sometimes even his lack of emotion), the singing seems so what-he-is. His pared-down technical machinery at times suggests a hip Alfalfa—he of "Our Gang"/"Little Rascals" fame—a little kid from a more innocent time singing grown-up songs, not screeching (like Alfalfa himself) but playing boy crooner, cooing up to the mike and making believe he's Bing or Frankie. Like a little girl putting on her mother's formal gown, the precious precociousness of it all is what makes Baker so endearing. He's not only deep and romantic—or, as on "My Buddy," swinging—he's cute, like a puppy or a kitten.

Many consider the initial phase of Baker's popularity—the years 1952–1957—when he recorded for Pacific, the height of his career. It is perhaps the greatest period of consistently excellent work, particularly when one factors in the material he recorded with Mulligan. The vocals in particular are pristine and perfect in these years, and consistent in quantity and quality. It's kind of a mystery why Baker recorded so few vocals over the years; out of the two hundred or so albums believed to exist, not more than five or so are primarily vocal. Even when, in his early live recordings, he performs his signature song, "My Funny Valentine," it's usually the instrumental arrangement, similar to the way he recorded it with Mulligan, rather than the vocal treatment he had recorded with his own quartet. In the 1960s, various record labels had him record anonymous dreck like *Blood, Chet and Tears,* and ten years later, label hacks made him do all-star dreck like *You Can't Go Home Again.* Both generations of hacks were trying to elicit a "commercial" product from Chet. If they had merely recorded a few inexpensive sessions of him singing and playing standards with a rhythm section, they would have produced masters of genuine commercial worth that would have been bringing back dividends decade after decade.

Baker's biography in the years following his "discovery" is better laid out in geographical terms: When was he in Europe? When was he in America? Baker toured the United States for the first time with his own group in 1954 with Russ Freeman, and while in Boston he met a brilliant young pianist (a gig documented on *Chet Baker, Boston, 1954* on Uptown Records) named Richard Twardzik. It's Twardzik who accompanies Baker on his first tour of Europe, or rather who starts the journey, because by the time the group finishes what has since become the longest-ever tour of Europe by an American band, the pianist has died of an overdose.

Rather than learning from Twardzik's example, it's when the band returns home to the States that Baker starts using heroin himself. At the same time, he forms another very strong working group of his own featuring Phil Urso on tenor and introducing Bobby "Moanin' " Timmons on piano, and in addition to recording with that group makes all kinds of interesting dates for Pacific with everything from a trio to a big band to an inspired team-up with Art Pepper and a reunion with Gerry Mulligan. In New York in 1958 and 1959, he makes four outstanding albums for producer Orrin Keepnews and Riverside Records, including one of his best vocal albums, *It Should Happen to You.* By the time he arrives back in Europe in 1959, he's a confirmed addict, a fact the

Italian authorities can't ignore. He is detained in an Italian prison from 1960 to 1962. Among other indignities, the guards subject him to repeated requests for "Cherry Pink and Apple Blossom White."

But despite his run-in with the European penal system, in light of what happened in America, he would have been much better off remaining far away from home in the late sixties. In the States, he is stuck recording jazz-Muzak treatments of contem-pop hits by the Lovin' Spoonful, the Beatles, and the Tijuana Brass—not to mention *Blood, Chet and Tears*. Worst of all, he is the victim of a mob hit—when he neglects to pay for his habit, he isn't killed but after the crap is beaten out of him, his teeth are scattered all over the Bay Area. It will be four years before Baker, who is not yet forty, gets a set of dentures and begins to play again.

It was Dizzy Gillespie who helped him get his "comeback" gig, at New York's Half Note Club in July 1973. He spends the next fifteen years working and recording prolifically, mostly in Europe, occasionally in New York, and on one rewarding occasion in Tokyo. "I work for a lot less than most people," he says, "but then again, I work a lot more." He sings in many concerts, and plenty of later live recordings have been issued commercially. There's no shortage of Baker vocals from 1973 to 1988, but there are very few projects that spotlight his singing in a focused way.

While Baker experimented with dozens of new instrumental compositions in these years, he stuck to a considerably smaller repertoire of vocal numbers—lots of "My Funny Valentine" and "But Not for Me." The major exception to this rule is "Almost Blue," by rock-pop singer-songwriter Elvis Costello. Costello didn't write this specifically for Baker, but by the time the trumpeter was finished with it, he might as well have had.

The visually stunning *Let's Get Lost* was released shortly after Baker's death, and did much to serve the cause of those who loved to look at Chet Baker, from the proto-cool hunk of the early fifties to the withered shell of the late eighties, and listen to him sing (even if his image received more attention than his music). That movie brought Baker's name to countless new lips and afforded further commercial credibility to the cottage industry that issuing Chet Baker records soon became. These were also the early years of the compact disc, and due to these various factors, the recently deceased trumpeter-singer was one of the more prolific recording artists of the late eighties and early nineties.

Baker's final recording is believed to be *My Favorite Songs: The Last Great Concert* (a two-CD package from Enja), from Amsterdam, on April 28, 1988. However, although it was taped only two weeks before his death, because so many new Baker discs constantly spill forth from Europe and Japan, one never knows what the "last" concert may turn out to be. (As of 2010, nothing has been released from the final weeks of Baker's life—between April 28 and May 13—at least according to Tom Lord's *Jazz Discography*.) If the "last" part of the title is up for grabs, however, the "great" moniker indisputably applies: Alternating between a twenty-piece jazz big band for up-tempos and blues and a full symphony with strings for the ballads, the album captures some of Baker's most poignant playing.

Leave it to Baker to climax the concert—and with it, his entire career—not with the loudest or most dramatic moment, but with the most lyrical. On his final vocal on the song that made his initial reputation, "My Funny Valentine," Baker not only sustains one note (on pitch) for so long it puts the lie to the idea that he had no technique, but exposes so much tenderness and pathos that he couldn't possibly fail to break the heart of anyone listening.

What exactly happened that morning in Amsterdam, Friday the 13th of May, 1988? Shortly after Baker's death, Bruce Weber visited that balcony, and in his opinion, it would have been impossible for anyone to have simply fallen off it—even someone stoned (and the autopsy revealed that Baker was—for once—not), and especially someone who was stoned more often than not. Weber also feels that suicide was unlikely: He never detected any suicidal vibe from Baker in all the time they spent together, and his feeling is that if Baker had decided to end his own life, he would have done it in some sort of spectacularly dramatic fashion—something, say, involving a motorcycle. The only explanation, Weber feels, is that some drug dealer, of the same sort that deprived Baker of his teeth twenty years earlier, sent him flying off that balcony—and into the ages—as payment for an uncollected debt. Jim Gavin, in his definitive biography, *Deep in a Dream*, makes the educated guess that Baker deliberately jumped.

Who knows? Chance is the fool's name for fate. Black's white today and day's night today: that fall, paradoxically, elevated Baker to a whole new level of "lost," sending him out even further beyond the reach of those guardians of standards and boundaries, both musical and moral, who could never quite entreat Chet Baker to stay, little valentine, stay.

Tony Bennett (born 1926)

Tony Bennett is the Pangloss of pop. The spirit of Dr. Pangloss, that learned pedagogue who taught the title character of Voltaire's *Candide* that we are living in "the best of all possible worlds," pervades Bennett's outlook on many levels. It is a guiding force, to begin with, in his interpretation of the songs themselves. "Who Can I Turn To?," lyrics by Leslie Bricusse and music by Anthony Newley, who introduced it in the London musical *The Roar of the Greasepaint, the Smell of the Crowd*, is a pretty bleak message. As sung by Newley in the show, the title isn't so much a question and the message is more like "there is no one to whom I can turn." Set in a roughly ABAB construction, the song doesn't have one note of optimism until the second half begins, at which point Bennett comes to the words "And maybe tomorrow . . ." It's only a brief section, following which the text goes back to dwelling on the darkness.

But this, for Bennett, is by far the most important part of the song; hearing him sing it, you wouldn't necessarily think it's cheerful or upbeat—there's nothing Pollyanna about Bennett—but it's uplifting. He also makes the song into more of a declarative statement than a question. His message is "I can turn to *you*." He manages to find the one major chord in a sea of all minor, and make that the most important part of the piece: "Maybe tomorrow, I'll find what I'm after." In Bennett's music, anything is possible, hope is never lost.

The Panglossian spirit also influences Bennett's large-scale view of his own life and career. From the beginning, when he first decided to try his luck as a popular singer as a teenager, Bennett has consistently proved that by giving the world the best performances of the best songs, he can touch the hearts of all who listen to him. And through this miraculous process, both the singer and the sung to are elevated. The better we communicate, the better we can understand each other, and the more we pursue excellence in our lives, the better things become. If you know anything about Tony Bennett, you know this: He truly believes in his heart of hearts that Cole Porter and Duke Ellington can save the world.

Bennett continued to put on a happy face even when, in the late seventies, his career underwent a major derailment when he became involved in a disastrous record venture that it took him years to buy his way out of. Fortunately, by the early eighties, partly through the efforts of his son Danny Bennett who took over as his manager at this time, Bennett Senior was back on his feet again. At this point, Tony could have played it safe: He had standing offers to work for as many weeks a year as he wanted in Las Vegas and Atlantic City. But he couldn't be content to continue preaching to the converted—in other words to go on concentrating on his traditional Tony Bennett market, those middle-aged fans who had been following him since "I Left My Heart in San Francisco" in 1962 or even "Because of You" in 1952. Rather, he wanted to reach the widest possible audience—not just his traditional followers, but their kids. Bennett is like the baby who can fly because he refuses to believe that it's impossible.

That he even thought he could do so was a strictly Panglossian conceit. Only in the best of all possible worlds would it be possible—after forty-five years of the singer-songwriters, hillbillies, British invaders, hard rockers, metallic rockers, punkers, and disco dancing queens who have dominated popular music for most of Bennett's life (his breakthrough hit happened only five years before Elvis). The idea that someone who sang the great show tunes of the Eisenhower era and earlier could compete with heavy metal and rap would have previously seemed fodder for one of those rapidly aging comics who opened for Sinatra, somewhere between the jokes about mothers-in-law and impotence.

But people who thought that way didn't reckon with the power of the Panglossian attitude that suggests that if you present people with the best music, a significant percentage of them will respond to it and flock to it. Some people (even some people who have worked with Bennett) believe in the lowest common denominator mentality, which postulates that no one ever went broke underestimating the taste of the average Joe. Some people are happy thinking that the only kind of culture that the great unwashed American public can accept is crap. But some people ain't Tony Bennett.

The key difference between Bennett and Pangloss is that the latter is ultimately exposed as a naïf and even a figure of ridicule. Voltaire uses the good doctor to make his point that the world is not a reasonable, rational place. In Bennett's universe, though, good things happen to good songs. Bennett, too, might seem naive if the world didn't keep proving him right, or had he not succeeded beyond his wildest dreams, giving him the opportunity to enjoy what Gary Giddins calls "the longest last laugh in history."

The supremacy of American music, Tony Bennett has repeatedly insisted, has been due to the dominance of two subcultures: black musicians and Jewish songwriters. There is yet a third group, one that he would seem to be deliberately omitting out of modesty. After Sinatra, Bennett is the greatest of the Italian-American popular singers who dominated American vernacular music after the war. The great Italian-American singers, almost exclusively male (unless you count Joni James or Connie Francis), however, are hardly a uniform species. The true forefather of the Italian school was actually Bing Crosby, who recorded albums of Irish, not Italian songs, and some of the greatest practitioners of the Italianate bel canto tradition were African Americans like Johnny Hartman and Billy Eckstine.

For all of its importance, music was hardly the only Italian tradition to impact upon Tony Bennett: There was also the Catholic Church. When we talk about the religious influence on American music, we're almost always referring to the stream of African American spirituals into gospel, blues, jazz, and eventually mainstream pop, or we're talking about composers like Duke Ellington, Mary Lou Williams, Dave Brubeck, or Leonard Bernstein who write music for church performance. For most of the twentieth century, many of the great black singers—from Dinah Washington and Sarah Vaughan on—evolved their styles out of the gospel and spiritual tradition. It stands to reason that Tony Bennett's music could also be, to a degree, shaped by his own religious experience.

Tony Bennett is the Sultan of Strain; where Crosby and Sinatra advocated a smooth, invisible vocal technique, Bennett, more like Sarah Vaughan, makes his breathing apparatus part of the act. Specifically, he takes the sound of himself straining, holding a note, almost extending to the point where it becomes a moan, and makes that beautiful. One obvious explanation for this approach is the impact on him of African American influences and the blues tradition (as well as the gospel tradition). But it also seems as if Bennett's straining and moaning are part of his own religious experience, out of the chanting practiced in the Catholic Mass.

Another one of the key features of his music is his penchant for big endings. This is one element that keenly distinguishes him from Frank Sinatra, who preferred to climax most songs about 80 percent of the way through, with maybe two or three lines to go, and then end softly and subtly. Bennett likes to go out with a big, boffo ending. This is partly the influence of Judy Garland, a singer who meant as much to him as anyone. But when one listens to him doing the ending of "How Do You Keep the Music Playing," you hear it all at once, the unbelievably big ending, with Bennett straining and belting for what seems like an eternity. It's not merely that he makes straining and belting sound beautiful, which indeed he does, but it's part of his way of achieving a catharsis with his audience. In a traditionally Catholic way, every time Bennett does one of those amazing, gut-busting ballads, he is, in a sense, symbolically dying and being resurrected. Steve Lawrence once pointed out that every Sinatra performance is like a three-act drama with a beginning, a middle, and an end; each Bennett ballad is more like a passion play, in more than one sense of the term.

It was around the time of Bennett's seventieth birthday, during the waning months of station WQEW, the last gasp of intelligent pop music in traditional radio broadcasting (in New York, at least), that the question was asked, "What is it that makes Tony Bennett so special?" "Apart from his great voice, his warmth and his swinging style," the answer came back, "I think what makes Bennett great is the way he simultaneously embodies two distinct kinds of musical cultures. On the one hand, he celebrates the jazz tradition, from Louis Armstrong and Miles Davis on down. Yet at the same time he's also Mr. Show Business, the living heir to such greats as Judy Garland and Jimmy Durante. There's no one who lives up to either heritage—let alone both—as wonderfully as Bennett." Shortly afterward, Danny Bennett was asked the same question—and his answer was remarkably similar: "Tony is the only artist who's a jazz singer and a pop singer at the same time. You can say that Sinatra is a pop singer with some jazz in him, or that Mel Tormé is a jazz singer with a pop side, but Tony's the only artist who's always both pop and jazz."

How fortunate for us, then, that historical circumstances dovetailed with Bennett's own ambition to mold him into the perfect representative of both cultures. Tony Bennett was born in the perfect place—Astoria, New York City—and time (August 3, 1926)—to absorb all the right influences. As a child he studied and absorbed the high styles, one by one, of the three great male singers who preceded him: the bravura of Al Jolson, the easy swing of Bing Crosby, the sensitivity of Frank Sinatra. His sister, Mary, told a story about how, at the beginning of the "Sinatrauma" movement, she once made a disparaging comment about the Voice and how Tony, who was about fourteen or fifteen at the time, proceeded to give her a lecture about what made Sinatra so great in specific, technical terms: breath control, timing, and so forth. Barely a teenager, he was already taking the craft of popular and jazz singing very seriously.

In 1944, Bennett reached draft age and went through some of the most disturbing experiences of his life during World War II, first as a foot soldier in the Battle of the Bulge, then as one of the GIs sent to flush Nazi soldiers out of their hiding places as the invading Allies came through, then as part of the forces that liberated the concentration camps. The upshot was that after VE Day, the army allowed him to pursue his musical leanings. In addition to his knowledge of the great pop singers, Bennett also was a child of the big band era. In fact, it wasn't until he sang with the 314th Infantry Orchestra (a successor to the famous Glenn Miller AAF Orchestra) over the armed forces network in occupied Germany that the young singer enjoyed what could be considered his first extended professional engagement. (Also his first recording: An aircheck survives of the very young Bennett singing "St. James Infirmary Blues" with the 314th Infantry band.)

By a coincidence, most of his early professional engagements involved famous black swing musicians. Before the war, he sang very briefly with altoist Earle Warren, well known for his years with Count Basie, and after the war, he worked as a singing waiter in an Astoria emporium that featured future Ellingtonian Tyree Glenn (vibes and trombone). He spent the immediate postwar period assembling all the elements necessary to launch his professional career and make the bells ring for him. He studied music and theater (courtesy of the GI Bill), auditioning all over the place and singing in any joint that would let him near the microphone.

In these years Bennett began working with his first manager, Ray Muscarella, and his piano-playing alter ego, Tony Tamburello, who became Tony B's musical director and coach, and reinforced Tony's own determination to concentrate only on songs of the highest quality. In 1949, Bennett, who for a brief while worked under the name of Joe Bari, made his first recording—for a very short-lived label named Leslie Records. The disc itself, produced by critic George Simon, has not been heard or seen in more than sixty years, although a collector on the West Coast claims to have a copy.

Bennett landed his first big break when he had the opportunity to appear with entertainer Pearl Bailey at a nightclub in Greenwich Village. While there, he was heard by comedy superstar Bob Hope, who helped him pick his stage name and invited him to join his troupe for a tour that started at Manhattan's celebrated Paramount Theatre. His recording career began in earnest when, in 1950, he began singing a rather melodramatic Harry Warren tango (introduced by nonsinging movie star Constance Bennett—coincidentally—in a 1933 picture called *Moulin Rouge*) titled "Boulevard of Broken Dreams." The twenty-three-year-old Bennett gave it a belting, dramatic rendition. When a demo of Tony doing the song found its way into the hands of Mitch Miller, the newly appointed head of pop singles for Columbia Records, the bearded producer signed him sight unseen to a year-long contract. In April 1950, Bennett made his first commercial recording for Columbia, with Marty Manning arranging and conducting a more polished reading of "Boulevard of Broken Dreams."

A year later, however, as Tony tells the story, he still hadn't made much money for the label, not yet having landed any kind of hit record of consequence, and was in danger of being dropped. Almost randomly, maestro Percy Faith picked "Because of You" for him, a song by Oscar Hammerstein's uncle, Arthur, better known as a Broadway producer from the early years of the century. "Because of You" was the breakthrough hit that Bennett, Miller, and Columbia had been waiting for, and it at last established Bennett as one of the biggest names in the music business. He was twenty-four years old.

Getting to the top was hardly easy, yet staying there was harder: Even in his first twelve months of glory, Columbia tried to upstage him with two other megablockbusters, "Come on-a My House" by friend Rosemary Clooney and "Cry" by then rival Johnny Ray. Yet for Bennett, "Because of You" was only the beginning: The early fifties saw "Cold, Cold Heart," "Rags to Riches," "Stranger in Paradise," and other chart hits. Today, he doesn't like the sound of his voice on his early records, and beyond a few hits hasn't approved any of his fifties singles for rerelease. Which is a shame, because although the early singles are not a patch on what he would achieve from the mid- to late fifties onward, the great albums and the mature hits, they are important documents of the beginnings of a great American artist, and they deserve to be heard.

Even as Bennett was racking up hit after hit, he was never completely at ease in the role of pop star. Teenage girls were putting his picture under their pillows and swooning over him as they had with Sinatra a decade earlier. But, like Sinatra, Bennett wanted to be something more. He found himself frequently at odds with his producer, Mitch Miller, who had specific ideas as to the kind of songs the singer should be recording, whereas Tony had his own plans. Miller had a proven track record with songs that many considered novelties and gimmicks, while Bennett insisted on singing material that meant something to him: first-class show tunes, songs by quality composers. He wasn't going to waste his breath on anything but the best. Occasionally, Miller would get his way and twist Bennett's arm until he agreed to do a goofy novelty (among them two sticky-sweet pieces, the quasi-R&B "Cinnamon Sinner" and Ervin Drake's mockalypso "Shoo-Gah"). However, Bennett gives credit to Miller for bringing him "Rags to Riches" (by future Broadway princes Richard Adler and Jerry Ross) and "Cold, Cold Heart" (the first time a country song became a mainstream hit). Bennett acknowledges that Miller was right about these, but what matters to him is not that they were hits, but that they were great songs. "We were always fencing," he said. "I always had the sword out."

Another area where Bennett and Miller were "always fencing" was on the subject of albums. Back then, the producer felt that albums by pop singers were a waste of time; they were strictly something for classical artists, and not enough people in the country actually owned long-playing phonographs to make them worthwhile. By the start of the 12" LP era, in 1954, Columbia lagged behind the competition in this regard; Capitol Records was releasing albums by Sinatra and Nat Cole, and Bennett wanted to catch up. He also intended to use the album format to expand beyond pop into the realm of jazz singing. The result was the 1954 *Cloud 7*, which was both his first original album and his first foray into small-group jazz settings. *Cloud 7* is the earliest recording of Tony, other than one or two of the better early hits, that the singer professes to actually like, and it was finally reissued on CD in 2004.

By the late fifties, Bennett was concentrating on albums, almost all of which had a jazz bias. *The Beat of My Heart* (1957), for instance, was notable as the only instance in which a major pop (and increasingly jazz) singer such as Bennett recorded an album based on percussion and emphasized the different approaches to swinging rhythm, as varied as Candido and Art Blakey. *Beat of My Heart* was also Bennett's first notable collaboration with British-born modern jazz pianist Ralph Sharon, who would serve as his musical director for most of his career. Over the course of their first stretch together (1957 to 1965), Bennett would make two other classic albums that focused on Sharon's keyboard work, *Tony Sings for Two* (recorded 1959, released 1961), a superlative collection of duets, and *When Lights Are Low* (1964), an even better pairing of him with his regular working trio led by Sharon. (Bennett and Sharon recorded a number of extra tracks for both albums, and some of the trio leftovers were used on the LP *A Time for Love*. These albums scream for a definitive CD reissue.)

Most of the full orchestra albums also have a definite jazz angle: *Tony* (1956), which I like even better than *Cloud 7*, gathered first-rate standard songs with charts by such luminaries of jazz orchestration as Neal Hefti, Marion Evans, and Gil Evans. On the surface, *Hometown, My Town* (1959) was a concept album of songs meant to reflect the glory and splendor of New York, even though only a couple ("Penthouse Serenade" and Gordon Jenkins's "Skyscraper Blues") were songs that specifically referred to New York. Yet *Hometown* was also a decidedly experimental package, centered on extra-long tracks and extra-lavish accompaniments from an extra-large orchestra (thirty years earlier it would have been called "symphonic jazz"). It was superbly arranged by Ralph Burns, who performed the same chore equally well on the more conventionally jazzy *My Heart Sings* (1961), another sublimely swinging set of standards with big band.

Then, too, there are Bennett's two albums with Count Basie, the Count's first full-length collaborations with a headlining vocalist: *In Person! With Count Basie* (1958) and *Bennett-Basie: Strike Up the Band* (1959), both largely arranged by Sharon and Marion Evans. The first was originally intended as a double whammy, not only combining Bennett with Basie, but capturing the singer for the first time in front of a live audience. According to Bennett, Columbia taped him and the band in mono at the Latin Casino, Philadelphia, but producer Al Hamm decided he wanted a stereo album, so he rerecorded the tracks in the Columbia studio with a small crowd applauding and cheering. The tracks have been released both with and without the crowd noises, but it's an exceptional package either way, climaxing in Sharon's marvelously up-tempo orchestration of "Lullaby of Broadway," with its famous vamp.

The second Basie album is perhaps even better. Mitch Miller, who still ran the show at Columbia Pop, was opposed to the enterprise, mainly because Basie was under contract to Roulette and the deal meant that the second Bennett-Basie had to be on Roulette. Yet the Basie influence is a key component of Bennett's musical makeup, manifesting itself in his flawless sense of dynamics. No one, not even Sinatra, has made greater use of the dramatic possibilities inherent in loud and soft: how he can do a whole number exceedingly sweetly, sotto voce, or use his soft voice for most of a song, and then Pow! Bam! Zonk! Some of his best concert specialties of the last twenty years have been based purely on dynamic expression, like "A Foggy Day" and "Speak Low." If you've ever heard the famous Basie dynamics in action, as on Billy Byers's arrangement of "All of Me," you'll know where Bennett gets his capacity for whispers and shouts.

Not all of Bennett's early albums were jazz projects: *Tony Bennett Sings a String of Harold Arlen* (1960) is a lush, semi-symphonic songbook built around Broadway's jazziest composer with arranger Abe "Glenn" Osser. There also were three pop albums with Frank DeVol using a rather insistent choral background: *Long Ago and Far Away* (1958), *Alone Together* (1960), and *To My Wonderful One* (also 1960). The last includes one of Tony's own favorite performances, his version of "September Song." The three DeVol albums are not the most exciting of his career, but they're consistent—which is more than can be said of many of his albums of the sixties.

Like Sinatra, Bennett has spent his career battling what has traditionally been perceived as the ephemeral nature—the planned obsolescence—of pop music. In the early fifties, it seemed for a brief while that he would be bypassed by Johnny Ray, before Bennett had that remarkable string of megahits from 1951 to 1954. In the late fifties, he had to worry about another Johnny-come-lately on Columbia, namely Mathis, who took most of the singles play away from him while he concentrated on classic albums. In the early sixties, the chief competition was no longer other traditional pop singers of his approximate generation, even though the dreaded Andy Williams was moving vinyl in quantities that were positively obscene. By now, Bennett and his generation were worried that the kiddie pop culture would start to overtake them as the record industry was beginning to have less and less use for traditional concepts like quality and durability.

It was then, with the barbarians about to cross the moat and ransack the castle, that Bennett fought back with his strongest suit yet: another, completely unanticipated, stream of boffo hit singles, delivered as a sort of eleventh-hour reprieve to stay the execution of quality pop. "The Best Is Yet to Come," originally written for Sinatra but by far the most successful of the many songs Bennett has sung by his close friend Cy Coleman; "I Wanna Be Around," a title and premise concocted by an amateur tunesmith from Ohio and fleshed out into pop song greatness by Johnny Mercer; two French imports, "The Good Life," a chanson delivered to Tony by song plugger Duke Niles, who found himself on Tony's A-list for the rest of his life, and "Watch What Happens," based on changes similar to "Take the A Train," and which cemented a solid relationship between Bennett and Michel Legrand, and later Allan and Marilyn Bergman; two West End–to–Broadway imports, "Who Can I Turn To" and "If I Ruled the World," both with lyrics by Leslie Bricusse. The latter two exemplified Bennett's long tradition of making hits of show tunes before the shows had even opened, from "Stranger in Paradise" (*Kismet*) to "Once Upon a Time" (*All American*), and "Love Look Away" (*Flower Drum Song*). In all, Bennett's was the first voice the world heard singing approximately fifty Broadway ballads that eventually became hits and standards.

Bennett's early career as a pop star climaxed in 1962, almost a decade after the naysayers would have left him for washed up, with "I Left My Heart in San Francisco." This was one of the biggest hits of the

Kennedy era, an early Grammy winner and probably the best-known performance of his sixty years in the music business. Ralph Sharon years before had actually stashed "San Francisco" in a clothing drawer underneath some shirts when he and Bennett were about to perform in the City by the Bay, and decided on the spur of the moment to take the tune with him. It got a favorable reaction in that town when Bennett and Sharon performed it, and the singer convinced Columbia to let him record the song, arguing that it had great possibilities as a regional, West Coast hit—at the very least. Both he and Columbia were completely unprepared for the runaway success of the single.

Right when "San Francisco" was at the top of the charts, Bennett became the first major male pop singer to do an entire evening at Carnegie Hall. The results were then issued as a two-LP set and eventually expanded to a very full two-CD package (released on the thirty-fifth anniversary in 1997). It's one of the most captivating two hours of music ever recorded, and a potent document of what Bennett's live appearances were like then. (As a concert performance, it was an anomaly: For another ten years his primary venues were large nightclubs like the Copa, the Waldorf-Astoria, and the various Vegas rooms. He would make the transition to formal concert halls beginning in the seventies.) *Tony Bennett at Carnegie Hall—The Complete Concert* climaxes with a spectacular showpiece, "De Glory Road," originally sung by Metropolitan Opera baritone Lawrence Tibbett and fashioned as a show-off piece for a virtuoso voice (such as Tibbett, Paul Robeson, or Bennett) out of elements of traditional Negro spirituals.

Thus Bennett was flying high in the mid-sixties. His mass-pop status was assured by all of his hits, but especially by "San Francisco." It became one of those songs that everybody knows, part of the collective consciousness, and audiences are just as likely to knock themselves out applauding for it (even though, unlike 99 percent of pop singles, it starts with an out-of-tempo verse) in Singapore, Moscow, or Florence, or even Brooklyn. Respect for Bennett as a serious artist was also accumulating, thanks both to the Carnegie concert and to a widely repeated pronouncement by Frank Sinatra. When the Chairman said that Bennett was the best singer around, nobody disagreed.

Yet there were dark clouds on the horizon. His first marriage was ending unpleasantly, and, culturally, inmates were now running the asylum. By this time, the tables had turned somewhat; ten years earlier, Bennett had to practically force Columbia to let him do a full-length album. By now, the corporation was releasing two or three Tony Bennett LPs a year. Paradoxically, however, where the pre-"San Francisco" albums were artfully crafted (even the compilations, like *Mr. Broadway*, had a deliberate theme to them), the mid- and late sixties albums were increasingly unfocused. Almost every year

brought a new volume of *Tony Bennett's Greatest Hits,* and even *Yesterday I Heard the Rain, I Gotta Be Me,* and *For Once in My Life* seemed somewhat randomly programmed, with various arrangers and conductors. Make no mistake, these are all terrific albums of wonderful songs, brilliantly sung and arranged, and that was already nothing to take for granted. But there's little rhyme or reason to most of his late sixties LPs; they don't lodge themselves in the memory as well as the great Sinatra concept albums or most of Bennett's earlier long-playing projects.

There were occasional coherent concept albums still, including two of his most beautiful: *The Movie Song Album* (1965), his last major project for fifteen years with Ralph Sharon, in which a gathering of the most distinguished composers in Hollywood—most notably Johnny Mandel—conducted Bennett in their own themes, and *Snowfall: The Tony Bennett Christmas Album,* his first meeting with Robert Farnon, the British "guv'nor" of "light music" (which compared to most pop is, indeed, pretty heavy). He also continued to craft outstanding collections of superior songs, in which he explores various moods with a single musical director, such as *Who Can I Turn To?* with George Siravo, *Tony Makes It Happen* with Marion Evans, and *Something* with Peter Matz.

By 1970, Bennett was competing at Columbia Records with Andy Williams and Johnny Mathis, who were, with Clive Davis's encouragement, making what was called middle-of-the-road or easy listening music, which wasn't all that different from the unobtrusive sounds that the Muzak corporation was already piping into supermarkets and elevators. A steady diet of Williams and Mathis could lead rock listeners and young people in general to regard all pre-rock pop as Muzak.

But if there's one thing that Bennett could never be, it was middle-of-the-road. Rock 'n' roll was supposed to be the music of rebellion, but the real rebels of American music were Artie Shaw, Frank Sinatra, and Tony Bennett, who continually bucked the status quo of the recording industry and stood up for what they believed in. Rather than capitulate, Bennett continually fought off the attempts by Clive Davis and the rest of the company's upper brass to transform him into an easy listening jukebox. With Mitch Miller, Bennett "always had the sword out"; with Davis, it was more like a bazooka.

The parting in 1971, after twenty years, between Bennett and Columbia Records was not, as is widely believed, the company's idea. Columbia, on the verge of ousting Davis, wanted him to stay. They still wanted him to record jukeboxy pop hits, but one way or another they wanted him on the label. Bennett elected to leave of his own accord after his contract expired. However, he ended his relationship with the label—for the time being—with two exceptionally beautiful albums, both recorded in London with Robert Farnon: the studio *Tony Bennett with*

Love and the live *Get Happy*, done with the Royal Philharmonic Orchestra at Albert Hall. For the next seven years or so he went on making records, first for MGM (the label formerly known as Verve) and producer (later turned politician) Mike Curb, then for his own boutique label, Improv Records. His work in the immediate post-Columbia period was of an extremely high caliber: In terms of his own vocals, he sounded better than ever—after twenty-five years at the top he had refined and polished his singing to an incredibly fine point. He also had the benefit of an extremely gifted musical director named Torrie Zito. Zito wrote hundreds of charts for Bennett at this time, most of which, unfortunately, were never documented in any form.

His orchestral albums from the seventies, from Columbia, MGM, and Improv, are generally overlooked. As it turns out, he did some of his very best work in this period, including first-rate albums with arrangers Farnon (*The Good Things in Life*, 1972), Don Costa (*Listen Easy*, 1973, marred only by the pretentious and overlong "Tell Her It's Snowing"), and Zito (*Life Is Beautiful*, 1975). The last, quite possibly the best of the bunch, is highlighted by an excellent title tune from habitual songwriter Fred Astaire, then Bennett's Hollywood neighbor (Tony lived in La La Land briefly in the mid-seventies, as a result of his disastrous second marriage, and the only thing he liked about being there was getting to spend time with Astaire). There's also an exquisite vocal version of the Ellington piano solo "Reflections."

The Improv period also signified the first occasion in over a decade on which Bennett had the opportunity to record with small groups. His two-LP (single-CD) *Rodgers and Hart Songbook* started life as a special concert at Lincoln Center. Beyond being notable as only Tony's second songbook package, this 1973 recording presented him in the most unusual setting of his career, a quartet of cornet, bass, and two guitars, led by Ruby Braff.

Bennett's other major small ensemble project of the era also resulted in two albums, his 1976 and 1977 meetings with Bill Evans. At the time, most of the world still regarded Bennett as a chart-topping pop singer with little connection to jazz—never mind those albums with Count Basie and many concerts with Duke Ellington. Evans was one of the supreme piano masters of modern jazz, a music that's supposed to be intellectual and, in Evans's case especially, introspective. Bennett is essentially an outwardly driven artist, the kind who would embrace the entire audience in his arms if he could; "gregarious" is one of his favorite terms of praise for people and it perfectly describes the singer himself. Evans, by further contrast, was so inwardly directed that our most famous mental image of the pianist has him bending his head into the keyboard as he plays, as if he wants to catch every single sound emanating from the instrument; it almost seems as if he

has forgotten the audience—not true, by the way—and has created a personal dialogue strictly between himself and the piano.

How to bridge this gap? Not surprisingly, Bennett and Evans find a common ground in their mutual love for the Great American Songbook and the jazz tradition, yet there's no attempt by Bennett to sound more "jazzy" than he does usually (he sounds considerably more swingingly jazzy—as the term usually is understood to mean—on *Beat of My Heart, Tony Makes It Happen,* the Basie albums, etc.). What one might not expect is that Bennett and Evans are further united by their mutual roots in the classical tradition: Bennett is a Verdi aria, Evans is a Chopin nocturne, yet they are fellow travelers on a long road of endless lyricism. I don't advise it, but if you were to pin Tony to the wall and make him name his favorite album ("San Francisco" would still reign as his favorite single), the two Evans albums *The Tony Bennett/Bill Evans Album* (1976) and *Together Again* (1977) would probably be his answer, and most of his fans would agree.

It was a fitting way for Bennett to climax the "classic" period of his career, although the major disappointment of said career is that it had to be ended at all. Bennett was never singing better than in his fifties, as surviving videos and concert tapes (none of which have been legally issued) testify, yet he barely entered a studio for that entire decade. He had other things on his mind in these years: He entered into a second messy divorce, his record company went bankrupt, and his career management was, to put it mildly, inadequate. He was working hard and continuing to earn top dollar playing the major rooms all over the world, but there was no one minding the store. In the early eighties, Bennett moved back to New York around the time that two people reentered his life and helped him get back on track: pianist Ralph Sharon, who climbed back on the piano bench as his musical director, and his son Danny Bennett as his manager.

From the beginning of their professional relationship, the Bennetts were very tightly focused on one goal: Tony wanted to bring the best music that he knew—the music that he had been singing all his life, the music of Gershwin and Basie, of Bobby Hackett and Cy Coleman—to the greatest number of people. The two Bennetts achieved this by gradually making Tony seem hip to the twentysomething and thirtysomething audience. He appeared on the MTV Music Video Award shows (in the company of the Red Hot Chili Peppers); he would do sets at alternative rock (a term that seems something of a misnomer) concerts; he appeared on *The Simpsons,* the David Letterman show, and every other TV series he could where Generation X, as it had recently been dubbed, was watching.

Yet he would have been unable to do any of this had his recordings not been gradually upgrading his profile. By 1985, the Bennetts had engineered a reunion with Columbia Records—a wise choice, considering that's where the bulk of his catalogue resided—and his first album in nearly a decade was the much anticipated *The Art of Excellence*, released in 1986. This was a pivotal recording, an outstanding collection of both swingers and ballads, not to mention those patented Tony Bennett medium tempos (like "City of the Angels," another Astaire original), and the seductive "What Are You Afraid Of?" *Excellence* is the album that was worth the wait, the one that made us fall in love with Tony Bennett all over again.

Bennett's albums over the last twenty-five-plus years have also been artful and excellent. Rather than exhaust my already overtaxed vocabulary of superlatives, let me just say that there's not a project from this period that's less than excellent. There are some I don't play as often as others, like his Irving Berlin centennial homage, *Bennett/Berlin* (1987), although the premise of both Dexter Gordon and Dizzy Gillespie guesting on a Bennett session is irresistible. Others I listen to so often that they've practically spent more hours in my CD player than on my shelves, like the 1989 *Astoria: Portrait of the Artist*, which weaves fourteen great songs into a de facto autobiography, much like friend Rosemary Clooney's later similar series of self-reflective albums on Concord; the 1998 *The Playground*, his only collection of children's songs; and 1999's *Hot and Cool: Bennett Sings Ellington*. The Berlin and Ellington sets represent his only composer-driven packages of the modern era; most of the other sets are tributes to various performers: Sinatra (*Perfectly Frank*, 1992), Astaire (*Steppin' Out*, 1993), Holiday (*Bennett on Holiday*, 1997), Armstrong (*A Wonderful World*, 2002), and the overall species of female singers (*Here's to the Ladies*, 1996).

Hot and Cool: Bennett Sings Ellington is my favorite Bennett record at least since *Astoria*— maybe since *Excellence*. Back in 1960, Bennett gave the semiclassical treatment to Tin Pan Alley's jazziest resident, Harold Arlen, and forty years later, he takes the works of jazz's leading composer and puts them into an unfamiliar context, a string orchestra (charts by Jorge Calandrelli, who has supplied most of Bennett's string writing since *Excellence*). Half of the album is done with a jazz big band, marking the last time Bennett would collaborate with Ralph Burns, who died two years later. "Do Nothin' Till You Hear from Me" is a minor miracle. Both of the two major Ellington–Bob Russell songs, "Don't Get Around Much Anymore" and "Do Nothin'," tend to be done as bright, upbeat bouncers, yet if you listen to the lyrics, they're actually quite morose. Bennett is one of the few who address the undercurrent of melancholy in "Do Nothin'," yet at the same time he turns it into a positive message. He's telling the object of his love, "You will never 'hear' any bad news from me because I will always love you."

The album that got the most attention, however, was Bennett's first live-in-concert project since 1971. As the singer was getting more and more attention at alternative rock concerts, his two albums of the early nineties, *Perfectly Frank* and *Steppin' Out*, were so successful that the whole music industry was taking notice. Pop singers of the pre-rock era weren't supposed to sell that many records to so many young people, especially if they sang only quality music and refused to cheapen their principles. Attention from MTV resulted in a Tony Bennett music video on "Steppin' Out with My Baby," written by Irving Berlin for Astaire in the 1948 *Easter Parade* and which Bennett used to honor both men. The video was so well received that MTV invited him to do an entry in its *Unplugged* series, a show normally reserved for superstar rock acts. Bennett's appearance, and the resultant album, were to be the most successful event in his entire career. Within a short while, the CD *Tony Bennett MTV Unplugged* had sold nearly a million copies and earned the Grammy for Best Album—not just best traditional pop album, a category that he generally won in the face of competition with Rosemary Clooney, but overall album of the year, the category that Michael Jackson, Bruce Springsteen, and Madonna competed in.

Around the same time, colleague and inspiration Frank Sinatra was attracting attention in the twilight of his career for his *Duets* albums, which can charitably be described as rehashes of his greatest hits with kiddie pop stars stitched in—many of whose fifteen minutes of fame seemed to be over even before the albums were released. What's remarkable about the Bennett MTV project isn't merely that Tony Bennett sold a million albums and won the big Grammy, but that he did it merely by being himself, by coming out with his trio—no additives—and singing the same songs he was singing every show for three or four nights a week, about forty-five or so weeks a year.

As it happens, two contemporary pop stars, k.d. lang, who sang beautifully, and Elvis Costello, who did not, joined Bennett on the MTV album, but these duets were merely the icing, not the cake itself. Bennett's 2001 *Playin' with My Friends: Bennett Sings the Blues* is a duet project, but one also done with considerably more class than the Chairman's comparable albums. Unlike Sinatra *Duets* and *Duets II*, Bennett's album is distinguished by three factors: one, that these are songs new to his career and not remakes of old hits; two, that these are real duets, with both performers in the studio at the same time; three, while I can't say that all the somewhat contemporary singer-songwriter types who share the mike with Bennett are to my personal liking, I do feel that all of them have earned the right to sing the blues with him—there are no embarrassments like Sinatra and Bono.

The best track on the album is one that he continues to perform as a solo on the road, "New York State of Mind" (I don't know about you, but I don't miss Billy Joel at all). Although Bennett hasn't actually landed any chart hit singles in the digital era, songs like "How Do You Keep the Music Playing" (*Excellence*) and "When Do the Bells Ring for Me" (*Astoria*) have become the equivalent of modern-day hit singles for him: the crowds cheer madly when he sings them, just as they do for "San Francisco" and "I Wanna Be Around." "New York State of Mind" shows every sign of becoming the latest of these—when he sings it, especially in the aftermath of 9/11, audiences react as though they are hearing a Tony Bennett classic. And, in fact, they are.

I mentioned Bennett's hiatus from recording from 1978 to 1985 as one of the major disappointments of his career. There's one other artistic catastrophe that's worth addressing here: only half a dozen of Bennett's classic albums of the fifties and sixties are in print on compact disc. As an artist, Bennett is in a class with Sinatra and Ella Fitzgerald—or something very near it—and like them, he deserves to have most if not all of his catalogue made available, even if briefly, in the CD era. I know it may be too much to expect Bennett himself to sanction the release of a complete recordings package—as has been done for the Columbia output of Sinatra, Clooney, and Doris Day. There are singles from the Mitch Miller era that he never wants to hear again. But though I don't care for "In the Middle of an Island" any more than he does, in this case I disagree with the artist himself in his decision to suppress large chunks of his own catalogue. The very few missteps he made should be heard if only because of the way they illuminate the great records that constitute the vast majority of his output.

Regardless of what one thinks of the early singles, it's a crime that one can't acquire definitive CD editions of such masterpieces as *When Lights Are Low, Tony, Tony Makes It Happen, Cloud 7, Long Ago and Far Away, Hometown, My Town, Life Is Beautiful, For Once in My Life, I've Gotta Be Me, A Time for Love, My Heart Sings.* . . . The list goes on for days, and Sony is also sitting on two amazing, unissued live albums by Bennett from 1964 (Las Vegas) and 1968 (Los Angeles) that demand immediate release.

Shortly after the death of Frank Sinatra, in 1998, Bennett was invited to help Rosemary Clooney celebrate her seventieth birthday at Rockefeller Center's Rainbow and Stars. She introduced him with the traditional English line regarding the succession of the monarchy: "The king is dead, long live the king." In 2002, with the deaths of Peggy Lee and then Clooney herself, Bennett's position as the last of the great singers of his era—or indeed, any era—is, alas further secured.

Andy Bey (born 1939)

A couple gets into the habit of spending one evening every week in Chinatown. Increasingly, they find themselves drawn into an exotic and, implicitly, erotic netherworld. The more time they spend down there, the more their belief system starts to change: The familiar starts to become strange and surreal to them, while what once seemed bizarre and far-out starts to look like normal. Within a short time, they grow gradually less sure of what they think they know.

That's the rough "plot," as it were, of "Tuesdays in Chinatown," a song that was the most prominent number in the repertory of the jazz singer Andy Bey in the first few years of the new century, a period that was probably the most productive of his entire long career. It was also the title song of one of his strongest albums (released late 2001). I heard him sing it a lot in 2001 and 2002, at shows at both the Kaplan Penthouse as part of Jazz at Lincoln Center's "Singers over Manhattan" series and the Blue Note.

Yet it's also a description of Bey's music: in the way he takes a song everybody knows and completely retools it via harmonic redecoration and elaborately conceived vocal effects. After listening to Bey's treatments of chestnuts like "You'd Be So Nice to Come Home To" and "Pick Yourself Up," even such old friends as Cole Porter and Jerome Kern start to seem like strangers in a half-remembered dream. The day of the week and the geographical location of the couple's descent into delirium are the only thing that Bey is specific about: Otherwise, he keeps everything vague and ambiguous. We don't know exactly what happens to them, if their worlds are rocked by sex, opium, or egg foo yong.

Maybe it had something to do with the Clinton era. Three of the major jazz vocal stars of the nineties were not newcomers but rediscoveries: Bey, Shirley Horn, and Jimmy Scott (the artist formerly known as "Little"). Bey, who was brought into the spotlight shortly before he turned sixty in 1999, was the youngest of the triad. They all have this thing about time: Each was willing to take every second it took to sing a love song in the most effective way—even if it meant dragging out "Someone to Watch over Me" for nearly ten minutes of just voice and piano. Likewise, they were willing to wait until they were ready for Social Security before being appreciated by the jazz world at large. (David Ritz's biography of Jimmy Scott is appropriately titled *Faith in Time*.)

In addition to his elastic, Monkish sense of time, Bey's greatest strength is his remarkable range: As a young pianist, he learned early on that one can go all the way from deep, sonorous notes in the bass to tinkly high notes in the treble, and it was only a minor leap to the conclusion that he could do the same with his voice. Not surprisingly, both Fats Waller and Sarah Vaughan, Bey's two major predecessors as explorers of the high-to-low vocal connection, were also accomplished keyboardists. Bey can challenge Billy Eckstine one minute, crooning in a deep basso profundo, and the next intrude into the airspace of

Pha Terrell or Stevie Wonder, yelping in a high falsetto. He's like all of the Ink Spots at once, contrasting Bill Kenny's stratospheric tenor with the Hoppy Jones talking bass, and bridging the difference in yet a third voice, a comfortable baritone, and employing an attractive rapid vibrato in all three.

If today Bey is a one-man vocal trio, it's partly because he started as a member of a three-person trio—one that fit the classic description of three people singing with a single voice. Born in Newark in 1939, Bey began his professional life as a child prodigy on the rhythm and blues circuit, playing piano and singing on the same bills as such legends as Dinah Washington and Louis Jordan by the time he was twelve. In 1956, he and his sisters Salome and Geraldine formed a vocal trio, billed as "Andy and the Bey Sisters," which toured the world nonstop over the next three years (like Jerry Lewis, they were especially beloved in France, where they first recorded) and made three albums. Both that first French session (as yet only issued on an EP), and the first album, an unreissued RCA LP, seem to have fallen off the face of the earth.

However, both of the group's other two recordings are handily available on a single CD, *Andy Bey and the Bey Sisters* on Prestige, which documents the combination of snappy rhythms and deep, gospel-style harmony—not to mention eclectic song choices (from Horace Silver to Anthony Newley)—that made them perhaps the best jazz vocal group since Lambert, Hendricks & Ross. Throughout, their sound is deeply rooted in African American religious music, in the churchy timbre of their voices, as well as the wide spacings between the three singers—unlike the Andrews Sisters, there's a lot of air in there. This is evident when they're singing three separate lines, as in much of "Sister Sadie," or even when they're comparatively closer to one another in something more like conventional harmony, as on "A Taste of Honey."

Eventually, Salome and Geraldine retired to start their own families back in Chicago, and Bey went out as a solo attraction, accompanying himself on the piano. Like Shirley Horn, he managed to attract the attention of a lot of jazz-and-song cognoscenti without getting anywhere near the big time. His first solo album, the 1974 *Experience and Judgment*, is a fusion-and-world-music-influenced mistake, considered a disaster even by his fans. Apart from guest appearances here and there, most notably with Gary Bartz and Silver, he didn't get another album until 1991's *As Time Goes By*, a live set from Zagreb distributed pretty much only in the Balkan states.

Bey finally began to record regularly in 1995, and his most important work consists of five albums recorded between then and 2003. *Blues, Ballads & Bey* (Evidence) is exclusively voice and piano, and *Shades of Bey* (Evidence) employs a small ensemble (including longtime collaborator Gary Bartz on alto and a string quartet). The 2001 *Chinatown* (N2K)

again ups the instrumental ante (Andy?) with a fuller ensemble that varies from track to track. The most recent performance is *American Song* (Savoy) from 2003. In 1997, Bey taped a live set at Birdland with the rhythm section of the Bill Charlap Trio—bassist Peter Washington and drummer Kenny Washington—titled *It Ain't Necessarily So* and released (on 12th St Records) ten years later.

Shades of Bey opens with Dori Caymmi's "Like a Lover" intoned by Bey at his bass-baritone best, which he improves by removing almost every trace of Brazilian rhythm, using only Paul Meyers's guitar for accompaniment. He heads for the bass-ment again with "Dark Shadows," his homage to Charlie Parker and Earl Coleman. Bey makes the song sound like a predecessor to such later, better known soul ballads as "Since I Fell for You" and "Please Send Me Somebody to Love"—one wishes he would tackle Ernie Andrews's "Soothe Me" and Cecil Gant's "I Wonder, I Wonder." There are two Billy Strayhorn items, "Star Crossed Lovers" and "Blood Count," and in general, his sensitive rendition does more than anyone else's (with the possible exception of the younger, more aggressive Allan Harris) to make the case for singing both of these instrumentals as popular songs. Supported by the strings, he also makes an eloquent case for "River Man," by the short-lived British folk-pop singer-songwriter Nick Drake.

On *Shades of Bey*, Bey's singing is considerably enhanced by the guitar, the strings, and the solos and obbligatos of Bartz—one of the best saxists of our time. The joy of *Ballads, Blues & Bey* is the absolute purity of Bey's voice and piano. It starts with his six-minute "Someone to Watch over Me," followed by a masterful, achingly slow eight-minute version of "So Nice to Come Home To." Unlike *Shades*, almost all of *Ballads, Blues & Bey* is overfamiliar songs from the basic jazz singer's repertoire (there's more Ellington-Strayhorn: "Day Dream," "I Let a Song Go Out of My Heart," "In a Sentimental Mood"—a song not performed often enough by singers—and "I'm Just a Lucky So and So"). He intones "Willow Weep for Me" with considerable authority, which is understandable since he's been singing about that weeping willow for almost forty years. "Willow" is the first track of the first Bey Sisters album, and when he sings it without Salome and Geraldine, he now uses his high voice to simulate the willow's wailing and gnashing of teeth.

The 2001 *Tuesdays in Chinatown* includes, in addition to the gnomic title track, the finest version of Milton Nascimento's haunting "Bridges" (jazz writer Gene Lees's best lyric) since Tony Bennett. The lyric's stated ambition, to build "a bridge made out of love," seems congruous with the nature of Bey's music, in which he has bridged the sounds of jazz, soul, scat, theater music, bossa nova, and his characteristic anguish-filled super-slow ballads. Only Bey could take "In a Mist" by jazz Gatsby Bix Beiderbecke and make it sound, in a haunting rendition, more like something written thirty years later by Billy Strayhorn.

Though it sometimes seems as if it takes Bey forever to get through a song (his whole set encompasses only six tunes and an encore), his show literally flies by. At the Blue Note, in 2002, the crowd had probably come to see the young headliner Jane Monheit, who was on the other half of the bill (I'd rather look at her myself, now that you mention it), but Bey made them his own with his first tune alone, "You'd Be So Nice to Come Home To." At the club, he sang it with only minor support from bass and drums; on the album it's no less effective by Bey completely solo. He punctuates the whole piece with a percussive, catchy riff, playing in one tempo while singing in another. He intones "breeze on high" in an Arthur Prysock pedal note and "sang a lullaby" in a Cleanhead Vinson squeak; then the second time he sings the chorus through, he completely reverses the trajectory. After an expert piano solo, he sings the chorus again, in yet a third way.

In fact, the only time you're aware of in a Bey performance is the time between his all-too-infrequent appearances in New York (he continues to perform despite being diagnosed HIV-positive). Otherwise, Andy Bey plays and sings like he's got all the time in the world.

Connee Boswell and the Boswell Sisters

Martha (1905–1958)
Connie (later Connee) (1907–1976)
Vet (Helvetia) (1911–1988)

Gary Giddins recently described the Boswell Sisters as jazz's answer to the Brontë sisters. Like Anne, Charlotte, and Emily, Connie, Vet, and Martha were strikingly original thinkers whose work has little or no precedent. Like the Brontës, the Boswells created a literary language all their own. Like the Brontës, the Boswells permanently influenced the course of their art form—American music rather than English literature. And like the Brontës, the Boswells' career was short (none of the Brontës lived to reach forty; the Boswell trio broke up around the time the oldest sister turned thirty) and their output was frustratingly small. Yet neither of these mediums, the jazz vocal group and the novel, was ever quite the same after these sister acts got through with them.

When we talk about the Boswell Sisters having a language all their own, we mean that both literally and figuratively. The Boswells created their own nonsensical musical vocabulary. Boswellese was essentially a variation on the concept of pig latin that utilized a combination of "G" and "L" sounds, and the insertion of such phrases as "oggle," "iggle," and "eggle." Researcher David McCain, who has spent a lot of his life tracking down the Boswells (making himself the Boswell of the Boswells), once transcribed, with the help of Vet Boswell herself, one of the Boswells' scatlike exercises in gibberish.

The song—"That's Love," written by Buddy DeSylva and Lew Brown (words) and Ray Henderson (music) for *George White's Scandals of 1931*—opens with the line "When a bull looks at a cow," which the trio sings as follows: "Wheggle-den a buggle-dull looks at a coggle-dow." The start of the second A section is "When two cats upon a fence," which comes out of the Boswell hopper as "When two caggle-dats upoggle-don a feggle-dence."

The iggle-diggle folderol was, however, hardly one of their more important musical innovations (for that matter, neither was their propensity for changing lyrics to something that makes less sense than the original, most notably on "42nd Street"), and it's safe to say that after the trio broke up, no one ever iggle-diggled again. Yet their more strictly musical innovations were a major influence on jazz vocal groups from that point on, from their slightly younger colleagues the Mills Brothers to their successors the Andrews Sisters and all kinds of swing era threesomes, foursomes, and fivesomes, like the Modernaires, the Pied Pipers, and many others.

The Boswells developed a new sound that was startlingly fresh. With the exception of Duke Ellington, no other jazz or pop music arrangers of the prewar era, especially the pre-swing era, so thoroughly recomposed the music they interpreted. Generally the major occasion when a band completely transformed a piece of music into something unrecognizable and new was when they were "swinging a classic." But by and large, when one band did a new song it didn't sound all that radically different from all the other dance band versions of said song.

When a pop song like Harry Warren's "Rose of the Rio Grande" enters the Ellington universe, it still retains its original outlines, but these outlines are filled in with a startling array of tonal colors. The Boswells gave Warren the same treatment when they addressed his 1932 movie musical anthem "42nd Street." The melody has little in common with that sung by Dick Powell in the picture, the rhythmic emphasis is in entirely different places, different phrases are set out and isolated, melodic lines that one expects to go up will go down instead, there are stops and starts where you least expect them. For the most part, you can only comfortably recognize the song by listening to the lyrics, although "42nd Street" represents a case where the sisters played around with those as well. "Where the underworld can meet the elite" becomes "Where the whole world meets success and defeat." (I don't know where those words came from, but I do know when I first heard this rendition on a scratchy 78, it sounded as if they were singing "Where the whole world meets excepting the feet." It was more charmingly self-referential when they changed "Jelly roll blues" to "Heebie jeebies blues" in "Darktown Strutters Ball.")

Warren and lyricist Al Dubin ended the song with a dramatic cadenza—"Naughty, bawdy, / Gaudy, sporty / Forty-second Street"—which, in the film, Dick Powell takes to the very top of his tenor head tones. Instead of rendering this 6-bar phrase as a traffic-stopping high-note affair, the Boswells reconfigure it for exclusively rhythmic purposes. Where Powell (and his Broadway heirs) shout it out with exclamation points at the end of every adjective, the Boswells retool it by rushing and then waiting ("*Naughtybawdy . . . Gaudysporty*, making two words into one each time) as they lay down rhythmic cells that are the quintessence of swing. Some of the more extreme Boswell performances—like "42nd Street"—anticipate the bop era reworkings of classic songs by Charlie Parker and his followers. In fact, Parker's "Bird of Paradise" is, after its distinctive opening vamp, easier to recognize as "All the Things You Are" than the Boswells' "42nd Street" is easy to recognize as "42nd Street." The Boswells also touch on the process of harmonic substitutions, to the point of taking major chords and making them minor and vice versa.

The Boswells were avant-garde and mainstream at the same time. Unlike, say, Gil Evans, who spent the better part of his career writing orchestrations and leading bands in dusty dives, the Boswells performed these radical recompositions in your better theaters, on top-rated radio shows, and even in movies. It was to be expected that they would occasionally encounter a radio listener who couldn't make head or tail of what they were doing. Yet by and large, the big radio audience couldn't get enough of them. They were by far the most popular female group of the Depression era—in fact, the only one to be remembered by subsequent generations.

If little they did sounded like what you would expect from a pop trio of the thirties—the kind that are always re-created in more modern pop representations, like "the lovely Boylan Sisters" in the Broadway musical *Annie*—there was a corner of the Boswell brain that had much in common with other heavyweight jazz singers of the era, like Ethel Waters, fellow New Orleanian Louis Armstrong, and co-star Bing Crosby. Sometimes instead of overhauling melodies and trashing lyrics, the Boswells merely reinterpreted them with the same degree of soul and swing, retaining the original shape of the tune as published. This aspect of the Boswells' legacy comes through in the solo passages in the sisters' sides, normally sung by Connie, and in Connie Boswell's own solo sides, done at the same time (and for about thirty years afterward). With her sisters, Connie Boswell is something else again, but even without them she's easily one of the top vocalists of the thirties, in a class with Mildred Bailey and Lee Wiley (as well as Billie Holiday, Maxine Sullivan, and Waters).

One younger singer who appreciated the dichotomy between the two poles—Connie's solos and the trio as a unit—was Ella Fitzgerald. Late in her life, Connie (who then spelled her name Connee) gave a somewhat self-aggrandizing interview to radio host Rich Conaty in which she claimed that in the early thirties, bandleader Chick Webb was such a Boswell fan that the drummer put the word out that he was looking for a black female chirp who could sound like Connie Boswell. And so: Ella!

Perhaps it's not a coincidence that Fitzgerald's own recording rabbi was also the redoubtable Jack Kapp. In spite of the way Kapp's musical conservatism gradually took hold, he was responsible for the preservation of at least a hundred classics of the jazz vocal group idiom by the trio. The Boswells made a lot of records in a comparatively short time, enough to fill five compact discs, yet one still wishes that, like Ellington, Fitzgerald, or the Mills Brothers, they could have gone on for decades.

The Boswell Sisters were eternally identified with New Orleans, where they grew up at the very moment that the new music from the Crescent City was taking the world by storm. Martha was born in Kansas City in 1905, and Connie two years later in that same town. By 1911, when Vet (her full name was Helvetia, which sounds suspiciously like a font) came along, the family had moved to Birmingham, Alabama. By the time the third baby was three, the family had settled in New Orleans.

The girls were raised not only by their parents but by an aunt and uncle who lived under the same roof—a quartet of adults who were actually a pair of sisters who had married a pair of brothers. The whole family was intensely musical: At the time of World War I, the little girls were playing chamber music in a string trio (Martha, piano; Connie, cello; Vet, violin), but as New Orleans jazz began leaving its imprint on the rest of the world, the threesome became more of a "hotcha" trio (Martha, still piano, but Connie, saxophone, and Vet, banjo). Sadly, the family lost two sons (one in the war), and the middle daughter, Connie, was stricken with polio as a child, and would be confined to a wheelchair for her whole life. Yet by all indications they were a happy and loving family.

Like jazz itself, the sisters' music was the product of a melting pot of Crescent City influences. The Boswell family, despite the very Anglo name, was primarily Italian, and thus part of the nation's single largest Italian-American community. In the teens and twenties, there was almost as much good jazz to be heard in the Italian parts of town as there was in the black neighborhoods, and there was frequent intermingling between the two groups. Obviously, the girls' musical education, as overseen by a German-born professor, was entirely slanted toward the European classics. Like Armstrong and their childhood friend Louis Prima, they grew up surrounded by the diverse musical influences of the city—everything from the funkiest blues imaginable to the opera house (unlike Armstrong, they were actually permitted in there).

The group was open to every kind of influence, race, and religion. "I remember we would park our car outside black churches and listen," Vet said in 1981. "Mama believed in finding out what other religions were doing. We'd hear some of the most wonderful Gospel. One song I remember which became our lucky song, 'The Heebie Jeebies,' we heard outside a black bar." "We [started singing] at church affairs," Connie told Conaty. "We sang at everybody's church."

And, like Crosby, they were part of the first generation raised with the phonograph. "I had all the solo records made by the various cellists in those days," said Connie, "and we listened to the Caruso records, we listed to [Amelia] Galli-Curci, the whole gamut in the '20s. But we also liked jazz music and swing and ragtime. Wc bought all kinds of records. I had Paul Whiteman, Gene Austin, Nick Lucas, we had the Wolverines [with Bix Beiderbecke] which was a real hot group." The combination of local and national influences was extremely important, and Connie relates that even as tots they were combining (national) mainstream pop songs with local music traditions, specifically jazz. No less important was the blending of classical techniques they studied at school with the jazz elements they picked up everywhere else. As Connie said, "We would take a jazz number of some kind, something that was real good with a good solid beat. We would slow it down and maybe put the major tune in a minor, and we would make almost a semi-classical number out of it."

By the early twenties, the chamber music trio that had evolved into a miniature jazz band had become a vocal trio. In 1921, a group called the Brox Sisters appeared on Broadway in Irving Berlin's *Music Box Revue*, and helped popularize the format. Connie dated the birth of the Boswell Sisters as a professional act to 1925; there was an unexpected, last-minute opening in the bill at the Orpheum Theatre—the most important vaudeville theater in town—and, as Connie tells it, the sisters had to get permission from their school in order to fill it. (Actually, only Vet would have still been in school, as Martha and Connie would have been twenty and eighteen by then.) The whole town turned out to see them—their school even closed so classmates could attend—not only because they were hometown faves, but because they were a sensation.

Thus by 1925 they were already local legends. Later that year, a mobile unit from the Victor corporation came through New Orleans, and did two sessions with the sisters, resulting in two issued tracks (the remaining three have never been found). The voices sound extremely young and chirpy, a quality that is exacerbated by the acoustic recording technology, but the two sides—"Nights When I'm Lonely" (the trio) and "Cryin' Blues" (Connie solo, both tunes credited to Martha)—are important as the first documents of the Boswell Sisters. Van and Schenck (who were, with the Happiness Boys, the most famous singing duo of the time, in the classic twenties tradition of tenor and baritone) made them

an offer to come on the road with them, which their father refused, but in 1928 he finally agreed to let the girls take an offer to sing in Chicago. They worked at the Grand Riviera in Detroit, and then, like Nat Cole ten years later, joined a fleabag vaudeville troupe that left them broke and stranded on the West Coast. And that was where things started to really happen for the Boswell Sisters.

In Los Angeles they came to the attention of agent Harry Leedy (Connie's future husband), who helped them build up an increasingly big following via radio. They made their second record on the coast, "Highway to Heaven" and "That's What I Like About You." Their voices have lowered to a more sonically pleasing contralto range, and the rhythm is relentlessly snappy-peppy in the manner of the better early thirties West Coast dance bands, like Gus Arnheim or Abe Lyman. In addition to appearing live on the air five times a week, they recorded a series of transcriptions for radio airplay produced by the Continental Broadcasting Company, of which about two dozen titles have survived. (Most of these are on two CDs: *The Boswell Sisters*, on Take Two, and *The Boswell Sisters: Air Shots and Rarities*, Retrieval.)

The Los Angeles transcriptions reveal that the sisters' mature style is almost fully formed—it's about 75 percent of the way there. "Song of the Dawn" opens with Connie giving this *King of Jazz* movie tune religious overtones by singing it slowly and soulfully. The other two don't contribute much until the second chorus, where the trio takes over and makes it more swing than spiritual. Another 1930 title, "When the Little Red Roses Get the Blues for You," is very close to the mature sound. They were already both speeding up and slowing down on unexpected passages, and playing up the contrast between the two, and also alternating between the three voices and Connie's solo.

In October 1930, still on the coast, they cut four titles ("My Future Just Passed," "Heebie Jeebies," "Gee but I'd Like to Make You Happy," and "Don't Tell Him What's Happened to Me") for Okeh that amount to the first recordings with the mature, fully developed Boswell Sisters sound. These, and all the threesome's commercial recordings, are included in *The Boswell Sisters Collection*, a definitive five-volume series from Jazz Unlimited, Denmark. *The Boswell Sisters: That's How Rhythm Was Born*, from Sony Legacy's *Art Deco* series, is probably the best American anthology, even though it doesn't include any of the 1931 MCA-owned material.

The big breakthrough came the next year. When Bing Crosby signed with CBS and became the biggest thing on the air in the fall of 1931, he opened the door for a pantheon of new-style singer-entertainers like the Boswell Sisters, the Mills Brothers, and Kate Smith (who seems less modern in retrospect than she did at the time), who followed him to CBS radio (and William Paley), Brunswick

Records (and Jack Kapp), and Paramount Pictures. Crosby was close to both the Millses (with whom he worked on records) and the Boswells (with whom he mostly worked on radio). The singer and the sisters would intersect in all three media, on the 1934 *Woodbury Soap* series, on several all-star Brunswick discs (usually 12" medleys and concert items), and in the 1932 Paramount musical *The Big Broadcast*, which represented a feature film debut for all of them.

In most of her interviews—not that there are very many—Connie Boswell tended to overstate her case, not only claiming that the Boswell Sisters were the first great trio (which they were), but that she was the first great solo jazz singer and even that her older sister, Martha, was the first great jazz pianist. Yet George Simon once documented a conversation with Connie in which she was surprisingly level-headed. "We didn't sing everything straight, the way other groups did. After the first chorus, we'd start singing the tune a little different. You know, with a beat, the way jazz musicians would." This is actually a better description of her own solo records, where she sings the first chorus somewhat straight, then throws in playful, jazzy variations after that, in the classic Ethel Waters mold. On the trio sides, the group often starts by throwing the composer's melody right out the window, and coming in on the very first chorus with what is pretty much a completely original tune. "Louisiana Hayride" opens with a melody that doesn't even seem remotely related to the Arthur Schwartz–Howard Dietz show tune from *Flying Colors*. We don't hear the familiar melody until it trots in instrumentally in the second chorus, an interlude dominated by trombonist Tommy Dorsey and violinist Joe Venuti. In the Boswells' topsy-turvy universe, singers take all kinds of liberties with the melody and jazz musicians play it comparatively straight.

"Shuffle Off to Buffalo" marks an especially radical treatment: This was a hit song (also from *42nd Street* and again by Warren), and even though it was new, the Boswells knew people would realize what the melody was supposed to sound like. Yet listeners were apparently delighted when the Boswells super-charged the song and completely recomposed the tune. Contrary to Connie's description, the first chorus here is a total recasting of the musical material—poor Harry Warren wouldn't even know it. Here the second chorus comes closer to the familiar tune. It starts with the verse, heard in dance tempo (not rubato), and then comes a solo chorus by Connie, which stays closer to the movie melody. Yet for the third chorus, they take off in blasting swing time.

Other numbers find the Boswells introducing melodic interludes from way out in left field. After the first chorus of "Old Yazoo," the sisters diverge into something completely different, an interlude not even hinted at in the original song (at least not in the song as recorded by Fred Waring's Pennsylva-

nians). They introduce a succession of regulation 12-bar blues choruses in which Connie sings the main line ("My Aunt Matty, she told me not to go") and the others answer back the resolution ("Now she's listening on the radio").

"Mood Indigo" also contains a "bonus" extra 12-bar blues passage, instead of the standard second strain as written by Duke Ellington ("always get that mood indigo"). Connie sings her own blues ("Blues all on my mind, / Blues all around my head"), followed by a solo from Tommy Dorsey that illustrates his influence on Ellington trombonist Lawrence Brown. There's at least one instance where the sisters so completely retool a song that Kapp felt obliged to change the title of the tune. Neil Moret and Jo Trent's "Swanee Woman" was released by the group on Brunswick as " 'Swanee Mammy'—Boswell Sisters version of 'Swanee Woman.' "

At around the time of their breakthrough, newspaper columnists wrote about an alleged feud between the Boswells and "portly warbler" Kate Smith (who, it was said, weighed as much as the three girls put together). Supposedly, Smith and the Boswells were vying to be thought of as the number-one songsters of the Sunny South. Smith, who was at the time billed as "The Songbird of the South and Her Swanee Music," was actually born in Greenville, Virginia (in 1907, the same year as Connie), and raised in Washington, D.C., which, in the opinion of some, didn't earn her the right to bill herself as a Southern songbird. (Turkey is more like it, said some.) The Boswells' Southern credentials were doubted by no one. It seems like a rather trivial pursuit, and indeed it was, but at the time, at the height of the Great Depression, nostalgic songs of home were among the most popular of pop music genres, and songs about the South were big business—as Frank Trumbauer told Hoagy Carmichael (as quoted by Richard Sudhalter), "No one ever went broke writing songs about the South." In the 1935 Fox musical *Every Night at Eight*, Alice Faye, Frances Langford, and Patsy Kelly play the Swanee Sisters, a singing trio who become a hit on the radio in obvious homage to the Boswells.

No one ever went broke singing about the South either. In a 1954 article in the British *Melody Maker*, Martha Boswell claimed that she picked the sisters' songs by means of astrology. "Martha has an uncanny ability to pick hit tunes," her husband, George Lloyd, reported. "In her system, she is helped by dreams and the stars." For Kapp, who probably actually picked most of the girls' songs, it was much simpler mainly to give the Dixie born-and-bred trio whatever new mammy and Swanee songs crossed his doorstep that day. For Kapp and the Boswells, as I've mentioned earlier, such songs were bread-and-butter. This was the greatest era of the American songbook, but you won't find much in the way of Gershwin, Porter, or Kern in their output—the only major standard from a Broadway show in their repertory was the previously mentioned "Louisiana Hayride," chosen more for its Louisiana relevance than its Broadway status. Yet I'd rather hear the Boswells do semi-forgettable songs about their paradise back home in the antebellum South than, in fact, almost any other singers doing Rodgers and Hart.

Perhaps Kapp sought to counterbalance their musical progressivism by assigning them songs with socially conservative, even backward content. A song like "That's How Rhythm Was Born" has the lassies shouting "Yowsah, yowsah" as if in some supremely hip minstrel show. In "42nd Street," the voices sound geographically neutral; on "Old Yazoo," they all sound as if they come from L.A.—Lower Alabama.

"Down on the Delta" suggests the rhythmic trajectory of Duke Ellington's "Daybreak Express," starting slowly with Connie singing the melody solo—rather heartfully, though not sentimentally—about how she wants to be down on the bayou (rhyming "bayou" with "friends that I knew") and how she misses the times her mammy used to spank her for playing in the muddy waters. The thing kicks into tempo after a transitional passage led by Tommy Dorsey, and the two sisters come in. After another half-chorus with the sisters, Connie sings a fast solo, followed by a still faster passage by the trio, with a rocking, steady locomotive rhythm that suggests the Daybreak Express plowing down the Yazoo delta where the Southern meets the Dog. Through tempo and rhythm, they render the text and its rather dated preoccupations completely irrelevant.

There seemed to be no limit to the Boswells' inventiveness. There are plenty of Boswell Sisters records with wordless and scat episodes, and others, like "There'll Be Some Changes Made," "Why Don't You Practice What You Preach," and "If It Ain't Love," where they briefly sidestep through instrumental imitations à la the Mills Brothers. They were among the first North American pop stars to employ the newly imported Cuban rhythm known as the rhumba—heard to great effect in "Whad'Ja Do to Me," Richard Whiting's "Don't Let Your Love Go Wrong," and most noticeably in a remarkable interlude on "The Darktown Strutters Ball"—they sing "I want to be there when the band starts to rhumba!"

The only records on which they sound less than brilliant are those big Kapp productions for which they were recruited for their star power, not for their musical acumen, as on the 12" super-special-production discs of "Star Dust" (1931) and "Lawd, You Made the Night Too Long" (1932). The first is the sisters' own fault; as Vet told David McCain, they were interested in writing their own symphony at this time and somehow that was reflected in this grandiose "concert" treatment of the Carmichael classic. The "Star Dust" chart is attributed to Vet, but it's hard to believe the sisters had anything to do with it. "Lawd, You Made the Night Too Long" is a wasted opportunity on several levels. The threesome sounds

generic here, as if they could be any vocal group of the period. If they had been singing it on their own—without benefit of the concert production—they might have been able to make this Tin Pan Alley spiritual sound like the real thing (which is exactly what they do on "The Lonesome Road" and Clarence Williams's gospelly "Shout Sister Shout").

On "Lawd," they don't get to interact with Crosby, and singing someone else's chart makes them boring. In fact, Crosby's solo on "Lawd" is much more lusty and passionate than their own. Yet on a certain level, to have Crosby singing directly with the Boswells would be too much of a muchness; it would be overkill. (Crosby and Connie Boswell singing together, however, would be sheer magic.)

Beginning in 1934, the Boswells—with Kapp's cooperation and perhaps even at his instigation—launched what might be called a jazz repertory series, in which they thoroughly reimagined a number of standards of the jazz and pop worlds, such as "Alexander's Ragtime Band," "The Darktown Strutters Ball," "Dinah," "St. Louis Blues," the folk song "Goin' Home," and the pseudo-folk spiritual but genuine jazz classic, "The Lonesome Road." This was a bit early even for a 78 album, but one wonders if the sisters or Kapp might have had something like this on their minds. These are probably the climax of the sisters' career. Yet there were still some great tracks ahead of them, particularly in songs from the new films: *Top Hat* ("Cheek to Cheek," "Top Hat, White Tie and Tails"), *Follow the Fleet* ("Let Yourself Go," "I'm Putting All My Eggs in One Basket"), and *Sweet Music* ("Fare Thee Well, Annabelle"); collectively, this is some of the trio's very best music.

In *Radioland* magazine, December 1934, Connie denies rumors that the threesome was disbanding, and offers proof of this by pointing out that they had just signed a new contract for the trio to co-star with Crosby on the *Woodbury Soap* program. But a little more than a year later, the split happened. Writing fifteen years ago, I espoused the theory that the sisters broke up because Connie simply wanted to work as a solo act, and so far no one has come up with a better explanation. The sisters themselves attributed their early retirement to their marriages—like Adele Astaire, they got married and they got out of show business. Vet was expecting her first child at the time the group stopped working in the spring of 1936. She had married a Canadian businessman named John Paul Jones, and Martha married one George L. Lloyd, an air force major who sat on Decca's board of directors.

However, Connie, who married manager Harry Leedy around the same time, went on working—more than ever, in fact. Perhaps the marriages provided the other girls with a convenient excuse to step out of Connie's way. Five years earlier, the Rhythm Boys, the group that introduced Bing Crosby to the big audience, had split up for what seem like similar reasons. Yet unlike the Rhythm Boys, the Boswell

Sisters never atrophied, never jumped the shark. Perhaps that was just it. They didn't want to become like Clayton, Jackson, and Durante, or, later, the Will Mastin Trio starring Sammy Davis Jr.—one big-hearted superstar sentimentally lugging two useless ex-partners around for no reason other than not wanting to appear callous. The Boswell Sisters exited the stage in the best vaudeville tradition: leaving us wanting more.

Technically, Connie Boswell's first recorded solo disc was "I'm Gonna Cry" aka "Crying Blues," recorded in New Orleans in 1925, which actually preceded the first recording by the Boswell Sisters trio by three days. Her solo career—on records—began in earnest in the fall of 1931, a few months after the trio signed to Jack Kapp's Brunswick label.

It certainly says something about Kapp's musical acumen that he was the first to record all three of the great female singers of the early thirties—Boswell, Mildred Bailey, and Wiley (and Fitzgerald, soon enough)—and both of the major males as well—Crosby and then Armstrong. Boswell was hardly a newcomer in 1931, but by the end of the year anyone listening would have immediately put her in the front rank with Bailey and Ethel Waters.

As with Bailey and later Wiley, Kapp teamed her with his star studio players, principally the Dorseys and Brunswick's number-one hot white road band, the Casa Loma Orchestra. English scholar Eric Woodward has compiled a discography that very informatively shows that Connie's solos were often recorded at the end of trio sessions—not strictly as an afterthought, but clearly the sisters were still the big attraction for most of the pre-1935 period. Yet even though Connie's features were obviously of secondary importance, it was in these years that she made her most consistently excellent solo recordings. Her solo sides in the Brunswick period place her very nearly on the same level as Crosby and even Armstrong.

No less than with the trio, Connie constantly animates otherwise forgotten material, starting with her very first Brunswick session. The term applies to such early Boswell solos as "I'm All Dressed Up with a Broken Heart" and "What Is It," the latter written by ex–Rhythm Boy Harry Barris, which Crosby sang on the radio but apparently didn't like enough to record commercially. She takes some liberties with the written tunes, as on "I'll Never Have to Dream Again": Although it was written as a waltz, she smooths it out into an even four in the second chorus. Also as with the sisters, Connie does even better with songs that have a Southern feel, a blues feel ("The River's Takin' Care of Me"), a dance feel ("Cariocha"), and upbeat pop items with a two-beat traditional jazz feel, like "Me Minus You." She described her own voice as "low and foghornish"; it was deep and sultry, highly sensual, no stranger to the blues. In all of these attributes, Boswell was a perfect female counterpart to Bing Crosby. She was

the flip side of Mildred Bailey, a petite femme with a deep throaty sound as opposed to a plus-sized gal with teensy girlish pipes. As the famous journalist Ernie Pyle described Boswell, "so much noise out of such a little package."

(There are a few decent samplers of Boswell's solo sides; *They Can't Take These Songs Away from Me* is a recommended two-CD set on the British Jasmine label that highlights the 1931–46 period, while *Moonlight and Roses* on ASV is a good single disc. Unfortunately, no CD has supplanted the two best LPs of Boswell solos, *The Early Solos 1931–'35* and *Under a Blanket of Blue*, both on Take Two, which include most of the best Brunswicks. What is desperately needed is a good Mosaic-style complete box, which may not be possible since her catalogue is divided up—no longer between Brunswick and Decca but between Sony and Universal/MCA. My dream package would include all of the sisters' sides as well as all of Connie's solos that are owned by both corporations.)

In the late thirties, the Goddamnedest thing happens: The Boswells follow Kapp from Brunswick to Decca in 1935 (around the same time they do a very successful European tour, and record and broadcast, both as a trio and solos, in England and Holland) and in 1936 the trio cuts its last sides. From 1936 to the 1942 ban, Connie's Decca sides are surprisingly double-jointed: She made semi-hot and semi-swing sides with a fabulous array of guest stars and accompanists, but at the same time, her regular "mainstream" pop sessions become increasingly dull. This was by no means limited to Boswell; many vocal records of the late thirties are not as exciting as we'd like them to be—arrangers and producers had not figured out a way to transmute the energy of the great swing bands into the discs made by the few star singers of the era.

It's not merely that not every side of the era is a gem—Connie's just as likely to find a buried treasure ("Stra-Va-Na-Da [The Double Talk Song]" is a very funny parody of "place" songs, whether set in the Sunny South or an island in the West Indies, and "The Clock Song"—"I Wish We Had a Clock That Had No Hands"—is a touching ballad that never made it). But a certain blandness has set in that is not to be found in the early thirties sides, which can be heard not only in Boswell but in the first few seasons of discs by newcomer Dinah Shore, to Crosbyites Buddy Clark and Dick Todd, to Tony Martin and even, on admittedly rare occasion, to the Mighty Crosby himself.

The pop sides Connie made in these years with the brilliant Victor Young are a bit more distinctive. Young directed two of her best ethnic items in 1941, a lightly swinging, wee-bit-o'-schottische treatment of the traditional Irish "The Kerry Dancers" (later a favorite quote reference for Charlie Parker) and the radically un-PC but delightful "The Gay Ranchero"—at once swinging and Latinate. But the bulk of the pop dates were done under the generally generic batons of Harry Sosnik, Ray Sinatra, and an unbilled studio orchestra. On the whole, the vocal discs of the prewar period illustrate how completely Frank Sinatra reinvigorated popular singing just a few years later, not just in his own vocals but in the intensely interesting and supremely supportive orchestrations of collaborator Axel Stordahl. (Boswell later claimed to have helped discover Sinatra; he filled the funeral hall with flowers when she died.)

There seems to be a dichotomy between vocalists who were billed on their discs as singers "with orchestral accompaniment" and those who were billed in the same way as bandleaders, as in "Mildred Bailey and Her Orchestra" or "Billie Holiday and Her Orchestra." The discs by the singers billed as leaders are never less than scintillating, largely because they keep the jazz and hot solo content very high. At the same time Boswell's making sleepy sides with Harry Sosnik, she's also cutting a series of brilliant, hot sessions with the best bands that Decca had to offer. The spirit of the Boswell Sisters is more than alive and well whenever Connie teams with Ben Pollack, Woody Herman, and the Crosby brothers. The Crosbys in particular ignited the best in Connie: She has the same freewheeling, improvisatory energy as on the classic trio sides. Bob Crosby's big band was full of New Orleanian star soloists who never fail to bring out her competitive spirit, and she was incontestably the best of Bing Crosby's female duet partners (even though Judy Garland was a challenger). Spokane Records did posterity a major favor in collating an entire LP of their *Kraft Music Hall* radio duets entitled *Bing and Connie*. Their rapport is remarkable, even on nonsense like "Rose O'Day" and "The Hut-Sut Song," a classic slice of Boswell gibberish that they make even more nonsensical via a Chinese menu.

Even though Boswell was the first—and finest— female singer to follow Crosby into the lower registers, Kapp would never succeed in making her into a female equivalent of Crosby. She was too much a jazz gal; she couldn't animate and personalize jazzless pop with the same charisma. Crosby almost revels in second-rate songs—sometimes I'd rather hear him sing "Poor Old Rover" and "Just a Kid Named Joe" than "Bewitched"—while Boswell is defeated by them.

Boswell peaked during the war, making one of her best and hottest platters for servicemen with an all-star unit billed as Connie Boswell and Her V-Disc Playfellows, of "Shine on Harvest Moon" and "Goodnight Sweetheart"—first chorus straight, second chorus Dixie-style. A made-to-order role model for the disabled, she tirelessly toured army bases and hospitals. By the late forties, when Crosby was hitting his own high point, she had already crested. Unlike Crosby, who kept socking out number-one hits until the very end of the decade, Boswell now

came across like your father's jazz-pop singer. Unlike Crosby, Boswell's career was not driven by chart records, but by overall, consistent steady selling of her whole catalogue—which did not endear her to the increasingly cutthroat postwar record business.

Yet, like several other artists of her generation, including Crosby and Wiley, Boswell enjoyed a technologically inspired resurgence in the early years of the 12" LP and hi-fi. She made a 10" LP for Decca, *Singing the Blues with Connee Boswell* (not a typo— by this time she had changed the spelling of her Christian name), but her major output from the postwar era consists of four 12-inchers, *Connee Boswell and the Original Memphis Five in Hi Fi* (RCA), *Connee Boswell Sings Irving Berlin* (Design), *Connee Boswell Sings the Rodgers and Hart Song Folio* (also Design), and *Connee* (Decca) with Sy Oliver. Crosby's great late fifties albums—particularly *Bing with a Beat* and *Fancy Meeting You Here*—represent a new peak for the legendary singer. Boswell's, by contrast, do not—fine as they are, they seem more like a great old gal (only about fifty) enjoying a final fling, a last hurrah, one more walk around the garden. Boswell's voice has deepened and darkened, and seems rhythmically stiffer, now that she's competing with younger-generation jazz-pop femmes like Clooney and Fitzgerald. Still, all four of these albums are worthy ventures, as fine as they can be (the best is the team-up with the Original Memphis Five, even though Boswell only sings on half the tracks); even the songbook albums are hot and jazzy.

For perhaps the last time the other sisters made the news: Martha's husband was ousted from the board of Decca in 1954 and tried to sue to reclaim his position, telling the press that Martha had made an invaluable contribution to Decca's fortunes by picking hit songs with her astrologically based method. Yet, *Melody Maker* reported, "Despite Martha's metaphysical aid, Connie didn't come up with a single hit, said [Decca president Milton] Rackmil." Martha died at the young age of fifty-three four years later. Connee's husband and manager, Harry Leedy, died on New Year's Day 1975, a year before what would have been their fortieth anniversary. Connee herself died of cancer at sixty-eight in 1976, and her illness and death were surprisingly big news in the age of disco. Vet lived to experience the Boswell Sisters revival—groups all over the world that re-created their original arrangements and an off-Broadway show, *The Heebie Jeebies*, before she died at seventy-seven in 1988.

About the cruelest thing one could say about Connee Boswell's postwar work is that it was superfluous because Boswell herself was no longer the most important beneficiary of the great work she had done in the thirties, both as a member of the threesome and as a solo act. That crown had been passed to her major successor, Ella Fitzgerald. In a sense, the two extremes of the Boswell canon replay themselves in Fitzgerald's career—her classic scat features

("Air Mail Special," "Lullaby of Birdland," "How High the Moon") represent, to a degree, her extension of the Boswell Sisters influence, whereas her songbook and more pop-oriented projects more directly indicate the influence of Connie's solos. Fitzgerald was once asked who inflenced her, and she answered, "There was only one singer who influenced me. I tried to sing like her all the time, because everything she did made sense musically, and that singer was Connie Boswell."

Al Bowlly (1899–1941)

At his short but prolific peak, Al Bowlly was easily the best male band singer of the thirties—not counting Crosby—on the entire international playing field. Across the pond, there were plenty of capable Americans—Chick Bullock, Scrappy Lambert, Smith Ballew, Dick Robertson, and slightly later, Buddy Clark—but not one who had that combination of swing and soul that distinguishes Bowlly.

There's a Monty Python sketch that always makes me think of Bowlly—a family of upper-class twits is discussing the merits of words that sound warm and "woody" as opposed to cold and "tinny." Bowlly has a very woodlike sound. He came to maturity in an age when voices were high, tenory and often tinny, and generic. Yet his sound was deeper, lower, and completely idiosyncratic—without any kind of identifiable non-American accent, yet certainly not American. There's a gray quality about it that reminds me at times of both Al Jolson and Jack Teagarden.

Al Bowlly made a treasure trove of high-quality recordings in London in the early thirties, the best being done under the baton of two superb arranger-bandleaders, Ray Noble and Lew Stone. Although he's underappreciated today, he was one of the finest swinging jazz singers of any era, and like Django Reinhardt, one of the first Europeans to understand the blues. But the basic idiom he worked in was not necessarily a jazz-oriented one, and many of his most outstanding vocals—things like "Hang Out the Stars in Indiana" and "Midnight, the Stars and You"—have little jazz content. (Which may be *why* he's underappreciated.) Yet his presence on a dance-band disc by Ray Noble, Roy Fox, or Lew Stone is enough to make the difference between good and great.

Like the young Crosby, Bowlly excelled at both ballads and swingers. There's a 1931 version of "Dinah," in fact, in which Bowlly sounds more as if he, rather than Nat Gonella, deserves the title of the "British Louis Armstrong." He also was, like Armstrong and Crosby, a clear predecessor of Sinatra's Swingin' Lover style. Since he worked in the dance band idiom, nearly everything he sings is in a foxtrot tempo—he's rarely if ever permitted the luxury of singing in a slow rubato. Yet he's one of those rare artists who make this potential liability seem like a virtue. His great strength, in fact, is love songs sung at a semi-fast clip.

He's learned what Crosby's learned: that jazz-style rhythm is the key not only to giving a performance more zest but to personalizing a lyric, to making it sound more spontaneous and believable; he's proving what Crosby and Armstrong had already proved and what Sinatra would reestablish a decade later—that the human heart is not only an instrument of emotion but of rhythm.

It's not too much of a stretch to say that in Bowlly's musical development he reinvented the wheel. He was born in 1899 and raised in South Africa, although both his place and year of birth are sources of controversy: The area has changed names at least once, and is now known as Mutapo, Mozambique. He grew up in Johannesburg, listening to the indigenous music he heard from black mine workers as well as European and perhaps even American entertainers and bands he saw in the variety halls. Is it taking things too far to infer that he might personally have combined these influences in a way that approximated the origins of jazz in the southern United States, or that his keen sense of rhythm derived from these African roots?

Like Perry Como, he worked as a barber until he was able to support himself by playing guitar and singing. He spent the twenties—his twenties—trekking around the globe and performing with a veritable League of Nations of musicians, many of whom were also continually in transit.

In London, he first began attracting attention from the British musical fraternity when he served as guitarist and singer with the Spanish-born, Cambridge-educated Fred Elizalde, whose orchestra at the Savoy Hotel was considered a breakthrough for British jazz, and included such American stars as Adrian Rollini and Chelsea Quealy. It seemed that Bowlly was always surrounded by fellow travelers—Anglo-Americans and American-Anglos. Within a short while, he would collaborate with Roy Fox and Carroll Gibbons, two Americans who spent their careers in England, and Ray Noble, a Briton who eventually became a major American bandleader.

Some of his first sessions, particularly in London, drew on his background. He worked regularly with other South Africans, making tons of sides that are fairly dreary. The notable point about these discs is their multiculti nature. Here was British and American pop performed in Hawaiian style by two South Africans billed under such pseudonyns as the "Honolulu Serenaders" and the "Brooklyn Broadcasters," including such regional airs as "Just an Old Italian Love Song" and "Love Made a Gypsy Out of Me." Bowlly also made records of Western hits for the South African market in Afrikaans.

But soon he was working in the mainstream of dance bands for his musical ability rather than his background. Bowlly hit Berlin and then London just at the height of the Jazz Age record boom. He was incredibly busy in Germany, recording mainly with Briggs and Adeler, and even more so in England. As soon as he arrived in London, he was in instant demand as a studio freelance vocalist, and sang with every conceivable subspecies of dance orchestra, which in England as well as in America were divided between studio-only ensembles and regular working bands (hotel-based bands and touring bands).

He quickly became one of the finest of all masters of the vocal refrain; like the younger Helen Forrest, he understood the discipline of saying all that needed to be said in a single-chorus vocal that usually lasted less than a minute, and he could say more in one chorus than most singers could in a whole record. Small wonder record producers utilized him on over a thousand discs.

Like Forrest, who created substantial bodies of work with three of the top leaders of the era (and unlike, say, most of Duke Ellington's outstanding singers, who worked only with him), Bowlly reached a pinnacle with several different groups. Where Forrest went from Artie Shaw to Benny Goodman to Harry James, Bowlly worked with two major bands, those of Lew Stone and Ray Noble, simultaneously, in the years 1930 to 1934. It was possible for him to sing with two bands at once since one of these played in a prominent nightclub and broadcast in the evenings, and the other existed only in the recording studio and worked only in the afternoons. No one considered this a conflict, even when Bowlly recorded the same titles, like "Brighter Than the Sun" and "I Love You Truly," with both bands.

Musically, the two bands were more alike than they were different. For starters, they were both led by extraordinarily astute orchestrators and occasional pianists, who had, obviously, identical good taste in band singers. Yet there were differences between the two, which have a lot to do with the traditional perceptions of his work. American fans tend to prefer Bowlly's work with Noble, which is understandable, since from almost the beginning American RCA regularly issued the Noble-Bowlly sides in the United States. After Noble himself relocated to the States, he continued to build up a following here, and was to all intents and purposes an American bandleader. But British fans and scholars favor Bowlly's work with Stone, who became an institution of British music.

Bowlly worked with Noble from 1930 to 1935 and with Stone from 1931 to 1934. The Stone association was centered around the Monseigneur Restaurant in Piccadilly Circus, which, despite its name, was apparently more like an American nightclub, since the resident band was a greater attraction than the food. The band was enormously well received, and recorded prolifically—approximately 150 titles under the name of Roy Fox, a star cornetist imported from America. Yet the match between bandleader and management was not a happy one, and lasted only four months. When illness caused

Fox to take a protracted sabbatical, the management seized the opportunity to appoint Lew Stone as the new bandleader. The Monseigneur band with Bowlly stayed intact for another two years, until July 1934, when the restaurant was sold and converted to a cinema (as the Euros say). The timing was actually good for Bowlly, who had one more stop to make on his itinerary: He had an offer to appear in the New World with his "other" bandleader, Ray Noble.

The Fox/Stone–Monseigneur recordings add up to an extremely classy batch of wax. For one thing, the quality of the songs is generally well above average, and Bowlly manages to work wonders even with a bizarre number like "Mediterranean Madness," which rhymes "through your shadows I grope" with "you mesmerize me like dope." There also are wild production numbers, like the ersatz Polynesian "Mauna Loa," and "Laughing at the Rain," which features wind sound effects, and Bowlly actually getting a sound in his voice as if he's outside, belting in the middle of a thunderstorm.

There are some exceptional ballads with Stone and Fox, or as close to balladry as you could get in foxtrot tempo circa 1931–34, like "Please Handle with Care," Jerome Kern's "Lonely Feet," and the haunting "Riptide." Yet on the whole it's the hot titles that really stand out. One of the first entries in the Fox series is a rendition of the future hot standard "Them There Eyes" that doesn't completely suffer in comparison with the more famous Gus Arnheim–Rhythm Boys–Bing Crosby version of the same tune. Both versions feature their stars as members of trios and as gifted scat singers, but where Crosby is already somewhat cool, Bowlly is red-hot here and full of energy in his scat solo. I actually prefer the Stone-Bowlly version of "My Woman" to Crosby's; Bing is slow and dramatic, but Al is hot and torchy at the same time—"lusty" is the only word for it.

"Junkman Blues" and "Balloons" are both production numbers built around the cries of street vendors, but while both are insinuatingly catchy, the first is also blazingly hot. "Junkman" is one of several Fox-Stone titles in which Bowlly shares the vocal action with Nat Gonella, the Satchmo of Bow Bells. Bowlly plays a supporting role while Gonella is the star of "Kickin' the Gong Around," an audio escapade that literally acts out the Harold Arlen–Cab Calloway specialty as if it were a radio drama. The two of them interact in a way that anticipates Crosby and Armstrong (as well as Armstrong and Teagarden) on "I Got Rhythm," "Tell Me, Are You from Georgia," "How'm I Doin'." He also sings a hot-and-lusty chorus on "Nobody's Sweetheart" over a trumpet obbligato from Gonella.

The meat of the matter was dance music, and Noble and Bowlly produced well over two hundred sides together in about five years—enough to fill a fourteen-LP box in the early eighties and a nine-CD series today. Considering that the New Mayfair

Orchestra was completely anonymous, and that both the Ambrose and Jack Hylton bands had first choice of new songs, Noble's achievement seems miraculous.

Bowlly and Noble (like the Boswell Sisters and Dean Martin) worked wonders with absurd songs that no one remembers otherwise. The Anglo-American Harry Woods was no Richard Rodgers—although he was called in to write additional songs for the film version of Rodgers and Hart's West End hit *Evergreen*—but he wrote two Bowlly-Noble classics that manage to be homey and celestial at the same time. "Hang Out the Stars in Indiana" and "Midnight, the Stars and You" (the latter featured in the Stanley Kubrick horror epic *The Shining*) both have a heavy camp factor that doesn't deter Bowlly in the least.

Many of the very best Noble-Bowlly tracks are the work of two composers, both of whom were also pianists, arrangers, and bandleaders—Johnny Green and Noble himself. Green wrote "What Now," "Not Bad," "Oceans of Time," and two of the strongest entries, the aforementioned "Weep No More My Baby" and the equally classic "You're Mine You." It's hard to sing lines like "we're chained and bound together" and not sound heavy, but Bowlly and Noble keep it simple and flowing, rhythmic and romantic.

Unlike Stone, Noble was a highly successful songwriter, responsible for at least ten fine tunes he recorded with Bowlly that did not survive the period, and four more that can be considered standards: "Goodnight Sweetheart," "Love Is the Sweetest Thing," "Love Locked Out," and "The Very Thought of You." (Later, in America, he would write several more standards, most notably "I Hadn't Anyone Till You" and "Cherokee.") "Goodnight Sweetheart" was an immediate transatlantic hit, recorded by Crosby, among other American stars. But my favorite is "Love Locked Out," if for nothing more than the way Bowlly illuminates Noble's rather fanciful lyrics, which anthropomorphize the emotion of love into some kind of vaguely Cupid-like figure who goes around beating his tiny wings on the doors of unsuspecting victims, blessing all those who have the good sense not to lock him out.

The Noble-Bowlly relationship was blessed from the git-go. The Noble-Bowlly ballads are generally in strict foxtrot tempo—no Sinatra-style rubato here, mate!—and yet the ballads with Noble sound more intimate than what anyone else was doing with a dance band. He wasn't afraid to reduce the band to a single section, a few tightly muted trumpets, an extended trombone solo ("Hiawatha's Lullaby"), and in general he exploited the superior ability of the HMV engineers to capture a dynamic range unheard of elsewhere in pop.

The short vocal on "Standing on the Corner," a 1933 song so obscure that it can't even be described as forgotten, is a thing of rare beauty: Bowlly knows exactly which words to emphasize, which to hold, which to sing louder; but more remarkably, he knows to underplay the lyric. When he does stress a word, it has a powerful effect, particularly as he achieves this emphasis in a characteristically subtle fashion—singing the phrase ("And I've got no—body") just slightly louder, but mainly calling attention to it by dragging the beat just the slightest bit and widening the pause between syllables. He sings some passages staccato, emphasizing the beat; others legato, letting the rhythm flow freely.

This attention to nuance, using rhythm and dynamics to make every word count, reminds us most obviously of Frank Sinatra. In fact, Ray Noble himself later spoke of a long-standing disagreement he had with Bowlly over the singer's insistence on singing behind the beat for emotional effect; Tommy Dorsey later had exactly the same beef with the young Sinatra. Lew Stone once told interviewer Cliff Harvey, "I used to be very worried about this in the early days. But I soon understood that this was an integral part of Al's technique—it always came out right and added a fuller dimension to the song."

As fine as the ballads are, most of the Noble-Bowlly titles that would accompany me to the desert island would be the hot sides. Some of these pieces are purely rhythmic novelties, including one of the earliest, the hot Hawaiian "Makin' Wickey Wackey Down in Waikiki." "Shout for Happiness" has Bowlly in a musical dialogue with muted trumpeter Max Goldberg, while the euphoric "You Ought to See Sally on Sunday" has him egging on a baritone sax solo by the excellent British reed virtuoso Freddy Gardner. Bowlly could even syncopate a tango, as on "Goodnight Vienna," and best of all are those torch songs that he puts over in an unexpectedly red-hot fashion, like the 1932 "Must It End Like This?" The arrangement on the first two (instrumental) choruses is merely peppy, Noble providing in this case an almost passive background over which Bowlly can really go to town, throwing in all sorts of Armstrongian interjections.

This was the height of Crosby's influence, yet Bowlly digs beyond Bing to the American singer's own influences, especially Armstrong (also plainly heard on "Hustling and Bustling for Baby," a performance that can stand comparison with Armstrong's own version) and Jolson (acknowledged in the cry of "Mammy" that Bowlly apparently ad-libs at the end of "My Hat's on the Side of My Head"). Bowlly could also get close to the edge of the blues on "Blues in My Heart," "Seven Years with the Wrong Woman," and "Who Walks in When I Walk Out?" In all, there are more than enough of the purely jazz titles to fill a disc all by themselves.

Although the years 1931–34 were Bowlly's pinnacle, this isn't to imply that the later work was not good. The best titles with Noble and Stone have a magical quality about them, a spell that was broken when Bowlly traveled to New York at the end of

1934. Ray Noble was brought over to form a band for the newly opened Rainbow Room at the top of Rockefeller Center, and another rising arranger-composer-bandleader, Glenn Miller, put it together for him. Noble and Bowlly recorded extensively with the American group in 1935 and 1936; though this was a band filled with present and future stars (starting with Miller himself, and including Bud Freeman, Will Bradley, Johnny Mince, Claude Thornhill, and Sterling Bose), Noble's Rainbow Room unit had neither the style nor the spirit of the New Mayfair organization. The Rainbow Room band sounds best on purely swing specialties, like Miller's charts on "St. Louis Blues," "Chinatown, My Chinatown," and "Way Down Yonder in New Orleans," but Noble has apparently lost his knack for turning grade-B tunes (such as "You Opened My Eyes") into grade-A records. The chief attraction here is Bowlly, and he is actually better served on a series of recordings he made under his own name in New York, accompanied by both Noble and Victor Young's Decca house band.

Back in the day, they referred to these as "personality" records, where the singer was featured most prominently, as opposed to dance band records where the singer usually only sang one chorus with the band, if that. Bowlly had recorded sporadically as a soloist up to the New York sojourn, but he would do many more solo sessions both in America and afterward.

By now, he regarded London as his permanent home, and when in 1937 Noble relocated once more—this time to Hollywood—Bowlly returned to Mother England. He had a difficult time reestablishing himself in his adopted country, however, especially since he went through a series of vocal problems in that first year back. He continued to guest with the leading British bands of the late Depression and early wartime era, such as Geraldo, Felix Mendelssohn, and Ken "Snakehips" Johnson, the last being a black West Indian who worked with Bowlly on two slices of swinging Shakespeare in the spirit of Maxine Sullivan.

Some of the later solo sides are quite lovely, even though a lot of the time he was saddled with dreary songs ("Romany," "Somewhere in France with You"). Worse, as was the case with many solo singers in the immediate pre-Sinatra era, such as Dinah Shore, Connie Boswell, and even the Mighty Crosby, the orchestrations on most of his vocal records of the late thirties are fairly formulaic and unimaginative. Yet there are some terrific solo titles from the last few years, especially "South of the Border," "Marie," "Bei Mir Bist Du Schoen" (intriguing, quasi-up-tempo treatments of songs that were swing band hits in the United States), "A Man and His Dream" (one of the nicest Crosby movie songs), and "Moon Love" (a Tchaikovsky adaptation). The best is his haunting, melancholy treatment of "Over the Rainbow," which opens with a paraphrase from

the bridge (played on celesta), then goes into the verse, and then the chorus, in which Bowlly finds a completely different meaning from that of the young Judy Garland. Garland sings it like a wide-eyed ingenue, dreaming about the land over the rainbow. Bowlly sings it like the voice of experience, like an old-timer who's been there and back.

In 1938, Bowlly reunited with ex-boss Lew Stone for approximately two dozen titles that, overall, are the most consistently good of the post-American recordings. A lot of these are heavy on the sentiment ("Little Lady Make Believe," "The Girl in the Alice Blue Gown," and especially "Penny Serenade"), while "The Frog on the Water Lily" is rather juvenile and the evocative "Moonlight on the Highway" recaptures the feeling of the pre-1934 discs. The best are a subseries of titles that show that he had everything it took, vocally and rhythmically, to keep up with the best band vocalists of the swing era: "Georgia's Got a Moon," "Down and Out Blues," and the wild scat feature "Mama I Wanna Make Rhythm." He is positively radiant on two outstanding Jerome Kern–Oscar Hammerstein titles from the film *Joy of Living*, "You Couldn't Be Cuter" and "Just Let Me Look at You," which show that despite career and personal setbacks, he still had lots of great music left in him.

At the end of his life, he teamed with a fellow guitarist and singer named Jimmy Mesene in a duo billed as "The Radio Stars with Their Guitars." They cut four songs together, all fairly uninspired sides, hardly a fitting conclusion to a spectacular recording career. Bowlly's last record was Irving Berlin's love song to Adolf Hitler, "When That Man Is Dead and Gone" in which he looks forward to the day when "Satan with a small mustache / Is asleep beneath the lawn." (All four titles are reissued at the end of one of the more comprehensive Bowlly CD reissue packages, *The Al Bowlly Story*, a series of three individual CDs that samples his whole career in England and America from 1928 to 1941, on the British Avid label.)

It's difficult to imagine what would have happened to Bowlly had he survived the war. The tide of popular entertainment had already turned, if not against him, then at least away from him; with a few exceptions, the dance band era did not lead to a period of superstar pop singers in Britain the way it did in the United States, and he was already going through a rough patch at the time of his death, in April 1941. Bowlly was regarded by his friends as a bit of a naïf, and God only knows what he was doing in his apartment during an air raid; it's not as if the Londoners hadn't constructed shelters precisely for such occasions. The bombs fell, and his flat, as they say, was instantly flattened by what the London papers called "the German murder gang."

Most of Bowlly's fans over the last seventy years associate him with a very particular time and place—thirties London. His life was much broader than that. His reissues are often packaged as mere nostalgia, an insult never handed to Armstrong but one that the reputations of Crosby and Jolson are only now transcending. Bowlly is simply one of the finest spirits ever captured on record. With his slightly husky timbre that anticipates Tony Bennett as much as it echoes Crosby, he is a genuine, three-dimensional personality that speaks to us across the generations on shellac surfaces that spin at 78 rpm. Journalists at the time tended to use the term "crooner" and "jazz singer" as if they were interchangeable. In later years, this was proven not to be apt, but, in Bowlly's work, the two roles are one and the same.

Dee Dee Bridgewater (born 1950)

There's a curious chronology at work in the development of important singers. The cultural holocaust known as the late sixties completely scuttled at least one whole generation, with the result that virtually no notable singer of jazz or standards would make his or her entrance in these years. It might be said that not even one important artist was born in the entire decade of the forties, so crushingly complete was the influence of baby boomer pop.

It's hard to name even a single world-class jazz diva born between Nancy Wilson (1937) and Dee Dee Bridgewater (1950). However, in recent years it's becoming increasingly apparent that there is a new gold standard of jazz singers, and that Bridgewater is at its epicenter—along with Cassandra Wilson (born 1955) and Dianne Reeves (1956). (Diana Krall, born 1964, surely deserves honorable mention at this point, but even though she has made significant strides in recent years, both artistically and professionally, and even though her album sales are the biggest of all, she's not quite yet ready to be placed in the same pantheon as Bridgewater, Wilson, and Reeves, who have been working at it ten to fifteen years longer.)

If Wilson is the most introverted of the three, then Bridgewater is the most extroverted, while Reeves takes the middle ground. As good as Bridgewater sounds on her records, she's also the one who most needs to be experienced live to be fully appreciated. She depends a great deal on visual presentation—not just the way she looks but the way she moves (undulates would be a better word). In both big concert halls and more intimate nightclub settings, she quickly transcends the barrier between the merely flirtatious and the openly seductive. Not content to overexcite the men in her audience, she seems intent on giving us all heart attacks. She's not just in your face, she's practically in your lap. Clearly, she thrives on the interplay and reaction from the crowd, and at least at one point in her career, her willingness to do anything to please the audience led her down some ill-advised paths. (Did someone say "disco"?)

As is also true of Reeves, the very elements that are supposed to make jazz singing obscure and esoteric—scatting and severely rewriting familiar melody lines—are the principal tools that Bridgewater uses to enchant an audience. It's all about energy, musical as well as erotic. She's irresistible when the tempo is fast and the chords are quickly changing—more than Wilson or Reeves, she excels at taking the really overdone basic jazz warhorses and subjecting them to the kind of workout that a first-rate jazz tenor saxophonist or pianist would, as on the live "All of Me" and "Just Friends" on her 1990 *In Montreux* and "Fascinating Rhythm" on *Keeping Tradition*. She just takes these tunes and runs up and down them with relentless invention, riffing on both the melody and the harmonies, the rhythm, anything she can get her hands on.

One thing Bridgewater rarely does is sing a classic love song in an intimate, open, and vulnerable way. This is actually one of the things she manages somewhat more frequently on record—perhaps it's easier for her in the isolation of a studio with no audience present. When she appeared at the Iridium around Valentine's Day 2002, the only time she reduced the tempo was for "Come Sunday," thereby establishing a mood of reverence rather than romance. She slows down on *In Montreux* for "A Child Is Born" (in honor of her first major bandleader, Thad Jones) and then for "Strange Fruit," a pair of songs about birth and death rather than the boy-girl thing. The major romantic number on *Tradition* is a medley of two Sinatra-associated songs about vulnerability and the frailty of emotions, "I'm a Fool to Want You" and "I Fall in Love Too Easily," yet here the medley is set up so that one pays more attention to the bright way in which the two tunes are overlaid than to the emotional content. Likewise, on "Stairway to the Stars" (on *Live at Yoshi's*) heartfelt expression takes a back seat to a very entertaining routine in which she mimes the sound of a muted trumpet by moaning (I'm guessing) into her hands.

For all her female wiles, Bridgewater's key strength is a very direct muscular modernism—in other words, hard bop. It's no surprise that after including several compositions of Horace Silver's on *Tradition* and *Montreux*, she would build an entire album around his music, entitled *Love and Peace*. Like others from the hard bop movement of the late fifties and early sixties, Bridgewater was essentially a jazz artist with strong ties to blues and gospel, as well as what later became known as soul and funk—not for nothing was the term "soul jazz" generally interchangeable with "hard bop." In these years, Silver and Ray Charles could have played with each other's bands and few listening would have noticed the difference, and certainly nobody would have complained. Equally certainly Bridgewater could have served as girl singer with either band (she has, in fact, performed with both of these iconic pianist-bandleaders).

She was born Denise Garrett on May 27, 1950, in Memphis, Tennessee, and was precisely the right age to participate in the beginnings of the formal jazz education system. As a burgeoning musical talent growing up in the sixties (a decade in which the music gained few converts), she might somehow have missed jazz altogether had it not been for her father. Professor Garrett was a music teacher and a trumpeter whose pupils included many of the brilliant young men of Memphis who made an important impact on jazz during the hard bop era, including Booker Little, Charles Lloyd, and George Coleman. Dee Dee, as she was nicknamed, was singing professionally in Michigan by the end of the decade, and in 1969 had joined the University of Illinois Big Band in time for a tour of the Soviet Union.

The next year, Garrett married a talented young trumpet player named Cecil Bridgewater (born 1942), and the two of them came to New York to seek their fortunes. Both their careers did indeed take off, even if the marriage only lasted a few years. Between 1972 and 1974, Bridgewater sang with the premier large jazz ensemble of the day, the Thad Jones–Mel Lewis Orchestra, permanently ensconced on Monday nights at New York's Village Vanguard. She turns up on several of the Jones-Lewis band's recordings, most notably on "The Great One," a movement from the 1971 *Suite for Pops*.

Around the same time, Mrs. Bridgewater toured Japan with the Vanguard Orchestra and, while in Tokyo, recorded her first album, *Afro Blue*, on the Japanese Trio label. The album featured her husband, Cecil, as well as tenor saxist Ron Bridgewater (no relation, apparently), pianist Roland Hanna, and bassist George Mraz; the set was widely regarded by the jazz community as an auspicious debut. She opens in an unexpected way for a future star singer: The first track, Mongo Santamaria and Oscar Brown Jr.'s "Afro Blue," starts with a long, meandering intro, an amorphous, directionless blob of sound in which her voice is one of many sonic elements. This particular idea seems rooted to its time and place, yet when she finally starts singing the song, everything works. (She uses a variation on the idea in the intro to "Love for Sale" on the *Live at Yoshi's* album.) Unfortunately, *Afro Blue* has yet to be made available on a domestic CD.

The jazz world had by now accepted Bridgewater as a budding star and, as a result, we were collectively disappointed when she left us. Nobody minded when, in 1974, she joined the cast of Broadway's *The Wiz* as Glinda (the part Lena Horne played in the movie), and especially not when she won a Tony Award. But most of her other work over the next ten years or so seemed to involve every kind of music except straight-ahead jazz and standards; instead, she turned out albums of disco, fusion, kiddie pop, and other regrettable distractions.

If there's one track from this period that's worthy of our attention, it's the final cut on her final pop album, from 1989. The album is titled both *Victim of Love* and *Precious Thing* in different releases, and the song itself is titled "Till the Next . . . Somewhere" on various issues, but the important thing is that this is her duet with Ray Charles (who himself was also known under several different names in his career). I would rather they were singing "Let's Call the Whole Thing Off" or "Two Sleepy People," but still the two of them have an amazing chemistry. I'm not crazy about the song—whatever you want to call it—but this twosome could make anything sound good.

In the eighties, Bridgewater relocated to Paris and since then has made Europe the center of her operations. She has remarried and raised Franco-American children, and she has also become a hero to jazz lovers across the French-speaking world (as I experienced firsthand when I caught her at the Montreal Jazz Festival in 1997). Equally important, she has been able to put together and work with her own full-time rhythm section. She was gradually coming back to the jazz orbit, although she also enjoyed several further triumphs on the musical theater stage: playing the title role in the London production of Stephen Stahl's *Billie Holiday*, a role that earned her a Laurence Olivier Award nomination (though the extroverted Bridgewater doing the dark, mysterious Holiday seems, on the surface at least, not what I would consider a good idea), and starring as Sally Bowles in *Cabaret*.

By the turn of the nineties, Bridgewater, who was still based in Paris, was at last ready to make a full-time commitment to jazz. In 1990, she recorded her "comeback" album, *In Montreux*, announcing the return of the prodigal in one of the most famous jazz festivals in the world. Over the last twenty years, her output has not been huge (the meat of it consists of seven studio albums) but every one of her projects has been a success. One point that's as unusual as it is commendable is that there has been only one general purpose studio album, the 1993 *Keeping Tradition*; every other Bridgewater release has been driven by a concept. There are two homages to pantheonic diva foremothers: *Dear Ella* (1997) and *Eleanora Fagan (1915–1959): to Billie [Holiday] with Love from Dee Dee* (2010); two songbook projects, one devoted to a comparatively traditional Broadway songwriter (*This Is New*, a collection of Kurt Weill songs; 2002) and the other to a composer-instrumentalist-bandleader whose music is only rarely sung (*Love and Peace: A Tribute to Horace Silver*; 1995); and two geographically inspired collections, *J'ai Deux Amours* (2005) and *Red Earth: A Malian Journey* (2007). In addition to *In Montreux*, there is another live album, the Grammy-winning *Live At Yoshi's* (1998). Two additional concert performances have been released on DVD: *Dee Dee Bridgewater Sings Kurt Weill Live at North Sea Jazz* (2004; mostly songs from *This Is New*) and *Live in Antibes and Juan-Les-Pins* (2005; mostly songs from *J'ai Deux Amours*).

Yoshi's in particular was a powerhouse of a project that not surprisingly garnered the Grammy for 1998, a disc of long improvisations that, like the best of Betty Carter, thoroughly justify their time allotment. Bridgewater's highly developed sense of humor and playfulness come to the fore here more than anywhere else, especially when she apparently spontaneously scats out "Sex Machine," and then offers her impression of how Ella Fitzgerald would sing that James Brown hit, as well as the improvisation that precedes the melody and lyrics to "What a Little Moonlight Can Do," and the way she frames Ray Noble's "Cherokee" with the dancing infidels theme of Dizzy Gillespie's "Shaw Nuff."

If I play *Dear Ella* less than the other tribute sets it's because in doing an album of songs associated with Fitzgerald (a swell marketing hook, by the way) she sets herself up most determinedly for a comparison with the First Lady of Song. I feel the same way about Dianne Reeves's 2001 tribute to Sarah Vaughan, and sometimes I think I enjoy Ann Hampton Calloway's Fitzgerald tribute album more because AHC sounds less like Ella. It was singularly classy of Bridgewater to recruit and feature two of Fitzgerald's favorite musical collaborators, pianist Lou Levy (who shines on "Mack the Knife") and the Great Lady's bassist and husband, Ray Brown.

Keeping Tradition, the themeless studio album, is also highly enjoyable. Still, none of these projects accurately captures what Bridgewater achieves in person, in a club or concert hall. The two composer-driven packages may well be Bridgewater's most wholly successful records, because they provide her with another dimension to work with. On most jazz vocal albums, everything is all *about* the singer; here everything is also *about* the composer, which gives us a point of reference, something else to think about.

You can't quite capture her spontaneity and presence, even in a live recording, so the best option is to go the other route—for a carefully prepared program rather than a singer whose greatest achievement may be her illusion of impulsiveness. Since Bridgewater has already proven herself in musical comedy and pop as well as jazz, it's only natural that she should also use an approach from the world of cabaret. In the cabaret world, artists are often expected to stick to one theme or songwriter for the whole evening; in jazz and related pop, not so much. Just as recordings can't capture what's freshest and most vital about a live performance, a live performance shouldn't try to indulge in a single theme for a whole evening like a record—note that Sinatra never did *Only the Lonely* in concert, and neither did Ella Fitzgerald do *The Rodgers and Hart Songbook*. Yet Bridgewater, like a jazz-cabaret hybrid, has done the whole Weill project, *This Is New*, as her act.

The Silver and Weill packages bring out the very best in her. The Silver set (*Love and Peace*) for the most part uses the composer's own lyrics, which, as is also true of the late Benny Carter, probably represent the least of his many talents. Yet this deficiency doesn't slow Bridgewater down in the least. As with Ivie Anderson singing Ellington or Ethel Merman doing Irving Berlin, the voice sounds tailor-made for the material, perhaps the result of growing up in the same environment as George Coleman and Booker Little.

Throughout, Bridgewater is backed by trumpet and tenor (the French Belmondo brothers, Stephane and Lionel), a sound intended to echo the famous Silver Blue Note–era quintet. The presence of two hard bop keyboard masters, Jimmy Smith and Silver himself, on two tracks each, also lends the album an air of authenticity. Bridgewater is everything that the music of Silver is supposed to be: tight, swinging, and sexy. She told me that she initiated this project after she had come back to jazz after Broadway and pop: She wanted to show off her jazz chops with a catalogue of music that only a 100 percent simon-pure jazz singer could do. And she succeeded.

On the other hand, *This Is New*, though undeniably the work of a superb jazz singer, also calls her theatrical side into play. Kurt Weill was a German-born composer of avant-garde classical music who ultimately found his greatest success writing show tunes on Broadway. Bridgewater is an American jazz singer who wandered through show music and kiddie pop before finding her jazz roots again in a foreign land. By now, too, a Bridgewater production was a family affair: her ex-husband did the arrangements, her current husband served as co-producer, and two of her daughters served in the vocal backup group.

Though *This Is New* draws on Bridgewater's Broadway background, it's no less thoroughly a jazz project than *Love and Peace*. She starts by treating the title song to tropical rhythms, while "Alabama Song" becomes a rowdy blues, one that marches through references to the Jazz Messengers and Benny Golson. "Lost in the Stars," normally rendered as a kind of musical oratory, is here intoned surprisingly tenderly and personally, while "Bilbao Song" (the first performance that springs to mind by a major jazz diva) juxtaposes flamenco and tango and other Spanish rhythms. Even at ten minutes—not a second of which is wasted—"Bilbao" is so compellingly sung and surreally imagined that one wishes this song would replace Jobim's over-performed "Waters of March" as the number-one foreign art favored by jazz vocalists.

The last ten years have been especially rewarding for Bridgewater. The four excellent albums she's released (plus the two live sets on DVD) follow a clear trajectory. The first track and title song of *J'ai Deux Amours* is Josephine Baker's theme, known in English as "Two Loves Have I" (thankfully she avoided the original English lyric, "Give Me a Tune"). Like Baker before her, Bridgewater means it: She is equally a product of both America and

Europe, and with strong African roots as well. (Somehow "J'ai Trois Amours" doesn't sound right.) Appropriately, *This Is New* and *J'ai Deux Amours* showcase her European side (although the first highlights her Broadway side as well), while *Red Earth: A Malian Journey* explores her African ancestry, and *Eleanora Fagan: To Billie with Love* honors a great American forebear.

J'ai Deux Amours consists of familiar French songs (only a few of the eleven tracks are sung even partially in English) that are interpreted in a new way musically, blending accordion, guitar, and other traditional sounds of French pop with state-of-the-art jazz textures. It sounds very contemporary, and, for once, I genuinely intend that as a compliment. On "Ne Me Quitte Pas" she makes Jacques Brel sound musical (practically a first), while in "Dansez Sur Moi" (a.k.a. "Girl Talk") she proves that Bobby Troup's infamously chauvinistic lyric sounds better in French, spiced up with fender bass and funk beats. "La Mer (Beyond the Sea)" swings in the original language and in a way that's totally different from Bobby Darin (or even Kevin Spacey). *Oui, oui, madame!*

Perhaps it's not a coincidence that Bridgewater is the only singer I can think of whose name is a scat phrase. I don't mind hearing Bridgewater sing in languages I don't know (which is virtually all but one of them); make no mistake, she's all about the groove rather than the lyric, and she could tell a story in Swedish or Swahili and be completely comprehensible. *Red Earth* is an album of irresistible grooves; most of the album consists of Bridgewater singing over different implements of percussion (lots of pan-African marimba) and a wide range of beats and time signatures. I knew only a few of the thirteen songs beforehand (this is not the Great American, or even European, Songbook), but the whole set is compelling. Two 1960s jazz standards are here: "Afro Blue," which is an appropriate opener, and Wayne Shorter's "Footprints." Both are reconfigured to sound completely different from any previous version, vocal or instrumental. She supplies a whole new melody to Nina Simone's "Four Women."

Simone did it as a performance art monologue: Bridgewater sings the piece rather than speaking it, but still makes it dry and understated and highly moving. The most impressive track is the finale, "Compared to What," which was also the basis for a rather amazing lavishly produced video (viewable at youtube.com). Bridgewater belts out the tongue-twisting, rappish lyrics with incredible passion; this is highly inspired funk, funk with a purpose, funk with a mission. Compared to what? Compared to anything.

After Bridgewater visits Broadway, Berlin, Paris, and Mali, she goes to her roots as a jazz singer from the American South with *Eleanora Fagan*. She portrayed Billie Holiday onstage throughout Europe in the late eighties, but here she's not impersonating the legendary diva so much as showing how her music is still relevant in the new century. She proves that her strengths are stronger than anyone else's and her weaknesses matter less and less. Holiday was the master of almost suicidally despondent love songs, and this is still the weak spot for Bridgewater, but it never stops her: She does "Lady Sings the Blues," for instance, in a hard-hitting 6/4. This is a defiant and upbeat description of the blues. Bridgewater focuses on the playful and jubilant side of Holiday's legacy. "Your Mother's Son-in-Law" is a frisky frolic between voice and bass with Bridgewater and Christian McBride, while "All of Me" and "Miss Brown to You" are also joyful rompers. "God Bless the Child" and "Strange Fruit" are obviously more serious, but since they're not supposed to be intimate (one person communicating directly to another) Bridgewater is all over them. The cover shows her naked from the shoulders up (except for an emblematic high gloss gardenia), looking like one of *Goldfinger*'s victims covered in metallic body paint—not to mention that she's the world's sexiest sixty-year-old.

The shame of Bridgewater's career is that even though she started early, she didn't hit her stride until her fortieth year. The few projects she's released since then, however, prove that Dee Dee Bridgewater was well worth waiting for.

C

Cab Calloway (1907–1994)

What a piece of work is Cab Calloway and His Orchestra! Seventy years after the fact, it's hard to imagine such an amalgam of talent in one place. Just consider the name itself—Cab Calloway *and* His Orchestra. Either half of the equation makes it worthwhile, but together they're unstoppable. The greatest singing, swinging, strutting, jumping, and jiving entertainer, and one of the best large-format jazz or pop ensembles of all time. On occasion, you'll find the relationship between the two referred to as "fronting"—a somewhat condescending term that

gets employed whenever a nonmusician is put in front of a band: a Bob Crosby say. Calloway couldn't play and he didn't compose, but he was hardly a mere front man—with his electrifying personality and dynamic performances, he both inspired and truly led his band, which, as it happened, was one of the most formidable aggregations of sidemen, soloists, and arrangers ever assembled.

When we listen to the best singers of the thirties, we can single out and praise artists like Mildred Bailey and Maxine Sullivan for the remarkable subtlety of their work. At the same time, we can also derive pleasure from Calloway for precisely the opposite reason—his complete and utter lack of understatement. Calloway's appeal is perhaps more subjective than that of any other major figure in jazz or pop singing: To some, he is simply a great vocalist, to others he's a parody of the expected roles of both jazz-pop singer and bandleader. Certainly he relies heavily on extreme exaggeration: His high notes are higher, his low notes are lower, his long notes are longer, his emotional highs and lows are more heightened and lowered. His entire act could be harshly judged as being more about effect than substance. Take his scat singing: Sometimes he's almost conventionally tasteful in the Armstrong mold, cleverly paraphrasing a familiar melody with genuine musicianship. At other times, he seems to be merely exaggerating the exaggeration—what we might call pure "Trickeration."

Musicologist Gunther Schuller wrote that Calloway "never left the bounds of good taste." Others would disagree. I would argue that, like jazz's other great showmen—Louis Prima, Fats Waller, Sun Ra, and even Armstrong himself—Calloway's performance art renders the entire concept of taste irrelevant. Whatever transgressions he may commit, he keeps fundamentally true to the two most important elements of jazz—swing and the blues. Among his first recordings are treatments of two venerable blues classics, "St. Louis Blues" and "Downhearted Blues." Both are outrageous, the first including one of the wildest and furthest-out scat solos he would ever perpetrate, but both are essentially true to the material and to the impulse of the music. Likewise, "Is That Religion," "Harlem Camp Meeting," Harold Arlen's "Save Me, Sister" (which he sang with Jolson in *The Singing Kid*), and "Hi-De-Ho Miracle Man" are gussied up but fundamentally sound elaborations of church music themes, many of which have the orchestra doubling as church choir. The first of these, the 1930 "Is That Religion," goes even further by bringing in female voices to make the band chorus sound even more churchy.

In jazz, time is taste: if something swings, to paraphrase Duke Ellington, it's got to mean something. We only care whether it's got that swing—who's going to bother to ask if it's in good taste on top of that? Anita O'Day didn't have any pipes to speak of for her last twenty years, yet she remained a great jazz singer because she could swing like crazy. Likewise, Billie Holiday could still achieve an emotional impact at the end of her short life despite a shortage of chops. We should be equally forgiving to those who might be judged as having an overabundance of chops—particularly Calloway, as he's always right in the groove. His vocals swing just as hard as his amazing orchestra. It's hard to imagine someone so allergic to the very concept of humor and good times that he couldn't derive enormous fun listening to him.

Calloway is a visual trip as well as a musical one:

I would love to see a top dance critic do a choreographic analysis of Calloway's performing style. At times he moves like a man in slow motion, other times he moves as if he were encased in Jell-O, or walking on the bottom of the ocean floor; the deliberate slowness simulates the feeling of being stoned, and this is a crucial aspect of Cabell Calloway. Indeed, where later funsters like Louis Prima and Louis Jordan primarily sing about food—with a more than occasional reference to getting drunk (particularly true of Jordan and Dinah Washington)—no other major figure in jazz celebrated the use of narcotics so openly and irreverently as Calloway.

Unfortunately, far too many major jazz figures were done in by the use of the very substances that Calloway celebrates. Not Calloway. He became rich and famous, one of the most celebrated American (and especially African American) entertainers, beginning well before the big band era and then decades and decades after it. And he owed it all to a gal named Minnie the Moocher. One shudders to think where Calloway would have been without her.

Calloway had, in fact, lived all of twenty-four years before "Minnie the Moocher" hi-de-ho'd her way into his life; he'd already starred in a Broadway revue and was by then leading his own orchestra, recording and headlining at the Cotton Club. But it was that song about Minnie, and the way he sang it, that made the Calloway orchestra something special. Even without Calloway, the band formerly known as the Missourians was first-class—on a par with, say, the Mills Blue Rhythm Orchestra (another group managed by Irving Mills, the business force behind both Calloway and Ellington). But with Calloway in front of the band, they were unstoppable—a too-much-of-a-muchness combination that couldn't help but rocket to the top of the entertainment industry.

Cabell Calloway was born on Christmas Day 1907, in Rochester, New York, and shortly afterward his family moved back home to Baltimore, where Calloway was raised. Although from an early age he strove to make music, he attended law school in Chicago. But, like Bing Crosby before him, he gradually abandoned this study when he realized that he was bringing in more money singing in nightclubs than he was likely to earn practicing the law.

His sister, Blanche (1904–1978), was a headliner before him, having starred in black revues, recorded as a blues singer (accompanied by no less than Armstrong himself), and fronted her own orchestra. Cabell's first notable show business gig was as a member of a vocal quartet in the traveling show *Plantation Days*. In Chicago, he worked variously as singer, drummer, and emcee at various clubs, including the Sunset and Dreamland cafés. In 1929, he was offered the chance to serve as front man for a band called the Alabamans, which brought him to New York. There, he landed a prominent spot in one of Broadway's most important black revues, *Connie's Hot Chocolates*, and after scoring a hit, he was given the opportunity to lead a band of his own on a permanent basis, a first-rate territorial group called the Missourians, who had already recorded for RCA Victor. Around the same time, he hooked up with entrepreneur (talent manager and music publisher) Irving Mills, who arranged for the new combination to replace Duke Ellington at the Cotton Club, the number-one showcase for black talent in the country. By this time they were already known as Cab Calloway and His Orchestra.

"Minnie" came along in 1931. In his 1976 autobiography, *Of Minnie the Moocher and Me* (what clsc?), Calloway is very clear about his sources: The piece has a blues feel, being roughly inspired by his rendition of the old-time blues number "St. James Infirmary Blues." "Minnie" is also clearly based on "Willie the Weeper," a folk song about a chimney sweeper "who had the coke habit and he had it bad," and who is here given a sex change. The name "Minnie" itself came from a 1930 song entitled "Minnie the Mermaid (A Love Song in Fish Time)" as recorded by Bernie Cummins and His Orchestra. Like Willie the Weeper, Minnie suffers from severe substance abuse problems. Someone once described "Minnie" as a song about "a good girl who becomes addicted to cocaine," but it's more celebratory than forlorn. As singer-songwriter, Calloway positively revels in vivid descriptions of Minnie's cocaine-induced hallucinations.

Apart from the subject matter, "Minnie" introduced other elements, both musical and thematic, into Calloway's musical makeup. "Minnie" brought the sing-along and the call-and-response pattern into jazz and pop in a big way, although it had long been one of the most basic aspects of African American music, especially in black religious music. Well before Calloway, the idea of a soloist going back and forth with the whole ensemble or one instrumental section responding to another was a fundamental component of big band jazz—very famously in Fletcher Henderson's treatment of Jelly Roll Morton's "King Porter Stomp."

Surprisingly, Calloway informs us, he first got the idea of having the band answer him vocally from a number of white orchestras he heard in Chicago in the mid-twenties: Benny Meroff, Paul Ash, and Fred Waring. Although Waring did do some very clever things with unison group singing (as did Bernie Cummins in "Minnie the Mermaid"), none of these bands sounds anything like Calloway. The scat episode in "Minnie" is directly anticipated by a wordless sequence in "Willie the Weeper," but Calloway developed it into the *Gone With the Wind* of scat performances. You know the routine: He sings "hi-de-hi-de-hi" and the band—and presumably the crowd—answers back "hi-de-hi-de-hi." Whatever scat phrase he sings, it comes back at him from band and the crowd. "I would have the whole damn place echoing with 'Minnie,'" Calloway wrote. "I could feel the mood of the crowd even in a huge auditorium. And it was a ball, me just swinging and swaying with my hair flopping down on my forehead and my arms stretched out, singing my heart out."

"Minnie" provided Calloway with the three signature elements of his canon: the characters of Minnie and her even more perpetually stoned boyfriend, Smokey Joe; the incessant references to drug culture; and the call-and-response sing-along. Throughout the rest of his career, the thirties in particular, he would continually find new plot lines for the characters Minnie the Moocher and the coke-happy Smokey Joe. They reappear next in two songs written by Harold Arlen and Ted Koehler for him to sing at the Cotton Club revues, "Kickin' the Gong Around" and "Minnie the Moocher's Wedding Day." In the first, Koehler's lyric uses both verse and chorus to depict Smokey's mission to Chinatown, in search of the wandering Minnie; the second describes in elaborate detail their impending nuptials. "Kickin'" is somewhat grimy, describing Smokey as if he were going through painful withdrawal symptoms ("He was sweatin', cold and pale / He was looking for his frail [slang for "woman"] / He was broke and all his junk ran out"). "Wedding Day" employs the fanciful, psychedelic imagery of a really wild trip ("the Prince of Wales said he would get away / For Minnie the Moocher's wedding day"). In short, the two most famous sequels to the original "Minnie the Moocher" depict the lows and highs of the addict's mental state.

Minnie and Smokey make guest appearances in songs not otherwise about them, such as "Zah, Zuh, Zaz" and "The Lady with the Fan." Minnie even turns up in "Growlin' Dan," a 1931 record by Calloway's sister, Blanche, who at the time was recording with her own orchestra for Victor. Minnie's also the inspiration for one of Groucho Marx's best lines in *A Night at the Opera* (1935). Why pay big money to hear a famous opera singer when, for 75 cents, you can get a record of Cab Calloway singing "Minnie the Moocher"? Then comes Groucho's punch line: "And for a buck and a quarter, you can get Minnie!" Everybody in the thirties would have known who Minnie the Moocher was.

In Calloway's mythology, Minnie and Smokey were more like underground cartoon characters, forerunners of R. Crumb's Fritz the Cat and Mr. Natural. Calloway himself participated in three classic animated one-reelers (and was referred to in many more) with Betty Boop, in which the surreal imagery of the Fleischer brothers matched the hallucinogenic quality of the music. Curiously, the Fleischers did not specifically depict animated versions of Minnie and Smokey: That would come a few years later in the MGM cartoon *Swing Wedding*, in which the saga of Minnie's wedding day is enacted by a cast of frogs who impersonate Harlem celebrities: Armstrong, Fats Waller, Bojangles Robinson. Smokey Joe himself turns out to be a caricature of Stepin Fetchit—who was a caricature to begin with, even in live action—although the use of drugs may explain why ol' Step was so lazy and slow in all of his movies: He was obviously smashed. Calloway himself is caricatured as an interloper who would seduce Minnie away from Smokey.

On Planet Calloway it seems everybody is stoned all the time, even in songs like the infamous "Reefer Man," which makes no mention of cokedom's most famous power couple. The record opens with a bit of dialogue ("I think he's lost his mind"), which is re-created when Calloway and band performed the song in *International House*. Then, too, when Calloway performed "Kickin' the Gong Around" in *The Big Broadcast*, his dance included—in addition to spins, splits, and slow walking—a pantomime of the action of sticking powder up his nose. In 1934, he sang of the "Jitterbug," one of the first times the term was used in a song title, yet it doesn't quite mean what it would a few years later. Rather than describe a jitterbug as a dancer or swing fan, Calloway depicts the guys in his band as such because of their self-medicating habits; it's drinking the "jitter sauce" that causes these bugs to jitter. In fact, the first line is "If you'd like to be a jitter bug / The first thing you must do is get a jug."

Calloway kept the original "Minnie" song alive as his theme song, with its famous moaning, minor key introduction, but by the forties sequels were less forthcoming. It was plain that by 1938, Calloway was milking things a bit too far when he came up with "Mister Paganini, Swing for Minnie," in which the Moocher makes a request of a famous radio maestro. A year later, in 1939, Calloway effectively ended the series with "The Ghost of Smokey Joe," which establishes both the mortality and the immortality of the characters. Yet they continued to return from beyond the grave: 1940 brought forth "Hi De Ho Serenade," in which Calloway, singing in the first person as Smokey Joe, and the band sing a lullaby to Minnie as she drifts off to dreamland, or perhaps shuffles off her mortal coil. In 1941, the King Cole Trio recorded their own addition to the series, "Smokey Joe," who is here described not as a drug addict but as a "gigolo."

Drug references became less rampant in Calloway's songs, too, as Smokey and the Moocher faded. As the thirties wore on, booze became legal (and the socially acceptable method of getting bombed), marijuana became officially taboo, and heroin became the black plague of jazz, but by then the entire subject seems to have lost its appeal for the Cabster.

One device that Calloway kept milking for all it was worth was his famous call-and-response bit, which remained integral to what he did for the rest of his career. "Eadie Was a Lady," written by Richard Whiting for Ethel Merman to sing in the Broadway

musical *Take a Chance*, shows the influence of Calloway and Minnie in spheres beyond jazz and big bands. The song was obviously inspired by "Minnie," so in his version Calloway takes it upon himself to transform Eadie into Minnie in whiteface. "Eadie," like "Minnie," tells a very distinctive story about a special lady, as lovable as she is trashy, whereas the rest of Calloway's call-and-response songs are pure nonsense, with little attempt at narrative. In the 1933 "Zah, Zuh, Zaz," he just gives us the call-and-response without any plot at all. Some of the other call-and-response arias include "You Gotta Ho-De-Ho" (1932), "Wah-Dee-Dah" (1932), "The Scat Song" (1933), "Hotcha Razz-Ma-Tazz" (1934), "Keep That Hi-De-Hi in Your Soul" (Arlen, 1935), "The Hi-De-Ho Miracle Man" (1936), "Mama I Wanna Make Rhythm" (1937), "Hi-De-Ho Romeo" (1937), "Hoy Hoy" (1937), "Hi-De-Ho Serenade" (1940), "Are You All Reet" (1940), "Foo-a-Little Ballyhoo" (1944), "Hey Now, Hey Now" (1946), and "Hi-De-Ho Man" (1947).

These are just a sampling of the titles that combine scatting, nonsense expressions, and call-and-response chanting-and-answering with the band. Calloway also finds opportunities for hi-de-ho that other bandleaders miss: Glenn Miller performed "Boog-It" as a straight vocal by Marion Hutton, but Calloway does it with the band hi-de-ho'ing back and forth.

There's also a subseries of kosher hi-de-hos, from the 1933 Victor remake of "Minnie the Moocher," to Calloway's interpretations of the Yiddish songs "Utt Da Zay (The Tailors' Song)" and "A Be Gezindt," to his wildly cantorial wailing 1947 "Hi-De-Ho Man." To judge by this strain of Calloway's work, it's clear that Minnie is no shiksa.

By the early thirties Calloway was one of the very top black entertainers and bandleaders in the country, on a par with Duke Ellington, Louis Armstrong, and Ethel Waters—in addition to the cartoons, he was featured in a steady series of live action short subjects and feature films. And despite his songs of drug addiction, he was, no less than Ellington, concerned with being a positive role model and presenting a positive vision of the black experience, consistently depicting Harlem in a celebratory light: "Harlem Camp Meeting," "Harlem Hospitality," "The Man from Harlem" (who at one point advises a couple of girls to "smoke these weeds and get high!"), "Harlem Holiday," and even "Tarzan of Harlem." There are exceptions: "Yaller," an excessively melodramatic song about a tragic mulatto (it's a male equivalent of Andy Razaf's "Black and Blue"), and "Papa's in Bed with His Britches On" and "Oh Grandpa," which depict those paternal figures as general lowlifes. Still, almost all these songs promote a positive view of the black experience.

With Calloway, scat and slang are instantly interchangeable, almost different words for the same thing. As is true of Louis Prima, the closest thing he would have to a white counterpart, Calloway is also concerned with ethnicities other than his own. Like other bands, Calloway's occasionally played Latinate numbers—"Doin' the Rhumba" (1931), "The Congo Conga" (1938), "Chili con Conga" (1939), "Rhapsody in Rhumba" (1940, which is just a straight-ahead swinger with no Latin musical content whatsoever), "Yo Eta Cansa" (1940), and "Goin' Conga" (1940). Other cultures are even better suited to the Calloway canon. Smokey and Minnie are forever running off to Chinatown to score some substances, but "Chinese Rhythm" (1934) and "Chop Chop Charlie Chan (From China)"—for once—don't even mention drugs, but rather afford Calloway the apparently welcome opportunity to hi-de-ho in ersatz high Chinese. These songs, like his Yiddish numbers, give him the chance to show how other languages can be converted to scat and hi-de-ho.

To his credit, Calloway never viewed his orchestra as a mere backdrop for his antics: Even when he narrates an otherwise instrumental disc and goes so far as to talk over other musicians' individual solos, he's still trying to showcase both the whole ensemble and each individual player. He deliberately put together the best band he possibly could, and his orchestra was one of the finest in jazz, on a par with Lunceford, Basie, and even his colleague in the Irving Mills office, Duke Ellington. (Over the years Calloway frequently recorded Ellington material, such as an outstanding "Take the A Train" and a "Creole Love Call" with a bizarre lyric, as well as a very obscure 1945 entry called "Afternoon Moon.") Like Sinatra—and unlike Ray Charles—he took a special pride in getting the best possible treatment for his men. He also showcased them extensively, even to the point of Ellington-like concertos that spotlighted individual talents for an entire side, such as "Paradiddle" for Cozy Cole, "Pluckin' the Bass" for Milt Hinton, "Jonah Joins the Cab" for Jonah Jones, and "Willow Weep for Me" for Hilton Jefferson. The most famous of these instrumental features was "Ghost of a Chance," which established Chu Berry as perhaps the first contender to Coleman Hawkins's throne as King of the Tenors, recorded around the same time as the emergence of Lester Young and Ben Webster.

The "serious" jazz aspects of Calloway's orchestra during the Chu Berry years, 1937–41, are celebrated in *Best of the Big Bands—Cab Calloway Featuring Chu Berry* (which mysteriously omits "Ghost of a Chance"). Another Sony Legacy release, *Are You Hep to the Jive*, was not included in the "Best of the Big Bands" series but rather in the corporation's "Rhythm and Soul" series, which makes a claim for Calloway as part of the world of R&B and postwar pop. Calloway's forties recordings were certainly heading in that direction, the basic texture of the ensemble on numbers like "The Honeydripper" being as much R&B and bop as traditional big band

swing. Certainly, many mid-forties pieces, like "Don't Falter at the Altar," "The Jungle King," "The Calloway Boogie" ("Keeps you groovy, twenty-four hours a day"), and "Everybody Eats When They Come to My House," all sound as if they could have come from the repertoire of Louis Jordan.

Calloway's voice was, if anything, getting stronger around the time of his fortieth birthday—the 1947 "Hi De Ho Man" opens with what might be Calloway's most extravagantly exhibitionist series of cantorial wails, yet delivered most effectively in a wild cadenza that frames the piece at the beginning and end. In addition to all that hi-de-ho, Calloway always had been a fine ballad singer, and that aspect of his music is also heard more frequently in these years. The 1944–47 Columbia sessions include at least three superior ballads: "Let's Take the Long Way Home" (Arlen again), "All at Once" (a Kurt Weill–Ira Gershwin obscurity, from *Where Do We Go from Here*), and "Afternoon Moon" (an Ellington song never recorded by the Maestro). There's also a swinging, Sportin' Life–type reading of "Necessity," from *Finian's Rainbow*.

As a vocalist, Calloway wasn't entirely dependent on the orchestra. Therefore, it's surprising that once he finally had to break up the permanent, full-time working big band, he didn't record more as a single. The fifties were an odd time, in which his main predecessor, Louis Armstrong, was triumphantly reborn as a pop singer. Yet Calloway's successors, like Louis Jordan, were falling from favor at least as fast as Cab himself. The new thing Calloway found to do was Broadway. He was offered the role of Sportin' Life in the Robert Breen production of *Porgy and Bess*, which extensively toured the forty-eight states and then the world. Calloway had always claimed that he had been the original inspiration for the drug-pushing Sportin' Life—he surely did inspire "It Ain't Necessarily So," with its wild hi-de-ho–like call-and-response section—and now it was time for Sportin' Life to give a little back to Calloway. This was the production that established the Gershwin opera as an American classic, and also revived Calloway's own fading fortunes.

His other big stage role in later years was as the senior male lead (Horace Vandergelder) in the all-black version of *Hello, Dolly!* which starred Pearl Bailey. Surprisingly, neither of these very successful productions yielded a cast album, although Calloway did appear on the sound track album of the 1959 film of *Porgy and Bess* because Sammy Davis Jr., who essayed Sportin' Life in the film, was under contract to another label. More important, he recorded a new album for RCA, in which he remade twelve of his thirties and forties classics with a superb studio band.

Calloway kept busy until the end, most famously in the 1980 car-crash comedy *The Blues Brothers*, which also featured cameos by Ray Charles and Aretha Franklin. In later years he worked extensively with his daughter Chris, who in 2000 led a revived Calloway orchestra at the JVC Jazz Festival.

When Cab Calloway died in 1994, I sat next to Harold Nicholas, who shared the screen with him in the 1943 all-black classic *Stormy Weather*, at the memorial service held at St. John the Divine on 112th Street. (Best line of the evening was Gregory Hines's "I never saw a brother who had hair that moved before.") It was amazing to see what Calloway still meant to the black population of New York, sixty-five years after he had first arrived in this city. Even in death, he had us hi-de-ho-ing and zah-zuh-zas-ing along with him via old film clips. In all, we had to echo the sentiments of Cole Porter in his 1936 song "Red, Hot and Blue" in which he tells us of his preference for swing over Wagnerian opera: "I'd throw my best pal away for Calloway." He was right: "hi-de-ho" beats "yo-ho-to-ho" anytime.

Eddie Cantor (1892–1964)

Jolson is the guy that everybody else tries to imitate. I don't want to mention any names—a guy with five daughters has got trouble enough as it is!
—George Jessel (on a 1937 radio program)

Considering the high percentage of early sound films that no longer exist, the 1930 *Whoopee!* could well have been a lost film—which would be a tragedy. Apart from being the major cinematic record of a Florenz Ziegfeld show (it had opened on Broadway two years earlier although the title of Ziegfeld's show lacked the exclamation point; Sam Goldwyn added it for the movie), *Whoopee!* contains the two most amazing numbers ever documented of Eddie Cantor, which are a wonderful microcosm of this long-running multimedia star at his pinnacle.

"My Baby Just Cares for Me" has a lot stacked against it, visually: Cantor sings it in blackface, which doesn't endear him to contemporary audiences, and he's performing in front of a very stagey-looking cast of characters (including singer Ethel Schutta in nurse drag and a chorus line of cowgirls—supposedly including the young Betty Grable—who aren't dancing but just standing around and looking as if they don't know what to do with themselves). Then, the second verse has him dropping the names of thirties movie stars mostly forgotten today ("My baby's no [John] Gilbert fan / Ron[ald] Colman is not her man . . ."). As currently seen on YouTube, "My Baby Just Cares for Me" is only a minute and a half long, but Cantor's energy and personality are nothing short of miraculous: He just comes bounding out at you, with a charm that's impossible to resist. Where blackface makes Al Jolson seem surreal, like a harlequin figure, Cantor comes across like a real person, one with contagious enthusiasm, bouncing all over the stage like a man on a trampoline.

The title song, "Makin' Whoopee," is even more impressive. In "My Baby," Cantor is an active partic-ipant in the middle of a love affair; in "Makin' Whoopee" he's observing from the sidelines, firmly taking the position of one who declines to partici-pate. Instead of jumping up and down in your face, here Cantor is subtle: He underplays every humor-ous twist of the lyric, every motion—even of his eyes, which are among the most expressive, not to mention the largest, in all movie history. Briefly interacting with a dancing chorus of bridesmaids, he even executes a few somewhat athletic steps, but very slowly. (It's all so subtle that, for some reason, he sings a completely different lyric from the one he sang in the show, or at least from the familiar words he recorded in 1928.) Cantor is bursting with per-sonality of an entirely different kind, and his laid-back, semi-sung approach is a textbook model of how to put over a lyric. In both numbers (not to mention another comedy song, "The Girlfriend of a Boyfriend of Mine") Cantor seems completely three-dimensional on every level, musically, emo-tionally, even physically—even in two-strip Techni-color.

As a comic, Jolson was nonhuman, peering at us from behind blackface or some other kind of harlequin-like mask. It wasn't until much later, when he went into pictures, that he was required to function as a conventional leading man—on Broad-way he was always "Gus," a mischievous Puck-like figure who comments on the action from the side-lines and steals the show without actually participat-ing in the plot. One of the reasons his movies aren't as effective as one would like them to be is because Jolson himself could never serve as a figure of identi-fication.

Cantor, on the other hand, was one of us. To use a Yiddish phrase that he himself certainly employed, he was a mensch—a real human being. Consider his resources: His comedy wasn't exactly side-splittingly funny, and his dancing depended more on sheer exuberance than technique. As for his singing, it was hardly that of a Jolson-level virtuoso. His voice, which gradually evolved from a low tenor in the acoustic era to a high baritone in the age of electric-ity, had a slightly nasal rasp to it; it would be fair to call it pleasant. But when you put it all together—the singing, the comedy, the hyperkinetic strutting across the stage—Cantor was a great entertainer, a colossal figure in American vernacular culture who served as a major player for almost fifty years. When Cantor sang "What a Perfect Combination," in the 1932 musical *The Kid from Spain*, he might have been talking about himself.

In some respects, he may well have been as much of a monstrous egomaniac as everyone else in show business (though no competition for Jolson in this department either), but, unlike Jolson, he had a sense of humor and objectivity about himself. It's impossible to imagine Jolson parodying himself the way Cantor does in *Thank Your Lucky Stars* (1943). In this wartime musical, Cantor plays "Eddie

Cantor" as a bombastic, domineering egotist who tries to control everything and everybody. When he's asked to perform in a revue, he immediately tries to take it over and run the whole show, which means forcing his bizarre ideas on everybody, such as having all the chorus girls dress up like boiled potatoes and jump into a giant pool of sour cream.

Yet if Cantor had an ego like Jolson's, he also had a social conscience like Paul Robeson's. Hard as it may be to believe about a public figure who was best known, for a period, for appearing in blackface, Cantor was a humanitarian above and beyond the call of duty. Among other things, he was virtually the only entertainer who had the guts to publicly denounce Joseph McCarthy at the height of his evil influence and was also one of the first to bring African American entertainers onto his TV show and treat them like equals.

Also unlike Jolson, Cantor had a large family, and his five girls were the topic of as much radio banter as Crosby's four boys. Today, his legacy benefits keenly from the efforts of his grandson Brian Gari, the child of his youngest daughter, Janet Cantor Gari. Where most reference books state that Cantor was born Edward Israel Iskowitz on the Lower East Side on January 31, 1892, Gari tells us that his real first name was Isidore and that the actual date of his birth is not known. But all sources agree that Cantor, like most performers of his era, started as a child performer. A half-generation or so younger than Jolson, he wasn't actually born in the Old Country, but was the child of first-generation immigrants from Russia. Not that his parents were much of an issue—they died when he was three—and Isidore was raised by his grandmother. Like many minority children at the turn of the century, a talent for singing and *shpieling* at first served as his protection from tough guys on the streets, and then served as his exit visa from the rougher neighborhoods.

In the early years of the new century, Cantor was working as a singing waiter in an only slightly less tough Coney Island saloon, where the pianist was an equally young James Durante (a scenario that they would re-create on radio show sketches). By the end of the first decade, Cantor was rising slowly to the top of the vaudeville world. Playing Hammerstein's Victoria Theatre in 1909, he sang "My Wife's Gone to the Country, Hooray, Hooray," and put both himself and the song's composer, the not yet established Irving Berlin, on the map.

For a time he toured with songwriter and impresario Gus Edwards, along with George Jessel and Walter Winchell (who started his career as a hoofer before he hit the jackpot with a different kind of song and dance); he played London with the Edwards troupe in 1914. Having climbed to the top of the Palace two-a-day world, Cantor helped blaze the trail out of vaudeville and onto the "legit" stage. By the end of World War I, he was a fixture on Broadway, thanks to the era's supreme producer and talent broker, Florenz Ziegfeld. He spent the Jazz Age as a Broadway headliner, starring in seven major musicals between the *Follies* of 1917 and Ziegfeld's *Whoopee* of 1928.

Cantor began his recording career with two sides for Victor in 1917, the same company where Jolson had cut his first sides six years earlier. After that first Victor session, he recorded prolifically for the Emerson label (his complete output has been collated by Gari on the recommended *Eddie Cantor: The Early Days, 1917–1921*, a forty-five-track, two-CD set on Original Cast Records). In 1922, he switched to Columbia Records, and continued to turn out discs regularly through the end of the acoustic era. After 1925, he recorded less frequently, first a few early electric sides for Columbia, then nine sides for Victor between 1928 and 1931, and then roughly two dozen titles for ARC (the once and future Columbia) and Decca between 1932 and 1942. Though he only recorded sporadically after his first Columbia contract (1922–25), the sides he did make are of a very high quality, and the bulk of these, the ones currently owned by Sony, are available on *Eddie Cantor: The Columbia Years, 1922–1940*, which is probably the most essential Cantor reissue package.

Just a few more Jolson parallels: where Jolie hit his stride in the World War I era, Cantor reached his peak in the early to mid-twenties. At a time when Jolson was already starting to sound vaguely anachronistic, Cantor, then in his thirties, came off as precisely the perfect singing comic for the Roaring Twenties. We think of Jolson as the ultimate "Mammy" singer, though obviously he was much more than that, but Cantor, who was even younger than Jolson when his mother died, sang of different kinds of relationships. His discs would be of as much interest to a sociologist as to a musicologist (and possibly even a gynecologist): Cantor's records are a kind of *Sex and the City* for Mongrel Manhattan in the Terrible Twenties. Cantor's Jazz Age is an era completely distinct from earlier generations. All of a sudden members of the fair sex were voting, working in offices, and earning regular salaries. At the same time, the Nineteenth Amendment (which essentially legalized the concept of breaking the law), technology, and economic prosperity all contributed to making the holding company known as old America into a brave new world, and no one captured the mood of the era more vividly than Cantor.

The series is nicely prefaced by the two 1917 titles, "That's the Kind of a Baby for Me" and "The Modern Maiden's Prayer." These songs work on several levels. One of them is that, Cantor seems to be griping about these newly liberated ladies, who, unlike his sainted grandmother, do not pray for virtue and moral purity but offer up prayers to God for material goods and as much fun as their female frames can withstand. But Cantor's complaints are offered strictly with tongue in cheek, because he knows the upside of woman's liberation is that sex will flow as freely as Prohibition hooch.

In almost every song, Cantor portrays himself as a horny young swain, dying to go around with as many beautiful girls as possible. When most of these lasses turn out to be more interested in finance than romance, he doesn't regard this as a nuisance—his attitude and exuberance are of a piece with the boom years leading up to Black Friday; he sings as if he knows there's no shortage of money or liquor to go around, and he's just dying to shower both on the fair sex.

He's hungry for love, and the dames are hungry for his money. Songwriters presented him with dozens of variations on this theme, and he wrote more than a few himself. Cantor's switch to Columbia occurred around the time he was opening in *Make It Snappy*, a revue that played for a respectable three months in the spring of 1922 (in those days before air-conditioning, even the most successful shows rarely ran through July and August), for which Cantor served as book writer, co-lyricist, and leading performer.

The first of the Columbia sides, "I Love Her (She Loves Me)," co-credited to Cantor himself, finds his character attracted to the unnamed object of his affection primarily for her father's money ("he has dough . . . And lumbago"). The flip side, "I'm Hungry for Beautiful Girls," introduces an idea he elaborates upon later in the 1928 "Hungry Women" from *Whoopee*. The idea in both songs is that these modern maidens view him strictly as a meal ticket (an interesting choice of subjects for an entertainer supporting a wife and five daughters). Both include the line "I feed 'em and weep," a play on the card-playing expression "read 'em and weep." As always, though there might be an element of a complaint, Cantor still seems happy to fulfill his function as a link in the food chain. ("My Wife Is on a Diet" has Cantor, conversely, complaining about women who *don't* eat enough.) A Jewish icon for a later generation, Woody Allen, would quote from "Hungry Women" in the 1975 *Love and Death*: When Diane Keaton tells him that she's "half-saint and half-whore," Allen replies, "I hope I get the half that eats."

Cantor sings of sexually aggressive young men and women in a way that's impossible to imagine anyone doing a decade earlier—even under the protective mask of blackface and minstrelsy. Cantor's 1922–25 late acoustics are especially strong in the subgenre of name songs. He sings of hungry women named Sophie ("I go so far with Sophie / And Sophie goes so far with me"), "No, No Nora (Nobody but You)," "Ritzy Mitzy" ("Ritzy Mitzy don't ritz me"), and "Row Row Rosie" ("Don't let him rock the boat / It's mighty hard to float").

Cantor would find his signature song early on, courtesy of the hungriest woman of them all, "Susie," heroine of the 1922 "Susie" and the 1924 "If

You Knew Susie." "Susie" looks to the past via a quote from "Ida (Sweet as Apple Cider)," a reference to Cantor's wife as well as the nineteenth-century minstrel and vaudeville star Eddie Leonard. "If You Knew Susie" was actually introduced by Jolson (in *Big Boy*), and soon it was being heard in five Broadway shows at once, but the performer who made the greatest impression with it was Cantor in *Kid Boots*. Cantor would sing "If You Knew Susie" again and again for the rest of his life—"Susie" was his "Mammy," his "April Showers," his "Waitin' for the Robert E. Lee" all at once, and also served as the title of his last starring film, in 1948.

Cantor's voice was, like those of most popular tenors of the acoustic era, high and androgynous enough for him to go in vocal drag—to sing from the female perspective in "Joe Is Here," "Eddie (Steady)," "Oh Gee Georgie," and virtually the only guy song to survive the Jazz Age, "Charley My Boy." These are sung by, rather than about, hungry women, who rave about the charms of their hip-flask-bearing sheiks. Unlike the output of most singers of the era, Cantor's includes only a token amount of exotica, like the jungleicious "Monkey Doodle," the mock tango "Those Panama Mamas (Are Ruining Me)," and the ersatz island "On a Windy Day 'Way Down in Waikiki." Other singers recorded tons of these in the teens and twenties—Jolson had a particular flair for faux espagnole—but not Cantor.

In 1928, Cantor was in *Whoopee*, which would be his best-remembered vehicle, first as a Broadway show, then as a film; it would be the only Cantor vehicle that would survive him, being revived on Broadway fifty years later with actor Charles Repole doing a convincing Cantor. (The 1940 *Banjo Eyes* would seem a fine candidate for revival. Despite the Cantor-specific title, this was in fact a musical adaptation of the popular comedy *Three Men on a Horse* with an exceptional score by Vernon Duke. Unfortunately, Cantor didn't record any of it.)

Whoopee's big song was "Makin' Whoopee," by Walter Donaldson and Gus Kahn, which challenges "If You Knew Susie" as the piece of music most identifiable with Cantor. Where "Susie" is typical of Cantor's high-energy set pieces, he deliberately undersells "Makin' Whoopee" in both the 1928 Victor disc and the 1930 Goldwyn film, singing it slowly and slyly, in a way that would not have been possible in the acoustic era. He gets maximum mileage out of every *entendre*, and within the course of 32 bars, a typical twenties boy and girl progress from sweethearts to man and wife to parents, yet by the second chorus hubby is now making whoopee with another sweetie. By now, the love-and-money cycle has evolved to the point where the Boy has to pony up in divorce court to get rid of the Girl. Clearly, the eco-socio-sexual boom of the twenties has reached a point of no return.

Cantor himself served as the oracle who prophesied the end of the Jazz Age. He commemorated the egg laid by Wall Street with "Eddie Cantor's Tips on the Stock Market," a spoken monologue recorded on October 29, 1929, the day after Black Friday. In it he observes that women's hemlines are falling at the same rate as stock prices—another money-sex metaphor. He was right in the short run, but soon enough the era of women in the workforce—or anybody in the workforce—as well as of casual love and loose securities was over, even with the repeal of Prohibition in 1933.

After *Whoopee,* Cantor's recording career also peaked. Up to 1925, records were more of a focus, but by the thirties his records were running a distant third to pictures and radio work. In fact, several recordings, "What a Perfect Combination" and "The Man on the Flying Trapeze," are direct spin-offs of his extremely popular *Chase and Sanborn Hour,* a radio institution practically on the order of *Amos 'n' Andy.* Both tracks begin with a crowd chanting "We Want Cantor," and he makes his entrance with his audio signature, a kind of bizarre spitting noise that he also used for a gag effect in several films.

Unlike Crosby, who made three or four films a year, and more like Astaire, who appeared in just one big movie per season, Cantor starred in a series of major musical spectaculars between the 1930 *Whoopee!* and the 1937 *Ali Baba Goes to Town,* namely *Palmy Days* (1931), *The Kid from Spain* (1932), *Roman Scandals* (1933), *Kid Millions* (1934), and *Strike Me Pink* (1936). All of these except the last were Samuel Goldwyn productions, and all of these through 1933 were distinctly pre–Production Code epics, with lots of scantily clad chorus girls—manipulated by Busby Berkeley no less—and sexual innuendo.

He was no longer doing Broadway and was recording only sporadically, but between pictures and especially radio work, he was more popular than ever during the Depression, even into World War II. The records, however, continue to provide the best evidence of what he was singing like. His "Hello Sunshine Hello," made early in 1929, is typical of the sort of song that became popular in the early thirties, as was "Making the Best of Each Day," recorded in London in 1934. His most successful Depression songs were "Cheer Up" (from a revue called *Ballyhoo,* which he sang on a 25-cent "Hit of the Week" disc) and "When My Ship Comes In" (from *Kid Millions*). They both make for a pertinent comparison with "Look What You've Done" (from *The Kid from Spain*).

"Look What You've Done" is perhaps Cantor's only completely straight love song, without any gags, any irony, or any reference to how either of the two lovers stands to benefit financially from the relationship. It's a fine song, yet it makes for one of Cantor's least interesting records; unlike Jolson, Cantor just doesn't cut it as a completely straight singer of love songs. His voice isn't attractive enough, and by emoting it out—he talk-sings the second chorus—

he doesn't make it any more interesting. It's not nearly as entertaining as "The Girlfriend of a Boyfriend of Mine," an entertaining parody of a lachrymose love lament (such as "Here Am I, Broken-Hearted"), which he put over with devastating acumen in the film version of *Whoopee!*

Likewise, the straight Depression songs "Hello Sunshine Hello" and "Making the Best of Each Day" aren't nearly as interesting as those that come loaded with irony and self-parody, like "When My Ship Comes In." The latter is a witty list lyric detailing the simple pleasures that poor slobs dreamed about while they waited on breadlines, and "Cheer Up" is an outright attack on Depression anthems—"Cheer Up, Smile, Nertz!" Where Jolson is a blackface harlequin, Cantor comes off like a wiseass kid; in "When My Ship Comes In" most of the pleasures he dreams about are those of a ten-year-old: buying an ice cream factory (which he eventually does in *Kid Millions*'s climactic number) and banishing spinach.

"What a Perfect Combination" and "There's Nothing Too Good for My Baby" are two rare examples of Cantor teaming with first-rate jazz-dance orchestras, Ben Selvin's and Gus Arnheim's, respectively. Back in 1924, he had teamed with the Georgians, an excellent hot jazz combo of the mid-twenties that actually was a small group out of the larger Paul Specht Orchestra, for the excellent "Oh Gee Georgie" and "If You Do What You Do." They all show that Cantor doesn't actually swing à la Armstrong or Crosby, but when motivated by strong accompaniment, he performs with a driving rhythm that's certainly the next best thing.

What's unfortunate is that since the bottom had dropped out of the record business, Cantor didn't make commercial records of most of the key songs from his films—only one from *Palmy Days* and two from *The Kid from Spain,* nothing from *Roman Scandals* or *Strike Me Pink* (a real shame in that the scores for these were by Harry Warren and Harold Arlen, respectively) or *Ali Baba Goes to Town.*

His last really significant recording project may have been done in fall 1934, when he cut all four of the excellent songs from *Kid Millions,* the Goldwyn film that reunited Cantor with his *Whoopee* words-and-music team of Kahn and Donaldson. "When My Ship Comes In," reissued on the Columbia package in two takes recorded a month apart, is one of his best Depression songs—a sterling example of how to face adversity with a sense of humor. "An Earful of Music" (sung in the picture by Ethel Merman, who, in a delightfully surreal touch, passes herself off as Cantor's mother) and "Okay Toots" are classic Cantor anthems of energy, "Toots" being a worthy heiress to the legacy of Susie and Ida and Nora and company. The equivalent of an Act One curtain closer is a minstrel show co-starring a blacked-up Cantor and a real African American dance team, the very young Nicholas Brothers. The two key numbers here are Irving Berlin's 1918 "Mandy" and a new song Burton Lane called "I Want to Be a Minstrel Man," which itself was later relyricized by Alan Jay Lerner as "You're All the World to Me" (and reimmortalized by Fred Astaire in *Royal Wedding* and re-re-immortalized by Tony Bennett throughout the nineties).

If *Whoopee* climaxed Cantor's Broadway career, *Kid Millions* was the apogee of his period as a movie and recording star. There were other highlights in the musical career, but, like Jolson after 1940, he spent most of the postwar period revisiting the past. He didn't always remake his old numbers strictly; sometimes he offered new twists and updates on the older songs, like "Now I Always Have Maggie Alone," from 1950, an update on a twenties song he hadn't previously recorded, "I Never See Maggie Alone." There was also a swing era reinterpretation of "Margie," a girl's name tune he cut for Emerson in 1920 and remade as his last Columbia side twenty years later. The swinging 1939 remake of "If You Knew Susie" may be even stronger than the original of fifteen years earlier, boasting a wild double-time patter chorus. Near the end of this later "Susie," the forty-seven-year-old singer asks, "Not bad for a grandfather, eh?" He's right, it isn't, but the comment can't help instilling in us the feeling that Cantor had already done everything he was going to do. From now on, we would have to judge him by a different set of standards, grandfather standards.

As with many grandfathers, the later work is more self-referential. There would be one more important show (*Banjo Eyes*) and several decidedly lesser films. The last celluloid project was his biopic *The Eddie Cantor Story*, which starred Keefe Brasselle, an actor who was otherwise best known for the classic *A Place in the Sun* (in which he's supposed to look like Montgomery Clift, playing Clift's cousin—it's a funny world where an actor can be hired for his resemblance to both Montgomery Clift and Eddie Cantor).

In 1950 Cantor appeared in a one-man show at Carnegie Hall, with much reminiscing and showbiz anecdotage, and re-created that event for records a decade later (the actual concert, in which Cantor courageously denounces Senator McCarthy, was more recently issued on CD by Original Cast). He continued recording sporadically, and did several full-length albums, generally remakes of old favorites. He continued to headline on radio and then television, and helped to launch the careers of younger performers like Dinah Shore, Bobby Breen, Deanna Durbin, Joel Grey, and Sammy Davis Jr.

He was slowed down by a heart attack in 1952, but just the same he wrote the second of his two autobiographies in 1957 (both recently reprinted in a single volume by Cooper Square Press). As grandson Gari reports, Cantor was severely demoralized by the death of his daughter Margie in 1959 and then of Ida, his wife of nearly fifty years. When he

died, on October 10, 1964, Eddie Cantor had clearly outlived his time. But not by much.

Betty Carter (1929–1998)

Betty Carter died on September 26, 1998, at the age of sixty-nine. At almost any point between the mid-seventies and the mid-nineties I would have had a much easier time writing about her. When she recorded what turned out to be her final album (in 1996), the perspective on her was very clear; I have no doubt it will be so again ten years from now. Yet roughly ten years after she stopped performing, the consensus on her seems hazy. Perhaps not enough time has passed to give an objective assessment of her contributions to the art of the jazz vocalist.

For at least twenty years, Betty Carter was by far the most celebrated female vocalist in jazz. The only singer who possibly got more attention was Mel Tormé, but even he wasn't as universally beloved among hard-core jazz critics and listeners as Carter. While Mel was regularly seen with Johnny and Merv, Carter was universally championed by the alternative media (especially *The Village Voice*) and jazz press gatekeepers. Even though Ella Fitzgerald, Joe Williams, Anita O'Day, Carmen McRae, and others were still active through most of these years, Carter seemed to be virtually the only jazz singer who was regarded as up-to-the-minute and cutting-edge. Everybody on Planet Jazz knew who she was and had an opinion regarding her, which was usually overwhelmingly positive.

However, after 1996 (the year Fitzgerald died, coincidentally), both Carter and Tormé became too ill to work, and as soon as they ceased performing, instead of their going on to legend status (as was happening concurrently for Sinatra), we just stopped hearing about them. Perhaps they had been too celebrated in the immediately preceding years. Then, too, perhaps there was a downside to the renewed popularity of the standard—by the late nineties we were hearing more about Diana Krall and Tony Bennett (again). In that context, Tormé and Carter started to seem too abstract and stylized, especially since they weren't in a position to speak for themselves.

There never was a convenient pigeonhole for Betty Carter. She said repeatedly that she hated being pegged with the term "bebop," which Lionel Hampton labeled her during the three or so years (1948–51) that she sang with his band. Perhaps she had more in common, musically, with the instrumental beboppers than any other group, but she was much further "out" than any other singer who worked in the company of Dizzy Gillespie or James Moody (both fine singer-funsters themselves). Did she belong to the jazz avant-garde? Carter herself repeatedly said no—she employed familiar chord changes and regular, metrical rhythms. Her use of very long, very abstract improvisations seemed to place her on the fringe rather than in the mainstream. Yet her instrument was not the equal of Fitzgerald's or Tormé's, and she occasionally hit notes that were under pitch. Even this, though, was a matter of perspective. Did she have her own, highly personalized intonation (as is frequently said about Jackie McLean), or was she just singing flat? With a singer as consistently challenging and exciting as Carter, did it even matter?

Thank God for amateur contests. It seems sometimes as if most of the major African American singers sprang from them. Those who didn't emerge from amateur contests inevitably worked with Lionel Hampton (or, in many cases, Earl Hines). Carter did both. She was born Lillie Mae Jones in Flint, Michigan, on May 16, either 1929 or 1930 (most sources give 1930, but *The New York Times* obit said 1929). She grew up in the early modern jazz scene in Detroit, the same musically rich backdrop that produced the Jones brothers (Hank, Thad, and Elvin) and a disproportionate number of top bop pianists such as Roland Hanna, Barry Harris, and Tommy Flanagan. Carter herself studied piano at the Detroit Conservatory, but became a professional singer after winning a contest at the Paradise Theatre.

She sang with Hampton for three years (using the stage name Lorraine Carter), and several things about her musical relationship with the euphoric vibesmaster are important. They only cut a handful of recordings—which may seem odd but is consistent with the fate of the other singers who toured with that band. We can count everything Carter officially recorded with Hampton on one hand: two Decca sides, "Benson Boogie" and "The Hucklebuck," and one short TV clip, "Cobb's Idea."

However, if Hamp failed to give her a break on records, he provided her with something equally valuable: her stage name. The bandleader billed Lorraine Carter as "Bebop Betty," and though she professed to hate the "Bebop" part, the "Betty" stuck. Hampton also schooled Carter in the importance of finding sympathetic sidemen: Dozens of the best modern jazzmen learned much of what they knew (except how to earn a living wage) under Hamp's tutelage. But the main thing that Bebop Betty seems to have learned from Gates Hampton was showmanship. This orchestra combined blues, pop, and all varieties of jazz in a way that inspired a following that can, without exaggeration, be called fanatical. This is a crucial element in Carter's musical makeup. To her, bebop wasn't esoteric, it was mainstream; when she scatted and squealed with Hamp's seventeen honkers and screamers, the crowds roared. Carter is the foremother of the contemporary Cassandra Wilson and, especially, Dianne Reeves, in the way she used the language of modern jazz to excite a crowd.

Certainly the stuff she sang with Hampton didn't err on the side of the intellectual. "The Hucklebuck" and "Benson Boogie" are novelty songs—ephemeral but catchy. "Hucklebuck" was a perfect tune for Carter to record with Hampton, as was "Red Top," which she sang with King Pleasure.

The Hampton period was important, but Carter made so few recordings with the band that it seems more like a minor prelude to her discography, which divides roughly into three areas. The first period really has to begin with her early solo albums of 1955–70. These are all for semi-independent labels, companies that were at the time subsidiaries of larger corporations (like her first album, *Meet Betty Carter and Ray Bryant*, on Columbia's Epic imprint, or *'Round Midnight*, on Atco, a subdivision of Atlantic) or firms that were eventually acquired by big corporations. The second period is from 1970 to 1988, when she produced her own records on her own Bet-Car label, and these were later absorbed into the Verve catalogue. In 1988, she began her alliance with Verve, and had the best of both worlds—she was free to do whatever she wanted but with the resources of a major conglomerate to back her up. One would think that she would have shone in this later period, but while everything she recorded in these years is worthwhile and listenable, it is not the artistic climax of her career.

Critical distance and the perspective of time are especially important in evaluating Carter's work, because no other singer I can think of, and precious few instrumentalists, has inspired such polarized opinions. I observed in the eighties that there was no middle ground with her, only extremes of adoration and repulsion. The last ten years of her life not only failed to produce a consensus of critical opinion, but only heightened the extremely polarized nature of the general reaction to her singing. There were those who loved her and those who hated her, but even those who professed to love her couldn't agree on anything—do you like the earlier Carter, where she kept her avant-garde tendencies relatively in check, or the later Carter, where she was inclined to go off into outer space for long stretches? (*Out There with Betty Carter*, a comparatively conservative early album, had a cover featuring her head shot plastered on an artist's depiction of Sputnik in interstellar flight.)

It's the early work that does, in fact, manage to please almost everybody; I can't imagine anyone claiming to enjoy and understand hard-core jazz singing who couldn't appreciate her albums of 1955 to 1965:

- *Meet Betty Carter and Ray Bryant*, which was also released as *Social Call* (1955, Epic)
- *Out There with Betty Carter* (Peacock, 1958)
- *The Modern Sound of Betty Carter* (ABC-Paramount, 1960)
  (The latter two were reissued on a single CD, *I Can't Help It*, Impulse!)
- *Ray Charles and Betty Carter* (ABC-Paramount, 1961)

- *'Round Midnight* (Atco, 1962–63)
- *Inside Betty Carter* (United Artists, 1964–65)

Carter's music isn't the only thing about her that's occasionally hard to understand: Even her discography is far from straightforward. After 1965, she was out of the studio until the end of the decade, when she produced an album appropriately titled *Finally*. This was first released by Roulette, a major label, but since it was produced by the lady herself (in 1969), it belongs to the middle rather than the early phase of her career. More confusing is that she apparently recorded two albums titled *'Round Midnight*, the first listed above (Atco, 1962–63), the second being a live album from 1969 released both on Roulette and Bush Records. She sings the song "Do Something," written by Bud Green and Sam Stept, on another live album, the *Live at the Village Vanguard*, but it's here titled "Please Do Something," and credited to B. Carter. One of her favorite songs, apparently, was "This Time," a lovely ballad by arranger and occasional composer Paul Weston. "This Time" is sung by her on *Inside Betty Carter*, but is listed as "Beware My Heart" by Sam Coslow. It appears again on her last album, *I'm Yours, You're Mine* (1996), and this time "This Time" is correctly titled, but credited to Jule Styne. Either way, it's a beautiful song and the important thing is that Carter sings the hell out of it.

Carter's first album isn't even exclusively her first album. This was a marvelous LP, originally titled *Meet Betty Carter and Ray Bryant*, that consisted half of vocal tracks by Carter and half instrumental tracks by the Ray Bryant Trio. Later, it was reissued as *Social Call* with four previously unreleased songs by Carter, and the current Sony Legacy CD version includes all of the material recorded by both Carter and Bryant. The album is worth the fuss—this is a Betty Carter album that even listeners on the "nay" side of the Betty Carter fence could love. She reached something of an early peak in her mid-twenties, and this first album is one of her most satisfying. Ironically, Carter is most stellar when she's most firmly grounded on planet Earth. As on "Moonlight in Vermont," where she actually gives you a feeling of being in that state in the middle of the night; you can practically feel the telegraph cables singing down the highway.

Even better are her next two albums, both currently owned by Universal Music and wisely reissued on a single CD, entitled *I Can't Help It*. These 1958 and 1960 productions show how great Carter could be with a small band including horns, even as the 1965 *Inside* is the best of her albums with just rhythm section.

A major delight is her propensity for finding great, not overdone songs. When profiled in *Down Beat* in 1965, Carter said that she didn't want to do more than one original tune per album or set. Though she generally kept that tendency in check,

more originals do turn up on the later projects. It should be mentioned that Carter's original words-and-music efforts are better than those of most singer-songwriters. However, unlike those of Abbey Lincoln, her songs (other than "Tight") are rarely revived by other vocalists.

In this regard, Carter is the most bourgeois of avant-gardists. She not only celebrates such decadent (and then not yet dead) white males as Cole Porter, she mines the most obscure nooks and crannies of the Great American Songbook almost as thoroughly as Michael Feinstein. Part of the reason there was so much confusion regarding the songs "Do Something" and "This Time" is that Carter is the only major jazz singer of her generation to perform either one. Her albums are rife with such discoveries: "Isle of May," virtually abandoned since the Sinatra-Dorsey days, "Something Big" and "Nothing More to Look Forward To," two gems by Richard Adler from his 1961 *Kwamina*, a Broadway flop with a sumptuous Afrocentric score, "Some Other Time"—not the well-known Comden-Green-Bernstein *On the Town* anthem but an almost completely forgotten Styne-Cahn ballad sung by Sinatra in an early flick but never recorded by him. In her song selection as well as her interpretations, Carter is presenting herself as an artist who may attract a radical following, but who has, at heart, extreme respect for Tin Pan Alley and the classic song form.

On the *Out There/Modern Sound* combo, Carter tackles everything from blues (the Randy Weston–Jon Hendricks "Babe's Blues") and ballads to European classics. "Isle of May" is credited to Tchaikovsky, "My Reverie" to Debussy, while "Bluebird of Happiness" is a semiclassical tenor showpiece (Jan Peerce popularized it) by the Hungarian composer-conductor Sandor Harmati.

The early records also illustrate Carter's propensity for playing with time: "All I've Got" employs a Caribbean polyrhythm—rather like a Sonny Rollins calypso—while "Isn't It Romantic" starts and ends South of the Border but takes a side trip to Swingville along the way. Likewise, "Remember" and "My Favorite Things" are waltzes transmuted into a solid four.

In dealing with an artist who for years was regarded as being beyond the fringe, is it even relevant to think in terms of aural pleasure and musical comfort zones? The Carter album that most elicits that question is the 1961 *Ray Charles and Betty Carter*. How it ever got made is a curiosity—the album is barely mentioned in either of the two books on Charles and neither he nor she ever talked about it much. I still have no idea how it was that Carter entered Charles's orbit, although at around the same time this most popular of great singers produced another album involving an artist who could be called the least popular of great singers, Little Jimmy Scott. In the notes to the contemporary reissue of *Ray Charles and Betty Carter*, annotator

Alan Swyer quotes the Genius as saying "The problem with most love songs you hear is that they're either sung by a man or a woman." Charles wanted to do an album of love songs by a man and a woman singing together, and, as he put it, "no singer on earth is more woman than Betty Carter."

It's significant that Charles, who could have picked any singer in the world, from Sarah Vaughan or Peggy Lee (who had already recorded several of his songs) to Kate Smith or Helen Traubel, picked Carter. More people probably know her from this one record than from anything else, and during the thirty or so years when it was completely unavailable, the original LP was in constant demand from used vinyl vendors.

The wonderful thing about *Ray Charles and Betty Carter* is that neither one of them is exactly Nelson Eddy or Jeanette MacDonald. Here you have two of the most distinct voices in American music, his high and squeaky, hers higher and squeakier—and both are completely disarming. The two are mournful on the opening "Ev'ry Time We Say Goodbye" (an unusual opener, you will admit) and jubilant on "Side by Side," while "Baby, It's Cold Outside" and "Two to Tango" (both he and she have listened to Pearl Bailey on these last two) are charged with erotic energy. (He drops down to low baritone register on "Two to Tango," perhaps to avoid conflicting sonically with Carter.) Their extra-long "Alone Together" plumbs emotional depths of the great unknown unsurpassed by anyone on this Schwartz-Dietz perennial this side of Judy Garland.

Although Charles—who took Carter on the road with his troupe for a time—brought her to an even bigger audience than Hampton had, she was unable to take advantage of it. The 1965 *Down Beat* profile talks about her feuding with various managers and, in general, not winning too many friends in the business side of the music world. By the seventies, Carter, like Anita O'Day and Blossom Dearie—the only singer in the jazz world with a voice even higher than either Brother Ray's or Bebop Betty's—had marshaled her resources well enough to produce, manufacture, and distribute her own product on her own label, Bet-Car Records. As with O'Day's Emily Records and Dearie's Daffodil label, a significant percentage of the Bet-Car product was recorded live. The Bet-Car releases document her progress musically as well as socially, as she gradually reemerged from the underground.

In the seventies and eighties, Carter produced the following, all of which were originally released by Bet-Car and later issued on CD by Verve:

- *Betty Carter* aka *At the Village Vanguard* (1970)
- *The Betty Carter Album* (1972)
- *Now It's My Turn* (1976)
- *The Audience with Betty Carter* (1979)
- *Whatever Happened to Love* (1982)
- *Live at the Great American Music Hall, San Francisco (The Carmen McRae/Betty Carter Duets)* (1987)

My favorite among these, and my least favorite, are, respectively, the second to last and the last from this group, both live albums. The duets with McRae (originally released on Great American Music Hall Records) were ill-conceived; McRae and Carter were not exactly the Ethel Merman and Mary Martin of bebop. Taped live at the Bottom Line, *Whatever Happened to Love* features her usual stellar rhythm trio (Khalid Moss, piano, Curtis Lundy, bass, Lewis Nash, drums) plus, on four tracks, a string section masterminded by *Manchurian Candidate* composer David Amram. Like nearly all her albums, *Whatever Happened to Love* is a happy mix of standards and originals, as well as a mix of tracks with the regular rhythm section and with the string. The nine tunes include three new offerings written by her, "With No Words," "New Blues (You Purrrr)," and "Abre la Puerta." There's also "What a Little Moonlight Can Do," associated with Billie Holiday but sung in a slow tempo that recalls Thelonious Monk, and a reading of Gordon Jenkins's "Goodbye" that's sung even slower. She repeats two tunes from the Ray Charles album, "Cocktails for Two" and "Ev'rytime We Say Goodbye," and redoes Gigi Gryce's "Social Call," which she sang on her 1955 debut album. Plus one pop surprise—something Carter's discs often have—a 1960 Burt Bacharach–Hal David–Dionne Warwick hit entitled "I Cry Alone."

The four string selections also feature a tenor saxophonist—whose name isn't listed anywhere in the package—who paraphrases the melody of "Cocktails" while Carter runs the changes. As already mentioned, she first recorded "Cocktails for Two," a highly effete 1934 movie song best remembered for being savaged by Spike Jones, with Charles. For Bebop Betty and Brother Ray to sing this song to begin with amounted to an act of parody, yet they did it completely straight and very beautifully. Carter's solo version, which might be called "Cocktails for One," is an even more exquisite *chansonette*. Rather than being too jazzy and abstract for the casual, non-hard-core listener, Carter abstracts the tunes by singing them almost painfully slowly; I can't imagine anyone who loves jazz or standards not enjoying everything on *Whatever Happened to Love*.

Of the three originals, two are all-scat features: the aptly named "With No Words" and "Abre la Puerta." The most controversial work of the Bet-Car period is on the immediately previous album, *The Audience with Betty Carter*. This two-LP concert recording opens with a twenty-six-minute, almost entirely wordless piece—part improvisation, part composition—entitled "Sounds Movin' On." Now the point isn't whether or not "Sounds Movin' On" is a good wordless work. It is, in fact, quite brilliant; anyone willing to pay attention and listen all the way through will be rewarded. The point is that to expect audiences to listen to a sixteen-minute scat solo is, to put it bluntly, self-indulgent. I can't think of any improviser who should just go on at this length— even such modern era works as Coltrane's *A Love Supreme*, Sonny Rollins's *Freedom Suite*, and Charles Mingus's *Cumbia and Jazz Fusion* give the listener a little textual variety, a few signposts to travelers on their way across. Like "Sounds Movin' On" these are extended works for smaller ensembles, but none of them expects the listener to listen to the same thing for so long. Yes, it is brilliant, and no, I won't hold it against you if you don't have the fortitude to get through it.

In 1987, Carter joined the recently reactivated Verve label, now part of Polygram (all of which became, around the time of her death, part of MCA and Universal Music). Between that year and 1996 she released the following albums:

- *Look What I Got* (1987)
- *Droppin' Things* (1990)
- *It's Not About the Melody* (1991)
- *Feed the Fire* (1993)
- *I'm Yours, You're Mine* (1996)

Look What I Got is positioned at the crossroads of Carter's career: She sounds the same as on the Bet-Car albums; the voice has deepened but still has that tight, pinched, almost Blossom Dearie–like sound that made her early work so appealing. She continues to juxtapose unfamiliar tunes ("That Sunday That Summer," recorded earlier by Nat King Cole and later in tribute to the King by his daughter) with astoundingly original treatments of overdone warhorses. For instance she and tenorist Don Braden completely overhaul "The Man I Love." There's a remake of "All I Got" that is about twice as fast as the original, and a tune called "Mr. Gentleman," which is described as a sequel to "Tight" (her most appealing original composition, first heard on *The Audience with Betty Carter*).

By the last ten years of her career, Carter was almost as famous as Art Blakey for nurturing young talent. But most of her discoveries were pianists who went on to big careers like the two who are heard on *Look What I Got*, Stephen Scott (later with Sonny Rollins) and Benny Green, who still seems too young to have ever worked with her. Three of the best pianists of the nineties are featured throughout *It's Not About the Melody*: Carter's old cohort John Hicks, Mulgrew Miller, and youngster Cyrus Chestnut.

The title, *It's Not About the Melody*, is something of a declaration of war—the best defense is a good offense, and it seems as if Carter had grown tired of musical prudes telling her that she didn't sing Cole Porter's melodies exactly as he wrote them. Nonetheless, her music, on this album no less than others, is rife with melody, if not Mr. Porter's (on "In

the Still of the Night"), then her own. It makes one want to reprise Mr. Babcock (Fred Clark)'s line about Agnes Gooch in *Auntie Mame*—"She's a member of *somebody's* family." Betty Carter is certainly singing *somebody's* melody, even if it isn't Cole Porter's.

The album, however, does not open promisingly. The first tune is a Carter-Hicks original, "Naima's Love Song"—possibly inspired by John Coltrane's first wife and the famous tune he named after her. It's a convoluted line, designed more for playing than saying, and Carter's voice is mixed so far down in the ensemble that it's impossible to make out the words. Yet the bulk of the package is standards, generally less obscure than usual. "Stay As Sweet As You Are" opens with a longish episode between Mulgrew Miller's piano and Christian McBride's thunderous bass—before Carter enters, singing a thoroughly recomposed treatment; you wouldn't have recognized it if not for the words. Other standards include an homage to the greatest crowd-pleaser of them all, Satchmo Armstrong, via his theme song, "When It's Sleepy Time Down South." Not all of the songs are treated in an abstract fashion—"I Should Care" is recognizable, short, and not at all indulgent, with Carter finding plenty of opportunity for her patented, tightly pinched vowel twists, "I should let it upset meeeeeeeee . . ." "and I dooooooooooo . . ." The song where the melody is most front and center is Michael Legrand's beautiful "Once Upon a Summertime" (her dip to a low note on "let you buy me" recalls Sarah Vaughan in her basso phase). Considering that the French were infamous for writing (with exceptions) tuneless repetitive music, it seems oddly perverse for Carter to make the one French song here into the most hummable, conventionally melodic item on the album.

Melody's cover shows her looking thoroughly feminized in a long red, flowing dress (multiple images yet); however, she looks rather butch on the front of *I'm Yours, You're Mine*, which has her in loose-fitting male suit drag. There's only one original (the title song)—an example of Carter returning to her quota promise of the sixties—and there are only seven songs, about half of her usual number. Should any of these elements be taken as a sign that she was saying goodbye? It's impossible to answer. The mood is predominantly slow; we don't get any swing time until it's almost over. Sung mostly in Portuguese (small wonder the title is so awkwardly translated), "Useless Landscape" is a downer of a bossa nova. Taken in this context, "East of the Sun (And West of the Moon)" can perhaps be taken as a metaphor for heavenly ascent. At least it brings her back to a swinging groove. The closer, "September Song," does indeed have a feeling of finality—one that would be impossible not to read into the last episode of a great diva's final statement. Carter's entrance is bleak, almost atonal; the performance is, if not an explicit message of goodbye, a vocal that's so far down that nothing could follow it.

She died of pancreatic cancer in Brooklyn, about two and a half years after recording *I'm Yours, You're Mine.* Was it about the melody? Or did it have something more to do with what Carter brought to the melody? Perhaps, after four decades of essentially singing the melody, Carter felt compelled, in her last years, to offer her audiences something else.

Ray Charles (1930–2004)

There's no music we hate so much as the pop music that's foisted upon us as kids. The cartoonist and philosopher R. (Robert) Crumb, for instance, grew up in the early fifties, and he can't stand the mainstream pop singers of that era, and will only grudgingly admit that someone like Sinatra deserves to be taken seriously as an artist. I feel the same way about the pop of the seventies; in fact, one of my earliest memories of music is the song "Wichita Lineman," a hit for Glen Campbell written by Jimmy Webb. Not only could I not stand the song, but it left me with the distinct impression that all people who live in Kansas were hopeless retards. It wasn't just the song itself that I found irritating, but it seemed to represent all the things that I disliked about contemporary pop music—in other words, everything.

And then, more recently, I heard Ray Charles sing "Wichita Lineman" on his 1971 album *Volcanic Action of My Soul,* and all of a sudden this nothing, piece-of-junk tune became the greatest song I ever heard. Graceful, poetic, eloquent—Jimmy Webb was instantly a greater composer than Cole Porter, Duke Ellington, or Verdi. Now the song was suddenly graceful, eloquent, and poetic, taking the most trivial of ideas ("I think I need a small vacation") and somehow transforming them into something with universal significance. (Ray Charles even made me love Glen Campbell.)

As with Sinatra, the innovations of Ray Charles operate on several distinct levels. They tell me God is in the details but when I want to find him the first place I look is in the big picture. Charles totally changed our notion of what the human voice should sound like, and what it was capable of. Extending the legacy of Armstrong, Charles showed us that there was beauty in all kinds of sounds that were previously thought to be extraneous to the vocalist's art: gasps, wheezes, grunts, squeaks, moans. Sometimes these sounds are delivered in conjunction with the text—like those unbelievable squeaks on "Ma, She's Makin' Eyes at Me" (on *Have a Smile with Me*). At other times, they're just purely nonverbal sounds: the gospel choir chants and moans in "What'd I Say?" and the shrieks in "Hit the Road Jack" ("What you *sayyyyy*?"). One thing he has in common with Tony Bennett is the way he revels in the rapture of the sound of strain—like an alto saxist struggling for a high F. And one thing he has in common with Ornette Coleman and Albert Ayler, two bluesmen in

a different kind of music, is that he challenges our notion of sound itself.

Sometimes these sounds are given in a comedic context, as on "Ma," but other times he makes them work for dramatic purposes as well: "Here We Go Again" has Charles adapting a completely different voice than anyone had ever heard him use before, not just using the squeak—a whole new kind of squeak, in fact—for additional coloring on the sidelines, but making it the heart of the matter, literally squeaking out the words and notes in harmony with the Raelettes. Fats Waller and Dean Martin both incorporated all kinds of extracurricular noises into their vocals, but Ray Charles alone has completely shattered our conception of what singing is and what it isn't.

And like Sinatra, Charles focused on the big picture, and gave us a whole new way to think about pop music. In a sense, he took the multiculti, polygeneric influences of his youth—jazz (both traditional and modern), the big bands, hillbilly music, blues, and gospel—and transformed them into the multiculti, polygeneric music of his own. "My ears were sponges," he said; "soaked it all up."

At times, Charles is genre-specific: When he sings "Drown in My Own Tears" with his eight-piece blues band, that's pure R&B (unless you want to call it soul or, to get fancy, proto-soul) in the spirit of Louis Jordan or Dinah Washington. When he sings "Georgia on My Mind" with Ralph Burns and strings, that's what the Grammy people call "traditional pop" in a class with Sinatra and Cole. And when he sings "Two Old Cats Like Us" with Hank Williams Jr., it's classic Nashville in the spirit of both of the two old cats named Hank Williams. Other numbers, like "Early in the Morning" and "Mary Ann," use a rhumba rhythm imported from Cuba—in fact, one of his last appearances on record found Charles reprising "Mary Ann" with Latin bandleader Pancho Sánchez.

All these are amazing accomplishments in themselves, but Charles rose to even greater heights when he mixed the disparate elements together: The classic 1963 "Busted" is everything at once—blues, soul, big band swing, all set to an up-tempo three-four rhythm that seems to have equal roots in modern jazz (Cannonball Adderley) and country ("The Tennessee Waltz"). As a teenager, he played piano for a while in an otherwise all-white hillbilly band, and sang the 1946 Bill Monroe hit "Kentucky Waltz." ("Busted" had actually been introduced by Johnny Cash.) One couldn't imagine Milt Jackson or Betty Carter working with country and western icon George Jones, and yet Ray Charles sounds completely natural with all of them.

In "Busted," Charles jubilantly sings of incredible privations—the contrast of upbeat attitude and miserable circumstances that are at the heart of the irony that's known as the blues. Yet nothing he has ever sung about can ever match the poverty and hard times that he himself had to deal with at the start of his life—in fact, perhaps the reason that he sang the blues so joyfully is because the situation that the protagonist of "Busted" has to endure is a walk in the park compared to Charles's own.

He was born Ray Charles Robinson in Albany, Georgia, on September 23, 1930. He had no father growing up, but he did have two mothers, Aretha and Mary Jane, who, as he told biographer David Ritz, "loved me and gave me what I needed to get by." His father had been married to Mary Jane at the time he conceived Ray with Aretha. After Ray was born, the deadbeat dad split and the two women set up housekeeping together, and raised Ray and his half-brother (Mary Jane's son), George.

Perhaps only a man with the love of two mothers could have overcome the adversity that Ray Charles Robinson did, being born at the absolute bottom of the social food chain, looked on with derision not only by the white race but by most of the "colored" folks as well. He grew up in miserable poverty, then lost his brother at age six, his eyesight at seven, and his biological mother at fifteen.

But he was naturally bright, even a savant; he had already mastered the piano before he left his hometown. Shortly after he lost his sight, Aretha took elaborate steps to ensure that young Ray could get an education, sending him to the state school for the blind. "Mama knew I needed the tools of education," he said; "Mama knew I didn't have those tools, but she knew where to find them for me." He noted that the school itself was rigidly segregated—by afflictions (deaf and blind kids), by gender, and by race. "Imagine separating kids according to color when we can't even see each other? Ain't that a bitch!" Yet like Louis Armstrong at the colored Waif's Home, young Ray flourished at the school, both as a scholar (he learned Braille and developed a lifelong passion for literature) and a musician.

As the movie *Ray* (one of the best musical biographies ever filmed) accurately showed, Charles first learned to play from the blues-based backwoods pianists found all over the South during the Depression. But Charles himself was far from a musical primitive—just the opposite: He was a thoroughly schooled musician. He not only could read music, he could read it in Braille, which is considerably harder. His later achievements were dependent on his thorough, technical knowledge of musical theory—and one ironic point that the movie omitted was that had he not been blind and not been entitled to attend that school, he might never have gained that knowledge, which made his subsequent career possible.

His earliest influences were such blues-and-boogie stylists as Albert Ammons and Pete Johnson. His next heroes were Artie Shaw ("that perfect tone, that sweet sound"), who inspired him to play clarinet and then saxes—and Art Tatum ("I wasn't good enough to carry Tatum's sh*t bucket, but that didn't stop me from trying"). He left the school in 1945, not long after his mother died, and began working around various cities in Florida as an itinerant piano player.

When he heard the smooth-toned Nat King Cole and Cole's immediate disciple, the rougher, more blues-based Charles Brown, Charles realized that he could sing as well as play the piano. "I could actually imitate them. I'm not talking about stealing a lick here but flat-out copying." One of his first records, made in Los Angeles circa 1949 and released under at least three titles, "Crazy About Me," "All the Girls in Town," and the mysteriously titled "Ego Song," has him sounding almost exactly like King Cole (he also sounds like Cole on such horn-driven blues numbers as "For You My Love"), while "Someday" and "Baby Tell Me What I Have Done" find him imitating Brown. (Charles's 1956 pianocentric instrumental version of "Ain't Misbehavin' " is particularly rife with keyboard licks that he learned from Cole.)

One session from this period, which produced Charles's first genuine hit, "Baby Let Me Hold Your Hand," has him not only working in a piano-guitar-bass trio à la Cole, but with the most famous of the King's own men, guitarist Oscar Moore and bassist Johnny Miller (Moore had also worked extensively with Brown). If Charles can come this close to Cole and Brown on these tunes, one can only imagine how much he sounded like them when he deliberately imitated them on live gigs, singing their own songs. As he put it, "I'd sing their hits at little clubs, and people would hardly know the difference." Charles later recorded some of their signature songs, such as Cole's "Gee Baby Ain't I Good to You" (1967) and Brown's "Drifting Blues" (1967), but by then his style had evolved to the point where listeners could certainly tell the difference.

The development of the Ray Charles style—or styles—is extensively documented on the several dozens of records he made in Los Angeles and then Seattle, the next stop of his early geographical and musical evolution, between 1949 and 1952. These years, in which he recorded for Swing Time and other independent "race" labels and toured as pianist, vocalist, and musical director with blues bandleader and guitarist Lowell Fulson, can be viewed as roughly the equivalent of Sinatra's incubatory period with Harry James and Tommy Dorsey. For all of the raw, primal energy of his music, it can't be stressed often enough that Charles is a schooled, trained musician, who arrived at his conclusions scientifically, through trial and error, like Miles Davis, Ellington, or Sinatra. His contract was picked up by Ahmet Ertegun of Atlantic Records—itself then a struggling independent "race" label. Each of the first few Atlantic sessions finds Charles getting closer and closer to what we would come to think of as the classic gospel + blues = soul Ray Charles sound. After years of experimenting, in 1954 Charles finally recorded his break-through hit, "I Got a Woman."

Between 1954 and 1959, he turned out a slew of

purely R&B hits ("This Little Girl of Mine," "Drown in My Own Tears," "Hallelujah I Love Her So," "What'd I Say, Parts I & II") for Atlantic, which began coming more frequently after he persuaded his booking agency to subsidize his dream of an eight-piece touring band. He was also at the center of the movement that was becoming known as rock 'n' roll—with one important difference: R&B was made for black adults and rock was aimed strictly at white teenagers (and younger). Charles never stooped down to the younger audience and never sang the kind of material (the songs about hound dogs and teddy bears) that even such worthy colleagues as Elvis Presley were lowering themselves to in pursuit of the youth market. In the fifties, his audience was primarily black, but the developments of the next few years would lead to his becoming an inter-everything star: interracial, international, and intergeneric. Working from a blues center, he quickly moved to the left and right to encompass pop standards and show tunes on the one hand and country-western music on the other. He'd added a female vocal quartet, the Raelettes, to his entourage, and soon would expand to a full-sized big band.

Charles's first album of standards—in fact, it was his first specifically planned original album (as distinct from a collection of singles)—was a set of jazz piano instrumentals from 1957 released as *The Great Ray Charles*. The first package in which he addressed the standard repertory as a vocalist came two years later with *The Genius of Ray Charles*. This was a dual-faceted project, done half with a studio orchestra of top jazz players (from both the Basie band and Charles's own working unit) and half with a string orchestra conducted by Ralph Burns. Half the songs were standards by the likes of Irving Berlin ("Alexander's Ragtime Band") and Gus Kahn ("It Had to Be You"), and the other half were standards from the world of the blues, such as Louis Jordan's "Let the Good Times Roll" and Lil Armstrong's "Just for a Thrill."

But *Genius*'s standout is its closing track, Harold Arlen's "Come Rain or Come Shine," which may be the first time he revealed his now perfected style, with its moans, shrieks, and other elaborate ornamentations. Arranger Burns uses a song that is equal parts show tune and blues lament to contrast Charles's voice beautifully with both the string section and the moaning trombone of Bob Brookmeyer. Even the first two bars are miraculous: Charles rushing the opening phrase, "I'm gonna love you," then pausing for what seems like an eternity before the second phrase, "like nobody's loved you." The track became an instant Ray Charles classic and even a minor hit single, proving that there was indeed an audience for Charles doing this kind of material. This was a major transition, in which Charles went where no R&B star had yet gone.

Genius was a notable preamble to Charles's shift of allegiances the following year from Atlantic Records to ABC-Paramount. ABC was still another start-up operation, but thanks to an influx of movie money, it was quite a well-financed one. These were the years when rock 'n' roll was supposedly taking over from traditional adult pop, but it's in this period that Charles chose to perform traditional pop standards. Both the quality and quantity of the material that he records in this amazing four- or five-year span is enough to establish him as one of the most important interpreters of the Great American Songbook.

His first four ABC albums were all primarily devoted to standards: *The Genius Hits the Road* (1960), *Dedicated to You, Genius + Soul = Jazz*, and *Ray Charles and Betty Carter* (all 1961). (Note the recurrence of the "genius" motif, an extension of the original 1959 *Genius* album.) Many of the standards albums were linked thematically—they're what might be called "concept albums." "[I] started fooling around with the idea of a whole album strung together by a single idea," Charles told David Ritz. "Couldn't call my ideas great. Might even call 'em jivey, but they were mine. They were little ideas and I liked them. The first one was an album of songs with the names of the states. Corny? Hell yes, but I'm a corny cat." The Charles albums generally consist of songs with similar programmatic subject matter but a variety of moods and tempos. On the whole, his approach to the songbook is much more irreverent than Sinatra's—he loves the great songs, but they're not a religion to him.

Genius Hits the Road is the one with all songs about the states—not metaphysical states of being, but the United States. He varies between up-tempos ("Alabamy Bound") and ballads (most famously "Georgia on My Mind"). Undoubtedly, he was inspired by two widely known travel albums, Sinatra's *Come Fly with Me* (general travel) and the Bing Crosby–Rosemary Clooney–Billy May *Fancy Meeting You Here* (mostly exotic locales, like "Hindustan" and "Calcutta"), but *Genius* offers only domestic destinations, with Ralph Burns once again serving as navigator. "Georgia on My Mind" is Charles's and Burns's follow-up to "Come Rain or Come Shine," substituting a choir for the trombone. Though it was originally planned as just another cut on the album—as opposed to a potential hit single—it became the biggest-selling song of Charles's entire career. "Georgia" was the number with which Charles went mainstream—without compromising any of his virtues, his vocal trademarks, his style.

As mentioned above, *Genius Hits the Road* was followed by other brilliant albums of standards that balance various tempos and yet stay consistent within themselves and with one another.

Each of these albums offers something in the way of an unexpected bonus: *Genius Hits the Road* has "New York's My Home," a song with a series of spoken recitatives that's one of several numbers going back to the dawn of his career ("Shoulda Been Me,"

"Greenbacks," and the 1967 "Understanding," with its sermonlike monologues). *Dedicated to You* has one out-and-out comedy number ("Hard-Hearted Hannah") and one instrumental ("Josephine," a hit for Tommy Dorsey way back when). *Sweet and Sour Tears* has one tune ("Baby Don't You Cry") in what Charles called the "new Swingova rhythm," a groove that's sort of half-shuffle (think Louis Jordan or Louis Prima) and half–bossa nova (even though it's unlikely that Ray Charles would have heard this brand-new Brazilian beat in 1961). These all amount to "extras," and show that he was not constructing albums strictly by formula.

There are at least two more albums that could be described as part of this period in that they're unified by tempo and mood: *Crying Time* (1966), for instance, isn't a sequel to *Sweet and Sour Tears* but simply a set of sad songs. *Have a Smile About Me* (1964) doesn't include either "When You're Smiling" or "Let a Smile Be Your Umbrella." Rather, it's all comedy numbers guaranteed to raise a gaggle of giggles, including lots of novel turns from the twenties. On the English "I Never See Maggie Alone," Charles demonstrates enough dry, understated wit to rival Jack Buchanan or even Sir-bloody-Noel himself. "The Man with the Weird Beard" has Charles describing the titular character ("seven robins live in there . . . ," "there's more on his chin than he's got on his mind . . . ," "straggly, raggly . . ."), while a femme choir chants "Beaver."

The 1963 *Ingredients in a Recipe for Soul* may be Charles's finest album—not just of standards, but of anything. He starts with two songs by Mel Tormé, "Born to Be Blue" and "Stranger in Town." There are two extras here, meaning songs from non–Tin Pan Alley sources, the aforementioned "Busted" and "In the Evening (When the Sun Goes Down)," a traditional blues, recorded to great effect by Count Basie and Joe Williams.

At the same time Charles was singing Hoagy Carmichael and Harold Arlen, he was enjoying equally great success with Eddy Arnold and Hank Williams. The two *Modern Sounds in Country and Western Music* albums were as much big band jazz as they were hillbilly, since the songs came from Nashville but the orchestral style was strictly Swing Street, alluding as much to Tex Beneke as to any cowboy named Tex. He also integrates country songs in other contexts, having earlier recorded "I'm Movin' On" with his regular R&B octet, and having put the country "Busted" in the middle of the otherwise noncountry *Ingredients*.

Producer Jerry Wexler has described Charles's classic R&B hits of 1954–59 as "gospel groove" numbers, but it occurs to me that his treatment of pop songs is no less driven by religious inspiration. "Georgia on My Mind," the megahit follow-up to "Come Rain or Come Shine," is even more hymn-like, even though there's nothing in the song as written to indicate anything remotely theological. There

continues to be some confusion as to whether authors Hoagy Carmichael and Stuart Gorrell were referring to "Georgia" as a place or a woman (Carmichael's sister was so named). In fact, in the song's most expressive passage, they deliberately blur the distinction between love for one's home and love of a lover—"other arms reach out to me, other eyes smile tenderly"—but Charles expresses it as a devotion to the Almighty. When he sings of visions seen in "peaceful dreams" he might as well be singing of the hereafter.

Just as he had already done for blues and jump numbers, in *Ingredients in a Recipe for Soul*, he takes the final step in his transformation of pop standards into a combination of hymn and anthem. Fully half of *Ingredients* consists of Charlesian anthems, each more devotional than the next:

- "Where Can I Go?," a Zionist tract by singer-songwriter Leo Fuld celebrating the founding of Israel, which was also recorded to great effect by Steve Lawrence and Fuld himself.
- "Ol' Man River," heard in the most moving performance since Paul Robeson and Sinatra.
- "Over the Rainbow," performed definitively by Judy Garland as a song of yearning and hope, is herewith reconstructed by Brother Ray as an anthem of spiritual inspiration. Where Garland sang of romantic or familial happiness—she could be looking for either a lover or a mother—Charles leaves no doubt that the land beyond the rainbow is a city called Heaven.
- "That Lucky Old Sun" was actually established as a faux-anthem/hymn by Frankie Laine in 1949, and Laine's record is actually better than Sinatra's cover version from that year, though not up to Louis Armstrong's. However, neither Frank, nor Frankie, can top Charles, who elevates it to spiritual heights that none of the others can imagine.
- "You'll Never Walk Alone": Speaking of Louis Armstrong, the Reverend Satchelmouth treated Rodgers and Hammerstein's show tune as a religious piece. By the time Charles (and Elvis) sang it in the sixties, "Walk Alone" had already been adopted as an unofficial mantra of the civil rights movement. Yet Charles took it a step further and made it even more explicitly religious.

On "Sun," "Rainbow," and "River," arranger Marty Paich brings in the Jack Halloran Singers, the blandest choir imaginable. It's almost as if Paich is trying to highlight Charles's blackness, depth, and feeling by contrasting it with the whiteness and blandness of the chorus. It more than works, particularly with Charles's slow, deliberate phrasing, and his determination to keep using his spoken asides ("now you sing . . ."), lyric changes ("drink a little scotch and you gonna land in jail"), and many melodic alterations and ornamentations even in a "serious," nonjazz context. (At times, he seems to be influenced by the quasi-gospel style of his fellow blind vocal icon, Al Hibbler.) The overall effect is devastating. Paich's arrangement of "Without a Song" (also issued as a two-part 45 rpm single) allows Charles to take full advantage of Edward Eliscu's spiritual allusions: Both singer and lyricist use music and spiritual devotion as metaphors for each other. Charles takes it to the max in an ultra-deluxe, extended arrangement—again with choir—originally released as a two-sided 45 rpm single.

Over the years, Charles continued to apply the hymn/anthem treatment to appropriate material: While his 1972 "America the Beautiful" has been appropriated by both Democrats and Republicans for their own purposes, his 1977 "Oh, What a Beautiful Mornin'" (on *True to Life*) is more moving; as biographer Michael Lydon has pointed out, when Brother Ray sings "The sounds of the Earth are like music," he means it like no sighted performer ever could. (Incidentally, this is one of the only essential Charles performances that's missing from *Genius and Soul: The 50th Anniversary Collection*, a deluxe box compiled by Rhino Records in collaboration with Charles himself that otherwise does an admirable job of encapsulating the Charles career in a mere five discs. Most of the quotes here from Ray Charles are taken from David Ritz's essay in the *Genius and Soul* booklet, and from *Brother Ray* by Charles and Ritz.)

Although the sixties were the glory years of Ray Charles as far as soulful standards were concerned, he continued to include selections from the Great American Songbook at every concert appearance and on almost every album. There's a tour-de-force treatment of "Am I Blue" from his 1975 *Live in Tokyo* that even surpasses his classic 1959 *Genius* version, and the same album also has a knockout "Till There Was You."

To a degree, the act of looking at Charles's career in its final thirty-five years (1970–2004) from the point of view of his work with Tin Pan Alley standards—as opposed to other kinds of material—almost seems beside the point, when he has the power to make even the lowliest kiddie pop or hillbilly trifle take on the significance of Gershwin or Ellington. He makes marvelous music with the likes of Melanie's "Look What They Done to My Song, Ma," Robert Guidry's "The Jealous Kind," Carole Bayer Sager's "Don't You Love Me Anymore," Barry Manilow's "One of These Days," Leon Russell's "A Song for You," Paul Simon's "Still Crazy After All These Years," and many others. Unlike my experience with "Wichita Lineman," I've never heard the original versions of any of these, which may mean it's somewhat unfair of me to suggest that these songs are only worth hearing when Ray Charles sings them. But I'll stick to my guns; Ray's records of these are the only ones I need.

I've spent a lot of time comparing Charles to Sinatra; I'd like to finish by comparing him to Duke Ellington. Ellington was the quintessence of jazz and so many other things, just as Charles is the quintessence of soul (or whatever you want to call it) and so many other things. Yet Ellington was always somewhat tangential to the jazz mainstream, always doing his own thing whatever the prevailing mood, and Charles is the same way: He's never completely in step with whatever's going on in the pop world. If he were, he might have burned himself out and worn out his welcome with the public early on. As the man himself once said, "Every music has its soul. If you're really sincere and ready to explore it, it's all soulful."

June Christy (1925–1990)

Consider, if you will, the last eight bars of June Christy's version of "All God's Chillun Got Rhythm." The arrangement starts with a familiar pattern: It's a fast rhythm number that utilizes the time-honored ploy of making a fast tune seem that much faster by prefacing it with a slow introductory verse, much like the original "Rhythm" song (the one by the Gershwins). Christy herself employs roughly the same idea on "It Don't Mean a Thing (If It Ain't Got That Swing)."

Yet Christy's "All God's Chillun" is something unique. The actual verse that Christy sings ("Children, listen here to me / This is my philosophy . . .") appears to be original with her, or at least isn't the one that Ivie Anderson sang when she introduced the song in *A Day at the Races* (that verse goes "I got a frown, you got a frown . . ."). For Christy to use the slow-then-fast opening isn't surprising, but what is unusual is that she repeats the idea of contrasting tempos. After the first chorus, she reprises the bridge slowly, as if it were a verse, and then sings the last eight bars back up to tempo. Then, following the last chorus, she sings a sort of epilogue via an original tag, somewhat in the spirit of Billy Eckstine ("Cottage for Sale" and "Sophisticated Lady"). The words themselves aren't much ("All God's children shout about / The things that we can't do without"). But she uses the tag to transform—and transcend—the song itself.

Some backstory: "All God's Chillun Got Rhythm" was inspired by a traditional African American spiritual adopted by three Hollywood Jews (one, Gus Kahn, from Chicago; the other two, Bronislau Kaper and Walter Jurmann, respectively, Polish and Austrian refugees from Hitler) into a movie song. The basic model for it was "Gonna Shout All over God's Heaven," a spiritual that had already provided the inspiration for an earlier pop song, "You Can't Get to Heaven That Way." "All God's Chillun" became a familiar jam session vehicle in the swing and early modern era. By the late fifties, when Christy recorded it, it was beginning to be replaced by "Green Dolphin Street," another movie theme by Kaper.

"All God's Chillun" thus already had two identities—production number spiritual and jam session fodder—but Christy turns it into something it had never been before, and would never be again. In the four bars of that original tag, she makes it into something vulnerable, something tender. As performed by everyone else, the lyrics are something of a parody of a religious song—meaning, they're at least vaguely about man's relationship to God—but the way she sings it, the song is about man's relationship with his fellow man. In fact, she's transformed it into something entirely unique: an intimate spiritual, a song about people needing people that is considerably more moving than the other, more recent famous song about people who need people.

Yet when I listen to it, my first reaction, to the fast choruses at least, is that either Anita O'Day or Ella Fitzgerald might have sung it at a faster clip and, perhaps, would have made those particular parts more exciting. Which brings me to one of the central issues concerning June Christy. I doubt that there's anyone reading this who has spent more time listening to Christy than I have, or who owns more of her albums in more confusing formats (I have *Something Cool* alone as a 10", a 12" mono, and a stereo LP, not to mention two vastly different compact disc reissues). Yet I confess that all my intense concentration has led to naught. Asked to explain why she's so good, and why her recordings are so worthy of attention, I still can't provide an easy answer. Maybe it's because the music of the late June Christy reflects the complications and contradictions of life and love so brilliantly that her artistry can't be summed up in a sound bite.

Perhaps a comparison with some of her contemporaries will prove useful—even if, at first, it hardly seems favorable. June Christy had less of an amazing vocal instrument than Jo Stafford, less of an incredible ear than Ella Fitzgerald, less grandeur than Sarah Vaughan, less vulnerability than Judy Garland, less high tragedy than Billie Holiday, less rhythmic recklessness than Anita O'Day, less of a feeling for the blues than Dinah Washington or Peggy Lee, less charisma and a comfortable way with an audience than Dinah Shore, less earthy optimism than Doris Day, less showbiz than Lena Horne, less in the way of visual attributes than Julie London, and less of an actress-y way with a lyric than Mabel Mercer. I don't think there was any one quality that June Christy had in greater supply than her colleagues, unless it was taste and intelligence.

It was the last-listed elements that gave her recorded works an edge that virtually no other singer's had. Further, she had the good fortune to be supported by a team of arrangers and producers who were eager to give her whatever it took to help her turn out a superior product. Capitol Records was ground zero for intelligently assembled LPs; that was where Frank Sinatra perfected the concept of the concept album, and the behind-the-microphone staff at the label was able to create worthy projects even when they worked with second-tier jazz or pop vocalists.

For much of her career, Christy was dismissed as a bargain-basement Anita O'Day. She replaced O'Day in Stan Kenton's orchestra, and, according to O'Day, she herself picked Christy as her successor. Christy's first and possibly biggest record with Kenton was "Tampico," which was a virtual rewrite of O'Day's hit with the band, "And Her Tears Flowed Like Wine." In the long run, however, Christy sounds little like O'Day. While O'Day's dramatic abilities, I think, are somewhat underappreciated, her style is chiefly high swing—"I go for the music more than the poetry of it all," as she once said. With Christy, the emphasis was the other way around; she could and did swing, but the chief point of interest was the way she told a story. Magnificent as O'Day was at her height, she was only occasionally interested in conveying a sense of tenderness and vulnerability the way that Christy was in all of her classic albums. (Chris Connor, the third and last major vocalist to come out of the Kenton band, was equally her own woman, even though she was beholden to both her predecessors.)

To a certain degree, it was ironic that Christy ever sang with Kenton to begin with—especially in that she became the singer most identified with his orchestra. The band was often characterized as the most intellectual of all jazz organizations. One of the chief accusers was Anita O'Day herself, who said that the band's music was so cerebral you couldn't dance to it, and that the Kentonians spent their free time reading books rather than scoring dope and getting laid, as most self-respecting band sidemen were expected to do in the forties. O'Day was only half-right about this: The band was not only brainy, it was brawny as well, with big-toned tenorists and trumpeters in trusses straining for stratospheric high notes. This was a band of both brains and muscle, but instrumentally, in the forties at least, it didn't have a lot of heart, and that's where Christy came in. It was also ironic that one of the most sensitive of all singers got her start in a band that was anything but. O'Day may have suited the band better, in that she, too, was unsparingly unsentimental, even "masculine" in her approach, yet she was perhaps too much of a piece with it—the Kentonites needed Christy for contrast. They needed something soft and feminine and tender—the kind of appearance Harry James, Duke Ellington, Tommy Dorsey, and the rest of the bands had—and that was the one thing that O'Day couldn't give them.

Stan Kenton's orchestra was many things to its millions of fans—brash, audacious, and exciting, and above all loud, as in *loud*—but sensitive was never one of them. Christy's singing, on the other hand, represented the summit of thoughtful introversion. Kenton may have initially selected her for her vocal resemblance to predecessor O'Day, but Christy had much more in common with one of O'Day's own stylistic antecedents, Billie Holiday. And like another Holiday descendant, Frank Sinatra, she was primarily concerned with the song as narrative process, which stressed the romantic as much as the rhythmic, achieving a oneness between song, singer, and arrangement.

Christy also shared Sinatra's preoccupation with finding precisely the right kind of material—all her songs not only tell a certain kind of a story, they depict a very particular character. That character was paramount—and was even reflected by the images of her on her album covers. And this in a hyper-glamorous era when even the tomboyish O'Day was dolled up with platinum hair, formal frocks, and opera gloves. Yet though Christy labored at the most high-glitz label of them all, she's invariably depicted in ultraconservative schoolmarmish outfits, which seem to have been calculated to make her laments of loneliness appear all the more believable. (This attire was not in keeping with her working wardrobe: According to one anonymous annotator, "Inside her immense kitchen closet there are net and sequined gowns that June wears to her concerts and nightclub engagements.")

Christy was also, after Sinatra, the most active purveyor of the "concept" album. Most of her classic albums were orchestrated by a giant in the field, Pete Rugolo, who had previously been Kenton's chief arranger. The only two exceptions in the series of her ten or so best albums come from near its end, *June's Got Rhythm* (1958) and *Ballads for Night People* (1959), which both featured the writing of Bob Cooper, an ace orchestrator who doubled as tenor sax obbligatist (most effectively on "My Ship" from *Ballads*) and tripled as her husband and father of her daughter. Each of the classic Christy albums—and there are only a couple of nonclassic ones—is a triumph of creating and sustaining a distinct mood. Only her children's album (*The Cool School*) and her Christmas album (*This Time of Year*) are organized programmatically, around a distinctly concrete extramusical peg. Most, like *Something Cool*, *Off-Beat*, and *The Misty Miss Christy* are held together only by a consistency of feeling. Emotion is the central element of Christy's recordings—what it feels like, how it sounds, where it comes from. It is not something abstract that you relate to in Christy's work. Rather, it's so real you feel you can pick it up and hold it in your hand.

"All I ever wanted to be was a girl singer with a jazz band," Christy once said. She was born Shirley Luster in Springfield, Illinois, on November 20, 1925. From her teens onward, Shirley was singing with dance bands around the state capital as well as the broader playing field of nearby Chicago. After working with Boyd Raeburn's local society-style orchestra (years before he launched a national unit in the progressive mode), Christy learned that Kenton was coming to town and in need of a replacement for the departing O'Day.

"I knew Stan was booked with General Artists Corp.," she later told disc jockey Gordon Spencer. "I naively thought the first thing he would do was go to GAC. So I went to their office and I sat in the outer lobby. They never allowed me anywhere other than that. But I had my little test record with me, and miraculously, Stan did come in. And what's more, he did need a singer. He listened to the record and then came out and said, 'I would like to try you out for a few days, and we'll see how it works out.' "

The newly rechristened Miss Christy soon became the voice most associated with the band (apart from the leader's own booming baritone pronouncements), over roughly five years of working steadily with him and another dozen or so occasional reunions. She had first joined Kenton on March 22, 1945. "I can't remember my own birthday, but I'll never forget that date," she later told Kenton scholar Michael Sparke.

Now officially O'Day's successor, Christy would also be, for the rest of her life, dismissed by the tin-eared as a mere O'Day imitator. Yet her singing style was born of many parents. Further, a great deal of the similarity in the sounds of these successive Kenton kanaries springs from the coincidence of their shared Illinois background. (In fact, considering that Mel Tormé also hailed from Chicago and Chris Connor from Missouri, one can make the point that the California vo-cool sound grew up in the Midwest.) Like O'Day, Christy employs a husky timbre and an even, vibratoless tone. It's not much of a stretch to call them both "cool," but the similarities end there.

It was also while employed by Kenton that Christy met her lifetime partner, tenor sax star and arranger Bob Cooper, whom she married in 1946 (Kentonites have long contended that Stan himself performed the ceremony) and also began collaborating with Pete Rugolo. She recorded roughly thirty-eight titles with Kenton, of which slightly more than half are on a Capitol special markets issue called *June Christy and the Stan Kenton Orchestra: The Complete Recordings*. It's a good sampling of twenty-two of the best K-C titles, even if the "complete" part is way out of order. (For completists, all of her studio tracks with the full Kenton band are on Mosaic's *The Complete Studio Stan Kenton on Capitol, 1943–1947*; three more tracks from 1950 are on *The Innovations Orchestra*.)

Her earliest recordings with Kenton—from "Tampico" onward—are in a very O'Dayish vein. There would be more band-chant numbers in "The Tears Flowed Like Wine"–"Tampico" vein (a hit formula for Kenton similar in spirit to Tommy Dorsey's "Marie" cycle), such as "I Been Down in Texas" and "Rika Jika Jack." The three are, in a sense, a kind of travelogue, in which the band-chant idea travels northward from Mexico to Texas to Iceland—a suitable destination for cool jazz. "His Feet Too Big for de Bed" is a calypso detour that uses a professional vocal group (Dave Lambert and the Pastels) in place of the chanting bandsmen.

Her second title with the band, "It's Been a Long, Long Time," one of the songs that heralded the end of the war (and lingered on through several future wars to become a standard), shows a hint of sentiment, but she's still more rhythmically motivated. The bandleader's own arrangement uses two vocal choruses, separated by a marvelous saxophone section chorus. Christy has been carefully written into the arrangement, and at this early stage, she almost seems more like an instrument than a human being, especially when, in the second chorus, she becomes part of Kenton's harmonic and melodic variations on the tune.

Yet she gets the hang of it fairly quickly—"Just a Sittin' and a Rockin' " finds her beginning to explore the dimensions of a song about loneliness, and even on "Easy Street" she starts to convey a sense of wanting and yearning. It's that wanting-yearning thing that would eventually do the most to distinguish her from O'Day. Christy's treatment of the blues in this period is especially instructive in this regard. O'Day was a colossal blues performer, whose colleagues in this area were not necessarily Bessie Smith or Ethel Waters but Ben Webster and Illinois Jacquet. Yet if O'Day is a master of the form, Christy is likewise a master (or mistress) of its meaning: To Christy the blues are a narrative element as much as a musical one. Kenton-Christy numbers that refer to the blues, whether lyrically or musically, include "Soothe Me," "I Never Thought I'd Sing the Blues," "Four Months, Three Weeks, Two Days, One Hour Blues," and "Ain't No Misery in Me." The latter, paradoxically, uses something closer to genuine blues form but to express an upbeat message, while "Soothe Me" (the Ernie Andrews hit) is openly erotic. She's not as thoroughly seductive as, say, Dinah Washington would have been (pity the Queen never recorded it), but when she sings "Make me feel good inside," we believe her.

Christy's last studio recordings as a regular member of the Kenton band are with the 1950 "Innovations" orchestra, the double-sized edition with a full string section. By this point, she's grown considerably as an individual voice, even if, as it happens, she still seems more like the vessel of Kenton's arranging crew in the three sides in which she's featured with the Innovations unit—two wordless works, "Conflict" and "June Christy," and a very avant treatment of the standard "Lonesome Road." Kenton himself wrote "June Christy," one of many vehicles for the singer that blur the distinction between scatting and improvising (as elsewhere, she sings wordlessly, but unlike O'Day's scats, hers are generally prewritten rather than improvised).

Although it was named after her, "June Christy" reflects the composer's rather than the singer's personality. The same is true of another of her features, "This Is My Theme" (1947), which isn't a song at all, but a rather abstract poem by one Audrey Lacey that Christy recites over an equally abstract background. It anticipates the jazz-and-poetry movement, of Charles Mingus, Vampira, and others, yet sounds disastrously dated today. Christy later told Michael Sparke that she agreed to record it with the band on the condition that Kenton wouldn't ask her to perform it live. Small wonder—the piece is awfully self-conscious. "June Christy" and "Conflict" have her performing music without words, and "This Is My Theme" has her reciting words without singing any music. Obviously, her own style would require both words and music.

Even as early as December 1945, half a year after she joined the band, Christy was recording under her own name, first for Capitol's transcription service, and then for commercial Capitol singles in 1947. The Capitol transcriptions, twenty-seven songs altogether, are on *The Complete Capitol Transcriptions of Peggy Lee and June Christy* on Mosaic, while her early singles are on *Day Dreams*, a 1995 CD collection. There are also a hundred or so tracks that she recorded for Thesaurus, a rival transcription company owned by RCA-NBC, in the late forties, done in New York with pianist Johnny Guarnieri's quintet, which were recently commercially issued on a series of CDs (titled *A Friendly Session*) from the British Jasmine label.

"Sweet Lorraine," from the first transcription session, is about the closest Christy, or anyone else, ever came to sounding like Anita O'Day; she has that same dark, husky timbre—as she became June Christy, her sound would lighten up somewhat. And the mere act of singing this particular jazz standard was in itself O'Dayish: By singing a lyric written clearly from a male perspective, without bothering to change any names or pronouns (granted that "Sweet Larry" wouldn't work), she was signaling that, as with O'Day, the rhythm and the swing are the only elements that are important to her, the "poetry of it all" and lyrics are insignificant.

Christy would find her own path first by mastering basic Tin Pan Alley irony, those songs where the protagonist professes to say one thing but actually means another, as on "Don't Want That Man Around" (done with Kenton). The first thing she leads us to believe with the lyric is that she can't stand the guy, but she gradually reveals that she doesn't want him around because she loves him too much. Likewise, on "I Got a Guy" (a Capitol transcription and a song she learned from Ella Fitzgerald), she starts by telling us what a lunkhead the guy is ("He don't dress me in sable / He looks nothing like Gable"), but in spite of spending more time with his liabilities than his assets, she's crazy for him, she's funny that way. "What's New?," the last title from the Capitol transcription series, is the forerunner of later half-a-conversation songs like "Something

Cool" and "Angel Eyes." She's broken up with the guy and is fine with that—or is she, delaying the punch line, as it were, to the very end of the song: She hasn't changed, she still loves him so. The way Christy has been singing for the 30 bars up to then, she doesn't even need that final line, it's already more than clear from the tone of her voice, the anxiety in it.

Yet she was also singing rhythm songs convincingly. "Skip Rope," as the title implies, is an elaboration on a child's rope-skipping chant and is a swinging nursery rhyme out of the "A-Tisket, A-Tasket" tradition, yet even when she sings nonsense like "I asked my mother for fifty cents / To see an elephant jump the fence," she sings it less like purely rope-skipping rhythm and more like she's telling you a story. On "Get Happy," first recorded in 1949, an early career staple, she comes alive not so much in the rhythmic department but when the piece slows down and she, again, focuses on putting across a narrative.

"Somewhere (If Not in Heaven)" is a somewhat awkward song—it could be the work of a newcomer—but it's more ambitious than most; the story and the language are less than straightforward. In that respect, it's an archetype of the classic June Christy kind of a song.

It's also the harbinger of the future in that this September 1949 session represents the first of many dates that Pete Rugolo arranged and conducted for her. Rugolo was Kenton's chief arranger throughout the Christy years, and they both went out on their own when he disbanded in 1949. Together they gradually became one of the top singer-orchestrator combinations. Like Nelson Riddle, who was much influenced by Rugolo and the other Kenton arrangers, Rugolo proved a master at using the language of modern jazz in a highly sensitive and supportive fashion.

From 1949 to 1955, Christy and Rugolo mostly worked on singles together—although most of the songs ("Magazines," "Kicks") done in this fashion in these years were, in fact, a decided step down quality-wise from the 1947–49 singles. As a team, they had two breakthroughs in these years: "My Heart Belongs to Only You," a 1952 hit single albeit a song that wouldn't make it to standard status, and the album *Something Cool*. It's safe to say that if Christy had never done anything else—never sung with Kenton, even—she would have earned her place in this book, on the honor roll of great jazz and standards singers, with this one album alone.

I have written so much on *Something Cool* over the years that it's difficult to resist the temptation to go off for five thousand words talking about it again. But in a vain attempt to put it into as few words as possible: *Something Cool* was the album on which June Christy consolidated her achievements and put it all together—that strikingly cool voice, her penchant for unusual narrative, her flair for mystery, the subtle drama, and the decidedly original orchestra-

tions of Pete Rugolo. The combination of the voice, the brain, the background, and the tunes seems amazingly fresh fifty years later—*Something Cool* is a better jazz vocal album than anything made in recent years. In fact, from the film noir of the title track and "Lonely House," to the amazing optimism (tainted with worldly wisdom) of "This Time the Dream's on Me" (with its telling modulation), it's closer to being a perfect album, in every respect, than most of the albums made by superior jazz singers, like O'Day and Fitzgerald.

It starts with Billy Barnes's title track, a structurally complex, philosophically deep saloon song that captures the essence of a Tennessee Williams heroine. The title itself has a double meaning, between cool in a sense of an icy drink and cool in the sense of West Coast jazz. Before *Something Cool*, most singers and listeners alike assumed that Johnny Mercer's lyric to "Midnight Sun" (another inflection of coolness) was merely a romantic story set at the North Pole, yet Christy and Rugolo make it sound like arctic symbolism—an Ingmar Bergman approach to a love song. Her skill at narrative is second only to Sinatra's, and like Sinatra she imbues her fast numbers with an undercurrent of melancholy. What Pete Hamill once said about the Chairman— that his upbeat swingers are primarily a release from the angst of his slow sad songs—applies equally to Christy. *Something Cool* was put together piecemeal over a two-year period, during a time when few realized the potential for the jazz-pop vocal album. She had considerable time to experiment, and wound up putting together a perfect sequence of eleven songs.

The record was a commercial hit, and thus Capitol gave Christy and Rugolo license to keep going. She became almost exclusively an album artist, particularly after the release of the 12" LP edition of *Something Cool*. She and Rugolo would collaborate again on *The Misty Miss Christy* (1956), *Fair and Warmer* (1957), *Gone for the Day* (1957), *The Song Is June!* (1958), and *Off Beat* (1960). There were also a couple of albums of remakes—*June Christy Recalls Those Kenton Days* and the 1960 stereo version of *Something Cool*, but the titles listed above are the core of their collaboration: six albums that could easily fit onto three CDs (if you left off the stereo *Something Cool*); in fact, four of them are already on doubles.

The Misty Miss Christy was quite possibly an even more well-rounded album than *Something Cool;* it seems less schizophrenic in its juxtaposition of fast and slow, uppers and downers. It may be that part of the appeal of *Something Cool* is that radical contrast, which seems to reflect the mind-set of a disturbed woman. *Misty* isn't quite so dramatic. It lies somewhere between a love song and a blues, a gray area of pop song that's both happy and sad. Rugolo has brought the two extremes together by covering them all in a light coating of strings. On the one hand,

"The Wind," with a melody by West Coast pianist Russ Freeman, is the most ambitious tone poem of the set; at the other end, Herman Hupfeld's "Sing Something Simple," despite the lyric's sarcastic but eloquent plea for pop song naïveté, is actually anything but. The last tune is especially ambivalent: "There's No You," associated with the young Sinatra (he would remake it a year after Christy), was written as a melancholy song, but Christy's treatment is surprisingly upbeat and defiant—at least until the tag, in which she switches moods completely and slows back down into ballad time.

The remaining four Christy-Rugolo albums (which have been collected in chronological order on two Capitol–Blue Note CDs) are also essential: *Fair and Warmer* was an attempt to showcase a lighter, swingier Christy, and opens with "I Want to Be Happy," another twenties show tune that would replace "Get Happy" as her perennial opener. She's especially strong with two relatively recent tunes by Irving Berlin, "The Best Thing for You" and "Better Luck Next Time," and swings another tune normally done slow, "I've Never Been in Love Before." The standout ballads are the lesser-known "Irresistible You" and "Beware My Heart." *Gone for the Day* has a stronger programmatic theme, being twelve songs loosely about its being so peaceful in the country, love turning winter to spring, the seasons—which is quite a departure for the protagonist of "Something Cool," who seems to have spent her entire life in a dimly lit saloon. Yet even here there's an undercurrent of melancholy: You get the feeling that the Christy character is spending all this time in the country to get away from the travails and tragedies of city life. (Perhaps she's at a sanatorium, drying out?)

Was the cycle beginning to wind down with the final two Christy-Rugolo entries, *The Song Is June!* and *Off Beat*? Yes and no. One wonders if the two could have kept going, but this was a hard act to keep following, finding standards and new tunes, familiar works and obscurities, that suited the Christy character, and which she and Rugolo could then reinterpret in new arrangements that were as warm and friendly as they were unconventional. The title song of *Off Beat* has her phrasing in a way that must have been difficult for anyone with big-band training, while it's the opener, the Kern and Fields "Remind Me," that gets the tone poem treatment, with Christy sticking (with difficulty, one imagines) to a tempo that's not quite rubato—over a section of flutes and oboe.

The non-Rugolo classic Christy albums are also Kentoncentric; the two with bands spotlighted the orchestrations of her husband, Bob Cooper. *June's Got Rhythm* is a set of mostly swingers—including a very moving "Easy Living"—and that surprisingly dramatic "All God's Chillun Got Rhythm." *Ballads for Night People* comes closest to *Misty Miss Christy* in spirit since it combines not overly mournful ballads with not overly frantic up-tempos, mostly with light strings.

There are also three small group sets, the most powerful of which is *Duet* (done right after *Something Cool* in 1955), a set of voice and piano encounters between Kenton and Christy that might have been inspired by the Ella Fitzgerald–Ellis Larkins albums. Benny Carter's "Lonely Woman" (a superior remake of a song she had recorded in 1947 with the full Kenton orchestra), Joe Greene's "Come to the Party," and Bobby Troup's "Just the Way I Am" are just about the saddest things Christy ever sang. Kenton's usual idea of great music was overbearing, but here he surprises us by showing he also appreciates the value of understatement. The starkness of the accompaniment and the exposed, vulnerable nature of Christy's singing effectively foreshadow Tony Bennett and Bill Evans twenty years later.

The remaining small group albums are the 1960 *The Cool School*, a set of generally rhythmic children's songs, and *The Intimate Miss Christy*. The latter has her voice in surprisingly good shape for 1963. It's a very gentle set, done with just flute (Bud Shank, playing pseudonymously as "Bud Legge") and guitar (Al Viola), perhaps influenced by the voice-guitar-sax bossa nova hits of Stan Getz, and the minimal instrumentation of Julie London. *Intimate* was Christy's last really worthy album. She also did a set of swinging big band charts (*Big Band Specials*) that wasn't as good as it should have been; a package self-described as *Something Broadway, and Something Latin*, which actually contains one or two decent charts, particularly "Do I Hear a Waltz." (In 1960, she had done half a Broadway album with Bob Cooper of the score to *Do-Re-Mi*, which consisted of five Christy vocals and five Cooper instrumentals.)

Christy wasn't even forty, but already she was in decline. It was a convergence of unfortunate events: For one thing, she hadn't really achieved any notable album sales since *Something Cool*. As Capitol president Alan Livingston told me, "*Something Cool* was a hit, but that was the only one of her albums that amounted to anything sales-wise." Then, too, by the mid-sixties the industry was beginning to shift away from even the bigger-selling artists of ten years previously—both O'Day and Chris Connor were soon looking for new homes. But the major issue was Christy herself. "When she got offstage, she'd be shaking and just a nervous wreck," her daughter Shay Cooper told writer Jim Gavin. The only thing that helped was scotch. By the time her career was fading, so were her pipes—there's decay evident on many of the sixties albums, although, surprisingly, she sounds fine on *The Intimate Miss Christy*, one of the very last and the one that leaves her voice the most exposed.

She worked only occasionally in the seventies and eighties—she reunited with Kenton at the Newport Jazz Festival in 1972 (one track, "Remind Me," shows up on a bootleg) and a decade after that she briefly toured Europe with other Kenton vets, Shorty Rogers and His Giants. On all these occasions, it was reported, Johnnie Walker and Jim Beam were in the house, cheering her on. She made a new album in 1977, *Impromptu*, for the independent, West Coast producer Albert Marx's Discovery Records. Her voice had deteriorated to a mere echo of its former self, thanks to alcohol and lack of work. Yet her conviction was there, and so was her ability to tell a story. For that matter, so was the support of old friends, such as musical director Lou Levy, Cooper, Frank Roslino, and Shelly Manne. And so was songwriter Matt Dennis, who obliged her by writing a verse for "Angel Eyes" (the song had never previously had one) especially for the occasion.

Song titles like "Midnight Sun," with its arctic connotations, and "Something Cool" referred to the California cool texture of Christy's accompaniments—although with her unsentimental, vibrato-less timbre, she shouldn't have been surprised that people applied the terminology to her singing itself. Right up until her death in 1990, Christy bristled whenever anyone confused the cool epithet for a description of her vocal style: "The one criticism that I've never been able to agree with is that I sing coldly," she said in 1956. "Warmth is the one quality I do think I have. Gosh, if I don't have that, I might as well give up." She never did.

Buddy Clark (1912–1949)

Buddy Clark is my favorite singer. He has the sweetest voice of them all. Let me tell you, Frank Sinatra couldn't shine Buddy Clark's shoes.

—Al Jolson

Buddy Clark was the original retro crooner. He had been recording and broadcasting since 1934, which makes him a member of the first post-Crosby generation, but Clark didn't become a big star until after the first wave of Sinatra hysteria ten years later. In an age when the Voice's more avant-garde rhythms and harmonies seemed to be pushing pop singing in unforeseen directions, along came Buddy Clark with what might be called a "neo-romantic" style. He not only made listeners think of Crosby as Bing sounded earlier in his career, to many he also evoked Crosby's pop predecessor, Al Jolson. Clark's hard-won and long-awaited success can perhaps be attributed to this remarkably personal distillation of Crosby's warmth and natural ease combined with Jolson's bravura radiance.

Where Sinatra and his musical director of the forties, Axel Stordahl, were exploring whole new territories in terms of tempo, orchestration, and harmonies that owed much to twentieth-century classical music, Clark continued to kick it old school. Yet he was also distinctly a phenomenon of the postwar era; in fact, he was one of the few veteran band vocalists of the thirties to enjoy a bigger and better career in the brave new world for pop singers that Sinatra opened up.

Clark was no renegade innovator: His vision of postwar pop was that it would sound a lot like prewar pop—but that itself was a kind of distinction. The late forties was an era in which pop music was beginning to get goofier and goofier even before Mitch Miller arrived. Clark sang some goofy novelty songs—"I'll Dance at Your Wedding" and "Apple Blossom Wedding" are hardly Cole Porter—but he sang them beautifully, and the very traditional style of both his voice and his orchestrations gave such songs a cachet they didn't have when, say, Evelyn Knight sang them. If Sinatra sings about the thrill of romantic discovery, Clark sings about weddings—apple blossom, dancing, and otherwise—as a further way of aligning himself with tradition. Where Sinatra sings about the beginning of the romantic chase, Clark sings about its inevitable end. Sinatra affectionately parodies the tender trap, but Clark glorifies it. He wants to be caught in it.

Where Sinatra is a lover, Clark is a husband. Further, he's the kind of husband who would have become an archetypal fifties sitcom father had he lived a little while longer. "I'll Dance at Your Wedding" begins with a spoken dialogue between himself and Anita Gordon (the object of his chase in "Linda") in which he insists on wearing his comfortable old shoes when he dances at their wedding—this is the kind of TV dad who has a favorite chair. The responsiblities cut both ways, too—"Ballerina" makes it clear that this traditional husband expects a traditional prewar wife. This Bob Russell–Carl Sigman hit (the Vaughan Monroe version was number one for ten weeks) has a husband and future dad telling his intended spouse that she'll have to choose between showbiz and him. It's a perfect postwar song: Rosie the Riveter gives up her career to become a domestic diva. Nat King Cole later reinterpreted "Ballerina" with both irony and heavy swing, but Clark sings it completely straight and makes it work that way.

Above all, Buddy Clark's music was remarkably beautiful—his voice was lovely above and beyond the call of duty, and he had warmth and personality to spare. He was always the extra man. In 1934 the kings of pop vocals were Crosby, Russ Columbo, and Vallee; in 1948, they were Crosby, Sinatra, and Como. Yet like the younger Dick Haymes, Clark could put over a love song with the best of them. A master balladeer, he could also be loose and swinging when the material called for it, as on "I'll Dance at Your Wedding," while "South America, Take It Away" shows that he had a sense of humor in addition to a sense of rhythm ("aye yi yi!"). When he was killed in a plane crash at the peak of his career at age thirty-eight, Buddy Clark still had charm he hadn't even used yet.

If Dick Haymes and Johnny Desmond might be said to represent a halfway point between Crosby and Sinatra, Clark is the link between Crosby and Jolson. ("Sincerely Yours," a lyric written in the form of a lyric, has a spoken recitative in the middle similar to what Jolson and Elvis Presley later did on

"Are You Lonesome Tonight?") Like Jolson, Clark was the child of a Russian Jewish couple, though unlike Jolson's Mammy and Pappy, Clark's parents had immigrated to the New World a few months before the arrival of their son. He was born Samuel Goldberg in Boston on July 26, 1912 (not in Dorchester in 1911, as previously reported). His father was a tailor, and as a boy Sammy worked in the family shop. By the time he attended Washington Grammar School, he had become both an ace athlete and a budding musician, studying clarinet and later the saxophone. The superb Boston-born jazz trumpeter Max Kaminsky remembered the nine-year-old Sammy Goldberg singing "mammy songs" (this was at the height of the Jolson era) at community social clubs.

Goldberg sang professionally for the first time at age eleven when he handled the tenor part at a local wedding for the princely sum of three dollars, and he frequented a Boston boys club called the West End House where he appeared in his first production. "I had the pleasure of directing a minstrel show in which Buddy Clark was the star," his friend Allie Coles recalled in 1970. "It was in June of 1923. He sang 'Way Down Yonder in New Orleans' and he actually tore the house down." (Coles added that twenty-five years later Clark did the same thing while performing the same song at a club reunion.)

He enjoyed early successes in showbiz, such as a week's engagement at Boston's Metropolitan that quickly extended to two, for which he would drive up every night in a truck bearing the device "Goldberg the Tailor." Still, Goldberg Senior insisted on having a lawyer in the family, and after Sammy graduated from Boston's High School of Commerce (where he had been president of the dramatic club), he was sent to Northeastern College, where he lasted three years. At around this time, Boston brahmin businessman David Lilienthal heard him sing and was so impressed that he not only arranged for Clark to continue taking music lessons but gave him a break on local radio by having his company sponsor Clark's programs. Buddy went on singing with local bands around Boston, including one group that played at the Mayfair Club led by pianist Sammy Liner. It was Liner who around this time suggested Goldberg's professional name, Buddy Clark, which became his legal appellation in May 1938.

It's not known when Clark began turning up in New York, although his first wife, whom he married in 1935, supposedly convinced him his career wouldn't start happening until he moved to the Big Apple full-time. He was certainly already regularly shuttling between New York and Boston when he made his first records, three 32-bar vocal refrains with Freddy Martin's sweet orchestra in September 1934.

Between 1934 and his induction at the end of 1942, Clark was essentially a studio freelance band vocalist, who worked with a great variety of dance bands on broadcasts and record dates. In the years leading up to the swing era, dance bands were still coming to grips with the idea of singers. Bing Crosby had put band vocalists on the map a half-generation earlier, but still most bands either didn't have regular vocalists or, if they did, didn't use them when they made records. Instead, virtually every band that recorded utilized the same small pool of studio singers. These included both real "working bands" (Eddy Duchin, Xavier Cugat, Wayne King) and bands that were put together only for record and radio sessions (led by house music directors like Freddy Rich and Nat Shilkret), and both white and black bands.

Between 1934 and 1942, Clark's voice could be heard in textures as disparate as Xavier Cugat's lightly Latin orchestra to Johnny Hodges's jumping little blues band to schmaltzy Mickey Mouse organizations, and lots and lots of dance bands that could play it either straight or swinging.

On his early band vocals, such as "Stars Fell on Alabama" (his first recording, done with Freddy Martin's band), Clark doesn't sound substantially different from the way he did at the end of his career in 1949. From the beginning, he combined Crosby's basic sound with Jolson's urgency. In fact, along with Al Bowlly, Clark is easily the best of the baritones of the era, the first generation of new crooners who matured under Crosby's influence. His first "solo" disc, recorded at the end of 1934, can safely be described as a Crosby cover. He recorded two songs from Crosby's picture *Here Is My Heart*, "June in January" and "With Every Breath I Take" for the ARC corporation, and he sounds closer to Crosby here than he ever would again.

The Take Two CD *Band Vocals from the Thirties* is a good sample of his work from the era, featuring Clark vocals recorded with no fewer than eight different bands. Like Bowlly, Clark was as versatile as he was sincere, and could handle sentimental as well as hot numbers. More than most of his colleagues, he had a gift for working in different kinds of rhythms. His vocals underscore how diverse dance bands were in the prewar era: He sang rhumbas and sambas not only with Cugat but also with Bud Gluskin; he sang waltzes not only with Wayne King, who was billed as the Waltz King, but also on a whole session of songs in three-four time with Cugat for Victor. He sang swing numbers not only with Benny Goodman and Johnny Hodges but, surprisingly, with Wayne King. On the 1941 "He's My Uncle" with King, he's so jaunty that no one could recognize the King band in a blindfold test. "Tia Juana" is an unlikely amalgam of talents, being an authentically ersatz *Spanglais*-style bolero written by Raymond Scott (like Clark, an American Jew who changed his name for showbiz).

Clark also showed some skill early on in a jazz vein, especially working with the fine jazz guitarist Dick McDonough, whose studio band was loaded with hot soloists, but his jazziest work as a freelancer was done on a 1937 session featuring sidemen from the Duke Ellington Orchestra, recorded under the leadership of star saxophonist Johnny Hodges, with the Maestro himself serving as pianist. "Foolin' Myself," "You'll Never Get to Heaven (If You Break My Heart)," and "A Sailboat in the Moonlight" have Clark getting hot and lusty in the manner of early to mid-thirties Crosby (as on "Sweet Georgia Brown").

In 1934 and '35, Clark also got in at the birth of the swing era by working briefly with Benny Goodman. This appears to be a rare case of Clark actually serving in a semi-permanent position with a real working band, even though Goodman hired him primarily for radio work.

"Buddy must have come to Benny on an audition," Goodman's wonderful female vocalist Helen Ward told me in the early nineties, "and he liked what he heard, and hired him. When we worked together, we got along fine and we had a lot of fun. He was very, very nice, we always exchanged pleasantries and some laughs. Strangely enough, in the beginning, he sang sharp. It wasn't until later that he really did his thing, which sounded so well and so good. In the beginning, Benny let him go because he was just a bit off. I don't know what caused it or how he got rid of it, because [being consistently] sharp or flat is something you don't acquire, you either have an ear or you don't, and I never could figure that out."

Yet Clark certainly doesn't sound off-key on his vocals with Goodman or anyone else of the period. He only recorded two vocals with Goodman, "Like a Bolt from the Blue" and "Livin' in a Great Big Way," but the latter in particular shows that he was a perfect singer for the band, capable of singing a melody straight but swinging in a way that that the leader must have appreciated. (He also turns up on additional tunes on *Let's Dance* airchecks, such as "Not Bad," "The Object of My Affection," and "Love Is Just Around the Corner.")

In 1935, Clark eloped with the former Louise Dahl Hitz, much to the annoyance of her society blue-blood parents. It's doubtful that they changed their tune, even when Clark was offered an opportunity that could potentially make him one of the best-known voices on the radio—a bigger prize even than the exposure that Goodman could have given him. From 1936 to 1939, Clark starred as the principal male singer on *Lucky Strike's Your Hit Parade*. Even so, although by the end of the decade millions of listeners knew Clark's voice, few knew his name. Most of his records were still in the dance-band format, in which the singer was secondary, and even the *Hit Parade* had a format that was designed to showcase the song and not the singer—the program never made a star out of anybody.

In 1937, Clark took his first shot at Hollywood and a film career. He was quickly told he was overqualified as a vocalist but underqualified in the looks department. He wasn't homely or unattractive, just average-looking, but he certainly didn't have the romantic leading-man appeal of Russ Columbo or Cary Grant.

Once in Hollywood, Clark wound up dubbing for established stars, most famously comic Jack Haley in *Wake Up and Live* (1937). This was the oddest example of art imitating life that Tinseltown knew before *Singin' in the Rain*: Jack Haley plays a reluctant singer who can only perform when no one is watching and who becomes a "mystery crooner," whose voice is celebrated but whose face and name are unknown. Clark provided his singing voice. Both the picture and nearly every song in it ("It's Swell of You," "Never in a Million Years," "There's a Lull in My Life," and the title number, all by Mack Gordon and Harry Revel) became a hit. Yet to his frustration, Clark was contractually obligated to keep quiet concerning his contribution to the picture. He later complained, "Radio fans write me and ball me out for imitating the singing style of Jack Haley, and it was my voice all the time!"

Despite a substantial role in making a success out of *Wake Up and Live*, he was not invited to work on any other pictures until 1942. Shortly before he went into the service, he had a part in a B vehicle, *Seven Days' Leave*, with Victor Mature.

Fortunately, Clark wasn't depending on Hollywood for his bread-and-butter. In the early war years he was recording and broadcasting like crazy, for sponsors selling everything from mattresses to coal. Indeed, he seems to have hit a sort of vocal apogee around 1941: His voice was never smoother, his style never more aggressively insinuating.

Beginning in 1938, Clark had begun to record under his own name on a semi-regular basis. His earliest sides suffer from the same maladies that plague many vocal records of the prewar and pre-Sinatra era, namely generic orchestrations and a tune selection that seems completely random. But there's a lot of promise in his work of the 1938–42 period, particularly as he begins the first session of the period with two blissful future standards by Rodgers and Hart from *I Married an Angel*, the title song and "Spring Is Here."

Clark would spend nearly all of his solo career with Columbia Records, first with its corporate predecessor ARC and its budget subsidiary, Okeh Records. However, in 1939–40 he also did a lot of excellent work for two smaller concerns, Associated Transcriptions and Varsity Records. There are some first-rate sessions for Varsity, including five songs from Walt Disney's *Pinocchio* and an all-star jazz date with the Varsity All-Stars, whose ranks included Bud Freeman and Pee Wee Russell. Between the dance bands and the transcriptions, it often seems as if Clark recorded every good song of the 1930s—and most of the second-rate ones as well.

By the time of his induction, Clark was quickly coming into his own as a solo artist. His principal recording activity was a set of twenty-four generally outstanding solos cut for Okeh, which included some workaday pop songs, ranging from the dreadful "A Feller and a Girl" to the delightful "Lamplight" (aka "A Boy, a Girl, the Lamplight"). He had the good luck to draw four terrific new songs by Cole Porter, among them "Let's Be Buddies," "Dream Dancing" (the best period recording after Fred Astaire's), "I Hate You Darling," and "Ev'rything I Love"—which has to be more than a coincidence, since these are from three different scores.

There are also a number of war songs, including Irving Berlin's jingoistic "When That Man Is Dead and Gone," in which he fantasizes with genuine conviction about the death of Hitler, and "Honorable Moon," which manages to salute the fighting Chinese for standing up to their invaders, and at the same time patronize them. The best is Berlin's "A Little Church in England," scarcely revived since 1941: It's a peace song on the level of "The White Cliffs of Dover" and Berlin's own "White Christmas." (The church may not be "white," but it is specifically Anglo.)

Nineteen forty-two was a busy year: In April, his wife, Louise, the mother of his first two children, received a divorce in Reno. In August, he married Nedra Sanders. (To describe the second Mrs. Clark as unlucky in love would be a gross understatement: She, too, had been married before, but her first husband had murdered both her mother and their baby son, for which he was given a double life sentence. Her second marriage, to Clark, would also end tragically, as we shall see.) In the fall of 1942, the newly remarried crooner traveled to Hollywood for *Seven Days' Leave*. In November, he entered the service. He most likely had volunteered: He was thirty-one, above draft age, and the father of two—in fact, his third child and second daughter, Penny, would be born in May 1943.

Private First Class Buddy Clark went through basic training in Staunton, Virginia. "His singing talent was so great that a large part of his non-training time was devoted to entertaining wounded soldiers" (at nearby Woodrow Wilson General Hospital), as Second Lieutenant Leo Lyons remembered. "Buddy was a 'good soldier' and did not seek or expect any special treatment," Lyons continued. Clark only made one recording during his whole three and a half years of service—a V-Disc of the Carmichael-Mercer "How Little We Know," accompanied by the 344th Army Special Services Orchestra.

When he was discharged in April 1946, he must have been in doubt as to whether he could earn his old spot back. He couldn't have imagined that now, after all these years, he would finally make it to the top. Two men were particularly responsible for his postwar "overnight success story." Paul Willis of the Carnation Milk Company signed him as star singer and emcee on the *Carnation Contented Hour*, which quickly became a top-rated program. Around the same time, Clark's records became more important partly because records themselves were once again

becoming a mass medium and he had the good fortune to get in on the postwar boom. Manie Sachs, who also shepherded the careers of Sinatra and Dinah Shore on vinyl, not only honored Clark's prewar Okeh contract, he improved on it by moving him over to the more prestigious red Columbia label.

At his fifth session after the war, in November 1946, along came "Linda," and his life was changed. The song had its origins with the songwriter Jack Lawrence and his lawyer, Lee Eastman. Lawrence already had a long list of successful songs; in fact, his songs were good-luck charms that had provided breakthrough hits for such singers as Sinatra ("All or Nothing at All"), the Ink Spots ("If I Didn't Care"), and Shore ("Yes, My Darling Daughter"). As Lawrence told me, it happened that everyone else in the Eastman family had a "name" song—his wife, Louise; his son, Johnny; his daughter Laura—everyone except his other daughter, Linda. (Actually, Harold Arlen had written a song called "Linda" in 1931, but it was long forgotten by the forties.) Lawrence relished the challenge, and wrote both the words and music by himself, but the song he came up with was initially rejected by every publisher. (Linda Eastman, as is well known, later became world famous as the wife of Paul McCartney.)

Finally, the trumpeter-bandleader Charlie Spivak agreed to publish and record the song, and it also came to the attention of the English émigré bandleader Ray Noble. Between Noble and Sachs, somebody got the idea of having Buddy Clark sing "Linda" with prominent backing by Noble. The arrangement was by Jack Anderson, but one aspect of it seems like a Noble idea. It was the kind of device that he had frequently employed in his 1931–34 New Mayfair Orchestra sessions with Al Bowlly. After a string intro and eight bars of melody divided between brass and reeds, we hear the speaking voice of Buddy Clark:

He: Hello cutie, what's your name?
She (played by Anita Gordon): Fresh! I don't talk to strangers.
He (sincerely): I'm no stranger. Been waitin' every evening for you to walk by.
She (cheekily): Keep waitin'—I'm still walkin'.
He: Aw . . . what's your name?
She (annoyed): None of your business.
He (with surprisingly little sarcasm): Pretty name! But I'll just call you "Linda."
She (surprised): Well! How did you guess?

Thanks to "Linda," Clark, after a dozen years in the upper rungs of the music business, and after having made enough records to go around Kate Smith, was suddenly a star. "Linda" provided him with his biggest hit and his signature song—not to mention jukebox immortality. "Linda" is one of the all-time top pop records, on a par with anything done in the period by Sinatra, Crosby, Como, Haymes, or any of his other rivals.

From "Linda" on, Clark would be a constant presence on the charts. Like Haymes, he made a specialty of sentimental old-timers, of which "Peg o' My Heart" was also a number-one hit, and "I'll Get By," "That Old Gang o' Mine," "When Day Is Done," "Girl of My Dreams," and "I'll See You in My Dreams" also did well for him—and he by them. He also put over "How Are Things in Glocca Morra" (and its *Finian's Rainbow* flip side, the cartoony "If This Isn't Love") by making it sound like an authentic, traditional Irish ballad. He did the same for the Scottish-inspired "Come to Me, Bend to Me" (from *Brigadoon*) and the enthusiastically ersatz "My One and Only Highland Fling." There was even a sequel to "Linda," entitled "I'll Dance at Your Wedding." In this scenario, Buddy and Linda, once again portrayed vocally by Anita Gordon, are preparing for their nuptials, and she entreats him: "You oughta be brushing up that new suit and new shoes instead of dancing around the room like a goon!"

Clark's final reputation rests on his 1946–49 red Columbia discs (which were interrupted by the 1948 AFM ban) and, fortunately, a large number of surviving airchecks from the *Contented Hour* (which were not). While there is much to like in his thirties band vocals and the prewar transcriptions and solos, it's the postwar material that is most likely to be heard. The singing is warm and robust; in his mid- to late thirties, the voice has deepened though not necessarily darkened, and the singer himself is rife with pep and personality. To a certain extent, his records help illustrate just how avant-garde his label mate Sinatra was at this time, but Clark's performances are endlessly pleasing in themselves.

Over a period of four years (1946–49), he recorded about a hundred songs for Columbia, enough for four very full CDs. (American Columbia has done at least two official Clark collections, with a lot of duplication between them—*16 Most Requested Songs* and *The Buddy Clark Collection*—and other titles are available on the British Vocalion *Encores* in more echoey sound.) Ever the perfect record husband, Clark co-starred in a series of duets with Columbia's two leading female singers, Dinah Shore (including a lovely "Summertime" by two singers as Jewish as Gershwin himself) and Doris Day (lots of hits, including "My Darling" and "That Certain Party"). There were more outstanding show tunes, including most of the good songs from the scores of the Broadway shows *Inside USA* (1947) by Arthur Schwartz and Howard Dietz and *Miss Liberty* by Irving Berlin.

Clark also continued to score with Latin and faux-Latin laments, some eight titles once again with Cugat (including the commercial jingle "Chiquita Banana"), and "Serenade," arranged by Ray Noble as a big fat pasodoble in the tradition of the Noble-Bowlly "Lady of Spain." "The Story of Sorrento" has

Clark and Cugat rendering a traditional Italian song as a Cuban rhumba. His single loveliest record may well be a song often done in a salsa tempo, "The Night Has a Thousand Eyes." Where Sinatra embodied the errant lover—the kind of swain who goes around seducing every señorita in sight—Clark is very convincing as he tries to talk his lover out of screwing around on him. It's a hokey, melodramatic idea ("words deep down inside can be seen by the night"), which he makes sound completely convincing.

Clark was no longer anonymous, but still he remained invisible. He got to sing "Linda" on-camera in a Columbia Pictures one-reeler, which seems to be the extent of his onscreen career in his glory period. He made three more films, which all somehow kept him out of the spotlight. *I Wonder Who's Kissing Her Now* (1947) and *Father Is a Bachelor* (1950) had him again dubbing the singing for onscreen actors—Mark Stevens in the first, William Holden in the second. You would think that somebody must have recognized his voice now that he was one of the most popular singers in the country. He also narrated *Melody Time* (1948), a Disney animated omnibus that he carried off with Crosby-like insouciance.

In September 1949, Clark at thirty-eight had reached the peak of his career, having landed six chart hits (including "My Darling, My Darling") in the past year while the *Contented Hour* continued to pull in big ratings. He and Nedra had set up housekeeping in California in 1948 with their five-year-old daughter, and he had also made a belated "legit" theater debut the previous summer in a revival of *Girl Crazy* at Los Angeles's Greek Theatre. A dedicated sports fan, Clark routinely flew from one city to another to catch an important game—publishers and song pluggers could always catch his attention by flashing box seat tickets in his face. On October 1, he was returning home from a football game in Palo Alto. The plane ran out of gas and crashed into a residential street in Los Angeles; the pilot and five other passengers survived, but Clark was fatally wounded from a head injury.

He died on October 1, 1949, even as one of his final recordings, "A Dreamer's Holiday," was on the hit single charts. Within a few months, both of his closest collaborators at Columbia, Manie Sachs and musical director Mitchell Ayres, left CBS for RCA Victor, where they transferred their energies into exploring new directions for Clark's former rival Perry Como. Within several years Clark's daughter was killed in a car crash, and his second wife, who married for a third time (movie producer Albert Broccoli), died in 1958.

"Buddy Clark is the finest voice around," Bing Crosby said in 1948, and it still holds true. It would be a miracle for any sound so sincere and tender to survive for more than sixty years, but, as Clark sang in "Linda," "miracles do happen."

Rosemary Clooney (1928–2002)

In 2001, Rosemary Clooney turned seventy-three at roughly the same time that she released her final studio album. By then, she had long been recognized as an institution, among an elite group of pop-jazz singers whose ranks included Peggy Lee, her friends Tony Bennett and Frank Sinatra, and precious few others. In June of that year, she was presented with the equivalent of a lifetime achievement award by the Manhattan Association of Cabaret (an event that was also significant in that it marked the final occasion in which she performed in New York City). It's clear that the cabaret world regarded Clooney as one of its own kind—one of the best, if not *the* best.

As much as any of the great goddesses of cabaret—Mabel Mercer, Julie Wilson—Clooney made a lyric come alive (she was also praised for this aspect of the art by younger masters like Mary Cleere Haran and Susannah McCorkle, and by veterans like Wilson). She could take 32 bars of some song you'd heard a thousand times sung by everybody and his brother and turn it into a fresh and intensely personal testament. One late-life album, *Brazil*, a collection of Latin American songs and rhythms, prompted another pianist-singer, Eric Comstock, to report that "She even made me cry with 'Brazil' for Christ's sake!" For those who only know the song through Clooney's recording, it should be stressed that this 1942 South American import was never intended or interpreted (even by Frank Sinatra) as anything other than background for shaking Brazilian booty. When Bob Russell wrote the English lyric, he wasn't aspiring to set hearts moving so much as to get toes tapping—Clooney was the first to prove that "Brazil" could not only be physically moving but emotionally moving as well.

Even though Clooney was accepted as cabaret royalty, it should be noted that cabaret singers do not, as a rule, make albums with the likes of Duke Ellington, Benny Goodman, Woody Herman, and the Basie band. I was always disappointed that she wasn't more widely recognized as the great jazz singer she was: She didn't show up on the *Down Beat* poll, wasn't nominated under Best Jazz Vocal at the Grammys, and didn't appear regularly at the JVC Jazz Festival. Clooney herself never remotely forced the issue, but to anybody who was paying the slightest attention, she was easily one of the leading contemporary jazz singers, no less so than Abbey Lincoln or Cassandra Wilson.

Nor do cabaret singers usually have their sense of rhythm extravagantly praised by hard-core jazz musicians. Scott Hamilton, who played tenor on many of Clooney's records from her last twenty years, told Peter Straub, "She has really great time. It's just there. You wouldn't believe how helpful that is when you're playing behind her. The other thing about Rose is that she's so strong, as a musician, that she can shape the whole way we're going to do a song in the first three notes. She can shape everything in a *pick-up*."

There is a word for this kind of music, but it's somewhat antiquated and I'm reluctant to use it: When you take cabaret singing and give it a beat, or when you take jazz singing and invest it with a profound sensitivity to the lyrics, then you have a kind of music that was once commonly known as pop singing. That's what Clooney's approximate contemporaries, like Margaret Whiting, Doris Day, Steve Lawrence and Eydie Gormé, Buddy Greco, Jack Jones, and most importantly Tony Bennett—just to name a few who are living—all managed to do. As much as I admire some of the younger vocalists in the jazz and cabaret fields, I'd have a hard time naming any who are able to do what these artists did so matter-of-factly, back in the day.

I've only heard jazz musicians praise two other pop singers with the enthusiasm that Scott Hamilton lavished on Clooney, namely Crosby and Sinatra. Clooney is obviously the singer who's learned the most from those two icons, and the female vocalist who was most closely connected with them both. She shared an idea that is central to the work of both men: that you don't have to sacrifice the narrative in order to get the beat, and that you don't have to stop swinging in order to put the love story over. If either of these men, both of whom were profoundly inspired by Louis Armstrong, contributed any one thing to American music, that was it.

Clooney always had a foot in two worlds: In the years of her emergence, when she spent the entire 1950s giving birth to even more hit records than she did babies (no mean feat), she worked with Mitch Miller, the pop-music mastermind who masterminded the very concept of the pop-music mastermind. During the height of Miller's reign—which was roughly a decade—there were two ways for pop singers to work with him: Either you completely went along with what he wanted and let him create a career for you, as did Johnny Ray, Frankie Laine, and Guy Mitchell, or you stood your ground and tried to bring as much of your own taste to the mixture as you could, as did Tony Bennett and Jo Stafford. Clooney questioned some of Miller's ideas, but quickly thought better of it when one of the absolute goofiest songs he trotted out was the blockbuster "Come on-a My House," which she received requests for over the next fifty years. From that point on, she sang along with whatever Mr. Sing Along told her to.

Today, Bennett and Stafford are regarded as great artists and major figures in the overall development of pop music, while Ray, Laine, and Mitchell, who certainly made plenty of hits in their day, haven't fared as well in the cold light of history. Each is remembered, at best, as a one-dimensional act. Clooney was every bit as malleable with Miller as these three gentlemen, and just as susceptible to such Miller gimmicks as echo chambers, sound effects, and multivoice overdubbing, not to mention silly tunes. It was only later that she achieved immortal status through talent, hard work, and a conscious desire to sing the best songs with the best bands.

Once when I disparaged some of her early Mitch Miller productions, Rosemary gave me a look that said she agreed with me but told me in no uncertain terms that I was wrong to suggest that all the changes for the worse that happened to pop music in the 1950s—from swing to novelties to rock 'n' roll—could be laid at Miller's doorstep. She was right; and by the same token, not all of the Red Scare (which happened at the same time) could be blamed on Joe McCarthy. Even in Clooney's earliest recordings, made with Tony Pastor's band, well before either she or Miller came to Columbia or had heard of each other, there's a significant percentage of inane material.

Yet Clooney's overall body of work, particularly in her last twenty-five years, has been so strong that no one holds the worst excesses of her early records against her. This is nothing to take for granted: Doris Day, for example, is still more closely associated with contemporary singles than the first-class albums of standards that she also recorded. Perhaps the woman who would later earn accolades for her albums of Richard Rodgers and Ira Gershwin had to start out by singing "Sailor Boys Have Talk to Me in English" and "Canasta," and only gradually raising herself up by her bootstraps.

After their parents broke up, Rosemary (born 1928) and her younger sister, Betty, were raised by their grandparents in Cincinnati. Like most kids at that time, the two Clooneys were swing-crazy, and like many future professionals got their start singing unpaid at nonprime hours on local radio. In 1945, saxophonist-vocalist-bandleader (and Artie Shaw alumnus) Tony Pastor played through Cinci, heard Rosie and Betty and liked them so much he decided to add them to his band. They were underage, and had to be chaperoned by an uncle. The Clooney sisters lasted with Pastor's band for four years and two dozen recordings, with the older Rosemary asserting herself as the dominant half of the team.

As with Doris Day and Dean Martin, we're fortunate to have all of Clooney's early work collected on a series of lavish boxes produced in Germany by the Bear Family label. The three Bear boxes gather all her recordings, for every label, up through 1968, including her early sides with Betty and the Pastor band, as well as a number of noncommercial items and other rarities. The box opens with thirty tracks by the Pastor-Clooney combination, starting with a session for the independent label Cosmo Records. (This short-lived operation was best known for recording Art Tatum and had no connection either to the cocktail or to Helen Gurley Brown.)

The Cosmo session rather deceptively gives us hope: Pastor's band was one of the star attractions on such a small label, and it had first crack at the new songs and thus was able to do a whole album of the music from the latest Disney musical, *Song of the South* (1946). The songs aren't quite Gershwin, but at least they're solid, catchy novelties (unlike some of the fifties Columbia material like "Cheegah, Choonem"). You don't have to feel embarrassed if you find yourself humming *Song of the South* tunes like "That's What Uncle Remus Said" or "Sooner or Later," Rosemary's first solo.

Starting with her second session with Pastor—the first for Columbia—the material follows a more predictable pattern. At Columbia, Pastor was a smaller fish in a bigger pond, and top tunes like the *Song of the South* score went to better-known bands, like the Les Brown–Doris Day combination. As it happens, Day and Brown also recorded "Sooner or Later," and their version is only slightly better than Pastor and Clooney's. Even so, as hinted above, the worst of the Pastor-Clooney numbers—"The Chowder Social," "The Click Song," "I'm My Own Grandpa" (based on a minstrel routine reprised in Spike Lee's *Bamboozled*), and the lowest of the lot, "It's a Cruel, Cruel World"—predict her subsequent work with Miller to a remarkable degree.

I wonder. Can it be a coincidence that Clooney recorded so many ersatz ethnic songs both with Pastor and with Miller? There's a very funny calypso comedy song, "Bread and Butter Woman." There's a Scotch-Irish cocktail called "My O'Darlin', My O'Lovely, My O'Brien." And there's "A Boy from Texas, a Girl from Tennessee" and other pieces that foreshadow her later work with country songs. On "Tira-Lira-Li (The Song of the Gondolier)," Clooney even introduces the mock-Neapolitan accent she would later employ on the blockbusters "Come on-a My House," "Mambo Italiano," and "Botch-a-Me." What distinguishes the cheesy songs with Pastor from the cheesy songs with Miller is that this is still the swing era, and a second-rate novelty like "The Click Song" could still be saved by a jazzy arrangement. Miller's introduction of goofy instruments—harpsichords and French horns—was still in the future.

Unlike Day with Brown, Clooney didn't enjoy any major record hits with Pastor, and was almost exclusively featured as half of the Clooney Sisters. Just the same, Columbia's Manie Sachs spotted possibilities in her and signed her to an independent contract. Even at twenty-one, she had an effectively dark, somewhat sultry contralto—it's interesting that fifty years later, her voice didn't really sound older or deeper than it did in 1949; it just sounded fuller, with essentially the same timbre.

Clooney did two sessions as a solo act for Columbia in 1949, and these consist of fairly decent songs, some new ("Don't Cry Joe"), some old ("Chicago," "Oh You Beautiful Doll"), a few surprises ("The Kid's a Dreamer"), and one country novelty ("Why Don't You Haul Off and Love Me"). Clooney then cut her first session with Mitch Miller.

As Rosemary told me in 1998: "I knew from the time I was a child that I would make my living singing. There was no question in my mind. My sense of where it would be didn't matter. I was happy in Maysville, I could make a living there. I was happy in Cincinnati singing on the radio, I could make a living there. I was happy on the road with the band because I could make a living there. All I was trying to do was put food on the table, you know. It didn't even occur to me that I would make records, make movies. . . . I never thought in those terms at all. I was satisfied with all the steps along the way. And therefore the object of it was to please the people that were paying the money. So when Mitch would give me a song called 'Canasta,' I'd say, Sure, I'll do it. You can't believe how bad it is—Oh, God. It was just awful!"

What's surprising is that it took Miller a whole year and a half—until June 1951—to find Clooney a breakthrough hit. This was "Come on-a My House," written by two Armenian-Americans, playwright William Saroyan and future Chipmunk impresario Ross Bagdasarian, who conceived it as an Armenian dialect song. The story goes that the very night Miller first heard it he cut it with Clooney.

This account is slightly at odds with the memories of the late Louis Prima, who told his fan and friend Bob Pepitone (who told me) that he had heard the song and wanted to record it for Columbia. It may have been Prima who first conceived of singing it in an Italian accent; when Miller gave the song to Clooney instead, Prima was so teed off that he didn't renew his contract with the label. Clooney herself was less than enthusiastic. When Miller brought the song to her, she asked him, " 'If I sing this song, do you think that people will understand that I can do other things?' So Mitch put it to me in an interesting way, he said, 'Well, you don't *have* to show up for this session, but if you don't, you're fired.' And I got the message, there was no ambiguity about that."

At least five years of singing professionally, and it was "My House" that made her an "overnight" sensation: All of a sudden she was one of the hottest acts in the country. And everything followed: offers from top-flight theaters and clubs, movies, TV, a marriage to noted actor José Ferrer, five kids, and many more hit records. Clooney was the archetypal working family woman who had everything—too much of everything, in fact. If her round-the-clock career and supersized family weren't enough to keep her busy, she also maintained a long-standing extramarital affair with arranger and soul mate Nelson Riddle. She was so overworked and overextended in the fifties and early sixties that it's not surprising she wound up with a substance abuse situation and other psychological problems.

As with the other artists on his roster, Mitch Miller viewed Clooney as primarily a singles artist. Her hit singles can be easily divided into two categories: songs where she makes like a hillbilly and those where she goes ethnic. The first category includes such real and fake country airs as "This Ole House," "I Wish I Wuz," "Beautiful Brown Eyes," and the Hank Williams hit "Half As Much." The latter category includes the faux-Italian "Come on-a My House," "Botch-a-Me," "Mambo Italiano," and two ersatz Island songs from 1957, "Mangos" and "Who Dat Man, Mom?" Other songs aren't even ethnically specific but just seem to be making fun of foreigners in general, like "Dot's Nice Donna Fight" and "Sailor Boys Have Talk to Me in English."

What's surprising is that Clooney also cracked the charts with some high-quality standards, present and future, like "Tenderly," "Mixed Emotions," "Hey There," "Blues in the Night," and "You'll Never Know." Even in the face of less than inspirational material, she is too much the professional to give anything less than her best shot. Bob Merrill's "Mambo Italiano" is hardly "Blues in the Night" (as an Italian-American novelty, it's about as good as Harry Warren's "That's Amore" or any of Louis Prima's zooma-zooma tarantellas), but this is a superior pop vocal, and Clooney renders it with a deep chesty voice and a lot of gusto.

The first two Bear boxes cover her complete Mitch Miller–Columbia period. Like all complete sets—in pop even more than in jazz or the one-hundred-CD epic *Complete Bach*—the Bear boxes make for fascinating musical archaeology, as much for what's bad as for what's good. There are some howlers in there—that very first Miller-Clooney collaboration, "Canasta," isn't even the worst of them. But there are some surprising standards—an excellent swinging "Lady Is a Tramp" from at least five years before Sinatra or Mel Tormé, Alec Wilder's "While We're Young" and "I'll Be Around." (Miller also got Wilder to supply such novelties as "Good for Nothin' " and "Too Old to Cut the Mustard," Clooney's hit duet with Marlene Dietrich.) Most interesting are the experiments: There's a country-jazz crossover, "Shot Gun Boogie," the Tennessee Ernie Ford hit covered by Clooney with an outstanding jazz tenor solo by Budd Johnson, and, on the eve of the rock 'n' roll era, a swinging update of the original rock 'n' roll song of twenty years earlier, "My Daddy Rocks Me (With One Steady Roll)" retitled "My Baby Rocks Me" by Columbia and saddled with French horns and harpsichord (which make it difficult to sing the blues). There are a lot of surprises in terms of first-rate, little-known songs by well-known authors, such as Frank Loesser's "Why Fight the Feelin'?" The Columbia period also includes two full CDs' (fifty-four tracks) worth of children's songs; Clooney was certainly an expert on the listening tastes of grit dribblers and rugrats, and much of this material is delightful to adult audiences even fifty years later.

In 1953, Clooney moved to Los Angeles. The Ferrers bought a house big enough for the five kids they were going to have (and where Clooney would live for the rest of her life) at 1019 North Roxbury. The house was haunted by two legendary figures who died mysteriously young, Russ Columbo (who lived there shortly before he died in 1934, although he wasn't killed there, as Clooney always believed he was) and George Gershwin (who stayed there with his brother, Ira, and sister-in-law, Lenore, in the last few months of his life); it was also owned in the forties by singer Ginny Simms, whose career, though not her life, ended prematurely. For roughly thirty years, Rosemary's next-door neighbor was Ira Gershwin, who resided on North Roxbury from 1940 to his death in 1983. The house was the one thing in Clooney's life that was stable, and she was obviously thinking about it when she sang "Come on-a My House" and "This Ol' House" over the decades.

The most immediate result of the move to L.A. was that Mitch Miller gradually phased out of her life and Nelson Riddle gradually came in—although the two were in no way equivalents. There was a falling out between Clooney and Miller when he disparaged her marriage to Ferrer to a journalist who quoted him; Miller denied ever making the remark, but as Rosemary told me, the reporter actually had Miller's comments on tape and played it for her. When she stopped working with Miller, the hits stopped coming, but she gradually switched her focus to long-playing albums. The hit singles made her a star at the time, but the albums, especially *Blue Rose*, are remembered much more fondly by posterity.

Her first notable album was the 1952 *Hollywood's Best*, a collection of Academy Award winners recorded with Harry James and His Orchestra— surely an impressive entry into the long-playing format. If everything Clooney had recorded was on this level, this period of her life would be held in much higher regard, but had she never recorded all those ethnic and hillbilly hits, she would never have been a superstar to begin with. There was also a fascinating live album done at the London Palladium in 1955, which was only released in England until the Bear box.

After the Harry James album, Clooney teamed up with two even more celestial bandleaders, Benny Goodman and Duke Ellington. The three tracks with Goodman and the album with Ellington are not only milestones in her career but in Goodman's and Ellington's as well. Her marvelously woody contralto is a perfect match for BG's clarinet, and one wishes they had cut an entire twelve-track package together. However, BG was always reluctant to share his spotlight with a star singer, and this may well be his most significant meeting with a heavyweight vocalist (other than those who had worked under him), apart from a 1940 meeting with Fred Astaire.

The 1956 *Blue Rose* album was Ellington's first full-length collaboration with any vocalist. Clooney's darker tone also perfectly suited Ellington, who had a habit of hiring singers with deeper and more idiosyncratic sounds (e.g., Betty Roche and Al Hibbler) than most of his fellow bandleaders. She even sounds sultry and cool on "It Don't Mean a Thing (If It Ain't Got That Swing)," a tune usually sung as a super-fast flag-waver. In 1956, she was still a superstar and Ellington was just beginning to come out of a fallow period—Rosie was doing Duke a favor by making the album, not the other way around. Producer Irving Townsend planned *Blue Rose* as Ellington's comeback album for Columbia—his first project for the corporation since 1952. But there was one major problem: geographical logistics, since Clooney (pregnant again) couldn't travel and Ellington couldn't get to the West Coast. Thus *Blue Rose* would seem to be one of the rare major jazz-pop albums in which the singer worked to pre-taped backing tracks.

Ellington put his most reliable deputy, Billy Strayhorn, in charge of the project and Strayhorn wrote the orchestrations and then flew to Los Angeles to work with Clooney on recording the vocals. When she sings, on the opening "Hey Baby," "You're just the type to bring out my attributes and my good looks," she might as well have been talking strictly to Strayhorn. It's to her credit, as well as to Strayhorn's mastery of the art of orchestration, that though this was relatively early in her career, she's never overshadowed by these veterans. The lyrics of Strayhorn and Ellington have also never received a better hearing, and she even intones some slightly obtuse "Dukespeak" in a way that makes perfectly clear even such offbeat slanguage as "Goo'm Bye" and "As long as there's three heavens above" (I still can't figure out what that means). It's hardly surprising that the singer on *Blue Rose* would resurface in later years to begin a long history of recording with jazz groups.

Another result of the move to California, apart from her four-picture film career, was her involvement with Riddle. At first this was a clandestine collaboration on both a personal and professional level. Ultimately they turned out to be the great loves of each other's life, but since each was married to someone else, they had to meet on the sly. Coincidentally, it was the same in the studio: Riddle wrote arrangements for Clooney's Columbia sessions, but since he was under contract to Capitol Records, they also had to keep their professional relationship a secret. His most famous chart for her at this time (later reprised for Judy Garland) was a wild, polyrhythmic treatment of "Come Rain or Come Shine" in the same general vein as his famous recasting of "I've Got You Under My Skin" for Sinatra. In 1956, Clooney and Riddle collaborated—for all to see—on *The Lux Show Starring Rosemary Clooney*, a weekly TV series; in 2004, Concord Records released twenty-six audio tracks from the show (produced for release by Michael Feinstein) that now amount to one of the best of her fifties albums.

In 1958, Clooney left Columbia and spent the years before her breakdown at a succession of labels: RCA, Coral, MGM, Reprise. Those two facts—that Clooney "changed lodgings frequently" label-wise (never a good sign), and then completely fell apart in the mid-sixties—might lead us to assume that her work was suffering. Far from it; in fact, the classic *Love* album shows that her immediate post-Columbia work was far more erotic than erratic. In the late Columbia period, Clooney and Miller switched from making fun of Italians to ridiculing Islanders: "Mangos" (a Riddle arrangement of a song also recorded by Sonny Rollins), "A Bunch of Bananas" (we can only guess what her duet partner, husband José Ferrer, thought of that title), and "Who Dat Mon, Mom?" Yet the singles ship had already sailed. She was, by now, firmly an album artist; there were no more chart hits, but the albums were superb.

Don't confuse *Ring Around Rosie* (1956), one of the later Columbia projects, done with the Hi-Los, the very nerdy vocal group from her TV series, with *Swing Around Rosie* (1958), a Coral set that reestablished her jazz chops by putting her in the context of a bluesy organ trio. In 1959, she recorded a rather astonishing album entitled *A Touch of Tabasco;* taped with Cuban superstar Pérez Prado, *Tabasco* was perhaps the first full-length pairing of a major North American pop vocalist with a major Latin orchestra (from the same era as Peggy Lee's *Latin à la Lee*). Clooney's big band training and Bing Crosby's example serve her well here, as she fits seamlessly into a groove that's not strictly North American jazz or pop.

She also frequently teamed with Crosby himself, in every kind of media, beginning with her appearance as his singing leading lady in *White Christmas*, one of the most widely loved mediocre movies of all time (the songs and performances are great, the script banal, and the sentiments cloying even to those of us who frequently cry at old movies). Then came the albums *Fancy Meeting You Here* (1958) with Billy May, *How the West Was Won* (1960), and *That Travelin' Two-Beat* (1965). The first is rightfully regarded as one of the best duet vocal albums ever (at least on par with Ella and Louis or Steve and Eydie), but the latter two are underappreciated— *West* being a kind of musical documentary and *Travelin'* being a Dixieland follow-up to *Fancy Meeting You Here* (Rosie and Bing also paired up with each other on radio and TV).

Clooney's best work may well be the two albums with Riddle, the up-tempo *Rosie Solves the Swinging Riddle* and the ballad-driven *Love*. The latter, recorded by RCA in 1960 but released by Reprise in 1963, is as stunning a collection of love songs as was ever recorded by anyone. That Clooney picked the songs herself, and chose some fairly offbeat stuff, such as "I Wish It So," from *Juno* (Marc Blitzstein's

major attempt at composing a mainstream Broadway show on his own), illustrates how much her heart was in this project. Everything about *Love* is perfect: Along with *Hollywood's Best*, *Blue Rose*, and *A Touch of Tabasco*, this is the climax of her early career. Here is art pop of the highest order.

The events in Clooney's life during the mid- and late sixties are tellingly documented in her two autobiographies, *This for Remembrance* and *Girl Singer*, and were, not surprisingly, the central focus of a TV movie made at around the time the film *Will There Really Be a Morning?* made the idea of celebrity crack-up stories a hot topic. Clooney's TV biopic illustrates how the entertainment business drives artists nuts and then profits again by turning their stories into maudlin movies of the week.

There were a few albums between 1967 and 1977, including at least one officially recorded concert from her 1976–77 concert tour with Crosby. That tour turned out to be Crosby's farewell and the start of Clooney's comeback, a comeback that was much enhanced by the start of a long association with Concord Jazz Records, and resulted in roughly thirty releases in twenty-five years. (The relationship didn't end with her death in 2002—Concord has since posthumously released her *Last Concert* from 2001 as well as the previously mentioned disc of sound tracks from *The Rosemary Clooney Show*, plus a tribute album from the seventies pop star Debby Boone, who was Rosemary's daughter-in-law.)

In many ways, the early Concord period was the absolute peak of her career: At fifty, her voice was as strong as it had ever been, she considered herself more free emotionally than she had ever been as a young woman, and Concord founder Carl Jefferson, if he didn't give her total carte blanche, at least was only interested in high-quality songs and quality projects. Having said that, I have to acknowledge that, like everyone else, she had to deal with the effects of aging. There was some loss of wind, some deterioration of the chops, particularly as the millennium rolled around. But it wasn't as if she started falling apart physically as soon as she got her act together mentally. And even when her chops aren't there, her heart and brain are, and in these moments her storytelling ability more than sustained her. There was never a point, never an album, never an appearance at Carnegie Hall, Park Ten, Rainbow and Stars, or Feinstein's at the Regency (to name the New York venues she regularly worked at in the eighties and nineties) when it seemed that Clooney had come to the end. The very last time she played the New York area, in October of 2001, was one of the greatest performances by her I ever had the privilege to experience.

Those thirty Concord albums are roughly organized along very distinctive lines. The two main themes were seven songbook albums—that is to say, songs organized by author—and autobiographical collections, a concept I'll explain more fully later.

There are two smaller themes, namely tributes to other performers (Bing Crosby, Billie Holiday) and collaborations (Woody Herman and His Thundering Herd, the Count Basie Orchestra). There were also sets of ballads, show tunes, and Christmas songs.

Obviously, there's a lot of overlap: The tributes and songbooks are all dedicated to music makers with whom she had a close personal relationship (Billie Holiday was the godmother of one of her children; Crosby was the godfather of her comeback.) This also holds true for the writers: There's a tribute to Ira Gershwin, her neighbor for thirty years, and not his more famous brother, George, whom she never met. The autobiographical albums also contain a lot of songs by the same authors featured on the songbook sets—for instance, *Girl Singer* has a treatment of "From This Moment On" as good as or better than anything on the Cole Porter album.

The songbook sets seem like sweet revenge—the girl who was forced to sing "Canasta" in 1950 is now recording entire albums by Ira Gershwin, Cole Porter, Irving Berlin, Jimmy Van Heusen, Johnny Mercer, Rodgers, Hart, and Hammerstein. The songbooks, which generally come from the earlier part of the Concord association, usually feature her working band of the period—three or four rhythm plus trumpeter Warren Vache and tenorist Scott Hamilton, two younger swing masters Clooney helped launch as stars. There are exceptions—the Richard Rodgers collection, the last in the series, utilizes the L.A. Jazz Choir. The nonsongbook albums, which include three packages built around team-ups with the big bands of Woody Herman, Count Basie, and Matt Catingub (that rare artist who made the retro swing trend seem like a genuinely musical movement), use a wide range of accompaniments, from solo piano to full orchestra.

Those recordings I'm referring to as Clooney's "autobiographical" albums are very special latter-day slices of this art form that used to be known as pop singing. I'll say it again: One of the major misconceptions that has sabotaged music in the last forty years is that performers are now expected to write their own songs in order to sing of their own experiences. (This has inevitably led to an era in which both writing songs and singing them has become, by and large, the province of amateurs.) In classic pop, however, artists are faced with the challenge of personalizing material not only written by others but that may already be closely associated with other singers. In such albums as *Do You Miss New York?* and *Still on the Road*, Clooney blurs the distinction between autobiography (in the singer-songwriter tradition) and interpretation, as she takes both classic and obscure songs and forges them into comprehensive programs that reflect her own personal history. *For the Duration* consisted of songs from her childhood; *Girl Singer* reflected her two

years on the road with the big bands; *Do You Miss New York?* began with the idea of reflecting on the four years at the start of her career in which she called Fun City home. The 1996 *Dedicated to Nelson* has obvious personal and professional relevance.

The scope is somewhat broader on her 1995 *Demi-Centennial*, which commemorates various landmarks in the then-fifty-year Clooney career: her Irish roots (a "Danny Boy" that would make any folksinger jealous), a song re-creating the Clooney sisters with Betty Clooney's daughter ("The Coffee Song"), a Louis Armstrong favorite done in honor of Satchmo disciple Tony Pastor ("I'm Confessin'"), a song for her number-one mentor ("White Christmas") and one for her lifelong buddy Tony Bennett ("I Left My Heart in San Francisco"), not to mention one for Dante DiPaolo, her companion since the seventies ("Mambo Italiano," a song she probably never wanted even to hear again, let alone sing, but was particularly appropriate since her second husband was not only Italian but a professional dancer who did a mean mambo). Not all the albums in this series are this specific, but you get the idea.

There are other elements running through the breadth and length of the entire series, not to mention recurring characters, principally John Oddo. The last important pianist and arranger to emerge from Woody Herman's Thundering Herd, Oddo first met Clooney during the recording of *My Buddy*, her 1986 album with the Herd, and then served brilliantly as her musical director for the remaining fifteen years of her career. By the nineties she had a regular East Coast rhythm section of Oddo, guitarist Bucky Pizzarelli (sometimes replaced or abetted by his son John Pizzarelli on both guitar and vocals), bassist Jay Leonhart, and drummer Joe Cocuzzo.

One of the most important contributors to the nineties albums is Dave Frishberg: Through most of the nineties, Clooney made a point of including an original tune by this singer-pianist-songwriter in almost every one of her albums. She didn't quite do enough of these for Concord to compile a *Rosemary Clooney Sings the Dave Frishberg Songbook*, yet in listening to the Clooney-Frishberg songs together, it becomes abundantly clear not only how fine the songs are, but how thoroughly Clooney has succeeded in transforming them, like everything else she sings, into autobiography. "Side Man" (on *Finally*, with the Basie orchestra) was, in the author's opinion, specifically written from a male point of view. As if that mattered—Frishberg could have written it from a canine or Martian point of view, and Clooney would still make us feel exactly what she wants us to feel.

Although Frishberg's best-known songs ("Peel Me a Grape," "I'm Hip") are usually sung for their wit, Clooney concentrates on the composer's sweetly nostalgic side, like "Heart's Desire" and "Dear Departed Past" on *Demi-Centennial*, "Let's Eat Home" on *Still on the Road*, and the title song on *Do*

You Miss New York? Most touching of all may be "Sweet Kentucky Ham" (on *Girl Singer*). Frishberg and Clooney are masters at turning the specific into the universal and back again: Kentucky ham triggers a sense memory of the past, but it could be Alabama fried chicken or Famous Ray's Pizza.

In 1980, she bought a house in her home state, Kentucky, and began spending some of her time there, nearly all of it with Dante DiPaolo. The two were married in 1997 (in her hometown of Maysville, Kentucky), but by the end of the nineties she was frequently in the hospital. Her second autobiography, *Girl Singer*, was published in 1999, and with it came a companion two-CD set (the first covers 1946–63, the second 1977–98) with the same title. Twenty-nine tracks are hardly enough to do justice to a career of this importance, yet the *Girl Singer* CD set is thus far the only retrospective package that attempts to cover Clooney's entire career comprehensively.

By the turn of the millennium, the city of Maysville had already dedicated an entire annual music festival in her honor. Several tracks on *Sentimental Journey,* the last album to be released in her lifetime, were recorded live at the Rosemary Clooney Music Festival. In October 2001, she played the Westbury Music Fair in Long Island; it was the final occasion on which she performed in the state of New York and the last time I saw or spoke with her. A few weeks afterward, in November, she gave the same show in Honolulu in a performance that was taped by Concord and posthumously released as *The Last Concert.* The Hawaii show was especially moving for Rosemary in that her "kid" brother, TV host Nick Clooney, and his wife, Nina, were in the house, which prompted Rosie to share a few self-deprecating anecdotes about how a new generation of fans— particularly young girls—were becoming interested in her, but only after learning that her nephew (Nick and Nina's son) is George Clooney.

At most of her later concerts, Clooney had a standard line: As she was taking her final bows, she would say to the crowd, "Thank you—this has been the best night of my life." Then she would pause and say under her breath, "I know Liza Minnelli says that *every* night, but I mean it!" At Westbury and Honolulu, she simply said, "Thank you for one of the best nights of my life," without the punch line. She continued to perform through December, but was hospitalized and given surgical treatment for lung cancer in January 2002; apparently, she never sang again. She died on June 29, 2002, about a month after her seventy-fourth birthday.

Both the Westbury and the Honolulu concerts were unbelievably moving, the first one especially so. A lot of us were aware, even if we didn't want to admit it, that this was going to be a farewell appearance, and we were also on edge because this was very shortly after the tragedy of September 11, 2001. Rosemary had been ending all her concerts that fall

with "God Bless America," and, as she told me afterward, she had been inviting the audience to join her for the second chorus. In New York, however, no one waited; the crowd started singing along with her from the first note. Rosemary was visibly moved, as was everyone else. She obviously was thinking about that when she got to the conclusion of the Honolulu show. If you thought her version of "Brazil" was heartbreaking, you should hear what she does with "God Bless America"; if anything, it's even more amazing in that she reminds us that Irving Berlin's number is not an institution, not an anthem, but a song, to be interpreted and sung from the heart like any other. You feel, as always, as if she's singing about something that means everything to her. It doesn't matter whether it's a country, a child, a lover, or sweet Kentucky ham.

Nat King Cole (1919–1965)

Nat King Cole achieved the most adroit balance of simplicity and depth of any performer of his century. His artistry operated on all levels at once. For starters, one could take Cole's sincere, seemingly uncomplicated depiction of life at face value and appreciate his music strictly for its sheer beauty.

He made accessibility his first priority; his was the art of the artless. Job one was hiding the hard work that it required to make his music so easy to listen to. Yet if you wanted more, it was there. Harder listening revealed layers of artistic mastery—the more attention you paid, the more you were rewarded. Ultimately, one finds in Cole's work a passion that bespeaks a design so accomplished that it seems the product of an inspiration beyond the quiet, unassuming man who created it.

Perhaps by steadfastly refusing to admit that there was any artistry to his singing, Cole made it possible for everyone to enjoy it. Talk to anyone who knew him, from a casual acquaintance and admirer like late-night guru Johnny Carson, to Alan Livingston, who ran Capitol Records during most of the years Cole recorded for the label, on to his pop star daughter, Natalie. Their first remark will inevitably be something about what an angel the man was. Virtually no one, it seems, has a bad or even remotely critical word to say about Cole. Then they'll tell you, with no small degree of astonishment, that the most popular vocalist of his day hardly considered himself a singer, much less a vocal artist of the highest magnitude.

The perceptions artists have of their own work— or want you to think they have—can be very much at odds with the way their audiences receive them. Cole always conceived of himself as a pianist; he studied and woodshedded on the keyboard until his fingers were bony. In contrast, he insisted the singing was something that just happened to happen, this despite the fact that by the time he died in 1965, he was selling approximately seven million records a year—nearly all of them as a pop vocalist.

It could have been that it was this very matter-of-factness that made his singing so appealing to so many people. To some he sounded untrained—to all he seemed devoid of artifice—yet he sang with flawless intonation and unerring time, and in fact had far greater technique than most professed vocalists, classical or popular. Largely considered a great "natural" talent, Cole nonetheless developed finely crafted mannerisms that further distinguished his sound and his approach.

He preferred to speak of the major artistic choices of his career—the forming of the King Cole Trio, the gradual decision to feature his own singing, and nearly all of his record hits—as lucky accidents. But no one could make millions from so many mere mishaps and not know exactly what he was doing all along. Whether he admitted it or not, at every stage of his career Cole was precisely aware of what he was about.

Cole triumphs as perhaps the only star of his caliber who was exclusively a musician. By and large, Crosby, Sinatra, and Doris Day came to be regarded as movie stars who also made records, and the greatest part of their energies and their income revolved around films. Cole made nothing except music. His busiest year may well have been 1958, during which he recorded no fewer than seven albums:

- *St. Louis Blues* (January): Probably my single favorite Cole album, featuring stunning treatments of classic blues compositions by W. C. Handy, and Cole's single finest full-length collaboration with Nelson Riddle.
- *Cole Espanol* (February): The first of Cole's three widely successful Spanish-language projects, arranged and conducted by Armando Romeu Jr.
- *The Very Thought of You* (May): One of the most influential albums of his career, and the second of his three superlative collections of love songs with that sentimental genius Gordon Jenkins.
- *To Whom It May Concern* (June and August): A lovely set of newly written songs, none of which grew up to be standards but all of which are eminently worthy of Cole and Riddle.
- *Welcome to the Club* (July): Cole only made a handful of all-swinging, big band vocal albums, most of which were collaborations with arranger Billy May. This fine set, however, was produced and arranged by longtime Capitol Records stalwart Dave Cavanaugh and utilized what was essentially the entire Count Basie band (minus its contractually excluded leader). Reissued on CD as *Big Band Cole*.
- *Every Time I Feel the Spirit* (September): One of the last Cole albums to be reissued on CD, this is a set of gospel music done with an authentic gospel choir in Chicago, with Gordon Jenkins, of all people, conducting.
- *Tell Me All About Yourself* (November): A low-key set of swinging standards—maybe "bouncing ballads" is a better term—also masterminded by Dave Cavanaugh.

Cole also kept up his output of 45 rpm singles that year, including some treatments of standards ("Sweethearts on Parade," "You're My Thrill") that seem to have been intended for an uncompleted album.

We've mentioned that he had next to no acting career; this was, to a degree, the result of the racist attitudes of an unenlightened era. But Cole also had comparatively little interest in that area, being a pianist who modulated to singing, rather than a singer who also acted. In surviving concert recordings, for instance, he rarely speaks directly to his audience when introducing songs, and when he does talk, he doesn't seem particularly comfortable—in this respect he has much more in common with fellow "serious" instrumentalists like Jascha Heifetz or Benny Goodman than he does with fellow great singers like Crosby or Sinatra.

As an interpreter, he rarely engaged in emotional soul-baring to the same degree as Sinatra or Billie Holiday. However, on the rare occasions when he does, like "Lush Life" and the entire *Where Did Everyone Go* album, the results are all the more moving. Cole simply never found it appropriate to parade the specifics of his own life in the lyrics he sang, and the overwhelming warmth that emanated from both his playing and singing proved so irresistible that he didn't have to. Where Sinatra was unabashedly personal, Cole lets you in more discreetly.

He possessed an almost saintly charisma, which endeared him to the same listeners who were attracted to the touch of the rogue in Sinatra. Beyond that, almost all of Cole's appeal can be attributed to the ravishing beauty of his sound and his supreme capacity for melody. Some of the songs he sang could get pretty heavy, like the chorus-happy hits "Faith Can Move Mountains," "Answer Me My Love," or "The Sand and the Sea." (Reissue producer Michael Cuscuna has described these as Cole's "Cecil B. DeMille numbers.") Likewise, his keyboard improvisations often were as intensely complicated as they were technically difficult. He could throw down chords on top of other chords, changing sometimes on every beat of the bar; his solo on "What Is This Thing Called Love" is mesmerizingly complex; this is anything but cocktail piano. Yet whether applied to playing or singing, his deft, feathery touch made even the most mountainous epic production or intricate piano passage sound light and easy.

Cole operates at his lightest when, with breathless accuracy, he depicts falling foliage in "Autumn Leaves," "Blue Gardenia," or "A Blossom Fell." Yet even in these fragile airs of plummeting petals, there's a rhythmic awareness to his singing that stems directly from his experiences in jazz. He knows exactly what to do with the beat, even when it's barely there, as in the rubato passages of "Lush Life" or Gordon Jenkins's faux-European legion-of-string sessions. It's perfectly natural, in the middle of *Nat King Cole Sings for Two in Love*, a set of ballads as genteel and lush as "Love Is Here to Stay," for him to swing into a rip-roaring up-tempo like "This Can't Be Love." Once you control the beat, Cole proved, you can do anything you like with it.

Whatever Cole played or sang he transformed into pure melody. Like Louis Armstrong, he could do plenty with a great Broadway-born standard by the Gershwins or Porter, yet he made equally marvelous music with the most minimal tunes Tin Pan Alley imposed on him, imbuing them with his magical stamp of sincerity and meaning. He could make any tune sound good, even if it was below or above the heads of his public—in the latter case with his many excursions into both modern jazz and semi-classical sounds.

And what applied to individual songs also held true for entire genres of music. We knew we could trust Cole no matter what new material he unearthed for us or what original avenues he chose to lead us down. And those included, in the last few years of his career, such departures from his own well-defined channels of mainstream pop as gospel, South American, and country and western music. From jazz trio to full symphony orchestra to sounds outside the Western tradition, the boundaries of Cole's music expanded in direct proportion to his fame, as he himself rose from beer joints (in godforsaken Los Angeles, no less) to international celebrity.

In the very beginning, Nat Cole was strictly a pianist who, if we believe the written evidence and not our ears, rarely if ever sang. When he made his first recording, at age seventeen, he was so far removed from contemplating a career as a crooner that his older brother Eddie (the date's bassist and leader) sang the lyrics Nat had written. The fourth of six children born to the Reverend and Mrs. Coles, Nathaniel Adams Coles (the original family name) arrived on Saint Patrick's Day, March 17, 1919. Both the South and the Windy City can claim him as one of their own: He was born in Montgomery, Alabama, but from the age of four grew up in Chicago. He matured in the roaring inferno of Jazz Age activity in the toddlin' town, cut his teeth at the Windy City's monstrously fierce jam sessions, and studied at the feet of Chi-town's jazz legends, particularly piano great Earl Hines. He later said, "Everything I am I owe to that man."

Cole's may have been the only career in history to benefit from making the wrong move at the wrong time. In 1936, the brothers Cole and Nat's future wife, dancer Nadine Robinson, took to the road with an all-black revue, which left them stranded and broke in Los Angeles. The King Cole Trio was born when the Swannee Inn in Los Angeles hired him to assemble a four-piece band of piano, bass, guitar, and drums. Supposedly Cole contacted Lee Young, but he missed the opening night (Cole later also said that there just wasn't room for a trap kit in the minuscule nightclub). "I always wanted to have a big band, never thought of a trio, particularly as there were no small groups playing on the coast," Cole remembered in 1945. "It was Bob Lewis of the Swannee Inn who suggested that I add guitar and bass and bring the trio into his place. I figured it would last just a few weeks and look what happened."

The King Cole Trio employed at least eight other master musicians from 1937 to 1951, the years in which it served as Cole's primary vehicle, among them bassists Wesley Prince, Johnny Miller, and Joe Comfort, guitarist Irving Ashby, Latin percussionist Jack Costanzo, and, most crucially, his co-star for a decade, Oscar Moore, who was as much an innovator on the guitar as Cole was on the piano. The group began recording radio transcriptions as early as 1938, and by 1940 made its first records for a national firm (Decca), although its sides for both that label and the fledgling Capitol Records (beginning in 1943) were initially aimed at "race," or black, audiences. "For seven years we each knocked ourselves out," Cole later said, "until something happened."

Cole had gone on to conquer the entire market, black and white, long before he abandoned the trio format. Thus, the major schism in his career isn't art versus commercialism or jazz versus pop, but Cole the leader versus Cole the star. During the fifteen years in which he led the most enduring small group of its day, Cole was chiefly concerned with the remarkable level of empathy he developed with such long-standing sidemen as, in the classic edition of the trio, Moore and Miller. Loaded with a surplus of harmony and a shortage of rhythm instruments (Cole never regularly employed a trap drummer), the threesome brought the art of interplay to a whole new level.

Throughout the forties, the King Cole Trio kept getting more and more popular as they relied more and more on the leader's singing—particularly on smooth love songs. Even by 1943, when they signed with Capitol Records, a new label, whose emergence paralleled Cole's own, they were already at the top of the African American market. With the resources of the new operation behind them, Cole and the trio were able to tackle the mainstream "white" demographic as well. Their first Capitol date yielded "Straighten Up and Fly Right," a number-one hit on the "race" chart and a number-nine hit on the mainstream list. Within a few years, that gap would be closed. In 1946 they added strings to the mix for the first time on the hit "The Christmas Song," while continuing to attain the upper brackets with the unadorned trio on such sensational sellers as "Route 66" (also 1946). In fact, "(I Love You) For Sentimental Reasons," done without strings in 1946 (again), was Cole's biggest hit yet. (Most of the trio's best-known numbers are on a Blue Note CD entitled *The Best of the Nat King Cole Trio—Vocal Classics*.)

His piano style was growing ever more sophisticated: From the beginning he was an influence on the burgeoning modern jazz movement (Illinois Jacquet said that Cole was the first to transform "How High the Moon" into a jazz anthem), and by the end of the forties there was more bop than ever in his playing. At the same time, his singing was becoming more and more refined, and by 1949 he had become one of the great living balladeers—only Sinatra and Eckstine were in his class.

Between "Nature Boy" (1948) and "Mona Lisa" (1949) the handwriting was clearly on the wall: Nat King Cole doing romantic ballads with strings was a more commercial proposition than the Trio. The transition, which was greatly encouraged by Cole's second wife, Maria, and by his manager, Carlos Gastel, took place gradually over the next few years. Much of the changeover, recording-wise, would be made smooth by arranger Pete Rugolo, who did the charts on most of Cole's early orchestral dates, including many that were done by the combination of the King Cole Trio with a big band and/or strings, such as his remarkable treatment of Billy Strayhorn's "Lush Life." In this period, Cole also experimented with adding a vocal group to the trio ("Who Do You Know in Heaven") and combining the threesome with the entire Stan Kenton contingent, both vocally (the hit "Orange Colored Sky") and instrumentally ("Jambo," actually the Swahili word for "hello"). In his personal appearances, he continued to tour with a core unit of guitar, bass, and occasionally drums (which worked with a local orchestra in larger venues and by itself in smaller ones) and he began to be billed as "Nat King Cole" rather than as "The King Cole Trio."

He had already begun working with the man who would shape the course of much of his later musical career, the most brilliant orchestrator in the history of American pop, Nelson Riddle. Riddle had already anonymously done the chart for "Mona Lisa," and in 1951 he began arranging and conducting most of Cole's charts. The very first song on the very first date (August 17, 1951) Cole and Riddle did together proved that theirs was going to be an "Unforgettable" partnership. Riddle devised a unique introduction of keyboard and vibes in tight harmony, and no one's been able to forget the song ever since. Ten years later, Cole again sang Riddles's arrangement of "Unforgettable," this time in stereo, as one of three dozen works in his autobiographical *The Nat King Cole Story* album. Thirty years after that, Nat and Maria's daughter, R&B star Natalie Cole, remixed those 1961 stereo tracks along with her own voice to simulate a duet, and created the most surprisingly successful album and single of 1991.

In contrast to the softer, Shearingesque sounds of "Unforgettable," many of the earliest Cole-Riddle hits extended the Eurocentricity of "Mona Lisa." The approach rang true since a number of these songs came from far beyond U.S. borders: "Answer Me, My Love," a secularized German hit that translates more accurately as "Answer Me, My Lord," and that masterpiece of fractured *franglais*, 1935's "Darling, Je Vous Aime Beaucoup," written by Hildegarde's manager and associated with both that pianist-singer and France's own Jean Sablon. Riddle and Cole approached both as epic productions, complete with large mixed choruses, and Cole also selected "Darling" as the climax of his amiable two-reel autobiopic *The Nat King Cole Musical Story in Technicolor*.

Yet not everything Cole and Riddle recorded was heavy and dramatic. Hits like "Somewhere Along the Way," "That's All," and the haunting "If Love Is Good to Me," on which Riddle mixes in offbeat electronic keyboard touches, all point to a lighter and brighter artist-arranger collaboration.

Ten years after Cole joined Capitol, his singing, especially on ballads, had grown so amazingly in confident, expressive artistry that he almost made all the vocalizing of his entire trio period seem an immature affectation. He was now a pop singer of the very highest rank, one who, with Ella Fitzgerald, was one of the few who ever gave Sinatra a few sleepless nights. Not only was his voice fuller and deeper than it had been ten years earlier, his emotional approach to his music had correspondingly matured as well. The 1953–55 Cole-Riddle singles "My One Sin," "If I Give My Heart to You," "A Blossom Fell" (another jolly-good English import), and "Blue Gardenia" (sung by Cole to Raymond Burr in the movie mystery of the same title), which were all collected in two LP anthologies of predominantly Riddle-arranged hits, *Top Pops* and *Ballads of the Day*, beautifully showcase him as one of the great crooners of all time.

In 1953, Cole and Riddle collaborated on their first pop vocal "concept" album, *Two in Love*. That same year, Riddle also began working with Capitol's newly signed "other" male vocal star, Frank Sinatra. In fact, Riddle helped that superstar singer to a second career no less brilliant than the one he had already helped create for Nat Cole. Whereas working with the two best and most prolific vocalists of their era might have spread a less imaginative arranger too thin, Riddle thrived on the challenge—both his artistry and his productivity increased exponentially from that year onward.

In his sessions with Cole and Sinatra, the arranger perfected what came to be known as his signature sound, beginning on *Two in Love* and perfected by 1956 on such singles as "Night Lights" and "To the Ends of the Earth" (which makes imaginative use of a deep-voiced male choir). In addition to a highly sophisticated harmonic sense, Riddle relied heavily on explosive orchestral colors, dynamic rhythm effects, and distinctive instrumental voicings, employing such star soloists as Harry Klee on flute, George Roberts on bass trombone, and Harry "Sweets" Edison on usually muted trumpet.

"Love Is Here to Stay" offers the most tender singing Cole had yet committed to wax, while "This Can't Be Love" shows how well he fit into the mold later defined by Sinatra and Riddle as the Swingin' Lover school of up-tempo romantic singing. The original 1953 10" album did so nicely that in 1955 Capitol assigned Cole and Riddle to add an additional four tracks to bring it to 12" proportions.

Cole and Sinatra complemented each other in that both insisted on high levels of quality control; yet while Sinatra developed the long-playing album as a vehicle for time-proven standards, Cole concentrated on making first-rate singles of new songs. This was a conscious artistic decision on his part, and the success he continued to achieve with the singles medium certainly proved him right.

Despite the obvious triumph of *Two in Love*, Cole correctly viewed his 45 rpm releases, most of which were arranged by Riddle, as the real meat of his work. The two men would not make another original vocal album together until nearly the end of the decade. In the meantime, Cole continued to find other uses for the long-play format: for collections of hit singles, like *This Is Nat King Cole, Top Pops*, and *Ballads of the Day;* in special collaborations with guest-star orchestrators, most spectacularly Gordon Jenkins and Billy May; and as a showcase for his piano.

In these years, he made three very different albums spotlighting his still formidable keyboard technique: *Penthouse Serenade* (1952 and 1955) was a small combo piano exercise, while *The Piano Style of Nat King Cole* (1955) had Riddle's full orchestra accompanying Cole's instrumental solos as if he were backing a singer. In 1956 he recorded the album of his that is most beloved by the jazz community, *After Midnight*, which augmented the King Cole Trio format with drums and a rotating cast of stellar soloists: Ellingtonian valve trombonist Juan Tizol, Basieite trumpeter Sweets Edison, Swing Street star violinist Stuff Smith, and the star alto saxist of many bands, Willie Smith. Personally, I don't find that the interplay and group dynamics here are at the same level as most of the classic forties sides by the original trio, even if the fidelity has improved considerably. But this is an album that, like *John Coltrane and Johnny Hartman*, every young jazz singer of the last forty years knows intimately.

In addition to his work with Riddle, Cole also made over forty tracks with the marvelous swinging orchestrator Billy May. The two went way back together, back to the days when May still toured as trumpeter and increasingly active arranger with the big bands (Charlie Barnet, Glenn Miller) and when the King Cole Trio was just beginning to gain a reputation. They began working together occasionally

in 1951, at a point when each was individually establishing himself as one of Capitol's strongest assets. May's righteous sense of rhythm and raucous humor fit Cole like an Italian suit, while Cole's silken sound slides smoothly among the slurping saxes in "Walkin' My Baby Back Home." Humor was clearly what was called for in the rarity "Open Up the Doghouse," the result of a once-in-a-lifetime meeting between King Cole and that Viceroy of Vegas, Dean Martin, as presided over by May.

May was no less a master at slower tempos and steamier moods, as he and Cole prove on the chart hit "Angel Eyes," with its film noir background and witty, electronically induced diminuendo in the coda. In their first album together, 1957's *Just One of Those Things*, Cole and May treated torch songs with a swing band format. The sultry "Don't Get Around Much Anymore" bespeaks both Cole's and May's mutual admiration of the great Duke Ellington, who served as a boyhood idol for both men. Can't you hear that hot marimba, as Irving Berlin would say, which May unexpectedly employs to fill in the breaks originally assigned to Johnny Hodges? On "I Should Care" and "The Party's Over," Cole and May no less astutely balance the generally downbeat message of the songs with their own struttingly brassy attitudes.

In 1961, Cole and May reunited for *Let's Face the Music and Dance*, a strictly-from-Swingville session. They highlighted an already great set with one of the last of Cole's hard-swinging classics, "Day in, Day Out," which May had already arranged definitively for Frank Sinatra on his 1958 *Come Dance with Me* album. Only a master like May had it in him to produce two such completely different yet equally spectacular arrangements of the same song in nearly the same metronome reading. The set also contained a bonus from God in the form of five tracks with electric organ solos by Cole, his only recordings on the instrument.

The third master arranger Cole collaborated with in the fifties—after Riddle and May—was Gordon Jenkins, who was actually responsible for Cole's first "original" 12" vocal album, 1956's *Love Is the Thing*. Never as harmonically profound as Riddle or as rhythmically witty as May, Jenkins possessed a strong sense of texture and a songwriter's capacity for melody that complemented Cole's own. In his albums with Cole and then Sinatra, Jenkins favored string-heavy lushness, which sounds cloying on paper but beautiful on vinyl. His keen sense of drama always kept a performance at high pitch, maintaining a perfect balance between tension and release.

Cole and Jenkins followed this first album, which was also Cole's first stereo set as well as his only album to chart at number one, with *The Very Thought of You*, in 1958. In songs like "When I Fall in Love," the opener of the first set, and the equally lustrous "Star Dust," as well as "But Beautiful" by Cole colleague Johnny Burke, Cole and Jenkins concocted the sweetest-sung set of love songs since the Sinatra-Stordahl sessions of a decade earlier. The two men hit upon the G-spot of precisely the most rapturous moment of romance, viewing love with an uncritical eye that sees nothing beyond its blithe beauty. Passion is a misty, dreamlike haze of violins, which can perceive nothing in more than two dimensions.

(Later in 1958, Cole and Jenkins reunited for one of the most obscure projects in the Cole canon: *Every Time I Feel the Spirit*, a collection of traditional spirituals that was as authentic as this preacher's son could manage. Cole went back to his roots, taping the project in Chicago with the First Church of Deliverance choir. He sounded even better singing genuine gospel music than he had earlier on Tin Pan Alley's ersatz religious confections such as "The Greatest Inventor of Them All" and "The Lighthouse in the Sky.")

With the final Cole-Jenkins album, 1962's *Where Did Everyone Go?*, the two men add the third dimension, lowering the tone of romantic ecstasy down a half-step into an emotionally dissonant note. "I Keep Going Back to Joe's" may be Cole's greatest accomplishment as a dramatic performer, as the singer sets up a pain-stained narrative of heartbreak that he gradually lets unfold, achingly slow and mesmerizing, in a single devastating chorus.

Cole's remaining major albums of the fifties were his team-ups with Dave Cavanaugh, mainly *Welcome to the Club* and *Tell Me All About Yourself*, two of the seven albums Cole recorded in 1958. Primarily a producer and A&R man for Capitol, Cavanaugh contributed solid, workmanlike arrangements to his projects with Cole, beginning with 1952's "Rough Riding." For *Welcome to the Club*, Cavanaugh patterned tense, exciting charts in the style of the current "Atomic" period Basie band, and then contracted the Basie crew—minus its leader—to accompany Cole on the sessions. The results were explosive, as evidenced by "Avalon," one of Natalie Cole's favorite of her father's recordings, and Dakota Staton's hit, "The Late, Late Show." Cole mixed new songs and standards liberally in both albums, succeeding strongly on the second with a zippy treatment of Irving Berlin's "The Best Thing for You (Would Be Me)." (Cavanaugh also worked with Cole on one of his three albums for the Spanish-speaking market, *A Mis Amigos*, as well as his only officially sanctioned live recording, *Nat King Cole at the Sands*, recorded in 1960 and issued in 1966.)

It should be stressed that all of these projects—with Jenkins, May, and Cavanaugh—as successful as they were, amounted to mere sidelines to his main business, which continued to be making pop singles with Nelson Riddle. The hits kept coming without a letup: "Ballerina" (1956), a swinging update of a 1947 Vaughn Monroe hit, and "Non Dimenticar" (1958), his latest European import, which he sang on his short-lived TV series as guest star Pearl Bailey

scarfed down a pizza. (Later slices of world music include "Madrid," a fast-moving pop update of the habanera from *Carmen*, and "In the Cool of the Day," a sample of Greco-pop that shared the same mood for oud as "Never on Sunday.")

There were also three original albums with Riddle, all of them brilliant, although none of them was a collection of great American standards in the Sinatra-Riddle mold. There was *St. Louis Blues* (1958), the only positive result of Cole's disastrous single starring role in a major motion picture; Cole and Riddle make W. C. Handy's classic blues of the teens and twenties breathe in whole new ways. *To Whom It May Concern* (yet another album from 1958), rates as something of an "un-concept" album, since its only unifying element was the undeserving obscurity of the twelve new songs it presented, like a litter of doe-eyed puppies panting to be taken home. Their final project, *Wild Is Love* (1960), was pure concept, being an attempt at a cycle of twelve songs about the ups and downs of a modern-day love affair written by two relative unknowns, Ray Rasch and Dotty Wayne. Riddle's arrangements, which involved nearly forty musicians and another big choir, fared considerably better than the songs themselves, which, with titles like "Hundreds and Thousands of Girls" and "Pick Up," skirted the edge of high camp. As ever, though, the singing and the orchestrations were ace and the end result was a superior album—as well as a hit.

From 1961 on, Cole used Ralph Carmichael (who later became prominent in the world of Christian pop music) as his regular musical director, filling the same function in Cole's career that Don Costa did for Sinatra—being the strongest of each man's post-Riddle partners. Carmichael never had as easily identifiable a sound as Riddle, May, or Jenkins, but his work with both ballads and swingers was so uniformly excellent that this seems a pedantic nit to pick. Their first album, taped in July 1960, was a set of traditional and sacred Christmas carols and hymns. That December, Cole and Carmichael turned to a Gordon Jenkins–like kind of love song album, *The Touch of Your Lips*, in which Carmichael showed his mettle with such exquisite charts as the title track and "A Nightingale Sang in Berkeley Square." Cole worked harder and sang sweeter than ever before, as if to make his new partner look good—at his job, that is, of making Cole look good.

Between March and July 1961, the two labored on Cole's most ambitious album, the three-LP, thirty-six-track *Nat King Cole Story*, remaking in state-of-the-art technology and singing voice all of the singer's hits and personal favorites. For their next project, Cole and Carmichael prepared a three-layer sandwich of aural textures: Cole's voice, Carmichael's orchestrations, and the George Shearing Quintet. In theory, it harked back to the Rugolo days a decade earlier when Cole's own piano-dominant small group was frequently accompanied by a string section. In actual practice, *Nat King Cole Sings/George Shearing Plays* turned out to be Cole's mellowest album ever. "What an amazing man he was," Shearing told me recently. "That's one of my all-time favorite albums."

The next few years saw Cole and Carmichael at work on the last of his Spanish albums, *More Cole Español*, while in 1963 the team experimented with yet another new format. Cole patterned *Those Lazy-Hazy-Crazy Days of Summer* (1963) after the highly successful sing-along sets with which Mitch Miller had topped the pop album charts in the late fifties and early sixties. Cole held court over a large choir in a set of, as Louis Armstrong used to say, good old good ones—simple songs in easy-to-follow tempos and keys, presented in such stereophonic presence that they seemed to be in your living room. Though the campy title track (kind of an Anglo-polka) became one of Cole's best-remembered hits, the gem of the album was actually "That Sunday, That Summer," a ballad so poignant it makes you want to turn around and give a big wet kiss to whoever happens to be sitting next to you.

Nat King Cole Sings My Fair Lady was Cole's only album of songs from a single score. Not all its numbers worked as well as others outside the context of the show, but Cole shone especially brightly on "The Street Where You Live" and on a newly sensitized interpretation of "Show Me." He also landed another chart-busting hit with "L-O-V-E," by German songwriter–producer–pop icon Bert Kaempfert, which titled an album of hard-swinging material, much of which was suitably Eurocentric in one way or another.

But in general, Cole's last few years would be remembered for his quasi–country and western records. In these years he also dabbled a bit in what we could call rhythm and blues (most notably on a beautiful treatment, albeit with a heavy rock beat, of the 1949 movie song "Again," and on his Grammy-winning hit "Looking Back"). But none of these came anywhere near the success of his country-tinged megahit, "Ramblin' Rose" (1962).

In another time-honored Cole tradition, "Rose" was a freaky fluke: a country song that had taken "two Jewish boys from Brooklyn," as Cole described them, all of eighteen minutes to write and about fifteen minutes for Cole to record at the end of a date in June 1962. Here, as on the later "Lazy-Hazy," Cole used a big choir and sing-along style—even inviting the audience to chime in on the last chorus—and gave the whole works a Nashville-style backing. Belford Hendricks, the arranger responsible for acres and acres of Dinah Washington's worst records, did the chart, both on the single and the *Ramblin' Rose* album. He quickly followed *Rose* with more country-choir laments on *Dear Lonely Hearts*, recorded at about the same time, also with Hendricks. Luckily, Cole made the final album in his

country series (*I Don't Want to Be Hurt Anymore*, 1964) with Ralph Carmichael.

At the end of his life, Cole was staggeringly popular, probably the most successful male vocalist of the 1950s, and his career showed no sign of slowing down. He continued to make high-class albums and singles, like *L-O-V-E*, and was accommodating contemporary tastes as tastefully as possible on the country records; further, cuts like "Looking Back" and "Again" proved that he could sing to a rock beat better than any other major vocalist of his generation. (Just listen to the dozens of standards done schlock 'n' roll style by Dinah Washington and Belford Hendricks by way of comparison.)

Cole was probably also the most prolific recording artist of his generation. He didn't just make albums, he made entire cycles of albums: three classic sets of love songs with Gordon Jenkins, three Spanish-language albums, three country-choral albums, three sets with Dave Cavanaugh, two swing sets with Billy May, three pianocentric projects. By the end of 1964, when cancer put him in the hospital, Cole was an entire recording industry unto himself. He died on Valentine's Day, a month or so before what would have been his forty-sixth birthday. A few days later in his hometown, Chicago, a few old friends—Tony Bennett, Bobby Hackett (playing ukelele instead of his customary cornet), and the excellent jazz clarinetist Joe Marsala—got together and recorded "Sweet Lorraine," the song that helped inspire Cole to become a musician to begin with, and then became one of his first hits. At that time, there was an organization in Hollywood known as the Losers' Club, which normally selected a certain individual as its Loser of the Month. For February 1965, the Loser of the Month was given as "Music."

Cole's influence on other singers, especially those who play the piano, has been immeasurable—Buddy Greco, Johnny Hartman, Johnny Mathis, and such contemporary singer-pianists (and even guitarists) as John Pizzarelli, Peter Cincotti, Tony DeSare, Loston Harris, Eric Comstock, Allan Harris, and especially Diana Krall are just a few who've been influenced by him, without even mentioning the dozens of Cole-inspired trios that proliferated following his example in the forties, or even the other members of his family who extend his legacy into the dynastic level. Yet there has never been another Nat Cole: No one else ever sang like that, that combination of a voice as smooth as ice and a heart warm enough to melt it.

Perry Como (1912–2001)

To what extent is great music technologically driven? I wouldn't want to imagine what Bing Crosby's career would have been without the microphone, and while Sinatra would have been great even had the LP record never been invented, the perfection of the long-form pop statement remains one of his signature achievements. Now take Perry Como. His early recordings and work on radio were enough to establish him as one of the top pop singers. But make no mistake: It was television that made him into a national institution.

I happened to be speaking with Bud Granoff, who worked as one of Sinatra's press agents in the early years and then helped steer the career of his wife, singer Kitty Kallen. We were talking about Sinatra's unsuccessful TV series of the early fifties, and Bud ventured, "I'll tell you something interesting: High-powered performers always failed on television. Lena Horne. Sammy Davis. Frank Sinatra. These are all high-energy, intense people, none of them could make it on TV. Because you're not comfortable with them on television, that kind of performer. You want somebody who's almost like a sleeping pill. It's true." I mentioned Como, and Bud responded, "You want somebody like Como who could just wander around casually. When somebody is high-energy, you just get the frenetic quality, but you don't get the fire. Something is diluted."

Yet it would be a mistake to suggest that Como was popular—or even immortal—strictly because of television. His voice was smooth and velvety, but beyond its sonic quality, he had a warmth and a down-to-earthness that's less evident in the voices of his competitors, and because his career lasted so long, those competitors range from Buddy Clark to Dick Haymes to Vic Damone to Johnny Mathis and even John Denver. Como was at once the most successful of Crosby's disciples and the next major Italian-American crooner after Sinatra. Even on the tackiest tunes—and he recorded more of them than anybody—Como has soul and he has humanity, and that's more important than all the technology in the world.

Sinatra, in his famous 1986 interview with Sid Zion, recalled that the main reason he was determined to break from Tommy Dorsey in 1941 was fear of the potential competition: "The reason I wanted to leave the orchestra was because Crosby was number one, way up on top of the pile. In the field, in the open field, you might say, were some awfully good singers with the orchestras. Bob Eberly with Jimmy Dorsey's orchestra was a fabulous vocalist. Mr. Como was with Ted Weems and he still is such a wonderful singer. And I thought, if I don't make a move out of this band and try to do it on my own soon, one of those guys will do it and I'll have to fight all three of them, from Crosby all the way down to the other two to get a position."

However, within ten years none of the three younger men whom Sinatra mentioned could be regarded any longer as rivals. Eberly never made it as a single, and Dick Haymes, essentially, didn't survive the forties. Como, however, was more popular than ever in the mid-fifties, at the time of Sinatra's comeback, yet he and his fellow *paesano* were no longer perceived as competitors in the same field. Sinatra

had mastered all the "hot" mediums, especially film (an area where Como would never amount to anything), while Como exuded mid-century cool. He employs a post-Crosby sense of informality, as well as an easy intimacy that identifies him as a member of Sinatra's generation.

Like Sinatra, Como ascended from the big band era to dominate small screens and jukeboxes alike, and reigned for over five decades as one of the most familiar figures of American popular culture. Deep into his eighties, Como continued to enchant audiences with his warm casualness and deep, lightly nasally tinged voice. We place Sinatra by what he does emotionally—he riles us up, he makes us cry, he makes us feel romantic. Nearly every article on Como, in contrast, begins by celebrating this Italian-American crooner in terms of his economic achievements, such as landing a staggering 147 hit singles, Nielsen ratings that pronounced him broadcasting's most popular singing variety show host, and the longest-ever relationship between a popular star and a record label (fifty years with RCA Victor). His appeal, though, can't be discussed entirely in terms of statistics. Mere numbers never tell the whole story.

A first-generation American, Como held down one of the most famous day jobs in show business history, working as a barber in his native Canonsburg, Pennsylvania. His first important musical job was as boy singer with a prominent local bandleader named Freddy Carlone from 1933 to 1936. These were the years of Crosbymania, and Como said later that in this period his goal was to sound as close to Crosby as possible. "I think if it hadn't been for Bing," Como said in 1980, "I'd still be cuttin' hair somewhere." In 1936, the twenty-four-year-old boy singer went from a local band to the nationally famous Ted Weems and His Orchestra, and by this time a more identifiable Como sound had emerged. In the late thirties, he sounded a bit more like Crosby, the same basic approach and sound, but somewhat hotter and lustier than Crosby was by that point or than Como would be later on. His first session, in fact, produced a swing number, "You Can't Pull the Wool over My Eyes" (1936).

The Weems orchestra had been one of the hot dance bands of the twenties, and they still maintained much of their previous popularity—especially in Chicago—during the swing era. The band could hold its own in the age of Goodman and Basie, but still must have seemed vaguely anachronistic; its listeners were probably slightly older than the teenage jitterbugs who shrieked over Benny G, yet Weems's Chicagoans could play swinging dance music with the best of them. The band still featured whistling solos (by violinist and sometimes vocalist Elmo Tanner), which were popular then but sound contrived today. If the whistling routine sounds archaic, the vocals by Como and the marvelous clarinet solos by Rosie McHargue serve as modernizing forces.

Supposedly the Kapp brothers, who ran Decca Records, hesitated to use Como as much as they might have because of his sonic similarity to Crosby, their star attraction, yet even on his very first dates in 1936, Como immediately establishes himself as just about the best male singer in the band business at the time—I certainly prefer him to either Eberly-Eberle brother or to Tommy Dorsey's Jack Leonard. One of the earliest and best Como-Weems tracks is "Darling, Not Without You," also recorded by Artie Shaw, a wonderful Edward Heyman item that didn't live beyond 1936 but which is eminently revivable. Even one of the more comparatively questionable songs of the Weems-Como collaboration is one with a solid pedigree, "Ad-De-Day (Song of the Cuban Money Divers)," written by one of the most enigmatic figures in pop, "As Time Goes By" author Herman Hupfeld.

At both these key leaps in his career, from Carlone to Weems and then from Weems to solo status (necessary when Weems joined the army in 1942—the band's last recording date was two days after Pearl Harbor), Como was even more cautious than he was casual. The story usually goes that he had to be pushed into soloing. Post-band success wasn't a sure thing—Como had sung on fewer hits with Weems than Sinatra with Dorsey or Eberle with either Miller or Jimmy Dorsey. Curiously, Weems landed his two biggest hits years after the fact: In 1947, a reissue of his 1933 disc of "Heartaches" went to number one, and later the 1939 Weems-Como recording of the 1909 "I Wonder Who's Kissing Her Now" became another blockbuster hit. By that time, however, Como was long established on his own.

Although he was both personally and professionally three years older than Sinatra, Como would spend most of the mid- to late forties—his postwar, pre-TV career—in the shadow of the Voice. Sinatra, as he himself had predicted, was indeed the first major male band vocalist to go out and "get a position" for himself as a solo attraction. Como was the next Italian-American (followed by the young Vic Damone in 1947) to graduate from big bands to a radio show of his own, to successful gigs at the Copacabana and various theaters (complete with screaming bobby-soxers), and then into films. Sinatra made light, frivolous MGM musicals, yet Como's Twentieth Century Fox vehicles were even lighter; unfortunately for him, Fox also had Dick Haymes, who sounded better reading scripted dialogue, and got the better and more Technicolorful roles.

Like Sinatra and Haymes, Como began his solo recording career in the middle of the 1942–44 AFM ban, working with a cappella vocal groups, and then with conventional orchestras once the ban ended. Like Sinatra and Haymes, from the beginning Como was a solid hit maker, landing hits in the top ten with predictable regularity. From one point of view, early Como was comparatively a highbrow; two of his biggest early hits were based on Chopin: "Till the

End of Time" (based on the Polonaise in A-flat) and "I'm Always Chasing Rainbows" (based on the Fantasie Impromptu in C-sharp minor). Another of his biggest early hits was "Prisoner of Love," already long regarded as a classic. In 1945, he landed the first of his nonsense blockbusters, the swinging "Hubba Hubba Hubba," an Adamson-McHugh number that takes a rather bloodthirsty delight in the destruction of Tokyo.

The transition from the forties to the fifties was not a smooth one for male singers: Haymes and Eckstine didn't make it, while Cole and Sinatra had to completely reinvent themselves, and even Crosby entered a new phase. Perry Como is perhaps the only major singer who made a smooth passage from Truman to Eisenhower without needing, in World War II parlance, a major reconversion. The medium was indeed the message: He was the same singer in the thirties and forties that he was in the fifties and sixties, but he had to find a way to help that musical persona make the changeover from radio to television. Beginning in 1948, his thrice-weekly radio series, *The Chesterfield Supper Club*, could now be seen as well as heard. Thus he got in on the ground floor—the basement, even—of the new medium. By the time other singers were first figuring out what to do, Como was already a veteran. "There was continuity in my career," he said. "I owe television everything."

As more and more Americans were able to afford sets, the Como show quickly became a cultural phenomenon. One thing that pop music has traditionally done over the last fifty years is divide up generations: On *The Simpsons*, thirty-nine-year-old Homer, a child of the sixties and seventies, listened to The Who and Queen; his son, ten-year-old Bart, hangs out with N-Sync. Since 1960, pop music has been the one area where the generations will never meet; it is traditionally ground zero for the generation gap. Como's show, like Crosby's and his fellow video icon Ed Sullivan's, was about providing entertainment for the whole family. A typical show featured Henry Fonda for those in their twenties and older, shapely dancer Vera-Ellen and sexy sci-fi star Anne Francis for Dad and postpubescent Junior, and her *Forbidden Planet* sidekick Robbie the Robot for the kiddies. His music was the same: a mixture of classic standards ("My Heart Stood Still"), contemporary show tunes (he touched on virtually every new Rodgers and Hammerstein production), and a long string of nonsensical novelties for the younger jukebox set. There's a photo from 1958 (reproduced in *Yesterday and Today*, the three-CD set that RCA issued to commemorate Como's fiftieth anniversary on the label in 1993) that shows him in a group hug with movie star Ginger Rogers, Borscht Belt wisecracker Jack Carter, and Pearl Bailey. Talk about something for everybody! And just in case that collection of talents and ethnic groups wasn't diverse enough to pull in a suitably wide demographic,

Miss Bailey in this photo is wearing Mickey Mouse Club ears.

As we've seen, stylistically Como came out of Crosby, and in the beginning his career ran parallel to Sinatra's. When television happened, he became one of the hottest things in show business just at the point when Sinatra was taking his famous career nosedive. On several occasions, both on radio and TV, Sinatra actually served as guest host for Como; when, in 1951, Como actually appeared on Sinatra's show, it was a very supportive gesture of Italian-singer solidarity, since Como was the king at that point and Sinatra couldn't get arrested. (Thirty years later the two also appeared together at a private White House concert hosted by President Reagan for the president of Italy.) What's interesting is that Como is no more or less energetic than any other post-Crosby crooner throughout the forties—on radio shows, and in his biggest picture (*Words and Music*, MGM's biopic of Rodgers and Hart). It wasn't merely that his "walking sleeping pill" style just happened to be supremely suited to television, but rather that he refined that style in response to what he brilliantly realized that the medium demanded.

By the great years of his weekly hour-long variety show of the mid-fifties to the mid-sixties, the Como sound was perfected—and words like "relaxed" and "casual" don't even begin to describe it. Sinatra was a stimulant, Como a relaxant; Sinatra was caffeine to Como's Nyquil, coffee to Como's cocoa. It wasn't even a matter of Como being personable or charming, and it was irrelevant whether you even liked him or his singing. It was just simply impossible to feel upset, worried, or depressed while Como was on. Sinatra made you feel you could go out and conquer the world, Como made you feel you didn't have to do anything. Still on the road at eighty, Sinatra went out and faced crowds down as if they had never heard of him and he had to win them over all over again. Como was also still on the road at eighty, yet he sang like a man who felt he didn't have to prove anything to anyone.

By the mid-fifties, most of his hit songs didn't even mean anything: "Hot Diggity," "Zing, Zing, Zoom, Zoom," "Chi Baba" (Como could sing nonsense in Italian)—these were songs you didn't have to think about, and rather than pondering their meaning, you just lay back and let that magnificent voice roll over you. His biggest latter-day song, the 1970 "It's Impossible," was about inevitability: He's not suggesting that one should actually attempt to keep the ocean from rushing to the shore but rather offering it as an example of the power of love.

Like Dean Martin, Como had an astute sense of humor about himself: Even before "Perry Como-tose" became a tag line among comedians, he was parodying his own persona. "Hubba-Hubba-Hubba" (1945) is a song so outrageous it could be in a Tex Avery cartoon, and Como climaxes it by taking

a poke at his own hit "Till the End of Time." Comics could joke about his semi-somnambulant manner, but it was funnier coming from the man himself. In "I Can Almost Read Your Mind," a piece of special material written by choral director Ray Charles for his 1970 concert tour, Como sings:

> From my publicity
> I bet you'd like to know
> If I'll stay awake
> Through the entire show

A few lines later, he adds:

> You wonder what it takes
> To make him lose his cool
> Does he have Holy Water
> In his swimming pool?

Como was generally regarded as one of the real Mr. Nice Guys of Show Business—in Television Land, where all those nuclear family sitcoms starred actors who were on their third or fourth wife, anyone who keeps the same spouse for sixty-five years is automatically a saint.

Como was undoubtedly inspired by Crosby, but he didn't ramble quite as far over the musical map. Taking "I Wonder Who's Kissing Her Now" (which he rerecorded for Victor in 1947, "covering" his own reissued hit with Weems) as an omen, Como recorded all kinds of even-then oldies, like "Carolina Moon" (a 1928 early hit for Lombardo that he imbues with understated nostalgia), "When You Were Sweet Sixteen," "That Old Gang of Mine," "Me and My Shadow," and "A Garden in the Rain." In the forties and early fifties, he was doing the old songs very straight, with full orchestra, and very effectively. By the mid- to late fifties, on the albums *We Get Letters* and *Sing to Me, Mr. C*, Como was giving these numbers more of a small combo bounce.

For even more conservative listeners, Como also sang religious music, both traditional and contemporary, and recorded far more of it than any other pop star in his league. He did two albums of sacred songs, *I Believe* and *When You Come to the End of the Day*, in which he was nondenominational enough to include such Jewish prayers as "Eli Eli" and the "Kol Nidre." (No Islamic or Buddhist chants the last time I looked, however.) Religious songs, like "I Pass This Way but Once," may be the only occasions from 1950 on when you hear Como really raising his voice and dramatically straining to hit a note—almost belting.

Sometimes his blend of sacred and secular material got a little bizarre: On one hit single from 1960, Como backed "Delaware," a sub-vaudeville, low-brow novelty ("What did Della wear? / A brand new jersey") by the composer of "Unforgettable," with something called "I Know What God Is." When he sang Paul Simon's "Bridge over Troubled Water"—a five-minute epic he taped in 1971—it wasn't necessarily out of any tradition of covering contemporary hits but rather out of his history of gut-busting religious belters.

And what of those novelty songs? Standard histories of pop music will tell you that rock 'n' roll grew out of rhythm and blues. The truth is, rock 'n' roll comes just as much out of Mitch Miller and Perry Como (not to mention Louis Prima) as it does out of Louis Jordan and Muddy Waters. Mitch Miller is infamous among pop historians as being the nabob of novelty, yet as he once told me, "Como made hits out of songs I wouldn't even touch!" Como's relationship to these songs is the same as Clooney's to "Come on-a My House" or Tony Bennett's to "In the Middle of an Island." He hated them, couldn't stand them, practically had to be forced to sing them. "I'd tell the A&R man, 'I can't sing that garbage!' " Como told Colin Escott, "and he'd say, 'Just do one take—one take for me.' And I'd say, 'I'm gonna get ill if I do two!' " Como is best remembered as a balladeer, yet the biggest percentage of his chart hits are these rhythm numbers, nonsensical and even nonverbal as most of them are. One song he really had to be pressured into doing was "Hoop-Dee-Do," which is surprising, as it's a rather innocuous polka. Or maybe not: Kay Starr was importuned to cover "Hoop-Dee-Do" for Capitol Records, and told an interviewer at the time, "Do you think I *like* singing a song like 'Hoop-Dee-Do'?" It was a number-one hit for Como and a number-two for Starr.

Songs such as "Chincherinchee" and "Chee-Chee-O-Chee" (apart from the alphabetical similarity, both are, I am given to understand, references to nonhuman noises produced by plants and animals) are often described as "forgettable novelties." The problem is that they're just the opposite: Once you get one of those stuck in your head you can't ever stop humming the damn thing. Inane, yes, but Como obviously believed that there are different kinds of music for different occasions—and if people wanted to pay money to hear him sing things like "Hot Diggety" he wasn't about to turn them down. Como once said Elvis Presley's "Hound Dog" made him vomit, and, to be fair, he said the same thing about a lot of his own hits.

Yet this area of the Como canon is hardly a wasteland: "Papa Loves Mambo" is a totally amusing song. Nat Cole's Capitol cover of this Como hit is pretty spectacular, too, but the song is eminently suited to Mr. C's laconic style. It's a supremely catchy tune—the kind you don't mind humming: The title phrase is primarily repeated notes, and the main melody goes up and down in thirds—first D-F-A-C and down again, then C-E-G-B and down again. The bridge is four bursts of three notes, each followed by a long rest, and at the end there's a place to grunt, à la mambo master Pérez Prado. The high-powered "Jukebox Baby" is pop music of a high order: rock 'n' roll energy channeled through adult

pop sophistication. As with his TV show, Como was bridging generations and proving that you *can* please everybody: He could sing real oldies like "I Wonder Who's Kissing Her Now" for Granny, "If I Loved You" and other roughly contemporary show tunes for Mister and Missus, and "Jukebox Baby" for Junior and Sis.

"Ko-Ko-Mo" is everything that has been vilified in histories of early rock. The song was originally recorded by an obscure R&B duo named Gene and Eunice on a small label called Combo; somehow it got into Como's hands and he made it the number-two song in the nation. This is technically a cover of the worst kind, not just one star borrowing a song from another, but an established white artist stealing a hit from an obscure black artist. (In this case, however, half of the team didn't mind, since Eunice Levy was a co-writer and her share of the author's mechanical royalties must have been sizable.)

Recorded in January 1955, "Ko-Ko-Mo" (not "Ko-Ko-Como") is occasionally cited as RCA's first rock 'n' roll hit (Kay Starr's "Rock and Roll Waltz" vies for that honor). "Ko-Ko-Mo" is a genuine 12-bar blues, a form that wasn't exactly Como's forte. Crosby had a greater empathy with the blues than either Sinatra or Como, yet while I wouldn't want to hear Como tackle a slow, depressing "woke-up-this-morning" kind of blues, he does just dandy with the jubilant, up-tempo mode of the 12-bar format. (The album *Como Swings* contains a way-over-the-top Hollywood production number version of "St. Louis Blues.") Yet he does have considerable rhythm: "Ko-Ko-Mo" and "Jukebox Baby" show that he has much better time than Pat Boone, Paul Anka, and most of the other early white rockers. The 1958 "Kewpie Doll" (backed by a superior show tune, "Dance Only with Me," from *Say, Darling*) is exactly the same kind of song that Elvis was singing that year, except that this Como record has more modulations.

The whole industry was paying attention to "Ko-Ko-Mo." Two months later, in March 1955, Sinatra went into the studio and recorded two slices of R&B himself ("Two Hearts, Two Kisses," which isn't too bad, and "From the Bottom to the Top," which is). In 1959, Como went after Sinatra's territory with an album entitled *Como Swings* (the cover showed him doing just that, with a golf club), an approximation of his fellow *paesano*'s Swingin' Lover albums with Nelson Riddle. It has to be admitted that he fared no better at Sinatra-style swinging standards (the best tracks on the album are the slower ones, like his very effective "Mood Indigo") than Sinatra did at doing Como-style proto-rock rhythmical nonsense. Como's "I've Got You Under My Skin" is no better than Sinatra's "Two Hearts, Two Kisses."

When Como did an up-tempo standard, he was better advised to stick to a gentler, less abrasive approach—"It's Only a Paper Moon," which combines combo and big band, is a fine example. Como's best album of all, *We Get Letters* (1955), swings in an intimate fashion, relaxed and jazzy at the same time, positing Mr. C in front of a rhythm section anchored by Como's rock-solid guitarist Tony Mottola and three rotating horns. In its quiet, unassuming way, *We Get Letters* is a very fine pop vocal album, nearly on a par with *Bing with a Beat*. Like the classic Sinatra albums, it can be played over and over. *We Get Letters* does everything that classic pop is supposed to do.

As late as the early sixties, Como was still producing well-arranged albums of quality songs, *Sing to Me, Mr. C* (1961) and *By Request* (1962). The latter was an exceptionally beautiful collection of his singing one great song after another, even turning in a lovely reading of the Presley hit "Can't Help Falling in Love." *The Songs I Love* (1963) had an unexpected bonus: In 1962, John Kander and Fred Ebb were writing special material for the Como show at the time they came up with their first hit, "My Coloring Book." It was supposedly written with comic-balladeer Kaye Ballard (who appeared with Como on his album of songs from the Irving Berlin flop *Mr. President*) in mind, while vocalist Sandy Stewart (mother of Bill Charlap) introduced it on the show, and Barbra Streisand had the big hit. Como, however, also recorded it for RCA and had the definitive version: He's understated and subtle, letting the words tell the story without a lot of angst. He just suggests an emotion, rather than hits you over the head with it, and you can't help feeling it all through your body.

Unlike Crosby, Como didn't tend to branch out into such detours as Hawaiian and cowboy songs— "Don't Let the Stars Get in Your Eyes" had begun life as a hillbilly song, but Como tamed it into a suburban mainstream hit. "Wild Horses" actually sounds like a country song trying to hide its roots, but on closer examination, this 1953 cowboy classic turns out to be based on a theme by Robert Schumann. After closing out his weekly series in 1964, Como (like Ray Charles) began moving in a more westerly direction. His mid-sixties albums, actually recorded in Nashville, might be called countrified pop, but by now the backgrounds in Como's albums had generally descended to the level of elevator Muzak, if that isn't mixing a metaphor.

However, the Nashville elements did help keep Como current. In 1965, he recorded "Summer Wind" well before Sinatra, but the Como version, a German-Italian-Western amalgam that includes a rarely heard second chorus, is just about the dullest record ever made, especially compared to the classic, unbelievably exciting Sinatra-Riddle version. Yet he continued to be superior in terms of inferior material: His reading of "For the Good Times" is much more convincing than Sinatra's *Trilogy* version.

Although fans of classic pop (me in particular) despise such terms as "easy listening" and "middle-of-the-road," those expressions are appropriate for the recordings of the sixties and seventies. Having explored the boundaries of American pop, for his best albums of the sixties Como began visiting other countries, recording both *Lightly Latin* and *Perry Como in Italy* in 1966. The former generally meant bossa nova and Brazil, although he also found room for a lightly Latin treatment of his first Beatles song, "Yesterday." The latter album included traditional Neapolitan and recent international hits—unlike Sinatra, Como could sing a piece of Europeana like "Forget Domani" without sounding as if he was stooping down to it. The sixties was an abrasive, violent era, especially for music, but these were two of the softest, gentlest albums of any era.

Como stayed on the charts. "Seattle" combined a semi-psychedelic background (including harpsichord), while the jingoistic bent of "Old Cape Cod" and "(Theme from) New York, New York" seem as if they were written by the local chamber of commerce (at least "I Left My Heart in San Francisco" has some kind of a narrative beyond an idealized depiction of local life). Erwin Drake's "The Father of Girls" (1968) is a singularly touching song, and two songs by the Mexican Armando Manzanero, "Yesterday I Heard the Rain" and "It's Impossible," constitute the most memorable of Como's latter-day recordings. If anyone understands the concept of inevitability, it's Como. Even in the eighties he was still lending considerable cachet to semi-country songs like "Wind Beneath My Wings," as well as contemporary show tunes like "Song on the Sand" and "The Best of Times Is Now" from *La Cage aux Folles* and "Not While I'm Around" from *Sweeney Todd*. There were still easy listening radio stations back in those days—it seems like a million years ago—and Como continued to be all over them.

After his decision to end his weekly show in 1963, Como spent much time over the next thirty years on the road. He kept going until he was finally stopped by Alzheimer's disease in 1994. When Sinatra died in 1998, the more reserved Como, as much as he was aware, was probably aghast at all the weeping and moaning he witnessed during the weeks-long grievathon enacted by the media. When he himself died, on May 12, 2001, a few days short of his eighty-ninth birthday, his passing was noted with quiet dignity. Newspapers reported that two hundred people attended the funeral, held in Jupiter, Florida, his home since the sixties. However, according to one attendant, the church actually had a capacity of seven hundred and was completely packed. He was understated to the end. It was a fitting finale for a modest giant of American pop.

Chris Connor (1927–2009)

Everything about "When the Wind Was Green" is subtle. The song is buried at the end of side one of Chris Connor's first Atlantic album (titled simply *Chris Connor*), which is probably the last place on a traditional twelve-song vocal album where one expects to find an important song (they are usually placed closer to the start of the sides). Ralph Burns's orchestration opens with a big string introduction, after which Connor enters discreetly. It's a lyric that takes us through the four seasons, and Connor ever-so-carefully modulates her emotional level as spring gives way to summer, winter, and fall.

The first 16 bars find her phrasing slightly behind the beat, as if she's got a very deep secret that she would just as soon keep that way. When she reaches the end of each of the first two 8-bar "A" sections, she lands solidly on top of the pulse, as if to finally let it out of the bag and directly inform the object of her affections why those long-ago yesterdays of green wind are so special to her. It's because, she sings, "*You* were there." The speaker grows increasingly direct as the song progresses. In the second "A," the wind changes color from green to red, and the love affair she's singing about develops into a deeper, more passionate experience—the red breeze reminds her of lips on other lips and the wind itself caresses her face and tosses her hair. But as soon as she attains this interpersonal confidence, the whole situation is threatened by the coming of the fall in the bridge. The protagonist, building to a peak of pitch, volume, and feeling, again echoes the wind and the leaves in "crying, dying" in a brown wind, as she changes her emotional keys from major back to minor. In the last 8 bars, the season changes from autumn to winter and the wind becomes snow-white. Even though the lyric ends on a down note, informing us that we'll never again see the days when the wind was green, Connor somehow ends the song on a note of optimism, as if to say that the memory of those days and that wind will be sufficient to comfort her in the long years of white winters to come. (It's the same concept as the ending of "I'll Remember April.")

It isn't just that she only needs 32 bars to blow us away—without the assistance of a verse or second chorus. Rather, the key thing is the indirect way she makes the power of this story sneak up on you. Both Eydie Gormé and Sinatra later recorded fine treatments of "When the Wind Was Green," but even they couldn't match Connor for feeling or subtlety of delivery. The word "subtlety" isn't subtle enough to describe her. You could almost call Chris Connor a stealth singer. Like the Pentagon's latest trillion-dollar project, she sneaks past the radar of your expectations to drop an emotional bomb on you. (Talk about stealth: Her entrance in "Angel Eyes" is so discreet you almost don't notice the point at which she starts singing.)

To her vast annoyance, Connor was always lumped in the same category as her predecessors in the Stan Kenton band, Anita O'Day and June Christy. "I had to be my own woman and do it my way," she told Marc Myers (of Jazzwax.com) in an interview about a year before she died in 2009. "I was influenced by June Christy and Anita O'Day, of course, but I never tried to copy them." Connor, O'Day, and Christy all sang with a so-called cool

tone (meaning without a lot of vibrato, by which definition neither Mahalia Jackson nor Ethel Merman could be considered "cool") and a Midwestern sound (Connor from Missouri, the older two from Illinois). I don't think they resemble one another sonically any more than Lee Konitz does Art Pepper or Paul Desmond.

Not that these great ladies didn't influence one another, but rather Connor stood on the shoulders of many giants, not just the white and cool ones. Her ability to paraphrase a tune brings to mind Sarah Vaughan—on "What Is There to Say" and "Time Out for Tears," she interprets the melody so personally it sounds like a whole new song. "Misty" suggests Peggy Lee, as Connor floats over a lightly Latin (à la Lee) beat, both the voice and the message appearing to be out-of-focus, opaque even. Like an image shrouded in gauze, it's a "misty" sound indeed. Other songs, like "Only the Lonely" and "You Make Me Feel So Young," suggest that she's been keeping up with Sinatra. Throughout her classic albums of the mid-fifties to the mid-sixties, she echoes Ella Fitzgerald's swing, Sinatra's drama, Judy Garland's directness, and Billie Holiday's honesty.

By the time Connor began working with Kenton, she had already sung with a number of major bands and musicians, among them Claude Thornhill, Herbie Fields, Jerry Wald, and Bob Brookmeyer. Born in Kansas City, Missouri, on November 8, 1927, Connor, whose father played violin, studied clarinet as a youngster. Her family moved to Jefferson City when she was thirteen, and a few years later she attended the University of Missouri, where she worked with a college band that was (like so many in the postwar era) patterned after Kenton's. Returning to Kaycee, Connor gigged with friend Bob Brookmeyer's combo before trying her luck in New York.

After only seven weeks Connor, landed the chance to join her first big-time band, onetime Kenton "rival" Claude Thornhill. In January 1949, she made her first recordings, primarily as a member of the pianist's vocal group, the Snowflakes, but also as a soloist on "There's a Small Hotel." That fall she left Thornhill to join multisaxist Herbie Fields in his short-lived orchestra, but returned to Thornhill for a year and a half after Fields disbanded. When Thornhill, too, broke up his band, Connor went to work for dance band leader Jerry Wald, a clarinetist (and onetime competitor of Artie Shaw) whose unit at one point also included the young Bill Evans. It was while broadcasting with Wald in 1952 from the Hotel Roosevelt in New Orleans that Connor happened to be heard by former Kentonite June Christy. According to a contemporary press release, Christy at first thought the singer she was hearing was, in fact, Ella Fitzgerald. According to Connor herself, however, Christy was "actually shocked by the similarity" of their voices.

Whatever the case, when Stan Kenton had an opening for a singer a few months later, Christy recommended Connor for the job. Said Kenton, "June told us about a girl by the name of Chris Connors [sic]—and I figured if anyone knew what we wanted it would be June. I got hold of a record Chris had made and agreed 'this was it.'" Connor came on board on January 16, 1953, and first turns up on the band's Capitol record session of February 11, 1953, at which she was featured on three tunes: "And the Bull Walked Around, Ole," "Jeepers Creepers," and "If I Should Lose You."

In a July 1953 magazine article, Kenton was again quoted: "In the few months Chris has been with us she's made great strides and I'm convinced she'll soon be one of the great song stylists of our day." (The piece offers further statistics: Connor was then five feet six and a half inches tall, 125 pounds, a natural blonde, and "her only hobby is singing.") She was featured on only four more recordings with the band (including "All About Ronnie" and the unissued "Nobody Knows the Trouble I've Seen"), most of which were arranged by William Russo. However, she was featured extensively on the band's widely heard "Concerts in Miniature" broadcasts, from Birdland and other prime spots. Unfortunately for Connor, she took sick before the band toured Europe that September, and the Misty Miss Christy was pressed back into service as touring thrush.

The Kenton exposure led to a solo gig in Birdland, and one night Gus Wildi, president of the independent label Bethlehem Records, walked in. Up till that point, the fledgling company had been floundering with poorly distributed pop singles. Liking what he heard, Wildi signed Connor as the label's first major jazz artist, and in December 1953, he recorded her in the pop context of Sy Oliver's orchestra and tunes like "Miser's Serenade" (aka "Mad Miser Man"). "Sy had me do a couple of ridiculous tunes," she told Marc Myers, "probably because Anita or Ella or June was singing novelty stuff like that at the time. I don't know. The songs certainly weren't my choice."

With Kenton, she had continued the band's long-held custom of goofy novelties for female singers but these first Bethlehem songs made even the lousiest of her Kenton material look like Cole Porter by comparison. "Chiquita from Chi-Wah-Wah" is perhaps the worst thing she ever sang, although it is in the tradition of Latinate comedy songs that often hit for Kenton, such as Christy's "Tampico" and Connor's "And the Bull Walked Around, Ole." "Mad Miser Man" would seem to be a direct swipe of the Kenton band's ensemble-chanting formula. It opens with a whole chorus of the band, and Connor is backed by a singing chorus of bandsmen in the style of Anita O'Day's "And Her Tears Flowed Like Wine," and "Tampico," again.

In August 1954, Bethlehem tried again, this time wisely setting her in the most intimate of settings, the superb accompanist Ellis Larkins's drummerless trio. Now they struck gold: *Chris Connor with Ellis Larkins*, the label's first jazz LP (BCP 1001), quickly sold forty thousand units, establishing Bethlehem as an important jazz label. Before August ended, Connor went back into the studio to tape *Lullabies for Lovers* with bassist Vinnie Burke's quartet. In April 1955 she recorded *This Is Chris* with a group of Bethlehem regulars led by pianist Ralph Sharon, a recent arrival from London, and featuring the already legendary tandem-trombone team of J. J. Johnson and Kai Winding. The CD reissue of *Lullabies of Birdland* is in the original LP sequence—which is usually a good thing, but not here. You're in the middle of such exquisite standards as "Spring Is Here" and "Why Shouldn't I" when all of a sudden you're forced to listen to such woofers as "Blue Silhouette" and that godawful "Chiquita."

Those few pop disasters aside, the twenty-six or so tracks she cut for Bethlehem are superb. When Doris Day first started, one critic supposedly compared her to the Anita O'Day of the same period: In 1953–55, Connor shows similarities to both Day and O'Day (could their professional names be a coincidence?), combining the dry, cool tone of the latter and the sunny optimism of the former. At this stage, Connor is best at barking bright bouncers. The talent for heart-stopping ballads would come shortly, with her arresting 1954 version of "Lush Life" being a harbinger of things to come. The Bethlehem sessions also include "He's Coming Home," Connor's first of several songs by the underappreciated pianist-singer-songwriter Charles DeForest, although it's not up to the slightly later "A Good Man Is a Seldom Thing," "Don't Wait Up for Me," and "Ballad of the Sad Cafe."

Connor's first albums for Bethlehem had been 10-inchers, but the introduction of the 12" format a few months later inspired another independent label, Atlantic Records, to launch an ambitious line of jazz LPs. Masterminded by Nesuhi Ertegun, the sagacious older brother of Atlantic founder Ahmet, the new jazz line quickly presented the succinctly titled *Chris Connor*, recorded in January 1956. It would be the first of twelve albums she would make for the Erteguns over the next six years.

These twelve albums are, as a whole, among the best works of the jazz vocal canon, fully on a par with—to cite two obvious points of comparison— the Anita O'Day Verve albums and the June Christy Capitols. The premier entry, *Chris Connor*, set the pattern for the series in varying among three instrumental formats: a foursome that was actually half of the Modern Jazz Quartet (John Lewis and Connie Kay); a jazz nonet consisting of trumpet, four saxes (a format employed again on *Free Spirits*), starring tenor colossus Zoot Sims, and four rhythm; and a string orchestra helmed by master arranger Ralph Burns.

The remaining eleven projects would vary among these formats, and add a few others to the mix as well: four rhythm plus vibes, trumpet, and tenor (*A Jazz Date with Chris Connor*) or one reed and rhythm (*Chris Craft*); piano trio or quartet (*Chris in Person*, the only live album in the series); a lush string ensemble (*He Loves Me, He Loves Me Not, I Miss You So, Ballads of the Sad Cafe*); a jazz big band (*Double Exposure, Witchcraft*); or all of the above on the ambitious *Chris Connor Sings the George Gershwin Almanac of Song.*

The 150 or so songs that she recorded for Atlantic—roughly 25 percent of which are anthologized on *Warm Cool* (a double CD released by 32 Jazz in 1999, programmed by Chris and myself)—gave Connor a capacious canvas on which she could show virtually everything she could do with a song. While "When the Wind Was Green" illustrates her subtlety, "Something to Live For" shows that for all her tact, Connor can be no less effective when she's very direct. (Connor had quite an affinity for Billy Strayhorn; she would cut at least seven Elling-Stray songs in this period, having already laid down the definitive female reading of "Lush Life" in 1954.) When she stretches the "oooohhhh" before "what wouldn't I give for," and then rushes ahead on the last "be my something to live" just so she can have the luxury of extending the final "forrrr . . . ," we know we're in the presence of someone who can express want and yearning like no one else.

Connor's mature ballad style comes to the fore on the string albums, particularly *I Miss You So* with Ray Ellis, and *He Loves Me, He Loves Me Not*, again helmed by the very brilliant Burns (the counter-riff he inserts throughout "But Not for Me" is especially on target). The first is her most poppish affair, boasting full strings and wordless choir; yet the setting is tasteful overall and Connor's restraint is as impressive as ever. Making the point that a pause can say as much as a whole sentence, Connor inserts a thoughtful fermata at a crucial moment in "Oh, You Crazy Moon" (on *He Loves Me Not*)—right before the payoff phrase "what did you do?" and all of a sudden the question seems so much more imperative. "Angel Eyes" and "I Wonder What Became of Me" are classic saloon songs on the order of "Lush Life" and Mercer and Arlen's own "One for My Baby." Most of the admittedly few other singers who've sung "Became of Me" (excepting the superb Joe Mooney) make it seem curiously cryptic; Connor, conversely, makes you feel you know exactly what's going on.

At this time, Ralph Burns was making the switch from big band arranger to jazz vocal orchestrator supreme. When Atlantic producer Jerry Wexler sent a copy of *He Loves Me* to fellow Atlantic artist Ray Charles, the Genius was so impressed with what he heard that he soon began his own, even more memorable, collaboration with Burns. Throughout 1956, Connor's regular accompanist was Ralph Sharon, who said recently, "We worked everywhere together, New York and out of town. I used to do all kinds of charts for her, little charts for combos and orchestra-

tions for full big bands. She's really an absolutely fine singer!"

Sharon put together the jumping charts for Connor's first all-swinging album, aptly titled *A Jazz Date with Chris Connor,* collating such big jazz personages as Joe Wilder, Al Cohn, Eddie Costa, and Oscar Pettiford. Sharon dips into his Anglo heritage for Noel Coward's "Poor Little Rich Girl," on which Connor swings firmly on the beat, still finding enough emotional space to conclude with Sir Noel's warning to the Poor Little Rich Girl not to strip for action all too soon. Costa and Wilder are most prominent on Irving Berlin's underperformed "It Only Happens When I Dance with You," the trumpet and vibes accentuating Connor's rhythmic playfulness—as in the way she soars straight up in the first line of the second chorus. "My Shining Hour" emphasizes the twin-tenor team of Cohn and Lucky Thompson in some marvelous two-sax riffs scored by Sharon, who supplies Latinate piano (enhanced by bongos) throughout.

But just because this is a *Jazz Date* doesn't mean ballads are unwelcome. "Lonely Town" opens like "Misty," with Connor at first "out of focus" in an ad hoc verse (the title repeated), then coming clearly into view in the refrain. Here, the interplay of piano and vibes recalls the Modern Jazz Quartet (albeit with flute added). Connor and Sharon made their strongest ballad statements on their 1959 reunion, *Ballads of the Sad Cafe.* On "These Foolish Things" and "The End of a Love Affair," Sharon takes the opportunity to write for his favorite kind of unit, a trombone section, in this case, supplemented by strings, rhythm, and the flute of Bobby Jaspar. Those trombones get a marvelous countermelody to play throughout "These Foolish Things," yet no matter how distinctive they sound, dem bones never steal the spotlight from the star at the center. "The End of a Love Affair" is virtually two arrangements in one, the first the song's rarely heard verse, the second revving the refrain into an up-tempo.

An album of nothing but highlights, *Sad Cafe* sports a pair of ringers, the title song (by Charles DeForest) and "Lilac Wine," an extra-long, quasi-folkish opus from a 1950 revue entitled *Dance Me a Song.* For a song about drinking, "Lilac Wine" is more delicate than boozy, yet it's entirely within the comfort zone (as is "One for My Baby") of the *Sad Cafe.* Rather than coming off as a delusional barfly, Connor sounds like a young girl who's just had her heart broken for the first time and is getting looped because someone snuck a little crème de menthe into her Shirley Temple (oh she's a big girl now). Which illustrates another major aspect of Chris's talent: her knack for finding intriguingly offbeat songs by little-known writers that tell unusual stories rarely presented by other singers.

"High on a Windy Hill" had been broadcast, but not recorded, by Glenn Miller's orchestra. Connor renders it dreamily, making the song relevant again even after its title line had been appropriated into the Oscar-winning "Love Is a Many Splendored Thing." Twice, she discovered composers who would later be a major asset to Sharon and Tony Bennett: Charles DeForrest ("Ballad of the Sad Cafe"), who later penned the memorable "When Will the Bells Ring for Me," and Douglas Cross and George Cory ("Harlequin"), who later wrote a little thing called "I Left My Heart in San Francisco."

"I always chose material no one else knew about," Connor said in 2008. "You know, all those times that I appeared at Birdland in the fifties I used to go over to Colony Records [on the other side of Broadway] and pick out-of-the-way songs that I thought would be good for me." Yet she hardly required offbeat material to keep her audiences guessing, as she proved when she put her stamp on two LPs' worth of the best-known numbers in the Great American Songbook in *Chris Connor Sings the George Gershwin Almanac of Song*. (Although even here she finds worthwhile esoterica, such as "Little Jazz Bird," introduced by Ukelele Ike in the 1924 *Lady, Be Good*.) Coincidentally, Connor went to work on this project right around the same time that Sarah Vaughan was recording her own double-LP Gershwin project for Mercury Records (both sets predated Ella Fitzgerald's five-LP package by two years). Connor and Sharon had gotten about halfway through the eight dates it would take to tackle the *Almanac*'s thirty-four songs (the 1989 CD added four more slices of Gershwiniana from other CC albums) before Ralph left Connor's convoy to join Bennett's bunch in March 1957. He was replaced by Hank Jones on one date and then by Stan Free as the lady's traveling accompanist.

Although Sharon wasn't able to play on the remaining sessions and Ray Ellis took over as arranger, the ensemble of three trombones and a tenor heard on "Jazz Bird" sounds like one of the pianist's arrangements. So, for that matter, does the ornithological reference to "Lullaby of Birdland" on "Jazz Bird," and the way that "Strike Up the Band" parades down South Rampart Street with a martial swing. "Foggy Day" and "S'Wonderful" spotlight Sharon's playing in trio format, with Connor speeding up and slowing down in an exciting fashion that's more Copacabana than Birdland. The *Jazz Date* team of Al Cohn, Joe Newman, and Eddie Costa further spices up "I've Got a Crush on You" (she sings the verse on virtually every item in the GG package, although here she truncates it down to the last two lines) and "I Got Rhythm," on which the verse is the only section Connor sings relatively straight, devising her own boppish paraphrase on those much mined chords.

A Portrait of Chris teamed Connor with Jimmy Jones and Ronnie Ball, and was highlighted by what amounts to a series of duets, with sterling instrumentalists. *Free Spirits*, with Al Cohn at the podium, put the focus on jazz composers, from the tried-and-true, like Ellington's "Jump for Joy" and "I'm Gonna Go Fishin'," to the unexpected, such as Leiber and Stoller's blues "Kansas City," to the experimental, such as a set of lyrics by one Margo Guryan to the Modern Jazz Quartet's classic "Milano." Nothing ever got more offbeat than Miss Guryan's attempt to pin words to Ornette Coleman's free jazz dirge "Lonely Woman."

Free Spirits would be Connor's last album for Atlantic. Apart from the essential twelve albums, she also recorded enough singles and odd tracks to fill a Japanese LP collection entitled *Misty*. That set includes Atlantic studio versions of both the title song and "All About Ronnie," which were otherwise only on her live album *Chris in Person*. One surprise on *Misty* is "Flying Home," a sensational "vocalese," in the Jon Hendricks sense of the term, inspired by the swing classic by Lionel Hampton and Illinois Jacquet. Connor also joined Bobby Short, Herbie Mann, and LaVern Baker in Atlantic's "after-theatre version" (Atlantic's term for an all-star covers album) of Richard Rodgers's *No Strings*.

Although the Atlantic albums are the centerpiece of Connor's career, she recorded considerably more, starting with two albums for Morris Levy's FM label: *Chris Connor at the Village Gate* (1963) and *Weekend in Paris* (1964), taped in the City of Light with a French orchestra. The *Village Gate* album seems like a direct extension of her 1959 Village Vanguard album—if anything, Chris is even better here, especially on a thoughtful arrangement of "Old Devil Moon" that uses Dizzy Gillespie's intro vamp to "Night in Tunisia" as a countermelody. The latter is highlighted, fittingly, by a French song, Charles Trenet's "I Wish You Love"—in contrast to the Sinatra-Basie version of the same year, this one seems much more melancholy, and, somehow, more *French*. She also scores heavily on a lush ballad treatment of the Mathis hit "Chances Are," which, naturally, I prefer to the original.

By the mid-sixties, producers impelled Connor to try to join the ranks of those holdovers from her generation (like Mathis and Andy Williams) who routinely covered the new hits, good, bad, and indifferent. Beware of albums like *Now!*—Chris Connor's 1966 effort for the ABC-Paramount concern. It was a great idea to bring her to ABC, but why did they try to make pop records for the main label when she could have been making brilliant jazz albums on the Impulse! subsidiary, the way Johnny Hartman and Lorez Alexandria were doing? Don Sebesky had done some fine straight-ahead charts for Connor's two albums with Maynard Ferguson, but here the order from on high was obviously to make these cuts as jukebox-level junky as possible, in a manner that trashes even the good songs. "Strangers in the Night" is a surprising combination of flamenco and kitsch; "Never on Sunday," done in a *Greek au go-go* style, isn't even amusing camp.

Yet her interpretation of Lennon and McCartney's "Nowhere Man" has a poignant, literal quality that makes it more directly emotional (in spite of the presence of a pseudo-psychedelic harpsichord in the mix) than the Beatles original. There's a major difference between Connor being forced to cover a contem-pop hit and being allowed to interpret the material. Her only American album between 1966 and 1976 was *Sketches,* an unfortunate collection of current hits for other people on Rod McKuen's Stanyan label, which found her struggling with "We've Only Just Begun" and "Make It with You." (There also was an album for Japanese RCA in 1969 with a considerably more sympathetic tune stack, which I've never been able to hear.)

Yet when given her own space to treat a song—even at times, an unpromising one—in her own way, the results could be magical. On her 1983 *Love Being Here with You,* she took Peter Allen's disco hit "Rio" and swung it like a forties Hollywood South-of-the-Border dance number, boom-chica-boom and all that. Further, she followed it with the authentic period Latin classic "Baia" (also on *Love Being Here with You*) and then the grandmother of them all, "Brazil" (on the 1986 *Classic*); these are three of her most satisfying later tracks, and it makes one regret that she never did a whole album of Pan-American rhythms, *Cuba à la Chris* or something like that.

Many of her recordings of the seventies, eighties, and nineties find her repeating songs from the Bethlehem-Atlantic period: There's a 1978 set issued under multiple labels and titles (*Sweet and Swinging* and *Chris' Corner* among them) that finds her in fine voice, although it's hard to be excited by a program of virtually all repeats (with the exception of "I've Got You Under My Skin"). There are more new numbers to be heard on the 1984 *Love Being Here with You,* whose title cut is one of many songs she's recorded over the years in homage to Peggy Lee, another long-running thread through the Connor career. This album is also notable for "Anyone Home," a hauntingly arty torch song by Richard Rodney Bennett (not yet Sir).

Much of the best work in her last quarter-century has been done primarily for the benefit of Japanese listeners. The 1976 *Chris Moves* includes two unpromising songs, "Feelings" and "The Way We Were," but since the rest of the album is so much better I suspect those stinkers are present only to make us realize that even comparatively obscure songs from the great years are better than the biggest hits of more recent vintage. A series of four albums from the early nineties produced by Todd Barkan—*Blue Moon, Angel Eyes, My Funny Valentine,* and *As Time Goes By*—contrast overly familiar mega-standards (as suggested by the album titles) with some offbeat choices: "Wild Is the Wind," "The Crying Game," "Beauty and the Beast," "Singin' in the Rain," and Elton John's "Can You Feel the Love Tonight." Again, considering the quality of the musicians and in particular arranger-directors such as Bennett and Mike Abene, the results are very fine

indeed. *Angel Eyes* and *As Time Goes By,* which were both taped over the same sessions in spring 1991 with the amazing accompaniment of pianist Hank Jones and the supremely sensitive bassist George Mraz, are particularly noteworthy.

Her overall best and most heralded later albums were the two on Contemporary, *Classic* (1986) and *New Again* (1987), which gave her everything she needed: two gifted musical directors, Abene and Bennett, sympathetic musicians (trumpeter Claudio Roditi on both, reed stars Paquito D'Rivera on the first and Bill Kirchner on the second), and first-rate songs. *Classic* is highlighted by a wonderful "Laura" with the intriguing verse (previously mainly sung by June Christy), and a tuneful slice of *Latin à la Lee,* "Sweet Happy Life" (aka "Samba de Orfeo"). The voice is still remarkably close to her work of the sixties. She also put together an emotional medley that began with "What Is This Thing Called Love?" and then proceeded to answer that question with "You Don't Know What Love Is" and "Love."

The latter period is, overall, a tangled mix of new songs and remakes (one reason that *Classic* and *New Again* were especially welcome is that nearly every song on them is a new arrival in her discography), American and Japanese independent labels, studio and live recordings. There are two club sets worth finding, Sweet Basil in New York in 1981 and Pizza on the Park in London in 1990. The New York set does not include the song "Lover Come Back to Me" but the album is titled *Lover Come Back to Me* (it was released on the Japanese Alfa label and the American Evidence); the London set does include the song "Lover Come Back to Me" and the album is titled *The London Collection* (on Audiophile).

Confusing, yes. But her singing makes it worthwhile. In her last forty years, Connor was intermittently prolific: She would stay out of the studio for long stretches, and then turn around and make a whole batch of new albums for various labels. As mentioned, she was very busy in the late eighties and very early nineties, but then, mysteriously, was out of the studios for almost a decade. She made a last stand at the turn of the new century, when HighNote Records (the final resting place of many a great singer) released three newly recorded Connor albums: *Haunted Heart* (2001), *I Walk with Music* (2002), and *Everything I Love* (2003).

In her mid-seventies, Connor still had most of her vocal power. (Despite catty comments by Dinah Washington—"I sing bad when I have a cold, but this?"—who should have had the class to know better, or at least to keep her big trap shut.) She could still bring a lyric to life and still swing, and she continued to find good songs—the titles of the three HighNote albums alone prove that—and she was still recognizably Chris Connor. The middle set, *I Walk with Music,* is especially satisfying: She maintains a subtle theme of traveling, beginning with "Route 66" and ending with "On the Road Again," and from Nat Cole to Willie Nelson, it's a fascinating journey, stopping at Peggy Lee ("Where Can I Go Without You") and even lunar travel along the way. Her ballad "How High the Moon" is certainly a geographical high point; she does it as a slow ballad, with the rare verse, and though she seems to have trouble staying in tune, she sings with feeling to spare. Hoagy Carmichael and Johnny Mercer's title song, another traveler, "I Walk with Music," is another Connor gem (also with a rare verse); she takes it as a medium-fast foxtrot, but still slow enough to get the lyric across, and leaving us no doubt that, after well over fifty years as one of the top singers in the jazz business, she continued to walk with music.

Even pushing eighty, Chris Connor could still make your hair stand on end whenever she sang "Lush Life." She made her last major appearance in New York at a memorial tribute to Peggy Lee at the JVC Jazz Festival. She lived long enough to see the fine contemporary singer Dominique Eade invoke something of that power in *When the Wind Was Cool*, her 1997 tribute to Connor and June Christy. At the time of Connor's death, on August 29, 2009, nearly all her classic Bethlehem and Atlantic albums had seen the light of day again on CD. (In 2006, Collectables put seven of the Atlantics on a four-disc set, having previously done another six of them on three twofer CDs in 1999–2001.)

It was an entirely different world in 2009 than in 1959, when Connor was at the height of her career, yet they still have much to say to us, those classic recordings made when the 12" LP was brand-new and the compact disc not even a gleam in the inventor's eye. That is to say, back in those days when the wind was green.

Bing Crosby (1903–1977)

Sure, I'm a Crosby fan. Everybody's a Crosby fan.
—Frank Sinatra

"One of those unbelievable manifestations impossible to explain," was how Bing Crosby once characterized the allure of a film actress he admired. The description applies even more to the inexplicable appeal of Crosby himself. Perhaps a first step in understanding Crosby's fifty-year reign as a multimedia superstar is to approach his persona, and his career, as a deliberate creation. To put it another way, Ray Bradbury once introduced his young son to animator Chuck Jones as "the man who draws Bugs Bunny." The lad corrected his father: "No, he draws pictures of Bugs Bunny." If the author had ever introduced his offspring to Der Bingle, he could well have described him as "The man who plays Bing Crosby."

The on-mike, on-camera Crosby was a carefully cultivated extension of the private Crosby. The persona he embodied in films and broadcasts, though based on who he was in real life, was as artfully crafted as any fictitious character. Bing Crosby was so believable as "Bing Crosby" that after a while almost no one knew or cared that there was a difference.

The perfection of the Crosby persona was part and parcel of two other innovations that made his career perhaps the most crucial in twentieth-century popular culture. All at once, Crosby hit on both the elements that were to make American pop unique: jazz and the mass media.

In a sense, his predecessor Al Jolson had been the Moses of show business. "No man in my memory could generate such electricity in the theatre," Crosby later said. However, while Jolson led us to the promised land of electronic reproduction, like Moses he could not enter: He never learned how to fine-tune his wattage for proper projection into people's living rooms. Crosby, however, had the benefit of growing up with the phonograph and, to a lesser extent, the wireless.

Crosby's career essentially began when he left home in 1925 to make it in showbiz, but it could be more accurately said that his musical evolution began approximately fifteen years earlier, on the day his dad brought home a windup gramophone. "We must have been the first in the neighborhood to have such an instrument," he later reminisced. Similarly, around 1917, his older brother Ted built one of the first radio sets in the area—this being well before the advent of commercial broadcasting. Bing realized early on that a performer couldn't adjust a current approach for the recording medium. No, you had to create a new sound specifically designed to fit the parameters of what the apparatus could capture.

What enabled Crosby to achieve this was the other half of his equation, the parallel development of jazz, which, partially thanks to him, provided the foundation for much of American popular music. He realized that the very informality of jazz made it the defining element of an intimate style that was all but designed for media reproduction. Jazz made it possible to celebrate the feeling of the moment; the technology made it possible to capture that feeling and project it. And the vocabulary that Crosby developed in tandem with Louis Armstrong ensured that its mood could be romantic as well as danceable.

Crosby also elaborated on an idea that he most likely gleaned from Jolson, one that Frank Sinatra would extend even further. Jolson and Crosby were the first pop singers to make a song's lyrics seem like a sort of reality. You didn't have to treat a Sammy Cahn song as if it were Keats; the important thing was to make the words ring true. "I used to tell [Sinatra] over and over," said Tommy Dorsey, "there's only one singer you ought to listen to, and his name is Crosby. All that matters to him is the words, and that's the only thing that ought to matter to you too." The first step in making a song believable was making sure that each text he sang, no less than his screen roles, was congruent with the context of his character.

"Cozy virtuosi" was the phrase that Cole Porter penned for Crosby to describe Louis Armstrong's All-Stars in *High Society* and, again, the phrase perfectly describes Der Bingle himself. The greatest trick of his virtuosity was covering it up. It's often said that he made his singing and acting "look easy," but more to the heart of the matter, he made it look as if his work was no work at all. Audiences assumed that Harry Lillis Crosby simply was the character he portrayed, and his singing a lyric or reading a line of dialogue was as natural to him as breathing. He was so thoroughly convincing in his art of the artless that it's still hard to convince some people that there was any kind of craft to what he did.

That idea accounts for the greatest part of his popularity at his zenith in the thirties and forties. It explains how he could deliver a message of middle-American morality without being immediately rejected by his target audience. We'll defeat the enemies of happiness, Crosby is telling us, be they the downward winds of Wall Street or the Axis superpowers, simply because the capital G is on our side. Since Crosby never had to hit anyone over the head with this theme and refrained from preaching (as close as he came was in "Ballad for Americans" and "Old Glory"), both the man and his message were always eminently believable.

In his 1953 memoir, *Call Me Lucky* (which is more of a warm and witty assembly of anecdotage than a soul-baring confessional), Crosby points to a further corner-turning revelation that might be deemed the actual start of his career. Born in Tacoma, Washington, on May 3, 1903, he had thought of music as something that was in his blood but nothing more than an avocation until around 1924. Having vaguely set his sights on becoming a lawyer, Crosby had made it as far as his third year of college and was working—"interning," they would say now—one summer in a Spokane law office. "But it began to dawn on me that I was making as much money on the side, singing and playing the drums, as an assistant attorney," he wrote. "This gave me to think: What was I doing studying the law when singing offered fatter financial possibilities?"

Crosby and his bosom chum Al Rinker were the sole remaining members of a semipro band called the Musicaladers that had worked around Spokane, and now they decided to strike out for the big time. That meant Los Angeles, to which late in 1925 they headed in a decrepit jalopy that, Crosby reported, was held together mainly by youthful enthusiasm. It's no small indication of both their talent and their ability to assess the showbiz market that within a few months, Crosby and Rinker were pulling in as much as $400 a week in vaudeville. And within a few months of that, the team had been absorbed into the aggregation of bandleader and musical magnate Paul Whiteman. (In this era, full-time band singers were such a novel commodity that, between vocals, our boys had to sit in the bandstand holding dummy instruments.) Working with Whiteman initially necessitated a cut in pay, but Crosby realized that the value of linking their names to the Everest of music men (in reputation as well as girth) was well worth it.

Crosby and Rinker were a hit with Whiteman across the country until the combination orchestra and theatrical revue reached New York where, anticipating Wall Street by several years, the act mysteriously "laid dinosaur eggs." However, the King of Jazz kept the pair on the payroll, realizing that Crosby's voice was a major asset in the recording studio. Many of Whiteman's orchestrators insisted on utilizing Crosby as their main solo voice even though in Whiteman's stage shows he was often buried in larger vocal groups.

Musicians of the late twenties, from the Whiteman band clear to Harlem, collectively identified Crosby as the first to "sing like a man"—with something like a modern idea of naturalism—in an age of fey falsettos, tenuous tenors, and belting bassos. As Mel Tormé later described it, "Bing was undoubtedly the first song star to do away with the accepted stance, feet close together and pointed at a 45 degree angle, hands clasped prissily and resting on the abdomen. Instead, he exuded a casualness which won America's heart."

Winning America's heart was still several seasons away from those first months with Whiteman when the bandleader himself came up with the idea that signaled Crosby and Rinker's future success. "Pops" teamed them with the energetic pianist, vocalist, songwriter, and oral effects specialist Harry Barris, who was to remain in Crosby's clique for many decades to come. Crosby, Rinker, and Barris became Whiteman's Rhythm Boys, an immediately popular trio that performed both with and without the full orchestra both in theaters and on wax. Barris's own "Mississippi Mud," originally recorded in 1927 and re-created for a 1943 broadcast, illustrates the kind of high jinks that made the Rhythm Boys a hit: witty arrangements (mainly by Barris himself), a sense of humor, and solid musicianship, heavily rooted in the syncopated and "modernistic" jazz of the late twenties.

However, if all was harmonious as far as the music was concerned, the Rhythm Boys had a lot to learn offstage. As Whiteman put it, although they were never hard to handle, they were often hard to find. Crosby later described the threesome as hard-drinking hotheads who cared more about raising hell than such minor matters as showing up on time—or even at all. The topper came in 1929, when Universal Pictures summoned Whiteman and company to Hollywood to star in an early talkie extravaganza entitled *The King of Jazz*. The Jazz King had promised Crosby a solo spot in the picture, but the occasionally out-of-control young crooner forfeited this potential break when he wound up in the cooler after an alleged drunk driving accident.

However, he had already cut his first sides as a solo act several months earlier and knew that this was the direction he would ultimately take. When Whiteman returned to the road, Crosby, Rinker, and Barris elected to remain in the film capital. At first, the Rhythm Boys worked at the Montmartre club and then in tandem with local leader Gus Arnheim's band at the Cocoanut Grove, but by now it was obvious that Crosby was outshining his partners. He was beginning to appreciate the wisdom of Kipling's dictum, "He who travels fastest travels alone."

Crosby was singing more and more solos, and by virtue of the band's nightly remote broadcasts was becoming known all over filmdom's capital. He sang one solitary song in the Bebe Daniels–Douglas Fairbanks picture *Reaching for the Moon*, and also starred in a series of slapstick musical comedy shorts produced by tobacco-chewing old-timer Mack Sennett, leading him to conclude, "Working in pictures looked like easy money." As Crosby's star was rising as a solo attraction, he gave considerable credit to Barris's efforts as a songwriter, citing "At Your Command," "I Surrender Dear," and "Wrap Your Troubles in Dreams" as bringing repeated requests from customers both in person and over the ether. Yet "Even in those days, you knew there was something special about Bing," Artie Shaw, who was then playing around Los Angeles, later recalled. "He was doing something special that hadn't been heard before. It was his own."

In 1930, Crosby married Dixie Lee, a rising though reluctant Twentieth Century Fox ingenue. Miss Lee's friends had warned her against marrying him, since judged on Crosby's performances to date, he was not much of a prospect. However, she was soon to fall into line with a famous one-liner of the era, "Prosperity was just around the crooner." Nineteen thirty-one was the year that it was due to arrive, when Crosby, thanks to his older brother Everett, who had stepped in as his manager, made contact with the men who would, at long last, "discover" him for radio and records: William Paley and Jack Kapp.

What had initially convinced Paley, the big man at CBS, to try Crosby were the remarkable recordings the crooner had begun making for Jack Kapp, head A&R man of the Brunswick label, beginning in March 1931. Starting with the crooner's premier side for the label, the ironically titled "Out of Nowhere," the Crosby Brunswicks had been both musical groundbreakers and top sellers. Of the twenty-two sides he recorded for the firm that first year, nearly all were at least minor hits.

What so appealed to those early Depression audiences is a combination of qualities that still resonates almost eighty years later: Crosby's radical reconciliation of rhythm with romance. He uses the ingredients of jazz as elements of a hotter, sexier sound than anyone had achieved before. As one contemporaneous columnist observed, "Bing Crosby succeeded Rudy Vallee as [broadcasting's] first male, and radio suddenly went masculine."

The 1931 Brunswicks display a more emotionally intense sound than we associate with Crosby, which in some ways seems to have rubbed off on him from his admiration of Jolson—witness the exclamatory cries on "At Your Command." At the same time, he is more deliberately jazzy, dishing out heavy doses of scat and improvisation, expressed in the vocabulary that he and another of his idols, Louis Armstrong, were simultaneously bringing to popular song. "I Found a Million Dollar Baby" boasts an especially loose second chorus and a scat sequence so Satch-mofied you almost expect Crosby to conclude with an "Oh, yeahhh!"

Crosby's use of scatting, whistling, and melodic paraphrasing derives from his sense of drama, which you might expect a former band singer (for years confined to a single chorus) to appreciate. He utilizes these devices as ways to make his second chorus different from the first—something he realized from the very first solo records he made apart from Paul Whiteman's orchestra in 1929. In the 1931 period, the second choruses of "Just One More Chance," "I Apologize," "Out of Nowhere," and others are especially hot (a lesson reinforced by study of Ethel Waters, a further fave), but throughout his career Crosby makes a point of justifying the extra vocal space allotted to him.

"I tried to vary my humming by imitating the saxophone," Crosby later explained; "my notion was to make a sound which resembled the human voice with a bubble in it." "Just One More Chance" proffers the single most notorious of Crosby's wordless vocal effects, the infamous "boo-boo-boo" of legend. Unlike the apocryphal culture clichés, "Play it again, Sam," "Judy, Judy, Judy," or "Come up and see me sometime," Crosby actually did boo-boo-boo at least this once, at the start of the second 32 bars. The only occasions when he used the phrase again were in self-parody, as on "Sing Soft, Sing Sweet, Sing Gentle."

"I Apologize," "Dancing in the Dark," and "At Your Command" represent the more dramatic early Crosby, displaying an intensity later expanded upon by Billy Eckstine, who made a hit out of the first tune again twenty years later. Crosby's tenderness strikes a riveting note of contrast with the martial mood of "Apologize," while he turns "Dancing in the Dark" into an example of Depression desperation that's culturally as well as sexually charged.

He put such a definitive stamp on "Star Dust" that, with this one record, he transformed friend Hoagy Carmichael's theme from a hot instrumental into the best-known popular song of all time. Crosby still clings closely to the song's jazz origins, starting with the verse—taken firmly in tempo—which, combined with the chorus, is so long that the singer only has time for a brief call-and-response episode with Jimmy Dorsey's alto sax and a reprise of the final line before the coda.

"I needed a theme song," Crosby later said in his album *Musical Autobiography*, "and Turk and Ahlert wrote me a good one." "Where the Blue of the Night (Meets the Gold of the Day)" has more to do with the thirties and forties tradition of slow, nostalgic theme songs than with anything in Crosby's own musical makeup. The original 1931 recording, done very strictly in 3/4 time, included the verse, which he apparently never sang again, but he did retain the whistling chorus, which could be heard at the start of countless Crosby radio shows.

When Bing and Everett received one of their first big checks, their younger brother Bob recalled, Bing instructed Everett to "book as many of those" as he could, because he couldn't foresee his popularity lasting beyond another sixteen weeks. As we've seen, he had done some odd jobs in Hollywood in 1930 and 1931, but when he returned to the movies in 1932, initially in Paramount's *The Big Broadcast*, it was as a star. Crosby topped the bill in two more features in 1933, and by the time of his fourth starring feature film, 1933's *Going Hollywood*, he had made it to the list of the ten most popular picture performers. Bing and Everett began to take steps toward long-range career planning, the first act of which was importing the rest of the Crosby clan to Los Angeles, putting most of the remaining siblings to work for them, as well as their father.

Nineteen thirty-four was also the year that Jack Kapp, Crosby's main man at Brunswick, decided to start a record label of his own. Armed with the promise that where he went Crosby followed, Kapp was able to secure backing from Decca Records in England to start an American subsidiary. The new firm would bear the parent's name, but Kapp was to have total control and, against the insecurity of striking out with a new concern, he rewarded Crosby with both a higher royalty rate and first crack at the choicest new songs.

It was an unlikely time to announce a major new venture in a business that was suffering from Depression doldrums. In fact, in 1935 Crosby apparently contemplated giving up recording altogether, as he waxed almost nothing but his songs from his films that year. "I Wished on the Moon," from *The Big Broadcast of 1936*, reflects his reluctance to record at this time as he insisted on doing the song as a dance band disc by the Dorsey Brothers, limiting his own contribution to a brief vocal chorus.

However, with Kapp at the helm, the new label led its bigger brothers in the gradual resurgence of the platter trade. Decca gave customers top stars—starting with Crosby—for the budget price of 35 cents. At the same time, Crosby stabilized his radio career. Where he'd had several sponsors up until then, in December 1935 he began an eleven-season association with NBC and the *Kraft Music Hall*.

Later on, he gave considerable credit to Kapp and radio writer Carroll Carroll for helping him reimagine himself and expand from simply a singer of jazz-and-romance into a fully rounded shpieler and personality. Crosby eventually got to the point where he had it both ways. He turned the whole

world into a collective Crosby fan club for his relaxed insouciance and happy-go-lucky attitude, while at the same time the sheer quantity of records, broadcasts, and films (not to mention children) that he produced, as well as his well-known exploits as a golfer and sportsman, must have tipped the public off to the hardly hidden truth that here was a man who had not only talent but brains and dedication.

The Crosby character that developed in the Kraft-Decca years was a direct extension of his singing. He was an easygoing casual character who, only at the end of pictures like *Rhythm on the River, Holiday Inn,* and *Blue Skies,* is reformed by his leading ladies into a more serious nose-to-the-grindstone type; in *Pennies from Heaven, Sing You Sinners,* and many others, the happy wandering troubadour becomes a happy, stationary family man. (One of the most appealing things about the *Road* movies with Bob Hope is that the two principal characters are never "reformed" and continue in an enviable existence of eternal adolescence.) The Crosby character, like that of John Wayne, Clark Gable, or Humphrey Bogart, was consistent, in that he was essentially playing the same role whether the picture called for him to be a songwriter, a doctor, or a priest.

The radio "Crosby" involved a small continuing cast, which began with Ken Carpenter and John Scott Trotter, respectively his announcer–straight man and bandleader–straight man of many years, and included recurring characters like Hope, Jolson, and Jimmy Durante. There was a series of frequently employed subjects that were regularly milked for laughs on the air: Crosby's horses, the baseball team he partially owned, his color-blind yet colorful sense of fashion. Crosby surely had a monopoly on making fun of his own family, starting with his many brothers, principally Everett (who allowed the Kraft writers to depict him as a loafer—and laughed all the way to the stockbroker) and bandleader Bob ("your brother—you know, the one who works"). When all four of his sons, long the butt of Hope's one-liners, began making semi-regular appearances on his radio and then TV shows, the line between sitcom and variety show, as well as between carefully cultivated image and actuality, completely disintegrated.

Together with Jack Kapp, Crosby gradually molded his recording career into a parallel concept: Crosby singing a Hawaiian song or as an Irishman was as believable as the screen Crosby playing a cop, a cowboy, or a traveling salesman. Crosby sings a comedy song, a kiddie song, or a Christmas song: They all wind up being a combination of the elements you associate with the context as well as the setting-to-setting characteristics of Der Bingle himself. "Jack wouldn't let me get typed," he explained. "He kept me spread out. I sang hillbillies and blues, ballads and Victor Herbert, traditional songs and patriotic songs, light opera and even an opera aria or two."

One of his first hits for Decca, "Two Cigarettes in the Dark," and the quasi-tango and later Sinatra perennial "The Moon Was Yellow," retain the hot-and-heavy emotional power of the Brunswicks. The sensuality and rhythm we associate with early thirties Crosby never actually disappeared, they simply diminished in importance, and shared the audio stage with many other characteristics of his music that gradually emerged.

Crosby's evolving attitudes toward both rhythm and romance can be followed through the songs from his first Decca-era film, *Here Is My Heart*. This cinematic bauble accomplished even more for Decca Records than it did for Paramount Pictures, in that all three of its songs—"June in January," "With Every Breath I Take," and "Love Is Just Around the Corner"—became hits and standards. In the picture, Crosby, playing a radio crooner (admittedly not much of a stretch), sings a duet with his own recording of "June in January," and the use of two Crosby voices inspires him to perform obbligatos to his own main melody lines. He does the same thing on both of the two "straight" ballads here, "Love Is Just Around the Corner" and "With Every Breath I Take," in which he musically comments on his own performance with jazz phrasing, never more effectively than in his telling insertion of the line "you keep it awake"—an Armstrongian repeat done Crosby style—on the second.

An excursion into out-and-out jazz, "Love Is Just Around the Corner," which Crosby later described as "a pretty good jump tune," outswings anything he had tackled either for Whiteman or for Brunswick. Crosby, at his most aggressively amorous, even makes the verse swing ("cop a look at that moon") and whistles energetically back and forth with a Joe Venuti–like hot violin. In the final few lines, he gets the beat going really strong with staccato syncopations attached to extra syllables ("let's go cuddle in a cozy little corner . . .").

The same can be said for the three hit tunes from Crosby's next film and first costumer, *Mississippi*, which offered an unusually politically correct story line aimed at debunking Confederate chivalry as well as the only occasion when Rodgers and Hart wrote for him. "Down by the River," "Soon," and "It's Easy to Remember" contain the same kind of hot-and-heavy romance as his early thirties crooning, still leavened with a touch of jazz.

Crosby's singing was at its heaviest and most Jolsonian at the start of the Decca period in 1934, gradually lightening as the Depression gave way to the war. In the first years of the *Kraft Music Hall*, Jimmy Dorsey, who had taken over the Dorsey Brothers Orchestra after his younger brother, Tommy, had walked out, served as Crosby's conductor in residence. But this amounted to merely a temporary measure since Crosby required a full-time conductor for his radio and recording work and Dorsey was obviously destined to become a star bandleader in his own right. While it lasted, though, the Crosby-Dorsey pairing was a fortuitous one; their most notable team-ups were the frantically swinging "I'm an Old Cowhand" (from *Rhythm on the Range*), in which Crosby's interjections are accompanied by frenzied cowbells and wild scatting (even the vocal group is hot), and the smooth and stylish "Too Marvelous for Words" (both the work of Johnny Mercer).

In 1936, John Scott Trotter trotted into Crosby's life. The large-named and large-framed conductor was, at the time, best known for his ten-year stretch as pianist and head arranger for college chum Hal Kemp's top-rated dance band. Since leaving Kemp in November 1935, Trotter had served as house musical director and A&R exec for the corporate ghost of Brunswick Records, the American Recording Corporation. Trotter's old friend the lyricist Johnny Burke had persuaded Crosby to let Trotter arrange several songs from his 1936 picture *Pennies from Heaven* as a freelance assignment.

The title song of that film, "Pennies from Heaven" itself, which may be one of Trotter's arrangements, exemplifies lyric interpretation at its finest. Crosby, at his most soothing and reassuring, sings thought by thought rather than word by word. He and lyricist Burke together make "Pennies from Heaven" not only an archetypal anthem of the Depression, but one of the cornerstone concepts of the country's collective consciousness.

By the following season, Crosby was so impressed with Trotter's work and personality that he decided to put him on permanent salary. "The Moon Got in My Eyes," which derives from the first Trotter-directed Crosby session, displays the partnership at its early apogee. Anticipating Sinatra and his various arranger collaborations, the treatment of this song from Crosby's *Double or Nothing* begins with a delightfully flutey introduction from out of left field, while Crosby himself never runs out of different ways to phrase the word "moon"—he doesn't let a single one get away.

"It's the Natural Thing to Do" is also from the first Crosby-Trotter session and sports an even more distinctive Trotter introduction. The song is another Johnny Burke text from *Double or Nothing*, and along with "Remember Me" and "I've Got a Pocketful of Dreams," it shows how Crosby and Trotter contended with the coming of the swing era proper. Crosby did little that could be described as straight-ahead, 4/4 swing in the manner of Benny Goodman (in fact, when he sang Goodman's "Don't Be That Way," he sang it slow and bluesy rather than up and swingy). Instead, he and Trotter reinvented the schottische, formally defined as a nineteenth-century dance found in both Germany and Scotland, similar to a polka. Merging their respective backgrounds in jazz and dance music, Crosby and Trotter updated the schottische as a way to sing contemporary songs in a bouncy dance tempo.

Harry Barris, playing a bandleader in both *Double or Nothing* and *Sing You Sinners* (two of many Crosby pictures in which the former Rhythm Boy gets a minor speaking role), gives the downbeat to his orchestra in the latter picture by announcing it as "a wee bit o' schottische." The schottische also worked perfectly with the quasi-Dixieland polyphony of the sort that Crosby loved. As a result, his uptempo numbers of the late thirties are some of the most appealing music of his whole career. "Pocketful of Dreams" is the very picture of a bouncer for unusually astute businessmen, and the schottische tempo makes his improvisations and jazzy variations seem even more comfy: They veritably trip off his tongue.

While conventional wisdom has it that Crosby was more of a "jazz singer" in the earlier part of his career, he kept making hot sides at every stage. And not only when he teamed up with a swing group: He himself was often the major jazz element of his recordings (as in his free-flying 1940 version of "You Made Me Love You" with the Merry Macs). His very style was rooted in jazz, and elements of it can be found in everything he sings—from "Pistol Packin' Mama" to "Blue Hawaii" and even "Adeste Fideles." The very device that identifies Crosby, the "trill" or syncopating mechanism that produces a catch in his voice (called grace notes, satellite notes, or mordents), amounts, in point of fact, to a jazz-derived element.

Composers writing directly for him via his film scores quickly learned to take advantage of the specific qualities of his voice. For the first bridge on "Be Careful, It's My Heart," Irving Berlin even set up a rhyme to contrast high and low trills on the same descending phrase that accompanies the words "quickly burn" and "never return." Note also that even in a ballad, Crosby always lets you know exactly where the beat is. One of the ways Sinatra in the forties distinguished his singing from Crosby's was by suspending the beat and spending as much time as he could in rubato.

Lyricists penning words for Crosby took even greater advantage, and, like the film and radio writers, enjoyed the head start of a predetermined persona to write for. While in the Brunswick era he expressed an eroticism so hot it would have been verboten under the Hollywood Production Code, he gradually let the fire relax from roaring flames to radiantly glowing coals. Eventually, he reached the point where, as Rosemary Clooney has explained, he was uncomfortable directly saying the three little words "I love you" in a song. Johnny Burke, one of Crosby's best friends and his most trusted scribe, often triumphed by working around this stipulation. Clooney cited the line "If I say 'I love you' " in "Moonlight Becomes You" (from *Road to Morocco*, 1942) as the definitive Crosby-Burke exhibition of indirect amour. (Another example might be ". . . and I'm thinking 'if you were mine, I'd never let you

go' . . ." in "But Beautiful"—the protagonist is deciding he loves her but not stating it outright to her.)

Which isn't to suggest that Crosby was afraid of emotion. He simply realized that by refusing to indulge in sentimental excesses he could address the widest range of material without turning off any element of his audience. The Burke ballad texts typed specifically for him, such as "Only Forever" (from *Rhythm on the River*, 1940) and "But Beautiful" (*Road to Rio*, filmed in 1947), work perfectly, as you'd expect. However, "found" texts, like the two very successful traditional Irish airs, "Too-Ra-Loo-Ra-Loo-Ra" and "Galway Bay," are no less effective. They're already wringing-wet with bathos, and for the singer to subject them to yet more sentiment would be to push them way past the edge of believability. Someone once wrote about Barbra Streisand, "If she were to sing with a little less emotion, there wouldn't be a dry eye in the house." Crosby did precisely that. And there wasn't.

His attitude toward emotion even worked when he put it in reverse. The one major American songwriter whom, by the luck of the draw, he almost never sang was Cole Porter. It might have been that Porter was too pointedly passionate for Crosby. Yet, together, Crosby and Porter landed two of the biggest hits of the war era—in the number-one hits "Don't Fence Me In" and "I Love You." Both were departures for the two men in other ways: Crosby had certainly sung cowboy songs before ("San Antonio Rose" had been an earlier blockbuster), but this particular "trunk song" (written for an unproduced film ten years earlier) was certainly atypical of Porter the Broadway sophisticate. On the other hand, Porter had written heart-on-sleeve love songs before, but Crosby had never sung them. Perhaps, as with tough guy Jimmy Cagney becoming a song-and-dance man in *Yankee Doodle Dandy,* the public appreciated the break from personal tradition.

By the end of the thirties, Crosby had marshaled all the resources necessary to fulfill Jack Kapp's vision of the ultimate musical Everyman. "Jack saw to it," as Crosby said, "that I achieved a musical variety very few other recording artists were able to." Hawaiian music, for example—who would have thought, at the time of Crosby's breakthrough in 1931, that he would have aspired to transporting listeners as far away from the mainstream—culturally and geographically—as songs of the Islands? (Although his single favorite song, he said on several occasions, was "My Isle of Golden Dreams.") Or that the first-recorded of Crosby's twenty-one million-selling songs would wear a Hawaiian shirt?

Crosby's multidecade Island excursion began with the coincidence of Mr. and Mrs. C taking a Hawaiian holiday shortly before he was scheduled to start filming *Waikiki Wedding*. While in Honolulu, the Crosbys danced at the Royal Hawaiian Hotel to Nebraska-born Harry Owens and His Orchestra, and were particularly taken with the bandleader's own composition "Sweet Leilani," named after his daughter (the dialect denoting "flower of heaven"). Crosby then had to convince Paramount Pictures, who had already commissioned a sumptuous score from longtime Crosby compadres Leo Robin and Ralph Rainger, as well as Owens himself, that "Leilani" belonged in the picture. The song wound up doing better than the movie—and the movie didn't do badly—winning the Academy Award for best screen tune and hitting seven figures' worth of sales by 1946.

Of Crosby's many albums full of hula music, the best songs are "Blue Hawaii" (later revived by Sinatra and Presley), the flip to "Leilani," and another chart-topper, "Trade Winds" (also sung by Sinatra and Bugs Bunny). They all gleam as brightly as a Technicolor travelogue, or, even as brightly as one of those proto-psychedelic shirts that were part of Crosby's characteristic costume. Where Crosby functions as a mere guest at the poi party in "Leilani," not sticking his head in until the second chorus, he has more to do on the others. On all three, the throbbing guitars match his own vibrato beautifully, and the minimal background brilliantly showcases his near-perfect pipes. (In 1964, Crosby anticlimaxed his Hawaiian series with *Return to Paradise Islands,* a singularly disappointing effort that was also his only full-length collaboration with Nelson Riddle.)

What Crosby did for Hawaiians and ukeleles, he could also do for cowboys and their twangy guitars. He had included Western material in his repertoire ever since he first recorded FDR's favorite song, "Home on the Range," for Kapp in 1933, and his many forays back to that home on the range resulted in a long, long trail of chart-toppers. "Sierra Sue" had been written by a cowboy named Shapiro in 1916, and it became a hit for both Crosby and Glenn Miller in 1940, and was subsequently used by Gene Autry (and his horse) as the title song for one of his B Westerns. Crosby takes it straight, affording old "Sue" the same respect he offers the best of Porter or Gershwin, singing over a lightly stringy background from Trotter. ("He's no hillbilly," the singer once said of his corpulent conductor, "but he's quite a hill.")

However, Crosby's best-remembered horse operas inevitably called on his deeply felt interest in jazz. "San Antonio Rose," with Bob Crosby's first-rate band, and "Deep in the Heart of Texas," with Woody Herman's Woodchoppers, dig deep into the heart of Western swing. (If Bob Wills and His Texas Playboys had been on Decca at the time, Crosby would have recorded with them, too.) Brother Bob's outfit supports his senior sibling with a considerably more punchy background than Trotter does, incorporating a beat from New Orleans rather than San Antonio. Likewise, Woody Herman's small band also boasts a Bobcats-styled Dixieland beat on "Deep." In 1946, "San Antonio Rose" became the first (though not the earliest recorded) Crosby disc to sell a million units, and it did even more for the burgeoning country music market than for the singer himself.

Bob Crosby, youngest of Bing's six siblings (coincidentally, Bing himself also sired seven kids), made it on his own as the singing front man for one of the best groups of the swing era. Bing himself really shone in front of the orchestra's band-within-a-band, the Bobcats, since both singer and the unit's New Orleans–oriented sidemen came from the same place in the soul, rhythmically and otherwise. Properly propelled by the relaxed yet potent drumming of Ray Bauduc, Crosby really rocks on both 1938's "You Must Have Been a Beautiful Baby" and 1941's "When My Dreamboat Comes Marching Home." On both, he demonstrates the side of his singing that blues giant Jimmy Rushing so admired and also shows where later bluesmen like Bobby Darin and Fats Domino learned these tunes.

As must be clear by now, Crosby's key strength was diversity—it's hard to imagine any piece of music that couldn't qualify as a Crosby song. He transforms "Swing Low, Sweet Chariot" into an intimate experience, backed by an a cappella choir and making his own appoggiatura congruous with the melismas and "flowers" of the traditional spiritual. "You Belong to My Heart," from Disney's *The Three Caballeros,* finds him teaming up with longtime amigo Xavier Cugat (imported from Columbia Records); the Spaniard backs Bing, who hits an exquisite long note at the capper, with smoothly sweet marimbas, maracas, and strings. A session with rhythm and blues trendsetter Louis Jordan produced two agreeably rhythmic novelties, "Your Socks Don't Match" and "My Baby Said Yes," and was mentioned in nearly all of the saxophonist's publicity materials as the high point of his career. Crosby easily essays the Tympany Five's famed shuffle rhythm, trades phrases with Jordan's own alto, and harmonizes vocally with the leader, becoming in effect the sixth guy named "Moe."

Note that Crosby encounters all these respective idioms on their own turf. He also enjoyed quite a few duet partners closer to home, one of the first being Mrs. Crosby, the former Dixie Lee. "No one will ever know the ordeal I went through to persuade her to cut a couple of records with me," Crosby later reminisced about his chronically reticent, ex–film star wife. "Building the pyramids would have been easier." The missus certainly sounds tense on "A Fine Romance," and even Mr. Casual himself, singing in an unusual key to accommodate his partner, seems less comfortable than usual. Still, the real-life chemistry they shared comes through, as does Jerome Kern's classic melody.

Crosby sounds better singing with ladies he wasn't married to, particularly Connee Boswell (on "Bob White") and Mary Martin, who both made frequent appearances with him on the *Kraft Music Hall.* Long before she embodied Richard Rodgers's moral and musical ideals by becoming the androgynous knucklehead Nellie Forbush, the almost-nun Maria von Trapp, and then Peter Pan, Miss Martin was quite a hip Hollywood chick. She shared the limelight with her "Dream Man" (as she called Crosby) on three records and two films, *Rhythm on the River* and *Birth of the Blues*; a generation or two later, their children, Larry Hagman and Mary Frances Crosby, would enjoy a soapier, and more violent, relationship on TV's *Dallas*. *Birth of the Blues* produced "Wait Till the Sun Shines Nellie," on which Crosby helps Miss Martin to sound, if not actually jazzy, at least somewhere in the proximity of the groove.

He also brought out the best in the ultimate pop diva, Judy Garland, who sounds even more of a mensch than usual when singing with Crosby, and is calmer and less intense than usual in their duets. Always one of La Garland's staunchest supporters, Crosby kept her and many another artist's career going during the lean years when they were between comebacks: In this case, he gave Garland (like Boswell and Martin) work as a semi-regular on his radio show in the era just before *A Star Is Born,* when Hollywood had excommunicated the often undependable Little Miss Showbiz. "Mine" (from Broadway's *Let 'Em Eat Cake*) is George Gershwin's most notable attempt at a double-melody contrapuntal cadenza like those of his hero, Irving Berlin. It's the best of their four commercial sides, and gives one cause to regret that Crosby and Garland never appeared onscreen together.

Unlike Sinatra, unfortunately, Crosby only occasionally recorded the major Broadway-oriented standards of Gershwin, Rodgers, Porter, Kern et al., although he certainly sang as many samples of the Great American Songbook as he did Hawaiian and cowboy songs. Sinatra made a point of quality, while Crosby stressed diversity—and the two goals were not necessarily in conflict. Like Nat King Cole, Crosby recorded a wider range of music than the mainstream-oriented Sinatra, whose discography includes far more revisits to the same material.

On the one hand, "I Got Plenty o' Nuttin' " doesn't necessarily qualify as a standard since *Porgy and Bess* had only closed on Broadway a few weeks before Crosby recorded it in March 1936; on the other hand, "Somebody Loves Me" had reached the decade-and-a-half mark when Crosby cut his definitive reading in 1939. He approaches both Gershwin classics with the aid of outstanding orchestrations by longtime comrade Victor Young. His interpretation of "Nuttin' " addresses the discrepancy between religion and morality, and illustrates how piety isn't necessarily the same thing as "a-frettin' 'bout hell." The record starts in the realm of the theatrical, but singer and arranger gradually shift it over to Crosby country by the time they're done, the star making us overlook the text's dated "dese and dose" dialect with his carefully focused, reverential attitude. Young and Crosby do equally well by "Somebody Loves Me," one of the crooner's high-water marks, which caps

in an especially stunning out chorus that Crosby accelerates and ritards at precisely the right moments for just the right dramatic effect.

It was through a number written by a stellar Broadway tunesmith, Irving Berlin, and not with one of his regular writers that Crosby established his all-time best-known song, "White Christmas." The song has its roots in Kapp's insistence from the mid-thirties onward that he should regularly tackle seasonal material. Crosby, a devout Catholic who was known to "bend a pious knee," at first resisted the idea that a pop crooner should involve himself with any kind of sacred music, and at that stage of the game there was actually very little popular Christmas music to speak of. Still, he agreed to cut "Adeste Fideles," which Kapp convinced him had become secularized enough over the centuries, and "Silent Night," the profits of which went to benefit American missions in China.

To those who've never heard these records, it's somewhat startling to hear Crosby addressing such material in the huskier voice we associate with his earlier jazz-and-gin period—"Oh, Come, All Ye Faithful" ain't exactly "Moan You Moaners." However, despite a somewhat scrappy-sounding little choir on "Silent Night," Crosby sings both carols with heartfelt reverence, and actually manages to make the phrase "tender and mild" sound like something other than a cigarette commercial. "Adeste Fideles" became a Crosby tradition: Each year on his Christmas show he would sing the first chorus in Latin, and the audience—both in the studio and at home— would sing along in the vernacular on the second.

"White Christmas" only came into existence through a plot convention for the film *Holiday Inn,* which required one song for every major nonworking day of the annum. In 1942, it was almost as likely for a popular songwriter to pen a song about Washington's Birthday as about Christmas. In fact, Berlin had written an Easter song many years earlier. Still, when he finished "White Christmas" he realized he had written something special. The songwriter was a genuine neurotic New Yorker and quite excitable, whereas the singer tended to be more laconic, which made for quite a contrast when Berlin presented what he considered his masterpiece to Crosby. "Of course, he's not the one to throw his arms about and get excited," Berlin later reported, "he just took his pipe out of his mouth and said, 'I don't think you have to worry about this one.' "

Crosby introduced "White Christmas" around the time of the attack on Pearl Harbor in December 1941, some time before *Holiday Inn* was released the following year. The record sold phenomenally from the start, although Crosby was not to realize the pure power of "White Christmas" until deep into the war, when he made a tour of U.S. bases in England and France around the time of the D-Day invasion in the summer of 1944. More potent than the most sacred of carols, Berlin's deceptively simple tune was embraced by soldiers everywhere as not only a song of seasonal warmth and nostalgia but a hymn for peace.

By 1954, when Crosby and Berlin were making their third movie together, "White Christmas" not only served as its title, but a scene in which Crosby sings the now classic song to a troopful of homesick GIs (an amplification of a shorter but similar scene in 1946's *Blue Skies*) became the central image of the film. By the nineties, the song had inspired well over four hundred different recordings (including, for reasons nobody knows for sure, a Crosby remake in 1947), and Crosby's version alone had sold into the hundreds of millions. To this day, Bing Crosby's "White Christmas" is the single biggest event in the history of recorded sound.

By the time of the war, Crosby had long since become one of the dominant presences of American culture. He felt warmly enough about the GIs to cross an ocean infested with U-boats and then perform perilously close to the front because he realized what he meant to them—which was possibly even more than Bob Hope's jokes or Betty Grable's tush. During the war years, he reached the pinnacle of popularity—he was the industry leader for all of showbiz, tops in pictures, broadcasting, and recording; his name was known to more Americans than that of Franklin D. Roosevelt. When he won the Oscar for the 1944 *Going My Way*, he was now officially recognized as a major actor as well as the greatest of entertainers.

The records made by Crosby, now known affectionately as Der Bingle to both Allied and Axis servicemen, became even more meaningful during the war. In fact, it took the coming of conflict to elevate the 1938 "I'll Be Seeing You" from obscurity to megahit, while "I'll Be Home for Christmas" operates as a seasonal variation on the same theme. No other singer could so effectively portray so ineffable a sense of absence and loss, down to the ironic twist endings on both sets of lyrics.

Not all songs of the period directly referred to the war: Two hits—"Sunday, Monday, or Always" (from Crosby's *Dixie*) and "On the Atchison, Topeka and the Santa Fe" (from Garland's *The Harvey Girls*)—were from Americana costume films that, like Broadway's contemporaneous *Oklahoma!*, reaffirmed traditional American values at a time when they were being fought for. There's nothing old-fashioned, however, about Trotter deputy Billy May's smooth-groove arrangement of "Atchison," which takes Crosby on a swinging railroad ride, suggested mainly by trainlike vamping from the individual instruments of the rhythm section: guitar, piano, and bass. "Sunday, Monday, or Always," unfortunately, is the product of another conflict. Made during the 1942–43 strike by the American Federation of Musicians, Kapp and Crosby were forced to use only an a cappella chorus trying to trick listeners into thinking they were listening to an orchestra.

Still, most of Crosby's war-era opuses were nei-

ther patriotic jingles nor teary ballads but jaunty, lively songs designed to take the minds of civilians and soldiers off their considerable hardships. Johnny Mercer's marvelous mock-spiritual "Ac-Cent-Tchu-Ate the Positive" and the Western swingers "Don't Fence Me In" and "Pistol Packin' Mama" are just a few of the hits that combine Crosby with the famous Minnesota-born trio, the Andrews Sisters. Like Abbott and Costello, or Betty Hutton and Red Skelton, the Andrewses were brash and unsubtle and immensely appealing, exactly what the doctor ordered for a loud and boisterous era of entertainment; they caught on big-time during the frantic forties, generating more firepower than a munitions factory.

First teamed in 1939, Crosby and the Andrewses made a perfect match, combining the coolness of the one with the high energy of the other; the sisters were sensitive enough to Crosby's nuances to match his vibrato and replicate his trills. Thanks also to ace Andrews accompanist Vic Schoen, the combination perfectly captures the decade's manic mood, with their tempo changes, choppy rhythm, and allusions to boogie-woogie like those the trio had popularized in their "Boogie Woogie Bugle Boy."

Crosby not only reigned as the definitive American voice of the war years, but held his throne long into the atomic era. Three songs in particular capture the mood of the immediate postwar period. "San Fernando Valley" spoke to the same westward-bound future homeowners as "Route 66" (introduced by Nat Cole but also recorded by the Crosby-Andrews combination). Fairly dripping with Trumanesque optimism, this bouncer by Gordon Jenkins encouraged the idea of relocating oneself physically and reinventing oneself, identity-wise. "It's Been a Long, Long Time" boasts a text that lyricist Sammy Cahn immodestly though accurately described as being so powerful that the words actually were the music. With the help of Les Paul, back in the days when the guitar wizard studied jazz and Django Reinhardt, the song helped convert America from a nation of fighters to one of lovers.

There was yet one more step in Crosby's cultural evolution. Although "Swinging on a Star" came from the 1944 *Going My Way*, this Burke–Van Heusen standard actually anticipates a postwar direction. The idea for "Swinging on a Star"—like that of "Pocketful of Dreams," "My Heart Is Taking Lessons," and "Only Forever"—had been inspired by one of Crosby's own phrases: Johnny Burke claimed he actually heard Papa Bing scolding one of his boys with the admonishment, "What do you want to be, a mule?" Crosby recorded it with the Williams Brothers, including future Hawaiian-wedding flower boy and easy-listening composer Andy Williams. With "Swinging on a Star," Crosby's war cycle comes to a climax as his position as pop music's supreme patriarch is reaffirmed: He has now transformed us from fighters to lovers to parents.

Another development that came with the end of

the war was a newfound prosperity and the opportunity to travel, which many Americans indulged in wholeheartedly. Crosby had already visited the American West, Hawaii, Ireland, Paris, and practically every place else where songs were either written or had been written about: "Rose of Mandalay," "Mexicali Rose," "San Antonio Rose." Now in the late forties, the semitropical, nostalgic hit "Now Is the Hour" (aka "Haere Ra" aka "Maori Farewell Song") whisks listeners off to far-flung New Zealand, where the song first became popular (even though it had originally been published in Australia in 1913), while the no less haunting "Far Away Places (With Strange-Sounding Names)" symbolically schleps to exotic locales all over the globe. Another postwar travel piece, Arthur Colahan's "Galway Bay," comes off as similarly sentimental despite the political themes it touches on.

Two other travel pieces, "South America, Take It Away" and "MacNamara's Band," are hardly so solemn. Coming from the other way around, "South America" makes fun of the North American's propensity for foreign fads. Crosby and the Andrews Sisters enter babaluing à la Desi Arnaz, and Harold Rome's combination of hot Latin rhythm and esoteric vocabulary fit El Bingo (who spoke fluent Spanish) perfectly.

"South America, Take It Away"—which sounds like a *Road* movie song but is actually from a smart postwar revue entitled *Call Me Mister,* starring Betty Garrett, ranks as one of the funniest recordings in the Crosby career, and the competition is formidable. "MacNamara" is another one of those Crosby discs that's guaranteed to put a smile on any face.

Crosby's interest in comedic sides stepped up in the late forties, in keeping with the public's accelerating appetite for novelties. While most of his teamups with female singers leaned toward the romantic (and, in the case of Connie Boswell, the rhythmic), when he crossed cadenzas with male performers, the results were more on the comedic side. His first series of duets with a male singer were with the songwriter and occasional singer Johnny Mercer—and they weren't necessarily all Mercer's songs. The most successful of these was "Small Fry," a Frank Loesser–Hoagy Carmichael collaboration written for a production number in the 1938 film *Sing You Sinners* that Crosby, in senior-citizen drag, performed in a broad burlesque fashion with Fred MacMurray, in old-woman drag, and Donald O'Connor. The Crosby-Mercer recording was more memorable.

Crosby's most celebrated partner, musical or otherwise, was Bob Hope, although unfortunately they only recorded together on a handful of occasions; their most pleasing disc was the title song of the third entry in their two-decade-long series of *Road* movies. Crosby had originally recorded "Road to Morocco" as a solo around the time that he was shooting the picture of the same name in June 1942, but several years later Decca decided to have him

remake it, this time in tandem with Hope. By this third stop on the *Road* tour, Hope and Crosby already have all the outrageous elements of the series perfected, and it all comes through on this recording, as the two rib everything from Crosby's notoriously tardy nags, Dorothy Lamour's costumery (or lack thereof), Paramount Pictures, the Hays Office, and most of all, their own physical attributes, from Hope's ski-snoot to Crosby's thinning thatch. One of only two Hope-Crosby teamings for Decca, "Road to Morocco" also benefits from an appropriately capricious arrangement by Vic Schoen.

Whenever Hope sang with Crosby, in addition to slipping his big shoes on, he inevitably retrogressed to his vaudeville roots and wound up throwing in a Jolson impression (particularly in "Appalachicola, Fla" in *Road to Rio*). Crosby, who had first caught Jolie's act as a teenager back when he worked as a flunky at the Spokane auditorium in the late teens, had idolized the World's Greatest Entertainer for thirty years when he finally got to split a mike with him in January 1947. They had already co-starred on two out of the twelve radio shows they would make history with together when they cemented their relationship with a Decca session that March, consisting of two antique arias.

"Alexander's Ragtime Band" has Jolson asking Crosby, "Don't tell me the first time you heard this song was when your Mama had you on her lap you know, listenin' to me singin'?" The two old pros and old hams engage in faux–noblesse oblige as each tries to goad the other into becoming the bill's opening act; when beauty ultimately precedes age, Jolie responds by comparing Crosby to a canine. The contagiously robust "Spaniard Who Blighted My Life" (which Jolson first recorded in 1913) has the two men echoing each other at different points rather like Jimmy Durante and Eddie Jackson, with Jolie moaning bizarrely in a send-up of a flamenco pattern.

Jolson and Crosby almost immediately became a magical mano a mano recording team because of their mutual belief that music and comedy represent but different sides of the same coin. Yet for all his manic energy, Jolson, as Joe Louis would say, can run but he can't hide. Wherever he dashes—high notes, low notes, a silly mood, a serious moment—Crosby, neither too aggressive nor too casual, is already there waiting for him. Jolson's long series of radio appearances with Crosby did as much to establish his comeback as *The Jolson Story*, yet Crosby always insisted that "Jolson did as much for me as I did for him." The two Crosby-Jolson Decca duets are just the tip of the iceberg. One yearns for Universal Music to issue more of their duos from the *Kraft Music Hall* and *Philco Radio Time* broadcasts.

Crosby's single funniest Decca duet also originated on a live broadcast: "Sing Soft, Sing Sweet, Sing Gentle" with Jimmy Durante, originally issued as part of the debonair Mr. D's *Club Durante* album. The first of two crucial elements of Durante's shtick was the merciless deflation of pomposity wherever he could find it, and the second was coaching people. No less than he did with Jolson, Crosby fit in perfectly with Durante's agenda, primarily because they employed the English language equally creatively, Crosby exalting it, Durante delightfully butchering it.

Making this track all the more ludicrous, here Professor Durante constantly exhorts Pupil Crosby to make like the title says: Sing soft, sweet, and gentle. Yet Durante's own approach, as radio listeners well knew, was to belt out every tune at the very top of his gravelly chops—as they both demonstrate with a hyperthyroid, inky-dinky-doo version of Crosby's theme "Blue of the Night." On an earlier program, Durante opined that he and Crosby had the potential to become the next Nelson Eddy and Jeanette MacDonald. Crosby responded, "I don't think that there's enough hair between us to play either part."

Before 1950, however, Crosby would have been surprised to know that his biggest-selling man-to-man duets would be labeled as by "Gary Crosby and Friend." Papa Bing put his four sons to work each summer on the Crosby ranch in Nevada, and one year before heading north, the Old Man and his firstborn casually stopped in at Decca. There they cut "Sam's Song," a contrapuntal comedy caper named after song plugger and publisher Sam Weiss. For a flip side, the two Crosbys ran through "Play a Simple Melody," a 1914 Irving Berlin antique that Crosby Senior and Groucho Marx had played around with at parties and on the air. Gary promptly put the session out of his mind, and when he returned home at the end of summer, he was astonished to learn that both of the songs had hit the top of the *Billboard* charts.

Gary later remembered that "the hour and a half it took to record the two sides was one of the best times we ever had together." That fun comes echoing through on the finished product—in spades. Innocuous little ditty that it was, "Sam's Song" was also reprised with other partners on the air—Bing sang it with Nat King Cole, Gary sang it with Frank Sinatra, and there's a later single of the tune by Rat Packers Dean Martin and Sammy Davis Jr.—but none of these compares with the father-son warmth that Bing and Gary apparently could only express when performing together. The two inspire each other to dizzy heights of jolliness, whether they're singing in harmony or—in the best-remembered episodes of both songs—where they sing different melodies and lyrics on top of the same chord changes. Dad takes the slower stanzas while the young upstart races through a mile-a-minute marathon of snappy patter. In addition to launching a wonderful cycle of Senior-Junior duets, the two sides launched a substantial career for Crosby Junior, who eventually evolved not only into Elvis's sidekick in several movieland Pelvis-fests, but a very

talented rhythm and blues singer. "I don't have to work," Crosby Senior quips in "Gone Fishin'," "I got me a piece of Gary!"

The other ingredient that had made "Simple Melody" such a rip-roaring success was that Crosby had also gotten a piece of the Dixieland revival bandwagon of the late forties and fifties. Not that he participated in such sounds strictly to follow a trend: As he wrote at the time, "when all is said and done, my favorite music is dixieland." The traditional jazz sound, with some minor modifications, helps him make "Chattanoogie Shoe Shine Boy," a hillbilly hit by Red Foley, his own. In singing the praises of this footwear engineer, Crosby flies into a veritable verbal tap dance. In "Sunshine Cake," he rattles his vibrato a bit, and the result anticipates Elvis Presley by half a decade; in "Shoe Shine Boy," he launches into a rap episode that shames the entire hip-hop movement. "When you goes / Man! You're twinkle-toes!"

"In the Cool, Cool, Cool of the Evening" was introduced by Crosby and co-star Jane Wyman in the Frank Capra picture *Here Comes the Groom*. The naturalistic way it was staged in that film won a Best Song Oscar (the fourth Oscar winner introduced by Crosby), but the record was even better, with Crosby, Wyman, the Four Hits and a Miss backup group, and traditional jazz backing by Matty Matlock. Johnny Mercer's lyric portrays a party and a picnic with guests who amount to a merry menagerie of beasties (grizzly bears, jackasses, prairie hens, and even a dinosaur) who could have stepped out of Walt Kelly's *Pogo* comic strip. Yet another duet partner made to look good by Crosby, Miss Wyman, then known primarily for not speaking (as in *Johnny Belinda*), gains both a voice and a musical presence. Playing Crosby's dubious dinner partner, the former Mrs. Ronald Reagan holds him down to terra firma when he affects a comically grand tone and threatens to lay a little Leoncavallo on us.

In "Play a Simple Melody," Gary Crosby briefly digresses into an approximation of Louis Armstrong, who had been the major favorite of both son and father for most of their lives. "Mr. Satch and Mr. Cros" had been friendly for nearly twenty-five years, when, as with the Crosby-Jolson date, the two wanted to put something down on wax in the middle of a spell when Satchmo was appearing frequently on Papa Bing's radio show. "Gone Fishin'," which could be sung as a countermelody to "Small Fry," perfectly delineates the Crosby persona: Our boy was, as the lyric suggests, rarely actually "tied up at the studio" since no microphone could ever compete with a golf club, and the fishing tackle lured him even more effectively than it did the fish. Several takes have been officially issued on different CDs, and though most of the "ad-libs" in "Gone Fishin'" were prewritten, the timing and delivery differ drastically. Between the pair of them, the two founders of the modern American vocal style scat and enthuse

("Oh yeah!") with enough warmth to heat all of Manhattan.

As Crosby approached his third decade at the top, he continued to explore his familiar subgenres, as well as investigate a few new ones. He enjoyed a string of country hits in 1949: "Careless Hands," "Riders in the Sky," "Mule Train" (which actually sold better than Frankie Laine's version), and "Dear Hearts and Gentle People." The last had been inspired by a phrase on a slip of paper found among the effects of Stephen Foster after he died penniless in New York.

Crosby was also still making hits out of Christmas songs, even one introduced by Bob Hope (in *The Lemon Drop Kid*). Carol Richards, who had served as Sinatra's co-star on *Your Hit Parade* in 1948, helped Crosby put over two hits of the period, "Sunshine Cake" and "Silver Bells." As songwriter Roy Evans said to me, "Crosby singing a Christmas song? It would have been unpatriotic not to buy it!"

Another Sinatra co-star, and a far more substantial one at that, helped Crosby achieve one of his most beautiful ballad renderings, the 1950 "Autumn Leaves." Axel Stordahl had been the Voice's musical director throughout the forties, and here Crosby gets the benefit of the arranger's impressionistic string textures. Since it's Crosby, the beat is a bit more pronounced than in the classic Sinatra-Stordahl sides, although he drifts ever so slightly out of tempo for a moving second chorus—hear the way he slides into "old winter's song" before an equally fitting, typically "small" Stordahl ending.

Which isn't to say that the home team couldn't hold its own. In 1951, Crosby and Victor Young commemorated their twentieth year of occasionally working together with a winning quartet of tunes from the current Rodgers and Hammerstein smash, *The King and I*. Crosby proves that "Getting to Know You" was wasted on all those stiff-upper-lipped British babes who've sung it in the show's various incarnations. Rather, he approaches it so easily and so convincingly that it's not difficult for us to believe that it's precisely his cup of tea.

It's a little known fact that Crosby sang songs from nearly all the Rodgers and Hammerstein shows, and a lot of other classic musicals from the R&H era. Jack Kapp had been the pioneer of the original cast album and so could give Crosby the inside track on a lot of superior songs from shows like *Bloomer Girl* and *Song of Norway*. My particular favorites are a pair of songs from Kurt Weill and Maxwell Anderson's *Lost in the Stars*, "Stay Well" and "The Little Grey House." (I wish he had also cut "Lost in the Stars" and "Thousands of Miles.") Of all the many lesser known Crosby performances, particularly from the postwar era, these are the ones that most deserve to be heard by everyone.

"Watermelon Weather," taped with Peggy Lee, weighs in as Crosby's most remarkable duet of the late Decca period. Crosby and Lee had sung together dozens of times on the radio but, thanks to competitive label affiliations, had not gotten the chance to do so commercially until 1952. Laid back as an old hound dog, these countrified cadenzas could be described as "Gone Fishin' " spelled sideways. Crosby and Lee animate it so vividly you can practically taste the watermelon juice as it drips.

When Dixie Lee died in 1952, it was the first time any of Bing's sons saw their father cry. Jack Kapp, his close friend and record guru, had died in 1949, and the team of Burke and Van Heusen, who had written twenty film scores for him (Burke had previously written another six) went their separate ways in 1953. All these events conspired to make Crosby uncomfortable with his old routines, as he acknowledges in *Call Me Lucky*.

In 1946, Crosby had left his long-standing association with the *Kraft Music Hall* in order to do a transcribed program (he had subsidized the development of recording on tape and was the first star to make use of the new technique) for whatever sponsor bid the highest: After several seasons with Philco, Chesterfield and then General Electric picked up the pre-taped Crosby half-hour. He eventually began freelancing with his recordings (and then films) along the same project-by-project basis (just as friend Louis Armstrong was doing), producing the masters himself and selling the tapes to various labels.

By the end of his regular contract with Decca in the mid-fifties, Crosby had been relieved of his responsibilities as the record industry's central hit maker and revenue producer. Far from being bitter, Crosby seemed positively liberated by the transition. For the last twenty or so years of his career, he no longer had anything to prove or any mountains to climb, and continued to sing just for the pure joy of it.

In fact, he so leaned on his own musical preferences that he returned to certain themes repeatedly. In the post-Decca years, he recorded four kinds of albums: Dixieland albums (*Bing with a Beat*), travel-theme albums (*Fancy Meeting You Here*), duet albums (*Bing and Louis*), and Dixieland-travel-duet albums (*That Travelin' Two-Beat*). Along the way he also recorded the memorable *Bing Sings Whilst Bregman Swings*, done in the general mold of the Sinatra–Nelson Riddle Swingin' Lover series.

Crosby later described *Bing with a Beat* (1957) as "the album I always wanted to make," and it's easily his finest effort of the entire album era. Taking the title literally, *Bing with a Beat* starts on an incredibly fresh note—or rather, not a note at all, but a beat. We begin with a few telling rimshots from drummer Nick Fatool before Crosby enters with the verse to "Let a Smile Be Your Umbrella." He starts nearly a capella, with drums only, in a dazzling (and for Crosby, almost exhibitionistic) display of his rhythmic virtuosity: New Orleans–style jazz is both a heterophonic and a polyrhythmic music, thus while

Fatool is playing at least two different beats on various parts of his kit, Crosby is singing to yet another. The whole album is full of such ingenuity and musical wit. Crosby is brimming over with enthusiasm throughout all twelve tracks; he's clearly having the time of his life.

It was apparently Crosby's own idea to cut this album with trumpeter Bob Scobey and his Frisco Jazz Band. Although this was a regularly working and touring group, riding the crest of the fifties Dixieland revival, for the purposes of the album the band was bolstered with several prominent Los Angeles studio players, most notably clarinetist and arranger Matty Matlock. After more than twenty years of working with both Crosby brothers (starting from within Bob's band), Matlock had come up with a perfect approach toward using traditional jazz to back a vocalist: Both the ensemble and Crosby himself sound at once spontaneous and controlled. He also put together an irresistible program of tunes from the Jazz Age—songs that are wonderful partly because they're not standards on a Gershwin–Rodgers and Hart level. Many of these songs ("Whispering," "Mama Loves Papa," "Last Night on the Back Porch") were associated with his ex-boss Paul Whiteman, but few of them had been heard since the Coolidge era. Instead of trying to find the most popular songs he could, he delighted in their obscurity. Crosby was no longer trying to compete with other singers for chart positions or box office receipts; this one was on him, and his joy is apparent in every note of this classic album.

He recorded a long series of intimate tracks with the backing of longtime accompanist Buddy Cole and his trio, primarily for his ongoing radio series, but also releasing many of the best of these on LPs like *Some Fine Old Chestnuts* and *New Tricks*. (In 2009, 160 of these CBS radio songs were released in a seven-disc boxed set by Mosaic Records.) "Softly, as in a Morning Sunrise" comes from the swingingly successful *New Tricks* (1957), an album whose cover—a very Bingish basset bearing a Crosby-style pipe, hat, and even eyes—had won listeners over even before they dug the disc. Although Cole's electric organ wheezes unattractively, "Softly, as in a Morning Sunrise" works as a ballad with both a jazz feel and a tango feel, Crosby and Cole somehow making it both fun and serious at the same time.

Another later album, *Songs I Wish I Had Sung (The First Time Around)*, was essentially Crosby's way of acknowledging that he wasn't the only male singer to create hits and standards. Longtime Decca associate Milt Gabler came up with the idea, and also that of using musical director Jack Pleis. Crosby offers "Thanks for the Memory" in recognition of the singing skills of Bob Hope and, ignoring the song's transformation into a Madison Avenue jingle, restores the bittersweet feeling Hope had projected when he introduced it in his movie debut, *The Big Broadcast of 1938*. In lines like "no frills, no fuss—hooray for us," Crosby shows that he fully appreciates the song's melancholy ironies. However, in retrospect the album makes it plain that Crosby introduced more great songs into the cultural bloodstream than everybody else put together.

He still made first-rate singles, some of which were even hits. The waltz "Around the World" (which led to a Crosby Decca LP of the same title) has Cole accompanying the singer with a full orchestra in a tribute to their late friend Victor Young, who had died a few months earlier and won a posthumous Oscar for this movie theme. My favorite later single is "Gigi." This rates as a Crosby sleeper—not an important song for him, or a sample from a well-remembered album, the Lerner-Loewe movie tune amounts to just a superbly sung single that beautifully closes the great years. In a stellar performance from yet another stellar Crosby era, he oozes with charm as he thanks heaven for little girls in a way that's half-husbandly and part paternal. He so easily enunciates the differences between "warmth" and "desire" that he really makes you feel it.

Crosby dominated popular music as no one else had before him; for more then twenty years no one came close to his pinnacle of mass popularity in all the mediums of the entertainment industry. His legacy was so capacious, in fact, that when he retired as undefeated champion, it took two subsequent superstars to carry the keys to his kingdom: Elvis Presley swept up the youth market with his spectacularly selling singles, even as the rejuvenated Sinatra made off with their parents via the new medium known as the concept album. Crosby represented the era of the unified, nondysfunctional family. He had started as something of a cutting-edge avant-gardist, musically and technologically speaking, but he quickly settled into a familial niche. Even before the war, he had become a paternal figure as much as a romantic leading man, the idealized superdad, lovable even in his foibles. There's still something about him that represents home, hearth, parents, traditions, continuity. He managed to please virtually everybody, and he did it without patronizing anybody.

In his mid-life and late-life performances, Crosby sounds as strong as he had twenty years previously—stronger, in fact, than in the war years when his voice was so overextended (with so much volunteer war work on top of his already full schedule). He kept recording at the same quality and quantity levels into the early sixties, and then took a few years off to concentrate on raising a second family. Then he surprised everyone by de-retiring in the seventies, leaving the world behind with a series of extended concert appearances and ten new albums between 1974 and 1977. Even though his death in October 1977 was largely overshadowed by Elvis Presley's six weeks earlier, Crosby's passing was still a very big deal. In the mid-1970s, Crosby's audience was still going strong; the World War II generation was only in their fifties. He was, in fact, in the middle of a sold-out world tour when he collapsed on a golf course in Spain. His widow, Kathryn, pointed out that he went out the way he would have wanted to. But he wouldn't have been pleased when, a few years later, his reputation suffered an enormous blow with the publication of *Bing Crosby: The Hollow Man.* This was a scandal-mongering, mudslinging volume that succeeded in doing to Crosby's image what *Mommie Dearest* had already done for Joan Crawford. Two years later, his eldest son, Gary Crosby, published his own memoir, *Going My Own Way,* which was a considerably more nuanced but still largely unflattering depiction of the man who was, for several generations, probably the most beloved figure in America.

The shock was not in the specifics of Crosby's relationship with his children, but that he had a dark side at all, and that his family with Dixie and his four sons was much more dysfunctional than the world had ever imagined. It took a long time for Crosby's status to recover—if indeed, it truly has—and not until Gary Giddins's 2001 biography did a balanced portrayal come to light. Crosby was, in fact, a very strict Catholic parent (if hardly a child-beating sadist) who treated his own sons as his mother had treated him, while Dixie was a lifelong alcoholic, and it was a disturbing combination. Yet Crosby learned from his mistakes, and when he raised the three children he had with his second wife, he apparently did not repeat them.

None of this detracted from his professional achievements: Thirty-plus years after his death, Bing Crosby remains the definitive voice in all of recorded sound, even more so than Armstrong, Sinatra, Presley, the Beatles, or Michael Jackson. When, in 1962, the National Academy of Recording Arts and Sci-

ences decided to create a lifetime achievement award, they not only made Crosby the first recipient, they named the award after him.

Crosby had, however, received a far greater commendation some decades earlier, one that he was decidedly not present to accept in person. In 1941, the nation of Japan declared war by scattering much of the old Third Avenue elevated subway on Pearl Harbor. Four years later, the emperor of the Land of the Rising Sun stood on the deck of the United States battleship *Missouri* and prepared to sign a treaty of surrender. As pen hit paper, a General Kenny turned to a Colonel Carter and said, "Well, now, if we only had Bing Crosby here to sing a few songs, this would be perfect."

Why was Crosby so widely loved that his name was evoked at an event that signified one of the greatest triumphs in the history of the American nation? Was it because Crosby could sing better than anyone else? Because he was more charming? Because he was funnier or more lovable? Because we envied his ideal existence, working at what he so obviously loved, siring not one but two adorable families, and finding time to indulge in every pastime that caught his fancy?

It was all of these things—but it wasn't because he was ever thought of as being superhuman. Rather, he was supremely human. There's a moment in his 1939 remake of Harry Barris's "Wrap Your Troubles in Dreams" when our man makes a wrong reentrance for his out chorus. Still singing, he proceeds to spontaneously describe his blunder in verse, using language that's a little strong for Father O'Malley but still tame by Tipper Gore standards. It's not only very funny, it's perhaps the most human moment ever captured by the microphone. And Crosby was simply the most human and most believable performer our age has known.

D

Vic Damone (born 1928)

If you look at a photo of a father and son together, you'll notice that the son doesn't necessarily look the way the father did thirty years earlier but rather looks like a younger version of the father today. It's a very subtle difference: For instance, in pictures of Bing and Gary Crosby together in the fifties, Gary doesn't look like Bing did in the twenties—and in his twenties—but rather like a younger version of the fifties Bing.

I use this example to suggest that Vic Damone sounds like an older version of the young Sinatra. If Sinatra hadn't gone to hell and back, hadn't done that whole Ava Gardner–Lee Mortimer–Mitch Miller–Harry Cohn *From Here to Eternity* thing, had he never changed his basic style from what he was doing in the forties—and had he kept his voice—he might have sounded like Vic Damone.

Which isn't to say that Damone didn't evolve over the years—he, too, dropped in register from a violin to a cello, to borrow Sammy Cahn's metaphor. And he also had to adapt to changing times. Yet Damone clearly started with forties Sinatra and never completely left that model behind. He was consistently able to stick to that pure early Sinatra; even in the age of philistinism, he never failed to adhere to the basic principles he gleaned from Young Blue Eyes's early work—the beautiful voice, the light clear sound, the precise articulation, the impeccable phrasing. In interviews, Sinatra occasionally used the term "bel canto" to describe, if not his own work, at least the ideal to which he aspired. However, the term applies much more consistently to Damone's singing. It's doubtful that such aggressive Sinatra items as "That's Life" and "I've Got You Under My Skin" could be described as "bel canto," yet virtually every note Damone ever sang, whether it was written by Cole Porter or Lennon and McCartney, was precisely that.

Damone's specialty has always been the semi-slow love ballad. I say semi-slow because there's always a touch of the forties dance band to his numbers; he would never attempt anything as fast and jazzy as Sinatra on the *Swingin'* or Basie albums or anything as suicidally slow as *In the Wee Small Hours* or *Only the Lonely*. Damone doesn't necessarily swing, but that's beside the point—he probably could if he wanted to. Rhythmic placement is just as important in a love song as in an up-tempo, and Damone's phrasing is just as sure-footed as his extraordinary intonation. (And yes, there are some singers, even beyond Eddie Fisher, who have no rhythm whatsoever, no matter what the tempo or the time signature.)

Damone never tried to be as emotionally deep as Sinatra, whose favorite expression concerning an exceptionally great song or a performance was that it would make somebody want to "run out and get drunk over it." I don't think anyone ever ran out and got drunk over something that Damone sang. Nor was he as intellectually motivated as Sinatra, who was continually pushing the envelope of what popular music was and what it could be. While Sinatra was a visionary, Damone was exclusively a singer, and an extremely good one, who could make virtually any set of words and music sound beautiful.

Vic Damone has also succeeded in being a class act for virtually the entire fifty years of his career—something that you can't say about Perry Como, for instance. (Vic did a few corny singles early on, but Como recorded enough cheese to fill every *fromagerie* in France.) And he is, at the very least, an extremely fine singer. And he was singing magnificently as late as 1999, at the age of seventy-one.

Damone's early biography is often compared to Tony Bennett's; they were born in the outer boroughs of New York two years apart in the late twenties (Damone in Brooklyn on June 12, 1928) and both came into this world with monikers considerably more Italian than their later stage names (Damone was born Vito Rocco Farinola); both also came to the music business just a little too late to get in on the big band era; and both were, in Bennett's term, "street kids," who learned to protect themselves with both their brains and their fists.

Both also grew up under the spell of Frank Sinatra. Damone can even remember the first time he actually heard the Voice. He's said he was thirteen or fourteen, but actually he must have been more like sixteen or seventeen, since this was on a WNEW radio program called *The Battle of the Baritones* that offered recordings by Sinatra and Bing Crosby, and he remembers that the disc he heard was "Ghost of a Chance," which Sinatra cut in 1945. Damone had already been taking music and singing lessons, but upon hearing Sinatra, he became obsessed with learning to sing like him. "That's when I knew that singing would be my life. . . . I wanted to be Frank Sinatra. For weaving a spell, interpreting a lyric, Frank stands alone. Just listening to him sing, I learned voice control, placement, breathing, phrasing, intonation, timbre." On a *Merv Griffin Show* in 1973, Damone referred to Sinatra as his god.

Around this time, the young Farinola worked as both usher and elevator operator at the Paramount Theatre, where he had the opportunity to study many of the top singers and bands of the day (including, possibly, Sinatra, who returned to the site of his first solo triumph for one week in November 1945). According to legend, Damone was transporting Perry Como from one floor to another when he imposed on the established star to stop, look, and listen to a sample of his own crooning. Como was most encouraging, which led to a long friendship between the two singers (the older man served as godfather to Damone's son, who was named after Perry). The one time I met Mr. Damone in person, he introduced himself to me as Perry Como.

Como wasn't the only major celebrity in Damone's camp. Things started to happen quickly for Farinola after he won the talent competition on *Arthur Godfrey's Talent Scouts* in 1945 or 1946: Milton Berle was present, and he was enough taken with the young singer's talent to set up an audition for him at La Martinique, a Copacabana-style "niteclub" in Manhattan. His two-week engagement there was his professional singing debut, and possibly the first time he was billed as "Vic Damone"—the latter being his mother's maiden name. Berle also saw to it that Damone participated in an album of Rodgers and Hart songs that was being produced by RCA Victor; thus, the young singer's premier recording was a collective affair in which he shared the spotlight with Berle and singer-actress (and future Sinatra co-star) Betty Garrett. Around this time, another venerated show business figure, New York talk-show host Barry Gray, also took Damone under his wing, frequently featuring him on his highly rated program.

By this point, Damone himself was a fixture on radio: He appeared on a program called *The Gloom Chasers* (WHN), and in late 1946 began recording an extensive series of songs for radio play only for the Associated transcription service. Commercial-record-wise, he did several sessions for Silvertone, an independent label owned by the Sears corporation, and then in April 1947 began recording for Mercury Records, which at the time was another indie, but one that, thanks to such talent as Damone, Frankie Laine, Tony Martin, and Dinah Washington (and producer Berle Adams), would quickly emerge as a major player.

Damone's first session for the new label commenced with an Italian song, "I Have but One Heart" ("O Marenariello"), a song that had been cut by Sinatra two years earlier, but not issued. When the Damone disc was released and landed on the

Billboard charts, Columbia followed by issuing Sinatra's 1945 version—kind of a before-the-fact cover. Damone reached number 7; Sinatra, number 13. Damone's "O Marenariello" sounds almost exactly like Sinatra's, which is remarkable, since he obviously couldn't have heard the as then unissued Sinatra disc. Over the years, Sinatra made a point of praising Damone's voice and technical ability, stating consistently that the younger singer had "the best pipes in the business." He once told Larry King, "If I had one wish, it would be for Vic Damone's tonsils." Damone is more than just pure chops, though as a storyteller and dramatist he wasn't Sinatra's equal (who was?), but he more than knows how to phrase, where the beat should be, and how to put a story and a song over.

On the strength of "O Marenariello" and the early Mercury hits, Damone landed a regular series of his own, *Saturday Night Serenade*, on the Mutual Network (10:00–10:30). Former Benny Goodman vocalist Helen Ward was a producer, PET Milk was the sponsor, and this initial series lasted for two seasons. By this point, he was a bona fide headliner, and was able to remain one for the rest of his singing career, roughly fifty years. He was a star, but never a legend: There would be no sensational fall and rise, no nosedive and no comebacks, although there would be several marriages and a hint of scandal here and there (particularly in his relationships and breakups with such stars as Pier Angeli and Diahann Carroll). His name would sell albums and seats in a nightclub but not newspapers. It's been an admirably straight-ahead career: He worked steadily from the late forties to the millennium, playing important clubs and halls all over the globe, and he recorded nearly every kind of song for nearly every major label: Mercury (now part of Verve), MGM (ditto), Columbia, Capitol, Warner Bros., RCA, and many independents.

He was never a larger-than-life figure like Sinatra, or an icon who stood for something beyond a voice itself, like Bennett, Laine, or Darin. Perry Como's music, overall, was not as consistently good and tasteful as Damone's, but Como had a stronger, more clearly defined musical personality. Yet Damone sang a ton of classic songs and made a lot of beautiful recordings: Anyone who wants to hear the Great American Songbook performed at a level close to its best could do a lot worse than to put on such albums as *That Towering Feeling!* or *Strange Enchantment*. If Damone can't really challenge Sinatra or Fitzgerald, his work remains eminently satisfying for what it is.

In one major respect, Damone, even more than Sinatra, was a perfect singer for the early postwar period: He was part of an era; Sinatra created one. Damone was much more likely to sing Italian songs, both traditional and contemporary, than Francis Albert, and Mercury producers Berle Adams and Mitch Miller gave him quite a few: "You're Breaking My Heart," "Just Say I Love Her," "Here in My Heart," "To Love You." The late forties and fifties were the international years of pop, in which songs from all over the globe landed on American charts.

The war had made Americans conscious of other cultures—and Damone, like Crosby, Armstrong, and Cole, scored a fair number of hits with international origins. In addition to Neapolitan love songs, there were all kinds of exotic items, such as the Spanish "My Bolero" (not to mention "Laroo, Laroo, Lilli Bolero"), the Portuguese "April in Portugal," "An Old Sombrero," "Tzena, Tzena, Tzena" (an Israeli folk song done in response to the Weavers' chart hit), and "Calla Calla," a song that seems to be "Tzena" translated into Italian and from there into English. He even sang the Xavier Cugat–Desi Arnaz hit "Babalu"—a track that has yet to be issued.

In the Mercury years, Damone played both sides of the fence: He had a number 11 hit with a *trayfe* novelty called "Cincinnati Dancing Pig," a stinker of a porker if ever there was one, and around the same time sang the Israeli hit "Tzena" for the kosher crowd. If I were Damone, I would be insulted that Polygram included "Dancing Pig" on the only widely available collection from the period, *The Best of Vic Damone—The Mercury Years*, but most of the rest of the CD is marvelous: Damone had hits with quite a few high-quality songs in this period, such as "April in Portugal," "Ebb Tide," "The Breeze and I," "Again" (a million-seller), and his jazziest early hit, "Vagabond Shoes." Most of *The Best of Vic Damone—The Mercury Years* lives up to its title, but unfortunately the producers included that dreadful pig song and a couple of meaningless covers of Guy Mitchell pseudo-folk hits. I offer these yet again as evidence that these collections should never be compiled strictly by chart hit numbers—you've got to actually listen to these records once in a while, guys.

The Mercury years (1947–55) also encompassed two key distractions: In 1951, Damone was drafted and served for two years in the army during the time of the Korean War; apparently, he was stationed stateside and had occasional leaves to pursue civilian activities, as he seems to have held recording sessions regularly during this period. He was also drafted, as it were, by Metro Goldwyn Mayer, for his good looks and smooth pipes. He appeared in six musicals during this period: *Rich, Young and Pretty* (the title could have described Damone, but in fact it referred to star Jane Powell, 1951), *The Strip* (1951, in a cameo as himself), *Athena* (the all-time classic mondo bizarro Metro musical, 1954), *Deep in My Heart* (the Sig Romberg bio, in which Damone goes operetta, 1954), and two Broadway adaptations, *Hit the Deck* and *Kismet* (both 1955). The latter was Damone's best picture appearance, in which he struck a perfect note as the idealistic young Caliph (a role created on Broadway by Richard Kiley, in his own juvenile phase). In this elaborate musical fantasy set in ancient Baghdad, Damone not only gets

Ann Blyth, but he also walks away with all three of the score's great romantic numbers: "Night of My Nights," "Stranger in Paradise," and "This Is My Beloved." Like many singers, including Sinatra, Damone often knocked his picture work and said that he didn't have the faintest idea how to act. Together with the occasionally naive quality of his singing, this actually proved an asset in building the Caliph's character in *Kismet*.

The MGM detour left Damone at the greatest period in his career, a magical ten-year span in which he recorded twelve albums for Columbia and then Capitol Records, nearly all of which have been reissued on English CDs or on Collectables in the United States (customarily with two LPs on each CD). The Columbia period begins with Damone's third million-selling single (after "Again" and "You're Breaking My Heart"), the 1956 "On the Street Where You Live." As with the Caliph's songs in *Kismet*, the naïveté of Freddy Eynsford-Hill in *My Fair Lady* proved a perfect vehicle for Damone's chops and his attitude. In concert, he often told a long, rambling story about how he and producer Mitch Miller had selected this song for him out of the Lerner-Loewe score. In retrospect, the choice seems predestined, and it's entirely fitting that Damone's single biggest hit—possibly the best-remembered song of his entire career—should be not a crass novelty or a jukebox-directed anthem but a show tune on the classiest level. In fact, something else that Damone has in common with Sinatra (and not, say, Cole or Como) is that neither depended on hit singles for a career foundation.

The Columbia and Capitol LPs are the high point of his fifty years in front of the public. There's not a weak album—not even a bad song—in the entire bunch. Damone officially announced that he was on a roll with the first in the series, *That Towering Feeling!* (1956, in which, oddly, "On the Street Where You Live" is not heard, even though the album title is taken from a line of that song). Talk about starting with a bang—it's tempting to call *Towering Feeling!* the single best album of Damone's entire canon. The set consists of twelve great standards rendered with utter sincerity and the sweetest voice imaginable. Even if one hesitates to label Damone a jazz singer or *Towering* a full-fledged jazz album, here he comes pretty close.

In the late fifties, there was a tradition of male pop stars briefly detouring into jazz territory, largely inspired by Sinatra's *In the Wee Small Hours, Close to You*, and the series of "chamber sessions" he'd been doing since the mid-fifties: Consider Billy Eckstine's *Imagination*, Frankie Laine's *Jazz Spectacular*, Dick Haymes's two Capitol albums, Nat Cole's *After Midnight*, and others. In all of these cases (except for the unrelentingly bombastic Mr. Laine), the use of a smaller setting and the showcasing of prominent instrumental soloists made the proceedings at once more intimate and more swinging than the standard pop-singer-with-orchestra format. Damone's *Towering Feeling!* is one of the very best of these, alternating between smallish big band, strings, and rhythm section with alternating soloists—most notably Buck Clayton playing Sweets Edison–like muted trumpet on the opener "You Stepped Out of a Dream" and trombonist Urbie Green on "Wait Till You See Her." Conducted by Tutti Camarata and arranged by a variety of writers, *Towering* was, simply, the most appealing platter that Vic ever Damoaned.

Still, the other eleven albums from the 1956–64 period were not far behind. *Closer than a Kiss* (1958), which takes its title from a little-known Cahn and Van Heusen gem, was a collection of ballads from the baton of Frank DeVol, climaxing in the most romantic reading of Ellington's "Prelude to a Kiss" I ever want to hear. *This Game of Love* (1959), orchestrated by the little-known Robert Smale (and featuring Damone with a model who looks mysteriously like the young Rosemary Clooney on the cover), picks up the tempo somewhat with "Alone Together" and backs Vito with harpsichord, of all things, on "My Romance." "Am I Blue," done with just rhythm section and solo guitar, is flat-out jazzy, as is "I Like the Likes of You," which sports a full-chorus solo by a xylophonist (not a vibraphonist, possibly Tyree Glenn) who has Red Norvo's percussive touch.

The pace gets faster still on *On the Swingin' Side* (conducted by Jack Marshall, 1960). Still, Damone knows his own strengths and weaknesses enough to stick to doing ballads with a beat, as opposed to out and out up-tempo singing in the Sinatra Swingin' Lover tradition. He's most convincing on the rhythmic "When My Sugar Walks Down the Street," which has a verse not even co-composer Gene Austin ever sang. *Young and Lively*, arranged by Johnny Williams (he of future *Star Wars* and *Jaws* fame) completed the Columbia series in 1961.

The six Capitol albums are *Linger Awhile with Vic Damone, Strange Enchantment, The Lively Ones, My Baby Loves to Swing, The Liveliest,* and *On the Street Where You Live. Linger Awhile with Vic Damone* and *My Baby Loves to Swing* both employ guitarist Jack Marshall (best known for his work with Peggy Lee) as musical director, and both picture Vic being fondled by babelicious brunettes on the cover. *Strange Enchantment* and *The Lively Ones* are by Billy May (with Marshall pinch-hitting here and there on the latter set). *The Liveliest* was taped live at Basin Street East "with a band conducted by Joe Parnello," and many of the charts were by Johnny Mandel.

On the Street Where You Live collates fifties show tunes under the baton of Pete King, including some breathtakingly lovely treatments of the major songs from *West Side Story*. Interestingly, Damone's "One Hand, One Heart," the tenderest treatment of that tune I've ever heard, seems only to have been released as a single and not on the album (it is on the

1997 Reader's Digest box *The Legendary Vic Damone*). Even better, in 1963 Damone appeared on *The Judy Garland Show* and sang medleys from *West Side Story*, *Porgy and Bess*, and *Kismet* with Garland herself. Both the duet medleys with her and his solos on these shows make these the finest representations of Damone on film or video.

The one drawback of the Capitol years is that the tracks are often super-short, as if the producers don't trust the listener's attention span or the singer's ability to sustain the listener's attention. The two packages with Jack Marshall remind one of the equally brief cuts on *Latin à la Lee*. (Peg, more than anyone else, could say a whole lot in a very brief amount of time.) Similarly, Marshall's cha-cha-cha chart on "Baby Won't You Please Come Home" from *My Baby Loves to Swing* sounds like a bonus track from *Latin à la Lee*. With the shorter playing time, there are accordingly fewer instrumental solos on the 1961–64 albums. Apart from that, the Capitol discs generally continue the swing-based feel of the 1956–61 albums; almost every track here is in a distinct dance tempo.

The most ballady of the bunch is the exotic *Strange Enchantment*, which, as song titles such as "Beyond the Reef" and "Hawaiian Wedding Song" (as well as two titles from Frank Loesser's Paramount Pictures period, "Strange Enchantment" and "Moon of Manakoora," written for sarong queen Dorothy Lamour) suggest, seems like an attempt to bring Damone into the realm of tiki room titans like Martin Denny and Les Baxter. Yet merely by bringing in Damone and May, Capitol got more solid musical values than either of those lounge masters ever bargained for. *Strange Enchantment* winds up with a masterful "Ebb Tide"—in which the old Vic soars up to a falsetto note at the climax—that's even better than the version he cut for Mercury a decade earlier.

The Lively Ones is mainly a collection of songs based on girls' names, and contains gems such as "Ruby" (which is also an improvement on a tune he had cut earlier for Mercury), Irving Berlin's "Marie," and two of Erno Rapee's twenties movie waltzes, "Charmaine" and "Diane," and what must be the only crooner version of "Cherokee," this time with the "brave Indian warrior" transformed into a maiden. On a similar note, *My Baby Loves to Swing* consists almost entirely of tunes with "baby" in the title, including "Is You Is or Is You Ain't (Ma Baby)." Bobby Troup's "Baby All the Time" gets an odd (but not unappealing) military press roll and lots of modulations, ending with Damone socking it to a real high tonic note. There are also two Cahn and Van Heusen originals, which sound like leftovers from a Sinatra concept album, "My Baby Loves to Swing" and "Make This a Slow Goodbye." *The Liveliest* is generally fine, but it also contains an ill-advised treatment of "Fascinating Rhythm" where anyone short of Mel Tormé himself would get tangled in the

tricky metronomic configuration. Between *Young and Lively*, *The Lively Ones*, and *The Liveliest*, one gets the feeling that Capitol was trying to employ the word "lively" as a slogan for Damone the way that Louis Prima had done with the phrase "The Wildest."

"Fascinating Rhythm" (which was, unfortunately, included in a Capitol Gershwin collection) amounts to one of the few missteps in Damone's golden decade of 1956 to 1964. In 1965, he taped two albums with producer Jimmy Bowen at Warner Bros., *You Were Only Fooling* and *Country Love Songs*, which were less successful either aesthetically or at the cashbox than Bowen's attempts to get the individual members of the Rat Pack back on AM radio at the time. Between 1966 and 1968, Damone switched to RCA for four albums, which, with the exception of the excellent *That Damone Type of Thing* (which tosses an electronic organ into the string and horn mix very nearly as successfully as Sinatra and Riddle do in *Strangers in the Night*), were a decidedly mixed blessing.

Generally, these discs are a combination of new tunes and standards, but one can't always assume that the new tunes are inevitably lousy and the standards are always classy. On *Why Can't I Walk Away?* (the title being a worthy song from the flop musical *Maggie Flynn*), the inclusion of "If You Are but a Dream" gives one hope, but then the track itself utilizes an annoying 16th note backbeat and irritating, R&B-like strings. It sounds as if someone wanted to recast this classically based love song as a rock 'n' roll power ballad. However, the next tune, "Star Dust," is one of the loveliest renditions ever made of that classic ballad. Unfortunately, not all of the really good ideas come out all good, like *Stay with Me*, a collection of Brazilian material in which the better charts are the work of the gifted Don Costa but a significant number of the tracks are butchered by arranger Ernie Freeman.

On the South Side of Chicago is mostly junk and *The Damone Type of Thing* is mostly excellent, although both intermingle good stuff and bad. There's an abundance of foreign songs on *Chicago* (e.g., "You Don't Have to Say You Love Me" aka "Io Che Non Vivo Senza Te," one of Elvis Presley's Italianate hits), a number of which sound like title themes from bad British spy movies. Even worse, "Ciao Compare" amounts to ersatz Eurojunk—a faux-Italian love song from an aborted Broadway musical (Bob Merrill's *Breakfast at Tiffany's*) rendered like a Nashville sing-along such as Nat Cole's "Rambling Rose," with lots of key changes to make the melody sound more memorable. "It Makes No Difference" and "I'll Sleep Tonight" are vaguely psychedelic, vaguely 2/4 in the "New Vaudeville" manner of "Winchester Cathedral."

And so it goes. Damone's recorded work since 1970 has been similarly inconsistent. A 1969 collaboration with future Sinatra conductor Joe Parnello (issued on various labels under various titles) yielded disasters like "MacArthur Park" and triumphs like "They Call the Wind Maria." The trivial content of the "MacArthur" lyrics makes Damone sound silly, particularly when he rambles on about cakes in the rain. "Maria" may refer to an element rather than a person, but Damone can sing about anything with a girl's name in it and make it sound attractive.

As inconsistent as these projects are, Damone's own singing is never a letdown, even when the material is. By the seventies and eighties, listeners came to expect a mixture of quality and questionable songs on Damone's albums and live appearances; suddenly he was trapped in an alien universe in which he was equally likely to sing "How Deep Is Your Love" as "How Deep Is the Ocean?"

In the second half of the nineties Damone reentered our consciousness on a significantly higher level. After a protracted absence from New York, he was suddenly appearing regularly at Carnegie Hall (both in various all-star tribute concerts and in a solo show) and at Rainbow and Stars. He was singing extraordinarily well, and not just for a man on the cusp of seventy—smooth and clear with a voice that had deepened, perhaps, but hadn't exactly darkened. The delivery was smooth and the pitch was effortless, as proved by a package of thirty standards that he recorded in 1996.

These tracks were released by two mail-order labels, Reader's Digest (in a three-CD box along with such welcome early sixties Capitol masters as *The Legendary Vic Damone*) and QVC (on the two-CD *Greatest Love Songs of the Century*). Alas, the string orchestrations of conductor Bebu Silvetti are often excessively Muzaky. (Somehow the dreaded "Feelings," on which Damone had already wasted his energy twice in the eighties, also snuck in here.) On at least a few of the charts, however, such as "Night and Day," which contrasts Damone's pipes with a booming baritone sax and lightly Latin rhythm, the arrangements are as inspired as the singing.

On January 24, 1998, Damone appeared at Carnegie Hall, and, as with most of his shows in the late nineties, used just a rhythm section, with pianist Roy Cohen and the fine jazz drummer Terry Clarke. His ballads were beautiful and his other numbers relaxed and jazzy. Since this concert was officially part of the Concord Jazz Festival, I had hopes that Damone was making a new album for Concord Records in the style of Rosemary Clooney's Concords, with rhythm section and perhaps one or two horns—Ken Peplowski on reeds, and maybe Randy Sandke on trumpet; such an album would have been very much in the tradition of Cole's *After Midnight* and Damone's own *That Towering Feeling!* It didn't happen. But it would have provided the perfect note on which to close one of the really admirable careers in American pop singing.

In 2002, Damone gave what was announced as his final performance, and in 2009 he released an autobiography, *Singing Was the Easy Part*.

Bobby Darin (1936–1973)

When Bobby Darin died of a heart condition at age thirty-seven on December 20, 1973, *Time* magazine resurrected an oft-repeated boast the singer himself had made fourteen years earlier in a *Life* magazine profile. His goal, the then-twenty-three-year-old pop star had said, was "to establish myself as a legend by the time I'm 25." *Time*'s obituary writer concluded, "He never achieved [this] outspoken ambition." Wrong! A legend is in fact about the only thing we can agree that Darin actually was, other than the most electrifying entertainer of his generation.

Rock star and friend Dion DiMucci has described Darin as "an original." This is no less a misinformed judgment than that of the Luce empire's anonymous hack. Bobby Darin was many things, perhaps too many, but an "original" was not one of them. In fact, he was everything but: a teenybopper idol, a crooner, a jazz swinger, a hillbilly, a rhythm and blues shouter, an Oscar-nominated movie actor, a cowboy, a TV personality, a songwriter, a political activist, a grassroots folkie, a psychedelic hippy-dippy, a composer, a multi-instrumentalist, a music publisher, a producer and impresario, a Vegas lounge lizard, or all of the above. An original? No. Rather he was pop's first great mix-master, the first to explore the varying strains of pop music, sometimes separately, often bringing two or more of them together.

Like the Borg of *Star Trek*, Darin went around assimilating the styles of whatever truly legendary entertainer happened to strike his fancy. At different times in his career—sometimes in different songs in the same show—Darin could be Frank Sinatra, Buddy Holly, Bob Dylan, Ray Charles, and all three guys named Louis (Armstrong, Jordan, and Prima). Yet somehow he was never more himself than when he was being someone else, almost always with enough vitality and swing to equal his inspirations. The late Harriet Wasser, Darin's onetime press agent, told me that the singer thought of himself, culturally, as much Jewish as Italian; it wouldn't have been surprising for him to refer to his music as a *patchkarye*—a polyglot of styles through which he was somehow able to create something that, if not "original," was undeniably new.

Darin dabbled in every genre short of opera and zarzuela, but in the end, his major achievement seems to have been rejuvenating classic pop with the rabble-rousing energy of rhythm and blues. In a sense, he was like a cultural commentator able to draw connections between various styles. For a brief shining moment he presided over a détente in the cultural war known as the Generation Gap, in which the two sides were presided over not by Elvis Presley (who treated his elders with respect) but by Alan

Freed, who encouraged the youth of America to listen only to what he told them was "their music," and Frank Sinatra, who, rather than trying to make peace with the other side, characterized all those who listened to the new youth pop as "side-burned juvenile delinquents." Darin was the first to build on the elements that the two factions had in common, that both Sinatra and Presley (in performance, though not offstage) had: a swagger and an attitude that were highly informed by erotic energy and the blues. Darin's own swagger, his cockiness, were equal parts Sinatra and Elvis. Unlike Presley, Darin showed his respect for Sinatra by using his *Songs for Swingin' Lovers!* as a starting point for his own best music; but also unlike Presley, who never said a bad word about Sinatra (even in private or off the record, apparently), Darin dissed the Chairman in print by boasting that he was going to do it better. Darin's bad-ass attitude can be described as being equal parts the offstage Sinatra and the onstage Elvis.

Sinatra supposedly said he would send Darin to do his prom dates. Obviously he recognized in him something of his own youthful zeal and obnoxiousness. There's a late concert where Sinatra sings one of his trademark songs, "It Was a Very Good Year," with an ad-libbed opening line: "When I was seventeen / I was a pain in the ass." (He then asks the audience, "Isn't everyone at seventeen?") Sinatra seems to have regarded Darin as a younger, pain-in-the-ass version of himself.

The word "diverse" hardly begins to describe Darin. As biographer Jeff Bleiel pointed out, a listener unfamiliar with Darin's work could sample the albums *Hello, Dolly!* and *Commitment* and have no idea they were by the same artist. Sinatra could be himself with Count Basie or Antonio Carlos Jobim, Crosby likewise with Louis Jordan or Jascha Heifetz. With Darin it was never an issue—he never had to worry about being himself. The question was which one of his selves to be. Darin was the original method actor of pop: When you look in his eyes you see a cowboy, a doo-wopper, a Swingin' Lover. You see everything but Bobby Darin.

He was born Walden Robert Cassotto in the Bronx on May 14, 1936. Even his childhood was filled with excitement and danger of the sort that makes the recent (and almost perversely disappointing) movie of his life look tame by comparison. (For starters, his uncle-stepfather was named Charlie Maffia.) He grew up being told that his actual birth mother was his sister, that his grandmother was his mother, and to this day no one knows the identity of his father.

At age eight, Darin was stricken with rheumatic fever, which doctors predicted would end his life before he reached sixteen. "You better believe he was a man with a mission," said his son Dodd Darin (born in 1961). "He had not a moment to waste. All [his] drive was because he realized he was not going to have a full life." Perhaps this obsession with death

accounts for Darin's gleefully morbid "Artificial Flowers," "Clementine," and his hall-of-fame anthem, "Mack the Knife," which were characterized by writer Darcy Sullivan as "a victory shout into the nuclear abyss by a little guy with a date-stamped heart."

The teenaged Darin learned several instruments as well as singing and songwriting (which he practiced with fellow Bronx boy Don Kirschner). These talents contributed to his early rock 'n' roll hits, beginning with his own "Splish Splash" and "Queen of the Hop." To a certain extent, the concept of mix-mastering is a foundation element of rock 'n' roll. One of Darin's contemporaries, the songwriter and occasional singer Neil Sedaka, has elaborated on the genesis of his 1959 hit "Oh Carol." He made a rough survey of all the hit singles from all over the world and combined their most memorable components: He borrowed the vamp from this one, the break from that one, the string line from a third, the horn passage from yet another one, and put it all together and crafted a paint-by-numbers hit. Stitched together, Frankenstein-like, from the bodies of other people's hits, "Oh Carol," naturally, got on the charts; some might even say it was good pop music.

Even in Darin's earliest rock 'n' roll work, there's an element of collage. The breakthrough hits, "Splish Splash" and "Queen of the Hop," are both replete with references to other early rock hits, like Little Richard's "Good Golly, Miss Molly" and Buddy Holly's "Peggy Sue"—there's also an homage to Dick Clark's *American Bandstand* in obvious hopes that Darin's records would turn up on that trendsetting program. "Early in the Morning" was so much like Buddy Holly that Holly himself had a hit with it. "Bullmoose" owes much to Bo Diddley's bump-and-grind, while the backing on "Multiplication" sounds exactly like Ray Charles's band, and the background riff could be a cousin of "What'd I Say?" (Darin exploited his ability to mimic Ray Charles for a whole album, *Bobby Darin Sings Ray Charles*, in which he doesn't pay homage to the Genius so much as mimic him—and very convincingly at that.)

"Even then, you could tell that Darin had more on his wish list than being a teen idol," as Dion DiMucci further noted. Darin, who loved old-school show tunes as much as he did the blues, taped his first album of standards, *That's All*, in 1959. The set yielded "Mack the Knife," one of the biggest-selling singles of all time, the overwhelming success of which earned Darin two Grammy Awards and a headliner's berth in Las Vegas. From there he hopped to Hollywood and a film acting career, which began with 1961's *Come September* (in which he met his first wife, teen actress Sandra Dee, who described him as "the brightest person I've ever known") and climaxed with his Oscar-nominated role in *Captain Newman, M.D.* (1963).

When Darin switched from youth pop to adult pop, one wonders if he was less switching genres than adding colors to his palette of personalities: not just a little Buddy Holly here and some Ray Charles there. Now he could be the whole Rat Pack, swinging like Sinatra, goofy like Dean Martin, and versatile like Sammy Davis. (Like Davis, he incorporated his multi-instrumental skills into his act as well as his ability to do impressions.) Singer Cary Hoffman has speculated that Darin's central role model could easily have been Buddy Greco as much as Sinatra. Darin, like Greco, never had the chops of a Sinatra; neither of them could sustain notes like the Voice, so the key question for them both was how and when to cut each note off. Sinatra had a lot of options; Darin and Greco didn't, yet they always managed to cut off their notes in a way that accentuated the positive, swinging beat.

The basic template for Darin's entry into classic pop was Sinatra's *Songs for Swingin' Lovers!*, specifically "I've Got You Under My Skin." The most spectacular example of this was "Mack the Knife." The two records have the same idea: starting slow and building, building, building to a musical/emotional climax. Yet Darin and arranger Richard Wess brought much that was new to the mix on "Mack," one element being the shuffle rhythm, which he could have picked up from Louis Jordan, Louis Prima, or the comparatively obscure white, Philadelphia-based bandleader Jan Savitt.

Another is the old showbiz trick of modulations. Sinatra, like most members of the big band and/or jazz fraternity, achieved most of his excitement without having to raise the key a half-step for added effect. I've met purists who regard the act of modulation as something of an artificial stimulant—a musical steroid. Darin, on the other hand, modulates copiously and shamelessly: "Mack" goes up a half-step with every 8-bar segment. The trick became a signature: "Artificial Flowers," "Hello, Dolly!" (which ends with a variant on "Mack's" tag, "Look out ol' Dolly's back!"), "Gyp the Cat" (Darin's own bald-faced "Mack" rip-off), "Mame" (still another high-octane show tune), "Beyond the Sea," and "Roses of Picardy" (more hyper-swinging updates of old European standards) were all songs for modulating lovers. By the mid-sixties, Darin was throwing in gratuitous modulations even where they weren't needed, as in "Work Song" and "The Good Life."

All those key changes and the repeats of the "Mack" formula start to seem boring after a while (sort of in the way that one or two sex scenes in a movie can be exciting, but too many dull the senses). Perhaps boredom with this device led to his eventually deserting the Great American Songbook idiom. Instead of following Sinatra's example, of consolidating his accomplishments and becoming a better version of himself, Darin chose to keep flitting from genre to genre without doing as well in any one of them as he might have done. He just wouldn't commit. Perhaps in the long run his versatility was a liability rather than an asset.

Yet the evidence shows that he could have been one of the most essential singers of the Great American Songbook. While his earlier albums with Richard Wess are fine, his best album in the genre is easily the 1962 meeting with Billy May, *Oh Look at Me Now* (his first project in a three-year association with Capitol Records), which is a deep, adult project all the way. In fact, there's even a key change in "A Nightingale Sang in Berkeley Square"—but unlike the modulation in "Gyp the Cat," it hardly seems like an immature affectation. (The song has a key change of its own, when it goes down a minor third, from Eb to G in the bridge in concert key and then back again. May enhances it with a customary shift between choruses.) Darin recorded a total of fifteen tracks with May for the *Oh Look* sessions, which, to the best of my knowledge, have yet to be released all together in one CD package. These include several tracks that weren't issued at all until thirty years later, as well as the very exciting "As Long as I'm Singin'," a self-penned, autobiographical single that borrows chord changes from "Let's Fall in Love."

"Mack," as I've said, was one of the biggest hits in the history of the record business—for the last time in American pop, someone had found a way to unite the generations: the parents who watched Frank Sinatra on TV and the kids who listened to Alan Freed. Darin's great years were from 1959's *That's All* to 1966's *In a Broadway Bag*. (Although both albums were for Atlantic, there was a three-year sojourn at Capitol in the middle of that period.) Not everything he did in those eight years was golden, but it was the period in which he did most of his best work. Sometimes he sang straight Sinatra-style pop standards, sometimes he laced the standards idiom with rock 'n' roll elements, and sometimes he went in other directions, like folk and country.

Often his mixing of the adult and youth idioms was done in a very hip, very entertaining fashion, as when he turned out a series of updated revisions of classic Tin Pan Alley tunes, such as a version of "Bill Bailey" made with only a rhythm section and a heavy shuffle beat. There are also more insidiously rockish treatments of "You Must Have Been a Beautiful Baby," "Minnie the Moocher," and "There's No Sweet Man That's Worth the Salt of My Tears." Wildest of all is an unbelievably bizarre "Nature Boy," with a wildly chanting femme backup chorus, which can only be described as Middle Eastern doo-wop.

Yet on other occasions Darin was clearly bending over backward to try to please everybody. *You're the Reason I'm Living* (1963) and *I Wanna Be Around* (1964) can only be described as middle-of-the-road music in the most accurate and the worst sense of the term. People who don't know what they're talking about have described Tony Bennett and Peggy Lee as "MOR," whereas they make their own music their own way, without regard to what road anyone thinks they ought to be on. Darin, however, is trying to walk down the middles of many roads. *Reason I'm Living* is halfway between country and Muzak, the title track being almost a paraphrase of the Ray Charles smash "I Can't Stop Loving You." *I Wanna Be Around* goes from contemporary hits to old standards rendered rockishly with 16th note phrasing. "Venice Blue" from that album (a surprisingly mediocre song by Charles Aznavour with English text by Gene Lees) is exactly the kind of thing that might have been sung by Al Martino.

Darin was actually making better traditional pop in his early excursions into folk music, *Earthy!* and *Golden Folk Hits*, two Capitol albums from 1963 that were recently reissued on a twofer (on Exemplar Music). Here he's concentrating on the showbizzy sides of the folk boom, and, unlike what he does on his later, ill-advised detour through protest music, here he is still focused on entertaining his audiences. Later on he would try to be Bob Dylan, but in 1963, although he includes Dylan's "Blowin' in the Wind," he does just as good a job at being Harry Belafonte (even to posing like him on the album cover) as he already had done in becoming the Chairman and the Genius.

Some of these mixtures, like "Nature Boy," are ludicrous—at times enjoyably so—while others, like "Lazy River," are superb. His treatment of the Carmichael classic, done around the same time that Ray Charles put Carmichael's "Georgia" back on everyone's mind, is a thoroughly successful slice of standard tune revisionism, with a beat that perfectly straddles swing and R&B. "Clementine" takes a traditional American folk song and shuffle-swings it, much the way both Sinatra and Ella Fitzgerald would soon be swinging "Ol' MacDonald." There's a TV appearance in which Darin introduces his version of a Ray Charles hit by saying, "I got a woman, way over town, she's good to me, and feeds me *kreplach*"—a wonderfully silly line in which he combines black, Italian, and Jewish references, but he could only juggle so many balls in the air for so long.

As Tony Bennett (supposedly) once elaborated, there was at least one thing that Darin couldn't do very well: "I used to worry about this guy," Bennett said, "until I found out he couldn't sing slow." The matter of Darin's ballads is indeed a problem. His whole shtick, whether he's being Buddy Greco or Buddy Holly, is rhythm, and without that steady pulse, he's lost. Ballads are the weakest link in Darin's chain. It's hard to tell whether his heart might not be in the right place (a deliberately ironic description, considering his cardiac situation) or if he just doesn't know what to do when he doesn't have the beat to egg him on.

At times it seems that he goes to elaborate lengths to avoid singing a slow ballad from the heart. Take his interpretation of the Bernstein-Sondheim "Somewhere": While it may not be a swinger, he inflates it into an anthem and loses whatever tenderness that another singer might have brought to it—

not through rhythm, but through sheer size. The way Darin sings it, it's less a song of boy-girl love than a rallying cry for a people, like the theme from *Exodus*.

There are exceptions—some credible conventional ballads like "The Curtain Falls," which he sang only on *Live at the Flamingo* (a set recorded in 1963 and not issued until nearly forty years later) and which uses showbiz terms as a metaphor for a relationship in the tradition that culminated in "Send in the Clowns." Exceptions aside, by universal consensus Darin wasn't much of a ballad singer.

Having broken through as a rock 'n' roller, Darin supercharged his career in 1959–60 by graduating to adult pop standards. His "defection," as it were, was a factor that drove a nail in the coffin of rock 'n' roll, which was a fairly dead music by 1959—by this time it seemed like virtually the whole first generation of rock 'n' roll stars were either in the army, in jail, or in the ground. The early sixties were rock 'n' roll's most fallow period—the dead spot between Elvis and the Beatles—and Darin was the music's most high-profile deserter. Still, he kept some rock and blues elements in his music even when singing standards with Billy May; and when rock made a comeback in the mid-sixties, it seemed obvious that Darin would himself come back to it as well. But before he left the traditional songbook, he made three more notable albums (all of songs from recent films and shows): *The Shadow of Your Smile*, *In a Broadway Bag*, and *Bobby Darin Sings Doctor Dolittle*.

The first is a mixed bag—lots of singers had done and would do albums of movie songs, from Tony Bennett's *The Movie Song Album*, Frank Sinatra's *Academy Award Winners*, Steve Lawrence's *Academy Award Losers* and an even better collection of movie songs with Eydie Gormé. Darin took the gimmick a step further in recording all five songs that had been nominated for Academy Awards from films released in 1965. It was a clever marketing strategy that resulted in lots of radio play and sales in the few months between the nomination and the ceremony. Unfortunately, that side of the album doesn't hold up very well, particularly "The Sweetheart Tree" (from *The Great Race*), despite a lyric by Johnny Mercer, and "The Ballad of Cat Ballou" (which worked for Nat Cole in the movie *Cat Ballou* but not for anyone else). Side two of the album is a blast, though, containing five strong swingers, plus the semi-slow, semi-sweet "Rainin'" (with a beautiful tenor sax solo by Eddie Miller).

In a Broadway Bag and *Doctor Dolittle* are both much more skewed toward balladry than previous Darin product. In a format somewhat unique for the LP era, *Broadway* consists of one side of six swingers, starting with "Mame," the latest entry in the "Mack"-"Dolly" stakes, and ending with one of the great self-affirmation anthems of the decade of self-affirmativeness: "Don't Rain on My Parade" (the way Darin sings it, you won't be tempted even to drizzle). Side two, surprisingly, is entirely ballads. The *Doctor Dolittle* album mixes fast and slow arrangements, but all from the same score. On these two albums, we finally get a sense that at last the singer is developing something that might be considered a Bobby Darin ballad style. Just as his up-tempo style is based on various elements of other icons he likes and assimilates, starting with Sinatra but not limited to him, the developing Darin ballad style is also built on Sinatra, Ray Charles, and others.

On "Once upon a Time," "Try to Remember," "I'll Only Miss Her When I Think of Her," he's working toward a romantic approach that's muscular yet tender. The two songs that work the best for me just happen to be a pair of songs that other singers hardly ever recorded, both from flop ventures, "The Other Half of Me" from *I Had a Ball* and *Dolittle's* "Something in Your Smile." He could never be as open and as vulnerable as Sinatra or Bennett, and he isn't trying to be, yet he's clearly on to something. Given time, he could conceivably have perfected a ballad style that might have made a lasting contribution to the literature of the Great American Songbook. He might have become a superior balladeer in his forties. He could have been a contender.

The one thing that Darin did not have, however, was time. Time in the sense of rhythm, yes, but not time in the sense of life expectancy. He would make five more albums after *Dolittle*, all of which were variations on the rock-folk-soul thing. He became heavily involved with the concept of protest music and with writing his own songs, which are both didactic textually and uninspired musically. His 1963 detours into folk-pop were solidly entertaining, but his late sixties protest music is heavy-handed and boring when it isn't irritating. He was trying to be Bob Dylan—even billing himself as Bob Darin—but he shows no comprehension of what Dylan's best music was all about.

It's our loss that he abandoned the standards-and-ballads idiom just when he seemed to be on the verge of getting it right. It's an even greater loss that he died, at the age of thirty-seven, before he could switch genres once again and return to the idiom of Johnny Mercer and Sinatra, an idiom he could finally have made his own. As we've seen, Darin was told by a doctor that he would never live to see sixteen; he got the laugh on that doctor by about twenty-one years. In a sense, his whole career was a bonus from God.

Even from beyond the grave, Darin's vivacity is impossible to resist. His finger-snapping, tie-loosening, Swingin' Lover personality, powered by what producer Ahmet Ertegun describes as his "profound and genuine blues base," was potent enough to resonate through whatever stylistic wardrobe he chose to dress it in. Renewed interest in the singer inspired two boxed retrospectives, Rhino's four-CD *As Long as I'm Singing* and Reader's Digest's triple *Bobby Darin*. There have also been several books—

Dodd Darin's very personal *Dream Lovers: The Magnificent Shattered Lives of Bobby Darin and Sandra Dee*, and two standard biographies, *Borrowed Time* and *Roman Candle*, and Jeff Bleiel's professional study *That's All! Bobby Darin on Record, Stage and Screen*. (There's also *Beyond the Sea*, Kevin Spacey's dreadful biopic of 2004.)

Darin's ongoing popularity might have surprised even him. In the twenty-first century, he is a disproportionately large influence, especially on such younger Italo-styled boy crooners as Tony DeSare, Peter Cincotti, and especially Michael Bublé. "Bobby didn't have Nat King Cole's voice and he didn't have James Dean's looks," as Darin's longtime colleague Nick Venet put it, "but he would step out onstage and become everything you ever thought was a star."

Sammy Davis Jr. (1925–1990)

Heard any good jokes lately? Sometimes it seems that Sammy Davis Jr. was so determined to entertain his audiences with songs and jokes that he eventually decided to become a joke himself. Lord! The man was multiculti all by himself, a built-in ethnic joke that, even decades after his death, no one can resist. Back in the Reagan era, Johnny Carson told one of the most memorable: When James Watt, secretary of the interior, made a politically incorrect statement that managed to offend blacks, Jews, and the handicapped in a single sentence, Carson quipped, "Sammy Davis Jr. is not too thrilled with this guy." In a spoken ad-lib on *Live at the Sands* (1967), Davis paraphrases a famous quote from James Baldwin: "That's all I need—to be a colored, Jewish fegela!" Here, Davis makes fun of the idea that he might be gay for the same reason that Baldwin had said that the last thing he needed was to be Jewish (after being black, gay, "short and ugly"). Davis's best line, however, may have been, "I'm black, Jewish, and Puerto Rican. When I check into a neighborhood, *everybody* moves out!"

In the big picture of Davis's career, these one-liners about his polyethnicity offer not only minor yuks but clues as to the actual identity of the Great Entertainer. This concept of multiple identities is central to any understanding of Davis. As he said, he was an African American whose mother was of Cuban descent (not Puerto Rican, as he claimed), who later converted to Judaism, and who lost one of his eyes in a car crash. On another level, he was a professional dancer who also sang well enough to become one of the top pop vocalists of all time (and a major chart hit maker), an actor and significant film and Broadway star, as well as a world-class impressionist and a multi-instrumentalist musician. If he had told the world that he was also a South American Hindu who could play the spoons, make balloon animals, and fly through the air with the greatest of ease, no one would have been surprised.

Davis anticipated the era when the concept of self-transformation became a style unto itself: He foreshadows Michael Jackson and Madonna, who had little to say musically but sustained the public's interest by constantly altering their images—Madonna by dyeing and redyeing her pubic hair, Jackson by, as another joke goes, being born a poor black boy who made himself into a rich white woman. The critic Clive James has, in fact, characterized the eighties, the moment of Jackson's and Madonna's greatest popularity, as the decade of transformations—an era whose leading icons constantly reshaped their images. In fact, if memory serves, the eighties was the era when we started to refer to these performers not as "singers," "entertainers," or even "superstars," but as "icons," which is a distinctly visual term.

Two of Davis's influences, Frank Sinatra and Nat King Cole, had sustained their careers by reinventing themselves at key junctures. But Davis, and later his virtual protégé, Bobby Darin, were the first major entertainers to make a point of assuming multiple identities—not only over the course of their whole careers but often in a single evening. Davis's style wasn't mere quick-change artistry, but a process of continual artistic metamorphosis. I don't mean merely in terms of surface considerations—although he did switch to hippie ephemera and let his afro expand to the point where it added another foot to his diminutive height in the psychedelic sixties—but in the content of his music. As with Bobby Darin, Davis's virtuoso versatility was at once a blessing and a curse—he could do so many things so well that he never seemed to settle on who he really was.

In Davis's music, transformation was the most direct kind of artistic renewal. It's also a key element of the experience of immigrants and minorities in the New World: In a nation of immigrants, adaptability was a necessity, as one ethnic or national group followed another along the assimilation food chain. An amateur psychologist would also put forward the notion that Davis's talent was an extension of his small physical stature: In Hollywood, tall, dark, and handsome guys can just stand there, but five-foot-three types like Davis had to do something to attract attention.

Davis was a charter member of Hollywood's pint-sized dynamo club—a fraternity that includes such multitalented near-midgets as Mickey Rooney, Mel Tormé, and Buddy Rich, all of whom were child prodigies who grew up to act, sing, dance, write (songs, books, or both), do stand-up comedy, and play several instruments, including drums; in addition, both Davis and Rooney were accomplished impressionists. Where you or I can summon up Jimmy Durante, Jimmy Cagney, or Jimmy Stewart with an "inky dinky doo," "you dirty rat," or "well, uh, ah . . . ," no one but Davis could flawlessly replicate both the vocal and terpsichoreal styles of Fred Astaire.

His gift for mimicry was another clue to his musical schizophrenia: Rather than be overshadowed by some of the *machers* he consorted with, Davis, like a musical Zelig, *became* them. He hung out with Sinatra, and he wanted to be Sinatra—and not just onstage, either. That is, when he wasn't being Nat Cole, Frankie Laine, or Huckleberry Hound. Being other people was easy—Davis already had the raw talent, it was easy for him to absorb their styles; the hard part was being himself. Davis had enough trouble figuring out who he was even before he started standing in the shadow of the most dominant personality of twentieth-century popular culture, a problem that then got mixed up in the confusion caused by his multiple racial and ethnic affiliations. A standard nightclub joke at the time (preserved for us by that acute cultural historian Earl Wilson) went that "Sammy isn't sure whether he wants to be the black Sinatra or the Jewish Sinatra." It's a rude (not to mention non-PC) gag—and precisely the kind you'd find in one of the Rat Pack's routines or one of Davis's voluminous autobiographies.

Davis wrote three books, the first of which, the enormous *Yes I Can*, makes him the Marcel Proust of showbiz. No other superstar (certainly not Sinatra) had such a capacity for self-reflection: He details his thoughts and reactions to a thousand events and micro-events. The book is touching, harrowing, shallow, and self-congratulatory in equal parts. A year before the book was published, that title, "Yes I Can," was first heard as the name of a song written for him by Charles Strouse and Lee Adams, originally as part of the score to *Golden Boy* but dropped before that musical opened on Broadway. Davis's own career peaked even as the civil rights movement was gaining momentum, and his cry of "Yes I Can"—both musical and literary—inspired the whole world. It would be hard to imagine anyone seeking to climb to the top of the show business heap with more strikes against him: He was born poor and black at a time when an African American had as much chance of becoming an international superstar as he did of walking on the moon. In addition, as noted, he was short and possessed something less than movie star looks. Born a member of a racial minority, he would eventually join a religious one as well. Yet as we've seen, his assets were also considerable, meaning his talents and, equally important, his tenacity.

Unlike Sinatra, Davis did not graduate from a big band. Rather, like Nat King Cole, he came out of a trio. This was the Will Mastin Trio, earlier the Will Mastin Gang, with which, for the first thirty years of his life, the young Sammy barnstormed all over the country in the company of his father, Sam Davis Sr., and his unrelated "uncle," Will Mastin. Born in 1925, in Harlem, Davis had little contact with his mother, who outlived him by ten years (dying at close to one hundred in 2000), being raised first by his grandmother, then by his dad on the road. His father and uncle shielded him from racism, which actually worked against him when he discovered it in a brutal way (or rather, bigotry discovered him) during World War II. He served as part of an early integrated unit in the army—and found out that "integrated" hardly meant enlightened. (The bigots made Davis's hitch such a living hell that he frequently wished he could have joined his brothers in the segregated services—integration be damned.)

Embittered by the war, Davis was more determined than ever to become a star. By the late forties the act was called "the Will Mastin Trio featuring Sammy Davis Jr."; and thanks partly to influential friends like Sinatra and Rooney, the group gradually climbed the showbiz ladder. The breakthrough came in 1952 when the WM3 opened for Janis Paige at Ciro's in Hollywood; Paige was a Broadway and movie star, but she couldn't compete with "three strong, hungry men giving the show of our lives," as Davis later wrote. "It was the most glorious moment I'd ever known."

Even after Davis became widely acknowledged—by both the media and the showbiz community—as the most dynamic young entertainer around, every step upward was a fight. Yet he was doing TV variety shows, playing the top clubs, starring in two Broadway smashes (*Mr. Wonderful* and *Golden Boy*, plus the hit revival of *Stop the World—I Want to Get Off*), and handling dramatic as well as musical roles in film. If he had been a white entertainer, it would all have come a lot easier, but if he'd been white, he wouldn't have been Sammy.

Davis's earliest records, made for Capitol in 1949, were generally "novelty" throwaways that emphasized his tap dancing (as on "Smile, Darn Ya, Smile"), his impressions ("Can't You See I've Got the Blues?"), and more or less everything but his singing. It would be thirty years before the cycle would turn and Davis would make the decision to abandon all of his "sidelines" and concentrate exclusively on singing. Though "Smile, Darn Ya, Smile" is one of his earliest records, earlier performances do exist on film. The most surprising of these is a pair of 1933 Vitaphone two-reelers in which the seven-year-old Sammy appears with Lita Grey, a singer famous for being married to Charlie Chaplin, and Ethel Waters, famous for being Ethel Waters. He can also be seen on a 1947 Paramount short featuring the Mastin trio.

It's not for a while that he sounds anything like Sammy Davis. On "Smile, Darn Ya, Smile," with its overemphasized hard consonants, the twenty-three-year-old Davis sounds as if he's still imitating Billy Daniels or Frankie Laine. "Gypsy in My Soul," one of four sides made for an obscure operation that rereleased these tracks (combined with a bunch by former Ellingtonian Joya Sherrill) in a million supermarkets, shows the influence of Billy Eckstine, particularly in the low vowels. Indeed, Davis was so anonymous on these early sides that Capitol could easily get away with billing him pseudonymically

on the labels as "Shorty Muggins" and "Charlie Green."

Finally, on "Hey, There," made not long after he began recording for Decca in 1954, Davis starts to sound like Davis, a fact the public responded to in sufficient numbers to make this *Pajama Game* show tune his first hit. The Adler-Ross song and "Birth of the Blues" (both on his first album, *Starring Sammy Davis Jr.*) would both become Davis perennials.

Although he made "Birth of the Blues" his own, the arrangement is clearly inspired by Frank Sinatra's 1952 recording; both treatments are very dramatic, employing exaggerated brass obbligatos at the end of each line. The chart fits Davis's high-energy style more comfortably than it did Sinatra. Not yet thirty years old, Davis still seems as if he's working to stir up excitement. He's got to nurse it and rehearse it, but soon he would reach the point where it would just happen, with the illusion of spontaneity. Davis would continue to perform these songs long into the Summit years, during which time Sinatra and Dean Martin would "spontaneously" supplement his voice with theirs on the harmony line "better forget her," Davis's famous comeback after the bridge on "Hey, There."

A lot of things were happening at once in 1954 and 1955—his signing with Decca, the first albums, the first hits—and this was only the beginning. That same year, he was nearly killed in the car crash in which he lost an eye, and it was in the hospital afterward that he began the course of his conversion to Judaism. He entered the mid-fifties as one member of a dancing trio and came out a recording star; he was only the fourth major black male star to regularly make it to the mainstream hit chart, after Armstrong, Cole, and Eckstine.

Davis came into his own vocally partly through the influence of Sinatra. Just as Duke Ellington once encouraged his "boy" singer, Herb Jeffries, to become himself through imitating Bing Crosby, Davis found himself by studying the Chairman. The two had known each other for almost ten years, but they became closer after the accident. (Sinatra was not, however, the first celebrity friend to visit Davis in the aftermath—that was Eddie Cantor. Sinatra famously had a phobia regarding hospitals and doctors.)

Davis was the keenest of Sinatra's students. Generally there are two camps of singers who followed in the blue-eyed footsteps: first, the "pretty" voices, like Vic Damone and Jack Jones, who have beautiful pipes and Frank-like phrasing but who could never approach Sinatra in terms of animating a song's lyrics; then Tony Bennett and Mel Tormé, who possess comparable capacity for interpreting words and music, but who, although they don't sound anything like him, could never have happened if Sinatra hadn't happened first.

Davis fits into both categories—at times he sings deliberately like Sinatra, using very similar phraseology, yet he also maintains the individuality of a Bennett or a Tormé. Most importantly, the greatest gift the "Leader" handed down to his most reverent follower is an unfailing sense of excitement. Nothing that either Sinatra or Davis does is ever done by rote; there are a million things going on in every line they sing—numerous tiny pauses, unexpectedly emphasized syllables, shadings, and accentings, and no end of surprising twists and turns. No matter what Davis or Sinatra do, they never fail to keep your attention riveted.

At one point in *Yes I Can*, Davis reports how Sinatra cautioned him to work harder at his singing and also to avoid sounding too similar to Old Blue himself. But in terms of Davis's efforts strictly as a singer, as Marty Paich, the best of his many arranger-conductor-collaborators, has confirmed, Davis was perpetually both inspired and overwhelmed by Sinatra. A few of his fifties Decca sides contain specific Sinatra references and mannerisms: "All the Way," "They Can't Take That Away from Me," and "Just One of Those Things."

Other hallmarks of the Sammy Style were already being introduced. Throughout "Birth of the Blues," he seems just on the edge of a shout, as if he's only a few decibels away from tearing his tonsils out. As early as "Gypsy in My Soul" (on the *Sammy Jumps with Joya* collection) we can hear the beginnings of a vocal device that we might call the "Sammy Surge." Instead of belting out a note, like a gospel (or even a musical comedy) singer, Davis developed a trick of starting with a pitch and pushing it up a half-step or so even while he continues to hold it, surging into a grace note without cutting off from the original note. Examples of the Sammy Surge can be heard through any random sampling of his work, as when he stretches "although the la-augh's on me" in "Bewitched" (on *Mood to Be Wooed*) and elsewhere on "My Romance" (on *Sammy Davis Jr. Belts the Best of Broadway*), "As Long as She Needs Me" (on *As Long as She Needs Me*), "Blame It on My Youth" (*The Wham of Sam*), and many other numbers. There's even a variation on the Sammy Surge on his 1972 blockbuster hit "The Candy Man" (on *Sammy Davis Jr. Now*).

The opposite of the Sammy Surge is a no less ingenious knack for emphasizing a word by driving it through the floor with a super-low pedal note. He hits those dark notes most dramatically at several points on "*you*'ve been locked in his arms" on "Change Partners" (*Sammy Awards*) and on "With a Song in My Heart" (*That's All!*) when he gets to the lines "*when* the music swells" and "it tells me you're standing *near*." Much as Davis worshipped at the shrine of Saint Sinatra, this device, reminiscent of Al Hibbler, shows his willingness to experiment occasionally with the kind of vocal colors that were outside Sinatra's stylistic realm.

Between 1955 and 1960, he recorded roughly fifteen albums for Decca. Many were random collec-

tions of songs; some, like *Mr. Entertainment* and *Sammy Awards,* were very loosely themed to the idea that since Davis could do anything, the lack of a specific concept was concept enough. Some were also Sinatra-style concept albums, and packages like *Sammy Swings* were even more upbeat and frenetic than *Songs for Swingin' Lovers!* or *A Swingin' Affair!* During the Decca period, he recorded two treatments of "That Old Black Magic," which, like "Birth of the Blues," was a showstopper for him in clubs. The first, from 1954, is wild enough, but the second, three years later, is so frantic it almost borders on the psychotic. He throws in random, irreverent quotations from all over the map of pop culture, from Western movie clichés to children's taunts, and is so hyper that the performance as a whole seems like Tourette's syndrome set to music.

The 1957 *It's All Over but the Swingin'* is a marvelous album, inspired by Sinatra but not directly imitating him; conceptually, it's sort of halfway between *Wee Small Hours* and *Songs for Young Lovers* in that it consists of torch songs—songs about the end of a love affair—but done medium-up-tempo, with a pronounced swing. Our protagonist here has been wounded in love but is trying to chase away his blues by confronting them with rhythm. I can't think of a case where Sinatra ever attempted a whole album of swinging-but-sad songs. The topper is a five-minute reading of "Can't Help Lovin' Dat Man" ("Gal"), which seems kind of hokey at first but allows Davis to build to a big bluesy climax—behind which a Sweets Edison–like trumpeter plays a tightly muted obbligato that quotes "Ol' Man River," an even more famous song from the *Show Boat* score.

Davis's other most memorable albums find him going in directions that suggest he learned the proper message from Sinatra, as if the man he called the Leader had said to him, "Do concept albums like I do, but find your own concepts." He made a voice-and-guitar project in the fifties, *Mood to Be Wooed*, with Mundell Lowe, and another in the sixties, *Sammy Davis Jr. Sings, Laurindo Almeida Plays*, an album with the Basie band for Decca (*I Gotta Right to Swing!*) and one for Reprise (*Our Shining Hour*), and his first live album for Decca (*Sammy Davis Jr. at Town Hall*) before taping a whole slew of them in the sixties, including two at the Sands alone (both of which are wonderful). He certainly beat Sinatra to the punch, live-album-wise, but then Sinatra was among the last major artists to release a concert album.

The two guitar albums offer ample proof that Davis could sustain interest as a pure vocalist and interpreter, singing love songs completely straight and from the heart, without the support of his usual well-crafted arrangements or such distractions as his extra-vocal abilities. Here he sounds more like Tony Bennett than Sinatra, anticipating Bennett's intimate meetings with Ralph Sharon and Bill Evans. Anticipating the Bennett-Evans encounter, Davis's voice is like an orchestra all by itself here, getting high and happy, low and dark, and all points in between. Whereas the guitar albums suggest Bennett, in 1961 he recorded twelve tracks with the Marty Paich Dektette that were clearly inspired by that arranger's work with Mel Tormé. That they were nearly all show tunes suggests that Reprise was planning a project along the lines of the Tormé-Paich *Shubert Alley* album. However, the sessions were scattered to the winds until not long after Davis's death, when reissue producer Greg Geller collated them onto a CD entitled *The Wham of Sam* (a great title, but one that invited confusion with the LP *The Wham of Sam*, of which it was not a reissue). Marty Paich once told me that Davis wasn't quite the vocal virtuoso Tormé was, nor was he as aware of musical minutiae. (He didn't necessarily know the name of one chord from anoher.) Even so, Davis's chops are flexible enough to get through these intricate charts, and his dancer's sense of rhythm is strong enough to make us forget how tricky they are.

If pressed to name the single best album of the Decca period (1954–60), I would have no problem selecting one of his last, the 1960 *I Gotta Right to Swing!* which is even more exciting and considerably more keenly focused than the earlier *Sammy Swings*. Like Nat Cole's *Welcome to the Club, Gotta Right to Swing!* employs the full Count Basie orchestra, although not billed as such, minus the Count himself. On *Gotta Right to Swing!* the charts are credited to Sy Oliver, then on staff at Decca, but they sound more like the work of Basie's own Ernie Wilkins, whose writing for the Basie band was a key factor in the Joe Williams success story—and of the "New Testament" Basie band in general. More than is true of Cole or Sinatra, the way Davis fuses himself with the swinging sixteen men sounds less like a celebrity guest star and more like an actual touring Basie vocalist, like Williams himself. A special bonus is four songs from the Ray Charles songbook—Davis and Peggy Lee were among the first old-showbiz stars to acknowledge the Genius. The way he gets in the groove on "I Got a Woman," "This Little Girl of Mine," "Mess Around," and especially on the dynamic "Get on the Right Track, Baby," Davis foreshadows the way in which Ray Charles himself adapted the Basie idiom for his own purposes when shortly afterward he expanded his touring group into a big band.

By the end of the fifties, Davis was growing both artistically and commercially—becoming a reliable hit maker—as well as growing closer, personally and professionally, to Sinatra. By the time that John F. Kennedy, who represented the political wing of the Rat Pack, was elected, Davis and Sinatra were working together regularly. When his Decca contract expired in 1960, Davis was anxious to switch affiliations to Reprise, the new record company recently founded by Sinatra.

Yet the closer he grew to Sinatra, the more he came into his own. This was the decade that popularized the concept of individuality—and who was more of an individual than this one-man Rainbow Coalition? Yet "individuality" was, in fact, merely a marketing concept in the sixties, when "nonconformity" became the new conformity. Madison Avenue was pushing love beads and long hair, and it was as rigorously enforced a dress code as gray-flannel three-piece suits had been a decade earlier. Likewise, the youth-driven pop music of the sixties was less concerned with the uniqueness of the individual than with pushing the values of the new community.

As we've seen, Davis's whole career up to this point was a walking identity crisis. Who better than he, then, to become one of the most appropriate (though in some ways unlikely) icons of sixties philosophy? There's no one who celebrates the self as gloriously as Sammy Davis Jr. Virtually all of his hits from the sixties pivot around this theme: "Once in a Lifetime" exalts the power of self-discovery, the thrill of testing one's capabilities and pushing them to the limits. Likewise, "If I Ruled the World" and "Gonna Build a Mountain" are both moving hymns to the capacity of the determined individual—the second, in particular, is half-boast and half-prayer. Sung by any other singer in any other decade, "I've Gotta Be Me" might have an edge of irony to it (that was how Steve Lawrence introduced it), along the lines of Sinatra's "Why Try to Change Me Now." But Davis performs it as an unabashed anthem of self-affirmation—it isn't that he *gotta* be he, as if he has no other choice in the matter; no, he *wants* to be he, he wouldn't have it any other way. Even "What Kind of Fool Am I?" is about self-examination and doesn't necessarily reach a negative judgment. Davis stresses the "I" more than the "Fool," and gives more weight to the possibilities for self-improvement than he does to whatever shortcomings this internal scrutiny may have revealed.

Armed with such material, Davis became the perfect performer for an era of Camelotian ambitions. His recording career thrived in the sixties not because he stooped to the lowest common denominator (in fact, it was later, when he began capitulating to the youth pop movement, that he began losing his grip), but because his message of "Yes I Can" was so in tune with the period. Both young people and their parents could find something to love in in these "133 pounds of suntanned superman." Logistically, he also found himself perfectly positioned to take advantage of every positive trend of the era—he was Vegas, he was Harlem, he was 42nd Street, he was soul, and he was schmaltz. He was Ray Charles and he was Kate Smith and he was Don Rickles—not to mention Charlie Broadway. This was the last era in which the great Broadway musicals had a pipeline into the pop music mainstream, and, for many shows, Sammy Davis was that conduit.

When I say "Broadway," I also mean the musical

theater of London's West End. Emphasizing his international appeal, Davis enjoyed a particularly rewarding relationship with the British team of Anthony Newley and Leslie Bricusse, whose productions were the most successful of all Anglo imports of the pre–Beatles and Lloyd Webber days. Indeed, Davis so helped their shows become hits that one could almost imagine that he had a piece of the publishing action. (As far as I know, he didn't.) He sang everything that could be sung from the two principal Bricusse-Newley shows (which both had longish titles) *Stop the World—I Want to Get Off* and *The Roar of the Greasepaint—The Smell of the Crowd.* He also made a point of recording songs from later projects by Bricusse (normally a lyricist) himself, like the more succinctly titled London musical *Pickwick* (music by Cyril Ornadel, which produced the hit "If I Ruled the World"), and the movies *Doctor Dolittle* and *Scrooge* (music and lyrics by Bricusse). It was obviously through his influence that Bricusse was commissioned to write the title song for Davis's 1968 film *Salt and Pepper*, and in 1971, the original threesome of Newley, Bricusse, and Davis was reunited for the widely successful single "The Candy Man" from *Willy Wonka and the Chocolate Factory.* He also starred in a Broadway revival of *Stop the World* in 1978 (for which he recorded a new cast album of the score—and no one made a more convincing Littlechap, I'm sure).

"Someone Nice Like You" could have used a minor lyric rewrite so that the song could stand on its own (unless you know the show, you won't know why he's singing to someone named Evie—not coincidentally, the name of Mrs. Bricusse). But the arrangements are gloriously free and not tied to the Broadway orchestrations. "Gonna Build a Mountain" is an amazing chart, especially for jukebox pop. ("What Kind of Fool" was a top 20 hit, and "Mountain" was on the flip.)

The spectacular "Once in a Lifetime" and "What Kind of Fool Am I?" contain everything Davis needs to command our attention. Both songs open with dramatic interval leaps: "What Kind" jumps up a 4th from "what" to "kind," and then, in the next line, up a 6th from "it" to "seems." Even more effectively, "Once in a Lifetime" zooms up almost an octave between its first two notes (and reaches its lowest point, intriguingly, on the phrases "giant" and "soar like an eagle"). These are all tools ready-made to help the singer send out a big, dramatic statement, and Davis milks them for all they're worth. While "Fool" contains hints of the quasi-rock underpinning that would eventually prove his undoing, "Lifetime" and "Mountain" revel in the glorious Paich Dektette sound.

Yet "Who Can I Turn To" shows us a completely different Sammy. In contrast to the brash bravura of the above numbers, here he's humbly introspective, as if praying for the strength to carry on. He brings that same level of internal examination to a non-

show ballad, "Lush Life" (from that first Reprise album). Being such a terrific dancer not only endows Davis with a knowledge of what to do with rhythm, here he shows he knows what to do without it, taking most of Billy Strayhorn's classic ad-lib and with just Tony Rizzi's guitar for accompaniment.

After Bricusse and Newley, the songwriting team that contributed most to Davis's Reprise output was that of Lee Adams and Charles Strouse. Their Broadway vehicle for Davis, the 1964 *Golden Boy,* was their third big Broadway show, following the 1960 *Bye Bye Birdie* and the 1962 *All-American.* Where Davis's previous Broadway production, *Mr. Wonderful* (1956), had been a lighthearted rags-to-riches show business story, *Golden Boy* was a musical tragedy based on Clifford Odets, filled with racial tension and epithets. (*Mr. Wonderful* had also been radical in its day, being one of the earliest racially mixed productions, showing black and white performers interacting together as equals.)

The *Golden Boy* original cast album came out on Capitol Records, but Davis reprised the score's two brightest gems, "I Want to Be with You" and "Night Song," in superior, straight-ahead pop versions for Reprise. The entertainer recorded many albums of show tunes for both Decca and Reprise, the best of which may have been the 1965 *Sammy's Back on Broadway.* German-born arranger Claus Ogerman's use of light Latin rhythm and tasteful sheen of strings makes "I Want to Be with You" (the show's big love duet) a forerunner to the arranger's classic 1967 encounter with *Francis Albert Sinatra and Antonio Carlos Jobim.* "Night Song" had been Davis's "establishing" number in the show, and here it's treated more intimately, as an introspective ramble.

A Broadway show was something that Sinatra never did—although it could be argued that his films of *On the Town, Guys and Dolls, Pal Joey* (and even *Robin and the Seven Hoods*) were his way of addressing that heritage. TV producer George Schlatter, who worked with both men, has stressed how Sinatra remained Davis's role model both on and off the stage; that Davis would try to emulate Sinatra's lifestyle ("Frank would buy a plane and Sammy had to have a plane too"), even though he hardly had pockets deep enough to cover such extravagances. As a result, while Sinatra left a fortune for his heirs to squabble over, Davis left his wife in debt.

Davis is at his most interesting when he's doing stuff Sinatra never quite did, and the sixties Reprise albums (nearly all of which have recently been reissued on CD by Collectors' Choice Music) elaborate on the fifties Deccas. The best concepts take him far afield from the Sinatrasphere: There was a second guitar album (*Here's That Rainy Day,* with Laurindo Almeida), a second Basie album (*Our Shining Hour*—the only "official" one), and some brilliant live albums, particularly, as we shall see, *The Sounds of '66.* He did one tribute album for another performer, and not Sinatra, surprisingly. *Sammy Davis Jr. Sings the Nat King Cole Songbook* varies between strict re-creations of King Cole hits—like the Billy May arrangement of "Walking My Baby Back Home"—and new arrangements of Cole classics, including Claus Ogerman's carefully considered semi–bossa nova version of "Unforgettable." A "Broadway" album was a natural and an inevitable idea, as he had done several for Decca (and not only that, but he had recorded "Stand Up and Fight" from *Carmen Jones* and "Gesticulate" from *Kismet* in the original Broadway orchestrations). Reprise released a Sinatra-Broadway compilation (as did Columbia), but it was a fairly slapdash, secondhand affair, and not in the same class as the superb *Sammy's Back on Broadway.*

There were two exceptional team-ups, both recorded in Las Vegas. *When the Feeling Hits You* (1964) was taped at a point when both Davis and Louis Prima were working in Nevada, and Davis made use of Prima's backup band, Sam Butera and the Witnesses. *The Sounds of '66* was recorded live at the Sands, where Davis had already done a live album, according to discographer Jamie McGregor, earlier that same month. In June 1966, Davis recorded enough material for *That's All: Live at the Sands* (which was already his second live double album on Reprise, following a 1962 set from the Cocoanut Grove). *That's All!* was done with Davis's own touring rhythm section and the regular Sands house orchestra; however, within a few weeks he returned to the Sands (of which Sinatra was part-owner) and made still another live album, *The Sounds of '66*—this one with Buddy Rich and His Orchestra.

Both *When the Feeling Hits You* and *The Sounds of '66* find Davis in exceptional spirits, literally supercharged. The title track of *When the Feeling Hits You* (apparently only otherwise recorded by the Four Freshmen) has him digging into a soul-gospel groove that uses some Butera-Prima-isms (such as an elaborate series of stop time breaks), but the album as a whole is more reminiscent of Ray Charles back in his octet days.

Likewise, both of the Sands live albums from June 1966 (a total of three CDs' worth of material) are first-rate Sammy. It's plain that he's most inspired by superlative drumming. Both in the 1962 *Cocoanut Grove* album and the first 1966 *Sands* set, Davis does a longish medley with his drummer Michael Silva, in which he semi-spontaneously hops from song to song, with a kind of planned randomness, the various tunes running in and out of each other with a wonderful intuitive logic. In both cases, the sequence starts with "I've Got You Under My Skin" and at one point has him running through the country hit "Big Bad John."

Sounds of '66 has everything going for it, not least of which is that Buddy Rich has never played better. It's also the best work I've ever heard by arranger Ernie Freeman, who normally had the thankless task of making the Rat Packers sound jukebox-savvy in the late sixties. Most of his charts represent the worst things ever recorded by Sinatra and Dean Martin, but the writing credited to Freeman here is so good that I almost think someone made a mistake and that the charts are actually by Ernie Wilkins. These treatments of Sammy perennials "Birth of the Blues" and "What Kind of Fool Am I?" are the best of the many that he preserved on vinyl. And there is a generous batch of show tunes and standards that he never addressed anywhere else, preserving them in definitive treatments here, starting with "What Did I Have That I Don't Have?" and "Come Back to Me" from *On a Clear Day You Can See Forever*. Every track on *Sounds of '66* finds Davis giving everything he's got to give, and that's more than enough.

Davis's 1966 "drums" medley most humorously detours "Ugly Chile," a rather derogatory tune New Orleans jazzmen like George Brunis and Wingy Manone used to play ("I really hate you, you alligator-bait you, you some ugly chile!") that suggests Davis still had self-esteem issues. Perhaps that's what gives his anthems of self-congratulation such a kick: He doesn't take it for granted—no man who suffered through the institutionalized racism that Davis did ever could—that he's great; he has to work up his egotism and self-congratulation, projecting the idea that he has fully earned the right to pat himself on the back. In songs like "I've Gotta Be Me," he seems to be struggling with the idea, but you can easily regard "Once in a Lifetime" and "Yes I Can" as songs through which he does more than celebrate himself, but tells the larger white world that black is beautiful.

In 1999, Rhino Records released a four-CD box entitled *Yes I Can! The Sammy Davis Jr. Story*, which includes nearly all Davis's hits and samples most of his albums. It's good to report that Collectors' Choice Music has generously reissued nearly all the Reprise albums on CD; unfortunately the Deccas remain very hard to find (there are scarce Japanese and British issues of only a handful), and the seventies albums are even rarer.

Oddly, most of the anthologies that sample his later albums concentrate on the more embarrassing tracks, covers of seventies pop hits and TV show themes (he did a whole album of these, *Sammy Davis Jr. Sings the Great TV Tunes*—this was a heckuva way to sell records). All of which conspires to cover up the fact that Davis's recording career continued to prosper in an unlikely era. "The Candy Man," the latest Davis-Bricusse-Newley confection, was the most successful recording of Davis's whole career, and he continued to find opportunities to record good standards—along with the other stuff. The best was a 1974 Davis LP entitled "*That's Entertainment*," a whole album of songs from classic MGM musicals, which was Davis's way of expressing his love for old Hollywood. There's a good anthology of his Polygram-owned material, *Mr. Bojangles*, titled after his pseudo-autobiographical hit of 1972, but on the whole one wishes that more of the seventies material, as well as the fifties, would find its way onto CD.

In 1966, as we have mentioned, Davis paid tribute to his friend Nat King Cole with a full-length album. Ironically—or just stupidly, depending on how one looks at it—Davis would die too young, like Cole, from an excess of cigarettes. Certainly, by that point the long-term risk of cigarette smoking was widely known, and Davis had plenty of warning. Yet he continued to use cigarettes with such rapidity that Sinatra found it excessive and taunted him by calling him "Smokey the Bear" in an unsuccessful effort to shame him into quitting the habit. Ultimately, Davis died of smoking too much, at the age of sixty-four in 1990.

"I think his ending was less than marvelous," the late Anthony Newley told me. "When you think of how much pleasure he gave everybody with his singing, and then for him to get cancer of the throat, that was just vicious. Fate was not kind to him. I was glad that just before he died, I had a chance to tell him what he meant to me." Even the man who had triumphed over racism—the colored, Jewish non-fegela who made himself into one of the most celebrated entertainers in the world—couldn't conquer cancer. There were, apparently, some things even a suntanned superman couldn't do—although you would never know it to listen to him.

Doris Day (born 1922)

The world of pop music is a funny place—perhaps the only area of our culture where someone can be rich and famous and still be considered "underrated." Doris Day is known to the world not just as a hit-making singer and a major movie star but as an American institution—yet she's never been properly acknowledged as the great artist she is.

Part of the issue is the way the pantheon of singers is organized in most of our brains. There's a Mount Rushmore of female jazz pop singers, namely Billie-Ella-Dinah-Sarah-Carmen, whom we can all agree on, and a comparable cavalry of male pop jazz singers: Bing-Frank-Nat-Tony (give or take a Mel or a Big Joe). But who are the major female pop singers in the Bing-Frank category? Do we go by record sales? In that case Patti Page and Joni James, or possibly Jo Stafford, would top the list. Do we judge on the basis of long-running popularity on radio and TV—the winner would be Dinah Shore. Sheer class? And career longevity? It's got to be Lena Horne . . . or maybe Rosemary Clooney. A taste for the exotic or even the blues? Peggy Lee. Pure Sex? Julie London. Pure power, in terms of emotion and chops, balanced with comparable vulnerability—Judy Garland, of course. The great lady who's done the most to inspire and encourage young talent? Margaret Whiting. Granted, Doris Day could perhaps win on

the basis of her being the only former band chirp who had a cinematic career on the same level as Crosby and Sinatra. But the point is: Doris Day can be considered the best just because she's as great as a pop singer can be.

The albums *Day by Night* and *Day by Day* contain twenty-three examples of the most erotic vocalizing you'll ever hear. A formidable arsenal of techniques has been deployed to put the listener in the most romantic mood possible: an angelic voice, note-perfect pitch, and a capacity for phrasing that's entirely at the service of the lyric—the story comes first, yet musical values are never ignored. Both the singing and arranger Paul Weston's orchestrations, which are appropriately light on the strings and heavy on the use of jazz solos, are steeped in romance, yet circumvent sentimentality. (Likewise, the repertory consists of songs like "I See Your Face Before Me" and "Under a Blanket of Blue," which are first-rate yet not overly familiar.)

Then there's that voice—Doris Day has a sound like bottled sunshine. It's hard to think of another human voice that's so luxuriously sensual. One would almost have to go into the tenor sax kingdom—to Stan Getz or Ben Webster—to find a sound that melts the soul so movingly. Ballads aside, tracks like "Close Your Eyes" (the opener to her *Duet* album with André Previn) reveal that Doris Day can also swing something fierce.

At her very best, Doris Day is worthy of being mentioned in the same breath as Frank Sinatra or Ella Fitzgerald, yet though she'll hardly die broke, she's never gotten a fraction of their respect. "It took me a long time to appreciate Doris Day," the late but still contemporary jazz-and-standards singer Susannah McCorkle once told me. "I loved her movies as a kid, but when I started to become a singer myself, I didn't like anybody unless they were black or very jazzy." There are an embarrassing number of reasons why not enough people appreciate Doris Day, starting with the way her film career overshadowed her recordings, and including how next to none of her best albums were in print for decades.

"I knew Doris Day back before she was a virgin," Oscar Levant once wisecracked. ("It's a little known fact that Doris Day used to date Santa Claus—before she was a virgin," said contemporary singer-songwriter Nellie McKay in introducing a Christmas song in Day's honor. She released her tribute album, *Normal as Blueberry Pie*, in 2009.) It's also easy to confuse Day the recording artist with the sanitized, irrepressibly perky heroine she played in a series of nostalgic movie musicals in the early fifties. We think of her screen persona, as another singing scholar, Mary Cleere Haran, says, "as so sunny and bright, but she's different when she sings. She can be dark and mysterious, and there's a wistfulness and a yearning in her voice."

It also works against Day that while her intonation and rhythm are consistently beyond reproach, her musical output isn't. Her professional mentors, husband and manager Marty Melcher and Columbia Records A&R guru Mitch Miller, who ran the singles department at Columbia Records, were both essentially interested in fast-buck hits; she didn't have the inner conscience of Sinatra (or the outer conscience of Fitzgerald's producer Norman Granz) egging her on to try to make albums of standards that would have stood the test of time. There's a vast polarization between Day's pop 45s fodder (including many of her biggest hits) like "A Guy Is a Guy" and "Everybody Loves a Lover," and what might be called her "art records," like *Day by Night* and *Duet*.

I couldn't say how Day's self-imposed musical exile affects our perception of her. Like Artie Shaw, she stopped making music in her forties. They cited different reasons for this decision, but the outcome, a wall of silence, remains the same. Ms. Day is only a few years older than Keely Smith and the late Rosemary Clooney, and it's a shame that she didn't share the impulse of those two great ladies to go on making incredible music well into their seventies. But then again, neither Clooney nor Smith had created a body of work as large and imposing—and as thoroughly satisfying—as Doris Day's.

In 1956, she introduced her most famous hit song, the Academy Award–winning "Que Sera Sera." The song amounted to a trim microcosm of her belief in the inevitability of fate. She was born Doris Von Kappelhoff, and her first ambition was to become a dancer—but her dance career was finished thanks to a car accident that temporarily cost her the use of her legs. Just to have something to do while she was recuperating, she began spending a lot of time listening to the radio and eventually noticed that she was singing along with Ella Fitzgerald's vocals with the Chick Webb Orchestra. Inspired by Fitzgerald's example, Day began taking singing lessons, ostensibly to break the monotony of the long healing process. As soon as people heard her sing, doors began opening for her. The first door opener was Barney Rapp, a local Ohio leader who led one of the most important bands in the Midwest.

Rapp not only gave her near-national exposure on the radio, he also came up with a stage name for her that was a bit easier to pronounce and write out than Von Kappelhoff. It so happened that her specialty with Rapp's orch was a little-known pop song called "Day After Day," and from it came the name Doris Day. Rapp also inadvertently helped launch a tradition of alliterative names for white female pop and band singers: Soon to come were Georgia Gibbs, Kitty Kallen, Patti Page, Joni James.

"I first heard her in Cincinnati," Les Brown told me in 1989. "She was there with Barney Rapp and she was working at WLW, which at that time had 500,000 watts—it could be heard in China! It covered the whole country and Mexico and everything. Bob Crosby heard her, came through Cincinnati and liked her and hired her, and two weeks later they were at the Strand Theatre in New York. I found out from a song plugger that she had given her notice [to Bob Crosby] for some reason or other. I went to see her because I liked her looks and her singing, her intonation, her voice and everything about her. I went backstage and hired her."

My conversation with Brown then went as follows:

Me: Why did she leave Crosby?
Les: That is X-rated! That's as much as I'll say.

In the beginning, singing with Les Brown and His Orchestra (the appellation "Band of Renown" would come later) must have seemed like a mere consolation prize. Bob Crosby had one of the top bands going, and probably even Barney Rapp was better known in most of the country. Still, Day made her first records with Brown and some of the results were impressive.

When exactly did they realize what a miraculous collaboration the Day-Brown combo was? Said Brown, "After she made her first records with us, I knew we had something pretty special there." Her first extant performance is a radio aircheck in which the Brown band sounds as if it's going through a Glenn Miller phase. It wouldn't succeed until it found its own style, but the Miller analogy is appropriate, in that of all bandleaders, Brown would come closest to succeeding Miller, not as a copycat but as perhaps the most widely beloved of straight-down-the-middle great American swing dance bands, equal parts pop and jazz.

On her first commercial session, Day and Brown chart the course of what would be one of the great careers in the recording industry, starting with "Dig It," a jive tune in which her vocal is introduced by the band chanting "Dig it, Doris!" on the vocal chorus, and dig it she does, showing herself already the equal of Miller's Marion Hutton (who also recorded it), Tommy Dorsey's Connie Haines, or the other Dorsey's Helen O'Connell, or any other perky canary who specialized in rhythm numbers. And she gets a groove going in Cole Porter's "Let's Be Buddies."

Her first big ballad, "While the Music Plays On," sounds like something Joan Crawford would sing in an MGM mellerdrammer about a torchy *vocaliste* who gets seduced into becoming the kept woman of the honorable Mr. So & So and discovers God in the final reel. While Day makes what she can out of the overbaked lyrics, the reed section digs into a hypnotic minor mood, sounding like Glenn Miller in concert at your local synagogue. She would record a total of ten tunes with Brown at this time, including a bizarre vocal version of Will Bradley's catchy instrumental "Celery Stalks at Midnight."

The Brown-Day combination was getting off to a fine start when it looked like a start was all they would get off to. In 1941, having just gained a toehold in the music business, Day left it at the age of nineteen to start a family with her first of four husbands and her only child. That idea lasted about three years: Husband number one, trombonist Al Jorden, turned out to be a psychopath. The marriage left her with her son, Terry, who, for the next sixty-two years (1942–2004), would be the closest long-term relationship of her life.

When Terry was two, she fled with her life, and reconnected with Les Brown; fortunately, the 1942–44 AFM ban was also about to end. It was during this second tenure that the Brown-Day combination really took off. They recorded forty-two songs together, all of which were gathered into a marvelous complete double-CD package, *The Complete Doris Day with Les Brown*, released by Collectors' Choice Music under license from Sony in 1998.

The collaboration was distinguished firstly by many fine up-tempo records like "Aren't You Glad You're You," introduced by Bing Crosby as Father O'Malley in *The Bells of St. Mary's*, and about which Brown said, "Oh God, that's a great record! She sang that beautifully!" The Brown crew reconceives the Jimmy Van Heusen melody as a Baroque fugue, voicing the instruments—including altoist George Weidler (Day's second husband) and bass clarinet (a rare instrument indeed in the swing era)—in round harmony. "Booglie Wooglie Piggy," another homage to Will Bradley, fairly grunts with style. Only she could combine cartoon character cutesiness with jumpin' jive jargon, and—heavens to hamhocks—"oink, oink!" from her sounds like Shakespeare from anyone else. One can't help feeling it's a good thing Father O'Malley never knew of the virtues of eight-to-the-bar swine, or else he might have decided that he'd rather be a pig.

It was the ballads, however, that advanced Day to the top of the band business, particularly the lovely "The Christmas Song," the best big band version of this Mel Tormé–authored Nat Cole hit. She and Brown also landed the hit on one of the best songs of the late band era, "My Dreams Are Getting Better All the Time."

Yet no Day-Brown platter had the impact of "Sentimental Journey," with music by arranger Ben Homer and Brown himself. More than a massive hit, it was a song that helped define an era. We can argue from here until D-Day about what the definitive war song might have been (the two strongest contenders were written well before World War II, namely the 1931 "As Time Goes By" and the 1938 "I'll Be Seeing You"), but there's no doubt that the definitive end-of-the-war song was Brown and Day's "Sentimental Journey." By 1946, she was drawing a salary of $500 a week and was simply too big a talent to remain under Brown's wing. Offers were already coming in from Hollywood while she was still under contract to the band, but she wasn't interested. Not yet.

Around this time, Day began recording for Columbia Records, Brown's label, on her own. She did some radio work, too (establishing a long professional relationship with Bob Hope and a shorter but rewarding one with Frank Sinatra), and played one important engagement at the Little Club, which, small as it may have been, was an important New York nightspot. She was thinking about her career, and her son, but was more preoccupied with the breakup of her second marriage. At around this time, lyricist Sammy Cahn recommended her for a forthcoming Warner Bros. musical, *Romance on the High Seas,* and both Cahn and director Michael Curtiz had to coax her into doing the test and then the movie itself. (The vocals on her first three starring films have been collated onto one outstanding CD, *It's Magic,* on Rhino.)

Doris Day was an instant success in pictures: It's no exaggeration to say the public took one look (and one listen) and she could do no wrong. Not just beautiful, not just a great singer, she possessed that kind of charisma that could be choreographed but not created. Day launched a film career that was, ultimately, more rewarding for us than it was for her. She remained one of Hollywood's top leading ladies for the next two decades, spending roughly ten years as the girl next door and an additional ten as the girl next door who might just sleep with you if you had a name like Rock or Cary and had some kind of a gimmick to trick her into it.

With the start of her movie career came Marty Melcher into her life—first as general manager and then as husband number three. Miss Day elaborated on the nature of this relationship in her very moving memoir *Doris Day, My Story,* but one anecdote that specifically regards her film and recording careers is worth detailing here.

Romance on the High Seas yielded her first post-Brown megahit, Cahn and Styne's lovely "It's Magic," which had been arranged for Columbia by George Siravo. Then—as is pretty much true today—costs for recording sessions were indirectly charged back against artists' royalties, and in general, the less expensive the sessions were, the more money they stood to make. When "It's Magic" was charting, Melcher took George Siravo out to lunch. Aware that the expenses of the orchestra were being indirectly charged off to the artist, Melcher wondered why they needed a full twenty-six-piece orchestra. Couldn't they do just as well with a rhythm section and a choir? In fact, Melcher reasoned, why did they even need a whole choir? A trio was really all Doris needed. Or maybe just an organ, which could simulate an entire orchestra with only one musician.

To put the rest of the story in Siravo's own words:

"So now my eyes are starting to go through my head, and I looked around, and I took a deep breath, and I said, 'You really wanna know what I think, Marty?'

"He says, 'Yeah!'

"I said, 'I have a better idea!'

"He says, 'What's that?'

"I said, 'Why don't you play the fucking organ yourself—that way you won't have to pay anybody!'

"I didn't hear from Marty for over a year and a half after that."

In spite of Melcher's machinations, Doris Day was probably the biggest female multimedia hit maker of the fifties, steadily turning out chart singles and top-grossing pictures. Dinah Shore, who had been around longer, had a bigger broadcasting career, but couldn't touch Day in pictures; Judy Garland had a shorter but more spectacular film career, but wasn't utilized as much on recordings and radio as she should have been. Paramount tried to make Rosemary Clooney the next Doris Day, but she never caught on in pictures. Day was the sole female singer to come from the band world and make the transition to solo stardom and pictures.

The two would be intertwined for most of her career. In fact, her four biggest songs would all derive from films, starting with "It's Magic" and then the Academy Award winners "Secret Love" from *Calamity Jane* and "Que Sera Sera" from *The Man Who Knew Too Much*, and even her last significant seller, the kiddie-poppish title song from *Move Over, Darling* (co-credited to her son, pop producer-writer Terry Melcher). Those four songs are also the titles of the four Bear Family boxes that collect her complete recordings, a total of twenty-three CDs of material that encompass everything she made after leaving Les Brown, including a self-produced album from 1968.

Twenty-three German CDs is a lot—especially seeing as how Herr Bear squeezes roughly twenty-five tracks or at least two LPs' worth of music on each volume. This is certainly one of the most prolific recording careers of the mid-forties to the mid-sixties, on a par with Sinatra, Cole, Como, Fitzgerald, or Vaughan. But no other major recording artist had a career so sharply polarized between high-road and low-road pop. One who is in a position to know is saxophonist Ted Nash, who worked with her closely in the Brown band, appeared on her first Columbia date, and was her favorite soloist all through her years in the studios, much as he was for Sinatra during his Capitol years.

Nash told me that Day was one of two extremes he witnessed in star singers: She would leave all decisions in the hands of those around her—her producers and Marty. In her memoir, she talks about questioning Melcher's taste and decisions, but it never seems to have occurred to her that she had the right to insist on doing things any other way; she would, according to Nash, sing anything that Melcher or Mitch Miller chose for her. Nash contrasts this with another singer he worked with, namely Barbra Streisand, who earned a reputation for insisting on doing *everything* her way, to the point where she completely stifled the creativity of orchestrators, musicians, engineers, and anyone else unfortunate enough to work with her. (Sinatra, Nash said, was Mr. In-Between.)

Even the recorded work of Perry Como didn't exhibit such a gap between the inane novelties she cut for singles and the high-class standards she put on albums: Think about "Tic-Tac-Tic (The Geiger Counter Song)," "Mr. Tap Toe," "Rickety Rackety Rendezvous," and "How Lovely Cooks the Meat" (not to mention "Let the Little Girl Limbo"). Como's novelties are at least nonverbal nonsense (as if it were an insult to real words to put them in such inane combinations); Day's aren't even that. "I thought she could have been a great singer," says Nash, "if she had been given the right material. She sounded like Lena Horne in those days. But all of a sudden they started giving her this crap, which made her a big star. But it took away from her singing ability, because everyone thought of her as a trite 'Que Sera Sera' type of singer from then on. [Essentially] all her stuff with Columbia was just garbage."

Nash is exaggerating, but only slightly. "Greatest hits" compilations tend to showcase the "crap" that sold millions, but the Bear boxes tell the whole story, and reveal that she cut an awful lot of first-rate songs in addition to all the cheese—in fact, the *Day by Day/Day by Night* albums, which extensively feature Nash's tenor solos, are only the tip of the iceberg. The 1947–50 period (before Mitch Miller took over at Columbia) is particularly rich in outstanding small-group sessions that reveal how the capacity for swing that she developed with the Band of Renown continued to serve her well. Her second solo date for Columbia, in June 1947, featured a catchy rhythmic treatment of a timely novelty by Cahn and Saul Chaplin, "I'm Still Sitting Under the Apple Tree." Central Avenue star Red Callender was on bass, and Nash got off a fine tenor solo—but no one swung harder than Day herself. The first date, incidentally, done in New York that February, included an outstanding reading of the minor Ellington song "Tulip or Turnip."

She also made a series of sessions with the King Cole–styled Page Cavanaugh Trio in three different media—commercial recordings (on Columbia, collected on the first Bear box), radio transcriptions (issued on Soundies), and picture sound tracks (released on Rhino). Day sings and swings superbly with this understated, drummerless group, especially on the Cole–Stan Kenton hit "Orange Colored Sky," on which she is light, sweet, and irresistible.

She is also hep to the jive laid down by the somewhat more aggressively swinging Harry James and His Orchestra, who were co-featured with her in *Young Man with a Horn,* a disappointing film of the most famous jazz novel of all time, yet which yielded an amazing sound track album. She comes off brilliantly with the full James orchestra, but is especially effective on an octet session featuring four horns and four rhythm. If there's a more convincing version of "Too Marvelous for Words" out there, I don't know it. Unlike a lot of so-called jazz singers, she tends to stay right on top of the beat. With Day, even sunshine swings.

Even some of Day's novelties have more substance to them than you might guess by the titles. In addition to championing Hank Williams and Alec Wilder, Mitch Miller also deserves credit for recording the music of Josef Marais, the South African singer-songwriter. Miller had many of his Columbia contract artists, including Jo Stafford, Frankie Laine, and Johnny Ray, cover songs by Marais. "Around the Corner" was done by both Stafford and Pete Seeger and the Weavers (on Decca). Thanks to Miller's efforts, Marais had at least half a dozen hit songs in the early fifties. Day recorded four songs by him: "The Cherries" was a solo, and the three others were duets, "Ma Says, Pa Says," "How Lovely Cooks the Meat," and "Sugarbush." These duets—the first with Ray, the other two with Laine—were amazingly successful, and are consistently reissued on *Greatest Hits* collections. Miller's productions are somewhat ostentatious and very similar to those that he employed on Guy Mitchell's long and profitable series of manufactured folk songs. However, the songs are wonderful upbeat music for children (lots of marching around and clapping hands is involved), and this quality is reinforced by the marvelously cheerful, spirited way that Day sings them. (I wouldn't want to hear Billie Holiday sing any of these songs.) I suspect that these discs were either purchased by or for nine-year-olds who, four years later, were listening to Elvis.

Even after Miller took over at Columbia, he didn't stand in the way of Day's recording many albums of standards—most of which were themed to her films. Considering that Garland had been excommunicated from Hollywood by the time Day's star ascended, there was no one to challenge her as the singing queen of musicals, and as with Garland, most of Day's pictures of the period were all-singing, all-dancing Technicolor costumers. But even more than Garland, she was the queen of the catalogue musical. *Young Man with a Horn* was more contemporary and gritty (and black-and-white), but most of her pictures took place in a more innocent era (*Tea for Two, By the Light of the Silvery Moon, On Moonlight Bay, I'll See You in My Dreams*) or in a present that's so sanitized it just seems like the past (*Lullaby of Broadway, April in Paris*). They all relied extensively on songs written prior to World War II—as did even the two somewhat heavier dramas she appeared in during this period, *Young at Heart* and *Love Me or Leave Me.* (The latter could be described as Day's answer to Garland's *A Star Is Born*, in that it was a dark drama about the seamy side of showbiz that gave her the chance to sing and dance as well as turn in an Oscar-level acting performance.)

If one considers the songs from these ten or so films—all of which were also represented on Columbia albums and singles—there's no denying that Day recorded an awful lot of top-level songs. The studio monopoly system, about to tumble and fall, helped her more than it did any other great singer, since her studio, Warner Bros., owned the most extensive publishing interests of any multimedia conglomerate, and in addition to controlling the copyrights from twenty-five years of Warners musicals (and the Harry Warren catalogue), they also had extensive holdings by songwriters like the Gershwin brothers and Vincent Youmans.

Sure, she recorded "Ooh Bang Jiggly Jang" (by Bob Merrill, no less), but thanks to the Bear boxes, we know that she also did more than thirty songs by Richard Rodgers, almost that many by Irving Berlin, a dozen each by the Gershwins, Porter, Mercer, and Loesser—figures that, I would think, are roughly comparable with those of virtually any other singer of the period excepting Sinatra and Fitzgerald.

Apart from the classic songs that she sang in her films (and recorded for Columbia), she also sang dozens of worthy new show and film songs: "Let's Take an Old Fashioned Walk" (a duet with Sinatra) and "You Can Have Him" (a duet with Shore) from Irving Berlin's *Miss Liberty*; "Something Wonderful," "We Kiss in a Shadow," and, later, "I Have Dreamed" from Rodgers and Hammerstein's *The King and I*; offbeat but worthy Johnny Mercer numbers, like "Oops" and "Baby Doll" from *The Belle of New York,* and "Love in a Home" from *Li'l Abner;* and superior Disneyana like "Very Good Advice" from *Alice in Wonderland* and "Your Mother and Mine" and "Second Star to the Right" from *Peter Pan*. She had also done two fully realized (nonbackstage stories) Broadway-style musicals, the adaptation of the stage success *The Pajama Game* and another adaptation of sorts, *Calamity Jane*, which was a better film version of *Annie Get Your Gun* than the actual film version of *Annie Get Your Gun*. The songs for all these projects were uniformly excellent.

In many ways, the 1955 film *Love Me or Leave Me* represents the simultaneous apogee of both her acting and singing careers, with Day delivering an electrifying performance on both the screen and the sound track. She plays Ruth Etting, singing star of the Jazz Age, catapulted to fame via a deal with the devil, in the form of her manipulating gangster husband, Marty (sounds familiar), played to perfection as the Gimp you love to hate by James Cagney. The score consists almost entirely of classic twenties songs, and these vary between Broadway-style showstoppers and some of her most effective ballads ever, such as "It All Depends on You" and "I'll Never Stop Loving You." The sweet voice of the band years and the early fifties now has a harder edge to it.

Following the success of *Love Me or Leave Me* and Hitchcock's *The Man Who Knew Too Much*, it was difficult for Day to go back to being a virgin (to echo Oscar Levant's famous wisecrack) and keep making nostalgia-oriented family fare, although she would do a few more musicals (most notably the 1962 *Billy Rose's Jumbo*). Fortunately, the late fifties were the burgeoning years of the 12" LP and the concept album, and Day recorded more than her share. We've mentioned the exquisite *Day by Day* and *Day by Night* duo with Paul Weston. There were also

Show Time with Axel Stordahl, *Bright and Shiny* with Neal Hefti, and *Cuttin' Capers* with Frank DeVol, not to mention a deluxe double package of film songs with DeVol entitled *Hooray for Hollywood*, which is highlighted by a slow and sexy reading of the Mercer-Warren title song (usually done as a rah-rah sarcastic anthem). Much of DeVol's writing for Day in this period is especially Nelson Riddle–esque. "Easy to Love" (on the *Hollywood* double) even sounds as if it could be Riddle himself working under a contractually stipulated pseudonym.

Her last overtly jazzy project was her finest album ever: the 1961 *Duet* with pianist André Previn. Technically, it isn't a duet, since Red Mitchell, bass, and Frankie Capp, drums, are on hand, and likewise, although most of the numbers on *Duet* are in a slower tempo, we shouldn't assume that this is anything other than a pure jazz record. It seems that after cutting so many Melcher-selected singles inanities, each set to a relentless businessman's bounce (Melcher was partial to shuffle rhythms of the corniest kind), she relished this opportunity to work in languorously slow tempos and this most intimate of settings. Only by listening to the Bear boxes does it become clear that Day concentrated on the slower speeds on her albums as a respite from the relentlessly peppy novelties inflicted on her on the singles dates. When she includes Alec Wilder's "Give Me Time" (a song introduced by Mildred Bailey, obviously a major favorite), the title has a double meaning. As we've seen, Day's ballads are one of the wonders of mankind: There's no one who sings a love song more tenderly and convincingly.

Her singing remained nonpareil in the early sixties, the years covered by the fourth and final Bear Box, *Move Over, Darling*. She had cut some R&B-style singles in the late fifties, but now all her singles were exclusively jukeboxy, with little likelihood of a good show tune finding its way in. As far as the sixties albums went, there was a collection of songs about dreams (*I Have Dreamed*), an exceptional collection of religious hymns and prayers (*You'll Never Walk Alone*), a children's album (*With a Smile and a Song*), and a bossa nova set (*Latin for Lovers*).

Two of her final Columbia albums make a convincing argument that Day should never have retired from recording; one looks backward, the other at the current pop scene, and she makes both the vintage and the contemporary music into something entirely timeless. The 1964 *Sentimental Journey* was done in a period when many of Day's colleagues—including Sinatra, Stafford, and Cole—were creating autobiographical projects, and is a highly simpatico collection of songs from the big band–World War II era that were not exclusively her own. Surrounded by what sounds like the largest string section ever to accompany her, these are Day's most intimate vocals yet—she's stunningly direct and personal throughout, particularly on the profoundly moving "I Remember You."

On the 1963 *Love Him*, Day's son, Terry Melcher, succeeded in bringing Mom (who was all of forty-one) up to date with a program of newish songs from Broadway, Hollywood, European, and even country and pop sources, done in an old-school orchestral setting and sung with complete compatibility and credibility. She's amazingly strong on the old blues ballad "Since I Fell for You" and two songs that had been hits for Elvis, "(Now and Then) There's a Fool Such as I" and "Can't Help Falling in Love." The climactic piece is Willie Nelson's "Night Life," which begins with an elaborate spoken and orchestral intro similar to Nat Cole's "Wild Is Love," and is seemingly designed to make the song sound as urban and uncountry as possible. No matter—when Day gets to the song itself, her vocal is so warm and heartfelt that it transcends any notion of genre. It could have been the work of Willie Nelson, Ozzie Nelson, Oliver Nelson, Nelson Riddle, Nelson Eddy, or Nelson Mandela.

After *Duet*, which Columbia executives probably considered Day's least-commercial album ever, her most memorable project of the sixties was the package they might have welcomed as the most potentially commercial: Columbia's 1962 studio cast album of Irving Berlin's *Annie Get Your Gun,* in which she shared top billing with Robert Goulet as a suitably stiff and sympathetic Frank Butler. This is the sound track for the greatest Doris Day movie that never was, far surpassing the 1949 film of *Annie* with Betty Hutton and even *Calamity Jane*, Day's own take on the concept of the Wild West tomboy. Day plays *Annie* like a coming of age story, as much Eliza Doolittle–goes–West as Annie Oakley, and she brings such depth and dimension to the songs that we barely miss the visual element. Apparently Day and Goulet recorded their vocals together with just piano, and then arranger Franz Allers added the orchestral parts later—which may explain why this *Annie* album feels more intimate than many cast recordings, and why Day and Goulet relate to each other so well.

As with any of the greats, this is a career that encompasses too many highlights to cover them all. As Mary Cleere Haran points out on her *Personal Christmas Collection,* Day "makes even 'Toyland' sound sexy." And she does the same with "Nearer My God to Thee" on *You'll Never Walk Alone*. As Haran puts it, "Doris Day embodies a song—she inhabits it—like no one else. She has a very internal approach, she isn't trying to dazzle you, she's just a real communicator. When the elements were right, she always delivered, because she had the goods. Sometimes I think that she's the absolute best. Even if her records weren't always as good as she was, she can make a song come to life better than anybody. You can listen to things like 'I Had the Craziest Dream' [on *Sentimental Journey*] over and over again, they're so perfect."

In all, hers is one of the richest catalogues of any

vocal icon, one that's fully worthy of the completist treatment it finally received after so many years of neglect. Doris Day's singing is among the most moving experiences that American pop has to offer. To paraphrase something else that Ted Nash said to me, Doris Day sang like she had nothing to prove.

Appreciation of Doris Day's singing has, appropriately, escalated in recent years: I've seen at least two full-length cabaret show tributes to Day, by cabaret singers Karen Oberlin and Mary Cleere Haran, and two albums in her honor, *Hearts Desire* (2007), by the more jazz-oriented West Coast–based singer Sue Raney, and *Normal as Blueberry Pie* (2009) by the uncategorizable Nellie McKay.

At first the connection between Day and McKay (their names, incidentally, do not rhyme) seemed obscure—beyond their mutual blondness and animal rights activism; least of all in that McKay, who was twenty-six at the time of the album, more customarily writes her own songs. Those songs are generally brilliantly arch and full of irony, with lines like "Feminists don't have a sense of humor." Whereas McKay gets her point across by means other than stating it outright, Day, for all of the profundity of her best music, is nothing if not incredibly straightforward. When Day sings "Close Your Eyes" or even something as surreal and poetic as Johnny Mercer's text to "I Remember You," there's never any doubt that she means exactly what she says.

Yet to hear McKay sing the Doris Day songbook is to realize that she more than gets it, and when she praises Day for being as "normal"—not to mention as straightforward and direct—"as blueberry pie," she is not being the least bit sarcastic. In fact, McKay has taken advantage of the opportunity, when singing the "songbook" for the first time, to treat these classic songs with a forthrightness that Day would surely find admirable. "Black Hills of Dakota," a song of "the beautiful Indian country" that Day introduced in *Calamity Jane*, is rendered like a genuine Native American chant, with an Indian tom-tom and wooden flute.

"Crazy Rhythm" becomes an homage not only to Day (who recorded it in 1950), but to the great female jazz-pop singers of the Roaring Twenties, like Ethel Waters and Annette Hanshaw, replete with syncopation, a Gershwinesque piano part, and finger-wagging spoken asides. When she sings "Close Your Eyes," with an affecting modal-style vamp, there's no doubt that she's singing with her eyes closed. On "Send Me No Flowers," McKay does her inspiration one better: there's nothing wrong with this movie theme by Burt Bacharach and Hal David, but it was sabotaged over the 1964 film of the same title by an annoyingly gimmicky and immediately dated arrangement that someone forced on Day. McKay sings it straight ahead, with minimal accompaniment and total earnestness (not to mention originality, especially in the combination of uke and trombone); it's actually more Doris Day–like

than Day's own version. In her original song, "If I Ever Had a Dream," McKay further shows that she completely understands Day and her idiom; harmonically and lyrically, it's an irresistible invitation to dream a little dream of her. I have a surprisingly easy time imagining Day herself singing it. Stranger things have happened. If Day ever makes her long-awaited return to performing and recording, maybe the first project she'll do is an album of songs by Nellie McKay.

Blossom Dearie (1924–2009)

As everyone says, it's a baby voice. And a lot of us first heard it as children. Most of us now bald-headed Gen Xers grew up with Blossom Dearie telling us exactly what we could do with the number eight and where we could stick our conjunctions in *Schoolhouse Rock,* a series of highly entertaining instructional musical cartoons shown on Saturday morning TV in the seventies, alongside such uplifting fare as *Scooby Doo* and *The Banana Splits.* Most of Dearie's music concerns itself with multiplication of a different sort, yet this may be the primary attraction of her art: this juxtaposition of the preadolescent charm of her voice with the distinctly adult agenda of the songs she sings.

We always knew that a seventy-minute set with her would be rife with mysteries and revelations. Dearie, who spent the final part of her career doing five or so shows per weekend at the now defunct Danny's on West 46th Street in New York, never gave you the whole story at once. As in that famous existentialist essay about the art of the striptease, Dearie's brand of storytelling is all about giving up secrets only slowly and reluctantly.

This is true whether she's going for laughs, as on "Someone's Been Sending Me Flowers" (on her 1995 collection *Our Favorite Songs*), or for something more serious, as on "Bye, Bye Country Boy," both of which stayed to the end in her tune stack. Jack Segal's lyric to "Country Boy" describes the end of a weeklong romance between a peripatetic chick singer and a local yokel she meets on the road; the irony arrives in the form of what she tells us but doesn't tell him, that she'd be willing to chuck the whole showbiz deal and settle down in No-wheresville if only he had chutzpah enough to ask. The professional woman who seems steely and flip on the exterior has a sentimental streak as big as New Jersey underneath.

Sheldon Harnick's "Someone's Been Sending Me Flowers" is just the opposite: What starts out sweet and tender soon turns out to be scathingly goofy. Our immediate impression is that a romantic young swain is doing the sending-of-flowers bit as a token of his sweet affection; however, we gradually learn that she is in fact being harassed by a wack job who hurls horticulture at her in various decrepit forms in a manner more like a weapon than a gift. "Besides being gray," she says of the foliage, "they were papier-mâché." And then there's the rock garden, which arrives "one rock at a time." Like much of her music, both "Country Boy" and "Flowers" are all about stripping away layers of facade to get at the truth.

Yet there is no deception or role playing with regard to Blossom Dearie herself—another fact that surprises observers is that what sounds like a stage name is, in fact, her actual given birth name. She was born in East Durham, a small town in the Catskill Mountains of New York, in 1924. "I feel like a true New Yorker," as she put it, "in the sense that I was born in New York state and live in New York City."

Dearie has also said, "My early roots in music came from listening to Ella Fitzgerald, Frank Sinatra, and George Burns and Gracie Allen," a statement that speaks volumes about the nature of her music and the importance of humor therein, particularly the mischievous, impish humor of Mr. (and especially Mrs.) Burns. In a brief autobiographical account, Dearie described herself as being attracted to the piano while still a baby. According to the lady herself, she was playing Debussy at the age of four months, adding dryly (and Gracie Allen–like), "this was before I had piano lessons." By the time she first took a crack at New York (the city within the state) twenty years later, she was, again by her own testimony, an accomplished pianist in an Art Tatum vein.

It's not known when Dearie began singing, but most of the work she found upon arriving in New York was as a vocalist. In two cases, she sang in vocal groups led by established big band leaders who shared a fixation with the word "blue": Woody Herman's Blue Flames and Alvino Rey's Blue Reys. She also fell in with members of New York's burgeoning modern jazz scene, or that particular sect of the bebop movement that was instigating the next big development in jazz, the Birth of the Cool. Both black (Miles Davis, John Lewis) and white (Gerry Mulligan, Lee Konitz) musicians, who would all be major figures in the jazz of the fifties, were constantly congregating in Gil Evans's apartment on 55th Street, and Dearie seems to have been the only female singer among them.

She didn't play or sing with the Miles Davis "Tuba" Nonet (later called the "Birth of the Cool" band), even though she was prominently mentioned in the official history of that group written (as liner notes for a reissue) by Mulligan, one of its founders. Along with Evans, another one of the central idea men of the proto-cool salon was Dave Lambert, who was constantly experimenting with new uses for the human voice much the way Evans himself was looking for new textures in instrumental jazz. Earlier, Lambert had recorded some very boppy vocal duos with Gene Krupa's band and his partner Buddy Stewart. In 1948, with Al Haig on piano, Lambert experimented with a trio by adding Dearie's voice to the duo on several titles (such as "In the Merry Land of Bop" and "Hot Halavah"); Lambert, Stewart, and

Dearie could be considered a predecessor to Lambert, Hendricks, & Ross. She turns up a year later scatting with guitarist Jimmy Raney on an early Prestige session done under Haig's leadership.

Dearie got in on the ground floor of the "vocalese" movement in other ways, too. In February 1952, she sang the "piano" part on the most successful vocalese record of all time, King Pleasure's "I'm in the Mood for Love." (That's her singing "What is all this talk about loving me?") Less than six weeks after that, she supplied the piano part again (playing, not singing) behind vocalist Annie Ross in her initial solo session, for DeeGee Records, run by Dizzy Gillespie and producer Dave Usher. The rest of the accompanying quartet was essentially the embryonic Modern Jazz Quartet: Milt Jackson, Percy Heath, and Kenny Clarke.

Later in 1952, Dearie moved to Paris, where American artists always seem to go after wars to find themselves. Her chief accomplishment there was serving as a moving force behind yet another "blue" vocal group, the Blue Stars. She recorded frequently in various capacities both with and without this group, as group singer, pianist, arranger, and occasional vocal soloist. Discographies list two French albums from this period that would appear to feature her more prominently, a set called *Bobby Jaspar and Blossom Dearie* (1956), co-starring her then husband, the French multireed player, and, apparently her own album, *Blossom Dearie Plays for Dancing* (1955).

Paris was an unlikely place for Dearie to network with an American record producer, but that's where she came into contact with Norman Granz. The famed impresario heard her playing and singing in Parisian hot spots and was so impressed that he extended her an offer to record for his new Verve label if she ever decided to return stateside. She came home to New York, more or less permanently, to cut her first American album in 1956.

On paper, Dearie's six early Verve records have much in common with the equally classic sessions Jeri Southern was cutting for Decca at the same time: pianist-singer, with a soft sweet voice, an understated style, super-intimate settings (usually just bass and drums), and extraordinarily high-class songs. Southern, on the whole, is a more dramatic singer; Dearie, with her baby voice, is more playfully kittenish, almost coy. There are far more Dearie discs in swinging tempo, while nearly everything Southern does is angst-fully slow.

All six of the Dearie Verve LPs—*Blossom Dearie* (1956), *Give Him the Oo-La-La* (1958), *Once Upon a Summertime* (1958), *Blossom Dearie Sings Comden and Green* (1959), *My Gentleman Friend* (1959), and *Soubrette Sings Broadway Hit Songs* (1960)—have been reissued on CD someplace in the world, the first four in the United States. Most also find her in the company of Oscar Peterson's rhythm section—Ray Brown, bass, and Ed Thigpen, drums, sometimes with Kenny Burrell or Mundell Lowe on guitar and Bobby Jaspar on flute; the only big band title is the last, the *Broadway* collection, which backs her with Russ Garcia's orch. Because they're all so similar (only the last two have any kind of theme), and so consistently excellent, it's easier to talk about the Verve work as a group rather than dealing with individual albums.

Dearie's autobiographical press release includes a statement regarding her early ambitions that's worth quoting at length:

"When I reached New York City, I discovered two different worlds of popular music, both of them using almost the same repertoire of songs, which were later labeled as standards (if these are 'standards,' what do we call the exceptional songs?) but different musical conceptions. If you heard Sarah Vaughan sing 'Embraceable You' at Birdland, then rushed over to hear Mabel Mercer at the By-Line Room, it was like listening to one singer from Mars and another from Pluto. The appreciation of the rhythm above all was definitely West Side. And utter disregard for rhythm and concentration on the lyrical content was definitely East Side. Mark Twain said they would never meet and I think he was ahead of his time. I tried putting them both together, with what I learned from Erroll Garner and Gracie Allen. When I was working upstairs at Julius Monk's in the late '50s, the juxtaposition of working there and recording in the afternoons with great swinging jazz musicians like Ray Brown, Herb Ellis and Jo Jones, was a perfect example of this. Here am I still sitting on that boundary line, loving every minute of it. It leads to many enlightening discussions." ("Mark Twain said they would never meet" is a quintessential Gracie Allen–esque misquoting of the famous Kipling line.)

Given that Dearie's work is a perfect synthesis of what she identifies as East Side and West Side ambitions—the desire to tell the story versus the idea of keeping the beat going—it's hardly surprising that she should name Frank Sinatra, who combined the musicality of Fitzgerald with the interpretive skills of Mercer, as a major inspiration. On *Give Him the Oo La La*, Dearie renders Cy Coleman and Carolyn Leigh's "I Walk a Little Faster" as pure, effortless balladry, at a slow tempo but with a definite beat. In contrast, one of her most convincing, purely rhythmic performances is the same team's fanciful piece of fluff, "The Doodlin' Song" (on *Once Upon a Summertime*), in which Coleman himself participates as duet partner.

She uses rhythm itself to tell a story very convincingly on one of the all-time Dearie perennials, "Surrey with the Fringe on Top," on *Summertime* and virtually every show I ever saw her do. In her treatment, the *Oklahoma!* opener becomes a slow and gently swinging jazz waltz. As she later wrote, "I love that song, and my interpretation sort of conjures up upstate New York rather than Broadway or Oklahoma." Another Richard Rodgers melody, "Everything I've Got Belongs to You," is another perfect juxtaposition of wit and swing, with Dearie missing neither a beat nor a punch line, while "Just One of Those Things" (on *Oo La La*) has her rocking with Ray Brown.

The Verve albums also display a penchant for songs that are French-leaning. She performs several *chansons* in the original language, the best of which are the strongly rhythmic "Tout Doucement," by Monsieurs Clausier and Mercadiers (on *Blossom Dearie*), and Charles Trenet's "Boum" (on *Gentleman Friend*), with an especially appropriate Jaspar flute solo. She also helped Michel Legrand break through to the American market; he was completely unknown when Dearie brought his song "La Valse des Lilas" ("The Waltz of the Flowers") to Johnny Mercer, who gave it an English lyric and American title, "Once Upon a Summertime." This haunting, minor-key waltz is a classic example of Dearie in high narrative style.

As good as she is with genuine French songs, she's almost better with *faux-franglais*. It's not known how Paris-ites would react to the likes of Cole Porter's "Give Him the Oo-La-La," Murray Grand's "Comment Allez Vous?," and Coleman and Leigh's "The Riviera," a tale of Americans vacationing in France who get fleeced by the locals. Dearie makes Oscar Hammerstein sound more romantic by singing his words in French on two selections on the original *Blossom Dearie* album, "I Won't Dance" and "It Might as Well Be Spring."

Both of those French translations were the work of her friend Bob Haymes, which brings up a key aspect of her fifty-year career: She was notoriously loyal to her songwriting pals. She recorded five songs by the obscure Haymes in the Verve years. The younger brother of crooner Dick Haymes, he had an off-and-on career as a singer before launching an off-and-on career as a songwriter. Haymes's only standard was "That's All," but Dearie showed that he had other good songs in him, particularly "They Say It's Spring" (on *Oo-La-La* and as a previous unissued bonus track on the *Blossom Dearie* CD), and another seasonal ode, "A Few Spring Mornings."

She was equally faithful to Betty Comden and Adolph Green, featuring their work for an entire album, the only songwriters to be given that full treatment. Likewise, almost all of her classic discs contain at least one song by Cy Coleman and Carolyn Leigh. In more recent years, Dearie clung just as loyally to the songs of Dave Frishberg and Bob Dorough, as well as to Jack Segal and Francesca Blumenthal, a contemporary New York songwriter, whose "The Lies of Handsome Men" was a Dearie favorite for many of her final years.

One wishes that the Dearie-Granz relationship had lasted longer: Six albums in five years hardly constitutes an abundance of riches. The quantity of first-rate Dearie on disc is as rare and precious as her baby voice itself. She appears to have left Verve after Granz sold the label and the new owners evidenced little interest in maintaining the relationship. Her output was minimal in the sixties, and what there is isn't always very good: One item is an obscure record called *Blossom Dearie Sings Rootin' Songs,* apparently issued as a promotional LP from a root beer company, which consists of her doing hit songs, from the early sixties.

Her last "classic" album is *May I Come In?* recorded for Capitol in 1964. Where the Decca executives had regarded Jeri Southern as a worthy label mate for the established Peggy Lee in 1951, the Capitol staff now seems to have regarded Dearie as the Peggy Lee for the sixties. The cover has Blossom all minked out, and, for that matter, so do the orchestrations. Onetime Lee collaborator Jack Marshall arranged and conducted in the same style that he brought to his work with Lee in 1958–59—and even included "I'm in Love Again," a Lee–Cy Coleman compilation. Apart from one standard ("I'm Old Fashioned"), the rest is mostly newish material of a very high caliber. There's more Mercer (the contemporary "Charade"), her first of many bossa novas ("Corcovado"), and another French import, "I Wish You Love."

The mere presence of an orchestra indicates that this is more of a pop project, employed with such subtlety that it's no less intimate or jazzy than any of Dearie's trio albums. No fewer than four songs here are by the gifted underdog team of composer Marvin Fisher and lyricist Jack Segal (who would later write many songs with Dearie herself): "Something Happens to Me," "When Sunny Gets Blue," done as a gently swinging waltz, "Love Is a Necessary Evil," and the title song, "May I Come In?" Apart from guitarist Marshall's sprightly arrangements, the package is also enlivened by the spry trumpet solos of the excellent Jack Sheldon, who confesses to having been "madly in love" with Dearie at this time. The way she's singing here, it would be hard not to be.

Sadly, *May I Come In?* was both a beginning and an end for Dearie at Capitol—not to mention being her last work for an American major. She spent a lot of time in England in the sixties, and doesn't turn up again on records until 1966, when she cut the first of four LPs for the English label Fontana. *Blossom Time at Ronnie's* (Ronnie Scott's, that is) and *Sweet Blossom Dearie* (both 1966) have worthy songs and trio accompaniments, while *Soon It's Gonna Rain* (1967) uses a full band.

Soon It's Gonna Rain is, in a sense, a follow-up to *May I Come In?* in that it combines gently swinging orchestrations, this time with a big string section, and as many better, newer songs as she can find. There are only two standards, both by Oscar Hammerstein: "A Wonderful Guy" (in an understated 3/4) and "Folks Who Live on the Hill." The landscape has changed: There's Burt Bacharach ("Trains and Boats and Planes," "Alfie") instead of Cy Cole-

man. Instead of four songs by Fisher and Segal, there are that many by Jobim. The most successful song is Jones and Schmidt's title tune "Soon It's Gonna Rain" from *The Fantasticks,* a nursery-rhyme-like ode of optimism that perfectly suits her voice and attitude, with a fine string orchestration by Reg Guest. That song is followed by "Sunny," a pop hit that here functions as a meteorological follow-up to "Rain" as well as the Fisher-Segal song about Sunny getting blue.

In their own way, *May I Come In?* and *Soon It's Gonna Rain* are both nearly as good as the classic six Verve albums. In 1970, her last Fontana album was *That's Just the Way I Want to Be,* which shows that the concept of what pop music was had done a complete turnaround even since 1967: The whole album is substandard contemporary songs dressed up in dreadful pseudo-psychedelic orchestrations. What's really disappointing is that the title isn't entirely a lie. This is at least partially the way Dearie wanted it to be, since most of the songs on it are hers. She chose this period to assert herself as a songwriter; it was, after all, the era of the singer-songwriter, and I wish I could report that her efforts in this area were any better than the average second-rate singer-songwriter pop song of the period. What's especially strange is that three of the songs are tributes to the talents of prominent British pop stars, including "Dusty Springfield," "Sweet Georgie Fame" (why she chose to honor this quickly forgotten English R&B singer I'll never know), and "Hey John," meaning Lennon. The only one of these songs to survive the era is the last. Dearie rerecorded it and continued to sing it over the years, and it went over well not because of the quality of the tune but because of her accompanying anecdote about Lennon being a fan of hers. (Personally, I never cared for "Hey John"— even though it was inspired by Lennon's and Dearie's mutual admiration for each other, it always seemed like she was sucking up.) Surprisingly, she never revived the best song on *That's Just the Way,* "I Know the Moon," with its catchy bass lines.

In 1973, Dearie began producing her own albums on her own label, Daffodil Records; unfortunately, the first of these more modest productions is sabotaged by the same problems as the 1970 album. She seems to feel the necessity of sounding "contemporary," and to think that the way to do it is to concentrate on original songs and to use electric rhythm sections.

The double LP *My New Celebrity Is You* (1976) has some brilliant tracks, especially the title—a particularly witty lyric by Mercer, one of his last, set to a melody by Dearie. But she also employs a rather irritating electric piano on many cuts and even attempts to sing Roberta Flack's hit "Killing Me Softly with His Song." Not an inspired idea. As late as the 1991 *Tweedledum and Tweedledee,* a collaboration with the gifted pianist and musical director Mike Renzi, Dearie is still relying overheavily on junky synthesizer sounds. However, the subjects of the album's tribute songs, "Everybody Loves Jobim" and "Fred Astaire," are more worthy *objets au hommage* than Georgie Fame or Dusty Springfield; there's also an original called "Blossom," in which the lyrics are more floral than autobiographical.

Dearie numbered her Daffodil albums, e.g., *My New Celebrity Is You* was subtitled "Daffodil Vol. 3." But just the same, nothing she ever did—even simple arithmetic—was totally free of ambiguity: The 1987 *Songs of Chelsea* was volume 10 and, what appears to be the next release, the 1991 *Tweedledum and Tweedledee,* was volume 15. What happened to volumes 11 through 14 remains a mystery.

Further complicating matters, not all of the Daffodils have been released on CD, but in 1995, Dearie compiled a selection of her best and most requested songs on a disc fittingly titled *Our Favorite Songs,* which includes most of the highlights from the series. *Our Favorite Songs* is notable in that it consists entirely of Dearie signatures composed by friends and colleagues; no Cole Porter or "Surrey with the Fringe on Top." Her single favorite would appear to be Dave Frishberg and Bob Dorough's "I'm Hip," which she apparently recorded on three separate occasions: In 1966 she sang it live at Ronnie Scott's; in 1975 (on *From the Meticulous to the Sublime*) she made her only studio version, which, alas, was something of a self-inflicted train wreck, in which she subjected the song to electronic textures and overdubbed several vocal tracks quoting other songs; in 1979 she did it live again, this time at Reno Sweeney (on the album *Needlepoint Magic*), and that is the rendition she reused on the *Favorite Songs* anthology.

The *Meticulous* album does contain at least a few sublime moments, particularly the closer, "How Do You Say Auf Wiedersehn?," which, for both Dearie and lyricist Johnny Mercer, serves as a Teutonic sequel to "Once Upon a Summertime." Yet the most salient feature of "Auf Wiedersehn" is that it features Dearie's solo acoustic piano accompaniment, which, by the seventies, had reached a new plateau. Dave Frishberg has written about a conversation he had with Bill Evans circa 1969, in which the late piano icon told him that Dearie "really knocked him out" and that he learned his device of "piled-fourths voicing of chords" from her and, further, that he named her as one of his inspirations. At a memorial held four months after her death, occasional collaborator Mike Renzi spoke about her unique harmonic voicings and reported that Dearie commissioned him to transcribe some of her solos for a songbook. Even though he got the notes down exactly right, he said, he couldn't come close to capturing her essence when he played them himself.

The last decade of her career found Dearie consolidating her accomplishments. From roughly 1998 to 2004 she appeared most weekends at Danny's Skylight Room on West 46th Street; from that point on, she slipped out of the limelight until her death at age eighty-four in February 2009. During the entire Danny's period, Dearie offered an extremely consistent program, which I must have heard at least a dozen times, and which was a live equivalent to the *Favorite Songs* collection. Throughout these years, her repertoire seemed to be permanently *pre-fixed.* You could always count on her to sing her hypnotically slow "Surrey with the Fringe on Top" and her three Frishberg specialties, "I'm Hip," "Peel Me a Grape," and "My Attorney, Bernie." She was the ideal interpreter of Frishberg, primarily because of the contrasts she brings out, in that she's so subtle and understated and Frishberg's characters are so outrageously broadly rendered: An overstated, self-proclaimed hipster who turns out to be a clueless clod; an Eartha Kitt–like sex kitten and gold digger lording it over one of her romantic conquests; a boorish businessman trumpeting the savvy of his solicitor—Dearie just naturally seemed funny embodying these personae even before she sang word one. (She was exquisitely understated with regards to everything, including the size of her voice and even her body.)

On *Our Favorite Songs,* Dearie introduces "I'm Hip" as the most requested song in her repertoire, and she always gives full credit to Bob Dorough, who wrote the music, and Frishberg, who did the words. Yet whenever Dorough himself plays and sings it, he inadvertently underscores what made Dearie so special. He tends to pound every note and pounce on every word, as if he were laboring hard to make it sound funny; Dearie knows that it is *already* funny—that she didn't need to do anything more to it. Likewise, John Wallowitch's "Bruce" starts out completely sincere, but turns out to be a hilarious description of a ghastly hag of a drag queen ("lacking allure"), and Dearie delivers lines like "undersize, thunder thighs" completely without any hint that the thing is supposed to be a gag. There was no one better at playing straight man to her own material.

Dearie was funny because of the contrast she brought out between herself and Bernie's client Brucie's friend. The same balance of the sublime and ridiculous informed her delivery of two of Sheldon Harnick's funniest efforts, "Someone's Been Sending Me Flowers" and "The Ballad of the Shape of Things"; she simply refuses to acknowledge that there's a joke until she and the audience are knee-deep in it. Sondheim's "Ladies Who Lunch" is in a sense the opposite of "I'm Hip"; instead of impersonating a buffoon of a hep cat who takes himself too seriously, Dearie shoots holes in the egos of women of a certain age and social station. They may think their busy little lives have meaning, but Dearie, by way of Sondheim, shows them otherwise. In *Company,* the song was poignant because Elaine Stritch's character turned out to be singing about herself, but Dearie's rendition is even more touching, at once comic and tragic, without needing to resort to Stritch's famous spoken asides, like the one about the hat.

Whether she's going for tears or laughter, there is, if not a formula, a dependable ratio: The less Dearie actually sings, the quieter and more understated she keeps everything (in that remarkable whisper of a voice), the more meaning she extracts from a text.

"Ladies Who Lunch" is a highlight of the following Daffodil release, the 1999 *Blossom's Planet*, which appears to be her final album (although who knows what's in the vault). The electronic strings are, at last, very tastefully deployed and even welcome, given the vast improvement over the technology of the seventies. There's also Dearie's final swinging waltz, "Bluesette," which is also one of her two final *franglais* songs, the other being "La Belle Dame Sans Regrets," by the British rocker Sting, and her latest bossa nova, "Love Dance," and an ultra-long, very slow, and very stringy "Wave."

She also does Francesca Blumenthal's "The Lies of Handsome Men." Another one of those Dearie classics that work on several levels, "Lies" has her finding mysteries to explore even where there apparently aren't any. She's not deceiving herself that the "Lies of Handsome Men" are anything other than lies, yet we're instantly hooked and want to stick with her to find out why a woman insists on believing them. We're determined to follow her trail of logic wherever it leads, much as we do with every Blossom Dearie song.

Matt Dennis (1914–2002)

As a performer, Matt Dennis only made about a half-dozen albums. As a songwriter, even though he worked steadily for several decades, he crafted perhaps a mere dozen songs that qualify as standards. Neither one of these statistics is particularly staggering, not compared with, say, Hoagy Carmichael or Johnny Mercer, both of whom wrote hundreds of songs and recorded steadily from the twenties to the fifties. But Dennis's output, both as a composer and as a singer-pianist, is of such high quality that even though his is not a vast legacy, it is nonetheless a major contribution to American popular music.

It's his singing that we're primarily concerned with here. Just as virtually every male singer who's stood in front of a band at any time in the last sixty years has dreamed of being Frank Sinatra (who, by the way, deserves credit for putting Dennis on the map as a songwriter), anyone who has ever played piano and sings in a small club wants to be Matt Dennis, whether he knows it or not. Bobby Short was too specialized, Nat Cole was too superhuman, Joe Mooney was too way out, Fats Waller hardly a romantic. Matt Dennis was the ideal role model.

Unlike Cole, Matt Dennis's strength was not godlike musical prowess, but like Bing Crosby, he made it look easy. It was only once you tried to do what Dennis did that you realized how tough it was. How hard it was to duplicate his rich piano technique,

that impeccable time with such a strong capacity for the right chords. And that voice, a dark, burntumber timbre, with a very quick vibrato that's especially evident on slow tempos. He's always on pitch, but at the same time he always sounds slightly on the "under" side; likewise, he keeps beautiful time, but he also rushes slightly. Both these characteristics only make his singing that much more appealing. Like Fred Astaire, Dennis uses an advanced sensitivity to time to compensate for what he perceives as deficiencies in terms of vocal range, and it's this capacity for singing around the tune that makes them two of the most interesting singers ever to tackle the Great American Songbook.

Dennis was born February 11, 1914, in Seattle. His father sang and his mother was a violinist, and the two of them worked in vaudeville in an act called the Five Musical Lovelands. When the troupe left the road, the Dennises settled in Los Angeles, just at the time the city was becoming a showbiz capital. Young Matt was singing and playing while in high school, by which time he was already directing his own dance band.

At nineteen, he became part of Horace Heidt and His Musical Knights, which had begun as a straightdown-the-middle dance band but by the midthirties was specializing in sweet music and novelties. He apparently sang with the band, and probably also wrote arrangements for it. By the late thirties, Dennis was freelancing as an arranger, accompanist, and songwriter around Hollywood, working with various singers and also playing and singing on his own in clubs. One of his first charges, in this early period, was writing words and music for what was billed as the theme song for the vocal group the Six Hits and a Miss, a snappy aria called "Relax," which the 6H&M recorded on Vocalion and which he himself later included on his 1955 album *Dennis, Anyone?*

While working in saloons at around this time, he met two gentlemen who would have a major impact on his career: NBC's Gordon Jenkins gave him work writing special material for that network and Tom Adair suggested that they write songs together. Adair was an aspiring lyricist who already had published poems in *The Saturday Evening Post*, but who was then holding down a day job with the L.A. water company.

Thanks to his connections with vocal groups, Dennis was already friendly with the rising singer Jo Stafford, and wrote for her both as a member of the Stafford Sisters and as a Pied Piper. When the Pipers joined Tommy Dorsey's orchestra, the Sentimental Gentleman also put Dennis on his payroll. Ever the astute music businessman, Dorsey thus ensured himself of first-rate exclusive material for both his band and his publishing company. With Dorsey's encouragement, the songwriting team of Matt Dennis and Tom Adair was launched in a big way.

"Tom was a very talented man," Dennis told me

fifty years later, "and I actually picked him out to go with me. Tommy Dorsey said bring along your favorite lyric writer, when I first signed with Tommy." According to Dennis, Adair had already written the lyric to "Will You Still Be Mine" (band singer Connie Haines's best record ever) when they first met; Dennis quickly came up with a tune to go with the text, and then they just as speedily knocked out "Everything Happens to Me" (an ironic, happy-sad concoction worthy of Rodgers and Hart) and "Let's Get Away from It All" (a two-sided extravaganza for all of the band's vocalists). Thus, the partnership gave birth to three of its most popular standards within a few days. Said Dennis, "It was a hell of a week!"

Dennis wrote about ten tunes for the Dorsey band, most of them instantly immortalized by the emerging Sinatra, as well as by Jo Stafford, Connie Haines, and the Pied Pipers. These comprise just about the most impressive collaboration between a songwriter and a bandleader in the swing era. In addition to the three above, there were also "Let's Just Pretend," "The Skunk Song" (admittedly not a classic), "Little Man with a Candy Cigar" (Stafford's first solo vocal), "Violets for Your Furs" (a major early solo hit for Sinatra), "Free for All" (a wartime patriotic number for the whole cast), "The Night We Called It a Day" (one of the most touching torch songs of any era). (Without Dennis, Adair wrote two outstanding additional songs for Young Blue Eyes: "In the Blue of Evening" and "There's No You.")

The Dorsey organization put Dennis on the map as a songwriter, so it's somewhat surprising the leader never elected to feature him as singer or pianist, even though he was going places in these departments as well. According to Dennis, he would demonstrate his songs to the band and Sinatra "would flatter even me 'cause he would listen to the way I phrase my songs. They were my songs, and he would interpret them much like I did, you know, like when I was doing a personal appearance." When we hear Dennis sing his own songs, we hear a smooth approach roughly in the same ballpark as Sinatra's, although without the Voice's enormous chops and amazing breath control. The Dennis-Dorsey relationship ended somewhat abruptly when Dennis joined the air corps, where he spent the bulk of the war years.

Upon returning to Los Angeles, Dennis went back to playing and singing in Hollywood watering holes. Now established as a composer (though he doesn't seem to have worked with Adair after being in the service), he was about to become better known as a performer. In January 1947, he sang with Benny Goodman on both a radio show and a Capitol side (an obscure alternate take of Kurt Weill's "Moon-Faced, Starry-Eyed"; Johnny Mercer sang the issued version). He also sings on six 78 singles by Jo Stafford's future husband, Paul Weston, including Carmichael's hit "Ole Buttermilk Sky" and the aquatic novelty "A Trout, No Doubt."

The earliest extended series of Dennis recordings is a group of radio transcriptions made for the MacGregor corporation on several dates in the late forties and early fifties. (The latest song included is "Angel Eyes," first heard in 1953.) There are at least two groups of sessions, as most of the titles have Dennis accompanied by his own orchestra, while several of the songs (most notably his own "Everything Happens to Me") feature a small orchestra conducted by transcription bandleader Eddie Skrivanek. So far, selections from these have been issued on several LPs, among them *Saturday Date* on the rack job label Tops and *The Original Matt Dennis* on Glendale.

It goes without saying that the Dennis-MacGregor material deserves to be collected on a comprehensive CD reissue: The piano sides are especially worthy, probably the most intimate setting in which this most intimate of performers ever recorded, and there are a lot of songs Dennis never sang elsewhere on disc. Most notable of these is his own "Natch," a very agreeable rhythm song and a prime candidate for a Matt Dennis songbook album. (So far, the only important all-Dennis projects have been jazzman Dave Brubeck's 1962 *Angel Eyes* and, more recently, cabaret singer Mary Foster Conklin's *Blues for Breakfast*.)

The sweet spot of Dennis's work as a recording artist consists of five albums made in the mid- to late fifties (I have yet to find a discography that accurately dates these LPs), for three different labels:

- *Matt Dennis Plays and Sings Matt Dennis* (Trend, 1954)
- *Dennis, Anyone?* (RCA, 1955)
- *She Dances Overhead* (RCA, circa 1956)
- *Play Melancholy Baby* (RCA, circa 1958)
- *Welcome Matt Dennis* (Jubilee, circa 1958 or 1959)

As it happens, Dennis's two finest albums are the two most different albums in the quintet: *Plays and Sings Matt Dennis* on the one hand, and *She Dances Overhead* on the other. They may be classified as extremes in several senses, firstly in that *Plays and Sings* uses just a trio (recorded live) and *Dances Overhead* (made in the studio) employs a full symphonic contingent: big band, strings, and woodwinds. Further, as the title suggests, *Plays and Sings* is all Dennis's own compositions while *Dances Overhead* is the only album he ever made that's entirely written by others—specifically, a collection of mostly well-known songs by Rodgers and Hart.

She Dances Overhead is an album that a lot of pubescent male record collectors have purchased without even knowing who Matt Dennis was—or, in a lot of cases, without even having heard of Rodgers and Hart. The cover is one of the major accomplishments of the great early years of the LP: a beautiful shot of a woman from the waist down, resplendent in shiny gold high heels, stockings, and garters. The model's legs are in full color, and positioned above a superimposed shot of Matt Dennis's face, in such a way as to suggest the actual act of dancing on the ceiling. Such subtleties were lost on most of us, who only cared about the gams and garters. Thank God some of us actually played the record when we got it home, because we then fell in love with the voice of Dennis and the songs of R&H as much as we had with the faceless babe on the cover (or what we could see of her—for all I know, she actually had a face like Shrek).

The program deftly switches between ballads with strings, among them a stunning "Isn't It Romantic" (with verse) and up-tempos with horns and rhythm ("Mimi," "I Married an Angel"). Former Goodman and Shaw trumpeter Harry Geller conducted the band, which appears to be playing orchestrations by several unnamed but top Hollywood arrangers. The charts are superb and suit Dennis superbly, while his mellow baritone has never been more appealing. This is virtually the only modern version of "Give Her a Kiss," an obscure song from the obscure film *The Phantom President* (George M. Cohan's only movie, and his first of two politically oriented collaborations with R&H), and Dennis turns it into a fifties swinger of the highest order.

Likewise, there's a lovely ballad rendition of "This Funny World," not notably done again until Tony Bennett twenty years later. Dennis also manages to put his stamp on some of the more familiar Rodgers and Hart chestnuts, like "Mimi," de-waltzed into a swung 4/4, and "I Didn't Know What Time It Was," in a slow three. "Have You Met Miss Jones" (from the second R&H/Cohan collaboration, *I'd Rather Be Right*) is a surprise in that most jazz-pop singers of the era did it as a swinger. Dennis makes it a danceable ballad, again with verse. The climax is side two, track one, a magnificent "Mountain Greenery" in which Dennis excels on both a scat and a piano solo.

I wouldn't be happy if forced to choose between *Dances Overhead* and *Plays and Sings*, but at gunpoint I would have to pick the latter. This wonderful album's history is somewhat confusing. *Matt Dennis Plays and Sings Matt Dennis* was originally produced in 1954 by Albert Marx for his Trend label, which was, not long after, absorbed into Kapp Records, who issued it with a different but, subsequently, more familiar cover. Since then, through many subsequent absorptions, it's become part of the Universal Music Group, and was issued with the original Trend cover on a Japanese Universal CD in late 2002, the year that Dennis died. In 2005, it had one more incarnation, as half of a Spanish CD with the longish title of *Matt Dennis Plays and Sings Matt Dennis Live in Hollywood*. This latter disc turns out to include the 1954 live album as well as the complete *Dennis, Anyone?*, another live album, this one recorded a year later.

Dennis never sounds more warm, intimate, and swinging than when he's doing his own material. Even though Sinatra returned time and again to "Violets for Your Furs," "Let's Get Away from It All," "Everything Happens to Me," and "Angel Eyes," among others, even the Chairman had a hard time topping Dennis when he plays and sings Dennis. This live set, taped at an obscure L.A. nightspot called the Tally Ho, adds more fuel to the fire; Dennis (or someone) announces several tracks with audible slate/take numbers ("T-72, take two"), yet somehow this makes the program even more up close and personal; rather than breaking the spell, you really feel you're there, present in the club with him.

Dennis performs virtually all his best-known compositions here, and makes even his lesser efforts, such as "Junior and Julie," sound great. (It was doubtlessly on the strength of this performance on this album that the song was revived by the young contemporary singer Erin Bode in 2004.) Also heard here is Dennis's wife and singing partner, Virginia Maxey, a veteran of the Charlie Barnet, Tony Pastor, and Bob Crosby orchestras (or so the liner notes tell us), who sounds something like Margaret Whiting but without quite so much in the chops department. Maxey joins him on two other lesser-known songs, "We Belong Together" and "When You Love a Fella." The major surprise here is "It Wasn't the Stars" with a lyric by one Dave Gillam, which turns out to be a minor Dennis classic that somebody ought to revive. It's hard to believe Nat Cole never got around to it.

Matt Dennis Plays and Sings Matt Dennis also includes the definitive version of what is probably the finest song in Dennis's canon: "Angel Eyes." Dennis and Earl Brent (a Hollywood lyricist and arranger credited on around thirty films) wrote it in 1951, and two years later he sang it himself in an obscure Ida Lupino film noir called *Jennifer* (1953). The promotional tagline for the film was, "Did Jennifer fear his fingers at her throat . . . or the burning caress of his lips?" Yet the real mystery here is why Dennis and Brent didn't go on to write a ton of songs together, because, Your Honor, on the evidence of "Angel Eyes" they could have become another Burke and Van Heusen. I rest my case.

According to Dennis, the premier recording was by his friend Herb Jeffries, but the song's first "real champion" was Ella Fitzgerald: "I was playing in a little nightclub in Reno, Nevada, in 1951, around Christmas, and Ella came there, too, to perform at a hotel there, and Hank Jones was her accompanist at the time, a wonderful pianist. I played 'Angel Eyes,' which was still unpublished at the time, for her, and that was the first time she heard it. This was on a Monday, I think, and she was opening two days later on a Wednesday, and she said, 'I'd like to open with that song, use it as my opening number.' I said, 'Of course!' So Hank Jones learned the song overnight. I went to her opening night, and she introduced me on the floor and said 'I'm going to record this.' That was very nice! She recorded it with Sy Oliver [June 1952]. The interesting story there was that she recorded for Decca, and Decca had a strange policy at that time. Even though Decca had a wonderful catalogue of wonderful artists, they were not too oriented with the blues and jazz, and they didn't think the song was too commercial. They held up her record for a year, and she was so mad, she quit Decca because of that, and went with Verve. She recorded the song four times after that. One time I was shopping in a mall out here, years ago, and in the window of one store there was a TV set, and I just happened to walk by, and there was Ella being interviewed by Mike Douglas. He asked her, 'What is your favorite song of all time?' and I heard her say, 'Angel Eyes.'" (It should be noted that Matt's was one of several explanations as to why Ella parted company with Decca in 1955.)

As I've said, although the competition was steep—Cole, Fitzgerald, and Sinatra (among many others)—the definitive version of "Angel Eyes" is the songwriter's own. Sinatra liked to refer to himself as a "saloon singer," which was true in the sense that he usually sang saloon songs, not songs in a saloon. "Angel Eyes" was the ultimate saloon song—its only possible rival was "One for My Baby." Both are half-a-conversation songs that communicate even more with what they leave unsaid. Neither song tells you explicitly what happened in the relationship, that's not important; what's important is that the guy is dealing with his pain through self-medication of the kind that's available in a saloon. In "One for My Baby" he's just drinking; in "Angel Eyes," he's more social and proactive. He's operating on the pretense that he's looking for his Angel Eyes, yet he's also more delusional if he thinks he's going to get her back. When Dennis sings the song, he becomes every pianist-singer in every saloon that ever was, trying to realize that love's not around, yet knowing on some unspoken level that it's uncomfortably near.

The other two RCA albums, *Dennis, Anyone?* and *Play Melancholy Baby*, are a notch below the Rodgers and Hart and the live at the Tally Ho recording. *Dennis, Anyone?* is also a live album, but for nearly fifty years it was a mystery: There's no mention of this in the liner notes (by columnist Jack O'Brian) or anywhere else in the packaging. It wasn't until the 2005 Spanish Fresh Sounds CD that it was revealed that *Dennis, Anyone?* was recorded in 1955 at an obscure Hollywood club, the Encore.

The cover of *Dennis, Anyone?* is another superimposition involving Dennis's face, this time with a cartoon tennis ball. It is a follow-up to the Trend album not only in the sense of being taped in a club but also in that it consists entirely of Dennis's own songs, none of which is repeated from the 1954 album.

Where *Plays and Sings* can truly be called *The Best of Matt Dennis*—as both a performer and a songwriter—*Dennis, Anyone?* is mostly Dennis's

grade-B material; every song here is about on the level of "Junior and Julie." "Old Uncle Fud," for instance, is ersatz Johnny Mercer and Hoagy Carmichael, while "Devil Talk" would have made good material for Harry Belafonte, a kind of a calypso-mambo with bongo drums. The twelve songs here are all good, but hardly classics on the level of "Angel Eyes" or the splendid songs of the Dennis-Adair-Dorsey era. None of the ballads really stands out in a positive way, but several of the faster pieces do: "Relax" (which he does much more convincingly than the Six Hits and a Miss) sets a modest goal and achieves it, and "Show Me the Way to Get Out of This World (Cause That's Where Everything Is)" is the closest thing to a standard here, being a tune also recorded by Harry James, Peggy Lee, and Ella Fitzgerald; Dennis's reading is rife with energy, as evidenced by a good scat interlude and piano solo.

What's really confusing is that *Dennis, Anyone?* is a live album packaged like a studio set, whereas *Play Melancholy Baby* is a studio set presented like a live album—the cover shows him singing (presumably in a saloon) while a model, wearing a low-cut gown and looking like a sorority sister of Lauren Bacall or Betty Page, listens enraptured. Yet despite the misleading imagery, no one would be the least bit disappointed in *Play Melancholy Baby*, which consists of two songs with melodies by Dennis and ten by others, both standards ("My Funny Valentine" and "Spring Is Here," which were not on the Rodgers and Hart album) and obscurities ("Heart of Stone"). Backed by a zippy vocal group (also better than the Six Hits and a Miss) and the fine West Coast trumpeter Don Fagerquist on different tracks, Dennis also turns in stunning readings of the early Arlen classics "Between the Devil and the Deep Blue Sea" and "I Gotta Right to Sing the Blues." Of Dennis's own songs, "This Is My Story" is a little melodramatic, while "For the Losers" is a sort of prequel to both "Everything Happens to Me" and "Angel Eyes."

The first two songs on side two are one of the most and one of the least performed songs of all time. "Heart of Stone" is a thirties antique, done only by bands like Hal Kemp and Harry Roy—an obscurity here saved from oblivion. His treatment of the barfly's perennial "My Melancholy Baby," with an original verse, is one of the most sincere and touching renditions of that saloon singer's staple, which at one time—no longer—was famous for being overdone. (In all my years of hearing songs in saloons, nightclubs, and cabarets, I don't think I've ever actually heard anyone sing "My Melancholy Baby.") Dennis has written his own autobiographical verse to the song, which talks about "When the crowd thins down, and the hour gets late and the customers are cryin' in their beer." That's when they come to him and request this pre–World War I perennial. With this verse, he transforms "Melancholy" from a saloon song to a saloon song about a saloon song, showing that the song's power isn't necessarily in its lyrics but in its legacy as the ultimate request of melancholy barflies. (I also love what he does with the Cuban song "Quizás, Quizás, Quizás [Perhaps, Perhaps, Perhaps].")

After *Melancholy,* there's one final studio album, *Welcome Matt Dennis,* recorded for Jubilee, on which he's backed by an orchestra arranged and conducted by Sy Oliver, an old friend from the Dorsey days. Where *Play Melancholy Baby* is mostly soft and intimate, *Welcome Matt Dennis* is loud and brassy and in-your-face. As annotator Mort Goode points out, Oliver used Dennis's trio as a core unit, a section unto itself (which indeed it was), and then augmented it with two different instrumental groups, one of five reeds, the other of eight brass— four trumpets and four trombones.

The title is to be taken somewhat literally (the cover shows him in formal evening wear opening his door and eagerly laying down a welcome mat for a hot-looking dish in fancy calico). The songs—three new originals and the rest from the Jazz Age and the Depression—all concern themselves with couples and families staying home and enjoying themselves romantically and otherwise: "My Blue Heaven," "Let's Put Out the Lights (And Go to Sleep)," and "By the Fireside"—only "Cheek to Cheek" describes an activity taking place elsewhere (although plenty of folks used to dance to the radio in their parlors), and it's done as a piano-orchestra instrumental. Even the one saloon song in the set concerns itself with heading in a hearth-bound direction: "Show Me the Way to Go Home," in which Dennis coyly omits the word "drink" whenever it occurs.

Yet most of the album is upbeat. The few ballads here are in semi-slow dance time—but generally it's all either biting brass or scintillating saxes. As with "Melancholy Baby," Dennis has a gift for reanimating the hoariest of chestnuts; this "Blue Heaven" is one of the most swinging I've ever heard, the interplay between his trio and the unified brass is remarkable. There's a full chorus of piano leading to a scat sequence, then he jumps back into the lyrics for the last 16 bars. The three new Matt Dennis–Bob Russell songs—"You Make Me Feel at Home," "Welcome Mat," and "Your Family"—are all worthy additions to the catalogue. "Cheek to Cheek" finds the trio playing against the eight brass instrumentally, in a manner similar to but perhaps even superior to the Nat Cole piano-and-orchestra album, *The Piano Style of Nat King Cole*—Dennis and Oliver show how words are often unnecessary when two are dancing cheek to cheek.

Dennis started his career, more or less, with Tommy Dorsey and Sy Oliver; in 1956 he guested on Dorsey's TV show, and it seems fitting for him to have reunited with Oliver for his last classic album. For many years, he went on playing all the top rooms across the country, often in tandem with his singing wife, and made dozens of TV appearances— memorably on Rosemary Clooney's 1957 series, and

on his own show, on which he was introduced by Frank Sinatra, who (according to Jack O'Brian) "proudly announced that he was speaking as the 'President, Hoboken Local, Matt Dennis Fan Club.'" (There was at least one more record, though: *Matt Dennis Is Back!,* made in 1981 when he was pushing seventy.) In 1965, jazz great Dave Brubeck showed his admiration for Dennis with *Angel Eyes,* a quartet album with seven of the composer's most famous songs.

On "Will You Still Be Mine," his first important song and the first track of his best album, *Matt Dennis Plays and Sings,* he predicts a time "When Miss Monroe gets old and flat," and then quickly mock-corrects himself with "fat!" Marilyn Monroe, unfortunately, did not live long enough to attain either state of existence. Matt Dennis, however, did live to the age of eighty-eight, and by all the evidence, he never became either. He died June 21, 2002, a few days before his longtime friend Rosemary Clooney.

A year or so after that, the New York–based Mary Foster Conklin did a fine program of Dennis songs at Danny's Skylight Room later released as the album *Blues for Breakfast.* Around 2000, however, another New York singer, Carol Fredette, included one of his songs at a show in New York's Birdland. Fredette is one of those singers I'm always hoping will yet be discovered in a big way, like Shirley Horn or Carol Sloane. Her most recent album at that time was a collection of songs by Dave Frishberg and Bob Dorough, both highly talented latter-day descendants of Dennis.

Unexpectedly, about halfway through, Fredette announced that she was going to take a break from the expected program and, instead, sing "Angel Eyes." All I can say is that it was hard to go back to the rest of the show. You just don't make other songwriters look good by forcing a comparison with Matt Dennis.

Jimmy Durante (1893–1980)

Back in the days of Napster, I once downloaded an MP3 file that purported to be Louis Armstrong singing "As Time Goes By." This was of great interest to me, because, to the best of my knowledge, Armstrong never sang "As Time Goes By," not in any format of sound recording, from cylinder to acoustic disc to LP, mini-disc, CD, or MP3. When I played the track, I wasn't too surprised to find that the raspy voice singing "As Time Goes By" wasn't Armstrong's at all but Jimmy Durante's. This was and is a very familiar track, originally released on his LP *Way of Life* and long available on the CD compilation *As Time Goes By: The Best of Jimmy Durante.* To someone who has no idea what he's listening to, like the rock 'n' roll computer kids who were the primary users of the once dreaded Napster, the rasp of Durante is identical to the rasp of Armstrong.

And yet I understand the mistake, especially since Durante and Armstrong had more in common than gravelly voices. Both were arch satirists who employed rhythm as a weapon as well as the music of words. There were other entertainers—most of them ethnic types, like Desi Arnaz (supposedly Durante's best friend in his post-stroke old age)—who used mispronunciations and malapropisms to gleeful comic and even chaotic effect, but Armstrong and Durante elevated these ploys to a grand art.

Both of them mangled the English language with a razor-sharp satirical wit that, in Durante's case especially, bordered on the anarchic. There are too many great Durante lines to quote, but I will share a couple of Armstrong's, as when he described the medical condition known as "very close veins" or when he referred to bandleader Guy Lombardo as his "inspirator." When you attack language, you undermine the very basis of civilization—this and nothing less seemed to be Durante's intent.

Yet Durante and Armstrong each played by the rules, too: Despite their unconventional voices, they both sang absolutely in tune with nearly perfect intonation. Both men were eventually absorbed into the mainstream, and, parallel to each other, evolved from revolutionary harlequin to cuddly establishment figure without losing any of their comedic edge but while gaining considerable coinage (both cultural and otherwise). One ethnic instrumentalist-vocalist who learned from both was Louis Prima, who absorbed from Durante the use of a relentless, nonstop tempo and a show that was constantly in motion. Another Italian disciple, Tony Bennett (who lists Sinatra, Armstrong, and Durante as his three favorite performers), once described Durante in action as "the greatest entertainer I ever saw. I never saw so much energy onstage!"

James Francis Durante was born on the Lower East Side of Manhattan on February 10, 1893. His parents were immigrants from Salerno, Italy; his father was a barber, and his mother, according to his biographer, David Bakish (*Jimmy Durante: His Show Business Career*), was a mail-order bride. Jimmy and three older siblings grew up amid the squalor of the slums, but in later years he insisted that his family was better off than most because his father had a profitable trade. "My dad made a good livin'," he said. "We were born in the back of the barbershop." After the young James had been studying piano for a number of years, the family was actually able to buy one. "I think we were the only ones with a piano," he put it. "We were the aristocrats of the neighborhood."

In the very early years of the twentieth century, Durante, already a first-generation American, also became a first-generation participant in the newly emerging American style of popular music. His parents and his professor gave him classical works (and light classical, but nonetheless socially acceptable, pieces like Von Suppé's *Poet and Peasant Overture*) to learn, but he was immersed in ragtime. By 1908, the fifteen-year-old "Ragtime Jimmy" was playing semiprofessionally all over New York and filling requests for sentimental songs of the nineties and "aughts" in every rough Tenderloin area in the city: the Bowery, Coney Island, Chinatown. In the early teens, he worked frequently with a young and energetic entertainer named Eddie Cantor.

As a pianist Durante had the good fortune to be in exactly the right place at the right time. Right after World War I, that is, when the original jazz boom was launched by the Original Dixieland Jazz Band, who inspired a mania for five-piece bands playing in the New Orleans style. Then again, when Mamie Smith's 1920 "Crazy Blues" opened up the "race" records market, Durante was also right there, an enterprising player who was almost preordained to succeed in the postwar climate: He was not only a more than competent pianist, steeped in the developing African American idiom, but he could write songs and he could put together bands.

Durante's bands are of special interest to jazz history because of his employment of authentic New Orleans players. From 1918 to 1922 he recorded prolifically, initially as the leader of the Original New Orleans Jazz Band, a five-piece unit very much in the style of the ODJB. In 1921 and 1922, he also recorded extensively with Lanin's Southern Serenaders, under the direction of Sam Lanin, and Ladd's Black Aces, two bands that more or less evolved into one of the most important and prolific groups of the early jazz era, the Original Memphis Five.

For worse or for better, this prehistoric period would be Durante's most prolific as a recording artist—unfortunately, he would never record nearly as much in his later guise as a singing vaudevillian. By 1923, he had made the transition: He was already opening his own speakeasy, the Club Durant, and working with his two partners, Lou Clayton (born Louis Finkelstein) and Eddie Jackson. The short-lived Club Durant (it was closed by the police before the end of 1924) would be endlessly mythologized and re-created for the rest of Durante's life. This was where he perfected his comedy style, both as a soloist and as part of the trio. After working in nightclubs and speakeasies for most of the twenties, Clayton, Jackson, and Durante made their vaudeville debut in 1927. Two years later, they made their legit—Broadway—debut in Florenz Ziegfeld's production *Show Girl*, sharing the stage with Ruby Keeler and Duke Ellington's orchestra, while Al Jolson sang from the audience for the first week.

It wasn't until 1929 that the trio left the first extant document of Clayton, Jackson, and Durante in action. This was a two-sided Columbia 78 of "Can Broadway Do Without Me" and "So I Ups to Him," two CJ&D specialties that were also performed by the threesome in *Show Girl*. The Durante voice is, though no less raspy, considerably higher pitched (he was thirty-six) and the tempo is more gentle and less frenetic than the Durante we know from the forties and fifties. But all the trademarks are there, starting with that familiar combination of self-deprecation and exaggerated braggadocio. The first cut has the threesome proclaiming Durante the biggest star there is ("Throw in the other knee and Jolson is out"), the second has him declaring himself a tough guy. In both cases the other two cheer him from the sidelines ("Sing it like you're getting paid for it, Jimmy!"), simultaneously encouraging and undermining him.

Between 1930 and 1940, Durante would appear in six more Broadway shows, justifying a well-earned boast he later made to Tony Bennett that he had had songs written for him by George and Ira Gershwin (*Show Girl*), Rodgers and Hart (*Billy Rose's Jumbo*, as well as the Paramount Picture *The Phantom President*), "Cole Porter and Cole Porter" (*The New Yorkers, Red, Hot and Blue*). Durante explained that he mentioned Cole Porter's name twice because "he wrote both woids *and* music." He could have also listed Arthur Schwartz and Dorothy Fields, who wrote *Stars in Your Eyes* for him, and Lew Brown and Ray Henderson (*Strike Me Pink*) and Jimmy McHugh and Al Dubin (*Keep off the Grass*), the latter two both being revues. Songwriter Ervin Drake also had the brilliant idea of writing a comic musical version of *Cyrano de Bergerac*, with Durante in the lead (which has been performed in cabaret by Durante impressionist Ricky Ritzel) but was unfortunately never produced because MGM wouldn't allow him enough time between pictures for an extended Broadway appearance.

Hollywood was quick to tap Durante in the early days of talking pictures, first recruiting the entire CJ&D trio in *Roadhouse Nights* (actually filmed in Astoria, New York), which contains the earliest use of the Durante catchphrase "I gotta million of 'em!" All his other films feature him as a solo attraction, even though he continued to split his MGM paycheck with Clayton and Jackson. For a time, MGM made him a co-lead with former silent comedy star Buster Keaton, a partnership that served neither well, as Keaton's passive style didn't mesh with Durante's in-your-face antics.

He appeared in an average of one film every year in the thirties and forties—pictures that were both good and bad, the best remembered being a series of lavish largely Technicolor musicals done at MGM after the war. After that, he most frequently appeared in all-star spectaculars, like *Pepe* and *It's a Mad Mad Mad Mad World*, and special productions, such as his best movie, the 1962 film of *Billy Rose's Jumbo*, which teamed him with another wonderful singing comic, Martha Raye, and leading lady Doris Day, who said, "Jimmy can do no wrong. Everybody loves him and his singing is just plain beautiful." His work is often brilliant in pictures, although he's generally only kept around as comic relief, rarely getting more than one or two numbers to himself in each film.

(Time Warner would do well to issue a best-of-Durante—*That's Durante!*—DVD collecting all his best bits from all the MGM pictures.)

Yet though his film legacy is rich, his overall output of commercial recordings is rather disappointing: He recorded only sporadically during his Hollywood years. There's a pair of sides including his theme "Inka Dinka Do" for Brunswick in 1933, then one 78 for Majestic in 1946. The rest of his career wasn't much: about nineteen titles for Decca and another nineteen for MGM Records done between 1944 and 1955. In all, it's a very modest catalogue, considering that Durante possessed one of America's most familiar voices.

But where Durante really shone, apart from nightclubs, was radio and, later, television, where he was at the center of the action, not relegated to the sidelines. At one point, Decca supplemented the smallish Durante discography with a glorious nine-track LP taken from radio shows entitled *Club Durant*. Not only was this Durante in front of a live audience, but Decca wisely selected tracks on which he interacts with a bevy of co-stars. Some of these partners were the old-school showbiz types you would expect, like Cantor, Jolson, and Sophie Tucker; others were more surprising: Peter Lawford, Ethel Barrymore, and Metropolitan Opera star Helen Traubel. In the post–*Sleepless in Seattle* years, a number of other radio tracks were issued on CD, on the collections *September Song* (Natasha Imports), *Durante: The Patron of the Arts*, and *I Say It with Music* (both on Viper's Nest).

Club Durant is perhaps the most essential Durante release of them all. In the music of Jolson, Crosby, and Sinatra, duets are a secondary consideration, but it's in his duos that one finds the purest essence of the great Durante. When he plays off another singer, that's when we get him at his most extreme: Durante the enemy of pretension, the saboteur of overblown high culture, the assassin of all things hoity-toity. He frequently achieves this by posing as a sage who's forever coaching his fellow thespians in the finer theatrical arts, informing Ethel Barrymore that there's a place in the theater for her, advising Bing Crosby that he should sing soft, sing sweet, and sing gentle, or telling Frank Sinatra (in the film *It Happened in Brooklyn*) that the song has to come from the heart. A big part of Durante's shtick, contributing to his self-deprecating/self-inflating image, is passing himself off as a guru.

There are times when he completely eliminates even the most rudimentary use of language—like Armstrong scatting "Heebie Jeebies," Durante uses a vocabulary all his own, running around shouting things like "Inka Dinka Do" and "Chidabee." In the same way that most Durante lyrics are about how great he is, delivered in what could be called tongue-in-cheek fashion, the lyrics to Durante's musical nonsense songs tend to be concerned with how great these songs themselves are. Most famously, "Inka

Dinka Do" starts with an introductory verse that places the song in the larger context of musical nonsense, like "Vo De Oh Do" and "Boop Oop-a Doop." Then in the chorus Durante informs us how "Inka Dinka" has got the whole world ("woild") croonin', and that even "Eskimo belles up in Iceland" are digging it. "Chidabee" promises its listeners that "someday even Frank and Bing will sing Chidabee Chidabee Chidabee . . .'"

He also makes frequent references not only to Clayton and Jackson but to an only slightly more fictitious character named Umbriago, which as many listeners knew was the Italian word for "intoxicated." Durante delineates his exploits in "Umbriago" (his first Decca disc, in 1944), which he later develops into a dance called "The Umbriago," which was copyrighted in 1952 as "The Dance of Umbriago." (In still another incarnation, he cites *Forever Umbriago* as his favorite novel. "Ah, literature!") In fact, social dances in general were a big part of the Durante mythology: Here was yet another way for the professor to bark instructions and coach from the sidelines on still more quasi-nonsensical arias like "The Hot Pattata," "Do the Strutaway," "Again You Turn-a," and others.

The war and postwar years, when he was in his fifties, were Durante's apogee, particularly the radio work—Marshall McLuhan's "hot medium"—with its lightning-quick tempos. In 1941, Warner Bros. tried pairing him with Phil Silvers, another fast-tongued comic who did his own variation on Durante's "teaching bit" ("Round tones! Round tones!"). The resulting film, *You're in the Army Now*, survives more as a curio than a resounding success. Durante made a major hit on the radio as half of a team with Garry Moore, who was too funny to be a mere straight man yet who wasn't quite funny enough on his own to be thought of as a major comic talent. (Moore later said he didn't feel he rated title billing at all, but Durante insisted they receive equal status.) In subsequent shows, with the likes of Victor Moore, Arthur Treacher, and even Peggy Lee as his co-stars and comic foils, Durante fared equally well.

The late forties shows are fast, fast, fast, and the tempo suits Durante perfectly. He still has that razor-sharp sense of timing and the explosive sense of humor—he's practically a one-man Spike Jones. In a parody of bandleader Phil Spitalny's *Hour of Charm* radio shows featuring "Evelyn and Her Magic Violin," Durante announces the appearance of "Morris and His Magic Kazoo." He's also surprisingly political, writing a song that declares that the country can achieve political unity if only they could physically move "The State of Arkansas." On another show, he remarks that his orchestra, which is comprised entirely of musicians named Petrillo (which happened to be the name of the head of the musicians union), will be the one band permitted to make records during the 1948 musicians union strike. On another show, he sings of "The Day I Read

a Book," and asks the crowd, "What did Napoleon do for relaxation? He read a book. What did Lincoln do for relaxation? He read a book. What does Congress do for relaxation? They book a red!," a surprising reference to the early days of HUAC.

That cool medium, television, immediately softened both Durante's humor and his timing, but he was still continually evolving and probably would have changed anyhow. By the end of the Eisenhower era, Durante was no longer singing things like "It's My Nose's Birthday Today," and he would no longer sit on the keyboard and exclaim "That's strange—I usually play by ear!" In fact, his humor no longer centered on his nose or his rear end; in the sixties the part of his anatomy featured in his music was the place where his songs had always come from: his heart. Now instead of relocating the state of Arkansas or going around "ups"-ing to people, he was telling us that fairy tales could come true, it could happen to you, that it was so important to make someone happy, and that a song of love was a sad song, hi-lilli, hi-lilli, hi-lo.

He announced this new transition in a series of LPs. The 1961 *Jimmy Durante at the Copacabana* offered a more traditional Durante, documenting him performing his familiar nightclub act with Eddie Jackson. Said act was pretty much the same as it had ever been, except that a new boy crooner named Sonny King had taken the place of Lou Clayton, who had died in 1950. The 1959 *Jimmy Durante (In Person) at the Piano* (Decca), however, signaled the beginning of a sea change. This wasn't a live album but the first program of songs on which Durante sang mostly straight, although there were a few humorous specialties and novelty songs like "Take An 'L'" and another "Inka Dinka Do." Here, he was featuring his vocals and his own piano, backed only by longtime drummer Jack Roth. Approaching his seventieth birthday, he was forging a new Durante, more intimate than archaic.

After paring Durante down to his barest essentials, the voice and the piano, his next move was to go in the opposite direction. From 1962 to 1967, Durante made five albums for Warner Bros. Records that featured him exclusively as a balladeer, a sentimental singer of sentimental old songs: *September Song, Hello Young Lovers, Jimmy Durante's Way of Life, One of Those Songs,* and *Songs for Sunday.* All these albums were recently reissued by Collectors' Choice and Collectables, and all but the last are sampled on *As Time Goes By: The Best of Jimmy Durante.* (The only album not represented in the *Best of* collection is the last, *Songs for Sunday,* a collection of religious songs like "His Eye Is on the Sparrow." When Durante refers to "Him," he's not talking about Umbriago.)

Like Louis Armstrong, the onetime subversive has now become a lovable grandpa figure with a raspy voice. As a comparatively young man in early talkies, Durante had seemed somewhat grotesque; as an old man, he seemed warm and cuddly—an American institution, even. It didn't matter that he was no longer on the cutting edge of comedy, because his singing was so beautiful—that's the word that Doris Day used and ultimately the only word that really describes his music—and the records, for all their sentimental excesses (the heavy strings, the heavy choirs), are wonderful. The jewel in the crown here is *Way of Life,* five tracks of which are on the *Best of* compilation, which teams Durante with the greatest sentimentalist of them all, the redoubtable Gordon Jenkins—the same arranger-conductor had aided Armstrong in his transition from outsider to mainstream pop star fifteen years earlier.

From a purely vocal standpoint, Durante is one of the greatest: His timing, his phrasing, his ability to sell a song, to put his heart into it and make everyone listening believe it, are on a level with Sinatra and Jolson. And that voice gives him a sonic identity like no one else in the history of Western music, with the exception of Louis Armstrong. (In 1965, Durante and Armstrong finally got together for an episode of *The Hollywood Palace* in which they duetted on "Old Man Time," which has a claim to being the single greatest two minutes in the history of television.) When Durante, on *Hello Young Lovers,* exhorts us to "Smile," he's clearly too late: We've been doing that all along.

I think Durante would have been pleased to learn that it is this aspect of his long (sixty-year) career that would be how he is best remembered—that is, after a stroke he suffered during his eightieth (in 1973) year more or less put him out of show business, and then after his death in 1980. This is the Durante that baby boomers remember, especially filmmakers like Nora Ephron and Ron Underwood, who heavily relied on Durante in their films *Sleepless in Seattle* and *City Slickers,* both released in time for Durante's centennial. (*Sleepless,* in particular, stirred such an interest in him that Warner Bros. released the *Best of* CD and Decca reissued *Club Durant* for a hot minute.) Whether being silly or sentimental, Durante, as Bakish notes, "offers a counterpoint to the slickness that has obscured the roots of many Americans."

For all their professionalism and their impeccable technique, slick is one thing that Armstrong and Durante never were.

Good night, Mrs. Calabash, wherever you are.

E

Billy Eckstine (1914–1993)

Everything about Billy Eckstine was profound, starting with his deep blue dream of a voice, the only sound in vernacular music capable of suggesting high notes and low notes at the same time. Then there was the sense of time that enabled him to take some of the slowest tempos in jazz and still make four minutes fly by like four seconds. And finally there was his career, in which the comparatively "frivolous" profession of pop singer carried with it social responsibilities akin to those of a civil rights leader. Before Louis Armstrong or Nat King Cole dared sing anything other than the blues or novelties, Billy Eckstine was among the first to show the world that the black man could be intellectual, passionate, sensitive, literate, articulate, proud—and profound.

At the crest of Frank Sinatra's first wave of popularity, the singer was known as the Voice. What, one wonders, does that make Eckstine? Superchops? The initial reaction that one experiences upon hearing the music of Billy Eckstine for the first time is pure rapture: God, what a voice! Eckstine's voice is a bit like Greta Garbo's face or the Grand Canyon, it's just so unendingly beautiful, rich and full, that one has a hard time believing that something so perfect can exist in the natural world. This is an instrument of melody fully as stunning as the tone of Lester Young or even the Great Caruso—the perfect instrument to convey the often extreme metaphors of the Great American Songbook: the depth of the ocean, the height of the sky, the distance to the moon. Here is a sound so moving that God must have worked overtime when He created it.

Eckstine is notable as more than a sonic marvel: Throughout the fifty-plus years of his career, he was a pop and jazz singer of rare intelligence and taste. Not only was his voice rich, but by using the tools of the jazz singer he made it sound richer. Without his use of harmonies, in which he sings chordal circles around notes, and his entrenchment in the blues, Eckstine might have been just another pretty-voiced, deep-chested Broadway-style baritone like, say, Gordon MacRae or Robert Goulet. Yet his consistent application of jazz vocal techniques is especially valuable when he's working in nonjazz contexts (as he did for most of his years at the top). The cliché is that jazzmen avoid the written melody, yet by his continual harmonic noodling and supplementation, Eckstine makes any song he sings sound better and melodically richer than it was before he first heard it.

"A remarkable artist," as Duke Ellington once described him, "the sonorous B." He was born William Clarence Eckstein in Pittsburgh on July 8, 1914. For a while he worked under the name X-Tine (now that sounds like a hip-hopper) and he later settled on Eckstine because he thought it was easier to spell. He started taking singing seriously at the age of seven, at least as seriously as a seven-year-old can. He followed the usual route: singing to entertain his family and friends, then at amateur shows (including one where he did an impression of Cab Calloway), and gradually worked his way up the music-biz ladder. Eckstine, however, did not study music formally in school. "With my gang," he told *Metronome* magazine in 1948, "anybody that did anything musical was considered more or less on the lavender side. So I stuck to football."

By the late thirties, still known as Eckstein, he was singing at the Club De Lisa in Chicago when he ran into an old friend, tenorist Budd Johnson. Johnson was at that time part of Earl Hines's reed section at the Grand Terrace Ballroom, and he was so impressed with the young man's singing that he invited Hines to come have a listen. Before long, Eckstine was singing with the legendary pianist and his big band at the Grand Terrace.

Eckstine recorded for the first time in February 1940 with Hines; twenty-five was comparatively old for a band singer's debut in those days, and thus, Eckstine had been a professional, working vocalist for some time before he began recording. As a result, we don't really have any documents of his voice in development; the sound we hear on the thirteen titles he recorded with Hines is essentially a slightly higher-pitched version of the sound that made him a superstar within a few years. (While on the road with Hines, the enterprising singer also began to study trumpet and valve trombone, eventually becoming an adequate soloist on both, and learned to read music.)

The baker's dozen of Eckstine-Hines tracks make for a body of work that's as satisfying as it is brief. "Water Boy" is a traditional black folk song, and is precisely the kind of thing that black concert singers like Paul Robeson and Jules Bledsoe would include in their acts; Eckstine and Hines show that they want to put a new spin on tradition by doing it in swing time. Eckstine later professed to dislike the blues, but he created two very successful statements in that format with Hines as co-author. The minor key "Stormy Monday Blues" is remorseful and emotionally "down," in contrast to the openly erotic "Jelly, Jelly," which is "up," both attitudinally and anatomically. Even this early on, Eckstine would make his greatest impression as a ballad singer, and three exceptionally beautiful love songs from this era would stay with Mr. B for the rest of his life: "Somehow," "Fool That I Am," and "I'm Falling for You."

He landed a surprising amount of attention in his three years or so with Hines—it was said at the time that his record of the Carmichael-Mercer instant classic "Skylark" actually outsold both Bing Crosby and Glenn Miller. Thus it wasn't surprising that he would find industry support for whatever venture he wanted to tackle once leaving the Great Fatha of the piano. The idea of a black man singing contemporary, sophisticated love songs was still a bit in the future (somehow, love songs were acceptable coming from black quartets, like the Mills Brothers and the Ink Spots, but not from solo baritones). Eckstine decided that his best shot at making it on his own was as the leader of his own big band.

Talk about being ahead of one's time: Within a few years, both Woody Herman and Stan Kenton would mix increasing amounts of modern jazz into their music, and the co-founder of the music, Eckstine's longtime compadre (and fellow former Hinesite) Dizzy Gillespie, would launch his own amazing bop big band. But in 1944, Eckstine was out there all alone, leading the first and at the time only modern jazz orchestra. It might have been a different story had someone at RCA, Hines's label, thought to sign the Eckstine unit; instead, the best offer came from Herb Abramson of National Records, a small independent, who couldn't supply very good sound quality or halfway decent distribution, but at least seems to have permitted Eckstine to record anything he wanted—which both was and wasn't a good idea.

Even nearly sixty years later, the music of the Eckstine orchestra sounds startlingly new and fresh. One would think that the lush, rich sound of the leader's voice might not be well served by the angular, boppish sound of the instrumental ensemble, but Eckstine's arrangers, in particular Jerry Valentine and Budd Johnson, ensured that the two textures complemented each other amazingly well. (Both the voice and the orchestra have to compete to be heard over the surface noise, but that's another story.) The modernist touches, in effect, strip off the sentimental edge that affects most love songs (heard to a degree on Eckstine's later recordings with strings) and thus make his ballads extremely effective, especially "A Cottage for Sale."

While not neglecting his specialty ballads, the band also featured Eckstine in the role of a bandleading "rhythm" singer on blues-based novelties. He didn't quite "hi-de-ho," but nonetheless his Cab Calloway skills came in handy on "Lonesome Lover Blues," "Rhythm in a Riff" (the latter distinguished not only by the leader but by amazing big band drumming by Art Blakey and a heavily Lestorian tenor solo by Gene Ammons), and "The Jitney Man." Indeed, most rhythm singers in big and small bands were usually gravelly types à la Armstrong, Louis Prima, Wingy Manone, Red Allen, and Tony Pastor; Eckstine and Calloway were the only smooth crooner types who could also scat and wail.

Eckstine would always speak of his orchestra as a failure; it was too far ahead of its time not only for the mainstream public, but also for the black audience, which should have been its core support group. Even the music press at the time, which had yet to catch up to bebop in general, couldn't comprehend what Eckstine was trying to do, and the poor pressings provided by National (exacerbated by wartime shortages of materials) certainly didn't help. Eckstine also seems to have insisted on not playing new "plug" tunes; what contemporary material there was in the band's book was all pretty much his own originals. While it's good that no overzealous A&R man foisted any dogs on the band (of the kind the bands on the major labels, even Goodman, Basie, and Ellington, were importuned to play), Eckstine surely would have had more hits had he done some current Broadway and movie songs.

Even so, it's hard to think of the band as a flop: The Eckstine orchestra left us about forty uniformly excellent titles (none, thanks to Petrillo, from the period when Gillespie and Charlie Parker were actually in the band) as well as a series of Armed Forces Radio Service *Jubilee* airchecks and a film sound track. It furthered the careers of at least a dozen major musicians, among them Bird, Diz, Ammons, Blakey, Dexter Gordon, Sonny Stitt, Budd Johnson, Fats Navarro, Kenny Dorham, and Wardell Gray. And, considering the difficulty in competing with the likes of Columbia and Victor, the fact that National managed to get no fewer than five Eckstine orchestra titles in the top 15—this at a time when interest in bands was rapidly declining—shows that the public demand for Eckstine's singing must have been very great indeed.

After the band broke up in 1947, the singer recorded sixteen titles for National, billed as the Eckstine orchestra but which were in fact solo vocal records of the singer with two brass, two reeds (Sonny Criss and Wardell Gray, no less), and rhythm. Shortly thereafter, MGM Records approached Eckstine with a solo contract. The movie studio had begun to formulate plans to launch its own record label in the early forties, and had made overtures to Tommy Dorsey and Frank Sinatra. However, after Pearl Harbor, MGM decided to wait out the duration before proceeding with their record venture. In 1947, Eckstine and former Goodman vocalist Art Lund became MGM's first important signings. Both Mr. B, as he had recently been christened by Fred Robbins, one of the early jazz disc jockeys, and the label were launched in style; the first session, from April 1947, contained one of his biggest hits, "Everything I Have Is Yours," which had been written fourteen years earlier for *Dancing Lady*, a *42nd Street*–inspired musical in which MGM's major romantic team, Joan Crawford and Clark Gable, reinvent Dick Powell and Ruby Keeler.

In 1951, *Down Beat* ran a profile of the singer headlined "I Refuse to Sing Any Bad Tunes, Says Billy Eckstine." Eckstine must have been something of a headache to his A&R crew in that, like Frank Sinatra at Columbia, he would sing only a certain number of new, potential hit songs, insisting on doing older songs, of the sort that would later be labeled classics and standards. His track record was even greater than Sinatra's in that virtually all of his hit records were of songs from the 1930s. That includes his five National hits, "I'm in the Mood for Love," "You Call It Madness," "Prisoner of Love," "Cottage for Sale," and "Sophisticated Lady," the last two of which boast ingenious extended codas arranged for Eckstine by Jerry Valentine.

The backbone of the Eckstine canon is his string of "revival" hits made for MGM between 1947 and 1955; even more than the first-rate Eckstine orchestra tracks of 1944–47, it's these MGM sides on which his reputation as one of the century's finest vocal artists rests. Among the best remembered are: "Everything I Have Is Yours," "True," "Blue Moon," "Somehow," and "Caravan" (the Ellington-Tizol classic, known only as an instrumental until Eckstine taught the world the words, although it's not known who actually wrote them).

Eckstine also put both "I Wanna Be Loved" and "Body and Soul" on the charts, which must have been satisfying for composer Johnny Green, then a top musical director at MGM, who conducted for Eckstine on another of his classic songs, the highly possessive "You're Mine You." B did yet a fourth Green song, "Coquette," for MGM with Nelson Riddle's orchestra, one of a series of songs he cut with a vocal group called the Quartones who recall the sound of Sinatra and the Pied Pipers. However, whereas the young Sinatra led his quartet from the top with his high, baritone-tenor voice, Eckstine leads from the bottom, with his low, baritone-basso voice.

It's almost as if Eckstine thought that there weren't enough good new songs from the period—as he suggested in that *Down Beat* article. It's unfortunate that he waited until 1986 to take on Frank Loesser's fine "(Where Are You) Now That I Need You" instead of doing it when the song was new in 1949, when he might have had a hit with it. Among the new tunes he did sing were many of his own compositions (like Mel Tormé and Peggy Lee, who were well known as singer-songwriters), but this aspect of his talent is rarely discussed. Which is a shame, as he wrote at least a dozen or so memorable songs—latter-day disciples like Milt Grayson, Kevin Mahogany, or Allan Harris could easily fill an album called *The Billy Eckstine Songbook*. Such an album would start with his Hines era hits "Stormy Monday Blues" and "Jelly, Jelly," as well as such worthy blues and rhythm numbers as "Lonesome Lover Blues," "Rhythm in a Riff," "It Ain't Like That," "Mr. B's Blues," and "Second Balcony Jump" (a memorable instrumental for both the Hines and Eckstine bands). Eckstine also wrote several outstanding ballads, especially "Last Night," "Mister, You've Gone and Got the Blues," and his most famous composition, "I Wanna Talk About You," which became a regular feature in the repertoire of John Coltrane and, following that (not surprisingly), a jazz standard.

While critics at the time failed to appreciate Eckstine's big band, jazz scribes ever since have taken too many potshots at his post-band career. *The New Grove Dictionary of Jazz* describes his achievements as "inconsistent"; it applauds the orchestral period but lambastes him for singing "conservative popular ballads," which, as I hope we've established, is a charge so wrong-minded that it's not even worth addressing. Eckstine's post-orchestra recordings contain at least as much jazz-oriented material as those of his musical soul mate Sarah Vaughan. As it happens, most reissues of Eckstine's MGM material reflect a jazz bias, which is fine, as these sessions contain some of his absolutely finest singing.

Among the Eckstine dates that have pretty much consistently been available are his 1951 meeting with George Shearing (the legendary pianist's first encounter with a star singer), which yielded two superb titles, "You're Driving Me Crazy" and "Taking a Chance on Love." Next are four equally terrific tracks with a studio group led by Woody Herman and arranged by Kenton vet Pete Rugolo, among them a deluxe treatment of Wynonie Harris's "Here Come the Blues" and an amiable duet with Woody himself on "Life Is Just a Bowl of Cherries." The singer cut his first of several pure jazz albums in 1952, *Tenderly*, which co-starred Eckstine and his musical director and sidekick for more than forty years, Bobby Tucker, and his quartet. (Tuck had earlier worked with an equally famous Billie, namely Holiday, and later with another famous B, as in Tony Bennett.) Throughout all eight songs, Eckstine is not only as mellifluous as we've come to expect, but there's a new level of intimacy and sensitivity in this, his most outstanding small group project.

Yet it wasn't just the setting or the material. Eckstine's singing itself was just as inherently jazzy as that of Vaughan—and the comparison is relevant because he was essentially her mentor, the man who heard her at the Apollo and brought her to the attention of Hines, then brought her along as his girl singer when he started his own band and continued to share the mike with her for years to come. Like Vaughan, Eckstine rarely sings a melody completely straight as written, but consistently enhances the tune with his sagacious harmonic know-how, singing around the melody and hitting other, even more sonorous notes in the chord change. His 1949 "Body and Soul" is one of his most outstandingly jazzy records, a melody that was earmarked for melodic and harmonic variation ever since John Green had written it twenty years earlier. What's more, apart from being a magnificent jazz vocal, Eckstine's record was a chart hit, too.

His abilities as a pure jazz singer come to the fore in a series of duets with Vaughan, done between 1949 and 1957, that are even hipper than his encounter with Woody Herman. Sarah Vaughan is routinely considered one of the great jazz singers; Eckstine is not, yet he seems every bit her equal here. It's especially moving when, on Cole Porter's "I Love You," their voices meld in delayed harmony over the final series of "I love you's." "Dedicated to You" contains another magical moment in the coda, when she takes a note in the line "If I should find a *twin*kling star" and he answers by taking the corresponding note in the next line, "one half as lovely *as* you are," a smidge and a half higher than that.

For the most part, the MGM recordings suc-

ceeded on every conceivable level, and were as satisfying musically as they were at the cashbox; by 1950, RCA was promoting Johnny Hartman (who had also tenured in Hines's band) to their distributors as their answer to Billy Eckstine, and Columbia had signed B's old colleague Herb Jeffries as *their* response. The very early fifties seem to represent Eckstine's peak, when *Down Beat* described him as singing for a "frantically appreciative audience. There was squealing from a starry-eyed set, and it reminded you of another singer and another time." (Ahem!) Many (including David Hajdu in his book *Heroes and Villains*) feel that the defining moment—the point at which he hit the glass ceiling—was on April 27, 1950, when Eckstine was pictured in *Life* magazine, surrounded by a group of young white women (not bobby-soxers but full-grown ladies), one of whom is burying her head in his manly chest with obvious adoration. That was further than any African American entertainer had ever gone, or would go again for at least a generation. A few years later, Nat King Cole, Johnny Mathis, and then any number of early doo-woppers and soul singers (Frankie Lymon, Sam Cooke, Ray Charles) would rescale those same heights, but Eckstine had gone as far as a black man was allowed to go in 1950. He would continue to have hits and do some, even most, of his very best work, but the plateau had been reached.

If anything, Eckstine's singing grew even stronger as the fifties wore on; in his last few years at Metro, he made a pair of remarkable two-sided discs with the Metronome All-Stars (the sound of Eckstine's baritone backed by Lester Young's tenor is in itself remarkable) and a stunning new/old show tune, "Lost in Loveliness" (written by Sig Romberg, who had died several years earlier, but just introduced on Broadway) from *The Girl in Pink Tights*. The latter MGM projects also include two other superb 10" songbook LPs, *Love Songs by Rodgers and Hammerstein* (1952) and *I Let a Song Go Out of My Heart* (a collection of Ellingtonia from 1953), both arranged by Nelson Riddle. In 1956, Eckstine left MGM for a disastrous tenure at RCA, where he failed to find a sympathetic producer and made the mistake of continuing to concentrate on singles, and not very good ones at that. The only notable result of this fortunately brief artist-label relationship was the hysterically awful "Condemned for Life (With a Rock-and-Roll Wife)."

From this point on, there seems to have been a consensus that B's days as a maker of hit singles were over, and for the rest of his career he would concentrate on albums. He would record approximately thirteen classic original 12" albums (as opposed to singles or hits collections), nine for Mercury, who had him under contract from 1957 to 1958 and then again from 1961 to 1964; between the two Mercury periods he made one album in Europe (*Mr. B in Paris*) and three for Roulette. All of these consist almost exclusively of standards, hardly a surprising move considering that he had concentrated on standards even in his singles days—well before it was hip to do so.

In 1957, Eckstine joined Vaughan at Mercury, quite literally, as his first project under the new contract turned out to be a set of duets with the woman he referred to as his "little sister." The perfect Eckstine-Vaughan project would have been a two-voice version of *Porgy and Bess*, which would have surely rivaled and possibly even surpassed the colossal Ella Fitzgerald–Louis Armstrong version of that same year. Yet the album they did make, *The Best of Irving Berlin* (which anticipated Fitzgerald's *Irving Berlin Songbook* by a year and boasted four charts by Billy May), was pretty terrific; while the B-Sass duets are perhaps a tad less magical than their 1949 session, Eckstine's solo track, the little-known "All of My Life," is one of his most magnificent.

But then nearly all the solo albums consist of magnificent singing. At every stage of his career, the voice got deeper and richer—with Hines, then his own orchestra, MGM, then Mercury. His vocals became more intense, his musical intelligence ever sharper. The solo Mercury albums start with what may well be his two finest, *Billy's Best* and *Billy Eckstine's Imagination*—apparently Mercury wanted people to think of the two as a unit, because they not only assigned Pete Rugolo to orchestrate and conduct both packages (a smart move), but they put the exact same picture of Eckstine, looking over his shoulder at the camera, on both covers (not a smart move). *Billy's Best*, the title of which misled some buyers into thinking it was a collection of greatest hits (also not a smart move), was a brand-new full-orchestra package, with B's singing reaching nearly operatic heights on a well-selected set of tunes, starting with an amazingly mellow, distingué treatment of Harry Warren's *franglais* "Boulevard of Broken Dreams," and including "Where Have You Been," a 1930 Cole Porter marvel done by almost no one. (This song is so obscure that even Barbara Carroll had to ask me what it was when we heard Bill Charlap play it at the Vanguard.) *Imagination* was a very loosely done jazz-oriented set, with generous solos by a contingent of West Coasters (Gerry Wiggins, Red Callender, Pete Candoli, Don Fagerquist, Bud Shank et al.); Eckstine is at his most relaxed here, but his singing is no less majestic.

Eckstine's first contract with Mercury involved only three albums, plus a smattering of singles (most memorable is a dopey theme song from Alfred Hitchcock's *Vertigo*). In 1959, he taped his rarest album, a set of French songs, *Mr. B in Paris*, for the European Felsted label (produced by Quincy Jones, featuring expatriates Don Byas, Billy Byers, and Kenny Clarke, as well as Bobby Tucker). Then there were the three albums for Roulette. "Roulette, at that time, had all of our clique," Eckstine told me in 1992. "They had Sarah, they had Basie, they had Dinah.

Then they got me. I was the only one they didn't have and they wanted me. You know, Morris [Levy] was an egomaniac. That was just an insult—he had to have me over there. I only stayed about a year, maybe two."

Thirty years after the fact, Eckstine complained that he had never received a dime from Roulette (hardly an isolated experience), but his three albums for the company are all superb: *No Cover, No Minimum* is his first of two notable live recordings, and *Once More with Feeling*, though marred by a bizarre treatment of "That Old Black Magic," is an otherwise fine set of ballads with Billy May. The album that everybody remembers, however, is *Basie-Eckstine, Inc.* B and Basie, like B and Ellington, were friends since the thirties, and Eckstine had helped the Count out in his lean years in the early fifties by taking him on one of his tours; an Eckstine-Basie pairing was inevitable. The package is also Eckstine's strongest statement as a composer, since six of the eleven songs have his name on them, including the comedy blues "Little Mama," and there are definitive readings of tunes he'd been doing since his big band period and earlier, like "Stormy Monday Blues." Above all, the Basie package is Eckstine's strongest effort as a blues-based singer, since all eleven songs are in the general vicinity of the blues. On the faster numbers, like "Lonesome Lover Blues," he's exceeded only by Joe Williams, who had recently left the band, and on the slow tunes, like "Jelly, Jelly," "I Want a Little Girl," and "Song of the Wanderer," Eckstine is outclassed by no one.

Between 1961 and 1964, Eckstine made another six albums for Mercury: a Latinate collection of show tunes, *Broadway, Bongos and Mr. B*, a bit more showy outing that misses the effectively minimalist approach of Peggy Lee's Broadway-Goes-Mambo offerings; his second live album, *At Basin Street East*; another superb set of mostly ballads, *Don't Worry About Me*; a newly recorded stereo retrospective of his *Golden Hits*; an outstanding collection of cinematic themes, *Billy Eckstine Starring in Twelve Great Movies*; and, lastly, *The Modern Sounds of Mr. B.*, ostensibly devoted to the best contemporary songs ("Beautiful Friendship," "Wives and Lovers") but also including the likes of "Sweet Georgia Brown" and "A Garden in the Rain"—both from the twenties—among the "modern sounds." Quincy Jones was now head of A&R, and he and his stable of arrangers were responsible for most of the charts here, along with Hal Mooney. As a whole, the arrangements on the later Mercury albums are almost as excellent as those of Pete Rugolo on the two 1957–58 Eckstine solo albums (*Billy's Best* and *Imagination*), and the singing is just as good.

Taken in toto, this is the last major body of work out of a mighty career: Approaching fifty, Eckstine had by now built himself up into just about the most perfect singing machine ever devised. The voice is deeper and more resonant than ever, not to mention more just plain beautiful, and his singing has more emotional and interpretative resonance as well. *Don't Worry 'Bout Me* includes the definitive reading of his own "I Want to Talk About You," a song he was likely inspired to revive by John Coltrane, who recorded it on the 1958 *Soultrane*. In rerecording the song, Eckstine shows us not only that Coltrane got more than this one tune from the singer, but that B may well have provided a crucial template for Coltrane's overall sound, which, like Eckstine's, was high and low, fast and slow at the same time. *Modern Sounds* contains "What Are You Afraid Of?," a stunning Bob Wells–Jack Segal song of seduction that lay otherwise neglected until Bennett tackled it in 1985 (it was then revived again by Freddy Cole twenty years after that). Eckstine sings it not only with that amazingly rich voice, but with a tenderness and warmth uncommon even for him.

Golden Hits includes his third, last, and best reading of "Somehow." From listening to the 1941 and 1948 versions, I always thought it was a vaguely optimistic song, but the way Eckstine sings it in 1963 makes it clear that it can be even more effective as a downer. If "Somehow" were more sentimental, as doubtless it would be in the tonsils of another, lesser vocal artist, it could be considered a torch song. With Eckstine, it's just incredibly poignant, a song of love and loss and too-late realizations. He comes out of the bridge and puts an extra emphasis on "*Some way*" in a way that makes it seem even more like an internal monologue in the best Sinatra tradition. It ends on a note that could conceivably be considered upbeat, but in his interpretation, somehow that faint hint of light at the end of the tunnel doesn't illuminate the darkness, it just makes it seem darker. Eckstine ends on a long, sustained note; it's quite a feat of vocal prowess, and few vocalists have chops Eckstineian enough to pull it off. Still, it's not the least bit showy, it's all in the service of making that last note sound more movingly melancholy.

The last thirty years of Eckstine's life left virtually nothing that compares with his classic work of 1940–64. Perhaps the great failing of his great years is that his singing and his music were just so ineffably perfect; perhaps if he had had more of a concept of what imperfection was he would have been better able to adapt to changing times. As it was, he couldn't constantly reinvent himself like Sinatra or Nat Cole, nor could he constantly refine and rerefine his art, like Bennett, or keep finding hit songs that didn't compromise his artistry, also like Bennett. One asset that might have helped him in the later period was his underutilized capacity for singing in other languages: The Felsted French album is altogether credible, while one of the most successful tracks on *Billy's Best* is the Cuban "Babalu"—he has far more powerful chops than Miguelito Valdés and Desi Arnaz put together. *Twelve Great Movies* has two Brazilian songs—the first actually recorded in Rio—"A Felicidad" and "Manha De Carnaval" (both

from *Black Orpheus*) that are probably the two most compelling Portuguese-language performances by a major American star. Why Quincy Jones failed to produce an album called *B Goes Brazilian* is anybody's guess, but in hindsight it seems clear that if Eckstine had persevered in this area, he could have been the boss of the bossa nova, and completely revived his career. It never happened.

The good news was that Eckstine was back in the studio within a year or so of the last Mercury album, *The Modern Sounds of Mr. B.;* the bad news was that he was now recording for Motown. The sad thing is that he still had his chops in the sixties and early seventies, but the albums he made in this era—three for Motown, four for Stax—were a complete waste of his time. Even when he gets a song that has some possibilities, like Stevie Wonder's "My Cherie Amour" (another foreign language allusion, included on the 1970 *Stormy*), the tempo and orchestration completely defeat his purpose; if he had sung it slowly and romantically (the way Bennett recorded it), as make-out music instead of a dance piece, he might have had a shot. Ironically, by the time Eckstine was able to get back to standard songs and what was basically a jazz background for his last two records, *I Am a Singer* (1984) and *Billy Eckstine Sings with Benny Carter* (1986), he didn't have any chops left. Carter, who was seventy-nine at the time of the album, sounds as great as he ever did, but, at seventy-two, Eckstine's once mighty instrument was now a tremolo in search of a voice, his so-called steamship vibrato was now all vibrato and no steamship. In performance, Eckstine was still remarkable, but unfortunately his final recordings seem to capture all of his shortcomings and little of his elder statesman majesty.

By most accounts, Eckstine's last years were not happy ones: Problems with the IRS and ex-wives saw to that. He lived in Las Vegas, and worked mostly in the lounges there and Atlantic City, although he could play what big jazz rooms there were around the world, like the Blue Note in New York. Whenever I spoke with him after a gig he always seemed a little standoffish; probably at this point in his life, performing took a lot out of him. However, the one time he spoke with me on the phone, he was as warm and avuncular as people like Tony Bennett and Sarah Vaughan had always told me he was.

"Woody, that's cool philosophy," Eckstine says in his 1951 record of "Life Is Just a Bowl of Cherries"; "You've got to love it [life], 'cause when you leave it, you're a long time gone." He died in his native Pittsburgh at seventy-nine, not long after Dizzy Gillespie, on March 8, 1993. There are those who regard Billy Eckstine as something of a tragic figure. The number-one bone of contention among his fans, particularly young white ones, is about how far he might have gone career-wise had he not been black. It's a pointless discussion: Blackness for Eckstine was more than the color of his skin. Rather, his African

American identity was a key element in the formation of his talent and a major ingredient of his music. If he had been white, he might have gone further, at least temporarily. He would have made more movies, possibly even starred in one. But, as with a lot of singers of that era (such as his unfairly neglected label mate at MGM Records, Art Lund), we probably wouldn't be listening to him today. In the end, it's both pedantic and pointless to speculate about what his life and career could have been, when what he did achieve, and the legacy he left us, are so incredible.

F

Ella Fitzgerald (1917–1996)

When Duke Ellington came up with the phrase "beyond category" to describe Ella Fitzgerald, he had no idea that those two words would take on a life of their own. However, in his most famous live appearance sharing a stage with her, their 1966 engagement at the Côte d'Azur in France, Ellington didn't employ his famous encomium. Instead he introduced Fitzgerald with a variation on her standard billing enhanced with what in any other case would have seemed like classic Ducal hyperbole, describing her as "the very, very, very First Lady of Song." Ellington's use of the triple "very" echoes Johnny Mercer, and indicates that Fitzgerald is not only beyond category, she's too marvelous for words—and he outdoes Mercer by one "very."

She had been known as the First Lady of Swing, the First Lady of Jazz, and the First Lady of Song for nearly her entire career, and posthumously she seems to have become the First Lady of the entire American Musical Experience. It's important to remember that people started calling her this back when the most celebrated first lady of all time was incumbent in the White House—and Fitzgerald was even then setting standards of excellence and achievement that were nothing less than Eleanor Rooseveltian. It wasn't Lester Young who gave her the "First Lady" moniker—his personal nickname for La Fitz was "Lady Time"—but Fitzgerald's "First Lady" made a fitting counterpart to Young's status as "the President." It was no coincidence, perhaps, that she recorded songs like "Vote for Mr. Rhythm" and "F.D.R. Jones" back in the day.

I can't see Billie Holiday, Peggy Lee, Sarah Vaughan, or even Kate Smith, for all her patriotism, ever being billed as "the First Lady." Yet Fitzgerald's status as such doesn't exempt her from a certain uninformed strain of criticism, since there are those who might consider her as sexless as Eleanor Roosevelt. In fact, there's a part of the American psyche that likes to reach instantly for the negative. Mention Frank Sinatra and they'll tell you what a horrible person he was. Mention Bing Crosby and they'll tell you he beat his kids (again a grotesque exaggeration and distortion of the truth). Mention either Judy Garland or Billie Holiday and their artistry will be ignored while you're told that they were both self-destructive, self-medicating nut jobs. Somehow pointing out the flaws, real or imagined, of these larger-than-life icons makes people feel better about themselves.

Perhaps the most irritating thing that Fitzgerald had in common with Sinatra (who was born two years before her and died two years after) is that both were, for all their fame and popularity, resoundingly underappreciated in their lifetimes. When she was still performing, the gossip among so-called connoisseurs went along the lines of "Oh, she doesn't really sing the words" or "She doesn't really know what she's singing about." The singer-pianist Jeri Southern, as quoted by her daughter Kathryn King, was once distressed to hear Fitzgerald sing the opening line of "Don't Get Around Much Anymore" as follows: "Mister Saturday Dance / Heard they crowded the floor," as opposed to "Missed the Saturday dance."

It's a funny turn of events when the first thing you hear about Ella Fitzgerald is that she didn't sing the words. Once, in the early nineties, I felt hackles starting to rise when I happened to be talking to one of her contemporaries, Jo Stafford. (If Fitzgerald had the loveliest voice in popular music, Ms. Stafford comfortably ties with Sarah Vaughan for the number-two spot.) She put it this way: "I would say that of the two elements, words and music, she gave more weight to the music than to the words." I went into my kneejerk-reaction defensive mode and vigorously denied it: "But it's not like she didn't understand the words or ignore the lyric." "Of course not," said Stafford, as calm as I was growing agitated, "she just gave more weight to the music."

When I calmed down, I realized not only that Stafford wasn't slamming Fitzgerald, but that she was right. Fitzgerald was an essentially musical interpreter, and the melody was, in fact, more important to her than the words. But as Stafford also said, that hardly meant that she didn't know what she was singing about. It might be fair to say that Sinatra and Mabel Mercer sang Lorenz Hart, but no one surpassed Fitzgerald at singing Richard Rodgers.

Although she was never as textually specific as Sinatra nor as "sad" as Holiday, Fitzgerald was always *emotionally true* to whatever she was singing: She could make you walk on air with a happy song and want to walk on razor blades on a downer. She sang the lyrics of Lorenz Hart, Oscar Hammerstein, Ira Gershwin, Johnny Mercer, Sammy Cahn, Johnny Burke, and any other Tin Pan Alley poet at least as well as anybody else in the canon of great jazz and pop singers, and there's no indication that any of these gentlemen was anything but delighted with the result. In 1961, she made a single of "You're Driving

Me Crazy" backed with "Mr. Paganini (You'll Have to Swing It)" for the German market and in that country's language, and even listeners who were unfamiliar with the English words to these jazz standards knew exactly what she was singing at every moment.

I'm dwelling on this particular aspect of Fitzgerald's artistry because all the other important elements of her music are so universally recognized. One favorite story of mine was told to me by pianist and accompanist Hal Schaefer. In 1953, he was faced with a challenge that was as daunting as it was delightful. He was then on the musical staff of Twentieth Century Fox Pictures, and the studio was about to cast their newest starlet, Marilyn Monroe, in her first major musical, *Gentlemen Prefer Blondes*. Monroe had sung a little, danced a little, but was at this point clearly not adequate to pulling off the lead role in a major musical comedy, and Schaefer was hired to bring her up to speed.

His first move: He went out and bought his protégée all the Ella Fitzgerald records that could be found in Hollywood. He then instructed her to listen to Ella as often as she could, night and day, day and night. His message to Monroe was simple: *This* is what it's all about. *This* is why it's worth taking the time to learn to sing in tune. *This* is what great pop singing sounds like. If you need a reason why it's worth the effort to develop a beautiful voice, achieve perfect intonation, and swing like nobody's business, here it is. Schaefer's plan worked even better than he could have imagined. She got it. Monroe did a more than passable job with the singing in *Gentlemen Prefer Blondes*, which became her most iconic role. And subsequently she became both a great fan as well as a friend of the woman who was already known as the First Lady of Song.

Fitzgerald provided the ultimate inspiration for numberless singers over the years, both as a role model and as a standard-bearer for anyone who would sing the great American popular standards. Her message was clearly "This is the limit—this is as great as these songs can possibly sound." As Carol Sloane put it, "She taught me my ABCs: intonation, diction, and swing." It's difficult to see, however, who taught Fitzgerald. Almost from the beginning she was more than the sum of such inspirations as Connie Boswell, scat master Leo Watson, and even Louis Armstrong.

She was born on April 25, 1917, in Newport News, Virginia, and as was true of both Mabel Mercer and Billie Holiday, her parents were not married at the time of this event. Fitzgerald's father was history soon enough, and so was her brief residency in Virginia, as her mom moved the two of them up to Yonkers, New York. For the next fifteen years, Fitzgerald grew up on the periphery of New York City and of the world of jazz but was enamored of the burgeoning music scene. She was especially keen on two New Orleanians, Armstrong and Connee Boswell, the gifted jazz-pop singer who appeared both as a soloist and as one of the three Boswell Sisters.

She never met her father, and her mother, according to most biographers, died when she was fifteen in 1932. By her mid-teens, Fitzgerald was on her own. In 1934, she tried her luck at the world's most famous amateur talent contest, the one held on Saturday nights at Harlem's Apollo Theater. According to Fitzgerald's own mythology, she had originally intended to perform as a dancer, but as it happened a very accomplished dance act went on immediately before her, so at the last moment she decided to give it a shot as a vocalist. She had no training or experience as a singer, but she liked the way Connee Boswell sang the Hoagy Carmichael song "Judy." (Or so Fitzgerald later said; there's no evidence that Boswell ever sang that particular song—she certainly never recorded it.) Ralph Cooper, the emcee at the contest that night and many others, later distinctly remembered Fitzgerald singing another Boswell-associated song, "The Object of My Affection." Whatever it was she sang that night is immaterial: The point is that she won the contest at the world-famous Apollo.

As a result of the attention, Fitzgerald was soon singing with drummer Chick Webb and His Orchestra, an outstanding aggregation that served as house band at the no less world-famous Savoy Ballroom, roughly twenty blocks north of the Apollo. Long before she was twenty, Fitzgerald was regarded as a cultural and musical leader by her fellow Harlemites. She cut her first of hundreds of recording sessions in June 1935 with Webb's band, singing on two titles, "Love and Kisses" and "I'll Chase the Blues Away."

Chick Webb himself was universally regarded by his fellow drummers as the hardest-swinging percussionist of a hard-swinging era—and the overall best at propelling a big dance band. Even so, the Webb orchestra was only one of many rhythmically inspired groups that were competing for the attention of black dancers and not even dreaming of catching on with the mainstream public south of 110th Street. However, when he latched on to Fitzgerald, he realized that here was the attraction that could help make him a potent force in the pop music business. Almost overnight, her singing began to dominate the band's music, on records and broadcasts. Before long, the combination of Webb's drumming and band and Fitzgerald's voice *had* boosted the band's popularity to the point where it was rapidly gaining on Ellington, Basie, and Calloway.

In 1938, the team rose even higher, thanks to the breakthrough hit "A-Tisket, A-Tasket." It was the singer herself who had the idea to do a swinging treatment of the traditional nursery rhyme, which she worked out with the help of staff arranger Al Feldman (aka Van Alexander). This would be virtually the only blockbuster jukebox hit that Fitzgerald would ever land, but it came at a time when she needed it most. "Tisket" made her into a household name in white homes as well as black, a status she would never relinquish. There had been success-ful attempts at swinging nursery rhymes before, such as Benny Goodman's "Yankee Doodle Never Went to Town" and "Peter Piper," and Jimmie Lunceford's "Rhythm in My Nursery Rhymes," while Maxine Sullivan's very successful "Loch Lomond" of 1937 can be considered part of the same moment. But "Tisket" put the concept solidly on the map in such a way that people quickly forgot it had ever been tried before. (Fitzgerald would do that a lot—with other ideas—throughout her career.)

Fitzgerald resonated with "Tisket" for various reasons: The song was pure hard-swinging rhythm with negligible emotional or lyrical content, yet when she sang of how she missed her little yellow basket, it sounded as if she really meant it. Here she was, half-girl, half-woman (at twenty-one), doing a song that was half–children's rhyme and half–grown-up dance number, with a text that was silly but also, deep down, almost serious. It was the perfect song for her at the perfect time. No wonder she had thought of it herself.

Over the years, she kept singing "Tisket," with partners ranging from Perry Como to Abbott & Costello. Not only was she doing sequels—"I Found My Yellow Basket" and other antic juvenilia, such as "Organ Grinder's Swing"—but so was everyone else. When Nat King Cole did his own swinging-nursery-rhythm version of "Three Blind Mice," he made it into a virtual paraphrase and tribute to "Tisket." It impelled Decca Records, Webb's label, to begin recording Fitzgerald under her own name (which is how "Organ Grinder" and "Bei Mir Bist Du Schoen" were done) and, in general, it raised the stock of female band singers everywhere. Lena Horne later observed, "A whole generation of us went looking for that little yellow basket."

The Webb-Fitzgerald records proved so popular that there was a backlash in certain circles: Hard-core jazz fans resented how Webb was turning over so much of the band to what they deemed a "com-mercial" attraction (the term was not a compliment among thirties hepsters), and higher-minded song buffs resented how many of the Webb-Fitzgerald records were novelties like "Chew, Chew, Chew Your Bubblegum" and "My Wubba Dolly."

In truth, while the 114 sides Fitzgerald recorded between 1935 and 1941 are not, on the whole, on the same level as the mostly amazing sides Billie Holiday was making at the same time with Teddy Wilson, or that the more experienced Mildred Bailey was making with Red Norvo, they are overall an auspicious and appropriate beginning for one of the greatest talents in the history of recorded sound.

Fitzgerald's big band experience lasted six years, the last two of which found her fronting the orches-tra after Webb's death, at the age of thirty-four, in 1939. Generally speaking, the weakest period of her career is the war years and their immediate after-math. Like such approximate contemporaries as Eckstine, Cole, Sinatra, and Shore, Fitzgerald would

spend the early to mid-forties helping to redefine the notion of the modern jazz-pop singer, and to rein-vent herself in the process. At that time, the popular music business was almost entirely predicated on singles, and Fitzgerald (like Sinatra later on) was just not a hit-singles artist. Despite the overall excellence of her output, which kept getting better and better as the forties rolled on, and her fierce allegiance to Decca Records and her producer, Milt Gabler, she cracked the top 10 only rarely.

Yet she achieved for herself what Tony Bennett later stated to be his only goal: Rather than the occa-sional hit single, Fitzgerald created a hit catalogue. "Ella Fitzgerald never had a hit after 'A-Tisket, A-Tasket' but she sold a lot of records," as Mitch Miller, a producer for a rival label, observed to me. "What single did she ever have on the charts?" Miller dis-missed "My Happiness"—a 1948 hit that was one of the few times Fitzgerald made the top 10—as a mere "cover." And he was correct.

On a TV interview with Edward R. Murrow in the early rock 'n' roll era, Fitzgerald lamented the fate of singers who are propelled to the top on the strength of a hit record, but then, when expected to do a full set in a nightclub or wherever, "all they have to offer is the hit." In spite of never recording a career-long signature song, like "Come on-a My House," "Fever," or "I Left My Heart in San Fran-cisco," she was one of the consistently biggest-selling female singers of all time; in 1954, Decca claimed that she had sold a staggering 22 million records for the company.

Interestingly, however, no singer ever seemed more conscious of other singers and their hits than Fitzgerald: She would occasionally treat crowds to her impressions of Louis Armstrong on "Basin Street Blues" and others, including Rose Murphy doing "I Can't Give You Anything but Love" with a signature "chi chi" interjection. (Indeed, more people have probably heard Fitzgerald's imitation of the now obscure singer-pianist than have ever heard Murphy herself.) "St. Louis Blues" from her 1958 Rome concert is a typical example of Fitzgerald affectionately referring to one of her peers, as she drops a nod to Peggy Lee's current hit, "You give me fever!" "I Can't Give You Anything but Love" has her interjecting the words "Elvis Presley—all shook up" while doing an Armstrong impression. Her treat-ment of Lee's "I Love Being Here with You" from the 1964 Juan-les-Pins show is a veritable catalogue of salutes to contemporaries, including Tony Bennett's "I Left My Heart in San Francisco," Nat King Cole's "Nature Boy," and Lee's "Fever" again.

Even before Fitzgerald began working with Gabler, she had begun following Bing Crosby's example in teaming up with a wide range of bands and singers. There were solo stars, most notably Louis Armstrong; vocal groups, like the Mills Broth-ers and the Ink Spots; and sometimes a whole band, like Louis Jordan and his Tympany Five. The meet-ings with the two Louises were especially fine.

With Armstrong in 1950 she laid down the definitive version of "Dream a Little Dream of Me." While that 1930 song eventually became a standard, their treatment of the unrevived "Can Anyone Explain" is no less warm and wonderful: After Fitzgerald sings the opening chorus over a prominent obbligato by Armstrong, she playfully admonishes the trumpeter, "Say Pops! Oh Pops, put that horn down and listen!" When Armstrong sings his chorus, the tempo picks up slightly and she accompanies him with a scatted ob-li-de obbligato. The eight big band–backed singles they did between 1946 and 1951 for Decca neatly anticipate the three equally marvelous full-length LPs they did for Verve in 1956–57, most of which were more informal, small band affairs (excepting their monumental reading of Gershwin's *Porgy and Bess*).

The meetings with Armstrong gave Fitzgerald the chance to explore that aspect of her music that had been directly inspired by the Mighty Man himself—in other words, her own roots and musical past. Louis Jordan was also a part of her past—he played alto for Chick Webb and on Fitzgerald's Savoy Eight series—together, the two stars examined the present and future of pop music. Jordan was the central figure in the new African American pop music not yet known as rhythm and blues, yet few of their six duets were strictly R&B of the kind that Jordan specialized in. "Baby, It's Cold Outside" came from the traditional great American show tunes songbook, while "I'll Never Be Free" was one of those songs that provided an early definition of the term "crossover." Written by Tin Pan Alley–ites Bennie Benjamin and George Weiss, it was a duet hit for Tennessee Ernie Ford and Kay Starr in the country field, for Paul Gayten and Annie Laurie in R&B, and Fitzgerald and Jordan in whatever field one chose to classify them.

The 1946 "Stone-Cold Dead in the Market" took the twosome to the Caribbean a decade before Harry Belafonte and became one of Fitzgerald's biggest-selling singles. Anticipating Peggy Lee's ersatz-Latin-American "Mañana" from a year later, a mainstream jazz-pop singer struck gold by visiting Pan-America. In both cases, the outrageous accents affected by the singers—North American stars caricaturing South American and Caribbean cultures—have troubled later generations, although where Lee's "Mañana" was her own original (to her great profit), Fitzgerald's was an authentic calypso by the master Wilmoth Houdini. It should be noted that the gruesome details of the text were not cleaned up for mass-market conception, as often happened when such material was translated into pop.

But beyond swing and the songbook, the new music with which Fitzgerald most effectively reenergized her career was the emerging jazz known as bebop, which she gradually discovered in the late forties. Born in the same year as occasional collaborator Dizzy Gillespie, by the late forties Fitzgerald was incorporating more and more of bebop harmonic and rhythmic conventions (meaning fast as a

bastard) into her music, in particular into her scat singing. She was building on the groundwork she had laid down a decade earlier with the swinging nursery rhymes, which, infused with the boundless imagination she channeled in her scat singing, elevated nonsense and even doggerel into art. She advanced from these to full-blown, purely wordless scat epics based on swing standards like "Flying Home" (1948) and "Air Mail Special" (1952). From there she progressed even further into bop classics, like Tadd Dameron's "Cool Breeze." However the best of her mature scat epics would be based on standards like "Lady, Be Good" and "How High the Moon" and would utilize at least a one-chorus run-through of the lyrics before flying home.

In 1954, Gabler compiled what is probably the single most exciting record of Fitzgerald's career, the 12" album *Lullabies of Birdland*. The set collects the eleven scat features she recorded over her second decade at Decca. These are not just free-blowing improvisations, Ella cutting loose with the trio the way she would do on many later live recordings, but carefully orchestrated affairs. Sometimes there's an orchestra, sometimes there's a vocal group, but in every case there's a tightly worked out balance between what's improvised and what's prearranged, as delineated partially by her special material intro to "How High the Moon" and other recurring signposts (the quote from the 1926 "Horses" in "Flying Home"). When Fitzgerald scats over this particular type of canvas, it doesn't feel like some avant-garde jazz experiment, it feels like great pop music.

Fitzgerald's swing and her time are perfect—astonishingly so, almost superhuman; you can't find a metronome with time this good. That's probably the key reason why her scatting uninterrupted for three to five minutes is so vastly entertaining. There are only a handful of vocalists who could sustain interest with a scat solo that lasts a whole chorus or more: Mel Tormé, Leo Watson, Sarah Vaughan, Anita O'Day—even Louis Armstrong almost never scatted for a whole chorus (he could have if he'd wanted to, though). Fitzgerald is the only one who could scat for an entire album without becoming boring or self-indulgent. Pieces like the amazing "Later" are the kind of music that give "rhythm" tunes a good name. The song has no melody or lyrics ("Later for the hap'nings, baby!") to speak of, it's just a pure exercise in swing, a launching pad for a journey that's strictly star-bound. It's no coincidence that so many of her songs have a celestial destination: "Airmail Special," "Flying Home," "Angel Eyes," "How High the Moon."

Yet at the same time that she was venturing away from traditional song form (not just with bebop, but with R&B and calypso), she was also helping to preserve the Great American Songbook. In 1950, Fitzgerald made her first songbook album, an eight-song, 10" LP collection entitled *Ella Sings Gershwin*, accompanied by Ellis Larkins, one of the most sensitive pianists ever to accompany a singer. Working with

Larkins, both in 1950 and on the 1954 *Songs in a Mellow Mood*, a varied set of twelve voice-and-piano duets, Fitzgerald offered a more emotionally open and vulnerable kind of singing than she had previously presented on disc. (The twenty tracks with Larkins were later collated by GRP-Decca into a CD called *Pure Ella*.) Here she made people forget that the songbook album idea had ever been tried before (in a four-composer series of limited distribution by Lee Wiley, and a little-known Capitol album by Margaret Whiting of Rodgers and Hart songs), and in general laid the groundwork for her monumental songbook series of later in the decade.

The 1950 Gershwin album makes for a notable contrast with her Birdland lullabies. Here she sings the melodies as written, with only slight harmonic and melodic variation. There are videos of Fitzgerald in concert where she reaches a fever pitch of excitement in the middle of a scat solo, drenched in perspiration (at one point she would spontaneously quote from "Smoke Gets in Your Eyes" but substitute "Sweat" for the first word), with no touch of formality, absolutely exposed to the audience without words or music to hide behind. Yet the cover of her 1950 *Ella Sings Gershwin* shows the completely opposite Ella, much as the music inside the jacket does. She's looking as formal as a Cafe Society singer like Mabel Mercer or Lena Horne or Alberta Hunter: gown, hair coiffed neatly in a bun. With the scat epics, she proved herself an improviser on the level of Gillespie or Charlie Parker; with the Ellis Larkins projects she gave the great lyric interpreters like Mercer, Billie Holiday, and Frank Sinatra something to worry about.

Sadly, there is no comprehensive collection of Fitzgerald's Decca recordings—in the nineties, MCA issued a bunch of titles that can be charitably described as half-assed, in terms of both compilation and sonic production. (I should know, I worked on the first installment.) Only the last volume, *The Final Decca Years*, is as good as the whole series should have been. What is really needed is a complete mega-box or series of boxed sets of Mosaic or Bear Family ambition. As of now, the best account of her 1935–55 work is on the Belgian Classics series, which is at least complete if sadly lacking in terms of packaging and sound quality.

One of the mysteries of pop history is why Decca Records allowed Ella Fitzgerald to leave in 1955 and begin recording for Norman Granz's newly formed Verve Records label. Why release an artist who, according to Decca's own figures, had sold 22 million records for them? The only possible answer is that Fitzgerald really wanted to work with Granz, and they let her go out of deference to her wishes.

It had been Decca's Milt Gabler who initiated the transition from singles to LPs, most famously on the celebrated *Ella Sings Gershwin, Lullabies of Birdland,* and *Songs in a Mellow Mood*. There were also the lesser-known but marvelous *Miss Ella Fitzgerald and Mr. Gordon Jenkins Invite You to Listen and Relax,* a superlative set of mostly ballads with strings, and *Sweet and Hot,* in which the most prominent arranger was Sy Oliver and the material was later expanded into the essential CD *The Last Decca Years, 1949–1954*. The last climaxes in an epic, double-length reading of "You'll Have to Swing It (Mr. Paganini)," originally written for Martha Raye but ultimately associated with Fitzgerald, who first recorded it with Webb in 1936.

In many ways, Granz followed Gabler's lead: *Ella Sings Gershwin* led to the wonderful voice-and-piano package *Let No Man Write My Epitaph* (an unwieldy title with a film tie-in, more widely known on CD as *The Intimate Ella,* 1960), as well as to the monumental *Ella Fitzgerald Songbook* series. Granz also produced over a dozen nonsongbook albums, with both big bands and small, which, no less than the songbooks, contained one great standard after another. In the early fifties, she teamed with brilliant orchestrators like Sy Oliver, Gordon Jenkins, Benny Carter, Bob Haggart, and André Previn. The Verve years got off to a slow start in that the arrangements for the first two songbook projects, *Cole Porter* and *Rodgers and Hart,* were not up to those of her earlier collaborators. Soon, however, Granz was acquiring the services of Nelson Riddle, Billy May, Paul Weston, Frank DeVol, and Marty Paich to work with her.

Fitzgerald was also a perfect fit with the Verve organization because Granz was generally indifferent to the singles market: It would release occasional 45s by its artists (Fitzgerald's have been collected in a CD series entitled *Jukebox Ella*), but the label's primary focus was on the long-playing album format. They were going after the highbrows who had heard of Jerome Kern and Charlie Parker, not kids dropping nickels in malt-shop jukes. The LP medium would become for Fitzgerald what television was for Perry Como: Both were veteran artists who had been around a while at the time of these technological sea changes, and both of them got in on the ground floor—well before the transition—and gave their careers a virtual B_{12} shot. As the album format became more and more important to the music business, Fitzgerald was perfectly poised to assume her position as queen of the long-playing disc.

The songbook albums were the most viable expression of the renewed vitality of traditional American pop: These were not only high class, but almost militantly so—not just good songs but good songs packaged with their composer as the selling point, guaranteed to appeal not only to the cognoscenti but proving in the process that the market for such "high-brow" material was bigger than anyone had imagined. As noted, while the first two songbooks were somewhat subpar, at least in terms of contributions other than the singer's, by the third entry, *Ella Fitzgerald Sings the Duke Ellington Songbook,* the series really caught fire.

It would be Ellington's most ambitious collaboration with a star singer, and overall the most exciting of Fitzgerald's songbook projects—proving that not only was traditional pop commercially viable in what has been wrongly portrayed as strictly the rock 'n' roll era, but so, too, was Ellington's blend of orchestrated jazz. Varying between the full-size Ellington aggregate (with special guest Dizzy Gillespie making his presence felt on "Take the A Train") and a Dukish small group (co-starring Ben Webster in his only studio appearance with Miss Fitz), she offers a full-scale exploration of all dimensions Ducal.

The Duke Ellington Songbook (1956–57) and *The Irving Berlin Songbook* (1958) show the songbooks hitting their stride. Oddly, the most exciting track from the *Berlin* sessions, arranged by pop music veteran Paul Weston, was omitted from the original release of the two-LP set and not restored to its proper place until the most recent CD edition. This was Fitzgerald's all-scat version of "Blue Skies," and one can only imagine that it was left off to please the songwriter, who probably did not enjoy having his lyric neglected even if his classic melody never sounded more glorious. (She had long been using the tune as a scat vehicle, as on a 1947 radio duet with drummer-vocalist Buddy Rich.)

The pace really picks up with the final four entries: *George and Ira Gershwin* (1959), *Harold Arlen* (1961), *Johnny Mercer* (1963), and *Jerome Kern* (1964), three of which were arranged and conducted by Nelson Riddle, greatest of all pop-jazz orchestrators, the exception being the Arlen set, which represents Fitzgerald's major meeting with Billy May. Granz seemed determined to make the world forget that Fitzgerald had done a Gershwin songbook nine years previously. But while the 1950 meeting with Ellis Larkins and the brothers formerly known as Gershovitz represented the ultimate in intimacy, the 1959 project—recorded in ten sessions over eight months—was a spectacle of Cecil DeMille–like proportions: not just a single or even a double LP, but a boxed set of five 12" albums; not just a big band but something very near a full symphony, all spectacularly packaged at a premium price. Fortunately, Granz had absolutely the right man at the podium—there was no one who could have more effectively kept the proceedings from getting too overdone or bombastic than Riddle, who helps keep the project every bit as personal, even intimate, as the earlier Ella-Ellis project. With these eight sets (released in a sixteen-CD box in 1993) Fitzgerald left a definitive record of virtually every song that anybody would ever sing—and to a vast extent defined the parameters of what was becoming recognized as the Great American Songbook.

While there were some precedents for the songbook album format, the other kind of album that Fitzgerald specialized in during the Verve years was rightfully recognized as a Granz innovation. He had been producing a series of jam session concerts at formal halls all over the country and then the world since 1944, which was then as radical an idea as his policy of recording the results and releasing highlights of these on disc, first in 78 albums, eventually on 10" and then 12" LPs. It was only natural that Granz would record Fitzgerald's in-person appearances as well, and, eventually, release the best of those commercially.

Live recordings of Fitzgerald exist going back to the Webb days (in 1999, I worked on a CD of hi-fi airchecks cut by the Webb orchestra under Fitzgerald's direction from sixty years earlier, *I'm in the Groove*, on BMG). Granz was, in fact, recording her as part of the Jazz at the Philharmonic series and on other occasions even when she was still under contract to Decca. Some of her appearances with JATP exist on tape from as early as 1949, even though he was not contractually free to release these performances on records for years to come. In fact, it's the pre-Verve live tapes of Fitzgerald, from 1949 to 1955, that mark what may be her all-time greatest live recordings. There are concerts from Carnegie Hall (1949), Tokyo (1953), and Connecticut (1954) that are positively transcendent. On the last—unfortunately, not yet available on CD—Fitzgerald finds the blues and the abstract truth at the heart of, of all things, "Hernando's Hideaway." Great as her classic later live albums are—especially *Mack the Knife, Ella in Berlin* (1960), and *Ella at Juan-les-Pins* (1964), not to mention a revelatory series of concerts with Duke Ellington in 1966—one would be hard pressed to say that she ever really topped these early live documents. (*The Enchanting Ella Fitzgerald*, another amazing collection of live airchecks from Birdland and the Apollo, circa 1950–52, was issued on the Canadian label Baldwin Street Music.)

It was an arrangement that also suited Fitzgerald and Granz very well: Contrary to how it might seem, the songbooks were somewhat mass-produced—she did two and a half of these multivolume packages in 1956 alone. Yet the live sets were painstakingly planned, as one can hear in the instances where multiple nights in the same engagement have survived. The live albums required almost more planning than the songbooks, except that the planning was entirely on the part of the artist, not the producer. Fitzgerald gave as much thought to selection and sequence as, say, Sinatra and Peggy Lee; Granz, on the other hand, just had to send a crew and turn on the tape deck. He simply set up engineers wherever she appeared, and released the results; the final product was like a photograph, an authentic sample of what Fitzgerald was doing in clubs all over the world, almost three hundred nights a year, through decade after decade.

Two further points regarding the live albums stand out. Although earlier on, a few sets were taped in the continental United States—there are albums from the Hollywood Bowl (1956), the Newport Jazz

Festival (1957), and the Shrine Auditorium in Los Angeles (also 1957)—the live albums that resonate most strongly long term are the slightly later ones taped overseas, in the years when Fitzgerald was as much a globe-trotting cultural ambassador as Louis Armstrong, Duke Ellington, or Dizzy Gillespie.

One other aspect of the live albums has been especially marked in the compact disc era: Granz, obviously, recorded much more live material than the market could bear, given how prolific Fitzgerald was in this period. The live tapes, more than the studio albums, tend to have lots in the way of unused material. *Ella in Rome: The Birthday Concert* was recorded on that occasion in 1958 but not issued until thirty years later, while an equally impressive show from Hungary in 1970 had to wait the same amount of time before being eventually issued as *Ella Fitzgerald Live in Budapest*. The 1964 *Juan-les-Pins* concert with Tommy Flanagan has been expanded to a two-CD that's well more than twice the length of the original single LP. The payoff is *The Ella Fitzgerald and Duke Ellington Côte d'Azur Concerts on Verve*, an extravagant package that justifies the length of the title: The original two-LP package has been more than quadrupled to an eight-CD box, containing 110 tracks and nearly nine hours of music—much of which is instrumentals by the Ellington band. But there's no shortage of Fitzgerald.

So much worthwhile Fitzgerald concert material has been released, starting just around the time the lady herself was making her last original albums, that it almost seems as if she never stopped singing. It also begs the question: Since Granz only released a fraction of this music back in the day, are the copious amounts of unissued recordings up to the same quality levels as the stuff that was issued? Having listened to all these CDs many times, I can only speculate that either the catalogue producers at Universal Music (which owns Verve) are still cherry-picking their material or, more likely, Fitzgerald simply never had an off night—at least not in the many representative nights when she was being taped. One can only hope that the flow of new live material never lets up: 2006 saw the release of a wonderful DVD of Fitzgerald in concert in Belgium, followed a year later by a wonderful two-CD set from Chicago in 1958.

In 1959, Granz sold his interest in Verve Records—less than four years after he founded it—but continued to produce Fitzgerald's recordings and serve as her personal manager. By this time, she—like Sinatra, Peggy Lee, Nat Cole, and at most one or two others—was now a cottage industry. She was constantly touring, appearing on every TV variety show in existence, and continually releasing new albums—as many as five or six a year.

While the songbooks and the live albums continued to occupy her attention, there were all kinds of other projects, some of which could be considered "theme" albums—*Ella Sings Broadway* (1962), for instance. Like Mel Tormé's earlier *Shubert Alley* (and using the same orchestrator, Marty Paich), it addresses twelve of the great songs of the postwar, post-*Oklahoma!* era (as opposed to the prewar-based songs and writers that were the subject of the songbook series). There were two other notable albums with Paich, the jazzier *Ella Swings Lightly* (1958), which utilized the arranger's famous Dektette, and the straight-down-the-middle *Whisper Not*, plus two "bonus" albums with Nelson Riddle, in addition to the three songbook projects in 1961–62, *Ella Sings Gently with Nelson* and *Ella Swings Brightly with Nelson*.

These five packages can generally be viewed as "bonus" albums to the songbook series, since they consist primarily of work by Broadway-oriented writers (generally of the thirties) who weren't fortunate enough to rate a full-length songbook. Had the series gone to, say, another three or four volumes, doubtless Fitzgerald and Granz would have chosen Harry Warren, Hoagy Carmichael, and perhaps one of the Jimmys—Van Heusen or McHugh; yet it's unlikely they would have gotten around to Gordon and Revel, Johnny Green, or Frank Loesser, good as they were. I'm grateful to these lesser-known projects for giving us such terrific tracks as Fitzgerald's hard-swinging "Steam Heat," her masterful ballad treatment of "Body and Soul," her jazz waltz treatment of "Matchmaker," and many others.

The live albums are perhaps most widely enjoyed for her ecstatic up-tempos and scat adventures. Yet she sings some of her best ballads and blues in these concert recordings. In the studio she spent time with these formats only sparingly; there are merely two albums each of blues material and another two purely of traditional romantic ballads. *These Are the Blues* (1963) consists of the most classic sort of 12-bar blues with Roy Eldridge and a small group; *Rhythm Is My Business* (1962), a set of what might be considered more up-to-date blues-oriented material with honky-tonkin' organist Bill Doggett leading a big band in the mold of Buddy Johnson or Lionel Hampton. Fitzgerald is hardly a specialist in the classic blues of Bessie Smith and the other twenties blues divas (mostly also named Smith), but *These Are the Blues* is far from a disappointment—in this period, she was often including the perennial "St. Louis Blues" in her live shows. The Doggett album is also a marvelous curio. When I hear a track at random, my first thought is that it's a Decca session from the late forties. It takes a while to realize this was actually 1962—it sounds decades away from what Riddle or Paich were writing for her, but superb just the same.

Curiously, Fitzgerald made only two albums of purely slow, romantic ballads with strings, both of which were the work of arranger-conductor Frank DeVol: *Like Someone in Love* (1957) and *Hello Love* (1959). Ballads are strewn throughout the songbook series—the live albums as well—and she sings them so well, one wishes that she had done even more. When she sings "I'll Never Be the Same," there's no doubt that she means it—and every word of it.

DeVol, who did his best work with Fitzgerald (their five or so projects together are at a much higher level than the three or so he did around the same time for Tony Bennett), seems to have been Fitzgerald and Granz's go-to guy for ballad albums: Much of *Get Happy* (1957–59) and *Hello, Dolly!* (1964) consist of DeVol's ballad charts for Fitzgerald and strings. The 1964 package might be Fitzgerald's equivalent of Sinatra's *It Might as Well Be Swing* from the same year in that a great deal of it is other people's hits—"Hello, Dolly!," "People," "Can't Buy Me Love," "Volare"—although Fitzgerald spends as much time "covering" herself, doing new and superior versions of tunes already long associated with her: "Miss Otis Regrets" (with strings, as opposed to just piano on the 1956 Porter collection), "Pete Kelly's Blues," and best of all, a new "How High the Moon" done not as a scat extravaganza but as a romantic ballad with verse (following the outline of Tormé's 1960 treatment). Yet DeVol also delivered the goods when asked to supply jazzier charts for the big band–styled *Ella Fitzgerald Sings Sweet Songs for Swingers* (1959) and the exceptional *Ella Wishes You a Swinging Christmas*. The latter was no mere capitulation to commercial considerations but one of her most inspired albums. It begins with a high-octane treatment of "Jingle Bells" that employs Fitzgerald's pet "horses" lick with reference to the "one-horse open sleigh" (Diana Krall heavily referred to this track in her own swing version of "Jingle Bells") and recasts Jimmy Rushing's "Good Morning Blues" (with its reference to "Santy Claus") as a seasonal aria.

If DeVol and Paich were considered Fitzgerald's fall-back arrangers—neither of them was given the chance to work with the First Lady on one of the high-profile songbook entries—it's a remarkable reminder of how gifted even journeyman orchestrators were in these years. Russ Garcia, who was trusted with the *Porgy and Bess* project by Ella and Armstrong—and did a highly commendable job on it—wasn't even given the chance to do another entire album with her, just a couple of singles sessions.

There's just no let-up: There are what might be called her "pure jazz" albums, among them the modest though marvelous *Clap Hands! Here Comes Charlie*, a 1962 session backed only by rhythm section led by Lou Levy (one of several master accompanists, along with Tommy Flanagan, to follow in the footsteps of Ellis Larkins). As I say, it's a jazz album, but the most effective track for me is Leonard Feather's ballad "Signing Off," an otherwise forgotten opus from the early bop era in which a radio sign-off serves as metaphor for the end of a love affair. When Fitzgerald died in 1996, this was the first cut I rushed to listen to.

The jazz team-ups, with Armstrong, Ellington, and Basie, more directly prefigure her later seventies work, except that the three meetings with Armstrong represent her only full-length collaborations with another singer. God knows every major male vocalist of the period was dying to have the chance: Sinatra, Crosby, Bennett, Tormé, Cole, and Joe Williams all sang with her here and there (mostly on TV), but none got into the studio with her for any real time. This was probably more Granz's doing than Fitzgerald's—he wanted to make sure the world knew she was kept at a level above every other singer who ever lived, with the exception of Armstrong. Here, Granz was once again following the example of Milt Gabler, who had teamed Fitzgerald and Armstrong on eight tracks, which serve as a suitable prelude to the three Verve projects: *Ella and Louis* (1956), *Ella and Louis Again* (1957), and *Porgy and Bess* (1957).

Even more than on the Doggett album, Fitzgerald builds up an incredibly swinging momentum with Basie on the 1963 *Ella and Basie* (essentially produced and conducted by Quincy Jones and arranged by his posse, including Billy Byers). One factor that makes this package different from most of the Basie band's other team-ups with star singers is that the Count, not Fitzgerald's accompanist of the day, is actually at the piano. The blending of singer and band is especially miraculous on a shuffle rhythm treatment of "Into Each Life Some Rain Must Fall"—a 180-degree turnaround from the hit single she had made nineteen years earlier accompanied by the stiff crooning of the Ink Spots.

If any one event climaxes Fitzgerald's Verve years, it's her team-up with Duke Ellington, which began with the songbook sessions in 1957 and resumed with new projects in 1965–66. They made a new studio album (*Ella at Duke's Place*) that serves as a marvelous postscript to the earlier *Ella Fitzgerald Sings the Duke Elllington Songbook* and, no less importantly, they hit the road together. Their 1966 tour resulted in live recordings from Sweden and Los Angeles, and, most famously, in the *Côte d'Azur* box. Good as the *Songbook* album is, Fitzgerald and the Ellingtonians seem much more comfortable with each other in the mid-sixties, and the studio set is considerably more relaxed and intimate—and features a bonus in that the singer and band don't duplicate any of the 1956–57 tunes, and so consists primarily of slightly more offbeat Ellington and Strayhorn items. Among these are "I Like the Sunrise," two flowers from Strayhorn's bouquet series ("Passion Flower" and "A Flower Is a Lovesome Thing"), one of Ellington's moods indigo, "Azure," and a sophisticated lady of a specific color, "The Brownskin Gal in the Calico Gown."

In 1967, Norman Granz decided to retire temporarily from the music business, leaving Fitzgerald to fend for herself. The late sixties would be the least-rewarding chapter of her career. When she did get into the studio, those sessions were sabotaged by lame ideas (Fitzgerald singing gospel, Fitzgerald singing religious Christmas songs, Fitzgerald covering lousy contemporary hits). *Thirty by Ella*, a Capitol album produced by veteran jazz chronicler Dave Dexter, is easily both the best and worst from the period: She does great songs with a great band (musical director: Benny Carter). The problem is that she does too many—two minutes of each, in a format derived from the Bing Crosby sing-along discs of earlier in the decade and anticipating the *Hooked on Swing* series of the eighties. Yet even amid this decidedly barren spell, there were bright moments.

There are two albums on Reprise, the 1969 *Ella* and the 1970 *Things Ain't What They Used to Be*, that are much better than they're cracked up to be. The second, which was produced by Granz (who put his name on the front cover) and arranged and conducted by the simpatico Gerald Wilson, is a particularly strong example of how well Fitzgerald keeping up to date could work. They're not exclusively current songs—her treatment of the blues-driven "Black Coffee" and the essential Ellington riff "Things Ain't . . ." are especially powerful, and she shows how "Got to Get You into My Life" (which sounds like Lennon and McCartney writing for Motown) fits into the same tradition. Overall, Fitzgerald sounds amazingly convincing on the contemporary pop songs they've picked, even the schlocky "A Man and a Woman" and Burt Bacharach's "I'll Never Fall in Love Again," both of which give her the chance to play around in interesting time signatures. Most surprising is "Savoy Truffle," George Harrison's gastronomic driven lyric, which appears on the album after "Black Coffee," indicating that Ella is still in the diner. As a piece of funky, swinging nonsense, Fitzgerald makes it into a sort of updated "A-Tisket, A-Tasket."

The 1970 *Live in Budapest* shows that Fitzgerald hadn't yet come down from her pinnacle, and here she works wonders with "Spinning Wheel," while "This Guy's in Love with You" and "Raindrops Keep Falling on My Head" make me yearn for an album of *Ella Fitzgerald Sings the Burt Bacharach Songbook*.

Order was restored in 1972 when Norman Granz formed a new label called Pablo Records, even more of a jazz concern than Verve had been. Pablo released virtually nothing that could be considered a pop project, and even her one album with a large ensemble and strings—*Dream Dancing*, a revisit to Cole Porter country with Nelson Riddle at the helm—had been originally released by Atlantic Records (before it found a permanent home at Pablo). By the time Fitzgerald was pushing sixty, the pace had slowed somewhat, down to a mere album or two a year. There continued to be great studio albums and even greater live projects. Indeed, *Dream Dancing* is virtually the only Pablo album that even remotely feels like a *production*.

The bulk of the new label's releases, by Fitzgerald

and everyone else, don't make the slightest concession to any kind of showbiz prettification. Fitzgerald was not an unattractive woman, and she always tried to dress as nicely as she could for her audiences. When she came to the studio to work, there was no need for such niceties, thus the covers of the Pablo albums inevitably portray her as *hamish* as possible, completely without showbiz-industry glamour. Even if they're not as visually attractive as they might have been (as the Verve and Decca albums are, for example), there's a special kind of honesty about Fitzgerald's seventies and eighties releases.

Likewise, when Old Man Time came a-callin' and her chops began to fall away from the mountaintop of perfection, as even the greatest voices (which hers was) will inevitably do, rather than cover up her gradually diminishing pipes with larger ensembles, Granz seemed determined to expose her more than ever, in ultra-intimate settings with longtime piano pal Oscar Peterson (*Ella and Oscar*) and guitar virtuoso Joe Pass (*Take Love Easy, Easy Living, Fitzgerald and Pass . . . Again,* and *Speak Love,* plus *Sophisticated Lady,* a posthumously issued addendum of live performances by the two from Japan and Germany). The Ella of the later years was even less phony, less glamorized, less insincere than all previous Ellas.

By and large, the later studio albums are excellent, but most of the real magic of these years was captured live in front of paying audiences. *Ella: The Concert Years* is a simply titled four-CD package that collates as much pure magic as can possibly be compressed into four and a half hours. It's that great rarity, a box set that one will play from start to finish over and over. It doesn't hurt that the first disc consists of earlier live concerts, with Jazz at the Philharmonic (1953) and Duke Ellington (1966 and 1967). The remaining three volumes come from the Pablo years proper, 1972–83, and a generous number of these co-star the finest of all Fitzgerald's accompanists (with the possible exception of Ellis Larkins), the remarkable Tommy Flanagan. The vocal deterioration increases as the seventies give way to the eighties, but the electricity that Fitzgerald (especially as empowered by Father Flanagan) communicates back and forth with a cheering crowd—even whatever percentage of it could be captured on tape—is wondrous to behold. Overall, this is the most compelling document of Fitzgerald's later years.

There are yet still more first-rate studio albums: *Ella Abraca Jobim* (only available on CD in truncated form, alas) is a worthy postscript to the songbook series, with an ensemble directed by Erich Bulling that combines elements of Brazilian contempop and great jazz soloists in the persons of Pass, Toots Thielemans, Clark Terry, and Zoot Sims. One wishes it hadn't stopped there—just as I wish the original songbook series had continued on to Harry Warren and Jimmy Van Heusen, I wish there had been a full-length follow-up series that would have included the major songsters of the seventies, such as Cy

Coleman, Michel Legrand, Henry Mancini, Burt Bacharach, and perhaps even *Ella Abraca Sondheim,* all of whom were at least as worthy of her attention as Jobim. Alas, the only other songbook-oriented projects from the seventies have to be considered sequels to earlier albums, such as *Nice Work If You Can Get It,* which revisits Gershwin in the company of André Previn, and *Dream Dancing,* which reunites the First Lady with both Cole Porter and Nelson Riddle. Not that I'm complaining—these postscripts are fine, and *Dream Dancing* is, in fact, vastly superior in every way to the 1956 songbook, so much so that one merely wishes they hadn't stopped there.

She found other different things to do: *Lady Time* is a full-length meeting with organist Jackie Davis that contains the only occasion when she got through all the lyrics of "Mack the Knife," while *Fine and Mellow* is a blues-oriented package, also with Sims, Terry, Pass, Flanagan, and Sweets Edison, climaxing in a superb "I Can't Give You Anything but Love." Still, the majority of her later albums find her reexploring older concepts, most notably team-ups with worthy constituents—in addition to Pass and Peterson, there are two superlative sets with the full Basie ensemble, *A Classy Pair* and *A Perfect Match.* The latter two titles represent stunning examples of truth in advertising, but *The Best Is Yet to Come* did not—the best was already here, this being her final meeting with Nelson Riddle (from 1982). No more, alas, was yet to come. This was a stunning large-ensemble set that would be Riddle's last great project (too bad that fate wouldn't allow him to reteam one last time with Sinatra before cancer claimed him in 1986).

Tony Bennett once compared Fitzgerald's discography to those of Crosby and Sinatra, who are generally regarded as the two most popular and prolific singers in American music (Nat Cole sold more records in a shorter amount of time, but alas, didn't enjoy a long life span). Fitzgerald's output, Tony observed, was just as impressive in terms of both quality and quantity as Crosby's and Sinatra's. "She's right up there with 'em!" is how he put it. Not only is he right, but both gentlemen had fallow periods—Crosby in the sixties, Sinatra in the seventies; only Ella kept steadily turning out new albums, generally great ones, through to the start of the nineties. She sounds better than she has to on the 1989 *All That Jazz,* a set with two rhythm sections (one spotlighting Kenny Barron) and four horn soloists in Terry, Al Grey, Benny Carter, and Sweets Edison. As it happened, she revived one song from her very first session under her own name, the 1936 "My Last Affair." The title turned out to be prophetic. Even so, about to turn seventy-two, Fitzgerald was still the voice of jazz.

Fitzgerald and Granz remained active participants in the Pablo operation for roughly twenty years. They were about the same age, and they were both ready to phase out at approximately the same time; within a few years of *All That Jazz,* which would turn out to be her last album, Granz, too, threw in the towel, and sold all his Pablo assets and interests to Fantasy, which was, in turn, absorbed into Concord Records a decade after that.

On that last album, she also recorded Johnny Mercer and Jimmy Rowles's memorable "Baby, Don't You Quit Now," and indeed she didn't. I saw her live on only one occasion, I am sad to admit, in 1991 at the JVC Jazz Festival (at Avery Fisher Hall), and at the end of the concert, I and everyone else wandered out of the enormous room somewhat dazed. The only thing we could be sure of was that we had just witnessed the greatest performance of our lives—if probably not of hers. It was hard to imagine that she had ever sounded any better or held an audience more firmly in the grip of her hand. She entered and left in a wheelchair, but she remained the First Lady of jazz, of song, of music, of spiritual essence. As great as she was on records, in person she had a warmth and a glow that were not reproducible by electronic media of any sort.

I already knew that Fitzgerald was the greatest female singer who ever sang the American songbook. Her voice was pure silk, it was perfume, it was a frothy pink cloud, it was champagne, it was the stuff that dreams are made of; her intonation and her time were unimaginably astonishing. Above all, she knew how to sing a melody: Even when she played with one, she never screwed around with it; even when she was scatting for chorus after chorus, she never made herself more important than the song. Like Sinatra, she was the beginning and the end, setting an impossibly high bar for jazz singers and female singers in particular that could never be exceeded or even matched.

By the mid-nineties, her diabetes made it impossible for her to work, especially when part of one leg, then the other, had to be amputated. She died in June 1996. As a singer, Fitzgerald is clearly one of the godlike mortals, perhaps the only vocalist with chops to rival Charlie Parker, Art Tatum, Benny Goodman, or Buddy Rich—she does things with her instrument that are simply not humanly possible.

Perhaps altogether logically, Fitzgerald's least-known live album, the 1961 *Ella in Hollywood,* was the one that came directly after the spectacularly successful *Ella in Berlin—Mack the Knife.* But if *Ella in Hollywood* was overlooked when it was first released, in 2009 those same tapes were greeted with overwhelming enthusiasm by critics and fans. Universal Music, corporate heir to Verve, released four full CDs' worth of previously unheard live Fitzgerald from the same 1961 dates at the Hollywood Crescendo (as well as additional material from the same club in 1962), and it turned out that they had been sitting on yet another buried Fitzgerald masterpiece for nearly fifty years. Released as *Twelve Nights in Hollywood,* the four-CD box contains seventy-seven tracks, and, remarkably, no repeated songs—Fitzgerald and Granz had planned to do different songs every night, including a great many that she had never recorded live, and some she hadn't performed at all. It's yet five more hours of live Ella, adding to the already copious pile, and yet every one of these seventy-odd songs is worth owning, capturing the First Lady at her most dynamic, her most intense, and yet also her most intimate. It's yet another big box of Fitzgerald that merits playing again and again, and makes you wonder why we would ever waste time listening to anyone else.

Aretha Franklin (born 1942)

What's the difference, in popular music, between an artist for the ages and a flavor of the week? Whatever it is, the answer to that first question leads to others: What will it take to convince Aretha Franklin that she is, in fact, a great artist, and not a fly-by-night hit maker? Why does she consistently act as if she's in the same league with Mariah Carey and Whitney Houston when she actually deserves to be classed with Ella Fitzgerald and Rosemary Clooney?

Ms. Clooney once said that she realized she had moved into a higher category than your average pop singer when she was invited to make an album with Duke Ellington. Alas, Aretha Franklin seems to have enjoyed nothing like a comparable epiphany. One thing that never helped was awards and accolades: Franklin's record still stands as the single most Grammy Award–decorated woman in the history of the National Academy of Recording Arts and Sciences. In the very first year the academy created the category of Best Rhythm and Blues Solo Vocal Performance, Female, Franklin easily won that award— and went on to cop it for eight years in a row. In 1994 she won the Kennedy Center award, and around the same time received the NARAS Lifetime Achievement award, which was originally named after Bing Crosby; the trophy for best female R&B singer was given to Franklin so frequently that it's still referred to as the "Aretha" award.

Arista Records, Franklin's label in the eighties and nineties, commemorated the event with the release of a new CD compilation entitled *Aretha Franklin Greatest Hits (1980–1994)*. However, Franklin's other release of 1994, her one-track guest appearance with Frank Sinatra on his *Duets*, carried a more significant object lesson for the great soul diva. Like Sinatra, she is the undisputed leader in her field, yet while Sinatra lived long enough to claim the privileges of legend status, Franklin persists in acting as if she's just another ephemeral pop star of the moment. Both the music industry and the media support the misconception. Every time she made the charts in the eighties and nineties, the trade press called it a "comeback." An artist of Franklin's stature, no less than Sinatra, is timeless. In the same way that a new production of *La Bohème* should not be referred to as a "revival," Franklin transcends the term "comeback," which should be reserved for such

lesser figures as Neil Diamond or Frankie Laine, trying to grind out a few more minor chart-denters before joining the nostalgia circuit.

Does it make any difference, this concept of labeling, in terms of an artist's self-identity? In her case, yes, because in identifying with Whitney Houston rather than Sarah Vaughan, Franklin has habitually denied herself and her fans the benefits of her stature—which is not to have to worry about charts and hits and MTV. She should be making great music. Instead, ever since the seventies, Franklin has been singing almost nothing but ephemeral junk. When she came to Arista in 1980, the label's two shining lights were Barry Manilow and Melissa Manchester. The Arista albums of all three artists, including Franklin's, are long deleted both from the catalogue and the collective consciousness. Besides which, both Manilow and Manchester have attempted albums of standards—the kind of music Franklin was recording at the start of her career; in fact, apparently everybody has but Franklin. In 1993 and 1994, while she was being honored not only with the NARAS Lifetime Achievement award but the Kennedy Center award, her major release was a dreadful pop single called "A Deeper Love." There's something embarrassing about witnessing the depths to which she was willing, even eager, to stoop—still trying to work it, still trying to hustle up a hit.

The gap between creativity and commerce needn't be so precarious. In Fitzgerald's and Vaughan's heyday, there was no appreciable difference, and a great album—like the Gershwin songbooks they both made—could also be a hit. In her glory years, Franklin maintained a similar equilibrium: While she occasionally made an "art" album, like *Unforgettable: A Tribute to Dinah Washington* or her gospel project, *Amazing Grace*, this didn't mean that pure pop items like "Respect" and "I Never Loved a Man" were the least bit inferior artistically. There might be some justification for things like "A Deeper Love" if such records were actually big hits, but the fact remains that Franklin's biggest-selling music is pretty much her best music, her classic singles and albums of the sixties. If there's anything that her work of the last thirty years proves, unfortunately, it's that she can no longer depend upon the equation of art and pop that once sustained her.

Perhaps she'd be more widely appreciated as an artist, not merely a hit maker (or worse, an "oldies" artist), if she could prove herself in more widely varying subgenres. She also might invest her talent in more "concept" projects exploring different kinds of themes—the only notable such projects she's ever made are *Unforgettable* and the gospel albums. It's been fifty years since she made her first recording in her father's New Bethel Baptist Church in Detroit, so she's obviously recorded in a lot of different contexts, but ultimately there isn't a lot of variety to her singing. She attacks virtually every number in the same way, particularly on the classic Atlantic sessions. Generally she varies between two approaches: slow tracks on which she starts comparatively small and builds to a climax of euphoric, head-thrown-back ecstasy, and fast tracks where she starts out that way.

Franklin's artistry is a virtuosity of excess: She just piles on more, and more, and yet more screaming and screeching and gospel embellishment, somehow never wearing out either herself or her listeners. She is excessive in the same way that Ben Webster and Sarah Vaughan are excessive. There's a highly developed sense of musical taste at work here. Barbra Streisand, Franklin's fellow Columbia discovery and Sinatra *Duet* partner, never fails to sound as if she's oversinging, no matter whether she's supposed to be intimate or larger than life. Yet Franklin can rant and rave her fool head off from here to Calvary, not only throwing in the kitchen sink but the bathtub and any other plumbing you've got lying around as well, yet it never sounds like too much. With Franklin's music, "too much" is an irrelevant concept.

Franklin's father, the late Reverend C. L. Franklin, may have understood the talent of the most prodigious of his five offspring better than his fourth child herself. "If you want to know the truth," as the good reverend exhorts in his speech on Aretha's classic 1972 gospel album, *Amazing Grace*, "she has never left the Church." Franklin's origins and her strengths are one and the same, and that's the gospel truth.

She was born in Memphis, Tennessee, on March 25, 1942, and grew up in Detroit, where she spent most of her childhood in her father's New Bethel Baptist Church. The music of the church, as the Franklins understood it, not only had all the eroticism—and then some—of secularly sensual sounds, it also had all the glitz and glamour of show business. Likewise, Aretha's own act, with its evangelical-style climaxes—everything but speaking in tongues—and its widely criticized costumery, grows directly out of the colorful pomp and pageantry of a Sunday service.

Aretha's father and mentor wasn't any ascetic, cloistered, vow-of-poverty Holy Hairshirter, but more like the Lionel Hampton of Baptism. "C. L. Franklin was a national leader, a charismatic character who reputedly took an occasional walk on the wild side," said Jerry Wexler, Franklin's key collaborator at Atlantic. "He'd been busted for pot possession, and he liked to party."

Reverend Franklin was also a prolific recording artist, and black audiences bought his syncopated sermons by the thousands. (He recorded for "race" labels like Gotham and JVB, the latter eventually bought by Chess, which itself was later absorbed into MCA and is now part of the Universal Music Group.) In 1955 or 1956, the fourteen-year-old Aretha recorded nine soul-stirring hymns singing lead with the New Bethel Baptist Church Choir, and these qualify as the first-ever Aretha Franklin records (now available as *Aretha Gospel*). Within a few years of making those sides, Franklin would have her first child (at fifteen), rise to the top of the gospel pecking order (or get as high as you could go without breaking out, like Mahalia Jackson), and then, eventually, be "discovered" by John Hammond of Columbia Records.

Franklin recorded virtually all of her best work between 1960 and 1972. When she first came to Columbia, she hadn't yet found her identity, so it's understandable that her producers and other collaborators would experiment with her, in some cases trying the same approaches that had already worked for other artists. On the album known as *Aretha: The First 12 Sides*—John Hammond applied the method he perfected with his most famous "discovery," Billie Holiday: He had Franklin informally sing standards and blues with a jazz rhythm section plus a couple of horns and a complete absence of prewritten arrangements. She also worked with the gifted, short-lived arranger and conductor Robert Mersey, best known otherwise for his work with Andy Williams and Mel Tormé. In their major project together, *Unforgettable*, Mersey backs her the way he would have backed Vaughan or Fitzgerald, like a mainstream pop-jazz professional. Both of these projects—even the sessions later reissued as *The First 12 Sides*, taped when she was eighteen—are among her finest albums. No one could complain that either one suffered by comparison to her Atlantic albums.

Even the Atlantic gurus Ahmet Ertegun and Jerry Wexler have acknowledged that the Columbia period is far from the disaster that most observers (who say things like "Atlantic was where 'the real Aretha' emerged") would have you believe. Apart from *Unforgettable* and *The First 12 Sides,* unfortunately, most of her 1960–66 sessions have only been reissued over the last forty years on hodgepodge collections, both on LP and CD. The liner notes of these collections invariably commence with an apology. The latest (2002) such anthology (or anthology-apology) is even titled *The Queen in Waiting*, as if to convey, well, we failed to make her a star, but here she is anyway. In retrospect, however, the only sin of the Columbia sides is that they sound nothing like the records that eventually made Franklin famous. The dismissal of the pre-Atlantic material amounts to confusing the job of a critic with that of an accountant. Yet even by those standards, with Franklin not achieving any really big numbers in terms of singles or albums on either the pop or R&B charts, she clearly had something Columbia wanted, and the label offered to renew her contract when it expired in 1966. How many jazz, blues- (real blues, that is), or gospel-oriented singers even had major label affiliations in the dim dark days of 1966?

Franklin herself might be amused to discover that

a subset of her fans actually prefer the Columbia period, mainly because these records boast so many first-rate renditions of great American standards. And these don't only include show tunes and pop standards—you haven't lived until you've heard her transform the show tune "Once in a Lifetime" into a working model of pure soul—but blues classics, too, like "Trouble in Mind" and "I'd Rather Drink Muddy Water." This use of time-honored compositions is the major tactic that Franklin retained in the Atlantic years, when she recorded R&B mainstays like "You Send Me" and "Drown in My Own Tears." "Beyond the hits," Wexler explains, Franklin's albums "demonstrated both the cutting edge of contemporary soul and its strong continuity with the past."

Interestingly, the success of her first album, produced by Hammond and originally titled *Aretha* (reissued as *Aretha Franklin: The First 12 Sides*), is slightly compromised by the producer's inclusion of too many undistinguished pieces by the now forgotten blues-pop writer Johnny Leslie McFarland. It would doubtlessly surprise both Hammond and Clyde Otis, two producers highly involved with various subgenres of the blues, that Franklin's most memorable venture into the realm of jazz and classic blues is easily the 1964 *Unforgettable: A Tribute to Dinah Washington*. The lush string backings don't challenge her quite as excitingly as the later Jerry Wexler–Arif Mardin material, but producer Mersey's charts are beautifully subtle and suit her superbly. Furthermore, there are masterful obbligatists like trumpeter Ernie Royal and vibraphonist Teddy Charles (an instrument that Queen Dinah also played), who exquisitely occupy the vacant spaces Franklin was still too withdrawn to fill herself. Above all, the great blues spirit of Washington (a friend of her father's and, with Mahalia Jackson and Clara Ward, one of Franklin's sweetest inspirations) provides a perfect model for Franklin's gospel inflections in a string setting. Even though Washington's strength was basically blues and Franklin's was gospel, as one Columbia producer told Franklin biographer Mark Bego (in *Aretha Franklin: Queen of Soul*), "Aretha ached in the same way that Dinah did."

One aspect of Washington's legacy proved a detrimental factor in Franklin's career. *Unforgettable* didn't achieve big sales—unlike Streisand, Franklin wasn't an instant success—but received encouraging reviews, inspiring Columbia to put her in the hands of Clyde Otis and Belford Hendricks, producer and arranger, who proceeded to surround her with the same overdone string and cloying choir backings that they had imposed upon Washington in 1959 and 1960. Hendricks had also done the same for Nat King Cole at Capitol and, as with Washington's "What a Difference a Day Made," proved that tacky arrangements can yield big bucks.

Otis himself produced another of the all-time best Franklin albums, namely her only other small

group set, the concisely titled *Yeah!!!* This was originally issued as a "live" album, which, in a sense it was: Annotator Dan Morgenstern remembers that even though it was taped in Columbia's 30th Street studio, a live audience was in fact present at an adjacent studio. Thus the applause heard on *Yeah!!!* is genuine, even though on many occasions, tracks have been reissued with the applause track removed. Unfortunately, as far as I can tell, the complete album has only been reissued as it was originally meant to be heard by CBS France. Which is a shame. This is one of Franklin's all-time greatest, a package on which Harold Arlen, Pete Seeger, traditional blues, Cole Porter, and even Steve Allen (represented by not one but two songs) all get equal time.

The most rewarding of her early sides are not the R&B items that come closest to her Atlantic hits, but the more traditional songs, the standards and show tunes (like "Once in a Lifetime" from *Stop the World* and "If Ever I Would Leave You" from *Camelot*). In the early years of soul and Motown, Otis had Franklin do covers of contemporary hits that could be gathered into a compilation called *Other People's Money*. Many of these are lame, pallid imitations, but some are beautiful: I vastly prefer Franklin's reading of "My Guy" to the Mary Wells hit version, mainly because Franklin sounds like a real person singing about another real person. Franklin and Otis did two whole albums of early soul in 1965, *Runnin' Out of Fools* and *Soul Sister*. These are generally frustrating to listen to today because of what we can hear in hindsight that wasn't apparent then: Franklin and her producer are headed in the right direction, but they can't quite put their finger on how to get there.

Paradoxically, the funkiest cut from the whole period, "Lee Cross" (a song credited to Ted White, Franklin's first husband), was not produced by Otis at all. This hymn to a legendarily potent Lover Man, in the tradition of those mythical characters Stagger Lee and Stavin' Chain, had been supervised by Mersey on the same sessions as the *Unforgettable* album, although Columbia didn't release it until 1967, after Franklin began bringing in the big hits on Atlantic. (It is today available on the CD issue of *Unforgettable*, a bonus track in the sense that it's a song not associated with Washington.)

On the whole, Columbia, still under the sway of Mitch Miller, showed much more interest in developing talent in the established, adult-oriented pop forms than in the new baby-boom-directed field. When it signed Franklin in 1960 and Streisand two years later, Columbia must have felt it had cornered the future of female singers in pop music. They had the two biggest-voiced divas in pop history, one representing blues, jazz, gospel, and the Chitlin Circuit, the other covering Broadway, TV variety showbiz, the Borscht Belt, and the Matzoh Ball Circuit.

After cutting her final session (which concentrated on Jolsoniana like "Swanee" and "You Made Me Love You") for Columbia in October 1966,

183 / **Aretha Franklin**

Franklin declined to renew her contract and instead signed with Atlantic's Jerry Wexler the following month. At that time, she and Wexler were longtime fans of each other's work. Franklin had grown up on Wexler's classic R&B singles with Ruth Brown and Ray Charles, and Wexler had been following Franklin since hearing her 1956 gospel album.

As Wexler had first encountered Franklin in a gospel context, not adult pop or R&B, his initial impulse was perfectly natural and utterly brilliant. Hammond, Mersey, and Otis had realized that Franklin was the one to take Dinah Washington's legacy (and that of such Washingtonians as Dakota Staton and the equally gospel-saturated Della Reese) and move it a step further. He concluded that her gospel roots enabled her to succeed Ray Charles and her fellow New Bethel Baptist Church congregationalist Sam Cooke in the evolution of gospel to soul. Wexler himself had been the sage who had coined the term "rhythm and blues" as a staff reporter for *Billboard* back in 1948, yet obviously he realized that, future Grammys aside, Franklin had nothing to do with R&B. Happy or sad, the blues are ultimately a response to hard times; no matter how jubilantly they may be performed, there's always an undercurrent of bad news. Characters in R&B tales are traditionally lowlifes—even those portrayed in the songs of Louis Jordan, the mos' happy fella of the forum.

In keeping with the resounding earthiness of the "Natural Woman" that Franklin proclaims herself, her music preaches the gospel of optimism. Her Christian name may be semianagram for "Earth," but she embodies an underlying message of heaven-bound hopefulness. Even the lyrics of "Respect," "Good to Me as I Am to You," "Do Right Woman— Do Right Man," and others decline to dwell down in the dismal dumps of despondency. Louis Jordan portrays a character who wants to eat as many chitlins, drink as much cheap wine, and chase as many women as possible. Franklin's songs are words to the wise, and advice on how to behave in an admirable, decent fashion—in other words, how to be a mensch. These songs are proverblike sets of instructions on proper behavior, accentuating the positive aspects of human interaction.

Franklin brilliantly completed the process that Charles had begun, and in so doing demonstrated that simply by virtue of her sex, she had amply upped the ante. When Charles and Franklin sing of redemption, both are not only referring to the afterlife but demanding deliverance from white oppression. And when Franklin sings of freedom (as in "Think"), she's also making a case for the liberation of women from the subjugation of persons whose pants zip up the front. The cover of *Young, Gifted and Black* says it all: a multiple image of Franklin in militant-looking African headdress, posing defiantly underneath the stained glass window of a church. And she's not just asking: When she yells, "Save me," that's not just a suggestion, it's a commandment. She

yells not only because of gospel fervor but because she wants your attention: You better damn well do as she says.

"Save Me," along with a great deal of Franklin's repertoire—particularly her own compositions—can be described as gospel songs with minor modifications implemented for pop purposes. Conversely, the many pop songs with spiritual allusions that she has recorded offer other clues to the inner meaning of her music. She can take a pseudo-spiritual—from Gershwin's "It Ain't Necessarily So" to Elton John's "Holy Moses"—and make it sound like the real thing. Like Armstrong, she also makes one sound as good as the other.

When Johnny Mercer utilizes biblical allusions ("Ac-Cent-Tchu-Ate the Positive") he leavens them with wit, and likewise, in "God Bless the Child," Arthur Herzog (writing for Billie Holiday) put a wryly ironic twist on the familiar spiritual metaphors. In contrast, "Holy Moses," the Band's "The Weight," McCartney's "The Long and Winding Road," and Simon and Garfunkel's "Bridge over Troubled Water" have no great depth to them; the most they can hope for is what, thanks to Franklin, they finally receive. They are not much in and of themselves, but thanks to her, they get what they need: That a "stone singer" (in her father's words) like Franklin will come along and authenticate them. If you were to transcribe her own lyrics to "Spirit in the Dark," you might be surprised to see that they're essentially just quotes from nursery rhymes: She makes them sound spiritual just with her voice. Speaking of stone singing, Franklin can also take contempop hits, by the likes of the Rolling Stones ("Satisfaction" and "Jumpin' Jack Flash") and the Beatles ("Eleanor Rigby") and make you think you're hearing genuine soul music.

And yet how irrelevant are the distinctions of category—especially in Franklin's case. Dave Marsh and other commentators have complained that her well-won and well-worn title of "Queen of Soul" ultimately sells her short, implying that she only reigns over this one specific musical domain. If we don't want to call what she does "soul," then we have to call it "Franklin Music," because there *sure* ain't no other word for it.

Unlike Bobby Darin or Sammy Davis, who could hop from Soulville to Tinseltown without missing a beat, Franklin doesn't have to flit from genre to genre. She sings the same way regardless of the material or the context, and these two latter factors determine the label. When she sings a Harold Arlen song with just a rhythm section and two Ellingtonian horn voices, we have to consider that jazz. When she does a Thomas A. Dorsey perennial like "Precious Lord" with her father's New Bethel Baptist Church Choir, then that's obviously gospel. And, likewise, sure as grits is groceries, when she renders a Curtis or Percy Mayfield song with the Muscle Shoals house band, she isn't likely to be confused with Julie Andrews. Her intergenre pieces are something else again. What are we to make of her bringing the Broadway-born "Somewhere" (from *West Side Story*) and juvenilia like "I Say a Little Prayer" and "Spanish Harlem" into her characteristic soulful setting? The answer is that we have to regard everything Franklin does as soul, and if another artist does anything the least bit different from her, then that must be categorized as something else. She simply is what soul is, and vice versa.

Jerry Wexler never claimed that he did anything extraordinary with Aretha Franklin. Atlantic was in a better position to get her records to the black pop market, which Columbia was essentially out of touch with. Franklin was almost predestined to become a superstar in 1967–68. Her time, and the time of new soul music, simply had come. In certain respects, Franklin seemed like a latecomer to the soul party, but she emerged just at the critical moment. If she had sung "Respect" and "Dr. Feelgood" and "I Never Loved a Man" in 1960, most likely they would have had little impact—the world just wasn't ready. But it was 1967.

It was thanks largely to Franklin that the soul revolution—when the music spread beyond its hard-core black constituency and became the product of choice for white teenagers—was able to happen. Whatever it was, Franklin showed the public that there was a whole world of color beyond what they had been listening to, the unexplainable trend of young whites (and still whiter Englishmen) imitating rednecks and fifties R&B bands, and of Detroit-manufactured, carefully choreographed (and even more carefully *coiffed*), assembly-line bubblegum music.

Wexler's other crucial revelation was that Franklin's talent went way beyond singing—her active participation in the music-making process bucked the trend of the all-controlling producer, synonymous with postwar pop. Ted White, who for a time served as husband, manager, and co-writer, told biographer Bego that in the Columbia period Franklin never worried that she wouldn't make it. "She was born with a Cadillac in the driveway, and had never been hungry," White feels. "It was just a matter of time. So she let other people worry about the semantics."

How different is Wexler's description of her production process: "When she arrived at the studio, she had already worked out her piano part, the lead and background vocal arrangements, the keys and hand-crafted the grooves," as the producer observes in his autobiography (titled, appropriately, *Rhythm and the Blues: A Life in American Music*). Franklin also wrote many of her biggest hits, and often sang her own background vocals via overdubbing. As in Nat Cole's early work, the star's keyboard work is as vital a musical and emotional centerpiece as his or her voice. "The arrangements would stem from the way Aretha played the tune," Arif Mardin recalled.

"Her left and right hand patterns would generally determine the bass and guitar parts, respectively. Similarly, her pauses and breaks would define the drum part." There was churchy piano on her music from the beginning: On the two Franklin albums supervised by John Hammond, who also knew the value of her gospel experience, the producer brought in soulful jazz keyboardist Ray Bryant to supply exactly the same kind of down-home, churchy keyboard that Franklin herself later played on most of the Atlantic hits.

Most important, where Franklin's earlier Columbia sessions attempt a kind of across-the-map experimentation, her work with Wexler focused on a very few specific elements. There's her matchless voice, a church-style vocal group (usually the Sweet Inspirations, led by Cissy Houston, mother of Whitney), a rock-solid rhythm section, usually including two acoustic (bass and drums) and two electric (piano or organ and guitar) instruments. On top of that basic formula, house orchestrator Mardin generally added texture via some quickly sketched horn section parts. He also occasionally brought in the likes of Ralph Burns when a string section was required.

Mardin and Franklin's deployment of these primary colors shattered all the rules of arranging for vocalists. "Write a fill for the band when I'm not singing," Sinatra instructed Nelson Riddle the first time they worked together, "but don't put a concerto behind me." That's always been Job One for pop vocal orchestrators—to create as few distractions as possible and not step on the star's toes. Earlier, at Columbia, Franklin had already tried that more traditional approach: Bob Mersey's string orchestrations and John Hammond's small-group productions succeed, at the very least, in keeping out of her way. Hammond even took pride later on in how the *Aretha/First 12* album utilized "an almost complete absence of arrangements." Hammond's heart was in the right place, but he missed the point. On the Wexler-produced sides, the brassmen and the wailing Arethettes behind Franklin do, in fact, intrude on her musical space. But in the process of competing with her, they also egg her on to greater heights of rafter-raising grandeur. Mardin and Wexler invariably all but bury Franklin in the mix, putting both that heavy horn section and as many as five or six Aretha sound-alikes (often including her younger sister Carolyn Franklin, 1944–88) way up front with her. While this would completely overwhelm a singer of any lesser power, Our Lady of Soul eats that kind of thing up for breakfast.

Serving as star singer, as well as her own key accompanist and co-arranger, Franklin completely overhauls every piece of material, reworking a tune from start to finish in a way that's no less original and personal than Billie Holiday or Mel Tormé. She virtually recomposes the hillbilly classic "You Are My Sunshine" to the point where it becomes even more concerned with perdition and deliverance than her own "Spirit in the Dark." She starts with a super-long-and-slow introduction, rendered all but a cappella and totally tempo-less, and it isn't until two minutes into this 4:19 track that we hear anything even remotely recognizable as something that had been once sung by Gene Autry.

By 1968, she had evolved to the point where she could completely remake any song in her own image: In 1964, she had sung a cover version of the Burt Bacharach–Hal David–Dionne Warwick hit "Walk On By," and the best thing one can say about the vocal is that it's much better than the original record; unfortunately the production and the arrangement, done under the supervision of Clyde Otis, come too close to the Warwick version. Four years later, when she sang the same team's later hit "Say a Little Prayer," she so thoroughly saturated it with soul that Bacharach and David must have thought they had somehow written a real prayer. Despite the title, there ain't nothin' little about it. About the only familiar song she doesn't totally rewrite is "Let It Be," which McCartney strung together out of some old gospel clichés ("words of wisdom") he had lying around. Franklin vastly improves on the Beatles original even while closely following the contours of that record.

Franklin casts (and recasts) an even stronger spell on material from sources closer to home: Her classic record of "Respect" owes little indeed to Otis Redding's original. In fact, most of her biggest hits derive from rather unspectacular songs, which owe their success entirely to the way Franklin "sells" the crucial hook line of each tune—how she stresses it both as singer and arranger.

Sung from a male point of view, "Respect" is a request for compassion in a relationship; when a woman sang it, the song automatically became an early feminist anthem through Franklin's attitude alone, even though her delivery is rarely about extracting any literal meaning from the lyric itself. When Redding sang his own "Respect," it sounded like a complete song with coherent words, but in Franklin's blockbuster hit, she broke it down, as it were, into a set of phrases—not only nonsensical but almost nonverbal in some aspects. What made Franklin's "Respect" into a blockbuster—while Redding's version was merely a hit—were Franklin's own additions. She added the "spelling" section ("R-E-S-P-E-C-T"), and then almost randomly interjected a couple of contemporary urban expressions that didn't make any literal sense. Her next line was "Take care of T-C-B," which meant "take care of business." It's got nothing to do with the concept of respect, and is doubly confusing coming after the word "respect" has been spelled out. The expression "sock it to me" means even less in the context of the idea of respect for women, but is merely one in a long line of pop-culture catchphrases ranging from "Open the door, Richard" to "Go ahead, make my day." It's the feeling, the power, the passion that puts Franklin over—the words themselves don't mean anything. You would think that her 1970 song "Spirit in the Dark" is about a religious experience, but it's not about anything at all: She just throws words around, chanting back and forth, even quoting nursery rhymes ("Little Sally Water"). Even in her famous 1971 live duet with Ray Charles from the *Fillmore West* album, they merely improvise jive around each other. They could be singing the ingredients in a recipe for bouillabaisse or the names of the streets in Kokomo, Indiana, for all it matters.

As the live documents *Aretha in Paris* and the landmark *Aretha Live at Fillmore West* (now available on a Rhino/Atlantic CD) of this period attest, when Franklin performed these pieces in person it amounted, in the best Louis Armstrong tradition, to variations on variations. For all her R&B Grammys, Franklin belongs just as much to the jazz tradition as to any other. Blues and gospel both dwell in houses next door to jazz. While she may not pay a formal visit very often, she frequently strolls across the alley, if only to borrow a cup of sugar. In a 1986 *Interview* interview, Franklin (who seems to describe virtually all her relationships in terms of food) refers to the spontaneous alterations she makes in concert, like flying into "Respect" at quadruple time, as "dessert."

Unfortunately, most pop music listeners born in the last fifty years are on a very strict musical diet. They only want to hear, Franklin says, "just what is on the record." In other words, no improvisation, no spontaneity, but mere rock 'n' roll recapitulation. Perhaps that's why she's been so gun-shy about jazz. In 1969, she moved a little closer to the form by using a full Count Basie–style big band in tandem with her familiar soul-style material. The Basie beat may be tap-your-feet where Franklin's is clap-your-hands, but between your feet and your hands, she gets your whole body moving, and the resulting album, inexplicably titled *Soul '69*, is Aretha at her Franklinest. In 1973, she started another jazz project, this time in conjunction with Basie graduate Quincy Jones, but it got sidetracked into a substandard, rather soulless set containing only a couple of juicy tracks, among them a blistering treatment of Leonard Bernstein's "Somewhere," with a burning alto solo by Phil Woods.

"I understand you!" Franklin hollers to Fathead Newman after his tenor explosion on *Soul '69*'s "Rambling." Her understanding of jazz is greater than she cares to explore or even admit. Her 1965 treatment of "Misty" ranks as no less of a jazz masterpiece than Sarah Vaughan's 1958 recording. The singing of both is highly mannered and thickly stylized, and delightfully so. Both furnish the place with so much ornamentation that you can barely discern the original layout of the room underneath, but it's an entirely different type of decorating. Vaughan is all dreamy wisps of aural sensation, and Franklin is stinging, blazing, and incineratingly intense.

Vaughan is more bop and Franklin is more blues, but they're both great ladies of jazz.

It may be that, for all her much discussed weight issues, Franklin could use a little more dessert. The soul revolution has come and gone, and it's now been fully thirty years since the magic stopped happening for Aretha Franklin. Franklin and Wexler peaked with the 1972 *Amazing Grace*, one of the most powerful albums of pure gospel ever recorded (and which digresses delightfully through such adjacent and appropriate pop detours as Rodgers and Hammerstein's *Carousel* anthem, "You'll Never Walk Alone").

Unfortunately, the Atlantic period, Franklin's peak years, went through a process of diminishing returns. Her music peaked with the *Amazing Grace* album, but by the mid-seventies had run out of steam. The four-CD *Queen of Soul* collection, put out by Rhino/Atlantic in 1992, collects virtually all of her essential music for that label, with a few exceptions. (Among these are her ball-busting treatment of "That's Life," available on *Aretha Arrives*, which makes even Sinatra's peacock-strutting hit seem comparatively lifeless.) It's instructive that the box contains sixty-five tracks from 1967 to 1972, eleven tracks from 1973 to 1976, and none at all from that point to the end of her Atlantic contract in 1979.

Franklin left Columbia Records shortly after corporate lawyer Clive Davis assumed control of the company. However, she went to work for Davis upon his relocation to Arista Records in 1980. By the mid-nineties, she had produced nine albums for Arista, and the news is more bad than good. There have been some hits, most notably the album *Who's Zoomin' Who?* and its big single, "Freeway of Love." She's also made one record with ears toward something other than the marketplace, her third all-gospel set, a paean to monotheism called *One Lord, One Faith, One Baptism*, from 1987.

The best we can say about the Arista albums is that a few contain a single spectacular track. The first, *Aretha* (1980), concludes with a swinging update of Gus Edwards's "School Days," which extends the Franklin tradition of soul-edifying children's songs, like "The House That Jack Built" and the nursery rhyme tangent in "Spirit in the Dark." Franklin's biggest-selling more recent album, *Who's Zoomin' Who?* (1985), contains a triumphant redo of Van ("The Hustle") McCoy's "Sweet Bitter Love," which she had first recorded in 1964. The later version is so moving, even more so than the original, that it overpoweringly puts the rest of *Zoomin'* to shame, even the tight-trousered "Freeway of Love." Further, there's a heart-stopping "It's My Turn" on *Love All the Hurt Away*, an electrifying rendition of an otherwise forgettable movie theme.

Aretha Franklin's Greatest Hits (1980–1994) can be described as remarkably consistent in that it doesn't contain a single one of these standout tracks.

What happened to "Look to the Rainbow"? Two years after the death of her father (who had been shot twice in a burglary), Franklin had cut this, his favorite song, as the climax to her 1986 release *Aretha* (the third Franklin album to bear that pithy if not especially informative title). Previously recorded by Dinah Washington in 1955, "Look to the Rainbow" rates as one of her strongest ballad performances ever. Along with her 1960 reading of lyricist E. Y. Harburg's thematically similar "Over the Rainbow" (on the first *Aretha* LP), this reading of the *Finian's Rainbow* anthem shows how Franklin can spiritualize even songs that have no ecclesiastical intentions, real or phony, serious or mock. "Look to the Rainbow" may amount to the most explosively over-the-top exhibition of her entire career; it's a cinch no leprechaun or munchkin ever beheld a rainbow quite like this one.

But apart from this unrepresentative sample, most of the Arista work fails to satisfy the demands of either art or pop—let alone both. No full-length production since 1976's *Sparkle* qualifies as an essential Aretha Franklin album, and most have also failed to keep her on the charts. By and large, the songs and backgrounds of the eighties and nineties sessions amount to a mushy amalgam of funk, disco, and TV movie theme music. In other words, ersatz soul; and if you think that's a contradiction in terms, you're right.

In the sixties, Franklin was associated with the likes of Otis Redding and King Curtis, while today she's paired with piddling descendants and copycats. The Arista *Greatest Hits* includes a trio remake of "Natural Woman" with Bonnie Raitt and Gloria Estefan, a track that illustrates the difference between making music and just hobnobbing with one's fellow celebrities. There wouldn't be anything to complain about if Franklin had just become a latter-day imitation of herself, but, as "Rainbow" indicates, her voice is deeper and more powerful than it ever was. The crime is that you'd hardly know it from any of the recent material, the stuff is so desouled it doesn't have to be Franklin singing it. It could be anybody, and she has as much business singing over these warmed-over dance tracks as Ethel Merman had on her notorious disco album.

Aretha Franklin remains apparently clueless about the dimensions of her talent. Being completely unself-conscious about her art helps her in many respects, because it means she's closer to her emotions, but it also prevents her from seeing the big picture of who she is, and the kinds of things she's capable of doing.

Yet how could she recognize her unique qualities, when even one of her producers and duet partners was quoted as naming the three great ladies of soul as Franklin, Dionne Warwick, and Diana Ross—which is a little like listing Faulkner, Jacqueline Susann, and Dan Brown as the three great American novelists. There's no reason Franklin couldn't go on turning out trendy, dance-mix tracks (like her single "A Deeper Love," available in four different mixes) while crafting quality albums in between. Yet she fails to realize that she's this generation's Ella Fitzgerald.

In the last dozen or so years, Franklin has released four more new albums: two basic sets, *A Rose Is Still a Rose* (1998) and *So Damn Happy* (2003), and two specialty items, *Jewels in the Crown: All-Star Duets with the Queen* (2007) and *This Christmas* (2008). The two new studio albums both take care of business, featuring Franklin doing decent if not especially memorable newly written songs, and bring her up-to-date, so to speak, with what R&B or soul music sounds like in the millennial era. Unlike some of the 1980–94 music, there's nothing embarrassing here. But they're occupied with making Franklin sound contemporary rather than classic.

Jewels in the Crown and *This Christmas* have Franklin doing what old pop stars do in this day and age: singing duets and holiday songs. In the spirit of Sinatra, Tony Bennett, and Ray Charles, *Jewels* has her remaking her essential songbook with both approximate contemporaries (George Benson, Luther Vandross) and newcomers (John Legend). It's an interesting assemblage—fascinating in its inconsistency—of fiber-optic duets collaged from tracks recorded separately (like her now-famous 1992 teaming with Sinatra on "What Now, My Love?") as well as performances with the participants obviously performing together (as on "A Natural Woman," done live in concert with Estefan and Raitt). *Jewels* ends, curiously, with a track that's a mite too classic, "Nessun Dorma" (from *Turandot*). This isn't exactly what I would have picked for her when suggesting that she record more standards, but her heart is truly in it and she gives it all she's got—alas, not nearly enough. There are also operatic moments throughout *This Christmas*, especially in the opener, "Angels We Have Heard on High," which have her doing the high, angelic vocalise passages with similar gusto.

There's only one recent Aretha Franklin release that's an absolutely essential addition to her canon. In 2005, Rhino Records issued a limited edition four-CD boxed set of Franklin's famous 1971 concert at the Fillmore West. The original ten-song LP issued at the time was classic enough, but this sixty-one-track package is nothing less than a landmark. It consists of three complete concerts from the same run, all of which she shared with co-star and band-leader King Curtis (in one of his final recordings, made a few months before he was murdered), and one never minds hearing the same songs several times since Franklin is so overwhelmingly spontaneous, in her singing as well as in her banter. ("Good thing I had chitlins this morning," she says at one point.) For instance, in the middle of "Dr. Feelgood," on the second night, she starts preaching an inspirational message. It's usually a sexy song, but here you get the impression that Dr. Feelgood is none other than Jesus Himself. All the sets climax with "Spirit in the Dark," which she starts slow and builds to mountainous proportions. Even when Ray Charles shows up and makes his famous guest appearance at the end of the final show, it takes everything he's got to ratchet the level of excitement any higher than Franklin has already. Alas, Rhino manufactured a mere five thousand copies of the package, *Aretha Franklin & King Curtis Live at Fillmore West: Don't Fight the Feeling*. I just checked online, and Amazon.com is getting $415 for a new copy, and even at that price it's an amazing value for your money.

We should give the lady the r-e-s-p-e-c-t she deserves and not wait until she qualifies for postage stamp status. Aretha Franklin may no longer be at the pinnacle of her powers, as her rendition of "My Country 'Tis of Thee" at the Obama inaugural painfully illustrates—but apart from being the only performer who can make salvation seem as tempting as sin, she's a great American artist. Say amen, somebody.

G

Judy Garland (1922–1969)

I have the tenacity of a praying mantis.
— Judy Garland (1963, private tapes on *Judy Garland Speaks!* CD)

Size does matter. Music consists of a series of agreed-upon elements, which can be defined as a series of contrasts: high versus low, short versus long, loud versus soft, fast versus slow, a full orchestra or just piano, major versus minor, happy versus sad. In the art of Judy Garland, these components can be reduced to a single consideration: big versus small. There are big notes and small notes, a big line in a song or a small line, and, as sure as there are

good witches and bad witches, there are great big noisy songs and little intimate ones.

Size isn't everything, though. Garland's voice is, more than any other performer short of Louis Armstrong or Jimmy Durante, a direct manifestation of who she is and what she represents. She has an amazing instrument at her disposal—an overwhelming that seems miraculous coming from such a small woman. She can sing as loudly and as powerfully as the occasion calls for, yet she's never more effective than when she seems to falter, when she lets us hear her gasp for breath, when she puts in a tremolo, making a tone quiver instead of hitting it straight. Her voice, even more so than those of the other major song stylists of her caliber, is immediately identifiable—it throbs like no one else's, cries like no one else's, even, in her low moments, cracks like no one else's. The voice is big, or at least it can be big when she wants it to be, yet even when she's belting at the top of her lungs, there's an incredibly personal quality to it.

Which brings us back to the matter of size. One of the more thought-provoking statements I've read on this subject was an essay in the *Gene Lees Jazzletter* by a self-described gay jazz fan who made a point of letting us know that he did not care for Judy Garland. His chief argument was that both Garland and her daughter Liza Minnelli were in his opinion incapable of sounding "small." This may or may not be true with regard to Minnelli, but in the case of Garland, it's simply wrong. For Garland, those big, bravura numbers like "Zing! Went the Strings of My Heart" are only half the experience. In fact, as Pete Hamill once said of Sinatra (an observation that's even truer with regard to Garland), the big, fast, exuberant numbers work so well because they offer a letup from all the pain and heartbreak of the slow, sad, melancholy songs, like "Here's That Rainy Day" and "Memories of You." By referring to these as big songs versus small songs, we can summarize all the more specific components of music—tempo, dynamics, coloration, orchestration, pitch, harmony, rhythm—into a single pair of words.

For years I actually believed our anonymous gay jazz fan, but now I know that both his key points were wrong. Apart from making the bizarre claim that Garland couldn't be intimate (if I ever meet him, I'll play him Garland's reading of André Previn's "Yes" on the *That's Entertainment!* album), he also insisted that gay people, himself aside, did not like jazz. From my own experience, I can tell you that the percentage of people who like or dislike jazz is exactly the same in both the gay and the straight communities. The gay men and lesbians I know listen to symphonies, jazz, folk songs, Barbra Streisand, Art Pepper, Bobby Darin, Charlie Parker, Tony Bennett, Hank Williams, Ray Charles, Leonard Bernstein, Oscar Peterson, Eddie Condon, Bruce Springsteen, and others.

I hope our gay jazz fan doesn't mind me making a sexual-orientation-related observation of my own. I'm willing to admit that it's possible he really doesn't like Judy Garland: Some people honestly don't like Louis Armstrong, Ella Fitzgerald, or ice cream. But it could also be that he's rebelling against the stereotype. For decades, Judy Garland and musical theater (be it Broadway or opera) were considered the sum total of so-called gay musical taste. Even in the new millennium, this stereotype, to some degree, persists.

No matter whom you sleep with, or whether you're a fan of the Metropolitan Opera or the Grand Ole Opry, practically everybody in the second half of the twentieth century (in America and around the world) has grown up with Dorothy and *The Wizard of Oz*; just as Garland was the major musical icon who started as a child star (even more than a headliner, like Sammy Davis Jr. or Buddy Rich), she's the only performer in the Sinatra-Fitzgerald-Crosby league who captures most of her audience while they're still little kids. Everybody knows who Garland and Dorothy are by the time they're ten, even before they know who Elvis (or, more recently, Lady Gaga or Eminem, not to be confused with Auntie Em) is—she's the one adult pop icon who has instant name-brand recognition with an even younger demographic than most kiddie pop stars. Like a favorite aunt or a best friend, Garland is part of our childhoods.

Yet she's also part of a unique musical aesthetic. One is tempted to describe it as a jazz-based tradition, but clearly it's larger than that. You can't describe it as purely an American phenomenon, since it also includes such overseas artists as Edith Piaf. Indeed, Garland, Piaf, and the more purely jazz-and-blues-based Billie Holiday form a unique triumvirate of female vocalists. Theirs was a bittersweet legacy of happy songs (even from the often gloomy Piaf and Holiday, particularly in their early years) tainted by short lives crammed with abusive relationships. Perhaps the price for moving an audience is a penchant for self-destruction. If their songs told us to get happy, their lives told us otherwise.

Garland's performances were emotionally explosive, often to the very edge of hysteria, yet even her highest moods were undercut by an undercurrent of melancholia. She was one of the great musical presences of all time, yet unlike her friends Bing Crosby, Frank Sinatra, and Doris Day, she wasn't a band singer or a recording star who graduated to film stardom, nor, like Ethel Merman, was she a Broadway headliner who took a fling at Hollywood. Rather, Garland was—other than Astaire—the only great vocal artist whose primary medium was the motion picture, whose gifts were not only purely aural but also visual and dramatic.

It's hard to think of a screen-sound track performer—perfect in her acting, singing, and dancing—who, as a consummate craftswoman, created more perfect and endearing characters. None but Garland could have made convincing all those little Lily Marses filled with adult aspirations, those Dorothys yearning for over the rainbow, those teenage Esthers who never seem more innocent and naive than when they're trying to act sophisticated. America watched Garland grow up, but at every stage she experienced a new plateau of misfithood: the "little in-between" too old for toys and too young for boys, from Betsy Booth, who wants Mickey Rooney to take her seriously as a romantic partner and not just treat her like a kid sister, to Dorothy, looking beyond the rainbow to a land beyond childhood's end and yet also to a kind of eternal childhood.

Garland shared with Sinatra a capacity for making every song sound like a chapter in an autobiography. Her "Born in a Trunk," a dreadful song that she transforms into a classic, describes a born trouper's backstage childhood, and becomes her equivalent to Sinatra's "My Way" (come to think of it, another dreadful song): a vividly personal depiction of triumphs and travails both on stage and off. Garland really did grow up in the equivalent of the "Princess Theatre, Pocatello, Idaho." She was born Frances Ethel Gumm on June 10, 1922, in Grand Rapids, Minnesota. Her mom played piano, while her dad both managed theaters and performed. At age three, "Baby Gumm" joined her two older sisters in a singing trio that played vaudeville theaters and movie houses across the country.

The Gumms settled in California when "Baby" was four, which put them at ground zero of the impending media revolution. In addition to their consistent theater work, "The Gumm Sisters Kiddie Act" were recruited by early Hollywood radio stations and, eventually, by some of the first talking pictures. By the time she was ten, the youngest Gumm had become the focal point of the act, and the family, acting on a tip from trouper supreme Georgie Jessel, had changed its name to Garland. In 1934, Hoagy Carmichael's song "Judy" would have a profound effect on show business history: This was the first song that Ella Fitzgerald sang professionally (or so she said), and the same tune that inspired Frances Ethel (or so she said) to become Judy.

Just as the trio was beginning to crack the big time, it was becoming increasingly apparent that the youngest Gumm was, in fact, the whole act. Her two sisters stepped out around the time that Judy was jointly signed to contracts to cut discs for Decca Records and to do nobody-quite-knew-what for MGM Pictures (the latter coming about as the result of a personal audition for megamogul Louis B. Mayer). Fortunately, Judy reached adolescence during a brief period when, for a few years, little girls were ruling the roost in Hollywood. In the mid-thirties, Shirley Temple was the single highest-grossing star in pictures, and Garland's early colleague Deanna Durbin went on to save Universal from bankruptcy. In an age of Depression, sunshiney moppettes singing sunshiney songs supplied a much needed message of optimism. With Garland, however, Hollywood got much more than it had bargained for.

Unfortunately, developing Garland's persona took longer than perfecting Temple's toddler optimism and Durbin's sunshine soprano. The studio wisely assigned her to Roger Edens, the musical guru who'd previously worked with Ethel Merman. At the very beginning, the most impressive aspect of the Garland-Edens relationship was its constant experimentation, even if not every avenue they explored would pan out.

Edens couldn't have known it, but he was helping shape a musical icon. It was key for Garland to find a way to channel her offstage personality into her performance style. Other icons were all around her: Bing Crosby was the ex–bad boy who became Mr. Home-and-Family and, later, Dean Martin was the happy-go-lucky tippler who couldn't bring himself to care about anything—even where his next drink was coming from—while Sinatra was the guy who loved and lost, lost and loved, and took it all the way. Garland's original musical and screen personality was the misfit, while Sinatra was to a certain extent the outsider—at least he gave the impression of wanting to be the defiant one who shook things up. Garland was the outsider who wanted to fit in: As a child she's the one who wants to be accepted by the other kids; then she's the kid who wants to be taken seriously by the grown-ups and accepted as one of them; and finally, in the fifties and sixties, she becomes a mature woman who wants nothing more than to please her man and take care of her kids. The central element of her character is the act of wanting. All Garland ever wanted, she tried to tell us in her music (and in a rather bizarre series of taped ramblings released surreptitiously as *Judy Garland Speaks!*), was to be a normal woman with a normal family. The major thing that stopped her was a virtuoso talent for self-destruction that, in the end, outshone even her talents as a performer.

The songs from Garland's poor-little-in-between phase, composed by Edens and others, have dated badly. They are, in fact, among the few entries in her entire canon that are less than delightful today. However, they serve a key function in her musical development in that they establish her not just as a singer of songs—as were any of the female band singers of the era—but as a precocious talent who was quickly developing a fully formed musical and showbiz persona. "In Between" (from *Love Finds Andy Hardy*) directly expresses the young singer's early identity crisis, thereby establishing her predilection for musical autobiography. By 1940, Garland was actually able to make the state of misfit-hood seem attractive with "I'm Nobody's Baby" from *Andy Hardy Meets Debutante*.

She was a recording artist even before her film career took off. As we've seen, the young singer was scouted out by the recently formed Decca label before MGM came a-callin'. The first four Decca sides (starting with "Stompin' at the Savoy" and "Swing, Mr. Charlie") were made a few days after Garland's fourteenth birthday, even though the label billed her as a "thirteen-year-old swing singer." Her major predecessor had been a prepubescent "swing singer" named Baby Rose Marie. Though barely out of diapers, Rose Marie was a hot and lusty and throaty vocalist with amazingly good time. She was a headliner in vaudeville, radio, and talkies—and had also made a few records—at the time the Gumm Trio and Garland the soloist were getting started. It was probably the success of Baby Rose Marie, soon to drop the "Baby" from her billing, that inspired Decca and then Metro to promote Garland as a "swing singer"—plus that this new thing called "swing" was in 1936 the musical craze beginning to sweep the nation.

In retrospect, this was a major miscalculation. Producer Joe Perry backed Garland with one of Decca's top swing bands, Bob Crosby's orchestra, and supposedly the band's manager (not Crosby himself) rankled at the thought of playing second fiddle to a fourteen-year-old newcomer (especially one passing herself off as thirteen). And so the Crosby band itself was not credited on the label of "Stompin' at the Savoy" and "Swing, Mr. Charlie." Judy had her own revenge, however, when just a few years later Bob Crosby and His Orchestra were delighted to get a very minor guest spot in her starring vehicle *Presenting Lily Mars*.

Garland's first four sides, done on a one-shot, session-by-session basis (Victor or Columbia could have come in and snatched her up anytime they wanted) serve mainly to illustrate to history that as vastly talented as Garland was, even at this very early stage of the game one of the things she definitely was *not* and never would be was a swing singer like Ella Fitzgerald. She was a belter, not a swinger (although the two ideals wouldn't always be mutually exclusive). Garland just doesn't have a jazz rhythmic sense, and when she does "Savoy," which referred to the ballroom where Fitzgerald reigned supreme, she doesn't know where to cut off her notes. Most of these very early recordings have Garland trying to establish herself as a swing singer by merely shouting the word "swing" over and over.

Garland had her own sense of time, informed more by the Broadway stage than by the jazz-dance bands of the era, though this, admittedly, was an age of considerable overlap, when nearly all the major show tunes of the era were reinterpreted in swing time by the leading bands, and when Benny Goodman himself appeared onstage in two Broadway musicals. Garland could certainly sing fast, although with her, "fast" was obviously a variety of "big." As early as 1939, the year Garland recorded "Zing! Went the Strings of My Heart," she had perfected her own rhythmic style. Sung by the sixteen-year-old in *Listen, Darling* (1938), this was the first of the great Garland belt numbers. "The Jitterbug," a number cut from *The Wizard of Oz* (which features composer Arlen singing Ray Bolger's Scarecrow part on the Decca recording), shows that if she wasn't swinging in the Count Basie sense, she could certainly sing *about* swing.

The best of Garland's numbers in a swing-band vein is "F.D.R. Jones." Harold Rome, a progressive-minded songwriter out of the same school as Yip Harburg, originally wrote it for a 1938 revue called *Sing Out the News*, and it was recorded that year by Chick Webb and Ella Fitzgerald. Edens apparently thought it would be a great number for Garland to do in a minstrel-show sequence in *Babes on Broadway* (she also recorded it for Decca). Rome probably thought he was furthering race relations by showing that black people could be patriotic and name their offspring after the president. Edens, on the other hand, saw the song as part of the minstrel-show tradition—the act of naming a black baby after the president was an extension of the minstrelsy practice of low-class colored clowns affecting grand names and airs for themselves as part of a comically inflated sense of self-important grandeur. As had already become her custom, Garland transcends any kind of political consideration, instilling in the song an exuberance that's irresistible. The politics of the song become as dismissable as the musical specifics—what's important is the way that Garland makes us all want to shout "Yessiree! Yessiree! Yessiree!"

In 1937, Garland launched a major phase of her movie career with *Thoroughbreds Don't Cry*, her first appearance in a picture with Mickey Rooney. This was the start of a ten-film partnership (three Andy Hardys, four Mickey–Judy–Busby Berkeley spectaculars plus *Thoroughbreds Don't Cry*, and guest shots in *Words and Music* and *Thousands Cheer*), which took second place only to the Astaire-Rogers partnership as the most exciting in celluloid musical history.

However, the major turning point of her pre-*Oz* existence was "You Made Me Love You." By the time of *Broadway Melody of 1938*, Garland and Edens were on the right track. Like many Garland landmarks, it's an old, old song (like 1914 old), sung in the teens by Al Jolson, who, like Merman, was a Garland role model. The inclusion of a chorus of special material, a whole song in fact (the semispoken "Dear Mr. Gable," Edens's homage to the celebrated Clark), harks back to the acoustic era, when comics like Jolson and Eddie Cantor included spoken monologues in the middle of their discs. It also looks ahead to such mature Garland spectaculars as the geographically driven "Chicago" and "San Francisco," which combine song, arrangement, and speech.

"Dear Mr. Gable/You Made Me Love You" (in *Broadway Melody of 1938*) was followed by "In Between" in *Love Finds Andy Hardy*, and then "Sweet Sixteen," which wasn't sung in a film, though it's easy to visualize Garland as Betsy Booth singing it in a Hardy Family comedy. Instead of singing of Mr. Gable, she tells us that she "wouldn't trade places with Shirley Temple" and explains that she was all set to join a monastery until she realized that this would make it impossible for her to listen to Bing Crosby (whose influence led to her subsisting on a diet of Kraft cheese).

In these early songs, Garland has already found the persona of a little girl with big dreams, a starstruck fan who pines after legendary leading men and fantasizes about going over the rainbow into adulthood. The ability to sing about big dreams would be even more crucial to Garland's success than her big voice, and by projecting these dreams onto Gable and Crosby (who would himself become one of her saviors later on when she needed all the support she could get) she was anticipating the moment when she herself would become the object of those same kinds of dreams and longings. With "Dear Mr. Gable" she struck a nerve; MGM started looking for bigger parts and songs for her, and Decca, at last, signed her to a regular recording contract.

Then, in 1939, Garland not only became an emerging star but shot to the upper pantheon of the immortals with *The Wizard of Oz*, not only the major vehicle of her career, but quite possibly the greatest of all movie musicals (and in my opinion the greatest film ever made, thank you very much). With "Over the Rainbow," Garland took the art of yearning to new levels. The notes themselves, with their operatic octave leap in the first interval, symbolized a reaching out, an optimistic striving for a greater good. Surrounding the seventeen-year-old trouper with three of the world's finest song and dance character men and a top score by lifelong friend Harold Arlen, *Oz* showed the world how good the movie musical could be. One of the tragedies of Garland's life is that she never surpassed *Oz*; still, after this she was the preeminent leading lady of the Hollywood musical. No woman in Hollywood—not Alice Faye, Betty Grable, Rita Hayworth, Ginger Rogers, Eleanor Powell, or Betty Hutton—could possibly compete with her.

It was an astonishing achievement, especially considering that she had yet to play an adult role, participate in a love scene, or share an onscreen kiss. Her early post-*Oz* roles weren't all that different from the prior ones: Her parts in *Ziegfeld Girl* and *Presenting Lily Mars* come directly out of her earlier Andy Hardy picture roles, except that in some of these, Betsy Booth finally scores a little romantic action. *Girl Crazy* (1942) may have been the first vehicle to present Garland as a genuine object of desire, while *For Me and My Gal* from that same year completed the process, with Garland emerging as a full-fledged romantic heroine in a period romance with leading man Gene Kelly as a nogoodnik (in his first movie part, and essentially reprising his *Pal Joey* character from the 1940 Rodgers and Hart show that brought him to Hollywood's attention). In *Girl Crazy*, for the first time, Garland and Rooney get a genuine boy-meets-girl (meeting cute) scene that seems more like the Astaire-Rogers films than anything in the previous Garland-Rooney entries.

After *The Wizard of Oz*, Garland's most perfect performance was in the 1944 *Meet Me in St. Louis*. We should rejoice that the twenty-one-year-old star went against her initial decision not to revert to teenhood in *Meet Me in St. Louis*, because the resulting role (with three career perennial tunes, "The Trolley Song," "The Boy Next Door," and "Have Yourself a Merry Little Christmas") was an instant Garland milestone. The conflict of the story is allegedly the Smith family's decision whether or not to leave St. Louis, but the real drama is all within Esther herself, a veritable case study in Freudian repression: a young woman with the usual raging hormones who's trapped in the strictures of the turn-of-the-twentieth-century bourgeois society around her. Throughout, she endeavors to keep any show of feeling as tightly restricted as her corseted torso—or her pretty little neck in her high starched collar. Even here, playing a young adult, she makes herself seem more immature by overdoing her attempts to act like a grown-up—never more so than by treating her little sibling Tootie (Margaret O'Brien) as if she were some sort of species of sub-infant.

Tellingly, the big climax of emotional release is not a love scene between Esther and the Boy Next Door, but a musical number, in which she lets her feelings explode in a flurry of notes and Technicolor. In Garland's hands, "The Trolley Song" isn't just about a chance encounter on the mass transit system, it's a musical foreshadowing of James Dean's "You're tearing me apart" speech in *Rebel Without a Cause*. Both cultural demands and her own desire for decorum, as well as a fear of embarrassment, force her to rein in her feelings, but by the high point of "The Trolley Song," she tells us she knows "how it feels / When the universe reels" (if that's not a euphemism for an orgasm I don't know what is). The contradiction isn't just an element in the performance, it's the whole show, the driving force. When Garland is later shown in a proper clinch with leading man Tom Drake, it seems anticlimactic compared to the emotions she's already triggered in "The Trolley Song." By then, we all know how it feels when the universe reels.

The "mature" phase of Garland's MGM years yielded one high point after another. The major Judy vehicles were produced by Arthur Freed, generally credited with shepherding Garland to stardom as well as with making a mature, salient art form out of the movie musical itself. The classic Freed-Garland efforts, *Meet Me in St. Louis* (1944), *The Harvey Girls* (1946), *The Pirate* (1948), and *Easter Parade* (1948), were all, like *The Wizard of Oz*, thoroughly integrated assemblages of song and story. Each boasted a complete, Broadway-style score, and on the whole they were all more intellectually ambitious than the backstage stories still dominating most of Hollywood song and dance productions. In each venture, Garland's character is about wanting—wanting to find a place to fit in and a place to find love, whether she's a mail-order bride who becomes a wild west waitress and reforms the bad guy with love, a chorine who becomes a dance star by being allowed to be herself, or a sheltered Island beauty who idolizes cutthroats but learns that politicians are really pirates and vice versa.

Garland also participated to great effect in several

Freed all-star productions: the producer's biopics of Jerome Kern (*Till the Clouds Roll By*, 1946) and Rodgers and Hart (*Words and Music*, 1948). Throughout the forties, she'd gone on recording for Decca, and her film songs were generally at the center of her recording career. While singers who had come up from the world of big bands and radio (Crosby, Sinatra, later Doris Day) were constantly in the recording studio, those who were essentially a product of Broadway or Hollywood (Merman, Astaire) were, alas, not nearly so copiously documented. Garland recorded about eighty titles for commercial release between 1936 and 1947, which was only a fraction of what comparable stars like Ella Fitzgerald cut in those same years.

On occasion, Decca did record her singing numbers other than those from her films, including a number of Gershwin standards that anticipate her 1943 appearance in the definitive film of the composer's *Girl Crazy*, as well as a trio of Rodgers and Hart songs, done with twin pianos, in advance of her guest spot in *Words and Music*. There also were duets with Johnny Mercer, Dick Haymes, and Bing Crosby (their "Yah-Ta-Ta, Yah-Ta-Ta [Talk Talk Talk]" is a charmer that foreshadows a routine on *Seinfeld* by about fifty years). There are also a few surprising standards, like Noel Coward's "Poor Little Rich Girl," and some very rewarding treatments of movie musical songs other than her own: "No Love No Nothin'" and "A Journey to a Star" from *The Gang's All Here*, "This Heart of Mine" and "Love" from *Ziegfeld Follies*, "Poor You" and "The Last Call for Love" from *Ship Ahoy*. Unfortunately, Garland's relationship with Decca Records ended with the American Federation of Musicians ban of 1948.

Proving that Garland's brilliance was not Freed's exclusive province, producer Joe Pasternak employed her with excellent results in two less ambitious vehicles, *In the Good Old Summertime* (1949) and *Summer Stock* (1950). Apart from summery titles, the key element to both films was the music of Harold Arlen; she hadn't worked directly with him on a project since 1939 (in addition to *Oz*, Arlen had written a song for *Babes in Arms*), but she had recorded his hits "Buds Won't Bud," "Blues in the Night" (on which she seems to be mimicking the composer's own vibrato), and "That Old Black Magic" for Decca. *Summertime*'s highlight was actually cut from the original release but was included, luckily, on home video issues: Garland singing "Last Night When We Were Young," a 1934 composition that further expresses Arlen and Harburg's epic side.

Likewise, *Summer Stock*, despite an excellent new score by Harry Warren, was climaxed by another Arlen oldie, "Get Happy." There was gender bending afoot, as Metro decked Judy out in a man's tuxedo jacket and fedora, yet somehow neglected to supply her with a pair of pants (which would have made her look something like Eleanor Powell in male top-hat-and-tails drag). She danced surrounded by a male chorus line, displaying shapely gams that went on for days—somehow putting on a man's formal jacket made her look more sensually feminine. Now that she was in-tux-icated, Garland could become the object of our erotic dreams. Clearly, she wasn't in Kansas anymore.

Nor would she be at MGM any longer. For Garland, the demands of stardom were too much for her to take, and before long her self-destructive reaction to those pressures was more than the front office at MGM could take. Garland's post-1950 career is inconsistent: She continued to excel in several mediums she'd long since conquered—phonograph recordings and radio—and even found new ones, such as an outstanding career on television and on the concert stage, live appearances being something she'd barely tackled since the Gumm Sisters days. Yet she was generally excommunicated from working in the medium where she did her best work, the motion picture musical.

Cast out of paradise, Garland was most steadily employed during this dry spell by old friend Bing Crosby. They had already duetted together for Decca, but their rapport on the air was even greater than on disc; a number of their exchanges have been released on two English CDs, *When You're Smiling* (Parrot) and *All the Clouds'll Roll Away* (Parrot). (On one program, she jokes about having been bitten by Metro mascot Leo the Lion.)

Yet even if she hadn't been cast out of MGM, it was clear that she couldn't have gone on making forties-style movie musicals, excellent as they were. In 1948, she began work on Metro's film of the Broadway hit *Annie Get Your Gun*, which, had it been completed as planned, might have provided Garland new direction. She would have been the perfect star to essay the great Broadway leading roles for Hollywood. Think about it: Garland as Julie Jordan in *Carousel*, Garland as Laurey in *Oklahoma!*, Garland as Nellie Forbush in *South Pacific*, Garland as Ella Peterson in *Bells Are Ringing*, Garland as either Magnolia or Julie in *Show Boat*. I can also imagine Garland as the climber of every mountain in *The Sound of Music*. Most of all: Garland as Mama Rose in *Gypsy*. In fact, apart from *Fiddler on the Roof* and *Zorba*, it's hard to imagine any traditional musical comedy that wouldn't have been much improved by Garland's presence. Alas, it was not to be.

Still, the 1954 *A Star Is Born* cut deeper than anything Broadway had attempted. In retrospect, it seems perfectly fitting that Garland's most significant production in her thirties or forties was a picture that glorified old-school Hollywood while at the same time exposing its dark, seamy underside. Far from the optimistic days of *The Harvey Girls* and *Meet Me in St. Louis*, here was a brooding noir drama that happened to be about movie stars, replete with some of the finest musical numbers of her career—again the work of Harold Arlen, this time in a one-off partnership with Ira Gershwin—

particularly the devastating "The Man That Got Away" and the lively "Gotta Have Me Go with You."

It was four years between *Summer Stock* and *A Star Is Born*, but it proved to be worth the wait. The same could hardly be said for the six years between *A Star Is Born* and the disastrous *Pepe* in 1960, an all-star flop highlighted only by Garland's reteaming with former Metro orchestrator André Previn, who supplied her with a haunting ballad called "The Far Away Part of Town." This excellent, overlooked song ensures that at least three of the 195 minutes of this clambake are worth watching (or at least listening to, since Garland is only heard on the sound track and not seen on the screen).

A Star Is Born aside, her Capitol albums were her most rewarding work during the fifties. As during the Decca years, she recorded considerably less than her colleagues: Sinatra and Nat Cole were, in spite of demanding movie, concert, and TV schedules, releasing new full-length-album masterpieces every three or four months. Garland turned out only one studio album a year for Capitol between 1955 and 1959, with two in 1960:

Miss Show Business (1955), Dick Cathcart,
  Harold Mooney
Judy (1956), Nelson Riddle
Alone (1957), Gordon Jenkins
Judy in Love (1958), Nelson Riddle
The Letter (1959), Gordon Jenkins
Judy: That's Entertainment! (1960), Jack Marshall
Judy in London (aka *The London Sessions*)
  (1960), Norrie Paramor

Miss Show Business, the first of the Capitol albums, suggests that she was on her way to becoming something like Al Jolson and Sophie Tucker in the second half of their careers: a walking nostalgia machine, re-creating old hits over and over—"You Made Me Love You" (she leaves out the special material concerning Mr. Gable), "A Pretty Girl Milking Her Cow," and even "Over the Rainbow." What makes Garland a special case is that, as we've seen, she was tapping into the nostalgia market at the height of her career, and *Miss Show Business* would seem to be offering not only nostalgia for Garland's earlier output, but for that of Jolson and Tucker as well, as evidenced by such signature songs as "Rock-a-Bye Your Baby with a Dixie Melody" and "Some of These Days." She was not only re-creating her own past triumphs, but everybody else's as well. You might say that she was offering nostalgia for nostalgia.

Overall, *Miss Show Business* was a cautious entry. It captured a large part of her 1952 Palace act, and served as a tie-in to her first TV special in 1955 on CBS. The album plays almost as a live performance, with musical transitions between the cuts rather than silent spreads. Considering that she was simultaneously moving into two new mediums at once with the project (LP and TV), it was perhaps under-

standable that no new musical ground was broken on this venture. She was on home turf here in more ways than one: The set was conducted by her brother-in-law, Jack Cathcart, and the pleasant, but hardly particularly innovative, arrangements (actually written by Harold Mooney) did not give her cause to stretch or leave her comfort zone.

Her finest moment here is comparatively the most modern, "Happiness Is Just a Thing Called Joe." Garland had already inspired many a great musician (Harry James was motivated to record "You Made Me Love You" after hearing her homage to Gable, thus landing the trumpeter one of his first and biggest hits) and, conversely, Garland was inspired to do "Happiness" after hearing Woody Herman play it. Her last child and only son, Joey Luft, was also born in 1955, and Garland certainly sings with so much tenderness and vulnerability that there's no way this can be a coincidence.

"Happiness" is also the track that points ahead to the three major masterpieces of her late fifties studio albums, both of those with Riddle and the first with Jenkins. Garland has a way of moving forward even while traveling backward into her own past: "Happiness Is Just a Thing Called Joe" (from the film version of *Cabin in the Sky*, directed by second husband Vincente Minnelli) is from her most reliable source of great songs, Harold Arlen, and thus leads directly into two of the highlights of *Judy*, which are two additional songs by Arlen from another all-black production, "Any Place I Hang My Hat Is Home" and "Come Rain or Come Shine" (both from *St. Louis Woman*); she also honors the operatic side of Arlen with "Last Night When We Were Young."

Although it, too, was released in conjunction with a TV special (her last one until 1962), *Judy* was different in every way. With arrangements by Nelson Riddle, who had midwifed the rebirth of both Sinatra and Cole, *Judy* offered a new Judy, a more exciting, more mature, more sophisticated version of the Judy everybody already loved; Dorothy Gale, Esther Smith, Betsy Booth, and Lily Mars had all grown up; no more a mixed-up little in-between. She still sang the old songs, and she still had that vaudeville two-a-day in her soul, still channeled the spirits of Jolson and Tucker, but now she did it to exciting new rhythms, modernistic new harmonies, and fresh orchestral colors, vividly documented, for the first time, in high fidelity. On "Dirty Hands, Dirty Face," she seems to throw the gauntlet down in front of the ghost of Jolson (who is listed as one of the four composers); as a love song to a male child it's presumably a direct follow-up to "Happiness Is Just a Thing Called Joe." Yet Riddle and Garland also seem to be thinking of Sinatra and the "Soliloquy" from *Carousel* as an intimate anthem of parenthood, and Riddle closed with the same sort of classical coda harmonic twinkling he would later put behind "Soliloquy" on *The Concert Sinatra*.

Judy begins with Garland singing "Come Rain or

Come Shine," almost a cappella, accompanied only by a bongo drum in the distance (a recording that made use of acoustic space in a way that wouldn't have been possible a few years earlier), with a hint of Cuban rhythm that no one until then would ever have dreamed of using behind a mainstream singer doing a show tune. *Judy* and its follow-up with Riddle, the 1957 *Judy in Love*, easily amount to the high point of Garland's recording career. The use of Afro-Cuban polyrhythms in "Come Rain or Come Shine" was only the beginning; even more remarkable was the second chorus, in which Garland played with the Arlen-Mercer song in a way that was so personal they couldn't even be labeled jazz. These variations (like repeating the phrase "let me" over and over) were not strictly spontaneous; they were part of the chart, and had probably been worked out in advance by Garland and Riddle, yet when she performed the chart on other occasions (as on the London sessions and at Carnegie Hall), she did variations on the variations. As time went on, Garland dropped the reference to Cole Porter ("one of those crazy things!") but continued to add more and more "let me's" to the end of the bridge.

Judy in Love, arranged by Riddle, and *Alone*, by Jenkins, were flip sides of each other: The first featured all optimistic, even erotic love songs, not all of them fast—in fact, the slow "I Can't Give You Anything but Love" (one of many Garland standards incorporating special material lyrics, probably by longtime mentor Roger Edens) and "I'm Confessin'" are two of the warmest, earthiest, and sexiest vocals ever captured on recording tape. *Alone* consists of eleven songs (one added only in the CD era) about strolling with one's shadow, sitting there and counting fingers and raindrops (not to mention a million sheep), about getting the right to sing the blues when it rains. Yet in Garland's musical universe, no less than Sinatra's or Holiday's, even the happy songs have more than a hint of melancholy, like a spice in a stew, and some of the sad songs, like "Mean to Me" and "By Myself," are delivered with a brassy beat.

The only disaster of the period is *The Letter*, not only arranged and conducted by Jenkins but also, too; in 1945, the composer-conductor had struck gold with *Manhattan Tower*, a sort of hybrid song cycle and musical theater for a narrator, male and female soloists, orchestra, and choir. The original Decca recording was a blockbuster and so was the 1955 LP remake for Capitol; both Capitol and Jenkins were hoping that this very similar work, also with a metrocentric theme and adding Garland's star power, would cause lightning to strike twice. Capitol heavily bankrolled this pseudo-sequel, with the first vinyl copies released in lavish packaging that included a "letter" in an envelope. Garland is in excellent form on the disc, but this music drama is far from Jenkins's best work. In 2007, DRG records reissued the album for the first time on CD, and included four bonus tracks, which

sound like the same tracks prepared for singles release. The songs, especially "That's All There Is" (later recorded by Nat Cole), sound considerably better without the dialogue, narration, and extraneous dramatic business.

The Letter was a misstep, but *Judy: That's Entertainment!* is an underrated gem. The arrangements, by Jack Marshall (best known for his work with Peggy Lee), are less distinctive than those by Riddle or Jenkins, but are suitably either jazzy or old-fashioned as the material demands. He, too, found new beats for Garland to groove to, including a Dixieland "Puttin' on the Ritz" and a campy mambo clave for "You Go to My Head" (his use of Latin rhythms is hardly as subtle as Riddle's). Apart from these rhythmic explorations, *That's Entertainment!* contains several of her most effective, understated ballads: "I've Confessed to the Breeze," a delightful, forgotten song from *No, No, Nanette* that remains obscure despite Garland's championing of it; André Previn's "Yes" is one of Garland's most touchingly intimate performances, and a stunning example of how she didn't have to get big and loud to move an audience; "It Never Was You" shows that Kurt Weill was just as good at writing sophisticated Broadway love songs, in the tradition of Kern and Rodgers, as he was at declaratively antibourgeoisie battle cries.

She made two studio albums in 1960 because no one had expected to release the London recordings as an album. (On the other hand, if *Judy in London* qualifies as a "bonus" album, then it's only fair that the dreadful *The Letter* should qualify as a "minus" album.) In fact, it's hard to say exactly why Garland did those London dates: She was making a concert tour of England with the well-known British bandleader Norrie Paramor conducting, and for some reason the two of them decided to get together in the studios of EMI, which by then had become the parent company of Capitol Records. The odd thing is that 1960 is supposed to be one of the low points in her career. Photos reveal that she was extremely overweight; she was chronically mismanaged (as usual); and, in general, she was in a very depressed state both personally and professionally. Yet somehow in London she rallied; some of these were songs she'd already been doing for twenty years or more, and the arrangements were ones that had been written for her previous six Capitol LPs.

The recording quality was superb and Garland herself was somewhere beyond inspired. The high point from the sessions is a city song that she seems to have recorded only this one time in a studio, Cole Porter's 1930 "I Happen to Like New York," which is embellished by a special material verse written for her. To hear her sing it, one has a hard time believing that she wasn't born in a trunk in the middle of Times Square. The use of a semisymphonic arrangement and angelic choir (not to mention the subject matter) puts us in mind of *Manhattan Tower* and *The Letter*; the way she steadily grows louder and modulates higher is at once operatic and old-school showbiz. This is an anthem, plain and simple, evoking the same spirit of stand-up-and-salute that Ray Charles later brought to "America the Beautiful." What makes it work is the contrast between Porter's dirgy melody and the sense of humor of the text, which is amply amplified by Garland. Porter doesn't idealize New York, but rather embraces the city for all its failings as well as its virtues, the "sight and sound and even the stink of it." It's a performance that never fails to give me goose bumps.

At thirty-eight, then, Garland was hardly wiped out; rather, she was ready for a last hurrah, a comeback that would put her entire career in perspective.

During her lifetime, Capitol also released three live concert recordings:

Judy Garland at the Grove (1958), with Freddy
  Martin and His Orchestra
Judy at Carnegie Hall (1961)
*Judy Garland and Liza Minnelli, Live at the
  London Palladium* (1964)

Carnegie Hall is just about the single greatest live album by a singer of popular American standards, the other major contenders being *Ella in Berlin* (although there are several other Fitzgerald packages one could also name), *Tony Bennett at Carnegie Hall* (done a year after Garland and almost as exciting), *Nat King Cole at the Sands* (released posthumously), and *Sinatra at the Sands* (with Count Basie, and a very late entrant in the live album stakes, but nonetheless superb). There were also several exciting live Mel Tormé albums, although all of Peggy Lee's "live" recordings turned out to be studio fakes.

Garland was in fine fettle as part of an extended concert tour that climaxed on April 23—when she became the first major pop singer to fill an entire evening at Carnegie (unless you count fifties chart divette Joni James). She was on fire from start to finish, fully in touch with The Force throughout, the bright side on "San Francisco" and "Zing!," the dark side on "Alone Together" (the one tune on the original double LP from a studio session). She also showed she had a sense of humor about herself—a whole other kind of camp that's completely different from that which is usually associated with her—when she belted out a red-hot mambo treatment of "You Go to My Head." (Having led in the live album stakes, it's too bad she didn't join Lawrence, Gormé, Lee, Reese, Tormé, and Clooney and later Sinatra and Jobim in the pop-singers-go-Latin category.)

Judy at Carnegie Hall was a blockbuster concert and a blockbuster album and launched an upward spiral for her. She followed Carnegie with a TV special, which she shared with guests Frank Sinatra and Dean Martin, and the results were so successful that CBS gave her a shot at a weekly variety show. In 1963, *TV Guide* called it "the Great Garland Gamble." *The Judy Garland Show* was indeed a crap shoot, in which CBS bet a heavy bundle both that the allegedly unreliable superstar, whose penchant for self-destruction was already legendary, would behave herself and that *any* program could challenge NBC's Sunday night blockbuster, the Western series *Bonanza*. Within six months, the stress of the weekly series left her again in a state of physical breakdown (Sinatra learned from her experience when he elected to make his ultimate television statement in a series of annual specials), and the mighty Cartwrights of the Ponderosa Ranch still had all their wagons in a circle.

In the meantime, however, Garland and her crew created twenty-six generally brilliant hour-long shows (most of which have been made available in a highly recommended series of DVDs from Pioneer Home video, while a number of the sound track vocals are on the four-CD box *Judy,* produced in 1998 by 32 Records). *Bonanza* be darned! From the vantage point of forty-five years, *The Judy Garland Show* was a triumph. That's not only because of the supercharged dynamo at its center, but for the quality of the writing, the orchestrations by Mort Lindsey, and the special vocal arrangements by Mel Tormé. In the lineup of guest stars, including Tormé, Peggy Lee, Vic Damone, Jack Jones, Steve Lawrence, Martha Raye, Lena Horne, and Tony Bennett, *The Judy Garland Show* amounts to a nearly definitive visual library of great American pop. Nearly every minute of the twenty-six hours—even the frequently dated comedy bits—is worthy of preservation.

CBS kept insisting that the star had to be showcased as "the girl next door," which presumably meant like Dinah Shore—a fine, cheerful, and decidedly nonthreatening singing star who hosted a nonthreatening show. The producers, however, starting with George Schlatter, wisely followed their own artistic consciences, and presented Garland as the marvelous monster that she was: the greatest of all pop superdivas, at once larger than life and supremely mortal in her wounded glory. At times she seems to burst with so much emotion and intensity that the small screen can barely contain her, yet for the most part, the television medium affords us a chance to witness a more intimate and personal side of the unique singer's personality than movies or even live concerts ever did.

Garland's numbers, which include her only performances of many wonderful songs, make the point convincingly that her pinnacle years were here in the early sixties and not, as most people assume, the golden age of movie musicals twenty years earlier. Any singer can make her strengths work for her—a beautiful voice, for instance—but it takes a master like Garland to turn a liability into an asset. On "Moon River," Garland's throat sounds drier than usual. Yet she uses her shortness of breath to help her tell the lyric's now familiar tale of yearning, to make the story even more poignant, even to the point of desperation, and every gasp, wheeze, and broken note makes her that much more convincing.

For Garland it was all about getting and keeping your attention: From one point of view, she was seen as a musical conservative—hell, a lot of her big numbers were songs that Al Jolson made famous long before she was born—but her arrangements were always innovative. She was the master of using the verse to a song as a way to heighten drama, and when Sinatra, Bennett, Fitzgerald, and Tormé did this, it was something they had learned from her. Garland often relies on the idea that an audience might not be familiar with the verse even to a song whose chorus they knew by heart (she's the only one I've heard sing the intro to "I May Be Wrong"—it's on a V-Disc with Tommy Dorsey), and in those cases, the leap from one to the other is always suspenseful. Garland takes this a step further in several cases by commissioning all new introductory verses to songs that already had perfectly acceptable ones. There are original intros to one of the oft-performed pieces of her career, "I Can't Give You Anything but Love" (no, Dorothy Fields was not writing about Thunderbird automobiles back in 1928), as well as to a song that she only sang once (so far as anybody knows), "Just One of Those Things," recorded live at her London debut at the Palladium in 1951.

Garland consistently sang verses to songs—more so than nearly any other singer in her class, including Sinatra—but the one verse that was conspicuous by its absence was that of her major mantra, "Over the Rainbow." As Mel Tormé and others have observed, Garland regarded that song as something sacred, and was hesitant to tamper with the arrangement. It would have been like messing with a religious text. There is a radio performance where she actually sings the verse to "Rainbow," and others where she does parody lyrics, but these are rare exceptions to the rule. Ella Fitzgerald, Frank Sinatra, and more recently Tony Bennett have all included that verse in their recordings of the Harold Arlen perennial, at once in tribute to Garland and in an attempt to put their own stamp on her property. In addition to the radio reading with the verse, there are two from the 1939 *Good News* program, which premiered the *Wizard of Oz* score: a truncated reading with Arlen himself "coaching" her from the piano, and a fuller run-through from the same show where she fudges one of the lines coming out of the bridge. Most sacrilegious of all is a politically motivated parody version recorded in conjunction with a 1944 fund-raising event for the Democratic Party.

Between Roger Edens at MGM and Mel Tormé at CBS, Garland had the benefit of working with two of the all-time best writers of special material, which was one of the essential elements that made Garland Garland. Edens had instilled in her a reliance on unique orchestrations as early as "You Made Me Love You"/"Dear Mr. Gable," and for her 1963–64 CBS TV series she went so far as to hire Tormé as a sort of hipper, heterosexual heir to Edens. Her radical revision of "San Francisco" owes only the central 32-bar chorus to the song introduced in the picture of the same name by Jeanette MacDonald in 1936. For starters, there's another one of those great new Garland verses, which plays on the song's history by poking fun at Miss MacDonald and the aforementioned movie. After the refrain, there's a set of variations in the form of a patter chorus (similar to those Garland employs on another city song, "Chicago").

But it's the tempo change that really brings it home. The classic jazz-pop ideal, perfected by Louis Armstrong in the twenties, is to increase excitement by making a song go faster and faster—think Sinatra's "I've Got You Under My Skin" and Bobby Darin's "Mack the Knife." Garland achieves the same effect by slowing things down to a crawl. But it's a crawl tempo that's at once sexy (in something of the mold of "The Stripper," the hit instrumental by her ex-husband David Rose) and classic showbiz, with a very dramatic emphasis on the second and fourth beats of every measure. (It's less pronounced in "San Francisco," more so in the ingeniously hoked-up Sousa-esque march "Hey Look Me Over.") When Garland gets all of it working at once, as indeed she did almost all the time, she's impossible to resist.

At the time, the Carnegie and CBS period (1961–64) seemed like a short-lived comeback for the singer. In retrospect, it may well have been her pinnacle, more of a career climax than even the amazing arc of films and recordings from *The Wizard of Oz* to *Summer Stock*. There were later films: The 1962 animated feature *Gay Purr-ee* brought Garland back to *Oz* territory in that it was ostensibly children's entertainment, but it boasted decidedly adult laments in a fine Harold Arlen score.

Unlike Sinatra, Garland was not able to reinvent herself as a nonsinging actor, even though she proved herself dramatically in the nonmusical *The Clock* (1945) well before Sinatra did in *From Here to Eternity*. (She did it again in a supporting role in *Judgment at Nuremberg*, 1961.) In 1963, she starred in two dramas with music, *A Child Is Waiting* and *I Could Go On Singing*. Fans found joy in the latter in that it boasted three excellent Garland numbers, two oldies plus the new title track, which would be the last of the major songs written for her by Harburg and Arlen. A further reunion with André Previn would mark her final appearances on a Hollywood soundstage; she recorded a vocal of "I'll Plant My Own Tree," which might have rescued *Valley of the Dolls* (1967) in the same way that "Far Away Part of Town" saved *Pepe*, but it didn't make the final print. Two years later, in 1969, she died at the age of forty-seven. "She was a good friend," as Tony Bennett put it, "but she couldn't be helped."

We launched this love letter with the observation that size was the most important consideration of Garland's singing; whether it was a big number or an intimate one ultimately mattered more than whether it was fast or slow, or loud or soft. But perhaps size didn't really matter after all. Whether Garland was blasting or whispering, she always seemed so much bigger, and more wonderful, than life.

Buddy Greco (born 1926)

When Buddy Greco walks out on stage, he's likely to start with an introductory move that's somewhere between cute and obnoxious. For instance, when Carnegie Hall mounted an all-star tribute to Nat King Cole in July 1997, Greco, an obvious disciple of the departed King, was fittingly on hand. Whereas everyone else on the bill introduced his segment by complimenting Cole, Greco elected to start his spot by saying something flattering about *himself*. "Nat and I had a lot in common," Greco told the Carnegie crowd, "we both had perfect pitch."

Greco is so *simpatico* with audiences (even when he's being antipático) that it makes sense that a significant number of his many albums were made in front of live audiences. At all the sets I've experienced, whether in person or via vinyl, he throws in at least one minor move calculated to give a little *zetz* to his listeners, a little dig, a twist, something to give us pause. It's a strategy, I suspect, calculated to get us interested, to make sure we're paying attention, because once he's got us listening, he knows it's just a matter of a song or two before he's won us over. We listen to his smooth vocal delivery, his excitedly aggressive swing numbers and surprisingly sensitive ballads, his virtuoso piano playing, and his relentless sense of rhythm, and how can we not be captivated?

Sometimes he starts by irritating us—as on "Baubles, Bangles and Beads" (*On Stage!*, 1964), in which he makes it look as though he can't even take his own arrangement seriously enough not to giggle through the thing. Or on "To Each His Own": Where the lyric calls for the title phrase to be repeated in a singsong fashion, Greco, instead of doing the repeat, simply shouts, "Same thing!" Yet even if he starts by teasing us with a little minor annoyance, he's more than able to deliver the goods. No performer works harder at pleasing his crowds.

He's a veritable study in high energy. The classic Greco tracks, like "This Could Be the Start of Something Big" (on *Buddy's Back in Town*), have the artist slowly gathering in both momentum and machismo, something his dual citizenship as musician and singer allows him to do. He varies between holding back and belting, and with every chorus he pushes the whole works just a little bit noisier and more exciting.

Many keyboardists will add the occasional vocal to their act, but they tend to have minimal voices and sing in an offhand, spare fashion, like Joe Mooney, Barbara Carroll, or Dave Frishberg, or even, in his early years, Nat Cole. Not Greco: It's not enough for him to be playing and singing at the same time, he has to totally occupy every space in the performance. Why should he let even a rest go by, or a fill between lines, when there's a potential opportunity to turn on a crowd—he'd much rather

let a consonant ring (or should I say, "ring-ah"—as in "It happened in Monterey-ah") than let there be any kind of letup in the music.

Greco's biggest accomplishment may be his perfect synthesis of the two greatest male jazz-pop artists of the mid-twentieth century, Frank Sinatra and Nat King Cole. He has the confidence, the charisma, the swagger, the Swingin' Lover machismo of the former, as well as the piano chops, the vocal and instrumental precision of the latter. For a period in the late forties, when Greco was serving as boy crooner with Benny Goodman, he also seemed to be making a move on Billy Eckstine's territory.

In discussing the influences on Greco, it wouldn't be fair to leave out the singers he himself has inspired, most notably Bobby Darin. Indeed, Darin's blending of Sinatra's Swingin' Lover school and rhythm and blues is in many ways anticipated in Greco's work, and Greco also foreshadowed his younger *paesano* in his employment of a Louis Jordan/Louis Prima shuffle rhythm. Greco's grunted use of nonverbal noises (those "ho"s and "hup"s) also found a place in Darin's art, but most notable is his overall phrasing. Also anticipating Darin, he tends to use modulations more frequently than Sinatra, a technique that obviously grows out of Greco's skill as a pianist—as indeed, it may well have also for Darin, an accomplished multi-instrumentalist himself.

The contemporary, Sinatra-styled singer Cary Hoffman and I have both noticed that Bobby Darin tended to cut off his notes in a jazzy, hard-swinging fashion that's obviously patterned after Greco. When I pointed this out to Buddy, he responded, "I had to cut my notes like that—I don't have any voice. After all, I'm not Sinatra, you know." It's as rare to find an artist who can put his own craft into perspective as it is unusual to find Greco acting humble—even if, in this case, he sells his talent short.

As with his hero, Nat Cole, for Armando Joseph Greco (born on August 14, 1926, in Philadelphia) it all started with the piano. In fact, his father, a devoted opera buff, made him practice on a "virtual keyboard" made out of cardboard long before the family could afford their own piano. And though he normally worked as what Greco called a "hardwood finisher," at one point Greco Senior pooled enough of his resources together to open a record shop, and future pop star Al Martino, then holding down a day job as a bricklayer, worked at the front of the store. At this point, in the early forties, Greco was able to hear the earliest releases of the King Cole Trio, and was soon to absorb the great jazz piano tradition of Tatum, Waller, Hines, and Wilson. "But the guy that really did it for me," as Greco has written in "I Had a Ball" (the working title of his unpublished autobiography), was not a pianist but the great Louis Armstrong. "When I first heard [him] play, he not only made me feel good, he made me happy and he made me laugh. I knew then and there that I was going to be exactly what I am."

However, he wasn't working the small-time circuits for very long. Around 1945, Greco came to the attention of Elliot Wexler, a well-connected talent agent. First, Wexler brought him to Musicraft Records, for whom he recorded his first hit, "Ooh, Looka There Ain't She Pretty?" a Fats Waller–esque tune done within a King Cole Trio–style rendition. Some of the early articles and liner notes on Greco state that this disc sold over a million copies; while it seems unlikely that the tiny independent Musicraft could have marketed or even manufactured a million-seller, "Ooh, Looka There" is, surprisingly, listed as a certified gold disc on the *Billboard* charts (according to Joel Whitburn's *Pop Memories*).

Equally important, Wexler brought him to the attention of Benny Goodman, who, even several years after what was considered the end of the big band era, was still one of the central figures in showbiz. Greco was hired ostensibly as a pianist, but he also served as the band's major male singer and on occasion he even fronted the band. (Greco also relates that one Norma Jean Baker auditioned for the band as a singer, but BG advised her to consider some other line of work.) Goodman's own sentiments were, at the time, somewhat divided: On the one hand, he was deep in a love-hate relationship with the new music known as bebop, and had assembled an outstanding ensemble that was more than capable of playing it. At the same time, he was continuing a love-love relationship with the big band classics he had already been playing for a decade. Goodman was also keen to satisfy the dancing public's hunger for pop music, which was generally achieved by featuring Greco's singing on contemporary numbers like the forgettable "Having a Wonderful Wish (Time You Were Here)."

When Goodman broke up the bop band, Greco went out on his own with a small combo just at the time that Nat Cole was deemphasizing his own jazz trio and featuring himself almost exclusively as a pop singer. Today, we think of Greco as exemplifying the better class of artists working in Vegas and Atlantic City, but in the fifties and sixties, he headlined at increasingly prestigious nightspots all over the country. He never quite made it to the superstar level of Sinatra, Cole, or Tony Bennett—he didn't have the multimedia career of the first or the propensity for hit singles of the latter two. It may tell us something that he spent his glory years under contract to two major recording concerns, MCA and Columbia, but that in both cases these companies assigned him to their subsidiary operations: Rather than appearing on Decca or Columbia, Greco's albums were released on Coral and Kapp (in the late fifties) and then on Epic (in the early to mid-sixties). Yet he recorded what seems like thousands of albums for these corporations, most of which hold up very well forty to fifty years later, and all of which are deserving of CD reissue. At the same time, he enjoyed a long run at the very top of the nightclub world during the Eisenhower, Kennedy, and Johnson years.

Greco did nearly all of his classic work for Coral/Kapp and Epic. For a time, Coral had the idea of presenting him as a romantic crooner, and released a number of ballad singles, nearly all of which went nowhere at the time and don't sound any better now. By the start of the LP era, he had come back to the King Cole–style pianist-singer and hot combo format that would serve him satisfyingly, with occasional exceptions, from that point on. The earlier albums tend to use small combos more consistently, most notably his own working group (including his brother, the talented saxophonist Al Taylor, who used that stage name to avoid charges of nepotism). The Epic albums often use full orchestras and team Greco with some of the best pop orchestrators in the business. Both corporations have released anthologies that I would endorse as well-chosen samples of the best of his work in those years. *Talkin' Verve* (don't ask me to explain the title) covers the fifties, and *16 Most Requested Songs* lives up to that title's promise of delivering most of his best-remembered tracks of the Epic era. He made live albums in both periods; the earlier ones, like the 1955 *Buddy Greco at Mister Kelly's*, appear to be genuine location tapings. However the sixties projects, such as *My Buddy* (1959) and *On Stage!* (1964), tend to follow Columbia's baffling—yet consistent—policy of crafting bogus live albums.

Although the 1958 *Buddy* (half of which, including all the vocal numbers, is included on *Talkin' Verve*) was neither a live album nor a pseudolive one, it seems to be a fairly accurate representation of what Greco and his group were doing live in the clubs at the time. *Buddy* uses Greco's working quartet, featuring Taylor on various saxophones (and taking a very creditable flute solo on "That's All") and is divided between vocal and instrumental numbers. By the end of the decade, and the switchover from MCA to Columbia, his style was practically perfected.

"Yes Sir, That's My Baby" is light and swinging, yet at the same time dense, with Greco shtick at its most endearing: He starts with a rap ("I met a chick / The other day . . . ") similar to that used by Ray Charles in "Greenbacks" or by Sam Butera in "Next Time," and from there goes into "I Love to Love" (an amorous anthem of the era associated with Peggy Lee and Lena Horne), and just when we're convinced that "Love to Love" is, at last, the song he's going to stick with, he leads us into the long-awaited "Yes Sir, That's My Baby." Such side trips would become part of Greco's formula: The thoroughly de-waltzed "It Happened in Monterey" finds him detouring through Billy Eckstine's "Stormy Monday" and Nat Cole's "Calypso Blues," while "The Rules of the Road" (on the 1964 *On Stage!*) takes us to "The Man That Got Away."

"Shtick" is often perceived as excluding jazz.

However, while Greco's bits of business are undeniably shtick, they are mightily swinging shtick. The most purist of jazz purists (the same ones who pooh-pooh Louis Prima) could conceivably object to Greco's highly animated offerings, but they'd be tapping their feet four beats to a bar while they did so.

It's Greco's unfailing sense of swing that makes his act musical. Following the examples of Sinatra and Tormé, "It Happened in Monterey," Mabel Wayne's ersatz Mexican waltz from 1930, is now no longer in 3/4 time: Greco's group has invested it with genuinely exotic rhythms, complete with flute and bongos. The same can be said for Irving Berlin's 1919 "I'll See You in C-U-B-A," only there it's a case of a comic faux-Latin song—as opposed to a romantic one—being made at once more authentic and more swinging. Likewise, Greco opens his sambafied "All of You" with a "Peanut Vendor"–like moan. Even when he's not folding songs into other songs, he and his groups have a great gift for finding suitable countermelodies, like the insinuating, country and western style vamp that emerges out of the lower registers to accompany "One for My Baby" and the catchy tenor sax introduction to and vamp behind "The Party's Over." And Greco doesn't always sound like a lounge lizard on steroids. Ballads like the sensitive "Here Am I in Love Again" reveal that he has—who'd'a thunk it?—a sensitive side.

My Buddy (1959) launches Greco's run of Epic albums, as well as several titles that play off his stage name—e.g., *Buddy and Soul.* Although ostensibly "recorded at Le Bistro, Rush Street, Chicago," the package seems to have been done in the studio with applause and other live effects added later. But the two Epic "live" sets—the other is *On Stage!*—are two of the singer-pianist's most essential packages. Although the applause may have been phony, Greco's swinging style was decidedly not, and a number of his classics were first documented on this set—the opener, "Like Young," André and Dory Previn's ode to swinging beatnikism, for instance. On "The Lady Is a Tramp," Greco (like Ella Fitzgerald in her live treatments of the sixties) concentrates on Larry Hart's fourth verse; even though Lena Horne, Frank Sinatra, and Mel Tormé had all made a career peg out of this song, Greco manages to imbue it with his own personality and becomes yet another performer identified with this Rodgers and Hart hit.

Where *My Buddy* includes a tender treatment of Erroll Garner's well-known "Misty," *On Stage!* (1964) has him doing that hit song's less-successful follow-up, "Dreamy," which he smartly introduces with a Garnerlike piano flourish. The two "live" albums also include what may well be Greco's two greatest wise-ass anthems: The 1959 set has "That's What I Thought You Said," an ingenious exercise in avoiding the issue of a significant other's rather extravagant demands, and the 1964 set has "The Best Man." This piece was earlier immortalized by the King Cole Trio (from whom Greco doubtless learned it) and has been revived more recently by singer-pianist Eric Comstock as well as by Cole's talented younger brother Freddy. But only Greco projects the perfect balance of ego and insecurity; only he sings it as if he really believes he *is* "The Best Man"; only Greco has the cojones to throw in a coda in which the ex-girlfriend comes to the conclusion that he (and not his best friend, whom she married) is "the best man in the end."

During the years 1959–64, Greco recorded seventeen LPs for Epic—it seems unlikely that the whole bunch will come out on CD, but I can dream, can't I? Of the ones I've heard, only a few can be called disappointing, and even those are far from worthless. Apart from the live albums, there are a number of other concept packages—four sets of ballads, one of Italian songs, one most unusual composer-driven songbook album, and an instrumental/all-piano package.

There are some surprises, and not all good ones. The Neapolitan package, *My Last Night in Rome* (1964), is, frankly, lame. Perhaps out of not wanting to screw around with his ethnic heritage, he sings most of these songs too straight—as if he were Al Martino, Jimmy Roselli, or Jerry Vale. One wishes that the whole thing had been done in Italo-American Swingin' Lover style, like Dean Martin or Louis Prima, or the way that Greco himself sang Rodgers and Hart (and, for that matter, the way he does the Italian song "[I Don't Care] Only Love Me" on *My Buddy*). Although the songs are suited to him, most of the discothequey arrangements just sound corny. The most engaging performance here is the opener, "It Had Better Be Tonight" (included on *16 Most Requested Songs*), written by Henry Mancini and Johnny Mercer for *The Pink Panther*.

On the other hand, there are some excitingly irreverent orchestrations, credited to Greco himself, and the singing to go with them, on *Modern Sounds of Hank Williams* (also 1964), Greco's one songwriter-tribute project. The great country composer's hits are solidly situated within a contemporary jazz-pop framework; for instance, "I'm So Lonesome I Could Cry" is a jazz waltz in the manner of Ray Charles's "Busted" (most of the others are in a solid four), "Jambalaya" employs a vaguely Latin beat, and "Hey Good Lookin' " has Greco soloing on a funky Hammond organ. (The only letdown is Williams's gospel number "I Saw the Light," which is sung by a Disneylandish choir interacting with Greco's piano improvisations, but, alas, no vocal from Greco himself.)

The love song albums are *Songs for Swinging Losers* (1960), a set arranged and conducted by Chuck Slagel that's different in tone from any of Sinatra's downer albums. A better comparison would be the Nat Cole–Billy May *Just One of Those Things*, which similarly intersperses up-tempos (like the highlight "By Myself") with down moods; the comparatively dull *Buddy Greco Sings for Intimate Moments* (1963), conducted by future bigwig Dave Grusin, which has Buddy belting "If Ever I Would Leave You" against a syrupy choir; and the superior *Buddy and Soul* (1962) and *Soft and Gentle* (1963), both of which also mix slow and fast moods in a general love song context. The inspired orchestrations of the short-lived Robert Mersey greatly enhance these last two, as does a good selection of tunes (especially an "After the Lights Go Down Low," in which he grunts like Al Hibbler). On his best ballads, Greco is nearly competition for such masters as Vic Damone, and frequently puts the lie to his own contention that he doesn't have any chops.

Ballads are all well and good, but there's no debating what Buddy Greco does best: swing. Pure swing. Explosive, relentless, insensitive sometimes, almost even annoying swing. This is precisely what he achieves on *I Like It Swinging* and *Let's Love*, the two albums that very well may represent the apogee of his entire career. Both are from 1961 and both are arranged and conducted by Al Cohn, the star jazz saxist.

Greco classics abound here: In "Around the World," he reinvents the Victor Young movie waltz as a killing swinger saturated with Prima-style shuffle rhythm. Instead of ending his first chorus with "for I have found my world in you," as written, Greco throws in a whole bunch of "I like it! I like it! I like it!"s as he lunges into a modulation. He even reanimates the normally tender and sensitive "Surrey with the Fringe on Top" and "Secret Love" with testosterone to spare. He gives the Greco treatment to two Peggy Lee signatures, "Fever" and "I Love Being Here with You" (wisely employed as a closer rather than an opener), and very nearly wrests them away from that great lady, while his "Roses of Picardy" is a blueprint for the famous Darin–Billy May treatment of a few years later. He also invades blues territory, in Jackie Wilson's "You Better Know It," Ray Charles's "Hallelujah I Love Her So," and Willie Mabon's 1953 "I Don't Know," which amounts to the latest in the ongoing line of Greco raps.

The Epic series ends with an instrumental album with the beguiling title *From the Wrists Down* (1965). Continuing the parallel with Cole, this package has more in common with *The Piano Style of Nat King Cole* (piano solos with orchestral accompaniment) than with *Penthouse Serenade* (piano solos with trio backing). That in itself is not necessarily a bad thing, nor was the decision to subject only contempo hits to this treatment. Greco's digits and the accompanying orch do fine with the bossa novas "So Danco Samba," "Carnival," and "Corcovado," although it's hard to see why producer Tony Palmer wanted a piano-orchestra instrumental of "What's New Pussycat?," "Sweet Pussycat" (I'm detecting a theme here), "Help!," or the Herman's Hermits hit "Henry the Eighth." (Throughout the early sixties,

Greco scholar Tony Sachs informs me, the pianist-singer recorded a steady stream of fascinating and diverse material for Epic singles, which have never been collated on LP or CD, ranging from Lennon and McCartney to Swingin' Lover Rat Packer finger-snappers like the marvelous "To Be or Not to Be in Love.")

Cole also echoes throughout *Big Band and Ballads* (1966), the first and best of three albums Greco recorded for Sinatra's Reprise label, produced by Jimmy Bowen. *BB&B* opens with two songs from Cole's concept album and TV special *Wild Is Love*—the title track and "It's a Beautiful Evening." (He also performs two other songs from the Cole songbook here, "L-O-V-E" and "Funny.") *BB&B* marks one of the few straight-ahead packages ever produced by Bowen, already famous for "contemporizing" the Rat Pack. Ironically, nothing that Bowen ever produced for Sinatra is as good as *Big Band and Ballads*.

The other Greco-Bowen-Reprise collections are not up to that level: *Buddy's in a Brand New Bag* (1967) fails for all the wrong reasons, and *Away We Go* (1967) fails for all the right ones. *Brand New Bag*, as the title hints, attempts to foist Greco on the jukebox crowd with songs by Leiber and Stoller and Italo-pop-like "You Don't Have to Say You Love Me" (already a hit for Dusty Springfield and later for Elvis Presley). On *Away We Go*, the title being taken from a summer replacement TV series that Greco shared with another pugnacious Buddy (namely Rich), the songs are generally of a higher class, but it was a mistake to try to update Greco with bossa nova hits: Unlike Sinatra, he is just too aggressive to work with those gentle, undulating rhythms. Sam Cooke's "Good Times," Greco's latest reconstruction of a rhythm and blues hit, works much better—thanks partially to an arrangement inspired by the Sinatra-Riddle *Strangers in the Night* album. (Greco's attack on "Summer Wind" is far from magical, alas.)

Away We Go seems to be Greco's last major label venture, though he's recorded about a dozen albums since 1967. There's some confusion about who he is and what he should be recording: The seventies and eighties albums are generally divided between him doing remakes of his past triumphs ("Around the World," etc.), and someone—sometimes the pianist-singer himself—trying to be contemporary with current hit songs and rock and/or disco rhythms. "Those awful eighties albums are, I believe, the brainchild of Buddy, much as I wish someone else had put him up to them," as Buddy's rabbi, Tony Sachs, put it. "He's very proud of, for instance, his cover of 'Me and Mrs. Jones.' "

But Greco never faltered in live performance, and when he brings that same clarity of focus to his recorded work, the results are memorable. For instance, the 1994 *Route 66*, with his quartet, is an admirable tribute to Nat Cole. ("Moonlight in Vermont" was never associated with Cole, but who gives a paper moon?) *'Round Midnight* (1992) was a concerted attempt to make a jazz album with a capital J, and while the arrangements are a little on the jazz-lite side, there are copious solos from such West Coast luminaries as Jack Sheldon, Terry Gibbs, Ernie Watts, Grover Washington, and Toots Thielemans. Jazzier still is *Jazz Grooves*, an all-instrumental package (only Greco's second) with challenging charts by guitarist Joe Lano.

'Round Midnight is one of several successful projects resulting from the union of Greco and producer-arranger Alf Clausen. (Unfortunately, while Greco and Clausen are obviously best buds, Clausen has never engineered an appearance by Greco on his most famous venture, the music for *The Simpsons*. Too bad—Greco would make a great replacement for the late Phil Hartman as the voice of Lionel Hutz.) Clausen also contributed to *It's Magic* (1990), *In Style* (1996), and *MacArthur Park* (1996).

The song "MacArthur Park" has been Greco's most reliable showstopper over the last few decades. Other singers, particularly Italianate crooners looking for the youth audience (Sinatra, Bennett, Damone), have sung it, but only Greco can claim that the song was written on his own piano: According to him, songwriter Jimmy Webb was crashing on the Greco couch at the very time he left his famous cake out in the rain. Only Greco renders it as an instrumental, which, given the autobiographical specificity of Webb's text (even after Sinatra and Bennett, I still can't quite bring myself to care about either that cake or that rain), is probably for the best. Greco generally uses it as his show closer—as with Bennett and "How Do You Keep the Music Playing," one gets the impression that nothing can follow it—

and even though my rational mind can't stand the song, I always find myself applauding wildly and leaping to my feet whenever I hear Greco play it.

I had occasion to do so one day in 1985, when Eric Comstock and I hopped a Greyhound down to Atlantic City to catch Greco, Billy Eckstine, and Tony Bennett, who were all appearing at the same hotel. Tony was in the main room, while Mr. B and Mr. G alternated in the lounge. Needless to say, it was one of the greatest marathons of jazz-pop singing I've ever experienced, and Greco easily held his own with these two big-voiced vocal athletes. He made a triumphant New York appearance in March 2001, a few months before his seventy-fifth birthday, and was next seen in these parts in summer 2005—at which point he announced that he was about to open his own club outside Palm Springs, California. Greco and his fifth wife, the talented Peggy Lee–styled vocalist Lezlie Anders, kept the club going for a few years in the mid-oughts before moving to the U.K. in 2009. His most recent vocal albums are a fine big band set called *Like Young* and a marvelous jazz combo album called *Back to Basics*. Greco sounds so good on this latter album, recorded in 1999, it's a small tragedy that he hasn't cut another one in the last ten years.

Both *Back to Basics* and *Like Young* are fitting titles and even mantras for an artist who, after well over sixty years in the business, is still as irrepressible, as charming, and as irritating as ever. Greco has all the finger-popping shallowness we associate with lounge lizards, but at the same time there's a sincerity and even a purity to his work that's quite remarkable. There's no one quite like him. Like, I'm hip.

H

Johnny Hartman (1923–1983)

When asked why it was that Johnny Hartman's success was never commensurate with his talent, Tony Bennett didn't have an answer. Ralph Sharon, who (a year or so before becoming Bennett's musical director) played piano on one of Hartman's finest albums, *Songs from the Heart*, couldn't explain that one either.

TV impresario Steve Allen, who had been in a position to give Hartman's career a real boost, later lamented that he didn't discover Hartman until years after the singer's death in 1983. "In the years when I was working every day or every night on television, I could have been some help to him. But he was never brought to my attention."

Of all the major male singers, Hartman was by far the least prolific—not counting his pre-LP singles, Hartman recorded a grand total of sixteen albums. Which is roughly the equivalent of what Nat King Cole or Frank Sinatra taped in any one phase of their careers. Those of us who make it a point to own all sixteen of them like to dwell on the conspiracy theory that Hartman must have committed

some unpardonable faux pas: He slept with the wrong big shot's wife, he punched the wrong columnist, he hesitated to denounce Eleanor Roosevelt, he gave the finger to Ed Sullivan, he wore white after Labor Day. Surely the world's refusal to make Hartman a star could in no way have been a reflection on his talent.

Hartman was one of the greatest of all interpreters of love songs. It wasn't just a question of a deep, sensual voice, which he surely had; it was his romantic attitude. "There was a sentimentality to him," as longtime accompanist Tony Monte put it. "He was in love with the idea of being in love, and he [continually] expressed that idea. He would sing about it, and he would speak about it in his patter. He would look out wistfully in the audience and say he was going to dedicate the rest of the show to the beautiful women out there and to the men who brought them, and who were paying such great attention to them. And it wasn't just a little piece of theater, he meant what he was saying." Hartman always made it clear that he meant what he was singing; like Cole and Sinatra, he had the gift of making you feel every word.

Hartman favored a more positive kind of love song—although he was a first-generation disciple of Sinatra's, he never followed the older singer down the abyss of despair into which the Voice often led his listeners. As Monte observed, "What I didn't realize about Johnny until I had been with him for many years was that he didn't do any songs about victims, songs that said 'Poor me, I was left out in the cold.'" Even when Hartman sang "Lush Life" with John Coltrane, it's torchy and sad but not despondent. "I wasn't influenced by the way Nat Cole sang it," Hartman once pointed out. "It took on a different meaning when I did it." Hartman's "It Never Entered My Mind" (on *The Voice That Is!*) is nowhere near the suicidal tract that it becomes on Sinatra's *In the Wee Small Hours*. And the same can be said for Hartman's interpretation of "In the Wee Small Hours" itself (on *I Just Dropped By to Say Hello*). When Sinatra sings "The End of a Love Affair," he really makes it sound as if it's the end of the whole wide world, whereas when Hartman sings it, he brings to it the particular kind of melancholy that one associates with the end of a love affair.

Hartman once told researcher Herb Kurtin that his favorite singers were Como, Haymes, Bob Eberly, Joe Williams, and Mel Tormé, but that his number-one fave, always, was Sinatra. Billy Eckstine also occupied a special place in his affections. As he once said, "Billy has always been one of my favorites, but if I find myself slipping into too much of an Eckstine bag, I rehearse myself out of it." Yet Hartman also said that he studied instrumentalists—naming Johnny Hodges as an example—more diligently than he did other singers.

"I was a cool singer, even when I sang in church," Hartman said in an *Essence* interview, reflecting upon his early days in Chicago. Singing "cool" may have been a deliberate measure to avoid competition with the woman who played piano for his church choir, Ruth Jones (later known as Dinah Washington), who was as "hot" as they come. "That was just me, my style of singing," he said. "It wasn't none of the hollering and screaming, [like] the old ladies [who] used to shout. And I got my message over."

Hartman apparently told historian Leonard Feather that he was born on July 3, 1926 (the same year as Bennett and Coltrane), in Chicago, although the program distributed at his funeral says he was born in Louisiana in 1923. If he was indeed born in the Deep South and then raised in Chicago, that provides a further parallel with Nat Cole, Joe Williams, and choirmate Dinah Washington.

Apart from singing in church, Hartman performed in school. As a kid, he took singing lessons, sang in his high school glee club and with the school's resident dance band. His original plan was to join his father in Hartman Senior's Pepsi-Cola distribution business, and with that in mind, he studied accounting at Wilson Junior College. However, fate took a hand when the seventeen-year-old happened to enter an amateur contest at Chicago's El Grotto supper club. He won first prize: $25 and a week's engagement with the resident group, Earl Hines and His Orchestra. The week became a year with Hines at the El Grotto, and then he took to the road with that legendary pianist.

That's one telling of the story, as the singer recounted it to the *New York Times*' John S. Wilson in 1982. On another occasion, however, Hartman told Leonard Feather that the first time he sang in what might be called a professional context was during World War II, when, as an infantryman, he managed to be transferred to the entertainment division, aka Special Services. Hartman also sang on the early TV show *Arthur Godfrey's Talent Scouts*, and became the first black singer to win that competition.

Hartman spent most of 1947 with Earl Hines, and recorded what is believed to be his first side with the Fatha in November: a slow boogie-blues original by the leader entitled "Midnight in New Orleans" for MGM Records. Hines also featured Hartman on an elaborate concerto grosso version of "Ain't Misbehavin'." "Earl's piano relaxes you and covers you up so nicely," Hartman told George Simon in 1949.

Mystery surrounds the first recordings made under his own name, ten sides cut for the Regent label in 1947 or 1948, which were presumably issued as singles, although the earliest documented issue of these is a Regent LP (followed by a Savoy LP) from years later.

The singer's combination of ease and inexperience shows itself in his version of Sinatra's first hit, "I'll Never Smile Again." Appropriately, Hartman can be heard beginning to learn some of Sinatra's lessons, although throughout these early sides his intonation is not what it would become later on. He later spoke about his early stiffness in this period: "When I was an amateur, I sang with both hands in my pockets. People remarked on it, but Earl said, 'He'll take his hands out of his pockets when he feels it. If I tell him to do it, he'll destroy himself.' And sure enough, one day one hand came out. It felt okay and pretty soon the other hand came out."

Hartman's emotional "coming out" occurred along similar lines—from the restrained sound of these early sides to the more outgoing balladeering of his mature work. The four early sides with Hines and the Regent/Savoy sessions could be compared to his singing with both hands out of sight, while his four tracks with Dizzy Gillespie (especially "I Should Care") and the other singles circa 1948–50 suggest him singing with one hand still in the pocket. After Hines broke up his orchestra to join Louis Armstrong's All Stars, Hartman went solo for six months. In summer or early fall of 1948, he was working at the Club Harlem in Atlantic City when Dizzy Gillespie came in to hear him. A week later, the trumpeter-composer-bandleader sent Hartman a telegram from California inviting him to join his bebop big band at the Clique in Philadelphia.

In his successive associations with Hines and Gillespie, Hartman was following in the footsteps of Billy Eckstine. "Dizzy played a very different kind of music from Hines," Hartman said. "Dizzy had an audience that had found bebop. I didn't fit in with bebop, so I just went on doing ballads like 'I Should Care' and 'That Old Black Magic.'" Which is a fairly apt description of Hartman's four vocals from Gillespie's Victor sessions. The loud, dissonant (for the time) bop orchestrations make a fairly odd frame for the romantic picture Hartman paints inside them.

At times, the contrast actually helped his style. Hartman said, "It didn't affect me at all working with a band that basically played bebop. But just listening and working with 'the Diz,' the kind of musician he is, was helpful to me, influencing my style, breaking and executing different kinds of musical phrases."

The Gillespie period also marked the beginning of the debate as to whether or not Hartman was a "jazz singer," which became more and more of a sore point to him as his career progressed. He eventually concluded that it was just as impossible for a black vocalist to be classified as anything other than a jazz singer as it was for a white singer to earn that label. "I'm an all-around singer," Hartman insisted to the day he died. "I studied classical music. I go back to the heavy spirituals." His thoughts on the subject of phrasing echoed Frank Sinatra's: "I hear some singers break up sentences in the wrong places. Phrasing is like talking. I think you should sing like you talk. If you do that, the song comes out right."

The issue of jazz versus nonjazz was not, however, raised when Hartman did four sides in 1949 with the marvelous pianist Erroll Garner and his trio. Unfortunately, although there's already a very attractive purity to Hartman's singing, unlike the six later Coltrane-Hartman performances these four titles never quite catch fire; Hartman is still more stiff at this early stage than related and romantic. One hand remains pocketed.

He fares better in a more conventional big-band date from July 1949, with Budd Johnson, Ray Brown, and Bobby Tucker (Eckstine's pianist for many a decade) on hand. Both dates were for the Mercury label, where Mitch Miller, then just beginning his career as a prince of pop, was the first to see the commercial possibilities in Hartman's crooning. These two sessions, done while Hartman was still touring with Gillespie, are diametrically different from the archetypal Miller oeuvre in that all eight sides are classic standards, not even one a novelty bid for a hit.

The big issue in the earlier part of his career, which came to the fore when Gillespie broke up his band and Hartman took a solo gig at New York's Cafe Society in January 1950 (and did his first post-Gillespie record date for Apollo that May), was whether a black man could be a pop singer at all. "I've seen times when I couldn't go into white clubs and sing my style of singing," he later said. "You either buck danced or sang a real gutbucket blues, and then they would let you in. But to go in with a shirt and tie and stand there clean and sing like Perry Como or anybody else, they didn't want you to do that. You get the feeling that you're never supposed to be serious or be a man who could fall in love."

Yet Hartman benefited from the pioneering efforts of Eckstine and Cole, who were the first black male singers to become widely accepted as mainstream pop stars. RCA Records was looking for star power of that magnitude when they signed him in 1951. The sales department even sent out an announcement to the distributors brazenly trumpeting Hartman as their own answer to MGM's Eckstine, proclaiming him a "singing gold mine."

RCA's commitment to Hartman lasted one year and sixteen songs. It was probably the single biggest missed opportunity of his career. It would be his only extended stay at a major label, back when it was still possible for someone who sang what the Grammy people now call "Traditional Pop" to land a hit. Unfortunately, his producers couldn't come up with any song that was good enough to compete with Eckstine and Cole or even a catchy novelty that was bad enough to go toe-to-toe with some of the junkier hits of the era. For some reason, the RCA producers had Hartman singing overbaked orchestrations of religious songs, like "Battle Hymn of the Republic" (heard with choir, and, God help us, Civil War sound effects) and "My Task."

The one song from his RCA period that went anywhere was "Wheel of Fortune," but RCA sat on it for so long that the competition—most notably Capitol Records and Kay Starr—quickly eclipsed him. Understandably, Hartman was bitter about "Wheel of Fortune" as well as about "I Ran All the Way Home," by the same composers, Bennie Benjamin and George Weiss; that time, Sarah Vaughan beat him to the punch. Musically speaking, his most memorable session in the 1951–52 RCA period resulted in a pair of sides with Pérez Prado's orchestra, an early example of a mainstream pop singer going mambo (predating Como's hit "Papa Loves Mambo" by three years).

In a more conventional vein, Hartman's best RCA sides were "Out of the Night," with its light Latin beat, and the whimsical and welcome "Worry Bird," his first two titles for the company, and two other titles with an all-star band featuring old friends Tyree Glenn and Budd Johnson, "Black Shadows" and "I Feel Like Crying."

By 1952, the "singing gold mine" had failed to pan out. The RCA debacle finished Hartman's chances of making it in the mass-market music business; none of the sixteen titles made any impact, or has ever been reissued. Hartman's only other record for the next few years was a guest appearance with old boss Earl Hines on a pair of easy listening style sides with a Mitch Miller–like choir and the Fatha in a Liberace mood: "I Dream of You" and Irving Berlin's "A Pretty Girl Is Like a Melody."

Around this time he began finding steady work overseas, starting with a two-week gig in London that eventually lasted two years. He later claimed that he was working in clubs, concerts, and making records (none of which have ever come to light), and even had a TV series in England. He said, "Then the English labor department complained that I was doing too many things. I came back to the United States and found that I'd been forgotten."

That changed in 1956. With the release of *Songs from the Heart*, Hartman was instantly elevated from an Eckstine/Cole/Sinatra wannabe to the pantheon. This was his first complete album and his earliest fully mature effort, and would also be one of the best ballad albums either he or anybody else would ever make. His ability to inject tenderness and sensitivity into a love song and make it believable were by now unparalleled. At long last, both hands were permanently out of their pockets.

Around 1970, Hartman appeared in a play (presumably off-Broadway) called *The Duplex*, in preparation for which he took acting lessons for a month at the Herbert Berghof studio. He said later that studying acting "gave me a different insight into lyrics. I could emote more." Yet a single listen to *Songs from the Heart* reveals that even by 1956 Hartman already knew all there was to know about emotion, especially where music was concerned. It's particularly crucial on "I See Your Face Before Me": the lyrics talk about the difference between the "unreal from the real thing" and Hartman ever so articulately enunciates that duality, offering the sincerity of his interpretation as an unmistakable example of "the real thing."

The minimal background of a quartet, piloted by Ralph Sharon, a recent immigrant from England, and veteran trumpeter Howard McGhee, a first-generation bop master second only to Gillespie himself, makes Hartman's performance even more convincing. Everything about his singing and musical acting is completely believable; the only unbelievable aspect of *Songs from the Heart* is how it failed to establish him as a star. Unfortunately, he was stuck singing second-rate material like "Lemme Go" for a major label like RCA and then, conversely, singing classic songs and weaving them into a supreme statement like *Songs from the Heart* for the small independent Bethlehem Records, which hadn't the business and marketing resources to do for Hartman what he needed.

Songs from the Heart established a pattern that would continue for the rest of his life. He would find a label, record a classic album or two, and then, when nobody bought them, go back to scuffling for a few years until he found another company willing to take a chance. He followed *Songs from the Heart*

with *All of Me*, an orchestral package for Bethlehem, taped later that year with fellow Earl Hines veteran Ernie Wilkins, and *And I Thought About You*, done for Teddy Reig's Roost label circa 1959.

"End of a Love Affair," from *All of Me*, is certainly first-class pop singing, with Hartman realizing that it's inappropriate for him to try to cut as deep on this faster tempo and with a larger ensemble. "Mamselle," in which Hartman's rendition was undoubtedly inspired by Dick Haymes, and the title track from *And I Thought About You*, find a middle ground of ensemble size and emotional expression. Using what we could call a chamber group of a rhythm section plus occasional reeds or woodwinds, Hartman gets a larger canvas that doesn't fence him in.

The three albums of 1956–59 show that he had fully arrived, musically if not professionally. The stiffness and occasional intonation problems of a decade earlier are a distant memory; now he can sound emotionally intense without turning up the volume, and can work within a very narrow space melodically, sticking close to the tune as written, and at the same time personalize it intensely. He can achieve that most difficult of musical feats: to make a tune his own without altering it. Yet despite a few lesser singles, notable mainly as Hartman oddities (for Jubilee and ABC), it looked as if his first albums would also be his last.

The next scuffling period between commercial recordings lasted four or five years, during which time he again worked overseas. He was in Japan in 1963 when Bob Thiele of Impulse! Records tracked him down and informed him that John Coltrane, then probably the number-one star of the jazz world, wanted to cut an album with him.

"I had never heard of Coltrane playing ballads, so I was a little reluctant," Hartman said. The singer first had to be assured that "it wasn't gonna be a lot of wild stuff going on." He later elaborated, "I was a Coltrane fan, and although I'd never met him, I'd been listening to him for years. I didn't think we'd fit too well. But Bob told me to go to Birdland when I got back to the States and listen to him. Then, after the show, when the place had closed, I tried a couple of tunes with him. I did—just me, Coltrane and his pianist, Cedar Walton. [Walton may have been subbing for Coltrane's regular pianist, McCoy Tyner.] A week later we went out to Rudy Van Gelder's studio to make the album."

That album, *John Coltrane and Johnny Hartman*, has become, along with Sinatra's *Songs for Swingin' Lovers!* and Cole's *After Midnight*, the *Kind of Blue* of vocal albums. It would be hard to think of a vocalist of the last forty years or, for that matter, an instrumentalist who has worked with a singer who hasn't been profoundly influenced by this classic record.

John and Johnny taped it in a single session, on March 7, 1963. Hartman had originally "lined up ten songs to do. But as we were driving out, listening to the car radio, we heard Nat Cole sing 'Lush Life.' I said, 'That is a fantastic song' and I started singing it in the car, although I didn't know all the words." As the session started, someone managed to locate a complete set of Billy Strayhorn's lyrics. Coltrane already knew the tune: He had recorded it earlier as an instrumental, although in both versions he used incorrect chord changes (or so Strayhorn himself charged).

Including "Lush Life," Hartman and Coltrane considered a total of eleven possible tunes. Of these, they recorded seven, one of which, Oscar Brown's lyric to Mongo Santamaria's "Afro Blue," has never been issued. "We did everything in one take," Hartman said, "except 'You Are So Beautiful.' We had to do two takes on that one, because Elvin Jones dropped a drumstick on the first take." While all seven tracks were recorded in the same session, with Hartman singing live with Coltrane and the rhythm section, the tenor saxophonist returned at a later date and overdubbed a few additional obbligatos behind the singer. All six issued tracks are masterpieces, yet the two that stand out are Hartman's homages to his mentors, Cole on "Lush Life" and Sinatra on "My One and Only Love."

With *Songs from the Heart* and then again with the Coltrane collaboration, Hartman had succeeded in something few artists in any medium manage to pull off—the creation of a genre that was distinctly his own. There had certainly never been a record like either one before, and if there haven't been many since it's because later singers have not dared to invade Hartman's turf.

When Hartman started in the forties, his goal was to be a straight-down-the-middle mainstream pop singer. Fortunately for us, although perhaps not so much for Hartman himself, economics forced him into what he very likely regarded as a "jazz ghetto." We can only surmise that he'd rather have been getting rich with hits (albeit with the kind of material he liked, not novelties or rockish tunes) with big orchestras, than making exquisite albums with intimate (and not coincidentally, low-budget) combos. Hartman also had the taste in songs of a Cafe Society *chanteur*, and forged a repertory of tunes like "Down in the Depths," "I See Your Face Before Me," and "The End of a Love Affair," all generally associated with posh East Siders like Bobby Short or Mabel Mercer. He stuck to what he described as "all standards, songs I like, songs that meant something to me, songs like 'More Than You Know' or 'How Deep Is the Ocean.' Not fly-by-night songs."

In short, Hartman was as much at home at the Blue Angel as at the Blue Note. The basic sound of a Johnny Hartman performance touches on all three sources: jazz, adult pop, and cabaret. "There's good news and bad news when you do an album with McCoy Tyner and John Coltrane," says accompanist Tony Monte, echoing Hartman's own belief that classifying him strictly in the jazz category was a limiting factor, both musically and professionally. "Nobody knew that this was going to become this monster album that's been selling since 1963. So what happened there was that Johnny had been singing and recording with big orchestras, with Frank Hunter, who was a commercial arranger and wonderful orchestrator; and Gerald Wilson did a lot of orchestrations for Johnny and arrangements. And they really worked, and Johnny sounded great with orchestras, especially with strings. But once he was tagged as a jazz singer, that was over. And places like the Copacabana in New York and the big hotel rooms around the country were not going to hire a jazz singer, so he lost a great deal of money from not being able to sing at places like the Persian Room and the Empire Room at the Waldorf." Hartman himself added, "In supper clubs, they don't even want to hear the word 'jazz,' so in that way it hurts my career."

All true (except that the big band album with Gerald Wilson actually came three years after the Coltrane album), but there were benefits to the association with jazz. Hartman would never play the high-profile mainstream nightclubs. But, as it turned out, after still more years of scuffling around, in the final years of his life he found himself working primarily in jazz clubs like the Blue Note and Fat Tuesdays (to name just two in New York) on the strength of that record. Later he even made an album in Japan, *Hartman Sings Trane's Favorites* (most of it appeared in the States as part of *For Trane*) to appeal to fans who knew him primarily from the Coltrane association. As Monte concedes, *John Coltrane and Johnny Hartman* "certainly put him on the map, but it took him off another map. He went from one map to another, I guess." At one point, Hartman also admitted, "Jazz has been successful for me and good to me, so I have no qualms about being classified as a jazz singer."

Indeed, the Coltrane album was so well received that Bob Thiele would produce another four albums with Hartman, two more for the jazz label Impulse!, *I Just Dropped By to Say Hello* (1963) and *The Voice That Is!* (1964), and two for that company's parent pop label, ABC Paramount, *Unforgettable* and *I Love Everybody* (both from 1966). The five albums for Thiele constitute the largest and most consistently excellent body of work in Hartman's career.

I Just Dropped By to Say Hello employs a core rhythm section beginning with Coltrane's celebrated drummer, Elvin Jones, and his older brother, the highly esteemed pianist Hank Jones. Half of the album also features another tenor colossus, Illinois Jacquet. Both Hartman and Jacquet shine on "Don't You Know I Care" (associated with Al Hibbler and Ellington) and "Stairway to the Stars" (which Coltrane and Milt Jackson had made into a jazz standard) breathily introduced by Jacquet in a Ben Webster bag. "In the Wee Small Hours" evokes Sinatra, but Hartman again takes it at a slightly faster tempo, and doesn't dive for the Chairman's suicidal depths. Just before hitting the last note in the first chorus, he cleverly switches to the verse, never sung by FS. "Stairway" is sheer perfection: Both voices, Hartman and Jacquet, are deep and rich, the mood is slow and sensual, and the baritone and the tenor phrase it as if they're in no hurry to get to where they're going—Hartman's rhythmic placement is somewhere beyond immaculate. He knows exactly where to drop each note for maximum rhythmic and romantic effect and there isn't so much as a beat out of place.

Hank Jones returns for *The Voice That Is!* (still another evocation of Sinatra, known as "the Voice"), beautifully outlining the harmonies in single notes (doubled by guitarist Barry Galbraith) behind Hartman on the bridge to "My Ship," which the singer makes sound like the greatest love song ever written. "The More I See You" picks up the pace a bit, going into a gently rocking tempo, with Hartman supported on the first eight bars only by bassist Richard Davis. *The Voice That Is!* is unquestionably a jazz album, yet there's no strong horn soloist—no Coltrane, Jacquet, or McGhee—and much of the album doesn't use anything that sounds remotely like a jazz background. For half of it, Hartman is accompanied by what seems more like a classical chamber group with no strings, instead using double reeds (bassoon, oboe) and marimba. The tunes, too, aren't jazz standards but include a few contemporary show and film songs, like Henry Mancini's marvelous, underperformed "Slow, Hot Wind" and *Fiddler on the Roof*'s "Sunrise, Sunset"—not only does he refuse to jazz 'em up, he ends the latter with a cantorial wail that would make Al Jolson *kvell*.

Fortunately, Thiele also brought Hartman to Los Angeles to tape a pair of more pop-oriented projects, *Unforgettable* and *I Love Everybody*. It was an inspired idea, especially the first album, which is classic Hartman all the way through, even if a couple of cuts and arrangements on the second album are below Hartman's usual standard. Interestingly, the three sets on Impulse! consist primarily of slow ballads, while *Unforgettable*, ostensibly a pop outing, has him conforming even more to the archetype of a "jazz singer" than he does on the Coltrane album. The title track, already a hit for Nat Cole and Dinah Washington, is rip-roaringly up, and both this and "The Very Thought of You" find drummer Stan Levey supplying a steady dance beat.

I Love Everybody was a two-sided album both literally and metaphorically, the second side consisting of a "live" session (the audience noises were actually overdubbed, according to annotator Patricia Willard) orchestrated by Oliver Nelson, and the first sporting six studio cuts from Jack Pleis's baton. Even though the arrangements are a trifle jukeboxy and the beat is rather businesslike, this is superior pop music. The Pleis tracks included three excellent standards, the British "If I Had You," Johnny Green's "I Cover the Waterfront" (a particularly juicy Pleis chart that includes the verse), and "As You Desire Me," written by "Gone With the Wind" composer Allie Wrubel (and recently revived by Peggy Lee and Sinatra).

On the one hand, it's hard to believe that, given the quality of his output, ABC let Hartman go after 1966. But in the larger context of his career, it's even more astonishing that he was actually able to find a major label willing to let him make five whole records—especially in the mid-sixties, when singers who sang standards were finding the rug being pulled out from under them. Says Monte, "In 1966, when I met Johnny, the great songs, from people like Gershwin and Cole Porter, were still in vogue—you could still turn on the radio and hear them. By 1968 it was over for that and for about ten years the culture didn't want to hear those songs anymore. They weren't played, except in jazz clubs. Johnny survived during the seventies by going to small jazz clubs in the black upper-middle-class neighborhoods in Philadelphia, Baltimore, and Washington."

He also took to the international road again. "I had to skip all over the world in order to make a living," he said. Landing in Australia in 1968, he was popular enough to star in his own television special (still never shown in any form in his native country) and to make a pair of albums in Japan for their branch of Capitol in 1972, *Trane's Favorites* and *Hartman Meets Hino.*

Both were spin-offs of the Coltrane album, the former being dedicated to the late great tenor (although it did include a few songs never performed by Trane) and the latter reprising the format of the 1963 album in teaming Hartman with a rhythm section and a leading jazz horn, in this case Tokyo trumpeter Terumasa Hino. Generally, the Japanese rhythm section seems to be trying to push him into more conventionally jazzy tempos and he sounds uncomfortable throughout, although there are some exceptional moments. "On a Clear Day," "Fly Me to the Moon," and "The Shadow of Your Smile" all give us the chance to hear Hartman put his tonsils to three standards new to his discography.

Hartman still had eight albums left in him, three of which were, to be blunt, atrocious. *Today* (1972) and *I've Been There* (1973), both on the Perception label, find him in the company of an excellent band (including two more top tenors, Jimmy Heath and George Coleman) doing inappropriate contemporary hits (like "Betcha Golly Wow"). However, when an independent producer-songwriter, Gene Novello, hired him to do an album of his own inferior material, titled *The Many Moods of Johnny Hartman* (Musicor, 1976), the results were even worse.

But all was not lost: Another package from Japan, *Live at Sometime* (1977), was the best of his later projects and was later rereleased with live tapes from Boston. He works in his most intimate setting ever, just piano and bass, which is fine because the musicians playing those instruments are Roland Hanna and George Mraz. Hartman doesn't need drums or anyone else to sound great, in spite of the fact that he's working with dated, meager material like "Feelings" and "The Way We Were." The title of *Once in Every Life* (Beehive, 1980), which gave him an all-star group with Frank Wess and Billy Taylor, proved prophetic as it earned Hartman his only Grammy nomination. *This One's for Tedi* (Audiophile, 1980), Hartman's final session, was a fittingly sentimental dedication to his wife, who, at the time of the singer's death in 1983, had been married to him for twenty-six years.

Hartman never exactly had a "comeback" because he had never exactly "arrived" to begin with. However, by the end of the seventies, it became clear that although the kind of standard songs that he had championed for so long would never regain their popular status, they were at last beginning to be taken seriously as a genre of art music. Hartman benefited from the exposure given to him by the *Times'* John Wilson as well as composer-critic Alec Wilder. Wilder also wrote a song for Hartman, although it wasn't surprising that the singer elected not to sing it, given the composer's penchant for depressing songs and Hartman's insistence on avoiding same. (With a new set of lyrics, the same melody became the Sinatra masterpiece "A Long Night" on *She Shot Me Down*.)

By the early eighties, Hartman was working in all the major jazz rooms, as well as the city's two priciest cabarets, Michael's Pub and Marty's; earlier, he had headlined in two concerts at Town Hall. Interest in both jazz and the great standards was increasing again, and had Hartman lived a few more years, he would have doubtlessly been snapped up by one or more of the major labels that were rediscovering jazz at that time.

In February 1983, he played New York's Blue Note, and in April announced that he had signed with another independent label, Stash Records, this time to record an album of Harold Arlen's songs. Then, around the time of his sixtieth birthday in July, Hartman arrived in England only to realize that he was too ill to work, and was forced to cancel all of his engagements there. In August, a benefit was held in Greenwich Village both to pay tribute to Hartman and raise money for his medical costs. He died of lung cancer on September 15.

It wasn't until nearly fifteen years after Hartman's death that he achieved the kind of success that had been denied him in his lifetime, when movie auteur Clint Eastwood employed liberal excerpts from Hartman's *Once in Every Life* album in his hit romance *The Bridges of Madison County*. All at once his name was being dropped in all sorts of major magazines, and virtually all sixteen of his albums, even the dogs of the mid-seventies, were restored to print via CD. The "discovery" occurred too late for

Hartman himself to enjoy it, although Tedi Hartman is still alive to enjoy it for him. Just the same, it's good that it happened. His was a talent that realized its full potential artistically, even if the world gave him far too few opportunities to display it.

Dick Haymes (1916–1980)

Special thanks to Dr. Ruth Prigozy, who, in a happy instance of author-to-author generosity, shared with me information from her book, The Life of Dick Haymes, *well before it was published in 2006.*

Dick Haymes's talent seems beyond reproach—without a doubt he was one of the best ballad singers ever heard in American popular music—but his career choices beyond music often seem questionable. Most of the pre-Prigozy literature concerning Haymes dwells on his spectacular series of failures—that string of flop marriages (most infamously to movie star Rita Hayworth), problems with alcoholism, the Internal Revenue Service, the Immigration and Naturalization Board, and the most fearful phenomenon of them all, Hollywood mogul and godfather Harry Cohn.

It makes more sense to concentrate instead on what Haymes did right. Along with Sinatra, Peggy Lee, Perry Como, and a few others, Haymes was an archetypal example of a pop singer who had the good sense to apprentice with a big band and absorb its musical values. In fact, apart from his frequent duet partner, Helen Forrest, no singer chose better in the succession of bands that he appeared with: Harry James, Benny Goodman, and Tommy Dorsey.

Haymes is often characterized as spending his career in Frank Sinatra's shadow. Sixty years after the fact, that may seem like a logical conclusion, since he followed Sinatra first into James's band, then Dorsey's, and then into a solo career. But at the time, Sinatra viewed Haymes not as a follower but as a real threat: One of the reasons Sinatra broke his contract with Dorsey—getting himself into a world of legal trouble—was that he wanted to beat Haymes to the punch in establishing himself as a solo act. Yet Haymes had already worked as a single in early 1942, before Benny Goodman and then Dorsey beckoned. He chose to go back to working as a band vocalist because Dorsey made him an offer he couldn't refuse. A few months later, when both Haymes and Sinatra were on their own, Haymes was the first of the new generation of postband pop singers to make solo recordings.

It's easy to see why Haymes would have been so popular, between his smooth style, robust voice, and Irish good looks; but it's hard to see what history has against him. Whenever his name has appeared in print in the last forty years, he's dismissed either as a crying drunk has-been who used Rita Hayworth as a punching bag or as a wannabe Sinatra rival deservedly dispatched by the future Chairman. Despite his megastar stature in the late forties, he is perhaps the least well remembered pop star of his caliber and his era. Even Buddy Clark, who certainly can't be said to sound more "contemporary" than Haymes, is considerably better represented in the CD market. (Haymes's music is relegated to his underground fan base of dedicated buffs who are unfailing in their devotion, publishing a quarterly journal and regularly issuing semiprivate CDs of broadcasts and other rarities.)

None of which seems to matter to Universal Music, which controls the vast bulk of his catalogue (his Decca sessions of 1943–52) and which, even at the height of the CD reissue boom, had zero faith that Haymes might sell well enough to justify even a comprehensive double-disc set of greatest hits. Whereas considerably lesser talents such as Johnny Ray and Frankie Laine rate Bear Family box sets, Haymes doesn't have the rock or country connections necessary for consideration by that label (which has more of a fifties than a forties orientation). Perhaps a full evaluation of Haymes will not be possible until the hundreds of 78s he cut for Decca in that decade (roughly the same years as Sinatra's stay at Columbia) are reissued in toto, an occurrence that, well into the new millennium, seems unlikely. (Even Dr. Prigozy, admittedly not a musicologist, hardly analyzes any of her subject's many records.)

Yet, musically, Haymes made the right decisions, and chose the right people to learn from. He's best remembered as the most prominent of a number of former band singers who went solo during the Second World War. They had all grown up on Bing Crosby, and it's easy to hear that Bing was their primary influence. Yet by the early forties, Frank Sinatra was fast emerging as the dominant voice of American pop and it was impossible to ignore him. Singers like Haymes, Johnny Desmond, David Allyn, Bob Manning (the latter two being highly indebted to Haymes), and others reveal some of the deep, rich baritone sensibility of Crosby, tempered with the heightened sensitivity of Sinatra. Haymes was going for the best of both worlds. He couldn't quite do as many different things as Crosby and Sinatra—his up-tempo singing was nothing to speak of (he could get through a fast up-tempo song, although it was hardly his forte). But when it came to singing a love song, there was practically no one who did it better.

This most all-American of success and failure stories was actually born in Argentina, in 1916. His father had been a rancher, his mother a concert singer and voice teacher. His parents separated when he was a toddler—he never saw his birth father again—and his mother relocated with him to the United States, where she remarried and had a second son (Robert, better known as the songwriter Bob Haymes, author of the standard "That's All"). The two brothers were raised both in the States and in various parts of Europe, including France and Switzerland. From an early age, both Richard and Robert wanted to make it in music and showbiz,

and in the mid-thirties, as a teenager, Haymes sang on local gigs with bandleader Johnny Johnson.

He spent the late thirties bouncing back and forth between the two coasts. At seventeen, he headed for Hollywood, where he managed to get some extra work in pictures and make a few radio appearances in Los Angeles. He returned to New York, but a few years later moved back to L.A., this time with his family, and in 1938 landed a bit part in a movie called *Dramatic School*. Back in New York a year later, he sang a few gigs (not recorded) with trumpeter Bunny Berigan's orchestra. The band was never a roaring commercial success, but at least by working with Berigan, however briefly, he attracted the attention of other, more successful bandleaders: Goodman, Dorsey, and James.

Then, a few months later, Haymes made contact with James, who, as it happened, wasn't doing too much better than the hapless Berigan at that early point. The story goes that in early 1940, Haymes, having tried both band singing and movie acting, was trying to make it as a songwriter; supposedly, he auditioned some of his compositions for James, who rejected the material but was impressed with Haymes as a vocalist. And, coincidentally, James had an opening for a singer in his band, which was still less than a year old.

Despite the leader's obvious charisma—not to mention his superb musicianship—and his high visibility as a former star of Benny Goodman's orchestra, the James band faltered in its first year out. Within a few months, his two star singers—Sinatra and Connie Haines—left to find greener pastures with Tommy Dorsey. Things grew especially bleak for him when he was temporarily dropped by Columbia and had to sign with Varsity Records, Eli Oberstein's bargain-basement label. For James, Haymes was a perfect replacement for Sinatra, and for the singer it was a job, and he abandoned the idea of being a songwriter. (His brother, Bob, went through a similar process but in reverse, having started as a boy singer with Bob Chester and Freddy Martin, and then gone on to his career as a composer.)

Haymes cut his first vocals with James for Varsity on March 18, 1940, two songs about ambition (which could be construed as either romantic or professional) and about taking risks, the quickly forgotten "You've Got Me out on a Limb" and the future jazz standard "How High the Moon." In the next two sessions, he recorded, among other tunes, some of the earliest versions of the standards "Fools Rush In" and "The Nearness of You." "Mister Meadowlark," best known for the duet recording by Crosby and lyricist Johnny Mercer, is notable for Haymes in that it's the first song he recorded by Walter Donaldson, the composer responsible for what would be the singer's biggest-ever hit, "Little White Lies," and for James in that the introduction anticipates the opening vamp to his classic "Cherry."

There's a touch of the tenor in these very earliest sessions, done when the singer was twenty-one and twenty-two, which makes him sound a little bit like Glenn Miller's Ray Eberle.

The Haymes-James recordings fall into three categories: the Varsity sides (roughly fourteen), a number of World transcriptions, and the twenty-five sides James made featuring the singer upon his return to Columbia. Haymes had the distinction of being part of the James crew when the trumpeter finally broke through to the big time. The first James-Haymes session for Columbia occurred on January 8, 1941—and the first thing that listeners both then and now noticed is how much better the recording quality is, and that both the band and the singer sound much more confident and assured. The first two Columbia sessions include some interesting diversions for the singer: There's the exotic "Montevideo" (later revived by Bobby Short) and the most extreme swinger Haymes would attempt in his entire career, a riotous and somewhat schizophrenic "Ol' Man River."

Neither of these approaches would prove long-term career paths for Haymes. However, on the third Columbia date, James adds a four-piece string section to the band for the first time and things really start to happen. Haymes's first sides with the expanded orchestra are nice but not outstanding. The singer and the band were solidifying their style, and both were steadily rising in popularity, even though none of their records together was an overwhelming hit: The most successful was "I'll Get By," cut in one of the early string sessions but which, like the James-Sinatra "All or Nothing at All," didn't catch on until the war and the recording ban.

The James-Haymes combination improved tremendously over the course of less than two years. Neither of their final sides together, "Rancho Pillow" (like "My Little Buckaroo," a song about a little kid dreaming of being a cowboy) and "Minka" (another of Tin Pan Alley's many ersatz-Russian songskis), is a standard, but the twosome makes great records of them just the same. Especially on the well-recorded Columbia sides, Haymes sounds marvelously confident, relaxed, and assured. As noted, his mother, Marguerite, was a vocal teacher, and from almost the beginning Haymes's voice sounds well trained and comfortable in all registers. He almost sounds too assured and confident: On "All or Nothing at All," done as a World transcription roughly two years after the James-Sinatra Brunswick recording, and on the future classic torch song "You Don't Know What Love Is," he sounds more robust than vulnerable, and it would take him a long time before he made any significant headway in that area. (The fittingly torchy remake on *Moondreams* is a considerable improvement. In 1941, he sounds as if he literally doesn't know what love is. By 1957 he sounds as if he's learned the hard way.)

Like Sinatra with Dorsey, Haymes in those days was an all-purpose vocalist, doing all kinds of songs in all kinds of tempos. But it was on the ballads such as "Lament to Love" (by a young singer who had considerably more success than Haymes as a composer, Mel Tormé), "You Don't Know What Love Is," "My Silent Love," and "Day Dreaming" that Haymes found his stride.

Nineteen forty-two was a busy year: He left James, ostensibly to form his own orchestra, but like many fledgling leaders, wasn't able to keep it together as the draft was heating up. (Haymes himself avoided the service through his resident alien status, which became a bone of contention ten years later.) He did radio work, and appeared briefly with Charlie Spivak's orchestra, and then accepted a spot with Benny Goodman. He sang with Goodman at the New York Paramount, home of Sinatra's past triumphs with Dorsey and future triumph as a soloist. And he also did one Columbia session with the clarinetist, resulting in the four most consistently excellent titles of his early career, all first-rate songs marvelously played by this near-greatest of BG bands and brilliantly sung by Haymes: two BG covers of Glenn Miller hits, "I've Got a Gal in Kalamazoo" (you wouldn't think he would do so well with a rhythmic novelty, but he does) and "Serenade in Blue" (as with Glenn Miller, it's more danceable than torchy or blue), "Take Me" (again, not quite as vulnerable as Sinatra and Dorsey's version), and jazz-blues composer Jesse Stone's "Idaho" (the inspiration seems to be any one of Crosby's late thirties schottische-swing concoctions). (All Haymes's 1940–42 recordings are, fortunately, available on CD, the Varsitys on the Belgian Classics label, the World transcriptions on Circle, and the 1941–42 James and Goodman sessions on an excellent two-CD set from Sony Special Products and Collector's Classics.)

Haymes left Goodman when the very persuasive Tommy Dorsey came a-callin' in search of a replacement for the departing Sinatra. He actually sang on at least one broadcast with Dorsey in August 1942, when Sinatra was allegedly down with laryngitis, before permanently succeeding him a few weeks later. The Dorsey-Haymes tenure, which lasted roughly six months, was not a particularly happy one, not least because the infamous AFM recording ban had already begun and Haymes was prevented from doing any commercial sessions with the band. (BMG is in possession of a number of live recordings of Haymes with Dorsey from 1942–43, and it's hoped that these will someday see the light of day.)

After replacing Sinatra with James and then Dorsey, Haymes appears to have been in a neck-and-neck race with the Voice; an article on the singer in the October–November issue of *Bandleader* magazine is titled "Challenge to Sinatra." Both men were basing the rough outlines of their careers on Crosby, in a rush to conquer recordings, radio, and motion pictures—although unlike Crosby, both Haymes and Sinatra still toured and made personal appearances.

Like Sinatra, Haymes was initially on CBS, with a show called *Here's to Romance*, and like Crosby, he was recording for Decca Records, but like neither he was signed by Twentieth Century Fox. The Decca deal turned out to be crucial. That label, the youngest of the three majors, was the most competitive, and willing to buck the American Federation of Musicians' ban by recording their new star singer with an a cappella choir. Thus, Haymes's first solo recordings were out a few weeks before Sinatra. Decca was also the first of the three to come to terms with the union, giving Haymes the opportunity to record a full year's worth of releases with full orchestral accompaniment before his rivals could catch up.

It's been noted—by Billy May and others—that Sinatra was keen to distinguish his early solo work from his earlier big band work by working with a lush string section and a semiclassical sound. Haymes and Perry Como were following a similar path, Como landing some notable hits with classical adaptations, while the textures of Haymes's accompaniments owed more to Brahms than to Harry James. Sinatra's musical director was the very classically grounded Axel Stordahl, while Haymes's most frequent orchestrator was Gordon Jenkins. Whereas Stordahl owed more to Ravel and Debussy, Jenkins sounded more like Chopin. When Sinatra, ten years later, wanted to return to what was essentially a new version of the Stordahl big string sound, he in turn recruited Jenkins.

Still, there were differences: Sinatra had his roots in Crosby, but he clearly represented a break from the Crosby technique, the start of something new, while Haymes's stylistic allegiance to the older style was always front and center. Both Haymes and Sinatra sang old songs, but much of Haymes's material seemed like sentimental oldies. Sinatra, on the other hand, sang primarily one- and two-decade-old works by the likes of Rodgers and Hart and Jerome Kern, which were not nostalgic favorites but had lyrics that delivered the multidimensional irony that Sinatra required. Both Haymes and the forties Sinatra came off as clean-cut, romantically motivated young swains, but Sinatra almost always had that ironic edge that cut a little deeper.

Fans of Haymes, naturally, could not have cared less: There was no beating him on something like "Little White Lies," a blockbuster hit that supposedly sold two and a half million singles for him. It's hard to imagine Sinatra being able to sound naive enough, even in 1946, to effectively sing such retro faves as "Back Home in Indiana" and "Let the Rest of the World Go By" (not to mention "'Twas Only an Irishman's Dream"). Such tentative texts as these would have crumbled at the first hint of irony; what they require is an interpreter like Haymes, who sings them exactly on their own terms, updated to the mid-forties sonically but with the age-old sentiment still intact. The combination of that deep, resonant voice and that unquestionably romantic attitude made Haymes irresistible to nearly as many bobby-soxers as swooned for Crosby and Sinatra.

It's in the Decca sessions of 1943–52 that one hears the essential Haymes, mostly with Jenkins but also with the brilliant Victor Young (who not only accompanied Haymes on Irish songs but on "When a Gypsy Makes His Violin Cry") and a charming 78 album of Irving Berlin songs with cocktail keyboardist Carmen Cavallaro. In addition to all those oldies, Haymes also introduced a number of future standards, among them "The More I See You" and "I Wish I Knew." The latter two, by Harry Warren, were from the Fox film *Billy Rose's Diamond Horseshoe* (1945), that rare example of a Haymes starring role that was not a period piece—most of the time he seemed to be done up in turn-of-the-century drag.

The best of all Haymes's classic recordings may well be his opulent series of eighteen duets recorded in the late forties with Helen Forrest. The two singers complement each other brilliantly—her overdoing it just a little bit, him playing it just a little bit cool, and the two voices meeting each other halfway. This is one of the finest series of boy-girl duos ever laid down on wax, ranking with the best of Lawrence and Gormé as well as Bing Crosby and his various female partners. (Unfortunately, the series of sides Haymes cut with Decca contractees the Andrews Sisters—who did their best work with Crosby—isn't nearly as good.)

As the forties progressed, the Haymes-Jenkins relationship matured into one of the outstanding singer-arranger combinations in pop music. When Jenkins backed Martha Tilton in 1942, he sounded just like any other prewar house bandleader—say Harry Sosnik or Leonard Joy—but by 1946–47, the classic Jenkins style (best heard on albums like Sinatra's *September of My Years* and Nat Cole's *Love Is the Thing*) is complete. One wishes Haymes had done more of Jenkins's own compositions, since their team-up on his "Skyscraper Blues" (a sort of bonus track to the conductor's extended work *Manhattan Tower*) is one of his nicest sides. In general, they did fine on better, newer songs like "Stella by Starlight," but really shone on older titles like "My Silent Love." Somehow, the classic status of these familiar songs enabled Jenkins to view them almost as much as orchestral as vocal records, and many of them begin with comparatively long orchestral preludes. (Haymes isn't heard at all until twenty-four seconds into "Silent Love.")

Haymes and Jenkins share a penchant for old-fashioned simplicity, which comes to the fore especially when they go to work on older songs by Irving Berlin—say, the ancient waltzes like "What'll I Do." Everything fits into place on this masterful 1947 interpretation—Haymes's stunning baritone, the leader's sobbing strings; they make the song work all over again without substantially changing it. On one singles session in 1947, Haymes and pianist Cavallaro recorded eight Berlin songs for a 78 album, which was later expanded with additional Haymes-Berlin tracks (mostly conducted by Jenkins) into a British 12" LP. He recorded a number of songs from Berlin's comparatively unsuccessful *Miss Liberty* as well as from the Berlin blockbuster *Call Me Madam*. In fact, I'm sure there are some musical comedy buffs who only know of Haymes for his role in *State Fair* (Rodgers and Hammerstein's only original movie musical score), and as Ethel Merman's Decca duet partner on "You're Just in Love."

Haymes sang as many substandard songs as Clark or Como or Crosby, but his proximity to Jack Kapp, the first mogul of the original cast album, led to his recording a great many interesting tunes from Broadway musicals. He is among the few nonshow singers to ever tackle Morton Gould and Dorothy Fields's "A Cow and a Plow and a Frau" from *Arms and the Girl* and Kurt Weill's "Thousands of Miles" and the title song from *Lost in the Stars*. Decca Broadway (the show-music division of Universal Music, which controls Haymes's MCA catalogue) owes it to the world to release a CD of *Dick Haymes Sings Irving Berlin* as well as *Dick Haymes Sings Broadway*, which would include his stunning renditions of two *Finian's Rainbow* hits, "How Are Things in Glocca Morra" and "When I'm Not Near the Girl I Love." Here, Haymes finds the perfect halfway point between the proscenium arch and the jukebox.

On the eve of the 1948 AFM ban, Haymes and Jenkins recorded their biggest hit—the track one most frequently encounters on anthologies of forties gold records. Originally published in 1930, "Little White Lies" was one of composer Walter Donaldson's major efforts at writing lyrics as well as music, and Haymes recorded it a few months after the songwriter's death in July 1947. Apart from the seventeen-year-old song itself, the arrangement seems to be reliving the past—not Haymes's, but Sinatra's. The chart seems exactly like one of Sinatra's Dorsey-era hits with the Pied Pipers, like "I'll Never Smile Again," with Haymes singing very slowly, surrounded by a close harmony group, the Four Hits and a Miss; he actually sounds several years younger and higher than on most of his other recordings from the period, as he occasionally sticks his head over the group. The baritone is more like a tenor here, and he continued to use that slow harmony sound in subsequent sessions.

"Little White Lies" was Haymes's last huge hit. It was also extremely popular in England, where in the early fifties it caught the ears of a pair of teenaged guitarists and songwriters, Paul McCartney and John Lennon. "One of John's favorite songs was called 'Little White Lies,' and that always surprised me," McCartney said in a *New Yorker* profile in 2007. "When I met him, I went, 'Oh wow! That's something we have in common.'" (The article didn't get any more specific, but it was obviously Haymes's recording that McCartney and Lennon had to have heard.)

Some of the later Haymes Deccas are among his very best, such as "Count Every Star" with Artie Shaw's accompaniment, and "Here's to My Lady." However, more often he sounds increasingly anachronistic. Even in 1945, he was somewhat behind the times, albeit charmingly so, but he was entirely unable to compete with the oncoming wave of novelties and general loudness that was overtaking American pop as it began the transition from a music for grown-ups to one for children. He addresses the young Tony Bennett's melodramatic "Boulevard of Broken Dreams" in 1950, while his "David and Bathsheba" sounds as if he's trying to come up with a Frankie Laine–style mock-gospel tune, the sort of thing that could serve as a theme for a Cecil B. DeMille movie. Al Martino's first hit, "Here in My Heart," is singularly unsuited to the combination of Haymes and the Andrews Sisters.

The final parallel with Sinatra is that both careers went south in the early fifties. Both men suffered through scandals and ignominious divorces, and in both cases it seems clear that the public simply got tired of their vintage World War II heroes. Sinatra was able to slowly and painfully pick himself up, dust himself off, and start all over again with a whole new musical persona; Haymes wasn't. Still, he produced some outstanding work in the last twenty-five years of his life. He sings with greater maturity and prowess as the years go on, even if, unlike Sinatra, he doesn't sound like a whole new singer—he sounds like an older, and in most cases better, version of his younger self.

Paradoxically, while the vast majority of the classic Haymes material, the Decca singles of the forties, has never been on any long-playing medium, virtually everything from the fringes—the beginning and end of his career (before and after Decca)—has seen the light of day on compact disc. All the commercial big band material from prior to 1943 is available, as are the majority of his post-Decca sessions.

Later albums include two swinging projects done in close collaboration with songwriter and pianist Cy Coleman, *Oh Look at Me Now* (1958, on CD as *Swinging Session*) and *King Richard the Swing Hearted* (1962), the first of which featured Coleman's quartet and orchestra conducted by Maury Laws, the second under the command of Ralph Burns, both featuring several tunes by Coleman. Both were done for rack-job labels, and though they don't quite make the point that Haymes could compete with Sinatra or his disciples as a Swingin' Lover, they're enjoyably classy sets nonetheless.

Still later Haymes LPs include two packages of contemporary songs, *Now and Then* (1968–69, reissued as *The Great Song Stylists Volume One*), featuring one of the more ambitious arias of Haymes's career, "My Favorite Color Is Blue," which sounds as if it came from Russia with love, recorded in England, and *Live at the Cocoanut Grove* (1973) with Les Brown's Band of Renown. Haymes doing Jobim's

"Wave" was an inspired idea (a whole album of bossa nova would have been even better), and his treatment of the Mancini-Mercer "Whistling Away the Dark" was masterful, but Haymes doing "Me and Bobby McGee" was not. Now a fixture on the nostalgia circuit, and no longer even claiming to attempt a "comeback," Haymes recorded two albums' worth of material for George Buck's Audiophile label in October 1976, and finished his recording career with a package produced by longtime fan club president Roger Dooner.

In listening to these various packages from his last decade, one can only conclude that they all offer pretty fair singing for an alcoholic has-been who died a thousand deaths before he closed his eyes for the last time in 1980. Although his voice did darken in the fifties and sixties, he didn't live long enough—and he had enough technique—to avoid major register descents of the sort that affected Jolson and Sinatra in their later years. His voice on the seventies recordings (his fifties) still sounds light and agile.

It's Haymes's first two long-playing projects, produced by Capitol Records in 1955 and 1957 (*Moondreams* and *Rain or Shine*), that offer what is easily the finest singing of his entire career. When Capitol gave him a shot, he was offered his choice of musical director, and while he could have gone with such established greats as Nelson Riddle (who had actually directed a few of his final Decca dates in 1952), Billy May, or longtime collaborator Gordon Jenkins, he instead recruited a young Canadian conductor named Ian Bernard. Featuring a small string section and prominent clarinet solos from the raspy-toned Jimmy Giuffre, these two sets offer Haymes at his deepest, singing ballads at a gut level reminiscent of Sinatra on *In the Wee Small Hours* and the best of Billie Holiday. Even though he flies at an altitude very close to Sinatra here, I don't think that Haymes has ever sounded more like himself.

This was as open and as vulnerable as it was possible for him to get. On "The Way You Look Tonight," he sounds incredibly exposed—like Sinatra on *Close to You*—and anticipates the best of Johnny Hartman. At the end of the track he builds to an optimistic, somewhat robust closer, but I prefer the first chorus, where, without altering the grammar of Dorothy Fields's lyric, he changes the whole meaning of the song—instead of being in the moment, thinking about how he will reflect on "the way you look tonight" in the future, it becomes a meditation on love and loss in which the speaker is thinking back on the past. I'm sure that Sinatra heard this album, just as he knew Nat Cole's "Stardust," and I can't help wondering if in both cases he deliberately decided to make very different treatments of these songs to avoid comparison—which might be why his own "The Way You Look Tonight" is a swinger and his "Stardust" includes only the verse. Unfortunately, like the Decca material, *Moondreams* and *Rain or Shine* have never been on an American compact disc, although they were reissued on a second British CD package in 2006.

In the absence of a comprehensive collection of the bulk of Haymes's work (in his native land at least; there are a number of British imports, including a four-CD retrospective on Jasmine), it should be noted that his fans have made a goodly amount of his radio and transcription material available, including an ongoing series on the all-Haymes Ballad label and a sampling of his World transcriptions on Audiophile. (One of the better releases issued by the Haymes Society is their *On the Air Vol. Three*, which includes radio performances—which offer an interesting supplement to the two great Capitol albums.) His is one of the richest legacies in all of pop singing; it's a shame that no one can hear the richest part of it.

Bill Henderson (born 1926)

Never underestimate the power of the rasp. However, you wouldn't be the first if you did—the rasp is a traditionally neglected element of jazz and pop singing. There have been dozens of female singers who followed Dinah Washington's lead in taking the techniques of church music and applying them to popular songs, but only a couple of major male singers who have utilized the virtues of the rasp, most notably one of the best known of all pop stars, Ray Charles, and the lesser known Bill Henderson. (Louis Armstrong, of course, had a rasp that was all his own.)

The rasp or the wheeze can make a love song more romantic and a soulful number more passionate. Billy Eckstine never rasped, his voice was always perfect and smooth. Yet Ray Charles and Bill Henderson use the rasp as a key to sounding tender and vulnerable. So, for that matter, did Sarah Vaughan and Judy Garland in their very different ways. All of them realized that the occasional gasp for breath gave a more human dimension to their work.

The rasp—as opposed to the gasp—is related to character singing, as in the distinct voice of Al Bowlly or Jack Teagarden. You'll also hear the rasp in the singing of Johnny Mercer, whom Henderson once honored with a songbook album. Once Mercer himself told Henderson, "You sing like me, only better," and he was right. Only Henderson and Charles have unlocked this particular code. When Henderson goes for the high notes on "You Make Me Feel So Young," you're just waiting for the instant when his voice will crack. Charles might have dropped the other shoe and let that happen, underscoring it with a shriek, but Henderson stays on pitch.

Henderson's first album, straightforwardly titled *Bill Henderson Sings*, recorded in 1959 (and included on the CD *His Complete Vee-Jay Recordings, Volume 1*) opens with another Henderson trademark. He starts with "Bye Bye Blackbird," a 1926 song so beloved of jazz and pop performers that it has practically become a folk song. Henderson makes it sound even more like one. Like many songs of the era, it's about avoiding one's troubles by going back home, and Mort Dixon's lyric starts with the line "Packed up all my care and woe." I always thought that was odd, in the sense, Why would you want to pack up all your care and woe to take them with you? Shouldn't you be leaving them behind? However, Henderson makes it sound as if he wants to be handed his cares and woes in order to confront them.

There are only a few really important male jazz-pop singers I regard as chronically underappreciated: Johnny Hartman, Jackie Paris, and Bill Henderson. (You might add Andy Bey, Freddy Cole, and Little Jimmy Scott to the list, but they at least enjoyed a proper moment of discovery and were recorded more extensively later in their lives.) Henderson's professional career parallels that of his fellow Chicagoan Lorez Alexandria. Like Alexandria, he was hard to pigeonhole. She wasn't strictly from Dinah's church, and Henderson likewise is positioned between the crooners and the blues shouters. Like Alexandria, he cut his first albums for a local Chicago label, including one with Ramsey Lewis, and then eventually settled in Los Angeles, where early on he made a classic album (she had made two at that point), and then, after the mid-sixties, was hardly heard from again. He also became a fixture on the local City of the Angels jazz scene, and cut a few further albums for producer Albert Marx of Discovery Records. Unlike Alexandria, however, Henderson supported himself very comfortably as an actor.

His birthday is generally given as 1930, but he admits to four years earlier. His father, a member of Chicago's black professional class, taught him the value of singing softly. He later told Jim Gavin (quoted in the notes to the Vee-Jay reissue) that his father's favorite song was "There's Danger in Your Eyes, Cherie," a 1930 piece recorded memorably by Al Bowlly. Henderson sang as a child vaudevillian, but spent the years after that fluctuating between school, "day jobs," and trying to make it as a singer. A stint in the army, surprisingly, provided him with musical opportunities, when he was assigned to sing with an army band that also featured Vic Damone (already the voice behind several hit singles). Throughout the 1950s he scuffled across Chicago looking for a chance to be heard, often unburdening himself to friend Joe Williams, who was in the same boat and a decade older on top of it.

There never was a breakthrough for Henderson, the way there was for Williams when he joined Count Basie in 1954. Yet plenty of people were willing to put themselves on the line to give him a chance: When he came to New York in 1958, Billy Taylor introduced him to all the independent jazz producers in town, which resulted in a few singles on Riverside and Blue Note, which co-star keyboardists Taylor, Horace Silver, and Jimmy Smith—some

seven sides altogether. He actually played the Vanguard as a solo at this point, to little attention, but back in Chicago in 1959, Sid McCoy of Vee-Jay finally produced Henderson's first album when he was thirty-three.

Bill Henderson Sings consists of thirteen titles recorded over two sessions, one with the Ramsey Lewis Trio, the other with an all-star group directed by Benny Golson (not playing, unfortunately), including Booker Little, Yusef Lateef, and Miles Davis's rhythm section of 1959—Wynton Kelly, Paul Chambers, and Jimmy Cobb. Accompanied by either group, Henderson is solidly in a hard bop mode: He sounds undeniably modern, yet firmly rooted in the blues and the church, evidencing approximately the same timbre as the equally underrated prince of hard bop tenors, the late Hank Mobley. Like Mobley's, Henderson's music is anatomically specific: He kicks ass on swingers and tears your heart out on love songs. Norman Mapp's "Free Spirits" and especially Bobby Timmons's "Moanin'," which fuse bebop with gospel, are perfect songs for him. But so for that matter are Rodgers and Hart's "My Funny Valentine" and "It Never Entered My Mind"—he renders these two with a poignancy rarely heard in this music apart from Johnny Hartman. "Love Locked Out" is also a killer ballad, done so slowly you can practically hear love knocking, in a treatment that bears comparison with Sinatra's (on *Close to You*).

The album also introduced two all-time Henderson favorites, which he would reprise on subsequent recordings and many, many times in performance: "Joey, Joey, Joey" and "Sweet Pumpkin." It's fitting that one is slow and the other fast. Like a considerably more tender "They Call the Wind Maria," Frank Loesser's "Joey, Joey, Joey" is about a man communicating with that element, and Henderson makes it sound considerably more elemental. He opens singing, as if to himself, over Chicagoan Eldee Young's walking bass, suspending the time and virtually all the accompaniment when he stops to ponder what the wind reminds him of ("Oregon cherries, Texas avocados . . ."). With the exception of those singers who specialize in extremely slow tempos (Jimmy Scott, Shirley Horn, Andy Bey), I have heard few vocalists who are so willing to put their trust in silence—it's at moments like these, especially combined with the raspy, vulnerable timbre of his voice, that Henderson comes as close as anyone to being a vocal equivalent of Miles Davis. When he comes to the chorus, the time picks up much the way a breeze might pick up, and it seems like the most natural thing in the world for the thing to kick into tempo, and equally so for the time to completely drop out again so he can stop and think: a bit of calm in the eye of a hurricane.

Where "Joey, Joey, Joey" is elemental, "Sweet Pumpkin" is terpsichorean, Henderson's timing working like that an expert dancer. His "Sweet

Pumpkin" is light, upbeat, dancing, and while it's actually not all that much faster than "Joey," Henderson makes it seem much more optimistic with his attitude. Instead of stopping the tempo to make a dramatic point, he pumps up the volume and rides the tempo as it surges—the feeling of getting louder and heavier somehow makes the thing more airbound. It almost sounds as if he's leaping in the air when he leans down on the beat and emphasizes, "*Come on admit it* and we'll walk down the aisle" and "*Say 'yes' good-lookin'*, let me share your life"; it both surprises and delights the listener.

The two CDs that comprise the *Complete Vee-Jay Recordings* series also include a number of delightful odds and ends, almost all of which are team-ups with various guest stars. There are a pair of marvelous sides by the singer with a string orchestra under the baton of Jimmy Jones; these were allegedly done for a 45 rpm single, but at nearly four minutes each, it's hard to imagine any jukebox operator or patron with the patience to get through them in an age when pop hits were generally half that length. But for the patient listener the rewards are tremendous: This is some of the most effective balladeering Henderson has ever done. He also meets pianist Harold Mabern, that young man from Memphis (as one of his albums was titled), and his group the MJT (Modern Jazz Trio) for a hard-edged Jazz Messengers–like treatment of "Sleepy."

Indeed, Henderson's most successful subsequent trips to the studio inevitably involved team-ups. His best album—at least on a par with the original Vee-Jay package—is his 1963 *Bill Henderson with the Oscar Peterson Trio*, originally released on MGM and reissued on Verve. Here is one of those perfect jazz vocal albums where everything works. Henderson once again opens with a slow, declarative melody; this time it's "You Are My Sunshine," which, like "Bye Bye Blackbird," straddles the fence between pop and folk song, and both singer and pianist employ a variety of gospel cadences. The absence of bass and drums makes this opening track sound less jazzy; in fact, when they do appear, as played by Ray Brown and Ed Thigpen, making this the very best of Peterson's ensembles, they make these tracks sound boppish.

The original album concluded with two especially strong tracks, the folk blues "Baby Mine" ("You get a line, I'll get a pole"), on which the primary accompaniment is supplied by Brown, strumming his double bass as if it were a guitar, and "Wild Is Love." The CD edition is fairly essential in that it contains four more songs, bringing the total up to sixteen. These continue the album's dichotomy of European versus jazz conceits, especially with another waltz, "Charmaine," which is not French but was written for a Hollywood silent film with a World War I setting; "Young and Foolish" (the best version before Tony Bennett and Bill Evans); and a show tune from *Plain and Fancy* that takes place in an American community modeled after very old Europe. Lastly, "Stranger on the Shore" is the Anglo-American hit by Mr. Acker Bilk, the crossover star instrumentalist who played clarinet like New Orleans by way of old London; Mr. Henderson's baritone is even raspier than Mr. Bilk's reed timbre.

The original instrumental record of "Stranger" has been recognized as the start of the British Invasion, and it was such developments in pop music that would at first sweep up Bill Henderson and then, as happened to so many other singers of his genre and generation, push him aside. He would participate in two more projects for Verve in the mid-sixties, both of which were symptomatic of the era. One of these was a brief collaboration with Count Basie. If Henderson had toured with Basie in 1960, one likes to think that they would have done a whole album together; however, since their collaboration took place five years later, and the world was a very different place by 1965, all that resulted from it (studio-wise at least) was a single track, and that was the Beatles song "Yesterday." It's surprisingly affable.

Two years after the Oscar Peterson album, Henderson made one more full-length project for Verve's Creed Taylor. This was *When My Dreamboat Comes Home* (1965), an album that has taken me at least twenty-five years to appreciate. When I first heard it, it struck me as a decidedly mixed bag, and not in the best sense of the term, yet I've gradually come to marvel at its multicultural diversity. *Dreamboat* is succinctly described as Bob Dylan meets Ramblin' Rose. This is as close as Henderson ever came to making a pop album, and it's hard to imagine what everyone was thinking: He sings over a large folkish choir doing simple, folklike songs, not one of which is actually an authentic American folk song. Instead, there are vintage twenties Tin Pan Alley songs that have, with the passing of time, assumed the patina of folk music (like "June Night," "Who's Sorry Now," and the title track, "When My Dreamboat Comes Home," beloved of country and R&B performers). There are also three contemporary show tunes ("People," "Matchmaker," and "Who Can I Turn To") that, for no reason other than Henderson's singing and the thoughtful orchestrations of Jimmy Jones and Bobby Scott, just happen to work in this folksy fashion (though the choir is generally absent on these).

Bobby Scott, who had already enjoyed a major hit with a song that everybody assumes is Brazilian ("Cast Your Fate to the Wind"), here supplies an original song that sounds as if it could easily be the work of either Woody or Arlo Guthrie, "This Is My Country." But *Dreamboat* opens with a mind-blowing interpretation of a contemporary folk song, "Lay Down Your Weary Tune"; Bob Dylan wrote and recorded it for his 1964 album, *The Times They Are A-Changin'*, but his version wasn't issued until about thirty years later (although the folk-rock group the Byrds included it on their very successful *Turn Turn*

Turn album). This is one of those early Dylan songs that really sounds as if it had been written two or three hundred years ago, and while Dylan recorded it with just his own guitar and voice, the Henderson track is a major production with orchestra and choir. Yet, for what it is, it's miraculously tastefully done. Henderson's bluesy rasp certainly qualified him to sing folk songs, no less than blues, and "Weary Tune" is an amazing performance. Verve had the good sense to issue it as a single, and you can hear why Taylor thought it had the potential to capture the folk-loving college kids as well as their parents. This is the kind of offbeat thing that should have been one of those unexpected sixties hits, like "Hello, Dolly!" or "Is That All There Is" (not to mention Tiny Tim's "Tip Toe Through the Tulips"). In the end, unfortunately, all that the *Dreamboat* album seems to have accomplished was to alienate Henderson from his core audience—the same audience that bought Oscar Peterson records.

When My Dreamboat Comes Home became even more valuable in that it was Henderson's last album for a decade. Now a Hollywood resident, he pursued a modest though successful career as an actor, with generally small speaking parts in about forty films and TV shows in the seventies, eighties, and nineties, most memorably *City Slickers* (1991), *White Men Can't Jump* (1992), and the TV special *Weird Al Yankovic: There's No Going Home*, in which he played the legendary blues singer "Blind Lemon Yankovic."

He returned to recording with three albums for Discovery Records, most notably his in-concert album *Live at the Times* (1975), followed by *Street of Dreams* (1979) and *A Tribute to Johnny Mercer* (1981). The live album opens with another roughly contemporary song, the *Midnight Cowboy* theme "Everybody's Talkin.'" It's a jazzier and more aggressive Henderson who sings it, liberally recasting the melody, swinging it more assertively than I've heard anyone else ever sing it. Henderson ends the live performance with a nonsensical, rather bizarre scat sequence in which he seems to be offering his approximation of the confusion that ensues when "everybody" is "talkin'" all at once. Otherwise, there are repeats of some Henderson perennials here, like the fifteen-year-old "Kiss and Run," "Joey," and "Pumpkin." Of the new songs, Henderson is aces on "Watch What Happens," winning the crowd over by pointing out to them that he sang a wrong note on the opener. He ranges from the very new, as in his stark and bluesy "Send in the Clowns" (with lovely piano accompaniment from Joyce Collins), to the very old, as in his opulent and bluesy "Roll 'Em Pete" (listed on the album simply as "Blues in B Flat").

After 1981, Henderson's career is even more scattershot. His most visible appearance on record is four guest vocals on *The Art of the Song*, a 1999 project by the outstanding bassist-bandleader and album conceptualist Charlie Haden and his Quartet West. This ensemble was and is an amazing amalgam of contemporary talent with the masterful pianist and accompanist Alan Broadbent and the fine tenor saxophonist Ernie Watts, abetted by a string orchestra. At seventy-two, Henderson still has that deep, chesty soulful sound, and continues to use the rasp as one of the most potent weapons in his arsenal, without it ever sounding as if the rasp is controlling him. He shines on two standards, "Why Did I Choose You" and the Van Heusen–Sinatra movie song "You My Love," and two Haden originals, "Ruth's Waltz," dedicated to Mrs. Haden, and "Easy on the Heart," both with texts by Arthur Hamilton, who was never quite able to come up with another classic song after "Cry Me a River."

Henderson is in amazingly good form on *Art of the Song*, and was equally so when he came to New York that summer for a JVC Jazz Festival concert with Haden's Q-West and a local string orchestra, and then two years after that, to play at the Algonquin as part of the jazz-Hollywood crossover revue *Made for the Movies,* with singer-pianists Eric Comstock and Dena DeRose. He did surprisingly well at both appearances, in spite of how each show was beset by disasters: I remember the 1999 JVC show, which took place on the most humid day of the summer in a former synagogue–cum–performance space that was so hot and sticky that all the violins were going out of tune. (Even so, Henderson insisted on wearing his trademark fedora.) Then, in 2001, Henderson and the *Made for the Movies* show had the misfortune to open on Tuesday, September 11. (It fared well even though few New Yorkers were going out cabareting that month.)

After the *Art of the Song* appeared on the resuscitated Verve label, Ken Druker, who then ran the reissue department of that corporation, dragged all the big wigs at Universal Music down to hear the Haden-Henderson-strings combination in concert at the Montreal Jazz Festival. Yes, Bill Henderson did a great job on the album. Yes, Henderson sounded wonderful. However, no, Verve Records was not interested in doing a new album with him. What's even more surprising is that no independent label— not Joe Fields, or Fantasy, or Telarc—stepped up to the plate, even though everyone agreed that he never sounded better.

That observation has been since verified by several additional guest shots on albums by pianist Mike Melvoin and drummer Chico Hamilton. Finally, in March 2007 a group of interested parties (including the singer's daughter, Mariko Mrakich) got together and independently produced a new CD of Henderson performing at a Santa Monica jazz club, released in 2008 as *But Beautiful: Bill Henderson Live at the Vic.* It was done as a sort of eighty-first birthday present to the singer, and on the most immediate level it's an astonishing document. The voice sounds roughly half the age it's supposed to be and you wouldn't be surprised if someone proved via carbon dating these tracks were actually recorded in 1967, not 2007. The voice is amazingly rich and full, and the rasp is as effective as always, completely under control.

He repeats a few songs—this is his third recording of both "You Are My Sunshine" and "Kiss and Run"—but that William Engvick lyric is such a classic and his performance of it (complete with a long high note that would floor a younger man) is so moving that I could listen to a whole set of him singing it over and over. He breaks ground, so to speak, in an unusual way with his vocal take on "Royal Garden Blues," an oldie from the early days of jazz associated with King Oliver (although, come to think of it, it's only a few years older than Henderson himself), a song that has hardly ever been sung by anyone. At the other end of the spectrum, and bringing him more up to date, Henderson does wonderful things with Elton John's "Sorry Seems to Be the Hardest Word." No less than "Royal Garden," "Never Make Your Move Too Soon" (suitably different from Ernestine Anderson's signature version) is still another new Henderson blues classic.

Bill Henderson is in his eighties and his rasp is still a sound for sore ears, a balm for a modern-day Gilead, and, above all else, easy on the heart.

Woody Herman (1913–1987)

Woody Herman enjoyed one of the least predictable careers in all of American music. Yet there are some aspects of his professional life that seem, in retrospect, both natural and inevitable. The basic facts are that his mom and dad, especially his father, Otto Herman, were archetypal stage parents. It was hardly the scenario of *The Jazz Singer:* Herman Senior loved show business, was excited by the idea of singing and dancing, and was completely infatuated with the idea of getting up on a stage and entertaining people. A shoemaker by trade, Otto realized that he had no talent in this area himself, but continually encouraged his son Woodrow in that direction, not that young Woody needed much pushing. By his early teens Woody was already a vaudeville veteran, bringing in a very respectable $50 a week. Then something completely unexpected happened: On his own, Woody discovered jazz, blues, and dance music, and announced to his parents that this was what he wanted to be doing.

Throughout Herman's career, those two identities worked together in perfect synchronization: Woody Herman the entertainer, the song and dance man, the crowd-pleaser, and Woody Herman the jazz innovator, the clarinet and alto soloist, the envelope-pushing purveyor of what was always the latest thing in hot jazz. He could keep the crowds thoroughly entertained while at the same time making them love whatever new form of jazz was supposed to be uncommercial. If Donald O'Connor and Stan Kenton were the same person, they would be Woody Herman.

Herman was by far the best of the singing band-leaders. That may not sound like much today, when there are precious few traditional pop singers or jazz bandleaders of note, but such characters were an important trend in the swing era. Quivering-voiced Skinnay Ennis left Hal Kemp to start a band of his own (which he acquired from Gil Evans); Bing Crosby's younger brother Bob was recruited to front an aggregate of mostly New Orleans jazz greats; board-stiff Vaughn Monroe put together a band that was much hipper than he was; and both Dolly Dawn and Ella Fitzgerald were top-drawer canaries who graduated to the roll of singing front person. That's not counting the more heavy-duty singing horn-men, like those Italianate Armstrongs, Tony Pastor and Louis Prima.

But none of them could match Woody Herman's achievement: keeping one of the finest ensembles in American music together for fifty years, while at the same time remaining one of its greatest assets. Ella Fitzgerald was a better singer, but her band was never as interesting or creative; Bob Crosby had a great band, but, sad to say, he was hardly the best singer even in his own family. Cab Calloway and, to a lesser extent, Billy Eckstine were the only singing bandleaders to match Herman on both counts. But even they were unable to compete with him in terms of longevity.

Even his name was something special: Whoever heard of a guy with two middle names? Woodrow Charles Thomas Herman was born in Milwaukee, on May 16, 1913. The first notable bands he worked with were essentially based on the West Coast, starting with Tom Gerun's, a California band that was trying to go national at the time Herman joined. (Gerun's other singers included Tony Martin, né Al Morris, and Ginny Simms.) At age nineteen, Herman sang his first recorded vocals with Gerun, "Lonesome Me" and "Sentimental Gentleman from Georgia." The latter, a rhythm-Mammy song that inspired Tommy Dorsey's nickname, is the height of hotness 1932-style, prominently featuring Herman throughout. He soars over the ensemble with his clarinet for the first chorus, and sings the second, hot and lusty in the classic Armstrong mold. Over the next few years, he also played and sang with Harry Sosnik (later to become a house conductor for Decca Records) and the very popular Gus Arnheim, then in residence at the Cocoanut Grove.

His most important apprenticeship was with Isham Jones, the songwriter who led what many regard as the greatest dance band of them all, a highly respected straight-down-the-middle band-leader who could play both hot and sweet. On Herman's first session with the band, October 1935, he is featured, appropriately, on a song that became a jazz standard, "If I Should Lose You." He sings on half a dozen titles with the Jones orchestra, among them the leader's own standard "(There Is) No Greater Love" (which Herman would readdress in 1947). Herman again breaks a familiar pattern: Most premier recordings of singers who later became famous sound higher and squeakier than their mature work (as in the case of Sinatra and Crosby); Herman, on the other hand, sounds deep and robust in his Gerun and Jones sessions, and certainly no higher than he would sound with his own band.

Most of the Jones sides spotlight Herman as a balladeer, but "The Day I Let You Get Away from Me" gives us Woody the swing singer. He really comes into his own on vocals recorded over two sessions in March 1936, done with a small hot combo drawn from the Jones ranks that Decca billed as Isham Jones' Juniors. Three titles in particular— "I've Had the Blues So Long," "Take It Easy," and especially "Fan It"—introduce Woody the blues singer, the most outstanding white vocalist to specialize in the form since Jack Teagarden. "Fan It," which became one of his signatures, is a classic call-and-response blues feature associated with Chicago-based Frankie Half-Pint Jaxon, who yelped the blues in a high falsetto that anticipated both Herman and Little Jimmy Scott.

When Jones retired—temporarily, it turned out—his label, Decca, informed Herman that they were happy with the sales of the blues-oriented sides he had been making and wanted to continue working with him. With support from MCA as well, Herman was able to put together his own dance band at the end of 1936. This was a cooperative group (like the Casa Loma) with Herman as leader, star singer, and clarinet and alto soloist, plus a core of five fellow former Ishamites.

This first Herman band (not yet a "Herd") was billed as the Band That Plays the Blues, and the blues were indeed Herman's stock-in-trade. The band played a lot of them, most with excellent vocals by him. When one listens to them consecutively, it becomes clear that he was the original rock 'n' roller, the first man to package and perform the blues and race music for white people. Unlike most later rock stars, however, he was never tempted to dilute the blues or compromise their integrity; even on the long, two-sided "Blues Upstairs"/"Blues Downstairs," he doesn't fancy them up or dumb them down.

The playing of this early band is well up to the level of most black bands of the era, such as Erskine Hawkins or Al Cooper, though not quite up to Basie or Ellington. Old and new blues (and similar pieces) like "Doctor Jazz," "Chips' Blues," "Jumpin' Blues," "Bessie's Blues," Andy Razaf's "Peach Tree Street," and many others, are all outstanding examples of the form. Even such novelty pieces as "Calliope Blues" and "Laughing Boy Blues" (which has Herman singing the blues while composer Sunny Skylar chuckles maniacally) are superior slices of blues-driven pop music.

At first glance, it may seem as if Herman's vocal ballad features with the early band were also blues-driven, in such titles as "Blue Evening," "Blue Pre-lude," "Blue Dawn," even "Don't Be Blue, Little Pal, Don't Be Blue" and "It's a Blue World." Indeed, Decca seems to have given Herman every title they could think of with the word "blue" in it, much as RCA gave Glenn Miller every title that came along with the word "moon" in it. But Herman had long since developed into one of the best all-purpose boy singers in the music business, and the blues were only one of many strings to his bow. By 1940, he was an especially accomplished crooner; for instance, he sounds considerably more poised than Frank Sinatra (two years his junior) on "The Sky Fell Down" and "The Isle of May," which young Blue Eyes recorded with Tommy Dorsey.

Herman would reach his peak vocally in the postwar period, but the early Deccas have much to offer vocal fans. Three recommended samplers are *Blues on Parade* (Decca Jazz), *The Band That Plays the Blues, 1937–1941*, and *At the Woodchopper's Ball*, (ASV Living Era). The band's female singers are not notable, and Herman himself wisely sings most of the better songs, ballads as well as blues. He also collaborated with a wide range of big-name guest stars: the Andrews Sisters, Connee Boswell, and two memorable dates with Bing Crosby, which yielded one of Burke and Van Heusen's most touching (and little known) songs, "Humpty Dumpty Heart."

There's also a very strange series with Broadway/film star Mary Martin, in which they address traditional material like "The Mockingbird" and "Il Bacio"; strange because they begin in a classical vein and then start radically swinging, and Martin wasn't the ideal artist for either half of that equation. (In hindsight, it would have made much more sense to record Martin and Herman together doing hip treatments of show tunes.) Wildest of all is his 1941 number-one hit recording of "Blues in the Night." In his brief memoir, *At the Woodchopper's Ball*, Herman remembered that both composer Harold Arlen and lyricist Johnny Mercer were in the studio that day, and that Mercer himself sang the obbligato part. He was almost right: The voice responding to Woody's calls on "hooey-da-hooey" is actually Arlen's.

By the end of the war, the Band That Plays the Blues had evolved into Woody Herman and the Thundering Herd (titled by band buff and writer George Simon), which in turn led to the equally amazing Second Herd. All of Herman's bands were terrific, but the first two Herds are rightfully regarded as being among the greatest in history, fully on a par with Basie, Ellington, and Goodman. Woody's singing was still one of the major features of the band, especially as far as the commercial aspects of the music business were concerned; at this time, his vocals still sold more records than any of the instrumental features, even Stan Getz's solo on "Early Autumn." Yet by the era of the Herds, there has been a shift in the band's dynamic—Herman continues to sing blues and ballads, and the crowds continue to eat them up, but his singing is no longer musically the hippest thing about the band.

Herman did some of his very best singing with the First and Second Herds. In addition to ballads ("I've Got the World on a String") and blues ("Panacea," the classic "I've Got News for You," and "Caldonia"), he sang a great many of what were then known as novelty songs. He and Nat Cole, that other paragon of postwar pop, were the two masters of taking songs that could charitably be called ephemeral and making immortal music with them. (Both men made a swinger out of the traditional Russian folk song "Katusha" and sang Ervin Drake's adaptation of "Humoresque," titled "Mabel, Mabel.") Herman could work wonders with songs I wouldn't want to see Crosby or Sinatra go near, like "Atlanta, GA," "Put That Ring on My Finger," "I Told Ya I Love Ya Now Get Out," "If It's Love You Want (Baby That's Me)," and "I Ain't Gettin' Any Younger." None of these are strictly the blues, but they treat postwar relationships with a healthy element of cynicism that seems closely related to the music of Louis Jordan and other early R&B giants. (Both Herman's and Cole's so-called novelties seem like high-art music compared to the novelty songs of the Mitch Miller era just a few years later.)

It was Herman, surprisingly, who made a hit out of "Laura." According to legend, he was all set to record David Raksin's movie theme as an instrumental, but Johnny Mercer had written a set of lyrics to the tune and taught them to Herman in the taxi en route to the session. ("Laura" and "Blues in the Night," Herman's two biggest hit vocals, were both Mercer movie songs.) Herman was also perfectly in step with the postwar penchant for exotica and travel songs, as with "Jamaica Rhumba," "The Crickets" (making him probably the first major American star to record the music of South African songster Josef Marais), "Johannesburg" (more Africana), and "House of Bamboo." He also cut two very funny South American specialties, "Pancho Maximillian Hernandez" and "My Pal Gonzales," which make Peggy Lee's "Mañana" seem politically correct by comparison. None of these are exactly Cole Porter, but in the hands of Herman and the Herd, they're outstanding pop music just the same.

Herman was easily the most successful and longest lasting talent scout in the history of jazz, having nurtured literally hundreds of the most important players the music has known—the tenors alone range from Flip Phillips to Joe Lovano, in addition to the famous Four Brothers (whose ranks over the years included Zoot Sims, Al Cohn, Stan Getz, and Gene Ammons). His arrangers deserve special credit for helping him shape his material, especially Ralph Burns, Neal Hefti, Al Cohn, and Shorty Rogers. (The best sampler of the band's greatest years, the height of the First Herd and the start of the Second, is *Blowin' Up a Storm!*, an excellent-sounding compilation of the best tracks from the Columbia period, 1945–47. Happily, in 2005 Mosaic Records compiled all of Herman's great 1945–47 Columbia material in an essential box.) Like Ella Fitzgerald, Herman could move with ease from the most sublime of sophisticated standards, like "Laura," to the nuttiest of novelties in the Second Herd's bop extravaganzas, like "Lemon Drop" and "Lollipop," which feature a vocal trio of Herman and two singing sidemen (Shorty Rogers and Terry Gibbs) scatting in unison over the chords to "I Got Rhythm."

What Herman achieved vocally with his big band—and the numbers he didn't sing were done by Mary Ann McCall, who proved to be one of the best band singers—was remarkable. Yet from the war on, his singing was no longer the central feature of his big band, and accordingly he increasingly participated in a whole bunch of special vocal projects outside the Herds. There were many such sessions, usually coming between Herds. After disbanding the musically and commercially successful First Herd at the end of 1946, Herman spent most of the following year working as a solo act, singing and playing in a variety of contexts, among them a radio series with Peggy Lee.

Had he never gone back to bandleading, these Columbia sessions of 1947 establish that he could have easily made a living—and, in light of future developments, probably a more secure one—as a bandless singer-entertainer. He made a number of dates by Herman with a Los Angeles studio orchestra, and in his various inter-Herd periods he would cross cadenzas with Nat Cole, Duke Ellington (the unremarkable "Cowboy Rhumba"), Billy Eckstine, and Dinah Shore.

Unfortunately, most of the inter-Herd vocals on Columbia from the 1946–47 period have been scarce since the 78 era (with the exception of *Eight Shades of Blue*, a 78 album reissued on British Vocalion). Columbia's A&R staff was apparently concerned that he hadn't recorded enough songs with the word "blue" in the title for Decca, so they had him cut eight more with a full orchestra and strings. These are mostly pop songs with a touch of the blues in the music as well as the title, including new, improved readings of signatures such as "Blues in the Night" (with Woody's alto) and "Blue Prelude" (with Woody's clarinet) but also the ballad "Under a Blanket of Blue."

Johnny Mandel told Doug Ramsey that "you could name a number of clarinet players who were better, but I'll tell you one thing, Woody never played a note that didn't swing." The same thing applies to his singing: He doesn't have the chops and polish of a lot of full-time singers, but his deep baritone voice (which he loved to push into falsetto yelps on a comedy blues like "Caldonia") is warm and attractive, and he sings every note, every word, as if he means it.

He made more oddball vocal projects after folding the Second Herd at the end of 1949, this time for Capitol, but these were not on the whole as memorable. Ironically, though the Capitol vocal items aren't as good as the Columbia sides, they've all been reissued on CD, as part of a complete Mosaic collection of all of the Capitol items. There's a novelty Dixieland session done in 1950, issued as by "Chuck Thomas" (Herman's two middle names), deliberately hoked-up to grab a share of the market for the kind of music that the label had opened up with Pee Wee Hunt. All the tunes come from Herman's early years as a jazz fan and young musician in the pre-swing era, especially "My Gee Gee from the Fiji Isles" and "Jelly Bean," a thirties oddity that might be the original Gay Lib anthem. Even a session with the Nat King Cole Trio, who shared a tour with the Second Herman Herd in 1949, isn't as good as it might be; the standard "My Baby Just Cares for Me" is fine, but their *verkakte* parody of Frankie Laine's blockbuster "Mule Train" is a waste of their talent. On the other hand, Woody sang and played on a 1950 MGM date with Billy Eckstine that's among the best either man ever did; their sole duet, "Life Is Just a Bowl of Cherries," is a most welcome slice of cool philosophy.

Herman's popularity peaked with the First Herd of 1944–46, and for the rest of his life he was cursed with incompetent (and downright evil) managers and accountants who conspired to ensure that he would spend the next forty years trying in vain to play catch-up with the IRS. Virtually all of the bands feature his singing—in May 1950, he sang three beautiful standards with his Bop City Band (an early incarnation of the Third Herd) and the King Sisters: "Pennies from Heaven," "You're My Everything," and "I Want a Little Girl"—and he continued to pursue extra-Herd vocal projects, now mostly albums.

One of the oddest and yet most surprisingly satisfying ventures Herman was ever involved with was the beginning of the calypso movement in America. Nat Cole's 1949 "Calypso Blues" was probably the first song in the genre done by an American pop star, but in the early fifties Herman embraced it with both hands, and all on his own nickel. In 1950, he took an all-star octet to Havana, and there recorded two lively tunes, "Tasty" and "Old Pail," a major foray into Island music. Bop guy goes calypso.

Late in 1952 he formed his own label, Mars Records, which lasted roughly two years. He later said he must have been on Mars to enter into yet another money-losing venture (Norman Granz ultimately bailed him out by buying the masters), but at least one of the few Martian albums was music that could easily have been a mass-market hit had it been properly promoted. This was the 10" LP titled *Woody Herman Goes Native*. The cover was ghastly, amateur kitsch, Woody's head shot with a Carmen Miranda tutti-frutti hat drawn on cartoon-style. But the music inside was splendid: Herman and his "New Third Herd" swinging through Island favorites like "Never Mind the Noise in the Market," "Go Down

the Wishing Road," and "Run Joe" (also recorded by Louis Jordan). This was, in best Herman fashion, pop-jazz at its finest, full of swinging riffs and catchy Island rhythms and, even though the political edge of the texts has been diluted, the lyrics are very funny. Woody bet on the right horse but too early: The Cuban-style mambo was going to be the exotic flavor of the mid-fifties (in 1958, Herman would make a Latin jazz album with Tito Puente), followed by calypso, ushered in by Harry Belafonte (doing many of the same songs Herman had already recorded) at the end of the decade. Both of these very colorful, ethnic, jazz, and Afro-influenced forms would mysteriously be succeeded by the rather colorless and rhythm-less Anglo-style folk music in the early sixties—but the mambo and calypso were what grown-ups were dancing to while the kiddies were buying rock 'n' roll singles.

Herman recorded four predominantly vocal albums in the mid-fifties, all of which were excellent, and two of which were directly aimed at various sorts of lovers: *Music for Tired Lovers* (1954) and *Songs for Tired Lovers* (1957). The first (recorded by Columbia in Detroit, of all places) is the more intimate, combining Herman with the classic edition of the Erroll Garner Trio. It's all slow love songs with Herman just singing. Once in a while I would like a little more variety in the tempos, and it would also have been nice to have him play a little alto or clarinet, but it's a lovely record, with Woody singing outstandingly well on twelve classic songs ("You've Got Me Crying Again" and "I'll See You in My Dreams" by Herman's late boss Isham Jones), four of which are combined in a longish medley.

Two years later, he cut *Blues Groove* for Capitol, not crooning ballads but shouting the blues in a most assertive—yet still subtle—fashion. He sings blues from all over the history of the music, even revisiting his own past on "Dupree Blues" (aka "Betty and Depree"), a "Frankie and Johnny" variation that he first recorded with the original Band That Plays the Blues nearly twenty years earlier. While "Smack Dab in the Middle" is a contemporary R&B hit, "Pinetop Blues" is the work of legendary Chicago blues pianist Pinetop Smith (1904–29), and Herman squeaks it out in a falsetto manner reminiscent of both Smith and Eddie "Cleanhead" Vinson. He delivers "I Want a Little Girl" and "Trouble in Mind" in his usual, more manly baritone. *Blues Groove*, which also included one extralong blues instrumental bearing that title (which the Herds kept playing for years to come), marked the first of only a handful of vocal albums Herman made with his own band. (*Blues Groove* is available on the 2000 Mosaic box *The Complete Capitol Recordings of Woody Herman*, including two R&B-tinged bonus tracks not on the original vinyl.)

Come the next year, Herman taped two all-vocal albums for Norman Granz and Verve Records. *Songs for Hip Lovers* is a fine jazz-oriented collection, while

Love Is the Sweetest Thing Sometimes is a less interesting orchestra-and-strings foray with pop maestro Frank DeVol. *Hip Lovers*, which has been reissued on CD, is the jewel, mixing in two sessions, one done in L.A. with two horns (Ben Webster and Sweets Edison) and four rhythm, like most of the Granz Billie Holiday dates. *Sweetest Thing* was done in New York with a ten-piece band: trumpet, trombone, four saxes, and four rhythm, arranged and conducted by Marty Paich. It's a wonderful, relaxedly swinging collection of great standards ("Moon Song" and "Willow Weep for Me," with Woody pushing the high note on "Weep" right up to the cracking point of his voice). Even though, once again, all the songs are in the same tempo (this time they're all medium-fast), the record is consistently exciting, even thrilling.

As a music maker, Herman kept incorporating new trends into his mix, from "MacArthur Park" to "Giant Steps." After the fifties, his singing grew increasingly secondary, now that traditional songs and singers were no more popular than big bands. In the early sixties, he presented his best band since the 1947–49 Second Herd, an orchestra he christened "the Swinging Herd." (On a WNEW broadcast he explained, "We've given up the numbers," to which host William B. Williams responded, "That'll be news up in Harlem!") Herman's most important vocal feature in this period was the revived "Caldonia," a Louis Jordan specialty he had already been singing for twenty years.

His last album-length effort as a vocalist was still another surprise, a 1966 Columbia LP with the Swinging Herd titled *The Jazz Swinger*, which as the title suggests (sort of) is a collection of up-to-date Herman Herd arrangements of songs associated with Al Jolson. Lord knows who came up with that one, but then again Herman's career was predicated on taking chances with one apparently nutty idea after another.

Alas, jazz's supreme talent scout, the man who knew exactly whom to hire for every section in his band, completely fumbled the ball when it came to choosing business associates. Tragically, Herman had to pick up the check for their incompetence and criminal negligence, and the IRS held him responsible even though Herman was, in essence, the victim of embezzlement. The situation gave him even more right than he already had to sing the blues. Woody Herman kept leading great bands until his seventy-fourth year, and when he died on October 29, 1987, his place in American music was totally secure.

Billie Holiday (1915–1959)

Well, it was painful to see her so near the end; it's still painful to me now to think about it. She seemed so out-of-it she had to grab on to her chair to keep from falling over. And my heart would go out to her, because the piano player would be playing the wrong key for her, or the tempo might not be right, and then he'd be in the way. These kinds of things turn me inside out. I tried not to let it upset me, to force myself just to listen to the music, and I did. And the music was wonderful. It wasn't like the early Billie Holiday, but the feeling was the same—she just gave you so much heart and soul, good Lord! She didn't lay it on and fool around and all that kind of stuff like some singers, but she just stands there and sings. Sings a song, paints a picture, lets you know everything that was going on, so you could sort of see into what her life was like. Well, even with her being half out-of-it, it was very moving. Actually, I cried.

—Shirley Horn (interview with the author, 1997)

Billie Holiday sang as if she were aware that her music had so much emotional power that she had to distance herself from it. Her eyes are closed, her body is motionless, and her head is almost always leaning to a slight angle away from the microphone. It's almost as if she were positioning her body like an antenna. Perhaps she wasn't actually singing; perhaps she was merely channeling a greater force. Maybe this incredible music wasn't coming out of her, but coming through her, as if she were the transmitter for some higher power. It's almost as if she wanted to disassociate herself from the creation of her music. If Holiday wanted it to appear that she was not an active participant in her singing, she also took similar pains to ensure that it would appear that her nonmusical life was likewise driven by circumstances out of her control. Even the songs she chose depict her as fate's eternal victim, helplessly trapped by her race, her gender, and the unorthodox nature of her talent, into a series of destructive relationships with both men and substances.

In this respect, Holiday is the diametric opposite of the character usually played by Judy Garland, her sister in self-destruction. In countless films (*Presenting Lily Mars*, *Ziegfeld Girl*, and *A Star Is Born*, not to mention the *Babes* movies), Garland embodies an eager young show business hopeful, desperate to sing for people and willing to give up anything to become a star. Far from being ambitiously determined to sing, Holiday tells us (in *Lady Sings the Blues*, a memoir that manipulates the facts of her life almost to the point of fiction) that the very fact of her career came into existence entirely by accident. The seventeen-year-old Holiday tried her hand at performing, she would have us believe, merely because she had failed at every other occupation she had tried (some menial, others sexual). It was winter, and Holiday was out of work and desperate for rent money; as a last-ditch effort, she tried singing at various restaurants around Harlem, hoping to raise some spare change. From there it was just a short time before producer John Hammond, who frequented uptown nightspots in search of new jazz and blues talent, came in. In the parlance of a later generation, Hammond was blown away by what he heard.

Thus her whole career, she seemed to say, was out

of her hands: Her talent was a gift from God, and she doesn't ever seem to have nurtured it in any conventional way (she didn't exactly spend hours at Juilliard learning to read music and sight sing); her professional success was merely a matter of being heard by the right people. In her book and in many of her songs, Holiday portrays herself as a perpetual victim; in her artistry and career, it was just the opposite: Holiday is the perpetual beneficiary of her own and everyone else's good taste. Far from suffering for her art, almost from the instant that anybody first heard her, she was immediately recognized as one of the major jazz-pop-blues singers of all time. The suffering she did was as a woman rather than an artist (if the two are separable).

Before she was twenty-five, Holiday had collaborated (at various lengths) with four of America's most important bandleaders: Duke Ellington, Benny Goodman, Count Basie, and Artie Shaw. Only two performances with Basie survive, taken from a live broadcast at the Savoy Ballroom in 1937, and they are among the most remarkable (and most frequently reissued) items in her entire canon: "Swing, Brother, Swing" and "They Can't Take That Away from Me." During the broadcast, the rather unctuous announcer exclaims, "Well, Mother, burn my macintosh!" It was an obscure expression even at the time, but to experience the Holiday-Basie combination is to know exactly what it means.

Her first song here, "Swing, Brother, Swing," is a miniature mystery. This is an eminently forgettable rhythm number, with lyrics so minimal it may be a stretch to describe them as nonsense. Like "Sing, Sing, Sing," it's a riff tune with a doggerel lyric that was designed for musicians to sing: It was first recorded in early 1935 (shortly before the official start of the swing era) by trumpeter Wingy Manone and pianist Willie "the Lion" Smith. Logically, it would make sense that the song's entire history would be over by the summer of 1935, but for some reason, two years later Holiday chose to sing it on her famous (surviving) broadcast with Count Basie and then, two years after that, she recorded it for Vocalion.

Holiday's 1939 commercial recording is a disappointment: The arrangement behind her is distractingly choppy, and as a result her performance is simultaneously subdued and agitated. However, as I say, the live track from 1937 is one of the finest moments in her discography. It's a feature for her throughout—she comes in right after the introduction, and then sings two whole choruses. There's no shortage of great swinging numbers in her catalogue, but even so, you've rarely heard Holiday let go with so much confidence and exuberance. At the start of the bridge, she sings, "Rarin' to go, and there ain't nobody gonna hold me down," completely capturing the mood of the text (such as it is) and at the same time transforming the words into a perfect expression of what she's feeling. She's at once relaxed

and excited, and swings with an easy groove—not dragging the beat, but not in a hurry either. She knows exactly which notes to stretch out ("*Cannn't* help but swing it, boy" / "*Doooon't* stop to diddle-daddle") and which ones to quickly drop, as if they were hot to the touch. Indeed, they are.

On "They Can't Take That Away from Me," from the same broadcast, the mood is similar, with a perfect tempo (slightly slower than "swing") and the band supporting her while staying out of her way. She had recorded the Gershwin brothers' classic two months earlier, but this live reading with Basie is, again, the one with the magic. Like Armstrong before her, Holiday is one of the great equalizers of American music—she makes a dumb little ephemeral ditty like "Swing, Brother, Swing" sound just as good as this classic by the Gershwins. On both songs, you instantly know that you're in the presence of one of the all-time musical minds; every note she sings, and even the rests and pauses, is charged with an ineffable sense of purpose. Far from seeming like a victim on these two tracks, Holiday seems completely in charge.

These two tracks—which were heard live on the radio just once, in 1937, and then not again until after her death—may be highlights of her recorded output, but they're hardly atypical. Nearly everything she recorded in her early years is this swinging, this infectiously charismatic, and this good. (The later work is excellent, too, but in a different way.) Tracks like these show why Holiday is held in such high regard more than fifty years after her death at age forty-four; she has the musicality of Ella Fitzgerald, the passion of Judy Garland, the sheer invention of Louis Armstrong, the soul of Bessie Smith, and more sensuality than any of them—but she has overwhelming individuality as well. It takes about thirty seconds of listening to any of her classic recordings to dispel the notion that Billie Holiday's reputation might somehow be inflated. She pays her dues every time you listen to a single track.

Holiday's musical genealogy—Louis Armstrong and Bessie Smith, with more than a drop of Ethel Waters (an influence that she would never admit to)—is rather straightforward. But her family genealogy is one of the more confusing in the annals of jazz or pop music: The infamous opening line of her autobiography notwithstanding, it's difficult to ascertain how old her parents were—and how old Holiday was—at the time of their marriage, or if they were ever legally wed. The girl went by a succession of family names (Eleanora Harris, Eleanora Fagan) even before she entered show business. At that point, she combined the family name of her birth father (Clarence Holiday, a guitarist best known for playing with Fletcher Henderson) with the first name of Billie Dove, a silent film actress whom she had admired growing up in the twenties.

Holiday seems to have spent her first eighteen or so years committed to exploring the seamy side of life. After being abandoned by her father, she bounced between convents, whorehouses, and prisons, and was even ritually molested at the House of the Good Shepherd for Colored Girls. It was all perfect training for a life of substance abuse and brutal treatment at the hands of the various characters she called Lover Man. Her one salvation, artistically, was early exposure to the recordings of Louis Armstrong and Bessie Smith; she later said that her own music was an attempt to merge the two—the feeling of the first with the power of the second.

The actual "discovery"—when Hammond met Holiday—apparently occurred in late 1932 or early 1933, and everyone who was there at the time remembered it differently. Holiday said it happened at Pod and Jerry's, where she was sitting in, hoping to pick up (literally) some loose coin. Hammond said the discovery transpired at a club operated by singer Monette Moore, where Holiday was formally hired to perform because Moore was then appearing on Broadway in a show with Clifton Webb. There's still a third point of view: Until the day he died, the vibraphonist and bandleader Red Norvo insisted that it was his wife, singer Mildred Bailey, who first noticed Holiday and pulled Hammond's coattails to her.

The *Rashomon*-like nature of this event also has a parallel in Holiday's music: In a sense, the two choruses of "Swing, Brother, Swing" are like two slightly different views of the same scenario. You hear the song once, and then when you hear it again, it's similar, but not exactly the same. There has been a slight phase shift—different words are emphasized in different ways, different meanings are drawn out, different conclusions are arrived at. This idea of singing multiple choruses of the same song, and then varying them from one to the other, comes very directly out of Ethel Waters and Louis Armstrong.

It was Hammond who opened the first doors for Billie Halliday (as she then spelled her name) when he wrote about her in the British music journal *Melody Maker* in April 1933 (describing her as being "over 200 pounds and incredibly beautiful"). More important, Hammond placed her as a guest vocalist on two Benny Goodman titles recorded in November. (According to some accounts, Billie and Benny dated for a while. Try imagining a more unlikely couple.)

Holiday left us only one surviving performance from 1934, but it's a doozy: Somehow, she wound up being hired by Paramount Pictures for a guest spot in *Symphony in Black*, a one-reel short starring Duke Ellington. Ellington used this film as an opportunity to put together one of his earliest extended works, a seven-minute suite of "Negro Moods" (in the same vein as "Creole Rhapsody," "Black, Brown & Beige," and "Harlem"), and the result is perhaps the single most moving visual manifestation of Ellington's artistry. *Symphony in Black* far surpasses anything else the Maestro did on film or television and even

(as far as I can tell) onstage. In just these few minutes, he depicts four powerful and distinct vignettes of contemporary African American life: labor, love, worship, and revelry. It's with deliberately Dukish deviousness that the church service he shows us is the funeral for a child (a preacher who looks like a black Moses delivers the rites over a tiny casket), and that the romantic relationship he depicts is a triangle, with Holiday as the unhappy frail whose man has left her for another woman. She's shown stalking Lover Man on the street, and then he knocks her down to the sidewalk.

She raises her head and sings "Saddest Tale," an Ellington original the band had recorded a month earlier (in September 1934). The commercial recording has Ellington himself speaking two lines at the beginning and end: "Saddest tale told on land and sea / Is the tale they told when they told the truth on me." The film version, however, has Holiday singing a full-scale blues vocal; more accurately, it's one of the many works in both the Ellington and Holiday canons that alludes to blues form and tonality without strictly conforming to the 12-bar pattern. Ellington adroitly frames Holiday's guttural, down-and-out blues statement with contrastingly grandiose semiclassical brass fanfares. It's a shame that after this film, neither Ellington nor Holiday returned to the song, or to each other. They shared the same bill on a few all-star concerts, but this remains their only true collaboration. (For my money, Holiday's interpretations of "Solitude," "Do Nothing Till You Hear from Me," and other key Ellington songs are as close to definitive as it is possible to get.)

After these early team-ups with Goodman and Ellington, Holiday's recording career truly gets under way with a series of small group dates done for the American Recording Corp., launched by John Hammond in the summer of 1935. Initially, Hammond had the brilliant idea to combine Holiday with another of his discoveries, pianist Teddy Wilson, and as her popularity increased, starting in 1936 the label also simultaneously released a series of discs under Holiday's own name. Hammond had started the ball rolling, and then another producer, Bernie Hanighen, picked up that ball and ran with it. Hammond was rigid and dogmatic, but Hanighen, in Holiday's own words, was "a great guy." (He also had a concurrent career as a songwriter, and Holiday recorded at least three of his tunes: "If the Moon Turns Green," "When a Woman Loves a Man," and "Yankee Doodle Never Went to Town"; alas, she never sang his most famous work, the lyric to Thelonious Monk's "Round Midnight," which would have been ideal for her.)

Teddy Wilson was, at the time, a considerably bigger name than Holiday—two weeks later he participated in the first date by the Benny Goodman Trio, the beginning of the most celebrated small jazz group of its time, and practically of all time. Wilson, incidentally, did not consider himself a fan, apparently regarding Holiday as a mere Louis Armstrong imitator with little of her own to offer. It certainly didn't help his opinion of her when, from the fifties and sixties onward, many of his sessions were reissued on LP under Holiday's name. The Wilson discs were originally released on Brunswick, while the Holiday titles came out on Vocalion; although the Holiday titles are more likely to open with the singer (rather than stating the main melody instrumentally), both series draw on the same pool of musicians and are generally indistinguishable.

In 2001, Sony (the corporate heir to Columbia Records) gathered all of Holiday's early masters into a spectacular ten-disc set titled *Lady Day—The Complete Billie Holiday on Columbia, 1933–1944*. At the time, Sony Music Legacy issued a press release comparing these sessions to the celebrated Louis Armstrong "Hot Five" recordings in terms of their importance to American music. In spite of Holiday's allegiance to Armstrong, it's hard to compare Holiday's work here to anyone else's—she's just too unique; she has no equal and no parallel. The 1933–44 recordings are unlike anything else, even her own later work. Many singers over the last seventy years have tried to replicate Holiday's seminal sessions of this period, and none of them, including the Lady herself, was able to pull it off.

"She had the world on a string, being beautiful, having a hell of a figure, and a style that no one could steal," bassist John Williams, who worked with Holiday at Cafe Society, told her first biographer, John Chilton. "Lady Day was a beautiful woman and it's a shame that hot pants were not in style, for the boys really missed something."(Yes, this interview took place in the early seventies.) The point is that her voice was correspondingly round and full in the mid-thirties, a far cry from the markedly undernourished sound and look that she had at the end of her life. The voice is sharp, somewhat pinched, and angular (though not as much as it would become in the forties and fifties), anticipating that of Dinah Washington, but also deep and full, with a lot of bottom (hot pants aside).

Hammond deserves credit for the idea of teaming Holiday with her peers—the major soloists from the leading big bands of the day—and placing them all on a level playing field. On that first date, July 2, 1935, Wilson's boss, Benny Goodman, sits in, and most of the rest of the band consists of players then associated with Fletcher Henderson, particularly the two other horns, trumpeter Roy Eldridge and tenor saxophonist Ben Webster. "Miss Brown to You" opens with Goodman stating the melody, and, at thirty-one seconds in, the sound of an auto horn is clearly heard in the background; no one bothered to cut another take, and I can't say I blame them—the Goodman-Wilson interplay is so perfect that Hammond rightly wanted to leave everything as it was. So too is Holiday's vocal; she's marvelously relaxed and secure, even when singing in what amounts to male drag, a dude bragging about his hot girlfriend. She's "baby to me," the lyrics tell us, but you, on the other hand, you pathetic slob, you can call her "*Miss Brown*." Wilson follows with a whole chorus of his own, before Eldridge leads the whole ensemble in a tutti that progresses into a coda and takes us out.

Three out of four tunes recorded on that first Wilson-Holiday date would become all-time Holiday signature songs: "Miss Brown to You," "I Wished on the Moon," and "What a Little Moonlight Can Do." The last song gave birth to something else, unfortunately. Nearly everyone who has written about these sessions—particularly jazzcentric historians who don't know much about the American songbook—has gone out of his way to dump on the overall quality of songs Holiday recorded in these years. I've even read attacks on "What a Little Moonlight Can Do" by Harry Woods, who wrote the words and the music to this song. Sure, the lyric "Oo-oo-oo / What a little moonlight can do" wouldn't give Oscar Hammerstein any sleepless nights, but it's an exceedingly cute song. Countless singers—mostly female—have followed Holiday's example with it (in 2003, Dianne Reeves released a whole album titled *A Little Moonlight*—and it wasn't even a Holiday tribute package), and the one thing that they have in common is that they all sound cute. "Moonlight" is a highly rhythmic tune with the scat sequence built right in. All I can say is that it takes better ears and more astute judgment than mine to classify this as a lousy song. "Moonlight" never fails to bring out the best in everyone who sings it, and that's what counts.

On most of the 1935–39 material, even on those titles where her vocals come first, Holiday is literally just one of the boys. Look at the rough outlines of two songs from a March 1937 session led by Wilson and featuring three key soloists from the Ellington band:

"Carelessly": alto sax (Johnny Hodges), then piano (Wilson), vocal (Holiday), muted trumpet (Cootie Williams)
"How Could You?": piano intro (Wilson), trumpet (Williams), baritone sax (Harry Carney), trumpet (Williams), vocal (Holiday), with prominent clarinet obbligato by Carney, alto (Hodges), piano solo (Wilson)

As you can see, the voice does not stand out more than any of the other instruments. Holiday can't even really be described as a band vocalist here—when Helen Forrest sang with Benny Goodman or Harry James, she certainly received more of a spotlight. The best word to describe Holiday's role on the 1933–38 recordings is "sideman": Even though her instrument is her own voice, this doesn't bring her any special treatment or afford her any more or less attention than is received by the other musicians present. Beginning around the end of 1938, the freewheeling jam session feeling of the earlier work is increasingly embellished with what sounds like prewritten arrangements. There are still generous solos from all the instrumentalists—not only Lester Young, but also Harry James and Benny Carter, who are all over the late 1938 sessions.

Not that there was any shame in being a sideman. That first date, as mentioned, had Benny Goodman returning the favor to Holiday and guest-starring on one of her sessions—and not for the last time, either. The idea that the King of Swing should defer to one of his own men and happily serve as a mere bandsman illustrates the democracy of the classic thirties Holiday sessions: the most sublimely musical of singers working with the other leading improvisers of her day in a state of pure equality.

Famously, the musician with whom she made the most beautiful music was the brilliant saxophonist Lester Young. Holiday was a greater musician with her voice than most musicians were with their instruments; Young was a far better singer with his horn than nearly every singer out there. A year after the release of the big ten-CD box, Sony came out with a sixteen-track collection featuring Holiday and Young. The idea for the compilation was to be applauded. Unfortunately, Sony titled this set *A Musical Romance*, then used "The Man I Love" as the first song, and in the promo copy on the back of the package they compared Holiday and Young to "Romeo and Juliet . . . Eloise and Abelard . . . Tracy and Hepburn."

The singer and the saxist were, in fact, very close personally; when the Basie band arrived in New York, Lester moved in with Billie and her mom before he found a place of his own. Famously, they gave each other the nicknames that are still associated with them: "Lady Day" and "Pres." (Though, of course, if he was "the Pres," he should have been married to Ella Fitzgerald, who was billed as "the First Lady" very early on.) But no, Lester Young was not the man that Holiday loved. (She made little secret of how she had little use for nice guys.) Packaging their professional partnership as a musical romance is deliberately misleading. Everyone who knew them, including John Hammond and Buck Clayton, states plainly that the singer and the saxophonist were never erotically involved. Not that I'm the most politically sensitive soul around, but it seems to me patently sexist to package their music this way, simply because she happened to be a she.

When Holiday sang about her relationships— which she did with an openness that seems astonishingly candid, even in our tell-all era—she wants us to know that she was perennially subservient to "her man." In her music it's just the opposite—what made the partnership with Young work so beautifully is that the two are equals on every level; if anything, she's the more dominant partner, since Young, in addition to being featured on his own solos, often plays behind her vocals in a supporting role. Young

may have, in fact, been the one man in her life who didn't boss her around.

Their premier session together (January 1937) starts with two first-rate Irving Berlin songs (from the contemporaneous *On the Avenue*), "He Ain't Got Rhythm" and "This Year's Kisses." The first (which is not, alas, on the *Musical Romance* CD) begins once again with Benny Goodman—it was as if Benny knew that the first meeting of Lady Day and Pres was going to be a historic event and he wanted to tell his grandchildren that he was there. "Kisses" gets under way with a gorgeous, laconic melody solo from Young. He seems to inspire Holiday, in her vocal chorus that follows, to sound more laid back and mellow than she usually does in this period. By contrast, on "The Man I Love," Young's tenor sound is darker and more full-bodied, more conventionally "masculine," but the arrangement on the whole is somewhat more formal and concertlike. "Me, Myself and I" opens with Young playing a brief intro before Holiday's entrance, but the real charm is Holiday's second vocal chorus, in which the two are on together—it's more than an obbligato, it's practically a duet; here they're like a considerably hipper Nelson and Jeanette or Fred and Ginger, singing and/or dancing around each other. It's not just that he's filling in behind her; she's also responding to what he's playing.

One happy consequence of the "Holiday" series, as opposed to the "Wilson" series, is that the singer was increasingly allowed to do two vocal choruses, and, as on "Me, Myself and I," these second choruses were where the hot obbligato activity was—on "Who Wants Love" and others. In the Roosevelt era, Holiday was queen of the jukeboxes; when the jukes and the roadhouse joints that sheltered them began to proliferate in the mid-thirties, the record industry responded with stacks of discs of mostly contemporary songs played by small bands for dancing, with both hot solos and vocals. Fats Waller's stardom in this period was based equally on his juke activity and his radio appearances. ARC survived largely by selling Holiday and others to the juke joints for thirty-five cents a pop; for a nickel, customers got a three-minute dance. You and your date could have a swell evening out for a couple of bucks, tops.

But Holiday was too special to stay in any one place. By the end of the decade, as she grew increasingly popular as a vocalist, her records came more and more into line with those of other singers, with more formal arrangements like those of Bing Crosby. (Even so, there's a considerable amount of give and take on the 1940–44 dates.) The main event that kicked her up the stairs, from being just another guy in the band to a Ladylike diva, was her relationship with Barney Josephson and the release of Commodore C-526.

Where Hammond was a WASP record producer, Josephson was a Jewish nightclub impresario, and they both were equally committed both to African American music and the cause of integration (well before it was called that). Holiday had previously sung successfully on Fifty-second Street (at Kelly's Stables and elsewhere), but Josephson, who opened Cafe Society in 1938, was the first talent presenter to take a long-term interest in her career, and her sustained appearances at Cafe Society did as much as anything to make her a star.

It was there that Holiday began singing "Strange Fruit," with words and music by Lewis Allen, a poet and schoolteacher who was so far to the left that he made Hammond and Josephson look like Fox News pundits. (Yet even he hesitated to put his real name, Abel Meeropol, on the song.) There had been other so-called protest songs (to use a later terminology) with regards to the so-called race issue in the mainstream before, some of them ambiguous. With "Strange Fruit," though, the meaning was explicit, and there were no other options or interpretations—there was only one way to sing it and only one way to listen to it. This was a lament about a lynching; there was no way it could possibly be construed as being about anything else. Holiday was hardly the type to confront controversy—no Nina Simone, she. She sang "Strange Fruit" only reluctantly but became committed to it when she witnessed the amazing effect it had on Cafe Society audiences. It was only natural that the song had to be recorded, but the American Recording Corp., which by now had morphed into Columbia Records, said thanks but no thanks.

Thus Hammond arranged for Holiday to do a session in April 1939 for Milt Gabler, who ran America's first independent jazz label, Commodore Records. "Strange Fruit" took Holiday out of the juke joints—there was no way you could dance to it, unless you happened to be Martha Graham. But the flip side of Commodore C-526 brought her back, at least temporarily. This was "Fine and Mellow," and it was more typical Holiday fare, a sexy blues credited to the singer herself.

At the time, as Gabler told me (and other interviewers), "Fine and Mellow" was the big hit, mainly since he was able to get it onto jukeboxes and tap into the burgeoning market for the blues. In later generations, "Strange Fruit" achieved a significance it didn't have or couldn't have had in its day. Apart from Holiday, virtually no one else sang it for at least a decade. "Love for Sale," "Body and Soul," and "Gloomy Sunday" all caused scandals in the 1930s for their allusions, respectively, to prostitution, physical love, and suicide, but "Strange Fruit" didn't even get far enough out of the gate to be banned in Boston, not to mention Birmingham. (Call it a coincidence, but Holiday is the only artist I can think of who recorded all four songs.)

Holiday's final sessions for Columbia are so amazingly good that when the Danish label Jazz Unlimited put out two whole volumes of alternate takes, you actually want to listen to them all the way through, even when sometimes hearing as many as three or four takes of the same song. The bulk of the 1940–42 dates feature her with bands directed by composer-arrangers Benny Carter and Eddie Heywood, who both struck an agreeable balance between Holiday and the band. There is still no shortage of terrific solos, but now it does seem more as if everything else is secondary to her. Though these sides are less democratic, they're no less delightful.

As Holiday ascended the ladder, and was given the star treatment more and more, something was gained as well as lost. If the 1940–42 sessions don't have the loose spontaneity of the earlier music, the compensating factor is that Holiday is given a better class of song. In this period, standards tested by time (even by then) are the rule and ephemeral new tunes are the exception. The songs she does here are almost all classics: "I Cover the Waterfront," "Love Me or Leave Me" (both with the verses), and even "Gloomy Sunday," the aforementioned Hungarian suicide song that had infiltrated the English-speaking world (via Paul Robeson and Hal Kemp) five years earlier. The 1936 "It's a Sin to Tell a Lie" is an unexpected choice; it's a rather old-fashioned song that sounds more like 1916. Fats Waller made a terrific record of it swinging and gagging it up (exactly what the song needed), while Ruth Etting did a lovely version that's completely straight. Sung in medium dance time, Holiday's treatment is somewhere in between; she doesn't jazz it just for the sake of it, but she isn't afraid to interpret the song and personalize it either.

She's especially winning on two old-timers by W. C. Handy (supposedly the start of an aborted album of Handy à la Holiday), "St. Louis Blues" and "Loveless Love." The latter is no less a traditional blues than the one named after St. Louis. The 1941 "Solitude" marks the first Ellington song she'd sung since "Saddest Tale" seven years earlier, and she renders it as much like a prayer as a torch song; Eddie Heywood backs her here with a sonorous "choir" of three saxes and a trumpet. She sings the phrase "mem-or-ies that never die," slowly, stretching out each syllable, as if she were truly savoring a memory. Heywood tinkles on the piano to make it sound like a celesta, giving it a more spiritual quality, and when she leaves the bridge and reaches the line "In my solitude I'm praying," it's hard to resist the compulsion to fall down on your knees.

Furthermore, the new songs that she did introduce in the immediate prewar period have an amazingly high batting average. "I Hear Music" is bright and upbeat, almost more of an Ella Fitzgerald number. It's hardly the fastest thing that Holiday ever sang, but she really swings. "Mandy Is Two" represents a case of literal reporting for lyricist Johnny Mercer, since his adopted daughter Amanda had just reached that age. The song represents the major expression of parental devotion for both Mercer and Holiday; she invests it with a kind of affectionate, cheeky impudence that, to me, portrays childhood much more endearingly than a pile of sappy sentiment.

Clearly, when Holiday wasn't singing classics in this period, she was making them: The "Solitude" date also includes one of her most identifiable numbers, "God Bless the Child," which uses the horns-as-choir sound to great effect. Both words and music, as Donald Clarke's *Wishing on the Moon* (the second of three recommended full-length biographies of Holiday) reveals, were written by Arthur Herzog based on a title and an idea from Holiday, who received half the credit and royalties. Holiday gifted Herzog with an old southern expression, the original meaning of which has long been eclipsed by the popularity of the song, but essentially describes self-sufficient offspring who are innocent of the sins of the father. At one point in *Lady Sings the Blues*, Billie has an argument with her mother and snaps back at her, "God bless the child that's got his own!"

As material specifically written for Holiday, it's a marvelous piece of performance art. Like "Mandy Is Two," it's about childhood; like "Solitude," it has a religious aspect. The song is written in a combination of biblical phrases and Southern slang: the opening line, "Them that's got shall get," is apparently what Herzog imagined people spoke like in a black church. Ray Charles, who knew a thing or two about the subject, later spun that line into a whole song by itself called "Them That Got." It seems at once reverent and sacrilegious—you're not quite sure what's going on. I wouldn't have a hard time believing it exerted an influence on the young Bob Dylan, whose songs have a similarly mysterious quality.

After Holiday's first chorus, Roy Eldridge plays what is, for him, a very brief and subdued muted passage. Holiday then wraps it up with a beautiful and carefully considered coda: Instead of doing an out chorus (everything from the bridge on), she sings just the key lines again, "Mama may have, Papa may have / But God bless the child that's got his own." She finally finishes with a tag that may have been written by Herzog: "He just don't worry 'bout nothin', 'cause he's got his own." Holiday didn't always use this line when she sang the song again (you can hear her rehearsing it a few dozen times on a 1956 private tape), but it actually anticipates the signature tags of Billy Eckstine. More than almost anything else from the 1933–44 period—even "Strange Fruit"—"God Bless the Child" became an all-time Holiday classic, one that she sang at nearly every concert and rerecorded for both Decca and Verve. There's also a wonderful film of her singing it, accompanied by a Basie small band in 1950, around the same time that she rerecorded it for Decca.

In 1942, she made the first recording of another song by a sagacious lyricist who completely captured her essence, "Trav'lin' Light." Johnny Mercer not only wrote the text, he produced the session for his newly incorporated Capitol Records. "Trav'lin'

Light" does a brilliant job of depicting someone trying to put a brave face on a breakup, a façade that you're supposed to be instantly able to see through—what Hammerstein would call "an air of resignation."

Holiday recorded "Trav'lin' " with old-timer Paul Whiteman's Orchestra on a sojourn to the West Coast. Although this transpired a few months after her final session for Columbia, she was apparently still under contract to CBS, as Capitol was obliged to credit her under the alias of "Lady Day." Earlier, Mercer had sung with Holiday (sort of) on a Benny Goodman program; later, he would introduce her at the Newport Jazz Festival. One wonders if it ever occurred to him to sign her to Capitol, seeing as she was about to be at liberty. Since the AFM ban was about to start in July 1942 and continue for two years, it was a moot point. In 1944, Holiday would begin a seven-year relationship with producer Milt Gabler, first at Commodore Records, then at Decca.

From a distance, it looks as if Gabler was planning a specific album of Billie Holiday on Commodore. She did three dates in a relatively short time span (two weeks) that produced twelve tracks, all of which are roughly uniform in the same tempos (only a few, like "I'll Get By," are slightly faster) and all are vintage standards (like "Lover Come Back to Me" and "He's Funny That Way"). On the whole, Holiday is much more subdued than on her earlier work, and there's even less interaction or active participation from the sidemen (including Doc Cheatham and Vic Dickenson, trumpet and trombone) than the 1940–42 sessions. Gabler wisely brought back Eddie Heywood as musical director, yet his arrangements here also seem much less exciting. It's almost as if they're all taking Holiday's status as Diva with a capital D so seriously that they're less inclined to take risks and have fun. One can't argue, however, with the best singer in jazz doing such great tunes (including a couple of older songs that were revived during the war, "I'll Be Seeing You" and "As Tme Goes By") with such a terrific band.

Holiday began the postwar era in a curious position: Was she a jazz diva, who primarily sang old songs with small bands in small clubs for a niche audience (as they say in the twenty-first century)? Or could she be what she had been in the late thirties, trying to reach the mass market with a mix of material, old and new, blues and novelties, happy songs and sad songs and whatever? The greatest strength of Holiday's work in the mid- and late forties was that Gabler was committed to creatively exploring these issues and seeing what they could come up with. Not all the Decca sides are on the same level, but that's what's bound to happen when you're willing to experiment. On the whole, this is a very listenable catalogue of thirty-six songs, with a fair share of Holiday standards: "Crazy He Calls Me," "Don't Explain," "Good Morning Heartache," and the song that launched her relationship with Decca, "Lover Man."

Gabler had started Commodore Records in 1938 (an offshoot of his jazz specialty record shop on East Forty-second Street), and in 1941 he went to work for Jack Kapp at Decca Records. The delineation between what he was doing for the two labels was clear cut: Commodore was hardcore jazz for specialists, whereas at Decca he produced a wide variety of pop, blues, and even country material. Hence, with the spring 1944 Commodore sessions, Gabler felt obliged to stick with jazz standards. But then along came "Lover Man," written expressly for Holiday by a soldier named Jimmy Davis and Harlem pianist Ram Ramirez. Holiday later said that she wanted to record it, but Gabler also said that when he heard her doing "Lover Man" on Fifty-second Street, he knew at once that it had the potential to be a "smash hit." When he and Holiday talked about recording it, she told him, "I want fiddles!," which solidified the decision that it had to be for Decca, not Commodore. (As she remembered, "I took the song to Milt Gabler at Decca and I went on my knees to him, I loved it so. I begged Milt and told him I had to have strings behind me. . . .")

If the strings themselves were Holiday's idea, it was prescient of Gabler to go along with it; few, if any, black or jazz (or blues) singers had yet recorded with strings—not Armstrong, not Fitzgerald, and certainly not Bessie Smith. This was the first major example of an undeniable jazz voice (in a way that, for instance, Lena Horne was not) set against a lush string section. Even Holiday herself was overwhelmed. Tutti Camarata, who arranged and conducted the October 1944 session, told Steven Lasker (who produced the recommended 1991 reissue *Billie Holiday: The Complete Decca Sessions*), "She came into the studio, turned around and walked right out! I went after her and asked her what was wrong. She said, 'Oh man, these strings hit me pretty hard!' "

Downbeat described the record as a "surprise," which was putting it mildly. It was something that no one had heard before. Purists charged that the strings were a commercial affectation that compromised the jazz integrity of Holiday's singing, but I feel just the opposite. It's worth remembering that even in straight-ahead mainstream pop, there was precious little like this—Bing Crosby and Kate Smith never sang with this kind of big orchestral backdrop. (The closest thing was Artie Shaw's string sessions.) In 1944–45, the use of a classical string section was also one of the ways that Sinatra (who was going regularly to hear Holiday on Swing Street) was beginning to try to distinguish himself from his predecessors.

Which is not to imply that the strings on "Lover Man" suggest Mozart; they're much more like Miklós Rózsa or any of the leading film score composers. "Lover Man" and "No More" (the other tune from the first Decca date) both have a distinctive noir sound, dark and pensive and maybe slightly melodramatic. The strings frame Holiday's performance in such a way as to make it more intimate and personal, even more sensual. Compared to her erotically charged delivery here, the vocals on "I'll Be Seeing You" and the other spring Commodore titles sound almost detached.

Holiday recorded five titles in October and November 1944 (including her own "Don't Explain") with Camarata's orchestra for Gabler, and Decca released "Lover Man" backed with the equally excellent, only slightly less iconic "That Ole Devil Called Love." But Gabler apparently viewed this as a one-shot deal, not a long-term relationship, and didn't bring her back into the studio for another nine months, following which she didn't return until 1946. The bulk of the Decca sides would be done between then and 1949.

As a producer, Gabler had big ears and big eyes, and was open to a wide range of possibilities. Among other things, he produced some of her best up-tempo swinging numbers with big band accompaniment: Her 1949 "Them There Eyes" is much more exciting than the Vocalion original of ten years earlier. The band is loud and lively, and the tenor sax solo by Budd Johnson even more so, very much in the honking fashion of Illinois Jacquet. Holiday is incredibly playful: In the first 4 bars, she pauses for what seems like forever between "I fell in love with you the first time I looked into . . ." and "Them there eyes," waiting for a whole beat to fall. It's as if she's toying with our expectations before she's conditioned us to expect them.

The form is ABAB, and on some of the A sections (particularly the line about her heart going "jumping") she's choppy and staccato, right on the beat, until she gets to the bridges, whereupon she stretches out and lets the words flow smoothly into one another; both approaches are miraculously swinging, the juxtaposition of them even more so. Sy Oliver's arrangement elaborates on the looser 1939 chart and has an ingenious second vocal chorus in which Holiday literally sings rings around the band: She sings the first two lines of each A, they come back blasting the title phrase at her instrumentally—as a kind of tutti—but the brassier they get, the hipper and subtler Holiday seems by contrast. In subsequent live performances, she would keep playing with the tune—sometimes deliberately squeaking on the high note on "bubble." The studio version ends with another personalized coda, "I'm looking for the boy with the wistful eyes," that she would vary over the years, sometimes using a spoken aside instead.

"Good Morning Heartache" represents the dark side of Holiday's force, packing the kind of emotional wallop we expect from Garland or Piaf. The title seems distantly inspired by the Count Basie–Jimmy Rushing "Good Morning Blues," in which the blues or heartache is characterized anthropomorphically, like a physical entity with whom one could have a conversation: "Good morning, blues,

blues how do you do?" "Good morning, heartache, sit down."

When Holiday cut "Heartache" in January 1946, the lyricist, Ervin Drake, was sitting in the main room between Holiday and the string section, so close that he could have reached out and touched her—which he was tempted to do. "She did it in one take," he told me, "and it was marvelous." According to the discography, there are only four strings on the session, but they're still a significant presence. As for Holiday herself, this is as sublime an interpretation as anyone has ever delivered on a song; she's capable of communicating profound levels of feeling that are entirely unprecedented anywhere in pop music, an ever churning mixture of protest, frustration, and resignation. The closest thing that I can think of is the happy/sad nature of one of Lester Young's classic tenor solos, like "Sometimes I'm Happy." She addresses the presence of heartache almost affectionately, "you old gloomy sight," kind of the same gentle put-down one would extend to an old friend. When she sings "I turned and tossed until it seemed you had gone," she inflects those words in such a way that you actually feel her turning and tossing. She's capable of extracting every single nuance out of Drake's lyric, yet you feel she doesn't need the words at all. No wonder Sinatra called her "the single greatest influence on me"—and that was in 1958, while she was still alive.

In trying to sell Holiday's records, Gabler, commendably, did not forget about the black audience. Holiday seems to have recorded more blues and blues-related material in the forties than during any other period; Gabler was concurrently producing Louis Jordan's records, and he was keenly aware of what was going on in the "race" market. Where "Billie's Blues" and "Fine and Mellow" were in traditional 12-bar blues form, many songs in the Decca period, like her own "Now or Never," freely drew upon both blues and pop elements, and were the same sort of thing that the early R&B stars like Dinah Washington and Jordan were doing. Both Holiday and Washington recorded Leonard Feather's "Baby Get Lost," a rather impudent blues in C that gets downright vituperative in the stop-time bridge. "The Blues Are Brewin'," which Holiday sang in the forgettable *New Orleans* (in which she played, as she told Feather, "a really cute maid"), is a phony-baloney Hollywood version of a blues, written by veterans Louis Alter and Eddie DeLange, who should have known better.

More creatively, "Big Stuff" was another Leonard's idea of the blues: Leonard Bernstein, who wrote both words and music as part of his 1944 ballet *Fancy Free,* the predecessor to *On the Town.* Holiday made a special recording of the song (accompanied by Bernstein's sister, Shirley) that was used as a prologue before the dance started. She also cut the song for Decca, a process that somehow took four sessions over sixteen months. On the 1991 *Complete Decca* package, there are two alternate takes with full orchestra and strings, although the issued take utilizes just a quintet featuring Holiday's current paramour Joe Guy on trumpet. We can be glad they persevered: "Big Stuff" is an ingenious variation on the blues with elegant words and music by the Maestro. Holiday adroitly follows Bernstein's emotional trajectory—haughty and defiant in the central section (sort of an A) and more compassionate and inviting in the equivalent of the bridge. I almost think she's too lovey-dovey on the big band version; in the small group take, the song gets treated rough, and it likes it.

In fall 1949 Holiday explored yet another kind of blues in the form of four songs closely associated with Bessie Smith. Gabler consistently denied that he was considering an album of *Billie Sings Bessie,* but the evidence is pretty clear; in any case, the project never got beyond these four songs, which were not issued at the time as an album. Two of the four, "Gimme a Pigfoot (and a Bottle of Beer)" and "Do Your Duty," were from the final session of the Empress of the Blues, which was masterminded by Hammond three days before Holiday's first recording in 1933. Sy Oliver's arrangements are very hard and angular, with boppish overtones, and much more intense than Smith's original accompaniments, although Holiday herself is remarkably subtle and highly nuanced, giving the songs a word-by-word interpretation of the sort I can't imagine Smith doing in the twenties. Holiday isn't entirely in her comfort zone: Some of the jazz age references seem anachronistic, particularly in "Pigfoot"—Holiday was a sophisticated lady and it's hard to imagine her getting excited over pig's feet and beer. (If only! What did turn her on, alas, was far more worrisome.)

But one of the things that make this quartet of songs great is that they show us another side of her. In "Do Your Duty," she plays a woman pleading for her man to give her some attention (my word, not hers), while "Keep's on A-Rainin'" is sung from the perspective of a man named "Big John" (obviously the same character whom Dinah Washington refers to as "Long John"), whose romantic inclinations are disrupted by the inclement weather. "'Tain't Nobody's Business If I Do" is a whole other story. It's telling that when dealing with matters of race, Holiday was eventually impelled to take up the torch of protest and rail against such matters as lynchings. Yet when it comes to the politics of gender, she's disturbingly acquiescent. Instead of protesting the inequality of the sexes, Holiday seems to be celebrating the lengths a long-suffering woman will go to for her man—unless, as some feminist might argue (and this is a stretch), these songs are actually her way of speaking out against these conditions.

A friend of Holiday's once said that she could walk into a room of respectable, good-looking, well-mannered young men, and walk out with the only wife-beating, parole-breaking, low-life, alcoholic reprobate in the bunch. Likewise, in her music she gravitates repeatedly toward what scholar Farrah Jasmine Griffith has identified as "masochistic love songs." "When a Woman Loves a Man," "She's Funny That Way," and "Jim" are the mildest; in these Tin Pan Alley songs, the male partner is merely insensitive. In "No Good Man" and her own "Don't Explain," Lady is thoroughly resigned to the idea that Lover Man will be serially unfaithful to her, and these are among the most moving performances she put on record—she's almost frighteningly believable when she sings that she doesn't care how her man treats her or what he does to her as long as he takes her in his arms.

The most extreme are the French "My Man" and "Ain't Nobody's Business If I Do" (from a traditional folk blues source), in which she accepts physical violence as a normal part of man-woman relations. Even "Jim," who doesn't bring her pretty flowers and try to cheer her lonely hours, is practically a saint compared to "My Man," who isn't true and beats her, too. When Bessie Smith sang "Ain't Nobody's Business If I Do" in 1923, she had a haughty, defiant air about her, leaving you with the distinct impression that no man could ever get away with anything that she didn't want him to do. Holiday is going for some of the same attitude, but let's just say that she's insufficiently empowered—she sounds as if she's making excuses for his abuse. The issue isn't whether Lover Man beats her or not; she's arguing that it's her constitutional right to let him do whatever he wants. (Talk about a pyrrhic victory.)

You don't need a degree in psychology to see this theme—womanly devotion far beyond the call of duty—running throughout her repertoire. "You're My Thrill," sung definitively by Holiday and echoed in her own way by disciple Peggy Lee, is clearly a song of erotic obsession, while in "Lover Man" she all but worships the second-person protagonist ("Oh where can you be?") as if he were the Greek god Eros. "Billie's Blues" includes the truly harrowing line "I've been your slave ever since I've been your babe," which she follows with "But before I'll be your dog I'll see you in your grave." It's true there's a note of defiance there, suggesting that even a doormat of a woman has some limits and draws a line somewhere, but ultimately it's a token gesture—the distance between acting as a man's slave and being his dog seems too minimal to fight over.

One of the most rewarding things about listening steadily to Holiday's output is that it's full of surprises (except, perhaps, when you go through the surviving tapes of live concerts from the fifties, which inevitably all contain the same half dozen songs). There are two amazing documents from 1949 and 1951 that are worth discussing, although it makes more sense not to talk about them in chronological order.

In April 1951 Holiday, again working under the name "Lady Day" (I'm not sure exactly why, since she doesn't seem to have been under contract to anyone else at the time), made one session for Aladdin Records. The fascinating thing about these four orphan sides (issued on the Blue Note CD *Billie's Blues*) is that they offer a hint as to what her subsequent career might have sounded like had she gone in a rhythm and blues direction. Backed by a sextet led by guitarist Tiny Grimes (who, throughout his long career, consistently demonstrated that there was little appreciable difference between jazz and R&B), all four songs impinge upon the blues in some fashion. Two are outright 12-bar I-IV-V melodies, "Be Fair with Me Baby" and "Rocky Mountain Blues," and two are ballads, "Blue Turning Grey Over You" (written by Fats Waller), which alludes to the blues in its title at least, and "Detour Ahead," which has a blues feel.

On the whole, the production sounds like what Dinah Washington or Ruth Brown were doing at the time. The sides made no impact on the market and, other than doing "Detour" (a song that was ideally suited to her) at a couple of live shows, Holiday never sang any of these again, even "Blue Turning Grey," which she learned from her hero, Louis Armstrong.

Obviously, the song-songs are excellent, no surprise there. But the two "pure" blues are also delightful, and they're the real thing—handy proof to have around in case anyone is foolish enough to claim that Holiday wasn't a genuine blues singer. More than jazz, the blues is almost never about composition; it's about the feeling you can come up with on the spot and about using the words and music as a conduit for that feeling. "Rocky Mountain" uses the metaphor of scaling a cliff for dealing with a bad relationship, and here she clearly communicates that even though she's currently down in the dumps, "I will climb this mountain / If it's the last thing I do." Even on "Be Fair," she feels she at least has a chance at getting Lover Man to treat her respectfully—or else why ask? There's no air of resignation here. It's easy to extrapolate a larger meaning from these four titles: On the more mainstream Tin Pan Alley pop songs, Holiday is more likely to be downtrodden and hopeless; on the blues, she's just as likely to be defiant and empowered.

But not on, along with other exceptions, "I Wonder Where Our Love Has Gone." Holiday sang that 1947 blues-inflected song by bandleader Buddy Johnson just once, in a live recording from California in June 1949. (Or at least, it was recorded or documented only on this occasion.) The details of the performance are unknown: Ten songs were used on the Armed Forces Radio Services show *Just Jazz*, produced by Gene Norman, a local radio personality who later became an important producer. We don't know the location, or even whether it's a nightclub or a concert hall (a lot of the *Just Jazz* shows were recorded at the Pasadena Civic Auditorium or at the

Shrine in Los Angeles); eight of the ten *Just Jazz* songs have been bootlegged and rebootlegged all over the world many, many times on LP and CD, but there is no complete issue with all ten tracks in good-quality audio.

The *Just Jazz* tracks are worth our consideration because this is an exceptionally good live performance from a comparatively early period, with pianist Jimmy Rowles, one of Holiday's best later accompanists. There are also three songs that she would never record commercially, including "You're Driving Me Crazy," the Basiecentric jazz standard. Holiday does it as a swinging riff in the "Them There Eyes" tradition—Rowles is especially helpful here—which she ends by reprising the title line in kind of a ballad coda, one of her famous descending slide notes. "Maybe You'll Be There" is the torch song from 1947 by pianist Rube Bloom; although this is the only trace of her doing it, it's clear it could have easily been one of her regular songs of love and loss.

"I Wonder Where Our Love Has Gone" is an absolute treasure. It's nearly four full minutes long, essentially just Holiday and Rowles (the bass is barely audible), equal parts magic and tragic. It's thrilling and devastating. It even helps that Johnson, who also wrote the lyrics, wasn't a super-polished wordsmith of the theater variety (he rhymes "more" and "go"); it makes the text and the delivery that much more direct and human. Traffic seems to stop around it, time just stands still, Holiday transports you to a whole other place when she sings—when the crowd applauds at the end (and well they should) it abruptly jolts you back to reality. No one has ever sounded so open, so alone, so fragile, so exposed, and so vulnerable. In anyone else's discography, this would be a high point; in Holiday's canon, it's merely a throwaway.

In terms of her relationship with her repertoire, Holiday was unique. She had a distinct body of songs associated with her that fans wanted to hear and that she sang at virtually every show. They weren't chart hits (like Peggy Lee's tune stack) and they weren't songs identified with her from shows or films (like Judy Garland's songbook). They were simply songs that she had sung over the years that seemed to fit her—they formed her own personal mythology. Michael Brooks, who produced the *Complete Columbia* box, is one of many advocates of the opinion that "much of [Holiday's material] was bad." While we're on the subject, not every one of the thirty-six she recorded for Decca is exactly "Embraceable You" either—"Girls Were Meant to Take Care of Boys" is just plain sappy, the kind of old-fashioned thing that they should have saved for Dick Haymes. Likewise, no one could have redeemed "This Is Heaven to Me," the last song in the Decca contract. (No one was more surprised than I when latter-day Holiday accolyte Madeline Peyroux revived it.) Yet both these eras yielded numerous wonderful, obscure tunes that never quite crossed over into standarddom, like the delightful "Here It Is Tomorrow Again," Hoagy Carmichael's "April in My Heart," and two songs by George Cory and Douglass Cross (the team who later wrote "I Left My Heart in San Francisco") in 1946–47, the beautiful "I'll Look Around" and "Deep Song." To me, the gems outnumber the dogs.

By contrast, when she recorded exclusively for producer Norman Granz from 1952 to 1957, she sang almost nothing but time-tested standards. No dogs here. Granz also backed her with nothing but excellent musicians who were worthy of the honor, in groups that generally consist of trumpet (usually Sweets Edison or Charlie Shavers), sax (Ben Webster or Vice President Paul Quinichette), and four rhythm (led by Oscar Peterson or, better yet, Jimmy Rowles). As with the 1944 Commodore titles, everything about the best of the Granz-Holiday sessions (originally released on Clef and then Verve) is practically perfect. Almost *too* perfect.

The only thing not to like about the 1952–57 sessions is the producer's unwillingness to take chances. Every tune is either a proven standard or a long-established Billie Holiday classic. It's a funny thing to complain about. Admittedly, these are some of the finest jazz vocal sessions ever made, and one feels like an ingrate complaining that the material is too uniformly excellent—or rather, that there are too few surprises. I can listen to the ARC material a thousand times and continually hear something marvelous I never noticed before, and this is less likely to happen on the Clef and Verve sessions. The major revelations, such as they are, derive mainly from the taped rehearsals, such as the aforementioned session with Tony Scott in which Holiday is obviously on a Sophie Tucker kick, singing "My Yiddishe Momme" and "Some of These Days," and another private tape with Jimmy Rowles. (All this material is included on another ten-CD set, Polygram's 1992 *The Complete Billie Holiday on Verve, 1945–1959*.)

If you want classy singing, even from well after the point where she begins to lose her chops, this is it. It's amazing how consistent the results are, given the carefully controlled circumstances. I doubt that Berlin, Arlen, Porter, Kern, and Rodgers have ever been subjected to a more thorough workout. (There's also a marvelous reading of Matt Dennis's "Everything Happens to Me"; would that catching colds and missing trains were the worst of Lady Day's problems.) This is a less frantic, more relaxed and mature Holiday that we hear in her late thirties and early forties. Her improvisational style has also settled down—you'll hear fewer instances of her radically rewriting a melody or, as in the case of the 1937 "I Can't Get Started," the lyric. These sides are less urgent than the thirties recordings, accomplishing in four or five minutes what she usually did in two or three in the early days, but that relaxed quality can be attractive, too.

In one sense, the 1950s recordings are the best of her entire career: Producer Granz was deliberately trying to re-create the freewheeling sound of Holiday's 1935–38 dates, the jam sessions from before she began using prewritten charts, but with uniformly better songs. He used small groups—not orchestras with strings—and encouraged full-length solos of several choruses each from at least two or three sidemen on almost every number. He couldn't entirely erase her more divacentric work of the forties and go back to the freewheeling thirties, but he gave it his best shot.

In spite of the long-term success of the Decca and then Verve releases, by 1950 Holiday was nowhere near as recognizable a black superstar as Louis Jordan, Louis Armstrong, Billy Eckstine, or Ella Fitzgerald. She was widely loved in Harlem and among jazz fans, but even her two most popular discs, "I Cried for You" and "Fine and Mellow," were mere minnows compared to a blockbuster like Ella Fitzgerald's "A-Tisket, A-Tasket." In the forties, her reputation as a cult favorite strengthened with songs like "God Bless the Child," "Lover Man," and "Good Morning Heartache," but she wasn't a consistent enough seller to remain on Decca after the shakeup that occurred following the death of founder Jack Kapp. She had her following and her fans, but was rarely popular enough even to get on the cover of *Down Beat*, and her final long-term producer-and-record-company affiliation with Norman Granz and Clef could be construed as a step back to the minors.

But in 1956, something happened that boosted Holiday's star power considerably. This was the publication of her autobiography, *Lady Sings the Blues;* she dictated her story to journalist William Dufty, who took considerable liberties with her words and the facts, but the result was a highly readable best seller that earned her considerable money and late-in-life fame. Sadly, it wasn't until the loathsome film of said book, which was released in 1972, thirteen years after her death, that Holiday became a pizza parlor perennial. (Diana Ross gives a surprisingly moving performance as some kind of bedraggled, drug-addicted torch singer, but neither she nor anything else in the picture seems to have anything to do with who or what Lady Day actually was.)

In writing *Lady Sings the Blues,* Holiday made the transition from a mere singer to a performance artist. In November 1956 she even did a full-length solo recital at Carnegie Hall, which could have been titled "Lady Sings the Blues—the Concert." She sang her now-familiar songbook (along with one of her few new songs of the period, "Lady Sings the Blues," with music by modernist Herbie Nichols) interspersed with readings from the book by Gilbert Millstein, the *New York Times* lit crit.

In a sense, she had found a way to profit from her misfortune—what Arlene Croce would later describe as "victim art." By now music was no longer her only art; her life itself had become an artistic statement. When the 1956 concert was released some years later as *The Essential Billie Holiday,* Millstein wrote, "It was evident, even then, that Miss Holiday was ill" and "I was shocked at her physical weakness . . . but I will not forget the metamorphosis that night. . . . She was erect and beautiful; poised and smiling. And when the first section of narration was ended, she sang—with strength undiminished—with all of the art that was hers." The recording bears him out: She is in incredibly good shape for this period in her life (she sounds better here than on most of the 1955 studio dates). This is one of her most powerful readings yet of "Fine and Mellow," for instance. Obviously, she was reenergized by the occasion.

The book and the concert were Holiday's ultimate confessional. Holiday was raised Catholic, and some observers (including the priest and jazz scholar Father Peter O'Brien) have noted the recurrence of Catholic themes in her art. She didn't write most of the songs she sang, but there was, shall we say, a certain consistency in her material, not only what she recorded but what she kept in her act for years and years, and many of her perennials have a confessional quality. Holiday even brings that spirit to the most ungoyish performance of her career, "My Yiddishe Momme," which was recorded under informal circumstances at the home of co-memoirist William Dufty, accompanied by Tony Scott (customarily a clarinetist, here playing piano). This 1925 song finds Holiday and Scott taking a break from working out routines and keys in order to sing a lullaby for the Duftys' fifteen-month-old son, Bevan. For her, "Yiddishe Momme" is not a gag. She really sings her heart out, and lines like "Ask her to forgive me for / Things I did to make her cry" suggest a solidarity between Catholic confessional and Jewish atonement merging into Holiday's tough love—in the toughest sense of the term.

Interestingly, Holiday didn't get along with most of her fellow singers. They tended to make her insecure and therefore jealous. Tony Bennett and Rosemary Clooney (who both recorded albums in tribute to her decades after her death) were exceptions. It may be a coincidence that they're both Catholic, however Holiday and Clooney can be said to have bonded over religion in that Holiday offered to serve as godmother for one of Rosemary's children. This was Holiday's own idea—it was too outrageous for Clooney to have suggested—but Holiday reasoned, "Well, I think that it would be a good thing if I was her Godmother because it takes a bad woman to be a good Godmother."

Clooney recalled an incident that more typically describes Holiday's relationships with other singers:

> I remember once when Billie was singing at a little place down on Hollywood Boulevard. Joe [Ferrer, Clooney's first husband] and I went to see her with Dinah Shore, who was a friend of

mine, and her husband George [Montgomery]. We had been at the tennis matches and Dinah said, "Let's go hear Billie Holiday." And, you know, I thought it was a fine idea because Billie and I had been friends for a while by that time. Well, I already knew that Billie could be brutally honest under certain circumstances. And her set was coming up and she stopped at our table before the show and said to me, "What are you sitting with her for?" meaning Dinah. And now I'm smiling and laughing and, like, "Isn't this a funny joke?," like I was trying to pretend Billie wasn't saying that. So I said, "Oh Billie you know Dinah here, you know George and you know my husband Joe and you know what fans we are of yours, and we just can't wait for your show. . . . What are you going to sing?" I was babbling, talking nonsense just to shut her up because I knew what the next words were going to be. She said, "Don't sit next to her. You could catch bad singing." My God, I just wanted the floor to swallow me up! But Dinah was ever the lady, you know, she acted as if it just never happened. She didn't hear it, and that was the end of it.

It was not yet Lady's last stand. Now that the book and the Carnegie concert had elevated her profile once more, the phone was ringing again; in December 1957, she made her most celebrated television appearance, singing "Fine and Mellow" on *The Sound of Jazz*. Two major labels wanted to do albums with her, and the results were *Lady in Satin* for Columbia (1958) and *Billie Holiday*, more often referred to as "the MGM Album" (1959). There also was a technological motivation behind *Lady in Satin*, in that the combination of the long-playing record and the new high-fidelity and stereo recording processes were making it possible and desirable to record ever larger and more opulent orchestras and string sections for what was starting to be classified as "mood music." Then thirty-four, Ray Ellis was one of Columbia's up-and-coming purveyors of the emerging genre; Holiday supposedly had heard and liked Ellis's first album, the very successful *Ellis in Wonderland*, and contacted producer Irving Townsend about doing an album with him.

Lady in Satin was an instant classic, capturing Holiday in remarkably good vocal form with excellent tunes and sympathetic string orchestrations. She obviously had heard Nat Cole's recent albums with Gordon Jenkins and the classic Sinatra-Riddle records and wanted a big hi-fi string section. Columbia originally released *Lady in Satin* on two very different LP editions (the mono and the stereo versions utilize different takes and even different songs) and, later, three equally different CD editions. The most recent of these, supervised by Phil Schaap, at least collates all the various material, and straightens out such matters as the absence of a stereo mas-

ter on the last tune, "The End of a Love Affair." (The credits of the second CD edition state that the arrangements themselves were actually the work of the young German composer Claus Ogerman, who would later collaborate with Sinatra, Stan Getz, Wes Montgomery, and others.)

Holiday had only a year and a half to live when these songs were recorded, and the voice was obviously far less palatable than it had been in her prime. (Although she actually sounds stronger on these February 1958 sessions than she did in many of her 1955–57 Verve sessions.) Yet what Holiday had lost in chops, she more than made up for in ability to move an audience. The dramatic contrast between her hoarse and passionate sound and the orchestrations (whether by Ogerman or Ellis) also helps make this one of the most moving collections of pop standards of its time—or any other.

Lady in Satin is a classic in spite of how the background music is truly "background music"; it doesn't sound like classical music, it doesn't sound like film noir, it really sounds like Percy Faith or Ray Conniff or the other purveyors of what was becoming known as "easy listening." *Lady in Satin*, indeed; you could call it *Lady on an Elevator*.

One of the set's major strengths is the way Holiday sings the verses to "Glad to Be Unhappy," "For All We Know," and others. She was reluctant to sing them; like many who had grown up in the band era (including Sinatra), she didn't care for verses as a rule. "I finally realized she had never learned the verses," said Ellis, "so I gave the orchestra a break and had her sit down with her pianist, Mal Waldron, and learn them." We're glad that the director insisted and that the star acquiesced. "For Heaven's Sake," though bereft of the verse, is an obvious highlight. The background voices hold back somewhat on this one, and a flute figure recalls Nelson Riddle, but more important, Holiday's storytelling abilities are at full throttle. She uses some of her trademark mannerisms, twisting the high notes on "Just *hold* me tight / We're alone *in* the night," but otherwise it's amazing how spare and reserved her singing is—as if she refuses to depart from the melody unless she feels she absolutely must. As with the best of her students, including Sinatra, this is a clear illustration of how Holiday's singing was not about her mannerisms, her personal life, or even the woman herself— the only thing that mattered to her was the song and the story.

A year later, in March 1959, Holiday sounds several decades older on the album released shortly after her death as *Billie Holiday*, which was also conducted by Ellis. These final two albums contain songs associated with Nat King Cole ("For All We Know"), Johnny Mathis ("It's Not for Me to Say"), and especially Sinatra ("I'll Never Smile Again," "All the Way," "Violets for Your Furs," and others); would that she had also done "Over the Rainbow." Holiday's vocal power has decreased, but fortunately so has the size of the orchestra, and the three wordless sopranos from *Lady in Satin,* saints be praised, have been locked in the ladies' room. Both *Lady in Satin* and *Billie Holiday* are of a piece with Louis Armstrong's *Satchmo Under the Stars* and Crosby's *Bing with a Beat.* Here we have three of the absolute primary colors of American culture keeping up to date with the times and making contemporary music in the style of their disciples, like Fitzgerald and Sinatra. Holiday was part of the younger generation chronologically, but in experience and wisdom she was by far the oldest of them all, and would be the first to go—only four months after these sessions.

It's all too apparent that Holiday is very close to the end here, and it comes through especially in her few faster tempos; she seems overwhelmed and underpowered, making her attempts at happy songs the saddest thing of all. On "Sometimes I'm Happy" you think, No, she doesn't sound as if she could ever be happy. On "You Took Advantage of Me" you think, Yeah, someone obviously did.

"When It's Sleepy Time Down South" is also very sad, but in a good way. The inclusion of the verse (the only time I've heard it) to Louis Armstrong's signature song heightens the emotional impact. The refrain itself describes a pastoral scene of the gallant South, but the verse establishes what the rest of the song does not implicitly state: that the singer is speaking from somewhere up north, where she's homesick for old Virginny. Holiday makes clear that the song is about going home, and in the context of where she was at this point in her life, that means a multitude of things. Home is the South, where she grew up (born in Philadelphia but raised in Baltimore). Home is the ideal of Louis Armstrong, the man whom she consistently acknowledged as her key inspiration ("I copied my style from Louis," she says in a 1956 interview with Willis Conover) and who made her want to sing to begin with. And lastly, home is the hereafter. When we pass from this earth we return to the cosmos or the happy hunting ground or the big bandstand in the sky. Whatever. Wherever she's going, it's not going to be long before she goes.

Armstrong is all over "Sleepy Time" and Sinatra is cited directly in a piece of special material for "There'll Be Some Changes Made." Following the dropping of his name, she continues, "I must make some changes from the old to the new / I must do things just the same as others do." Holiday, unlike Sinatra, was powerless to change anything about herself, whether it was good or bad. On the ten-CD *Complete Verve* box, the MGM album is sequenced in original recording order, which illustrates how some sessions are jazzier than others, particularly the final date, which employs three brass, two reeds, and four rhythm—no strings. Had *Lady in Satin* been Holiday's final album, she would have gone out with a big dramatic exit. *Billie Holiday* makes for a

much subtler coda, and it's not a bad note on which to conclude a great career.

Mel Tormé was one of the few younger singers who was mentioned in Holiday's book, and whether it was Dufty or Lady herself who put him in ("He wasn't imitating anybody and he had that beat," true, true), it was a singular honor that Mel was always proud of. Mel was fond of likening the sound of Billie Holiday's voice to the taste of spinach: "It may not taste good, but it's so good for you." I have to admit that for the longest time, I thought Mel was selling Holiday short. He himself had a smooth, beautiful voice, but I couldn't imagine that he could only appreciate smooth-voiced singers like, say, Vic Damone or Sarah Vaughan; he couldn't possibly fail to appreciate the beauty of the sound of Holiday, Armstrong, or, for that matter, Thelonious Monk. Stupid me. It wasn't until after Mel died that I finally figured out what he was talking about: It wasn't her voice that didn't taste good; it was her message that, like medication, was often difficult to swallow. Mel was referring to the often-horrific content of her music, her tales of lovers being pushed to the very precipice of human emotion, the most remote peaks of human feeling, the uppest ups and the downest downs that we are capable of feeling. Perhaps Holiday is telling us that it's only when we're subjected to these extremes that we can truly appreciate life. Even when she's mired in the dregs of human weakness and failings, she is, in the end, celebrating the human condition.

Shirley Horn (1934–2005)

Understatement is overrated. Most of the time, less is not more, as the minimalists would have you believe, but less is actually less. Musically speaking, who wouldn't prefer the art of maximalists like Oscar Peterson or Judy Garland, whose work is crammed to the breaking point with musical and emotional resonance? The pianist and singer Shirley Horn is a rare example of an artist who might convince you that less really is more.

Yet I still can't think of the music of Miss Horn as "minimalist" in the way the term is generally used. It's true that, like Count Basie, she employed as few notes as possible—never playing two notes when one would do, never sustaining them for two beats when one was sufficient. Yet she was never making a conceptual point, she was simply trying to keep her artistic canvas from getting overcrowded, knowing full well that too many notes on one's plate could easily get in one another's way, compete with one another, overpower one another.

When she sings Johnny Mandel's "Close Enough for Love" on her 1988 album of the same title, each gorgeous note and each well-placed idea has plenty of room to resonate. She keeps the harmonic backdrop wide and open so there's always plenty of room up front for the melody. Even when she employs a Latin rhythm, as on "How Am I to

Know?" (on the 1992 *Here's to Life*), she does it subtly and gently, and refuses to let it overwhelm the piece as a whole.

It's not that she never built to a loud climax—she did occasionally, as on "Georgia on My Mind" on her 1981 *Violets for Your Furs*. But when she does it's particularly effective, simply because she made it a point never to overuse this particular device—in fact, never to overdo anything. But we shouldn't make the mistake of thinking that Horn did as little as she could get away with. Just the opposite: She sang and played as much as she could, belted as loud as she could, played as many breathtaking fast arpeggios as she felt the music would allow. But her innate artistic tolerance of such things had a very low threshold. She knew exactly the point of no return at which too many notes or syllables would start to cancel one another out. In a sense, she was a musical maximalist who squeezed as much music as possible out of every precious note.

Horn could be sultry and mysterious, yet for the most part she was direct and forthright. She eschewed the tricky arrangements, so common to music today, that are complicated for no reason other than to declare the so-called cleverness of the performer or arranger. As she once told me, "I think a ballad should be sung slow, I don't think a ballad should be sung like a foxtrot. That bugs me. If you're going to do a foxtrot, do a foxtrot. Slow down and interpret the lyric and try to paint a picture, tell a story. If it's a love song, do it that way."

In jazz, tempo is an essential part of an artist's musical personality: As critic Francis Davis has said of Bud Powell, speed is a key part of stylization, and the lack of speed is likewise an artistic statement. If slowness was a driving force of her artistry, it was correspondingly slow to pay off for her: In June 1992, she opened for Mel Tormé at Carnegie Hall during the JVC Jazz Festival. The crowd was primed for Mel's high-energy presentation and had no idea what to make of this extremely subtle, extremely slow pianist and singer (whom nobody there had ever heard of), who, in a manner diametrically opposed to the headliner's, never seemed to reach out to them. They all but ignored her, acting as if she weren't there—or worse, as if she were just there to supply cocktail piano as a background to their conversation. And I can't only blame the callousness of the crowd, or even the technicians at Carnegie who left the house lights on during her set. For her part, Horn refused to do anything to attract attention, she just kept playing and singing her usual nightclub material—which included long solos for her bassist—and seemed not to care whether anyone was paying attention or not. Yes, the crowd was acting as if she weren't there, but she was acting as if the audience weren't there. This was undoubtedly one of her first appearances at Carnegie and it gave her a good chance to win over several thousand people who had probably never heard her before. The way

in which she was unable to make the most of this opportunity provides a clear illustration of why it took the world so long to appreciate her.

As noted earlier, time is a key concept both in the music and the career of Horn—as is also true of Andy Bey and Jimmy Scott. Horn, especially in the latter part of her career, phrased so slowly that the thirteen-year-old son of a friend of mine referred to her as "Shir . . . Lee . . . Horn." For all three artists, the concept of slowness works on several levels: Just as Horn, Bey, and Scott have never been in a rush to get through a song (Scott in particular can take "Try a Little Tenderness" and make it seem as long as *Gone With the Wind*), none of them was in a hurry to be appreciated by big, mainstream audiences. All three were around for many decades before they began to be noticed by more than a few hard-core cultists.

Shirley Horn lived virtually her whole life in Washington, D.C., where she was born on May 1, 1934. She was attracted to music and songs as a very young girl. "My family loved music and there was always music around from the greatest singers and bands," she said. "Usually, I just learned the songs my mother used to sing around the home. I would ask her, 'What's the name of this one, what's the name of that one?' because I'd have the melody in my mind. I remember hearing Peggy Lee singing 'Why Don't You Do Right?' In fact, probably 75 percent of the songs I do are ones I heard at home." "What I remember first in my life is playing the piano. That's when I was four years old. I'd go to my grandmother's home. She had a parlor with a great big piano. The parlor was for company, and it was closed off with French doors. It was always cold, but I didn't want to do anything but just go in there and sit on the piano stool. I wasn't interested in playing with the kids outside. After several years of this, my grandmother told my mother to get me lessons."

Horn's two biggest influences as a pianist-singer were Nat Cole and Ray Charles, and like them, she described her whole singing career as "an accident." At seventeen, she was working at a local Washington restaurant. "One night close to Christmas, this older gentleman who would regularly come in for dinner came with a teddy bear as tall as I. Somehow I knew that [bear was a gift] for me," she recalled. Soon enough, the customer sent her a note saying, "If you sing 'Melancholy Baby' the teddy bear is yours." "I was very shy and it was hard for me to sing, but I wanted that bear." Early on, she was particularly attracted to "You're My Thrill," another standard associated with Peggy Lee. Horn would play it and sing it at the Step Down, which she remembered was then considered D.C.'s "best jazz joint." The owner would repeatedly insist, " 'You've got to record that song,' " she remembered, "and I said, 'I'm going to do it once I've made up my mind.' " In the early fifties, she went to Howard University and supported herself and her education by working in local jazz clubs.

Around 1959, by which time she was married and about to give birth, she had the opportunity, for the only time in her life, to hear another favorite performer of hers in person. "I heard that Billie [Holiday] was going to be in Baltimore at the Tijuana Club," Horn told me. "So I said to my husband, 'We're going to see her.' I was practically in labor at that time, but I had to see her! I said, 'Do what you want to do, but I'm going,' and I did, and we went and I saw her for the first time. I was the biggest thing in the world and I insisted on sitting right in the front seat, and everybody just moved and let me have it!

"Again, I was very, very, very pregnant and was about to have a ten-and-a-half-pound baby. So they told me I couldn't go back to the dressing room, but I said, 'I'm going,' nobody stops me! I was terribly upset because she was in another world. But she was very kind to me, the way she looked at me! She said, 'I'm gonna give you my seat!' I sat down and I don't think I said anything to her, but she just talked to me. I was in a trance just looking at her, it was easy to see she had been a very beautiful woman, and no longer able to function very well."

Horn was at first more successful at starting a family than at launching a career: She was teaching music and playing in smaller clubs, but it seemed as if she would never progress beyond being a local favorite among the black population of Washington. In 1959, she recorded for the first time as a sideman to the pioneering jazz violinist Stuff Smith. Verve Records, recording in D.C., intended to do a Gershwin jazz album featuring Smith's hot violin as well as vocals by both Horn and the leader, but unfortunately most of the session was released only many years after the fact as part of a Mosaic box. A year or so later, she had the chance to make an album for the tiny independent label Stereo-Craft, a concern mostly known for albums by traditional jazzmen like Ruby Braff and Pee Wee Russell.

Almost no one heard the resultant record, *Embers and Ashes*, but one of the few who did was Miles Davis, who liked it so much that he brought Horn up from Washington to New York to open for him at the Vanguard in 1961. It's said that a number of the standards Davis recorded on his next album, *Seven Steps to Heaven*, were directly inspired by Horn; he obviously recognized that she shared his distinct aversion to throwing too many extra notes around.

Between an album, even on an itty-bitty label, and sharing a bill with Davis at the Vanguard, Shirley Horn now had a foot in the door. However, like Jimmy Scott, her history over most of the next three decades would be one of getting an occasional break (generally meaning a chance to do an album), but then not being able to capitalize on said break and falling back into obscurity. The exposure from the Vanguard brought her to the attention of Quincy Jones, then at Mercury Records. In 1962 and 1963, he produced two albums with her: *Loads of Love*, on which another Jones, pianist and arranger Jimmy Jones, conducted an all-star band (including Gerry Mulligan), and *Shirley Horn with Horns*, done under the baton of Q himself. It's overstating the obvious to declare that neither of these early efforts made Horn into a star, and today they serve mainly as historical documents of her early style.

The best of Horn's sixties studio albums is the last, the 1965 *Travelin' Light*. Unlike the Mercury sets, *Travelin'* wisely employs Horn's regular working rhythm section plus a group of major jazz instrumentalists. Not surprisingly, she sounds much younger than the familiar, widely heard Shirley Horn of the nineties, and consistently sings in much faster tempos. However, she had already developed a deep, burnt umber sound, and a way of suggesting a melody, of outlining it, rather than filling in each little note. Even by the age of thirty-one, in 1965, she had perfected the art of giving the listener just enough information to follow either a story line or a melody line.

Travelin' Light is a sensational album. Nearly thirty years later, Horn would record a tribute to Ray Charles, *Light out of Darkness*. Songs that she obviously learned from him are scattered throughout her discography—like "Georgia on My Mind" on *Violets for Your Furs* and "New York's My Home" on *A Lazy Afternoon*. The influence of Miles Davis (which she acknowledged in a full-length tribute package, the 1998 *I Remember Miles*) is readily discernible in terms of her use of timbre and tempo; Horn's debt to Ray Charles is buried a bit deeper—you'll never hear her screaming and squealing like Brother Ray. Yet particularly on Marvin Jenkins's "Big City" and "Don't Be on the Outside," Horn and her eight-piece ensemble capture the spirit of the great, compactly swinging octet Charles led in the 1950s, before he expanded to orchestral proportions.

Throughout, from the Broadway-saucy "Confession" (from *The Band Wagon*) to the blues-saucy "Some of My Best Friends Are the Blues," Horn found the perfect balance of sultriness and coolness. Unlike most singers of her genre and generation, she even made an early and most admirable peace with the rival camp by doing a tender, personal, and highly jazzy treatment of the Lennon-McCartney "And I Love Her."

Travelin' Light is our first full-scale glimpse of the mature Horn style. Thirty years later, her message caught on, in that the most successful singers (in jazz or genres adjacent to it) of recent years have all been, to a certain degree, sultry and understated: Cassandra Wilson, Madeline Peyroux, Diana Krall, Patricia Barber, Norah Jones. The best of them have learned Horn's lesson: Don't just sound detached and dispassionate, as if you couldn't give a darn, but make an emotion more powerful by bringing just enough energy to it. Less, as we have seen, is not more, but just enough is perfect.

Travelin' Light, which, like her other early works, was in the catalogue for roughly a day and a half, would be her last full-length album for seven years (and her last project with an ensemble larger than her trio for almost thirty). *Where Are You Going* (1972, Perception) is a quartet album that points to her future work with her trio, including several Horn classics that would remain in her repertoire for years, the Arlen-Harburg "The Eagle and Me" and Marvin Fisher's scintillating "Something Happens to Me," a tune prized among pianist-singers following the Cole brothers, Nat and Freddy. The most familiar piece is the Gershwin brothers' "Do It Again" (with a marvelous spoken verse) and the most esoteric is a rather unexplainable piece of performance art entitled "Consequences of a Drug Addict Role," a longish and bizarre polemic against substance abuse, in which Horn uses electronic effects to phase in and out—and in general sounds completely stoned.

The two most ambitious pieces on *Where Are You Going* are the least successful: The title track lives up to its name by being a rather directionless melody, and "Drug Addict Role" can only be considered a success in that no one who hears it would ever want to go near drugs or drug addicts. Yet her use of the quartet format presages her classic later albums with her trio, and the tempos are slower than her earlier recordings, also pointing forward to the nineties more than back to the sixties. Most innovative is a treatment of Bobby Scott's "A Taste of Honey" that uses Miles Davis's "All Blues" as a framing, contextual vamp.

The big news in Horn's career in the early seventies was not this comparatively lesser album (by her standards), but the entrance into her life of the bassist Charles Ables. Ables, a steady, supportive player who wore oversize glasses that made him look like Louis Jordan playing Deacon Jones, would be her partner on the instrument for the next twenty years. Her classic trio finally coalesced a few years later when drummer Steve Williams, the only surviving member of the group, came on board. The Shirley Horn Trio was such a perfect mini-ensemble, it's not surprising that just as the group was reaching a pinnacle, they were heard and signed by the recently reestablished Verve Records. Horn's "mature" period, therefore, can be easily divided in two distinct portions: pure trio (that is, trio-only) albums, and those where the trio interacts with larger and more ambitious studio-based ensembles.

The Shirley Horn "trio" albums include the following (only the first doesn't feature Ables or Williams) and *Where Are You Going*, which is technically a quartet date, albeit one that establishes the later sound of her working band:

A Lazy Afternoon (1978, Steeplechase)
All Night Long (1981, Steeplechase)

Violets for Your Furs (1981, Steeplechase)
The Garden of the Blues (1984, Steeplechase)
All of Me (1986, CBS-Sony), the trio plus Frank Wess on tenor and flute
I Thought About You (1987, Verve)
Softly (1987, Audiophile)
Close Enough for Love (1988, Verve)
I Love You, Paris (1992, Verve), taped live in Paris

The following projects utilize accompaniments beyond the trio (all of these are on Verve):

You Won't Forget Me (1990), with Miles Davis, Wynton and Branford Marsalis, and Toots Thielemans
Here's to Life (1992), with Johnny Mandel and His Orchestra
Light out of Darkness (1993), with Gary Bartz and various Ray Charlesian additives, among them a vocal group dubbed "The Hornettes"
The Main Ingredient (1995), with Joe Henderson, Buck Hill, Roy Hargrove, and Elvin Jones
Loving You (1997), a more contempo-poppish project, utilizing various combinations, including Steve Novosel on bass and synthesized strings
I Remember Miles (1998), with Roy Hargrove, Toots Thielemans, Ron Carter; her only Grammy winner thus far
You're My Thrill (2001), with Johnny Mandel and His Orchestra

Admittedly the distinction is in many cases elastic. *Close Enough for Love* uses the trio plus guest star Buck Hill, the finest of Washington-based tenors (what Von Freeman is to Chicago and Teddy Edwards was to Los Angeles), who was so much a part of Horn's musical family he could well be considered the fourth member of the trio; he guested with her again at the Au Bar in 2005 on what is believed to be her final recording. *Loving You* substantially reworks both the personnel of the trio, with Steve Williams in his familiar place at the drums but Steve Novosel in for Ables. *You Won't Forget Me*, *Light out of Darkness*, and *The Main Ingredient* all do use the familiar trio as a core group; still, the emphasis here is on the guest stars.

The trio albums have a purity that makes them unique; in a sense, it should be no surprise that Horn doesn't alter her performing style whether she's in a comparatively intimate room like Maxim's, a now defunct East Side spot where she played several times in the mid-nineties, or whether she's in Carnegie Hall. Naturally, like most singers Horn was better experienced live than on disc, but it's mainly because of the context, not because she does anything different. The intimate trio albums are the recordings where she comes closest to sounding the way she did in person.

Nearly all the trio discs have the same general assortment of tunes that she performs in a typical club set; the only one that qualifies as a concept album is *Garden of the Blues*. This is her only songbook package—a collection of works by a single composer. It's completely consistent that she elected to devote her only songbook album to a writer considerably off the beaten path, one Curtis Lewis. Like Marvin Fisher, Curtis Lewis is a favorite among jazz musicians. He also has some blues and soul credentials (Helen Humes and Aretha Franklin both recorded his "Today I Sing the Blues"), and as with Willard Robison, most of the inspiration for his lyrics derives from contrast between rural and urban, the traditional and the newfangled, and at least every other song seems to be about the loss of innocence. Though short (thirty-eight minutes), the live *Garden of the Blues* is a singularly ambitious and very satisfying project. In fact, all four of the albums she recorded for the Danish Steeplechase label are live, this one taped at a concert in Miami in 1984.

In 1986, Horn made another live album (from a club called Vine Street in Los Angeles), *I Thought About You*, but with a difference: This would be the first of eleven albums for Verve.

The concepts for her albums were often vague, but it didn't matter. *I Remember Miles* is essentially just a collection of standards with guests Thielemans and Hargrove, and if you heard the album without knowing the title, you might not guess it was a Davis tribute. Although, inspired by Horn, Davis recorded Spencer Williams's "Basin Street Blues" along with Clarence Williams's "Baby Won't You Please Come Home" and "I Fall in Love Too Easily," I don't think anybody associates those songs with him. It's all exquisitely done, and the very fact that Horn doesn't have to go out of the way to evoke Davis illustrates how essentially similar their slow ballad styles are. Her burnished tone and reliance on crawl tempos are just two qualities that make her voice closer than anyone else's to capturing Davis's very vocal Harmon-muted trumpet timbre.

The Miles tribute record arrived seven years after Horn had recorded with the trumpeter himself, on the title cut of *You Won't Forget Me*. Thirty years earlier, he had been one of Horn's early boosters, and roughly a year before his death, he consented to appear with her on what was probably his final studio session. At the time, it seemed as if the superstar Prince of Darkness was helping his onetime protégée by lending her his marquee value and presence, but in retrospect it was clearly the other way around. In giving Davis a chance to show that he could still play beautifully on standard changes, and that his chops hadn't completely eroded from decades of chemical and musical abuse, Horn was doing Miles a favor.

She never got to record with Ray Charles, but she did record a tribute album to him. When *Light out of Darkness* (1993) first came out, the only projects I could imagine that were less likely were *The George Shearing Quintet Plays Leadbelly* or *Lennie Tristano*

Plays Louis Jordan. Both Charles and Horn sang and played the piano, but at first glance that was all they seemed to have in common. The album juxtaposed the most raucous and rocking R&B shouter with the quietest and most intimately reflective singer-pianist ever to tiptoe across a keyboard. Bill Evans once observed, "You don't go to a Keith Jarrett concert to yell, 'yeah!'" We normally listen to Shirley Horn for different reasons than we listen to Ray Charles—for meditative rumination rather than romping and stomping; for thoughtful introspection rather than butt kicking. In *Light out of Darkness*, Horn moves several tunes from Charles's domain into her own territory, such as her spare, minimalist treatment of "Drown in My Own Tears," and "Georgia on My Mind." She likewise underplays "Hard-Hearted Hannah," a jazz standard usually treated with much wailing and gnashing. On other pieces, like the extroverted "Hit the Road, Jack!" she finds a halfway point between her own idiosyncratic sound and Charles's. When she unexpectedly essays a genuine rockhouse flag-waver like "I Got a (Wo)Man," she doesn't exactly rock but she proves that the uptempo Horn is no less engaging than she is on one of her more characteristic snail-tempo hypnotic spells.

The 1992 *Here's to Life*, a collaboration with arranger-conductor-composer Johnny Mandel, may well be my favorite of all Horn albums. That year, Verve sent out an advance promo disc on *Here's to Life* that came in a little cardboard case, with the silhouette of a piano in front; when you unfolded the piano cutout, you found a picture of Horn underneath, glamorized more like the other Horne (Lena) and sporting opera gloves she could have borrowed from Hildegarde. The idea of hiding Horn's portrait behind the outline of a piano is an ironic one. The risk of giving her a larger ensemble to work with is that her style is so subtle and quiet that a traditional jazz big band would bury her completely; even a string section would have to play extremely pianissimo. Few besides Mandel could have so adroitly used a symphony-sized ensemble to more fully expose Shirley Horn's brilliance, to praise her rather than to bury her.

Mandel worked on *Here's to Life* not long after participating in Natalie Cole's 1991 megahit *Unforgettable with Love*. It would be enough if *Here's to Life* were just Horn's best trio-plus project (Ables and Williams and her own piano are at the core, abetted by Mandel's strings and guest soloist, trumpeter Wynton Marsalis). Yet it's more: This is one of the triumphant works of an era that was just rediscovering the art of jazz-influenced standards. Like Nelson Riddle before him, Mandel has mastered the art of taking a big orchestra and making it light and subtle, turning a studio full of musicians into an extension of Horn's own playing. One never feels there are any incongruous or foreign elements behind her—the strings apparently emerge from Horn's own sensibility and artistic consciousness.

(The orchestrations were, in fact, recorded after the trio tracks and then added to what Horn had already laid down.)

Over the years, Mandel was supported more by the movies than by the pop music industry, and between his own songs and two by Russian composer Dimitri Tiomkin, there's a lot of cinematic material here. Horn's reading of "Wild Is the Wind" is less flamboyant than Johnny Mathis's and less tortured than Nina Simone's, while "Return to Paradise" restores a worthy slice of Island exotica to the public consciousness. (Like Nat Cole before her, she can take a line like "Evil turns to love" and almost make you take it seriously.) Mandel's own songs— "Quietly There" and "Where Do You Start"—have never sounded better, while his classic "A Time for Love" sounds better here than in any treatment since Tony Bennett's.

The maestro's "Where Do You Start" doesn't quite belong here, since it's a downer of a dirge concerning a divorce and therefore out of place with the reserved yet upbeat overall mood of the project. For that matter, had you read me the lyrics of "Here's to Life" before Horn or Joe Williams sang them, I would surely have vetoed it for inclusion, since the song is the latest in the adult pop music world's long string of attempts to re-create Sinatra's "My Way"— a series of heavy-handed self-celebratory anthems that have seemingly been omnipresent since the sixties. It's the kind of thing that Barbra Streisand should sing, yet Horn, like Joe Williams, has managed to make quite a convincing soliloquy of introspection out of otherwise unpromising material.

In 2000, Horn and Mandel reunited for *You're My Thrill*, an album that's a worthy sequel if not quite a full-fledged return to paradise. One would have thought that on *Here's to Life*, Horn would have exhausted Mandel's supply of good original songs (she had already used his collaboration with Paul Williams, "Close Enough for Love," as the title of her second Verve album in 1988), but no, he surprises us by unleashing another one, "Solitary Moon," a classically Horn-like melancholy mood with a lyric by the Bergmans. She starts with the title track, with a burnt tone and breathlessness that implies that she first learned the song from Peggy Lee. (She also honors Lee on "Why Don't You Do Right?," on which she updates the year mentioned in the lyric from "1922," as Lee sang it with Benny Goodman, to "1942," the year Lee and Goodman recorded it.) "Solitary Moon," the slightly faster "Sharing the Night with the Blues," and "All Night Long" are all "Wee Small Hours"–type arias of love, loss, and trying to make it through the long nights. Even though "Sharing the Night" is in a kicking tempo, Horn leaves us in a quandary as to whether she's trying to confront the blues by singing about them, or if she's just resigned to the fact "That night will fall / And deepen my despair." The title of "All Night Long" may suggest an erotic romp, as in, "I want to love you all night long,"

but no! This Curtis Lewis song is more in the spirit of never-had-no-kissin'-ooh-what-I've-been-missin' all night long.

The best thing about *You're My Thrill* is that it displays every side of Horn's music. There are the expected slow numbers and a quota of faster tunes ("Rules of the Road," "You Better Love Me"), as well as numbers by the trio, or close enough to it. "Solitary Moon" further marks her first important performance with someone else playing piano, in this case the remarkable Alan Broadbent. Yet what's perhaps most rewarding about the album is that it contains a generous amount of the Horn piano. Sadly, for two tragic reasons *You're My Thrill* was the last time we would ever hear the classic Horn trio on record: Within a few months in late 2001 and early 2002 she lost one of her feet to diabetes, and her longtime bassist, Charles Ables, to cancer at the age of fifty-eight. The loss of the second upset her even more than the first.

Horn was out of commission for almost two years, but in November 2002 she appeared at the San Francisco Jazz Festival, with bassist Eddie Howard, and George Mesterhazy (described in a local paper as a Horn "disciple") on piano. For a year or so, she worked strictly as a singer, and recorded one album in this fashion, the 2003 *May the Music Never End*. Her three major appearances in New York in that year were especially triumphant, a sold-out week at the Iridium and two shows at Carnegie Hall as part of the JVC Jazz Festival. Her devastatingly perfect "The Folks Who Live on the Hill" was the high point of a tribute to Peggy Lee, and a bill she shared with the Dave Brubeck Quartet was no less mesmerizing. The Carnegie shows were especially rewarding to those few of us who had been present at her disastrous Carnegie appearance eleven years earlier: Whereas the crowds all but ignored her in 1992, in 2003 they were hanging on to every word and every note, breathing along with her and feeling along with her. If anyone in the hall had so much as coughed, the crowd would have stoned him.

Halfway through 2004, she also began playing piano again, this time using a prosthetic foot to work the sustaining pedal. In 2004 and 2005, she found a new home in New York, and played three engagements at the Au Bar on East Fifty-eighth Street. As great a self-accompanist as Horn had been, she was actually better when Mr. Mesterhazy played, as this freed her from the difficulty of the artificial appendage, which occupied too much of her diminishing resources. With him playing, she could concentrate on putting everything she had into her singing.

Obviously mindful that she would not be able to make a new recording, Verve Records, her label for the most rewarding part of her career, put together a compilation, *But Beautiful: The Best of Shirley Horn on Verve*, and released it, it turned out, only a week before her death on October 20, 2005. The *Best of* concludes with three tracks recorded at the Au Bar in January 2005. (Let's hope more will be issued in the near future. As of 2010, nothing more has been released.) There are two Richard Rodgers songs familiar to Horn fans: "I Didn't Know What Time It Was," co-starring trumpeter Roy Hargrove, and "Loads of Love," one of the many medium-up numbers with comic overtones that she would employ to give audiences a respite from her devastatingly moving slow ballads. Strangely, none of the three Au Bar numbers is one of those classic Horn torch songs, but this subset opens with Billy Eckstine's "Jelly, Jelly," one of the strongest traditional 12-bar blues numbers she ever sang, and with a spot for an old friend, the tenor saxist Buck Hill.

Her greatest moments were the slow love songs, with which, at the end of her life especially, she could get a crowd—whether several thousand in a concert hall or several dozen in a club—following her en masse. The title of the more famous of those Rodgers and Hart songs to the contrary, it wasn't that we didn't know what time it was, but that Shirley Horn made it seem as if time, somehow, had ceased to exist.

Lena Horne (1917–2010)

Lena Horne, like her contemporary and sometimes friend Frank Sinatra (born eighteen months before her), has demonstrated a recurring tendency toward premature autobiography. In 1965, Sinatra turned fifty and used the occasion to proclaim that he had reached the September of his years. In that same year, Horne, who was then only forty-eight, published her memoir *Lena*. A decade and a half later, she made an even more emphatic autobiographical statement in her one-woman Broadway show, *The Lady and Her Music* (the title borrowed from Sinatra), which ran thirteen months and closed on her sixty-fifth birthday. In both cases, Horne insisted on telling her life story at a point when she still had a lot of living left to do; however, she'd already lived enough experiences, both good and bad, to fill a dozen books or shows.

Still, we should be glad that Horne wrote *Lena*. For me, there's one detail that is particularly revealing about the lady's commitment to her music, even though when she wrote it, she was obviously thinking about something else entirely. She was discussing the song "Penthouse Serenade." The lyric depicts a romantic, idyllic fantasy of existence at the top of a Manhattan skyscraper. The text is the height of fanciful Depression-era escapism: "Just picture a penthouse way up in the sky / With hinges on chimneys for stars to go by." Anyone else might approach it as pure fantasy, yet Horne questioned her ability to sing this song properly. It's unlikely, she reasoned, that she'd ever be permitted to dwell in this oh-so-serenade-able penthouse, because like most first-class buildings in New York at that time, even a fictitious penthouse was subject to the heinous yet legal racially based restrictions designed expressly to keep black people out of these midtown Manhattan towers. How could she invest "Penthouse Serenade" with the level of credibility and total belief that she brought to all the songs in her repertoire when, as an African American, it was beyond her ability even to imagine herself living in one?

Horne was making a point regarding the racial situation she had been subjected to for her entire life, but to me this observation says much more about her approach to her music, about how very deeply she thinks about the words and the music of every song she sings. She has to thoroughly believe a song herself before she can sing it; she can't just knock out a number that doesn't mean anything to her. Once she believes it, it's a logical progression to convincing her audiences to believe it as well. But if she can't feel it, she won't sing it. That's all there is to that.

There were other black performers of Horne's immediate generation who were singing, for lack of a better word, "mainstream" love songs—particularly Billy Eckstine (older) and Nat King Cole (slightly younger); Cole even made an album called *Penthouse Serenade*, in which he doesn't sing the lyric but plays the tune as a piano instrumental. Yet more than anyone else, Horne gives the impression of having lived in two worlds at the same time. She alone seems to have been scarred by the idea that here she was, a movie star—never a leading lady, unfortunately, but still a movie star—whom MGM was packaging as one of the most glamorous women in the world, as instantly recognizable as her friends Judy Garland, Ava Gardner, or Lana Turner. Yet if she wanted to live in a penthouse, there was a lot more standing between her and that piece of real estate besides the asking price. One thinks about Sammy Davis Jr.'s observation at the time that the biggest dream that there was for a black person circa 1950 was not to have money or fame or power, but simply to be able to walk into any public place that he wanted to.

The confusion and hurt that Horne felt were part of the price she paid to help change things for the better. It was in 1942 that Lena Horne and MGM changed the world; that was the year they filmed and released *Panama Hattie*. On the surface, this was hardly a significant event. *Panama Hattie* was Hollywood's treatment of a 1940 Cole Porter musical that had starred Ethel Merman on Broadway (with Merman's part, as usual, going to a Tinseltown stand-in). Ann Sothern played the title role and Horne only got one number. But once the world got a look at, and a listen to, Lena Horne in this film, both American culture and the civil rights situation in America could never be the same.

It's not too much of an exaggeration to suggest that this film marked the mass-media debut of the concept of the African American as a real person. Before Lena Horne, blacks in films were depicted as, if not subhuman, then certainly as something inferior to white folks. Roles for African Americans ran the gamut from A to B, from servants on the plantation to "ooga-booga"-chanting natives in the *Tarzan* flicks: If they weren't carrying a tray, chances are they were carrying a spear. In her memoir, Horne recounts a crucial conversation she had with friend Count Basie at the start of her Hollywood experience. The issue was whether, as Basie explained to her, "they [white America] could learn to see me as he [Basie] saw me, as a woman first, a Negro second. If they could do that, maybe they could see him as a man and all of us as individuals." Lena Horne was the Jackie Robinson of show business.

Sixty years later, the battle with racism is hardly won, even if we do have a black president. However, we have come so far that it's difficult to fathom the magnitude of Horne's achievement. It should be stressed that, just as when Benny Goodman hired Teddy Wilson and Lionel Hampton for his band several years earlier, MGM had no interest in furthering the cause of race relations. Producer Arthur Freed and musical supervisor Roger Edens had no political purpose in mind; they simply wanted Horne for the studio because she was the classiest musical presence around. Metro's talent roster already included more stars than there were in heaven, but it was incomplete until they annexed this celestial performer. It's to their great credit that they weren't about to let the color line (this at a time when the military, pro sports, and even the Los Angeles musicians' union were still separate but unequal) stop them.

What might be regarded as Metro's one concession to the era's bigotry was their decision to present Horne exclusively as a musical and sexual object; in other words, she would never be shown mingling, plot-wise, with the white leading men and women who populated the rest of her pictures. The motive for this strategy wasn't entirely political: As it happens, almost all the musical numbers in *Thousands Cheer, Two Girls and a Sailor, Till the Clouds Roll By,* and *Words and Music* have nothing to do with the stories (such as they are), while *Ziegfeld Follies* has no plot whatsoever.

This may be too charitable to Metro's failure to let Horne have even a line of dialogue in any picture other than the all-black *Cabin in the Sky.* In this way, as she has often pointed out, exhibitors in the Southern states could scissor out her scenes and not risk getting lynched by their patrons. Perhaps this same backward thinking kept the studio from giving her any kind of screen credit in that first film, *Panama Hattie.*

Yet, in a sense, MGM's policy of segregation contributes less to Horne's exploitation than to her deification: In virtually all her dozen MGM films, Horne is completely unconnected to such down-to-earth concerns as plot and characterizations. She only flies in from the Planet Heaven to whet our collective appetites with a single sublime number and then vanish as mysteriously as she appeared. Beaming in and out like the otherworldly entity she was and is, Horne remains unidentified by anything other than her beauty and her magnificent music. If the color bar denied her the right to participate in the plot, and, in a sense, prohibited her from being seen as human, it also added credence to her divinity.

Consider that first film, *Panama Hattie,* in which Metro presents Ann Sothern as a floozy with a heart o' gold. For all the studio's fear of negative repercussions from more reactionary quarters, Horne comes off with considerably more dignity than the picture's star. Although Arthur Freed saw fit to transform one of Broadway's more sophisticated Cole Porter soirees into what quickly becomes an ersatz Three Stooges vehicle (with such colorful comics as Red Skelton, Ben Blue, and Rags Ragland falling all over one another in pursuit of enemy spies), Horne emerges untainted.

As Horne's daughter, Gail Lumet, documented in her book, *The Hornes,* their family had been among the leaders of the black bourgeoisie since the beginning. When Lena Horne entered life on June 30, 1917, she was the scion of the closest thing that Negro America had to royalty. After her parents separated, Horne's father's mother and family raised her in genteel Brooklyn society for the earliest years of her life. She then spent most of her teens living with her rather paranoid mother in a fast-paced succession of Southern towns. Horne went to work in the Cotton Club at sixteen, where she helped introduce Harold Arlen's "As Long as I Live"; she wasn't singing yet, but she danced around headliner Avon Long.

She was singing by 1936, however. In that year, she took to the road for several months with the orchestra led by Noble Sissle, a revered lyricist, singer, and bandleader who had been a pillar of black showbiz society since serving in World War I with Jim Europe's band and co-writing the 1921 *Shuffle Along,* the first wildly successful all-black Broadway show of the modern era. It was a good foundation for her: Unlike, say, Basie's band or Ellington's, Sissle's was regarded as the black equivalent of a society band, playing waltzes and sweet music in addition to straight-ahead jazz (boasting such notables as Sidney Bechet). Horne would likewise develop into an all-around pop singer, one of the few performers who seemed equally at home on the Broadway stage and in front of a swing band. At the age of eighteen, she made her first recordings, a pair of Deccas with Sissle: "That's What Love Did to Me" and the jaunty "I Take to You."

At nineteen, largely to escape her family, she married a friend of her father's named Louis Jones and settled with him in Pittsburgh. It was quickly evident that the marriage was a mistake, but Horne stuck with it through the birth of two children. While still married, she returned to the boards when given the opportunity to star in her first film (the all-black B quickie *The Duke Is Tops*, 1938) and her first Broadway show (the flopperoo revue *Lew Leslie's Blackbirds of 1939*). By 1940, she and Jones had separated and she returned to New York to resume her career full-time. Whether by accident or design, she would no longer confine herself to the "ghetto" of all-black show business: She went on the road with Charlie Barnet's orchestra (with whom she landed her first hit record) and then gained fame as a solo star at Cafe Society, Barney Josephson's cross-racial nightclub. (At which point she appeared in her second film, the short subject *Boogie Woogie Dream*, in 1941.)

By then, when she was performing full-time again, it was apparent that Horne was an artist who came off extremely well in an age of electronic reproduction: The camera loved her looks and the microphone loved her voice. Five years after her Sissle session, she returned to the recording studio, this time as a regular vocalist with Charlie Barnet and as a special guest with Artie Shaw and Teddy Wilson. She also appeared, both on the air and for RCA Victor, with the rather oddball ensemble from the NBC Radio series *The Chamber Music Society of Lower Basin Street*; the W. C. Handy classics she cut with the CMSLBS ensemble are perhaps the finest tracks ever recorded by that studio band.

The earlier recordings, especially the big band selections like "Love Me a Little, Little" and "Don't Take Your Love from Me" with Shaw, and "You're My Thrill" with Barnet, spotlight Horne as a goddess-in-training, displaying a wide-eyed ebullience that came naturally enough while she was still in her mid-twenties. Yet she would never lose that ability to convey love in its most purely euphoric state—as witnessed on such later performances as "It's Love," "Let Me Love You," and "At Long Last Love" (which she recorded with a rare verse). Horne never lost anything; she merely gained the ability to convey defiance ("Love Me or Leave Me"), obsession ("Mad About the Boy"), heartbreak (the 1941 solo side "What Is This Thing Called Love?"), and resignation ("I'm Through with Love").

At the end of 1941, the NBC-RCA organization was impressed enough with Horne's work to record six solo titles with her. By an apparent coincidence, she cut her first of many versions of the song that would become her theme, "Stormy Weather," as the first title on the first date. She renders it in a moody, semiclassical treatment that's somewhat reminiscent of the Chamber Music Society approach.

By that time, she was in the midst of a very successful nightclub engagement; in fact, within a few months she was the sensation of Hollywood. The film studios obviously were well aware of her, but the only one who was bold enough to show some interest was MGM, at that time the number-one producer of movie musicals. "I was 'discovered' singing in a nightclub called the Little Troc by Roger Edens," Horne said in a 1992 interview. "I wasn't

impressed because I didn't want to be in California, and I hadn't ever thought about the movies. The next day [the studio] called and asked me to come in, I said I had to get my father first. So, he flew in from Pittsburgh and we sort of laughingly went to the studio. My father was, in fact, fighting against the idea of my going into the movies, because neither of us liked the roles that we Afro-Americans were obliged to play at that time."

At this point, Horne, her father, and longtime friend Walter White of the NAACP helped the studio devise a strategy by which Lena would be afforded the same star-making treatment as any of Metro's white stars—and avoid being presented in the traditionally demeaning light afforded black entertainers. In *Cabin in the Sky*, for instance, Ethel Waters, Eddie "Rochester" Anderson, Butterfly "Prissy" McQueen, and Horne are all presented as social equals. Yet in the films immediately surrounding that 1943 blockbuster, all except Horne revert to playing servants—Waters as a maid in *Cairo* (a role Horne rejected), Anderson in *Broadway Rhythm*, and McQueen in *I Dood It*. Horne, who also appears in the last two titles, is seen as a singing siren, opening herself up to be judged only on the basis of her talent and not her racial identity.

At several points early in her career, Horne was confronted by managers who insisted that she "pass"—not necessarily for WASP but for Spanish. Metro may have had that in mind when they had her perform two ersatz-exotic numbers, "The Sping" (no, that's not a misspelling) in *Panama Hattie* and "Brazilian Boogie" in *Broadway Rhythm*. Just as likely, they may have been cashing in on the vogue for Latinate novelties, as "Sping" suggests via its rhyme of "propaganda" with "Carmen Miranda" and by dressing Horne up in a seashell equivalent of the Brazilian Bombshell's banana republic outfit. Though neither amounts to a great song—which becomes criminal when you consider that these two pictures have their roots in shows composed by Cole Porter and Jerome Kern—she works wonders with both.

Phil Moore was responsible for virtually all the accompaniments on her mid-forties sides. He was likely responsible for directing her to the Black & White label—oddly, in the years when she was getting the most exposure as an MGM star, she was under contract to an independent label rather than the better-known RCA. The Black & White recordings, which were all directed by Moore, are among the most consistently excellent sessions of her career—almost from the beginning she was an artist who stuck to first-rate material. Label executives at every stage of the game recognized that she was a class act and never stooped to sully her reputation, even in pursuit of the all-mighty hit single. The Black & White years climaxed in a deluxe production number built around the traditional "Frankie and Johnny," with Horne and a full cast of actors;

issued on both sides of a 78, this musical drama is equal parts Busby Berkeley and Gordon Jenkins, though Horne and Moore are considerably hipper than either. Next, she recorded sixteen tracks for Metro's own fledgling record label, which were reissued as *The MGM Singles* in 2010.

She would spend occasional periods with other labels (Twentieth Century Fox) but for the most part her home base, record-wise, was the label formerly known as RCA. (Unfortunately that corporation has never seen fit to provide any kind of comprehensive overview of her work on the label.) In contrast, two other outfits she sang for in the mid-forties, Black & White and MGM, have issued complete, single-disc packages of her work for them: *The Complete Black & White Recordings* (Simitar) and *Lena Horne at MGM* (Turner-Rhino, which contains all of her sound track vocals for the studio) are recommended reissues, and one wishes Victor would follow suit. The bulk of her best-known recordings were done for RCA in the fifties, most notably *Lena at the Waldorf Astoria*, which for many years was the biggest-selling album by a female vocalist in the history of the corporation.

For an artist of her stature, Horne recorded surprisingly little. She spent the bulk of her glory years at RCA, and was under contract to that corporation in three (nonconsecutive) periods. From the birth of the LP (the first Horne long-play, the 10" *This Is Lena Horne*, was released in 1952) to 1963, when she left for the second time, she released a total of only eleven albums, of which the first two were largely made up of existing singles.

It's difficult to make the claim that Horne is a jazz singer in the sense that Ella Fitzgerald or Sarah Vaughan was, or that she's a pop singer like Doris Day, since she didn't make what could be easily classified as pop records either. It's a stretch to call her a movie star (although I do not hesitate to do so), and she only had one important Broadway leading role to her credit apart from her one-woman concert show. Her stock-in-trade was a room that pretty much no longer exists: What they used to refer to as a nightclub was somewhere between the jazz clubs or cabarets of today and a Las Vegas showroom. Most of these nightclubs, for lack of a better word, were situated in hotel ballrooms like the Waldorf-Astoria, although there were non-hotel-affiliated joints like the Basin Street clubs in New York, the famous Copacabana, and Ciro's and the Mocambo in Hollywood. (As a general rule of thumb, nearly all the nonhotel venues tended to be under the control of organized crime, either of the Jewish or the Italian mafia variety.)

Aside from that warm, familiar vibrato and Henry Higgins–like articulation, there's not one overwhelming standout characteristic we can instantly point to, like Fitzgerald's swing, Billie Holiday's vulnerability, or Vaughan's virtuoso impudence. In fact, one of the traits we treasure in Horne's performances is her simplicity and the absence of stylistic devices. She has her tricks to be sure (I keep swearing I hear tinges of a Southern accent so sweet it could charm the honeysuckle off the magnolias, even though I know darn well she spent most of her youth in New York), but they ultimately contribute to her naturalness.

Horne's specialty is the bravura opener: There's no one else who can so grab your attention with just a couple of notes, and then hold it like a dog clutching a bone. Some of her albums seem to consist entirely of openers. She's especially convincing when she does this with one of the great songs, say Cole Porter's "From This Moment On," a song she has recorded at least four different times. Yet she works magic even with material by the decidedly less charmed team of Matt Dubey and Harold Karr (the team, somewhat further down on the Broadway food chain, who wrote Ethel Merman's most notable flop, *Happy Hunting*): "A New Fangled Tango" and "I'd Do Anything." On the second of these in particular she effortlessly tackles all the notes that the tune throws at her, and goes for the high ones excitingly and dramatically without resorting to screeching or belting. She also phrases just a hair behind the beat, again without making a point of it.

A master at building and sustaining a mood, she never fails to evoke precisely the right attitude for each song. She's sultry without overdoing it on "Love Is the Thing" and "I Get the Blues When It Rains," exuberant without being Pollyanna on "It's Love," resigned without being maudlin on "Fun to Be Fooled" and "Rules of the Road," kittenish without being coy (well, not overly coy, anyhow) on "I Let a Song Go Out of My Heart" and "Paradise." On "It's Love" (by Bernstein, Comden, and Green, from *Wonderful Town*, a song that deserves another airing today), she's so upbeat that one can practically hear the smile on her face, and muted trumpeter Shorty Baker gleefully reinforces the feeling.

Both "It's Love" and "Love Is the Thing" (the latter introduced by Ethel Waters, who wasn't particularly gracious to Horne when they worked together on *Cabin in the Sky*) employ a backing reminiscent of the great trio led by Horne's friend Nat Cole. While guest pianist Billy Strayhorn completes the King Cole Trio allusion by comping behind Horne with Coleish block chords, an orchestra stays very piano in the background, excepting a standout trumpet solo by Joe Wilder.

By the fifties, Horne had close personal relationships with many of the great songwriters. As early as the thirties she was part of Duke Ellington's inner circle, and through him she met Strayhorn (she described him as looking like "a beautiful brown owl"), who quickly grew closer to her than anyone. In addition to the songs he wrote for her, like "You're the One," she also recorded near-definitive readings of classic Strayhorniana like "A Flower Is a Lovesome Thing." The poignantly touching "You're the One" (arranged by Joe Reisman), with its wonderfully descriptive (and "Lush Life"–like) verse, was not only written for her but, it seems, about her, and may best be interpreted as an expression of the bond between them. Perhaps that same sense her romping treatment of Ellington's "I Let a Song Go Out of My Heart" can be viewed as the result of her relationship with the Maestro. Although studio virtuoso Bernie Leighton played for Horne on "You're the One," Strayhorn himself plays on "Fun to Be Fooled," "It's Love," and "Love Is the Thing."

Horne's career intersected with Harold Arlen at several points: When she first broke into the chorus line at the Cotton Club, Arlen was already the in-house songwriter at that legendary nitery. Ten years later, she recorded his "Stormy Weather" for the first time (for Victor) and when, several years after that, she starred in a Twentieth Century Fox musical using that same title, the song became the Lena Horne national anthem. Arlen also contributed songs to the MGM film of *Cabin in the Sky*, in which she made a notable impression as the heavy. (With Horne in the devil's corner, the good guys haven't got a prayer.)

Arlen does not seem to have been offended when, in 1946, Horne turned down the lead in his show *St. Louis Woman*; it was the book she rejected, not the score, and certainly not the composer. Though she declined to do the show, she later gave wonderful readings of its two best songs, "Come Rain or Come Shine" and "Any Place I Hang My Hat Is Home." Horne and Arlen would get together on Broadway in 1957 for *Jamaica*, which featured the long-delayed debut of "Ain't It the Truth," which Arlen had written for both her and Louis Armstrong to sing in *Cabin in the Sky*, but which went unheard until *Jamaica*. That show was a hit, thanks mainly to Horne's star power, but it wasn't the Broadway blockbuster Arlen dreamed of (and ultimately never had). Much later, Horne's positively sizzling treatment of "I've Got the World on a String," another Cotton Club song, climaxed her 1976 *Lena: A New Album*.

Many of the composers whose works she exalted were, like Arlen, Ellington, and Strayhorn, personal friends. One of her very best albums, the 1959 *Songs by Burke and Van Heusen*, grew out of the relationship she and her second husband, Lennie Hayton, enjoyed with that songwriting team. Whereas Strayhorn was the great platonic love of her life, there's little doubt that Hayton was closer to her than anyone else has ever been. By the time she became Mrs. Hayton, in 1950, Hayton had superseded Phil Moore as Horne's key musical partner.

As her musical director, Hayton wrote outstanding charts for her and also commissioned other arrangers to do the same—like Ralph Burns, who came up with some brilliant writing on the Burke and Van Heusen album (especially "It's Anybody's Spring," which buffets Horne's chops with an especially springy flute solo by Phil Woods). Other Van Heusen songs abound in the Horne canon: "Darn That Dream," on which, as free from shtick as ever, Horne sparkles especially brilliantly. "Dream" also testifies to the remarkable craft of the RCA engineers at this time—the amount of reverb with which they decorate her already shimmering voice is precisely perfect. Van Heusen's "Come on Strong" isn't one of his best melodies; the A sections are indulgently long and the payoff phrase at the ends of each section could be a little stronger—but Horne turns it into a tour de force of self-affirmation. (Something that she was amazingly good at, insecurities aside.)

Matty Malneck, another friend of Hayton's from Paul Whiteman days, wrote "I'm Through with Love." Horne and conductor Marty Gold take it much faster than usual, and observers will note that she's in particularly excellent voice on this date. She doesn't have to occasionally strain to reach any notes (she's never been a vocal virtuoso); here they just seem to be waiting for her to hit them, like petunias in a flower box outside her window anticipating their inevitable plucking.

It's hard to think of a major songwriter whose work Horne didn't exalt. There are at least three near-definitive renditions of Gershwin biggies, beginning with a 1941 treatment of "The Man I Love," which finds the young singer appropriately moon-faced and starry-eyed, while on her 1961 "Someone to Watch over Me" she seems acutely conscious of the consequences of allowing someone to watch over oneself—and of the consequences of not finding someone to perform said task. It's an ever richer and more rewarding experience. Her "I Got Rhythm" of 1962 is particularly brilliant, as she avoids this very familiar tune itself and instead sings a countermelody in the foreground while the ensemble plays the original Gershwin line behind her.

These are just a few of the high points from the several hundred tracks she recorded for RCA over the decades. Beginning in 1963, she worked for a variety of other labels, including two film companies then getting into the LP racket, United Artists and Twentieth Century Fox. My favorite album of the sixties was the second of two that she made for the little known Charter label (both of which, fortunately, are available on a single CD from DRG Records), *Lena Sings Your Requests* and *Lena Like Latin*. The *Latin* (arranged by Shorty Rogers) album is a minor gem, showing that time is indeed one of her strengths. Here she catches the Latin groove, alternating between bossa nova and mambo (that is, between Brazilian and Cuban) like the accomplished master that she is. The set climaxes, for me anyhow, with "Island in the West Indies," a neglected jewel introduced by Josephine Baker in the 1936 *Ziegfeld Follies* whose Ira Gershwin lyric is as knee-slappingly funny as Vernon Duke's melody is rhythmically contagious.

The other Charter album, *Requests*, alternates outstanding charts by another superb modern jazz arranger (Marty Paich) with some really tacky singles-like tracks aimed at the youth pop market, saturated with annoying 16th-note patterns (including a discothequey treatment of her immortal "Stormy Weather"). She fared better than many singers of her generation in the sixties, at least philosophically: The politics of the era made many other artists seem old-fashioned, but Horne, who had always stood in defiance of the racist status quo, at last seemed vindicated. In fact, she has written that one of the more personal consequences of the civil rights revolution in the sixties was that it gave her permission to go beyond her traditional role as a "symbol" of African American achievement. Now she considers herself "free merely to be human, free to speak frankly as an individual, not as an example, not as a 'credit to my race.' " (The last phrase being a reference to Hattie McDaniel's famous Oscar acceptance speech in 1939—for playing a maid in *Gone With the Wind*—and how several years later Horne became the first Hollywood black to appear, in Langston Hughes's term, "without benefit of apron or bandana.")

Still, at the close of the sixties, both her finest hour and her darkest moments lay ahead of her. In 1967, Billy Strayhorn died of cancer at the age of fifty-two, and his passing set the scene for the deaths of the three other most important men in her life: her father, her husband, and her son, who all died in 1970 or 1971. Not long after, however, she was on the road as half of a two-star show with longtime colleague Tony Bennett. He described her professionalism with a curious term: "frightening." Bennett was amazed that even while she was recovering from such a tragic blow as the departure from her life of almost everyone she loved (only her daughter, Gail, remained to her), she still could go out and give a hundred percent every night. She may have been feeling incredible pain, but the crowds who paid good money to see her never knew it.

She adapted to changing times, back in those years when it was customary for show business veterans to refer to themselves as "survivors" and nearly every fifty-plus-year-old diva could have sung Sondheim's "I'm Still Here" (from *Follies*). One of her Twentieth Century Fox albums, *Here's Lena Now!* circa 1965, had her essaying a butt-kicking, Basie-like version of Bob Dylan's "Blowin' in the Wind." But there was little that was notable for the next ten years. A one-shot project for the Gryphon label resulted in *Watch What Happens!* (1969), for which the jazz guitarist Gabor Szabo was billed as a collaborator (even though he doesn't get a whole lot of solo space) and the outstanding jazz orchestrator Gary McFarland was at the podium. Alas, the album was a major disappointment: Horne could deal with inappropriate tunes or weak arrangements, but even she couldn't contend with an entire album of both.

Yet she entered into a new winning streak starting with the 1976 *Lena: A New Album*, released around the time of her sixtieth birthday. It's a career triumph for both Horne and her collaborator, the superb orchestrator Robert Farnon. The two of them stuffed the LP with the works of old friends like Strayhorn (a heart-stopping "Flower Is a Lovesome Thing"), Gershwin (an even better "Someone to Watch over Me"), and Arlen (that Cotton Club song, "I've Got the World on a String"). Unlike Szabo on the 1969 album, alto saxophonist Phil Woods is all over the place here. He starts "World on a String" with a ballad solo so strong that you fear for the sanity of any singer who tries to follow him, but Horne manages to wrest the crowd's sympathies back just the same.

The major triumph of her later career was *Lena Horne: The Lady and Her Music*, the stage show that led to an equally successful double LP "original cast" album. Much of the album is good, but twenty-five years later a lot of it sounds much more dated than her forties and fifties recordings. Horne claimed to be playing herself here, but she also seems to be playing the role of angry black woman to the hilt, throwing in post–Aretha Franklin gospelisms of the kind that you don't hear in any of her earlier work. It seems like a minor issue, but she even addresses her audience as "y'all," and you wonder exactly when she lost her capacity for perfect English. At one point she tells the crowd, "I gotta right to be as trashy as I want whenever I want."

Horne has released only five full-length albums since the show: *The Men in My Life* (1988), *We'll Be Together Again* (1994), *An Evening with Lena Horne* (1995), *Being Myself* (1998), and the 2005 *Seasons of a Life*, which was drawn from previously unissued sessions done in the mid-nineties. They're all excellent—the product of a woman whose recorded output was devoted, corny as it sounds, to the concept of quality over quantity. The first, done for the otherwise unknown Three Cherries label, has some dispensable songs and rockish arrangements but also some beautiful duets with Joe Williams and Sammy Davis Jr. (possibly his final recordings), while the other four packages, all done for Blue Note, are uniformly excellent. Horne sounds older than she did in the sixties, but one would never guess that she was pushing eighty. Not even Sinatra attempted so ambitious a project so late in life, featuring so many new songs and the backing of loose, mostly small group arrangements that leave the star vocalist with no place to hide.

In the middle of her Blue Note period, she appeared at Lincoln Center's Avery Fisher Hall as part of the JVC Jazz Festival. She told the crowd that she was surprised to have been called for a Jazz Festival (apparently her first), and that she hoped producer George Wein didn't expect her to become a jazz singer all at once. Whatever kind of singer she was, she sounded great. She had trimmed out the pseudo-soul excesses of the *Lady and Her Music* period and still had the energy and the drive of her fifties and sixties work. The album that will likely be her swan song, *Seasons of a Life*, concludes with what will probably be her final recording of "Stormy Weather," and she has never sung it any better than she does here at age eighty-something.

Thus, at the point when Lena Horne believed that she had completed her social mission—to serve as a role model for black America—by the end of the sixties, her musical career was in a sense only beginning. The last fifteen years alone saw her four outstanding Blue Note albums, as well as a reexamination of her early work, both in film (as in 1994's *That's Entertainment III*) and recordings (2004 also saw the publication of the definitive Lena biography, James Gavin's *Stormy Weather*). In 2000, EMI classics released *Classic Ellington*, a celebration of the Maestro's music by Simon Rattle and the City of Birmingham Symphony Orchestra, which featured two guest vocals by Horne. Assuming these were actually recorded in 2000, they qualify Horne as virtually the only leading jazz or pop vocalist to have recorded in eight decades, from the thirties to the millennium. It's fitting that her final project involved her dear colleagues Duke Ellington and Billy Strayhorn. She died in 2010—aged ninety-two—of a heart problem.

Most performers sing only with their voices, but Horne sang with her whole being: not only with her head and with her heart, but with her whole body. The flashing eyes, the graceful hands (whether clenched or unclenched, in motion or still), the commanding chin, the towering hair—even her teeth radiated with purpose. Like Sinatra, she inhabited a song and embodied it. The one time I was lucky enough to meet her in person, I was astonished to realize what a tiny woman she was close up, and how she made herself seem so much larger than life in performance through sheer willpower. She did the same thing with her voice: She never had the pure chops of Judy Garland or the miraculous musicality of Ella Fitzgerald, to name two of her peers, but she could take a tune and sell it like no one else. Sometimes even within the course of a single song she could be defiant and vulnerable, ecstatic and melancholy, serious and girlishly whimsical, seductive and spiritual.

We'll let Ellington have the final word: Lena Horne, he once said, "is an American standard."

Helen Humes (1909?–1981)

Surprisingly, there were several musical trends that Helen Humes was never involved with: She was never in a Broadway show, nor did she find fame in prewar Europe, like many of the black female singers from the generation immediately before her; and (paradoxically) unlike many ladies from the next generation, she was not specifically part of the church music or gospel movement.

But these are virtually the only aspects of African American music in which Helen Humes did not participate. In the twenties, she sang what later became known as classic blues, which was roughly the same idiom as Bessie Smith and the other Smith girls. In the late thirties, she established herself as one of the very finest of all female big band vocalists. In the forties alone, she worked in three different areas: the chichi New York nightclubs, the more visceral, hands-on jazz of Norman Granz's Jazz at the Philharmonic company, and the even earthier strains of the brand of black pop that was about to erupt as rhythm and blues. That was all before the end of the 78 era and before Humes herself was even forty; she would spend the next thirty years exploring these genres—not in isolation from one another but rather by mixing them all together.

Through it all, Humes had a style that was at once sweet and swinging. Even more than Mildred Bailey, an obvious influence, Humes demonstrated how the act of creating jazz and blues could be a classically feminine, even dainty activity. She had a delicate squeak of a voice, yet far from tiptoeing through a song, she practically belts it out, making her understated and overstated, introverted and extroverted, subtle and in-your-face all at the same time. (Among many other things, she was the foremother of such cherubic cuties as Rose Murphy and Blossom Dearie.) Her feet were firmly planted in the blues even as her voice soared into the stratosphere; her style was perfectly described in a blues sung by her Basie band mate Jimmy Rushing: "Low and lean and built up from the ground."

The best interview with Humes was conducted by Stanley Dance and included in *The World of Count Basie*. As she tells Dance, she did in fact start singing in church, and as a child, she played piano and sang in a Sunday school band. She said that she was born in Louisville on June 23, 1913, but scholars today, including Dan Morgenstern and Bob Porter, believe the actual year was more likely 1909, which makes her 1927 recordings more plausible.) Her family was part of the local gentry: Her father owned property and was one of the first black attorneys in Kentucky. In all her interviews and in every profile, she always stressed that she had a very happy childhood, and insisted on describing the rest of her life and her career the same way. (She would, however, have problems with alcohol and gambling.)

By the time she was twelve or thirteen, Humes was playing and singing on a semiprofessional level with several local bands of musical youngsters. She also performed at amateur shows, and at one of these was heard by a guitarist named Sylvester Weaver, who recorded for the Okeh Records's "race" line, and who alerted his producer, future management giant Tommy Rockwell, about this remarkable young blues singer he had just heard in Louisville. Even at the height of what has become known as the "classic blues" era, good blues singers were at a premium. (As a result, many fairly dreadful singers were offered the chance to record, often with first-rate jazz musicians.)

In April 1927, when Humes was still only thirteen (or seventeen), Rockwell had her and her mother come to St. Louis, where Helen cut two sides, both credited to her as composer, "Black Cat Blues" and "A Worried Woman's Blues." In November, Rockwell brought the two Humeses up to New York, where Helen recorded an additional eight sides.

Was Helen Humes the Charlotte Church of the blues? Not exactly. Part of Church's multiplatinum appeal is that she sounds like a very polished little girl, whereas there's nothing about the ten sides Humes made in 1927 that gives even the slightest hint that the singer is below the age of consent. Age is never an issue with Humes—in fact, the longer she worked, the more she mastered the technique of bringing a childlike innocence to her singing, so that, essentially, the older she got the younger she sounded, and she was never more girlish than when she was in her sixties.

The ten 1927 sides are sterling examples of the classic blues genre near its zenith—she sounds so good she might well have changed her last name to Smith. Even in "Everybody Does It Now," when she sings about how "Grandpa" is "putting new tunes in this old trombone" or how that venerated gentleman is "taking monkey glands" (a hormonal therapy that was the twenties equivalent of Viagra), she doesn't miss a single subtlety. At thirteen and fourteen (or whatever), Humes was already competing in the big leagues.

Unfortunately, she wasn't allowed to continue on this path—her mother insisted she go back to Louisville and finish school. By the time she graduated, the first "race" records boom was over. Humes went to work as a waitress, but happened to be visiting an old friend in Buffalo, New York, when said friend's husband encouraged her to sit in with Buffalo bandleader (and future Ellington tenor) Al Sears. Humes spent her early twenties bouncing back and forth between her hometown and upstate New York, and also worked—again with Sears—at the Cotton Club in Cincinnati. She later told the story of how Count Basie heard her for the first time with Sears in Cinci, circa 1937, and tried to induce her to join him on the road, replacing the departing Billie Holiday. Unfortunately, the pay Basie was offering was the same as she was making with Sears, and she saw no reason to take to the road for the same amount of coin.

Later in 1937, Sears brought his band, including Humes, to New York, but soon after disbanded it, at which point he and she both joined the house band at the Renaissance Ballroom in Harlem. By now, Humes had been heard by the eminent talent scout John Hammond, who seconded Basie's notion that she was just right for the Count's band. Just around the time she joined Basie, she was recruited, along with most of Basie's key soloists, for several sessions produced by Hammond and starring trumpeter Harry James, at that time still a sideman with Benny Goodman. These dates include some of the best music of the swing era, with James and the Basie men completely inspiring each other—anticipating the day some twenty years later when James would lead a Basie-based band on a permanent basis.

In 1927, Humes was very nearly in the same class as Bessie Smith and Ethel Waters; by 1938 she's worthy of being mentioned in the same breath as Billie Holiday and Ella Fitzgerald. (She also had the good fortune to land four absolutely first-rate songs: "Jubilee," "I Can Dream, Can't I?," "Song of the Wanderer," and "It's the Dreamer in Me.") Yet these are, in a sense, just a warm-up for the twenty-six superb sides she cut with Basie between 1938 and 1941. It's instructive that the four James sides precede the twenty-six Basie titles, because they show us that it wasn't merely the Basie platform that empowered Humes to become one of the swingin'est singers around. She was already deeply in the groove.

Humes recorded with Basie himself for the first time on an unusual Kansas City Six–style session in January 1938, semiprivately produced by Hammond, featuring trumpeter Buck Clayton and tenor saxophonist Lester Young. In his autobiography, Hammond writes of a rather elaborate ruse, involving an Apollo Theater amateur contest, that he concocted to shoehorn Humes into the band and not offend its resident singer, Jimmy Rushing. (This in itself is strange: Every band of the era had a female singer, as had Basie with Billie Holiday.) As she told Stanley Dance, "Jimmy Rushing sang all the blues and originals with the band, so I got mostly ballads and pop songs, some good, some not so good." In 1974, she recorded the Rushing-Basie classic "Goin' to Chicago" under the title of "Tribute to Jimmy Rushing."

All the numbers Humes mentions in the interview are, in fact, very good: "Dark Rapture" (her first actual commercial record with the full band), the Johnny Mercer standard "Don't Worry 'Bout Me," and a number of songs associated with other bands and singers: "All or Nothing at All," "And the Angels Sing," the Ink Spots' "If I Didn't Care," "Moonlight Serenade," as well as the song that soon became her own signature, "If I Could Be with You." On Glenn Miller's theme, "Moonlight Serenade," she sings the rather pedestrian lyric by Mitchell Parish, which Miller himself never recorded, and she and Basie also make Parish's "The Moon Fell into the River" into a moony melody of considerable worth. There also were two specialty blues custom-made for her, "Sub-Deb Blues" (a societal predecessor to Rushing's more collegiate "Harvard Blues") and "My Wandering Man."

Even more than her predecessor Billie Holiday, Humes was the note perfect female singer for the Basie organization, light on her feet and supremely swinging—the female vocal counterpart of Lester

Young (who especially shines on the bridge to "Don't Worry 'Bout Me," immediately before Humes's out chorus reentrance) or Sweets Edison. Basie was eventually able, if not to replace his great blues shouter Jimmy Rushing, at least to find in Joe Williams a successor worthy to fill Rush's big shoes, but he never had another female vocalist who could live up to Humes. Practically no one else did, either.

All in all, it was a very satisfying three years that Humes spent with Basie. She said she left because "I got tired of doing the same songs year after year." This statement is not supported by the song lists we have from records and broadcasts; however, the last session she recorded with Basie is a curious example of the negative results of singing the same song too many times. The first of the two songs is a typical swing era jive novelty entitled "It's Square but It Rocks." After singing two perfectly acceptable takes, Humes starts a third run-through, gets as far as the bridge, and then proceeds to forget the lyrics and completely mangles those words she does remember. It's curious in that one imagines that Humes, or any other singer at a recording date, would have had the words in front of her when she sang. She returns for a fourth take, on which she gets everything right. As a parting joke, after finishing the four extant takes of "It's Square but It Rocks," Humes's final Basie side is a ballad titled "I'll Forget."

Now on her own, Humes again trailed Holiday, this time from the Basie band to a solo spot at New York's Cafe Society. She owed this gig at "the Right Place for the Wrong People," as it was billed, to Hammond, who served as mentor and advisor for the club's owner, Barney Josephson. There, she was accompanied by both Teddy Wilson and Art Tatum—as she put it, "That wasn't bad at all!" New York was her home base for most of the war years, although she occasionally toured the South as a solo act. In 1944, she relocated to California, where Norman Granz's Jazz at the Philharmonic troupe became the center of her activities for the remainder of the decade.

After Hammond and Granz, the next producer-benefactor to take an interest in Humes was Leonard Feather, who'd already written for her in the Basie period. While, unfortunately, Granz never did record her, Feather did, and was responsible for her first two post-Basie recording dates. These were done in early (preban) 1942 and late (postban) 1944, and both utilized a combination of swing, bop, and blues musicians. Feather and Humes brilliantly launched the singer's solo career; Feather later wrote that, "with her high-pitched timbre and high spirits, Helen was a natural for the lighter side of the blues."

The bulk of these numbers were, like "My Wandering Man," written for her by Feather, although the funniest is "Fortune Teller Blues," credited to "Coots and Davis." Here, Humes pleads with a Gypsy fortune-teller to inform her as to "where my papa was last night / He plays hot fiddle in a band

uptown / Oh tell me can it be that he's been fiddlin' around?" She's particularly effective on the bridge, delivered in quasi–stop time, and then in an interjection near the climactic line, "Don't tell him where I was!" No one else before Dinah Washington, who would emerge a few seasons later, could have delivered that line with exactly the right amount of urgency, lyricism, and humor as Humes does. The other prize of the two Feather dates is "Mound Bayou," a poem by Andy Razaf set to music by Feather. As with the best of Willard Robison, both Razaf's words and Humes's interpretation take the considerably overused song peg of "going home to the South" and invest it with more poignancy than perhaps the genre deserves.

As it happens, the 1942 Feather session, done for Decca, would be Humes's last for a major label for roughly thirty years, and the 1944 date, with a band billed as Feather's Hiptet, would be her first commercial session under her own name since 1927. It was also the first of several dozen titles done for the independent labels (Savoy, Philo, Aladdin, Mercury, Modern, Discovery) that sprang up to service the "race" market with blues and jazz product in the immediate postwar years. (All of this material is included on a recommended three-CD box import, *Helen Humes Complete 1927–1950 Studio Recordings,* on the French label Jazz Factory; the set contains all her early recordings with the unfortunate exception of her Basie vocals. The addition of those would have made for a perfect four-CD collection.)

Between leaving Basie and the end of the 78 era, she recorded roughly fifty tracks, half of them salacious blues numbers (not all that different from her 1927 sides in terms of content) and half of them heartfelt ballads. For Humes, singing the blues means lots of different things. It means fast and snappy quasi-nonsensical things like "Be-Baba-Leba," "Be Ba Ba Le Ba Boogie," "Flippety Flop Flop," and "Be-Bop Bounce." (These songs were apparently written by passersby.) It means her classic double entendre theme blues, like "Airplane Blues" ("First he turns me over and he starts to loop the loop / It takes a long, long time before his wings begin to droop"), or even "Jet-Propelled Papa" ("He don't need no refueling / He can even burn air") and "They Raided the Joint," where for once she isn't singing about sex but describing the addictive effects of gambling and virtually every brand of cheap liquor known to man (Sneaky Pete is probably the classiest of the beverages that she lists). Likewise, on "Knockin' Myself Out," a tune similar to the Duke Ellington–Ivie Anderson "Killin' Myself," she expresses her determination to commit suicide one glass at a time, "gradually by degree."

Humes contrasted her blues numbers with ballads. There's even one 1948 date in which she's backed up by a vocal group called the Contrastors (not the snappiest of names). The best titles from this period are those where she combines the power of the blues with the sensitivity of a love song, and this she achieves quite often, especially on "Today I Sing the Blues," which she apparently co-composed with Curtis Lewis. "Every Now and Then" is the work of a different Lewis (Al), and she sings this 1935 song both so poignantly and yet so rhythmically that it became her most repeated signature after "If I Could Be with You." (At the time she cut her second version of "Every Now and Then," in 1961, she named it as her favorite song.)

In 1950, Humes briefly reunited with Count Basie; the renewed association left no recordings, but it did result in the major visual document of Humes, two Snader Telescriptions of her doing the standards "I Cried for You" and "If I Could Be with You" with Basie's sextet, featuring Wardell Gray. Later that fall, she cut eight especially successful sides for Discovery: "Sad Feeling," which commences with a wild, Johnny Hodges–ian blues wail from Marshall Royal, is one of her hardest-hitting blues, a composition and arrangement that sounds more the province of Dinah Washington, while the next number, Benny Carter's "Rock Me to Sleep," is a riff romper of the kind that Ella Fitzgerald frequently essayed. The next, "This Love of Mine," is a love song associated with (and co-written by) Frank Sinatra.

Then, too, there are some Humes specialties she perfected in her thirties that she would keep singing for the rest of her life, especially her elaborate semi-comic paean to relationships of extreme contrast (young-old, rich-poor, you get the idea), recorded both as "Helen's Advice" and "Million Dollar Secret." What she does best is revel in the dysfunction of love, both its comic and tragic implications, even celebrating such unconventional situations as menage-à-trois in "Married Man Blues" and another original she recorded under two titles, "He May Be Yours" and "He May Be Your Man." Humes can be subtle even when she's shouting, and the November 1950 session with tenor colossus Dexter Gordon spotlights the singer at her loudest—and most exuberant.

Her work in the album era is considerably quieter. She returned to the jazz-and-standards audience when, in the mid-fifties, Red Norvo invited her to tour Australia with his band as a de facto replacement for the vibraphonist-bandleader's longtime collaborator—and Humes's original inspiration—Mildred Bailey. Even better, RCA Victor had the brilliant idea of rerecording a number of classic Norvo-Bailey big band charts with Humes taking the vocals. The set was titled *Red Norvo in Hi-Fi*, and it was a blessing for all concerned.

Humes's career hit its next of many high points between 1959 and 1961 when, in her mid-forties, she cut three wonderful LPs for Contemporary Records in Los Angeles: *'Tain't Nobody's Biz-ness If I Do, Songs I Like to Sing!*, and *Swingin' with Humes*. The first

positions the singer with three horns and three rhythm, and though two super arranger-conductors are playing, Benny Carter (here on trumpet and officially leading the sextet) and André Previn, there's nothing in the proceedings to contradict annotator Nat Hentoff's claim that the sessions were completely ad-lib. *Songs I Like to Sing!* sports Humes in a prom dress on the cover, and decked out with more formal but no less swinging arrangements within, the work of the brilliant Marty Paich. *Swingin'* returns HH to the small group context, this time with a few more modern players.

The ad-hoc small group format was a distinct throwback to the thirties sessions of Mildred Bailey and Billie Holiday, a setup often credited to John Hammond. It works so well for Humes that one wonders why other pop-jazz singers of the fifties, such as Ella Fitzgerald or Sarah Vaughan, used it so sparingly if at all. Their output was polarized between extremely small bands (trios) and extremely large ones (string orchestras), instead of finding the sweet spot in the middle, as Humes does.

Humes recaptures the upbeat spirit of the best small group swing and, like Bailey, thrives in a context in which her swingingly cherubic voice is juxtaposed against such soloists as Carter, tenor saxophonist Teddy Edwards (on both albums), trombonist Frank Rosolino, and trumpeter Joe Gordon on a level playing field. She even swings "Someday My Prince Will Come," something few other singers have ever tried, with Wynton Kelly, the pianist who had played it with Miles Davis a few months earlier. She's especially impactful when radically reconfiguring the traditional phrasing on two twenties apostrophe songs, "I'm Confessin'" and "S'posin'."

After the 1961 sessions, Humes, like many other singers of her generation, became rather scarce and wouldn't be rediscovered for another twelve years (until she came, once again, to the attention of Barney Josephson and John Hammond). There were a lot of lean times in the interim. Her personal troubles are suggested by a headline in *Jet* magazine from 1953: "Singer Helen Humes arrested in gambling raid." That she already had experience with such matters is indicated by one of her 1947 blues titles, "They Raided the Joint," in which the lyric goes "They took everybody down but me / I was over in the corner just as high as I could be." (Nor was she an innocent bystander; according to the *Jet* story, the Los Angeles police found "Miss Humes and five other women playing blackjack at a white-covered table.") The cop who raided her joint was none other than Tom Bradley, the future mayor of Los Angeles. She had also developed a fondness for rye whiskey.

Humes had already created enough essential music for three careers, and she still had another twenty years to go. After another protracted absence from the studio, she cut ten more albums (mostly for various European and American independents), beginning in 1973. By now she had carved out yet another identity for herself, this time as a grand sex-agenarian of swing. The later work features a lot of familiar material, as well as a singer with diminished vocal ability but an increased determination to put a song over. Oddly, the 1975 *The Talk of the Town,* which was the one album for a major label and her reunion with John Hammond, is not the high point of the later career. The sets she taped in France, like the earlier *Let the Good Times Roll* and *Sneakin' Around,* are stronger, as are such later efforts as *Helen Humes and the Muse All Stars,* and her final album, the 1980 *Helen.*

Humes died in 1981 at the age of sixty-eight. Her work of the years 1973–81 essentially constitutes a fifth career (counting her 1927 juvenilia as the first), and any one of her five distinct bodies of work would be enough to earn her a place in the hall of fame. At every step in the evolution of jazz and the blues, Humes was able to communicate her message to a whole new generation of listeners. Thirty years after her death, it seems likely that her music will continue to speak to one new audience and generation after another.

J

Al Jolson (1885 or 1886–1950)

After Duke Ellington, the most quotable man in American pop may well be Bing Crosby, who came up with the definitive one-sentence summations of the artistry of Louis Armstrong ("the beginning and end of music in America"), Paul Whiteman (who "towered above other bandleaders the way Everest towered above other mountains"), and Ella Fitzgerald ("Man, woman and child, Ella is the most!"). Crosby's description of Al Jolson seems especially insightful: Der Bingle said of Jolie in action that "no man in my memory could generate such electricity in the theatre." It was an especially apt comment, considering that electricity was at the heart of Jolson's greatest triumph. Indeed, Robert Benchley hit upon a similar concept in reviewing a Jolson show in 1925, when he wrote, "When Jolson enters, it is as if an electric current has been run along the wires under the seats where the hats are stuck." Twenty years later, the arranger Gordon Jenkins compared Jolson to Sinatra and Garland, and concluded, "Neither had the electricity that Jolson did." Yet, as it turned out, the very concept of electricity would also prove Jolson's undoing.

The electricity that runs the computer that this is being written on also makes it possible to pinpoint the exact moment when Jolson "happened," when he crossed the boundary from being merely a great entertainer to a legend, a figure who completely transformed American culture. We may not know the exact date, though it had certainly happened by the mid-teens, but we do know *what* it was. In retrospect it sounds simple enough: In mid-performance, Jolson leapt off the stage and into the audience. He later refined this practice, so that instead of simply parading down the middle aisle, he performed on what came to be called a runway, a part of the stage that extended deep into the middle of the audience. When Jolson made that leap, the whole concept of popular entertainment leapt right along with him, out of the nineteenth century and into the twentieth.

Jolson was a harbinger of a new intimacy between performer and audience—a legacy that was extended considerably by Crosby and then perfected by Sinatra. From the vantage point of the twenty-first century, Jolson's brash bravura may seem anything but intimate, but at the turn of the previous century, the act of breaking that barrier and rushing into the faces of his listeners was startlingly new and original. In a sense, the impact of that moment has made possible everything that's come since. Seventy years after his moment passed, Jolson probably remains his century's greatest all-around entertainer; if he wasn't Bing Crosby, Fred Astaire, Elvis Presley, and Bob Hope all rolled into one, he laid the groundwork for all of them and dozens more besides. Dizzy Gillespie once said of Louis Armstrong, "No him, no me." Without Jolson, there would have been no Armstrong, no Crosby, no Sinatra, no Garland, no Darin, and, as Gary Giddins has noted, his influence can even be tracked through early rhythm and blues headliners like Jackie Wilson. Jolson may not have been a god himself; in the classical sense of the term, Jolson was a Titan, a forerunner of the gods.

Asa Yoelson was born in Srednik, Russia (now Lithuania), on a date that has been approximated as May 26, 1885 or 1886. Seven years later, the family immigrated to Washington, D.C., where Asa's father, the Rabbi Moisha Reuben Yoelson, had been appointed to a prominent synagogue. Shortly after they arrived, Asa's mother died, screaming in agony, too consumed by her pain even to see her little son in front of her. Small wonder that years later, in the song "Mammy," the mature Jolson confronts his long-lost mother with the phrase, "Mammy! Don't you know me? It's your little baby!"

Jolson would spend his life forever in search of love and approval. None was forthcoming, obviously, from his mother, who had died when he was eight. What was equally painful to Jolson at every stage of his life was that his father was also never to give his blessing to his son and his chosen profession. The rabbi not only disapproved of the theater and of practically all music (except that made in the synagogue), but he seems to have taken a special dislike to anything his son was ever involved in.

The outlines of Jolson's life story are essentially similar to those of the protagonist in Jolson's breakthrough talking picture, *The Jazz Singer*. The basic plot is something of a morality play (filmed no fewer than three times) for the early twentieth century, regarding the assimilation of ethnic groups into mainstream American culture and the conflict between the ways of the old country and those of the new. It's far from strictly a Jewish issue, and echoes of this plot can be found as late as the fifties, not only in the first remake of *The Jazz Singer* (with Danny Thomas as a Lebanese cantor's son) but in *St. Louis Blues*, which jazz cinema theorist Krin Gabbard has identified as a black version of *The Jazz Singer*. (The Rodgers and Hammerstein musical *Flower Drum Song* is also essentially a variation on this immigrant assimilation story.)

The Jazz Singer is only one of several Jolson films that give us insight into the singer's mind-set; another is, not altogether surprisingly, *The Jolson Story*, which demonstrates that massive egomania is merely the flip side of massive insecurity. He played to an audience as if he were making love to it, and constantly needed approval—whether a departed mother, a lover, or a capacity crowd of ten thousand—the way that other human beings needed food and shelter. *The Jolson Story* may be completely ludicrous in terms of the so-called facts of Jolson's life, but it struck a true note in its depiction of Jolson as a man who would sacrifice anything (even, in the last scene, the love of his wife, Julie Benson, i.e., Ruby Keeler) to hear that applause. Having never received the love he needed from his parents, he found it in the adulation of an audience—it was the only thing that could fill the hole in his heart.

It was indeed a dilemma: He desperately needed parental approval, and yet he chose to enter the single profession that was most likely to earn his father's scorn. At twelve, he began singing professionally as a "shill," paid to start "spontaneously" vocalizing along with the artist onstage in the audience as part of a carefully prepared maneuver to get the crowd singing along. In 1899 he appeared in *The Children of the Ghetto,* and through the first decade of the new century, he worked in tandem with his brother, Harry, and in various minstrel companies. In the years 1910–26, Jolson conquered and then dominated Broadway in such shows as *Vera Violetta* (1911), *The Honeymoon Express* (1913), *Dancing Around* (1914), *Robinson Crusoe, Jr.* (1916), *Sinbad* (1918), and *Bombo* (1921). He also became one of the first Broadway headliners to double as a star of the fledgling recording industry.

In 1911, as biographer Herb Goldman has noted (in the definitive *Jolson: The Legend Comes to Life*), Jolson's Broadway career began in earnest with *Vera Violetta*: He only had two numbers, but by all accounts he was the hit of the show, and to capitalize on his success, the Victor Talking Machine Co. had him record both songs, "That Haunting Melody" and "Rum Tum Tiddle." (Rumor says he made two Edison cylinders in 1910, but no trace of them has ever surfaced.) Over the next two years, as Jolson continued to ascend the showbiz mountain, he made a total of thirteen sides for Victor (three were never issued).

In 1913, the young entertainer made it to a new career pinnacle when for the first time he received sole top billing in a Broadway show. This was a revised edition of *The Honeymoon Express*, which opened at New York's Winter Garden Theatre on Monday, April 28. To complement his more exalted status, Jolson upgraded to a long-term contract with the Columbia Graphophone Co., the first session transpiring on June 4 and including the future standard "You Made Me Love You." Jolson would remain at the label for a full decade, and the statistics of his Columbia output immediately identify him as one of the most successful and prolific recording artists of the era. Sixty-something issued masters in ten years may not seem like a lot of music—Jolson would record more than that in less than half that time for Decca in the late forties—but for the period it amounted to a significant stack of wax. In fact, the only artists of the time who surpassed Jolson's output were full-time recording vocalists like Billy Murray and Henry Burr.

As musician and scholar Loren Schoenberg points out, one of the chief preoccupations of Jolson buffs is scouring the existing documents of the man in performance, looking for clues as to what Jolson was actually like onstage. Sonically speaking, the bitter truth is that the recording technology of Jolson's greatest years only captures a faint echo of his voice; the most authentic representation of what he sounded like was only achieved in the final phase of his life in the virtual hi-fi recordings made for Decca Records and Columbia Pictures' two Jolson biopix.

Even though the equipment used for Jolson was state-of-the-art for the teens and early twenties (especially compared with that used to record King Oliver and other early black jazz bands), it had severe limitations. As Goldman has noted, the orchestral accompaniment often sounds like a Xerox copy of itself, while the reproduction of Jolson's voice is also compromised: His high notes tend to splatter above the range of the acoustic horn. In general, the richness of his voice is only hinted at—and even then, only in spurts—while the great "bottom" quality that thrilled Broadway audiences (and could not even be completely captured with the more advanced audio techniques of the post–World War II era) is all but absent.

In the teens, the medium of recording itself was still evolving into both an art form and a big business. The industry as a whole was a much smaller deal back then. Before the big boom of the twenties, phonographs were far from a mass medium, on the whole only in the hands of the upper middle class and higher. A talking machine cost less than a piano, but a purchase was not to be undertaken lightly. When Bing Crosby's father brought home a phonograph during this period (Bing was still a youngster), this was a luxury not entirely within the family's means, and an indication of how much Crosby Senior valued music and wanted to have it in his home.

While Jolson amounted to a bigger fish in a smaller pond, many of the amenities that his successors would take for granted just didn't exist. Whereas Crosby and Sinatra would employ their own musical directors on recording dates, Charles A. Prince, one of Columbia's in-house baton wavers, conducted on most of Jolson's sessions for the label. Though a fine director of military music like Sousa's, Prince unfortunately was not as sensitive a conductor for Jolson's purposes as the two musical directors who accompanied him in live appearances, Al Goodman and Lou Silvers, who gave him more tempo and spontaneity. When Jolson sang a standard pop song of the day, apart from his elaborate parody routines, the "arrangements" often hardly justified the name, mostly being nothing more than reproductions of the notes found on published sheet music transposed into the singer's key. Nearly all the musicians employed on studio orchestras like these had been classically trained and felt it was a comedown to be playing pop songs behind a vaudevillian rather than dishing out Beethoven for Toscanini.

The question begs an answer: Should we even bother with Jolson's recordings if they're only vague shadows of his genius? Can we reconstruct what Jolson meant to his generation any more than we can David Garrick, Henry Irving, Edwin Booth, or Jenny Lind? The answer is that Jolson's records offer far more than fragments from lost Greek plays or amateur tapes of Charlie Parker solos. Despite the limitations, there's a certain irresistible magic in these early recordings. More than the other World's Greatest Entertainers of the Jolson era—George Jessel, the dynamic Sophie Tucker, the impeccable, peppy Eddie Cantor, even the brilliant Bert Williams—Jolson is more than an entertainer, more than a comic, more than a shtickmeister; he is a great musician, with a beautiful deep voice and an endless capacity for melody. In fact, the bulk of his early recordings are just plain wonderful—the best of them have a sparkle and a vitality that all but defy the passage of time. For all his high-energy antics, the voice is perfectly suited to the acoustic equipment—indeed, by all accounts, perfectly suited to the Winter Garden Theatre. Heard today, Jolson's singing on the acoustic sides is positively mellow.

Making pronouncements from the vantage point of nearly a century is dangerous but, from the evidence available, Jolson, from the very beginning, seems to have made one apparently unprecedented contribution to the concept of what a popular singer was. In the earliest years of the talking machine, a recording of a song was generally as generic as the sheet music, and was sold in much the same way. The song itself was everything; the artist was incidental. Middle-class young ladies and gentlemen would take their horses and buggies to their local music emporium and request "Shine On, Harvest Moon" and probably not even specify an artist. Many records issued in the early days didn't even list a singer, simply "tenor" or "soprano." (In fact, even on Jolson's one release on the Little Wonder label, he was identified simply as "baritone.")

Chances are, when somebody brought home a new record of a new song, the artist turned out to be Billy Murray, perhaps the most prolific, and most anonymous, recording artist of all time. He sang virtually every song ever written in the acoustic era, yet one can't imagine anybody going into a shop and asking for a Billy Murray record. Murray exemplified the overall style of the acoustic era more completely than anyone else of the period, yet compared to Jolson, his thousands of discs, enjoyable as the best of them are, seem generic. Jolson brought style and personality to the art of recording and, particularly after he switched to Columbia in 1913, record buyers would approach their dealers asking for the new Jolson record—the song was starting to become secondary.

In 1930, Jolson's fourth feature film, *Mammy*, was released with a score principally by Irving Berlin. *Mammy* contains the one tune that comes closest to qualifying as Jolson's theme song—his mantra, even: Berlin's "Let Me Sing and I'm Happy." In it, Berlin, astute musicologist that he was, identifies four types of song as being Jolson's bread-and-butter: a happy song ("with crazy words that roll along") to get the audience laughing, a "sad refrain" (with "broken hearts that loved in vain") to get 'em crying, a "lowdown blues" to start them tapping their shoes, and lastly a song about the South to get his audience homesick and missing their mammies. (I know that I miss mine.)

Which is, in fact, a pretty reliable breakdown of the kind of songs Jolson—and presumably everybody else in the era—was singing, although for some reason Berlin omits the genre of happy, upbeat love songs, of which Jolson sang quite a few; he was never more convincing than in the 1917 "N'Everything," a bright and catchy trifle that's also one of many songs that bears his name as co-composer (both he and Rudy Vallee were notorious for demanding to be cut in on the songs they plugged and recorded). There are comparatively few love songs of the broken-heart variety. Even songs bemoaning the lack of love—such as "Don't Write Me Letters" (1916), which has Jolson yearning for a specific absentee lover, or "Wedding Bells" (1917), which finds him wondering when the titular tones will sound for him—contain more than a note of optimism.

Not surprisingly, considering Jolson's minstrel-show background (he toured with Lew Dockstader's Minstrels in 1908 and 1909) and his longtime affinity for the blackface tradition, there are an awful lot of nostalgic songs about going home to the land of Mammy, King Cotton, and dat ol' boll weevil. To name just a few, not even hitting all the famous ones: "Back to the Carolina You Love" (1914), "I'm Saving Up the Means to Get to New Orleans" (1916), "Down Where the Swanee River Flows" (1916), "I'm All Bound 'Round with the Mason-Dixon Line" (1917), "There's a Lump of Sugar Down in Dixie" (1917), "Rock-a-Bye Your Baby with a Dixie Melody" (1918), and "Coal Black Mammy" (1923). In later years, Jolson would refer to the whole genre as mammy songs. In 1917 and 1918, he channeled some of that nostalgic sentiment, combined with a patriotically jingoistic attitude, into a brief series of songs about the conflict then known as the European War: "Hello Central, Give Me No Man's Land," "Tell That to the Marines," and "On the Road to Calais" (in 1919, Jolson recorded Berlin's postwar comedy piece, "I've Got My Captain Working for Me Now").

But the biggest portion of Jolson's recording schedule was devoted not to sentimental songs or romantic songs about either mother or lover, but to comedy numbers. It is here that Jolson immediately moved as far as possible from the notion of the record being as generic as sheet music. Who would think of buying the printed music for a song like "Sister Susie's Sewing Shirts for Soldiers" and trying to replicate it at home? From the beginning, one of Jolson's key strengths was his aptitude for what later would be called special material, elaborate routines that simply could not be notated in published music and then reproduced by amateurs standing 'round the pianola. If one goes along with the aural scenario of "Sister Susie's Sewing Shirts for Soldiers," the performance transpires in a vaudeville theater in which Jolson actually interacts with the audience (he stages a singing contest halfway through the side). There's even more evidence in the earliest sides that, for a while at least, Jolson was a harbinger of the new, as he proceeds to blithely parody all kinds of material that was taken quite seriously just half a generation or so earlier, such as the even-then-hoary "Asleep in the Deep" and *The Mikado* (in "Tillie Titwillow").

Although identified with blackface and mammy songs, Jolson incorporated all sorts of ethnicities into his act: "Scandinavia" (1921) and the so-called Eskimo love song "Oogie Oogie Wa Wa" (1922) take Jolson about as far away from the Sunny South as imaginable, while the no less nonsensical "Ding-a-Ring a-Ring" (1921—not to be confused with Sinatra's "Ring-A-Ding Ding") finds him in the Fiji Isles. Island music had landed on Broadway in the 1912 *Bird of Paradise*, which launched a national craze for Hawaiian harmonies, and Jolson was happy to oblige with "Yaaka Hula Hickey Dula" and "I'm Down in Honolulu Looking Them Over" (both 1916), the latter boasting a priceless text by Irving Berlin ("Try and guess the way they dress; / No matter what you think, it's even less").

Jolson's most elaborate cycle of parodies is his Spanish quintet: "The Spaniard Who Blighted My Life" (1913), which goes after Bizet's bullfighters; "I Wonder Why She Kept Saying Si Si Si, Senor" (1918); "That Wonderful Kid from Madrid" (1920); "Wanita" (a tale of a carnivorous *muchacha* from 1923); and "Tillie Titwillow" (1917). The latter savages Gilbert and Sullivan with castanets as well as pretentious coloratura shenanigans (best line: "Her husband has no friends except Haig & Haig, / His breath has a dialect Scottish"). Even when he's in the midst of one of these intricate soliloquies, Jolson has no qualms about breaking character and leaping through the fourth wall, as in "Titwillow," to address the conductor Charles Prince. "From Here to Shanghai" (1916) is an Oriental fantasia, also by Berlin ("I'll get my mail / From a pale pigtail"), while "My Yellow Jacket Girl" (1913) is a true tale of culture clash. Jolson had originally sung "Yellow Jacket" in *The Whirl of Society* (1912); he then sang the rewritten version in *The Honeymoon Express*. Inspired by a hit play called *Yellow Jacket*, it concerns a homeboy who grows so obsessed with Asian ephemera that he wants to bedeck his honey babe in chinoiserie drag.

At the end of 1923, Jolson's contract with Columbia expired after ten years, and he was offered a better deal by Brunswick; "California Here I Come" and "The One I Love Belongs to Somebody Else" come from the first Brunswick session, in January 1924. Thus he was ensconced at Brunswick when the industry made the switch to electrical recordings the following year, and he made about three dozen sides before 1932. The electric Jolson is decidedly a mixed blessing. The reproduction of the voice is undoubtedly more accurate, and the new label also had the good sense to team him with name bands (as opposed to the anonymous Columbia studio orchestra) like Isham Jones (composer of "The One I Love"), Abe Lyman, Ray Miller, and Gene Rodemich. The Jolson voice itself was still in excellent condition as he turned forty. His first session in the new process, done on Christmas Eve 1925, includes the typically boisterous future Jolson standard "I'm Sitting on Top of the World" and Berlin's lovely waltz "Remember."

Vocally, Jolson sounds as good as ever on the exuberant up-tempo as well as the sentimental ballad. Yet sometimes it feels that he's somehow started to feel self-conscious in this age of new technology. For whatever reason, the extreme comedy numbers of the previous decade have completely disappeared: no more parodies, no more ethnic send-ups, no more savaging of operetta or opera, no more wacky asides to the conductor or the audience.

In retrospect, the sonic ambiguity of the earlier

acoustic technique may actually have been an asset; in listening to the World War I–era Jolson, it's possible to picture the World's Greatest Entertainer in the mind's eye as performing live at the Winter Garden or some other enormous old theater, and Jolson does everything he can to maintain the illusion—the singing contest in "Sister Susie," for example. Yet on the electrics, one can't visualize him as being anywhere but in a recording studio, performing his antics in front of an orchestra cold, with no audience. The more accurate recording process somehow makes everything more literal.

For whatever reason, whereas his performances seemed so free and effortless on the earlier discs, in the electric era Jolson is beginning to seem forced (on some tracks more than others, especially so on the 1926 "I Wish I Had My Old Gal Back Again"). He came up with some minor variations on old themes. In the twenties, he was now singing about the West more than the South ("California Here I Come," "Golden Gate," "Avalon," and "Pasadena," all of which anticipate his imminent conquest of Hollywood) and about Sonny Boy more than Mammy ("Sonny Boy" is the subject of a showbiz legend about how songwriters De Sylva, Brown, and Henderson were trying to come up with a song too maudlin even for Jolson), but in general, the old formulas were becoming stale. Had the Great Jolson, to use an anachronistic term, begun to jump the shark?

Yet the new technologies of the late twenties gave Jolson's career a tremendous boost. The invention of electrical microphones gradually made possible the widespread acceptance of radio and talking motion pictures. In 1927 and 1928, he starred in the first widely successful talkies, *The Jazz Singer* and, even more so, *The Singing Fool*, which put him at the absolute zenith of his career. To this day, the image of Jolson in blackface, arms outstretched as he pleads to Mammy on bended knee, is the dominant icon of the beginning of sound cinema. Whenever a new medium is introduced, it takes an established figure from an older medium to put it over; it makes perfect sense that the leading figure of the new genre known as the movie musical had already been Broadway's greatest star for fifteen years.

At the start of the Depression, Jolson was by far the most popular entertainer in the world; millions more were now seeing him in films than could ever see him on Broadway or on the road. Yet most of the other recording stars of the era were about as different from Jolie as imaginable—singers like Gene Austin, Rudy Vallee, and Nick Lucas, who contrasted Jolson's increasingly deep baritone with their own somewhat effeminate tenors and falsettos. Where Jolson blasted and bellowed, the likes of Whispering Jack Smith and Little Jack Little tiptoed their way through the tulips—as well as through the lyrics. It would take the coming of Crosby at the turn of the thirties to remind people how much they liked rich, deep voices, and then of Ethel Merman and Judy Garland to bring back the big open sound with plenty of projection.

Jolson had begun his career as an instigator of change, and in the first twenty or so years of the century, he left the older vaudevillians of earlier eras behind in the dust. Now it was his turn to be the victim of both changing times and changing technology. Sooner or later, he would have been superseded anyhow, but now the specific refinements in recording reproduction were sealing his fate. That's why Crosby's "electricity" comment regarding Jolson is especially apt, as it was becoming increasingly clear that WGE was unable to fine-tune his wattage so as to be best received by the microphone. Despite Jolson's first few films being so popular (until the novelty wore off), and despite his intermittent radio career (most famously on the *Kraft Music Hall* in 1933–34 and again in 1947–49), he was becoming passé by the time of the Depression.

By way of comparison, Jack Benny and Bob Hope could switch between different speeds of comic tempo on radio and television; Tony Bennett (a Jolson fan since he saw *The Singing Fool* at the age of two) gestures altogether differently in Carnegie Hall than he does on *The Tonight Show*. Yet Jolson, who, unlike Crosby, didn't have the benefit of growing up listening to recordings, was simply too set in his ways to make any kind of adjustment. On Broadway, too, the idea of the integrated story-song musical was becoming increasingly popular after *Show Boat* (1927). Jolson sang the hell out of "Ol' Man River" on his Brunswick recording, as if it were the greatest mammy song ever written, but book shows would never be his meat. He was out of place in any show in which he couldn't freely break character and converse with the conductor or directly address his audience as "folks."

Yet the power of the man will still occasionally come through. Like a mighty river breaking down a dam, Jolson just can't be contained by any kind of technological conceit, as on his 1928 record "There's a Rainbow 'Round My Shoulder" and occasionally in his films. The best of these is easily the 1926 *Al Jolson in a Plantation Act* (his earliest surviving film), an utterly convincing, not to mention mesmerizing, one-reeler that seems to come closest to documenting the same Jolson that Broadway audiences saw. And there are great moments throughout *Big Boy* (the all-blackface epic), *Mammy* (his and Irving Berlin's homage to the minstrelsy tradition), *Hallelujah, I'm a Bum!* (his most sensitive performance, set in the context of a pop operetta experiment by no less than Richard Rodgers and Lorenz Hart), *Wonder Bar*, and *The Singing Kid*. The last two find Jolson surprisingly adapting very well to mid-thirties style—and, no less startlingly, to the idea of playing in an ensemble rather than having a one-man show entirely to himself.

Jolson seems to have given up on the idea of making records in early 1930, but in 1932 he came back to the studio for two sessions, primarily for the sake of his longtime pal Joe Schenk, producer of *Hallelujah, I'm a Bum!*, as well as for electrical remakes of two of his standards in the company of Guy Lombardo. Jolson's recording career essentially went into a deep freeze because he began demanding a better deal from Brunswick head Jack Kapp, a counterproductive move in an era when the Depression pretty much put the kibosh on the entire record business. The major loss in Jolson's thirteen years of not recording is that no document exists of his performing the excellent score written for him by Burton Lane and Yip Harburg for his 1940 "comeback" show, *Hold On to Your Hats*.

Jolson resumed his recording career in 1945 in anticipation of *The Jolson Story*, which, when released a few months later, became the hit of the 1946–47 season. Lip-synching to Jolson's prerecorded tracks, Parks has some of Jolson's warmth but not his depth—not his sly, arch take on everything. Considering that the biggest pictures of the immediately previous years were *Going My Way* with Crosby and then *Anchors Aweigh* with Sinatra, it almost seemed as if Jolson had somehow become the New Bing, or even the New Frankie.

Jolson's first side for Decca, in August 1945, proved so successful that he and Jack Kapp buried their hatchet, rolled up their sleeves, and went to work. The postwar era was by far his busiest period, discwise, yielding seventy-one titles in a little over five years. After *The Jolson Story*, Columbia released a sequel that was nearly as popular entitled *Jolson Sings Again*; as Oscar Levant punditted on the radio, "They oughta call it, *Try and Stop Him!*" Around this time, Decca released a 78 rpm album, *Al Jolson in Songs He Made Famous*, which sold over a million copies—a staggeringly large sale for an album at that time, and a figure that, again, boosted the sixty-year-old WGE into Crosby and Sinatra country.

Jolson even introduced one last major hit, "The Anniversary Song," adapted by Saul Chaplin from an older, traditional waltz, "Waves of the Danube." This was a theme by an Italian composer (J. Ivanovici) inspired by a German river that immediately became the number-one song of choice at Jewish weddings. "The Anniversary Song" is one of the most beautiful recordings Jolson ever made, sung entirely in his lowest register, which is deep and rich and beautifully documented by 1946 hi-fi equipment; his intonation and style are even more Semitic here than in "The Cantor" (aka "A Chazend'l Ohf Shabbes"), a remarkable 1932 recording he made of a traditional prayer, actually sung in Hebrew.

On some of the up numbers, the backgrounds tend to date more severely than Jolson himself; generally, the ballads hold up better. The 1945 "April Showers" is a darn sight better than either the 1921 original or the 1932 recording with Lombardo; likewise, the long slow intro that opens "Liza" is more effective than the fast segment into which it leads.

There's also an unexpected bonus in two duets with Bing Crosby, who helped restore Jolie's radio career and eventually handed the keys to the *Kraft Music Hall* kingdom back to him. "The Spaniard Who Blighted My Life," a 1947 remake of his 1913 classic, and "Alexander's Ragtime Band" find both old pros sounding remarkably fresh and spontaneous, and recapture the fun of early Jolson more than any of his electric era recordings.

Thus Jolson started as a groundbreaker and style-setter in the teens and arrived at an uneasy maturity in the twenties and thirties. Happily, he was able to conclude his career with a rewarding happy final act in which he accepted his role as a figure of nostalgia—to the tune of millions of dollars—who was delighted to re-create his former triumphs for fans old and new.

Jolson died at age sixty-four or sixty-five on October 23, 1950—much too young—simply because he was too popular in his final years. He loved entertaining too much to take it easy, doing too much radio, too many record dates, and way too much shlepping over foxholes and trenches to entertain young soldiers—who weren't even born when he was at his height—in World War II and Korea. As off-again, on-again friend Georgie Jessel said in his eulogy to Jolson: "And not only has the entertainment world lost its king, but we cannot cry 'The king is dead, long live the king!' For there is no one to hold his scepter. Those of us who tarry behind are but pale imitations, mere princelings."

Jolson's impact on American performance traditions can be discussed in terms of his sheer physicality, as distinct from his singing. Jazz scholar Loren Schoenberg has identified Jolson's movement style in two numbers in the film *Mammy* in particular, "Why Do They All Take the Night Boat to Albany" and "Who Paid the Rent for Mrs. Rip Van Winkle?," as being key to an understanding of his art. "He's making a real attempt to recapture his early, possibly even prerecording-era style. Look at the hand gestures, and the sway of the hips in the last eight bars of 'Albany.' This is as close as we get to seeing the minstrel era Jolson." Jolson does a similar "sway" in "Toot Toot Tootsie" (in *The Jazz Singer*) on the line "If you don't send a letter then I'm goin' to jail . . . hey-hey!" Schoenberg notes that that this particular movement is directly linked to Jolson's bluesiest, most African American–styled singing.

Even here Jolson was widely influential: Irene Dunne moves as if she's studied Jolson in "Can't Help Lovin' Dat Man," her minstrel-style number in *Show Boat* (1936), and Judy Garland, singing "FDR Jones" in *Babes on Broadway*, could easily be Jolson on amphetamines. Wearing blackface and minstrel drag, she flings her elbows, waves her hands (talk about jazz hands), bounces her knees, shakes her head from side to side, cocks her hat, and performs with an in-your-face intensity that's like Jolson to the nth power. More than anyone else, Garland was

Jolson's greatest heir. She never stopped singing the Jolson repertoire—"Swanee," "Rock-a-Bye Your Baby," "California, Here I Come," "You Made Me Love You." And the two of them later sang together on the radio. One can only wonder what he thought when he saw *Babes on Broadway*. For the only time in his career, the World's Greatest Entertainer found himself out-Jolsoned.

Jack Jones (born 1938)

Jack Jones is one of the major singers of our time.
—Frank Sinatra

For all the protesting, the wailing, and the gnashing of teeth that went on in the sixties, it was essentially a decade of optimism. This upbeat feeling is reflected in both varieties of pop music of that era—that directed at teenagers and that aimed at adults. Yet there's a difference between optimism and naïveté, and it manifests itself in the cultural Generation Gap. In retrospect, much of the youth-pop of the mid- and late sixties (all that singer-songwriter and hippy-dippy stuff) seems, from the distance of forty years later, impossibly naive. Somehow, the kids of that era thought they could actually change the world by lighting up and writing and groaning three-chord subpop songs; the answer, my friend, might indeed have been blowin' in the wind, but it was of little help to those of us here on planet Earth. The adult pop of the era was far more realistic in its optimism. The music of Jack Jones, an artist who was in his twenties throughout the sixties and who has spent much of his career occupying that crevice known as the cultural divide, speaks to a generation that was trying to end the cold war being waged between men and women rather than that which existed between Washington and Moscow.

No one embodies the optimism of those years better than Jones. Some may think of him as an anomaly—why would someone younger than Elvis Presley and even most of the second-generation rockers want to concentrate on sounds other than the youth music of his era? Jones (born 1938) is young enough to actually be the child of Frank Sinatra (or Perry Como or Billy Eckstine). Yet he was precisely right for that decade—and all of those that have come since—and the classic albums he made back then will probably be prized and listened to longer than nearly all of the so-called in-the-moment pop acts of the time.

Even at his sweetest and tenderest, Jones is never merely sentimental or naive: In "My Best Girl," he slyly shifts the relationship implied from maternal to matrimonial (in the show *Mame* it's sung from child to mother figure; Jones sings it as from boy to best girl). And for all of Jones's polish, there's never an instant when he comes off as merely slick. He returns to the roots of the great baritone tradition, the rich romantic singing style that briefly flourished after the war (before it was overtaken by novel-

ties and worse), and reinvents it. He is part of the continuum that includes Sinatra, Eckstine, Haymes, and Cole—there are similarities between his sound and what they sounded like at the beginning of their careers—but his music is fundamentally in touch with his own era, just as they were with theirs.

No one else could do what Jack Jones does. Sinatra's cover of Jones's hit "Wives and Lovers" is, naturally, an excellent record, but by 1964 Ol' Blue Eyes had lost too much of his youthful innocence to truly embody the song the way that Jones did. In trying to find his own take on the piece, Sinatra comes off like a patriarch passing on advice to his offspring, the Godfather on the day of his daughter's wedding. Jones, on the other hand, can take this Bacharach bacchanal exactly at face value, with its primal explanation of how to keep amour alive between young, recently married couples. There's also more than a hint of a nudge-and-wink in the Sinatra version, while Jones has mastered the trick of sounding sexy without coming across as salacious.

For that matter, can you imagine Sinatra singing "Lollipops and Roses"? He would just overwhelm it. First, you require exactly the right technical equipment to create a very specific kind of gentle-yet-masculine audio persona. Jones has this by the carload, boasting one of the prettiest and strongest voices ever raised in song. But that's only the beginning. The Tony Velona tune is so simple and so sweet, an ounce of irony would just deflate it. "Lollipops," like so many Jack Jones hits, requires precisely the right emotional perspective. Jones had years of training and study, all of which he funnels toward the goal of sounding as if he just happens to embody the young lover described in the text.

"Lollipops and Roses," recorded in 1961, was Jack Jones's first big hit and his first song of note under his contract for Kapp Records. (A full four minutes, the disc must have been a pop epic in those days of 120-second jukebox singles.) At the time he was twenty-three and had already been around the block quite a few times, as well as being the second generation of a prominent Hollywood family. Whereas most of his fellow pop baritones were Italian (or occasionally black or Jewish), Jones is one of the seemingly few midcentury pop stars of Celtic stock: His grandfather was a Welsh coal miner and his father, Allan, worked himself up by his bootstraps from the coal mines of Scranton, Pennsylvania, to the salt mines of Hollywood. Allan Jones (1907–1992), one of the major leading men of the golden age of the movie musical, is best remembered for playing the lead in Hollywood's versions of two classic operetta-styled musicals, Rudolf Friml's *The Firefly* (1937) and Jerome Kern's *Show Boat* (1936). Allan Jones is also justifiably celebrated for serving as a simpatico singing straight man for such zany madcap comedy teams as Abbott & Costello (*A Night in the Tropics*), Olsen and Johnson (*Crazy House*), and especially for the Marx Brothers in two of their classics, *A Night at the Opera* (1935) and *A Day at the Races* (1937). In all his films, Jones Senior proved that he was not only a looser and more human leading man than Nelson Eddy but that he was funnier, more sympathetic, and a considerably greater asset to slapstick antics than Zeppo Marx.

It's showbiz custom for performers to cover up their actual age, yet the birth date of Jack Jones is part of his mythology: He was born on January 14, 1938, the day his father recorded the disc that was to be his greatest hit and his theme song, "The Donkey Serenade." (This was his big number from *The Firefly*, and a tenor showpiece that composer Rudy Friml had adapted from an earlier instrumental composition, "*Chansonette*.") By the mid-forties, Allan Jones was primarily appearing in B musicals while he was still starring on the radio, and in the late war years he shared the *Wildroot* series with Woody Herman. This was Herman's greatest band— the fabulous original Thundering Herd. It would be exaggerated to suggest that this one season on the airwaves had much impact on Jones's seven-year-old son, but Jack's long-term evolution would, in fact, suggest a balance between the pure classical technique of his father and the swing of Woody Herman's big band.

Jones Senior insisted on formal opera training for Jones Junior, but the youngster also grew up immersed in American pop, specifically the great singers Frank Sinatra, Mel Tormé, and, later, Tony Bennett. Jack made his official debut at the age of nineteen when he joined his father on the stage at a nightclub-casino in Elko, Nevada. At around this time, he was signed to Capitol Records, where "they tried to make me into what they thought was a rock 'n' roll singer, but it didn't work and I wasn't really into it." He cut kiddie-pop singles for Capitol, none of which was even up to the level of those being recorded by his slightly older contemporaries Steve Lawrence and Bobby Darin; unlike them, he was not an established star in the youth pop world when he made the transition to adult pop.

However, he did cut one album of grown-up material for Capitol: Produced by Voyle Gilmore, *This Love of Mine* boasted an intelligent concept—it consisted entirely of songs written by great singers not generally known as composers, such as Nat Cole's "With You on My Mind," two by Peggy Lee, and the title track by Sinatra—with a delightfully banal cover, depicting Jones as a caveman, complete with puppet brontosaurus and cutie in fur bathing suit.

Also like Lawrence, Jones was inducted into the service at the dawn of the sixties. While still in air force uniform, he signed with Kapp Records, named for the founder of Decca and all-around record biz guru, Jack Kapp, and run by his younger brother, Dave. The younger Jones and the younger Kapp decided to take Jones's career in the direction of standards and ballads. Jones was able to record while

on leave, and the album, *This Was My Love*, consisted almost entirely of familiar standards, except for one comparatively new and very obscure number by the otherwise unknown songwriter Tony Velona. It was "Lollipops and Roses." "The record came out in the fall," said Jones, "just as I was getting out of the service. It was a helluva way to get back into civilian life!"

The album was a resounding hit; the single even more so. With a few more albums and a few more hits, Jones was a bona fide recording star, one of the big sellers of the era. He was also one of the most prolific artists of any generation: He would spend most of the sixties at Kapp, releasing some twenty-seven albums, and then the seventies at RCA, where he cut twenty-three vinyl LPs (the total on his Web site is something like seventy-five LPs and CDs). By 1962–63 Jones was headlining at all the big rooms across the country, especially on the two coasts and in Las Vegas, and appearing on every TV variety show of the period—his stints on the amazing Judy Garland series are especially memorable (including a Christmas episode where he sings "Lollipops").

"Lollipops" was followed by "Wives and Lovers." "At this time," Jones recalls, "we had two songs that we really liked and wanted to record, 'Wives and Lovers' and 'Toys in the Attic.' However, the company felt that because 'Toys' had a tie-in to a big movie with Geraldine Page and Dean Martin, it had a better chance. So they put 'Toys in the Attic' on the A side and made 'Wives and Lovers' the B. 'Wives' was inspired by a movie, too, but it wasn't actually in the film. When [composer] Burt Bacharach heard that Kapp had put 'Wives' on the B side, he went into a studio and recorded another version with Vic Damone to cover it, just to make sure the song got out there! Fortunately for me," Jack said, "before Vic's record could catch on, the deejays started turning my record over, because they liked 'Wives and Lovers.' So they played that and it became the hit."

The two initial Jones hits (both beautifully arranged and conducted by Pete King) afford equal time to both partners of the traditional marriage equation, "she" in the first and "he" in the second. Unlike most love songs, they're not so much about initiating a romance as maintaining one, keepin' 'em rather than gettin' 'em. Unfortunately, we're almost at the point in these oversensitive times where the word "girl" will be considered politically incorrect, and at least three of Jones's biggest hits employ that word in their titles ("You're My Girl," "Real Live Girl," and "My Best Girl"). It doesn't matter: Jones is so loving, so tender, so absolutely believable in his advocacy of love as a way of life and marriage as an institution that sexism never becomes an issue. (In fact, he even wrote special lyrics for a feminist response to "Wives and Lovers," which begins, "Hey little boy, cap your teeth, get a hairpiece. . . .") Even when singing the movie title theme "Love with the Perfect Stranger" he makes it sound less like a one-night stand than a relationship of considerably more depth.

When Jones discusses his recordings, particularly the early hits of his breakthrough years, he stresses that the essential quality that made them successful is their simplicity and straightforwardness. "Call Me Irresponsible" is a good example: The song was written—originally for Fred Astaire—by Sammy Cahn and Jimmy Van Heusen for *Papa's Delicate Condition*, a picture that was eventually produced with Jackie Gleason in the lead. It was a mess of a movie but a terrific song, which eventually won the Academy Award. Naturally, Sinatra, who had a long history with Sammy and Jimmy, recorded it, and his version was primed to be a hit. "I was given the song after Frank Sinatra had recorded it," says Jones. "Sammy had me over to his house and said he wanted to cover that record with me. Whatever reasons he had, I was thrilled that he did! Frank did a very good characterization on his record, he sort of sang it as if he [actually] were a little bit drunk, as if he were the [irresponsible] character that the song is about. It was a great record, but it wasn't very commercial. Mine was totally pure and right out there. I did it straight, and I think I got the hit because mine was simpler."

More than many artists, Jones seems to have struck a happy balance between singles and albums: Singles were the primary product that kept his name before the public, but at the same time his albums sold well (seventeen of them made the *Billboard* Top 200). Like his hero Tony Bennett, his singles were of extraordinarily high quality, and his focus, like Bennett's, was on the best contemporary show tunes: "My Best Girl" (from *Mame*), "Real Live Girl" (*Little Me*), "She Loves Me" (*She Loves Me*), and "A Lot of Livin' to Do" (*Bye Bye Birdie*). And the lion's share of songs that aren't from shows are almost all movie title tunes, like *Wives and Lovers, Toys in the Attic, Alfie, Love with the Proper Stranger, Dear Heart*, and "You're Sensational" from *High Society*, as well as "Call Me Irresponsible" and "The Impossible Dream."

Sacrilegious as it may be for a Sinatra fan to admit, Jones's big hits are sometimes more tasteful affairs than Sinatra's major sellers of the sixties: His "Strangers in the Night" sounds more like a classic pop record—a traditional Sinatra record, in fact—than the Chairman's own version, which, with its Jimmy Bowen–Ernie Freeman production, is entirely discotheque-directed. (Sometimes Jones himself succumbs to temptation, as on the hillbilly-styled "The Race Is On.")

Sometimes Jones's pop records are so good—"You Better Love Me," "A Lot of Living to Do," "Alfie"—that listening to them today it seems hard to believe that they were once marketed as pop music as opposed to jazz (which isn't really marketed at all) or some other esoteric art. When Sinatra sang Burt Kaempfert, which he often did in the six-ties, he was trying to match what Jones had already achieved in bridging the difference between youth and adult pop with the music of Burt Bacharach.

"Alfie" was Jones's second Bacharach-penned hit after "Wives and Lovers," and I have to admit that he was the first singer who actually got me to acknowledge that Bacharach's metronomically intense melodies could be more than mere bubblegum fodder. In playing the role of the narrator-protagonist in Hal David's lyric, Jones becomes, to use Oscar Hammerstein's phrase, an "untutored philosopher." Aided by a lightly dissonant orchestration by Marty Paich, Jones elevates a series of portentous pontifications into a potent piece of spontaneous, intimate philosophy. Further, he shows that the quality of what's being said doesn't matter when the person saying it is so absolutely sincere. As he nears the finish and repeats the phrase, "What's it all about" and goes up on "ALL about . . . ," it's a moment as breathtaking as the best of Sarah Vaughan or Ella Fitzgerald.

Saying that his pop singles were of an extraordinarily high quality is another way of saying that they had a lot in common with his albums. One of the great joys of discovering the LPs by way of the hit singles is realizing that there are whole albums of such material. "She Loves Me" is a contemporary show tune that Jones swings lightly but unmistakably in an irresistible Brazilian beat, and it provides the leadoff to a whole album of bossa-styled swinging show tunes, of which the two other highlights are both from Cy Coleman's *Little Me*. "On the Other Side of the Tracks" swings gently in a manner recalling Maxine Sullivan or Mildred Bailey. Likewise, "Real Live Girl," which is performed as a waltz with an element of self-parody in *Little Me*, is done by Jones in his typically sincere fashion here on *She Loves Me*, swinging firmly yet sensitively, balancing youthful innocence with youthful horniness. Jones's partner in this classic 1963 album was arranger-conductor Jack Elliott, later a Hollywood big shot.

Elliott's name is not widely known to jazz aficionados, but Jones also worked with such celebrated auteurs as Marty Paich—a stickler for rehearsal and careful preparation, something that did not always endear him to record company executives. "A Lot of Livin' to Do" and "Alfie," says Jones, "were both orchestrated by Marty Paich. I wouldn't say that they were quite jazz records, but they had that influence because of Marty—he's just tremendous!"

The material with Elliott and Paich is so outstanding that one of the best compliments one can pay it is that when Jones was able to work with Sinatra's two finest collaborators, the two albums he cut—*Shall We Dance* with Billy May and *There's Love & There's Love & There's Love* with Nelson Riddle—aren't that much better than the normal terrific Jack Jones albums of the early to mid-sixties. The May package is a top-notch follow-up to

Sinatra's *Come Dance with Me!* but even more specific—every song describes some kind of terpsichorean approach, from the tango to the two-step. *There's Love & There's Love & There's Love* is a collection of mostly classic ballads, blessed with an especially winning title song by Cahn and Van Heusen. *There's Love* opens with a modern, down-to-earth treatment of Dana Suesse's operettaish melody "The Night Is Young and You're So Beautiful." If *Shall We Dance* is Jones's answer to *Come Dance with Me!*, *There's Love* is his response to Sinatra and Riddle's *Nice 'n' Easy.*

It would take far too much space to list even the highest of the highlights from the classic Jones sixties albums—the good news is that there are so many, the bad news is that only a handful have been released on CD, and almost all of those as imports. (There are at least three essential twofers from British MCA, *She Loves Me/There's Love*, *Wives and Lovers/Dear Heart*, and *Where Love Has Gone/My Kind of Town.*) As late as the mid-nineties, when I first discovered these records, it was still possible to pick up most of the Jones-Kapp series for a buck or two at Sixth Avenue flea markets, provided one still had a working turntable.

Like all his contemporaries, Jones had to contend with the sea changes in the music industry in the late sixties. Unlike his inspirations, such as Tony Bennett and Mel Tormé, Jack Jones did not head for the tall timber when someone suggested he include more contem-pop numbers in his albums. Thus, also unlike Bennett, Tormé, Sinatra, Lawrence, Damone, and many others, there was absolutely no lull or gap in his recording career during these years. Jones, who turned thirty in 1968, switched to RCA Victor in time for the seventies: As with Steve & Eydie's albums for the label, the series starts off great but tanks pretty quickly. The first few, like *Without Her, If You Ever Leave Me*, and *Where Is Love*, feature good standard tunes and charts by such stalwarts as Paich and Pat Williams. And they also show Jones with short hair and in a tuxedo—before long, he was sporting a David Cassidy moptop, bell bottoms, and love beads.

What's surprising is that all was not dross—there are a couple of what could be called "highbrow" projects mingled in with the likes of *L. A. Break Down*—albums such as *Jack Jones Sings Michel Legrand* (a beautiful album that did for my appreciation of that French composer what Jones had already done for my opinion of Bacharach and Mancini). Even less predictably, there's an RCA package called *Write Me a Love Song, Charlie*, which consists entirely of words and music by that other famous Frenchman Chuck Aznavour. But Jones also recorded a songbook album called *Bread Winners*, composed entirely of ditties by David Gates of the pop group Bread (they made plenty). This is a period when Jones was more likely to be singing the Little Feat swamp rock hit "Dixie Chicken" (which he actually did) than Jerome Kern, or even Cy Coleman or Jerry Herman. In this decade, Jones attracted his greatest notoriety for singing the theme for the TV series *The Love Boat*. As Mel Tormé put it, "Jack's forte is the singing of contemporary songs, and in these choices I do not always agree with him." No kidding.

Jones never came back because he never went away—but his work in the nineties does amount to a renaissance. There were at least four classic Jones projects in that decade, one for Sony, *The Gershwin Album*, and three for the independent label Honest Music (later taken over by pop star Pat Boone): *Music of the Night* (1995), *NEW Jack Swing* (1997), and *Jack Jones Paints a Tribute to Tony Bennett* (1998). The *Gershwin* set, produced by Mike Berniker, is primarily ballads, with Jones's now deeper, fifty-something voice backed by a lush symphonic orchestra.

There's some jazz content on the *Gershwin*, but it's pretty much window dressing; on *NEW Jack Swing*, the emphasis is on swinging all the way through. While Jones is going for a hip big band sound, he feels no obligation to limit his repertory either to traditional standards or even to younger writers who work in that tradition. As a result, there are agreeably swinging treatments of Lennon and McCartney's "She's Leaving Home" and Sting's "Every Breath You Take." The most surprising entry in the package isn't any of the pop-rock items, however, but a swinging recasting of the dreaded *Love Boat* theme, as if to thwart those of us who would prefer to distinguish between Jones's classy material and his cheese. The only thing tacky about *NEW Jack Swing* isn't any of the selections; it's the use of synthesized horns rather than an actual big band. However, this criticism doesn't apply to Jones's 1997 gig at New York's Blue Note in which he was accompanied by the all-female Diva big band. At the Blue Note, it seemed as if he had found a perfect balance between new and old pop.

In the sixties, while Jones's slightly younger contemporaries were singing about tearing down the establishment, Jones was singing about changing the world one broken heart at a time. One of his most compelling later performances is an ambitious, eight-minute medley of John Lennon's "Imagine" and "From a Distance," an AM radio anthem that, pre-Jones, always seemed hopelessly disingenuous. Despite how the messages of the two texts would appear to be contradictory ("Imagine there's no Heaven" versus "From a distance, God is watching"), by combining the two songs he makes them much stronger jointly than they ever were individually. In truth, he has no business singing either one of them, but he and arranger Matt Catingub have forged the two songs into a veritable "Impossible Dream" for the millennial era.

Apart from the Honest albums—of which we can hope more are forthcoming—Jones's major successes in the last dozen years or so are his appearances in several touring productions of Broadway shows. He was a masterful Sky Masterson in *Guys and Dolls* (and sang a "Luck Be a Lady" that brought the house down at a Carnegie Hall tribute to Sinatra in 1995) and, more recently, went on the road as the title character in *Man of La Mancha*. Thirty-five years ago when Jones made a hit out of "The Impossible Dream," he thought he was too young to fully appreciate all the subtleties inherent in the Don Quixote character. Now he not only still sings it with incredible chops but with the voice of considerably more experience, a voice that has hardened and deepened with age and battle scars, now capable of extracting all the Quixotic meaning of the song.

I had the chance to hear this at first hand in 2005 and then again in 2007 and 2009 (and hopefully every two years from here on) when Jack Jones returned to New York at the Oak Room. Every one of those shows, alas, opened with "I Am a Singer" (including his tribute to Alan and Marilyn Bergman, who, to their credit, did not write it), a somewhat stoic, self-congratulatory anthem in the "My Way" vein. It's a showoffy piece of self-celebration, and I can happily live without ever hearing it again—but there's no denying that Jones sings it like he means it.

Exhibitionistic as he can be, Jones is still amazingly hip musically, continually doing things one would never expect, like putting the classically derived "Stranger in Paradise" into jazz time and revamping "Wives and Lovers" into a modal waltz—it now sounds more as if it was composed by Bill Evans than by Burt Bacharach. It's easy to get distracted or just plain dazzled by what he does with rhythm alone. In "Just in Time," Jones sings the line "I was lost" rubato, as if he can't find the beat, but then he pounces on the pulse when he gets to the phrase "now you're here." He takes "Just One of Those Things," usually done in 4/4, and puts it in a jazz 3/4, and does just the reverse with "Falling in Love with Love," written as a waltz, and now a straight 4/4.

But all this musical sleight-of-hand rarely detracts from the way he communicates a lyric, particularly his deeply felt, deeply sung songs of love and loss, like the little-known Michel Legrand tune "One Day at a Time" or Cy Coleman's "It Amazes Me." Even if you don't want to dig that deeply, it's possible to enjoy Jack Jones on a surface level, just listening to that remarkable voice and those amazing chops, effortlessly hitting notes that others couldn't find with a metal detector and a seeing-eye dog. He hardly needs to tell us that he is a singer.

Louis Jordan (1908–1975)

I really want to be an entertainer, I want to play for the millions, not just a few hepcats.

—Louis Jordan

From a distance, it may appear that Louis Jordan instigated the most important transition of Ameri-

can pop music, that from a swing–and–show music foundation to a rhythm and blues foundation. But Jordan, who was himself also displaced when blues-driven pop took over the marketplace in the mid-fifties, was too idiosyncratic, too individual, and too flat-out swinging—too *Petootie Pie*—to represent various kinds of cultural forces impacting upon one another. More than that of any other figure, Louis Jordan's music belongs equally to the worlds of swing and the blues, but in the end it's wrong to try and make it part of a larger equation that explains the ebbs and flows of pop music. It's just too singular.

And Jordan's Tympany Five's output seems today as entertaining as it ever was—in fact it seems even more so, especially after experiencing several generations of one watered-down Jordan disciple after another. Thirty-five years after his death, Louis Jordan has yet to be outdone: No one's comedy is any funnier, no one's blues are any bluer.

Jordan was a dazzling, high-energy entertainer who dominated the "race" record charts for nearly a decade. He was also, well before Billy Eckstine or Nat King Cole, the first major crossover artist since Cab Calloway and Jordan's onetime boss Louis Armstrong (and, in a different way, Ethel Waters). He was one of the first black entertainers whose music was embraced without reservation by white America. He worked both the black and the white "time" (circuit), he made special films for theaters in black neighborhoods at the same time he appeared in Hollywood features. He was all over the radio, both in band remotes with just his own group and as a guest star on all the mainstream variety shows. His songs were covered constantly at the height of his popularity during World War II: "Is You Is or Is You Ain't (Ma Baby)?" was performed by Bing Crosby, the Andrews Sisters, Glenn Miller. Even Frank Sinatra, who pooh-poohed junky novelty songs in the late forties much the way he blasted rock 'n' roll ten years later, felt no compunction about singing Jordan's "Is You Is?" The ultimate sign of mainstream acceptance was his co-starring on a Decca disc with Crosby himself. By the standards of midcentury America, this was as far up as it was possible to go.

Louis Jordan, who was born in Brinkley, Arkansas, on July 8, 1908, once said of his father: "My papa was a fine musician, and he played just about all the horns, he would teach all the youngsters who needed lessons. I started off playing with [his band] myself when I was about seven, playing clarinet." Both Jordans played with a succession of vaudeville troupes and minstrel shows, but although Louis grew up playing professionally, he somehow managed to attend both high school and college. In the late twenties and early thirties, he traveled as far north as New York, where he worked with one of the first bands led by virtuoso drummer Chick Webb. In his sideman years, Jordan toured and recorded with Louis Armstrong (he's in the sax section on the famous 1932 Victor medley of Armstrong hits), Clarence Williams (he's prominent in the vocal trio on Williams's 1934 "I Can't Dance, I Got Ants in My Pants"), and others, playing clarinet and alto.

In 1936, Jordan rejoined Webb, whose band, thanks to the burgeoning popularity of Ella Fitzgerald, was fast approaching Calloway's and Duke Ellington's as one of the top "colored" orchestras in the country. At this time, Webb employed three musicians who would radically change popular music in the postwar era: Fitzgerald, high priestess of popular song; Mario Bauza, a founding father of the Latin jazz movement; and Louis Jordan, the first superstar of rhythm and blues. In 1937, Jordan cut three solo vocals with Webb, which represent the first real recordings of his voice. Two of these are contemporary pop songs (from the Fox film *Wake Up and Live*), "Gee, but You're Swell" and "It's Swell of You," which find him singing in a "swell" tenor voice. Why Webb used Jordan rather than Ella Fitzgerald on these two tunes is a puzzler, especially since he already had two regular male singers: the very straight tenor Charles Linton and the Armstrong-inspired singing trumpeter Taft Jordan (no relation). Obviously, Webb saw the same kind of potential stardom for Jordan that he had already helped create for Fitzgerald.

Swell as the two charts may be, it's the remaining Webb-Jordan item that is the harbinger of things to come: "Rusty Hinge." It's not much of a song, but it's the first indication of what Jordan would be singing about for most of the rest of his career. The meaning is a little more obscure than most of the Tympany Five lyrics on the same subject, but "Rusty Hinge" is the first song in which Jordan presents himself as a good-for-nothing lowlife who likes his liquor hard and his women easy. "Rusty hinge / On a binge," he sings, "I'll be drinking my corn / Until Gabriel blows his horn."

Roughly a year before Webb's untimely death, in the summer of 1939, Jordan left his big band to organize a small group of his own to play at a Harlem joint called Elk's Rendezvous. Before the year was up, J. Mayo Williams, the "race" records impresario for Decca, utilized Jordan's "Elk's Club Rendezvous Band" on several sessions backing up a singer named Rodney Sturgis. Decca was a likely place for Jordan to wind up. The newest of the major labels, the company had an aggressive "race" roster that in the late thirties would include a number of groups that blended swing and blues in very different ways: Al Cooper and the Savoy Sultans (in residence at the Savoy Ballroom, not far from the Elk's Rendezvous), Skeets Tolbert and His Gentlemen of Swing (who were based on Fifty-second Street), and especially the Harlem Hamfats (who, despite their name, were based in Chicago).

You can hear the roots of the Tympany Five all over the map of prewar black music, especially in the vaudeville-style comedy blues of such husband-

and-wife teams as Butterbeans and Susie, the more comic songs of twenties classic blues singers like Bessie Smith, as in "Put It Right There" or singing of having a good time in "Gimme a Pigfoot," which is a virtual blueprint for "Let the Good Times Roll." There were also any number of washboard and jug bands that specialized in punchline-driven comic blues, many involving songwriting magnates Thomas A. Dorsey and Clarence Williams.

The first Elk's Rendezvous disc, in which Jordan sings behind Rodney Sturgis, is something called "Toodle-oo on Down," which describes a dance (as in Ellington's "East St. Louis Toodle-Oo"), which, like the many tunes composed, published, and recorded by Clarence Williams a decade earlier, is kind of an advertisement for itself. The relevance of dancing can't be overstated: We don't think of either Bessie Smith or Robert Johnson as performing for dancers, but there was considerable rhythm in rhythm and blues. The vaudeville blues divas of the twenties worked primarily in theaters and tent shows, but virtually every other kind of blues, from New Orleans to the Mississippi Delta to Chicago to the Kansas and Missouri territories, was driven by dancing. Louis Jordan's breakthrough beyond dance music came later, when customers who were already dancing to his music stopped to listen to his tall tales of Deacon Jones and Five Guys Named Moe.

Jordan's original Elks band, like the Savoy Sultans, was a full nine pieces. The idea was to deliver the gutbucket blues with some of the energy and drive of Southern and Western players but with something of the sophistication and polish of the big urban swing bands.

Jordan knew he needed a gimmick, and early on he had a drummer named Walter Martin who specialized in the tympani, a percussion instrument employed regularly in symphonic music but rarely in jazz. Thinking that this would be his signature, Jordan christened his group "The Tympany Five," and kept the name even after he dropped the tympani and carried more than five men. (It could be that "Tympany" was also Jordan's shorthand for his trademark shuffle rhythm.) It would take a while for him to realize that it would be his own singing, comedy, and general carrying on that would be the band's calling card to fame.

The first Jordan group lacked the precision and well-drilled section work of the Savoy Sultans, and it couldn't match the gritty authenticity of the Harlem Hamfats. But it had an asset that no other black band had enjoyed since Armstrong and Calloway: a leader with star power up the wazoo. As an alto saxophonist, he was a few notches short of Benny Carter or Johnny Hodges; as a singer, he wasn't an athlete like Calloway or an innovator like Armstrong. But Jordan had incredible charisma and dynamic energy. When he was onstage, as his many films prove, you couldn't keep your eyes off him. It wasn't so much that he was both a singer and an instrumentalist; what was important was that he was a comic and a blues singer, a lover and a lowlife, a sophisticate and a slob, a showman and a shaman.

It was a particularly fortunate moment for such an entertainer. Come the Second World War, African Americans were gradually allowed to have a more positive image of themselves. The war served to unify all Americans as never before, especially as blacks were expected to serve both in the military and in the defense industry. It was still a long way from equality or integration, but it was a major step forward from what had been before. Jordan was the perfect, high-polished singer-bandleader for the era. He may not be singing about the finer things in life, the kind that the black bourgeoisie aspired to, but he made it clear that he was not a reprobate rascal himself; he was quick to distance himself from the low-class characters who populated his narratives. He and the Tympany Five wore immaculately tailored suits (he was the Miles Davis of his day), he was learned and articulate in his interviews, and in general he carried himself like a man everybody could be proud of. His was the kind of blues that had been to college.

The two major singing bandleaders of the era were Cab Calloway and Woody Herman. Jordan's singing voice, unlike Calloway's, was unexceptional. Rather, as with Herman (who helped make "Caldonia" into a standard), it was what he did with his voice that was remarkable. He sings in a comfortable high baritone, in addition to which, like Herman, he's not afraid to shriek and squeal and, like Fats Waller, puts flesh and bone on a wide variety of character voices. He employs one particular timbre when he's embodying a faux-hipster, a cat who's too hip for the room (you dig?), another when he's supposed to be drunk, still another when he's an exasperated down-and-out, down to his last wooden nickel. And he has other approaches when he wants to enumerate the charms of his latest lady friend, whether she might be slender, tender, and tall, or—as he likes 'em—fat like that.

His subject matter was hardly a point of pride for the African American middle class—just the opposite. Like Richard Pryor, Jordan continually immersed himself in what was, at the time, commonly considered the worst nightmare of upper- and middle-class African Americans. He sings of the lifestyles of the horny and the inebriated, reveling in every conceivable vice, from substances to illicit sex to overindulgence in food and even chicken stealing, something that neither black nor white comics had addressed since minstrel days. He affectionately savages all the institutions of African American life: family life, business, education ("Teacher, Teacher"), the law, and even the church. The message seems to be that you can't trust nobody—even distinguished businessmen and clergymen forget themselves and get messy around gin, women, and music, especially at a Louisville Lodge Meeting or a Saturday night fish fry.

The extreme consequences of that message were graphically depicted in the 1982 play *A Soldier's Play*, which concerns a murder conspiracy in which a group of bourgeois-wannabe black officers do away with a low-class, blues-singer "geechie" type because they think he makes them—and all black people—look bad. That's exactly the type that Jordan played: a low-life country cousin who spends his days, if he works at all, with his overalls covered in mud and animal feces, and his nights getting drunk, chasing women, and beating his wife. The only time he doesn't indulge in such low-life behavior is when he's "Locked Up." The latter is one of Jordan's most extremely unacceptable texts: Both here and on "Gal, You Need a Whippin'" (both are from 1954), Jordan's character—the lovable carouser—sings about wife beating as if it were a harmless vice, just another aspect of what makes him charming.

When Jordan wasn't writing songs on this topic (most of them, unfortunately, published under the name of his wife, Fleecie Moore, who not only stabbed him and nearly killed him, but wound up Fleecin' him of all his royalties), he was singing comparable ones written by other folks. One of his most famous was "Open the Door, Richard," which became a national catchphrase in 1946. Chitlin Circuit performer Dusty Fletcher devised and introduced this combination comedy routine and pop song, but Jordan had the biggest hit with it. He recorded his version in two takes, and in the first and less frequently heard of these, he specifically acknowledges Fletcher by name. ("I met old Dusty Fletcher standing on the corner the other day. . . .")

The two most popular black combos of the forties were easily Jordan's Tympany Five and the King Cole Trio. The chief difference between the two was that Nat Cole exemplified the urbane ideal that black men were encouraged to aspire to. Even when Cole's character is faced with hard luck, as in "Now He Tells Me," he never gets his suit dirty or ends up with mud on his shoes. You would never catch King Cole in a barnyard, and when he does go there, as in "Old MacDonald" on *King Cole for Kids*, he turns it into a Disney cartoon. In Jordan's music, the barnyard is the nexus of commerce; in Cole's, it's a quaint place to bring one's children, rather like a petting zoo. Cole's relatively early "Bring Another Drink," in which a couple of desperate dudeskis try to get a pair of hip chicks intoxicated for some unspecified but certainly immoral purpose, is a rare example of the King addressing Tympany Five–like subject matter.

Jordan spends rather a lot of time immersed in animal husbandry: "Show Me How You Milk a Cow," "Barnyard Boogie," "Cock-a-Doodle Do," "Chicken Back," "A Chicken Ain't Nothin' but a Bird," "Chicky-Mo, Craney-Crow," "That Chick's Too Young to Fry," and his masterpiece of poultry in motion, "Ain't Nobody Here but Us Chickens." In the show *One Mo' Time*, Vernel Bagneris played a vaudeville entertainer in New Orleans in the twenties who was horrified at the blow to his dignity at having to wear blackface and a chicken suit. It takes a man mighty sure of his own worth and place in society, as Jordan obviously was, to get up on a stage and sing "Cluck cluck, bow wow, there's boogie in the barnyard."

Most of the food and drink songs, like "Saturday Night Fish Fry," are about that which can be consumed at a party where well-dressed people are dancing and drinking and having a good time. The acts of eating and drinking are directly intertwined with both music-making and merrymaking. One of Jordan's most durable hits, "Five Guys Named Moe," sprang from all these impulses. The songwriter Larry Wynn, otherwise best known for Billie Holiday's "I'm All for You," later recalled that the idea for the song came to him when he was unable to recall the complete personnel of that Holiday recording session, and off-handedly described most of the band as "Five Guys Named Moe." This idea for a comedy song delighted Jordan: Each member of the group (which was still a quintet in 1942) was identified as a different Moe—Big Moe, Little Moe, Four-Eyed Moe, No Moe, and Brother Eat Moe, the last being portrayed by the leader. The song was a hit in its day but, oddly, Jordan never remade it for any of his post-Decca labels. When it served as the title for a successful Broadway revue of his music in the nineties, subsequent reissues of his music became increasingly Moecentric. (Not a case when less is Moe.)

Comic insults, "ranking," and "signifying" are a major stock-in-trade of African American comedy, and, as with Redd Foxx and Moms Mabley, this is one of Jordan's key strengths. It was highly appropriate that Louis Armstrong should reprise "(I'll Be Glad When You're Dead) You Rascal You," his 1931 hit and the original "ranking" song, as a duet with Jordan in 1950. Jordan had already offered such variations on the "You Rascal, You!" theme as "Friendship" (conspicuously not Cole Porter), "Dad Gum Ya Hide, Boy" (which could have been sung by Gabby Hayes), and "Do You Call That a Buddy" (a variation on the spiritual "Scandalize My Name" and also recorded by Armstrong).

Jordan also made a specialty of comedy songs that the term "misogynist" doesn't begin to describe. "Caldonia," with her great big feet and big hard head, is merely the most famous of Jordan's lopsided lovers and low-rent romances. Sometimes the ladies are overachievers in the corpulence department. Although he may sing "I Like 'Em Fat Like That," elsewhere he tells his woman, "You're Much Too Fat and That's That." Similarly, his desire to pick chicks who are "Slender, Tender and Tall" would seem to be at odds with his enthusiasm for gals whom he describes as "Reet, Petite and Gone." Sometimes he's merely getting on the cases of these big fat mammas (with the meat shakin' on their bones), but usually he mixes in a little sentimentality with the insults: "Caldonia," "Messy Bessie," "Tillie," "Crazy Baby" (which paraphrases "Ornithology," obviously equat-

ing women with "birds" and "chicks"), and "Honey Chile" are all ladies with various shortcomings, from oversized pedal extremities to false teeth and wooden legs, yet they float his boat just the same.

Overeating is a logical consequence, since Jordan sings even more lovingly of food and drink than he does of women (whatever their size): "Cole Slaw," "Fat Back and Corn Liquor," "Texas Stew," "Beans and Cornbread," not to mention all those chickens boogieing in the barnyard and other items on the "Boogie Woogie Blue Plate." Jordan's titles read more like a menu than a track list. The 1949 "Hungry Man," an early hit by Bobby Troup, is another Jordan classic, a witty text that rhymes foods with cities in a manner that presages Dave Frishberg. Jordan's characters manage to keep feeding their faces even when wartime shortages made food hard to come by, as in "Ration Blues" and "You Can't Get That No More." Lord knows this barely begins to scratch the surface of Jordan's subject matter, and one could certainly listen for hours to his various songs about achieving a state of inebriation, most notably "What's the Use of Getting Sober (When You're Going to Get Drunk Again)" and that epic drunken rant, "Open the Door, Richard" (which contains Jordan's most aggressive falsetto vocal).

"Beans and Cornbread" obviously belongs to the category of songs about food and drink, but it's as much about religion as it is about food. Jordan most famously assumed the clergy robes and oversized spectacles in "Deacon Jones," a tale of a misbehaving church elder of the sort that goes back to minstrelsy. His ribald reverend is a direct descendant of the comic preachers previously portrayed on recordings by Armstrong and Bert Williams. One of Jordan's many original compositions, "Beans and Cornbread," starts by describing a fight between these two foodstuffs—one imagines them being depicted anthropomorphically, perhaps in some Pixar-like animation technique. But the piece climaxes in the most animated of Jordan's sermons: He goes on a spirited—to say the least—diatribe delineating how beans and corn bread should follow the example of brotherhood set by other food pairings, such as hot dogs and mustard, wieners and sauerkraut, liver and onions, ham and eggs. The other Tympanists assume the role of the various members of the congregation, egging the Deacon on, you should forgive the expression. (Best line: "It doesn't matter at all what you think about me. But it matters a whole lot what I think about you!")

Jordan's deployment of different rhythmic approaches is every bit as deserving of attention as his subject matter. He was, along with Louis Prima and mainstream bandleader Jan Savitt, one of the early avatars of the beat known as the shuffle. Like Prima, Jordan recorded a lot of boogies and woogies. "Caldonia" was originally titled in full "Caldonia Boogie," and there was "Ching Ching Boogie," "Choo Choo Ch'Boogie," "Saxa-Woogie," "Tambaritiza Boogie," "Boogie Woogie Come to Town," "Pine-top's Boogie Woogie." Then there's the famous boogie that transpires in the barnyard and the one named after the blue plate.

The two post-Armstrong Louises, Prima and Jordan, found other interesting things to do with the shuffle, both of which were closely related to their ethnic backgrounds. Prima combined the shuffle with the Italian tarantella and Jordan merged it with various pan-Afro-American rhythms, most notably samba and calypso. "Early in the Morning" is an early example of a blues, or almost any kind of non-Latin tune, to utilize bongos and a distinct samba rhythm, and to do it subtly, without hitting you over the head with the fact of its having a Latin underpinning (except for a spoken reference to somebody named "Pedro"). Jordan's blend of Latin and blues very specifically anticipates the way Ray Charles would employ samba and shakers in R&B numbers. (The major songs Charles would glean from Jordan would be "I'm Gonna Move to the Outskirts of Town" and the ballad "Don't Let the Sun Catch You Crying." B. B. King later recorded an album-length tribute to Jordan.)

Beginning in the late thirties, Decca Records maintained a very busy ethnic division that extensively recorded the early, authentic calypso bands and singers (such as the Lion), from Kingston and Trinidad. In 1941, Jordan recorded "De Laff's on You," which may have been his first full-blown calypso, and in 1943, he accompanied the calypso singer Duke of Iron on an Armed Forces Radio Service *Jubilee* broadcast. Calypso suited Jordan's purposes on several levels—rhythmically, certainly, as well as in content. Jordan's calypsos were populated by scoundrels and rascals who were even seedier than those appearing in his other songs—presumably because the West Indies are, geographically, even farther south than Alabama or Louisiana. In these songs, West Indians are portrayed as even more country and geechie than those African Americans who were still trapped in the South, thus even more embarrassing to assimilated urbane Northerners: "Junco Partner" is an intoxicated Caribbeanite who gets locked down. "Run Joe" depicts a couple of skanky characters who run afoul of the law by telling fortunes, which, though it may seem harmless, was apparently illegal (perhaps it was regarded as an offshoot of voodoo). "Push Ka Pee She Pie" ("it's the new calypso bebop") tells of a country bumpkin who comes up North and gets taken by a slick city woman, who sells him the Brooklyn Bridge. The character is a "Saga Boy" (pronounced "Psycho Boy"), which was a genuine fashion trend among young men in postwar Trinidad and Tobago, similar to the Mods and Rockers in England a generation later.

"Stone Cold Dead in the Market," words and music by the pioneer calypso singer Wilmoth Houdini, was one of the greatest of Jordan's hits, but is often left out of latter-day re-creations (like the London and Broadway musical *Five Guys Named Moe*), perhaps because it's too gruesome even in the age of Tupac and Eminem. A husband comes home drunk and starts beating his wife even more savagely than usual, so she retaliates by bashing his head in with a rolling pin. (Why the corpse turns up in the market is one for Columbo.) "Stone Cold" was one of a series of duets by Jordan with his former Webb-mate Ella Fitzgerald, the flagship artist of all jazz-pop female singers in the postwar era (who had a lot of prestige, and sold a lot of records overall, but, unlike Jordan, had very few chart hits). "Stone Cold Dead" is, overall, much more joyous and funny than grisly, sort of like a bloodthirsty calypso Punch-and-Judy show. Today it would be hard to say which would be regarded as more insensitive—the horrific tale of spousal abuse that ends in a crushed cranium or the hysterically insensitive caricatures of Caribbean accents by Jordan and Fitzgerald.

Jordan remained with Decca for roughly fifteen years, his last session being in January 1954. He recorded 216 masters for the label in this time, all of which are included in Bear Family's *Let the Good Times Roll*. (When originally issued, the set included eight CDs and a bonus LP containing Jordan's duets with Fitzgerald. Later, the set was reissued with the Jordan-Fitzgerald cuts now on a short bonus ninth CD.) The Bear set also includes an excellent biographical sketch by Peter Grendysa, from which most of the facts in this essay were taken. (Also recommended is John Chilton's fine full-length biography, *Let the Good Times Roll: The Story of Louis Jordan and His Music*.)

The Bear box, like the King Cole Trio Capitol (Mosaic) box and the Dinah Washington complete Mercury series (Japanese Polygram), is one of the very few massive complete packages where nearly every track is worth owning, not merely to satisfy the collector's urge to acquire everything, but because they're all good. There are plenty of formula songs, numbers where Jordan or someone else just took a current expression or slang phrase and quickly built a song around it, like "There'll Be No Days Like That," "Put Some Money in the Pot, Boy" (a catchphrase from the final years of radio), "I Know What You're Puttin' Down," and "I Love That Kind of Carryin' On." While I can't imagine anybody reviving them, they are nevertheless first-class samples of Tympany Five rhythm and raillery.

As Grendysa estimates, there was an eight-year run in which approximately one-third of all the hit records on the "race" (R&B) chart were Jordan's. What was especially remarkable was that the Tympany Five was a one-man show; in a sense, it was the forties update of what Fats Waller and His Rhythm achieved a decade earlier, but Waller's sidemen were more important to the overall mixture. In general, few people can recall an outstanding trumpet solo on a Jordan record, or a statement by a reed player other than the leader (who alternated between clarinet, alto, and tenor, as on "Five Guys Named Moe"). The rhythm section was another matter, and Jordan had any number of future stars on piano (Wild Bill Davis, Bill Doggett, John Malachi) and a first-class drummer in Chris Columbus.

As good as the band was, Jordan knew that the Tympany Five format couldn't sustain him forever. In the early fifties, not long after Nat King Cole began moving away from his very successful trio, Jordan began tinkering with the formula. He began including numbers by bright new writers, such as Jon Hendricks ("I Want You to Be My Baby," "I'll Die Happy," "Messy Bessy") and Bobby Troup ("Hungry Man"). Like Cole, in 1953 he recorded as a crooner with a string orchestra (using Cole's musical director, Nelson Riddle), with mixed results: "Just Like a Butterfly That's Caught in the Rain" was too obvious an attempt to mimic Cole, being the kind of sensitive, sweet, caressing love song that Cole did so well, but "It's Better to Wait for Love," a less ambitious ballad, fared better. In 1952, Jordan had briefly experimented with his own big band; the records were good and the critics (particularly Leonard Feather) were kind, but the time for big bands had passed. And, increasingly, it was clear, so had Jordan's.

The reasons were racial and generational—and also both and neither. Jordan, who was a founding father of the music now being known as rock 'n' roll, was being upstaged by a bunch of his own disciples. First among these was guitarist Bill Haley, about whom, producer Milt Gabler remembered, "All the tricks I had used with Louis Jordan, I [re]used with Bill Haley." Most of the early rockers, both black and white, learned from him, including Chuck Berry and Bo Diddley, who said, "Louis Jordan is one of the cats I tried to be most like." However, within a short time the lot of them—Jordan, Haley, Berry, and Bo—were all pretty much a thing of the past. Jordan's star was fading by the mid-fifties, and even his rock-era followers were out of the picture by the early sixties.

It's too easy, and misleading, to say that the public would by now accept Jordan's antics coming from a bunch of young ofay imitators but not from their middle-aged oxford gray originator. While that's partly true, it fails to explain how many of Jordan's contemporaries, including Nat King Cole, Louis Prima, and even one of his key inspirations, Louis Armstrong, were all successful in reinventing themselves for a new generation. Prima, in fact, broke through all over again, ironically, by making his act more like Jordan's Tympany Five—though, unlike Jordan, Prima had the good sense to surround himself with musicians, and even another singer, with whom he could share the workload and the spotlight. (Perhaps Jordan could have used a Keely Smith equivalent.) After 1954, he continued to record prolifically in the Tympany Five format for the independent, black-oriented label Aladdin (for whom he cut one of his very best ballads, "Hurry Home") and

then for RCA and Mercury. He worked and recorded sporadically in the sixties and seventies, as his health would allow. He still had some of his songwriter's royalties, and he sold a house in Phoenix (to Elijah Muhammad). He hardly starved; he had enough beans and corn bread to last him for a while.

He cut albums for various independents, including one for disciple Ray Charles's Tangerine label. The best of the latter recordings is one of his last, cut in 1973 for the French jazz label Black & Blue. Here he sounds nothing less than remarkable. Both his voice and his alto hardly seem to have aged at all, even though he was in his sixty-fifth year. The voice is the same high baritone, squeaking occasionally into falsetto for comic effect, and surprisingly it hasn't even deepened in the slightest. These later versions of "Caldonia," "Saturday Night Fish Fry," and "I'm Gonna Move to the Outskirts of Town" are not in the least outclassed by the originals. ("Caldonia" now encompasses a long talking routine that rhymes "turban" with "bourbon.") Jordan also laid down two jazz and blues classics he had never hitherto recorded, "Take the A Train" and Gene Ammons's "Red Top." Most notably, there was a dynamic, even thrilling treatment of a contemporary country-pop tune by Mac Davis, "I Believe in Music," which also served as the album's title.

Louis Jordan died less than two years later, on February 4, 1975. His influence was vast, yet, sadly, he was completely ignored by the classic rock generation of the sixties and seventies. Both British and American rockers mistakenly identified the source of their inspiration as the very country types that Jordan made fun of, all those out-of-tune Mississippi Delta guitarists with mud on their overalls. Mick Jagger and Keith Richards called their band the Rolling Stones after Muddy Waters, not Five Guys Named Moe or Beans and Cornbread.

Jordan began to be rediscovered in the eighties when a now mostly forgotten British rocker named Joe Jackson (who looked eerily like a six-foot Mel Tormé) began covering his stuff. At the beginning of the nineties, there was a full-fledged Jordan revival, which climaxed in nearly all of his music being reissued on compact disc (most ambitiously on the Bear Family compendium), in John Chilton's biography, and in the hit musical *Five Guys Named Moe*. *Moe* originated in London and came to Broadway in 1992, where it ran for over a year at the Eugene O'Neill Theatre, with an original cast album on Sony. The principal six singers were all ace balladeers and comics: The highlight is an animated "Ain't Nobody Here but Us Chickens," which Milton Craig Nealy, essaying the role of Four-Eyed Moe, performs in an expert chicken voice. However, none of them, even collectively, could swing with anything approximating the authority of Jordan. The revival of interest in both him and Louis Prima led directly to the retro-swing phenomenon later in the nineties.

The good times, it seemed, were rolling again, even if Louis Jordan himself—along with Deacon

Jones, Brother Eat Moe, and the Saga Boy—was reet, petite, and gone.

Sheila Jordan (born 1928)

On January 25, 2010, at Town Hall, Sheila Jordan was presented with the New York Nightlife Award for best jazz vocalist. It was a proper capper for a decade, if not a career, of achievement: In her seventies, Jordan has released four new albums, toured continually, and played many important engagements, including a week with a full string section at Jazz at Lincoln Center in 2008.

At Town Hall, Jordan sang "Autumn in New York." Can she have been conscious that she was working in a house full of cabaret- and theatergoers, not her usual hardcore jazz audience? One can't be sure if she deliberately reined in her jazzier techniques, or—just as likely—simply felt like singing the song this way. Despite her very small range and chops that certainly aren't helped by being eighty-one years old, she is sonically still more or less where she was fifty years ago. In "Autumn in New York," she didn't go off on any tangents, there was no scatting, and while she mixed in a little stream-of-consciousness free-associating—though in a very musical way—she stayed on-message throughout. And it occurred to me that even when Jordan is giving full vent to her jazz side, she's never trying to run all over the place just to show how hip she is; that even when she's drifting and dreaming hither and yon, all of it is done in the service of the song. As formidably idiosyncratic as she may seem from a distance, she is above all a storyteller.

What are we to make of Sheila Jordan? This question is strictly our problem—not hers. Jordan's music has been remarkably consistent, from her first appearances on records (guest shots with Peter Ind and George Russell and her premier album, the 1962 *Portrait of Sheila*) to her most recent studio album, *Little Song*, recorded in 2002. (There have also been two recent live sets, the 2005 *Celebration: Live at Triad* taped in New York and the 2008 *Winter Sunshine: Live at Upstairs* from Montreal.) This might be because she was already well past thirty when the first document of her voice was made, and her style was fully formed. Had she recorded in her teens or twenties, she might have sounded quite different. In any case, she's changed remarkably little over the course of forty years. Compare Jordan to Rosemary Clooney, who was born in the same year (1928) and who never stopped evolving over those same forty years, or even with Jordan's younger compadre, Mark Murphy, who alters his sound and approach with every album—almost with every song.

But a better point of comparison might be Betty Carter, who was born half a year later. In the early eighties, when I started listening to both Jordan and Carter, they struck me as peas from the same iPod. Both were grounded firmly in the classic bebop idiom and both had sung informally with Charlie Parker himself. Both evolved to highly individual, idiosyncratic musics of their own that at one point I felt were best described as being part of the jazz avant-garde—only in free jazz did one get such long, wordless, "free"-sounding improvisations—as well as a penchant for indulging in often exceedingly odd original songs. Carter eventually came back into the mainstream or, rather, it came over to her. Not only did she land a much deserved spot at a major label, but her bands produced a slew of talented musicians who literally became the jazz mainstream.

Carter was able to reshape the mainstream around her, but Jordan, even in her "Grand Old Lady of Bebop" phase, remains an outsider. She has never been a full-time singer: During the golden age of jazz in the fifties, she supported herself by working as a typist while she raised her daughter. More recently, her "day job" has been serving as one of jazz singing's most illustrious teachers, sharing the same pool of students and the support network that backs up Mark Murphy.

Like both Carter and Murphy, Jordan is often described as a "musician's singer." This is one of those alleged compliments that no one wants: Who would want to be appreciated only by other musicians? Yet the term is usually applied by one singer to another in relation to pure technique—Jo Stafford, Mel Tormé, and Ella Fitzgerald might be called "singer's singers," not because their fellow singers are the only people who appreciate them, but because their intonation is so amazingly good.

In that sense, the term doesn't apply to Sheila Jordan. Her sense of pitch is all that it needs to be, but it's not in a class with, say, Nat King Cole's. In her late seventies, especially, the voice occasionally comes up short, especially on ballads like "Fair Weather." Jordan doesn't follow all the conventional rules of singing in pitch any more than she follows any other set of conventional rules. In a sense, one wouldn't want to set her up as a role model for other singers, unless it were in the abstract sense. Other singers shouldn't be encouraged to do specifically what she does, but her example should inspire other vocalists to find their own way, as she has.

She has recorded sparingly, only about fifteen albums, which is just about as many as Murphy has made in any one decade in his career. Yet there are several advantages to her having kept her discography small and manageable. For one thing, it means she had a greater shot at staying consistently inventive: It's not going too far to say that almost every track on almost every album contains something new. In fact, even on *Little Song* (recorded in June 2001), every track seems to contain something that's at least slightly out of the ordinary.

Track one is "Blackbird" by the Beatles, which in itself is far from common in jazz circles, but what's considerably more unusual is that she sings it in something like a medley, introducing it and then weaving in a Cherokee chant, or rather an improvised approximation of one. She has quite a bit of Native American blood in her background, apparently, and so starts the album with an appropriately autobiographical note; her grandfather (she explains to Kirk Silsbee in the liner notes) gave her the Indian nickname Little Song.

Track two is "Autumn in New York," which serves as a representative example of Jordan's offbeat, highly personal approach to the Great American Songbook. It's a slow and moody treatment that begins with the last line of the verse. In this case, Jordan isn't radically reshaping the melody or putting it in a nutso time signature; but by opening this way, she ensures that you pay attention. After which, "Barbados" springs from Jordan's long-standing fascination with the music and legacy of Charlie Parker; twenty years earlier (on the album *Old Time Feeling*), she recorded this Parker tune with just bass accompaniment. (The 1982 version, however, was only issued on the later CD edition of the album.)

Little Song does contain several samples of Jordan taking songs at surprising tempos: Frank Loesser's "Slow Boat to China," despite the title, is normally done fast and zippy (as in Billy May's cartoonish arrangement for Crosby and Clooney); here it becomes slow and sensual, in a way that seems so natural you wonder why nobody thought of it before. Likewise, "Something's Gotta Give," normally rendered fast-fast-fast by dudes like Sinatra, Greco, and Tormé, here becomes slow and meditative, with Jordan letting her pitch wobble all over the place on lines like "so en garde"—and never has the "vast mysterious sky" seemed quite so mysterious. (She changes "But how long can anyone try" to "But how long before I give in.")

"If I Could Lose You" starts as a Latin lament, a treatment appropriate for a song first heard in a picture called *Rose of the Rancho*, but which I can't say I've ever heard before. After the first chorus, done Latin-style, she surprises us with the verse. That passage is in turn followed by a scat chorus, followed by improvisations from guest trumpeter Tom Harrell and pianist Steve Kuhn, the latter her most frequent accompanist through the last forty years. Rodgers and Hammerstein's "Hello, Young Lovers" was written in 3/4 time, and that's how Jordan sings it, but it's an off-kilter, Monkish kind of a slow jazz waltz, not quite like any other version of the song—jazz, pop, or musical comedy—that I've heard before. Even when she's adhering to tradition, Jordan is anything but conventional.

She was born Sheila Jeanette Dawson, on November 18, 1928, in Detroit. She grew up in a mining town called Summerhill, Pennsylvania (near Altoona), amid abject poverty and alcoholism. Her mother had a drinking problem, but apparently didn't let that interfere with her maternal duty of singing to her baby daughter, and Jordan included "When I Grow Too Old to Dream" on *Little Song* because she remembered it from those occasions. She obviously had her mother in mind in her 1977 album *Sheila* when she transitions from Steve

Kuhn's "Hold Out Your Hand," which concerns itself with, as she says, "someone who drinks," into Billy Strayhorn's "Lush Life."

In essence, her deep, sometimes rough voice (she's not smooth and sultry, like Julie London or Diana Krall, say) seems to come straight out of an Appalachian coal mine. It's to her credit, though, that she doesn't rely on this aspect of her music, limiting it to an occasional reference to country and folk styles, as with "You Are My Sunshine" and on "The Water Is Wide" on *Lost and Found* (1989); the latter is one of the most beautiful performances of her career. (The Canadian soprano saxophonist Jane Bunnett apparently agreed, for she had Jordan sing it again on a 1993 CD titled *The Water Is Wide*.)

By the time Jeanette Dawson was in high school, the family had moved back to Detroit, and she was already singing jazz. In the mid- to late forties, she was thoroughly immersed in the Motor City's modern jazz scene, which was richer in great bop pianists than any other metropolis: Tommy Flanagan, Barry Harris, Hank Jones. She was also singing in a trio called Skeeter, Mitch, and Jean (her) that adapted jazz instrumentals into vocal terms in a manner that she claims anticipated Lambert, Hendricks & Ross. (The lyrics she still sings to Parker's "Confirmation" and "Barbados" come from this group.)

Charlie Parker had a major fan base in Detroit among both musicians and listeners, and he played there regularly, often encouraging local talent to sit in. It was Jean Dawson's (as she was then known) first encounter with Parker, but it wouldn't be her last. As she later told critic Don Heckman, "When I first heard him do 'Embraceable You,' I used to sing the lyrics just straight with him. I became so familiar with his music that I'd know when he substituted another bridge or used altered chords. I could hear his chords." Parker supposedly told her, "You really hear those changes for a kid." (She was around twenty at this time, but Jordan has the advantage of looking younger than she is—today she certainly doesn't look eighty-something.)

Here comes Mr. Jordan: A few years later, Charlie Parker reentered her life when she married Bird's pianist Duke Jordan. This was not a match made in heaven; Jordan, by all accounts, was not one of nature's noblemen. The marriage ended after seven years, but left Mrs. Jordan with three things: her daughter, Tracy (born 1955); her professional name, Sheila Jordan; and the occasional opportunity to sing informally with the Parker Quintet. It's safe to say that no singer has sung the glories of Bird more expressively or more frequently: Parker's Caribbean melody "Barbados" is performed on *Old Time Feeling* and *Little Song*; "Anthropology" is on *Lost and Found* and in a medley with its source, "I Got Rhythm," on *Songs from Within*; she sang "Confirmation" both on *Confirmation* and on the 1979 *Lennie Tristano Memorial Concert* album; she also sings "Little Willie Leaps" (written by Miles Davis but associated with Parker) on both *The Crossing* (1984) and *Winter Sunshine.*

As Jordan has said in interviews, she was especially fascinated with Parker's variations on "Embraceable You." Parker (accompanied by Duke Jordan) recorded the Gershwin brothers' classic twice for Dial in 1947 and neither of his recordings directly states the Gershwin melody. The first, from October, is a ballad that uses the original title (producer Ross Russell had to pay the Gershwin estate a royalty, but Bird wanted people to know what his source material was and what he was doing with the tune). The second, from December, is a medium-tempo bop number, which has been issued as both "Quasimado" and "Quasimodo" in various performances by Parker, Jordan, and others. Jordan has recorded at least four different sets of variations on Parker's variations: Her lyrics to the fast variation appear as "Tribute (Quasimodo)" on *Old Time Feeling,* in a duet with bassist Harvie Swartz, and as part of a medley with another Parker composition, the 1949 "The Bird" (itself a variation on the Count Basie standard "Topsy"). On the 1991 *One for Junior,* she expanded that medley into a larger medley that includes "The Bird" as well as "Quasimodo" and "Embraceable You" sung simultaneously, Jordan singing her words to Parker's melody and Mark Murphy singing Ira Gershwin's original lyric. In 1997, she included both songs as part of a massive memorial medley she titled "Mourning Song": "Tribute," "Quasimodo," "Embraceable You," "Goodbye Porkpie Hat" (Charles Mingus's memorial to Lester Young), "Good Morning Heartache" (one of Jordan's many Billie Holiday homages), "I Got Rhythm," and "Listen to Monk."

When Duke and Sheila Jordan parted company in 1959, to support her daughter, she went to work as a typist in an ad agency. By the early sixties, she was singing frequently at a club called Page Three in Greenwich Village, and came to the attention of two composer-arranger-pedagogues and musical theorists, Lennie Tristano and George Russell. In 1960, a group of Tristanoites, led by bassist Peter Ind and including pianist Ronnie Ball, recorded Jordan for the first time on *Looking Out,* the first release on Ind's label, Wave Records, singing "Yesterdays." George Russell eventually got to hear her sing, and was so taken with what he heard that, at the age of thirty-four, she made what is usually listed as her debut on records with "You Are My Sunshine" on his 1962 album *The Outer View.*

"You Are My Sunshine" tells us several things about Jordan, first that her Appalachian accent was uniquely suited to songs with folk or country origins (this song was also political in its circumstances, if not content, having been credited to Governor Jimmy Davis of Louisiana). And by going on for ten minutes, in which she contorts the familiar melody into no end of surprising new shapes, it showed us that Jordan has a gift for extremely personal inter-

pretations—interpretations that are so idiosyncratic that they might as well be new songs. "Sheila's singing," Russell said (as quoted by Nat Hentoff), "made my skin crawl."

"Sunshine" led to attention from several members of the jazz press, as well as from Blue Note Records. Even more than the other jazz labels—Prestige, Riverside, Contemporary—Blue Note was resolutely dedicated to hard-core instrumental jazz, and Jordan remains the only important vocalist to have done an album for the label while it was still owned by Alfred Lion and Frank Wolff. *Portrait of Sheila,* cut in the fall of 1962, is a magnificent record, with Jordan backed by a pianoless rhythm section of Barry Gailbraith, guitar; Steve Swallow, bass; and Denzil Best, drums. It's the kind of record even a non–Sheila Jordan fan could love: She keeps her proclivity to personalize—some would say distort—melodies in check, and there are no tracks longer than five minutes. The absence of a piano, which would be a recurring theme in her discography, helps give the set a wide-open feeling harmonically. She constantly displays her melodic ingenuity, especially on Tadd Dameron's "If You Could See Me Now," in which she takes the line "The way I feel for you I never could disguise" and phrases it to the melody of Fats Waller's "The Jitterbug Waltz." *Portrait* contains some offbeat choices (from Alec Wilder's "Who Can I Turn To?" and the twenties antique "Laugh, Clown, Laugh" to Oscar Brown Jr.'s "Hum Drum Blues") but no originals.

In general, as good as *Portrait of Sheila* is, it sounds less like Jordan's way-far-out later recordings than "You Are My Sunshine." All the more disappointing, then, that Nat Hentoff's prediction did not come true: "She's waited a long time, but I'll be very surprised if Sheila soon won't have to leave that day job and spend all her time at doing what she is best at—being herself through music." Unfortunately, her wait was just beginning. Blue Note was hardly the label to launch a singing star and, despite write-ups in jazz magazines, Jordan continued typing by day and singing at the Page Three by night. Apart from beginning her four-decade collaboration with Steve Kuhn, the next event of note in her career occurred in 1966. That was the year when, thanks partly to George Russell, who was then living in Stockholm, she started appearing regularly in Scandinavia. In 1968, she began working with Swedish bassist Arild Andersen, the first of her long-term partnerships with bass players; the two did duet concerts together both at home and abroad.

By the mid-seventies, the situation began to improve for her; for one thing, her daughter was now grown up. Although Chris Sheridan, writing in 1977, observed that her whole working schedule was four or five concerts and three or four club dates a year, Lee Jeske, writing about the same period, points out, "Her luck started to turn around. Members of the so-called avant-garde, Roswell Rudd and

Carla Bley, for example, were using Sheila Jordan's vocals, and her singing began to expand." She was working overseas more than ever, which led to her second and third albums—respectively, *Confirmation* (1975, for a Japanese label) and *Sheila* (1977, done in Denmark).

Both were brilliant. *Confirmation* backed her, for virtually the only time in her career, with a full jazz quartet, tenor sax and three rhythm, in what was a clearly defined program in the LP age: Side One was all songs associated with childhood, like Frank Loesser's "Inchworm" (brought into the jazz universe by John Coltrane) and Frederick Hollander and Dr. Seuss's "Because We're Kids" (from *The 5000 Fingers of Dr. T*), plus "God Bless the Child" and "My Favorite Things"—songs for some pretty hip children. In all of which she may be contemplating her own long-departed youth, or perhaps the more recently departed youth of her daughter, Tracy Jordan, but more likely she is just having fun with the songs in the most joyous, playful manner possible. Side Two lives up to the album's title, *Confirmation*, and is her usual mixture of bebop and nuttiness, expertly done, including her first recordings of songs by Parker and Kuhn.

Sheila is her first of many voice-bass albums, done with Andersen. *Song of Joy* would have been a better title for this expressive opus, as that song (by R&B star Billy Preston) begins and ends the album in two very different readings. What is surprising is one of the best versions of "Better Than Anything" (introduced in a 1963 album of that title by Irene Kral), a swinging waltz with music by David Wheat, words by Bill Loughborough, that's become one of the more important vocal jazz standards of the postmodern era.

Usually Jordan doesn't miss an opportunity to work the names of musicians she admires, especially Parker and Holiday, into her songs. This is one of the more pedagogical aspects of her music; it's one thing to sing jazz, but quite another to sing *about* jazz. "The Lady" (on *Sheila*, credited to one R. Stevenson) is a didactic homage to the white gardenia lady in a sort of "I Remember Clifford" way. The Parker tribute on *One for Junior* works a bit better because it's less serious and tragic: Jordan congratulates Clint Eastwood on his movie *Bird* ("Thank you Mr. Clint Eastwood for making my day, by letting Charlie Parker play"), but half-kiddingly chides him, "What about Max Roach, what about Tommy Potter, Miles Davis and my ex-husband, Duke Jordan? Well that's okay, I don't get alimony anyway." These tribute things work better when the likes of Parker and Holiday are not presented as martyrs or saints to be worshipped.

Unlike Betty Carter, Jordan has never enjoyed a breakthrough moment when all of a sudden she becomes accepted and starts touring and recording regularly. She has come close several times: In the eighties, the quartet she co-led with Steve Kuhn, which recorded for the comparatively well-distributed ECM Records, garnered more press attention than most of her previous ventures. The 1984 album *The Crossing* was also well received, and in 1985 and 1987 Jordan came in ahead of Carter in the *Down Beat* poll, placing second after Sarah Vaughan; Jordan has, in fact, won the *DB* poll for "talent deserving of wider recognition" a total of nine times, a record for a vocalist.

For the last twenty years she's continued to make a living through a combination of teaching and touring. She's too feisty and too unconventional to be recognized by normal outlets, but considering the offbeat nature of her talent, she's shown remarkable resourcefulness in getting her music in front of the people that want to hear it. As discographer James Coffey has pointed out, even though Jordan has barely done more than a handful of albums under her own name, she appears on several dozen by other musicians as guest vocalist, among them Carla Bley's classic *Escalator over the Hill*, four albums each by trombonist Roswell Rudd and German big band composer George Gruntz, and a wide variety of postmodern players from all over the world.

As noted, since *Sheila*, one of her favorite formats on both disc and live appearances is the voice-bass duo, as heard on *Old Time Feeling* (1982), *The Very Thought of Two* (1988), *Songs from Within* (1989), and the aptly titled *I've Grown Accustomed to the Bass* (2000). All are with Harvey Swartz except the last, which teams her with Cameron Brown. Considering that her entire discography isn't much more than a dozen releases, five whole albums of bass and voice duets is quite a lot.

Lost and Found (1989) is one of the few Jordan albums (*Little Song* is another) to use a conventional jazz rhythm section, and she's also recorded with longtime collaborator pianist Steve Kuhn, most recently *Jazz Child*, which by their standards is a comparatively conventional outing with voice, piano, bass, and drums. Other Jordan-Kuhn projects (which are generally billed as Kuhn-Jordan efforts) include *Home*, bassist Steve Swallow's cycle of musical settings of poems by Robert Creeley; *Last Year's Waltz*; and *Playground*. Despite the title, the last is not another collection of children's songs in the tradition of *Confirmation*, but rather a gathering of offbeat Kuhn originals; as the billing implies, the emphasis on most of these is on Kuhn as a pianist, composer, and bandleader, with Jordan's vocals taking a secondary role.

The Kuhncentric projects are atypical of Jordan's output in that while she's not above writing a song herself occasionally (or more often a lyric to a famous jazz line by Parker or someone else, or singing a song by Kuhn or another musician friend), this is the only album she's ever made without one standard on it. This is probably the most conventional aspect of Jordan's music, that she can be far-out and even avant-garde, if that word means anything anymore, but likes to be firmly rooted in the Great American Songbook.

Other albums utilize the classic jazz quartet format of one horn plus trio; *The Crossing* teams her with the brilliant trumpeter Tom Harrell, who reappears almost twenty years later on parts of *Little Song*. *Body and Soul*, which was taped in 1986 for Japanese Sony, is perhaps her most mainstream album yet, combining a comparatively old-school rhythm section with a program of familiar standards. In contrast, the least likely album in the Jordan discography is one of her nicest: *Heart Strings* (1994), which backs her with two violins, a viola, and a cello, the familiar Harvie Swartz on bass, young power-drummer Smitty Smith, and Alan Broadbent as string arranger and pianist. This Los Angeles–based musical director is one of those godlike accompanists who can make anybody sound good and the good, needless to say, sound better. He's the perfect intermediary between the "outside" elements (Jordan herself) and the "inside" ones (the string quartet). *Heart Strings* is an album with an opening track, "Haunted Heart," so strong that the rest of the record doesn't have to do anything, it can just sit there. As it happens, the strings allow her to shine like a classic jazz-pop singer of standards, like Sarah Vaughan and her beloved Holiday. Broadbent's string orchestrations make her improvisations and variations seem all the more special and at the same time they make her more accessible.

The strongest track after "Haunted Heart" is an eleven-and-a-half-minute medley of the Jordan fave "Inch Worm" and another text that uses an insectoid metaphor for human behavior, "The Caterpillar Song." She starts the Loesser song slow, going back and forth with the strings pizzicato, almost treating it as a verse. This opening section—one minute ten seconds—is a gem all by itself: In the lyrics, the speaker takes the titular inch worm to task for looking at life from a strictly "businesslike" perspective, without stopping to take in the beauty of the world; appropriately, Broadbent's strings are resolutely businesslike, rigid in their rhythm, while Jordan herself is warm and effusive and resolutely human.

Then the strings drop out, and Jordan kicks it into tempo with the rhythm section, treating it as a Coltranesque modal vamp, using both scat phrases and the Loesser lyrics. This is a full song within the larger production of the medley, with solos by Broadbent, who ends the "movement," as it were, by slowing down into a solo transitional passage that abruptly stops at about 6:30; it's almost like the first side of a two-sided 12" 78. The strings come in, followed by Jordan, with a metaphoric text about caterpillars, cocoons, and butterflies, spreading your wings and taking to the sky, that sort of thing ("I'll meet Heaven's inhabitants / Take naps on exotic plants / Give rides to deserving ants"). It's a wonderful performance of an otherwise unknown but beautiful song, which concludes with Jordan going back into "Inch Worm" for the coda.

It's surprising that my favorite track by the jazziest of all jazz singers should be a ballad, two ballads even—and with strings, no less. But then, there's nothing about the music of Sheila Jordan that doesn't keep us in a constant state of surprise.

K

Eartha Kitt (1927–2008)

Every Eartha Kitt performance works on at least two levels: She's always completely serious and yet constantly making fun of herself—and everything else. She sings a song of seduction and pulls out all the stops; she poses with her voice (even on a recording you can see her batting her eyes and undulating her torso), while at the same time she lets you know that she's not only in on the joke, she *is* the joke. Just because she's sexy doesn't mean she can't be funny, and just because she's funny doesn't mean she isn't sexy.

Because she's primarily an "entertainer"—a term that some of our more high-minded individuals (the Artie Shaws, for instance) have used to define someone who is not an "artist"—doesn't mean that there isn't a lot of art to what she does. Throughout her career, Kitt had amazing vocal technique: Her high, sharp voice, as nearly everyone has pointed out, was indeed in the feline register but with strong projection and impeccable intonation. Her father's family name, apparently, actually was Kitt, and she embodied a catlike persona both physically and vocally for at least fifteen years before she became Batman's sexiest arch-nemesis, the Catwoman. If a *Felis domesticus* could sing in tune, it would sound like her.

The voice itself is remarkable, but what she does with it is even more so. She said that when she learned to speak French in her early twenties, she figured out that she could make the guttural rolled-*r* sound, so necessary to the language, essentially through what she described as "gargling." Gargling was only the beginning—her singing encompasses a wide range of vocal effects. Inspired, to a degree, by her immersion in the musical styles of different languages (it was said that she could sing convincingly in seven, and speak and read in at least four), Kitt was able to do things with her voice that no English-language diva ever dreamed of. She incorporates the throaty noises of a French chanteuse like Juliette Gréco or Edith Piaf, as well as the vocal effects you expect of a Brazilian bombshell like Carmen Miranda or a Cuban *cancione* like Celia Cruz. Nor is she limited to sounds from the human world: She not only purrs like a cat, she chirps like a bird. On the whole, she uses her voice—the different registers, the different kinds of sounds, those vocal gyrations and ululations, gargling noises, vibrato, and tremolo—as creatively and surprisingly as Fats Waller, Dean Martin, and Elvis Presley. In one French song, "Le Danseur de Charleston," she even hiccups expressively.

I was fortunate that I got to see la Kitt live at least four times in her final years—in *The Wild Party* on Broadway (2000), in an all-star concert at Town Hall, at her big eightieth-birthday party at the JVC Jazz Festival in 2007, and at her one-woman cabaret show at the Café Carlyle. But even those who are reading this in decades to come, who weren't as fortunate, can get the full impact of Eartha Kitt in all her glory, because her artistry transfers very well to recordings. Future generations won't be missing out on anything—except her gorgeous looks.

She told her story in at least three autobiographies (*Thursday's Child*, 1956; *Alone with Me*, 1976; *I'm Still Here: Confessions of a Sex Kitten*, 1989) and countless interviews, but apparently she didn't learn the exact details of her birth until she was about seventy, when for the first time she saw her birth certificate. The major surprise was that she had been born on January 17, 1927—she had always thought that she was a year older. Her mother had both Native American and African American blood, and her father was Caucasian, of German and Dutch lineage; she was conceived when her father "forced himself" (as the singer consistently reported) on her mother.

If one could choose the circumstances of one's upbringing, I don't think anyone would pick what she was stuck with: growing up a part-black, illegitimate, virtual orphan in abject poverty at the absolute bottom of the social ladder, in the Deep South in the 1930s. As an adult, Kitt was understandably bitter about her childhood, which seems like a reasonable response (more so than for Nina Simone or Lena Horne, who both had it considerably better than she did). Rather than hating the world, Kitt grew up with a desire to entertain—to make everybody happy and make herself rich and successful in the process.

She spent her first eight years in South Carolina. A potential stepfather refused to have a "yellow" girl in his house, but fortunately she was later sent to live in Harlem with a woman who may or may not have been her actual mother. The first way she got anybody to notice her was through dancing; modern dance innovator Katherine Dunham offered her a scholarship at her studio and eventually a spot in her troupe. The Dunham company brought Kitt to England shortly after the war, and from there she somehow landed a spot in a nightclub in Paris singing Cuban songs (most notably "Tierra Va Temblar," which she later recorded). People started to pay attention to her—the way they had to Josephine

Baker a quarter-century earlier—and she made her recording debut (which consisted of three standards and the contemporary blues ballad "Since I Fell for You") with trumpeter Doc Cheatham in Paris in 1950. Most important, she was spotted by Orson Welles—still regarded as a boy genius—who cast her in his European production of *Doctor Faustus* and encouraged people to think that they were having an affair (which she later denied).

By now Kitt really was a sensation in Europe. She then enjoyed a triumphant run at Churchill's, a nightclub in London, followed by a similarly successful engagement of twenty-five weeks at the Blue Angel in New York. Then the Broadway revue *New Faces of 1952* cemented her popularity in the United States. Among other things, the score provided her with her first classic set pieces, "Bal Petit Bal" and "Monotonous." These two songs laid a foundation for much of her subsequent career. The first was a genuine French song performed by Kitt with a genuine French singer, Robert Clary. By then, she had spent most of her adult life in Europe and was more French than anybody. What was remarkable wasn't that she was believable as a French girl, but rather that by restraining her tigress attitude and killer vibrato, she managed somehow to sound like a virgin. "Monotonous" broke new ground; it was among the first songs to create Kitt as a man-eating—but nonetheless self-mocking—femme fatale diva. Even more than Dolores Gray or Gwen Verdon, Kitt would spend most of her career as a glamour girl in a tight dress.

By now she had begun her long-standing relationship with RCA Victor Records. "I had a hard time getting a record contract," she said in an interview with the Associated Press circulated at the time of her death. "They said, 'She's too strange, she's too weird, her voice doesn't sound like anything we know.'" Kitt told historian Jim Gavin that her agency, William Morris, had tried to interest the record labels in her by prodding her to sing a so-called commercial novelty with a line that went "My ma gave me a nickel / To buy a pickle." "The maitre'd [at the Blue Angel] came to me one night and said that Dave Kapp of RCA was there and that he wanted to see me after the show. I said, 'Well, that's gonna be a waste of time, because five companies have refused me.' . . . But I saw him anyhow, out of courtesy. I said, 'Mr. Kapp, there's no point in talking to me. . . . I know what you're gonna say, you saw my act and you want me to sing some stupid song. . . .' He said, 'No, we'd like to record you exactly as you are.'" Thanks to Kapp, she wound up recording 132 tracks in the period (for RCA and then for the producer's own Kapp Records), all of which were collected in *Eartha Quake*, a five-CD boxed set released in 1993 by Bear Family Records of Germany.

"Monotonous" really started something: She would thereafter spend the largest portion of her time onstage and in the studio singing about what a hot-stuff sugar baby she was. Obviously, Kitt was playing a version of this character in her club act even before *New Faces,* but by the mid-fifties, the fine points of her extreme-capitalist man-eater persona had come into focus. She was in precisely the right place at the right time. These songs captured the imagination of a materialistic era. Men and women alike found them sexy and hysterical, comically exaggerated but all too real, and they laughed uneasily but hard at what the songs said about gender roles in the larger society.

Kitt constantly sang of love and avarice. "Mink, Schmink" atypically promotes the message that love is more important than money—but she gives every impression of not believing it. In another variation she sings of being "Just an Old-Fashioned Girl" whose only dream in life is to marry "an old-fashioned millionaire." "C'est Si Bon" (a record famously parodied by Stan Freberg, though I would argue that Kitt's original is even funnier) is a landmark in that even though it's entirely in French there's never any doubt what she's singing about. In "If I Can't Take It with Me (When I Go)," she would appear to be seducing God into letting her take her ill-gotten gains when she ascends in that heavenly elevator toward the penthouse apartment in the sky.

Kitt's most extreme song for greedy lovers was a Christmas tune. Kapp's faith in her was rewarded when "Santa Baby" became one of the major holiday hits of the era. Composed by Philip Springer, the song is similar, melodically, harmonically, and philosophically, to Bobby Troup's early hit "Daddy." "Santa Baby" showcases the lady as a sex kitten making out her Christmas list and requesting, in a remarkably understated tone, exaggeratedly luxurious goodies, such as a duplex apartment and the deed to a platinum mine, from the man with the bag. (Good luck with that—how's that going for you?)

In a way that must have surprised both Springer and Kitt, the song became a seasonal perennial; as of 2010, it appears on more than five hundred compact disc albums, by Kitt and dozens of other female singers. (Which I myself think is a major mistake. No other singer should do "Santa Baby" for the same reason that no one other than Peggy Lee should do "Fever." These aren't songs that anyone can interpret but are essentially special items specifically tailored for particular artists.) The song led to a sequel, "This Year's Santa Baby," as well as a subsequent comic Christmas caper, in which Kitt bemoans she's getting "Nothin' for Christmas" precisely because she *didn't* put out.

Apart from songs of romance with finance, Kitt's other specialties were exoticism and continental sophistication—the legacy of "Bal Petit Bal." Her global musical travels vary in quality and authenticity as much as in geography. The mid-fifties was an international era in American pop music, and, per-haps coincidentally, most of the leading exponents of pop internationalism were African American, most notably Louis Armstrong, Nat King Cole, and Kitt. A disproportionate share of their hits and even nonhits originated in places other than North America.

Kitt sang far too many of these to catalogue here—at least half the Bear Family box seems to be international or exotic material; the titles that follow are just a few standouts. An obvious starting point was French songs—both genuine and faux—"Je Cherche un Homme (I Want a Man)" and "Après Moi," among many others. "Vid Kajen" and "Rosenkyssar" are a pair of actual Swedish serenades, while "Jonny" is one of Marlene Dietrich's *Blue Angel*–era Weimar seductions. Kitt sang waltzes ("Under the Bridges of Paris"), tangos ("There Is No Cure for l'Amour"), boleros ("No Importa Si Mentí"), and en clave ("Oggere"). There's probably even a polka or two in there.

After France, her second favorite locale was the Latin world: Her pan-Spanish pieces were serious ("Angelitos Negros") and frivolous ("Señor") and everything in between—including some authentic foreign songs with suspiciously wacky English lyrics. The mid-fifties saw two Portuguese songs become hits in North America. Both were instrumental singles for famous arrangers, Les Baxter's "April in Portugal" and Nelson Riddle's "Lisbon Antigua"—and Kitt, not surprisingly, did vocal versions of each.

Certainly more than any other American-born pop singer, she spent a lot of time, musically, even beyond Europe. "Uska Dara" was an authentic Turkish song that came her way, and became her biggest hit single after "Santa Baby"; it was so popular by the time of the 1954 movie version of *New Faces* that it had to be inserted into the film. She sings entirely in Turkish, but the record does feature her speaking in English, as if she were narrating a travelogue or a foreign film—the aural equivalent of subtitles. Like most of Kitt's best music, "Uska Dara" is both funny and sensual, a sexually charged, minor-key tour of the exotic East. She followed it with other nonwestern laments such as "Shango," "Sholem" (both of which have more spoken narration from Kitt), and "Torah Dance (Ki M'Tzion)."

"African Lullaby" is sort of a Swahili update of Louis Armstrong's "When It's Sleepy Time Down South." Although Kitt sings in authentic Swahili for part of the disc, it's still possible for future generations of Afrocentrist PhDs to view it as patronizing (though no less than "Sleepy Time," which was, after all, written by black songwriters). Kitt risks less criticism from future generations when she's striving for humor rather than authenticity: Two of her funniest songs are about musical culture clash, "Honolulu Rock and Roll" and "Mambo de Paree"—the latter a much bigger laugh than Rosemary Clooney's earlier (and more successful) "Mambo Italiano." Clooney is a game girl when she sings the novelty songs foisted on her by Mitch Miller, but Kitt is really into it. She sings these dopey little European songs with immense conviction, tearing into them and extracting every last ounce of humor or rhythm or what have you. Whatever is to be gotten out of them, she gets.

"Mambo de Paree" is an especially witty three minutes, with quotable lyrics: "Just like a Yank mambos / sometimes a Franc mambos / old George the Cinq mambos." The melody pivots around the by-then-essential mambo "grunt," which Perez Prado had perfected—at stop-time intervals, the bandleader grunts his approval. The device was long a signature of Cuban music by 1955. In "Paree," the Prado grunt is supplied by a choir of high-voiced maidens typical of France who chant "oui!" at the appropriate moments. It's a funny, funny record—and, you can, in fact, do the mambo to it. "Honolulu Rock and Roll" by Dick Manning (who wrote a ton of novelty songs, many involving parents and islands and animal noises, such as "Mama Will Bark," "Papa Loves Mambo," and "The Pussycat Song") isn't quite on that level—the best that can be said for it is that it anticipates Elvis Presley's "Rock-a-Hula Baby."

The fifties were Kitt's pinnacle years as a recording artist. (She was then so popular that she wrote her first autobiography before she was thirty, although not many people bought it.) According to Gavin, in his notes for the Bear Family box, in 1954 RCA listed her as one of their five best-selling artists, and the label's publicity made the unlikely claim that every one of her singles was selling at least 600,000 copies. "Honolulu Rock and Roll" shows that like a lot of classy popular singers of the era—including Cole, Como, and Day—Kitt had arrived at an interesting place. Considering that she started her recording career with a refusal to sing a song about nickels and pickles, she was now barking quite a few woofers that made the "nickel"/"pickle" lyric seem like Keats.

But there were compensating virtues. In the years following *New Faces,* she appeared in two other Broadway shows, both unsuccessful, starting with the dreary *Mrs. Patterson* (1954–55), which Kitt and everybody else regarded as a disaster, yet which was recorded by RCA (you can tell the plot is dopey, but James Shelton's score isn't bad). In 1957 came *Shinbone Alley* (with a book by Mel Brooks), which was a great idea, at least, for a show: It was based on *archy and mehitabel* by Don Marquis, a fanciful tale of a typewriting *cucaracha* and a superannuated femme fatale feline (guess which part Eartha played); Kitt recorded only three of Joe Darion and George Kleinsinger's songs for RCA. She was a hit again in the film of *New Faces.* Then there was a very obscure B picture with Sidney Poitier called *The Mark of the Hawk* (1957), about African independence.

The big payoff was Kitt's involvement in the 1958 *St. Louis Blues.* The film itself was far from the triumph that everyone was hoping for, but the music—liberally adapted from the works of W. C. Handy (no less "adapted" than the way the script bore little resemblance to Handy's actual life)—was glorious. Handy's classic songs resounded brilliantly, not only in the film sound track itself but in three companion albums by Nat King Cole (in the lead, as Handy himself), Pearl Bailey (as "Aunt Hagar"), and Kitt, as a femme fatale of a siren (does anyone see a pattern here?) who lures a blues-curious preacher's son away from the church and into the saloon. Around the same time, she made a highly entertaining appearance on Cole's NBC TV series (it's on YouTube); forty years later, she gossiped about Cole during her show at the Café Carlyle, telling us how the man himself was a dreamboat and an angel and that the only thing that came between them was his wife.

Kitt's *St. Louis Blues* album on RCA is almost unquestionably the best studio album of her entire output (the other high points of her recording career were singles and live albums). The idea was to take Handy's classic blues and bluescentric songs of the jazz age and update them. Kitt had sung variations of the blues before. "The Blues" (from *Black, Brown and Beige*) is Duke Ellington's meditation on the concept of the blues, which is famously not in blues form; neither is "Way Down Blues" from *Shinbone Alley.* "My Heart's Delight" by Charlie Singleton is pure R&B that could have been sung and arranged for Ruth Brown and Dinah Washington. "A Woman Wouldn't Be a Woman" is straight up doo-wop, rather like Nat Cole's "If I May," with a chanting vocal group and 16th-note triplets.

St. Louis Blues is a whole different shade of blues. RCA chose to back her with modern jazz arranger–trumpeter Shorty Rogers and his group, the Giants, which is as fine an example of thinking out of the box as I've ever seen. Both Kitt and Rogers are removed from their traditional comfort zones; you'd expect her to show up with a more theatrical musical director, and him with a more boppish singer (like Mel Tormé). Yet somehow they meet in the middle and totally pull it off, aided by the high quality and infinite malleability of Handy's music, which is theatrical enough for Kitt and swinging enough for Rogers. His arrangements sound modern and hip with just enough of a twenties two-beat that they never break character with the era.

Kitt herself is a total delight throughout; "Long Gone (from Bowling Green)" is Handy's most ambitious comic narrative, the tall and winding tale of a Kentucky-based bank robber on the lam, which Kitt intones with a mixture of respect and reproach. The opener, "Careless Love," has her artfully combining self-deprecation and remorse over a bouncing beat and an unobtrusive male vocal quartet. On "Beale Street Blues" and elsewhere, she suppresses the purrs, rasps, and comically rolled *r*s, and just sings the blues as straightforwardly as possible, without the special effects. She's also very evocative on one of

Handy's most sophisticated songs, the Creole love call "Chantez les Bas"—she begins with a vividly sung verse and slowly rocks through the central refrain, as if she were somehow singing a lullaby and performing a striptease at the same time. The album ends movingly with two traditional spirituals heard in the film, "Steal Away" and "Hist [Hoist] the Window, Noah," which offer evidence that anytime she wanted to Kitt could have had a whole other career as the world's sexiest gospel singer. More than anywhere else in her recorded output, Kitt totally rocks throughout this album.

In 1959, Kitt followed Dave Kapp to his own label, Kapp Records, where she recorded *The Fabulous Eartha Kitt* (new stuff) and *Eartha Kitt Revisited* (new versions of mid-fifties hits and signature songs); these two albums conclude the *Eartha Quake* boxed set. Her best recording of the 1960s was *Eartha Kitt in Person at the Plaza*, an absolutely sensational album that gives you a proper sense of what she was like live at her peak. (It was released by GNP Crescendo Records, and I've seen the year given as both 1961 and 1965.) She opens with a "real" song of seduction, "Sell Me," followed by a parody of one, her classic "I Want to Be Evil" (her idea of evilness isn't drinking and screwing or even drowning kittens, but rather such activities as changing her seat in the theater and stepping on everybody's feet), which is done with even more evil energy than the two previous studio recordings. Likewise, the Lerner-Lane song with the famously long title "How Could You Believe Me?" (that's just the beginning) is a way for her to uphold her evil seductress icon in a vaudeville humor way, outfitted with a long, funny monologue delivered in a mock Southern accent.

All the Kitt trademarks are here: the femme fatale numbers, such as "Champagne Taste" (which includes the great line "You'll have to work on / something better than a zircon"), as well as the exotic ones. Kitt was sharp enough to use the international songs for two purposes. Naturally, they make her seem sophisticated and worldly, but at the same time they're as rhythmic and bouncy as any bubblegum hit on the charts in the early sixties. "Waray, Waray" is a Philippine folk song but it's also catchy as hell. Her international streak lets her be high class in a way that simultaneously appeals to the lowest common denominator. The most vivid illustration of that is her show-off version of "Come on-a My House" sung in high Japanese. "Zhara Bee, Zha Zha" is a Pakistani song that she sings with such a sense of fun that it could be "Come on-a My Harem."

Her climax is a total surprise: the klezmer classic "Rumania, Rumania" sung in Yiddish. Like a true Klezmorim, she squeezes the notes in and out of all kinds of kinky pentatonic places. Kitt renders the traditional song with such spirit and even fury that she leads the patrons of New York's Plaza Hotel into a veritable frenzy. She's so convincingly Yiddish that

she could have appeared in *Fiddler on the Roof* if only there were a character in Sholem Aleichem sexy enough for her to play.

Kitt achieved a new height of fame in 1967–68 when she played the Catwoman in the third season of *Batman,* one of the TV shows that defined the era. It was a moment when the culture caught up to her, since she had already been embodying Catwoman for her whole life. Kitt was built less like a conventional supermodel than the previous women who played the role, Julie Newmar and Lee Meriwether (and, more recently, both Michelle Pfeiffer and Halle Berry), but nevertheless Kitt was the Catwoman that you remembered. She inhabited the character so vividly that the costume almost seemed superfluous, even though she was certainly something to see in a shiny, form-fitting catsuit.

But fate also taketh away. Nineteen sixty-eight was the year of Kitt's unfortunate remark at the White House; it was one of those watershed disasters, like Jackie Mason giving the finger to Ed Sullivan, that derailed a career and the full facts of which are much debated. Just let it be said that she made a few pointed remarks regarding the Vietnam War to First Lady "Lady Bird" Johnson, which were not appreciated by the president. In "Monotonous," a generation earlier, Kitt sang of how "Harry Truman plays bop for me," but in 1968 the Democratic Party was not quite so accommodating. By Kitt's account, she was unofficially blacklisted and barred from working in her native country for about a decade.

After spending most of the 1970s in Europe, she returned to Broadway in *Timbuktu!,* an Africanized version of *Kismet.* She was now fifty, and her last three decades were full and rewarding ones, notable for two further important appearances on Broadway in *The Wild Party* (2000) and *Nine* (2003). There were also memorable guest roles in a number of later films, all of which seemed to be the work of writers and directors who'd grown up with Kitt on *Batman.* She played a sexy, helpful witchy woman in the Ernest P. Worrell comedy *Ernest Scared Stupid* (1991), a predatory older woman warm for Eddie Murphy's form in *Boomerang* (1992), and an evil sexy witch woman in *The Emperor's New Groove* (2000). In all of these flicks Kitt rather easily stole the whole show—she had grown from Catwoman to queen of the cougars.

There also were latter-day records: To her own surprise, she was on the charts again with a series of disco hits in the mid- to late eighties, such as "Where Is My Man" and "Cha-Cha Heels." She also did two later albums of standards for DRG, the studio *Back in Business* (1994) and *Live from the Café Carlyle* (2006). Both these sets confirm my memories of her at the Carlyle, particularly "Let's Misbehave" on the first, which opens with her purring the verse. She's all over it, but she still withholds something. She doesn't give the whole show away; you still get a sense that she's keeping something to herself. Overt as she is, she still has a sense of mystery.

"I invented myself," Kitt sings in *The Wild Party*. Seeing her up close at the Carlyle was an experience that permanently burned itself into the brain of everyone lucky enough to be there; for a short woman, she was incredibly leggy—those amazing legs seemed to go all the way up to her neck. At seventy-nine, she was the sexiest entertainer I've ever experienced. She made all the other high-glam nightclub queens—from Ute Lemper to Dee Dee Bridgewater—look like mere poseurs. I've no doubt that all the other men in the room were also fantasizing about her, even the gay ones.

She died on Christmas Day 2008, which some found fitting since "Santa Baby" was still her all-time biggest hit. Her last project, recorded shortly before she died, was a guest shot on *The Simpsons*. The episode was eventually aired more than a year after her death, in January 2010, as the show's twentieth-anniversary special. She plays herself, Eartha Kitt, the fifteenth wife of Krusty the Clown. The story line: She's already deceased but is seen as part of a prerecorded video deposition that Bart Simpson uses to try and break up Krusty's latest marriage. Krusty and Eartha were only married for six hours, we learn, and Kitt, on videotape, tells us "Krusty was asleep for five of the hours—and the one he was awake for was a cat-tastrophe!" At this point she makes a cat growling noise and flashes her claws. Only Eartha Kitt could find a way to both turn us on and make fun of herself from beyond the grave.

Diana Krall (born 1964)

In general, there have been three kinds of reactions to the amazing success that Diana Krall enjoyed in the final years of the nineties and into the new century: First, that she's really great, and deserves all the attention and acclaim that she's received. (This is not exactly my opinion, but I do have to respect the taste of some of those who have expressed it, such as Johnny Mandel and Tony Bennett.) Second, that she's a total sham in a little black dress and high heels, foisted on the public by astute promoters, largely by virtue of her supermodel appearance. (This opinion is inevitably put forward by other, less successful would-be singers, whose mouths are so filled with sour grapes that they can hardly sing themselves.) Third, that she's somewhere in between the two poles—that she is, if perhaps not the greatest thing since sliced bread, certainly one of the more wonderful (and, correspondingly, more popular) performers of jazz and standards currently active; that she not only has a lot of talent but works hard and is constantly improving her craft, and further, that her success bodes well for the future of this music. Speaking personally, I started with the second opinion, have been very comfortable with the third for a few years now, and am starting to veer toward the first.

I used to think that Krall was purely a product of promotion and public relations, but I have since come to feel that the larger public buys her CDs and attends her concerts in huge numbers because they genuinely like her. If they were exposed to Catherine Russell or Paula West or some other comparatively young female jazz singer they would doubtless feel the same way about them—that they haven't been is not Ms. Krall's fault. I used to hold it against her that promoters were so keen to exploit her glamour-puss looks: Like Julie London's LPs, Krall's CDs are loaded with hubba-hubba pictures of her, and one year, her label, GRP Records, even sent out a calender with twelve sexy shots of Miss K. (I still have it . . . right here, in fact.)

No one ever sent out a calendar for Nina Simone or Ma Rainey (not to mention Betty Carter or Sylvia Syms), but we shouldn't let this focus on her looks detract from the obvious fact that Krall (no less than London) can, in fact, actually sing. She has a low voice and can sound sexy and sultry—as much so as she looks—without trying particularly hard; in fact, this apparent absence of effort is one of her most appealing characteristics. She achieves an immediate intimacy with her voice, as well as her direct to-the-point style. She is also a talented and well-studied pianist, though it's unlikely that Universal Music will ever record her doing an album of piano instrumentals.

Yet talented though she undeniably is, one can't deny that astute marketing has played a large part in putting her where she is. Most of what's written about her stresses her youth and beauty, to the point where few of her press releases mention her actual age. Most of her early press releases shave a few years off her age—it wasn't until she turned forty in the same year that she got married (to the rock star Elvis Costello) that her record company began owning up to 1964.

Krall grew up in Nanaimo, British Columbia, Canada, and was first attracted to music by her father, an avid buff of jazz and the songbook; her grandmother gave her her first piano lessons. She describes her father as collecting everything "from the time when recording began" onward, and who exposed his daughter to artists ranging from Claude Thornhill and Thelonious Monk to Paul Whiteman. (In one interview, Krall even mentioned Bill Challis! Now this is a well-contemporary-schooled jazz singer.) Her father played stride piano and turned her on to Fats Waller. Even though Krall's performance style is hardly similar to that of the late Fat One, this proved to be the most important discovery of Krall's career—that it was possible to sing and play piano at the same time.

Krall arrived in the United States to study at the Berklee College of Music in her early twenties. Back in British Columbia, she met two pivotal Los Angeles studio musicians, drummer Jeff Hamilton and bassist-composer-orchestrator-bandleader John

Clayton. At their incentive, she ended up spending three years in California, where her two godfathers were pianist Jimmy Rowles and bassist Ray Brown. After leaving Los Angeles, where she cut her first album. *Stepping Out*, for the Canadian label Justin Time in 1992 (with the Clayton-Hamilton rhythm section), she would live in both Toronto and New York. After arriving in NYC, Krall came into contact with Mary Ann Topper, a manager largely given credit for masterminding the careers of three of the biggest-sellers in recent jazz history in Krall, Joshua Redman, and, later, Jane Monheit (all young and attractive).

Krall's first album was originally distributed by GRP (already part of MCA), and the label signed her directly to produce her second, *Only Trust Your Heart*. The other most important person in her professional life was producer Tommy LiPuma, who took charge of her recording career at this point. Of her early American (and major label) efforts, the track that affords me the most pleasure is the title cut to that first Universal Music album, "Only Trust Your Heart." It's a Sammy Cahn lyric to a Benny Carter melody (the combined age of the two collaborators at that point must have been well over 160) on which Krall conveys exactly the right amount of distrust, and it's one of the few pieces of material from this period that completely suits her rather emotionally distant attitude.

It was her second GRP album, *All for You*, released in 1996, that made Krall a star, selling 100,000 units within a matter of months, but unfortunately established her in my mind as an artist I couldn't take seriously simply because she seemed to be taking herself entirely too seriously. The album was a tribute to the King Cole Trio, and while the ballads sound better now than I remember them sounding then, it was the up-tempos that put me off. The point of the actual King Cole Trio was to take flippant novelties and have fun with them; here was Krall intoning things like "Hit That Jive Jack" as if it were a funeral speech. She succeeded in taking the most fun music ever made and draining all the laughs out of it. Even the cover of *All for You* was a tip-off—they take a beautiful woman and pose her as if she's in agony, hunched forward as if, as a friend of mine said, her neck was broken.

Yet it was this very element of Krall's work that helped make her a star: Not only was she beautiful and talented, she was cool. She perfectly epitomized the distingué attitude displayed by posers in bars who don't know the first thing about jazz or the songbook but think it's hip to be cool and show as little emotion as possible. (Obviously they never heard of Ben Webster—not to mention Nat King Cole.) "Cool" was a euphemism for a state of emotional detachment—at times she seemed to be cool and disassociated from her work in order to save herself the trouble of having to figure out ways to invest her feelings in an interpretation. (Krall was the most visible of a school of megacool stylists,

whose numbers include the San Francisco–based Ann Dyer and Chicago chanteuse Patricia Barber.)

Krall followed *All for You* with *Love Scenes* in 1997, which was an improvement, singing-wise, as well as the best document of her best trio, with two absolutely rock-solid rhythm players for support in guitarist Russell Malone and bassist Christian McBride. But to me her breakthrough came with the 1999 *When I Look in Your Eyes* (kudos for finding an excellent neglected Leslie Bricusse song from *Doctor Dolittle*) and even more so with the 2001 *The Look of Love*. In both cases, she put her piano playing and her trio temporarily on the back burner. By focusing on her singing alone, she was becoming better and better at injecting more emotion into her music. In this she was aided by the decision to make these large-format old-school jazz-pop albums, big projects with string orchestras and two veteran arranger-conductors, Johnny Mandel and Claus Ogerman. Her cool sound was perfectly offset by the strings—her singing was still slightly on the detached side, whereas strings, by nature, are certainly on the sentimental side. By putting these two elements together, her arrangers found the sweet spot in the center.

In 2000, Krall toured with Tony Bennett as his opening act (no bandwagon jumper he, Bennett had been inviting her to share his stage at least as far back as 1997, when I saw them together at the Montreal Jazz Festival); I'm not sure if her proximity to Bennett made me want to like her more, or if it made me that much harder on her because of the inevitable comparison. Although I had already seen her in person a number of times, it wasn't until the new millennium that she seemed warm, relaxed, and swinging. As it happens, her earlier trio, with Malone and McBride, may have the edge over the more recent edition, with Anthony Wilson (who is an excellent guitarist to be sure, it's just that Malone is a hard act to follow) and bassist Robert Hurst. But on her recent work Krall herself sounds much more like what a jazz singer is supposed to sound like, with another less-well-known bassist and guitarist. About the only dumb thing that Krall has ever done is decline Tony Bennett's generous offer to share an album with him, something that no other vocalist had the opportunity to do up to that point. (Bennett eventually made an album with another Canadian superstar, k.d. lang, who has a beautiful voice, but, alas, doesn't seem to have the faintest idea of where the beat is supposed to be, something of a hindrance in a supposed jazz project.)

As far as I'm concerned, since then Krall has been on a virtually unstoppable winning steak. After the breakthroughs of the two "look" albums, *When I Look in Your Eyes* (which was nominated for a Grammy in the mainstream album competition, not relegated to the jazz or traditional pop categories) and *The Look of Love*, Krall consolidated her gains with *Live in Paris* from the next year. As with *When I*

Look in Your Eyes, the settings alternated between her trio by itself, with drums and occasional vibes, and this rhythm section with a full string orchestra. Well into her forties, Krall is both a better balladeer and a stronger swinger than she ever was, and now she seems so much more invested in the material; it's impossible to imagine the Krall of six or seven years earlier making a Tony Bennett–like aside the way she does in "Let's Fall in Love"—after asking, "Why be afraid of it?" she answers her own question, "I'll tell you why!" It's taken her all this time to be able to get deep inside a song; now, at last, she has earned the right to momentarily climb out of it and wink at the audience.

In 2004 and 2005, Krall released two very different, and equally satisfying, albums showing two sides of her personality, although both were, in a sense, retro. *The Girl in the Other Room* harked back to the singer-songwriter era of the early seventies, whereas *Christmas Songs* was strictly a traditional pop album of the kind Jo Stafford, Eydie Gormé, or Kay Starr made in the early years of the 12" LP—not to mention *Ella Fitzgerald Wishes You a Swinging Christmas.*

The assumed backstory behind *Other Room* was that it reflected the influence of Krall's new husband, the very well-respected rock-singer-songwriter Elvis Costello (who had himself sung a duet or two with Tony Bennett). Whether or not this is the case, *Other Room* is a project of the kind that Krall was bound to want to try sooner or later. (The fine jazz-and-standards singer Karin Allyson released a similar seventies-centric album that same season—and she never married Mr. Costello.) In any case, *The Girl in the Other Room,* which combines "classic" singer-songwriter material by Tom Waits ("Temptation"), Joni Mitchell ("Black Crow"), Bonnie Raitt ("Love Me Like a Man"), with new original songs by Ms. Krall (some written with Mr. Costello), is, even to my ears (and I am not predisposed toward liking this type of thing) an unqualified success. I like that she included one song from as far back as 1940—"I'm Pulling Through," one of the more obscure numbers in the Billie Holiday songbook—and also that she included one by Mose Allison, "Stop This World." I also like that in the piano solo of "Love Me Like a Man" she quotes from the Count Basie "Splanky," thereby transforming singer-songwriter pop into something more like the blues. The most touching ballad in the set is, surprisingly, Costello's "Almost Blue," one of his most effective songs, and one of the few that could be confused for a traditional pop standard.

The Girl in the Other Room can't be described as an attempt to go contemporary—the seventies are only slightly more relevant than the fifties—but *Christmas Songs* is resolutely old-school. This is the first time Krall has been presented as a traditional jazz-pop diva, both in terms of Jeff Hamilton's swinging arrangements and the art direction, which shows her with open-mouthed smiles in green and red holiday gowns. Universal even released an LP edition—talk about taking it old-school—in which the green-colored vinyl is, I hope, a metaphor for the performer wearing green lingerie beneath her red dress (and vice versa). Though there are one or two tunes in her traditional melancholy approach—that's the only way to do "Have Yourself a Merry Little Christmas" and "I'll Be Home for Christmas"—most of the album is joyously upbeat and swinging. She's so carefree and unfettered that she even throws in a nutty tag—"I'm just crazy 'bout horses" (one of Ella Fitzgerald's signature quotes)—at the coda to "Jingle Bells." Everything about *Christmas Songs* is cause for celebration.

In the discographies of most major singers, the Christmas albums are just a side dish, a Lucky Strike extra, but Krall's is absolutely vital because it adds an ingredient that had been lacking in her earlier work: fun. Her next two albums went back and forth between the two extremes, in that *From This Moment On* (2006) showcased her apparently trying to sound like a classic jazz singer in vaguely the manner of Sarah Vaughan or Anita O'Day—swinging, yes, but also distorting melodies and adding scat sequences here and there, none of which really is her forte. She sounds most assured on "Exactly Like You," and with good reason: The arrangement is literally lifted from the 1949 treatment by King Cole and His Trio (like Cole, Krall uses bongos throughout), and Krall's swinging here is so natural and unforced that it's obvious that she's spent a lot of time listening to the Cole record.

Quiet Nights (2009) brings her back to the opposite extreme; it's a large semisymphonic program masterminded by Claus Ogerman. Overall, it's uncomfortably reminiscent of both her own *The Look of Love* and the classic Sinatra-Jobim-Ogerman album. The arrangements are almost too mellow and laid back; where Sinatra had the bite and the aggression (even in reflective mode) to cut through, Krall just seems kind of blissed out. Still, all her albums contain cuts I enjoy, and here those I find myself playing repeatedly are "Walk on By," a Burt Bacharach hit not often enough done in the traditional pop style. There's also a treatment of the 1971 Bee Gees anthem "How Can You Mend a Broken Heart" that reminds me that this too can actually be treated as a song for singing (as opposed to whatever it was the Bee Gees were doing).

I had caught Krall live here and there over the last ten years, following her Radio City show of 2002. There were several guest appearances at Jazz at Lincoln Center, at one of which, a 2005 benefit for victims of Hurricane Katrina, she delivered a wonderfully cool and bluesy treatment of "Basin Street Blues" that was the highlight of a long and moving evening. But in Carnegie Hall in June 2009, she came across like never before. Seven years earlier she seemed like an in-person version of one of her albums, somewhat aloof (probably out of shyness) from the crowd and even from her own musicians. Now she had developed a marvelous rapport with her audience—she was jokey and dishy and very down to earth, hardly the unapproachable diva. Both her jazzy numbers and her ballads were precisely on target, with no polarizing distance between them, as there seemed to be on her studio albums.

Maybe what's needed is a new live album—I certainly would love to have a CD or DVD of the show I saw at Carnegie. Throughout, she added another element that was new, or at least in quantities I hadn't experienced before: charisma. It looks good on her, you know?

L

Lambert, Hendricks & Ross
Dave Lambert (1917–1966)
Jon Hendricks (born 1921)
Annie Ross (born 1930)

Lambert, Hendricks & Ross: Hip doesn't get any hipper, cool doesn't get any cooler, and jazz vocals don't get any more swinging.

Their first Columbia album was titled *The Hottest New Group in Jazz*, which succinctly sums up their status. Bix Beiderbecke once defined jazz as "musical humor," and from Armstrong to Thelonious Monk, the great soloists have all known how to tell any kind of story—especially a joke. Lambert, Hendricks & Ross created a level of verbal humor to supplement the musical proceedings, in the process establishing that words could suit jazz as swingingly as notes.

Jazz and pop singing had been harmonious though somewhat strange bedfellows ever since the twenties, when Louis Armstrong and Bing Crosby introduced the two mediums to each other and created modern popular music, but their relationship had to wait thirty years to be completely consummated. Tin Pan Alley borrowed from jazz both musically and philosophically, and in return, jazz's great soloists and arrangers dined at the table of Broadway and Hollywood like starving men at a buffet. But while singers interpreted mainstream songs with varying degrees of jazz influence, the repertoire of singers in and around jazz was strictly a hand-me-down one: Major artists like Louis Armstrong and Billie Holiday could import the musical comedy songs of Jerome Kern and Richard Rodgers into the jazz canon, but no one had ever devised a words-and-music aesthetic reflecting a strictly jazz sensibility. No one wrote "jazz songs" per se, in the sense that Duke Ellington and Benny Carter, to give two examples, were writing material for jazz instrumentalists.

LHR essentially merged two traditions: the vocal group and what had come to be known as "vocalese." Multivoice groups had been singing jazz almost since the beginning, most successfully the Boswell Sisters and the early Mills Brothers. Vocalese had been around almost as long, starting with various experiments from the twenties in which words were attached to Bix Beiderbecke's celebrated solo on "Singin' the Blues." To elaborate: In jazz, an improviser traditionally starts with a chord sequence to a familiar song, which he uses as the basis for an original melody. The vocalese singer-songwriter would pick it up from there, taking these spontaneously created tunes and penning lyrics to them—re-creating the solo vocally and lyrically, trying to follow every note of the improvised melody and every inflection of the original soloist.

Before LHR, vocalese's major moment in the sun was the hit record "Moody's Mood for Love," in which the mysterious singer King Pleasure sang words to a tenor sax solo improvised in Sweden by James Moody. But the whole vocalese movement would likely have been a one-hit wonder and a quickly forgotten gimmick had it not been for Dave Lambert, Jon Hendricks, and Annie Ross.

Each brought to the group exactly what it needed. Like every first-rate jazz soloist, Hendricks, who wrote most of the lyrics, told a fully realized story with each text. Even on a simple travelogue like "Charleston Alley," Hendricks paints the scene so vividly you can practically smell the catfish frying. For his part, Lambert crafted brilliant vocal arrangements in which the three voices would meld as a unit but also could assert their individuality without leaving the ensemble—never more so than on his transmutation of the Miles Davis–Gil Evans revamp of "Summertime." And Annie Ross gave the group both elegance and lung power; who else could vocally re-create the treble-to-bass pyrotechnics of a Horace Silver piano explosion as she does on "Come on Home"?

Not that everything that they did was vocalese. One of Hendricks's first breaks was writing rhythmic raillery for the great jazz-R&B comic Louis Jordan, and pieces like "Gimme Dat Wine" are cast exactly in the Jordan mold—without any kind of instrumental prototype. (And, in the best Jordan tradition, a disproportionate number of LHR classics are preoccupied with the pursuit of food and drink.) "Cookin' at the Continental" features a rudimentary set of words written for another Horace Silver "head." Following these, rather than re-create the horn solos, Hendricks and Lambert have at each other in an all-scat cutting contest (similar to the ones Lambert had sparred in ten years earlier in Gene Krupa's band with his first partner, supreme scatter Buddy Stewart). Both Ross's "Farmer's Market" and Hendricks's "Cloudburst" (the latter a holdover from his and Lambert's early, pre-Ross days) employ carefully considered language to tell very specific stories; in contrast, "Popity Pop" is pure nursery nonsense from the maniacal mind of Slim Gaillard.

Ross's sumptous high and low registers supplied the trio with its real vocal muscle, but leave us not overlook the with-it wailings of the way-out Mr. Hendricks. It's hard to imagine anyone else articulating the tongue-twisting tenor tones of Sam the Man Taylor on Hendricks's own larynx-locking libretto and windpipe-whacking words on "Cloudburst," the LHR masterpiece based on a now forgotten hit by the pseudonymous "Claude Cloud and the Thunderclaps." The breakneck speed of some of these through-composed pieces (i.e., no part of the text is ever repeated), containing two or three times the standard single chorus of words, always separates the diehards from the dilletantes in the inevitable latter-day re-creations of the group. Hendricks never shined brighter as either screenwriter or star than on "Cottontail," achieving the impossible in reconciling Duke Ellington with Beatrix Potter, doing justice to both and matching perfectly the climactic moments of Ben Webster's much memorized solo with the high points of this skirmish in the rabbit-farmer wars.

Dave Lambert, Jon Hendricks, and Annie Ross first worked together on the 1956 *Sing a Song of Basie*, which was to be one of the most influential albums of an extraordinarily productive era of jazz and pop activity. The fifties were the first years of the long-playing record, and the second half of the decade, in particular, saw a whole series of albums that changed the way we think about music. It was impossible, for instance, to consider the popular song in the same way after Frank Sinatra's "concept" albums and Ella Fitzgerald's "Songbook" series. Miles Davis did it twice: With *Miles Ahead*, he created a whole new context in which jazz musicians could play, and in *Kind of Blue*, he created a whole new way for musicians to play, in any kind of context. *Sing a Song of Basie* had the same kind of impact. After that album was released in 1956, our perception of the human voice, its use in jazz, and its relationship to instrumental music was permanently altered. That relationship, we learned, was far deeper than we had ever imagined.

Jon Hendricks had been writing vocalese lyrics all his life, just as Dave Lambert had been continually experimenting with new ways to use the human voice. Hendricks had known about Lambert since the mid-forties, when Lambert and Buddy Stewart were practically the first vocalists to work in the new idiom of modern jazz. And most likely, Lambert knew of Hendricks as an emerging lyricist who had some well-regarded R&B hits to his credit.

When Hendricks and Lambert started working together, their first project was based not on Basie but on Woody Herman's "Four Brothers." Hendricks had written lyrics to that pivotal big band instrumental, and a friend put him in touch with Lambert. "So, I went down to Dave's house," said Hendricks, "and he was there with [the arranger] George Handy. I said, 'I got this little thing I want you to hear.' And he said, 'Okay, put it on.' So I sang 'Four Brothers,' and Dave jumped up, grabbed one of those big pads of manuscript paper and wrote the arrangement right then and there! It took him about fifteen minutes—it's the most amazing thing I ever saw in my life. He wrote arrangements like you write letters." (Perhaps not coincidentally, Annie Ross uses that same phrase to describe Hendricks's skill and speed at writing lyrics.)

From that point on, Lambert and Hendricks were a team, and their early projects included not only "Four Brothers" but their famous take on the R&B hit "Cloudburst." Eventually, those two songs came out as a Decca single. "We didn't know what to do next until Dave said, 'Well, we both like Basie, so why don't we put some words to some Basie things and see if we can sell them to somebody, get a record date or something.' So, I said, 'Do you know how long it takes to write *one* lyric like that?' He says, 'You got something else to do maybe?' So I wrote four things and we peddled them all around." Eventually, Lambert and Hendricks found themselves standing in front of the desk of Creed Taylor, a fresh-faced recent college grad who had been put in charge of a brand-new "start-up" label called ABC-Paramount. Taylor was intrigued by what he heard, and offered them a budget to produce an entire album of Basie material.

At this point, Hendricks and Lambert were thinking in terms of larger ensembles: If one singer represented one instrument, then it followed that a whole choir would be needed to translate the entire Basie big band into vocal terms. In 1956, however, it proved to be impossible to put together twelve genuine jazz singers who could work together as such a choir. Furthermore, classically trained singers were needed who could sight-sing (read music) and clearly articulate Hendricks's fast-moving lyrics. The team decided to contract a contingent of studio singers, the kind who backed up pop stars on TV and records and sang on jingles for radio and TV commercials. Studio singers, however, couldn't be expected to sing with a jazz rhythmic feel, and so they got in touch with Annie Ross.

At twenty-six, Ross, who had considerable experience both in jazz and theater, was then primarily known for having sung with Lionel Hampton's band as well as for "Twisted," the second major vocalese hit (based on a solo by Wardell Gray). She was in New York when Jon and Dave turned up. "I had heard of Dave, of course, but I didn't really know Jon," she says today. "They arrived and they started talking about this album of Basie music that they were doing, and they sang some of the lyrics. They wanted me to come to the sessions—to help coach the singers they'd hired. I was a little miffed, because

I had hoped they wanted me to sing, so when they mentioned the coaching thing I just laughed, because you can't teach someone the Basie feel in half an hour! But they wanted studio singers who could sight-read and all that, which I couldn't do."

Even with Ross coaching the choir, the results were disastrous. "I did the best I could," says Ross, "but it was awful, they couldn't swing one iota." Hendricks agrees: "We sounded like the '*Moron* Tabernacle Choir.' They would have been okay for the *Perry Como Show* and *Your Hit Parade*, but they couldn't swing if you hung 'em!" They certainly couldn't come anywhere near capturing the Basie feel, even though, Hendricks notes, one of the singers was a young man named Mark Murphy.

Thus, after the dates with the actual choir, Hendricks and Lambert had nothing that could be released. "When we got through with that date we were $1,250 in the hole," says John, "and Creed was about to be fired." "We were desperate," Annie agrees. "Then Dave got the idea of multi-tracking. I said 'What's that?' But Creed went along with it. We would have tried anything! We made a test, and when we finished the first little sample and then listened back to it, we knew that we were on the right track—or multi-track."

It was exacting work. Overdubbing was a fairly new practice then, and there was no guidebook of do's and don'ts. Says Jon, "We had the rhythm section lay the parts down first. That was intelligent, but then everything we did after that was so stupid, because we did the lead voices first. Then, when we added layers and layers on top of it, the lead voices, which were supposed to be the most prominent, just kept getting dimmer and dimmer. After three months, we could no longer hear the first harmony parts! They were buried under all those multi-trackings put together on one tape. So we realized we had to start all over again and reverse the process and put the least prominent voices first. So that took us another three months in the studio."

Hendricks's strongest memory of the sessions is that "we were not on salary at the time. We were literally starving, it was hard because we had to work hungry. We used to be able to borrow money from Creed once in a while and then Dave knew a restaurant, Joe's, down in the Village that let us run a tab until the album was finished. They said we could have lunch or dinner, but not both, so we'd always eat lunch and then try to get an invite from somebody to dinner."

Hendricks has also spoken of the craft of writing vocalese lyrics: "I write in a kind of a shorthand. I go phrase by phrase. I get the story from the title and then I get what I want to say and I listen to the phrase and then I find the words that fit that phrase and forms into the thought from the sentence before. It's a strange process because describing it takes more time than it does to do it." Thus, "Blues Backstage" became a sort of *Pagliacci* story set in modern showbiz terms, and "Fiesta in Blue" puts the blues in actual physical form and then proceeds to throw a party for them.

Ross remembered that although she didn't read music, she didn't have to, since she already knew the original Basie records and already had the right rhythmic feeling: "What we couldn't do by reading, we made up for in interpretation." Ross stresses that in singing a solo by, say, Buck Clayton, you have to find a halfway point between yourself and the original musician. It's Clayton's phrasing, his improvised melody line, but Annie Ross's soul.

After the recording was finished, Ross accepted an offer to go to France. When the ten tracks were finally released as *Sing a Song of Basie*, the album was an instant smash, one of the big jazz albums of the era. Ross then found herself the frequent recipient of transcontinental calls from Jon and Dave. "They kept saying, 'Come home and sing with us, we have an agent, we have offers for work!' I thought that they were nuts! I thought that trying to do that album live would be like Les Paul and Mary Ford or something." Soon, they put it to a test drive at the Banker's Club, a little joint in West New York, New Jersey, and from there worked in several spots with the Buddy Rich group, which qualify as the first live appearances of the trio now and forever known as Lambert, Hendricks & Ross.

At last working as a trio, sans overdubs and additional voices, the group recorded two more albums over the next two years. The original *Song of Basie* made such a hit that Basie's manager, the infamous Morris Levy, recruited the trio to do an album with the band itself. And so, the trio recorded *Sing Along with Basie* (1958) for Roulette, which combined the threesome with the entire Basie band, including Basie's own star vocalist, Joe Williams. While in Los Angeles in March 1959, LHR cut most of *The Swingers!* for Pacific Jazz, for which label both Hendricks and Ross also recorded solo albums. The presence of bassist Eddie Jones, guitarist Freddie Green, and drummer Sonny Payne lent a continued Basie feel to the proceedings, yet this was the first occasion in which the trio explored other areas of the jazz repertoire, most notably the contemporary Randy Weston ("Babe's Blues," "Little Niles," and "Where") as well as such bop classics as Sonny Rollins's "Airegin," Miles Davis's "Four," and Charlie Parker's blues "Now's the Time."

Later in 1959, the group switched to Columbia for what, at last, turned out to be a long-term affiliation. The three albums and eight or so miscellaneous tracks for Columbia (plus their guest appearance on Dave Brubeck's *The Real Ambassadors*), as Hendricks later put it, "represent the high point in our career."

Their first set for Columbia, *The Hottest New Group in Jazz* (later reissued as both *The Best of Lambert, Hendricks and Ross* and *Everybody's Boppin'*) showed the world the outer limits of what Lambert,

Hendricks & Ross could do: Charlie Barnet's "Charleston Alley" had never been a hit like the bandleader's "Cherokee," yet LHR made it into a jazz standard. Then, with "Moanin'" and "Sermonette," they shifted gears from swing to hard bop spiritual. "Twisted" and "Cloudburst" were superior remakes of items from earlier in the careers of Ross and Hendricks, both inspired by tenor sax stars—Wardell Gray in the first and Sam the Man Taylor in the second.

Composer Ralph Burns had originally subtitled "Bijou" as "Rhumba à la Jazz" when he wrote it for Woody Herman, but LHR bring it to even more exotic climes, situating the titular lady as a belly dancer from Istanbul. "Centerpiece" was trumpet guest star Harry Edison's treatment of a familiar blues line. "Gimme That Wine" and "Summertime" modulate between the vocabularies of the Tympany Five and the Metropolitan Opera, while "Everybody's Boppin'" is a flat-out all-bop scatfest (Ross's sideline squeaks show that she can hit 'em even higher than Edison).

Having earlier given the full treatment to Basie, LHR's second Columbia album put the "sing a song of" spotlight on another jazz icon with *Lambert, Hendricks and Ross Sing Ellington* (1960). Here the team was especially astute in translating the complexities of twelve remarkably lush Ellington and Billy Strayhorn orchestrations into three-voice LHR terms. "All Too Soon," "I Don't Know What Kind of Blues I Got" (with Lambert reprising Herb Jeffries), "What Am I Here For?," and others have Hendricks weaving new material (in the case of the second, also singing Ben Webster's classic tenor solo) around familiar lyrics that had been pinned to Ellington instrumentals many years previously. "Things Ain't What They Used to Be" and "Rocks in My Bed" elaborate on Ellington's take on the blues, while "Happy Anatomy" and "Midnight Indigo" spring from Ellington and Strayhorn's then contemporaneous score for Otto Preminger's *Anatomy of a Murder*. Best of all are "Cottontail" (in which Hendricks assumes Webster's mantle once again) and "Caravan," wherein the threesome spins some of its most convincing yarns in the carrot patch and then head out through the desert and over the sands.

The third Columbia set, *High Flying* (1961), returned the team to hard bop territory, most notably with three works by Horace Silver: "Come on Home," "Home Cookin'," and "Cookin' at the Continental." Other tunes here are also based on compositions already well known as instrumentals, including Randy Weston's "Hi Fly" (Hendricks's lyric would help make it a well-known vocal standard). Yet there are more complete originals here than on any other LHR release: "With Malice Toward None," "The New ABC," "Blue," and a decidedly different holiday song, "Halloween Spooks."

Thirty-five years after the fact, Columbia collected these three LHR albums in a double-disc

package that utilized *The Hottest New Group in Jazz* title and cover. This set included everything the group did for the label, with the exception of their participation in *The Real Ambassadors*, a concept-driven project written by and starring Dave Brubeck (in which the trio backs up their heroes, Louis Armstrong and Carmen McRae). Some of the extra tracks in the two-CD set seem to have been intended as singles, including several fascinating attempts at combining jazz with the Twist, and there are a bunch of other new lyrics to famous instrumentals that indicate that the group was starting work on a fourth Columbia album. The most exciting of these is bassist Oscar Pettiford's "Swingin' Till the Girls Come Home." Hendricks not only pays tribute to the composer here, but, in a section in the middle, he does brilliant impressions of a whole generation of great jazz bass players: Percy Heath, Paul Chambers, Ray Brown, and just plain "Mingus."

That March 1962 date represents the final studio session by Lambert, Hendricks & Ross. Miss Ross unfortunately left the group that summer. Various reasons have been given for the group's breakup—conflicting egos, Ross's health problems, collective weariness from the grind of touring—but they all boil down to one thing: The threesome simply amounted to too much talent to be contained in a single unit. Lambert and Hendricks then worked together for about two years with a very theatrical singer named Yolande Bavan, who had some of Ross's class but not her rhythm. Carol Sloane, who had subbed for Ross during a Philadelphia engagement (and to this day performs a treatment of "Cottontail" second only to Hendricks's) would have been a better choice.

As Lambert, Hendricks & Bavan, the group recorded three live albums for former Columbia producer George Avakian, now at RCA. Everything is terrific about these later albums until the female vocalist is heard, and one realizes again how essential Ross's contribution really was. Lambert and Hendricks remained close until the former's death in a road accident in 1966. Hendricks and Ross have occasionally reunited in the years since, for one-shot engagements in the early seventies and mid-eighties. They teamed up on a semipermanent basis for an extended period in the late nineties and early 2000s, which turned out not to be a good idea; the two ex-partners were just no longer on the same page.

Before Lambert, Hendricks & Ross, there were certain preconceived notions of what the human voice could do and what instruments were supposed to do. LHR showed how an instrumental, big band performance could be translated into vocal terms—not only with voices, but with words. In the process, they became the greatest jazz vocal group that ever was. More than half a century after they began, Lambert, Hendricks & Ross are still *The Hottest Group in Jazz*.

Steve Lawrence (born 1935) and
Eydie Gormé (born 1931)

"One of the major cultural pre-occupations of the '50s," writer Diana Loevy once observed, "was wondering why Steve and Eydie, those two nice Jewish kids from New York, didn't get married." And once the couple did marry, which happened in 1957, Lawrence and Gormé succeeded in fostering an even deeper sense of connection, to each other and to their audiences. Separately, either would have been regarded as one of the finest contemporary pop music performers, but together, the Las Vegas Lunts (as they were called a long time ago) are something beyond that.

But then show business is a perverse thing. Sometimes the factors that work in your favor can also turn against you. In 2002 and 2005, respectively, Gormé and then Lawrence turned seventy—which by the standards of their music isn't very old. The year 2002 also marked the fiftieth anniversary of their first encounter, which occurred rather casually, in front of the old Brill Building in 1952, so the legend goes. In 2003 they marked the fiftieth anniversary of their first getting to know each other and to begin working together on *The Tonight Show*, then hosted by TV pioneer Steve Allen. In 2007, Lawrence and Gormé celebrated the fiftieth anniversary of their marriage, and in 2010 they celebrated their fiftieth anniversary as a permanent act.

Time is a wonderful and a terrible thing: Like Perry Como, but unlike their idol and longtime colleague Frank Sinatra, Lawrence and Gormé owe the biggest part of their career to television. When they first started in that medium, they were precisely what the small screen called for: bright, fresh-faced, squeaky-clean, good-looking young talents—no one knew then that they would develop into such outstanding vocal artists. (One commentator observed early on, "The camera is a restless beast with huge eyes and small ears, more often interested in visual gimmicks than in the glories of sound.") Both were national celebrities by the time they were in their early twenties and stars well before they hit thirty.

Yet the problem with making it so early and being around so long is that people begin to take you for granted. To most people, Steve and Eydie seem as if they've been around forever. If they had been born in the teens—like Sinatra, Haymes, and Fitzgerald—they would have had time to flourish in the very different musical world of the thirties, forties, and early fifties. As it is, they both barely had the chance to reach musical maturity before their kind of music was overtaken in the cultural disaster of the sixties. (Which is an oversimplification, since, as we shall see, both in the fifties and the seventies, the two singers also recorded a lot of lesser music in the youth pop style.) Unlike Sinatra, Fitzgerald, and even Bennett (born in 1926) and Clooney (1928), Lawrence and Gormé had made all their classic recordings before they were forty.

These considerations seem beside the point, however, when one considers their talent. Both are genuine vocal virtuosos: They have extraordinary range and they have extraordinary control, in the same sense that we might say a major jazz saxophonist or concert violinist has extraordinary control of his instrument. They both know their way around the beat and can swing with the best of them. Gormé can attribute her sense of time to her apprenticeship as a big band singer, and perhaps also to her experience in the field of Latin music, yet of the two, Lawrence is the harder swinger. Like Sinatra, both are master storytellers and interpreters, and both have a sense of humor and genuine love for what they're doing (not to mention each other) that energizes their best work throughout their fifty-year careers, individually and as a team.

During the cultural divide of the sixties, the music of the older generation became associated with "the establishment" and the patriarchal white-bread culture—yet Gormé and Lawrence were born and raised multiculti. They grew up under the pervasive influence of two cultures—in Gormé's case, three. As indicated, they were nice Jewish kids from the outer boroughs, he from Brooklyn and she from the Bronx, where they were reared amid the soul and schmaltz of traditional Jewish life. From the beginning, though, they were immersed not only in traditional Jewish music but in the bands and singers of the thirties and forties. Gormé was nurtured in the big bands, Lawrence first achieved fame as the only Jewish R&B star I can think of (unless you count the Hebrew Pentecostal Marvin Gaye). There were plenty of jazz instrumentalists, from Benny Goodman and Stan Getz on down, who reflected this double mix, bringing a Jewish sensibility to American pop and jazz (or the other way around), yet for some reason, it's hard to think of other singers who fit this description. Among the major Jewish vocalists of American vernacular music, Mel Tormé was swinging but not schmaltzy, while Eddie Fisher was schmaltzy but not swinging. For whatever reason, only Gormé and Lawrence were both consistently finding the intersection where Fifty-second Street meets the Borscht Belt.

On top of which, Gormé is just as Spanish as she is Jewish, and Latin music is just as much a part of her upbringing and her musical profile. (Indeed, the wailing cadenza that opens their duo version of "Bésame Mucho" can be described as pentatonically Spanish and Hebraic at the same time.) And finally, the Lawrences are the only outstanding American vocalists who have jointly made it to the inner circle of pop paradise both as individuals and as a team (with the exception of Louis and Keely), and are the longest-lasting duo in any kind of popular music. Mix it all together, and in Steve and Eydie you have a total package of very rare value indeed.

Early in their relationship, Steve and Eydie decided that, in the showbiz tradition of Burns &

Allen and Ozzie & Harriet, Lawrence would be billed first. Sidney Liebowitz was born July 8, 1935, in Brooklyn. He grew up in the Brownsville district, the second son of a cantor who brought home much needed extra bacon (not the phrase he would have used) by painting houses. "My parents were so poor," he said later, "they were thinking of moving in with *Eydie's* parents!" Both Sidney and his older brother Bernie sang from a very early age with their father in his synagogue choir. Edith Gormézano was born in the Bronx on August 16, 1932 (or 1931, according to some sources), the youngest of three children of Nessim Gormézano, a tailor and Sephardic Jew of Spanish descent by way of Turkey. Lawrence's neighborhood was strictly Jewish, but Gormé grew up in a typical New York mix of ethnicities. Supposedly, the Gormézanos lived in a twelve-story walkup—which seems incredible (I had no idea there were such things)—and she later said it "was like walking from Hungary to Africa to Italy," but she also acknowledged that this rather breathless climb helped strengthen her lung power.

In his early teens, Lawrence's voice began changing and he decided to cease singing for a few years until it settled down. At roughly the same time, at Taft High School in the Bronx, Gormé had become the star singer with her high school band and was elected "prettiest, peppiest" cheerleader in a high school popularity contest. During his sabbatical from singing, Lawrence kept his hand in music by playing piano for his brother Bernie. In her teens, Gormé took a desk job at a company that exported theatrical supplies (which made use of her bilingual skills), and by hanging around show people she gradually gained the confidence and ambition to shoot for a singing career. In their early twenties, they both changed their names for showbiz. Edith first became "Edie," but promoters kept adding an extra "D" and making her into "Eddie," which is why, she said, she inserted the "Y." As for Sidney, as it happened, brother Bernie had two young sons named Steve and Lawrence, so he combined their Christian names (you should forgive the expression) into his stage moniker.

In 1952, an old schoolmate of Eydie's named Ken Greengrass put together a dance band that worked around the outer boroughs, including a gig he later remembered in Brooklyn's Prospect Park (he also remembered that the young band canary looked and sounded so good that she stopped all kinds of traffic). Greengrass was so convinced Eydie had a future that he disbanded his orchestra and became her full-time manager. He helped her get a demo disc together, and then got said disc into the hands of nationally known sweet band leader Tommy Tucker, who employed her briefly. Her next step was upward to Tex Beneke. Three Beneke transcription tracks with vocals by Gormé have come to light (probably recorded in 1950 and issued on the British collector's label Magic, on a CD entitled *Dancer's*

Delight)—"Baby O, Baby O," "Orange-Colored Sky," and "If I Were a Bell"—and they all show what an outstanding vocalist she already was, even at eighteen or nineteen. After her band experience was over, Gormé was hired by the Voice of America to serve as singing host for a good-will (or "propaganda") program to be broadcast to Spanish-speaking countries, entitled *Cita con Eydie* ("A Date with Eydie").

Around 1950–51, Bernie Liebowitz was drafted, which prompted Steve Lawrence (now) to begin singing again. He auditioned several times for the *Arthur Godfrey Talent Scouts* TV show and finally made it—and won. The prize was a week of appearances on Godfrey's widely popular regular show, for which he had to beg and borrow the appropriate suits from friends. He attracted the attention of another Sidney, the infamous Syd Nathan of King Records in Cincinnati, which was a surprise, in that the King label was primarily known for its catalogue of "race" (R&B) and "hillbilly" (country) records. Nathan signed Lawrence, and his first record, an ultradramatic rendition of "Poinciana," was an immediate hit. For a few years Lawrence carefully balanced gigs around the country with his final semesters of high school. By this time, Gormé was under contract to Decca subsidiary Coral Records.

As we have seen, the two made contact for the first time in 1952, when they were formally introduced by singer (and Dick Haymes sound-alike) Bob Manning. For the next few years their paths crossed occasionally and randomly: They both appeared in Telescriptions (early music videos) for the Snader Corporation. Lawrence looks so young in these that he could be singing at his own bar mitzvah. In 1953, they had begun getting to know each other better when they were hired, still individually, as regular singers on Steve Allen's *The Tonight Show*, which at that time was only broadcast in the New York area. The program would go national the next year, and the first coast-to-coast episode opens with the towering Mr. Allen strolling out, flanked by the considerably shorter Steve and Eydie at either side. Apparently they sang together occasionally, but they were far from an act, either on-camera or off—not yet. In 1955, they appeared separately in a Universal Pictures two-reel short subject called *Ralph Marterie and His Orchestra with Eydie Gormé, the Hi-Los and Steve Lawrence*. It seems to have dawned on them only gradually that this could be the start of something big.

Lawrence's entry in the *Current Biography* of November 1964 states that Gormé was "five years his senior"—which could mean either that she was actually born in 1930 or that he was actually born in 1936 or 1937—but the difference in their ages meant that her first exposure on the national scene came with big band swing, while Lawrence's King singles were backing, rather maladroitly, into rock-pop and doo-wop. For a while, King seemed to specialize in crummy arrangements of standards like "Poinciana" and "King for a Day" (although there is a more subtle and more mature treatment of "With Every Breath I Take"); nearly all of Lawrence's arrangements in this period suggest the overdone, overbaked style of such belters as Al Martino and the young Tony Bennett. Lawrence's "Poinciana" uses a heavy bolero rhythm, and features an overbusy mixed choir and too much belting and straining from the lead singer himself—though it's still remarkable, considering that Lawrence was only sixteen at the time it was on the charts.

By the mid-fifties, his singles were solidly in a 16th-note-based doo-wop vein (a less tasteful scribe than I might describe this music as "Jew wop," thereby offending no fewer than three ethnicities at once). The best thing about Lawrence's youth pop work of the fifties and early sixties is that some of it reveals a sense of humor: "Girls, Girls, Girls," for instance, is a commentary of sorts on the Tin Pan Alley practice of using female names as the basis for songs. At this point, Lawrence was also crooning the classics in a manner suggestive of Tony Martin (another Jewish Italian). "Mine and Mine Alone" is taken from Saint-Saëns's "My Heart at Thy Sweet Voice" (from *Samson and Delilah*), while "My Claire de Lune" (done for United Artists Records in 1961) adds words to Debussy's piano piece. The first is fairly straightforward, the second is so outrageously bad (the text and the orchestration, not the vocal) that one feels it must be a *Producers*-like parody on the very idea of adapting a pop song from the Old Masters.

For whatever reason, Bobby Darin has gone down in history as the only artist able to move freely back and forth between the genres of youth pop and adult pop, yet both Lawrence and Jack Jones were singing quite a bit of jukebox pop before they established themselves in the grown-up market. Indeed, Lawrence was something of a staple at the Brill Building in its early years, with songs by the likes of Neil Sedaka, Barry Mann, Cynthia Weil, Teddy Randazzo ("Pretty Blue Eyes"), and company. Gormé, too, was churning out jukebox singles in the mid-fifties, though less successfully—dreadful, forgettable songs like "I Want You to Meet My Baby" and "The Dance Is Over." In the very beginning, she'd dented the charts with "Climb Up the Wall" and "Fini," but in the fifties, music industry commentators were wondering why she hadn't yet landed a substantial hit. That was to change in 1957 with "Mama, Teach Me to Dance," a single that anticipated her dance-directed blockbusters of a few years later. On December 29 of that same year, Lawrence and Gormé were married at the home of Rabbi Bernard Cohen in Las Vegas.

In 1956, Gormé switched from the singles-oriented Coral to the album-oriented ABC-Paramount and that year made what is regarded as her debut album, *Eydie Gormé*. Remarkable as it was for Lawrence to land a hit single at age sixteen, it's even more of an accomplishment for Gormé to have recorded such a perfect album at age twenty-four. She's accomplished and poised, and sophisticated enough to tackle such a complex slice of musical acting as "Guess Who I Saw Today?" Immediately she's in the category of such masters as Doris Day and Margaret Whiting. She also has miles and miles of chops, which she displays with a wild wailing high note that takes on a life of its own at the very end of the first track, "I'll Take Romance."

Between England, Japan, and even the United States (thanks to Taragon Records), at least five of Gormé's early ABC albums have been available on CD, including *Eydie Gormé, Love Is a Season, On Stage, Eydie in Love . . .* and *Eydie Swings the Blues*. This is about half of her late fifties long-playing output, and it must be noted that all the ABC albums are consistently excellent, partly due to the presence of the brilliant orchestrations of Don Costa. Although Sinatra later hired Costa on the strength of what he had arranged for the Lawrences, little of Costa's work for Sinatra—excepting *Sinatra and Strings* and *The Present*—was up to what he had earlier arranged for Steve and especially Eydie. Most of these employ some sort of loose concept—"love songs" is about as loose as concepts get. She also makes things interesting for pop music buffs by singing the obscure verses to famous songs, such as those for Irving Berlin's "Better Luck Next Time" and "Be Careful It's My Heart."

Eydie Swings the Blues is a title that stands for a lot of ribbing among record collectors (What's next? *Muddy Waters Sings Steve Allen?*) since it suggests that Gormé is a blues singer (which she isn't); not enough people realize that she can really swing (which she does). The package doesn't consist of genuine 12-bar blues, obviously, but rather pop songs with a blues element—or what they used to call torch songs. She handles them all remarkably well, but the single best of her early albums is the unlikely *On Stage*. This package is a curiosity in that the title and jacket photos promise a live recording, yet what's contained is clearly a studio product—there's no applause (even of the canned variety). Yet the charts are the slightly scaled down ones a singer of the era would customarily use on the road, utilizing a regulation-sized big band (such was once the norm) rather than the fuller, roughly thirty-plus big band with strings used at record sessions. All the tracks here are bright bouncers, and Gormé's singing is looser and jazzier than usual. There's even a treatment of the Basie-associated blues "All Right, Okay, You Win" that's hotter and bluesier than anything on the *Blues* album. If you are ever subpoenaed and need to produce an exhibit A to prove to a court of law that Eydie Gormé is a jazz-tinged pop singer of the very highest order, here it is.

Meanwhile, Lawrence's primary business, even after he, too, switched to ABC-Paramount (which seems to have happened after he got back from his year's hitch in the army in 1958–59), continued to be kiddie pop singles, such as "Why, Why, Why," "Come Back, Silly Girl," and "Footsteps." Lawrence was the only Jewish member of the school of largely Italian pretty-boy teenybopper idols who dominated the charts between Elvis and the Beatles, the most substantial of whom was Bobby Darin, and the most infamously untalented of whom was something called Fabian. On "(I Don't Care) Only Love Me" Lawrence seems to be trying to establish an Italianate identity for himself.

Even as late as 1963, his biggest singles continued to be Brill Building fodder like "Everybody Knows" and most especially "Go Away, Little Girl." By this time, the triumvirate of Gormé, Lawrence, and Don Costa had switched from ABC-Paramount to United Artists, another movie studio–owned label, and then to Columbia Records. Lawrence may have been singing to grown-ups staying up late to watch *The Tonight Show,* but his recordings were still aimed at their baby-boomer brats. When Gormé recorded Neil Sedaka's "Breaking Up Is Hard to Do," she crafted a literate, "adult" version of it. (In Gormé tradition, she includes the verse, and imbues it with harmonies similar to those in "Since I Fell for You" and "Please Send Me Someone to Love," and a great payoff modulation as she leads into the final eight.) Lawrence, by contrast, recorded a doo-woppy arrangement of Rodgers and Hart's "You're Nearer," of all things.

To a certain extent, this duality was inspired by Sinatra, who recorded the great standards on his long-playing LPs and more ephemeral material on his singles. Lawrence took it one step further and more schizophrenically, in that his singles were for kids, but even as Bobby Darin jumped into competition with the Chairman with "Mack the Knife" and *That's All,* Lawrence began at last to make albums of adult popular standards. *Swing Softly with Me* (1959), which boasted marvelously jazzy arrangements by Billy Byers above and beyond the call of duty, was Lawrence's leap into the fray (as well as his equivalent of Gormé's *On Stage*). *Swing Softly* established him as a Swingin' Lover of the highest magnitude, a pop crooner with a beautiful voice and with rhythm like nobody's business. He didn't have Darin's bad-boy attitude (though as early as *Lawrence Goes Latin* he showed an aptitude for some of the funniest and most irreverent asides ever), but he could match Darin for time, and beat the pants off him for chops and vocal technique.

In 1960, Steve Lawrence and Eydie Gormé officially announced their status as a permanent, professional team: Since that time they've worked together exclusively in all their in-person appearances. There had been pop duet albums before, such as Sammy Davis Jr. and Carmen McRae, Bing Crosby and Rosemary Clooney, the amazing team of Louis Armstrong and Ella Fitzgerald, and later Ray Charles and Betty Carter. But Steve and Eydie's only real competition, particularly among permanent married duos, was with Louis Prima and Keely Smith (not as permanent a team as Prima's fans had hoped). The Lawrences had cut their first album together, *Steve and Eydie,* in 1958, but in 1960 they cemented their partnership with two masterpieces, *We Got Us* and *Eydie and Steve Sing the Golden Hits.*

It's clear from the opening track of *We Got Us,* their boss Steve Allen's only substantial standard composition, "This Could Be the Start of Something Big," that this is a duo of rare ability. Not only are we experiencing double the aural pleasure of two beautiful voices but double the musicianship—as when he sings a harmonic variation ("This could be the start of something very big . . .") and she literally sings rings around him. *We Got Us* sets the stage by revitalizing a number of established tunes for boy-girl duets from Broadway and film sources: "Baby, It's Cold Outside," "Side by Side," "No Two People" (from *Hans Christian Andersen*), "Together Wherever We Go" (*Gypsy*), "I Remember It Well" (*Gigi*), and "Two Lost Souls" (*Damn Yankees*). The set also includes two songs associated with long-running movie teams: "Cheek to Cheek" (homage to Fred and Ginger in *Top Hat*) and the rarely revived "Harmony" from *Variety Girl* (homage to Hope and Crosby). It's as if by doing songs associated with established duos, Lawrence and Gormé are marking their territory.

Their four other finest albums take their songs from clearly defined sources. *Golden Hits* is all big sellers from the big band era, including two Yiddish-derived blockbusters, "Bei Mir Bist Du Schoen" and "And the Angels Sing," and the Latin "I Hear a Rhapsody" and "Green Eyes." Costa's arranging style in *Golden Hits* recalls Billy May, a likely role model in that May was the acknowledged master of making pop singers swing, especially in tandem. *Two on the Aisle* (1962) and *Steve & Eydie Together on Broadway* (1967) are comprised entirely of show tunes and, as the title indicates, *Steve & Eydie at the Movies* (1963) is all from Hollywood. Their sense of humor runs rampant: When Lawrence sings "I Believe in You" from *How to Succeed in Business Without Really Trying,* he sings the title line once, at which point Gormé answers, "That's very nice, dear," and then he repeats his line, as dictated by composer Frank Loesser, causing her to comment (in rhyme no less), "You've said that twice, dear." The second Broadway collection is a scorcher, with rousing treatments of "Mame" and "Sunrise, Sunset."

The Columbia years—the mid-sixties—would seem to be the highlight of the Steve and Eydie story, individually and as a duo, with Don Costa as well as with other musical directors. In 1964, Lawrence did something few other pop singing stars (except Sammy Davis) had attempted—that is, star in a Broadway musical. *What Makes Sammy Run?,* with a superb score by Ervin Drake, gave Lawrence what must be his first grown-up pop hit song and perhaps his most memorable single ever, the irresistibly erotic "A Room Without Windows." Album-wise, he scored high points with intelligently produced and brilliantly sung concept packages: *Steve Lawrence Conquers Broadway* (1962) was an appropriate forerunner to the two Steve and Eydie Broadway albums, and the *Sammy Run* project (he had already recorded one of the most beautiful show tunes ever in Styne, Comden, and Green's "Long Before I Knew You" from *Bells Are Ringing*).

Also from 1962, *Come Waltz with Me,* a set of ballads in 3/4, took as its point of departure a Cahn–Van Heusen song commissioned by Sinatra but rejected by him, while *Academy Award Losers* (1964) both anticipated and offered a wry preemptive strike on Sinatra's *Academy Award Winners* of the following year; *Swinging West* (1965), a collection of cowboy classics in big band treatments, was a concept Sinatra wouldn't have touched with a ten-foot lasso. Lawrence's single best ballad album was *Sings of Love and Sad Young Men* (1967) in which he was the only major male pop star to bite off Fran Landesman's harrowing "All the Sad Young Men" (from *The Nervous Set*). Lawrence explored every conceivable concept—with the exception of a package entitled *Lawrence of Arabia: Songs for Swingin' Saudis.* (The ballad "Desert Moon," from his second Broadway show, *Golden Rainbow,* would have fit perfectly here.)

Meanwhile, Mrs. Lawrence also had a few surprises up her sleeve, establishing herself as the first American pop star to make a mint off the new Brazilian beat, a move that should have surprised no one, given her rhythmic fluidity and Latin background. "Blame It on the Bossa Nova" (1963), along with Tony Bennett's "I Left My Heart in San Francisco," is virtually the last time an adult-oriented singer could come up with a mass-market hit that, unlike Sinatra's "Strangers in the Night," the artist him- or herself didn't find embarrassing. "Blame It on the Bossa Nova" is still de rigueur in dance studios across the country, and though there's certainly an element of camp about the thing, Gormé could still sing it with her head held high. The sequel, "Can't Get Over (The Bossa Nova)," is, if anything, even better. A song credited to the Lawrences themselves, it finds Gormé affecting in a smaller, more pinched voice that could be an in-tune version of Astrid Gilberto, complete with an unidentified tenor soloist making like Stan Getz. The lyrics are sort of an optimistically twisted update on "South America, Take It Away," and the harmony and melody suggest "Baubles, Bangles and Beads."

The high points of Gormé's career are probably her major ballad packages for Columbia of the mid-sixties, most notably two LPs titled after hit songs associated with other artists: *Softly As I Leave You* (Matt Monro, Sinatra) and *Don't Go to Strangers* (Etta Jones, Vaughan Monroe). Apart from those two prior chart hits, there's a preponderance of first-

rate Broadway ballads, particularly "If He Walked into My Life" from *Mame*. Gormé's songs of love and loss here are a perfect balance of the very subtle and understated with the outsized and melodramatic: She never soars for a high note or a big emotion without making us feel she's really earned it. As a great Jewish American songstress, Gormé is the missing link between Helen Forrest and Barbra Streisand, yet her output is ultimately more satisfying than that of either of the other two: She's more prolific and diverse than the former and considerably less bogged down in pure ego than the latter. (Dinah Shore, for her part, was rarely publicly identified as Jewish.)

As a team, the Lawrences' joint career climaxed in the 1968 *Golden Rainbow;* where *What Makes Sammy Run,* with Lawrence alone, was a hit, it stood to reason that Steve and Eydie together in a Broadway show would do even better. Thanks to the changing climate, *Golden Rainbow* (based on a play that had been filmed with Frank Sinatra as *A Hole in the Head*) wasn't quite as golden and didn't run as long as *Sammy,* but was a success just the same. Like *Sammy, Rainbow* was also considerably boosted by a Steve Lawrence hit single—in this case it was "I've Gotta Be Me," which became an even bigger seller for Sammy Davis. Walter Marks's score for *Rainbow* wasn't quite Lerner and Loewe, but the original cast recording (there are a couple of numbers by other performers, but essentially it's a Steve and Eydie album) is one of their very best.

Even at the time of this pinnacle, changes were in the air. The team switched to RCA at the end of the sixties, where Gormé landed her last big chart hit, "Tonight I'll Say a Prayer." Their first few albums under the new contract, such as *On a Clear Day Steve Lawrence Sings Up a Storm* (1970), maintain the same level of quality as the Columbia and earlier releases. Yet even the orchestrations to *Golden Rainbow* are rife with sixties-isms—not necessarily the Rolling Stones but echoes of Burt Bacharach and other Austin Powers–era icons. It seemed as if Lawrence had only graduated from fifties kiddie pop for a few years before the pressure was on the duo to incorporate more and more elements of sixties and seventies kiddie pop. Like Streisand, Mathis, and other stars of their generation, they responded by subtly working soft rock sounds into their mix.

As a result, the few records that the Lawrences did make, individually and as a team, sounded increasingly like the genre already known as easy listening or MOR, something that the classic Steve and/or Eydie records of the fifties and sixties most definitely were not. "Can't Stop Talkin' About You" was hippy-dippyish but also somewhat endearing (though not enduring), in the manner of Sinatra's "Somethin' Stupid." "We Can Make It Together" (MGM), their last chart entry, was and is fairly unlistenable—not least because the duo is accompanied by the bubblegum singing group the Osmond

Brothers. Over the years the team had only occasionally addressed overtly Jewish material, such as "Sunrise, Sunset" and "Where Can I Go?," an anthem of Israel that Lawrence interpreted as a megadramatic showstopper and cantorial wail in the tradition of his father. In the seventies, their big rouser was "Hallelujah," not Vincent Youmans (or even Handel) but an Israeli item that always brought down the house—and not just with Jewish audiences. The recording, though, is too much a part of its era, and can only be described as *Jewzak*. This is the song you would expect to hear if Steve and Eydie had ever gone to Tel Aviv to guest-star with the Brady Bunch on *A Very Brady Pesach*. Whether singing Jewish songs or working with a Mormon backup group, the Lawrences' recordings had by and large lost their bite—a sad state of affairs for two singers with miraculous chops who were barely forty.

There were some bright spots—Lawrence made one of his very best albums in 1972 with *Portrait of Steve*, his only collaboration with the greatest orchestrator of them all, Nelson Riddle. The team found a few more opportunities to make their kind of music in their original medium, television. In 1969, they starred in an original television musical entitled *What It Was, Was Love*, with words and music by Gordon Jenkins.

In the seventies, the Lawrences' starred in a series of specials devoted to the great songwriters, most notably the Gershwin brothers, Irving Berlin, and Cole Porter. Both extremes of the Steve and Eydie oeuvre are represented here: Some may find these medley-heavy events a little overburdened with Vegas glitz. Content-wise, they're a bit wider than they are deep in the effort to include as many classic songs as possible. At the same time, *Steve and Eydie Celebrate Gershwin* features several numbers backed by just a jazz rhythm section with Ray Brown and Shelly Manne, with some of the loosest singing they've ever done: he on "Bidin' My Time," she on "But Not for Me," the two of them on "They All Laughed." The core of these productions is totally sound: Two of the best voices in pop tackling the best songs ever written. A number of these sound tracks have been released on CD, but one would like to see all the specials restored to DVD, particularly *Steve and Eydie Celebrate Gershwin*, with special guest Gene Kelly, and *Steve and Eydie Celebrate Irving Berlin* (1978), with Sammy Davis and Carol Burnett, not to mention Oscar Peterson (singing).

Most of Gormé's recordings of the seventies grew out of her extracurricular career: She has kept one foot in two worlds for most of her professional life. Since the fifties, she has continued to record collections of *canciones* for Spanish-speaking audiences all over the globe; she's been perhaps an even bigger star in the Latin world than she is with North Americans. Though this aspect of her work is essentially outside the scope of this volume, most of her albums since the seventies—such as *Tómame o Déjame*

(1982), *De Corazón a Corazón* (1988), and *Eso Es el Amor* (1992)—have been both *en español* and uniformly excellent. In 1977, Lawrence released *Tú Serás Mi Música*, no doubt with Mrs. Lawrence coaching from the sidelines. In their sixties, the Lawrences released their most recent duo project, *Alone Together* (from the mid-nineties), which cannily sprinkles in a few agreeable new songs ("I Dreamed a Dream" from *Les Misérables*; the pop hit "That's What Friends Are For") into a program of first-rate standards, like "Again," "I Can't Give You Anything but Love," and "My Shining Hour." In 2003, Lawrence released a new album, *Steve Lawrence Sings Sinatra*, in which Mr. Lawrence's singing is as superb as ever; the album only suffers from the decision to use Sinatra's actual arrangements, which make it more of a re-creation than the reinterpretation it should have been.

For most of the digital era, their recorded legacy has been in their own hands. Having had bad experiences with the major labels, the Lawrences gained control and ownership over most of their own vintage masters. In the 2000s, they have made a sizable portion of their best post-1960 albums available on CD, even though those on the G&L label (at last, she gets top billing) are primarily sold at gigs and on their Web site (steveandeydie.com). One wishes they would allow a Bear Family or some other such organization compile a complete or at least comprehensive package of their best work. In 2003, they announced they would no longer tour, although they continue to perform occasionally, especially in places where people shoot crap and pull levers on slot machines. Their chops are in near-perfect condition: It doesn't seem like too much to wish that they might resume making new albums and perhaps even play New York again. Both in terms of the past as well as (hopefully) the future, Steve Lawrence and Eydie Gormé are well worth everyone's attention. Individually, they are amazing; together, they are everything that great American pop is supposed to be.

(Over the fifty years of their collective career, Lawrence and Gormé have had countless hit singles, best-selling albums, and long runs in nightclubs. They co-starred on Broadway and opened for Sinatra on his Diamond Jubilee tour. But as successful as they have been, you can't help thinking that if talent, intelligence, charm, and endurance were the only factors in a career, they would be even better known and celebrated than they are. Why is that? The only reason I can think of is that neither of the voices, strong and appealing as they are, is immediately distinctive. When you hear Tony Bennett or Peggy Lee—let alone Sinatra or Garland—you don't even have to think about who it is, you know instantly. When you hear Steve by himself, you usually have to figure out who it is by process of elimination ["It's not Frank, it's not Vic . . ."]. The same with Eydie: "It's not Doris, it's not Jo . . ." If either one of them had a truly unique sound, they would have surely climbed even higher in the pantheon.)

Peggy Lee (1920–2002)

There are essentially two camps of great American female singers, which are not always separate and also not always regarded as equal. You might think of them as twin Rushmores or dual pantheons: When we think of the major jazz singers, we start with Billie Holiday and move on to Ella Fitzgerald, Sarah Vaughan, Carmen McRae, Anita O'Day, and Dinah Washington and perhaps one or two equally unimpeachable others. Then there's the list of the great female pop singers: Doris Day, Margaret Whiting, Rosemary Clooney, Jo Stafford, and Dinah Shore. The lists are flexible: We might even add a Bessie Smith to the first group or a Judy Garland to the second. They are not strictly racially divided: O'Day belongs unquestionably to the jazz faction just as Lena Horne rates as one of the leaders of the pop group. There's also considerable crossover: Fitzgerald and Vaughan had pop hits and a considerable pop following, Stafford and Clooney have spent a lot of time in the jazz world—they've visited so frequently that they've earned green cards and resident alien status.

But there's only one singer who can be said to truly belong to both groups: to be considered one of the all-time pop superstars as well as genuine jazz royalty. Only Peggy Lee rates as both at the same time. Is she a jazz singer? If she isn't, it would be hard to imagine who would be. She is thoroughly steeped in the vocabularies of the blues and the great jazz soloists. When she sings a song, she always personalizes it, generally liberally but always very subtly. When Frank Sinatra would change a word or a note, Ira Gershwin would moan, "If we wanted it that way, we would have written it that way!" But when Lee makes her melodic alterations, it's so subtle that even though the songwriters themselves would certainly notice, they would feel like nitpickers for making any objection.

When Lee sings "Stormy Weather" (as she did in 1947, later issued on *Rendezvous with Peggy Lee*), she's singing an interpretation of the melody that Harold Arlen wrote, with some of the notes and rhythms adjusted. The tendency for most singers is to emphasize the last note of the first line, "Don't know why," but Lee places more of an emphasis on "know," and cuts the "why" off surprisingly quickly, letting it fall away like a blues singer would. It's hard to imagine any other pop-based vocalist of her generation changing a familiar tune to such a degree.

The only reason not to classify Peggy Lee as a jazz singer is because she was so successful as a pop singer, and it's widely believed that whatever is pop cannot be jazz. Lee was pop in the most basic sense: Unlike Fitzgerald and Vaughan, who sold a lot of records but didn't have a lot of hit singles, Lee was continually on the charts. At the same time, one often finds a discrepancy in the music of pop singers of Lee's approximate generation, such as Day and Clooney (both also big band vets) in that there's a marked difference in quality between their hit singles and the "art" music they were sometimes permitted to sing on albums. So many of Lee's bona fide chart hits—"Why Don't You Do Right?" "Fever," "I'm a Woman," to name one song each from the forties, fifties, and sixties—were based in jazz and blues, and were at the same time superior pop music. Unlike Clooney or Day, Lee never had a hit song that she had to be ashamed of.

As with Sinatra, all the elements—psychological, musical, and personality—fit together perfectly. Her way of reshaping, perhaps minimizing, a melody often gives a tune a chantlike quality, and that in turn adds to the mystical quality of her singing. The older she got, the more she emphasized this element of her music, not only in the way she phrased a tune, but the way she stood, the way she moved, the way she made eye contact—or didn't—with the crowd. More than that of any other singer, with the possible exception of Nat King Cole, the music of Peggy Lee is about casting spells. When I finally got to see her live, in the eighties (usually at New York's Ballroom), she seemed like some kind of hip Gypsy fortune-teller, with blond wig and shades, and hands darting every which way, like a belly dancer who never revealed or even moved her belly.

As was Clooney's, Lee's time was impeccable. The bassist David Finck has characterized Sinatra's sense of time as being incredibly metrically precise, so much so that you can feel exactly where every beat is all of the time. Lee, on the other hand, is more of a "floater"; she doesn't try to get down into that precise groove rhythmically, but flies over the ground beat, particularly on her trademark rubato ballads. Yet her music is, overall, just as swinging and satisfying as Sinatra's. Her floating sound at times reminds me of Lester Young, which isn't surprising considering her fondness for Billie Holiday, and it parallels the way Miles Davis phrases a ballad.

Lee was also flexible enough, rhythmically, to experiment with different kinds of beats: Twenty years before Sinatra's encounter with Jobim and the bossa nova, Lee was singing to rhythms from Cuba, Brazil, and the rest of Latin America. Here, too, she works with the rhythm by working against it, not emphasizing all the beats in a measure but continuing to drift over them. On the polyrhythmic "You Stepped Out of a Dream" (on *Olé ala Lee!*) there are three strains going at once: a ground Latin beat voiced on bongos and congas, then a small reed section playing a repetitive, rather droning background pattern, and on top there's Lee singing the Nacio Herb Brown melody—or rather her own take on it. The three strains operate roughly independently of one another, yet they work together beautifully. For a while, the reeds are supplemented by a very subtle male chorus, and then by blasting Cuban brass, yet still the multileveled polyrhythmic texture of the performance remains intact. In the classic Sinatra-Riddle orchestrations, most of the interesting instrumental stuff happens when Sinatra is not singing: the intros, the closings, the instrumental breaks, and especially in the fills between lines. With Lee, all this stuff is happening even as she's singing. She exists in the same sonic space as the instrumental components of the performance.

If that helps make the argument that Lee should be regarded as a jazz vocalist one doesn't require nearly as much ammunition to make the point that Lee is equally a pop singer. Indeed, she's one of the most consistently popular female singers the music industry has known. She was a headliner from the forties to the nineties, and she had a run on the charts longer than any other femme singer I can think of, landing hit singles as late as the seventies. Who else could bridge both the generation gap and the stylistic gap between Benny Goodman and Leiber and Stoller?

In the end, the major factor that accounts for Lee's jazziness is the same element that explains her sustained popularity: her affinity for the blues. she, in fact, sang the blues more frequently and more meaningfully than most black female jazz singers of her era (with the exception of Dinah Washington). In her final appearance in New York in 1996 (at Carnegie Hall, as part of the JVC Jazz Festival), she announced to the crowd, "I've always loved the blues," and she then elaborated, "When I was a little girl, I used to read about Leadbelly, and that kind of music always fascinated me." The second part of the story is at least a little apocryphal—nobody had much heard of Leadbelly until the forties (by which time Lee was hardly a little girl anymore)—but it illustrates the depth of her feeling for the blues.

Is Peggy Lee a pop singer with a strong sense of the blues, or is it the other way around? We think of her as having a soft, sensuous sound, yet no other pop singer can so skillfully switch to a hard-edged blues timbre when the material demands it. Where Sinatra was the first singer to show the world that there was such a thing as what we now call the Great American Songbook, Lee was the first to explore the other Great American Songbook, and show that the music of Big Bill Broonzy and Willie Dixon held just as much value for singers as that of, say, Burke and Van Heusen. "Why Don't You Do Right?" the song that launched her career, was a thoroughly blues-drenched mantra that gave her both a solid hit with Goodman's band and the legs, as it were, to stand on her own as a solo act. And "Do Right" was hardly an anomaly—over the next few decades one Lee hit after another would be cast from a blues mold.

Lee has exalted many traditions over the years, from South American music (from her blockbuster "Mañana" to her celebrated *Latin ala Lee* album series) to Oriental poetry (*Sea Shells*) and, naturally, the Broadway-based tradition of Berlin, Rodgers,

Kern et al. But the blues have held a prominent part in her repertory—she's included a blues-tinged pop tune, at the very least, in practically every album, and twice recorded entire sets devoted to the form (*Blues Cross Country* and the later *Miss Peggy Lee Sings the Blues*).

If the blues are the music of a suffering people, then they must have provided a much needed outlet for the young Peggy Lee, who grew up amidst deprivations and cruelty second only to those of Oliver Twist, including an alcoholic father and a wicked stepmother who made Cinderella's look like an amateur. (Lee later wrote an autobiographical song about her relationship with her father's wife, entitled "One Beating a Day.") Born on May 26, 1920, Peggy Lee was originally, as the title of her final Capitol album proclaimed, *Norma Deloris Egstrom from Jamestown, North Dakota.* Although Norma/Peggy had six older brothers and sisters, her childhood was a desolate and lonely one—until she discovered the wonder of radio. Tuning in bands from faraway Kansas City (she liked to brag that she had heard Bill Basie on shortwave remotes well before he was canonized as the Count), Lee discovered that music was in her blood, and what she had to do was sing.

She first performed professionally on Valley City (North Dakota) radio KOVC with local bandleader Doc Haines, who referred to the fledgling vocalist as "my little blues singer." She soon was given a regular show on KOVC, which was sponsored by a local restaurant that paid her in chow. During and immediately after her high school years, Lee took whatever jobs she could get around North Dakota, both musical (singing for next to nothing on more local radio stations) and otherwise (waitressing). Along the way, the program director of WDAY Fargo (the most widely heard station in the state) changed her name to Peggy Lee. She also did paperwork for the station, including ASCAP reports, an activity that helped inspire a lifetime fascination with the songwriting side of the music industry.

Broke and alone, and still only seventeen years old, Lee headed to California, where, among other jobs both musical and nonmusical, she sang at a noisy joint in Palm Springs called the Doll House. It was there that she made a remarkable discovery. "In a moment of intense fear, I discovered the power of softness," she recalled in 1984. "I was thinking people didn't want to listen to me, so I'd just sing to myself. They immediately stopped talking." Around this time, she also came across a singer whose work would inspire her to put this principle into action. "People say I emulated Billie Holiday," Lee remarked to *The New York Times* in 1988. "Although that is a great compliment, it isn't true. I wasn't drawn to any particular singer until I heard Maxine Sullivan. I liked the simplicity and economy of her work. She communicated so well that you really got the point right away. Later, when I came to New York, Mel Powell [Benny Goodman's pianist] introduced me to Billie Holiday, and I loved what she did, although we never became terribly close." Lee was being cagily diplomatic—most of the time, when people mistakenly said that she "emulated" Billie Holiday, they didn't necessarily mean it as a compliment.

It wouldn't be in Tinseltown that Lee herself would be "discovered" but closer to home. She'd returned to North Dakota for a tonsillectomy, and from there lined up a gig at the Buttery, a nightclub in the Ambassador Hotel West in Chicago, hometown of Benny Goodman. As Miss Lee recalled, "Benny's then-fiancée, Lady [Alice] Duckworth, came into the Buttery, and she was very impressed. So the next evening she brought Benny in, because they were looking for a replacement for Helen Forrest. And although I didn't know, I was it."

Lee joined Goodman in 1941 and stayed for two years. By and large, it's a much more mainstream Lee you'll hear here than the one who became a star and a diva years later. The ambiguous rubato tempos that mark her mature ballad singing would evolve out of a more solidly grounded, dance-driven 4/4 approach to time—as established by Goodman, the man who put swing on the map to begin with—even on slow pieces like "How Long Has This Been Going On" and "Ev'rything I Love." The soft and sensual tone had to develop from what was originally a firmer, more clearly focused contralto.

Likewise, Lee's later penchant for exotic sounds would be arrived at after thoroughly checking out the domestic product first. Yet among the Lee-Goodman titles (issued in their entirety by Sony Music Legacy on a two-CD set, *Peggy Lee and Benny Goodman: The Complete Recordings, 1941–1947,* you will find her first explorations of Latin rhythms ("Full Moon" and "The Lamp of Memory") and Jewish melodies ("My Little Cousin," based on the Yiddish song "Greena Cousina"). There's also John Latouche's lyric to "Not a Care in the World," which affords Lee, quoting Catherine the Great, the opportunity to sing in Russian.

"Blues in the Night" offers a hint of her developing blues style, which also informs her performance of "That Did It, Marie." The latter is a typical swing era concoction of riffs and jive that prompted no less than Count Basie himself to inquire, in sincere (though today politically incorrect) terms, "Are you sure you don't have a little spade in you, Peggy?" But with "Why Don't You Do Right?" Lee establishes herself as one of the most credible blues singers, white or otherwise, working in any band at that time, not far behind Count Basie's Helen Humes.

"Why Don't You Do Right?" began life in 1936 as "The Weed Smoker's Dream," by the remarkable and underappreciated band known as the Harlem Hamfats. It was later recorded by blues diva Lil Green, then a major star on the "race" circuit. "I was and am a fan of Lil Green, a great old blues singer . . . ," Lee said in a 1984 interview with journalist George Christy. "I used to play that record over and over in

my dressing room, which was next door to Benny's. Finally he said, 'You obviously like that song.' I said, 'Oh, I love it.' He said, 'Would you like me to have an arrangement made of it?' I said, 'I'd love that,' and he did." While Lee utilizes blues inflections that are not necessarily part of the Scandinavian-American experience, it's unfair to accuse her of simply covering Lil Green (who, by that same logic, was herself covering the Hamfats). For starters, Lee and Goodman take the tune about four times as fast as either previous record. Lee uses an African American–influenced style informed by such giants as Billie Holiday and Ethel Waters.

Thanks to "Do Right," when Lee and Goodman parted company in 1943, she left the band with three things she didn't have when she first came onboard: a national name, a hit song, and a husband, Goodman's guitarist, Dave Barbour. "David joined Benny's band, and there was a ruling that no one should fraternize with the girl singer. But I fell in love with David the first time I heard him play, and so I married him. Benny then fired David, so I quit too. Benny and I made up, although David didn't play with him any more. Benny stuck to his rule. I think that's not too bad a rule, but you can't help falling in love with somebody."

When Mrs. and Mr. Barbour left the band, the idea was that he would work in the studios and she would content herself with keeping house and raising their daughter, Nicki. "I tried to retire when we got married, but it didn't work. David didn't want me to [give up singing], either. He said that later I might resent not having used the talent I'd been given. I guess that was true. I was very happy, though." Lee was too drawn to music to stay tied to her own apron strings for very long—she preferred preparing songs to preparing meals. As she once remembered during a show, "David would come home at night and say, 'Where's dinner?' and I would answer, 'Well, I didn't get around to it . . . But the song is finished!'" From songwriting she gradually drifted back to singing at the occasional recording session for the fledgling Capitol Records.

Lee's first session after leaving Goodman was with an all-star band titled the Capitol Jazzmen on January 7, 1944; from that point on until 1972 (with the exception of a five-year sojourn at Decca), she recorded continually and prolifically for Capitol. There's no complete package—no Bear Family box—of Lee's output either for Capitol or Decca, but there are some recommended samplers and several definitive collections of smaller chunks of her career. The previously mentioned *Peggy Lee and Benny Goodman: The Complete Recordings* includes all the 1941–42 Columbia sides plus the three reunion tracks from 1947. Also highly recommended is *The Complete Peggy Lee and June Christy Capitol Transcription Sessions* on Mosaic, a five-CD package that includes all of Lee's radio-only recordings of the late forties, including many excellent small group–accompanied performances of pop and jazz standards. (The three and a half CDs' worth of transcriptions were also sampled in a single-CD package called *Travelin' Light*.) There are also two recommended double-disc samplers of highlights from her Decca period, *Black Coffee and Other Delights* and *Classics and Collectibles*. The CD era has also seen two four-CD retrospectives of the Lee career, *Miss Peggy Lee* (the art direction of which has led fans to refer to it as the Pink Box) and *The Singles Collection*. The second goes beyond Capitol to include a handful of Goodman and Decca tracks.

Both of these four-CD sets are generous in that they fill each disc up to its full seventy-nine-minute capacity: By the LP era, Lee was prone to short tracks, thus the four-volume *Miss Peggy Lee* (the pink one) package contains nearly 125 tracks. Disc one is mainly given over to her big hits, and in that respect covers a lot of the same turf as the 1990 collection *Peggy Lee: The Capitol Collectors Series*—in both cases, the idea is to include only items that appeared on the charts. This is normally a fairly reprehensible practice—chart status and enduring quality are two often unrelated issues. With Doris Day, for instance, a collection that genuinely consists of "The Best of Doris Day" would have almost no songs in common with a package entitled "Doris Day's Greatest Hits." With Lee, luckily, there's less of a discrepancy—most of her hits are actually good music, a generous number of which are the lady's own compositions, such as "It's a Good Day," "I Didn't Know About You," and the blockbuster "Mañana." The lowest point of either collection is the completely inappropriate "Ghost Riders in the Sky"—just because it was briefly a number-two hit doesn't mean it qualifies as the best of Peggy Lee, deserving of being reissued on two CDs.

Volume two of the Pink Box is considerably stronger, consisting largely of vintage forties Lee recordings of standards. Actually, this disc dovetails nicely with *Rendezvous with Peggy Lee*, which was just about her earliest 12" album, a collection of singles gathered in 1952. The very fact of Lee's having sung so many standards in these years is part of her spiritual kinship with Frank Sinatra, whom she had first gotten to know in 1943 when both were at the New York Paramount (she with Goodman, he experiencing his solo, post–Tommy Dorsey breakthrough).

Indeed, the singer that Lee has the most in common with philosophically (though not in terms of vocal quality or this emphasis on the blues) is not one of her own gender, but Sinatra, who was a close friend (and, according to various accounts, an occasional lover) from her Benny Goodman days onward. In talking to Alan Livingston, the longtime president of Capitol Records, who knew both Lee and Sinatra well, the impression one gets is that she was the first major singer to follow Sinatra's example of taking charge of her own musical destiny. Livingston acknowledges that Lee, like Sinatra (and completely unlike Day and Clooney), worked with her producers (most famously Dave Cavanaugh) in planning every detail of her sessions, from the songs themselves to the outline of the arrangements and the musicians involved. She was even more fastidious, in her live appearances, planning sets meticulously and also in charge of wardrobe and lighting. Livingston remembers that Lee's instincts were right at least 80 to 90 percent of the time (as opposed to Sinatra, who was always right) but that her collaborators had a hard time getting her to go with one of their suggestions on those rare occasions when they could offer an idea that was an improvement. The overall impression was that she was not always the easiest woman to work with. Still, she inspired tremendous loyalty in musicians and co-workers.

Although she sometimes denied having imitated Billie Holiday, Lady Day herself was generous with her praise for Lee. Holiday, who could be cruel to singers she didn't like or was jealous of, was quoted in *Metronome* magazine in 1950: "I've always loved Peggy, ever since she first started, and she's been very fortunate. She's always had the kind of background every singer needs." Only Holiday, who built a career around bad luck both on- and offstage, could view Lee's success in terms of songs and accompaniments as luck. "All girl singers are a pain in the ass, and she's no exception, but she knew what she wanted," Billy May told me. The choice of words is revealing—to May, the ultimate "pain in the ass" was an artist or producer who had no idea what he or she wanted, and made him write a chart a dozen ways before figuring it out. May went on, "Like Frank, if she made a change, there was a good musical reason. So, you respect people like that."

More than any other singer of the forties—perhaps even Sinatra—Lee's music represents a complete and total stylistic universe, a world unto itself. No doubt this is partially because she was the only singer of the period who was also a first-rate songwriter; the only one who comes close was Mel Tormé, but unlike Lee, Tormé did not keep writing songs throughout his career. Like Tormé, however, Lee did write the majority of her most successful songs in the forties. She co-composed 18 of the 170 songs that she recorded between 1944 and 1952. (She almost always wrote lyrics, but she generally had a hand in the melody as well.) That's only a small percentage of her recorded output, but a higher than average percentage of her own songs were hits for her, songs that were widely recorded by other artists. (Sarah Vaughan sang Lee's "What More Can a Woman Do," Doris Day covered Peggy's "Just an Old Love of Mine," and, in what must have been a major thrill for Lee, Duke Ellington and Al Hibbler recorded "Don't Be So Mean to Baby.") There's a recent CD package of the music of Hoagy Carmichael that describes that composer as *The First of the Singer-Songwriters*, but with no disrespect to Carmichael, it seems that the term applies much more accurately to Peggy Lee—Carmichael's career as a performer was ultimately far less important than his contribution as a writer of music. Yet Lee had enough successful songs in the immediate postwar era to rate as one of the most decorated women in ASCAP. She was easily the most successful female singer-songwriter until the sixties.

Lee's affinity for the blues is a key part of her composing skills. The blues tend to be written by the people who sing them; the act of interpreting and personalizing a basic 12-bar blues is fundamentally a compositional process. To come up with "You Was Right Baby," "Everything's Moving Too Fast," or "Whee, Baby," Lee started with an understanding of how the blues works, much as Louis Jordan did when he wrote his concurrent early R&B hits. To know the blues is to have a template, a mold from which a wide range of compositions can be created.

The blues were merely one of many unique aspects of her music from the beginning—aspects, again, not found in the music of any other singer in her era. As singer as well as songwriter, she traversed the globe, both literally and metaphorically; Planet Peggy was a vast enough world to encompass many subcontinents. Apart from the blues, she wrote and sang country (hillbilly) songs, folk songs, and what could be called Americana. "Wandering Swallow" was an early example of a Peggy Lee folk song, which could have been sung by the Weavers or, later, the Kingston Trio. Her 1950 original "Neon Signs" was a square-dance-ready Western number of the sort that Spade Cooley might have played, and she also recorded Cooley's "Cry, Cry, Cry" in the time shortly before Mitch Miller and Tony Bennett brought Hank Williams's songs into mainstream pop.

Lee's interest in Americana encompasses a large amount of material by Willard Robison, who wrote rustic American airs that don't sound in the least like either conventional country music or Tin Pan Alley either. Robison was a close friend, and it's said that she actually wrote "Don't Smoke in Bed," their biggest hit together, because he was too drunk to write it himself. "Don't Smoke" was recently revived by k.d. lang, who also straddles the worlds of hillbilly and pop music. Yet, as touching as Lang's rendition is, she can't lay a glove on Lee, who knew firsthand that the expression "Don't smoke in bed" usually referred to drunks who had a tendency to pass out while holding a glass in one hand and a cigarette in the other. Both of the two most important men in Lee's life, her father and her husband at the time, were hopeless alcoholics; Lee sings this song with the resignation of a survivor who's been there and done that.

Another Robison composition, "Run for the Roundhouse, Nellie," took its place in the long list of Peggy Lee train songs. Her fascination with trains goes back to her childhood; as one of the songs from her autobiographical musical *Peg* proclaimed,

"Daddy Was a Railroad Man." All the genres of American music that interested her—blues, country, and folk songs—used the railroad as a reference point and a symbol for distant dreams. In 1961, she combined both subtopics with "The Train Blues" on *Blues Cross Country:* This was a disappointing album with too many original songs that were not up to her highest standard. Still, "Train Blues" was one of the best of the new numbers, using modal harmonies that were in vogue in modern jazz at the time to tap into the power of the train metaphor as well as the deep well of the blues.

By 1950, Lee was all over the map, not only of American music, but the world. She explored Latin rhythms very successfully on her self-composed 1947 blockbuster "Mañana," which combined Carmen Miranda's rhythm section with Mel Blanc's faux-Mexican accent. "Golden Earrings" took her into the realm of faux-Gypsy music for another major hit (which she followed, eventually, with "The Gypsy with Fire in His Shoes"—tap dancing by Sammy Davis Jr.—and "I Love Your Gypsy Heart"). She also found success with Italian songs both real and ersatz: the lullaby "Chi-Baba, Chi-Baba (My Bambino Go to Sleep)," the love song "Bella Notte," and the novelty "Who's Gonna Pay the Check," singing the latter in an accent that anticipates Carmela Soprano. She also took a traditional Yiddish melody and sang it in two different pop song adaptations with different lyrics, Mel Tormé's "Once in a Lifetime" and Sammy Fain's "I Hear the Music Now." (The same song is also known as "Hushabye.") Still later she sang in French and even Japanese. Then there are songs like "Similau" and her own "Sans Souci" where she travels to places that are so bizarre and offbeat that they're not even on the map. You can tell Lee was a movie buff—these latter two titles sound as if they were written for some crazy Technicolor jungle epic with Maria Montez and Jon Hall.

The visual-audible influence was a key factor in Lee's biggest musical breakthrough, the 1952 "Lover." Although "Mañana" and "Golden Earrings" were megahits, "Lover" has had the widest influence on subsequent jazz and pop. It also was the reason she switched labels from Capitol to Decca in that year—or so she said, claiming that she left Capitol when they refused to let her record it. "Lover" was cinematically linked to the image of a team of horses; this typical Richard Rodgers waltz was introduced by Jeanette MacDonald singing in a horse-drawn carriage (a surrey with no top to hang a fringe on) in the 1932 *Love Me Tonight;* twenty years later, Lee was inspired to devise a radical new interpretation of the song when she watched a team of horses charging across the desert in some other old movie she happened to catch on TV.

In viewing this tits-and-sand adventure epic ("Death to the infidel!"), Lee conceived of redoing "Lover," which had already been swung by Gene

Krupa and Frank Sinatra, as an explosive pasodoble that steadily mounted in tempo and tonic key and gets more and more exciting as it progresses. Since her contract with Capitol was almost up, rather than renew, she succumbed to the enticement of Milt Gabler to sign with Decca. There, an immediate benefit was the opportunity to record duets with Bing Crosby (with whom she had already worked extensively on the radio and in a film), as well as a green light to do "Lover." She spends more time in her memoir talking about the recording of "Lover" than about any other song, even those she composed herself. Even if she exaggerated a bit—this obviously wasn't the sole reason she left Capitol Records—it's telling that she wanted people to know that this song was that important to her.

The finished "Lover," conducted by Gordon Jenkins, who followed Lee's guidelines for the arrangement, was considered somewhat shocking in 1952. The resulting hit was publicly dismissed by both the composer, Richard Rodgers, and by musicologist Sigmund Spaeth, among others. It was polytonal (starting in F, then modulating to G and finally to A flat), polyrhythmic, polycultural, polyeverything. This "Lover" is indeed a very mad affair, boasting a satanically cacophonic instrumental orchestration as well as the male chorus in the background, wordlessly holding the tonic note of each chord, and even further-out fever-pitch phrasing from Miss Lee, who all but breathes flame.

"Lover" was a hit—the biggest of her five years at Decca. But it signified something much deeper. This wasn't the first time anyone had taken a standard song and given it a whole new feeling—a new time signature, a new tempo, a new cultural context—but it *was* the first time that a major artist created such an impact with such a reinterpretation. Jazzmen and big band arrangers had taken sentimental old songs and even classics and swung them, but it's hard to think of anything like this before "Lover." Even Lee's previous Latin-oriented recordings were either actual Latin compositions or South-of-the-Border-style novelties that she'd written herself. (On a similar note, she brought a folk treatment to the pop standard "Bye Bye Blackbird," and again it's hard to think of a precedent.)

With "Lover," Lee was anticipating a period when singers of both the jazz and pop varieties would transform all kinds of standards into sambas, to bring the rhythms of Rio and Havana to music from Broadway. Around the time of "Lover," she applied a similar treatment to "Just One of Those Things" (also done with Jenkins). From there she continually refined the idea: In 1955, she crafted a mambo treatment of "Ooh, That Kiss," a long-forgotten pre-Hollywood Harry Warren song. The orchestration includes Latin percussion, flutes, a male chorus of bandsmen chanting "cha-cha-cha," and a modulation near the end, but it's still a much simpler and subtler treatment than "Lover" or "Just One of Those Things." By continuing to pare down, Lee gradually brought this ideal of Latinization to a new level.

This was beginning to happen in jazz and instrumental pop, as when George Shearing added Latin percussion to his famous quintet on Warren Covington's dance hit "Tea for Two (Cha-Cha-Cha)," but Lee was way ahead of the curve. She consolidated her accomplishments with her widely successful 1959 album, *Latin ala Lee*, which transforms contemporary show tunes into sambas and mambos (there was also a sequel, *Olé ala Lee*, 1960; the third album in the series, was *Guitars a la Lee*, 1966). It was a brilliant idea for the album era, and soon enough everybody was doing it: Billy Eckstine's *Broadway, Bongos and Mr. B*, Steve Lawrence's *Lawrence Goes Latin*, Mel Tormé's *Olé Tormé*, Rosemary Clooney's *A Touch of Tabasco*. When the bossa nova came in, even more singers got on the now Brazilian bandwagon, and when Sinatra and Jobim sambafied Cole Porter and Irving Berlin, they were, in a sense, following the trend that Lee had begun with "Lover."

Lee's Decca years, 1952–57, were a period of artistic refinement. Following Sinatra's lead, she used the new 10" and then 12" LP format to bring her artistic ambitions to a whole other level. More than any other time in her life, the mid-fifties were years of cultural diversity: *Black Coffee* (1953), with a quartet featuring trumpeter Pete Candoli and pianist Jimmy Rowles, was her finest album of pure small group jazz, while the sound track album for *Pete Kelly's Blues* (1955) took her to the traditional jazz of Chicago in the twenties, and *Miss Wonderful* (1955) was big band swing, in an occasionally Basie-esque bag, from the pen of the brilliant Sy Oliver. She also worked with two major arranger-conductor-composers and string stylists in the person of Gordon Jenkins on *Lover* (1952–53) and Victor Young on *Dream Street* (1957). *Dream Street* also includes a really juicy trio date with the group that by 1956 had established itself as the definitive Lee rhythm section, Lou Levy (piano), Max Bennett (bass), and Larry Bunker (drums). From a career perspective beyond her work as a singer and recording artist, Lee also created her most successful project as a composer in these years, the full-length dramatic score for the Disney classic *Lady and the Tramp* (1955), a collaboration with composer and arranger Sonny Burke.

And there was *Sea Shells*, her New Age–style album of meditation music and Chinese love poems (not to mention courteous friends preparing cooling drinks). The fact of the album is more interesting than the record itself. The idea that she would even think of it is something that links her to a later generation rather than her own. Try to picture Sinatra or Fitzgerald becoming interested in alternative philosophies or religions like the Science of Mind. (These are precisely the kind of groups that Elvis Presley later got involved with.)

In 1957, Peggy Lee returned to her alma mater, Capitol Records, where her first projects were collaborations with Frank Sinatra and Nelson Riddle. They would join forces for a miraculous ménage à trois titled *The Man I Love*, which set the bar for slow, lushly orchestrated treatments of standard ballads. Produced and conducted by Sinatra (with input from Lee), and arranged by Riddle, it's interesting that Sinatra never quite did an album like this of his own singing (the closest he ever came was the 1959 *Nice 'n' Easy*): When he sang slow songs in this period, they were at least torchy if not suicidal. This collection of basically happy but slow songs about love had more in common with Nat Cole's albums of the era. Interestingly, Sinatra himself never recorded most of the songs here, especially the album's highlight, "The Folks Who Live on the Hill." As George Shearing, who would collaborate with Lee on her first live album, the 1959 *Beauty and the Beat*, told me, "Take Peggy's record of 'The Folks Who Live on the Hill' with Nelson Riddle and Sinatra conducting . . . I could listen to that at least six times in a row without getting tired of it."

Lee's emphasis for the remainder of her career would be on albums, starting with *The Man I Love*, although she continued to score hit singles as well, beginning with the biggest of them all, "Fever" (1958). Again, like Sinatra (and Tony Bennett as well), Lee flourished throughout the sixties, a decade when many jazz-pop singers (Tormé, O'Day, Christy, Clooney) found the going increasingly tough. As with Fitzgerald, it would take a full-length book to examine even just the high points of all her albums in these fifteen years (1957–72).

Any quick list of highlights from Lee's mature years would start with *Jump for Joy* (1957–58), which was the up-tempo companion to *The Man I Love*, also arranged and this time conducted by Riddle. For several projects she collaborated with guitarist Jack Marshall, who served as arranger and conductor on *Latin ala Lee, I Like Men,* and *Things Are Swingin'*, until the two had a falling out; one gets the impression that Marshall, even more than Riddle or Billy May, was entrusted to orchestrate the sketches that Lee had given him up front.

Around 1960, she was making one of her regular appearances at New York's Basin Street East when she heard a cut with Ray Charles with a big band. Duly impressed, she tracked down the arranger, who turned out to be Quincy Jones, then still living in Paris. She wound up doing two albums with him in 1961, one blues and one of ballads, *Blues Cross Country* (which, unfortunately, was not the Peggy Lee blues album of our dreams) and *If You Go*. (Lee's daughter, Nicki, has said that her mother and Jones enjoyed rather more than a professional relationship.)

She teamed up with the outstanding veteran Billy May on the all-ballad *Pretty Eyes*, the holiday album *Christmas Carousel* (1960), and parts of both *In the Name of Love* (1964) and *Guitars a la Lee* (1966). The even more venerated arranger-player Benny Carter was responsible for *Sugar 'n' Spice* (1962) and portions of *Mink Jazz* (1963). There also were three LPs originally released as "live" albums—all of which intermingled elements of genuine location recordings with doctored studio performances: *Beauty and the Beat* with George Shearing (1959), *Basin Street East* (1961), and *Two Shows Nightly* (done at New York's Copacabana in 1968). In the case of the Basin Street performance, the actual performance taped at the club in 1961 was finally issued over forty years later.

Dizzy Gillespie once said that his greatest accomplishment was bringing Latin rhythms into jazz, and in the same sentence he said that the greatest strength of his partner, Charlie Parker, was the blues. Lee's mastery of both forms—Latin music and the blues—enabled her to keep her audience long beyond most other singers of her generation. When Capitol, in the late nineties, asked me to put together a compilation called *The Best of Peggy Lee: The Capitol Years,* I was able to do so using exclusively blues-oriented material, mostly from the sixties, including such hits as "Fever" and "I'm a Woman," Ray Charlesiana like "Hallelujah! I Love Him So" and "Just for a Thrill," prehistoric blues like "Mama's Gone Goodbye" and "See See Rider," contemporary but at the same time traditional blues like Willie Dixon's "Seventh Son" and B. B. King's "The Thrill Is Gone," pop blues like Billy May's hard swinging arrangement of "Call Me," sophisticated and jazzy blues like Benny Golson's "Whisper Not" and Duke Ellington's "I'm Gonna Go Fishin' " (which Lee herself adapted into waltz time and song form from Ellington's *Anatomy of a Murder* theme), Basie blues like "All Right, Okay, You Win" and "Goin' to Chicago," and classic blues like Percy Mayfield's "Send Me Someone to Love."

Lee was reaching a new peak when so many were starting to lose it. She was blending traditional pop (Broadway and Tin Pan Alley), Latin, and blues with amazing skill and utter transparency. As with Bennett but not Sinatra, most of her albums from the mid-sixties were not comprehensive packages with a coherent theme—or even the same arranger-conductor throughout. Sets like *Big Spender* and *Extra Special* seem randomly thrown together, but there was a kind of beauty in that, their emphasis on diversity over cohesiveness. Even her arrangements of new show tunes, like "Come Back to Me" (from *On a Clear Day You Can See Forever*) combine these elements: There are bongos as well as a trace of electric funk in the rhythm section.

By the sixties, Lee could seamlessly add Latin rhythms without making a big deal of it. Charles Strouse and Lee Adams's "You've Got Possibilities" (from the *Superman* musical) is a strong enough melody on its own, but by adding Latin accents to it, she makes it irresistible. I've noted how Lee, especially in her slow ballads, flows over the beat in a tempoless, rubato fashion: In her Latin numbers, she sings precisely *on* the beat, singing everything with sharp accents, and cutting off notes in a way that makes them swing even harder. As on "Possibilities," she's even swingier and jazzier in a Latin framework than she is with a Benny Goodman– or Count Basie–style regulation swing band.

The blues also ennoble much of Lee's post-1974 recordings, including "Some Cats Know," which is the highlight of *Mirrors* (1975), an all-original concept album written for her by rock songwriter-producers Jerry Leiber and Mike Stoller. *Mirrors* is an outgrowth, in a sense, of her last big hit single, the 1969 "Is That All There Is?" (which sounds more like Weill and Brecht than Louis Jordan or Dinah Washington). I've always found *Mirrors* to be somewhat dreary—except for "Some Cats Know"—but the album has become a latter-day cult favorite; it's widely admired by rockcentric connoisseurs of pop exotica and esoterica, and has even been performed in toto as a song suite by the contemporary cabaret singer Mary Foster Conklin. In 1988, Lee built another whole album out of the blues, titled, straightforwardly enough, *Peggy Lee Sings the Blues*. The key strength of her last worthy album, the 1992 *Love Held Lightly—Rare Songs by Harold Arlen*, is the affinity that both the singer and composer share for the blues.

Lee's very sporadic final twenty-five years of performing and recording include some nonblues highlights as well. One of her post-Capitol triumphs is a longish medley of Rodgers and Hart songs on the 1977 *Peggy Lee in Concert at the London Palladium*. This concludes with a stunning treatment of "Who Are You?," a song from *The Boys from Syracuse* almost completely unheard in the jazz-pop sphere, which demonstrates that Lee knows her Richard Rodgers as well as her Ma Rainey.

Lee recorded her final studio performance in 1995, at the age of seventy-five, a single song called "I See You" done in honor of longtime friend Benny Carter (who turned ninety that year and actually outlived Lee by several seasons). The singer, with her voice that seemed so delicate and fragile, with a career that at the beginning (at least at the start of its post–big band phase) seemed so tentative, proved to be one of the most resilient forces in the entire jazz-pop continuum. Lee was never exactly part of either the jazz or the pop mainstream, yet she drew on both—and emerges, nearly a decade after her death, as more influential than nearly any of the more easily categorizable divas on either side of her.

Peggy Lee died in January 2002, at the age of eighty-one, shortly after winning the second of her two epic lawsuits against the megacorporations that controlled her work. In 2003, the JVC Jazz Festival mounted a full-length concert tribute to her, of which the undisputed highlight was Shirley Horn's touching, high-Lee-inspired rendition of "Folks Who Live on the Hill." Even while Lee was still alive, tribute albums began to appear, such as *Some Cats Know—Songs of Peggy Lee* by the excellent young jazz singer (and daughter of Dizzy Gillespie) Jeanie Bryson, from 1995. As of 2009, Lee discographer Ivan Santiago has noted no fewer than seventeen Lee tribute albums, but the quantity is less impressive than the diversity: She has been honored by pop divas (Bette Midler), folk-blues singers (Maria Muldaur), musical theater actresses (Jessica Molaskey), cabaret artists (Mary Foster Conklin), jazz singers (Connie Evingson and Bryson), and, in at least one case, a fellow jazz-pop legend, Buddy Greco in conjunction with his wife and musical partner, Lezlie Anders; both Madonna and k.d. lang have also paid homage.

Obviously, Peggy Lee spoke to a great many people—no end of contemporary artists want a piece of her magic. Yet it is her own recorded legacy that will be giving listeners fever for generations to come.

Abbey Lincoln (1930–2010)

In 1956, Liberty Records introduced recording artist Abbey Lincoln as a high-glamour black counterpart to their star sexpot, Julie London. Then, like a sixties honor student who drops out to join the radical underground, Lincoln reemerged at the end of the decade as a socially significant songstress advocating musical and political reform in the company of Sonny Rollins, Kenny Dorham, and her then husband, Max Roach.

That was in the fifties and sixties. Throughout the nineties and into the new millennium, Abbey Lincoln reigned as one of the most imposing presences on the jazz scene, both for *how* she sang and *what* she sang: The magnificence of her musical style was enhanced by the consistently high quality of the songs she wrote. Her sound is something way beyond special: Like Billie Holiday, Lincoln has a dark, hypnotic timbre, and while her range may be limited, her intonation is more than sufficiently accurate within it. More important, she has a dramatic ability to command a listener's attention that's far in excess of raw vocal technique (the ability to hit and sustain notes).

Lincoln possessed an equally remarkable asset in that her original songs both showcased her sound and gave her singing a compositional context. Both jazz and pop have known songwriters whose singing was good enough for them to enjoy parallel careers as performers—such as Johnny Mercer, Jon Hendricks, and Dave Frishberg—as well as performers like Billie Holiday and Lee Wiley whose name occasionally turns up on a song. But even Mel Tormé and Peggy Lee, who had substantial careers as composers, wrote most of their best-known songs in the earlier stages of their careers. No major vocalist has written more excellent songs in her sixties and seventies, and in the recent history of this music, than Abbey Lincoln. (When Lincoln began reemerging as a major contender in the early nineties, one phrase she often used in interviews was "I'm a late bloomer.")

In the past I have tried, for the purposes of discussion, to consider Lincoln's twin achievements as if they were distinct from each other. But—as she sings on *Over the Years*—it's impossible. The sound and approach that she has perfected as an interpreter of songs is part and parcel of what she has achieved as a composer of songs. She created a distinctly Lincolnian sound, which went hand in hand with her songs of philosophical ambitions expressed in abstract lyrics, the better to ponder the big questions of God, man, and the universe but in a down-to-earth way. Making her writing more individual still, many of these songs are cast in a vaguely waltzish meter and make use of a vaguely bluesish harmonic texture. She doesn't exactly pivot around in a strict 3/4 gait, but her songs turn in on themselves like a carousel that happens to be shaped like an oval rather than being strictly circular: The ride is smooth until you get to the bump. After those first few bumps, you start anticipating the rest, and that expectation makes you hold on tight to the painted horse as you feel the wind on your face and start to smell cotton candy.

At times her singing seems to leave the confines of either a Western or an African pitch mode; she prefers instead to temper the notes she sings in terms of a scale tuned purely to their emotional significance. Listening to her sing her lyrics to Freddie Hubbard's melody to "Up Jumped Spring" on *A Turtle's Dream* is instructive: Hubbard played it as a hard bop barn-burner—a hard-hitting jazz waltz—with a touch of a whimsical gait; Lincoln reconceived it as a loping three with just the slightest touch of aggression, more like "Up Crouched Spring."

The remarkable nature of Lincoln's twin achievements can't be overstated. Since the fifties, nearly all jazz singers have inevitably stuck to two kinds of material: overdone old songs and neglected old songs. The big exception is Abbey Lincoln. Apart from being the last of a sorority of great jazz ladies that extends from Billie Holiday to Betty Carter, Lincoln is the only artist to effectively make the point that the jazz singer's repertoire is a living, breathing organism. She provided us with a thrill taken for granted in other genres but virtually nonexistent among jazz vocalists: We eagerly anticipated her new releases not least for the excitement of hearing her new compositions. A telling indication of how impressive her originals are is that they're frequently taken up by other singers.

Abbey Lincoln was born Gaby Wooldridge on August 6, 1930, in Chicago, and she grew up in Kalamazoo, Michigan. Her first important gig seems to have been a two-and-a-half-year stint in Honolulu. Upon returning to the States, she settled in Los Angeles, where she met Max Roach, then on the brink of forming his famous quintet with Clifford Brown, and worked as what they used to call a "production singer" in a stage show at a nightclub called the Moulin Rouge. While trying to establish herself as a solo artist, she came to the attention of Bob Russell, the gifted lyricist who had written words to Duke Ellington's most successful popular songs and who was at this time trying to establish himself as a talent agent. Between Lincoln's looks and talent—she seems to have started using the emancipated name of Abbey Lincoln at this time—and Russell's connections, things started happening for her. She headlined at Ciro's, she appeared on Oscar Levant's talk show (what I wouldn't give for a YouTube of that), and she had a guest appearance in the Hit Parade–oriented movie musical *The Girl Can't Help It.*

It should be noted that Russell wasn't interested in molding her as a jazz singer, à la Fitzgerald or Vaughan, but rather, following the example of impresario-coach Phil Moore, as a black pop singer and nightclub headliner in the vein of Lena Horne and Dorothy Dandridge. This approach is reflected in *The Girl Can't Help It,* in which she sings a very Hollywoodized treatment of a traditional gospel song. Profiles of Lincoln invariably mention the skintight red dress she wore in the film—which was supposedly also worn at some point by either Jayne Mansfield or Marilyn Monroe.

Still, Lincoln's one album for Liberty, *Abbey Lincoln's Affair,* is more than a fashion statement. Three superior West Coast–based jazz arrangers—Jack Montrose, Marty Paich, and Benny Carter—supplied the orchestrations, and both the woodwind and the string charts are thoroughly straight-ahead, if not swinging. All the songs are first-class, especially the roughly half that contain lyrics by Russell, who, in addition to managing Lincoln's career, produced the album (under the pseudonym Russell Keith) and wrote a new title song for the package as well as the liner notes. "You know why I chose the songs I did?" Lincoln once asked me. "Because my manager had written all of them." The most interesting of these is an obscure Russell lyric to the Ellington instrumental "Warm Valley." Liberty did try recording a pop single with Lincoln, a forgettable entry called "The Answer Is No," but they thought better of it, and this song lay unissued until forty years later when it surfaced as a bonus track on the CD release of *Affair.* Throughout all the tracks of *Affair,* Lincoln already sounds like Lincoln: That precise, dark-hued sound and hypnotic timbre are already in place, and so is some of her phrasing. She's already starting to think *slow*—for the rest of her career rarely did swingingly fast up-tempos—even if it's not exactly the same kind of slow she would perfect later on.

She talked to the *New York Times*'s Peter Watrous in 1996 about *The Girl Can't Help It.* "I hated that dress, and everything it meant," she said. "Nobody had the courage to tell me it was wrong to do something like that except Max Roach, who said to me, 'Abbey, that dress isn't right for you.' All the attention that I was getting wasn't for my work; it was for the way I looked. I wasn't running for Miss America. I wanted to be taken seriously." She and Roach became romantically involved around 1957, married in 1962, and stayed together until 1970. Roach, the pioneering bebop drummer and a major bandleader for nearly fifty years, became the dominant philosophical and musical influence in her life, and as a Henry Higgins–like figure, he represented a 180-degree turnaround from Bob Russell. Where Russell wanted to package Lincoln for the white mainstream audience, Roach helped her to evolve into a highly politicized jazz poet. The three most famous works she participated in with Roach advocated both progressive politics and progressive music: *We Insist! Freedom Now Suite*, *Percussion Bitter Sweet*, and *It's Time* (the last featured a large classical choir along with Roach's quintet and Lincoln), although the lesser known *Moon Faced and Starry Eyed* was a more traditional collection of standards.

These projects reflect Roach's ambitions more than Lincoln's, but at the same time, she was developing as a sonic auteur all her own who reflected the influences of both Roach on the left and Russell on the right. The concept of balance is, in fact, the guiding force on the milestone achievement of her early career, namely, the three classic albums she made for Riverside Records. Everything about these three— *That's Him* (1957), *It's Magic* (1958), and *Abbey Is Blue* (1959), all produced by Orrin Keepnews—is perfectly aligned: the balance between the dominant element, Lincoln's singing, and the band in the background, as well as between the ensemble writing and the horn solos, and between well-chosen standard tunes and newer material from the fields of both jazz (Jon Hendricks, Oscar Brown) and cabaret (Murray Grand).

To listen to these albums again fifty-plus years after the fact is to hear the beginning of many careers—not only Lincoln's. The three Riversides were so influential that they could be said to have started the ball rolling for Dianne Reeves, Dee Dee Bridgewater, and Cassandra Wilson (whose status as a leading contemporary jazz singer-songwriter was especially informed by Lincoln). In many ways, the signature of the series is "Afro Blue," which opens *Abbey Is Blue;* the song was written by Cuban percussionist Mongo Santamaría, and first recorded by him with vibraphonist Cal Tjader's band earlier in 1959. It was originally something more like a Latin impression of Africa, but when Oscar Brown Jr. added words and Lincoln sang them, it became highly African, set in a very fast, almost militant 3/4 tempo that could in no way be called a waltz. In more recent years, Reeves, Lizz Wright, and dozens of other singers have learned the song from Lincoln and recorded it, usually very early in their careers,

indicating that Lincoln exerted a significant influence on their work.

There's little else in the series that's explicitly African, but nearly everything is rendered in a way that carries an implicit message of liberation. The first album, the astutely titled *That's Him*, is particularly filled with traditional songs of female subservience—"When a Woman Loves a Man," "I Must Have That Man, "Happiness Is a Thing Called Joe"—which Lincoln turns into anthems of empowerment. Even the most politically extreme of these songs, "My Man" (introduced in France in 1916 as "Mon Homme"), which was famously sung as a lament with a heavy air of resignation by Fannie Brice and Billie Holiday, is delivered defiantly by Lincoln as a combination of a threat and a promise.

She offers variations on that idea in *It's Magic*, as in "'Tain't Nobody's Business," associated with both Bessie Smith and Holiday (Holiday was already an overwhelming influence on her work), a blues-based song which deals with gender rights in an almost perversely original fashion. She juxtaposes this with several American songs that affect a continental air—"I Am in Love" (from Cole Porter's *Can-Can*) and "Music, Maestro, Please." Somehow the idea of Lincoln as a jaded club-goer who tries to drown her sorrows not with another old-fashioned, please, but by having the bandleader play a succession of fast and snappy dance tunes seems especially ironic. It's even more so that she winds up with "Little Niles," Randy Weston and Jon Hendricks's African-style ode to parental responsibility. *Straight Ahead,* her 1961 album on the Candid label, also has much to recommend it, and had she never recorded anything after the three 1957–59 albums, she would still be remembered as one of the finest jazz vocalists of the era.

It would take a while for Lincoln to reemerge, but when she did her mature material was even stronger. Between 1961 and 1983, she would make only three albums (*Caged Bird, People in Me,* and *Painted Lady* aka *Golden Lady,* all done overseas). Her most significant achievement in the late sixties was co-starring with Sidney Poitier in the independent feature film *For Love of Ivy* (1968). In 1970, she separated from Roach and seems to have voluntarily entered into a period of personal and professional withdrawal: She left New York and moved to California, where she and her mother took an apartment over a garage. She kept singing, however, but strictly on a local level, and doesn't seem to have been noticed by anybody.

In 1981, Lincoln returned to New York, and two years later made what might be considered the first "modern" Abbey Lincoln album, *Talking to the Sun,* taped in New York City for the Dutch label Enja. In it, the Lincoln sound has almost finished developing, and the disc is also notable for the presence of emerging saxophone savant Steve Coleman. Her only other recordings from the eighties are curiously retro: *Abbey Sings Billie,* volumes one and two, were taped live at New York's Universal Jazz Coalition (I was there) in 1987. Lincoln had heard Holiday live in Honolulu around 1953, and as with Carmen McRae, Chet Baker, Rosemary Clooney, Ruby Braff, Johnny Griffin, and many others before her (and Tony Bennett after her), the idea of doing a collection of standards associated with Holiday is something she apparently felt compelled to work through. There was a lot of sonic similarity between the two voices, which increased as Lincoln grew older; *Affair* had already included two Holiday songs, "Crazy He Calls Me" and "No More," both of which were written by Bob Russell. Although Lincoln was given a fine quartet for the 1987 album, which featured veteran tenorist Harold Vick, this is not a distinctively Lincolnian project—it's just a good bop quartet with a good jazz singer in front of it. Lincoln is recognizable by her distinctive voice, but there isn't the aural presence that would be unmistakable a few years later.

If the two Holiday albums were a step backward, Lincoln was soon headed in the right direction. In 1989, she began a new arrangement with French producer Jean-Philippe Allard, under which her albums would be produced and released internationally by Polygram France and issued in America on the recently revived Verve label. The breakthrough release was *The World Is Falling Down,* taped in February 1990. Now, just in time for her sixtieth birthday, all the elements were in place: the characteristic Lincoln backdrop, the presence of heavy-duty guest stars, and a new commitment to original compositions. These achievements were consolidated in her major New York appearance in support of *The World Is Falling Down,* a 1991 concert at the Promenade Theatre. As she alighted on stage in a blaze of red satin topped with African dreadlocks, it was clear that she had merged both of her earlier identities—the high-glam cover girl and the cutting-edge radical—into a single sensibility, a unified outlook and vision.

Lincoln's best-known early lyrics were those to Thelonious Monk's blues "Blue Monk" and Freddie Hubbard's waltz "Up Jumped Spring." Like singing songs associated with Billie Holiday, this also proved to be a dead end—she was not a Jon Hendricks, whose mission was to pin words to melodies that already existed. Lincoln's strength was constructing music and words, and, more important, fundamental philosophies, from the ground up. With *The World Is Falling Down,* Lincoln established herself not only as a composer but a sonic auteur—you can tell an Abbey Lincoln record from anybody else's even when she isn't singing.

Although she was not at her best when dealing with the melodies of musicians like Monk and Hubbard, she was a master at incorporating the solo styles and sonic timbres of major players into her work, starting with Clark Terry and Jackie McLean

on *The World Is Falling Down.* Both of these jazz giants blend their sounds and their presences into Lincoln's overall texture—and the specific arrangements by bassist Ron Carter—deferring to her role as guiding force the same way they would with Gil Evans or any other great orchestrator, finding a perfect balance between their sound and hers.

On her two-song guest shot on Frank Morgan's *A Lovesome Thing* (also from 1990), Lincoln asserts her own authority without challenging Morgan's. Neither alters style one iota: The sly, modal-tinged alto and Lincoln are already two of a mind. The same could be said for Steve Coleman, who was the sole horn at the 1991 Promenade concert. In 1983, he was an unknown sideman; ten years later, Coleman was one of the hottest names in jazz, and it was clear that Lincoln was a primary inspiration for the young altoist and the other musicians in his circle, such as saxist Greg Osby and singer Cassandra Wilson. Both the album and the concert were unqualified triumphs. Though Lincoln may have pointed out that the world was falling down, in her assemblage of totally new sounds and structures she had already erected a better one.

Subsequent Lincoln-Allard albums continue the pattern established by *The World Is Falling Down,* stressing original compositions amid a fascinating array of guest stars. *You Gotta Pay the Band* (1991) spotlighted Stan Getz (the final studio recording, supposedly, by the great tenorist) and Hank Jones, while *Where There Is Love* (1992) is a collection of duets by Lincoln and Jones. *Devil's Got Your Tongue* (1992) and *A Turtle's Dream* (1994) feature a brace of guests, J. J. Johnson and Stanley Turrentine on *Devil's* (which also backs Lincoln with a children's choir on several numbers) and Roy Hargrove, Pat Metheny, and bluesman Lucky Peterson on *Turtle's.* On *Who Used to Dance* (1996) Lincoln works with tap dancer Savion Glover and three different alto saxists, while *Wholly Earth* (1999) teams her with mallet master Bobby Hutcherson. *Over the Years* (2001) recruits the tenorist Joe Lovano, one of the most imposing musicians of our era, while *It's Me* (2003) co-stars multireed player James Spaulding, whose sound is nothing if not distinctive.

Equally important, as we shall see, Lincoln continued to develop as a composer. There would be two or three really good Lincoln originals on every album—which is a fairly high batting average. Her songs have been picked up by such perceptive fellow vocalists as Baby Jane Dexter ("Throw It Away," "Painted Lady," and "I Got Thunder"), Kendra Shank, and Freddy Cole (who both did "Should've Been"). In fact, her compositions are, more often than not, the strong points of her mature albums. *You Gotta Pay the Band* and *A Turtle's Dream* are especially rich in outstanding originals. Each opens with a classic Lincoln anthem—the first with "Bird Alone," the second with "Throw It Away." Both also have excellent title tracks: She moves from using music as a metaphor for existence (a recurring theme) in *Band* to a contemplation of the universe from a shell-bearing reptile's point of view in *Turtle's Dream*. *Band* also includes the excellent title track and what she tells us is her first own recording of "Up Jumped Spring," while *Turtle's Dream* also has the amazing "Should Have Been." Each also includes one killer rendition of an offbeat standard, "Brother, Can You Spare a Dime?" on *Band* and "Nature Boy" on *Turtle's Dream.*

You'll note that none of the above tunes, whether originals or standards, is a song of romantic love. As Lincoln has said to me—and to virtually every other interviewer—"I like to sing about subjects other than a man and a woman—sometimes." Indeed, most of her originals are driven more by philosophy, as distinct from religion, than the boy-girl thang. She said that the motivating factor behind the 1994 *When There Is Love* was to do a whole album of love songs, seeing as there had been none on her immediately previous album, *Devil's Got Your Tongue.* *When There Is Love*, her set of duets with Hank Jones, is also Lincoln's only album in her last twenty years in which her original compositions are secondary. The lineup is almost entirely standards, and this package contains some of her best work in that area, such as a stunning reading of "I Should Care" with the verse, and "Can't Help Singing," a little-known Kern-Harburg masterpiece introduced by Deanna Durbin, and a "Nearness of You" almost as good as Sarah Vaughan's. She also bests another old friend on one number here: There's a treatment of Fats Waller's "The Jitterbug Waltz" that's superior to the one on *Dinah Washington Sings Fats Waller*, not least because this one has an improved lyric by contemporary Broadway pro Richard Maltby.

Who Used to Dance boasts five numbers by Lincoln (out of a total of nine) from the melancholy opener, "Love Has Gone Away," to the optimistic "Love What You Doin'" to the evocative title tune. All of these retain her trademark haunting, medium-slow tempos, reflecting the lingering influence of Billie Holiday (neither one of them was afraid of open spaces or silence). Of the four non-Lincoln songs, only one, "Street of Dreams," is the kind of American standard you expect to encounter on a jazz vocal album. There's Bob Dylan's "Mr. Tambourine Man," which may qualify as about the least likely item imaginable in this context. Yet the transmutation of unlikely material is the jazz singer's birthright no less than it is of her instrumentalist brethren. After all, as Lincoln once pointed out to me, Dinah Washington sang Hank Williams's "Cold, Cold Heart." (I rather think Dylan would relish that comparison.)

On *Who Used to Dance*, three individualist altoists, Steve Coleman, Oliver Lake, and Frank Morgan, submerge their own identities into Lincoln's musical vision. Coleman, for instance, has eschewed the contempop-hip-bop rhythms he usu-

ally prefers on his own albums, such as *Drop Kick*, in order to fit in with Lincoln's engagingly lumpy, rolling sense of the beat. The sound collage piece "The River" suggests that the saxist's use of this technique may have been partly inspired by Lincoln. The most surprising sideman is Savion Glover, who may be able to tap in *Da Noise*, but who convinced me for the first time that he can actually dance with grace, charm, and rhythm. Serving as pedal percussionist in the rhythmic title track, Glover shows that, in a Lincolnian context, he can swing. Who knew?

Lincoln's song "Wholly Earth" was the focal point of her live shows in the spring of 1999 and the title of her seventh Verve album. The lyric is suggestive of Wayne Shorter's *The All Seeing Eye* in that Lincoln describes planet Earth from what she postulates is God's own point of view. By now, all of her songs were focusing on philosophy (as in "Conversation with a Baby," "Look to the Star," and "Another World"), as expressed in a tightly crafted marriage of words and music. At the same time, she continued to interpret other folks' music, which is another way of saying incorporating other kinds of melodies into her stylistic universe. On *Wholly Earth*, she works this magic on "If I Only Had a Brain" (complete with verse) and the psychedelic imagery of "Midnight Sun" and "Mr. Tambourine Man"—all subjected to that familiar Lincoln rhythmic groove, which is sort of a chromatic half-step between 3/4 and 4/4 time— you might call it $3\frac{1}{2}$ time.

It's often reported that most jazz artists, singers in particular, have less impact on record than they have in person. Lincoln is an exception to that truism, especially since, as we have seen, she is keen to gather instrumental (and sometimes even vocal) guest stars and share the spotlight with them. *Wholly Earth* not only featured trumpeter Nicholas Payton and vibes master Bobby Hutcherson, but the latter amounted to virtually a co-leader, who gets almost as much microphone space as the star singer. Hutcherson primarily backs her on marimba, an older mallet instrument heard much more often in classical and world music, giving the group the exotic texture Lincoln needs for her blend of jazz and world music. Surprisingly welcome is a second voice belonging to one Maggie Brown, who helps Lincoln emphasize the title phrase of *Wholly Earth*'s opener "And It's Supposed to Be Love." Given its catchy hook and erotic imagery, Universal-Verve could have marketed "Supposed to Be Love" as Lincoln's breakthrough pop single.

In her early sixties, Lincoln was coming out with a new album every year—in 1992, she even released two, *Devil's Got Your Tongue* and *When There Is Love*. One suspects she was able to do this at least partially because she had a backlog of songs saved up from the many years when she wasn't recording at all. By the end of that decade, as Lincoln neared seventy, we were lucky to get an album every two years: *Who Used to Dance* (1996), *Wholly Earth* (1999), *Over the*

Years (2000), and *It's Me* (2003). (In 2007, Verve released *Abbey Sings Abbey,* a disappointing retread of some of her finest songs. If she had wanted to make a record without writing anything new, a new album of standards would have been a better choice.)

The new songs on *Wholly Earth* and *Over the Years* are especially fine, perhaps Lincoln's all-time peak as a composer: "I Could Write It for a Song," "Blackberry Blossom" (which opens with a duet between Kendra Shank, normally a vocalist herself but here playing flamenco guitar, and tenor saxophonist Joe Lovano), and "I'm Not Supposed to Know." On the 2001 set, the nonoriginals are also compelling, especially "Somos Novios" (the original Mexican title of the Perry Como hit "It's Impossible"), "Windmills of Your Mind," and Leonard Bernstein's "Lucky to Be Me." On familiar show tunes, Lincoln sounds more like a traditional jazz singer, who we are generally aware is interpreting someone else's work; on the songs by foreign composers, the opposite happens—Lincoln makes them sound so much like her own work that we tend to forget they had a life before her.

When first released *It's Me* seemed like a late-in-life statement: For the first time, she looked like an older woman on the cover, sporting glasses and letting a few wrinkles show. You can hear the wrinkles in her voice as well. She uses a string section for several tracks here (arranged alternately by the fine French orchestrator Laurent Cugny and the exceptional Alan Broadbent) for virtually the first time since her first album, which may indicate the closing of a cycle. The instrumental co-stars are James Spaulding on alto and flute and the wonderful pianist Kenny Barron.

Interestingly, for the first time in the Verve series, the Lincoln originals do not pull focus—there are two songs about the nature of music, "They Call It Jazz" (which must have been inspired on some levels by "Now They Call It Swing," which Billie Holiday recorded) and "The Maestro." It's distressing that the only word Lincoln can rhyme with jazz is "razz-a-ma-tazz," a phrase we might accept from Jerry Herman but not from Abbey Lincoln. She also uses musical references in "Through the Years," a song that sounds as if it belongs on *Over the Years.* Normally she writes about God better than she does about music or love, but here the most memorable original is the brief and to-the-point "Love Is Made."

However, the covers are outstanding beyond the call of duty. For any other singer, the title song, "It's Me," would immediate suggest a swinging, snappy Sammy Cahn–like rhythm song, such as "If you're looking for someone who loves you / It's me!" That's the kind of song that Nat Cole would have done. In Lincoln's stylistic universe, "It's Me" turns out to be her distinct adaptation of the traditional spiritual "Standing in the Need of Prayer" (coincidentally also recorded by Cole) aka "It's Me, O Lord." While Barron lays down major key gospel chords, Lincoln

interprets these with both rhythm and reverence. She also swings, convincingly and in the conventional sense, on the Roaring Twenties jazz anthem "Runnin' Wild" (in ABAB form).

Most surprising is "Yellow Bird," which most of us grew up with as a piece of folk-pop-Muzak. Lincoln, who doesn't sing the familiar pop lyric written by the Bergmans but a text credited to one Don Burgie, reminds us that the yellow bird hatched from an authentic Caribbean song. "Yellow Bird" becomes especially important in this context, considering that *It's Me* begins with a minor miracle, "Skylark"—Lincoln and the string section actually make this terminally overdone standard sound fresh and new. Both songs complete a cycle of Lincolnian ornithology that began with the 1991 "Bird Alone" and the 1999 "Caged Bird," which was inspired by the African American poet Paul Laurence Dunbar. Lincoln's best song of music and spirituality is the 1999 "Learning How to Listen," a song about getting in tune with one's inner self as well as the universe— "learning how to listen to the melody that flows." Yet this, too, brings us back to the high-flying metaphor: "Music is a lover / With shiny golden wings." Hope, it seems, is still the thing with feathers.

Lincoln released *It's Me* in 2003; it would be her last album in the classic Verve series. The same year, she was named a Jazz Master by the National Endowment of the Arts—one of less than a handful of singers to receive that honor. In 2007, two newly recorded retrospective albums of Lincoln songs were released, the singer's own *Abbey Sings Abbey* and Kendra Shank's *A Spirit Free: Abbey Lincoln Songbook,* a highly original take on eleven Lincoln originals. In 2010, Lincoln died, shortly after her eightieth birthday.

The always interesting material and the constantly changing array of guest stars and instrumental contexts combine to make Lincoln's gorgeous singing sound more arresting and incisive than ever. She was, with Tony Bennett and Rosemary Clooney, one of the most consistently satisfying vocal artists of the last two decades. Even in the audio-only medium of the compact disc, Lincoln seems to be looking you dead center in the eye as she sings.

Julie London (1926–2000)

A new millennium demands new gods. Twenty years ago, if you had asked me who the most influential female jazz singers were, I would have said, without hesitation, Billie Holiday, Ella Fitzgerald, and Sarah Vaughan. Yet lately, answers to that question provoke a wholly different response: The two most impressive contemporary singers right now, without getting into an argument, are Cassandra Wilson and Dianne Reeves, and the next two, especially in terms of popularity, are Diana Krall and Jane Monheit (although Monheit has been less visible in recent years). As Reeves once told me, speaking both for herself and for Wilson, the number-one influence on those two outstanding divas is Nina Simone. Equally surprising, although neither Krall nor Monheit would necessarily agree with this observation, it seems clear to me that the biggest influence on these two is Julie London. By virtue of the effect she's had on them, Julie London (who died in 2000) must be regarded as one of the most influential stylists of the early twenty-first century.

The "serious" pop song community, myself included, has been unjustly tardy in acknowledging London's status as an influential jazz-pop stylist. To be sure, even her biggest fans wouldn't rank her at anywhere near the level of Ella Fitzgerald, Jo Stafford, or Judy Garland. But she deserves to be taken seriously, perhaps not on the basis of her raw talent, but because she made several dozen first-rate albums, singing almost nothing but the best standards from the Great American Songbook.

Much of the reaction to London has to do with qualities beyond her musical ability. Her high-glam looks made her a natural for the LP era: The cover designers at Liberty Records, for whom she made all of her classic albums, were never at a loss as to what to use. Each album showed the drop-dead gorgeous *La Jule* in one amazingly sexy outfit after another, always looking like the dream date about to be chauffeured to the most expensive restaurant in town. Yet though these album covers have a pinup quality, there's nothing remotely pornographic about them; London's oomph-girl form is always draped in yards of shiny satin, acres of pink tulle, barrels of old lace, and absolutely no arsenic. The most notable departures to this rule—where we see more than the average amount of legs or cleavage— were made for purposes of camp humor, like the antiquated bathing costume on *Swing Me an Old Song* and the twelve sexily seasonal poses on *Calendar Girl*. The albums inside these sexy album covers are just as tastefully erotic as what's up front, and her singing leaves just as much to the imagination.

I am sure there are many who purchased *Calendar Girl* primarily for those twelve cheesecake shots of London, including that amazing shot of her as Miss September, gone fishin' and getting the hook caught on her little denim short-shorts, or that unbelievable shot of her as Miss July, wearing an Uncle Sam top hat and a two-piece red, white, and blue chorus girl outfit, balancing a enormous firecracker on her knee—not to mention holding an enormous phallic firecracker practically between her legs. And then there's London as Miss December, posing amid luggage in a red bathing suit with Kris Kringle trim, the very thing for sunbathing at the North Pole. Even if you bought the album for those very good reasons, when you eventually got around to playing it, you heard some very credible singing indeed, not to mention first-rate songs and orchestrations. Her sexiness never seems contrived or forced; it works because it comes off as extremely natural, unforced, and honest. It's who she is.

As you might predict from her album artwork, London does indeed have a very sexy voice and a very sensual singing style. She could hardly complain if anyone confused her with one of those tone-deaf glamour girls turned would-be siren. Apart from her looks, her gifts were modest at best: Although the voice was beautiful, her vocal range was minuscule, and she barely had any chops at all in terms of sustaining notes. On "It Never Entered My Mind" (on her hit first album, *Julie Is Her Name*) she apparently ignores Sinatra's famous rules about phrasing and breath control, and sings "and wish that you / were there again / to get into my / hair again." Likewise, on "The Lonesome Road," she barely has the lung power to sing the four notes of the title phrase on one breath. Yet London was a credible singer—a respectable middleweight, whose many albums are worth our attention forty to fifty years after the fact—both in spite of and because of her technical limitations. As she herself acknowledged: "It's only a thimbleful of a voice, and I have to use it close to the microphone. But it is a kind of over-smoked voice, and it automatically sounds intimate."

She was born Julie Peck on September 26, 1926, in Santa Rosa, California, and was raised in San Bernardino, where her family moved when she was three. The Pecks were performers who sang and danced in vaudeville and also, as is frequently recounted in biographical accounts of her life, were early pioneers on the radio. They had their own regular series (presumably on a local California station), and some of Julie's earliest performances were delivered as a precocious youngster on her parents' program. By fifteen, she was a scuffling hopeful in Hollywood, where she first found work as an elevator operator and was soon singing with a dance band led by violinist and composer Matty Malneck. She attracted the attention of budding actor Jack "Just the facts, ma'am" Webb and Sue Carol Ladd, wife of star Alan Ladd, who contrived to set London up with a screen test. With her looks and charisma, she had no trouble breaking into pictures, and started as a bit player in such films as *Nabonga* (aka *The Girl and the Gorilla*) and *Billy Rose's Diamond Horseshoe*.

Her career took a brief hiatus, however, when she married Webb in 1947 and began raising a family (she doesn't seem to have stopped entirely—her filmography lists about one entry per year from 1947 to 1951). In 1954, she and Webb divorced, and she may well have considered remaining a full-time mom until she met the songwriter and occasional pianist-singer Bobby Troup (1918–1999). A composer with several big hits to his credit, Troup also performed in nightclubs and acted in several films. If Webb encouraged her earlier acting career, it seems that Troup was the Svengali of her singing. They were married on New Year's Eve 1959. But well before then, she had become a star.

In 1955, London made a notable debut at the 881 Club in L.A., and soon after recorded four standards that eventually wound up on the Bethlehem label; this was around the same time that Troup was making two excellent albums of his own for Bethlehem (*The Distinctive Style of Bobby Troup* and *Bobby Troup Sings George Gershwin*). Since she only made four sides for Bethlehem, the label, eager to capitalize on an asset, frequently reissued them along with eight tracks they owned by Carmen McRae. The eight sides McRae did for Bethlehem (also her first recording under her own name) are a decidedly mixed bag, and even though McRae was a better and more musical singer and a considerably more experienced musician, her Bethlehem sides are not up to the level of London's—which clearly illustrates the value of a superior producer-collaborator like Bobby Troup.

London's four tracks include two well-known standards, "Foggy Day" and "Don't Worry 'Bout Me," the slightly more obscure "You're Blasé," and a modern but very sensitive arrangement of the traditional "Sometimes I Feel Like a Motherless Child," which she makes sound more like an earthy folk song than a spiritual. In every respect—the repertoire, the accompaniment, and the singing itself, soft and understated—the Bethlehem date is a pilot session for London's subsequent career as an album-driven artist.

London and Troup had the chance to make a full-length album just a few months later when they went to work with another independent label, Liberty, which had been founded a few months earlier in 1955. Liberty apparently let them do whatever they wanted, and Troup took the idea of intimacy several steps further. From a quintet, they pared down to the most minimal accompaniment imaginable: just a guitar (Barney Kessel) and bass (Ray Leatherwood). By doing this, they were cleverly taking advantage of the new possibilities of the 12" LP. The very idea of recording a low female voice with just bass and guitar is the kind of thing that could have been done only with difficulty in the 78 era, and which worked so much better with the improved dynamic and frequency range of tape recording and microgroove reproduction. Secondly, but even more obviously, the 12" LP made it possible for every London album to advertise itself with a stunning, four-color miniposter of the toothsome vocalist herself.

The first album, *Julie Is Her Name*, launched the London album series with a bang, thanks to what would be her biggest hit, "Cry Me a River." With words and music by Arthur Hamilton, "River" seems like a highly original variation of the archetypal torch song, "I Cried for You," updated to sound slinkier and more erotically minor-key. The song put London—and with her, Liberty Records—on the map in a big way. She was even featured singing it in the movie *The Girl Can't Help It* (holding her own amid a plethora of bombshells that also included Jayne Mansfield and Abbey Lincoln). Featuring eleven well-chosen standards ("River" was the only new song), *Julie Is Her Name* (according to some contemporary accounts) quickly sold three million copies.

In retrospect, it seems amazing that, fine as the song, the singing, and the arrangement were, "River" could have caught on. In 1955, rock 'n' roll was taking over the singles market, and even the hits of Cole, Bennett, and Sinatra (like "Learnin' the Blues" and "Hey Jealous Lover") were loud and boisterous. "River," on the other hand, was both intimacy and simplicity itself: One single slow chorus of words and music, then a brief guitar interlude with Barney Kessel playing a repeat of his guitar intro, and then London returns to reiterate the title phrase several more times over a board fade. (By which I mean a fade created by the engineer—the singer and the accompaniment didn't actually get softer and softer in the studio.) The mood is torchy and personal, as London suggests, but this was also as close as a female singer had come to achieving the Sinatra ideal of sounding vulnerable yet tough, even aggressive, at the same time.

This would be the one and only song associated with Julie London, though virtually all her records are, at the very least, well-crafted "concept" presentations; there's always a consistent mood and atmosphere, and quite often a thematic concept as well. She's generally able to sustain our interest, despite her narrow range of notes and tempi—she rarely sings anything really fast (although many of the tracks on *Whatever Julie Wants*, 1961, are an exception).

The bulk of songs on London's LPs are standards from the Great American Songbook, Kern, Porter, Berlin, et al. She sang almost nothing but superior songs, almost always in a way that was straightforward and organically sexy. Although from a distance London seems like the archetypal nightclub singer from a fifties crime or war movie, there's nothing generic about her. Her singing is at times reminiscent of Doris Day (on up-tempos such as "S'Wonderful" on the original *Julie Is Her Name*), and like Anita O'Day on her more toasty, sultry numbers (like "Makin' Whoopee" on *Your Number Please . . .*), and here and there like Peggy Lee and June Christy as well. The 1956 *About the Blues* was the album that accompanied her with what sounded most like big swing band orchestrations, although here the writing of arranger Russell Garcia sounded remarkably close to that of Stan Kenton and Pete Rugolo.

Julie Is Her Name Vol. 2 was every bit as good as the first, especially "Blue Moon," where she boasts a Doris Day–like timbre and several well-handled tempo changes. There are a couple of worthy obscurities in "Too Good to Be True" and "Hot Toddy," a very soft yet not Frank-ly tragic "Spring Is Here," plus a nicely defiant "Goody, Goody" and a wryly ironic "The One I Love." One of her better later albums, *Nice Girls Don't Stay for Breakfast* (1967), as orchestrated by bassist Don Bagley, emphasizes string bass and guitar over a light string background in a manner that anticipates Krall's *The Look of Love.* On "When I Grow Too Old to Dream" and "I've Got a Crush on You" she shows that slow tempos can be not only sexy but swinging.

Whatever Julie Wants (1961) is a thematic collection of twelve songs of coy seduction, with London looking fetching in a lush mink (wearing who knows what underneath), clutching jewelry, banknotes, and champagne. Yet even here, she never quite crosses the border into camp, finding instead lightly swinging humor in songs like "Hard Hearted Hannah" in which she sings of a man-eating siren in the third person, not necessarily making herself into one. She's also perfectly attuned to the comic nuances of "Take Back Your Mink" (from *Guys and Dolls*), even deliberately hitting a few flat notes for comic emphasis on the phrase "flat as all that." *Whatever Julie Wants* also provided her with the long-awaited opportunity for her to sing Troup's first hit as a songwriter, "Daddy," which was introduced in 1941 but sounds as if it were written expressly for her.

Arranged by Pete King, the 1963 *Love on the Rocks* is a subtly orchestrated collection of torch and saloon songs: "Willow Weep for Me," "A Cottage for Sale," "Guess Who I Saw Today" (done as much seductively as ironically), and two newbies entitled "Where Did the Gentleman Go?" and "Love on the Rocks." *About the Blues* (1957), with the underappreciated Russ Garcia, is precisely that, especially on her husband's "The Meaning of the Blues." *Send for Me* (1960) could be viewed as a sequel (it could be titled *About the Blues II* or even *More About the Blues*), with such Basie-based material as "Evenin' " and "Every Day (I Have the Blues)" and Lunceford's "Cheatin' on Me" and " 'Tain't What 'Cha Do (It's the Way That 'Cha Do It)."

While the above three are lush and stringy, there are also more jazzily backed packages, including three that heavily feature the superb pianist Jimmy Rowles in various capacities. He's officially credited as conductor on *Julie* (1958) and on *Swing Me an Old Song* (1959) and was probably responsible for the bulk of the less-formal arrangements played by the jazz sextet that backs her on the wonderfully loose *Julie . . . at Home* (1960). The two larger ensemble albums are definitely of a piece, with *Old Song* taking material from the turn of the century up through the twenties and *Julie* focusing on songs from the twenties to the forties. The idea of filtering archaic material through London's sex-kitten persona (not to mention modern swinging rhythms) could, again, potentially lead to camp, but rather than taking the long way around to avoid this, London and Rowles confront it directly. The use of a male chorus—voiced like a hip barbershop quartet—contributes to that quality; however, both

participants quickly diffuse it with their coolness, London with her understated attitude, and Rowles with the California cool textures of the ensemble.

Both *Swing Me an Old Song* and *Julie* are high in jazz elements, particularly a reed player (probably Bud Shank) who seems to be doubling on alto and flute throughout, while on "Indiana," it seems to be Shank playing a baritone sax solo. *Julie . . . at Home* is better still, showing that somewhere between the lushness of the big string albums and the minimalness of the guitar and bass, London shines especially brightly in a jazz context using a full, George Shearing–like five-piece rhythm section. All three of the Rowles albums make the point that London could have earned the credentials to be considered a jazz singer had she wanted to compete in this area. I've certainly heard a lot of self-described "jazz singers," especially in recent decades, who are significantly less swinging and musical than London is throughout these three packages.

All Through the Night served a double purpose in being her only songbook album (Cole Porter) as well as a meeting with Shank (doubling on alto and flute again) and his quintet. Guitarist Joe Pass comps especially nicely behind London on the only slow sexy ballad version of "At Long Last Love" that I've ever heard. "My Heart Belongs to Daddy" is sexy and swinging even in 5/4 time.

London was highly productive—certainly enough so to qualify as one of the more solid middleweights of the era, releasing nearly thirty albums between 1955 and about 1969. The majority of these are collections of sultry standards on the subject of loving and losing, most typically *London by Night* (1958, with Pete King). This is an especially classy album, perhaps to counterbalance the questionable cover (Julie as a hooker—why did the Troups go along with that idea?); it's highlighted by Troup's own terrific "Just the Way I Am" and "Well, Sir." The latter is the couple's own contribution to the classic torch song literature. In the spirit of "Angel Eyes" and "Something Cool," this is a lyric that presents itself as half of a barroom conversation, one which seems tailor-made for London and in which she's completely believable, and which poignantly establishes that surface glamour is no guarantee against heartache.

Your Number . . . Please (1959) is themed to songs associated with the great male singers, in her only collaboration with André Previn. London's third album, *Calendar Girl* (1956), arranged by Pete King, is a distraction if not a disappointment. For the only time, the musical content was actually driven by the cover, with one song for every month of the year. The good standards, such as "I'll Remember April" and the neglected "Memphis in June" and "Sleighride in July," are up to London's usual high-level mainstream pop, even with the presence of an unnecessary male choir on "June in January." But somehow they ran out of songs—they should have fired their researcher—

and had to commission new monthcentric songs for at least half the year. Although they contacted such classy writers as Arthur Hamilton, Dory Langdon (not yet Mrs. Previn), and Bob Russell, not one of the new songs is the least bit memorable.

More than many of her colleagues, London maintained a high level of quality and taste in her work up through the late sixties. *The End of the World* (1963), one of her few albums of contemporary (as opposed to standard) material, is actually a lot better than it had to be. This is an "Other People's Money" album (like Sinatra's *It Might as Well Be Swing* and Nancy Wilson's *Today, Tomorrow, Forever*, and practically every album by Andy Williams) of cover jobs of recent hits by other artists.

Nice Girls Don't Stay for Breakfast (1967) is a classy offering from way late in the game. It's almost as if Liberty realized that London couldn't beat the rock 'n' rollers and decided to let her keep on doing what she did best: subtle and lightly swinging treatments of standards, e.g., "When I Grow Too Old to Dream." Once in a while the organ gets too funky, lousing up "Baby Won't You Please Come Home," but overall it's a remarkably unsullied production. Further, London also takes two classic slices of Disneyana and gives them an R rating: the "Mickey Mouse Club March" (the ending version) as a closer, which she transforms into something as affecting as "Ev'ry Time We Say Goodbye," and her sensual treatment of "Give a Little Whistle," which owes less to *Pinocchio* than to Lauren Bacall in *To Have and Have Not*.

Yet even London succumbed to the Dark Side of the Force: One of her very final albums, *Yummy, Yummy, Yummy*, had her covering bubblegum pop like the title hit by the Ohio Express, "Light My Fire," "Stoned Soul Picnic," and even the Bob Dylan–Manfred Mann hit, "The Mighty Quinn (Quinn the Eskimo)."

London more or less stopped recording by the start of the seventies. The Troups weathered the decade safely thanks to regular roles on the long-running TV series *Emergency!* This was a family show and a family affair: She played Nurse Dixie McCall and he was Dr. Joe Early, and the entire clambake was produced by her first husband, Jack Webb. The show lasted six seasons, 132 episodes, and was a big hit in syndication. As Billy May, who scored background music for some of the episodes, once told me, "That fucker's still selling peanut butter somewhere at three in the afternoon!" Her last recording was a special version of "My Funny Valentine" taped for the sound track of the Burt Reynolds movie *Sharkey's Machine* in 1981. Troup lived to the age of eighty before dying in 1999, and London died at seventy-four one year later, on October 18, 2000.

London offered proof that taste and class can be as valuable to a performer as raw talent, especially when combined, as in her case, with an extra helping of visual appeal. The taste exhibited on her albums (much of which has to be hers—not everything that's good about her music can be attributed to Troup and the various arrangers and producers) is more than in inverse ratio to the size of her voice. I've compared her singing to that of Doris Day at several points, but in one key aspect, the two singers are precisely opposite. Day was a great singer who was too often given lousy songs and backgrounds and only rarely allowed to function at her best; London, by contrast, was a second-tier vocalist who routinely made excellent albums precisely because she worked with sympathetic producers who gave her excellent songs and suitably excellent accompaniment. Blessed with minimal chops and technical ability, she nonetheless made some of the better pop-jazz vocal albums of the early LP era. She was more than a pretty face, a pretty body, or even a pretty voice.

M

Dean Martin (1917–1995)

Never treats me like a gentile . . .
—Dean Martin, singing the opening line of Duke Ellington and Paul Francis Webster's "I Got It Bad (And That Ain't Good)"

The most talked-about celebrity biography of 1992, Nick Tosches's *Dino: Living High in the Dirty Business of Dreams,* didn't even get mentioned that year in *The New York Times Book Review.* The *Times* somewhat atoned for that oversight by commissioning Tosches to write an "Arts and Leisure" think piece after Dean Martin's death on Christmas Day 1995; it was *fortuna* that the ultimate party animal somehow checked out on a day when everybody was celebrating. However, it doesn't take Sherlock Holmes to figure out why the paper of record saw fit

to overlook Tosches's full-length opus on Rat Pack existence. It wasn't merely that too much of the book was in Italian or even, to use an archaic euphemism, the kind of "French" that generally has to be pardoned. What the *Times* probably objected to was the author's attempt to tell Martin's story from an interior point of view, his use of a stream of consciousness that purported to reflect what his subject was actually thinking at every stage of his life. The author's outrageousness and his extremely thorough research combined to produce the kind of book that resists being put down, even if the copious sources listed in the appendix would seem to be at odds with the notion that Tosches had created some kind of a reality-inspired novel.

It's also one of the most entertaining showbiz books I've ever read. Still, it concentrates on Martin's personal life and his films, giving his musical career third priority at best. In reaching this conclusion as an author, Tosches is elaborating on what he concludes is the central tenet of Martin's existence—that it was his lifestyle and personality that made him an icon, and that the actual work itself was merely secondary. Martin's greatest achievement was not his body of work, it was himself.

The most quotable line Tosches extracts from Martin is "I hate guys that sing serious," uttered during a nightclub appearance at the Riviera, Las Vegas, in December 1971, so to study Martin's canon as if he were a "serious" singer may well be to miss the point. Yet there's a lot to be said about his music. Despite the singer's own attempts to dissuade everyone from taking his work the least bit seriously, he turns out to be, in retrospect, one of the major popular singers of his generation.

Bing Crosby once described Perry Como as "the man who invented casual," although that term applies more accurately to Bing himself. Still, neither Crosby nor Como had anything on Martin in the casual department. Before Martin, pop singers may have been relaxed, but Martin brought "casual" to new heights of alcoholic insouciance. He blurred the distinction between the merely cool and the totally indifferent. Martin was casual almost to the point of unconsciousness, projecting the idea that he never had to put the least effort into his work; that he could just fall out of bed in his immaculately pressed tuxedo, roll toward the microphone, and open his mouth—and not even have to stay awake long enough to get through a whole chorus. Does it matter if this was actually true—that Martin really couldn't care less—or if it was all carefully calculated showmanship? No more than it matters whether Martin really was as much of a lush as he wanted audiences to think. Tosches repeatedly invokes the Italian concept of *menefreghista*—of being simply incapable of giving a damn.

He was born Dino Paul Crocetti on June 7, 1917, in Steubenville, Ohio, a first-generation American. Steubenville was foremostly a steel mill town, but it was just as much in the business of entertaining its hardworking metal-helmet men with nightclubs, bars, gambling houses, and brothels. As a young man, Dino realized that there were ways to get by without having to follow the traditional route: hard work, first in the classroom, then on a job. Deciding he was smarter than his teacher, he quit school at the age of ten, and as a teenager worked in gambling halls and, briefly, as a professional boxer. He was singing professionally by 1934, with such local bandleaders as George Williams (at Craig Beach, Ohio), Ernie McKay (Columbus), and Sammy Watkins (Cleveland).

Later in life, Martin acknowledged that his two biggest influences were Bing Crosby and Harry Mills of the Mills Brothers, whose long legato lines anticipated Sinatra's. In movies like *Pennies from Heaven* and *Blue Skies*, Crosby plays a carefree troubadour—a character directly in opposition to the role model of the typical American males of the Depression and war years, who were told that to beat the wolf at the door and the Nazis, they had to knuckle down and be responsible and hardworking. Crosby's character is more like that described in the Italian folk song "The Happy Wanderer," who travels around from town to town with a song in his throat, a smile on his lips, and not a care in the world. Dean Martin would take that idea several steps further: Not only couldn't he be bothered to hold down a job, he wouldn't even stay awake or get sober. He wouldn't even put any effort into partying. He would make himself into the Antichrist of bourgeois respectability and responsibility.

The earliest recording by Dino Crocetti that's known to exist is a demo of "I Surrender Dear" (not coincidentally, one of Crosby's first hits), probably recorded in Ohio in the late thirties, done well before the singer changed his name or his nose. Martin sings the main melody à la Crosby, while behind him a four-part vocal group harmonizes the tune in an arrangement that owes much to the Millses. The backup singers sound as if they could be Martin himself, via overdubs, which was a rare practice before the advent of recording tape, but which was certainly technologically feasible.

In 1943, Martin hit New York, following Frank Sinatra at the Riobamba, but not quite cracking the big time. He sang all over town, landed a local radio show in the mid-forties, and screen-tested for MGM, but nothing much happened until he met Jerry Lewis. That was in 1946, when the twenty-nine-year-old Italian crooner and the younger Jewish comic happened to be booked on the same bill at the 500 Club in Atlantic City. The two started improvising bits together, and somehow they seemed to fit—before they knew it, they were a team. Inspired by Bing Crosby and Bob Hope, who reached their zenith in the war years, Martin and Lewis reinvented the Crooner-and-Stooge duo for the Age of Anxiety.

Martin later said, "Two of the greatest turning points in my career were, one, meeting Jerry Lewis and two, leaving Jerry Lewis." However, in the ten years they were together they became one of the biggest acts across the entire panorama of mass media—nightclubs and theaters, radio and TV (especially the latter), motion pictures and recordings.

Martin's first commercial waxings were made for a series of independent labels, Diamond, Apollo, and Embassy, in 1946 and 1947. Then in 1948 he was signed to Capitol, not on the strength of his earlier recordings but because of the boffo business he was doing with Lewis, and his first session for the label was as half of Martin and Lewis. A year later, they made their first of sixteen movies, *My Friend Irma;* their longtime producer, Hal Wallis, later said that no one ever lost money on an Elvis Presley picture, but he could have just as easily said the same thing about Martin and Lewis.

Jerry Lewis has been extremely generous to his former partner in histories edited by others—not only to Tosches but to Bob Waldman, who wrote the excellent documentary on Martin for the A&E TV *Biography* series (and in his memoir, *Dean and Me*, written with James Kaplan). In both these accounts, Lewis all but gushes with praise—how Dean was the whole act, how Jerry would have been nothing without him, etc. But Lewis's own compilations of highlights from the team's *Colgate Comedy Hour* appearances tell quite a different tale. There are three video compilations of the team's best television moments, all produced by Lewis and shown on the Disney Channel, and in all of them, Martin is even more marginalized than he was in the team's original films and TV appearances. By way of example, in one of Lewis's early post-Martin films, *The Geisha Boy*, his co-star is a rabbit named Harry Hare, and this rabbit gets considerably more to do than Martin does in most of their films together.

Martin later said that, out of necessity, the M&L films were 65 percent Lewis and 35 percent Martin, and that the only way he could grow as an actor was to get out of the partnership. Such a move was even more necessary to accelerate his growth as a vocalist. Nineteen fifty-six would seem an unlikely time for him to relaunch his career as a solo pop singer: He was pushing forty, and rock 'n' roll had already taken over the singles market. Yet even as his number-one disciple, Elvis Presley, was increasingly gearing his music to teenagers, Martin, in distancing himself from the childlike idiot-savant Lewis, was establishing himself as the most adult-oriented of pop stars. As the fifties gave way to the sixties, he exemplified how the older generation let loose, with a martini in one hand and a cigarette holder in the other, never seen in anything less than a tuxedo; always slightly buzzed if not totally *umbriago*.

Martin remained somewhat relevant to the younger generation, however—some kids must have thought he was Elvis's Italian uncle. Indeed, all three Rat Packers—Sinatra, Sammy Davis, and Martin—would consistently hit the charts in the age of flower power. Martin was gradually introducing a kiddie pop element to his music in such singles as "Let's Be Friendly," and 16th-note-based quasi-rock, as on "Just Kiss Me"—in fact, he did both at a single session in August 1956.

If you take Martin's usual singing and apply a little more vibrato to it, you end up with something that sounds suspiciously like Elvis. Founding father Bing himself did this in a patter chorus on his 1950 hit "Sunshine Cake," as did the Four Freshmen in their atrocious version of "Mood Indigo." For much of his career, Martin also predicts Presley—and when his producers started giving him rock 'n' roll-ish backgrounds after "Memories Are Made of This," it was hardly surprising that he should appeal to the Presley market.

Presley admitted trying to copy Crosby in his most musically successful early ballad, "Love Me Tender," and "It's Now or Never," based on the old Italian folk song "O Sole Mio" (which both Dean Martin and Tony Martin had sung as "There's No Tomorrow"), marks Presley's most Dinoesque performance. Martin would later spend most of the sixties in pseudo-Nashville, under the guidance of producer Jimmy Bowen, a onetime Elvis-inspired rockabilly singer who had graduated to producer and who would later make his mint in Christian rock. It's worth noting that around the same time as the initial "Memories Are Made of This," another hit maker of an earlier era, the somewhat-folky Mitch Millerite Guy Mitchell, landed an immediate post-Elvis hit in 1956's "Singin' the Blues." Where rockers of the Nixon era (and later rappers) cursed and swore onstage, Tosches depicts Martin and company as uttering an unending stream of profanity whenever they're off it. Where the rock 'n' rollers wore leather jackets and tried to look like juvenile delinquents—and in more recent years evolved into gangsta rappers—Sinatra and Martin hung with real-life gangsters like Sam Giancana, who proved that not all menaces to society are hip-hoppers.

The Rat Pack experience has, on the whole, been greatly overstated. Although Martin and Sinatra were friends for forty years, the part of their career where they occasionally worked as a trio with Sammy Davis Jr. (and occasional hangers-on like Peter Lawford or Joey Bishop) was only a minor chapter in their careers. The collective is probably best remembered by their two films, *Ocean's Eleven* and *Robin and the 7 Hoods*—both of which boast ingenious twist endings. Despite their ideal of spontaneity, the Pack came off best when sticking to a script. Even their most carefully edited best in-person moment, a five-minute segment released as "The Summit" on Sinatra's 1965 *A Man and His Music*, is the only unlistenable portion of the Chairman's career compilation album.

In the mid-nineties, around the time Martin and then Sinatra went to the big saloon in the sky (and the original Sands was razed), there was a revival of interest in the Rat Pack, along with what marketing geniuses chose to repackage as "lounge music" and retro swing. In retrospect, most of the Rat Pack's surviving performances, when listened to in the sober light of history, are deadly dull. Like the Nixon tapes, the unedited reels of the Rat Pack tell the whole story. Two and a half hours of the Rat Pack in full flight, not in Vegas but at the Villa Venice in Chicago, at the height of the Kennedy era in 1962, were released in semi-under-the-counter fashion on the Jazz Hour label in 1993. Divided onto two discs, the first, which contains most of the music (and the least time of the threesome onstage simultaneously), is actually quite bearable—particularly Martin's segment—but the second is devoted almost exclusively to lame drunk/sexual/ethnic jokes.

At least in "The Summit," producer Sonny Burke deemed it more acceptable that Davis should be the one to deliver the ethnic (referring to Martin and

Sinatra as "jolly Neapolitans"), religious ("They sing good for goyim, don't they?"), and sexual (affecting a gay lithp) jokes. At the Villa Venice all three indulge in almost nothing but. (Martin's "Do you know how to make a fruit cordial?" is the *best* of them!) It isn't merely that you had to be there—I know people who were there who found the Rat Pack antics tiresome—you had to be drunk, too; in fact, the more you drank, the funnier the Rat Pack seemed. Perhaps their most noble accomplishment was increasing our admiration of Sinatra. He may not have been as funny as Martin or as animated as Davis, but as a singer he has them both beat by more than a mile—where Davis tries too hard and Martin not enough, Sinatra is the most keenly aware of when you should jump in an audience's face and other moments when you should play it cool.

But Martin was by far the funniest member of the Rat Pack in a way that Sinatra obviously envied. As good he was with Davis and Sinatra or Lewis, Martin was truly at his best by himself—and he was virtually the only major traditional pop singer whose forte was *not* the Great American Songbook; he did much better with ephemeral novelties than he did with Cole Porter. He preferred to use the great works of Broadway and Tin Pan Alley as fodder for his parodies (such as the immortal "You made me love you / I didn't want to do it / You woke me up to do it"). He was also, by and large, a much stronger singles singer than he was an album-oriented artist. Martin's best "concept" LP in the traditional sense was more or less his first, the 1955 *Swingin' Down Yonder*, a Dixieland set inspired by Bing and Bob Crosby.

This becomes obvious in the two most widely available compact disc anthologies of Martin's Capitol work, both of which were part of the mistitled *Capitol Collectors Series,* a collection of hit singles, and the *Spotlight on Dean Martin* disc, which is all standards. Martin proves himself the instant opposite of, say, Doris Day: His goofy little jukebox songs are superior pop music, whereas when he sings Rodgers and Hart or Gershwin he seems well aware that he can't compete with Frank or Ella. As mentioned above, he is much better in the smaller scale of the 45 rpm single, where he has to tell a whole story in three minutes, than on the more ambitious canvas of a full twelve-song, 12" LP. Most of the *Spotlight* collection is, in fact, culled from two albums, *Sleep Warm* and *This Time I'm Swingin'!,* and even though the former is conducted by Sinatra and the latter is arranged by Nelson Riddle, I would rather hear Dean Martin sing "Tona Wonda Hoy" or "The Sailor's Polka." The same material that would bring out the best in a Jo Stafford or a Steve Lawrence doesn't even begin to float Dean Martin's boat. ("Is that a U-boat?" "That's notta my boat!") He doesn't even sound perfunctorily romantic on many of these songs—he may be heading for the bedroom, but as album titles like *Sleep Warm* and

Dream with Dean indicate, it's only so he can sleep it off.

Martin's number-one strength is Italian songs—both real and ersatz; in all of American pop, there's no one who sings them better, with the exception of fellow *paesano* Louis Prima. His work with this material extends to a certain strain of American pop songs that depict foreign lands and cultures, though he doesn't go quite so far afield as the Chinese and jungle exotica that Peggy Lee sang. Martin's *menefreghismo* functions best when he stays closer to home with pseudo-Europeana—his songs of Italy spill over into similarly genuine and faux-songs from France (like "Relax-Ay-Voo") and the Spanish-speaking ("Belle from Barcelona," "The Peanut Vendor") world as well.

Martin's best music recalls the old joke about the drunk in an earthquake: The only time he can walk like a normal person is when the earth is shaking all around him. Martin is at his best in contexts that would make most straight-down-the-middle singers toss their tequila. For instance, Sinatra seems as if he's stooping to something beneath him in his few recordings in Italian, which were over with very early in his career; in contrast, Martin's Italianate items are the high points in his career. He's more convincing in that medium—the same way that Marlene Dietrich can sing in tune in German but loses her intonation in English.

In the classic mob movie *Donnie Brasco*, the title character (played by Johnny Depp) uses the Italo-American slang term *fugazi* to distinguish between a real diamond and an artificial one. Some of Dean Martin's Italian songs are the real thing, others are *fugazi*. Even so, when he sings a genuine Italian song, he often Americanizes it: One of his very earliest sides is "Oh, Marie," done in 1947 for Apollo with a small band led by swing saxophonist Jerry Jerome. Surprisingly, this is mostly a swing version of the traditional Italian song, with a Goodmanesque clarinet solo by Johnny Mince. Even though both choruses are in Italian, the first is hot and lusty, and as close as Martin ever came to making a jazz record, and even though the second chorus is much straighter, he sings it robustly and convincingly. It doesn't matter whether the songs are real or *fugazi*, or whether he sings them old-school or modernizes them in some way, it's the spirit of Italy that inspires him, not the specifics.

No other form could so perfectly have accommodated the specifics of Martin's chops. For a resonant baritone, Martin had a way of hitting high notes in something like falsetto, almost as if he were cracking through his range to emit endearingly squeaky sounds. In fact, on his second country album, *Dean "Tex" Martin Rides Again*, Marty Paich's arrangements make him sound suspiciously like pop's other great squeaker and rasper, Ray Charles, on the latter's *Modern Sounds in Country & Western Music* album (also orchestrated by Paich). With Richard

Rodgers such squeaks would sound inappropriate, although Martin makes them work on silly twenties and thirties baubles like "Who's Your Little Who-Zis?" (not exactly a standard) as well as on "An Evening in Roma," "Volare," "Buona Sera," and what sounds like a vocal flaw becomes a bona fide technique.

"That's Amore," a Hollywood hit (from M&L's *The Caddy*) by the Italian-American Harry Warren, is quintessential Dean Martin. The song had a revival in his lifetime, when it was used over the main titles of the hit 1987 film *Moonstruck,* and it perfectly set the mood for that Italo-American-themed romantic comedy. "That's Amore" has him bringing his massive sense of humor as well as all of his considerable charm to the fore, and his high-low voice never sounded righter. The very pasty, *Americano*-sounding chorus contributes, on some level, to the camp atmosphere, as does the *concertina* and all the men with those *mandolinos*. However, the climactic moment is breathtaking: just before the last chorus, Martin, in cahoots with the choir, relaxes, then ritards—like a pitcher winding up for a throw—and then just lunges into it.

Another Italo-American cocktail, "An Evening in Roma," is equally good. If there were an Italian-English equivalent of *franglais* or *spanglish* this would be it. The lyric cleverly offers words in both languages, translating as it goes along: "Down each avenue or *via* / Street or *stretta* . . ." Martin hits precisely the right tone and character, part affectionate, part leering, part lecturing, part wishing to participate himself ("On each lover's arm / A girl I wish I knew"), and how can you not love a text that rhymes "espresso" with "I guess so"? Both are exhilarating discs—and nothing less than classic American pop.

It's surprising, then, that Martin recorded only one all-Italian album, the 1961 *Dino: Italian Love Songs*—and it's particularly disappointing that he didn't cut an Italian set for Reprise, especially as he would do Latin-style collections for both companies. (He switched to the Sinatra-owned label in 1962.) He was almost as good with mambos and other Pan-American rhythms: It was Martin's recording of the Cuban "Sway" that inspired his younger Italianate disciples Peter Cincotti and Michael Bublé to sing the praises of those marimba rhythms more than forty years later.

Dino: Italian Style was, in fact, his farewell to the Italian format, his biggest and final statement in that medium. Yet it's not nearly as good as the various Italianate singles he'd been recording—nearly two dozen of them—over the previous fourteen years, from the previously mentioned 1947 "Oh, Marie" onward. Tosches is right when he claims that these earlier singles are considerably more powerful than the later album, and of the several songs he remade in 1961, particularly "Sorrento" (rendered with a different set of English words on the remake), the originals are superior. *Dino: Italian Style* also makes

a point of including only genuine Italian tunes, yet producer Dave Cavanaugh should have realized that with Martin the difference is strictly academic. In fact, with Martin the ersatz can have even more impact than the authentic; the *fugazi* are more meaningful than the real stones from Harry Winston.

Some of his ventures into other musical territories are equally rewarding. Martin's best French song isn't genuinely French at all, but "Relax-Ay-Voo," a glorious piece of ersatz by Sammy Cahn with a melody by Arthur Schwartz (they made a fine team) from one of the final M&L pictures, *You're Never Too Young* (1955). The movie version has Lewis, as usual, pulling focus with his spastic dancing, but the Capitol "Relax-Ay-Voo" is a Martin masterpiece, duetted with the charismatic French actress-singer Line Renaud. (*Dino French Style* should have been titled *In the Oui Small Hours*.)

The two Latin albums, *Cha Cha de Amor* (1961) and *Dino Latino* (1962), are also superior Martin, making the case that he's better at South American songs than North American ones. He sounds especially fine on the Brazilian "Amor" and "Let Me Love You Tonight," and there are also appealingly Latinized versions of American tunes. He also renders French songs, "I Wish You Love" and "Two Loves Have I," very expressively here with a Latin background. The *Cha Cha* album climaxes with the Yiddish "I Love You Much Too Much," which he puts over so convincingly and with so much chutzpah (not to mention *nachus*) that one wishes his next album had been *Dino Hebrew Style*.

Unfortunately, Martin had generally given up the Italian and other ethnic songs by the mid-sixties; by then his most consistently excellent and successful recorded work had a Nashville accent. His biggest songs of the sixties, like the simple and memorable "Houston" and the more complex "Little Ol' Winedrinker Me" (kind of a country "One for My Baby" with a shitkicker sense of humor), are first-rate period pop. Producer Jimmy Bowen cast him as the first Spaghetti Western crooner and Gucci cowboy, crafting a pop sound for him that was equal parts Texas and Brill Building, which the two of them also applied successfully to such older songs as "In the Chapel in the Moonlight" and "Everybody Loves Somebody," the latter generally regarded as his greatest hit and theme song. They don't approach the level of "That's Amore" and "An Evening in Roma," yet they hold up better than a lot of other hits of the L. B. Johnson years.

Within a few years of Martin's death, the German label Bear Family had begun producing a massive, four-box (thirty-two-disc) series covering his complete recordings. *Memories Are Made of This* contained all of his earliest work, including the Martin and Lewis years, while *Return to Me* covered the rest of his work for Capitol Records, 1955–62. (The first box is particularly valuable in that not only does it contain Martin's ultrarare pre-Capitol singles, it also includes a fair amount of sound track, radio, and transcription material.) Two additional boxes, *Everybody Loves Somebody* and *Lay Some Happiness on Me,* finished off the Reprise years and beyond.

In addition to Bear's complete studio recordings, several live recordings have been released since Martin's passing, most valuably two shows: *Live at the Sands* in 1964 and 1967 (the latter issued as *Live in Las Vegas* by Capitol in 2005). The difference between Martin's live and studio performances is overwhelming; it seems impossible that anyone could resist his personality and charm on these two live sets.

Martin's contributions to American pop music were so idiosyncratic that they're difficult to assess, and the comparison to his colleagues (like Sinatra), his influences (like Crosby), and his stylistic successors (like Presley) perhaps only adds to the confusion. Yet it would be a mistake to dismiss Dean Martin's music as mere cocktail kitsch. Just because it ain't serious doesn't mean it ain't art.

Mary Martin (1913–1990)

I find it ironic that Mary Martin's original goal was to make it in the movies. When Martin, who was born and raised in Texas, originally left her native Weatherford, it was to travel west to Hollywood, not east to Broadway. When she did hit it big on Broadway in the 1938 *Leave It to Me!* she followed this up not with another musical comedy on the Great White Way but with a short but busy film career. She wouldn't be seen on the stage again for another five years (and after starring roles in feature films). By that standard, her entire Broadway career was merely a consolation prize.

Yet by the time Mary Martin was finished, she had become perhaps the most exclusively theatrical of all Great American Divas. Even more than was true of the Mighty Merman, the magic Martin created on a stage was never reproduced elsewhere, certainly not in films. At least we have one movie—*Call Me Madam*—of La Merm at her best and in one of her classic vehicles, and through other appearances we can get at least a vague idea of what she must have been like in a theater. Martin goes down in history for creating the two most important female roles in Rodgers and Hammerstein—Nellie Forbush in *South Pacific* and Maria in *The Sound of Music*—yet you'll have to take the word of the critics (and listen to the cast albums) to realize how good she was. I don't say this merely to rave about Mary Martin, I say it because I cannot tell a lie.

The most valuable visual documents of Martin come from television. Merman wisely used the small screen merely as a vehicle for her considerable talents as a comedienne—she never had the chance to attempt anything as finely nuanced as her Mama Rose characterization in front of a camera of any kind. Martin, on the other hand, utilized television

as the perfect balance between Broadway and Hollywood, combining the intimacy of the one with the immediacy of the other. She took her *Peter Pan* repeatedly to television, and did it so successfully that even though James M. Barrie's character has been played in every medium from Barrie's original children's play to his print adaptation to silent films to animation, the character is permanently identified with Martin. Very nearly as valuable, if less widely seen, is Martin's 1957 television production of *Annie Get Your Gun.* She was one of the greatest of all Annies, easily outshooting the MGM Annie played by Betty Hutton (Judy Garland would have proven tougher competition), or Bernadette Peters or any of the Broadway-revival Annies of recent years.

Martin's career was all about bridging extremes, starting with her voice—a comfortable low soprano or high alto, roughly in the precise midpoint of the female range. Likewise, few other performers seem as ageless—as simultaneously young and mature—as Mary Martin. That may be because she never got to finish her childhood: She was an adult by age sixteen, the year when she married for the first time (she gave birth to her only son, actor Larry Hagman, two years later). She was equally ageless at the other end of her career: Not only did she keep working into her late seventies, especially on television, but she never quite seemed like anybody's grandmother.

Her finest achievement may well have been reinventing the classic character of Peter Pan for the postwar world. She played him with a warmth and believability that made both the character and the play more than just a simple exercise in nostalgia and nonsense for the Age of Anxiety. It seems almost beside the point that she first played the most famous boy in literature as a forty-one-year-old woman (who was just four years away from her first grandchild). Thanks in no small part to Martin, Peter Pan became the symbol of eternal youth, the boy who won't grow up (not he). Likewise, the name of the character Peter Pan has come to exemplify a state of pan-sexual ambiguity, not quite boy, not quite man, and never more successfully played than by a grown-up woman. It's hard to escape the conclusion that her other best-remembered roles— Nellie Forbush and Annie Oakley—are also sexually ambivalent, tomboyish women who do a man's job. No wonder no one could out-Pan Mary Martin— even down to her alliterative name: Who else could be male and female, young and old, alto and soprano, even Mary and Martin, at the same time? As Peter Pan puts it, "It's just that I am what I am, and I'm me."

She was born on December 1, 1913, in Weatherford, Texas; her mom taught violin and her dad practiced the law; her first husband (Larry's father) was a district attorney. She studied singing and dancing as a youngster, but (like Lena Horne) she interrupted her career to get married and start a family at a very young age. At the time that Larry was old enough to go to school, she began making the rounds in Hollywood, getting some work in clubs and on radio and doing screen tests and auditions for the various studios. Eventually she came to the attention of producer Vinton Freedley in New York, who'd discovered Ethel Merman (and put her in *Girl Crazy*). And again paralleling Merman in that Gershwin hit, Martin was given the big number in Cole Porter's *Leave It to Me!* and wound up stealing the show. After the success of *Leave It to Me!* Martin spent the next five years in Hollywood, where she starred in eight films.

In this first phase of her career, Martin was presented as something of a love goddess (not in the least bit androgynous), which is literally what she played in the 1943 *One Touch of Venus* (her second show and her first starring role). In *Leave It to Me!* she made her impact by singing "My Heart Belongs to Daddy," the Cole Porter classic whose modulations between major and minor paralleled Martin's fluctuations between Virgin and Venus. She sings "Daddy" in what accounts describe as a "mock" striptease, lascivious and innocent at the same time. "When I first sang 'Daddy,'" she later wrote, "it never entered my mind that it was a risqué song." Yeah, right! She reprised the innocent striptease bit in the 1941 movie *Kiss the Boys Goodbye*, in which she gradually sheds her clothing down to a bathing suit. Despite the title, the movie has nothing to do with the war in Europe or the draft. Rather, it's a song by director Victor Schertzinger (music) and Frank Loesser (lyrics), which is a pretty neat sequel to "My Heart Belongs to Daddy." Addressing her main squeeze as "Daddy," she explains that the other "boys" she's been seeing don't mean a thing to her, she's just kissing them goodbye before she marries Sugar Dad. Yes, she's always true to Daddy in her fashion. "My Start" (aka "That's How I Got My Start") is another mock striptease, with Martin sarcastically describing her fall from virtue in such a squeaky-clean way that the Hays Office couldn't possibly complain.

During her Hollywood years, Martin also established herself as a recording artist, if not quite a record star. She cut her first session, her two main songs from *Leave It to Me!*—"Daddy" and "Most Gentlemen Don't Like Love" (which she had performed with a bunch of other goils onstage, although she had the vocal all to herself on record)—accompanied by pianist and bandleader Eddy Duchin. From 1939 to the end of the war, she would record sporadically but exclusively for Decca, including the cast albums for *One Touch of Venus*, *Lute Song*, and her participation in a cast album of *On the Town*, although she wasn't in the original show. (The bulk of her 78-era waxings are included on the Columbia *16 Most Requested Songs* and *The Decca Years: 1938–1946*, reissued on Koch.)

For her first dates on Decca, producer Jack Kapp tried an interesting though unsuccessful idea: Kapp was a great one for diversity and unusual team-ups, and his first thought was to combine Martin with young bandleader Woody Herman. (Unfortunately, the only thing that they had in common was that they were both twenty-six.) Kapp tried to take advantage of her gender—and genre—ambiguity not only by combining with her the Band That Plays the Blues but by having her swing the classics, somewhat in the way Maxine Sullivan had done the previous year with "Loch Lomond." Martin and Herman used traditional and classical material—two oldish parlor songs, "Listen to the Mocking Bird" and "Who'll Buy My Violets," and two lite classics, "Il Bacio" and "Les Filles de Cadiz," rendering them first straight and then in swing time. The problem is that Martin doesn't do either of those things particularly well, being neither a swing jazz singer nor an opera singer. (However, "Les Filles" would be successfully brought into jazz by Miles Davis and Gil Evans, while "Il Bacio" would become the Spike Jones canine classic "Il Barkio.") None of these four cuts (which manage to be ersatz-jazz and ersatz-classical at the same time) was included on the *Decca Years* compilation, even though there was plenty of room for them.

In Hollywood, Martin was pleasantly paired with strong and mellow leading men like Bing Crosby (*Rhythm on the River, Birth of the Blues*), Dick Powell (*Happy Go Lucky, True to Life, Star Spangled Rhythm*), Fred MacMurray (*New York Town*), Don Ameche (as Lloyd Lloyd, in *Kiss the Boys Goodbye*), and even Jack Benny (*Love Thy Neighbor*). She was a perfect Crosby leading lady in their two films together: Like most of his female co-stars, she's a civilizing influence. He wants to wear mismatched socks and go fishin', she wants him to knuckle down and straighten up and fly right. Hilarity ensues.

In late 1942 Broadway beckoned, and she had two good offers on the table to return to the stage in musical shows written by veterans Vernon Duke and Richard Rodgers. For whatever reason, she chose Duke's *Dancing in the Street*, which closed out of town, over *Away We Go*, which became *Oklahoma!* However, she had a major hit of her own in her thirtieth year with *One Touch of Venus*, in which she was paired with tenor Kenny Baker, another singer known more for his work in radio and movies than on the stage.

At the time, Baker was best known for predating (and outsinging) Dennis Day as the star tenor on the *Jack Benny Program* (he later resurfaced as the juvenile tenor in *The Harvey Girls*). *One Touch of Venus* was one of two very successful Broadway musicals written by the German composer Kurt Weill, who, at different points in his career, was both the most experimental of European avant-gardists and the most melodic of Broadway tunesmiths. By the 1960s, with the posthumous revival of his Berlin-written *Threepenny Opera*, Weill's name itself became a selling point, but during the composer's short lifetime, he achieved his greatest success by writing for two legendary name-above-the-title divas, Gertrude Lawrence in *Lady in the Dark* and Martin in *One Touch of Venus*.

Originally the producers wanted Marlene Dietrich, who would have made a more characteristic Goddess of Love than Martin, as well as fitting in with Weill's Weimar background. Dietrich would never make it to Broadway (her inability to sing in English and in tune at the same time was undoubtedly a factor) except in her own one-woman shows. Martin, however, was a sensation as a statue that becomes inhabited by a mythological muse and comes to life. She introduced three well-remembered standards: "Speak Low," which became an instant jazz perennial, soon to be recorded by everyone from Glenn Miller to John Coltrane, and "That's Him" and "I'm a Stranger Here Myself," which were kept alive by the cabaret intelligentsia. (She also sang a lovely Weill waltz, "Foolish Heart," a song eventually overtaken by the superior Victor Young–Ned Washington "My Foolish Heart.") "That's Him" and "I'm a Stranger Here Myself" are particularly striking pieces of musical acting, hitting the same emotional notes Martin would later refine in her *South Pacific* triumphs, "A Wonderful Guy" and "I'm Gonna Wash That Man Right out of My Hair."

One Touch of Venus ran until 1945, and Martin's next Broadway success was not until *South Pacific* in 1949. But she was far from idle throughout the early postwar era. A year after *One Touch of Venus* closed, she was back on Broadway with the ill-fated *Lute Song*. This was a decidedly odd book show out of the post-*Oklahoma!* land rush for integrated story shows. Somehow producer Michael Meyerberg and director John Houseman were convinced that the next Broadway bonanza was this unlikely Chinese fable, which, from the descriptions, sounds as embarrassing as Katharine Hepburn wearing slant-eye makeup and trying to portray a Manchurian peasant girl in the dreadful film *Dragon Seed*. *Lute Song* had two saving graces, though: Mary Martin and the very capable score by two songwriters who neither before nor after came anywhere near Broadway, Raymond Scott, the bandleader and composer of offbeat, cartoony instrumentals (and, in the eyes of many, a genuine musical visionary), and record producer–lyricist Bernie Hanighen, who'd collaborated on several standards with Johnny Mercer and Thelonious Monk.

"Ah so!" Apart from all the chinoiserie, *Lute Song* was unusual in other key aspects, beginning with the show's very long three-act format. Rather than sporting a full cast of singing actors, virtually all the singing seems to have been done by Martin—who was occasionally joined by her own discovery, the future King of Siam himself, Yul Brynner, playing opposite her as "Tsai-Yong, The Husband." There was also a lot of orchestral music, but Decca only recorded six tracks from the show, two of which were instrumentals. Martin did a lovely job with the only song to survive the show, "Mountain High, Valley Low," whose strong minor key melody transcends faux-Asiana. The song turns up instrumentally on many a late fifties LP of so-called hi-fi exotica.

Later in 1946, the thirty-two-year-old Martin was called upon to relive her own past, reprising "My Heart Belongs to Daddy" in *Night and Day,* Warner Bros.' highly fictionalized biopic of composer Cole Porter. More often, however, she would be called upon to re-create other people's careers for various purposes. In 1943, Decca decided to do an album of the music for the hit show *On the Town,* but instead of doing a proper cast recording, they brought in the three comedy leads from the show—Nancy Walker and lyricists Betty Comden and Adolph Green—and had Martin sing the two major "serious" songs, "Lucky to Be Me" and "Lonely Town." She's very strong on both, though "Lucky to Be Me" is particularly non-Broadwayish, done in a chart that goes from medium fast into swing time. In the fifties, Martin would appear in other studio cast albums for shows she'd never otherwise had anything to do with, including *Girl Crazy* (in which she's convincingly laconic on "Bidin' My Time" and rousing on "I Got Rhythm") and *The Band Wagon.*

In late 1946 and early 1947, Martin ran for three months in another unsuccessful show, this one in London: Noel Coward's semioperetta "musical romance," *Pacific 1860,* which inserted her into another exotic setting. Neither side of the Coward-Martin equation (Coward's partner, Graham Payn, played Martin's leading man) was happy with the outcome, but she and the future Sir Noel would get together a decade later for a very successful TV special. That 1955 TV show, *Together with Music,* included Martin's last attempt at classical music, in a straightforward reading of one of the most famous of all operatic arias, the "Un Bel Di" from *Madama Butterfly,* during which Sir Noel rather ungallantly interjected disapproving commentary from the sidelines.

In October 1947, she got into costume for a third occasion in two years, but this time with considerably more success, in what would turn out to be her most famous secondhand role, Annie Oakley in *Annie Get Your Gun.* Dallas turned out to be a doubly appropriate spot for her to launch her association with that role: Not only was this her home state, but it perfectly suited the show's wild Western setting. (Irving Berlin even wrote a special chorus of "There's No Business Like Show Business" for Martin to sing in Texas.) She toured into 1948 in the American road company production, even as Ethel Merman continued to play Annie on Broadway, and was so well received in the part that she and Annie would be reunited even more meaningfully a decade later. This was also the first time she worked with Rodgers and Hammerstein serving as the producers, rather than the composers, of *Annie Get Your Gun*. In the long run, Dick and Oscar were actually delighted that she had turned down *Oklahoma!*, because her presence would have compelled them to rewrite it into a star vehicle for her.

Between 1949 and 1959, Martin would create the three central roles of her career — Nellie Forbush in *South Pacific*, the title character in *Peter Pan*, and Maria von Trapp in *The Sound of Music*. Ensign Forbush has the distinction of being virtually the only Rodgers and Hammerstein leading lady who's a career gal, or something other than a wife and homemaker. (Aha! I hear you say, But don't both Anna in *The King and I* and Maria in *The Sound of Music* work outside the home? Yes, says I, but their jobs are, in fact, taking care of children.) Perhaps because they were trying to create a believable working woman, a female executive type, they deliberately wanted a leading lady who was in touch with her masculine side, a tactic that came to a head in the cross-dressing number "Honey Bun," in which Martin pranced in male sailor drag. Surely no other Rodgers and Hammerstein leading lady (such as Jan Clayton, Shirley Jones, or Barbara Cook) could have pulled that off successfully, although Martin's Broadway replacement was the more conventional glamourpuss Janet Blair, who must have made a very different knucklehead Nellie (as was Mitzi Gaynor in the 1959 film). Likewise, the male romantic lead was the "cultured Frenchman" Emile de Becque (opera basso Ezio Pinza), a very different, less conventionally physical type than Curley in *Oklahoma!* or Billy Bigelow in *Carousel*. In fact, de Becque is the sort who would hire Curley or Billy Bigelow to do his heavy lifting for him while he sat around drinking French wine and reading Proust (and teaching his mulatto offspring to sing "Dîtes-Moi").

Coincidentally, as was true with Kurt Weill, Mary Martin and Gertrude Lawrence were the only name-above-the-title headliners to loom large in the Rodgers and Hammerstein universe. In fact, after their seven classic shows had been established on Broadway, none of the many revivals has been dependent on star power; the name recognition of the shows has been more powerful than that of anyone in the cast. Yet they provided both *South Pacific* leads, Martin and Pinza, with a generous supply of showstoppers, particularly for Martin: "A Wonderful Guy," and "I'm Gonna Wash That Man Right out of My Hair," in which she actually dumped water and shampoo through her tresses for six nights a week plus matinees—a bit of stagecraft that was as celebrated in its day as Peter Pan's magical flight.

Rodgers and orchestrator Robert Russell Bennett supplied some musical stage magic as well: Because Martin's voice was lower than most R&H sopranos, she was afraid that between herself and Pinza the show would be stuck with "two bassos" for leads. Thus there's no classic boy-girl duet like "People Will Say We're in Love" or "If I Loved You"; when Nellie and de Becque do get together musically, they don't so much sing together as sing around each other, in "Twin Soliloquies." Nellie is introduced with "A Cockeyed Optimist," in which Hammerstein employs whimsical metaphors more in the style of Johnny Burke or Yip Harburg.

South Pacific was Martin's greatest triumph yet ("Hers is a completely irresistible performance," the *New York Post* raved, summarizing the opinion of most critics). There were more minor successes in the next few years, such as a well-received nonmusical comedy on Broadway, *Kind Sir* (1953), in which she played opposite Charles Boyer. In the studio, Columbia's Goddard Lieberson had her record four albums of four classic show scores of the thirties: *Anything Goes, Babes in Arms, The Band Wagon*, and *Girl Crazy*. With *On the Town* a few years earlier, Martin had already shown how a single performer could do a substitute cast album all by herself— perhaps Lieberson thought that Martin was androgynous enough to be equally believable in songs written for both male and female characters. She was far from absent from the public eye—but her biggest blockbuster of all was just ahead of her, second star to the right.

Peter Pan is the central role of Martin's career, and as noted, over the last hundred years, Martin has faced a lot of stiff competition. The character, created by Scottish playwright Sir James M. Barrie, and known as "The Boy Who Wouldn't Grow Up," was already immortal. *Peter Pan* made his Broadway debut in 1905, with the universally adored Maude Adams, and there were many revivals going up to 1928, as well as one of the most elaborate of all silent film fantasies, in 1924. Pan seems to have been forgotten in the rough years of the thirties and forties, but returned just as the baby boomers were old enough to appreciate him in the mid-fifties. Pan and his colleagues were revived with a vengeance in the postwar era, when three very different treatments were produced within a few years—and the only thing the three had in common was that, for the first time, the Barrie story was now serving as the basis for a musical.

In 1950–51, a partial-musical version (with songs by Leonard Bernstein) made it to Broadway with Jean Arthur (then pushing fifty) in the lead and none other than Boris Karloff in the dual role of Mr. Darling and Captain Hook. (The show is a Freudian bonanza: Pan and the lost boys worship the very concept of "Mother," but Barrie, from the beginning, envisioned the father and the principal villain as one and the same role—a concept that predates the morphing of the farmhands into fantasy characters in the movie versions of *The Wizard of Oz*.) The Arthur-Karloff adaptation of *Peter Pan* had only about five songs, which also marked one of the rare attempts by Bernstein to write lyrics to his own music. Then, in 1953, Walt Disney unveiled his animated version, with a decidedly more masculine boy as Pan (not voiced or acted by a grown woman, as had been the custom since 1905) and a fine, full score by two multiple Oscar winners named Sammy: Sammy Fain and Sammy Cahn.

At roughly the same time the Disney studio was finishing its feature cartoon treatment, a pair of virtually unknown songwriters named Mark "Moose" Charlap and Carolyn Leigh—both of whom would have tragically short lives—were working on a full musical theater production of the play. This incarnation had its tryout in California, the land where people fly, and where director-choreographer Jerome Robbins insisted on beefing up the score by bringing in more practiced hands: composer Jule Styne and lyricists Betty Comden and Adolph Green. As a result, each songwriting team—Leigh-Charlap and Styne-Comden-Green—wrote about half the score. And if that wasn't enough, Hollywood composer Elmer Bernstein was recruited to supply "incidental music."

It turned out to be more than worth the effort: Between Martin's performance, the magical stage effects, and the efforts of the five songwriters, this is the best remembered of all *Peter Pan*s, the definitive musicalization of Barrie (you'll note that no one has come along and written another one in the last half-century). When people talk about *Peter Pan*, this is the incarnation they mean. The characters and the story are inseparably identified with such songs as "I Won't Grow Up," "I'm Flying," and "Never-Never Land," just as the characters and the story of *The Wizard of Oz* are inseparably identified with "Over the Rainbow" and "If I Only Had a Brain."

In 1905, Maude Adams created such an impression that she was still identified with the character fifty years later. Even before Martin and company started, *Peter Pan* was already an amalgam of British and American stage traditions, which Charlap, Leigh, Comden, Green, and Styne elaborated upon by setting the score in a wonderful variety of moods and tempos—mimicking Gilbert and Sullivan in the pirate songs, while Hook himself (Cyril Ritchard, the swishiest pirate in all pop culture before Johnny Depp) cavorts in tangos, tarantellas, and waltz time. "Ugg-a-Wugg" holds the record as the most gloriously politically incorrect of Native American love calls. "Mysterious Lady" is a surprise; cast roughly as a Spanish pasodoble (à la "Granada"), it allows Martin to parody a classical coloratura. Pan himself/herself fluctuates between playing Peck's Bad Boy and father and teacher to the lovable little scamps whom he induces to fly away with him/her to Never-Never Land.

As Pan, Martin embodies the very essence of self-esteem and human empowerment in "I've Gotta Crow" and "I'm Flying." No one could better personify the soul and spirit of Peter Pan than Martin in "I Won't Grow Up," refusing to put away childish things and clinging to bad grammar, and making the notes rise and surge on the words "never grow *uh-up*," thereby stretching the humble "up" into two ascending notes—notes that literally "grow up" before our ears. Her Pan still strikes resonant chords in audiences, not because of the man-woman or even mother-child thing, but by continually appealing to that little bit of Peter Pan in each of us.

In its first run on Broadway, *Peter Pan* played only 152 performances but, again like *The Wizard of Oz*, Martin-as-Pan became a television phenomenon. Martin and the original cast performed it live on NBC on March 7, 1955; five years later, she donned Pan's hose and fly-wires once again for the production that most of us know, which was made in full color and on videotape and was rebroadcast regularly from 1960 on. Between *Pan*'s two TV incarnations, Martin enjoyed still another teletriumph with *Annie Get Your Gun* in 1957. Having done the road company production a decade earlier, Martin, playing opposite one of the all-time most imposing Broadway leading men—John Raitt as Frank Butler—now took *Annie* to every medium between (but not including) Broadway and the movies: a sixteen-week run on the West Coast (Los Angeles and San Francisco), an NBC TV production, and an outstanding hi-fi Capitol album. Martin's Annie Oakley—"Peter Pannie Oakley"—like Nellie and Pan, also moved beyond traditional gender roles: She's the woman who can outshoot a man but eventually throws a match and accepts second-best position to marry him. (I personally prefer the revised nineties ending, in which the shooting match ends in a draw.) In either case, Annie thus breaks the jinx she had delineated in her opening scene: She can indeed get a man with a gun, but only when she suppresses her own talents with it.

It's been said that Martin is a more feminine Annie than Ethel Merman—which is kind of unfair. La Merm, blustery and brassy as she was, never struck me as butch. Could there be a more extreme way for a woman to prove her heterosexuality than to marry Ernest Borgnine? It would be more appropriate to say that Martin was both a more vulnerable Annie—"I Got Lost in His Arms" is probably the most tender song Irving Berlin ever wrote—and a more subtle one. Martin finds all the nuances Berlin wrote into "You Can't Get a Man with a Gun," which might be his cleverest piece of wordplay, proving that he was fully the equal of such specialists in tricky wordage as Noel Coward, Lorenz Hart, and Cole Porter.

In "I'm an Indian Too," Martin ran afoul of future Native American antidefamation leagues for the second time in three years. But though it may be politically indefensible, here Berlin and Martin rattle off the names of several dozen American Indian tribes in a manner every bit as clever as the way Ira Gershwin and Danny Kaye utilized the names of

Russkie composers in "Tchaikovsky (And Other Russians)," employing the names of "Chippewa, Iroquois, Omaha" for their sonic value, the tongue-twisting novelty of the way these names *sound*. (Blane, Edens, and Martin utilized the same idea around the same time for "Pass That Peace Pipe" in the MGM version of *Good News*.) Martin doesn't sing the verse to "I Got the Sun in the Morning" but uses the chorus like a verse, first slow like a ballad, then taking the second chorus in a rousing dance tempo. (The orchestrator isn't credited, but whoever he is, he supplies some jazzy big band dissonances in the brass voicings here.)

As Annie Oakley–as–an–Indian, Martin sings of having "three papooses on the way." The third papoose would arrive in 1959 (after Martin had appeared in a limited-run revival of *The Skin of Our Teeth* in summer 1955; this also was televised) and be titled *The Sound of Music*. This was the third project in a row in which she toted around a bunch of toddlers, following after the lost boys in *Peter Pan* and the brood of little brothers and sisters who help her do what comes naturally in *Annie*. It would also be the final blockbuster megahit for Martin, as well as for Oscar Hammerstein (who died shortly after it opened) and, surprisingly, also for Richard Rodgers. There are those who feel that history robbed Martin of this triumph by casting Julie Andrews in the 1965 movie version, but Andrews was not only younger and more European but more believable as a twenty-something Austrian novice-turned-nanny. In the vast scheme of things, the part of Maria does seem to belong more to Andrews than to Martin. The show cast the Jewish folksinger Theodore Bikel (an Austrian refugee like Von Trapp) as her lead, whereas the movie cast a Brit and a Canadian, Andrews and Christopher Plummer, as Teutonics.

The Sound of Music was fundamentally different from the six other widely successful R&H productions in the way it has been received by its audiences. The other six seem more like classic Broadway shows that were eventually filmed, and though these movies are loved by millions, they seem like afterthoughts—the stage productions are the meat of the matter, and are constantly revived, both on Broadway and regionally. However, *The Sound of Music*, in the eyes of the zillions of people who love it, seems more like a classic movie musical that went through an intermediate step on Broadway before arriving on celluloid. The film of *The Sound of Music* was so overwhelmingly successful that people essentially forgot the show ever existed and that someone else had actually created the role of Maria. It's seen relatively little attention on the revival circuit—there wasn't even a full-dress Broadway revival until 1998: It's as if no one wants to compete with the movie.

Yet Martin was by all accounts (and on the evidence of the Columbia cast album) marvelous as Maria, helping establish the story of the Von Trapp family singers, complete with nuns and Nazis, as one of Broadway's great musical vehicles. Her opening number, cavorting on an Austrian Alp, was, if not quite a Dionysian dance of ecstasy, certainly an exuberant celebration that instantly grabbed the audience and set the tone for the piece. *The Sound of Music* presented Martin with her greatest kids' songs, the solfeggioistic "Do-Re-Mi" (in which she teaches children to sing in a musical universe bereft of accidentals) and the story-song "The Lonely Goatherd." She also introduced what may be the most enduring jazz standard associated with her (along with "Speak Low" and "Never-Never Land"), Rodgers's evocative, minor key waltz "My Favorite Things." Andrews gained a few choice songs in the film production, "I Have Confidence" and "Something Good," for which Rodgers later wrote both words and music, but "An Ordinary Couple" and "No Way to Stop It," which were not used in the film, remains the property of Martin and Theodore Bikel.

It seems unfair that Martin's last triumph should be taken from her—especially since a few months earlier the film version of *South Pacific* had been released, with the more hubba-hubba Mitzi Gaynor as a suddenly sexy Nurse Nellie. Following *The Sound of Music*, Martin returned to Broadway in *Jennie* (1963) and *I Do! I Do! Jennie* was a quick flop, illustrating the failure of composers Arthur Schwartz and Howard Dietz to move from revues (like the classic *The Band Wagon* and *Inside U.S.A.*) to book shows (*The Gay Life*, with Barbara Cook, was another, but at least that had one great song in "Magic Moment"). *I Do! I Do!* was a two-character exploration into the magical world of marriage. It ran for more than a year and a half, but didn't present Martin with any of her great songs or moments, and it would be hard to include *I Do! I Do!* in a list of Martin's major career highlights.

Mary Martin was never regarded as one of the theater's great voices—unlike her friend Ethel Merman—but it was a combination of charm and chops that made her an essential presence. In the sixties and seventies, she enjoyed some reunions: There was a television special with her old Paramount co-star Bing Crosby, and a well-received joint benefit concert with fellow Annie Oakley Ethel Merman (their names were dropped together to humorous effect in the "Rin-Tin-Tin" number in *Bells Are Ringing*) in 1977. A year later she appeared briefly in a short-lived romantic comedy entitled *Do You Turn Somersaults?* She kept going, even after the death of her second husband and occasional producer, Richard Halliday, in 1973 and a dreadful taxi accident (in San Francisco) a decade later that all but incapacitated her. There were more TV appearances, including, as Martin neared seventy in 1981, a special that was announced as the farewell performance for soprano Beverly Sills. But Mary Martin herself never gave anything like a farewell performance: She remained a powerful presence on TV (even as her son, Larry

Hagman, found a genie and later became the most famously "shot" actor on the tube) and elsewhere until her death in 1990, as befitting a career that was always straight-ahead, second star to the right and straight on till morning.

Susannah McCorkle (1946–2001)

"Hi, it's Susannah." As if she had to say the name. Like Blossom Dearie, Sarah Vaughan, even Tony Bennett, Susannah McCorkle not only had one of the most distinctive voices of any singer, but a trademark sound that carried over into her speaking voice. You knew who it was with the first word—like Tony and Louis Armstrong, she had a slight rasp to her voice, a catch to it (sometimes even a cry that could be heard on an up-tempo number like "It's All Right with Me") that gave her immediate distinction. McCorkle would have made a terrible undercover agent—there was no way she could hide who she was. Or so I used to think. After she died, those of us who knew her found out that she was more adept at hiding things than we had ever imagined.

When the phone rang on the morning of Saturday, May 19, 2001, it wasn't Susannah herself, but rather news about her. When I learned that a few hours earlier she had jumped out of her sixteenth-floor apartment on the Upper West Side, I, like most of her friends and fans, immediately started playing all my Susannah CDs. My immediate assumption was that her songs of love and loss would assume greater significance with her death—that now every song of goodbye, every "They Can't Take That Away from Me," every "Ev'ry Time We Say Goodbye," and every "You Will Remember Me" would seem that much more poignant. How naive of me—and how unfair to McCorkle's memory. She was enough of an artist not to need the boost of this extramusical circumstance to make her sad songs so effective. Besides which, she dealt in honest emotion, not sentimental excesses, and she'd have been the first to insist that maudlin mourning—even that inspired by her own demise—would have compromised her singing, not enhanced it.

The issue of Susannah's voice is part and parcel of who she was and where she came from. Once, after a show at the Oak Room, I cornered her about her accent, explaining that I was no Henry Higgins but I thought that I could at least tell North from South, or New England from merry old England, yet when she spoke I hadn't a clue as to what region could possibly claim her as its own. Now the Algonquin lobby, postshow, is no time to do this—it's a moment when a performer needs to meet and greet, and to autograph, and more important, to sell product (CDs). However, she took pity on me and resignedly raced through a two-minute summary of all the places she had lived in as a child and an adult, and how her speaking voice was an amalgam of all of them. Within about ten seconds she had completely lost me, covering so much geography I couldn't even

begin to keep up. "And that," she concluded, "is why I talk funny."

In his obituary, *The New York Times*' Stephen Holden appropriately used the word "peripatetic" to describe her childhood. She came from an academic family—her father was a professor who went wherever the higher-education grass was greener. In a certain sense this constant travel had its impact on her career. Firstly, in that having seen every university in America by the time she was a teenager, she decided to go to college in Europe when the time came. Secondly, in that her career as a singer likewise took her all over the musical map while remaining roughly in the area of jazz and the Great American Songbook. The titles of her albums tell it: *From Bessie to Brazil, From Broadway to Bebop, From Broken Hearts to Blue Skies*.

Because of her upbringing, and because she did happen to be a child of the sixties, McCorkle did get caught up in the movement that renounced traditional American values. For a lot of young people of that era, this was a kind of collective and extreme self-deprecation: The culture that produced me can't possibly be of any value. Thus it seems perfectly fitting that she discovered jazz and the American songbook in Europe, where such art forms were not taken for granted the way they are here. McCorkle later identified Billie Holiday's treatment of Harold Arlen's "I Gotta Right to Sing the Blues" as the record that did it for her, the one that turned her around and made her love the music. She was not only hooked by the jazziness of it all and the blues feeling of the song and the performance but by the profound sadness that Holiday had in her voice. As she once later told me, it took her considerably longer to appreciate Ella Fitzgerald, since Fitzgerald never exhibited that same kind of innate melancholy.

McCorkle had originally aspired to a literary life (an ambition she at least partially fulfilled), but on hearing this music she became determined to sing it. Her first gig of note was with trumpeter John Chilton, who, prophetically enough, is himself a musician and scholar-historian who specialized in both performing and documenting the older styles. She said that it was while hanging out with musicians, particularly those who specialized in the great songs, that for the first time in her life she felt a sense of community. London was where she met her first husband, the British pianist and arranger Keith Ingham (who, for some reason, was excluded from most of her obituaries). Ingham served as musical director for her early albums, which began with *The Music of Harry Warren* (1976) and *The Songs of Johnny Mercer* (1977), both taped in London.

At that point, it seemed as if Susannah McCorkle was virtually the only singer—particularly the only young singer—on the planet who made a practice of singing the Great American Songbook. (Even the great Carmen McRae, who employed that very phrase, was at the time recording Stevie Wonder songs with electric pianos.) McCorkle was so unusual in those days that her Harry Warren album was released on the World Records label, a subsidiary of EMI that specialized in reissues of thirties dance bands. The idea of old was new and radical then.

I first met Susannah around 1980, when she and Keith had relocated to New York from London; both she and I had lots of hair then. She was being interviewed by a friend of mine who did a show tunes program on WNYU, our college radio station, and I vaguely remember that the three of us drove to Harlem for dinner afterward. The inevitable question then, and for years to come, was, Why sing these songs? Why bring back the music of her mother's generation? Why revive 4/4 time and swing-style 8th-note triplets? Why revive the AABA form and the 16-bar verse? Yes, she evoked the idiom, singing wonderful songs in a swinging fashion, but she was never merely retro. She never performed in period drag or acted as if she was trying to re-create the past. Instead, she made it live and breathe again in the present.

In her first American recordings, McCorkle continued her songbook series with two underanthologized lyricists, E. Y. Harburg (*Over the Rainbow*, 1980) and Leo Robin (*Thanks for the Memory*, 1983–84). She also made several albums consisting largely of newer songs in the standard tradition, *The People That You Never Get to Love* (1981) and *How Do You Keep the Music Playing?* (1985).

In 1988, she taped the first of what would be eleven albums for Concord Jazz, *No More Blues*, and that song (which she had earlier recorded in 1981) and her next album, *Sabia* (1990), consummated her love for Brazilian music. This often seemed to be the only material written after 1950 that excited her. She spoke fluent Portuguese and loved the bossa nova. Two albums and three years later (on *From Bessie to Brazil*, 1993) she recorded Antonio Carlos Jobim's "The Waters of March," which became a kind of signature song for her. She could be doing a whole program of Cole Porter or Irving Berlin at the Algonquin, yet her encore was always "The Waters of March." Jonathan Schwartz once described "The Waters of March" as "the greatest song ever written"; it was a typical slice of Schwartzian hyperbole, but Susannah certainly brought the "Waters" into circulation among jazz and cabaret singers, and is responsible for Rosemary Clooney, Cassandra Wilson, Paula West, and others singing it.

"Waters of March" became so closely associated with her that, like a pop star endlessly reprising his biggest hit, she must have certainly grown tired of it. It was as if it was the only thing of hers that people wanted to hear—they wouldn't leave until she sang it. The lyrics to the song are cryptic, even in the English translation, and according to Mark Murphy, Jobim wrote the song about the murder of a friend of his in Rio. When listened to with that in mind, the abstract, fragmented text ("a stick, a stone" . . . "a life, a death") becomes somewhat more concrete. In the light of McCorkle's suicide, it makes one wonder if future generations will treat her performance of "Waters of March" in the way we regard Bobby Darin's "Artificial Flowers," a song that directly foreshadows the singer's own tragically early death.

From Broadway to Bebop from 1994 is probably my favorite McCorkle album. She's got a little bit of everything on there, and even when some things don't work as well as others, you still applaud the effort. There are classic tunes by the canonical show writers, all done with a little bit of a twist: an unusual treatment of Cole Porter's atypical "Don't Fence Me In," Frank Loesser's title song from "Guys and Dolls" done in flat-out swing and with the unusual "female" lyric (rare but not completely unprecedented), Rodgers and Hart's "It's Easy to Remember." There's also some exotica: a French song by Legrand and the Bergmans I've never heard anyone else do, "Once You've Been in Love"; a Broadway calypso, "I Don't Think I'll End It All Today" (about which more later); and "Chica Chica Boom Chic," a forties Hollywood approximation of a Brazilian song from the Carmen Miranda songbook, which she makes swingingly authentic. "One of the Good Guys" (feminized as "girls") had struck me as whiny and obnoxious in the off-Broadway revue *Closer Than Ever*, yet McCorkle made me love it; "Friend Like Me" was then a new Disney song in the classic Broadway tradition that she made work in the classic swing tradition. The only two tracks that don't quite work are the two direct odes to the jazz heritage, "Moody's Mood for Love" and Don Sebesky's maudlin "I Remember Bill" (a soppy homage to Evans in the approximate style of "I Remember Clifford"). However, her vocalese homage to Chet Baker on "My Buddy" is winningly hip—so much so that she repeated the compliment in 1999 on "Look for the Silver Lining" on *Hearts and Minds*.

In 1995, McCorkle, who hadn't made a songbook album in a decade, returned to the format. Having already tackled three songwriters who were almost never given the songbook treatment—Warren, Robin, and Harburg (Ella Fitzgerald ignored them all, songbook-album-wise)—she turned to the three most celebrated composers of the golden era: Porter, Berlin, and Gershwin. (If anyone cares, the Berlin album marks the only time I ever did liner notes for Susannah—I'm grateful she gave me that opportunity.) These albums are examples of how to make even much-sung writers sound new and exciting. All three sets contained little-known songs by these big boys that hadn't been heard in eons. No one had sung Berlin's "Love and the Weather," "Everybody Knew but Me," and "When You Walked Out Somebody Else Walked Right In" since the Eisenhower administration at least. Porter's 1929 "Why Don't We Try Staying Home" anticipates Dave Frishberg, and Gershwin's "Will You Remember Me" (which

McCorkle combined in a haunting medley with the little-known "Drifting Along with the Tide") had never previously been published or recorded.

She also made very familiar songs sound as if we'd never heard them before, usually by means of rhythm: Berlin's terpsichorean tunes "Easy to Dance With" (not all that familiar, actually) and "Cheek to Cheek" now became Latin dances, making you wonder what set of cheeks were being referenced. "Suppertime" is reborn as a blues, a feeling that also permeates "It Ain't Necessarily So"—which McCorkle opens with one of the lesser-known verses, just to throw us off guard. "Anything Goes" is treated as a jazz waltz, and the national anthem of Broadway, "There's No Business Like Show Business," here becomes slow and melancholy. "You Do Something to Me" contains echoes of "Miles Ahead," while the Gershwin album is laced with hints of John Coltrane's "Giant Steps." She worked out these arrangements with pianist Allen Farnham and drummer Rich DeRosa, but certain touches are distinctly her own, as on "I Got Plenty o' Nuttin'" wherein she takes part of the choral episode ("Porgy changed . . . ") and works it into an extra patter section in the middle of the song.

McCorkle, who wrote articles on Bessie Smith and others for *American Heritage*, was enough of a scholar of American culture to work a few of these albums into cabaret shows at the Algonquin, where for a decade she headlined annually. Her performances there were equal parts cabaret and jazz; in fact, the major difference, it seemed to me, was not in the music itself, but in the talking between the songs—most jazz singers, particularly younger ones, tend to say as little as possible, whereas cabaret singers prepare an elaborate script and concept. In the nineties, McCorkle was one of three star-singer-scholars who regularly worked the Oak Room, the others being Andrea Marcovicci and Mary Cleere Haran. All three of them would blend anecdotes and music into a seamless tapestry; still, I always felt that Marcovicci and Haran were somewhat better at that particular approach. McCorkle, however, had a much more substantial recording career, since her overall effectiveness was not predicated on patter and the in-person experience.

As devoted a researcher as McCorkle was, she was much better at talking about herself—strangely enough. Some cabaret artists are so self-centered that the last thing you want to hear them do is talk about themselves, and doing a historical show gets them away from that. With McCorkle just the opposite was true: She was so caught up in pop music history that it was a welcome stretch for her to get up and talk about her experiences. This she did very movingly in her final two shows for the Algonquin, the songs from which were captured on her two final albums, *From Broken Hearts to Blue Skies* (1999) and *Hearts and Minds* (2000). Both shows were light-hearted looks at contemporary life, about losing one love and finding another, which had recently happened to McCorkle, who had separated from her second husband. She set both shows in the second person ("Then you try something else"), but they were clearly autobiographical. These last two albums were among her very best, and McCorkle was never more effectively emotional than when singing Fran Landesman's "Scars" ("Don't be ashamed / Everybody's got scars")—both in person and on the CD, she really made you feel it. Even though the songs were old, she made them contemporary, and in general they reminded me of the romantic comedies of the nineties starring Meg Ryan and written by Nora Ephron in that old-fashioned romantic sentiment suddenly seemed relevant.

"Did you know Susannah?" many people asked me in the weeks after she died. I'm sure all her friends had the same answer, "Not as well as I thought." I knew she'd had a bout with cancer about the time she turned fifty, and had gone through her second marriage and divorce. Only those closest to her knew that she suffered from chronic depression.

There were professional setbacks: After thirteen years, Concord decided not to make a new album with her in 2001. Likewise, the Algonquin had decided not to book her that year. She had been on medication for her psychological condition, which it seems she thought she could stop taking—apparently she was off it before the bad news arrived. This was hardly the end of the world professionally—plenty of former Concordites had found homes at other labels, and I can't imagine that Telarc, Arbors Jazz, Fantasy, or Nagel-Hayer wouldn't have been interested. Nor was the Algonquin the only game in town—she could have almost certainly gotten a booking at Feinstein's, the Café Carlyle, or one of the upscale jazz clubs, like the Blue Note.

She wasn't as well known as Bobby Short or Michael Feinstein, but she was indeed a superstar in the little world of jazz singing and cabaret. Like a lot of people, she saw only her failures—it infuriated her when she sensed that other singers were doing better than she—even though most of them weren't. In fact, Susannah was the envy of most other singers of her generation—for her talent, for her identifiable voice, for the range and depth of her knowledge of music, for what she had achieved: a discography of eighteen albums and a total of a year's worth of nights at the Oak Room. She seemingly had it all together and was so amazingly organized. Her gigs were always well publicized and well attended; she seemed to know what she was doing on every level. She even carried a note advising that in case anything happened to her, she had two cats who needed to be fed.

Again, in the light of what happened in May 2001, it's difficult to listen to those two final albums and resist the temptation to find new meaning in songs like "Something to Live For" and "Down," another recent Fran Landesman offering that could well achieve standard status, particularly thanks to McCorkle's rendition of lines like "There's something irresistible in down." The major song that does take on a new meaning is "I Don't Think I'll End It All Today," a little-known Arlen and Harburg comedy calypso that McCorkle exhumed from the 1957 *Jamaica* for *From Broadway to Bebop*, which, as the title suggests, is about *not* committing suicide. The day before Susannah died, I happened to run into Yip Harburg's son, Ernie. We were both being interviewed by the BBC for a documentary about Lena Horne and, since Horne had starred in *Jamaica* on Broadway, we started talking about "End It All"—how Susannah was apparently the only contemporary artist who had been hip enough to sing it. Harburg's lyric specifically mentions the "fall from the building tall" as one of the ways in which the protagonist is not going to take her own life. How we wish she'd taken those words to heart.

Audra McDonald (born 1970)

Audra McDonald is something of a paradox: She is, by general consensus, the best singer-actress Broadway has produced in the last four decades or so, since the great years when Julie Andrews and Barbara Cook trod the boards; yet she has, as of this writing, somehow failed to have a major hit in a major new show or create a role on the level of Annie Oakley, Liza Doolittle, or Marian the Librarian. McDonald has thus far won three Tony Awards, including one for what was regarded as a brilliant revival of *Carousel*, and another for *Master Class*, essentially a nonmusical play that required her to sing. Her most important Tony may have been for *Ragtime*.

At the end of the first decade of the new millennium, McDonald has moved on to a successful career as a TV actress, and her years as a Broadway leading lady may be behind her. But the main reason I've given her more space in this volume than other musical theater stars of her generation has less to do with her succession of Tonys than because between 1998 and 2006, she released four thoroughly brilliant albums of both standards and new show tunes more or less in the classic tradition; this is an achievement matched by none of her contemporaries. (And there are many excellent Broadway leads, such as Christine Ebersole, Kelli O'Hara, Christine Andreas, Melissa Errico.)

McDonald has ceaselessly championed the cause of young musical theater composers—Adam Guettel, Michael John LaChiusa, Ricky Ian Gordon—with the sound logic that unless living writers are supported, the art form as a whole will eventually die out. Naturally, our heads approve of this course of action, yet our hearts and our feet respond more fully to McDonald when she sings the great standards. Her three solo albums of 1998–2002 (*Way Back to Paradise, How Glory Goes,* and *Happy Songs*) offer a clear-cut trajectory: The first is all contemporary songs, the second is roughly half old and half new, and the third is all standards. Although McDonald's desire to support emerging composers is commendable, it must be admitted that the more frequently she violates this policy and sings the Old Masters, the more listenable her albums become.

That was my reaction when these albums were new, yet listening again years later (and listening to the four albums as a coherent whole), I note that the then new songs sound better now than they did at the time and some of them have even become somewhat familiar on the cabaret and songbook circuit (especially "I Won't Mind"). The second album, *How Glory Goes*, is particularly well organized in that the new and the old songs complement each other: "I Won't Mind" is an intriguing musical monologue that is well placed a few tracks after "Bill" (from *Show Boat*), while "Come Down from the Tree" is a catchy item by *Ragtime* writers Ahrens and Flaherty from their previous show, *Once on This Island*.

The 2002 *Happy Songs*, which consists of twelve classic and two new numbers—which do not suffer at all by comparison—consistently entertains. Perhaps it's all a matter of how one defines art: If one wishes to see the envelope pushed by doing—or singing something—that's never been sung before, then the first album, *Way Back to Paradise* (the title presumably refers to a new golden age of popular songwriting), is the most successful. If one's idea of art is music that you can listen to for unadulterated pleasure, to hear songs you already know by heart in interpretations worthy of comparison with the great vocalists of a bygone era, then *Happy Songs* is the McDonald album to choose.

Broadway's most acclaimed new talent of the nineties was raised in Fresno, California. She came to New York to study classical singing at Juilliard at Lincoln Center, and not long out of college she landed the role of the secondary female lead (the one who sings of "Mister Snow") in the revival of *Carousel* at Lincoln Center's Vivian Beaumont Theatre. Over the course of the next decade she was a smash success in *Master Class* (playing opposite Greek singer-actress Patti LuPone as the great Maria Callas) and *Ragtime,* in which she made an indelible impression with her solo lullaby, "Your Daddy's Son."

The same can't be said for *Marie Christine— Medea* in black Broadway drag—which was a flop with the critics, the public, and the theatrical community as well. It was notable not only as the first attempt to build a major role and a great show around McDonald, but also as her first big Broadway venture not to win a Tony. Apart from the Broadway stage, she has chiefly appeared in new productions of classic works: *Wonderful Town* (an RCA cast album), *Sweeney Todd* (a concert version at Lincoln Center, also with LuPone), *The Cradle Will Rock* (a threatrical film about the show), *Annie* (the 1999

Disney–ABC TV movie of the Charnin-Strouse show), the successful 2007 revival of *110 in the Shade* (also recorded), and the classic African American drama *A Raisin in the Sun*. She has also done a number of TV musical specials and some nonsinging dramatic TV and theater roles.

Everything about *Way Back to Paradise* screams ambition: Clearly, McDonald and producer Tommy Krasker were determined not to do anything the easy way. As noted, this set is nearly all premieres, including a few selections from the as-yet-unopened shows *Parade* and *Marie Christine*. More important, despite the variety of genres (including some attractive settings for the poetry of Langston Hughes and Thackeray), each selection here tells a very specific story, or at least is full of ideas, both philosophical (addressing issues from politics to theology to "Mistress of the Senator") and musical. That McDonald's voice is an incredibly rich, not to mention stunning, soprano seems less important than her determination to fully inhabit these song stories, and to transform each into a moving slice of reality set to notes. At the time, I noted that it was a remarkable album, yet it's pretty much remained in its jewel case ever since.

The 2000 *How Glory Goes* offers a lot more pure-entertainment value, and kibitzers on both sides of the argument could hardly complain that there weren't enough standards or enough premieres—it contains plenty of both. In this approach, familiar songs, among them no fewer than five Harold Arlen classics, gain a new freshness, while contempo works like Adam Guettel's title track get a little of the old-fashioned stardust rubbed off on them. Where *Paradise* has a few tracks that were somewhat experimental (a kinder way of saying "tuneless"), some of the new material on *Glory* is almost as captivatingly melodic as the standards. As alluded to earlier, by so thoroughly investing herself in "I Won't Mind," an intriguing ode sung by a doting aunt to a young baby, McDonald makes us hungry to hear the entire work it came from, the little-known *The Other Franklin*.

If *Glory* is a marked improvement over *Paradise*, *Happy Songs* is the payoff. This is the record that those of us who loved Audra McDonald's voice but wanted to hear her address the standard repertoire were waiting for, the album that was as listenable as the previous two were commendable. She doesn't just sing any old standards here, the focus is appropriately on songs from the African American theater of the twenties to the fifties. As usual, that expression means specifically one thing: Harold Arlen, the man who composed virtually every black show of the era. One could easily gather the nine Arlen songs from *Glory* and *Happy* into a very delightful nine-song minialbum (which, at thirty-five minutes of music, would actually be longer than many Peggy Lee LPs). Other such songs and productions represented are "I Must Have That Man" (*Blackbirds of 1928*), "More

Than You Know" (*Great Day*), and "Suppertime" (Ethel Waters's standout from *As Thousands Cheer*).

On *Happy Songs*, McDonald's coloratura chops are lusher and more lavish than ever, making it even clearer that she has one of the richest and most glorious voices currently being applied to the popular song. The orchestrations (which one assumes were written by Ted Sperling, credited as conductor) are equally sumptuous, with an authentically art deco feeling to them. The only inauthentic note is a modulation between choruses of the opener, "Ain't It the Truth," the kind of device one would not likely hear in a thirties or forties arrangement—yet, this minor cavil aside, the key change does, in fact, make the track even more exciting. Otherwise, McDonald, Sperling, and pianist Lee Musiker were fastidious enough to replicate the two-piano accompaniment originally played by Eadie & Rack on Judy Garland's 1947 Decca disc of "I Wish I Were in Love Again."

As for the two newer items, "Beat My Dog" (the wittiest of bassist-songwriter Jay Leonhart's originals and one he's been doing for decades) and Michael John LaChiusa's "See What I Wanna See"— all I can say is if *Marie Christine* were anywhere near this much fun and swinging, I can't imagine why it wasn't a smash. Even the apparent departures from the format work perfectly, such as the traditional Afro-Brazilian "Bambalele," which is certainly happy. The only tune that doesn't fit the bill is "Suppertime," one of the grimmest of all protest songs; doubtless it is included here to remind the listener that the black experience in the thirties wasn't all *Happy Songs*.

Even though it has no lyrics, Duke Ellington's "On a Turquoise Cloud" is every bit as artful and ambitious as any of the art songs on *Way Back to Paradise*. This wordless piece, which combines Sugar Hill with Rachmaninoff (in the sense of "Vocalise," his wordless art song of 1912) was originally written for Kay Davis's soprano, and McDonald doesn't need lyrics to interpret it even more sensually and soulfully than any of the tunes with texts here. Sometimes one can say more, especially in this area, without words. Larry Hochman's orchestration, which must be the first time this lesser-known Ellington work has been rendered with strings, is extremely beautiful. Talk about ambition: No other piece I've ever heard merges the worlds of jazz and classical music as artfully as this one simultaneously blends the dual aspirations of vocal and instrumental music.

In the last ten years, McDonald was brilliant in revivals of both *A Raisin in the Sun* (2004, in which she was handicapped by having to play opposite Puff Daddy, the nonacting, nonsinging rap star making his Broadway debut) and *110 in the Shade* (2007). In 2006, she released her fourth album, *Build a Bridge*, an entirely appealing amalgam of mostly newish material. The bridge being built would seem to be connecting current generation musical theater composers, like old friend Adam Guettel ("Dividing Day"), to folk-oriented singer-songwriters, old (Laura Nyro's "Tom Cat Goodbye") and new (Rufus Wainwright's "Damned Ladies" done as an evocative tango). The virtues of eclecticism are worthwhile in that the most entertaining show-tune-type song is by the uncategorizable Nellie McKay, "I Wanna Get Married," a contemporary song witty and ironic enough to share the title of Gertrude Niesen's classic showstopper (from the 1944 *Follow the Girls*). McDonald is especially excellent on the opener, Elvis Costello and Burt Bacharach's "God Give Me Strength," soaring with her considerable chops over mountainous high notes in a love song she transforms into a prayer. Between pop songwriters of disparate continents and time periods, and McDonald's own Broadway–opera house hybrid singing style, a bridge has indeed been built.

The year after *Build a Bridge*, McDonald began work on the TV series *Private Practice*, a medical soap opera so entirely preoccupied with matters gynecological that I can't refer to it as anything other than *Private Parts*. As a result, many more people know her as a soap star than as a Broadway leading lady and recording artist. Yet these four albums, as noted, constitute a unique body of work, unmatched by anyone else in the contemporary era.

Carmen McRae (1920?–1994)

A gross oversimplification: Louis Armstrong is the wellspring, the primary source of all jazz singing, and the two greatest prodigies of the next generation, Billie Holiday and Ella Fitzgerald, amplified contrasting components of Armstrong's genius. Holiday picked up on his emotional and dramatic side, while Fitzgerald elaborated upon his musical and improvisational side. This is a bit too pat, since Holiday was also a great musician and Fitzgerald also a brilliant interpreter, but we'll continue the conceit to say that it wasn't until the forties and fifties that singers began to put both halves of the Armstrong equation together again. Among the great ladies of jazz, no one was better able to do both things at the same time than Carmen McRae. An arresting stylist, McRae is at once stunningly musical and lyrically emotional, her sound biting, sharp, and astoundingly clear, full of pure jazz variations and brilliant melodic paraphrases that never undercut her masterfully dramatic, interpretive style.

When one considers the career of Carmen McRae, two facts immediately present themselves, and the more one tries to make sense of them, the more they continue to contradict each other. The first: Carmen McRae is indisputably one of the very finest vocalists the idiom known as jazz has ever produced. The second: She was also one of the oldest singers to gain a major reputation. It wasn't until she was in her early thirties that she sang in major clubs and recorded, a good ten years older than such peers as Holiday, Fitzgerald, Sarah Vaughan, and Dinah

Washington. How can this be? Was she that unlucky? Were the gatekeepers of talent, the producers and agents, so tone-deaf? Was the jazz world, which knew about McRae years before the larger public, so greedy that it wanted to keep this major revelation all to itself?

It's also easy to divine what side of the fence she lands in: Where Ella Fitzgerald and Sarah Vaughan had "round," full voices, Billie Holiday (her earliest influence), Dinah Washington, and Carmen McRae had "sharp," precise voices that place them closer to the blues than pop or opera. McRae was also in Fitzgerald's and Vaughan's class as a pure musician, with a larger gift for melodic invention and improvisation than the other great ladies of the jazz pantheon share. Like Vaughan, she was an expert pianist (as one can tell from "Perdido," one of the rare instances when she documented her instrumental ability in the recording studio), and was thoroughly immersed in the workings of harmony that are the jazz singer's prerequisite. Mel Tormé once singled her out as one of the all-time great scat singers, which is surprising since she didn't do it very often. (The 1981 *Live at Bubba's*, taped in Fort Lauderdale, includes one of her most brilliant scat episodes on "I Concentrate on You.")

Along with Holiday (who could turn any song into autobiography), McRae had a gift for putting over a lyric and making it believable which far exceeds that of most of her sister singers—how many of her colleagues even sing a single song (other than "Mad About the Boy"), much less a whole album's worth of material, by Noel Coward, and make it completely consistent with her overall musical character? She once, famously, declared that "lyrics are more important than melody." Which makes it all the more baffling that she was the oldest of the big six pantheon (Holiday, Fitzgerald, Vaughan, Washington, and O'Day) to make it; as with her contemporary, Joe Williams, it took her a long time to be heard.

In truth, we don't know exactly how long it took. At the time of her first notable recording, in 1954, she was thirty-two, thirty-four, or thirty-six, depending on what date you believe. The year of her birth has generally been given as 1922, but she told friend and interviewer James Gavin that the year was actually 1918 (at the time of her death, she was "older than the Pope," as she memorably put it). In any case, she was raised at the height of the Harlem Renaissance and came of age musically in the swing era. McRae learned piano as a child and her parents encouraged her to study the classics, but the world of jazz and what would later be called the Great American Songbook was beckoning. For a time she also wrote songs, and as a teenager she came to the attention of one of the power couples of the jazz world, keyboard star Teddy Wilson and composer Irene Kitchings Wilson. Thanks to the influence of the Wilsons, one of McRae's early songs, "Dream of

Life," was recorded by the pianist's longtime collaborator Billie Holiday. It became kind of a mantra in McRae's own career; she herself occasionally sang and recorded it over the decades.

Unfortunately, this early breakthrough did not lead to a career as writer or performer, and McRae spent most of the forties scrabbling as a pianist-singer. She achieved her next public notice in 1946 as girl singer with the orchestra briefly led by Duke Ellington's son, Mercer. Around this time she married drummer Kenny Clarke, who was then playing with Ellington the Younger and was himself one of the founding fathers of bebop; she later told Gavin that she was never in love with him.

As Carmen Clarke, she cut her first disc with this particular Ellington orchestra: the ballad "Pass Me By," for the start-up label Musicraft. By the late forties McRae was well known among the cutting-edge musicians who gathered at Minton's, Harlem's most famous after-hours joint, as well as at the Onyx, another mecca for swing-style jam sessions on the city's famed Fifty-second Street. She even sat in with Charlie Parker, whom she doubtless met through Clarke, and he taught her a song he had written some years previously known as "Yardbird Suite" or, with the lyric, "What Price Love." (After her death, four fragments of McRae performing the song with Parker at the Onyx in 1948, as recorded by Birdmaniac Dean Benedetti, were issued on Mosaic's Parker-Benedetti collection.) By 1953 McRae was no longer playing and singing but was working as a fully fledged "stand-up" singer. The late pianist Dick Katz has described what it was like to play for her in her earliest stand-up engagements at Minton's. According to Dick, McRae already was mature and polished (an observation supported even by her earliest recordings), and playing for her, even then, was "a crash course in professionalism."

It was, however, neither her regular engagement at Minton's nor her sitting in at the Onyx that would turn the tide for her, but a gig in Brooklyn. There, she happened to come to the attention of the record producer, songwriter, and publisher Chuck Darwin. The exact circumstances (and dates) of what they did together remain vague, but some tracks were issued on singles on the Stardust label and others were first released as an LP, titled simply *Carmen McRae*, on Bethlehem.

The effort and the confusion were justified by the results. Unlike the first recordings of a lot of artists, these cuts are not mere embryonic samples of a future great: At age thirty-three (or near), McRae's development is nearly complete. The various Darwin sessions are a worthy sample of the singer at an early peak. Nearly all the fifteen songs involved are composed by either him or the participating musicians, including one title, "Last Time for Love," by McRae herself. The loveliest of the originals is "If I'm Lucky," credited to Darwin, and a worthy song. While it may or may not be considered a standard,

two other superlative standards do stand out among the Darwin material, "Old Devil Moon" and "Easy to Love." McRae's voice is lighter and clearer here—it would get considerably heavier and darker by the nineties—but essentially she sounds fully formed.

The Bethlehem titles are indisputably jazz—unusual jazz at that, featuring accordion, flute, and clarinet. When the venerated producer Milt Gabler brought her to Decca at the end of 1954, he had her record pop as well as jazz, and her first session included a memorable pop treatment of the Gershwin standard "They All Laughed," backing her with big band and mixed chorus. She is remarkably accomplished here, tart and swinging, full of rhythm and personality that already put her in a class with major pop divas such as Doris Day and Jo Stafford. In fact it's hard to imagine even Ella Fitzgerald doing better. When Jack Pleis's chart calls for her to be irreverently cheeky in a series of asides (Ira Gershwin's famous line about Mr. Whitney and his cotton gin is followed by "but nobody laughed when they found they couldn't drink it"), she's more than up to the task. This was probably the first recording of McRae's to be heard widely by the general public.

For five years, McRae recorded steadily and consistently for Gabler in an outstanding series of albums released first on Decca and then on Kapp (and today all owned by Universal Music). Making up for lost time, she recorded frequently and prolifically, launching a forty-year career that would prove one of the richest in the history of jazz. Virtually every other jazz or pop singer of her approximate generation was doing his or her best work in the late fifties, from Sinatra to Tormé to Vaughan to Fitzgerald to O'Day to Connor to Christy to Cole to Stafford. What is surprising is that a virtual unknown could come out of the woodwork and compete with all these established heavyweights—overnight, McRae went from dark horse to contender.

The first of her twelve albums in the Decca-Kapp series, *By Special Request*, was a purely jazz project. Fortunately, the twelve standards included here are considerably better than most of the songs from the Darwin dates. Better still, *By Special Request* includes two selections, one of them them a standout "Suppertime," which are among the very few occasions when McRae recorded accompanied by her own piano.

By Special Request, essentially a first album, is an amazing effort: McRae is accomplished, poised, and in control. One track in particular showed that she already had the support of the mainstream jazz community: "Something to Live For," one of Billy Strayhorn's major compositions, is accompanied by the composer himself. In "I Can't Get Started," she sings "Frank Sinatra had me to tea," and you can't help thinking that she was already worthy of such an invitation.

Like most singers of the era, McRae and her producers, from Gabler on, followed the Sinatra example of using the LP medium for what Capitol president Alan Livingston called "standard product"; at the same time, she cut a series of 45 rpm singles that utilized more contemporary songs which the A&R staff had earmarked as potential hits. With McRae, however, even the tritest of jukebox ephemera sounds positively sterling. While neither Decca nor its corporate heirs, MCA and Universal, have shown much interest in reissuing her singles, in 1989, the Danish label Official released *Invitation*, which contains the bulk of her fifties 45s.

These one-off tracks include a few dogs, but in the main consist of respectable if lesser known items. There's "I Guess I'll Dress Up for the Blues" and Livingston and Evans's neglected "As I Love You," as well as a few numbers that eventually caught on, such as Bronislau Kaper's film theme "Invitation," and a terrific reading of the Artie Shaw semi-standard "Moon Ray." The two biggest surprises are "You Don't Know Me," a mainstream pop version of the Eddy Arnold country song later immortalized by Ray Charles, and "It's Like Getting a Donkey to Gallop," which, despite a beastly title, turns out to be a swinging, witty novelty by Johnny Burke with a suitably brassy orchestration by Jack Pleis.

McRae's five-year association with Decca (and its brother label, Kapp) served to make her a bona fide singing star as well as to yield what time may prove to be the most consistently excellent series of recordings of her entire career. These twelve 12" LPs, indeed, rank among the best of all vocal records. It's tempting to discuss McRae's work in terms of record labels, especially in that Pleis, who wrote many of McRae's orchestrations in these years, also did the same for Decca's two other leading African American artists of the period, Sammy Davis Jr. and Al Hibbler. Yet as with Chris Connor at Atlantic, Ella Fitzgerald and Anita O'Day at Verve, Sarah Vaughan and Dinah Washington at Mercury, June Christy at Capitol, and Mel Tormé at Bethlehem, the excellence of McCrae's work in this period isn't so much due to the label or even the producer. To take a longer view, this was simply an amazing era for jazz and intelligent pop music, in which the confluence of technological, artistic, and economic imperatives made it the only time in history when conditions encouraged the recording of great albums—and lots of them—by major pop artists. Suffice it to say that the dozen McRae albums from the 1955–59 period take a back seat to no one.

On the Decca-Kapp series, McRae puts across all kinds of material in all kinds of settings. The legacy of *By Special Request* was extended in various ways. For instance, another small group album, *After Glow* with the Ray Bryant Trio, and *Carmen for Cool Ones*, utilized unusual instruments and combinations even further out than the accordion-flute combination. Yet in these years, McRae was also wisely teamed with four of the finest jazz vocal orchestra-

tors involved in full-length projects: Jimmy Mundy and Tadd Dameron on *Blue Moon*, Ralph Burns on *Torchy* and *Birds of a Feather*, and Ernie Wilkins on *Something to Swing About*. She also utilized a full-sized string orchestra on *Book of Ballads* (conducted by Frank Hunter) and *When You're Away* (Luther Henderson). Two of the more mainstream pop projects involved concepts rarely addressed by anyone from either the pop or jazz spectrum: *Mad About the Man* collects the songs of Noel Coward and *Birds of a Feather* spotlights tunes about our feathered friends.

The series is loaded with so many superb moments that it's frustrating to concentrate on just a couple of highlights. Each of the albums balances well-known standards with excellent songs just bubbling under: On *Book of Ballads,* her stunning reading of the verse to "How Long Has This Been Going On" (the chorus has been done a million times and the verse maybe half that, but this still has to be the loveliest it's ever been sung), which is followed immediately by "Do You Know Why?" a lament to lost love by Burke and Van Heusen. *Blue Moon* includes the title track as well as "My Foolish Heart," and such worthy obscurities as Joe Mooney's "Nowhere" and Jack Segal's "Laughing Boy." *Blue Moon* also contains Peter DeRose's rare and beautiful "Lilacs in the Rain," which could have been a key track in a collection of songs about either flowers or different atmospheric conditions.

The two packages with Ralph Burns are singularly outstanding: *Torchy* is just that, and the *Birds* collection is both swinging and sentimental, put together with a sense of humor that was rare in jazz even then. There's a major instrumental guest star here, in the person of tenor great Ben Webster (billed pseudonymously as "A. Tenorman"), who appears as well on "Georgia Rose," a single from the same sessions. The latter is a song from the African American vaudeville tradition that both McRae and friend Tony Bennett (who learned it from her) reinterpreted as a black-is-beautiful anthem.

The concept of *Mad About the Man* is also out of left field, but the record itself is marvelous, although it took me years to fully appreciate it. After McRae, you don't want anyone else even to try to sink his teeth into the line "Play me some barbaric tune" in Sir Noel's mock-Gypsy waltz, "Zigeuner." *Carmen for Cool Ones,* arranged by cellist and contemporary classical composer Fred Katz, is perhaps a touch arch, or at least that's true of "All the Things You Are." She also addresses "Any Old Time," which Artie Shaw had written and which Billie Holiday had recorded while she was with his band—a worthy song rarely included in Holiday tribute sets. For the most part, both the charts and the songs here are refreshingly straight-ahead, and McRae's singing is up to its usual high standard.

Something to Swing About is another extraordinary release. Ernie Wilkins, best known for his arrangements for Basie and Joe Williams and for Dinah Washington's *Fats Waller* album, was, surprisingly, only rarely given the chance to show what he could do with a top-flight swing singer, and this is one of his finest efforts. Nearly every cut here is worth singling out. "Sleepin' Bee," with an exceptional piano solo by Dick Katz, is a high-powered romp through a tune that's usually treated more sedately; neither the insect nor anyone else is likely to get much sleep with all this excitement going on.

The only note of discord arrives with "So Nice to Be Wrong," a 1957 single that contains the briefest hint of the 16th-note rock 'n' roll beat that had already conquered the 45 rpm singles market. The boom falls with a one-shot singles date for Mercury, masterminded by producer Clyde Otis and arranger Belford Hendricks. This was the same dreaded team that was then sabotaging Dinah Washington (all the way to the bank) and they brought the same formula to McRae, combining a top singer with top songs but absolutely subputrid pseudo-R&B arrangements. Who would have believed that Carmen McRae singing "The Very Thought of You" and "Oh Look at Me Now" could be so dreadful? The intrusion of rock-pop-soul elements in her work, from this point on, would be a recurring theme almost until the end of her life.

Luckily, this issue would not surface in the next major phase of her career, though it lurked in the background, like a cobra waiting to strike. Between 1960 and 1962, McRae made four albums (three and a half, actually) for Columbia. Much of the Columbia work is highly jazz-oriented, starting with her most famous album of the period, *Carmen McRae Sings Lover Man and Other Billie Holiday Classics*, and including parts of three projects with Dave Brubeck: all of *Take Five*, parts of *Tonight Only*, and a couple of tracks of *The Real Ambassadors*. The Holiday album in particular has McRae, obviously inspired by Lady Day, liberally reshaping the melodies in a far jazzier fashion than anything she recorded in the fifties. Done with her own rhythm section at the time (Norman Simmons, piano; Bob Cranshaw, bass; Walter Perkins, drums) plus three guests (Nat Adderley, cornet; Lockjaw Davis, tenor; Mundell Lowe, guitar), this tribute collection to her late mentor (who had died only three years earlier) is a pinnacle in an outstanding career, in which McRae literally wrestles Lady Day's signature songs into her own image. "Billie Holiday is the greatest influence in my life," McRae often said, usually adding that if Lady Day "had never existed, I probably wouldn't have either."

Her other album from this association, *Something Wonderful*, goes to the opposite extreme: This is a purely pop project—pop of the show tunes variety, that is. An album of Broadway music with a vengeance, orchestrator (and apparently producer) Buddy Bregman conceived the package as a tribute to various Great White Way leading ladies, and it lays out, for the most part, in a series of medleys. On the minus side, the idea of McRae singing a tribute medley to Ethel Merman seems bizarre, and nearly all the tracks are frustratingly brief (as is the set as a whole); what's more, the Bregman charts are serviceable but uninspired. Still, McRae's singing doesn't disappoint, and any concept that gives her the chance to sing such excellent songs as "Long Before I Knew You" (from *Bells Are Ringing*) is to be enjoyed. When the set was reissued in 2001, several singles were added, and these, at least, give McRae a chance to do a few songs at proper length, as opposed to the medleys, which are not very adroitly arranged and feel unnecessarily truncated. Show buffs will take delight in hearing rare songs from flop productions with terrific scores: *All-American*, *Nowhere to Go but Up*, and, best of all, "How Does the Wine Taste?" from *We Take the Town*, which McRae sings with so much vivacity you can practically taste the wine yourself.

McRae's work from later in the sixties is a mixed bag: She made several sets of chintzy, backbeat-driven arrangements, particularly during her association with Atlantic, as well as some wonderful, straight-ahead packages on both that label and Mainstream. Without a doubt, the best release of these years—indeed, possibly her finest ballad album of all—is a 1964 Mainstream well titled as *Second to None*. Arranged and conducted by Peter Matz, *Second to None* consists largely of new songs—proving that they were still writing 'em at the dawn of Beatlemania (in fact, McRae was among the first American stars to record a Lennon-McCartney tune: "And I Love Her," heard here), such as "The Music That Makes Me Dance" (from *Funny Girl*) and "Where Did It Go?," an early English lyric for the 1959 Brazilian theme "Manha de Carnival" (from *Black Orpheus*) that later became known in the U.S.A. as "A Day in the Life of a Fool." Her singing is no less jazzy than usual, while Matz's orchestrations (reminiscent of Don Costa at his very best) are lush and yet superbly subtle and tasteful.

There isn't a wrong move on the entire package, and it's a sheer delight to hear her sink her teeth into Marvin Fisher's "Cloudy Morning" and Michel Legrand's first American crossover, "Once Upon a Summertime," the Frenchman's only significant song with Johnny Mercer. There are also superlative readings of "My Reverie" and "Blame It on My Youth." "The Night Has a Thousand Eyes" is a special treat: I've heard it performed by pop singers (Buddy Clark) and also by jazz musicians (Sonny Rollins, Stan Getz), but for some reason it was largely overlooked by the upper pantheon of heavy-duty jazz divas. McRae's reading is the rendition that I always want to hear.

Subsequent sixties and seventies projects were both dreams and nightmares. Most of the Mainstream works fall into the first category, particularly a series of about four live albums taped mostly in San Francisco (*In Person/San Francisco*, *Live and Doin' It*,

Live and Wailing, Woman Talk). These were all made with her regular accompanist, Norman Simmons, and her regular rhythm section, as was the studio package *Bittersweet. Haven't We Met?* is another lush orchestral album, this time arranged by Don Sebesky, which comes in second to *Second to None.*

Her work for Atlantic Records is decidedly uneven: There are several albums with fine orchestrators and worthy material, specifically *For Once in My Life*, done in London with Johnny Keating in 1967, and *Portrait of Carmen,* done later that year on the West Coast with charts by Gene DiNovi, Shorty Rogers, and Oliver Nelson. McRae also recorded live with small group accompaniments, as was the custom at the time: *Live at Century Plaza* (taped in 1968 but not released for another seven years) with Simmons, and the double-length *The Great American Songbook*, done at Donte's in Los Angeles in 1971, with the outstanding Jimmy Rowles.

The studio albums were increasingly oriented toward pop-rock material, but gems surface here and there: *Portrait of Carmen* contains one of her all-time best ironic torch songs, "I Haven't Got Anything Better to Do," which surely provided the template for Natalie Cole's 2002 treatment (also a wonderful performance, but clearly based on McRae). McRae's 1968 *The Sound of Silence* and 1970 *Just a Little Lovin'* are hardly a waste of time, especially the first. There contain a few contemporary chart items, like the Paul Simon title song and Jimmy Webb's "MacArthur Park," yet though I might rather hear her sing Cole Porter, she certainly does an outstanding job with these and I'm pleased to hear her sing them. There are other surprises: "I Sold My Heart to the Junkman" has more of a rockish backbeat than I'd like, whereas Della Reese's Italian import "And That Reminds Me" is done in much more of a traditional swinging four than we might expect. And there are lots of worthy standards here, notably a moving "Stardust" and a harrowing "Gloomy Sunday."

Oddly, McRae had not recorded live at all before 1961 when she taped a set in England released as *Carmen McRae in London*, a rare LP that subsequently became an equally rare CD, but from that point on she made up for lost time, beginning with two of the Brubeck collaborations on Columbia. From the Mainstream and Atlantic periods onward, she rivals Ella Fitzgerald as one of the major singers who recorded most frequently in concert. The title of the Atlantic live album *The Great American Songbook: Live at Donte's* (which is not to be confused with *At the Great American Music Hall*, another live album, from five years later, released by Blue Note), is indicative of the times. By putting the songbook in the title of her albums, she was precisely telegraphing her intentions to her traditional audience, and distinguishing her live albums from her increasingly contempo studio projects. (Atlantic recorded hours and hours of McRae singing live at the Century Plaza in Japan that will seemingly never be heard.)

As she got deeper into the seventies, she continued to do her best work in live albums. *Live at the Dug*, also from Japan, is a complete surprise, and not merely in its curious title (which refers to a club in Tokyo). This was the only time McRae recorded an entire set working with just her own piano accompaniment, and the highlight is her killer treatment of "As Time Goes By" (the album was also released under that title). Apart from this once-in-a-lifetime event, she also recorded for the last time with her ex-husband Kenny Clarke on *November Girl:* This excellent package, taped in London in 1970, is a set of offbeat, interesting songs with the first-rate European-based big band Clarke co-led with French pianist Francy Boland.

In 1975 and 1976, McRae recorded a series of albums for Blue Note, the once venerable jazz label that was then entering into a state of corporate limbo and trying to conquer the as-yet-unnamed smooth jazz field. There were two largely forgettable studio projects, *Can't Hide Love* and *I Am Music*, which drew heavily on synthesizers and Stevie Wonder (not necessairly a terrible thing), but there also was still another excellent live album, *Carmen McRae at the Great American Music Hall* (1976). (She also guest-starred on two all-star projects for the label, *Live at the Roxy,* 1976, and *Blue Note Meets the L.A. Philharmonic*—who knew they even had one?) In 1995, Blue Note issued *The Best of Carmen McRae*, which, as promised, collates most of the good stuff for that label, including an outstanding Bill Holman arrangement of "Star Eyes," which makes one yearn to hear the live material, at least, in complete form.

McRae sounds completely convincing on the likes of "The Man I Love" (consistently credited by Blue Note to Cole Porter). "Miss Otis Regrets," with a muted trumpet obbligato by no less than Dizzy Gillespie, marks one of the few times that any major singer since Ethel Waters had taken this authentic 1934 Cole Porter classic completely seriously. The *Roxy* album contains the amazing sound of 1976 Los Angelinos cheering wildly as McRae explains why it's her feminist right to get beaten up by her papa should she so desire on the Bessie Smith classic "'Tain't Nobody's Business If I Do."

By the seventies and eighties, McRae's voice had lost some of its youthful freshness, and much of the time she seemed to be singing with what could only be described as a bitchy, Miss Thing attitude. Like Lena Horne's attempts to "sound black" during this period, McRae occasionally overuses gospel and soul effects. Her last widely heard recordings were a series for Concord Jazz and then BMG (the label formerly known as RCA Victor). All of these were projects in which she shared billing with another performer, either living or dead. *Two for the Road* (1980) was a long-awaited teaming with George Shearing, just voice and piano, highlighted by two first-rate songs from their friend Marvin Fisher, "Cloudy Morning" and "My Gentleman Friend," while *Heat Wave* (1982) auspiciously teamed her with Latin jazz giant Cal Tjader.

The best of the tribute albums was the first, the outstanding *You're Lookin' at Me (A Collection of Nat King Cole Songs)* (1983). She went on through the curious *Carmen Sings Monk* (1988) and her final album, *Sarah—Dedicated to You* (1992). The Cole set is wonderfully lively and animated, the Vaughan tribute is oddly lifeless. The *Monk* set is a mixed blessing. McRae still sounds great, as does the backup band, but most of these pieces are instrumentals that were not meant to be sung, and—with the exception of the vocalese standard "'Round Midnight" and several texts by Jon Hendricks—especially not with these lame lyrics.

She had done the same thing much better nearly thirty years earlier with the delightful *Take Five* and *Tonight Only* with Dave Brubeck and his quartet. The McRae-Brubeck collaborations were far more enjoyable, largely because the pianist-composer and his lyricist wife, Iola, were active participants, and also because Brubeck's melodies were more conventionally lighter and more singable. One doesn't feel that anybody was defiling masterpieces on the Brubeck-McRae tracks the way that the after-the-fact lyricists on *Monk* are. Further, McRae's voice itself was lighter and friskier in the early sixties, and she was better able to capture Brubeck's whimsy and capriciousness, whereas in 1988 she only seems to get Monk's heaviness and not his antic wit.

The *Monk* and *Sarah* albums were hardly ideal notes to end on, which is a shame, since she was generally sounding fine in these years, was being managed by the resourceful Larry Clothier, and overall was in good shape. Luckily, since McRae's death in 1994 there have been numerous releases of live performances, generally from the eighties with her at the top of her form. Quincy Jones released *Dream of Life*, an outstanding live concert from 1989 with the WDR Radio Big Band of Cologne. She returned to her roots with *For Lady Day*, two volumes of Billie Holiday songs taped at New York's Blue Note with guest Zoot Sims. There are a lot of songs not on *Lover Man*, and those that are repeated here are considerably darker, deeper, and more moving than on the 1962 album. McRae had by now come full circle.

Few singers, even among the upper reaches of the pantheon in whose company she walked, were more consistently excellent than Carmen McRae.

Mabel Mercer (1900–1984)

It took me a long time to "get" Mabel Mercer. For years, I went with my first impression: that she understood a lyric better than anyone, but that she interpreted the words to the detriment of the music and was completely unmusical. The lyric was everything to her—all other considerations, melody, rhythm, harmony, tempo, time signature, were strictly secondary. Yet I've come to see that there are indeed musical values in her singing.

For years, Mabel Mercer seemed more of a monologuist—as they used to be called—rather than a vocalist. She told stories with music but never much concerned herself with carrying a tune. Before I really listened to her, I sort of assumed she was a kind of Margaret Dumont—or maybe even Eleanor Roosevelt—with musical accompaniment.

I was wrong. And I first began to realize that there was more to Mercer than had previously met my ears when I began listening to a set of live recordings from the sixties (released on Harbinger Records as *The Legendary Performers*). It immediately became apparent that a great many of her numbers were done in waltz time. Why, I wondered? I couldn't think of any performer in cabaret, jazz, pop, musical theater, or even opera or lieder, who did so many songs in three-quarter time (not even Patti Page). That she was paying so much attention to the time signature indicated that there must be *something* going on in the musical department.

It's quite odd to conclude that the singing of Mabel Mercer is actually driven by rhythm. After all, swing time isn't the only valid rhythm in American music, and Mercer may not swing like Ella Fitzgerald, but she's nonetheless well aware of where the beat is; she doesn't parade it up and down and sideways and crossways, or turn the beat back around on itself like Anita O'Day, but she's far from ignorant in the ways of time. It should be obvious that, perhaps even more craftily than Sinatra and Holiday, Mabel Mercer is the master of subjugating her musical strengths to the narrative. For example, on "Everybody's Looking" and "Trouble Comes" (both included in the Harbinger live set), she employs repetitive rhythmic phrasing to underscore a repeated dramatic concept in the text. Unlike Holiday and Sinatra, she doesn't drop the tempo entirely for rubato or stop time effects. She keeps the tempo going—you don't think of her as performing for dancers, but she certainly could have. Surely she would have never attempted "From This Moment On" (which, in a sense, was Cole Porter's answer to "I Got Rhythm") if she didn't know where the beat was. (Her "Moment" includes what must be a rare instance of the great lady addressing someone as "Babe!")

The lady herself and everyone around her insisted that her work couldn't possibly be appreciated by the great masses. Everyone in her immediate circle took it as gospel that her music would only be popular with a small crowd of cognoscenti. God knows how that rumor got started: She has about the fruitiest English accent you can imagine, and her enunciation is even more so, but her work is more about passion than pretension; she never gets so sophisticated that anyone capable of understanding the English language couldn't understand exactly what she's doing—and enjoy it.

To me, Mercer is not so much an elitist artist as a universal one. Even when she was born, in Burton upon Trent, Staffordshire, England, on February 3,

1900, she was many things at once: English and American, black and white. Her parents were of different nationalities and races, but they had showbiz in common: Her mother was a singer of English-Welsh stock who worked in music halls and her father was an African American tumbler visiting from the States.

A valid point of comparison might be with Billie Holiday. The circumstances that Holiday was raised under undoubtedly pointed her to the blues and her becoming enmeshed in a self-destructive pattern that led to drugs and an early death. The privations of Mabel Mercer's life were every bit as devastating and demoralizing as those of the young Eleanora Fagan, yet she grew up singing "Just One of Those Things" and lived into her eighties. As was true of Holiday, Mercer's parents had not enjoyed the benefit of clergy.

Mabel never met her father, Benjamin Mercer, and her mother was only in her life until she was seven, at which point Mom took to the boards and the road once again and was gone. She did, though, give Mabel some singing lessons in church, in which, it's said, she stressed volume and clarity and volume again: "All right, sing! And I want to understand every word!" Until the age of fourteen, the girl was known as Mabel Alice Wadham; at that point, she learned her father's real name, and claimed it for herself. As she later said, it was the only thing she ever got from her father, and even then it wasn't freely given.

Holiday later talked and wrote (or rather, her ghostwriter William Dufty wrote) about encountering rampant racism and sexism in both the North and South. One can only imagine how much worse the young Wadham-Mercer's life was, who, growing up in England at the turn of the century, probably never came into contact with another person of color. Raised by her mother's parents, Mabel was constantly ridiculed by the white English children around her for the tone of her skin, the "Negro" quality of her hair, her illegitimacy, and even for being left-handed.

Like her mother, she was determined to make it as a singer. None of her jobs lasted particularly long in the teens and twenties, because she would be fired the instant the theater managers realized that she wasn't entirely Caucasian. She gained her most valuable early stage experience thanks to an aunt, who led a traveling music hall troupe that, billed as the Five Romanies, passed themselves off as Gypsies. She also teamed up with a "cockney" song and dance girl named Kay and worked across Europe, entertaining Allied troops during the First World War.

It was during this period and immediately after it that Mercer began to benefit from the vogue for "colored" entertainers on both sides of the Atlantic. Though never a star like Josephine Baker, she finally began to reap some of the benefits of her Afro-European status. She appeared with such troupes and shows as the Chocolate Kiddies, *Coloured Soci-*

ety, and eventually in the London production of *Lew Leslie's Blackbirds of 1926*. It was while working in these shows that, for the first time, she came into contact with other black people. Up until this time, she had only been exposed to music hall songs and other varieties of turn-of-the-century and Edwardian Britpop. Now she gained familiarity with the entire spectrum of American and African American musics—spirituals, pop, blues, and eventually jazz; the *Coloured Society* show even featured black performers doing arias from Italian opera.

By the end of the twenties, however, Mercer had found her niche: Singing the great American show tunes in small nightclubs in London, Paris (where she sang at Bricktop's, a cross-racial, multinational gathering place for Lost Generation expatriates), and, eventually, New York. At this early stage, she sang softly, employing a megaphone when necessary (before electric microphones and sound systems began to be installed in clubs), making her, in a sense, a pioneering crooner along the lines of Bing Crosby and Rudy Vallee.

By the thirties, Mercer was beginning to be recognized as a vocalist of uncommon sensitivity: This, incidentally, at a time, when singer-actors in Broadway and West End musicals were more prized for their ability to project (like Ethel Merman) than to animate a lyric. (The Mabel Mercer Web site also proclaims, "Unjudgmental depths of understanding won her a devoted following, especially among homosexuals.")

In 1938, surprisingly, Mercer made contact with her mother again, and moved to New York to be closer to her. However, Ms. Wadham, who lived upstate, was reluctant to introduce Mabel—now a full-grown black woman—to her white neighbors as her daughter. So Mabel settled in Harlem, and began singing at Le Ruban Bleu at 4 East 56th Street.

Around this time, two events occurred that changed her life. First, she underwent a tonsillectomy, which lowered her voice to the deeper mezzo-soprano register, and gave her a unique, throaty sound. Second: World War II. Mercer happened to be working in the Bahamas at the end of 1941 when war was declared, and was temporarily trapped there by immigration restrictions until Kelsey Pharr of the Delta Rhythm Boys offered to facilitate her permanent settlement in the United States by marrying her. Throughout the forties her home base was Tony's on West Fifty-second Street, proving that there was more than swing on Swing Street. There, Mercer was discovered by a generation of homecoming New Yorker GIs. When Tony's was razed at the end of the decade, she traveled a few blocks east to the Byline Room; by then, she was a favorite of reporters and other media insiders.

Her visibility increased when, in 1950, she appeared in *The Consul*, a new, Pulitzer Prize–winning opera by contemporary classical composer Gian-Carlo Menotti; she didn't herself sing any opera here, but performed a traditional French street song called "Tu Reviendras." Mercer's stock also ascended when, not long afterward, she began recording for Atlantic, then a label that concentrated almost exclusively on R&B and black pop. Ahmet Ertegun himself produced her sessions for the label, this being long before his brother, Nesuhi, returned east from Los Angeles to run Atlantic's jazz division. The relationship began promisingly with *Mabel Mercer Sings,* originally released as a 45 rpm extended play disc, which was soon expanded into the 10" LP *Songs by Mabel Mercer.*

In 1954, Mercer recorded her definitive studio album, *Mabel Mercer Sings Cole Porter* (also first heard as a series of 45 rpm EP discs, and two years later collected onto a 12" LP, the same year that *Ella Fitzgerald Sings the Cole Porter Songbook* was recorded). This was indeed a fortuitous combination of singer and material: Mercer's singing was a juxtaposition of rolled R formality ("in love with the night mysteRRRRious . . .") and casual intimacy; like Porter's lyrics, Mercer's singing combined straightforward sex with suave sophistication. On Porter songs that were both famous (the then brand-new "It's All Right with Me," from *Silk Stockings*) and obscure ("Looking at You" and "Experiment"), she's constantly meeting the songwriter halfway and finding the midpoint where the intentions of performer and composer dovetail perfectly.

The accompaniment of the twin-piano team of Stan Freeman and Cy Walter helped immeasurably; at this time, they were probably better known to most record buyers than Mercer, having starred on their own radio series (*Piano Playhouse*) and long worked as an act in their own right across Manhattan. Other Atlantic albums also used suitably minimal backgrounds: *The Art of Mabel Mercer, Midnight at Mabel Mercer's, Once in a Blue Moon,* and *Merely Marvleous.* She also made an album for Decca, *Mabel Mercer Sings,* in which her characteristic intimacy was not compromised by the use of a small orchestra. (Nor is it by the string section on her later Atlantic album *Once in a Blue Moon.*)

Mercer was probably the most emblematic figure of the golden age of the New York cabaret scene, and is justifiably celebrated as such in the history of that epoch, James Gavin's *Intimate Nights* (she's also the subject of two biographies, notably *Midnight at Mabel's* by Margaret Cheney). Her friend and agent, the remarkably coiffed Donald Smith, has, for the last quarter century, run a foundation in her name that produces what has become an annual institution he calls the Cabaret Convention. Every year every kind of chanteuse and chanteur (not to mention chantootsies and chanteusettes), the famous and the infamous, the good and the great, the bad and the lousy, all gather in her memory.

Mabel Mercer is a role model for cabaret singers not only for her singing itself, but for her persistence, weathering the gradual closing of the once lively cabaret scene. As one club after another shut its doors, Mercer fell on tough times but kept on

working: In 1968 and 1969, she co-headlined with fellow cabaret star Bobby Short in a pair of legendary concerts at Town Hall produced by Newport Jazz impresario George Wein. She semiretired to a farm (near Chatham, New York) and seemed contented to charm the birds off the trees. In the seventies, Smith helped resuscitate her career by booking her in plush rooms and concert halls across the country, and she was able to spend her last decade as a grand dame of American music, her seventy-fifth birthday in 1975 cause for celebration: The St. Regis hotel named a cabaret room after her, *Stereo Review* commenced an annual award in her name, and in 1983 President Reagan bestowed upon her the Presidential Medal of Freedom. She died on April 20, 1984, and was buried beside her longtime lover and manager, Harry Beard.

About all that most people know about Mabel Mercer is that, as with Billie Holiday, Frank Sinatra regularly named her as one of his favorite singers and key influences. *McCall's* magazine quoted him as saying, "Mabel Mercer taught me everything I know." It's occurred to me that one way to introduce Mercer to Sinatra listeners is by invoking the 1965 album *September of My Years*, which is the Sinatra project that comes closest in spirit to Mercer's musical ethos. Not that Mercer ever sang in these painfully slow crawl tempos, or worked with a symphony-sized string orchestra constantly going in and out of major and minor, but the feeling of the songs on *September* is close to much of Mercer's material.

Put another way, virtually all of Mercer's most poignant performances could be described as fitting into one of two patterns: first, songs of introspective reminiscence on past loves and lovers ("It Was a Very Good Year") and second, advice to romantic young hopefuls ("Hello, Young Lovers"). If her songs aren't strictly one or the other, chances are they're some combination of the two. "Everybody's Looking," "Trouble Comes," and "More I Cannot Wish You" all find La Mercer in the position of the romantic guru dispensing not mere Ann Landers–style "advice" but true wisdom to the lovelorn.

On the other hand, "When the Family Is Home," "When the World Was Young," "While We're Young," "They Were You," "Mira" (a beautiful song from *Carnival*, a show with a Bob Merrill score sadly neglected by singers), "Days Gone By," and "Once upon a Time" all have the singer gazing inward and reflecting on episodes in her own life.

Which brings us to the central irony of Mercer's work: She's generally regarded as the Queen of Cabaret Singers, and therefore, by extension, one of the most sophisticated individuals ever to prance upon the planet. She's the very type for whom Cole Porter wrote such highfalutin arias as the perennial bittersweet farewell song "Ev'ry Time We Say Goodbye." Yet at the same time, her most memorable performances are the ones in which she retrogresses to young girlhood, all those songs listed above with the word "Young" in the title. She sets up all this sophistication and urbanity expressly so she can cut through it and dispense with it: Suddenly it's not about how she rolls her Rs or whether she says "to-*may*-toe" or "to-*mah*-toe" but how she transports us back to another time, another place, and makes us all feel young and foolish.

And this explains the preponderance of songs in 3/4 time. The waltz is the time signature of the fair and the merry-go-round, saturating these songs with a feeling of innocence and naïveté by harking back to a time when the world was so much younger than we and merry as a 3/4 carousel. These contradictions are what give her work layers, what provide it with texture. Mabel Mercer is, like Holiday, Sinatra, or Edith Piaf, one of the primary colors of twentieth-century music. A Mercer performance is like the blues in that everything is distilled down to its purest essence—there's no wasted motion, no unnecessary frills or extravagances. She doesn't embellish a tune the way Sarah Vaughan does because that's not her way of telling a story. In the highly musical art of Mabel Mercer, everything is exactly where it should be.

Ethel Merman (1909? 1984)

The parts I played upon the stage
Were cast in a similar mold
Brassy and classy and tough as nails,
But always with a heart of gold.

—From special material written for Merman's nightclub act by Roger Edens, included on *Mermania!, Volume 2*

There's *no* business like *show* business. On October 14, 1930, a musical called *Girl Crazy*, with songs by George and Ira Gershwin, opened at Broadway's Alvin Theatre, and a miracle was born. Near the end of the first act, a twenty-four-year-old virtually unknown singer, who until very recently had been known as Ethel Agnes Zimmermann, came out and sang "Sam and Delilah." "The audience yelped with surprise and pleasure," she later recalled. "To be honest, I thought my garter had snapped or something." A few minutes later, she lunged into "I Got Rhythm," and the crowd's mood shifted from mere "surprise and pleasure" to total hysteria. It wasn't only their delight at their first exposure to the song that would become a national anthem of American pop and jazz, it was the earthquake level of intensity that the singer projected. When she finished the first chorus, instead of reprising the melody for a second time through, she simply belted a single high C for an entire 32-bar chorus. The show was officially stopped. Even by the end of "Sam and Delilah," the audience knew that a star had been born. By the time the first act concluded with "Rhythm," the crowd realized they were in the presence of something even bigger than a star: a bona fide showbiz legend. (It's actually a matter of conjecture among contemporary scholars as to whether Merman really held that legendary single note in "I Got Rhythm" for a whole

32 bars. And in any case, it doesn't seem like that big a deal—"Rhythm" is a rather fast song, and one chorus of it could easily fly by in thirty–forty seconds.)

Ethel Merman possessed the biggest and most powerful sound ever to emit from a Broadway theater, and she had charm, chutzpah, and emotional warmth to match. Those chops were even more powerful than Mother Nature herself: When "Iron Lungs Merman" (as she referred to herself) played *Panama Hattie*, she projected with a force strong enough to flatten Central America like a tropical hurricane. Her chops were so overwhelming that, in the plots of her shows, they became an engine of transformation and social change, powerful enough to vanquish all kinds of class distinctions: In *Anything Goes*, Reno Sweeney is a former evangelist turned nightclub headliner; in *Call Me Madam*, Merman is Sally Adams, a dirt-poor farm girl turned society hostess turned diplomat; in *Annie Get Your Gun*, Annie Oakley is an illiterate backwoodswoman who rises to the top of American showbiz and hobnobs with royalty merely by "Doin' What Comes Naturally."

Even time itself bends to the will of the Mermforce: In *Du Barry Was a Lady*, when she played a thirties showgirl who morphs into the legendary eighteenth-century courtesan, you really believed that her vocal powers enabled her to traverse the generations. Which, of course, they have; Merman's singing made her immortal, and her recorded performances seem as fresh and vital in the twenty-first century as they did during the Golden Age of Broadway more than half a century ago. Merman's greatness consistently transcends genre and generation; in 2000, the contemporary jazz singer Dianne Reeves (who has more chops than anyone else singing today) acknowledged that she studied Merman's singing "for projection."

Projection was only the beginning: There was her amazing enunciation, and the miraculous clarity of her voice—she did more than project to the back of a theater; even in the cheap seats you could easily comprehend every nuance and every gesture. Merman has been compared to the greatest of Wagner sopranos, the similarly iron-lunged (not to mention iron-helmeted) Kirsten Flagstad; neither icon had to do anything other than remain motionless onstage, and stand and deliver.

It's rightfully asserted that no one introduced more of the great American standards than Fred Astaire, but Merman came closest. Indeed, she premiered far more Cole Porter classics than any other artist and she did the same for Broadway's other great composer-lyricist, Irving Berlin: Hard as it may be to believe, the great man only had two major hits in the age of modern book musicals, *Annie Get Your Gun* and *Call Me Madam*, and Merman was the force behind both of those. She also originated more of the great musical comedy heroines than any actress or singer, not only the aforementioned Reno Sweeney, Sally Adams, Annie Oakley, Panama Hattie, and

Madame Du Barry, but her favorite and most revived role, Mama Rose in *Gypsy*.

The sum of Merman's achievements is much higher than if she had been merely a "belter"—as she often described herself—and nothing else. Her voice had the power and volume, but she also had a tender and vulnerable side. When she sang "Down in the Depths (On the 90th Floor)" in *Red, Hot and Blue* or "Make It Another Old-Fashioned, Please" in *Panama Hattie*, she displayed pathos as well as power. She characterized her characters as "invulnerable dames" or "tough brassy broads," but all of them, from the hard-edged Hattie to the Medea-like Mama Rose, who will stop at nothing short of eating her young, had a sentimental side. Merman both acted and sang them all with total believability and conviction. And from the beginning, she had an ear for timing that served her both as a musician and a comic, and an uproarious sense of humor. In fact, the reviews that pleased her the most were the ones that implied she could have succeeded as a comedienne and actress even without those miraculous pipes.

The young Ethel Agnes Zimmermann first began to realize her power while entertaining at army camps during the First World War. Singing a sentimental song about her mother, she discovered that "an awful lot of those big tough fighting men had mysteriously got something in their eyes." She had been born in Astoria, Queens, on January 16—that much is agreed upon. She later said the year was 1912; most sources say 1908 or 1909; her most recent biographer, Geoffrey Mark, has established the year as 1906. While Merman was frequently taken for Jewish (and was discriminated against because of it), she was actually a devout Episcopalian. She grew up hooked on vaudeville, sneaking into shows in local theaters as often as she could get away from school, and she soon began to enter that world by winning a series of amateur contests.

Meanwhile she was also studying to be a secretary, learning to type and take dictation, and she later spoke more proudly of these achievements than she ever did of her considerably less formal musical education. Her father played a little piano, and constantly encouraged her to sing out "Louise" as he pounded the Steinway. George Gershwin himself later concurred: "Never go near a singing teacher," he told the young singer, "and never forget your shorthand." She went to work as a stenographer, but after business hours, she continued to haunt theaters for singing work. While still holding her day job, she sang at parties and restaurants and met her lifelong pal Jimmy Durante when working for the singer-pianist-comic at his famous club, Les Ambassadeurs. By 1930, she and pianist Al Siegel were performing at the top houses in vaudeville, such as the Brooklyn Paramount, and while still in the outer boroughs, appeared in a few very early talking picture short subjects filmed in Astoria.

Around this time, another rising young star—Virginia Katherine McMath, already known as Ginger Rogers—caught Ethel Zimmermann's act in White Plains, New York. "She strode forcefully to the front of the stage and began to sing," Rogers later wrote. "She was sensational. Her voice was clear and brilliant and every word could be heard in the far reaches of the theatre." A few months later, Rogers was signed to play the ingenue in the Gershwins' forthcoming *Girl Crazy,* and producer Vinton Freedley needed a girl singer for a secondary lead who would be responsible for putting over three key songs. Rogers and her mother suggested that they go and listen to "the girl from White Plains." And that was it.

It was to Merman's great regret that, as close as she became to the Gershwins, circumstances prevented her from doing another show with them. After *Girl Crazy* ran for nearly a year (which constituted a major hit in those days), she moved on to the most celebrated edition of *George White's Scandals.* With Rudy Vallee, Ray Bolger, and such songs as Merman's standout "Life Is Just a Bowl of Cherries," that show was also a winner. She followed it in 1932 with another success, *Take a Chance* (titled *Humpty Dumpty* out of town), in which she introduced "Eadie Was a Lady."

In 1934, Merman made a major breakthrough, creating the first of the many characters that established her as an actress and comic as well as a pair of tonsils. This was Reno Sweeney in *Anything Goes,* who, thanks to Merman, quickly entered the collective consciousness. She made instant standards out of "I Get a Kick out of You," "You're the Top," "Blow Gabriel Blow," and the title song.

For the next ten years, the Cole Porter–Ethel Merman collaboration continued unabated over five successive and successful shows: *Anything Goes* was followed by *Red, Hot and Blue* (1936, which yielded "It's De-Lovely") with Jimmy Durante and Bob Hope, *Du Barry Was a Lady* (1939) with Bert Lahr, *Panama Hattie* (1940, in which "I've Still Got My Health" and the torchy "Another Old-Fashioned, Please" were the standouts), and *Something for the Boys* (1943). (The pattern was interrupted only for a 1939 flop called *Stars in Your Eyes,* with songs by Arthur Schwartz and her dear friend Dorothy Fields.)

Apart from Broadway, where the hits far outnumbered the flops, she didn't score highly; Hollywood, where they liked girls with big eyes and small voices, had no idea what to do with her. Merman made her earliest feature, a cameo in the deadly dull *Follow the Leader,* back in 1930, and also starred in two pictures each with Bing Crosby and Eddie Cantor. She apparently wasn't ever considered glamorous enough to play a romantic female lead, although *Strike Me Pink* with Cantor actually cast her as a femme fatale. Twentieth Century Fox put her in two big musicals, but was equally clueless, although *Alexander's Ragtime Band* gave her all the best songs and the first chance to work with her postwar savior, Irving Berlin.

Merman reigned unchallenged as the supreme voice of Broadway in two distinct eras of that great street's history. Most musicals in the thirties, including the five classic Merman-Porter shows, were built around songs; the plots of these were mere devices upon which to string a series of potential Hit Parade entries. It's telling that the last of these productions, *Something for the Boys*, opened two months before *Oklahoma!* heralded a new kind of musical comedy, one in which song and story were more integrated.

Merman created three of the great musical comedy roles in the modern era. It turned out to be prophetic that she and Porter had earlier described "a Berlin ballad" as "the top," because her postwar career got under way with Irving Berlin's two greatest heroines, the lead characters of *Annie Get Your Gun* (1946) and *Call Me Madam* (1950). The two shows created an endless list of hits: "I Got the Sun in the Morning," "Doin' What Comes Naturally," "Anything You Can Do," "You Can't Get a Man with a Gun," and "There's No Business Like Show Business" in the first, and "The Hostess with the Mostes' on the Ball" and "You're Just in Love," among others, in the second.

She also starred in Berlin's last top film, the beguiling and delightful *There's No Business Like Show Business* (1954), which didn't quite compensate for her not being asked to re-create her role as Annie in the 1949 MGM film of *Annie*. Show-wise, Merman was next sidetracked by a minor undertaking called *Happy Hunting* (1956), which, although described by its star as "a jeep among limousines," actually ran 412 performances (and produced the immodest and memorable "Mutual Admiration Society"). She rightfully admitted, "Most critics attributed the fact that so many people were willing to shove $8.05 under the ticket wicket to my efforts."

Finally, La Merm climaxed her career in 1959 playing Mama Rose in the "Musical Fable" *Gypsy*, perhaps the greatest female role in all of musical comedy. Based rather loosely on the story of stripper and monologuist Gypsy Rose Lee, *Gypsy* may have been the title character, but the star turn was actually Lee's mother, who overshadowed her both in real life and in the show. More than any other vehicle, *Gypsy* gave Merman the chance to show everything she could do, both as an actress and a singer. As the most ambitious stage mother of all time, Merman was by Rose's turns domineering, romantic, tender, and savagely aggressive. Her Mama Rose was one of the supreme characterizations of the American stage.

As always, she did much of her best acting in song, particularly with Jule Styne and Stephen Sondheim's exuberant "Some People" and the double meaning of "Everything's Coming Up Roses." Most meaningfully, Merman's musical soliloquy "Rose's Turn" exhibited a hitherto unrevealed reflective side. Subsequent Mamas Rose—Rosalind Russell (in the Warner Bros. film), Angela Lansbury, Tyne Daly, Bette Midler, and many others have played the character in revivals, foreign casts, films, and TV productions—have grown increasingly carnivorous, but none displayed the sensitivity and depth that Merman brought to Mama Rose when she created her for the stage. The widow of German playwright Bertolt Brecht even tried to get her to play the title role in *Mother Courage*.

Merman had already forfeited many a movie role to a Hollywood regular (Hattie to Ann Sothern, Du Barry to Lucille Ball, and Annie to Betty Hutton), but she came closest to being bitter when producer Freddy Brisson snatched up the movie rights to *Gypsy* as a vehicle for his wife, Roz Russell. Merman had every right to be upset, not least for the way Russell actually plays the part in the film, which is like a high-class dame gone slumming. (Russell was even more out of place in *Gypsy* than Merman would have been in *Auntie Mame*.) Indeed, the 1936 film of *Anything Goes* (even with its truncated score) and the excellent 1953 film of *Call Me Madam* are, regrettably, the only two cinematic records we have of Merman preserving her great roles for posterity. (There's also a live TV production of *Anything Goes* from 1954, which is a mere footnote but a much better visual record of the classic 1954 show than either of the two films of it. Frank Sinatra and Bert Lahr co-star as Merman's romantic-musical and comic leading men, respectively.) Hollywood only discovered her late in life as a brilliant, nonsinging comedienne in the slapstick spectacular *It's a Mad Mad Mad Mad World* (1963) and *The Art of Love* (1965). She also made self-parodying appearances on TV's *Batman*, *The Muppet Show*, and in the 1980 spoof movie *Airplane!*

After *Gypsy*, Merman more or less considered herself retired from the eight-shows-a-week grind of Broadway. Still, she deigned to appear in two revivals, starting with a 1966 revamping of *Annie Get Your Gun* done at Lincoln Center complete with a new Berlin ballad about an old-fashionied wedding. In 1970, she essayed the role of Dolly Levi in *Hello, Dolly!*, a vehicle she had turned down in 1963—which technically wasn't a revival, as the show had been running continually since Carol Channing opened it in 1964.

It's difficult to fully assess the achievements of Ethel Merman, who more than two dozen years after her death on February 15, 1984, remains the single most dynamic icon in the history of musical theater. Not long ago, *The New Yorker* ran a cartoon in which a large chorus is shown belting out "There's NO business like SHOW business" and they're billed as—what else—"The Ethel *Mormon* Tabernacle Choir." At least two New York cabarets were named after Merman characters, Reno Sweeney's and Rose's Turn.

Merman is perhaps the only major twentieth-century popular vocalist who emerged at the dawn of mass media—electric recording, radio, and talkies—whose career was largely unrelated to any of these technical developments. She was a natural for Broadway with her outsize voice and personality; yet the fact that she could reach the upper rafters without benefit of amplification didn't mean that her voice didn't record well. She could and did: Her voice rings pure and true on all her studio records, from the first sides of 1931 to the dread—but well-sung—disco album of the seventies.

Recording-wise, one wishes that she'd come along either earlier or later. If she could have caught the recording boom of the twenties, she probably would have made dozens of discs of all kinds of tunes. If she'd started during the war or later, then all her important roles would have been documented on original cast albums (as indeed all her postwar parts are). But she made it right at the start of the Depression, and her 78 rpm activity is embarrassingly scattershot. The record business was in such a depressed state in the very early thirties that, sadly, she did not make any recordings of the songs from *Girl Crazy*—what I wouldn't give to have a disc of her doing "I Got Rhythm" with Gershwin on piano (as he had done for Fred Astaire)! In 1931, she test-recorded seven songs (including three from *George White's Scandals*) for three different labels, but these have yet to be unearthed and issued.

Her earliest issued session, done for Victor, consists of four songs none of which, oddly, are from any of her shows, although she did document "Eadie Was a Lady" from *Take a Chance*. Yes, she did two songs from *Anything Goes* and all four of her biggies from *Red, Hot and Blue*, but nothing from *Du Barry Was a Lady*. Yes to *Stars in Your Eyes* and *Panama Hattie*, but no, strangely, to *Something for the Boys*. It wasn't until 1947 that Decca invited Merman to document the eight biggest song hits of her prewar shows on a 78 album called *Songs She Made Famous*. What was the record business looking for? A bigger star? A bigger voice? Ha! Not bloody likely.

For a very brief while around 1950, Decca—with *Annie* already a top-selling album and *Madam* on the horizon—treated her like a bona fide recording artist, and actually let her do a few singles of songs that she didn't introduce on Broadway. No one was more surprised than Merman herself when she landed a hit record with "Dearie" (from the *Copacabana Show of 1950*). Done as a duet with the old Scarecrow, Ray Bolger, her former *Scandals* co-star, the disc sold 200,000 copies in a month. A follow-up with Bolger, "(If I Knew You Were Comin') I'd've Baked a Cake," a cover of Eileen Barton's hit, also dented the charts. She and such colleagues as Bolger and Durante could create memorable moments out of every kind of triviality—songs that made "Baked a Cake" (by Bob Merrill, then in his novelty phase) look like Rodgers and Hart, things like "The Lake Song" and "A Husband, a Wife." A few years later,

Merman became the only artist after Louis Armstrong and Bing Crosby to record a *Musical Autobiography* for Decca. Like Armstrong for jazz and Crosby for pop, she was the industry leader in her own field, yet she had never been the colossus that her talent warranted in the world of recording. (In recent years, Universal Music collected these 45 rpm tracks on a welcome package titled *The World Is Your Balloon: The Decca Singles 1950–1951*.)

The irony is that Decca was by far the most supportive label of her career, and even they failed to do what they should have done, which was to have her in the studio day and night—or at least fairly regularly. She should have recorded every show tune that ever was, every big song from every Rodgers and Hammerstein or Hart hit, every song ever written by Jerry Herman, Jule Styne, Bob Merrill, Comden and Green, every song from *Fiddler on the Roof, Cabaret*, even *The Wiz*, or any other musical comedy you can think of. Merman starred on a short-lived national radio series in 1949, and surviving airchecks have her singing such unexpected songs as "Some Enchanted Evening." It sounds exactly the way you would expect.

In 1961, Merman taped a bunch of staples with zingy, Sinatra-age arrangements by Billy May for the Chairman's own label, Reprise (*Merman . . . Her Greatest!*), and ten years later she re-re-created them with a disastrous contemporary sound on *The Ethel Merman Disco Album* (released in 1979 on A&M). There was also *Merman Sings Merman*, a beautifully recorded set of oft-sung Merman perennials taped in London in the late sixties. As an illustration of what a cockeyed (not at all optimistic) world this is, the wonderful *Merman . . . Her Greatest!* has yet to be reissued on CD while the ghastly *Merman Disco Album* is readily available. The message is clear: Merman fans are not permitted to have taste of any kind.

Two collections contain the bulk of the recordings that she did make. *Doin' What Comes Naturally!* (on the British Jasmine) has most of the prewar sides, and *There's No Business Like Show Business: The Ethel Merman Collection* (Razor & Tie, licensed from Decca and Columbia) has all of her big numbers from the postwar shows (although for some reason the *Annie* masters have artificial stereo echo). Both are generally recommended. More recently, Harbinger Records has released two CDs of material from her private holdings. It's almost as if the great lady has come back from beyond the grave to make sure that some of her best music is available.

Mermania!, Volume 1 is a combination of demos and private tapings of songs she never recorded elsewhere, while *Volume 2* is a full-length document of her 1964 nightclub act, recorded live in an undisclosed location. (The only thing they tell us is that it's not Las Vegas.) *Volume 1* is principally for collectors, but *Volume 2* is the live album that one of the majors should have released forty years ago. This is a very stirring performance indeed, very nearly in a class with the great Carnegie Hall albums by Judy Garland (1961) and Tony Bennett (1962). There's a particularly poignant reading of "Everything's Coming Up Roses" here, in which one can almost discern something of a Jolson-like tear in her voice, as if all this in-your-face brassiness is just a façade to hide a sentimental and vulnerable soul—or that she wants you to think it is. Yet, enjoyable as the *Mermania!* series is, we still feel as if we're rooting around in the closet looking for scraps, looking for something to fill in the gap, anything to take the place of the "real" records that she should have made.

In all of show business, only Jolson and Judy Garland had chops comparable to Merman's, and neither of them intruded on her territory: Jolson dwelt in Broadway's prehistory, and would have found it inconceivable to play any role other than himself. Garland was exclusively a creature of Hollywood and blew her chance to play the musical theater's great heroines (beginning with Merman's own Annie Oakley).

Call her Madam. Call her Zimmermann or Merman. Call her Episcopalian, or, if you must, Jewish. Call her a singer, an actress, a comic, a diva, or an American icon. Call her whatever you wish, but precious few performers beyond Merman can accurately be described as a genuine force of nature.

Helen Merrill (born 1930)

Is Helen Merrill a major jazz singer? She is certainly an important singer in many respects. Her major vote of confidence comes from the recording industry. As I write, Merrill reaches her eightieth birthday and her fiftieth album. Needless to say, that's an imposing statistic—even such indisputably colossal artists as Anita O'Day or Joe Williams never made it to fifty albums. More amazing, Merrill managed to keep recording steadily in the seventies and early eighties, a period when most jazz singers were having a hard time of it.

A second factor in support of Merrill comes collectively from jazz musicians. For reasons I don't fully understand, no singer has performed or recorded with more major jazz musicians—particularly of the bop generation. Clifford Brown, Gil Evans, Kenny Dorham, John Lewis, Oscar Pettiford, Bill Evans, Jimmy Giuffre, Thad Jones, Stan Getz, Jim Hall, Lee Konitz, Gary Peacock, and Pepper Adams are, no exaggeration, just a handful of the important musicians who rarely appear with singers yet have all recorded with Merrill—often on more than one occasion. And then there are the outstanding pianists who have made a specialty of backing singers and who have worked with her, such as Dick Katz, Hank Jones, Jimmy Jones, and Tommy Flanagan. (And finally, let us also consider the musicians whom Ms. Merrill has married: the fine reed player Aaron Sachs and the outstanding pianist-arranger Torrie Zito.) Jazz musicians, it's safe to say, just plain like her.

Another way of measuring importance is influence. Martin Williams famously argued that influence is not necessarily a measure of quality, giving the example of Jelly Roll Morton: No one else tried to compose or arrange like Morton or lead a band similar to his Red Hot Peppers, but that doesn't take anything away from the overall excellence of his music. Up until the last ten years or so, I wouldn't have thought Merrill was influential either. Even now, it's not that anyone tries to sound like her, but that the concept of emotional detachment, which Merrill seems to have pioneered, has in recent seasons caught on in a big way in the jazz world. Diana Krall, Norah Jones, and many others all employ the concept of detachment in a way that points directly back to her.

So there are many reasons to listen to Helen Merrill albums, another one being her uniformly excellent taste in songs, which fully matches her capacity for working with superior sidemen. She sings the higher-minded works of the songbook, as well as many compositions by jazzmen (like Thad Jones's "A Child Is Born").

But all of these are secondary reasons. The main question remains, Is her singing any good? We would listen to Ella Fitzgerald singing the worst dreck in the dreariest possible accompaniments. It's a complicated issue for me. I enjoy Merrill when I hear her, but I rarely go out of the way to listen to her either on disc or in person: A little of Merrill goes a long way with me. She's not one of those singers—such as, say, two of her approximate contemporaries, Jackie Paris or Chris Connor—whom I enjoy listening to for more than a single album. Perhaps the most remarkable thing about her is that she has, as we shall see, improved with age, and the albums of the nineties and aughts represent a dramatic improvement over her vintage work.

Jelena Ana Milcetic was born on July 21, 1930 (some sources give 1929), the daughter of immigrants from Croatia. By the time she began infiltrating the jazz world, she was already known as Helen Merrill.

The first major musician she recorded with was Earl Hines, the pioneering pianist who had surely employed more important singers than any bandleader other than Tommy Dorsey. She was twenty-two and already a veteran; six years earlier, she'd won an amateur contest and sung professionally with the dance band led by Reggie Childs. She also hung around the old Nola Studios—then a rehearsal as well as a recording facility—where she got to meet musicians and other music industry folk. She had frequently sat in at a club called the 845 in Brooklyn, which seems to be the first place she worked with nascent bop stars like Miles Davis and Bud Powell. It was there she met her first husband, Aaron Sachs, who—befitting his name—played tenor and clarinet.

In 1952, both Sachs and Merrill joined Hines, who had left Armstrong's All-Stars shortly earlier and was leading a particularly outstanding group. The normally prolific pianist hadn't recorded in two and a half years, but, after Merrill had been with him a few weeks, he went into a studio. As we'll see, one of the chief characteristics of Helen Merrill's artistic output is an unfailing consistency, which is both a good thing and a bad thing. She sounds as mature as she would ever sound on her first recording, "A Cigarette for Company," which establishes several other precedents in her work. As the title suggests, she already has the dry, ashen, and smoky sound that she retains to this day, even though she didn't smoke—which in itself was somewhat unusual for 1952.

She made a few singles for Teddy Reig's Roost label, which are extremely rare, but her recording career began in earnest when in 1954 she came to the attention of producer Bob Shad (and Quincy Jones) of Mercury Records. She started with what amounts to a test date in February, in which she sang four songs (including two alternate takes), of which two were issued on a single at the time, accompanied by arranger Johnny Richards. Shad may well have thought of her as Mercury's equivalent to June Christy, who was currently a solid seller for Capitol. Even before her first album was released, Leonard Feather had proclaimed Merrill "The Best New Jazz Star of 1954." Presumably he made that decision on the basis of her work in clubs, as well as her Hines and Richards sessions.

The first Merrill album, titled simply *Helen Merrill*, consisted of seven longish tracks, all standards familiar to the jazz audience, for which Shad and arranger Quincy Jones paired her with the single most dynamic figure in jazz of the mid-fifties, the short-lived trumpeter Clifford Brown. A week earlier, Brown had cut a small group jazz album with Sarah Vaughan, and the previous summer had participated in a Mercury jam session that starred Dinah Washington.

The date is similar to the Brown-Vaughan session in that Brown is the essential secondary voice on both. There are woodwind instruments present on both sessions: Vaughan had flute and tenor behind her, Merrill has Dannie Bank doubling on flute and baritone. In both cases the woodwinds aren't there as soloists but more for atmospheric backing and obbligato behind the spotlighted female voices. Merrill's musical relationship with Brown is unique: He plays with passion and fire, while she supplies exoticism and mystery; Brown puts everything out there, Merrill holds plenty back. They're almost like Billie Holiday and Lester Young, but in reverse—the singer is cool, withdrawn, and introverted, and the horn soloist is up-close and personal. Solo-wise, Brown has "Yesterdays" on his mind—he begins his solo on Holiday's "Don't Explain," the first tune of the first of two sessions, with a Kern-el of that classic melody. Then he plays something entirely different on the second session when Merrill formally sings "Yesterdays"—but

returned to the Kern melody a month later when he plays the song on his classic album *Clifford Brown with Strings*.

Shad then assigned Hal Mooney, a very talented "commercial" arranger, to work with Merrill, but what seemed commercial then seems avant-garde now—Mooney's charts are only slightly more conventional than those of Johnny Richards and Gil Evans. They did two albums for Mercury, *Helen Merrill with Strings* (1955) and *At Midnight* (1957). Merrill's ethereal voice and playful jazz phrasing ensure that these are more jazz than pop projects, even given the strings. In fact, the comparatively plainer backdrop sometimes makes her seem even jazzier (again, much the way Mooney's contemporaneous writing for Sarah Vaughan did). "Just You, Just Me" is a comparatively lighthearted treatment of the jam session standard, whereas "When I Fall in Love" finds her reminiscent of Jeri Southern.

After the Clifford Brown album, Merrill's most celebrated recording was *Dream of You,* her 1956 collaboration with Gil Evans. Although he arranged tracks here and there for various singers like Tony Bennett and Johnny Mathis, *Dream of You* was Evans's most notable collaboration with a vocalist, and, as Dan Morgenstern points out, the first full-length album that the notoriously difficult arranger-conductor created. In her notes to the 1992 CD reissue of that album, Merrill recalled that Shad was opposed to using Evans—who, like Charles Mingus, was clinically unable to finish projects in time and insisted on endless takes, even rehearsals in the studio—but that she stuck to her guns.

After Miles Davis, Merrill may be the most compatible solo voice that Evans ever arranged for; like Davis, whom she had sat in with as early as the forties, Merrill is a very astute artist who knows what not to sing. Her knack for leaving things out and understating emotions meshes perfectly with Evans's sonic textures, as does the smoky, surreal quality of her voice. She seems to have been the first jazz artist to do "A New Town Is a Blue Town," put over convincingly by John Raitt in *The Pajama Game* a short while earlier on Broadway. But she stands out the most on songs like "By Myself," "Alone Together," "Dream of You," "I'm a Fool to Want You"—she's at her best when singing of a lover who isn't there. He may have left her, he may never have been there to begin with, he may only exist in a dream, but wherever he is, he isn't where she is. Merrill's vocals consistently convey a sense of absence; whenever you hear her you get the distinct feeling that something or somebody is missing. It's always about less rather than more.

"Any Place I Hang My Hat Is Home" and "Where Flamingos Fly" speak to a related theme in Merrill's music. "Flamingos" was sung by Peggy Lee about a month before the Evans-Merrill session, and would become an Evans perennial—he would play it many times and on several other albums over the next thirty years. His arrangement for Merrill features quasi-Iberian passages similar to what he would write for Miles Davis a year later on "Blues for Pablo." It's easy to see how other singers could interpret "Where Flamingos Fly" as merely exotic, a song about longing to be somewhere else, but Merrill makes it a characteristic song of loss and absence. As with "Key Largo" (a song she should have done) the lyrics suggest a Humphrey Bogart–style exotic noir, but Merrill makes it clear it's the other person, the perennial absentee, not the faraway place, that she longs for.

Songs that evoke far-off places and, occasionally, times would continue to be important in Merrill's music, but even more so were the least exotic, plainest songs and images you can imagine. As far as I know, she's rarely been given credit for being one of the first jazz singers to incorporate folk and occasionally country songs into her work. In fact, that first Mercury date (with Johnny Richards) included "How Is the World Treating You," a country-politan tune by guitarist and producer Chet Atkins. "Troubled Waters," which Gil Evans undoubtedly remembered from the Ellington–Ivie Anderson recording, is a Sam Coslow movie song that uses folk-blues imagery, including a reference to the traditional spiritual "Scandalize My Name."

The second album with Mooney, *At Midnight*, introduced a Merrill standard, her treatment of "Black Is the Color of My True Love's Hair," a folk song first documented in the southern Appalachian Mountains at the turn of the century, which is believed to have evolved out of an older English ballad. Singing folk-derived material, Merrill early on perfected a taut monotone sound: She sings in slow, measured phrases in which the dynamic level is essentially even and one word or idea rarely gets more attention than another. In both her singing of folk songs and her use of monotone, Merrill anticipates the slightly younger Nina Simone.

At times, Merrill and Simone seem to have arrived at a similar place via completely different routes. Merrill, with her stone-white hair and pallid sound, is the epitome of whiteness—or perhaps colorlessness is a better way to put it. Whereas Simone is one of the most Afrocentric performers American culture has produced; it isn't only her true love's *hair* that's black. Merrill sang both "Black Is the Color of My True Love's Hair" and "Lilac Wine" well before Simone did.

In Merrill's hands, as in Simone's, the monotone is a powerful thing. Film critic Jim Hoberman once described the emotional presence in Chet Baker's singing as a seductive void, and Merrill's effect is similar. She leads us to think more than we want to think, and she leaves so many spaces unfilled that active listeners can put whatever meaning they like into them, and make her music mean whatever they want it to mean. The slo-mo quality of her work sometimes makes me think that she really has been partaking of lilac wine, or perhaps some other variety of depressant.

Merrill completed her three-year, five-album association with Mercury with *The Nearness of You*, taped half in Chicago (Johnny Frigo plays an extended bass obbligato behind her on "Softly, as in a Morning Sunrise" and "Summertime") and half in New York. The New York date features a typically astute amalgam of players, including young pianist Bill Evans and composer-theorist George Russell on guitar, plus Oscar Pettiford and Jo Jones, bass and drums.

Still not yet thirty, Merrill taped two albums in 1959 for two other labels, *You've Got a Date with the Blues* on MetroJazz (the MGM subsidiary) and *American Country Songs* on Atco (the Atlantic subsidiary). Both represented key steps in her evolution. The latter seemed like an obvious step forward from the country and folk material she'd already been doing. The former was a collection of blues-tinged material with, like most of the albums on MetroJazz, copious input from producer-songwriter Leonard Feather (who wrote "Signing Off" and the title song) and pianist-arranger Jimmy Jones (returning from the Clifford Brown album).

Date with the Blues is crucial to her development, not because of the blues material (not one piece of which is a traditional 12-bar blues), but because of the international presence on the album. There are French songs sung in English ("When the World Was Young"), but, more unusually, there are two American songs sung in French, "You Go to My Head" ("Vous m'Eblouissez") and Ellington's "Just Squeeze Me" ("lorsque tu m'embrasses"). They show that Merrill with her detached monotone has arrived at a state of pure sound. It no longer matters what she's singing—the songbook or folk-country music, English or some other language, something happy or something sad—her singing has evolved into an amorphous soundstream, which communicates whatever the listener wants to read into it.

And that very quality has been one of the sustaining forces of her long career. It makes perfect sense that she spent most of the sixties and early seventies living and working in Europe and then Japan. She was that rare jazz singer whom it was possible to fully appreciate no matter what the listener's command of English, or even if one hadn't the slightest idea what she was saying. Her singing, even more so than Vaughan's or Fitzgerald's, was never lyric-specific: She sings mostly sad songs and she sounds undeniably sad when singing them, but that's about it—it's never about taking a text and extracting nuances of meaning out of it.

Merrill was amazingly prolific in the sixties, recording constantly in Rome, Paris, Milan, Berlin, Tokyo, Hilversum (The Hague), and occasionally New York. In 1960, for instance, Italian RCA released a Merrill LP entitled *Parole e Musica;* from my meager knowledge of Italian, it seems to be the sound track of a television drama. Each track is an American pop standard ("Night and Day," "Everything Happens to Me") sung by Merrill in English, but which opens with a local narrator who recites part of the lyrics in an Italian translation (e.g., "Notte e Giorno"). Unless you've listened to the album, you can't possibly imagine what the lyrics to "Why Don't You Do Right?" sound like recited in Italian.

The areas of Merrill's recorded legacy that interest me the most are her earliest and her most recent releases—in other words, the fifties and the nineties. It's hard for anyone but a die-hard Helenist to wend his way through her copious sessions of the sixties, seventies, and eighties. She was so prolific that despite singing superior songs (including songbooks of Rodgers and Hart, Kern, Gershwin, Cole Porter et al., as well as collections of folk music and bossa novas) with the best musicians in the international forum, her work was bound to get a bit generic. Even though the quality of the soundstream never changes, she starts to sound a little self-consciously arty and pretentious. I heard her once in the mid-eighties (I wish I could remember where), and she seemed detached to the point of boredom. (Drummer Mel Lewis looked as though he wanted to be someplace else too, but then he frequently did.)

Two albums that stand out from the sixties are her team-ups with Dick Katz, a keyboardist of uncommon sensitivity and harmonic acumen: *The Feeling Is Mutual* (also released as *Something Special,* 1965) and *A Shade of Difference* (1968), both on Orrin Keepnews's Milestone label and both with Thad Jones, cornet, and Jim Hall, guitar, among others. Katz served as producer as well, which presumably means he picked the songs with Merrill—the only one that doesn't work is "The Winter of Our Discontent," in which the combination of Shakespearean snobbery and downer message could only be the work of Alec Wilder. In 2008, Mosaic Records thoughtfully reissued the two albums together on a single CD titled *The Helen Merrill–Dick Katz Sessions.*

Around the same time, Katz participated in several projects with Lee Konitz, and even though I wouldn't suggest that Merrill was directly influenced by that brilliant alto saxophonist, the way she shapes and phrases a melody seems distinctly postmodern. As with Konitz—particularly in the more recent part of his career—her approach to a song can safely be described as abstract. On "It Don't Mean a Thing," the one distinctly up-tempo track on *The Feeling Is Mutual,* Katz weaves his own piano and the cornet of Thad Jones into a pointillist arrangement that shatters the Ellington tune into a thousand fragments and sticks them back together in reconstituted form. Even though it's not exactly swinging, it nonetheless means something. The most intimate track in the Merrill-Katz collaboration is "You're My Thrill," which, as the younger singer Jeanie Bryson once pointed out to me, is a song of psychological extremes (and even more obsession than "Night and

Day"), which Merrill and Katz perform accompanied only by bassist Ron Carter.

In 1976, Merrill made another major collaboration with a pianist on *John Lewis Helen Merrill.* Lewis was, as always, best known as the musical director of the Modern Jazz Quartet, and the running motif of his career was the conjoining of jazz with classical music. The two Lewis originals that appear here, the wordless "Django" and "The Singer (La Cantatrice)," both have European overtones and are vaguely Baroque; so too is the contrapuntal fashion in which they splinter the melody to "Alone Together." Six of the nine tracks are unaccompanied duets, and Merrill is comparatively extroverted in this context; Lewis is often thought of as a spare piano player who never played so much as one note too many, and Merrill seems to be taking the opportunity to meet him halfway. There's an undercurrent of Bach in Lewis's keyboard style, and while this would normally not augur well for a jazz vocal album, *John Lewis Helen Merrill* doesn't have a pretentious moment on it.

If the John Lewis album represents Merrill's most intimate setting, her best full-scale orchestral album of the period is the 1980 *Casa Forte,* which teamed her for the first time with her future husband, the exceptional arranger and pianist Torrie Zito. As the Spanish title may indicate, this is an album of Latin songs and Pan-American rhythms, mostly from Brazil—although there's a bossafied treatment of Mercer and Warren's "Too Marvelous for Words." Even with the big string section, it's an extraordinarily intimate album, especially so on the two duets, "Like a Lover" with guitarist Bucky Pizzarelli and "Wave" with Zito's solo piano, on both of which Merrill's phrasing is refreshingly direct and straight ahead. *Casa Forte* is among the least typical albums of her career, one of the few that could easily fit in on a WNEW-like adult standards radio station, if such a thing existed anymore.

In the eighties and nineties, Merrill worked frequently with several overseas producers, most notably Kiyoshi Koyama, all of whom had some connection to the corporate vestiges of her original label, Mercury. Koyama is also a historian who specializes in the Mercury label, and as such produced as many new albums as he could with the major jazz singers who had been on it, including Jackie Paris and Billy Eckstine (in fact, Merrill sings two duets with Mr. B on his album *Billy Eckstine Sings with Benny Carter,* 1986). *John Lewis Helen Merrill* was also released on the reactivated Mercury imprint, and at the dawn of the CD era, Koyama oversaw a four-LP/CD box reissue of all of Merrill's fifties Mercury albums.

Koyama and Merrill's oddest project was *Collaboration,* her reunion with Gil Evans in 1987, less than a year before the composer-orchestrator's death. Because Evans's eyesight was failing and he was finding it impossible to write anything new, the two of them rerecorded the same charts they had used for *Dream of You* in 1956. Academically it's interesting: The charts in and of themselves, like nearly all of Evans's work (except his dreadful *Jimi Hendrix* album), are never less than inspired, and Merrill, pushing sixty, hasn't lost anything vocally. But it's hard to consider *Collaboration* a success. Even though Merrill's phrasing is looser and more playful than usual, I can't think of her singing as an improvement on what she had done thirty-one years earlier. Evans had crafted those arrangements for a very young woman in 1956, perhaps wise beyond her years but comparatively inexperienced. He also wrote for a sunnier, more optimistic voice than it was possible for Merrill to be in 1987. Obviously, given his druthers he would have preferred to write new orchestrations of different songs, which would reflect where the two of them now were. (They did do one "new" piece, a treatment of "Summertime" obviously derived from the Miles Davis–Evans version with Steve Lacy on soprano sax.) As I say, *Collaboration* is academically interesting, but that's all—*Dream of You* is still the classic.

In addition to Koyama, Merrill also worked with several French producers, such as Jean-Philippe Allard and Daniel Richard, from the other side of the conglomerate then known as Polygram. Both Koyama and Allard are credited as co-producers of *Just Friends* (1989), which teams her with Stan Getz. The album, unfortunately, has too many remakes, among them "It Don't Mean a Thing" (which she'd already done with Katz and which didn't suit her to begin with) and her third recording of "Yesterdays" (having already done it with both John Lewis and Clifford Brown). *Just Friends* should have been better—the Merrill-Getz combination never quite jells.

Surprisingly—or maybe not so much, given Merrill's career-long capacity for surprise—my favorite of all Merrill's recordings may turn out to be her last (it's her only album of the twenty-first century, at least as of 2010). *Lilac Wine* was taped fifty years after her first recording session and released two years later when she was approaching her seventy-fifth birthday. In some senses it's a follow-up to the singer's previous release, *Jelena Ana Milcetic aka Helen Merrill* (taped in 1999 and released in 2000), in which she intermingled a few Croatian folk songs alongside American standards. To my knowledge this is the first time she's actually recorded a Croatian folk song, "Ti Si Rajski Cvijet (You Are a Flower from Paradise)," in that language.

In both albums, *Jelena Ana Milcetic aka Helen Merrill* and *Lilac Wine*, the focus is autobiographical. For several reasons, it became a convenient coincidence that Merrill's roots are in Croatia. For a time in the post–Cold War era, it was both economically and politically expedient to record sessions with large string sections in the former Yugoslavia. By a further coincidence, one of the finest living bass players, George Mraz, was born and raised in the

Czech Republic, which imbues his playing with a Slavic sensitivity. It was a masterstroke to title the album *Lilac Wine*, which is a song that not only comes from her own past but, by yet another coincidence, happens to concern itself with the loss of youthful innocence.

After many decades of many albums in small group settings with great jazzmen (here the major trumpet soloist is Lew Soloff), and in spite of many often brilliant pianocentric collaborations (Dick Katz, John Lewis, Roger Kellaway), *Lilac Wine* confirms what *Dream of You* first showed us well over fifty years ago: that Merrill's voice is essentially an orchestral instrument, and that she works best accompanied by a lush contingent of strings. Even though Soloff is a powerful presence, the album benefits most from the contributions of Torrie Zito. She has recorded with some outstanding arrangers—Gil Evans, to name one—but Zito may be the most perfect of them all for her. He made a substantial contribution to Merrill's songbook series of the eighties, as well as various other albums going back to the 1980 *Casa Forte*. His string orchestrations for her are nothing short of spectacular; his custom-tailored outfits for her voice suit her better than any other collaborator, even Evans. Zito has achieved the near-impossible in crafting string arrangements that somehow sound lush and spare at the same time.

Still, it's Merrill who has improved the most. She can no longer keep doing the amorphous soundstream thing; rather, age has given her voice a new texture, a new depth. The voice is no longer anonymous and androgynous or neutral. She always sounded at least vaguely pained and anguished, and now the craggy, crackling sound of her voice makes her sound that way whether she wants it to or not. Like *Jelena Ana Milcetic*, the album is full of inner reflection; in fact, she even convinces me that I've heard her sing "Wild Is the Wind" before (another folklike song associated with Nina Simone) even though the discography tells me that this is her first recording of it. Her treatment has a bittersweet, nostalgic quality that's new in Merrill's music, and totally welcome.

"Wild Is the Wind," in fact, now becomes classic Helen Merrill, much like "Lilac Wine." The third song, "Pierre," is something of an oddity, by the late and very iconic French singer-songwriter Barbara (aka Monique Serf, 1930–97), and it's both hummed and sung in French by Merrill. This is a typical singsongy chanson, done with Soloff playing muted and Zito chiming in on electric piano. The combination of Barbara's song and Merrill's stark delivery has a Brelish quality, but Merrill is ultimately much warmer and life-affirming than Brel. Most American listeners, myself especially, will have no idea what the lyric's about, and thus context is everything, and it's easy to imagine it's another aria dealing with wind and wine, lost youth and first love.

"Something I Dreamed Last Night" is a rarity for Merrill, a fully formed old-school torch-and-saloon song. The dramatic action actually transpires in a bar—thanks to the verse ("Scotch and soda for the gentleman"), and in Merrill and Zito's interpretation, it alludes equally to Sinatra's "One for My Baby" and June Christy's "Something Cool," replete with Eugene O'Neill–like allusions to love and other pipe dreams in a bar. The Elvis Presley hit "Love Me Tender" is done as a medley with "How Sweet You Are," an obscure Frank Loesser–Arthur Schwartz movie song (from *Thank Your Lucky Stars*, 1943)—I can't imagine how they ever came up with this juxtaposition, but darned if it doesn't work perfectly. She next tackles Ivan Lins's "The Island," a song that was seductive in the hands of the middle-aged Sarah Vaughan; with Merrill it seems less romantic than nostalgic, a reflection on past romantic rendezvous on all kinds of islands, both geographic and metaphoric.

"One More Walk Around the Garden" is the true climax of the record. Two tracks come after it, the string instrumental "Portrait of Helen Merrill" (a title and idea inspired by "A Portrait of Ella Fitzgerald," which Duke Ellington wrote for Fitzgerald's Ellington songbook), a collaboration between Marian McPartland and Zito, and something called "You" by someone called "Yorke," a disappointing duet with guitarist-vocalist Alan Merrill (apparently a relative).

The best way to listen to the album is to concentrate on tracks one through seven, "Lilac Wine" through "Walk Around the Garden," two very compatible songs about the transitions of time and young/old love in rural (read youthful, innocent) settings. "One More Walk Around the Garden" comes from the flop musical *Carmelina* by Alan Jay Lerner and Burton Lane, and although it was done by theater and cabaret dudes around New York in the mid-nineties, Merrill's treatment is the first I've heard by either a woman or a jazz-oriented singer.

"One More Walk" dovetails perfectly with "Lilac Wine." In 1955, Merrill sang that James Shelton show tune from the perspective of a young woman who had only recently made the rite of passage out of childhood—it ends with her being ready for love. In *Carmelina*, "Walk" was sung by a quartet of old studs who wanted a final youthful fling before being resigned to senility. Merrill instead seems to be more interested in reflecting on those original walks around the garden of her childhood. In both songs, however, Merrill (whose husband and musical director, Torrie Zito, died in December 2009) is not merely reflecting on the transitions of her earlier life, she also sounds as if she's preparing herself to accept the one big lifestyle change that is still to come.

The Mills Brothers

John Junior (1911–1936)
Harry (1913–1982)
Herbert (1912–1989)
Donald (1915–1999)
John Senior (1882–1967)
John III (born 1957)

"You can't imagine the impact that the Mills Brothers had in the early thirties," said James Maher, the venerated historian who recalled that era firsthand. "They just turned everything upside down!" Before the Millses, no one imagined that a vocal group could "fit in so well," as Maher put it, with the jazz and hot dance music of the early thirties, which was already well on its way toward exploding into the swing era. The four brothers not only captivated America's Depression-weary youth, Maher adds, but "they took all the generations in their stride. It wasn't only kids that loved them, it was everybody's entire family." Like their occasional partner Bing Crosby, the Mills Brothers exemplified the best of popular music in the years before the Generation Gap, when grandparents and grandkinder listened with equal interest to essentially the same popular music.

Spiritual cousins of the Boswell Sisters (whose rapid tempo changes made them less suitable for dancing) and forerunners of Lambert, Hendricks & Ross, the Mills Brothers were the first to transmute ensemble jazz into vocal (if not necessarily verbal) terms. They were among the earliest to master the wordless scat singing style, so it's no surprise that they provided perfect quartet counterpoint for both fathers of jazz-pop singing, Crosby and Armstrong. The act was originally billed as "Four Boys and a Guitar" (not altogether condescendingly, since in the beginning the younger brothers still qualified as boys), and the Mills method of impersonating instruments was soon imitated far and wide. Tony Bennett, who grew up in the multiculti neighborhood of Astoria, Queens, remembers that it was the Irish families in particular who, on warm Sunday nights in the thirties, would sit on their porches and give out with their imitations of the latest Mills Brothers hit. Lester Young would often refer to his quartet—and the saxophone-plus-rhythm-section combination in general—as the Four Mills Brothers.

Groups of all races and sexes and nations (including a distant quartet known as the African Mills Brothers) were soon mimicking the patented Mills wa-da-da-da-de's. Indeed, the earliest extant performance by Frank Sinatra is an unabashed cloning of the Crosby-Mills classic "Shine." Likewise, the group's beautifully extended bass lines, initially sung by its original guitarist, John Mills Jr., have also been cited as a forebear of the later Sinatra-Dorsey legato style. Dean Martin in particular was profoundly influenced by the group. When Bennett met Martin for the first time, he told the older Italian crooner, "I can tell that you grew up listening to the Mills Brothers." An early private recording exists that is believed to be Dean Martin's first demo, and it contains a tinny-sounding treatment of "I Surrender, Dear" in which he imitates both Crosby and the Millses.

The brothers' technique and their sound were so unprecedented that, in the way Armstrong claimed to have accidentally started scatting when he dropped his sheet music in the middle of a take, they felt compelled to rationalize their approach with an explanatory story. Harry Mills once recalled, "There was a seven-piece band that used to play in our hometown. They played 'Tiger Rag,' this fast little tune that didn't have words. That's how we got the idea of trying to sound like a band. We took the song home and started playing with it." On another occasion, Harry claimed, "We [originally] copied musical instruments with a kazoo. But one night, I forgot the kazoo and we made the imitations with just our own voices. And it was better!"

The brothers were born between 1911 (basso and guitarist John Junior) and 1915 (lead tenor Donald), tenor Herbert and baritone Harry coming along, respectively, in 1912 and 1913. Like their father, all four of the brothers were born and raised in Piqua, Ohio. In 1925, when the youngest was only ten, the legend goes, they first starting singing together as the Mills Brothers. Coincidentally, showbiz columnist Earl Wilson, who happened to be in Piqua that year, didn't get to hear the youngsters in their early teens, but he did encounter a barbershop quartet called "The Kings of Harmony," comprised of the previous generation of Mills Brothers—father John Senior and various uncles of Harry, Herbert, Donald, and John; their mother, Ethel, was supposedly a trained opera singer.

It's no coincidence that the brothers began to work professionally in the same year that electrical recording was perfected. There's no way any aspect of the brothers' music—especially the instrumental imitations—could have worked before the invention of the microphone. As John Junior stated in a rare interview (quoted by Peter Grendysa in the notes to the recommended *The Mills Brothers: The Anthology, 1931–1968*), he could only make his patented tuba sound by doing his oom-pah thing right up close to the microphone. Harry reported that he made his trumpet sound by cupping his hands around his nose and lips, and Herbert came up with the saxophone sound by manipulating his mouth muscles just so. The youngest, Donald, had the highest, purest voice, and generally sang lead, but also engaged in the instrumental imitations, performing whatever "horn" was required.

The group got started in local vaudeville, and then got in on the ground floor of the radio boom by singing on local stations. Soon they were being featured on the most important radio station in the Midwest, Cincinnati's WLIW. They sang on many different programs, under a variety of pseudonyms; occasionally the station had them work completely nonverbally, so that those at home would assume they were listening to an instrumental band, not a vocal group. These stations certainly never drew attention to the fact that the brothers were black.

They hooked up with the well-connected Tommy Rockwell, who for a time managed Louis Armstrong and dozens of other major black and white bands and attractions.

Through Rockwell, the Millses became an essential part of the new wave that revolutionized pop music in the early thirties, thus laying the ground for the swing era: Bing Crosby, the Boswell Sisters, Cab Calloway. All of these acts, including the Mills Brothers, were signed by William Paley to CBS Radio and by Jack Kapp of Brunswick Records, and all four acts also made movies for Paramount Pictures (they're all in Crosby's first starring feature, *The Big Broadcast*). And all four acts were profoundly influenced by Armstrong. "I just remember my mom was sitting in this room in New York with this fellow who I found out later was William Paley," said Harry. "She made a three-year deal for us." (Paley may have socialized with Ethel Mills, but it seems more likely that Rockwell would have worked out the deal.) The brothers caused an instant sensation on CBS in 1930 and 1931, particularly when they co-starred on the widely popular *Fleischmann's Yeast Hour* hosted by Rudy Vallee. (A later aircheck survives of the foursome on Vallee's show, introduced by the bandleader host and then singing their famous arrangement of "Dinah" with co-star Alice Faye.)

The young brothers recorded for the first time in 1930, at the facilities of the independent Gennett label, the results of which are unissued and are lost. Their recording career begins in earnest with Kapp and Brunswick in October 1931, and in many ways the group's very first recordings are their most radical. The first order of business was a brilliant series of sides that completely challenges accepted notions of what vocal and instrumental jazz were supposed to be about. At a time when the record industry was almost entirely predicated on new hits—the current songs from films and shows that the publishers were pushing, the pluggers were plugging, and all the bands and singers were doing—the Mills Brothers recorded almost nothing but jazz standards for their entire first year; one suspects that a lot of these were the arrangements they had been perfecting since 1925. Throughout 1931–32, they concentrated on what would today be called repertory jazz classics: a great many songs that were already the staple of what hot bands were playing, songs that generally had only existed instrumentally, beginning on their first date with "Tiger Rag." (If you have any doubt that the brothers were well versed in the jazz canon, you need only listen to their quotation of Jimmie Noone's "Apex Blues" in the middle of the Carmichael-Mercer "Lazy Bones.")

Even though "Tiger Rag" has no lyrics to speak of—none are necessary—other than "Where's that tiger?," the hoary old feline comes alive in a way it never had before. It should be stressed that even apart from the instrumental-to-vocal conversion, this is a superb rearrangement of a familiar piece.

The Mills version of "Tiger Rag" is a daring reconstruction in form as well as in its vocal texture: It doesn't follow the four or so very formal strains of the ancient New Orleans warhorse; no traces linger of the original French source material. Rather, the Millses open with the most familiar section, the "Hold that tiger" line, after a series of variations, some closely tied to the established song, some not. Then they return to the same "Hold that tiger" sequence at the end, phrasing and voicing it completely differently. In a mere ninety-four seconds, this new quartet has managed to totally rock our world.

A great many of their earliest recordings may be taken almost as an homage to the man who most inspired them—and with whom they would later make some of their most memorable music—Louis Armstrong. "St. Louis Blues," "Shine," "Dinah," "Chinatown," "Rockin' Chair," and "Sweet Sue" are all jazz standards and material associated with Armstrong (which are two different ways of saying the same thing); on "Rockin' Chair," Harry Mills does an extraordinary impression of Armstrong's vocal style, while singing all of his variations ("What cabin jokin' father?") in a high tenor rather than mimicking Armstrong's baritone. It's not until 1934 that the brothers begin recording new pop songs with any regularity.

Where the Boswells specialized in elaborate extravaganzas with elaborate key and time signature changes, the overall shape of the Mills Brothers' arrangements was somewhat simpler. Rather than impressing us with their ability to stop on a dime and start again in a whole new tempo, the brothers were masters at locking into a specific groove and sticking with it, making them far easier to dance to than the Boswells. Where the changing of tempos in a Boswells production points to their indoctrination in the European classics, the way the Millses lock into a groove and hold it (especially effectively on "Digga Digga Do") shows their fundamental foundation in the blues. And where Armstrong tended to get more ornamental in his second choruses, the Millses get more ascetic and streamlined—they drop any word or note that might get in their way. The second choruses of "Put On Your Old Grey Bonnet" and "Chinatown, My Chinatown" find them dropping irrelevant articles, as if they were whittling the melody down to its bare essentials.

It's this blues-jazz-Armstrong-informed sensibility that allows them in many cases to transcend their material. Unlike the way Kapp dealt with the Boswells and their Swanee-Mammy extravaganzas, he doesn't seem to have any specific content agenda concerning the Millses. However, the brothers, while rarely heading south to Boswell territory, do take a Tin Pan Alley view of the rest of the world. They travel to "Chinatown, My Chinatown" to get a look at those "almond eyes of brown" (and treat us to an extended "tuba" solo by John Junior) and also to "Nagasaki," where they sing of Fujiyama mamas. In "Jungle Fever" (which they introduced in the 1934 MGM Civil War epic *Operator 13*), they sing of a dusky maiden, a brown-eyed siren, and a native dream girl. In "My Little Grass Shack In Kealakekua, Hawaii," a track not issued until the CD era, Donald sings of being "a homesick little island boy" who wants to go back to his fish and poi. On Dorothy Fields's lyric to "Digga Digga Do," done with Duke Ellington, they ponder the double meaning of the term "Virgin Isle."

It's not as if the lyrics don't matter, but, as with Armstrong and Crosby, the Millses have developed a means of singing that lets you hear the integrity of the music without it being compromised by the banality of these outdated racial references. Even more politically out-of-touch is "Smoke Rings," in which the brothers heartily endorse the medicinal powers of tobacco. One way to avoid such messages was to avoid the words altogether, as they do on the jazz classic "Some of These Days," which ends with Donald doing a double time scat before Harry enters with his "trumpet solo."

(Incidentally, in addition to the double disc, career-long MCA retrospective, I can also recommend two sets of singles from their 1931–34 Brunswick material, *Four Boys and a Guitar: The Essential Mills Brothers* on Sony Legacy and *Sweeter than Sugar* on English ASV. Better yet, go all the way with *The Mills Brothers: The '30s Recordings*, an ace six-CD box from English JSP which covers their chronology up through 1938, with superb sound by John R. T. Davies. The JSP-Nostalgia series is especially good at capturing all their team-ups of the early days, including previously unissued radio and sound track performances.)

At their fourth session for Brunswick, Bing Crosby dropped in and became the first and most important of many guest stars who crossed cadenzas with the brothers over the next twenty years or so. There would be three especially brilliant Crosby-Mills titles, "Dinah," "Shine," and "My Honey's Lovin' Arms." Early on, the brothers also worked with guest artists on Kapp's epic *Blackbirds of 1928* album, on which they shared space with Cab Calloway and the orchestras of Don Redman and Duke Ellington. As it happens, they don't sing with the Ellington band per se, but rather are given an extended interlude (accompanied by John Junior's guitar, as usual) in the middle of an Ellington instrumental of "Digga Digga Do." It's a particularly astute pairing on Jack Kapp's part: to combine the band with vocalized instruments with a vocal group that specialized in instrumentally styled singing.

There were other, even more attractive combinations ahead, after the Millses followed Jack Kapp to his berth at the new Decca Records in 1934, including four sides with Ella Fitzgerald (1937 and 1949) and an especially glorious eight-song teaming with Louis Armstrong himself. The brothers had already done right by Irving Berlin's classic waltz "The Song

Is Ended" at a session a few months earlier in London, done with Harry's hand-made "trumpet," but upon returning stateside, they cut an even better treatment with Armstrong, his distinctive voice, and an actual metal instrument. What's amazing is that the London recording reveals how thoroughly the brothers had worked out the arrangement, even to the point of composing what later became Armstrong's trumpet solo. Louis essentially just plays on his horn what Harry had already laid down on his simulated trumpet solo. The Armstrong-Mills team-ups are surprisingly politically charged, varying between songs of the Abolitionist movement that still carried some juice in the twentieth century ("My Darling Nellie Gray") and the extremely topical "W.P.A.," a very mean-spirited attack on President Roosevelt ("Sleep while you work . . .") that I can't honestly believe either Armstrong or the Millses actually endorsed.

In April 1933, John Junior was diagnosed with what was then called "double pneumonia," and his illness prompted the quartet to take a few months off from working. He temporarily rallied, but by the time of their 1935 tour of Europe, he was in bad shape again. He died at the age of thirty-four in January 1936, at which point his father, John Senior, took over his place in the vocal quartet. "Pennies from Heaven" may be the first masterpiece by the new lineup; perhaps the presence of the elder Mills led them to a slightly more conservative approach, as they phrase the first statement of the melody in more of a traditional glee club–barbershop quartet fashion, with very dramatic speed-ups and slow-downs, and a striking contrast between their gorgeous sustained harmonies and the choppier, swinging instrumental imitations at the center. John Senior shone especially brightly on his featured solo on the foursome's swinging treatment of the traditional basso sailor's air "Asleep in the Deep."

The next big change came in 1940, when they formally abandoned their famous hand trumpets, tubas, and saxophones and instead became something closer to a conventional vocal quartet. Their harmony and the attractive, dark timbre of their voices were now so refined that perhaps they felt they no longer needed the instrumental imitations. Or maybe they were afraid that they would feel silly, now that they were gradually turning thirty (John Senior was almost sixty), cupping their hands and blowing into them. The imitations do appear again, but only occasionally, and rather mildly, as on their 1942 "I'll Be Around."

In the immediate prewar period, the act was facing a greater transition than the one from John Junior to Senior, or even from the Four Boys and a Guitar sound to a more mainstream pop background. When the quartet first started, it was the sound of the group itself that was everything—in fact, they sounded so fresh and radical that perhaps Kapp thought they would be best appreciated when they sang well-known jazz standards. After ten years on the market, their sound itself was no longer novel. At the same time, the commercial music industry itself was transitioning to a state in which an individual sound was gradually becoming less important than a hit song; in 1940, *Billboard* for the first time began charting which records sold the most—in all parts of the country and from all labels—as an indication that the business as a whole was changing.

Incredibly, the career of the Mills Brothers was just really taking off at this point. Though not quite as frequently on the charts as the Andrews Sisters, they soared to new heights of popularity during the war—with three top hits ("Paper Doll," "You Always Hurt the One You Love," and "Till Then"), and then did even better in the late forties and fifties, a period when they were almost never off the charts. They landed two of the all-time best-remembered songs of the war era in "Paper Doll," a 1930 opus that had never quite caught on but which became suddenly relevant in light of the war as a song of fantasy lovers. Like virtually all artists talking about the biggest song of their career—Clooney and "Come on-a My House," Sinatra and "My Way"—the Millses claimed they couldn't stand "Paper Doll" at first, but gradually warmed up to it. Good thing, as it turned out to be their equivalent of "White Christmas" (indeed, it's said to be the single biggest song of the era after Crosby's Christmas hit), the biggest number of the group's career (twelve weeks at number one), and a song that they reprised in performance every night for the rest of their lives. "Till Then" was an even more potent song of separation that grew out of the current tradition of dramatic English war songs like "The White Cliffs of Dover" and "When the Lights Go On Again."

Which brings up one quality the Mills Brothers had in common with the Andrews Sisters, only more so, which was the art of sounding traditional and cutting-edge at the same time. By the end of the war, the brothers had a sound as familiar and reassuring as Bing Crosby's, or, for that matter, Guy Lombardo's. But they were still bending notes in unforeseen directions, still sustaining harmonies that never grew stale, still offering challenging bass lines and effortless modulations, as on "Glow Worm." And they could still swing like crazy, particularly on the series of hit singles they recorded with Sy Oliver in the fifties. Small wonder the Mills Brothers continued to be so popular: They still appealed to both the kids of draft age and younger, as well as to their parents. Only the Millses could sound old-fashioned enough to find their last great singing partner in Al Jolson on "Is It True What They Say About Dixie?"—leave it to Jolson to take them down to Dixie at long last. Yet they also sound hip and swinging and completely contemporary on the Stan Kenton specialty "Across the Alley from the Alamo." The four boys—men now—and a fifth on guitar were still taking entire generations in their stride. They offered musical comfort food that was never less than substantial and nourishing.

Indeed, the vast bulk of the tracks on the *Anthology* double disc are from 1945–68. They continued to compete in the pop stakes, practically the last of their generation to do so—even Crosby was no longer trying as hard. By the fifties, the dichotomy between the Millses with just guitar and instrumental impressions, which was supposed to be more jazzy, versus the Millses as a vocal group with accompanying orchestra, which was supposed to be mere pop, was completely irrelevant. They landed many original hits, in such irresistibly catchy items as "The Jones Boy" (cool key change before the bridge) and "Be My Life's Companion," a terrific Nuclear Age courtship dance on which the brothers outsold emerging canary Rosemary Clooney.

Most of their big chart toppers, however, remained swinging updates of older material. "Glow Worm"—Johnny Mercer's revamp of a 1908 operetta showpiece, "A Carnival in Venice"—was a turn-of-the century brass virtuoso piece, while "Pretty Butterfly" was Tin Pan Alley's latest take on Antonín Dvořák's "Humoresque" (the previous one had been Ervin Drake's "Mabel, Mabel"); "Lazy River," "Say 'Sí Sí,' " "I've Got My Love to Keep Me Warm," and "Nevertheless" were supercharged updates of thirties songs. "You're Nobody Till Somebody Loves You" and "Opus One" were decade-old swing-era remnants when the Millses put them back on the map.

One consequence of having started so young, when the eldest was barely twenty, was that their longevity became something wondrous to consider. They were the major male vocal group of all time, there's no doubt, yet in the thirties they competed with the Boswell Sisters, in the forties with the Andrews Sisters, and in the fifties with the McGuire Sisters, the Four Aces, and other current fave raves of the Eisenhower era that threatened to make the very concept of intonation obsolete. Even in the late fifties, after the pop singles market had changed radically, the Millses were still in there pitching. They appeared with Fats Domino (not to mention Harry James, George Shearing, and Cal Tjader) in the 1958 musical quickie *The Big Beat,* released in the same year that the seventy-five-year-old John Senior left the act, leaving the Mills Brothers a trio once more.

The quartet, still with paterfamilias singing bass, continued to keep up with the changing generations. On "Standing on the Corner" they competed with Dean Martin and the Four Lads, while "Queen of the Senior Prom" was designed to give Bobby Darin's "Queen of the Hop" a run for its money (Darin would soon be going into Mills territory on "Lazy River"), and their cover of "Get a Job" is far more sublimely harmonized than the original by the Coasters. Likewise, "Smack Dab in the Middle" is, to paraphrase Artie Shaw, better rock 'n' roll than most real rock 'n' roll. With the understated Island rhythms of "Yellow Bird," an early hit by Alan and Marilyn Bergman (with choral director Norman Luboff), the mix starts to get a little more Muzaky, but it's still the Mills Brothers.

Long-distance running was already one of their strengths, but no one could have predicted that the three remaining Mills brothers would have one last chart hit around the time their father and longtime fourth voice, John Senior, died at eighty-five in 1967. This was "Cab Driver." To be honest, the statistical achievement—of charting steadily for thirty-plus years—was more of a point of pride than the record itself, which isn't particularly good: It's a quasi-hillbilly, quasi–youth pop item written by Carson Parks, author of the Frank and Nancy Sinatra hit "Somethin' Stupid." It wasn't a spectacular hit, like "Hello, Dolly" or the Rat Pack resurgence, but it got the threesome up to number 23 on the charts—not bad for three old-timers who were stars when Frank, Sammy, and Dino were kids, and when the *parents* of the Beatles and Herb Alpert were still young. Yet the Mills Brothers went out on a high note, as they had recorded a long and successful string of albums for Dot Records as a trio in the sixties, including two memorable meetings with the Count Basie Orchestra.

Their work of the seventies was less distinguished, but still they persisted. Between 1970 and 1981, Paramount Records and then Ranwood Records released another ten or so albums by the Mills Brothers, now a trio before Harry Mills's death at age sixty-nine in 1981. At this point, Donald's son, John III, then about twenty-four, stepped in as the third voice. After Herbert died in 1989, father Donald and son John III continued as a duo for a full ten years more. In 1998, the two Mills brothers were presented with a Grammy lifetime achievement award, but a year afterward Donald Mills, the youngest of the original brothers, died at the age of eighty-four. The cab driver had finally come to take the last of the Mills brothers home. (As late as 2009, John Mills III continues to tour under the Mills Brothers name, usually in a duo with Elmer Hopper, formerly with the Platters, sometimes with a third member.)

Matt Monro (1930–1985)

Whenever Frank Sinatra was accused of being too cozy with the mafia, the singer responded that he was singled out for such a charge because of his ethnic background. He wouldn't have been in so much trouble, he once said, "if my name didn't end in a vowel." Terry Parsons took the stage name "Monro" at the suggestion of a friend, the pianist Winifred Atwell, who borrowed it from her father's first name. One can't help but feel that Parsons (perhaps even subconsciously) responded well to the proposal of "Monro" as a last name because it sounded somewhat Italian—it ended in a vowel. Perhaps Parsons wanted to get into a little of the trouble that Sinatra always seemed to find himself in. Monro also consistently cited Perry Como as his primary influence, and "Monro" is very much like "Como." It seems possible that Parsons wanted some Italian-American good luck to rub off on him. (Paradoxically, just a few years earlier, Italian-American singers were pressured to make their names more Anglo.)

At the dawn of the twentieth century, Mother England was the center of all culture—theatrical and musical—in the English-speaking world. By the Jazz Age, the Brits had ceded to the Yanks, but they kept pace: British pop competed respectfully with America, at least up to the start of the Second World War. During the thirties, big dance bands thrived in England no less than in the States, even though by the time of the war the British bands were sounding less and less British and more and more like cockney imitations of Benny Goodman and Glenn Miller. When Major Miller himself initiated a long London residency with his Army Air Force band, that was, in fact, the end of the native English big band style. (Robert Farnon once told me that the British musicians were put off by Miller himself, who supposedly pulled rank and acted every bit like a snobby major. But both Miller's orchestras are, in fact, still worshipped in the U.K.)

There were relatively few major British "modern" swing bands (the Squadronaires, Ted Heath, and Vic Lewis were exceptions) and, surprisingly, there were even fewer notable British pop singers. I say surprisingly because American-style postwar pop singers were amazingly popular in the British Isles: Crosby, Sinatra, Eckstine, Haymes, Stafford, and Fitzgerald all had big followings and fan clubs in Old Blimey. When the King Cole Trio first played England in 1950, the group didn't go over as well as Cole would later on, as a single, because the trio was still a largely instrumental act and the Britishers wanted to hear more of his singing.

Perhaps the popularity of American singers in England was precisely the problem for local talent. The avalanche of Americans was too much, for other than Dame Vera Lynn; it's almost impossible to think of a Brit pop star between Al Bowlly and Anthony Newley (and Matt Monro) who could compete on an international level. In America, almost without exception, the major postwar pop singers graduated from the big bands; in England the major band singers, like Sam Browne and Elsie Carlisle (and even Al Bowlly, who was born before the turn of the century) were perhaps too old to start new careers as bobby-sox idols after the war. (The one important exception was Lynn, whose major contribution to music would seem to be bringing monotony to a whole new level.)

Yet the British *were* consistently producing excellent jazz, from Humphrey Lyttelton to Tubby Hayes and Ronnie Scott, and in the late fifties, the local trad scene, a mixture of Dixieland, R&B, and instrumental pop, began yielding international hits: Kenny Ball's "Midnight in Moscow," Monty Sunshine's

"Petite Fleur," Acker Bilk's "Stranger on the Shore." (One would have a hard time naming an American Dixieland group that sold records like these British trad groups, excepting the Village Stompers, a Dixieland band marketed to a folk audience.)

One looks in vain for the English equivalents of Dick Haymes or Billy Eckstine. Perhaps the most telling thing about Matt Monro's career was that before he emerged, the closest thing to a major male singer in his genre was the Liverpudlian Frankie Vaughan, who was not so much an English equivalent of Sinatra or Como as the U.K.'s version of almost any of those Mitch Miller acolytes (Frankie Laine, Guy Mitchell, Johnny Ray) singing a similar species of quasi-novelty material in a highly mannered, exaggerated style. Yet even though Vaughan was prominently placed in one of Marilyn Monroe's last big pictures, the 1960 *Let's Make Love*, and though he had a more durable career than many crooners of the era (such as Alan Dale and Richard Hayes), he never caught on in America.

There almost always were English songs and English artists on the American charts, but the term "British Invasion" refers specifically to the rock bands that sprang from the U.K. in the wake of the Beatles in the mid-sixties. The one traditional pop singer to play a significant role in that invasion was Matt Monro, who kept his hair short and generally fit in better with the Rat Pack than the Fab Four.

Monro was part of the great flowering of adult pop talent that blossomed after the first wave of rock (Elvis) ended and before the second wave (the Beatles) began. Back in the U.S.A., Jack Jones, Steve Lawrence, Bobby Darin, and others (all born in the 1930s) came into their own in this era, while Bennett and Greco got a second wind. The standard story you expect to read about a traditional pop singer is that he came of age in the fifties and peaked in the early sixties. Monro, on the other hand, didn't really get anywhere until the peak years of rock 'n' roll, and then he quite comfortably coexisted with that style for the rest of his career.

The definitive collection of Matt Monro's career, despite a rather lugubrious title, is *Matt Monro: The Singer's Singer*, a four-CD box set released in 2001 with a very generous booklet and an equally generous hundred or so tracks, compiled and annotated by the singer's daughter, Michele Monro. According to the notes, Terence Edward Parsons was born on December 1, 1930, in Shoreditch, London. His was not an easy childhood. His father died when he was three, his mother took sick shortly thereafter, and the five siblings were scattered among foster homes. Terry quit school at fourteen to work in a cigarette factory, which was not a good move for his long-term health. Still in his teens, he worked a variety of manual jobs, ranging from the railroad to a custard manufacturer, and, motivated by a desire to travel, he lied about his age and joined the British Army. Travel he did: After being stationed in the U.K., where he learned how to drive and repair a tank, he spent three years in Hong Kong.

Apparently it was in the service that Parsons first began to take the idea of singing seriously. He started making the rounds of talent shows for servicemen and other Englishmen living in Hong Kong. When he won too often and was barred from the competitions, he was offered his own radio show, first strictly for the British military and then for civilians. Demobilized in 1953, he returned to London, where he put his tank-piloting skills to work driving a city bus.

For years his very brief tenure as a "singing busman" became the bread-and-butter of feature writers across the country, much like Perry Como's stint as a singing barber. He drove a bus in the day, and he sang with bands in the clubs at night, including a brief nocturnal stint with veteran dance band leader Harry Leader, who was then leading one of the more popular postwar orchs. Parsons also came to the attention of conductor Al Jordan, with whom, in 1955, he recorded a song called "Strange Lady in Town" on the obscure Solitaire label.

A demonstration disc by Parsons fell into the hands of singing pianist Winifred Atwell. (The Trinidad-born Atwell, 1914–83, seems to have been the rough British equivalent of those black American ladies who specialized in raucous piano and an engaging blend of blues, boogie, and standards, such as Julia Lee, Nellie Lutcher, Rose Murphy, Martha Davis, et al.) Atwell was so taken with the young singer that she forwarded his demo to her record company, British Decca, and the label shared her enthusiasm. Decca signed Parsons immediately and put him to work making singles and albums; the story goes that when he did his first Decca session he was still wearing his bus driver uniform. The record company also decided that Terry Parsons was an unsuitable name for a pop star, and Miss Atwell helped him come up with "Matt Monro." "Matt" was a journalist who had given Parsons one of his first write-ups and "Monro" was the first name of Winifred Atwell's father. As Michele Monro remembered, her father used to say, "It's an anagram of 'moron.'"

Parsons, Monro, or moron: It didn't make much difference. Heard today, the Monro Decca sides (including his marvelous premiere album, *Blue and Sentimental*) reveal an emerging talent, but they completely failed to make any impact at the time. The same thing was true for the recordings he made after Decca dropped him and he made a second album and a few singles for Fontana. Still, he had reason to be optimistic: He was signed as the principal male singer on a much listened to BBC series, *The Showband Show*, and went over well there; it was now a matter of putting the right combination of elements together.

In the mid- to late fifties, Monro was married twice, briefly to the mother of his "fine young son," and then for considerably longer to Miss "Mickie" Schuller. The second Mrs. Monro was a music business insider who worked for the London office of the publisher Mills Music, and who in addition to becoming his second wife (and the mother of his daughter and son) also served as his manager. The late fifties were musically frustrating although professionally rewarding, in that he paid the bills mainly by singing jingles in TV and radio commercials.

How he turned the tide from zero to hero is a tale like no other. In 1960, producer George Martin (not yet *Sir* George Martin) was crafting a very successful series of comedy albums for EMI with Peter Sellers, the comic actor and man of a thousand voices. For one particular bit, they needed a singer to do a send-up of Frank Sinatra, and Martin hired the still unknown Matt Monro, who sang on the LP *Songs for Swinging Sellers* under the pseudonym of "Fred Flange." (The song—"You Keep Me Swingin'"—a very well-turned slice of ersatz Cahn–Van Heusen–Riddle, is included on the *Singer's Singer* box.) The identity of Fred Flange immediately became a subject of much discussion in the British press. Some listeners thought it was the Swinging Sellers himself, others thought it could only be the real Sinatra, who was then still under contract to EMI's American arm, Capitol Records.

Martin and EMI were so pleased with all the attention Fred Flange was receiving that they offered Monro a contract to make real singles under his own name. Starting at the top, Monro's first Parlophone release was the Gershwin brothers standard "Love Is Here to Stay." This fared no better than his Decca or Fontana efforts. But his next Parlophone release proved that the third label had the charm. Where he had not been able to make an impression singing a classic American song, it was somehow fitting that he should land his first hit with a homegrown song, "Portrait of My Love," by Cyril Ornadel.

Not only was it fitting, it was the start of a trend: Virtually all of Monro's most notable songs and hits were British or European. After the British "Portrait," there was "Softly (As I Leave You)" based on an Italian song (originally called "Piano") with which, for a time, he succeeded in becoming more Italian than Sinatra himself. Monro gave Leslie Bricusse his first notable hit with "My Kind of Girl," and when *Stop the World* and then *Roar of the Greasepaint* opened in the West End, Monro was the first to come out with definitive pop versions of the Bricusse-Newley hits "Gonna Build a Mountain," "Who Can I Turn To?," and "On a Wonderful Day Like Today."

When the James Bond film series was launched, in 1962, the larger world learned that Englishmen (even though both Sean Connery and the Bond character were actually Scottish) could actually be macho and sexy—and have lots of groovy toys, baby! It was Monro who christened the tradition of having a cool title song for each super spy epic, starting with Lionel Bart's "From Russia with Love." He also had first crack at several hits by songwriter Don Black (also doubling as the singer's personal manager), among them "Walk Away" (a German import) and the blockbuster "Born Free" (co-written with *Bond* musical director John Barry). When Monro's producer, George Martin, achieved even greater success with the Beatles, it was Monro who first showed the parents of the world what a pretty song Paul McCartney's "Yesterday" actually was. He also later sang a beautiful and profound interpretation of "The Long and Winding Road."

It's also fitting that all of these songs were covered, as it were, by local artists in the United States. Sinatra got back on the charts with "Softly," while he and Count Basie—as well as Nat Cole and Buddy Greco—jumped on "My Kind of Girl."

While American stars were singing Monro's signature songs, he in turn made a point of recording virtually all the major American adult pop hits. He did especially well with the songs of Henry Mancini, the Hollywood composer whose appeal was most international, not least because he wrote the theme songs for so many films set in Europe, such as *The Pink Panther* and *Charade,* even though the hazily alcoholic "Days of Wine and Roses" and the Nashville-styled "Dear Heart" were resolutely American.

The music of the Italian-American Mancini was just one example of how Monro reigned as the postwar pop singer most associated with the international experience. Too often inaccurately cited as the British Sinatra, Monro can be better positioned as the British successor to Nat King Cole, in that his two specialties were movie songs and international songs. He had hits in Italian ("*Come Sta*"), ersatz–Middle Eastern ("Mirage"), Spanish ("*Todo Pasará* [All of a Sudden]" and "*No Puedo Quitar Mis Ojos De Ti* [Can't Take My Eyes off You]"). He even did Cole one better in recording three pop slices of heightened Hebraica: "Theme from Exodus," "Sunrise, Sunset," and even "Hava Nagila."

Monro only did one songbook album devoted to a major American writer, and that was Hoagy Carmichael, who was never the focus of such a project from an important American star. *Matt Monro Sings Hoagy Carmichael* drew praise from the songwriter, not surprisingly, especially for his rendition of a Carmichael–Mitchell Parish rarity of 1934, "One Morning in May," while Crosby himself singled out Monro's reading of "I Get Along Without You Very Well." It's not surprising that he's so good on the classic Carmichael love songs like "The Nearness of You," but he's also aces on such unlikely numbers as "Small Fry" (learned from Crosby), and he makes "Memphis in June" sound like "Mayfair in June."

Perhaps Monro's point was that he wanted to associate himself with the most thoroughly American of all major songwriters. Remarkably, he captured the New World at the same time he conquered

the Old: The Americans were just a heartbeat behind the British in accepting this "Italian" singer from Central London. Indeed, Monro spent most of the second half of the sixties operating out of Los Angeles, where he was able to collaborate with such inspired American arranger-conductors as Sid Feller and Billy May, and where he also did a TV special (recently issued on CD) with Nelson Riddle.

Monro had what Pete Hamill would call an "area code 800" voice: Bereft of accent, he sounded as if he could have come from anywhere in the English-speaking world—Cambridge, Massachusetts, or Cambridge, England, Wales or New South Wales. Terry Parsons might have been born a cockney—Shoreditch is within the sound of Bow Bells—but even Henry Higgins himself couldn't have told where Matt Monro hailed from; when he opened his mouth, no Englishman despised him. Even his second son, Matt Monro Jr., had more of a sharply pronounced English accent when he duetted with his dad on the Italian import "More."

Monro's vocal quality was slightly generic (perhaps a bland title like *The Singer's Singer* may actually suit him). When he sings "Spring Is Here" or "I'm a Fool to Want You" it's lovely, but unlike Sinatra, Matt Monro never made you want to go and down a few pints and plunge off London Bridge (and he never claimed to; as mentioned above, Monro always cited Como as his primary influence). Nor could he, on an up-tempo like "Let Me Sing and I'm Happy," lift you out of your seat like Jolson. His voice didn't have the combination of beauty and depth that Nat Cole's had, but his "When I Fall in Love" was quite effective, especially in that it catches one off guard by opening with the verse. Compared to Sinatra's version, his "My Way" is relatively shallow and singsongy, but as with the best of Vic Damone, great beauty doesn't always need additional depth, because when you reach a level this rarefied, beauty is in itself a kind of profundity. The *Singer's Singer* box wanders quite far afield: There are readings of Como's Chopin-derived hit, "Till the End of Time," and "The Green Leaves of Summer," Dimitri Tiomkin's faux folk song (conceived along the model of the famous passage from Ecclesiastes that later became Pete Seeger's "Turn, Turn, Turn") that are both surprisingly stirring; he does the same with "If I Were a Carpenter," nudging that folk-pop hit with considerably more emotional impact than Bobby Darin was able to manage.

Perhaps the most obvious reason why Monro didn't make it in the fifties had nothing to do with managers or records or songs or other circumstances, but simply because his style and sound were so right for the sixties. His was the perfect voice for and the living embodiment of a nation that was just stepping into the spotlight: "It's a Breeze," "Here and Now," "The Good Life," "This Is the Life" are all fairly ecstatic songs of conspicuous consumption, which, although some are from France and America, celebrate the awakening of newly swinging Britain. At times his up-tempos seem like slightly forced stepchildren of the best Sinatra-Riddle singles, but his best swing numbers, like "My Kind of Girl" and "You've Got Possibilities," excite and stimulate largely through the use of Bobby Darin–like modulations (and modulations and modulations).

Monro's most frequent collaborator was arranger and conductor Johnny Spence, who began working with him from the start of the EMI period. Thanks to Spence as well as to Martin—and of course to Monro's chops and taste—he emerges in retrospect as one of the classiest acts of the sixties. With the exception of Tony Bennett, virtually all the major male singers of the sixties made a great many lousy records. (Sinatra made only a few lousy records, and Andy Williams made only a couple of nonlousy records.) But Monro perhaps had the greatest gift for taking a lousy song and, through the strength of his singing and the orchestration, making it nonlousy. Williams had the hit out of "Music to Watch Girls By," but despite his attractive voice at the time, that single sounded indescribably junky, and it hasn't improved with age. But Monro's treatment is surprisingly palatable; he makes it sound, in fact, like a real song, something a singer could actually sink his teeth into and not sound as if he's insulting the intelligence of his audience.

The same thing goes for "You've Made Me So Very Happy," "Can't Take My Eyes off You," and "Bridge over Troubled Water." I wouldn't want to hear Sinatra or Sammy Davis do any of these, but, as far as Generation Gap crossovers go, in Monro's tonsils they certainly are not a disgrace. One song that sounds amazingly good is "He Ain't Heavy, He's My Brother," a slice of pseudobiblical flower-childism that was a hit for the Hollies, another band of British Invaders. In fact, there is only one track in the whole *Singer's Singer* box that I have to skip past: "I Don't Want to Run Your Life," a dreadful, anthemic disco disaster. I've even grown to love the hippie-dippie "We're Gonna Change the World."

To get through the sixties without embarrassing oneself was difficult enough. By the seventies, it had proved impossible. By now, Monro's hits had stopped coming, even in the U.K., and the record industry had achieved the ultimate triumph of effectively neutralizing any trace of taste and intelligence. Fortunately, by that time Monro — like Jones (Jack, not Tom), Greco, Damone, Lawrence, Gormé et al.—had built enough of an international audience base that he could keep touring as long as his health held up. Today, he's justly celebrated in any number of British Web sites and reissues, such as *Matt Monro Sings Standards* and the four-CD *Singer's Singer* set. Three recommended American releases may be easier to find stateside: *Gentlemen of Song: Spotlight on Matt Monro*, and two packages on Collectables, the excellent single LP on one CD, *My Kind of Girl*, and a two-LPs-on-one-CD set *Walk Away/Born Free*.

The artist formerly known as Terry Parsons (not to mention Fred Flange) continued to tour and record throughout the seventies and early eighties (long enough to record a half-decent treatment of Andrew Lloyd Webber's horrible "Memory" from *Cats*). In 1984, he was diagnosed with liver cancer, which, his family maintained, was caused by excessive smoking—something else he had in common with both Nat Cole and Sammy Davis Jr. Like Cole, he had even, earlier on, joked about his dependency on the drug; when, as a teenager, he held down a job at Imperial Tobacco, he stated that the cigarette shortage in postwar England was entirely due to his own "consumption from source." A few years earlier, he had bought a home in Florida, where he lived part of the year, but it was in London that he died on February 7, 1985.

Joe Mooney (1911–1975)

Shakespeare wrote great comedies in addition to his classic tragedies, but in general, we don't expect our supreme comedians to double as tragedians, or vice versa. In jazz and popular music it's different: Musicians like Fats Waller, Dizzy Gillespie, and all three guys named Louis (Armstrong, Jordan, and Prima) could make you cry as well as laugh you into good (or bad) health. Likewise, Nat King Cole was a master comic when he played piano with his trio and a romantic leading man when he became a solo stand-up singer.

Joe Mooney was a classic example of this—the work he did with his quartet was devastatingly funny. On the strength of his classic set of variations on "Tea for Two" alone, Mooney deserves to be rated as one of our chief musical/comic minds. At the same time, his "serious" songs, particularly his large-format orchestral records of the sixties, make the point that Mooney was one of the finest dramatic storytellers. And like all of the musicians listed above, he was a virtuoso instrumentalist as well as a more than convincing singer.

Mooney was also a pioneer on his instrument: As one of the first and best jazz accordionists (indeed, one of the only jazz accordionists), he was able to wring sounds from the device that led some to describe him as the Art Tatum of the squeeze box. In fact, long after the deaths of both Tatum and Mooney, a private tape was discovered and issued of the two of them playing five tunes together, with Tatum on piano and Mooney on organ. Most of the time, Mooney plays a really lovely background to Tatum, which can't have been easy since Tatum, as always, was playing everything that could possibly be played, but on "I'm Confessin'" Mooney grabs off a juicy solo for himself, and Tatum supplies a fitting background for him. It's to Mooney's credit that he was even able to keep up with Tatum, let alone complement him so perfectly.

Mooney was known for two further things: his gargantuan sense of humor and capacity for pranks, and his achieving all this despite having been blind since his teens. He was born in Paterson, New Jersey, on March 14, 1911, and began studying the piano at age six. In the mid-twenties, he and his brother Dan, also blind, formed a singing duo that eventually became known as the Sunshine Boys. Between 1929 and 1931, the Sunshine Boys recorded seventeen titles for Columbia Records and the American Recording Corp., nearly all of which are accompanied by Joe's piano, a major guitarist, and often a major brass player for added spice, such as trombonist Tommy Dorsey or trumpeter Manny Klein.

The Sunshine Boys' routines were obviously inspired by Bing Crosby and the Rhythm Boys, yet one would be hard-pressed to say that their recordings are not every bit as good. Most of the Sunshine Boys' tracks can be described as highly rhythmic and harmonically hip vaudeville turns. Like the R-Boys, the S-Boys excelled at swinging examples of group singing laced with comic banter. On "I'm Croonin' a Tune About June," sentimental gentleman Tommy Dorsey reveals a comedic capacity when he participates in a routine with the brothers, "speaking" his punch lines through his trombone. The Sunshine Boys' output, which also includes band vocals with the orchestras of Ben Selvin and Irving Mills, has been collated on the CD *The Sunshine Boys (Joe Mooney and Dan Mooney) 1929–1931—The Complete Set*, on the Challenge label in 2003.

According to Dieter Salemann, author of a bio-discography on Mooney (published in Germany), the Sunshine Boys continued to perform on radio as late as the mid-thirties, but by that time Mooney himself was regularly being offered work as an arranger for swing bands, including two relative newcomers, Les Brown and Larry Clinton. He also seems to have been sought out by old-time bandleaders like Vincent Lopez and Paul Whiteman, who were then trying to be up-to-date and add the swing style to their repertoire. Another veteran who used Mooney's arrangements was Buddy Rogers, who for a time took over the house band at the famous Meadowbrook Ballroom in New Jersey.

Paul Whiteman in particular seems to have kept Mooney busy: In the late thirties, the corpulent conductor was constantly dividing his equally elephantine ensemble into a series of smaller bands-within-bands, and Mooney wrote for both Whiteman's more compact Swing Wing and for his vocal group, the Four Modernaires (who dropped the number from their title when they switched allegiance to Glenn Miller). In 1941, Mooney formed his first quartet, which went on the road as part of the entourage of that most undistinguished of big bands, Russ Morgan and His Music in the Morgan Manner. Around 1942, he was nearly killed in a car accident, which left him permanently disabled in addition to being blind.

After spending a year and a half in the hospital, Mooney began putting together a new combo to work around his native Paterson, which he originally called the Jersey Skeeters. By the end of the war, he was able to get exactly the musicians he wanted as they were gradually mustered out of the service, and he formed the Joe Mooney Quartet. The use of jivey vocals backed by a combination of two chordal instruments, keyboard and guitar, and the absence of drums, gave the quartet a sound similar to that of the King Cole Trio. At the same time, the use of clarinet in the quartet made some listeners think of the Benny Goodman and Artie Shaw small bands, although the clarinet here plays much less aggressively than either of those leaders.

The group coalesced at Sandy's Bar in Paterson, but by early 1946 they were ready to crack the big time across the Hudson River at Dixon's on Swing Street. For about three years, Mooney and his quartet were in the spotlight, recording for Decca and playing major clubs across the country. Fortunately, nearly all the essential material by the JM4 has been collated onto two absolutely essential compact discs on the Scottish Hep label (*Do You Long for Oolong?* and *Joe Breaks the Ice*, both also available from eMusic.com). The Fifty-second Street period was easily the height of Mooney's celebrity; it's said that both Frank Sinatra (sitting in the back, hoping not to be recognized) and Tony Bennett (who could barely afford the price of a beer in those days), along with dozens of other singers, both emerging and established, came in to see him as often as possible, to listen and learn. In the Fifty-second Street days, Mooney also made a prominent guest appearance with Ella Fitzgerald and Buddy Rich on their famous V-Disc of "Budella."

In December 1946, the quartet recorded its acknowledged masterpiece, "Tea for Two." The 1924 Youmans-Caesar show tune is only a starting point for one of the most ingenious packages of words-and-music-and-riffs in all of jazz. The entire three minutes or so is a set of jive variations on the concept of tea and twosome: Irving Caesar's original 1924 lyric merely serves as point of departure. Mooney's embellishments describe a young married couple who are infatuated with, respectively, tea (the kind one sips rather than smokes, surprisingly), sugar cakes (the "knocked out" variety), and each other, and not necessarily in that order. This teasome twosome doesn't just drink tea, they long for oolong and are gone on Ceylon, until they are up to their "eyeballs in teaballs" (I have yet to learn what teaballs are, but it's still a funny line). Elaborating on Caesar's famous "We will raise a family," Mooney describes his couple as starting "to raise a family / But the kids left home at the age of three / Singing 'Oolong! Too much of that oolong!' " Apparently the offspring do not share their parents' obsession with the beverage in question.

There are other jivey variations on standards, such as "Just a Gigolo" ("Every night a different chick / makes him sick / but he can't kick!"), which, coincidentally I imagine, also starts with a famous lyric by Irving Caesar. And there are Mooney's semi-novelties, some written by Mooney himself, like "A Man with One Million Dollars," and by other writers that almost seem like special material written exclusively for the quartet, like "Warm Kiss and a Cold Heart," "I Can't Get Up the Nerve to Kiss You," and "Meet Me at No Special Place." Mooney's own "Nowhere" (which he remade ten years later on the *Lush Life* album) and "Have Another One, Not Me" are both torch tunes with a sense of humor, in which the message would seem to be, "The chick left me and broke my heart, but, like, man, I'm much too cool to care—or am I?"

In most of these rhythm pieces, the vocals are by the quartet in unison—an approach which the Cole trio had largely given up by 1945. On Mooney's ballads, though—meaning the ones, like "September Song," that he doesn't jive up—he sings solo. His ballad singing is intriguingly legato and staccato at the same time: The tempo is slow, but he doesn't have enough breath or chops to extend a line in ballad time like Sinatra, so he delivers each phrase in what amounts to a staccato burst, and then fills in generously at the end of each phrase with his accordion (or organ, on the beautiful 1951 "We'll Be Together Again"). Technically speaking, Mooney isn't playing and singing at the same time—he's singing the melody and only playing in the fills—but either way the effect is quite splendid.

From the age of James P. Johnson and Earl Hines onward, jazz pianists have been been described as either orchestral or hornlike, what Hines called "trumpet-style piano." The sonic nature of Mooney's instrument gives his playing a hornlike approach, which he used to brilliant advantage in his sing-and-fill style. His approach is attractive enough on the fast tunes, but when he stretches out on the slow numbers, his chords become lush and especially lovely. In 1957, when he was living in Miami, he briefly served on several gigs as accompanist for Tony Bennett, who described his chordal backgrounds as "the most sublimely musical thing you could imagine. He put you right in heaven."

The classic Mooney quartet seems to have recorded only about twenty sides for Decca; the group wasn't going over well in clubs outside the New York area, and the label dropped them when all contracts were canceled by the second AFM ban, in 1948. With the quartet breaking up, Mooney continued to work primarily in the Northeast, and made four titles for an obscure concern called Carousel Records, taped in Hackensack in 1951, featuring the twenty-five-year-old Bucky Pizzarelli on guitar. (Appropriately, in recent decades, both Pizzarelli *père* and his son John Jr. have been among the biggest champions of the Mooney legacy.)

In 1952 and 1953, Mooney entered into a frustratingly brief collaboration with the orchestra led by veteran arrangers Eddie Sauter and Bill Finegan.

Considering that all three individuals had a penchant for quirky and offbeat sounds, this was potentially a *pas de trois* made in heaven. The combination of the singer, the band, and the song "Nina Never Knew" led to a number 12 *Billboard* chart hit. That wasn't exactly Sinatra-Cole-Eckstine territory, but it wasn't bad, and RCA wanted more. Mooney would go on the road with the Sauter-Finegan Orchestra for several months and record four more tracks before he reached an impasse with the company.

The Mooney/Sauter-Finegan combination works marvelously because of the extreme contrast between the two halves of the equation. The delight and the defect of Sauter and Finegan's music is that everything they did sounded like a couple of ingenious orchestrators, now freed from the constraints of being dictated to about what they could and couldn't write by the likes of Benny Goodman and Glenn Miller and given license to put anything they wanted into a chart, usually for their own amusement—or to keep other arrangers guessing. Every Sauter-Finegan chart sounds overdone or at least overstuffed; they can't give you two bars of melody without throwing in this device or that one, or, more often, both. Mooney, however, is a less-is-more kind of artist, and the contrast between these minimalist and maximalist approaches makes for fascinating listening.

"Nina Never Knew" opens with what sounds like a dream sequence in a Hollywood movie: Flutes, harps, and a choir introduce the melody in a blurry, out-of-focus fashion—as if you've been slipped a mickey in your Shirley Temple. Mooney makes it work because he's precisely the opposite: He sings with no wasted motion; he doesn't hold a single note for even a fraction longer than he has to, and he gives out in a voice that's as quiet as it can possibly be. At its most extreme, the Sauter-Finegan Orchestra comes off like a bunch of effects spiraling around a tune, both musical effects and sound effects, but Mooney makes the whole mess sound warm and human.

Mooney's other best-remembered tune with the group was "Love Is a Simple Thing" (a show tune from *New Faces*) in which he sings around cuckoo clock effects—like Béla Bartók meets Leroy Anderson on Fifty-second Street. The Arlen-Mercer standard "Hit the Road to Dreamland" and the new "Time to Dream" both sound more like hallucinations than dreams, despite all the ethereal vapory voices floating around Mooney, and "It's Mutual" (co-credited to Mooney) is another worthy current song. Mooney sounds as cool and relaxed as ever. Most of the time, when we listen to Nelson Riddle and Ella Fitzgerald, for instance, we feel that the arranger is making the singer sound better; with Mooney and Sauter-Finegan, it's the other way around. He gives their music a soulfulness that it wouldn't otherwise have, and sorely needs.

Unfortunately, RCA was not giving Mooney

what he sorely needed. There was talk of him doing more for the label or at least more with the band, but, it wasn't to be. A disagreement about money got in the way.

In the mid-fifties, Mooney made two major transitions: He switched to electric organ and, according to Salemann, "seldom if ever touched the accordion again." He also relocated to Florida, where he spent the last part of his life in even more obscurity than he had spent the first forty years. There were, however, brief forays back into the mainstream, as with the Tony Bennett gig at the Americana in Miami Beach and at the Copacabana in New York. He was, as a *Variety* review of one show specifically noted, playing accordion on these dates, probably at Tony's encouragement.

In 1956, he recorded *Lush Life: Joe Mooney's Songs* for Atlantic Records. It's a sumptuously beautiful album, alternating between fast and slow songs, with his own electric organ and an all-star rhythm section of Milt Hinton (bass), Osie Johnson (drums), plus a guitarist credited as "Lonesome Jimmie Lee Robinson." Mooney is working as a soloist here, not as the leader of a quartet, so not surprisingly he no longer has his unison vocals and special double-talk routines going for him. He plays the organ rather than the accordion, but other than that he is still doing the same stop-and-start vocal thing. There's a lovely, wry song that combines his ballad sensitivities and his ironic approach, "The Kid's a Dreamer," credited to the Snider brothers; it was earlier recorded by Rosemary Clooney and later by Bennett, but Mooney's version is the standout.

Bennett remembers visiting him in Florida in the sixties. He was continually trying to perfect the electric organ to his own taste, which meant eliminating the vibrato so it could have a hip, cool sound. Said Bennett: "Here's this blind guy working inside this organ for years and years. For about five years I kept asking him, 'How's the organ coming?' He would say, 'Well, it's coming; I still haven't got it yet.' Finally, I asked him about it and he says, 'I didn't get it!'"

In these years, Mooney fell into the company of four dynamic entertainers who were known as the Vagabonds; this was the kind of high-energy quartet popular on *Ed Sullivan* and other early TV variety shows, singing, dancing, playing instruments (their main musician, known simply as Tellio, happened to play accordion, the kind of keyboard one could play while standing up), telling jokes, and also doing physical comedy. The Vags, as *Variety* nicknamed them, seem to have taken Mooney under their wing. They operated their own nightclub in Miami, where Mooney was pretty much permanently in residence.

Their audacious sense of humor complemented Mooney's own, and he was not shy about making jokes about his sightlessness. Both Tony and his sister Mary Chiappa remember well what had to be the most outrageous, not to mention dangerous, stunt ever pulled by Mooney and the Vags. They would all pile into a car and put Joe at the steering wheel; the others would scrunch down so that they couldn't be seen. Neither Tony nor Mary was clear about whether Joe was actually driving, or whether the Vags were somehow steering unseen. In any case, the startled denizens of Miami's famous main drag were startled, to say the least, at the sight of the legendary blind musician piloting a Thunderbird.

Mooney had one more stab at the limelight: In 1963 and 1965 Columbia released two complete 12" albums: *The Greatness of Joe Mooney*, with a full orchestra arranged and conducted by guitarist Mundell Lowe, and *The Happiness of Joe Mooney*, which backs him with a small group consisting of flute, vibes, Lowe's guitar, and three more rhythm. These final two projects represent the ultimate distillation of Mooney's art. Now into middle age, he had no voice left to speak of, but his storytelling abilities had mushroomed in the years since 1956.

When he sings "Lollipop and Roses" (on *Greatness*) he's got a lot less vocal power than the young Jack Jones, but as much I like Jones, he could never move me to tears with that song the way Mooney does. He also swings like crazy on "This Is the Life," the last track on *Happiness*, showing that sheer swing isn't a matter of chops so much as smarts, knowing where to cut off a note; he could give lessons in swinging to all the members of the Rat Pack, including Sammy Davis, who sang "This Is the Life" in *Golden Boy*, and Sinatra, who, as he grew older and his vocal resources diminished, seemed to be following Mooney's example ever more faithfully.

My favorite of these sixties tracks is a pair of especially introspective Johnny Mercer lyrics, "Once upon a Summertime" on *Happiness* and "I Wonder What Became of Me" on *Greatness;* both lend themselves easily to Mooney's singspiel style. It was never about chops but about placement, knowing exactly where to put each phrase in relation to the beat, how to talk one's way through a lyric and make it all seem incredibly hip. Joe Mooney had those kinds of chops in spades.

That, sadly, was the end of it. After 1964, he doesn't seem to have been heard from again. He lived out the rest of his years in Florida, and died there of a stroke at the age of sixty-four in 1975. The Pizzarellis keep alive his memory and have recorded several of his songs, and in 1997 Terry Teachout wrote an affectionate, suitably laudatory essay about him for *The New York Times*. At long last, the bulk of his recordings became available in the late CD era: the two collections of his 78 rpm work on Hep Records (assembled and instigated by Dieter Salemann), and two CDs on Koch Records, containing his Atlantic and Columbia LPs.

People use words like "subtle" and "tasteful" when describing Mooney's music, and while they're certainly correct, we shouldn't lose sight of other aspects of his work, namely that he was wild, swinging, and outrageous, and in that respect should be considered an Irish *paesano* of Louis Prima (they independently discovered the comic possibilities of "Just a Gigolo" very early on). Which isn't to make a comparison between the two—who are as different from each other as they are from everyone else in this music. In the entire history of jazz and American pop, there's been no one even remotely like Joe Mooney.

Mark Murphy (born 1932)

Throughout the nineties and the aughts, Mark Murphy sang frequently in New York, and every time he appeared, it was almost impossible to get in. Whether it was Birdland, the Jazz Standard, the Blue Note, the Kitano, the Iridium, or the teeny-tiny Danny's Skylight Room, the place was always packed with fans who usually happened to be practically every jazz singer in New York (and who were also, often as not, Murphy's own students). His life in those years was an endless trek around the globe, not only to perform but to teach others how to sing jazz. And the most important lesson he imparts to his students is the one he never has to come out and explicitly utter. Murphy's lore is a lesson that he teaches through the example of his own life: Pay your dues and stay true to your artistic conscience, and eventually the world will catch up with you, even though it may take forty years.

Murphy and Betty Carter were the co-founders of the school of swinging eclecticism in jazz vocals, major influences on virtually all the well-regarded singers of the current generation: Cassandra Wilson, Dianne Reeves, Dee Dee Bridgewater, and especially Murphy's sort-of-protégé, Kurt Elling. Although the nineties and later may be remembered for more conservative younger singers who brought forth a retro counterrevolution (the return to normalcy instigated by Diana Krall and Jane Monheit), there were, at the same time, a number of post-Murphy and post-Carter vocal artists who were gloriously eclectic.

Still, even though his stylistic descendants may incorporate repertoire and other elements from wide-ranging, far-flung sources, it would be hard to say that anyone has ever out-eclecticed Mark Murphy. The man simply never stands still long enough for anyone to peg him. Just as there are younger contemporary musicians who make a point of being able to play in every jazz style that exists, like the multifaceted Joe Lovano, Murphy seems determined to use every tool in the jazz singer's kit: from swinging in 4/4 to Latin rhythms, vocalese, scat singing (of which he is one of the major masters), the blues (of which he has considerably more than a passing knowledge), and spoken recitations of poetry. Yet he can also just plain old sing a happy song so that it makes you feel happy, or do a love song in a way that makes you feel love. He is something that the jazz world could use more of: a hipster with heart.

Murphy pushes the edge and goes beyond the fringe, yet at the same time he celebrates the mainstream: He has an encyclopedic knowledge of songs, singers, and popular culture. He can not only sing "When to Say When," but tell you that it's from the somewhat obscure show *Goldilocks* and that it was introduced by Elaine Stritch.

Like Betty Carter (especially on her early records), Murphy comes up with more good, not overdone tunes than just about anyone else. As a teacher, however, this sometimes works against him: As soon as he started singing "The Peacocks," Jimmy Rowles's Billy Strayhorn–like ballad with a lyric by British avant-garde vocalist Norma Winstone, virtually every singer in New York started singing "The Peacocks." Within a short while I was sick of those goddamned "Peacocks"—it took seven years after that album (*Some Time Ago*) was released before I could bring myself to listen to it again.

His performances are rife with references, both literary and lowbrow. One of the first times I saw him, at Fat Tuesday's in the mid-eighties, he revived Louis Jordan's "Ain't Nobody Here but Us Chickens" (not to be confused with "Ain't Nobody Here but Us Peacocks") with a slew of chicken-crossing-the-road jokes of the kind your five-year-old might tell. He ends other songs with an in-person representation of a device usually created electronically, a board fade (meaning gradually lowering the volume), which he simulates vocally with a dramatic diminuendo. But before he went into the fade, he craftily paraphrased the last line of Robert Anderson's *Tea and Sympathy:* "When you talk about this—and you will—tell them you saw Murphy *fade . . .*"

Mark Murphy (his real name) was born March 14, 1932, in Syracuse, New York. His parents both sang, and his brother led a six-piece dance band in high school. Murphy himself started studying piano at age seven, and made his "professional" debut with his brother's band very early. When he was seventeen, his aunt played him some records by Art Tatum, thereby exposing him to jazz. In his late teens, he acted in summer stock productions of various musicals in the evening and studied the great jazz and pop singers in the daytime: Ella Fitzgerald, Frank Sinatra, Peggy Lee, Jeri Southern, Nat Cole, Sarah Vaughan. He toured singing in the Northeast and Canada for a few years in the early fifties, before he settled in New York in 1954.

Murphy was young, tall, dark, and had matinee-idol good looks. He didn't have a hard time finding opportunities to sing. It did, however, take him a while before he figured out exactly what he wanted to be singing, and how to support himself by singing it. Had he wanted to go the mainstream pop route, it's not hard to imagine that he would have been a major success fairly expeditiously. Making a place musically, and commercially, in the jazz world has been much more of a challenge.

It wasn't long before he had landed singing spots on some TV talk shows, which impressed Milt Gabler of Decca Records enough to give him a chance. He made two albums in the mid-fifties for the label, *Meet Mark Murphy—The Singing M* (it was a pretty lame marketing concept) and *Let Yourself Go*, both with Ralph Burns arranging and conducting. Neither of these albums made much of an impression, except on Capitol Records producer Tom Morgan, who signed Murphy to a contract for three albums when he was out on the West Coast in 1959–60. Of the three Capitol LPs, *This Could Be the Start of Something*, *Hip Parade*, and *Playing the Field*, the first and last have title songs by Steve Allen, on whose show he frequently appeared, while the second and third, more importantly, have arrangements by the exemplary Bill Holman.

The five albums in Murphy's crew-cut period are well sampled on two contemporary CD collections. The two Deccas are heard almost complete on *Crazy Rhythm: His Debut Recording* (GRP) while the three Capitols are anthologized on *The Best of Mark Murphy: The Capitol Years* (Blue Note). (The two with Holman, *Playing the Field* and *Hip Parade*, were more recently reissued complete on one CD by DRG-Koch Records.) Murphy was already keen to do something interesting and different with familiar songs, but also, when the occasion called for it, to be true to their traditions: "Limehouse Blues" on *Meet Mark Murphy* uses Asian-style minor harmonies, while "'Tain't No Sin" (on *Let Yourself Go*) refers to twenties jazz bands, and "Heart and Soul" (on *Playing the Field*) opens like a Lombardo-like thirties sweet band.

The five 1956–60 albums reveal a young singer with a strong, dark, attractive voice, with a lot of good ideas and an obvious commitment to the jazz idiom—but one who stops just short of having a sound and a style of his own. On many tracks, like "Put the Blame on Mame" and "Swinging on a Star" he's constantly modulating, like Bobby Darin (he once referred to these as having "Bobby Darin endings"), giving the impression that he's almost trying too hard to come off like Mr. Hip Young Jazzy Dude. *Hit Parade* was an idea Murphy regretted almost immediately: swinging jazzy versions of contemporary hits like "Catch a Falling Star" (a hillbilly song gone Como) and Frankie Avalon's "Venus." As Murphy himself noted, the audience for these songs just wasn't his, and vice versa—even though he succeeded in doing something aesthetically interesting and indeed hip with material that no one would have thought could lend itself to such a treatment; this could be the start of something eclectic.

Murphy, now pushing thirty, finally begins to sound something like his mature self on his first two albums that can be considered genuine Murphy classics. *Rah* and *That's How I Love the Blues* were done in 1961 and 1962 for the smaller, jazzcentric concern Riverside Records. These are the signature works of his early career. Both back the singer with an all-star contingent of terrific New York jazzmen, under the direction of two superb arranger-conductors who didn't get enough chances to work with great jazz singers: Ernie Wilkins and Al Cohn.

Murphy now had crossed into the happy place where, instead of trying to sound hip, he *was* hip. Hip for Murphy is not merely an attitude or a frame of mind, it's a state of being. The songs are hip, and the backgrounds by Wilkins and Cohn are especially so, but Murphy himself is now so thoroughly indoctrinated in the jazz feel that he could sing any song in any setting and it would still be a jazz performance—just as Lee Konitz could play any piece of music in any context and it would almost automatically be jazz.

Rah—the title alludes to Riverside's apparent attempt to market Murphy to college students—has Murphy picking songs from sources ranging from the jazziest (Fran Landesman's "Stoppin' the Clock" and "Spring Can Really Hang You Up the Most") to the most jazz-hostile (Rodgers and Hammerstein's "My Favorite Things"). *That's How I Love the Blues* is what would today be called a jazz repertory project, offering twelve variations on the blues, from every corner of the jazz world—Count Basie, Horace Silver, Joe Williams, Harold Arlen, Tin Pan Alley ("Everybody's Crazy 'Bout the Doggone Blues"), Broadway ("That's How I Love the Blues" from *Best Foot Forward*), Earl Hines and Billy Eckstine, and Benny Carter. The only aspect of the blues that he overlooks, surprisingly, is the massive contributions to the form by Ellington and Strayhorn. (He would later record over a dozen of their compositions.)

"Everybody's Crazy 'Bout the Doggone Blues" comes from the dawn of the Jazz Age, a work by Henry Creamer and Turner Layton, who were among the very first African American songwriters to be accepted in the fraternity of Tin Pan Alley. Cohn's chart and Murphy's vocal are precisely perfect, finding the balance between the Dixieland staccato of the twenties and the stop-and-go dance rhythms of the sixties. The most represented writer on both albums is, not surprisingly, Jon Hendricks, whose lyrics are heard on "Going to Chicago Blues," "Fiesta in Blue," "Doodlin'," "Li'l Darlin' "—between those four songs and Annie Ross's "Twisted," Murphy stakes his claim, not merely to become a one-man version of LH&R, but to expand the jazz tradition from the inside. Indeed, on "Doodlin' " (the Horace Silver blues, which is on *Rah* but could have easily been on the blues album), Murphy has almost as much personality as LH&R combined, especially when he assumes a whole other voice, that of the waiter in the restaurant who hassles the protagonist for doodling (for which he uses a voice borrowed from Hungarian character actor S. Z. "Cuddles" Sakall).

Murphy told me that when he went to California in 1959 and 1960, he was primarily looking for places to work. Instead, to his surprise, instead of getting gigs, he got the chance to make the three albums for Capitol. Around 1963, the Riverside albums were being so well received overseas that he started receiving offers to work in Europe. He spent most of the sixties living and working abroad in precisely the opposite of the West Coast situation: He found enough gigs to support himself, but recorded only infrequently. Those albums that he did record in the years 1963–71 have been hard to find on CD, even on European labels. *A Swingin', Singin' Affair*, done in London in 1964, has a contemporary jazz-pop crossover feel—it sounds like a Jack Jones album with vocals by Murphy, as on a Basie-inspired treatment of "I Left My Heart In San Francisco." The best known of his mid- and late sixties albums is *Midnight Mood*, done in Cologne in 1967 with an all-star band of mostly European jazzmen. Here, he sounds exactly like his mature self, especially on the partially scatted opener, "Jump for Joy," and "Sconsolato," which may be his first bossa nova.

In 1972, Murphy began working with the independent New York–based producer and entrepreneur Joe Fields, a relationship that so far has lasted over thirty-five years, off and on. He has done roughly twenty albums for Fields's labels Muse (1972–94) and then HighNote Records (since 1999). There are also at least a dozen other projects for other labels, both bigger and smaller, such as *Night Mood* (1986, Milestone) and *Song for the Geese* (1997, BMG, his first album for a really major major since Capitol), and several especially worthy sets for foreign labels, like the Canadian *Mark Murphy and Benny Green: Dim the Lights* (1997, Millennium) and the Austrian *Very Early* (1993, West & East Music).

Murphy's basic sound has not fundamentally changed since 1972. A higher baritone in his twenties, in his forties his voice settled down into a deeper, gray, wood-toned timbre. The tone itself is sometimes similar to Jack Teagarden's, but without the trombonist-singer's somewhat nasal quality. It's easier to identify whom he doesn't sound like than whom he does, and it's quite striking how little he sounds like the important male singers who have made a point of swinging the Great American Songbook—specifically, the school of Italo-American jazz crooners and even the few non-Italian Italians (Lawrence, Davis, Jones, Monro). His vocal range is admirably wide (though not as wide as the range of his musical imagination), beginning deep in the basso basement and peaking with falsetto yelps that he sometimes uses for effect in scat episodes.

As of this writing, the Muse catalogue seems to be in limbo (although the five HighNote albums are easily available). Most of the Muse albums were individually issued on CD by Fields himself, in the late eighties and early nineties, and then, when a new company called 32 Records bought out Fields's holdings, four double disc anthologies were issued of the Muse material: *Stolen . . . and Other Moments, Jazz Standards, Songbook,* and *Mark Murphy Sings Nat King Cole & More.* Between these eight, gener-

ously long discs, a great deal of Murphy's Muse material was sampled. There are cases, one very strong one in particular, where one does miss the sequencing of the actual albums (especially the classic *Bop for Kerouac*, about which more later), but just the same, these double sets provide such rewarding listening that it would be pedantic to complain.

Those who might have heard Murphy live or on the radio before buying one of his albums, or know him by reputation, would expect his output to be diverse. One point that the four 32 Jazz anthologies make immediately is the astonishing range and scope, not to mention sheer size, of the singer's seventies and eighties output. Other than Helen Merrill and Sheila Jordan (neither of whom is quite as consistently interesting as Murphy), no other pure jazz singer was so prolific in these years. Even those three grand dames who launched their own labels—Blossom Dearie, Anita O'Day, and Betty Carter (all of whom, theoretically, could turn out albums as frequently as they wished)—didn't produce such an amazing body of work in a period that was generally considered to be such a lean one for jazz.

Listening to the 32 Jazz series feels a lot like having a stack of Muse CDs in a multiple-disc changer with the button set to random play. (With some exceptions: The first double, *Stolen . . . and Other Moments*, ends with three of Murphy's Kerouac pieces in a row, and the first disc of the last double, *Mark Murphy Sings Nat King Cole & More*, includes all seventeen of the Cole tribute tracks by Murphy, originally released on two LPs.) Murphy has, by now, preconditioned us to expect variety, but the 32 series may surprise many in that it reveals that his output has been so consistently excellent—that so many of these records deserve to be regarded, in retrospect, as classics of the jazz vocal genre—and that even his occasional missteps are instructive. Much of his second Muse album, *Mark II* (1972), is a waste; someone had the misguided idea that he could sell more records by doing tunes by Stevie Wonder and other contempopsters. Several seventies albums make rather too much use of electronic keyboards, although Murphy fortunately never fully plunged into fusion or smooth jazz. (For a time, though, he was taken up by the acid jazz movement in nineties London.)

The first tracks that are likely to catch one's fancy are those on which he does what essentially every jazz singer does: take those standards collectively referred to as the Great American Songbook and reinfuse them with swing, energy, and feeling. The first Muse album, *Bridging a Gap*, reinvents "As Time Goes By" for the seventies, done in a surprisingly hard-swinging treatment with the Brecker Brothers; and early in the Muse series you can also hear straight-ahead treatments of "I'm Glad There Is You" and "Young and Foolish." In all three cases, Murphy sings the verse, a component of the songs not frequently heard on bebop treatments.

Over the course of the series he also cut "Body and Soul," "We'll Be Together Again," and any number of familiar faves from Broadway biggies like Gershwin, Kern, and Rodgers and Hart and Hammerstein. Like any singer with a catalogue as copious as Murphy's, he has recorded enough standards by most of the canonical composers to fill entire albums; there also are a handful of songbook albums, like *Mark Murphy Sings Dorothy Fields and Cy Coleman* (little known even to Murphy fans, done for Audiophile in 1977), *The Latin Porter* (Go Jazz, 2000), a wittily titled collection of Cole Porter songs done as bossa novas, and, also in a Brazilian vein, *Night Mood: The Music of Ivan Lins* (Milestone, 1986). He's as interested in paying tribute to performers as to composers, and there are collections dedicated to Joe Williams (*Memories of You*, 2003) and Miles Davis (*Bop for Miles*, 2004), in addition to the Nat Cole material.

The second of the Muse/32 doubles is called *Jazz Standards*. While for the purposes of this discussion, I may draw a distinction between standards written by jazz composers and those from pop and Broadway sources, this compilation rightfully suggests that there's no need to. Over the years Murphy has recorded dozens if not hundreds of songs that have originated within the world of jazz itself, including many that graduated from the jazz world to find pop success—like Don Redman's "Gee, Baby, Ain't I Good to You" (he does it really slow and funky) and Tadd Dameron's "If You Could See Me Now" (surprisingly, he rocks it, with a loping back-and-forth rhythm and grabbing scat interjections—talk about "being brave").

There is literally no important writer of the modern and postmodern ages he doesn't include somewhere along the line: Benny Golson ("Along Came Betty," "I Remember Clifford"), McCoy Tyner ("Effendi"), Sonny Rollins ("Doxy"), Bill Evans (who himself played on *Rah*—"Two Lonely People," "Waltz for Debby"), Charles Mingus ("Goodbye Porkpie Hat"), Wayne Shorter ("Beauty and the Beast"), Freddie Hubbard ("Red Clay"), and two tunes from Herbie Hancock's pivotal jazz suite *Maiden Voyage*, the title cut and "Cantaloupe Island."

There are also snippets of Ellington and Strayhorn, particularly the latter: "Take the A-Train," "Lush Life," and "Blood Count," a tune that several gay jazz singers (among them Andy Bey) have invested with new meaning in the age of AIDS. He has also honored the Maestro with Charles Mingus's dedicatory hymn, "Duke Ellington's Sound of Love." The Ellington-Strayhorn canon, in fact, is an obvious idea for an album that Murphy has never made—I would love to hear him sing some of Ellington's Sacred Songs as well as the Duke's hipster nonsense.

He has been clever enough to find the great lyricists of the jazz song genre—*Jazz Standards* has

three Lambert, Hendricks & Ross classics in a row ("Charleston Alley," "Farmer's Market," and "Bijou"), and he's also sung Abbey Lincoln's "Living Room." He's sung what few vocalese standards there are as well, mostly from the King Pleasure–Eddie Jefferson axis, "Moody's Mood for Love" and "Parker's Mood," and even a dedication piece to Jefferson himself. Unfortunately, a lot of the time the lyrics Murphy sings to these amazing melodies are hardly worthy of the tunes, or of the singer. Some are by Murphy himself, some almost seem to be the work of passers-by. On a triumvirate of songs associated with the Miles Davis–Gil Evans union, "Boplicity" (given a pro-jazz lyric and renamed "Bebop Lives"), George Wallington's "God Child" (bizarrely renamed "The Odd Child"), and "Miles Ahead," one is so grateful to hear what he does with the melodies that the words themselves are secondary.

When it comes to the bossa nova, no other American jazz singer can touch Murphy. He recorded *Brazil Song*, his first all-Brazilian album, in 1983. For at least a decade, in his engagements at Birdland, the singer initiated a policy of doing his customary mix of different styles in his first set of the evening but then concentrating on Brazilian rhythms for the late show. "The Waters of March" might as well be "The Waters of Mark," as he is the earliest American jazzer to sing it. His treatment of "Waters" has an urgency, a dynamism not heard in those of other singers, North or South American. His great service to Braziliana was *Night Mood*, probably the first full-length songbook by an American jazzer of the music of Ivan Lins, including an English text to "Magdalena" not heard anywhere else. On the other hand, his reading of "Nothing Will Be as It Was" (which I've heard him do live but which is regrettably not on this album) is kinder and gentler than the other, more militant treatments of this song one customarily hears (Nnenna Freelon's, for instance).

When Murphy travels beyond these regions, it's also always interesting. He actually doesn't do Michael Franks any favors by putting "Satisfaction Guaranteed" on the same album with "All the Things You Are"—we already know what a paltry songwriter Franks is; forcing us to compare him with Jerome Kern is just plain cruel. In contrast, Murphy gives James Taylor some jazz credibility he might not otherwise have on "Long Ago and Far Away," in which he combines the Kern–Ira Gershwin classic with a newer song of that title by Taylor, making Taylor seem like a response to, or an extension of, Jerome Kern. But only a naïf would think Murphy was actually telling us that Franks and Taylor are in a class with Kern. As usual, he's being provocative—he always has some kind of a point to make.

Murphy's most successful concept album is his extraordinary *Bop for Kerouac* (1981), which was followed five years later by a worthy sequel, *Kerouac, Then and Now*. As much a cultural critic as performer, Murphy had obviously taken the decades since the Beat Generation to formulate his ultimate statement on literary and musical beatnikism. The two sets constitute a moving meditation on the subject, focusing on Kerouac as a pop culture hero, and dwelling on the music of Charlie Parker and his inner circle of bebop heroes, such as Charles Mingus and Sonny Rollins. There are vocal versions of jazz instrumentals that might have been better left wordless—"Bongo Beep," "Goodbye Porkpie Hat." The best moments are the ballads of the forties and fifties, such resolutely Kerouacian torch songs as the Jeri Southern–associated "You Better Go Now" and the Sinatra-identified "The Night We Called It a Day" and "There's No You" (two texts by Tom Adair).

The very highest points, though, are the recitations of Kerouac's prose (two on each disc), artfully juxtaposed with an appropriate song. For supremely hip comedy, Murphy has memorized the most famous monologue by the greatest of all beat comics, the legendary Richard "Lord" Buckley, which translates Marc Antony's funeral oration from *Julius Caesar* into hep-cat lingo ("Caesar has goofed to Wig City"). The four Kerouac pieces may well be the most moving things Murphy ever recorded. Anybody else would sound forced here, particularly in Kerouac's description of Anita O'Day and George Shearing sitting in at a Chicago club in "November in the Snow," although the portrayal of Bird himself in "Parker's Mood" is a bit more personal.

The ending of the original *Bop for Kerouac* is stunningly perfect. Murphy sings "The Ballad of the Sad Young Men," by Fran Landesman and Tommy Wolf. The vocal is moving enough, but he introduces it with one of the most famous passages in modern literature, the ending of *On the Road*, with its cryptic, run-on sentences and obscure metaphors describing "all that road going, all the people dreaming in the immensity of it, and in Iowa I know by now the children must be crying in the land where they let the children cry, and tonight the stars'll be out, and don't you know that God is Pooh Bear?" Both the recitation and the vocal are delivered atop a backdrop of shimmering notes played on a for-once-welcome electric keyboard by musical director Bill Mays, which twinkle like little stars. After thirty years in the business, Murphy had indeed found his own thing, and it's as beautiful as anything by Vaughan, Tormé, or anyone else who was making music at the time.

Murphy's continuing commitment to eclecticism makes me think of the Monty Python slogan, "And now for something completely different"; Murphy's fans have long become accustomed to the completely different. *Dim the Lights* teams him with Carter veteran Benny Green, and with his usual plethora of ideas, some brilliant and some bizarre (like overlaying three different vocal tracks of three different songs at once), it is so far Murphy's only

full-length duet project. By contrast, *The Dream*, with the Dutch Metropole Orchestra, and *Very Early*, with a Viennese nonet known as "Nine," are his best projects with a large ensemble—especially *The Dream*, which was recorded in bits and pieces over a twenty-year period.

For a while, it looked as if Murphy was catching on with a whole different audience: In "Ding Walls" (from his 1990 *What a Way to Go* on Muse) Murphy talks about how his recording of "San Francisco," from the second *Kerouac* album, was catching on with kids in acid jazz clubs in London. Apparently there was a sect of real, Old Skool hippetty-hopping and dancing intellectuals in Blimey who anointed the Murphy-Kerouac recordings as early examples of rap. Murphy capitalized on this trend when, in 1997, he made his first album for an American major since Capitol in 1960, *Song for the Geese* (BMG). There are standards, there are ballads, there are jazz numbers, and yes there are bossa novas, and there is also a treatment of the British standard "You're Blasé," which begins with a Kerouacian rap, and ends with a "rant" of the kind that Kurt Elling learned from him. And there are tasteful, even welcome elements of deejay culture, sampling, overdubbing, electronica, breaks, and beats. It was nominated for a Grammy.

When, in September 2005, Murphy played Birdland again, there was an even greater buzz than usual among the throngs of acolytes who came to hear him. A new album was coming soon, which in itself was no big deal: According to the singer's own Web site, he had released seven CDs (not counting reissues) since the start of the new century. But there were two special things about this set, *Once to Every Heart*: first, that it was his first major label project since *Song for the Geese* eight years earlier; more important, it was Murphy's first album of standards and ballads in at least twenty years.

In his more-than-fifty-year career, Murphy has done just about everything except what people expect of him. *Once to Every Heart* (Verve) came about because of Till Bronner, a best-selling jazz trumpeter in Germany (although not as known in this country as he might be). The latest of many jazz musicians (not only singers) who came under Murphy's spell, Herr Bronner decided he personally wanted to produce a new Murphy album, of the kind that hadn't been heard before. The album pivots around "Once to Every Heart," an obscure song recorded by Jo Stafford and composed by her husband (more customarily a conductor and arranger), Paul Weston. Murphy's one original here, his most successful such effort in recent memory, is "I Know You from Somewhere," a love song in the time-honored half-a-conversation format of "Guess Who I Saw Today?" and "Something Cool." The piece caught me by surprise and moved me even before I heard Murphy's spoken introduction to it at Birdland, in which he explained that he wrote it in the immediate aftermath of 9/11 and that it described two people encountering each other again in this frightening new world.

Murphy characteristically has the good sense to feature original songs only sparingly, and more generally concentrates on reworking the Great American Songbook. There is no one better at taking a familiar or even unfamiliar old song and turning it inside out, spilling its guts and finding the feeling underneath. What has never been clearer than now is that at his best, Murphy does not abstract and skewer a song merely for the sake of being different, but to get at its inner meaning. By making you think differently about a song you've heard before, he makes it relevant and meaningful all over again.

Murphy's other major showpiece here is "I'm Through with Love," the 1931 Bing Crosby hit better known to subsequent generations courtesy of the Little Rascals. Mr. Murphy is a veritable quartet by himself: He starts in a straight-ahead chest voice, drops down to a deep basso as he heads for the end of the first A section (and the first utterance of the title), switches to a lacy filigree for "keep my feelings there," and for the end of the next A section (and hook), instead of diving low, as he's got us expecting him to do, he goes way up high into falsetto—this may be the most creative use of the falsetto in jazz singing since Cab Calloway.

When he sang it at Birdland, he concluded with a long, piercing head tone, but then reinforced the message by detouring through a spoken rap in which he delineated at greater length just how through with love he is—even to the point where he now strolls the boulevards "holding my own hand." It was highly effective in person and is no less so on the recording, especially since on the record he has the additional support of a full string orchestra playing an arrangement by Johnny Mandel's protégée Nan Schwartz.

Murphy also has the benefit of the playing of producer Till Bronner, joining his customary quartet of Misha Piatigorsky (piano), Max Vader (bass), Obed Calvaire (drums), and Gilad (percussion).

With Murphy at least, Bronner's playing recalls the line of lyrical trumpeters who worked with Charlie Parker: Miles Davis, Kenny Dorham, and Chet Baker. The Milesian mode is especially in evidence on "It Never Entered My Mind," in which Bronner employs a metal Harmon mute and which was directly patterned after Davis's famous 1954 recording, which in turn had been inspired by Frank Sinatra's astounding 1947 version of the great 1940 Rodgers and Hart show tune. Of all the thousands of times I have heard this song, I never realized before how lyricist Lorenz Hart used the line "to get into my hair again" to contrast with what's going on in the speaker's mind—as a way of differentiating between the internal and external mechanisms of the human head.

Murphy's rap at the end of "I'm Through with Love" contains the admonition: "LOVE is a four-letter word, after all." But he can't fool us: After so many years of singing about it, he still believes in it. Murphy long ago resigned himself to the idea that he would never be a household name. Yet his is one of the most consistently prolific and rewarding careers in modern music. As fellow singer Sheila Jordan told deejay Michael Bourne, "What's not to like? What singers do what Mark Murphy does?"

Rumors about Murphy's health were circulating in spring 2009, but he played in New York in the summer and San Francisco in October; according to his Web site, he is currently residing at an assisted living facility in New Jersey. That July I caught a late show at the Kitano on Park Avenue; his powers were somewhat diminished (he was seventy-seven at the time), but he was still Mark Murphy. Unlikely though it may be, I like to think that he will soon be back at Birdland in a few weeks, still saving the second set for bossa novas, still packing the place with aspiring chirps, still sporting that bushy handlebar mustache and that amazing hair (how I wish he would lend it to me sometime), still reassuring all of us balding beatniks and sad young men that God is Pooh Bear.

O

Anita O'Day (1919–2006)

"There are three sexes: women, men, and singers." It's a quote often attributed to Billy May, and which has been much bandied about the music industry ever since Bing Crosby and Frank Sinatra established the primacy of the vocalist in popular music well over half a century ago. Singers, particularly outside the jazz area, have an unusual relationship with the rest of the music scene. They're often stereotyped as knowing less about music than anybody else in the band. (The old joke goes: How do you know when a singer is ringing your doorbell? When she doesn't know when to come in.) Yet fans

of, say, the Benny Goodman Orchestra are much more likely to know the name of the girl vocalist than the bassist. As Dee Dee Bridgewater once put it, when the singer is on, there's no way anybody else is getting any attention. No wonder, as Billy Eckstine once explained, so many musicians resent the hell out of so many singers.

Anita O'Day, in a kinky way that seems completely characteristic of her life and music, both supported and challenged this kind of thinking. On the one hand, if any singer has earned the privilege (if indeed it's a privilege) of being labeled a "musician," it's O'Day. She distrusted the term "singer," but for her own reasons, claiming that since she had so little in the way of traditional voice or vocal chops, she should be described as a "song stylist" instead. In O'Day's way of thinking, apparently a singer is someone with a pure voice who really sings the melody as written. By contrast, in O'Day's own music the emphasis isn't on voice or melody, it's about taking a song and styling it: swinging it, improvising on it. Yet even though she didn't have the pure power of an opera singer (or of Ella Fitzgerald or Sarah Vaughan), her voice was one of the most efficiently musical instruments in all of jazz. O'Day always regarded herself as a musician. She may not have played piano, like Carmen McRae or Vaughan, but she had more than a working knowledge of the technical side of music: She could read a score, wrote songs, and generally worked out her arrangements in collaboration with her accompanists and musical directors (in the sixties, she also learned to notate her own ideas).

And as her improvising shows, she knew her harmonies: Her scat solo on "Night and Day" (1959) is a typically brilliant O'Day invention, with the singer leaping over Porter's chromaticisms like Tarzan swinging through the trees. What makes this an especially notable jazz statement is that in this particular case she wasn't even supposed to be making a pure jazz album—this was an album of Cole Porter songs aimed at the same mass-market audience that had made Ella Fitzgerald a mainstream pop star. She was also working in collaboration with Billy May, who, like her, was a veteran of the pinnacle years of the swing era, and what the two of them came up with together was just as modern and innovative as anything written by any of the somewhat younger, more bop-oriented arrangers she also worked with—Johnny Mandel, Bill Holman, Jimmy Giuffre.

In 1941, the twenty-one-year-old Anita took to the road for the first time, as the chick singer with the nationally known Gene Krupa and His Orchestra. At that time, "chirps," as they were affectionately if condescendingly named, were essentially a kind of window dressing for a big band. They were expected to glamorize the bandstand in their frilly gowns, to give the boys dancing out front something to look at, and likewise to decorate the melody in a pretty voice, with little interpretation on either a musical or a lyrical level. O'Day was one of the first band singers to declare emphatically that she was, in fact, a genuine musician, a real soloist, comparable to Roy Eldridge, the trumpet god who would shortly join her in the Krupa band.

Early in her Krupa days, O'Day made a decision that was at once a fashion statement and a musical one: Instead of the de rigueur high-glamour togs worn by most bandstand chirpers—think of Helen Forrest in her elaborate gowns—O'Day insisted on wearing a band uniform (albeit with skirt instead of slacks) like the rest of the musicians. She explained, "I believe what you hear is more important than what you see." It's not that she completely ignored the presentation side of performing—she had showmanship in abundance—but her whole shtick, as it were, was designed to put the focus on the music above all else.

Even the essence of her singing, the sonic quality of her voice, is about pure essentials: When O'Day hits a note, you just get the pure note and no vibrato. She claimed that when she first began singing professionally (around 1936), she discovered that some years earlier a careless doctor had sliced off her uvula while he was removing her tonsils. This also made it difficult for her to sustain notes, which indeed she did only very rarely: When she holds a note at the end of "Travelin' Light," it's to achieve a special effect, and it works because it's such a departure for her. "I can't get a sound with the air back there because there's nothing to vibrate it," she wrote. "That's the reason I got into singing eighth and sixteenth rather than quarter notes. Instead of singing 'laaaaa' I'd sing 'la-la-la-la' to keep it moving." She used syncopation to break up long laaaaa's into short la-la-la-la's in a way that's sublimely rhythmic and swinging.

Her greatest period, recording-wise, is the decade or so in which she worked with producer Norman Granz (and then, briefly, with his successors at Verve). You can hear her applying this technique on practically every song, as when she turns "who will buy" into "who-oo-oo will buy" in the last 8 bars of "Love for Sale" (also on *Anita O'Day Swings Cole Porter with Billy May*) or "Speak Low" (1952) into "Speak lo-ho-ho" and likewise in the coda ("myself to you-hoo-hoo . . .") of "Body and Soul" (on *Anita Sings the Winners*, 1958). Nearly every musician she worked with praises her remarkable *time;* it's something they comment on even more than on her off-beat personality. When she sang at Avery Fisher Hall in 1999 (in the JVC Jazz Festival), she asked the band to give her a "Lunceford two"—I can't imagine that her accompanying musicians, generally half her age, would have had any idea what she was talking about before they started working for her. She's also said that in order to get the most out of her relatively narrow vocal range, she had to break the scale up into her own microtones within the scale—to create new notes in places where there never were any notes before.

In matters of keys, chord changes, and tempos, O'Day knew way more about music than your average horn player. But at the same time, much of what she does communicates that she's not of the same breed as ordinary musicians—that she does, in fact, belong to another group entirely. When Johnny Mandel says that "Anita is a true original," he knows full well he's risking a redundancy—there's no such thing as an untrue original; you either are an original or you're not—but rather that O'Day's originality is so striking that it bears underscoring. It wasn't only that she launched a trend, or started a whole new school of singing (which indeed she did). The truth is that while some singers both in the States and around the world were profoundly influenced by O'Day's compelling tone, her way with a song, and her unique approach to improvisation, these factors were just too personal for anyone else ever to successfully imitate.

Not that anyone so individual and idiosyncratic is going to be to everybody's taste. Once, the late Gene Lees, a critic I would have thought would be of the age and mental disposition to appreciate O'Day, made a point of dissing her to me. He referred to her disparagingly as "that O'Day woman" and went on to dismiss her with "she sings out of tune and has a funny sense of time." The first complaint is answered by her recordings themselves, in a way that's not really debatable. Many years later, once she had passed the seventy-year mark, intonation became less important to O'Day, as it must to nearly all singers. But in her recordings from the forties to the seventies (especially the 1952–62 period with Granz and Verve) you won't hear many flat notes, if any.

Now about that "funny sense of time" thing. You'll notice that he didn't say "she doesn't swing." You don't need a PhD in music theory to know that O'Day can't help swinging; swinging is part of her, no less than her arms, her lips, her hips, or any other part of her anatomy. She's so perfectly in time that one imagines she must have been conceived and born on the beat. No other singer, not even Ella Fitzgerald, has so effectively and so frequently employed the device of trading phrases with her accompanying musicians. When she trades fours, twos, or even ones with the band, as in "Tea for Two," she might be thinking of spontaneous phrases, paraphrasing the tune, or quoting some other melody, yet she's always completely at one with the time. "Tea for Two" was documented on two famous live occasions in 1958: at a performance in Chicago released as *Anita O'Day at Mr. Kelly's,* and at the Newport Jazz Festival, included in the film *Jazz on a Summer's Day.* "T42" reveals that O'Day's relationship with the beat is so rock-solid that she can completely trust it—she doesn't have to hug it constantly out of fear that it will get away from her. In the coda, she slips briefly into waltz time (sounding as if she's about to go into a 3/4 reading of "Stranger in Paradise") and then suspends the beat altogether, finally leaping back into swing time for the closing fanfare.

Everything O'Day did, both in music and in her often equally unconventional extramusical life, seemed designed to convince us that she wasn't part of the same continuum as the rest of us. Not that she thought she was superior—just different. Whenever I (or presumably anyone else) met Anita in the eighties and nineties, one of the first points that she wanted to impress you with was that she hadn't read her own autobiography, *High Times, Hard Times.* She dictated her story to writer George Eells in a series of interviews, but she never actually read it herself. Or at least, that's what she told most people who asked. In reality, according to longtime manager Alan Eichler, she started to read her book several times but

gave it up because it forced her to confront her own past; it brought her down and moved her to tears.

As O'Day herself said in that book, there's a "Good Anita" whom you get most of the time, but there's also a "Bad Anita, who wants to shock, mock, and put everybody and everything down." If you really want to live adventurously, just try dining with Anita when she's in one of her moods. I've never seen a woman so accomplished in the art of making grown waiters cry. Even before the soup comes around, you're thinking you're trapped at dinner with a bebop Norma Desmond. When fans approached her after concerts with ephemera to sign, or just wanting to tell her how much her music meant to them, she could be either nice or gnarly depending on how she was feeling at that moment. What you saw was what you got, with no diplomacy or artifice.

This kind of thing is probably what led O'Day (or more likely, Eells) to open her book with a judgment rendered by her onetime agent Joe Glaser: "Anita, you've got a million dollars' worth of talent, but no class." Yet—no matter how much O'Day strikes terror in the hearts of maîtres d'hôtel—Glaser's statement ultimately leaves one scratching one's head (unless we consider the possibility that the lack of class refers more directly to Glaser himself).

How could he say that Anita O'Day has no class? It's hard to imagine how anyone could describe her music, ballsy and direct as it is, as anything but the epitome of classy singing. Was he talking about stage patter like "Thank you very much, ladies and gentlemen. At this time, I'd like to tell you a joke, but I don't know any clean ones"? Was he talking about her deglamorized outfits? Was it without class to wear those band uniforms instead of glamour gowns on the road? In fact, when she became a headliner in the fifties, and was playing weeklong engagements in jazz clubs rather than one-nighters in ballrooms, O'Day did indeed switch to the high-maintenance satin-doll drag that the other female singers in nightclubs wore (including long opera gloves, which she later admitted were primarily there to hide the track marks in her arms). Her album covers, too, in the Verve years were impeccable. So where's the no-class?

Perhaps one man's no-class is merely what another would describe as a penchant—or, more strongly, a firm commitment—to the unusual, the unexpected, the original. You just don't expect singers to do what O'Day does. For example, in "Can't We Be Friends?," she revs up the tempo at the bridge of the second chorus, then slows it down with something of a boogie-woogie feeling in the last 8. Next, she suspends the time altogether before the last line, at which point she goes into harmony with the band as it plays a paraphrase of the final 2 bars. She uses that trick, unexpectedly harmonizing with the ensemble in the tag, a number of times in the Verve sessions—"Frenesi" is another example. The device may not or, considering that O'Day had a hand in most of these orchestrations, may in fact be in the written charts, but the point is that it almost always catches listeners off guard.

Speed is another facet of O'Day's stylization skills: Surely no other singer, not even the great Fitzgerald, has sung so many songs at such a lightning-fast pace and yet so intelligibly. I don't even want to know what the metronomic count is on "From This Moment On," yet rather than just singing it fast, O'Day sings it brilliantly, with every word making sense, and the singer herself sounding confident and even relaxed no matter how breakneck the pace. On "Old Devil Moon," she takes the second chorus at a blistering tempo, crunching all the words and notes so they're barely distinguishable from one another, yet the narrative remains crystal clear. She's neither racing ahead of the band nor lagging behind it, she's just perfectly in sync with the ensemble at all times. "I listen to Anita for speed," the singer Ernestine Anderson once said; "She can sing faster than any jazz singer I know and will still make sense."

O'Day almost never sings the melody exactly as written—particularly after the first chorus. Yet what she sings can't be described as a completely original improvisation either. At the age of fifteen, she met Redd Evans, later a songwriter (author of "Let Me Off Uptown," "No Moon at All," "Slow Down," and other works recorded by her, as well as many of Nat Cole's hits) but then playing ocarina with Horace Heidt and His Musical Knights. This hardly qualifies Evans as a jazz expert, but O'Day credits him with introducing her to the existence of riffs, which she defines as a "repeated musical phrase." Virtually everything O'Day sings is a riff, and usually these riffs are ingenious paraphrases of the melody— something between the written tune and her own invention. Whether paraphrasing or improvising, O'Day is always on the chord, carefully sticking to the notes that are prescribed within the changes.

O'Day's relationship with lyrics is another issue. She once said, "I go for the music more than the poetry of it all," and there's no doubt that the words are far less sacred to her than they are to, say, Mabel Mercer. Yet note that she'll change a melody much more readily than she alters words. At times it may seem as if the lyrics have no more meaning to her than nonsensical scat phrases, but no matter what she's singing, you can feel the underlying message behind it. The happy songs sound happy and the ballads and torch songs communicate the melancholy. "The most important thing," as she has also said, "is to never lose the story."

All these differences—between the lyrics and scatting, the melody and improvisation—may be important with some other singers, but with O'Day they're just academic. The wonder in the music of Anita O'Day is how outrageousness somehow becomes the epitome of pure class.

The jazz establishment has been enthusiastic about constantly recoronating Anita O'Day as the queen of a select group of singers (most notably Chris Connor and June Christy) who are admittedly cut from the same cloth. This is all fine and dandy, but way too little thought is given to placing O'Day in the bigger picture, which is in the major leagues— in the same breath with the canonical figures Billie Holiday, Ella Fitzgerald, and Sarah Vaughan. Indeed, she does everything that those great ladies can do— scat like crazy, exchange phrases back and forth and hold her own with the fiercest of jazz horn combatants, sing the blues like nobody's business, and, from time to time, put all her soul into a ballad. And like them, she sounds like nobody else. It could be that O'Day is just too far out, too much of an individual, even for a music that prizes those very qualities.

In a career that long ago surpassed all rivals, becoming the longest of any jazz singer (sixty-five years easily), O'Day's entire modus operandi is predicated on the notion of spontaneity. Everything in an O'Day performance has the element of happening ad-lib, with as little preparation as possible, therefore making even routines that she's done in some cases since the fifties seem fresh and spontaneous. Everything she sings is animated by spur-of-the-moment invention. Equally important, her vocal style stresses rhythm above everything: Her singing tone is sweet enough, but she'll happily sacrifice whatever beauty there might be in an extended legato note in exchange for the more strongly swinging momentum of a series of jazzy staccato bursts. Given her dedication to the twin gods of improvisation and swing, she may be the most firmly committed of all jazz vocalists.

O'Day was an important figure in the jazz world ever since she first went to work in the big-time jazz clubs in her native Chicago around 1939, about the time of her twentieth birthday, and along with colleague Lena Horne she would become one of the only major artists to work steadily from the thirties into the new millennium. She burst upon the national scene in 1941, when, as chief chirper with Gene Krupa, she and trumpet guru Roy Eldridge duetted on "Let Me Off Uptown," one of the signature hits of the entire swing era.

Her big band years, 1941 to 1946, were the first of her two prime periods, at least as far as the latter-day evidence of recordings suggests. (Secondhand sources tell us that she must have been singing equally well, for instance, in the late forties but unfortunately she left us with virtually nothing to listen to in those years.) It was an age of great band singers—from those who took you on a musical tour de force (like Ella Fitzgerald) or an emotional one (Helen Forrest) or even a sentimental journey (Doris Day). But there was no one who could do what Anita did. Even the magnificent Fitzgerald had never achieved anything in her dance band days that compared with O'Day's early output.

Up to that point if, say, Benny Goodman wanted to play one of his superfast rhythmic numbers (or flag-wavers, as the jitterbugs called them then), that was exclusively an instrumental domain. Even the most swing-happy of the pre-1941 band singers couldn't hope to fit in with Goodman's "Clarinet a la King" or Ellington's "Rockin' in Rhythm." Fitzgerald could and soon would, but even the biggest Fitz fan would have to admit that O'Day's big band sides of 1941–46 are on the whole far better than most of Fitzgerald's big band work of 1935–41. (O'Day had been deeply inspired by the slightly older Fitzgerald, but she has consistently named the entertainer Martha Raye as her greatest influence.)

With the arrival of O'Day, for the first time a vocalist had a real place in even the fastest and most intricate or even unsingable of flag-wavers. The band could play it as fast, as tricky, as loud, as rhythmically supercharged as they wanted, and they would never lose her: If it were a race, she'd be standing there at the finish line waiting for the rest of the ensemble to show up—and not even breathing hard.

The Krupa recordings (eighteen of which are sampled on a highly recommended Sony CD, *Let Me Off Uptown*) are distinguished by near-definitive readings of two of Hoagy Carmichael's greatest, the vintage "Georgia on My Mind" and the brand-new "Skylark"—surely O'Day had a lot to do with making the latter an all-time favorite of female jazz singers. Even more than on songs with literate lyrics, O'Day excelled at a series of flag-waver-like vehicles that were essentially purely rhythmic exercises in which the lyrics, and often the melody as well, are purely incidental and nonsensical: "Slow Down," "Stop! The Red Light's On," and "Thanks for the Boogie Ride."

Her first two recordings with the Krupaites, done in New York on March 12, 1941, lay out the pattern for the thirty-six generally excellent sides to follow: a pure rhythm piece, "Alreet," and a jazz-friendly Tin Pan Alley work, "Georgia on My Mind." (Needless to say, if the pieces fed to O'Day were not intrinsically hip to begin with, she would instantly rectify that.) Of the rhythm numbers, "Kick It" from early in the relationship (June 1942) is fairly typical: The melody is a series of phrases the likes of which musicians might improvise in a jam session; the lyrics generally are slang phrases of the day. When O'Day sings "Kick It," she's at once exhorting the musicians to play harder and faster and the dancers on the floor to do likewise.

Similarly, "Bolero at the Savoy" may not be a masterpiece of songwriting in the tradition of Cole Porter (although in this particular case the tune was inspired by no less than Ravel), but is the most appropriate raw material imaginable for the Krupa-O'Day combination. Again, the whole shebang of "Bolero" is a paean to the concept of dance—or any other kind of movement that turns you on. The idea of a classical Spanish dance catching on in Harlem in 1940 may leave us, like the square "ickies" O'Day sings of, wondering "what it's about," but nothing here is meant to be taken too literally. Surely, no bolero ever jumped like this. It's hard to imagine even the most vitamin-energized, swing-crazed

stomper at the Savoy moving this fast; surely, no singer besides O'Day could have not only sung it but put it over so convincingly at this clip.

In 1943, Krupa was arrested for narcotics possession (he is generally believed to have been set up, as they said in the crime movies of the day) and was forced to disband his group. O'Day sang very briefly (unfortunately) with Woody Herman; a single broadcast survives of her with the First Herd, which includes a performance of "Let Me Off Uptown" with Herman singing Roy Eldridge's part in the duet. She also cut a fascinating session (in spring 1944) for the MacGregor transcription label in which she was backed up by the King Cole Trio, another amazing one-shot combination. O'Day laid down five jazz standards with the trio (which have only been released on semilegitimate issues) and here is indeed the foundation of much of her work of the following sixty years. These provide our first glimpse of Anita O'Day the hip singer with the hot small group, coming up with infinite variations on very well known jazz classics: "Ain't Misbehavin'," "When We're Alone (Penthouse Serenade)" (with a juicy solo by guitarist Oscar Moore and a modulation before the final eight), "The Lonesome Road" (which speeds up for Cole's short solo and then slows down again for O'Day's reentrance), "I Can't Give You Anything but Love," and "Rosetta." The interplay—the trading of 4- and 2-bar phrases—isn't quite there yet, but everything else is, most notably her constant reshaping of melodic lines, as dictated by a keen sense of harmony.

Her next steady gig with a band was with the relatively new outfit led by pianist Stan Kenton, whose group was emerging as being harmonically more sophisticated than your average swing outfit, although significantly less rhythmically propulsive than the mighty Krupa crew. O'Day and Kenton only left a handful of documents of their few months together—commercial recordings (Capitol), studio transcriptions (MacGregor), and airchecks (live remotes from various ballrooms across the country). But while her output with the band was small, many of the Kenton-O'Day performances would prove vital: "Gotta Be Gettin'," their first side for Capitol Records, is a slangy rhythmic number that contains some of the first stirrings of the poignancy she would later bring to jazz-tinged ballads like "A Nightingale Sang in Berkeley Square." By contrast, the hit "And Her Tears Flowed Like Wine" would launch an entire series of rhythmic novelties for Kenton in which the solo singer (in an O'Day-like mode) would alternate episodes of comic interplay with the bandsmen doubling as Greek chorus in a variation, of sorts, on Tommy Dorsey's "Marie" cycle. In January 1945, while still touring with Kenton, O'Day did an extracurricular session of four inspired "solo" titles for Capitol Records (using L.A. studio players rather than Kentonites), which are also highly prophetic of her mature albums of a decade later.

There's no doubt that her big band period was an essential part of her development. It reached a climax in 1945: She started the year with Stan Kenton, and in the summer returned with Gene Krupa's reorganized orchestra for roughly six months. During this second tenure with that drummer's band, she helped concoct an ingenious set of variations on the 12-bar blues, with the startlingly unoriginal title of "Boogie Blues," which became a career perennial, like "Let Me Off Uptown" and "And Her Tears Flowed Like Wine." During this reunion period with Krupa, O'Day also devised the embryonic version of her future milestone "Tea for Two." Both this title and at least one of the 1945 titles, the poultry-specific novelty "Chickery Chick," are features for the singer all the way through; like Helen Forrest's work with Harry James, these are more like vocal records with orchestral accompaniment than regulation big band records with vocal refrain.

O'Day's next batch of commercial recordings, a short series for Bob Thiele's independent Signature label, is, in a sense, an extension of the Krupa years in that the songs are generally purely rhythmic baubles designed to show off her speed. Several of the Signatures are comic novelties ("I Ain't Gettin' Any Younger" and the serio-campy "Ace in the Hole"), and there's at least one exotic ballad (Benny Carter's "Key Largo," heard in a lovely arrangement by Ralph Burns), but on the whole, the emphasis here is on rhythm. "Hi Ho Trailus Boot Whip" is a showcase for her scatting ability of the sort that she had done with Krupa, and "Malaguena" is a significant breakthrough, being, as far as I can tell, her first total scat feature, in which she improvises nonsense syllables from beginning to end, anticipating her later "Four Brothers" and "Slaughter on Tenth Avenue"; all of them are vocal instrumentals, so to speak, of well-known melodies that were iconic in different ways.

In 1949 and 1950 O'Day would record a series of pop titles for the London label (owned by Polygram but never reissued by that corporation—and perhaps only of interest to O'Day completists) in which both the comic and dramatic material is distinctly second-rate, although there are three excellent semi-standard ballads, all of prewar vintage, "Something I Dreamed Last Night," "Black Moonlight," and "I Apologize." What the postwar recordings do document, in a rough parallel to the more copiously recorded Ella Fitzgerald, is O'Day's unmistakable immersion in the burgeoning bebop movement.

She only recorded sporadically and inadequately between 1946 and 1951. Luckily, she would compensate spectacularly in the decade to follow. Her relationship with Norman Granz would be the most fruitful of her long career. The roughly sixteen albums she would make in the twelve years of that association would, beyond the shadow of a doubt, establish her preeminence in the very uppermost bracket of jazz vocal stylists.

It was in these years that O'Day set forth many of the basic building blocks of her repertory, classic arrangements that she continued to perform for decades. On all the O'Day classics, the interplay's the thing: "Honeysuckle Rose" and "Sweet Georgia Brown" start small, with O'Day sexily insinuating the melody with just bass or drums, then gradually letting the full ensemble collect around her. "Sing, Sing, Sing" and especially "Four Brothers" find her translating classic big band instrumentals into the vocal idiom, while "Anita's Blues" encapsulates her mastery of that form as well. "The Ballad of the Sad Young Men" and "The Party's Over" reveal that jazz's nerviest, hardest-swinging hip chick also has a sentimental side.

Impresario Norman Granz, one of the few men who made a million dollars in the jazz business, built an empire through a combination of concert tours and recordings (and only a few musicians I have spoken with have suggested that he ripped them off—very rare indeed). His strategy, with a few exceptions, was: He who produces least produces best. He was principally responsible for signing great talent and letting it do what it wanted, only rarely imposing his own taste on his artists. O'Day has said, somewhat in the form of a gripe, that Granz would show up at her dates but with his head buried in a newspaper. Yet I can't imagine that she actually wanted him to take charge and start telling everyone what to do. If she had never met Granz, she would doubtless have been stuck doing pop singles and would, at best, have only occasionally been given the chance to make a straight-ahead all-jazz album. Instead, O'Day's fifties catalogue is just the opposite, and perhaps is even purer than Dinah Washington's, Sarah Vaughan's, or Carmen McRae's, none of whom were on Verve and all of whom went back and forth between pure jazz and semipop projects.

Her association with Granz began with three sessions in 1952, which were eventually gathered into the 12" LP *The Lady Is a Tramp*, then another three in 1954, which later became *An Evening with Anita O'Day*. In 1955, Granz formed the Verve label—a much more mainstream affair than his previous label, Clef. But even though this enterprise was inspired mainly by his signing of the bigger-selling Ella Fitzgerald, the first major singer to record for the new outfit was Anita O'Day.

While the 1952 and 1954 albums were mainly small group affairs (although there was one string session in 1952), the first two Verve releases hewed closer to mass-market pop—but of the most intelligent kind. Her arranger and conductor here was the industry insider Buddy Bregman, not a Nelson Riddle or a Billy May, perhaps, but a smart cookie with just enough musical know-how to give O'Day what she needed. The two chose a brilliant array of standard songs that were not overdone in that early stage of the 12" LP, and varied the orchestration between rhythm section, big band, and string orchestra. Of the two albums by O'Day and Bregman, *Anita* (1955) was an instant classic and *Pick*

Yourself Up (1956) a worthy sequel. The two sets contain the definitive readings of two major "production numbers" that would be O'Day's mega-perennials, "Honeysuckle Rose" and "Sweet Georgia Brown," in what I believe are essentially her arrangements but filled out for big band by Bregman.

Where the Bregman albums effectively contrast backing groups of different sizes, most of her remaining albums of the period divide themselves between big bands and small bands. Next came *Anita Sings the Most* (1957), a quartet project co-starring that most popular and prodigious of jazz pianists, Oscar Peterson, leading his own quartet with the addition of O'Day's longtime drummer and collaborator John Poole. "When I got deeply into improvising, that's the way I thought of each number, as a horse race," was how O'Day herself put it. "I put myself on the line. Sometimes I win, sometimes I lose, sometimes it's too close to call." From the opening tune, "S'wonderful," onward, *Anita Sings the Most*—which she once named as among her favorite albums—is the most exciting horse race of her whole career. The real speed demons here are "S'wonderful," "Love Me or Leave Me," and especially "Them There Eyes," which builds to a masterful scat exchange of fours with guitarist Herb Ellis and drummer Mr. Poole. As superfast as the Peterson digits lay down the chords, he can never lose O'Day.

In the late fifties, O'Day's popularity among jazz fans—and lovers of the Great American Songbook—was actually growing; at this early stage of the game, the dominance of rock 'n' roll over the singles market was by and large not yet a threat. Since 1952, she had only done one 12" LP a year for Granz (and nothing at all in 1953); from 1958 on, she doubled her output. That year she recorded both an ambitious big band album, *Anita Sings the Winners*, and an excellent live small group set, *Anita O'Day at Mr. Kelly's*. The *Winners* was her first orchestral project without Bregman, and she made the most of the opportunity, with a program of songs associated with legendary jazz greats that helped establish her place in that pantheon. Among other gems, there was an Artie Shaw–inspired "Frenesi," a Gerry Mulliganesque "My Funny Valentine," and vocal adaptations of two big band milestones that, for anyone else, would have been unsingable: Stan Kenton's cacophonic "Peanut Vendor" and Benny Goodman's "Sing, Sing, Sing." The second has O'Day assuming the clarinetist's role in the climactic trade with the drummer (Alvin Stoller filling in for Gene Krupa).

With *The Winners*, Granz and O'Day were putting their best foot forward, in that the producer hired two major modernist arrangers, Russ Garcia and Marty Paich, to do the charts. With a few exceptions, the bulk of O'Day's final Verve albums (1958–62) were high-level collaborations with similarly brilliant orchestrators who had also grown up steeped in the language of bebop. A few weeks after *The Winners*, O'Day taped her live album in Chicago, *Mr. Kelly's*, an essential offering in that it would be her only in-person recording of the era. A year after that, in April 1959, she taped her first meeting with Billy May, *Anita O'Day Swings Cole Porter with Billy May* (1959), and her only team-up with the very modern Jimmy Giuffre, *Cool Heat*.

She got even busier in June and August 1960, recording three worthy projects in those two months: *Anita O'Day and Billy May Swing Rodgers & Hart*, *Waiter, Make Mine Blues* with Russ Garcia, and *Incomparable!* with Bill Holman. The two songbook albums seem, in retrospect, the kind of thing that would have been Granz's idea, since he very successfully masterminded the concept of the songbook album with Ella Fitzgerald, yet 1959 and 1960 were the years in which he was selling the company and phasing out his involvement. Even in the way their last names rhyme, O'Day and May are ideally suited to each other. Although these are supposed to be mainstream pop projects, as opposed to the more modernist work of Giuffre and Holman, May abounds with brilliant ideas here, and these two projects represent some of the freshest and most inspired writing of his career. The Rodgers project includes one of O'Day's finest comedy-narrative songs, "To Keep My Love Alive," which completely puts the lie to the singer's claim that she didn't care about lyrics—here she proves herself one of the most astute interpreters of the song ever, and doesn't take a back seat to any musical comedy star in terms of getting laughs. On the other end of the spectrum, "Little Girl Blue" is perhaps her single finest ballad. She wrings all the emotion possible out of one of Lorenz Hart's most poignant texts—and she does it without missing a beat. Ella Fitzgerald and Buddy Bregman had beaten O'Day and May to the punch by three years with both the Cole Porter and Rodgers and Hart projects, but in these two instances, I will take Anita's over Ella's anytime.

Her most modern-sounding album was *Cool Heat*, arranged by Jimmy Giuffre at the same time he was recording with his third stream–style chamber jazz trio, and in which O'Day and the arranger-instrumentalist update a program of songs mostly from the twenties and thirties with icy-cool sonorities. In *Mr. Kelly's*, she included a camp treatment of the twenties show-tune dance "The Varsity Drag," with Looney Tunes references; here she takes a couple of songs from the same era that one would assume are resolutely unupdateable, and does precisely that with "Hooray for Hollywood" and the theme song to the popular radio show *Little Orphan Annie*, which climaxes with the boys in the band collectively supplying the "arf" of Orphan Annie's dog, Sandy. Those "boys," incidentally, include perhaps O'Day's most stellar cast of sidemen, including altoists Bud Shank and Art Pepper, trombonist Frank Rosolino, guitarist Jim Hall, and drummer Mel Lewis.

Winners, *Cool Heat*, and *Incomparable!* are each graced with a wordless vocalese by O'Day, in which she hums the melody to a famous composition and then improvises on it—doing precisely what a trumpeter or saxist would do. "Four Brothers" was written by Giuffre but arranged for O'Day by Marty Paich, "Hershey Bar" was composed by Johnny Mandel but arranged for O'Day by Giuffre, and "Slaughter on Tenth Avenue" is one of the more famous instrumental themes by Richard Rodgers but is heard on *Incomparable!* rather than O'Day's album of Rodgers songs. *Incomparable!* is mostly high-octane swingers, delivered with the bop era voicings of the outstanding big band orchestrator Bill Holman. The big numbers are the main attraction here, but there are some nice intimate ballads, too, particularly "The Party's Over," from *Bells Are Ringing.* Yet even on this swingcentric project, O'Day ends "If I Love Again" by ritarding briefly into waltz time. It's virtually the same ending that she had used on the Richard Rodgers waltz "Falling in Love with Love" with Billy May—making it obvious that in both cases she had a lot of input in the arrangements, even when working with luminaries like May and Holman.

Waiter, Make Mine Blues is a similar idea in reverse, a torchy album of songs about love and loss yet with room for jazzy up-tempos. Russ Garcia's arrangements are more forties-swing-based than those of Giuffre or Holman, but there's nonetheless a wailingly boppish alto solo by Shank on "Whatever Happened to You?" The 1961 albums, *Trav'lin' Light* and *All the Sad Young Men,* extend the idea of doing mostly prewar songs in defiantly postwar style charts. The first is a tribute to Billie Holiday, taped roughly a year and a half after Holiday's death, and six months before Carmen McRae's Holiday tribute. "She didn't copy Billie Holiday," as arranger Johnny Mandel told me. "She didn't sound at all like [Holiday], although that was obviously the main source of inspiration." Mandel supplied light and tasteful modernistic touches throughout this set of mostly ballads and torch songs; Holiday was only four years older than O'Day, and Mandel's charts sound like the kind that the Lady herself would have used had she ever wanted to go in more of a modern direction. In fact, one of Holiday's cohorts, Ben Webster, is prominently featured.

All the Sad Young Men, for which arranger Gary McFarland recorded the orchestral tracks in New York before O'Day added her vocal parts a few months later, was the most modern she ever got, using dissonant, semiclassical voicings of brass and reeds, not to mention tricky rhythmic patterns well beyond 4/4 swing that made even Stan Kenton's orchestrations seem conventional by comparison. Yet at the same time, this album contains more examples of O'Day doing the old-fashioned blues than any other album, including the semiscatted but comparatively straight 12-bar blues "Up State." There are songs that allude to the blues, such as Horace Silver's "Señor Blues," John Benson Brooks's

"You Came a Long Way from St. Louis," and Willard Robison's "A Woman Alone with the Blues." There's also a dynamite 3/4 time jazz waltz arrangement of her Krupa specialty, "Boogie Blues"; O'Day would keep this treatment of the blues in her book for many years to come.

All the Sad Young Men was the first O'Day album produced by Creed Taylor, who was now running the artistic side of Verve, which had recently been purchased from Norman Granz by MGM Records. *Sad Young Men* was also the last purely jazz album she would do: The next two packages combined her with two jazz-pop acts, one successfully and one disappointingly. *Time for Two* co-starred O'Day and the very popular Latin vibraphonist Cal Tjader in a generally exciting program in which she once again responds to a whole new kind of rhythmic stimulus—and made Dave Frishberg's "Peel Me a Grape" into a jazz standard. On the other hand, *Anita O'Day and the Three Sounds* teamed her with that popular lounge jazz trio to generally dismal results. It was an inauspicious way to wind up the climactic period of her career.

In 1960, she had recorded a tender and touching yet still swinging treatment of "The Party's Over," on *Incomparable!* and two years later, for some reason, she sang it again, in the Latin treatment on *Time for Two.* Perhaps this was her way of signifying her realization that within a few years the party would indeed be over.

By 1962, Norman Granz had long since departed from Verve Records (even though, apart from the misfire with the Three Sounds, the rest of Anita's later albums with the company maintain their usual high standard). After the end of the relationship with Verve, the sixties would be a blank to O'Day: She was mired in her addictions, which may have made little difference career-wise since the commercial music industry was hardly breaking down her door in any case.

In the seventies, O'Day suffered from any number of personal problems, including alcohol abuse, but fortunately heroin was no longer among them. She would continue to work steadily through the seventies, eighties, and nineties, and her recording career was rejuvenated, for the most part, thanks to her fans in Japan. Shuttling regularly between the States, the Far East, and Europe, she recorded a dozen or so projects for various independent Eastern concerns, mostly from the mid-seventies to 1981. A number of the Japanese-produced albums, both live and studio affairs, were released in the United States by O'Day herself on Emily Records, the label operated for the singer by her longtime drummer John Poole and his wife, Elaine.

It's easy to overlook the seventies recordings because, on the one hand, they lack the diversity of the Verve albums, they don't have arrangers like Johnny Mandel and Bill Holman, and O'Day almost never sings with anything larger than a trio. At the same time, while being less diverse, they're also less consistent, particularly in terms of sound quality. Yet albums like *Live in Person* offer some of her most inspired and exuberant performances. That particular live session, taped in Vancouver in 1976 and featuring the gifted Canadian tenor saxophonist Fraser MacPherson, is one of her best—on the up-tempos, especially, O'Day is as animated as she ever was (which is considerable) and her ballad singing has matured considerably since the fifties. Interestingly, the second half of the set is mostly vintage standards, but she gets under way primarily with newer material. Seeing Anita myself around this time, I was annoyed that she chose to do music by Leon Russell and Stevie Wonder and their ilk (even that word "ilk" sounds perjorative), but thirty years later, "A Song for You" and "You Are the Sunshine of My Life" sound like all-time Anita classics.

Two projects of the period stand out and come closest to the "concept" albums she made for Verve: *Mello'Day*, as the title (ungainly as it is) promises, is a set of mostly slower, comparatively romantic material, aided by the presence of the heavyweight accompanist Lou Levy on piano. I'm especially enamored of her treatment of "On the Trail," the American light classic (from Ferde Grofé's *Grand Canyon Suite*) much beloved of beboppers. In 1981, she taped a very special set with pianist Don Abney, issued at different times under two titles, *Misty* and *The Night Has a Thousand Eyes*. Bereft of bass and drums (but not necessarily of tempo), the program naturally settles into a mostly ballad groove. She sings "You Go to My Head" with the worldly wisdom of a gal who has had a lot of things go to her head over the course of a lifetime, and her "Am I Blue," which opens with the verse, is clearly inspired by Ethel Waters. It's an overlooked gem of a session that should have been released as *The Intimate Anita.*

Unfortunately, the 1981 duo session may be the last Anita release that's without question worth listening to (then again, some of those seventies and eighties projects are very hard to find—I don't claim to have heard them all). The next major album, somewhat easier to find, is the 1989 *In a Mellow Tone*, which has its moments but is clearly a step down. The biggest disappointment is the 1993 *Rules of the Road*, a long-awaited reunion with Buddy Bregman (arranger of *Anita* and *Pick Yourself Up*) in

which O'Day sounds as if she's singing over big band instrumentals for which the orchestrator neglected to leave a space for the vocalist. The biggest surprise is the 1996 *Swing Time in Hawaii*, a collaboration with the jazz ukulele virtuoso Herb Ohta.

I first began catching O'Day in the early eighties: From that point on to the mid-nineties it seemed as though she was gradually losing more and more of her sparkle. She never had much of a voice in those years, at least not the way she did in 1955, but it was distressing to note the diminishment of her energy and chutzpah. In the mid-nineties, O'Day was hospitalized, and it looked as if she would never be heard from again. According to longtime manager Alan Eichler, it seemed as if the entire medical fraternity of Southern California was out to get her. Fortunately, as Eichler told me at the time, that hospitalization, disastrous and nearly fatal as it was, resulted in her freedom from substances.

Around 1999–2000, O'Day enjoyed something of a brief Indian summer, yet one more time. Around the time of her eightieth birthday, she was rejuvenated, partly because she was out of the hospital and not drinking anymore, and also because a new boxed set on Mosaic Records (*The Complete Anita O'Day Verve/Clef Sessions*) was bringing her renewed attention and reminding everyone of how great she was.

In summer 1999, O'Day opened for the Manhattan Transfer in a concert at Avery Fisher Hall that provided a perfect example of what makes Anita O'Day great. When the headliners were on, you felt as if your foot was nailed to the floor; when O'Day sang, even as incapacitated as she was, your foot went up and down in time with joyous abandon. Even with barely a breath left in her body, O'Day had swing and style to spare.

In her final years, she participated in the making of an excellent documentary titled *Anita O'Day: The Life of a Jazz Singer,* produced by her last manager, the inexhaustible Robbie Cavolina. She continued to perform until 2003, long after she could remember any lyrics or even knew where she was; she died on Thanksgiving Day 2006. Ironically, the most self-destructive of the canonical jazz singers turned out to be the one who lasted the longest, proving that God enjoys a joke as much as anyone.

P

Patti Page (born 1927)

She is the most popular female vocalist of all time. Who am I talking about? This claim has been made for at least three singers of the forties and fifties: Jo Stafford, Joni James, and Patti Page. Stafford is surely unchallenged as by far the classiest member of this trio, and the earliest, while James is probably the last widely popular prerock female

singer. In more recent years, Celine Dion, Aretha Franklin, Madonna, and Mariah Carey could also be hailed as the biggest-selling female pop star ever.

But in the big picture, it makes the most sense that the title would go to Patti Page, and probably the major reason for that is that she has never depended on just one area of the overall pop music audience for support. The Oklahoma-born singer has been just as beloved by people who otherwise listen to Rosemary Clooney and Benny Goodman as she has by the fan base of Loretta Lynn and George Jones. She "crosses over" genres in other ways, too, and is one of the few singers who appealed equally to pop music listeners in 1950 and also to those in the very different kind of music that was nonetheless also known as pop ten and fifteen years later. Page is known for so many kinds of music, from the hard-luck blues to songs about doggies in windows and mama dolls to crossing over bridges to salvation in Old Cape Cod, that it's hard to imagine how anyone could compete with her.

In 1997, Page celebrated the fiftieth anniversary of her first recording with a concert at Carnegie Hall and a lavish, four-CD box set (the booklet of which, written by pop music historian Colin Escott, is the source for most of the facts in this essay). Each of the eighty tracks on this very well produced package shows that she has what it takes to be a superior pop singer. She has a beautiful, deep voice, wonderful intonation, solid time, an often surprising capacity for the blues, and a gift for putting over a song in a particular way that, opines Escott, is philosophically (and often musically) related to the country-folk tradition. If everything Page sang were worthy of her gifts—or even if market success were the sole criterion for inclusion—she might well be mentioned in the same breath as Stafford, Lena Horne, Doris Day, Judy Garland, or even Ella Fitzgerald.

Yet Page rarely is regarded as one of the all-time giants of popular singing, partly because there are so few absolutely essential Patti Page records, and also because she tends to be remembered for the million-sellers rather than the lesser-known but superior songs that might better make her case. It's not just that she sang a lot of lousy songs—so did Doris Day and Rosemary Clooney—but at least Day and Clooney sing well even on inferior material. Page has an outstanding voice, but it's the way that voice is treated that adversely affects our ability to enjoy her records fifty to sixty years after the fact. Like Day and Clooney, she often had to contend with inferior songs and formula orchestrations, but the bigger problem is the way the actual sound of her voice itself is manipulated. I'm speaking, of course, of multitracking; the gimmick that propelled her to the top of the charts was the electronic technique that turned her into a one-woman vocal group. One can get around the gimmicks on Day or Clooney records, but on Page's biggest hits, the gimmick is the tricked-up quality of her voice itself.

Unfortunately, there's no escaping it—except on those comparatively rare records Page made which don't use the multitracking gimmick. On the very few where she has good songs, good charts, and doesn't use multitracking, Patti Page flies in a very high orbit indeed. She has elements of Doris Day's sunny, middle-American sound, Dinah Shore's Southern cooking, and Jo Stafford's California coolness, but Page's sound is ultimately no one's but hers. Much of the time, she's a gimmick-driven hit maker, whose records are almost better enjoyed for cultural and anthropological reasons (e.g., what does "Doggie in the Window" tells us about pre-Elvis America?) than musical or artistic ones. Yet in the course of her long career, Page recorded more than enough presentable albums and singles to earn a place in the annals of the better interpreters of the American songbook. Ironically, while no one disputes her amazing success at the cash register, her many good records are chronically underappreciated by the cognoscenti who love good pop singing. She is somehow both amazingly successful and chronically underrated.

In the 1947 "Oklahoma Blues," Patti Page sings about "goin' back to Oklahoma, goin' back to my old hometown / Where folks all take it easy and never race around." In actuality, Page raced around quite a bit as a child. As was true of Peggy Lee, her father worked for the railroad, and the family lived all over Arkansas, Kansas, and Oklahoma; she spent the biggest chunk of her childhood in Tulsa. "Oklahoma Blues" was deliberately autobiographical in other respects: She sings "got eleven in my family"; she actually did grow up surrounded by seven sisters and three brothers.

Born Clara Ann Fowler, she started singing in school, and like virtually everyone else who began in the thirties and forties, found her first professional opportunities to perform on local radio. As a sixteen-year-old, Fowler sang on Tulsa radio KTUL with the early jazz organist Glenn Hardman, and eventually landed a sponsored show with the Page Milk Company (at the same time, under a different name, she also sang on a country program for the same station). More than ten years earlier, in 1935, Helen Fogel (who eventually became Helen Forrest) appeared on a local show on the East Coast entitled *The Blue Velvet Hour*, on which she was billed as "Bonnie Blue." When Fowler sang for Page Milk, she was introduced as "Patti Page," and in her case (unlike Forrest's), the name stuck. The idea of naming performers after products apparently led indirectly to a long-standing tradition of white female pop singers with alliterative names such as Doris Day, Joni James, Kitty Kallen (her real name), Georgia Gibbs, and Patti Page. In a sense, these names don't just sound like artists or even real people—more than anything, they sound like commercial products.

In the mid-forties and in the Midwest, Page was gradually singing her way up the radio food chain when she met saxophonist Jack Rael in Chicago in 1946. He was, at the time, playing with territory bandleader Jimmy Joy, yet Rael had been so taken with Page's singing that he forsook his own career as a musician in order to earn 10 percent of her pay as an emerging vocal star. Rael helped her land appearances on a Chicago radio series, and then gained her an entry to Mercury Records, then a start-up operation based in the Windy City. Page's first session included "Every So Often," an independent (not from a show or film) song by Johnny Mercer and Harry Warren. She later dismissed it—"Nothing much happened with those first records, my family bought them, and they had to order them"—yet compared to some of her hits, "Every So Often" is a masterpiece.

Somewhere along the line, somebody got the idea of having Page sing in multiple voices. Overdubbing of some sort had been going on for decades, even in the pretape era. There was Sidney Bechet's famous one-man band recordings of 1941, and, at around the same time as Page, guitarist and pop maverick Les Paul was also tinkering with ways to superimpose one level of sound upon another. This is precisely the sort of idea one would normally associate with Mitch Miller; though the producer was actually working for Mercury at the time, based in New York, he has never claimed credit for this particular technological brainstorm. It was probably Jack Rael who thought of the multivoice technique. "It was just logical that it could be done," Rael told Escott; "we were desperate and had no budget."

Their initial experiment was "Confess," which charted first for Doris Day and Buddy Clark. Page's "Confess" featured its two voices in counterpoint, answering each other back and forth like a real pop duet (supposedly the label billing was "Patti Page and Patti Page"). Their next attempt with the technique was "With My Eyes Wide Open I'm Dreaming," a 1934 movie song that Page had heard sung by Don Elliott. On this second overdub session, the irritation level grew proportionately higher when Page doubled the stakes from two to four voices. Instead of counterpoint, now the four Pages sing in tight harmony—harmony that's tighter than a toreador's trousers. As she upped the ante, sales rose correspondingly. The sound of Page as a one-woman quartet is grating and artificial (granted, it got smoother as the technique improved, as on "Once in a While" and "Tumbling Tumbleweeds"). Patti Page's voice sounds much more beautiful by itself, but millions upon millions of record buyers disagreed with that opinion, and responded in overwhelming numbers when the overdub discs began appearing.

Page continued doing double duty as a country singer, and early on she turned to readings of such C&W standards as "Detour," "San Antonio Rose," and "Tumbling Tumbleweeds." Thus, by 1950, Patti Page had two factors going for her: the overdubbing gimmick and her potential to appeal to both mainstream and country audiences. It stood to reason that if she and Rael could combine these two factors—in other words, record a country song with multiple voices—they could produce one of the biggest blockbuster hits of all time.

The result was "Tennessee Waltz" (which even contained what could be called a jazz element in the form of Buck Clayton's trumpet solo, although I don't think that anyone bought it for that). It was a perfect disc for the era of Truman-style moderation: *Everybody* liked it, from the sophisticates at the Copacabana (where she was appearing at the time the disc was released) to authentic Tennesseans and Oklahomans, to mainstream urban pop record buyers in their fedoras, to prairie record fans in their saddles and ten-gallon hats. All in all, it was a hit of "White Christmas"–like proportions.

Page had a gimmick that no one could beat; the closest contender was Les Paul, who also struck gold by overdubbing levels of a country-style voice (his then wife, Mary Ford) with his own multiple guitar tracks for a series of hits in the early to mid-fifties. In the output of both Page and Paul, we have superior talents laboring hard to make inferior music; the hits of both of them were immediately successful in their time, but more or less forgotten even a few years later. In the case of Page, the multiple voices tend to instantly dominate every song they're on, and it's impossible to register subtleties or nuances when she's singing in this format. The moment you start hearing the one-woman quartet, nothing else matters; you don't have to worry about anything in the orchestration—tonal color, interesting harmonies, modulations, instrumental solos. The only thing that anybody hears is those damned voice tracks.

Nearly all of Page's dozens of hits employ the device. In fact, I find this the most annoying aspect of Page's most infamous hit, Bob Merrill's 1952 "Doggie in the Window." I don't know why everyone pounds the poor "Doggie" (pun intended); it's often held up by rock 'n' roll revisionists as endemic of the blandness of mainstream pop in the years immediately before the transformation of youth music. Actually, one could point out that in its youth appeal, its use of sound effects (the dog barks), "Doggie" sounds a lot more like what Mel Tormé would describe as the "puerile, vapid, crappy music" that belongs to the late fifties as much as to the early fifties. It's hard to see how rock-biased historians could claim that "Doggie in the Window" is either a worse or a better piece of music than Elvis Presley's "Teddy Bear." "Doggie" is, in fact, nothing more than a lesser children's song that inexplicably caught on in the big pop stakes of the immediate prerock era. (Even more than "Tennessee Waltz," "Doggie" was notable for the parodies it inspired, most hilariously Mickey Katz's "How Much Is That Pickle in the Window?")

"Doggie" is also in waltz time, and that was Page's other gimmick. She followed "Tennessee Waltz" with "Changing Partners," a song that's little more than a virtual paraphrase of its predecessor—it could be called "The Nashville Waltz." Next came "I'll Remember Today," in which an Edith Piaf chanson gets the overdubbed waltz treatment. In 1958, Page recorded *The Waltz Queen*, an entire 12" album of songs in 3/4. For most of the fifties, her drummer was Stanley Kaye, who earlier served as deputy percussionist in Buddy Rich's big band and later became a successful talent manager. "We played so many damn waltzes," Kaye told me, "that I almost forgot how to play in four!"

I don't think it's being too elitist to say that the vast bulk of Page's hits—she had seventy-eight chart entries between 1947 and 1962, her first tenure at Mercury—are not exactly music for the ages. "Mister and Mississippi," "I Went to Your Wedding," "Mockin' Bird Hill," "Allegheny Moon," "Whispering Wind," and "Old Cape Cod" (a jingle I find particularly cloying)—all use the multitrack technique. As much as "Doggie," they're emblematic of how quick adult pop music was to sell itself out, and how the takeover of kiddie pop music in the late fifties wasn't that much of a step down. And compared to Page's "The Mama Doll Song" from a year later, "Doggie" is positively Leonard Bernstein.

Fortunately, the four-disc *Golden Celebration* includes more than just the chart hits; volume four, which is subtitled "The Singer," collects twenty exceptional pop standards, including composers as removed from the world of doggies and Mama dolls as Duke Ellington and Noel Coward. The set ends with eight selections from Page's finest straight-ahead albums, *Patti Page in the Land of Hi-Fi* (1956), *You Go to My Head,* and *Manhattan Tower.* Parts of these were arranged and conducted by Pete Rugolo, already known for his outstanding work with both June Christy and Nat King Cole. These are easily the most memorable of Page's recordings, signifying almost the only time when she competed in the world of good songs and gimmick-free arrangements. It seems pointless to compare her to Rosemary Clooney or Doris Day or Lena Horne here. Featuring such supperior songs as "Spring Is Here," "The Lady Is a Tramp, and "Mountain Greenery" (to name three by Rodgers and Hart), these are virtually the only Patti Page albums we can listen to all the way through—without apologies.

In spite of the badly dated quality of many of her hits, Page deserves a Bear Family–style complete collection of all her Mercury recordings. Who knows how many decent songs are buried in their vaults, waiting to be exhumed and appreciated? The good songs, which didn't sell then, would sound great now, in contrast to the hits, which are best forgotten.

The most surreal, and perhaps even witty, of all of Page's hits is "Mama from the Train," written by Irving Gordon, a prolific songwriter who wrote classy songs ("Prelude to a Kiss," "Unforgettable") as well as shlock ("Delaware"). Yet another novelty waltz, this 1956 gem is built around a spoonerism supposedly uttered by an old Pennsylvania Dutch lady. In her backward sentence construction, the request to "throw a kiss to your mother from the train" becomes "throw Mama from the train / a kiss." It's also one of the last ethnic hits—a final vestige of what the old neighborhoods were like before we all

moved out to the suburbs—although the Dutch Uncle phraseology could just as easily be Yiddish or Italian. (The song's other quotable line is: "and eat Mama up all her pie.")

Page has consistently claimed that she never realized it was a gag; I personally think that she's been pulling our collective leg. The song is so bizarre that it almost didn't need anyone to parody it, although in 1987 Billy Crystal and Danny DeVito appropriated its title for a rather dark and very funny movie comedy called *Throw Momma from the Train.* Thirty years earlier, "Mama from the Train" received the ultimate accolade when it was singled out for ridicule by Frank Sinatra, who was never shy about denouncing songs he didn't like. At a 1957 concert (available on CD), the Chairman went out of his way to put down this song, spontaneously launching into it in the middle of his show, but giving it a different sort of ethnic imperative. He sings: "Throw Yer 'Mudder' off the Train, but Quick, but Quick." In his own perverse way, just by acknowledging that the song existed, Sinatra imbued it with a kind of immortality.

Jackie Paris (1924–2004)

Fifteen years after the death of Lenny Bruce, Sally Marr, the comedian's mother, happened to come across an unmailed letter among her son's effects. Upon opening the envelope, she found a three-page testimonial to the talents of Jackie Paris, the jazz singer who'd shared a bill with Bruce for several months in 1959.

The comic was writing to implore his agent to sign Paris to a long-term contract. "[My last gig in] New York was a gas, and the biggest thrill was working with Jackie Paris," Bruce wrote. "You know how much I dug him before, well, I find out he tap dances great and plays 'the end' guitar. . . . To make a long story thrilling, [he's got] a beautiful act [and it's] commercial, because it's bright and original. And he is cute as a button and the audience loves him and he gets laughs. Toooo muccchhh!" Bruce continues, "I dig his talent, and I know he could be a star. I've never seen a singer that could talk and command the audience['s] attention like this kid, except Sinatra or Dean Martin, and they talk about booze and broads. This kid [actually Bruce and Paris were both thirty-three at the time] is a hip Pat Boone."

Bruce was convinced that Paris was going to become the next big singer—in fact, at different points in Paris's long career, many people would have put money on that happening. Little could Bruce or any of the others know that Jackie Paris was fated to spend almost sixty years strictly as an insider's favorite, known to the cognoscenti and the converted but to hardly anyone else. Paris wasn't even a pop singer with jazz influences—like, say, Steve Lawrence or Billy Eckstine. Rather, he was an uncompromising jazz singer who happened to have potentially enormous—albeit unrealized—pop appeal.

Paris was also the favorite singer of Charles Mingus, who had worked with him in Lionel Hampton's band in 1948 or 1949, and three years later wrote several compositions expressly for the singer, which they recorded together on Mingus's own Debut label. Further, Paris was the only singer ever to tour with Charlie Parker (in the famous Parker quintet with Miles Davis and Max Roach). He also was the vocalist selected by producer-critic Leonard Feather (and presumably, Thelonious Monk) to introduce the now famous lyrics to "'Round Midnight."

It's easy to hear what Bruce, Mingus, and Parker found so appealing in Paris's singing. He was a thorough musician, saturated with the virtues of modern jazz—the harmonic sophistication, the cool attitude, the bright, clean tone—who never sounds as if he's doing anything way-out or complex. He can sing the oddest and most original harmony lines exactly where we expect to hear the straight melody-as-written. Yet nothing he ever sings strikes us as weird, unfitting, or anything but exactly what it ought to be. One of his key strengths, in fact, is his fundamental grounding in the blues. He may be a "Skylark," to quote the title of one of his signature songs, but his feet are rooted deeply in the ground even as his head pokes high into the stratosphere.

Most of Paris's repertoire consisted of very familiar standards that he consistently managed to make sound fresh. He considered it a point of honor that he didn't drastically alter a songwriter's words or music. Still, he personalized each tune, not only through rhythm and phrasing but also by paraphrasing each line from its harmonies outward. More intimate than, say, Sarah Vaughan's very cerebral inventions, Paris's lines remain close enough to the original tune for one to recognize it even without benefit of the words.

Paris, who was born in Nutley, New Jersey, in 1924, was dancing and singing from the time he was two years old. (For most of his life, Paris gave 1926 as his birthday; this was hardly the most significant example Paris bending the truth.) As an eight-year-old dancer, he tapped his way across the Northeastern vaudeville circuit. Even before he sang, Paris told me in one of our many conversations and interviews, he always had *time*. "I would say rhythm is 99 percent of what I do," he said. "I had that from birth. I was always working with all the black guys all the time, and they flipped over my rhythm. They would say: 'Man! Dig this kid, he's got rhythm.' " At one point, the young Paris shared the stage with the legendary Bill "Bojangles" Robinson, who told him, "Son, you sure got rhythm for a white boy." It would not be the only instance of racial blur in his career.

Paris also started playing the guitar as a youngster, following the encouragement and the inspiration of his friends the Mills Brothers (whom he had met on the vaudeville trail), and under the tutelage of his uncle, who had played bass with Paul Whiteman's Orchestra, Jackie said. After serving in the army from 1944 to 1946, Paris enjoyed his first burst of fame when he formed a trio that worked at New York's Onyx Club. The Jackie Paris Trio played there for twenty-six weeks, supposedly one of the longest-running gigs in the history of Swing Street. Following the example of the King Cole Trio, Paris's threesome sported piano, bass, and himself on guitar. "I remember listening to Nat when I was a little kid," he said. "I think I knew Nat's records before almost anybody else did. I think that's when I loved him the best [the early trio period], things like 'I Can't See for Looking' and 'I Realize Now.' "

Paris recorded his first singles with this trio in 1947 for MGM Records. The eight sides (two unissued) he cut at this time included two numbers from the Cole trio's repertoire, "I've Got a Way with Women" and "Your Red Wagon," as well as two tunes that would become Paris perennials, "Skylark" (earlier done by Billy Eckstine, Anita O'Day, and Helen Forrest with Harry James) and Eckstine's "Lonesome Lover Blues," which Paris still kept in his act well into the nineties.

It was while working on Swing Street that the singer was first heard by Hampton as well as Charlie Parker. Paris remembered that Parker first heard him scatting at the Three Deuces on "The Street" around 1947, and that Bird immediately invited him to go on the road with him. "The first job was Boston Symphony Hall in Boston," said Paris. "That was the first concert I ever did with him, and that was a big deal to me, because I hadn't played for that kind of an audience. He'd call out 'Get me Jackie P!' and I'd come out and do three ballads with Bird and Miles and Max. Then I would wail along with the band on 'Anthropology,' and 'Scrapple from the Apple.' " Unfortunately, Paris never recorded with Parker, and, alas, there also is no aircheck or location recording that documents his tenure with the quintet (although there is a beautiful photo of Parker and Paris together on the bandstand, with a very young Miles Davis in the background).

A short while after his stint with Parker, Paris was rehearsing with bassist Red Mitchell at Nola Studios when Gladys Hampton walked in and asked him to join the band. He appears to have toured with Hampton's big band for about three months in 1948 (this was the year of the second musicians' strike, thus Paris didn't get to make any records with Hampton, either). Fifty years later, Jackie remembered two key points about this tour: the grueling difficulty of doing seventy-eight consecutive one-nighters without a letup—and the wardrobe. Paris was the only white member of the band at the time and certainly the first white vocalist Hampton ever hired. For some reason, this inspired Mrs. Hampton to give him an all-white gabardine suit to wear, which was actually an improvement over the rest of the band, who were forced to perform in shocking orange-gold tuxedos.

The tour started at the Strand in Times Square

and then played all the famous black theaters, including the Earle in Philadelphia and the Howard in Washington. Once, down South, a couple of racist cops started harassing the Hamptonians, and Paris in particular. When they asked, "Hey, what are you?"—presumably meaning, "Are you black or white?"—Paris answered, "I'm one of the guys," and let them make of that what they wanted.

Paris was back in the studio in 1949, working for the first of several occasions with Leonard Feather, who got Paris a session for Herb Abramson's National label (two of the tracks were issued in 2003 on the Savoy Jazz compilation *All That Jive*). This session marked the vocal debut of an important standard, Bernie Hanighen's lyric to Thelonious Monk's " 'Round Midnight." The date also included the pop-religious "The Old Master Painter," which became a widely covered pop hit for other singers on bigger labels.

In 1953, Paris was named "Best New Male Singer of the Year" in *Down Beat*. By that time, he had already begun collaborating with two other long-time supporters, bandleader-composer Charles Mingus and producer Bob Thiele. The latter documented him on about twenty tracks (recorded between 1953 and 1955), including a brief series of singles as well as his first two LPs, the 10" *That Paris Mood* and the 12" *Skylark*. This second version of "Skylark" is probably the definitive one, as both the song's creators acknowledged publicly.

Yet their voiced approval didn't result in the album becoming a hit. One of the reasons Paris often had to wait so long between singing gigs is that he never had a big hit song that the public could automatically identify with him. He came close in 1953, when songwriter Redd Evans, who had written many notable songs for Nat King Cole and Anita O'Day, presented him with an exclusive on a new tune called "If Love Is Good to Me." The song had a simple, elemental message and a directly folkish feeling that perfectly suited Paris's style.

In those days before singer-songwriters took hold, the way to pop music success was to get an exclusive. Being the first to record a potential hit gave you an edge. Then, once your record came out—and caught on—the other singers would be the ones trying to catch up with you. Evans promised that he wouldn't let any other singer make a recording of "If Love Is Good to Me," and when the single was released, various trade magazines began predicting that it was going to be a hit. However, Paris happened to be singing the song at the Flame Bar, Detroit's most famous black club, when Nat King Cole himself came in and heard it. The King asked Redd Evans for the music and even though the songwriter had promised Paris an exclusive, he had to give in. "I introduced that song [on Brunswick] and my record had just started to sell. The next thing I know, Redd told me, 'Listen, Nat Cole wants to do the song and I can't turn him down.' " Cole had already made hits out of half a dozen of Evans's

songs. "So Nat recorded it, and though *Cashbox* picked mine over his, Nat's became the biggest record in the country." (According to other accounts, Cole always felt somewhat guilty about it.)

Paris solidified his relationship with "If Love Is Good to Me" by rerecording it in 1962 for his Impulse! album (also produced by Bob Thiele), *The Song Is Paris*; Evans's tune remained perfect for Paris's sweet yet achingly soulful sound. This is what Sarah Vaughan meant when she described him as a "kissy" singer.

In 1955, Paris recorded his next album, a package of thirteen superb songs (in its most recent incarnation on Japanese CD), released under at least three different titles: *Paris in Swingtime (Jackie That Is); Can't Get Started with You—Songs by Jackie Paris*; and *Jackie Paris*. Whatever you call it, this album is one of those fortuitous occasions when everything came together—the singing, the basic material, and the brilliant orchestrations of Manny Albam, in what might be his most impressive writing. Like Nat Cole, Paris was especially partial to songs by the Fisher clan, a key dynasty of Tin Pan Alley, who are represented by "Cloudy Morning" and "Strange" (by Marvin Fisher), "That Ole Devil Called Love" (by Marvin's sister Doris Fisher), and "Whispering Grass" (by Doris and Fred Fisher, their father). Unlike Nat, Paris actually married into the Fisher clan—his first wife was Marvin Fisher's sister-in-law.

Jackie Paris was Paris's first of a handful of classic 12" LPs. Manny Albam alternates between a smallish string band and a strings-and-woodwinds combination with prominent oboe. Paris has never sounded more convincing and his velvet voice has never been more suitably accompanied. "That Ole Devil Called Love" is a particular triumph, on which he shows he's in the same class with the song's other two most famous interpreters, Billie Holiday and Tony Bennett. He's never sounded more tender, more assured, more "kissy," and his time and intonation have never been better.

Paris's next two releases were *The Jackie Paris Sound* (1957–58), a quintet session for Atlantic's East-West subsidiary, featuring tenorist Eddie Wasserman and four rhythm, and *Jackie Paris Sings the Lyrics of Ira Gershwin* (1960), for the smaller Time label. Even considering that Paris was a walking definition of the term "underrated," these two albums are underappreciated even by Paris-ians. Both have the usual well-selected array of tunes, the first being highlighted by "Someone's Rocking My Dreamboat" and "It Could Happen to You." The *Gershwin* package, Paris's only songbook album, was musical-directed by Irv Joseph, a pianist generally considered to be part of the cabaret rather than jazz world.

In addition to these three albums from the early 12" LP era, Paris would make a number of guest shots on other people's records (as well as earlier and later stints with Mingus): He sang the blues "Big Fat Nothin' " with bassist Chubby Jackson's big band on the Argo LP *I'm Entitled to You* in 1957, and he scatted his way through several instrumentals with the all-star band led by Donald Byrd and Gigi Gryce on *Jazz Lab* (also from 1957). A few months later, he was prominently featured by Feather on a jazz cover album of the Broadway show *Oh Captain!*, which teamed him with an all-star band (directed by Dick Hyman and featuring Coleman Hawkins) and the Billie Holiday sound-alike vocalist Marilyn Moore.

In 1962, Paris climaxed the first half of his career with his finest-ever album, *The Song Is Paris*, which reteamed him with one of the more hyphenated individuals in American music, Bobby Scott, the pop singer–jazz pianist–arranger–songwriter. Here was the album in which Paris, not yet forty, showcased everything he had learned up to that point. Paris sounded amazing on two kissy ballads with strings, Scott's own folkish "Jenny" and "If Love Is Good to Me," both suggesting a very pleasing hybrid of jazz and folk singing. " 'Tis Autumn," which would later become a Paris signature as well as the title of the documentary on his life, is a similarly elemental song, about the birds, the trees, and the passing of the seasons, animated by composer-lyricist Henry Nemo's fanciful anthropomorphism. They also included several very down-to-earth, blues-driven numbers, such as the wordless "Thad [Jones]'s Blues," Don Redman's "Cherry," "Duke's Place" (aka "C Jam Blues"), and "Nobody Loses All the Time." Then there are more fanciful and/or metaphoric pieces like "My Very Good Friend in the Looking Glass" and "Cinderella (Stay in My Arms Tonight)." Neither Paris nor Scott missed a trick.

Another Bobby Scott original on *The Song Is Paris* was "Nobody Loses All the Time"; within a few years of the release of the 1962 album, that song title was starting to seem ironic. When the disaster known as the sixties occurred, it was hardly a surprise that Paris, who wasn't a top seller to begin with, would become even more marginalized. He cut only one album between 1962 and 1981, and that was a very atypical package of duets with his then wife, singer (and later teacher) Anne Marie Moss. The two worked as a duo and spent a lot of time playing in Playboy Clubs in the seventies. *Live at the Maisonette* (1974) is far from classic Paris, but shows these two talented individuals trying to come up with their own take on the duo of Jackie and Roy and the trio of Lambert, Hendricks & Ross (with whom Moss had briefly sung); sadly, these efforts are compromised by wishy-washy contemporary songs and even wishier and washier contemporary-style arrangements of good songs. Their treatment of "Mountain Greenery," which survives in a video clip, is very clever—but Jackie just didn't do "clever."

In that same year, Paris renewed his association with Mingus. The two had met in the Lionel Hampton Orchestra, and over the years Mingus recruited him on three different occasions; overall, Paris is the vocalist the bassist-bandleader relied on most regularly. "Charlie could be a bit of a bully," says Paris,

"but he respected me, because I stood up to him. Which in a way was kind of stupid, he could have flattened me." Paris inspired some of Mingus's most songlike compositions, such as "Paris in Blue" from 1952 (produced by the composer himself on his Debut label) and "Duke Ellington's Sound of Love" (1974), which feature some of Mingus's most singable melodies and lyrics, written specifically for Paris.

Mingus also came up with some of his more formless and abstract pieces for Paris, such as "Portrait" (also from 1952, and like "Paris in Blue" included on Fantasy's *Charles Mingus: The Complete Debut Recordings*), knowing full well that Jackie could "sell" the number more convincingly than anyone else. "Paris in Blue" veers off into all kinds of odd directions, yet Paris effectively anchors all narrative and melodic motion to the blues framework that the piece begins and ends in. The piece—as much dramatic narrative as musical composition—presents Paris as actor and narrator, playing a guy in a club, both pissed-off and drunk off his ass, listening to a singer announcing that he's going to do the blues. He tells us that he could do a better job of it ("I'm the guy who should be cryin' the blues around here!"), and proceeds to prove his claim.

For several months during the sixties, Paris worked steadily with Mingus's Jazz Workshop group. He recalled one night at the Village Vanguard in which he witnessed Mingus's vitriolic temper in full force. "Once he was so upset," Paris recalls, "that he chased everybody off the stand except [drummer] Paul Motian and me. The three of us just wailed on the blues for about an hour and a half before he called the other cats back." Twenty-two years after their 1952 sessions, Mingus (in his four roles as composer, bandleader, bassist, and producer) recruited Paris to introduce "Duke Ellington's Sound of Love."

Paris worked infrequently in the eighties and nineties. I saw him at an engagement at New York's Tavern on the Green and a concert for Jack Kleinsinger's "Highlights in Jazz" series, and supplemented his income by teaching voice and guitar at the New School. He made four albums in these years, two for George H. Buck's Audiophile label, *Jackie Paris* (1981 and 1993) and *Nobody Else but Me* (1988), and two for Japanese producer Kiyoshi Koyama on the reconstituted Mercury label, released in Japan, *Lucky to Be Me* (1988) and *Love Songs* (1989). It seems almost cruel to compare these to such earlier triumphs as the 1955 *Jackie Paris* and the 1962 *Song Is Paris*: It's not just that the voice is heavier, but the backing is altogether more serious and more conventionally like late-modern jazz. All four albums concentrate on Paris's specialty, the luxuriously slow ballad. He still sings well, even if his voice isn't quite as rich and juicy as it was in the fifties and sixties. The more tightly budgeted later trio albums also suffer in comparison to the variety of group textures heard on such earlier sets as *I Can't Get Started* with You, The Jackie Paris Sound, and The Song Is Paris. Even so, all four eighties and nineties sets contain outstanding balladry: "More Than You Know," with its anguished, forlorn, and particularly compelling treatment of the verse, which, though rubato, he invests with as much melody as the central refrain, makes for as classic a Paris perennial as "Skylark." Still, the Paris albums of 1953 to 1962 possess both a tenderness and a whimsicality that's hard to hear in these later recordings.

Strangely, his best album of this period is You and I, a 1987 project with a full sixteen-piece big band. The producer found an angel to underwrite the recording sessions, but so far no label has ponied up the funds necessary to release it—at least as late as 2010. You and I balances exciting if typically busy up charts by Michael Abene with haunting and sensitive string arrangements by Bobby Scott, including a loving treatment of Jule Styne's "Small World" that'll tear your guts out. Also in the can somewhere is another completed but unreleased album project, tentatively titled Paris 'Round Midnight (which features his third recording of the Thelonious Monk classic), with Paquito D'Rivera (alto) and Lew Soloff (trumpet).

Of the later recordings that have been released, the best by far was his final project, The Intimate Jackie Paris, produced independently by Seth Cooper in 1999. The singer is not given a driving rhythm section as he is on the Audiophile and Japanese Mercury albums, nor does he have the larger format accompaniment of the classic fifties and sixties albums. Instead, the album lives up to its title and presents him with only bassist Mike Richmond and his own guitar. Paris may have been seventy-five at the time of these sessions, but he still has a youthful exuberance. More remarkably, here he comes closer to regaining the glories of his early career than on any of the albums he made in his fifties and sixties.

Paris was singing remarkably well in his midseventies; in October 2001, he appeared at the resuscitated Birdland (he had played the original Birdland hundreds of times), and he sounded better than at any other occasion that I'd ever heard him. As always, the ballads brought out the best in him, starting with his set opener (and longtime Paris classic), "But Beautiful," as well as a pair of new discoveries, both co-credited to the otherwise unknown J. Robert Harris, "Too Soon" (with Sunny Skylar) and "Lovelight" (with Redd Evans). Both The Intimate Jackie Paris and the Birdland gig served notice that the "kissy singer" was back in town.

Although his ratio of talent to success seems highly disproportionate, it was impossible to feel sorry for Jackie Paris, mainly because the singer and his music were so upbeat. Fans and friends felt until the end that Paris had so much voice and charisma that "it" could still happen for him. I reviewed him the last time he played in New York, perhaps any-place, and said I had hoped his story wouldn't be a replay of the Johnny Hartman scenario—meaning posthumous recognition. Paris died in June 2004.

Still, better late than never—especially since mainstream movie director Raymond De Fellita filmed several long interviews with Jackie (as well as a set at the Jazz Standard) that became the basis for the excellent documentary 'Tis Autumn: The Search for Jackie Paris, which has been shown at film festivals across the country and released on DVD.

When I had formally interviewed Jackie about ten years earlier, Paris had only two major regrets in decisions he'd made along the way. Around 1949 or 1950, he turned down Duke Ellington's invitation to join his band because he had just come off that particularly exhausting road tour with Lionel Hampton; the Maestro's son, Mercer Ellington, later described Paris as "the only guy that ever turned down my father." Then, in the mid-fifties, as Jackie remembered, Dave Lambert and Jon Hendricks tried to recruit him for the jazz vocal trio they were forming, but he—foolishly, he said forty years later—didn't want to be part of any group. The idea of sharing the spotlight rankled his ego, and he thereby lost out on the chance to be part of history with Lambert, Hendricks & Ross.

But Jackie was upbeat until the end. "I never gave in," he told me. " 'Cause I love it, man! What am I gonna do, get bitter and hate the world and kill myself? For what? I had a lot of fun. I loved every minute of it."

Louis Prima (1910–1978)

He's so delightfully low!
—Henry Higgins, Pygmalion

It's long been a dream of mine to write a doctoral thesis entitled Louis Prima: The Life, the Legend, the Linguini. For all of his zooma-zooma zaniness, Prima is worthy of such serious, even scholarly attention, because he was such a unique figure in American music. First, he was a brilliant musician, an inspired trumpeter, and a superlative singer. Even if he were just another singing hornman—on the level of such Crescent City colleagues as Red Allen or Wingy Manone—Prima would easily have earned a place in the jazz history books. But he was something more: Like Frank Sinatra and Artie Shaw, Prima had an intrinsic belief in the value of pop music—that it was no less capable than, say, opera or lieder of moving the heart and stirring the soul, and no less worthy of a permanent place in our collective consciousness. Yet though he had the equipment, both technically and mentally, to produce superior "straight" pop, he was too much of a wisenheimer ever to play it completely straight. He could appreciate the value of a classic pop song like "That Old Black Magic," but his way of exalting the tune, extracting as much pleasure from it as possible, and turning on an audience with it, was to take the song and tear it limb from limb, making fun of it in order to make fun with it. On second thought, maybe I should title that dissertation *Deconstructing Louis*.

Louis Prima wasn't merely a satirist but a genuine satyr, a Dionysian figure who combined music and comedy to revel in the glories of lovemaking and Italian food, and not necessarily in that order. There were times when he was a romantic, but for most of his career he employed a succession of lady friends—such as Gia Maione and, most famously, Keely Smith—to handle the sentimental love songs. Prima himself was charged with erotic energy, and his music was rich in testosterone and tomato sauce.

Smith, his fourth wife and most celebrated partner, once said that the man could have had any woman he wanted. When Prima helped launch the swing era in 1935 at New York's Famous Door, the joint was packed with debutantes and dowagers alike. As owner Sam Weiss reported, "When he shouted [the song] 'Let's Have a Jubilee,' a lot of those sex-starved dames would practically have an orgasm on the spot. I think they thought he was shouting 'Let's have an orgy' in that hoarse, horny voice of his." Prima's sidekick for twenty years, Sam Butera, remembered how Prima's double entendre blues numbers "used to knock 'em out in the black theatres [and] had the women screaming from the balcony."

Where some of Louis Armstrong's more strait-laced biographers have a problem with the Great Man's occasional "lapses of taste," Prima reveled in vulgarity of the most glorious sort. Italian pop singer–cum–historian Billy Vera has identified him as the key musical icon of what he characterizes as *carfone* culture, or what non-Sicilians might call *goombah*. Vera describes a *carfone* as "a loud, uncouth male, given to wearing flashy continental suits made of mohair or shark skin, gaudy initials-in-diamonds pinky rings, and too much cologne. His taste in automobiles runs from black Cadillacs to red Cadillacs."

Prima throws in every gloriously cheap gag his fertile mind can latch on to, from singing an entire chorus of "I Don't Know Why" backward to, thirty years before rap, blurting out the street invective "Your mother!" as part of a scat line on "Margie." His "Sheik of Araby" contains a barely concealed counterlyric—"with no pants on" (for recording purposes he softened the line by switching the garment to "turban," though anyone listening at the time would have known what he meant). In "Five Months, Two Weeks, Two Days" Prima explores the fine line between scatting and belching. But he wasn't necessarily pushing the boundaries of taste as much as he was constantly coming up with new stuff to do what was always uniquely his, as on a 1954 single in which he sings two pop hits (both recent revivals of songs of a certain age), "Paper Doll" and "The Dummy Song," in Italian.

Prima is a head honcho in two distinct areas of popular musical culture, the first being the tradition of the Crescent City cutup. In his early work, especially, the influence of Louis Armstrong saturates much of his singing and playing, but it would be a mistake to dismiss him as a white Xerox of New Orleans's other trumpet-playing Louis. There's reason to believe that there was a long-standing tradition of New Orleans player-singer-funsters, and though Armstrong was by far its greatest exponent, it did not originate entirely with him. For Prima to participate in this tradition did not mean that he was merely copying his fellow Louis; he was part of an entire generation of trumpeter-singers, and not just in New Orleans, who learned to play through the processs of *Satchmosis*.

By the end of the war, Prima had become central to another strain of pop. While the years 1945 to 1955 are often described in histories as the era of pop vocalists, it also was the grand era of novelties, when singers and bands alike tried relentlessly to outsilly one another with the most inane tunes imaginable. Frank Sinatra, who actually recorded a few novelties even before falling into the clutches of Mitch Miller, was the first to tell the world that there was a better kind of pop music, that Artie Shaw and Cole Porter were better in the eyes of God than Arthur Godfrey and the "Too Fat Polka." Yet in this period there was also an elite handful of brilliant, innovative performers who took silly songs seriously and transmuted novelties into art, specifically, Louis Prima, Louis Jordan, Spike Jones, and Mickey Katz. At the heart of their art was a shared ideal of taking middle-American culture and setting it askew, often with an ethnically driven motivation. The combination of ethnicity and silliness meant that the usual concerns of the pop song—love, love, and more love (the list goes on)—took a back seat to other imperatives: usually food. They sang of beans and corn bread (Jordan), chicken schmaltz and lox (Katz), and lasagna and pasta fazool (Prima) as all-consuming objects of desire. In ethnic America, a menu is a political and cultural statement.

From the beginning, Prima drew in equal parts on his Italian heritage and his New Orleans upbringing. Immigration patterns are often directly horizontal: Middle Europeans, French, and English traveled directly west to North America and Canada, and Spaniards wound up in Mexico and Central America. Likewise, at the turn of the twentieth century, more Italians were living in New Orleans than in any other part of the Western Hemisphere, where the balmy weather was most similar to Rome, Naples, and Palermo; it took New York (not to mention New Jersey) and Chicago a few decades at least to catch up. Italians were the first nonblack group to participate in the evolution of jazz as it was being developed by various forces, mostly by people of color, around 1900 in New Orleans. Black culture and Italian culture were rubbing up against each other in productive ways: As is well known, the teenaged Louis Armstrong listened carefully to Italian opera, and the influence is undeniably present in his solos.

Likewise, Louis Prima, born in the Crescent City on December 7, 1910, grew up in such close proximity to the black and Creole population of New Orleans that jazz was always his native language. He began playing at the insistence of his mother, Angelina, whose love of music and skill at preparing Sicilian dishes (her parents had emigrated to New Orleans from Palermo) were known across the city. She forced instruments on all three of her surviving children: a cornet on Leon, a piano on Elizabeth (who later became a nun), and a violin on Louis. Around the time that Leon, who later owned a successful jazz club in the French Quarter, began to play professionally, little Louis had started to fool around with one of his big brother's discarded horns. Not long after, by the start of the twenties, Louis began getting paying gigs with a kids' band. There was a viable Italian jazz scene in the city, and both the trumpet-playing Prima brothers were soon working with the cream of New Orleans's Italianate jazzmen, including Irving Fazola, Leon Roppolo, and Sharkey Bonano.

Prima's cultural connections, though, go well beyond Italian and even African American influences. He shares with fellow *Siciliano* Frank Sinatra a predilection for all things Jewish. Songs of Semitic origin are second only to Italian in Prima's repertoire—songs like "Meshugah," "Mahzel" (which he performed earlier and with considerably more Yiddish gestalt than Benny Goodman), "Shepherd Boy," "Hitsum Kitsum Bumpity Itsum," "And the Angels Sing," "A Good Time Was Had by All," and "Bei Mir Bist Du Schoen." When Prima solos on these pieces, he becomes a *freilach* trumpeter every bit as convincing as Ziggy Elman and Manny Klein (to name two inspired swing era trumpeters of Jewish extraction). In Prima's mature art, his ethnic dance card was filled with numbers (not to mention dinners) from every conceivable background: "I Love to Polka," "Bring Forth the Light" (a calypso), "Jamaica Shout," "Chinatown," "Chop Suey, Chow Mein, Tofu and You," "Chili Sauce," "In a Little Gypsy Tea Room," "The Gypsy," and the ersatz-Hawaiian "Beloved."

Prima crossed chronological boundaries as well as ethnic ones—indeed, he always had an innate gift for knowing what was precisely right for each successive generation. Although his penchant for novelties and general silliness runs through his entire career, his professional life divvies up into three distinct phases and ensembles: his "New Orleans Gang" of the thirties, his big band of the forties, and the Witnesses, his rhythm and blues–based group of the fifties onward. The first phase is synonymous with New York's "street of swing," a throughway that Prima put on the map much as he would do for Las Vegas Boulevard twenty years later. Prima had first come to New York at the encouragement of Guy Lombardo (rarely regarded as a connoisseur of hot talent), and initially worked as a sideman with the trumpeter Red Nichols, the violinist Joe Venuti, and the pianist and composer David Rose.

The New Orleans Gang is the only Prima band that has been taken seriously by jazz scholars; Richard Sudhalter in *Lost Chords* appropriately praises both the ensemble and Prima's playing. That judgment is supported by the legion of top-drawer improvisers who passed through the ranks of the New Orleans Gang, including such homeboys as Sidney Arodin, Eddie Miller, and Nappy Lamare. The two most illustrious musicians to work in the the New Orleans Gang may well have been hired because of their entertaining—if hardly glamorous—faces: The brilliant clarinetist Pee Wee Russell was famous for contorting his puss into the most extreme expressions imaginable. Likewise, sour-pussed pianist Claude Thornhill is addressed by Prima on one disc as "Baboon-faced Thornhill."

Prima's hot and raspy voice never sounded better than on "Lazy River," his 1934 homage to Louis Armstrong's 1931 treatment of the Hoagy Carmichael–Sidney Arodin classic. Prima's horn work is brilliant enough, but his singing, which artfully blends the Carmichael lyrics with an imaginative scat and a long passage introducing Russell ("Oh . . . Pee Wee . . . Hoddle-doddle . . . Pee Wee!") is even more astonishing, with a floating, levitating quality, firmly establishing Prima as one of the best scatters and jazz singers of the early post-Armstrong era. (In 2003, all of the band's recordings from 1934 to 1937 were included in the Mosaic box *The Complete Vocalion and Brunswick Recordings of Louis Prima and Wingy Manone*.)

The New Orleans Gang was indeed one of the great jazz groups of a great jazz era. The Mosaic box, which includes sixty-four selections by Prima, makes it clear that the trumpeter-singer's first national identity—long before he became known as an Italo-American wildman—was as the leader of one of the country's finest jukebox combos of the late Depression–early swing era. The New Orleans Gang recordings even hold their own when compared with such other juke leaders as Fats Waller and the Teddy Wilson–Billie Holiday sides; Prima's version of "(Looks Like I'm) Breakin' the Ice" is, if anything, even more irreverent and energetic than Waller's. As with Holiday and Waller, the mid-thirties sessions are a succession of one terrific tune after another, most of which have never been revived— "Danger—Love at Work," for instance. He sang this minor Mack Gordon–Harry Revel gem with Alice Faye in the Fox musical *You Can't Have Everything*, but his solo commercial version with the New Orleans Gang was even more inspired.

One song that Prima himself returned to was "The Lady in Red"—it had come from a Warner Bros. film (*In Caliente*), but it was Prima, not any of the performers in the picture, who had the hit record. Within a short while, Prima himself would be appearing in the movies, and he would continue to do so over the next thirty years: "band" shorts in the thirties and forties, guest appearances in features (like *You Can't Have Everything,* 1937, and *Rose of Washington Square,* 1939, both starring Alice Faye), and eventually starring in two B-level features of his own (*Hey Boy! Hey Girl!,* 1959, and *Twist All Night,* 1961).

He was always looking for new venues and formats. Having helped open the door for Swing Street, and, to a certain extent, the swing era itself, he was keen to get in on the big band boom. The first Prima orchestra, introduced at Chicago's Black Hawk in 1936, was not a success, but a few months later he recorded two sessions in Los Angeles with larger (eleven- and twelve-piece) ensembles, including one title, "Let's Get Together and Swing," in which his singing was backed up by Jo Stafford and the Stafford Sisters, making their recording debut.

In 1940, he introduced what he called his "Gleeby Rhythm" orchestra. The name, which referred to a specific beat that later became known as the shuffle, didn't last long, but the big band itself did. The large-format jazz-pop ensemble would be the focus of Prima's professional life for the next dozen years. Most of his big bands—unlike those of, say, Cab Calloway (another extravagant singer-entertainer)—were neither stuffed with major improvisers nor technically outstanding. As historian Rod Baum has noted, the band didn't always consistently play in tune, and the overall sonic quality of the sections was not helped by the poor technical quality of his releases on the Majestic label (which he recorded for during the World War II era). But as a whole, every edition of the many bands Prima directed going up through the early fifties was galvanized by the leader's electrifying personality, and he made sure that they provided the backdrop he needed.

During the big band era, Prima consolidated his position as a jazz-pop superstar and refined his arsenal of shtick. Up until this point, he publicly identified with his origins as a Crescent City jazzman—his most famous band, after all, had been titled the New Orleans Gang. It was during World War II, when the United States, home of the Prima family for several generations, had entered into a state of war with Mussolini and the family's ancestral homeland, that Prima, for the first time, publicly identified himself as an Italian. These were the years when he began singing Neapolitan novelties, beginning with the blockbuster "Angelina." Before Prima, only two popular culture stars, Rudolph Valentino and Russ Columbo, even had Italian names—it was only a short while earlier that Prima's friend Bing Crosby began to publicly identify himself as Irish; at this point, it was still de rigeur in showbiz to have a WASPy name.

Hardly a single Italian word appears in Prima's first ten years of recording—even when he mentions "spaghetti" on the 1934 "House Rent Party Day," it's on the same menu as "pig feet and chitlins." From "Angelina" on, a significant portion of his act was devoted to both traditional and fake Neapolitana, including such great moments in music as "Please No Squeeze da Banana" and rhyming titles like "Josephina Please No Leena," "Felicia No Capicia," "Baciagaloop (Makes Love on da Stoop)," and "For Mari-Yooch I Walka da Pooch."

"Angelina" represents the first instance of Prima incorporating the *tarantella* into his music; what the polka is to Slavs and the tango to Argentines, the tarantella is to traditional Italian dance music. To later generations, Italo-Americanness represented smooth, powerful characters, be they mobsters or crooners. At this early stage of the game, Prima is singing of very early, unassimilated Italians who live in overcrowded urban environments, work as manual laborers, and never have any money.

His characters are country cousins—*greena cousina,* in the words of a Yiddish song he could have sung—who show up from the Old Country and embarrass their more assimilated *famiglia.* Both "Josephina" and "Baciagaloop" have no place to take their paramours, so they are forced to entertain them in semipublic spaces, usually on the front steps of the tenement. Prima's amorous young suitor takes both "Angelina" ("the waitress at the pizzeria") and "Felicia" (who doesn't speak English) out to eat and worries what he's gonna do when the check arrives—he feeds 'em and weeps. Prima always casts himself as the *schlemiel,* but he's sublimely hip—there's a live version of "Felicia" from a 1945 Frank Sinatra show where he's positively electrifying, with a charisma and sex appeal that suggest the Sinatra of 1955 rather than 1945. (It's also amazing to hear the crowd roar every time Prima drops a phrase in Italian.)

In fact, food is as much of a preoccupation in Prima's Italian songs as sex. Prima's "Angelina" (1944) anticipates Cab Calloway's "Everybody Eats When They Come to My House" by devising as many rhymes as could be found for various Italian delicacies. He sings:

I eat soup and *minestrone,* just to be with her
   alone,

and

I eat cutlet *parmesan* / Just so I can gaze upon
   /Angelina,

not to mention

I'll be having matrimony / with the girl who
   serves *spumoni.*

"Angelina" is Prima's ultimate aria of sex and food: Our hero yearns to get laid—and get fed—by "the waitress at the pizzeria," and the lyric shoves that very Italian girl's name down the listener's throat. If ever a man were obsessed with a feminine appellation, it is Prima's Italian protagonist, who repeats the name of his lady love (and the song title) over and over. WNEW deejay Martin Block even held a contest asking listeners to count the Angelinas (the correct tally being thirty-one).

"Angelina" is also the first of Prima's juxtapositions of Neapolitan jolliness and Harlem jive. Where Armstrong gets serious the minute his horn touches his lips, Prima has the band extend the madcap mode even as he solos; in a takeoff on the black dancer John Bubbles's catchphrase, "Shoot the liquor to me, John Boy," Prima's band chants, "Shoot the vino to me, Angelino" behind the boss's trumpet solo. Even when Prima sings of women, they have to "put out" in a very specific way; for example, "Pizza and Beer" finds him craving a *signora* who supplies him with those delicacies. "Angelina" concludes in a triumph over both social and class distinctions—the hero announces, "I'll be dining at the Astor with the waitress from the pizzeria."

After the war, the energy of the big band era splintered into many different factions, and Prima gave his listeners a sampling of all of them: dance music, his own jazz and comedy singing, romantic numbers from singer Lily Ann Carol, Dixieland from a small band within the orchestra for followers of the traditional jazz revival, and even a smattering of modernistic charts with vaguely beboppish harmony. Prima had spent most of the thirties with the American Recording Corp. (which later became Columbia Records) and briefly at Decca, and the war years with the independent labels run by Eli Oberstein (Varsity, Hit, Majestic). In the latter part of the band era he seems to have been determined to hit every label under the sun: RCA, Mercury, Columbia, Decca, and his first attempt at a self-owned operation, Robin Hood Records.

Prima's output from label to label was remarkably consistent; at RCA, the home of Spike Jones and Mickey Katz, in 1947–49, he seems to have been encouraged—even more than usual—to turn out novelty material, resulting in the hits "Civilization" and "The Thousand Island Song." His most outrageous record of this period may well have been 1947's "The Bee Song." Opening with a piano allusion to "Flight of the Bumble Bee," this piece of "bee-bop" (my pun, not theirs) shows what happens when Bobby, a busy he-bee, meets Bebe, a dizzy she-bee (their pun, not mine). She gives him the heebee jeebees (what else?), and eventually they settle down and raise a family of wee-bees. Various members of the band portray the male and female bee voices in basso and falsetto, and it ends with a dramatic sting (ouch!). Yet for all the shenanigans, there's solid musical value throughout, not the least of which derives from a swell sax solo in the Italian (as in Charlie Ventura) tenor tradition. Keely Smith began singing with Prima's big band during this period, although her days as his deadpan musical foil and personal and professional partner were still a long way off.

In 1951–52, Prima collaborated with Mitch Miller, the grand guru of postwar pop and the nabob of novelty himself, when the trumpeter briefly signed with Columbia. Two of his zaniest singles of the era, "Basta" and "The Bigger the Figger" (based on *The Barber of Seville*) were written, paradoxically, by one of the major intellectuals of the popular music business, Alec Wilder. Miller, the future father of the sing-along record, collaborated with Prima on the most gloriously whacked-out, surreal sing-along disc ever, in which Prima urges a WASPy, stiff-as-starch choir to sing "Oh Marie" with him in the original Italian.

According to the entertainer's number-one fan, the late Bob Pepitone, Prima and Miller parted company over the song "Come on-a My House." When the number, an adaptation of an Armenian folk song, came to Columbia, Prima begged Miller to let him record it—it was a natural for his Italianate *tarantella* style—and Rosemary Clooney, conversely, begged Miller *not* to make her sing it. When Miller forced the song on Clooney, Prima cried *"Ah fan-gool!"* and left the company. Prima was right to be so fixated on the song, which soon made a superstar out of Clooney. (Later, he "covered" it for his own Robin Hood label, using his own Italian accent but mimicking the harpsichord backing of the Clooney-Columbia single.)

By this point, he was already investigating rhythm and blues—he recorded the R&B standard "One Mint Julep" very early on. Along with Louis Jordan and Philadelphia bandleader Jan Savitt, Prima had been an early advocate of the shuffle beat that later became a cornerstone of the rock 'n' roll era—the beat that propelled Bobby Darin's "Mack the Knife," for example, can be heard on dozens of earlier discs by Prima, Jordan, and Savitt. For a brief interval around 1953–55, he ran his own label, Robin Hood Records, and an even more short-lived subsidiary called Happiness Records (which released Keely Smith's first solo sides). Most of the Robin Hood releases were big-band R&B, such as "Oh Babe," "Dig That Crazy Chick," and (ten years before the Beatles) "Yeah, Yeah, Yeah." Prima was immersed in R&B, and paying close attention to Louis Jordan as well as the Treniers. Many stars present and future were also learning a lot from Prima; "Elvis told me he got some of his moves from Louis, which doesn't surprise me," said Keely Smith, adding in her characteristically ribald fashion, "Louis had some great moves—I mean, it was my pleasure!"

By the end of 1954, the Louis Prima Orchestra had gone the way of most of its big band brethren, and it was up to him to reinvent himself yet again. We can look at the transformation and rebirth of Prima from several perspectives, and the one that was probably most important to the trumpeter-singer at the time was essentially a matter of geography or, rather, as real estate agents say: location, location, location.

Twenty years earlier, he had helped transform

New York's Fifty-second Street from a back alley into the most happening highway in all of jazz. Now in the mid-fifties, it was Prima, more than any other entertainer, who turned Las Vegas into the epicenter of show business. "When Louis caught on in Las Vegas, all the celebrities started coming in to hear him," friend and fan Tony Bennett has recalled. "When you came to Louis's shows, you might turn around and see that you were sitting next to Fred Astaire! Pretty soon, audiences started coming to his shows not only to hear Louis, who was the greatest, but just to be part of the scene."

Prima's Las Vegas music was about making connections. This jumping little combo bridged many gaps, between jazz and rhythm and blues as well as between generations. Even as the baby boomers were being encouraged to discover a music that they were told was as different as possible from that of their World War II–era parents, Prima began bridging the Generation Gap even as it was being formed.

The Prima-Butera band played adult pop standards old and new on a level playing field with blues and R&B, without making any stylistic distinction—or judgment—about either. The self-same parents who complained that their kids were rotting their minds by listening to rock 'n' roll were actually getting off on the very same thing—only better. The major difference was that Prima was playing a fundamentally superior—a hipper and deeper—brand of rock 'n' roll. It was musically richer, harder-driving, and had a lot more energy, despite the fact that the leader was pushing fifty. It was bluesier and at the same time more sophisticated. Even Prima's sexually charged double entendre semidirty novelties like "Scuba Diver" and "The Pump Song" were comparatively classy pieces of work.

The two key players in the new Prima lineup, after the Godfather of Goofiness himself, were Keely Smith and Sam Butera. Smith, who was part-Irish and part-Cherokee, joined the band in 1947 and became the fourth Mrs. Prima six years later. At first she seemed to be an odd replacement for Lily Ann Carol: Carol was a perfect singer for the band in the war years, and her sentimental warmth made her a particular favorite of the GIs. Keely was always considerably cooler. In the big band period, Smith, then still in her teens, looked to Doris Day and cool canary June Christy for inspiration. However, Prima, who had used Carol as a "straight man" to his wacky antics for some years, gradually figured out how he could use Smith's icy attitude to mold her into his best foil ever. While he would be all but bouncing off the walls, his wife would stand motionless and expressionless with what the arranger Nelson Riddle called "this dumb, deadpan look." It was a perfect juxtaposition of a minimalist and a maximalist.

Butera, a young New Orleans *paesano* who played tenor, was recommended to Louis by his brother Leon—Butera had been playing in Leon's club for years. Butera was one of a school of Italian-American tenor colossi who came out of Coleman Hawkins and Ben Webster. More than most, he leaned toward the honking, R&B style pioneered by Illinois Jacquet; he would have fit right in with Lionel Hampton's band. Butera was already on his way to becoming a name in his own right, having worked extensively with New Orleans celebrity Paul Gayten and done four sessions for RCA and Groove Records, its subsidiary.

As Keely Smith later admitted, "Louis and I were flat on our rears until he sent for Sam." With Butera and a band of similar-minded Crescent City players aboard—an entire band equally conversant in blues, swing, bop, and traditional New Orleans jazz—the elements were in place. Within a matter of months, the Prima-Smith-Butera combination was the hottest in Las Vegas, and soon all of showbiz. According to legend, Prima said, "You guys are all witnesses to what's happening here." Christening the group the Witnesses was a ballsy reference to the well-publicized involvement of Italian-Americans in both organized religion and organized crime.

These are Prima's most celebrated recordings, done between 1956 and 1961 for Capitol Records (plus a few postscripts for Dot Records). Perhaps the single most electrifying side in the bunch (issued in toto by the German label Bear Family, in an eight-CD box licensed from Capitol) is "That Old Black Magic." This amazing treatment of the Harold Arlen–Johnny Mercer tune is a study in creative contrasts: The drummer starts with a shuffle pattern, the pianist tinkles a trebly riff over and over, Butera enters with a honk and plays yet a third rhythmic figure on tenor. Then Prima launches the lyrics with his rough-edged, husky vibrato, followed by Smith, whose contralto is as smooth and cool as a cuke.

The most celebrated performance by this combo is their first for Capitol, Prima's medley of "Just a Gigolo" and "I Ain't Got Nobody," later imitated by rock star David Lee Roth, who copped Prima's licks note for note but couldn't begin to approximate the Sicilian's throaty charisma. Smith doesn't sing solo here but forms part of Prima's vocal group background along with Butera, who gets in a wild chorus in tandem with trombonist Red Blount. The four-and-a-half-minute Primasterpiece climaxes with Prima hyperventilating and ecstatically screaming phrases in Italian, while the ensemble honks and cheers him on. Black Magic indeed.

For about seven years, the Prima-Smith-Butera-Witnesses combo, whose repertory included not only the two leads' solos and duets, but features for Butera (like "Night Train" and "Next Time") and other members of the Witnesses (particularly trombonists Lou Sino and Red Blount), ruled in Las Vegas and on *The Ed Sullivan Show*. The new group, however, didn't make any records until April 1956. As Smith told me, "The producers from Capitol Records came out from Hollywood and they wanted to record us. Louis said, 'Fine, but you also have to give Keely her own contract to make her own albums, too.' But they didn't want me and refused.

So Louis just waited." Finally the company resigned themselves to the fact that to get Louis and Keely they were going to have to make solo records with Ms. Smith as well.

Though Smith's first few singles (among them "Rock-a-Doodle-Doo") were in the doo-wop mold, Capitol quickly realized that she was (and still is) a superior singer of the Great American Songbook. She made three Capitol albums that have been much reissued: *Politely* with Billy May, and *Swingin' Pretty* and *I Wish You Love* with Nelson Riddle. The latter yielded a hit single in its title track, a translation of a French song with words by Charles Trenet, which has been Ms. Smith's signature ever since.

By the end of their association with Capitol in 1961, Smith had matured into a first-rate pop singer, worthy of comparison with Margaret Whiting and Jo Stafford, as well as that other distaff half of a famous ethnic singing team, Eydie Gormé. Prima then switched to a smaller label called Dot Records, part of the deal being that he was allowed to own his own masters. Said Keely, "It was a mistake to leave Capitol for Dot. [Label head] Randy Wood was a nice man, but nothing at Dot was as nice as Capitol, the arrangers, the studios, the distribution, none of them were on the same level." There are roughly a dozen Dot albums, about half by Louis (most with Keely) and half by Keely solo. On most of the Capitol LPs, Smith is merely the most prominent member of Prima's troupe; on the Dot albums she receives equal billing.

Smith is right in terms of Dot's production values and the overall quality of the Dot arrangers, especially with regard to the very Muzaky Billy Vaughn, who arranged several solo ballad albums for her. But even though Vaughn was hardly Nelson Riddle, Smith's singing has gotten even better than in the Capitol years, and on the up-tempo albums, at least, the label provides her with arrangers that help rather than hinder her—as on *Swing, You Lovers*. The best of the Dots is *Cherokeely Swings*, which, disappointingly, contains no Native American content but has Smith vigorously swinging through a dozen standards, both likely and unpredictable. She is one of the few female singers who can appreciate the antic wit of a Prima or a Billy May and use it to enhance her own performance. Even the album that should be her worst, *Twist with Keely Smith*, is surprisingly good—she sings R&B hits with an exaggerated shuffle beat better than any female singer of her approximate generation. I can't even imagine Peggy Lee or Dinah Washington, to name two major singers well versed in the blues, doing as well.

Fortunately, most of Prima's own Dot records don't use any staff arranger but rather the dependable backing of Sam Butera and the Witnesses. There's a particularly fine live album called *On Stage*, which is fully the equal of any of the Capitol releases. *Return of the Wildest* has a drawing of a theater on its cover, leaving us to assume it's another live recording, even though it's a studio set mostly with fairly dull orchestral backing. There's a fine, heavily spirited reading of "Sorrento" done with the Witnesses in two tempos and two languages—slow but swinging in Italian and faster and more swinging in English: It's one of my favorite Prima solos. Yet even on the big band tracks, both here and on *Louis Prima: Greatest Hits* (which features new versions of Prima perennials going back to the 1935 "Lady in Red"), there's a considerable amount of humor to be derived from the contrast between his outrageous antics in the foreground and the bland backdrop.

Around 1961 or 1962, the Prima-Smith combination broke up, and the two were divorced both personally and professionally. Prima replaced Smith with Gia Maione, whom he duly married in 1965. It was never Prima's idea to turn his fifth wife into a second-rate version of his fourth, and this twosome found its own dynamic: It wasn't wildman-and-deadpan, but more like sweet young thing–and–crazy horny old guy. When Prima revived some of his major hits of a decade earlier, like "That Old Black Magic," Maione sang the female part her own way, without mimicking Smith's stone-face bit. Maione also made a crowd-pleasing specialty out of Jon Hendricks's tongue-twister, "I Want You to Be My Baby."

Smith briefly remained at Dot while the Prima-Maione-Butera combination made a brief return to Capitol, where they made an outstanding live album recorded in Lake Tahoe. After that last Capitol project, Prima essentially produced and manufactured his own albums on his own label, Prima 1 Records, with the exception of a few stray projects for Disneyland, United Artists, and Buddha (for whom he recorded a single named after his youngest daughter, "Bald Headed Lena"). Prima enjoyed controlling his own means of production and putting the profits directly into his projects. The move to self-production may well have hurt his reputation, as it led some observers (even the usually right-minded Billy Vera, for instance) to surmise that his career went downhill after Keely left the act. It's a logical conclusion, but still a mistake. Prima continued to thrive (as did Smith on her own), despite the competition from kiddie pop, mostly by concentrating on his core audiences in Las Vegas and New Orleans.

It would also be a mistake to assume that Prima lost any of his ability or appeal in his last decade. His ongoing vitality is documented in a series of a dozen or so albums for his Prima 1 label, most of which were reissued around 2003 in a series supervised by Gia Maione Prima. The Prima-Maione-Butera combination went on appearing on *Sullivan* and other top-flight variety shows, and he entered into a very productive relationship with the Walt Disney organization. He did an album of the *Mary Poppins* score and made his best-remembered movie appearance as the voice of the ambitious orangutan King Louis in the 1967 feature cartoon *The Jungle Book*.

Of the later recordings, nothing tops *Louis Prima*

on Broadway, a 1967 United Artists album that consists of gonzo, mondo-bizarro treatments of contemporary show tunes. (Alas, as of 2010 it's not yet on CD.) Over an orchestral background that's part-Dixieland, part-Muzak, part-psychedelic, and just annoying enough to contribute to the perverse atmosphere, Prima renders timely hits such as "Sunrise, Sunset" (another Jewish number), "Illya Darling" (the title song from the Broadway version of the film *Never on Sunday*—Louis goes Greek!), and strangest of all, "Poor Old Marat" from *Marat/Sade*. The disc's pinnacle is "The Impossible Dream," the most portentous and overblown of all sixties Broadway anthems, which the trumpeter-singer deftly deflates with his manic irreverence.

Prima kept going until 1974 when he was diagnosed with spinal meningitis, and an operation that was supposed to cure him instead left him in a coma for the remaining four years of his life. He died on August 24, 1978. His appeal transcends generations—putting him in a class, longevity-wise, with Armstrong and Crosby. And time has been powerless to erode his appeal. Perhaps it's part of his charm (and anticharm) that his magic seems beyond the grasp of both history and historians. Perhaps he was neither a satirist nor a satyr, after all—satire generally involves taking something serious, like opera or literature, and making it into something silly. Prima did just the opposite: He took grade-Z novelty songs and rendered them with such sensibility. No one else could so rapturously sing about sex and *scungilli* and, in the process, subvert lowbrow culture into high art.

Arthur Prysock (1923?–1997)

We tend to group singers by color, by which I mean the specific tonal "color" of a singer's voice. Thus, those deep-voiced African Americans who occupy the low end of the sonic scale could be classified as a group that some years ago I began referring to as the "Black Baritones." That term actually takes in a lot of territory: The spiritual father of the movement is Paul Robeson (1898–1976), who was an extremely popular singer for a long time, although not exactly what one would call a pop singer. (In fact, he was also a basso rather than strictly a baritone.) There were two gentlemen born in the mid-teens who were the first to take pop music and jazz into the deep, deep end of the pool: Billy Eckstine and Al Hibbler. (Herb Jeffries and Johnny Hartman also emerged around the same time, and while they were certainly fine baritones, they were not members of the ultradeep bass-baritone school.)

Eckstine and Hibbler were the two major bass-baritones who followed the same essential career path as other singers of their generation, black and white, male and female, from out of the big swing bands and into solo careers. They were followed by several generations of top baritones, most importantly Arthur Prysock, Lou Rawls (1933–2006), and Barry White (1944–2003), who also represent the evolution of black pop music from Fifty-second Street to Motown.

Oddly, these men have no Caucasian equivalent. There was Vaughn Monroe, whose barrel-chested bleating was less remarkable than the overall quality of the bands he led. There was also Don Cornell, who left behind one or two memorable hits ("It Isn't Fair," "Hold My Hand") but who would be regarded by few as a pop singer of significance. Both Monroe and Cornell had impressively low voices, but that was about it—for whatever reason, no white male made a great impact on the singing of standards or jazz in the bass-baritone register.

It's widely acknowledged that Bing Crosby was the first singer to popularize the baritone register, but while this is true, it can't be said that there was no turning back, especially in the black community, where high-pitched tenors and falsettos were always prominent. (Think Little Jimmy Scott.) Big bands like those of Claude Hopkins and Andy Kirk landed their biggest-selling hits with ultrahigh singers like Orlando Robison and Pha Terrell. When the Ink Spots appeared at the end of the thirties, they established what would be the building blocks of black pop singing in the duality between the irritatingly stratospheric tenor of Bill Henry and the no less exaggerated basso of Hoppy Jones. For the next few decades, virtually no black male singers would reside on the main floor: They would be either up on the roof or down in the bass-ment.

Working separately, Prysock and Scott carried that contrast of high and low forward into the postwar period. Likewise, Eckstine and Nat Cole, the first two black male singers to be widely accepted by white audiences, represented the same sort of dichotomy. The contrast between Eckstine and Cole, obviously, was not as extreme as that between Prysock and Scott, because both were essentially baritones; Eckstine a bass-baritone and Cole a tenor-baritone. Yet one sang deep and soulfully, the other high and true. Likewise Herb Jeffries and Al Hibbler, even though they both sang with Ellington, were on extreme ends of the baritone range. At the start of the sixties, when R&B was evolving into soul music, the high-low contrast was embodied by Sam Cooke and Lou Rawls.

Arthur Prysock's voice may be ultradeep, but he encompasses many textures within it: Sometimes that voice is as smooth as satin, at other times it's as rough as shoe leather. It seems that Prysock's vocal basement is a big, roomy place, and there's space for all sorts of tactile materials down there. As with Eckstine and Hibbler—and most of all, Sinatra—his singing is emotionally multidimensional. Prysock will try a little tenderness even in the hardest, least-sensitive blues lyric, and likewise will invest a touch of poignant cynicism in the most romantic love song.

With Prysock, size matters. His voice is so big that bigness kind of becomes an end in itself. In the same way that dancers who are statuesque or large-framed tend to move about less than those who are itty-bitty, Prysock typically sings at glacial speeds. The second tune on his best-known album, *Arthur Prysock—Count Basie*, is "Ain't No Use," a song about running out of options, yet Prysock was never one to confuse an issue by offering too many choices. The Basie album makes it especially clear that when Prysock is placed in a jazz context, he dances so slowly that sometimes he hardly seems to be moving at all. The familiar Basie reed and brass sections swirl right around him, but Prysock stays where he is, the prototypical eye of calm in the center of the Basie hurricane. In a sense, he's following the Basie example of minimalism: He knows how to put a melody over by using the least amount of motion and effort. "I Worry 'Bout You," my favorite song on the album, conveys the essence of Prysockism: He doesn't walk the floor or tear his hair out when the one he loves gives him cause for concern, he's just a-sittin' and a-worryin'.

At some point, Prysock made himself younger— it wouldn't do for lover boy to be pushing seventy. At the time of his death it was widely reported, even in *The New York Times*, that he was born in 1929. That struck longtime fans (myself included) as somewhat odd: tenor saxophonist Red Prysock was usually described as Arthur's younger brother, yet Red's year of birth was generally given as 1926. However, the producer and blues scholar Bob Porter, who worked with Prysock on his final three albums in the mid-eighties, has fixed the date of the singer's birth as 1923, a full six years earlier than Prysock himself was to claim. (Other experts disagree: In different liner notes, Steve Cushing says 1925 and Lee Hildebrand says 1924.) Arthur was born in South Carolina, but the family had moved to a farm in North Carolina by the time his brother, Wilbert (later nicknamed Red), was born several years later. Both brothers would grow up there. Arthur left home at age sixteen, and wandered as far as Hartford, Connecticut, where he worked as a cook (or, in some accounts, in a defense plant) and sang with a local band.

In 1944, Buddy Johnson and His Orchestra came through Hartford. Woodrow "Buddy" Johnson was a pianist and composer whose band had been steadily growing in both size and popularity since his first sessions, done for Decca, in 1939. Unlike Louis Jordan and Lionel Hampton, whose core demographic also consisted of what was then called the "race" audience, Johnson never seems to have put much energy into the idea of crossing over (and, over the long haul, neither would Prysock). The Johnson orchestra was a family affair in that Johnson's younger sister, Ella Johnson, was the band's primary vocalist.

By 1944, Johnson seems to have decided he needed a male singer, and was apparently in search of a deep-voiced crooner in the mold of Billy Eckstine, already widely popular with Earl Hines's band. There are at least three different stories as to how Prysock and Johnson began working together, but

the upshot is that Prysock sang with Johnson's band for eight years.

The Buddy Johnson Orchestra was one of the real success stories in the music soon to be known as rhythm and blues. In the mid- to late forties, Johnson had hit after hit on the "race" and then R&B charts, including "They All Say I'm the Biggest Fool," Prysock's first recorded vocal. He sounds abnormally deep for a young man—it's hard to believe he's only twenty-one here (he's certainly not fifteen!)— but then he sounds so deep on all his earliest recordings that almost every time I hear them I assume that the turntable is running too slow; only Prysock could make 78 rpm sound like 33⅓. Like Lionel Hampton, who didn't give his singers enough space on wax, Johnson was at first loath to take recording opportunities from his sister, and even after "The Biggest Fool," Prysock didn't get another record with the band until 1947. In the meantime, however, he had already done his own featured session in 1946 (for the very obscure Haven label), which included the Eckstine-Hines hit "Jelly, Jelly."

Together, Johnson and Prysock were the progenitors of what properly should be called the "soul ballad." Among Johnson's best-remembered compositions (he usually wrote both words and music) were "They All Say I'm the Biggest Fool," "I'm Just Your Fool," and two classic songs done by a range of both jazz and pop singers, "Save Your Love for Me" and "Since I Fell for You." Within a short time, the soul ballad was well on its way—soon Percy Mayfield's "Please Send Me Someone to Love" and Jimmy Scott's hit "Everybody's Somebody's Fool" would both be in this small but growing canon. Johnson's greatest accomplishment as a composer is probably "I Wonder Where Our Love Has Gone," which Prysock introduced with the bandleader in 1947. Prysock recorded it again in 1963 (on *A Portrait of Arthur Prysock*). By the third time he recorded it, in 1986, "I Wonder Where Our Love Has Gone" had become as close as he would have to a theme song, and that final version, on his penultimate album, *This Guy's in Love with You* (1986), is by far the most moving.

These songs aren't exactly the Gershwins—"I Wonder Where Our Love Has Gone" could use a few more actual rhymes—but it's the directness of the lyrics that makes them sound so soulful. The soul ballads employ similar lyrical ideas, including, as we've seen, a frequent use of the words "fool" and "cry." They also make use of similar chord changes—it's hard to tell "Save Your Love for Me" from "Please Send Me Someone to Love" by the changes alone. Within a few years, Nat King Cole would transport a number of older standards by white composers, most famously "For All We Know" and "When I Fall in Love," into the realm of the soul ballad. Where a "white" saloon song, like "Angel Eyes," could have something of a sense of irony, the soul ballads are generally more directly melodramatic. These are all simply defined as songs associated with torch singers of a certain type. Prysock also deserves credit for introducing the Glenn Miller hit "At Last" into this realm, singing it almost a decade before Etta James made it a soul standard.

Virtually every song Prysock recorded with Johnson was a soul ballad—they cut about twenty tracks altogether, all on Decca, including "As I Love You," "Lovely in Her Evening Gown," "I Cry," and "We'd Only Start It All Over Again." Very few, if any, of these are in the standard dance band vocal refrain format; rather, they feature Prysock from beginning to end, like regulation vocal records. Decca's Milt Gabler recognized Prysock's hit-making potential and featured him as a solo act on an additional twenty-one titles between 1951 and 1953, backed up by the pioneering jazz organist Bill Doggett and the ace arranger Sy Oliver—both of whom were working frequently at the time with Ella Fitzgerald. Prysock's biggest hit in this period was "I Didn't Sleep a Wink Last Night," a characteristic soul ballad with blues changes (and no connection to the earlier Sinatra hit) with a little more tempo than usual. The contrast with Doggett's organ makes Prysock's voice seem slightly higher than usual, and the backup vocal group sounds exceedingly Caucasian. "Baby, Don't You Cry" reapplies the soul ballad formula with greater production values, notably a string section.

Gabler discovered what Prysock and his future producers would later learn, that this singer was fundamentally an album artist, and that he would never mean much in the world of singles. Prysock knew how to capture romance on records, and he wasn't offering a three-minute quickie but an entire forty-five-minute session of slow lovemaking. Yet even as late as 2010, few of his complete albums have been reissued. (Fortunately, there are three recommended compilations from the label formerly known as Polygram: *Compact Jazz, Jazz 'Round Midnight,* and the especially recommended anthology *Morning, Noon & Night: The Collection.*)

Gabler tried steering Prysock toward a hit by having him record cover versions of songs that were already hits for other singers, and in many cases Prysock's treatment is superior to the original—his "(It's No) Sin" is, for me, way more convincing than Eddy Howard's. His "Wheel of Fortune" is as different from Kay Starr's as his "Blue Velvet" is from Tony Bennett's Lanza-like tenor of the time. "A Man Ain't Supposed to Cry" fits the soul ballad context remarkably well, especially considering it was co-written by Frankie Laine, who (as I've said before and will say again) made his greatest contribution to quality pop music as a composer. Joe Williams's more famous later treatment of "Ain't Supposed to Cry" is definitive, but Prysock's is no less so—it's hard to believe it wasn't a hit for him. Prysock also recorded a lovely "I Cover the Waterfront," which opens with atmospheric sounds evoking a dockyard

scene before the verse; it's no surprise that his voice is several octaves lower than the foghorn.

By 1954, Mercury Records was emerging as a force in the R&B market, having had Dinah Washington under contract for almost a decade, and now Buddy Johnson and both the Prysock brothers were there as well. "Morning, Noon and Night," a ballad, was Prysock's biggest seller on Mercury. The *Morning, Noon & Night* collection contains only three Mercury tracks—the title, and two oddities. "Woke Up This Morning," taking its title from one of the most familiar phrases in all the blues (and its subgenres), is a B. B. King composition, and one of the few examples of Prysock singing in the classic 12-bar format. He carries it off rather well, abetted by a tenor solo from his brother ("Go, go, Red!" Prysock exhorts). "Show Me How to Do the Mambo" is even more unusual; here's Prysock doing an ersatz-Cuban novelty in the same general coordinates as Perry Como's "Papa Loves Mambo"; Prysock's approach to the mambo is to tell us all how he can't do it.

The Mercury association didn't last long—perhaps the label envisioned him as a male counterpart to Washington or as their answer to Eckstine, but Prysock was gone by the time Eckstine himself arrived at Mercury in the mid-fifties. Then, in 1958, the singer hooked up with the producer-entrepreneur Hy Weiss, who had founded the independent label Old Town Records four years earlier. Old Town had begun life with singles for the R&B market, and when the label landed Prysock, he became its passport into the long-playing album business in a big way. Prysock would cut dozens of albums for Old Town over the next fifteen years or so, into the early seventies.

He was the leading purveyor of old-school soul, selling albums to the parents of the kids who were buying Motown 45s. The Old Town LPs represent Prysock's biggest and best body of work, the recordings for which he will most be remembered. It's not surprising, though, that none of these LPs has been reissued in its entirety on CD: For all the records it sold, Old Town never seems to have gotten the concept of concept albums—all the Prysocks consist of just one love song after another, mostly varying tempo-wise between slow and slower. But Prysock is a superior artist who can sustain interest without a lot of variety—one never feels the absence of swingers or comedy songs.

Most of the Old Town albums are the work of three different arrangers, and the songs derive from widely varying sources as well. There are no songbook albums, or even something as obvious as "Prysock Sings Movie Hits" or "Prysock Sings Broadway's Best" or "Prysock Sings Hits of Today"—there's almost nothing to distinguish one album from any other. Even for Prysock fans, it's hard to remember what song comes from what album. As a result, the catalogue is well served by the three compilations listed above. If anyone ever does release a boxed set called "The Complete Arthur Prysock Old Town Recordings"—and I hope someone does—it would make just as much sense to group the songs alphabetically as in original album sequence.

Prysock suffered from some of the liabilities of being on a smaller label—most of the Old Town albums have very amateurish graphics, cover shots that show him, with his square jaw and rugged mustache, looking like a sepia Robert Goulet. He's generally displaying a big smile that looks somewhat forced. Occasionally the grade-B atmosphere pervades the music itself—there's a fair share of substandard songs in the mix, many of which are forgettable foreign imports, songs that Old Town must have picked up cheap overseas. Occasionally, the arrangements are pedestrian—you'll almost never hear a treatment of a song that strikes you as particularly interesting or unusual. Prysock doesn't take you by surprise.

Yet there are exceptions, and even when there aren't, there are still many valuable performances scattered across the Prysock Old Town catalogue. He addresses a number of songs from the Buddy Johnson days, including Johnson's best ballad, "I Wonder Where Our Love Has Gone" and "I've Got the Blues So Bad." There are some outstanding new works in the soul ballad style, like "It's Too Late Baby, Too Late" and "I Worry 'Bout You." He also sings the hits of other proto-soulmen, like Hibbler's "Unchained Melody" and gives an excellent reading to "Everybody's Somebody's Fool" that examines it from the opposite end of the sonic spectrum from Jimmy Scott.

Occasionally the label caught important orchestrators on their way up or down. Yet some of the ideas on Prysock's records are almost too corny for words, as in a series of songs that he introduces by reciting the verse, rather than singing it: "When I Fall in Love," "I Left My Heart in San Francisco," and "Ghost of a Chance." Some of these recitative performances are so extreme that they're almost beyond any concept of camp. "The Working Man's Prayer" is a completely spoken recitation that delivers exactly what the title promises, the words of a humble man speaking directly to God, ending with the following lines:

> Make my days a little shorter,
> And my nights a little longer.
> Make my hammer a little lighter,
> And my arms a little stronger.

At the end of 1965, the singer recorded his finest album, *Arthur Prysock—Count Basie*. Everything came into place here: eleven first-rate songs (expanded to fourteen for the CD) and the accompaniment of the greatest band in the universe, with excellent arrangements by longtime Basie stalwarts Frank Foster and Billy Byers. Dick Hyman also made a substantial contribution to the album, both as arranger and deputy pianist. Throughout, Hyman and Basie switch off between piano and organ, playing together on the different keyboards on various

tracks. Prysock never had a better program of songs, including "What Will I Tell My Heart?" which Billie Holiday established as worthy material for black singers, a function that Etta Jones fulfilled for "Don't Go to Strangers" (a song that always sounds somewhat creepy when a man sings it), also heard here. Other songs identified with comparable black masters include the Nat Cole–associated "I'm Lost," the Fats Waller favorite "I'm Gonna Sit Right Down and Write Myself a Letter" (which Sinatra had earlier recorded with Basie), and Duke Ellington's "Do Nothin' Till You Hear from Me." The last is one of many tracks that feature Basie's outstanding tenorist Eddie "Lockjaw" Davis soloing in a manner reminiscent of both Ben Webster and Red Prysock.

The set includes further soul ballads, like still another Buddy Johnson song, "Come Home," as well as his contemporary Lionel Hampton's "Gone Again," and a mess o' songs he could have learned from Sinatra: "Where Are You?" "I Could Have Told You," "I Could Write a Book." The standout for me is "I Worry 'Bout You" (as always, he drops the "A" in "about," as in "Don't Worry 'Bout Me"). Prysock hits precisely the right note of deep-chested, laid-back soulfulness and concern. The arrangement is fundamentally the same as the one he'd recorded several years earlier, but it's delivered much more convincingly both by Prysock and the Basieites. There's a sweeping countermelody, which dances around Prysock with considerable aplomb.

Arthur Prysock—Count Basie was released on Verve; Prysock's contract and some of his Old Town masters were picked up by the bigger label (at the time owned by MGM). The Verve–Old Town albums released over the next few years don't sound any different (among them *Art and Soul, To Love or Not to Love*, and *A Portrait of Arthur Prysock*), but the packaging is substantially more attractive. Then, around the turn of the seventies, Prysock recorded several albums for King Records, including *Fly My Love*, which has some outstanding tracks on it— Prysock delivers credible treatments of contempo songs like Bobby Hebb's "Sunny" and the relatively recent "Our Day Will Come." The winner on this album, however, is "I'll Get Along Somehow," a kiss-off aria from circa 1940 that was immortalized earlier by Ethel Waters and Julia Lee.

Prysock's overwhelming consistency, which is another word for lack of variety, meant that he was one of the few traditional pop-jazz singers whose recordings of 1970 are not noticeably crummier than those of 1960, but within five years that was no longer the case. After managing to keep his head above all the forgettable trends of the sixties, Prysock was now ensnared in the worst of the seventies. *Arthur Prysock '74* (Old Town) does feature some good songs, including "Good Morning, Heartache" and the similar "Good Morning Blues" (not the Jimmy Rushing–Count Basie classic, but a soul ballad Prysock had recorded earlier), "A Day in the Life of a Fool," and Perry Como's hit "And I Love

You So"; unfortunately, the backings make the album all but unlistenable. In the sixties, he had already done at least two surprisingly agreeable treatments of Beatles songs—"A Hard Day's Night" on A *Double Header* and "Yesterday" on *Fly My Love*—but his reading of George Harrison's "My Sweet Lord" here is dismal. In 1978, Prysock came out with *Here's to Good Friends* (bearing both Old Town and MCA logos), which opened with Carole Bayer Sager and Melissa Manchester's "Midnight Blue" and reaches a nadir with a dismal disco opus by Melanie (Safka) entitled "Spunky."

Yet, unbelievably, Prysock achieved something in this period that he almost never had before, even when his voice was younger and his traditional crooning was still in style: a chart hit—"When Love Is New." This came about, he said, when his daughter asked him for a song that she could dance to. Around the same time, he reattained the upper brackets in a different sort of a way. Madison Avenue, apparently under the impression that African Americans needed more alcohol in their lives, hired him as the voice of the Löwenbräu beer jingle "Here's to Good Friends," and the singer reached a bigger audience in thirty seconds than he had in thirty-five years. The one attractive feature of the *Here's to Good Friends* album is the chance to hear him sing that number—which anybody who owned a TV set in the seventies and eighties will be familiar with—all the way through. Surprisingly, it's not a bad song: I'd rather hear it than most pop songs of the era. The line "Tonight, let it be Löwenbräu" is decommercialized, so to speak, on the album into "Tonight, let's begin again."

Prysock kept on keepin' on. He continued to play one-nighters across the country, appearing in front of increasingly older black audiences. By now, he was known on that circuit as "King Arthur." In 1985, Bob Porter brought him to the attention of Fantasy Records, which resulted in three new albums (and two Grammy nominations) on the Milestone label: *A Rockin' Good Way* (1985), *This Guy's in Love with You* (1986), and *Today's Love Songs, Tomorrow's Blues* (1987–88). Even though his ferocious vibrato tends to vibrate a little excessively, the voice still retains much of its majesty. Porter went with one idea so obvious that it was hard to believe it had never been done before, namely for Prysock to record with his regular working band, which for fifteen years had been helmed by his brother, Red.

The three Milestone albums, effectively sampled on *The Best of Arthur Prysock: The Milestone Years,* are a solid catalogue of old-school soul, such as Sam Cooke's "Bring It on Home to Me," Roy Brown's "Good Rockin' Tonight," and, of more recent vintage, "Everything Must Change." Here Prysock also renders a number of other songs that had long been considered part of the black pop experience, like "Teach Me Tonight" and "It's All in the Game." An additional two tunes honor Prysock's spiritual descendant, the deep-voiced talk-singer Brook Benton: "A Rainy Night in Georgia" and "Baby (You've Got What It Takes)," the latter one of several duets with Betty Joplin, who occasionally helps spell Prysock from his vocal chores throughout the second album.

The 1986 "I Wonder Where Our Love Has Gone," which Porter reports was done in a single take, is the most poignant version of this or practically any other song Prysock sang in his entire long career—just like Jimmy Scott's late-in-life remake of "Everybody's Somebody's Fool." Like Oscar Peterson playing with only half of his technical ability after his stroke, senior citizen Prysock sounds more tender and perhaps even more sincere at this stage in his life than ever before. King Arthur, aka Old Leather-Lungs, the mountain-voiced iron man, for once sounds absolutely vulnerable, as if he really was wondering where his love and his life had gone.

Prysock's road ended in Hamilton, Bermuda. He had been suffering from Alzheimer's for some time when he died at King Edward Hospital on June 21, 1997. When *The New York Times* ran his obituary, the paper of record chose not to begin by telling us that Prysock had recorded nearly sixty albums, that he had introduced many classic songs and made many more into standards, helped invent a whole genre of pop music, and was virtually worshipped in the black community for several generations. Instead the lead item in the *Times* obit was that the singer had "coaxed listeners to 'let it be Löwenbräu' in a popular beer commercial." Prysock deserved to be remembered as something more than a booze pitchman. Perhaps he had done too good a job on the jingle, because he sang of Löwenbräu as convincingly as he had done about everything else. Whether croonin', cryin', or just plain carryin' on, Arthur Prysock always sang it like he meant it.

R

Martha Raye (1916–1994)

It's a showbiz cliché that all clowns want to play *Hamlet.* According to legend, when John Barrymore made this suggestion to Jimmy Durante—that he should consider playing this greatest of the stage's tragic roles—the Great One's answer was: "Nah, I don't like ta woik in dem small towns!"

Clowns apparently also want to be regarded as serious musicians: Charlie Chaplin wrote a few pop songs in the twenties, but, as it happened, it wasn't until thirty years later that an old film theme of his was adapted into "Smile," which became his only enduring musical work. To this day, Jerry Lewis likes to brag that his album *Jerry Lewis Just Sings* sold eighty gazillion copies. Sure. (The album's title is a clue that there's a gag afoot: "Jerry Lewis just sings," as opposed to "Jerry Lewis jumps into Dean Martin's arms with a goofy look on his face and shrieks, 'OH LADY!!' ") Then, too, Bob Hope, Danny Thomas, Danny Kaye, and many other comic leading men have also worked as vocalists both straight and silly.

The output of Martha Raye, however, when considered in the context of magnificent clowns who were also magnificent musicians, takes us way up into the stratosphere, approximating the orbit of Jimmy Durante and Louis Armstrong. Durante was a great comic who, later in life, revealed himself as a great singer; Armstrong was a genius of a musician who throughout his career never hid his talents as a comic and entertainer under any kind of a bushel. Raye had a lot in common with both of them and perhaps even more with Fats Waller, who throughout his short career was never less than a master musician and a master clown at the same time.

It won't do to describe Martha Raye as being both a great comedienne and a wonderful singer, as if those were two entirely unrelated fields of endeavor, like a champion golfer who can also dance the rhumba, or a prizewinning chemist who can also do a mean impression of Groucho Marx. What makes Raye so remarkable is the way she's consistently both at the same time. Yet it's hard to imagine her as a major comic who also happened to be, say, an opera singer; Raye was essentially a jazz singer. She fits any imaginable definition of that carefully applied term, and she used the medium of jazz to connect the two hemispheres of her talent.

Bix Beiderbecke was once quoted as saying, "Jazz is musical humor," and eighty years later, it's not hard to see what he meant. There is a lot of humor in other musical genres, too, such as country music and classical, but in these cases, the humor usually comes from the words—it's the libretto, not the notes, that makes us laugh at *Die Fledermaus, HMS Pinafore,* or *The Barber of Seville.* But apart from "Mr. Paganini," Raye rarely sings an overtly funny song—not "The Major General's Song" or "Mama Will Bark." With Raye, humor, like jazz, is mainly a matter of interpretation. She was able to find humor in "Ol' Man River" and "Body and Soul." She finds humor, drama, and most of all exhilarating rhythm in every number she sings—her "Gone With the Wind" packs as much punch as Rhett and Scarlett could muster with a cast of thousands and three hours of Technicolor. Her impeccable sense of rhythm empowered her to make a dramatic number swing and to make a silly song supremely musical.

Raye was a significant presence in the pop culture of the thirties and forties—particularly on the radio and in films. Yet because she was known more as a comic than a singer, she enjoyed relatively few opportunities to make records. Her only notable body of work as a recording artist is a scant twelve titles cut in 1939. They amount to barely thirty-five minutes of music altogether, yet this is an overpoweringly excellent, if frustratingly brief, canon of

music. Heard six decades later, the power of her voice and the skill of her musical and comic imagination make it hard to believe that she wasn't regarded more seriously as a musical artist in her prime.

Certainly no subsequent girl singer ever took Martha Raye for granted. Rosemary Clooney, Anita O'Day, and even Billie Holiday have all been especially vocal in their adoration of Raye's combination of megachops and limitless imagination. Ella Fitzgerald doesn't even have to say anything; if Raye's application of goddesslike intonation on top of brilliantly conceived scat singing may not have prefigured Lady Ella's whole career, at least it certainly gave her the perfect diving board from which to spring. Every time Fitzgerald performed "Mr. Paganini" from the thirties to the nineties, she was, in essence, raising her glass in a toast to Martha Raye.

Anita O'Day was very specific. Shortly after Fitzgerald died in 1996, I was assigned to interview O'Day to get her thoughts on Ella. However, every time I asked her about Fitzgerald, O'Day would bring up Martha Raye. "I loved Ella, I thought that everything she did was great," said O'Day, "but when I heard Martha Raye, I just said to myself, 'Well there's my singer!' " If anything, O'Day gave almost too much credit to Raye—to hear her tell it, almost everything she did was inspired by Mother Martha. (Interestingly enough, Raye was only three years older.)

Judy Garland, who married Raye's ex-husband David Rose, frequently sang a rather overbaked showbiz anthem called "Born in a Trunk." Garland was, in fact, performing professionally from a very early age, but the phrase applies even more literally to Raye. Margaret Theresa Yvonne Reed was born backstage in a vaudeville theater in Butte, Montana, on August 27, 1916. Her parents, dancers on one of the smaller-time circuits, only briefly took time away from work for the occasion. In fact, according to Raye, her mother was back onstage before little Margie was even forty-eight hours old. Not surprisingly, within three years Martha had become, as she later said, "hypnotized by the spotlight" and joined her parents in the act, singing "I Wish I Could Shimmy Like My Sister Kate." "I thought I was having a wonderful life," she remembered. "I never realized we were being culturally deprived."

As Raye and her younger brother, Bud, grew up in that trunk, their talent gradually surpassed that of their parents. The family act, which back in the teens had been known as "the Girl and the Traveler," now became "Bud and Margie." As the troupe became more and more polished, they began working with increasingly better-heeled vaude companies, including those headlined by Benny Davis and Ben Blue (who would later appear in Paramount's *Artists & Models* and *College Swing* with her). But just when things were going swingingly, the act did a major nosedive for no apparent reason. "We were just as good as we'd ever been, but nobody wanted us," said Raye. "Pretty soon we were working [only] one week out of three." (Likely, it was the combined onslaught of talking pictures and the Great Depression that put a lot of vaude houses out of business.)

But out of adversity comes opportunity: When things got so bad that Raye decided to strike out on her own, stuff started to happen. She managed to land an audition with the famous Chicago bandleader Paul Ash, who was then reorganizing his orchestra for a new radio show, and she wound up singing with Ash's Pabst Blue Ribbon Casino Orchestra in Chicago for eleven months. From there, she got her first break in New York, when she landed a gig with the house orchestra at the Paramount Theatre, as led by future Paramount Pictures music executive Borris Morros.

Nineteen thirty-two would be a breakthrough year: She would be seen for the first time in a film and make her first recordings, although nobody would actually hear these for more than seventy years. All three of these early appearances had her singing "How'm I Doin? (Hey! Hey!)," a current "rhythm" song that had been introduced by composer Don Redman with his orchestra just a few months earlier. She sang Redman's lament in her film debut in the short subject *Benny Fields' Musical Court,* although unfortunately she wouldn't make it into a feature film for another four years. She also made two test recording sessions in 1932, both with important guitarists: In August she sang "How'm I Doin?" and "Dinah" with Roy Smeck (for ARC, the American Recording Corp.); in November, she cut "How'm I Doin?" and "I Heard" accompanied by the famous blues guitarist Lonnie Johnson (for RCA Victor).

The November track has not surfaced, but—better late than never—the August 1932 test pressing was at last released in 2005. Although Raye is only two days past her sixteenth birthday, she's already a spectacularly accomplished rhythm singer, and though this was right around the time that Louis Armstrong began regularly singing on records, she has already fashioned an entire singing style out of what she learned from him. She sings and scats exuberantly, with precisely the same kind of manic energy found on Armstrong's pre-1935 recordings. Accompanied only by Roy Smeck's guitar, she offers a more convincing—and sublimely musical—display of scat fireworks than almost anyone in that decade, excepting Armstrong and Leo Watson, and possibly even including Ella Fitzgerald. Here, Martha Raye reminds me of Captain Miles Gloriosus's description of himself in *A Funny Thing Happened on the Way to the Forum:* She *is* a parade—all by herself.

In the mid-thirties, Raye alternated easily between singing with big bands and working as a single in vaudeville. Still a teenager, she appeared with a troupe of equally young aspiring entertainers that included dancer Hal Le Roy and the tapping team of siblings Vilma and Buddy Ebsen, all of whom would eventually wind up in Hollywood. She also worked three years in an act put together by impresario Will Morrissey. By now she had picked the name "Martha Raye" out of the phone book, and in April 1932 appeared in Morrissey's Broadway-bound flop play, *The Crooner.* In 1934 she made another short film appearance, in a Universal two-reeler entitled *A Night in a Night Club,* and that December made a major impression at the Hollywood Theatre in a stage revue called *Calling All Stars.*

By the time she turned twenty in 1936, Raye was established as a nightclub headliner. She would be sustained for the next sixty years primarily by personal appearances in clubs and, fortunately for us, she also enjoyed a brief but busy career in motion pictures. In 1935, executives from Paramount caught her act at Hollywood's Trocadero and enthusiastically signed her up for the next Bing Crosby picture, *Rhythm on the Range.*

On the success of her cameo in that movie, Raye was signed by Paramount and appeared in roughly four movies a year for them—a total of twenty features—between 1936 and 1940. Typically, she was third- or fourth-billed; she was never the leading lady but always the star comic and/or half of the secondary love team. (It's hard to think of any female comic who was top-billed at Hollywood's height; in those years even Lucille Ball was always cast as just another glamourpuss rather than the ace comedienne she later turned out to be.) Raye typically co-starred with Paramount's top leading musical and comedy men, starting with Bing Crosby (including her first, *Rhythm on the Range,* as well as *Double or Nothing* and *Waikiki Wedding*) and Bob Hope (including his first, *The Big Broadcast of 1938, Never Say Die,* and *Give Me a Sailor*) but never played their love interest. Even *Give Me a Sailor,* in which she was top-billed with Hope, had the lower-billed Betty Grable playing the ski-snooted one's girlfriend.

The Paramount pictures are filled with amazing musical moments that more than give Raye a chance to shine, particularly *Double or Nothing,* a generally forgettable Crosby programmer that all but explodes in a three-way scat shoot-out among Der Bingle, Raye, and deep-voiced pianist-singer Frances Faye. Her best moments on film are probably her signature song, "You'll Have to Swing It," in *Rhythm on the Range,* and *Artists & Models,* which climaxes in a spectacular duet with Armstrong on "Public Melody Number One"—she's probably the best female partner he ever sang with apart from Fitzgerald. Raye appears here in a comparatively tasteful form of blackface side by side with Satch, a rather conservative skin darkener that gives her something of a café au lait appearance. Between her swarthy appearance and soulful singing, Raye earned a most unusual compliment. Legend has it that Raye's landlord saw *Artists & Models* and was so convinced that she was black that he actually tried to evict her. At the time, the number was controversial because it showed a black man and a white woman (albeit one in tanface) singing together. Today the number is viewed as politically incorrect because of Raye's makeup.

Paramount's strategy typifies old-school Hollywood at its most abusive. For five years they overworked Raye until she could hardly stand up, then they unceremoniously dumped her: One day she found a note stuck under her door informing her that her services would no longer be required. (The upside was that she was free to co-star with Al Jolson in *Hold on to Your Hats* on Broadway in 1940.) However, her entire film career pales in importance beside the twelve sides she recorded in 1939, near the end of her association with Paramount. These twelve in and of themselves are more than enough to earn Raye a place in the pantheon of great jazz and/or pop singers.

The sessions were done at a transitional period in which the old ARC label, the same firm she recorded for in 1932, was being reorganized as Columbia Records. Raye's personal life, by contrast, was for a brief time *not* in transition: For three years, beginning in 1938, she was married to the conductor and composer David Rose, who served as a musical director on these sides. Later, he would write the well-known instrumentals "The Stripper" (which Raye's voluptuous figure could have certainly inspired) and "Holiday for Strings." Within a few months of divorcing Raye, he would marry Judy Garland.

The most notable of her recordings, done at the first 1939 session, is also the most notable of her picture songs (and pretty much the only recording she would make of any of her early film songs), known informally as "Mr. Paganini" although officially titled "(If You Can't Sing It) You'll Have to Swing It." According to Gary Giddins in his biography of Crosby, Sam Coslow had originally written the song for Raye to use in her initial screen test for Paramount and she wound up introducing it in her first film, the 1936 *Rhythm on the Range*. Coslow originally titled it "Mister Toscanini," which actually makes sense, because Mr. T was the leading classical conductor of the era. When Sophie Tucker recorded it in London in 1936, she addressed the maestro as "Mr. Toscanini." For fear that the Big T and his network, NBC, would not relish the compliment, Coslow changed the title to refer to the nineteenth-century violinist Niccolò Paganini. Signore Paganini was not particularly well known as a conductor, but his name, at least, scanned just as well as "Toscanini."

Ironically, just as the lyric's subject was changed from a living conductor to a dead violinist, its association was changed from one heavyweight jazz singer to another. Raye introduced "Swing It" in 1936, but didn't have a recording contract at that point. Ella Fitzgerald, however, did, and her performance of the song became much more widely heard by successive generations. Yet with no disrespect to the great Fitzgerald, Raye's treatment of the song is nothing short of rapturous. "Paganini" had already set the pattern in her work, in that many of her specialty numbers would juxtapose two tempos, starting in slow ballad time, either romantically or setting up a story (as in "Paganini"), and then, after the first chorus, exploding into a red hot, superfast killer-diller. In "Paganini," Raye sets up two radically different tempos and moods. It begins, in Coslow's lyric, with the end of a concert "at Carnegie Hall," at which "The Maestro" assumes the performance is over, having taken "bow after bow." But then there's an unexpected request for an encore "from the gallery way up high"—an anonymous girl (played by Raye in the first person) disrupts this classical affair by demanding that "Mr. Paganini" play her "Rhapsody." Taken literally, the song makes absolutely no sense. The girl in the gallery obviously loves European concert music, yet she demands he follow his classical concert with a swing performance of some kind—and it's never explained precisely what "rhapsody" this chick is talking about. The point is that Raye begins singing completely straight, the way one would expect to hear singing at Carnegie Hall in 1939. She even affects something of a hoity-toity upper-class accent as the conductor starts to exit the podium, declaiming, "Sorry, but it's all over now." The gallery girl wants the maestro to play her rhapsody, but "if you can not play it" (note the use of re-expanded contractions—how very formal), will he consent to sing it? As a last resort, she sings, "If you can not sing it, you'll simply have to swing it."

"Paganini" is laid out in the standard 32-bar structure (verse AABA) and each A segment ends with the phrase "swing it." Every time Raye reaches that "swing it" phrase she takes it very literally, contrasting the stuffiness of the longhair maestro's deportment with an increasingly wild, even deranged nonverbal solo. When she flies into these brief scat episodes, the whole complexion changes, her tone shifts from very proper to smeary and guttural and the tempo becomes hot and anxious. The bridge ("We've heard your repertoire / and at the final bar . . .") is almost entirely given over to pure scat ecstasy, as she keeps punctuating the rhythm with wild, almost random cries of "Zoot! Zoot!" One of her trademark ploys is to start to make a classical-style nonverbal noise, a soaring, birdlike trill out of the opera tradition (like the "Bell Song" from *Lakmé*), and even as she extends a beautiful high note shall take the same note and start twisting it, making it blue and growling like a tightly muted trombone.

The 1939 "Paganini" has been issued in at least two takes: the original 78 master take and an alternate first issued on the famous Martha Raye Epic LP, circa 1955. The alternate take (or LP take) has the musicians laughing audibly as the final A section approaches, the sidemen obviously unable to resist expressing their pleasure. It's completely appropriate, especially as Raye tries joshingly to silence them with an aside: "Quiet, fellas!" After a verse and one complete, extended chorus, the song ends with Raye delivering a gorgeous, completely straight ascending line leading up to a perfect high note: "Won't you play my little Rhap-so-*dy!*" David Rose might have titled this tour-de-force "Holiday for Chops," for it shows off everything that Raye can do in terms of ballads, jazz, and humor, and also allows the pretty side of her voice to come through. Raye would reprise "Paganini" in a second film, the 1944 *Four Jills in a Jeep,* and a different performance of the song by Raye (possibly from radio) would be issued for the benefit of American fighting forces on V-Disc.

Many of the eleven remaining Columbia-owned sides follow a similar trajectory: "It Ain't Necessarily So" contrasts pretty sounds and wild scatting in a predetermined script, this time by the Gershwin brothers. The "Sportin' Life" aria is recast by Raye as a swirling symphony of conflicting moods and textures, including a Cab Calloway–like squeaky high note pop, with Raye jumping all over the time signature, most effectively when she walks into the wind by going against the rhythmic grain.

Other Raye specialties combine different moods and tempos in a slightly more traditional fashion, according to the pattern established by Ethel Waters a decade or so earlier, in which the first chorus is done relatively straight while the second is rendered much more jazzy and playful. "Gone With the Wind" and "Yesterdays" are stunning examples of this format at its best, with the second chorus sounding especially frisky even within the confines of the overall minor mood. "Once in a While" and "Ol' Man River" are considerably wilder, with Raye completely changing directions from sweet to hot in the second chorus. "Once in a While" has her liberally rewriting the melody; it's written to end on the low tonic, but Raye concludes by taking it up, up, up! "River" starts out with Raye crooning the most romantic version ever of what was already a jazz-pop chestnut. Yet though it's sweet rather than hot, she isn't doing the melody straight, she's actually offering an angularly idiosyncratic paraphrase of Kern's iconic composition. She then spontaneously combusts into swing time with a cry of "Shoot the liquor to me, John Boy!," a swing era catchphrase associated with the song and dance team of Buck and (John W.) Bubbles. She explodes from sweet to hot and climaxes in the kind of riffs that Louis Armstrong would improvise or that Fletcher Henderson would orchestrate. In all of these, Raye swings as hard as a whole big band all by herself. She still is a parade.

In other tunes, she follows the patterns estab-lished by other singers. Stephen Foster's oldie-but-moldy "Jeanie with the Light Brown Hair," which Raye would also sing in her final film for Paramount, *The Farmer's Daughter* (1940), opens with her floating as a vapor on the soft summer air. The idea of swinging folk songs in this fashion was on some level inspired by the vogue launched by Maxine Sullivan in 1937; however, where Sullivan, or Mildred Bailey, or even the slightly more abrasive Connie Boswell would swing subtly, Raye generally explodes with pure energy and rhythm and is enormously exciting. But even on "Jeanie," she kicks into swing time for one line only. "Peter, Peter, Pumpkin Eater" is a hot treatment of a nursery rhyme, which doesn't take long to climax in a wild scat that echoes both Raymond Scott's "Christmas Night in Harlem" and Benny Goodman's "Down South Camp Meeting." We've heard her take love songs and swing them; here she takes a hot number and slows it down into ballad time while encouraging a hot trumpeter (identified by her as "Joe") and a tenor saxist. Both "Jeanie" and "Peter" demonstrate how the first generation of post-Armstrong scatters was likely to rely on nursery rhymes as source material, as demonstrated by the earlier works of Fitzgerald, the King Cole Trio, and the entire career of Leo Watson.

Raye's "straight" ballads are no less effective. Lest we fear that she couldn't sustain a romantic mood for the full three minutes without going into a hard-swing second chorus, she proves otherwise on "Stairway to the Stars" and "Melancholy Mood." In those pre-Sinatra days, the ballads were still strictly in dance tempo, and in Raye's case, they differ from the swingers mainly in that the former don't have her shouting "Zoot!" every eight bars. Almost all the non-"Zoot!" numbers tend to be the newer songs, such as "Stairway," a stunningly lovely reading on a par with Ella Fitzgerald and Johnny Hartman. It opens with two models of restraint. The first comes from a muted trumpeter (probably Manny Klein), followed by Raye in the verse, where, anticipating the mature Fitzgerald, she seems to hit the notes from the top down, as if she were indeed descending a stellar staircase. "Melancholy Mood" is a superior treatment of a tune that would otherwise be forgotten had it not been recorded shortly thereafter on Frank Sinatra's first session with Harry James. ("I Walk Alone," the least interesting of these twelve tunes, in fact, suffered from this very fate.) The major exception is the 1930 "Body and Soul," which she does as a straight ballad all the way through—I guess she figured that following the three key changes was enough of a workout for her choppers. Apart from the singing instrumentalists like Armstrong and Red Allen, Raye is one of the first leading singers to perform Johnny Green's classic—and she did it a month before Coleman Hawkins.

In 1955, when *The Martha Raye Show* was going great guns, Columbia gathered her twelve sides from 1939 into an LP on their Epic subsidiary called

Here's Martha Raye; at some point a few years later, they reissued the twelve masters with artificial echo meant to simulate stereo, and that LP was reissued in the early nineties as a Columbia Special Products CD with the same horrible engineering. Raye's progeny—younger singers like Anita O'Day and Tony Bennett—grew up with her on radio and later TV, and her recordings were almost beside the point. But subsequent generations have only been able to experience her through these twelve sides. It's hard to imagine that any singer could be so enormously influential with such a minuscule body of recorded work. (In 2007, Sepia Records issued *Martha Raye Swings*, which contains virtually all of her 78 rpm era works.)

Between 1940 and 1944, Raye made six films for Warner Bros., Fox, and Universal (including an underappreciated film version of *The Boys from Syracuse*, Rodgers and Hart's toga party take on Shakespeare, in which she stole the picture with "Sing for Your Supper." At Universal, she even outfunned the two zaniest comedy teams of the day, Abbott & Costello and Olsen & Johnson. But after that, as Raye put it, "I couldn't get arrested in Hollywood." She appeared in only four movies after the war, of which the only two worth mentioning are the 1947 *Monsieur Verdoux* (in her classic, nonmusical cameo as the woman Charlie Chaplin, as a profiteering blue beard, couldn't kill) and *Billy Rose's Jumbo* (1962). The latter, coincidentally, was also based on a Rodgers and Hart stage show—Stephen Boyd gets a solo number but Raye doesn't.

There were recordings after 1939, but they have never been properly anthologized or reissued. In 1942, she cut four sides for Decca, among them a fine recent movie tune, "Oh, the Pity of It All"; a contemporary hit based on a traditional Jewish theme, "My Little Cousin"; the wartime flag-waver "Three Little Sisters"; and "Pigfoot Pete," Don Raye and Gene DePaul's rewrite of their own "Beat Me Daddy, Eight to the Bar." Around 1945–46 she sang a couple of unbilled guest vocals with Woody Herman (on V-Disc) and Charlie Barnet (as "Margie Reed," her real name, on Apollo). The Herman sides primarily consist of two takes of "He's Funny That Way"; the Barnet sides include an over-the-top treatment of "Sweet Lorraine," wherein Raye mangles the words and, for once, sounds like she's laying the jazz mannerisms on a little too thick (restraint wasn't always her strong point). The best of these is the brilliant "As Long as I Live," in which almost any listener in a blindfold test would swear he's listening to Anita O'Day; although her contralto is deeper and her phrasing slightly less clipped, the overall delivery is amazingly similar.

In the late forties, Raye recorded one session for each of two independent concerns, Discovery and Mercury. She does one song about sex, a rather outrageous 12-bar blues called "Oh, Doctor Kinsey," which is more overtly salacious than anything recorded by Dinah Washington, and one that appears to be about drugs, called "Lotus Land," which contains a lot of slow-tempo atmospheric scatting and vocalese. There's also "Wolf Boy," about which I can only say that they don't write 'em like that anymore (good thing, too). Raye appeared on a few sound track albums, including *Billy Rose's Jumbo* (she played Jimmy Durante's love interest), and in 1969, she made her only original LP. This was a collection of duets in which she played second banana to Carol Burnett—two funny ladies alternating between silliness and seriousness. And that was all.

Despite her treatment at the hands of the moguls, Raye continued to thrive in nightclubs and, later, in Las Vegas. Her talents were also tailor-made for television, which was like vaudeville all over again. Raye headlined in one of the most popular variety shows of the Eisenhower era and later had memorable roles in the sitcom *Alice* (1982–84) and the Sid and Marty Kroft kids show, *The Bugaloos* (1970–72; she played the heavy "Benita Bizarre"). Virtually every presenter of comedy-variety had her on at one point or another: Bob Hope, Red Skelton, Merv Griffin, Mike Douglas, Ed Sullivan, Steve Allen . . . the list goes on. There's an especially rewarding guest shot on Judy Garland's CBS show in 1963. You would expect the two divas to do a medley of songs by their mutual ex-husband, David Rose, but instead what they do to the hits of Glenn Miller makes for one of the best musical moments ever captured on videotape. Still later, she appeared in the familiar Broadway vehicles for veteran divas: *Hello Dolly!* and the famous 1971 revival of *No, No Nanette*. She also stole the show in the video of *Pippin*, singing Stephen Schwartz's "No Time at All."

But Raye's greatest legacy, whether comic or musical, is that bunch of 1939 set pieces where she combines Broadway belting with Harlem swing, becoming the rhythmic shouter caricatured as "Moutha Bray" in the Looney Tunes. Even though Paramount ingloriously dropped her, Raye was even more at home in the atmosphere of the frantic forties than in the swinging thirties. She may have enjoyed her finest hour during World War II when she tirelessly entertained troops at the battlefields and in the hospitals, something she continued to do for the duration of her career. Innumerable fans knew her as a patriot whose primary achievement was entertaining wounded servicemen, who addressed her as "Colonel Maggie."

One of her biggest admirers, Noonie Fortin, a female Army Reserve first sergeant, put together both a Web site (www.colonelmaggie.com) and a book (*Memories of Maggie*) devoted to this aspect of her career. It was in this capacity that Raye was honored by everyone from General William Westmoreland to B'nai B'rith to the Motion Picture Academy (the Jean Hersholt Humanitarian Award) to Secretary of Defense Caspar Weinberger. Finally, near the end of her life, in 1993 Raye was awarded the Presidential Medal of Freedom by President Clinton. She was actually in the news quite a bit at that point; two years earlier, she got married (for the seventh time) to a bisexual cosmetologist thirty-three years her junior named Mark Harris. (Howard Stern had a field day; "Oh, Doctor Kinsey!") After her death, on October 19, 1994, Colonel Maggie was buried at Fort Bragg, North Carolina.

Della Reese (born 1931)

"If your niece is Della Reese," bellows Fred Sanford (aka Redd Foxx), "then my son is Attila the Hun!" That was how I first heard the name of Della Reese. While millions of fans discovered her not on this 1975 episode of *Sanford and Son* but on her long-running show *Touched by an Angel,* the point is that they know her from television, as an actress rather than a singer. To Generations X, Y, & Z, Reese is regarded not even as an actress but as a character in a dramatic series, a television institution who was endlessly rerun and thus never far from the consciousness of the average television viewer. Reese is perhaps the only jazz singer to achieve fame as another Captain Kirk or Archie Bunker.

Even if one can get beyond Reese's TV career, there are other distractions before one arrives at her music. The most important aspect of her life, she maintains, is her spiritual devotion. Reese does more than just pay lip service to the Almighty—shouting in the Amen Corner. She is a genuine ordained minister and runs a full-service religious organization in West Los Angeles: the Understanding Principles for Better Living Church (or UpChurch, as it's known on the Web). Between making money on TV and saving souls, there's not a whole lot of time left for singing "Baby, Won't You Please Come Home."

Perhaps because Reese herself apparently places so little priority on her music, the rest of the entertainment industry has followed suit. Considering that she has long been a highly familiar figure in showbiz, and that her catalogue of recordings is long and prolific, it's surprising how little of her music (particularly from her comparatively mature period in the sixties) has been available in the digital age. Which is a shame, because Reese is and was so very good, one of the most promising young vocalists to emerge in the fifties. She has a deep rich voice— which increased in depth and richness as she got older—and a gospel-derived penchant for ornamentation and melisma. Most important, she has a style and a sound that's pure excitement: She doesn't just come on singing or even swinging, she enters blasting, not just singing the song itself but singing everything all around it in a highly decorative, gospel-driven style.

Reese resonates pure energy, practically tearing into each tune like a hungry hound on a roast chicken. It's less a matter of hitting notes than biting into them, making it clear why the use of terms like "execution" and "attack" are appropriate to her music. By the sixties, Reese was digging into her notes with such ferocity that she virtually had to come up for air after each note—which frequently resulted in her adding a little echo effect after certain key words, a little vowel sound that follows the main note, as in (the 1959 *Della*) "You're driving me-*ah* crazy!" That biting-into-the-wind effect is so prevalent that one wonders who came up with the idea first, Reese or Buddy Greco, who was chomping into words with similar ferocity at the same time.

At the height of the popularity of the *Touched by an Angel* series, Reese published her autobiography, *Angels Along the Way,* and even as cynical a pundit as myself doesn't think she was just cashing in on the idea of angels—she's been believing in them all her life. One of the most poignant stories she tells in the book involves the dramatic recitations she would perform for her father as a very small child. When she was a youngster in Depression-era Detroit, the two major influences in her life were the church and the movies; not surprisingly, religion and showbiz would be her whole life. Her mom's only "temptation" was taking in double features at the local cinema, and young Delloreese Patricia Early (that was the name she was born with in 1931) would often act out scenes from these flickers for the benefit of her dad.

She reports that even when she was a two- or three-year-old, her father wouldn't tolerate her mumbling any of these lines in a childlike fashion; rather, he would stand over her and not let her off the hook until she clearly enunciated every line. As a professional singer, Delloreese grew up with a habit of almost ridiculously precise pronunciations, every word almost exaggeratedly articulated. It's no surprise that her favorite singer was always the great Ethel Waters, who on the one hand reflected blues and gospel influences, while also possessing fairly dicty, highfalutin rolled R articulation. Reese exemplifies a determination among black entertainers in the mid-twentieth century to transcend the stereotype of illiterate, transient, low-down blues singers and low-class mumblers who couldn't speak proper English. At times such vocalists as Reese, her one-time mentor Al Hibbler, Nat King Cole, and Bill Kenny (of the Ink Spots) sing with such precise diction that you can't help thinking of Henry Higgins and Liza Doolittle.

Delloreese was singing in the church at age six, and by thirteen had risen to the top of the gospel world when she was asked to join the choir that accompanied "the world's foremost Gospel singer, Mahalia Jackson." Within a short while, she was taking solos with Jackson's entourage, staying with the world's foremost for three summers. Soon she was pursuing her own career in the gospel field, joining a female quartet—regarded as the finest in Detroit— called the Meditation Singers, and quickly became the group's leading voice.

In her late teens there were a number of distractions that took her away from music. Some were good, as when she enrolled as a psychology major at Wayne University, but others were negative, like the death of her mother and the debilitating illness of her father, as well as an abusive marriage that lasted two years. By the time Reese returned to music, she was no longer singing the Lord's music exclusively. She had become a part of the waning years of the swing era by singing with long-running Harlem-based trumpeter Erskine Hawkins.

In the early fifties, Reese won a popularity contest in a local Detroit newspaper, and was voted the best young singer in town. First prize was a week-long engagement at the Flame, the number-one nightclub in the city, and just about the most crucial venue for black talent outside New York and Chicago. She wound up working there for eighteen weeks straight, serving as a house vocalist and opening act for all kinds of headliners, from jazz singer Sarah Vaughan to bluesman T-Bone Walker to song and dance act the Will Mastin Trio starring Sammy Davis Jr.

She also hooked up with the Ellington band, or at least part of it, and made her first records in 1953. Combining the pertinent information from three sources (the Tom Lord *Jazz Discography*, Reese's *Angels* memoir, and the online discography of the Great Lakes label), what seems to have happened was that she did a session in Chicago on June 30 of that year with clarinetist Jimmy Hamilton leading a contingent of Ellingtonians—possibly including trumpeter Dick Vance. Two vocals by Reese were issued on the very short-lived Great Lakes label, one of which was "Yes Indeed." The other was an original Vance novelty entitled "Blue and Orange Birds and Silver Bells," which Reese described as a knockoff of Nat Cole's "Orange Colored Sky."

One of the few people who actually heard the Great Lakes disc was talent agent Lee Magid, who soon became her regular manager. That, at least, is Reese's story; another Ellingtonian remembers it somewhat differently. "After Lee and I got together," Al Hibbler told me, "I went out to Detroit and heard Della Reese out there [at the Flame] and I said, 'Man, I'm bringing a singer with me back to New York!' So I brought her and gave her to him."

Magid was the one who began opening doors for her, most notably a recording contract with the scrappy independent label Jubilee. The company name, with its gospel connotations, must have seemed a sign from above to Reese, and her first album for the label was a collection of sacred music entitled *Amen!* She stayed with the company from 1954 to 1959, in which time she recorded roughly fifteen singles and six albums (of which one, *And That Reminds Me,* is a collection of twelve singles tracks). (In the late nineties and early aughts, nearly all of this material has been reissued on two collector's imprints, Westside and Collectables.)

Listening to the Jubilee singles (on the Westside

CD, *Della Reese: The Jubilee Years: The Singles, 1954– 1959*) is an unpredictable experience. Most of the titles are new songs that are just as bad as your average pop single of the early rock years, but there are notable exceptions. There are a few standards in the mix, like her first single, Cole Porter's "In the Still of the Night," and while some of these are also outfitted with the 16th note triplets and doo-woppy backup singers (I actually kind of like her Coasters-style "I Cried for You"), others are surprisingly on target. The best is a pair of duets with the pianist Kirk Stuart on two show tunes, "You're Just in Love" and "When I Grow Too Old to Dream," on which they reprise a popular jive routine on that Romberg classic (as previously recorded by the Cats and the Fiddle and Rose Murphy). Stuart is a fine, musicianly singer and a simpatico duet partner; one wonders why he didn't sing more often on records. The nice surprise is that some of the otherwise unknown singles tunes are quite good, like her own "Fine Sugar," a rockin', high-octane big band blues in the spirit of Lionel Hampton, while "How Can You Lose Whatcha Never Had?" is an appealingly and swinging gospel-rooted love song.

It's especially nice to have the Jubilee LPs on CD since the original LPs are invariably poorly pressed; these discs—recorded in "Superlaphonic Hi Fi"— must have sounded scratchy and poppy even when folks originally brought them home new from ye olde record shoppe. Reese recorded two exceptional ballad albums for the company, *Melancholy Baby* and *"What Do You Know About Love."* On the latter, the arrangements are credited to one Reg Owen, but sound exactly like the work of Gordon Jenkins, and by an apparent coincidence, one of Jenkins's rarer songs, "That's All There Is" (from *The Letter*), is sung by Reese here.

Many latter-day listeners may prefer the earlier Reese albums to the later ones in that she's significantly less mannered and stylized in the Jubilee years. *A Date with Della Reese at Mr. Kelly's in Chicago* is the first of many superlaphonic live packages that Reese would record throughout her singing career. It's a very honest, unaffected live set that, with the help of the Kirk Stuart Trio (and the excellent Johnny Frigo on bass), builds to a thoroughly earned climax as she makes Cole Porter rock on "Just One of Those Things" and keeps the momentum going through a conclusive "The Party's Over."

The Story of the Blues is the most ambitious of Reese's early projects: It's essentially a set of classic variations on the basic blues ("Daddy, Won't You Please Come Home," "Squeeze Me," and "Stormy Weather") done with backgrounds that reflect both New Orleans and Swing Street, all supplied by Sy Oliver. What makes it truly unique is the spoken narration, written by Mort Goode (who did the liner notes for all her Jubilee sets, not to mention almost every LP ever released); these recitations may signify the beginning of her career as a nonsinging actress.

The album is bookended by two original songs from the team of Joe Bushkin and Johnny Burke, "The Story of the Blues" and "There's Always the Blues." Throughout, Reese makes for a solidly rocking, earthy blues singer.

Between "Sermonette" and "How Can You Lose Whatcha Never Had?" Reese was establishing herself as a solid and swinging pop singer with a gospel and blues foundation. Yet for all the excellence of the Reese-Oliver combination, and despite Jubilee's pushing her toward doo-wop and R&B on her singles, Reese was about to strike gold by traveling in an entirely different direction. It wasn't American cheese that put Reese into the big time, it was European *fromage*. The song seems to have been written by a pair of Italians, Camillo Bargoni (music) and Dante Panzuti (words), and first published in Germany under the title "Autumn Concerto." When an English lyric was written by hit maker Al Stillman, the piece caught on in the States with competing versions by Reese on Jubilee, titled "And That Reminds Me," and Kay Starr on Capitol (whose disc was titled "My Heart Reminds Me"). This was the breakthrough hit that put Reese on the charts and escalated her to the big time and the big rooms across the country, the big shows on television, and soon enough, the big label, RCA Victor.

Before she left Jubilee, her final single for that label was a pop adaptation of Tchaikovsky's *Sleeping Beauty* waltz, recently reanimated for the 1959 Disney version of that fairy tale. Titled "Once Upon a Dream," today it comes across as a considerably more palatable Euro-hit than "Reminds Me." It didn't chart, but at RCA Reese soon struck foreign gold again with the rather ambiguously titled "Don't You Know?" based on the famous "Musetta's Waltz" from Puccini's *La Bohème*. "Don't You Know?" was the biggest hit of Reese's recording career. It led to a fairly dispensable album, *The Classic Della*, a collection of like-minded classical adaptations. In 1963 she followed it up with *Waltz with Me,* a set of mostly standards in 3/4 time and another misguided attempt to parlay the success of the waltz time "Don't You Know" into an album. (Sarah Vaughan's *Sarah Slightly Classical,* recorded around the same time, was somewhat more palatable.)

Reese was off to a flying start commercially at RCA, where she would record nine albums, and soon was at an equally high level musically with her first album for the corporation, the 1959 *Della.* (As late as 2010, this is the only one of her RCA albums to be easily available on domestic CD.) RCA immediately teamed her with the emerging production team of Hugo Peretti and Luigi Creatore, who were always credited on their albums by their first names, two producers who knew how to make both memorable albums and successful singles.

The hardest swinging of the RCA releases are *Della,* arranged and conducted by Neal Hefti, and *Special Delivery* (1961), with orchestra directed by

Duke Ellington's son, Mercer. Her singing is at its broadest here, the very essence of broadness. I can't think when I've heard a bigger, more aggressive sound from any kind of voice, male or female. She is overpowering on records, and at in-person appearances at the Copacabana or Las Vegas she must have been a firebrand, a real dynamo of explosive energy and excitement. Is she a bit much? Well, yes, but jazz fans are inclined to forgive singers their excesses as long as they're soulful and as long as they swing, and Reese easily achieves both these virtues with room to spare.

The notes for the 2002 BMG reissue are irritating in that they insist that this is her first album; it's actually her seventh—can't BMG afford a discography? But the CD reissue itself is especially desirable for the bonus material it contains. This being the first time Reese had worked with Peretti, Creatore, and Hefti, she was asked to run through the twelve tracks with just her pianist, George Butcher. This demo—actually more of a rehearsal disc—forms the second half of the BMG *Della* CD, and an extraordinary document it is. Reese interjects a steady stream of verbal notes to her producers, among them rejecting their suggestion to do the Dietz and Schwartz song "I Guess I'll Have to Change My Plan" because no one could think of a scannable lyric alteration that would make the song work for a woman. (She also adds, "A female *Lothario* would be ridiculous!")

The most interesting comparison is between the piano-only and the full orchestral versions of "And the Angels Sing." The demo treatment is a kind of medley, with Reese interjecting liberal snatches from "I Hear Music" into this Ziggy Elman–Benny Goodman–Johnny Mercer perennial; the orchestral version uses the "Music" melody, but only instrumentally. However, in her piano-only demo, Reese employs an introduction inspired by Charlie Parker's "Bird of Paradise," and Hefti not only uses this, he reprises the *freilach* section from the original Goodman hit record. Hefti had plenty of ideas of his own, however: It seems to have been the arranger's idea to embellish "You're Driving Me Crazy" with the Basie variation "Moten Swing." It would be a blessing if more of these demo/works-in-progress were unearthed and released commercially, like Peggy Lee's pre-orchestral sketches with pianist Lou Levy and Sinatra's early run-throughs.

Special Delivery extends Reese's history of circling around the general orbit of Duke Ellington; she doesn't seem to have ever worked with the full band proper, despite her early connections with Jimmy Hamilton and Al Hibbler. In the early sixties, Mercer Ellington toured with her as her conductor and musical director, and virtually all her albums include at least one Ellingtoncentric song: *Melancholy Baby* has "Mood Indigo" and "Monday Every Day," *What Do You Know About Love* has "I Got It Bad," *Della* boasts a riotous "I'm Beginning to See the Light" (one that actually makes me forget I've heard that song a few too many times), *Special Delivery* has "Just a Lucky So and So," and the 1966 *Della Reese Live* has "I Got It Bad (And That Ain't Good)." Most intriguingly, *The Story of the Blues* has an Afro-militant lyric (of unknown authorship) to the famous blues instrumental (credited to Mercer) "Things Ain't What They Used to Be."

In 1962, Reese participated in a series of recruitment transcriptions for the U.S. National Guard on a syndicated show called *Guard Session* (issued on a CD on the English Jazz Band label thirty years later). Duke Ellington and his orchestra are also present, but by and large it doesn't sound as if she and they are on the same tracks together—she appears to be backed by a conventional studio orchestra, and the "dialogue," by the three principals—emcee Martin Block, Ellington, and Reese—was obviously recorded on three different occasions and spliced together. However, there's a wailing treatment of "A Foggy Day" that features a tenor solo that's either actually by Paul Gonsalves or some studio saxist who does a great impression of Ellington's major tenor star of the fifties and sixties.

Other albums of the period explore different moods and, in fact, would be easily divided into packages of two-LPs-on-one-CD: There are the two semiclassical projects, *Classic Della* and *Waltz with Me,* as well as *Moody* and *Della by Starlight,* two sets of exceptionally well-sung slow love songs, and the two live albums, *Della on Stage* (done in a recording studio but with an invited audience present, 1962) and *Della Reese Live at Basin Street East* (1964).

The live albums would be especially welcome on digital disc, because the 1962 set includes the most moving of spirituals, a riveting treatment of "His Eye Is on the Sparrow" (which she may have learned from Ethel Waters). This leads to a red hot blues, "Mad About Him, Sad Without Him, How Can I Be Glad Without Him Blues," which has heavy echoes of Dinah Washington. The blues, in turn, brings us to "Ol' Man River," a Broadway anthem reborn as a jazz flag-waver, and then a very tender contemporary show tune, "If Ever I Would Leave You" (from *Camelot*). The disc concludes with one of Reese's extremely unceremonial songs of goodbye, namely the Mills Brothers' quasi-country hit "Someday (You'll Want Me to Want You)" (which she had already done in the studio on *Della*).

Della Cha Cha Cha mambos onto the same Cuban bandwagon as *Latin ala Lee,* Dean Martin's *Cha Cha d'Amour,* and the Rosemary Clooney–Perez Prado *Touch of Tabasco.* Featuring a vocal trio on "Tea for Two (Cha Cha Cha)," the piece that launched a thousand bar mitzvahs, the *Cha Cha* adds perhaps one genre too many to a career that already includes gospel and blues, jazz and pop. While not classic pop (the idea of Latin versions of "Come on-a My House" and "Why Don't You Do Right?"—the breakthrough hits of Clooney and Lee—is a little extreme), the album as a whole is, in fact, great campy fun.

In 1965, Reese began her last extended stay at a major label, ABC-Paramount, where she was very much in the shadow of Ray Charles—a rather comfortable place for her to be. At least three of Charles's associates turn up on her ABC albums: arranger-conductor Sid Feller (on the outstanding *Della on Strings of Blue*) and trumpeter Bobby Bryant (on the two live albums and *I Like It Like Dat!*), who was also the man in Reese's life at the time, as well as multireed player Clifford Scott (also on *I Like It Like Dat!*). Reese was at first produced by Bob Thiele on the inferior *C'Mon and Hear,* which, despite a well-chosen program of standards, was sabotaged by overdone strings-and-choir charts by Peter DeAngelis. Her longtime manager, Lee Magid, then stepped in as producer and the results were a distinct improvement, particularly on yet two more outstanding live albums, both from 1966, *Della Reese Live* (the first side of which builds to a slow and sexy, extended "Drifting Blues") and *One More Time,* both of which were conducted by Bobby Bryant.

I Like It Like Dat!, arranged by Bryant, is an occasionally overly jukeboxy attempt to bring out Reese's blues strengths, evoking Dinah Washington and Aretha Franklin as well as Ray Charles. Yet there are some outstanding ballads, too, like "If It's the Last Thing I Do," "Drinking Again," and Billy Eckstine's hit "Fool That I Am." Despite the charts of Oliver Nelson, *I Gotta Be Me . . . This Trip Out* is pretty much a complete disappointment, being all dreary bargain-basement Motown-wannabe tunes with board fade endings. There are two future hits here, the title track (from Steve & Eydie's Broadway vehicle, *Golden Rainbow*) and "For Once in My Life," but neither did anything for Reese.

The best of her studio albums from this period is the 1967 *On Strings of Blue,* which rates as a practically perfect Reese package. Sid Feller, who was responsible for most of Ray Charles's best standards albums, posited a perfect balance of ballad and blues style, the former represented by the strings, the latter by an all-star jazz rhythm section. The tunes are perfect—including a couple of overlooked gems from the early forties, "I Heard You Cried Last Night" (a song pretty much killed by the World War II–era recording ban) and "Walking by the River" (by "Body and Soul" co-author Robert Sour). She sings two songs by Bobby Worth (author of "Don't You Know?"), his 1940 hit "Do I Worry" and "I'm Coming Home, Los Angeles." She also bites off June Christy's "Something Cool," and even though it doesn't quite work for her, one is nonetheless glad that she was adventurous enough to try it. Reese sings it more like a song of failed love than as a tale of a delusional demimondaine. The two most winning tunes are both on side two: "Some of My Best Friends Are the Blues," by Woody Harris, and a tune later rediscovered by Lena Horne, and the most soulful treatment imaginable of "A House Is Not a Home"—or for that matter, virtually anything ever written by Burt Bacharach. The way Reese sings it, it ain't a home, honey, it's a church.

Nearly everything Reese has recorded since (and there hasn't been much) has sounded as if it belongs in a house of worship. Since the start of the seventies, she has recorded a couple of youth pop albums and a number of gospel albums, but only one I know of where she deals in the music that used to be her stock-in-trade, jazz and standards. This is a 1978 outing entitled *One of a Kind,* produced by vibraphonist Terry Gibbs for an independent Los Angeles label called Jazz a la Carte. It's not just her last worthy album, it's one of her all-time best. She's not only loose and swinging—including the only swing treatment I've ever heard of the Legrand-Bergman "Pieces of Dreams"—but there's a far greater sense of subtlety and restraint than when she was devouring the orchestra and spitting it out, entertaining as that was in the early sixties. On the one hand, you wish that Reese could have been signed to a label like Concord and done albums like those Rosemary Clooney and her friend Carmen McRae were doing, unpretentious gatherings of swinging small groups and great songs. On the other hand, you feel you should be grateful that we at least have this one album, which offers documented proof that Reese could still ring the bell.

Throughout her career, Reese had frequently appeared on TV, initially as a musical guest (there's a clip of her on the Dorsey brothers' *Stage Show* from the Jubilee years), but by the late sixties it became clear that she could do more than sing. Before the decade was over she became the first black woman to host a talk show—her original idol, Ethel Waters, was actually a guest—and by the mid-seventies she was garnering speaking roles on *Sanford and Son, Chico and the Man,* and, soon enough, dozens of other shows. In 1991, she co-starred with Redd Foxx in *The Royal Family,* a series ended by the death of its star in October of that year. In 1994, she returned with the extremely popular quasi-religious *Touched by an Angel,* a show that transformed her from a durable character actress and comedienne into a household name. The show lasted nine very successful seasons and 212 episodes before finishing its run in 2003.

In addition to television (and the 1989 Eddie Murphy movie *Harlem Nights*), for the last few decades Reese has been active in running her ministry. It makes one feel like something of a heathen to suggest that she should spend less time doing the Lord's work and more time singing the blues. And it would be gratifying to hear her do some jazz and the Great American Songbook again—perhaps an album of the Sacred Music of Duke Ellington? Lord knows she was—and is—a major singer. Now if only more of His People—which is to say everybody—would get the Word.

Dianne Reeves (born 1956)

Major artists can change the way one thinks about things. For instance, I've always enjoyed scat singing, but have long maintained that most of the

vocalists who've attempted it probably shouldn't have. After Louis Armstrong, who essentially invented the concept of scatting (but rarely did it at any length), there is only a very small list of comparably canonic figures identifiable by their first names—Ella, Sarah, Anita, Mel—who should be permitted to scat for a whole chorus or longer.

Most scatters I've heard turn off the crowd within at most 16 bars. Reeves, however, sounds as if she's just getting going at that point. Ella and the others of the classic pantheon only rarely made scat the absolute center of their focus. Apart from specialized features (Fitzgerald's *Lullabies of Birdland* LP, Vaughan's "Pinky," and Tormé's "Night and Day"), scat was essentially a flavoring for them, an extra added attraction. With Reeves, however, it's not a side dish, it's the main course. She'll start to take off on a wordless flight of fancy, and even five or six choruses later ladies of a certain age in big hats in the fourth row are still yelling, "You go, girl!"

It's not just a question of ability or talent—I've heard scatters even more technically gifted than Reeves put crowds to sleep—it's a question of context, intentions, and attitude. Everything about Reeves, both her presentation and her music, tells us that she's not there to indulge herself but to entertain, to communicate. From her resplendent costumerie to her equally resplendent intonation, the kind that puts bells to shame, everything about Reeves establishes her as the most expressively communicative of contemporary jazz performers. In certain circumstances, though, that's actually been something of a drawback—there are times when one gets the distinct feeling that she works too hard to please too many diverse groups of people.

I've interviewed Reeves on a number of occasions, once on the subject of Nina Simone. It was Reeves, in fact, who pointed out to me that both she and Cassandra Wilson regarded Simone as a key influence, in the same way that most female singers since the thirties have cited Holiday and Fitzgerald (as indeed, Wilson and Reeves also do). While it's easier to discern echoes of Simone's monotone in Wilson's understated sound, both younger singers have followed Simone's example of interpolating elements (specific songs as well as ensemble textures) from folk, pop, and international music sources. Reeves and Wilson are, along with Dee Dee Bridgewater and the younger Diana Krall, the only indisputably jazz singers of the current generation who could fill Alice Tully Hall.

Both Reeves and Wilson use Simone as a foundation; Reeves included an impressive reinterpretation of a Simone signature on one of her first albums, the 1984 *For Every Heart.* Yet it's fascinating to observe how they veer off into similar yet different destinations from that common starting point. Wilson is introspective; she's the kind of inwardly directed vocal artist who entreats the audience to come to her, to find her where she is. Reeves is gloriously extroverted, and when you catch her in concert, you feel she's trying to reach out to every last individual in all of Avery Fisher—and darn near doing it. Wilson is understated, Reeves can be somewhat excessive, albeit in a very cool and swinging way— stuffing every line, every note, with as much ornamentation and decoration as her considerable chops can muster. For much of her early career, she was reluctant to try a real slow, heart-on-your-sleeve ballad, preferring to do even such normally tender tunes as "The Nearness of You" (on *I Remember*) in a driving, rhythmic fashion. (Although in fact there were several very successful slow ballads on that same album—among them the title song—which amounted to a breakthrough.)

Reeves is a perfect voice for a twenty-first century that likes big voices: Note how nearly every female entrant on *American Idol* is an Aretha Franklin wannabe. The sound of American pop—and a great deal of jazz—is a warmed-over gospel sound inflated to an exponential power. Reeves sounds big and at times excessive—Sarah Vaughan was a major influence and a good comparison point—but even in her excesses, Reeves, like Vaughan, is utterly musical. Even when she fills the whole hall with sound or goes off on a wordless tangent for what seems like forever, there's a subtlety to her singing. Her chops are the engine of her interpretative skills, not the other way around.

One of Reeves's first good albums, the 1996 *The Grand Encounter,* surrounded her with an amazing band of old-timers, including Clark Terry, James Moody, Phil Woods, Sweets Edison, Al Grey (the latter two making what would be close to their final appearances on record), and the album opens with Curtis Lewis and Nat Adderley's "The Old Country," in which a young woman rather curtly admonishes an old man "sitting by the lonesome road." Normally, Reeves is more sensitive than that, particularly in her dealings with her elders. In "Better Days," an original song included on her first album, she sings of her grandmother, "What she told me / Would mold me / And hold me."

Reeves, who was born in Detroit (in 1956) and grew up in Denver, was surrounded by strong female role models, including her mother (a professional nurse), the grandmother she later sang about, and all kinds of aunties. "They're all fighters," she said of the women in her family. "They're amazing to me." Her musical inspiration, however, seems to have come primarily from the male side: Her father sang, her uncle played bass violin with the Colorado symphony, and her cousin George Duke (born 1946) is a mover and shaker in the smooth jazz market.

She grew up studying piano and, later, voice. As a young teenager, she sang at a school concert intended to promote better race relations (in junior high she participated in a busing experiment, and until this particular concert, the experiment was not a success) and listened to Motown and other pop musics. She first became attracted to jazz when she

heard Sarah Vaughan's 1972 collaboration with the French composer-conductor Michel Legrand. "My uncle gave me a bunch of records to listen to when I was singing with the high school band," Reeves recalled. "More than anything I was struck by the sound of [Sarah's] voice—its color, range, the places it went to create feelings. I didn't know the voice could do all that. She changed my way of listening, and all of a sudden I had a place to reach for in my own singing."

Reeves was one of the first emerging stars to benefit from the now-defunct International Association for Jazz Education: She sang with her high school band at the IAJE conference and caught the attention of the trumpeter Clark Terry, and, at sixteen, found herself singing with his band. At twenty, she moved to Los Angeles, where she first began working with Latin groups, electronics, and fusion, and she appeared with vocal groups and did incidental solos on albums by Eddie Henderson, Stanley Turrentine, and her cousin George Duke. In 1981, she sang "Ancient Source" with the electro-Latin-jazz-pop band Caldera on the album *Sky Islands,* a track that she regards as her first notable recording. Soon afterward, she was also singing with a band called Night Flight, in which she met Billy Childs, a pianist much enamored of Herbie Hancock. Childs accompanied Reeves for ten years, and helped bring her to the attention of Herb Wong, the writer, educator, and producer, and, through Dr. Wong, to the attention of the short-lived Palo Alto Records.

Apart from the guest appearance with Caldera, Reeves recorded two albums for Palo Alto, *Welcome to My Love* (1982) and *For Every Heart* (1985). This period in her life is summarized on the 1996 CD *Dianne Reeves: The Palo Alto Sessions, 1981–1985,* which includes "Ancient Source" with Caldera, all of *Welcome,* and three tracks from *Every Heart.* Judging by the material sampled, this seems to be a reasonable balance: *Welcome* is a listenable mix of straight-ahead jazz with some electronic elements, whereas *Every Heart* is pretty much fusion all the way.

In the early eighties, Reeves was being pulled in many different directions. She was then studying with Phil Moore, the vocal coach and orchestrator who had nurtured the careers of, among others, Dorothy Dandridge and Bobby Short. While Moore steered her in an old-school, jazz-and-standards direction, she was also touring with two international stars, Brazilian pop star Sergio Mendes (who gave her her first prolonged exposure to South American music) and Harry Belafonte. The two Palo Alto albums reflect what could be regarded either as her diversity or her lack of direction. "My Funny Valentine," on the first album, foreshadows much of her later work with standards, with Reeves encircling the melody with heavy harmonic ornamentation ("Is your mouth just a tiny bit weak, baby?"), although there's a thudding electric keyboard vamp that fortunately would be absent on her best later work. "Be

My Husband," on the second, is a compelling tribute to Nina Simone, sung with just Afro-Latin percussion and chanting choir.

In 1987, Reeves became the first vocalist signed by Bruce Lundvall to the newly reactivated Blue Note Records. Her first album for the new concern, *Dianne Reeves,* had some lingering fusion elements (supplied by George Duke), and I remember that I was at first unconvinced by it. I interviewed Reeves for the first time at this point, and was more impressed by her than I was by her music. She said of "Yesterdays" that she also felt she was too young and inexperienced to have accumulated enough yesterdays of her own to give the song the full dramatic treatment it required (she was actually older than Billie Holiday when Lady Day did just that, but no matter). Thus, rather than reflecting back on her own personal "Yesterdays," she decided to use the general concept of the past as her starting point, the "Yesterdays" when the song was written, rather than her own story. She plays with the melody, with allusions to the swing era and the beginnings of bebop. From that viewpoint, she succeeded admirably. Even though she couldn't yet sing a lyric with the depth she wanted to, at least she understood what it was. As she would have put it, "something to reach for." It would only be a matter of time.

It wasn't long in coming. Reeves's next album, *I Remember* (recorded between 1988 and 1990), showed that for the still young woman to achieve greatness, the deal-breaker was that she had to find the right material and ditch the electronic additives. *I Remember* was indeed the breakthrough that those of us who wanted to like her were waiting for. This becomes clear with the very first track, "Afro Blue." Where Abbey Lincoln's earlier treatment of the Mongo Santamaría–Oscar Brown anthem is a somber, low-moaning contemplation of the diaspora, Reeves revs it up as a celebration of Pan-African percussion. The combination of rhythm and choir makes it a kind of sequel to "Be My Husband."

Appropriately, *I Remember* was an album full of surprises: a medley of two ballads, "The Nearness of You" and "Misty," done in romping, stomping, swinging style, and the first performance of Sondheim's "I Remember" by a major jazz artist. There are two traditional extended scat features in which Reeves set herself up for comparison with the masters: "How High the Moon" (a regular feature of Ella Fitzgerald's) and "Love for Sale" (ditto for Mel Tormé)—and despite the competition, came out looking amazingly good. She sang a Brazilian song, Dori Caymmi's "Like a Lover," with hardly any bossa nova accoutrements, and three standout ballads: "I Remember," "For All We Know," and the treatment of "You Taught My Heart to Sing" (Sammy Cahn's words to McCoy Tyner's melody) that put that song on the map. The biggest surprise of all was that Reeves had now, in a manner that her previous work

had not led us to expect, shot to the uppermost rank of young straight-ahead jazz vocalists.

For a long time, it looked as if *I Remember* might be a one-off pinnacle. Still, it was admirable that when she participated in some more electronic-oriented projects, she issued the results on EMI rather than the more purely jazz-oriented Blue Note. There were *Never Too Far* (1991) with George Duke and *Art and Survival* (there's an instructive title) with Caldera keyboardist Eddie Del Barrio. In 1995, she recorded *Quiet After the Storm* (1995), which was part electronic and part straight-ahead. Then she took everyone by surprise again in the late nineties by dazzling us with two of the best jazz vocal albums of the era: *The Grand Encounter* (1996) and *That Day* (1997).

"Grand Encounter" refers to a series of all-star sessions, mostly with the senior swingers previously mentioned, as well as Kenny Barron (a comparative youngster in this company), Toots Thielemans (supplying a Belgian tinge to the Latinate "Bésame Mucho"), and none other than the master, Joe Williams (duetting with her on "Tenderly"). *Grand Encounter* grabbed me with "After Hours," a beautiful noir ballad recorded by Sarah Vaughan and Herb Jeffries early on but then largely ignored. "Cherokee" was clearly also learned from Vaughan, using the same tempo as the Divine One but adding Bobby Watson on alto. "Side by Side" is an amiable scat battle with New Orleans–based singer Germaine Bazzle that starts fine but goes on a little too long, and "Ha!" is a complete surprise. An "I Got Rhythm" variation from the early modern days by tenorist Charlie Ventura, "Ha!" finds Reeves leading the entire studio company as an ad-hoc bop-for-the-people choir (Moody's and Terry's voices are audible). "Some Other Spring" (for some reason, composer Irene Kitchings Wilson isn't credited) is another moving performance, showing that the song doesn't deserve to be restricted to Billie Holiday tribute albums.

That Day, from a year later, was as good or better, with no veteran stars but a solid contingent of ace younger players. When you look over the tune stack, you spy such familiar entries as Fields and McHugh's traditional jazz standard "Exactly Like You" and several tunes that originated in the jazz world: "Blue Prelude" (Gordon Jenkins and Joe Bishop when they were still with Isham Jones) and "Close Enough for Love" (Johnny Mandel with a lyric by Paul Williams, learned from Shirley Horn). She also takes on three slices of folkish material: the Johnny Mathis hit "The Twelfth of Never" (inspired by the old "Riddle Song"), "Morning Has Broken," and Joan Armatrading's "Dark Truths," and renders them in a style that bridges the gap between folk monotone and the more expressive colorations of jazz. She also includes two brilliantly jazzed and resensitized slices of Brill Building pop, the Goffin-King "Will You Love Me Tomorrow?" and the Mann-Weill "Just a

Little Lovin'," and then ends with Bessie Smith's anything-but-bubblegummy "Ain't Nobody's Business If I Do" (rewriting, thank God, those lines about how Bessie reserves the right to be beaten up by her man if she so desires), done with just Kevin Eubanks on acoustic guitar.

It's a glorious mixture, and the title track is the kindest cut of all. "That Day" is based on a text by the African American poet Yolanda Cornelia "Nikki" Giovanni, with a musical setting by Terri Lyne Carrington and Reeves. Given that literary source, you'd expect the piece to be lofty and poetic. Far from it. As sung by Reeves, "That Day" is at once the most erotic and the most innocent piece of exposition I can recall. "If you've got the dough, then I've got the heat / We can use my oven, till it's warm and sweet." Warm and sweet indeed she is, stretching that first word until it sounds exceedingly *warrrmmmmm*. She makes you tap your foot at the same time you're squirming in your chair for an entirely different reason. The record includes an overly long fade-out, which serves to remind me that she was even more effective when singing this song in performance (as at New York's Blue Note in 1998). As the rhythm section vamped, she would saunter along, throwing a semi-improvised stream of innocently erotic and erotically innocent epithets, including the prepubuscent cry of seduction, "You show me yours, I'll show you mine."

After the doubleheader success of *The Grand Encounter* and *That Day* within two years, Reeves appears to have become intimidated by her own track record. Almost anything that followed those two triumphs would have been a letdown, but the 1998–99 *Bridges* was especially disappointing: Here was her return to smooth jazz under the guidance of cousin George Duke. Still, although the production is overall very soupy—as electronic jazz (and for that matter, pop) generally tends to be—*Bridges* is an improvement over her earlier smooth-style music. (If jazz can be likened to peanut butter, I prefer the chunky to the smooth.)

Although Reeves's next two albums also involved Mr. Duke, both are substantial improvements. *In the Moment (Live in Concert)* revives a tradition of the early sixties, the live-in-the-studio album. Like Dave Bailey's *One Foot in the Gutter* and Aretha Franklin's *Yeah!*, *In the Moment (Live in Concert)* was taped on a Hollywood soundstage (as opposed to a club or concert hall) but with an invited audience of a few hundred, and their reactions are preserved along with the music. (Reeves had actually done a live album at the New Morning in Paris, but that set, titled *New Morning*, has so far only been released in France.) Among the principal delights of the L.A. package is Reeves's penchant for singing what are normally spoken passages: her spiels to the audience, her introduction of the band. There's also "The First Five Chapters," her autobiographical elaboration of a poem by musical-comedy leading-lady-turned-

cabaret-songwriter Portia Nelson, and the happiest version ever of Jobim's "Triste" (sad), done with just Romero Lubambo's guitar and acres of scat ornamentation—sort of minimal and maximal at the same time. The album could have been titled *The Best of Dianne Reeves—Live*.

The NARAS people certainly regarded it as her best. It not only won the 2001 Grammy for best jazz vocal album, but started Reeves on a remarkable winning streak. As of 2009, she has racked up four Grammys in eight years, which probably makes her second only to Ella Fitzgerald. The only case when my taste substantially differs with the committee's is in regard to Reeves's 2001 release, *The Calling*—which was good enough to have won in any other year except this one, when the trophy should have gone to Cassandra Wilson's masterpiece *Belly of the Sun*.

Still, *The Calling* is a fine album, even if I don't play it as much as I play *I Remember, Grand Encounter,* and *That Day*. Her third Duke production in a row, this 2001 release is so far Reeves's only all-standards project and her only set with something every jazz/pop singer once took for granted, a string orchestra. Producer Duke seems to have fixated on the extremely opulent side of Sarah Vaughan: Everything on *The Calling* is lush and excessive. He seems to have forgotten that Vaughan was also a singer of great subtlety. When the Divine One recorded Benny Carter's beautiful, exotic "Strange Cargo" she used just bass and guitar and stayed fairly close to the tune; Reeves and Duke inflate the accompaniment to what sounds like a symphony-sized pops orchestra. Vaughan originally scatted her famous intro to "Lullaby of Birdland" (a riff that other singers have been borrowing for years) in harmony with Clifford Brown; Reeves does the same riff with what sounds like a thousand violins. Every element on *The Calling* is at least five times as big as it ought to be. There isn't a melody she doesn't extensively rewrite or throw in five notes for every one the composer wrote. In Reeves's music, the original tune as written often seems like an afterthought.

In the first decade of the twenty-first century, Reeves went on to release four studio albums, all of which were outstanding and highly traditional, but in completely different ways. *A Little Moonlight* (2003) seemed to be deliberately pitched at moldy-fig fans like myself who wanted to hear her do a whole album of standards with a standard jazz trio. It pivots around "What a Little Moonlight Can Do," which, ever since Billie Holiday made it a jazz standard in 1935, most singers just assume is a given; few take the trouble to make it work on its own merits (rather than the strength of its associations). It's not much of a lyric, mostly just a lot of "ooh, ooh, ooh's"; yet Reeves in a sense reverses its polarities. The song is constructed ABAB, and the A sections are essentially just "oohs"; the Bs contain all the exposition, such as it is. Singers generally sound as if they're somewhat embarrassed by the A sections, like they're just rushing through them to get to the Bs, but Reeves takes it the other way around. She opens the song with just drums, telegraphing her intention to squeeze every rhythmic nuance out of the thing. By the third chorus, she's dispensed with the lyric altogether, and no one misses it.

With *Christmas Time Is Here* (2004), Reeves goes from Holiday to holiday. She has found a much more jolly way to rack up big sales by bringing her amazing sound to a very pleasing mixture of seasonal material. She varies from folk songs, like "Christ Child's Lullaby," to songs from jazz composers (Thad Jones's "A Child Is Born," Vince Guaraldi's "Christmas Time Is Here"), and one from the world of R&B (Brook Benton's "This Time of the Year"). Nor does she forget such familiar Christmas pop songs as "Let It Snow," "Have Yourself a Merry Little Christmas," and "I'll Be Home for Christmas." In blending Tin Pan Alley with folk, African, and singer-songwriter traditions, *Christmas Time* is close in feel to *That Day*.

Alec Wilder's lyric to "A Child Is Born" is, in its usual nonholiday context, a very pretentious text indeed, but by placing it on a Christmas album, Reeves justifies all the grandiosity—it's all right to get a little excited over the birth of the Savior. Here is the first recording I know of where "Christmas Time Is Here" (from *A Charlie Brown Christmas*) reaches its full potential, a brilliant song whose lyrics are greeting-card simple but whose harmonies are highly complex; the combination gives the piece a remarkable depth. *Christmas Time Is Here* is easily the best holiday album I've heard in recent decades, and it's no juvenile bauble or flimsy tree ornament—shiny on the outside but hollow. Rather, it's the most rhythm-driven of Reeves's projects, in which she not only plays with songs written in common and cut time, but takes songs in 3/4, like "The Christmas Waltz," and reconfigures them into odd-meter funk of the most joyous sort.

Still, her next album, *Good Night, and Good Luck*, was even more like a Christmas present. Officially the sound track to the 2005 film about Edward R. Murrow and Joseph McCarthy, it's a splendid and even more straight-ahead jazz project consisting of ten vocals by Ms. Reeves (and one instrumental) that can be enjoyed independent of the film. Rather than weaving her elaborate webs of harmonic and melodic embellishments, Reeves sticks to the written melody and concentrates on bringing out the meaning of the lyric in a manner inspired by Rosemary Clooney. The only major mistake on the album is that it features David Strathairn rather than Dianne Reeves on the cover; he may be the star of the movie, but it's her album all the way. Leave it to Reeves to go do something different by doing something comparatively conventional.

Good Night, and Good Luck was Reeves's fourth Grammy in six years; in 2009, the committee felt obliged to give the award to Cassandra Wilson's *Loverly*, but Reeves's 2008 release was also a strong one. *When You Know* was fully up to her usual high standards, starting with a protracted meditation on "Just My Imagination," the 1971 Motown hit. In concerts from the 2007–08 period (and I saw many), Reeves used the Temptations classic as the centerpiece of an extended meditation on life and love, in which she brilliantly interwove not only scatting and written words, but her own autobiographical narrative. In concert, by the time she finishes "Just My Imagination" you wanted to stand up and cheer. However, the album version—which wisely does not use Reeves's long spoken section (it would only work in a live album or video)—nearly makes you cry; it's one of the most emotional and moving things she's ever sung.

The rest of the album is just as good, and it proves that Reeves can make a Motown hit sound jazzy in the same way she makes compositions that were jazzy to begin with (like "Midnight Sun" and Benny Golson's "Social Call") sound contemporary.

When You Know marked Reeves's twentieth anniversary with Blue Note Records (*Good Night, and Good Luck* was her only project from this period on another label). She is unchallenged as the Voice of Blue Note, and to that extent has participated as a guest star in a number of other projects, such as singing "The Feeling of Jazz" on the opening track of Wynton Marsalis's 2004 *The Magic Hour,* and turning in a beautiful "The House I Live In" as part of *Higher Ground,* Jazz at Lincoln Center's 2005 benefit for victims of Hurricane Katrina. She has six vocals on the all-star album *Lush Life: The Untold Story of Billy Strayhorn* (2006), which amount to a brief but nearly definitive songbook of the composer's best-known works.

On the opposite side of the musical spectrum, she sang on three tracks on *Strawberry Fields,* a 1996 jazz tribute to the Beatles masterminded by arranger-producer Bob Belden, one of which is her long-awaited girl-girl duet with Cassandra Wilson on the Beatles' boogaloo "Come Together." Reeves's finest moment here is "Tomorrow Never Knows," in which the combined ingenuity of the singer and the maestro make for, in my mind, an even more compelling interpretation than the Fab Four original (on the 1966 *Revolver*). John Lennon based the original lyrics on psychedelic guru Timothy Leary's quotes from the Tibetan Book of the Dead, and nobody makes the Book of the Dead come alive more vividly than Reeves.

"Tomorrow Never Knows" is a comparatively faithful reinterpretation: Belden and Reeves take the ideas from the original track and simply do them better. Again and again, Reeves substantially rewrites the melodies and even the harmonies of the songs she chooses to sing, but I doubt that the original composers would complain. Instead, I expect they would applaud if they could hear what she's doing with their music. The whole point of writing music is to communicate something to someone, and what she does, as with the enhancements of Sinatra and Fitzgerald, only helps the song drive its message home. Dianne Reeves is one of contemporary music's great communicators. I for one can't wait to hear what she's going to do next—whatever it is.

Jimmy Rushing (1902–1972)

My father, the late Herb Friedwald, went many times to hear Jimmy Rushing sing at the old Half Note down in the West Village in the late fifties or early sixties, where the great blues shouter worked frequently with the two-tenor team of Al Cohn and Zoot Sims. Rushing was infinitely approachable, according to Herb, who many years later told me that he happened to ask Rushing about one of his best-remembered blues lyrics. Rushing carefully delineated it for Herb: "Sent for you yesterday, here you come today—*repeat!*—Sent for you yesterday, here you come today. If you can't do better, then just stay away." The spoken emphasis was definitely Rushing's—he very clearly stressed the word "repeat" so there was to be no doubt that this was a classic 12-bar, three-line blues, in which the first line was reiterated.

That was Rushing to a T—singing the blues with both abandon and precision. He sang of sad times with a smile on his face. He sang of lowlifes and incorrigible behavior while all the time dressed like a fashion plate and, more importantly, with impeccable musicianship. He always stressed that he was more than a blues singer, but at the same time he did more for the blues than any other male singer of his generation, imbuing them with a dignity, a warmth, and a virtuoso technique that were all unique to him. Blues were like mother's milk to Rushing, but it's worth noting that even though at least one of every two or three tunes he sang in his sideman days, virtually all of the tunes he cut in the fifties and sixties, when he was presumably calling the shots and picking his own material, were standards and ballads.

Rushing came of age at a time when two things were happening to the blues: They were beginning to become a mass-market popular music, accepted by mainstream—meaning white—audiences at the same time that the black bourgeoisie was starting to shut them out. Rushing's music was in response to both developments: He sang the blues in a way that was uncompromised, full of genuine blues feeling, yet musically and professionally immaculate. On his first record, the 1929 "Blue Devil Blues," he threatens bodily harm to the other members of the band for not leaving his baby alone, but violence and infidelity are merely poetic extremes in Rushing's music. There was nothing untoward or messy about his blues—he was the kind of blues shouter you could take your church group to hear—but at the same time he never resorted to cleaning them up or

minimizing their power. He sang with perfect articulation, partly the result of his fondness for Ethel Waters, yet his flawless diction only meant that the power of the message of the blues came through that much more clearly.

Rushing's forty-year recording career divides fairly evenly into two halves—his years with the big bands (specifically Basie) and then afterward as a solo act; roughly twenty years each. He is an essential part of the Basie legend, easily the number-one vocalist in the Basie experience (even ahead of the very worthy Helen Humes and Joe Williams). In the Basie universe, everything swings—all other considerations are secondary to swing. The ornamentations that other bands might employ have all been streamlined away like so much unnecessary wind resistance, the notes are clipped and the phrasing is staccato, everything is reduced to sheer rhythmic momentum. Yet, at the same time, there's plenty of room for emotion.

This description could apply to Basie's own playing, the sound of his band, or Rushing's singing. The difference between Basie's piano work and Rushing's singing is that the Count's keyboard artistry is always feather-light, even when he's swinging hard. Rushing, by contrast, was a big man with a big sound—he's like the Hulk dancing *en pointe*. His deep, soulful sound was somehow rough and scratchy yet smooth and polished at the same time. He managed to maintain an illusion of lightness by keeping that voice in constant motion, the same way a multiton jet plane stays in the air by hurtling forward. Were the thing to stop moving, it would plummet earthward. With Rushing, that never happened.

Rushing and Basie were the advance men for a new style of jazz that sprang up in the South and Midwest beginning in the twenties, more streamlined and economical than the ornate New Orleans and Jazz Age styles of the period. Their new approach to rhythm would become a cornerstone element of both the swing and bop eras. The music they played wasn't always blues, but as Rushing himself put it, the blues was the foundation for nearly everything they did.

Rushing was born in Oklahoma City, not long after the turn of the century (early sources say 1902; he himself, in later interviews, said 1903). His father played trumpet in brass bands, his mother sang in church, and his uncle played bluesy piano and sang suggestive songs in local houses of ill repute. Little Jimmy was attracted to music at an early age, not least because he saw how much money his uncle raked in. He may have been the first blues singer to go to college; he attended Wilberforce University in Ohio, the oldest private African American school in the country, but his early biography is so crowded with other activities it seems unlikely that he stayed there long enough to get a degree. Like Jelly Roll Morton, with whom he worked in California in the early twenties, Rushing was literally all over the map of early jazz: Texas, Chicago, Missouri, Los Angeles, New Orleans.

He worked most frequently in Kansas City in the mid- to late twenties, where he became a member of a band regarded as one of the wellsprings of the new Midwestern jazz: Walter Page and the Blue Devils. It was Rushing who first talent-scouted Bill Basie, a young pianist from Red Bank, New Jersey, then still many years away from being christened "the Count," and brought him into the band. The two would be a working partnership for the next twenty years, and when the Blue Devils gradually disintegrated, both men moved into the more upscale Bennie Moten Orchestra.

Rushing was doubtless happy to be given some pop tunes to record with Moten, even the undistinguished "Sweetheart of Yesterday." He does get to sing one first-rate future standard in Hoagy Carmichael's song about that quaint old Southern city "New Orleans" (the last of his twelve 1929–32 tracks); here the band has an appropriately dark quality, one that easily matches Rushing's baritone and also resembles the texture of such stylish contemporary dance orchestras as that of Isham Jones. Apart from "New Orleans," the best of the Moten-Rushing sides are the blues, especially "That, Too, Do," in which the first 12-bar chorus contains the embryonic version of the later Rushing signature, "Good morning blues, blues how do you do?," and the no-less-famous "Sent for you yesterday, here you come today."

The Count Basie Orchestra was already gradually evolving out of the Bennie Moten band before Moten's death in 1935. When Basie broke through to the national scene the following year, thanks largely to advocate John Hammond, Rushing was one of the band's star attractions. In that year, the singer participated in two sessions that set the stage for the rest of his work with Basie. Basie's first date as a leader was made with a quintet out of his larger band (including Lester Young on tenor) in Chicago in November, with Rushing prominently featured on two of the four titles. "Evenin' " was a pop song in rough AABA (standard) form, and Rushing sings two full choruses. (A remake of the side, done four years later with the full Basie band, is just as good.) The second Rushing vocal was on "Boogie Woogie (I May Be Wrong)," which was even more of a harbinger of things to come. The day before New Year's Eve 1936, Rushing guest-starred with Benny Goodman's orchestra in New York, on a new Irving Berlin movie tune, "He Ain't Got Rhythm"—BG had the smarts to nab Rush for a date even before the full Basie big band had made it into the studio.

The total output of the Jimmy Rushing–Count Basie combination is roughly one hundred songs, about eighty of them from commercial 78s and perhaps twenty more that are fortunately preserved via radio broadcasts. That's just about the most prolific of any African American singer-bandleader combo.

The great bulk of these are blues and rhythm songs—which belong in two rough categories, as distinct from the latter single category of music, which they anticipate in many ways, called rhythm and blues.

Almost all the pure blues numbers that Rushing sang with Basie, starting with the 1936 "Boogie Woogie," are 12-bar tunes of the most deliberately rudimentary sort. "How Long Blues," "Blues I Love to Hear," "Sent for You Yesterday," "Don't You Miss Your Baby?," "Blues in the Dark," "I Left My Baby," "Goin' to Chicago," "Nobody Knows," and "Blues (I Still Think of Her)" all sound as if Rushing could be improvising the lyrics as he sings, semirandomly throwing together phrases and ideas that were already familiar to most listeners. In fact, as Rushing sang different versions of the same blues numbers over the years, the lyrics often differ radically—as if these pieces were not set in stone but were evolving from night to night.

It would seem logical that throughout his career Rushing sang at least one fast 12-bar blues and one slow 12-bar blues in every performance: The tempo and the feeling were the important thing, the actual lyric content was secondary. Certain choruses reappear as part of different songs: One of Rushing's favorite couplets was a 12-bar epigram concerning one "Miss Thelma Lee" ("The poor girl's gone, but she sure was good to me"). Miss Lee turns up in both "Don't You Miss Your Baby" (1937) and the V-Disc of "Jimmy's Blues" (1945). Rushing and Basie recorded "Jimmy's Blues" twice in that year, once for a red-label Columbia 78 and once for V-Disc, and the two versions are substantially different. The Columbia version opens with "I've got a mind to ramble," a chorus later reprised by Rushing himself (on his 1959 album *Little Jimmy Rushing and the Big Brass*), as well as by Joe Williams and Jon Hendricks in tribute to Rushing; the V-Disc opens with Rushing belting, "Did you ever dream lucky, baby, and wake up cold in hand?" This is a reference to the dream books that were utilized by gamblers playing the numbers, and it's a standard blues line heard in the music of Taj Mahal and others that Rushing also sings in "Blues in the Dark." You can't trust these blues singers: Rushing portrays himself as a no-account gambler on the V-Disc, but on the Columbia he sings with alarming flippancy about oversensitive women who "scream bloody murder" when he "raises his hand" to them.

Doubtless, Basie's musicians were much inspired by Rushing's example of seamlessly and spontaneously crafting and inventing these choruses—improvising on the blues. The slower blues tend to be sadder, and almost always concern somebody leaving somebody, the two most famous of which are "Goin' to Chicago" and "I Left My Baby." In both cases, his protagonist, although hardly oblivious of the sadness he's inflicting upon the woman he's leaving, is not sad himself. (Incidentally, when he describes his soon-to-be ex-lover as a "monkey woman," he's probably not talking about her looks but to her having a "monkey" on her back; this was already slang for a drug problem.) The 1947 "Don't You Want a Man Like Me" is one of Rushing's many slow, confident blues, where he sounds like even if the "little girl" doesn't want him, it won't ruin the rest of his day.

"I Left My Baby" is by far the saddest of Rushing's leaving-my-woman blues. He and Basie recorded it in 1939 and revived it memorably almost twenty years later on the 1957 *Sound of Jazz* TV show. Basie's piano opens as if he's about to play the Chopin "Funeral March," then trumpeter Buck Clayton growls while Earl Warren plays an obbligato around him. When Rushing sings, Lester Young blows a blues obbligato behind him, of the sort that the Pres famously supplied for Billie Holiday. But even though the instrumentalists are indescribably mournful, there's no one more filled with the dark spirit of the blues than Rushing. He sings slowly and deliberately, making every line count—making you feel every little nuance of the blues; why he's sad that he has to leave his baby but knows it's what he must do. He is to the blues what Sinatra is to love songs—and Rushing sang those pretty well, too. His last line is movingly bleak: "Where there ain't no love / There ain't no getting along."

If his slow blues are for the most part far from morose, his fast blues are nothing short of jubilant. When he sings "If you catch me stealing" in "Baby, Don't Tell on Me" (performed as "Stealing Blues" at John Hammond's famous "Spirituals to Swing" concert) he's swingingly defiant, making a pun on the word "stealing" to indicate not thievery but stealing away in the sense of Arabs-and-tents ("I'll be stealin' back to my old-time used-to-be"), stealing away on tiptoe. Both here and in "Rusty Dusty Blues" there's an undercurrent of a thinly veiled threat. The blending of aggression and eroticism is unmistakable, as is the influence on such future Swingin' Lovers as Sinatra (a lifelong Basie buff) and Bobby Darin—as well as on Ray Charles and the entire soul movement.

One of Rushing's best unrecorded features with Basie—preserved, fortunately, thanks to a 1937 aircheck—is "Rhythm in My Nursery Rhymes." Rhythmic nursery rhymes are a key component of Rushing's music. The concerns in the basic blues tunes are decidedly adult, dealing with mature relationships, breakups, infidelity, substance abuse, physical abuse, gambling. In "Take Me Back, Baby" and "Tricks Ain't Walkin'," the object of Rush's affection or, at least, attention, is clearly a streetwalker. But content-wise, the "rhythm" songs are just the opposite. Even before Ella Fitzgerald and "A-Tisket, A-Tasket," Rushing and Basie were swinging nursery rhymes and children's songs, often recast in the form of a popular song, like "Stop Beatin' 'Round the Mulberry Bush (Come Out and Say You Love Me)," and "London Bridge Is Falling Down."

From the title of "Listen My Children," you might naturally assume it's one of those hysterical history songs, like Andy Razaf's "Christopher Columbus." However, this 1937 pop song, written by Burton Lane and Ralph Freed for Martha Raye to belt in the 1937 *Double or Nothing,* turns out to have nothing to do with Longfellow or Paul Revere. "Listen" gives Rushing the opportunity to explain how he was "born to swing," and grew up to be a jitterbug because his mother rocked him to sleep with "Muddy Waters." As 1936 audiences would have been aware, "Muddy Waters" is a blues-inflected popular song associated with Bessie Smith (who recorded it in 1927), which would later provide a stage name for the superb blues singer formerly known as McKinley Morganfield; Rushing himself recorded it in tribute to Smith in 1960. Other than the title, there's nothing in it that refers to American history; the songwriters—and Rushing and Basie—are merely riffing with the opening line of a poem that schoolchildren were once forced to memorize. In Rushing's idiom, children's songs are a lot like the blues: The lyrics are often strictly secondary. The words to both "Listen My Children" and "One-Two-Three O'Lairy" (1940) are nonsensical rhymes that kids would chant while playing jacks or skipping rope, mere placeholder syllables to mark the time.

Rushing mixes the adult and the infantile in other, more subtle ways, too. One of his most famous blues features, "Good Morning Blues," is all about how he misses his baby, how he's got to see her again, but in this particular instance he expresses this desire in the form of a request to Santa Claus—thus, even a serious blues about adult concerns has something of a childish capriciousness to it. The two are similarly mixed in "Mama Don't Want No Peas 'n' Rice 'n' Coconut Oil," in which Rushing's own grammar is considerably better than that of the lyricist. Here "Mama," for once, refers to a maternal rather than romantic relationship. Speaking from the perspective of a little child observing his parents, Rushing points out how "Mama she likes her rum / She says it fills her soul with fun" and that the reason Mama felt cold last night is because "Papa must be getting old." It's all good clean fun.

When Rushing sings standards, he picks tunes that were already time-honored and timeworn: "Somebody Stole My Gal," "Gee Baby, Ain't I Good to You," "I Want a Little Girl," "After You've Gone," "Blue Skies," and the like. Here, the implication is that the listener already knows the words and therefore Rush can play with them as he chooses.

Basie and the A&R directors at Decca and then Columbia only rarely gave a contemporary pop song (other than a blues or a novelty) to Rushing. In some ways, that was a good thing, since he was spared some of the egregious dogs recorded by other bandleader-vocal combinations. Earle Warren, one of the linchpins of the Basie reed section, also occasionally sang something new in a straight tenor voice, serving as Basie's equivalent of Andy Kirk's Pha Terrell, but most of the best new songs went to Basie's girl singer, the wonderful Helen Humes. Good as Humes is, one would occasionally like to hear Rush get a crack at Rodgers and Hart ("Sing for Your Supper") and Cole Porter ("My Heart Belongs to Daddy"). One of the rare new songs he tackled was his first recorded vocal with the full Basie big band, "Pennies from Heaven," which, along with his heroes Crosby and Armstrong, he helped transform into an instant jazz standard.

On some songs he only sings a chorus, in the traditional big band vocal refrain style; on others, he dominates the record almost all the way through. "Harvard Blues" is an extraordinary piece of material, written for Rushing by jazz writer and college graduate George Frazier. Obviously, somebody thought it would be funny to play up the apparent contradiction between a low-down blues singer and the conventions of Ivy League existence, employing such fanciful language as "think checks from home sublime." The joke seems less funny in our politically enlightened era, even more so given our knowledge that Rushing did, in fact, enjoy a degree of higher education. I disagree with Gunther Schuller's opinion that "Rushing [may not have] really understood what he was singing about" (and that's even though I personally don't get a lot of the references, like "Reinhardt, Reinhardt, I'm a most indifferent guy"). However, there's no debating the quality of his own performance on "Harvard Blues," that of the leader on piano, and especially the outstanding tenor saxophonist Don Byas, taking his finest solo with Basie. The inherent message is abundantly clear—that college students are the same sort of shiftless lowlifes normally portrayed in the blues. (There's a V-Disc version from several years later that's longer and juicier, and with Buddy Tate taking the tenor solo, but the original is still more powerful. By contrast, the V-Disc version of "Gee Baby, Ain't I Good to You," arranged for the band by composer Don Redman, is one of the very best of the Basie-Rushing features, offering an extralong vocal that starts with the only reading of Redman and Andy Razaf's introductory verse.)

By the early war years, when Humes had left the band, Columbia's producers were steering more topical material toward Rushing, such as "Draftin' Blues," "For the Good of Our Country," and "Lost in the Blackout Blues." He also shines on another politically oriented piece, "It's the Same Old South," by the liberal songwriting team of Jay Gorney (who had written "Brother, Can You Spare a Dime?") and Edward Eliscu. Like Duke Ellington's "Jump for Joy," Eliscu's lyric skewers the conventions of Southern racism (sharing with the Ellington song a reference to "the bloodhounds who once chased Liza / Chased a poor CIO organizer") in such a way as to point optimistically toward a more tolerant future.

The most complete edition of the entire output of the original "Old Testament" edition of the Basie orchestra is a series of comprehensive CDs from the French Masters of Jazz label. This includes four hours of live radio performances from 1937–39, which are intermingled chronologically with studio sessions (granted, not always the best way to hear them all). These airchecks are justly prized, firstly because they offer the only document of Billie Holiday with Basie, but also because, as we've seen, there's a lot of especially rewarding material from the band's longer-lasting vocalists, Rushing and Humes. They sang many songs and arrangements from these years that never made it onto Decca or Columbia. The live material has Rush singing "St. Louis Blues," "Rhythm in My Nursery Rhymes," "When My Dreamboat Comes Home"—a song that became immediately beloved of traditional New Orleans jazzmen—and "Dinah," an older song that already was. The airchecks also document two Rushing items that, in retrospect, seem absolutely essential to his canon, "I Let a Song Go Out of My Heart," one of his rare performances of an Ellington piece (twenty years later, between 1958 and 1960, Rushing would make several guest appearances with Ellington himself, most famously at the 1959 Newport Jazz Festival), and "The You and Me That Used to Be." The latter was, by all accounts, one of Rushing's most popular features with the band, but for whatever reason they weren't given the chance to do it for Decca (although Rushing did record it in 1971 as the title of his last album).

As early as the Moten period, Basie and Rushing were perfecting their amazingly propulsive brand of 4/4 swing, showing that the blues and the popular song could be even more powerful over a solid four beat. This comes especially to the fore in the live performances, in which the band's time is simply irresistible. In a sense, it's almost better that "The You and Me That Used to Be" survives as an aircheck rather than a commercial disc, despite the lesser sound quality, which means it will probably never be available on an easy-to-find American major label. In "You and Me," Rushing puts over a story very convincingly; a tale of love and loss—he paints a vivid picture of what used to be—rendered in a swinging up-tempo.

Rushing and Basie stopped working together when Basie broke up his big band around 1950 (he could have kept Rushing on; instead he rehired Helen Humes). Apart from a few memorable reunions, most notably the amazing TV show *The Sound of Jazz* in 1957, Rushing was not to be a part of the second half of Basie's career, when he went back on the road with his equally remarkable "New Testament" orchestra. Still, the singer who did fill Rushing's very large shoes was the magnificent Joe Williams, who frequently acknowledged his predecessor.

Rushing's first recording sessions apart from the Basie band are very much in the Countish style. In

1946 he did a date of his own for Excelsior, still a member of the Basie entourage and with lots of Basieites for support; remarkably, it took this long for Rushing to be given a record date under his own name. Between then and 1953, the singer made a short series of singles for small labels like Excelsior, Parrot, and King aimed at the "race" (later rhythm and blues) market. One of his most imposing R&B-style numbers is the tune called "Go Get Some More, You Fool," in which he sings his characteristic 12-bar blues, talking about a girl who took all his money, while what sounds like a vocal quartet chants the title phrase behind him. "Hi Ho Sylvester" is R&B of the sort that Big Joe Turner was then cutting for Atlantic, parodying the "Lone Ranger" catchphrase ("Hi-Yo Silver!") with hoofbeat sound effects, a wailing tenor, and the same choir. "Where Were You," though still in the 12-bar blues format, uses pan-Caribbean-calypso rhythms. (In 2004, the Belgian Classics label collected all twenty of these sides on *Jimmy Rushing, 1946–1953;* although one would like to hear better source material and engineering, this will have to do until the real thing comes along.)

Rushing would never have a hit on the R&B or soul charts, but he didn't have to; by the start of the LP era, he had transitioned from the blues to the jazz market. He began this phase of his career with the help of Basie's original benefactor, producer John Hammond, with three albums on the Vanguard label: *Going to Chicago* (1954), *Listen to the Blues* (1955), and *If This Ain't the Blues* (1957). Hammond, who would also later make new albums with Helen Humes, exhibited a curious tendency in his work with both of these vocalists in their post-Basie careers in that he seemed completely determined only to have them repeat themselves. Virtually every song Rushing sang for Vanguard was a new version of something he'd done in the Basie years. These are outstanding albums, and Rushing sings wonderfully in the company of fellow former Basieites led by tenorist Buddy Tate (on the first and third albums), but even so there's a feeling of déjà vu here.

Hammond also favored longish jam session–style tracks. Everybody in the band takes long solos, and the background on the third album, *If This Ain't the Blues*, is rather cluttered by the use of three chordal instruments going at once, Clarence Johnson on piano, Marlowe Morris on organ, and Roy Gaines on guitar. The proceedings are extremely informal; at times, it seems that no one's sure who's going to solo next, or even when Rushing is due to reenter. The extended jam format also ensures that we hear comparatively little of Rushing himself—he essentially serves as a framework for long-form instrumental blowing, and actually only sings for perhaps ten minutes on each of these albums. But what's there is choice.

Rushing would make his most successful later recordings in collaboration with producers who had grown up on the Basie band: George Avakian, Irving

Townsend, Bob Thiele, and Don Schlitten. Although they also generally preferred to reteam Rushing with onetime Countsmen, the albums they made are not limited to the Basie style and canon. At Columbia, he recorded frequently with trumpeter-bandleader Buck Clayton, with whom he also toured Europe in 1959. The best of the 1955–71 LPs use the Basie legacy as a cornerstone but not as a millstone.

The Columbia albums collectively offer a stimulating and varied program, starting with *Cat Meets Chick* (1955), a curious package from the dawn of the 12" LP with Rushing and Ada Moore as guest vocalists with Buck Clayton's big band. The album's high-concept sets up the blues shouter and the trumpeter as competing with each other for the affections of Miss Moore. The problem is that the music is so good it makes the narrative look insignificant by comparison.

The other Columbia albums are more conceptually successful. *The Jazz Odyssey of James Rushing, Esq.* (1956) is equally geographically and autobiographically driven, with four different bands and different approaches to songs themed to four different cities where Rushing worked in his early career. The high point is easily "Tricks Ain't Walkin' No More," a bordello song taught to him by his uncle, in which he sings the parts of both pimp and prostitute (in a squeaky yelping falsetto), accompanied by his own piano. It's the kind of thing I can envision some contemporary rapper picking up, but no way would a hip-hopper be able to tell the tale as vividly as Rushing. (These first two Columbia albums were reissued on a Collectables CD in 2002.)

In 1957, Rushing would make a Columbia single ("My Last Affair"/"Don't Tell on Me") that represents another marginal attempt to reconcile his style with rock 'n' roll. The next two albums, *Little Jimmy Rushing and the Big Brass* (1958) and *Rushing Lullabies* (1959), are so amazingly appealing one can easily imagine them being played on every kind of radio format, from jazz to standards to blues. The *Brass* album, as the title indicates, is Rushing with a modern swinging big band and charts by three Basie arrangers in Jimmy Mundy, Nat Pierce, and Buck Clayton. He starts off by blasting "I'm Coming, Virginia," a thunderously declamatory statement, sounding not just as if he's traveling to the state but determined to raze it to the ground, like Sherman marching through Georgia. He also reclaims "Mr. Five by Five," a pop song hit of the World War II years that was famously inspired by his own nickname, and he reprises his already famous statements on "Harvard Blues."

Rushing Lullabies (1959) is mostly funky blues, and may have been an attempt to package Rushing for the younger generation. It wasn't much of a compromise—merely adding electric guitar (Skeeter Best) and electric organ (Sir Charles Thompson) to a standard accompaniment of tenor (Buddy Tate), piano (Ray Bryant), bass (Gene Ramey), and drums

(Jo Jones). The ensemble never sounds too busy, even with both organ and piano going at once (a convention of the gospel music world). Likewise, "Russian Lullaby" becomes autobiographical: Irving Berlin's minor key, 16-bar lament gets reoutfitted in basic blues, with longish choruses from everybody in the ensemble. Rush skillfully blends standards of the jazz, pop, and R&B worlds, such as Joe Liggins's "Pink Champagne" and even the early rock anthem "Good Rockin' Tonight." There's also a new song in a blues-gospel mode by beatnik songwriter Fran Landesman, "Travel the Road of Love," not issued until the CD era. (Sony Music Legacy has conveniently combined *Big Brass* and *Lullabies* onto one disc, with the bonus track.)

In the Columbia years, Rush worked live and on record with old friends Count Basie and Benny Goodman, as well as making several appearances (on record and live) with Duke Ellington's orchestra, but his only full-length recorded encounter with a major instrumentalist was, surprisingly, with one of Columbia's major modern jazz stars, pianist Dave Brubeck and his celebrated quartet with Paul Desmond. Produced by Teo Macero, *Brubeck & Rushing* was entirely agreeable on every count, showing that Rushing could keep up with a bop-based combo and that Brubeck could stick to the fundamentals. The standards like "Ain't Misbehavin' " are exemplary, but what really makes the pot cook is the way the Brubeck-Desmond group plays the blues, particularly on "Evenin'," a slow and resigned reading that compares favorably with the faster Basie-Rushing readings. "Blues in the Dark" finds Brubeck, often the heaviest keyboardist in all of jazz, outlining a simple, effective blues chorus with Basie-inspired minimalism. By the time Rushing gets to the repeat of his oft-asked question, "Did you ever dream lucky, baby, and wake up cold in hand?," raising his voice into another one of those mother-grabbing shouts, it's clear that this is one of the most powerful blues performances Rushing left for us.

Jimmy Rushing and the Smith Girls (1960) is the final Columbia album and was at long last issued on the Spanish label Lone Hill Jazz (on a twofer CD with *The Jazz Odyssey of James Rushing, Esq.*) in 2008. It's another skillful blending of the old and new, using mostly Basieites, including Clayton and trombonists Dickie Wells and Benny Morton, and, as a special guest, tenor champ Coleman Hawkins. This is Rushing's most blues-driven package and, conversely, also the one that features the most new material. The idea of having Rushing sing numbers associated with the four classic blues singers of the twenties who were named Smith—the unrelated Bessie, Clara, Trixie, and Mamie—was an inspired one. It's a fairly perfect matching of man and material. Rush is practically the only singer of the modern era to resurrect Mamie Smith's ur-blues hit "Crazy Blues," and he fully addresses the odd, psychological manifestations of some of the hoarier

twenties blues items like Clara Smith's "Shipwreck Blues."

The Rushing Columbia albums are, overall, the high points of his post-Basie career. Not only do they feature him belting the blues like no one else ever could, but in *Brubeck & Rushing* in particular, these performances are distinguished by what Billy Strayhorn once characterized as the intimacy of the blues. Rushing would continue to make excellent albums in the sixties, most notably *Five Feet of Soul* (Colpix, 1963), *Every Day I Have the Blues* (ABC Bluesway, 1966), and *Livin' the Blues* (ABC Bluesway, 1968), but while these are far from disappointing, they lack the subtleties and intimacies of the 1955–60 work. Still, all three of these sixties sets are exciting and hard-swinging projects that make tasteful use of a Hammond organ, and *Five Feet of Soul* and *Every Day I Have the Blues* had the benefit of being orchestrated by two outstanding saxist-arrangers who were steeped in the Basie canon, Al Cohn and Oliver Nelson; *Livin'* is a small group package co-starring Dickie Wells and Buddy Tate.

The accompaniments on all three albums sound as if they could have been written for Ray Charles in his early sixties standards-concept packages. In 1967, in between the two Bluesway albums, Rushing participated in two uneven jam sessions for the Connoisseur's label Master Jazz, *Who Was It Sang That Song* and *Gee, Baby, Ain't I Good to You,* both apparently done on the same date, with Clayton and Wells.

It's his last recording, made in 1971, a year before his death, that's the charmer. Rush at last sounds elderly here and beyond his prime, in a way he never did on any of the sixties projects. He no longer has the raw power he had even a few years earlier on *Five Feet of Soul.* But we never miss it. Perhaps it was no coincidence that producer Don Schlitten titled this album, done for RCA, *The You and Me That Used to Be.* Now when Rushing sings of the you and me that used to be or about growing too old to dream, there's an introspective quality to his work, as if he were giving his own testimonial to himself. By now, even the kids who had grown up on Basie, Pres, and Rushing—players like tenor sax stars Zoot Sims and Al Cohn (who played with him frequently at the Half-Note)—were pushing fifty, and Rushing was about to pass his legacy on to still another generation.

He also sings several especially touching duets with Dave Frishberg, including "I Surrender, Dear." Drummer Mel Lewis later said that whenever he listens to the final track, "Thanks a Million," he feels Rushing is saying goodbye. I myself get that feeling from "More Than You Know," the voice-piano duo. It's as if, after a lifetime of pondering the meaning of life through the blues and the Great American Songbook, Rushing is telling us that there's still more out there than he will ever know.

"Even today," Ralph Ellison wrote in 1958, Rushing "seldom comes across as a blues 'shouter,' but maintains the lyricism which has always been his way with the blues. Indeed, when we listen to his handling of lyrics we become aware of that quality which makes for the mysteriousness of the blues:

their ability to imply far more than they state outright and their capacity to make the details of sex convey meanings which touch upon the metaphysical." That's Jimmy, all over.

S

(Little) Jimmy Scott (born 1925)

Jimmy Scott, who for most of his career was officially billed as "Little Jimmy Scott," is the living embodiment of what novelist Nick Hornby identifies as the central dilemma of pop music. To paraphrase the opening of *High Fidelity:* "Did I start listening to Little Jimmy Scott to help me deal with my heartache, or did I get my heart broken by listening to too many Little Jimmy Scott records?"

Sometimes when you're feeling down, you have the mistaken idea that things can't possibly get any worse. Well, you're wrong—they can, and probably will. By the time you get all the way down to miserable, then even bad starts to look good to you.

Jimmy Scott can capture that feeling like no one else. Sometimes when he'll come, say, to the word "love" at the end of a line in a slow, sad song (and the way he sings them, they all are), he sings it as something more like "lo-uh-ve," and he'll take that long "uh" sound in the middle and just twist the hell out of it. By twisting I mean that he not only emphasizes it, he injects it with a certain slight flatness, lets the pitch apparently just drop and fall to the ground. The way Scott sings "love," he makes it sound as if it has three distinct syllables. Far from taking a sad song and making it better, Scott will take any kind of a song and break your heart with it. He could make "Three Blind Mice" sound like "One for My Baby."

Like Al Hibbler, Jimmy Scott has a bluesman's sense of distortion. Neither of them hardly ever sang an actual 12-bar blues, but the way they sang standards and ballads led people to believe they were closer to the stylistic universe of B. B. King than that of Frank Sinatra. Also like Hibbler, Scott can articulate with impeccable diction in what sounds like a falsetto (technically, it isn't—he sings in his natural voice, the same one he uses for everyday speech), but then he'll personalize a phrase so emphatically it sounds as if he's gargling it. There's his 1952 record of "Why Was I Born?" on which he just ever so slightly rushes and mangles Oscar Hammerstein's lyric so that it comes out like "Why wazza born." (It helps that he sings the melody correctly, so that the "I," on a high note, is at least implied though not explicitly stated.) Likewise, on "I Wish I Didn't Love You So" and "I Wish I Knew" he repeatedly mispronounces the second word as "I *Wished*" or "I *Wish't*," and somehow makes that reinvented pronunciation sound so impeccably right.

Scott also puts one in mind of Thelonious Monk in the way he reinvents melodies—and often a

lyric—in his own image. You're going along, following the tune the way you're used to hearing it, and boom! Here comes the zinger, that little twist of pitch and inflection that stabs right into your heart, just the way Monk's funky little chromaticisms occur right where you least expect them. Time-wise, Scott is no less devastatingly original—he basically sings slowly and legato, yet he unexpectedly clips his phrases in an idiosyncratically staccato fashion.

More than any other upper-echelon vocal artist in jazz or pop, Scott deals exclusively in heartbreak. His tempos are almost always the slowest in music, and his albums almost uniformly contain nothing but one killer-slow, heart-wrenching ballad after another. It's something of a shock to listen to *Live in New Orleans* from 1951, one of the earliest location recordings of any vocalist, and to realize that he opens with "All of Me" in a bright, bouncy tempo. Not that it's the only nonballad in the entire Scott catalogue, but bright bouncers would never be his preference. His later albums sometimes include one faster track for the sake of variety, like "Blue Skies" on *Mood Indigo* and "Pennies from Heaven" on *Over the Rainbow*. When Scott picks up the tempo, it seems to be primarily for contrast—and even a respite—from all the anguish of his torturous torch songs. Yet he never completely submerges himself in self-pity; there's an ironically upbeat side to every sad song he sings. Even those two contemporary masters of the snail's-pace tempo, Andy Bey and the late Shirley Horn, have felt a greater need, at least once or twice an evening, to speed things up a little bit for the sake of variety. Not Scott.

Billy Vera has for years served as Scott's number-one advocate in the music business (he's had many more, as we shall see). In his many annotations of Scott reissues, he often addresses the question, "If Jimmy Scott is as great as you say, why isn't he the major star he should have become?" The answer is that Scott is just too unique, too idiosyncratic, too personal. Every fan of his realizes that by the very definition of who and what he is, he's not going to appeal to everybody, not even within the unfortunately already limited demographic of people who like jazz, standards, and blues. The more people who hear him, the more people will get caught up in his magic, but he's not going to be like Sinatra or Fitzgerald, both of whom were blessed with a sound and style that virtually everyone takes to instantly. For those of us who do love Jimmy Scott, though, the rewards of his music are endless.

Vera has stated that he considers Scott "the world's greatest jazz singer," yet Scott's high-pitched, near-falsetto sound fits more easily in the context of black popular music. He comes out of the tradition of Ink Spot Bill Kenny and Andy Kirk's Pha Terrell, but he's earlier than their doo-wop progeny. He has also been described as a blues singer, but though he boasts a greater depth of feeling than any dozen genuine Delta blues guys with "Big" in their names, he rarely sings the purely blue I-IV-V chord progression product. He prefers Tin Pan Alley ballads, which he sings in a way that some have described as transforming them into the blues, but he also sings R&B and soul numbers as if they were traditional love songs. When he gets through any piece of material, it is neither a blues nor a ballad—it's now a Jimmy Scott song; he is a genre unto himself. The glory of all great song texts, be they ballads or be they blues, is the balance between the specific and the general. "Time After Time" is a very personal statement about a specific relationship that Scott makes sound universal, whereas "Without a Song" and "How Deep Is the Ocean" are big songs that invoke the cosmos itself—and which Scott makes you feel are more intimate than grandiose.

At times Scott is broad and exaggerated—as in the coda of "Without a Song," wherein he sings the last "without" three times, sounding progressively more anguished; never has the word "without" seemed so desolate, so empty, so just plain without. Yet at the same time he's also subtle—consider the ending of "Time After Time" (a song originally tailored to Sinatra's stealth singing), and the way that he ever-so-gently tiptoes into the concluding tonic note. But most of the time he's both things at once, broad as well as intimate, finding new details in songs you've heard a hundred times. Just before the bridge on "Imagination," librettist Johnny Burke writes, "Has you asking a daisy what to do," and then reiterates those last three words. Most singers just state that second "what to do" as a simple repeat, but Scott mines all kinds of meaning from it. He takes this second "what to do" further downward, and slyly suggests that this three-word phrase may be a sentence in itself, one with a question mark on the end of it. Near the end of "How Deep Is the Ocean," he rewrites a line as "How far would I travel to be near a star," and then proceeds to emit the longest and most bone-chilling "annnnnd . . ." that you will ever hear.

The sight of Jimmy Scott is as unique as his audio presence. The term "Little" isn't just for a catchy nickname, nor is it, as in the case of Little Jimmy Rushing, intended sardonically. Rushing was anything but little, but Scott is anything but big. He was eventually diagnosed as suffering from a hormonal deficiency, a condition known as Kallman's syndrome, which caused his body to stop growing at the point when it reached adolescence—his voice never changed but remained at a high, boyish tenor (some would say soprano), and his body froze at the height of four foot eleven. He has excessively soft, almost feminine features, and as he's gotten older his voice has come to sound more and more like an old lady blues singer (in contrast with such masculine-sounding ladies as Frances Faye and Nina Simone). The most egregious case of Scott being confused with a woman occurs on what is almost his first recording, a June 1950 Birdland performance of "Embraceable You" with the Charlie Parker quintet, on which the issuing producers (the track was first released in the 1970s) misidentified Scott as an obscure female blues singer named Chubby Newsome. (One discography simply describes the singer as "unknown female vocalist.")

Scott was often challenged to prove his masculinity, which he did by getting into bar fights and by using his romantic voice to make conquests of more women than you can shake a stick at (if that's your idea of a good time). His arms are disproportionately long, and he tends to use them most dramatically and effectively to help underscore lyrical points (as you can see on any of a number of songs from a 2000 Tokyo concert, thankfully viewable on YouTube); producer Joel Dorn described him as a "mocha-colored marionette." Reprehensibly, several of his record companies have decided that he was too much of a funny-looking duck to rate getting his picture on his own albums: *Falling in Love Is Wonderful* shows a black makeout man about to go to work on what looks like an unconscious Asian chick (both are sprawled out on the floor listening to records), and *The Source* shows a sexy black babe sporting a big old funky afro.

Scott was born on July 17, 1925, in Cleveland. He was one of ten siblings, most of whom were raised in foster homes after their mother was killed in a car accident. Most of those who have sketched out his biography have taken pains to point out two things. First, that he got the bug for performing while portraying Ferdinand the Bull in a school play. As portrayed in the Disney cartoon from 1939 (when Scott was fourteen), Ferdinand is the pacifist bull who refuses to act like a bully and declines to fight and gore matadors. (What this has to do with Scott's later gender-confusion issues, I don't know.) Second, that his original showbiz mentor was a lady contortionist named Estelle "Caledonia" Young (she probably took her stage name when the Louis Jordan record of "Caldonia" became a hit), who shepherded a series of tent shows for black audiences across the South and Midwest. Supposedly Little Jimmy was already singing in that high-pitched, piercing voice and doing songs of heartbreak.

In 1948, he signed on as boy singer with Lionel Hampton, a post filled earlier by Joe Williams. While Williams never had the chance to record with Hampton, Scott fortunately did, but this was near the end of his tenure with the band and resulted in a total of only four titles. Quincy Jones, who joined Hampton's trumpet section shortly before Scott left, described the singer in performance to James McDonough: "It was dramatic when Jimmy came out in the solo spot. He'd just stand there with his shoulders hunched, his eyes closed and his head tilted to one side. He sang like a horn—he sang with the melodic content of an instrument. It's a very emotional, soul-penetrating style. Jimmy used to tear my heart out every night."

It's recently been revealed that he recorded for the first time in 1949, for Universal Records, an even then obscure concern based in Chicago; the sides were never issued and the masters are lost. The next year, however, one of his four vocals for Hampton's orchestra was the song that would be his biggest ever, "Everybody's Somebody's Fool." According to McDonough, the song began as a rather rough, unpolished lyric that a fan brought backstage to Scott; he and organist Doug Duke reworked it into its familiar form. At some point, Gladys Hampton, Lionel's wife and general business manager, got her name on it as a co-author; Scott did not.

It's not too much of a stretch to rank Scott as one of the forefathers of the soul movement. Ray Charles was later justifiably celebrated for bringing techniques associated with gospel music to rhythm and blues and then mainstream pop, and though Scott doesn't go as far with the idea as Charles later did, there's undeniably a gospel flavor to much of his music. Charles is said to have done as little as to substitute "baby" for the original word "Jesus" in his gospel-to-pop transformation, and Scott is on a similar path. In his hands, "Time After Time" (on *Mood Indigo*) becomes an almost religious experience. When he finishes a number, you want to say "Amen."

Take "Everybody's Somebody's Fool": The lyric is a philosophical warning to those who would toy with other people's hearts and make a game of love; most songs that do, "Goody Goody" and "I Wanna Be Around," for instance, would simply suggest that the tables will turn on the second-person cad—meaning that some hot chick will come along and break *his* heart. However, the bridge to "Everybody's Somebody's Fool" suggests that this particular romantic ne'er-do-well will get his come-uppance from no less than "The One Above" Himself. Scott sings it less like a crooner than in the declamatory fashion of a sundown deacon preaching to his flock—even addressing them as "sisters and brothers."

When he gets to the line "Making fools of others / And pretending that it's love," he injects a character-istic Scottian twist to make it really dig into your heart. It's a classic record and his best-known song, yet every other time he sang it it got better—there's a live version from 1951 where the fidelity is terrible but the performance is even stronger than the 1950 Decca; there's a remake for Savoy done with strings in 1960 (on which the tune is credited to two completely different songwriters—go figure). Lastly, his 2000 album, *Over the Rainbow,* contains the most

gut-wrenching "Everybody's Somebody's Fool" you can imagine. If Scott is capable of wringing more emotion out of this song—which is to say out of the audience—I don't think I could handle hearing it.

The song was something of a hit in the "race" market and gave Scott a calling card to go out on his own as a single. He also wanted to get away from the Hamptons' low salaries and they, in turn, wanted to get away from Scott's excessive drinking, which was compromising his singing. At this point, he became a featured attraction with the troupe led by R&B leader Paul Gayten.

Also around this time, Scott began a multi-decade, on-again, off-again relationship with pro-ducer Fred Mendelsohn, one of the few characters in his life who wasn't bent on robbing him for all he was worth. Though Mendelsohn had musical taste and ability, he seems to have been less gifted in a business sense, and the one who most often suffered because of this was Scott.

In 1952, Coral Records added Scott to their ros-ter, in a situation that roughly paralleled Johnny Hartman's short-lived association with RCA Victor at the same time: Cult artist gets major label con-tract, but is stuck with crummy songs and wannabe hits that don't quite make it (neither one managed to make "Wheel of Fortune" pay off for them, even though that turned out to be one of the biggest gold mines of the decade). Only a few of the Coral songs are memorable (all are on the CD *Everybody's Somebody's Fool*); one that leaves a favorable impres-sion is "Take a Lesson from a Fool," if only because it's such a close reworking of the original "Every-body's . . ." and it's almost as good.

Once the Coral deal was over, Scott resumed his relationship with Fred Mendelsohn, first on Roost and then on Savoy. The label was in a good place to establish him, if not as a crossover superstar, at least as a leading figure in the black market—and this it did. Some of the Savoy products are beautiful; some are more than a bit tacky because of what McDon-ough has described as "laughably cheap string over-dubs." On occasion, Scott's kind of hard-luck singing almost sounds better the worse the material and the worse the accompaniment, as if fighting his own musical circumstances is part of what his art is about—perhaps being surrounded by mediocrity makes his sad story more believable.

Thanks to Mendelsohn, however, Scott was all-owed to record a higher percentage of standards than he had been at Coral, and some of these are among the highlights of his entire career: "Please Be Kind" (oh yeah, you better believe he means it), "Time on My Hands," "Imagination," "Laughing on the Outside (Crying on the Inside)"—although with Scott it could be retitled "Crying on the Outside (Crying on the Inside)"—"Street of Dreams," "Someone to Watch over Me," "Smile," and especially two older songs that became minor hits and career pegs, "When Did You Leave Heaven" and "I'm Afraid the Masquerade Is Over." (All the Savoy-owned material was collated into the essential *Little Jimmy Scott: The Savoy Years and More . . .* , a three-CD box prepared in 1999.)

Scott and Mendelsohn left Savoy in 1957 to do a very rare album for King, but returned the following year. Still hopping from club to club all over the country, Scott recorded for Savoy from 1958 to 1960. But this time Lubinsky seemed bent on shoving him into the kiddie pop market, and thus inflicted the most miserable trappings imaginable upon him, with ricky-tick 16th-note triplet rhythms and irritatingly tightly pitched string sections. These brutally awful orchestrations were deployed even when he was doing superior songs like "The Way You Look Tonight" and "Time on My Hands." Apparently he made the mistake of complaining about the overall ineptitude of his output to Savoy label owner Herman Lubinsky, who at this point assumed the role of Scott's Moriarty, his Judas, his Lex Luthor, his mortal nemesis, and who apparently committed himself to doing anything he could to sabotage Scott's career.

The story goes that Lubinsky held Scott to his contract—he couldn't record for anyone else—but was now so angry at Scott that he refused to let him make a record—for Savoy or anyone else. When Scott did sessions for other labels, Lubinksy threatened lawsuits, so that the results would either be withdrawn or never released. When Ray Charles formed his own imprint, Tangerine Records (a subsidiary of ABC-Paramount), the first artist he signed was Scott. In 1969, Joel Dorn produced an album with him for Atlantic. Alas, in both cases Lubinsky took these labels to court, claiming that he still had Scott under exclusive contract, and succeeded in having these two records taken off the market. This may be the greatest tragedy of Scott's professional life, because the Tangerine and the Atlantic projects are easily the finest albums of his whole career.

The 1962 Tangerine album, *Falling in Love Is Wonderful,* is indeed wonderful. It consists of ten exceptional standards arranged and conducted by the superior orchestrators who were, at the time, also doing executive producer Ray Charles's own albums. As Dorn says, this was the first time that the real Scott, the one he had heard at the Apollo two years earlier, actually got captured on record. Among other songs he absolutely sings the hell out of—and I do mean the *hell* out of—is Frank Loesser's "I Wish I Didn't Love You So."

The strings have a little more of an R&B tinge on 1969's *The Source,* but are still far superior to the ass-end tackiness of the 1960 Savoy dates. *Falling in Love* attempts to do in the classiest way for Scott what Ray Charles's crossover ballads ("Come Rain or Come Shine," "Georgia on My Mind") did for him. *The Source* brings more of a blues and soul feel to the proceedings, as evidenced by the opening three tracks, starting with "Exodus," an Israeli-inspired movie theme that black performers (Billy Eckstine, Eddie Harris) had appropriated as a soul anthem. This is followed by two numbers that had earlier been hits for doo-wop groups, "On Broadway" (the Drifters) and "Our Day Will Come" (Ruby and the Romantics). Both were somewhat optimistic, even cheerful in their original incarnations as 45 rpm hit singles. Not anymore; Scott sings them both, especially "Our Day Will Come," slowly and painfully, as if he were trying to extract every last gasp of angst out of them.

The Source has an amazing postscript: Atlantic signed Scott to do two albums, and Dorn and Nesuhi Ertegun decided to go ahead and do one session for the second album in 1972 even though they already knew Lubinsky wouldn't let them release it. Five songs from that date were at last issued in 1990 (on *Lost and Found*), and though they may not be quite up to *The Source* material, they are still essential LJS. We can assume that on the proposed album they would have been interspersed with other material, because as heard by themselves they are just too similar: Each is an excruciatingly slow ballad made to seem even slower by the inclusion of the verse. Even the normally upbeat "For Once in My Life" now sounds like the saddest, saddest song you ever heard, as if were titled "Not Even Once in My Life." Even more moving is "I Have Dreamed," taken at an impossibly slow, mournful tempo; at one point Scott sings "I have dreamed what a joy *it* be." It's one of the most arresting performances of his oeuvre, particularly when it shifts upward for the final 8 bars (starting with "in these dreams I've loved you so . . .").

In 1975, his fiftieth year, Scott made one more album for Savoy, which was now free of Lubinsky, who had gone to his final reward, such as it was, a year earlier. *Can't We Begin Again* combines contemporary hits by Alan and Marilyn Bergman with standards and two selections credited to pianist Ace Carter; it has its moments, but it's neither the best nor the worst of his albums.

And for a while, that was it. For most of the late sixties through the eighties, Scott was no longer working in music but as a shipping clerk at the Sheraton Hotel in his native Cleveland. For years the songwriter Doc Pomus (who wrote virtually all the early rock hits not written by Leiber and Stoller) had been unceasingly beating the drums for Jimmy. (Doc even called me at Stash Records, where I was working in the eighties, and tried to get us to record LJS—much as it pains me to admit it, I was in my early twenties, still in school—in more ways than one—and had never heard of him. As they say, everybody's somebody's fool.) When Pomus died in 1991, all the bigwigs turned out for the funeral and listened to Scott sing "Someone to Watch over Me." At last, he had the collective ear of the music industry. Sure enough, someone signed him to a major label contract, and that was Seymour Stein of Sire Records (a division of Warner Bros.).

Scott's deal with Sire started with the excellent *All the Way* (1992) and continued through *Dream* (1994) and *Heaven* (1996). Even with major label support, and ringing endorsements from rock celebrities like Madonna and Lou Reed, it was plain that he was never going to be a mass-market superstar; for Warners to keep the deal going for three albums and five years was a valiant effort on the part of the conglomerate. In 1998, Scott made *Holding Back the Years*, a one-shot project for the Artists Only label, and then in the years at the immediate start of the new millennium there were four excellent studio albums for Milestone—*Mood Indigo* (2000), *Over the Rainbow* (2001), *But Beautiful* (2002), and *Moonglow* (2003)—and lastly, so far, two live sets recorded in (and thus far released only in) Japan, *Unchained Melody* (2001) and *All of Me: Live in Tokyo* (2004).

Ten albums in less than fifteen years is more than Scott had recorded in his whole lifetime up until then, and in a sense it's fitting that his later years should be so productive. As with Sinatra, Scott's chops were diminished by age, but his other dramatic resources had grown more than compensatingly deeper. His vocal equipment itself, in his sixties and seventies, was comprised of a weather-beaten voice, a capacity for breaking down a melodic line into the most curious phrase patterns you're ever going to hear, a tendency to sing so far behind the beat as to risk being arrested for tailgating, a vibrato that could eat Cincinnati, and intonation that is surely not the most precise you're ever going to hear.

Rather, as producer Todd Barkan says, "With Jimmy, it ain't about the notes—it's about the way he writes his name in our hearts." Scott has often averred that the key factor in his choice of material is whether the song affords him a powerful enough story to tell. It's merely secondary if the piece has an intricate melody, or whether the chords resolve on an augmented ninth, or whether the lyricist rhymes "heaven rest us" with "asbestos." Likewise, he makes his artistic resources add up to a formidable storehouse of techniques—a recipe guaranteed, after sixty years of seasoning, to reduce the human heart to a mound of jelly.

He also stresses that his primary directive is to respect the composer's intentions. "I feel that if I were to destroy his concept, then why bother to do his song? I want to enhance what the songwriter has given us." To place this observation in a larger context, it's certainly true that Johnny Burke and James Van Heusen wrote the title of "Imagination" (one of their first major songs, on *Mood Indigo*) as a single word, whereas Scott sings it as "i—mag—gin—a—shun" so that it sounds more like five. And yet few singers have ever made Mr. Burke and Mr. Van Heusen's story come alive so vividly—in Scott's soul-saturated universe, even the most whimsical ideas seem real.

Nearly all the tunes on the later albums are in Scott's patented crawl tempo—one can almost feel the breeze from the snails whizzing by. He sustains speeds that are so slow, you can hear every nuance and feel every note; it's impossible to miss *anything*. Not only can he sustain the same funereal tempo for most of an album without it ever getting tiresome, he can even do the same song twice and not sound as if he's repeating himself—*Mood Indigo* actually contains two very different versions of the title song, one with a quartet led by Cyrus Chestnut, the other done totally impromptu as a duet with guitarist Joe Beck.

Of the later albums, the first, *All the Way* (Sire), is the most effective, while the 1998 *Holding Back the Years* (Artists Only) is the strangest project of his entire career, consisting almost entirely of songs by contemporary rockers like Elvis Costello, Bryan Ferry, and Prince; it almost seems as if the producers were in agreement with my theory that Scott thrives in adverse circumstances and wanted to supply him with the material least likely to inspire a good performance from him. He does his best with all of it, but one would still rather hear him singing "All the Way" and "Over the Rainbow."

As already noted, it's the 2001 "Everybody's Somebody's Fool" (on *Over the Rainbow*) that's the most devastating of the three studio recordings of his signature song. And "Without a Song" (*Mood Indigo* again), in particular, is one for the ages, right up there with longtime colleague Ray Charles's as one of the all-time great slow versions of the Vincent Youmans classic. For most of his seventy-five years Scott had a hankering to put "Without a Song" on record (he's loved it since both he and the tune were youngsters). It's an anthem of ambitious aspirations, demonstrating how music is the spiritual force of the universe. Love ("there ain't no love at all"), the weather ("what makes the rain to fall"), and life itself ("what makes the grass grow tall") are all motivated by song. The way Jimmy Scott sings, who are we to doubt it? As of this writing, Scott is scheduled to headline at a benefit concert for the Apollo Theater in May 2010. He hasn't been in a recording studio in almost a decade (although a live album was recorded in Tokyo in 2003, and, so far, released only there, on Venus Records) but there is some amazing recent footage up on YouTube. One event easily worth watching is a number of songs from a 2000 concert, also in Tokyo (but apparently not the same as issued by Venus), in which Scott is performing at full throttle, completely animated and alive on "I Cried for You" and others. There's also a handheld camera clip of him singing "Embraceable You" in an open-air concert in Las Vegas, dated 2007; he seems decades older, but still vital. The downside of this being a park amphitheater concert is that you can feel the mugginess and even hear a helicopter chopping by—doubtless it's Donald Trump, trying to get a closer view.

I caught Jimmy most recently in the spring of 2008 at Dizzy's at Jazz at Lincoln Center. At eighty-two, he was in a wheelchair, which actually was a good thing, in that he wasn't worrying about appearances—or even standing up—but rather devoting all of his energies to singing (reading the lyrics off a music stand). His body was frail, but his voice was incredibly strong. In recent years, he had been letting his accompanying group, billed as the Jazz Expressions, do more and more of the work, playing longer solos and taking more instrumental features. But this night Scott sang almost every number, and sounded remarkably good. His most moving performance was "The Folks Who Live on the Hill," which he sang with such passion that the hill of the title might just as well have been in Heaven and the house upon it, a Cabin in the Sky.

Now and forever, the music of Jimmy Scott is the sound of one heart breaking.

Dinah Shore (1916–1994)

Dumb joke from the movie version of *On the Town:* Our hapless sailor heroes somehow wind up at the Museum of Natural History and accidentally knock over the skeleton of a dinosaur. A pair of cops are summoned to the scene via the police radio, which orders them to investigate the collapse of a dinosaur. "That's terrible about the collapse of Dinah Shore," says one cop, with a perfectly straight face. "She's my favorite singing star."

In a kooky way, that's as good a description of Dinah Shore's career as anyone has offered. She was indeed a "singing star," a star who happened to sing, as opposed to someone like Jo Stafford, a singer who happened also to be a star. Without demeaning Shore's vocal abilities, she lasted at the top for so many decades primarily because she was selling personality first and music second. The important thing with her was that you liked her; more than anything, she was a warm and friendly person whose company you wanted to be in. You wanted to be around when she chatted with her guests—whether it was on her variety show of the forties, fifties, and sixties (first on radio, then TV) or her afternoon talk show of the seventies and eighties. If she could capture our attention with a song, so much the better. But no one was shocked when she launched her own talk show and put her singing on the back burner. She was just as engaging when she was stir-frying with Sinatra in the mid-seventies as when she was singing with him in earlier decades.

Broadcasting was always Shore's thing: She made movies, but they never amounted to much. She was more than attractive, but never movie-star glamorous like Doris Day. As she once said, "A singer [in the movies] was usually 'pretty pretty' [like Alice Faye] or a comedienne [like Martha Raye], and I was neither." Still, this didn't seem to hurt her longevity on television, a medium that relied at least partly on visual appeal. Where you spent time with Doris Day on two or three occasions a year, when her new movies were out, Shore was a consistent presence in your home on the radio, not only starring on her own shows but appearing as a guest on everyone else's; you spent time with Dinah at least two or three nights a week, and she continued, without a letup into television, variety shows and then talk shows, for an unabated run of over forty years. Chances are that when anybody, not just a dumb cop in a movie, said "singing star" for the whole middle of the twentieth century, they meant Dinah Shore, who exemplified that ideal more than anyone else.

Shore isn't associated with any particular innovations; she left it to Sinatra to experiment with long-breath phrasing, the discovery of the standard songbook, the invention of the concept album. Yet darned if Sinatra didn't delight in being in her company, working with her on radio and TV (and several famous Columbia recording sessions) every chance she gave him. She had a warmth and a charisma that were distinctively feminine, not necessarily hubba-hubba or funny, as she suggests, but with at least a little of both.

Her career parallels that of Perry Como in that both singers went from big bands to huge solo careers and then made the small screen safe for pop. Compared to Como, she had fewer blockbuster hits and signature songs, but she was a powerful force in the recording industry.

"People forget this about Dinah Shore," Mitch Miller said, rather undiplomatically, a few years before her death in 1994. "She's had only two hit records in her whole life, 'Buttons and Bows' and 'Sweet Violets'!" There were actually four number-one hits from the period between 1940 and 1955: "Buttons and Bows," "The Gypsy" (eight weeks!), "The Anniversary Song," and "I'll Walk Alone," which is surprisingly few for a star of her magnitude. But at the same time, one feels that there might be an element of sour grapes to Miller's statement, since he never got the opportunity to work with her; when he came to Columbia in 1950, Shore had already left to follow her mentor Manie Sachs back to RCA. In the forties especially, Shore was a constant presence on the *Billboard* hit singles charts—landing there with at least seventy-five different songs. Her discs sold consistently well in both single and long-playing formats; at her peak, it was said she was selling two million pieces of vinyl a year. No one ever went broke putting out Dinah Shore records.

Shore doesn't belong in the ranks of all-time top record sellers, or in the ultimate top bracket of female pop singers—like Jo Stafford or Doris Day—but she had a highly distinctive and appealing voice. Content-wise there are no shortage of first-rate Shore records out there. Unlike some of the top "pure" jazz singers, like Sarah Vaughan or that other Dinah, Washington, who sounded great no matter how bad their material or their accompaniment, Shore wasn't always able to transcend her circumstances. But give her a good tune and a good chart and she'll do just fine. She's particularly excellent when she's working with someone a little extra special, a duet partner or an especially good arranger or instrumentalist. When she has a Buddy Clark, a Red Norvo, a Nelson Riddle, an André Previn, or, best of all, a Crosby or Sinatra to inspire her, she will, without fail, rise to the occasion and attain the upper brackets of pop royalty.

One element that generally jogged her interest was jazz and sometimes even the blues. Before becoming a solo star in her own right, Shore appeared as an incidental singer on a wide variety of radio shows, including NBC's *Chamber Music Society of Lower Basin Street,* a show that presented traditional jazz—usually incredibly hoked-up, but sometimes not. She later observed that while her stay on that program was not long, "More people seem to remember the *CMSLBS* than anything else I did on radio." By 1939, virtually every band in existence would have added Shore to its payroll in a heartbeat, but she wanted to avoid being identified as a canary with a swing band. Yet she was a long-term fan of hot music, who went out of her way to bring Gerry Mulligan and Ben Webster onto a high-profile TV special. She not only sang with Duke Ellington on-camera at a time when white and black did not mix on screen or anywhere else, but, when she had Ray Charles on her show, she shattered a a few taboos by putting her hand on his shoulder—something white chicks just didn't do at that time, especially if they were from Tennessee.

If the name "Dinah Shore" has inspired many a Jurassic pun (e.g., "When Dinah Shore Ruled the Earth"), her given name—Frances "Fanny" Rose Shore—is capable of setting off wordplay of an even gnarlier kind (frequently concerned with levitating buttocks). She was born in 1917, the youngest daughter of the only Jewish family in Winchester, Tennessee. When she later described her childhood to friend George Simon (she wrote the introduction for his 1979 book, *The Best of the Music Makers*), she remembered that there was as much jazz and "black music"—swing, blues, gospel—on the air in Tennessee in the thirties as there was mainstream white pop. Shore grew up enamored of black music, and later cited Billie Holiday and Maxine Sullivan as early favorites (although it seems unlikely that she would have heard much of them before moving to New York in 1938).

Before she left Tennessee, she had already been singing professionally over Nashville station WSM. According to some sources, it was there that Shore, inspired by Ethel Waters, sang the 1925 jazz standard "Dinah" and adopted that as her professional name. According to other accounts, it was WNEW's Martin Block, the most famous deejay of his era, who gave her the new first name; this would have happened around 1938–39, when she began doing a sustaining (nonsponsored) show for the network. She was paid bupkis, but she gained exposure and, occasionally, the chance to work with Sinatra, then in the same position career-wise, who became a lifelong friend.

Shore never did accept a long-term position with any of the major dance bands, but she did one-shot engagements with several, such as a theater date at the Strand with Leo Reisman and a short-lived radio spot with Ben Bernie. She made her first recordings in 1939 when Latin lothario Xavier Cugat needed an American chirp for a series of sessions for RCA Victor (she was supposedly credited as "Dinah Shaw"). She sang with various *Chamber Music Society* aggregations on the air and for Victor. Earlier, she had auditioned for Jack Teagarden (supposedly he turned her down because he resented her choosing to sing his signature, "Basin Street Blues"), but when in 1940 Tommy Dorsey made her a generous offer to come on the road with him, she told him that she was committed to remaining in radio.

She began making records of her own in 1939 for RCA's subsidiary Bluebird, and she recorded frequently for Bluebird and then Victor until well after the end of the AFM ban in 1945. These early recordings for Victor (which are sampled on the CD *You and I* on the English Conifer label) show, among other things, that the art of accompanying pop singers was virtually frozen in the decade between Crosby and Sinatra. The arrangements, even when by the emerging Paul Weston (then Wetstein), are very much in the manner of John Scott Trotter's work for Crosby. Yet where Der Bingle could rise above those rather uninspired, plain-vanilla backgrounds, Shore, as we'll see throughout her career, needs a little more to get her juices flowing. Even when the songs are good, and they frequently are, the 1939–42 recordings tend to be on the tepid side. Between her two-month stint on the *Chamber Music* show, then an even more high-profile spot on Eddie Cantor's top-rated program, she scored increasingly prestigious spots of her own. Now headlining on a national show, Shore was given a high-glamour makeover, and now sported a honey-colored blond "do" to match her honey-tinged contralto.

Her first big record hit arrived in 1940, "Yes, My Darling Daughter," adapted by Tin Pan Alley pro Jack Lawrence from an old Ukrainian folk song. But what really cemented her stardom was World War II: After Crosby and Sinatra, Shore was easily the most popular singer with service audiences, and her work was steadily distributed through GI channels such as V-Discs and the AFRS. She tirelessly toured army hospitals, and her voice was recognized as the aural equivalent of the famous pinup of Betty Grable sticking out her tush. One soldier described her as having "the kind of voice you'd like to take home to Mother."

In 1943 she landed her first important sponsored series, the *Birds Eye Open House,* and also co-starred on a summer replacement series with Paul Whiteman. Her movie career then got under way, thanks again to Cantor, with *Thank Your Lucky Stars* (she looked lovely in lamé, and her big number, "The Dreamer," was a fine, sentimental war song by

Arthur Schwartz and Frank Loesser). In her next film, *Up in Arms* (Danny Kaye's debut was the big news here), Shore introduced another hit, "Tess's Torch Song," this time in Technicolor. She was one of the few singers who recorded a cappella sessions with choir during the 1942–44 recording ban, but her work in this period is better represented on CD samplings from her broadcasts, such as *When Dinah Shore Ruled the Earth, The Dinah Shore Memorial Album,* and *Dinah's Showtime '44–'47.* There are also four masters with Glenn Miller's AAF band, recorded between blitzes in London, that haven't sufficiently circulated; and she sang in phonetic German as part of propaganda broadcasts to the Axis.

By war's end she was ensconced as the number-one female singer in the country. Soon there would be lots of competition from Stafford, Day, Whiting, et al., but Shore's untouchable success on the broadcasting front and with the Allied forces put her in a class by herself. Having been the sweetheart of the service during the war, Shore—who was now very publicly married to movie star (and ex-GI) George Montgomery—had become the perfect picture of postwar domesticity. In addition to Montgomery, two other men were by now permanent fixtures in her life: Pianist and songwriter Ticker Freeman had become her longtime accompanist and musical mentor, and her career rabbi, as he was frequently called, was CBS's Manie Sachs, who arranged for her to come to Columbia Records in 1946. She then followed him when he changed teams from CBS to NBC/RCA in 1950.

The late forties saw her bringing her Tennessee Southern tones to quasi-hillbilly songs for the first time—songs like "Buttons and Bows," "Doin' What Comes Naturally," "Lavender Blue (Dilly Dilly)," "Shoo-Fly Pie . . . ," and "Dear Hearts and Gentle People." As always, a fair number of standards and first-rate new show tunes turned up in her repertoire, although she never made as much of a point of them as Sinatra. While there is a fair amount of unmemorable material in the late forties and early fifties, she did especially well with Cole Porter in this period, being a bit excessively girly on "Always True to You in My Fashion," but just right on "So in Love," and deserving considerable credit for having the smarts to do "Nobody's Chasing Me" from *Out of This World.* (Two recommended samples of the postwar era are *16 Most Requested Songs,* despite its dreadful cover, on Sony, and *Love and Kisses, Dinah* on BMG.)

She was always a game participant in duets—"Tallahassee" with Woody Herman, a long-running series with Buddy Clark (including the hit "Baby, It's Cold Outside" and an outstanding "Summertime"), and "A Penny a Kiss" with Tony Martin. She got in on some girl-girl action, a great rarity in pop, when she and Doris Day sang together on "You Can Have Him" (from Irving Berlin's *Miss Liberty*). She and Sinatra did some of their best boy-girl work together

on the famous 1946 Columbia disc of "Tea for Two" and "My Romance." There's also a V-Disc of the two of them doing "The Night Is Young (And You're So Beautiful)," which is even better, and, more important, they appeared frequently together on radio and then television and were always a magical duo. He brought out the best in her, and vice versa. (There's a bootleg disc for collectors out there entitled *Blue Eyes and the Dixie Flyer* that makes this point perfectly.)

Shore's peak years as a TV star were 1951 to 1961, during which she headlined on *The Dinah Shore Chevy Show,* which, like Perry Como's programs, consistently finished at the top of the ratings for an entire decade. In the mid- to late fifties in particular, her recorded work was rarely consistent, neither consistently bad nor consistently good, but in 1959 she rejuvenated her singing career by switching to Capitol. Now the emphasis was on long-playing albums: The first major Capitol LP, *Dinah, Yes Indeed!,* served as a welcome wagon in which Sinatra and Nelson Riddle brought her into the Vine Street fold, Riddle arranging and conducting and Sinatra supplying a cheeky endorsement: "This is the Thin One saying 'Welcome to the swingin'est label of them all.'"

The five major albums she recorded for Capitol are undoubtedly the high point of her career as a singer, perhaps because nearly all of them give her an extraspecial collaborator to work with. After *Yes Indeed!* with Riddle, she made two projects with André Previn—*Somebody Loves Me,* with full string orchestra, and the remarkable *Dinah Sings, Previn Plays,* with trio; even better was *Dinah Sings Some Blues with Red* (Norvo, that is). Even the overtly "commercial" *The Fabulous Hits of Dinah Shore,* a collection of stereo remakes of hit singles from over the previous twenty years, has more than its share of moments. She's never been in better shape sonically than in the early sixties, and her commitment to the material seems total. *Dinah Sings, Previn Plays* is light and jazzy, while *Somebody Loves Me* offers heavier ballads, and she doesn't overdo either extreme, not trying to be as hard-swinging as Sinatra on the first or as exactingly emotional as, well, Sinatra, on the second. On each, she and Previn find a perfect balance.

Following the Norvo and Previn projects, her most interesting album of the sixties is *Lower Basin Street Revisited* (1965). This was a time when other singers of her generation were revisiting their big band roots, such as Sinatra's and Stafford's tributes to Tommy Dorsey and Doris Day's *Sentimental Journey.* Thus Shore paid tribute to the institution that she viewed as having launched her career, which, in her case, was not a big band but a radio series, NBC's *Chamber Music Society of Lower Basin Street.*

This would have been the ideal opportunity for an album of Dixieland and blues, and there are tracks when *Lower Basin Street Revisited* is exactly that: The most straightforward and successful number is "Nashville Blues." However, much of the music on the original *CMS LBS* was hokey and gimmicky, and some of *Lower Basin Street Revisited* is, unfortunately, faithful to that tradition as well. Still, the album is worth hearing for compelling readings of blues-oriented material by Arlen ("I Had Myself a True Love") and Gershwin ("My Man's Gone Now"). Surprisingly, one of the most exaggerated charts is one of the most listenable. This is a Ray Charles–influenced "jazz waltz" treatment of the 1930 pop standard "Bye Bye Blues"; Shore does it as a variety show–style duet with herself, overdubbing a countermelody. There are also warm and winning renditions of "Nobody Else but Me" and the much covered megahit Italian movie crossover theme "More." She ends with one of the ultimate songs of the South, "Chloe," which starts straight and then changes horses midstream, going into a swing treatment with bongos that seems closely modeled on the Nelson Riddle (Judy Garland and Rosemary Clooney) version of "Come Rain or Come Shine."

Lower Basin Street Revisited has enough successful tracks on it to make it well worth hearing; *Yes Indeed!*, though, is Shore's single most perfect album, from alpha to zed. On so many of her bread-and-butter singles of the fifties, she sounds professional but not completely committed. What a difference when she was really "feeling" her material. The word for the way she sings on *Yes Indeed!* is "excited": She sounds so happy to be singing these first-rate Riddle arrangements of these excellent songs and she effortlessly passes that enthusiasm on to the rest of us. The album contains a medley that she had introduced in Vegas (unbelievably, and unlike Como and Crosby, she still found time amid all her activities to continue making personal appearances) consisting of four songs that have no real reason to be sung together—"Where or When," "Easy to Love," "Get Out of Town," and "They Can't Take That Away from Me"—other than that she obviously enjoys singing them; as such, the medley sounds better than most medleys constructed along more rigorously thematic lines. Stuck in the middle of side two are a pair of superstandards that open with the verse rendered in tempo, "I'm Old-Fashioned" (introduced by the familiar sound of Harry Edison's muted beeping trumpet) and "Love Is Here to Stay," which in themselves are enough to place Shore as one of the great pop singers.

Just in time, too: The gold rush years of traditional pop music were about to come to an end. Shore wound up the weekly *Chevy Show* in 1961, after a staggering 599 appearances, and the next year divorced her husband. There would be other TV ventures, most notably a series of specials (including one that featured Gerry Mulligan, Ben Webster, and Sinatra all in the same sixty minutes) and other men and marriages, but an era had ended. In the seventies she was famous both for her long-running

afternoon chat show (at a point where daytime talk was dominated by former band era singers, the others being Mike Douglas of Kay Kyser's band and Merv Griffin of Freddy Martin's) and for keeping company with Burt Reynolds. In 1976, she recorded an album of contemporary pop material for Reader's Digest, *For the Good Times,* which only became widely available thirty years later from DRG Records; it wasn't Rodgers and Hart, but it was as well arranged and well sung as an album of covers of the mid-seventies could possibly be.

She is one of the few figures in all of American popular culture who managed to keep current for more than five decades—from the big band era to years as a chart-topping solo headliner to reinventing herself as a variety show diva in the early years of TV to re-reinventing herself as a talk show hostess. She's been likened to Como in some of these aspects, and the comparison has also been made to Loretta Young (who had a whole other career on television after the Golden Age of Hollywood movies was over), but in truth, Shore did more different things and lasted longer than anybody.

When she died in 1994, ex-boyfriend Burt Reynolds told the press that she had been the great love of his life. Whether we knew her as a band vocalist, a TV icon, or a singing star who collapsed at the Museum of Natural History, when Dinah Shore died, it seemed as if we'd all lost part of our family.

Bobby Short (1924–2005)

The word "cabaret," like the word "jazz," means many things to many people—yet I know I'm safe in saying that when most people think of a combination of musical and performance style associated with the East Side of Manhattan, the late Bobby Short is the first name that comes to mind. He is the gold standard of the genre, the alpha and the omega. This is entirely appropriate, since it acknowledges Mr. Short as the archetype, the man who defined the entire style as we know it today.

Short was an institution for a long time: He was a headliner in the black vaudeville circuit; he recorded in the 78 era; his initial albums were in mono; and when he first sang Victor Schlesinger's faux-Cuban classic "Sand in My Shoes," it was so long ago that this *rhumba* described an island nation that was still not yet under the *thumba* of a communist dictator. Bobby was around so long (even by the time he cut those first albums he had already been a professional musician for nearly twenty years) that it was easy to take him for granted.

We're not trying to prove that he was a radical— the Ornette Coleman of cabaret, as it were (although Nesuhi Ertegun discovered both of these influential musicians in Los Angeles at roughly the same time). But we would do well to remember that before Bobby Short, your typical cabaret pianist-singer didn't sound anything remotely like Bobby Short. The evidence of recordings shows that for most of the major cabaret stars of the pre-Short era, time—meaning rhythm—is almost immaterial. A jazz artist and a cabaret artist can be doing the same songs with the same background, and the only thing that distinguishes one from the other is the use of rhythm. The great majority of rank-and-file cabareteurs and cabareteuses have absolutely no concept of it; as polished as they may be, they wouldn't know a rhumba from a waltz.

With Short it's just the opposite. It's not as if he's a rhythmic virtuoso like Sinatra or Fitzgerald, but he realizes that he can really make things happen with a strong driving beat behind him. He knows how to use rubato for contrast, and whether it's a slow love song or a fast and bouncy up-tempo, you know exactly where the beat is. It's significant that for the whole of his career he consistently made a point to work with the best bassist and the strongest drummer he could get.

With Short, time is indeed everything—or practically everything. When he sings Rodgers and Hart's "The Most Beautiful Girl in the World," it's still a waltz, but now it's a rather more aggressive, driving waltz than it had ever been before. Even the verse isn't, as you'd expect, out of tempo but is delivered by Short with a solid beat. Time doesn't always mean speeding things up. As producer Nesuhi Ertegun once observed, "I'll never forget when he did 'Bye Bye Blackbird.' I think we did only one take. It was so perfect, so *right*, although it was a totally new approach to this standard. Bobby chose a much slower tempo than usual and he imbued the song with melancholy and despair. When he finished I was speechless. It was a triumph, one of the greatest moments of music I had ever heard." It's well known that Short's landmark performance of the Mort Dixon–Ray Henderson jazz standard was the one that motivated Miles Davis to record his own, even slower, interpretation.

Like two of his heroes and role models of musical sophistication, Cole Porter and Fred Astaire, Bobby Short was from a town in the Midwest. As Rogers Whitaker, one of his early champions, put it, few of his listeners "could ever be persuaded that Bobby was not a big-town boy."

Robert Waltrip Short (born September 15, 1924) never claimed to be the only celebrity from Danville, Illinois: When he was growing up in the thirties, the pride of the town was Miss Helen Morgan, then headlining on Broadway and in Hollywood; later on, a schoolmate of Short's named Dick Van Dyke also made it big. In 1971, Short (still in his forties) wrote *Black and White Baby,* a very personal memoir of his childhood. He starts with a vivid description of his life as a so-called ordinary child in your average African American family in the Midwest during the Great Depression. Then he details his early experiences as a babe in the woods of prewar black showbiz, in the years when he played piano and sang on the vaudeville circuit as the twelve-year-old king of swing. (In 1995, Short published a second memoir, *Bobby Short: The Life and Times of a Saloon Singer,* a more formal, full-dress autobiography. This covers the seventy years of his life up to that point but is far more cursory and less intimate.)

Short, who was one of ten children born to Randall and Myrtle Short (six of whom lived to adulthood), was a professional entertainer by the time he was ten. Later in his life, the name "Bobby Short" became a brand name, synonymous with ultra-sophisticated Upper East Siders, TV commercials (most famously a campaign for a perfume called Charlie), and movies like *For Love or Money,* which capitalized on his stature as an distinctly metro-centric icon. Yet for the first forty years of his career, Short was perhaps more peripatetic than anyone else in the music business. In his preteens, he played mostly the Midwest and the South; then he left show business for a few years to finish high school. When he trod the boards again, starting in his late teens, he worked primarily in Chicago and Cleveland; he supposedly did his first recording session in Chicago in 1944 (for Herb Abramson's National Records), but the results were unissued.

Short first became a star not in New York but in Los Angeles; by the turn of the fifties, he was a Hollywood institution. Still, even at that time he was identified with Manhattan; in fact, he embodied the Californian's idea of New York elegance. He headlined at a Hollywood hot spot called the Gala, which Whitaker describes as "the only place that expatriate New Yorkers swore was home to them." He quickly became a favorite of the Hollywood community, a little slice of home for all the émigrés, and even landed a memorable number in the film version of Broadway's hit revue *Call Me Mister.* In the mid-fifties, he let his coastal sophistication go continental when he worked an extended gig at the Mars Club in Paris. Even though he spoke French like a native (he later recorded in the language, including "Bedelia" and "Pilot Me"), he still seemed like an especially recherché Manhattanite.

Back in Los Angeles by 1955, Short was by now working with Phil Moore, the musical Svengali who normally coached impressionable deb stars (most famously Dorothy Dandridge, who never had much of a singing career). For a few years, he steered Short's career both musically and professionally, and Short later acknowledged that he was Moore's most notable male "discovery." Short cut a four-song EP for Albert Marx's Discovery label (arranged and conducted by Buddy Bregman) around this time, and then, fortuitously, at the start of the 12" LP era, came into contact with the Ertegun brothers, who would be the angels of his recording career.

Atlantic Records had made its first fortune by recording black pop music (R&B) for adult black audiences, but with the coming of the long-playing disc, Nesuhi and Ahmet were encouraged to indulge more fully in their love for jazz and standards. Self-proclaimed lovers of the Great American Songbook, the Erteguns had also recorded cabaret entertainers like Mabel Mercer and Sylvia Sims almost from the beginning. It's easy to see how Bobby Short—a cabaret star with, by now, something of a following all over the world, and who played and sang the essential songbook with considerably idiosyncratic diversions in an especially aggressive and rhythmic fashion—would have been precisely their meat.

Short's recording career begins in earnest with the early Atlantic albums, especially the two cut in Los Angeles, *Songs by Bobby Short* (1955) and *Bobby Short* (1957). These laid the foundation for much of the rest of his recording career: "I Like the Likes of You," "Manhattan," "From This Moment On," "Island in the West Indies," "Sand in My Shoes," "Down with Love," "The Most Beautiful Girl in the World," "At the Moving Picture Ball," and others. Any subsequent singer who wishes to do a tribute to Short (as Jane Schecter did in 2006) had better start with these songs.

Short's initial association with Atlantic ran for eight albums—all of which can justifiably be called classics—ending in 1963: There was *Speaking of Love* (1956, the first to be taped in New York), *Nobody Else but Me* (1957), followed by *Swing Me a Sing Song* (1957), *The Mad Twenties* (1958–59), *On the East Side* (1959), and *My Personal Property* (1963). Few singers have created a more rewarding body of work. The symmetry of eight years and eight albums is impressive (even though two of these projects— *Nobody Else but Me* and *My Personal Property*— lingered in the vaults until the seventies).

Truth to tell, the more traditional male cabaret stars of earlier times sounded nothing like anything we would recognize today. Your classic cabaret, upper-crusty, nightclubbing pianist-singer who concentrated on Cole and Noel and Dick and Larry was a lot closer to George Feyer, the man he succeeded at the Café Carlyle. Before Short, most cabaret piano singers were effete and haughty, which was a pose he adopted only for comic purposes; in fact, he reserved his dictiest tone (to use a piece of Harlem Renaissance slang) and his grandest demeanor for Randy Newman's vaudevillian turn "Simon Smith and His Dancing Bear." Certainly, one can't imagine Feyer or Mabel Mercer or any other pre-Short cabarateurs essaying Bessie Smith's "Gimme a Pigfoot" or the Coasters' "Down in Mexico."

For many generations, world citizens regarded Short as Mr. East Side Cabaret, but he was more than that—he was vaudeville, he was the Apollo Theater, he was big bands, he was Broadway, he was Borscht Belt, he was the blues. There was no one better at finding the common ground where these musics meet, as in the scores of the great black songwriters who wrote for Broadway like Andy Razaf and Eubie Blake, as in the songs of Harold Arlen, or anything that was ever sung by Ethel Waters.

Just at the time that Sinatra and Fitzgerald were defining the boundaries of the standard American songbook, Short was pushing back its parameters in unexpected ways. Though Rodgers and Hart, Cole Porter, Irving Berlin, and the brothers Gershwin were his essential bread-and-butter, he also explored a surprisingly wide range of unread pages in the songbook: The first album, for instance, was predominantly the work of Vernon Duke, who composed dozens of standards but wrote only one classic show, *Cabin in the Sky*; Ella Fitzgerald would never do a Vernon Duke songbook album, but Short practically did. He was equally sensitive to contemporary composers: Both Peggy Lee and Tony Bennett were personally close to composer Cy Coleman (as was Short), but Short beat them all to the punch when he cut his own collection of Coleman classics, the aforementioned 1963 *My Personal Property*.

There are strains running through the eight original Atlantics which suggest that the actual albums could be broken down into comprehensive subcollections, and which, when tallied, add up to a remarkable picture of Short's diversity. My favorite imaginary Short album is *Sand in My Shoes*, a collection of Latinalia and exotica, which would start with that tune from the second album and go on to the Duke-Gershwin "Island in the West Indies," "Carioca" (performed in a slow, undulating manner more suggestive of a tango from the Argentine than a rhumba from Rio), "Montevideo," "Hottentot Potentate," "Delia's Gone" (a "Frankie and Johnny"– like Caribbean folk song), "I Left My Hat in Haiti," and "Nagasaki," which, though it heads to another part of the globe, is equally exotic. Both real and ersatz exotic effects turn up in the strangest places, such as the melody to "When Yuba Plays the Rhumba on the Tuba" as an intro to Cole Porter's implicitly Latin "Dream Dancing." As Short himself once described this aspect of his work, "Surely you remember those days in which everyone was calypso mad?"

However, the jury is out as to whether "Down in Mexico" belongs in the Latin collection or in a subsequent set entitled *Bobby Blows the Blues*. "Down in Mexico" is set in a Latin locale, but otherwise is an R&B hit by the Coasters, and therefore would be equally at home on either collection. I once received a press release describing Bobby Short as coming "out of the blues tradition." That's pushing it too far—I wouldn't want to hear Short sing Otis Redding's "Sittin' on the Dock of the Bay" or Robert Johnson's "Hell Hound on My Trail," any more than I want to hear Blind Lemon Jefferson sing "Miss Otis Regrets."

Yet Short's first album concluded with "Gimme a Pigfoot," which was the last song Bessie Smith ever recorded, but which I can't imagine Mabel Mercer singing even if it were the last song on earth. Short virtually never addressed the regulation 12-bar, three-chord blues out of the Mississippi Delta; nor did he follow *Bobby Short Loves Cole Porter* with

Bobby Short Is Ka-Ray-Zy for Leadbelly. Yet he sang any number of songs that bridged the gap between "race" music and Broadway: Clarence Williams's "I Got What It Takes (But It Breaks My Heart to Give It Away)," Willard Robison's gospel-inflected "Wake Up, Chillun, Wake Up," Duke Ellington's blues-tinged "I'm Checkin' Out, Goo'mbye" and "Rocks in My Bed," and later, Big Bill Broonzy's "Romance in the Dark," Rosetta Howard's "You're a Viper," and "The New Orleans Hop Scop Blues," "Four Walls," and "Roller Coaster Blues" (the last three done consecutively on his 1973–74 *Live at the Café Carlyle*).

It's precisely because he's in touch with the blues that he can make camp and even kitsch palatable. *The Mad Twenties* is perhaps his best statement of both driving rhythm and outrageous humor. In singing quasi-novelty songs of the Jazz Age—"Don't Bring Lulu," "Laugh, Clown, Laugh" (a song that brought Leoncavallo's *Pagliacci* into the pop mainstream much as "Poor Butterfly" had already done for *Madama Butterfly*)—Short doesn't even have to exaggerate their silliness to make them funny; nor, for that matter, does he play them entirely straight.

Conversely, when he takes the "sophisticated" route, he makes it clear that he's merely indulging in his Anglophilia, his love for English songs and mannerisms. We've heard him sing in French, and when he sings material associated with Jack Buchanan ("You Sweet So and So," "Her Mother Came Too," "It's Not You") and Leslie Hutchinson ("The Wind in the Willows"), he is best described as singing in *British.* Carmen McRae—surprisingly—was probably the first major African American star to do an album of Noel Coward songs, but even if Short didn't get there firstest, he got there with the mostest on his 1972 double LP *Bobby Short Is Mad About Noel Coward.*

As already mentioned, Atlantic didn't release Short's last album of the period, *My Personal Property,* until a decade or so after it was recorded. In one sense, he was more fortunate than other recording artists of his genre and his generation in that he hit his dry spell (everybody has one sooner or later) and then moved beyond it relatively early. In the mid-sixties, as he told writer Jim Gavin, "It had really begun to hurt. If I told you some of the situations that I found myself in looking for a job, you would not believe it." Around this time, Short went to the Erteguns with the idea of doing a Cole Porter songbook and was rebuffed with, "Who wants to hear Cole Porter?"

However, in 1968, things began to come his way again. He began working at the Café Carlyle, at first as a seasonal replacement for George Feyer (in residence since the venue opened thirteen years earlier), but he quickly made the room his own. Before Bobby, the Café was known only to East Side habitués, jaded roués, and gay divorcées. But with Short installed, the joint became a national shrine for lovers of this music: The Great American Song-

book at last had an address, a place it could call home and weather the storms of changing fashions.

The buzz prompted Atlantic Records to once again come a-calling; this time they were being prodded by Jazz Festival majordomo George Wein, who produced the first of two headline-making Town Hall concerts co-starring Short and Mabel Mercer. In selecting Short as Mercer's co-star, Wein was officially anointing him as the King of Cabaret. The May 1968 concert, followed by a sequel a year later, led to a successful live double album on Atlantic.

In between the two Town Hall shows, Short also did a new studio date for Atlantic, comprised of songs from Ervin Drake's Broadway musical *Her First Roman.* The six songs were never released as a unit, but two of them were mixed in with ten other songs recorded the following spring to form *Jump for Joy,* the first all-new all-Bobby album since 1959. (The Koch reissue, from 2002, unfortunately does not include the additional four *Her First Roman* songs, which should have been included as bonus tracks.) Short's second tenure with Atlantic lasted until 1975, at which time the label finally released *Nobody Else but Me* and *My Personal Property,* along with four new songbook double albums—Cole Porter, Noel Coward, George and Ira Gershwin, Rodgers and Hart—as well as a new in-person album, *Live at the Café Carlyle,* also a double.

In a period when Sinatra, Bennett, and Tormé were all relegated to the sidelines, Bobby Short was suddenly Mr. American Songbook. A mere decade after being forced to do things we don't want to know about, he was incredibly chic—and any other French word you want to throw in there—all over again. He was constantly seen in *New York* magazine, a publication by hip New Yorkers to tell other hip New Yorkers exactly who is hip and who is unhip. He was considered one of the in crowd at the ultra-trendy Elaine's. He was constantly seen with heiress and fashion mogul Gloria Vanderbilt (an even greater friend was and is Jean Bach, one of the great ladies on the sidelines of jazz and later the force behind the award-winning documentary *A Great Day in Harlem*), to the point where it was widely assumed that they were engaged. (In actuality, Short remained a bachelor to the end of his days; if he ever actually cohabited with anyone, it never made the papers.)

On the whole he survived the seventies remarkably well. There are photos of him wearing badly dated turtleneck sweaters and sporting a handlebar mustache, but the music he recorded in these years is still classic Bobby; there would be no Lovin' Spoonful covers or "Abraham, Martin, and John" for this Phy. *Jump for Joy* (1969) is one of Short's finest albums, seamlessly blending superior new songs with the cherished classics. The first category includes the two by Drake, one each by Bacharach and David and Jones and Schmidt, and "Simon Smith and the Amazing Dancing Bear" by Randy Newman, which anticipates the composer's superior recent work for Pixar cartoons. The old songs include two blueses, "Romance in the Dark" and "If You're a Viper," and two Frederick Hollander love songs (both written for Marlene Dietrich) in a medley, "I've Been in Love Before" and "Falling in Love Again," smoothed out from waltz time to common time.

Perhaps it was too much product in too little time: In all, thirteen LPs (a tally that doesn't include the Town Hall–Mabel Mercer recordings) of new Short found their way onto the market, including the five double albums, *Jump for Joy,* and the previously unissued older projects. For whatever reason, Atlantic stopped recording him in 1975. The label might have regretted that decision when, shortly afterward, he began appearing on a long-running national TV campaign for a perfume called Charlie. Between the media coverage, the Charlie commercial, and the reflected glory of Miss Vanderbilt, Short was almost as instantly recognizable as any of *Charlie's Angels.*

There would be two more Atlantic albums as postscripts: *Moments Like This,* recorded in 1981 on the West Coast (his only all-orchestra-and-strings project), and the finest of his songbook projects, *Guess Who's in Town,* a 1986 collection of lyrics by Andy Razaf. He spent most of his remaining career recording regularly and highly satisfactorily for the Cleveland-based Telarc Records, which up to then had been primarily a classical concern. Between 1992 and 1999, he would complete six albums, all first-rate, for Telarc: *Late Night at the Café Carlyle,* with his long-running colleagues bassist Beverly Peer and drummer Robbie Scott (1991); *Swing That Music,* with the Dan Barrett–Howard Alden Quintet (1993); *Songs of New York: Live at the Café Carlyle,* with an another all-star jazz group including trumpeter Warren Vache (1995); *Celebrating 30 Years at the Café Carlyle* (1998); *How's Your Romance?* (1999) and *You're the Top: Love Songs of Cole Porter* (1999), both with Loren Schoenberg's fifteen-piece jazz big band.

The nineties recordings find Short's accompaniments growing more and more ambitious; he began the Telarc association with the familiar backing of just bass and drums, but soon expanded into two configurations of all-star combos. Around the time of his thirtieth anniversary at the Carlyle, in 1998, he began working with his "orchestra," which consisted of eight pieces plus himself, led by musical director Loren Schoenberg. Supposedly, the Café paid Short the same fee whether he employed a trio or big band or even his solo piano, but he brought in the full band anyway, because he figured he'd earned it, and all the music lovers who clustered to him like moths around a flame have benefited from his self-indulgence.

His final recording stemmed from an indulgence of a different kind. The 2000 *Piano* (on the Audiophile label Surroundedby Records) is a set concentrating on his piano playing. Most fans at the time wanted to hear more of his singing, but in the larger context of his career, *Piano* was as welcome as it was inevitable. Besides which, *Piano* is one of his smoothest recordings, the only flaw being the packaging, which somehow omits all the composer credits—a major faux pas in Shortland (as if Bobby or his fans don't care who wrote the songs). Strangely, so does *50 by Bobby Short,* a recommended four-LP box released at Atlantic at the dawn of the digital era—the CD edition is somewhat rare—which samples his career from 1955 to 1975. However, at least here one can read the songwriters' names as they spin 'round on the LP labels. Between Atlantic, Rhino, Koch, and Collectables—as well as the original (and hardly negligible) six CDs of the nineties on Telarc—the bulk of Short's recordings is currently available.

In 2000, Bobby Short was officially recognized as a "living legend" by the Library of Congress. He lived long enough to celebrate several important anniversaries: He made it past his eightieth birthday and he reached the thirty-fifth anniversary of his tenure at the Carlyle. In 2003, he had actually announced that he was retiring from the club after that season—a nice round number—but then a year later he returned. He was set to appear at the Café again in the spring of 2005, but he died on March 21.

Cabaret singing is often depicted as excessively formal, full of classical and even bourgeois effects—like Mabel Mercer's rolled Rs and English accent (both of which were normal to her—not affectations—but that's another story). Yet Short never sounded remotely artificial but brought to cabaret an easy, intimate, persuasive sound, free of anything that vaguely hinted of phony effects.

It would be an overstatement to announce that Bobby Short was the greatest artist ever to sing the Great American Songbook. But not by all that much. Billie Holiday had her own approach to the material that was just as valid, so did Frank, so did Ella. It's all a matter of taste: These various styles are not in competition or conflict; rather, they complement one another. It is, however, safe to say that when Bobby Short was in full throttle, the songbook never sounded better.

Nina Simone (1933–2003)

Some of the most effective singing isn't necessarily singing at all, but what might better be described as a kind of chanting, in a slow, grinding monotone. Sometimes the best way to express an emotion is not to fully state it but to hint at it, to suggest it, to point your listeners toward a certain feeling without spelling it out for them. Sometimes the best way to be sensual is not by letting everything hang out, so to speak, but by holding more than a little back. Sometimes the best way to appreciate the joy of human existence is by dwelling on the dark side.

The only element that Nina Simone does not understate is her intensity; every single number, even when she's having fun, is as serious as your life. And speaking of seriousness, late in her own life Nina Simone was awarded an honorary doctorate, and from then on insisted on being addressed at all times as "Dr. Nina Simone." Her Web site is known as the Dr. Nina Simone Web site, her fan club is called the International Dr. Nina Simone Fan Club.

Somehow the academic honorarium seems especially appropriate in that, by any stretch of the imagination, Simone is both the most serious and the darkest of all divas: Try to imagine a "Dr. Dakota Staton" or a "Dr. Helen Humes"! There would seem to be little joy in what at first seems like a repertoire of pain-etched laments. Yet never make the mistake of pigeonholing Dr. Simone as the black, American, female equivalent of Jacques Brel, all gloom-and-doom, because she'll surprise you. This is the same woman who manages to make "Trouble in Mind" (on *Pastel Blues*) and "Mood Indigo" (on her first album, *Little Girl Blue*) into cheerful songs; in fact, there's an even peppier "Mood Indigo" on her 1966 *Let It All Out*, in which, when she sings the famous opening line "You ain't been blue," she truly sounds as if she hasn't.

Like many African American singers of her generation and earlier, she grew up immersed in gospel and blues, and first established herself in the jazz world. Where she differs from nearly everyone else is that as early as her second album, she began mixing in liberal amounts of "traditional" (i.e., American) folk music, then bringing worldbeat (i.e., international folk music, often related to the lands of the African diaspora) to her mix. In the process, she wound up a pop icon. Obviously, most of her dyed-in-the-wool jazz fans prefer those performances of hers (e.g., "My Baby Just Cares for Me") that are based in the jazz-and-standards repertoire, but the inclusion of all this folk material allowed her to participate in the hootenanny boom of the early sixties—like Odetta with better chord changes. At the same time, it's easy to see how Simone's diversity, her insistence on a wide range of options and directions, have made her an ongoing influence on contemporary generations.

In the mid-nineties, it seemed as though the most important living influences on the better younger jazz artists were those two pure jazz eclectics, Betty Carter and Mark Murphy. In the twenty-first century, it seems as if Nina Simone has become more important than anyone—at the very least because of her impact on Cassandra Wilson and Dianne Reeves. These are the two ladies who are generally most regarded (along with Dee Dee Bridgewater and Diana Krall) as the gold standard of the contemporary generation of jazz singers.

Although Reeves and Wilson perhaps more than Simone are comfortably classified as jazz artists, the influence of Simone on them can be measured in all kinds of ways: They both—Wilson especially—use something of her chanting monotone and they both use material from folk (both Western and non-Western) and pop sources.

One area, however, where no one touches Nina Simone is in the area of attitude: She was the most confrontational of performers, not only aggressive but sometimes outright hostile. The character she plays in the song "Dambala" (on the 1971 live album *It Is Finished*) addresses those listening to her (i.e., the audience) as "slavers." She represented a voice of the civil rights movement for blacks and a expression of liberal guilt for whites.

In *Princess Noire*, the well-researched biography of Simone by Nadine Cohodas (published in 2010), the author quotes an interview from 1965 in which the singer-pianist rather incredibly compares herself to Billie Holiday: "I have gone through things that she went through, both musically and personally; always pushed down, rejected." The reality, as the facts that Cohodas presents make clear, is precisely the opposite. It's true that Simone worked tirelessly to become a concert pianist and never achieved that goal, but once she switched to vernacular music—jazz and pop—she was almost instantly embraced by the commercial music business. Within months, not years, club owners and concert promoters were fighting to book her and record companies were almost literally lining up to make albums with her and continued to do so, even though she never was a top seller. She was also immediately beloved of the leading black intelligentsia—Langston Hughes, James Baldwin, Lorraine Hansberry.

She was born Eunice Waymon in Tryon, North Carolina, in 1933, the next to last of seven children. A classical piano prodigy born to a poor family, the young, gifted, and black little Miss Waymon was given the chance to study formally when her piano teacher started a special fund to subsidize her education and local citizens chipped in with hard-won Depression dollars. In her teens, she came to New York to attend Juilliard and eventually she rejoined her family in Philadelphia, where she found work teaching piano and began working as a pianist-singer in Atlantic City in the early fifties. She had never taken singing seriously before, but, like Jeri Southern, when she was offered a job that paid more if she sang, she took it. Still ashamed of working in the popular music world, she decided to take on a stage name, which she concocted by combining the Spanish word for "little girl" with the surname of French actress Simone Signoret.

Within a very short time, Nina Simone was playing and singing in increasingly important clubs. In 1957, Bethlehem Records recorded fourteen tracks by Simone with a trio of Jimmy Bond (bass) and

Albert "Tootie" Heath (drums), which they spread over two albums, *Jazz as Played in an Exclusive Side Street Club* (aka *Little Girl Blue*) and *Nina Simone and Her Friends* (an anthology). The twenty-four-year-old pianist-singer hit the jackpot on her first shot right out of the box when one track from the album, her slow, sensual four-minute treatment of the Gershwin brothers' "I Love You, Porgy" was released as a single, and became a genuine chart hit. (It's been claimed that "Porgy" sold a million copies. This seems unlikely—few pure jazz piano trio records without Belford Hendricks–style strings or dopey choirs ever sold in that kind of quantity, and Bethlehem hardly had the resources to promote, distribute, or even manufacture a million-seller.)

"Porgy" was undeniably a hit, though, and there were follow-ups: The first side of the *Exclusive Side Street Club* album concluded with two Gus Kahn–Walter Donaldson songs from the 1928 *Whoopee!*, "Love Me or Leave Me" and "My Baby Just Cares for Me." The former was one of several early Simone tracks (the opener, "Mood Indigo," was another) that included a long Baroque section. That fugal variation would remain intact when she performed "Love Me or Leave Me" on *The Ed Sullivan Show* in 1960 as well as when she rerecorded the song on her 1966 *Let It All Out*. "My Baby Just Cares for Me" was something else entirely. She rendered this novelty-rhythm song in a half-fast medium-shuffle beat that was similar to—but slower than—most of Louis Prima's arrangements of the period. In 1987, "My Baby Just Cares for Me" was heard in an English TV commercial and then it, too, turned up on local charts. (Originally it was a career signature for Eddie Cantor.)

The Bethlehem tracks, about 50 percent of which are instrumentals, constitute her most purely jazzy recordings. Even if she had never sung a note, Simone, like Nat Cole, could certainly have scored as a mass-market pianist like Ahmad Jamal or Ramsey Lewis. After Bethlehem, between 1959 and 1964 she recorded ten LPs for Colpix, a label originally founded by Columbia Pictures to exploit movie- and TV-oriented properties. She then did seven albums for Philips from 1964 to 1967. These seventeen albums constitute the bulk of her work in the field of jazz and standards. In 1959, practically everything she did could be considered jazz; by 1969, the jazz elements are few and far between, though not totally gone.

The 1962 *Nina Simone Sings Ellington* is perhaps the closest she ever came to an album that consists entirely of jazz and/or the Great American Songbook, and parts of it are also her most traditional pop-oriented project, one that employs a full studio orchestra with strings plus choir. Yet she's still determined to give listeners something out of the ordinary, and surprises us with four really unusual Ducal items: "Hey, Buddy Bolden," "You Better Know It," "The Gal from Joe's" (unsung since Ivie

Anderson, though later remade by Simone), and "I Like the Sunrise." Simone brings out the religious overtones of "Sunrise" in a very unusual choral arrangement that's more like Bach than Mahalia Jackson. Her version suggests that "Sunrise" could serve as the spirtual section for *The Liberian Suite*, much as "Come Sunday" does for *Black, Brown and Beige,* and that both pieces rank among Ellington's most significant religious statements prior to the Sacred Concerts. In the best tradition of Billie Holiday, Simone also turns "Solitude" into a prayerlike invocation.

Around this same time, another African American pianist-singer and musical iconoclast, Ray Charles, was recording a lot of standards, and the difference in their approaches is illuminating: Charles did whole albums of standards, whereas, with the exception of the Ellington package and the Bethlehem album, Simone kept mixing things up. Likewise, when Charles addressed the idiom of Mel Tormé or Tony Bennett, he never attempted to sound like them, but he did do albums in collaboration with their most famous orchestrators, Marty Paich and Ralph Burns. As a result, such Charles albums as *Genius Hits the Road* and *Sweet and Sour Tears* don't sound like the Genius's earlier soul-R&B work, but have more of a big band sound that complements the traditional adult pop repertoire. Simone, on the other hand, essentially sings Cole Porter ("The Laziest Gal in Town") and Irving Berlin ("You Can Have Him") with the same basic approach that she brings to Screamin' Jay Hawkins's "I Put a Spell on You" or folk sources ("Black Is the Color of My True Love's Hair").

Thus, while she always performed an eclectic mix of material—there are folk songs in the early as well as the later periods—there is a general trajectory in her music, from jazz and traditional adult pop to something closer to rock and youth pop. There's more Cole Porter in the early period (especially on Colpix) and more Bob Dylan in the later (on RCA); the middle years (on Philips) are probably the most diverse. Some of the more Broadway-oriented sessions of the mid-sixties use lush string orchestrations by Hal Mooney, who had fulfilled the same function for Sarah Vaughan, Kay Starr, and other "conventional" jazz-pop singers. Many of Simone's late sixties sides for RCA take the opposite tack and are totally psychedelic, pitched at the youth market with 16th-note rhythms and yeah-yeah-yeah backup vocals. But by and large, Simone offers a unified sound, whether she's singing Bob Merrill or Bob Dylan, Vernon Duke or Duke Ellington. The overall consistency of her approach empowered her to address a diverse range of material.

In 2005, two years after Simone's death, a large group of her early Colpix albums were at last reissued by EMI U.K.; this was probably the last major section of her discography not yet on CD. It's well worth owning all of Simone's albums in digital sound file (iTunes) format, because her packages are so overwhelmingly diverse that it often makes more sense to hop around from one track to another than it does to listen to one whole album in sequence as originally released. She will leap from a tender ballad to an R&B jump tune to a calypso to a civil rights anthem in a heartbeat, from Leonard Cohen or Bob Dylan to Jule Styne without even that. Nina Simone isn't just eclectic, she's all over the place, and yet at the same time she's remarkably consistent.

Some singers (Frank Sinatra, Ella Fitzgerald), as we've seen, are about albums, others are about singles (Sam Cooke), but Nina Simone is something else entirely. She recorded relatively few unified concept albums—*Nina Sings Ellington* and *Nina Simone Sings the Blues* are the two that stand out, although her many live concert recordings should perhaps be considered thematic packages (especially in that her 1963 performance at Carnegie Hall yielded two albums' worth of material, the second of which was a program of traditional folk songs released under the title of *Folksy Nina*). With Simone, it's instructive and useful to deconstruct the CDs into playlists organized around different genres: Nina Simone Sings Broadway, Nina Simone Sings Spirituals, Nina Simone Sings the Blues.

In 2006, the producer Richard Seidel assembled eleven tracks from the RCA period in *Forever Young, Gifted and Black: Songs of Freedom and Spirit,* which encompassed most of the material from the years 1967–69 that directly addressed the civil rights movement. It was an inspired compilation, one that shows that listening to Simone genre by genre can be even more pleasurable than listening to whole albums.

I would love to see a *Simone Sings Broadway* compilation that would include such well-known songs as "Ain't Got No" from *Hair* (a chart hit for her in the U.K.—and also a civil rights song), "Feelin' Good" from *Roar of the Greasepaint,* and such obscure ones as "Beautiful Land" from the same show, not to mention "Marriage Is for Old Folks" from *The Secret Life of Walter Mitty* and "Who Am I?" from Leonard Bernstein's version of *Peter Pan.* A new blues collection—a supplement to the blues album she did for RCA in 1966 and 1967—would include mostly songs with blues elements and blues associations, such as her oft recorded "Sugar in My Bowl" (her variation on a Bessie Smith double entendre), "Trouble in Mind," and "Nobody Knows You When You're Down and Out."

There also should be a collection of Simone doing traditional spirituals and religious songs: One of her most enjoyable performances is the rollicking children's counting song "Children Go Where I Send You," and in contrast, her reverential reading of Thomas A. Dorsey's archetypal gospel song "Take My Hand, Precious Lord." "Children Go Where I Send You" turns up in a short and sweet studio version on *The Amazing Nina Simone* and in a long and

drawn-out version on *Nina at the Village Gate,* and it's hard to say which treatment is the more satisfactory. The song already does double duty, as a spiritual that satisfies in an earthly way, more rhythmic than religious; the studio version gets right to the point, but the *Village Gate* version climaxes an outstanding live set. Coming after a string of downers, it lets us leave the club with a shot of adrenaline.

She took the traditional "Balm in Gilead" and set it to something of a disco beat—but surprisingly it works. And she did a rousingly traditional version of "Sinnerman," a fire-and-brimstone sermon set to music that finds her in a characteristic mood of "J'Accuse!" There's even more fire and brimstone in "Go to Hell," which is not a song of defiance but a cautionary tale, telling the listener where he'll wind up if he doesn't straighten up and fly right. You could also construct a whole album of folk songs, both American and international, even avoiding those on *Folksy Nina.* In fact, you could put together an album of traditional American and European songs (i.e., from the white world), and another of traditional music from the African diaspora, songs from Africa and the Caribbean, like "West Wind Woman," and "See-Line Woman." The latter is a Simone signature (from the 1964 *Broadway-Blues-Ballads*) that anticipates virtually the entire career of Cassandra Wilson.

The title of *Broadway-Blues-Ballads* might lead one to believe that it contains more standards, but, unfortunately, there are five generally undistinguished contempop tunes by Bennie Benjamin, a former Tin Pan Alley–ite gone rock 'n' roll; his "Don't Let Me Be Misunderstood" turned out to be a Simone classic, but his other four songs on the CD are best forgotten. Yet the rest of *Broadway-Blues-Ballads* is Simone at her absolute best, including "The Laziest Gal in Town" (a Cole Porter song from 1927 made famous by Marlene Dietrich in Alfred Hitchcock's 1950 *Stage Fright*), which she intones with a lazy, Southern accent and Billie Holiday–like emphasis; "Night Song" from *Golden Boy;* "Something Wonderful" from *The King and I;* and her infectiously rhythmic calypso "See-Line Woman." Even once she has conditioned us to expect the unexpected, she manages to surprise us: She follows Rodgers and Hammerstein with "Nobody," a comedy monologue by Bert Williams from 1906.

By the mid- to late sixties, her work was sounding less as if it belonged on jazz or traditional pop radio stations than as if it were being packaged for classic rock formats. Yet at the height of this occasionally overproduced period, she recorded her simplest, starkest, and, in many ways, most moving album, the aptly titled *Nina Simone and Piano!,* a set for just voice and keyboard. Although concentrating on contemporary songs (including "I Think It's Going to Rain Today" by the then virtually unknown Randy Newman, which Simone inspired Norah Jones to sing thirty-five years later), she treats us to an exceptionally chilling reading of Hoagy Carmichael's "I Get Along Without You Very Well (Except Sometimes)" as well as "Who Am I?," that rare song with both words and music by Leonard Bernstein.

The CD edition of *Nina Simone and Piano!* is even better than the LP in that it annexes four previously unused songs from the same period with the same voice-and-keyboard setting, three of which are from the standard songbook: Kern's "In Love in Vain," "Man with the Horn," and "I'll Look Around." Around the same time, Simone recorded a partially live album called *Emergency Ward,* which opens with a twenty-minute track called "My Sweet Lord—Today Is a Killer" (not exactly a medley; the two songs just kind of run in and out of each other) that illustrates her ability if not to pad a song, then certainly to stretch it as far as it will go. *Nina Simone and Piano!* makes the opposite point, that she's never better than when she cuts to the chase and concentrates on the bare essentials.

In 1960 she was unique among singers in jazz clubs by singing folk songs (like "House of the Rising Sun," made into a hit by the British band the Animals), but by 1970 she was moving counter to trends by continuing to do the occasional song by Porter or Berlin. She had a particular genius for finding material that fits into both categories, like "Wild Is the Wind," a movie theme by Russian-born composer Dimitri Tiomkin written to sound like a traditional American folk song. "Pirate Jenny," from *The Threepenny Opera,* is a show tune by white German males that, as performed by Simone, rather violently protests the conditions that both people of color (blacks) and people of gender (women) are forced to put up with.

It's Simone's habit to ignore the distinction between songs of love and songs of freedom: In "Night Song," from *Golden Boy* and sung by her on *Broadway-Blues-Ballads,* when she sings "Where do you go when your brain is on fire," is it because her man done her wrong or because she's forced to drink from a water fountain labeled "Colored"? She's forever finding a note of Afro militancy in unlikely places. *Broadway-Blues-Ballads* opens with "Don't Let Me Be Misunderstood," on which she also blurs the distinction between the suffering one person does for another in a dysfunctional relationship and the suffering that black people have endured since they were dragged here in chains four hundred years ago. That 1964 album is the one that contains Bert Williams's "Nobody," the most famous piece of material by the first African American superstar, who performed it in the 1906 *Abyssinia.* Allen Woll, in his *Black Musical Theatre,* acknowledges that this early all-black entertainment was far from your average "coon"-minstrel show and presented a comparatively enlightened view of black culture, at least for the period. Still, before Simone did it, "Nobody" could have imagined what Simone

would do with the song, transforming what was once a comic complaint of Williams's low-life character—griping that there's no one to soothe his "thumpin', bumpin' brain"—into a plea for black solidarity. It's as if she's asking: Who, among the white people, gives a Mississippi Goddam about the rest of us? Comes back the answer: Nobody.

If she can take lighthearted—sometimes even silly—pieces like "Nobody" and make them deadly serious, she can also take the opposite tack: Some of her most politically charged pieces are also her most entertaining. "Go Limp," an adaptation of the old English folk song "Sweet Betsy from Pike," is a comedy piece about a mother cautioning her daughter not to go on Freedom Rides for fear that the sit-in will become a love-in and that the young virgin will "give her nuclear secrets away." Here, Simone savages the conventions of the pop-folk movement, describing the proceedings as a "hootenanny" and berating the audience to sing "too-ra-ly-ay" along with her. From the titles, Simone's originals, "Old Jim Crow" and "Mississippi Goddam" (both heard on *In Concert,* 1964), may sound like searing indictments of white prejudice—and in fact they are—but she's set them to melodies that are catchy, upbeat, even jocular. Simone even describes "Mississippi Goddam" as a "show tune," but the musical comedy to which it belongs "hasn't been written yet."

The last album of Simone's pinnacle years was titled, appropriately, *It Is Finished* (RCA, 1974). By the mid-seventies, Simone was known as a black militant who sang, although the recordings from her early (pre-1965) period, before she was totally swept up in the movement, show that she was an outstanding artist well before her music became so politically charged. What is particularly unfortunate is that Simone was possibly the only jazz singer of her generation who had the potential to keep on headlining straight through the seventies and eighties: Unlike the Great American Songbook, Simone's unique mixture of jazz, folk, gospel, and soul essentially never went out of fashion.

Yet as Cohodas shows us in *Princess Noire,* Simone's last thirty years were generally miserable ones. Characteristically, she tended to blame her problems on the white establishment, yet she also railed against black audiences when she felt they didn't appreciate or support her enough. Cohodas provides dozens if not hundreds of examples: At the beginning of her career, Simone admonished club audiences for talking during her show; later, she verbally attacked crowds when they weren't vociferous enough in their applause and enthusiasm. "You know, being black lends to one's paranoidness," she said on the stage of the Apollo Theater. But it was her own mental issues, not racial conspiracy, that held her back, as Cohodas lays out in painful detail.

As many as twenty Nina Simone albums may have been released after the RCA period; it's hard to tell which of these recordings are live and which are studio recordings (and which are bootlegs). However, I have heard three later studio sessions that can be described as classic Nina. The 1978 *Baltimore,* despite a bit more electronics than I would prefer (typical of the era and the CTI label in general), has several absolutely essential tracks, starting with Randy Newman's title song, which like many on the album, uses a heavy electric bass backbeat in a quasi-reggae rhythm. Her singing on Bernard Ighner's "Everything Must Change" is stark and understated, using primarily her own acoustic piano and a comparatively subtle hint of strings, and generally shows why this much-covered song was on its way to becoming a contemporary standard. As she had with many other songs, Simone sings it like a prayer—and, likewise, the traditional spiritual "Balm in Gilead," also delivered with a Bob Marley beat, is church music for the postmodern era.

Fodder on My Wings was produced in New York in 1982 for a French label: The overall beat this time is not reggae but calypso, and in the tradition of the great calypsonians, most of the lyrics are very personal and topical. She rewrites the 1972 Irish pop hit "Alone Again (Naturally)" into an autobiographical account of her relationship with her father. The traditional Trinidadian "Run Joe" becomes a memoir of a trip to an African discotheque retitled "Liberian Calypso." "I Was Just a Dog to Them" and "Color Is a Beautiful Thing" (kind of an updated "Mississippi Goddam") are two additional diatribes, albeit highly catchy ones. Curiously, she repeats two spirituals from *Baltimore,* "Balm in Gilead," here sung in French, and "If You Pray Right," which had evolved from an African chant and is here titled "Heaven Belongs to You."

Taped the year that Simone turned sixty, *A Single Woman* is a marvelous late-in-life statement and career capper. It's also thoroughly personal and autobiographical; she almost sounds as if she's mellowed with age and, by now, years and years of behavioral meds; adding to the mellowness, this was her only album with full orchestra and strings in almost thirty years. The centerpiece here is three songs by poet-composer Rod McKuen that she might have heard on Frank Sinatra's 1969 album *A Man Alone.* "A Single Woman," "Lonesome Cities," and "Love's Been Good to Me" (an even more folky paraphrase of "It Was a Very Good Year"): All of these sounded slightly peculiar coming from Sinatra—as if they took him out of his milieu—but seem just right from the sixty-year-old Simone, whose comfort zone was the whole world. "Papa Can You Hear Me?" was written for Streisand in *Yentl;* in the film, it's very specific to the story, but Simone, once again bemoaning her own late, lamented father, makes it universal—it's no longer just Yentl's song (or even Babs's song), it's everybody's story. But when Simone begins with "Swing Low Sweet Chariot," we know we're not in the land of Isaac Bashevis Singer anymore.

She spent most of her later years in France, where she died in 2003, aged seventy. These three studio albums were among the few high spots in a long, three-decade period of decline, of failing to show up for major concerts and then being erratic and undependable even when she did make it on stage. Still, Simone's legacy is secure—there have been no fewer than four books on her, starting with the lady's own somewhat-skewed memoir, the 1992 *I Put a Spell on You,* and including, most recently, Ms. Cohodas's highly recommended *Princess Noire.* There have been tribute albums and shows by Nina's daughter, Lisa Stroud, who works under the name Simone, and the fine British "alt cabaret" singer Barb Jungr. I noted at the beginning that at least two of the gold-standard jazz singers of recent decades, Dianne Reeves and Cassandra Wilson, name her as a major influence.

In the twenty-first century, that influence has spread and multiplied. Simone's model of mixing genres—a little pop, a little folk, a little soul—has become widely prevalent, and you can hear Nina Simone variations in everybody from Norah Jones on sideways. (There even was a house music–style album that sampled her original master tapes, *Remixed & Reimagined,* released by Sony in 2006.) In 2010, almost every movie comedy or TV drama has a snippet of someone doing a Nina Simone imitation somewhere on its sound track. Yet Simone's own singing remains inimitable: an auditory balm in Gilead, a sound to heal a sin-sick soul.

Frank Sinatra (1915–1998)

No other artist was so wide-ranging in his scope, so expansive in his vision, so far-reaching in his accomplishments as Frank Sinatra. In over sixty years of singing before the public, there was hardly an area of American music that Sinatra didn't conquer. Nor was there a performance medium immune to his dynamic energy, as evidenced by his multimedia success in radio, recordings, film, and television. (Even many items in the local bookstore were driven by him, to the endless annoyance of the singer and his family.)

The essential appeal of Sinatra comes from the way he was able to put so much of himself into every performance, into every song, on every level; he simply covered more ground, both stylistically and philosophically, than anyone else. Like Ella Fitzgerald, he possessed impeccable musicianship, and like Mabel Mercer, he could make you feel every syllable. He integrated music and emotion to such a degree that they're impossible to extricate from each other in his performances. Sinatra elevated pop singing into a rarefied level of musical acting.

Sinatra achieved living legend status long before he turned thirty, and well before 1950 the first of many generations began growing up not just fascinated but mesmerized by him. He turned his private life into his own personal mythology: We were entranced by his affairs and his high-rolling, high-living bachelor lifestyle (as in "Luck Be a Lady"), and we also admired his paternal, familial side (as in "Soliloquy"). We admired his campaigning for civil rights as well as his connections with presidents from Roosevelt to Kennedy to Nixon and Reagan. We envied his unending list of boudoir conquests and even though we hardly approved of his consorting with notorious figures of the underworld, we still couldn't take our eyes off him. He was everything we wanted to be: swinging, romantic, erotic, melancholy, and even a little bit dangerous.

Sinatra employed all the tools available in both drama and music, leading Duke Ellington to famously describe him in performance as "the ultimate in theatre." He could render "One for My Baby" or "Angel Eyes" in the most intimate fashion, making the listener suspend all disbelief and engage in what Sinatra made us all feel was a one-on-one discourse with him. Then, he would immediately turn 180 degrees and launch into the brashly extroverted "My Way," in which we would empathize with him in an entirely different way—this time in a mass celebration of our collective self. He could be swingingly exhilarating, then, in the blink of an eye, switch to a saloon song so convincingly morbid he underscores the hopelessness of novelist Patrick White's declaration that "only those who suffer can understand what life is about."

Sinatra could treat "Spring Is Here" more sensitively than even librettist Lorenz Hart could have envisioned, as an exquisite vehicle for self-examination of the most personal kind—with his heart as exposed as a plumber's *tuchus*. But if Sinatra knew exactly which texts to take very seriously, he also knew which ones were strictly for fun. He plays with the nonsensical lyrics of the likes of "Ring-a-Ding-Ding!" and treats the songs on his 1955 masterpiece *Songs for Swingin' Lovers* like purely rhythmic baubles. It's true that if tenderness were a crime, Sinatra would have been on death row, yet at the same time he had a black belt in swinging, taking a jazzy big band chart and making it move.

In the fall of 1942, not long after he had parted company with Tommy Dorsey, Sinatra had a conversation with publicist and journalist Gary Stewart. "Frank outlined everything he wanted to do in his career," Stewart later recollected. "He said, 'I want to make records, I want to do radio, I want to go to Hollywood and make pictures.' He even said, 'And someday I'd even like to win an Academy Award.'" It wasn't only Sinatra's friends who observed this determination; Mitch Miller, the singer's onetime producer—and sparring partner—stressed the same point: "Sinatra had a direction, he knew where he was going, come hell or high water."

By the late 1950s, Sinatra's vision was even more overtly ambitious than it had been since the beginning—by now "the Chairman of the Board" (who had since won two Oscars) sought to own his own record company, to control where he sang, and produce his own motion pictures. But then his career had always been marked by outsized aspirations: Sinatra started with the drive to transform himself into the greatest singer of popular songs that ever would be, and eventually made himself into something even bigger than that. Still, he never grew too big to forget that he started as a "boy singer" in the big band era.

According to legend, the Sinatra career begins when the teenaged Hobokenite catches Bing Crosby live at the Paramount Theatre in the early 1930s. Crosby, whom Sinatra later deemed "the father of my career," inspired him in two distinct areas—the multimedia aspect (making it simultaneously in radio, pictures, and recordings), and in pioneering the idea of intimacy in popular singing. Radio writer Norman Corwin once described the new kind of relationship between performer and audience made possible by radio, the new medium of the twentieth century: "You're talking to a great many people, [but] in their homes. It's at once public and yet private."

Sinatra was born on December 12, 1915, in Hoboken, New Jersey, an only child. Both he and his father, Martin Sinatra, were to a large extent dominated by the oppressively matriarchal Dolly Sinatra, who not only ran the family with an iron hand but also held most of Hoboken and the local wing of the Democratic Party in her grip. Like most middle-class kids of the twenties and thirties, Sinatra grew up exposed to pop music through 78 rpm recordings and the burgeoning medium of radio. As much as he furthered the art of popular music, he also remained firmly grounded in the classic American songs of his youth: He was not only faithful to the major stars like Cole Porter and George Gershwin, but continued to sing the glories of any number of first-rate but less celebrated Tin Pan Alley craftsmen like Walter Donaldson and Jimmy McHugh.

Apart from canonizing the Great American Songbook, Sinatra's entire motivation, from his earliest amateur appearances onward, was in finding a way to establish an ever more direct connection with audiences. Other inspirations helped: the jazzy vocalizing of Louis Armstrong, the broadened emotional canvas of Billie Holiday, and numerous attributes of two notable employers, Harry James and Tommy Dorsey (the latter being announced on radio shows as "the star maker of the music world"). From trumpeter James, Sinatra gleaned his bravura, his swaggering style; from trombonist Dorsey, the singer learned how to, in the words of essayist Wilfrid Sheed, "hold a note, hold his liquor and hold a grudge."

Sinatra's own accounts of the Dorsey apprenticeship center on his absorption of what has come to be referred to as the trombonist's "long breath" technique. This enabled him to communicate an entire phrase of a song on a single breath in order to make his singing more conversational. Prior to this time, singers were prone to chop up a line into several breaths, thus hindering the listener from following the thread of the story. Sinatra has repeatedly cited this as the single most important characteristic of his own style—the element that allowed him to create such a sensation upon going out as a solo act at the end of 1942.

He was studying Dorsey's legato style long before he actually joined the orchestra of the "Sentimental Gentleman of Swing" at the start of 1940. Indeed, the young singer's most notable record of his six months with Harry James was "All or Nothing at All," which shows him already beginning to lean toward the long breath sound. However, under Dorsey's genius tutelary, Sinatra's use of the technique blossomed. It's particularly evident in the single most famous product of the Dorsey-Sinatra collaboration, "I'll Never Smile Again," which introduced the "Sentimentalist" sound, a combination of super-close harmony and superslow tempo.

Dorsey here dispenses with the full band, using only Sinatra and the band's vocal group, the Pied Pipers (including another future star, Jo Stafford), backed by a rhythm section (including a celesta that Sinatra asked pianist Joe Bushkin to play) and his own trombone. "We were rehearsing on a Saturday afternoon, at the Astor Hotel," the singer later recalled, "and Tommy asked Joe Bushkin to play the song. I noticed that everybody suddenly was very quiet. There was a feeling of a kind of eeriness that took place, as though we all knew that this would be a big, big hit, and that it was a lovely song."

The synergy between Sinatra and Dorsey was wondrous to behold. On "Say It," one of the earliest TD-FS titles (and a performance that inspired John Coltrane several decades later, and Kurt Elling several more generations after that), the give and take is remarkable, especially considering that the two voices never actually interact. The arrangement is so simple as to be almost nonexistent: We open with Dorsey playing the melody, then Sinatra sings the chorus, then there's eight bars of the band before Dorsey and his trombone take it out. Dorsey's playing is so tightly focused, warm, and human that he sounds almost like a human voice; Sinatra's singing has such control and musicianship that he sounds almost like a virtuoso instrumentalist—a classical violinist. They're so in sync with each other that they might as well be the same person, like Louis Armstrong playing, then singing. They're erasing the distance between singers and instrumentalists, making you forget that there's a difference between voices emanating from flesh and blood and those emanating from metal implements.

The classic Sinatra-Dorsey ballads like "Fools Rush In," "I'll Be Seeing You," "Without a Song," and especially Sinatra's own "This Love of Mine" would have an immediate impact on his career. Even at this early stage of the game, he's one of the few singers of the period (and practically the only one working with a swing band) who is able to tell a complete story, with a beginning, middle, and end, in the scant space of a single chorus and sixteen lines of text. Still, he was feeling increasingly constricted by the dance band format—the rigid foxtrot tempo, the three-chorus structure, the tradition of confining the vocalist to a single 32-bar "refrain" in the center.

"Everything Happens to Me" (from February 1941) shows how Sinatra was beginning to make things go his way even while he was still an employee of the Dorsey organization. Here's a dance record that's practically a vocal record, in which Sinatra is no longer a humble band vocalist but a headlining star while the Dorsey orchestra is relegated to his accompaniment, a setup that predicts the entire development of postwar pop. By January 1942, he was able to take things even further: In his "pilot" session as a "single" act (done while still under Dorsey's employ), Sinatra waxed four exquisite arrangements by longtime musical director Axel Stordahl (most notably his first of six completely different record arrangements of "Night and Day"). Both the superlative results and the promising sales boded well for his leaving the band for a solo career.

That career only happened after Sinatra was able to extricate himself from his contractual obligations to Dorsey, a feat of legal maneuvering that seemed to occupy half the lawyers in the country for several years. It's a common mistake, when examining the entire course of the Sinatra story, to write off Sinatra's "sideman" period, from 1939 to 1942, as a mere prelude to his mature career. Rather, the James and Dorsey years are a great and fruitful Sinatra era just like any other. In fact, throughout the sideman period, we hear foreshadowings of later phases: "I'll Never Smile Again" and "All or Nothing at All" point to the classic love songs of the mid-forties, while "The One I Love Belongs to Somebody Else" and "Oh Look at Me Now" anticipate the songs for swingin' lovers of the fifties. Sinatra's four years with James and Dorsey weren't just the equivalent of his college education, they were the foundation of the most remarkable career in all of American popular music.

As early as the World War II period, the press had a name for it: "Sinatrauma." No one ever documented the first Sinatra swoon, although it's rumored to have happened as early as his 1935 tour with the Hoboken Four and Major Bowes's amateur troupe. Already in his Dorsey days, Sinatra was being bannered as "the Voice That Is Thrilling Millions," and by the time he opened in his breakthrough solo engagement, at the New York Paramount at the end of 1942, the billing had come true. Female fans mobbed the theater, and when he launched into one of his classic love songs, like "Where or When," "These Foolish Things," or "Someone to Watch over Me," hordes of pubescent girls would swoon and shriek en masse. As the singer himself described it, "If I bent a note, looped a note, they went wild."

The reaction of young women to Sinatra was so unprecedented that not even George Evans, Sinatra's press agent supreme and the Napoleon of the news media, could have thought it up. Evans eventually began choreographing and stage-managing the swooning and screaming, but it started as a genuine grassroots movement. The hysteria surrounding Sinatra was like nothing that had ever been seen before, and in its day far more shocking than that which later greeted Elvis Presley or the Beatles. They were liked only by kids, in the beginning at least. Yet while a few grown-ups recoiled at the fanaticism that Sinatra inspired, almost no one professed to not liking his singing. As *The New York Times* reported in 1943, "Mature ladies are as apt to grow as hysterical as teenagers."

And it wasn't only females who got so excited, as Tony Bennett, who was sixteen at the time of Sinatra's initial triumph, recalls. "I was one of the original Sinatra groupies. I used to get out of classes to see him at the New York Paramount. I would stay for seven shows a day at the Paramount, and just watch him over and over again. I didn't even mind having to sit through the movie seven times." According to a report from Auckland, New Zealand, "Tests at dairy farms where radios are played show that cows produce the most milk when listening to recordings" by Sinatra.

What was it about Sinatra's singing that inspired this reaction? In leaving his dependable weekly paycheck with Dorsey, he was gambling his future on the idea that the world was ready for a new, romantic sound. No pop singer had captured the public's imagination so vividly since Bing Crosby a decade earlier. And Sinatra took the concepts of naturalism and intimacy that the Old Groaner had pioneered and took them to the limit. Where Crosby, as friend Rosemary Clooney has pointed out, was uncomfortable with the direct statement of "I love you" in a song, Sinatra's singing was always charged with an unmistakable erotic energy.

Sinatra only started showing his rough side later on; he was tender long before he was tough. This was in an age when even the romantic leading men of the era were rarely sensitive in the way we use the term today. When girls of the war generation were exposed to the new and heavily romantic sound of Sinatra, they couldn't help responding dramatically. As Clooney said, "I think that it was just a very appealing, personal sound that girls my age just adored."

The Sinatra sound was no accident: The singer, working in conjunction with musical director Axel Stordahl, crafted it slowly and carefully. The first step was to distinguish him from the other singers of the period, both those still singing with the bands and those who were following Sinatra's lead out of them. Sinatra and Stordahl developed a lushly ro-

mantic, almost semiclassical sound that relied heavily on violins. As longtime Sinatra arranger Billy May later observed, it's important to point out that Sinatra insisted on using twelve strings at a time when Crosby was employing only four. The heavy reliance on "strads" helped Sinatra create a lushly sensual atmosphere, one that had little in common with the characteristic dance band sound of the era.

Very early in the game, it occurred to him that the basic musical repertoire afforded to pop singers and bandleaders would not be enough for him to both develop and apply this miraculous talent. In those days performers sang current hits almost exclusively: Sinatra was the first singer to make a conspicuous point of going back to the great songs of Cole Porter, Rodgers and Hart, Jerome Kern, the Gershwin brothers, and the other canonical musical comedy composers of the interwar years. In doing so, he established the basic parameters of what later became known as the Great American Songbook, leaving everyone else to rummage through his leftovers. Sinatra's influence in determining what singers sang after him is immeasurable.

It's true that no one introduced more standards than Fred Astaire, but no performer made more existing songs into standards than Sinatra—including a great many of the songs written for Astaire. "If you look at songs like 'Glad to Be Unhappy,'" Frank Military, Sinatra's assistant for most of the fifties (and longtime head of Warner-Chappell Music New York), points out, Sinatra brought them into the mainstream. "He even took songs out of flop shows, like 'Guess I'll Hang My Tears Out to Dry,' and made them into important standards." Sinatra almost singlehandedly invented the concept of the popular song standard. Great as Nat King Cole was, the best that he could do for "Angel Eyes" was to make it a hit; it took Sinatra to turn it into a classic.

Sinatra called it his "Year of Mondays," yet it lasted much longer—he started his downward slide around 1948 and didn't climb back on top until 1953. The reasons were manifold: musical, cultural, and personal. It was a one-man confluence of disasters.

On the most basic level, audiences were gradually tiring of the lushly romantic Frank Sinatra–Axel Stordahl sound of the forties. Sinatra had inadvertently launched an entire epoch of pop by inspiring dozens of singers to leave the big bands that spawned them and take to the hit singles charts on their own. Yet most of the hits of the postwar era were hardly in Sinatra's image—where he was singing Cole Porter, the airwaves were filled with novelty songs that predicted the coming of the rock 'n' roll era a decade later. Where Sinatra was singing "It Never Entered My Mind" and "Embraceable You," the hits of the age were more like "Bongo! Bongo! Bongo! I Don't Want to Leave the Congo (Civilization)" and even "How Much Is That Doggie in the Window?" Though regarded across the music industry as the classiest of class acts, Sinatra was also increasingly regarded as a leftover of the war years. He had reached an early peak in 1945, the year of his MGM musical debut, *Anchors Aweigh,* one of the most successful films of the decade, and one that also linked him to a wartime image.

Then, too, his personal associations were turning various factions against him: His support of President Roosevelt and his campaign against bigotry and intolerance led the conservative press (from William Randolph Hearst on down) to put him on their enemies list. In those pre-TV and pre-Internet days, newspapers ran the world, and when Sinatra belted a columnist (the obnoxious Lee Mortimer, who, by all accounts, deserved it), the entire news media turned on him. Therefore, when the press uncovered some genuine dirt on him, like his insistence on socializing with mafiosi, they didn't pull their punches either. By the end of the decade, Sinatra was enmeshed in another kind of scandal of the type that ruined more than a few careers back then, when he left the mother of his children (his first wife, Nancy Sinatra) to chase after the most glamorous movie star of that or any other era (Ava Gardner).

Sinatra was no longer believable. In films and radio shows, his character had been a shy, skinny, retiring wallflower, the kind that teenage girls, used to all kinds of aggressive male wolves, found irresistible. But that characterization—Clarence Doolittle in *Anchors Aweigh*—was no longer credible in the face of Sinatra's relationships, either with Lucky Luciano or Gardner. "People forget the climate in those days, when Frank started running around with Ava," as Columbia Records producer Mitch Miller pointed out. "Ingrid Bergman had a child out of wedlock, she was banned from movies in America. When Sinatra left his wife, the priests told the kids, 'Don't buy his records.' "

Not that the kids were buying his records anyway. The period is generally remembered for Sinatra's unfortunate efforts, many shepherded by Miller, to come into step with the novelty-conscious public of the period. "Mama Will Bark," a Miller production in which Sinatra imitates both dogs and Jimmy Durante, is merely the most infamous. Miller, who had enormous success with this kind of material in the hands of Guy Mitchell and Rosemary Clooney, also steered him to such howlers as the pseudo-Nashville "Tennessee Newsboy" and the pseudo-Hebraic "Feet of Clay."

To make matters worse, Sinatra's professional and personal disappointments were taking their toll on his voice; while doing a daily radio show and three sets a night at the Copacabana in early 1950, his throat went totally silent. "He was under a lot of pressure," trumpeter Chris Griffin told me. "That's the only time I ever saw him tight [forties slang for drunk] on a few record dates."

Yet the amazing thing about Sinatra's work in this period isn't the depths to which the singer sank but the heights that he still could reach under the right circumstances. Indeed, the forties-style Sinatra-Stordahl magic could still work wonders with material like the key songs from Rodgers and Hammerstein's *The King and I,* especially the miraculously effective "We Kiss in a Shadow" and "Hello, Young Lovers." There was also "I'm a Fool to Want You," in which Sinatra put all the pain he was feeling into one of the most harrowingly effective ballads of his career—a torch song that's more like a forest fire.

Miller made one surprisingly positive contribution to Sinatra's recorded legacy when he encouraged the singer to do more up-tempo jazz numbers—starting with "American Beauty Rose," the first song produced after Miller took over Columbia Records. "I loved the way Frank did rhythm songs," said Miller, "and I thought he should do more." George Siravo, an ace big band writer who'd already been working for Sinatra (as well as Glenn Miller, Charlie Barnet, and many other bands), was given the task of arranging and conducting an entire album of swing numbers. The result was *Sing and Dance with Frank Sinatra,* Sinatra's first original long-playing release, which, though later acknowledged as one of the very best jazz vocal albums, made little impact at the time.

The doldrums that inflicted his career were, with some big exceptions, not permeating his music. The early fifties should be regarded as a primarily experimental era in which he continued to record show tunes, ballads, and swingers, but also tried novelties, folk songs ("Good Night, Irene"), duets (like "Peach Tree Street" with Rosie Clooney, and a radio series in which he teamed up with opera diva Dorothy Kirsten), more of his superintimate chamber ensemble ballads (like "Nevertheless"), large-scale snappy productions with choruses ("Life Is So Peculiar," "Chattanooga Shoe Shine Boy"), Italian songs (like the exquisite though hopelessly faux-"Stromboli"), Western songs ("When the Sun Goes Down"), and all kinds of fascinating attempts at finding a new sound. In fact, as records like "Birth of the Blues" exhibit, Sinatra was well on the way to discovering the style and the sound that would bring him back with a vengeance. All that was missing was the fresh orchestral backdrop of Nelson Riddle and the event that would restore the public's faith in him, which would arrive with *From Here to Eternity.*

"I did lay down for a while and had some large bar bills for about a year, I think," as the singer later told friend Sidney Zion. "But after that I said, 'Holiday's over, Charlie, let's go back to work.' "

During the recording of the title song from *From Here to Eternity,* Sinatra, who was just beginning his climb back to the top, was so "down and out" and "insecure" that he had to lean on lyricist Bob Wells for constant reassurance. "At the end of the date he asked, 'Was that all right, Bob?' and I said 'That was great, Frank.' " But *Eternity* was such a sensation, not only catapulting Sinatra back to the pinnacle of fame but earning him both an Oscar and a new career as a dramatic actor, that when Wells ran into Sinatra a mere few weeks later, he greeted him with a "Hello, Frank," and the singer responded with a boisterously confident, "Hi, kid!"

It's an oversimplification, though, to say that *From Here to Eternity* was solely responsible for the Sinatra "comeback." (In 1954, *Good Housekeeping* ran a story titled "The Rise and Fall and Rise Again of Frank Sinatra," while *Time* magazine's headline was, more simply, "Back on Top.") In the wake of that film, Sinatra enjoyed two of the biggest hit singles of his career, the bright and optimistic "Young at Heart" and the jazzy and bluesy "Learnin' the Blues." Would they have been such spectacular successes without *Eternity*? Mitch Miller opines, "By getting stomped to death in that movie [referring to his character, Maggio's, famous death scene], Frank did a public penance. From the day it came out, his records began to sell."

Without question, the major factor in the latest and greatest phase of the Sinatra success story was arranger and conductor Nelson Riddle, almost certainly the finest orchestrator in all of popular music. Riddle had a control of harmony and melody, as well as an emotional depth and sensitivity, that were equally inspired by Duke Ellington, Billy Strayhorn, and Debussy. Sinatra once described himself as "an 18 carat manic depressive" because of his equal capacity for both "sadness and elation." Riddle was the ideal collaborator for him because he alone could follow the singer into these extremes.

Sinatra had already been making full-blown concept albums—collections of songs unified by mood and tempo, in roughly the shape of a narrative—since the mid-1940s, first in 78 album format and then on early 10" long-playing discs. With Riddle at Capitol, he kept going, beginning with the romantic *Songs for Young Lovers* (1953) and the upbeat *Swing Easy* (1954). From there, the ballad albums grew progressively moodier and sadder, to *In The Wee Small Hours* (1955), *Close to You* (1956), and *Frank Sinatra Sings for Only the Lonely* (1957), while the swing albums became ever more jubilant, from *Swing Easy* to *Songs for Swingin' Lovers* (1956) and *A Swingin' Affair* (1956). (Sinatra would also make other melancholy love-song albums with Gordon Jenkins and up-tempo, dance-driven projects with Billy May, but these seven albums with Riddle form the core of his canon.)

In the process, Sinatra and Riddle perfected the modern pop album (aka concept album). Back in 1945, three years before the introduction of the long-playing record, Sinatra showed how individual songs could flow into a cohesive whole with *The Voice*, a package that not only led to Sinatra's fifty or so subsequent concept albums but to the best works of Miles Davis and the Beatles. "He sat down and

carefully planned his albums, and lyrically they had to make sense," Frank Military recounts. "They had to tell a story. He'd spend days and weeks just preparing this album. Each song would be hand-picked, it had a reason for being in the album."

Not surprisingly, the first mood Sinatra wanted to tackle in this brave new era was fast and swinging, jazz numbers having been one avenue that he had rarely traveled in the previous decade. "Sinatra in the forties was the crooner with the bow tie," as guitarist Al Viola, who worked with him in both eras, puts it. "We hardly did any up-tempo things. When he came back in the fifties, I noticed right away that he was now *the* swinger, like 'Lady Is a Tramp' and all those things with Nelson. The ballads were still strong, but he got more into the jazz stuff."

"I've Got You Under My Skin" from *Swingin' Lovers* resonates as the definitive Sinatra swinger, and a more perfect, more powerful, or goose-bump-raising track there never was; Sinatra and Riddle build from tender whispers in a lover's ear to primal, orgasmic screams. Sinatra combines pure swing with caveman machismo, capable of grabbing even the most Frank-resistant listener way down at the bottom of the soul.

He once stated, "There are times if I want to do something that has a lonely effect, we go back to the [solo] piano, or an alto saxophone as part of the orchestration." He was undoubtedly speaking of "One for My Baby (And One More for the Road)" from *Only the Lonely,* which rates as the perfect Sinatra saloon song. The piece is essentially a combined couple of conversations: The lyrics depict half a dialogue between barfly and barkeep, the music gives us a comparable duet between Sinatra and accompanist Bill Miller, who plays barroom piano of the gods. Riddle drapes the efforts of the two men with a bluesy alto solo by Gus Bivona and the lightest possible shimmer of violins, which are felt more than heard, and effectively underscore the emotional content of the performance sound even starker. "One for My Baby" marks the finest piece of musical acting Sinatra has ever turned in. He has never sounded closer to the end of his rope, and he makes the lyric come alive, word by painful word, in an intimate reality that's as disturbing as it is believable.

Still, there was even more to Sinatra's eight years at Capitol Records (1953–61), which are by and large considered the pinnacle of the singer's career. Apart from his work with Riddle, Sinatra collaborated on a series of sessions, by turns humorous and swinging, with the era's greatest funster arranger, Billy May (*Come Fly with Me, Come Dance with Me, Come Swing with Me*), as well as a succession of sentimental, sad, and gloriously schmaltzy sets with the lovingly lachrymose Gordon Jenkins (*Where Are You?, No One Cares,* and the perversely titled *A Jolly Christmas*). Then there were nearly a hundred singles, almost exclusively with Riddle, which covered the cream of contemporary songs as adroitly as the albums defined the standards.

Sinatra's work with Riddle ultimately posed an unusual problem: Their seven classic Capitol albums of the 1953–58 period represented an insurmountable peak. Where could Sinatra go—where could *anyone* go—after *Songs for Swingin' Lovers* and *Only the Lonely*? That was the peak; that was as good as pop music would ever get. In order for the form to progress, it's not surprising that, rather than try to top what Sinatra had done, the next generation decided to invent a whole new form of pop music instead.

In 1943, Sinatra ushered in the age of the solo vocalist as the dominant icon of popular music. In 1960, he helped change the face of the entertainment industry once again by becoming the first pop star to launch his own high-profile record company, which he called Reprise Records. More than any other pop star of his generation, Sinatra would always be in control of his music: picking his songs, hand-selecting his arrangers and musicians, outlining his arrangements right down to the individual measure. Now he was seeking ownership as well.

In his work for his own label, particularly in the few years before he made a major killing by selling both the company and his own services to Warner Bros., Sinatra was making another point as well. The debacle of a decade earlier, when he was still pushing his forties style after the public tired of it, was still fresh in his mind, and he determined never to let that happen again. Although the classic Sinatra-Riddle sound showed no sign of running out of steam, he wanted to keep both himself and his listeners on their toes by trying one new sound after another: In the really great years of the early sixties, Sinatra would often be working on ten different concepts with ten different collaborators at the same time.

To start with, he extended his associations with his Capitol cohorts Nelson Riddle (with whom he recorded five new albums that are nearly as amazing as the classics of 1953–58), Billy May (most notably on *Sinatra Swings,* which takes both the singer and the arranger's taste for hard-driving swing, exotic rhythms, and whimsical humor to marvelous extremes), and Gordon Jenkins (on *All Alone,* a stunning statement in 3/4 time, and *September of My Years,* Sinatra's haunting if somewhat premature contemplation of old age, which brought forth a masterpiece in Ervin Drake's "It Was a Very Good Year"). Looking further back, he concluded his collaboration with Axel Stordahl (on his final Capitol disc, the 1961 *Point of No Return*), and returned to the very beginnings of his career on *I Remember Tommy* with fellow former Dorseyite Sy Oliver.

However, most of the classic Reprise albums (from 1960 to 1968) found Sinatra reaching into the future rather than reflecting on the past. Early on, he taped a pair of albums with two younger, more bebop-oriented arranger-composers, Johnny Mandel (*Ring-a-Ding-Ding!,* the set that was Sinatra's first for the new concern) and Neal Hefti (*Sinatra and Swingin' Brass*). Hefti also served as orchestrator on what was Sinatra's own most eagerly anticipated project, *Sinatra–Basie* (1961), a dream collaboration that the singer had his heart set on for years. It was followed by a second Basie set, *It Might as Well Be Swing* (1964). (Sinatra also stretched his wings, jazz-wise, in two live concerts with swinging small combos that were first issued legally many decades later: *With the Red Norvo Sextet in Australia, 1959* and *Sinatra and Sextet in Paris* from 1962.)

The first of the two Basie albums (with Hefti) found the singer tackling familiar standards, climaxing in a hard-swinging "Pennies from Heaven" that ends on a rollicking high note. The second Basie set (conducted by Quincy Jones) addressed the better contemporary hits of the early sixties and allowed Sinatra to put his unmistakable stamp on "Fly Me to the Moon" and "The Best Is Yet to Come." All these projects showed how his prowess as a jazz singer had grown even since the heights of the classic Riddle and May swing albums. As jazz clarinetist Ken Peplowski observes, "Sinatra started more implying beats rather than stating every single one. He has a unique way of sometimes leaving out whole sections of lyrics, or perhaps punctuating them with just one word, and you know exactly what he means." The second chorus of "I'm Gonna Sit Right Down and Write Myself a Letter" (on *Sinatra–Basie*), for instance, finds him outlining entire lyric lines with only a single syllable. As a postscript to the two studio collaborations with Count Basie, Sinatra also toured extensively with the band in these years, and brought the band as his accompaniment to his long-awaited first-ever live recording, the 1966 *Sinatra at the Sands.*

Nineteen sixty-seven saw the climax of this fruitful period in two of Sinatra's most remarkable (and similarly titled) collaborations: *Francis Albert Sinatra & Antonio Carlos Jobim* and *Francis A. and Edward K.* Neither was characteristic Sinatra, and the latter, Sinatra's long-awaited encounter with Duke Ellington, wasn't classic Ellington either. Still, thanks to guest arranger Billy May, the two found a common ground in an underappreciated sleeper of a set highlighted by a beguiling opener. This was "Follow Me," a show tune from *Camelot,* the Broadway musical that titled a cultural and political era in which Sinatra had played no small part. The Jobim encounter yielded some of the Chairman's softest singing ever, not to mention some of his most tender, as he addressed both Brazilian originals and a few American standards in a bossa nova context, masterminded by the brilliant German composer Claus Ogerman. Unfortunately, these two sets might also be described as the final two classic Sinatra concept albums.

Even by 1967, such high-minded undertakings as

team-ups with Jobim and Ellington were becoming increasingly uncommon, even in the rarefied, high-class world of Sinatra's music. In the mid-sixties, he began working with producer Jimmy Bowen and musical director Ernie Freeman, both of whom had already enjoyed considerable success in the field of youth-oriented pop, with the goal of creating juke-box singles for the kids to dance to. And in fact, Bowen gave Sinatra a contemporary sheen with "Softly," "The Impossible Dream," "That's Life" (with its Ray Charles–inspired hard-biting edge), "The World We Knew" (a considerably softer and sweeter duet with daughter Nancy), and, most successfully, "Strangers in the Night" (1966). The most important benefaction of the last was that it led to an album which, apart from the opening title track, would prove to be the last and almost the greatest of his albums with Nelson Riddle, reaching a new level of perfection in another German-born song with an English lyric, Johnny Mercer's "Summer Wind."

The Bowen singles served their purpose, which was to keep Sinatra on the charts. The same couldn't be said of his later efforts to stay contemporary, like the 1969 "rockoncept" album *Watertown*, a thought-ful song cycle and Sinatra's attempt to keep pace with a genre he had been instrumental in inspiring, the pop concept album. Although *Watertown* was not a commercial success, some of it is beautiful. This is also true of *A Man Alone*, a generally preten-tious album of poetry and songs by pop poet Rod McKuen.

Still, Sinatra could not escape the feeling that he was losing touch with the pop music audience—his audience. In the mid-sixties, Sinatra had it both ways: He was still creating classic albums for the ages at the same moment he was producing jukebox hits. By 1971, he was producing neither. Not knowing what to try next, Sinatra then both rocked and shocked the world by announcing his retirement. Even though said retirement didn't take, it was clear to all that an era had ended.

In 1974, Sinatra was at it again. In his first season back on the boards, he told the story many times about how he gradually eased back into full-time activity after twenty-nine months of retirement. First, President Nixon entreated him to perform at a White House gala in honor of Prime Minister Giulio Andreotti of Italy, on April 17, 1973. Then, urged on by fan mail, he began to consider the idea of just doing an album or a TV special—without making live appearances. Finally, he realized he could never work without performing in front of flesh-and-blood crowds, and he finally came around to the idea of touring full-time.

Ironically, now Sinatra would be making more live appearances than ever before, especially since his Hollywood career was essentially over. He con-centrated almost exclusively on touring, in a way that he never had before 1970. The key to this new phase of his renewed career was his transformation from saloon singer to stadium singer—the idea that he could play the same sports stadiums that the major rock acts played.

"When Frank started doing stadiums, he didn't know if he would draw," recalled guitarist Al Viola. "He was going to have to pull in fifteen thousand people or eighteen thousand every place he went. But Jerry Weintraub handled the promotion and booking when he started to tour. Jerry was involved with rock groups, he knew all the stadiums from one part of the country to another and he knew what he could sell. But in '74, neither Frank nor anybody else had any idea what he could actually do in a room where they sold hot dogs."

The theme song for this era was "My Way," which, though Sinatra had first recorded it in 1968, proved absolutely essential to the concert era that began in 1974. In his famous *Main Event* concert at Madison Square Garden that year, he refers to "My Way" as "the national anthem." Yet as pretentious and self-aggrandizing as the song was, Sinatra never missed an opportunity to put it—and himself—down. At his 1974 Carnegie Hall concert, Sinatra tells the crowd that although the English lyrics were written by pop star Paul Anka, the original French chanson was the work of a young Parisian named "Jacques Strap."

Anka wrote the familiar lyric with Sinatra in mind, and our appreciation of the song is fueled by the belief that Sinatra is singing about his own life; knowing that he's telling us his own story, he seems to extract a doubly cathartic response from concert audiences. When he sings of the dejection and fail-ure that led to his transforming tragedy into tri-umph, we not only feel it along with him, we give vent to our own inner longings to redirect rejection into redemption. Here he becomes living proof that a nobody from nowhere can not only become the single most significant figure in American popular culture, he can, in fact, do it twice.

Usually, Sinatra would very cagily position his "saloon song," most often "One for My Baby" (or occasionally "Angel Eyes") right before "My Way." He would immerse you in his most intimate moment, a performance so direct he would practically be engaging each member of the audience in an indi-vidual, one-on-one dialogue, and animating it so vividly that we can't help visualizing a bartender with bent ears wiping clean his shot glasses. Then he would turn 180 degrees and into his most extro-verted, bravura, and self-aggrandizing number. Audiences would be overwhelmed by the transfor-mation: Right before their eyes he becomes bigger than life. It's as if you're standing in front of Macy's on Thanksgiving morning, watching the Sinatra bal-loon float by.

As impressive as "My Way" was and as successful a concert attraction as Sinatra became, he hadn't fin-ished wrestling with the demons that had pressured him to retire in the first place: He still wasn't sure if he should be singing Cole Porter or Barry Manilow. His concert repertoire generally consisted of familiar material, although he made a point to include at least several contemporary items in each show. Throughout the seventies, the singer relied on Don Costa, a talented younger orchestrator (who would die young), as the envoy between the Sinatra generation and the baby boomers he wanted to reach.

Millions of fans now had the chance to see Sinatra live in person, fans who never could have gotten into the smaller rooms in Vegas before 1970. Yet though his live performances were a sure thing (Elvis Presley was going through a parallel career transformation at the same time), Sinatra remained unsure of what he should be recording. Classic songs? Potential hits? Trendy new songs? (He even reworked a pair of his signature songs into disco arrangements.) Album concepts that he hadn't made use of before? (There were precious few of those.) Sinatra barely made it into the recording studio at all throughout most of the seventies. The unretirement began with a bang and a good start in two brand-new albums recorded within a heartbeat of each other, *Ol' Blue Eyes Is Back* and *Some Nice Things I've Missed;* he followed those with an exuberant concert album (actually a hodgepodge assembled over several concerts), *The Main Event.* (Both *The Main Event* and *Ol' Blue Eyes Is Back* doubled as TV specials.)

But it turned out to be a false spring: For the rest of the decade there was only silence. Sinatra recorded interesting singles, and started work on several albums, but never finished any of them. His absence from the studio was especially regrettable because issued and unissued concert tapes from the decade reveal that his voice was in better shape than ever. In the forties, Sinatra had been billed as "the Voice"; his chops were at their strongest in his twenties and thirties, when he had a range comparable to some of vernacular music's most well-endowed stars, such as Ella Fitzgerald and Sarah Vaughan. The singer's personal collapse of the early fifties cost him some of those pure chops, but he continued to gain in emotional range; even if he couldn't hit some of his earlier high notes, he could express much more complex and detailed emotions as he grew older. Sammy Cahn famously likened the young Sinatra of the Dorsey and early postwar period to a violin, and the deeper, darker Sinatra of the post–Ava Gardner years to a cello. The all-time sweet spot may have been when his voice hadn't yet deteriorated from the effects of age. In fact, in the late seventies and early eighties he approached singing athletically, taking his daily warm-ups and vocal exercises as seriously as a prizefighter training for a title bout. His interpretive prowess grew sharper even as his pitch grew darker and deeper.

Finally, at the end of the seventies, Sinatra climaxed the decade with a spectacular three-LP package that was worth waiting for: *Trilogy*. He solved his repertory problem by devoting one disc to contemporary songs, arranged by Costa (highlighted by "Summer Me, Winter Me"). Another disc, batoned by Billy May, was for the most part previously unrecorded standards. The third LP was the most controversial, a generally overwrought and overambitious all-original song suite by Gordon Jenkins that attempted to predict *The Future.* (It didn't succeed as either philosophy or music.)

Excited by new marriages both personal (his fourth wife, the former Barbara Marx) and professional (his conductor Vincent Falcone), Sinatra was never in better shape, vocally and spiritually, than at the start of the eighties. He followed *Trilogy's* sensational success with a brilliant album of ballads, *She Shot Me Down,* which captured the singer at his most intense. Not long afterward, old friend Quincy Jones shepherded an all-star aggregate of champion sidemen and arrangers for a jazz-oriented album entitled *L.A. Is My Lady.*

Like *Strangers in the Night* almost twenty years earlier, *L.A. Is My Lady* was an outstanding jazz album with a pop title track. Unfortunately, the single "L.A. Is My Lady" was not the hit to rival "Strangers," as Sinatra had been hoping it would. The early eighties, with *She Shot Me Down* and *L.A. Is My Lady* following the three-LP *Trilogy*, would be Sinatra's last major era of recording. Still, he was touring constantly, and concert recordings, such as an amazing show from Tokyo in 1985 (legally issued on home video in Japan only), reveal that he was still at the top of his game. In 1988, his son, Frank Sinatra Jr., took over as his father's conductor on the road, and he made a valiant but fruitless effort to induce the Old Man to return to the studio.

In the early nineties, Sinatra was still on the road, although by now pundits were increasingly grousing that he was losing his wind power and was reduced to following TelePrompTers for his lyrics. Yet even if he became somewhat erratic in his final years, his performances retained almost all their potency. So did his ability to move product: All four of the labels he had recorded for began issuing mammoth box sets of his output (he became the first singer of his magnitude to have virtually every note he ever sang made available on CD). At the same time, Sinatra created his own retrospective of his most memorable musical moments: In *Duets* (1993) and *Duets II* (1994), he reprised many of his signature songs in the company of some of the biggest contemporary pop stars of the era. In the event, the two *Duets* albums amounted to a triumph of technology (using digital editing to make it sound as if Sinatra and his co-stars were actually singing in tandem), sales (moving over seven million units worldwide), and, in some cases, even music. "Where or When," with Steve Lawrence and Eydie Gormé, was every bit as good as one would expect, and "Come Rain or Come Shine" with Gloria Estefan was even better.

He continued to tour up to the end of 1994, and

in February 1995 gave his last public performance. It was a brilliant but short six-song set mounted as part of his annual charity golf event, which proved he was more than ready to return to the road anytime he wanted. It was just like Sinatra, who famously described himself as "a symmetrical man, almost to a fault," to pick 1995 to end an era: In addition to marking his eightieth year on the planet, that season also signified sixty years since he first "went pro" with the Hoboken Four. Now he was ready to retire for real. As critic David Hajdu once wrote, "To hell with the calendar—The day that Frank Sinatra [is finished], the 20th Century is over." It also seems typical of Sinatra that he managed to take the millennium with him.

"He gave pop singing something it never had before—style," as Jule Styne put it. "Before Sinatra, songs were just sung straight and without much panache. Crosby had a little sense of style, but Sinatra was the one who went the whole way."

As the first singer of the swing era to break away from the big bands that spawned him—yet keeping something of that swing sound in his music throughout the rest of his career—Sinatra launched the era of singing stars that followed. Yet he then transcended that period, doing his best work in the late fifties and the sixties, long after rock had become entrenched. He began his career billed as "the Voice That Is Thrilling Millions," a public relations slogan soon shortened to simply "the Voice," a term indicative of his formidable vocal technique at that early stage. Yet by the time he reinvented and re-reinvented himself several times and several generations over, he was no longer simply a voice. In so eloquently and poignantly expressing what the rest of us could only feel, Sinatra had by now become our collective heart and soul as well. In all eras, in all mediums, and whether singing or acting (the two were ultimately indistinguishable), Sinatra was, in the phrase of the Irish pop star Bono, "the Big Bang of pop." It's impossible to imagine what American music would have sounded like without him.

Carol Sloane (born 1937)

In an article for *Down Beat* in the late sixties, Carol Sloane's main piece of advice to young singers was "Think of the lyric at all times and forget attempts to emulate trumpet or saxophone sounds you may have heard, no matter how appealing they may be. It is essential to be constantly aware of the story and the words, not the sound you create." I quote that statement not because it unlocks any particular key to Sloane's work, but because to me the truth about her is just the opposite. When I listen to Sloane, the first thing that occurs to me is the instrumental nature of her singing. You couldn't say it's specific to any particular horn, but Sloane likes to play with melody and sound in a way that allies her more with Ella Fitzgerald than with Mabel Mercer.

You never feel that she is exclusively concerned with words.

Like Fitzgerald, Sloane can be warm and winning on a slow love song—and really make you feel it—yet her attention to lyrics seems generally secondary to what she does with melody, tone, and rhythm. Surely she was thinking of a trumpet when she interjected one of Clifford Brown's pet quotes (from "All This and Heaven Too") in the middle of Tommy Dorsey's theme "Getting Sentimental over You" (as she did at Rainbow and Stars in January 1998); I have also heard her utilize John Coltrane's "Giant Steps" as intro music.

For years Carol Sloane used to confuse me when I heard her on the radio—I would hear that voice scatting, stretching notes, slowing down and speeding up tunes—and, thanks to the imprecision of AM (or even FM) radio, I would assume that I was listening to Ella Fitzgerald. A friend of mine had a similar reaction: He would hear that sharp biting tone, that crafty way with a lyric, and thought it couldn't be anybody but Carmen McRae. The point isn't that Sloane, in the cold clear light of day, sounds like either Fitzgerald or McRae—two divas who certainly don't sound anything like each other—but rather that she belongs in the same territory that they occupy.

She was born Carol Morvan in 1937. As a little girl in Providence she was drawn both to music and the lure of New York, particularly when she heard radio remotes from such jazz joints as Birdland. She was born too late to participate in the swing era; nonetheless she developed her style by working in big bands—first in local groups in her native Rhode Island. "I started singing when I was fourteen," she told Suzi Price in a 2000 interview, "and for money too! I made nine dollars a night. Can you imagine when you are fourteen years old and you hear a woman singing [from Chris Connor's signature, "All About Ronnie"] 'We'll drink from dry glasses . . . There's no need for wine . . . the champagne is Ronnie'? Hey, I'm a Catholic girl going to Catholic school. Can you imagine? Who the heck ever heard of anyone drinking wine from a dry glass? I was so fascinated by the lyrics. I mean it makes more sense than someone singing 'Come-on-a my house, I'm gonna give you candy.' "

In 1953, a pair of songwriters happened to hear her, and bused her down from Rhode Island to Manhattan so that she could record one of their songs. This was "So Long," backed by "Strange Power," released as a single on the obscure Cadillac Records under the name Carol Vann. Two years later, Sloane was married for the first time, and two years after that went on the road in Europe as a singing actress in a USO-style touring company of *Kiss Me, Kate* that played U.S. army bases in Germany. In 1958, she made New York her semipermanent center of operations, and worked primarily with saxist and society bandleader Larry Elgart. It was Elgart who helped her come up with the name Carol Sloane, and produced a number of early sides featuring her, including several tracks released by RCA. Elgart also produced a full-length album demo of Sloane that was eventually released briefly in Japan, almost thirty years later, under the title *Early Hours.*

Also around this time, she substituted for an ailing Annie Ross with Dave Lambert and Jon Hendricks in Philadelphia, for which gig she was compelled to memorize the trio's book of very complicated arrangements in a single night. (Jon and Dave would have done well to make Sloane the permanent Ross replacement when she eventually left the trio.) In August 1961, Sloane had her first major solo gig in New York, opening for Oscar Peterson at the Village Vanguard. That summer she also made a triumphant appearance at the Newport Jazz Festival at a special showcase for emerging talent (in those days they were billed as "lesser" artists). She went over so big at the festival that she attracted the attention of critic George Simon and eventually that of producer Mike Berniker at Columbia Records.

She would make two albums at Columbia, *Out of the Blue* (reissued on CD by Koch Jazz) and *Live at 30th Street* (issued on CD only in Japan). Although, as we've seen, she had recorded some bits and pieces here and there, these two projects are her first real recordings—and *Out of the Blue* resounds as a knockout of a debut. It remains one of the finest works of her entire career. The voice is lighter and higher than we know it from the eighties and nineties recordings, but it still sounds like her. She's also generally taking fewer liberties with the melodies than she would later on, but she plays with the tunes more than enough to qualify as a dyed-in-the-wool jazz singer. The arrangements, mostly by Bill Finegan, are equally outstanding. Oddly, the two tracks with the biggest impact are the ones that were added to the 1995 CD issue: "April in My Heart," a little-known Hoagy Carmichael song that Sloane might have remembered from Billie Holiday's record, and "I Want You to Be the First One to Know." This was a revue song, from *New Faces of 1962,* by Arthur Siegel and June Carroll. It's a wonderfully warm and witty tune—and performance—that Sloane ought to revive, and it shows her early mastery of lyric interpretation; another plus is trumpeter Clark Terry's outstanding obbligato.

In the early sixties, Sloane was flying high. Although *Live at 30th Street* was apparently taped with an audience in Columbia's Thirtieth Street "church," she headlined at, among other spots, Mr. Kelly's in Chicago and the Hungry i in San Francisco, and was seen on Arthur Godfrey's show and on many occasions early in the life of *The Tonight Show* with Johnny Carson. But this was far from an opportune time for a new singer of jazz and standards to launch a career. *Live at 30th Street* wound up being her last official album for about fifteen years. (One unauthorized exception: In 1964, some-

one made a live recording in a club in Pawtucket, Rhode Island, in which Sloane jams with a fellow New Englander, pianist Mike Renzi, and tenor legend Ben Webster; this was later issued on the mysterious label Honey Do Records.)

Eventually, work dwindled down to nothing, and Sloane took a day job as a legal secretary while still keeping her hand in music. In the late sixties she was living and singing in Raleigh, North Carolina, her home for most of the seventies and early eighties. She enjoyed a long, ongoing gig at Raleigh's Frog and Nightgown, and in 1977 began recording again. Her return to the studio was *Sophisticated Lady,* which was not only the first of two entire albums she would make of Duke Ellington's music, but the first of ten or so recordings she would cut either in Tokyo (usually with American musicians) or for the Japanese market.

Among her other Japanese albums are *Spring Is Here* (1977), *Carol Sings* (1978), *As Time Goes By,* which is one of the few that have been commonly available in the United States (1982), *Carol Sloane Live with Joe Puma* (1982), *Three Pearls* (1983), *Summertime* (1983), *A Night of Ballads* (1984), and *But Not for Me* (1986). *A Night of Ballads* and *As Time Goes By* both prominently feature Don Abney, an ace accompanist who had long served Ella Fitzgerald, the latter album being issued on an American CD by a budget label called Four Star.

The major difference between Sloane's Japanese albums and her later projects for American independents is that the Japanese market seems to prefer only the most familiar of standards, while her albums for Contemporary Records (1988–90) and Concord Jazz (1991–97) generally include a few more offbeat items.

Apart from a poorly distributed album on the Choice label (the 1977 *Cottontail,* which contains a kickass version of Jon Hendricks's lyric to the Ellington title song) and the 1978 *Carol Sings* (originally released as *Carol Sloane Loves Cats* on Progressive), Sloane hadn't recorded for an American label in more than twenty-five years by the time she made *Love You Madly* for Contemporary in 1988. By then, she'd settled in Stoneham, Massachusetts, and remarried, to a New Englander with the unlikely name of Buck Spurr.

Her artistry was steadily growing: *Love You Madly* and the second Contemporary package, *The Real Thing* (1990), were probably Sloane's best work to date. The 1990 album ends with a CD-only bonus track, "Maybe You'll Be There," a song that became one of her most outstanding ballad vehicles. She uses pitch and rhythm but keeps her dynamic level fairly even. Whether she's swinging a fast rhythm number ("Until I Met You," on the 1993 *Sweet & Slow,* is a prime example of a soft, subtle swinger) or crooning a slow ballad, she rarely gets louder or softer. Although she continues to cite Carmen McRae as her greatest influence, this is a trait more commonly found in such cool singers as Chris Connor. Like Connor, Sloane can also sometimes be described as a stealth singer—her very specific use of dynamics makes her seem even more subtle. She's not as militantly monodynamic as, say, Nina Simone, but I wouldn't be surprised if Cassandra Wilson were to cite Sloane as an influence.

While some singers—Vaughan and often Fitzgerald—always seem to be giving everything they've got, Sloane always seems to be holding just the slightest bit back, giving every line she sings a feeling of mystery. This is a trait she could have inherited directly from McRae. As she once told Jim Gavin, "As much as I adored Sarah and Ella, Carmen had a voice I could really understand. The way she read a lyric made much more sense to me, because she sounded more human. I thought, that's what I have to aim for when I sing—to make someone share a moment with me."

Sloane was already well known in Japan, and the success of the two Contemporary CDs led to an offer to sing at the Concord-Fujitsu Festival. At this point she was approached by Carl Jefferson, head of Concord Jazz records, who asked, "So when am I gonna record you?" Between 1992 and 1997, she made six albums for Concord: three general interest sets, *Heart's Desire* (1992), *Sweet & Slow* (1993), and *When I Look in Your Eyes* (1994), and three tribute albums, *The Songs Carmen Sang* (1995), *The Songs Sinatra Sang* (1996), and *The Songs Ella & Louis Sang* (1997). (There also were two multiartist projects, *The Concord All-Stars on Cape Cod*, 1992, and *A Concord Jazz Christmas*, 1993.)

The Concord albums are the most consistently excellent and rewarding work of Sloane's career. She has never sounded better, and as a bonus, on the first three especially, she's permitted to indulge her talent for unearthing exceptional but somewhat out-of-the-way material not done to death by other chirps. That describes the title tracks as well as virtually all the others on *Sweet & Slow* and *When I Look in Your Eyes*. Both are terrific songs that haven't been heard to the point of overkill, the first being a little-known Warren and Dubin movie song recorded by Fats Waller and British bandleader Harry Roy, the second a gem by Leslie Bricusse from *Doctor Dolittle* that Sloane rediscovered in advance of Diana Krall. Sloane's romantic side comes to the fore in "An Older Man Is Like an Elegant Wine," a sentimental concept that she makes into a compelling experience. (I'm rather like a manishevitz on the rocks myself.) Her sense of humor is the main focus on "I Was Telling Him All About You," a vintage slice of tongue-in-cheek drollery from Moose Charlap, father of Bill Charlap, Sloane's accompanist at the time.

The other aspect of Sloane's music that repeatedly asserts itself is her capacity for cultural history, specifically of the Great American Songbook and the people who sing it. When she sings June Christy's signature "Something Cool" (on both the 1994 *When I Look in Your Eyes*, in which she adds an original spoken introduction, and a lesser-known 1978 album called *Something Cool*) or "A Woman's Intuition," inevitably associated with Lee Wiley, she does it with a full sense of the history of her art form, to complement rather than compete with the famous originals. She's enough of a scholar of pop culture that when she sings "As Time Goes By" (on an album of the same title), she accurately quotes the introductory line from *Casablanca* and correctly attributes it to Bergman rather than Bogart. (Sloane's scholarship also often comes to the fore in the Songbirds mailing list at yahoo.com, an Internet chat group in which she is one of the star participants.)

It's altogether appropriate that she would make three albums that paid tribute to three—or actually four—of the archetypal performers in the jazz-pop spectrum. The business of tribute albums is tricky: Carmen McRae recorded full-length tributes to Nat King Cole, Sarah Vaughan, and did several Billie Holiday songbook projects. So when Sloane, in turn, pays homage to McRae, she includes songs from those albums; in other words, Sloane's tribute album, *Songs Carmen Sang*, includes tracks from Carmen McRae's tributes to Nat King Cole.

No matter: All three of Sloane's tributes to jazz vocal icons are first-rate offerings. Although there have been almost as many Sinatra tribute albums as actual Sinatra albums, Sloane's *Sinatra* set is especially welcome: Concord's Japanese affiliate requested it, and apparently was willing to pony up the yen for a larger-than-usual ensemble, which includes such stars as Bill Charlap, trombonist Steve Turre, and multireedist Scott Robinson.

Singing the songs of these artists, she shows us, doesn't necessarily mean aping their styles—as when Sloane and company come up with a nine-minute version of "One for My Baby" that's twice as long and more ruminative than anything the Chairman ever attempted, even in this, his most famous of monologues. The Fitzgerald-Armstrong salute, too, is outstanding, in that Sloane recruited a partner for it. On *Out of the Blue*, thirty-five years earlier, Clark Terry had been a prominent trumpet soloist in the accompanying orchestra. Here, he's recruited as a frontline co-star, sharing both the spotlight and the microphone with Sloane. This is probably the most extended example of Terry's singing yet heard, though his opening chorus—on trumpet—on "Stars Fell on Alabama" is the most memorable moment on the package. Throughout, his singing is warm and appealing, and the two singers have lots of chemistry together, particularly when Terry recreates the Armstrong special lyrics from "Blueberry Hill" ("Come climb the hill with me . . .").

(Sloane also has amazing chemistry with singer-drummer Grady Tate, who joined her for a medley of "Makin' Whoopee" and "The Glory of Love" on *The Real Thing*. Together, they also did a slightly ribald and hysterical take on "Baby, It's Cold Outside" with Tate ad-libbing at a 1997 Christmas concert at Avery Fisher Hall.)

In the twenty-first century, Sloane, who turned seventy in 2007, is indisputedly one of the elder stateswomen of jazz and the American songbook—in a class with Barbara Cook, Freddy Cole, Tony Bennett, Marilyn Maye, and Jimmy Scott. She continues to assert her status with excellent albums, including *I Never Went Away* (HighNote, 2001), *Whisper Sweet* (HighNote, 2003), and two collections of Ellingtonia, *Romantic Ellington* (DRG, 1999) and *Dearest Duke* (Arbors Jazz, 2007). She goes on touring regularly, including, in New York alone, appearances at Dizzy's Club Coca-Cola, the Village Vanguard, and one particularly rewarding engagement at the Oak Room, ground zero for worshippers of the text of the great American lyric.

If her object was to convince us that she's just as outstanding at singing slow, sensual love songs as she is at doing anything else, she succeeded. The two latest Ellington albums (making a total of three, thus far) are particularly effective, since the *Romantic* title applies equally to both. She sings ballads with an especially jazzy and musical sense. On the 1999 album, musical director Mike Renzi divides the action among three settings—Sloane and Renzi, solo; Sloane and Renzi with bass and drums; and Sloane and Renzi with trio plus string quartet plus Benny Golson on tenor. (Unbelievably, after forty years of recording this was apparently her first session with strings.) The backing on *Dearest Duke* is more pared down: It's just Brad Hatfield on piano and the brilliant Ken Peplowski on tenor saxophone and clarinet, yet the proceedings are no less rapturously romantic.

For much of her career, Sloane may not have sounded distinctive enough to carve out a place for herself in the upper echelon. But by the time of the second decade (2010), her skills have sharpened even as the competition from her own generation has thinned out. She continues to make excellent recordings, and also to sound even better in person. Unquestionably a jazz singer, she is one of the major living masters who continually prove that using a jazz approach to a song doesn't have to entail a lot of nonverbal fuss and extraneous overdecoration; rather, she employs jazz techniques to get to the core of a song's meaning. I most recently heard her at the 92nd Street Y's Jazz in July series in summer 2008. A year later she recorded her most recent album, *We'll Meet Again* (released in early 2010 on Arbors Jazz). As with *Dearest Duke*, it's primarily an unusual trio of Sloane, Peplowski, and, this time, guitarist Bucky Pizzarelli; once again she thrives in the intimate setting. For me, the standout track is her duet with another guitarist, Howard Alden, on "Something to Remember You By." It makes clear that she has never sounded stronger, never "jazzier" or more personal, never more sincere or direct, yet never more individ-

ual or idiosyncratic. It rarely takes more than one song to remind me that at least one member of jazz singing's elite old group is still very much at the peak of her powers.

Kate Smith (1907–1986)

If ever anyone was an unfortunate victim of changing attitudes, it's Kate Smith. By the sixties, she was routinely derided for her musical and political conservatism—not to mention her obesity. Other than those who would make her the rather large butt of such ungallant humor, who remembers Kate Smith today? Mainly grandmothers with first names that have fallen off the face of the earth—names like Mabel, Gertrude, and Edna. Yet at the height of her career, during the World War II era, Smith was one of the most respected women in America. In a nationwide poll conducted in 1942, only Eleanor Roosevelt and Helen Hayes rivaled her for overall popularity. Three years earlier, the Roosevelts summoned her to the White House to sing for the king and queen of England, and introduced her simply with: "Your Majesties, this is Kate Smith. This is America."

Smith got started during the Jazz Age, reached her peak during the Great Depression, and, perhaps surprisingly, sustained her stay at the top throughout the swing era and especially the war. Stylistically, she had the most in common with the jazz singers of the thirties (like Ethel Waters and the comparably corpulent Mildred Bailey) and the great pop singers of the postwar era (Margaret Whiting, Jo Stafford), but professionally her appeal presages the subsequent rise of country music. Years before Nashville became mainstream, Smith was the direct conduit from Tin Pan Alley to the heartland. (Perhaps it's not a coincidence that her TV show contains the only surviving film footage of C&W legend Hank Williams.)

She was far from a song stylist, even though her best records occasionally find her singing in swing time or using jazz-derived devices. Her strength lay in her singing's very plainness, a generic quality that allowed her to appeal to everyone. Likewise, she never went for the highbrow; she reigned in the thirties and forties, the golden age of the popular song, yet she rarely expended her breath on the tonier new Broadway songs—of the Lorenz Harts, the Cole Porters. She concentrated on songs that were, increasingly, as plain-vanilla as possible. (Which makes Bing Crosby's achievement seem all the more remarkable by comparison—he managed to appeal to everybody but without sacrificing his distinct style and personality.) She sang your basic love songs with an emphasis on songs of loneliness, most famously her theme, "When the Moon Comes over the Mountain," and "We'll Meet Again," which made her particularly relevant during the war, when separation was the prevailing musical and cultural mode. Smith's medium-deep contralto voice just rang out sweet and clear, free from nuance, reassuring middle America that contemporary pop didn't have to be jazzy or flashy or even clever to be good.

Plenty of performers became big names thanks to radio, but with Kate Smith it was more the other way around: With her strong and clear voice, she helped make a national institution of the new medium. Many performers contributed what they could to the defense effort during the war, but Kate Smith both raised more money for war bonds and entertained more troops than virtually all the other stars combined. Other singers sang about America, but only Kate Smith put over a song so effectively that it launched a grassroots movement—still active to this day—to make the song "God Bless America" the new national anthem. If Mrs. Roosevelt was the first lady of these United States, and Ms. Hayes was first lady of the American stage, Kate Smith ruled virtually unchallenged as the first lady of the airwaves and the musical world.

Later billed as the "Songbird of the South and Her Swanee Music," Kathryn Elizabeth Smith was born in Greenville, Virginia, on May 1, 1907, and raised in Washington, D.C. From her childhood she knew she wanted to sing, and gained valuable experience during the First World War by performing for soldiers under General Pershing, for which, the story goes, the eleven-year-old was personally commended by Black Jack Pershing himself. The legend also informs us that while still a teenager, she sang for Presidents Wilson and Harding, anticipating her later relationship with the Roosevelts. Despite this early success, her family had little faith in the long-time security of show business and pressured young Kate to enter nursing school. After a year, she gave up health care and headed to New York to try her luck on the boards.

Back in Washington, a visiting producer hired her for the Broadway show *Honeymoon Lane,* where—in wise-guy contrast to her already imposing physical characteristics—she was given the role of "Tiny Little." By all accounts, her singing and dancing made her the high point of the production, which she remained with for its yearlong run on the Great White Way as well as with the touring company. But even before *Honeymoon Lane* opened, when she was still completely unknown, there was interest in recording her from both of the major labels of the day, Victor and Columbia. Both corporations brought her into the studio to record her singing three songs from *Honeymoon Lane,* but only the Columbias were issued. The most memorable song of the show, "The Little White House," suggests that at this very early stage Smith was possibly being groomed as a female Gene Austin, singing a song of domestic bliss (à la "My Blue Heaven") in a simple, straight-ahead voice—at a time when Annette Hanshaw and Ruth Etting were considerably more stylized.

Smith released more than a dozen discs in the twenties, and, as in much pop of the era, there was a strong jazz element to her work, both in her singing itself as well as the settings Columbia put her in. There also was a sardonic tinge that was nowhere to be heard in her later work, as when she recorded "In the Baggage Coach Ahead" in 1932. The title refers to a little girl riding in a train while the body of her dead mother is as described. (Why this morbid 1890s song was revived in 1932, I can't imagine.) Columbia also recorded her singing "Frankie and Johnny" and "St. Louis Blues," and although those two particular sides were never released, her treatment of "I Got Rhythm" was riotously red-hot, and almost in a class with the superb version by Ethel Waters done around the same time and also on Columbia. Unfortunately, there's no comprehensive collection of any period of Smith's recorded output. Sunbeam Records released two fine LPs of her earlier sides, which is how I first heard them, but these have not been reissued on CD. Take Two Records does offer a nice assortment of twenty tracks from the thirties titled *Emergence of a Legend,* which is much recommended.

When *Honeymoon Lane* closed, Smith had no other Broadway show lined up, so she returned to Washington, where she sang in local vaudeville theaters. In 1929, she was brought into a stock company of Vincent Youmans's *Hit the Deck,* in which she appeared in blackface, and, upon returning to New York, she resumed recording for Columbia. Her fame gradually began snowballing, and around this time she was filmed for an early Vitaphone movie short subject. Her real breakthrough came in 1930 with the Broadway musical *Flying High,* a major hit in the early Depression thanks to the combination of legendary funnyman Bert Lahr and her own song and dance work. By that point, Lahr's jealousy and insecurity—not to mention competitiveness—were also legend; by Smith's later account, he was continually trying not only to upstage his co-star but to humiliate and ridicule her. It's a tribute to her show-biz acumen that she was able to hold her own against this comedy master.

The experience soured her on Broadway; she was afraid that if she stayed in the musical theater, the only thing that lay in store for her was a succession of low-comedy fat-girl parts. Her records were selling, but now that the Depression had arrived, the phonograph industry was no longer a way to make a living. Smith was at a loss until she met Ted Collins of Columbia Records, who became her manager and partner, and helped her grasp the possibilities of radio. Initially Collins got her on Rudy Vallee's very important *Fleischmann's Yeast Hour* on NBC, and she was so well received that NBC soon gave her a fifteen-minute tryout spot of her own beginning in March 1931, at a time when she was also singing days at New York's Capitol movie theater. However, NBC failed to sign her to a permanent series—mainly because CBS's William Paley moved in and beat them to the punch.

The Kate Smith CBS program quickly became

one of the most popular shows on the air, challenging even the unchallengeable *Amos 'n' Andy*. The following year she made her first feature film appearance, in *The Big Broadcast*, which also launched fellow Paley protégé Bing Crosby in his film career. Later in 1933, Paramount featured her in her only starring movie role, *Hello, Everybody!*, which contains the sole cinematic sample of the dancing routines that helped make her a success on Broadway. But *Hello, Everybody!* was both the high point and the *only* point of her Hollywood career, while she went on going great guns both in vaudeville and radio. Also in 1933 she headlined with her own revue, the format of which was transferred to CBS in 1935. When supermarket chain A&P sponsored the series that fall in order to push its brand of coffee (*Kate Smith's Coffee Time*), the company reported an astounding 25 percent increase in sales nationally—and Lord knows how many more wide-awake Americans.

Early in her CBS radio period, Smith introduced her theme song, "When the Moon Comes over the Mountain." The melody to "Moon" was supplied by the well-known Harry Woods and the lesser-known Howard Johnson, but the words were based on a poem by Smith herself, who received one-third credit. Her performance of "Moon" revealed a new maturity; it wasn't Ira Gershwin, but it tells a poignant story of love and loss, ending with the touching line "I'm alone with my memories of you." Smith never married and even in *Hello, Everybody!* (titled after her radio opening line) she wasn't cast as the romantic leading lady; it's her sister who lands hunky Randolph Scott while Kate is busy holding family and community together. (And solving everyone's problems, sort of like a singing Angela Lansbury in *Murder, She Wrote*.) There's a melancholy ache in the best of her singing, a bittersweet longing for romantic happiness that's forever beyond her reach.

As it happened, Smith became a star on CBS at about the same time that Columbia Records temporarily severed its connections with the Columbia Broadcasting System. She continued to record for the label and its subsidiaries under the American Recording Corp. until May 1932, and for the rest of the decade her disc output was sporadic. ARC brought her back to do the four songs from *Hello, Everybody!* in 1933 and then a year later she did six sides for Decca. Somehow, she then stayed out of the studio for three years before cutting a mere dozen sides for Victor between 1937 and 1939. The *Hello, Everybody!* songs, composed by Sam Coslow and Arthur Johnston (who were writing some great things for Bing Crosby, Mae West, and other Paramount stars at the time), are disappointing, although some might enjoy "Pickaninny's Heaven" for its camp value, and the future standard "Moon Song" is an excellent follow-up to "When the Moon Comes over the Mountain."

Smith still showed a hearty sense of humor in the early thirties: In a Vitaphone short circa 1932, she's shown bounding into a room wearing a riding habit. In those days, horseback riding was regarded as a way for the landed gentry to lose weight. When someone asks her, "Well, did you reduce?" Smith answers, "No, but the horse sure did." The six songs that she recorded for Decca in 1934 are very much in that exuberant, wacky spirit: She sings peppy orchestrations with a very peppy vocal group billed as the Three Ambassadors. The harmonies are exhilarating and the tempo just won't quit—and she modulates to a big note in the climax of "The Continental." There are other occasions in the early forties where Smith does something like swinging, but the Deccas, particularly "The Continental," are maybe the last time she's genuinely exciting with a capital E.

The Victors begin in 1937 with the very sentimental "There's a Goldmine in the Sky," and in 1939 she first recorded her best-known song, "God Bless America." Irving Berlin had written it during World War I, but shelved it, lest it be buried in an avalanche of patriotic airs at the time. In 1938, he decided that its time had come at last as war threatened in Europe, and he somehow knew that Smith, who heretofore had never recorded anything particularly patriotic, was the perfect singer to introduce it. He was right. With "God Bless America," Smith became something even more than the most popular female singer in the country. It was the beginning of her transformation from entertainer to an American institution.

Her recording career began again in earnest in 1940, not long after CBS and Columbia Records merged. Naturally, an institution can't be expected to keep up with changing times or even to swing, and there are increasing instances from 1937 on when Smith sounds more like an institution than a pop singer. But there are also many exceptions: The Victors include a lightly jazzy "I Cried for You" where Smith shows that she knows how to phrase behind the beat and even suspend the rhythm in a stop time break.

At least a few of the Columbias—nearly all of which were done under the baton of her musical director, Jack Miller (and many of which are on Sony's 1991 *Kate Smith: 16 Most Requested Songs* and the more generous *Kate Smith: The Columbia Years, 1940–1946*) have some oomph to them. She didn't hesitate to tackle big band era novelties, like "Rose O'Day (The Filla-da-gusha Song)," Glenn Miller's "I Got a Gal in Kalamazoo" (done as a dance record and opening with a Milleresque instrumental chorus), and her best up-tempo of the period, "One Dozen Roses." Here and on the slightly later "On the Atchison, Topeka & the Santa Fe," Smith shows that even if she doesn't exactly swing like Jimmy Rushing, she comes close enough. There's also a memorable session in which she cut all four of the principal songs from Berlin's *Louisiana Purchase*—perhaps as repayment for "God Bless America." The mature Columbia period also encompasses no shortage of effective ballads, like the lovely South American "Time Was."

With her patriotic attitude and penchant for songs of separation already in place, Smith was more popular than ever during the war. Besides "God Bless America," she sang such red, white, and blue–colored arias as "We're All Americans (All True Blue)" and even "A Merry American Christmas," not to mention songs that saluted our Allied allies, like "A Little Church in England," "The White Cliffs of Dover," "Don't Cry, Cherie," and "The Last Time I Saw Paris." She also was a perfect purveyor of the many songs written for Americana-type productions (which began with *Oklahoma!*). She had already been singing of romantic isolation for a decade—ever since "When the Moon Comes over the Mountain" (which she rerecorded on Columbia in 1941), and virtually all of her final sessions before the 1942 AFM ban consist of songs about being alone and apart: "I Don't Want to Walk Without You," "There Are Rivers to Cross (Before We Meet Again)," "I Threw a Kiss into the Ocean" (a love song to an absent sailor in his blue jacket), the more sarcastic "Somebody Else Is Taking My Place," and the extravagantly sentimental "We'll Meet Again" from England.

The war, then, served to extend Smith's stay in the spotlight, but she was destined to be outclassed by the onslaught of new popular singers that took over in the late forties, your Dick Haymeses, your Ella Fitzgeralds, your Perry Comos. She was, to an extent, a vocal equivalent of what Guy Lombardo was to dance music, and in fact, one of her two biggest hits (listed as number one on the charts in Whitburn's *Pop Memories*)—"River, Stay 'Way from My Door" (1932)—was backed by Lombardo. Like the Royal Canadians, she would hold on to her large traditional audience for a long time, deep into the television era. But she didn't expand it. Unlike Crosby, Smith didn't continue to land big hits in the Truman era and then enter a period of renaissance and resurgence under Ike. Yet as it happens, most of her work in the LP era—the fifties and sixties—is quite good; there's an especially excellent 10" LP on Capitol done under the baton of Nelson Riddle.

By the sixties, Smith comes across like a *Twilight Zone* character transported to an era not her own and a world she never made. Now recording albums for RCA, she began the decade with superior material like "I Left My Heart in San Francisco" (another song of separation) and "My Coloring Book" (ditto). (Both are on *The Sweetest Sounds,* reissued by Collectors' Choice as half of a double-length CD also featuring her later religious album, *How Great Thou Art.*) In 1965, RCA released *The Best of Kate Smith,* but it wasn't a reissue or a greatest hits compilation: There were a couple of new treatments of old signatures, like "When the Moon Comes over the Mountain" and "There Goes That Song Again." But she also sings "Born Free" and "The Impossible Dream"

and even does a credible job on "That's Life," apparently recorded a year before Sinatra.

Her mistake, as Michael Feinstein put it, was sticking around for too long. By the end of the era, though, when Smith was singing about riding in a beautiful balloon, it seemed as if she had lost whatever musical integrity she ever had—as if her career no longer had any reason for existing. New listeners might have confused her with the hilariously horrible Mrs. Miller, although, because Smith had considerably better intonation, her later records are not, in fact, as entertaining as those of that delightfully dreadful amateur yodeler.

In the seventies, Smith somehow became aligned with the Philadelphia Flyers; the hockey team came to regard her as a sort of good luck charm, claiming, "The game ain't begun 'til the fat lady sings!" After her death in 1986, the team erected a statue of her outside their arena. Today she almost seems to be better remembered in the world of pro sports than in American music or media. (Her Wikipedia page currently contains considerably more verbiage about the Flyers than about her radio shows or recordings.)

By the time Ronald Reagan awarded her the Medal of Freedom, the poignancy of "When the Moon Comes over the Mountain" had long been forgotten. All that remained were innumerable and interminable renditions of "God Bless America." Decades after her death, people who may never have heard her name can recognize her voice singing Berlin's great anthem—singer and song joined together to create an imperishable emblem of America.

Jeri Southern (1926–1991)

Cool? Compared to what? Coolness in jazz never implied the total absence of emotion, as with Mr. Spock or the Sharks in *West Side Story.* Somehow the absence of vibrato in the voice of Anita O'Day and those who followed her was taken as a sign of emotional restraint, one that happened to parallel the tremolo-free textures of the bands and soloists inspired by the 1949 Miles Davis tuba band. The same way that a "cool" tenor saxophonist, like Bob Cooper, would never get as hyper as Ben Webster (in his more frantic moments), O'Day sounds "cool" only compared to Ma Rainey. (You don't hear Helen Merrill pleading "Send Me to the 'Lectric Chair"!) Yet Mel Tormé can interpret lyrics no less thoughtfully than Sinatra, and June Christy's "Something Cool" is an epiphany of acting as well as singing.

Jeri Southern was both immersed in and apart from what we might call the "vo-cool school" of such Kentoncentric singers as Anita O'Day, June Christy, and Chris Connor. She was accurately described by *Down Beat* as "calm, cool, and collected," yet she effectively communicated oceans of feeling by conveying that what she was letting out was merely the tip of the emotional iceberg. The lyrics to "Fire Down Below," one of her few hit singles, could have been a personal mantra: "Keeping the temperature so low . . . is a work of art. / For there's a fire down below . . . in my heart."

As close friend and student Ruth Cameron Haden puts it, "I think her emotion went inside rather than being projected out. So as a listener, you would have to go to her to find the emotion. It would draw you to her when she was singing, she would keep it all within herself. She had this paradox within her: Jeri was a very analytical person who at the same time had a lot of passion for life. She was able to control it and center it."

Southern's tone is far more "warm," with an unmistakable vibrato (more apparent on her later sides), than any member of the O'Day gang. She acknowledged that her placidity was one of the major factors in her success. Pop singing in the early fifties was dominated by chart-topping tonsil-tearers, whose collective success morphed into the even more hysterical pop of the late fifties. In the context of all this overwrought belting, Southern and the cool school were an oasis of sanity.

In November 1955, Southern headlined at Birdland, and one of the accompanying acts was the recently revitalized founder of the cool, Miles Davis himself, then introducing his quintet with John Coltrane. Within a few months, the Davis-Coltrane fivesome would be one of the most important bands in American music, but at the time of that gig, Southern was the big news. When Nat Hentoff reviewed the bill (which included yet a third group, the Terry Gibbs Quartet) for *Down Beat*, most of his column inches went to Southern; he noted that this was her first Birdland appearance in six years (possibly meaning her first ever, since the club only opened in 1949), comparing the event to a "warm sunny day in the dead of winter." Contrastingly, Hentoff's praise for Davis was mainly limited to how the trumpeter's group "made for a generally effective complementary billing with Jeri."

Duke Ellington's later comment about Miles Davis—he applauded Miles for having the wherewithal to inform listeners that his was not a passive pop music—applies equally to Southern. As with Davis, her music requires active, attentive listening: You can't just turn her on in the background, and listen casually. You also have to listen to the right records: The later Roulette and Capitol albums are fine if you're already a fan, but unless you start with the exceptional Decca releases of 1951–57 you'll probably be wondering what all the fuss was about.

Her art also requires intimacy. Even Birdland must have seemed on the cavernous side for her; by consensus, Southern was at her best in really intimate rooms. When she did play Birdland, normally the home for such louder acts as the Basie or Kenton big bands, a banner with the following device was placed on all the tables: "Cognoscenti of the Birdland Arts are hereby importuned to forgo requisi-tioning of *vins et viands* during the recital of Miss Jeri Southern to effectuate the maximum benefits from her volatile variations in vocalizations. There will be a hiatus in service, seating and side issues during Miss Southern's renditions, with full restoration of such facilities following the *dénouement* of her inimitable delineations." (French words italicized by *moi*.)

This was the work of the club's loud, falsetto-squeaking host, Pee Wee Marquette, who signed the card "William Crayton Marquette, curator"; even a parody of dignity was more dignified than most acts received at Birdland, and seemed appropriate for this pianist and vocalist who started out in classical music.

Southern was born Genevieve Hering in 1926 in Royal, Nebraska (which, as all of her liner annotators can't resist pointing out, had a population of 190). She began studying the piano at five, and began formally teaching music ten years after that. Shifting from instructing to performing, Southern initially had eyes to make it as a classical pianist, but soon found herself hooked on jazz and pop songs. While she was playing piano in a club in the late forties, the manager offered her an extra $10 a week if she would also sing. She took up vocalizing on the spot, throwing herself into learning her new "instrument" with characteristic dedication. "I tried to sing in my speaking voice," Southern recalled in 1956. "It was pretty bad, because I had no vibrato. But I kept practicing my low voice and in about two months I sang well enough not to sound ridiculous."

By 1950, Chicago had become her home base, and there she made several important contacts. Like other Windy City jazzers, she became a favorite of the *Down Beat* staff, and would be regularly covered in that bible of the band biz; they were always anxious to put a good-looking white woman on the cover (where she appeared as early as 1951), so much the better if she had talent, better still if she could play as well as sing. Southern also became a favorite of Peggy Lee's, who generously brought her to the attention of her own producer, Sonny Burke, and label, Decca. At least this makes a good story, and although it's widely repeated in press releases and articles from the fifties, Milt Gabler, who ran Decca in those days, remembered it somewhat differently: Gabler told me in 1996 that he was turned on to Southern by her agent, Dick La Palm.

As Hal Webman, who produced her 1956 *When Your Heart's on Fire*, later recalled to me, the label initially concluded that her "soft, husky-voiced sexy thing" made her an ideal "Peggy Lee competitor"—even to the point of hiring Lee's ex-accompanist and husband Dave Barbour for Southern's *Southern Hospitality* album.

Southern made her best records for Decca between 1951 and 1957, the years when she had producers—most often Gabler, but also Burke and Webman—who were intelligent enough to let her do whatever she wanted, and encouraged her to play piano on most sessions. When she elected to do "Something I Dreamed Last Night," Gabler assigned Sy Oliver to do a chart for her. Since the arranger didn't know the song, Southern played it for him on a tape. "When Oliver brought back the arrangement," columnist Ralph J. Gleason reported, "it was merely an extension of her piano part."

The bassist-leader Charlie Haden, a longtime friend and fan, describes these sides like this: "She sang the way she spoke, in the most pure, honest, and vulnerable way. She bared her soul in her singing, and just gave everything she had, [expressing it all with just] this whisper in her voice. I especially like the first part of her career, when she was singing with [guitarist] Dave Barbour's trio. Those sessions were the most beautiful time for her."

Southern's recording career is comparatively small—about eleven LPs and some scattered singles—but, fortunately, she doesn't waste a lot of time. Her style sounds absolutely perfect and fully formed on one of her very first sides, "You Better Go Now." The idea for her to sing that particular song was very likely Gabler's; he had produced Billie Holiday's classic recording. Southern recorded two other songs out of the Holiday-Gabler collaboration, "No More" and "That Ole Devil Called Love." He's to be commended for not trying to make her into something she wasn't: Almost any other label would have tried to squeeze some hit singles out of her (can you imagine if she had recorded for Mitch Miller at Columbia?), and while she did cut 45s for the label, on the whole Gabler seems to have encouraged her to do what she did best.

"I always wanted her to do interesting songs," Gabler said, which also were appropriate in "the kind of room she worked in, in those years. She had a great style and she liked the kind of songs I liked, the Mabel Mercer school and the stuff I used to do with Billie Holiday and Peggy Lee." Southern told Ralph Gleason, "I've been collecting songs for years. People suggest them to me. Obscure tunes, stuff from old shows."

The 1957 *Southern Hospitality* (an expansion of her 1954 10-incher *Warm . . . Intimate Songs in the Jeri Southern Style*) is archetypical Southern, starting with its backing of Barbour's understated trio behind the star's own piano. She sings old songs almost exclusively, and these fall into two categories: standards you've heard (she was very big on Rodgers and Hart) and worthy old-timers that never quite caught history's ear, like "Have You Forgotten So Soon" and a lot of other thirties Crosby items. Even when she renders a familiar standard like "Until the Real Thing Comes Along" or "Something I Dreamed Last Night" or "The Gypsy in My Soul," she'll throw listeners off guard by starting with a verse that only the most indefatigable of tune detectives will have heard before.

Southern's specialty is understatement; some might even call her a minimalist. She combines Mabel Mercer's intelligence, taste, and narrative ability with Julie London's va-va-voom sensuality and attraction to the smallest possible accompaniment (usually a trio with her own piano or a small orchestra with a soft string section). To me, her understated erotic warmth is even more of a turn-on than London's more obvious bombshell sexiness, and her storytelling on the whole seems less mannered, more direct, and therefore more effective than Mercer's. Both of those other fifties stars had a talent for intimacy, but, in my opinion at least, neither could touch Southern in this quality. She communicates more meaningfully in part because of the very untrained informality of her voice. She's not only right in your face, she's practically sitting in your lap.

Does Southern only seem more sophisticated than London because her material is generally more melancholy? When Leonard Feather played her Billie Holiday's recent Clef recording of "Come Rain or Come Shine," she gave it five stars but with the caveat "I really would rather hear Billie sing sadder songs than this, but it's a great record," and also added, "I like that little way she has of sometimes sounding like 'I hate you,' you know?"

Southern could even turn "Too Marvelous for Words" and "Cross Your Heart" into a gut-wrenching experience. Bill Coss, talking about a Birdland appearance in 1956, reported, "As Jeri left the bandstand, a quiet, large man announced to no one in particular that he was going to commit suicide." (Coss added, "It was an idle threat.") Southern herself said in *Down Beat*, "It used to bother me when people would come up after a set and ask me if I was really as unhappy as I looked. There are very few happy ballads written, and if you understand the story each song tells, you're bound to appear unhappy."

At her best when she was both playing and singing, Southern attains a level close to that of her idol Nat King Cole, and she admitted to being inspired by the King's success with comparatively thoughtful, tasteful numbers (she cited "Too Young") in the face of the noisy competition. In a *Metronome* profile from 1956, she listed her favorite performers, the first and last being pianist-singers: Nat Cole, Frank Sinatra, Ella Fitzgerald, Peggy Lee, Mel Tormé, and (surprise!) Buddy Greco. In at least one case, she herself may have influenced Cole and in the process helped make a song into a standard: Southern recorded "When I Fall in Love" not long after Victor Young wrote it (for the 1952 *One Minute to Zero*), and her record, done with Young himself arranging and conducting and with her own piano, is remarkably similar in feeling and mood to the classic Cole–Gordon Jenkins record that made the song a standard a few years later.

Quoted in a 1951 *Down Beat* article, Southern chastised singers in general for not paying enough attention to the words: "I don't see how anyone can hear a song and not be conscious of the lyrics, but I'm always surprised at the number of singers who seem to sing without that same consciousness." (Not many singers or musicians or even writers were using words like "consciousness" in 1951.) "It's possible to sing a shaky lyric and to sing it well. I've heard Nat Cole transform a very ordinary song into something special, but few singers can do that. I've also heard singers wreck a fine ballad because they didn't understand what it meant, or perhaps they'd never really thought about it."

From her selections, we can gauge that Southern wasn't only big on solidly constructed words-and-music assemblages, but was partial to texts that told an unusual story. Who else would revive "I'm in Love with the Honorable Mr. So-and-So," Tin Pan Alley's most melodramatic soap opera portrayal of a kept woman in the back streets of a married man's life? This she contrasts with the equally unwieldy title "Miss Johnson Phoned Again Today." In this "Miss Otis Regrets" variant, the long-suffering mistress dumps her two-timing, not-so-honorable Mr. So-and-So in a message relayed via his secretary. (He's probably banging her on the side too, the rat.) The tune was one of many arty items written for Southern by a coterie of high-minded songsmiths, the most famous of whom were Tennessee Williams and Paul Bowles, who collaborated on "Cabin" (admittedly not one of her more memorable numbers) on the *Southern Hospitality* album.

Even when annexing a big band to Southern, as on *When Your Heart's on Fire* with Tutti Camarata and *Jeri Gently Jumps*, on which the superb Ralph Burns employs, of all apparently unhip things, an accordion, her album work of the mid-fifties maintains Southern's prerequisite intimacy. So do many of her singles. Said Gabler, "We used to put out singles in the 78 days, and then the 45s, but she wasn't big on the coin machines, we very seldom did pop tunes, if we ever did any. But as an artist I loved her!" (Southern actually endorsed a jukebox in the mid-fifties, and the magazine ad described her as a "comely young singer who combines pulchritude with fine voice projection. Her wistful, velvet soft manner is both new and neat. 'A lush thrush' say popular music enthusiasts.")

Some of the songs Gabler assigned her for singles did indeed have hit potential, particularly show tunes. "Show tunes," said Southern, "usually not the top hit for a show but an equally good though neglected number, form a large part of the songs I sing." Southern must be the only pop singer ever to have recorded the title song from *Bells Are Ringing*, backed by "Just in Time," which was indeed a hit (but not for her, as Ira Gershwin would say); "Nothing at All" from *Ankles Away;* "We're Not Children" and "Life Does a Girl a Favor" from *Oh Captain!,* "Do I Love You Because You're Beautiful?" from *Cinderella,* and "Married I Can Always Get" from *Man-*

hattan Tower. Only a few of the forty or so songs Southern cut as singles qualify as dog tunes; the single doggiest title would have to be something called "You're Gonna Flip, Mom," which, in the Southern style, isn't nearly as horrible as it might have been.

Around 1958, Gabler recalled, there was a shakeup at Decca; he himself had been transferred to Coral and was no longer able to look after Southern. That year, *Down Beat* announced that Roulette had signed her up as part of a "pacting spree" that included lots of major jazz vocal stars. In about two years she cut three albums for Roulette: *Coffee, Cigarettes & Memories* with Lennie Hayton, *Southern Breeze* with the Marty Paich Dektette, and *Jeri Southern Meets Johnny Smith*.

There are moments on all three of these: the title song from *Coffee* and "I'll Be Tired of You" with Georgie Auld's tenor solo on *Breeze*. But on the whole, this is not first-rate Southern; compared with the languorous moods of the 1952–58 recordings, she sounds less assured, possibly because the Roulette producers kept her away from the piano, which undercuts both her intonation and confidence. In spite of the presence of first-rate writers like Hayton and Marty Paich, she rarely achieves the oneness with the musicians that she had attained on the earlier discs. In her 1956 blindfold test with Leonard Feather, she praised Mel Tormé ("I think Mel is the most sensitive, artistic singer in the country or elsewhere"), but was herself unable to attain the compatibility that Tormé enjoyed with Paich. The two are like chalk and cheese.

"Later on I think producers started telling her to add more vibrato and get more of a guttural sound," says Charlie Haden, "more of a belting sound to her delivery," and her work suffered because of it. In 1960, Southern, now living in Los Angeles and married to bassist John Kitzmiller (who plays tuba on the Paich album), relocated label-wise again, this time to Capitol. The association started with a single of Southern singing Horace Silver's "Señor Blues." She made her only songbook album, a collection of Cole Porter songs, with the most audacious arranger working at the time, Billy May. It's my favorite of the later albums precisely because it makes good use of May's characteristic antic wit and can't necessarily be compared to the classic work because it doesn't even attempt to re-create the earlier intimacy—and it's filled with seldom heard songs like "Which."

She also recorded her in-person album, *Jeri Southern at the Crescendo*. Unfortunately, the Crescendo engagements of 1959–60 would not be high points in her personal or professional life. "The pace had been hectic for several months," *Down Beat* reported, and, according to the paper, she suffered a series of nervous breakdowns as well as the Asian flu. She was ill in November 1959, and collapsed on stage while working at the Crescendo in March 1960. Southern was set to do an English tour that year, but it was canceled after what *Melody Maker* described as three nervous breakdowns.

She was ready to quit by now anyhow. "She just stopped singing," says Ruth Cameron. "One day in the middle of a set, she just walked off and took a plane back to L.A. She hated the music business, and she said she had sung everything she wanted to sing and she didn't want to repeat herself." For the last three decades of her life, she devoted herself to playing, arranging, composing, two husbands (Kitzmiller and then arranger Bill Holman), a daughter (Kathy King), writing a piano-method book, and, most of all, teaching. She died at sixty-four in 1991. Two months later, her greatest latter-day exposure came when Charlie Haden incorporated her vocal "Ev'ry Time We Say Goodbye" in his remarkable Quartet West album *Haunted Heart*.

A lot of people got the point then: No one could move you like Jeri Southern.

Jo Stafford (1917–2008)

Maybe it's me, but as much as I love Jo Stafford, I find that of all the major jazz-influenced pop vocalists, she's the hardest to talk about, or, rather, the nature of her appeal is the hardest to pin down. In a way, it's easier to talk about what Jo Stafford isn't rather than what she is: She isn't warm and friendly, for instance, like her contemporaries Rosemary Clooney or Doris Day—there's no mistaking that they sing so obviously from the heart and never leave us wondering why we like them so much. Neither does she belong with Ella Fitzgerald and Sarah Vaughan, two great jazz singers who, in Ms. Stafford's description of Fitzgerald, "give more weight to the melody than to the lyric." Perhaps she is the spiritual foremother of those cool and reserved singers like Chris Connor and Jeri Southern, who make you look a little harder to find the emotion; it's there all right, but, like the silver lining, you have to look for it.

When we try to decode the emotional relationship Jo Stafford establishes with a song, it soon becomes plain that we can't use the patterns established by any other singer as a precedent. It's apparent, from her very first note, that she's one of the greats, but her emotional approach to a song makes me think of her as the *Mona Lisa* of pop music, happy and sad at the same time. Even after years of listening closely, I find that it's almost as impossible to identify the source of her greatness as it is to deny the beauty of her voice and the haunting quality of her singing.

There's no one who can sing "Haunted Heart" like Jo Stafford, as bassist-bandleader Charlie Haden acknowledged when he sampled her 1947 vocal of that song for his 1991 Quartet West album *Haunted Heart*. Haden exploited the ethereal quality of her singing: Of all the best of her generation and ever since, Stafford seems the most like a disembodied voice. We don't really think of her as a live performer: There's no famous album of Jo Stafford live

at the Waldorf or Carnegie Hall. She was never widely known for her work in nightclubs, and even though she appeared frequently on television in the golden age of that medium, few videotapes or DVDs of her have circulated.

If there's a single word that sums up the source of our attraction to Stafford, it would be "paradox." There's something joyous about her, which comes through particularly in the up tunes, but it would be hard to find her doing a purely optimistic love song—there's always a hint of melancholy. Surely no other pop star sounds at once so intimate and yet so distant, so emotionally forthcoming and yet so completely in control. While Stafford can be sexy, she doesn't have to be; while she's always feminine, she's rarely erotically steamy. I could never imagine her singing one of those masochistic I-must-have-that-man-or-I-will-die extreme torch songs; she's just too smart for that particular genre.

One of the few songs that doesn't suit her is "Homework," an Irving Berlin opus from *Miss Liberty*, which is mainly notable in its antifeminist viewpoint (somehow "misogynist" doesn't quite describe it). Dinah Shore's Columbia version was coyly girly-girly, but the only way Stafford can do it is to downplay the lyric altogether and make it into a toe-tapping swinger. Unlike Sarah Vaughan (who later recorded "Homework"), Stafford is incapable of playing it cute. She was never the girl next door, like Doris Day. She is somehow familiar, but with an inexplicable air of mystery. She's the beautiful divorcée down the street, sophisticated, wise, and hot; you don't know anything about her but you can't take your eyes off her.

Jo Stafford instantly overwhelms the listener with the magnitude of her gifts. First, there's that steely-perfect intonation, which immediately locates her in the same high-rent district as Nat Cole and the superhuman Miss Fitzgerald. Then there's the perfect rhythmic sense, which knows exactly what degree of slow to bring to the stately "Whispering Hope" and precisely what gradation of swing to give an up-tempo number like "The Gentleman Is a Dope." And though she's never been as lyric-literal as some of the other ladies, she shares with Fitzgerald the gift for projecting immeasurable kilowatts of radiant warmth.

(A note on reissues: There are two three-CD packages that offer a well-chosen sampling of Stafford's best work. *Her Greatest Hits and Finest Performances*, from Reader's Digest, concentrates on the big sellers, while Sony Music's *The Portrait Edition* offers superb songs, chosen irregardless of chart placement, and samples almost all her albums as well as the entire career, from the first Pied Pipers [octet] date of 1939 to the last Darlene Edwards date of 1979. Both sets are essential and complement each other well.)

"There was always singing around the house," Stafford told researcher Gino Falzarano. "When I was still a kid in high school, my sisters Christine and Pauline, who were eleven and fourteen years older than I, were in radio as the Stafford Sisters—a very original name. We did a lot of harmonizing, so when I graduated it was just very natural for me to go with them." Though the Staffords were originally from Tennessee, the family had settled in Coalinga, California, by the time their youngest daughter was born in 1917; she would grow up in Long Beach. Mr. and Mrs. Grover Cleveland Stafford must have had some sort of musical or showbiz aspirations for their three daughters, which is the only explanation as to why they gave their girls the euphonic rhyming names of Christine, Pauline, and Josephine.

By the mid-thirties, the Stafford Sisters had clearly made it beyond the amateur level; as scholar Henry Schmidt has discovered, the trio made what must be their first record in the company of Louis Prima when the trumpeter-funster was on the coast in 1936. The tune is the forgettable but catchy "Let's Get Together and Swing," and the label states clearly "Louis Prima and his New Orleans Gang, vocal by Louis Prima and The Stafford Sisters." Schmidt has also unearthed four tunes by the Stafford Sisters (billed as "girl's quartet," rather than a trio, curiously) recorded in summer 1939 and issued on a 16" commercial transcription produced by the Standard Corporation. As a solo vocalist she also recorded several transcriptions with Frank Trumbauer's Orchestra.

The Stafford Sisters were particularly active on live radio and in pictures—supposedly they're the off-screen "madrigal" singers heard behind Fred Astaire in *Damsel in Distress*. While recording various vocals for *Alexander's Ragtime Band* (1938), the youngest Stafford joined forces with two male groups, the Four Esquires and the (three) Rhythm Kings, merging into an eight-voice supergroup called the Pied Pipers. Early on, the octet attracted the attention of Tommy Dorsey, and he brought them east to appear with him on a broadcast from New York. Stafford had the good fortune to be in New York at the early peak of the Swing Street era, as she later recounted to Gene Lees: "In 1936, my sisters and I used to frequent a place called the Famous Door. It had jazz players. It got to be where we were there every night. We got to be the house singers, practically, the three of us. And one night, all of a sudden, there sits Johnny Mercer. I almost went out of my skull. I was such a fan." (It's a strange anecdote—Mercer was hardly widely known in 1936.)

The Pipers hustled all over New York looking for gigs and also traveled to Chicago for another radio show with Dorsey. By the end of 1939, the Sentimental Gentleman had made up his mind to permanently annex the Pied Pipers to his orchestra, but on the condition that they cut down from eight singers to four, three men (one of whom was Stafford's first husband) and a girl (Stafford). It's an unwritten law of vocal groups that great voices eventually rise to the top; Stafford was distinguished within the Pieds from the beginning in that she was the quartet's only female voice, but it became clearer and clearer that she was the dominant talent in the quartet.

She consolidated her position as a rising star—within the Pipers quartet and the entire Dorsey orchestra—with her ties to the songwriter Matt Dennis. She had known him for several years already, since, in his role as pianist, he had accompanied the Stafford Sisters. When the Pipers were situated with the Dorsey band, she recommended him and his songs to her boss, and pretty soon the astute bandleader and publisher put Dennis under contract to several of his various music publishing houses. In return, Dennis singled her out to handle the solo vocal on what was for them a rather atypically sentimental aria entitled "Little Man with a Candy Cigar."

Stafford was an excellent choice—only the most straight-ahead of voices could have put over "Little Man" without descending to the maudlin. It wasn't a blockbuster hit on the level of Sinatra's big numbers with Dorsey from the same period, but it was a record that got noticed. "One of the greatest vocals in the world is 'Little Man with a Candy Cigar,' " said band singer Kitty Kallen (of Jack Teagarden, Jimmy Dorsey, and Harry James fame). "It changed my approach to singing pop music. I think every singer should listen to that song." It could be argued that this was the birth of the cool—the best band singers up until that time, like Helen Forrest, were openly warm and even hot and sensual, whereas Stafford always seemed to be holding a bit back, with something of the even, monodynamic edge of a folksinger.

After "Candy Cigar," Dorsey featured Stafford increasingly as the central voice, both with and without the other Pipers. (All of her commercial vocals with Dorsey have been collected on *For You*, on the British label Memoir, but dozens of airchecks spotlighting her still linger unheard in the BMG-NBC transcription vault.) These vary between ballads ("Who Can I Turn To?"), rhythm numbers ("What Can I Say, Dear, After I Say I'm Sorry"), and some red-hot rhythm numbers—"Whatcha Know, Joe?," "Margie," and "Swingin' on Nothin' "—the last of which is somewhat remarkable in that it's probably the first ever recorded duet between a white woman, Stafford, and a black man, arranger-composer Sy Oliver doubling as rhythm singer.

The Pied Pipers left Dorsey not long after Sinatra did, at the end of 1942, and Stafford gradually emerged from the quartet. By this time, Johnny Mercer, who had long been a mentor, was encouraging her to go solo, and now was in a position to offer her a recording contract with his new label, Capitol Records. Stafford immediately established herself as a potent force in the record and radio business (and later televison, although, unlike Doris Day, she never bothered much with movies). From the start of her solo career, Stafford was a formidable hit maker: The big chart-toppers started coming as early as the war years—she would be known as "GI Jo" to the veterans of both World War II and Korea.

Stafford and arranger-conductor (and occasional composer) Paul Weston had known each other since the earliest days of the Pied Pipers. They first became close personally and professionally in the mid-forties, as Weston gradually assumed musical directorship of Stafford's career. Within a few years, they were inseparable, and they were married in 1952. Two years before that, however, they demonstrated their allegiance to each other by jointly relocating from Capitol—mentor Mercer was now gone—to Columbia.

In 1952, Stafford established her worth to Columbia with "You Belong to Me," one of the biggest hits of the era. The story goes that it was the work of a Kentucky-based female songwriter, Chilton Price, who shared the credit with two established male writers (one of whom was Pee Wee King, writer of "Tennessee Waltz") because she was convinced a lady composer wouldn't be taken seriously. It sort of makes sense that a song about romantic possession would be written by a composer who was afraid that she would be penalized for being a woman.

"You Belong to Me" traveled up the food chain from Sue Thompson, a second-tier country artist, to Patti Page, and then to Stafford on Columbia, and was also successfully recorded by Dean Martin on Capitol. All three of these later recordings were successful, but Jo Stafford's was an absolute blockbuster: It was on the U.S. hit singles charts for an amazing twenty-four weeks and topped the listings in Britain as well. Soon there were doo-wop versions by the Orioles and the Duprees and a rockabilly treatment by Gene Vincent (all of which, surprisingly, kept the modulation at the end of the bridge). The song so permeated postwar pop culture that it was one of the few mainstream standards to be recorded by Bob Dylan.

The Stafford version begins with a multiple-voice intro (actually one voice with lots of reverb and echo—like a sonic equivalent of a hall of mirrors), similar to the kind of thing that Patti Page (the one-woman vocal group—although, oddly, Page does not use that gimmick on her version), and uses a marimba backing that sounds like the kind of off-beat instrument Mitch Miller might throw into an orchestration, different for the sake of novelty. But Stafford and Weston are much more thoroughly musical than either of these comparison points. The tune keeps rolling out with a distinct countermelody that heightens the tension, although on the whole it's less dramatic and more intimate than the Page version. Stafford sounds warm, yet reserved, motherly and loverly at the same time, as she informs the object of her affection that it's all right for him to go gallivanting all over the globe as long as he remembers, "when a dream appears," that he belongs to her. There still is something of a country feel to the thing, and a doo-wop/R&B thing as well (a hint of triplets); it's one of those rare records that is everything at once. It's a classic example of Stafford at her very best; she uses her amazing voice like an instrument, a saxophone playing with absolute purity and perfect intonation, and amazingly bell-shaped notes like no horn I ever heard. But the amazing thing is that she's never just being an instrument and concentrating on the melody to the exclusion of the words; she always makes the song and the narrative the most important thing.

Stafford came to Columbia an established star, and, being based on the West Coast, she generally avoided having to do the bidding of Mitch Miller, the label's head of pop singles, who was based in New York. Miller seems to have been the force behind Stafford's long series of duets with Frankie Laine; obviously it was Miller who insisted that they record a trilogy of songs about food: "Chow Willy," "Piece a Puddin'," and "Hambone." On the plus side, though, it was also Miller who motivated Stafford to record a trio of classic country songs by country savant Hank Williams: "Hey, Good Lookin'" and "Settin' the Woods on Fire" as duets with Laine, and a big-selling solo single of "Jambalaya," which proved an appropriate seafood-specific companion to her equally successful "Shrimp Boats" (Weston's top-selling adaptation of a folk song).

Even with Miller's occasional input, Stafford and Weston seem to have controlled their own musical destinies. Essentially they recorded whatever they wanted, particularly in terms of albums (Weston was, for a time, put in charge of Columbia's pop album division). She earned the right to control what she put on her albums by continuing to turn out an unstoppable stream of hit singles. Like Sinatra—and virtually no one else (unlike, say, friend and sometimes radio co-star Dick Haymes)—she was one of the few singers of her generation to lose no ground between 1945 and 1955. Stafford is frequently named as one of the biggest-selling female vocalists of all time, and certainly of the decade between the war and Elvis. There's no debating that between her vast popularity and the consistent astoundingly high quality of her work, she is one of the most important pop singers of all time.

In one respect, Stafford is a sort of an un–Peggy Lee. Lee reaches outward to other cultures, going beyond Tin Pan Alley and even Western music itself. Stafford, too, goes beyond Tin Pan Alley, but instead she turns inward to the riches of the Anglo-Saxon poetic tradition. Where Lee indulges in Japanese haikus and Jewish wedding songs, Stafford reanimates American and Scottish folk songs and traditional spirituals. Her *American Folk Songs* album was considered a classic even in its own day, so much so that Stafford and Weston remade the whole project in stereo in the early sixties. Then, too, the single most beautiful album she ever made may well be *My Heart's in the Highlands.* Lee's thing was Asian love poetry, Stafford's thing was musical settings of the work of the great Scottish poet Robert Burns. (The recommended three-CD retrospective, *The Portrait Edition,* made something of a musical wisecrack when it followed "My Heart's in the Highlands" with "My One and Only Highland Fling," a slice of ersatz Scottish poetry by the Jewish Ira Gershwin and the Italian Harry Warren from *The Barkleys of Broadway.*)

If there's such a thing as Anglo-Saxon soul, this is it. Unlike Lee and their other Capitol co-star of the late forties, Kay Starr, Stafford projects nothing even vaguely black about her singing. People have mistaken Peggy Lee for Billie Holiday and Kay Starr for Dinah Washington, but Stafford is far more Anglo than Afro. Yet when she sings a blues, she sings it with authority: Her 1955 "St. Louis Blues" can be charitably described as overarranged, but the vocal itself is fine; likewise, her 1959 "Blues in the Night" is way overdone compared to the wonderfully subtle reading of the Arlen-Mercer standard she cut in 1941 with Tommy Dorsey. She's even more convincing on the blues-tinged "Smoking My Sad Cigarette" (1952) as well as on Richard M. Jones's old blues song, "Trouble in Mind" (1947). She even participated in an extended song suite, *Ballad of the Blues,* assembled by Weston, and whether or not one cares for this concert-style presentation, her vocals are superb.

What she did for folk songs, she also did for traditional spirituals. "Whispering Hope" was Weston's brainchild—he remembered this old religious song from an acoustic record he had owned as a child. It was the work of one Septimus Winner (1827–1902), who wrote under the name Alice Hawthorne. The composer originally conceived of the song as a duet for two female voices, alto and soprano; Stafford and the superb Broadway-styled singer Gordon MacRae refitted it for alto and baritone—and made a chart hit out of it—though Stafford returned to it in Winner/Hawthorne's original format with her daughter, Amy, on one of her final recordings, in 1978.

It was Weston who reimagined "Whispering Hope" as a duet for Stafford and MacRae, although he noted that he personally didn't know anyone who had bought it or any deejay who had played it—presumably because it was too square. No such disclaimer was necessary: It was and is a beautiful record, and became a million-seller in the Bible Belt, where people weren't afraid of an honest religious sentiment sincerely expressed. MacRae is, not surprisingly, a bit of a stiff, and while I wouldn't want to hear him sing "Whatcha Know, Joe?" with her, he is just perfect on this traditional material. The Stafford-MacRae religious duets (collected on a British CD, *The Old Rugged Cross*) are indeed rather rigid but beautiful, proving that not all great American pop has to have a jazz component in even the

loosest definition of the term. Yes, music can mean something even if it doesn't swing.

The twosome also recorded enough duets of secular material to fill a CD (another British compilation, *Down Memory Lane*). Their pop sides have a retro feel, including, as they do, a lot of older songs ("Tea for Two") as well as newer songs—some from Broadway ("Wunderbar," "My Darling, My Darling"), some not ("Dearie," "Say Something Sweet to Your Sweetheart")—with an old-fashioned feeling. "Tea for Two" had already been swung and parodied to well beyond the breaking point, while "Wunderbar," Cole Porter's send-up of a Viennese operetta waltz, was usually delivered with, if not sarcasm, at least a hint of irony. The twosome even did a full 10" eight-tune LP of all the major *Kiss Me, Kate* songs (reissued, at last, shortly before Stafford's death in 2008). Stafford and MacRae sing Cole Porter's score completely straight, and the results are gorgeous. (The Stafford-MacRae duet sessions continued until 1951, which was some time after she had already relocated from Capitol to Columbia—apparently there was a special clause in the new contract that allowed her to continue the series. Later, she would record a very different series of boy-girl duets with rhythmic belter Frankie Laine.)

Stafford can go completely the other way as well. In July 1949, at roughly the same time she was visiting the tightly corseted past, she cut a remarkable two-sided bebop gem, on which the billing read "Jo Stafford with Dave Lambert and His Vocal Choir Plus Paul Weston and His Orchestra." One side is a bop version of the old-time tune "Smiles." The tempo is fast and boppy, the orchestration (which sounds more like Pete Rugolo than Paul Weston) is angular and dissonant, like Dizzy Gillespie's big band, and after Stafford's 32-bar opening chorus with the choir, Dave Lambert takes an extended scat vocal that's at least as prominent as Stafford's part in the proceedings. Eventually she joins and blends in with the choir, also scatting all the way.

The other side is even wilder. Credited to Lambert, the composition is titled "M + H + R x 3ee—oo (over) 4/4 aa3 X (times) 32 = BOP (JOLLY JO)." This was the early age of wordless scat features, and "Jolly Jo" was Stafford's answer to Lambert's own "What's This" with Gene Krupa (and "That's What," the King Cole Trio's answer), Mel Tormé's "That's Where I Came In," and the big Ella scat features like "Flying Home" and "How High the Moon." There's no familiar melody (although the tune is similar to "Blue Lou") and there are no words, nor is Stafford featured much as a soloist—she blends in with the choir, although she's obviously the dominant voice, and there's a lengthy scat exchange with Lambert. Considering that Stafford is not generally regarded as a pop singer with jazz capabilities, "Jolly Jo" and "Smiles" are a revelation. Probably she took a chance on this experiment because she was a softie for vocal groups of all stripes.

While "Jolly Jo" and "Smiles" (the latter is currently available on *Jo Stafford on Capitol*, on Collectors' Choice Music) lay buried in the vault, Stafford trumpeted her jazz intentions on one well-known, long-playing album, the brilliant *Jo + Jazz*. This 1960 project found her in the company of five of the top soloists of the Ellington orchestra: Ben Webster, Ray Nance, Lawrence Brown, Harry Carney, and, making what so far as I know is his only appearance with a major girl singer outside the Ellington fold, Johnny Hodges. Johnny Mandel did the orchestrations with more than a slight nod to Duke, and the tunes include "Day Dream," "I Didn't Know About You," and "Just Squeeze Me" from the Ellington-Strayhorn catalogue. Stafford looks wildly seductive on the cover, like a cougar who means business (with bright red lips and exaggerated eye shadow). When she later reissued the album on her own Corinthian label, she unfortunately replaced the sexy original shot with a considerably more demure portrait.

Stafford's singing, low and sultry, is perfect throughout. The Ellingtonians—the saxists in particular—take center stage, and West Coasters Don Fagerquist (trumpet) and Jimmy Rowles (piano) are along for more than just the ride. The stereo recording is superb, what with Hodges coming at you from one channel, Webster and Stafford, technically and spiritually, right down the center. This is one of the crucial Desert Island Discs in jazz history—I'm comfortable asserting that no one except possibly Fitzgerald with *Lullabies of Birdland* or Holiday with *Lady in Satin* ever made a better jazz vocal album. The fact that it wasn't made by a full-time jazz vocalist is miraculous. Had Stafford made more records like this, surely she would be regarded as one of the greatest of jazz singers. But her heart was in more places than just jazz: It was up in the Highlands, and down in the valley, the valley so low.

Other Stafford long-playing albums, were very nearly as jazzy as *Jo + Jazz*. *Swingin' Down Broadway* puts just as much emphasis on the swingin' as it does on Broadway, and she's astute enough to include "Tomorrow Mountain," another slice of Ellingtonia, this one from the Duke's short-lived 1946 show, *Beggar's Holiday*. "Old Devil Moon," on the same album, is as fine a swing treatment as any version of that song since the Sinatra-Riddle version that inspired it. Likewise, *I'll Be Seeing You* (1958), also released as *GI Jo*, which concentrated on songs of the World War II era (including, but not limited to, remakes of her wartime hits), was primarily a swinging assemblage of terrific songs. We've seen that Jo Stafford can be very genre specific—you won't find a jivey track in the middle of *American Folk Songs*—but on other occasions the theme is more flexible. For instance, a number of tracks originally released on *Swingin' Down Broadway*, ostensibly a show tunes collection, turned up on CD in a collection called *The Big Band Sound*, ostensibly a swing collec-

tion. She also made an outstanding all-swinging set with the jazz accordionist Art Van Damme titled *Once Over Lightly*; if you don't believe me, listen for yourself.

"The voice says it all, beautiful—pure—straightforward—no artifice—matchless intonation—instantly recognizable," said Rosemary Clooney. "Those things describe the woman too." But then she added, "You think you really know her, then she becomes Darlene Edwards." Stafford's sense of humor seems partly connected to her capacity for making extraordinary music in tandem with the most unlikely of male co-stars. You can't work with Gene Autry, Nelson Eddy, Frankie Laine, or Liberace (just to mention a few) without developing a grand sense of irony. This ties into her cool-yet-savage sense of humor—in her alter egos as hillbilly hollerer Cinderella G. Stump or café society chantootsie Darlene Edwards, Stafford further mystifies one's already futile attempts to make sense of her. Another pop star might incorporate gags into her regular act (as, early on, she did when the Pied Pipers incorporated Ravel's "Bolero" into "In a Little Spanish Town") or occasionally stoop to a Mitch Miller inanity. For instance, when Doris Day does a comic song, she does it in the same persona—Doris Day doing "The Geiger Counter Song" or "Mr. Tap Toe" or "Rickety Rackety Rendezvous" is still Doris Day. But for Stafford to get silly, she has to, in effect, morph into a whole other character.

She saves up her comic talents like a squirrel his nuts, until she's piled up enough purely comedic albums to suggest that she's as much a comedienne, in the great tradition of femme funsters Martha Raye and Betty Hutton, as she is a balladeer. And what makes the Darlene Edwards performances so scathingly funny is how incredibly close they come to being just regular pop records. In her own way no less a superb satirist than Spike Jones or Stan Freberg, Darlene Edwards presents a view of the workaday world of straight pop that's skewed just slightly off-center. Somehow it seems altogether appropriate, given the wit and wisdom of the music industry, then and now, that Darlene Edwards should win a Grammy Award before Stafford.

Jonathan and Darlene Edwards, the hilariously inept piano and vocal team (he was portrayed by Paul Weston), and Cinderella G. Stump were to Stafford what Charlie McCarthy and Mortimer Snerd were to Edgar Bergen, alter egos that took on a life of their own. Indeed, Darlene Edwards maintained a completely separate recording career for nearly two decades; I once asked Paul Weston, "What's Jonathan Edwards *really* like?," and Paul answered, "He's a pain in the ass!" The Edwardses Cinderella G. Stump (the "G." apparently stood for "Goofy") came from a long-ago era when, unlike today, the pop music industry had the healthy capacity to laugh at itself, and these parodies were often divided on ethnic lines. Spike Jones would famously do "Chinese Mule Train" (Western song goes Asian) and "Japanese Skokian" (African song also goes Asian); Mickey Katz would make everything Jewish (e.g., the Brazilian "Tico Tico" into the Yiddish "Tickle, Tickle"). There were other acts during the forties who did hillbilly parodies of mainstream pop songs, such as the team of Abigail and Buddy, billed as "the Goon Holler Twins," and not much later, country and western comics Homer and Jethro. As early as 1940, Tommy Dorsey had famously recorded a "hillbilly"-style version of Cole Porter's "Friendship," with Stafford on hand. The results were issued as "Dorsey Family—Mountain Branch."

Capitol's contribution to the country comedy stakes was Red Ingle and His Natural Seven, led by the veteran reed player and vocalist, who had enjoyed long tenures with both Ted Weems and Spike Jones. The story that she always told was that Stafford invented the Stump character on the spot when she was asked to fill in for Red Ingle's missing vocaliste. In 1947, "Timtayshun" was Miss Stump's "Mountain Branch" version of "Temptation," a melodramatic tune often performed as a tango. She takes the very serious and makes it downright silly. Remarkably, real-life country singers were not offended by the parody; June Carter Cash and Johnny Cash included "Temptation" on her final album, and they re-created the Cinderella G. Stump–Red Ingle banter word for mispronounced word.

By the time the public figured out who "Cinderella" really was, the record had become a number-one hit. To me, the mystery is why Stafford confined the business of pseudonymous activity to her comedy recordings. She would later sing "straight" country material, from Pee Wee King's "Tennessee Waltz" and "You Belong to Me" to Hank Williams's "Jambalaya" and Paul Weston's faux-folkie "Shrimp Boats." (Weston once told me that the song was the number-one hit for so many weeks that the choreographers on *Your Hit Parade* went out of their minds trying to come up with a new dance number for it every week.) Why didn't she record these as "Josephine Weston"? She could have sung Scottish and Irish numbers as Josie MacStafford and done Yiddish records with Mr. Katz as Yosela Wetstein (Paul Weston's given name).

Weston also once told me that Jonathan and Darlene Edwards emerged out of the Westons' dealings not only with Mitch Miller ("You can't believe the crap he wanted us to record!") but as a confrontation with the whole wide world of mediocre music. Yet where Cinderella G. Stump could be taken as an assault on what some might (condescendingly) think of as lowbrow culture, Jonathan and Darlene Edwards were an attack on the pretentious. Darlene is sort of a Tin Pan Alley version of Florence Foster Jenkins and a predecessor of Mrs. Miller (the infamously out-of-tune Capitol artist of the sixties who recorded hysterically dreadful versions of popular songs). People debate whether or not Mrs. Jenkins or Mrs. Miller were in on their own joke—if they actually were aware of how godawful they were—but as portrayed by Stafford, Darlene Edwards is obviously a deliberate joke rather than an unintentional one. She has a flawless talent for hitting flat notes at the most excruciating moments and singing with the most infirm sense of rhythm possible. Weston mentioned that Mr. and Mrs. Edwards evolved partly out of Miller's dreadful novelty songs, but actually they are at their funniest when doing a dreadful version of a great song like "April in Paris" or "Sophisticated Lady." Then, too, they're particularly amusing when doing a completely inappropriate song, like "Tip Toe Through the Tulips," "Stayin' Alive," or "I Am Woman."

Darlene Edwards shadowed Stafford around for the final portion of her career. By the end of the fifties, Stafford and Weston had decided to move on. Their initial stop was Capitol again, where their primary business seems to have been making stereo remakes of Stafford's earlier mono hits. Other albums from the same period also caught her in a reflective mood: *Getting Sentimental over Tommy Dorsey* was a marvelous homage to the Smiling Irishman. Her most original project during this period was *Do I Hear a Waltz?* Where both Sinatra (*All Alone*) and Steve Lawrence (*Come Waltz with Me*) had made entire albums of mostly slow waltzes, Stafford had the idea of doing a set of largely jazz numbers in a swinging 3/4 time. The set wasn't a Stafford masterpiece on the level of *Jo + Jazz* or *Swingin' Down Broadway*, but it had some outstanding tracks, such as the title cut, "Do I Hear a Waltz?" (the title of the only collaboration between Richard Rodgers and Stephen Sondheim) and the *Finian's Rainbow* standard "When I'm Not Near the Boy I Love." The early sixties was ground zero for swinging and modal waltzes, à la Ray Charles's "Busted," and Stafford's hip and happy waltz employs a Charlesian electric organ and a muted trumpet reminiscent of Nat Cole's "L-O-V-E."

By this time Stafford was easing from semiretirement to full retirement. A few of the later tracks on *The Portrait Edition* with trombonist Warren Covington and his Dorseyesque orchestra (produced by Reader's Digest recording division), "Ghost of a Chance" and "The Party's Over," where Stafford sounds better than ever. One can't help regretting that she didn't press on until the bitter end, like Sinatra and Clooney.

Upon leaving Columbia, Weston and Stafford assumed the ownership of their masters, an occurrence supposedly made possible by Doris Day's husband and manager, the infamous Marty Melcher. Apparently, the contract Melcher negotiated for Day gave her the option of owning her own masters at the eventual end of her deal with Columbia. When Stafford and Weston signed with Columbia in 1950, they asked for, and received, favored-nation status, giving them any beneficial arrangement that any other Columbia artist had in his or her contract. Day never exercised her option to take her own masters with her, but Weston and Stafford did. By the seventies, the Westons were pressing their best-remembered Columbia masters on their own Corinthian label. Stafford also made several original recordings for Corinthian: Her last recording project was a trashing of six Duke Ellington classics by Jonathan and Darlene Edwards, done around 1982.

After that, Mrs. Weston (I always addressed her as such when we spoke) claimed, she wasn't even remotely tempted to sing again; certainly whatever thoughts she might have had about going back to work were banished from her head when Weston died in 1996. She told Gino Falzarano that she refused to sing for the same reason that Lana Turner wouldn't pose in a bathing suit in her seventies—in other words, because she no longer had the technique. She was being modest on several levels—not the least of which is the idea that we would only or even primarily listen to Stafford's singing for technique alone. We listen for that Anglo-Saxon soul. We listen to decode the mystery of her vocal equivalent of the *Mona Lisa*'s smile.

She died in July 2008, aged ninety. When all is said and done, who was Jo Stafford? A pop singer and a comic, a ballad singer and a folksinger, a band singer and a group singer, a swinger and a mourner (not to mention a radio and TV star, wife, and mother). She's a riddle to be solved, with no simple answers, and she haunts you so that after hearing her just once, you can't ever unhear her.

Kay Starr (born 1922)

The word "jazz" applies to a very specific kind of music, no matter what subgenre of jazz we may be talking about, and the same thing goes for "country," "opera," and "blues." But the phrase "pop music" has more to do with a set of cultural and economic circumstances than exclusively musical concerns. Otherwise, how could Al Jolson, Benny Goodman, and Sting all be considered pop stars?

The state of pop, like the state of Texas, is a vast one, and no one covers more of its territory than Kay Starr. Oklahoma-born and Texas-raised, Starr is the only major pop personality who is equally at home with Harlemites and hillbillies, and who can jump over the boundaries of genre like a Kentucky thoroughbred leaping hurdles.

It isn't that Starr leaps from style to style—although she has made albums that are exclusively jazz, country, and gospel—but rather that every note she sings encompasses all this music simultaneously. Surely no other vocalist has been able to combine a country tone with a swinging beat, or to match the immediacy of pop with the intensity of the blues, and wrap it all up in one of the greatest careers in pop music. It speaks acres about her style that as a youngster in her mid-teens, jazz violin pioneer Joe Venuti heard her singing with a local hillbilly band and somehow divined that, among all those twangy guitars and banjos, here was the vocalist he needed for his swing band.

Starr is undeniably a jazz singer—one of the very best ever—yet the essential tone of her voice, divorced from her swinging sense of time and her reliance on the jazz repertory, might be considered country. The same way that her contemporary Dinah Washington starts with a blues sound but uses jazz techniques, Starr starts with a country timbre and makes it jump through jazz hoops. She's the only major jazz singer, unless you want to count Bessie Smith, who has a distinctly nonurban timbre. And, like another contemporary, Anita O'Day, she ascended to the ranks of exalted jazz royalty (if not quite on the same level as Fitzgerald or Vaughan, not far from it) without the slightest tinge of anything that could be considered an African American sound.

We can give some credit to the fortunate circumstance that Starr happened to be born in 1922. Had she come along twenty or perhaps only ten years later, she would have been too late to have been caught in even the aftershock of the big band boom. Starr sold a lot of records in the forties and fifties, but probably could have done even better as a beehived C&W Nashvilleite in the sixties and seventies, to be compared to Patsy Cline rather than Sarah Vaughan. Had that been the case, the loss to jazz and standards would have been inestimable.

Still, throughout Starr's generation and earlier, record sales were strictly a secondary consideration—it was on the radio that pop singers made their careers. It was certainly central to Starr's success: In her earliest days, her radio enabled her to sample and take in all the styles that would influence her, from the Grand Ole Opry to Benny Goodman band remotes. By the time she started singing professionally in her teens, radio was the means by which she was letting the rest of the world hear her. There doesn't seem to be any time in Starr's life when she wasn't singing in front of audiences, although at the very first stage in her career (when her age was not yet in the double digits) the beneficiaries of her talents were the feathered denizens of her family's henhouse.

Starr's official biography, which resides on her Web site, informs us that her mom was Irish and her pop was 100 percent Iroquois; researcher Ted Ono, however, insists that Starr herself was 75 percent Cherokee. She was born Kathryn Starks in Dougherty, Oklahoma, in 1922; by 1931, the family had moved to Dallas, and in that year she won a talent contest sponsored by a local Dallas radio station at a local theater (singing "Now's the Time to Fall in Love"). The station awarded the young Kathryn Starks her own regular fifteen-minute slot three nights a week, which lasted until the family moved to Memphis. In Tennessee, she again landed a regular spot on local radio, doing both pop and hillbilly songs.

Radio also helped Starr to land her first gigs with important bands; she seems to have enjoyed brief stays with more important bandleaders than any other singer, starting with Joe Venuti. In 1937, the famous jazz violinist and his orchestra played at the Peabody Hotel in Memphis. He was, at that moment, lacking a girl singer, and the Peabody, the swankiest establishment in town, regarded his band as being incomplete without a "femme chirper" (as *Down Beat* used to call them). Fortunately, the band's manager happened to hear Kay Starr (as she was now known) on a local broadcast. She served as Venuti's girl singer during the summers of 1937, 1938, and 1939 (she was legally required to remain in school during the rest of the year). According to some accounts, Gil Rodin, the power behind the throne in the highly successful Bob Crosby Orchestra, heard her on the air with Venuti and signed her from there. However it's equally possible that the very generous Venuti (who seems never to have recorded with any of his working bands) himself brought her to the attention of Rodin and the Crosbyites.

Given that Crosby's was the only swing band with a down-home Southern feel, it's disappointing that Starr only spent two weeks with the band when the network decided to replace her with the more seasoned and better known Helen Ward. She apparently only made one broadcast with Crosby, on which she tells host Johnny Mercer that she comes from Memphis (not entirely true) and then launches into an amazingly polished rendition of W. C. Handy's "Memphis Blues," including a very sensual, nonverbal humming chorus, which is pretty darn amazing for a sixteen-year-old. A few days later, she was tapped by Glenn Miller, then leading the most popular band in the business. This particular relationship was also preordained to end quickly, since Starr was only brought in to fill in for Marion Hutton, who was out with a sinus infection. "I had to sing in Marion Hutton's key," Starr told me in the early nineties. "They would ask me, 'Is that in your range?' and I didn't know so I just said yes because I only knew two kinds of ranges—one of them you cooked on and the other was where the cows were. I said, Why not? God, when you're young you think you can do anything, you're invincible. Ignorance is bliss, when you don't know that something is too high for you, then you just go for it; sometimes I hit it and sometimes I didn't. I had the attitude that if I can't sing it I'll whistle it. I just loved music and I thought as long as I can start and end with the band I've done my job."

Only one tune ("Memphis Blues") exists from her two weeks with Crosby, and a mere two songs ("Baby Me" and "Love with a Capital You") resulted

from her brief liaison with Miller (both were on Bluebird 78s). In the early forties, Starr resumed her off-and-on relationship with Joe Venuti, and an aircheck survives of her singing "Slowpoke" with the violinist's 1942 band. For a while, she worked even more casually with the Dixieland-style combo led by the New Orleans trumpeter-singer Wingy Manone. She waxed a single side with the one-armed Manone, "If I Could Be with You" on ARA Records, in which the combination of a Crescent City trumpeter-funster and a Native American girl singer anticipates Louis Prima and Keely Smith. Starr happened to be rehearsing with Manone in early 1944 when fate, once again, took a hand, as she told me: "A guy who turned out to be Charlie Barnet's manager stuck his head in the studio and listened to me singing with Wingy, and he said, 'Hey kid, Charlie Barnet is auditioning for a singer, you want to come down?' I thought that Wingy was going to brain him with his horn, he chased him out of there so fast! Anyway, later on when everything was over with, I went by the ladies' room and passed by Studio A. You could hear the Barnet band playing clear through the wall, even though it was soundproofed. I was just thinking, 'Oh God, isn't that wonderful?' and I peeked my head in. The manager saw me and motioned for me to come in. I just stood with him, and on the other side there were about four or five girls with little attaché cases and folios full of music to audition with. I guess the manager had told Charlie how close he came to getting brained by Wingy for talking to me, and Charlie thought that was funny.

"He said, 'I understand you sing with Wingy Manone?' I said, 'Yeah, every chance I get.' He said, 'Have you got any music?' I said, 'No, haven't you got any?' I didn't know any better, I wasn't trying to be smart. He said, 'Yeah we got some, you know this one?' I said yeah, I think I know that—remember there are all these girls waiting to sing—and he said they'd try it and he would point to me when I'm to come in. I sang for about thirty minutes, not quite realizing that I was auditioning. When it was over they told me I had a job. My first reaction was, Who's brave enough to tell Wingy? That's the only time I ever auditioned for anything."

Her tenure with Barnet ran from March 1944 to April 1945. Even though she lasted fourteen very busy months with the tenor saxophonist, her stay with that band unfortunately coincided with the fatal recording ban of 1942–44. As a result, there are less than a half-dozen commercial sides by Starr with Barnet, among them excellent renditions of "Into Each Life Some Rain Must Fall," "You Always Hurt the One You Love," and the intensely playful "Come Out Wherever You Are." Fortunately, there are also assorted airchecks of her with the band, including three excellent standards, "I Can't Get Started," "The Very Thought of You," and a hard-swinging treatment of the Garland signature "The

Trolley Song." Starr and Barnet also recorded two sensational four-minute special tracks for V-Disc, an expanded version of Willard Robison's "Sharecroppin' Blues" (done in a shortened version for Decca) and a marvelous big band orchestration of the spiritual "Nobody Knows the Trouble I've Seen" in which Starr's plaintive alto interacts with Barnet's own mournful soprano sax.

Starr left the Barnet band when her throat just plain gave out; she gradually recuperated in New York but then settled in Los Angeles. Immediately she began singing in increasingly important nightclubs on the Left Coast and broadcasting regularly. After six years and five important bandleaders (Venuti, Crosby, Miller, Manone, and Barnet), Starr was at last beginning to get her name and sound out there. Although, she said, "people kind of knew me from working with Charlie Barnet for so long," her earliest breaks, record-wise, came from two producers who had first heard her with Manone: Dave Dexter, of Capitol Records, and Ben Pollack, the former drummer and bandleader, now manager and A&R man. Dexter utilized her in a series of all-star jazz sessions he was producing for the label, including a memorable version of "Stormy Weather" with no less than Nat King Cole on piano. She also sang with all-star jazz groups at impresario Gene Norman's *Just Jazz* concerts and on *Jubilee,* the Armed Forces Radio Service's flagship program for black servicemen.

Two years later, Capitol would sign Starr to an exclusive contract, but during this interval she recorded for several short-lived independent concerns based on the West Coast, namely Ben Pollack's Jewell and Ted Yerxa's Lamplighter Records. These masters were acquired, issued, then deacquired, reacquired, reissued, and re-reissued by all kinds of equally untraceable recording concerns before being comprehensively collated into *Kay Starr: The Complete Lamplighter Recordings* (Baldwin Street Music). (Two other highly recommended collections of early Starr were issued from the British Isles, *I've Got to Sing, 1944–1948* on Hep, and the two-CD *Rising Starr* on Jasmine.)

These early sessions, particularly the dates for Lamplighter, show what an amazing, hard-core jazz singer Kay Starr was. This is especially clear when she's accompanied by ace players like clarinetist Barney Bigard and giving her all to jazz standards like "After You've Gone," "Stardust," and "St. Louis Blues." Surely, somebody at the company was a jazz history buff: Starr reprises one of Billie Holiday's very first recordings, the existentially ephemeral "Riffin' the Scotch." Starr changed the title to "Frying Pan," which is actually more accurate than the one that Holiday used in 1933. (It gets even more confusing: Starr also sang an original blues that was titled "Frying Pan," in its slow incarnation, but when she sang it fast, it was announced as "Garbage Can Blues.")

At the time Starr was recording for these indies, she also cut an extended series of transcriptions for the Standard Transcription Service, which was also based in Hollywood. Although these approximately eighty titles were produced exclusively for radio use, they have been issued commercially (with Ms. Starr's participation) on LP and then on CD on the Hindsight, Stash, and Soundies labels. The Standard sessions, in fact, continued into her early Capitol period.

It's worth paying so much attention to Starr's recordings from the late forties—the studio sessions, the Standard transcriptions, and the live performances—because they're so uniformly excellent. This is a remarkable body of work: Starr was easily one of the finest jazz singers in the world during this period. Peggy Lee and Sarah Vaughan had not yet hit their stride, and Anita O'Day was between pinnacles, which left Starr in a class with Ella Fitzgerald, Billie Holiday, and very few others—mighty rarefied territory. The Standard transcriptions are particularly valuable in that they have been available in the CD era, providing testimony to her remarkable powers at this point. Alas, the only reissues of her Capitol 78s are "greatest hits" collections driven more by chart position than the intrinsic quality of the music. (As of 2010, the world still badly needs a box of Kay Starr's complete forties Capitol sessions from Mosaic or Bear Family.)

By the late forties, Starr's mature style was in place: Her voice itself is extremely appealing, with its country-blues timbre and technique of stretching and bending notes like a hillbilly, combined with the rhythmic strengths and matchless swing of an Ella Fitzgerald. In fact, her primary strengths are rhythmic, and that's putting it mildly; Starr is one of the hardest-swinging jazz vocalists of all time. When she starts in on swinging, particularly on the best of these early sides, her rhythmic drive becomes positively spiritual. Listening to her kick into high gear, you feel you could positively levitate from the sheer momentum she generates.

Transcribed for Standard, "Tell Me How Long the Train's Been Gone" is a masterpiece. Starr recalled that it was written by her manager Hal Stanley, although it's officially credited to swing era character Henry "the Neem" Nemo; in either case, it seems to be adapted from a traditional spiritual. The arrangement starts with a spoken intro, which is as cute as it's alliterative (although it secularizes the titular locomotive from the gospel train into just another Chattanooga choo-choo), and from there it's basically a very simple phrase repeated over and over, plain as vanilla as written but with infinite variations thrown in. It ain't the meat, it's the motion. Starr rocks so hard here she could be inventing rhythm and blues all by herself. (Curiously, the record of hers that most appealed to the rock generation was far from her most rocking, except in the title, a dreary novelty entitled "The Rock and Roll

Waltz" from 1955—an aria of generational and cultural conflict if ever there was one.)

The allusions to gospel are but one additional ingredient in her vocal mix: As we've seen, Starr has an undeniably country sound, but at the same time she has a searingly intense blues sound that stylistically allies her with Dinah Washington and her gospel- and blues-injected followers, as well as to Sister Rosetta Tharpe, who combined big band with gospel. None of them, not even Washington, outswung Starr. "Tell Me How Long" is already jazz and pop at the same time, and it also contains intimations of gospel, blues, and country.

Starr was a formidable adversary when it came to the blues. But most of her best work relied on a very specific genre of popular song. She tells a great story, worth quoting at length, about how she arrived at this particular musical policy. As she recalled, it was not long after she was signed to Capitol in 1947, at which point, the corporation—aware that the musicians' union was going to declare a strike at the end of the year—informed her that if she wanted to make any records, she'd better come up with some songs. As she told me: "The only things I knew were standards, because I didn't have somebody scouting through all the new tunes for me the way the stars did. And Capitol didn't have any time to look for songs for me, since I was only going to be an also-ran in the company anyhow.

"So I kept passing in these lists of standard tunes for their approval, but what I didn't realize for the longest time was that they had to show these lists to their top-rank girl singers, like Peggy and Jo. They had the authority to pass on them or not, as I could only do songs that they didn't want to record, since I was the new kid on the block. The label figured they couldn't put out two versions of the same song by girl singers. So I'd get these lists back and there would be a line through every song title. What I was doing, it turned out, was finding songs for these girls! Everybody was trying to record as many numbers as they could and get them in the can.

"It was getting closer and closer to the time when the strike was supposed to start, and I was just getting more and more depressed. They couldn't set a date for me because I didn't have any songs. So I wandered into a place that I used to go to a lot, where Red Nichols had a steady gig. I was young but I could go there by myself because the bartenders knew me and watched out for me. It was down on Vine Street en route from Glenn Wallich's to Billy Berg's. We used to call it the Hymn and Hangover Club.

"Ordinarily, I'm a pretty happy sort. But when I walked in this night, when the set was over, all the guys walked up and said, 'My God, who died?' They thought sure as hell there'd been a death in my family, because I really looked terrible. I explained to them what was going on, that I wasn't getting any closer to making this date with Capitol Records.

"So Red Nichols asked me, 'Have you got any wheels?' I said, 'No, but what have you got in mind—I'll find some.' He said, 'If you come out to my house, I have the proverbial piano bench with all the songs in it.' So I went to his house and sure enough, he found me all these songs like 'Lonesomest Gal in Town,' 'Poor Papa,' 'You Gotta See Mama Every Night,' 'Mama Goes Where Papa Goes,' all those kind of songs. They had these pictures of all these girls in their boas and with old-fashioned hats and these old unsanitary curls hanging down.

"I had never heard of any of these ditties, but I thought, well hell, it's worth a try. And when I got the list back from Capitol, it was pristine! There wasn't even a fingerprint on it. . . . So I brought this list back to Red's house and he had to teach me all the songs.

"But then 'Lonesomest Gal in Town' was the first tune that I did which became what we called then a regional hit for me, it got a little business going around California. It made Capitol think, Hey, maybe we didn't make a mistake here.

The ungrammatical "I'm the Lonesomest Gal in Town," written by Albert Von Tilzer and Lew Brown in 1912, was part of a trend for Starr since she also recorded songs with titles like "I'm Oh So Lonesome Tonight" and just plain "Lonesome" around the same time. It didn't actually show up on the national *Billboard* charts; her first entry there is "You Were Only Fooling (While I Was Falling in Love)," while her second chart entry, "So Tired," a touching tune composed by bandleader Russ Morgan, reached the top 10; according to Starr it was actually recorded while the ban was still on, in the company of a bunch of trombone players who were sworn to secrecy, in an office temporarily converted into a sound studio.

While starr's recollections of the success of "Lonesomest" may be accurate, she had been making a specialty of singing vintage chestnuts long before the 1948 AFM ban and that fortunate encounter with Red Nichols amid hymns and hangovers. In fact, her very first record under her own name was the 1929 "Should I" on Pollack's Jewell Records; her Lamplighter sides are predominantly older songs, like "Baby Won't You Please Come Home" and "I'm Confessin'."

Starr had also already made a specialty of "Honeysuckle Rose," waxing a treatment that positively defies gravity for the AFRS *Jubilee* in 1945. That track features two sax masters then with Harry James's orchestra, Willie Smith (alto) and Corky Corcoran (tenor). In general, her early recordings co-star (co-Starr?) a brilliant array of master instrumentalists. There are an amazing ten titles done with a four-piece rhythm section led by emerging guitarist Les Paul (who would never surpass his playing here) and featuring Kay's old mentor, Joe Venuti—the two got to record together at long last. She made ten Standard transcription tracks (presumably done at a single session) with the Paul-Venuti group; all ten of these are currently on *Kay Starr: The Best of the Standard Transcriptions*, a double-disc collection of the first two-thirds of Starr's complete Standard output, released in 2000 by Soundies.

Starr believes that finding these little known antiquities gave her a foot in the door at Capitol. Yet most of her hits from this point on derived from a variety of ethnic and cultural sources in this most diverse era of pop music: "Hoop De Doo" was a polka that had already proved a hit for Perry Como, and this now Slavic-Italian-hillbilly concoction got her as high as number 2 on the charts; "Bonaparte's Retreat" had been an old "fiddle tune" instrumental she had heard back home, and she found it so irresistibly catchy that she prevailed upon publisher Roy Acuff to supply some lyrics for her; "Mississippi," one of several songs that humorously spells out that most un-phonetic of states, this time referring to the letter "S" as a "crooked letter," was a pure Nashville novelty with big band backing.

Starr also had hits with two songs written by the highly successful team of Bennie Benjamin and George Weiss. "I'll Never Be Free," a duet with Tennessee Ernie Ford, was a pure country ballad, which just happened to be by these two Tin Pan Alley hit makers. In 1952, Benjamin and Weiss's "Wheel of Fortune" looked like a surefire hit, and every label tried to push its own version: Competing contenders included Sunny Gale and Frankie Laine; for some reason, it was particularly popular among African American singers like Arthur Prysock, Dinah Washington, Johnny Hartman, the Four Flames (a doo-wop quartet), and Little Jimmy Scott.

Yet the wheel of fortune spun 'round and 'round and it landed on Kay's number. "Wheel of Fortune" would be Starr's blockbuster, her "Come on-a My House," "Tennessee Waltz," and "You Belong to Me." The arrangement includes a few gimmicks: It opens with the sound of a roulette wheel doing its thing, and for the central hook of the song, Starr's voice is heard in multiple layers (a device borrowed from Patti Page), and the chart is highly melodramatic, punctuating the lyric with sharply aggressive brass stings.

But it's Starr's intense vocal that seizes the day. She sings of "yearning for love's precious flame" with such tightly focused conviction that, combined with her amazing voice and musicianship, the disc had no choice but to go gold and spend ten weeks at number one.

In the next few years, Starr would be wresting hit singles out of more twenties chestnuts, such as her zesty two-beat treatment of "Side by Side," which also features Patti Page–style multiple voice tracks; old and new gospel (the excellent "The Man Upstairs," by Hal Stanley); at least one Dixieland standard favored by New Orleanians ("When My Dreamboat Comes Home"); French chansons (Piaf's "If You Love Me [Really Love Me]"); and Cole Porter's "Allez-Vous-En," which was, to all intents and purposes, a Broadway show tune and a *chansonette* at the same time.

By the mid-fifties, Starr was beginning to feel that her multiculti diversity was working against her. Even though she had proved herself one of the biggest-selling artists in the short history of Capitol Records, she felt that the label regarded her as a "utility" singer, who could take anything they could throw at her and turn it into a hit. When her contract was up in November 1954, she switched to RCA in January 1955 and launched the new association with her second biggest hit, the infamous "Rock and Roll Waltz." The sheet music of that song announced, "Introducing the brand-new rock and roll in waltz time." The idea never quite caught on, even if the song did; although this was one of the least rocky songs in Starr's catalogue, its success prompted RCA to go out and hire their own rock 'n' roll star, the Hillbilly Cat, Elvis Presley.

While there was some dreck on RCA ("Flim Flam Floo," anybody?), in general the new contract christened Starr's second golden age. If 1945–54 were the years of Starr's wonderful jazz sides and hit singles, the years 1954–62 were the era of classic albums, first for RCA and then again for Capitol. Between 1950 and 1954, Capitol issued about six long-playing collections of mostly previously released material, but her first all-original album seems to have been *The One—The Only* (1955). The other classic RCAs include *Blue Starr* (1957), *Rockin' with Kay* (1958), and *I Hear the Word* (1959). The new albums for Capitol after she returned there are *Movin'* (1959), *Losers, Weepers . . .* (1960), *Movin' on Broadway* (1960), *Jazz Singer* (1960), *I Cry by Night* (1961), and *Just Plain Country* (1962).

The ten or so albums that Starr made in these years are among the essential treasures of American pop and jazz: an amazing voice doing great songs, backed up by generally worthy accompaniment. The jazz albums—*Rockin' with Kay, Movin', Movin' on Broadway*, and *Jazz Singer*—spotlight her at her rhythmic best, in every way living up to the potential that she'd displayed in her forties big band and jazz sessions. The ballad albums—*In a Blue Mood, Blue Starr, Losers, Weepers . . . , I Cry by Night*—show that she had developed a surprising capacity for intimacy once she hit her peak in her mid- to late thirties, a tenderness and a vulnerability that no one expected.

Starr's canon includes two "specialty" albums—*I Hear the Word*, an exceptional collection of swing time spirituals, and *Just Plain Country*, which is highlighted by a slow and smoldering treatment of Guy Mitchell's hit "Singin' the Blues"—which are also worthy entrants. But the best of all is *I Cry by Night*. Everything comes together here: It's a jazz album, done with a small combo led by the West Coast–based pianist Gerald Wiggins and spotlighting tenor champ Ben Webster, yet it's also a ballad album. It's as fine a sampling of a great singer in a jazzy-yet-intimate setting as Tony Bennett's *When Lights Are Low,* Nat Cole's *After Midnight,* and the famous *John Coltrane & Johnny Hartman.* Though it's a small group jazz album, there are also overtones of country and the blues—in fact, Starr winds up with a smoking, smoldering rendition of T-Bone Walker's signature ballad, "I'm Still in Love with You." Her singing has never been more powerful, more entrenched in the blues, and more moving than here—this has got to be the most moving treatment of the oft-recorded Vincent Youmans standard "More Than You Know" ever committed to vinyl.

Thus Starr's career had reached its pinnacle before she turned forty. She kept singing, especially in areas where legalized gamblers appreciated the irony of "Wheel of Fortune," and she tended to her daughter and to her husbands (six of them altogether). Of all the major singers of her generation, Starr had the greatest propensity for blues (her only rival was Peggy Lee) and country music, two qualities that should have served her well in the sixties and seventies, yet, curiously, she totally dropped out of sight in these years. There was no late career comeback hit for her, no "Is That All There Is?" or "My Way."

Although *I Cry by Night* (1959) was an all-time pinnacle, there were several postscripts. In 1968 she finally made an album with Count Basie and His Orchestra, issued under several titles but best known simply as *Kay Starr/Count Basie* (released on Gold Star and MCA). Whatever the title, the album had some exceptional moments ("I Get the Blues When It Rains"), but on the whole was not as good as the very many little tributes she had paid to the Count and his men over the years, such as her earlier "What Comes Up, Must Come Down," "Blue and Sentimental," and "Goin' to Chicago."

Starr did three studio albums in her fifties: the forgettable *Country* (1974, GNP Crescendo, which isn't nearly up to her 1962 *Just Plain Country*), the highly obscure *Kay Starr* (1981, Glenn Productions), and in between them there's *Back to the Roots* (1975, GNP Crescendo). This is a brilliant album of standards drenched in jazz and blues, with an ace backup band featuring hard bop trumpet star Blue Mitchell, tenor sax giant Georgie Auld (playing in a Ben Webster vein), legendary accompanist Jimmy Rowles on piano, and the masterful vibraphonist Red Norvo. Although I regret that a lot of the songs are repeats in her discography, Starr sounds as great as ever, giving "Mean to Me" the blues treatment and swinging like mad on her oft-recorded "What Can I Say After I Say I'm Sorry?" If *I Cry by Night* is her masterpiece, *Back to the Roots* (lessened only by a substandard cover) is the neglected jewel of her later catalogue.

In 1986, Kay Starr played New York for the first time in a long while, at a soon-to-be-defunct watering hole called Freddy's (a gig that represented the only time that I had the good fortune to experience her in person). Fortunately, the Japanese-born producer and historian Ted Ono recorded one of her shows there, and released that tape eleven years later as *Live at Freddy's.* From her entrance number, Ray Charles's "Hallelujah I Love Him So," Starr sounds as compellingly jubilant as ever. Apart from a few early airchecks, this is Starr's only live album, and it was worth waiting for. Unfortunately, the *Freddy's* project represented both her final album and her final appearance in New York.

Early in 2001, I received a call from Danny Bennett, Tony Bennett's manager and son. Tony—who had appeared with Starr on a TV special forty years earlier—was doing an album of duets based on the blues, and wanted to include Kay Starr. What Danny wanted to know was, could she still sing? I hadn't heard her in person since Freddy's, and that had been fifteen years earlier. So I put the word out and heard from a few people who had seen her in the last few months. Yes, the answer came back, she still sounded wonderful. Thus Tony and Danny followed through, and lo and behold, Starr wound up duetting beautifully and touchingly with Tony on her old Basie favorite "Blue and Sentimental." Starr was the only performer of Tony's approximate generation on his Grammy-nominated set *Playin' with My Friends—Bennett Sings the Blues,* which turned out to be one of the biggest-selling albums of his entire career.

In the last few seconds of the track, you can hear Starr ad-libbing the line "one more for the road"—an appropriate coda and last hurrah for one of the most distinctive stylists American music has ever known.

Dakota Staton (1931?–2007)

Dakota Staton was the last of the three Ds, following Dinah (Washington) and Della (Reese). These three large-framed, big-voiced ladies not only had similar first names (they could be a sister act) but each combined gospel, blues, and jazz influences into sturdy careers in the pop mainstream, and all broke through at around the same time. (Even though Washington was a half-generation older, and had been a star among black audiences in the late forties, she didn't cross over to the white mainstream until roughly the same moment that Reese and Staton emerged.) Like Dinah (1924–63, raised in Chicago) and Della (born in 1931, according to most but not all sources, and raised in Detroit), Dakota (raised in Pittsburgh) has a big, soulful sound. The voice of Barbra Streisand has been famously likened to butter (or "buddah"), but Dakota, like Dinah and Della, has a bluesy attitude and the kind of chops that could cut through steel. Like a lot of jazz singers—particularly those who came up in the big band era—she liked to decorate a song with additional notes taken from the music's harmonic underpinning. But unlike, say, the bebop-inspired Ella Fitzgerald or Anita O'Day, the D-Girls don't come out of a tradition of instrumental jazz but from the melismatic heritage of gospel and the interpretative imperative of the blues.

Staton was the most capricious of the three; although not lacking in gospel and blues significance, she was the one who sounded the most girlishly playful, particularly on her early records, the classic Capitol albums of 1954–62. "My Funny Valentine" was a big number for her; she recorded it at least twice (in 1957 and 1963) and kept it in her working book for several decades. Her treatment is as whimsical as it is soulful, displaying not only light gospel and blues inflections but a constantly surprising tendency to chortle "ha ha!" every time she informs her lover that his looks are laughable. In her girlishness, Staton reminds us of Rose Murphy cooing "chi-chi," Sarah Vaughan singing coyly of a cunning cottage, or even Helen Humes or Blossom Dearie (singing just about anything).

Where Washington and Reese had a sense of humor, you wouldn't call either one of them coquettish, which Staton certainly was. On "Little Girl Blue" from her 1958 album *Dynamic!,* she repeatedly reverts to a childlike voice, one who can't resist counting her "itty bitty little fingers." Staton has a much lighter, sweeter sound than Reese or Washington—at least it was in the fifties and sixties—yet she's no less authentically soulful and jazzy.

Born in Pittsburgh on June 3 (the date is variously given as 1930, 1931, or 1932), she wanted to sing from an early age even though her parents were not very encouraging. "When I was four years old, I started singing and dancing like Shirley Temple," she told annotator Joe Laredo. According to the notes for her breakthrough album, *The Late, Late Show* (1957), Staton "began her career at seven, singing with her two sisters. When they married and the trio dissolved, Dakota went on as a 'single,' attending high school by day and performing in a Pittsburgh night club in the evenings."

Unlike Washington or Reese, Staton had formal musical education, at Pittsburgh's Filion School of Music; instead of singing semiprofessionally in church settings, she came of age musically in a Broadway-style musical revue and from there served as girl singer with a local dance band. The show was *Fantastic Rhythm,* originally written by Billy Strayhorn in his own Pittsburgh youth, which had been running since in 1935. She then went on the road with Joe Westray, a Pittsburgh-based bandleader.

After several years with Westray, Staton gradually began to work as a solo act in black nightclubs, crisscrossing the country, touring the Deep South and also the Deep North (meaning Canada). She was particularly well received by two of the country's premier showrooms for black talent, Maurice King's Flame Show Bar in Detroit and the Baby Grand in Harlem. It was in the latter venue that, in 1953, Staton was heard by Dave Cavanaugh of Capitol Records. He tried her on a singles session, then another, and then another. The bad news was that

the songs were mostly ephemeral trifles fit only for 45s at best; the good news was that one of these early dates was done with Nelson Riddle arranging and conducting. (Her first date included "What Do You Know About Love?," coincidentally recorded at the same time by Della Reese for Jubilee. Eventually, a number of Staton's 1954–55 singles were combined with some standards recorded in 1958 to fill out an album called *Crazy He Calls Me.*)

Where Reese had some powerful hit singles, Staton was primarily an album artist. She gathered a fan base in several different areas: She appeared in Alan Freed's rock 'n' roll revues (even though she was singing standards, not R&B or R&R), and also attracted the attention of the jazz fans who voted in the *Down Beat* magazine reader's polls and who elected her the most promising newcomer of 1955. After twenty or so singles tracks, she made her first real album, *The Late, Late Show,* and that did the trick. Competing against such blockbuster artists as Sinatra, Cole, Mathis, and Fitzgerald, Staton's watershed disc made it all the way to number 4 on the album charts—a formidable achievement for a relative newcomer.

The Late, Late Show is a terrific jazz album, one that, like June Christy's *Something Cool* and the classic Sinatra and Cole records (some of them, anyway), stayed in the Capitol catalogue through the seventies, almost until the end of the LP era. The notes state that "the background was conceived and conducted by Van Alexander"—Fitzgerald's "A-Tisket, A-Tasket" collaborator—but there wasn't much in the way of actual orchestration to be heard. This was a small group affair all the way, with pianist Hank Jones and trumpeter Jonah Jones (no relation) credited on the jacket, and an outstanding unidentified trombone soloist also livening things up on "Broadway," "Trust in Me," and elsewhere. With the opening track, the Count Basie perennial "Broadway," Staton effectively telegraphs her intention to swing lightly yet strongly in the Basie manner, and proceeds to live up to that ambition throughout the remaining eleven tracks.

Throughout *The Late, Late Show,* Staton is right on the money (or right in the pocket, as musicians say), getting playful on "Funny Valentine," bluesy on "Ain't No Use," soulful on "Summertime," swinging on "Give Me the Simple Life," scatting on Artie Shaw's "Moon Ray," and misty on "Misty." The best remembered track of this, her best remembered album, is the title. "The Late, Late Show," credited to one "Murray Berlin" (believed to be one of several pseudonyms used by producer Dave Cavanaugh) and also recorded by Nat Cole, is an endearing romp inspired by the late-night old-movie phenomenon that was becoming a staple of early local television.

The Late, Late Show was her only real hit album, but it was far from a singular pinnacle—nearly all her Capitol LPs are just as good. A few months later, the label released *In the Night,* a Cavanaugh production that featured Staton as a special guest with the George Shearing Quintet. Earlier, on MGM Records, Shearing had worked with both Teddi King and Billy Eckstine, but *In the Night* was apparently his first meeting with a star vocalist in his relatively new contract with Capitol, anticipating the piano superstar's future meetings with Peggy Lee, Nat King Cole, and Nancy Wilson. It's somewhat disappointing that Staton only sings on half the twelve tracks here—it would have been especially good to hear her on Horace Silver's "Señor Blues," which is played only instrumentally—but the quintet's playing is so outstanding here that it's impossible to complain.

Staton and Shearing are remarkably simpatico: "Confessin' the Blues" is her outstanding first performance of a traditional-style blues, and the two of them get a rocking good beat going both here and on Benny Carter's similarly tinged "Blues in My Heart" and "I Hear Music." The pair also score points for including "I'd Love to Make Love to You," a romantic romper that unfortunately had gone unrecorded since the King Cole Trio.

From 1958 on, arranger Sid Feller was responsible for the bulk of Staton's Capitol albums. But despite the change in personnel, the team maintained the same direction—both *Dynamic!* (1958) and *Time to Swing* (1959) have Staton swinging standards with essentially small group backing, one or two horn soloists with rhythm section; overall the backing is just as on-target as *The Late, Late Show,* with classical-style woodwinds, rather than strings, brought in as accompaniment for slow love songs.

There are more opportunities for her to show her coquette side ("Little Girl Blue" on *Dynamic!*) and to scat lightly ("Anything Goes" on *Dynamic!* and "Gone With the Wind" on *Time to Swing*). *Time to Swing* co-stars such soloists as Phil Woods (identified as "Bill Woods" on the jacket) on alto, two terrific trumpeters in Taft Jordan and Joe Wilder, and a sterling rhythm section with Hank Jones, George Duvivier, Don Lamond, and "Ken" Burrell. Unfortunately, the only musician identified on *Dynamic!* is Sweets Edison, but it does sound like the same rhythm section.

With *More Than the Most!* (1959), Feller stepped up the accompaniment to a full big band, a very happy decision considering his skill as an orchestrator and Staton's remarkable chops. The band is again uncredited, but I'm again willing to believe it's the same rhythm guys plus Phil Woods, who makes his presence felt even more keenly here. The repertoire is equally worthy of praise, from the very familiar—the opening "September in the Rain"—to two underperformed Sammy Cahn items, "I Could Make You Care" and "It's You or No One," and a previously unswung prewar ballad (done more sentimentally by both Glenn Miller and Stan Kenton), "High on a Windy Hill."

The bulk of these early Capitol albums are up-tempos—with the tracks generally kept under two

and a half minutes for radio play. On these swinging numbers, Staton is fast but never furious. The singer has considerable drive, but even at breakneck tempos both her diction and her intonation are impeccable: She's never remotely off pitch or imprecise. She's also very strong on "blue ballads," those slow love songs generally written in the late forties and beyond by black composers (Buddy Johnson, Percy Mayfield) that incorporate blues elements into the traditional Tin Pan Alley love song framework, like "Ain't No Use" on *The Late, Late Show* and "Baby, Don't You Cry" (later done by Ray Charles as a wild swinger) on *Time to Swing*. She sings the latter with considerable compassion: He's dumping her, but she's worried about his feelings. Yet Staton may be at her best on the slow ballads, nearly all of which are love songs that have traditionally been favored by jazz musicians and singers: The ballads on *Time to Swing* include "Willow Weep for Me," which is also endowed with a blues sensibility, enhanced considerably by Phil Woods; "If I Should Lose You" and "You Don't Know What Love Is" are both slow and powerful, with woodwindy backing that's at once classical and funky. "You've Changed" (with prominent flute obbligato) was not included on the original *Time to Swing* (it was first released almost forty years later on the Capitol anthology *Spotlight on Dakota Staton*), which is a surprise, because it's one of her most moving ballads.

Wisely, after five sets of pretty much unrelenting swinging, Staton decided to slow down the pace a bit with a run of ballad-oriented projects: *Dakota Staton Sings Ballads and the Blues* (1959) and *Softly* (1960). The former was handled partly by Feller, who presided over a string and woodwind section on four ballads (including "Someone to Watch Over Me" and Frank Loesser's "I'll Know," the latter with a fine Ben Webster–like tenor obbligato). The bulk of *Ballads and the Blues* falls into the latter category, including tunes by Willie Dixon and Robert Johnson, as conducted by Eddie Wilcox. Wilcox directs a regulation jazz big band—reeds, brass, and rhythm—and Staton is especially convincing on Lil Green's "In the Dark" and Dixon's "My Babe." She combines the two genres on "My One and Only Love" and the exotic "Where Flamingos Fly," two songs that are bluesy as well as bally, and as sultry as they're sentimental, showing that she's learned the lessons of Dinah Washington.

Benny Carter took over the reins as arranger-conductor on her next two Capitol albums, *Softly* and *Dakota* (both 1960). *Softly* is all ballads and no blues, done in a very big-string style, with no pronounced jazz elements other than Staton's imaginative phrasing. Consisting mainly of pop standards frequently found in the jazz and soul gene pool—"Body and Soul," "Dedicated to You," "Old Folks" (along with the Ink Spots' "Whispering Grass" and Dinah Washington's "Congratulations to Someone")—this is clearly Staton's most romantic effort ever. *Dakota* intermingles fast and slow numbers, all with a big band backing, starting with an appropriately rocking reading of Carter's own "Rock Me to Sleep," in which she is surrounded by trombones and muted trumpets. A few of the highlights include two further nods to Washington, "Make Me a Present of You" and "I'll Close My Eyes," and one to Little Jimmy Scott, a gentler, less intense "Everybody's Somebody's Fool."

That wasn't it for Staton on Capitol. There was a small group album, *'Round Midnight,* and a live set wih Simmons, *Dakota at Storyville* (1961). Apparently she never cracked the top 10 after her first album, and the title of her last studio album, *'Round Midnight,* seems to complete an arc suggested by her two Capitol LPs, *The Late, Late Show* and *In the Night.* In 1962, Staton did a final session for Capitol under the direction of Simmons; there were some singles tracks, but also a pair of excellent ballads, "You'd Better Go Now" and "Detour Ahead" (included as bonus tracks in the 2009 CD of *Time to Swing*), which suggest that she may have started—but never finished—another album for the label.

More than likely, her relationship with Capitol had just run its course. In 1958, Staton married the trumpeter Talib Ahmad Dawud, a West Indian–born player originally known as Al Barrymore before his conversion to Islam. Under her husband's encouragement, Staton also joined the Nation of Islam, and took the name of Aliyah Rabia. Although many male black musicians of this generation (famously Yusef Lateef and Ahmad Jamal) converted to Islam, Staton is the only female singer headliner who comes to mind, although, as far as I know, she never worked under her Muslim name.

By 1963–64, around the same time as Malcolm X's departure from the organization, Dawud and Staton were also going through their own period of disillusionment with Elijah Muhammad and the Nation of Islam. Still, her career was in good shape. In 1963 she starred at the Newport Jazz Festival, and that year began an excellent series of three albums for United Artists: *From Dakota with Love* (1963), *Live and Swinging* (1963), and *Dakota Staton with Strings* (1964).

Live and Swinging was a follow-up to the 1961 *Dakota at Storyville,* not only in that both albums were recorded in front of a live audience but that both were done in venues operated by impresario George Wein, the *Swinging* album originating at the 1963 Newport Jazz Festival. Rather than merely use her regular working band and book, Staton and Wein commissioned new charts from star arrangers Howard McGhee and Melba Liston, and then put together a killer eleven-piece band of modern jazz stars to play it, with McGhee as director, sharing the trumpet section with Snooky Young. *Live and Swinging* is perhaps her most exciting record: Where the later Capitol albums focused on her sweet, romantic sound, this live package has her kicking

butt. The LP climaxes in "Rhythm in a Riff," her most concentrated, high-octane scat workout. Even apart from that, this live album is a peerless mixture of fast and slow numbers, ballads and blues.

Slow love songs come to the fore once again on *Dakota Staton with Strings,* a set that may be even better than any of her previous ballad-driven projects. For whatever reason, though there are indeed a lot of strings, there's also no shortage of bluesy piano, breathy tenor, and growling trumpet—this is a jazz album through and through.

In 1965, Staton and Dawud moved to England for a few years; possibly for professional reasons, possibly to get away from the situation with the Nation of Islam after Malcolm X was assassinated in February. Staton's last project of the sixties, *Dakota '67,* was done in London with an all-star aggregate of British players, including three different arranger-conductors. It's also a stunningly well-chosen amalgam of tunes, including "The Midnight Sun Will Never Set," for which Quincy Jones served as intermediary between a traditional Swedish folk song and a new lyric by French singer Henri Salvador. Here, more than on any other Staton project, a Billie Holiday influence prevails, particularly on "You Go to My Head" and Artie Shaw's "Any Old Time," which Holiday recorded definitively, and on "A Sunday Kind of Love," which Lady Day never sang at all.

The dozen years from 1954 to 1966 amount to Staton's glory period. Yet she kept on going for another thirty years. The seventies to the nineties were hardly as consistent and prolific as the fifties and sixties, but there is some great stuff in there. After returning from England, she made an album of contemporary hits for Verve in 1970 called *I've Been There,* recorded in Los Angeles.

Then in the early seventies, she taped three LPs for the Groove Merchant label that continue to explore the boundaries between jazz and soul: *Madame Foo-Foo* (with Groove Holmes, organ, 1972), *I Want a Country Man* (with Manny Albam leading a band of mostly Thad Jones–Mel Lewis dudes, 1973), and *Ms. Soul* (1974). Not every song is a gem on these three, but one would be hard pressed to think of another major jazz singer who was flourishing on this level in a very difficult period. Eleven tracks from the first two LPs were included on a CD called *Congratulations to Someone,* and seventeen cuts from the three packages are on *Dakota Staton: The Sonny Lester Collection.* These three albums all deserve to be reissued in toto—two CDs would easily do it.

Ms. Soul, which is partially reissued on a disc called *Moonglow,* is also more than worthy of our attention. Once again, Staton, accompanied by the indefatigable Norman Simmons and a quintet (tenor plus rhythm), hips us to some very cool tunes. The standout is Buddy Bernier's "Hurry Home," which had been done by Buddy Stewart, Louis Jordan, and Ella Fitzgerald without ever becoming a standard, even though it deserves to be one; Staton reminds us that more people ought to sing it, though perhaps omitting the line about "gaining weight."

"She's very underrated," said Sid Feller, who orchestrated most of her Capitol albums. "I don't think that Dakota ever got the breaks she deserved that would've helped her become a major pop singer, but I know she's always been very well respected in the jazz community." Maybe yes, maybe no. Compared to Ray Charles—with whom Feller also worked extensively—Staton qualifies as somewhat neglected, but there doesn't seem much point in complaining, since she recorded more than two dozen first-rate albums, nearly all for major labels. Even if she's underrated, as Feller suggested, she was hardly underrecorded. Unfortunately, at the time of her death in 2007, only roughly half of the Capitol albums and none of the United Artists LPs had ever been reissued on CD. (Capitol released a decent compilation in their *Spotlight* series—aka *Great Ladies of Song*. One yearns, as always, to see Mosaic Records do a complete box of her Capitol and United Artists recordings, 1954–66.)

By the late seventies, Bross Townsend, another blues-driven pianist, was touring with Staton as her musical director, and filled that function on a rare album called *No Man Is Going to Change Me* as well as a shared set with Freddy Cole (both for a very obscure firm called GP Records). Staton continued to tour but didn't record in the eighties, but fortunately came back to the studio in 1990 for three albums on Joe Fields's Muse label.

The Muse period starts with the simply titled *Dakota Staton* (1990), on which tenor champ Houston Person does double duty as producer and primary soloist, giving Staton the same glorious support he provided Etta James, his longtime partner, followed by *Darling Please Save Your Love for Me* (1991), *Isn't This a Lovely Day* (1992), and *A Packet of Love Letters* (1996, on Field's HighNote label). Around the time of her death in 2007, a really obscure company called Caffe Jazz released *Dakota Staton Live at Milestone's*, a club tape from an unknown year, with Staton in good shape but substandard audio.

By the nineties—her sixties—Staton's voice had darkened considerably, although the new lower sound was still attractive—and brought her closer to her original inspiration, Dinah Washington. Now old enough to be a grandmother, she stopped playing the coquette—but still was girlishly frisky on the old torch tune "Jim." Yet if Staton could no longer be coy, she was still funny and bluesy in equal parts. Although a couple of the songs on *Dakota Staton* aren't quite worthy of her, on the whole it's a classically Statonian blend of ballads and blues—and ball-busters.

There are two classic songs titled "The Thrill Is Gone"—one is a 1931 pop song by Lew Brown and Ray Henderson, the other is a blues written in 1950 by Roy Hawkins, which became a major hit for B. B. King twenty years later. Staton is the only artist I can think of who could and did do an equally marvelous job with both tunes. She cut the earlier song on her 1957 *In the Night* with George Shearing, and then did the Hawkins blues on the 1990 *Dakota Staton*. Blues or standards, it was all the same to Staton, she was equally at home in both.

Her last studio album, *A Packet of Love Letters* (1996), reunited her with Houston Person for what turned out to be a moving farewell. The opener, "More Than You Know," is one of her most touching ballads and renditions of that oft-recorded archetypal love song. "Remember" and the closing "You'd Better Love Me" (from *High Spirits*) are both done as medium rompers, but it's the slow tunes on which the sparks really fly—in some cases literally. "Night Life," which opens with a gutsy guitar solo by Melvin Sparks, is the Willie Nelson country-blues classic, which Staton makes sound considerably more blues than country. Both Staton and Person are on fire here, yet even at her most extreme, Staton never overdoes anything, and always sounds more like an influence on Aretha Franklin than an imitator of her. As fiery as she is on this hot blues, the most impressive track is the blues-tinged ballad "Trav'lin' Light." Here the voice sounds exactly like it did on one of her Capitol albums of forty years earlier; only her tenderness and interpretive skills have noticeably increased.

Would that Washington, or, for that matter, Della Reese, had recorded as satisfying a late-career statement as *Dakota Staton*.

Barbra Streisand (born 1942)

In the words of *South Park*'s Eric Cartman: "Damn your black heart, Barbra Streisand!" The French use the expression "sacred monster" to describe larger-than-life legends like Judy Garland and Frank Sinatra, and in a caricature of Streisand that appears in an early episode, *South Park* takes that phrase rather literally. At first the show's portrayal of her may seem rather mean-spirited, but it's so completely over-the-top, it doesn't really lay a glove anywhere near her.

If this cartoon caricature were toned down a bit, it might be more effective as parody; likewise, if Streisand could tone down what she does vocally, she might be regarded as an artist to be mentioned in the same breath as Sinatra and Garland. But *South Park* did her a favor in presenting her as a showbiz superstar with a taste for world conquest: In a parody of Japanese big-lizard movies that's probably lost on most Streisand fans (or indeed, anybody who didn't grow up with Gamera, MechaGodzilla, and the Peanuts), the show's Streisand-figure transforms herself into a hundred-foot-tall robot version of herself called Mecha-Streisand. The more the *South Park* animators can portray Streisand as a black-hearted sacred monster, the bigger favor they're doing her.

South Park contains a lesson that one wishes Babs herself would take to heart: Although the show is hysterically outrageous, often dealing with extreme sexual and scatological humor, its funniest moments are often the smallest—even the most intimate. In the Mecha-Streisand episode, several middle-aged suburban women talk about having watched the singer's HBO special. A pudgy, Jewish mother walks up to Mecha-Streisand and asks for her autograph, and we next see the skyscraper-sized sacred monster temporarily interrupting her rampage of mass destruction to take out a tiny, human-sized pen and sign the woman's tiny, human-sized autograph book. I personally would enjoy Streisand's music that much more if only it suggested she was capable of an act that intimate, human, and personal.

Streisand's 1994 concert special is a much more frightening depiction of monster-sized ego than *South Park*. Compare it with Frank Sinatra: Your typical Sinatra concert of the late seventies onward would generally climax with "My Way," if not at the very end, then right before "New York, New York." The bulk of each Sinatra performance, though, consisted of love songs—some would be fast and swinging, some would be slow and melancholy, but the entire impulse behind Sinatra's music is this idea he has of reaching out to another person. Sometimes you win, sometimes you lose; to paraphrase Stephen Sondheim in *Company*, the tragedy about love isn't that it isn't perfect, the tragedy is when it just *isn't*.

Thus, after Sinatra has been singing for an hour or so about love for another human being, it's collectively understood that he has earned the right to sing about self-love, to do a song that says "Applaud me, you bastards, applaud me!"—hence, "My Way." But Sinatra was never a self-love kind of a singer: That was really Sammy Davis Jr.'s forte, as reflected in "Once in a Lifetime," "Gonna Build a Mountain," "I Gotta Be Me," and other songs of self-aggrandizement written well before Paul Anka penned the English lyric to "My Way." And even when Sinatra sang "My Way," he went out of his way to undercut its egocentric message by telling audiences that he hated the song, never enjoyed singing it, and, in fact, was only doing it because we, the audience, liked it. The message was clear: He was only glorifying himself because we wanted him to.

Streisand knows better than anybody that an audience loves self-aggrandizement, that once they've accepted you as a sacred monster, it's simply impossible to lay it on too thick, to exceed the limit. In fact, there *is* no limit. Instead of starting with songs about love for others and then moving on to self-love, Streisand's concerts typically begin with what seems like a dozen "My Way" clones of the crassest sort. The 1994 show, issued as a double CD entitled *The Concert*, begins with an Andrew Lloyd Webber anthem of self-aggrandization titled "As if

We Never Said Goodbye" (from *Sunset Boulevard*) and then quickly moves to three similarly themed show tunes: "I'm Still Here," "Everybody Says Don't," and "Don't Rain on My Parade." All these songs, from the depths of Lloyd Webber to the heights of Styne and Sondheim, have the same message: "It wasn't easy. The odds were stacked against me, but I made it—now applaud, you bastards, applaud!" Her 1975 film *Funny Lady* climaxes Fanny Brice's life story with a resolutely Streisandian anthem, "Let's Hear It for Me"—the kind of song that the self-deprecating Brice wouldn't have sung in a zillion years.

Streisand's voice and her raw talent really are at least a hundred feet tall (at times it seems that her ego is even taller, but that's another matter). In the late fifties, impresario Max Gordon opened the Village Vanguard on Sunday afternoons for a special series of shows for teenagers; soft drinks were served and headliners like Anita O'Day were presented at popular prices. "There were lots of kids who came in to listen to jazz stars," O'Day later wrote in her autobiography. "I wish I could tell you one girl stood out in that crowd. I can't." Ten years later, O'Day was appearing in Vegas when one of the most famous women in the world approached her; even though she was wearing a scarf and dark glasses—clearly not wanting to be recognized—O'Day could see that it was Barbra Streisand. She came up to O'Day and said, "Teacher, I've come for my singing lesson!" It turned out that the teenaged Babs had been one of Anita's Sunday afternoon regulars at the Vanguard.

There's no reason to doubt O'Day's story; it's not as if she were claiming that John Lennon and Bob Dylan were coming to hear her in the West Village in 1958. Yet whatever lessons Streisand learned from O'Day must have been rather abstract ones. O'Day triumphed as one of the all-time most important singers (jazz or otherwise) of the songbook despite her small vocal range. Streisand's situation was precisely the opposite: O'Day, at least, never had to worry about oversinging. It would be less surprising to learn that Streisand had spent her Sunday afternoons listening to and learning from Sarah Vaughan. Like Streisand, Vaughan has a big, big voice and an amazing musical range, and was frequently accused of overdoing things; to love Sarah is to love the excess.

In 1962, Streisand recorded "My Coloring Book" on one of her first commercial recording sessions for Columbia Records. The song quickly caught on with female vocalists of all genres and generations: Aretha Franklin, Julie London, Brenda Lee, Dusty Springfield . . . and, importantly, Sarah Vaughan, on her 1963 album *Vaughan with Voices*. Clearly, the two who have the most in common—and the most pure chops—are Streisand and Vaughan. Both singers imbue "Coloring Book" with nothing less than epic grandeur. The lyrics make clever use of irony (the smaller-voiced Julie London sings it the most intimately) but Vaughan and Streisand employ melodrama on a scope that's positively operatic. But it's the differences between them that are crucial: Vaughan is excessive, yes, but she tempers that excess with elements of gospel, blues, and jazz style, so that even though it's big, big, big, it still seems cool and hip. Streisand is ultrastylized, with each syllable painstakingly articulated, each emotion artificially inflated, each vocal movement deliberately jagged and angular. Even, for instance, Eydie Gormé's most emotional number, "If He Walked into My Life" (to compare Streisand to another singer with chops galore), seems comparatively understated. No one would call Streisand cool or hip, but who cares? If you want angst and you want bigger-than-life feelings right up in your face, here they are.

One of Streisand's most important early TV appearances, on Judy Garland's short-lived but brilliant variety series (October 1963), contains a moment that's as disturbing as it is thrilling. The two divas launch into a medley of two Depression ditties, "Happy Days Are Here Again" and "Get Happy," both done in a moving, minor key fashion. At forty-one, Garland, as usual, comes off as a needy, self-destructive waif—she seemed to need everybody and everything. By comparison, Streisand, even at age twenty-one, had already perfected the ability to sing as if she doesn't need anybody, and we can all go to heck as far as she's concerned.

The contrast between the two is almost scary: The most vulnerable soul in creation belting her lungs out side by side with the most impervious. You want to take Garland in your arms and protect her, to make all the hurt go away. As for Streisand, you only want to be protected *from* her. Her blockbuster hit "People" (from *Funny Girl*) would have been a perfect song for Garland, who needed boyfriends, managers, lovers, husbands, children, doctors. Garland never stopped needing people, whereas Streisand gives every impression of never needing anybody whatsoever. After all these years of hearing her sing that song, I remain completely unconvinced that she's a person who needs people—except, in Norma Desmond's phrase, all of those "wonderful little people out there in the dark."

To her credit, Streisand didn't wait for Hollywood to mythologize her life story, like Larry Parks discovering African American culture in *The Jolson Story,* or Judy Garland as Madame Crematante in *Ziegfeld Follies* inventing the safety pin. With the take-charge tenacity typical of her career, Streisand has personally exploited her own personal morality play in every possible medium. She's ingeniously cast herself as the eternal little girl from Flatbush with a big nose, a bigger voice, and even bigger dreams. Everyone, most infamously a rather insensitive stepfather, tells her she'll never make it because she's too homely, because she's too ethnic, too *hamish,* and too just-plain-Barbra. Her stepdad is anything but supportive, and her mom is absolutely no help either.

Radio commentator Howard Stern, who has carefully cultivated a bad-boy image of his own (and who claims to say what we're all thinking—Christ, I hope not!), said of Babs's paterfamilias, "Well, he may not have been the most tactful guy, but you can't fault his judgment." (I disagree—I always thought Babs was kind of, well, *hot.* I had no trouble believing, watching either *The Owl and the Pussycat* or *For Pete's Sake,* that somebody would pay to have sex with her.)

This is the foundation of the Streisand saga: that she succeeded despite her lack of conventional, Julie London–like glamour, despite her oversized schnoz, her Brooklyn-Jewish accent. She never changed her name or her nose, never hid who she was, even spelled her name "Barbra," rather than the more familiar "Barbara," because it made her sound even more New Yawkish. She came out of an age when no one was supposed to be ethnic—when the Italians were anglicizing their names and the African Americans were still years away from saying black is beautiful—and she became bigger than everybody.

Streisand was already a sensation in nightclubs and on Broadway in *I Can Get It for You Wholesale* and then *Pins and Needles* as early as 1962, the year she turned twenty. In the nineties, she was even reenacting her childhood as part of her concerts; a child actress played the young Barbra, while the adult Barbra encouraged her from the spiritual sidelines, rather like Obi-Wan Kenobi or the ghost of Hamlet's father. This little playlet-within-a-concert would conclude with both Streisands raising their voices together, as if in a Battle of the Barbras. Likewise, in another concert, she projected images of herself in *Yentl,* the ultimate cinematic Babsfest, and would climax this portion of the show by joining forces with herself in a duet with the onscreen Barbra. Fans who couldn't get enough Barbra were flying out of their seats at the thought of two Barbras singing at once (Lord knows she has enough voice and ego for any two performers). And she achieved the same state of karma in 1997 with "Tell Him," her duo with Celine Dion, which in a sense was Streisand duetting with her own clone. After thirty-five years in the big time, she had at last found someone she could relate to, even if it was, well, Barbra Streisand.

With the exception of several original cast and sound track albums, Streisand has been under contract to Columbia Records for her entire career, releasing her first record, *The Barbra Streisand Album,* in 1963. It was, by all accounts, the album of the year, a smash at the cashbox and the recipient of two Grammy Awards, a foreshadowing of things to come. In the beginning, some saw her as a jazz singer, but whether she is or isn't is completely irrelevant.

It's kind of a stereotypical view of the careers of several major pop stars—particularly Bing Crosby and Nat King Cole—that they started out as jazz singers but grew less and less jazzy as they became more and more popular. I've also heard that said about Streisand—that she, too, started out as a jazz singer in the early, pre-*Funny Girl* period. There are two live documents currently in circulation of Streisand at the start of her career, both from 1963: eight tracks from the Bon Soir in New York (in excellent sound and included on her 1991 anthology *For the Record*) and fourteen cuts from the Hungry I in San Francisco (in lesser sound, and only issued on a bootleg). But rather than making the point that Streisand was jazzier early on, they show that her signature mannerisms were in place from the very beginning. She almost seems to start swinging in "Keepin' Out of Mischief Now" at the Bon Soir, but just when you start to think she might be relaxing into the groove, she abruptly switches tempos and revs into a dreadfully unswinging superfast tempo, which is hardly the same thing as swinging.

"Cry Me a River" is another song that appears on all three of these early 1963 projects—the first album and the two live tapes (from the Hungry i and the Bon Soir). It's essentially a woman's song: The only meaningful recording by a dude is by Ray Charles, and he did it as part of a concept album (*Sweet and Sour Tears*). It's a song of feminine empowerment, but when Julie London sang the original hit single, she was as dainty as she was defiant: The absolute worst thing a beautiful woman can do is leave you, thereby depriving you of her beauty. London doesn't need to threaten anything worse than that. When Streisand sings it—and the live tapes are even more unrestrained than the studio version—she really sounds as if she's going to kick your ass. Not getting any is the least of your worries; you really have one pissed-off lady on your hands here, brother! You feel she's going to stalk you and cut your brake wires, put a snake in your boots, and rocks in your cornflakes. The damage she threatens to inflict is more physical than emotional. This isn't a song about heartbreak and disillusion, this is a song about calling 911 and filing a restraining order.

So can Streisand swing? Technically speaking, she can sing with a fast rhythmic drive that has plenty of energy and that at least approximates swinging. Indeed, her voice is so perfect she can do virtually everything she makes up her mind to do. When she sings "Down with Love" on the Garland show, she goes in for jazzy effects, a kind of sonic playfulness inspired by Sarah Vaughan. But in order to truly swing, one has to lighten up and let go, to achieve a state of looseness and relaxation—like Lester Young, who was always so thoroughly chilled out that he seemed as if he would find it too much of an effort *not* to swing.

Streisand, by contrast, is incapable of easing up—whether on a note, on the beat, on the band, on the words, on anything. Everything is pounce, pounce, pounce all the time, in a way that such belters as Garland, Jolson, and Merman never did. From time to time, they all sang *at* you rather than *to* you, but Streisand nearly always sounds as if she's attacking you with a song, as if she's bludgeoning you to death. When she sings "Bewitched" in concert (and on *The Third Album*), it's a tour de force: She takes the Lorenz Hart lyric and runs it through a whirlwind of emotions both happy and sad, with sharp, dramatic movements, both vocally and visually. (I feel exhausted when she's finished—and can't even imagine how *she* feels.) In her singing, even her small moments are overstated; she's grandiose even when being intimate, and she overdoes everything, even when she's being comparatively subtle. To create jazz, you have to be able to cut loose and let things happen spontaneously, even with a degree of randomness. Streisand's just too much of a control freak.

The major area where Streisand shows restraint is in her album titles: Her first three releases were *The Barbra Streisand Album* (1963), *The Second Barbra Streisand Album* (1964), and *The Third Album* (1964); her first two television specials were *My Name Is Barbra* (1965; Columbia released a companion album with that title, which was followed by a sequel, *My Name Is Barbra, Two*, released that fall when the special was rerun), and *Color Me Barbra* (1966). Following that pattern, you would expect her first film to be called *The Barbra Streisand Movie*. Somehow these titles manage to be simple and self-aggrandizing at the same time: The message is that you don't need to know anything about these releases other than that Streisand is in them. Who cares what she's singing—it's a Streisand album.

She was in control of her image from the start. She was the first and perhaps the only pop star to come along who was actually younger than her target audience. By way of contrast, in their early days both Crosby and Sinatra shaved years off their biographies to make them more appealing to younger audiences. Yet Streisand wisely knew that most kids her age were buying Connie Francis or Chubby Checker, that her real support group wasn't the baby boomers but their parents, the people who bought Bobby Darin's *Love Swings* rather than his "At the Hop." With a kind of ingenuity that time would reveal to be characteristic, she brilliantly exploited her youth image—almost every TV appearance has her coming out in a sailor-suit top, like a grown-up version of what a little girl would wear. (She's wearing a white sailor's middy blouse on the cover of *The Third Album*, as if her tailor had been Donald Duck.) At the same time, said top was well stacked with what were decidedly a grown woman's . . . attributes. All in all, it was a most attractive package.

Her first two TV specials are, in fact, almost Freudian representations of her dreams and ambitions. *My Name Is Barbra* (1965), which won Streisand every Emmy in the book, has her singing every song of youthful naïveté she could find: "A Kid Again/I'm Five," "I've Got No Strings," "If You Were the Only Boy in the World," "I Can See It," "Jenny Rebecca," "My Name Is Barbra," "My Pa," "Someone to Watch over Me" (delivered à la Gertrude Lawrence, like a child in search of a parent figure), "Sweet Zoo," and "Where Is the Wonder?"—it's a veritable concept album of songs about lost innocence and preserving a childlike sense of wonder. She even had the good luck and intelligence to find a Leonard Bernstein song for children that just coincidentally happened to be called "My Name Is Barbara." The first album also included the Disney classic "Who's Afraid of the Big Bad Wolf" (introduced by that decidedly *trayf* trio, the Three Little Goyish Pigs), which opens with a snatch from Prokofiev's *Peter and the Wolf*. Using a number of children's songs written for Danny Kaye, Streisand is a mature young woman pretending to be a child pretending to be every beast in the zoo. The cover even shows her at about five or six, looking out at us (in a photo taken by her brother), telling us with her eyes that she wants "Much More" out of life.

Even the title of that first breakthrough recording, *The Barbra Streisand Album*, tells you it's not going to be about love, about the songs, about anything else but her. As we've seen, it opens with a defiant declaration of independence, the ultimate "fuck you" anthem, "Cry Me a River," which says "I no longer need you" in no uncertain terms. Both the first album and the first special contain a perfect "My Way" variation for a twenty-one-year-old sensation on the verge of becoming a living legend: "Much More." As introduced in *The Fantasticks*, "Much More" is the ultimate "I Want . . ." song, anticipating well in advance precisely the sort of accomplishments that Sinatra would later sing about in "My Way" (not to mention Jimmy Webb in "MacArthur Park"): "I will live, I will suffer, there will be times when I will be down, but I will ultimately be triumphant." Quite possibly, Sinatra learned everything he eventually knew about self-celebration from her.

My Name Is Barbra and its 1966 sequel reinvent the musical TV concert-special in a way that made Streisand's older colleagues take note. As late as 1962, Judy Garland had made a marvelous TV special in the conventional way, singing songs, chatting, and duetting with all-star guests—in this case, Sinatra and Dean Martin. Streisand began by asking the question, "What do I need with guests, hey?," immediately reconceiving the TV special as a strictly solo outing, the musical equivalent of a soliloquy or monologue. Within a few years of *My Name Is Barbra*, veteran stars such as Sinatra, Ella Fitzgerald, Tony Bennett, and Peggy Lee would all make what were essentially solo concert specials.

Much of *Barbra* is surreal, a prelude to the psychedelic era, and during the major sequence—Streisand wandering about a Victorian mansion in a manner reminiscent of Alice in *Through the Looking-Glass*—you almost expect her to wake up at the end as if from a dream. As she roams from one room to the next, you're struck by the coincidence that absolutely none of these tableaux requires her to interact with other human beings. When she encounters a percussionist playing a kettle drum, he moves in a dehumanized fashion, like a robot. In fact, the whole room is full of automatons. Even later, when she at last sings in front of a full flesh-and-blood orchestra, the conductor—presumably offscreen—is never shown. The musicians are looking one way, she's looking another, and there's never the least hint of eye contact between the two.

The 1966 special, *Color Me Barbra*, isn't quite as much fun, being a more highbrow event that has Streisand schlepping around a fine arts museum, highlighted by her spirited rendition of "The Minute Waltz" as Marie Antoinette about to be led to the guillotine. The final sequence has her sounding quite jazzy in Harold Arlen songs (like "Any Place I Hang My Hat Is Home") with a touch of the blues and a handful of Lena Horne mannerisms. Sometimes she almost seems to settle into a groove, to relax, lighten up a little, and almost swing, but a heartbeat later she's pouncing down on the beat again, like a drill sergeant in hobnailed boots.

Even when she sings "It Had to Be You," it sounds like a personal revelation, as if she's singing about herself, infatuated by her own self-discovery, rather than expressing love for someone else. (Her diction is so impeccable that she's virtually the only singer I've ever heard who sings "some others I've seen . . ." instead of "some mothers . . ."). Most singers, especially musical theater–oriented ones, strive to hide their modulations, to make that aspect of the musical process invisible, but Streisand loves to parade her key changes in plain sight, making sure no one misses them. She wants you to be conscious of her technique at all times. Every number seems to be a final number, every concert is a concert of nothing but climaxes. "Where Am I Going?" (from *Sweet Charity*) is a song made for Babs (on *Color Me Barbra*), particularly with lines like, "No matter where I run / I find myself there," except that she's running toward herself rather than away, as Charity is in *Sweet Charity*.

Occasionally there's evidence that her total self-confidence is, in fact, a good act. Engineer Frank Laico has said that when the singer recorded her *Classical Barbra* album in 1976, she had absolutely no faith in her natural ability to sing: Rather than simply singing a number straight through, she instructed the engineer to splice it together note by note. According to Laico, virtually no two notes in that album are heard as actually recorded; it was all assembled—precomputer—with a razor blade. Ironically—or not—*Classical Barbra* is one of her best albums. She realizes that she isn't well versed enough with the music of Carl Orff and Gabriel Fauré to overwhelm it the way she abuses Broadway and pop songs (familiarity breeds contempt). For once, she's actually humbled by the material.

According to producer-demagogue Mitch Miller, Streisand already had a reputation as a take-charge kind of a gal when she first came to Columbia Records at the age of twenty. "Goddard [Lieberson] brought her to Columbia, and she wanted me to produce her," the veteran A&R man recalled, "and I said to Goddard, 'No, I can't, because she demands *all* your time. She wants you there, to do this, to do that, to hold her hand. And then afterward she says, 'I did it all.' What do you think everybody in Hollywood hates her guts for? Because she uses people and spits them out and shoves them away.'"

"I wrote for her in the late sixties and seventies," the late arranger-conductor Billy Byers told me in 1995. "She's not pleasant to work with. I already knew she was impossible. I saw her embarrass [arrangers] Ray Ellis, Peter Matz, Don Costa, and I told her up front, 'I worked with you and you always seem to change your mind. I'm up for small fixes, but if you want major changes, let me do it overnight or it'll be a major catastrophe.' We decided what we were going to do, and she said, 'Oh, this is it.' I went to rehearsal and she changed her mind, first about little things, and when it got to be major, she said, 'Isn't this fun?'"

The violinist Dave Frisina was yet another studio musician who volunteered his impression of Streisand without waiting to be asked. "She's rough to work with, she's tough," he said, around 1991. "She's temperamental, she's got her own ideas about music and she's not happy unless it's done exactly the way she wants. I only had a couple of sessions with her and found her difficult to work with, but then so does everybody else." Then he added, "But she's a talent and has a helluva voice, she's a good actress."

Ted Nash, a fine tenor saxophone soloist who worked in Hollywood for many years, drew a contrast between Streisand and Doris Day. "Doris wouldn't have that much to say about it. Whatever the leader would recommend, do this and do that, she'd just go ahead. Whereas somebody like Streisand comes in and takes over the whole scene. From then on, no one else has anything to say. She dictates the whole policy of the date." (Nash suggested that Sinatra was a perfect balance between the two extremes.)

It's also true that any woman in the entertainment industry who had a definite idea about what she wanted—and how to get it (including, to name one, Peggy Lee)—is labeled a bitch, even today. Forty years ago it was even more difficult to know where to draw the line between feminine assertion and bitchiness. Byers also told a story about meeting a painter who was hired to paint one of Streisand's houses, a job that lasted exactly two days. "The first day I showed her how I mix my paints and apply my brushstrokes," the painter said, "and the second day she showed me how to mix my paints and apply my brushstrokes."

The days when Streisand would use orchestrators

like Billy Byers and jazz musicians like Ted Nash were numbered. Her primary studio albums for this period (not counting Broadway original cast albums and movie sound tracks) are:

The Barbra Streisand Album (1963)
The Second Barbra Streisand Album (1964)
The Third Album (1964)
People (1964)
My Name Is Barbra (1965)
My Name Is Barbra, Two . . . (1965)
Je m'appelle Barbra (1966)
Color Me Barbra (1966)
Simply Streisand (1967)
A Christmas Album (1967)
A Happening in Central Park (1968)
What About Today? (1969)
Stoney End (1971)
Barbra Joan Streisand (1971)

This marks the end of the period when Streisand regularly sang the Great American Songbook—and actually the last two albums don't qualify, and are listed here for completeness' sake. Her sales were supposedly on the downslide at the turn of the seventies, but Clive Davis, the soon-to-be-deposed head of Columbia Records, knew why. As he revealed in his book, *Clive: Inside the Record Business* (the *Mein Kampf* of the music business, if ever there was one), it was because she was under the mysterious impression that Rodgers and Hart were better songwriters than Laura Nyro. Needless to say, Davis felt personally impelled to correct this fallacy. Streisand had already done an album called *What About Today?* that included some songs by Burt Bacharach and the Beatles, and, rather than boosting her career, it was her poorest-seller yet—the only one of her albums thus far not to go gold or platinum.

However, two years later, when Davis and producer Richard Perry put together a program of soft, Muzaky rock songs entitled *Stoney End*, it completely turned Streisand's career around, moving her from the AM audience (read, Sinatra and the Rat Pack) to the FM one (read Joni Mitchell, Carole King). The prettiest cut (and, several generations later, the least embarrassing) is "Just a Little Lovin' (Early in the Mornin')" (Barry Mann and Cynthia Weil), but the one that sticks in your brain is "Time and Love" by Laura Nyro. The rather left-field reference to Jesus seems like a response to Leonard Cohen's "Suzanne"; however, the major key, hand-clapping feeling sounds like revival night at the Osmond household, or *King of Kings* enacted by Kermit the Frog and Miss Piggy: *The Muppet Messiah* anybody? *Stoney End* immediately went platinum. Columbia Records took out ads pointing out that Streisand was still a young woman in her twenties, and the message was implicit: Just because your parents like her doesn't mean that you're not allowed to like her, too. At twenty-nine, she finally began selling records to fans her own age or younger. And she has rarely looked back.

Yet you can never tell where a great Streisand performance will turn up. Apart from "Bewitched," there are three performances of far more obscure Rodgers and Hart songs that she does brilliantly: "I'll Tell the Man on the Street" (on the first *Album*) and particularly "Quiet Night" and "Where's That Rainbow" (both on *My Name Is Barbra, Two*). She keeps it subtle, and even though I expect her to start blasting, as she almost always does just when I find myself liking her, everything stays under control—these are remarkably subdued performances. Her "Where's That Rainbow" is equally marvelous, building to a Garland-style half-time chorus, getting big but never over-the-top, never shifting the focus from the song to the singer. No wonder Richard Rodgers offered a spoken testimonial to her (which is included as a track on the *Just for the Record* collection).

Yet "I Got Plenty o' Nuttin'," which comes right after "Quiet Night," is just the opposite, self-conscious all the way, in a dreadful boogaloo arrangement; she may approximate swinging from time to time, but one thing she should never try to be is funky. As far as I'm concerned, she's the last person in the world who should be taking a pop standard and trying to funk it up. On the other hand, there's at least one example of her taking an R&B hit and making it into something more like a traditional ballad. One of her comparatively lesser-known packages, the 1974 *Butterfly* (the cover shows a housefly on a stick of butter; this was years before her voice was famously compared to the stuff) ends with a pair of beauties. Buck Owens's "Cryin' Time" is clearly based on the hit Ray Charles arrangement, but she sings it directly and straight-ahead, with comparatively little unneccessary cuckooness. She also recorded the song in a duet with Ray Charles himself (included on her 2002 album *Duets*), but, disappointingly, the presence of another pop icon brings out her competitive edge here, and she lays on the ersatz-soul extra-thick, almost as if she's trying to out–Brother Ray Brother Ray.

On *Butterfly*, her superior solo reading of "Cryin' Time" is followed by the 1956 rock 'n' roll hit "Let the Good Times Roll" (the Shirley and Lee single, not the very different Louis Jordan song of ten years earlier). For her first chorus at least, "Let the Good Times Roll" is an amazing example of Streisand singing more subtly than I could have ever imagined, as if she's not trying to force the song into doing anything it doesn't want to do; as if for a change she's letting the song itself dictate how it wants to be sung. It's too good to last; after the first chorus, a gospel choir comes in and everything kicks into tempo, and Streisand now sounds as if she's trying to out-Aretha Aretha. For a minute or so, though, she really had me going.

There's no one album, even in the early period,

where she's on target all the way through and that I can unhesitatingly recommend. However, one major surprise arrived in 1975. This was *Funny Lady,* her sequel to *Funny Girl,* the 1968 film of her 1965 Broadway sensation. *Funny Lady* continues Fanny Brice's life story, and it's a mediocre movie, closer to Streisand's worst than her best. Yet the sound track is an unexpected delight, starting with the way the singer switches between vintage songs of the Fanny Brice era (the twenties and thirties), such as "It's Only a Paper Moon" and worthy new ones by John Kander and Fred Ebb (especially "How Lucky Can You Get?").

"More Than You Know" and "If I Love Again" are two of Streisand's most believable ballads, while "I Found a Million Dollar Baby (In a Five and Ten Cent Store)" is a delightful period piece, much wittier and less overdone than such earlier over-the-top swipes at Brice such as "Sam, You Made the Pants Too Long" and "Second-Hand Rose." Unfortunately, the *Funny Lady* album offers evidence of the career that might have been, rather than what was fast becoming one of the biggest disappointments in American music. (Though, to be fair, not more so than the seventies recordings of Aretha Franklin and Nancy Wilson, in comparison to their earlier work.)

Streisand has occasionally sung good songs since then. Since *What About Today?* she has followed every trend that came down the pike, from quasi-disco to watered-down country and western to duets. It's unfortunate that such a major talent has chosen to be a follower rather than a leader, but she continues to gross millions. And, by a fluke, once in a while, these trends include the Great American Songbook. In the wake of Linda Ronstadt, she recorded *The Broadway Album* (1985), then, after Natalie Cole's *Unforgettable* proved a sensation, Streisand retaliated with *Back to Broadway* (1993). In these two sets, she has, unfortunately, considerably enriched the already overflowing coffers of the dread Andrew Lloyd Webber. Considering that in the sixties, she championed *The Fantasticks* and *The Yearling* (an unsuccessful show containing two classic songs, "Why Did I Choose You?" and "I'm All Smiles"), this is a painful reminder of how low this once promising talent has sunk.

When Streisand first emerged in the sixties, the phrase "middle-of-the-road" was used by musical fascists (or, at the very least, fashionistas) like Clive Davis to describe anything that was popular to the generation of record buyers over, say, twenty-five. Today, the term "middle-of-the-road" implies something entirely different, and Streisand is the only artist to dominate both generations of MOR. She rules over such a vast dominion that she's inspired two disciples in entirely opposite fields: Julie Budd and Celine Dion come out of, respectively, the early and late eras of Streisand, which is to say before and after she began wasting her chops on pseudo-soul.

In 1997, Streisand released an album with a

subject that was, at last, so big that both her voice and her ego paled in comparison to it: God Himself. This was her long-awaited religious album, *Higher Ground*. It was a brilliant idea that, with a few exceptions, and like almost everything else after 1970, was ruined by all kinds of electronic accoutrements and forgettable songs. Her duet with Celine Dion, "Tell Him," was truly one for the fast-forward button; here was a singer (also accurately portrayed on *South Park*) who embodied the worst aspects of the Streisand legacy, starting with a voice like a big empty house, not to mention the overdone mannerisms, the monumental ego, the towering insincerity. More's the pity, because for the only time in three decades, Streisand had found a subject matter to match her own pretensions: big, profound, religious, and quasi-gospel songs that ponder the nature of God and the universe. Only when she sticks to straightforward treatments of comparatively traditional items, like Ervin Drake's "I Believe," "Deep River," and the Hebrew prayer "Avinu Malkeinu," does the majesty of the celebrated Streisand instrument peek through. (The cabaret singer Julie Budd continues to make albums that sound like early sixties Streisand—this is what Babs might sound like today had she never succumbed to the dark side of The Force.)

As Streisand sings on *Higher Ground*, "Everything Must Change." In 1976, her career turned one more time. That was the year she made *A Star Is Born*, a dreadful rock-era remake of one of the most oft-told tales in Hollywood history. Streisand and her boyfriend at the time, hairdresser-boxer dude Jon Peters, took over the production. Pretty soon the whole industry was predicting the imminent downfall of the vehicle, based on Streisand's having the temerity to proclaim herself a producer. When the film was finally released, the negative word of mouth regarding the producer-star herself was exceeded only by the negative opinions of the reviewers. (Her next album, *Streisand Superman*—there's a title— included a response to what was being written about her at the time, "Don't Believe What You Read," co-written by the singer.) Virtually everybody in show business, not just the critics, was looking forward to dancing on Streisand's grave.

And they were disappointed. *A Star Is Born* was not only a blockbuster, but the main song, "Evergreen" (written by Streisand and Paul Williams), also became a smash, winning both a Grammy and an Oscar for best movie song. The more the world thought she was a bitch, the more they loved her. And the more she tried to do everything—produce, write, direct—the more she dominated a production and stretched the outer limits of bitchiness, the more fanatical her following became.

It was only logical that after that she would proclaim herself a director, and the result was the even more successful *Yentl*. *Yentl* was also a logical follow-up to Streisand's role in the 1969 film of *Hello,*

Dolly!, a movie that, viewed today, actually seems like two movies in one. Half of it is a very watchable film of the 1964 Broadway musical; the other half seems like a Streisand solo concert. Director Gene Kelly keeps cutting between the two (almost like the interwoven stories of *Intolerance*), but the two halves seem to have nothing in common. Streisand does nearly all her big numbers without the other cast members; her only notable interaction with another human being is not a performer playing a character, but the great Louis Armstrong (who is only making a cameo, and is otherwise not visible).

Yentl takes things a giant step further: Leave it to Streisand to pioneer the concept of solo musical theater. The whole sound track could be one of Streisand's one-woman TV specials, with Streisand singing one anthem of self-discovery, self-exploration, self-aggrandization, self-determination, self-self-self after another. The songs, independent of one another and of Streisand, represent some of the best work of the formidable, long-standing collaboration of composer Michel Legrand and lyricists Alan and Marilyn Bergman. Streisand's demo of "Papa, Can You Hear Me" with just Legrand on piano (included in the *For the Record* package) is devastating all by itself, and much more personal and moving than the full orchestra version on the sound track. Yet taken all together, what Streisand has come up with is an entire score filled with nothing but "I Want" songs, as if *The Fantasticks* had consisted of nothing but variations on "Much More."

With the success of *A Star Is Born* (her first film as producer) and *Yentl* (which marked her debut as director), it was inevitable that she would continue doing both—it seems a natural outgrowth of her goals in her musical career to be the woman who had to have total control of everything. She went on to produce, direct, and star in the very successful *The Prince of Tides* (1991) and *The Mirror Has Two Faces* (1996). She was already virtually the only pop singer of her generation to follow Sinatra, Crosby, and Doris Day in their paths from pop singers to film icons; perhaps even more than Sinatra and Crosby, she succeeded in making herself into a mogul as well, and a veritable industry unto herself. (Surely the leading female singers of more recent eras— Cher, Bette Midler, even Mariah Carey—have sought to emulate her in this regard, with varying degrees of success.)

Streisand's most recent album, the 2009 *Love Is the Answer*, is another example of her by now long-standing practice of making traditional Barbra Streisand music primarily when she's following a trend inspired by someone else. Her major standards albums in the eighties and nineties were done in the wake of Linda Ronstadt and Natalie Cole, and *Love Is the Answer* is an obvious attempt to capture some of the market carved out in the new century by Diana Krall's very successful albums of songbook standards done with a big, almost symphonic strings section; Streisand even telegraphed her intentions by inviting Ms. Krall to produce the album and play piano on the sessions. (No surprise: The result sounds exactly like one of those big-selling Krall albums produced by Tommy LiPuma.) My first reaction—or at least that of the pundit in me—was to wonder why Streisand needs Krall; she was making this kind of album well before Diana was born. Perhaps Streisand just needed Krall in order to give her a trend to follow.

Still, I'm inclined to suppress my inner pundit, because *Love Is the Answer* is Streisand's best album in forty years, possibly ever. She sings with a subtlety and reserve that, in her canon, is rare if not unprecedented. For once, she doesn't sing as if she's trying to beat a song to death, to overwhelm it with sheer chops. For once, she doesn't express every emotion with an outrageous stylization that nearly negates it, or makes it seem like so much empty posturing. There are times here when Streisand is so laid back, particularly by her standards, that it almost seems like a Diana Krall record with Streisand's vocals electronically inserted. (No one was denying that there was electronic tampering in the album—Columbia released a deluxe double-disc edition, in which one volume features the vocal tracks with full orchestra, the other with Krall and her quartet. I actually like both.)

If Streisand was tempted to sound, well, like Streisand—to belt and blast all over the place— you'd never know it. Even "Here's to Life," easily the most self-aggrandizing anthem since "My Way," is comparatively subtle (particularly on the quartet version, although both are primarily voice-and-piano duets). The song was famously identified with Shirley Horn, the most withdrawn, subtlest singer of them all, and Streisand has clearly paid attention. When she sings "The Gentle Rain" (credit Krall for unearthing a sixties bossa nova standard that hasn't been overrecorded) it makes me think that she's actually capable of being gentle. I can live without "If You Go Away"—Jaques Brel doesn't exactly compose melody; what he writes is a script for pop song divas to get all Medea on our ass—but I listen to the whole track, waiting for Streisand to drop the bomb, and, to my surprise, she never does. The suspense actually keeps me going. "Spring Can Really Hang You Up the Most," is almost the "Lush Life" of the twenty-first century. I hear a lot of singers (Jane Monheit among them) trying to bite off this long rambling melody and inevitably they're not up to it—it gets boring long before it's finished—but Streisand, old pro that she is, actually sustains interest throughout.

There are moments when she just lets go and releases the Streisand within, as on "Smoke Gets in Your Eyes," but within this context, you feel she's earned the right to do so. Although the album title proclaims that *Love Is the Answer*, this recent album actually raises more questions than it answers. Con-

sidering that it was and is a breakout success—it debuted at number one, and was generally regarded as the album of the year—one has to wonder if this marks a new beginning for the singer (and even Krall), or if, on her next project, she'll just go back to yelling. Surely it's clear to her that the public and the press alike approve of her new direction; now it's up to her.

South Park aside, Streisand never needed the Triangle of Zinthar to turn herself into a hundred-foot sacred monster bent on world conquest; she had become that long before *A Star Is Born* or *Yentl*.

Maxine Sullivan (1911–1987)

"I had no choice, I had to swing it." It was a story that Maxine Sullivan told thousands of times, especially in her later years, when she was frequently profiled and interviewed. (This particular quote is from a write-up by John S. Wilson in *The New York Times*.) The year was 1934, and the twenty-two-year-old Sullivan had been asked to perform at a Pittsburgh establishment called the Benjamin Harrison Literary Society. The name sounds like a front for a speakeasy, and, in fact, it was likely a holdover from Prohibition, which had ended only a year earlier. Although this was strictly an after-hours joint, it did indulge in a few literary pretensions. Sullivan would have preferred to sing a pop song or blues, but instead she was asked to perform Joyce Kilmer's famous poem "Trees." What to do with "Trees"? The poem was only twenty years old in 1934 but already something of a cliché. Obviously Sullivan couldn't sing it straight—at least not with a straight face. This is a text that has defeated many an interpreter: The only way to make it palatable is to goof it up à la Spike Jones (with bird-call sound effects) or at least to undercut its excesses by rendering it in a semiparody treatment, the way Al Hibbler did later on. Then, too, one can always repeat the famous schoolchild's dyslexic spoonerism, "God can only make a tree."

Sullivan, however, found another approach. She swung it—not a fierce, hard swing, like Jimmy Rushing with Count Basie or Ella Fitzgerald with Chick Webb, in which one little girl armed with just her voice proved that she could swing seventeen grown men with an arsenal of horns into bad health. Rather, Sullivan employed a soft, gentle swing, very much influenced by Mildred Bailey (perhaps the number-one jazz-pop singer of the thirties) and Bailey's own chief inspiration, Ethel Waters.

"I just couldn't sing it straight," said Sullivan. By refashioning "Trees" into a relaxed and swinging 4/4, Sullivan made Kilmer bearable. Fittingly, this engagement was the one she regarded in later years as her first important professional gig. For most of her career, Sullivan's calling card would not be singing blues or ballads, even though she had few peers when she sang either W. C. Handy or Cole Porter, but material like "Trees." She made a specialty of folk songs, classical tunes, iconic poems, and ancient airs that she revived with her lightly swinging style. On the one hand, the practice had a novelty value and certainly couldn't be classified, as Sullivan made clear, as singing things "straight." Yet she never played these songs for laughs or for camp value; she retained some of their lyric value as love songs, and in that sense, she might be considered a key player in the development of the Swingin' Lover style later perfected by Sinatra.

Swinging traditional material like "Trees" and her breakthrough hit, "Loch Lomond," immediately gave her a unique identity: There were plenty of blues singers, big band singers, and torch singers in the public eye during the swing era, but there was no one else who specialized in swinging Shakespeare, Stephen Foster, Robert Browning, and medieval and Renaissance poetry. In a sense, Sullivan practiced a kind of reverse racial profiling: If Mildred Bailey and other white vocalists could sing Handy, Ellington, and the blues, there certainly was no other artist like Sullivan, black or white, who could breathe life into the Anglo-Saxon repertoire or even those traditional songs from the antebellum South that could be construed as glorifying slavery.

Some singers, like Sarah Vaughan (positively) and Barbra Streisand (negatively), make a specialty of embellishing a song. Sullivan, like Mildred Bailey before her and Peggy Lee after her, did just the opposite. With her cool, honey-flavored contralto, she trimmed off everything nonessential from a melody, reducing it to its bare minimum by dispensing with anything that remotely suggested exhibitionistic pyrotechnics.

Although Sullivan's gentle swing and unique repertoire gave her a distinct identity, even when she departed from both she was still one of the finest singers to work in the great jazz or pop tradition. But for circumstances, she might well have reached the uppermost pantheon of American vocal artists; in fact, at several different points in her career, she did.

Maxine Sullivan was born Marietta Williams on May 13, 1911, in Homestead, Pennsylvania. She rarely spoke about her first twenty-three years, and although she was evidently successful singing around Pittsburgh by the early thirties, there's little on the written record about her life before the Literary Society gig of 1934. However, it's known that while she was singing at that club, she was heard by a white pianist named Gladys Mosier, who recommended her to the young Claude Thornhill, at that time something of a hotshot piano player, arranger, and conductor for radio stations and in recording studios. By the mid-thirties, Thornhill had played in several outstanding bands, including Louis Prima's New Orleans Gang and Ray Noble's all-star orchestra at the Rainbow Room.

Thornhill was so impressed with Sullivan that he took over as her manager. This seems odd considering that, over the arc of his career, he was proven time and again to be anything but a businessman (as his attempts to manage the business of his own orchestra subsequently proved). Thornhill introduced Sullivan to bassist and bandleader John Kirby, and the three musicians—Sullivan, Thornhill, and Kirby—were quick to realize that they all had something in common: They all were interested in expanding the repertoire of the jazz performer by going beyond pop songs and blues and into the European repertoire, both classical and vernacular. What Sullivan would do with Scottish folk songs both Thornhill and Kirby would also do, in their very different ways, with Tchaikovsky and others.

"Loch Lomond" was shorthand for "The Bonnie Banks o' Loch Lomond," a traditional Scottish folk song that dates back to the uprising of 1745 led by Bonnie Prince Charlie. The text is sometimes credited to Robert Burns, and was later included in a collection of Burns songs by Jo Stafford. (Unlike Sullivan, however, Stafford sang it straight, and didn't swing it at all.) Apparently, the first vocalist to swing it was the Scottish entertainer Ella Logan, who had performed with big bands in the U.K. before coming to America and establishing herself as a Broadway star. Even if this is true, the idea of a Scottish woman swinging a Scottish song was bound to have less of an impact than an African American woman swinging a Scottish song. Indeed, Sullivan may have sought to heighten the novelty by picking an Irish-sounding stage name for herself.

Sullivan's arrival in New York seems to have provided Thornhill with the impetus to do his first record date as a leader in 1937. Using a band that sounded more like Prima or Kirby than his own orchestra of the forties, the pianist recorded four current pop songs, two of which featured Sullivan: Burton Lane's "Stop, You're Breaking My Heart" (later remade by the singer on an entire album of Lane's songs) and Allie Wrubel's future standard "Gone With the Wind." Shortly afterward, Thornhill and Sullivan reconvened for a second session, the results of which would be released under the singer's name. This time she sang two decade-old pop songs that were already regarded as jazz standards, "I'm Coming, Virginia" and "Blue Skies," as well as two Scottish folk songs, "Loch Lomond" and "Annie Laurie." Thornhill presided over the marriage of singer, instrumentation, and material, devising an ensemble (four horns, four rhythm) and an orchestration that suited her perfectly. Often when small bands play tight arrangements they sound stiff and stilted (a charge that was frequently leveled against the John Kirby Sextet); this was hardly the case with the Sullivan-Thornhill sessions, in which the light and lilting sound of the ensemble perfectly complemented Sullivan's own.

"Loch Lomond" was not only a near-perfect record, but the combination of its excellence plus the novelty of the idea—a black swinger doing a swing treatment of a familiar song—resulted in one of the big hits of 1937. The song was all over *Your Hit Parade*, and Sullivan herself was all over the radio, as well as appearing in clubs and movie theaters—she turned up in several feature films, among them Warner Bros.' *Going Places* and Paramount's *St. Louis Blues*. Considering that no one in the general public had remotely heard of Sullivan or Thornhill and that the song was hardly a hot plug item from a film or show, the hit took everybody by surprise. "Loch Lomond" also turned up in two film short subjects without Sullivan, as swung by Ella Logan's eight-year-old niece, Annabelle Logan (later known as Annie Ross) in the "Little Rascals" two-reeler *Our Gang Follies of 1938*, and by Louis Prima, sans Thornhill, in a Vitaphone short.

The song associated with a Scottish prince and an African American vocalist underwent a further cultural crossover when it was appropriated by the Jewish King of Swing. Benny Goodman, knowing a good thing when he heard one, commissioned an arrangement from Thornhill for his full fifteen-piece big band, which was sung memorably by Martha Tilton at the famous January 1938 Carnegie Hall concert. Yet even the talented (not to mention "liltin'") Miss Tilton failed to supplant Sullivan as the Loch Lomond lass in the public's eye. Sullivan herself soon appeared with Goodman in the short-lived Broadway show *Swingin' the Dream* (1939).

Thornhill had connections with the Onyx Club on Fifty-second Street, where the raucous, wild-man antics of in-house bandleader Stuff Smith ("and His Onyx Club Boys") were about to be supplanted by the more sedate sounds of John Kirby's newly formed sextet, which, as we've seen, had more than a passing interest in swinging the classics. Sullivan and Kirby were married for three years beginning in 1939, at which time she also made a series of commercial recordings and radio transcriptions with the sextet. (These were almost all folk airs from the British Isles: "If I Had a Ribbon Bow," "Molly Malone," "Who Is Sylvia?," "Barbara Allen.") Her husband's soft-swinging combo suited her just as well as Thornhill's band had, and she fit into the group as expertly as did the more experienced Mildred Bailey, who was also recording with the Kirby unit at around the same time. The Sullivan-Kirby combination also starred on a nationally broadcast radio series, *Flow Gently, Sweet Rhythm*, one of the first national musical programs built around black performers.

Meanwhile, Sullivan had launched a trend for swinging the classics, a bandwagon that many singers and bands, both black and white, jumped onto. While Goodman swung "Loch Lomond," Jimmie Lunceford did a stunning treatment of "Annie Laurie." Even Ella Fitzgerald's biggest hit and earliest signature song, a swinging version of the traditional nursery rhyme "A-Tisket, A-Tasket" from 1938, can be said to have been motivated by "Loch Lomond." (Fitzgerald also recorded one ersatz-Scottish song,

"MacPherson Is Rehearsin'," an unmemorable offering no doubt also inspired by Sullivan.) In fact, Fitzgerald's producers continued to feed her children's songs (such as "Melinda the Mousie" and "I Got Me a Pebble in My Shoe") even as Sullivan continued to sing and swing folk songs, from "Dark Eyes" to "A Brown Bird Singing." A generation later, when Peggy Lee performed traditional folk songs, she was undoubtedly also reflecting the influence of Sullivan, whom she more than once cited as her biggest inspiration.

Sullivan was so hot in the prewar era it seemed as if all the major labels were fighting for her contract, and she bounced back and forth among the American Recording Corp., Victor, Columbia Records, and Decca. She was also all over the map stylistically, singing not only the folk songs that made her famous but a mixture of contemporary pop songs and jazz standards, often performed with the chamber-group-style accompaniment of the Kirby Sextet. Yet somehow she failed to find another hit.

The swinging folk song bit was beginning to wear thin, at least as far as the major labels were concerned—they seem to have lost interest in her by the end of the 1942–44 recording ban. Sullivan was by now represented by the Moe Gale Agency, and, as she told historian Ted Ono, she had begun to feel as if they were working against her rather than for her. She broke with Gale at this time, representing herself in all negotiations for the rest of her career. Perhaps a black woman had to eat a certain amount of crow—Jim Crow—to keep working in the male white world, but whereas Fitzgerald and Billie Holiday, soon to be joined by Sarah Vaughan and Dinah Washington, were able to keep going, Sullivan was not. Both Fitzgerald and Holiday had the good fortune to hook up with Milt Gabler and then Norman Granz, two producers who profitably served the singers' best interests.

However, Sullivan did cut twenty-two generally excellent sides between 1944 and 1949, all of which are included (along with five bonus radio tracks) on the much recommended CD (produced by Mr. Ono) *Maxine Sullivan: The "Le Ruban Bleu" Years*. Her track record in terms of the quality of her material is amazingly high. The closest thing to a disappointment in these years is a 1944 date in which the four songs (all credited to publisher Joe Davis) fall short of her customary high standards. Yet everything else she sang from this period—and pretty much every part of her career—has certified brand names stamped on it, names like Warren, Gershwin, Porter, Mercer, Arlen, and even Noel Coward.

The bulk of the late forties recordings are second to none in Sullivan's, or practically anyone else's, output. She sang two excellent sides with Teddy Wilson and Red Norvo (Mildred Bailey's two favorite accompanists), and two equally outstanding ones with Benny Carter. In 1946 and 1947 she made two 78 rpm albums (six songs each) with two remarkable backup groups. The second utilized a trio led by pianist Ellis Larkins (who would later distinguish himself with Mildred Bailey and more famously with Fitzgerald), which echoed what she sounded like in clubs of the period (she was a regular at the New York cabaret Le Ruban Bleu in these years). The use of piano, bass, and guitar gives the proceedings a King Cole Trio–like intimacy.

The first album (from 1946) pairs her with a string ensemble known as the New Friends of Rhythm, who, like John Kirby, were also determined to combine jazz and classical music. But where the Kirbyites were black jazzmen playing what later became known as chamber jazz, the New Friends were white classical string players who were getting hot.

No less than Sullivan and the Kirby Six, Sullivan and the New Friends were an excellent combination. The string arrangements were much gutsier than the very effete jazz violin ensembles on the more famous NBC's *Chamber Music Society of Lower Basin Street,* and the addition of clarinet soloist Buster Bailey and a saxophonist made it even better. This wonderful session, which consists mainly of folk material, was yet another Sullivan high point. The six sides with the string ensemble and the six with the Ellis Larkins Trio (both released on the short-lived International Records label) are among Sullivan's finest, and, like virtually all of her output, deserve to be better known.

Sullivan seems to have kept working steadily and making excellent sides, even if they were for dinky labels with poor sound quality and poorer distribution. In 1950, she married for the fourth time (in all the years I knew her, she never mentioned husbands two or three, except to say that the second was the father of her daughter, Paula), this time to the well-known pianist Cliff Jackson (who had led the Krazy Kats, one of the hot Harlem bands of the twenties), and they stayed together until his death in 1972.

In the fifties, Sullivan entered into a period of semiretirement, emerging only sporadically; none of that "show must go on" nonsense for her. In 1955, a longtime fan, the critic and producer Leonard Feather, brought her into the studio for several projects. He assembled a re-creation of the Kirby Sextet, with bassist Aaron Bell representing Sullivan's late first husband, and hired Sullivan to sing two more Anglo-Saxon folk songs, "Molly Malone" and "If I Had a Ribbon Bow." The tracks were well enough received for Feather to produce two full-length Sullivan LPs for the same company, Period Records: *Maxine Sullivan 1956* and *A Tribute to Andy Razaf* (1956), both with pianist Dick Hyman as musical director. These are two sumptuously fine albums, probably her two all-time best, if only for the obvious reason that she still has her "young" sound but now captured in the modern tape-era fidelity of the fifties.

Hyman and Feather achieve further continuity with Sullivan's past by devising small band orchestrations that are faithful to the tradition of Thornhill and especially Kirby—with two ex-Kirbyites, Buster Bailey and trumpeter Charlie Shavers, on hand to ensure authenticity. Throughout, Sullivan keeps in check her perfect balance of swing and restraint, control and release. The *1956* album looks to Sullivan's past, in that the bulk of it is traditional songs (among them her fourth, I think, commercial recording of "Loch Lomond"), and a few standards she'd previously recorded, such as the Kern-Hammerstein "Folks Who Live on the Hill" (she'd done it back in 1937, when it was new, and her versions were undoubtedly an influence on Peggy Lee's definitive reading, from 1957).

Even though the *Andy Razaf* album celebrates a superb Harlem lyricist of the prewar era, it can be said to look to the future, since her most memorable albums of the later years would largely be in the songbook format. Hyman and company evoke a variety of swing era styles from Waller ("Honeysuckle Rose") to Basie ("Stompin' at the Savoy"), yet of all involved, no one swings harder than Sullivan. The album also provides a fascinating counterpoint to the Fats Waller collection recorded a year or so later by Dinah Washington and Basie arranger Ernie Wilkins; as magnificent as Washington is, it's hard to say she's better than Sullivan on the songs that overlap, like "Christopher Columbus."

Sullivan turned forty in 1954; her forties and fifties would have been an ideal time for her to make more albums on the level of the two Period projects (which were reissued on numerous labels, including a 1991 CD on the Spanish Fresh Sounds that includes all twenty-six tracks; there's also an easier-to-find edition on the American label DCC that includes only the *Razaf* LP and uses the original cover). Alas, this was not to be. The *1956* album contains one of her most powerful songs, "Raggle-Taggle Gypsies," a traditional song found all over the British Isles. It has its origins in the 1624 execution of a Scottish Gypsy chieftain charged with the crime of seducing an English lady and enticing her to ride away with him, leaving His Lordship (her husband) and their castle behind. At this point in her life Sullivan made just the opposite decision: She stayed behind with her Lord and her daughter in the home she titled "The House That Jazz Built" and vowed nevermore to take to the open road with the Raggle-Taggle Gypsies, ho.

Sullivan's retirement was, alas, only temporarily interrupted by the Hyman-Feather projects; otherwise she barely sang at all again until 1968. Whenever I spoke with her, she was never quite clear: Did she want to keep singing and had no opportunities, or did she just want to leave music behind for a while? It's hard to believe that impresarios like George Wein and Norman Granz wouldn't have come up with work for her had she approached them. Feather and Hyman, in fact, included her in their famous *Seven Ages of Jazz* concert in 1956. Whatever the case, Sullivan spent a dozen years focusing on family, especially her daughter (then in her "difficult years," she said), as well as on community service and a subsequent career as a registered nurse. In fact, her major musical preoccupation in those years didn't involve singing at all; instead, she taught herself how to play the valve trombone.

In 1968, Maxine Sullivan was ready to sing professionally again, and accepted a spot with trumpeter Bobby Hackett's band at the Riverboat, near Grand Central Station in New York. Before long she was touring once more, often in the company of the former Bob Crosby–ites who then made up the World's Greatest Jazzband. In 1969, she recorded two exceptional albums with the WGJB's Bob Wilber, a brilliant multireed player and arranger. Hyman and Wilber were the first of many new collaborators for Sullivan who, in this phase of her career, were generally at least a few generations younger than she.

The two Sullivan-Wilber albums, *The Music of Hoagy Carmichael* and *Close as Pages in a Book*, both showcase her at her very best—my only disappointment being that *Hoagy Carmichael* features her on just four of its twelve tracks; on the whole, Wilber's arrangements spotlight the singer just as effectively as Hyman's. Monmouth-Evergreen Records also had the smarts to capitalize on her past by reteaming with Hyman for a program of swinging Shakespeare. (She and Hyman would cross paths for the last time on *I Love to Be in Love*, another excellent, well-rounded collection from 1985.)

Sullivan turned sixty in 1971, the year that *Maxine Sullivan—William Shakespeare—Dick Hyman* was recorded, at which point the floodgates were just about to open. It's as if she were determined to make up for lost time. She appeared more and more frequently at traditional jazz festivals all over the world, especially after she began working with Alan Eichler, a talent manager and booker who specialized in legendary older divas. Along with all this work, Sullivan also found increasing opportunities to make records. She seems to have agreed to record for any producer or label willing to put a thousand bucks or so in her purse, and as a result made nearly thirty albums in the seventies and eighties. There were three for the Fat Cat Jazz label (all recorded live at the Manassas Jazz Festival), and six for George Buck's Audiophile label. The enterprising Mr. Buck seemed determined to corner the market on Maxine Sullivan: In addition to the half-dozen Audiophiles, he acquired the catalogues of both Fat Cat and Monmouth-Evergreen; further, he released two CDs of vintage 1940–41 transcriptions by John Kirby featuring her.

Many of her seventies and eighties albums were essentially swing-style jam sessions built around her voice, such as *Something to Remember You By* and *Uptown*, both made with Scott Hamilton during a 1985 tour of Japan. The most ambitious of her later projects was a series taped in Jarfalla, Sweden, which apparently was produced so expeditiously that there wasn't even time to give them proper titles; they were simply released as *The Queen,* Volumes One through Five. At the same time, she did three songbook albums produced by Harbinger Records that were ambitious in a different, but complementary, fashion. On the Swedish records, which yielded five CDs and a total of nearly eighty tracks, Sullivan seems to be singing virtually every song she learned in her life. She lays the songs down jam-session style with a rotating series of young Scandinavian soloists who are consciously striving to re-create the small group style of the thirties (as in Teddy Wilson, Fats Waller, and Billie Holiday), and the format, overall, is very loose and swinging.

The Harbinger projects, in contrast, were carefully planned songbooks devoted to the works of Harold Arlen, Burton Lane, and Jule Styne, and are tightly arranged in the grand tradition of her work with Thornhill, Kirby, and Hyman, in accomplished arrangements for small band by pianist Keith Ingham. I'm personally biased toward the Harbinger albums since I attended these sessions and was thus able to spend time with Maxine and talk about her life and career. But objectively speaking, she blossoms in both of these settings. Perhaps not coincidentally, the best of her Audiophile albums, particularly from the later period, was *Spring Isn't Everything: The Music of Harry Warren*, another well-organized songbook project.

In 1986, she taped a live album, *At Vine Street*, the Jule Styne album, then the Harry Warren project, and the second of her Tokyo albums with Scott Hamilton—among other projects. Not a bad year. On March 12, 1987, I saw her at the *Highlights in Jazz* concert series at New York University, where she had appeared more or less annually since producer Jack Kleinsinger had launched it fifteen years earlier. Fortunately, the show was taped and later released on the Danish label Storyville. Sullivan was looking and sounding as spry as ever, and went on joking with the emcee and the audience as she always had. As with most jazz concerts, there was no rehearsal, so Sullivan and the rhythm section (helmed by pianist Derek Smith, a virtuoso Brit in the Hyman league) simply laid familiar standards in familiar keys. What makes the concert so superb is that this was one of the few later occasions on which she worked again with old friends from her own generation: tenor saxophonist Buddy Tate and trumpeter-singer Doc Cheatham. Their presence enhances the feeling that Maxine was coming home. The love exchanged between her and the crowd is palpable on the CD, even to those who weren't there in 1987.

Maxine Sullivan died less than a month later on April 7, aged seventy-five. Me and my true love will never meet again.

Her loss was a major one for the jazz community, and the world had signaled its appreciation by giving her several Grammy nominations, such as for the 1984 *Cotton Club Songs of Harold Arlen and Ted Koehler*. (As an actress, she had also received a Tony nomination for her role in the 1979 play *My Old Friends*, in which she co-starred with Imogene Coca.) Along with Ella Fitzgerald and Lena Horne, she was a rare link from the jazz world of the thirties to the modern scene of the eighties. Had her career only suffered from a little less *interruptus*, she might well be more frequently held up for comparison with Fitzgerald and her fellow über-divas. As with all the great ladies of jazz, Sullivan's diction was miraculously precise, her intonation—even in her seventies—was impeccable, and her time was something to be reckoned with. Like Holiday and Sinatra, she can be moving even in swing time: "Raggle-Taggle Gypsies" (on *1956*) makes one's heart pound and feet tap in rough synchronization. She was always incredibly warm, and her music was awesome in its very gentleness.

Sylvia Syms (1917–1992)

In talking with and listening to contemporary cabaret singers, the four names that emerge as the most influential on singers working now are the late Mabel Mercer and Sylvia Syms, who were both active well into their seventies, and Margaret Whiting and Julie Wilson, who both turned eighty in 2004. Syms and Wilson can be described either as cabaret singers (since that was and is how they worked) or as jazz singers (since they often sang with jazz accompaniments, and sometimes with a jazz sense of time).

I hope the reader won't mind if I interject a few personal experiences. I never quite *got* Sylvia Syms while she was alive, and I still don't completely understand why some musicians and critics rate her so highly and regard her as one of the finest interpreters of the American popular song. To me she always seemed a bit off-center. It's certainly my loss that I never caught a whole solo set by her: I saw her at numerous multiple-artist, all-star shows, and met her on several occasions, but in those days when I had to pay to get into clubs I had to think carefully about which cover charges I was willing to endure. Both Mel Tormé and Rosemary Clooney introduced me to her, and I also heard her praises sung by Tony Bennett, as well as scribes I respect, like Whitney Balliett, Rex Reed, and Jim Gavin. The notes to her 1965 *Sylvia Is!* are comprised of testimonials from Bennett, Woody Allen, Erroll Garner, Jack Jones, and others, all wholeheartedly admiring. Frank Sinatra paid her the ultimate compliment of producing and conducting a whole album for her, something he had only done previously for Peggy Lee and Dean Martin.

Perhaps meeting Syms in person was not a good idea: Whenever I spoke with her, she had a strange, glazed expression, and she immediately struck me as something of a loose cannon. An hour or so after meeting me for the first time (at Tormé's opening at the Park Ten, circa 1985), she told everyone present that she wanted to hire me as her manager. (Which, she couldn't have realized, would have been career suicide; I couldn't manage my way out of a paper bag, or even into one.)

Even today when I listen to her albums, I don't completely understand why so many worthy judges of talent regard her as among the great. Good, certainly, even very good, but why would Tormé, Clooney, Bennett, and Sinatra all regard her as an equal? I had the same feeling when I attended a tribute show (at Highlights in Jazz) staged in her honor by two of her closest friends and musical associates, the pianist-singers Daryl Sherman and Barbara Carroll. The salute was very personal, as indeed such a show would have to be, and very well done, but it didn't leave me convinced that Syms was worthy of such adulation. I could only conclude that she was like a lot of major figures in pop culture—either you got her or you didn't.

But she was certainly very, very good on her first three albums, *Songs by Sylvia Syms* (Atlantic, recorded in 1952 and 1954), *Sylvia Syms Sings* (1955), and *Songs of Love* (1957), the latter two both on Decca. The voice keeps reminding me of Judy Garland—perhaps a calmer, less dramatically high-pitched Judy Garland. In fact, on Syms's fifties recordings, she sounds curiously like the sixties Garland. As with both Garland and Billie Holiday, her strengths are at slow and medium tempos, but unlike both of those superdivas, she often sounds awkward at faster speeds, albeit sometimes charmingly so.

Art Tatum, who played piano on a private recording session with Syms in 1953, called her "Moonbeam Moskowitz—the Jewish Indian" (in fact, she played a Native American in the 1958 cult favorite Broadway show *Whoop-Up*), which led a lot of people to assume that her birth name was actually Moskowitz. (Just to confuse matters further, Duke Ellington addressed her as "Lady Hamilton.") In fact, she was born Sylvia Blagman, on December 2, 1917, and grew up in Brooklyn. Her parents weren't particularly musical, but Blagman—who first worked under the name Sylvia Black—was attracted to music and song as a child, and was just the right age to experience the glories of Fifty-second Street. She met and hung around with Billie Holiday ("I copied everything she did, excluding the drugs and booze," Syms told Whitney Balliett—but it was she, Syms also said, who gave Holiday the idea of using a white gardenia as a trademark).

She also hung out with Mildred Bailey. "She was a domestic lady, and she loved to eat and so did I. She thought I looked like her and she'd tell people I was her little sister. She told me I'd be a star, but I'd be very unhappy getting there." Needless to say, looking like Mildred Bailey was not an asset when one's goal was to succeed in showbiz. (Looking like Julie Wilson would have helped her a bit more.) This was another factor in her never becoming a household word, even though she was old enough to have lived through the golden years of radio, the medium in which oversized chanteuses such as Bailey and Kate Smith became famous. Both Wilson and Syms appeared in films and shows—in fact, Syms had a bigger career on Broadway—but always as a character actress, never as a leading lady.

Syms was singing around Fifty-second Street as early as her early twenties, and had a few good breaks in 1947. That year she was offered a tour of Scandinavia with bassist Chubby Jackson's band, which she had to decline for health reasons, but she was able to make her first discs. Between then and 1952, she made over a dozen very rare singles for independent labels like Version, Deluxe (which wasn't), and Bell. Nineteen forty-seven was also the year she met Barbara Carroll, who would be a close musical and personal associate for the rest of Syms's life. "When I first met Barbara, it was like seeing my reflection in a mirror," she told Balliett (in a statement that could be called self-flattering—Carroll was and is as lean as Syms was corpulent—but one trusts that she didn't mean it literally). In 1949, she appeared on Broadway in a successful revival of Mae West's hit play *Diamond Lil.*

In March 1952, Ahmet Ertegun of Atlantic Records decided to include her in a series of 10" LPs he was making to document the major East Side cabareteurs of the era. He hired the Barbara Carroll Trio for accompaniment, and cut all eight songs on a single night, after Carroll had finished work at the Embers.

From the beginning, Syms was at her most effective when she was being wistful and nostalgic—as on "There's Something About an Old Love." She strikes precisely the right note here, as indeed she does on Porter's "Down in the Depths," being subtle and evocative, suggesting the outline of a faded love. In contrast, the melodramatic lyric of "Lonely Woman" doesn't work for her, despite the fine melody by Benny Carter, who had encouraged her on Swing Street years earlier. "Can't You Just See Yourself" is a Rodgers and Hammerstein–like song by Sammy Cahn and Jule Styne, from their Americana show *High Button Shoes,* and where one would expect Syms to sound stiff here, somehow she's amazingly loose—perhaps even giddy. After all, it was near the end of an all-night session—and propelled by Carroll's boppish notes and chords. Two years later, Atlantic brought Syms back for four more tracks, this time accompanied by a seven-piece band featuring saxists Al Cohn and Danny Bank, multi-instrumentalist Don Elliott, and trombonist Kai Winding.

Her next two albums, *Sylvia Syms Sings* and *Songs of Love*, are probably her overall best, and they were combined onto one very desirable compact disc by the British Jasmine label. Both were arranged and conducted by Ralph Burns, and the Burns-Syms scores are so understated that they establish the notion that there's almost no such thing as being "too subtle." In a manner that recalls the best of his work with Jeri Southern, Burns's writing has a semi-classical, chamber music feeling, making use of a small woodwind section (flutes predominate) and strings.

Nothing on these albums is obvious, overt, or overstated. On later recordings, from the sixties, seventies, and eighties, Syms sounds more heavily stylized and mannered. Here she seems utterly natural. The voice may not be particularly attractive; in fact, it's just plain-vanilla. But pushing forty, Syms has mastered the art of disappearing into a song—you barely feel she's there at all; it seems that the song is singing itself, the story is telling itself. She has perfected the illusion in a way that few singers beyond Sinatra and Peggy Lee ever managed to do. When we hear Sinatra at his ballad best, as on "In the Wee Small Hours," even though the story is completely convincing we never forget who is singing it to us. On "A Woman's Intuition," however, Syms seems notably less stylized than Lee Wiley, who wasn't exactly Frankie Laine either and who sang with a distinctive, burnished tone. Syms stays completely out of the way of the song, and one can only speculate on how difficult that is to achieve; how much labor and craft is required to create this illusion.

The particular highlights are two story-songs from a short-lived 1950 revue entitled *Dance Me a Song:* "I'm the Girl" and "Dance Me a Song." The first is a well-constructed torch song in the classic mode, the second is what used to be called an "art" song, set mostly in long meter with a longer-than-usual verse, and an involved narrative about love and alcohol. Another cabaret classic, Bart Howard's "Let Me Love You," has Syms sounding loose and jaunty, whereas both Victor Schertzinger's "I Don't Want to Cry Anymore" and Cole Porter's "Experiment" benefit from her willingness to take her time and stretch the verse out to the point where it seems like a song in itself. "Experiment" has a bit more brass and more of a jazz beat, but nothing so severe as to undermine Syms's singing.

The arrangements and singing on *Songs of Love,* from two years later, are remarkably consistent, so much so that the album could be a direct continuation. The grouping of small string section, four-piece rhythm section, and occasional horns (like trombones on "Can't We Be Friends" and "Isn't it Romantic") appears to be inspired by Sinatra's chamber settings with Axel Stordahl on *The Voice* and Nelson Riddle on *Close to You.* Here, "Hands Across the Table" invites comparison with the young Lee Wiley, with Syms again succeeding in coming darn near outsubtling her.

Clearly Syms (rightfully) regarded Arthur Schwartz as one of the major composers. The 1955 album opened with a wise, knowing "I'll Be Tired of You," and the 1957 album includes both "Dancing in the Dark" and "Alone Too Long," a rarity from *By the Beautiful Sea* otherwise recorded only by Nat Cole.

"Dancing in the Dark" is done in a deliberately old-fashioned and melodramatic style, in 3/4 time, apparently so that she can waltz in the wonder of why she's here, and with a tinkly pianist who suggests a Victorian parlor recital. She milks the song's upward melodic trajectory, and ends, uncharacteristically, on a gut-busting high note—it's a break with character, but it works.

She's is also completely convincing on "What's the Use of Wondering," the Rodgers and Hammerstein *Carousel* aria that allows her to illustrate the idea of thinking aloud in song—almost the best version before Barbara Cook. Backed by bongos and more trombones, she sings Cole Porter's "I Am Loved" in a way that suggests and combines Sinatra's vulnerability with Garland's exuberance. "Don't Ever Leave Me" goes along great for a while, then hits a misstep, in that somebody decided to overdub a second Syms voice in the second chorus. It's tastefully done, harmonically, electronically, and otherwise, but who the heck needs it?

She gets the album back on track with the closer, "I'll Be Seeing You," starting slowly with the verse, and gradually unraveling the story, a treatment that seems like the archetype for many LP-era renditions of this prewar chestnut. There's a moment near the end when she builds up expectations that she's going to go for a big high note on "when the night is *new*," a note that Sinatra could hit, but which we know is out of Syms's range. She very cleverly deflects it, going down instead of up, a move that effectively colors the melancholy mood of the piece. It's a perfect ending.

The late fifties were Syms's best years: Decca released an up-tempo, dancey single of "I Could Have Danced All Night," and it became one of the jukebox hits to spin off the *My Fair Lady* score. Syms told Balliett that Milt Gabler, her producer, was dead set against it, especially at double time, but he eventually went along with her idea and was rewarded with a hit. Not a blockbuster—it only reached number 20 on the *Billboard* chart—but enough to keep Decca interested. She charted twice more that year with a pair of novelty items titled "English Muffins and Irish Stew" and "Dancing Chandelier."

In 1957 both *Songs of Love* and the Atlantic 12" album were released, and Leonard Feather, in the notes to the latter, put a positive spin on her career by opining, "Sylvia Syms is now a familiar name to disc jockeys who dig Gogi Grant." In fact, Syms's up-tempo work has more in common rhythmically (though not interpretively) with that class of four-square fifties pop chantootsies that includes Grant, Jane Morgan, Teresa Brewer, and Joni James than it does with post–big band singers like Stafford, Clooney, or Lee.

"The truth is," as Barbara Carroll told Gavin, even when Syms was at her peak "she never really worked a lot. She was sitting in that apartment waiting for something to happen." Syms elaborated to Balliett how even in the "I Could Have Danced All

Night" days she managed to shoot herself in the foot: "I got offers from hotels and nightclubs all around the country, and it practically destroyed me. They expected Miss America, but they got me." She could sing, but according to her own account, she knew nothing about presentation, how to dress, how to look good onstage. Perhaps it's not surprising that she fared better in musical comedy, when she was able to take advantage of professional makeup and costume people, as she did in *Whoop-Up* and various productions of *South Pacific*. Alas, she never participated in a cast album of that Rodgers and Hammerstein classic, but I like to think that she reimagined Bloody Mary as a yenta.

To me, none of the later albums has the sincerity and directness of the 1952–57 recordings, even *Torch Song*, her 1960 reunion project with Ralph Burns, done for Columbia. Carroll says, "Her sense of time was absolutely perfect. She was a jazz singer, truly." But attempts to work in a pure jazz idiom accentuated her weaknesses rather than her strengths. Her mid-sixties albums are heavy on guitar: *The Fabulous Sylvia Syms* (1964) and *Sylvia Is!* (1965) both co-star the outstanding Kenny Burrell. *Fabulous* also features three exceptional horn obbligatists in trumpeter Joe Newman, trombonist Urbie Green, and the one and only Ben Webster on tenor; yet somehow it's one of Syms's least-appealing efforts.

In 1965 and 1967 she cut two albums for producer Cal Lampley at Prestige, the above-mentioned *Sylvia Is!* and *For Once in My Life*. She has remarkable accompaniment here, particularly the supportive and swinging guitarists Kenny Burrell, Bucky Pizzarelli, and Gene Bertoncini—each album backs her with a guitar-centric rhythm section and no piano. She's at her best on ballads like "Smile." When one of the guitarists tries to egg her on into swinging, she's game enough to give it a go but, at the risk of contradicting Ms. Carroll, Syms never seems to know what beats to emphasize or what notes to hold, and she loses her control of the lyric when the tempo picks up. The idea of her doing Brazilian songs and bossa novas—there are four on the 1967 disc—must have seemed a good one on paper, but on the record it just doesn't work.

One wishes that rather than give her three first-rate guitarists, Lampley would have done the conventional thing and just brought in one superlative pianist, which is what Nesuhi Ertegun did on the 1976 *Lovingly, Sylvia Syms*. Give credit to Atlantic Records for bringing her back after twenty years for an encore and also for not censoring her remark quoted in Rex Reed's liner notes that the label had never paid her the first time around. *Lovingly* benefits from wonderfully intimate, chamber-style charts by Dick Hyman and, perhaps more important, the piano playing of Ellis Larkins, an accompanist who could do no wrong. "I Get a Kick out of You" is her most appealing up-tempo, and even though one might assume it wasn't a good idea to remake both "Lonely Woman" and "I'm the Girl" from the first

Atlantic album, the new performances are highly credible.

The gems here, however, are two excellent ballads by Cy Coleman: "On Second Thought," an independent song from 1961 with a lyric by Carolyn Leigh, and "Pink Taffeta Sample Size 10," a cut number from *Sweet Charity*, lyric by Dorothy Fields. These are both moving story-songs, monologues set to music in the tradition of "Lilac Wine," although in the case of "Pink Taffeta," a bit more innocent and less alcoholic. Both are slow and suspenseful, with Syms grabbing us in the first bars and never letting go, and both reestablish that her home turf is Broadway, not Swing Street. The label put the bulk of its eggs in one basket with the song "The Long Lonely Season," by the chalk-and-cheese team of Paul Anka and Sammy Cahn, but nothing tops these two Coleman classics. (In 2001, Collectables licensed *Lovingly* and issued it on CD. Two years later, they would do the same with her Columbia tracks. I wish they had been able to include a further Atlantic session from 1976, which contains "Nobody Else but Me," and is listed in the discographies but is so far unissued.)

Whereas *Lovingly* may or may not be the most satisfying of Syms's post-1960 albums, there's no argument as to which is the worst: the 1977 *She Loves to Hear the Music*, produced by Don Sebesky, with Dee Anthony credited as executive producer. This is Syms's equivalent of *The Ethel Merman Disco Album*, but where that record is at least mildly entertaining for its camp value, *She Loves to Hear the Music* doesn't even have that going for it. I can't begin to re-create the thought process that led to its creation. Here was a woman who had a hard enough time capturing the attention of the very small jazz-cabaret show tunes market—a tiny ghetto of the music industry that could have sustained her had she played her cards right. Why Sebesky and Anthony and A&M Records somehow thought she could appeal beyond that audience, even beyond grown-ups, and come up with a record that would be treasured by the kids who were dancing to the Bee Gees is completely beyond comprehension.

The most ambitious project from her last decade is *Syms by Sinatra* (1982). As the title implies, the set was conducted and produced by Sinatra, who is, as usual, to be commended for sharing something of his star power and, presumably, his bank account in order to help out a friend. Here was a rare case of a celebrity willing to put his money where someone else's mouth was. As with his collaboration with Peggy Lee, *The Man I Love*, the results sound more like other Sinatra albums than like anything else by the chanteuse in question, but unlike the way it turned out with that superb 1957 album, here I keep wishing it was Sinatra himself who was doing the singing. Syms's voice had aged significantly since 1976, and for all the efforts of Sinatra and musical director Don Costa, as well as the fine pianist Vinnie Falcone, she never sounds totally comfortable. An orchestra this big, whether emphasizing soothing strings or swinging brass, was just not her thing. The tracks that work best for me are two songs Sinatra himself should have done at some point, Johnny Mandel's "Close Enough for Love" and Michel Legrand's "You Must Believe in Spring," which Syms cut again seven years later with a small group, and one Sinatra classic, "All My Tomorrows," which features a prominent and sensitive tenor obbligato by Al Klink.

Following the Sinatra encounter, Syms, sounding older and older, recorded two tribute records for Hugh Fordin's DRG label: *A Jazz Portrait of Johnny Mercer* (1984) and *Then Along Came Bill: A Tribute to Bill Evans* (1989). Just as Duke Ellington and other songwriters had "Broadway envy," figuring that the world wouldn't take them seriously as creators of words and music unless they could create a hit musical, Syms seems to be the archetype of those cabaret singers who have "jazz envy," who sometimes ignore what they do best in order to gain the respect of the jazz world. Her last album was *You Must Believe in Spring*, from 1991, accompanied by the outstanding trio of Mike Renzi (piano), Steve Laspina (bass), and Terry Clarke (drums). Six months later, Sylvia Syms was singing at the prestigious Algonquin when she suffered a heart attack just after finishing a set.

She had long since reached the point where she was an icon in the saloons and songcentric rooms around New York and the world. Her music wasn't perfect, but it was clearly close enough to it for the world of cabaret.

T

Jack Teagarden (1905–1964)

Singing musicians were especially relevant in the earlier decades of the twentieth century—the period roughly known as the premodern era of jazz. Even into the swing era, bandleaders were less likely to hire a full-time singer than to try and recruit one of the trumpeters or saxophonists for that purpose. Indeed, plenty of leaders would have preferred doing without the vocal chorus whatsoever, but were compelled to include them, on records and broadcasts especially, at the insistence of A&R men and radio sponsors under pressure from the music publishers, who wanted the dancing public to hear the lyrics as well as the tunes.

Of all singing horn players after Louis Armstrong, there was simply no one greater than Jack Teagarden—even more so when it came to singing the blues. There were plenty of other singing musicians who had their own thing, but none of them had the talent, the depth, the distinction, or the rich, long career of Teagarden, whose overall output was second only to the Mighty Satchmo's.

Teagarden sang in a deep, wide Texas accent—he follows Bing Crosby by only two years as one of the first popular singers to concentrate on the baritone register. His voice has been described—by me among others—as a whiskey-soaked tone, but even though he certainly drank enough of the stuff I don't think it could have affected his actual vocal quality. A lifetime of strong drink would obviously affect one's phrasing, although it's hard to imagine how it could have an impact upon Teagarden's timbre itself—especially since he has something of the quality even in his earliest recorded vocals. Yet that is the somewhat romantic, somewhat insulting way that most of us who love Teagarden invariably remember him.

In the context of Teagarden's early career, then, his voice sounded more alcoholically altered than it actually was: At a time when Armstrong and Crosby were both still newcomers, most singers were much more high-pitched and peppy; to sound as deep and relaxed as Teagarden, even in his early twenties, would have required a considerable amount of Prohibition hooch. Yet I can't help feeling that if he had drunk tea (rather than smoked it) he would still sound the same.

Like his trombone playing, Teagarden's singing was deep, rich, and expressive, and thoroughly saturated with the blues. He could do a marvelous job on a ballad, like "One Hundred Years from Today" or "Under a Blanket of Blue," but of all the singers active in the thirties through the fifties, his is the voice that best suits the classic blues concoctions of W. C. Handy, especially the Handy works that tell of "Beale Street" and "Aunt Hagar." In Teagarden's playing and singing, the blues are full of possibilities, nuances, emotions; an endless wellspring of inspiration. He had a vibrato as broad as the Rio Grande—the kind better described as big rather than "rapid" and a soul as big as the blues itself.

"I learned all that I know about the blues when I was pretty young," Teagarden states in a 1941 profile in the *Milwaukee Journal* (unearthed by the late Teagarden scholar Joe Showler). "There was a negro section in Vernon [Texas, his home town] and they used to have big camp meetings, and I used to sit out back and listen. They had some wonderful singers, and their music just seemed to fit in with what my idea of music had always been."

One wonders what kind of blues he was hearing in turn-of-the-century Texas—certainly this was well before the relatively new form had come into contact with traditional black religious music (i.e., spirituals). He probably didn't hear anything like New Orleans jazz until the first recordings of the Original Dixieland Jazz Band in 1917.

Teagarden arrived in New York in 1927, and by the time he made his first record date, at the very end of that year, he was already on his second wife. That premier date, done with RCA Victor bandleader Johnny Johnson, did not include any solos from the precocious twenty-two-year-old, but it did help introduce two significant show tunes, the Gershwins' "My One and Only" and Rodgers and Hart's "Thou Swell." He'd spent the earlier years of his career playing in Southwestern territory bands, most notably that of boogie-woogie piano legend Peck Kelley (who played the best piano by far in a little honky-tonky village in Texas).

Within a few months of landing in New York, Teagarden was in the big time, appearing with such established bandleaders as Roger Wolfe Kahn (with whom he recorded his first classic solo, on "She's a Great, Great Girl"), Willard Robison, the Dorsey Brothers (no small feat, considering that Tommy was probably the finest trombonist in the city prior to Teagarden's arrival), and soon Red Nichols, who employed only the crème de la crème of New York jazzmen. Teagarden's first steady gig with a major band was that led by drummer Ben Pollack, whose ranks at the time also included Benny Goodman, Glenn Miller, and other future swing-era stars.

As with Armstrong and Fletcher Henderson, however, Pollack was reluctant to let Teagarden sing as often as he should have. Pollack had a different reason from Henderson's, though: He was promoting himself as a drummer-bandleader-vocalist-entertainer, and thus was reserving the vocal privileges for himself. The Pollack men also recorded frequently in pseudonymous pick-up dates arranged by impresario-publisher Irving Mills (the Whoopee Makers, the Hotsy Totsy Gang, etc.) and here, too, Mills, much as he did with Ellington, liked "to play boy singer" (in Gary Giddins's memorable phrase). In a 1929 Vitaphone one-reel short subject, Pollack generously features Teagarden's wonderful singing on what he describes as "our Negro spiritual version" of the current pop tune "My Kinda Love"; on the Victor recording, which has been reissued countless times, Teagarden takes a marvelous trombone solo but Pollack, unfortunately, reserves the vocal for himself.

The fall of 1928 would appear to be the height of the immediate pre-Depression recording boom: In that one season alone, Teagarden participated in dozens of sessions. The most important of these by far was "Makin' Friends" from a session led by Eddie Condon, which established many precedents—to begin with, this was Teagarden's first recorded vocal. The song itself was a basic blues that he would record three times under that title (once with Condon and twice with Mills) that season alone. (It would also be known as "Dirty Dog" and "I'd Rather Drink Muddy Water.")

It was also significant that a second voice was heard on the original "Makin' Friends," that of clarinetist, raconteur, and marijuana merchant Mezz Mezzrow, who surely knew ways of making friends. A precedent was set: For the rest of his career, Teagarden would do much of his best singing in the company of male vocal partners. In the beginning it seemed as if Condon was the only bandleader who appreciated Teagarden's singing, featuring Tea three months later on two terrific titles, "I'm Gonna Stomp Mr. Henry Lee" (whoever thought up that title must have been smoking Mezzrow's wares) and "That's a Serious Thing."

Teagarden's next major vocal refrain on record was "The Sheik of Araby," a career-peg routine he introduced in 1930 that also involves a second male voice, that of sometime trombonist Treg Brown (who later came into his own as a Looney Tunes sound effects wizard). Brown starts by singing the even then ancient standard in a completely straight fashion, before Teagarden comes in and does with his voice what he normally did with his trombone, which is to run rings around the melody, and, in this case, the words, too. "Sheik" was done under the direction of bandleader and cornetist Red Nichols, who was the next important impresario after Condon to fully appreciate Teagarden's singing.

Nichols himself wasn't much of a blues player at this early stage, but in featuring Teagarden so extensively, he revealed a keen appreciation of the form. Teagarden recorded "Basin Street Blues" for the first time with a Nichols band (as the Louisiana Rhythm Kings), and this, too, is something of an evolving mystery. The Spencer Williams tune was already a jazz classic, and it would later be a Teagarden perennial, but whatever Teagarden is singing here it is not Williams's famous blues-song-form hybrid but a straight 12-bar blues with lyrics about Basin Street—in fact, it is practically identical to the later Jimmy Rushing–Count Basie "Goin' to Chicago."

More important, Teagarden continued his series of double-voice recordings under Nichols's direction. On the concert-style arrangements of "Some of These Days" and especially "Sally, Won't You Come Back," Nichols contrasts Big Tea's rough, blues-hewn tones with the straighter singing of Scrappy Lambert, one of the better studio tenors of the era but clearly no competition for Teagarden. Lambert sings the song itself, which is a remake or a rip-off of the old chestnut "I Wonder What's Become of Sally," but then Teagarden offers what sounds like a gutsy ad-lib blues on the subject of Sally in our alley.

The most elaborate Nichols-Teagarden item is the 1930 "On Revival Day," an extralong, two-sided production number, which recruits the Foursome, the vocal quartet that had worked with Nichols on Broadway in *Girl Crazy*, and features Teagarden in the role of "Mr. Parson."

Through the early thirties, while Teagarden remained with Pollack as his day job—or night job, as it were—he continued to appear on records with a variety of different leaders and other musicians. He kept right on makin' friends, one of his closest being Fats Waller. "He used to call us every night and say—when you boys get off work, come on up to Harlem," Teagarden recalled later. "They used to take me places I don't think any other white boy had ever been—Fats was just as close to me as any friend I ever had." Teagarden was the rare musician—ofay or Oxford gray—who could keep up with Waller's drinking and appetite for nonstop action. The two made several sessions together, and actually did sing in tandem on one memorable occasion, on a 1931 date, in which the twosome do delightfully goofy songs of male bonding. "You Rascal You" and "That's What I Like About You" have Teagarden singing the central words and melody while Waller heckles prominently and irrelevantly from the sidelines.

Other duets followed: As a member of Paul Whiteman's Orchestra in the mid-thirties, Teagarden sang many memorable vocals with Johnny Mercer, then better known as a boy singer than a lyricist, most famously on two songs with a distinctly ebonic perspective, Mercer's own "Fare Thee Well to Harlem" and Raymond Scott's "Christmas Night in Harlem." In 1934, he also cut "Fare Thee Well to Harlem" and "Ol' Pappy" with Bob Crosby's future singing banjoist Nappy Lamare doing the heckling and mugging. Both Teagarden and Mercer guested with Wingy Manone, who is obviously stewed to the gills on a 1935 date that centered on the energetic rhythm song "I've Got a Note."

Leading his own streamlined swing orchestra at the finish of his Whiteman contract, Teagarden would reprise "Sheik of Araby" with band vocalist Meredith Blake singing the "straight" intro—a rare example of his duetting with a female singer. He and his orchestra would also form a trio with Mary Martin and Bing Crosby on "The Waiter, the Porter and the Upstairs Maid" in the 1941 film *The Birth of the Blues*. All these duets and trios, needless to say, pale behind his classic duets with Louis Armstrong during the six or so memorable years when the trombonist was the most prominent sideman in the trumpeter's All-Stars.

Not that Teagarden's solo vocals weren't equally remarkable. Most of his 1930–33 sessions still feature past and present members of the Pollack band, such as Goodman and various future stars of the Bob Crosby orchestra. By December 1933, when Teagarden joined Paul Whiteman, he kept on playing and singing on dozens of sessions for dozens of leaders, sometimes doing the same songs for two or more, making even more music than a Mosaic box could contain. The sessions he made under his own name are, naturally, the most likely to feature him in both capacities.

Oddly enough, one of the earliest recordings of Hoagy Carmichael's "Rockin' Chair" was released under Teagarden's name, yet the producer didn't see fit to let him sing on it. Before long, even the dumbest A&R man realized that no one could touch Tea on the blues and on material with a Southern or Western flavor. Within a short while Teagarden had already made multiple recordings of such

Dixiecentric signatures as Spencer Williams's "Basin Street Blues" and W. C. Handy's "Beale Street Blues" (and the same composer's "Loveless Love"). He sings "Ol' Pappy" rather straight, while Nappy Lamare plays the cutup, proving that there was already more to Teagarden than the blues and Mammy (not to mention Ol' Pappy) songs. On "Emaline" and "Ol' Pappy," two songs fairly dripping with moonlight and magnolia, Teagarden is singing sweetly and tenderly; as with Armstrong, his use of jazz devices and phrasing enhances rather than undercuts the tenderness of his performance.

Still another producer-bandleader-impresario—Victor Young—had the brilliant idea of presenting Teagarden as a star singer on four sides in which the vocals take priority and the trombone rides in the back seat. All four open with Tea singing the verse and then the chorus and then an instrumental break, just like Bing Crosby's Brunswicks of the period—in fact, even Armstrong would not be presented this way, essentially, until the postwar period. Young arranges and conducts, as he often did for Crosby, and he also composed three out of the four songs: "Love Me," "Blue River," and "One Hundred Years from Today."

Teagarden's vocals are superb, with a slightly underpitch sound that's more like an especially expressive Texas drawl than an intonation problem. He's equally winning on a 1934 session with other Whiteman and Goodman men, including BG himself, especially on a song of Southern romance—combining both of his specialties—Mitchell Parish's "Stars Fell on Alabama." Alas, Teagarden doesn't get to sing on "Junk Man," a blues torch song by the young Frank Loesser that would have been Teagarden's meat. (Instead, the pioneer jazz harpist Casper Reardon takes an extended solo.) He sang two of his very best nonblues numbers with an early BG lineup in 1934, "I Ain't Lazy, I'm Just Dreamin'" and Harold Arlen's future standard "As Long as I Live."

As it happened, his colleague Benny Goodman featured him more than his regular boss of the mid-thirties, Paul Whiteman, did. Apart from the two duets with Mercer, in July 1935 Whiteman used the Teagarden voice most effectively on two then-standards of the jazz world, "Ain't Misbehavin'" and "Nobody's Sweetheart Now." Unfortunately Whiteman, unlike Victor Young, didn't have the foresight to put Teagarden to work on nonjazz material such as basic bread-and-butter pop tunes and ballads. Whiteman had a variety of straight crooners and band singers to handle such chores, none of whom were a patch on Teagarden.

However, the Whiteman tenure included a brilliant series of recordings—some of the best of the trombonist's entire career—made under the leadership of saxophonist Frank Trumbauer while both were still with Whiteman. These are all included—along with some other fine samples of early Teagardenia—on the Mosaic box *The Complete Okeh and*

Brunswick Bix Beiderbecke, Frank Trumbauer and Jack Teagarden Sessions (1924–36). (Teagarden is featured only on the last half of the seven-disc set, but I heartily recommend it anyway.) There are six sessions from 1934–36 under Trumbauer's name that extensively feature Teagarden in both his capacities, including a pair of Gershwin standards, "S'Wonderful" and "Somebody Loves Me" (unfortunately he only sings on the second), and such engaging ephemera as "Long About Midnight" (another trip to Harlem in ermine and pearls) and "Emaline" (more courtship, Southern-style, yowsah). "I Hope Gabriel Likes My Music" and "The Mayor of Alabam'" find Teagarden and Trumbauer, who speaks on both cuts, addressing such buzz topics—talking points, if you will—as religion and politics.

Apart from the Trumbauer sessions, Teagarden was of two minds about the Whiteman experience: He realized that there was a lot he could learn about music beyond jazz from the veteran leader—about pop, classical, and show music, and how to put together a musical aggregation—but at the same time he found it stifling. More to the point, he was beyond the stage where it made sense for him to serve as a sideman to anybody. Joe Showler reports that the minute his contract with Whiteman ended—they were playing an event that extended past midnight—Teagarden packed up his horn and strolled right off the bandstand in midgig. He led his own big band from then until the end of the swing era, when many other bands were also breaking up. The Teagarden big band is often described as a musical failure, and it's almost always described as a financial one, even though the leader did manage to keep it going for pretty much all of seven years, which hardly rates as a failure in my book.

His first own big band session included his new streamlined version of the now-ten-year-old routine "Sheik of Araby," the one with the "straight" vocal sung by band canary Meredith Blake. Teagarden's voice had sounded so perfect in the mostly Pollack-ian settings of the early thirties that it takes a little time to get acclimated to that warm, nasal baritone in the new setting: state-of-the-art big band swing circa 1940—a reed sound like Glenn Miller here, some Dixieland polyphony à la Bob Crosby there, some futuristic and semiclassical textures like Claude Thornhill here and there. On one of the band's earlier broadcasts, they even do a treatment of "One O'Clock Jump" that's more elaborately orchestrated than the Count Basie original. Teagarden hired some outstanding arrangers (such as Phil Moore), but unlike his very successful colleagues from the Pollack and Nichols bands (such as Miller, Goodman, and either Dorsey), he never led a band that was as good as he was.

During the big band years, Teagarden, like any other commercial dance band, traveled with a girl singer and, at least part of the time, a boy singer too, and he chose his band vocalists very well. For a time in 1939 he carried two canaries, Dolores "Dodie" O'Neill, who, within a few months, made a big hit with the Bob Chester Orchestra, and Kitty Kallen, who, after subsequent tenures with Jimmy Dorsey and Harry James, would become an important hit maker in the postwar era. Teagarden's most notable male singer was David Allyn (a very talented Dick Haymes disciple whose career was scuttled at numerous points by his substance problems) in 1940–41. One wishes that Teagarden had been as egocentric as his own former bandleader Ben Pollack; instead of hogging the best tunes for himself, he doled them out all too generously to the rhyming team of Kallen and Allyn. Ms. Kallen does a fine job with the better class of tune, especially "The Lamp Is Low" and "Stairway to the Stars," but one yearns to hear Teagarden's voice on these first-rate ballads.

Still, Teagarden was no fool. No one was going to sing the blues in his band but he himself, and he played and sang almost as many with the big band as Woody Herman or Basie. He also sang most of the rhythmic novelties, which is some consolation—though I would rather hear him singing "All the Things You Are" instead of "The Little Man Who Wasn't There." The Teagarden orchestra played all the latest plug tunes as well as any other A– level band (if not quite on the level of an absolute A+ unit, like Goodman), but also gave Teagarden ample opportunity to record souped-up, swinging treatments of his traditional blues specialties, like "Aunt Hagar's Blues," "Muddy River Blues" (a particularly nice new blues for the leader), and "Beale Street Blues." Sony-BMG, in fact, could do worse than to put out a disc of the best tracks by the Teagarden band in the 1939–42 period.

His discography shows him participating in nearly as many special all-star dates (on V-Disc, Commodore, etc., with Louis Armstrong and Eddie Condon, and others) without his orchestra as regular business-as-usual big band sessions. It probably doesn't say much for Teagarden's business acumen that he did so much of his best playing and singing of the era away from his own orchestra—with Bud Freeman, Eddie Condon, and in small groups under his own name on HRS and Commodore.

One of the more rewarding aspects of Teagarden's orchestra phase is that a lot of extra material by the band has been issued from radio performances, both live and on studio transcriptions. Live remotes from such ballrooms as the Southland in Boston and Frank Dailey's Meadowbrook in New Jersey (on Vernon Music) and waxed for Standard Transcriptions (issued on Jass) complement the band's commercial 78 rpm output very nicely.

Only a few bandleaders survived the postwar crunch: guys for whom leading a band was everything, like Les Brown, Stan Kenton, Woody Herman, Ellington, and eventually Basie. Teagarden was not one of them. Many leaders cut back to smaller combos, but Teagarden elected to get out of leading

bands altogether. He worked as a soloist for a while (there are broadcast recordings from 1946–47 that find him in the company of such worthy if unexpected colleagues as Woody Herman—he and Tea sing the blues together on one Gene Norman–produced concert in Pasadena—Duke Ellington, Billy Strayhorn, and Wardell Gray. In 1947 he began working regularly as a member of Louis Armstrong's rapidly gelling All-Stars, most famously at the new band's very celebrated recitals at New York's Town Hall and Carnegie Hall, and Boston's Symphony Hall.

He remained with Armstrong until 1951. The war-era "Jack-Armstrong Blues" was an early example of their musical rapport and repartee, but their musical marriage was consummated with Hoagy Carmichael's "Rockin' Chair." The 1929 song had a jazz pedigree even before Mildred Bailey made it her signature song and Roy Eldridge also made it a regular feature. Yet "Rockin' Chair" was born to be a duet—Armstrong had recorded it previously as a duet of sorts with composer Carmichael, and Teagarden had done it in 1944 with Wingy Manone—and thus it was predestined that Armstrong and Teagarden would sing it together.

And together they were something even more magical. Armstrong is pure radiant energy, Teagarden is pure cool chic; he ain't lazy, he's just dreamin'. The routine was that one sings it straight and the other offers sideline commentary, and then they reverse roles. Teagarden was best singing the main melody with Armstrong chiming in with a vocal obbligato. They sang it together hundreds of times, none more memorable than on a December 1957 TV telecast, with the added advantage of cornetist Bobby Hackett playing behind both singing hornmen.

This is why God invented YouTube: To be able to see the two of them; what they do with their faces, mugging for the crowd and the camera, is almost as valuable as what comes out of their horns. When Armstrong sings "Remember my Aunt Harriet, how long in heaven she be," Teagarden quips "I knew her well," then pauses while Armstrong shoots him a rather inquisitive look—as if there might be something unkosher about this relationship with Aunt Harriet (who surely is a relative of the Aunt Hagar about whom Teagarden sang so often). Teagarden then responds to Armstrong's insinuation by saying, "Not that well," to Armstrong's apparent relief. We all laugh loudest about what worries us the most and Teagarden and Armstrong were able to create their most moving, tragicomic set piece in their forties and fifties—old for a jazz musician then—when what they were most afraid of was being put out to pasture and not being able to get in front of audiences and make music anymore. "Rockin' Chair" remains quite possibly the single most delightful mano a mano vocal duet in all of jazz.

Teagarden was usually given a solo feature in

addition to "Rockin' Chair" with Armstrong, but it was too much to expect him, now a living legend of jazz in his mid-forties, to play sideman, even in an all-star band led by the greatest living legend of them all. His main reason for leaving the All-Stars, however, was that the constant traveling was too much for him. From 1952 to 1963, he intended to stay as close to home as possible—but rarely managed it.

Teagarden alternated between leading his own bands and participating in special all-star events; in the studio, he often played in front of sympathetic orchestral ensembles of varying sizes built around him. On the whole, his working sextets and septets were not up to Armstrong's bands of the same period, even though he usually found good musicians to join him, and though his own playing and singing is always superb. In the studio, he often learned new material for special projects, whereas on live gigs and recordings he mostly sticks to the old favorites. He continued to team up with worthy constituents, particularly in impermanent settings, such as his two marvelous team-ups with trumpeter Bobby Hackett, the well-titled *Jazz Ultimate* and *Coast Concert* (which wasn't so well titled since it was a studio, not a live, album), and *Accent on Trombone*, a 1953 oddity co-starring young traditionalist Ruby Braff, Benny Goodman clone Sol Yaged, and bop era tenor Lucky Thompson (Tea turned in a beautiful rendition of "The Christmas Song").

Continuing the comparison with latter-day Armstrong, although Teagarden was steadily popular with traditional jazz audiences (and quite a few modernist fans and musicians as well), he never enjoyed anything like Armstrong's ever-increasing mass-market success as a pop singer. He had no hit singles—no "Blueberry Hill" or "Mack the Knife"—but he did make a series of what could be considered pop-oriented albums spotlighting his vocals, often with orchestral settings, and no one, at least, was accusing him of compromising. Or of getting rich. There are two, *This Is Teagarden* and *Swing Low, Sweet Spiritual,* both from 1956, on Capitol (included, along with the Hackett and other small group albums, on Mosaic's *The Complete Capitol Fifties Jack Teagarden Sessions,* a total of six LPs on four CDs), and three on Verve from 1961–62, *Mis'ry and the Blues, Think Well of Me,* and *Jack Teagarden!!!*

This Is Teagarden is a loose equivalent of Armstrong's *Musical Autobiography,* while *Sweet Spiritual* anticipates *Louis and the Good Book,* although in both cases the trombonist's albums are more big-band-driven than the trumpeter's. Teagarden's attempt to shout all over God's heaven is somewhat sabotaged by a very Caucasian-sounding doo-wop vocal group—at least Louis had something closer to a real gospel choir when he sang the glories of the Good Book. *Sweet Spiritual* is good, but *This Is Teagarden* is better: Teagarden revisiting twelve of the songs most associated with him from over the last thirty years (including not only the oft-visited "Beale Street," but also "If I Could Be with You," "Aunt Hagar's Blues," and even "Fare Thee Well to Harlem"), in splendid new arrangements by the sympathetic Van Alexander. Alexander, who started with Ella Fitzgerald and also provided brilliant support for Kay Starr, bridges the sound of Teagarden's own big band—particularly, in "Peg o' My Heart," getting the whole trombone section to phrase like him—and the Ben Pollack/Bob Crosby–style orchestrated Dixieland of the late thirties.

Throughout this later period—the five predominantly vocal albums of 1956 and 1961–62—Teagarden's singing on these dear old Mammy tunes has grown so mellow it's ripe. No vocalist, male or female, in any subgenre of American music, whether an instrumentalist-vocalist or a full-time singer, has ever explored the relaxed side of the blues more convincingly. By the time of the three Verve projects, Teagarden's last studio albums, his playing and singing have achieved a state of mellow-beyond-mellow. There's a transcendent tranquillity to this later work; who knew the blues could be so laid-back?

In one sense, Teagarden's career was coming full circle. At nineteen, Teagarden played briefly with an orchestra in Kansas City under the direction of composer-pianist-bandleader-vocalist Willard Robison; at twenty-two, he played his first solo on record with Robison in January 1928. As a composer, Robison pops up repeatedly in Teagarden's later work. *This Is Teagarden* contains one notable song that the trombonist had never recorded before, Robison's "Old Pigeon-Toed Joad," a typical Robisonian concoction of country-tinged nostalgia with a classical sense of irony and additional gospel flavoring. Two more Robison tunes appear on the first Verve album, *Mis'ry and the Blues,* namely "Don't Tell a Man About His Woman" and "Peaceful Valley," although it should be noted that virtually every other song on the record has a distinctly Robisonian flavor as well.

The payoff comes with *Think Well of Me,* a collection of ten songs by Robison (plus "Where Are You" by Jimmy McHugh). Backing Big T with superb arrangements by the imposing modernist Bob Brookmeyer and studio veteran Russ Case—two brassmen who achieved greater success as arranger-conductors—this is an essentially vocal album of tremendous sensitivity. (It's also the only time I know of that Teagarden did an album with a full string section.) It would be hard to find a record, particularly a songbook project, in which the three primary elements—the star (both playing and singing), the material, and the orchestrations—suit one another so superbly. Teagarden comes up with just the perfect blend of mournful blues and self-deprecating humor to make these beautiful if difficult songs work. Only he could bring a touch of optimism to such songs of love's dismal demise as "A

Cottage for Sale" and "Don't Smoke in Bed," while the essentially upbeat "I'm a Fool About My Mama" and "Guess I'll Go Back Home This Summer" have an undercurrent of melancholy. On his instrumental-orchestral album *Shades of Night*, Teagarden had played the Rosemary Clooney hit "Mixed Emotions." Here he illustrates exactly what that expression means.

His final studio project, *Jack Teagarden!!!*, despite the abundance of exclamation points, isn't quite up to the previous two, but it's an excellent album nonetheless. One has to admire Verve pres Creed Taylor for bringing Teagarden to the label at all, since he can't have been much of a cashbox draw in 1961–62. *Teagarden* seems like the album that the commercially minded Taylor would have probably wanted to make to begin with—not that there's anything wrong with that—a kind of jukebox-goes-Dixie project: sympathetic sextet arrangements from Bob Wilber, Teagarden, and an all-star group (Bobby Hackett, Bud Freeman, Hank Jones, and Wilber) address mostly contemporary hits of the past few years, from songs as appropriate as "Moon River" to off-the-wall items like "Never on Sunday." It's highlighted by five Teagarden vocals, four of which are major Sinatra standards: "Learnin' the Blues," "Time After Time," "High Hopes," and "All the Way." Hearing them is like hearing Billie Holiday sing Sinatra songs on her final two albums; as with the Teagarden-Robison album, there's a feeling of the past catching up with the present—something like a homecoming.

Teagarden was plainly exhausted at the time of his death in January 1964. Supposedly, he was mostly sober in his forties—for the only time in his life—but in his fifties he fell off the wagon and returned to his hard-drinking, rough-and-rowdy ways. Like Coleman Hawkins several years later, he seemed to know that the end was near, and drank to accelerate his decline, which was comparatively quick. He was only fifty-eight, but he seemed years older, his spirit withered away by the drinking and years of incessant touring. He would apparently never set foot in a recording studio again after the last Verve album, recorded in June 1962. By that time, Jack Teagarden had simply said all he had to say, and given everything that was his to give.

Mel Tormé (1925–1999)

There was a time, after the passing of Bing Crosby in 1977 and the general disaster area known as the sixties and seventies, that Mel Tormé came to be regarded as one of the greatest of all jazz and pop singers. It was as if the flood had just ended, Noah landed the ark, and the first singer to sprint out and claim a piece of dry territory for himself was Mel. This period was often spoken of as a comeback for him, but the truth is that he was now a bigger fish in a smaller pond than he ever had been before. Tormé was never the iconic figure that Sinatra seemingly always was, nor could he point to a career full of hit songs like Tony Bennett. But as the waters receded and the market began to grow slightly more receptive to forms of music other than baby boomer pop, Tormé was the only one of the three with new product on the market. While Tony and Danny Bennett were biding their time as they ironed out a reunion with Columbia Records, and the aging Sinatra was finding it increasingly difficult to get himself into the studio and sing a song (he would make only two albums throughout the eighties), Tormé was smart enough to affiliate himself with a series of scrappy independent labels, most notably Concord (then called Concord Jazz). They couldn't launch a media blitz the way Sony would later do for Tony, but they played a crucial role in getting Mel's name back on the map, in bigger letters than it had been before. He was on the talk shows, he was at the festivals, he was being written about in all the newspapers.

Perhaps even more than Concord founder Carl Jefferson, the most important player in the Tormé rebirth of the eighties was jazz-fest impresario George Wein, who realized early on what a killer draw Tormé could be. Wein chose him to open his flagship event, Night One of the New York (first Kool, then JVC) Jazz Festival, at Carnegie Hall. He could have picked Joe Williams, Peggy Lee, Betty Carter, Ella Fitzgerald, or any of the leading jazz-pop headliners, and yet the nod went to Mel. For roughly fifteen years, Tormé's Friday night concerts provided the Kool and JVC Fests with an opening salvo. The man was perfect in person; apart from Sarah Vaughan, no other JVC headliner found a crowd so eager to leap to its feet and rock the room with applause. In this same period, he could also be counted on to make an appearance every September at one of the posher clubs on the East Side, first at Marty's, then the Park Ten, then for about ten years at Michael's Pub. Although he resided in Beverly Hills (90210, no less), Mel Tormé was now a Big Apple institution, and a crucial part of every standard-loving New Yorker's internal calendar: Mel at Carnegie meant summer was a coming in, Mel at Michael's signaled the start of the fall season.

Both professionally and artistically, Tormé was at his zenith in the last twenty years of his career—say between 1974, when he recorded *Live at the Maisonette* (his first real album in about ten years) and 1996, when he was silenced, it turned out permanently, by a stroke. In the fifties and sixties, most of what was written about him described him as "underrated," and suggested that his was too specialized a talent to catch on like Sinatra's. In the eighties, he was at last getting his due—plus, perhaps, a little extra. In 1996, he was awarded the music industry's equivalent of a lifetime achievement award—not the actual citation from the Grammy people, although he did win a lot of Grammys, but a four-CD box from Rhino Records (*The Mel Tormé Collection, 1944–1984*) that summarized virtually the entire, rather confusing, panoply of labels for whom he had recorded.

By the time he died in 1999, however, he had been marginalized once more. Between Bennett, with his MTV coup and Grammy-winning marathon of albums, and Sinatra, with his mega-selling *Duets* projects and then the media barrage that followed his death in 1998, it seemed as if once again no one was talking about Tormé. The problem was exacerbated by his physical condition; once the stroke ended his singing career, he was out of sight and out of mind. Had Tormé died in 1989, it would have been front-page, stop-the-presses news. When he did die, ten years later, it was not the event of note that it should have been. It remains to be seen how his legacy will be treated by history; as of 2010, for instance, there's no official Mel Tormé Web site that I can find on the Internet. And yet virtually all of his albums were at one point or another released on CD, something that, unfortunately, can't be said for Bennett, or even Bing Crosby.

There are those who feel that Tormé's Indian summer at the top was limited by the man's own personality—charismatic as he could sometimes be, he was hardly the paragon of sheer lovableness that Tony Bennett was and is. Nor did he inspire the treatment accorded Sinatra, that combination of movie star, political bigwig, and American icon. I'm proud to say I knew Mel fairly well from around 1984, when he played New York again for the first time after a few years' hiatus, to his last gig at Carnegie in June 1996. Mel could be an absolute sweetheart, but he wasn't always the nicest guy in the world, and he was never the most modest. He could be charitable and generous and surprisingly petty in the same breath.

Above all, Mel was smart. Some old friends even regarded his considerable un-college-educated intellect as his worst enemy, that he was thinking too much and too often managing to mentally paint himself into a corner. He was extremely talented and he knew it. Perhaps it would have been illogical for him to be modest, yet his knowledge of how good he was at times tended to affect his performances. Audiences could sense his high opinion of himself, yet he didn't turn his cockiness into an asset, like Buddy Greco or Bobby Darin, whose anticharm became a kind of charm.

(Yet sometimes he displayed an uncharacteristically humble side. For instance, he attributed all of his later popularity to his recurring appearances on the now forgotten TV sitcom *Night Court*. He also didn't seem to mind the way he was treated in the show, in that Judge Harry, the leading character, was presented as an outright geek for being a fan of Mel Tormé.)

Tormé had a hard time accepting that Sinatra and Bennett were better known and better loved than he was, but he never seemed to begrudge that to Ella Fitzgerald. She was the only singer I absolutely never heard him speak of in tones anything other than reverential. In fact, hers was the one talent he graciously accepted as superior to his own.

Then, too, the completely creative part of Tormé's brain was at odds with the area of his psyche that enjoyed being a nerdy movie buff, record collector, musical savant, and general know-it-all. Even Tony Bennett, who more than once was the victim of Tormé's jealousy, had to admit that Mel was a walking encyclopedia of all things musical. Mel could be one of the funniest guys whose company I've ever had the pleasure of enjoying, but at the same time, in the words of longtime friend Margaret Whiting (who recorded an album of duets with him in 1960), he was "always caustic, even as a teenager." Still, his best music is also clearly the work of a man who is in touch with the joy in his soul.

A paradox, this Tormé.

Whenever Mel Tormé walked out on a stage anywhere in the world, he always came out "cold"—that is to say, without the benefit of an offstage announcer booming, "And now, ladies and gentlemen, the Velvet Fog, Mr. Mel Tormé." This was a kind of stagecraft, in which the singer-songwriter-orchestrator-actor-writer-drummer acknowledged his stature as, in the parlance of the George Jessel school of after-dinner speakers, a man who needed no introduction. Tormé's legacy, however, is so large and so diverse that he perhaps requires an inventory. To begin with, Mel was easily the best of all scat singers this side of Ella. At the same time, he amounted to one of the finest dramatic interpreters of the great American popular song to emerge after Frank Sinatra (the Chairman himself was proud to be counted as "both a friend and fan of Mel"). No other singer could embody the tenderest poetry of Cole Porter or Ira Gershwin one minute and then, a song later, ditch the words altogether to fly off into the scatosphere.

In the forties, Tormé was perhaps on the Hit Parade as a composer more often than he was a singer (as he still is every year with "The Christmas Song"). Among singer-songwriters of the period, only Peggy Lee rivals his record. He was also a more than adequate instrumentalist: a capable pianist (he also played ukulele for Ralph Gleason's *Jazz Casual* TV show) and drummer. He couldn't out-thunder his idol Buddy Rich, but he certainly was a professional-level player who could have held down the traps chair in any major-league band. In the fifties Tormé mastered the art of orchestration, attaining a level comparable to such collaborators as Marty Paich and Shorty Rogers. "When Mel is singing," friend Vic Damone points out, "his brain is working with more than the lyric and the story of the song. He's listening to every instrument and all the chords. He's fitting himself into an arrangement that he's usually written himself."

It's key that Tormé started out as a child star. The late vaudeville era produced a number of similarly schooled diminutive dynamos, among them Mickey Rooney, Sammy Davis Jr., and Buddy Rich himself. All began as preteen prodigies who achieved remarkable early virtuosity in multiple areas of show business: They each could sing, dance, act, play several instruments, and even do impressions. They could do all this, as David Letterman has observed, at an age "when most of us are sitting in mud." All four of them retained the high-energy personality so characteristic of child stars throughout their mature careers.

Tormé's career was born barely four years after he was (on September 13, 1925). For his whole life, this was a story he told in virtually every interview: The family scraped up enough shekels for an evening out to dance to Radio's Aces, as they were known—the Coon-Sanders Nighthawk Orchestra in residence at Chicago's Blackhawk Restaurant. Co-leader Joe Sanders overheard the precocious toddler singing along with a song that was to become a Tormé perennial, "You're Driving Me Crazy," and invited the youngster to clamber up onstage and sing it with the band. Not only that, the two leaders asked Tormé's parents to bring little Melvin back every Monday night to do a couple of songs with the Nighthawks, for the lordly sum of $15 plus dinner for the three of them. Even at four, the youngster was already addicted to music, and loved the sound of jazz and big bands. Although the family was Jewish (the name was originally pronounced "Torm-ah," before Melvin *franglicized* it into "Tor-may"), they resided in one of the Windy City's black neighborhoods.

Throughout the Depression, the young Tormé helped support his family by working as one of radio's busiest child actors. He continued studying voice, piano, and drums (playing in a school band with classmate Steve Allen), and initially infiltrated the big time as a songwriter. In his first year of high school, he penned "Lament to Love," a romantic ode to one Sophie Kostak, the unattainable girl of his dreams. When, in 1941, "Lament" became a hit for Harry James (who had tried to enlist Mel for his orchestra a year earlier but was prevented by child labor laws), Tormé became the youngest composer on the *Hit Parade* up to that time. His drumming was prodigious as well.

Tormé's first "grown-up" professional gig came in the summer of 1942 with Chico Marx. During the peak years of the big band craze, the pianist and pseudo-Italo-American comic fronted a dance orchestra in an attempt to make jazz safe for Marxism. Tormé had connected with Chico via drummer and agent Ben Pollack, then serving as the band's organizer and musical director. Now sixteen, Tormé's primary function was to organize and arrange for the band's vocal group, but he also sang solos and at one point replaced Marx's drummer, the formidable George Wettling.

Thanks to the 1942–44 musicians strike against the recording industry, Tormé never recorded with Marx, but one broadcast, made in Los Angeles, survives. Here, the youngster, introduced as "the latest Chico Marx discovery—he's a composer, musician, singer, arranger, radio actor, oh he's a lot of things, he's a very young fella too, only seventeen years old," gives out with "Abraham," in what is apparently the earliest document of the Tormé pipes extant. Although Irving Berlin wrote this tune (introduced by Bing Crosby in blackface in *Holiday Inn*) to commemorate Lincoln's birthday, the Marx band's performance suggests the Old Testament Abraham, with Tormé flying into wildly swinging cantorial wails over a choir of bandsmen. The older Tormé decried the "nanny goat vibrato" he heard in this aircheck, but considering his youth, it ain't bad.

By now tired of the touring band grind, Marx broke up the group in July 1943. Tormé was, and not for the last time, pulled in several directions. He was recruited as a juvenile song and dance man by RKO Pictures, and together with one of his favorite singers, Frank Sinatra, made his film acting debut in RKO's *Higher and Higher*. Although he went on to both featured and lesser parts in a dozen or so movie musicals of the era, Hollywood almost never seemed to know what to do with him. Fortunately, Ben Pollack, briefly Mel's manager, did. He put Tormé in front of an equally young vocal group known as the Schoolkids, which resulted in a new combination, Mel Tormé and His Mel-Tones.

The Mel-Tones vocal group was Tormé's first substantial contribution to music: In an age of swinging, big band–affiliated units like the Pied Pipers and the Modernaires, the Mel-Tones were even more superbly musical and of a piece with the jazz world. Tormé has said that he patterned his arrangements for the unit on the saxophone sections of Artie Shaw and Jimmie Lunceford, and it was appropriate that the group made some of its most memorable sides in the company of Shaw himself. The Mel-Tones were flexible and mightily swinging, in a way that connected the major units of the thirties, like the Boswell Sisters and the Mills Brothers, with the major jazz vocal group of the fifties, Lambert, Hendricks & Ross. When Tormé reorganized the quintet to do the album *Back in Town* in 1960, it became clear that his innovative charts hadn't dated at all. Indeed, Mel-Tone showpieces like "What Is This Thing Called Love?" and their intermingling of "It Happened in Monterey" with "Ramona," sounded better than ever—indeed, they still do, more than fifty years after 1960.

At the time, however, there was more interest in Tormé—particularly from the enterprising impresario Carlos Gastel—as a solo star attraction than as the leader of a group. The bulk of both the Mel-Tones sessions, as well as those of Tormé taking his first steps as a soloist, were done for the independent but temporarily well-financed Musicraft label.

Tormé's singing in the 1946–47 Musicraft period, including some of the most astute balladeering we have, would be remarkable even if he hadn't been a mere twenty-one and twenty-two years old at the time. In light of his nickname of the later forties onward, it's hard to resist applying the adjective "velvety" to such serenely sung laments to love as "It's Dreamtime," with the appropriately dreamy, theremin-like quality of Sonny Burke's string writing.

After Sinatra, Tormé was virtually the only artist of the forties to insist on singing quality standards as opposed to the novelty-oriented items that were becoming the bigger hits of the postwar era. He and his arrangers, in particular Sonny Burke (another conductor, composer, producer, and all-around saint of the West Coast music industry), devised a method for treating old songs as new: Whereas the likes of "Making Whoopee," "You're Driving Me Crazy," "Fine and Dandy," and others had for decades only been heard in double time, tap dance tempo, Tormé and Burke slowed them down for greater romantic effect—in order to make listeners take them seriously. Tormé's own career as a songwriter was going especially strong at this period, thanks to a fruitful partnership with lyricist Bob Wells, resulting in his major cash cow, "The Christmas Song" ("Chestnuts roasting on an open fire"), the widely recorded jazz standard "Born to Be Blue," and a more bucolic extended song composition entitled "County Fair" (written for an animated sequence in a Disney feature).

The most remarkable of Tormé's early solos is "Night and Day" (1947), a scat extravaganza clearly done in response to Ella Fitzgerald's breakthrough all-scat epics, "Flying Home," "How High the Moon," and "Airmail Special." The Cole Porter song finds Tormé flying across the chord changes over three flawless choruses: The first utilizes next to nothing of the melody, although it does quote a lick from "Stars and Stripes Forever" in deference to Fitzgerald's "Lady, Be Good." The third chorus finds Tormé dancing around the tune, commencing with call-and-response with the ensemble, then doing the bridge in close harmony with the band, and finishing by returning to the lyrics for the final 12 bars. Night or day, it's a spectacular flight. (His next all-scat features were "Stompin' at the Savoy" and "Sonny Boy," done three years later in wildly boppish homage to scatmaster Leo Watson, replete with quotes from "Yardbird Suite.")

After the 1948 recording ban, Carlos Gastel relocated Tormé to the label where most of his other clients (Nat Cole, Stan Kenton, June Christy) were recording, the burgeoning Capitol Records. At Capitol, Tormé had the benefit of an even finer pantheon of resident arranger-conductors to work with, including, once again, Sonny Burke, as well as Pete Rugolo, Billy May, and Nelson Riddle (the last collaborated with him on one of his favorite if most obscure singles, an adaptation of a traditional Russian song entitled "Love Is Such a Cheat").

Tormé grew in several directions at Capitol. As a composer he crafted his most ambitious work yet: *California Suite,* a full-length song cycle inspired in equal parts by Gordon Jenkins's *Manhattan Tower* and Duke Ellington's long-form works like *Black, Brown and Beige.* He recorded the *Suite* twice, once with multiple studio orchestras and choirs (including pseudonymous guest vocalist Peggy Lee) under the baton of various arrangers in 1949, and once in a more streamlined treatment with Marty Paich in 1957.

The late forties and early fifties were also Tormé's heyday as a pop star. Other than the slowly emerging Cole and the fading Andy Russell, Capitol seems to have had few important male singers on its roster in 1949. In Tormé they realized they had an artist who could compete with Sinatra on ballads and Fitzgerald on jazz. (Naturally, there was more money in the former than in the latter.) This is virtually the only extended stay in Tormé's career when his records sound like those of any other pop star—mostly new songs, good and bad. He was able to record a few of the standards he loved, particularly after his role in *Words and Music,* MGM's Rodgers and Hart biopic, helped push his treatment of "Blue Moon" onto the charts. There was one outstanding session of four superior standards, all with lush orchestrations by Pete Rugolo and Mel-Tones–like vocal support from the Dave Lambert Singers ("Bewitched," "Lullaby of the Leaves"). There also were superior new songs, like the country-styled "Careless Hands," and "Again," a movie song (like "I Only Have Eyes for You") that has since been embraced by singers in all genres, including rhythm and blues.

Under Gastel, Tormé also began working the more upscale joints, like the Copacabana, one of the most imposing bastions of old-time showbiz. It was hardly the home for a young upstart like Tormé; even Sinatra hadn't worked there yet. There was an extra outcome of the Copa engagement, in which the singer was thoroughly lauded by teenaged bobby-soxer fans who could barely make either the monetary or age minimums. This was when Tormé's nickname was coined by New York disc jockey Fred Robbins: the Velvet Fog.

In 1995, Tormé commented, "Artie Shaw says of my singing in that period, 'Mel didn't have a lot of projection in those days. He had to learn projection.' Artie was absolutely right! A lot of my records with Artie in that period were kind of wispy. They were kind of breathy . . . which probably contributed to why Fred Robbins wound up calling me 'the Velvet Fog.'" Tormé enjoyed a love-hate relationship with the phrase but eventually came to terms with it and titled his autobiography *It Wasn't All Velvet.*

Both Tormé and Peggy Lee, with whom he had sung four duets (in addition to *California Suite*), left

Capitol in the early fifties. The label doesn't seem to have been keen to keep them, and old friend Sonny Burke, by then an executive at the Decca corporation, was happy to pick up their options. Tormé was signed to Decca's subsidiary Coral, where he made a bunch of completely forgettable 45s (among them "How" and "Anything Can Happen Mambo") and two terrific albums, one of them his first live project (which yielded a hit single in Britain, "Mountain Greenery," to Mel's astonishment).

The second Coral album was given a title he detested, *Musical Sounds Are the Best Songs,* but had a concept that was near and dear to him. "I had an idea that I thought was kind of interesting. I'd start with all those gimmicky songs of the forties, like 'Tutti Frutti' and 'Cement Mixer' and 'Flat Foot Floogie,' all of those things. I said to them, 'What I want to do is take these dopey numbers into the studio and have each arrangement represent a major big band of the thirties and the forties.' That's why on 'The Hut Sut Song' you hear [Charlie Barnet's theme song] 'Cherokee.' And then on 'Hold Tight,' we have Al Pellegrini playing a clarinet solo in the style of Benny Goodman. We did that on each one of those tracks on that 10" LP. It was a lot of fun."

After the Coral albums *Musical Sounds* and *Live at the Crescendo,* that first live album, Tormé went independent. His first glory period was the span from 1954 to 1964, in which he cut just under two dozen albums, most of which are classics. This is the body of work upon which his larger reputation and his subsequent "comeback" rest:

Musical Sounds Are the Best Songs (1954, Coral), arranged by Billy May, Benny Carter et al.
Live at the Crescendo (aka *Mel Tormé in Hollywood*) (1954, Coral), Al Pellegrini
It's a Blue World (1955, Bethlehem), conducted by Al Pellegrini, arranged by Pellegrini, André Previn, Marty Paich, Russ Garcia, Harold Mooney, and others
Mel Tormé and the Marty Paich Dek-Tette (aka *Lulu's Back in Town*) (1956, Bethlehem), Marty Paich
Bethlehem Presents the Complete George Gershwin Porgy and Bess (1956), Russ Garcia
Mel Tormé Sings Fred Astaire (1956, Bethlehem), Marty Paich
Mel Tormé Live at the Crescendo (1957, Bethlehem), quintet with Marty Paich
Songs for Any Taste (1957; released 1959, Bethlehem), quintet with Marty Paich
California Suite (1957, Bethlehem), Marty Paich
Mel Tormé Meets the British (1957, Philips), Wally Stott
Prelude to a Kiss (1957, Tops), Marty Paich
Tormé (1958, Verve), Marty Paich
Olé Tormé (1959, Verve), Billy May
Back in Town (1959, Verve), with the Mel-Tones and Marty Paich

Mel Tormé Swings Shubert Alley (1958, Verve), Marty Paich
Swingin' on the Moon (1960, Verve), Russ Garcia
Broadway Right Now (1960, Verve), with Margaret Whiting and Russ Garcia
I Dig the Duke! I Dig the Count! (1960, Verve), Johnny Mandel
My Kind of Music (1960, Verve), Wally Stott, Geoff Love, and Tony Osborne
Mel Tormé at the Red Hill (1962, Atlantic), Jimmy Wisner Trio
Comin' Home Baby (1962, Atlantic), Shorty Rogers
Sunday in New York and Other Songs of New York (1962, Atlantic), Shorty Rogers, Johnny Williams, and Dick Hazard
That's All: A Lush Romantic Album (1964, Columbia), Robert Mersey

Apart from the first two (on Coral) and the last (on Columbia), these were all for independent labels: Bethlehem went bust early, despite releasing some of the finest jazz albums of the period, while Verve and Atlantic, which were absorbed into conglomerates, are still around today as corporate entities.

The last classic Tormé album is *That's All*, which completes a cycle: The golden age of Tormé is roughly bookended by his two finest ballad albums, *It's a Blue World* and *That's All*. If Mel were alive to read this, he would bristle at the suggestion that his best work was done in the years 1955–64, when he was in his thirties. He always professed to dislike his singing on the early albums and even offered, he told me, to rerecord the original Paich Dek-Tette charts free of charge.

There's a reason that Tormé's really great years coincide with those of Ella Fitzgerald on Verve (1956–66), Vic Damone on Columbia and Capitol (1956–64), and even Sinatra on Capitol and Reprise (1953–67); only Bennett kept making first-rate albums straight into the seventies, but then he suffered his own dry spell from 1977 to 1985. These were the halcyon years for virtually everybody born before Elvis arrived; Tormé was reaching a peak of artistic maturity at precisely the point when the economic-political circumstances that allowed adult pop singers to make first-class albums gave them the opportunity to work with full orchestral complements and their choice of brilliant arranger-conductors and musicians. It was only a brief era, lasting roughly from the dawn of the 12" LP to the final revolt of the philistines in the mid- to late sixties.

These were the years in which everything came together for Tormé: his voice (his own later opinion to the contrary), his musical know-how, and the affiliations with Bethlehem and Verve that allowed him to do whatever he wanted. No less important was the advent into his life of one of the most brilliant orchestrators ever to work in the popular and jazz fields, the remarkable Marty Paich (1925–1995). Tormé has said that when he heard Paich's writing for Shelly Manne and His Men, the pivotal West Coast group, he instantly knew that he had found the musical partner of his dreams. As it happened, the first project they worked on, and Tormé's first Bethlehem album, was *It's a Blue World,* a project that revealed how his understanding of the great American love song had deepened since the forties.

Then, in 1956, the team made, in quick succession, the original two Dek-Tette albums: *Mel Tormé and the Marty Paich Dek-Tette* (reissued as *Lulu's Back in Town*) and *Mel Tormé Sings Fred Astaire* (both for Bethlehem). The Marty Paich Dek-Tette was roughly inspired by Gerry Mulligan's Ten-Tette of several years earlier, and combined the power of a swing big band with the flexibility of a smaller combo. There were other variations on the instrumentation: The singer's first Verve album, *Tormé,* used what was essentially the Dek-Tette format abetted by strings; in contrast, the Tops album, *Prelude to a Kiss,* was pretty much all strings, without much Dek-Tette presence. The climax of the series was *Mel Tormé Swings Shubert Alley,* which billed the group, on the cover, as "The Marty Paich Orchestra."

All of a sudden, everything changed. This was a time of many revolutions in the age of jazz and pop singing: Sinatra's *Songs for Swingin' Lovers;* Lambert, Hendricks & Ross's first album, *Sing a Song of Basie;* and Tormé's first Dek-Tette album opened up whole new vistas in the jazz universe. Extending what Sinatra had been working on since the forties, Tormé showed that the voice could be completely immersed in the jazz ensemble and interact with jazz soloists on a level playing field. Together, Tormé and Paich constructed a new context for the human voice—not unlike what Miles Davis and Gil Evans were concurrently refining for the instrumental soloist and jazz orchestra—in which scatting, balladeering, and swinging were all congruent with trombone, trumpet, and saxophone solos.

These Dek-Tette sessions were logical outgrowths of the instrumental achievements of the Miles Davis Nonet circa 1949 (aka the Tuba Band) and the Mulligan Ten-Tette, which had given birth to the cool. Yet more than Davis, Mulligan, or Evans, Tormé and Paich were bringing the Great American Songbook into the mix: *Fred Astaire* and *Shubert Alley* were rigidly thematic, the former honoring the greatest of all song and dance men, the latter focusing on show tunes from roughly the first ten years following *Oklahoma!*

For years, Sinatra fans have debated which of the two classic *Swingin'* albums with Riddle is greater, *Swingin' Lovers* or *Swingin' Affair.* Likewise, for years I have similarly pondered which of the two Tormé-Paich albums I would take with me to a desert isle if I were allowed only one, *Shubert Alley* or *Lulu.* Ultimately, I decided I have to go with *Lulu.* First, the songs are more diverse, including such remarkable obscurities as Paul Weston's "When April Comes Again" and Vincent Youmans's "Keeping Myself for You." The moods and tempos are likewise more all-encompassing; in contrast to *Shubert Alley,* where everything is in a sort of cool school tuba-band medium gallop, *Lulu* ranges from fast and up to slow and moody, including Duke Ellington's so-named "The Blues" (which isn't even remotely a blues) from *Black, Brown and Beige.*

The opener of the first album, "Lulu's Back In Town," became a Tormé signature, probably the number most associated with him after "The Christmas Song." Paich's chromatically opening vamp is as distinctive and immediately identifiable among jazz fans the world over as Ralph Sharon's piano intro to "I Left My Heart in San Francisco" or Nelson Riddle's electric organ gambit on "Summer Wind."

The unchallenged classic from the premier Dek-Tette set is "Lullaby of Birdland," the most famous composition of Tormé's future partner George Shearing. It took chutzpah for Tormé to tackle the tune, seeing as it had already been made into a scat classic by Ella Fitzgerald. However, where Fitzgerald's version is a triumph of pure improvisation, the Tormé-Paich version is an archetype of how preplanned orchestration and an extemporaneous solo can interact and complement each other, and how the human voice can be used as part of a jazz ensemble.

"Lullaby" opens with Red Mitchell's bass, over which Tormé sings the first 16 bars, completing the chorus (from the bridge on) with the addition of Mel Lewis on drums. Tormé scats the second chorus brilliantly by himself (going into another lullaby—"Lullaby of the Leaves"—around bar 24), but it's the third and fourth choruses that truly amaze. Chorus three is a call-and-response episode with the two trumpeters: 4 bars of Don Fagerquist, then 4 bars of Tormé (doing "Love Me or Leave Me," the tune that supplied Shearing with the "Lullaby" chord changes), then 4 bars of Pete Candoli, then Fagerquist, then Tormé, then Candoli, and so on. The fourth chorus finds him doing the same with valve trombonist Bob Enevoldsen for the first half, occasionally making his entrance early to get in some harmony, while for the second 16 bars he trades 4s with the ensemble's four reeds, led by Bud Shank on alto. Along the way, Tormé also works in quotes from Gerry Mulligan's "Ontet," "Chloe," "Moon over Miami," and "Blacksmith Blues." With all this he creates what, by any standards, has to be considered a great jazz solo—a positively transcendental one, in fact. That it happens to be sung rather than played is irrelevant.

"Lullaby" is perhaps Tormé's single greatest recorded performance. In later years, he, like Peggy Lee, generally wanted it to be known that he was responsible for the arrangements on these albums: Even if he wasn't putting them down on paper himself, Paich was orchestrating Tormé's ideas. When I interviewed Paich toward the end of his life, the arranger remembered things somewhat differently: "I would write the arrangements—he would give me an idea of the tempo, but any singer would do that, I would pick the key, I would write the arrangement, I'd make any necessary modulations, and Mel would maybe say, 'How about modulating here?' Those arrangements are like 90 percent mine and maybe 10 percent Mel's."

Billy May, who worked with Tormé on three projects (parts of *California Suite* and *Musical Sounds* and all of *Olé Tormé*), put it this way: "[Mel] has great ideas. All I did was orchestrate his ideas [on *Olé Tormé*], and they all worked out very well. Of course, I contributed some things of my own to the charts, too. I always found working with him to be very enjoyable. He's a very talented man." Still, on another occasion May said, "Mel Tormé was a good musician, but he was a little too demanding. He wanted to make sure that every hot chord he knew was in there, and sometimes that gets in your way."

One can hear touches throughout Tormé's finest albums that are surely the singer's own ideas, such as that amazing coda to "I Like to Recognize the Tune." Here, he goes into waltz time, slows down and speeds up, then detours through a Dixieland band passage, and lastly a brief scat episode. It's undeniably Tormé's work when there are special material lyrics involved: the intro to "Lulu" ("You've heard about Margie, you've heard about Dinah . . ."); this is precisely the sort of thing he was recruited to write for Judy Garland on her CBS TV series of 1963–64.

Paich participated in nearly half of Tormé's Golden Twenty-three, including a pair of very short live sets recorded probably on the same evening at the Crescendo in 1957. (These two, *Live at the Crescendo* and *Songs for Any Taste*, could—and should—be combined onto a single CD, and you'd still have room left over for the *Rhapsody in Blue*.) The two Bethlehem *Crescendo* albums are bizarrely programmed: "Autumn Leaves" is divided between the two LPs, and the second includes a studio track from *Porgy and Bess*, ostensibly as filler.

That leaves a dozen Tormé albums from 1954 to 1966 that have no input from Paich, yet even these are definitively worth owning—with two exceptions, both of which attempted to fuse jazz with Broadway. There's the Bethlehem *Porgy and Bess* disaster (Mel himself, incidentally, was far more critical of it than I ever could be) and *Broadway Right Now,* although the latter did produce a beautiful duet medley with Margaret Whiting of two songs from *Wildcat* by Cy Coleman and Carolyn Leigh.

The remaining ten albums from the halcyon period include thematic packages: delightfully ersatz Latinalia with Billy May (*Olé Tormé*), positively ripping English yarns with Wally Stott (*Mel Tormé Meets the British*), songs about the moon with Russ Garcia (*Swingin' on the Moon*) and about New York

with three West Coast arrangers (*Sunday in New York*), and a set of modern jazz anthems with Shorty Rogers (*Comin' Home Baby*). There also were two half-songbooks: *My Kind of Music*, taped in London, featuring Dietz and Schwartz on one side and Tormé's own songs on the other. (Said Mel, "The madness of that album is it should have either been Schwartz and Dietz or Mel Tormé. But, to have both—it didn't make any sense. It's one of the things that drove me away from Verve. The thinking was so weird. So strange"), and the more sensibly combined canons of Ellington and Basie on *I Dig the Duke! I Dig the Count!* with Johnny Mandel.

As I've suggested, Mel would probably demand that I perform an anatomically impossible act if I were to imply that he recorded his last classic album a few months after he turned thirty-nine (the beautiful ballad set *That's All*). But circumstances were out of his control. The cultural nightmare had begun. He recorded occasionally over the next ten years, principally three crummy discs from Columbia (*Right Now*, a title that portended disaster) and Capitol (*A Time for Us* and *Raindrops Keep Fallin' on My Head*). Tormé accurately described Columbia and Capitol as "alter egos": " 'We want you to cover this, we want you to cover that.' I did 'Games People Play' for Capitol. I was nothing but a cover artist. And, it was demeaning. It was absolutely destroying to me. I just couldn't handle it." The worst was yet to come, namely the 1970 *A Day in the Life of Bonnie and Clyde* (Liberty), which offered half-baked, ersatz-soul treatments of great thirties standards. The best track of Mel's forties would be "Hurry on Down," a Basie-styled big band elaboration of Nellie Lutcher's erotic R&B hit of twenty years earlier.

The return to grace began in 1974, when he played an engagement at the Maisonette Room at New York's St. Regis Hotel. Former Kenton trumpeter Al Porcino led the band, and a friend of Porcino's made arrangements to tape the show; he then sold the tape to Atlantic, who issued it as *Live at the Maisonette*. Twenty years later Tormé was griping that he had never received a thin dime from either Porcino's pal or Atlantic, but he was grateful for what the album did for him. Neither Sinatra nor Bennett was doing much, record-wise, and few of the other old-guard artists (Jones, Lawrence, Damone, Vaughan, McRae, O'Day) were recording anything worthwhile. The *Maisonette* album didn't sell like "The Hustle," but it attracted a lot of attention, and he garnered a Grammy for his epic Gershwin medley. He was ending his dry spell precisely when everyone else's were just beginning.

Tormé, who had spent much of the previous ten years not only performing around the world but writing (novels, screenplays, a memoir of his experiences with Judy Garland), and acting, was now back in the singing business. Between 1974 and 1982, he would make *A New Album* (Gryphon, 1974), *Together Again for the First Time* with Buddy Rich and His Orchestra (Gryphon, 1978), *Mel Tormé and Friends* (Finesse, 1981), done live at Marty's, and *Encore at Marty's* (1982). It was exciting to hear these albums at the time, as Tormé was still the only singer of his genre and his generation (other than Ella Fitzgerald) who even made it worthwhile to visit your local record store.

Heard today, they don't hold up as well as they might, although all have at least a few good tracks. Tormé resented having to cover pop hits in the sixties, but there was a part of him that did indeed want to keep current. He had to be forced to sing "Raindrops Keep Fallin' on My Head" earlier, but now by his own choice he was singing "Stars," "Ordinary Fool," "You Are the Sunshine of My Life," "The First Time Ever I Saw Your Face," "All in Love Is Fair," and "New York State of Mind." It wasn't only the material, it was the writing: Many of the charts done even for classic tunes use seventies-style harmonies and tonal colors, and there's a vaguely disco sheen about a lot of this material, much the same way that rock elements compromise many of Buddy Rich's big band recordings of the seventies and eighties. These were also the years when the few good songs of what Mel called the RRP ("relatively recent past"), such as "The Best Is Yet to Come," "What Are You Doing for the Rest of Your Life," and "Watch What Happens"—and virtually everything else ever written by either Cy Coleman or Michel Legrand—were done so often and by so many singers that they were heard to death.

It was in 1982 that Mel started recording for Concord Jazz. The albums he began making for Concord—the era's equivalent of Bethlehem or Verve—showed that he was prepared to put the excesses of the sixties and seventies behind him, roll up his sleeves, and get back to some serious work. Between 1982 and 1985, he would make four albums (*An Evening with George Shearing, Top Drawer, An Evening at Charlie's,* and *An Elegant Evening*) with the star pianist George Shearing, an extraordinary musician who works the jazz circuit but utilizes a considerable amount of classical elements and techniques and has amassed what amounts to a vast pop following. In 1987 and 1990, Tormé and Shearing would turn out two more (*A Vintage Year* and *Mel and George "Do" World War Two*), and then, in 2002, Concord would release all six in a deluxe box with a seventh bonus disc of previously unheard bits and pieces. My own perspective on these records is somewhat skewed: I was listening to them at the same time as I was discovering the golden age Tormé of 1955–64. Compared to his amazing work with Marty Paich et al., the Shearing collaborations seemed rather pallid.

Listening to them again today, I couldn't disagree more. The seven discs of *Mel Tormé and George Shearing: The Complete Concord Recordings* are easily the best work of Tormé's career after 1964. These finely nuanced duets were just too subtle for me to appreciate in my twenties. On playing them for the first time in fifteen or twenty years, it's all I can do to marvel and ask myself which instrument is more expressive, the eighty-eight notes at Shearing's disposal or the infinite palette of emotions, tones, and time that Tormé's voice had become in his fifties and sixties. His range had dropped, deepened, and widened, had lost some of its youthful prettiness but gained in depth and expressiveness. There seemed to be no loss at the top end; he could hit notes as high as ever, whether for genuine dramatic effect or sometimes just to show off (and more power to him).

The impression Tormé tended to give to the uninitiated was of a guy who was trying to do everything at once, not only singing, orchestrating, and playing drums—apparently all simultaneously—but also trying to sing every song he had ever heard at once. The Tormé-Shearing duets show that he didn't have to overdo anything, that he could just pare down and concentrate on essentials, the simple purity of the voice and piano combination. Throughout the eighty or so songs that the pair recorded, sometimes backed by bass and drums, sometimes by just bass, or, on *An Elegant Evening*, the only studio session in the bunch, just the two of them, the beauty and charm of the voice-piano combination never wears off. Although there are some marvelous rhythm and scat numbers—in fact, the first album starts off with "All God's Chillun Got Rhythm"—the highlights are inevitably ballads. Tormé had done whole albums of love songs before—*It's a Blue World, That's All,* and most of *Prelude to a Kiss* and *Tormé,* but nothing equals the sensitivity he brought to the Shearing sessions; never before had Mel sounded so completely vulnerable.

The only downside of the Concord association was that producer Carl Jefferson was somewhat provincial and Californiacentric in his outlook. Virtually every album seemed to be taped in a vinery somewhere (which was ironic in that Tormé was the rare jazzbo who rarely drank), so that virtually the only small group projects he did for Jefferson were the Shearing albums. Concord missed a major part of Tormé's career in that it never documented the more aggressive, hard-swinging side he brought to his East Coast appearances, in particular the superb rhythm section that accompanied him at Michael's, primarily Mike Renzi (piano) and Jay Leonhart (bass), the same two gentlemen who made most of Peggy Lee's New York City appearances of the eighties so special. It wasn't until 1992, when Tormé switched briefly to the Cleveland-based Telarc Records, that he was recorded at Michael's. By then, a battle of egos had long since parted Tormé and Renzi (succeeded by John Campbell and John Colianni), and that album, titled *The Great American Songbook,* used a full-sized big band anyway.

Other live albums, like *Night at the Concord Pavilion* (1990) and the disappointing *Live at the Playboy Jazz Festival,* taped in 1993 and released in

2002, tend to be very medley-heavy. Heard live in person, Mel's medleys generally worked very well indeed; they don't translate quite so well to the living room, even when one is listening to a live recording. In the moment, it was exciting when Tormé switched from one tune to another, particularly in his adroitly organized minisuites done in tribute to George Gershwin, Duke Ellington, Benny Goodman, and Frank Loesser's *Guys and Dolls*; heard on record, they're frustrating—you don't get enough of each song!

The six (now seven) Shearing albums set the benchmark for the rest of Tormé's output in the Concord years. The closest he came to a genuine disappointment was *Nothing Without You* (1991), a set of duets with Cleo Laine, which possibly pleased fans of that British diva (I couldn't say). Other than that, there were four other exceptional larger ensemble projects: Two of which, *Mel Tormé, Rob McConnell and the Boss Brass* (1986) and *Velvet and Brass* (1995), combine Mel with Rob McConnell and the Boss Brass. The only thing tacky about this Toronto-based big band, led by trombonist-arranger Rob McConnell (until his death in 2010), was the name (it sounds like something led by Herb Alpert or Sergio Mendes). Instead, this Canadian ensemble challenges the Village Vanguard Jazz Orchestra for the crown as the most steadily working large jazz unit of the Western Hemisphere in recent years. The other two, *Reunion* and *In Concert Tokyo,* reunite Tormé with Marty Paich; these excellent sets from 1988 don't replace the masterpieces of 1956–60 but satisfyingly supplement them.

I saw Mel for the last time at Carnegie in June 1996, shortly after the passing of Ella Fitzgerald. Our conversation was mainly notable in that he told me that Michael's Pub had closed (it couldn't have happened to a nicer club owner), which I hadn't realized, and that for the first time in more than fifteen years he had no New York club lined up for his annual fall engagement.

What was notable was the music itself. For some reason, Donny Osborne wasn't there that night, and Mel was working instead with Lewis Nash, perhaps the best young bebop drummer of the day; also in the rhythm section was Mike Renzi, who after too many years returned to the fold. Their reunion portended great things. Tormé was on fire that evening, the best I had ever heard him. His ballads were never more intimate, his bebop was never harder or sharper.

It was a transcendent evening, but one that I knew was going to end on something of a sour note when I saw the *New York Times* reviewer leave before the preplanned last number. That night, there were three standing ovations and three encores, none of which was mentioned in the *Times* review. As I expected, I got a call from Mel that day, complaining about the review, which was good but not boffo. I couldn't blame him; he deserved an ecstatic review

for that performance. It had been a good year so far for him: The cable channel A&E had profiled him on their series *Biography,* something that they had done for precious few other singers of Mel's stripe, and the Rhino four-CD *Mel Tormé* collection had just been released. Yet none of this seemed to be making him happy; all he could think about was that sonofabitch from *The New York Times*. He went into his usual rant: He didn't have to do this for a living, he had tons of money from investments, he'd put his money from movies and television and song copyrights into the right places and could retire anytime he wanted. He still had "Christmas Song" money, for Christ's sake (literally for Christ's sake). So he didn't need the goddamned *New York Times*.

Tormé never had a problem with drugs or drink the way so many musicians of his generation did; he never smoked to excess like his colleagues Sammy Davis or Nat Cole. What felled him was his inability to control his diet; in the later years he was continually slimming down and fattening up (he even did commercials for Slim-Fast). In August 1996 he was beginning work on a tribute album to Ella Fitzgerald (who had died in June), working for the first time with arranger Ralph Burns. Tormé briefly passed out, and—with his lifelong aversion to doctors—tried to keep working when he revived. It was Ralph's opinion that if Mel had seen a doctor right away he might have been able to avert what happened. He pressed on, but then suffered what turned out to be a second stroke. Mel was permanently out of commission, never to sing again, but he hung on for three painful years until he died in June 1999.

On July 23, 1996, roughly a month after Carnegie Hall and JVC, Mel gave what is generally regarded as his last concert, a session at the Disney Institute in Orlando. Fortunately, A&E decided to complement their *Biography* documentary by videotaping and televising this performance, and Concord followed suit by releasing it on CD. It ends, prophetically, with "Ev'ry Time We Say Goodbye." At the time, the Disney performance seemed like just another Mel concert, but heard fifteen years later, it serves as an almost painful reminder of all the beauty and swing that were unleashed when Mel Tormé was at his peak. To think that we used to take it for granted.

Sophie Tucker (1884–1966)

I'm the last of the red-hot mamas,
I'm gettin' hotter every day!

—Jack Yellen and Milton Ager

She told us, over and over again, that she was "The Last of the Red Hot Mamas," and she sang it with such persuasiveness—not to mention sheer force—that we have no choice but to believe her. Few entertainers ever came up with a slogan and a theme song as memorable as that; one even imagines that Al Jolson, who was sometimes billed as "The World's Greatest Entertainer," would have loved to have a line as great as Tucker's to use as a calling card. In the parlance of the twentieth century, declaring herself the Last of the Red Hot Mamas was a combination shout-out, mission statement, and permanent, ongoing Tweet.

Jolson is an appropriate reference point for Tucker. It's possible to see her in the context of other major divas of her era and afterward—Bessie Smith and Judy Garland are likely candidates—but Jolson and Tucker were extrovert Jewish entertainers from the turn of the century whose careers ran parallel up to a point. Both professionally and stylistically they differed mainly in the details—and the nuances. In the late forties, when Jolson was enjoying a renaissance, he frequently made jokes on the radio about being as old as Tucker (she was actually one or two years older): "When I was a boy, I used to carve my initials in trees—AJ & ST—Al Jolson and Sophie Tucker."

After the release of *The Jolson Story*, however, Jolson was hot all over again. At the time he was making his well-intentioned wisecracks, Sophie Tucker was still doing very well, thank you very much, appearing at high-ticket nightspots like New York's Copacabana. Yet as wonderful as she was, and as popular as she continued to be with her audiences, one can't imagine Tucker doing what Jolson and then Jimmy Durante did, which was to reinvent themselves for a new era. She was still a household name, and working as much as she wanted to, but she was hardly competition on the *Billboard* charts for Dinah Shore, Margaret Whiting, Kay Starr, Doris Day, or Jo Stafford. Perhaps her way of getting back at Jolson was to sing "The Older They Get, the Younger They Want Them," all about how foolish older men seem when they chase after young *chiquitas*—she might well have been alluding to Jolson's recent success with bobby-soxers and jitterbugs (not to mention his substantially younger wives).

By the time of the age of anxiety, the final twenty years or so of her career, Tucker's Jazz Age prophecy had been fulfilled: There were no other red hot mamas in sight. Yet up until then, almost every part of that phrase is open to question. Born in 1884 and performing professionally at the turn of the century, Tucker could have rightfully claimed that she was the first and not the last of anything. It's also up for argument as to how "red hot" she actually was. She certainly was neither red nor hot in a jazz sense (you wouldn't compare her to Bessie Smith or Billie Holiday), even though she made some very credible sessions with genuine jazz musicians over several generations. She wasn't torchy and blue, or even remotely seductive, not in the sense of the female vocal style that predominated among white *vocalistes* form the early electrical age through the Depression.

Instead, and also like Jolson, Tucker wasn't "hot" in a musical sense, but she was red hot in a Marshall McLuhan sense—hot in the way that radio was a "hot" medium, compared to a "cool" medium like television. Tucker and Jolson had plenty of what the music historian David Wondrich has described as "drive," and both sang with such power that they pulled the crowds along with them—as she still does on recordings. They were like forces of nature, radiant fireballs of pure energy—they could *force* an audience to have a good time. Whatever you think you might want, Tucker just wants it more; she wants to entertain you much more than you might want to resist her.

The contemporary observer Carrie McLaren has identified Tucker as a protofeminist—which makes her "hot" in terms of gender politics. The 1928 "Aren't Women Wonderful," written for her by her longtime accompanist Ted Shapiro, could be employed on either side of the argument: She praises other members of her gender for being able to fly planes and climb mountains, while at the same time pointing out that they're still scared of mice. Sophie Tucker may well have been red hot in every sense of the word.

Tucker is also enjoying something of a renaissance more than forty years after her death. Around 2004, the scholar Brad Kay assembled a four-CD set containing nearly all of her prewar recordings, titled *The Complete Early Sophie Tucker (1910–1937)* (available most easily from squidoo.com/superbatone). At about that time, the team of Susan and Lloyd Ecker began researching her and gained access to the woman's copious collection of scrapbooks, which she had meticulously maintained throughout her long career. Their eventual goal is to produce a documentary and complete a formal biography, and in 2009 the efforts of their research began to bear fruit, when Archeophone Records released *Origins of the Red Hot Mama* (available from Archeophonerecords.com). This highly recommended CD not only contains her first twenty-one sides (from 1910–22) but a copiously illustrated seventy-two-page booklet as well. In their extensive notes, the Eckers make it plain that we'll probably never know the whole truth about Tucker's life and career. For one thing, her famous account (*Some of These Days: The Autobiography of Sophie Tucker,* published in 1945) is no more notably accurate than other showbiz memoirs of the period. But beyond that, in every article or profile written about her over a sixty-year period, writers just seem to have printed what she told them—to the extent that she might as well have been writing them herself. Thus, little written about her can be considered entirely reliable, with which caveat I acknowledge that most of the facts in the biographical sketch that follows come from her book.

Before she was the last of the red hot anythings, Sophie Tucker was a woman of many names—well before anyone had heard of her, she was already known as Sonya Sophie Kalish Abuza Tuck. Her account of her early years is roughly as follows: Her family's actual name, back in Mother Russia, was Kalish. However, shortly before Sonya (aka Sophie) arrived in 1884, the Kalishes had left the Old Country. Her father was fleeing forced induction into the Russian army, and she was born when her mother was en route to Poland. The family didn't reach New York until the baby was three, but by then a curious thing had happened: Tucker's father had become friendly with an Italian immigrant named Abuza, who died before he made it to the New World. Kalish decided to rename his family Abuza, and make the whole family Italian, just in case the Russian army was still on his trail. (As with much else in Tucker's own personal mythology, she told the story in different ways over the years. The Eckers, who have made a remarkable attempt at sorting it all out, report that it's no less likely that Kalish might have won Abuza's papers from him in a card game.)

Their daughter grew up with the name Sophia Abuza, a name that, in the earliest days of her career, might have given her something of an exotic appeal. With that name, she was tapping into the same Latin fantasy that she would later deflate in her 1928 record of "There's Something Spanish in My Eyes" ("My father is Jewish, my mother is Irish, which proves that I'm Spanish . . .") and "A Little Balcony in Spain." At the age of sixteen, she married a beer-cart driver named Louis Tuck. They separated almost immediately, but he left her with two things she would keep for the rest of her life: her son, Bert, whom she was now compelled to raise on her own, and her professional name. At this point Sophia Kalish Abuza Tuck became Sophie Tucker.

Even before the marriage, Sophia had worked as a singing waitress, initially in a humble emporium in Hartford, run by her father. In Connecticut, she befriended the comedian Willie Howard, who would later headline on Broadway, and he encouraged her to seek her fortune in Manhattan. She had her first taste of singing in the city at the Cafe Monopol, which is the first time she used the name Sophie Tucker.

She worked her way up from restaurants, like the famous Tony Pastor's, to the vaudeville circuit, which at the time still retained many vestigial traces of the old minstrel show tradition. To her great displeasure, she spent most of the first decade of the twentieth century performing in blackface, which, she said, theater owners foisted on her because she was so "big and ugly." One point she makes in her autobiography that seems inarguable is that she detested the then widely accepted convention of burnt cork and falsely darkened faces. This wasn't necessarily because she was an enlightened champion of racial sensitivity (in 1910 her act was billed as "a Revelation in Coonology"), but because, she said, she didn't want any kind of a mask to come between herself and her audiences: In 1929, she expressed this philosophy in a song called "Take Off Your Mask and Be Yourself." In Tucker's case, that

meant to be a self of one's own definition; she seems to have hated performing in blackface because she was more interested in wearing a persona of her own invention.

That persona is a key element of her recorded work, which began shortly after her Ziegfeld debacle (described below). Throughout the first decades of the commercial recording industry, the song was overwhelmingly regarded as more important than the singer, and a great many discs and cylinders were released of generic tenors and sopranos, each indistinguishable from the others. Tucker, along with Jolson and Bert Williams, was among the first to present a distinct personality, one that would have a profound effect on the subsequent development of popular songs and singers. It's easy to imagine youngsters like Louis Armstrong and Bing Crosby, who were introduced to a wide array of music via the phonograph, listening to Tucker's records as teenagers in New Orleans and Spokane.

In fact, in *Hear Me Talkin' to Ya*, Clarence Williams (pianist, composer, publisher, and producer of Bessie Smith, among others) talks about going to hear Tucker when she played the Orpheum Theatre in New Orleans in 1911, and being so thrilled with her and the song "Some of These Days" that he immediately went home and played it. It was recorded brilliantly by both Armstrong and Crosby, not to mention Judy Garland (in a famous medley), Rosemary Clooney, Tony Bennett, and hundreds of others including country and western pioneer Milton Brown. Clearly, Billie Holiday learned both "Some of These Days" and "My Yiddishe Momme" from Tucker. In 1964, two years before her death, the Beatles famously named Sophie Tucker as their "favorite American group," a reference to her iconic stoutness that would have seemed in bad taste had she herself not been joking about it onstage for fifty years by that point.

In 1909, Tucker was spotted by one of Florenz Ziegfeld's talent scouts, and that year made her Broadway debut in the third edition of that producer's legendary *Follies*. This was, supposedly, much to the chagrin of Ziggy himself, who prided himself on stocking both his professional and private lives with naught but beautiful girls. The producer was actually annoyed when Tucker stopped the show with "It's Moving Day down in Jungle Town" during the Atlantic City tryout. The story that Tucker told was that both Ziegfeld and the show's star, Nora Bayes, conspired to have her removed from the show when it reached Broadway. In the second month of the run, "Jungle Town" was reassigned to another major star, Eva Tanguay, and Bayes and Jack Norworth left the production entirely. Ironically, the very next year, in the 1910 *Follies*, Ziegfeld had to contend with another very funny (and not particularly glamorous) singing Jewish lady, Fanny Brice.

Also in 1910, Tucker returned to Broadway in the

nonmusical play *Lulu's Husbands,* and a year after that, headlined in her own productions, *Louisiana Lou* and *Merry May* (although apparently not on Broadway). In that same year, she began cutting cylinders for the Edison Company, and one of her very first was "Some of These Days," done in New York, shortly before she headed westward for an engagement in San Francisco. She beat Jolson to the punch record-wise, although he is also believed to have cut some unissued sides (apparently lost) for Edison later that year. Jolson flourished on discs throughout the teens, but Tucker didn't step into a studio again until the decade was almost over, in 1918. The early Edison recordings (1910–11) are the best documents of Tucker's early period, perhaps no longer working in blackface but a "coon-shouter" just the same. The 1911 Edison version of "Some of These Days" has her singing in more of a "Negro" dialect than any later recording. "Phoebe Jane" is entirely in the minstrel tradition of burnt-cork transformation, in which a Russian Jewish female sings from the viewpoint of an African American male.

Sophie Tucker's mature approach was a combination of a performing persona and a musical style—"The Last of the Red Hot Mamas"—that came into focus over the course of the teens and the end of the acoustic era in the early twenties. "When I started out, I had a distinctive style," she later wrote. "I never sang on the beat, but slightly after it." No longer confined to the minstrel tradition, she flourished in the years surrounding World War I. When she signed a new contract with Aeolian-Vocalion in 1918 the evolution of her sound was considerable: The early Edison cylinders are steeped in ragtime and minstrelsy, whereas her recordings of 1918 onward sound more like vaudeville and nightclubs.

Her first of four discs for Aeolian contains two songs that are fascinating footnotes to her career, specifically in that they show her learning what *not* to do—they're rare examples of Tucker stepping completely out of character and falling flat on her face. "Won't You Be a Dear, Dear Daddy to a 'Itta Bitta Doll' Like Me?" shows her rather coyly attempting to sing in baby talk—not exactly her forte. Nor is the language of mascochism: "I'm Glad My Daddy's in a Uniform" is a rather repulsive combination of female masochism and patriotism—the message is "It's okay that my man beats me up because he's fighting the Huns now." However, the next two titles are among the great gems of the Tucker canon. "Please Don't Take My Harem Away" depicts a Turkish sultan bargaining with his conquerors after having made the mistake of siding with the Germans rather than the British—it could be the big number in a period musical adaptation of *Lawrence of Arabia.* "Everybody Shimmies Now" shows Tucker getting hot and demonstrating the latest dance to the accompaniment of a group (billed as her "Five Kings of Syncopation") clearly patterned

after the Original Dixieland Jazz Band. (These four sides are apparently the rarest of all her recordings— Brad Kay was not able to locate them for the Super-batone set, although they were unearthed a few years later for the Archeophone CD.)

From 1918 to 1937, Tucker is in the recording studio fairly consistently. Unlike Jolson, however, she rarely appeared on Broadway. The legit theater, as they used to call it, was apparently too formal for her; Tucker is officially documented as being in only five Broadway musicals—*The Ziegfeld Follies of 1909,* the Shubert Brothers book show *Hello, Alexander* (1919), *Earl Carroll's Vanities of 1924,* Cole Porter's *Leave It to Me!* (1938–39), and *High Kickers* (1941–42). Not much for a fifty-plus-year career.

Hollywood was even less to her liking; she only starred in one film, the 1929 *Honky Tonk,* which cinemaphile Richard Barrios has identified as one of the post-Jolson rush of "Dueling Mammies," early talkies quickly built around famous, old-time vaudeville headliners like Harry Richman, Fanny Brice, Maurice Chevalier, and Ted Lewis. *Honky Tonk*'s plot foreshadowed the Frank Capra–Damon Runyon *Lady for a Day* (remade as *Pocketful of Miracles*), as well as the Doris Day picture *Lullaby of Broadway* (1951), in which a sheltered young girl who has been kept from her mother all her life has been led to believe that her old lady is a high-class society-type dame, see, but in reality she's either a lush, a tramp, a beggar, or, worse, a cabaret singer. Only the sound track of *Honky Tonk* survives, which no one seems to think is any great loss, since Tucker's singing and the five songs written for her by Jack Yellen and Milton Ager are the only things about the movie that were worth preserving.

Tucker flourished neither on Broadway nor in Hollywood, but in vaudeville and, later, nightclubs. She had to be the center of attention, and she had to be in a position to address the audience directly, with no other cast members in the way. She also had to have a degree of spontaneity, without being confined to a preset routine. Like Jolson's, her oeuvre was a potent combination of music and comedy, and also like Jolie's, her aesthetic was driven by issues of ethnicity and assimilation—although she was concerned with gender as well. Many of her recordings (and, presumably, her live performances) had some sort of Jewish reference, as in the 1931 "Make Yourself at Home," where she invites a prospective beau to come over for some good old kosher cooking. Likewise, in "I Don't Want to Get Thin," her accompanist challenges her to eat ham. In 1934 she recorded "Lord, You Made the Night Too Long," an ersatz religious song supposedly re-creating the lament of a poor Southern colored gentleman addressing de Lawd directly, and she makes it considerably more believable and touching by incorporating the authentic Hebrew prayer "Eli, Eli."

Even more of her recordings have Tucker jokingly describing herself as corpulent and unattractive, at once seductive and self-deprecating: "You gonna miss your big fat mama, some of these days." By the time she turned forty in 1924, Tucker was deliberately bucking the trends: The fashion for pretty girls in the Roaring Twenties was to be almost boyishly thin, like Colleen Moore, while the leading men were somewhat effeminate, like Charles Farrell or Buddy Rogers. It was the first era of gender blur. Yet in song after song, such as "It's a Pleasure" and "He's Tall, Dark and Handsome," Tucker tells us that she's a real woman in search of a real man. She was already setting herself up as somewhat anachronistic, which is how she remained for the next forty years. "Some of These Days" itself was the nexus of the Red Hot Mama style: It's at once a torch song and a threat—I'm not gone yet, but you'll be sorry when I am—and she all but shouts it so that there's no way her errant swain could fail to get her message.

Through her recordings of the twenties and thirties, Tucker combines humor and music in a way that's continually original. Some of her records are in a mostly talking, declamatory style, with a loose relation to the beat and very little regard for the notes. She learned early on that she could make a song either more dramatic or more comedic by delivering it with as minimal a melody as possible. When she does sing, it's in a deep, chesty contralto—almost a female baritone.

It would be a stretch to say that Tucker was a jazz singer in the mid-twenties any more than she was a true ragtime singer in the early teens, but there was an undeniable rhythmic momentum to her music that allowed her to fit in very well with jazz musicians, as when, in 1927, an all-star unit, under the direction of trombonist Miff Mole, and featuring the pioneering guitarist Eddie Lang, backed her on two exceptional titles: "After You've Gone" and "I Ain't Got Nobody." Tucker was keen to capitalize on her rhythmic compatibility with the new music, billing herself as "the Inimitable Queen of Syncopation" and later "the Queen of Jazz," and titling her band the Five Kings of Syncopation. The Five Kings (for a time, future bandleader Gus Arnheim was one) were eventually succeeded by Theodore Shapiro, who stayed with her for the lion's share of her long career, as accompanist, musical director, and virtual alter ego: Their musical-comic banter back and forth on "He's Tall, Dark and Handsome" is, if anything, even funnier and hipper than it must have seemed in 1928.

At the start of the electric period, in 1925, Tucker was maintaining her popularity at a time when Jolson (even though he was about to launch the talking picture medium) was beginning to seem irrelevant. There were other kinds of female singers by then, as Tucker observes in "I'm the Last of the Hot Red Mamas," a song written for her by Jack Yellen and Milton Ager to sing in *Honky Tonk*. She explains that she's not at all threatened by "debs, flappers, and

baby vamps," and even "collegiate charmers," asking us, "What do they know? / Come get your hot stuff / From this volcano." Where Ruth Etting and Annette Hanshaw were cool, Tucker was still red hot.

She first referred to herself as a "Red Hot Mama" when she sang a song with that title in 1923–24; according to the Eckers, she utilized props, lights, and stagecraft (paper flames and a red spotlight) to make it appear as if she were actually on fire as she sang. In 1928, she referred to herself as a "flaming mama" in the otherwise undistinguished song "Conversational Man." Finally, in 1928–29, Jack Yellen's "I'm the Last of the Red Hot Mamas" became one of the key numbers in her act, and, long after she stopped doing the song, the catchphrase remained.

Tucker had actually been, as I've pointed out, the first of the red hot mamas, but was now milking the benefits of being the last. She made fun of the microphonic subtlety of other, younger singers of the era, turning her anachronistic status into an asset, much as she had already done earlier with her body type. She had never been the object of seduction, and when she sang of herself as a participant in a love affair, it was always with a considerable amount of irony. She was hardly a singing femme fatale or even a victim of a dramatic heartbreak; she was more like a musical Texas Guinan, a Jazz Age hostess who was going to work every ounce of her oversized frame until you admitted, like it or not, that you were having the time of your life. And it paid off: By being an object of fun rather than of *l'amour*, she kept going for generations beyond all those flappers and vamps who were out of business by the swing era. Once she established herself as the ultimate red hot mama and, in a sense, built her career on the concept of being out-of-date, a holdover from an earlier era (kind of a preemptive strike), time proved powerless to stop her.

At her very best, as on the four sessions she did in 1927 (one of which was the classic date with Miff Mole), Tucker is one of the great singers of her era, in a class with Ethel Waters and Bessie Smith and, yes, Jolson. Indeed, Brad Kay was far from the first to describe Tucker as the "Jewish Bessie Smith." And back in the day, singer-actress Hattie McDaniel was billed as "the Colored Sophie Tucker." In Forbidden City, an Asian-themed nightclub in San Francisco's Chinatown, one entertainer billed herself as "the Chinese Sophie Tucker."

Like the Empress of the Blues, Tucker, who was certainly the empress of something, is a font of knowledge for future generations. While she was a part of the past, she also anticipated the women's rights movement: No less than the music of Smith and the classic blues singers of the twenties, Tucker's tunes take a hard-line I-ain't-gonna-play-no-second-fiddle stance. From "Some of These Days" onward, at least every other Sophie song seems to be warning her "Papa" (and not in the paternal sense) that he better watch his step because

Mama goes where Papa goes and he's got to see his Mama every night or he can't see his Mama at all. When Tucker sings "I Ain't Takin' Orders from No One," she becomes a role model for affirmative women.

Into the twenties, Tucker, like Jolson and Eddie Cantor, continued to sing traditional mammy songs. These were semicomic, semisentimental numbers that were frequently self-parodying even when they were new, about going home to the Sunny South and the dear and colorful characters who inhabit it. Typical are "Pick Me Up and Lay Me Down in Dear Old Dixie" (1922), in which she entreats listeners to "keep those darkies singing till I get back," and the later "There's a Cradle in Caroline," "Away down South in Heaven," and "Stay Out of the South" (both 1928).

One of the cleverest darkie-dialect songs is "Seven or Eleven," written by Lew Brown and Walter Donaldson, which was officially introduced by Cantor, although he didn't record it. Although this 1923 song draws on traditional stereotypes, which were already passé if not yet politically incorrect, it shows that there was life in the burnt-cork tradition yet: Tucker sings of one Rufus Johnson, a Southerner trapped up North, challenging Pullman porters to a series of crap games in order to win enough money to buy a ticket on the midnight choo-choo so's he can see his Mammy in Alabammy. Tucker sharply accents the staccato rhythms of the title, "seven—or—eleven," with pauses ("cutoffs," as Sinatra fans would later call them) between the words, in a way that anticipates swing. The accompaniment features the first superstar of the saxophone, the pioneer virtuoso Rudy Wiedoeft, as well as a creative drummer who approximates the sound of rolling dice with his trap kit. (In a sense, this was the *Wheel of Fortune* of its day.)

As the twenties progressed, Tucker also sang a fair amount of what would come to be known as torch songs, of the sort that Ruth Etting, Lee Morse, Frances Williams, and other torchy tessies sang, most notably "What Good Am I Without You?" (1931). She also sometimes sings straightforward songs about the object of her affection, such as "That Man of My Dreams" and the best early version of the Gershwin classic "The Man I Love." She's not at all bad at this sort of thing, but it really wasn't her bag: Rather than telling us that she's nothing without her man, in the torch tradition, she was better, as we've seen, at instilling these songs of love and loss with an implied threat, "Some of these days . . . You'll miss my huggin', you'll miss my kissin'," while in "After You've Gone" the message is similar: "You'll feel blue, you'll feel sad / You'll miss the dearest pal you ever had." These were not torch tunes so much as warning shots. In songs like "I Know That My Baby Is Cheating on Me" and "If Your Kisses Can't Hold the Man You Love," she becomes a one-woman support group for all those other ladies out there whose significant others are doing them dirt. A flapper, a

vamp, or a sweet young thing would cry herself to sleep, but not Soph; she advises that what's good for the gander is good for the goose. In "If Your Kisses Can't Hold the Man You Love," Tucker tells "neglected wives" not to worry, because "that's what God made sailors for."

The first thing one notices about Tucker's specialty songs is that, having invented herself as a Red Hot Mama, she's determined to corner the market on songs that confuse lovers and parents. Somehow, this seems consistent with a woman who had such a dysfunctional childhood and, by her account, a strained relationship with her own man and dad. "I wasn't a normal child. I didn't play. I had no playmates. I had nothing. I was four, five, six, and I had to make my own cup of coffee." Nearly every song she sang was Daddy this and Mama that, with a few babies thrown in for good mesasure: "Aggravatin' Papa," "Papa, Better Watch Your Step," "Red Hot Mama," "Mama Goes Where Papa Goes," "Nobody Knows What a Red-Headed Mama Can Do," "My Yiddishe Momme," "I'm the Last of the Red Hot Mamas," "Stay at Home Papa," and "I Know That My Baby Is Cheating on Me."

Tucker's relationship with her parents resulted in what is certainly her most ambitious and possibly her single greatest record, the 1928 "My Yiddishe Momme." Jack Yellen, who was the closest thing Tucker had to an on-call lyricist, wrote it for her with Lew Pollack, a composer best known for old-fashioned melodies, most famously the girl's-name-waltzes "Dianne" and "Charmaine." The piece also captures Tucker both at her most Jolsonesque and, somehow, also at her most Bessie Smith–like, delineating the words and music in dramatically slow, measured steps, using less to say more, putting it down with little embellishment in order to project as much dramatic power as possible. "My Yiddishe Momme" was, in a sense, the "Soliloquy" (from *Carousel*) of its day, or Tucker's equivalent of Smith's "Empty Bed Blues (Parts One and Two)," and like those two extended opuses, it occupied both sides of a 78 rpm single, the first in English, the second in Yiddish. (In 1924, Tucker had recorded the American pop song "Mama Goes Where Papa Goes" in Yiddish.) The verse, which sets up the narrative, tells of an assimilated immigrant, seated "in the comfort of my cozy chair," reflecting on her childhood "in a humble tenement, three flights in the rear" and reminiscing about "the dear little lady so old and grey." In Tucker's tonsils, "Yiddishe Momme" is one of the great songs of the American experience. Apart from the title, the English language lyric is not even specifically Jewish. There are no references to rabbis or *afikomen* or matzoh balls or seders. It could just as easily be "That Irish Mudder o' Mine" or "Italiana Mama Mia!" The record isn't like two takes of the same material in two different languages: Side two is actually quite different from side one. It begins with a spoken word speech in Yiddish, reviewing the material of side one in greater detail.

"Yiddishe Momme" marks Tucker's grandest foray into drama—and there's little that's "melo" about it. Normally, her specialty was comedy, with herself as the central figure in a sequence of comic scenarios. In Tucker's comedy, she shows a self-deprecating side that represents her major conceptual departure from Jolson. The World's Greatest Entertainer had a sense of humor about himself, but he would never go so far as to use his physical and mental shortcomings as running jokes. In this aspect, Tucker had less in common with Jolson and more with Jimmy Durante (who was almost a baby compared to Tucker, born a whole nine years later). Durante proclaimed he was the world's greatest lover, a "real piano player," and Jimmy the well-dressed man even at the same time he made jokes about how ugly he was and how-big-is-my-*schnozzola*. Apparently, one was supposed to receive and believe both sets of signals.

Tucker set up the same paradox: In song after song, too many to list, she tells us she was a red hot mama, that nobody could warm up a man like she could, that Eskimos leave her hut in their BVDs, that all the married men who chased after her had skinny wives back home. Yet at the same time, the underlying message is that she's insecure about being an overweight, none too attractive immigrant Jewish girl from a poor family. Tucker, like Durante, has appearance issues, and her girth was her equivalent of Durante's oversize proboscis. Eventually, in the sixties, Durante got all poignant if not quite sentimental in the albums of romantic standards he recorded as a sexagenarian. But when Tucker added issues of gender and ethnicity to her comedy mix, she imbued her comic songs with a sad undercurrent that gives them deeper dimension.

When she sings "I Don't Want to Get Thin," she brags about vanquishing slender mamas "who can fill my shoes but not my pajamas," but you get a feeling her braggadocio is a defense mechanism, putting on a brave front to hide her insecurity. In " 'Cause I Feel Low Down" (1928) she sings "I guess he feels I'm getting older," and while singing of "That Man of My Dreams," she mentions that this man "loves a lot of form." At other times, she'll catch us off guard and let it be known that most of her beaux are "Spaniards or Greeks" ("those darn Greeks" appear in a number of songs, like "He's Tall, Dark and Handsome"). These references, to the shape of her frame or the kosher status of her kitchen, are a way of making a Tin Pan Alley song, with its idealized depiction of love and life, more real, more believable, more down-to-earth.

They also give special poignancy to Tucker's exotica; the farther she ventured from home, the more resolutely herself she became. In 1922, Tucker made the first of many visits to London, and she would spend almost as much time in the theaters and recording studios of England as those of the United States. She appeared in several prominent West End productions, including the 1922 *Round in Fifty* (what the title refers to is obscure) and, more ambitiously, *Follow a Star*, a full-scale musical production written for her by famous songsmith Vivian Ellis in 1930. She also appeared in a British film, the 1934 *Gay Love*.

Most of her records from 1925 to 1936 were made in the U.K. Beginning with the 1923 "Old King Tut," Tucker began regularly singing about other times and climes. Even funnier was the 1931 "Egyptian Ella," in which she sings of an overweight dancer who ventures to the river Nile, where she becomes a local legend because "they like 'em plenty that way out there."

Tucker also took us to Hawaii via "Hula Lou" (1924) and "Makin' Wickey Wackey in Waikiki" (1931), and trifles with Parisian *lovairs* in "Fifty Million Frenchmen" (1927) and "I Never Can Think of the Words" (1930). She takes us to the land of Latin lovers in "On a Balcony in Spain" (1931) and the even more amazing "There's Something Spanish in My Eyes" (1928). These could be viewed as attempts at using the concept of travel as a means to escape herself, yet, as she is well aware, she is in fact reinforcing what she actually is. She never seems more like her zaftig, Jewish American self than when she's singing a special material line like:

> You know that my *pash* is
> For men with mustaches.
> How Sophie just crashes
> When she loves you.

She sings "A Balcony in Spain" convincingly straight until the last 8 bars. At this point, she is informed that her so-called Spanish lothario is, in reality, "a waiter from Alsace-Lorraine," and, as if on cue, her obese frame collapses that precarious Spanish balcony, thereby flattening her imposter of a Latin lover.

Apart from making her seem more American, the British sessions made her appear more down-to-earth, especially in their use of colorfully earthy language. Noting the frequent occurrence of the words "hell" and "damn" in her British sides (they're heard within a line of each other in "I Never Can Think of the Words"), historian Anthony Slide observes, "It is doubtful that most American [labels] would have risked marketing these songs, particularly one which hints at rhyming a word never used in polite society with the singer's last name." (Pucker? Sucker? Mother Trucker?) In England, she also recorded a typically aggressive treatment of Duke Ellington's "Sophisticated Lady," which she sings in the first person and includes a detour through "I've Got to Sing a Torch Song" in the process. Likewise, her 1934 London recording of "Louisville Lady" uses "St. Louis Blues" as a countermelody.

Slide also informs us that Tucker's popularity did not extend beyond the English-speaking world: When she sang "Yiddishe Momme" on a Paris stage, she was hissed off by local anti-Semites—the same

French fascists who would be collaborating with the Nazis a few years hence. In 1936, Tucker recorded one of the first pop songs of Israel, "My People," an early anthem of Semitic solidarity that still seems moving seventy-odd years later. When the singer was informed that her records were banned in Nazi Germany, she immediately addressed the problem by protesting it in a personal letter to Herr Hitler. No response was forthcoming.

Sophie Tucker wound up the international phase of her career with a marvelous session in 1936, which includes "My People" as well as "When a Lady Meets a Gentleman Down South" (somehow she makes it sound dirty), which, if not exactly swinging, comes close enough. Before and then after returning to America, she recorded two very up-to-date songs that might have seemed out of character, "You'll Have to Swing It," in which she addresses the beleaguered maestro as "Mr. Toscanini," and "The Lady Is a Tramp," both of which she puts over convincingly.

Tucker lived long enough to pass her torch on to other divas, such as Judy Garland in the MGM movies *Broadway Melody of 1937* and *Thoroughbreds Don't Cry* (1938) and Mary Martin in Broadway's *Leave It to Me!*, in all of which she played mother figures. She was beloved of both American and British troops during the Second World War, and made guest appearances as "Herself" in two wartime musicals, *Follow the Boys* (1944) and *Sensations of 1945,* in which she was co-billed with more modern entertainers such as Cab Calloway and Louis Jordan. After the war, her career actually expanded. She had never done much work on the radio, but in the postwar era she became a perennial presence on television, generally on variety shows like *Ed Sullivan* and *The Hollywood Palace.*

Tucker continued to record in her sixties and seventies, most successfully on a late forties date in which she does a marvelous "Louisville Lou" and her umpteenth version of "Some of These Days." She sounds as red hot and relevant as ever, and the jazz accompaniment—including such forty-something youngsters as Jack Teagarden and Bud Freeman—is particularly excellent. Certainly no one, least of all Tucker, sounds the least bit anachronistic.

She continued to appear regularly in England, making her last appearance there a year before she died, at the age of eighty-two, in 1966. By the fifties, Tucker had made an art out of self-referentiality, reliving her past on LPs, TV shows, and venues like the Copacabana (where she infamously dissed the young Mel Tormé) and Las Vegas. She supplemented her income by selling autographed copies of her book and records at club appearances; it's been speculated that she signed so many that copies of these are actually worth more on eBay if they're *not* autographed.

Writing her memoir was one of the many ways Tucker constantly fine-tuned her own mythology; another was in the song "Some of These Days" itself. In 1911, she sang it with the original two verses, an elaborate narrative in which a husband (presumably black) has to leave his wife (presumably temporarily) and she warns him that he'll miss her "some of these days." The tables are turned when the wife tells the husband that now it's her turn to go away for a while; now he's the one flipping out and begging her not to leave. She recorded the song again, in 1926, for her second electrical recording session—this time she doesn't sing the verse at all, but the band (Ted Lewis's, no less) plays it instrumentally. She tackled it again less than a year later, in a performance that wasn't issued for another forty years or so; this one is truly remarkable in that there's a new verse (by Tucker and Ted Shapiro) in which she sings of "being a young Connecticut lass" with "lots of nerve but no class." She has turned the song into her own autobiography, quite literally, and fixed it so that it's impossible to think of "Some of These Days" without thinking of Sophie Tucker.

Similarly, Tucker wove autobiographical rings of personal lore around the origin of the song. She consistently told an elaborate story about how her black maid, Mollie Elkins, pressured her to listen to a song by a friend named Shelton Brooks. When Sophie kept putting off the audition, Elkins read her the riot act: "'Now see here, young lady,' said she, hands on hips, 'since when are you so important that you can't hear a song by a colored writer?'" It's a colorful story, but one thoroughly debunked by the Eckers, who establish that Tucker first heard "Some of These Days" courtesy of the song's publisher. Now this is a comparatively pedestrian account—Tucker's is much more entertaining—but, alas, it's probably the truth. Because of Tucker, Brooks (who later wrote another standard in "The Darktown Strutters Ball") was among the very first African American songwriters to have a song go mainstream. It became one of the perennials of American music; the Tom Lord's discography lists 566 versions in the jazz vein alone.

As good as her later remakes of the song are, the original 1911 performance remains remarkable, and not just for its time. The setting and basic idea of the song—you won't leave me if you know what's good for you—use the vocabulary of minstrel shows and a white conception of black life. Tucker employs syncopation and other rhythmic devices associated with African American music, but at the same time she bends notes—as in the way she stretches that all-important word "days"—and throws in moans and cries out of the Jewish cantorial tradition. "Some of These Days" is one of the most dramatic illustrations of an Afro-Semitic stylistic alliance, and, at the same time, it's a defiant and empowering feminist anthem from a hundred years ago.

V

Sarah Vaughan (1924–1990)

The first time you hear Sarah Vaughan, you're immediately blown away by the unending lushness of the voice, the deep, rich beauty of the tone, the vocal agility and range that allowed her to hit a note from all directions, to swoop up to it or scoop down to it, that perfect intonation that assured that no matter where she came at it from, she always hit it square on like a champion archer. The standard initial reaction is to compare Sarah Vaughan to a great classical diva—she had technique on that level. She never quite sang *Madama Butterfly,* but on the many occasions when she performed her career perennial, the Tin Pan–Puccini "Poor Butterfly," she imbued it with nothing less than operatic grandeur.

Yet for all the chops she evidenced, Sarah Vaughan was hardly one of your more serious classicists. Indeed, onstage she had one of the most kittenish senses of humor imaginable. Like colleague Ella Fitzgerald, she had a coy demeanor that reminded fans of a little girl. Who could forget her patented rap in which, after introducing the members of her trio to the crowd, she would finish by declaring, "In case you don't know who I am—and maybe there are some of you who don't know who I am—my name is Della Reese" or, later, "Carmen McRae." Can you imagine Billie Holiday introducing herself as Maxine Sullivan? Not for all the white gardenias in the New York Botanical Garden.

Vaughan's deliberately whimsical moments endure in my memory banks just as much as her majestic ones: The first time I saw her, which was at a concert hall in her native Newark in the early eighties, she was about to go into "Moonlight in Vermont" when she stopped and addressed the audience directly, "I know the first word—'pennies'! You can't sing a song unless you know the first word." Then there's her 1954 "They Can't Take That Away from Me" (on *Swingin' Easy*) when she zings us with a frighteningly flat note on "the way you sing off-key" and interjects a few musical speed bumps into "on the bumpy road to love."

That impish capacity for fun was hardly confined to pure comedy: Her approach to a song was infinitely playful. She could scat and improvise (her knowledge of music and her ability to play the piano assured that), but it was even more rewarding when she took a familiar melody and stood it on its ear, letting you hear it every which way. Indeed, Vaughan's two nicknames indicate the range of her gifts: To those who worshipped her remarkable multioctave chops above all, she was known as "the Divine One" (a description coined by deejay and TV personality Dave Garroway). To the fans who prized her jazzy coquetry, she was simply "Sassy" (a nickname applied to her by pianist John Malachi). At her best she was both things at once, Sassy and Divine.

She was born Sarah Lois Vaughan in Newark, New Jersey, on March 27, 1924. She was making music from a very early age, first singing in her church choir, then studying piano, then playing organ in church, then singing around town with the New Orleans–style trumpeter and singer Jabbo Smith. At eighteen, she won the weekly amateur contest at Harlem's fabled Apollo Theater, an event that was attended by her future mentor and musical partner Billy Eckstine. Eckstine, who was then the star vocalist with piano master Earl "Fatha" Hines, recommended her to his boss, and Hines not only hired her as female singer for his big band, he made her his second pianist. (Like Carmen McRae, Vaughan was a professional-level keyboardist, and could have accompanied herself throughout her career had she chosen to. Her finest recorded moment as a pianist, or rather, a self-accompanied vocalist, occurs on "The Nearness of You" from the 1973 *Live in Japan*.)

When Eckstine put together his own famous big band of the mid-forties, which featured Dizzy Gillespie as musical director and Charlie Parker in the saxophone section, he brought Vaughan as well. Thus she was in an ideal place musically at the point when she graduated from the big bands to being a star singer in her own right: She was already immersed in the basic vocabulary of jazz techniques, but now she was in on the ground floor of the bebop revolution. Indeed, Vaughan sings on the very first recording of the bop milestone "A Night in Tunisia" (which, in its love song incarnation, was known as "Interlude") as part of a Gillespie-Parker group. Meanwhile, her new manager and first husband, George Treadwell, was pushing her in other directions. Treadwell liked to boast that he remade Vaughan's entire image, glamorized her, and made her marketable to major record labels, radio, and later television. No one—not even the vainglorious Treadwell—took credit for Vaughan's musicianship. However, Treadwell probably does deserve acknowledgment for making her more salable and showbiz-savvy, prompting her, for instance, to fix that considerable gap in her front teeth that would have kept her off magazine covers for life.

Being in the Hines and Eckstine bands clinched the role that Vaughan seemed destined to fill: leading female vocalist among the first generation of bebop pioneers (next on board was Ella Fitzgerald). Like Parker and Gillespie, Vaughan was championed and recorded by bop advocate Leonard Feather, and first appears on wax working for a variety of independent and regional labels (Continental, Guild, Crown). She then enjoyed a longer relationship with Musicraft, an art-minded little label attempting to get into the big pop stakes (Artie Shaw and Duke Ellington were also under contract) from 1946 to 1949.

Vaughan is sometimes described as a jazz singer who went pop, which ain't necessarily so. She is a product of the late big band era and, like her fellow ex-band canaries, kept pop and jazz strains going throughout her whole career. The emergence of bebop is not a point of demarcation for the two concepts in Vaughan's music. In fact, particularly in the Musicraft period, she sang pop songs, both classic and contemporary, with backing that includes some of the bebop harmonic language—much as the big dance bands of the time were already doing (not just Kenton, Herman, and Gillespie, but Barnet and even Beneke). One of the few notable occasions when her accompaniment is without a modern jazz influence is a 1947 date on which she sings two early ballads and two spirituals, "Sometimes I Feel Like a Motherless Child" and "The Lord's Prayer"—the idea was to suggest reverence by having her sing in front of the plainest, most neutral string background; she sounds remarkably reverent here, far more Divine than Sassy.

It's assumed that none of the original masters exist for her early 1944–49 recordings, and what's worse, the discs themselves were generally pressed on poor material and sound awful. What's needed is for an audio restoration specialist to collate the cleanest copies that can be found into a comprehensive package, much as historian Robert Sunenblick did for Charles Mingus's earliest, and even rarer, 78 recordings. Two European labels have done the most through job so far of assembling Vaughan's earliest work, Classics and Proper. The sound is about the same (not as good as it ought to be) on both, but the Proper effort, which collates virtually all her material up through 1950 into a four-disc box, is more convenient, easier to find (and cheaper), and includes considerably nicer packaging (a forty-four-page booklet).

The best-sounding document of the period is a remarkable concert recorded at Town Hall in 1947, in which Vaughan shares the stage with Lester Young. She sings nine standards here (all old-timers, excepting "Time After Time"), all songs otherwise recorded for Musicraft but in looser, freer, and better-sounding versions, climaxing in "I Cried for You," with Young. She's considerably friskier here, performing for an audience of New York jazz fans, than in any of her contemporary recordings, stretching every melody line as far as it can be stretched, and generally dwelling in the upper reaches of the chords. I agree that she would later refine this habit to the point where it was more easily digestible, but I disagree with those who accuse her of doing it to excess, especially here in the early part of her career. As one Dale Harrison griped in the *Chicago Sun*, "Vaughan's tempo drags unconscionably [and] the boys in the rhythm section have time to yawn between every beat." He wound up by denouncing her as "annoying and amateurish." This would prove to be a minority opinion.

Vaughan's first decade or so is highlighted by collaborations with superstar bebop trumpeters, of both the long-lived and well-documented variety (Dizzy Gillespie, Miles Davis) and a couple with short careers and small discographies (Freddie Webster, Clifford Brown). Gillespie worked with her on the *Interlude* session and with the Hines and Eckstine bands, and Freddie Webster appears on some of the Musicraft sides conducted by Tadd Dameron (whose "If You Could See Me Now" she made into a modern jazz standard). Miles Davis is prominently featured with Vaughan on a wonderful pair of sessions from May 1950, released with Treadwell's name as leader. This would mark the most notable occasion when that already famous trumpeter, who never played second fiddle, backed a singer. Columbia originally issued the eight titles as a 10" LP called *Sarah Vaughan* at the time, and then used them as the heart of the 12" set *Sarah Vaughan in Hi Fi.*

Somebody at Musicraft was picking hip songs for Vaughan—in addition to familiar jazz standards ("Don't Blame Me" and "I Can't Get Started")—and somebody was also creaming off some of the very best contemporary tunes from films ("Time After Time," "It's You or No One," and "It's Magic," the last a good seller for her) and shows ("Blue Grass" from *Inside U.S.A.* and "Gentleman Friend"). The label could have used a few more lowest common denominator hits, as by the time of the 1948 recording ban, Musicraft was going bankrupt (her last two titles for the label, the hit "Nature Boy" and "I'm Glad There Is You," were done with a large, nonunion a cappella choir). Still, there was rancor between the Treadwells and Musicraft, and by 1949 the two sides were suing each other. Treadwell moved Vaughan to Columbia Records. This was the big time, as far as any "colored" singer had thus far ascended, and a sign that the powers that be had faith that Vaughan could appeal to a pop as well as a jazz audience, to whites as well as blacks.

Which was both true and not true. Columbia, principally the new pop A&R man Mitch Miller, gradually realized that Vaughan, like Fitzgerald, was simply not a singles artist, although she lasted a full five years and some eighty masters on the label. The jazz and standards that she cut in the period, particularly the May 1950 titles with Miles Davis, have been almost continually in print, whereas the attempts to crack the jukeboxes have made themselves rather scarce. The pop hits that she would achieve in the fifties are notable for their utter lack of distinction. The songs are no better or worse than, say, Rosemary Clooney's or Doris Day's Columbia chart-topping singles; Vaughan's hits like "Make Yourself Comfortable" and "Broken-Hearted Melody" seem completely generic. These particular tunes, with the right amount of promotion, were perhaps destined to get to a certain place on the charts no matter who was singing them, but it's impossible to imagine anybody having any kind of emotional attachment to most of Vaughan's singles.

Mitch Miller even produced a single of Vaughan doing an ersatz ethnic number, "De Gas Pipe She

Leakin', Joe," which enabled her to do a funny accent that anticipated Clooney's Italian-Americanisms on "Come on-a My House" and "Mambo Italiano" and sing a rather violent calypso in the same vein as the Fitzgerald and Louis Jordan hit "Stone Cold Dead in the Market." In "De Gas Pipe" the theme is suicide rather than murder, but still nobody bought it. Her most experimental record of the period was "Pinky," Alfred Newman's lyricless movie theme (from a drama about race relations that was rather daring at the time). Singing wordlessly in front of a full studio orchestra, Vaughan articulates the difference between jazz-based scat and classical-style vocalese. She could have recorded many more of these wordless pieces and still not have exhausted all the possibilities of the form.

In fact, there is plenty of first-rate material from the 1949–53 period; Sony or Mosaic would do well to consider a definitive four- or five-CD box of Vaughan's complete Columbia recordings. Two tracks that beg to be widely heard are her 1940 spirituals, "Ave Maria" and "A City Called Heaven," which may have been inspired by her rendition a year earlier of the egregiously ersatz-religious song "That Lucky Old Sun," which somehow did make it onto the charts. (File under: "Cover Versions of Pretentious Hits of Bombastic Male Singers by Superior Female Singers," alongside Peggy Lee's even bigger-selling "Ghost Riders in the Sky.") This period gave us the classic recordings of Sassy standards like "The Nearness of You," "My Reverie," "Deep Purple," and one of the very best of her up-tempo big band features, Juan Tizol's "Perdido"—Fitzgerald and other jazz singers have done it memorably, but it still seems like Vaughan's private property. (Her best-ever Ellington ballad was the more obscure "Tonight I Shall Sleep," from 1949.) The May 1950 sessions are a marvel: Vaughan is every bit as frisky as on the Town Hall concert of two and a half years earlier, but her playfulness now seems more at the service of the song—still uncompromising, but less likely to offend musical conservatives.

In 1954, she switched labels again, this time to the aggressive Mercury Records, for six very productive years. Three decades later, at the end of the LP era and near the end of Vaughan's life, the Japanese producer-scholar Kiyoshi Koyama collated all of her Mercury recordings of 1954–59 (and then of 1963–66) into four box sets that reach a total of bearlike (or Bear Family–like) proportions of twenty-three discs. By any reasonable standard, this is a major blessing. We want every note Vaughan ever sang any way we can get them, even if the strictly chronological programming (session by session) forces us to act as editors and reassemble the tracks (on our iPods, anyhow) back into their original album sequences.

As early as the dawn of the fifties at Columbia, it was clear that there were at least two species of Sarah Vaughan record: jazz (as in the May 1950 sessions with Davis) and pop (the bulk of everything else she did on Columbia). In the mid-fifties, the album for-

mat was still viewed as a minority interest that happened to dovetail with the jazz market, thus Vaughan's first two Mercury albums (both from 1954) were hard-core jazz small group sets, *Swingin' Easy*, which remains the best document of her working trio with John Malachi, and *Sarah Vaughan*, which co-starred her with Clifford Brown, the brightest trumpet star of his generation. The Vaughan-Brown album, stage-managed by expert arranger Ernie Wilkins, is the more formal of the two, even though it gives a fittingly generous amount of solo space to Brown, Herbie Mann, and Paul Quinichette. The set even seems carefully organized on "Lullaby of Birdland," with its famous vamp intro and a marvelous trade of fours between the star singer and the horns of Brown and Herbie Mann (if flute can be considered a horn).

Swingin' Easy, by contrast, is so loose it seems as though Vaughan and Malachi and trio showed up without any previous preparation and just ran through seven standards and a scat blues. Casual is the word, even more so perhaps than Vaughan's club appearances at the time probably were. In 1957, she added four more songs (by now Jimmy Jones was on piano) to expand the collection to a total of twelve for a 12" LP, including an appealingly scatty "All of Me." In fact, although she would do two live albums in this period, *Sarah Vaughan at Mr. Kelly's* (1957) and *Sarah Vaughan After Hours Live at the London House* (1958)—Mercury was based in Chicago—nothing was as relaxed and informal as the well-titled *Swingin' Easy*.

In the fifties, Vaughan would regularly record purely jazz projects, including some of her sessions with larger ensembles, like *Sarah Vaughan in the Land of Hi-Fi* (1955), in which Wilkins gets to write for a full-sized big band. A lot of her jazz work over the next ten years would be very Basiecentric: there were the two albums with Wilkins, *Sarah Vaughan with Clifford Brown* and *In the Land of Hi-Fi*, recorded before and after, respectively, Wilkins wrote the most popular vocal chart of the era for Basie and Joe Williams, "Ev'ry Day I Have the Blues." A full-fledged Vaughan-Basie collaboration never materialized in the fifties because the Count was under contract to other labels (only Sinatra could break label affiliations, and that was years later). She was already appearing regularly with Basie on package tours, and several live location recordings of them together would eventually be released (Carnegie Hall and Birdland, 1954; Topeka, Kansas, 1955; Madison Square Garden, 1960). In 1958, there were two further Basiecentric offerings, *Live at the London House,* which featured four Basieites dropping in with Vaughan and her trio in Chicago (Basie was at the Holiday Ballroom at the time), and *No Count Sarah*, which featured the full band without its contractually obligated leader (similar to recordings made at the time by Nat Cole and Sammy Davis). In this case, the *No Count* title indicated that Basie himself wasn't actually at the piano, the usual circumstance when his band made an album backing a star singer.

By this point, Vaughan was mostly recording trivial novelties for singles ("The Bashful Matador"), some of which were actually hits. With friend Ella Fitzgerald, there was almost never any difference worth mentioning between her so-called pop and jazz projects. With Vaughan, there was a distinctly camp element to such chart hits as "Make Yourself Comfortable," "The Banana Boat Song," "Hot and Cold Running Tears," and "Broken-Hearted Melody." For some reason, Vaughan—unlike Sinatra or Cole—never seems to have landed a hit with any halfway decent song. "I hated 'Broken-Hearted Melody,'" she once said, "but it was the biggest thing I ever had." Yet it can't be said that the camp factor compromises the jazz value of her work. If she was to get through "The Bashful Matador" at all, the sassy side had to assert itself.

Like an amoeba, the music world continued to subdivide. By the end of the decade, not only was Vaughan making jazz albums and pop albums that were very different from each other, but now the pop world itself had split in two: high-road standards like her Broadway-oriented projects and increasingly inane singles like "Spin Little Bottle" and "Padre." Thus, by the end of the Mercury period, there were three kinds of Sarah Vaughan product: jazz albums, like *Swingin' Easy* and the two Ernie Wilkins and the two live albums; generally forgettable pop singles; and quality standards albums, most notably *Sassy, Sarah Vaughan Sings Broadway; Great Songs from Hit Shows; Sarah Vaughan Sings George Gershwin* (two LPs each); and *Sarah Vaughan and Billy Eckstine Sing the Best of Irving Berlin*.

The musical director for all four of these projects—a total of six LPs—was Hal (full name Harold) Mooney. Mooney's writing, unlike that of Ernie Wilkins, was not a jazz ingredient into itself, despite having come to prominence with Jimmy Dorsey's orchestra and his long collaboration with one of the greatest jazz singers of all time. He was, however, an excellent, straight-down-the-middle pop arranger, and he did a superb job in Vaughan's mid-fifties excursions into the Great American Songbook. His work is not, unlike that of colleagues Nelson Riddle or Billy May, the kind that stands out or that you actually notice behind a singer, but he gives both Vaughan and the tunes everything they need, writes with a light, deft touch—rarely if ever overdoing anything—and knows enough to stay out of their way. Here Vaughan's voice is undeniably a jazz instrument, while the occasionally slightly stiff charts are Broadway-cum-pop with something sort of classical grandish. The various elements are never in conflict, but blend together magnificently.

Sarah Vaughan Sings Broadway represents her finest work in this area. Every note is a sparkling gem and each track is a velvet cushion that sets her chops off perfectly. I can't imagine another arranger doing a better job, and I don't blame Polygram for, years later, extracting all the Rodgers and Hart tunes and putting them into an album of their own.

The Broadway album and its Rodgers and Hart spinoff represent the height of Vaughan and Mooney's collaboration; surprisingly, for the *Gershwin* collection, the two apparently couldn't resist the temptation to increase the heaviness quotient, and this set could use more of the light touch they brought to *Broadway*—it's still terrific, though, for the combination of Vaughan and Gershwin could hardly be anything but. *The Best of Irving Berlin* is a sleeper favorite that united Vaughan and Eckstine for their first duets since they cut four sides together for MGM in 1949. The mode is more pop than bop, but the two, with Mooney's support, get into some interesting melodic and harmonic variations, as on "Isn't This a Lovely Day?" and especially on "I've Got My Love to Keep Me Warm." At the same sessions, they also turned out a hit (non-Berlin) single, "Passing Strangers," which like much of the Vaughan-Mooney work somehow seems hip and corny at the same time, very melodramatic but musically aware. If Nelson Eddy and Jeanette MacDonald ever played Birdland, this is what they would sing.

In 1960, Vaughan (along with fellow Mercurians Eckstine and Dinah Washington) started the new decade with a fresh label affiliation by switching to Roulette, run by the world's foremost giant Jewish gangster, Morris Levy. To a certain extent, the careers of Vaughan and Washington, who were both born in 1924, parallel each other at this point, in that during the final seasons of their long affiliations with Mercury they recorded a fair amount of junk with the tacky orchestrator Belford Hendricks—stuff that you might diplomatically call low-road pop. In switching to Roulette, things could only get better.

Mosaic's box *The Complete Roulette Sarah Vaughan Studio Sessions* was released in 2003, and the eight-CD package makes concrete what was already apparent: Her output in the years 1960–63 was massive both in quality and quantity. In these four years, Roulette released thirteen full-length LPs by Vaughan, as well as enough singles to fill at least another three discs. If almost any other singer had done thirteen albums of this caliber in her entire career, we would have to assess her as a major artist. This is more, in fact, than Johnny Hartman and Jackie Paris were able to do in their whole lives. Yet with Vaughan, it's just a drop in the bucket in the context of her total catalogue.

Roulette was doing a brisk trade in kiddie pop music, yet the albums they made with Vaughan, Washington, and Eckstine were projects that shared all the pure-jazz trademarks of the best Mercury albums (particularly *Count Basie—Sarah Vaughan, After Hours, The Explosive Side of Sarah Vaughan, Sarah Vaughan Sings Soulfully,* and *Sarah Vaughan + 2*), as well as mainstream adult pop albums (like *You're Mine You, Dreamy, Snowbound, Star Eyes, The Lonely Hours,* and *Sarah Slightly Classical*), while *The*

Divine One and *Sweet 'n' Sassy* each consisted of a little bit of both.

Of the whole 1960–63 period, the sets that most stand out are her most personal, namely the two meetings with just guitar and bass. These sets were recorded on different coasts, using the best guitarist and bassist to be found in New York—Mundell Lowe and George Duvivier (on *After Hours*, 1961)—and Los Angeles—Barney Kessel and Joe Comfort (on *Sarah Vaughan + 2*, 1962), respectively. "My Favorite Things," from the first album, finds Vaughan approaching the *Sound of Music* show tune in a minor key manner that has more in common with Coltrane than Mary Martin or Julie Andrews. Benny Carter's "Key Largo" is also intriguingly exotic. If there's a difference between a jazz album and a ballad album, you'd never know it from Vaughan, whose "jazziest" statement is also her most intimate.

The Roulette years found Vaughan working with a fresh crew of first-rate orchestrators, surprisingly few of whom would be part of the picture with her after 1963. *Sarah Slightly Classical* (arranged by Marty Manning, who also handled *Star Eyes* for her, both in 1963, not to mention "I Left My Heart in San Francisco" for Tony Bennett), is a generally tasteful set of pop adaptations of classical compositions. *Star Eyes*, *Sweet 'n' Sassy* (arranged by Lalo Schifrin in 1963), and *Snowbound* (Don Costa, 1962) were all excellent ballad packages, the highlight of the bunch being Vaughan's killer treatment of "More Than You Know" with Schifrin.

Her longtime pianist Jimmy Jones arranged and conducted on the 1960 *Dreamy*, Vaughan's first album for Roulette. Benny Carter also crafted two albums with her in this period, including the ballad set *The Lonely Hours,* a noirish collection of downer songs that opens with a dramatic title number. Their other collaboration was the appropriately named *The Explosive Side of Sarah Vaughan*, a spectacular up-tempo set that reached a climax with the *Showboat* aria "Nobody Else but Me." The West Coast–based trumpeter, arranger, and conductor Gerald Wilson played on *The Lonely Hours* and also shepherded the singer through a jazz-oriented set of his own small-group arrangements, *Sarah Sings Soulfully.*

Where *Sarah Slightly Classical* played up the operatic overtones of her singing, the idea in *Sarah Sings Soulfully* was to go for the gospel. Backed by big band and organ, Vaughan explored her gospel roots (particularly on the down-home, churchy "Moanin'"), the funkier side of contemporary jazz, and a brace of current hit tunes that she hadn't yet gotten around to covering ("A Taste of Honey" and "What Kind of Fool Am I"). It always seemed cause for regret that she never did a full-fledged album of gospel songs and spirituals, and in that respect, *Sarah Sings Soulfully* could be viewed as a consolation prize.

Vaughan's church roots were, in fact, always evident in everything she sang. The melismas and other decorations of her singing have much in common with the gospel style. Martin Williams once referred to this aspect of her artistry as "an opera singer without an opera." He might just as easily have called her a gospel singer without a church—though hardly without a prayer. When she sings "Maria" from *West Side Story* (on *You're Mine You*), it's my idea of angels singing the "Ave Maria." It's instructive to remember that, in the first half of the twentieth century, traditional black spirituals were regarded as the first American "art" music, and that concert singers both black and white in the twenties and thirties—when Vaughan was growing up—were almost as likely to include "Motherless Child" as they were to sing Schubert lieder.

And although Vaughan holds one "Maria" for more measures than any other human being could count, let alone sing, the performance is more than operatic—it's downright spiritual. Lines like "The most beautiful sound I ever heard" take on religious overtones, and her reiteration of the word "Maria" (itself a distinctively Catholic reference) assumes the quality of a chant. When she gets to the line "Say it soft / And it's almost like praying," she takes lyricist Stephen Sondheim at his word, employing the aspect of her artistry that's usually reserved for ecumenical works like "The Lord's Prayer." (The way she expresses the same idea in a different song reveals an entirely different attitude. The line "I started praying" occurs in "Moonglow" and also on *You're Mine You*, but there the implications are far less ecumenical. As with other tracks on the album, such as the Cy Coleman hits "The Best Is Yet to Come" and "Witchcraft," the mood on "Moonglow" is light and swinging.) "Send in the Clowns," the super-spectacular set piece of her final decade, is also sung like a hymn, overdecorated to the hilt with melismas and flourishes galore.

Taking its title from a Johnny Green–Edward Heyman standard that Vaughan first made her own in 1949, *You're Mine You* is the best of the Roulette albums that employs a conventional studio orchestra with strings. The arrangements are credited to Quincy Jones, which, in reality, means that he should properly get credit as producer, since he was already boss of an operation in which most of the best New York arrangers (Billy Byers, Al Cohn, Ralph Burns) were doing charts for him. *You're Mine You* expertly balances light swingers like "So Long," a fine and mellow blues with a bridge, with heavier opuses like "You're Mine You" and "Maria," two secular items that Vaughan imbues, as we have seen, with the power and the glory of the best religious music.

The Roulette period also saw Vaughan renewing her association with Count Basie. The two teamed for the first time officially on the 1960–61 *Count Basie—Sarah Vaughan,* a high-powered hard-swinging set orchestrated not by Quincy but by Thad Jones (no relation). Quincy Delight Jones first collaborated with Vaughan on one of her best Mercury albums, *Vaughan and Violins* (1958), taped in

Paris, with Zoot Sims, and as the title indicates, a large string section; the set produced the heart-stopping "Misty," one of Vaughan's subtlest and most winning ballads. As wonderful as her classical-gospel diva mannerisms are, "Misty" (like the 1962 "I Remember You" with Don Costa) demonstrates that she didn't have to go the full monty every time out, and could be just as effective with a light touch of decoration. "Quiet Nights" (on ¡Viva! Vaughan) opens with the title phrase—three notes—sung in such an understated, minimal fashion it could almost be Blossom Dearie.

Quincy Jones would continue to play a prominent role in Vaughan's recordings, particularly when she returned to Mercury in 1963, where Q was by now ensconced as A&R head for all pop recording. He took an active hand in all her sessions during this second stint at the label (1963–67), particularly in the first few years, generally as executive producer. He put such brilliant writers to work for Vaughan as fellow Basieite Frank Foster, who masterminded ¡Viva! Vaughan, their 1964 answer to the bossa nova craze, and the famous Robert Farnon, on Vaughan with Voices, still another set of superlative balladeering including the colorful "My Coloring Book." That 1963 set was recorded in Copenhagen, where Vaughan also cut her first live album in a number of years, Sassy Swings the Tivoli, reissued as an especially generous double CD. Jones also oversaw Sarah Vaughan Sings the Mancini Songbook, which made her probably the first heavyweight to tackle the movie composer's songs so extensively (most of his biggest hits hadn't even been written by 1964).

Still, this was the mid-sixties, and the cheese factor was at work on Vaughan's sessions just the same as it was on everybody else's. She cut two albums of pop "covers," fairly dreadful ass-end pop albums, entitled Pop Art (1965) and The New Scene, primarily arranged by one Luchi De Jesus. "A Lover's Concerto," a piece best described as Bach au-go-go, made even "Broken-Hearted Melody" and "The Bashful Matador" look like Gershwin by comparison. Her last two albums of the classic era, It's a Man's World and Sassy Swings Again (both from January 1964), allowed her at least to end this era on a high note. Both utilized high-quality songs and the same top-notch contingent of star sidemen and writers that Jones typically employed on his jazz projects: J. J. Johnson, Thad Jones, Manny Albam, and even future smooth jazz giant Bob James, then in his straight-ahead period.

Vaughan was essentially out of the record business for nearly a decade—with a few remarkable exceptions—from the late 1960s to the mid-1970s. She was under contract to Mainstream Records, whose owner, Bob Shad, had been one of her producers at Mercury. Even so, most of her studio albums of the era are best forgotten. Drenched in ersatz-Motown pseudosoul, somehow even the future Vaughan classic "Send in the Clowns" doesn't sound good (but more about that shortly).

So what's worth listening to? She made two songbook albums dedicated to contemporary composers, Sarah Vaughan with Michel Legrand (arranged and conducted by the composer himself, for Mainstream, 1972) and Songs of the Beatles (arranged and conducted by Marty Paich, 1977). I totally failed to appreciate these when they were new, mainly because the songs of Legrand and Lennon and McCartney seemed unbelievably overdone at that time. Today, except for a few lapses in taste here and there (did Legrand actually want to underscore his amazing ballad "Hands of Time" with a boogaloo countermelody?), these two collections sound much better than they did then. Vaughan is especially expressive and effective on such comparatively grandiose texts as "I Will Say Goodbye" and "The Long and Winding Road"; it would seem that the trick for her in singing contemporary composers is finding songs that are ambitious enough to support the weight of her epic chops.

Yet even without these albums the early seventies are far from being a washout, since this is the period in which Vaughan recorded what might be her single greatest album. This was a live concert in Japan in 1973, which Mainstream was prescient enough to tape; the original LP (Live in Japan) was excellent, but the full two-CD version, issued in 2009 as Sarah Vaughan Live in Tokyo, is a career pinnacle. She's amazingly relaxed and energized at the same time, and she stretches out on nearly every song—she's one of the few singers who can take as long as she likes whenever she likes, and we don't mind. She reprises "Misty" here, and, while it may not be as direct and terse as the original studio version, she compensates with uncompromising depth.

"Wave" is also outstanding. The Live in Tokyo album cover shows Vaughan as I remember her, standing with her hands folded, holding the microphone with her eyes closed, as if illustrating the opening line of the song: "So close your eyes." Vaughan and her pianist, Carl Schroeder, have pretty much eliminated every trace of the bossa nova from this Brazilian standard, leaving Antonio Carlos Jobim's melody to stand on its own—which it unflinchingly does. At seven minutes long, this "wave" is in no hurry to get anywhere, and Vaughan creates a remarkable image of rhythmic stasis, as if an ocean wave were actually moving in slow motion, like a wave of Jell-O rather than water. No one has ever made Jobim's lyric (he seems to have actually written the English lyric, or at least no other writer ever gets credit) come alive more vividly—particularly the line "When your eyes met mine / It was eternity." The song loses no impact when Vaughan and the trio pick up the tempo in the second chorus.

Yet for me the most amazing track is "The Nearness of You," which Vaughan had been singing since 1949 and which here opens the second CD. It begins with bow music—the trio plays a fast riff that allows her to milk the applause—and then she coyly announces to the crowd that she's going to play the piano. Somehow she's at once defiant and self-deprecating, saying she's going to play simply because she wants to (so there!), but at the same time telling us, "They can just take it off the record." This turns out to be, in fact, the perfect attitude for the song. Vaughan puts over Ned Washington's gorgeous lyric with a perfect mix of reverence and humility, a love song that's also like a little prayer. She starts with an intro that seems ambitious for someone who isn't a full-time pianist, and then slowly eases into the rubato verse. You totally believe her when she says her heart's "in a dither, dear," when her love is "at a distance," but even more so when she sings "When you are near—oh-oh-oh my" and rises chromatically on each "oh." Somehow, the act of accompanying herself on the piano causes Vaughan to focus on the lyric; she delivers the notes and the words with utter clarity and transparency, and even when she plays with one or the other ("If you—if you—if you only grant me . . ."), she never lets the narrative get away from her. She's always in complete control.

"Nearness" is also seven minutes, although she doesn't start the song until a minute and a half into the track; however, because it's only one verse and one chorus, it may be the slowest and most intimate thing she ever sang—and it's unsullied by other musicians, just her own piano without any bass or drums. Vaughan stretches everything as far as it will go, but refuses to allow it to break. At the climax, she holds the final note for what seems like forever, with a big arpeggio underneath. "That was hard!" she says, but it turns out she was talking about her piano work. "I don't know how they can play and sing at the same time." The act of holding that unbelievable note apparently meant nothing to her, but it never fails to give me chills.

A number of other concerts—from London, Paris, and even Warsaw—were taped in the period but are only on very hard to find releases from those countries. The idea that there might be performances out there that are anywhere near as good as *Live in Tokyo* and are just waiting to be heard also gives me chills.

"Where have I been all these years?" Vaughan asks in the title track of her second Pablo release, *How Long Has This Been Goin' On?* Vaughan's final statement as a recording artist was a series of eight albums for that Norman Granz–owned label: There were two albums of Brazilian music, both recorded in Rio, *I Love Brazil* (1977) and *Copacabana* (1979); another album with the Basie band (her third); and *Send in the Clowns.* Even better were two albums with a four-piece rhythm section, *How Long Has This Been Goin' On?* (1978) and *Crazy and Mixed Up* (1982)—in fact, the latter contains her versions of two songs by Ivan Lins, "The Island" and "Love Dance," which are even more effective than anything on the two LPs that were done in Brazil. Vaughan had long been an Ellington fan (she recorded nine of

his songs for Roulette alone), but, though she toured with him in 1952, she never went into the studio with the Ellington band. She made up for this loss by taping her *Ellington Song Book One* and *Two* in 1979, and it was worth waiting an entire career to finally hear her go to work on "Day Dream" and "What Am I Here For?"

The Pablo sessions saw the culmination of several other longtime threads in the Vaughan canon: The wordless "Autumn Leaves" (on *How Long?*) and "Chelsea Bridge" (on *Ellington*) were the final entries in a long series of nonverbal performances that also included the orchestral "Pinky" (1949) and the small group scat "Shulie-a-Bop" (1954). "Body and Soul" (on *How Long?*) was perhaps her sixth recorded version of Johnny Green's jazz anthem, this one a duet with bassist Ray Brown. Vaughan could virtually do no wrong on these six releases.

It's tempting to describe the Pablo series—her last great recordings—as Vaughan's swan song, but she remained active for eight years after *Crazy and Mixed Up*, the final Pablo entry. She made nothing but one-shots in these years, encountering such characters as George Gershwin, Michael Tilson Thomas, and the Los Angeles Philharmonic (*Gershwin Live!*, 1982), which grew out of her work with symphony orchestras, the Mormon Tabernacle Choir, Barry Manilow, and the pope.

As she grew older, Vaughan's voice deepened, and she became ever more steeped in her mannerisms—to the annoyance of some pundits, but to the delight of most of her fans. In the seventies and eighties she explored new ways to grow as an artist that accommodated both sides of her nature: The Divine side found new outlets in a series of performances with full-blown symphonic orchestras and His Holiness; the Sassy side was indulged by new meetings with the leading jazzmen and by fresh musical challenges such as Brazilian music. The voice grew bigger, bolder, deeper, but never seemed strained—like Dizzy Gillespie's cheeks, it bulged larger and larger but never popped.

"Send in the Clowns" was the masterpiece of Vaughan's last decade. It was a standout for her in concert—like Sinatra's "New York, New York," this Sondheim show tune (virtually his only pop hit) inevitably closed the show for her. But for many years you couldn't get Vaughan's "Send in the Clowns" on a representative recording—even though she sang it twice on records. The first was on a dreadful album titled *Send in the Clowns* on Mainstream in 1974 (reissued by Sony on CD twenty years later)—a treatment that could aptly be called "Sondheim: The Disco Album." Then in 1981 she re-recorded "Clowns" with Count Basie's band, on another album also titled *Send in the Clowns.* This is the arrangement fans remember from these climactic years, but she still doesn't take it as far as she would later in concert. Besides which, the presence of the Basie ensemble is wasted; they sustain a chord here and there, but the orchestral treatment of her arrangement is nondescript. Overall, this studio recording just lacks *pizazz*. Mysteriously, Pablo's Norman Granz—who had made his initial reputation as a presenter of jazz concerts and concert recordings—did not document any of her appearances with a live album. At the time of her death from cancer in 1990, there was no definitive document of her rendition of "Clowns."

At last, in 1999 *Sarah Vaughan in the City of Lights* was released, a 1985 concert from Paris—the French city that the singer had named her daughter after. And at last, here is a valid record of her bravura concert showstopper: The first few notes are a little off-mike, but here is "Clowns" in all its excessive eminence, with Vaughan milking every melisma, squeezing every grace note, soaring to the rafters in all her gospel-cum-opera glory, all but shrieking into "in myyyyy careeeer . . . ," lightening up on "don't you love *farce*," and tumbling down on the last "but where are the clowns?" This is a "Send in the Clowns" to make angels tremble and grown men weep.

The most amazing thing about Vaughan's forty-year career was that she was all these things at once, jazz and pop, divine and sassy; there was no limit to things that she could do and ways she found to do them. Plenty of contemporary singers list her as a primary influence (Dee Dee Bridgewater and Dianne Reeves, to name two), yet in the twenty years since her death, no one has taken her place in American music, and no one ever will.

W

Fats Waller (1904–1943)

The pianist Marian McPartland has a sense of humor, but no one would ever accuse her of impudence. So there's only one way to explain her behavior at a jazz party at the White House in the fall of 1998 at which she had the temerity to dedicate "Ain't Misbehavin'" to the nation's commander in chief, our frequently misbehavin' president Bill Clinton. Obviously, this was not McPartland herself making a statement; rather, she was channeling the spirit of the song's composer, the Ayatollah of Irreverence himself, the great Thomas "Fats" Waller.

Waller speaks to the "naughties" in other ways: In the middle of a live 1938 version of another of his classics, "The Joint Is Jumpin,'" the Fat One goes into a spoken "rap" on the subject of violence against women: "No, don't hit her, that's my baby! No, don't do that, that's bad, son." Another line could be directed at P. Diddy (or whatever he calls himself these days): "Check your weapons at the door." Today, Waller likely would be billed as "Fat-C Wat-C," but this is no mere rapper, or even a lowly Prince: The man in charge here is none other than the King of the Ivories himself.

Fats Waller lived only thirty-nine years, and didn't become a star attraction and featured vocalist in his own right until his last decade. But ever since 1934, when the singer-pianist began his most celebrated series of recordings, the "Fats Waller and His Rhythm" sessions for RCA Victor, Waller has been a force in the parallel worlds of jazz and pop. His most important recordings have been in print in all formats from 78s to downloads (almost every note he ever recorded was reissued in the decade before his centennial). His songs have been endlessly sung by the great singers—even without the aid of the 1978 hit Broadway revue *Ain't Misbehavin'*—and his catalogue of songs (at least the ones that he didn't give away) is probably worth millions of times what it was in his lifetime. After Ellington, he has probably inspired more songbook and tribute albums than any other jazz composer. He is still regarded as one of the very greatest pianists ever to work in the jazz idiom, in a class with Hines, Tatum, Wilson, Powell, Cole, and Evans, and the infectious joy of his music has spread to players across the jazz generations, from Louis Prima to Louis Jordan to Marty Grosz.

Interest in Waller is not unique to the current era, even though it seems his spirit—as Marian McPartland demonstrated—is especially welcome in this age when jazz musicians, no less than everyone else, sometimes take themselves too seriously. Mama Waller's very own little Fatsy-Watsy was a genuine giant of jazz and jocularity. His only competition for the crown of jazz's number-one clown prince and comic genius was none other than Louis Armstrong; the sole pianist of his generation who could approach the fat man in sheer keyboard speed and precision and swing was Art Tatum. Like Armstrong and Dizzy Gillespie, Waller was at once a world-class clown and a true instrumental virtuoso; he was nothing less than a combination of Vladimir Horowitz and Buster Keaton.

Many were the resources that Waller had at his disposal. To begin with, there were always his piano skills. In an age when piano competitions between such eastern stride masters as Waller's mentors James P. Johnson and Willie "the Lion" Smith were the equivalent of climbing in the ring with Mike Tyson, Waller established himself as the fiercest fighter of all. His hands were the pianistic equivalent of a Joe Lewis knockout punch, being massive implements, each of which could span an entire octave or even a 10th all by itself, so that he could augment his chords with unexpected inner pitches. Bill Dobbins has observed that Waller's use of chromatic alterations and passing tones undoubtedly influenced even the titanic Tatum. In other words, when Fatsy-Watsy hit you with some of those big fat chords or those dramatic glissandos, son, you stayed hit. As friend and fan Dizzy Gillespie put it, "This nigger could eat up a piano!"

Then there were his songs. For Waller, it wasn't a question of trying to come up with a melody but for his collaborators and publishers to pin him down long enough for them to tap into the treasure trove of tunes that effortlessly sprang from him like water from a faucet. He was a veritable one-man ASCAP, from blockbuster copyrights like "I've Got a Feeling I'm Falling," "Honeysuckle Rose," "Squeeze Me," "Ain't Misbehavin,'" and the similarly themed "Keepin' Out of Mischief Now" to gems of the classic blues era like "Wildcat Blues" and "In Harlem's Araby" and more serious laments like "What Did I Do to Be So Black and Blue" and "Blue Turning Grey over You." Indeed, his catalogue as a composer was so capacious that it exceeded his vast discography as a performer, and includes many a lesser-known gem that he composed but never recorded, like "My Heart's at Ease" and "Ain't-Cha Glad?," not to mention "Since Won Long Hop Took One Long Hop to China." There was also "I Had to Do It," which he did, fortunately, perform on an extant radio broadcast. In 1955, when Louis Armstrong recorded his masterpiece album *Satch Plays Fats,* he was merely cementing a relationship of nearly thirty years; Satchmo probably recorded more compositions by Waller than by any other tunesmith, going back to the great Hot Five days and numbers like "Alligator Crawl" and "Georgia Bo-Bo." Then again, Waller's piano features, like "A Handful of Keys," "Clothesline Ballet," and "African Ripples," rival Ellington, Morton, and Hines as some of the most amazing music ever written for the jazz keyboard.

Not least of Waller's assets was his Rhythm, both in the lower- and uppercase senses of the word. "Fats Waller and His Rhythm" was a wonderfully tight band he maintained throughout his glory years on RCA Victor Records and NBC Radio. His sidemen were first-rate, particularly the brilliant trumpeter Herman Autrey and clarinetist and tenor saxophonist Gene "Honey Bear" Cedric, drummer Slick Jones, and the no less slick guitarist Al Casey, who survived well past the Clinton era, long enough to hear his name announced from the stage by the Squirrel Nut Zippers. They may never have gained the individual reputations of Duke Ellington's or Count Basie's sidemen, but they were all master players in the same class as the Duke's or Count's men. This was a polished yet swinging unit that perfectly complemented the leader's pianistic and vocal contributions.

The final ingredient in the Waller mix was his voice; you'll notice that his vocal contributions can't be limited to a conventional definition of the term "singing." Waller did so much more than strictly sing—he offered asides, often scathingly funny sideline commentary (the best lines may be in "Until the Real Thing Comes Along," "I'd work for you, I'd slave for you. . . . You want me to rob a bank? Well I won't do it! / I'd be a beggar or a knave for you . . .

whatever *that* is!"), he egged his soloists on ("Send me! Send me, son!" or "Beat it on *outsy-woutsy*!"); in short, he would stop at nothing to encourage his audiences to have fun. This is the hardest aspect of his music to take seriously—Waller's vocals in particular defy any notion of seriousness—but he was one of the most creative vocalists of his or any other era. He could switch from song to speech at the drop of a hat, and croon in every register from falsetto to basso. He would bat his eyes and sound like an effeminate, fey tenor at one moment, then drop to a basso profundo (anticipating Carol Channing) the next, and then, for something completely different, get all deep and bluesy on the next. "Stop Beatin' 'Round the Mulberry Bush," a bit of nursery rhyme nonsense from 1938, finds our hero extracting mucho comic mileage by overemphasizing the Bs in "berry bush."

It's often been observed that Waller's vocals amount to parodies of many of the "lesser" works of Tin Pan Alley that he was importuned to record. It should be noted that some of the so-called dross in his repertoire originated from his own pen—the sentimental "Old Grand Dad," for instance, turns out to be a Waller original. On the song "Inside," recorded in April 1938 for Victor, he finds it impossible to "seriously" sing the line "let me have my cry." I would instead suggest that the Fat Man's versatile vocalizing was merely his way of improving the written material, and that he wasn't so much making fun *of* those songs as *with* them. Waller had both a black belt in making merry and a PhD in having fun.

Born in New York on May 21, 1904, Thomas Waller began studying piano and organ at age six. Although his parents, a minister and a church organist, must be described as his first influence, Waller's mastery of the keyboard blossomed under the genius tutelary of the Harlem stride masters, most famously Willie "the Lion" Smith (born 1897) and James P. Johnson (born 1891). (Later, he would pass along his knowledge to the young Count Basie.) By every account one of the most lovable personalities in all of American music, Waller had no trouble finding professional gigs as early as the age of fourteen. He worked as an accompanist to vaudeville acts, did rent parties in Harlem and all up and down the East Coast, and played for silent films.

Under the aegis of blues and jazz impresario Clarence Williams, Waller made his first recordings in 1922, and a few years later began composing songs in collaboration with the master lyricist Andy Razaf. He went on performing and partying from the mid-twenties to the mid-thirties, his fame steadily increasing. He recorded frequently in these years— as a solo performer, a bandleader, and as a sideman with all the leading black as well as white musicians of his era, including Red Allen, Jabbo Smith, J. C. Higginbotham, Jack Teagarden, and Benny Goodman. He also cut a series of piano solos for Victor that are today regarded as some of the definitive examples of the vigorous, two-fisted, and heavily swinging school of piano playing later dubbed "stride." However, as pianist and jazz authority Dick Katz points out, "'Stride' is a slight oversimplification describing his work; close listening reveals subtleties that go beyond the mere bass-note-to-chord-and-back in the left hand that defines stride."

In 1932, Waller capitalized on the novelty of a new medium with a little known song entitled "Radio Papa, Broadcastin' Mama." He actually made his first radio broadcast as part of Clarence Williams's Blue Five in 1923. As Dan Morgenstern notes, Waller landed a regular show of his own on New York's WABC, but began to become a radio institution while broadcasting all over the Midwest from Cincinnati's WLIW in 1932. Once he started recording regularly for RCA (part of the same conglomerate that owned NBC), he launched a national series, oddly enough on CBS. When he made his first of several triumphant tours of Europe in the summer of 1938, he even appeared in an experimental television broadcast—he would have been a natural for that medium, even as he was for radio. By 1935, when Waller appeared in his first of three feature films, *Hooray for Love*, he had reached the pinnacle of his national popularity, which he would sustain for the remainder of his tragically short life.

The previous year, Waller had begun his most celebrated series of recordings, the Fats Waller and His Rhythm sides, done with a six- or seven-piece small band that perfectly framed the Great Man's antics. In these Victor recordings (many currently available on BMG-Bluebird), Waller's prodigious talent as a vocalist in particular came to the fore. His infectious joy and his irrepressible sense of humor transform many run-of-the-mill pop numbers into classics of jazz and jive. Then, too, Waller had a gift for lightly mocking the occasionally lachrymose lyrics he sang both by rendering them in various voices and by his irreverent asides. Although he became best known as a clown, both in his singing and playing, Waller could also function superbly as both a balladeer and a bluesman.

Fats Waller's voice can be heard on a record for the first time on the 1927 "Red Hot Dan." In the twenties, he had worked as accompanist for vocalists, from the great Ethel Waters to many obscure, long-forgotten femme singers then regarded as part of the classic blues trend of the era, as well as entertainers like his future partner Andy Razaf (recording under the name Johnny Thompson) and pioneering crooner Gene Austin. Waller began to assert himself as a singer beginning around 1931: That year he did a piano-vocal record of his own, "Crazy 'Bout My Baby," which he also recorded as pianist and singer with Ted Lewis's orchestra.

Dan Morgenstern feels that Waller would have made more vocal records in the early thirties—he certainly was singing frequently on the radio—but was avoiding entering the New York area lest his funds be attached by his ex-wife. Thus, unfortunately, he recorded comparatively little either vocally or instrumentally in the early thirties. Yet he certainly makes his presence known as a special guest on a 1931 date with Jack Teagarden, providing smart and snappy retorts to Teagarden's low-key, bluesy vocals on "That's What I Like About You" and Louis Armstrong's hit "You Rascal, You."

In the thirties, Armstrong and Waller reigned unchallenged as the two kings of music and comedy. Armstrong's vocals were recognized as outgrowths of his trumpet style: the same kind of attack, the same use of slurs and glissandi and other devices that were interconnected with his brass playing. Waller couldn't exactly approximate his piano style with his singing voice, but it seems appropriate that a pianist would have come up with the style that Waller forged: If he could go from very low to very high, from bass all the way to treble, with his frantic fingering, why not do the same with his titanic tonsils? If he could do several things at once, like play harmony and melody—not to mention rhythm—why not add one more with his voice? On most of the classic Rhythm sides, Waller has become a one-man equivalent of what it took both himself and Teagarden to achieve in 1931. He sings the main melody himself, while at the same time providing his own obbligato retorts. He's a one-man Abbott & Costello, comic and straight man at the same time.

Beneath all that kidding around, Waller was a fairly well-schooled singer. There are many records on which he parodies concert baritones by dipping down into the bottommost registers: "Let's Sing Again" and especially "The Curse of the Aching Heart" ("the soul [sole] within me died . . . not my shoes, though!"). Yet he could easily have done this "seriously," without the gags, and become the great black romantic baritone of the period—sort of an American Hutch. He also employs a high squeaky voice at times (as on a brief aside in "Who's Afraid of Love?") and sometimes will do a moronic, nutty voice. More often, he'll employ two or three different vocal registers on a single song, doing the main melody in his natural singing voice, jumping all around from high to low, stupid to wiseass, in his other vocal characters. He does so many voices on his classic "Christopher Columbus" he practically sounds like a one-man vocal quartet. (Indeed, some vocal groups, like the Ink Spots, at least in the beginning before they found their gold record formula, sound like an attempt to do with four jivey voices what Waller did all by himself.)

Often Waller will employ scatting, humming, or some other, unclassifiable wordless approach, as on the start of "The Old Plantation." Other times, he'll poke fun at serious, classical-style tenors by overenunciating his words, and sometimes he'll rush the lyrics so that they sound silly—he does both on the 1936 "You're Laughing at Me," pronouncing it as "yourelaughingatme." On the basis of the title alone, this Irving Berlin number (from *On the Avenue*) could have been Waller's theme song: After the bridge, which ends with the line "humor is death to romance," Waller interjects, "Ain't no undertakers 'round here!"

Thomas Fats Waller and William Count Basie were born within a few months of each other; can you imagine if Waller had had the strength of character to create as long-running and perpetually self-renewing a career as Basie's? Unfortunately, the undertakers would indeed be comin' 'round before too long. Waller sounds so alive and vital on his commercial recordings, as well as on the radio transcriptions and live broadcast remotes that have been issued over the last sixty years, that it's hard to believe he died while still a very young man. He announces on one 1935 radio performance, "Ladies and gentlemen: I want to let you know that I paid my alimony, and I ain't misbehavin'"; however, in real life, he spent far too much time doing just that. Waller's life was devoted entirely to playing and partying. As sideman Garvin Bushell put it, "Fats was a big baby. He never grew up." As such, he completely avoided all aspects of adult responsibility, much to the consternation of his wives, children, managers, and employers.

His career never slowed down: In addition to two further films (*King of Burlesque*, 1936, and *Stormy Weather*, 1943), he continued to broadcast, returned to Europe, recorded prolifically, concertized in Carnegie Hall, and even wrote a Broadway musical (the 1943 *Early to Bed*, which ran for more than a year), all while unceasingly touring the country. But Waller simply could not stop "carrying on," and was finally felled at the height of both his abilities and his fame. Substantially weakened by alcoholism, he died of pneumonia while returning from Hollywood to New York at the age of thirty-nine. At the end of "The Joint Is Jumpin'" the singer-pianist seems to be scolding himself when he says, "After all, we have to get serious once in a while." But Fats never did.

In September 1943, Waller recorded what must be the most unintentionally moving song in his oeuvre. This was his final studio session, in New York on September 16, a piano-and-vocal date for V-Disc. There's a famous story about the saxophonist Zoot Sims, who showed up at a gig completely inebriated but played brilliantly just the same. Asked how he could play so well when he was drunk, Sims replied "I *practice* drunk!" Waller is in a similar state here: He's positively drunk off his ass, but you can tell that performing in such a condition is hardly a new experience for him. On this date, he laid down several songs from his show *Early to Bed* as well as new treatments of long-standing signature tunes for the benefit of servicemen, and his playing is so sloppy and his speech so slurred that the performances would never have been released by a commercial label. Waller's GI audience, however, probably enjoyed how he was completely crocked and having such a good time.

"This Is So Nice It Must Be Illegal" is a terrific song from an excellent score. It's a classic Fatsy-Watsy ode to high spirits and good times, making merry and making love, with an especially witty lyric by George Marion ("Quick! Let us kiss before it's illicit / It can happen here!"). Waller had written and sung a million tunes like this before, but this recording is different. He's so perilously close to falling off the piano bench that in light of his death three months later, it's hard to enjoy the performance in the spirit in which it was intended. The forced jocularity makes the song almost painfully poignant. In retrospect, "This Is So Nice It Must Be Illegal" is Waller's "Vesti la Giubba." It's impossible not to hear the tear behind the smile. He sounds like a man literally partying himself to death.

In the words of Dizzy Gillespie, "Fats Waller was one of my idols. I dug the way he was a master musician and a master pantomime artist. I patterned my career after that. I loved him and he loved me. Fats Waller influenced me not only through his music, but his whole personality, because he was funny, and then you could sit him down at the piano and close his mouth and he'd play. Everybody respected him. Art Tatum, James P. Johnson, Earl Hines, all of them respected Thomas 'Fats' Waller. That's right! All you have to do is listen to 'Ain't Misbehavin'' or 'Honeysuckle Rose.' Those tunes will last forever. [Take] the bridge in 'Misbehavin'.' Where did he get that from? Boy, I bet all the piano players right now love it. I haven't heard anything in music since that's more hip, harmonically and logically."

Dinah Washington (1924–1963)

Dinah Washington had such a passionate and aggressive singing style that any attempt to describe what she does invokes a series of metaphors so active that they're almost violent: She *digs* into a song, she sings *the hell* out of a song, she *attacks* a song. Yet this kind of rough-and-rowdy treatment is hardly anti-social. Washington does right by her numbers by subjecting them to extremes of feeling, and she invariably leaves each piece of music better than when she found it. For all the vigor of her unsentimental approach, she does more to make a given song sound wonderful than any conventional chanteuse. When singing a love song, for instance, she's virtually the only pop songstress who can sound tender without getting soft.

And that's because she's more than a pop singer, a blues singer, or a jazz singer; she's one of the very few, very great vocalists who figure equally prominently in the development of all three of these genres of American music. She invests pop standards with a blues feeling, sings the blues with a jazz-based improvisational outlook, and can bring both a jazz and blues feeling into the most tepid of pop contexts.

Washington was the first artist who began with a blues foundation to eventually spread her wings far enough to conquer all of pop, transcending the boundaries of country music, gospel, and show tunes. Her major male counterpart in this area is Joe Williams, and both of them started in church music (although Williams in later years explained that he preferred to be thought of as a balladeer who also sang the blues rather than the other way around). Between the two of them they made it possible for artists of succeeding generations to slip more easily between the music of George Gershwin and Memphis Slim, and yet the only two successors who have produced a body of work even approaching Washington's and Williams's are Ray Charles and Aretha Franklin.

While Charles is given credit for "the Birth of Soul," there's no word other than "soul" that describes what Washington was singing in the forties and fifties—if Charles was the father, then surely Washington was at the very least the godmother. She was billed as "Queen of the Blues," yet she actually presided over an empire that covered the widest possible stylistic territory. Indeed, we can go so far as to say that Washington can be considered the first soul/R&B singer as we understand the term today, a link between the classic blues singers of Bessie Smith's era and the modern blues singers of the postwar era. Aretha Franklin made it clear how much Washington's influence meant to her when she recorded *Unforgettable,* an album-length tribute to the Queen, in 1964.

Washington's intonation is among the strongest in American music—like Fitzgerald, Stafford, Cole, and Tormé, she effortlessly hits every note dead-on. Unlike those other artists, she also has an arsenal of blues devices at her disposal—particularly growls and a wide range of darker tonal colors. Her time and her swing are faultless and yet her biggest asset isn't strictly musical but attitudinal: Washington has a remarkable kind of confidence that comes through in whatever she sings—there's always a feeling that she means every word. She can be haughty and defiant in one of her famous (and in some cases infamous) off-color 16-bar blues, she can be vulnerable in a traditional ballad like "More Than You Know" or a soul ballad like "This Bitter Earth." Unlike most of her descendants, she knows well the value of subtlety; even though she brings gospel and blues feeling to the popular song, she never overdoes it in the fashion of those all-power and no-taste screechers like Whitney Houston and Celine Dion.

Blues singers, from Bessie Smith onward, often use distortion, but generally the message is apparent even if the words are garbled. With Washington, the lyric is always crystal clear—she can sing show tunes with all the clarity of an Ella Fitzgerald or even a Barbara Cook. As friend and fan Abbey Lincoln put it, "She was a great storyteller, you could understand every word she said, and she told you what was on her mind and what was in her heart. And as she grew a little older, all of that was in her songs too. 'Cold, Cold Heart' took on a life of its own when Dinah sang it."

That confidence permeated her personal life as well. Washington knew exactly who she was, what she was capable of, and what she could expect. She didn't take any nonsense from lovers or co-workers, as her seven or eight husbands (sources do not agree), or Brook Benton (the soul singer who attempted to record a disc of duets with her in 1959) will attest. Dan Morgenstern has reported how even the notorious Pee Wee Marquette, the pushy Birdland emcee who typically lorded it over the musicians who played there, was relegated to a mere flunky when Washington was in residence at the club. (A set of brilliant location recordings from Birdland, taped in 1962, was issued some thirty-five years later.) Washington always insisted on being referred to as "the Queen," and had those words inscribed on her trunk. And that was even when she appeared in England, although "the English didn't think that was particularly funny," according to Abbey Lincoln. "But Dinah was a mischievous queen. Yes, she was, and it's all in her music."

Born Rutha (not Ruth, as historian Ted Ono has uncovered) Lee Jones in Tuscaloosa, Alabama, on August 29, 1924, the future Queen moved to Chicago with her mother at an early age, where she grew up playing piano and singing spirituals in church. Exposed to blues and pop songs through records and radio, Washington first worked in amateur shows in black neighborhoods around the Windy City. At the start of the forties, she spent several years with the famous gospel troupe led by Sallie Martin, eventually becoming the group's lead singer. On her own, she worked several small Chicago clubs (once sharing a bill with Fats Waller) before she came to the Garrick Club. There she was heard by Lionel Hampton, who invited her to try out with his orchestra at the Regal Theatre. When she joined Hampton's orchestra in December 1942, she also changed her name.

"It only took one exposure to the tart, take-me-or-leave-me Dinah Washington sound to realize that she had to be recorded," producer-critic Leonard Feather recalled, but both the AFM ban and the shortsightedness of Decca Records, who had Hampton under contract, prevented her from recording with the big band. Fortunately, she did cut a series of solo sides for Keynote (produced by Feather and with Hampton graciously participating as sideman) and Apollo Records while still with the band. Washington went out as a solo act in the fall of 1945, and began recording for the newly formed Mercury Records in January 1946.

At this point, Washington was at the crossroads of many movements in American vernacular music. Ostensibly, like Peggy Lee and Ella Fitzgerald, she was a former band singer now working as a solo act. In the mid-forties, for the first time, many pop and jazz singers were being recorded in significant quantities, the same way the big bands had been—which indicates that singers were being recognized as the bread-and-butter of the music business.

Like Louis Jordan, Washington was a key figure

in the evolution and gradual mainstreaming of the blues that occurred after the war. "Race" music, about to be rechristened "rhythm and blues," had always been marketed to black audiences, but now it was pushing away from the margins and toward the center, to the point where, in the late fifties, a liberally watered-down version of R&B would come to dominate the youth music market. She was a key player in both trends: the big-band-nurtured pop singers who took over in the late forties and the R&B artists who supplanted them ten years after that. When she signed with Mercury the company was essentially still a start-up, and she and the label more or less grew up together.

Washington's first session yielded results that were abnormally high even for her: two Ira Gershwin standards, "Embraceable You" and "I Can't Get Started with You," plus "When a Woman Loves a Man," a slightly lesser-known 1934 song by Johnny Mercer, Bernie Hanighen, and Gordon Jenkins, and one riotous blues, "Joy Juice." The next date, conducted by Gerald Wilson, yielded three titles: one new pop song, "You Didn't Want Me Then," another swinging blues, "Oo-Wee Walkie Talkie," and another Gershwin standard, "The Man I Love." (This last title has her altering the lyrics rather liberally: "We'll build a little home . . . from *whence* I'll never roam" and that "*all other things* aside, I'm waiting for the man I love.")

The point is that, overall, the general quality of Washington's output can be said to be somewhat higher than that of most female pop singers of the era. She did fewer forgotten and forgettable pop songs and a lot more blues. Indeed, her place at the crossroads ensured that every possible kind of song would turn up in her recording sessions—just looking at the years 1946 to 1952, we find classic pop standards along the lines of the Gershwin items I've already mentioned, as well as "I Thought About You," "Mad About the Boy," "Just One More Chance," "Stairway to the Stars," and "How Deep Is the Ocean." There were also songs by African American writers who were considered part of mainstream Tin Pan Alley (such as Fats Waller's "Ain't Misbehavin,'" and the René brothers' "I Sold My Heart to the Junkman") and songs by white writers that are generally considered part of the black experience, like "Stormy Weather," "Out in the Cold Again," and "I Can't Face the Music Without Singing the Blues" (which she recorded twice, both times incorporating Benny Carter's "Blues in My Heart").

What's most impressive is how she treats the blues songbook with the same respect and understanding that singers like Sinatra were just beginning to show the classic show tunes: She preserves the classic blues songs from the twenties and thirties that she must have loved since childhood—"Trouble in Mind," "When the Sun Goes Down," the Louis Jordan hit "Early in the Morning," the Bessie Smith–associated "'Tain't Nobody's Business but My Own," and two harmonically similar blues songs that she

helped to make into instant standards, Buddy Johnson's "Since I Fell for You" and Percy Mayfield's "Send Me Someone to Love."

Washington's penchant for the blues gave her recorded work a certain edge that other female pop (or even jazz) singers of the era didn't have. Gershwin was considered somewhat high-minded then, but at the same time she was recording him, Washington launched a series of somewhat lower-slung blues numbers of a more explicit nature than most Tin Pan Alley songs. "Joy Juice" was the first of a series of alcoholic-drenched blues opuses: Here Washington sings of trying to get her man stoned ("nice and stewed" is how she puts it) so she can have her way with him. "Juice Head Man of Mine," which might be viewed as a sequel, illustrates the downside of such a policy: By now her man insists on getting juiced all day long and comes home angry and disagreeable (not to mention "smelling like a skunk"); still, he does continue to satisfy her where it counts. "Lord, don't let him lose his mind," she pleads, "'Cause his juice-head love's so fine." (This from the same woman who sings Cole Porter's "Why Can't You Behave" and Rodgers and Hammerstein's "If I Loved You," albeit the latter with a schlocky intro.) On the other hand, in "Good Daddy Blues," another original, Washington boasts of how she got rid of "a no account, triflin' man" who would "come home stumblin' drunk," and replaced this loser with a "cool, kind papa." These songs belong in the same genre as Louis Jordan's "What's the Use of Getting Sober (When You're Gonna Get Drunk Again)?" and Lou Donaldson's "Whiskey-Drinking Woman."

As Leonard Feather, who composed more than few blues numbers for Washington, has observed, nearly all of these pieces use the strict 12-bar form and are in the key of C. In many cases, the meaning is overt, like the bedroom-based "Pillow Blues" and "Fine, Fine Man," but others manage something of a double entendre. In her own "Long John Blues," Dinah has eyes for a dentist built like a basketball player—over seven feet tall—who knows how to fill more than one kind of cavity. "You thrill me when you drill me," she sings, happily paying him $10 for the privilege. In 1954 she came back with a sequel; this time she's raving about her doctor, who happens to be named "Short John," who gives her "medicine" that would drive most women "stark raving mad."

In "TV Is the Thing This Year," Washington is visited by her television repairman, who knows all the ins and outs of the fine art of twisting her dials. When he's finished, she's left panting, "My TV's gonna need fixin' 'bout this time *every* night!" Most licentious of all is a tale of the trombone player who, well, er, um, *serenades* her with his "Big Long Sliding Thing." She likes him even better than the electric guitarist who plugs it into her amp or the pianist who tickles her keys. The most unlikely profession of all gets the double entendre treatment in "My Man's an Undertaker."

By the fifties, the pop business was becoming

increasingly splintered—there now were three distinct music markets in the United States: pop, which was by now mostly singers and the occasional dance band; R&B, which had replaced the thirty-year-old term "race" music; and country and western, until then known officially as "hillbilly." At the dawn of the forties, the big money was in pop, which was aimed at white people in urban, especially coastal, markets, but R&B and C&W were becoming increasingly profitable. For the most part, songs introduced in one market tended to stay there, but occasionally there were crossovers, which, at this early stage, occurred mostly in terms of songs rather than artists.

The most famous example was "Cold, Cold Heart": It was written by Hank Williams, greatest of all cowboy poets, and became a pop hit when Mitch Miller had Tony Bennett record it. When the song caught on in mainstream pop, Dinah Washington recorded it for the R&B market, with a bluesy tenor sax and an arrangement not all that different from the way she sang things like "Double Dealing Daddy." Bennett sang "Cold, Cold Heart" as if it had been written by Jerome Kern; Washington sang it as if it had been written by Buddy Johnson or Percy Mayfield.

Thus the same song had become a blockbuster in all three markets—with Bennett and Washington reinterpreting the song in their own way (Louis Armstrong's Decca version can be considered the fourth major treatment). And none of these versions should be regarded as covers in the Little Richard–Pat Boone sense of the term. For a brief shining moment in American pop, the marketplace actually encouraged diversity and ethnic identity. As no less an authority on the subject of the blues than B. B. King has observed, "I remember when Dinah was considered R&B or 'race,' but she sang anything that anybody else sang, she just sang it her way."

"Cold, Cold Heart" was only the most successful of Washington's often brilliant reimaginings of mainstream pop hits in the early to mid-fifties. If that Hank Williams classic was the best, the worst was another "heart" song, "My Heart Cries for You," orchestrated by Jimmy Carroll, more normally the right-hand man of Mitch Miller, who had produced the hit Guy Mitchell version for Columbia. Washington's treatment limps along in a very pedestrian 3/4 time: Apparently if there was one thing Washington couldn't sing, it was a second-rate waltz. Fortunately, other Washington covers of contempop hits were significantly better, such as her versions of two older songs very successfully revived by sweet bandleader Sammy Kaye, "It Isn't Fair" and "Harbor Lights," as well as Billy Eckstine's "I Wanna Be Loved" and "I Apologize," Sinatra's "I'm a Fool to Want You," and, among others, Kay Starr's "Wheel of Fortune." Washington also made excellent music with Clyde McPhatter's "Such a Night" (covered ludicrously by Johnnie Ray and later, superbly, by Elvis Presley).

Up through the mid-fifties, Washington's pop records, even those covering the tritest mainstream hits, could be things of extreme beauty. She also continued to do brilliant work in the R&B genre: There's a particularly exciting set of nine titles from 1953 in which Washington is backed by a combo based on organ (Jackie Davis) and tenor (Paul Quinichette)—Washington and Davis are relentlessly intense, but "Vice Pres" Quinichette counterbalances them with his light, ethereal tenor tone. This combination is especially effective on blues and bluesish numbers with a sense of humor, such as "Fat Daddy" and "Lean Baby," a Billy May instrumental outfitted with a witty lyric by Roy Alfred. Between "Long John," "Short John," "Fat Daddy," "Lean Baby," and the later "Fine Fat Daddy," there's something of an obsession with body size, which is ironic, considering how Washington died. In the last of these, with a tenor solo by her then husband, Eddie Chamblee, she tells her fine fat daddy *not* to reduce, because what matters "is the way you feel inside." (Make of that what you will.) Dinah has no qualms about the apparent contradiction between swooning over a slender swain in one song and caressing a corpulent Casanova in the other—she would return to the topic in her own good time. She not only sings lustily of her fondness for giants and midgets alike, she doesn't mind being an "Old Man's Darling."

Beginning in 1954, Washington began making records specifically for the jazz market. Supposedly this came about indirectly because of Norman Granz: In 1953, the famous impresario, who had been producing jazz sessions for Mercury since 1948, left the company and took his catalogue with him. Mercury then let producer Bob Shad start a new jazz subsidiary called EmArcy, and among his master strokes was the idea of recording purely jazz sessions with two of the greatest of all singers, Washington and Sarah Vaughan, who had more recently joined the label. The two singers recorded pop for Mercury and jazz for EmArcy.

Washington's most important projects for EmArcy were two all-star jam sessions, *After Hours with Miss D* and *Dinah Jams* (both 1954). The former, which was the second to be released, spotlights Washington with two nouveau Ellingtonians, alto saxist Rick Henderson and the brilliant trumpeter Clark Terry; the second positions her with the nucleus of the superb Clifford Brown–Max Roach Quintet. Yet even when she locks horns with two ensembles comprised of some of the finest of all jazzmen, it's clear that the swingin'est and the most intense musician of them all is Washington.

Curiously, "You Go to My Head," from the Brown-Roach session, is a rare example of Washington being thrown. She starts with two choruses, the first a medium-slow ballad approach that is classic Washington; for the second, the tempo kicks in and a lightly Latin polyrhythm is introduced, and Washington, though swinging, nonetheless sounds slightly stilted. When she reconfigures the rhythm, she sounds like one of those pop calypso singers of the late fifties who deliberately "put the accent on the wrong syl-LAB-ble." When singers like Billie Holiday and Frank Sinatra do "You Go to My Head," naturally enough they deemphasize the article "to." For some reason, Washington gives all five words in the measure equal stress, and the result sounds somewhat awkward and ungainly—it's hard to pinpoint what's throwing her, since she'd dealt with Latin rhythms before and after; the bongos are in full force throughout the Quinichette organ sessions. (Judy Garland would later pick up on the idea of doing "You Go to My Head" in mambo time to greater effect in her famous 1961 Carnegie Hall concert.) For the rest of the two records Washington swings effortlessly.

While the core of her support had always been the black audience, these two albums represent the first time a producer had deliberately tried to package her for the jazz market—by the mid-fifties that was no longer the same thing. Washington's vocals frame long tracks that are exclusively strings of extended solos by the heaviest hitters of the day; the format, right down to Bobby Shad's opening announcements, seems borrowed from Norman Granz's live and studio jam session recordings. This is a pure jazz format and Washington was one of the few divas of the jazz universe to try it. There are a few Ella Fitzgerald live JATP tracks scattered here and there that fit this profile, although I can't think of anything like this (hot singer framing longish horn solos by heavyweights) by Sarah Vaughan, Carmen McRae, or virtually any other singer.

If the two jam session dates are extreme jazz, there's a remarkable album from 1954, *For Those in Love* (another EmArcy release), that mixes elements of pure jazz and traditional pop. Here, she gives out with twelve first-rate standards, most notably a recent Nat Cole movie song now elevated to that category, "Blue Gardenia." There are very full solos by several musicians on each track, and the nonsensical but glorious "I Diddie" sports a tenor battle between Paul Quinichette and Budd Johnson, although none of the numbers is a ten-minute jam session. Further, there are also solidly arranged ensemble passages that showcase Washington spectacularly. The package was put together by emerging arranger-producer Quincy Jones. On "You Don't Know What Love Is," Washington goes down on "You don't know how hearts burn" in a way that minimizes the word "burn" yet somehow stresses it at the same time— just burnin' it up, baby. Coincidentally, each of the two sessions begins with Rodgers and Hart: "I Could Write a Book" and "This Can't Be Love."

After *For Those in Love*, Washington's next important albums (recorded amid an ongoing slew of singles) arrived in the form of a pair of outstanding big band albums from 1955 and 1956: *Dinah!* and *Dinah Washington in the Land of Hi-Fi*, the latter part of a Mercury series that also included albums with this title by Sarah Vaughan and Patti Page. Both

were conducted by Mercury house rabbi Hal Mooney, who saw to it that both the ballads and the swingers on each package were decked out in loud and bristling brass. There are no strings (except at the fifth and last of the sessions), and trumpets and trombones get most of the emphasis; these decorate her singing style like jewelry around her neck. The gem of the twenty-four tracks recorded at these sessions is "Nothing Ever Changes My Love for You," a classic Marvin Fisher song also recorded by Nat Cole and instrumentally by George Shearing. Of the three, Washington and Mooney are the only ones who treat it to a cha-cha beat—which, incidentally, Washington handles with so much authority ("You Go to My Head" aside) that once again she picks up the mantle of *La Regina del Mambo*. (There's an even better mambo from 1956, "Relax, Max," which she tosses off without apparent effort, even though the time doubles in the bridge.)

Washington's single best concept album is easily the 1957 *Dinah Washington Sings Fats Waller*, which includes tunes both written by and associated with the harmful little armful. The pairing of Washington with arranger-conductor Ernie Wilkins is an inspired meeting of singer and musical director, on a par with Wilkins's work for the Count Basie–Joe Williams combination. Wilkins gives these twenty- and thirty-year-old jazz standards a tough, biting edge that suits Washington sublimely. Over the years we've heard her in countless settings with every kind of material (and the worst was yet to come), from easy listening strings and choirs to pure jazz, yet this is the best showcase she ever had for her formidable talents. Better than any other arranger, Wilkins frames this great artist at the very pinnacle of her powers.

The closest thing to a drawback (apart from a lame lyric to Waller's "Jitterbug Waltz," which should have remained an instrumental) came from Washington's insistence on spotlighting her husband and primary accompanist, Eddie Chamblee, not only on tenor (on which he's not bad but still no Dexter Gordon), but as vocal duet partner on two tracks. Love can be a terrible thing—especially for Washington, who was by now doing her best singing on long-playing records, even though her relationships were barely even three-minute 45 rpm singles. It would be unkind to blame Chamblee, who is billed as musical director on *Dinah Sings Bessie Smith*, because that album isn't as good as the Fats Waller package. It was apparently the label's decision to back Washington with a quasi-Dixieland group that evokes the twenties (the worst offender is the ricky-tick drumming that persists throughout—especially since most Bessie Smith records don't employ drums at all).

Although the Bessie Smith album is not nearly as good as the Fats Waller album, it's still worth hearing, especially since, at times, the band almost anticipates the "avant-gutbucket" sound of Charles Mingus or David Murray. Washington's singing is still first-rate, and the Queen is immediately on the same page as the late, lamented Empress of the Blues. At their best, tribute projects like these establish a continuum—Dinah Washington saluting Bessie Smith in 1958, then Aretha Franklin saluting Dinah Washington in 1964. Too bad there isn't a contemporary blues-jazz-soul singer to honor Aretha the way Franklin did Washington or Washington did Smith.

Washington's career was thriving in the late fifties. By this time she was also working regularly in Las Vegas, where she appeared at the Thunderbird and became friendly with Tony Bennett. "She never had a regular contract," said Bennett. "She'd just show up one day, carrying her suitcases, and say, 'I'm here, boss.' And Dave Victorson, who ran the place, would say, 'Well, go to work tonight.' She'd go to the lounge, and the word would get out all over town, 'Dinah's here, Dinah's in town,' with no advertising or anything, and the place would be packed with all the gypsies, all the people on the Strip, the chorus girls and the chorus boys and all the guys that worked the tables. . . ."

In one of the great benefactions of the modern recording industry, the Japanese producer Kiyoshi Koyama gathered all of Dinah Washington's Mercury recordings into a comprehensive, complete package, which came to seven boxes of three discs apiece and which was released at the dawn of the compact disc era in the mid-eighties. There are other complete retrospectives of major female singers, such as Sarah Vaughan (also by Koyama), and the Bear Family collections of Doris Day and Rosemary Clooney. It should be noted that actually sitting down and listening to the complete works of no other singer—with the exception of Billie Holiday—is as rewarding as listening this way to Washington. Maybe it's due to her easy ability to switch between the blues and standards that her total output is just so listenable. Virtually everything on boxes one through five—1946 through 1958—is something to treasure and play again and again. Unfortunately, the average goes way down on box number six, 1959–60. In 1959, she began recording with producer Clyde Otis and arranger-conductor Belford Hendricks, whose mission apparently was to repackage Washington for the younger rock 'n' pop doo-wop crowd. He succeeded immediately: The second track on their first session together was "What a Diff'rence a Day Made" (which she changed to "Makes"), and it became the single biggest song of her career—a breakthrough hit.

Otis and Hendricks backed Washington with large doo-wopping wordless choirs, irritatingly high-pitched strings, obnoxiously heavy-handed drumming (usually by Panama Francis, a fine jazz drummer who could have done much better if given the chance) emphasizing the annoying 16th-note triplets that were an unavoidable element of first-generation kiddie pop. What makes the sessions with Hendricks (who later did the same for Nat King Cole) particularly painful is that they primarily use great standard tunes. A forgettable doo-woppy novelty would be easy to pass over, even with Washington, but when you see titles like "It Could Happen to You," "It's Magic," and "Unforgettable" (which became a hit for her) you simply have to listen. Washington's singing is exemplary on all of these tracks, and one yearns for the invention of some twenty-first-century super karaoke machine that removes the original backgrounds and inserts some more appropriate accompaniment. Anything would be an improvement.

Most of Washington's 1959–60 sessions are simply dreadful, although there are four marvelous duets with the Sam Cooke–like soul singer Brook Benton. The plan was to do an entire album of boy-girl duos, but the two singers had a falling out and were barely able to get even these four tracks in the can. Even so, the two voices get a very congenial vibe going on "Baby (You've Got What It Takes)" and "A Rockin' Good Way (To Mess Around and Fall in Love)," even if the backgrounds are as relentlessly annoying as ever. The seventh box is fairly dispensable for a different reason: Quincy Jones now replaces Clyde Otis as Mercury's main A&R man, and it seems as if the most profitable things he could think of for her to do were stereo remakes of earlier hits. All three discs of box seven—nearly seventy tracks—were taped in 1961, perhaps the most prolific year of her career, but at the same time the least rewarding.

Apart from the megahit "What a Diff'rence," the best-remembered song from the period is "This Bitter Earth," credited to Otis and recorded by the Washington-Otis-Hendricks trio in 1959. The Mercury track is one of Hendricks's more palatable arrangements, but there's a live version from Birdland in 1962 that's considerably better—and even more bitter. The studio single has a big string section, but the live one is simply Washington and pianist Joe Zawinal. Like all her live performances, the Birdland treatment is somehow looser yet at the same time more intense. It's less of a torch song than a *scorch* song—Washington is positively inflammatory. Her second chorus is more decorous, and Zawinal's playing stays even closer to the wellspring of the blues. If someone were to tell you it was Ray Charles himself playing for Washington, you'd have no reason not to believe it. In his music and lyrics, Otis aptly harnessed Washington's spirit; the mood is bitter but not self-pitying. At the end, she helps the song deliver a minor note of optimism, a hint of sunshine peeking through the clouds, with the line that "this bitter earth may not be so bitter after all." It was one of her most affecting performances, a song that everybody remembers. She sang it dozens of times in her last five years, and it's been performed in her memory by Aretha Franklin, Lou Rawls, Nancy Wilson, Etta James, and Jimmy Scott—and that's far from all.

In a nutshell, the received wisdom regarding Washington's post–"What a Diff'rence a Day Makes" and post-1959 career is that she did nothing worth listening to (like post-Riverside Wes Montgomery or Nat King Cole in his "Rambling Rose" period). In reality, this theory only holds water until you listen to the records. When she was lured away from Mercury to Roulette early in 1962, they had no intention of packaging her for lowest-common-denominator pop. Indeed, the point of albums like *Back to the Blues*, her fourth for Roulette, was to prove that her newfound pop audience wouldn't desert her if she returned to the hard-hitting sounds that had put her on the map in the first place.

In her two years at Roulette, Washington concentrated on albums as opposed to singles, and recorded a total of seven basic sets for the label; these have been frequently reformatted, rehashed, and reanthologized into dozens of compilations and "best of" collections over the last forty-five years, until Mosaic Records came out with a definitive, five-CD collection in 2004. Washington launched her association with Roulette with a set of swinging standards titled *Dinah '62*, which included such milestones as "Destination Moon," "Coquette," "Miss You," and "A Handful of Stars." She followed this with two collections of ballads orchestrated by the gifted Don Costa. *Dinah in Love* consisted of romantic numbers treated considerably more straight-ahead than "What a Diff'rence." *Drinking Again* was a more melancholy gathering, which introduced the titular Johnny Mercer classic and included an aching, blues-inflected "Lover Man" and "The Man That Got Away."

Nineteen sixty-three saw Washington's most powerful Roulette set, *Back to the Blues*, as her scorching treatment of "The Blues Ain't Nothin'" mightily testifies. The underappreciated arranger Fred Norman, who crafted both *Dinah '62* and its more pop-oriented follow-up, *Dinah '63*, here showed what he could do with an orchestra full of jazz all-stars and blues intentions. *Dinah '63* combined pop standards with contemporary hits, including a particularly earthy treatment of Mercer's "I Wanna Be Around" that likewise travels back to the blues.

Dinah '63, was, sadly, the last Washington release to come out during her lifetime. Billie Holiday and Judy Garland were probably the two most self-destructive divas of all time; Washington did not share that impulse, yet she died younger than either of them, at thirty-nine. It wasn't narcotics that messed her up, but legal substances from a drugstore and a liquor store taken in a lethal combination. Throughout her life, she was continually preoccupied with losing weight, and apparently no one ever told her not to mix alcohol and diet pills. Unlike many musicians, Washington didn't die trying to get high. She died trying to get thin.

When that happened, on December 14, 1963, Roulette still had two albums in the can. The first,

eventually issued as *In Tribute,* may have been planned as *Dinah '64,* since it consists primarily of more or less recent songs (as well as Jimmy Van Heusen's poignant, older "Funny Thing") and, like its annual predecessors, was arranged by Fred Norman. The final project, a third sublime collection of ballads with Don Costa, was released simply and appropriately as *Dinah Washington.* Although built around classic songs like "Just One More Chance" and "I'll Never Stop Loving You," it also included newer pieces such as "Don't Say Nothin' at All" and Washington's own "To Forget About You." "A Stranger on Earth" was a haunting track that, like "I Wanna Be Around," had morbid relevance after Washington's death.

"Dinah was strong-willed and forceful," as fellow Hamptonite Betty Carter once noted. "Her personality was such that whenever she was around, performing or not, you knew it." She was also the most soulful voice and persona that popular music has known. Even the lesser offerings of the Queen of the Blues deserve to be treasured.

In her own original blues "Love Me with Misery" (1950), Washington sings,

> Say you always tell me I'm evil and salty
> And got them old funny time ways
> But you're gonna miss my salty evilness
> One of these old rainy days.

She was right.

Ethel Waters (1896–1977)

> *It's a long, long story,*
> *Do you want to hear it?*
> *If not I'll tell it anyway.*
> —Ethel Waters, "Second Hand Man"
> (Easton-Waters, 1929)

By any standards, Ethel Waters was a pioneer, and generally speaking, there are two reasons why we listen to pioneers today. First, to see how much they influenced subsequent artists and gauge exactly what they introduced that was eventually adopted into the standard vocabulary. Second, to see what they did that didn't catch on, and experience whatever still remains unique to this artist and her or his generation. Ethel Waters doesn't lack for acolytes: Bing Crosby, Lee Wiley, Mildred Bailey, and Jimmy Rushing, among many others, named her as a direct influence, and one hears distinct echoes of her immaculate, precise articulation in the singing of Frank Sinatra; Bobby Short apparently memorized every note she ever recorded (most famously "Guess Who's in Town?"). All these are good reasons for listening to Ethel Waters. A better reason is that she is considerably bigger than the sum of those she influenced: Waters still has something to say to us, ninety years after she cut her first disc. The best reason is because most of her records still sound so good.

Apart from Sophie Tucker and some of the early classical divas, Waters may well have been the first truly great female vocalist to make a record, and many of the principles she developed in the early twenties took hold and influenced multiple generations of jazz, blues, and pop singers—indeed, are even in use today. And then again, many are not. As she sings in the 1929 "Better Keep an Eye on Your Man": "Everybody's not like me."

Waters showed us that there were two Great American Songbooks available to jazz and pop singers: One is Cole Porter, George and Ira Gershwin, and company; the other is Clarence Williams, W. C. Handy, and, later, Robert Johnson et al. In the work of both groups, the performance takes precedence over the source material. Yet, also thanks to Waters, we know that these two American idioms are deeply connected to each other: One of her descendants, Dinah Washington, can take a song by Rodgers and Hart and make it sound as if it were written by Memphis Slim. Although I've never heard her do it, I don't doubt that Eydie Gormé could take something by Muddy Waters and make it sound like Cy Coleman.

Yet although these two different songbooks exist, there are relatively few artists who take advantage of them equally—among the few who do are Washington (Waters's "Oh Joe, Play That Trombone" directly prefigures Washington's "Big Long Sliding Thing"), Joe Williams, Ray Charles, Etta Jones, Dakota Staton, and, among the few Caucasian artists who belong in this category, Peggy Lee and Kay Starr. Ethel Waters, to borrow Gary Giddins's very apt phrase, was the mother of them all. She was more than a jazz or blues singer; her many recordings of popular songs lacking those elements are no less remarkable than those that use them. Her treatment of "Love Is the Thing," formal yet funky, diction so impeccable it almost sounds like an English accent, illustrates her influence on Mabel Mercer.

It would almost be too trite to call Waters the original crossover artist, although she surely was the first African American female entertainer to completely be welcomed into the hearts of the great white audience: to sell to white buyers on the mainstream record labels, to headline on Broadway, to make talking pictures. It's all true, yet Waters was a crossover in a deeper, more important sense. Everything about her screams convergence. She emerged at the dawn of the Jazz Age, when jazz, blues, and the popular song were all being refined into their present forms and packaged for popular consumption, first black and then white. When both of the songbook traditions were in their embryonic form, Waters not only brought them together but helped influence the future shape of both, in terms of their interaction with each other and as distinct, individual entities. Even today, well after her centennial, she remains the only major vocalist who could sing the blues with rolled Rs.

Waters was born on Halloween 1896, in Chester, Pennsylvania. (She usually gave 1900 as the date, but 1896 is believed to be correct.) She talked about her early life with remarkable frankness in her 1951 memoir *His Eye Is on the Sparrow*, a book that surpasses Billie Holiday's better-known *Lady Sings the Blues* for candor and readability. (When first published, Waters's book was a best seller, although Holiday's book became more iconic in the long run.)

Waters first sang in church, and in her teens worked as a domestic. She began performing in amateur shows and saloons, first around her native city and then Baltimore, and began gradually working her way up the ladder of black showbiz. By 1917, when she moved to New York, she was already a headliner, regularly playing the "colored" vaudeville circuit. She got into a touring revue called *Hello 1919*, which initiated her gradual transition to what was then known as the legitimate theater. In 1920, the equally young Mamie Smith recorded "Crazy Blues" and thus launched the vogue for "race" records: black artists (usually women) singing songs by black composers for purchase by the emerging black middle class. Waters was in a good place, career-wise, to benefit from this turn of events, and in 1921 was recruited to make a commercial recording by a short-lived firm named Cardinal Records. Their association lasted exactly one disc, Cardinal 2036, containing two dance-driven titles, "The New York Glide" and "At the New Jump Steady Ball."

Not long afterward, she first met her longtime accompanist and friend Fletcher Henderson, who was then employed by Black Swan Records. Henderson later related, "I was walking along 135th Street in Harlem one night, and there, in a basement, singing with all her heart, was Ethel. I had her come down and cut four sides, of which two, 'Down Home Blues' and 'Oh Daddy,' became such hits that we were made."

The first thing one notices about the earliest Waters records, her acoustic era sessions for Cardinal and Black Swan, is how thin her voice sounds. At this time, she was nicknamed "Sweet Mama Stringbean" in vaudeville, and her voice was equally slender; given time, both her frame and her chops would fill out considerably. Even given the limitations of the technology, her high pipes reproduced well. It's been said that high voices reproduced better in the acoustic process, while electrical recording favored low ones, explaining why tenors were gradually superseded by baritones like Bing Crosby. Waters, like Al Jolson, was aware enough of the technological transitions to take full advantage of the difference; it's clearly more than an accident or even the natural process of aging that her voice is considerably lower in 1931 than it was in 1921.

Waters's career trajectory established a pattern that many other African American artists would follow—or at least aspire to: first, gaining the love and support of the black audience; then, using that as a platform to eventual acceptance by the larger white audience. (Her only notable predecessor in this accomplishment was Bert Williams, the short-lived Ziegfeld star.) Waters shows much of her mature style even in her first recordings; in her early acoustic period, the recording process wasn't sufficiently refined to capture nuance or vocal timbre, but she was astute enough to get her personality across in this primitive medium. She had the stuff in abundance. For one thing, she would cleverly refer to herself in her own records. On "No Man's Mama" (1925) she refers to herself as "sweet Miss Waters," while it's "Ethel" on both "Ethel Sings 'Em" (1925) and "You've Seen Harlem at Its Best" (1931). There was never any doubt as to who was singing.

As Henderson reports, her first pairing for Black Swan, "Down Home Blues" and "Oh Daddy," was an unexpected success, selling 100,000 copies. Despite the title of the first, neither of these two items was strictly a blues in the traditional sense, as the form would be defined and codified two years later by Bessie Smith; Waters herself describes Smith as "the Empress" in her 1925 "Maybe Not at All." But neither is "Down Home Blues" strictly a standard pop song—it pays to remember that both forms were still in the process of evolution in 1921; there are allusions to blues form, even if the second line isn't repeated exactly, and also to blues harmony. "Memphis Man" and "Midnight Blues" of 1923 come closer to the authentic blues requirements—one can even imagine them being sung by any of the Smith girls. But although Waters would cut relatively few numbers that were strictly in the classic 12-bar blues format, virtually everything she did sing had at least an element of the blues. Sometimes it was something inherently musical, but equally often it was found in the lyric content—a word or phrase in the text that spoke of the "race" experience.

The earliest Waters sides are divided not only between the blues and standard song form, but between those with band accompaniments and those with only piano. The band records, naturally, have been particularly prized by jazz fans over the decades, particularly the many titles with Henderson and his star players, most notably cornetist Joe Smith and tenor Coleman Hawkins. There are several sessions employing the rare instrumentation of piano, bass saxophone (at least once played by Hawkins), and trumpet.

It's a major disappointment, however, that Waters never recorded with Louis Armstrong. Oddly, even though the trumpeter seems to have accompanied every two-bit pseudoblues singer of the era—not to mention the great Bessie Smith—he never worked with Waters. However, in 1923 she recorded "If You Don't Think I'll Do, Sweet Pops (Just Try Me)," a blues song credited to Louis and Lil Hardin Armstrong and featuring his future nickname in the title. Waters would later make what might be considered the first two Armstrong tribute records, "West End Blues" (1928) and "I Can't Give You Anything but Love, Baby" (1932); in the latter, she launches into a full-scale Pops impression. She also recorded "When It's Sleepy Time Down South," already Armstrong's theme song, in 1934.

One shouldn't make the mistake of overlooking Waters's piano-only sessions; the acoustic years in particular are graced by any number of duets with such accompanists as Henderson, J. C. Johnson, Fats Waller (on Sidney Bechet's "Pleasure Mad" and his own "Back-Bitin' Mama" in 1924), and her longtime accompanist Pearl Wright. These voice-and-piano items directly anticipate such later jazz vocal-piano masterpieces as *Ella and Ellis* and *The Intimate Ella*, as well as the June Christy–Stan Kenton *Duet*.

On a similar note, in 1926 Waters recorded a fascinating series of sessions in collaboration with a group of well-known pianist-composers, both black and white, including Sammy Fain on "If You Can't Hold the Man You Love" and Maceo Pinkard on "Sugar" and "I Wonder What's Become of Joe." Best of all are the songs by and/or with Shelton Brooks, one of the first successful African American composers, in which she seems to be joined by the songwriter himself in a dialogue at the start of "Make Me a Pallet on Your Floor" and other arias of sexual humiliation such as "Throw Dirt in Your Face" (the title refers to a gravedigger's assignment, "a woman whose daily occupation is stealin' other women's men"), "After All These Years," and "Bring Your Greenbacks." A year and a half later, she completed her Shelton Brooks series with a rendition of his best-known work, "Some of These Days," that even Sophie Tucker would admire.

Waters herself sang a perfect description of what she did in "You've Seen Harlem at Its Best," a 1934 song by Cotton Club staff writers Dorothy Fields and Jimmy McHugh:

> Then when Waters croons
> Those slightly earthy tunes
> [spoken aside: You've had your money's worth!]
> You've seen Harlem at its best.

Crooning refers to a mainstream pop style identified most strongly with Bing Crosby, while "slightly earthy tunes" alludes to the risqué and openly erotic quality of many of the double entendre numbers that she sang. Waters was well aware that not all blues are sexual in nature and not all songs about sex are blues. Cole Porter and Noel Coward managed to indulge in all kinds of lusty lyrics without going anywhere near the 12-bar pattern; in fact, the next number to be recorded by Waters after "Harlem at Its Best" was "Miss Otis Regrets," a classic slice of Porter that deals with love in vain, murder, the heat in the kitchen, and hellhounds on the trail every bit as eloquently and explicitly as anything by Robert Johnson.

Neither the 12-bar blues form nor the standard AABA pop song were rigorously set in stone in these years, and neither were the boundaries between these two developing forms so rigid. For instance, "Sweet Man" (1925) and "Heebie Jeebies" (1926) both open with a full chorus of jazz band instrumental (future generations would put this break in the middle of the two vocal choruses), so that it blurs the distinction between the two basic species of mainstream pop record, the dance record (band—vocal—band) and the personality record (vocal—band—vocal). Convergence and crossover seemed perfectly natural, with Waters's jazz techniques as a common ground, an element that could be applied to either blues or pop.

Waters probably didn't invent the modern jazz vocal form, but she certainly perfected it and inspired many generations to take it up. She typically starts with the verse, sings the first chorus relatively straight and then treats the second chorus more playfully—jazzy, so to speak. It's so simple it's almost not worth being identified as a musical format, but that's just the point: This is the single most basic outline of how a jazz-pop singer operates. Doubtless, Armstrong would have been doing this had he been singing two choruses in the twenties, but as it happens, Waters was the one who popularized this approach, and everyone seems to have learned it from her, from the three major white goddesses of the thirties—Mildred Bailey, Lee Wiley, and Connee Boswell—to all the important black singers, such as Maxine Sullivan, Helen Humes, Ella Fitzgerald, and even Billie Holiday, although she denied it.

Waters went on experimenting, not only with song and blues structure but searching for novelty within the recording form itself. Both the 1925 "You Can't Do What My Last Man Did" and the 1926 "Pallet on the Floor" open with a patch of dialogue between Waters and a male speaker (in the first it's one "Slow Kid" Thompson), and "Last Man" on the whole is very dialoguey, with Waters blurring the distinction between speech and song. At one point, she affects an outrageously unnatural upper-class accent ("you just cahn't!"), and then follows this by exclaiming "Come get me, Ethel Barrymore!" She virtually invents rap on the 1924 "You'll Need Me When I'm Long Gone" (in which she refers to her misbehaving lover as "Rudolph Vaselino") and then again on "Weary Feet" (1926), in which she addresses a long speech directly to her overextended pedal extremities. The best of all Waters raps is the 1935 "Thief in the Night," a "signifying" and "ranking" series of eloquent put-downs that all but defies summarization; the best line is "You're everything that begins with the letter S and the letter B!"

If Waters's use of spoken raps can be described as words without notes, her use of scat singing amounts to notes without words. She hints at the technique as early as 1922 in "That Da Da Strain" and then develops it more fully, following Armstrong's example, in "Guess Who's in Town?" (1928),

"My Kind of a Man," and "I Got Rhythm" (1930), on which she exchanges phrases with trumpeter Manny Klein, in addition to the more directly Armstrongian "West End Blues" (1928) and "I Can't Give You Anything but Love, Baby" (1932). Speaking of impressions, the 1925 "Maybe Not at All" interpolates Waters's devastatingly on-target approximations of both Clara Smith (hot and staccato, clipped delivery) and Bessie Smith ("Get ready for the Empress," she avers as the tempo grinds down to a slow drag).

Waters even dabbled in spiritual music, anticipating the later gospel movement. "You're Mine" uses a church-style organ and several references to the Almighty, while "He Brought Joy to My Soul" is a pure spiritual, rendered with a male vocal quartet but otherwise a cappella in the down-home church tradition. On the other hand, "St. Louis Blues" employs the Cecil Mack Choir to humorously accentuate the spiritual side of the Handy masterpiece. Both of these selections prefigure Waters's last twenty years, in which she devoted considerable time to religious activities, including tours with the Reverend Billy Graham. Yet it must be confessed that she spent more time with the profane than the sacred.

Waters also all but invented the risqué double entendre blues—all those "slightly earthy tunes"—and no one ever did them better. She also was the master of the technological metaphor: the 1925 "Loud Speakin' Papa (You'd Better Speak Easy to Me)," which employs a radio conceit—"I'm gonna twist your aerial and bust your horn"—and the 1926 "Refrigeratin' Papa (Mama's Gonna Warm You Up)," in which she vows "Mama's gonna make you hot" and turn her ice-cold lover into a red-hot papa. Eventually, lyricist Andy Razaf became her principal accomplice in this pursuit, as on their all-time classic "My Handy Man," while the self-penned "Second-Hand Man" (1929) is nearly as suggestive. On both of these, the text is never directly dirty, yet Waters conveys a broad range of erotic expression purely through tone of voice, sly emphasis, and other kinds of innuendo. Then, too, she can do the same thing in reverse, taking something written to sound somewhat off-color and cleaning it up in grandiloquent fashion, as on "Take Your Black Bottom Outside," which she rephrases as "remove your dark anatomy outside."

Waters's self-satirizing sexpot was an obvious influence on Mae West. In fact, her records were so closely studied by other singers that it's hardly surprising she introduced many jazz standards, starting with "There'll Be Some Changes Made" in 1921. In the twenties alone, Waters put a whole lot of standards on the jazz map, songs like "Sweet Georgia Brown," "Dinah" (both 1925), "I Found a New Baby," "Sugar," "Heebie Jeebies," "I'm Comin', Virginia" (all 1926), "One Sweet Letter from You" (1927), and even "Am I Blue," which was written for her in her first film appearance, the 1929 *On with the Show!*

It's also easy to see what other singers learned from her: Billie Holiday claimed not to like Waters, yet she undoubtedly studied the 1922 "Ethel Sings 'Em" (the "'em" refers to the blues), which includes the line "Love is like a faucet, it turns off and on," which Holiday later worked into "Fine and Mellow." (Holiday's "Billie's Blues" also paraphrases from Waters's 1924 "Craving Blues" and 1925 "Down Home Blues.") Waters's "Sugar" was all but literally remade, almost inflection by inflection, by Lee Wiley, starting with the verse and two choruses, although the younger singer for some reason elected not to employ the witty special second chorus lyrics that Waters sang. Her 1927 "Someday Sweetheart" is the obvious model for the Bing Crosby version of seven years later, and likewise her "I'm Coming, Virginia" strongly influenced Crosby on one of his first solo vocals, while the 1925 blues "Shake That Thing" ends on a syncopated trill that can only be described as Crosbyesque.

In 1927 Waters made her "legit" Broadway debut in *Africana*, an all-black revue with a score written for the most part by black composers and longtime Waters associates such as J. C. Johnson, Andy Razaf, and Will Marion Cook. *Africana* gave her plenty of opportunities to ply her specialties, many of which did not originate in this production but were interpolated into the score. She returned to Broadway in *Blackbirds of 1930*; although this Lew Leslie revue did not duplicate the blockbuster success of his original *Blackbirds* two years earlier, it gave Waters the chance to introduce two Andy Razaf–Eubie Blake standards, "You're Lucky to Me" (another number Lee Wiley learned from her) and "Memories of You." *Rhapsody in Black* (1931) was her third all-black Broadway revue. She commissioned an outstanding score from Alberta Nichols and Mann Holiner, a gifted lyricist who would later work as radio producer for both Sinatra and Crosby. This score included their charming "You Can't Stop Me from Loving You" (with the line "You can put Lux in my cornflakes") and an early incarnation of "Until the Real Thing Comes Along" (which, with some additional kibitzing by Sammy Cahn and Saul Chaplin, became a blockbuster hit in 1936, though not, unfortunately, for Waters).

She would land her single biggest hit song not on Broadway but in Harlem. In 1933, she was asked to headline at the Cotton Club for their spring revue. At first, she turned them down (not a smart move, considering the wiseguys who owned it didn't like to take no for an answer), but changed her mind when she heard the song that Harold Arlen and Ted Koehler were then working on, which was called "Stormy Weather." She made a few changes to the rough draft of the piece, pruning away some extraneous material, and both Waters and "Stormy Weather" were an immediate sensation when *The Cotton Club Revue* opened. Eventually, three major black divas would make career pegs out of "Stormy Weather": Waters, Duke Ellington's number-one singer, Ivie Anderson, and, of course, Lena Horne, with whom in the long run it would be most associated. But it was Waters who put it over and made it one of the most popular songs of the entire Depression era.

The aftereffects of the success of "Stormy Weather" helped bring her to a level that no black female singer had ever achieved: She soon had her own radio series, and was perhaps the first black diva to headline an otherwise white show on Broadway. In 1929, she had recorded the finest version of Irving Berlin's original spiritual "Waiting at the End of the Road"; in 1933, the composer caught her at the Cotton Club and was so impressed that he brought her into his new revue, *As Thousands Cheer,* that fall. Although she had no interaction with any of the white headliners, she was given the full star treatment, with separate-but-equal billing.

She caused a further sensation with three all-time Irving Berlin classics: "Heat Wave" was pure tropicalia fluff, whereas "Harlem on My Mind" and "Supper Time" were specifically Afro in content. The first of those was comic, poking fun at a "colored" chorus girl turned toast of Paree, i.e., Josephine Baker; the second was scathingly tragic, depicting the aftermath of a lynching in the Deep South. It was the most stunning protest song since Razaf and Blake's "Black and Blue" (also recorded unforgettably by Waters) from the 1929 *Hot Chocolates*, and perhaps the most disturbing number in a Broadway musical until the sixties.

She continued to proceed where few, if any, black performers had been allowed to tread before. In 1933, she co-starred with the six-year-old Sammy Davis Jr. in the Vitaphone two-reeler *Rufus Jones for President*. It was a surreal, wild minstrel show of a short subject, only with authentic Negro performers (not corked-up Caucasians), but Waters was the acknowledged standout with a sensual and funny rendition of "Underneath the Harlem Moon" (in which she referred to her people as "we *schvartzes*") that truly transformed the ridiculous into the sublime. *Rufus Jones* was followed by another short subject (*Bubbling Over*, 1934), and then a speaking and singing role as well as a number ("I Ain't Gonna Sin No More") in the feature *Gift of Gab*.

But her biggest step forward at this point was returning to Broadway in 1935–36 in a second successful mainstream revue, *At Home Abroad,* with a score by Howard Dietz and Arthur Schwartz. She made a big impression with "Thief in the Night," the jungle-set "Hottentot Potentate" (in which she refers to herself as "the Empress Jones"), and the Jamaica-set "Steamboat Whistle." In both of the latter, she worked with scat savant Leo Watson and the Spirits of Rhythm. In "Got a Bran' New Suit," she did something even more radical in that the producers allowed her to share the stage with a white woman, dancer Eleanor Powell.

Waters next became just about the first pop singer of any race who succeeded in getting the world to take her seriously as a nonsinging actor in a non-musical drama, namely DuBose Heyward's *Mamba's Daughters* (1939). The play was well received at the time, but since then has been passed over along with the rest of Heyward's works; even *Porgy* is only remembered as the source of Gershwin's opera. Waters had already recorded a song called "Porgy" by Dorothy Fields and Jimmy McHugh, which had been directly inspired by Heyward's *Porgy,* years before *Porgy and Bess.* Aida Ward introduced it in *Black-birds,* but Waters made the definitive recording—actually she cut it both in 1930 and again in 1932 for the Brunswick *Blackbirds* studio cast album. There was, in fact, one song in *Mamba's Daughters,* "Lonesome Walls," with a lyric by Heyward (virtually his only non-*Porgy*-related popular song) and a melody by Jerome Kern (just about the closest that American classicist ever came to writing a blues), that she recorded marvelously for Bluebird in 1939.

At her pinnacle, Waters was earning $5,000 a week. It's hard to think of another big star from the early twenties who was doing as well decades later. Even Jolson and Bessie Smith were considered passé by then. Yet although Waters was one of the best-known names on Broadway, she was subject to the standard brutal treatment from the segregationist Jim Crow society, both in the South, where racism was overt, and in the North, where it was more subtle but nonetheless still omnipresent. (On "Georgia Blues," she sings with almost disturbing complacency about riding the "James Crow car" back home.)

Waters directly prefigured the success that black performers like Nat King Cole, Billy Eckstine, and Lena Horne would begin to have with regularity in the postwar era. Like Eckstine and Cole, Waters at the height of her career was largely recording songs by white authors accompanied by white studio orchestras. Still, no one could fail to recognize that she had reached a musical as well as professional peak. She recorded all the significant numbers from her revues and a great many other marvelous songs as well, being almost as responsible as Louis Armstrong for making an instant jazz-pop standard out of "When Your Lover Has Gone," and bringing her magical touch to "Please Don't Talk About Me When I'm Gone," "I Got Rhythm," "You Brought a New Kind of Love to Me" (this must be where Sinatra first heard it—forget Maurice Chevalier), and dozens of others. There are classic sessions from the early thirties with the Dorsey Brothers and Benny Goodman's first orchestra, and then in 1938–39 she made an amazing series of sides for the Bluebird label, using her husband, trumpeter Eddie Mallory, as leader of an all-star black orchestra featuring no less than Benny Carter. (My favorite of the latter batch is Hoagy Carmichael's catchy—and nourishing—"Bread and Gravy.")

All in all, Waters was the most popular African American female recording artist of the thirties, one of the few singers to keep going without a letup from the blues craze of the early twenties right into the swing era. Joel Whitburn, in *Pop Memories,* tells us that "Stormy Weather" and "Am I Blue" were both number-one hits for Waters (and "Dinah" made it to number 2), and while those songs, like everything else in the book (at least with regards to pre-1940 recordings), should be taken with a grain of salt, no one would argue that Waters was extremely popular in live appearances, radio, and recordings.

She may well have hit the high point in her career when she was given the lead in one of the first intelligent book shows written for an all-black cast, the 1940 *Cabin in the Sky,* in which black performers were, for the first time, allowed to do something other than minstrel-show-style antics. It was another hit, fortunately filmed by MGM, thereby providing us with an invaluable cinematic record of one of the most important of all American artists at her absolute pinnacle. Waters had been filmed before, but this was the first time an African American actor was allowed to be completely human, not just singing and praying, but shown as a three-dimensional (at least as much as anything was in Hollywood musicals) personage.

The audio portion of *Cabin* is itself no less invaluable; original Broadway cast albums were relatively rare then, and even though Waters recorded four *Cabin* songs for Liberty Music Shop with a small orchestra in 1940, those tracks pale beside her vocals of the same songs with the lavish MGM studio orchestra. Metro also improved upon Broadway by bringing in Harold Arlen to supply several new songs to supplement Vernon Duke's already excellent Broadway score, most notably one of Waters's biggest moments, "Happiness Is Just a Thing Called Joe." Duke's "Takin' a Chance on Love" is another Waters masterwork. Starting with an intro of single string guitar and whistling (from leading man Eddie "Rochester" Anderson), Waters shows how "special effects"—sighs, whispers, purrs like a muted trumpeter, and mild scatting—can enhance a lyric rather than detract from it. *Cabin* is one of the most remarkable documents of a classic performance by a major Broadway leading lady—there is no comparable movie of Mary Martin, Barbara Cook, or even Ethel Merman (except *Call Me Madam*). Waters is positively radiant in every shot of *Cabin;* even the luminous Lena Horne seems like a mere supporting player in her presence.

Cabin in the Sky was indeed Waters's pinnacle. Unlike most other black headliners, she at least got one starring vehicle. Around this time in the early forties, there were other, less substantial gigs in Hollywood. Like every other female black actress or singer of the period (except Horne, who flatly refused to) Waters was impelled to play a maid at one point (in *Cairo* with Jeanette MacDonald), but at least she got to sing the fine Harold Arlen song "Buds Won't Bud." Then there was one movie in which she sang without acting, *Stage Door Canteen,* in which she sang "Quicksand" accompanied by Count Basie's orchestra, and another movie in which she acted without singing, *Tales of Manhattan.* But by the end of the war years, her career seemed to have crested—all of a sudden no Broadway or Hollywood opportunities were forthcoming.

She describes the long, lean years quite movingly in *His Eye Is on the Sparrow,* published in 1951. The down period went on for too long, but happily ended when she reemerged as a dramatic actress, first in the nonmusical film *Pinky* (1949), then in the Broadway drama *The Member of the Wedding* (1950), starring Julie Harris, and later in the film of Faulkner's *The Sound and the Fury* (1959). She appeared frequently on TV, including a season of the sitcom *Beulah* in the role originated by Hattie McDaniel on radio, and often on Billy Graham's Christian crusades. She even wrote a second autobiography, *To Me It's Wonderful,* in 1972. By the time she died, on September 1, 1977, it might even be argued that it was forgotten by the public that she had even been a singer. Forgotten by everyone, that is, except by anyone who ever sang the blues or a popular song.

Margaret Whiting (born 1924)

It seems to me that rather too much is made of the simple fact that Margaret Whiting is, in Shakespeare's phrase, "to the manner born." W. C. Handy used this expression to somewhat diplomatically state that only black people were capable of singing the blues; the implication would seem to be that because Whiting's father, Richard Whiting, was a leading songwriter, that Whiting herself was genetically predisposed to make great music. (Her mother's sister, too, was a well-known singer: Margaret Young, one of the better female pop singers of the twenties.) I would be more inclined to think that Margaret Whiting's parental bloodline contributed to her talent if the daughters of other songwriters were equally talented. As it happens, a number of the female offspring of major songwriters are acquaintances of mine, among them Linda Emmett Berlin (daughter of Irving), Rory Burke (daughter of Johnny), Mary Rodgers Guettel (daughter of Richard Rodgers), Ellen Donaldson (daughter of Walter); in this random sample, only Margaret Whiting became a star singer and only Ms. Guettel had a career as a composer.

Whiting was one of six white female pop singers whose stardom was cemented during the war years and whose work is still listened to today; the others were Dinah Shore, Kay Starr, Peggy Lee, Jo Stafford, and Doris Day. (It's indicative of the talent-spotting abilities of Johnny Mercer that four of the six, including Whiting, were essentially launched by Capitol Records.) Kay Starr's singing was drenched

with Western jazz and blues, Peggy Lee's was no less jazzy or bluesy but with Scandinavian restraint, Doris Day's was pure sunshine, and Jo Stafford's favored reserved optimism with a touch of melancholy.

With her bright, clear contralto and flawless intonation, Whiting was a bit of all of the above. She was something of a swinger like Starr and Lee and also a storyteller like Stafford and Day. Excellent as she is, though, Whiting is the least distinctive of the major vocalists in this group—it's hard to identify her on the radio as quickly as you can Starr or Lee. She's also the least idiosyncratic, which can be a good thing.

Margaret Whiting's father, Richard A. Whiting, was born in 1891 in Peoria, Illinois. Unlike most major songwriters of the golden age of Tin Pan Alley (with the exception, as we shall see, of his future partner Gus Kahn), Whiting spent almost none of his career in the heartland of pop music, which, then as now, meant New York, New York. At the dawn of Whiting's career, several early efforts reached Jerome H. Remick, a publishing firm located in Detroit. The company not only agreed to publish the songs, they gave Whiting a job there in Motor Town. Before long, he was running the whole office. In those early days, his most frequent partner was Raymond Egan, a bank teller turned lyricist. The two of them had, among many other songs, substantial hits with the classic "Till We Meet Again," one of the best-remembered tunes of World War I, and "Japanese Sandman," which, thanks to Paul Whiteman's multimillion-selling disc, helped launch the dancing twenties.

It wasn't that Whiting didn't want to be recognized on Broadway; still based in Detroit, he submitted songs to different producers. Some made it into various shows, but none of these was even remotely a hit. Still, by the early twenties, he was regarded as a major songwriter and a local hero in Michigan. Around this time, he received a visit from two sisters from California, Margaret (1900–1969), a rising singer, and Eleanor Young (originally Youngblood), who was serving as her sister's agent. They came to Whiting for advice, and he quickly developed a crush on Margaret.

Shortly thereafter, the two Young sisters moved to New York, where Margaret Young did indeed become a headliner, a star of vaudeville and Brunswick Records. Heard today, her work holds up remarkably well, especially the many sides she cut in the early twenties with pioneering sax virtuoso Bennie Krueger. She was the kind of exuberant, jazz-and-blues-inspired vaudevillian who performed the same kind of semihot, seminovelty material as the more famous Marion Harris: "Louisville Lou," "Lovin' Sam, the Sheik of Alabam," and "Way Down Yonder in New Orleans." Like Harris, she was an acoustic age performer whose singing sounds considerably less dated than many of the early electric age singers. However, perhaps because her extroverted style was so rooted in the conventions of the early twenties, Brunswick didn't keep recording her beyond 1925. (She returned to the studio briefly in 1949, for Capitol, undoubtedly through the intervention of her niece, and also sang supporting roles on a few studio cast albums for budget labels.)

Margaret Young also recorded one of Richard Whiting's big hits of the era, the 1924 "Ukulele Lady." By that time, they were in-laws. After Margaret married a dancer she had met in New York, Eleanor returned to Detroit and married Richard. Their first of two daughters, Margaret Eleanor—named after her aunt—was born on July 22, 1924, in Detroit. (This is a date that's generally agreed upon, although various other dates have been offered over the years, some by Whiting herself.) She spent her childhood in Detroit, where she was raised completely immersed in music and songs. In the mid- to late twenties, Richard Whiting's career went from strength to strength, and he supplied the nation with a fair share of the hit songs that made the twenties roar: "Ain't We Got Fun," "Sleepy Time Gal," "Breezin' Along with the Breeze," and "Honey," to name a few.

Hollywood, then making the transition to talking pictures, took note. Paramount invited him to write the score for Maurice Chevalier's debut, *Innocents of Paris* (for which he wrote the standard "Louise"). In a story that still makes Maggie cry, before he left Detroit for this trial job at Paramount, he pinned a love note to his wife's pillow, and Eleanor took the initiative of submitting it to his publisher, where it was set to music by Neil Moret (of "Chloe" fame). It became possibly Whiting's most successful copyright, "She's Funny That Way," and his only notable effort as a lyricist.

Whiting made good in Hollywood, where, with lyricist Leo Robin, he wrote primarily for Paramount, most famously for stars Maurice Chevalier and Bing Crosby. He also enjoyed a brief sojourn at Twentieth Century Fox, where he wrote Shirley Temple's most famous song, "On the Good Ship Lollipop," and also took a breather to work on several Broadway shows, most notably *Take a Chance*. (Apparently, at least a few customers did—it was one of the bigger hits of the Depression.) For the last few years of his life, Whiting composed songs for Warner Bros., where he worked principally with the young Johnny Mercer (who was originally impressed by Whiting's golfing skills) for singer Dick Powell and choreographer-auteur Busby Berkeley.

It was in Hollywood that young Maggie got to meet the major music makers of the great years of songwriting, including George Gershwin, Lorenz Hart, and Jerome Kern, who would all be gone by the postwar era. Even granted that no other songwriter's daughter grew up to become a pop diva, it's a sure bet that long before Maggie was thirteen—the year her father died—she knew a good song when she heard one. Exactly what killed Richard Whiting on February 10, 1938, is still unclear; what's usually suggested is that, although a fun-loving, family guy, he was also incredibly high-strung and nervous, and suffered from acute high blood pressure. Undoubtedly, the stress of working in the Hollywood studio system was an important factor; he was also hit hard by the death of his friend George Gershwin a few months earlier.

Following Whiting's untimely death, his last major partner, Johnny Mercer, took young Maggie under his wing, both as a father figure and as a musical mentor. Sixty years later, she recollected that the most important piece of advice he gave her regarding her singing consisted of only two words. Apparently, as a young teenager she still sounded too immature for Mercer's tastes, and his pronouncement was that she should "Grow up."

Fast forward to just four years later, to 1942, when Mercer decided to form his own record company. At that stage in the development of pop music, roles were strictly regimented: Composers didn't sing professionally, few vocalists could actually write or even read music, and creative types almost never got involved on the business side. Yet Mercer would quickly prove himself one of the most astute music industry men of all time, with a keen knack for picking hit songs and launching or furthering the careers of major singers.

Capitol Records was launched in the months immediately following the attack on Pearl Harbor, and was almost put out of business by the 1942–44 AFM ban. Margaret Whiting recalls that during the window of those first few months, she was an extremely nervous seventeen-year-old waiting for her chance to make a record—like Ruby Keeler in *42nd Street*, setting foot onstage as a youngster and coming back a star. As she tells the story today, she had no idea what song Mercer would assign to her, and was completely floored when he brought out "My Ideal," a then forgotten song written by her father for Chevalier in the 1931 *Playboy of Paris*. She was even more surprised when the disc became a hit—number 12 on the *Billboard* charts.

Whiting had never worked on the road with any of the major big bands, but Mercer teamed her with two important orchestras for recording purposes. First she cut "That Old Black Magic" and "Silver Wings in the Moonlight" (a number 19 hit) with pianist Freddie Slack's band. Then, more successfully, Mercer backed her with a band identified as "Billy Butterfield's Orchestra," but which was actually Les Brown and His Band of Renown, recording under the pseudonym of the band's star trumpeter. With the Brown-Butterfield group, Whiting recorded "My Ideal," "There Goes That Song Again," and the song most identified with her, "Moonlight in Vermont."

Johnny Mercer actively managed Capitol's A&R department until the second record ban (1948), when the pressures of running the business drove him away, but Whiting remained with the label until the midfifties. During these years, she would land about fifty chart hits—not a bad track record—which makes it all the more mysterious that she's been pretty much ignored by the commercial music industry ever since. In the absence of a Bear Family box or some other comprehensive package, reissue coverage of Whiting's top years has been fairly negligible. Capitol has made two packages available, a two-CD set of hits, *The Complete Capitol Hits of Margaret Whiting* and a single of standards, *Great Ladies of Song: Spotlight on Margaret Whiting*. Apart from that, there are only a few odds and ends: some additional discs from England, such as *My Own True Love* (Vocalion), and a British EMI twofer CD containing two 12" Capitol collections, *Love Songs* and *Margaret Whiting Sings for the Starry Eyed*. All in all, it ain't much to show for a major hit maker.

Whenever you have the word "complete" in an album title, and even more so when you have the word "hits," you know you're in for trouble. As we've seen before, hit songs are not always the same thing as good songs, even in Whiting's case, and thus not everything on *The Complete Capitol Hits of Margaret Whiting* is worthy of being heard in the same package as such classics as "My Ideal" and "Moonlight in Vermont." In her case, as with a lot of other singers from her generation, it's a matter of diminishing returns. Nearly all of the forties sides are good, but as you get into the fifties, this is less and less the case.

Fortunately, Whiting's hits in the Mercer era (1942–48) were all good if not great songs, and as a result, the first disc of Whiting's *Complete Capitol Hits* set is not only highly listenable but essential. Her voice flows out sweet and clear on what can really be described as being as good as any of the best music of the immediate postwar era. Working with Mercer as producer, occasional songwriter, and duet partner, her output was skewed toward Broadway and its canon of major composers. Peggy Lee and Kay Starr may have charted with blues, country, and ethnic novelties, but Whiting was the fair-haired girl as far as show and movie tunes were concerned. Her single biggest hit, however, was a rather tepid British import called "A Tree in the Meadow."

For Whiting, "Guilty" was a blessing: another vintage song of her father's that charted all over again thanks to her. Richard Whiting wrote it in 1931, with Harry Akst and Gus Kahn, and it was popular enough and widely recorded at the time. Fifteen years later, it was apparently Tony Martin (who was old enough to remember 1931) who first had the idea of reviving "Guilty." Both Martin (on Mercury) and Whiting's friend Mel Tormé (on Musicraft) recorded it before she did, but it was her Capitol single that was the big hit. The song was relentlessly snappy and peppy in 1931, a true period foxtrot, but Whiting's treatment is slow (though still in a very danceable tempo). "Guilty" displays the

trademark sincerity of both Whitings at their most moving; she sings it without affectation of any kind, but with complete commitment to the material, totally caught up in the happy-sad nature of Gus Kahn's lyric.

Whiting also helped make Mercer and Arlen's "Come Rain or Come Shine" and "Black Magic" into hits and standards, and she gave "Uncle Jerry" (Kern) his last hurrah with "All Through the Day" and "In Love in Vain." Both were from *Centennial Summer*, and were so new that Whiting sings the latter lyric as "who wants to be in love *alone*." She also put over Burke and Van Heusen's "But Beautiful" (*Road to Rio*), Lane and Harburg's "Old Devil Moon" (*Finian's Rainbow*), Martin, Blane, and Edens's "Pass That Peace Pipe" (*Good News*), and Harold Rome's "Along with Me" (*Call Me Mister*).

However, the songwriter she best served was Richard Rodgers; apparently, she changed the very shape of "It Might as Well Be Spring." According to Margaret, the composer had envisioned this tune as a jaunty little schottische, a dance form much used by Bing Crosby in the late thirties, but when Whiting and arranger Paul Weston slowed it down to ballad tempo, Rodgers followed suit—as soon as his blood stopped boiling. In 1949, she recorded no fewer than three R&H classics from *South Pacific*: "Younger Than Springtime," "(I'm in Love with) A Wonderful Guy" (which she put on the pop charts), and "A Cockeyed Optimist"; Hammerstein's lyrics might have proclaimed that these songs were "a cliché coming true" but Whiting's straightforward, meaningful interpretations emphasize Hammerstein's truths rather than his clichés.

After Mercer left the A&R department, however, things went downhill fast. Her best record of 1949, paradoxically, is her major duet with Johnny himself, on Frank Loesser's "Baby, It's Cold Outside." Whiting has related that she heard Loesser and his wife, Lynn, sing it at a Hollywood party sometime around 1947 or 1948 and thought right away that it would make a great duet for her and Johnny; Loesser, however, was cagey, saying that he couldn't give it to them just yet as MGM had bought the rights for an Esther Williams epic. The song won an Oscar despite Ms. Williams, who sang it fully clothed and on dry land. However, while Whiting and Mercer waited for permission, Columbia Records got their version, with Dinah Shore and Buddy Clark, out first. (That's the way Maggie remembers it; according to Whitburn, the Whiting-Mercer version made it to number 4 on the charts while the Shore-Clark rendition also peaked at number 4.)

Whiting continued to be given good songs at least until the late forties, not all of which came from Broadway or Hollywood, like the zingy and catchy "Great Guns" (1949) and "Dime a Dozen" (both on the *My Own True Love* collection), which utilizes virtually the same arrangement and chord changes as Mel Tormé's "Careless Hands," right down to the handclaps, a quasi-country harbinger of things to come. By the early fifties, Whiting's Capitol hits grew increasingly unlistenable to, the worst offenders being a seemingly endless series of horrible hoe-downs with a half-baked hillbilly named Jimmy Wakely. The mystery is not what genius came up with this idea to begin with, but rather how on earth these dreadful sides could have been such blockbuster hits. Heard today, they are Exhibit A for the argument that the hits of yore are not necessarily music worth listening to after the fact. The series includes "Slippin' Around," a good country song though hardly suited to Whiting, the considerably worse "I'll Never Slip Around Again" (a sequel to a song that Whiting shouldn't have recorded to begin with), "The Gods Were Angry with Me," and "Let's Go to Church (Next Sunday Morning)." Few of Whiting's solos were any better, the dreadful "Good Morning, Mister Echo" is as bad as anything that Doris Day was singing for Mitch Miller at Columbia, worse even than "Rickety Rackety Rendezvous" and "Mr. Tap Toe," which at least are catchy and danceable.

One wonders how many terrific songs lie buried in the vaults while these appalling hits are ready for purchase on the Internet. One of the greatest mysteries is why her 1947 *Margaret Whiting Sings Rodgers and Hart* has never been available since the 10" LP era. As Whiting has said, this was Mercer's idea, and at the time it was radical. Previous to this project, only Lee Wiley had recorded a songbook album, and her four 1939–42 songbooks were hardly mass-market (they were sold only in specialty shops, mostly in Manhattan). Whiting was not only the first mainstream star to record a songbook package, Rodgers and Hart specifically (this was a decade before Ella Fitzgerald), but she also seems to have been the first star singer ever to record "My Funny Valentine." By the time she left Capitol, "Valentine" had assumed its place as one of the most recorded standards of all time.

"Valentine" is not on the *Spotlight* compilation, but everything that is on there is good. One of the better entries in that long—and not always imaginatively programmed—series, the Whiting collection starts with "Day In—Day Out," one of the most effective ballad treatments of that Mercer text from the days before Sinatra and later Cole taught it to swing. Whiting also shines on a previously unreleased master of Cole Porter's "I Get a Kick Out of You," which retains the quasi-Latin underpinning heard on many of the original 1934 dance band versions. There's also a reading of "I Could Write a Book," from a 1952 session with her then husband, pianist and conductor Lou Busch (father of her daughter, Debbie). Other highlights of the *Spotlight* collection include a heartfelt rendition of her father's classic "She's Funny That Way," a swinging "Gypsy in My Soul" (a song salvaged from a University of Pennsylvania Mask and Wig Club production), and a touching "I've Never Been in Love Before."

The bulk of her better songs from the late forties and early fifties were arranged and conducted by Frank DeVol, who was working occasionally with Peggy Lee during this period (and once with Nat Cole, on "Nature Boy"), but was reserving most of his dance card for Whiting. DeVol also conducts on the generally excellent full-length album *Songs for the Starry Eyed*, a first-rate set of ballads, including more worthy obscurities like "Love Can Happen Anytime" (by Josef Myrow) and "Young Man's Fancy" (from *John Murray Anderson's Almanac*). There's also a marvelously introspective, ruminative "Let's Fall in Love," complete with verse.

But key exceptions aside, Whiting never really made the transition from a singles artist to an album artist. Ultimately there was just too much of a sameness to her delivery: Everything sounded like everything else, and you didn't want to hear a whole album's worth. As Alan Livingston, then the president of Capitol Records, recalled: "It was painful for us, because she was one of the original Capitol artists, successful Capitol artists, and when rock came in, they didn't sell. Stan Kenton stopped selling. Peggy Lee stopped selling to an extent. Margaret Whiting wasn't selling. Her contract came up, and out of loyalty to her I said I would re-sign her. She sent in a lawyer to meet with me who made ridiculous demands, and I said, 'I'm not going to meet them. I can't. I will keep Margaret and make records with her, but not on that basis.' And he left. And poor Margaret, that was the end of her—on records, at least."

The end of her relationship with Capitol also marked the end of her years as a hit maker, but not quite of her career on records. She began recording for Dot, for whom she made the excellent *Goin' Places* in state-of-the-art 1958 stereo. Although most of her best-known hits were ballads, this album is primarily bouncers in the Sinatra-Riddle–style heartbeat tempo, starting with a Whiting favorite, the swinging "Gypsy in My Soul"; she also swings two Johnny Mercer classics usually done in slow blues or ballad tempo, "Hit the Road to Dreamland" and an especially Frankish "Any Place I Hang My Hat Is Home" with muted trumpet obbligatos. Other delights included "Song of the Wanderer" by her father's onetime partner Neil Moret, and the early R&B classic "I'm Gonna Move to the Outskirts of Town." *Goin' Places* again saw the light of day on a later LP (from the British Jasmine label), but it would be especially welcome on CD.

After Dot, Whiting moved over to Verve, recently annexed by MGM Records, where she made two albums, the largely disappointing *Broadway Right Now* with old friend Mel Tormé and the indisputably perfect *Margaret Whiting Sings the Jerome Kern Songbook*. Both were arranged and conducted by Russ Garcia, but the Tormé album has only a few moments of charm (among them Whiting's solo "Make Someone Happy" and the medley of two songs from *Wildcat,* "Far Away from Home" and "Angelina"); the *Jerome Kern* album is absolutely flawless.

Still only in her mid-thirties, by now Whiting had perfected her style: Where fellow Capitolians Lee and Starr were fine-tuning an approach that combined elements of jazz and pop, Whiting situated herself precisely between mainstream pop and Broadway-style emoting, juxtaposing the virtues of, say, a Barbara Cook with those of, say, a Jo Stafford. The proof is evident throughout the *Kern Songbook.* Whiting was virtually the only (comparatively) young major singer in the LP age who had actually known the Old Man personally. She had already sung more of her "Uncle" Jerry's music than most of her contemporaries, including three Kern classics on *Songs for the Starry-Eyed,* among them a wonderful "I've Told Every Little Star." Her 1960 album is easily the finest collection of Kern's music ever recorded by a singer, its only possible rival being the Ella Fitzgerald–Nelson Riddle album of a few years later.

Whiting is superb on Kern classics like "I Won't Dance" as well as worthy obscurities like "You Couldn't Be Cuter" (one of the only performances of this 1938 charmer, from *Joy of Living,* in the modern LP era). She's up to the task of making his heavier and more melodramatic songs, like "Smoke Gets in Your Eyes," seem believable, but she also makes light bouncers such as "Why Do I Love You" something more than frivolous. She's appropriately serious but not overly heavy on "Can't Help Lovin' Dat Man," the song that virtually defined the torch song era, and she meaningfully reanimates the long dormant "D'Ye Love Me" (from the 1925 *Sunny*) along with other worthy antiques, such as "Poor Pierrot" from *The Cat and the Fiddle.* If you want to hear the best work of Margaret Whiting's career, you needn't go all the way back to her mid-forties hits, wonderful as some of them are. You need only go to this classic album. (*Margaret Whiting Sings the Jerome Kern Songbook* was at last reissued on CD in 2002; let's hope it's still findable when you read this.)

It's indeed unfortunate that the 1960 *Jerome Kern Songbook* is Whiting's last classic album. But if she was going to go out on a high note, she couldn't have picked a higher one. She did continue to record into the sixties, but never again scaled the heights. After Dot and Verve, there were three albums for London, one of which included a hit that penetrated the lower (or is it higher) reaches of what was then being called the "adult contemporary" charts, a single with the uncomely title of "The Wheel of Hurt." In her cabaret phase, Whiting has recorded more recently for Audiophile and DRG, the latter a surprisingly good package for a seventy-year-old diva that guest-stars Gerry Mulligan, who obviously knows a good singer when he hears one.

Since the seventies, Whiting had enjoyed the company of Jack Wrangler, a former porn star who had since reinvented himself as a cabaret and musical theater impresario. I don't know why that should raise any eyebrows: Of Whiting's contemporaries, only Dinah Shore had the good luck to consort with major leading men of two generations, George Montgomery and Burt Reynolds. Otherwise, Peggy Lee was married to a drunk and Doris Day to a psychopath and then a con artist, while Kay Starr seemed determined to marry everybody who wasn't already married to Dinah Washington. So why worry if Mag wanted to marry a porn star? As far as I could see, they were happy together for thirty years, so more power to them.

After relocating to New York, Whiting has come to be regarded as a goddess of the New York cabaret scene, a diva who's always surrounded by other divas, except that there's nothing haughty or unapproachable about Maggie, in either her offstage presence or her singing. She worked around the country and the city frequently in the seventies, eighties, and nineties, and was a longtime member of the 4 Girls 4 troupe, the original edition of which combined her with Rosemary Clooney, Helen O'Connell, and Rose Marie. Whiting continued to perform until well into the twenty-first century, and she remained a vital presence in New York cabaret rooms even after she stopped performing. She ostensibly went to visit old friends and check out newcomers, but in the process she became the inspiration for hundreds of singers at all ages and career levels. After the death of her husband, Jack, in 2009, Margaret left her West Fifty-eighth Street apartment (she lived around the corner from Tony Bennett) to move into an assisted care facility in New Jersey. The fall and winter of 2009 into 2010 was the first season I could remember in which I didn't run into her at at least one show or another. Over a career that lasted more than sixty years, Margaret Whiting played a considerable role in making the Great American Songbook great.

Lee Wiley (1908?–1975)

Ecclesiastes 9:11 tells us that the race is not always to the swift nor the battle to the strong, but that "time and chance happeneth to them all." Time and chance have happeneth to a great many artists since I've been listening to music. I can't even remember the names of most of the pop groups my fellow students were abusing their eardrums with back in the days when I wore glasses and had long hair (I miss the second but not the first), but at the same time, tastes have changed among those of us who listen to the major singers and songs of the mid-twentieth century as well. Yes, Louis Armstrong, Billie Holiday, and Frank Sinatra dominated our tastes then, even as they do now, but other reputations have risen and fallen. For one, Mildred Bailey's: Most of her music was completely unavailable—out of print and out of mind—for the entire LP era. By the nineties, Bailey existed only in the memories of artists who grew up hearing her; finally, in 1999, with the release of ten CDs of her nearly complete recordings by Mosaic Records, we can all hear exactly why Bailey deserves her place in the pantheon.

Thanks to that reissue, Bailey's reputation has risen, yet I can't help wondering if that of Lee Wiley hasn't fallen a little, if only because she recorded so little for an artist of her stature. Lee Wiley lived considerably longer than her friend Bailey, yet her career in retrospect seems considerably smaller. Virtually everything she ever sang has been available one way or another, and it amounts to far less than we would like, in terms of quantity though not of quality. Yet she was a distinctive stylist, with a warm, smoky sound, and an obvious influence on vocalists of the swing era and the postwar era, too, from Billie Holiday, Kay Starr, and Peggy Lee on. More than Bailey, Wiley had an indisputably jazzy timbre—it wasn't just her phrasing and interpretation, it was the very sound of her voice itself. This was what a jazz singer sounded like, a bluesy, Midwestern drawl that was almost a feminine counterpart to Jack Teagarden. Hers is the sound of scotch and cigarettes, not to mention broken hearts.

It's clear that both geographic and temporal circumstances can affect an artist's reputation. After something of a career as a pop star, Wiley reinvented herself in the forties as roughly the only chick singer in the Eddie Condon Mob, which led to a later career very different from that of other vocalists. She wasn't jazzy in the scatting-and-improvising sense of an Ella Fitzgerald, yet her voice on its own sounded more like a jazz instrument than Fitzgerald's or anyone else's. Early on, fans of traditional and Chicago-style jazz recognized that she was something special. Geography is also a consideration: Wiley, like Kay Starr after her, was from Oklahoma, which was still a territory when Wiley was born. Yet it wasn't her Okie associations that marked her music, or even her alleged Native American bloodline (something also said of Starr and Bailey); Wiley was an indelible part of the jazz scene in New York and Boston in the forties and fifties. In those two towns there was almost always an audience for her singing. Boston was the center of master impresario George Wein's operations, and he became her biggest booster. It was no coincidence that both Teddi King and Barbara Lea, the two younger artists who rate as her finest disciples, also came from the Boston area.

Unfortunately, time and chance certainly did happeneth to Lee Wiley. One can only wish that she had been as prolific and consistent as Bailey or Holiday or Connee Boswell; it would be great, for instance, to have a ten-CD box of recordings of the prewar period. Even in the twenty-first century, the music that Wiley did leave us sounds as good as ever. She still has that cool, breathy sound, that knack for a well-placed passionate sigh at the end of lines (particularly on her earlier sides), that lightly swinging approach. Thirty-five years after her demise, her recordings continue to be well served by her career-

long penchant for wanting to work with the best musicians (even if they didn't always enjoy working with her). Her finest albums—*Night in Manhattan, East of the Sun, A Touch of the Blues*—are still among the most satisfying efforts ever by a female singer.

Wiley herself always said that she was born on October 9, 1915, which would make her a mere wisp of a girl, aged fifteen, when she made her recording debut as a vocalist with Leo Reisman's orchestra in June 1931. Few people believe that date, including her younger brother, Ted, who told me that it had to be at least four or five years earlier. More recently, researcher Ted Ono discovered that the date inscribed on her tombstone is 1908. In a seventies interview with Richard Lamparski, Wiley speaks vividly about growing up in the twenties in Oklahoma, about dreaming of being a famous singer, and discovering jazz and blues via "race" records— particularly those of Ethel Waters—which were sold only in a certain part of town. She also said that the influence of Mildred Bailey inspired her to make singing a career, but this seems like an attempt to convince the interviewer that she was younger than she actually was, since Bailey wouldn't have been widely heard on the radio until Wiley was an adult herself. Both of these ladies played fast and loose with their ages; it may not be a coincidence that Bailey always claimed to have been born in 1908, which apparently is Wiley's actual birth year.

From singing on a local radio station, Wiley made her way to St. Louis and then New York. There she attracted the ear of Leo Reisman, one of the most prominent bandleaders of the thirties, and made her first recordings as Reisman's vocalist in 1931. Recently, a company called Devil's Music (available from Baldwin Street Music) has begun a CD series covering Wiley's early recordings in what they call the *Completists' Ultimate Collection*. So far, the series has reached four volumes, and does a remarkable job of collecting all the commercial studio material (there isn't much), every master recording, every known alternate take, and every aircheck extant.

It's an interesting, wildly varied mix of material. In these years, Wiley was almost a serious contender in the mainstream pop stakes, along with Bailey, Kate Smith, and Connee Boswell, as one of the most recognizable female voices on the radio. She broadcast and recorded with big bands ranging from the hot and jazzy, like the Dorsey Brothers Orchestra and the Casa Loma, to those oriented toward concert and society listeners—Reisman, Paul Whiteman, Johnny Green, and Rudy Vallee. A considerable amount of her recording activity centers around Victor Young: She sang with his band on his records (most notably "You're an Old Smoothie"); he accompanied her with his studio orchestra on her records (there are superb sides from 1934 and 1937); they wrote songs together, most famously "Got the South in My Soul" and "Anytime, Any Day, Anywhere." Apparently, Young and Wiley were engaged in other activities together that were not entirely of a musical nature.

Wiley was terrific from the very beginning. Earlier, in the twenties, female pop singers were either flappers or girly, occasionally high-pitched squirrely types (be they as musicianly as Annette Hanshaw or as annoying as Helen Kane, or a little bit of both, like Ruth Etting), all very popular in the early years of electrical recording. By the onslaught of the Depression, the focus had shifted to what they then called torch singers, who took Broadway's Helen Morgan as their model. These were sultry, world-weary types, best exemplified by Claudette Colbert in the 1933 movie *Torch Singer,* in which she plays a young unwed mother who becomes the toast of Manhattan as a nightclub headliner. ("The worst woman in New York . . . sang the best love songs! Lips that had kissed more men than she could remember . . . crooned lullabies no one could forget!") The casting was ideal, except that it never seemed to occur to Paramount Pictures that Colbert couldn't sing a note. (They should have brought in Wiley to overdub for her; even Rita Hayworth or Vera Ellen would have sounded better.) But such was the norm with torch singers: Libby Holman, the real-life wounded woman who popularized the genre (Broadway headliner marries tobacco heir, accused of murder, vindicated) and introduced the ultimate torch song, "Body and Soul," also didn't have much to offer musically.

Wiley's contribution to popular music directly paralleled that of her friend and supporter Bing Crosby. If you could reduce Crosby's innovations to a single sentence, it would be that he combined the intimacy now being made possible with electrical recording with the energy and rhythm of jazz, as perfected by friends Louis Armstrong and Bix Beiderbecke—not to mention the high drama of childhood inspiration Al Jolson. Likewise, Wiley took the established genre of torch singing and infused it with a true feeling for jazz and the blues, which she learned from Ethel Waters and classic blues singers like Bessie Smith. Crosby was not the very first crooner, but he was the first singer of mainstream popular songs with genuine musicianship and an understanding of jazz and swing. Likewise, Wiley may have been the first torch singer who knew her way around jazz and the blues, expressing a genuinely erotic sultriness and sensuality that's nowhere to be found in most white female singers of the twenties.

It's not surprising that the thirties would be Wiley's biggest decade in terms of mainstream acceptance: She was essentially the only one combining jazz and torch at that time. But by the end of the decade, all kinds of singers were doing it, and Wiley had lost her uniqueness; what's more, contemporaries like Connee Boswell and Mildred Bailey were better equipped to keep up with the swing era.

Bailey sang more than convincingly with Benny Goodman in 1939 and Boswell recorded brilliantly with Bob Crosby, Woody Herman, and other top leaders, but it's impossible to imagine Wiley with any kind of a big swing band. "She could swing, every note she swung," as George Wein put it, "but she swung in a very sophisticated and very genteel way."

In 1940, however, the public wanted a heavy-duty, flat-out, no-holds-barred swinging singer like Ella Fitzgerald, and not the genteel and sophisticated swing that Wiley offered. Both Maxine Sullivan and Mildred Bailey have been described as genteel and sophisticated, yet they were both much stronger rhythmically than Wiley. Wiley was possibly too subtle for the war years, an era when brassy stars like Betty Hutton and the Andrews Sisters dominated; even before the war, Wiley's moment in the sun had passed.

That is, as far as the mainstream was concerned. Yet even if she would never be on the cover of a national magazine again, there were two smaller support groups who would keep her working for as long as she could keep her act together. The first was the cabaret and musical theater crowd, who bought the albums she recorded of the songbooks of the great Broadway composers, and the second, as already mentioned, was the group of Chicago- and New Orleans–oriented traditional jazz and swing players who congregated in New York and Boston around Eddie Condon.

Both groups were satisfied by a series of four remarkable songbook albums cut between 1939 and 1942, in which she was accompanied principally by Condonites (as well as major guest stars, like Bunny Berigan and Fats Waller). These were all eight-song collections of the music of, respectively, George and Ira Gershwin, Rodgers and Hart, Cole Porter (done mostly with members of Tommy Dorsey's band), and Harold Arlen. Of the composers represented, only George Gershwin was no longer living at the time; this is surely the only Rodgers and Hart album released while Lorenz Hart was still around to enjoy it.

In a sense, these four 78 rpm album collections laid the foundation for the groundbreaking LPs of both Frank Sinatra and Ella Fitzgerald. Yet while Sinatra and Fitzgerald were aiming at the American mainstream, Wiley was reduced to reaching for the margins: All four of her songbook packages were produced and sold by midtown Manhattan music shops like Liberty and Schirmer and so were largely available only to their theater-going cognoscenti clientele.

By 1943, Wiley was firmly a part of the Condon circle. He accompanied her on the Arlen album and officially labeled her "the greatest of all jazz singers." She was a regular guest vocalist on the guitarist-raconteur-producer's World War II–era Town Hall concerts (most of which have been issued on the

Audiophile label, the same label that has made the four songbook albums available), and it was clear that she could always count on Condon and the traditional jazz circuit for work.

Wiley escaped from cult status only twice: In 1950 and 1951, when she made three 10" LPs for Mitch Miller and Columbia Records, and then in 1956 and 1957 when she made two 12" LPs for RCA. By then, nobody was harboring any illusions about Wiley breaking through to the pop audience, or even to the bigger jazz audience that was supporting many singers. As pianist Stan Freeman told me, "I remember Mitch saying that he felt that Lee's records weren't going to be big sellers, but that he owed it to the public to record her, because she was so good."

Despite the smoky, burnished quality of her voice, it would be wrong to characterize her exclusively as a jazz singer. "I never thought of her as a jazz singer, she was a *great* singer," said Mitch Miller, by which he meant she was an essential artist with a profound gift for interpreting a lyric, and other skills, beyond rhythm and swing and the blues, that were not necessarily the exclusive province of jazz. Although there were some jazz elements to her work, she didn't belong in the same class with such pure, 100 percent jazzers as Ella Fitzgerald and Sarah Vaughan.

Conversely, in the forties, when you said "cabaret singer," chances are you meant someone very fancy and formal, with a touch of Old Europe, like the Incomparable Hildegarde. Mabel Mercer, with her rolled Rs and very proper diction, plus her Margaret Dumont–like deportment, was the ideal cabaret singer. Still, within a few years the archetypal image of the cabaret singer became someone more like Wiley than Mercer, a lot jazzier and looser and bluesier. In those days, there was more of a gulf between Birdland and the Blue Angel, but since Wiley's day, there has evolved a hybrid heritage, part traditional cabaret and part traditional jazz. Lee Wiley seems to be its principal foremother, along with her most important progeny, King and Lea—and their own latter-day stylistic descendants like Daryl Sherman. By the millennium, the principal difference between a jazz singer and a cabaret singer was that the latter talked considerably more and always thanked her lights-and-sound guy.

If Wiley's music was a potpourri, her personal life was also a mixed bag, filled with apparent contradictions. On one hand, she did have a few close friends, like pianist Joe Bushkin and his wife, Fran, who played on many of her most famous recordings, including *Night in Manhattan*. To the end of Joe's life, he defended her both professionally and musically. Other musicians got along with her famously. But not all. Wiley had a longtime drinking problem that worsened with age, and, to play armchair psychologist (you don't have to be Freud to dope this one out), it was exacerbated by an acute insecurity.

"The funny thing about Lee," Bushkin said to me, "was that she was perfectly relaxed and comfortable in the studio when the red light went on, but she was a nervous wreck whenever she appeared at the Pierre or different supper clubs. [Singing live] somehow or other rattled her, you know? It's the opposite with most musicians. They're relaxed when there are people around digging it. But in the studio, Lee was happy as a clam, and she sang so beautifully." There are also stories of Wiley being verbally abusive to her musicians, particularly when she was under the influence. To the end of *his* life, the always irascible Ruby Braff (hardly a paragon of upstanding behavior) went ballistic at the very mention of her name.

Alcohol wasn't the only thing she was addicted to. There is an unending supply of gossip from the musicians of a certain generation concerning Wiley's no less insatiable appetite for men: gentleman callers, beaux, boyfriends, lovers, whatever. Wiley's most famous lovers were Victor Young and Bunny Berigan, two married men who were thus unavailable on a permanent basis, but there were liaisons with many famous bandleaders, composers, and other celebrities. Artie Shaw also talked about her with surprising warmth and sentiment. Wiley could have easily been the inspiration for Ira Gershwin's "Poor Jenny": Had she ever published her memoirs, wives would have surely shot their husbands in thirty-three states.

Her first marriage was to Jess Stacy, a wonderful pianist associated with both Goodman and Condon, a relationship that ended acrimoniously. The second time around, she married one Nat Tischenkel, who owned a drugstore inside New York's posh Hotel Astor, and who made it possible for her to work or not work as much as she pleased in her final decades.

When Wiley sang Joe Bushkin's "Oh! Look at Me Now," for some unknown reason the original lyricist, Johnny DeVries, wrote a special set of lyrics for her—and how I wish he hadn't. The new text turns the protagonist from an optimistic lad into a gold digging hussy; the original hero sings of his desire to fall in love, the new heroine sings of her avaricious desire for checks and jewelry. I can only hope in my heart that the real-life Wiley wasn't anywhere near so mercenary.

As minimal as Wiley's overall output is, she does get better and better as the decades wear on: Her dance-band-oriented work of the thirties is superseded by her Condon-associated work of the forties (and the very best tracks from that association are, surprisingly, from the live concerts), including her appearances on the Condon Gershwin album for Decca. Then, too, the three major albums of the fifties, *Night in Manhattan*, *West of the Moon*, and *A Touch of the Blues*, are enough to turn anyone into a Lee Wiley convert.

In 1939, Wiley (backed by trumpeter Max Kaminsky) recorded "I've Got a Crush on You" in a classic performance on her original Gershwin album, one which, as Ira Gershwin readily acknowledged, completely changed the public perception of the song from a peppy foxtrot to a melancholy love song. In 1947, Sinatra, obviously inspired by Wiley, recorded his own treatment of "Crush." He slowed it down even further, adding a string quartet, and amplified the trumpet obbligato, now played by the superior Bobby Hackett. Three years after Sinatra, Wiley returned to "Crush" for *Night in Manhattan,* a performance with string section (and Bobby Hackett again) that seems equally based on her own 1939 performance and on Sinatra's in 1947. It's Wiley's 1950 recording that blows everyone away, even her younger self. If the word "crush" had previously been jazz slang, Wiley did more than anyone to make the word a permanent part of the English language. She invests so much feeling in the word "crush" that she could have inserted any jive phrase in its place and the meaning would still be crystal clear. (She does the same for the phrase "cunning cottage.") Wiley tells us that the world will pardon her "mush," but she sings so straightforwardly and movingly that there simply is no mush to pardon.

"Crush" is merely one-eighth of *Night in Manhattan,* in which the combination of string quartet and trumpet soloist is a direct reference to the earlier "chamber" sessions by Sinatra and Axel Stordahl. "I had done some piano 'mood music' for [Columbia]," as Bushkin recalled for me. "They were very pleased with the reaction to my trio and they said, 'Would you like to do an album?' I said I wanted to do one with Bobby Hackett. So I wrote some strings behind me and Bobby [to play behind Lee]." Apparently Miller, who ran the entire pop singles division of Columbia, George Avakian, who produced the jazz and pop albums, and Bushkin were all in agreement: The optimal project was a combination of Lee Wiley, Bushkin's trio, a string quartet, and Bobby Hackett. The four elements get along brilliantly on all eight tracks: Wiley shines in the elegant yet funky surroundings of Bushkin's keyboard, Hackett's horn, and the strings.

Wiley was certainly loyal: For this, her first major label project in a dozen years, she turns over fully half of the eight cuts to the love of her life, Victor Young, delivering definitive interpretations of three of his best-known songs, "Street of Dreams," "Any Time, Any Day, Anywhere" (co-written by Wiley), and "A Ghost of a Chance," and one of his worst, "A Woman's Intuition." Wiley's own woman's intuition should have scared her away from this puppy, which bears the cross of a convoluted lyric that one can't believe is the work of the normally excellent Ned Washington. Apart from "Intuition," the closest thing to a disappointment is the heinous revised lyric to "Oh! Look at Me Now." Despite that, this is nonetheless one of the finest albums ever recorded of the Great American Songbook, perhaps the most essential document of the jazz-cabaret style.

Wiley made two other 10" LPs for Columbia, also conceived and produced by Miller. These are songbooks, first *Irving Berlin* and then *Vincent Youmans,* and on both she's accompanied by the two-piano team of Stan Freeman and Cy Walters. This was a convention of theater music and cabaret at the time—Judy Garland and Mabel Mercer, among others, recorded in the two-piano format. It may well have been Miller's bid to pitch Wiley at one of her core audiences, the Liberty Music Shop crowd of song connoisseurs. There's some wonderful singing here, particularly on "Fools Fall in Love," a first-rate Berlin ballad from *Louisiana Purchase* done by hardly anyone else (except Teddi King, who learned it from Wiley, and Marlene VerPlanck, who learned it from King).

There's also some first-class Wiley on her 1954 Rodgers and Hart collection, produced by George Wein, despite some apparent hostility between her and Ruby Braff; "A Ship Without a Sail" is the standout. The mid-fifties also saw one rather disappointing date, apparently produced independently and sold to Coral Records, released as singles, which attempted to repackage her in pop trappings (even though the songs were from the thirties, including "Old Man of the Mountain") but instead only proved that this particular ship had long since sailed.

After *Night in Manhattan,* Wiley's worthiest effort was *West of the Moon,* another one of those rare jazz (or what have you) vocal albums that's so amazingly good one can't imagine changing a note. (It's hard to believe it took until 2007 for it to come out in a definitive American CD edition, from Mosaic.) Again we have Wiley, a tight rhythm section, and a bed of either soft strings or soft reeds, plus first-rank soloists: clarinetist Peanuts Hucko and trumpeter Billy Butterfield, under the baton of one of the finest of arrangers, Ralph Burns, who had the unique gift of writing charts that were at once sensitive and swinging. Wiley's voice is absolutely perfect. By 1956–57, the hi-fi recording technology was astute enough to pick up every exquisite nuance of her chops.

The second RCA album, *A Touch of the Blues,* is a bit louder and brassier—yet no less perfect—with orchestrations that seem more suited to a conventional definition of a jazz singer. *A Touch of the Blues* has Wiley backed by a studio group led by trumpeter Billy Butterfield with orchestrations by Al Cohn and Bill Finegan. Even though *A Touch of the Blues* is significantly less subtle, it's almost as good as *West of the Moon.*

And that was pretty much it. There's a rehearsal with Bushkin from 1965 (issued thirty years later on CD), and then in 1971 and 1972, she did a disappointing final album called *Back Home Again* followed by a disappointing "comeback" performance at Carnegie Hall (all three post-1960 recordings have been issued by Audiophile). Should we be angry that there aren't more albums up to *Night in Manhattan* and *West of the Moon* when Wiley was clearly singing brilliantly in the fifties, or should we be grateful for the albums that did get made?

Wiley died in 1975. As was true of Johnny Hartman, her career was one of fits and starts. It's amazing that she had the influence she's had, considering how small her recorded output is and how inconsistent her professional life was.

Ted Wiley recalled an incident that occurred one day when he was visiting his older sister at her suite at the Hotel Astor. There was a knock on the door, and in came Artie Shaw. "He wanted to show Lee some shirts that he'd just bought. After he left, she said to me, 'You know, he wanted to marry me.'" I then asked Ted if Lee had ever regretted any of the decisions she'd made in her life, or cried over the way things had gone. "No, she wasn't sentimental," he answered. "When she'd break up with somebody, it didn't faze her. She put her feelings in her songs. Friends of mine remark about that, that she sings the blues, you know? Maybe she was singing over lost loves, I don't know, but she never mentioned it. When she sang, you would think she was carrying a torch for the whole world."

Joe Williams (1918–1999)

In the latter part of his life, whenever Joe Williams got ready to sing a love song he would characteristically begin by quoting a description of himself by his friend Billy Eckstine: "Here comes Joe Williams," he would reminisce, dropping into a Mr. B basso, "singing a ballad and looking like the blues."

I heard Joe use this one-liner many times, in interviews with me and onstage, most memorably at what must have been his last big concert in New York, at Carnegie Hall at the JVC Jazz Festival, June 21, 1996. Eckstine's gag has less to do with a pejorative judgment of Mr. Williams's physiognomy (plenty of women would have disagreed) than it does about the dual nature of Big Joe's career. Sure, there were a few balladeers who were conversant with the blues (like Mr. B himself), and even bluesmen who could croon love songs (particularly in the tenor sax family—Ben Webster and such descendants as Gene Ammons and Houston Person).

Yet there's no one who's so completely at home in so many genres. Williams was among the first singers to completely integrate blues, jazz, and pop singing into a single seamless idiom. Longtime friend Ella Fitzgerald can detour into a "Happy Blues" for the sake of diversity, Big Joe Turner might belt out "Pennies from Heaven," but Williams is not merely proving he can do it; he is absolutely at home in both idioms at the same time. Williams could switch between Harry Warren and Bill Withers and still never sound like a visiting fireman. Indeed, it hasn't been until very recently that new male singers (in particular the talented Kevin Mahogany) have tried to do it all—to get all boppy and scatty like Jon Hendricks, belt the blues like Jimmy Witherspoon, and melt your heart with a Johnny Hartman–style

ballad. In doing all three, Mahogany is, in essence, trying to do Joe Williams.

Williams's colleagues in this accomplishment are two fellow Southerners who, like him, grew up in Chicago in the Jazz Age and the Depression: Nat King Cole and Dinah Washington. Both of them were younger than Williams, yet they both had recorded before Williams had achieved any prominence. On the flip side, Big Joe's career would last considerably longer than theirs: Washington checked out at age thirty-nine, Cole at forty-five, while Williams kept going until after his eightieth birthday. In the cases of Washington and Cole, there was no third act—whereas Williams's life had all sorts of extra acts, overtime innings, and encores. With both Cole and Washington, we have a considerable amount of prehistory—early, embryonic recordings that show how they developed before their stars rose and they hit their stride. Joe Williams emerged full blown and sui generis, with nothing like an incubatory period.

That was in 1954, when the thirty-five-year-old singer joined Count Basie's orchestra, an association that catapulted him to international acclaim and helped christen the amazing New Testament phase of the legendary bandleader's career. What's remarkable about Williams's life before Basie isn't that he never sang with anybody—far from it—but rather that despite having forged associations with such high-profile bandleaders as Jimmie Noone, Lionel Hampton, Andy Kirk, and Coleman Hawkins, his formidable light was hidden under a bushel for so long.

Like many musicians, Williams was born in the Deep South (in his case, in the lumber town of Cordele, Georgia, on December 12, 1918) but raised in Chicago. His mother, Anne Beatrice Gilbert, moved to the Windy City when her son was two. Joe always referred to his mother (as on his last album, the magnificent *Feel the Spirit*) as "Miss Anne." Contrastingly, he never referred to his father as anything; as he later told biographer Leslie Gourse, the absentee Willie Goreed was simply "never talked about" at all.

His earliest memories—of either Georgia or Chicago—all involved church. It was there that young Joseph Goreed undoubtedly enjoyed his earliest prolonged exposure to music. Early in his Chicago years, his mother's "lifelong companion," a Mr. James Mason (no, not *that* James Mason), began to expose him to the wonders of Chi-Town's rich musical heritage. By his teens, the youngster was hustling up singing jobs around town using the concocted name "Joe Williams."

But if work was immediately forthcoming, fame was not. Shortly before he turned twenty, Williams began singing with a band led by New Orleans clarinet legend Jimmie Noone, which held forth at the Hotel Vincent and broadcast over WBBM. In 1941, Coleman Hawkins hired Williams (for $80 a week) to sing with his own new big band, and a few years later he signed on as Lionel Hampton's "boy singer." Whenever I talked to him about this period, Joe stressed to me that in all these early gigs he was hired as a balladeer—not as a blues shouter. "Coleman Hawkins asked me to come and join him as a ballad singer," Williams recalled in 1994, and when he first joined Hampton in 1943, the vibist-leader informed him, "Gates, I want you to sing the pretty songs, and let Dinah [Washington, also touring with that remarkable ensemble] sing the blues."

It was apparently with Hampton that he played through Milwaukee in 1943, where he is captured in a private recording with Albert Ammons and Pete Johnson, the famous boogie-woogie four-hand piano duo from Kansas City. One can already sense that Williams is an artist being pulled in two directions, toward the blues and toward the songbook. He belts out "Roll 'Em, Pete" in a clear, high baritone, with much cleaner articulation than Big Joe Turner, the Kansas City–based blues shouter most associated with this fundamental blues; he then does the jazz standard "Basin Street Blues" not as a Southern bluesman but more like a crooner, even, at one point, accentuating one line with a scat extension in the manner of Louis Armstrong. In 1946, Williams appeared with another national touring orchestra, Andy Kirk and His Clouds of Joy, and with Kirk he made his commercial recording debut on two Decca sides, the medium-slow ballad "Now You Tell Me" and the catchy novelty "Louella."

Williams appears regularly on records beginning in 1950, when he hooked up with the talented and enterprising drummer-bandleader Theodore "Red" Saunders. Where neither of his recordings with Kirk was the least bit bluesy, Williams gave Saunders credit for encouraging him to concentrate on the blues. He recorded about a dozen sides with Saunders's band for Okeh (Columbia's "race" records imprint) in 1950–51, beginning with another novelty, "Blow Mr. Low-Blow," on a date that is listed in at least one discography as being with trumpeter Hot Lips Page's band.

It would be as a bluesman that Williams would finally begin to attract the acclaim that was rightfully his. Between 1950 and 1954, he was working with two of Chicago's most prominent R&B-oriented big bands, those of Red Saunders and trumpeter King Kolax. He also crossed paths with other extravagantly named celebrities, such as LaVern Baker, the future R&B star, then working under the name of Miss Sharecropper, and Herman "Sonny" Blount, a pianist, composer, and arranger then prominent on the Chicago blues scene, later to be known internationally and intergalactically as Sun Ra. With both Saunders and Kolax he recorded on several significantly smaller labels (masters that were later acquired by Regent and Savoy Records), which were also intended for the "race" market.

To the singer's own surprise, he would at last break through to the big national audience by singing the blues. In 1948, Peter Chatman, who worked under the name Memphis Slim, wrote a blues-based song that he first copyrighted under the title "Nobody Loves Me" and recorded under that name that year in Chicago for the Miracle label. In 1950, the guitarist and singer Lowell Fulson recorded it under the new title "Every Day I Have the Blues," and Williams must have picked up on the song around this time. The last two bandleaders whom he would apprentice with, King Kolax and Count Basie (each of whom sported royal monikers), both hired him on the strength of what he was doing with "Every Day I Have the Blues."

Williams and Basie joined forces officially on December 25, 1954 (the first recording sessions came in July of the following year), and their union was indeed a Christmas present for all concerned. Williams's presence was one of the most important factors that signified the revitalization of the Basie band in the mid-fifties. The Count's comeback, as it were, became official when he courted the Hit Parade with two best-selling singles, the instrumental "April in Paris" and the two-part band and vocal extravaganza "Every Day," as explosively sung by Williams and arranged by Ernie Wilkins. It was a surefire crowd-pleaser that both Basie and Williams could rely on to bring down the house for as long as they'd be performing, both together and separately.

Wilkins's chart of "Teach Me Tonight" and Leroy Carr's ancient blues "In the Evening," orchestrated by Frank Foster, are no less perfect demonstrations of everything that the thirty-seven-year-old Williams was capable of. "Teach Me" has him bringing his thunderous blues wailing to a ballad (albeit one that, as lyricist Sammy Cahn has observed, has a long history with blues singers). "In the Evening," like "Every Day," is a tour de force that builds and builds: The first chorus has him singing softly and sweetly, backed by Frank Wess's flute—more like a ballad than the blues. But then he contrasts this by switching to loud shout mode on the second chorus, starting with the line about hollering like "a mountain jack"—I'm not sure exactly what that is, but there's no doubt that Williams is hollering something fierce. The third chorus finds him aspiring for the operatic, hitting a high, high note on the phrase "in the *Eeeeve*-ning," and holding it for all of seventeen beats (each and every one of them clearly punctuated by Freddie Green's guitar).

This is undeniably showboating, using the song as a vehicle for showing off one's chops; but Williams already knew that this wouldn't work if he were singing Cole Porter: It obliterates the material. But as he makes clear, the blues isn't about the song but what you do with it—and Williams does more with it than anyone else. Just for contrast, he recorded another song with a similar title, "Ev'ry Day (sometimes listed as "Ev'ry Day [I Fall in Love])" by Irving Kahal and Sammy Fain, introduced by Rudy Vallee in the 1935 Warners film *Sweet Music* and later crooned by Nat King Cole. It's very much a sweet love song, in the best tradition of Vallee and Cole at their most romantic, and Williams does it justice. He uses the full range of his voice here, dropping to low basement tones, but this time it's done in a way that furthers the cause of the song and the story rather than simply vocal exhibitionism.

After what seemed to Williams like a lifetime of missing the boat, the Basie-Williams combination boasted absolutely perfect timing in that it coincided with the birth of the 12" LP era. The first album featuring Williams, recorded in mid-1955, was titled simply but appropriately *Count Basie Swings, Joe Williams Sings,* the cover of which featured a classic David Stone Martin illustration of Williams wailing while a giant, specterlike Basie head floats above him—like something out of *Watchmen*. This is one of those fifties vocal jazz masterpieces, like *In the Wee Small Hours, Lady in Satin, Bing with a Beat, Tony Sings for Two*—a perfectly scrumptious set on which every track is glorious. There isn't a single cut you can live without.

Unfortunately, the same cannot be said of the only other Basie-Williams album on Verve, released with the confusingly similar title *The Greatest!! Count Basie Swings, Joe Williams Sings Standards.* The idea portended greatness: Considering what Williams did with "Ev'ry Day (I Fall in Love)," which wasn't even a standard, there was every reason to believe he could scale those same heights with classic songs like "You Took Advantage of Me" and "Don't Get Around Much Anymore." This was a project apparently foisted on Basie by Verve; unfortunately, he and Williams were learning the hard way the wisdom of something Frank Foster told me many years later. According to Foster, when the Basie band played the arrangements of an outside orchestrator, the music invariably suffered. Instead of going to Foster, Ernie Wilkins, or Neal Hefti, Verve employed a journeyman Hollywood arranger-producer, with tellingly mediocre results.

The third relevant Verve album, *One O'Clock Jump,* seems to be a hodgepodge of Williams vocals and Basie instrumentals that the label threw together after the team had relocated to Roulette. However, *One O'Clock Jump* contains "Too Close for Comfort" (which Sammy Davis Jr. had recently introduced in *Mr. Wonderful*). This track ensures that the album is more than an ordinary hodgepodge, because this is one of three duets Williams waxed with Ella Fitzgerald.

The first magnificent Basie-Williams album also included "The Comeback," another Memphis Slim original, which could have served as Basie's theme song in the mid-fifties. Once during this period Duke Ellington, himself enjoying a resurgence, congratulated Williams by telling him, "You brought all this good luck to Count Basie." Williams found strength and guidance in his relationship with the older man: He had never known his biological father, yet now one of the greatest men in all of American music was referring to Joe as his "number-one son."

In 1957, Basie parted company with the only recently formed Verve label and producer Norman Granz and relocated to Roulette, an even newer and ambitious concern owned by Morris Levy, the force behind Birdland in New York, where the band had played regularly since the club's opening in 1949. On Roulette, the Williams-Basie association on disc blossomed even further, and the seventy or so cuts they made together there (spread over about a half-dozen albums) effectively document the apogee of that relationship. The Roulette association also marked the beginnings of Williams's subsequent breakthrough as a solo recording force, a development explored further in a series of albums he made on his own, minus the rest of the Countish contingent, although recorded while he was still on the road with the band. The Williams solo albums divide evenly into two categories: jazz sets usually done with trumpeter Harry "Sweets" Edison (a fellow Countsman) and ballad collections usually done with pianist and arranger Jimmy Jones.

Williams's Roulette albums provide a microcosm for his entire career in that they reveal his respect for the two crucial traditions of American songwriting: the blues and Tin Pan Alley. Blues composers are often less well regarded than their Broadway counterparts, mainly because they frequently double as performers and, not surprisingly, tend to stick to their own compositions. But as a bluesman who preferred to devote his attention to the efforts of professional songwriters, Williams was in a unique position to show that the efforts of Memphis Slim ("Every Day I Have the Blues") and Pete Johnson ("Roll 'Em, Pete") are just as expressive as Richard Rodgers and Jerome Kern. The two full-length albums that Basie and Williams recorded of this material, *Everyday I Have the Blues* (which yielded the definitive version of Williams's most durable hit) and *Just the Blues* (which opens with Jay McShann and Walter Brown's classic "Confessin' the blues"), constitute a veritable songbook of landmark compositions from the vital tradition of the basic blues.

Basie wasn't always receptive when his singer insisted on introducing romantic material into the band's book. Still, the two of them collaborated on a further two albums of popular standards, one with the full big band (*Dance Along with Basie*) and the remarkable *Memories Ad-Lib*, which placed the two of them in the intimate setting of quartets and quintets helmed by the Count at the organ. The latter album gave Williams the chance to explore a repertory of blues ballads that amounts to a subset of both traditions—songs like James P. Johnson's "If I Could Be with You" and Don Redman's "Cherry," which Jimmy Jones conducted in a meditative Frank Foster arrangement. In the same groove is Nellie

Lutcher's hit "Hurry on Down," which Williams recorded in 1966 with the band led by fellow Basieite Thad Jones and then later in 1992 with the Frank Foster edition of the Basie band.

With the exception of the occasional blues (such as another Williams-Basie perennial, "All Right, Okay, You Win") on his live set *A Swingin' Night at Birdland*, Williams's early solo albums explore the possibilities of Tin Pan Alley as a source material for jazz. The three sets with Harry Edison do this especially successfully—*Together* builds to a medium tempo yet ultra-cool treatment of the Schwartz-Dietz show tune "Alone Together." *Have a Good Time* included two items with Basie relevance, a romping "Sometimes I'm Happy," forever associated with Countsman Lester Young, and "Until I Met You," that rare pop song to be based on a Basie instrumental (guitarist Freddie Green's "Corner Pocket").

The potential conflict between Williams's desire to establish himself as a "legitimate" singer of ballads and show tunes, and the popular perception of him strictly as a blues shouter, came to a head in 1957, not long after he and Basie had relocated to Roulette. One of their first projects for the new label was a team-up with the vocal group of Lambert, Hendricks & Ross. Dave Lambert and Jon Hendricks put together a program of new vocal versions of Basie classics, with the full band in support, and with Williams singing the solo blues parts originated both by himself and his predecessor with Basie, Jimmy Rushing.

Everybody was happy with the idea, Basie and Roulette Records (meaning Morris Levy), as well as Lambert, Hendricks & Ross. Williams didn't object to sharing his vocal mike with the trio—hardly—but he annouced to all present that he was finished with the blues. He would sing anything they wanted, as Jon Hendricks told me in a 2000 interview, *except* the blues. According to Jon, Basie had to take him aside: "I don't know what he said to him, but I suspect it was 'What the hell is the matter with you?'" In any case, logic prevailed, and Williams sang the central parts on the album—blues and all—while the trio sang around him. And Joe, needless to say, continued singing the blues for the rest of his life, in one form or another.

Williams began to assert himself as a balladeer with his very first non-Basiecentric project, a collection of sad songs and love songs called *A Man Ain't Supposed to Cry*. The title track was already associated with two undeniably masculine men, singer-composer Frankie Laine and bass-baritone Arthur Prysock. Veteran arranger Jimmy Mundy did the marvelous string arrangements here, and though he had written for nearly every major band under the sun, including Goodman, James, and Basie, the results were as far away from the big band sound as possible. Mundy did a standout job, but for subsequent ballad projects, Williams switched to another Jimmy, his boyhood friend Jimmy Jones.

From the start, Williams is a balladeer of extraordinary sensitivity, and Jones matches him nuance for nuance. Together they turn what could have been exercises in pop music excess into some of the most haunting ballad collections of a great era. By excess I mean that *Joe Williams Sings About You* consists of twelve songs with the word "you" in the title, and *That Kind of Woman* used a Burt Bacharach title song to open twelve songs based on girls' names. The *You* collection opened with the ironic "I Was Telling Her All About You," a very funny lame-excuse lament in the tradition of "Don'Cha Go 'Way Mad," while "When Did You Leave Heaven" (a staple of the blues balladeer genre) features an added bonus in the presence of master obbligatist Ben Webster.

Williams had been working and recording on his own as well as with Basie at the end of the fifties and the beginning of the sixties. Even when he officially left the fold in 1961, he continued to carry the Basie banner by co-leading a five- or sometimes six-piece band with Sweets Edison. His half-dozen or so albums for RCA, made between 1962 and 1965, mark the first period in his career with no overt connection to the world of Basieana. Still, he would always be Basie's number-one son. The RCA series started with two excellent packages done under the helm of Jimmy Jones (though Oliver Nelson also contributes some excellent arrangements to the first), *Jump for Joy* and *Me and the Blues,* and there's an outstanding live session, *Joe Williams at Newport '63* (part of which, according to Williams discographer Denis Brown, was actually recorded in the studio).

The early sixties work is particularly notable for Williams's (and the producers') amazingly good taste in songs. *Jump for Joy,* for instance, carefully balances familiar standards ("Wrap Your Troubles in Dreams"), worthwhile older songs that might not be as well known ("My Last Affair"), jazz classics (two by Ellington out of the dozens of Ducal ditties he would disc over the decades, "Just a-Sittin' and a-Rockin'" and the title, "Jump for Joy"), and outstanding new works in both the jazz (Curtis Lewis's "The Great City") and pop idioms, including two by Williams's good friend Marvin Fisher ("A Good Thing" and "She Doesn't Know [I Love Her]").

Of the two albums with arranger Frank Hunter, *The Song Is You* is more of a mainstream pop project—and an excellent one—with a vocal group even on the Ellington standard "Prelude to a Kiss," while *The Exciting Joe Williams* employs more jazz elements. Williams later told writer Yvonne Tost Ervin, "They asked me years ago which albums I would like to have buried in a time capsule in Israel, and I said *The Exciting Joe Williams* with 'On the Sunny Side of the Street' on it was one of them. There wasn't a bad cut on the album; all of them are good." "Sunny Side" was rightfully Williams's favorite, with the combination of his own laid-back vocal, Hunter's string chart, and deft piano support from Hank Jones and a piercing tenor obbligato by Jerome Richardson.

After Roulette and RCA, it would be some time before Williams would enjoy another long-term relationship with any record label. As it happened, many years later, three CDs' worth of live and other noncommercial material from the mid-sixties were released as *Then and Now* (Bosco), *Havin' a Good Time! with Ben Webster* (Hyena), and *Chains of Love* (Natasha Imports). His next actual releases at the time were the two projects arranged by Thad Jones (*Presenting Joe Williams, Thad Jones, Mel Lewis and the Jazz Orchestra* [1966] and *The Great Joe Williams, Something Old, New, and Blue* [1968], both done for Solid State)—and the mistitled *Worth Waiting For*, on Blue Note (1970). The two Thad Jones projects are classic Joe Williams, vis-à-vis the wonderful "Hurry on Down" on the second and the outstanding "It Don't Mean a Thing (If It Ain't Got That Swing)" on the first. Here Williams uses Ellington's wordless passages as a launching point for a wild scat epic, showing how his technique in this medium had improved by the late sixties. His skill as a vocal improviser was never actually lacking; it's just that scatting was always one of the things that people tended to forget that Williams could really do.

While the Jones-Lewis projects maintain Williams's high standard, the ironically titled *Worth Waiting For* (arranged and conducted by one Horace Ott) does not. It's a lackluster collection of current hits that sound as if they've all been inflicted on him. The disc does contain the singer's only attempt at "Lush Life," but it's the most comically overarranged treatment you can imagine—Spike Jones plays Billy Strayhorn. Yet Williams was lucky—he had managed to get as far as 1970 before making his first truly embarrassing record. For nearly every major vocalist in both the jazz and pop spheres, it had happened much earlier.

For him to have continually made records that showed him at his best was further proof of the remarkable artist that Williams was—in one sense, the ideal of what every jazz singer wanted to be. When the youth base of pop switched from something like standards to something like rock in the fifties and sixties, it had no effect on Williams, who had never aspired to create hit singles (the only one that really made it, "Every Day I Have the Blues," was a royalty-earner for the Count, or rather for Basie's bookie, and not for Joe himself). He was well supported by the jazz audience, and unlike many jazz singers of whatever race, by the black audience. Between Las Vegas, where he eventually settled with his fourth and last wife, Jillean, and jazz festivals and clubs all over the world, he never had to worry about keeping busy. Most singers of Williams's generation worried a lot in their forties and fifties; Joe, on the other hand, had worried a lot in his twenties and thirties, but now was beyond that. As Jon Hendricks says, he was living the good life.

We've noted the absence of a full first act in Williams's recording career: His remarkably excellent and prolific output of 1955–70 constitutes a very solid second act. (It would seem even more so if a company like Mosaic would at last get around to collating his Roulette and RCA material into complete box sets.) The third act begins with a highly obscure set of songs with the word "heart" in the title: *The Heart and Soul of Joe Williams and George Shearing*, in which Williams was produced and accompanied by Shearing on the pianist's own Sheba label; a live set in Europe for the Japanese label Denon; two for the independent Delos (*I Just Want to Sing* and *Nothin' but the Blues*); and a one-shot for Fantasy done live in Berkeley with the Cannonball Adderley Septet. (Williams also played the title role in *Big Man*, the 1974 musical drama written by Cannonball and his brother Nat Adderley.)

Even throughout the seventies and early eighties, probably the all-time low point in the quantity and quality of recorded jazz, Williams never went long without making a record, including a number of guest spots with contemporary big bands such as the Capp Pierce Juggernaut, Frenchman Claude Bolling, and even Basie. He also was surely the only vocalist ever to appear with both Dave Pell's Prez Conference, a four-man saxophone section that re-created the solos of Lester Young (on *Prez and Joe*) and Med Flory's Supersax, a four-man saxophone section that re-created the solos of Charlie Parker (on *In Good Company*). There's also a marvelous live album from 1974, titled *Having the Blues Under a European Sky*, in which Williams not only belts more than enough blues to justify the album title but also treats us to Cole Porter's "Experiment," which he introduces as a "Gertrude Lawrence" song. It's far from obscure, but it's very rarely performed by blues (or even jazz) singers. He sounds equally convincing on a lovely medley of two ballads from the Nat Cole songbook, "Gee Baby, Ain't I Good to You"/"Come In Out of the Rain."

In 1987, Williams was an obvious signing for the reconstituted Verve label under executive producer Richard Seidel. His four projects done under that contract include the 1988 *Ballad and Blues Master*, which was a sterling example of truth in labeling; a Christmas album, *That Holiday Feeling* (1990), arranged by young alto prodigy Bobby Watson; and the meetings with singers and saxists on *In Good Company* (1988–89). His camaraderie with Shirley Horn is apparent from the start. Marlena Shaw is a little more problematic since the particular charm she has in front of an audience rarely transfers to vinyl, but she and Williams can back-and-forth with the best of them. The first of the new Verves is probably the finest, the 1987 *Live at Vine Street*, which shows how Williams's own charisma in a personal appearance loses nothing in the translation to one's CD player. The *Vine Street* set is highlighted by "A Dollar for a Dime," a wonderfully sentimental oldie by Eubie Blake. Joe sang it a lot in his later years, and with his characteristic subtlety never failed to put a lump in the collective throat of everyone listening.

It was fitting that Williams had one last chance to do a live album with his regular working trio, as he did at Vine Street. His last major albums, done for Telarc (kind of a major independent) between 1992 and 1994, were special projects in special formats, all of which broke new ground while at the same time returning Williams to his roots. *Live at Orchestra Hall, Detroit*, reteams him with the Basie band in a varied program under the baton of Frank Foster, while *Here's to Life* was a package of ballads done with the all-time master orchestrator of the form, Robert Farnon. Between the two of them, these albums show that Williams was in remarkable form vocally on the eve of his seventy-fifth birthday—consider the falsetto that he shoots up to at the start of "Hurry on Down" and throughout "Here's to Life." If there were an award for the all-round vocalist with the most chops at the latest stage in life, Williams would snatch it hands down.

The Basie-Foster set wasn't an all-blues album, but the blues tended to predominate, both the well-heeled modern variety, as in Stanley Turrentine's "Sugar" (done as an extended scat by Williams) and the traditional variety, like Eddie Miller's "I'd Rather Drink Muddy Water." The parameters of the moods therein were defined by two antique African American flowers—as Duke Ellington would say, "*Les fleurs africaines*"—the haunting ballad "Georgia Rose" and the wild scat feature "Honeysuckle Rose." Throughout the final recordings, Williams went back to his beginnings and even earlier in "Jimmy's Blues," a signature for Jimmy Rushing, his predecessor in the original Basie band, and a blues that took considerable nerve to sing in the politically correct nineties. Artie Butler's arrangement of "Lover, Come Back to Me" sums up Williams's achievements: Originally written for the operetta *The New Moon*, the piece had been a swinger ever since Mildred Bailey in the thirties, but in Williams's version the lover takes a side trip on his way back through Big Joe's risqué blues "Who She Do." In a single performance, Williams has gone from operetta to pop song to hard swing and even detoured through blues—all without missing a beat.

Here's to Life, the Farnon album, both began and ended with the title song, first with the full Farnon orchestra, then closing with just Williams and pianist George Shearing. It's a dreadful, maudlin piece of sentimental, even self-aggrandizing, junk, along the lines of "My Way," but Williams makes it sound like the most moving thing you ever heard, a powerful end-of-life summation, an anthem. In the mid-nineties, Bob Jones and other deejays on New York's WQEW played this track practically hourly, as if it were a hit single—it was almost annoying hearing it at eight every morning. But damned if Williams doesn't sing the hell out of it. "Between Joe and Shirley Horn," Mr. Shearing remarked to me, "I could say that song has been sung."

Feel the Spirit (recorded in 1994, released in 1995) took him way back. Williams, who had practically never recorded a religious song in his long career, was now returning to the church that had inspired him to begin with, seventy years earlier. For the first time, there are slight signs of vocal deterioration; he's playing it close to the vest vocally, not trying for loud and high notes he can't handle. Yet his singing is still never less than beautiful, whether he's intoning a spiritual sweetly and prayerfully ("In My Heart," "His Eye Is on the Sparrow"), sounding powerful and declamatory like a righteous reverend (on the opener, "In the Beginning," which was appropriately the final Ellington song he would record), or raising a ruckus with Marlena Shaw (a born rabble-rouser if ever there was one on "Feel the Spirit" and "Walk with Me"). It was a fitting final statement.

Although *Feel the Spirit* was the last Joe Williams album, he made guest appearances on other projects, including albums by old friend Benny Carter and new friend Dianne Reeves. He kept working regularly as late as 1998, including a triumphant appearance at the JVC Jazz Festival at Carnegie Hall in 1996. He had long since given up the original big band arrangement of "Every Day I Have the Blues"—at least as early as the mid-eighties he had been doing a less explosive treatment, a medley that folded his signature song into other blues melodies, most notably Miles Davis's "All Blues." The new treatment taxed his chops less and didn't require a big band, yet left the crowd no less satisfied, so that he could go on singing "Every Day" every night. He continued to appear with the Basie band, now under the direction of trombonist Grover Mitchell; luckily, one Basie-Williams show at New York's Blue Note (circa 1997) was broadcast, and may well be the last complete document of the great singer in performance. By 1998, the year he turned eighty, he was canceling concerts more frequently, and on at least one occasion Jon Hendricks subbed for him at the Blue Note. In early 1999 he was hospitalized, and according to the news, simply got dressed and walked out of the hospital. He died on his way home.

Despite the circumstances that robbed his career of its first act, and the long wait he had to endure before he made the big time, Williams still had a career and a life that were the envy of other singers. No one else could ever make "trouble and hard luck" seem so appealing.

Cassandra Wilson (born 1955)

Not all suspense is heavy and dramatic, like an Alfred Hitchcock movie or the Bernard Herrmann score that usually accompanies it. Cassandra Wilson, who in the opinion of many is the most important jazz singer of the current generation, learned a lot about how to create an understated kind of suspense from her two most obvious musical heroes, Nina

Simone and Miles Davis. It was the late trumpeter in particular who specialized in a cool kind of tension that was very much rooted in the blues. Both Davis and Simone showed Wilson that you didn't have to make a lot of noise to keep an audience riveted.

Dianne Reeves, Wilson's friend and contemporary, once told me that both she and Wilson were deeply influenced by Simone. Just as we can see how Nancy Wilson built on the basic sound of Little Jimmy Scott, it's easy to see how Simone's minimal approach, combined with Davis's incisive, understated tone, could have provided Cassandra Wilson with a starting point. Like both the late diva and the late trumpeter (who was a diva in his own way), Wilson favors an intense, mesmerizing vocal attack. There's a spiritual quality to her work: not the extroverted, jubilee, in-your-face-style gospel of say, Aretha Franklin, but a more inwardly directed sound. At times, her singing suggests incantation— as if she were repeating a mantra or a catechism to herself as much as singing to an audience.

As with Simone, Wilson's singing is essentially monodynamic; both singers might be described as the antithesis of Tony Bennett, who contrasts very loud louds with very soft softs in a manner inspired by Count Basie. The term "monotone" may seem a bit extreme, but then some critics (including Scott Yanow) regard her singing as boring. I prefer the term "stealth." I used that phrase to describe her in a review a few years ago and then was surprised, when I went to see her at New York's Blue Note in December 2005, to find that she herself was using that very expression to describe the playing of her longtime guitarist Marvin Sewell. The term applies equally to Wilson's entire band and most of all to the singer herself. She isn't necessarily holding back or suppressing an emotion, she's actually saving a carefully calculated outburst of feeling so she can lay it on you when you least expect it.

One of my favorite moments in my many years of listening to Wilson occurred in "Surrey with the Fringe on Top," a song she was doing frequently in 1997 and 1998 but that, to my knowledge, she has never recorded. In coming to the end of the chorus, she gets to Oscar Hammerstein's line, "Don't you wish you could go on forever," and states it very plain-vanilla, almost as if she were throwing it away. But when she begins repeating it for emphasis, she imbues it with so much strength that it becomes the most important part of the song. Every time she repeats the phrase, it grows more and more powerful. This idea doesn't come from show music or big bands; this is a direct application of a device found in the blues and gospel music, taking a phrase or a line that doesn't mean anything on its own and saying it over and over until the tension builds beyond belief. The idea of just going on forever is a crucial one in Wilson's music: She favors long, repetitive vamps that give her tracks both a dance feel and an improvisatory, jam session vibe.

In Wilson's music, a riff, an idea, a vamp, a feeling, an emotion can in fact go on forever. In the (comparatively) earlier part of her career, Wilson wrote most of her own material, but even when the melodies are familiar, the individual tracks tend to blur into one another. Throughout much of the playing time on her first eight albums, she instills the feeling that she's singing one continuous, forty-minute song. It's perhaps another way of luring the listener into her spell, capturing us with the intoxicating power of her riffs and vamps and refusing to let us go.

In 2002, Wilson recorded a bluescentric album called *Belly of the Sun*, laying down the basic tracks in her hometown, Jackson, Mississippi; what better place to explore the implications of the blues? She had been born there on December 4, 1955, and began studying music at age nine, taking piano, guitar, and singing lessons. At first, she was primarily drawn to blues and folk music, and by the age of twenty was working in what northern musicians call club-date bands, groups hired to replicate familiar hit records as closely as possible at weddings and other private functions. In her twenties, she was increasingly drawn to jazz, when she studied with the drummer Alvin Fielder and then, upon moving to New Orleans, with the saxophonist Earl Turbinton. In 1982, the trumpet player Woody Shaw encouraged her to come to New York.

By the mid-eighties, Wilson was appearing regularly with the loose collective of musicians sometimes known as M-Base, who were centered around alto saxophonist, composer, and bandleader Steve Coleman. Like Ornette Coleman (no relation), Steve Coleman (born 1956, raised in Chicago) had worked out an elaborate musical philosophy, one along the lines of the older Coleman's Harmolodic Theory and George Russell's Lydian Theory of music. Coleman insists that M-Base is not a style or a genre (e.g., like free jazz or Dixieland) but a philosophical approach to playing and thinking about music.

I can't go into all its implications here, so suffice it to say that Coleman's music is, in my uninformed opinion, the most palatable blend of jazz and rock (or whatever it is you may wish to call post-1955 pop music usually aimed at younger audiences) yet devised. Unlike such seasoned campaigners as Miles Davis and Ornette Coleman, Steve Coleman and Cassandra Wilson and their associates had the benefit of growing up entrenched in both rock and jazz, and their blending of the two seems altogether more organic and less forced than that done by older generations, even the likes of Weather Report, Herbie Hancock, and other Milesian descendants. As with earlier attempts at merging jazz with this kind of pop, the first step was juxtaposing acoustic horns and electric rhythm sections. That was generally as far as most fusion efforts took things, but Coleman and the M-Basers went on to incorporate something of the static harmonies and rhythms of the black-oriented pop forms of recent decades: soul, funk, hip-hop. The result is a highly original and compelling sound. Much of Wilson's eighties and early nineties albums utilized M-Base players and principles.

Although Coleman was based in Brooklyn at that time, the first producer willing to take a chance on the M-Base group was Stefan Winter of JMT Productions, a firm based in Munich. Coleman's *Motherland Pulse,* recorded in March 1985, was the collective's first album and featured Wilson on several titles, employing her voice as an element of the ensemble. In November of that year, she recorded her own first album, *Point of View,* which sounded almost identical to the first Coleman albums—the only concession was that her voice was featured slightly more prominently. Most of the tunes were Wilson-Coleman collaborations, and his co-leadership was felt throughout. (Wilson would also be heard on Coleman's *On the Edge of Tomorrow* and *World Expansion.*)

Both Coleman and Wilson were under the spell of Abbey Lincoln at this time, and it's safe to assume that Wilson's early penchant for composing her own material was at least partially inspired by Lincoln. In fact, as mentioned earlier, most of her 1985–92 albums consist primarily of original compositions. When jazz singers who are not primarily composers write their own songs, the results generally fall into three categories. One: The great majority of these original songs, unfortunately, are so unmemorable that they shouldn't be heard even once, even when performed by the artists who've written them. Two: There are a few that sound decent enough when they're being sung by the artist who composed them—like those of Betty Carter and, indeed, Cassandra Wilson—but I wouldn't want to hear anybody else attempt them. And three: There are those originals that are actually well enough written that a variety of performers can sound good singing them, a description that applies to Abbey Lincoln at her best (and Peggy Lee and Mel Tormé in earlier generations) and precious few others. Wilson's work falls into the second category: She has written and recorded dozens of her own songs, and while I can recall the titles and melodies of comparatively few ("Little Warm Death" comes readily to mind), her songs do at least sound good when she's singing them.

Point of View (1985) has two standards, "Blue in Green" (credited to Miles Davis but generally acknowledged to be the work of Bill Evans, with a new lyric by Wilson) and "I Wished on the Moon," which has the voice mixed deep in the band and is as much a Steve Coleman record as a Cassandra Wilson record. Yet on her second, *Days Aweigh* (1987), she is quickly crafting a unique personal sound. Where the M-Base ensemble is densely textured, with overlaying acoustic and electric instruments, *Days Aweigh* is a lot more open and spacious, in a manner that became an obvious influence on younger artists, especially Norah Jones. Although Coleman co-produced *Days Aweigh,* the dominant instrumental influence is Olu Dara, a cornetist and vocalist well schooled in the seemingly disparate disciplines of the most basic blues and the most avant-garde Knitting Factory–style downtown music. Prominent figures in the contemporary jazz scene abound, like composer-saxist Henry Threadgill, trumpeter Graham Haynes, and guitarist Jean-Paul Bourelly, who wrote the title track and would himself shortly become an important Wilson collaborator. For the first time, Wilson sings two standards, a swinging "Let's Face the Music and Dance" and a stark, emotionally naked "Some Other Time" (another Bill Evans heirloom) in a way that represents more of a compromise between the song's traditions (and the composer's intentions) and Wilson's proclivity to radically rethink them. The standout original is "Electromagnolia," a duet with composer Dara that contrasts her scatting with his yodels and cornet, both done against a background of Bourelly's mandolin-like figures and a choir of overdubbed Cassandras.

Her third album, *Blue Skies* (1988), was the one that first showed signs of establishing her as a breakthrough star. For the only time in her career, Wilson sang a whole program of great American standards in the company of a traditional, straight-ahead jazz rhythm section. Although her drummer (Terri Lynn Carrington) and bassist (Lonnie Plaxico, her most frequent fellow traveler on that instrument) were associated with M-Base, her principal accompanist here was the fine Mulgrew Miller. Wilson seems to have been determined to make a record for people who didn't otherwise like Cassandra Wilson records. Not only does she do only familiar songs and no originals, she sings them in the conventionally swinging fashion, utilizing such time-honored devices as, on the opener, "Shall We Dance," changing keys between choruses—hardly a Harmolodic device. On "Sweet Lorraine," a tune with a somewhat rudimentary lyric that's usually done with a strong rhythmic sense, she does just the reverse, takes away the time and sings ad-lib in order to make the words sound more tender than ever before. Yet even without electronics and radical arrangements that revamp well-known tunes to the point where they sound like original compositions, Wilson sounds terrific—a rare youngster, who at thirty-three was on her way to being able to compete with pantheonic masters like Vaughan, McRae, and Fitzgerald. *Blue Skies* seemed like a breakthrough at the time; heard twenty years later, much of it sounds as good as it did then, but in retrospect we see that Wilson, in 1988, was still formulating her approach to interpreting other people's music, and a lot of the time she sounds like she's trying to reconcile Betty Carter's energetic eclecticism with Nina Simone's monodynamics.

With her next album, however, *Jumpworld,* Wilson went out of her way to demonstrate to longtime fans that she hadn't gone completely old-school. *Jumpworld* (1989) was her most M-Base–based project yet, the group backing the singer with the thickest ensemble and most rigidly hip-hop–iest rhythms you can imagine. Largely a new collaboration with Coleman—all the tunes but one (by Graham Haynes) are by either him or Wilson, separately or together—the set heavily features such other leading M-Basers as Haynes, trombonist Robin Eubanks and alto saxist Greg Osby. (At around this time, Wilson also guest-starred on Eubanks's *Karma* and Osby's *Season of Renewal.*) The title track, "Jumpworld," is particularly successful in blending jazz with hip-hop, including a serpentine alto by Coleman, at least two levels of vocal track by Wilson, and a guest appearance by rapper James Moore.

In the eighties and early nineties, it seemed as if Wilson was burying her voice and herself in her ensembles—far from being a star or even the central attraction, she positioned herself as merely one of many (human or brass or electronic) voices in the mixture. Whenever I saw her in concert in these years she seemed similarly reluctant to step forward and interface, as it were, with the audience. The consensus at the time was that, apart from being a superb vocalist and a truly original mind, Wilson was a strikingly beautiful woman (in November 2002, at the age of forty-six, she became the first artist in this book to be photographed more or less topless in *Vanity Fair*—just be glad it wasn't Kate Smith) and that if she were to step into the spotlight a bit less reluctantly, she could accomplish more than any jazz singer had in several generations.

Whereas *Blue Skies* and *Jumpworld* (her last major collaboration with Coleman) were both uniquely Cassandra Wilson, they represented two polar extremes, and her mature sound would owe something to both. She continued to be prolific in the early nineties, releasing four albums in three years: *She Who Weeps* (1990), *Live* (1991), *After the Beginning Again* (1991), and *Dance to the Drums Again* (1992, this last one on DIW). Over the course of these four projects, Wilson begins gradually lightening up from the almost impenetrable density and "science fiction" sound of her earlier, M-Base–oriented projects.

She Who Weeps and *Live* (done in concert in Germany) are the most scat-oriented: *Weeps* is highlighted by a beautiful wordless rhapsody based on Billy Strayhorn's "Chelsea Bridge," while *Live* is rife with scat. Moving stealthily and without pause from one song to the next, in the tradition of a Miles Davis concert, *Live* is Wilson's most instrumental album yet. I have no idea if it was her intention, but she comes closer to capturing the sound of a horn here than any other singer I've ever heard, even such traditional divas as Fitzgerald and Vaughan; there are moments throughout the live album where you're likely to forget that you're listening to a singer. Some will find that making a sound so purely instrumental is a desecration of the human voice, a waste of its potential; others will deem it the highest honor a voice can receive: to be mistaken for a jazz horn. Either way, *Cassandra Wilson Live* is compelling listening.

Dance to the Drums Again is the only one of Wilson's albums not to contain at least two songs that could fit a generally agreed-upon definition of standards—although it does have the traditional hymn "Amazing Grace." Those standards, including the long, drawn-out, remarkably sensual readings of "Body and Soul" on both *Weeps* and *Live,* are obvious highlights for us more conservative listeners, but they're not the only ways that Wilson employs tradition. "New African Blues" (on *She Who Weeps*) offers a collective homage to all the great blues divas of the past, incorporating the line "Pack your razors and your guns" from Bessie Smith's final record, "Gimme a Pigfoot (And a Bottle of Beer)." "Redbone" (on *Beginning*) summons those traditional African jingle-jangle tunes that turn up in jingle-jangle American pop as "Hambone" (Red Saunders, Frankie Laine and Jo Stafford) and "Iko, Iko" (the Dixie Cups, Dr. John). Not coincidentally, *Drums* is the most conventionally fusiony-sounding of all her albums.

Drums was also the last of Wilson's albums for a foreign concern; her premier Blue Note projects, *Blue Light 'Til Dawn* and *New Moon Daughter,* were released in 1993 and 1995. Produced by Craig Street, these first of her ongoing series for the label have since come to define what most of us think of as classic Cassandra Wilson. Her sound is, more than ever, marvelously dark and sultry—not a Julie London/Diana Krall sultry, but an Afro-tribal-type sultry (particularly on the very dark "Children of the Night"). When clarinetist Don Byron plays a low-register obbligato behind her on "Black Crow," the two voices come from the same place sonically and spiritually. By now she's also mastered the art of emotional restraint, demonstrating that by holding back just a little, it seems as if she's actually giving more.

After 1993, she sounds like the mature Cassandra Wilson, having moved from dauntingly dense to loose, open-sounding ensembles, from electronics to acoustics, from hip-hop to blues. Even though by 1995 her records were being heard by listeners far beyond the rather limited confines of the jazz audience, the general sonic texture of both Wilson and her ensemble, from my viewpoint at least, is essentially a jazz sound, even though it's embroidered with elements of folk music, international music, Latin percussion, a heavy dose of blues, and a smaller amount of youth-oriented pop. As with the emotional content of her singing itself, the genre ingredients of her music left much to the imagination: Jazz fans like me heard enough jazz elements to satisfy us; so did pop, rock, and blues fans. Her repertoire is likewise eclectic. On both of the

Wilson-Street albums, she balances a wide but highly consistent range of material. Both sets open with traditional Tin Pan Alley standards—the kind that jazz singers usually do: *Blue Light* starts with "You Don't Know What Love Is" and *New Moon Daughter* with "Strange Fruit." (No, I wouldn't say that these are exactly two of the more cheerful entries in the songbook.)

The most consistent aspect of Wilson's Blue Note albums is her continual exploration of the blues. Even in this most time-honored of musical forms, Wilson's choices continue to surprise. She has made her stylistic allegiances not by gender but by geography: Rather than following the line of important female blues singers, from Bessie Smith to Dinah Washington, she prefers to address the legacies of the bluesmen from her native Mississippi Delta. When most jazz singers want to do the blues, they lean toward Harold Arlen, W. C. Handy, or Duke Ellington. Wilson, however, veers toward Robert Johnson, Son House, and Muddy Waters.

Blue Light 'Til Dawn set the tone for most of her work for the next decade. She starts with a foundation of the blues, including Robert Johnson's "Come in My Kitchen" and "Hell Hound on My Trail" and Son House's "Death Letter." Staying true to the blues impulse, she widens her net to include a number of contemporary pop/folk singer-songwriter songs (Joni Mitchell's "Black Crow" and Ann Peebles's "I Can't Stand the Rain"), a slice or two of country (Hank Williams's "I'm So Lonesome I Could Cry"), and R&B (Charles Brown's "Tell Me You'll Wait for Me"), and even out-and-out kiddie pop, U2's "Love Is Blindness" and the Monkees' "Last Train to Clarksville." The last is an especially compelling revision of a 1966 bubblegum hit: The mop-topped Monkees sang it as if Clarksville were somewhere in Orange County suburbia; Wilson's dark interpretation supports the notion that the song is about inductees leaving Clarksdale, Mississippi, and heading for Vietnam.

Interspersed amid this wealth of material, Wilson's own songs don't suffer by comparison. Rather, they are improved by the context. The intentions behind her original songs are illuminated when they're heard before and after "Hellhound on My Trail" and "Strange Fruit." Given the images of "Strange Fruit," "Death Letter," and "Little Warm Death," Wilson would seem to be among the most morbid of jazz singers—the Morticia Addams of jazz. However, the last title turns out to be rather jubilant: "warm death" seems to be a euphemism for physical love, and the tune may be Wilson's catchiest original, rendered with a bluegrassy feel enhanced by a solo violin. Her second version of "Redbone" proves that she subjects her own work to the same radical reconception that she brings to the songs of other composers, as this 1993 treatment sounds like a completely different song from the original recording (on *After the Beginning Again*).

Blue Light and *New Moon* served notice that at forty, Wilson was now a star who could command a substantial mainstream following. The changes were cosmetic as well as musical; the first two Blue Note albums were her best work yet, and among the best jazz vocal albums of the nineties. At the same time, Blue Note also played the glamour card, sporting images of Wilson on the cover that took full advantage of her face and figure. By now she was headlining at Carnegie Hall and opening for Ray Charles at Radio City.

Her follow-up release was *Rendezvous*, a collaboration with Blue Note star pianist Jacky Terrasson, produced by Bob Belden. The mostly standards set was considered something of a disappointment in 1997; it doesn't have the multigeneric excitement of her previous releases and the constantly shifting instrumentation: It's pretty much just familiar standards reinterpreted on the spot by voice and piano (generally with bass and percussion). The tracks seem to get slower and less exciting as the album progresses—even "Tennessee Waltz" doesn't provide the distraction that you'd expect from 3/4 time. Yet *Rendezvous* sounds better now than it did in 1997: In retrospect, this low-key collaboration seems like a perfect recess between the very exciting projects that came before and since, a pleasant time-out. Individual tracks are more impressive than the album as a whole: She plumbs extraordinary depths of emotion in "Little Boy Lost" (surely the finest recording of this Legrand-Bergmans tune since the title was changed from "Pieces of Dreams") and elsewhere transforms the quasi-nonsensical warhorse "Tea for Two" into something profound.

In her JMT/DIW years, Wilson was turning out one album a year, a figure roughly halved in her Blue Note years (six albums between 1993 and 2005). But she's not taking it easy; rather, *Rendezvous* aside, the Blue Note projects are so ambitious it makes full sense that it would take her two years to conceive and produce each of them. At the time *Rendezvous* was released, in the fall of 1997, Wilson was already deep into her Miles Davis project and premiered some of the arrangements at the end of the year at a concert for Jazz at Lincoln Center. The finished album wouldn't be released for another two years.

As promised, *Traveling Miles* was a celebration of the late trumpeter, bandleader, composer, and twentieth-century icon, not a re-creation of Davis's music or even an attempt to translate it directly into the vocal idiom (which had already been done by Lambert, Hendricks & Ross, Mark Murphy, Sheila Jordan, and, at album length, Dennis Rowland). Throughout, Wilson interprets the tunes from her source every bit as freely as Miles did from his.

Instead of simply resurrecting his music, Wilson explored the sonic similarities between her sound and the trumpeter's. In concert especially, she was cagey enough to realize that she could clarify the comparison by, paradoxically, avoiding the familiar trademarks of Davis's bands. She not only eschewed trumpet and tenor sax but brass and reeds altogether, concentrating on rhythm (piano, bass, and five percussionists including two vibraphones) and five strings (spotlighting the jazz chamber ensemble Quartette Indigo). Her regular guitarist, Marvin Sewell, was on hand, but he was hardly a smooth fusioneer like those in Davis's own bands, having the rough, raw sound of a Delta blues player. The ensemble reflected a concerted attempt to orchestrate the very idea of eclecticism.

Lincoln Center's raison d'être has traditionally been jazz repertory, and though it has occasionally given historically venerated figures (like the Bennys—Carter and Golson—and Wayne Shorter) a forum to present whatever music they like, this was virtually the first time they unleashed a young and contemporary artist (other than the institution's head honcho, Wynton Marsalis) into their playground. In juxtaposing Wilson with Davis, the Lincoln Centerians came up with a whole new take on jazz rep, namely, combining it with the cutting edge.

Wilson reveals how the Milesian mode had informed her sense of economy, a debt that's equally apparent on her trim melodic lines on "My Ship," the major Davis-associated track on *Rendezvous*. At Lincoln Center, she offered many arrangements different from those on the final album, as well as several entire songs that didn't make the final release. For "I Remember You" she gleefully garbled the lyric into what sounded like a scat solo and rendered "Surrey with the Fringe on Top" with a quirky, M-Base–informed stop-and-start pattern (sort of similar to "It Might as Well Be Spring" on *Rendezvous*). Appropriately, old friend Steve Coleman reunited with Wilson on the title track of *Traveling Miles,* a Wilson original. Cyndi Lauper's "Time After Time" was another highlight. It may be the most moving love song she has yet sung, both at Lincoln Center and at Carnegie in June 1998 (where she was joined by the composer herself, who was as white and blond-headed as Wilson was black and dreadlocked).

Wilson also made it plain that she prefers the rambling, meandering Miles of the modal and early electric eras to the terser, more direct Miles of the fifties. Indeed, instead of sticking with familiar ballads that Miles had made his own (like his Sinatra-inspired "It Never Entered My Mind"), Wilson relished the challenge of finding what was singable in melodies like "Miles Runs the Voodoo Down" and "Pfrancing" (the latter issued only as a bonus track on the Japanese edition); on these compositions, merely pinpointing the central melody takes some doing. Much of Davis's later compositions seemed like mere riffs that he vamped on, and in both the trumpeter's own performances and Wilson's reinterpretations, both artists deliberately hide the levels upon levels of control and skill that it takes to craft this music. When you're traveling Miles, Davis and Wilson are both telling us, the destination is secondary, the journey itself is all-important, and you want it to go on forever, like the surrey with the fringe on top.

The gap between *Traveling Miles* (1999) and *Belly of the Sun* (2002), when it finally came out, did indeed seem like forever. As with *Traveling Miles,* there's a loose umbrella of a theme: the blues, both as a concept and a specific musical destination. Still, Wilson incorporates the same wide range of blues-related genres that she addressed in *Blue Light 'Til Dawn* and *New Moon Daughter*. Her idea was to return to her native Mississippi, birthplace of both herself and the blues, both literally and figuratively. She recorded in an abandoned railroad station in which the Blue Note engineers set up rudimentary recording equipment—a parallel to the years in which white A&R dudes from the North would record the legendary Mississippi bluesmen in transportable disc-cutters hastily assembled in hotel rooms. She then assembled the material and added a few more elements and tracks in the climate-controlled comfort of a New York facility.

What she came up with after considerable time and effort was an hour-long meditation on the nature of the blues. Once again, her originals are well positioned in the midst of more familiar compositions that ponder the meaning of the blues experience: The opener, "The Weight," earlier immortalized by Aretha Franklin, examines it from a rock perspective, while "(When It's) Darkness on the Delta" does the same from that of Tin Pan Alley. The pure blues form itself is heard in Mississippi Fred McDowell's ur-gospel "You Gotta Move" and Robert Johnson's "Hot Tamales." The central peg of the album, however, is how Wilson accentuates the blues strengths in three well-known works by composer ideologues of the sixties: Antonio Carlos Jobim ("The Waters of March" further Africanized by a choir of children's voices from New York's M.S. 44), Bob Dylan ("Shelter from the Storm"), and, most unexpectedly, Jimmy Webb ("Wichita Lineman"). Both "Waters of March" and folkster James Taylor's "Only a Dream in Rio" would seem to connect the blues with Brazilian music, using the theme of water and rivers as a linking point.

"Darkness on the Delta" is easily the gem of the album. This 1932 pop song by Jerry Livingston (music) and Al Neiburg and Marty Symes (words), the same team responsible for "Under a Blanket of Blue" and "It's the Talk of the Town," was introduced by Mildred Bailey and movingly recorded by Isham Jones and His Orchestra. It's part of the last generation of pop songs to rhapsodize the racially divided South, and a subcycle that specifically celebrated the nocturnal habits of African Americans (which also included Louis Armstrong's theme "When It's Sleepy Time Down South" and "When It's Slumber Time on the Swannee"). Wilson records "Darkness" in a stunningly stark duet with unknown octogenarian piano bluesmaster Boogaloo Ames. In the bridge, lyricists Neiburg and Symes threw in the line "All God's chillun got someone to love," a reference to the traditional spiritual "Gonna Shout all over God's Heaven"; Wilson uses this as an excuse to instill the song with a bit of gospel feeling. Thus uniting the traditions of Tin Pan Alley with those of the Mississippi Delta (in the darkness or the daytime), "Darkness on the Delta" is Wilson's most successful traditional lyric interpretation. (As of 2010, my opinion hasn't changed. *Belly of the Sun* is, along with Barb Jungr's *Every Grain of Sand,* still my favorite vocal album of the last ten years.)

It was a surprisingly short wait for her next album, *Glamoured,* which may be her most consistent album yet. The title refers to a term from Irish folklore meaning "enchanted," or caught in a spell, which she indeed achieves. Traditionally, as on *Belly of the Sun,* Wilson varies the texture from track to track, maintaining a consistent combination of jazz rhythm section plus guitars plus Latin percussion. It may be that since Norah Jones achieved so much success with a sound fundamentally similar to Cassandra Wilson's very open-sounding blend of jazz, blues, country, and Latin textures (achieved partly in conjunction with David Street, one of Wilson's own producers), Wilson is more determined than ever to sound like herself. As before, she brings unlikely songs from the country ("Crazy") and pop ("If Loving You Is Wrong") genres into her territory. Her reading of "Throw It Away," by Abbey Lincoln, the premier singer-songwriter of our day, reveals how much she owes to Ms. Lincoln in both of those capacities.

At the beginning of December 2005, Wilson turned fifty and celebrated in her hometown; at the end of the month, she made her annual appearance at a special New Year's engagement at New York's Blue Note. On her opening set, it was clear that she was continuing to use the blues as the home base of her pan-stylistic musical explorations. After starting with a regulation 12-bar blues (Muddy Waters's "Honey Bee"), Wilson traveled all over the map of American vernacular music—from twenties and thirties jazz standards to sixties and seventies singer-songwriters, encountering bluegrass (represented by Brandon Ross's banjo solos) and Brazilian bossa novas along the way.

Her favorite device these days is a direct legacy of the blues: the stop time break. "Stop time" means just what it sounds like: When a blues musician or vocalist reaches a climactic moment in the tune, the instrumental backing just drops away and the melody or words are delivered unaccompanied. Wilson used this device in almost all nine of the songs in her Blue Note set, in a way that's closely related to her sense of dynamics. When she wants to emphasize a dramatic point, rather than actually getting louder herself, she has the band get softer—or drop out entirely. Like a movie director, she's controlling our focus without breaking the spell.

She began with "Honey Bee," a regulation 12-bar blues, and moved on to Antonio Carlos Jobim, with a subtly rhythmic reworking of "Waters of March" and a slyly seductive "Corcovado," Bob Dylan ("Lay, Lady, Lay"), and Joni Mitchell ("For the Roses"). Yet there continues to be an important place for the Great American Songbook in her act, and, in fact, there's no one who sings the songbook like her. When she finally gets around to Irving Berlin or Harold Arlen, she makes you feel that both you and she have truly earned the right to them. You can tell she learned "Them There Eyes" from Billie Holiday because of the breakneck tempo and the way she uses stop time in the bridge. She also made stop time the focus of Arlen's "I've Got the World on a String," reusing the bridge as a coda and repeating it over and over as the band came in and out, getting slower and slower and slower until she stopped entirely, making us really think about the last line, "I'm in love."

It seems likely that Wilson's last albums of the first decade of the new century will be the 2006 *Thunderbird* and the 2008 *Loverly.* The first was sabotaged by too much electronics and overproduction (although there is a harrowing treatment of the cowboy song "Red River Valley") and the second was redeemed by a refreshing lack of same. *Loverly* was not only acoustic but was subjected to as little postrecording tinkering as possible. It's marvelously spontaneous, especially on tracks like the opener "Lover Come Back to Me," which almost sounds more spur-of-the-moment than a live album, as if Wilson and trumpeter Nicholas Payton are truly rearranging the Romberg standard as they go along. Yet again, Wilson travels a wide range, from the high London sophistication of Ray Noble's "The Very Thought of You" to the deep Delta sophistication of "Dust My Broom" (she's running out of Robert Johnson classics). There are, in fact, more show tunes here than on any other Wilson project— "Spring Can Really Hang You Up the Most," "'Til There Was You," and "A Sleepin' Bee," as well as the opening "Lover Come Back to Me" and the titular "Wouldn't It Be Loverly?" Yet the set is, at the same time, drenched in the blues and the other non-Western (specifically non-Broadway) traditions that Wilson has reveled in, particularly in the texture of her voice and the wailing, often pentatonic playing of Marvin Sewell.

There isn't room here to go into all of Wilson's guest appearances, which, in the Blue Note years alone, include vocals on albums by Kurt Elling, Don Byron, Bob Belden, Dave Holland, and many others. (However, there are two cameos that number among my all-time favorite Wilson performances, both on soul standards: "Papa Was a Rollin' Stone," on violinist Regina Carter's *Rhythms of the Heart,* and "When Doves Cry," from producer-saxophonist Bob Belden's Prince tribute, *Purple Rain.*) Possibly even more so than Dianne Reeves or Dee Dee Bridgewater,

Cassandra Wilson is the contemporary artist whose appearances I most look forward to. She also may be the only major jazz singer since the golden years who, without compromising herself in any way, has managed to please almost everybody.

Julie Wilson (born 1924)

If there's a human being out there who's more of a class act than Julie Wilson, I'm not sure I want to meet her. The kind of class that Miss Wilson has is comparable to what she describes courtesy of Ogden Nash in "One Touch of Venus": "You either have it or you ain't." The late Mel Tormé once defined a gentleman as someone who can play the banjo but doesn't (George Shearing told the same joke about the accordion). By that same token, a true lady is someone who has the sheer class to outshine every other dame in the joint anytime she chooses but elects not to. Cabaret singers, perhaps even more than jazz musicians, routinely attend one another's shows. Sometimes they go to be supportive, sometimes to see and be seen, sometimes they go to network, sometimes to gnash their teeth. When Ms. Wilson attends the performance of another artist, which she does frequently, the last thing she wants is for her celebrity to distract from the performer she's there to support. Thus, she makes a point of not being seen: She comes covered in *schmata* and a babushka, as it were, so that you don't recognize that the little old lady sitting next to you is, in fact, the divine Julie Wilson. Julie Wilson reminds me of Rosemary Clooney's description of meeting Marlene Dietrich for the first time. A small, nondescript figure walked in out of the rain covered in slicker and galoshes, but as the rain gear came off, the goddess emerged.

Julie Wilson has less voice than any of her fellow cabaret immortals—less by far than Mabel Mercer, Sylvia Syms, or Margaret Whiting in their prime. In the famous profile of Wilson by Whitney Balliett, she talks about how, in the early fifties, she decided she wanted to develop a legitimate soprano singing voice. She auditioned for Richard Rodgers, who was then casting for *Pipe Dream*, and that most sensitive of composer-producers immediately pronounced her the worst soprano he had ever heard. Rather than being offended, Ms. Wilson apparently concurred with Rodgers's judgment and went back to cultivating her familiar singspiel style.

"Voice" is too broad a term; chops are measured in many ways. Wilson's voice itself is not particularly attractive, and her range is amazingly small; she rarely sings flat because she has the smarts to stay within that narrow range. But as she shows time and time again, there's a helluva lot more to singing than just hitting notes. There's a prime example on "Most Gentlemen Don't Like Love," the first track of her 1957 At the St. Regis album. Wilson isn't necessarily (or at least not exclusively) a jazz singer, but there's a useful comparison to a jazz trumpeter like Cootie

Williams, whose trumpet solos aren't mere strings of pitches; he takes a melody and personalizes it with growls and smears, rasps, and any other effects he can think of. Likewise, Wilson tells a story through the effects as much as through the actual notes—or even the words.

On "Most Gentlemen," she sings the first chorus briskly and straight-ahead, but her storytelling abilities kick into high gear when she slows down and heads into the verse. Cole Porter provided the song with a lot of comic detachment, contrasting, as he often did, the very proper, dignified ways of the upper-crusty set and the base desires that drive us all. This protagonist refers to her mother as "Mummy" and here, instead of referring directly to love and sex, she slips into highfalutin French—a sure indication of pretensions that are, as she leads us to expect, about to be deflated. She affects a very high-toned voice, which is only slightly exaggerated and emphasizes the word "mature" the way one does when one is employing a euphemism to cover up something untoward. She uses articulation for maximum comic effect, going over-the-top and cracking her voice at the edges, as if to suggest that the veneer of bourgeois respectability is chipping off, and then dips down for an accentuated low note. Wilson gets maximum effect out of Porter's comic contrast between the sophisticated and the gully-low: She's forever the virginal bride with the guy on the side, the coloratura who moonlights in a black-and-tan dive, Margaret Dumont and Groucho Marx rolled into the same person.

She was born Julia Mary Wilson—or Julia Mary Wilson Wilson, if you will, since both her parents were, coincidentally, surnamed Wilson—in Omaha, Nebraska, on October 21, 1924. As she told Whitney Balliett (who profiled all the major cabaret artists of the seventies and eighties in his highly recommended book *American Singers*, 1998), her mother was a hairdresser and her father, who sold coal for a living and was of Swedish descent, was a mean drunk. Julia started singing with local bands at fourteen and didn't last long after she enrolled at Omaha University. At around this time, according to an anecdote in the *St. Regis* album notes, she entered the Miss America contest and was chosen Miss Nebraska; unfortunately, she was forced to surrender the crown when it was divulged that she was not yet eighteen.

Wilson was tall, slender, and statuesque, and she could dance enough to hold a spot in the chorus of the road company of *Earl Carroll's Vanities*, which brought her from Nebraska to New York. In the big city, she worked at the Latin Quarter until the chance came to audition for Johnny Long and His Orchestra. This was a sometimes hip, sometimes corny, but generally grade-B dance band, which, like Hal Kemp's, Kay Kyser's, and Les Brown's before it, had originated as a college band in North Carolina. Wilson lasted only a few months with Long before the leader fired her, but still, this was an important chance to work with a relatively known touring band.

After Wilson's Johnny Long night of the soul, she transitioned from big bands to nightclub revues, such as the one at the Copacabana; during the war, the club sent her as part of a company of their entertainers, to entertain servicemen as a USO troupe. From nightclubs she moved to Broadway: She auditioned for *Angel in the Wings,* but the spot went to Elaine Stritch. (To think, it could have been Wilson who introduced "Civilization" aka "Bongo Bongo Bongo, I Don't Want to Leave the Congo.") However, she did get to the replacement cast (along with Ray Bolger and Gordon MacRae) of another hit revue, *Three to Make Ready*. She screen-tested for MGM, but didn't actually make it into pictures until ten years later, in 1957, when she appeared in two long-forgotten epics, *The Strange One* and *This Could Be the Night* (in which she was billed as the second female lead, after Jean Simmons and before the veteran Joan Blondell).

Wilson's career in movies, despite her looks, poise, and talent, didn't amount to much, but she spent the fifties and sixties productively, alternating between clubs and musicals, presented all over the world. She hit most of the major "nitespots," including, as she told Balliett, New York's La Maisonette (at the St. Regis Hotel), San Francisco's Mark Hopkins (back in the days when nightclubs were mostly in posh hotels), and was also a frequent attraction in Nevada's early days as an entertainment center. Trodding the boards, she played Bianca (sister of the famous Kate) in *Kiss Me, Kate* both in London and in the American road company, and also did *South Pacific* in the U.K. During the original 1953–55 run of *Kismet*, Wilson replaced Joan Diener as the grown-up lead, and what a Lalume she must have been; oh, that some genie could conjure up a cast recording of her doing "Not Since Ninevah." Over the years, she also appeared in one production or another of *Show Boat, Silk Stockings,* and *Panama Hattie,* among others.

Wilson did everything it was possible to do as a musical comedy leading lady, except that she never had the chance to create a classic role of her own in a great show. Well, I shouldn't say she never had the chance; she was, in fact, offered the lead in *Pajama Game,* but turned it down. "It was a terrible decision," she said. "It would have put me on the map." But I disagree; it's hard to imagine the ultrasophisticated Wilson as the simple factory girl Babe. In fact, I can't even imagine her wearing pajamas (or anything less than the most expensive negligee—and believe me, I've tried), much less making them. There was some TV work, including recurring parts in the American soap opera *The Secret Storm* and the long-running Australian medical soap opera *The Young Doctors*.

Wilson made at least three albums in 1956 and

1957: *Love*, which was done in Los Angeles with the arranger-conductor-pianist and svengali Phil Moore, for the very small Dolphin label, and two for RCA, *My Old Flame* and *Julie Wilson at the St. Regis*. The first of them, done in the studio, seems like an attempt to make Wilson into a regulation pop singer, with interesting results. The production and arrangements, by Moore, Russ Case, and Marty Gold, seem to have been conceived with some other singer in mind, or at least a Julie Wilson very different from the one we all know. The opening "You Don't Know What Love Is" is decidedly exotic, with bongo drums and bass clarinet contributing to the atmosphere; you not only don't know what love is, you also don't have the slightest idea which end is up in this arrangement. The desired effect would seem to be to make Wilson into the next Peggy Lee; the slow-tempoed, medium-sized ensemble mirrors Lee's late forties sound, and there's an echo of Lee's soft, smoky voice. It doesn't work all the way; Wilson's voice is thin and angular where Lee's is round and curvy, and Wilson is tense where Lee is relaxed. Still, *My Old Flame* is a very decent album of a fine singer doing fine standards and is nothing to be embarrassed about.

Yet the *At the St. Regis* album, also from 1957, is the real Julie Wilson, the one we can still hear today, more than fifty years later, the one who was still performing actively at least as late as fall 2010. By now, she was deploying her glamour-girl image as meticulously as her idiosyncratically trained voice: All of the twelve songs cast her in the first person as a femme fatale with a healthy sexual appetite; Hugh Hefner wrote the album notes. (Way to go, Hef!) The *St. Regis* album contains an interesting assortment of tunes. Not only are there few if any really well-known standards; there are only two tunes by canonical Broadway composers, Cole Porter's "Most Gentlemen Don't Like Love" and Harburg and Duke's "What Is There to Say"—and the latter is the set's only straightforward ballad. The only other two items by writers with any reputation are "I Refuse to Rock and Roll" by Sammy Cahn and Nicholas Brodsky, and Gordon Jenkins's "Married I Can Always Get." Otherwise, it's all pretty much special material, elaborate narratives that revolve around the subject of Topic A, mostly written for her by lyricist Allan Roberts. Basically, its songs are about women who seduce men or allow their virtue to be compromised in return for money, favors, and other considerations. The second track, "Twelve Good Men and True," details how she went through all the members of a jury in order to beat a murder rap. She affects a hillbilly accent here, with the attendant gasps and rasps, and does bluesy growls on "I Refuse to Rock and Roll" and to emphasize the punch line of "A Woman Without Experience." There's also a vintage novelty, "A Man Could Be a Wonderful Thing." When performed by other artists (such as Buddy Rich) about ten years earlier, it was merely another catchy rhythm tune, no more, no less; Wilson, by contrast, makes it sound as if it could be Cole Porter.

The *St. Regis* album turned out to be an early peak. Wilson would be less active in the sixties, after marrying producer Michael McAloney in 1961 and starting to raise a family in her late thirties and early forties. (There's an album listed called *Meet Julie Wilson* from 1961, but this may be a reissue of earlier material.) She participated in one of the oddest yet most satisfying projects of her career in December 1965: a live concert from Tampa by an assemblage of traditional jazz players, mostly from New Orleans. How she hooked up with these Crescent City Dixielanders is a mystery, but the results are marvelous. There were two albums, both pressed on what was apparently a semiprivate label from Tampa, H&H Records, and both the concert and the albums (as the LP jackets clearly state) were produced to raise money for the Hillsborough County Association for Mental Health.

The one that I've been able to hear, *Jazz: Bayou to Bay—Out of the Blues* boasts four vocals by Wilson: "I Ain't Got Nobody," "Sunday," "Sugar," and "Bill Bailey," the last three of which are essentially an extended medley spotlighting her, and the final title is a duet with guitarist and singer Doc Souchon. Here is still another side of Wilson: She's left the double entendres back at the St. Regis, and sings these four Dixieland standards in a swinging, straight-ahead fashion, emphasizing rhythm and melody, even when exchanging comic banter with the good doctor (not a nickname, by the way; Souchon was a genuine M.D.). Roughly thirty years later, Wilson played the Algonquin with another Dixieland band, Herb Gardner and the State Street Dixielanders, and those of us who at the time knew her only as an interpreter of Weill and Sondheim were surprised at how capably her appeal translated into the two-beat format. The two Tampa albums (which may or may not actually have been taped live—the applause sounds somewhat suspect) could and should be reissued in toto on a single CD.

At the turn of the seventies, Wilson appeared in two flop musicals, *Jimmy* and *Park,* but had better luck in the road companies of three classic Sondheim shows, *Company, Follies,* and *A Little Night Music.* By the latter part of the decade, Wilson, who had since divorced McAloney, was not only taking care of her children, now in their teens, but also her elderly parents. She took to the boards once more beginning in her sixtieth year. By then, the landscape had changed considerably, and she was among the first to fathom its implications. Like Mercer and Syms, Wilson was helping to define what contemporary cabaret is.

She quickly established herself as one of the leading lights of the resuscitated cabaret scene—cabaret in the eighties and nineties being something significantly different from what it had been in the forties and fifties. Back in the day, cabaret meant either small, intimate rooms like the Blue Angel and the Bon Soir, which had more in common with off-Broadway (as it stands today) than with contemporary cabaret, or it meant bigger rooms, like the Copacabana or the hotel showcases, like the Waldorf, where recording artists like Tony Bennett, Lena Horne, and Tony Martin worked (the forerunners of Las Vegas and Atlantic City).

Wilson helped invent what we might call "deep context" cabaret, which consists of intelligently themed shows, performed by a single singer and an accompanist, who sometimes joins in, and which are most often built around single composers. Modern cabaret leans heavily toward the big six of Broadway in the prewar years—Kern, Berlin, Porter, Gershwin, Rodgers, and Arlen—as well as toward authors like Weill and Sondheim who were perceived as having stretched the limits of what was possible in song form and in musical theater. Even more than Mabel (with whom she shared a certain fruitiness in her style, a kind of plummy, overripe sound) and Sylvia Syms, Wilson is the foremother of K. T. Sullivan, Andrea Marcovicci, Mary Cleere Haran, Maude Maggart, and the other standard-bearers of contemporary cabaret.

Over a little more than twelve years, Wilson recorded six songbook albums, with producer Hugh Fordin and longtime accompanist and collaborator Billy (William) Roy, a series that began and ended with the two youngest composers:

*Julie Wilson Sings the Stephen Sondheim
  Songbook* (1987)
Kurt Weill (1988)
Harold Arlen (1989)
Cole Porter (1990)
Gershwin (1999)
Cy Coleman (2000)

They all have tracks to recommend them. The Porter set, quite naturally, stresses his extended, talkier works like "The Tale of the Oyster" over his simpler, more conventional and tuneful pieces like "I Love You." The *Sondheim* is especially valuable since Wilson made no cast recording of the score to *Follies,* and her medley of four songs from that show— "Beautiful Girls," "Lucy and Jessie," "Losing My Mind," and "Leave You"—says in five minutes what it usually takes an entire cast two hours and an intermission to say. And on the disc's (and the show's) climactic song, "I'm Still Here," Wilson makes me understand the line "But someone said 'she's sincere,' so I'm here," more than anyone else.

On most of these canned cabaret shows, Wilson's voice naturally sounds discernibly older than it did in 1957 or 1965, but she hasn't lost anything that she needs to put these songs and entire songbooks over. We're less conscious than ever of the notes and more mindful of the narratives. If I were forced to pick one, it would probably be the Kurt Weill entry, which packs more of an emotional punch than most Broadway shows. Wilson and Roy open with "One

Touch of Venus," in which she bemusedly pats herself on the back for the success that she and her fellow goddess-divas have had with their control of the male gender, proving "that the panty is mightier than the pants." Conversely, in "That's Him" (also from *One Touch of Venus* and also with a lyric by Ogden Nash) she now sings in praise of men, showing that women may not be so doggone dominant after all.

Julie Wilson Sings the Kurt Weill Songbook is no less notable for showing that Weill's European songs can be included in the same context as his Broadway show tunes—a juxtaposition as unusual as combining Rodgers and Hart with Rodgers and Hammerstein. She's never more effective than on the two best-remembered songs from the 1929 *Happy End* (both with original German texts by Bertolt Brecht, translated by Michael Feingold), "Bilbao Song" and "Surbaya Johnny." Before replaying Wilson's treatment of these two numbers, I would have bet money that these songs, traditionally very overdone in New York cabaret circles, had been drained of their power, a couple of empty, bourgeois-savaging snarls that have long since lost their ability to shock us. Madeline Kahn even parodied the extreme Weill-Brecht torch tangos like "Surbaya Johnny" in such a crushingly funny way (as "Das Chicago Song") that I thought I could never take the song seriously again. Wilson shows me that I was wrong. In her hands, "Surbaya Johnny" is more devastating than I could have imagined, as she fluctuates between bipolar extremes of love and hate in reenacting what can only be described as a grandly dysfunctional relationship. This is a song that confronts the most brutal outer limits of gender politics, and in Wilson's hands it's as wrenching as the most powerful blues by Bessie Smith or Billie Holiday.

A duet between Wilson and Roy, "Bilbao Song" operates on several levels: Two old lushes wax nostalgic about the hedonistic pleasures of their youth, and we don't so much listen as participate by proxy as their reminiscence becomes ever more three-dimensional. I had never noticed previously that "Bilbao" is fundamentally two different songs stitched together, somewhat in the fashion of the more famous "Alabama Song" from *Mahagonny.* The basic sections, in which the two characters describe the action from an outside, objective perspective, are harsh and severe in the Germanic marching tradition, with rigorous oom-pah rhythm. This is in stark contrast, however, to what might be thought of as a song-within-a-song, which is an entirely different piece of melody, like a flashback within the main narrative. Using two voices and piano, Wilson and Roy conjure up an amazingly vivid scene, depicted more spectacularly in the mind's eye than anything experienced courtesy of narcotics or MTV (not that I've had enough first-hand knowledge of either to know what I'm talking about). Wilson and Roy knowingly emphasize the contradiction between the two melodies—the interior one sweet and sentimental yet equally laced with irony, the exterior gruff and jaded—making the performance into a veritable production number unto itself.

There are other great moments in the *Weill* album: for one, "What Good Would the Moon Be?," a rarely heard Langston Hughes lyric from *Street Scene.* Her "Sing Me Not a Ballad," rescued from the Weill–Ira Gershwin flop *The Firebrand of Florence,* is significantly more moving than the recording by Lotte Lenya, who introduced it. Equally commendably, she shows us that both "Trouble Man" and the lovely "Stay Well" do, in fact, have a life outside of *Lost in the Stars.*

At the end of the first decade of the new century, Wilson, now in her upper eighties, is still out and about. (There are also a few albums I haven't been able to track down, including a live set from the Russian Tea Room, supposedly from 1995.) I haven't seen her do a whole show of her own in a few years, but she does make special appearances at events like the 92nd Street Y's *Lyrics and Lyricists* series as well as at the Mabel Mercer Foundation's annual Cabaret Convention. Even so, it's not too fanciful to predict that some of her best work may still be ahead of her. You know the way you feel about "Rhapsody in Blue," or when a tooth stops aching, or when you sense autumn in the air? The way you feel that you really shouldn't feel? That's her. That's her.

Nancy Wilson (born 1937)

Searing, burning, and intense—not to mention swinging—from her first recording onward, Nancy Wilson immediately established herself as a top singer. At that time, the matter of whether she was a pop singer or a jazz singer was a subject of some discussion. "I don't like categories," she once said. "When I started, I was definitely a jazz singer to jazz enthusiasts, but strictly a pop singer to everyone else. Everyone wanted to put me in a category."

As with Dinah Washington and Joe Williams, her singing draws equally upon elements from the pop, jazz, and blues schools all at once, forged into a seamless blend. Wilson may be the first postmodernist of jazz-pop singing, the most important vocalist to come along after these three genres were codified and move freely among them. At the same time, it's hard to place her in the highest bracket of African American divas—Holiday, Fitzgerald, Vaughan, Washington, McRae. She may be a step down from the diva pantheon, yet her sound is immediately distinctive (you might say "stylized" or even "mannered") and she is, at the very least, a major stylist.

She is also one of the most prolific of all recording artists, the majority of her work is at an extremely high level. Almost all of her sixties albums are more than competent: They're expertly sung and orchestrated jazz-pop treatments of standards, contemporary hits, and show tunes old and new. If Wilson isn't up there with the Billies and Ellas and Carmens, it's because one rarely hears anything absolutely startling on a Nancy Wilson record: a slice of emotion so powerful it leaves you with your mouth hanging open, as with Holiday, or a melody line rewritten in such a brilliant fashion that it actually improves on Gershwin, as with Ella, or a little bit of both, as with McRae, or even a startling arrangement idea, like "My Favorite Things" done in 4/4, as by Betty Carter. Yet there's not a single record Wilson made in these years that I wouldn't want to own, that I don't feel is worthy of being reissued on compact disc.

At her peak Wilson made dozens and dozens of albums—as many as two or three a year. She continually mined the standard songbook, and, at the same time, sang virtually every half-decent song from every new show or film to come along, and also occasionally managed to uplift contempop hits into her own idiom. Wilson's sixties output is nothing less than overwhelming; she recorded so many albums, and virtually all of them are so remarkably good, that she obliterates the conceptual difference between quality and quantity.

While none of her sixties LPs is disappointing, there are at least a half-dozen that are jazz vocal classics, in which her own outstanding performance is enhanced by the presence of a superior collaborator, including *Nancy Wilson/Cannonball Adderley, But Beautiful* (with Hank Jones), *Yesterday's Love Songs, Today's Blues* (with Gerald Wilson), and *The Swingin's Mutual* (with George Shearing). In these, Wilson modulates from good to great.

From 1970 to 1980, Wilson, still recording for Capitol, worked primarily in the soul field, although it was a lighter and more urbane approach to the music (as opposed to, say, Isaac Hayes), in which she did songs like "Everything Must Change." In the eighties and nineties, however, her recorded work bottomed out when she switched to Columbia and began turning out a series of completely soulless albums. This is the only period of Wilson's work with virtually nothing to redeem it. Yet even if one only considers the early work, she recorded enough good music in her twenties to sustain a career-long reputation.

Wilson (born in 1937) and Jack Jones (born a few months later) were probably the last of the major jazz-pop singers of the golden age—anyone younger qualifies as a revivalist. The dawn of the sixties may hardly seem like the time to launch a career as a pop singer who directed her energy at the adult rather than the teen market. Even when she recorded more contemporary material, it was aimed at adult listeners. Whether in spite of or because of this, her music, intelligent and mature as it was, immediately found an audience, and it has never lacked for one.

Born in Chillicothe, Ohio, and raised in Columbus, Wilson grew up singing in church choirs and winning talent contests; according to one account, she starred on a local TV show at fifteen. Her most overwhelming influence, which to this day comes through loud and clear in her singing, is the Grandfather of Soul, Little Jimmy Scott. "I owe so much to him," she said in the early sixties. "I think he's fabulous. I guess you can say if anybody influenced me, it was he." And there are times when I feel that Wilson employs his emotional yet unsentimental sound to almost as great an effect as Scott himself does.

After high school, she sang in local clubs and enrolled in Ohio College, but one semester later said to herself, "Look, girl, if you're ever going to be a singer you've got to stop this stalling around and get out there and sing." In May 1956, Wilson joined the band led by blues tenor saxophonist Rusty Bryant, with whom she toured the States and Canada for two years and cut her first disc ("Don't Tell Me," a Dot single).

In 1958, Wilson left Bryant to follow a trail of solo nightclub engagements from Kansas City to Montreal. However, when she arrived in New York a year later, it was without a gig or even a place to stay. She took a day job in an office and held tight until she was asked to fill in for ailing singer Irene Reid at the Blue Morocco, a nightclub in the Bronx. It was there that Cannonball Adderley heard her, and soon the alto giant brought in Capitol producer Dave Cavanaugh, as well as his agent, John Levy, who still fills that function as Wilson's manager more than forty years later.

Before 1959 was over, Wilson had attracted record industry attention with one of her earliest singles, "Guess Who I Saw Today?," and her first album, the 1959 *Like in Love*. Although five of her platters wound up in *Billboard*'s pop and R&B listings, she would never be a chart artist. The record industry hadn't yet reached the point where a quick-hit fix was more important than developing a long-time career, and Wilson gradually racked up big sales—like many artists in the prolific fifties and sixties—partially because she recorded so prolifically.

Wilson's most frequent studio collaborator in the earliest years was the brilliant Billy May, with whom she cut at least five albums' worth of material, starting with *Like in Love*. With May she taped, among other projects, a set of ballads (*Tender Loving Care*), which included the comparatively bouncy "Like Someone in Love" and a jazz-oriented package (*Something Wonderful,* her second LP) that guest-starred Ben Webster. Webster's unmistakable tenor blows beautifully breathily behind Wilson on "He's My Guy" and "Call It Stormy Monday," the latter being a traditional blues associated with T-Bone Walker. Wilson and May later reunited for an entire album of similarly earthy material, *Nancy Naturally,* including "Just for a Thrill" (which had been brought back into circulation by Ray Charles) and a bluesified treatment of Frank Loesser's Oscar nominee "I Wish I Didn't Love You So."

After May, the big band arrangers who worked with Wilson most frequently were the very gifted pianist Jimmy Jones and alto saxophonist Oliver Nelson. Jones guided Wilson through two scrumptious sets that collected the best film and show songs, *Hollywood—My Way* and *Broadway—My Way*. In both of these, she makes a point of swinging songs written as ballads, such as Jerome Kern's "Dearly Beloved" and Rodgers and Hammerstein's "Getting to Know You." Jones also worked with Wilson on several individual-track excursions into bossa nova territory; a delightful treatment of "Wave" (the highlight of a set of later, lesser material called *Easy*) worked the best. The jazzy and moving "People" (from an equally unpromising compendium of hit singles called *How Glad I Am*) also suggests Jones's ace keyboard work.

Although, surprisingly, the bulk of Wilson's early work with May has yet to be reissued (there's at least enough for a superb and very full three-CD package), fortunately their last collaboration—about half of the 1967 *Lush Life*— is available. The emphasis here is on ballads, and they come from a wonderfully eclectic blend of sources, including many international items (like the French "Free Again" and "When the World Was Young" and the Argentine Lalo Schifrin's "The Right to Love"); undeservedly overlooked domestic product ("Over the Weekend," "Do You Know Why?"); and a contempop hit ("Sunny") elevated to the level of a standard. Still, no song brings out the best in Wilson as a dramatic interpreter more than Billy Strayhorn's titular classic.

Oliver Nelson, who arranged most of the non-May tracks of *Lush Life*, supplied many of the highlights of her catalogue in the late sixties, their best project together being *Welcome to My Love* (also from 1967). As with *Lush Life*, love songs predominate and the ratio is similar: unexpected movie themes ("In the Heat of the Night," "Theme from 'Hotel'"), transfigured chart items ("Ode to Billy Joe"), and neglected songwriters like Tommy Wolf ("I'm Always Drunk in San Francisco [And I Don't Drink at All]") and Joseph McCarthy ("Why Try to Change Me Now?"). By this point, the label was already beginning to saddle her with unsuitable chart-oriented material, but Wilson's and Nelson's blues strengths were able to work wonders with items as unlikely as "Ode to Billy Joe." "You're Gonna Hear from Me" was a worthy movie tune (from *Inside Daisy Clover*) by the Previns (André and Dory) with an outstanding guitar-only verse. Likewise, "You Don't Know Me," with its blues-drenched ad-lib sax section intro, shows how well the combination could move at full throttle. Tightly focused by Nelson's shimmering string arrangements, Wilson is riveting from start to finish.

For the most part, her more overtly jazzy works come from the early sixties: *The Swingin's Mutual* is an early collaboration for both Wilson and George Shearing. This generous 1960–61 set (twenty tracks,

five of which weren't issued until the CD era), shows that Shearing's cool is a perfect foil for Wilson's hot. This was her first teaming with a small jazz unit, prefiguring the Adderley team-up and collaborations with combos as late as the 1969 *But Beautiful* with the Hank Jones quartet. The movie theme–cum–jazz standard "Green Dolphin Street" is an obvious high light, as is Marvin Fisher's "My Gentleman Friend." As with the Adderley album, a handful of instrumentals provides a complement to Wilson's contributions. Shearing also worked with Wilson on *Hello, Young Lovers,* for which the pianist is credited with devising string backgrounds. "A Good Man Is Hard to Find," from the Bessie Smith songbook, is a singularly stunning slice of blues-with-strings.

Where *The Swingin's Mutual* with Shearing is soft and swinging, the albums with May and particularly *Yesterday's Love Songs* with Gerald Wilson are loud and swinging. Every track on *Yesterday's Love Songs* is first-rate and occasionally even more: When she holds a long high note on the word "key" at the climax of "Someone to Watch over Me," it takes your breath away, though she still seems to have breath to spare. (She reports that this was her manager, John Levy's, favorite of her recordings.) "Never Let Me Go" is one of the most emotional of all her performances, and her treatment of this Livingston and Evans movie song is second only to Nat Cole's. The CD issue is beefed up by a number of singles, most notably Wes Montomgery's "West Coast Blues," that, unlike some CD bonus tracks, really do contribute to the overall enjoyment of the total package.

Still, there's little doubt as to what Wilson's single most valuable album is: *Nancy Wilson/Cannonball Adderley*. Indeed, if there's someone out there who wishes to own only one classic Wilson album (I would also recommend the three-CD box *Ballads, Blues and Big Bands: The Best of Nancy Wilson*), the Cannonball album is the way to go. In some ways, this 1961 collaboration prefigures the more famous *John Coltrane and Johnny Hartman,* but where that 1963 masterpiece sticks to slow ballads, Wilson and Adderley mix jazz pieces (including several by Nat Adderley, the leader's cornetist-composer brother), contemporary show tunes (the superb "Never Will I Marry"), and blues ("Save Your Love for Me"), as well as one of Wilson's best slow love songs (the Jimmy Scott perennial "The Masquerade Is Over"). "Never Will I Marry," a performance that was singled out for praise by Wynton Marsalis on an NPR profile, has the combination working over their heads, starting with the inspired idea of treating this deliberately archaically worded Frank Loesser lament (from the flop *Greenwillow*) as a hard 4/4 swinger. It's an essential package, only marred by the producer's decision to limit Wilson's participation to six tracks (a seventh was recorded but not issued until the CD), meaning that half the album are Adderley instrumentals. Not that there's anything wrong with that, but the Wilson-Adderley combination works so well that one wishes they had done all twelve tracks together.

Those team-ups, with Gerald Wilson, the Adderley brothers, George Shearing, Hank Jones, and others, were significant events in Wilson's career. But what really made her early work special is, conversely, the very ordinariness of even her run-of-the-mill, bread-and-butter projects. The remarkable thing about her best years was how excellent even her throwaways were.

In 1964, she took two days to record a typical album called *Today, Tomorrow, Forever,* which, with the benefit of forty-five years of hindsight, turns out to be one of the most special nonspecial albums ever released by anybody. *TTF* was hardly high-concept: Producer Dave Cavanaugh seems merely to have looked at twelve of the recent biggest-selling songs and drawn his album from them. As a result we have everything from Tony Bennett ("I Left My Heart in San Francisco," "The Good Life"), Jack Jones ("Wives and Lovers," "Call Me Irresponsible"), Steve Lawrence ("Go Away, Little Girl," or, in Wilson's case, little boy), and the Newley–Bricusse–Sammy Davis combination ("What Kind of Fool Am I," done in a swinging 3/4 with Lou Levy on celesta) to Ray Charles ("Unchain My Heart," "I Can't Stop Loving You"), the Drifters ("On Broadway"), and Ruby and the Romantics ("Our Day Will Come"), not to mention the bossa nova ("One-Note Samba"). As with Sinatra's *It Might as Well Be Spring* or virtually any Andy Williams album from the Clive Davis Columbia period, this set could be subtitled "Other People's Money."

Cavanaugh produced the album in a quick-and-dirty fashion, basically using Wilson's traveling rhythm section, led by her musical director, drummer, and then husband, Kenny Dennis, and a couple of guest stars on a few tracks: Lou Levy on piano, Bill Perkins on tenor on two cuts, and Lou Blackburn on trombone on just one. There are only a couple of arrangements that could be described as anything beyond serviceable, so it may not be the most original album ever made, but who cares? It's amazingly good. Each track is well arranged, well sung, and Wilson extracts meaning from even the most overexposed pop hit. Occasionally it's even great: "Unchain My Heart," with just tenor, organ, and rhythm, might seem meager compared to Ray Charles's epic version with his orchestra and the Raelettes, but Wilson rivals him for power. The album's gem is "Our Day Will Come," which anticipates and rivals a far more harrowing rendition from 1969 by Wilson's hero, Little Jimmy Scott. Unlike Scott's, Wilson's treatment is not a trip to hell and back, but it's plenty effective just the same. If *Ella Fitzgerald Sings the George and Ira Gershwin Songbook* is an epic, *Today, Tomorrow, Forever* is a quickie—the whole package is less than twenty-eight minutes long—yet there's nothing about it that isn't eminently satisfying.

And yet *Today, Tomorrow, Forever* is hardly the classic that *Yesterday's Love Songs* and the Shearing and Adderley collaborations are. It's those team-up albums that became required listening for young jazz singers. Kevin Mahogany and Jeanie Bryson, who both sing "West Coast Blues," are only two of the contemporary vocal artists who grew up on the classic Wilson albums and regard them as essential works to study for aspiring vocalists—"Save Your Love for Me" is almost overdone by young singers who learned it from the *Cannonball* album.

One singer who for many years did not make records that sounded like classic Nancy Wilson was, unfortunately, Nancy Wilson. She did her best work with two producers, Tom Morgan (1959 to 1963) and Dave Cavanaugh (1964 to 1973). But by the late sixties, the times were changing. Wilson initially was an album artist for Capitol; as soul historian Dave Nathan notes, the label didn't release any singles at all by her until 1961. But by the Nixon era, the label seemed determined to market Wilson to the soul/R&B audience—which they did rather successfully.

In 1969, both Wilson and Cavanaugh were fully aware of the changes that were going on, and they seemed to have conceived of *But Beautiful* as a counterreaction. It's as if they knew this would be their last chance to make a great jazz-and-standards album before the gate closed, and they took full advantage. Working in New York, Cavanaugh rounded up an amazing rhythm section of all-star studio players, including Hank Jones, piano, Gene Bertoncini, guitar, Ron Carter, bass, and Grady Tate, drums. At one point, Bertoncini recalled, Cavanaugh seemed to have considered overdubbing strings on top of the voice-and-rhythm tracks, which he obviously realized would have been a mistake, for the album as recorded is perfect in itself. The standards here are generally very familiar, with the exception of "For Heaven's Sake," sung previously by Holiday and Tony Bennett but certainly not overdone, as well as "Oh! Look at Me Now." While "Oh! Look" and "Do It Again" (a Gershwin antique not often heard in modern circles) romp lightly, the basic meat of the matter is slow, angst-full ballads of the Jimmy Scott variety. Wilson reported that when she finished "Glad to Be Unhappy," everybody in the booth, including the producer, was in tears.

Nancy Wilson Anthology is a two-CD package that purports to offer the best of the singer's seventies recordings for Capitol—I have to assume it's representative, although I don't know enough about that music to fully judge it. After leaving Capitol at the end of that decade, she's recorded most notably for Columbia and, more recently, Telarc. The nineties works seem intended for radio stations that play what's sometimes known as fusion and sometimes referred to as Quiet Storm, a kind of black pop with light (or lite) jazz elements. There was at least one album of traditional material from the late eighties—just around the time that *But Beautiful* was reissued—and it was a reunion with Hank Jones no less, but it was recorded and so far released only in Japan.

It wasn't only the material she was singing that sabotaged most of Wilson's eighties and nineties albums; her singing itself had grown increasingly mannered and even pretentious. Typical of her later work is "A Lady with a Song," an anthem of self-congratulation out of the tradition of Sinatra's "My Way" and Billy Eckstine's "I Am a Singer." Even when she sang good songs in a straight-ahead setting, she risked sounding overstylized. Her physical mannerisms grew proportionately mannered as well: In 2007, Ms. Wilson was the focus of a seventieth birthday tribute at Carnegie Hall, and one of those paying tribute was the younger singer Nnenna Freelon. In both her singing and her physical deportment, Ms. Freelon is highly influenced by Ms. Wilson, and seeing them on the stage together made me think I was watching a pair of Balinese dancers.

In 1984, Nancy Wilson and funk-jazz-pop pianist Ramsey Lewis joined forces for *The Two of Us*, easily one of the worst records of her entire career: a soupy mix of smooth jazz and pop-fusion in which her vocals seem secondary and even unnecessary. Thus, in 2001 when Wilson and Lewis reunited for a sequel to this masterpiece, titled *Meant to Be* (she also guests on his 2003 *Simple Pleasures*), I didn't even bother to open the shrink wrap. My bad! I later realized with perfect hindsight that this album played a major role in her resuscitation. He isn't always the lightest-fingered pianist (Ramsey Lewis isn't John Lewis) and Wilson still tends to overenunciate, although she has a sense of humor about her own entrenched mannerisms. *Meant to Be* opens with her doing all her purrs, vocal smears, diminuendos, and other trademark shtick on "Peel Me a Grape," and at the end of the track, the producers left in a brief snippet of the singer laughing, apparently at herself.

Wilson seems to have spent most of the first decade of the new century receiving awards and testimonials. In 2003, she gave a big gala concert at Jazz at Lincoln Center, at the climax of which she announced that she was retiring. I assumed that this was sheer stagecraft, calculated to provoke a major response from the crowd. And although it did achieve precisely that, she turned out to be on the level. From that year on, Wilson has apparently not toured but only made special appearances—generally to receive an award. In 2004, she was named a Jazz Master by the National Endowment for the Arts (who had fortunately listened to *Nancy Wilson/Cannonball Adderley* and not *The Two of Us*), and in 2007, the JVC Jazz Festival paid tribute to her on the occasion of her seventieth birthday (the concert mentioned above).

For whatever reason, Wilson seems to feel that this will be the final phase of her career, and with

that, apparently, comes a desire to set the record straight. Starting with *Meant to Be*, Wilson has made four albums in which her goal seems to be to prove to her fans that she is capable of doing better than the generally inferior material that she's been recording for the last thirty years. She followed *Meant to Be* (which also includes a moving, if overdramatic reading of Allan Sherman's "Did I Ever Really Live?") with three albums on the Pittsburgh-based MCG label: *A Nancy Wilson Christmas, R.S.V.P. (Rare Songs, Very Personal)* (2004), and *Turned to Blue* (2004).

Nearing seventy, she sounds better than ever; the voice is still dark, in the sense of African American coloration, but light in the sense of weightless, as if she could take flight at any moment, and she still combines the best attributes of Jimmy Scott and Dinah Washington. The voice is still sharp, in the sense of accurate, and extremely lithe. For all her talk about retiring and unretiring, she has lost little if any power or projection since the 1960s.

The Christmas project is a fine, straight-ahead holiday package, but the other two (which both won Grammy Awards) are the albums most capable of restoring her reputation. *R.S.V.P.* and *Turned to Blue* may not quite be the full-fledged return to classic form that most of us longtime Wilson fans were waiting for, but both are closer than we ever expected: The backings are flesh-and-blood acoustics, not the electronic dreck she'd been subjected to (or subjecting us to) for far too long, and most of the songs are standards. (Between "Did I Ever Really Live?" and Carroll Coates's undersung "You'll See," Wilson reveals that she still has her 1960's knack for unearthing excellent neglected songs.) Even the new tunes, scattered among classics like "Be My Love" and Duke Ellington's "Take Love Easy," are worth a listen. Between old and new, there are a lot of self-reflecting songs about the aging process, from "This Is All I Ask" to the new "The Golden Years" and "Knitting Lessons"; the two albums also contain the ultimate farewell songs, "Goodbye" and "I'll Be Seeing You." Wilson very creatively uses the autobiographical angle to enhance the three-way relationship among the singer, the songs, and the audience. And that's a very good thing.

"I'm jazz-oriented, [but] I never professed to be a jazz singer," Wilson once said. "I'm not really a pop singer either. I'm one of those people in the middle. I'm a song stylist. I just like to sing good music, tunes that have good range and good lyrics, and I've never cared what anybody else calls it. My job is to take good material and deliver it. It's like being an actress, and that's really what I've been doing throughout my whole career."

What's amazing but not in the least surprising is the respect that Wilson commands in the black community. She has become a role model, and not only to singers but to the entire community, and a symbol of class and achievement second only to Lena Horne.

Multiple Artists

The Birth of the Croon

Cliff Edwards
Nick Lucas
Rudy Vallee
Russ Columbo

When you listen to the top male popular singers of the twenties and thirties, you know how the story's going to turn out: Spurred on by the influences of Louis Armstrong, Al Jolson, and others, Bing Crosby becomes the dominant voice of his generation, perhaps in all of American pop. Then Crosby will, in turn, be succeeded by Frank Sinatra. However, when we listen to the singers who preceded Bing Crosby or emerged around the same time that he did or even shortly after, we obviously know more about what happened to the music than the artists themselves did. If we listen to a 1925 cut by Cliff Edwards, we may hear two or three aspects of his performance that anticipate what we know to be the eventual development of the music, but we're just as likely to hear a number of things that didn't happen to go anywhere beyond him—Cliff Edwards wasn't singing as if he thought he was laying the groundwork for Crosby and Sinatra.

The twenties is an especially fascinating period in the development of jazz and popular singing. As it happens, not many major male singers emerged in the earlier half of the decade, although a few of the stronger representatives of the previous generation did some of their finest work in these years, among them Billy Murray and Jolson. In the very last gasp of the acoustic era, which ended in 1925, two new singers, Cliff Edwards and Gene Austin, came along as if to stake their claims and announce that they would be important voices in the age of electricity, which, as it happens, was just about to begin.

Entertainer-historian Ian Whitcomb makes a provocative point: From his perspective, the late twenties was the most interesting period in the history of popular singing. In 1931, Bing Crosby (even though he'd been on the scene and recording for five years by then) essentially established himself as the dominant voice of the mass media; from point onward, every new pop star who came along, black or white, had to absorb Crosby's influence—if not just flat out imitate him.

Everyone was defined, in a sense, by their stylistic relationship to Crosby. However, in the years between the introduction of electricity and the coronation of Crosby, there was more than one way to do things. (Whitcomb is especially fond of the subgenre of talk singers who proliferated in the era, most of whom, perhaps not coincidentally, seemed to bear such colorful appellations as Little Jack Little, the well-named Whispering Jack Smith, and the less-well-named Singin' Sam.) The early electric years, as we shall see, would be a period of much experimentation.

Cliff Edwards (1895–1971)

Martin Williams observed that Jelly Roll Morton wasn't particularly influential—if you want to hear the roots of big band jazz, listen to what Fletcher Henderson, Duke Ellington, and even Paul Whiteman were doing in the same period. Although everyone seemed to acknowledge that Morton's classic Red Hot Peppers sides were masterpieces, few people tried to compose or arrange like him, no one really played piano like him, and apart from "King Porter Stomp" (a tune he considered so unimportant that he never did a proper treatment with the Peppers), few of his compositions were even heard during the swing era.

By any standards, Cliff Edwards was a very big talent. At their best, his music and singing are so strong that even though we may recognize a device here or a tactic there that reappears later in the work of Crosby, they're almost beside the point. This is music, like Jelly Roll Morton's, that should be listened to today because it's so good, and whether or not it was "important," whatever that means, or anticipated certain developments in the history of pop music, is irrelevant. Even so, he was in fact quite influential.

There are two significant aspects of his early life. First, he was self-taught, in terms of a fundamental reading, 'ritin', and 'rithmetic education as well as in music. Clifton A. Edwards (even bio-discographer Larry Kiner couldn't figure out what the middle initial stood for) was born in Hannibal, Missouri, in 1895. "I didn't have a long schooling," he later told Richard Lamparski. "Used to pass by the high school but never got in." As an autodidact, he gradually invented himself into a completely self-contained musical act. In the early years, when he worked in saloons and other unsavory establishments, he couldn't count on the presence of a piano or anyone to play it, so he learned to accompany himself by banging out a few simple chords on the ukulele—the most rudimentary and least expensive musical instrument that would suit his purposes. Unlike Nick Lucas, Edwards was far from a string virtuoso, but his own accompaniments were eloquent in their simplicity. In later years, he would occasionally work with pianists and full bands, but the core of his act was just his voice and ukulele. Working in Chicago around the time of World War I, Edwards became known for the first time as "Ukulele Ike."

Seventy years later, Bobby McFerrin proclaimed "I'm My Own Walkman," but he had nothing on Edwards, who was doing essentially the same thing as early as the teens. Perhaps because he was his own Walkman, Edwards was determined to get as many different kinds of musical textures out of his voice as possible. As such, he was one of the first entertainers to popularize what later became known as scat singing—improvising nonverbal noises, growls, and various nonsensical syllables. He never made any claim for himself in this regard—nonsense singing seems to have been part of vaudeville and, in a sense, goes back even earlier than "hey nonny nonny" in Shakespeare's time. However, one couldn't really consider scat singing as a jazz technique until instrumental jazz itself had been introduced. Edwards had been enlivening his singing with goofy noises ever since his teenage years in St. Louis, when he was hired to supply music for silent films and threw in the sound effects as well. (I imagine it must have sounded something like his 1925 record of "Alabamy Bound," in which he not only sings of taking a train back home to his Mammy in the Sunny South, he throws in the sounds of the locomotive as well.) In the years before the term "scat singing" was coined, the term for these nonverbal noises—used by Edwards and others—was "eefin'." (I can only speculate that it has some connection with "F-ing," and it's easy to see what that, in turn, is connected with.)

By the end of the decade, Edwards was employing his eefin' technique in conjunction with the emergent strains of jazz and blues that were coming out of the South; by the time he begins recording in earnest in 1923–24, he's creating full-blown wordless improvisations that are scat solos in everything but the name. Indeed, his gift for scatting seems to have been his first ticket to fame. In 1918, he was working at the Arsonia Cafe in Chicago when pianist Bobby Carleton wrote a rhythmical piece of nonsense entitled "Ja Da"—the lyrics essentially went "Ja da, ja da, jing jing jing!" It was Edwards who put the song over, making it into a hit by plugging it all around Chicago and then the nation. It was too early for him to make a record of it or sing it on the radio (although he may well have gotten his picture on the sheet music cover), but a lot of people heard his name for the first time in conjunction with this song.

Between 1918 and 1922, Edwards worked consistently in vaudeville, and also made some headway in what was then known as the "legitimate" theater, or Broadway, appearing in the 1919 *Ziegfeld Midnight Frolic* and something called *Mimic World of 1921* at the Winter Garden. He formed partnerships with dancer Pierce Keegan and singer Lou Clayton (later part of Clayton, Jackson and [Jimmy] Durante), and was already married at least twice by the early twenties. In 1919, while still working with Keegan, Edwards recorded several sessions for Columbia, none of the results of which have ever surfaced (possibly because the act broke up shortly after); he left us our first tangible documents of his voice in 1922. This opportunity to record came about, once again, due to his scatting/eefin' abilities. Recording director Sam Lanin, then working for the Gennett label, seems to have heard Edwards doing his scat stuff in a show somewhere and brought him in as a guest star on three otherwise instrumental jazz records. He

creates full-blown scat solos on these records, which, like most jazz improvisations of the era, are based on the song's written melody but with considerable harmonic embellishment.

Edwards's recording career begins in earnest in late 1923, just around the time when he started appearing regularly on Broadway; in spring 1924, he was featured in Irving Berlin's *Music Box Revue*, and in fall of that year he headlined in a watershed production, *Lady, Be Good*. This was not only a breakthrough for him but also for two famous pairs of siblings. It gave Fred and Adele Astaire their first important, starring roles on Broadway, and it was also the first of many full-length collaborations between George and Ira Gershwin. The score included the title song as well as "Little Jazz Bird" sung by Edwards and "The Half of It Dearie Blues" by the Astaires; the standard "Fascinating Rhythm" was introduced in a production number featuring Edwards, Fred, and Adele, and, according to Astaire, "Ukulele Ike stopped the show." (In addition to the Gershwin brothers' songs, Edwards sang some of his own specialties, such as "Who Takes Care of the Caretaker's Daughter?") He would go on appearing in important shows throughout the decade, most notably *Sunny* (score by Jerome Kern and Otto Harbach, 1925) and *Ziegfeld Follies of 1927* (score by Irving Berlin), but in general he seems to have been making more money headlining in vaudeville than even producers like Charles Dillingham and Florenz Ziegfeld could pay him.

From December 1923 to December 1927, Edwards recorded prolifically for the Pathé Phonograph and Radio Corporation, based in Brooklyn. This is the most substantial body of work in his long career. His output is remarkably consistent, whether he's working strictly by himself or accompanied by a small jazz band billed as his "Hot Combination," and there's also a change in quality when he makes the transition from acoustic to electric recording in 1925. On the basis of the dozens and dozens of Pathé titles (also issued on the corporation's Perfect label), Edwards is easily the most impressive male jazz and pop singer of the twenties, the transitional figure between Jolson and Crosby.

What's most rewarding about the Edwards solo titles is the unstoppable energy and rhythm that he generates. Although a few of the titles feature additional accompaniment, generally he gets this remarkable beat going all by himself. The faster numbers are the thing here; the slow love songs are only modestly interesting. He gets excitingly hot and bluesy when telling his gal to take a hike on the up-tempo "I Don't Care Anymore" and "It's All the Same to Me," but more sentimental when pleading for her to return on "I'll Take Her Back if She Wants to Come Back."

Edwards is a veritable dynamo, and his use of a single string instrument not only anticipates the future of scat (Armstrong, Crosby, Fitzgerald) but specifically points to the great early recordings of the Mills Brothers. Like the Millses (and Bobby McFerrin), Edwards is a whole band in himself. It should be noted that he doesn't just scat sparingly—a phrase here, a line there; the bulk of the classic Pathé-Perfect titles are saturated with the technique: There's almost as much scatting as there is regular singing. Indeed, "I Don't Care Anymore" concludes with a longish "trumpet" solo that, in fact, really does lie on the ear like an actual horn statement on a 1925 blues record—as a trumpeter, Edwards has a tone and imagination worthy of the best brassmen of the day: Phil Napoleon, Red Nichols, even Bubber Miley.

Paralleling the development of instrumental jazz, his "solos" become less tied directly to the melody and more and more based simply on the chord changes in the manner of jazz solos of a later era. One might assume that when Pathé combined him with a genuine jazz band (essentially its cornet star, Red Nichols and His Five Pennies), the singer would feel less need to go on creating his instrumental scat solos. But, 'tain't so, honey, 'tain't so. On "Someone's Stolen My Sweet, Sweet Baby," done with the Hot Combination in 1925, he takes an extended scat solo over the rhythm section, and sounds no less compelling than he did when working with just his own uke. Even better, his "Dinah" features a brilliant chase chorus between himself, scatting, and cornetist Nichols, as well as a superlative reading of the verse and chorus, one that really puts him into competition with Ethel Waters.

On the whole, it would be difficult to choose between the solo sides and the Hot Combination sessions; it's not, however, much of a contest between the Pathé-Perfect sides and the Columbia discs he began making at the end of 1927 and going up to 1930. Both of his preferred backgrounds of the mid-twenties, his own uke and the Hot Combination, brought out the best in him. For some reason, Columbia gave him what discographies list as a "small instrumental group" that was neither as hot as the Hot Combination nor as inspired as his own uke work. There are a few excellent Columbia titles, such as "It Goes Like This (That Funny Melody)," but on the whole there's less spontaneity, less energy, and less scatting than on the earlier records (it was almost as if, now that Armstrong and Crosby were also scatting regularly on records, Edwards lost interest in it). Even when you're listening to the comparatively hotter Columbia sides, like "Anything You Say," "Sophomore Prom," "That's My Weakness Now" (which contains his best scat solo of the period), and his epic two-sided blues of 1928, "Stack o' Lee," you can't help thinking that they would have been better had they been recorded a year or two earlier.

Edwards's career was continuing to fly high, although, surprisingly, he never seems to have been much of a presence on radio (apparently he never had a major sponsored series of his own). But he did turn out to be a force in early talking pictures, appearing in more than thirty mostly A pictures, most of them for Metro Goldwyn Mayer. While his film work was, obviously, not as memorable as his recording career, there is some outstanding music here—in the 1929 *Marianne* he helps introduce the jazz standard "Just You, Just Me," and in *The Hollywood Revue of 1929* he does the same for a song that became a veritable anthem of the movie musical, "Singin' in the Rain." He also appeared in most of the early talkies starring Buster Keaton, the sublime silent comedian who was then making an uneasy transition to sound. Though these pictures (*Doughboys, Parlor, Bedroom and Bath, Sidewalks of New York*) don't feature Keaton at his best, it should be noted that Edwards is just as funny in them as the legendary stone-faced one.

Unfortunately, he was temporarily between recording contracts during his peak years in Hollywood. When he resumed recording, this time for Columbia's corporate successor, the American Recording Corp., he had already started sliding downhill. He was no longer the hottest, most jazz-inflected singer of popular songs around—that spot had been claimed by Crosby—and his career was overtaken by personal problems: an endless succession of wives, and what seems to have been a river of alcohol. Nineteen thirty-three marked the first of three occasions when he filed for bankruptcy.

Yet musically Edwards was not stagnating: At the height of the Depression, he made two dozen or so ARC sides in New York, Los Angeles, and London (there's a date in New York with a band billed as "the Californians," go figure), which are all consistently fine. The ballads have a bit more rhythmic bite to them than the 1927–30 recordings, and the faster numbers are, not surprisingly, superb: "Hush My Mouth (If I Ain't Goin' South)," "Old Fashioned Love," "St. Louis Blues," "Love Is Just Around the Corner," and "One Little Kiss" are all delicious.

He doesn't just rekindle the old fires but gets exciting in all new and contemporary ways, especially on two dates done with Mills Brothers–inspired vocal groups, the Eton Boys and the Four Blackbirds. Edwards is as hot as ever, scatting up a storm against their vocal harmonic backdrop. "Paper Moon" and "Night Owl" (a beautiful, neglected song by Herman Hupfeld) are two of his loveliest, comparatively slow pieces. "Hunkadola" (from *George White's Scandals of 1935*—he was in both the film and show, as well as the *Scandals* film of the previous year) is just about his funniest, being a parody of Astaire's early Latin dances, such as the Carioca, the Continental, and the Piccolino.

By 1936, Edwards had entered into a long spiral downward: trying to stay one step ahead of his ex-wives and the bottle (and other temptations) and being stuck in something of a rut as the singing sidekick in a long series of B Westerns, but nonetheless still working like crazy. There's an outstanding session done with a Hawaiian band, Andy Iona's Islanders, for Decca in 1936, which includes another "St. Louis Blues" as well as the operetta-like "The Night Is Young (And You're So Beautiful)." Around the same time, he did a session for the Hollywood Hot Shots label that's outstanding for different reasons, in that an anonymous Edwards recorded at least seven notably salacious "party" records—the disc equivalent of a stag film for a bachelor party, with titles like "When You Were a Buttercup (And I Was the Son of a Bee)" (aka "What an Insect!"), "Give It to Mary with Love," and "Take Out That Thing."

There were some major movies, a small but important role in the classic Howard Hawks comedy *His Girl Friday*, a nonspeaking bit in *Gone With the Wind*, and then in 1940 his career was temporarily thrown the first of several lifelines by Walt Disney. Already dubbed Ukulele Ike, he assumed the role by which successive generations would remember him, namely the singing and speaking voice of Jiminy Cricket (what an insect!), sidekick and conscience to Disney's Pinocchio, the little wooden puppet who wants to become a real boy. (He put over the picture's song "When You Wish upon a Star" so convincingly that it won an Academy Award.) Disney would give him more money to fork over to his ex-wives with *Dumbo* (a classic role as a black crow) and *Fun and Fancy Free* (reprising his role as Jiminy Cricket), and then kept him working in the fifties, both as the cricket and himself as a semiregular on *The Mickey Mouse Club* TV show. He also cut a 12" LP for Disneyland Records, the fine *Ukulele Ike Sings Again* in 1956.

In addition to working for Disney, like Jolson he spent most of the forties re-creating his earlier career for nostalgia-minded older audiences. He made a ton of syndicated radio transcriptions in these years, sounding almost as good as ever, thanks largely to a very hot and swinging backup group that featured guitarist Tony Mottola and old colleague Joe Tarto switching between string and brass bass (tuba). There's also a session from circa 1944 (no one seems to know why or for whom it was made) that includes some old songs and some new, in which "A Love Like Ours" and "Hold on to Your Heart" are very worthy additions to the Edwards canon. Pushing fifty, Edwards sounds terrific.

Given his talent, and the fact that audiences seemed to welcome him whenever he could get his act together enough to perform, Edwards could have sustained a career into his fifties, sixties, and seventies as a nostalgia act—but he could not, alas, get his act together. Apart from the Disney appearances, he didn't get much done in the fifties and even less in the sixties. In a children's record done for the Disneyland label, Edwards sings "Fools find out when it's too late that they don't live so long." He put the lie to that statement. He died all but forgotten in a home for aged actor dudes in 1971.

Nick Lucas (1897–1982)

It's impossible for anyone born after 1950 to listen to Nick Lucas and his most famous song, "Tip Toe Through the Tulips with Me," and not think of Tiny Tim. At first listen, it may seem as if Tiny Tim was barely exaggerating when he re-created Lucas for the psychedelic sixties. Tiny Tim, born Herbert Khaury, took most of his basic shtick from Lucas, a crooning idol of four decades earlier: the high-pitched tenor voice, which TT caricatured into a castrated falsetto; the guitar, for which TT, taking a leaf from Ukulele Ike's book, substituted a ukulele; and most of all "Tip Toe Through the Tulips with Me." It was this song, which Lucas introduced in the pivotal early talkie musical *The Gold Diggers of Broadway* (1929), that in retrospect has become the biggest number of the singer-guitarist's career. Forty years later, Khaury rejuvenated this number from the Herbert Hoover administration and made it a hit all over again in the age of Richard Nixon. (In 1976, he even released a single entitled "Tip Toe Disco.")

Lucas and "Tip Toe Through the Tulips" came from the age immediately before Bing Crosby introduced the concept of the robust baritone to popular music. Compared to what came after, both Lucas and "Tulips" must have seemed terribly, well, fey. How appropriate, then, that Tiny Tim should revive this approach when, in a turnaround following three decades of increasingly macho male singers, it suddenly became popular for boy pop stars to wear long hair and parade around in platform shoes and unisex garb.

Still, though Tim may have savaged Lucas, he hardly undermined the older artist's accomplishments. Lucas's voice may have been high-pitched, in the fashion of the early age of electrically recorded tenors, but he was far from a lightweight. He sang with conviction and style, and was able to bring sincerity and musicality to the best songs of a wonderful era of songwriting. As for his guitar playing, Lucas was one of the most advanced soloists in the entire family of string instruments in that pivotal early period. He only recorded two strictly instrumental guitar features, "Pickin' the Guitar" and "Teasing the Frets" (cut in 1922, then again in 1923 and 1932), but these alone are enough to place him in the pantheon of pioneering jazz guitarists.

After Tiny Tim recorded his two mondo-bizarro masterpieces (*God Bless Tiny Tim* and *Tiny Tim's 2nd Album*), he had pretty much shot his bolt. His popularity faded as quickly as it appeared, and nothing else he ever did measured up. With Lucas it was quite the opposite: Fifteen years after his peak of fame, he turned up again in a transcription studio and proceeded to make some of the finest recordings of his career. He concentrated on the best songs of his own glory years—the twenties—along with a few numbers of more recent vintage, and was able to document, thanks to high-fidelity recording techniques, that both his singing and guitar work were stronger than ever.

As historian Michael R. Pitts has noted, "Nick Lucas's long and illustrious show business career was filled with so many 'firsts' that it would take a large volume to do him justice." He was the first "guitar star," the first popular entertainer who made this instrument a part of his act (in the twenty-first century, Gibson Guitars is still offering a "Nick Lucas Special"), and the first Italian-American pop superstar. (Russ Columbo and Louis Prima subsequently became the first Italo-American pop stars not to change their names and their ethnic identities.) And if he wasn't the very first singer to make use of the three breakthroughs that revolutionized the mass media in the 1920s—the microphone, the radio, and talking pictures—he certainly was part of the first generation.

A first-generation American, Dominic Nicholas Anthony Lucanese was born in Newark, New Jersey, in 1897. He began playing and singing very early, while still in the single digits. He and his equally musical brother were busking on train cars for spare change. In his teens, Lucanese entertained in cafés around New Jersey and New York, and about the time he turned twenty, he joined forces with pianist and composer Ted Fio Rito to put together a vaudeville band called the Kentucky Five (a suitable monicker for a quintet of New Jersey Italians). Like Rudy Vallee, another instrumentalist of the period who became a superstar crooner, Lucas spent his early twenties working with a variety of dance and jazz bands, including the Original Memphis Five and Sam Lanin's (as Bailey's Lucky Seven, the same spin-off unit that had earlier worked with Cliff Edwards), as well as his old friend Ted "Toot Toot Tootsie" Fio Rito.

Unlike Edwards, but like Crosby, Columbo, and Vallee slightly later, Lucas was made into a star and a national name by radio. While working with the Fio Rito band in Chicago in 1924, he had the opportunity to broadcast on WEBH, and it was there that he gradually began to catch on. In 1922 and 1923, he recorded his famous pair of pioneering guitar solos, and he began to sing on records at the end of 1924 on the heels of his Chicago radio success. By 1925, he was broadcasting and recording with regularity, and from that time until around 1932 he moved from strength to strength.

Lucas was a tenor, more or less in the Vallee register but with a bit more of a robust quality; he was more of a lover than a vagabond, and never aspired to Vallee's college-boy kind of appeal. Lucas might be seen as a transitional figure between the twenties tenors and the later school of Italian baritones that began with Columbo, followed by Como, Sinatra, Damone, Bennett et al. In addition to selling an estimated 84 million discs for the Brunswick label (or so it was claimed), he headlined on Broadway in *Sweetheart Time* and *Show Girl*. He also appeared in two of the most important early talking pictures, *The Gold Diggers of Broadway*, which was advertised as the first all-talking, all-singing, all-dancing motion picture, with Technicolor sequences, and *The Show of Shows*, in which he paraded in Chinese drag with Myrna Loy and took away all her rice cakes. He and Edwards were probably the most significant talents to headline in the early talking picture revues, and between them introduced the best-remembered songs of the epoch, Edwards with "Singin' in the Rain" in *Hollywood Revue* and Lucas with "Tip Toe Through the Tulips with Me" in *Goldiggers*. When Lucas sang on his tiptoes, well, he wasn't exactly Oley Speaks doing "The Road to Mandalay" or Paul Robeson doing "Ol' Man River," but nonetheless he wasn't deliberately campy or effeminate; unlike Tiny Tim's exaggeration, Lucas's tale of walking *en pointe* through the flora comes off as sincere and genuinely romantic.

Apart from radio, Lucas's biggest medium was the then dying art form known as vaudeville. He would make personal appearances all over the globe, becoming an early international star, a favorite in London at the Café de Paris, the Alhambra Theatre, and the famous London Palladium. Lucas was part of that unique generation of entertainers that had it both ways: Radio and talkies were killing vaudeville, yet Lucas appeared in all of these media at the same time—essentially competing with himself.

His stardom gradually faded by the mid-thirties, and he stopped recording regularly in 1934; yet he was far from finished. Unlike Cliff Edwards, Lucas would never end up anywhere near Skid Row. He had a long and healthy career that kept him active almost until the time of his death, in 1982, continuing to work all over the world, making notable appearances in Hawaii and Australia in the thirties and forties, starring in nightclubs, and even doing television in the fifties and Lake Tahoe in the sixties.

In 1939, he recorded a series of eight lovely songs in Sydney, Australia, most of which came from the current Bing Crosby picture *The Star Maker*. Then, in the early war years, he laid down some of his absolute finest work in a series of radio-only transcriptions, which have, fortunately, been made available on CD. Both sets of material show that he had lost nothing in the decade or so since his peak of fame. His tenor is strong and true, and his guitar fingers as fleet as ever. The selections include some new versions of his hits ("Painting the Clouds with Sunshine") and other songs of the twenties ("I'll Get By," "Sleepy Time Gal"). It's especially rewarding to hear him tackle a number of songs of more recent vintage. Coincidentally, nearly all of these are North American songs with a South American flavor: "Tangerine," "The Gay Ranchero" (if there's such a thing as a Hispanic antidefamation league, surely they'll object to the line about "counting little chicos by the score"), "In a Little Spanish Town" (the oldest of this quartet, from 1926), and "Mexicali Rose."

Lucas is accompanied exclusively by his own guitar, the playing time is short, and the performances are wonderfully to-the-point. For those who like waltzes, there are two of Irving Berlin's finest,

"Always" and "The Song Is Ended." ("Spanish Town" is also in 3/4 time, although the feeling is more Madrid than Vienna.) Lucas is also obliging in terms of including the rarely heard verses to certain songs, such as the longish and interesting one to "Sleepy Time Gal" as well as "Three Little Words" and "I'm Looking Over a Four Leaf Clover."

As it happened, long after Tiny Tim had been forgotten, Nick Lucas enjoyed his last hurrah: On New Year's morning of 1980 he appeared at the Rose Bowl Parade on a float dedicated to his celebrated song "Tip Toe Through the Tulips," which he had introduced more than fifty years earlier. In short, although Tiny Tim deserves to be remembered as an inspired satirist and surrealist, from the vantage point of today it's Nick Lucas who stands out as the true class act. Yet Mr. Khaury never hesitated to acknowledge his inspiration. In fact, he was directly responsible for providing Nick Lucas with the single biggest audience that he ever had. On December 17, 1969, Tiny Tim married a seventeen-year-old girl live on *The Tonight Show*. On his wedding day, Khaury apparently decided it would be inappropriate for him to sing "Tip Toe Through the Tulips," so he graciously invited Nick Lucas on the program to sing it that night, along with an equally zesty and robust reading of "Looking at the World Through Rose-Colored Glasses." (When he sits and chats with Carson, the subject, naturally, turns to weddings, and Lucas confesses to having been married for fifty-two years by that point.) No less than forty million people were watching. More people saw Nick Lucas that night than in the previous fifty years of his career, thanks to Tiny Tim, who proved that he could also be a class act.

Rudy Vallee (1901–1986)

Vince Giordano—the bandleader, multi-instrumentalist, and historian—tells about talking with Rudy Vallee in the last few years of the pioneering crooner's life. In the twenties, Vallee became a superstar largely on the strength of his high, warm, nasal tenor; sixty years later, that sound had completely disappeared, and the elderly Vallee sounded like any gruff-voiced old geezer—he could have overdubbed for Popeye. Furthermore, his choice of words in this conversation also seemed like a deliberate attempt to distance himself from the sensitive, sweet-toned singer and conductor who named his bands after colleges and served as the mass media's first representative of the ideals of higher education. Giordano doesn't particularly remember asking Vallee the secret of his success, but Vallee made sure to tell him anyway: "The girls loved me," the eighty-something-year-old Vallee snarled in a voice that sounded like Louis Armstrong gargling with gravel, "because I had *cock* in my voice."

It's as if Vallee had grown so tired of playing the fresh-faced, clean-scrubbed collegian that he relished—even reveled in—the role of dirty old man. His summary of the secret of his appeal was simi-larly perverse: It was more likely the total absence of cock in his voice that made him the most popular vocalist, especially on the radio, in the period immediately before the emergence of Bing Crosby. It isn't exactly that Crosby knocked him off his throne, he just exemplified the start of a whole new era. Vallee personified the great economic boom years of the mid- to late twenties, a time when Americans were so rich that they could send their sons to college, and when the boy hero wasn't a manly cowboy-hatted Indian fighter but a slender, androgynous type bearing a mortar board.

By the sixties, Vallee was no longer the Vagabond Lover of 1929; he identified instead with the role of J. B. Biggley in *How to Succeed in Business Without Really Trying*, the lecherous old-timer who chases after curvaceous cuties half his age (specifically one Hedy La Rue). He may have been more of a comic figure than a romantic one, but he was a decidedly heterosexual one. Likewise, in real life he was anything but on the fence sexually, having married four gorgeous girls—Leonie Cauchois McCoy (1928), Fay Webb (1930–36), Jane Greer (1943–44), and Eleanor Norris (from 1946 on)—and doubtlessly bedded many more than he wedded.

The personification of the desirable male in the late twenties wasn't the rough-and-rugged type, like John Wayne or Clark Gable, but sensitive pretty boys like Charles Farrell or John Gilbert. At the end of the Jazz Age, Vallee was far from masculine, although he wasn't quite effeminate either, just sexually neuter, a voice that promised sweetness, holding hands, and pleasant stolls through lover's lane, a nonthreatening sound that was utterly cockless. He suited the late twenties perfectly, and was bound to be toppled by the realities of the Depression, when tough times called once again for tough types. In February 1929, Vallee recorded "My Time Is Your Time," which would go on to become a hit and a signature for him; yet within a few seasons it must have become clear to him that his time as the original American Idol was not going to be long, even before Crosby's big breakthrough in 1931–32.

The story goes that he never regarded himself as anything like a vocalist until one day in the fall of 1927, a few months after his graduation from Yale. He was invited to go to a recording session at the Edison studio in New York by a bandleader named Joe Herlihy, with whom he had worked some years earlier in Maine. There was a vocal trio with the band, but, after multiple takes, it just wasn't happening. Herlihy asks Vallee if he'd like to try singing in the trio, and Rudy is all like, "Dude, whatever, anything for a laugh." So he takes a hack at it, and Herlihy and the Edison people are so happy with the results that that they decide to issue this take, with Vallee singing in the trio. Herlihy encourages him to keep singing, Vallee does, and for the next four years or so he is like the Prince of Pop, the biggest name in American vernacular music.

Up until that time, Vallee had been strictly a saxophonist and bandleader. Vallee was a college boy, but not a bloodless rich man's son—he worked his way through college as a professional musician. He was born Hubert Prior Vallée (the accent became optional) in Vermont in 1901, and was raised in Westbrook, Maine, the son of a druggist. Even without radio or records, Vallee grew up totally enamored of music. At ten his dad gave him a snare drum and by his teens he had built it up into a full trap kit; he played with his high school band and then with the Westbrook City Orchestra. By this time, he was also begging his older sister to teach him what she knew about the piano. In 1917, he dropped out of high school to join the navy, but was summarily released when they realized he was underage.

In 1919, he heard a sound that changed his life: It was a record by the first superstar virtuoso of the saxophone, Rudy Wiedoeft, a vaudeville headliner who played both popular songs and tricky semi-classical showpieces and who was among the first to popularize this hybrid brass-reed instrument, invented by Adolphe Sax almost a century earlier. Vallee became obsessed with Wiedoeft, his horn, and his music. Apparently without any help—saxophone instructors were not plentiful in Maine in 1919 (although he probably received some instruction on the clarinet)—Vallee set about teaching himself to play the sax. According to his later testimony, Vallee locked himself in his room and spent upward of five or six hours a day trying to master Wiedoeft's finger-busting, tongue-twisting technique. By the time he began attending the University of Maine, in 1921, the other students had taken to calling him "Rudy."

Vallee worked his way through college by playing saxophone and leading bands at dances and other functions. After a year at Maine, he transferred to Yale. During this first college stint, he made a number of private recordings, all of them Wiedoeft-inspired saxophone solos. (One slightly later item from 1926 was a sax transcription of "The Swan" by Camille Saint-Saëns.) Going to school full-time and working full-time to pay for it was breaking his back, thus in 1924 he decided to take a year off from school, to work and save up enough money to finance the rest of his education. On the strength of one of his private recordings, which he used as an audition disc, he was offered a job with one of the leading dance bands in London, the (Hotel) Savoy Havana Band, where he worked from September 1924 to July 1925. The band recorded prolifically during the year Vallee served in its reed section, and also provided backup for musical comedy stars such as Beatrice Lillie and Gertrude Lawrence.

Vallee returned to Yale in the fall of 1925, continuing to play his horn and directing bands at football games and dances; he graduated in spring 1927. He was already leading bands on a semiprofessional level by that fall, when he sang for the first time on record on that aforementioned Edison session. He was also making the odd record here and there,

additional sax solos and sides with one of his early bands, the Westchester Biltmore Five. Soon, he was working regularly in New York with his own orchestra—first billed as "Rudy Vallée and His Yale Men"—and in the summer of 1928 he began a regular recording contract with the Columbia Corporation, which issued the results on Harmony, Diva, Velvet Tone, and other subsidiary labels. At the very beginning, the writing is not yet on the wall: A few of the earliest sides released under his name have vocals by other singers like Sleepy Ward and George Morrow (on the memorable "Salaaming the Rajah"), although most of these are probably not actually Vallee's band.

By late 1928, early 1929, Vallee was on his way: He was singing all the vocals with his band, which was now and permanently known as Rudy Vallee and His Connecticut Yankees. He was turning out new records virtually every week for the Victor label (beginning in 1929) and, most important, he was now on the radio. In later years, he tended to dismiss his movies, of which he made many, and records, of which he made many, many, many—but he never underestimated how important the radio had been to his career. By 1929, he had established himself as one of the very first superstars of the new medium; virtually everybody in the country knew who he was. He practically lived in the broadcasting studio, and was omnipresent on the airwaves. As the Roaring Twenties become the Depressed Thirties, he was seemingly on every station day and night.

Vallee was still essentially a bandleader; although he was frequently (and not favorably) compared to Bing in later years, he probably had more in common with Bob Crosby. The Connecticut Yankees have been described as a sweet band, but it was actually a straight-down-the-middle dance orchestra, a group that was equally indebted to Fletcher Henderson (Vallee even sings the "St. Louis Blues" on one 1930 disc) and to Guy Lombardo, which occasionally featured hot jazz solos and played everything in a solid, occasionally even swinging, dance tempo with a dependable beat. Virtually every record Vallee released in the twenties and early thirties was a dance disc, featuring the band first and Vallee second, the singer only taking a single chorus or vocal refrain on most of his hundreds of titles. Perhaps this was astute planning on his part; could it be that he realized that 32 bars of his voice was all people needed to hear? It can't be a coincidence that he didn't start singing for longer stretches on his own records until, as we shall see, his singing began to improve.

Vallee's early records (say, up to 1931) aren't as exciting as those made earlier in the decade by the more jazz-oriented Cliff Edwards—nobody was comparing Vallee to Ethel Waters—and few entries in his capacious output are in a class with even the most minor of Crosby's performances. Yet his singing has a certain charm, particularly as his deep-rooted background in dance bands (as musician more than vocalist) left him with a good sense of time and the ability to keep up with his band on even the punchiest of foxtrots. There are any number of worthy, highly listenable Rudy Vallee records even from the beginning: "Deep Night," an effective ballad he's given co-credit for as composer; his radio theme, "Heigh Ho, Everybody, Heigh Ho"; and "My Time Is Your Time," another radio theme and just about his best-known song. "Vagabond Lover" did provide Vallee with a slogan: The song, oddly enough, is about a lack of commitment; both the singer himself and the object of his desire appear and disappear in the lyric, rather like a voice on the radio.

Vallee's biggest hit was from one of his alma maters, "The Stein Song," a march from the University of Maine; the idea of college boys openly singing about getting plastered apparently held a certain risqué novelty—apparently there was no Prohibition against drinking songs. Vallee sang of boys who toted books rather than barges, but their love for strong drink and weak-willed women was the equal of any longshoreman's. Most college songs were about cheering a football team on to victory, but "The Stein Song" was a stirring call to arms for drunken frat boys, a rallying cry for the inebriated on campuses everywhere. Recorded less than six months after Wall Street laid an egg, it was a cry to go out and get bombed before the semester was over; Papa took a dive on Wall Street (in some cases literally), and there's no money for you to come back for your sophomore year.

Early on, it was part of Vallee's shtick to surround himself with college ephemera. At a time when every other band was the Varsity Six or the University Seven, the first band Vallee sang with was the Yale Collegians. He performed in his Yale sweater, and frequently sang through a megaphone; before this time, the only people who ever employed a megaphone were the coxswain on the Oxford rowing team and the cheerleaders rooting on the Yale footballers. Yet Vallee's college period didn't last long—a couple of traditional college march medleys, plus two songs about femme *collégiennes*, the ballad "Sweetheart of My Student Days" and the jaunty "Betty Co-Ed." That was pretty much it; with unemployment ravaging the country no one wanted to hear about carefree undergraduates whooping it up.

When Vallee returned to the college genre—as a graduate student, presumably—it was with an air of nostalgia. This was in the 1937 "Whiffenpoof Song," which he sang with the sentimental air of a thirty-something attending his ten-year reunion, waxing sentimental for the tables down at Mory's and the place where Louie dwells. One of his most effective sentimental songs, "The Whiffenpoof Song" was not a customary love song to a woman but a love song for a college, a nostalgic look back at one's youth inspired by Rudyard Kipling's barracks room ballad "Gentlemen Rankers" (the same poem that gave James Jones the title for *From Here to Eternity*, a

novel that figured big in the career of another male singer). Even long after the Depression made higher education little more than a fantasy for most Americans, Vallee—like Kay Kyser a little bit later on—remained a poster boy for college life.

Vallee was indeed a heartthrob, but one who refused to take himself too seriously. His many novelty and comedy records have held up well, although it must be admitted that his numerous waltzes are by and large dreary. On his first successful songs, "You'll Do It Someday (Why Not Now?)" and "Outside," he comes off like a horny frosh sweet-talking Betty Co-Ed (or Kansas City Kitty) into climbing into the rumble seat of his roadster. He's almost too innocent, too cockless, to be convincing as a cad; it's rather as if he wants to lose his own virginity as much as he's trying to persuade the girl in question to lose hers. Even on the rather rude "Kansas City Kitty," a narrative of considerable misogyny and sexism, Vallee is much too much the proper young man for the song to be as offensive as it might be. Even these backroom ballads resonate like college humor, naughty novelties of the sort that bored undergrads might recite to one another when the prof is momentarily called out of the classroom.

Which brings us to the main difference between Vallee and Bing Crosby: Both men were, at the point of Crosby's first starring feature film, *The Big Broadcast*, considered romantic crooners, yet Crosby was even then steadily fashioning himself into the ultimate musical Everyman—the kind of guy who could sing everything from "Empty Saddles" (which Vallee also recorded, come to think of it) to "MacNamara's Band" to even "The Whiffenpoof Song." Vallee was anything but a musical Everyman; he was far too idiosyncratic. There was a distinctly Rudy Vallee kind of a song, whereas Crosby could and did sing everything.

Vallee also maintained close ties to England, where he had worked in the mid-twenties and returned briefly for the coronation of His Royal Highness Edward VIII, at which point he also recorded several sessions for British Columbia, in 1937. Back home, both before and after, Vallee seems to have made a point of recording more British songs than any other American singer or bandleader. He must have been the only American bandleader who, in the age of Benny Goodman, recorded Noel Coward's masterpiece "Mad Dogs and Englishmen," thus introducing that wonderful patter song to even madder dogs and Americans. (He's probably the only performer to tackle "Mad Dogs and Englishmen" in rough foxtrot time—I can't think of a British dance band that ever played it that way.)

There was a deliberately camp side to Vallee: He made a specialty of taking some ancient sentimental song from the turn of the century and playing it for laughs. His contemporary, the American monologist Walter O'Keefe, had adapted two melodramatic songs of the Gay Nineties, "The Tattooed Lady" and

"The Man on the Flying Trapeze," for audiences of the mid-thirties; Vallee recorded both and followed up with his own adaptation of two other oldies-but-moldies, "He Wooed Her, He Wooed Her, and He Wooed Her" (1936) and "The Drunkard Song (There Is a Tavern in the Town)" (1934). The latter is possibly Vallee's funniest and most entertaining side. He took an ancient temperance air and revived it for the immediate, post-Prohibition era; Vallee seems genuinely unable to control his own laughter in the studio and kept cracking up throughout the take. Victor executive Ted Wallerstein thought that the breakup was so funny he issued it as a regular Victor pop-dance release, though in some cases with a note on the label alerting purchasers as to what was in store for them.

Indeed, Vallee may have had the last laugh after all. Even after Bing Crosby took over as pop music's man of the moment—and, quite possibly, of all time—in 1931, Vallee imitators were ensconced on the airwaves: Virtually all the session and studio vocalists like Scrappy Lambert and Smith Ballew had high, clear nasal voices like Vallee's, and they recorded thousands of discs in these years, no exaggeration. At the same time, at least two up-and-coming singing bandleaders clearly patterned themselves after the Vagabond Lover: Will Osborne and, more important, Ozzie Nelson, who went on not only to lead a terrific band but to found a show-biz dynasty. Vallee himself never quite made it as a movie musical leading man, but most of the guys who did, such as Dick Powell, John Boles, and Gene Raymond, sounded more like him than like Crosby.

Interestingly, though, at around this time Vallee started sounding less like the old Vallee (which is to say, the young Vallee); perhaps inspired by the competition from Crosby, both Vallee's band and the singer himself began to sound a lot less passive and tepid. In September 1931, shortly after his thirtieth birthday, he opened in his first Broadway show, *George White's Scandals,* having recorded the four main songs from the show (all by Lew Brown and Ray Henderson) a few weeks earlier: "Life Is Just a Bowl of Cherries," "This Is the Missus," "The Thrill Is Gone," and "My Song," which revealed a newer, hotter Vallee, one who sang with considerably more gusto-con-brio. For the remainder of the decade (at least), he was in a very good place musically. He was no longer the musical man of the hour, but he was singing better than ever, and remained a fixture on the airwaves.

In 1932, he left Victor for the first of many occasions and participated in two technological experiments. The first was a short-lived venture named Hit of the Week Records, which, in the depths of the Depression, sought to make its product more affordable by pressing records on chintzy cardboard (neither the idea nor the records themselves lasted long, but Hit of the Week cardboard discs are eminently collectable—see eBay for details). Vallee made only a handful of titles for Hot W, then switched from the low-slung technology of paper records to the opposite end of the spectrum, a set of deluxe discs pressed in stunning blue wax by Columbia, all of which bore Rudy's caricature on the label. He followed these with a series for Victor's new imprint, Bluebird Records; the records he made in these two years—1932–33—are the overall high point of his career, and, being for Blue Columbia and then Bluebird, might be considered his "Blue Period." RCA then moved him back to the main Victor label during 1934–36. Vallee's tenor is now growing ever more baritoney if no less nasal, while the band itself is exceptionally well polished, snappy, and peppy, not too hot, not too sweet, and Vallee's singing is filled with conviction and energy. The 1933 "My Dancing Lady"—not too fast, not too slow—just plain *kicks;* the band doesn't have quite the polish of Paul Whiteman's, but they play with unmistakable energy, particularly after the vocal chorus, when the singer-leader pushes them forward, like a Connecticut Caucasian Cab Calloway, shouting "Yeah, go!"

The tunes he plays and sings are also uniformly excellent. He had a particular liking for Herman Hupfeld, recording at least four songs by that worthy writer: "When Yuba Plays the Rhumba on the Tuba," "Let's Put Out the Lights and Go to Sleep," "Savage Serenade," and "Dodo" Hupfeld's great standard, "As Time Goes By." He also had a very high batting average as far as Rodgers and Hart were concerned, recording much of the score to *I'd Rather Be Right* (including "Have You Met Miss Jones?"), *The Boys from Syracuse,* and even the team's ambitious, two-sided "dramatic monologue," *All Points West.*

There was plenty of room on the airwaves for both Vallee and Crosby, and Vallee's recordings seem to spin off from his radio popularity—on most of his 1932–33 sides he provides a brief spoken intro before launching into the vocal refrain. Three of the Bluebird sides have an added bonus in vocals by rising star Alice Faye, who, like Crosby, would quickly surpass Vallee in the motion picture department. That was one area in which he just couldn't compete despite a few successful pictures—and even a few in which he's not at all bad (best are the Warner Bros. efforts *Sweet Music* and *Gold Diggers in Paris*).

As a bandleader, Vallee stayed on top deep into the swing era: He made some of his only excursions into the field of foreign songs such as "Hot Cha Cha" (a Latvian pop hit) and two faux-French songs he sang in the 1938 *Gold Diggers in Paris* (written by that genuine Frenchman Harry Warren), "Stranger in Paree" (in which he does an impression of Maurice Chevalier singing flat) and the absolutely adorable mock-*français* double-talk triple-rhyme song, "The Latin Quarter." In 1937–38 he and Benny Goodman (both on Victor) were competing with rival versions of the Neapolitan novelty "Vieni, Vieni." Vallee's record is one of the only pop platters of the period that contains a modulation midway through. He followed with another Italian adaptation, "Oh Ma-Ma," later immortalized by Louis Prima. Vallee's version utilizes a Spike Jones–like cast of characters and is quite the zaniest thing the crooner was ever involved in.

Vallee bounced back and forth between Victor and other labels, from Hit of the Week to Blue Columbia (1932–33) and Bluebird (1933), then Victor (1934–36), then the American Recording Corp. and British Columbia (1936–37), then Victor (1937–38) once more, then Decca and Varsity (1939–40), and then Victor for a fourth time—all before 1942. During World War II, Vallee, now forty, served his country by leading the Coast Guard Band—the most famous service band after Glenn Miller's AAF Orchestra—which featured semiclassical selections as well as pop tunes, and even some Rudy Vallee vocal features.

Even though he had never been a top movie musical leading man, in the forties he thrived as a character actor in such comedies as *The Bachelor and the Bobby-Soxer*. His finest moments as an actor-comic come in Preston Sturges's 1942 *Palm Beach Story* and the 1961 Broadway show (and 1967 film) *How to Succeed in Business Without Really Trying*. Like Harold Lloyd returning to his 1925 *The Freshman* twenty years later in Sturges's *Mad Wednesday* (aka *The Sin of Harold Diddlebock*), Vallee revisited and exploited his image as an old-money twenties collegiate in *The Palm Beach Story*, *It's in the Bag!* (a hysterical cameo), and *How to Succeed*. His big number in *H2$* was "Grand Old Ivy," sung with lead Robert Morse, which was less a parody than a sequel to the Maine "Stein Song" and all those other college songs he had made hits of forty years earlier. Vallee was also a familiar presence on television, on such shows as *Night Gallery, Alias Smith and Jones,* and even *CHiPs*. He achieved still another kind of immortality when, along with Ethel "Lola Lasagna" Merman (and Eartha Kitt) he played a villain on *Batman*, Lord Marmaduke Phogg, who was essentially Sherlock Holmes's evil twin.

On the whole, the well-educated Vallee, who actually changed the name of the street he lived on (in a mansion he bought in 1939) to the Rue de Vallée (arf! arf!), did considerably better than the uneducated Cliff Edwards, even though they both enjoyed long lives, chasing after beautiful women, and went through multiple marriages. (Incidentally, both Edwards and Vallee are well represented by highly recommended sampler CDs on the English ASV Living Era and the American Take Two labels.) Rudy Vallee died a few weeks before his eighty-fifth birthday in 1986. Few would claim that his was a major talent, yet he managed to make a major contribution to the American cultural landscape just the same.

Russ Columbo (1908–1934)

The resurrection of Russ Columbo occurred right after the Second World War: In the late forties, the long-deceased original Italian crooner was resurrected as a powerful influence on both young Italian- and African American singers—in particular Perry Como and Billy Eckstine. Both were just starting to sing professionally during Columbo's brief heyday in the early thirties, and when they became stars themselves, both Como and Eckstine saw fit to record Columbo's theme song—and life mantra—"Prisoner of Love," and had hits with it. (Later on, Crosby and Sinatra would record it as well.) Around this time, Eckstine told one of his own disciples, the comparatively younger Earl Coleman, what a profound influence Columbo had been. When Coleman said he didn't quite get it, Eckstine told him that Columbo's records didn't do him justice, but to have been around when the short-lived star was at his height, to hear him on the radio, was to realize that the man was indeed an important influence on the art of singing love songs.

The history of popular singing seems to have been written by Bing Crosby fans, and a lot of us have tended to fall in line with the idea promoted back in the early thirties, that Crosby and Columbo were rivals. (Rudy Vallee was regarded as one of the big three, but not really serious competition in the deep-chested romantic baritone department.) Even today, the reasoning would seem to be that to admit that Columbo was any good at all was to take something away from Crosby. Not true.

At the same time, as Gary Giddins and others have observed, there was something rather manufactured about Columbo—like the (often Italian) teen idols of the late fifties and early sixties, Columbo was annointed because of his Neapolitan good looks (appearance was more of a factor than one might have imagined in those radio days, although try telling that to Kate Smith), then carefully groomed as Crosby's competition. Columbo's short career wasn't so much a triumph for musical values as for marketing and publicity: He was managed by the songwriter and hustler Con Conrad, who stayed up nights dreaming of ever more outlandish ways to get his star client's name into the papers. By contrast, Crosby's career seemed like a natural, even organic and inevitable, occurrence; Columbo's stardom was more the result of artificial insemination.

One thing he didn't have to fake: He was genuinely Italian. His full name at birth was Ruggiero Eugenio di Rodolfo Columbo. He was born in San Francisco on January 14, 1908; with the exception of a few years in Philadelphia (where he first studied guitar as a youngster), he grew up on the West Coast, shuttling between San Francisco and Los Angeles. By his high school days, he was working as a professional violinist, playing in local dance bands. He also had a very early relationship with the movies: In the mid-twenties, he supplied mood music on the sidelines of sets for emoting silent stars. In this capacity he was first noticed by silent diva Pola Negri, who was then dating loverboy Rudolph Valentino. Struck by Columbo's Valentino-like looks, she arranged for the violinist to get small parts in various pictures.

However, he was rising steadily in the music world as well, joining increasingly important bands like Slim Martin's and Professor Moore's before he landed a spot in the string section of Gus Arnheim's Cocoanut Grove Orchestra, one of the first Los Angeles bands to land a coast-to-coast hookup and a national following. Sometimes dismissed as a sweet band, this was another of the excellent straight-down-the-middle dance bands at the time that could play everything from hot jazz (the second Columbo-Arnheim title, "Peach of a Pair," fits that description, being literally loaded with hot solos) to snoozingly dull waltzes. Playing arrangements by future bandleader Jimmy Grier, the Arnheim band had a swingingly loose and harmonically open sound that, to my ears at least, anticipates the California cool jazz of Shorty Rogers and Shelly Manne twenty years later. Although there's no evidence that Columbo had his eyes on a career as a singer at this time, he did sing occasionally with the Arnheim band; his then-high voice can be discerned in the vocal trios on several early Arnheim records, and he takes two vocal solos with the band: "Back in Your Own Backyard" (there's a Joe Venuti–like violin solo here that may well be Columbo himself) from 1928 and "Peach of a Pair" from June 1930.

On the early sides, Columbo sounds like a typical tenor of the era, a style brought to its peak by Rudy Vallee. By 1930, the voice sounds much lower and deeper, a high baritone, but a baritone nonetheless. Columbo had already discovered Bing Crosby—he probably was well aware of the slightly older singer from his recordings and his reputation—but in the summer of 1930, Crosby and his vocal trio, the Rhythm Boys, left Paul Whiteman to sing at the Cocoanut Grove, both as a solo attraction and in front of the Arnheim band. Columbo was thus the first of countless crooners, jazzers, and pop singers to follow Crosby down the scale to the lower registers ("Get your voice down here where the money is," Crosby once asserted to Irish tenor Dennis Day). According to legend, it was while listening to Crosby sing in front of the band night after night that Columbo decided that he could do it, too. The two were friends, as Crosby later told interviewer Mort Goode: "There were a lot of times we sang together in front of that band."

However, in the summer of 1930, there was not yet reason to do the Bing thing—Crosby was not a star, although he was clearly destiny's tot, a young man for whom things were going to happen. Columbo went on getting odd jobs in movies at this time, sometimes with the Arnheim band (he's plainly visible in several shorts and in the very strange feature *Street Girl*). In Cecil B. DeMille's first talkie, *Dynamite*, Columbo plays a convict—wearing a mustache, strumming a guitar, and singing Dorothy Parker's plaintive "How Am I to Know?" His song serves as accompaniment for a jailhouse wedding even as the carpenters are constructing a gallows for the groom; it's a brilliant early use of sound—the singing, the spoken marriage vows, and the pounding of the hammers are movingly overlapped. Columbo went with Arnheim on a tour of the East Coast but left when the band headed for Europe.

Back in Hollywood, Columbo did more picture work and tried organizing his own band and even became a partner in a fledgling nightspot (the Club Pyramid), but, according to legend, was broke and unemployed when he met Con Conrad. The latter was a talented composer—he would later win the first Academy Award for Best Song ("The Continental" from *The Gay Divorcee*)—occasional manager, and full-time huckster; there was little doubt what the nickname "Con" was short for. Descriptions of Conrad make him sound like one of those charismatic flimflam men so lovingly portrayed in Depression-era comedies by the likes of Lee Tracy, Roger Pryor, or even Robert Armstrong as Carl Denham in *King Kong*. Conrad happened to walk into the Club Pyramid and, supposedly, was the first to recognize greatness in the singing violinist-guitarist. From that point on the two were a team, Conrad making the deals and Columbo doing the singing. Conrad was astute enough to realize that radio was the medium where Columbo had the best chance of making it. Fittingly, he raised the dough for two train tickets to New York, center of the broadcasting industry, by selling his car to Bing Crosby. It wouldn't be the last time Crosby gave Columbo's career a push.

The odd thing was that once this peach of a pair arrived in New York, the silence was deafening. In his book *Let the Chips Fall*, Rudy Vallee claimed to have given Columbo's career a boost by introducing him to a showbiz mover and shaker at the Astor Roof. But even if this was true, despite Vallee's intervention and even with Conrad working all his classic huckster machinations, Columbo, at first, couldn't get arrested. NBC threw them a bone, a four-week sustaining show in the middle of the night, probably just to shut them up. However, at that time, both networks, NBC (Sarnoff) and CBS (Paley), were trying to land Crosby, and when CBS got the prize, NBC made the obvious decision to put some juice behind Columbo as a rival to Bing. RCA Victor Records followed suit and set him up to compete with Crosby on Brunswick.

This was where Conrad's con artistry began to pay off: He played up the rivalry between the two singers and got media attention; he played up Columbo's romances (both real and those he dreamed up) with various starlets and got media attention. Conrad used any factoid he could think of to generate buzz; even when he told the press that his boy was pocketing five or seven Gs a week, the figures made him seem even more glamorous at the height of the Depression (I wonder what they told the IRS). Soon—surprise, surprise—Hollywood was beckoning. Conrad made Columbo into a showbiz icon; the singing, it sometimes seemed, was only incidental.

Looking back at Columbo's small output from the vantage point of seventy years, it almost seems cruel to compare him to the Mighty Crosby—yet Columbo invited the comparison, even thrived on it: If Crosby hadn't made it first, Columbo would have never gotten anywhere. Crosby concentrated on semislow love songs in those years, interspersed with the occasional hot number, and from the mid-thirties on he would become Mr. Diversity. Columbo more or less did only what Crosby had done up until the early thirties, and less, in that there were few, if any, faster numbers. Columbo isn't as deep as Crosby, either sonically or in his interpretation of a lyric; in pieces like "Temptation" and "My Woman" Crosby could be hot and lusty. Columbo was romantic and sentimental but little more. Like Crosby, he embellishes his melodies with nonverbal humming and light scatting around the tune (even "bo-bo-bo"-ing à la Bing on "Paradise"), but his melodic invention is never in a class with Crosby's. The odd thing is that Columbo was a professional instrumentalist, while Crosby was, at best, a half-baked drummer (he certainly didn't have drum chops enough to work with a major dance band), yet Crosby was by far the greater musician.

Nevertheless, Columbo has a charm and a sincerity that have endured. Even the fact that his singing is considerably stiffer than Crosby's is somewhat endearing; like forties Sinatra and fifties Chet Baker and his contemporary Al Bowlly, Columbo had the ability to become part of his songs. In almost every lyric he ever sang, he assumes the role of a romantic, innocent young swain—something that was never part of Crosby's musical makeup—and plays it to the hilt. He doesn't even seem like he's acting: He sings "I Don't Know Why (I Love You Like I Do)" and you feel he genuinely doesn't. When he sings "Living in Dreams" or "Lost in a Crowd," you feel he really is. Perhaps the payoff for his somewhat limiting consistency was, in fact, a hard-won credibility.

Columbo's ultimate mantra was "Prisoner of Love," written for him by lyricist Leo Robin, who would pen some of Crosby's best movie songs of the thirties, and composer Clarence Gaskill, best known for working with Jimmy McHugh on the early jazz standard "I Can't Believe That You're in Love with Me." The harmonies of "Prisoner of Love," closely inspired by "Body and Soul," are rather complicated, but the melody and words are simple and soulful, in a way that not only inspired the Italian and black crooners of the postwar era but continued to be sung by R&B and soul singers into the sixties. The facts of Columbo's life—the way his career was carefully stage-managed, how even his love life was choreographed for the benefit of gossip columnists—somehow make his rendition ring true. From the vantage point of his centennial in 2008, he seems to have truly been a prisoner of love.

He would not be for very long, however. In 1932, he was flying high, and that spring Conrad hired no less than Benny Goodman himself to put together a band to back the singer on personal appearances. The clarinetist gathered a variety of jazz greats: Gene Krupa, Jimmy McPartland, Joe Sullivan, Babe Russin, and Crosby's own future guitarist, Perry Botkin. Unfortunately, Victor does not seem to have let Columbo use his real working band on any of his record dates, sticking him with the regular Victor studio orchestra instead. Also unfortunately, Conrad and Columbo decided to hold RCA up for more money when his first contract (apparently just for one year) was up, and then instead renegotiated a new deal with Brunswick. As it happened, Crosby had just left Brunswick for a contract with the new label named Decca; Crosby's first session for Decca and Columbo's first (and, as it turned out, last) session for Brunswick both transpired in August 1934. As a result, between the two contracts Columbo was out of the recording studio for nearly a year, which is a major loss, in that his total time at the top lasted barely three years. The gap is somewhat filled by a dozen or so individual songs that survive as airchecks, nearly all of which are first-rate tunes ("Star Dust," "The House Is Haunted," "I've Had My Moments," "Lover," "Time on My Hands," etc.), and which are generally superior to those he had been recording for Victor.

In 1933 and 1934, Columbo landed featured roles in four major motion pictures: *Broadway Through a Keyhole* (based on a story by Walter Winchell, allegedly inspired by the love triangle of Jolson, Ruby Keeler, and gangster Johnny Costello), which featured "I Love You Pizzicato," by far Columbo's best up-tempo performance; *Moulin Rouge* (in which Columbo should have introduced "Boulevard of Broken Dreams," an honor that for some reason went to the nonsinging Constance Bennett, no relation to Tony); *Wake Up and Dream;* and *That Goes Double.* The last was a Vitaphone featurette designed to spotlight Columbo's acting talents, but, alas, there wasn't much to show off. Especially considering that he had been involved in the movie industry for some ten years by that point, he was amazingly wooden in front of the camera.

On August 31, 1934, Columbo did his one date for Brunswick, and the four numbers he cut—"When You're in Love," "Too Beautiful for Words," "Let's Pretend There's a Moon," and "I See Two Lovers"—are among the most beautiful of his career. Still, it's doubtful he could have gone on to truly rival Crosby. More likely he would eventually have become a productive elder statesman like Vallee or at worst an alcoholic has-been like Edwards.

He did not, however, live. On September 2, Labor

Day weekend, Russ Columbo was visiting his friend photographer Lansing Brown when he was accidentally killed in an incident involving an antique pistol belonging to Brown. In the nearly seventy years since then, there have been all kinds of Columbo conspiracy theorists. In certain scenarios Columbo and Brown are gay lovers, in others the mafia is involved. There's no evidence to support any of these claims. Apparently it is true that Columbo's mother was tricked into believing her son was still alive for the remaining ten years of her own life, and that Rosemary Clooney eventually bought the house where Columbo spent that last summer of his life (which is not the house where he was killed).

It somehow seems fitting that twenty-five or so years later, Bing Crosby and Clooney actually recorded together in "This Ol' House" where Columbo had lived, and that when the funeral was held for his twenty-six-year-old potential rival in September 1934, Crosby was one of the pallbearers. Even in death, Columbo remained trapped in Crosby's shadow.

Torch Singers and Flappers

Marion Harris
Ruth Etting
Helen Morgan
Annette Hanshaw

The best jazz singing is a kind of a synthesis: If we hear a great jazz singer with poor accompaniment—like Sarah Vaughan on that horrible first version of "Send in the Clowns"—something major is lost. Even though Vaughan's vocal is perfectly fine, there's no way we can consider this an acceptable Sarah Vaughan performance. Likewise, when one hears a second-rate singer with a great band—like Eddie Fisher or Pat Boone struggling to sing with Count Basie—it couldn't possibly rate as credible music. (Not that Fisher or Boone is necessarily second-rate, it's just that they don't belong with Basie, he said, diplomatically.)

Synergy is one of the bywords of vocal jazz, and it happily exists in every period of the music, from the swing era onward: In the thirties, we hear Billie Holiday interacting with musicians who were her equal in every way, starting with Lester Young and other Basieites. In the forties, Ella Fitzgerald began a remarkable, multidecade series of relationships with superb pianists, among them Ellis Larkins, Tommy Flanagan, Paul Smith, and Lou Levy. In the cool era, one gets the combination of June Christy with Pete Rugolo, Mel Tormé with Marty Paich, Anita O'Day with Bill Holman, Jimmy Giuffre, and Russ Garcia et al., and more recent years saw Betty Carter working with her remarkable groups that launched such talents as Benny Green and Cyrus Chestnut. In all of these cases, we find the great jazz singers interacting with the great jazz instrumentalists and arrangers on something like a level playing field.

Do we find the same synergistic relationships when we look at the singers of the twenties? It's a tricky question, involving a shifting point of view between that time and the way succeeding generations have looked back at it. The tendency has been to refer to all black female vocalists of that decade as "blues singers" and all white female singers of the period as "torch singers." The term "jazz singer," apart from being the title of a Jolson movie, was not really widely employed before the thirties, at which point it heralded the arrival of Mildred Bailey, Connee Boswell, and Lee Wiley—and ultimately, Billie Holiday and Ella Fitzgerald.

The female vocalists of the Jazz Age were more appropriately described as pop singers, whether they were black or white, revealing varying degrees of jazz and blues influence. Many of the black women who were marketed as blues or "race" artists were vaudeville and cabaret entertainers who had scarcely even heard the blues much less sung them before Mamie Smith (not really a blues singer herself, good as she was) launched the blues record craze of 1920. On the other side, Annette Hanshaw is today lumped in with "torch singers"—the buzzword for white female singers of the Jazz Age—even though there's nothing remotely torchy about her singing. Even when she sings a sad song, it's impossible to picture her doing a Helen Morgan, sitting on a piano and crying her eyes out about some man who done her wrong.

The only female artist of the era who can safely be described as a great jazz singer, with elements of blues, torch, and pop, is the marvelous Ethel Waters. Although nobody called her a jazz singer at the time, she incorporated every style of the era, including Broadway and comedy, into her music, and was overall the most important female vocalist of the era, influencing subsequent girl and boy singers—Holiday, Wiley, Crosby, Jimmy Rushing—for decades to come.

It's hard to find another artist of the period, black or white, whose work so consistently satisfies the definition of jazz singer, but there are some key white singers of the era, generally classified as the torchy type, whose careers are well worth considering.

Marion Harris (1896?–1944)

I can't claim to be intimately familiar with every major artist of the acoustic era, which ended with the introduction of electrical recording in 1925. However, I've heard quite a few, and I've come across only one singer who fulfills every expectation of what a jazz singer is supposed to be. Marion Harris comes closer than anyone else to doing for the late teens and early twenties what Maxine Sullivan and Billie Holiday later did for Swing Street.

Harris is the vaudeville-jazz-blues-minstrel shouter of our dreams; she stomps and swings with as much energy and charisma as any of the best "jass" bands of the period. She has chutzpah and she has projection, and her sound is remarkably well captured by the acoustic recording technology. She's not the only singer of the era who sounds something like a modern pop-jazz artist (Margaret Young, who recorded for Brunswick, is another contender), but Harris is by far the best. She has the theater-filling excitement that we expect of artists in the preelectronic era, when live performance was the primary focus and the so-called mass media was just an afterthought. Yet she also has an understanding of shading and nuance far beyond what we would anticipate. In fact, one doesn't expect any subtlety whatsoever from performers of this period, who were told that the acoustic horn was only capable of capturing broad strokes, not tiny details. Yet Harris has these qualities in abundance.

The major source of information on Harris—in fact, the only one I have come across—is *Popular American Recording Pioneers* (Haworth Press, 2000) by Tim Gracyk, who, along with Tim Brooks, is the leading historian of the acoustic recording era. As Gracyk points out, there are few reliable primary sources on Harris, thus most of our information comes from press releases and newspaper accounts that were generally written by publicists with a tendency toward colorful, attention-grabbing anecdotage rather than the truth. For instance, there are unverifiable accounts that Harris was related to both Civil War general Benjamin Harrison and President William Henry Harrison. She was supposedly born Mary Ellen Harrison in Henderson, Kentucky, in 1896, but, all or none of these details may be true. When she was in her teens, her parents sent her to boarding school at a convent in Chicago, but supposedly she ran away and by the age of fourteen was appearing in local theaters, singing along with illustrated song slides. One story has a theater owner telling her to get rid of her pigtails, as they made her look too young to be working legally.

Another story that's frequently told about her is that she was "discovered" by Vernon Castle, the vaudeville star and leading dancer of the pre–World War I period. Castle supposedly brought her to the attention of producer Charles Dillingham and songwriter Irving Berlin, who then created a spot for her in Berlin's breakthrough "ragtime" Broadway show, *Watch Your Step*. By 1916, she had come into the orbit of the supreme producer of the age, Florenz Ziegfeld, and introduced Berlin's hit "I Love a Piano." By this time, her picture was appearing on sheet music covers, and she was already identified with the jazz movement: The sheet music cover of the 1917 "Sweet Daddy" advertises it as "the only real jazz song."

Harris began recording in 1916 for Victor. (These are among the few tracks by her that are commercially available on CD, having been collected on Archeophone's *Marion Harris: The Complete Victor Releases*.) A side benefit is that she had an extraordinarily good track record in terms of picking songs that would become standards, and a great many of these have jazz, blues, ragtime, or other African American relevance. She was also especially partial to the work of early black songwriters like Spencer Williams, Henry Creamer, Turner Layton, and W. C. Handy. Harris recorded "I Ain't Got Nobody," her signature song, more than three times in the acoustic era, as well as "After You've Gone" (Creamer and Layton, another early African American hit), "A Good Man Is Hard to Find," "Rose of the Rio Grande," "How Come You Do Me Like You Do," Irving Berlin's "Some Sunny Day," Sissle and Blake's "I'm Just Wild About Harry" and "Runnin' Wild," "It Had to Be You," "Jealous," "There'll Be Some Changes Made," "Somebody Loves Me," "I'll See You in My Dreams," "Who's Sorry Now," and even "Tea for Two."

Harris seems to have been the leading interpreter—of any race, of any era, practically—of the pioneering blues songs of W. C. Handy, as on "Memphis Blues" and "Beale Street Blues." She also laid down multiple recordings of his masterpiece, "St. Louis Blues," the Brunswick version co-starring early sax virtuoso Bennie Krueger. The labels consciously promoted the idea of Harris as a white interpreter of black music. The 1922 Columbia catalogue stated, "When asked how she came to choose Negro songs for her type, Miss Harris guessed, 'It just came naturally. When you first get over stage fright your one instinctive thought is to please. In order to please you must do your best, and you usually do best what comes naturally. So I just naturally started singing Southern dialect songs and the modern blues songs, which closely resemble the darky folk songs.'" Handy's songs never had it so good until the mid-fifties, when there was a flurry of Handy albums by Louis Armstrong, Nat King Cole, Pearl Bailey, and Eartha Kitt. In 1923, Brunswick Records anointed Harris as "the Queen of Blues Singers." Indeed, Harris seems to have been the world's number-one performer of "race" material for the mainstream audience.

Harris recorded for Victor (from 1916 to 1920, and again in 1928), Columbia (from 1920 to 1922), and Brunswick (1922–25). These discs are comprised of charming antiques, songs that bespeak the era, which are generally laden with jazz and blues references: "Paradise Blues," "My Syncopated Melody Man," "Everybody's Crazy 'Bout the Doggone Blues but I'm Happy," "Take Me to the Land of Jazz," "When I Hear That Jazz Band Play," "I'm a Jazz Baby" (which she sings with far more style than Carol Channing did when she reprised it in *Thoroughly Modern Millie*), and even "Cleopatra Had a

Jazz Band"—not to mention "I'm a Jazz Vampire"! During 1917–18, she recorded an especially important subseries of songs that describe, in exaggerated minstrel show style, the African American experience in what was then known as the European War: "When Alexander Takes His Ragtime Band to France" (apparently not by Irving Berlin), "Mammy's Chocolate Soldier," "Goodbye Alexander (Goodbye Honey Boy)," "At the Dixie Military Ball," and "Draftin' Blues."

Harris also had a winning way with a comedy number. In one 1923 catalogue, Brunswick reported, "Marion Harris, the ever-applauded Comedienne, is up to her habitual tricks of making the world laugh," even as they also ballyhooed her as "vaudeville's darling." Harris is especially funny on a comedy piece like the one describing "Fickle Flo (From Kokomo)," who breaks the hearts of beaux all over the world, including her ex-boyfriend Phil in Philadelphia, Louis from Louisville, Jack from Jacksonville ("who spent his *jack* so free"), Al from Alabama, and Vick from Vicksburg—not to mention a hobo from Hoboken, a rummy from Rome (a romin', and, while we're on the subject, a ham from Hamburg, a pest from Budapest, a barber from Seville, and a sissy from Sicily). It would be hard to maintain that any singer of the era had a more consistently excellent output, even the great Jolson.

After her early experiences on Broadway, Harris began headlining in upper-echelon vaudeville theaters like the Palace, making her a key player in the climactic years of the vaud medium. She recorded consistently up until the end of the acoustic era in 1925, at which point there's a break in her discography. (She married in 1924, and the year after she seems to have taken a maternity leave; her two children were born around this time.)

In 1927, Harris entered the electrical age, starting with two sides for Victor, and then resumed her association with Brunswick. She cut what may well be the premier recording of the Gershwin Brothers superclassic "The Man I Love," and another show tune that Victor was even more keen on, "Did You Mean It" (from *A Night in Spain*). The 1927–30 discs are, on the whole, slightly less exciting than the acoustic records. To her credit, Harris adapted to changing times and technologies, but perhaps she adapted all too well. The later sides have her sounding like a typical torch singer of the era—like Ruth Etting, Libby Holman, or Broadway's Helen Morgan. On the whole, these late twenties sides are significantly less jazzy than Annette Hanshaw at her best, and they're also less funny and less fun than Harris at her best. No longer would she sing of scintillating vampires and chocolate honey boys; now she sang of broken hearts, much like every other croonette of the Coolidge era. The "Southern" element of her early work, as represented by "Dixie Highway" and "Mississippi Choo-Choo," is gone. Even here, however, there are some jazz standards

and Afro efforts, like "Nobody's Sweetheart" (the best of her later sides) and Waller and Razaf's "My Fate Is in Your Hands."

Harris excelled in vaudeville and in acoustic recording, but by the late twenties, these forums were fast fading into history. She was importuned to try other mediums—Broadway, movies, radio—which she did only halfheartedly. Returning to the legit stage, she appeared in the Philadelphia production of Vincent Youmans's *Great Day*, where she apparently rewrote the ending of "More Than You Know" into the form we know today, as well as in the more obscure *Yours Truly, A Night In Spain*, and the better remembered *The Second Little Show*. In Hollywood, she supposedly turned down offers to dub her voice for nonsinging movie stars, but did appear in several short subjects (one entitled *The Songbird of Jazz*) as well as the successful period musical *Devil-May-Care* with Ramon Navarro. She also sang on radio, with her own spot on WEAF-NBC, and made guest appearances with Rudy Vallee and the Ipana Troubadours. She didn't flop in any of these attempts, yet she somehow failed to make a lasting impression in any of them.

One place where she did make a hit was London; she played long engagements at the Café de Paris and in the Rodgers and Hart show *Evergreen* (apparently replacing Jessie Matthews). Harris recorded her last eight sides in England, the most famous of these being her most outrageous and futuristic performance. This is "Singing the Blues," her very last record, cut in London eighteen years after her first one. Anticipating the careers of Eddie Jefferson, King Pleasure, and Lambert, Hendricks & Ross, the record is done in the style of what was later known as vocalese. Harris began with what at that time was one of the most famous of all jazz records, Frankie Trumbauer's 1927 disc of "Singin' the Blues," and wrote her own lyrics to the two classic improvisations of Trumbauer and Bix Beiderbecke. It's an astounding record; I had to hear it myself before I could actually believe that it existed.

Apparently Harris settled in England for most of the thirties, where she made appearances on the BBC. By the end of the decade, she seems to have stopped working entirely. She remarried, to a London-based theatrical agent named Leonard Urry, and her final performance seems to have been a monthlong engagement at the Café de Paris. At the height of the Blitz in London, Mr. and Mrs. Urry's home in Knightsbridge was blown to smithereens by a German bomb. The Urrys somehow survived the ordeal, but went home to New York to recuperate. She checked into the Hotel le Marquis on West Thirty-first Street, where she reacquainted herself with old friends. She wasn't to be home in the States for long, though. Having survived the Luftwaffe attack, Harris was killed on April 23, 1944, when she dozed off while holding a lit cigarette.

By this point practically nobody knew who she

was: Her passing only rated a minuscule mention in *The New York Times.* However, as more of her music is heard in the CD era (Take Two Records did an outstanding LP in the early eighties, which, alas, has yet to be made available digitally), it's a cinch that Marion Harris is a jazz-pop stylist whose music is ripe for rediscovery.

Ruth Etting (1896–1978)

Marion Harris's whole career was vaudeville and acoustic recordings; in contrast, Ruth Etting was a notable success in all the major media in which Harris failed to rate: Broadway, Hollywood, radio, and electrical recordings. Still, when we discuss the music of Ruth Etting, it's difficult to decide whether we're talking about a major artist or purely an icon of nostalgia. First off, we shouldn't hold it against her that, unlike Harris and Annette Hanshaw, she can't be judged by jazz standards—compared to Ethel Waters (the gold standard of the era), especially, Etting doesn't remotely cut it. And as a pop star it would take a rather extreme fan to put her in the same class with the heavy hitters of subsequent generations like Jo Stafford, Peggy Lee, Kay Starr, and especially Doris Day, who so movingly enacted her life story in the 1955 movie biography *Love Me or Leave Me.*

Yet Etting was a major figure. She sold more records than practically any other female singer of the early electric era, appeared in six Broadway shows, and was a consistent if modest presence in early talkie cinema. And *Love Me or Leave Me* is a terrific movie, one of the most riveting pictures Hollywood has ever made about the nature of what later became known as "codependency." Doris Day plays Etting as a showgirl with equal parts talent, sex appeal, and ambition, who will do anything, even cozy up to a slimy gangster, to further her career. Oddly, in the movie at least, Etting really is a major talent—she's Doris Day, for Chrissake! (In real life, Doris Day didn't have to sleep with anybody to get ahead—in fact, her choice of husbands actually hampered her professional life.) Etting's deal with Marty "the Gimp" Snyder is portrayed as something of a pact with the Devil: She gives up her soul in order to get ahead. Gifted though she may be, she is not redeemed by her talent; even when she falls in love for real with another man, she is understood to be beyond salvation. She's portrayed by Day—in the bravura acting job of the great singer's movie career—as a vaguely sympathetic character, while Jimmy Cagney's Gimp is just the opposite. Although he's outwardly repulsive, we at least want to admire him for his willingness to do anything for the woman he loves, but Cagney portrays him as such a thorough bastard we can't even feel sympathy for the Devil.

One comes away from the movie with the notion that Etting was both a major talent and very beautiful—like Doris Day. It becomes obvious, though, that Hollywood, even while immersing Etting's life story in seediness hitherto unseen in a Technicolor costume musical, overglamorized her to the hilt. In real life, she was kind of funny-looking, even a little homely. One probably couldn't tell in most of the cavernous theaters where Ziegfeld put her (she did have great legs, however), although her lack of looks is undoubtedly why she never had a leading role in a major motion picture.

Likewise, her singing is somewhat on the flat side; it's not that she doesn't make the notes, but rather that her voice doesn't have any kind of Lilt to it: Even when she hits the notes, they just sit there, they don't go anyplace. And she's at her absolute worst when she tries to get jazzy, as on "Exactly Like You," where she makes it clear she has no idea what syncopation and improvisation are supposed to be.

Why then is Etting—Doris Day and Jimmy Cagney aside—so important? Because she was the first major female singing star of the electrical age. She had the smarts to realize that an understated, intimate style was just what was called for in the new technology, and she more than delivered it. As she told George Eels in the seventies, "I had a big voice. I mean, you could hear me for blocks. But when I recorded or was on the radio, they didn't have to fool with the dials. . . . To me Sinatra was king, but he'd be singing so softly you could hardly hear him, and then he'd bellow out. In my day we couldn't do that. I learned to hold my volume steady. . . . The boys liked to work with me. I was a quick recorder."

The irony of Etting's career, which is not addressed in the movie, is that her talent and style would have easily made her a major asset to the recording industry even without the Gimp's strong-arm tactics. He infamously muscled other singers off the Columbia label (most notably the more talented Annette Hanshaw), but he wasn't going around door to door to the homes of thousands of fans across America and forcing them to buy Ruth Etting records. Ultimately, she probably didn't need the Gimp at all.

She was born in David City, Nebraska, in 1896, and her mother died when she was five, after which she was virtually abandoned by her father. She was essentially raised by her paternal grandparents; her grandpop owned a mill and the Ettings were considerably well-to-do. Her father, George Etting, was enamored of showbiz and music: He built the town's opera house and allowed traveling shows to pitch their tents on his land. Ruthie grew up fascinated with music, although she was not allowed to sing outside of church. "I sang in a high, squeaky soprano," she told Eels. "It sounded terrible, but I didn't know I could sing in any other range." Her other interest was clothing design, and at the age of twenty she moved to Chicago to attend that city's Institute of Fine Arts. When Prohibition arrived, she took a job designing costumes at a nightclub, and before long she was dancing in the chorus line at the Marigold Gardens.

Soon she was singing solo in several of the Windy City's top clubs, and at this time she came to the attention of the Gimp, so named because of his lame left leg. Marty Snyder was a prominent figure in the Chicago underworld, and his main function was to accelerate Etting's career to increasingly better spots in increasingly prominent nightclubs; given her talent, this probably would have happened anyway. In 1922, they were married, she saying later that what she felt for him was nine-tenths fear and one-tenth pity.

No less important than having a gangster for a manager and husband was Etting's awareness of the importance of new technologies. She made her first radio broadcasts in 1924, and saw the results immediately when she began to get bookings in better and better vaudeville theaters across the Midwest. In 1925, she came to the attention of Columbia, who began recording her regularly early the next year.

In 1927, the Snyders moved to New York, where Irving Berlin introduced her to Florenz Ziegfeld. Fifty years later Etting said that her audition for the impresario consisted mainly of her "walking around the room" and that he merely "looked at my ankles, and that was it. That was my audition. He wouldn't hire anyone, no matter how talented, with big ankles." Etting is selling herself short; for one thing, she had ankles and legs that ranked with the best of Ziegfeld's famous showgirls; for another, she was a Columbia Records recording star and surely a valuable property for Ziegfeld.

Hiring her was a whole new experience for the veteran showman. Over the previous twenty years, his elaborate revues helped put the medium known as musical theater on the cultural map; but it was too much to expect him to fathom the emerging equation of multimedia. He realized, though, that Etting's rising importance in these media would bring people into his theater, and that was something he could relate to. In all his years of producing *Follies* and *Midnight Frolics* and other shows, he rarely featured anybody who could be described as a major vocalist. When he later described her as "the greatest singer of songs" that he had ever presented in his forty years in the business, he might not have been exaggerating.

"I liked Ziggy, and he always treated me fair and square," Etting later told *Film Fan Monthly*. "I'd go out in front of the curtain dressed in one of those luscious creations that Ziegfeld always had for his girls. I was no actress, and I knew it. But I could sell a song. When I sang it was one of those opportunities for them to change the set and for the girls to get dressed . . . or undressed." For the next four years or so, Etting was a major force on Broadway, singing Irving Berlin's "Shakin' the Blues Away" in *Ziegfeld Follies of 1927*, Walter Donaldson's "Love Me or Leave Me" in *Whoopee!*, Harold Arlen's "Get Happy"

in *The 9:15 Revue*, and Rodgers and Hart's "Ten Cents a Dance" in *Simple Simon*. She also revived Nora Bayes's 1906 hit "Shine On, Harvest Moon" in the 1931 edition of *Ziegfeld Follies*, the last to be produced by the great impresario himself.

From purely musical, nonacting spots on Broadway, it was a minor step sideways to purely musical, nonacting spots in Hollywood feature films, such as *Hips, Hips, Hooray!* (1934) and *Gift of Gab* (also 1934), although she made her biggest impression singing Harry Warren's "No More Love" in *Roman Scandals* (1933), starring fellow ex-Ziegfelder Eddie Cantor. The number is less notable for Etting's vocal than for the presentation, staged by Busby Berkeley, which involves somewhat lascivious pre-Code scenes of nearly naked slave girls; it's one of the kinkiest things ever shown in a Hollywood musical. Three spots in three pictures was not a bad run for a pop singer, although Etting seemed disappointed in her feature career. "I always thought I might have made it, but they could only see me as a voice," she said in 1974.

Etting was, however, a major success in two other media that existed on either side of the feature picture business: She reigned on radio for the first ten years or so of that medium's existence, on a level very close to that of Bing Crosby, Kate Smith, and even *Amos 'n' Andy*. In New York, she'd starred on Chesterfield's *Music That Satisfies* and after moving to Hollywood, she headlined on *The Chase and Sanborn Hour* in the company of Jimmy Durante.

The other medium that suited her superbly was the motion picture short subject: Whether strictly singing or being featured in some minor plot built around her songs, Etting's short subjects are never less than charming souvenirs of a long-forgotten age. She claimed to have starred in thirty-four Vitaphone and other shorts, far more than any other musical performer. (The number may be vastly exaggerated; according to Vitaphone historian Ron Hutchinson, she probably made fewer than twenty, which is still the record for a singer, dancer, or bandleader.)

Throughout her career, though, recordings remained Etting's primary medium, and she was certainly Columbia's premier female vocalist. Having started for the label in Chicago, she wrote on a 1973 reissue, "I of course continued in New York, with only piano background, with such artists as Arthur Schutt and Rube Bloom. Gradually the background grew, adding a violin played by the greatest jazz man of all time, Joe Venuti, plus Eddie Lang on guitar and Manny Klein on trumpet." Over eleven years she recorded approximately two hundred sides altogether, a track record probably not as great as Marion Harris's, yet she made the definitive "straight" premiere recordings of many future standards.

Etting seems to have reached her pinnacle in her high Hollywood years, 1933–34, at which point she was voted the most popular female singer on radio.

It was at this time that she and Marty the Gimp split up. As was to be expected, it was not a cordial separation. She remained on the West Coast while he headed back to New York. Then, in 1936, like Marion Harris, she found renewed career interest in London, where she starred in the musical *Transatlantic Rhythm* and made six sides with Jay Wilbur's orchestra. The English recordings, as well as eight that she made for American Decca upon returning to New York, are probably the most pleasant of her whole career. She's especially convincing on "A Message from the Man in the Moon," a song dropped from the Marx Brothers picture *A Day at the Races*, and the Shirley Temple–associated "Goodnight My Love," in which she seems to be saying goodbye to her audiences and to show business.

In 1937, Etting and Snyder were officially divorced. By this point, she was involved in a relationship with her accompanist Myrl Alderman. In 1938, Snyder went ballistic, trekked back to Los Angeles, and fired a few shots into his ex-wife's boyfriend. There followed one of those big Hollywood trials, which dragged on for three months, and the Gimp ultimately took a rap for kidnapping and attempted murder. Although Etting's name was back in the papers, in those days this was the kind of publicity that could hinder rather than help a career. In 1939, she married Alderman and the two of them decided to call it quits career-wise.

Fortunately, unlike a lot of stars of the Jazz Age, Etting had managed to save some money and hadn't lost it all in the Crash. She bought a little ranch in Colorado Springs, and the Aldermans lived there without incident for the next forty years. She made a brief attempt to renew her career around 1947, when she appeared at New York's Copacabana (home of a lot of stars older than she was, like Sophie Tucker) and on Rudy Vallee's radio show, but, at fifty, decided that this was not a good idea.

The biggest Etting revival occurred, not surprisingly, in the wake of *Love Me or Leave Me*. As a result, she was afforded something neither Harris nor Hanshaw ever received, a full-fledged 12" LP reissue of twelve of her best Columbia sides, which remained in print for many years. She was fairly well served by reissues in the late LP era, particularly in a series on Take Two Records, but has been less covered in the digital age, although Neovox, an English firm that issued her complete output on cassette, has announced tentative plans to release the whole works on CD. The best individual collection of her tracks is *Goodnight My Love* on Take Two, which samples her thirties sides. It would have been more comprehensive had it included some of the 1925–29 recordings, but the later ones are, in fact, superior.

Etting died in 1978 at eighty-two. She was pleased to have lived long enough to enjoy the revival of interest in her old records, and gave several interviews in her final decade.

Again, it seems too much to claim that Etting was a superior singer, yet it's unfair to suggest that her records are only worth listening to for the quality of her songs and the excellence of her sidemen—something we can say about other twenties vocalists, but which seems too stringent to apply to Etting. If you're looking for a straight-ahead performance of a good song, without a lot of embellishment and also without a lot of histrionics or melodrama (or, for that matter, excitement) but with a large degree of believability, well, you could do a lot worse than reach for a Ruth Etting record.

Helen Morgan (1900–1941)

"I've never been a speechmaker," Helen Morgan says in a 1933 interview, "just a piano sitter and song singer." Early on, this business of sitting on the piano became a career signature—like Al Jolson's innovation of strolling down an extended stage into the audience—and a way for Morgan to get closer to listeners. Standing and posing in front of a microphone was too formal; sitting on the piano was more intimate, less like giving a concert recital and more like sharing secrets among friends.

The piano-sitting stunt would follow her throughout her short career. There's one tale told early in Gilbert Maxwell's *Helen Morgan,* the only full-length biography of the singer. The author presents it and then summarily debunks it even before it gets the chance to become an urban legend. As the story goes, Morgan started her career singing in dives so small that when the piano was onstage, there was no room left for a singer (even the diminutive Morgan), so she had to position herself on top of the instrument. The first time movie audiences saw Morgan was in 1929's *Glorifying the American Girl*, and there she is, wearing a black gown, seated on an enormous white piano being played by an accompanist in a white tailcoat, the whole works up in the air on a platform high above the stage.

Maxwell tells another story—which might actually be true—from about 1933. When *Show Boat* was on its national tour, the company played through Cleveland at a time when Louis Armstrong and his orchestra were working in a joint called the New Orleans Club. Armstrong spots Morgan in the audience, and is so delighted to see her that he pleads with her to sing "Bill." She begs off, claiming, "Louis, darling, I'd love to, but you're using a baby grand and I've always sung from an upright." She's obviously pulling Satchmo's leg—the piano in *Glorifying the American Girl* is as grand as grand can be. But Pops calls her bluff: He summons a pair of busboys, and from out of nowhere they produce an upright piano. Thus cornered, she has no choice but to sing. She gives out not only with "Bill" but also "What Wouldn't I Do for That Man?"—presumably with Armstrong playing hot obbligatos behind her. (What wouldn't we all do to have a YouTube video of that?)

That 1933 quote was part of a newsreel story

announcing Morgan's marriage to Maurice "Buddy" Maschke, Jr., a Cleveland lawyer. In the same clip (included as a "special feature" in the DVD of her 1929 film *Applause*), she also sings "What Wouldn't I Do for That Man?," which is described as her signature song. Actually, it was one of three songs that are inextricably linked with Morgan, the other two especially so posthumously: her big numbers from *Show Boat,* "Bill" and "Can't Help Lovin' Dat Man."

In these key songs, Morgan portrays herself as a romantic underdog, a woman slavishly devoted to her man, no matter how he mistreats her. That was the story of Julie LaVerne, the essential Broadway character she created in *Show Boat,* as well as of Kitty Darling, the central figure in *Applause.* In *Show Boat,* the advice that Julie gives the ingénue Magnolia is strictly from her own experience: Once a woman starts loving a man, nothing in heaven or on earth can convince her to stop loving him. That's the point of all these songs: Even though he's just an ordinary lug, who "can't play golf or tennis or polo / or sing a solo / or row," she can't help lovin' her Bill—what wouldn't she do for him, the big sap.

Not every song she sang in a show or a film or on a record told of submissive, myopic feminine devotion, but enough of them did. The term "torch singer" actually existed before Helen Morgan, but it might as well have been invented for her because she played the role so convincingly. Indeed, there are levels upon levels of torchiness: "Bill" is a song about an unnamed woman who remains faithful and loyal to her man against all odds, and it's sung by Julie LaVerne in a stage setting, a nightclub within the show. Miss LaVerne, Edna Ferber's story tells us, happens to be a woman who remains faithful and loyal to *her* man against all odds, and according to Morgan's biographer, she herself spent most of her off-stage life pining after a man who could never be hers (because he was married to someone else). Alas, she dug an early grave for herself—dying not long after her forty-first birthday, with the persistent help of Jack Daniel's and Jim Beam.

Born Helen Riggins in 1900, Morgan divided her early years between Toronto, Ontario, and Danville, Ohio. (Bobby Short, who grew up in the latter town in the 1930s, later wrote that Morgan was a major source of civic pride for Danvillians, black people especially, possibly because she had famously played a mulatto.) Her father died when she was a child, and her mother married Tom Morgan, a railroad worker who took a somewhat more passionate interest in gambling and who could be depended upon to walk out on the two of them at regular intervals. Around the time she was twelve, Helen was singing for the entertainment of her father's train yard co-workers when she was heard by Amy Leslie, a newspaper reporter and former actress, who became her first mentor.

In her late teens, Morgan found success in several beauty pageants, and eventually arrived in New York as both Miss Illinois and Miss Mount Royal. Even so, she had a hard time finding work in the theater, and supported herself by working as, among other things, a model at the Art Students League. In 1920, she got into the chorus of the Florenz Ziegfeld production *Sally,* which portended well for things to come but had no impact on her career at the time. She wasn't seen on Broadway again until *George White's Scandals* of 1925. Then she landed a spot in "a minor summer revue" (according to Maxwell) titled *Americana* (1926), and it may have been there that she sang her first torch song, "Nobody Wants Me." (Which no one seems to have recorded until contemporary cabaret star Maude Maggart, almost eighty years later.) Fate intervened in the form of Jerome Kern, who was already hard at work composing his masterpiece, *Show Boat.* After hearing Morgan sing in *Americana,* he knew he had found his Julie LaVerne. What's more, he was so taken by what he heard that he exhumed a trunk song of his, "Bill," dropped from a show ten years earlier, and retrofitted it for Morgan. He and lyricist Oscar Hammerstein also wrote "Can't Help Lovin' Dat Man" expressly for her. (The final libretto of "Bill" is essentially a rewrite—fully credited—of the original lyric by P. G. Wodehouse.)

Now, after getting nowhere in New York for almost seven years, Morgan's star was rapidly rising—and through rather unusual channels well before *Show Boat* finally opened at the end of 1927. In the fall of 1926, while she was still appearing in *Americana,* a well-heeled entrepreneur decided to build a speakeasy around her called Helen Morgan's 54th Street Club. She was hardly a Broadway headliner at this point, yet it seemed like a perfect fit; who better to sell bootleg hooch to the suckers than a gal already famous for sitting on the piano and singing of how her man done her wrong? The club was an immediate success, so much so that the police and the FBI began to take an interest in the kind of beverages that the joint was purveying. Morgan also did so well in her New York club that an offer came from England for her to headline in cabaret in a land where alcohol was refreshingly legal. She seems to have spent much of the summer of 1927 in London, until *Show Boat* was ready to go into rehearsal.

The most important aspect of the London trip was that it presented her with her first opportunities to record, and by September she had laid down twelve delightful titles for the British branch of Brunswick Records. Heard today, and compared with Harris, Etting, or Hanshaw, Morgan sounds somewhat trilly and classical. Yet no one would have thought that at the time: This was what a nightclub or Broadway singer sounded like. At age twenty-six, she's certainly a soprano, and the voice is a bit higher than we think of for Julie LaVerne. In 1929, Burns Mantle of the *Daily News* described Morgan as singing in a "brave little voice" when he reviewed her in *Sweet Adeline,* and that says it very nicely. There's also a hint of a catch in her voice, a little twist that she puts on the notes, of the kind that Bing Crosby was simultaneously developing.

The 1927 British recordings are among the high points of her career. For eight of the twelve, the accompaniment is provided by another emerging star, Leslie A. Hutchinson, then just beginning to establish himself in Britain as a singing pianist. "Hutch" actually joins her as a second voice on the first title, "Me and My Shadow," thus launching a tradition of having a black entertainer serve as the singer's shadow in that song. (John Bubbles later performed it with Judy Garland.) The other four titles use a hot little British jazz group led by yet another visitor to London, the Spanish pianist Fred Elizalde, and Morgan's vocal on "Lazy Weather" is spiced considerably by a hot, Bix Beiderbecke–influenced trumpet solo from future bandleader Jack Jackson.

Four of the British tracks are especially special—a pairing of songs by the Gershwin brothers from *Oh, Kay!* and two by Rodgers and Hart from *Peggy-Ann*. On "Maybe," Morgan is joined by a pair of male singers, and the tempo-changing arrangement sounds like a sequence in a Jazz Age revue, while the flip side, "Do, Do, Do," plays up Morgan's inter-action with Jackson and Elizalde; you wouldn't think of Morgan as a jazz singer (even by 1927 standards), but, game gal that she is, she's not at all afraid of the syncopations and slurred notes on "try-y again" and "fly-y again."

"Where's That Rainbow?" and "A Tree in the Park" show that Morgan has charm she hasn't even begun to use yet. "Rainbow" is a lament about the absence of love, but it is too witty and self-satirizing to be considered anything like a torch song; Morgan even chortles subtly after the line "But pardon my laughter." "A Tree in the Park" may be my favorite Morgan recording; again, as with most of Hart's lyrics, there's a lot more wit than sentiment, but while no one's looking, Morgan helps him smuggle in some deep romantic feelings just the same. She promises her lover she'll carve "I love you" in the bark of said tree, and I'm glad no one saw the need to change the lyric perspective from male to female. She ends by personalizing the last line in a way that I've heard no one else do (not that many singers have done "Tree" at all; it's a comparatively rare song by Rodgers and Hart standards), as she sings "Underneath our little tree / Inside the p-a-r-k park!" In Morgan's singing, wit and charm are often the same thing.

None of the British records, apparently, were issued in the United States, but they're proof that she was well on her way to great things even before *Show Boat*. That legendary production opened in December 1927, and in February 1928 she recorded her two big numbers, "Bill" and "Can't Help Lovin' Dat Man," for Victor. By that point, Morgan's bid for immortality was settled—she would forever be Julie

LaVerne, and Julie LaVerne would forever be her. (No other actress would come close; even the normally enchanting Ava Gardner, in the 1951 MGM film of the property, isn't in Morgan's orbit—it was probably the only time that Mrs. Sinatra had to settle for being a second-rate anything.) The fit was so perfect that from then on, virtually every role that Morgan played would be some variation on Julie, the ultimate tragic torch singer with a weakness for strong men and stronger drink. Immediately after she finishes singing "Bill" in the audition scene in the 1936 *Show Boat* film, the club owner observes to the pianist, "Queer how a woman goes all to pieces over a man. She was the best bet in Chicago until that big curly-haired tramp threw her down." This could be said about virtually every character she played.

Show Boat would define the contours of her career; it wasn't exactly her breakthrough, as we have seen, but it certainly was the vehicle that made her a legend. In 1932, she played Julie again in a revival, the last major production supervised by Ziegfeld himself, which was also a major success. It ran for five months on Broadway and could have gone on longer, but the producers decided to take the whole show on the road, where it also did incredible business. In 1936, she reprised her role for posterity in the classic Universal film directed by James Whale, and she played Julie yet again in 1940 in Los Angeles. Doubtless, she would have still been playing Julie into the fifties and sixties had she lived that long. You can virtually divide her career into two sections, those periods when she was appearing in (or filming) *Show Boat* and those when she was doing something else.

While the original *Show Boat* was still running on Broadway, Morgan was in the papers—the front pages this time, not the theater section. In 1928 she had been arrested and charged with violating the Volstead Act; it seemed that federal agents had raided her Fifty-fourth Street saloon and, anticipating Claude Rains in *Casablanca*, were shocked, shocked I tell you, to discover that alcohol was being sold and consumed on the premises. Gilbert Maxwell goes into considerable detail on the arrest and trial: It seems that Morgan had been fingered by a jealous little snit named Mabel Walker Willebrandt, a Linda Tripp–like character who took great delight in making sure that no one else had any fun either. The Feds, for their part, took great delight in sticking it to a celebrity (as when they busted Gene Krupa for smoking dope a generation later). Ultimately, Morgan hired a slick lawyer who was able to prove that she didn't actually own the joint, that she was just an employee, hired for the use of her name and her talent, and she beat the rap. (Alas, she probably celebrated her victory with a few belts.)

Maxwell feels that Morgan had an unconsummated crush on Oscar Hammerstein (she did have an actual and long-standing affair, he also tells us, with another married man, MGM executive Arthur

Loew), and the love that Kern and Hammerstein felt for her was just beginning with *Show Boat*. Instead, they followed it with *Sweet Adeline* (1929), the only musical that would ever be entirely built around Helen Morgan. Described as a "comic romance," the story featured Morgan as a beer-garden singer in the 1890s—she would never completely get away from the backstage showbiz setting, but at least here, for almost the only time, she played a singer less tragic than usual. The two main songs written for her, "Why Was I Born?" and "Don't Ever Leave Me," were every bit as good as her *Show Boat* standouts. They both were about devoted, loving women who, just this once, didn't seem eager to go to the extreme of selling themselves into white slavery for dat man. Burns Mantle, writing in the *Daily News,* felt that the question raised by the title of "Why Was I Born?" essentially answered itself: Why was she born? To sing songs like this.

The same year, Morgan starred in Rouben Mamoulian's *Applause,* which has often been cited as the first all-time classic, all-talking, all-singing—not to mention all-acting—movie musical. At twenty-eight, Morgan was much too young for the part of an aging burlesque queen (she was barely nine years older than Joan Peers, who played her daughter), but there was apparently no one else anybody would consider for the part. And she was brilliant. Other aspects of the story are less believable: Both a backstager and a maternal melodrama, *Applause* tells the story of Kitty Darling, a burlesque headliner (in the days when the form was more about tap dancing than lap dancing) torn between an abusive Mr. Man and her daughter, April. The heel in question is such an overtly slimy SOB that you can't believe someone as bright as Kitty couldn't see right through him. Still, thanks to Mamoulian and Morgan, there's not a shot or a note in the whole production that isn't eminently believable. And she sings throughout the whole film, on stage and off; it's a rich and magnificent tapestry in black and white and Vitaphone that remains today every bit as powerful and moving as it ever was.

Mamoulian makes amazing use of the audio track: There's a brilliant scene in which Kitty is putting April to bed while humming "Give Your Little Baby Lots of Lovin'," presumably a song from her show. It's a bouncy fox-trot, normally played in a fast 2/4 by all the bands of the day, but Morgan croons it softly and sweetly, like a lullaby. As Kitty sings, April recites her prayers, and the overlay of the two voices, one singing, one praying, carries a powerful emotional impact. Morgan sings at least three songs over the course of the story, but, curiously, the only one she recorded was "What Wouldn't I Do for That Man?," the same song that was her big number in the Ziegfeld film *Glorifying the American Girl*.

Between 1928 and 1930, Morgan recorded ten very attractive titles for Victor, nearly all of which were fairly heavy torch songs—including such all-time classics as "More Than You Know" (which includes an amazing reading of the verse) and "Body and Soul." When Annette Hanshaw sang "Mean to Me" it was teasing and pouty; when Morgan sings it, you want to just hang your miserable male head in shame for having been so gosh-darned mean to the poor girl. Amazingly, all ten of these Victor songs are future standards—they're all first-rate tunes from shows and films. The most cheerful of the lot is "Something to Remember You By," in which her lover is leaving (isn't he always?), but at least she has reason to hope that he'll someday return to dampen her bath mat again.

In 1930, she starred in a film called *Roadhouse Nights,* in which she seems to have gotten only one main song ("It Can't Go On Like This") and sacrificed most of her screen time to Jimmy Durante. For us Durante fans that's hardly something to object to, but as far as Morgan's career was concerned, she managed to get to Hollywood just in time for the industry to turn away from the musical genre, and it's not surprising that at this point they would have put the focus on a comic rather than on a diva. There was nothing for her in Hollywood in the early thirties, but Ziegfeld recruited her to co-star in the 1931 *Follies,* alongside Ruth Etting and Harry Richman. She also took part in two sketches, one in which she played a Russian ballerina named Polly Adlervitch (a rather risqué reference to Manhattan's most infamous madame) and another in which her character was described as a "Victim of the Talkies."

Her big number in the 1931 *Follies* (the last edition produced by Ziggy himself) was "Half-Caste Woman," but alas, she never had the chance to record it. A Noel Coward classic, "Half-Caste Woman" brought out the tragic mulatto side of Julie LaVerne. Coward's half-caste woman, like many a Morgan protagonist, is doomed from the start, in this case not because of men or booze, but simply because of who she is and the fact of her parentage. Anyone, in film or song, who is unfortunate enough to be part white and part something else is immediately asking for trouble simply by the act of being born.

In 1932, *Show Boat* was back on Broadway, and Morgan was better than ever in it. There also was a remarkable recording of the score produced by Jack Kapp of Brunswick Records. Just as *Show Boat* gets credit as the first modern American work of musical theater, this album is often described as the first major Broadway cast album. The producer included only two principals from either Broadway production, Morgan and Paul Robeson, and, more surprisingly, he commissioned all new concert-style arrangements from Victor Young. It's different from anything else that can be considered a cast recording before or since, flowing from number to number rather like a thirty-three-minute symphonic medley. Morgan sings her two numbers much more deeply and movingly than in 1928, but you really have to listen to all eight sides in sequence to get the total impact.

The best thing that happened to Morgan personally at this point was meeting George Blackwood, who played her love interest ("Steve Baker") in the 1933 revival of *Show Boat*. The two moved in together during the run and remained that way during the subsequent national tour. He lived long enough to share his memories with Maxwell, and they make up the most compelling part of the book. Blackwood proposed to Morgan at least three times, but she seems to have been interested only in cads, heels, and/or assorted bounders. Blackwood, for all his dashing good looks and kindness toward her, was a nice guy who finished last. Once he was really gone—he left the road company when Hollywood called—she inexplicably married Buddy Maschke, who, in Maxwell's portrayal, was a completely nondescript character who seems to have annoyed her relentlessly until the only way to shut him up was to marry him.

She divorced Maschke in 1935. Between 1934 and 1936, Morgan was busy in Hollywood. She made five feature films and recorded ten songs for Victor and Brunswick, mostly from those pictures. None of the films is either a buried gem or a hidden dog, or anything like a career milestone, even though there is some first-class male talent in them—Rudy Vallee, Al Jolson, and both Spencer and Lee Tracy. The first, *Frankie and Johnnie,* is the only one in the bunch in which she plays the full female romantic lead; in the others—*You Belong to Me, Marie Galante, Sweet Music,* and *Go into Your Dance*—she's always the second female lead. (Come to think of it, that was her role in *Show Boat,* too.)

Her rendition of "I See Two Lovers," a pretty if melodramatic song, is the high point of *Sweet Music;* she sings earnestly while Rudy Vallee conducts and looks on with sincere appreciation (he'd already been in *Glorifying* with her and would play himself twenty years later in *The Helen Morgan Story*). In *Go into Your Dance* she has the thankless task of playing the heavy—a troublemaker who comes between Jolson and Ruby Keeler, husband and wife, in their only film together. Yet when she sings "The Little Things You Used to Do," all sympathy goes to her—it's a superior song and a worthy addition to her canon of torch tunes. You immediately feel more for Morgan than you do for Jolson or Keeler.

But her big moment was yet to come—or come again, as it were. The 1936 film *Show Boat* superseded anything she'd done before, especially on-screen, with the exception of *Applause*. Considering that her career was so short, it's amazing that she was a vital part of two landmark musicals by two of Hollywood's most impressive directors, Rouben Mamoulian and James Whale. *Show Boat* was the climax of her career yet again. She was an important part of a brilliant ensemble cast—everyone, especially Paul Robeson, is exceptional. Truth to tell,

though, as much as I love Irene Dunne and I love Allan Jones, I can force myself to imagine another Magnolia or another Ravenal. As great as the movie is, it wouldn't be anything without Morgan; it's impossible to imagine *Show Boat* without her.

Considering that Morgan's great benefactor was Florenz Ziegfeld, it's ironic that her death knell—figuratively—was sounded in the posthumously produced *Ziegfeld Follies* of 1936. Fanny Brice, who'd sung "My Man," one of the first epic torch songs (in the 1921 *Follies*), spoofed herself by singing Ira Gershwin's scathingly funny "He Hasn't a Thing Except Me," the ultimate parody of all torch songs. In deflating herself, Brice let the air out of all the other torch singers as well.

It was now the swing era. Florenz Ziegfeld was long dead (even if a successful revue was being presented under his imprimatur), and the torch singer had become a cliché to make fun of. Brice didn't care; she had moved on to a whole other career as radio comic. Morgan didn't have that luxury. Nearly all the major femme singers of the twenties—Harris, Etting, and Hanshaw (even Bessie Smith)—were now on the way out. Morgan wasn't doing much in the late thirties—apart from drinking. The last known recording of her voice is a very nice radio transcription of her singing "Bill" on a 1938 Chevrolet program. In 1940, she married a man named Lloyd Johnson, who seems to have earnestly tried to help her get her career back on track. She appeared in *Show Boat,* one last time, in Los Angeles, and was getting ready to do a new edition of *Scandals* in Chicago when she had to be hospitalized. She died of cirrhosis of the liver on October 9, 1941.

Hers was a small but disproportionately iconic career. Obviously, if Morgan is remembered for only one thing, it's for *Show Boat*—in comparison to hundreds of headliners from the period who aren't remembered for anything. You have only to go to YouTube.com and type in "Helen Morgan—Bill—Show Boat" or any combination thereof to realize that what I say is true. Even viewed apart from the rest of the film, her performance is magical and riveting. The only little snippet of the plot you need to know is that Julie is being considered for a spot at the Trocadero nightclub. A bunch of jugglers and other performers are rehearsing, but Julie can't be bothered to audition—"I'd rather go off on a tear," she tells the manager, Mr. Green (Charles Wilson), with refreshing honesty. Green and Jake, the pianist (Harry Barris), implore her to sing anyway. She starts slowly, in tempo, and at this point she sings directly to Green and Jake, as if she were having a conversation with them. But even by the end of the first verse, her singing gets more and more internalized, as if she's having some kind of interior dialogue with herself, thinking over the pros but mostly the cons of her man, Bill.

Now, it's said that when Wodehouse and Kern wrote "Bill," the song was supposed to describe a character in *Oh Lady! Lady!* whose full name was Willoughby Finch. When Hammerstein and Kern resuscitated the song for *Show Boat,* they made the wise decision that "Bill" shouldn't be a song about an actual flesh-and-blood character, but rather about some dream man in Julie's head—even though the dream is almost nightmarish from the way she describes Bill's lack of talent. By the time she gets to the chorus, it's clear that Bill exists only in Julie's imagination, but Morgan makes him seem more real than Ravenal, Steve Baker, Cap'n Andy, or any other man in the show.

Hammerstein could have written the scene so that Julie sings "Bill" as part of an actual performance, but having her sing it at an audition allows her to get further lost in an alcohol-induced reverie. One whole chorus into it ("I love him . . . because he's wonderful"), Julie keeps singing, but she's clearly forgotten that anyone else is there. In fact, James Whale indulges in what would later be a familiar device in movie musicals: As she sings, everyone else in the Trocadero stops what they're doing and gathers round to listen. Jugglers put down their pins, dancers stop warming up, bartenders cease wiping their beer mugs, charwomen drop their mops and start to wipe tears off their weather-beaten faces. Julie, however, has no clue that anyone is listening, and she probably wouldn't care if she knew; she's not even conscious that she's singing, she's just completely wrapped up in her man, and thinking about him in such a way that others around her can hear. At the end of the second chorus, when she gets to the "because he's wonderful" line, she hesitates, as if becoming self-conscious for a fleeting instant and realizing that maybe no one else would think he's so wonderful, so she stumbles and says, "Because he's . . . I don't know . . . because he's just my Bill." As Touchstone says in *As You Like It,* "an ill-favoured thing, but mine own." At that point, Julie is so wrapped up in her thoughts and her dreams that she barely acknowledges it when the whole room full of people applauds her and Green confirms that he wants her in his show. Like he needed to say anything at this point.

No wonder Helen Morgan was the ultimate torch singer. She's singing as if for every woman who ever loved a man, or everybody who ever loved anybody. Talk about picking up the check for the whole table! I'll tell you one thing: It's the only time I ever cried while watching YouTube.

Annette Hanshaw (1901?–1985)

If you're a fan of twenties jazz, especially the white bands like those of Red Nichols, Gene Gold-kette, or the California Ramblers, chances are that Annette Hanshaw is your favorite singer. That opinion, however, is far from universal: Historian-archivist David J. Wiener has described her singing style as "squirrelly," while Dan Morgenstern has said that "she sounds like a virgin." But by and large, if you like Bix Beiderbecke, Adrian Rollini, or the young Tommy and Jimmy Dorsey, it's pretty much a given that you'll like Annette Hanshaw. That's not only because these musicians appear on her records—they may be heard on Ruth Etting's as well, as on those of a number of far less memorable artists of the era. But Hanshaw is the only major female vocalist of the era (again with the exception of Ethel Waters) to completely capture the jazz ethos of the day in her vocals; to swing, syncopate, and give out with the excitement and exuberance of the best instrumental soloists. At her worst, she can indeed be squirrelly and virginal, but at her best, she prefigures the top jazz pop vocalists of the rest of the century: Mildred Bailey, Connee Boswell, Peggy Lee, Kay Starr, June Christy, Rosemary Clooney, you name it. She may not be completely on their level, but she's a great opening act.

As we shall see, there is a major dichotomy at work in Hanshaw's music career, between how she was perceived in her own time and how later generations came to see her. This phenomenon becomes important at the very beginning: The lady herself pretty much let everyone believe that she was just sixteen when she was discovered by Pathé Records and began to record. To this day, 1910 is the birth date that appears in all the literature regarding her, but Joseph Woodruff, who has thoroughly researched her life and career, has found evidence that she was actually born in 1901, which makes much more sense, and places her in her mid-twenties at the time of her "discovery."

Like the young Bing Crosby on the other side of the country, Hanshaw was part of the first generation to grow up with the phonograph (unlike Crosby's family, Hanshaw's well-off merchant father had enough money to indulge her), and she was fascinated by early recording personalities—anyone who sounded a wee bit different, individual, and had a style of her own charmed her. If not rich, her family was at least upper-middle-class, and she had access to high society. In the mid-twenties, she was invited to all kinds of swell affairs and usually asked to sing. It was at one of these that she caught the attention of one Hermann Waldemar Rose, an artists' manager and talent scout for Pathé-Perfect Records. He arranged for her to make a test record, and though she was nearly frightened out of her wits—remember, she didn't come from a showbiz family or have any kind of stage background—the company was pleased with the results.

Between 1926 and 1928, Hanshaw was the major female vocalist on the Pathé and Perfect labels, where she seems to have reigned unchallenged. The voice is amazingly thin—almost nonexistent—in these earliest sides, but she clearly had something. She recorded approximately fifty songs in less than two years. When the company was about to fold, Rose and Hanshaw switched affiliations to the major conglomerate Columbia Records, which was a blessing, if a decidedly mixed one. The Columbia move coincided with an acceleration of the role of radio in her career, so that by the end of the twenties she was an increasingly important star in both mediums. But how big was she, really, back in those days? It's difficult to tell.

Hanshaw's most zealous supporters over the last seventy years have been English collectors and historians, most notably the premier jazz discographer Brian Rust, and they saw to it that in the seventies and eighties virtually every note she sang was made available on LP. (More recently, Sensation Records in Toronto started a planned eight-CD series. They made it as far as three volumes before the label founder died, but hopefully some other will continue the project.) Naturally, long-playing reissues are not necessarily an accurate picture of an artist's popularity at the actual time of her career: Vincent Lopez was a much bigger name bandleader in the twenties than Jelly Roll Morton, but because of Morton's importance to the subsequent development of jazz, one can readily purchase everything he ever recorded, which is as it should be, while you'd have to look high and low for a Vincent Lopez CD.

Thus, when we're considering Hanshaw's career, we have to ask ourselves: Is she only important to latter-day jazz collectors, or was she actually a major star in her day? The answer would seem to be a little bit of both: She wasn't a Ziegfeld headliner like Ruth Etting, and though Etting complained that she was essentially wasted in the three motion pictures she appeared in, that was three more than Hanshaw was asked to make. Etting also starred in a large number of short subjects; Hanshaw sang one number in a single short. Her career was also limited in that while she may have been among the first star vocalists to work exclusively in the medium of electronically reproduced sound, as far as is known, she didn't make personal appearances—she sang exclusively on radio and records.

It is in those areas that Hanshaw does stand out as an important star: Her recorded output confirms that she was a major artist, and clippings from newspapers and magazines make it clear that she was a significant presence on the radio. In these fields, she may well have been close to the upper rung of the most popular singers of the Hoover era, a notch or two below Ruth Etting and Kate Smith. She recorded copiously, yet there's some evidence that she was ranked as a B-level artist, or perhaps A-minus would be more fair.

During most of the time she was under contract to Columbia, though, the label only featured her on its budget imprint releases, such as Harmony and Velvet Tone, which was far less prestigious than being on the main label. (This was at least partly due to Etting's gangster husband, Marty the Gimp, ensuring that no chick singer but his Ruthie had the honor of appearing on the Columbia label itself.) Columbia also employed her as a utility vocalist

of sorts; they had her participating in some rather gnarly side ventures. When the label decided to produce Hawaiian band records (with Frank Ferera's Hawaiian Trio) of both Island and mainstream tunes, Hanshaw was recruited as vocalist (singing a South Sea Island version of "Sonny Boy"—just what the world needed). When rival RCA caused a short-lived sensation with the original boop-oop-a-doop singer, Helen Kane, Columbia had Hanshaw record pseudonymously as an ersatz-Kane, in what turned out to be an improvement on the original with a more musically motivated Betty Boop voice (in fact, her version of "Don't Be Like That" sounds notably more childlike than the contemporaneous reading by the four-year-old singing sensation Baby Rose Marie). Columbia also recruited her to handle dance band vocal refrains with their popular leader Sam Lanin and with a studio group led by her longtime accompanist Irving Brodsky. All of these extra-curricular ventures would have been regarded as demeaning and undoable by Etting, yet Hanshaw seems to have tackled them with relish. In all, Columbia got forty sides out of Hanshaw in the single year of 1929.

Excluding those boring Hawaiian and boop-oop-a-doop titles, Hanshaw is fairly consistently first-rate throughout the late twenties, in both the Pathé and the Columbia periods. From time to time she's placed in front of big dance bands, as on a 1927 session with the bandleader Lou Gold and, as we have seen, a 1929 session with Columbia house music director Lanin. The dance band dates aren't bad, but they are hardly Hanshaw's forte. The real treasures of her discography are the many small group sessions she made, usually with rhythm section and a few hot horns, especially the musicians associated with the Original Memphis Five and Red Nichols and His Five Pennies, including their cornetist leaders, Phil Napoleon and Nichols himself. She cut two particularly excellent sessions in 1927 that are blessed by the presence of pioneering violin and guitar duo Joe Venuti and Eddie Lang, on the second of which her accompaniment is listed as "Her Sizzling Syncopators." The first, in which her accompaniment is billed as "the Four Instrumental Stars," begins and ends with two superior swingers, "I'm Somebody's Somebody Now" and "Under the Moon," the latter of which is driven by the bass saxophonist Adrian Rollini to brilliant advantage.

Phil Napoleon shares honors with Hanshaw on "Daddy, Won't You Please Come Home," a Sam Coslow song from the picture *Thunderbolt*, which is a very strong contender for the title of her single best performance. On this perfect synthesis of jazz vocal and instrumental aspirations, both the background and the vocal are hot and lightly blue (justifying Hanshaw's oxymoronic billing as "Society's Blues Singer"). She's working in pure 4/4 swing, the kind heard more in jazz than in pop in 1929, though still hardly common currency. Hanshaw rides the beat confidently and gracefully, proving that although there were (and still are) such things as blues shouters, one could sing jazz and blues with understatement, even a hint of introspection. (Note one irresistible rhyme: "There are lots of other new sheiks / Who would like to be sheikin' / Haven't slipped yet / But I'm liable to weaken.")

By the very end of the decade, a number of factors—the evolution of the new genre known as torch singing, the start of the Great Depression, the acceptance of jazz, blues, and African American music—had led to ever increasing numbers of blues and Afro-associated songs. Hanshaw's records, like Harris's, were never aimed at the "race" market, but she does a number of songs with black and jazz relevance: "I Can't Give You Anything but Love," "I Must Have That Man," "Moanin' Low," "What Wouldn't I Do for That Man," and others. She's considerably earthier here than she is on "A Precious Little Thing Called Love." Still, she continues to address the issues of traditional Tin Pan Alley. You wouldn't hear Bessie Smith or even the more mainstream Ethel Waters sounding coquettish or vulnerable while asking a question like "You Wouldn't Fool Me, Would You?" While Hanshaw was pouting "My sin was loving you," Bessie Smith was pleading for a judge to send her "to the 'lectric chair." The intricacies of bourgeois relationships rarely found their way into the repertoire of black singers in those years; they were too busy demanding to know where their misbehaving gentleman friends had stayed the previous night when their hair was a mess and their clothes didn't fit them right.

As mentioned earlier, Hanshaw was frequently billed as "Society's Blues Singer" (and also as "the baby blue" singer) and she does indeed get everything that can be gotten out of such race-directed songs as "Am I Blue?" and Fats Waller's "I've Got a Feelin' I'm Fallin'." She challenges Waters herself on "Am I Blue?," the jazz standard written for La Waters in her picture debut *On with the Show*—Hanshaw even includes the second verse, "He's in Chicago . . . ," rarely sung by anyone other than Waters. Hanshaw's time is so self-assured that she can even afford to stop it, as she does near the end of "Am I Blue?" repeating "Only . . . only . . . only . . . one" for swinging emphasis. ("Lawdy!")

Hanshaw's "Big City Blues" is a perfect description of what she was achieving. The refrain is very general, as most pop songs have to be, but the verse is unusually specific: A modern, urban woman is by herself on Thanksgiving, friends and relatives are all out of town, and while alone she sings of lost loves. Another pop song with a similar reference, "I Get the Blues When It Rains," has our cosmopolitan lass lamenting that the rain makes her lose her rouge and splatters mud on her silk hose. Bessie Smith would laugh you out of the gin joint if you brought such a song to her, but Hanshaw makes it poignant, and even these somewhat trivial concerns somehow become important. (Even more so with a delectable little trill that she introduces at the very end of "Blues When It Rains.")

Hanshaw's recording career can be roughly divided into three periods: After Pathé-Perfect, she spent three very productive years at the "old" Columbia Records, as we've seen, being mostly heard on its second-tier labels. (The middle period is excellently sampled on *The Girl Next Door*, on Take Two Records.) After September 1931, when Columbia hit the depths of the Depression, Hanshaw stopped recording for almost a year, resuming in August 1932, this time for ARC a concern that could be described as a ghost of the once mighty Columbia. (Such were the times that by now even Etting was on ARC.)

If Woodruff's research is correct, Hanshaw would have been thirty-one in 1932. She recorded roughly eighteen sides for ARC from 1932 to 1934 that are less jazz-oriented than the late twenties work, but excellent nonetheless. Few of these are as unrelentingly hot as, say, "Daddy Won't You Please Come Home," but fortunately none of them, not even the juvenile "This Little Piggy," is as dumb as the pseudo–Helen Kane sides. Hanshaw has by now passed into the age of Mildred Bailey, Lee Wiley, and Connee Boswell, yet she still sounds relevant. She uses the idiom of her era just as creatively as the major jazz-pop singers of later generations— Peggy Lee, Kay Starr—use the idioms of their own generation.

"Fit as a Fiddle," a seminonsensical piece revived to great effect by Gene Kelly and Donald O'Connor in *Singin' in the Rain*, shows that Hanshaw's rhythm strengths are as astute as ever, while the great majority of the sides show that her abilities as a storyteller have grown considerably stronger. A couple of these tunes weren't worth her time, although I confess to actually enjoying several samples of ethnic multiculturalism such as the ersatz-Scottish "Sweetheart Darlin'" and the chinoiserie of "Sing a Low Down Tune." Otherwise, she has a pretty good track record here for picking superior future standards: "Say It Isn't So," "Moon Song," "I Cover the Waterfront," and "Don't Blame Me," a particularly poignant reading of "It's the Talk of the Town" (another song that could be described as a bourgeois blues). Her final commercial recording is also special: "Let's Fall in Love." Hanshaw opens intriguingly with the verse and it gets even better from there.

Her career kept going for a few more years after 1934, when she made her last record. She seems to have continued to be popular on the air, progressing from one top-flight radio program to another: *The Van Heusen Program*, *The Maxwell House Showboat*, and others, climaxing in *The Camel Caravan*. She remained a presence on radio throughout the early swing era—indeed, she shared the spotlight on the *Camel* hour with Glen Gray and the Casa Loma Orchestra.

One gets the impression that she gradually lost interest in the music business though she went on performing as late as 1941, her last program being for Chevrolet. (There's a Chevy transcription from 1938 of her swinging "Mama I Wanna Make Rhythm.") Even apart from the coming of swing, pop music had undergone many sea changes, and Bing Crosby was virtually the only artist of the twenties who stayed current—and stayed on top—into the war years and beyond. (Rudy Vallee survived as a comic, Jolson as a nostalgia act, albeit an incredibly potent one.) Ironically, Hanshaw probably had the physical and mental equipment to keep up—she certainly was no stranger to 4/4 swing time—but it would have meant work on her part. She doesn't seem to have had that driving ambition to stay in the public eye, and was content to phase herself out.

Ten years later, sometime in the mid-fifties, a friend of hers made a private tape recording of the singer, apparently accompanying herself at the piano, doing a variety of tunes. There were some old favorites of the twenties, as well as some newer items that she obviously liked, such as two Nat King Cole favorites, "Because You're Mine" and "Baby All the Time." There were a couple of late thirties songs she'd never done—"My Funny Valentine" and "I See Your Face Before Me." There's even a future hit in "Fly Me to the Moon (In Other Words)." Overall, the results were not encouraging. She was obviously out of practice, and the possibility of her resuming her career seems to be more her husband's idea than her own.

She kept busy, and took up the rich woman's burden of volunteer and charity work. For a while, she flirted with the idea of running her own talent agency in conjunction with her second husband, Herb Kurtin. She kept up with her many fans in England, as well as younger admirers like Roy Evans and myself in New York, where she lived on a pricey piece of real estate at Park Avenue and Thirty-fourth Street. She was surprised and delighted whenever she met anyone who knew her work; obviously, most of her remaining fans were forty or fifty years younger than herself.

Both Morgan and Etting were exonerated for their sins, as it were, in Hollywood biopics. Apart from that, Hanshaw was kept alive by hot jazz collectors, Etting by nostalgia buffs, Harris by no one. None of these women was remotely as important as Ethel Waters, Bessie Smith, or Mildred Bailey, but each of them has something to teach us, and their music, some seventy years after their last discs (all three recorded for the last time in 1934–36), still has something to say to us.

African Americans Abroad

Adelaide Hall
Josephine Baker
Elisabeth Welch
Alberta Hunter

Europe was the central event in the careers of Adelaide Hall, Josephine Baker, Elisabeth Welch, and Alberta Hunter. In turn, these four African American women played a central role in the changing ways in which American culture was perceived by the rest of the world during the interwar era. When Josephine Baker first appeared in Paris, in 1925, Europe was still the cultural center of the universe; but twenty years later, by the time the Allies drove the Nazis out of France, it had become a given that popular culture, no matter where it was produced, would have a distinctly American accent. The very term "popular culture," in fact, had become a synonym for "American culture." (And even, to an extent, "*African* American culture.") The influx of entertainers from Harlem and the Deep South into Paris and London would play no small part in helping to change attitudes.

These four women were not the only American music makers to be gainfully employed overseas in the interwar era. There were also songwriters: In the twenties, the opening of an American production in London's West End was at least as important as the Broadway edition. Rodgers and Hart, the Gershwins, Oscar Hammerstein, Jerome Kern, and others spent considerable time working on productions for English consumption, while several American songwriters were practically binational, like Eddie Pola and Harry Woods. There also were many musicians—both black, like Coleman Hawkins, Benny Carter, and Bill Coleman, and white, like Adrian Rollini, Jimmy Dorsey, Bunny Berigan, and the underappreciated Danny Polo—who had a deep impact on the development of jazz overseas. But no group of performers had such a profound effect on the entire development of cultural relations between the New and the Old World as these four women. When Miss Baker in particular alighted on the stage in *La Revue Nègre* and then in the Folies Bergère six months later, she appeared to be the very embodiment of everything African, everything American, everything feminine; she caused a sensation that in many ways has not abated eighty years later.

To a certain extent, the allure of Europe for these women was getting away from racism and the limitations imposed on black entertainers in the land of their birth. In Europe they could be divas, whereas in America, no matter how brightly their stars shone, they were still regarded as second-class citizens—they couldn't get a table in most restaurants, even in New York, they couldn't buy a house in a white neighborhood. But there were other enticements: To succeed in Paris in 1925 was to make it in the absolute epicenter of world culture—in fact, what

New York was about to become. By the post–World War II era, when the Germans had been defeated but France and England were a shambles, black Americans like Don Byas, Ben Webster, and Sidney Bechet regarded Europe as a safe haven and an escape from Jim Crow, but they knew they had retreated to cities that had by now taken a backseat to New York.

Thus for Hunter, Hall, Baker, and Welch, making a breakthrough in twenties Europe meant experiencing something that no one had ever undergone before—or ever would again.

Adelaide Hall (1901–1993)

Three of these superb African American singers abroad lived to a ripe old age, making it into their nineties. Yet it was Josephine Baker, who died at the comparatively young age of sixty-nine, who was the only one of the quartet to write her autobiography, which she actually did on several occasions. (Indeed, between Baker's own books and that of her adopted son, Jean-Claude Baker's *Josephine: The Hungry Heart,* among many other biographies, Baker lit has become an accepted field of literary study.) Between all the Baker books and Frank C. Taylor's *Alberta Hunter: A Celebration in Blues,* I thought I'd read everything that there was to know about this particular experience.

However, Iain Cameron Williams's *Underneath a Harlem Moon,* a biography of Adelaide Hall, which actually began as her autobiography, held quite a few surprises for me. Before this exhaustively researched biography was published, I had tended to think of Hall—apart from her brief artistic liaison with Duke Ellington—strictly in terms of the European exodus. After all, she settled permanently in England in 1938 (when Williams's book ends) and, like Baker, was a much bigger star over there than she ever was over here.

Or so I thought. Williams proposes that Hall was a major star in her native country, much bigger than the surviving evidence of recordings and films suggests, or than most historians realize. He suggests that with the death of Florence Mills, the short-lived first black superdiva, Hall enjoyed a long summer in which she was the most popular black entertainer in the land, for a time bigger even than Ethel Waters.

The recorded evidence rather literally points to Waters. She was a consistently successful recording artist throughout the twenties and thirties, one of the biggest of that era, whereas Hall barely recorded forty songs before she settled in England in 1938—a period during which Waters recorded several times that amount. Waters was also prominent on Broadway and in Hollywood, not only in *On with the Show!* but also in several two-reel featurettes. Adelaide Hall was filmed only once, a single captivating number in the Vitaphone short *An All-Colored Vaudeville Show.*

Yet this kind of evidence is not always conclusive. Williams doesn't go into specifics concerning Waters, but leaves you with the general impression that neither the 1927 *Africana* nor *On with the Show!* was all that important to her career—neither one put her on top. On the other hand, when Hall broke through, in *Blackbirds of 1928,* she became the biggest black star of the late twenties and early thirties. *Blackbirds* was, along with *Shuffle Along* (in which she also appeared), one of the most successful all-black shows of its day. Its songs, especially "I Can't Give You Anything but Love" and "Diga Diga Do"—both introduced by Hall—were massive hits, heard everywhere at the time, and which immediately became jazz standards. Furthermore, *Blackbirds* toured successfully overseas, where, for a time, Williams insists, Hall eclipsed even Josephine Baker.

Hall's star only began to fade as Waters's rose. Hall was making a fortune in vaudeville just at the time Waters was breaking through in the Cotton Club, and then in *As Thousands Cheer* on Broadway, and later in *Mamba's Daughters* and *Cabin in the Sky,* the latter for MGM Pictures as well as on Broadway. But for a generation or so, as pop musicologists count them, Adelaide Hall was the most important black female entertainer around. For her even to be considered competition for the mighty Ethel is amazing enough.

Adelaide Hall was born in Brooklyn in 1901, but grew up as part of the first generation of African Americans to call Harlem their home. Her dad, she always said, taught piano at Pratt University (Williams feels that he probably didn't). Both her father and her younger sister died around the time of World War I, leaving Adelaide and her mother, Elisabeth, to fend for themselves.

Early on, the young Hall made a strong impression on future producer Lew Leslie, who would later become the closest thing to the Ziegfeld of black talent, although his moment in the sun was considerably briefer. She appeared in the general chorus (listed in the credits as one of the "Jazz Jasmines"), along with many other black showbiz stars including Josephine Baker and Aida Ward, in the watershed 1921 production *Shuffle Along.* Over the next few years she appeared in several other black productions, including the revues *Runnin' Wild* (1923), *Chocolate Kiddies,* one of the first all-black efforts to enjoy a highly successful run in Europe (Berlin, actually), and the short-lived 1926 *My Magnolia.* In 1924 she married the onetime merchant marine and native Trinidadian Bert Hicks, who managed her career until his death in 1963.

In 1927, there was another, possibly even more significant breakthrough. As she later told the story, she was sharing a bill with Duke Ellington's fledgling orchestra, when the Maestro launched into a recent composition, "Creole Love Call," which was a variation on a melody King Oliver had recorded in 1923 as part of "Camp Meeting Blues." Listening from the wings, Hall began improvising a spontaneous countermelody, not intending to be heard, just humming to herself. Ellington, possessor of the sharpest ears around, heard her backstage singing from his piano bench. No mean improviser himself, he raced back into the wings and yanked her out onto the stage, insisting that she continue to hum and scat and otherwise weave her impromptu, wordless passage. It went over so well that he made her voice and her countermelody a permanent part of the song; "Creole Love Call" became one of the most notable early Ellington masterworks. In future years Ellington would perform the "Love Call" with other vocalists as well as instrumentalists (particularly trumpets) assuming Hall's wordless part.

Although "Creole Love Call" established Hall's place in jazz history, what happened the next year did considerably more to position her at the absolute pinnacle of the black showbiz world. This was Lew Leslie's blockbuster revue *Blackbirds of 1928*. It made her a star in her own right, and it led to her first chance to make a record under her own name. Hall is sometimes described as a jazz singer, but the truth is actually much more interesting: Jazz may be a useful catch-all phrase to describe her singing and the circles she moved in, but her vocal style includes elements of Broadway-musical-comedy style singing, blues, straight-down-the middle pop singing (the sort that Ruth Etting was then doing), scat, and more than a touch of classical style. Her voice sounds more like an opera singer's than a blues singer's. I wouldn't want to find her in *La Bohème*, but one could easily imagine her appearing in an operetta like *The New Moon* or a musical comedy like *Girl Crazy*, or doing a pop song with a contemporary dance band like George Olsen's or even a 12-bar blues with Lonnie Johnson.

The 1928 recordings from *Blackbirds*, Hall's first of many versions of "I Must Have That Man" and "Baby," show her moving through multiple genres even within a single track. "I Must Have That Man" opens with an introductory instrumental vamp in twenties Broadway style, with prominent violins and sounding similar to what one might hear backing Jolson or in an early talkie. After the verse, Hall sounds more like what they used to call a torch singer, dropping hints of blues inflections here and there. In the second chorus, she goes the full monty, launching into a wild scat sequence, a fully improvised line that could be called a countermelody or some other kind of wordless variation. At first, the scat is high and ethereal, almost like a classical *vocalise*, but when she reaches the breaks after each 8-bar section, she descends into a low growl in response to one of the trumpeters, also growling, muted in the style concurrently being perfected by Ellington's Bubber Miley.

Hall didn't record again for another three years. In the fall of 1931, she was headlining at the London Palladium—her first appearance in the U.K.—and she cut eight titles (one unissued) for the British Oriole label. These eight selections, backed by a four-hand, two-piano team, would have made a perfect 78 rpm album or 10" LP. As with the 1927–28 tracks, Hall continued to switch genres in midstream, from sweet to hot and back again: "Rhapsody in Love" starts as a ballad, but becomes a hot-cha number halfway through, with Hall scatting and playing with the melody.

The most outrageous number of the group is her treatment of Cab Calloway's "Minnie the Moocher"; but whereas Calloway first arrived as a master scat singer with this breakthrough hit, Hall had already been scatting for years. Apparently Oriole Records had some concern that British record buyers wouldn't know what a "moocher" was, so Hall commences with a spoken intro explaining that the term refers to a "young girl that's out stealing other girls' sweethearts." The duo-piano treatment suits her surprisingly well; instead of the whole band hollering back with the hi-de-ho's, chanting pianists Joe Turner and Francis J. Carter take on the task and are more than up to it. The two men also chime in with spoken asides, as when one inquires, "What'd she do?" as if to prod her into singing. "She had a dream about the King of Sweden." She describes the king's gift to Minnie as "a million dollars in shillings and pence," which rhymes (sort of) with "and she's been a-countin' 'em ever since." (She also includes the verse about Minnie's encounter with Deacon Lowdown, never sung by Calloway but apparently included in the published sheet music.)

Hall's pre-1938 recording career is superb but erratic—a handful of dates spread over the decade and two continents. In 1932, she cut four sides in New York (two of which marked the recorded debut of Art Tatum), and then at the end of the year there was a brief reunion with Ellington (as part of the Brunswick *Blackbirds* cast album). A year later, she cut two sides with the Mills Blue Rhythm Band, which would not actually be issued until many decades later and would constitute her last recording date in the United States. Between 1936 and 1938, Hall recorded more consistently in Paris, but also did one session in Copenhagen and another in Berlin; she was certainly one of the last African Americans to perform in Nazi Germany.

The French sessions co-star Harlemite bandleader Willie Lewis as well as the legendary French jazz violinist Stephane Grappelli. Around this time, Hall and her husband opened the Big Apple, one of the more successful jazz nightclubs of immediate prewar Paris, and they actually hired Grappelli and Django Reinhardt's Quintette of the Hot Club of France to work there, although, alas, she doesn't seem to have recorded with them. But trouble was already brewing in France, and she accepted an offer from C. B. Cochran, the British Ziegfeld, to appear in a London show called *The Sun Never Sets*. It worked out well, with the couple leaving France to settle in England two years before the Nazi invasion.

Hall began recording regularly for HMV in

August 1938, launching what would be a long relationship with a Harlem reunion. Old friend Fats Waller was in town, and the two cut the *Blackbirds* hit "I Can't Give You Anything but Love," along with a new song with built-in nostalgia, "That Old Feeling." Here, Waller not only accompanied Hall on the organ, he chimed in with the same sort of irreverent spoken asides he used on his own records.

Hall would call England home for the rest of her life. She left to entertain Allied troops in Germany even as it was being defeated in 1944–45, and then briefly returned to Broadway for a supporting role in Harold Arlen's *Jamaica,* which starred her old friend Lena Horne (who had been an anonymous dancer in the Cotton Club line when Hall headlined there in 1934).

Both her earlier (1927–38) and her HMV-era work deserve to be reissued more comprehensively. The post-1937 sides include many worthy jazz-oriented titles from the London period (heard on *Hot from Harlem,* a recommended anthology on Pearl Records): the Jimmie Lunceford hit "'TAin't What You Do (It's the Way That Cha Do It)," that swampland serenade "Chloe," Ellington's "Solitude," and two early Sinatra items, Jimmy Van Heusen's "Shake Down the Stars" and "Who Told You I Cared?" Many of the 1939–40 titles employ vaguely jazzy accompaniment—this was still the swing era, even in London—a relaxed, lightly rocking combination of Walleresque organ and New Orleans–style subtone clarinet.

Hall remained a major star in the United Kingdom throughout the war years and beyond. She sang a little bit of everything, from swing signatures to current U.K. and U.S. show songs (there's a terrific 1940 disc of Rodgers and Hart's "This Can't Be Love," with the verse), film songs, novelties, and even exotica, like "Tropical Magic," "Moonlight in Mexico," "Minnie from Trinidad," "Sand in My Shoes," "Pagan Love Song," and "Song of the Islands."

There were precious few straight-down-the-middle pop singers recording as solo acts in 1940, and Hall was certainly in the upper ranks. On mid-forties hits, like "I'm Gonna Love That Guy (Like He's Never Been Loved Before)" and "It's Been a Long, Long Time," she sounds a bit old-fashioned, still with a tinge of semiclassical style, but this hardly seems to have been a drawback in England. The recommended double-CD set *A Centenary Collection* (Avid) concludes with a charming transcribed broadcast in which Hall is introduced by a very fruity British announcer and sings a number of pop hits old and new, notably the French import "(All of a Sudden) My Heart Sings," accompanied by piano alone. By now, she was even starting to sound British.

She made other appearances in the upper levels of English showbiz, on screen and singing a wordless lullaby in the 1940 fantasy classic *The Thief of Bagdad,* and in the London production of Cole Porter's *Kiss Me, Kate.* Hall seems to have kept going without a hitch until she was past sixty, when her husband and manager, Bert, died in 1963. And that only slowed her down temporarily. For much of that decade, she went on working on the British nostalgia circuit. As she put it, "For many years I toured variety theatres in shows like *Thanks for the Memory.* I worked with so many stars: Frankie Howerd, Harry Secombe, Vera Lynn."

Then, at the start of the next decade, she was rediscovered by the jazz world, and her collaboration with Duke Ellington was recalled in time for the Maestro's seventieth birthday. She made several albums beginning in 1969 and 1970, including *The Wonderful Adelaide Hall* and *Hall of Ellington,* the latter a songbook collection devoted to the Duke—which included a new "Creole Love Call."

In 1982, Hall extended her Ellington association by appearing in a restaging of one of the Ellington Sacred Concerts, and in 1988 she returned to New York for the first time since *Jamaica* thirty years earlier and played a sold-out solo concert at Carnegie Hall. She appeared at Carnegie one more time in 1992, and died a year later in November 1993, a few weeks after her ninety-second birthday.

Josephine Baker (1906–1975)

Josephine Baker was the single most important American musical expatriate of the last century—especially African American—especially female African American. Historian Alan Eichler wrote that "she escaped her childhood and lived out the fantasy for black women back home," yet the life she lived in Paris was so far beyond the imagining of your typical black women from Atlanta or Chicago that they would have probably had an easier time believing they could ride in a rocket ship with Buck Rogers. For a person of color in interwar America, it was enough of a fantasy to imagine not having to drink out of a Jim Crow water fountain or even to enter a whites-only restaurant. To be worshipped by fifty million Frenchmen and become the idol of an entire nation was something beyond an impossible dream. In America, it would have been enough to be regarded as the equal of any white person; in Europe, Baker was as much of a celebrity as the royal family of any nation. She didn't just live out this fantasy; she created it and subtly crafted it. Indeed, as her biographers reveal, Josephine Baker's life was continually shaping, manipulating, and then moving in and out of one fantasy image after another.

It was all about image. Though she was a key player in terms of the way American music and songs were received overseas, the claim has never been made that Josephine Baker was an exceptional singer or recording artist, even though she did, in fact, make a lot of records. Her genius was in the icon she created, and how for the first time she made Frenchmen, Europeans, and other internationals think of the African American female as a love goddess. She didn't do that in terms of advancing the cause of jazz or the popular song; it was more about what music could do for her.

More than most stories in American cultural history, the biography of Josephine Baker has the quality of a morality play. It goes like this: She was born Freda Josephine McDonald on June 3, 1906, in St. Louis. Like Louis Armstrong, who would also be a sensation in Europe in the thirties, she grew up surrounded by dire poverty and racism. At eleven she found herself on the perimeters of the most horrible race riot the country had yet known, and at thirteen she got married for the first time—within roughly eighteen months she had parted from both her first and second husbands, the second having left her her stage name.

The woman who would eventually become immortal as a sexual icon gained her first showbiz notoriety as a comic. Like Adelaide Hall, she was part of the chorus line of *Shuffle Along*, the breakthrough all-colored Broadway production that helped ignite the Jazz Age in 1921. According to legend, Baker was originally turned down because her skin was too dark for the café au lait chorus line that producers Miller and Lyles wanted, and when she was hired it was only as a dresser. When one of the girls in the line took an unexpected maternity leave, Baker was quick to take her place, and even quicker to grab the spotlight with her clowning—deliberately doing the wrong steps, crossing her eyes and mugging, and shaking what the French would call her *cul* at the crowd. Composers Sissle and Blake enjoyed her antics so much that they gave her more to do in their 1924 *Chocolate Dandies.*

She appeared in prominent spots in several important Harlem clubs, including the Plantation Club and the Cotton Club, and in 1925, she was offered a turn in *La Revue Nègre*. America had been exporting black entertainers overseas ever since the Fisk Jubilee Singers decades earlier, but the trend reached a peak in the twenties: Even though black entertainers had now broken through on Broadway, Americans of all races were surprised to learn how astonishingly popular they could be in Paris and Berlin, where African Americans were considerably more exotic.

But there was simply no anticipating the sensation that Baker would cause in *La Revue Nègre*. Within hours of stepping on that stage, wearing only the slightest hint of a feather (placed strategically somewhere in between Germany and France), she was instantly the toast of Paree. From there she could only go up: Next year she headlined at the Folies Bergère, the traditional symbol of French cabaret culture, and after that she opened her own club and married a man claiming to be a count. The Parisians at the time viewed her as a symbol of everything that was hip and sexy and American, although when we look back at those miraculous photographs of her from that era, she has become a symbol of everything that was great about Paris between the wars.

It's important to remember that she was only nineteen when she first landed in Paris. Even prancing about in her altogether, wearing only a belt of bananas, Baker never came off like a seductress, or someone remotely experienced in the world of love. Her charm is her innocence. (This at a time when, Jean-Claude Baker tells us, his future *La Mère* operated a sideline in which she rented herself out by the hour for carnal purposes. The fee was 33,000 francs a night, and the line formed to the right, babe.)

There's a great shot of Baker in a man's tuxedo tailcoat in the early thirties. When Marlene Dietrich wore the same outfit, you somehow just knew it was a sex thing: It came across as erotically motivated cross-dressing. When Baker wears the tux, it seems a tomboy thing, like Eleanor Powell in the same outfit in *Broadway Melody of 1936*. Both Baker and Powell (who, unlike Dietrich, were real dancers) were sexy yet sexless.

Throughout the twenties and thirties, Baker still seems always ready to go for a laugh; when she uses her tongue, it's to make a silly face (generally accompanied by crossed eyes), and not for an erotic purpose. To the French, her innocence was part and parcel of her exoticism. Perhaps this helps explain why she was always doomed to be a prophet without honor in her home country. Just as Rudolph Valentino was, as he put it, "just another wop" when he visited Italy, Josephine Baker was merely another black American woman when she returned home to America. Both blacks and whites in her homeland failed to see what the fuss was all about; perhaps there was something in her dark-skinned charm that only continentals could appreciate. After flopping back home in Broadway's *Ziegfeld Follies of 1936*, she returned to France, and more or less forevermore stayed where she was appreciated. Still, she had a knack for getting into trouble: Not only did she remain in Paris during the German occupation, but by the time the Nazis marched in, Baker had managed to get herself married to a French Jew.

According to most accounts, she behaved gallantly in the war, supporting French freedom fighters. Exactly what she did do for *La Résistance* has never quite been determined, but the French were impressed enough to award her the Legion of Honor. Still, Baker always succeeded in saying or doing the wrong thing; though she probably wore the most expensive shoes in Europe, she couldn't help putting her foot in her mouth. At the time of the Italian-Ethiopian war in 1935, she made the mistake of praising Mussolini and pooh-poohing Haile Selassie; she did the same thing after the war when she lauded the regime of Eva and Juan Perón in Argentina at the expense of the United States. Even her friends agreed it was Baker's temperament that sparked a notorious incident at the Stork Club in 1950 that incurred the wrath of Walter Winchell. In terms of such screwups, Baker had a lot in common with that other icon of the Jazz Age, Charles Lindbergh. Just as Lindbergh should have kept his mouth shut when he was on the ground, Baker became decidedly less magical when she was fully dressed, or speaking instead of singing.

She could also be less magical when she was working in an audio-only medium like records. In 1926 and 1927, she recorded twenty-five titles for the French Odeon label; twenty of these are heard on *Josephine Baker: Breezin' Along,* on American Sony Legacy. She was only twenty and twenty-one when these were made. As Jean-Claude Baker says in the notes, "She is not yet the great chanteuse she would become." Leaving aside (for now) the question of whether or not she ever became a great chanteuse, it is perhaps charitable to say that these were made prematurely. Baker mostly yelps out the lyrics with little distinction, sounding less like a master than one of the many grade-B singers Louis Armstrong or Sidney Bechet accompanied on records in this decade.

It doesn't help that the acoustic recording technique and the rather stiff French "jazz" band accompaniment make these American pop songs of 1926 and 1927 sound as if they were recorded five or six years earlier. "I Wanna Go Where You Go" finds Baker experimenting with a mild scat episode; "Dinah" has her wailing and chirping. "That Certain Feeling" is amazingly amateurish—she completely mangles the melody and can't seem to find the beat; one has the feeling she's been rushed through the session without being given a chance to learn the tune properly. On the positive side, "I Wonder Where My Baby Is Tonight" includes an endearing Charleston episode; one gets the impression that she must have been delightful doing this number on the stage of the Folies Bergère.

On the whole, there's nothing to suggest that Parisians would have been remotely excited if they had only heard and not seen Baker. Yet this misses the larger point in the big picture of her career: As Gary Giddins writes, "Don't make the mistake of judging Josephine Baker by her records alone. She was a terrible singer, but look at her two movies from the '30s (*Zouzou* and *Princess Tam Tam*) and you'll see why she had Paris by the short hairs. She could hold the stage like few entertainers." Baker cultivated and controlled her image like no superstar before or since—the body, the facial expressions—it's amazingly evident why she captured interwar Europe with her "look" alone—sexy, playful, innocent, adorable, childlike, and knowing.

There are more pleasing platters out there as well. *Josephine Baker* is a recommended two-CD set on the American label DCC Classics, although one wishes they had released it as two individual discs. Disc one, regrettably, consists of the twenty-five 1926–27 tracks complete, and disc two includes her 1930–36 recordings virtually complete. For some reason, a few of the 1936 titles are omitted; one of the two sides she made with an innovative German vocal group, the Comedian Harmonists, "Sous le Ciel d'Afrique," is included, but the other is not. Perhaps the producers figured that by skipping a few titles in the chronology they could squeeze in "La Conga Blicoti," one of the two very nice titles she made with the Lecuona Cuba Boys.

It would have been preferable for the producers to simply skip the twenties titles altogether, since her thirties work is vastly superior. In fact, one wishes they had done a three-CD package, covering all of her 1936–39 titles as well. Baker did her best work in the decade leading up to the war, and even though she would never quite be a world-class singer or a history-class one, her best sides have a considerable amount of charm.

After a three-year absence, Baker resumed recording in 1930 for French Columbia, with whom she would stay for the rest of the decade. Her first side was "La Petite Tonkinoise," an utterly disarming French music hall song (later reprised by Luise Rainer in *The Great Ziegfeld*). This spirited 3/4 piece is delivered by an ensemble mimicking a toy orchestra or a music box, while Baker sings it with the innocence of a little French girl. It's difficult to reconcile what one hears on this record with the images of a performer who was still prancing about onstage clad in less than either the Lady Eve or the Lady Godiva.

Where the Odeons are an uncomfortable attempt at sounding American, the Columbias are a delightful mix of local French songs, as well as both American and British songs in both French and English. At the same session as "Tonkinoise," she recorded for the first time her theme song, "J'ai Deux Amours," a text that accurately represents her status as a woman caught between two worlds, France and America, innocence and experience. The 1930 record is still captivating. After the verse and first chorus, Josephine is joined by an unidentified *chanteur,* a French tenor who sings the melody straight, while Baker hums and scats an obbligato around him—an effective way of illustrating the difference between the traditional French and the hot American approaches.

Baker gets melodramatic in "King for a Day" and offers a touch of Harlem in Fats Waller and Andy Razaf's equally theatrical "My Fate Is in Your Hands." "You're Driving Me Crazy" and "Confessin'" were pop tunes that American jazz bands, following Louis Armstrong's example, were doing a lot—and serve to balance her loftier, artier pieces like "Love Is a Dreamer." Some of her most effective efforts are the exotic ones, like "Aux les Hawaii," "Sous le Ciel d'Afrique," "La Conga Blicoti," and "Haiti."

Following the retreat of the Nazis, Baker resumed her recording career in 1944, although apparently only intermittently. It's hard to ascertain how much she actually recorded in the second half of her career, since none of the Baker bios includes a comprehensive discography; apparently even her biographers don't regard her music as worth cataloguing. Still, there are worthwhile tracks going up to the early seventies. "Zoubida" is both exotic and semiclassical, with Baker doing some wild coloratura stuff, while "Brazil" is the South American song that would become the definitive samba for North Americans, just as "Bésame Mucho" took the Mexican ideal of romance all over the world. "C'est Ça la Vrai Bonheur" (aka "Esto la Felicidad") from 1953 is an especially exciting French-Cuban mambo, with Baker intoning wordlessly over bongo drums. "C'est Lui," which she sang in the 1934 Zouzou, was also done by Nat Cole on his series of Spanish and Portuguese albums, and sounds better in her 1953 recording. She is a far more accomplished singer by the forties and fifties, and though still not quite a "great chanteuse," she is especially believable when she slips into the exotic mold.

La Baker continued recording into her sixties, although by this point performing in general took a back seat (she was only in her forties when she started giving farewell performances) to her political activities, participating in marches on Washington, raising money for civil rights causes, and capturing the attention of the world with her Rainbow Tribe, a miniclan of children of varying ethnic backgrounds and skin tones she'd adopted as a symbol of racial unity and lived with in her château.

Unlike the younger Lena Horne, who conspicuously acted like a role model (at the expense of her own personality, she often felt), Josephine Baker was never held up by herself or anyone else as an emblem of African American achievement. She was too much of an individual for that, even though the power of her temperament, the ego of a superdiva, was often a powerful force in breaking down the barriers of racism. Yet though she could never stand as a symbol for anything beyond herself, Josephine Baker, who died in 1975, remains one of the great icons of the twentieth century, with or without clothing or even bananas.

Elisabeth Welch (1904 or 1908–2003)

Unlike Adelaide Hall or Josephine Baker, Elisabeth Welch was never a super-duper superstar; as far as I know, she never received sackfuls of fan letters and marriage proposals, nor did counts and diplomats act like bally alley cats and threaten to kill themselves unless she gave them a tumble. She simply was an extremely talented singer and actress who realized very early on that there were more opportunities for her in England than in her native America; there was both less racism and less competition on the other side of the pond. As with Hall and Baker, her singing contained elements of Broadway, the blues, and jazz, with a distinct classical sound as well. However, she didn't create wildly funky wordless improvisations like Hall or strut about clad only in produce like Baker.

Welch does point up the connections that all of these twenties Afro-American-European songbirds had with Mabel Mercer. All of them learned their music in the teens and earlier, before even most African Americans outside the Deep South had ever encountered jazz or the blues. Proper middle-class young women were taught to sing in a very proper way—there are times when all of them sound very British, with rolled Rs and precise diction, like Mercer herself who was born and raised in England. Much of the time, especially on her many excellent later albums—by which time she'd spent many decades in London—Welch sounds very much like Mercer only with considerably less hoity-toity-ness and a much stronger sense of the beat.

Although the year of her birth is sometimes given as 1904, it is generally thought to be February 27, 1908. Born and raised in New York, Welch worked for a time with poverty-stricken children in a local community center. Unlike her fellow early African American expat songbirds, she formally studied acting and stagecraft. In 1923, she appeared in Miller and Lyles's revue Runnin' Wild, and even though the cast also included the rapidly rising Adelaide Hall, Welch was the one picked to star in what would be the show's biggest dance number, "The Charleston." She wasn't much of a dancer (she was strictly a singer), but nonetheless she and the chorus more than put the number over, helping establish the Charleston as the most significant dance of the decade.

In 1928, Welch again crossed paths with Hall in Lew Leslie's blockbuster sensation Blackbirds of 1928. (Hall's biographer, Iain Cameron Williams, interviewed Welch in 1993, and Welch made it clear that Hall had been a major inspiration, and that she had been very proud to be in the same production with her.) She recorded for the first time that year, with a studio group produced by Irving Mills, publisher of the McHugh-Fields Blackbirds score. It seems as if record producer Jack Kapp was already thinking in terms of something like an original cast album; four years later, he would gather as many of the original Blackbirds stars to record as much of the show's score as he could, but as early as 1928 he recorded three of the cast doing various songs from the production, starting with Welch doing "Doin' the New Low Down" and "Diga Diga Do" (which had been Hall's big showstopper on Broadway).

Welch's two 1928 sides with Mills would be her only American recordings for many decades. She first traveled to Europe with the wildly successful Moulin Rouge production of Blackbirds, and in 1930 was back in New York to appear in that resolutely New York–ish show The New Yorkers, starring, among others, Jimmy Durante and Fred Waring's Pennsylvanians (yes, the Pennsylvanians were among the New Yorkers), with a score by Cole Porter.

How New York–ish and how American was it? Even as a star in a successful show, Welch was hardly immune to bigotry. As the production originally opened, white singer Kathryn Crawford sang "Love for Sale," backed by the Girl Friends, the vocal trio from Waring's band. This Cole Porter standard, which uses prostitution as a metaphor for jaded love, created an immediate controversy, and the lyrics were banned on the radio for years to come. When the show opened, it was considered unacceptable that a quartet of white women should sing a song of "Love for Sale," but when a few weeks later the producers replaced Miss Crawford with Elisabeth Welch, no one seemed to mind; for a black woman to sing of prostitution was perfectly acceptable. It probably pleased her that she helped make "Love for Sale" into one of the most famous of all Cole Porter standards, and that Porter himself at least once cited the song as his favorite among his own works.

Whatever the case, having already experienced Europe she next headed back to that continent, where there were, apparently, no different standards for women of different-colored skins. In spring 1933, she was in Paris again, recording vocals on two titles done under the leadership of expatriate American banjo player Maceo Jefferson; whereas Duke Ellington and Ivie Anderson had introduced "Stormy Weather" in England, Welch was apparently the first to sing it and record it in France. Later that year, she traveled to England, originally to do another all-black revue, this one with the rather eyebrow-raising title of *Dark Doings,* and before 1933 ended she starred in another Cole Porter show in London, *Nymph Errant.*

The move turned out to be permanent. Having settled in London, Welch recorded scattershot for HMV up to 1940, primarily doing songs from her films and shows, such as "Solomon" from *Nymph Errant* and several from the movies *Glamorous Night* and *Big Fella*. She co-starred with Paul Robeson in two of his British productions (*Song of Freedom* and *Big Fella*), and sang with him on his HMV recording of "I Still Suits Me." Otherwise, she participated in three medleys with the New Mayfair Orchestra, one in tribute to impresario C. B. Cochran, another a collection of recent pop hits (the "Soft Lights and Sweet Music Medley") in 1934, and, four years later, a twenty-minute Gershwin posthumous homage.

Welch also had cameo roles, at least, in half a dozen or so British comedies and musicals: She's torchy and melodramatic singing "Yesterday's Thrill" in the 1936 *Soft Lights and Sweet Music,* then saucy, rhythmic, and exotic—and in glorious Technicolor no less—enacting the role of "Red Hot Annabelle" (which is sort of a rough, British equivalent of a rhumba) in the 1939 *Over the Moon*. She's also both torchy and exotic in jungle drag (hardly as revealing as Baker's, and only in black and white) as an African slave in ancient Rome moaning "Drums in My Heart" in *Fiddlers Three* (1944). She's totally winning in all three numbers (and they're all in beautiful quality on YouTube).

Her most memorable early recordings are six songs done over three sessions in 1936 with Benny Carter, who, at the time, was another visiting Yank. These are the best early slices of Welch's style: She's formal yet flexible, proper but warm and relaxed. (Like Welch, Carter, born in 1907, was active even as he approached his century mark; more's the pity that they never reunited for an album titled *Life Begins at 90.*)

Welch remained active, primarily as an actress, over the next forty years. She's probably best remembered on the stage for Ivor Novello's musical play *Arc de Triomphe* (1943) in which she sang "Dark Music." During the war, she traveled widely to entertain British troops, and in 1945 starred in the revue *Happy and Glorious* at the London Palladium. Filmwise, she made a lasting contribution as the cabaret singer Beulah in the chilling *Dead of Night;* she also appears in *This Was Paris* (1942), *Alibi* (1942), *Our Man in Havana* (1959), *Girl Stroke Boy* (1971), and *Arabian Adventure* (1979). In Derek Jarman's 1979 film of Shakespeare's *The Tempest*, she plays a "Goddess" who sings a totally charming vintage deco rendition of "Stormy Weather," and in Blake Edwards's *Revenge of the Pink Panther* (1978), she plays Mrs. Wu.

If life didn't actually begin at eighty for Welch, her career certainly received a major boost between 1986 and 1996. In these years, she was regularly featured on British television, generally in specials devoted to the music of the great songwriters. More important, she also recorded half a dozen or so excellent new albums. Some were done in New York, like *Where Have You Been*, named after a lesser-known Cole Porter song from *The New Yorkers*, and *Live in New York*. The latter was recorded in Carnegie Hall in 1989, while the equally excellent *In Concert* was recorded in England a few years earlier. Her British studio albums include the catch-all *This Thing Called Love* and two first-rate songbook sets, *The Irving Berlin Songbook* and *Elisabeth Welch Sings Jerome Kern.*

One would be hard-pressed to think of another artist who so completely blossomed in her ninth decade. She still sounds like a more rhythmically driven Mabel Mercer—there's the same supercareful articulation and British accent lite—but she's so warm and human that she never comes off like a musical Margaret Dumont, as Mercer occasionally did. Throughout the series, she breathes new life into both very familiar standards and songs, usually by upper-echelon writers, that are somewhat off the beaten path.

The two songbook packages, *Irving Berlin* and *Jerome Kern* (Welch's *Kern* is the best since Ella Fitzgerald and Margaret Whiting), have outstanding big band arrangements by Gordon Langford and a tunestack for the *Berlin* that varies between the well known—"How Deep Is the Ocean" and "The Song Is You"—and the seldom heard—"Fools Fall in Love," "Snookey Ookums" (many of us know it from *Easter Parade*, but Welch, unlike Judy Garland and Fred Astaire, sings the verse). The *Kern* includes quite a few of the composer's rarely sung, quasi-operatic pieces, like "The Night Was Made for Love," "Try to Forget," and "Don't Ever Leave Me."

Throughout the series, Welch varies between giving us what we expect, namely songs from her generation, the twenties and thirties, and surprising us with songs of a more recent vintage: "Long Before I Knew You" from *Bells Are Ringing* shows that she was covering the waterfront in finding suitable songs from shows across the decades. So does "Losing My Mind" from *Follies*, while "Song on the Sand" from *La Cage aux Folles* will more likely raise an eyebrow or two. She sings Kern's "Yesterdays" on her *Kern Songbook* and Paul McCartney's "Yesterday" on *This Thing Called Love*.

Her success with the classic songs derives both from her eighty years of sharpening her skills and her authority and authenticity; she not only personally knew most of these composers, she was singing these songs when they were new. My favorite of her albums is *In Concert*, on which she renders "The Man I Love" in strict 1924 style, with the verse, but makes it sound so fresh that you could easily believe the ink was still wet on George Gershwin's manuscript, as well as "Love for Sale," "Solomon," and "Experiment," three arias of untraditional love that sound as if Cole Porter himself were looking approvingly over her shoulder.

Yet she was also resolute in her conviction that music is not a museum, never more so than when (on *In Concert*) she sings Lincoln Chase's "Such a Night." This jumpy, jittery R&B classic from 1954, which became a hit for the Drifters, Johnnie Ray, and Elvis Presley (my single favorite Elvis disc, in fact), is a perfect piece of Welch showmanship, an eye-opener and a crowd-pleaser. Welch is irresistible here—approaching eighty, she's rocking and rolling—and reeling with the feeling, like a squealing teenager. She's even more lovable on "No Time at All," the Stephen Schwartz song from *Pippin* (also sung memorably by Bing Crosby), a brilliantly self-deprecating narrative about growing older that doggedly refuses to get sentimental or self-aggrandizing—it's the philosophical opposite of "My Way" and "Here's to Life." In all of her later performances especially, Elisabeth Welch is never anything less than an utter delight.

Welch died in 2003 (she was either ninety-nine or ninety-five, depending on which birth date you believe). It isn't enough to say that there was no one like her, either in the unique trajectory of her career or the quality of her music. Elisabeth Welch was a glorious one-of-a-kind product of the twentieth century who was singing through practically all of it.

Alberta Hunter (1895–1984)

Like Adelaide Hall and Elisabeth Welch, Alberta Hunter was a long-distance runner who enjoyed a revival at the end of her life and kept performing until she was almost ninety. She lived long enough to be extensively interviewed by journalists Frank C. Taylor (who in 1987 published the only full-length biography of the singer, *Alberta Hunter: A Celebration in Blues*) and Chris Albertson, who also wrote extensively about her. (The biographical information in this essay is taken largely from these two writers.)

Of the four major African American chanteuses who traveled from what was then still the provinces (the United States) to what remained the center of world culture (Europe), Alberta Hunter was the most deeply immersed in the blues. She was the only one of the four who without question was a major figure in the classic blues movement. She would be worthy of history's attention even if the only thing she had done was to write (with pianist Lovie Austin) "Down Hearted Blues," one of the classic songs of the era, and the tune that launched Bessie Smith's recording career. But she herself also made dozens of the very best records in the form, including, in the finest classic blues tradition, sessions with the leading jazz soloists of the day, including Louis Armstrong and Sidney Bechet, under the direction of the two leading pianist-bandleaders of the Jazz Age, Fletcher Henderson and Clarence Williams.

Her total time in Europe was considerably shorter than that of Baker, Welch, and Hall, all of whom settled in London or Paris, yet Hunter had enough impact on the English music scene to be considered a very important part of the African American expatriate movement. In retrospect, the greatest mistake she made in her career was not staying longer on the far side of the Big Pond.

Alberta Hunter was a professional singer, well known in her own community, well before the blues or jazz had arrived in Chicago, let alone to London. She was born in 1895 in Memphis, Tennessee, and, according to Albertson, may have come to Chicago to become a professional singer as early as 1906—when she was eleven. As the young Alberta began singing for coins in the lowest of low dives, her repertoire consisted mainly of sentimental old faves like "Where the River Shannon Flows" (then a current hit), songs that moved the pimps, whores, and pickpockets—even the police—to tears.

She sang her way upwards to a succession of increasingly classy black clubs: Hoskins, the De Luxe, the Panama. At the Panama, she told Albertson, she sang "St. Louis Blues" to a celebrity-laden crowd—including Al Jolson and Bert Williams, who was hearing it for the first time. Her early arrival in the Windy City ensured that she would be in on the ground floor of the massive African American migration from the South to Chicago during World War I, as well as on the breakthrough of jazz and blues occurring around the same time. "I didn't really go to town," she said, "until I hit the Dreamland." At the dawn of the Jazz Age, the Dreamland Ballroom was the premium emporium for "colored" talent in Chicago. At the time Mamie Smith's "Crazy Blues" broke out, Hunter, billed as "the Southside Sweetheart," was singing there, backed for a time by New Orleans trumpet legend Joe "King" Oliver.

In 1921, Hunter, now living in New York, recorded for the first time, with a band led by Henderson—although the emerging bandleader was based in New York, the band was billed on the labels as "Ray's Dreamland Orchestra," so famous was Hunter's connection to the Chicago nightspot. She made her first two discs for Black Swan, where Henderson was musical director, and then spent most of the rest of the acoustic era recording for Paramount and (briefly) Gennett. After the release of her first Paramount, her own lyric to "Down Hearted Blues" (which she'd been singing and working on since she was a little girl), Frank Walker of Okeh Records tried to entice her to switch labels. When she couldn't, Walker satisfied his desire to record the song by cutting it with Bessie Smith. In other words, the entire recording career of Smith began with a cover of an Alberta Hunter song.

In 1925–26 Hunter did record for Okeh and after that did an exceptionally well-recorded series of sessions for Victor Records. She sang in a rich, deep voice but also had the ultraprecise articulation that we associate with prejazz singers of the Gay Nineties and the turn of the century—no doubt that helped endear her to early A&R men and made her that much more desirable an asset on a record company roster. Even on prehistoric equipment (and the stuff she was singing into for Paramount was far inferior to that being used at, say, Victor) it's impossible to miss a word of what she's singing.

The voice is robust and very warm, and certainly full of character. Perhaps it was an advantage that she was then pushing thirty, and was already a highly seasoned performer, when she began recording regularly. Even her first version of "Down Hearted Blues," done in 1921 with a band conducted by songwriter Eubie Blake, is good. She sounds a little like the rather stiff singers we associate with the acoustic era, but there's plenty of jazz phrasing, too, in the way she inserts pauses and rests and emphasizes certain notes over others. Then, too, there are no shortage of blues cadences throughout—this is no sanitized imitation of the blues, this is as close to the real thing as had yet been captured on wax. The accompanying band starts by sounding like one of those early march-dance orchestras so popular in the teens (Sousa, Prince), but as the record proceeds, they follow Hunter's lead and get looser and jazzier.

Her most frequently reissued vocals are her Gennett sessions, done in November and December 1924, under the aegis of producer Clarence Williams. She sounds better than ever, but the main selling point for most jazz collectors is the presence of Louis Armstrong (on all) and Sidney Bechet (on most) of these; now the band has more than caught up with her. She's down and despondent on the 16-bar blues "Nobody Knows the Way I Feel 'Dis Mornin',' " but a little more upbeat on "Early Every Morn" when she sings of how she likes "a little lovin' " at that particular point in the a.m., with Armstrong making his presence felt via a dynamite cornet break in the coda. On "Cake-Walkin' Babies from Home" she's downright exuberant, as half of a vocal duo with singer Clarence Todd, whom she immediately overshadows.

She also enjoyed a rewarding relationship with Fats Waller: The young pianist accompanied her on one of his very first sessions, done for Paramount in 1923, and they enjoyed a memorable reunion at Victor in 1927. Waller was playing pipe organ on that date, and there are not many singers with a voice powerful enough and diction clear enough to be heard against that overwhelming instrument. The titles include two jazz classics, "Sugar" and "Beale Street Blues," and while the third may sound like a dud, "I'm Going to See My Ma" is actually the fastest and snappiest of the bunch. Hunter is on the beat, and swinging. (In 1935, she recorded three titles with an unknown pianist. When he—whoever he is—solos on "You Can't Tell the Difference After Dark," she cheers him on with "Look out, Fats Waller!" High praise indeed.)

Hunter arrived in Europe for the first time in August 1927, initially to play several spots in Paris, Nice, and elsewhere in France. While there, she received an offer from another black American expat, songwriter Noble Sissle, who was then staging a revue in London. Now in England, she attracted the attention of Jerome Kern and Oscar Hammerstein, who were working on the London production of *Show Boat*, which had just opened very successfully in New York. In the choice of the two major black roles, Queenie and Joe, the London edition was a marked improvement over Broadway, in that Tess "Aunt Jemima" Gardella (a white entertainer who specialized in blackface) and Jules Bledsoe (regarded as a second-string Paul Robeson) had performed the roles in New York, whereas Alberta Hunter and the real Paul Robeson took over in London. The only regret is that she never recorded "Can't Help Lovin' Dat Man" or her other *Show Boat* numbers, which is strange, because even at this early point the English were usually very thorough about documenting notable West End performances.

For the next ten years she would be shuttling back and forth among the States, England, and France. There was a one-shot session for Columbia in 1929, and then in 1934 she turns up, most surprisingly, with Jack Jackson and his Hotel Dorchester Orchestra, one of the top British dance bands. This was a mainstream white orchestra that played hot dance music. She made twelve sides with Jackson, in which she moved from lines like "I got myself some pig meat and I don't want you no more" to songs that described sex and death no less vividly in lines like "Miss Otis regrets she's unable to lunch today." She had become so continental by this point that it's said Noel Coward wrote "I Travel Alone" for her.

The twelve Hunter-Jackson sides—including "Miss Otis Regrets"—are also notable in that they are the only recordings from her career that aren't featured in a five-CD series from the (Austrian, later Scottish) label Document Records that otherwise includes all her 78 era recordings. Document is a blues-driven concern and these are most decidedly Hunter's least bluesy records, although the Jackson group is a fine, hot band.

Back in New York, Hunter did three sessions between 1935 and the war (all on volume five of the Document series and most on *Alberta Hunter: The '20s and '30s* on Jass), all of a blues nature. These fourteen tracks contain some of the best work of her entire career. She starts with one of the most controversial titles, "You Can't Tell the Difference After Dark," which, like Razaf and Waller's "Black and Blue," discusses how dark-skinned women were somehow considered less desirable in the uptown pecking order. In the bridge she sings, "They say that gentlemen prefer the blonde-haired ladies / Tell me, am I out of style because my color's slightly shady?" "Send Me a Man" is a double entendre number that has been an eternal staple of classic blues revivalists, like the contemporary Carrie Smith.

Recording for Decca in 1939 (according to Taylor, her fees had gone way down by this time), Hunter cut six excellent sides with an all-star band of Charlie Shavers (trumpet), Buster Bailey (clarinet), Lil Hardin Armstrong (piano), Wellman Braud (bass), and no drummer, in the twenties style. She was the first artist after Billie Holiday to tackle Lady Day's self-penned Commodore hit "Fine and Mellow," which she renders very respectably—with somewhat more old-fashioned (not to mention better) diction than Holiday's. Likewise, "Down Hearted Blues" is a fine upgrade of Hunter's own biggest hit as a songwriter, while "Someday, Sweetheart" is essentially an adaptation by Jelly Roll Morton of an old folk blues called "Tricks Ain't Walkin'," which Hunter had recorded in 1921 for Black Swan.

Her final prewar date was also first-rate, done only with pianist Eddie Heywood (before "Canadian Sunset") for Bluebird, consisting of four of her own compositions. The ballad "The Love I Have for You" has Heywood making his piano sound like a harp, and "My Castle's Rockin' " may well be Hunter's most essential record. It's a declaration of a sensibility in the spirit of Fats Waller's "The Joint Is Jumpin'," Helen Humes's "They Raided the Joint," Nellie Lutcher's "Hurry on Down," Big Joe Turner's "Shake, Rattle and Roll," or even Bill Haley's "Rock Around the Clock." Hunter and Heywood create a festive, rowdy mood that's impossible to resist. Like these other, younger artists, Hunter makes a signature song out of a clarion call to party: to indulge in music, dancing, booze, or whatever else happens to rock your particular castle.

Then came the war, and Hunter spent most of the next dozen years entertaining American troops via the USO. Between 1946 and 1952 she did several dates for small labels, but nothing much came of them, the most memorable title being a "Fine and Mellow" blues variation entitled "He's Got a Punch Like Joe Lewis." In 1956, she left showbiz (she thought, at the time, permanently) and got her license to work as a registered nurse. Now sixty-two, she had to lie about her age to be allowed to receive her training and then to work, and twenty-one years later, she was forced to retire—which, again, would have happened a lot sooner had her actual age been known.

Of the four women in this section, Hunter was the only one who didn't remain in Europe, and the only one who was pressured out of the music business during changing times. For her part, Hunter never complained or said, "I'm quitting because I can't get any work." Rather, she explained that she had reached a point in her life where caring for her fellow man meant more to her than dealing with the frustrations of show business.

Yet Hunter had a comeback like no one else's. During her twenty-one-year absence from regular work, she actually recorded twice (notably the fine *Alberta Hunter with Lovie Austin's Blues Serenaders,* produced by Chris Albertson for Riverside Records in 1961). After involuntarily retiring from the nursing profession in 1977, she was asked by Bobby Short to sing at a party for Mabel Mercer. It was there that she met Charlie Bourgeois of Festival (George Wein) Productions, who subsequently introduced her to Barney Josephson. The veteran club-owner served as her manager for the remaining stretch of her career, and built his new establishment, the Cookery (on the corner of Eighth Street and University Place), around her.

Even more than Maxine Sullivan or Helen Humes, Alberta Hunter was very much a living legend in her last decade. Using the Cookery as her home base, she traveled all over the country and then the world. She was now a media event—her picture plastered in all the magazines, her story on TV news shows. Josephson negotiated as much well-paying work for her as possible. In a sense, he might have negotiated a bit too well: Humes and Sullivan worked for considerably less money, and as a result, made lots of records—mostly for small-budget independent jazz firms—in their last years. After her rediscovery in 1977, Hunter made only four albums, all for the considerably better-fixed Columbia Records: *Remember My Name* (1977), *Amtrak Blues* (1979), *The Glory of Alberta Hunter* (1981), and *Look for the Silver Lining* (1983).

As far as I can determine, only the second of

these, *Amtrak Blues*, has been made available on CD, and it may be currently out of print. But taken together, these four octogenarian statements form a strong last hurrah. Hunter's voice and style had aged remarkably well, and her spirit and personality were more powerful than ever. Largely produced by John Hammond, the four Columbia albums employ a well-chosen mixture of young and veteran swing-style players, presenting both old favorites and tunes new to Hunter. *Glory* has two particularly astute choices in the traditional hymn "Ezekiel Saw the Wheel" and the Yiddish love song "I Love You Much Too Much" (Ich Hob Dich Tzufil Lieb).

Alberta Hunter died after a long illness in 1984. When I saw her in those later years, she was a feisty old woman who delivered a song as if it was a sermon. In between songs, instead of talking about herself and her music, she would encourage her listeners to go out and help the sick and the poor. "Next time you see someone sleeping on the street, lend him a helping hand. Maybe he's not just drunk, maybe he's sick." Hunter's eighty-nine years among us are not only a monument to the healing power of music, but also to the indomitable nature of the human spirit.

There'll Always Be an England

Hutch (Leslie Hutchinson)
Layton & Johnstone
Gracie Fields

There were few major pop singers per se in thirties Britain, and they existed mainly as a subset of the two major entertainment forms, musical theater and dance bands. The three major mediums for disseminating pop music—recordings, radio, and talking pictures—were all invented in America, but the Brits glommed on to them with the speed of summer lightning. Yet in the U.K., the equation among the three was differently skewed. In America, the twenties recording boom ended with the Depression; by contrast, in England the record biz seemed to be just getting started as the twenties turned into the thirties. All the major British bands were incredibly prolific even in the depths of the Depression—Ambrose and His Orchestra released well over 350 sides between 1927 and 1932, and they weren't even the busiest. As popular as the name bands were in New York and Chicago, they seem to have been even more so in London.

The entire country was band-crazy; Britain had its share of song and dance stars, although, while British shows of the twenties and thirties were, by and large, as good as anything on Broadway, the British movie musicals could hardly compare with Hollywood, despite song-and-dancers like Jessie Matthews and Jack Buchanan. Nearly all the best singers were affiliated with the dance bands, even apart from Al Bowlly: Sam Browne, Elsie Carlisle, Pat O'Malley, Dan Donovan, and Australian-born Brian Lawrance.

Apart from the stage and the bands, the country's leading purveyor of song, without question, was Leslie Hutchinson, better known as Hutch. At the same time, the most popular—and distinctly British—figure throughout the Depression and the war, on both records and in a long series of films, was Gracie Fields, known to several generations of Brits as "Our Gracie." A look at the two of them reveals something unique about popular music—and about British taste on the whole.

Hutch (Leslie Hutchinson) (1900–1969)

Was Britain still setting trends in the entertainment world by the thirties? Not as much as at the turn of the century, but it still had at least a vestigial influence. One worthwhile point of comparison is the relationship among Jack Buchanan, Fred Astaire, and Gene Kelly. Kelly once supposedly described himself as "Fred Astaire for truck drivers," which meant that he did the song and dance stuff that Astaire did but without Astaire's sophisticated, debonair approach. At the same time, I can well imagine that Astaire thought of himself as "Jack Buchanan for truck drivers." Remember, Astaire never relished the whole romantic, partner-dancing thing; he thought of himself as a manly man who seems to have preferred his acrobatic solo dances to having to cope with a lot of silly females. In the same way that Sinatra repeatedly denounced "My Way," Astaire consistently said that he disliked getting decked out in top hat and tails; they may have been his signature, but they just weren't his thing.

To find the real sophisticated and debonair song and dance man, one must turn to Jack Buchanan. Before him, song and dance acts were generally on the lower rung of the British variety profession, pearlies and cockneys and provincials who made dancing something similar to slapstick comedy. Buchanan was the first to transform the song and dance man into a figure of romance, and whenever either Astaire or Kelly did romantic partner dancing, they were beholden to Buchanan, even though they did it so much better than he did.

Leslie Hutchinson did for the art of the romantic pianist-singer what Jack Buchanan did for the song and dance man. He was the embodiment of the combination cocktail pianist and crooner, best experienced late at night in a small club, having no problem being seen through the smoke and heard over the sound of glasses tinkling and martinis being shaken, not stirred. He was the archetype of the singing pianist, the foundation for Bobby Short, Nat Cole, Matt Dennis, Michael Feinstein, Eric Comstock and every other romantically motivated piano player–vocalist. The others could perhaps outswing him or outemote him, but no one could out-debonair him. Compared to Hutch, they were *all* truck drivers.

By a coincidence, the three most popular male singers in interwar England were born in neither America nor the U.K.: Richard Tauber, the widely loved operetta tenor, was a German Jew who fled that country in the wake of Hitler; Al Bowlly was a South African of Lebanese and Greek descent and came to London by way of Singapore, Calcutta, and Berlin; and Leslie Hutchinson was born and raised in Grenada. As Charlotte Breese noted in her 1999 biography, *Hutch*, being from the West Indies already gave him an advantage. For one thing, he grew up bilingual (he was "bi" in other ways, too, or so Ms. Breese informs us), and his ability to speak and sing in perfect French as well as the Queen's English would later serve him well. No less important was his West Indian attitude. The Grenadans had no heritage of slavery, and thus weren't precon-ditioned to accept the status of second-class citizen. He did indeed come to America in his late teens, but was quickly driven away by the racism he found here.

Leslie Hutchinson's father made hats and sold dry goods; Hutchinson Senior was also musical, and played the organ in church. As a youngster, Leslie operated the hand pump for the instrument and practiced keyboard on a harmonium the Hutchin-sons kept at home. When it dawned on him, at age sixteen, that a musical career would be impossible in Grenada, he left for New York, at first working as an elevator boy, and tried to acclimate himself to a North American winter. By then he was an accom-plished pianist, and gradually he started to penetrate black show business. He began working the private party circuit, primarily in Harlem, and made his first recordings in 1923 as accompanist for several vocal-ists, most notably the first famous blues singer, Mamie Smith. In 1924 and 1925, he played piano for banjoist bandleader Elmer Snowden (who had once employed the young Duke Ellington himself in that chair). When the band played a resort in Palm Beach, Florida, Hutchinson was dismayed to learn that he and his fellow Snowdenites were forced to lodge in the colored section of town and prohibited from mixing with the white guests. To make matters worse, the band was terrorized by the Ku Klux Klan. "I left America as soon as possible," Hutch later said, "and went to work in Paris."

The Hutch story really begins in Europe, which is where he began working under that name. At first he found work playing piano in dance bands and accompanying singers, while gradually establishing himself as a vocalist in his own right. Early on, he attracted the attention and support of Cole Porter just at a time when this wealthy young American songwriter was first coming into his own. At one point, Porter brought Hutchinson to Venice to lead a band in a particularly spectacular shindig he was throwing at the height of the Jazz Age and economic boom. Hutch was perhaps the first great interpreter of Porter's songs, and with his combination of mas-culine presence, delicate charm, and attention to detail he seems to have sung and played Porter's songs in precisely the way that the composer-lyricist himself would have wanted to.

Thanks both to Porter's help and his own relent-less ambition, Hutch rapidly rose in both European society and show business. C. B. Cochran, the Ziegfeld of England, hired Hutch to play in the pit band for the revue *One Damn Thing After Another* (score by Rodgers and Hart), and in the next few years he would also appear in shows by Noel Cow-ard (*This Year of Grace*, with Jessie Matthews and Sonny Hale) and Porter (*Wake Up and Dream* and *Cochran's 1930 Revue*). In 1927, he accompanied Helen Morgan on "Me and My Shadow," in which he joined the visiting American star briefly in song, and Jessie Matthews on "My Heart Stood Still." It was Matthews, Hutch later said, who encouraged him to sing: "But for this girl my career might never have happened."

At the start of the thirties, Hutch was no longer in the pit but onstage: He was a genuine star, on a par with, or even exceeding, the African American Ethel Waters on Broadway and the African Ameri-can Josephine Baker in Paris. He was quite possibly the most celebrated and respected black male enter-tainer in the world (on a par with Paul Robeson)—and he was the first and only African American male permitted to sing "sophisticated" love songs (and not "about work or blues or some dumb crap," as Billy Eckstine put it) until Nat Cole and Eckstine himself a decade later. Hutch was a star in variety, touring theaters everywhere, playing nightclubs in every spot on the continent that hadn't been con-quered by the Nazis, occasionally appearing on radio (which did not dominate in England as thoroughly as it did in the States) and recording. And recording and recording. From 1931 to 1940, he was under contract to Parlophone, for whom he cut an esti-mated four hundred songs. In this regard he approached Bing Crosby. (Though not with Bowlly, Buddy Clark, Dick Robertson, and others who recorded equally prolifically but only as semi-anonymous band vocalists, not stars.) Hutch seems to have documented every major song of the era, film or show or independent, American or English, sentimental or swinging.

In his love life, Hutch was equally democratic. Biographer Breese links him romantically to every-one from Lady Edwina Mountbatten to Cole Porter himself (no surprise there). He was actively involved with lovers of both sexes, poets and peasants, lords and ladies, losers and louses. He was the great heart-throb of his era, and he utilized an arsenal of tricks. He specialized in visual gestures, certain bits of busi-ness with his handkerchief, for instance, that were carefully calculated to make feminine hearts flutter. Bobby Short once recalled to me how Hutch's name came up in a conversation with the aging duchess of something or other, and she said, "Hutch? Oh yes, Father threw him down the stairs once." There was then a pregnant pause before her ladyship added, "Can't imagine why."

His most important element was his chops: Even sixty to seventy years later, that voice of his still drips elegance. No one pays as much attention to detail as Hutch does; no singer until Sinatra was as determined to extract every little nuance from a lyric and a melody. Given this description, one might expect him to sound effeminate or overly mannered. Far from it; although he doesn't have a character-type voice, like Louis Armstrong or some of the blues singers of the era, Hutch's baritone is deep and masculine, if a touch fruity. He sounds sensitive and tender, yet at the same time manly and robust. At his best, he combines a deep chesty sound, comparable to his friend and contemporary Paul Robeson's, with a zest for what Blossom Dearie would call "East Side"–style lyric interpretation that anticipates Bobby Short, his greatest and most direct heir. (Hutch made his records that much more enjoyable to future generations by including as much of each song as he could, which almost always meant verses, and, in the case of "Sophisticated Lady" and "You Go to My Head," additional lyrics of the chorus that I suspect must be original Hutch concoctions.)

Hutch's 1929 "What Is This Thing Called Love" (which Jessie Matthews sang in *Wake Up and Dream*, very likely accompanied by him) is perhaps his first perfect record. The disc opens with a Chinese-style gong (probably gonged by Hutch himself), which adds to the minor key mood of the piece. Early versions of the Porter song start with a distinctive vamp. Following the gong, Hutch elaborates considerably on the vamp, stretching it out with an insinuating stop-and-start rhythm, heightening the suspense with unresolved chords. He then takes us through the verse, ever stepping up the drama; back in 1929, the whole song was new and unfamiliar, and the verse is still pretty much unknown today.

With the record two-thirds over, Hutch still hasn't dropped so much as a hint of the now familiar words and melody, but finally resolves the tension by playing and singing the chorus. Throughout he uses both Porter's fascination with minor keys and a steady, undulating beat to create a mood of seduction, and like any good seducer, he leaves us (after a single run-through of the verse and chorus) wanting more. The voice is an octave or two higher than we're used to hearing it, a few steps closer to the tenor/falsetto range popular in the twenties, but otherwise this is quintessential Hutch, evidencing his classic blend of the highly sophisticated with the earthy, the primitive, and the sensual.

Hutch was occasionally accompanied by a small orchestra, sometimes billed as "Hutch and His Charm Music," more frequently so after he switched from Parlophone to HMV in 1940. (However, the first two in the new series, a pair of Porter songs heard in *The Broadway Melody of 1940*, "Begin the Beguine" and "I've Got My Eyes on You," use only piano.)

Two of my particular favorites from the early forties are songs more closely identified with other, younger, black male singers: "Flamingo," the theme song of Herb Jeffries, and "Sand in My Shoes," a signature for Bobby Short. On both of these, Hutch demonstrates his willingness to give his audiences a touch of Caribbean and South American rhythms—as if the sight of a six-foot-plus black man in an extra-large tailcoat wasn't exotic enough in wartime London. It's somewhat surprising to hear him do mid-forties and postwar hits like "There, I've Said It Again" and "Now Is the Hour" in a style that hadn't changed since before the Depression. He sounds less incongruous now, seventy years after the fact, than he did then—a good singer is a still a good singer and a good song is still a good song—but he was obviously becoming something of an anachronism, the symbol of prewar elegance carrying on into the era of postwar deprivation and shortages.

Hutch continued recording unabated until 1948; his total output is probably somewhere between six hundred and seven hundred masters. The capaciousness of his catalogue is both a blessing and a curse, the former in that, if one collects British 78s it is at least possible to hear Hutch performing virtually every major song of the golden age. The downside is that the sheer enormity of his work probably means that there will never be any kind of comprehensive collection. It's theoretically possible, since both Parlophone and HMV are today controlled by EMI, but it seems unlikely that any label will have such faith in Hutch's sales potential as to issue a twenty-five-CD box. Several dozen samplers and greatest hits collections have been made available (including the recommended *That Old Feeling* and *Leslie Hutch Hutchinson*, which draws from his forties sides; Living Era has also issued two collections, *Treasured Memories* and the generous double disc *Begin the Beguine*), but these constitute a mere drop in the ocean of Hutchinson.

If such a megaultimate collection is ever issued, I would accept it on whatever terms the record label chooses to give it to us. But I'd rather the compilers followed the format of the recommended collection *Hutch Sings Cole Porter, Noel Coward and Others* (Conifer). Rather than simply lay out the tracks in the order in which they were recorded, as most reissues of 78 era music do, why not organize them along thematic lines? Group the songs by composer and by source, do volumes of "Songs from British Shows" and "Songs from American Films." The Conifer disc starts with fifteen individual selections of Hutch doing Porter from 1929–43 and ends with his two-sided 12" Porter medley of 1940. It makes an articulate case that although Hutch's glory years were over by the time the long-playing album was perfected, his singles can, in fact, be compiled into comprehensive songbook packages.

He recorded only a dozen or so sides after 1948, although he continued to tour cabarets around the globe (spending lots of time in India in the fifties). When he died, in 1969, he was completely marginalized, a specialized taste rather than the epitome of mass appeal that he had been thirty years earlier. Supposedly there were only fifty people at his memorial service.

Yet in his day Hutch (who seems to have completely ignored America—at least after 1927—and vice versa) was a towering figure of Britpop. As mentioned, he was part of the worlds of both the musical theater, having appeared in many West End revues, and the dance band world, since he occasionally fronted such ensembles, was backed by them on record, and virtually every disc he made can be used for dancing purposes. Yet even when surrounded by a full musical cast or a whole orchestra, Hutch was essentially a solo performer; other artists were just so much window dressing to him. By the same token, it didn't matter whether he was playing before a packed house or for a single customer—or whether the chap he was performing for was some bloke who drove a lorry or the bloomin' Duke of Windsor.

Layton & Johnstone
Turner Layton (1894–1978)
Clarence Johnstone (1885–1953)

Hutch was a singularly unique figure: There was no one remotely like him anywhere in the world at the time. The closest thing he had to a competitor was Turner Layton, an African American songwriter, pianist, and singer, who worked in interwar England both as a soloist, and, most successfully, as part of a celebrated duo with singer Clarence "Tandy" Johnstone. Layton was the son of a music teacher in Washington, D.C. (making him part of the same general generation of black professionals as Duke Ellington); he went to medical school briefly before choosing a career in music. At twenty-four, Layton, along with his original partner, Henry Creamer, wrote their first all-time jazz and pop standard, the perennial "After You've Gone." In 1920, Creamer & Layton performed on Broadway and, in 1921, recorded for Black Swan Records (founded by W. C. Handy's former business partner, Harry Pace), and over the next few years they played in further all-Negro revues and wrote additional songs, including at least two other early jazz classics, "Way Down Yonder in New Orleans" and "Strut Miss Lizzie." In 1930, Layton would write still another jazz standard, "If I Could Be with You One Hour Tonight" (with James P. Johnson).

Around 1922, Layton met Clarence Johnstone, who was nine years older and at that time a veteran entertainer working as a songplugger for W. C. Handy's publishing company. (It's said in several sources that Johnstone was born in Harlem, which would make him a pioneer of sorts, since upper Manhattan was not yet a black neighborhood.) After meeting Johnstone, Layton decided to adjust his focus: from composing to performing, from Creamer to Johnstone as a partner, and from New York to London as a base of operations.

The new team found steady work together in Anglo nightclubs, and then made their "legit" debut in the 1924 revue *Elsie Janis at Home*. In 1924 they began recording steadily for Columbia Records' British imprint. Thus, they actually were big stars well before anyone had heard of Hutch, and, like him, they were among the most popular acts of the late twenties and early thirties. According to Peter Dempsey (in his notes to *Bye, Bye Blackbird*, a 2002 CD from Living Era, from which some of these factoids have been lifted), the team sold an estimated 10 million discs worldwide. As noted by John Norbury (on his Web site restoring78s.com), their versions of "All Alone" and "(You Forgot To) Remember" (both by Irving Berlin) sold three-quarters of a million copies each, while their single big hit was "Sonny Boy," which sold a cool mill. Not bad for that period—or any period.

Layton & Johnstone appeared at the very apogee of a unique showbiz phenomenon: tenor-baritone duets. These were especially popular in the early twentieth century and the pioneering years of sound recording. The early team of Arthur Collins (baritone) and Byron Harlan (tenor) were recording both together and separately at the very turn of the century, their own work often being steeped in burned-cork minstrelsy traditions. It might be said that the tenor-baritone duo was one of the first forms encouraged by technology: the combination recorded very well, and many teams were spontaneously put together for recording purposes—both Victor and Columbia used the format frequently, often with Henry Burr singing the tenor part. By the twenties, the flagship t&b team was Billy Jones and Ernest Hare, billed as the Happiness Boys (direct inspiration, on many levels, for the Rhythm Boys and the Sunshine Boys, among many others). Like Jones & Hare, Van & Schenk were also extremely popular, and sustained their stardom long enough to star in early talking pictures—most famously the 1930 *They Learned About Women*. Even Paul Robeson's famous early recordings of spirituals, in which he was accompanied by the piano and voice of Lawrence Brown, have a similar t&b feeling.

Layton & Johnstone were clearly in the Jones & Hare/Van & Schenk tradition; Johnstone sang in what was described as a "Negro *tenorino*," using the upper part of the harmony line, while Layton accompanied him with both a baritone voice and the piano. The two voices are highly distinctive: Johnstone is a delightfully old-fashioned tenor, while the younger Layton sounds more like a contemporary crooner. *The Times* of London described the two, beginning with the older man, as "an attractive figure, tall, with grey hair, [who] stood by the piano, which his partner played so pleasantly."

In fact, they both sound a lot like Hutch—Johnstone is a high Hutch, and Layton is a low Hutch. Compared to the earlier t&b teams, L&J on the whole sound much more like part of the modern, electrical era. Their work is much less vaudevillian: The Happiness Boys did a lot of comedy and topical songs, L&J were much more romantic—the *Bye, Bye Blackbird* compilation includes almost nothing but superior standards to be, many of which are show and film tunes: Irving Berlin ("Always"), Rodgers & Hart ("Blue Moon"), Arthur Schwartz ("Louisiana Hayride"), Vincent Youmans ("Time on My Hands") and some very European stuff ("Oh, Donna Clara," "Auf Weiderseh'n, My Dear"). Their work, at least the samples I've been able to hear, is excellent overall—mark them down as yet another Britpop act of the period (along with Hutch & Gracie) worthy of additional reissues and research. (Norbury estimates that during the eleven years of their collaboration, the team recorded 1,008 numbers—which seems extremely high.) The mere fact that they had charm and musicianship enough to compete with Hutch speaks volumes about them.

Sadly, the partnership ended ingloriously: Johnstone became enmeshed in a scandal that rocked British society almost as thoroughly as the debacle involving Prince Edward and Mrs. Simpson in 1936. The singer, who was already (and inconveniently) married, was named as the correspondent in a divorce case with a younger white woman, Raymonde Sandler, the wife of a famous violinist. Anyone who had made the mistake of thinking of Europe as being somehow more enlightened than the U.S.A. was in for a rude awakening. Layton & Johnstone were booed from the stage wherever they appeared, and their extant contracts were cancelled left and right.

Johnstone had no choice but to flee the country, and he headed back to Harlem, where the next catastrophe waiting to land on his head came in the form of the Internal Revenue Service. He married Mrs. Sandler, but she left him after eight years, and he died in total obscurity ten years after that. The irony is that Hutch was famously involved in dozens of affairs, with both women and men, married and single, white and whatever, but he was smart enough to make sure that they never blew up in his face. (Obviously, it helped that Hutch was a confirmed commitment-phobe—he certainly never married a white woman.) Possibly, Hutch's bad-boy behavior was part of his charm—like Sinatra a generation later, he was a glamorous antihero—whereas Layton & Johnstone were society's darlings.

Turner continued on as a solo act, vocal and piano, making (according to Norbury) an additional four hundred or so sides from 1935 to the postwar era. An anthology of his late thirties sides, *Thanks for the Memory* (Happy Days) shows that he sounds quite like Hutch—which is to say very good indeed—but while the later sides have many excellent moments, on the whole they lack the charm and originality of the best L&J titles. Turner apparently was not tainted by his ex-partner's scandal, and endeared himself further to the Brits by remaining in London during the war and the blitz, entertaining the troops and supporting the English war effort like a native son. Into the fifties and sixties, Turner remained a popular personality in Great Britain, first on radio and then on television. According to his official bio, the royalties of his songs are currently subsidizing a hospital in London.

Layton & Johnstone remain a morality play for the twentieth century—they make it clear why, for instance, Lena Horne and Lennie Hayton had to be married in total secrecy in 1947. In 1993, the BBC produced a radio drama on their lives, starring Lenny Henry and Clarke Peters. "It was a painful story, but the business of marrying a white woman struck a real chord," said Henry, whose own wife was the no-less-white comedienne Dawn French. "They went from being the nation's favourites to ruffians whom everyone felt should be kicked out of the country."

Bye bye blackbird, indeed.

Gracie Fields (1898–1979)

As I've stated, Leslie Hutchinson and Gracie Fields were the two most recorded stars of interwar England. They shared the bill at several benefits and all-star shows, but apart from how they were both beloved by British audiences, the two could not have been more different. Hutch celebrated the singularity of the British individual; as we've noted, you could see him surrounded by a full musical comedy cast or a fifteen-piece dance orchestra and yet not notice anybody else onstage—accompanying himself at the piano, he was essentially a one-man entertainment unit.

Gracie Fields, on the other hand, celebrated British solidarity and community. As the late British film historian William K. Everson (who grew up on Fields) pointed out, virtually every Gracie Fields film ended with her leading a sing-along with a chorus of jolly chums. The principal plot of all her films is her efforts to help others, often the entire community. *Sing as We Go* concerns itself with Gracie's efforts to get a factory reopened, and when it does, she and her mates break into the title song—and sing it as they go; in *Shipyard Sally* it's basically the same idea.

Fields was as widely beloved in her country as Kate Smith was in ours—and both were domestic faves who served their nations particularly well as morale boosters during the Depression and then the war. But the appeal of both Fields and Smith rarely crossed international boundaries. (I ask you, can one get any more British than a song like "I Like a Nice Cup of Tea"?) Smith is one of the few major American vocalists of almost any era who have never been the subject of a reissue series in England, Europe, or Japan, and Fields's recordings and films have rarely been experienced outside the U.K. Smith's one film, *Hello, Everybody!*, like most of Fields's, has her helping others to find romantic happiness rather than serving as leading lady herself. But despite its jocular title, *Hello, Everybody!* is rather melancholy; Sister Katie is pining for lost loves whereas Our Gracie revels in her role as Miss Fix-It. In songs like "Clogs and Shawl," Fields was virtually the voice of British industry, defeating the Depression by outshouting it.

Where Hutch's bread-and-butter was Cole and Sir Noel, Fields's repertoire wasn't quite so high-minded. I can well imagine that both he and Our Gracie attracted the attention of the censor, but Hutch was more likely to sing a Cole Porter lyric with a sensual underpinning, whereas the closest Fields got to the truly erotic was "What Can You Give a Nudist for His Birthday." Although she didn't share George Formby's penchant for lightly blue material or for songs that poked fun at hoodoo Hindus and Chinese laundrymen, like him she was up for any kind of comedy number. Many of her records weren't really songs, they were essentially comic monologues with musical accompaniment: "I Took My Harp to a Party," which she pronounces as "I Took Me 'Arp to a Party" (a song performed stateside by Ish Kabibble with Kay Kyser as "I Took My Cornet to a Party"), has her toting the bloody instrument to such an affair and being disappointed when nobody asks her to play. Hutch's songs set him up as the supreme lothario, Fields's make her out to be the butt of humor. Hutch was a romantic idealist, something to aspire to; Fields conspicuously never set herself as being high above the crowd, she was always just one of the mob.

Also unlike Hutch, whose music bespoke an Anglo-American (and occasionally French) alliance, Fields rarely recorded American songs. Indeed, it usually wasn't enough for her just to be British—as in "There's a Lovely Lake in London"; she had to get more specific, embodying a Lancashire lass in "In a Little Lancashire Town" and "Lancashire Blues," while "Mary Ellen's Hot Pot Party" naturally transpires in Lancashire. She also visits " 'Appy 'Amstead," the more famous "Lambeth Walk," and eventually turns to the north, singing of "Grandfather's Bagpipes" and "Laughing Irish Eyes." She positively reveled in being provincial.

In one of her songs, "The Rochdale Hounds," Fields sings of hunting in the Lancashire village where she was born. That took place on January 9, 1898, and she was originally named Grace Stansfield. How much more British can one be than to have been born over a shop that sold fish-and-chips?

Crikey! Young Gracie was sent to work in the local mill alongside her mother. As a child performer, she found work in several troupes that specialized in juvenile talent: Charburn's Young Stars and Haley's Garden of Girls. At twelve, she made her solo debut in the Rochdale New Hippodrome theater, and within a few years was touring the variety halls. In 1913, she made her only appearance in the traditional British theatrical form known as pantomine in *Dick Whittington's Cat*, and was first seen by London audiences in a revue entitled *Yes I Think So* in 1915.

It was in the latter production that she first ran into Archie Pitt, who at that time was a fellow performer, but was shortly to become her manager, producer, and first husband. Working with Mr. Pitt, Gracie Fields (as she was now known) appeared in a touring revue called *It's a Bargain* and then the wildly successful show *Mr. Tower of London*. This toured up and down the provinces for about four years beginning in 1917 or 1918, and when it finally made it to London in 1922, one might think that the sophisticated West Enders would consider it too hayseed. Far from it: Fields made such an impact that the London papers were immediately pronouncing her a new star. She spent most of the rest of the twenties doing variety, several more "legitimate" shows at the end of the decade, the "straight" (nonmusical) *S.O.S.*, *Topsy and Eva*, *The Show's the Thing*, and *Walk This Way* in 1931.

Fields recorded for the first time in 1923, an HMV test that has yet to be issued. She wouldn't return to the studio until deep into the electrical age, in 1928. Her first song was "Because I Love You," a little-known Irving Berlin item that she gradually worked up into a comic specialty. (Berlin would prove to be her favorite American songwriter: She recorded more than a half-dozen of his tunes.) Her first few sessions set a pattern, as she varies between straight-ahead pop songs ("My Blue Heaven," one of those domestic tranquillity songs that play up her similarity with Kate Smith), semiclassical soprano showcases ("Toselli's Serenade"), sentimental weepies ("Laugh, Clown, Laugh"), and Lancashire laugh riots ("Eee, by Gum") and other novelties that capitalized on her skill with regional accents. At the start of the thirties, Fields was as popular a recording artist in the U.K. as Smith would be on radio in the United States; she had sold nearly a million records in less than two years.

Fields's whole upbringing seems to have been in show business; nothing I've read about her gives any indication that she ever formally studied singing. This is rather astounding, because Fields's voice sounds extraordinarily well trained. There's a legend to the effect that she was once commended by none other than Luisa Tetrazzini, the Florentine Nightingale herself, who supposedly praised Fields's top C and D, and said that she could have easily succeeded as an opera soprano. However, to have sung Verdi and Puccini would have meant giving up arias with such deathless lines as "Walter, Walter lead me to the altar / And I'll show you where I'm tattooed."

Nevertheless, Fields does operatic stuff all over her pop records. Just about all her noncomic sides (and even a lot of the comedy numbers) have her trilling about in coloratura fashion. In 1937, she recorded Victor Herbert's "Ah! Sweet Mystery of Life" as well as Rudolf Friml's "Giannina Mia," and the following year she cut a medley of two operetta classics by Sig Romberg, "Will You Remember (Sweetheart)" and "When I Grow Too Old to Dream." She's also completely credible with that material, as convincing if not more so than an operetta diva like Jeanette MacDonald. At times, when doing a somewhat blue tune, Fields's wordless episodes blur the distinction between classical *vocalise* and American scat, as on "You're Driving Me Crazy" and "I'm Playing with Fire." She had such control over her intonation that she could play with it for comic purposes, making herself sound trembly and out-of-tune on numbers like "The One Little Hair on His Head" and "I Never Cried So Much in All My Life."

In 1930, Fields made her first appearance in New York, and the following year her popularity in her native land was cemented when she starred in her first film, *Sally in Our Alley*. As if she wasn't already beloved enough among the Britishers, it was in this picture that she sang "Sally," the song that was her "My Way" and "Over the Rainbow" combined. For the remainder of the interwar years she would make one movie a year. It's hard to believe she had the time to make even that many, she was so busy touring and recording. Like Hutch, she was constantly in the studio: In 1929 alone she recorded more than forty songs.

Her output was as diverse as it was prolific. In an age when singers like Annette Hanshaw frequently recorded under pseudonyms, Fields could easily have recorded under four different names, as there were four distinct types of songs in her repertoire; it would be difficult to ascertain which of her identities was the most popular. As the Lancashire Lassie, she recorded more songs than you've had hot dinners about little pudden basins, five-barred gates, Mrs. Binn's Twins, Obadiah's mother, Fred Fannakapan, the photograph of mother's wedding group, all with 'ardly an "H" in 'earing distance. Songs like "'Erbert, 'Enery, 'Epplethwaite," "In Me 'Oroscope," and "Turn 'Erbert's Face to the Wall, Mother" would have made Professor 'Enry 'Iggins unleash the bloomin' 'ounds on 'er. One of her more popular—not to mention unique—topics of humor was a somewhat obscure English potted plant known as the aspidistra; her songs on the subject range from "The Lovely Aspidistra in the Old Flower Pot" (1930) to "The Biggest Aspidistra in the World" (recorded for the first time in 1938 and redone in Los Angeles in 1941). Aye, her comic songs were

champion, I tell ye, champion! (One wonders if such songs provided the inspiration for George Orwell's early novel *Keep the Aspidistra Flying*.)

Closely related to her comic pieces were all those jolly community marching chorus songs—of which there was at least one in every film. The 1931 "Fall in and Follow the Band," which she sings with a chorus of little blokettes, set the tone, but it was the title song from *Sing as We Go* that solidified the trend. It sounds like an ancient British march—one can easily imagine chaps in pith helmets and jodhpurs chanting it as they trek about suppressing heathens in Injah. "Sing as We Go" was written expressly for Fields in that film and was recently revived by another British institution, Monty Python's Flying Circus, with the lyric "Sit on My Face (And Tell Me That You Love Me)." Four years later came another jolly-marching-chorus number entitled "The Trek Song" for Fields's 1938 film entry, *We're Going to Be Rich*, this one with a considerably less discreet imperialistic undercurrent, since it's sung in the film by Fields and her jolly chums in both English and Afrikaans. For the 1941 *Shipyard Sally* (more Depression-and-war material about putting unemployed shipbuilders back to work), she came up with her most memorable march yet, "Wish Me Luck (As You Wave Me Goodbye)." None of these is exactly Noel or Cole, but just the same, it's 'ard to stop 'umming the bloody things.

Mood seemed to be largely a matter of tempo: When the tempo was in 6/8 or march time, Fields was as jolly as jolly could be. Put her in waltz time though, and the pace got slower and the mood considerably more sentimental. Her sentimental waltzes were the polar opposite of her comedy and communal march numbers: Most of these songs, like "Sally," were utterly basic and old-fashioned. The best of them, though, are quite lovely; Geoff Clarkson and Peter Van Steeden's "Home" (1939) and Nat Shilkret and Allie Wrubel's "The First Time I Saw You" (1938) are beautifully realized combinations of pop and classical singing, with the latter becoming even more emotionally effective when Fields briefly breaks into dance tempo.

In 1934, Fields did a session accompanied by pipe organ in which she sang her most classical piece ever, "Ave Maria" (in the Bach-Gounod setting), and a medley of waltzes by "Sally" composer Will E. Haines, among them a new version of that song, which had already become a signature for her. One of her most remarkable assets was the ability to vary between singing a corny old song completely straight, such as "Play to Me, Gypsy," or camping one up for laughs, like "Because I Love You." She spent a lot of time sending up corny old musical melodramas like "Heaven Will Protect an Honest Girl" and "She Fought Like a Tiger for 'Er 'Onour," the latter perhaps the only song ever to rhyme "Tiger Rag" with "Egyptian fag."

Beyond provincial comedy songs, rousing marches,

and tear-jerker waltzes there was yet another genre of song that Fields excelled in, which, from the standpoint of history, seems the most satisfying: plain old, straight-ahead Tin Pan Alley pop songs. Fields is never better than when she's just singing a regular song, generally a love song, generally in foxtrot tempo. To hear her sing one of her bright and bouncy film songs like "Happy Ending" and "Looking on the Bright Side"—the former from *This Week of Grace*, the second from *Looking on the Bright Side*—is to realize that she wasn't merely Britain's most popular female vocalist of the thirties, she was also the best. Like all the superior singers, she can extract memorable music even from unpromising material; in 1935, she came up with a potentially dreadful bit of faux-Italiana entitled "The Organ, the Monkey and Me." Without Fields, it would be a ruddy joke, but she somehow manages to break our hearts with it.

After hundreds of sides for HMV, in 1935 she switched to the smaller Rex Records and introduced her first offering for the new label, "Turn 'Erbert's Face to the Wall, Mother," with the following greeting: " 'Ello everybody, I 'ope you're gonna enjoy me first Rex Record. It's all right, it's only a bob—money for jam!" After three years, she returned to EMI. As with Hutch, one yearns for some enterprising entrepreneur to bite off a *Complete Gracie Fields* megabox (we're talking another fifteen or twenty CDs), but also as with Hutch, it would make more sense for the set to be organized thematically rather than chronologically. I would hope that the comedy numbers would be separated from the marches, and the sentimental waltzes from the contemporary pop songs. I'd listen to the comics, the marches, and the waltzes (especially her beautiful 1935 reading of "When I Grow Too Old to Dream," perhaps the best treatment of it ever until the Cats and the Fiddle jived it up), but naturally I'd play the standard pop songs over and over.

This fictitious *Complete Gracie Fields* box set (the package would, of course, come in the shape of an aspidistra, and the letter H would ne'er be found anywhere in the accompanying booklet) would also include several discs including nothing but medleys. The Brits were much fonder of the medley format than the Yanks, and beginning with the "Gracie Fields Medley" and "Gracie's Christmas Party," both recorded in 1932, HMV was keen to use their star to help sell the 12" two-sided medley format. Indeed, her popularity inspired HMV to push the envelope of recorded sound in more ways than one.

Fields may well have been the first major pop singer to record an entire album. In 1933, EMI set up remote equipment and captured one of her London theater appearances, releasing the results in an album of three 12" discs (six sides) titled both *Gracie in the Theatre* and *Gracie at the Holburn Empire, 11 October 1933*. (There are editions of the show issued on both HMV and Regal-Zonophone that appear to

be different performances.) That this was a live recording made it doubly unusual. The sound is remarkable (especially as reproduced on the mid-seventies World Records LP, *Gracie Fields—Stage and Screen*), considering that this live recording is seventy-five years old, and that when performing in front of a live audience, Fields felt less impelled to stay firmly planted in front of the microphone (handheld and wireless mikes were decades in the future) than she did at a regular record session.

She frames the live set with two American songs, Billy Hill's very sentimental "There's a Cabin in the Pines" and Harold Arlen's bluesy "Stormy Weather," and she belts out both with a slight touch of camp. Apart from "I Can't Remember," another Irving Berlin obscurity in 3/4, the songs are all British. There's the usual assortment of extreme comedy numbers ("Whiskers and All" and "The Rochdale Hounds" expanded with a longish monologue, a semiparody of Denza's "May Morn"), one-steps or sentimentals—and a sentimental parody, "Out in the Cold, Cold Snow" that has the entire Holburn in hysterics. Before "Stormy Weather," she climaxes the whole works with her perennial "Sally." It's said that she had to sing this song so often in the thirties that she grew to hate it, but you could certainly never tell that here. It's not only intoned with much love, it's actually heard twice, the first time by Fields in solo, the second time in which she's outshouted by the audience in a palpable demonstration of how much she meant to them.

Gracie in the Theatre was hardly the end of it. Both EMI and Rex had her turn out a steady stream of medleys and other mostly two-sided 12" specials: A few weeks after the Holburn, she cut *Gracie at Home* (in which her family participated), and in 1934 it was her *Medley of Film Waltz Songs* (with organ), then a location recording from Great Ormond St. Hospital, *Gracie in the Children's Ward*. She made even more of these extravaganzas: *Old Soldiers Never Die* (a set of World War I songs), *Gracie's Request Record*, *Gracie and Sandy's Party*, and *Gracie and Sandy at the Coronation*. ("Sandy" was Yorkshire comic Sandy "Can You Hear Me, Mother?" Powell.) There were also numerous annual permutations of *Gracie's Hit Medley* as well as medleys of songs from the films *Show Boat* and the first three animated cartoon features, *Snow White and the Seven Dwarfs*, *Gulliver's Travels*, and *Pinocchio*.

From 1939 on, the Gracie Fields medleys take on a more militaristic tone. Not long after war was declared, HMV sent their location recording equipment to capture Fields in a barracks in Chelsea on *Gracie with the Troops*, which was followed by *Our Gracie with the Boys in France*, *Our Gracie with the Air Force*, and *Our Gracie with the Navy*. The second of these, *Our Gracie with the Troops in France*, was the most ambitious of these military medleys, indeed of all her recorded productions since the Holburn. It purportedly originated from an undisclosed location close to the enemy lines (poor P. G. Wodehouse was trapped on the other side), and consisted of four sides, a total of over twelve minutes (included on the closing track of *Looking on the Bright Side,* a 2002 CD). If anything, the affection exchanged between Fields and her audience has increased in the seven years since the Holburn—by now a generation of young tommies had grown up with Our Gracie—whose love for home was heightened by the war and their proximity to the front; Gracie meant to them what Bing Crosby meant to the Yanks.

The early years of the war marked the height of the British public's love affair with Our Gracie, but the relationship went south even before America entered World War II. In 1940, Fields, who had long since been divorced from Archie Pitt, married Monty Banks, an actor-director and general film industry factotum who had directed her three most recent films, *We're Going to Be Rich* (1938), *Keep Smiling* (1939), and *Shipyard Sally* (1940). The problem was that Banks, born Mario Bianchi, was an Italian immigrant who had neglected to file for British citizenship. When Mussolini sided with the Axis, Banks was considered an "enemy alien." Facing the threat of internment, Mr. and Mrs. Banks decided to leave the country. She spent 1940–42 shuttling back and forth between London and Hollywood, appearing in a few American films and recording for American Decca.

No big deal, you might think, marrying an "eye-tal-yan," but the way the notoriously fickle British press treated their once beloved Gracie, you'd think she'd gone and shacked up with Adolf 'Itler 'imself! According to historian Chris Ellis, Fields "was now regarded as a deserter and a traitor." (In Hollywood, Mario Bianchi had to de-Italianize his name even further, now to "Montague Banks.") Yet Gracie never served her country more unselfishly than during the war, a time in which she ceaselessly entertained Allied troops and campaigned to raise consciousness and money for British war relief.

After 1945, Fields and Banks returned, and Gracie was gradually reaccepted by her native land and recognized as the patriot she was. She launched a new BBC series and enjoyed a major comeback performance at the London Palladium. In 1948, to make her return to grace complete, she was awarded one final hit—her biggest ever, in fact, and the only disc of hers to become really big in the United States. This was "Now Is the Hour (Maori Farewell Song)," a suitably sentimental air from the further reaches of the empire formerly known as British. In the early postwar period, the Yanks were far more receptive to songs from Europe and the rest of the globe than at any other point in the history of American pop. "Now Is the Hour" became a number 3 hit on the charts for Fields; Bing Crosby took it to number one.

After Banks's death in 1950, Fields was married for a third time, to another foreigner, the Yugoslavian-born Boris Alperovici. The Alperovicis went into a period of semiretirement beginning in the fifties, spending most of their time on Capri—the isle that Fields had sung about in 1934. Although her last films were the Hollywood *Paris Underground* and *Molly and Me* from 1945, she occasionally appeared on television and in the recording studio in the fifties, sixties, and seventies. In 1960, she published her autobiography, *Sing as We Go.*

The last recording that I've been able to hear by Gracie Fields is *Hey There!*, an original album from 1962. It shows a very svelte sixty-something Gracie on the cover, looking rather like the Queen Mum, posing in front of a view of the Thames. I had assumed that her voice would grow deeper as she got older, but surprisingly she's very much up in the high alto–near soprano register, singing the way she looks, somewhat formal but very friendly and warm. The repertoire is entirely American pop hits, show tunes, and film themes of the previous decade: "Three Coins in the Fountain," "I've Grown Accustomed to His Face," "Small World," and even "Somewhere" (Our Gracie sings Sondheim). No comedy songs, no marches, and she even makes a point to clearly articulate the H sounds in "Wish You Were Here" and "Hey There!" She does, however, stay true to her own tradition by doing the last number with a big chorus, sort of like a de facto singalorg: "The Loveliest Night of the Year" (the old waltz "Over the Waves" adapted into song form for Mario Lanza), sung with "chorus of Guardsmen of Her Majesty's Forces." If she made other original LPs that are this good, I should jolly well like to hear them. Well I say! Rather!

Shortly before all the trouble started, in 1938, Fields was "created," as they say, Commander of the British Empire in the King's Birthday Honours List. Forty years later she was designated a Dame of the British Empire. The honor would have come a great deal earlier had it not been for the World War II business and for the fact that she was principally a comedian—it's a fact that dramatic actors and opera singers are recognized a lot earlier and more often than pop singers and comics. But though she was officially a DBE at the time of her death in 1979, several generations of Brits from Lancashire to Manchester to Liverpool would never be able to think of her as anything other than Our Gracie.

Female Band Singers I: Benny's Babes

Helen Ward
Martha Tilton
Helen Forrest

If you want to find the absolute epicenter of the swing era, you need look no further than Benny Goodman and His Orchestra. Not that there wasn't stiff competition: The rival orchestra led by Glenn Miller perhaps inspired a little more sentiment and, eventually, nostalgia. Likewise, BG's former trumpet star Harry James cut a somewhat more dashing figure in Hollywood. There are also a few wags who actually believe that Artie Shaw played better clarinet (I try not to associate with such people) and there's no doubt that the most distinguished composer of the era was Duke Ellington. But there was no one figure more crucial to the big band era as a whole than Goodman. He represented more than the sound of his music, or the history of his career and his band; indeed, the very cultural texture of an entire epoch was bound up in this unassuming, self-absorbed clarinetist from Chicago.

Goodman's band, from his 1935 "breakthrough," which officially launched the swing era, up to his 1938 concert at Carnegie Hall, which gave the era its prewar climax, is perhaps the most celebrated ensemble in the history of popular music until the arrival of the Beatles. As a musical force, Goodman was so all-pervasive that he not only bolstered the careers of not just one great arranger and/or soloist after another, but he continually spawned other major bands—like those led by Lionel Hampton, Gene Krupa, and Harry James—which themselves gave birth to yet other bands. Benny Goodman was a whole era of American music unto himself.

Thus, nobody had more to do with what pop sounded like circa 1940 than Goodman, whereas the bandleader who most anticipated what pop music would sound like in the postwar era of, say, 1950 was Tommy Dorsey. The trombonist's most famous band, which reached its peak between 1940 and 1942, included two future star vocalists who would dominate much of postwar pop, Frank Sinatra and Jo Stafford, plus other solid hit makers in the Pied Pipers, Connie Haines, and Dick Haymes.

Yet what of Goodman's vocalists? The big four were Helen Ward, Martha Tilton, Helen Forrest, and Peggy Lee. (This is apart from boy singers like Buddy Clark and Dick Haymes, neither of whom was with the band for very long.) All four names should be well known to anyone who knows anything about the swing era, but of the four, only Lee is remembered for being something other than Benny Goodman's band vocalist.

Not that being a lead singer with one of the great Goodman units during its peak years isn't enough of a claim to fame. (Or rather, at least it was for anybody but Goodman himself: "I don't think he was too thrilled with any girl singer," as Tilton told Dave Weiner, "but he knew he had to have one for the public. He liked playing the clarinet—period.")

Yet time and perspective change everything. Helen Forrest had just logged too much time with too many bands—Shaw, Goodman, James—for the public to welcome her into the new era of vocal-dominated pop that emerged after the war, while Peggy Lee was just getting started in her two years with Goodman, and she worked hard to develop an identity that had nothing to do with the big bands. Ward, Forrest, and Tilton were all excellent singers—in fact, their overall work with Goodman was considerably better than Lee's—but Lee, like Sinatra, had a larger musical vision, which carried her forth into a brave new world at least partially of her own creation. The point when Lee left Goodman happened to coincide with the first American Federation of Musicians ban of 1942–44; by the time of the second ban in 1948, she was well established as a solo star, and it was largely forgotten that she had ever sung with Goodman or any other band.

Tilton's story was somewhere in the middle: She flourished after the war, and successfully created a post-Goodman identity, but after a decade or so, she knew it was time to step down. Her good looks and bright sunny sound meant that she could compete very nicely, for a time at least, with such younger hit-makers as Doris Day, Margaret Whiting, and Dinah Shore. Helen Forrest more or less failed to create a postband identity (or hits) for herself, yet paradoxically, it was Forrest who had by far the longest career—she worked steadily from the forties to the nineties, though almost exclusively by continuing to re-create what she had achieved in the four or so years of her big band career.

Leaving Lee's work for its own chapter, we can see that the three main Goodman canaries all had musical strengths as well as career strengths. Helen Ward's were primarily rhythmic: She was the first girl singer BG found who could make ballads and pop songs credible in the new universe of solid 4/4 rhythm that he was defining. Forrest's strengths were primarily emotional; she could take a single 32-bar chorus and make an audience feel every word of it. (Little wonder that she flourished in the war period, when audiences were in particular need of such a cathartic release.) For Tilton, as we shall see, it was a bit of both. Yet it was Ward who was undeniably the woman who defined the role of female singer with a big swing band.

Helen Ward (1913–1998)

Helen Ward wasn't the first major girl singer, any more than Benny Goodman was the first universally popular bandleader. Those distinctions more properly belong to Mildred Bailey and the bandleader she worked with, Paul Whiteman. Yet just as Goodman (following in the footsteps of Louis Armstrong) popularized the concept of the bandleader as superstar soloist—not to mention the very format of the swing band itself—Ward was the one who defined what a band vocalist would do. She sang in a clear, straight voice, with a slightly burnished quality similar to Lee Wiley's, with little vibrato but plenty of warmth. (At least that's the way she sounds on most of her classic vocals with Goodman; scholar Bob Conrad points out that more vibrato is heard on her Columbia recordings, possibly indicating that she was singing the same way with Goodman but the Victor engineers failed to capture it.)

And, appropriately, as on something like "Feelin' High and Happy" with Gene Krupa, she offered plenty of energy and a very strong sense of time. She swings. Singers in jazz contexts would tend to diversify a bit more in later years, but Ward sounded equally strong on major love songs like Rodgers and Hart's "There's a Small Hotel" and "Blue Moon" and on nursery nonsense like "Yankee Doodle Never Went to Town" and "Eeny Meeny Miney Mo." She is the voice on songs like "You Turned the Tables on Me" and "Goody Goody" that were not only signatures for Goodman but for the entire early swing era. To this day, the voice of Helen Ward remains an indelible element of the early big band epoch; it's hard to imagine the breakthrough years of the big bands without her.

Born in 1913 in New York, Ward took piano lessons for many years but doesn't seem to have ever studied singing formally. Even so, by her teens it was obvious that she had both the voice and the perky, doe-eyed good looks to make it in the singing business. In the early thirties, she worked regularly with Burton Lane, a young pianist struggling to succeed as a songwriter at the same time Ward was struggling to make it as a singer. By her mid-teens she was singing professionally on the radio and at dances and other gigs with any band that would have her. In 1933, when she was twenty, she began recording as a freelance studio vocalist; her first disc was "This Little Piggy," a rather cloying attempt to turn an old nursery rhyme into a new pop hit. Ward would later find considerably more success when she began putting rhythm in her nursery rhymes—she sounded much more convincing when given a beat to work with, as on the other three tunes from this session, "Night on the Water," "Let's Put Two and Two Together," and the tango-foxtrot hybrid "Boulevard of Broken Dreams."

In this early period, Ward also recorded with the lightly Latinate society leader Enric Madriguera, and luckily these sides have been collected on the double-CD package *The Complete Helen Ward on Columbia* (Sony/Collectors' Choice Music), which includes, among other things, the pre-Goodman vocals as well as her embryonic work with the clarinetist. Though these were not great records, they were evidence that something new was in the air. Even as late as 1933–34, hearing a female voice was still a novelty on a dance record, most band vocals still being sung by tenors. Helen Ward and Benny Goodman were about to change all that.

Ward was working with Madriguera at New York's Waldorf-Astoria in 1934 when she first got the offer to sing with Goodman, who was making a valiant stab at starting his own band. She joined the fledgling Goodman group at Billy Rose's Music Hall that year and recorded with a version of that band, which was calling itself "Harry Rosenthal and His Orchestra." Without Goodman himself, this was a fairly standard sweet band, but Ward sounded fine on two new Cole Porter songs from *Anything Goes,* "You're the Top" and "All Through the Night."

Goodman's own early Columbia Records are somewhat schizophrenic, ranging from the purely sweet "Blue Moon"—Leo Reisman's or any other major mainstream dance orch could have cut this— to the purely jazzy numbers, from the Billie Holiday and Mildred Bailey vocals to the hot instrumentals like "Georgia Jubilee." The best of the early Goodman-Ward sides is Johnny Mercer's "The Dixieland Band," which prominently features the young singer in a very hip and swinging extended jazz-flavored narrative.

Ward's musical place in the band was well defined by the time Goodman made his breakthrough. In fact, everything was in place by then, including the band's Victor contract (the corporation was then taking a chance on what was still an unknown band, one whose radio exposure had not yet amounted to anything, or so they thought), plus its first key players, including trumpeter Bunny Berigan, who wouldn't remain very long, and drummer Gene Krupa, who would, and the band's amazing library of arrangements by Fletcher Henderson, Spud Murphy, and others. This was the perfect band to put swing on the map in a big way, which is exactly what it did in August 1935 at the Palomar Ballroom. By now the classic Goodman records were coming out left and right, not only terrific instrumentals like "King Porter Stomp," "Bugle Call Rag," and "Stompin' at the Savoy," but equally wonderful Ward features like "You're a Heavenly Thing" and "Restless." (The best of the lady's classic vocals with Goodman from the Victor period are on the collection *The Queen of Big Band Swing* from the British Living Era–ASV label.)

By now, Ward's voice has a deep, sultry quality that's surprising in a twenty-one-year-old band chirp. Goodman, like his rival Artie Shaw, regarded the great majority of his singers as mere commercial concessions, but he seems to have thought of Ward as something more. He not only featured her with the big band, but also brought her along to lend her musicality and popular appeal to three small group sessions from 1936: "Too Good to Be True," with his own trio; "Mutiny in the Parlor" and "I'm Gonna

Clap My Hands," done under Gene Krupa's leadership (with a combination of Goodmanites and Hendersonians); and "You Came to My Rescue" and "Here's Love in Your Eyes," with Teddy Wilson leading an octet of Benny's boys. What Goodman didn't do, to Ward's chagrin, was include her in any of the several motion pictures the band made in these years.

From the beginning, their relationship was personal as well as professional. She worked with the band for roughly two and a half years, from 1934 to 1936, during which time they were almost always an "item" in the Winchellian parlance of the day. (Or so Ward later told the best of Goodman biographers, Ross Firestone, for his 1993 *Swing Swing Swing: The Life and Times of Benny Goodman*.) Goodman and Ward would get together for a while, then fight and break up, then get back together again. (The romance anticipates that of Harry James and Helen Forrest, except that James was married at the time and Goodman wasn't.)

In summer 1936, a year after the legendary Palomar engagement, the band returned to that Los Angeles ballroom, upon which occasion Goodman "discovered" the soon-to-be-legendary vibraphonist Lionel Hampton. At this time, the singer and the bandleader's relationship came to a head: Goodman proposed to her, and while she knew that he "really liked" her, she also suspected that he was offering marriage just to keep her in the band. "After all, I did sing every other tune." She made her last sides with Goodman in December, the same month she married record producer Albert Marx (one of the men responsible for recording the historic Carnegie Hall concert of 1938) and announced her retirement at the age of twenty-three.

Even though the marriage didn't last, Ward's career never quite regained its momentum. Even had she hung on with Goodman until after the Carnegie Hall concert of 1938, this was still a little early for band singers to be going out on their own. However, with her charm and visual appeal, it's easy to imagine her getting a call from Hollywood— strangely, it never happened. Over the next few years, Ward, now Mrs. Albert Marx, appears only sporadically on our radar: "Day in, Day Out" with Bob Crosby; two standards ("I Cover the Waterfront" and "I've Got a Crush on You") with Chicago piano master Joe Sullivan; two dates with violinist Matty Malneck (most not known until the 2000 *Complete Columbia* package); and a tour with the Glenn Miller–associated altoist Hal McIntyre. Still, most of her output was distinctly Bennycentric: There are memorable sides with fellow ex-Goodmanites Gene Krupa, Harry James, Teddy Wilson, and Red Norvo, as well as several reunions with the mother ship, the Goodman big band itself.

In the late forties, she worked behind the scenes in the music business, as a radio producer whose charges included, among others, the young Vic Damone. Surprisingly, she enjoyed something of a resurgence in the fifties, starting with a pair of vocals with Chicago jazz trumpeter Wild Bill Davison in 1952 ("Goody Goody" and "I Can't Give You Anything but Love"). With the coming of the LP and the release of the Carnegie Hall concert in that format and then hi-fi, there was a revitalized interest in the swing era—prodded by Hollywood with their Miller and Benny biopics—and Ward, who was only in her late thirties, was perfectly suited to re-create the music of her teens. She was one of several key attractions on what was planned as a blockbuster tour combining the reunited Goodman orchestra and Louis Armstrong's All-Stars. Though that event was sabotaged by the clarinetist's ego, Ward came out smelling like a rose: She recorded new tracks for Columbia both with this edition of the Goodman band and at long last, as a star in her own right, accompanied by Percy Faith's orchestra. In general, she sounds fine on both sets of 1953 recordings, even though they're not as uniformly perfect as her prewar work. In 1935–36, she was as hip and swinging as anybody in the band; by 1953 the voice is heavier and less assured.

Re-creating the swing era continued to be Ward's stock-in-trade. In 1956 and 1957, she participated in a series of albums in the classic swing style led by clarinetist Peanuts Hucko (the arranger was Larry Clinton), as well as *With a Little Bit of Swing*, her second featured LP, with Hucko directing the big band accompaniment. Late in her life, she married again, to still another figure in Goodman's general orbit, Columbia engineer Dr. Bill Savory, and the two produced *The Helen Ward Song Book* on their own Lyricon label. Helen Ward survived Benny Goodman by a dozen years, and was eighty-four when she died in 1998.

Martha Tilton (1915–2006)

The career of Martha Tilton illustrates the old adage that out of print is out of mind. As I've mentioned, audiences in the mid-forties only dimly remembered that Tilton had been with Goodman's band. Yet from the fifties through today, the only Tilton recordings that have been consistently available are drawn from the stack of fifty or so vocal refrains she cut with Goodman between 1937 and 1939. In the late LP era, RCA rereleased the band's complete output for the label on a series of double albums, so, for a brief period, all of Tilton's Goodman sides were in the catalogue. Yet the perspective continually changes: In the CD era, reissues of classic Goodmania have tended to focus on the band's many hot instrumentals, and most of the more pop-oriented discs featuring Tilton are now no longer available. But at the start of the twenty-first century, two CD packages were released that drew attention to Tilton's post-Goodman work, namely *The Complete Capitol Sessions*, a two-disc set licensed from that label and issued by Collectors' Choice Music, and *The Complete Standard Transcriptions,* a collection of studio recordings made for radio use in 1941 and 1944. At the time of Tilton's death in December 2006, the focus was more on her post-Goodman work. It still remains for some enterprising concern to collate all of her BG vocals into a comprehensive double set.

Martha Tilton was born on November 14, 1915, in Corpus Christi, Texas, but she and her younger sister, Liz Tilton, were raised on Laurel Avenue in Hollywood. The two sisters were fascinated with the craft of pop singing and grew up listening to the likes of Ruth Etting and Connee Boswell. While attending Fairfax High in Los Angeles, Tilton fell in with a band of high school boys who had a daily sustaining spot on local radio. An astute manager happened to catch one of the broadcasts and "pacted" her, as *Variety* used to say, for what Tilton later implied was an exploitive seven-year contract.

Around 1935, she sang at the Cocoanut Grove (in Hollywood's famous Ambassador Hotel), and she made her first film appearance at the age of twenty-two as an unbilled lounge singer in the classic screwball spook comedy *Topper.*

In 1937, she was also singing with a quartet called the Three Hits and a Miss (Tilton was the latter). They landed a plum gig as the vocal group on the *Camel Caravan,* a show that had featured the famous Casa Loma Orchestra for many years but had been recently taken over by Goodman. Presumably, the vocal group sang commercial jingles and other bits but rarely if ever participated in the featured numbers with the Goodman band itself. For the first few months of the year, Goodman was frantically auditioning female singers to find one to fill the pumps of the recently departed Helen Ward. It was Goodman's manager, Willard Alexander, who suggested that he give Tilton a try.

In the world of band singers, almost everyone has a story about auditioning for Benny Goodman—even Anita O'Day. Tilton's tale is archetypal: The young girl starts to sing, she gets through several numbers, but all the while Benny looks preoccupied. He seems to be thinking of everything else in the world except the singing of the woman doing her best in front of him. Then, abruptly, he gets up in the middle of a song and leaves. Naturally, she figures she's been given the brush-off, goes home, and cries her eyes out to her mother. Shortly thereafter, Willard Alexander calls to tell her that she's got the job.

Tilton sang dozens of pop songs of the day with Goodman, around forty-five of which were commercially recorded by the band for RCA Victor. Almost an equal number were not and survive only on airchecks (such as the generous six-CD series of remote broadcasts from the Manhattan Room at New York's Hotel Pennsylvania in late 1937) or not at all. The great bulk of the Tilton-BG items were new tunes being fed to RCA Records, NBC Radio, and Goodman by the music publishers and their army of song pluggers. "A lot of what I recorded with Benny were lousy songs," Tilton told producer Billy Vera. "He picked everything. In those days, the songwriter would give him a piece of the tune to record it. He knew everything we did would sell a million, so we'd cut 'em and never do 'em again."

Tilton may be unduly harsh on the material she sang with Goodman; indeed, the first record she cut with the band was "Bob White (What'Cha Gonna Swing Tonight?)," a witty and entirely memorable rhythm song by Johnny Mercer, the man who would be the next most important influence in her life and music after Goodman. She and Goodman would record no fewer than eight songs by Mercer, three ("Let That Be a Lesson to You," "I've Hitched My Wagon to a Star," and "I'm Like a Fish out of Water") from *Hollywood Hotel,* a Warner Bros. feature in which he and his band were prominently featured but Tilton was nowhere to be seen. In fact, Tilton's other vocal on the first session was "I Can't Give You Anything but Love"—hardly what you would call a "lousy song."

Indeed, only a few of the dozens of tunes Tilton recorded with BG could be described as lousy: "Silhouetted in the Moonlight" (a rare guest vocal with the Goodman Trio) wouldn't strike anyone as a deathless air, but "You Took the Words Right out of My Heart," "Mama, That Moon Is Here Again," "True Confession," "Feelin' High and Happy," "Always and Always," "Don't Wake Up My Heart," and "What Have You Got That Gets Me" are all exceptionally good songs of the period. Even better are "Thanks for the Memory," "I Let a Song Go out of My Heart," "Please Be Kind," and "This Can't Be Love," which all became instant standards.

Tilton also contributed mightily to at least three all-time classics of the swing era, "Bei Mir Bist Du Schoen" (a two-sided 78 done with the BG quartet), "Loch Lomond," and "And the Angels Sing." Throughout, she sings in a light, clear voice, influenced as much by Helen Ward as by the leading subtle swingers of the era, Mildred Bailey and Maxine Sullivan. The most popular of all Tilton-Goodman sides was "And the Angels Sing," which had begun as a traditional Jewish *freilach* that was transformed by trumpeter Ziggy Elman into a swing number, and from there into a hit love song by lyricist Mercer (with an arrangement by the young Abe Osser). "We spent so much time on that one song," Tilton later told Billy Vera, "I said to Harry James, 'I don't think that song is going to amount to anything.' He never let me forget that I was no good at picking hits!"

In the famous 1938 Carnegie Hall concert, Tilton was more than a vital asset to the band: She literally stopped the show. After "Lomond," the crowd refused to let the concert proceed as planned until BG made an announcement promising that she would come back later.

The standard length of time for a Goodman

vocalist to remain with the band was two or three years: Ward (1934–37), Tilton (1937–39), Forrest (1939–41), Lee (1941–43). By 1939, Tilton, who was already all of twenty-four, left him, she later said, for health reasons, not personality issues. Essentially, she was worn out from the band's relentless touring. She freelanced between 1939 and 1942, recording with bandleaders Bob Crosby and Artie Shaw. Most famously, she supplied the singing voice for Barbara Stanwyck (whom, coincidentally, she closely resembled) in the Howard Hawks classic comedy *Ball of Fire,* singing "Drum Boogie" with the band of another Goodman vet, drummer Gene Krupa.

She dabbled in the movies. In addition to dubbing off-screen for some nonsinging actresses, she had onscreen guest bits in some A pictures, like the Fred Astaire–Rita Hayworth *You'll Never Get Rich* (in which she sang Cole Porter's "The Wedding Cake Walk," which she recorded for Decca), and starred in at least one B musical, *Swing Hostess* (which had featured the very first film score by Ray Livingston and Jay Evans, later to win three Academy Awards for best song). Tilton makes a bright and engaging— not to mention tuneful—leading lady here, so much so that it's hard to believe that none of the majors ever gave her a tumble. (In the eyes and ears of history, there was only one female band singer who graduated to pictures in the manner of Crosby and Sinatra, and her name was Doris Day.)

Tilton's 1941 Standard transcriptions are very much rooted in the swing era. Some (such as "Why Dream?") open with a whole chorus of band instrumental before her entrance, others have Goodmanesque clarinet solos. Tilton is in terrific form, and the band, a Hollywood studio orchestra under the direction of the otherwise unknown Don Allen, is just fine. What loused up this potentially terrific offering is the ASCAP-BMI war of 1941; for most of that year, radio broadcasters were forbidden to play songs controlled by ASCAP, which covered virtually every tune by every major composer. The songs that they could play, which were licensed by BMI, were notably second-rate. Tilton may have griped about the songs she did with Goodman, but compared to most of these later ones, her Goodman songs are masterpieces. The best is "My Sister and I," which was a hit at the time, but today is mainly known as one of the more overbaked oversentimental opuses of the war era.

However, apart from the seventeen 1941 transcriptions, the *Complete Standards Transcriptions* disc (on Soundies) is graced with eight additional— and superior—tracks. There are five superb transcription sides from 1945, with a very informal jazz combo (trumpet, tenor, and rhythm) and all good songs—four standards and Gordon Jenkins's fine "San Fernando Valley"—that show Tilton at her loosest. These are some of the very best sides she ever made. In addition, there are three fine live tracks from a 1948 show with long forgotten radio

tenor Jack Smith. Not readily available, unfortunately, is a series of very swinging duets of old jazz standards she made for V-Disc, singing with the surprisingly loose Jack Leonard (the former Tommy Dorsey crooner) backed by a Dixieland unit led by Lieutenant Bob Crosby.

Tilton seems to have worked with Johnny Mercer for the first time when the singer-lyricist briefly tripled as an emcee on Goodman's *Camel Caravan* in 1939. They renewed their acquaintance when he quadrupled as a record company executive and A&R man for the years 1942–48. According to legend, when Mercer founded Capitol Records around the time of America's entry into the war, the first artist pacted to the new firm was the lady long known as "the Liltin' Miss Tilton." The forty-four selections she recorded for Capitol between 1942 and 1949 (all collected on the *Complete Capitol Sessions* on Collectors' Choice) rival her forty-five vocals with Goodman as the most important component of her legacy.

We've seen how Tilton had no faith in "And the Angels Sing" when she first heard it. She wasn't one of those postwar hit makers who bombarded the charts with megasellers like "Too Fat Polka" or "Bongo! Bongo! Bongo!" Rather, she (and Mercer, who apparently actively produced her sessions) had an extraordinarily high batting average in terms of recording early vocal versions of future standards: "I'll Remember April" (with Gordon Jenkins's orchestra, featuring the conductor's famous onefinger melody piano solo), "Serenade in Blue," "I'm Old Fashioned," "I'll Walk Alone," "A Stranger in Town," "I Should Care," "You Make Me Feel So Young," and "How Are Things in Glocca Morra?" (On the last, she was apparently reading from a somewhat illegible handwritten lyric sheet; she sings of a "River Sharon breeze" instead of the river Shannon, and no one corrected her.)

The Capitol masters also include more obscure, though eminently revivable, items, including three of Mercer's own ("Moon Dreams," "Every So Often," and "The Angels Cried"), as well as "Does Everyone Know About This?," "The Last Time I Saw You," "Somewhere in the Night," "Where Flamingos Fly" (not the same tune later done by Peggy Lee and Gil Evans), and "What a Deal." Even the lesser songs, like "The Texas Polka" (in which country meets Poland to a Dixieland beat), are more than bearable. There's also a brilliant session from 1946—not issued until the 2000 double CD—in which she does four firstrate standards with a jazzy small group led by guitarist and Capitol producer Carl Kress. She also sang two duets with Mercer himself, on the classic older songs "If I Had a Talking Picture of You" and "A Fine Romance."

If Tilton isn't one of the immortals—a Doris Day or a Jo Stafford—she comes pretty close. Around 1947, she made a handful of sides for the short-lived Majestic label, but returned to Capitol for a few more dates after the 1948 AFM ban. Perhaps she needed a couple cheesy hits to keep the label people interested in her; after Mercer left Capitol, she departed for good as well, recording through the early fifties for Coral (highlights of which were issued on the British CD *Coral Treasures* on Sepia Records in 2007, including a nice pairing of duets from *Call Me Madam* with Kay Kyser krooner Harry Babbitt. There were frequent spots with Paul Whiteman and Frank Sinatra, plus a brief run on *Lucky Strike Presents Your Hit Parade* in 1947, and in the early fifties she enjoyed a long-running daytime series with actor Curt Massey. She had already done regular spots in the mid-forties and several appearances with Sinatra on his 1945–46 *Old Gold* show.

Tilton's solo career seems to have officially ended in 1955 after she reunited with Benny Goodman, first in the biopic *The Benny Goodman Story* (she was the only one of his singers to get the call from Universal Pictures—no Ward, no Forrest, no Lee; for that matter, Billie Holiday was still alive), and three years later guested with the re-formed band at the Newport Jazz Festival. Perhaps because she reteamed with Goodman as the last major act of her career, she ensured that her excellent solo work of the forties and fifties would be almost completely forgotten. Fortunately, CDs of her Capitol and other work started turning up in the late nineties, and in the years immediately before and after her death (at age ninety-one in 2006) more of her music was easily available than at any time in her life.

Helen Forrest (1917–1999)

Like Helen Ward, Goodman's other Helen, Helen Forrest had a far less substantial career after the big band era: Around the time she went out on her own as a single, Ed Sullivan (then with *The New York Daily News*) referred to her as "the Sinatra of femme singers." Her tenure with the big bands was twice as long as Sinatra's, which was probably not a good thing in the long run—Sinatra had the foresight to go solo as early as he could, even though it meant incurring the considerable wrath of Tommy Dorsey to do so. Forrest had more hits than any other big band vocalist—virtually every song she cut with Harry James was a blockbuster, and she ranks with Bing Crosby and the Andrews Sisters as one of the definitive voices of the World War II era.

Apart from the obvious comparison with Helen Ward, the contrasts between Forrest and Anita O'Day (born a year later) are instructive. When O'Day joined Gene Krupa in 1941, Forrest had already been headlining with bands for three years, first Shaw's and then Goodman's. Both women changed their last names for show business, but that's about all they have in common. Whether consciously or not, O'Day seems to have gone out of her way to do precisely the opposite of whatever Forrest did.

Helen Forrest—or at least those running her career—was keenly concerned about the visual aspects of her presentation. Artie Shaw once insisted to me that Forrest was the only female singer he hired for her voice rather than, Billie Holiday aside, her looks. In fact, there's a famous shot of the Goodman orchestra circa 1941: Charlie Christian and Cootie Williams, the only black faces in the band, are plainly visible over the leader's left shoulder; Helen Forrest, the only woman in the group, is equally easy to pick out, only here in this nonglamour photo she looks more like Benny's *Yiddishe Momme* than his chick singer.

Back in that pre-Streisand day, there was an awful lot of fussing about how both Forrest's nose and name (originally Helen Fogel) had to be changed to hide her Semitic origins. In the same spirit she was compelled to change the color of her hair to a bright shiksa blond and presented herself in the most extravagant gowns—Earl Wilson once devoted an entire column to describing how her costumery prevented her from sitting down.

Anita O'Day, as is well known, was the first singer to take a stand and say to heck with all that, and you accepted her strictly as a musician or not at all. Forrest was the embodiment of the pre-O'Day school for whom primping and preening for the gig—extremely difficult to deal with on the road—were as important as the music itself. As it happens, O'Day was hardly deficient in the attractiveness department (she cleaned up real nice) and Forrest was also a brilliant musician and interpreter.

Both ladies wrote autobiographies, and they're two of the best behind-the-bandstand looks at the swing era. In *I Had the Craziest Dream,* Forrest recalls how she was able to withstand the temptation to become romantically involved with the many nice, attractive men she worked with in the bands (even the remarkable Artie Shaw; Goodman was less of a lure). That is, until she ran smack into Harry James, the master seducer who completely derailed her heart. O'Day, on the other hand, was able to mess around with as many men and/or musicians as she liked without fear of anyone coming anywhere near her heart.

Born in 1917, Forrest got her start, like almost everyone else of her generation, singing on radio. In 1935, at eighteen, she landed an important stint on WCBS's *The Blue Velvet Hour* with (future *Hit Parade* conductor) Mark Warnow and His Blue Velvet Band playing "Blue Velvet Music" with vocals by "Betty Blue" (née Forrest, née Fogel). The only thing odd about this arrangement was that they weren't hawking any "Blue Velvet" product; this was a sustaining, or nonsponsored, series. After a fit of prima donnaism with Warnow, she left the show and received an offer from rising bandleader Ozzie Nelson. This she wisely turned down: Nelson's wife, Harriet, was already singing with the band, and Forrest realized that Mrs. Nelson would automatically get first crack at the best songs. It was an insightful move on Forrest's part, although she must have realized she could sing rings around Harriet Hilliard

Nelson, who was far from the world's greatest singer (although she's charming on her many duets with her Ozzie).

Forrest was brought to the attention of both Goodman and Shaw by Ziggy Elman (born Harry Finkelman), a *landsman* who had also changed his name for show business (he also changed his instrument, when he switched from trombone to trumpet). When she auditioned for Goodman, he rather rudely walked out in the middle of her number (as he had done with Martha Tilton), which turned out to be highly symptomatic of their relationship. Shaw, however, was the first to hire her, and for two years she served as star singer with Shaw's superb 1938–39 band.

But Forrest was more than just a singer with Shaw, Goodman, and then James; she was the singer who helped all three of these legendary leaders reach (or at least sustain) their commercial peaks. Like Ward with Goodman, Forrest and the Shaw band matured together, evolving into one of the best jazz-pop units of all time—you never forget your first love, and this one of many editions of the Shaw organization is probably the most widely beloved by fans, not least because of the contagious warmth of its girl singer. To reiterate what Shaw told me, he normally didn't dig singers of any kind, unless they were musicians like Tony Pastor or Hot Lips Page, who reminded him of his hero, Louis Armstrong (as did Billie Holiday). The major exceptions, Artie said, were Forrest and Mel Tormé. (For reasons known only to himself, however, Shaw neglected to include even a single Forrest vocal in *Self Portrait*, the five-CD retrospective boxed set of his career, which he compiled himself for release on the occasion of his ninetieth birthday in 2000.)

At the end of 1939, Shaw astonished the entertainment industry by breaking up his band, in a much discussed act of rebellion against what he perceived as the excesses of commercial music. Since Forrest was now famous, she wasn't surprised to get a call from Benny Goodman's office. Theirs was a passionless relationship: She happened to need a band, he needed a singer, and that one phone call was all it took. They didn't get along particularly well—she called him "one of the most unpleasant men I ever met"—and after less than two years, the leader so irritated the singer that she felt compelled to quit.

Forrest had an advantage over most of Goodman's singers—Ward, Tilton, the talented and underappreciated Louise Tobin, Peggy Lee, and the others—in that she was already a seasoned pro (all of twenty-two years old) when she came to work for BG. "We loved her, for the time she was great, and even now she'd be great," as the late trumpeter Chris Griffin, speaking for the Goodman sidemen collectively, said of her to me in a 1991 interview. "She always had a great sound, and excellent phrasing ability. Helen was just a naturally fine singer, probably the best band singer around at that time." Like

the immediate prewar Goodman band itself, Forrest is at once sexy and swinging, slick and polished yet constantly exuding warmth, at once an excellent musician and a terrific actress and interpreter.

By the time she joined Goodman in December 1939, she was, along with Count Basie's Jimmy Rushing and Ray Noble's Al Bowlly, one of the absolute masters of the 32-bar vocal refrain, and, as Mr. Griffin says, probably the best band singer of all time. (Decades before there was a pop-rock singer who called herself "Madonna," WNEW's Bob Jones dubbed Forrest "the Madonna of the Middle Chorus.") Two years after her death in 1999, Collectors' Choice Music issued *The Complete Helen Forrest with Benny Goodman*, a three-disc package that includes all fifty-five of the Forrest-Goodman tracks, beginning with "Busy as a Bee" from December 1939 and continuing through the provocatively titled "Down, Down, Down (What a Song!)" in May 1941; fifty-five titles in eighteen months is a goodly body of work.

Forrest provides the perfect balance for the other major "voice" of the Goodman orchestra at this time, arranger Eddie Sauter. For years Sauter embodied the ideal of progressivism in jazz, the slowly emerging movement that looked to incorporate the developments of modern academic music into the popular dance band, a trend that paralleled the rise of modern jazz. Sauter's writing, replete with brilliant modulations and harmonies that few dance band writers dreamed existed in 1940, achieved a stingingly serious "cold" sound, reminiscent more of the posttonal compositions of Bartók than of the more overtly romantic textures of Debussy or Delius. Yet Goodman initially assigned the high-minded Sauter the bread-and-butter role of writing most of the ballads for the new singer, Miss Forrest—despite his alleged insensitivity, Goodman knew that the two would, in a way no one else could have predicted, play off each other perfectly.

Forrest was never at liberty for long in the band era: Less than a month elapsed between Shaw and Goodman, and then between Goodman and James, even though she had not directly been poached by one bandleader from another. Because of the AFM recording ban of 1942–44, Forrest's two-year period with James (1941–43) was not nearly as well documented as her work with Goodman. There are only nineteen commercial tracks by her with James (all included on *The Complete Helen Forrest with the Harry James Orchestra*, Sony/Collectors' Choice Music), but the percentage of successful music—in every sense of the word—is extremely high.

As previously mentioned, Forrest was possibly the definitive voice of the American experience in World War II. Like the Andrews Sisters, she did those jingoistic songs that rah-rahed our boys on to victory rather like college football cheers: "My Beloved Is Rugged" and "That Soldier of Mine" and the almost comically propagandistic "He's 1-A in the Army and

He's A-1 in My Heart." But the most important hits of their time—the real substantial music of World War II that Forrest made immortal—were the sentimental songs of separation, such as "I Don't Want to Walk Without You," "I Remember You," and "I Had the Craziest Dream," all three of which were blockbusters. No one ever sounded better at addressing absent lovers than Helen Forrest. Billie Holiday could sing the same songs and make you think she was alone because her man had left her for another woman—or was dead. When Forrest sang them, you knew the absence was only temporary, that her man would soon be back with a medal on his chest as soon as it was over over there.

She left James in December 1943 to go out as a single—only a year after Sinatra—and made a string of singles for Decca (1944–46) and then for MGM (1947–50), as detailed in Bob Sixsmith's discography (in Forrest's book). She had a number of top 10 hits in the Decca period, but they were nearly all duets with Dick Haymes—there was nothing that established her as a solo act, and nothing that she sang in those years managed to find its way into the collective consciousness.

The duets with Haymes—she also was a regular on his Autolite-sponsored radio show—constitute some of the finest ever recorded by a boy-girl team (not to mention a Jewish–Irish/Argentine team). She's a bit perky, while he's a little on the mellow side; she has a little too much personality, he perhaps not enough; and together they're simply perfect. The eighteen songs that they recorded together (collected on the British CD *Dick Haymes and Helen Forrest: The Complete Duets,* Music Club) represent some of the very best of postwar pop. Haymes already had a taste for the better class of sentimental oldies, songs like "I'm Always Chasing Rainbows," "It Had to Be You," and "Something to Remember You By," but what's notable is that virtually every one of the new songs essayed by the duo is outstanding, including three of Jerome Kern's latest and greatest, "Long Ago and Far Away," "In Love in Vain," and "All Through the Day" (not to mention his 1920 "Look for the Silver Lining").

Although the bulk of the MGM and Decca sides (beyond the Haymes duets) have never been reissued, she also recorded fifty sides for World Transcriptions in 1949–50, which have come out on the highly recommended *The Complete World Transcriptions.* The songs are also first-rate standards, like "I Can't Give You Anything but Love," "I'm Confessin'," and the finest-ever treatment of Rodgers and Hammerstein's "What's the Use of Wonderin'?" The orchestrations, featuring a full studio orchestra and strings (conducted by Carmen Dragon, father of the first half of the Captain & Tennille) are sufficient, and the playing times are generally short—for the most part just around two minutes. While for most singers this would be a liability, for Forrest it's an asset. We like her better with a smaller canvas than a

larger one. We're already so used to hearing her with only a brief vocal refrain, or as half of a duo, that it's hard to get used to Helen Forrest having a whole three-minute side to herself. These short tracks are just perfect, and she's never been more appealing.

As good as her postwar work may be, there's a feeling in all of it that her moment had already passed, even though she was only thirty in 1948. In the early fifties, Forrest cut a few singles for the Bell label, a company concerned primarily with covering songs that were already hits. By 1955, she was no longer a current artist; almost everything else she would sing would be a remake of her big band era work. Even covering other people's hits was more creative than simply rehashing her own, and then rehashing them.

Yet her 1955–56 Capitol material is surprisingly fresh. Like Ward at RCA at the same time, the label was bent on rerecording many of the major hits of the swing era in hi-fi. Forrest cut four "reunion" sides with Harry James, of which only one prompted listeners to exclaim "I've Heard That Song Before." The others, "I'm Beginning to See the Light," "I Cried for You," and "It's Been a Long, Long Time," were all Harry hits that had not originally featured her. Her own Capitol album was similarly inspired, featuring mostly familiar songs, like most of the James-era biggies ("I Had the Craziest Dream," "I Don't Want to Walk Without You," etc.), as well as more obscure items from her big band days (like the melodramatic "I'm in Love with the Honorable Mr. So and So," which she'd earlier cut with Shaw). Even when the songs are very familiar, the arrangements by Billy May and producer Dave Cavanaugh are fresh and lively—more like 1955 vocal charts, with a full string section, than 1943 big band charts—and Forrest herself is at her absolute peak.

There were other opportunities to record, like an RCA album with the Tommy Dorsey ghost band, a by-product of a 1963 tour. But mostly she did and redid her old songs, as for Reader's Digest and Time Life in the late sixties, as well as for an unusual album with Buddy DeFranco, the third great clarinetist in her life. She doesn't sound at all bad on her final album (1983), *Now and Forever* (Stash), for which arranger Hale Rood put together an all-star octet to back her on yet another run-through of her familiar repertoire. Her final years were marred by a recurrence of the scarlet fever she had suffered as a young girl, which resulted in a partial loss of hearing. But even as her hearing was going, she was able to keep singing the songs she knew by remembering where the notes were.

She died in 1999, at the age of eighty-one or eighty-two.

Though Forrest had top-10 hits in her duets with Haymes, none of her postband songs made quite the impression that her great sides with Harry James did. Even "I'll Buy That Dream," which is as perfect an anthem of postwar optimism—romantic, economic, technological ("a honeymoon in Cairo / in a brand-new autogyro")—as the Forrest-James hits were of wartime separation anxiety, was not a tune that fans were requesting.

Forrest, like Ward and Tilton, had her big moment, but even though she went on singing almost until the end, like the others she understood that when it was over, it was over.

Sing a Song of Ellington

Ivie Anderson
Herb Jeffries
Al Hibbler

"In this country," Shakespeare wrote in *Othello*, "the Ducal word is law." So it was, too, in the world of jazz, where the word of Duke Ellington was law for the fifty years he led the greatest orchestra in the history of American popular music, and for all the decades since then as well. Describing Ellington is like the parable of the blind men and the elephant, in that you're dealing with a number of discrete entities at once: the bandleader, the pianist (who never sounded better than when he accompanied singers, as when he plays behind Ethel Waters on the verse to "I Can't Give You Anything but Love"), the songwriter, the composer of extended concert works. Each individual Ellington was a master of his art, and taken together, the parts add up to genius.

(In many of his spoken introductions from concerts, mostly from the latter decades of his long career, Ellington became enamored of the phrase "of course." Having broached the subject of his work with vocalists, of course, I have to state up-front that we're not just talking about Ellington himself, but also Billy Strayhorn, the most vital of all Ellington collaborators, whom for nearly thirty years the bandleader referred to as his "composing and arranging partner." Originally hired to help with vocal charts—although his responsibilities quickly expanded to include everything else—Strayhorn went on orchestrating a goodly share of the band's works involving singers and pop songs.)

Of jazz's major composers, it was Ellington who devoted the most energy to exploring the relationship between vocal and instrumental jazz. Very early on, he realized that jazz was a music in which instrumental solos were initially vocalized—that is, made to sound as close to the human voice as possible (a key factor in the genesis of jazz in New Orleans, particularly in terms of the influence of church music). Subsequently, much of vocal jazz was a matter of making the human voice sound like an instrument. The dichotomy—instruments as voices and voices as instruments—is perfectly realized in "On a Turquoise Cloud." On this 1947 classic, the two primary "voices" are a singer (the opera-oriented Kay Davis), who produces pure, wordless notes that sound exactly like a brass or reed instrument, and a trombonist (the smooth-toned Lawrence Brown), whose solo could easily be mistaken for a human voice.

Thus Ellington and Strayhorn moved in unique ways their wonders to perform. Adhering to the classical definition of the term "vocalise," the likes of Davis, Adelaide Hall, and Yvonne Lanauze could sing wordlessly like instrumentalists. But though they sang the tune without the words, as Emily Dickinson put it, they could hardly be described as scat singers in the tradition of Leo Watson or Ella Fitzgerald; within the context of the Ellington orchestra, those singers were Betty Roche and Ray Nance. Singers also occasionally participated in the extended works of the two maestros (such as *Black, Brown and Beige; The Perfume Suite;* and *The Liberian Suite*) as well as in the band's numerous shorter experiments in musical form, like "I Don't Know What Kind of Blues I Got" and "Lush Life." Even apart from Ellington's specifically theatrical works, like *Beggar's Holiday*, there were many longer pieces that extensively utilized the human instrument—pieces like *My People*, *A Drum Is a Woman*, and the three Sacred Concerts.

Ellington's choice of vocalists sometimes puzzled certain critics; even Stanley Dance, Ellington's own Boswell, who probably wrote more words on the Maestro and his music than any other scribe, hardly talks about the band's singers—Ivie Anderson and Al Hibbler are barely mentioned in *The World of Duke Ellington* and Herb Jeffries isn't even in the index. Still, from the perspective of history it's clear that the best of the bunch, Anderson, Hibbler, and Jeffries, were to other band vocalists what Johnny Hodges and Ben Webster were to saxophonists.

Ivie Anderson (1905–1949)

Of all Ellington vocalists, Ivie Anderson was the most versatile; her charismatic alto could address seminonsensical rhythm songs, scat episodes, and tender love laments with equal success. Although she didn't enjoy a lengthy post-Ellington career the way Herb Jeffries and Al Hibbler did, I don't think either of those two gentlemen would object were we to describe her as the most beloved of Ellington vocalists. Her stay (1931–42) was the longest of any singer in the band, and likewise her exquisite voice introduced more classic Ellingtonian songs, from "It Don't Mean a Thing" to "I Got It Bad," than any other. She was the ultimate voice of the Ellington experience.

Ivie Anderson was born on July 10, 1905, in Gilroy, California (although Barry Ulanov, in his *Metronome* obituary, says that "she was born in Oklahoma and educated at a convent in California"). She grew up in early black show business, working in those California venues that would hire black talent, and very early on acclimated herself to the rigors of the road (long before she joined the most famous traveling band in history). Anderson appeared in one of the many road companies of *Shuffle Along,* as well as the Club Alabam in Los Angeles, the Grand Terrace in Chicago, and, according to scholar John Chilton, even the Cotton Club in New York—well before her stint with Ellington. She also worked the Cotton Club in Culver City, California, was one of the first African American entertainers to tour Australia (in 1928), and appeared with Anson Weeks and His Orchestra at the Mark Hopkins Hotel in San Francisco, which would make her perhaps the first black vocalist to sing in public with a white group (not to mention one of the first women to sing with any dance band).

After a brief, unrecorded stint with Earl Hines in Chicago, Anderson joined Ellington's band at the Oriental Theatre in that city in February 1931; as band historian Klaus Stratemann has ascertained, the idea of adding a permanent girl singer to the band was originally the suggestion of theater owners Balaban and Katz, who had booked Ellington and company for four weeks in various Windy City theaters. The concept seems to be one that Ellington only accepted gradually: Anderson didn't record her first vocal with the band, "It Don't Mean a Thing (If It Ain't Got That Swing)," until a year later, in February 1932. Following her recorded debut, she didn't reappear on disc ("Delta Bound") until the end of that year. Ultimately, that monthlong tryout stretched into eleven years and several international tours.

Along with the rest of the Ellington aggregation, Anderson was a resounding success when the band played the London Palladium in 1933. Had she elected to remain in Europe, she could not only have easily found work but doubtless become a major star in her own right—tethered to no man's orchestra—along the lines of earlier Ellington voice Adelaide Hall. In fact, Anderson was unmistakably cut from the same cloth as that group of somewhat more formal-sounding black female entertainers who found success in Europe—Hall, Elisabeth Welch, and Alberta Hunter, not to mention Ethel Waters. Like Waters and Hall especially, Anderson could sound rather proper, with very accurate intonation and sharp verbal articulation. Unlike Waters, Anderson doesn't roll her Rs, though she comes close. She sounds as if she'd grown up in the tradition of opera and parlor-room ballads long before discovering Louis Armstrong and Bessie Smith as a young adult.

Which was precisely what Ellington wanted: a woman with a very proper sound who could also get low-down and funky—a lot of the material he laid out for her can be described as nonsense and/or jive. Her first recorded vocal, "It Don't Mean a Thing," quickly became the national anthem of scat and the archetype for hard-swinging, jive-inflected

numbers in the big band era. Over the years, Ellington hurled further slices of jump and jive in Anderson's direction, like "La De Doody Do." A number of these somewhat less-than-literary efforts, such as "I've Got to Be a Rug Cutter" and "Scrounch" (aka "Scrontch"), were attempts to launch new national dance crazes at the Cotton Club; "La De Doody Do" is pure rhythm, with next to no help from the lyric (which may be the only one ever to rhyme "Mozart" with "go-cart"), and it's the whole show again on "Scrontch," in which Anderson jumps down hard on the first beat of the measure—as if she were kicking a football—making that one note into a veritable symphony all by itself.

"Scrontch," along with the infrequently revived "Swingtime in Honolulu" and "Carnival in Caroline," were all written by the team of Ellington and lyricist (and frequent composer) Henry "the Neem" Nemo for the band to play as dance numbers in the 1938 Cotton Club revue. The three numbers embody very different aspects of Anderson's artistry. Ellington occasionally had her sing of foreign lands, like Hawaii in this case, or "Martinique Island" in the band's Liszt variation "Ebony Rhapsody." But more often he had her extol the charms of places closer to home. The most frequent kind of material that Ellington and Anderson addressed is mammy songs—airs of the Sunny South—and their efforts in this area represent the final surge of creativity to be devoted to this formerly formidable genre of popular music. Her second side with the band was "Delta Bound," which has her answering the call of the levee, while "Cotton," from 1935, finds her ruminating over the fact of how "darkies" were born to pick the stuff. And where there's cotton, can watermelon be far behind? The most unabashed of the Maestro's own mammy songs (apparently he wrote both words and music) is "Watermelon Man," a quick 16-bar chorus written not from the perspective of a watermelon consumer, as was usually the case in watermeloncentric literature, but from a vendor of the fruit.

Which was only the beginning: In quick succession in 1937 she recorded three mammy songs in a row: "Old Plantation," "All God's Chillun Got Rhythm," and "Alabamy Home." "All God's Chillun" is easily her best-known performance, since she sang it onscreen in the classic Marx Brothers MGM picture *A Day at the Races,* which, given the multiracial nature of the music, gives the title a double meaning. Written by two Jewish songwriters, the veteran lyricst Gus Kahn and the recent refugee from Hitler Bronislau Kaper, "All God's Chillun" was partly inspired by the traditional spiritual "Gonna Shout All over God's Heaven." Staged as a rather elaborate production number in the film, it gives Anderson her finest moments of screen time (there weren't many). The Ellington band is not seen: Although they recorded part of the instrumental material, their contribution was not included in the original film sound track but had to wait to be heard until a CD released in the year 2000. "Alabamy Home" celebrates the exotic and the familiar at the same time, simultaneously heading South and to the Far East. Even though the lyric praises Mammy and 'Bammy, the music (opening with Tricky Sam Nanton's divine trombone ya-ya's) paraphrases the slightly earlier "Caravan."

"Old Plantation" also features Nanton, this time stating the main melody, but Cootie Williams's tightly muted trumpet solo is even more to the point, as he introduces this Stephen Foster–style plantation-praising aria with a quote from "Dixie." Ellington offered a variation on that idea three years later on one of his last Dixiecentric discs, "At a Dixie Roadside Diner," which commences with the piano player paraphrasing "Old Folks at Home" ("Way down upon the Swanee River . . .") and includes rhumba rhythms; it's a sterling example of Ellington and Anderson levitating a fairly undistinguished song. As Bobby Short put it, "Like Gertrude Lawrence, she could sing the worst songs in the grandest way."

That trip to the Dixie diner occurred in 1940—late in the game for that kind of a song. Finally, the singer and bandleader effectively killed off the mammy song genre with "Jump for Joy"—the title song of Ellington's 1941 revue—which revels in the death of the symbols of servitude, such as *The Green Pastures* and the slave-chasing "hound dogs" from *Uncle Tom's Cabin.* Ellington recorded two takes of this song of his, one with Anderson, the other with Herb Jeffries, and ultimately elected to release the Jeffries version; perhaps Anderson had waxed poetical on the charms of "the beautiful South" so often that he feared no one would believe her if she started to criticize it. Another sequence in the show *Jump for Joy* was titled "Uncle Tom's Cabin Is a Drive-in Now," which similarly satirized and trivialized the clichés of the beautiful South.

"Carnival in Caroline" and "Let's Have a Jubilee" (the latter being a distinctly Southern social event) are vivid descriptions of party time in the beautiful Southland, which is only appropriate as Anderson was the original party-down signifier. Another number from *Jump for Joy,* "Chocolate Shake," is the best of her Ducal dances. And she's never more high-flyingly exuberant than on "So Far, So Good" and "Me and You" (her first two vocals after the band switched to RCA Victor in 1940), in which she perfectly nails the thrill of being in love not in vain. "The Five O'Clock Whistle" is the sort of song that Ella Fitzgerald was doing at this time in her wubba dolly–little yellow basket phase. Anderson's final vocal with the band, Erwin Drake's "Hayfoot, Strawfoot," makes even U.S. Army basic training sound like the most fun thing in the world. With Anderson exhorting us to get hep-hep-hep in our step, marching off to war becomes a real blast.

"Killin' Myself" pushes the party atmosphere to the very edge, with Anderson's protagonist determined to achieve a laconic hipness at any cost, even self-destruction. Likewise, she gets a party started even when the subject is giving the kiss-off to an abusive playmate, as in "You Gave Me the Gate (And I'm Swinging)" and "I'm Checkin' Out Goo'mbye," the latter of which is laid out in the form of a "Dear John" phone call as set up in a spoken introduction. These define the genre of swinging vengeful goodbye-and-fuck-you songs; Rosemary Clooney, who later revived the song in loving memory of Ivie Anderson on her 1956 album with Duke Ellington, praised the line "the cake is all dough."

Most of the time, however, when love has faded, the mood is far from jubilant. Anderson's greatest strength may not have been Mammy or nonsensical party songs but torch songs, sad songs of love and loss, many of which quickly became Ellington and Strayhorn standards. Hordes of singers have addressed "Mood Indigo," "Solitude," and "I Got It Bad" over the last seventy years—Sinatra and Holiday, in particular, made them their own—but Anderson's treatments remain definitive (even though she sings only half of "Mood Indigo," and messes up the last line at that). Anticipating Sinatra and Holiday, she was a master of the bittersweet torch song, self-pity with a touch of irony and just enough of the blues to prevent the whole thing from getting too much sentiment all over you. She was also particularly sensitive to the nuances of Billy Strayhorn's music, as in "Your Love Has Faded" and the obscure "Love Like This Can't Last."

The relationship between the singer and the bandleader climaxed, as it were, with the "revuesical" *Jump for Joy,* which ran from July to September 1941 at the Mayan Theatre in Los Angeles. This celebration of African American culture yielded the aforementioned "Jump for Joy," "Chocolate Shake," "I Got It Bad," and "Rocks in My Bed." These four songs effectively conclude the Anderson-Ellington relationship: "Jump for Joy" renders it impossible for Anderson, or anyone else, to ever sing a Mammy song again. "Chocolate Shake" is the best of the team's dance numbers, "I Got It Bad" is their ultimate torch song, and "Rocks in My Bed" is a blues like no other.

Anderson had suffered from asthma all her life, and by 1942 the rigors of twenty years on the road had worn her down considerably. She left the orchestra shortly after the first AFM recording ban went into effect that summer, settling in Los Angeles. The condition of her health meant that she could only work locally in the L.A. area, but, in addition to performing, she operated a successful restaurant (Ivie Anderson's Chicken Shack) and an apartment building. She also married, divorced, and married again. Her post-Ellington work is all but negligible: Known to survive is a single AFRS *Jubilee* broadcast with the Johnny Otis Orchestra, and eleven songs for two very obscure West Coast labels.

In 1946, she recorded eight songs for the L.A.-based Black & White Records. She is accompanied by an all-star orchestra, which includes the outstanding tenorist Lucky Thompson, future Ellington star altoist Willie Smith, and occasional Ellingtonian Charles Mingus, yet the first reaction one has to these sides is to miss the hands of Ellington and Strayhorn as musical directors. The backgrounds are lively but generic—here's none of the custom tailoring that she routinely received in the Ellington band. Their absence is particularly evident on "I Got It Bad," the only Ellington item in the bunch. Anderson herself at the age of forty-one sounds as terrific as ever, especially on three songs it seems she had been singing since the twenties: the jazz-pop perennial "On the Sunny Side of the Street" (bass solo by Mingus), and two semi-standards from the classic blues experience, "Big Butter and Egg Man" and "Empty Bed Blues."

The standout of the bunch is "Twice Too Many," a lovely ballad driven by a unique concept ("twice too many stars . . . twice too bright a moon . . ."); it also makes a vivid contrast with the old Bessie Smith number that deals precisely with the same issue using the invective of the blues, "Empty Bed Blues." "Tall, Dark, and Handsome" and "I Tho't You Ought to Know" show Anderson keeping up to date with postwar developments in two songs associated with, respectively, Louis Jordan and Nat Cole. These and the two hard-core 12-bar blues numbers, "Empty Bed Blues" (brilliant solos by Lucky Thompson and Irving Ashby) and "My Voot Is Here to Stay," show that with her sharp, hard tone and aggressive, kick-ass attitude, she could have continued to compete in the more aggressive world of postwar blues and black pop; these sides, along with her high-octane, fast and furious revamp of "Empty Bed Blues," compare favorably with anything Dinah Washington was doing in the late forties.

But, alas, it was not to be: Ivie Anderson died of an asthmatic condition on December 27, 1949, aged forty-four. At the time, Duke Ellington was on the other side of the country, heading from New York to an engagement in Toronto. Doubtless he wanted to be at Ivie's funeral, but the show, as they say, must go on. However, according to *Down Beat*, "he sent condolence in the form of a huge floral piece."

Herb Jeffries (born 1913)

Herb Jeffries and Al Hibbler were studies in contrast—the first was basically a smooth-toned balladeer whom Ellington occasionally put to work on the blues, the latter was steeped in funkiness yet could also put over a love song with the best of 'em. Jeffries exemplified the Ellington sound at its most finely polished, like Lawrence Brown, Otto Hardwick, or Ben Webster in one of his tender moods; Hibbler represented the band at its most raucous and low-down, like Tricky Sam Nanton, Bubber Miley, or Ben Webster getting hysterical. Jeffries only

stayed three seasons with the band (1940–42) before departing for solo success on the wings of his best-selling "Flamingo." Hibbler, whose inventive distortions led Ellington to describe his style as "tonal pantomime," lasted from 1943 to 1951 before he, too, graduated to the Hit Parade as a single.

After Ivie Anderson, Jeffries extended the tradition of Ellington vocal stars who got started with the Maestro's fellow pianist-leader Earl Hines (the next was Ray Nance). Based in Chicago, Hines was in a good position to scout out new talent from that city. The "Fatha" actually recorded twice with Jeffries, and both times he seemed to view him as a blues singer, on "Blue" with his own orchestra in 1934 and "Blues for You, Johnny" under Sidney Bechet's leadership in 1940. But both cuts illustrate, despite the allusions to the blues, that Jeffries is essentially a crooner at heart: "Blues for You, Johnny" may utilize something like blues harmony, but Jeffries croons it like a love song, romantic and mellow, without any of the invective that, say, Ivie Anderson would bring to it. In his solo career, in fact, one of Jeffries's best-known later numbers was a very romantic, showbizzy, and somewhat de-bluesed version of the Spencer Williams jazz standard "Basin Street Blues."

In the forties, vocalists would start leaving the big bands that sired them to make it on their own. In the thirties, singers, particularly in the black community, could be quite well known around black showbiz before they joined a nationally known big band; this was the case with Bon Bon Tunnell with Jan Savitt, and both Anderson and Jeffries with Ellington. In fact, Jeffries already had a film career before coming on board with the band, having starred in three all-black Westerns made for the circuit of theaters in Negro neighborhoods across the country.

He was born in Detroit, in a year now believed to be 1913, and came of age musically in Chicago. There he sang with bandleader Erskine Tate and then Hines, with whom he made "Just to Be in Caroline" and "Blue," his first waxing, in 1934. At this point, the twenty-something Jeffries sounds much like one of the many black tenors of the era, such as Orlando Robeson (who sang with pianist Claude Hopkins's orchestra), Pha Terrell (who made "Until the Real Thing Comes Along" into a breakthrough hit for Andy Kirk and His Clouds of Joy), or even falsetto-voiced Bill Kenny of the Ink Spots. Between 1937 and 1989 he starred in four all-black B Western musicals, produced in Los Angeles, most famously the 1939 *Bronze Buckaroo*. He joined the Ellington orchestra in October 1939.

Like Anderson, who was then still with the band, he came on board in Chicago and then had to wait awhile before making his Ducal debut on disc with the band. That was almost six months later, back yet again in Chicago, in March 1940 on "You, You Darling."

For Jeffries, the part of the "Bronze Buckaroo"

and the role of Ellington boy singer were only two of the identities he would have over the years; this to a degree reflected his own multicultural ethnic background, which, even though he continues to regard himself as Negro, also included French, Irish, and Native American ancestry. Appropriately, "You, You Darling," his first recorded vocal with Ellington, was an ersatz-traditional Irish ballad written for movie tenor Dennis Morgan (who, coincidentally, introduced the Ellington band at its 1943 Carnegie Hall debut). Jeffries had already been a tenor and a cowboy; now, singing an ersatz-Irish song was a logical reentry point back into the mainstream of American pop and jazz. This may have inspired Billy Strayhorn to note the potential similarities between Jeffries and Bing Crosby. At this point, Strayhorn and Ellington both encouraged Jeffries to take Crosby as his model: When the singer developed his own variation on Der Bingle's baritone, they liked what they heard, and told him to hold it right there.

Jeffries only sings on ten commercial sides with Ellington (plus an additional four songs on the Standard Transcriptions sessions), and his specialty is, obviously, lush romantic opuses. Strayhorn's arrangement of "There Shall Be No Night" is as close as the Ellington orchestra ever came to sounding like a sweet band like Wayne King's; although the piece is in 4/4, the opening melody is accented with waltzlike rests: 1-2-3-pause. Here and on "What Good Would It Do" (on which the band takes a back seat), Jeffries, Strayhorn, and Ben Webster make these long-forgotten songs sound as good as if the Duke had written them himself. Likewise, Jeffries sounds so rich, deep, and completely in charge on "I Never Felt This Way Before" and "The Girl in My Dreams Tries to Look Like You" (credited to the leader's son, Mercer) that one wonders why these two lovely slices of Ellingtonia are seldom if ever revived.

If Anderson's specialty in the mid-thirties was swinging mammy songs, Jeffries belonged to the realm of the exotic. His straight tone—far more flexible tonally than it was rhythmically—made him a kind of vocal equivalent of valve trombonist Juan Tizol. Had he stayed longer with the band, he would probably have done more of this material, but he's heard to great effect on "I Hear a Rhapsody," a quasi-Spanish tune by Latin bandleader Richard Gasparre. And, most famously, there was his big hit with the band, "Flamingo," one of the best-selling singles in all Ellingtonia. It was Strayhorn's adventurous arrangement and Jeffries's robust, lusty vocal—especially his wordless wailing, and his leaps from a low Bingish baritone to high falsetto trills—that put the song over, and became the foundation of his subsequent solo career. (Strayhorn reused part of the arrangement, including Jeffries's signature wails, on the band's transcription of "I Don't Want to Set the World on Fire.") Jeffries has spoken of how people love deep, rich voices like Crosby's, but black audiences in particular also love high Jan Peerce-ing

falsettos, from the Ink Spots to Jimmy Scott to Michael Jackson. On "Flamingo," Jeffries is a deep baritone and a stratospheric falsetto at one and the same time. As he has told every audience he's played to over the last sixty-five years, most people came to earth by stork, but he arrived on a flamingo.

Even though Jeffries appears on so few studio recordings with the band, these include several undisputed masterpieces of Ellington's writing for vocals, none greater than "The Brownskin Gal in the Calico Gown" from *Jump for Joy*. "Brownskin Gal" is Paul Francis Webster's most surreal lyric, this being a nonlinear sequence of unrelated images ("a penny for the moon . . . a jackknife for a song, a garter for the gal in the blue sarong"), tchotchkes of romance and whimsy that add up to the implication of a story, which Jeffries makes sound warm and erotic. That title tune, "Jump for Joy," incidentally, finds him doing surprisingly well with an up-tempo swinger.

Jeffries's last two sides with Ellington are the payoff, two songs that feature the composer-arrangers as first-rate writers of both words and music: "I Don't Know What Kind of Blues I Got" (words and music by Ellington) and "My Little Brown Book" (words and music by Strayhorn). "Blues" has Ellington the lyricist following Paul Francis Webster's example, this being another disjointed set of images, only this time instead of suggestions of romance, Ellington offers up verbal tableaux depicting the steamy underside of early African American culture: the slow-dancing blues and voodoo ("I'm going to see Snake Mary"). "Little Brown Book" may be Strayhorn's finest lyric, more mature, more sincere, and less melodramatic than his celebrated "Lush Life." Jeffries—marvelously understated here, not sounding just exotic but completely believable—helps Strayhorn finish the job of turning it into one of the all-time touching laments of lost love.

In 1959, Jeffries married the burlesque star Tempest Storm. (He's credited with writing, directing, and producing the 1967 "nudie mystery" *Mundo Depravado* starring Ms. Storm.) In her 1987 autobiography, *The Lady Is a Vamp*, Ms. Storm offered an interesting opinion as to why her husband never made it bigger as a solo attraction after leaving Ellington in 1942. According to the onetime Mrs. Jeffries, it wasn't racism or changing tastes that held the singer back, it was Jeffries's own relative lack of ambition. To be fair, he was forty-five at the time they wed, and may by then have wanted to slow down a bit, and it does explain why he never approached his contemporaries Billy Eckstine and Nat Cole in postwar popularity. Storm contends that he just wasn't hungry enough to keep working all the time, do all the gigs that were offered to him, or keep fighting his way up the showbiz mountain. And who could blame him? It's a mighty tough row to hoe.

Jeffries's recorded work of the last sixty-five years is erratic, but there are some marvelous pockets scattered throughout. He'll bounce between major and minor labels, singles and albums, and sometimes years will pass without his going into a studio—all of which would seem to support his ex-wife's contention. It would take more time than we have to track his path from label to label and project to project, but there are plenty of highlights worth noting.

Like Anderson, after leaving Ellington he first turns up on a black-owned West Coast label, Exclusive (aka Excelsior) Records, with a series of 78 rpm single masters that later appeared on 10" LPs on Mercury. The three best-known Mercury albums are *Magenta Moods, Herb Jeffries Sings,* and *Just Jeffries.* Thanks to him, Exclusive actually landed a number 21 hit on the national *Billboard* chart, "When I Write My Song," based on the melody to "My Heart at Thy Sweet Voice," the most famous aria from Saint-Saëns's *Samson and Delilah.*

If the material on the 10" LPs is indicative, the Jeffries Exclusive catalogue is of a very high caliber indeed, with a large percentage of first-rate standards, including some absolutely terrific treatments of the oft-performed "These Foolish Things" and "Body and Soul." The tracks certainly don't sound as if they were produced by a budget-conscious independent: The first cut on *Magenta Moods* is one of several remakes of "Flamingo," this time in a decidedly un-Ellingtonian arrangement with a lush string section. Flamingos are more typically found in the wetlands than in the desert, yet here the woodwinds play an exotic, faux–Middle Eastern figure that makes it sound as if the "murmuring palms" of the lyric were doing their murmuring in a sandy oasis. There are also top-grade production values, like the additional singers on "Basin Street" and the spoken scenario that introduces "Angel Eyes." The latter is worth quoting:

> George: I see you're alone, sir. Shall I serve
> the usual?
>
> Herb: Yes, George . . . ah . . . has she . . . ?
>
> George: No sir, she hasn't been in tonight.
>
> Herb (singing): Try to think that love's not
> around . . .

Jeffries also did a marvelous session with a trombone octet led by West Coast arranger Buddy Baker, which resulted in some of his jazziest numbers, like a Luncefordian "My Blue Heaven" and a casually swinging "Million Dollar Baby." On occasion, he swings in a relaxed, Crosbyesque fashion even without the trombones, as on the rarely revived Arlen-Koehler Cotton Club song "You Gave Me Everything but Love." Like Sinatra, Jeffries recorded an a cappella version of Nat Cole's hit "Nature Boy" (although unlike either of the other singers, Jeffries shared many of the same spiritual beliefs as the song's composer, the yogilike eden ahbez).

By the late forties, Jeffries no longer sounds as if he's cloning Crosby, if indeed he ever did; a trace of the high-toned tenor still lingers, as well as the Western-style feeling of the buckaroo balladeer. Had the racial climate been different, he would have been a natural for Broadway, as he has the equipment and attitude to compete favorably with stars like Alfred Drake and John Raitt (as well as leading man good looks)—I would love to hear him belting "They Call the Wind Maria" or cooing "I Talk to the Trees" from *Paint Your Wagon.*

Following the 1948 recording ban, three key figures at Mercury switched to the more upscale Columbia: Herb Jeffries, producer Mitch Miller, and singer Frankie Laine. Unlike Miller and Laine, however, Jeffries was only with the label a year or two, and the random sample I've heard suggests that the Columbia sides are not on the same level as the best of the Exclusive/Mercury material. He sang fewer really good songs on Columbia, fewer standards, and more contemporary items that Miller was obviously hoping had hit potential. The most horrendous of these wannabe drama-novelties is Ervin Drake's "The Flying Dutchman," which, unlike Herb's previous swipe at Samson and Delilah, borrows the philosophy but not the music of Wagner's *Die Fliegende Holländer.* There were more amusing slices of exotica, though, like the desert epic "Flaming Sands," and then there's "Swamp Girl," which is a pop record like no other.

Mitch Miller originally produced "Swamp Girl" for Frankie Laine at Mercury, then, after he switched affiliations, redid the song in an even more over-the-top reading with Jeffries at Columbia. "Swamp Girl" is a brutal tale of lust, betrayal, and murder in the bayou—the sort of scenario more customarily depicted in original paperback novels or B movies of the period. The Jeffries disc, personally conducted by Miller, is permeated with sound effects designed to simulate swampy ooze and animal noises. Written by one Michael Brown, it may actually be somebody's idea of an ambitious art song: The three-minute disc has Jeffries singing from start to finish without repeating a line. It's actually just a damn long song, ending with the rather foreboding bromide, "Come to the deep / Where your sleep is without a dream." All in all, it's rather lurid trash, yet "Swamp Girl" is one of the most oddly compelling pop records I've ever heard, and an interesting corollary to Jeffries's more highbrow semiclassical sides.

Not all the Columbia sides are so outrageous. His biggest charting single of the era was "The Four Winds and the Seven Seas," an early hit for lyricist Hal David, for which Miller conceived the gimmick of applying extra echo to Jeffries's readings of the title line—making it sound especially windy. There are some dreadful faux-religious songs, "My Mother Singing" and "Sunday Isn't Sunday," but there's a compensatingly first-rate date backing Jeffries with a loose small group featuring Bobby

Hackett, which included "Love Me Long—Hold Me Close—Kiss Me Warm," which is a decent song despite its unwieldy title. There are also two singularly swell but somewhat obscure ballads, "Baby, Won't You Say You Love Me" and "Count Every Star," a beautiful slow love song, recorded by Dick Haymes and Artie Shaw, Lester Young, and even the Ravens, but never more beautifully than by Jeffries.

His next stop after Columbia was Coral, where he did several sessions with Les Brown, then the top bandleader at that Decca subsidiary, including new treatments of "Flamingo" and "Basin Street." There also was *Time on My Hands*, an excellent small group 10" album on Coral, done with just a rhythm section. This and his subsequent 12" albums, *Señor Flamingo* on RCA and the RKO Records ersatz-calypso package *The Devil Is a Woman* (reissued as *Jamaica*), are among the rarest of Jeffries's recordings. Fortunately, the album that may be his best, the 1957 Bethlehem 12" *Say It Isn't So*, is not so hard to find, being available on a gorgeous CD from that label's current corporate heir. The gorgeousness commences with the cover, which features future *I Dream of Jeannie* TV star Barbara Eden, working as a model at the time, posing fetchingly in a nightie.

Arranged and conducted by Russ Garcia, *Say It Isn't So* reveals Jeffries singing at his deepest and most magisterial, exploring the lower ranges of the baritone register almost like a cross between Eckstine and Crosby. His phrasing and sensitivity are strictly his own, however, and they make these twelve love songs come alive. This is one of the finest slow ballad albums, comparable to the efforts of Cole, Hartman, Haymes (in this period), and Jimmy Scott, perhaps even Sinatra. Jeffries is especially convincing in two songs of love and eating and drinking, "Angel Eyes" and "Dinner for One Please, James."

If *Say It Isn't So* is the high point of Jeffries's career, it's far from his swan song. There were more singles, including a few on the very obscure Olympic label, in which the singer is backed by intelligent accompaniment from Pete Rugolo's orchestra and the vocal group the Hi-Los (the best I've ever heard them, in fact)—and very decent songs indeed (for mid-fifties singles) such as "Autumn in Rome" and "Love Me or Leave Me." There are also some dismal singles from this period, done in rock 'n' roll style or a caricature thereof, among them a hysterically awful doo-wop interpretation of Crosby's megahit "Sweet Leilani." (In 1957, he played the title character in another B movie, *Calypso Joe,* in which the leading lady was Angie Dickinson.)

Jeffries also sounds fine on three albums made in the eighties: *I Remember the Bing* and *If I Were a King*, honoring Crosby and then Nat Cole in the company of the Lou Levy Trio, as well as a set of Ellington standards done with just the guitar of Laurindo Almeida for accompaniment. Before the eighties were over, he cut *I've Got the World on a String*, a fine set of standards for Discovery, but the most amazing revival was yet to come.

Around 1995, I reckon, Jim Ed Norman, a record producer with three first names, had a hankerin' to bring Jeffries—who at the time admitted to being eighty-three—back to the very beginning of his career. The result was *The Bronze Buckaroo (Rides Again)*, in which Jeffries sings an assortment of countrypolitan material, in the company of special guests from both country (Michael Martin Murphey, the Sons of the San Joaquin—neither of whom I had previously heard of) and pop-jazz (Take Six and the final edition of the Mills Brothers). Jeffries sounds absolutely inspired; his articulation is somewhat slurred compared to what it is on *Say It Isn't So*, but his pitch is absolutely on the money, and he has the mental and vocal resources to firmly invest himself in this material, giving these songs the same benefit of his long years of experience as he would the music of Ellington or Arlen. As a result, "I'm a Happy Cowboy" becomes a sagebrush equivalent of "I've Got the World on a String." *The Bronze Buckaroo* is both a wonderful capper for an extraordinary career and a cowboy record that even a city slicker like myself can love.

But who says it's the coda? Jeffries, who has already gone beyond ninety-five as this is being written, is hardly down for the count. For an Irish tenor turned Bronze Buckaroo turned band singer turned Black Bing turned calypso movie star turned master balladeer turned colored cowboy all over again, maybe life begins at ninety.

Al Hibbler (1915–2001)

"Albert Hibbler! Albert George Hibbler." That's what Ellington would announce after Hibbler had finished a number. According to veteran vocalist Bill Henderson, this wasn't mere Ducal sophistry and flowery verbal embellishment, but rather served a very definite purpose. Hibbler was blind, and though he could hear the applause, when Ellington recited all three of his names, it was a tip-off to the vocalist that he was receiving a standing ovation. On surviving airchecks and concerts, we hear Ellington announcing "Albert George Hibbler" on almost every show.

Ellington knew how to use distortion on the bandstand—the ratty tone of trombonist Joe "Tricky Sam" Nanton, the jungle-style growlings of muted trumpeters Cootie Williams and Rex Stewart, the near-hysterical tenor climaxes of Ben Webster and his stylistic descendants. It's hardly surprising that he would eventually hire a vocalist who could offer the same kind of "tonal pantomine"—to use Ellington's own term—with his singing.

Of the five major African American male vocalists of his generation—Billy Eckstine, Nat King Cole, Herb Jeffries, Joe Williams, and Hibbler (all born between 1914 and 1919)—Hibbler and Williams were the most fully immersed in the blues. But Hibbler's brand of blues was a much grittier kind than Williams's—even when he sings a ballad, he sounds as if he's singing a love song for a rough character in a tough dive. He also has a considerable amount of gospel feeling, except that he's so funky I can't imagine any self-respecting church that wouldn't excommunicate him the second he started emitting those sacrilegious distortions. On "Monday Every Day" and other songs he seems to be singing a love song, wailing the blues, and bending his knees in prayer all at once. He's praying to the Almighty that he'll find a lover and/or salvation, but at the same time he's singing the blues because he doesn't think it's bloody likely.

I use the term "bloody" because it's the sort of expression Hibbler himself would have used with his mondo bizarro English accent, as in "After the loyts go down leowwww—uh uh!" There are times when he sounds so bloody English that he could be the American equivalent of Anthony Newley. For all his immersion in the low-down blues, there's a side of Hibbler that yearns to be fancy and formal—why else would he record "Dinner for One Please, James" and, heaven help us, Joyce Kilmer's "Trees"? These are not exactly the kinds of songs that one expects to hear in a Kansas City speakeasy. Or a Beale Street bucket-of-blood.

On one of several occasions when I interviewed Hibbler, the name of Herb Jeffries, his predecessor in the Ellington orchestra, came up. All of a sudden Hib grew dismissive, not to mention derisive. "Herb Jeffries?" Hib croaked. "He sings like a white man!" I wouldn't want anyone to think Hibbler didn't like the singing of white people, since he named many of them as his influences and favorites, but he clearly didn't feel it was appropriate for Jeffries, who was essentially black (Jeffries's ethnic makeup comes from many different nations and strains, as we have seen), to sing that way.

The late Mr. Hibbler might not have intended that comment for publication, and I quote it here only because it serves to illustrate a point about his own singing. Whatever he does sing like, even when it's somewhat like what producer Bob Porter has described rather colorfully as "a freakin' limey!," Hibbler most definitely does not sound like a white man. It's difficult to imagine Jeffries singing "The Blues Came Falling Down" as Hibbler does on his 1950 Atlantic sessions, this being the most gully-low of all blues, as sung by a lowlife in a prison cell. On the other hand, he sounds unconvincing on the next track, Willard Robison's "Old Folks," the kind of thing that Jeffries, following the example of Crosby, could have pulled off with ease. (Perhaps for that reason, Hibbler's "Old Folks" was left off the original LP edition of his Atlantic material and not restored until the CD era.) Likewise, Hibbler sounds out of place singing "Dinner for One Please, James" (on *Monday Every Day*)—a song that was Jeffries's meat, and when he gets to the second line, he ad-libs the word "the" at the start, turning "Madam" into "the Madam," completely altering the character of this woman, and, for that matter, James as well.

Hibbler was born sightless in Little Rock, in 1915 (sometimes the location is given as Tyro, Mississippi), and received his earliest musical training in an Arkansas school for the blind. In the thirties, he sang with territory bands around the Midwest and Southwest, such as the Dub Jenkins band in Memphis, the Jeter-Pillars Orchestra in St. Louis, and Boots and His Buddies in San Antonio. Around 1941, he hooked up with pianist Jay McShann, who seemed poised to be the next bandleader to follow Count Basie out of Kansas City and onto the national scene. McShann's orchestra, which also included the young Charlie Parker in its reed section, was possibly the only band to carry two full-time male vocalists, both of whom were primarily blues shouters: Hibbler and the well-known Walter Brown. Brown was the bluesier of the two, and his features with McShann such as "Confessin' the Blues" and "Hootie Blues" were almost as popular with "race" audiences in their day as Jimmy Rushing's features with Basie were. Only in comparison with the even rougher-hewn Brown would Hibbler be considered more of a balladeer. His singing survives on two performances with McShann: a commercial Decca disc of "Get Me on Your Mind" and an aircheck from the Savoy Ballroom, coincidentally, of Ellington's "I Got It Bad (And That Ain't Good)."

In the summer of 1943, Hibbler was on his own again in New York, and was invited by Ellington, whom he had first met about five years earlier, to sit in with the band at the Hurricane Club in Times Square. In a story that Hibbler would tell many times over the next sixty years, he sat in with increasing regularity until he finally informed Duke that he couldn't keep singing on love alone. At this point, Ellington told him he was already on the payroll and could pick up a paycheck anytime, which he did with regularity until leaving the band in 1951. Ellington, it seemed, had commitment issues with potential sidemen, and when he wanted Hibbler to sit tight and wait, he extended the instruction "Do nothing till you hear from me."

The singer would soon have two opportunities to prove how well he could do "nothin'." Impresario George Wein has written of how Ellington would occasionally pick out a less-than-attractive woman as his evening playmate because, as he told Wein, "We all have to dig the distortion once in a while." By all indications, Duke began digging Hibbler's distortion almost immediately: No one was better at singing an especially Ducal turn of phrase. The first case in point was "Do Nothin' Till You Hear from Me," a song born when Ellington and songwriter Bob Russell took an expression the Maestro had already been employing in his conversation and used it as the title for a song adapted from the earlier instrumental "Concerto for Cootie." "Do Nothin'" was Hibbler's first studio recording with Ellington, done in 1943 for World Transcriptions. When Ellington switched to Columbia in 1947, at long last they finally did "Nothin' " commercially.

Whereas Jeffries didn't know what kind of blues he had, Hibbler declared at the outset that he "Ain't Got Nothin' but the Blues"—the title of his first commercial disc with Ellington in 1944. This is an unusual kind of blues—it starts with a blasting, lightly polyphonic, New Orleans–style slow drag before settling into a familiar swing era blues groove, with Al Sears stating the melody à la Ben Webster in his lean mode. Then Hibbler sings the lyric while coloratura soprano Kay Davis hums an obbligato.

The same session produced Hibbler's first ballad for RCA, "Don't You Know I Care," a pretty tune, with Johnny Hodges at his most decorative. Both here and on "Every Hour on the Hour," a largely forgotten Don George lyric inspired by a train station timetable, Hibbler is already beginning to introduce those elements of distortion. "Nothin' but the Blues" was hardly the only time Ellington played Hibbler's beautifully guttural voice off that of a female singer. For a period in 1945, Ellington was carrying three distaff vocalists—Kay Davis, Joya Sherrill, and Marie (whose full name at the time was Maria Ellington, by coincidence, and who was soon to marry Nat Cole), all of whom appear on "Solitude," singing the Ellington perennial for the most part in round harmony. When Hibbler enters to cap the vocal, he injects a jolt of testosterone into the proceedings, asserting his manliness like the alpha male he is.

"Pretty Woman" is upbeat, in the sense of optimistic, with a heavy touch of the blues, opening with a dissonant intro from the Piano Player. The chart steers Hib through a series of stop time breaks in the bridge ("My heart's palpitatin' . . ."); even when he's happy, the blues manage to find him. "Strange Feeling" is one of Ellington's most successful attempts to bring blues feeling to an extended concert work, this being the sole vocal movement in the composer's *Perfume Suite.* Here he uses Hibbler's voice to convey a strange feeling of uneasiness, a premonition that something dreadful is about to happen. Another, less adventurous songwriter might resolve the strange feeling into something more cheerful, perhaps titling the song "That Strange Feeling Called Love." But Ellington, who again wrote both words and music, treats it like the main title theme for a classic film noir (starring Hibbler as a blind gumshoe who solves crimes that baffle the ofay opkays). Hibbler's other role in an Ellington concert work, "I Like the Sunrise" (from *The Liberian Suite*), is somewhat less of a downer.

Over the course of his eight years with Ellington, Hibbler's voice gets deeper and deeper and his mannerisms grow more and more pronounced. He recorded one of his most beautiful ballads with the band, "It Shouldn't Happen to a Dream," in 1947, and continued to turn out top-notch vocals under

the new Columbia contract, including Peggy Lee's blues-inflected "Don't Be So Mean to Baby," "It's Love I'm In," "Monday Every Day," and the definitive "Don't Get Around Much Anymore."

At the same time, Hibbler recorded more prolifically just a little to the left of the Ellington big band, in a series of small band dates done mostly for independent labels (Aladdin, Chess, Sunrise, Mercer). This material has been scattered to the winds for many years, but recently the Belgian Classics label has made a stab at collating it. *Al Hibbler, 1946–1949* and *Al Hibbler, 1950–1952* are far from definitive, but considering the rarity of these discs, and that even comparatively good-condition copies sound like hell, it's unlikely that there will ever be an ideal reissue.

However, it would be well worth the time for some patient producer-engineer to make the effort to restore these 1946–51 sessions, as they are overall the most outstanding recordings of the singer's long and distinguished career. The 1946–51 Hibbler "Ellington Era" (as opposed to "Ellington Orchestra") recordings are also the best postwar extension of the celebrated series of small group, vocalcentric jam sessions discs of the prewar period, such as those made by Billie Holiday and Fats Waller. "I Love You" is a particularly rewarding track: With Strayhorn at the piano and presumably directing the accompaniment, it opens with a tenor intro from Ben Webster, which quickly turns into a cadenza for tenor sax and baritone voice when Hibbler joins him. His treatment of the song, the Archer-Thompson 1923 *Little Jessie James* show tune (not the 1945 Cole Porter *Mexican Hayride* show tune or the Grieg aria from *Song of Norway*) is somewhat romantic and at the same time swings with a casualness that anticipates Frank Sinatra's classic 1953 Capitol single. Hibbler gets a similarly simpatico thing going with trombonist Tyree Glenn on "It Don't Mean a Thing," in which both men seem deeply inspired by the playing style of the recently deceased Joe "Tricky Sam" Nanton.

Most of these cuts were made for labels that didn't survive the decade. The next two concerns for which Hibbler recorded, however, were both nascent independents that would grow into multinational corporations, Ahmet Ertegun's Atlantic Records and Norman Granz's Clef. The Atlantic and Clef sessions were done between 1950 and 1954, when Hibbler was leaving the Ellington fold and establishing himself on his own. The Granz recordings maintain the Ellington connection: There are many Ellington songs, many Ellington sidemen, and two sessions in which Hibbler guest-stars with Johnny Hodges's own small band.

In contrast, the Atlantic sides, for the most part produced by Herb Abramson, generally remove Hibbler from the big band context and place him into the two major directions of postwar vernacular music: rhythm and blues on the one hand and mainstream pop on the other. Even when Ellingtonians appear here, like Tyree Glenn (this time playing vibes) on "Song of the Wanderer" and Paul Gonsalves on "This Is Always," there's little in the way of a Dukish texture to the proceedings. There are some first-rate ballads, like "This Is Always" and "Dedicated to You," and "Song of the Wanderer" is especially wonderful.

Hibbler is also especially fine on "The Blues Came Falling Down," a big band blues in the spirit of Jimmy Rushing. Hib chews up the carpet on "After the Lights Go Down Low," as pure and forceful a statement of rhythm and blues at its best as I have ever heard, with Hibbler declaiming his sexual aggression not only with words, delivered in alternately soothing and stirring tones, but with nonverbal grunts. Hibbler is probably the most famous grunter of the fifties after Pérez Prado.

Which is probably Hibbler's greatest strength—he's one of those individuals, like Dinah Washington, Joe Williams, and, to a degree, Jimmy Scott (who rarely sang an actual 12-bar blues), who belong equally to the world of the Great American Songbook and the world of the blues, which we might call the Other Great American Songbook. Hibbler was in a particularly good place at the start of the rock 'n' roll era, at which time he signed to the major conglomerate Decca; he was making sides that appealed to black buyers, to white teenagers, and, remarkably, to their parents, and was well equipped to satisfy the musical needs of pop music consumers on both sides of the rock 'n' roll divide. Indeed, his biggest hits, "After the Lights Go Down Low" (remade for Decca) and "Unchained Melody," combine mainstream pop, blues, and, in the case of "He," gospel aspirations. The Decca LPs, though, to put it in a way that Hibbler himself might appreciate, are surprisingly white-bread. Decca directed him toward the traditional pop demographic. In retrospect, it might have made more sense to keep the jazz and particularly the blues elements more prominent.

The best of his LP-era recordings is *Monday Every Day*, an outstanding package from 1961, arranged and conducted by veteran Los Angeles bandleader Gerald Wilson for Frank Sinatra's Reprise label. This is also Hibbler's most laudable effort in terms of mainstream pop and songs with some jazz relevance, like "Baby, Won't You Please Come Home" and "When the Sun Comes Out." The repertoire is a well-balanced blend of familiar Hibbler favorites, starting with the title; some Ellington songs not associated with Hib, such as "I Got It Bad"; and even a few Sinatra standards, like "I'm a Fool to Want You." The title track is one of the best performances of Hib's career. He had first performed this song in 1947, and there's a particularly fine live version from Carnegie Hall in 1948. But by 1961, Hibbler's voice had acquired an even rougher, more scabrous timbre that makes the song's message of the blues even

more convincing. This is one of the most powerful blues-inflected interpretations of a popular song, and it's hard to believe that the likes of Ray Charles or Kevin Mahogony never picked up on it.

From *Monday* on, an increasing degree of vocal deterioration would mar Hibbler's work. At only forty-six, he was already starting to lose some of the awesome command he had just a few years earlier—which is ironic, because he himself was in good shape, and lived to the ripe old age of eighty-six. His voice started to go long before he did.

Hibbler's next album, *Early One Morning*, was done in 1964 for a very obscure label in Los Angeles called LMI, with Roland Hanna at the piano. Although the vibrato is starting to vibrate out of control and the low notes are drifting out of pitch, essentially he still is singing well. He starts with "Believe It, Beloved," which he had previously cut with Johnny Hodges ten years earlier, this time trying—in a way that's bizarre even for him—to recreate the capricious singing style of Fats Waller, who is also summoned up in "I'm Gonna Sit Right Down and Write Myself a Letter." (He pronounces it "royt moyself a lettah.") There are two slices of Ellingtonia, the familiar "Lucky So-and-So" and the obscure "I Can't Put My Arms Around a Memory." The best moment is the title track, "Early One Morning," which is subtitled "Prison Bound Blues." It turns out to be the same song as "The Blues Came Falling Down," which he had recorded on Atlantic in 1950. Whatever you call it, it's one of Hibbler's most powerful blues performances, opening with a wordless, hummed introduction that's perhaps all the more moving precisely because he can't quite make all the notes.

None of his subsequent albums would reach this level. The most intriguing and ambitious was *A Meeting of the Times* (1972), an album by the equally adventurous blind Rahsaan Roland Kirk. As producer Joel Dorn has stated, both he and Kirk were hoping to create something as memorable as the classic *John Coltrane and Johnny Hartman*, but an overall lack of preparation and direction led to a disappointing meeting of the titans. In spite of all-star backing, neither *Christmas with Al Hibbler* (1981)—now that is one gnarly Saint Nick—nor *For Sentimental Reasons* (1982), the latter with Hank Jones and Buddy Tate, is anything like classic Hibbler.

By an odd quirk, the only members of Ellington's great band of the forties who lived to participate in the 1999 Ellington Centennial were all singers: not only Jeffries and Hibbler but all three of the ladies who toured with the band in 1945—Joya Sherrill, Kay Davis, and Maria Cole. Hibbler's appearances at the festivities mounted by Jazz at Lincoln Center were probably his last hurrah. The organization flew him in from Chicago, where he had been living, and he participated in a seminar and sang spontaneously at a party afterward. Ironically, he didn't do a song of Ellington's on this occasion; somehow the spirit moved him to sing "If You Are but a Dream," a classical adaptation Kay Davis had sung with Ellington. That was the last time I saw Hib; he died two years later, in 2001.

"We have been extremely lucky with our singers," Ellington once wrote. "Each seemed to join us at the right time when what they were doing with songs was just right for the places we were playing. They are virtually a story on their own." How true. While Anderson, Jeffries, and Hibbler are the most celebrated, mention must also be made of the multi-talented Ray Nance, one of the best of all the singing instrumentalists. Using Armstrong as a template, Nance broke it up both as a trumpeter and a singer, and was also one of the foremost violinists in jazz history. As George Wein has observed, Nance could have gone a lot further, both in the Ellington universe and outside it, had he not been mired down by addictions.

Beyond Anderson, other Ellington canaries had something special to offer: Where Betty Roché was pure bebop and Kay Davis was pure opera, Joya Sherrill came the closest to an Ellington equivalent of Lena Horne, a straight-down-the-middle sound that can be described as either jazz or pop. In addition to many outstanding vocals with the band, including her own song "Kissing Bug," she recorded an outstanding Ellington songbook album in 1965. Kay Davis was the most operatic of Ducal divas, and he used her most notably on his vocalise numbers. After she joined the band in 1944, Ellington not only revived his 1927 "Creole Love Call," but wrote several new features for her classically textured, wordless vocals, most notably "Transbluency" and "On a Turquoise Cloud."

Betty Roché probably went the furthest of the band's post-Anderson canaries, which is odd in that her tenure with Ellington was the least documented. But although she fell through the cracks of the 1942–44 recording ban, she made a considerable impact at the time, especially at the band's first Carnegie Hall concert in 1943, in which she premiered "The Blues," the vocal section from Ellington's most famous extended work, *Black, Brown and Beige*. Roché had a harsh and severe voice that cut somewhat like Dinah Washington, but her bop-based style suggested a bridge between Anita O'Day and Betty Carter. After a year and a half with the band during the ban, she returned for another brief stay in 1951–53, at which time her specialty was an extended scat on "Take the 'A' Train." After she departed, Ray Nance was designated to perform this set of variations, and in the early years of the twenty-first century I have heard several contemporary singers re-create this solo note for note—it's almost as popular among budding scatters as Ella Fitzgerald's "Flying Home." Roché also recorded three LPs: *Take the "A" Train* (1956) and *Singin' and Swingin'* (1960), a pair of exciting sets of blues and boppers, and *Lightly and Politely* (1961), an unsuccessful attempt to make a ballad singer out of her (she has the rare trait of sounding staccato even at slow tempos).

All of which only begins to document the dozens of chanteuses and chanteurs who worked in the most formidable orchestra of them all. Some lasted weeks, others stayed for decades, and he loved them all madly.

Sing a Song of Miller: Male (Mostly) Band Singers I

Bob Eberly
Ray Eberle
(Marion Hutton)
Johnny Desmond
Tex Beneke
Ray McKinley

In 1979, Frank Sinatra and Billy May were working on the album that would eventually become *The Past*, the first volume of his three-disc magnum opus *Trilogy*. Their original concept was to address classic songs from the war years and earlier, and somewhere along the way Sinatra decided to pay homage to both of the major bandleaders of the era who figured in his own past, Harry James and Tommy Dorsey. At one point, Sinatra and May also considered including a re-creation of the famous Glenn Miller sound. In several interviews over the years, Sinatra had expressed his admiration for the Miller band. He also related that back when both the young singer and the bandleader were getting started, around 1938, Sinatra tried to get Miller to hire him as a boy singer in the band; but that spot went to Ray Eberle instead. Eventually, Sinatra and May dropped the idea, since as May said, "that was pretty much an instrumental sound" and probably wouldn't work as well behind a vocalist.

Which brings to the fore a pertinent paradox regarding Glenn Miller and His Orchestra: Although he took his singers very seriously and took pains to hire those he thought were the best—his singers all won polls and awards as the most popular band vocalists of the day—none of them had substantial post–big band era careers. Conversely, it seems as if every important pop star of the postwar years had worked with either Harry James or Tommy Dorsey (and, in the cases of Sinatra, Dick Haymes, and Connie Haines, both). The only vocalists from the Miller fold who retained a degree of stardom in the ensuing decades were his two star singing instrumentalists, Tex Beneke and Ray McKinley, whose talents were far from exclusively vocal. Curious.

Bob Eberly (1916–1981) and
Ray Eberle (1919–1979)

Consider the case of the Eberle/Eberly brothers, Ray and Bob. (As we shall soon see, much of the history of band singing is a family affair.) For starters, even though they spelled the family name differently, Eberly and Eberle were, in fact, actual flesh-and-blood brothers. Ray, the younger and perkier of the two (as someone might write of the Hardy Boys), utilized the original spelling with an "e." According to historian Roger Kinkle, Bob had sought to make the name easier to deal with for showbiz purposes by changing the spelling to conclude with a more resolutely American "y." And as if that weren't confusing enough, in 1958, just as the Eberly/Eberle brothers were realizing that they were never going to set the world on fire as solo acts, along came a considerably younger pop-rock-country duo by the name of the Everly Brothers (not only with a "y" but with a "v") that instantly made the world forget that there had once been two other brothers with very similar names who sang popular songs. (Not confused enough? There was also an alto player who was a cousin of Bob's and Ray's in the Casa Loma band, circa 1929–30, by the name of Ray Eberle, when Glenn Miller's Ray Eberle would have been ten. Then there's the actor Ray Eberle, who appears in the World War I drama *Me und Gott*, 1918, released the year before our Ray Eberle was born.)

The Eberly/Eberle saga is closely connected to the story of two additional pairs of musical brothers: Bing and Bob Crosby and Tommy and Jimmy Dorsey. In the beginning, the Dorseys were closely bound up with the Crosbys. In the late twenties, when Bing Crosby (born 1903) and both Dorseys (born 1904 and 1905) were essentially sidemen, they were all part of Paul Whiteman's band, and the three of them appear on various recordings by Whiteman and other leaders. There's also a famous session from 1929 under the Dorseys' leadership that produced three titles, all with vocals by Bing. As the Jazz Age evolved into the swing era, the stars of all three artists, Bing Crosby and the two Dorseys, were on the rise: Crosby was by now the most popular singer of his generation, and the Dorsey brothers often directed his accompaniment; unlike the Crosbys or the Eberles, the Dorseys were, for a time, attempting to work together on a full-time, permanent basis.

On the eve of the big band boom, the Dorseys ventured forth from the security of their careers as freelance studio musicians to try establishing their own regularly working, touring dance band, though they still were happy to work behind Crosby, accompanying him on sessions for Decca as well as on his broadcasts. So enamored were the brothers of Crosby that they even instructed their chief arranger, one Alton Glenn Miller, to pitch the ensemble in a lower key than most other bands, to get a warm and masculine "baritone" sound like the one being popularized by Bing.

When it came to their own dates, the new Dorsey Brothers Orchestra hired Kay Weber as girl singer. For a boy singer, they would have liked more than anything to have been able to hire Bing Crosby, but by 1934 he was much too big a star to work as anybody's band vocalist. Thus, at Bing's suggestion, the Dorseys contacted his youngest brother, Bob. However, as Gary Giddins has recounted, this was perhaps intended as something of a prank on his two pals by the older Crosby. What Tommy and Jimmy didn't know was that Bob Crosby (born 1913) couldn't sing; or, to put it more charitably, had absolutely no singing experience and very little vocal chops. Just the same, the Dorseys went ahead and hired him. Bob Crosby's relationship with the Dorsey Brothers, predictably, was short and not especially pleasant; after just a few months, he leapt at the opportunity to lead his own orchestra. Which turned out to be a happy ending for all concerned: Even though the younger Crosby never developed into a world-class singer, he did become one of the best band front men, and Bob Crosby and His Orchestra featuring the Bob Cats was one of the most significant units of the swing era.

Thus the two Dorseys, who were constantly fighting and who looked as if they would split their own band in two at any second, were in need of a new male singer when they happened to be playing a one-nighter in Troy, New York. Someone told them about a local crooner from nearby Hoosick Falls who had recently won a radio amateur contest hosted by Fred Allen, and then they located the lad himself, who turned out to be Robert Eberly, the older of two singing brothers. Eberly went to work for the Dorseys, but just when he had somewhat settled into the job, the battling brothers finally had the much-predicted fracas that led to the end of their professional career as a team.

Jimmy Dorsey continued with what had been the Dorsey Brothers band, virtually intact, including singers Kay Weber and Bob Eberly, the band's library, the same personnel, and the Decca contract. He also continued the previous relationship with Bing Crosby. In fact, the most important early job by the new Jimmy Dorsey Orchestra was one that shunted Bob Eberly into the shadows. For the 1935–36 season, Jimmy served as the house band on Bing Crosby's Phenomenally successful NBC radio series, *The Kraft Music Hall*, and obviously there wasn't room on the program for Dorsey's own male vocalist. However, for the rest of the week the Jimmy Dorsey Orchestra toured and played one-nighters, with Weber and Eberly singing, the latter even using some of the Crosby orchestrations. The exposure to Crosby ultimately did Eberly far more good than harm, and even Bob Eberly never developed Crosby's versatility (not to mention flexibility), he did become one of the most popular singers of the band era.

As early as 1938, Eberly was regarded as one of

the best boy singers around and one of the key attractions of the Jimmy Dorsey band (later, he would sing duets with the band's girl singer, Helen O'Connell, and give Jimmy Dorsey several of his biggest hits). In fact, Glenn Miller, who left the Dorseys well before their breakup, was so keen on Bob Eberly that he pretty much went and hired Ray Eberle for the same reason that the Dorseys had hired Bob Crosby four years earlier—simply because he was Bob Eberly's younger brother, and talent, they all reckoned, had to run in the family.

The story goes that Ray was still living in Hoosick Falls when he came to New York to hear his older brother singing with Jimmy Dorsey at the Hotel New Yorker. Glenn Miller also happened to be there and, as Miller intimate and biographer George Simon told it, the trombonist couldn't believe his eyes: Right in front of him are two Bob Eberles—just what he was looking for. In years to come, Ray Eberle was always under the impression that Miller hired him strictly because of his physical resemblance to his more famous older brother; just the same, Miller went around boasting that he had hired the more talented of the two brothers. (In a similar manner, Miller also hired Marion Hutton, the older sister of Betty Hutton, who had already established herself as a name vocalist with Vincent Lopez.) Miller was then in the process of reorganizing into what Simon called "the band that made it," and Ray joined in time to sing "Don't Wake Up My Heart" for the new band's first session, which was actually the last in his old contract with Brunswick. Ray Eberle would remain with the band for virtually the entire extent of Miller's civilian career, leaving in 1942.

Most fans would hold with George Simon's opinion that Bob was by far the more talented of the two. His deep baritone voice was manly and robust, and, as Simon put it, Bob, "in his own quiet way, exuded confidence." Ray, on the other hand, while essentially a baritone, was a very, very high one, and he, "in his own quiet way, exuded trepidation." Having been a Glenn Miller fan all my life, I tend to think that Bob may be the slightest bit overrated and Ray may be a little underrated—that Ray is almost as good as Bob. It's easy to be prejudiced in Ray's favor, since even sixty-five years after Miller disbanded, there still is a rosy glow surrounding everything the band did, and Ray Eberle is obviously part of that. One of the major reasons that it's easy to appreciate Ray is that virtually every note that the Miller band ever played has been issued on some sort of compact disc somewhere in the world, which unfortunately is not the case with Jimmy Dorsey. Thus, even though Bob is by and large considered a better singer than Ray, paradoxically it's much easier to hear Ray's music than Bob's. (There is a recommended twenty-five-track compilation, however, *The Best of Bob Eberly with Jimmy Dorsey* on Collectors' Choice, but even that can't compete with Ray Eberle's participation in

BMG's epic thirteen-CD box *The Complete Glenn Miller and His Orchestra, 1938–1942*.)

Bob Eberly was a finer technician, had a better voice, much more personality, and a better way with a lyric, yet something about Ray is more interesting. Bob sounds more like Bing Crosby lite (or, if you will, like Bob Crosby heavy); he weds a Crosby tone to a more old-fashioned approach. In fact, he sometimes comes off like an old-time tenor who happens to be working in the baritone range. He has more of an operetta approach, along with his warmth and personality; he comes in between Crosby and the tenors who preceded him, much as Dick Haymes seems to split the difference between Crosby and Sinatra.

My experience has been that the more you hear the Miller-Eberle combination, the more you like it. Simon thought that Miller pitched most of Eberle's arrangements in keys that were too high to be comfortable for him, and he was probably right, yet one can hear what Miller was going for, and Eberle's voice blends beautifully with Miller's patented clarinet-led reeds and soft, muted brass. This was a romantic, ballad-driven band, and while Marion Hutton and Tex Beneke divided up the swing songs, Eberle was Miller's only balladeer. Simon is right—Eberle does sound as if he's straining, but that strain perfectly accommodates his role as the hopeful—albeit trepidatious—young swain: He's nervous and unsure, like all young lovers. Tony Bennett would later turn that sound of strain into an asset, and the young Mel Tormé, a rabid Miller-maniac, would be the jazz-pop singer to make the best of a superhigh baritone. When Eberle sings "Fools Rush In," he sounds as if he's genuinely afraid to hold his heart above his head; when he sings "Stairway to the Stars," it sounds as if he wants the city building commissioner to inspect the stairway before he'll risk climbing the darn thing; in "Dear Mom" he sounds as if he's embodying the character of the lyric—a nervous soldier, scared to be away from home, missing his mommy as well as the yet undeflowered girl he left back home. The young Sinatra, in his Dorsey and forties recordings, had an innocence he lost in his postnosedive recordings, but even he came off like Casanova compared to Eberle. Ray Eberle sings like a virgin, it's true, but he's highly effective on the right song, such as the celestial "A Handful of Stars," "Starlight and Music," "It Was Written in the Stars," "The Story of a Starry Night," "Shake Down the Stars," "The Starlit Hour," "When You Wish upon a Star," and especially the lovely future standard "Stairway to the Stars." His high voice sounded as if he was actually reaching for all those stars.

Ray left Miller because of a personal disagreement with the leader, despite the fact that Miller had been defending him to George Simon and everyone else for five years. The two parted company in June 1942, roughly three months before Miller disbanded to enter the service, and although Eberle also was inducted (briefly), the two did not work together in the military. Eberle turns up for just a few months at the end of 1942 with Gene Krupa's band, and, this being the height of the recording ban, there is no evidence of this tenure, other than a couple of airchecks.

Bob Eberly made his greatest impact with a series of real and fake Latin specialties delivered in three tempos. "Amapola," "Tangerine," and "Maria Elena," among others, all start with Bob rendering the first chorus very straight. Leader Dorsey then jazzes the second chorus up on his alto, and then Helen O'Connell enters and sings the third chorus at once sexy and comically goofy, girlish squeals and all.

Eberly stayed with Dorsey as long as he could, even after Helen O'Connell departed to go as a single. When he and Dorsey split up, it wasn't their idea but Uncle Sam's—Bob was inducted in 1943. Some of his last work with Dorsey—done after the start of the 1942–44 recording ban—was actually his best, as on the sound track to the 1943 Red Skelton film *I Dood It,* in which he sings one of his best up-tempos, the cowboy-styled "So Long, Sarah Jane," and what might be the best of his triple-tempo specialties with O'Connell, the future jazz standard "Star Eyes." (This material is on Rhino's excellent-sounding *Tommy and Jimmy Dorsey: Swinging in Hollywood.*)

After both Eberles got back from the service, they never quite regained their footing. In the case of Bob at least, this was especially surprising, since he was so gifted and had been so popular—like Helen Forrest, perhaps, he just seemed too linked to the band era, a link that the singers who made it big after the war, like Sinatra and Peggy Lee, had worked hard to break. Both brothers worked only sporadically through the postwar years. Eberle the younger led a Miller-style orchestra around 1945–47 (some of the airchecks of which are gathered on the CD *Ray Eberle and Ex–Glenn Miller Men* on Jazz Hour), did one commercial date for Bob Thiele's Signature, and turns up with various permutations of Miller ghost bands, earlier with Tex Beneke, later with Buddy DeFranco. In 1957, the Tops label hired him to front a Miller re-creation album, *Ray Eberle Plays Glenn Miller Favorites,* and while this was a rack-job or supermarket operation, the sound quality (as reissued on CD forty years later) was superb. For better or worse, Eberle's own singing hasn't changed at all; at thirty-eight, he is trying hard to do exactly what he was doing twenty years earlier. The strength of this album is the audio: This is perhaps the best-recorded example of the Miller sound that was ever made. There's an added bonus in Eberle's vocal on Miller's theme "Moonlight Serenade," which he sang on at least one rare Miller aircheck but never recorded commercially with the leader-composer. Ray Eberle died in 1979.

Sinatra has said that, along with Perry Como and Dick Haymes, Bob Eberly was one of the singers he regarded as his fiercest competition. He didn't give Sinatra many sleepless nights for long, however—by 1946 Bob Eberly was fast fading into the recesses of recent memory. What is surprising is that Ray actually did better in Hollywood than Bob. If nothing else, Bob really seems like a movie leading man—you would expect him to be playing a straight romantic lead with Abbott and Costello or the Ritz Brothers, like Dick Foran or Allan Jones. It was Ray, however, who appeared in a half-dozen or so B musicals and band shorts, including one with dancer and bandleader Ina Ray Hutton. Bob Eberly never made any films except with Dorsey: *The Fleet's In, I Dood It,* and he also, fittingly, was given a spot in the brothers' biopic *The Fabulous Dorseys.* However, Bob and Helen O'Connell were regulars on the 1953 summer replacement series *TV's Top Tunes,* a sort of *Hit Parade* knockoff. Eberly the Elder also made a few solo sides for Capitol, as well as a brief series of fresh duets with O'Connell (with whom he also re-created the Dorsey era for Warner Bros. Records). Bob, too, made an LP under his own name, the very scarce *Bob Eberly Sings Tender Love Songs* on Grand Award. He died in 1981.

Marion Hutton (1919–1987)

The Hutton sisters, Marion and Betty, parallel the Eberle brothers in instructive ways. The family lineage is equally confusing, not because the two sisters spelled their names differently (they didn't), but because the big band era brought us two distinct sets of Hutton sisters, Marion and Betty, and Ina Ray and June. As it turns out, the more famous Huttons (Marion and Betty) were not actually Huttons at all—their family name was Thornburg. The other Huttons—the actual Huttons—were born and raised in Chicago and were half sisters. Ina Ray (circa 1915–84) was a dancer who led her own bands, both all-female and all-male, and whose performances were better documented in film (such as the band short mentioned above with special guest Ray Eberle) than on record; she never made it to the upper echelon of the band business, but her gyrations were a source of delight for male band buffs both then and now—not to mention her own musicians. Her younger sister, June (circa 1920–73), started as a vocalist in Ina Ray's band, then went into Charlie Spivak's orchestra. June Hutton is best remembered as a member of the Sinatra circle: She replaced Jo Stafford as the lead voice in the Pied Pipers not long after the quartet left Tommy Dorsey, and eventually departed for a solo career as well as to marry Sinatra's musical director Axel Stordahl—and to work as regular female singer with both Stordahl and Sinatra on the singer's 1950–51 TV series. A gifted singer with a distinctive voice, somewhat in the Stafford mold (but higher), June Hutton also cut a memorable album for Capitol, the star billing of which she shared with Stordahl. For a while, Hutton and Stordahl were a sort of parallel to Jo Stafford and Paul Weston, an ex–Pied Piper soloist married to a prominent conductor.

Marion (Thornburg) was born in 1919 in Little Rock, and Betty (Elizabeth Jane Thornburg) came along two years later in Battle Creek. Sometime around early 1938, the two Thornburgs, now known as the Hutton Sisters (where they got the name, I don't know), were singing together with the dance band led by veteran leader and onetime Paul Whiteman rival Vincent Lopez. At that point, violinist Nick Pisani was playing in the Lopez band, and he pushed the two Huttons on Miller, who hired Marion. (Meanwhile, Betty Hutton stayed with the big bands only briefly: After leaving Vincent Lopez, she jumped to Broadway and then was discovered by Paramount Pictures, where she reigned as the studio's queen of musical comedy for the war years and well beyond. For more info, see the section in this book titled "Hollywood Divas.")

Having hired Marion, Glenn Miller doubtlessly went around bragging that he had snagged the superior sibling, much as he had with Ray Eberle. However, unlike Miller's experience with Eberle, neither Simon nor anybody else gave Miller an argument in the case of the Huttons. As with the later Clooney sisters, the younger of the two (also named Betty) was the one with the chutzpah and the drive, but the older daughter was the one with the real singing talent—and the one who had to overcome her shyness. Marion told George Simon how, during her first tour with Miller, she felt overwhelmed by her sister, now a star attraction with Lopez, and that Miller had to keep encouraging her. Marion Hutton sings on all the early Miller broadcasts, and first turns up on record on "Gotta Get Some Shut Eye." On this February 1939 disc Hutton really comes alive, especially on the unusually structured bridge.

Anyone who's heard Marion Hutton with Miller would have a hard time believing that she needed any coaxing to come out of her shell. Within a few months, she was one of the most popular and most extroverted canaries around; when she was relaxed and comfortable, she could really swing with the best of them, and contributed a lot to Miller's groovy way with novelty and rhythm numbers. I like her lots on "What Have You Got That Gets Me," "Why Doesn't Somebody Tell Me These Things?," "FDR Jones," "We Can Live on Love," "Back to Back," "Wanna Hat with Cherries," "Ding Dong! The Witch Is Dead," and "The Man with the Mandolin," to name just a few from 1938 and 1939, some of which were done only as airchecks, not commercial recordings. Hutton was certainly well ahead of most other perky chicks who sang rhythm songs with name bands, like Helen O'Connell with Jimmy Dorsey and Connie Haines with Harry James and Tommy Dorsey. She also had considerable chemistry with Tex Beneke, whom she later admitted she had a crush on—it comes through in their duets—but

none at all with Ray Eberle, who wasn't particularly good at the duet thing anyhow.

In July 1939, Hutton took sick and was very briefly replaced by newcomer Kay Starr, who made her debut on the band's commercial recording of "Love with a Capital You" (a song Hutton sang with the band on airchecks; her versions are possibly even better than the very young Starr's). In 1940, Hutton wed song plugger (and later TV producer) Jack Philbin, and in January 1941, she announced she was taking a maternity leave from the band. For two months, she was replaced by Dorothy Claire, a singer Miller had pilfered from his fellow trombonist Bobby Byrne's band, and who shines on the somewhat spooky "Swinging at the Seance" in February 1941.

At around the same time, Miller also hired a vocal group, the Modernaires, who had already served with the Paul Whiteman and Charlie Barnet bands. The Mods were an impressive foursome virtually on the same level as Tommy Dorsey's Pied Pipers; the only major difference was that they didn't have a soloist nearly as monumental as Jo Stafford to enhance their harmony (or like Sinatra to sing in front of them). When Miller heard Paula Kelly (1919–92), wife of Modernaire Hal Dickinson and former vocalist with Al Donahue, he knew he had his gal. Kelly was a more than credible band singer, if not quite the inspiration that Hutton was. She's especially good on "Sweeter Than the Sweetest," a song by pianist Willie "the Lion" Smith. Kelly became part of the Modernaires, and as a unit they enjoy the distinction of being the only genuine Miller band vocalists to appear in the 1953 *Glenn Miller Story* (no Marion, no Ray, no Tex). The previous year, the Modernaires had done a TV series with Lawrence Welk, illustrating that their taste in bandleaders had distinctly deteriorated since the war. Immediately after Miller disbanded, Hutton and the Mods would tour together throughout 1943.

Spring of 1941 was also when the Miller band made its first of two starring feature films, *Sun Valley Serenade;* Hutton missed that one completely, and she didn't fare much better in the second, *Orchestra Wives,* made a year later. *Orchestra Wives* may be the only Hollywood film that actually treats musicians like human beings, not a bunch of wise-cracking gum-chewers (or was it gum-chewing wisecrackers?); unfortunately, it instead treats women like some sort of subhuman species. In any case, neither Hutton nor Eberle had much to do in either film—the Miller band vocalist who shines the brightest in both, by far, is the highly cinematic Tex Beneke.

Hutton finally got a break in movies after Miller disbanded the civilian edition in September 1942, in *Babes on Swing Street* (1944). Even as kid sister Betty was exploding on the screen as Hollywood's most volatile singer-comedienne, Marion was paired with filmland's zaniest comedy teams: Olsen and Johnson, in the aptly named *Crazy House* (1943), which also featured the Modernaires in another guest bit; the Marx Brothers, in *Love Happy* (1949); and Abbott and Costello, in *In Society* (1945). In the latter she introduced "My Dreams Are Getting Better All the Time," which became a sizable hit, not for Hutton, alas, but for the Les Brown–Doris Day combination. The same A&C vehicle also featured a memorable novelty (more recently revived by Christine Ebersole) entitled "No Bout Adoubt It."

Marion Hutton recorded for MGM Records in the late forties, although by this time it seemed as if A&R men were thinking of her as a less famous version of her sister, giving her extreme novelty songs like "Borsht" ("It's a super soup"), "Okay Louie, Drop the Gun," and "A Brooklyn Love Song." It should be stressed, however, that although none of these songs is "All the Things You Are," Hutton is perfectly personable, pert, and swinging, as well as very funny, on all these numbers. Hutton would sing an even more horrific tune, the ghastly pseudo-spiritual "I Had a Little Talk with the Lord."

While neither of the Eberles went anywhere except downhill after the band era, at least Hutton continued to get better and better after 1942, as proved by some of the better songs she recorded in these years, and many of her MGM sides leave even her best Miller vocals in the dust. *Marion Hutton on the Air* (Collectors' Choice Music) is a short but highly entertaining compilation of miscellaneous Marion vocals from 1940 (with Miller) to 1948. Most of these airchecks are marvelous, especially a 1945 reunion with Beneke, a reprise of the Miller wartime hit "Don't Sit Under the Apple Tree" introduced by Milton Berle and accompanied by Benny Goodman's orch. There also are two rhythm-comedy tunes with a somewhat higher pedigree than most of either Hutton's material, Cahn and Styne's "Five Minutes More" and "Let's Do It," the Cole Porter classic with a new verse and with Hutton sounding somewhat like the Judy Garland of the mid-forties, only with a better sense of rhythm.

Her last notable performances were a Miller singers reunion LP in 1959 and a Miller band reunion TV special in 1984—on both of which she sounds as good as ever. Marion Hutton didn't seem to have much interest in continuing to sing beyond her twenties. Her son and her family—she eventually remarried, still in the music business, this time to arranger-conductor Vic Schoen—took up more of her attention. Then, too, her sister Betty's film career was beginning to peter out in the early fifties after ten years at the top: She simply was too much of a one-trick pony, a one-note samba, to keep going for more than one approximate generation. Plus, Betty was having mental problems—according to one biography, her father was a suicide and her mother suffered from alcoholism. At the same time that Betty was cracking up, Marion was working toward several degrees in psychology. She died in

1987, and Betty, who eventually saved herself by discovering Jesus, died twenty years later.

Johnny Desmond (1920–1985)

It was strangely appropriate when Ray Eberle joined Gene Krupa's band, since it meant that Krupa and Miller more or less switched boy vocalists. Krupa got Eberle, and Miller, who in 1943 launched his famous Army Air Force Orchestra, got the boy singer who had worked for Krupa for about a year, Johnny Desmond. Although I like Ray Eberle, I have to acknowledge that Glenn Miller easily got the best of that exchange. Despite a relatively small discography and an absence of major hit records, Desmond enjoys a rare position of respect among big band buffs and pop music fans. While Bob and Ray were among the first generation of male singers to grow up listening to Crosby, Desmond was young enough to have learned from Haymes, Como, and especially Sinatra. He was one of the smoothest and most sensitive of big band crooners, so much so that his nickname in the Miller AAF band was "the Creamer." Desmond seemed ideally poised to make it in the postwar environment—especially since he was yet another in the long parade of crooning Italian-Americans—and why he didn't remains a mystery.

Johnny Desmond was born Giovanni Alfredo Desimons in Detroit, where, unlike virtually every other singer of his generation, he studied formally at that city's Conservatory of Music. In his early teens, he put together a vocal group called the Downbeats, which came to the attention of bandleader Bob Crosby (him again); Crosby hired them as his vocal group, renaming the foursome the Bob-O-Links, heard on "Dry Bones" (and they're behind singing guitarist Nappy Lamare) and "Drummer Boy" (both from 1940), among others.

From 1941 to 1942, Desmond was the featured male singer in Gene Krupa's band, alongside such attractions as Anita O'Day and Roy Eldridge. (All of his vocals with Krupa are, fortunately, collected on *Johnny Desmond: The Complete Early Sides*, Sony Music Special Products/Collectors' Choice—where would we be without 'em?) Even as early as 1941, on Krupa sides like "This Time the Dream's on Me" and "Violets for Your Furs," Desmond is in the vanguard; he sounds well ahead of either Eberle brother and has clearly learned from Como, Haymes, and Sinatra even at this early stage, when all three of those future headliners were still apprenticed to various bands.

When he was drafted and went to work with the Miller AAF band in 1943, it was only fitting that this smoothest of all band crooners should work with the lushest of all swing era bands. The idea was to illustrate that the American way of life—and music—was superior to the enemy's; the Desmond-Miller combination served as a vivid illustration of the good life to be found in the American-style democracies, home not just of Mom and apple pie but of great swinging dance numbers and beautiful ballads. The Italian-American Desmond further infuriated Der Führer by crooning love songs like "Where or When," "Long Ago and Far Away," and "All the Things You Are" in German for Axis listeners, even as Major Miller himself promised that the Allies would provide home life and happiness by wiping out Nazi gangsterism from the face of Europe.

Back in 1938, Miller delighted in taking unproven talent such as Hutton and Eberle and shaping them into a band. In 1943, by contrast, Miller's key men—the soloists, arrangers, and vocalists—were all established stars, with proven track records in the band business: pianist-orchestrator Mel Powell and drummer–rhythm singer Ray McKinley, trumpeter Zeke Zarchy, and tenor and clarinet player Peanuts Hucko, already a veteran of two major bands at the age of twenty-three. It was an honor for the young Desmond to be included in their company. And Desmond, who was by then a sergeant, was regarded as more than a boy crooner. Like Helen Forrest with James, he rarely sang mere vocal refrains; his featured numbers were built around his singing. When the full Miller troop was ensconced in England, the company not only broadcast with the full AAF Orchestra, with its symphony-sized string section, but in various subsets drawn from the larger band: a program featuring the fiddles (*Strings with Wings*), a program featuring Miller's hot Swing Sextet (*The Uptown Hall*), a program featuring the big band playing regulation dance music sans strings (*The Swing Shift*), and a show built around Desmond variously titled *A Soldier and a Song* and *Sergeant Johnny Desmond Sings*.

One of the great benefits of listening to the many LP and CD reissues of the AAF band is the treat of hearing Desmond singing nearly all the key songs of the World War II era, such as "Going My Way" and "Long Ago and Far Away." There's one 1945 broadcast on which Desmond and Miller's vocal group, the Crew Chiefs, having just returned from the recently de-Nazified France, sing special lyrics about riding on the newly liberated Paris Métro to the tune of "The Trolley Song"—this from one of the band's final broadcasts done in New York, more than ten months after the disappearance of Miller over the English Channel. Desmond does very well with this tempo song, but creamy ballads were still his specialty, and he sang dozens of them during the two-year existence of the AAF band. None was creamier than the Brazilian import "Poinciana," which shows how well the trademark Miller reed sound could blend with a huge string section, reminiscent of Hollywood movie music, a jazz piano interlude by Mel Powell, a brief melody bit by a solo French horn, plus solos by tenorist Vinnie Carbone (who became Frank Sinatra Jr.'s manager in later years) and clarinetist Hucko, and the backing vocals of the Crew Chiefs—not to mention a bolero beat. Arranged by Jerry Gray at a length of five minutes, it's quite a production number, yet even amid everything that's going on here, the dominant feature is Desmond's baritone.

Again and again, the only sensible point for comparison is the Sinatra of the same period. Desmond, indeed, was known as "the G.I. Sinatra," but he doesn't necessarily sound like Young Blue Eyes (certainly not compared to Ronnie Deauville, a crooner who consciously imitated Sinatra in Tex Beneke's postwar band). Like Sinatra's, his singing is rich and full. He not only has a magnificent vocal instrument, he seems to understand that he's singing better than nearly any other band singer this side of Helen Forrest. Like Sinatra, he makes virtually every other boy singer of the period sound one-dimensional by comparison. Only a year younger than Ray Eberle, he seems to belong to a whole different generation. They are of the present, he is of the future. (*The Secret Broadcasts*, released in 1996 by BMG, is an excellent-sounding three-CD set of Miller AAF instrumentals and Desmond vocals.)

Or is he? Desmond differs from Kay Kyser's Harry Babbitt and the Eberles in that he had no commercial hits of any consequence, in his big band phase or beyond it. Although the Miller AAF band did broadcast for civilians, their focus was on entertaining the servicemen, inspiring the Allies and demoralizing the Axis, and Desmond never really got the chance to show what he could do in front of, say, screaming bobby-soxers. His work remains the exclusive province of the GIs who were lucky enough to hear him.

After the war, Desmond sang for Columbia, Victor, MGM, and Coral. According to Whitburn's *Pop Memories*, he once got as high as a number 9 hit but was generally bubbling around the teens, twenties, and thirties. He never seems to have found the right producer or the right song that could have put him over—there was never a defining hit, a "Because of You," a "Cry," or even a "Come on-a My House." Precious few of Desmond's post-Miller singles have been reissued, but among the ones I've heard "Sleigh Ride" on MGM is delightful, a hip, swinging treatment of the Leroy Anderson instrumental transformed, via Mitchell Parrish lyrics, into a holiday song. "Don't Cry, Joe" (a number 22 hit, also on MGM) is part of a series that he did with the brilliant cornetist Bobby Hackett. One yearns for an RCA/BMG disc of the best of Desmond's Miller and Victor performances, and likewise for Universal to collect all of his MGM and Coral recordings. (*C'est la Vie* [*That's Life*] on the English Vintage Jazz Band label is a generous sampling of late-forties sides.)

Alas, it seems that Desmond never rose higher than the rank of a grade-B pop singer; he had minor hits on his own, but whenever he sang a big song, it was almost always a cover of someone else's hit. He sang the mainstream pop covers, for instance, of the iconic country hits "Sixteen Tons" (Tennessee Ernie Ford) and "A White Sport Coat and a Pink Carnation" (Marty Robbins). Unfortunately, he spent too much time under contract to Coral Records, which, compared to Capitol or Columbia, seems like a poverty row producer; there are whole albums on Coral, like the 10" *Play Me Hearts and Flowers*, where he sings nothing but second-rate songs (the title track was almost an exception, as was his vocal on the hit theme from the film *The High and the Mighty*). One was even the singer's own indulgence: a Coral album called *Desmo Sings Desmond*, which consists entirely of his own compositions (the cover shows two Desmonds, one singing, the other reclining in a *Jetsons*esque chair obviously digging his own performance). One or two of these originals aren't too bad, but in general one wishes he'd concentrated more on finding some good songs rather than trying to roll his own.

Paradoxically, although Desmond never succeeded entirely as a pop star, he did rise to the top rank on a purely artistic level. There are at least four exceptionally good albums that make it clear we can talk about Desmond in the same way we talk about Dick Haymes or Vic Damone. His two best-known albums are probably the ones on Columbia, *Blue Smoke* and *Once upon a Time*, which were rereleased on a single CD from Sony's British wing. The main event is *Once upon a Time* (1955), in which for the first time he sang the Miller arrangements of a decade earlier for commercial consumption. Since the war, Desmond's voice had grown somewhat heavier and deeper, but at thirty-five, he did a splendid job of reverting back to his style of the war years. He was benefiting from a renewed wave of interest in the band, sparked by the 1953 biopic *The Glenn Miller Story*, which led to much reissue activity. Conducted by Norman Leyden, who had won his wings with the Miller AAF band arranging staff as well as the first postwar Tex Beneke–led Miller band, *Once Upon a Time* showed that the best of the Miller-Desmond works were more than nostalgia or wartime sentiment; they really were slices of terrific pop music that could stand the test of time.

The other big band album that's been reissued is *Johnny Desmond Swings*, which was originally released on a "rack job" (supermarket) label, but recorded in fairly spectacular early stereo; it's been reissued in a beautifully packaged CD on Simitar. This is Desmond with a regulation swing band (no strings, as distinct from *Once upon a Time*), arranged and conducted by Johnny Williams (who, as John Williams, would become the most decorated and famous composer of late-twentieth-century Hollywood). The mood is completely inspired by the contemporaneous Sinatra-Riddle albums, and Desmond is a Swingin' Lover to compete with the best of them: relaxed yet intense, urgent and erotic, with a beautiful baritone and a knowing attitude that makes him worthy of discussion even with Sinatra, Cole, and Eckstine. He's the only singer who ever got me (a confirmed Francophobe) to actually like Kern and Hammerstein's heavy-handed "The Last Time I Saw

Paris" by swinging it lightly but engagingly. (Perhaps he'd earned the right to the sentiment by being one of the first American musicians to enter liberated Paris at the end of World War II.)

There are two small-group albums that are, if anything, even more special: *Blue Smoke* (on the same English Columbia CD as *Once upon a Time*) and *Easy Come, Easy Go Lover*. The first is highly intimate: Desmond appears here with just Tony Mottola's guitar and Bob Haggart's bass. But he has chops and presence to spare. The voice is deep and secure and his phrasing utterly sure-footed. *Blue Smoke* shows Desmond looking like Jacques Brel or an existentialist in a blue sweater surrounded by dry ice fumes, with the painting of a mysterious woman's face obscured but visible in the background. Indeed, the whole thing is fairly existential—Desmond's voice seems to be drifting in space, unconnected to anything, his miraculously restrained emotions hanging suspended.

But I have to confess, I like *Easy Come, Easy Go Lover* even better. Here he works with a full jazz quartet led by pianist Dick Marx, featuring tenor sax (Mike Simpson) and rhythm (including the famous Johnny Frigo on bass); recorded in Chicago circa 1955, it's easily the best of his Coral albums and possibly my single favorite Desmond effort. The voice is light and airy, and somehow he's even more intimate and personal here than on the guitar-and-bass-only session. The songs are all excellent, and mix in a couple of interesting contemporary items (like Moose Charlap's "Here I Am in Love Again") alongside standards like "I'll Remember April" and "I Got It Bad." He somehow makes Johnnie Ray's lachrymose hit "Please Mr. Sun" sound palatable, singing it slow and easy, making it a real song, not merely an excuse for ranting and hair-pulling. *Easy Come, Easy Go Lover* is even more amazing for never having been reissued in any form for fifty-five years, yet I have no doubt that Johnny Hartman and other younger singers heard it and paid close attention.

In the late fifties, Sinatra was quoted as saying he was surprised Johnny Desmond didn't have a bigger career. In 1951, he had appeared on *Don McNeill's TV Club*, based in Chicago, and about the time Sinatra was making that statement, Desmond was beginning a minor career in B action movies—*Escape from San Quentin* (1957), *Calypso Heat Wave* (1957), *China Doll* (1958), *Desert Hell* (1958), *Hawk of the Caribbean* (1964), and *The Fantastic Invasion of planet Earth* (1966). He also tried Broadway, and played the male lead opposite Vivian Blaine in *Say Darling* (1958), described as a "play with music" rather than a full-blown musical comedy; it ran for ten months, but on the whole is better remembered by Broadway buffs than it was received by critics or audiences at the time. Six years later, he replaced Syd Chaplin as the leading man in *Funny Girl*—an Italian Nicky Arnstein. In a sense, it was another cover job.

Yet somehow all of this didn't add up to much. Desmond, who had never managed to make the real big leagues before the sea changes of 1955–64, would not have another chance to make a name for himself later on. His last big moment was *Glenn Miller Time*, a summer replacement variety series that ran for ten weeks in 1961, starring Desmond with Ray McKinley and the current Glenn Miller Orchestra. Fortunately, the ten episodes survive, and the clips that have found their way onto YouTube are well worth seeking out—especially a Desmond-McKinley duet on Johnny Mercer and Bobby Darin's "Two of a Kind." Throughout, Desmond not only sings beautifully, with that marvelous baritone we'd loved for two decades by that point, but is a loose and affable host. He and McKinley are a completely charming and disarming team.

Desmond kept working, and whenever he needed to he milked the Miller connection (Why not? He'd earned the right, certainly) on PBS specials going into the early eighties. Around that time, he played the Rainbow Room with a big band that included educator and historian Loren Schoenberg in the reed section. Although young, Schoenberg had already seen his share of star singers with big egos who liked to throw their weight around, but he reported that Desmond got along famously with the musicians, that he respected them and they, in turn, had tremendous respect for his musicianship. He died in 1985, only sixty-five years old. Sinatra was right; Johnny Desmond should have been bigger.

Tex Beneke (1914–2000) and
Ray McKinley (1910–1995)

The two most successful vocalists, in terms of postwar careers, to emerge from the entire Glenn Miller saga were neither Ray Eberle nor Marion Hutton, neither Johnny Desmond nor the Modernaires nor the Crew Chiefs. Surprisingly, they were a pair of musicians who doubled on vocals: the tenor saxophonist Tex Beneke and the drummer Ray McKinley. Apart from how they fulfilled parallel functions in the Miller civilian and service bands, they both were star singing sidemen who later established themselves as leaders—in fact, each of them led an edition of the postwar Glenn Miller Orchestra. Coincidentally, they both were born in Fort Worth, Texas, and they both lived into their eighties.

In the sixty-plus years since Miller's death, if there is any one musician who has been synonymous with the Glenn Miller franchise, it's Tex Beneke, who—though his existence was ignored in *The Glenn Miller Story*, the movie that inspired a whole new generation to hear that serenade in the moonlight—did more than anyone else to keep the Miller sound alive for decades and decades. It's a surprise to learn, then, that in early 1946, when the Miller estate decided to launch a new Glenn Miller Orchestra, their first choice was not Beneke but McKinley.

Tenor saxophonist Gordon Beneke had come up through a string of territorial bands. While playing in Detroit with a now forgotten leader by the name of Ben Young, he came to the attention of another star tenor player, Sam Donahue, who was then with Krupa (and later with Tommy Dorsey and others); between Donahue and Krupa, word of this prodigious Texas tenor eventually reached Glenn Miller.

Miller hired Beneke as his top tenor soloist when he was putting together his new band in March 1938, and four and a half years later, when Miller disbanded, Beneke was still there. In the intervening period, he had not only become one of the most popular stars of the saxophone, but an absolute asset to the band as a vocalist. A true son of Satchmo, Beneke sang in a warm, woody voice—with a very fast and recognizable vibrato—that made a lot of high-swing-era rhythm tunes sound better than they actually were. In the best jazz tradition, he was never better than when he had a partner to play off, be it Marion Hutton ("The Rhumba Jumps"), leader Miller himself ("When Paw Was Courtin' Maw" and many others), or the Modernaires, who back Beneke on the megahit "Chattanooga Choo Choo," probably the biggest-selling big band record of its day. Like Hutton, he was an expert at extracting all musical and emotional value from even a grade-B novelty, like "The Gentleman Needs a Shave" and "Papa Nicolini."

By June 1939, Miller deemed Beneke, with his Fred MacMurray smile, ready to handle a solo ballad vocal of his own, and he couldn't have done better than with Willard Robison's bittersweet "Guess I'll Go Back Home This Summer." Beneke was also, along with Jack Teagarden and Woody Herman, one of the finest blues singers then working with a white band, especially on Mary Lou Williams's "What's Your Story, Morning Glory." The West was to Tex what the stars were to Eberle; in fact, I wish that Miller had given Beneke all his quasi-Western ballads, like "Call of the Canyon" and "Prairieland Lullaby." (Much as I like Eberle, somehow I don't quite believe him when he tries to convince us that the prairie dust is in his soul, "like the dusty tumbleweeds when they roll.")

Come the war—and Miller's disbandment—Beneke and Miller, surprisingly, do not seem to have considered the idea of working together, even though both went into the service. From 1943 on, Beneke was a bandleader, and would never again appear as a sideman. He led a band under the auspices of the navy for the duration, on a considerably smaller scale than Miller's superambitious AAF project, while Miller focused his spotlight on another superb musician who doubled as vocalist, drummer Ray McKinley. Born three years before Beneke, McKinley had considerable big band experience. His first documented session occurs in 1931, under the leadership of Red Nichols, and fellow sidemen on the date include Jimmy Dorsey and

Glenn Miller, in both of whose bands he would later play. On that very first date, McKinley also establishes himself as a vocalist as well as one of the many Sons of Satchmo who were proliferating as the swing era approached, by singing one of Armstrong's early hits, "You Rascal, You."

McKinley's career paralleled Miller's for a time in that, like the trombonist, he worked with Red Nichols, singer Smith Ballew's band, and then the fledgling Dorsey Brothers Orchestra; he also played for Benny Goodman on a famous all-star jazz session. After the Tommy-Jimmy divorce, McKinley stayed with Jimmy's band when Miller left to work for Ray Noble. The drummer gradually established himself as the key rhythm vocalist with the Jimmy Dorsey band, singing things like "The Love Bug Will Bite You if You Don't Watch Out," "Cowboy from Brooklyn," and a deservedly forgotten slice of Johnny Mercerana entitled "Show Your Linen, Miss Richardson." Even though he sang on only half a dozen or so Dorsey Decca titles, he was, by 1939, one of the stars of the older brother's band.

In the late twenties, McKinley first worked with trombonist Will Bradley in a territorial group called Milt Shaw's Detroiters. In 1939, the agent Willard Alexander, one of the guiding forces of the swing era, decided to build a new band around the trombonist and the drummer-singer. They were conceding that neither one of them was enough of a name on his own to front a major-league band, but if they pooled their star power and musical know-how they might just about pull it off. Exactly how they were supposed to work together wasn't quite clear: McKinley's understanding was that they were full co-leaders, but the group was always billed as Will Bradley's Orchestra. He later explained to anyone who asked (including George Simon and myself) that he couldn't lead the band, sing, and play drums all at the same time (Buddy Rich brought in deputy drummer Stanley Kaye when he later tried to do that), and thus was happy to let Bradley stand in front of the band and conduct.

McKinley was a solid drummer, but he may have been an even better singer, and his vocals were a major asset to Dorsey, Bradley, and, eventually, Miller. The voice itself was thin and somewhat scratchy—in its timbre and approach, it was more like a higher-pitched, Texas-style version of Woody Herman's. Obviously, it wasn't the voice itself that was special, it was what he did with it, and McKinley, or "Mac," as he was nicknamed, was heavily featured with Bradley from the beginning.

The first session, in September 1939, featured one of the most cryptic titles Bradley and McKinley or anybody else ever recorded: "Old Doc Yak." After hearing this song for years, I'm still not quite sure what the lyrics are supposed to be about—my best guess is that it's the tale of a snake-oil salesman who travels out West, "where a quack's a quack," claiming to have "a cure for cancer." (No, there aren't many songs of the swing era that bring up the subject of curing cancer.) There are Indian-style tom-tom rhythms throughout, so perhaps it's another one of those Native American love calls so popular among the big bands, like Bradley's own swinging instrumental of "From the Land of Sky Blue Waters."

At first, the band seemed somewhat derivative: When Bradley is heard soloing on trombone, it all sounds a little like Dorsey or Miller (or even Teagarden, who was also establishing himself as a bandleader at this point). The reed section voicings likewise fluctuated between the creamy sound of Miller and the New Orleans retro of Bob Crosby. Although Bradley's horn continued to be a prominent voice, for the first time a drummer provided the inspiration for what major big bands became known for: boogie-woogie riff numbers, both instrumentals and novelty vocals. With his ability to kick the band as a drummer, McKinley could take a silly song and make it sound good, as in "I Get a Kick out of Corn," or sometimes do the reverse, as on the Jan Savitt–Bon Bon hit "It's a Wonderful World."

McKinley came up with the expression "Beat Me Daddy, Eight to the Bar"—a fairly accurate description of how boogie-woogie piano works, meaning to play twice as many notes per measure as the usual 4/4—and he just happened to blurt it out one evening. It began as a spontaneous vocal break in the middle of a number, something he said in place of a drum break, much the way "Oh, play that thing" became part of "Sugarfoot Stomp." The songwriters Don Raye and Gene De Paul were present, and they built a new song for the band around that title. Producer John Hammond was so impressed with the whole package—the song itself, the way the arrangement translated boogie-woogie into big band terms, and McKinley's vocal—that he encouraged the band to record it as a two-sided 78 single.

Big bands (Count Basie, Tommy Dorsey) had played boogie-woogie (which was always foremostly piano music) before, but here, for the first time, was a pop song with lyrics that celebrated the whole boogie phenom, expertly sung by a superb rhythm stylist, and a native Texan to boot. "Beat Me Daddy" became one of the big hits of the swing era, and there were all sorts of sequels combining McKinley's hip, jivey vocals with Freddy Slack's authentic, down-home boogie piano. There were "Bounce Me Brother with a Solid Four," "All That Meat and No Potatoes," "Rhumboogie," "Strange Cargo" (the latter two pieces combining the boogie beat with more exotic, quasi-Latin trappings), "Celery Stalks at Midnight," "Scrub Me, Mama, with a Boogie Beat," and even "Boogie Woogie Piggalie." Other artists got in the act, too, "Piggalie" being covered by Miller and the Les Brown–Doris Day team, with piggish squeals of delight, and the Andrews Sisters recorded dozens of ersatz boogies, many written by the team of Raye and DePaul, most famously the World War II hit "Boogie-Woogie Bugle Boy."

Bradley and McKinley broke up in 1942, not because of the war but because of a disagreement between the two leaders. As McKinley told me around 1990, Bradley wanted to abandon their string of boogie-woogie successes and come up with a band that essentially cloned the Goodman orchestra of the period. McKinley thought they should keep doing what had been successful, even though he, too, was aware that the boogie-woogie thing couldn't last forever. "After all," Mac asked me, "how much can you do with a three-chord tune?" (As it turned out, three-chord tunes of a decidedly less interesting nature would completely take over the music business a few years later.)

McKinley left and started his own band, a group that had time for just two commercial sessions in summer 1942. The ten issued titles include plenty of war-related material (like Mac's vocal on Irving Berlin's amazingly pro-Soviet "That Russian Winter") and two covers of Kay Kyser movie hits, "Who Wouldn't Love You" and "Got the Moon in My Pocket." The latter two were both duets with Imogene Lynn, who would soon attain movie immortality in a different way, as the singing voice of Tex Avery's Red Hot Riding Hood in a series of MGM cartoons. The most characteristic title is Mac's personality-filled vocal on the Jazz Age standard "Hard Hearted Hannah"; his singing is especially Johnny Mercer–like here.

With McKinley gone, Bradley so completely overhauled his existing unit that it could be described as an all new band. It didn't last for long, however. Within a few months, the draft had decimated both bands, and McKinley himself was soon annexed by the Miller AAF Orchestra. One has little doubt that Miller would have loved to have had McKinley in his civilian band from the beginning, even though his own drummer, Maurice Purtill, certainly became an essential part of the classic Miller sonic identity. McKinley could have doubtlessly kicked the civilian band even harder as a drummer, and contributed a lot as a singer as well.

McKinley was equally valuable as a vocalist to Miller, filling Beneke's big shoes—the astute leader had miraculously managed to replace one ace rhythm singer from Fort Worth with another. Mac was just as important to the 1943–45 Miller band as Tex had been to the 1938–42 edition. His infectious, heartily nasal whine figured especially well on propagandistic and war-specific numbers like "G.I. Jive," "There Are Yanks (From the Banks of the Wabash)," "A Hot Time in the Town of Berlin," and "Peggy the Pin Up Girl." He also reprised Beneke's vocal on "Chattanooga Choo Choo" as well as his own Bradley-era hits "Down the Road a Piece" and "Beat Me Daddy, Eight to the Bar."

After Major Miller died—or whatever—Sergeant McKinley was a natural to take over as front man. "When Glenn became lost, they stuck me in front of the group," he told historian Burt Korall, "with

everyone doing his job, just as if Glenn were still around." Therefore, after the AAF Orchestra disbanded in the fall of 1945, McKinley became the first choice to lead the new postwar Glenn Miller Orchestra, which the Miller estate sanctioned a few months later. However, he had already decided that he was going to resume his bandleading career with his own group, whereupon the Miller estate extended their string of pearls, as Gary Giddins aptly put it, to their second choice, Tex Beneke.

This was a good decision in that it led to two of the finest jazz-pop ensembles of the late forties, Tex Beneke and the Glenn Miller Orchestra, and Ray McKinley and His Orchestra. Although both were among the best of that or any other time, they have been overlooked by virtually everybody ever since—even the redoubtable George Simon, in *The Big Bands*, devotes less than a page to McKinley's late forties band, and not even that to Beneke's groups. Perhaps the McKinley band is largely neglected because he made the unfortunate decision to sign with Majestic Records, which couldn't do the band justice in terms of either recording quality or distribution, and by the time he upgraded to RCA (just in time for the 1948 AFM recording ban) it was too late: The band business was by then pretty much finished. Likewise, although the Beneke-Miller band was a popular enough attraction in its day, scholars ever since have dismissed it as merely a ghost band.

Yet both orchestras were sublimely musical. They each had a foot in the relatively recent past—McKinley kept playing "Celery Stalks at Midnight" and Beneke kept playing "Chattanooga Choo Choo"—and maybe both hands in the pop mainstream, but the toe on the second foot, at least, was pointed clearly toward the future. McKinley employed the progressive-minded Eddie Sauter (a direction that had been encouraged by Glenn Miller himself) as his principal writer, and Beneke brought in equally far-sighted writers like Norman Leyden (who'd written a lot of the best stuff for the AAF band), Henry Mancini, and Sauter's future partner, Bill Finegan.

The music press of the time tended to dismiss most of Mac's and Tex's vocals as mere "commercial novelties," but compared with the direction that much of postwar pop was about to go in, even the tritest of these seem like art music. Tunes like McKinley's "Have Ya Got Any Gum, Chum?" and Beneke's hit "The Woodchuck Song" ("How much wood would a woodchuck chuck if a woodchuck could chuck wood?") seem like the Gershwins compared to the increasingly subliterary music of the next few years.

I know music critics and historians aren't supposed to like so-called dopey novelties, but I really enjoy the many comedy pieces done by McKinley and Beneke, particularly as their bands are so musical, their arrangements so outstanding, and McKinley and Beneke themselves are such good singers.

Besides, both these bands really swung. Majestic and RCA took advantage of McKinley's and Beneke's Fort Worth origins and accents by assigning them a lot of Western-oriented material like "In the Land of the Buffalo Nickel," "Cherokee Canyon," and "Pancho Maximillian Hernandez." McKinley also kept singing his former boogie-woogies while Beneke also played material with a rhythm and blues tinge, like the hit "Hey Bop-a-Re-Bop," which he sang with at least as much conviction and credibility as Helen Humes or Lionel Hampton did. Both groups also made some outstanding transcriptions for the RCA-owned The-saurus concern (some of which have been issued on CD by the Hep, Viper's Nest, and Magic labels). The two bands were even better on superior songs; in three movie songs of the period—"My Heart Is a Hobo," "Gal in Calico," and "That's What Uncle Remus Said"—Beneke shows what a musically rich period the immediate postwar years were.

It was too good to last. McKinley kept going until 1950, when he gave up his touring band, although in the next few years he made a few studio dates as a leader. In that same year, the Miller estate and Beneke terminated their arrangement. What had made the 1946–50 Beneke-Miller band so terrific was the way the leader constantly varied the mixture, adding new material and even allowing the classic Miller sound to absorb the influence of such new developments as bop and R&B. This was precisely what the Miller estate objected to.

Beneke went right on with his own group, only now he no longer shared billing with his deceased ex-boss. He switched from RCA to MGM, making some decent sides, such as another amiable song of the South, "Nashville, Tennessee," and the King Cole standard "Unforgettable," with a Ray Eberle vocal that's pretty much only of academic interest (it con-tradicts its own title). The 1950–51 band is beauti-fully captured on a series of transcriptions issued on Magic as *Dancers' Delight*. Again, this is some of the best big band music ever recorded, and proof posi-tive that large ensemble pop still had a lot of energy and ideas even as solo singers were taking play away from them. Beneke sings wonderfully on the pop-gospel "Look Up," as well as on the jazz standard "I Never Knew" and the 1931 "Walkin' My Baby Back Home," recently restored to the Hit Parade by Cole and Johnnie Ray. (As a bonus, *Dancers' Delight* also contains four vocals by the nineteen–twenty-year-old Eydie Gormé, of which "Orange-Colored Sky," "Baby O," and "If I Were a Bell" make the case that Gormé may well have been the single finest vocalist ever to work with a Miller band or a spin-off.)

For several years there was no official Miller band. (There was a successful Miller knockoff band, led by arranger Ralph Flanagan, no relation to Miller arranger Bill Flanagan.) Then in 1956, inspired by the success of *The Glenn Miller Story* and the many 12" LP reissues of Miller's music (including, for the first time, live performances by both the civilian and AAF bands previously unavailable commercially), the Miller estate launched a new touring band.

This time, Ray McKinley was ready to accept their offer. The band under McKinley was also quite far from one of those ghost bands that sound as if they've given up the ghost: They played new Miller-sound-style treatments of other songs, both old and new, as well as old favorites, and the band's chief asset was the singing and drumming of its leader. He even revived "Pancho Maximillian Hernandez" and "Red Silk Stockings and Green Perfume." Still, the band didn't have quite the energy and panache of any of the four major editions of the Miller band up to 1950. When McKinley left after a decade, Buddy DeFranco took over, and his clarinet playing continued to spark the ensemble the same way that McKinley's drumming had. But with McKinley gone, the band was no longer interesting from a vocal perspective.

Beneke kept leading bands almost until the day he died, in 2000, though, as he got older and the times grew further and further away from the swing era, he grew more conservative rather than progres-sive, and in the final few years of his life he was pretty much playing only Miller civilian band hits circa 1939–42. It was increasingly apparent to him that the only thing people wanted to hear from him was the classic Miller sound. Yet he went on playing this music as if it meant something to him, and every time Tex sang "Chattanooga Choo Choo," he made it sound as if he really meant it—whatever "Chattanooga Choo Choo" was supposed to mean. So, too, did McKinley, although he rarely seems to have participated in Miller re-creations after three years of propelling the AAF band and ten years of leading the official ghost band. The drummer died at the age of eighty-four in 1995. As he told his friend the discographer and researcher Chris Popa, "I'm not sorry the way it turned out."

Singing Songwriters

Hoagy Carmichael
Harold Arlen
Johnny Mercer

The singer-songwriter is a concept that came to dominate popular music in the sixties, and therein lies an odd contradiction. Apart from the amazing achievements of a few ultratalented individuals (Dylan, Lennon, McCartney), pop had no choice but to dumb itself down when it became a given that an artist was supposed to write his own songs and sing them while accompanying himself on guitar (the music press of the late sixties was unkind, not to say savage, to pop acts like the Monkees, who by and large just sang and didn't play their own guitars or write the bulk of their material—as if singing were somehow a completely negligible talent). It stands to reason that if you're going to write, play, and sing, you're not going to be able to do any one of those three things as well as a professional who's dedicated his life to one of those individual pursuits. (Unless you are a genius. It pays to be a genius, of course.) In trying to do more, the singer-songwriters of the sixties actually wound up doing much less, and the overall quality of American pop has never recovered: The music wasn't merely compromised, it was downsized.

All the great songwriters of the age before Bob Dylan and the Beatles were keenly aware that they weren't the best interpreters of their own work—Richard Rodgers knew that he couldn't play piano as well as Teddy Wilson, and Jerome Kern knew that he couldn't sing like Helen Morgan (or even Irene Dunne). But there were notable exceptions. It seems almost unfair to bring Duke Ellington and George Gershwin into the equation, since they were both multifaceted in the extreme, being equally skilled at playing piano, conducting, and composing everything from 32-bar songs to extended works in classical forms as well as full-length productions for musical theater, even opera. It's hardly surprising that the whole of our music has only been able to produce one Gershwin and one Ellington; we should consider ourselves lucky to have even those two.

Of the upper, upper echelon of famous, name-above-the-title songwriters, only Gershwin had any noteworthy skill as a performer. Recordings of Richard Rodgers and Cole Porter exist, and an air-check survives of Kern, yet these documents are mainly interesting as historical curiosities.

This essay concerns itself with a few other exceptions. When we look at the three major singer-songwriters of the twentieth century—Harold Arlen, Hoagy Carmichael, and Johnny Mercer—certain shared qualities emerge. Most important: Not one of them wrote a show that might be considered a classic Broadway musical. Arlen and Mercer (together and separately) had successes on Broadway, but nothing to be considered part of the permanent repertoire of revivable shows. All three of them were heavily oriented toward jazz and other forms of African American music, including blues and minstrelsy. In a famous observation, friend Roger Edens spoke of Arlen's "super minstrel show attitude" and Ethel Waters described Arlen as "the blackest white man I ever knew"; then again, Waters presumably hadn't met Carmichael or Mercer, and might well have said the same thing about them.

And this, to me, is a mystery: Kern, Porter, Rodgers, and Berlin wrote dozens of songs that became part of the world of jazz and black music, but for some reason the four songwriters who were active performers for much of their careers—Gershwin, Carmichael, Arlen, and Mercer—were also the ones who considered themselves part of the jazz world from the beginning and pretty much through-

out their careers. In other words, jazz-oriented songwriters seen more inclined to perform than Broadway-oriented songwriters. Go figure.

It's also noteworthy that the three singers were professionally drawn to one another: Both Carmichael and Arlen were primarily composers, and Mercer, who was foremost a lyricist, worked with them. Indeed, he was probably the finest lyric writer to collaborate with either of them, even though Arlen wrote many classic songs with both E. Y. Harburg and Ted Koehler, and Carmichael also worked with a variety of talented wordsmiths.

Hoagy Carmichael (1899–1981)

Beginning chronologically: Hoagy Carmichael was born in Indiana in 1899 (eight years after Cole Porter) and had studied to be a lawyer before he became a full-time songwriter. In the mid-twenties, he was pursuing both practices, doing the law thing full-time while writing and publishing songs on the side. In the context of the period, it seems clear why he took so long to get into music on a full-time basis. He was so many things—composer, occasional lyricist, pianist, vocalist, arranger, bandleader—that he almost had too many options open to him. And it couldn't have been clear exactly how he could make a living in the music business. Yet by 1927, the twenty-eight-year-old Carmichael was clearly a man with a lot to say, and it's fascinating to hear the many ways in which he figured out how to say it.

We are indebted to the late Richard Sudhalter, not only for his definitive biography *Stardust Melody* but also for *Hoagy Carmichael: The First of the Singer Songwriters*. This is a four-CD boxed set issued by the English JSP label in 2003, and about which the only element that I can find fault with is the title, which uses a sixties term (no one referred to Hoagy as a "singer-songwriter" in 1930) to forge a link between Carmichael and his psychedelic successors. It also sells Carmichael short in that he does considerably more here than write songs and sing them: The set derives its great diversity from the variety of ways Carmichael performs on various sessions, playing keyboards, putting his own bands together, serving as guest vocalist with well-known orchestras, and even playing a cornet solo now and then. The JSP package also includes quite a few tracks featuring Carmichael's songs performed by others, like Louis Armstrong and the Boswell Sisters, in order to give a completely well-rounded picture of his songs in their era. (While the JSP package samples Carmichael's complete oeuvre, there's also a recommended single CD from Timeless, *Hoagy Carmichael, 1927–1939*, which covers all of the composer's early, jazz-oriented vocals.)

In both the book and the boxed set, Sudhalter concentrates heavily on the late twenties and early thirties, if only because there's so much variety here. Carmichael's earliest sessions, done in Richmond with various bands under the leadership of the composer and local friends, spotlight the recent college graduate (itself a rarity in the pop music and jazz community at the time) as composer, bandleader, pianist (offering an elegaic solo on the first version of "Stardust"), and cornetist ("Friday Night"). As a vocalist, Carmichael doesn't so much evolve as appear on records full-blown, on the 1927 Paul Whiteman Orchestra record of his "Washboard Blues." The lyric was written from the perspective of an African American woman, whose blues about having to "keep washin' dem ol' dirty clothes" gradually assumes the profundity of a spiritual. He very astutely juxtaposes two different meanings of the trip to the river—the literal, in the sense of washing clothes, and the devotional, which twenties listeners would be well aware of (a familiar image presented in such traditional songs as "Shall We Gather at the River?"); he's washing his clothes at the same time that he's cleansing his soul.

To paraphrase the title of a 1932 Carmichael song, Hoagy sings it way down low. Like colleague Bing Crosby, he was one of the few voices in the twenties pop period to sing in the baritone register, a deep, resonant sound that was encouraged by recent musical and technological developments. Yet compared to either Crosby or the popular tenors of the period (e.g., Gene Austin), Carmichael's is a brutally untrained voice. Like Chet Baker after him, he makes his lack of technique into an asset, an indicator of sincerity. The lack of artifice in his singing makes him more believable; he has to be exactly what he claims to be because, we think, well, he obviously doesn't have the craft to be anything else. Although he sings in a low register like Crosby's, the accent is distinctly Midwestern or Southern; at a time when the voices of pop singers were anything but regional, Carmichael has a nasal sound with a pronounced twang. He employs a lot of singspiel, but at the same time his pitch and rhythm are musically accurate, and his singing is never anything less than it ought to be.

"Washboard Blues" was cut in Chicago in November 1927; three weeks later, Carmichael surfaces in Kansas City, singing vocal refrains (and, Sudhalter believes, contributing at least part of the orchestrations) on two songs by other writers, "So Tired" and "My Ohio Home," with Jean Goldkette's orchestra. His singing on "Ohio Home" is a little too frantic (he just doesn't sound believable when he sings with this much animation), but "So Tired" is marvelously laconic; he never overdoes the understatement. This is inspired character singing, head and shoulders above most dance band vocals of the period. Where "Tired" and "Washboard" are wonderfully low-key, to connote both world-weariness and common garden-variety weariness, the scat vocal he offers on "Walkin' the Dog" (recorded in Richmond a few months later) is pure energy, with Carmichael leaping all over the place.

Also during that fateful season Carmichael worked on a series of sessions with Irving Mills, who was not only his publisher at the time but the general manager of a stable of important big bands and a busy record producer. Released under Mills's name, "Harvey" is one of Carmichael's best early vocals, and an original song ripe for revival in this age of gender politics. The title character is not a seven-foot rabbit but, equally fantastic, a Jekyll-and-Hyde. One side of him is rugged and masculine, the other simpering and effeminate; it's hard to believe, in the light of the last seventy-five years, how much things have changed. By 1929 standards, it's the pansy side of Harvey that's considered presentable, while his butch side ("always tight [meaning drunk], in a fight, shootin' craps and out all night") is the one he keeps under wraps. Carmichael's vocal, sung in two distinct voices, is so effective that I keep checking the label to make sure that he's really singing both parts by himself.

More's the pity that he elected not to sing both the male and female roles on "Barnacle Bill the Sailor" (1930), another early, hilarious gender-bending novelty. The country-pop singer Carson Robison essays the part of "the fair young maiden" here, while Carmichael, who leads the date, reprises his "Harvey" baritone as the eponymous sailorman who is nautical but not at all nice—like Harvey, he fights and swears and drinks and smokes. It tells us something—I'm not sure what—that this extreme novelty encompasses several generations of jazz greatness in that there are blisteringly hot solos from Bix Beiderbecke, Bud Freeman, and Benny Goodman. Maybe this is why it took so long for jazz to be recognized as a legitimate art form—somehow I can't imagine Wynton Marsalis and the Jazz at Lincoln Center Orchestra playing "Barnacle Bill the Sailor," especially with violinist Joe Venuti contributing to the vocal in his own way, singing in a voice that presages another famous Sailorman in language that would get an R rating today; Carmichael has transitioned from scat singing to scatological singing.

However, most of Carmichael's canon hinges on issues of race rather than gender. There's an interesting contradiction here. First, as is well known, Carmichael was an active participant in the prototypical cool jazz of the late twenties, and was famously identified with Beiderbecke and Red Nichols, two pioneering cornetists of the era who were among the first to record his compositions. Carmichael's career, and Beiderbecke's as well, can be said to begin with the 1924 "Riverboat Shuffle," which was Carmichael's first successful song and practically Beiderbecke's first great solo (from his second session, done with the Wolverines). Over the next sixty years, Carmichael did more than anyone to keep Bix's memory alive, even playing a character based on himself in the movie *Young Man with a Horn*, a highly fictionalized biography of the cornetist, and, for what it's worth, Hoagy also named his son Bix. Beiderbecke was the man who most encouraged Carmichael's writing career to begin with, and the composer also freely acknowledged that Beiderbecke directly inspired many of his best-known melodies, such as "Star Dust" and "Skylark." On many of Carmichael's own productions, like "One Night in Havana" and his early versions of "Star Dust," he fits in easily with the Midwestern-Caucasian sound of the period, as exemplified by Beiderbecke and Frank Trumbauer, with echoes of American impressionist composers like Edward MacDowell and Eastwood Lane (not to mention French impressionists like Debussy and Ravel).

But at the same time, Carmichael shares with his younger colleagues Arlen and Mercer an almost obsessive fascination with all things African American. There are elements in the songs of all three—as on Carmichael's singing on "Smile" (not his own song) and "Rockin' Chair," both of which find him casting himself as an elderly black man in a way that could be considered condescending by today's standards. (We've already witnessed him transforming himself into an older black woman in "Washboard Blues.") Yet all three men—Carmichael, Arlen, and Mercer—never meant to do anything other than celebrate black life, even when they're indulging in what today seem like burned-cork routines.

It's worth noting that black musicians at the time did not find these songs offensive. In fact, Louis Armstrong quickly became (with the possible exception of Mildred Bailey, who took up the tune as her theme song) the most celebrated interpreter of "Rockin' Chair." He was the first major artist to record it, with Carmichael himself supplying the other half of the duet, a role assumed quite spectacularly two decades later by Jack Teagarden. Carmichael's relationship with Armstrong became, over the decades, just as intense as that with Beiderbecke, Armstrong easily recording more songs by Carmichael than those of any other songwriter. Many of Carmichael's best songs were composed with Satchmo in mind, just as Ellington wrote for Johnny Hodges and Cole Porter wrote for Ethel Merman.

It's telling that Carmichael recorded "Rockin' Chair" both with Armstrong and with Beiderbecke, the latter in a session (one of Beiderbecke's last) under the composer's own leadership for Victor in 1930. By the early thirties, all the various elements of Carmichael's music—and his singing—had coalesced: the Midwestern twang and the Southern drawl, the Caucasian impressionism and Negro blues.

He did a particularly lovely series of sessions for RCA from 1929 to 1934, which offer our first extended visit with Carmichael the vocalist, and he comes through with flying colors. He's snappy and bouncy on "Come Easy, Go Easy Love," recorded with a territorial bandleader bearing the unfortunate name of Sunny Clapp, and a most convincing balladeer on his future standards "Georgia on My Mind" and "Lazy River." The 1933 "Snowball," also recorded by Bailey and Armstrong, is a traditional Mammy song in the strictest definition of the term, but handled with sensitivity, and, like "Georgia Rose" of a few years earlier, a song with a distinctly pro-black message.

"Sing It Way Down Low," with lyrics by African American songsmith Jo Trent, is a neglected Carmichael gem that he recorded memorably in 1932 under his own name. When Hoagy croons "Sing it . . . easy and slow," the verb "sing" would appear to be a euphemism for something else. The rest of the date features three more outstanding Carmichael songs, also surprisingly neglected: "Mighty River," "After Twelve O'Clock," and "Thanksgiving." Beginning in 1933, his writing and singing were enriched by the presence of Johnny Mercer as lyricist, and Carmichael made a point of recording their first important songs together, "Lazy Bones" and "Moon Country," even though he continued for a time to write outstanding songs with "Star Dust" lyricist Mitchell Parish and others, such as "One Morning in May."

There is a gap in Carmichael's discography from the last date in 1934 until four years later, when he cut a few sessions for ARC (Brunswick) and soon after began a longer relationship with Decca. The four-year silence represents Carmichael's transition from jazz jack-of-all-trades to Tin Pan Alley tunesmith to Hollywood songwriter, which he would remain from the mid-thirties to when he stopped writing twenty years later. The later recordings and songs find him less inclined to experiment than earlier, but not entirely so. In "Two Sleepy People" (1938), written as a duet for Bob Hope and Shirley Ross but also recorded by Carmichael and Scottish jazz singer–musical comedy star Ella Logan, there's a reference to the couple going out dancing, and the accompanying band plays a quote from "Star Dust," indicating that the song has already become something of an institution. However, when Carmichael recorded his best-known version of "Star Dust" for Decca in 1942 (the first time he sang the lyric on disc), he is still inclined to play around with the tune, at one point even swooping down a whole octave from the melody as written, meaning that "Star Dust" was not fixed in stone for him and was still something he could take chances with.

Interestingly, Carmichael chose this period to record "Hong Kong Blues," one of his most ambitious works (as both composer and lyricist). According to Sudhalter, who provides a convincing musical analysis, the composer first wrote it circa 1929, a dark narrative somewhat similar to Cab Calloway's tales of Minnie the Moocher and Smokey Joe kicking the gong around in old Chinatown. Carmichael casts both blacks and Asians in a none too favorable role here, and the principal difference between this and the Calloway pieces is that the hi-de-ho man distinctly celebrates the use of hallucinogens, whereas Carmichael's is more of a cautionary tale, albeit one that positively revels in its un-PC nature.

Carmichael obviously regarded "Hong Kong Blues" as one of his most important songs: He made at least five studio recordings of it and also sang it in his first major feature film appearance in *To Have and Have Not* (Hoagy meets Bogie). More specifically, he regarded it as his personal property; hardly any other artist of Carmichael's generation touched "Hong Kong Blues," the only notable cover version being by Tommy Dorsey's orchestra. All of Carmichael's own recordings liberally employ faux-Asian effects. The keyboard in the 1938 original Brunswick version sounds more like a harpsichord tuned to simulate a Chinese string instrument, and the guitar, clarinet, and arco bass solo produce similar effects. Here is Carmichael's most exaggerated singing: He sharply overemphasizes every consonant in a way that vaguely anticipates the unsubtle, overbaked vocalizing of Bob Dorough, who recorded what could be called a Carmichael caricature in his 1999 album *Who's on First?*

In "The Old Music Master," introduced by crooner (about to turn actor) Dick Powell, in one of his final musicals, *True to Life*, Carmichael and Mercer address the issue of generational conflict in music. Another ambitious narrative, this story concerns the meeting of a nineteenth-century composer who somehow meets "a little colored boy" born a hundred years later, who advises the music master to swing it, rock it, and jump it. Sadly, this too is a Carmichael casualty, recorded only by its authors, Carmichael with his own piano (and celesta), Mercer with Paul Whiteman's orchestra in a zesty duet with Jack Teagarden. Ideally, this would have been the perfect song for Carmichael and Mercer to sing together; more's the pity that it never happened. (There's a fine transcription by the King Cole Trio in compensation.) This meeting of different eras and styles of music threatens to tear apart the space-time continuum itself, when the music master hits a mysterious chord (paging Sir Arthur Sullivan) that rocks the spinet, causing him to disappear "into the infinite."

"The Old Music Master" (originally titled "Mr. Music Master") was one of six sides Carmichael cut for Decca in 1942, which also include that wonderful "Star Dust." These are comparatively intimate sides, which emphasize Carmichael himself (backed mainly by bassist Artie Bernstein and drummer Spike Jones, who had already begun his career as a novelty bandleader). For the rest of the decade, his recorded work would be much more extroverted and oriented toward mass-market pop.

From 1944 to 1946, Carmichael threw in his lot with ARA Records, a start-up operation that never quite got started. The ARA sides haven't been reissued in toto, although a few of the best are sampled on the JSP box. These sessions for the label were, in a sense, a throwback to the years 1929–32,

when the composer was presented as the leader of various dance orchestras; here he's fronting a big modern swing band. Even familiar Carmichael classics sound considerably more opulently produced than we're used to hearing them: "Doctor, Lawyer, Indian Chief" (which he wrote for Betty Hutton in *Stork Club*) opens with Native American tom-toms, and "Memphis in June" boasts strings and a romantic tenor sax solo. "Baltimore Oriole," a Carmichael-Mercer masterpiece, is especially interesting; subsequent singers (such as the talented Barbara Lea) sang this minor key ballad in a slow, thoughtful tempo, making it into the art song it is. The composer's own rendition, however, while slower than some other bands might play it, is still very much in dance time.

Carmichael also cut yet another swell "Star Dust" for ARA (not to mention "Hong Kong Blues"), this one being an especially Hollywood treatment, with strings and a full choir behind him. Several Carmichael tunes from the ARA period are very well suited to the hard-swinging attitude of the mid-forties: "Ginger and Spice" and "Billy-a-Dick" (a verbalization of a percussion pattern), which anticipates the later jazz vocalese movement. Likewise, "Walk It Off" and "It Aint' Gonna Be Like That" are endearing, well-crafted swingers that perfectly suit the era, the kind of thing that Woody Herman or the King Cole Trio would have recorded. Carmichael wrote "Ole Buttermilk Sky" for himself to introduce in a forgotten Warner Bros. effort titled *Canyon Passage*. While the hit went to the combination of bandleader Kay Kyser and singer (and future talk-show host) Mike Douglas, Carmichael's ARA version is singularly charming. "The Whale Song" is a truly adorable children's song; he should have written more like it.

The late forties were the high point of Carmichael's career as a performer, both in film and on record. He appeared in ten mostly major motion pictures, among them a few classics: *To Have and Have Not, The Best Years of Our Lives*, and *Young Man with a Horn*. (Supposedly, when *Best Years* won the Oscar, producer Sam Goldwyn referred to Hoagy as "Hugo Carmichael" in his acceptance speech.) Carmichael is a cool, understated presence in these films; so much so that some sources claim he was actually a key inspiration for the film version of the fictitious British secret agent James Bond. (No kidding—Hoagy was the original ole buttermilk spy.)

Befitting his increased visibility, he returned to Decca for the bulk of the 78 rpm era. Hoagy was perfectly in step with the postwar period, and was delighted to send more and more novelty songs toward the Happy Cat Hit Parade. His recordings in these years grew increasingly unsubtle (like much late forties pop music), as exemplified by his 1950 single "The Old Piano Roll Blues," a duet with Cass Daley, the female equivalent of a baggy pants comic, whose comedy was so broad (in every sense of the term) that she made Betty Hutton look like Gertrude Lawrence. Another trend that he participated in was the sing-along format, which was more or less pioneered by bandleader Art Mooney and led to the Mitch Miller TV and album series; "Happy Hoagy's Medley" features the Hoagster singing with a large choir in an arrangement that sounds borrowed from Mooney's "I'm Looking Over a Four-Leaf Clover."

Carmichael's biggest hit as a recording artist, oddly enough, was not one of his own songs, but "Huggin' and Chalkin' " by the San Francisco–based singer-banjoist Clancy Hayes. In 1947, radio personality Arthur Godfrey landed a number 2 hit with a complaint against corpulence entitled "Too Fat Polka." Three years later, Americans voted in favor of fatness when "Huggin' and Chalkin' " became a supersized hit and claimed the number-one spot. It's so un-PC—even more so than "Harvey," "Barnacle Bill," or Carmichael's 1930 "Jewish Boy Blues"—one almost feels embarrassed explaining the title. In Hayes's narrative, the object of his affections is so obese that he can't hug her all at once, he has to hug a little bit of her at a time, and employs chalk to mark his place. No, it's not exactly Noel Coward. In that sense, "Huggin' and Chalkin' " could be described as a sequel to "The Whale Song."

Carmichael's Decca remake of "Doctor, Lawyer, Indian Chief" uses an eerie-sounding early electric keyboard (possibly a Novachord), and, though less swinging than the earlier ARA version, has a certain amount of charm. His Decca "Old Man Harlem" is way more audacious than any of the recordings of the song from 1933, but it's also warm and engaging. His treatment of "In the Cool, Cool, Cool of the Evening" lacks the star power of the Bing Crosby–Jane Wyman–Matty Matlock hit version, but there's still a lot to be said for hearing the singer-songwriter himself do it in a comparatively intimate reading, if such a thing is possible of this highly extroverted party song. Much as I like Carmichael's solo version, the song represents another missed opportunity, in that "Cool, Cool, Cool" would have been another potentially perfect duet for the composer and lyricist, Carmichael and Mercer.

On the plus side, Carmichael had a voice and style that were perfectly suited to the Dixieland revival of the late forties. Sides like "Abba Dabba Honeymoon" (one of several lively laments of the Roaring Twenties successfully revived twenty years later), another duet with Cass Daley, feature a good deal of Bob Crosby–style traditional jazz. Along with Crosby, Carmichael also recorded one of the few vocal versions of the Dixie warhorse "That's a Plenty," as well as such stalwarts as "Coney Island Washboard."

There's a fair amount of second-rate material in Carmichael's post-1946 Decca sessions, some of it the composer's own, like "Who Killed 'Er" and "Shhhh the Old Man's Sleeping." Yet there are also lots of terrific underappreciated songs and performances here, the tune stack being fairly evenly divided between Carmichael and other authors, including Harold Arlen's beautiful "For Every Man There's a Woman" and many more that never became standards: "Casanova Cricket," "A Tune for Humming," "Ten to One It's Tennessee," "A Man Could Be a Wonderful Thing" (later revived by Julie Wilson), and "Some Days There Just Ain't No Fish." He also wrote and recorded a fair share of gems that deserve to be more widely performed, like "The Monkey Song," an elaborate story-song in the tradition of "The Old Music Master" and "Hong Kong Blues" (like the latter, it boasts the composer's own lyrics), and "My Resistance Is Low," which Bing Crosby had the good sense to sing, very late in his career. One would like to see the Carmichael estate, which is run by the composer's son, Hoagy Bix Carmichael Jr., join forces with Universal Music to produce a complete collection of the Decca output.

Like Crosby (in *Bing with a Beat* and other fifties albums), Carmichael made one of his most powerful statements as a vocalist just as he was getting ready to leave the world of active pop music making. This was *Hoagy Sings Carmichael*, which he recorded in September 1956, with producer Richard Bock and arranger-conductor Johnny Mandel. Things get under way immediately with Art Pepper and Carmichael shining brilliantly on "Georgia on My Mind"; fortunately, Pepper and Jimmy Rowles are generously spotlighted throughout. Arranger Mandel conceived of the charts less as star turns for a heavy-duty vocalist than as modern jazz mood pieces, in which the dark tones of Carmichael's not especially mellifluous voice interact with the individual horns. Overall, Mandel's work here offers early evidence that he was destined to become one of the best of all vocal arrangers. The orchestrator told Sudhalter that it was mutually decided to include only tunes that Carmichael could sing comfortably, and to avoid those that needed a more trained voice, like "One Morning in May" (which Carmichael had once named a personal favorite).

Carmichael and Mandel also avoid the really fast and overtly jazzy items, like "Riverboat Shuffle" and "Hong Kong Blues." These are all love songs, both to specific women and to places (or, in the case of "Georgia on My Mind," apparently both), and unlike nearly all of Carmichael's earlier sessions with full bands, the singer and the arranger keep everything intimate, up close, and personal. Even those songs about ornithological entities, all those skylarks and orioles, are no longer about birds, they're very much about human feelings. "Winter Moon," which features a solo by Pepper (who would return to the song over twenty years later in a devastating rendition with Bill Holman's string orchestra), is, in the hands of Carmichael and Mandel, nearly as moving as Sinatra and Riddle's "I Get Along Without You Very Well." *Hoagy Sings Carmichael* is a succinct, not to mention succulent, summation of everything Carmichael had achieved both as a vocalist and a songwriter.

In 1958, Carmichael recorded another original LP, *Ole Buttermilk Sky* on Kapp Records. It's not a bad effort at all, and if the masterpiece *Hoagy Sings Carmichael* had never been made, it would probably attract more attention. Where the World Pacific album concentrates on Hoagy's intimate and romantic songs, the Kapp project focuses on his upbeat showbizzy side—everything here is bright and bouncy and outgoing ("Doctor, Lawyer, Indian Chief," "Cool, Cool, Cool of the Evening"). In fact, it sounds like a late fifties TV special with lots of chorus girls in tights and feathers. The newest song is "Music, Always Music," a 1957 copyright with Carmichael's own lyrics that could easily have been a number on the Milton Berle show or the *Colgate Comedy Hour*. (The lyrics describe it accurately as "a crazy Latin thing"; Carmichael sang it on *The Rosemary Clooney Show* with the host—and the Hi-Los.) Throughout, Carmichael is spirited and engaging; he actually does some of his best singing here. And as a bonus for those who have followed his whole career, there are a few rarities, among them "When Love Goes Wrong Nothin' Goes Right" (which he sings better than Jane Russell and Marilyn Monroe do in *Gentlemen Prefer Blondes;* however, they looked better), "Rogue River Valley," and "Mediterranean Love."

"Music, Always Music" and "Mediterranean Love" are two of Carmichael's final songs. He had stopped composing regularly by 1960, but continued to make the occasional public appearance, even one in animated form on *The Flintstones*. (It was *The Simpsons* of its day.) There were other recordings, too, like a 1960 version of "Star Dust," again with his own piano. (It's included in the now out-of-print BMG CD *The Hoagy Carmichael Songbook*, along with Della Reese doing "Two Sleepy People." Reese may be many things, but sleepy ain't one of 'em.) He continued to turn up on TV, appearing with Louis Armstrong, Danish jazz violin star Svend Asmussen, and country singer Crystal Gale, to name a few. Carmichael's final commercial recordings appear on the 1981 *In Hoagland*, a British-produced tribute record starring two crossover artists: musical comedy and jazz singer Annie Ross and English blues and pop star Georgie Fame. The arrangements, though rockish, are not nearly as bad as they could have been. (This may sound like faint praise, but believe me, it's a compliment in light of how most of the music from this period was every bit as bad as it possibly could have been.) Carmichael's contribution was a thoughtful, contemplative "Rockin' Chair," accompanied by his own piano.

In all these later performances, even the *Hoagland* album, which was done just a few months before he died in December 1981, Carmichael's voice is only slightly lower and older-sounding than it was when he first began singing in the late twenties. (In fact, he sounds every bit as fresh and contemporary in 1956, 1960, and 1981.)

Apart from the issues of race and gender that we've seen in his songs, Carmichael also dealt with what would today be considered issues of ageism. So many things in his songs are old, a way of making them inherently nostalgic: "Ole Buttermilk Sky," "Old Man Harlem," "Old Man Moon," "The Old Music Master," "The Lamplighter's Serenade" (yes, the lamplighter himself is old, anticipating the even older "The Old Lamp-Lighter" by Charles Tobias and Nat Simon), apart from his two masterly portraits of the elderly, "Little Old Lady" and "(Old) Rockin' Chair."

At eighty-two, Carmichael sounds as capricious and charming, but also as dark and mysterious, as ever. Ol' Rockin' Chair hadn't quite got him yet, even as he was getting ready to meet the Old Music Master.

Harold Arlen (1905–1986)

It may be significant that Hoagy Carmichael never recorded one of his very best love songs, the 1938 "I Get Along Without You Very Well." This has always been the odd song out in the Carmichael canon: It began as a setting for a poem, and represents one of the only times Carmichael wrote a melody to fit an existing lyric. As a result, "I Get Along" sounds more like the work of one of the major writers in the Broadway fraternity: Most people would probably guess it was by Rodgers and Hart (or even Rodgers and Hammerstein), or Arthur Schwartz and Howard Dietz. On Sinatra's *In the Wee Small Hours*, it seems perfectly at home in the company of "It Never Entered My Mind" and "I See Your Face Before Me." This was the most Broadway-like, New Yorkish of Carmichael's songs, and its singing songwriter never sang it.

Much has been made (by myself, certainly) of Harold Arlen's involvement with the world of jazz, perhaps a little too much. He and Gershwin were the only members of the Broadway Big Six who were capable enough instrumentalists to support themselves as musicians before their ASCAP royalties began coming in. The comparison with Gershwin is revealing: The older man came up through the world of songwriters and song publishers, while Arlen entered the music industry by means of the dance bands, which at the time were very close to—and often indistinguishable from—hot jazz. Both men approved of and encouraged the use of their music in the jazz community: Gershwin was flattered when, even during his lifetime, jazzmen found endless new uses for his chord sequences (notably "I Got Rhythm"). On the other hand, they didn't have to rewrite Arlen's melodies: Just as Arlen wrote them they sounded jazzy enough.

For Gershwin, Broadway musicals were bread-and-butter; the prize he had his eyes on was academic respect, which he sought to achieve by writing rhapsodies, ballet, and an opera. He created some great music in the process, even if he failed to knock Mozart off his pedestal. Arlen, like Mercer and Carmichael, valued the respect he earned in the jazz and pop community (unlike, say, Richard Rodgers, who seems to have actively disdained it), but for him the goal was Broadway: Nothing could top the respect a composer earned by writing a great musical show. In America, that was the top of the food chain—and it's a sign of Gershwin's ambition that he sought to climb even higher.

Arlen, like Carmichael and Mercer, spent most of his career as a writer of songs for Hollywood films, and almost every time he wrote for the New York stage it was for a black-oriented show. *Life Begins at 8:40, Hooray for What!*, and *Saratoga* are among the few productions he wrote with all-white casts, and even in the long-running hit *Bloomer Girl*, the black characters get all the best songs. It's significant that we remember the subplot about the runaway slave more than we do the central plot about the girl who wants to trumpet her nineteenth-century liberation by wearing bloomers.

Arlen grew up immersed in both Jewish and black culture: He was raised in a two-family house in Buffalo, New York, in which one family was African American and the other was that of the Cantor Arluk, including his son Hyman. Hyman Arluk sang in his father's synagogue choir, studied piano, and by his teens was forming his own vocal groups and dance bands—he was a founding member of a popular upstate-based group called the Buffalodians. In 1926, they made it down to Manhattan, where they played the Silver Slipper Cafe and, fortunately for posterity, cut six sides for Columbia Records, two of which feature vocals by Arlen himself.

Thanks to the luck of the draw, we have Arlen vocals with the Buffalodians on two very good standard songs of the period: "Baby Face" and "How Many Times," the latter by Irving Berlin. It seems perfectly fitting that Arlen's premier recording, done well before he wrote his first song, is by Berlin, whose music had spoken to issues of racial integration in pop music a generation earlier. On "How Many Times," the first note is way high, and for a split second Arlen sounds like one of the stratospheric tenors of the era. This turns out to be a false alarm: His vocal is otherwise warm and deep; even if the jazz-blues elements that we will hear in his singing later on aren't quite there yet, there's definitely something different happening here. At the same time, there's a lot of the era in his singing, a bit of a Jolsonian cadence, perhaps, and the wide, rapid vibrato. He also tends to ac-cent-tchu-ate his high notes; in fact, it's this quality of exaggeration (which he shares with both Hoagy Carmichael and Bob Dorough) that undoubtedly contributed to Roger Edens's description of him as having a "minstrel show attitude."

Here's where Arlen the singer begins to lay down a foundation for Arlen the songwriter: He later wrote those very qualities into his music, as in "I Got a Song," written for Richard Huey and Dooley Wilson in *Bloomer Girl*, in which their voices go up at the end like a traditional field holler: "I Got a So-on-ong-*ah!*" Likewise, in the same score, "Man for Sale" (sung by Arlen himself on the *Bloomer Girl* cast album) has him employing the trick of rising at the end of a note in the auctioneer's spiel—he would incorporate that yelp into many of his melodies. These qualities would always be present in his vocals, even into the sixties. Later, this quality would make his singing sound dated, albeit charmingly so, but here in the late twenties he's perfectly in step with the period. In fact, if anything, he's ahead of the curve, along with Crosby and Cliff Edwards (and, as we've seen, Carmichael) as an early example of a white vocalist influenced by black jazz styles. (Speaking of race relations, it should be noted that "Man for Sale" isn't a metaphor for love and abuse in the mode of Cole Porter's "Love for Sale," but a literal description of a slave auction.)

The Buffalodians caught the ear of a considerably better-established bandleader named Arnold Johnson, a sort of lower-league Paul Whiteman. Like Whiteman and Vincent Lopez, Johnson could play hot music, sweet music, show music, or whatever was demanded, and was an important presence on the radio and even on Broadway itself. At the time Arlen joined, Johnson's orchestra was supplying the music for the current edition of *George White's Scandals*, much as Whiteman would soon be doing for Florenz Ziegfeld's *Whoopee*. Arlen joined the Johnson band as a triple threat: arranger, pianist, and vocalist. And, coincidentally, he wrote charts for several songs also recorded by Crosby and Whiteman, "American Tune" and "I'm on the Crest of a Wave."

Also like Crosby with Whiteman, Arlen sang many songs with Johnson, but with varying degrees of involvement and audibility. He participates in roughly a dozen Johnson sides, all from 1928, five of which have been reissued on the Canadian label Jazz Oracle in a three-CD collection (released under the name of trumpeter Jack Purvis). "After My Laughter Came Tears," which is typical of the Jazz Age in that it's ostensibly a sad song but is performed in a relentlessly energetic tempo, features Arlen as the central voice, abetted by a Rhythm Boys–like vocal trio, scatting and making hip vocal-instrumental noises as accompaniment. Arlen is often the dominant voice on these sides, although on Harry Woods's future standard "Together" (done more as a foxtrot than a waltz), he's merely audible in the chorus behind lead singer Roy Ingraham. His distinctive voice is also prominent on three trio numbers: "What's the Reason?" (which features a pennywhistle solo and an individual spot for Arlen in the coda), "Get Your Man" (in which he stays strictly within the trio), and "Georgie Porgie." The last also has a few solo moments for Arlen, who makes the other two members of the group sound antiquated by comparison.

Johnson kept Arlen busy—perhaps a mite too much so. He later told biographer Edward Jablonski that he couldn't keep up with the grind and quit in the middle of writing a chart. Arlen went out on his own as a singer (presumably accompanying himself at the piano) in vaudeville and a traveling revue called *Maytime*, showing enough promise that in 1928 the Victor Company gave him an audition session at which he sang "I Can't Give You Anything but Love." (He also recorded "Since I Found You" with the dance band led by former Whiteman trumpet star Henry Busse in 1929. Both these Victor masters were, unfortunately, unissued, and are lost.) In February 1929, Arlen wrote his first notable song, "The Album of My Dreams," with lyricist Lou Davis. Shortly thereafter he was hired as a sort of assistant to composer Vincent Youmans, then working on a show called *Great Day*, which, while a flop, would yield several notable standard songs.

As it happened, *Great Day* was an all-black show, featuring the leading black band of the Jazz Age, Fletcher Henderson's orchestra, and Henderson himself was playing piano. Arlen served as rehearsal pianist, and while playing for one of the dance routines, he had an idea for a melody that eventually became "Get Happy," and at the suggestion of Harry Warren, he began working with lyricist Ted Koehler. "Get Happy," recorded by, among others, the bands of Red Nichols and Frank Trumbauer, was an immediate hit, and almost instantly cinched Arlen's destiny as a leading songwriter. Arlen and Koehler wrote for several smaller Broadway revues, but found their niche when they began creating the scores for the elaborate shows staged at the Cotton Club, beginning in 1930.

Yet Arlen was far from finished with the idea of being a performer. He went on recording frequently throughout most of the years of his collaboration with Koehler, beginning with a series of sides with Red Nichols in 1930, some of which are historically significant in that they're Arlen's first recorded vocals of his own songs. "Teardrops and Kisses" and "Were You Sincere," the latter also cut by Crosby, are good straight-ahead ballads in dance time, while "Things I Never Knew Till Now" is considerably hotter. Arlen is immediately in a class with the best band singers of the day—not Crosby, perhaps, but certainly Chick Bullock, Smith Ballew, and Red McKenzie. Had he continued in this vein, it's easy to imagine him working steadily as a radio singer, at least until the end of the thirties. He certainly was good enough to croon and swing over the air and on a series of sides under his own name. On his two original sides, "Linda" (from the first Cotton Club show, *Brown Sugar*) and "Sweet and Hot" (from the successful revue *You Said It*), he's better still. The quirky, anxious, and undeniably hot quality of

Arlen's early melodies is directly related to those same qualities in his singing. He's likewise sizzling and lusty on the jazz standard "How Come You Do Me Like You Do?"

In June 1931, Arlen cut two of his very finest vocals, "Pardon Me, Pretty Baby" and "Little Girl," in a session with the long-standing team of violinist Joe Venuti and guitarist Eddie Lang. Arlen holds his own not only with those two formidable improvisers but also with the virtuoso multireed player Jimmy Dorsey, here playing clarinet and alto and baritone saxes. Inspired by the company he keeps, Arlen swings with an abandon I can't imagine coming from any other white male singer of the era other than Crosby and Cliff Edwards. "Pardon Me, Pretty Baby," which Dorsey opens on baritone, is exceptionally strong, and Arlen, after singing his regulation 32-bar vocal refrain, is given an additional 16-bar out chorus, after briefer statements from Lang, Venuti, and Dorsey (now on clarinet). Arlen has all the amorous energy that both songs require, in a way that has less in common with pop singers of the time and more with jazzmen like Armstrong and Red Allen.

Arlen must have realized, however, that he would never be as good a singer as Fats Waller or Jack Teagarden, who followed him on a 1931 Red Nichols date, telling us to "Keep a Song in Your Soul" right after Arlen asked us "Were You Sincere?" These eight sides from 1931 are probably the last in which Arlen was considered a professional vocalist: For the rest of his career, he would only be a visiting fireman, a songwriter who once in a great while recorded one of his own tunes.

In the fall of 1933, Arlen wrote his first film score, for a picture called *Let's Fall in Love* (released early the following year), which, though quickly forgotten, yielded one of his most beautiful standards in the title song. In November, he recorded it with RCA studio conductor Ray Sinatra, and the following month he appeared as a special guest on Paul Whiteman's radio show singing the same song. The rather unctuous radio announcer makes a big deal of ensuring that we realize how unusual it is for a composer to come on the air and actually sing one of his songs for the public. Songwriters would generally only sing for producers, for backers, or to demonstrate their wares for the stars who they hoped would be singing them for real.

Nonetheless, Arlen was comparatively busy in the Victor and then Brunswick studios between 1932 and 1934, resulting in fourteen released masters, the first and last four of which were done with the society-oriented orchestra of Leo Reisman. Reisman was the dance bandleader most connected to the Broadway pipeline; he frequently tapped stars from the shows for his vocal refrains (Fred Astaire, Clifton Webb), and occasionally even songwriters (Arlen, Arthur Schwartz) as well. Arlen sang two of his Cotton Club songs with Reisman, the jubilant "Happy as the Day Is Long," in which he also engages in vocal banter with the bandleader, and the most famous of them all—the biggest hit of the songwriter's career—"Stormy Weather," on which he's appropriately dark and bluesy. "Steppin' into Love" was subtitled a "Collinstone Fox Trot," a very unusual rhythm that kind of turns in on itself (almost the thirties answer to 5/4 time). "Smoke Rings" is the only item from the 1932–34 Victor sessions not composed by Arlen himself, and it's a gem indeed, being a rare vocal version of the theme song for the Casa Loma Orchestra, by the band's musical director Gene Gifford with an especially thoughtful lyric from the underappreciated Ned Washington.

Two of the Victor discs stand out—"Let's Fall in Love" and the lesser-known "This Is Only the Beginning" with Ray Sinatra's orchestra (both from *Let's Fall in Love*), and "Ill Wind" and "As Long as I Live" (both from the Cotton Club) with Arthur Schutt's piano—because these are, as far as I can tell, the only actual Harold Arlen records of the entire 78 era. That is to say, the only sides where Arlen himself is the featured attraction, and not a guest star or vocalist with some band or other. The prize of the bunch is "Let's Fall in Love," which he sings with an uncommon tenderness that makes the performance sound quite contemporary, as much of its period as it may be. Arlen starts with his own verse, which was hardly heard through most of the song's existence but was exhumed by Sinatra in 1961 and more recently re-exhumed by Diana Krall, inspired by Sinatra, and is currently being heard from singers all over New York, inspired by both Krall and Sinatra.

After the four solo sides (from fall 1933–spring 1934), Arlen cut a further two tracks ("Ill Wind" and "As Long as I Live") with pianist Eddy Duchin, whose band at the time was essentially a spin-off of Reisman's. Then in 1934, with Reisman himself again, Arlen recorded band vocals on all four principal songs from the score of the 1934 revue *Life Begins at 8:40;* three years later, the Arlen-Reisman team tackled two tunes from *Hooray for What!*, namely "In the Shade of the New Apple Tree" and "God's Country."

Virtually everything else Arlen subsequently sang on records would be of the surprise-guest variety: He turns up unannounced on the 1939 Decca album of songs from *The Wizard of Oz* (a studio recording, as distinct from the actual film sound track), and also unbilled as the second voice on Woody Herman's 1941 "Blues in the Night" (he's the guy who evokes the lonesome whistle singing "a-hooey da-hooey"), and briefly on two tracks on the *Bloomer Girl* cast album, "Man for Sale" and as one of the voices in "Sunday in Cicero Falls." There are also a few more radio and TV appearances, including a memorable spot on the *Colgate Comedy Hour* (1953) with the unusual trio of Eddie Cantor, Eddie Fisher, and Frank Sinatra, and, as with many songwriters, he left an estate of demos and private recordings that

cry out to be comprehensively catalogued and commercially released.

Toward the latter part of his career, Arlen also made three LPs worthy of discussion, all of which were arranged and conducted by Peter Matz, who was the composer's own choice as musical director ever since he orchestrated Arlen's score for the 1954 *House of Flowers*. Together, Arlen and Matz produced *The Music of Harold Arlen* (subtitled *The 1955 Walden Sessions* on its CD reissue on Harbinger Records), *Harold Arlen and His Songs* (also 1955, Capitol), and *Harold Sings Arlen (With Friend)* (1966, Columbia).

In the mid-fifties, the pop music scholar Ed Jablonski was operating an independent label called Walden Records, which devoted its resources to building multiartist songbook albums around the great composers. Ira Gershwin gave him Arlen's number, and to Jablonski's great delight, Arlen not only agreed to give his approval to the project, but to participate in it by playing and singing some of the tracks himself. He also refused to accept any money for his work, and the project as a whole, unbeknownst to Arlen, was largely underwritten by Gershwin (the two had worked together on *A Star Is Born* a short time earlier). Jablonski and Arlen grew so close personally that six years later Jablonski published Arlen's biography, *Happy with the Blues*. In that book, Jablonski suggests that at one point the Walden project and the Capitol album were planned to complement each other. The big-budget Capitol album had the more famous songs, while the shoe-string Walden venture consisted of worthy but more esoteric material.

Both albums are delightful, and must have seemed like a welcome deluge of Arlenia, since, unlike Carmichael and Mercer, Arlen had not made any commercial recordings (except for the aforementioned dribs and drabs) in twenty years. The Capitol set, *Harold Arlen and His Songs*, places the singer-songwriter with a small but adequately sized orchestra, and his own very stylized, still slightly exaggerated singing is beautifully balanced against Matz's marvelously subtle and tasteful charts. "The Gal That Got Away" is appropriately bluesy, with prominent alto, while others use a small string section.

As with the best of Carmichael's and Mercer's recordings, this is a project that proves, overall, how good composers doing their own songs can sound. The vocals and orchestrations are fine enough in their own right, and our enjoyment of the results is only increased by our knowledge that we're hearing these classic songs done by the man who wrote them. Arlen is sweet and optimistic on "Over the Rainbow" (like virtually every other non-Garland singer, he includes the verse) and both rhythmic and charming when affecting a Caribbean accent in "Two Ladies in the Shade of the Banana Tree"; his timing is as perfect as any professional entertainer's when interacting with the orchestra here, and his scatting is also up to snuff. He closes with his most famous song, but still in an understated fashion, by winding up with a low-key "Stormy Weather" and a final high note wail in falsetto.

The Walden project was released as a double LP (reissued as a single CD), featuring five additional singers (among them the vivacious Louise Carlyle). It was planned as a sort of revue in itself, with various singers doing various songs, but the composer ended up doing most of the numbers himself, and marvelously so. He performs on thirteen of the twenty-four selections, including two piano solos, "Minuet" and "House of Flowers Waltz," both of which allude to traditional dance forms, and one duet, "Can I Leave Off Wearin' My Shoes" (from *House of Flowers*). Arlen's vocals here on his lesser-known songs are no less valuable than those of his biggest ASCAP-earners, like "Come Rain or Come Shine" or "Over the Rainbow." In fact, there's nothing here from *The Wizard of Oz*—but there are some absolutely wonderful film songs, like "You're the Cure for What Ails Me" (introduced by Jolson in *The Singing Kid*), which I can well imagine the Cowardly Lion singing once he discovered his latent hypochondria, and "Halloween" (from *My Blue Heaven*), which we might think of as a song about the only holiday that Irving Berlin left untouched.

For me, the ringers here are the songs Arlen performs with his own piano, particularly the three selections in which he's unaccompanied by any other instrument—two relatively recent songs, "I Never Has Seen Snow," from *House of Flowers*, which was still running at the Alvin Theatre when Arlen recorded it for Jablonski, and "It's a New World" from *A Star Is Born*, and one all-time Arlen classic, "Last Night When We Were Young." "Moanin' in the Mornin'" (from *Hooray for What!*, 1937) begins with the composer and his piano, then adds an eight-piece ensemble that neither adds to nor detracts from the performance. Just as Carmichael offered his most emotionally direct performance on "Washboard Blues," using the guise of African American style, so, too, does Arlen on "Moanin' in the Mornin'."

Normally a track by a songwriter, with his characteristically untrained voice, accompanied only by his own piano, would sound like a demo disc, but these tracks by Arlen are complete performances. It's particularly telling that they are mostly ballads, and none of them is the easiest song in the world to sing. They've been recorded by the likes of Sinatra, Garland, and Fitzgerald, and yet the composer's own performance ranks with the very best of them.

Unfortunately, there are few such moments on the composer's last full-length album, *Harold Sings Arlen (With Friend)* (1966). Even though Matz is back at the baton, the arrangements are way overdone, especially in comparison to the exquisitely restrained work he turned in on the 1955 projects. Perhaps the arranger felt compelled to compensate because Arlen's voice had severely declined in the previous decade. Having Barbra Streisand (the parenthetical friend of the title) aboard only reinforces the notion that everything about this package is excessive, with the exception of Arlen's own chops. (Babs's solo on "House of Flowers" isn't bad, though not in the same class as Tony Bennett's 1960 recording.) However, the Arlen-Streisand duet on "Ding Dong! the Witch Is Dead" is, like the apples in the enchanted forest, not what it ought to be. Set to a mod-sixties beat, which makes it sound like "The Wizard of Oz à Go-Go," the attempt to be hip effectively sabotages what should have been a classic performance.

While the Columbia album is disappointing, Arlen had already left the world a valuable recorded legacy in his commercial recordings of 1931–37 and 1955. He was not in the studio nearly as often as his colleagues Carmichael and Mercer, but what he did leave us was of such high quality that he deserves to be ranked as one of the very best of singer-songwriters. At least, unlike Carmichael and Mercer, he never sang "Huggin' and Chalkin'," and for that we can be grateful.

Johnny Mercer (1909–1976)

Nineteen thirty-two was a helluva year for Johnny Mercer. Within the course of a few months, he wrote his first song with Hoagy Carmichael ("After Twelve O'Clock") *and* with Harold Arlen ("Satan's Li'l Lamb"). And, as if launching these two collaborations (perhaps the most significant of his career) was not enough, that selfsame "Satan" song would be the first Mercer lyric to make it into a Broadway musical (in *Americana*). Mercer would later collaborate memorably with many other composers, most notably Harry Warren and Henry Mancini (the two most celebrated tunesmiths in Hollywood history, although Mancini was famously famous and Warren was famous for not being famous), but I think that, without fear of contradiction, we can say that the ne plus ultra of Mercer's career was the dual catalogue of songs he wrote with Carmichael and Arlen.

Mercer's career has certain parallels with both men in that, as a singer and songwriter (and occasional actor), he set his sights on showbiz very early, and was less concerned with what he specifically became: He would have been just as happy competing with Bing Crosby as with Lorenz Hart or Ira Gershwin. Like Arlen, he was one of the few giants of Tin Pan Alley who grew up immersed in genuine African American culture and more than any of his colleagues he had a firsthand familiarity with the Sunny South that every songwriter was penning odes to in the teens and twenties. He was born in old Savannah (I said Savannah), Georgia, and originally came to New York in the late twenties with the intention of going on the stage, as they used to say. Unlike his older singing collaborators, Mercer had the advantage of being young enough to ingest the new jazz and pop of the electrical recording era, particularly that of Bing Crosby and Louis Armstrong.

However, 1932 was not only the year that Mercer had his first notable successes as a lyricist, it also saw him take his first successful steps as a singer. That was the year he followed in the footsteps of Crosby and went to work singing for Paul Whiteman and His Orchestra. According to Phil Furia's biography, Mercer hit the big time as a vocalist for the top band in the world all at once—without any notable previous band experience—when he entered an amateur singing contest. Pops Whiteman liked his invigoratingly high baritone and distinctive Southern accent, and he was in.

Over the next ten years, Mercer recorded a little over two dozen commercial tracks; most, with a couple of notable exceptions, were collected on the CD *Pardon My Southern Accent*, on the English Conifer label (which also includes a substantial bonus in three airchecks of Mercer singing on the BBC wireless in 1936). Mercer only remained with Whiteman for a brief period before he settled in Hollywood, and he recorded only a few tracks with the official, full Whiteman orchestra itself. Even so, virtually every side he made in this era has some Whiteman relevance: He sings with Frank Trumbauer, Jack Teagarden, Bing Crosby, Tommy and Jimmy Dorsey—past and present fellow Whitemanites all.

Mercer's initial recorded appearance is under Trumbauer's direction on a collage of jazz standards entitled "Sizzling One-Step Medley." It is not mistitled. Mercer's contribution to the medley is especially valid: On his 1931 recordings, he's especially hot and lusty, in a way that places him in a class with Arlen, Carmichael, and Crosby. He sings on two tunes, getting blisteringly hot on "Dinah" and offering up his most notable recorded scat solo on "My Honey's Lovin' Arms."

This disc set the tone for virtually all of Mercer's early recordings; just about everything he sang in the thirties would turn out to be a sizzling one-step. Whether singing his own lyrics or somebody else's, Mercer's whole repertoire in these years was Harlem this and hotcha that. His second record session was an audition date for Columbia, in which he sang an even then severely dated minstrel-type number called "Watch a Darkie Dance" (it shows up nowhere else, and is possibly Mercer's own words and music, however much I would prefer to think otherwise), accompanied only by piano and including a 16-bar scat solo. He follows "Darkie" on the test disc with Rodgers and Hart's five-year-old "You Took Advantage of Me," done in two choruses. This is virtually the closest thing to a ballad Mercer recorded in the early years, but even though the lyrics are for a love song, Mercer treats the melody very playfully in the Crosby-Armstrong mold, obviously inspired by the 1927 Whiteman version.

Columbia didn't release the side (it was issued sixty years later on the Conifer CD), but Mercer turns up on two band vocals, "Doin' the Uptown Lowdown," with Richard Himber's orchestra, and "Dr. Heckle and Mr. Jibe," with the Dorseys. These are both first-class examples of superior rhythm songs, neither credited to Mercer (the first is Mack Gordon and Harry Revel), but of the kind that Mercer would make a specialty of for the next thirty years. "Dr. Heckle" is credited exclusively to guitarist Dick McDonough, but it seems entirely plausible that Mercer might have written the text, which is precisely his blend of poetic jive ("The Pulitzer Prize for champion liar / Goes to Heckle, MD, and Jive, Esquire").

Mercer commercially recorded only four vocals with the Whiteman orchestra proper, and it's here that his talent as a duet partner comes to the fore. All four are vocal duos: "Fare Thee Well to Harlem" and its sequel, "Christmas Night in Harlem," with Jack Teagarden, and "Here Come the British" and "Pardon My Southern Accent," with Peggy Healy; all but the second are Mercer's lyrics. Whiteman's judgment appears to have been that Mercer, as good as he sounded on the Himber and Dorsey sides, wasn't quite strong enough to carry a vocal all by himself, and that he functioned better playing off another singer; indeed, as much as he recorded in the forties, there are precious few sides where he is the solo attraction—he's always sharing space with a name bandleader, a soloist, a vocal group, whatever. Even though many airchecks exist of the Whiteman band playing live in the mid-thirties, none of them features Mercer singing solo either (though there is a live version of "Christmas Night"). None of the four Whiteman-Mercer commercial titles is a traditional dance band or even hot dance side; they feature the singers much more heavily than that, and the Teagarden-Mercer duets are vocal records all the way through. "British" is actually a trio, with vocalist Johnny Hauser also playing a role: The threesome indulges in a vaudeville-like parody of a schoolroom scene, with some marvelous special material lyrics by Mercer.

He provides a welcome ingredient of spice on the two Healey duets—his singing is all tempo and energy. For the same reason, he also makes a very effective contrast with Teagarden; the trombonist's low baritone and laconic groove make for a fascinating juxtaposition with Mercer's high-pitched, high-voltage style. The two "Harlem" songs are not particularly good pieces of songwriting, but Mercer and Teagarden are a terrific team and make them memorable on their own. Mercer's closing comment on Raymond Scott's "Christmas Night in Harlem" is one for Ripley: "Man, you drooled a bibful!" In 1935, Teagarden and Mercer also joined with New Orleans trumpeter Wingy Manone on a lively novelty called "I've Got a Note," and the banter and horseplay seem more spontaneous here than on the Whiteman sides.

Teagarden also plays a prominent role on "Lord, I Give You My Children" and "The Bathtub Ran Over Again." These are on a 1934 Decca disc that marks Mercer's first-released solo effort. (He had previously cut "Lazy Bones" and "There's a Cabin in the Sky" in 1932, but those sides were only issued on a very obscure Varsity pressing four or five years later, and that pairing remains extremely rare.) As Furia details, at various points Mercer had ambitions to become a romantic crooner like Crosby (he appeared in one film as an actor, the 1935 RKO musical *Old Man Rhythm,* but he wasn't particularly effective onscreen, and though he recorded all four songs he wrote for the picture, these sides were never released). However, his first record under his own name is anything but a pair of love songs: "Lord, I Give You My Children" is a mock-religious effort that gives him the chance to spotlight various members of his small band, most notably Brother Teagarden; it's all very much in the style of Crosby's "Someone Stole Gabriel's Horn." "The Bathtub Ran Over Again" is closer to a conventional love song, but not by much—the bathroom overflows while our hero floats there oblivious, dreaming of his lost love. Somehow it makes me think of *Marat/Sade.*

As with Carmichael and Arlen, the big break in Mercer's career is the point at which he becomes established in Hollywood. For Mercer, this occurred not with *Old Man Rhythm* but when friend Crosby got him the opportunity to write "I'm an Old Cowhand," words and music both, for the 1936 *Rhythm on the Range.* It's a lively, jivey Western parody, which Mercer sang (verse and all) with a small band (muted trumpet and rhythm section) on the BBC, when he happened to be in London writing the *Blackbirds of 1936* revue. The BBC broadcast also included "Goody, Goody," one of the signature hits of the early swing era and long associated with Benny Goodman, and "I'm Building Up to an Awful Let Down."

Early in his Hollywood tenure, Mercer found two champions in Fred Astaire and Ginger Rogers. Rogers invited him to record his own "Eeny Meany Miney Mo" (a nursery rhyme variation and nonsensical precursor to "Jeepers Creepers") in a duet with her. Although they have a lot of charm, she wasn't a particularly strong vocalist (unlike Astaire). The best thing about the duet with Rogers was that Astaire supposedly came to the session, which led to the two collaborating on "I'm Building Up to an Awful Let Down" (credited to Astaire, but actually by Hal Borne, as Michael Feinstein has discovered). More important, Mercer would eventually write no fewer than five motion picture scores for Astaire, which is more than any other songwriter apart from Irving Berlin would do.

Now established in Hollywood, Mercer continued to record frequently but irregularly, and almost always with other singers. There was the duet with Ginger, then four yummy sides with Crosby (which,

happily, survive in two takes each), and one with Judy Garland (Cole Porter's "Friendship"). He also cut another session under his own name, backed by the Six Hits and a Miss. These are four of the most swinging sides ever done by the combination of a star singer and a vocal group, aided considerably by Mercer's proclivity for extending and customizing songs, both his own and others, with additional, special material lyrics. "The Murder of J. B. Markham" and "Jamboree Jones" are elaborate story-songs. While the first is forgettable, "Jamboree Jones," cut later by Crosby and still later by John Pizzarelli, is a swingingly substantial attempt at extending a mood and a tale beyond the usual 32 bars. "Bob White"— also cut memorably by Mildred Bailey and the team of Connee Boswell and Crosby, although the Mercer version contains more of the lyrics—is an ornithological entry à la Carmichael's "Baltimore Oriole" and "Skylark." Yet Mercer does his best work on "Last Night on the Back Porch," a Lew Brown lyric that he and Crosby both apparently remembered fondly from 1923; the vocal group adopts the flexibility of a big band sax section, which combined with Mercer's extended text gives the whole thing the feeling of a swing era Lambert, Hendricks & Ross number.

The four songs with Crosby represent a high point in the discographies of both men, and are among the most appealing mano a mano duets ever recorded. Carmichael's "Small Fry," from Crosby's picture *Sing You Sinners,* and "Mr. Crosby and Mr. Mercer," a big band–era update of the old Gallagher and Shean vaudeville routine, are early examples of Mercer updating an old tune with jivey new lyrics and swinging rhythms, as he would later do with "Glow Worm." Mercer wrote both of the 1940 sides, "Mister Meadowlark" and "On Behalf of the Visiting Fireman." All four are in the loose and playful style that the two men performed in private vaudeville–minstrel show productions staged at Crosby's house. Since both of them are expert duetists, these four sides are sterling examples of what Crosby called the crossed cadenza, combining rhythm and wit, classy singing and one-upsmanship. On "Small Fry," the semi-Southern, semi-Afro accent that Crosby employs from time to time is even more credible than Mercer's natural Georgia brogue. "On Behalf of the Visiting Fireman" has the two re-creating a pair of lowbrow entertainers in a down-at-the-heels roadhouse, with the bandsmen making crowd noises. At one point Crosby says, "And one for the road," forshadowing, a somewhat less jovial classic Mercer torch song of just three years later. "Mister Meadowlark" is the most elaborate, a fully worked-out scenario told in music that could have been a number from a film or show, with a narrative that flows in swinging, rhythmic dialogue from start to finish. Mercer only rarely created anything like this for his many musicals, although there are some very Gilbert and Sullivan– like interludes in his last Broadway show, *Foxy.*

(Mercer's duet with Garland on Cole Porter's "Friendship," from *Du Barry Was a Lady*, isn't quite up to this level of banter and interplay, though Garland holds her own remarkably well for a seventeen-year-old. Mercer and Garland would later do one of their best movie musicals together in the 1945 *The Harvey Girls*, and, as Furia tells us in perhaps too much intimate detail, they also had a very passionate affair.)

In 1942, Mercer, who hadn't yet won his first Oscar but was nonetheless a Hollywood power player, co-founded Capitol Records in partnership with a successful music retailer, Glenn Wallichs, and a well-heeled mogul and former lyricist himself, Buddy DeSylva. Although Capitol had an impressive lineup of big bands at the beginning, such as Benny Carter's, ex-boss Paul Whiteman's, and pianist Freddie Slack's, the label's strength would be pop singers. This was at a time, around 1945, when Dinah Shore was signed to Columbia and that label in turn dropped Ginny Simms, figuring that one star femme singer was enough. Mercer, on the other hand, was early in envisioning a pop music industry with plenty of room for talented singers, and within a few years most of the major ones recorded for him: Peggy Lee, Jo Stafford, Kay Starr, June Christy, Anita O'Day, and Mercer's own discovery, Margaret Whiting—not to mention Nat King Cole.

Almost as a bonus for doing such a good overall job with the company, Mercer permitted himself the luxury of regularly making his own recordings—although since many of his discs sold well enough to enter the *Billboard* charts, these were hardly vanity projects. There is still no complete collection (or even a published discography) of Mercer's own recordings, but in 2007, Mosaic Records at last came out with a three-CD sampling of seventy-nine of the jazzier titles in the series. If any artist deserves a Mosaic- or Bear Family–style supercollection, it is he. (Mosaic has also included a number of Mercer vocals on their boxed sets *Classic Capitol Jazz Sessions* and *Mosaic Select: Freddie Slack*. In the centennial year, 2009, yours truly was asked to compile *Johnny Mercer Sings Johnny Mercer*, a single CD containing all of his Capitol recordings of all his own songs.)

More than one employee described the early days of Capitol as being like a family, and many of the records Mercer produced and appeared on reflect that familial feeling. His first record, done in May 1942, a month or so after the company was officially founded, was his own "Strip Polka," a record that sixty years later seems more charming than risqué. The small orchestra approximates a grade-B band in a less than top-drawer nitery, replete with staccato trumpets and a swishy sax section, two clichés of Mickey Mouse band tradition. Capping the whole production is uncredited guest star Phil Silvers (who actually had a long career in burlesque) in a speaking role as a delightfully oily emcee.

Mercer's second date for the new company starred his musical "father," Paul Whiteman, who was star-billed on the best of Mercer's duets with "big brother" Jack Teagarden, "The Old Music Master"; the old master is played by Big Tea, and Little J plays the "little colored boy." Over the course of the decade, Mercer sang with the bands of Whiteman, Freddie Slack, Billy Butterfield, Bobby Sherwood, Wingy Manone, Cootie Williams, Benny Goodman, and with the King Cole Trio, among others—almost every band on Capitol at the time, with the notable exception of Stan Kenton.

Mercer reprised the Jolson standard "Waitin' for the Evenin' Mail," his own "The Air-Minded Executive," and another hit of the period, "The Salt Lake City Blues," with Slack. He also sang a few lines as a guest on the Ella Mae Morse hit "Mr. Five by Five," also with Slack. The song about the Utah town, which opens with the classic line "I left my sugar in Salt Lake City," features Mercer going into a monologue in which he recites Salt Lake City statistics in kind of a Bert Williamsy, deadpan minstrel voice. That voice is key to Mercer's ambitions—the idea wasn't to present himself as a star crooner like Crosby or the nascent Sinatra, but to play a character and tell a story. Even singing itself is less important than conveying a narrative, which he does more effectively by mimicking a comically exaggerated lazy Southerner of the type he might have encountered in minstrelsy when he was growing up in Georgia. Mercer plays that role all throughout "Sugar Blues," a devastating parody of old-school Mickey Mouse bands, and "Surprise Party," a comic turn in which he doesn't sing so much as wheeze out the notes.

Mercer had an affinity for guesting with trumpeters. He sang "It Ain't Necessarily So" with an all-star band led by Billy Butterfield (on the same session that yielded Margaret Whiting's hit "Moonlight in Vermont"), and covered Peggy Lee's "It's a Good Day" in the company of Bobby Sherwood, while he and Cootie Williams did the jivey "He Shoulda Flip'd When He Flop'd." There also were several reunions with Wingy Manone, most of which reveal a preoccupation with conveyance: "Tuscaloosa Bus," a witty follow-up to "Chattanooga Choo Choo"; "Box Car Blues," which is a genuine 12-bar blues, though far from a mournful one; and "Tailgate Blues," describing a traditional band parading through New Orleans on a horse-drawn wagon.

This Dixielanding was far from an indulgence, seeing as how Mercer's disc of the New Orleans standard "Ugly Chile" was a chart hit. Backed by the Skylarks and Ben Pollack's band, he sang four traditional titles in 1950. For this inspired session, included on the Mosaic *Classic Capitol Jazz Sessions* box set, he wrote new lyrics to the old-time warhorses "At the Jazz Band Ball" and "Royal Garden Blues."

In 1939, Mercer had served as the host of radio's *Camel Caravan*, which starred Benny Goodman's orchestra (and then Bob Crosby's). He sang three vocals with that fabulous Goodman band, "Cuckoo in the Clock," Jimmy Rushing and Count Basie's high-powered blues "Sent for You Yesterday," and "Show Your Linen, Mrs. Richardson," a song about lusty women kicking up their petticoats as they dance (I suspect that alcohol may have been involved; if so, Mercer could certainly relate), which Charlie Ryan of the Smoothies vocal group once described as "a Mercer stiff." Mercer and Goodman's best pairing, however, was on the 1947 "Moon Faced and Starry Eyed," a marvelous song by Kurt Weill.

Though Mercer recorded regularly for Capitol, even beyond the period when he was the label's hands-on artistic director, most of what he did on records in the forties, like that of the previous decade, falls into a certain pattern. Even as his own producer, he seems reluctant to feature himself as a star singer, even less a star singer of ballads and love songs. He would never be Frank Sinatra, although his 1947 recording of "Why Should I Cry over You" closely anticipates the later Sinatra-Riddle Capitol single. Mercer's version of his own "One for My Baby" is one of the very best after the Chairman's; he and Arlen wrote this song for Astaire (in *The Sky's the Limit*).

If Mercer isn't singing as the special guest of a famous musician or bandleader, then he's doing a duet with Jo Stafford, Margaret Whiting, or Nat King Cole, or performing with the Pied Pipers or some other vocal group. He also participated in multistar events and early concept albums, beginning with *Songs of Johnny Mercer*, the first-ever Capitol album, released in May 1944, and featuring the songwriter and various others he had under contract. Capitol and Mercer followed this up with albums of songs by Willard Robison, one of Mercer's heroes (he sang "Country Boy Blues" and "Don't Take Your Meanness Out on Me"), and an album of songs from Disney's *Song of the South* that yielded another top 10 hit for Mercer in "Zip-a-Dee-Doo-Dah." But surrounding himself with concepts and other stars seems to have been another way of ensuring that what he considered his substandard voice would not have to carry too much weight all by itself.

Mercer landed well over a dozen top 10 hits as a pop singer—"Ac-Cent-Tchu-Ate the Positive," backed with "Candy" by Mercer, Stafford, and the Pipers, was that great rarity, a single in which both sides went to number one on the *Billboard* charts, an even more amazing feat considering that Mercer not only sang but produced the sides for his own company, and wrote one of them. He also landed the number-one version of his first Oscar winner, "On the Atchison, Topeka and Santa Fe," despite tough competition from Bing Crosby and Judy Garland, who sang it in *The Harvey Girls*.

In all, Mercer the vocalist was as dependable a hit maker as most of the other artists on Capitol's roster. In the period before Nat King Cole established himself as a mainstream pop star, Mercer may have been the best male vocalist on the label. His popularity was underscored by consistent appearances on the radio: After the *Camel Caravan*, he starred as a talking and singing attraction on several other shows, most notably the Chesterfield-sponsored *Johnny Mercer's Music Shop*. The show, which co-starred fellow Capitolians Jo Stafford and Paul Weston, was especially popular with both American and English servicemen. (There's a good-sounding LP of excerpts from the 1943 and 1944 shows, *Johnny Mercer's Music Shop*, on the British Submarine label, that makes one wish that more of this material would find its way onto commercial releases.) As with Carmichael, people clearly wanted to hear him sing, yet he still seemed to lack faith in his own ability. Even when he wrote the classic score to the less than classic musical *St. Louis Woman*, Mercer was more likely to sing the Southern-style rhythm and character song "Little Augie Is a Natural Man" than his all-time masterpiece of a love song, "Come Rain or Come Shine."

In 1946, Mercer recorded what might be the most remarkable album ever of his own vocals. Alas, it was recorded only for Capitol's transcription series and not released on a commercial LP (hindsight) until four years after his death. Mercer sings sixteen Jazz Age warhorses (all included in the Mosaic select package) of the kind he grew up with in the twenties—including many great gals of the era, as in "Sweet Georgia Brown," "Margie," "Lulu's Back in Town," "Sweet Lorraine," and "Louisville Lou," as well as places like Indiana, Georgia, the river St. Marie, and Texas, where it's round-up time when the bloom is on the sage.

The sides were conducted by Capitol house musical director Paul Weston and feature the outstanding hot tenor sax of Herbie Haymer (who gets off a good solo on "I Never Knew"). The charts, many of which he also sings on the 1943–44 *Music Shop* series, were done in a roughly Bob Crosby-esque big band Dixieland style by clarinetist Matty Matlock. Mr. Mercer is consistently loose and swinging throughout, singing without a trace of self-consciousness or a care in the world. Often he confines himself to 32-bar band vocals, but sometimes he spreads out for the whole track. The most dated, politically offensive track is also the most endearing, namely Milt Ager and Jack Yellin's tale of that vampin' baby, that heart-breakin', shimmy-shakin' "Louisville Lou," who is the diametric opposite of Sam Coslow's later "True Blue Lou." Here Mercer ad-libs a minstrel show conversation with himself, as if he were playing both parts in "Small Fry," doing the other voice as Bert Williams.

Mose: Guess what [my boy] asked me for? An encyclopedia!
Jasper: Well, did you give it to him?
Mose: No! Let him walk, like I did!

One of Mercer's final chart hits was a duet with protégée Margaret Whiting on "Baby, It's Cold Outside"; Whiting has elaborated on how, in this instance, Mercer relinquished his identity both as songwriter and producer and put himself entirely under the direction of songwriter Frank Loesser. The result was a number 3 hit, the most immediately successful of the many versions of that great boy-girl party piece that were recorded that year. He charted for the final occasion with his swinging update of "Glow Worm," from an ancient German operetta; Mercer recorded the worm in 1949, but his disc only charted three years later in the wake of the very successful Mills Brothers single.

Unfortunately, when Mercer lost interest in actively running Capitol, he also put his singing career on hold, with occasional exceptions. The second half of his career, from the fifties to the seventies, centered around writing movie theme songs that became instant classics (leading to a total of four Academy Award winners) and Broadway shows that were decidely not. Like his frequent collaborator Harold Arlen, Mercer wrote many of his greatest songs for flops, most notably the infamous *St. Louis Woman*. Even when he wrote a show that enjoyed a run on Broadway, it never turned out to be a Rodgers and Hammerstein–level masterpiece. This was, unfortunately, also true of Arlen's Broadway career, one of epic flops and minor hits. It was no way to treat a great American songwriter; no wonder Hoagy Carmichael avoided the place altogether.

Mercer's post-1950 recordings were rather scattershot, but the few that he did make are generally of a high quality. The best known of the later recordings is also his only full-length duo album, *Two of a Kind*, done with rock star cum traditional pop singer Bobby Darin, and arranged and conducted by Billy May, who also presided over nearly all the important duet projects of the period. Some Darin specialists, like author Jeff Bleiel, tend to dismiss *Two of a Kind* as a Mercer project rather than a Darin effort: The songs are more from Mercer's era than Darin's, and several are his own work. Still, such a statement denies the formidable power of Darin's charisma—he doesn't have to worry about playing second fiddle to anyone. No matter how much Mercer content there may be, the Darin personality can't help but dominate.

The whole project certainly comes out of Mercer's long history as the duettin'est man in the record biz. Mercer's own tunes on *Two of a Kind* include "Bob White" (which Connee Boswell originally sang with Crosby, though it would have been a perfect Mercer-Crosby item), as well as a couple of relatively recent Mercer items from somewhat countrycentric productions, "Lonesome Polecat," from *Seven Brides for Seven Brothers*, and "If I Had My Druthers," from *Li'l Abner*. The rest of the tunes are, like the 1944 transcriptions, the hoariest of Jazz Age chestnuts: "I Ain't Gonna Give Nobody None of This Jelly Roll," "Ace in the Hole," "Mississippi Mud," "My Cutey's Due at Two-to-Two Today," and the like. I, for one, have always filed the album under D for Darin rather than M for Mercer, but perhaps I should put it under M for May instead, since the arranger-conductor often emerges as the dominant personality. Neither principal seems to have any faith whatsoever in his ability to sing ballads—and the idea of two dudes singing love songs to each other may not have been acceptable in 1960—so it seems to have been suggested to May that he make the album as noisy and raucous as possible. Although May himself was also a superlative orchestrator of love songs, you'd never know it here—every track is rollicking and jolly to the max. The disc is framed with an outstanding new title composition co-credited to the two principals, which beautifully captures their spontaneous banter and give-and-take.

None of Mercer's other album-era projects have achieved quite the notoriety of *Two of a Kind*, but there's a nice LP collection of miscellaneous, mostly radio material called *Jeepers Creepers* on Glendale, and a very interesting British CD with the ambiguous title of *Johnny Mercer Sings Johnny Mercer and Friends* on Memoir. This latter disc is the work of producer Ken Barnes (also known for producing the final sessions of both Bing Crosby and Fred Astaire), and its centerpiece is the nine tracks Barnes produced with Mercer in Los Angeles and London in 1971 and 1974. These are supplemented by two additional Mercer sessions, one much earlier, from 1956, and one slightly later, in 1974.

The 1956 material features Mercer with the unusual backing of a jazz piano trio and a vocal chorus—no horns or strings, just rhythm and voices. It helps that the pianist is the illustrious Paul Smith, and also that the choir, identified as the Notables, is surprisingly hip, somewhat like the Hi-Los, but less fussy and not exclusively male. This is only about six years after the Capitol era (if the date is to be believed), and Mercer is merely in his late forties, but the voice has deepened considerably. The treatment of "Blues in the Night" is actually more resonant than the earlier Capitol record, and Mercer is warm and avuncular on "Spring, Spring, Spring"; he also turns in a satisfactory blues on W. C. Handy's famous "St. Louis" excursion and makes "Java Jive," a great choice for him and the Notables, sound as good as his own "Jeepers Creepers."

The 1971–74 material is fascinating. Mercer is in his early sixties here. Barnes made the astute choice of Skip Martin, who had considerable big band and movie experience, as arranger-conductor. I don't know why Barnes and Mercer felt compelled to give the world a new reading of "Huggin' and Chalkin'," of all undesirable things, but the session is otherwise marked by the singer-songwriter's performance of many songs he never sang elsewhere. "Pineapple Pete" is a first-rate Mercer story novelty, being the tale of a hungry Hawaiian kind of a male answer to the chalkin'/huggin' equation—although considerably wittier ("When you say *Aloha* / he's reachin' for *samoa*"). "Shake It but Don't Break It" is still another early jazz classic that Mercer just had to sing. But at the opposite end of the spectrum he delivers a moving rendition of the hit "Gentle on My Mind," a Glen Campbell song for the man more normally associated with Glenn Miller.

The third session on the disc is very special indeed. I've more or less avoided demo recordings by these three singer-songwriters and concentrated on recordings made for commercial consumption. Barnes, however, filled out the Memoir CD with the demos made by Mercer and composer André Previn for the great lyricist's final show, *The Good Companions*. Mercer and Previn may never have intended these tracks to be heard by the general public, yet Barnes made the right decision to release them commercially.

Even though he was characteristically American, Mercer was the perfect man to write the lyrics for this adaptation of the British showbiz novel by J. B. Priestley. The songs aren't Mercer's absolute best, but they're pretty darn good, and they don't deserve the obscurity they fell into when the show flopped. "Slippin' Around the Corner" is a comic drinking song (which figures directly in the novel), "Susie for Everybody" is a production number dance for the ensemble. Had the show been a hit, Mercer might have recorded these songs commercially. And some of *The Good Companions* demo songs are very special indeed: "The Pleasure of Your Company" is cast in the same mold as "Two for the Road," and "The Dance of Life" is classic Mercer, related to "The Days of Wine and Roses."

But the gem of the seven Mercer-Previn songs is "Little Lost Dream." After forty years of Mercer records from all manner of sources, at last we have Johnny singing one of his own slow love songs—a genuine unfettered ballad. I admit that my appreciation of both the song and his performance is affected by the knowledge that he would be gone just a year or two later. Even so, this tale of a "dream that got away" is deeply moving, and makes you wish more than ever that Mercer had recorded all of his finest love songs.

Johnny Mercer, it turns out, was a great singer, even when he didn't realize anybody was listening.

Female Band Singers II: Big Bands into Pop

Edythe Wright
Bea Wain
Ginny Simms
Kitty Kallen
And others!

When we talk about the singers who worked with the big bands, principally in the central years of the swing era (generally accepted as 1935–45), there are useful subcategories we can break them down into. Back in the day, the obvious idea would have been to divide them racially, as in singers with white bands versus singers with black bands, or by gender, as in what they used to call "canaries" versus what some people still call "crooners." Today we'd probably start to think about ballad singers (Helen Forrest, Ginny Simms) versus rhythm singers (Anita O'Day), or blues singers (Jimmy Rushing, Ella Johnson) versus novelty singers (Marion Hutton, Wee Bonnie Baker) or singers who also played instruments (Tex Beneke, Tony Pastor), or singers with funny nicknames (Ford Leary, Bon Bon) versus singers with movie-star-like names (Bob Carroll, Bob Haymes, Bob Manning). Still, these dividing lines are not always quite so clearly drawn.

There is, however, one point of demarcation that should be even more apparent: There are many big band singers who remain tethered, in our minds, to the swing era, and also a few who went on to bigger, if not necessarily better, things after their band tenures. When I say better, I am, by defini-tion, talking in terms of career rather than strictly about music: Don Cornell, who started with Sammy Kaye's band and sold a lot of records in the fifties, is by no stretch of the imagination a more worthwhile musician than Helen Ward, best known for singing with Benny Goodman's breakthrough band of the mid-thirties, an artist as worthy on her "instrument" as Goodman, Gene Krupa, or Bunny Berigan were on theirs.

It's not altogether surprising to learn of the postwar fates of the major canaries: Helen O'Connell (1920–1993) fit perfectly into the Jimmy Dorsey band framework; she didn't have much in the way of chops but had plenty of charisma. (There are a couple of good compilations of her best Dorsey-era work, most notably *Especially for You* on the U.K. Flare label, and *Sweetheart of Song*, a short budget compilation from Collectors' Choice, both of which co-star O'Connell with her frequent duet partner, baritone Bob Eberly.) Owing to the visual appeal of her work, it's not surprising that she was one of the few swing band–era stars who actually fared better on TV than on the radio. No one else could make a flat note sound so sexy, not to mention cool and limpid.

Dolores O'Neill (sometimes spelled with one "L," born 1917), on the other hand, was a superb band singer who never made it into the history books, other than with a well-deserved mention in George Simon's essential *The Big Bands*. She sang briefly with Artie Shaw (1937) and Jack Teagarden (summer 1939), but then reached her peak with a band almost completely ignored by history, Bob Chester and His Orchestra. She was a terrific singer with a grade-B band, in an era when even grade-B bands could be marvelous. The three dozen or so vocals that O'Neill recorded with Chester between 1939 and 1941 are, by turns, swinging, sentimental, full of emotion and rhythm, and, in short, everything a great 32-bar vocal refrain ought to be. She married Chester's trumpeter Alec Fila (later she sang with Fila's own band), and left Chester (being replaced by the capable Betty Bradley) to spend a memorable season on NBC's *Chamber Music Society of Lower Basin Street*, a highly contrived jazzcentric program that boasted memorable guest stars and top girl singers (including Lena Horne and Dinah Shore), on which she was regularly introduced, presumably with good reason, as Dolores "Yum Yum" O'Neill. Should BMG ever come to me and ask which hitherto neglected band vocalist is most worthy of a reissue under her own name, you can bet I won't hesitate. (Ted Ono, of Baldwin Street Music, has announced a double-disc reissue package containing her complete recordings, both with and without Bob Chester, but it hasn't been released as of this writing.)

Edythe Wright (1907–1965)

By the end of 1936, when Helen Ward and Benny Goodman parted company, female singers were established as a permanent part of the big band artillery. Ward's earliest equivalent, apart from her Goodman successors, was Edythe Wright, who lasted for the first five years of the Tommy Dorsey Orchestra.

Between 1940 and 1943, Dorsey discovered more superpopular star singers than all the other bandleaders put together—not just singers who had postband careers but those who went on to megastardom: to begin with, Jo Stafford, Frank Sinatra, and Dick Haymes. Yet the two principal singers of Dorsey's first band, Edythe Wright and Jack Leonard, didn't fare nearly so well. Both recorded dozens and dozens of songs with TD between 1935 and 1939, and having listened to Dorsey's entire recorded output in that period, I find that Jack Leonard is best in short doses. In the 78 rpm era, no one could imagine listening to ten titles in a row by any band singer; live sets at ballrooms and radio remotes were planned accordingly. Leonard has a decent voice, something closer to a tenor than a baritone; at least he sings in tune, and he has fine breath control and something of the long-form phrasing that Sinatra later learned from Dorsey. You would think his singing would be easier to take, but I find his voice irritating. Major drawbacks to trying to listen to Dorsey's complete late thirties output is getting through one Leonard vocal after another.

With Wright, I have the opposite reaction: The more one hears her, the more she grows on you. She doesn't have Leonard's chops, and though her voice is roughly in the same range and honeyish timbre as Helen Ward's, her rhythmic skills aren't nearly as developed. Yet something about Wright remains appealing. Leonard's biggest hit with the band, "Marie," made an asset out of his lack of personality—he was essentially playing straight man to the amusing antics of the rest of the band singing around him, Abbott to fifteen Costellos harmonizing in wiseguy unison.

Wright is the diametric opposite: She has little voice but no shortage of pep and personality. In her early days with the band, the temptation must have been to assign her the romantic numbers, which corresponded with her sultry, smoldering good looks. However, as it worked out, Leonard was given the responsibility of handling most of the basic boy-girl love songs, while Wright sang more swing numbers and novelty songs, and most of the tempo vocals with Dorsey's small-band-within-the-big-band, the Clambake Seven. She doesn't have a killer-strong sense of rhythm or even of humor, but she is just right for songs like the minor-key "You Don't Know How Much You Can Suffer (Until You Fall in Love)" and the topical novelty "All in Favor of Swing Say 'Aye.' " It was Wright who was called upon to interact with the Clambake Seven's individual soloists on tunes like "At the Codfish Ball" and "Posin'." On "Well, All Right" and "The Jumpin' Jive," Wright engages band (and presumably audience) members in a hi-de-ho-style sing-along. She even sang the blues once in a while, as on "After You." In short, Wright was game for any kind of nutty idea that came along (even something that went "Be it ever so thrilling / There's no place like your arms"), and had the chutzpah to pull it off.

Of all the major singers with major bands, Wright may be the most neglected. We know that she joined TD in 1935, shortly after Tommy broke off from the Dorsey Brothers Orchestra and formed his own band; she's heard on the band's first session, for Victor, that September. It's impossible to find out anything about her, other than that she was born in Bayonne, New Jersey. The only birth year I have seen is 1907, which seems unreasonably early; 1917 might be a better bet. The few Internet sites that list her seem to have copied one another, probably using Roger Kinkle's *Complete Encyclopedia of Popular Music and Jazz, 1900–1950* as the original source. Even Levinson, in his Dorsey biography, doesn't add any new facts regarding her background, although he does confirm the long-standing rumor that Wright doubled as Dorsey's mistress on the road. In fact, even after Mrs. Dorsey (no fool she) learned what was going on and demanded that TD give Wright the sack and hire another femme singer, Wright continued to tour with the band for a few months, strictly for sentimental reasons.

After that, Wright presumably left the business; in any case, she is not known to have performed again. At one point, in the late fifties, when RCA had launched a series of new hi-fi albums of swing era classics by the original stars, there was talk of an LP of the Clambake Seven (minus the recently deceased Dorsey) with Wright, which never came to fruition. She died in 1965. Though she was far from a major talent, she deserves some credit, at least, for her contribution to some of the most enjoyable recordings of the early swing era.

Bea Wain (born 1917)

Larry Clinton and His Orchestra with Bea Wain represented a very special package indeed: After Duke Ellington, this was the most composer-driven band, in which the leader was celebrated as a swinging maestro. Clinton, who had been an arranger for the Casa Loma and Tommy Dorsey bands, won wide attention for his own pieces, which were clever and somewhat tricky, like those of Raymond Scott, but jazzy and danceable like that of any of the great big bands. Most of his energy went to writing hit instrumentals, like the easily hummable "Dipsy Doodle" (a hit for Tommy Dorsey before Clinton had his own band), "A Study in Brown," "A Study in Surrealism," "Satan Takes a Holiday," "Snake Charmer" (which, with its evocation of exotic lands, was especially Scott-ish), and so on; as a composer, he had something of the novelty flair of Scott, but wrote more in the danceable 4/4 swing of Ellington, Henderson, and Redman. The band was most famous for the leader's evocative instrumentals, but also recorded dozens of standard-issue pop songs, nearly every one of which had a vocal by Bea Wain. As Ted Ono has tabulated, in fifteen months of working with Clinton, Wain recorded no fewer than sixty-five songs.

Beatrice Wain was born in New York on April 30, 1917; her parents were music buffs and she studied voice and piano as a child. Throughout the early thirties she worked as a choral singer in radio vocal groups of varying sizes—and degrees of hipness—starting with a program called *The Children's Hour* when she was still in her very early teens. She also sang with Kate Smith, the Kay Thompson Singers (which included former Rhythm Boy Al Rinker), the Ted Straeter Chorus, the Fred Waring Glee Club, and her own quartet, Bea and the Bachelors. While singing primarily in groups on the radio, she was also building a reputation as a solo singer with big bands. She worked with the dance band led by Gene Kardos, both in person at Delmonico's in Manhattan and on wax on a dozen or so Melotone/ARC records. She also appeared in these early years on discs with trumpeter Manny Klein and emerging clarinetist Artie Shaw.

In October 1937, she joined Larry Clinton, a sort of an American Ray Noble: He had come up through the ranks as an arranger, working for all the Dorsey bands (Tommy's, Jimmy's, and the one they shared), Casa Loma, George Hall, Bunny Berigan, Leith Steven's *Saturday Night Swing Club* orch, and even Mezz Mezzrow. He also wrote hit songs and led a studio-only ensemble. And, like Noble, Clinton sported a dapper little mustache that made him look like a second-string movie lead, the kind of character who invariably loses the girl to Gary Cooper or Jimmy Stewart. (He was the Allyn Joslyn of jazz.)

In the fall of 1937, Clinton took the plunge as bandleader, with a regular touring ensemble. He needed a singer, and listened to Wain on the recommendation of publisher Chuck Rinker (Al's brother). "She only sang eight bars on a [Kay Thompson] radio show, but I knew immediately that she was what I wanted," Clinton told George Simon. Starting in October, the combination of the bandleader, with his clever humor and catchy riffs, and the vocalist, with her idiosyncratic voice (and strong New York accent) and her swinging style, was an instant hit. From their first side, "True Confession," onward, they landed dozens of top-selling discs.

Also like Raymond Scott, Clinton liked to adapt the classics into pop and jazz, both vocally and instrumentally. Wain's style was so warm, down-to-earth, and swinging—and so very human—that she proved indispensable in making the likes of Debussy ("My Reverie"), Von Flotow ("Martha"), Saint-Saëns ("My Heart Thy Sweet Voice"), and Tchaikovsky sound like Berlin and Gershwin, as well as the 1841 classic "I Dreamt I Dwelt in Marble Halls," and the traditional Irish "A Pretty Girl Milking Her Cow"—this was some years before Judy Garland began milking that particular cow.

(CD-wise, *The Very Best of Larry Clinton and His Orchestra*, Collectors' Choice Music/BMG, is a good, albeit Whitburncentric, compilation of the band's most popular tracks—if, perhaps, a little too indebted to the bogus listings in Joel Whitburn's *Pop Memories*. Also recommended are three discs from the Scottish Hep label, *Shades of Hades, Studies in Clinton*, and *Feelin' Like a Dream*, although Wain doesn't appear on the last. Numerous studio transcriptions of the Clinton-Wain partnership have also been released on the Hindsight and Storyville labels.)

While the sixty-five Clinton-Wain tracks offer some of the best singing of the period, in retrospect it's clear that she did her best work after leaving the band, in a series of thirty-eight solo tracks for RCA (all collected on *You Can Depend on Me* and *That's How I Love the Blues*, both on Baldwin Street Music). Her vocal sides are more listenable en masse than those of almost any other jazz- and/or band-oriented femme singer of the period (with the obvious exceptions of Bailey and Holiday). Wain received the pick of superior film and show songs and sympathetic backings, and the results show that she was indeed a heavy hitter: "Blue Rain" (remembered as the "other" Mercer–Van Heusen song after "I Thought About You") has her indulging in wild Crosbyesque trills; on "Nobody's Baby" the band backs her with chanting similar to the Tommy Dorsey "Marie" cycle; while on the Ink Spots' hit "Do I Worry" she surprises us with an unexpected way-high note on the ending "you know *darn* well I do."

She sounds good both on classic songs like "That's How I Love the Blues" (from *Best Foot Forward*) and buried treasures like "Hello, Ma! I Done It Again!" (which a boxer supposedly said on the radio after a knockout) and "Peekaboo to You," a two-minute delight and another slice of esoteric Johnny Mercer that shows that the Savant from Savannah could be razor-sharp even in a throwaway rhythm tune, with the line "Mama, hand me my fowling piece." (For your information, a fowling piece is a small gun used once upon a time by hunters for bagging certain species of birds.) She sounds equally terrific on two pieces based in both spiritual music and the blues, Arthur Herzog's "God Bless the Child" (written for Billie Holiday) and "Sometimes I Feel like a Motherless Child," done with the Deep River Boys, a very churchy black vocal quartet. One of her sweetest solos is on "Baby Mine," the lullaby from Walt Disney's *Dumbo*, done with a string orchestra.

One of the most striking characteristics of the Wain sides of 1939–41 is their relentless tempo. These are, in every sense of the term, big band dance records; even though the singer is more prominently featured than the band, they're designed primarily for dancing—in fact, some were released with the legend "vocadance" on the labels, beneath Wain's artist billing. She was one of the first jazz/band singers to make a record of the classic Rodgers and Hart torch song "Glad to Be Unhappy" and the only one to swing it in a solid four. Wain told me that when she was starring on *Lucky Strike's Your Hit Parade* in 1943, it was up to her co-headliner, Frank Sinatra, to break the tyranny of the tempo. Only Young Blue Eyes had cojones enough to tell George Washington Hill that when he sang a ballad, he was going to sing it slow, and if the infamously dictatorial Mr. Hill did not approve, Sinatra would not hesitate to tell him where he could stick his Lucky Strikes.

This may be one reason why Wain seems locked in the swing era: As Ted Ono again points out, while she made a fairly astounding 120 or so tracks in six years, from 1936 to 1941, she never made a commercial recording after the start of the war. She was, apparently, just too associated with that highly specific era. In a sense, she cemented that status by marrying the most famous of all radio announcers, André Baruch. Here was a power couple who, rather than moving on, made a lifetime career out of embodying the era of swing bands and radio to future generations.

Although she never recorded again—even when Larry Clinton recorded a hi-fi album for Victor in 1956, the bandleader hired Helen Ward instead—other noncommercial performances were preserved on V-Discs, AFRS transcriptions, and the like. Let's hope these will be commercially released by Baldwin Street Music (or somebody) in the near future.

Ginny Simms (1915?–1994)

In 1941, all bets were on that Ginny Simms would be one of the major female singers to make it. She didn't have the strong swing of Ward or the distinctive voice of Wain, but she was a gifted singer of ballads and she had been very prominently featured—"starred" even—with Kay Kyser's orchestra. Kay Kyser was more than just a bandleader who played ballrooms and made records and broadcasts, as most of them did; he was an entertainment industry unto himself—a veritable radio institution who helped popularize the medium of the game show (as well as the band remote and the variety show) and also starred, with his orchestra, in a series of mass-market feature films. As a star of the Kyser entourage—the main one, after the mortar-boarded bandleader himself—Ginny Simms was already a very well known quantity when she graduated from Kyser's employ.

That year she placed at the top of *Billboard*'s college poll as the most popular female band vocalist, and upon striking out on her own, she was offered a contract to record solo for Columbia Records (where Kyser was also contracted), and several movie studios beckoned; she was also given a spot on the popular radio program *The First Nighter*, which was soon followed by her own series. Ginny Simms seemed to have everything: In addition to a winning way with a ballad and a smile in her voice, she also had the high-glam looks to make it in Hollywood. All the singers in Kyser's band were identified with descriptive nicknames: "Sassy" Sully Mason, "Handsome" Harry Babbitt, and "Gorgeous" Ginny Simms. (Kyser probably figured that novelty vocalist Ish Kabibble already had a name that said it all.) Yet for various reasons that no one could have realized at the time, she became yet another casualty of changing tastes in the postwar era.

Virginia Simms was born in San Antonio, Texas, purportedly in 1915, and grew up in Fresno, California, where she attended Fresno State Teachers College; she sang in a female trio while still in school. However, she is known to have been in Tom Gerun's band in 1932 (alongside Woody Herman and Tony Martin), which could mean that she was actually born in 1912 or 1913. She did not record with Gerun, but she joined Kyser in 1934, and turns up on some of his first sessions (not counting Kyser's prehistoric sides as a college band in 1928–29).

Simms was thus part of the band as it evolved from the rather sticky-sweet unit of the mid-thirties to the red hot unit of the forties, which could compete with Charlie Barnet and Glenn Miller; she was also present as Kyser himself developed from a mere stick-waver into the most extroverted bandleader-entertainer-showman of them all. From the beginning, the Kollege was well staffed with vocal talent. Still billed as Virginia Simms, she sings "Wouldn't I Be a Wonder?" in a charming duet with Bill "Smiling" Stoker, who doubled on alto and clarinet and tripled as a credible crooner. Like Helen Forrest with

Artie Shaw, Simms and the Kyser band matured together, and she was quickly accepted as a top canary with a top band.

Kyser used her wherever necessary, as one voice among many in his novelty tunes and production numbers, and also as a soloist on superior love songs like "For Sentimental Reasons." She brings a touch of the blues to "Monday Morning" while on "You Don't Know How Much You Can Suffer," she gets perfectly into the minor key mood of the piece, bringing out the tune's similarity to a Jewish folk song. Even when the fine baritone Harry Babbitt joined the band as full-time boy singer, she still got her fair share of the action, both solo and joining with Babbitt in lovely duets like the *escapada* entitled "Her Name Was Rosita" and "Why Don't We Do This More Often," a hit that was as catchy as it was romantic. (In 2005, Collectables issued the recommended *Simple and Sweet: The Best of Ginny Simms with Kay Kyser and His Orchestra.*)

Simms was so popular that she was virtually the only singer that ARC (and then Columbia) recorded as a solo while she continued to serve as a big band canary. As Dave Weiner points out, this was also true of Billie Holiday and Mildred Bailey—two heavyweights to be sure. (Victor didn't record the highly popular Bea Wain on her own until after she left Clinton, and Columbia never recorded Helen Forrest on her own, even though she was making loads of hits for Benny Goodman and then Harry James.) Simms turned out a prolific stream of discs for Vocalion and Okeh during her Kyser tenure, most of which were accompanied by her fellow Kollegiates. With the exception of a short, ten-tune budget release from Sony Music Special Products (*Gorgeous Ginny Simms*), these have proved very difficult to find, although the ones I have caught are solid, artful slices of state-of-the-art pop singing circa 1940 (my favorite is "Chinese Lullaby," a well-sung slice of chinoiserie).

It's hard to put one's finger on what went wrong after she left Kyser in 1941: For a while she seemed like a natural for film stardom—for RKO (*Seven Days' Leave*), for Warner Bros. (*Night and Day*), for Universal (*Hit the Ice*, with Abbott and Costello), for MGM (*Broadway Rhythm*)—but there was never a solid vehicle for her. Even though studio mogul supreme Louis B. Mayer supposedly took a, ahem, personal interest in her career, she never landed the kind of roles that another musical starlet, the now forgotten Lucille Bremer, was garnering in more substantial pictures like *Ziegfeld Follies*, *Meet Me in St. Louis*, and *Yolanda and the Thief*. Much the same thing happened to her recording career: Columbia didn't have faith that they could actually support, just think of it, not one but two popular female singing stars, so when Dinah Shore switched from RCA to CBS in 1945, the label let Simms go. Shore's success, in fact, illustrates the wisdom of her early decision not to hitch her wagon to the star of a big-name bandleader.

Simms kept busy on the radio: *There Goes That Song Again: The Ginny Simms Memorial Album* (Viper's Nest), despite a rather ghoulish cover, is a fine collection of war-era airchecks from various shows, both civilian and AFRS, including her own CBS series. Even though her post-Kyser singles are difficult to track down, these radio performances provide documentation that she adapted, musically at least, to the role of solo vocalist. "It Could Happen to You" is perhaps the finest performance I've heard of that Burke–Van Heusen instant standard to include the verse, beginning with the line "Do you believe in charms and spells?," which she appropriately dresses up with humming that suggests mystical incantation. She also hums enticingly throughout the bilingual *Amor*, a song from her own film *Broadway Rhythm*, but unfortunately the hit went to Capitol Records newcomer Andy Russell. She does well on up-tempos, too, like "Gotta Be This or That," "Dance with a Dolly," and "When He Comes Home" (all wartime hits—for other people), but it's the low sultry ballads that we remember her for, like Cole Porter's "In the Still of the Night," with more sensual humming, and "You'd Be So Nice to Come Home To," which she reminds us is also a war song. Her most endearingly bizarre performance is "Holiday for Strings," a misguided effort to pin words to David Rose's famous instrumental.

Somehow Simms wound up recording for grade-B labels like ARA and Sonora, a beautiful and talented singer who found herself strangely adrift in a postwar world that was supposedly receptive to female singers. In the fifties, she married two real estate moguls, and both with them and on her own did very well in that field—an area where it was then even harder for a woman to succeed—and also ran resorts, hotels, motels, and restaurants. History has not recorded whether she missed show business, but in 1960 she, too, like Ward and Forrest (but not Wain, surprisingly), participated in the hi-fi nostalgia boom. She sang two vocals ("Why Don't We Do This More Often?," with Handsome Harry Babbitt and "Three Little Fishies," with the whole company) on Capitol's *Kay Kyser's Greatest Hits*. This was a re-creation in which Kyser's role was dually re-created by Billy May (as arranger and conductor) and Stan Freberg supplying the voice of the Ol' Perfesser, who had declined to participate but gave his blessing. (Kyser had since switched roles from teacher to preacher, as in doctor of Christian Science.)

Simms also made one LP of her own, *Ginny Simms: Love Is Here to Stay* (originally on Tops but very nicely reissued on CD by Simitar). The voice has lowered somewhat, from a low soprano to a high contralto, but she certainly doesn't sound like an ex-star who's fallen out of practice. As opposed to the Capitol album, the charts are not re-creations but brand-new arrangements of classic songs done by Kenton trombonist Harry Betts. It's a very classy package all around (especially on the CD edition), with Simms particularly convincing on the blues-inflected "Stormy Weather" and Leon René's ironically torchy "Salt Lake City Blues" (the one that begins "I left my sugar in Salt Lake City"). She also pulls off the folkish "Candle Song" particularly well, even though this wasn't the sort of subject that she ever studied at the Kollege of Musical Knowledge.

Perhaps she made the album just to prove that she could still do it—if that was the case, she certainly succeeded. Unfortunately, by then even those singers who hadn't been displaced at the end of the band era were themselves being marginalized by new musical trends. That album seems to represent Simms's last stand. Now pushing fifty, she continued in the real estate and resort business, and doesn't seem ever to have looked back. She died in 1994.

Kitty Kallen (born 1922)

For a few moments, at the very start of the postwar era, it looked like things would continue as before: One of the biggest hits of the war years was "I Don't Want to Walk Without You" by Harry James and His Orchestra, with music by Jule Styne; in 1945, James followed it with an anthemic hit that signified the conflict's end: "It's Been a Long, Long Time," with music by the same Jule Styne. By this time, however, Helen Forrest had gone out on her own and James had replaced her with the younger (but no less Jewish, and also from mid-Atlantic America) Kitty Kallen. Only twenty-two years old, Kallen, like Forrest before her, joined James as a veteran, having already sung with two major bands, namely Jack Teagarden's and Jimmy Dorsey's. Yet unlike Forrest, or, indeed, any of the other ladies profiled in these two sections regarding female band singers, Kallen would go on to a substantial career in the postswing musical world.

Kitty Kallen was born in Philadelphia in 1922; thanks partially to an aunt with showbiz connections, she grew up singing in movie theaters all over the City of Brotherly Love. Very early on, her path crossed with that of Philly's most famous bandleader, Jan Savitt, and she also came into contact with producer Manie Sachs (a native *landsman*) and onetime "King of Jazz" Paul Whiteman. She met Jack Teagarden while he was still serving in Whiteman's brass section, and when the trombonist's contract with Whiteman expired, he formed his own full-fledged big swing band. For a time, in the summer of 1939, Teagarden, who was never known for his decisiveness, briefly carried two girl singers, Kallen and Dolores O'Neill. Within a few months, however, Teagarden switched to the more conventional policy of carrying one crooner and one canary, these being a twosome with the rhyming surnames of Allyn (meaning David) and Kallen (as in Kitty).

Surrounded by such formidable vocal talent— and remember, her chief competition wasn't so much Allyn but leader Teagarden himself, one of the greatest of jazz singers—the very young Kallen couldn't help being overshadowed. She did, however, get in some adequate vocals on a few decent songs with the Teagarden orchestra, nine of which are on *Band Singer* (Sony/Collectors' Choice Music, along with fourteen tracks by Kallen and Harry James), like "Two Blind Loves," a lesser-known Arlen-Harburg movie song worthy of revival.

Kallen stayed with Teagarden until the very end of 1941—she was still only nineteen. Throughout 1942, she worked as a house vocalist on NBC out of Los Angeles, at which time she also participated in several sessions with trumpeter-guitarist Bobby Sherwood (Judy Garland's brother-in-law). In early 1943, she accepted a generous offer to go back on the road again, replacing Helen O'Connell with Jimmy Dorsey's band. She didn't enjoy her Dorsey experience, later recalling to annotator Gino Falzarano that the alto saxist–bandleader was a bitter and hostile man, jealous of the success of his younger brother, Tommy, and resentful that the hit records he did achieve were so dependent on the strength of vocalists like O'Connell, Bob Eberly, and Kallen.

Dorsey, however, gave Kallen what Teagarden couldn't: hit records. He was under contract to Decca, one of the first labels to make a deal with the musicians' union during the 1942–44 AFM strike, and thus Dorsey was one of the first bandleaders to come out with new records at the end of 1943. Kallen proved exceptionally winning on Frank Loesser's witty war song "They're Either Too Young or Too Old," the romantic Mexican future standard "Bésame Mucho," and one of the finest of love songs, "Star Eyes" (the latter two being duets with Bob Eberly). All were top 5 hits for Dorsey and Kallen. Helen O'Connell had been long on personality and short on chops and technique, and it's hard to imagine anyone who wouldn't feel that Kallen was a distinct improvement. Thanks to Dorsey, she became a name with the record-buying and radio public.

Kallen's star rose even higher with Harry James. With "I'm Beginning to See the Light" and "It's Been a Long, Long Time," Kallen was the voice on two of the best-remembered hits of the entire big band era. She was a perfect successor to Forrest: warm, emotional, and swinging, with a beautiful deep voice, although perhaps not quite as beautiful or deep as her predecessor's. It was perfectly fitting that Kallen should be remembered as the first major voice of the immediate homecoming period, just as Forrest was of the war years. With "I'll Buy That Dream," a song that perfectly captures the sheer optimism felt at the end of the war, James and Kallen were competing with the trumpeter's two former vocal stars, Forrest and Haymes. Indeed, the song was so omnipresent that radio pundit Fred Allen came up with his own tune, "I Take a Blank Check to Bed with Me in Case I Have to Buy That Dream."

Kallen remained with James until the end of 1945, but like Ginny Simms she discovered that even on the very eve of the vocal boom, opportunities for solo singers were still rare. Unlike Forrest, she wasn't offered a berth at a major label, but wound up doing some sides for the short-lived independent Musicraft. The few I've heard are quite good, particularly "Man with a Horn," accompanied by Sonny Burke's orchestra, and "My Heart Belongs to Daddy," with Artie Shaw. Kallen worked in a diverse range of areas in the late forties: a little recording, a little radio (there's a wonderful aircheck of her doing "I've Got a Crush on You" on the *Dave Garroway Show*), a little nightclub work (she played the Copa), and even a little Broadway—she replaced Ella Logan in *Finian's Rainbow*, making it into a Jewish-Irish affair. She also kept up a busy personal life: She became especially friendly with Frank Sinatra and his first wife, Nancy, and married Bud Granoff, who worked for Sinatra's publicist, George Evans; she and Granoff remained together until his death forty-four years later.

After Musicraft, Kallen moved on to another indie, this one with a little more staying power, Mercury, where she became one of the first pop singers to work with emerging giant Mitch Miller. She had some minor hits, all of them novelties, like "Kiss Me Sweet (Kiss Me Gentle)," "Juke Box Annie," and "Abba Dabba Honeymoon," the latter a duet with crooner Richard Hayes. By 1953, Kallen and Granoff, who was producing most of her sessions, moved to Decca, and they resented that she was typecast with what she described to Falzarano as "rhythm songs and cute songs." Because she couldn't persuade any record label to think otherwise, the couple decided to produce their own session, spotlighting two new songs of their own choosing, "I Don't Think You Love Me Anymore" and "Little Things Mean a Lot." Decca released the single with the first song on the A side and the second on the B, yet, as often happens, the B was the hit—not just the hit but one of the biggest records of the decade—a Clooney, Doris Day, Nat Cole, Sinatra–level supersized hit that spent nine weeks at number one.

As this summary suggests, Kallen had a most interesting career, climbing the rungs to the top of the big band ladder, then, ten years later, briefly reestablishing herself as a pop superstar. Her career is well sampled in the two-CD *Kitty Kallen Story* (Sony Music Special Products), with a thorough interview by annotator Gino Falzarano, while *I've Got a Crush on You* (Natasha) serves as a useful addendum; both sets were compiled by Kallen and Granoff themselves. Kallen's career momentum was ultimately sabotaged not by changing tastes but by her own health. She developed a mysterious condition that made her lose her voice in 1956; three years later, she began to work for a while, but by 1965 had developed blood clots in her throat that made it impossible for her to sing. She never performed professionally again.

Kallen's total output is a mixed bag: She was indisputably a major band canary, and a valuable asset to Teagarden, Dorsey, and James, but her fifties work doesn't hold up nearly as well. Although it was a huge hit, "Little Things Mean a Lot" is not a great or even good pop song; it is trite, oversentimental, and badly written; the infamous second line, "Say I look nice when I'm not," doesn't even make sense. It was written, according to a fan Web site, by "a Richmond, Virginia, disc jockey and a music editor for the *Richmond Times-Dispatch*" and is obviously not the work of professional songwriters, and in this it anticipates an era when unprofessionalism would become the rule. I can't imagine anyone ever reviving "Little Things" except for camp or kitsch value (as in the 1981 Lily Tomlin comedy, *The Incredible Shrinking Woman*). Kallen sings it very well, but the record is overproduced, making her voice sound biting and thin, even irritating.

For all her talent, Kallen became the epitome of a school of singing that dominated pop in the mid-fifties, a kind of overdone angst-ridden style that involved white female singers who were almost all big band veterans with alliterative names (Doris Day, Kitty Kallen, Patti Page, Georgia Gibbs, Joni James), a tradition that, as we've seen (with Helen Forrest as Betty Blue), grew out of the thirties custom of sponsors creating pseudonyms for girl singers based on their product (Clara Ann Fowler's stage name, Patti Page, was the creation of the Page milk company). Of these five gals, only Joni James was born too late to have any band experience; rather than being a sweetheart of the World War II era, James (born Giovanna Babbo) was the Helen Forrest of the Korean conflict.

Some naysayers might insist that Kallen's career would have been derailed anyway because of the changes in the music industry, but the one point common to virtually all the alliterative sisters of angst was that the takeover of youth pop (aka rock 'n' roll) didn't upset them at all; Georgia Gibbs made peace with the enemy by singing covers of protorock hits like "Tweedle Dee" and "Dance with Me, Henry," and Joni James, in particular, appealed to youngsters of the rock 'n' roll generation. More important, the major female singers who appealed to the younger generations, especially Connie Frances, and even most of the big pop divas of the sixties, like Petula Clark, Dusty Springfield, and Dionne Warwick, still sound like the worst of the early fifties chicks: forced, artificial, unnatural, and overwrought.

Not everything Kallen did—or indeed any of the others did—fits this description (especially Doris Day). In Kallen's case, the issue is compounded by her health; she wasn't given the choice between making more mediocre singles or striving for a better class of pop music; the question was whether she could even sing. Some albums, as sampled in *The Kitty Kallen Story*, are better than others, particularly the 1964 *Quiet Nights*, done for Twentieth Century Fox Records, arranged and conducted by Manny Albam with a very strong jazz rhythm section. She sounds fine on "If Someone Had Told Me" and "Let

Me Love You"—at least half the album is on the *Kitty Kallen Story* and *Crush on You*. The single most convincing track is the Johnny Mathis hit "It's Not for Me to Say," done with the verse and a strikingly simple accompaniment—just Jim Hall's guitar and

Richard Davis's bass, while Kallen's voice, for once largely free of that phony-sounding echo chamber resonance—has an appealingly dark timbre slightly reminiscent of Kay Starr. If Kallen made more albums of this quality, I would love to hear them.

Male Band Singers II: Exceptional Boychicks

Harry Babbitt
George "Bon Bon" Tunnell

By their very existence, male band singers—or, to use the technical term, boychicks—establish a line of demarcation among the great swing bands. Virtually all the big bands, even hard-core jazz units like those of Goodman, Basie, and Ellington, were forced by commercial circumstances to carry a female band singer. Even if they only wanted to play hot flag-wavers and feature instrumental soloists, their chances of getting a recording contract, a gig in a theater or ballroom, or a sponsored radio program were next to nil if they couldn't offer something attractive in a glamorous gown giving out with the hits of the day. Female singers were a minimum requirement, but boy singers were another matter; in the swing era, bands essentially only hired them if they were really trying to go beyond the minimum requirement and really be *commercial*. The mere fact that Ted Weems, Hal Kemp, or Kay Kyser carried a male singer meant that they were reaching for more mass-market success than Goodman or Artie Shaw were.

Like many of their female counterpoints, any number of major male band singers went on to impressive postband careers, starting with the founding father himself, Bing Crosby, and continuing through Frank Sinatra, Dick Haymes, and Perry Como. There are several outstanding male singers, however, who sang with the big bands and made some excellent recordings but never quite made the leap to solo stardom. (Those many exceptional vocalists who worked with Glenn Miller—male and female, such as Ray Eberle and Marion Hutton, not to mention their siblings—are dealt with in a separate essay.)

Harry Babbitt (1913–2004)

I'm somewhat surprised to find myself starting this section with Harry Babbitt, although he enjoyed one of the longer vocalist-bandleader relationships of the period. Babbitt sang with Kay Kyser for well over ten years, virtually the entire big band era, and was to Kyser what Jimmy Rushing was to Basie or Al Hibbler to Ellington. Yet for the longest time I couldn't get what Harry Babbitt was all about; undoubtedly, I was influenced by a rather harsh judgment from the dean of big band critics, the late George Simon. In *The Big Bands*, a tome of biblical significance for swing fans, Simon describes Babbitt as "a handsome man with an ingratiating grin, who never sang in an especially identifiable style, but who always sang well."

I knew George but, regrettably, never had the chance to debate him regarding the virtues of Mr. Babbitt. George had the benefit of experiencing the Babbitt-Kyser combination in live performance, but I didn't fathom Babbitt's appeal until I started watching the old Kay Kyser movies on AMC in the nineties. As documented in this series of B musicals, Kyser's ensemble was more than a dance band, more than a radio program, more than a film cast; they were a vaudeville troupe and sideshow set to a 4/4 foxtrot tempo. It had rhythm, in the form of outstanding jazz-oriented arrangers and hot soloists; it had romance, in the form of vocalists with equally attractive faces and voices, most famously Ginny Simms and Harry Babbitt; but it also had an abundance of novelty instrumentalists like Sully Mason and Ish Kabibble, who doubled as comedy vocalists and stooges, and the entertaining antics of the leader himself, the Ol' Perfesser, who was a kind of Cab Calloway and Danny Kaye combined—and with a deep Southern accent no less. The band carried with it all sorts of vaudeville stunts—everything but a dog act. In the thirties, it competed with Sammy Kaye (both leaders did a bit they called "singing song titles") in the sweet category, while in the forties Kyser flipped over to the hot side, with a troupe that competed with Shaw and Goodman and matched the Dorseys and Miller in alternating sentiment and swing.

"A beautiful thought, a plaintive melody, and the interesting voice of Harry Babbitt" is how Kyser introduces the baritone on the 1939 "I Promise You." Babbitt was born (in 1913) and raised in St. Louis, Missouri, and when he joined Kyser, in 1937, he was only one more performer in Kyser's three-ring circus, yet he held his own. He was there primarily to sing the romantic ballads—this was the basic function of all crooners in big bands—and he did it with the best of them. He's even convincing in unlikely circumstances: On Kyser's treatment of the British hit "He Wears a Pair of Silver Wings," Babbitt croons a lyric written for a woman, and makes it work, despite the awkwardness of having to sing it in the third person ("an ordinary fellow in the uniform she loves"). What's surprising is that although he was hired for slow, romantic love songs, Babbitt sounds both swinging and relaxed when Kyser started to cut loose, even during the World War II period when the tempos grew faster and the beat more frantic. Babbitt is at his studliest on Kyser's blockbuster hit "Jingle Jangle Jingle," in which he exemplifies the typical male who may be afraid of commitment but is never afraid of the beat. Very few crooners could do this besides Crosby—not Haymes or Como; even Sinatra had to grow into it.

But where Babbitt beats out nearly all his fellow crooner-boychicks is in comedy; he competed not only with Mel Tormé but with Mel Blanc. It's not Sully Mason or Ish Kabibble who supplies the demented baby-boy voice in "Alexander the Swoose" and "Three Little Fishies," it's Babbitt; he essays this awkward falsetto with perfect intonation, which couldn't have been easy. He also supplies the Jerry Colonna impression in "Who's Yehoodi," a novelty hit that was in the obituaries of composer Matt Dennis when he died in 2002. Babbitt refused to get lost in the shuffle of Kyser's Karnival, and he stood his ground not by acting like a straight man—no Zeppo, he—but by being sillier and funnier than anyone else. While all others about him were losing their heads, Babbitt lost his as well—and much more spectacularly.

Babbitt's performances are a special delight of the seven starring feature films made by Kyser and his group. He was a much more engaging leading man than a lot of the stiff, square-jawed movie leads you find in most musicals and comedies of the era. Indeed, why RKO never thought to build an entire musical with Babbitt and Ginny Simms as a singing romantic musical team is something I'll never understand. He would have also been a perfect singing straight man to work with zany funsters like Olsen and Johnson, Abbott and Costello, and the Marxes.

In 1944, after seven years, Babbitt left Kyser to serve in the navy. Kyser replaced him with one Don Leslie, a baritone with a voice very similar to Babbitt's, who was then succeeded by the somewhat higher-voiced Michael Dowd, renamed as Mike Douglas by Kyser—the Mike Douglas who later became a very successful daytime talk show host. Douglas was responsible for the only major hits by the Kyser band to involve a romantic crooner other than Babbitt, two beauties, in fact: "Ole Buttermilk Sky" and "The Old Lamp-Lighter." Just the reference to all that oldness in those titles indicates that postwar sentiment was indeed of the "old"-fashioned variety.

Meanwhile, after being discharged from the navy, Babbitt experimented with a solo career. He doesn't, however, seem to have gotten very far, and he rejoined Kyser for two years beginning in 1947. Back in the saddle, Kyser and Babbitt turned out one more really big hit: "On a Slow Boat to China." This would be the climax of the long relationship between the singer, the bandleader, and songwriter Frank Loesser. Kyser and Babbitt had already made hits out of Loesser's "Let's Get Lost," "Jingle Jangle Jingle," and "Praise the Lord and Pass the Ammunition." Gloria Wood, who later sang on Bing Crosby's show as a member of the Jud Conlon Rhythmaires, was the last of many notable KK girl singers to duet with Babbitt after the departure of Ginny Simms,

among them Julie Conway, Trudy Erwin (who also joined Crosby's radio cast), and Gorgeous Georgia Carroll, who became Kyser's wife, then widow. "Slow Boat to China" is Babbitt's meat: Both a love song and a swinger, rhythmic and romantic, it also gives him the chance to be funny—surely Loesser wrote the song's famous nonverse (which begins by announcing, "There is no verse to this song") with Babbitt in mind.

Kyser probably had more hits in the immediate postwar era, thanks to Douglas and Babbitt, than any other band, but the leader knew the writing was on the wall. In 1949, Babbitt left for the second time, and Kyser made the smart move of transferring the Kollege of Musical Knowledge to television. However, he had expended a tremendous amount of personal energy during the war; researcher Raymond Hair has documented that Kyser entertained more troops and sold more bonds even than Bob Hope or Glenn Miller. In 1950, he was ready to retire, and left show business to become a minister of Christian Science. (He was officially forty-five at that point, although scholar Bob Conrad believes the Ol' Perfesser was actually older than he let on.)

After 1949, Babbitt worked in nightclubs as a single. Recording-wise, his career trajectory was similar to that of Simms, in that the labels he was signed to got smaller and smaller: from Coral and Mercury to Seeco and Popular. The few of Babbitt's fifties sides that I've been able to hear have been surprisingly good: The 1951 "Shanghai" with the Modernaires on Coral is a swinging novelty that Babbitt sings with even more energy and panache than the hit Doris Day version. There are also two very nice duets with former Benny Goodmanite Martha Tilton, including a pairing from *Call Me Madam*, "You're Just in Love" and "It's a Lovely Day Today." He also sounds just fine, as do the whole gang, on the 1960 re-creation *Kay Kyser's Greatest Hits*.

Babbitt did some television work on Steve Allen's *Bandstand Review*, but in general his post-Kyser career wasn't what it should have been. In his fifties and sixties, he went into the real estate business (paralleling Ginny Simms at that point), but also occasionally led and worked with Kyser-style orchestras into his eighties. Harry Babbitt died at the age of ninety in 2004. A year later, Collectables released the long-awaited—at least by me—*Pocketful of Dreams: The Best of Harry Babbitt with Kay Kyser and His Orchestra*.

George "Bon Bon" Tunnell (1903–1975)

If the specifics of Harry Babbitt's career are a surprise, those of George Tunnell are even more so. Known simply as Bon Bon for most of his professional career, Tunnell is remembered on one level for a sociological rather than strictly musical reason: He was by far the most important African American entertainer to work for an extended period with a white band, Jan Savitt and his Top Hatters. Earlier on, Ivie Anderson had done a famous stint with San Francisco hotel leader Anson Weeks, June Richmond had toured with Jimmy Dorsey, and Billie Holiday sang briefly with Artie Shaw. But Bon Bon and Savitt were the only black singer and white bandleader to enjoy a long-lasting collaboration and to leave an important impression on the swing era. Perhaps it was because Savitt's Top Hatters orchestra was originally based in Philadelphia that Savitt and Bon Bon were moved to create a prototype of brotherly love. Not everyone shared their enthusiasm for racial harmony: In areas less brotherly than Philly, Tunnell was only allowed to stay in the same hotel as the rest of the band by posing as Savitt's valet.

Were that the whole reason for remembering Bon Bon, he'd be worth a paragraph at most in the history books. But the real justification for Tunnell's inclusion here is the overall excellence of his music. He's an appropriate act to follow Harry Babbitt in that he, too, was a high baritone who could also sing in the tenor range—or something very close to it—and that he could switch from ballads to bouncers without missing a beat. He was sort of like Ray Eberle and Tex Beneke combined, surpassing the former and challenging the latter, or, if you will, like Harry Babbitt and Sully Mason joined together—or even Herb Jeffries and Ray Nance.

Of all the important artists, there is the least amount of available documentation on the career of Bon Bon Tunnell. As far as I can tell, George Tunnell was born in 1903 in Reading, Pennsylvania. In the twenties, he made it to New York, where he led a band called Bon Bon and His Buddies. Closer to home, in Chester, Pennsylvania, Tunnell worked with the Three Keys, a vocal-instrumental combo that recorded sixteen excellent sides for Brunswick and Vocalion in 1932 and 1933. The Three Keys consisted of Tunnell on piano, Slim Furness on guitar, and Bob Pease on bass, with vocals by all three and Bon Bon singing lead; they are instantly one of the best vocal groups of their time—or any other time, in a class with the Boswell Sisters, the Mills Brothers, the Ink Spots (in their earlier, jazzier incarnation), or Leo Watson and the Spirits of the Rhythm. At the height of their popularity, in 1933, the Three Keys played the Palladium in London.

The group's first released side is an innovative transmutation of Duke Ellington's "Mood Indigo" into vocal terms, using their own set of lyrics (as opposed to the official text, which was, unofficially, the work of Mitchell Parish). The flip side, "Somebody Loses, Somebody Wins," also helps set the tone of the series, a well-balanced combination of trio harmony and solos by Bon Bon, clever jivey lyrics, and pure scatting, as well as inspired guitar solos by Furness. Like the Boswells, the Keys can make you feel good through their phrasing alone, especially with the wonderful syncopated accents they put on the titular phrase "Some*body* loses, some*body* wins."

"Jig Time," "Nagasaki," "Heebie Jeebies," and "Wah-De-Dah" are pure wordless euphoria. "Fit as a Fiddle," written by Arthur Freed for a *George White's Scandals* revue and later revised for *Singin' in the Rain*, shows that tunesmiths of Hollywood took a back seat to no one in their efforts to produce superior rhythm concoctions. "Someone Stole Gabriel's Horn" and "Basin Street Blues," respectively, find the threesome adding elements of gospel and blues to the mixture, while "That Doggone Dog of Mine" and "Rasputin (That Highfalutin' Lovin' Man)" are just plain funny. Likewise, "I Would Do Most Anything for You" (the theme song of pianist-bandleader Claude Hopkins) has Furness speaking a comedy version of the lyric in a deep monotone inspired by Bert Williams. The combination of unison vocals plus a star soloist and the piano-guitar-bass format anticipates the Three Peppers, a terrific unit of the latter thirties. More important, the Three Keys laid part of the foundation for the earliest incarnation of the great King Cole Trio, who pretty much picked up where the Keys left off.

Although the Three Keys pointed to the future of hot vocal groups, they did not, it turned out, represent Bon Bon Tunnell's own future. Their comedy song "Rasputin" concerned itself with a Southern sheik by the name of Rasputin Jones, not the infamous mad monk of czarist Russia, but Tunnell's destiny did indeed involve a Russian visionary. According to George Simon, bandleader Jan Savitt, born in 1913 in St. Petersburg (Russia, not Florida), heard Tunnell performing with the Three Keys and hired him on the spot. Savitt grew up a violin prodigy in Philadelphia, and put together a swing band in 1935, which made use of an early version of the shuffle beat.

This shuffle rhythm was somewhat relentless, especially on commercial 78s, so it is not advisable to listen to a lot of Savitt discs one after another. Savitt began his swing band career on Philadelphia local KYW and the station's wattage carried his sounds far and wide. Soon he was receiving offers to take his band, dubbed the Top Hatters, on the road. Savitt began recording, first for Irving Mills's Variety label, then for RCA Victor on their Bluebird imprint; later he switched to Decca and eventually back to Victor.

Bon Bon Tunnell was on board with Savitt from the beginning. Savitt obviously realized that there were few vocalists of any color who were rhythmically astute enough to handle both swingers and ballads and make them all sound meaningful in that shuffle beat; that's exactly what he had in Tunnell. Tunnell also was one of the keenest students of both Bing Crosby and his mellow crooning and Armstrong and his scat specialties. Bon Bon was known at the time for his expert work on rhythm-driven novelties like "The Paper Picker," "Shabby Old Cabby" (not promising titles, I will admit), and "How Warm It Is the Weather." Owing to Savitt's classical background, he was a major maven for swinging the old masters (even Paul Dukas's *The Sorcerer's Apprentice*), and while most of these were instrumental, Bon Bon contributed significantly to the Kipling-Speaks "Road to Mandalay."

The Tunnell-Savitt relationship continued with few interruptions from 1937 to 1941. Their two most famous tracks arrived in 1939, both credited to Savitt as co-composer, unanimously regarded as big band classics. One of them, "It's a Wonderful World," was probably the best example of the band's propulsive shuffle rhythm: the bright melody, the optimistic text, and that very danceable beat all coming together perfectly, not to mention Bon Bon's exceptionally clean, swinging vocal that suggests a perfect midpoint between Louis Armstrong and Frank Sinatra. If he anticipated Nat King Cole in his trio phase, other titles point directly to the Swingin' Lover style that Sinatra later perfected; there's an aircheck of "Mandalay" in which Tunnell embellishes Kipling as "come you back you swingin' soldier, swing it back to Mandalay," directly prefiguring Sinatra on *Come Fly with Me;* his was a smooth romantic voice that could really move in tempo.

Both "It's a Wonderful World" and "720 in the Books" were introduced as instrumentals, and lyrics were added before Savitt and Tunnell recorded them for Decca. The latter began as a swinging, bluesy riff; no one could decide what to call it, so eventually the song's number in the band library became the title. Veteran lyricist Harold Adamson came up with a text that foreshadows Sy Oliver's "Opus One" in that it essentially expounds on how the song doesn't have any words, or even a proper name. That other major singers listened to these records is evidenced by Ella Fitzgerald's recording of "720 in the Books" in 1958, and "It's a Wonderful World" was covered extensively: In 1939 it was done by Harry James, Charlie Barnet, and the Will Bradley–Ray McKinley combination, while Glenn Miller "borrowed" it for one of his famous medleys. In later years, "It's a Wonderful World" was recorded by Peggy Lee, Joe Williams, even Sinatra himself.

In 1941 and 1942, Tunnell recorded eight sides for Decca featuring an all-star lineup of jazz and other studio musicians, which may well be the highlight of his short but crucial career. Released as by "Bon Bon and His Buddies," these are absolutely delicious, with Bon Bon at last unshackled from the shuffle, even though he does remain within the confines of accepted dance band tempos. He's especially excellent on "I Don't Want to Set the World on Fire," which he sings much more swingingly and lustily than the Ink Spots, who made the song a hit. The first date uses a number of black musicians from the South and Midwest, including trumpeter Joe Thomas and Buster Smith on clarinet, both of whom get to solo on Cole Porter's blowing vehicle "Blow Gabriel Blow." They also help Bon Bon accentuate the blues strengths of "Sweet Mama (Papa's Getting Mad)," a tune associated with the Original Dixieland Jazz Band in the very earliest days of recorded jazz; here he foreshadows the blues-driven crooning of Nat King Cole and Joe Williams. Fats Waller's "All That Meat and No Potatoes" uses a tight, John Kirbyesque ensemble, and this feeling is even more pro-

nounced on the 1942 date, which features two Kirbyites, pianist Billy Kyle and drummer O'Neil Spencer, along with white studio men like trumpeter Red Solomon and guitarist George Van Eps.

Bon Bon went out as a single shortly before the war, and in the mid-forties began recording for music publisher Joe Davis, whom he had known since the early thirties and who branched out into recording in the early days of the postwar boom. Several dozen Bon Bon titles have been listed in various discographies on the Joe Davis label. Davis was essentially a music publisher who also ran his own label and occasionally managed black talent (and it's said that in all of these endeavors he made even Irving Mills look like the soul of benevolence by comparison). When he produced these sessions with Bon Bon, it's clear that Davis was primarily interested in promoting his copyrights rather than furthering the singer's career. Eight of the tracks were issued a 78 album (Davis Album D2), which includes a session wherein Bon Bon is backed by an outstanding traditional jazz group (featuring trumpeter Yank Lawson and clarinetist Bill Stegmeyer). Alas, none of these songs is remotely worth the effort. ("Crystal Gazing Mama," a Louis Jordan–like self-deprecating comedy piece, incorporates a reference to Bert Williams's "Cousin of Mine," and it's fascinating that this 1906 song was still a familiar expression to black audiences.) None of these titles is known to have charted, and none has since been reissued on CD or LP. At the end of the forties, Tunnell rerecorded "720 in the Books" and "What a Wonderful World" with clarinetist Tommy Reynolds's orchestra (originally released on the very obscure Derby Records and briefly released on a 10" LP by the supermarket label Royale).

Meanwhile, Savitt kept going despite some setbacks—in fact, he was aided by a boost from Sinatra, who chose the Top-Hatters to accompany him on a theater tour in 1945. Savitt died of a cerebral hemorrhage in 1948, aged thirty-five. By the early fifties, Tunnell, approaching fifty himself, was ready to retire, and spent the remaining twenty years of his life in various other businesses in Pennsylvania— although he was occasionally hired to put together new editions of the Three Keys for local gigs. Even today he remains unappreciated; while there are a few smallish samplers of Savitt sides (including *Shuffle in Style* on the British Jasmine label), alas, there's nothing like a basic batch of Bon Bon–Savitt sides to be found anywhere. There is, fortunately, a disc on the Belgian Classics label titled *The Three Keys, 1932–1933/Bon Bon and His Buddies 1941–1942* that contains all his prewar non-Savitt sessions, but the sound quality leaves a lot to be desired. Even so, as with a lot of other Classics releases, it's better than not being able to hear the music at all. But as disciples like Mel Tormé, Jon Hendricks, and (if not in so many words) Sinatra have acknowledged, Bon Bon deserves more and better. George Tunnell died in Philadelphia on May 20, 1975.

Hollywood Divas

Alice Faye
Dorothy Lamour
Shirley Temple
Betty Hutton

There are Hollywood divas and there are Hollywood divas. When we talk about the female singers who headlined in the major movie musicals, there are all sorts of variations on the theme. In retrospect, it seems safe to say that the number-one female actress-singer in the heyday of old Hollywood was Alice Faye; she would be somewhat eclipsed in the war years by Betty Grable, Judy Garland (whose shorter career as an adult lead was disproportionately valuable), and then Doris Day, but no other leading lady of her period made more important movies or introduced more great songs. Yet in the key years of Faye's popularity, the number-one star at the box office was actually her Twentieth Century Fox studio colleague (and occasional co-star) Shirley Temple.

Of all the dozens of women who sang and starred in the hundreds of musicals produced by the major studios in these years, I'm also including Dorothy Lamour and Betty Hutton, who were both outstanding vocalists: They had fine voices and solid technique, and they each had a musical and cultural idiom that was distinctly her own. They also deserve consideration because they were among the few Hollywood leads who enjoyed a recording career that ran parallel to their film work.

There were other Hollywood leading ladies who deserve mention, but of all the dancing divas, whose ranks include Ginger Rogers, Rita Hayworth, Vera-Ellen, Cyd Charisse, and Betty Grable, only the last is worth considering, and she had no singing career to speak of. Like Gene Kelly, Grable sings well within the context of her musical numbers, but it's understandable why neither she nor Kelly was pursued by the record companies. Hayworth and Vera-Ellen weren't singers at all; every time they opened their mouths in their films, someone else's voice came out. (Grable, at least, didn't require the services of an Anita Ellis, Annette Warren, or Marni Nixon.) The producers were extremely inconsistent in their approach. Nonsinging dancers Hayworth and Vera-Ellen were in the same boat as nonsinging (or semi-singing) dramatic actresses such as Joan Crawford, Ava Gardner, and, later, Audrey Hepburn. All three of them made a few musicals in the midst of what were, essentially, straight dramatic careers, yet audiences apparently never noticed that they had a different singing voice in every film—occasionally, it was even their own.

Then there's Mae West. Music is a key ingredient in her films, and she actually made a handful of recordings, both at the height of her career in 1933–34 (six titles for Brunswick) and then, thirty years later, as a camp attraction in the psychedelic sixties, when she was regarded as kind of a female drag queen. Yet more than nearly any other actress, West uses her voice really creatively: She colors each word in the script with every kind of inflection, and though she wrote her own dialogue, what she says is less important than the way she says it. West uses sighs, moans, groans, vocal grimaces—she establishes her character with her voice more than anything else (she never would have made it as a silent film actress). However, none of this constitutes singing—not exactly. In her use of a distinct voice as a means of creating a screen archetype, West should be considered in the same class as Cary Grant, Katharine Hepburn, James Cagney, Edward G. Robinson, Humphrey Bogart, and others on that exalted level.

In hindsight, history would appear to be a matter of somebody figuring out the right way to do something and then everybody else falling into line. Right? Wrong. After Bing Crosby divined the perfect synergy of mass media, perfected by the mid-thirties, it's surprising that no other performer followed suit. Crosby had shown that motion pictures, radio, and commercial recordings could work together—complement one another, even—but no one else seems to have gotten the message. (The closest was Judy Garland, and even so her recorded output was a fraction of what it should have been.) It's particularly odd that there was nothing remotely like a female equivalent to Crosby, especially in the thirties: a girl vocalist who starred in pictures, had her own radio show, and recorded regularly.

Just as there was enmity between the record companies and the radio stations (the labels didn't want their product played on the air), the megamoguls who ran old Hollywood viewed the other arms of the mass media with suspicion. Why would you pay 25 cents to see Alice Faye in her new movie, when for 35 cents you could bring her voice home and listen to her as many times as you wanted? That particular reasoning makes so little sense in the modern world that it's difficult to believe that it was the prevailing attitude in the days of the Hollywood star machine. Even Faye, who had built a major portion of her fan base through records, was apparently discouraged from making them. Because of this attitude, we have a rather skewed viewpoint on the major singing actresses who were Crosby's immediate contemporaries; for the most part, we get a few records here and a few records there. There's no comprehensive picture of what these stars were like as recording artists during their high Hollywood years, and most of them had retired or faded from view by the LP era.

The four leading ladies chosen for this section were selected both because they were primarily singers (which is why I'm not discussing Ginger

Rogers or Eleanor Powell) and because they were at once representative (what I say about Alice Faye would pretty much also apply to Betty Grable or June Haver, and probably also to Ann Sheridan and Ann Sothern) and yet distinctive; each of them had a style and an approach of her own, as well as a body of music that's uniquely hers. They all had huge careers, during a period when stars generally turned out three or four movies a year—that's a lot of songs in a lot of films, so this is a sketchy, informal survey at best. All four of these gals were also exceptionally musical in a way that you can't imagine a contemporary movie star being.

Alice Faye (1915–1998)

Alice Faye may be the single most significant female singer in Hollywood history; only Doris Day and Judy Garland rank as potential rivals. She was the number-one leading lady at Twentieth Century Fox; in fact, virtually every musical released by the studio in the glory years was either a real or virtual Alice Faye picture; even those that didn't feature Faye herself inevitably starred an Alice Faye type (like the aforementioned Grable and Havoc, and even the young Vivian Blaine). Faye herself starred in roughly thirty Fox films from 1934 to 1945, and she was the rare picture star whose popularity did not diminish between the height of the Depression and the war years.

Unfortunately her recording career only corresponds with the years of her ascent, a pair of band vocals with Rudy Vallee in 1933 followed by nineteen film songs waxed between 1934 and 1937. She sang in a low, throaty voice, and had plenty of pizzazz, not to mention wisdom in the ways of how to shade a text and utilize nuances in putting a lyric over.

A native New Yorker, Alice Jeane Leppert had worked her way up to the chorus of the annual *George White's Scandals* revues by the time she was sixteen. With her good looks and dark, smoky voice, she attracted the attention of *Scandals* star Rudy Vallee, who was impressed enough to bring Alice Faye (as she was now known) into his entourage.

Under the imprimatur of the singer, saxophonist, and bandleader, Faye made her first radio broadcast (on Vallee's *Fleischmann's Yeast Hour*), her first recordings (with Vallee's band on Bluebird), and her first film (*George White's Scandals*), the latter being done for the Fox Film Corporation shortly before it merged with Twentieth Century Pictures. The first *Scandals* film gave Faye third billing, following Vallee and Jimmy Durante. However, when Twentieth Century Fox produced the follow-up film a year later, *George White's 1935 Scandals*, Faye was now top billed, and Vallee was no longer in the picture. Faye, who had appeared in three other Fox films in the interim, was already a much bigger picture star than her mentor would ever be.

Yet Vallee may well be responsible for the early musical typecasting of Faye as a singing flirt. Her two recorded vocals with Vallee's Connecticut Yankees were "Honeymoon Hotel" and "Shame on You," and her big song from the 1934 *Scandals* film was "Nasty Man," a number similar in attitude and theme to "Shame on You." In fact, at one point in "Shame on You," one of the Yankees starts answering Faye back as she sings, and he even chants, "You nasty man!" (The expression was a catchphrase of comic Joe Penner.) "Nasty Man" was also her first recording under her own name for Brunswick, and it was backed by her next big song from a film (titled, provocatively, *She Learned About Sailors*), "Here's the Key to My Heart," in which Faye bats her eyes at the entire NYPD as well as the whole of the United States fleet. The verse to "Sing, Baby, Sing" has Faye explaining how she learned to sing from her "Harlem Mammy." All of her earliest songs are invested with a healthy sexual energy that translates into jazzy playfulness. Vallee generously allocates her plenty of space on the two Bluebirds: She sings two full choruses on both, and on "Honeymoon Hotel" the second run-through is saturated with the jazziness of Armstrong, Crosby, and Ethel Waters. A handful of airchecks of Faye on the *Fleischmann's Hour* have come out on a British CD (*On Screen and Radio, 1932–1943*, Vintage Jazz Band), one of which is a duet with Vallee on "You're an Old Smoothie," and it turns out that the Old Smoothie is the selfsame Shameful Nasty Man; it's yet another example of the flirty Faye wagging a finger, tongue-in-cheek, at a swinging seducer.

The earliest surviving performance (that I've been able to hear) is a *Fleischmann's* aircheck of "Hats Off, Here Comes a Lady"—yet another song that casts doubt on a woman's respectability. All these early songs (including "Young and Healthy") are sexy and perky (as opposed to sad and torchy), and a surprising number are by Harry Warren, who would write most of her forties film scores (Faye would help Warren win an Oscar for "You'll Never Know" in 1943). When she sings "Young and Healthy" on the air, Faye then goes into "Ooh, I'm Thinking" (a virtually unrecorded song from the 1932 *Strike Me Pink*) in which she launches into a full-fledged scat solo. Another hot item that turns up among the early airchecks is Faye singing lead with the Mills Brothers on "Dinah" and doing nearly as credible a job as Bing Crosby. At this early stage of the game, Faye was a red hot mama; in her first films, she was utilized as a kind of a singing Jean Harlow. In *Every Night at Eight*, which boasts an especially rich Fields and McHugh score, Faye is a hot honey—but also a sympathetic sweetie—who helps out as innocent ingenue Frances Langford gets the guy (George Raft).

As the decade wore on, Faye's simmering sultriness slowly subsided into worldly wisdom. In most of her movies, the hero never has to win her over: Usually she loves him from the beginning, but the big sap is too dumb to realize that she's the right one for him, see? He's so busy inventing popular music, creating radio, or running a boffo nightclub to pay much attention to her. Then, the guy is a success, and some society dame bats her eyes at him, until he realizes that she's not the one who really loves him, it was Alice all along! The Fox musicals are so similar that even buffs have a hard time remembering which is which, but this is the basic plot of both *King of Burlesque* (1936) and *Hello Frisco, Hello* (1943) (Faye and funny man Jack Oakie play exactly the same roles in both, only the leading man—the big lug—is different); in fact, this is pretty much the plot of *every* Fox musical.

After waxing one song each from *George White's Scandals* (1934) and *She Learned About Sailors* (1934), Faye made commercial recordings of the key numbers from most of her early films: *365 Nights in Hollywood* (1934), *George White's 1935 Scandals* (1935), *Every Night at Eight* (1935), *King of Burlesque* (1936), *Stowaway* (1936), *On the Avenue* (1937), and *Wake Up and Live* (1937). But it seems as if at precisely the point that Faye became established as the number-one woman in the Hollywood musical, Fox unexpectedly pulled the plug on her recording career. It's a major pity; *On the Avenue* and *Wake Up and Live* have particularly wonderful scores (by Irving Berlin and the team of Mack Gordon and Harry Revel, respectively). And Faye was still just getting started; there would be dozens of superior songs written for her between that point and the end of her picture career in 1945.

While thinking about the records that Faye should have made is merely frustrating, it's possible, to a degree, to enjoy her film sound track vocals as sort of faux 78s. Another British label, Jasmine, has issued four whole CDs of Faye sound track excerpts (divided into two double disc packages, *Got Music on My Mind* and *I Feel a Song Coming On*), which include virtually all of her movie vocals. The major drawback is that the audio was obviously taken from either 16mm prints or DVDs—in other words, the final film, which means that listeners have to deal with sound effects, occasional bits of dialogue, lots of overdubbed applause, and many vocals that were truncated because of their placement in the narrative context of the films. What's really needed is a restoration of the sort that Michael Feinstein did for the *Frank Sinatra in Hollywood* box and other projects, wherein the original component vocal tracks—without extraneous noise—are used.

Faye scholar George Ulrich, who maintains the official Alice Faye Web site, once issued several semi-private LPs of the sound track playback discs—it's well-nigh time for a digital release of same. Ulrich has also issued three CDs of excerpts from Faye's 1937 *Chesterfield Show*, which she shared with popular bandleader Hal Kemp. Presented in excellent audio quality, these outstanding discs enrich Faye's scant recorded legacy considerably. Faye and Kemp are not always a simpatico fit musically, and the charts occasionally interject his staccato, tukka-tukka sound as an unnecessary additive, as well as occasional concert-style tempo changes. There are a lot of overwritten production numbers with special lyrics, some of which are highly amusing. In fact, there appears to be a long-running gimmick of using one song to lead into another, as when "Remember" introduces "The You and Me That Used to Be" and another Irving Berlin tune, a much rewritten version of "He Ain't Got Rhythm," which leads directly into the then current Crosby film tune "Smarty." But overall, there's no faulting Faye's singing on standards like "The Lady Is a Tramp," "Once in a While," "You're the Top," and "Night and Day." She's never less than excellent, even on the unpolished rehearsal takes offered on the third volume.

In these 1937 airshots, Faye still has the smoky, smoldering sound we remember from her 1933–34 recordings, but now she's added lots of new tonal colors. Other than some of the hard-core jazz and big band vocalists from that time (Holiday, Fitzgerald, Bailey), it's hard to think of any female pop singer of the period who was more consistently terrific than Faye. She introduced "Goodnight, My Love" in *Stowaway*, and at the time it was sung by both Ella Fitzgerald and Helen Ward with Benny Goodman (as well as by Shirley Temple in the same film), but none of them has the warmth and expression and clarity that Faye does.

She brings the same musical intelligence to the sound track items included on the two Jasmine double sets; here, her singing is also consistently terrific, and so, too, are most of the songs that were written for her. In the thirties the reigning team at Fox was lyricist Mack Gordon and composer Harry Revel, who wrote most of the choice scores for both Faye and Temple (their four tunes for *Wake Up and Live* are especially exceptional, particularly the first-rate ballad "There's a Lull in My Life"). Around 1940, Harry Warren migrated from Warner Bros. to Fox, and immediately entered the most profitable phase of his long career. The scores he wrote for the two Glenn Miller movies alone were major blockbusters and, likewise, the Oscar-winning "You'll Never Know" (inspired by a racetrack bugle call and introduced by Faye in *Hello Frisco, Hello*) became one of the songs that defined an era.

Warren's score for *The Gang's All Here* (1943) is among the composer's very finest. The film itself is mainly celebrated for the hallucinogenic visuals of Busby Berkeley's production numbers, but the purely musical contributions of Faye and the Warren-Gordon team (aided by a cameo from Benny Goodman and His Orchestra, and, also on the sound track, the equally wonderful Benny Carter) are no less noteworthy. Faye has never sounded more luscious and sensual than on her two key ballads, "No Love, No Nothing" (aided by an equally sexy alto sax solo from Carter) and "A Journey to a Star"; she provides a bit of musical sanity in a movie that's otherwise so completely over-the-top you keep thinking it's going to fall over. She seems to have agreed to participate in only one example of Buzz Berkeley at his most delirious: "The Polka Dot Polka" has her sashaying across a ballroom floor surrounded by menacing-looking children of the darned in 1880s drag, lip-syncing to an off-screen choir of bassos and sopranos. Her vocal is notable for its raplike qualities (as she sings of how her "heart went wacky for a dapper whippersnapper"), but the chorus dance that follows, with dozens of dames in skintight leotards doing strange things with giant dots (that's right, I said dots) almost defies description.

After the gangbuster triumphs of *Hello Frisco, Hello* and *The Gang's All Here,* pretty much anything would have seemed anticlimactic; Faye made one last picture, the nonmusical noir drama *Fallen Angel,* and then abruptly left the studio and the picture business because it seemed that, all of a sudden, Hollywood was treating her as if she was over-the-hill—at age thirty. She continued to co-star with second husband Phil Harris on their long-running radio show (which was one of several satellite shows revolving around the monumental *Jack Benny Program*) and even sang occasionally. She made a brief return to pictures in the dreadful 1962 remake of Rodgers and Hammerstein's *State Fair* (and cut an album for Sinatra's Reprise label at the same time); approaching senior citizenhood, she was seen on Broadway in a revival of *Good News.* Faye died in 1998, three years after Harris and a week before Sinatra.

Most jazz fans know the song "One Never Knows, Does One?" from Billie Holiday's 1937 recording; this was a rare early example of Holiday leading her own session and getting to sing for most of the disc (as opposed to just a vocal refrain). And her vocal is, in fact, marvelously creative, one of her very best. "One Never Knows, Does One?," however, was written by Gordon and Revel for Faye to sing in *Stowaway,* and Faye's version is also worthy of history's attention. Holiday virtually rewrites the melody, twisting it here and there to reflect her own personality, but Faye personalizes it without changing it—and there's a lot to be said for that approach. Her vocal is shorter than Holiday's, only a minute and forty seconds (it's one of the dozens of first-rate songs written for Faye that she never got to record commercially), but she packs a lot of interpretation into that brief chorus. Her timing and her nuance are perfect throughout. I'm particularly taken by the way she goes up to a high note in the bridge, on "hope for *the* best" emphasizing "the," apparently the least important word in the line; it was a brilliant stroke. At the end, she sings the last line—the title line—as if it were simply "one never knows," but then there's a long and very pregnant pause before she returns with "does one." It adds to the unpre-

dictability of the tune, thereby reinforcing the message of the lyric.

Who knew? Scratch an old movie star and find a magnificent, underappreciated pop singer underneath.

One never knows.

Does one?

Dorothy Lamour (1914–1996)

In 1932, the pianist and bandleader Eddy Duchin (who had recently left Leo Reisman's orchestra to form his own band) was playing a show at the Hippodrome in Baltimore when he hired a singer from New Orleans named Dorothy Slaton. She was recruited primarily for her musical talent, but Duchin was certainly distracted, to say the least, by her appearance. A few years later, he wrote, "I told her she must do something with that figure. A scenario and a sarong must have overheard me."

Dorothy Lamour, as Slaton was later known, was a much better singer than she had to be: Paramount Pictures wanted her because of her exotic beauty and magnetic charisma. It was icing on the cake that she quickly proved herself to be a fine dramatic actress and an even better comedienne. And then it was icing on the icing that she was an inspired singer, possessing one of the very best voices and overall styles of any vocalist in the Golden Age of Hollywood. As a comic she could keep up with Bob Hope; as a singer, she was a worthy duet partner for Bing Crosby.

In 1948, Lamour participated in one of the funniest bits of self-parody ever pulled off by a movie icon when she sang "Queen of the Hollywood Islands," written for her (in the picture *On Our Merry Way*) by Frank Loesser. "She was born in New Orleans, ran an elevator in Chicago," Loesser's lyric begins, "but look what she's a native of now!" Mary Leta Dorothy Slaton was born in the Crescent City in 1914; she was raised primarily by her mother and her stepfather, whose name was Charles Lambour. The family struggled, and couldn't afford to keep Dorothy in school. Even after she won a citywide beauty contest and was crowned Miss New Orleans, she took a job, as the song suggested, running a department store elevator in Chicago.

Apparently Slaton never studied singing formally, but by 1932 the combination of her voice and her looks earned her gigs with Duchin (briefly) and Chicago-based bandleader Herbie Kay, who was also her first husband. She also met two of the Crosby brothers, Bing and Everett, in Chicago at around this time. Kay's orchestra broadcast out of Chicago under the sponsorship of Fleischmann's Yeast, and that was apparently how Slaton, like Alice Faye around the same time, came to the attention of Rudy Vallee. Vallee pulled a string, as he had a few years earlier for Faye, and landed her a spot singing at the famous nightclub El Morocco and then One Fifth Avenue. One night, Louis B. Mayer came in and got wise to the possibility of the singer with a scenario and a sarong, and arranged for a screen test.

However, it was Paramount Pictures that gave her a contract; she was now using the name Dorothy Lamour, a variation on her stepfather's name. Lamour immediately clicked, as they said back then, in the title role of *The Jungle Princess* (1936). From then on, she was Paramount's on-call gal whenever they had a character that was the least bit exotic: Hispanic, Caribbean, or from any island other than Manhattan. Much the same way that certain male actors were repeatedly expected to play gangsters, cowboys, or mad scientists, Lamour was usually cast as a jungle princess or a desert island dish (sometimes you expect her opening line to be "Me no use prepositions").

Thanks to her, the word "sarong" entered general usage; it became her visual signature. She was always up for kidding about it—and herself—famously in the "Sweater, Sarong and Peekaboo Bang" number in *Star Spangled Rhythm* (in addition to, as already mentioned, "The Queen of the Hollywood Islands" song). She similarly ribs herself, in the company of Crosby and Betty Hutton, in the 1947 all-star effort *Duffy's Tavern* (and dressed in a little girl's sailor suit, probably her single least sexy outfit). But contrary to popular belief, Lamour also had plenty of nonexotic roles, the most significant of which was as the top-billed leading lady in *The Big Broadcast of 1938*, in which Broadway comic Bob Hope made his feature debut.

A year later, Lamour's obvious assets—the exotic appeal, her comic ability, and her musical skill—led to her being cast in *Road to Singapore;* she obviously belonged on the road to any of these faraway places (with strange-sounding names) much more than Hope and Crosby did. The *Road* movies would comprise the most lasting part of her legacy: She may have been the third most important ingredient, but she was absolutely essential to their ongoing, classic appeal.

The downside was that once the *Road* series took off—and certainly by the time it reached a high point with the third film, *Road to Morocco* (1942)—Lamour had so effectively kidded her sarong roles into submission that neither she nor anyone else could take them seriously again. By the war, her output had become increasingly Hope-and-Crosby-centric; among her most notable non-*Road* pictures of the forties were *They Got Me Covered* (1943) and *My Favorite Brunette* (1947) with Hope, and *Dixie* (1942), in which she played Crosby's leading lady (described in the trailer as "a lovely, lively lady of old New Orleans") in crinolines and glorious Technicolor.

As with Faye, Lamour's movie career ran about a dozen years, from the mid-thirties to the end of the forties, with a few postscripts. But unlike Fox with Faye, Paramount doesn't seem to have put the kibosh on Lamour's recording career, and she did a healthy sixty or so songs for Brunswick, Vocalion, Bluebird, and other labels between 1937 and 1947. Her recording work roughly paralleled the film work in that there are a lot of exotic, Caribbean, Latin, tropical, and Island songs, but many excellent straight-ahead ballads and bouncers as well. In all, the combined titles of this ten-year period are a very respectable body of work. There's no comprehensive set of her sessions, but if you pick up *Thanks for the Memories: The Brunswick Recordings* (Collectables), *On a Tropic Night* (Conifer Movie Stars Series), *The Moon of Manakoora* (ASV/Living Era), and *Queen of the Hollywood Islands* (Sepia 1032), you will have a complete set of her 78 rpm era output (albeit with many tracks duplicated).

Coincidentally, the accompaniments on her 1937–38 Brunswick sessions (including one with then husband Herbie Kay) sound exactly like the kind of orchestrations that John Scott Trotter was concurrently using to back Crosby on his Decca dates—so much so that one has to wonder whether Trotter had any input in Lamour's sessions. As an offshoot of her role in *The Big Broadcast*, she recorded "Thanks for the Memory" long before it became Hope's theme song, and also duetted with him on "My Favorite Brunette" and "Beside You," from their 1947 Bing-less comedy-mystery *My Favorite Brunette*. She also recorded several songs from *Road to Singapore:* "Sweet Potato Piper," "The Moon and the Willow Tree," and "Too Romantic," some of which were done by Crosby in the film.

Lamour has a lovely voice, dark and sweet and a perfect extension of her onscreen persona. Just about everything she sang sounds good, including all those tropical and Island songs (generally done with American-style dance bands, not exotic instruments or steel guitars). "On a Tropic Night" is actually a mildly silly tango (in ABAB form) and sort of a countermelody to "Orchids in the Moonlight," while "Mexican Magic" and "Panamania" take her South of the Border. She continues to tour Pan-America with the dramatic "Perfidia" and "Adios, Marquita Linda," both of which back her with marimbas and more of a Latinate, Xavier Cugat–y feel.

She sang far too many Hawaiian and Island songs (both genuine and ersatz) to list, but some of the better ones are "The Moon of Manakoora," "A Song of Old Hawaii," "Lovely Hula Hands," "Hawaiian Hospitality," "My Little Grass Shack in Kealakekua, Hawaii," "My Tane," "Malihini Mele," and "Aloha Oe." "Moon of Manakoora" seems to be her signature: She recorded it with two very different accompaniments—once with a full orchestra and strings, and then with Island-style guitars. (In both, she beholds the moon in her lover's "dusky eyes.")

I have to admit that even I get a little tired of all these fish-and-poi arias after listening to too many of them in a row, but never tire of her other tunes, especially standards and future standards like "The Lamp Is Low," "The Man I Love," "I Gotta Right to

Sing the Blues," "It Had to Be You," "There's Danger in Your Eyes, Cherie!," and "I'm Getting Sentimental over You." She's delightfully zippy on Frank Loesser's "I Go for That"; her rendering is only slightly less hip than Mildred Bailey's.

Lamour's single most appealing disc may well be "Comes Love," introduced in the 1939 musical comedy *Yokel Boy*. This later became one of the national anthems of jazz singers (it's an agreeably swinging tune in minor key), sung by everyone from Sarah Vaughan to Joni Mitchell, but Lamour was virtually the only solo vocalist to make a record of the song when it was brand spanking new. As Lew Brown's lyric states, Lamour "knows just what to do" with this energetic list song. She plays with the time throughout: At one point it goes into a habanera section with congas and castanets, and at other points it slows down and speeds up dramatically while Lamour gets the most out of Brown's gag-laden text.

She made her last 78s prior to the 1948 recording ban for the independent Coast label, which were released in an album of four steel guitar songs titled *Queen of the Hollywood Islands*. This independently produced 78 album roughly coincided with her independently produced film *On Our Merry Way* (with Burgess Meredith, Paulette Goddard, James Stewart, and Henry Fonda, it was truly an all-star independent). Lamour also recorded four general-interest titles for Coast with a standard string orchestra, including the evocative "Ace in the Hole" and "Lulu Belle," which, despite the cheerful title, turns out to be a torrid tale of a swarthy siren. Unfortunately, she somehow missed the chance to make Decca discs of nearly all the exceptionally fine songs written for her by Burke and Van Heusen in the *Road* flicks, like "Constantly," in *Morocco;* "Personality," in *Utopia;* and "You're Dangerous," in *Zanzibar,* but overall her recording and film career left little to complain about.

By the time the 1948 AFM ban was finished, Lamour's recording was pretty much over. She made a few more films, but everything after 1949 was basically a special appearance, as in *The Greatest Show on Earth* and *Road to Bali,* the last of the original *Road* movies. When Bob and Bing reunited a decade later for *Road to Hong Kong,* they made the disastrous decision not to bring Dotty with them for the full ride. Instead, they relegated her to a somewhat demeaning guest shot, as if to imply that she was too old to play an enticing leading lady when she was, in fact, eleven years younger than the two leading men. Go figure. (Along the way there also was an original LP on the Design label, *Dorothy Lamour—The Road to Romance . . . for Bing, Bob and You!*)

Lamour could have been bitter about her treatment over *Hong Kong,* but she spent the last forty or so years of her life playing the role of an ex–glamour girl with considerable dignity. She did a cameo in the 1964 *Pajama Party,* and brought some unexpected class to the Annette and Frankie *Beach Party* series, and her number "Where Did I Go Wrong" cleverly compared thirties sarongs to sixties bikinis. (Regrettably, Lamour herself wasn't seen in either; she still looked amazing at fifty.)

After splitting from Herbie Kay, Lamour lived for nearly forty years with her second husband, William Howard (father of her two children), until his death in 1978. The personality that she presents in her autobiography, *My Side of the Road,* published in 1980, is consistent with the warm, generous, unpretentious person whom everyone remembers. The sarong-clad Queen of the Hollywood Islands was, by all accounts, remarkably down-to-earth. She died, almost twenty years after Crosby and seven years before Hope, in 1996.

Shirley Temple (born 1928)

Before we talk about Shirley Temple's singing, there are two facts we have to get out of the way. Number one: She is on a par with Fred Astaire and Gene Kelly as one of the greatest dancers in the history of cinema (I'd speak of her in the same breath as just about any female dancer, from Eleanor Powell to Cyd Charisse). To watch Temple move is just amazing. In the old VHS days, I would rewind the tape to try and get to the beginning of each number so I could watch it again and again, a task that's considerably easier in the age of DVD and YouTube. She dances with complete conviction and a kind of breathless athletic perfection. As with Astaire, to describe her as "poetry in motion" is to pay the medium of poetry a compliment it doesn't always deserve.

Number two: Temple ranks with Crosby and Astaire in that a remarkable songbook was created for her. Between 1934 and 1940, Temple, aged six to twelve, made roughly twenty starring pictures for twentieth Century Fox, each of which had a first-rate score of four or so songs, usually with words by Mack Gordon and music by Harry Revel. Although she didn't make any commercial recordings or do much radio work (thank you, Darryl Zanuck), the songs she introduced were heard all over the airwaves and widely covered by bands and singers on disc. Temple wasn't only the single most popular film star of the Depression era (or so it's widely reported), she was also a significant force in driving the entire music industry of the period.

Between those two factors, coupled with her industrial-strength cuteness and her adorability factor, one might assume that Temple had so much going for her that she didn't have to be a great singer. However, her singing is far from incidental. She sings in a high, bright, chirpy voice. The voice itself is kind of a fantasy version of what a seven-year-old should sound like, but other aspects of her singing are even more remarkable. Like all the great dancers, including her unfortunately underrecorded co-star Bojangles Robinson, Temple's time and rhythm are superb. Her phrasing and her interpretation easily make her one of Hollywood's all-time heavyweight singers. She was obviously coached by directors and conductors, but even as a toddler she can effortlessly extract the meaning of a text; even when the subject matter concerns ships named *Lollipop* sailing through soups alongside animal crackers and codfish balls, she makes whatever she's singing about seem like the most wonderful and important thing in the world.

Born on April 23, 1928, Shirley Temple—a rare film star who didn't change her name for showbiz—was the daughter of a banker father and a mother who had professional dancing experience. Long before then, there was an established tradition of child performers in vaudeville and Broadway, and little Shirley started taking dancing lessons not long after her third birthday. Soon after her fourth, she began appearing in a series of one-reel short subjects with all-toddler casts. Cursed by a poverty both of budget and imagination, these *Baby Burlesques* were bastard stepchildren of Hal Roach's brilliant, ongoing *Our Gang* shorts, apparently the brainchild of a maniacal pedophobe who, one can only hope, was suitably punished for his extreme cruelty to audiences as well as to child performers.

Temple's first feature, the 1934 *Stand Up and Cheer!*, wasn't much better (although it's hard to argue with a casting credit that reads "Stepin Fetchit as George Bernard Shaw"), but it gave her a good song, "Baby Take a Bow," and with it the chance to create a minor sensation. Within a few months, Temple was reunited with James Dunn (who played her father in *Stand Up*) for *Baby Take a Bow*; this picture didn't exactly set the world on fire either, but it was increasingly obvious that Fox had something amazing on their hands. With *Bright Eyes*, released in the final days of 1934, the Temple series was officially under way, and the film gave the six-year-old the first of her signature songs, "On the Good Ship Lollipop." Even here, her singing is something to listen to, as when she stretches the word "it's a *sweet* trip" over several notes and syncopates it.

Nineteen thirty-five began with a historical picture, *The Little Colonel*, which didn't feature any new songs but teamed Temple for the first time with the already legendary song and dance man Bill "Bojangles" Robinson. Their dancing together was even more magical than anything they did individually, and the two immediately became one of the top musical teams of popular culture, a veritable Fred-and-Ginger (or, for that matter, Pres-and-Lady). The string of original Temple musicals continued (although there would be other costumers, too, like *The Littlest Rebel*) with *Captain January*, which introduced another Temple classic in "At the Codfish Ball." By now, the seven-year-old was on a remarkable roll: From 1935 to 1939, Temple was virtually unchallenged as the top box office attraction in all of movies.

Disappointingly, she made no commercial recordings during these years; later, Fox issued snippets of her sound tracks on various LPs and one very rare CD (*Songbook* on Casablanca Records); the Temple issues to look for are *America's Sweetheart, Volume 1* and *Volume 2* on Flapper (another British label). As with Alice Faye, it's doubly disappointing that no one has collated her musical tracks without the sound effects and dialogue (scholar Dave Weiner reports that some of these discs include extra vocal and instrumental choruses not used in the final films).

Shirley Temple sings roughly two kinds of songs in her movies, the best remembered of which are her kid-song specialties such as "When I Grow Up" and "You Gotta Eat Your Spinach, Baby." (It would have been altogether fitting for her parents to throw a big party at which they served lollipops, spinach, codfish balls, animal crackers, and soup.) "Spinach" is one of her more ambitious production numbers from a purely audio viewpoint (this is an all-singing, nondancing number); there's an elaborately sung scenario in which the precocious moppet identifies herself as the duly appointed spokesman of "the kids of the nation" who pleads the case against spinach ("take away that awful greenery") to Alice Faye and Jack Haley (who are apparently the designated representatives of the grown-ups of the nation). What's wild is the way songwriters Gordon and Revel throw a bunch of references to black spirituals—"hosannas!" and "hallelujahs!"—into Temple's passionate plea for a spinach-free world. (In *Dimples*, she sings the traditional "Gospel Train.")

The closest that Faye and Haley can come to a logical retort is that "Children have to do what they are told / Or you will be a meanie when you're old." Which is another way of saying that the grown-ups don't present a particularly compelling argument; basically, children have to eat their spinach because adults tell them to. Kids could relate! Still, as both Maurice Sendak, who certainly knows a thing or two about childhood, and the late film historian William K. Everson have observed, Temple's pictures were aimed at parents rather than children. Sendak remembers that kids resented Temple because parents tended to hold her up as an unattainable ideal of perfection. While Temple was up there singing and dancing, most real kids of the Depression were sitting in mud. Temple made mothers dissatisfied with their children in the same way Clark Gable made them dissatisfied with their husbands. Who could blame them for being annoyed? Little girls were even more irritated when their stage moms ran curling irons through their newly peroxided locks and hauled them off to dance classes and auditions.

But the great majority of Temple's songs were of more general interest than "Animal Crackers in My Soup" (from *Curly Top*, and the most famous of her signature songs after "Good Ship Lollipop"). "Picture Me Without You" (from *Dimples*) was introduced by Temple and immediately taken up by leading bands and singers of the era, most notably Mildred Bailey, and, later, Bobby Short. "But Definitely" was covered by the bands of Hal Kemp, Charlie Barnet, Bunny Berigan, Ray Noble, Bob Crosby, and others; it's also sung in the film *Poor Little Rich Girl* by both Temple and Alice Faye, and I would be hard-pressed to choose who does a better job.

In the same way that many of Dorothy Lamour's songs are not exotica, most of Temple's songs are not age-specific and could thus be enjoyed by anybody: "This Is a Happy Little Ditty"—an example of truth in labeling if ever there was one—is the kind of insanely catchy song that Fox loved to cram into her pictures. You can't stop humming the damn thing no matter how hard you try; patrons undoubtedly went right out to their local music shops and purchased the sheet music (replete with Shirley's picture on the front) even if they couldn't buy a record of her singing it. For all the simplicity that the lyric ascribes to itself (with repeated quotes from nursery rhymes), it's a complex creation with a triple rhyme scheme: ". . . doesn't matter / . . . silly chatter / . . . to the patter." If Cole Porter had kids, this is the kind of nursery song he would have written for them.

"Happy Little Ditty" (from *Just Around the Corner*) shows the Fox team working overtime to sell a simple song: It's not only sung and danced by Temple, but she's joined by Bojangles Robinson, wisecracking Joan Davis, and Bert Lahr, bellowing in his mock-operatic lion-baritone and also playing the alto saxophone (who knew?). Lahr's contribution is more visual than vocal; here's another case where one wishes that Temple had also made a straight-ahead commercial 78 of the song.

Temple's greatest partner was, unquestionably, Robinson—Rogers to her Astaire—who appeared with her in four films, the two "Little" Civil War stories (*The Little Colonel* and *The Littlest Rebel*), *Rebecca of Sunnybrook Farm*, and *Just Around the Corner*. The two 1938 films are especially satisfying in that even though Robinson plays a dancing butler in the Civil War, in the two contemporary pictures he and Temple interact more like social equals. Robinson makes a marvelous contribution to "Happy Little Ditty" and especially to "I Love to Walk in the Rain," in which the two dance as true partners, with no visible trappings of hierarchy. "I Love to Walk in the Rain" has them frolicking not only in the liquid precipitation but across a magical landscape of mechanical and puppet animals—it's as close as Temple ever came to dancing in a cartoon setting à la Gene Kelly.

If Robinson was Temple's finest partner, it's worth pointing out that she danced brilliantly with any number of highly accomplished adults. In *Poor Little Rich Girl*, she gets to strut her stuff with Faye and Haley in "I Love a Military Man," where, curiously, the number is all dancing and almost no singing (as opposed to the "Spinach" number, which

is all singing and no dancing). The trio do a precision tap-and-march routine in toy-soldier drag, but an off-screen male quartet sings the main chorus in a manner obviously patterned after the Mills Brothers. (Temple would reprise the military man bit with Robinson to the staccato rhythms of Raymond Scott's "Toy Trumpet" in *Rebecca of Sunnybrook Farm*.) Between Lahr in *Just Around the Corner* and Haley in *Poor Little Rich Girl*, one doesn't have a hard time believing that Temple was considered, at one point, for the role of Dorothy in *The Wizard of Oz*. She also danced with Buddy Ebsen, the original choice for the Tin Man, in *Captain January*, and Toto, too—meaning that she shared the screen with Terry, the terrier who would gain canine immortality as Dorothy's dog in *Oz*.

Fox loved to team her with what were then known as "eccentric" dancers like Haley, Ebsen (in the "Codfish Ball" number), and leggy Charlotte Greenwood in *Young People*. "We Should Be Together," from *Little Miss Broadway*, however, is amazingly straight-ahead and decidedly noneccentric. Temple and George Murphy dance together with a sense of humor but without Temple being the least bit patronized because she happens to be nine years old and four feet tall. Except for the height proportions, it's exactly the same dance that Murphy would have done with Eleanor Powell (who supposedly paid a visit to Temple on the set of this picture) or any other full-grown dancing lady, and it's a singularly good song from the only score written for Temple by Harold Spina and Walter Bullock (who also wrote excellent songs for Faye in *Sally, Irene and Mary*, also produced by Fox in 1938).

Whether there was much chance that Temple might have gone into *The Wizard of Oz* is a matter of some debate; however, by 1940 Fox seems to have been looking for something new to do with their twelve-year-old star. They came up with *The Blue Bird*, an *Oz*-inspired big-budget fantasy, which completely failed to take the proper cues from either *Oz* or Temple's earlier films in that it didn't allow the star to do what she did best: sing and dance. The most egregious egg laid by this ninety-minute turkey was that there was barely any music in it. To watch *The Blue Bird* is to realize anew what a classic *The Wizard of Oz* is.

The studio quickly and wisely steered Temple back to formula with *Young People*, which was as entertaining as it was unambitious. This was probably Temple's last worthwhile project, and utilized a familiar showbizcentric story with another exceptional score, this time by Harry Warren, who had recently relocated from Warners and teamed up with the corpulent and capable Mack Gordon. *Young People*'s two key songs, "Fifth Avenue" and "I Wouldn't Take a Million," were widely done by major bands (including Glenn Miller's, Tommy Dorsey's, and Harry James's). "Fifth Avenue" is also a near-march, which provides an opportunity for an athletic tap sequence by the trio of Temple, Charlotte Greenwood, and Jack Oakie. "Tra-La-La-La," another ensemble number by the central trio, is one of Temple's many winning variations on nonsense and nursery rhymes. Alas, the title tune, "Young People," is a waste, predicated on the idea of a chorus of kids trying to act grown up; it's the kind of song that no one did well, but if I have to sit through something like this, the sixteen-year-old Judy Garland did it much better.

Between the faux-*Oz Blue Bird* and the "Young People" song, it looked as if Fox was now setting up Temple as a claimant to Garland's throne, rather than the other way around. But *Young People* also includes the marvelous "I Wouldn't Take a Million," one of Temple's best pure vocals; she talk-sings her way through a very grown-up lyric, interpreting it exactly as it ought to be interpreted, and putting all the emphasis in the right places. The vocal is only a minute long, but she handles it like a pro. It's a tantalizing suggestion of the way she might have developed had she been encouraged to grow into an adult dancer-singer.

Following *Young People*, Temple actually made a picture for Arthur Freed at MGM, the quickly forgotten *Kathleen* (1941), which also was almost completely bereft of music. If MGM was trying to sustain Temple's career, and Freed was the greatest producer of movie musicals that ever was, you have to wonder why he didn't make a musical with her when he had the opportunity. But even by 1941, both Garland and Deanna Durbin were making the transition from kid roles to grown-up ones; Temple, alas, wasn't even given the chance to move into the teen roles that Garland and Durbin had left behind. Still, in those twenty key films produced between 1934 and 1940, Temple had made more excellent music than most artists do in a lifetime.

In her teenaged years, between 1942 and 1949, Temple appeared in several important pictures, from the wartime dramas *Since You Went Away* and *I'll Be Seeing You* to the postwar comedy *The Bachelor and the Bobby-Soxer* (co-starring our old friend Rudy Vallee, as the district attorney—yeah, he turns up in her career too!), and the classic Western *Fort Apache* (as Philadelphia Thursday). Still, these failed to add up to a significant career as an adult actress. Temple would go on to a career in politics, business, and the occasional showbiz project. Appropriately, she added the name of her second husband (of fifty-five years), Charles Alden Black, and was known as Shirley Temple Black as an adult. Good thing, too. You can only be Shirley Temple once.

Betty Hutton (1921–2007)

The most famous quote regarding Betty Hutton comes from James Agee, who described the singer-actress in positively Nietzschean terms as being "Beyond good and evil." It's hard to argue with that: Hutton explodes on the screen. Where Dorothy Lamour or Marlene Dietrich smolders, Hutton combusts—small wonder she made a movie titled *Incendiary Blonde*. When Nat King Cole recorded "Orange Colored Sky," he used Stan Kenton's supersized, brass-heavy orchestra for accompaniment; when Hutton recorded the song for Victor, she somehow made more noise than the King Cole Trio and the Kenton orchestra put together. Hutton was one of the definitive female movie presences of the forties—brassy, then tender, then brassy again.

As we've seen in the discussion of Hutton's sister, Marion, in the section "Sing a Song of Miller," there actually were two sets of Hutton sisters, except that June and Ina Ray Hutton were only half sisters and Betty and Marion Hutton weren't really Huttons—their birth name was Thornburg.

By 1938–39, Betty Hutton was singing with the very popular and well-established orchestra led by Vincent Lopez, while Marion had joined a band led by a young upstart named Glenn Miller (whose first band had already flopped). In an unexpected reversal, Miller became the most successful bandleader virtually of all time—with Marion Hutton being a key part of that success story—and the Betty Hutton–Lopez relationship was over quickly.

Hutton recorded only three vocals with Lopez (on Victor), all of which are the kind of high-energy nonsense song that later became her stock-in-trade: "The Jitterbug," the famous cut song from *The Wizard of Oz*, is a very elaborate showcase for her. "Concert in the Park" is best known to cinema enthusiasts for the performance by Daffy Duck in *You Oughta Be in Pictures*, but compared to Hutton the little black duck is positively low-key. Crooner Sonny Schuyler sings the lyric relatively straight while Hutton heckles loudly from the sidelines in her best Brooklynese. Yet in many ways "Igloo" is the most prescient of the three. In this tongue-twister tune, Hutton machine-guns out a lot of rhymes in choppy staccato fashion, as in "Something he said turned her head in the igloo / For she changed her rude attitude in an igloo." She's at once hard-swinging and very funny, stretching the title word into three notes ("Ig-a-loo") and getting a laugh with the superhigh note on "atti*tude*." These are her earliest documented performances, and already they're classic Betty Hutton; if the official record is to be believed, she's all of eighteen years old here.

Hutton's most valuable legacy with Lopez was not commercial 78s but a series of short films the orchestra leader was making that, early on, brought Hutton to the attention of Paramount Pictures. As part of the bandleader's troupe, she sang in three Paramount one-reelers; a vocal from one of these is included on *The Blonde Bombshell in Hollywood* (a two-CD collection of sound track vocals from the British Jasmine label). Here Hutton sings a hot, swinging version of Louis Armstrong's "Ol' Man Mose Is Dead." "Sings" may not be the right word: She bellows, she blasts, she cackles like a chicken kicking the buck-buck-bucket. It's way excessive, even by Hutton's own standards, but no one can deny that she swings like crazy. Her wartime-era work, as hysterical as it often is, seems restrained by comparison.

Apart from Lopez, Hutton moved laterally into two featurettes for Warner Bros., the more ambitious of which was *Public Jitterbug No. 1*, a twenty-one-minute mini-epic with an actual plot, in which she co-starred with Hal Le Roy, one of the fine dancers of the era. Even though dancing was not her primary skill, Hutton began working under the billing of "America's Number One Jitterbug." As she later said, "It was just an unfortunate label that was pasted on. I was just a screwball. I sang crazy songs. I did just whatever came to my mind. They didn't know what to call me, so they called me a jitterbug."

Jitterbug or not, Hutton was now well known enough to attract the attention of a Broadway producer, and in March 1940 she opened in the revue *Two for the Show* (she sang "Calypso Joe," but co-star Alfred Drake wound up with the score's big standard, "How High the Moon"). That fall, producer and lyricist Buddy DeSylva put her in the Cole Porter–Ethel Merman vehicle *Panama Hattie*. Her big number was "They Ain't Done Right by Our Nell," a comedy duet with stuffy Englishman Arthur Treacher; the song was cut after the first night because, according to Hutton, Merman didn't want the competition. (Hutton would later exact her revenge.)

DeSylva knew a good thing when he saw it and heard it, and he reintroduced Hutton to Paramount for his production *The Fleet's In*, released shortly after America's entry into World War II. Hutton was the perfect role model for the aggressive working woman of the war years—she's the one who carries sailor Eddie Bracken up the stairs, and it's she who "mans" the oars when they go for a romantic rowboat ride, rather than the other way around. She also sings Johnny Mercer's zingy "Build a Better Mousetrap" and his elaborate story-song "Arthur Murray Taught Me Dancing in a Hurry" (in a singularly repulsive costume) in front of Jimmy Dorsey's orchestra.

From there, Hutton and Bracken were cast as part of the nonstar framework story for the all-star *Star Spangled Rhythm*. The twosome then served as the second-string couple (behind top-billed Mary Martin and Dick Powell) in the glorious Technicolor *Happy Go Lucky*. The film was remembered less than the song "Murder, He Says"—which launched her long-running relationship with lyricist (later composer) Frank Loesser and became a national hit (although she didn't herself record it until around 1950).

Hutton finally made it to full leading lady status opposite Bob Hope in *Let's Face It* (1943); as usual, Hollywood severely truncated the number-one asset of this 1941 hit show—the score, which was by Cole Porter, no less. However, they allowed Hutton to shine in one of the classic Porter patter songs, "Let's Not Talk About Love," which made her into a sort of female Danny Kaye (he had done it on Broadway). Not surprisingly, Paramount skipped Porter's famous line "They say Bucks County, Pennsylvania, is a nest of nymphomania," but the film did leave in one particularly provocative couplet that went, "Let's talk about drugs, let's talk about dope / Let's try to picture Paramount minus Bob Hope!"

Had Hutton done nothing else in her career, she would be remembered for her wonderful performance in Preston Sturges's classic (nonmusical) comedy *The Miracle of Morgan's Creek*. Here she played opposite Eddie Bracken for the fourth time. (Hope had played her GI boyfriend in *Let's Face It*.) By the height of the war years, she was fully established as Every Serviceman's wacky, jitterbugging sweetheart, capable of igniting explosive comedy numbers with all the firepower of a munitions factory. On one radio show, Bob Hope refers to her as "a vitamin pill with legs" and remarks that if the Allies could somehow capture her raw power and direct it against the Axis, Hitler would instantly throw in the towel. In her book *The Star Machine*, Jeanine Basinger observes that Hutton embodied "the high-octane fear and desperation that was inside everyone during the hard days of World War II, the insanity that had to be denied, repressed, lived with, and unleashed only on the dance floor." Hutton was pure energy—the high-powered comedy dame to end all comedy dames.

By the end of the war, Hutton had established herself as reigning queen of musicals at Paramount. The studio seems to have been aware that a little of her went a long way, and was careful not to overuse her. Fox could put Alice Faye or Betty Grable in at least three pictures a year, and by those standards, Hutton was underworked—she was in only one or two a year at most. These were generally big-budget, full-color musicals, and in 1944–45 the studio was varying her between contemporary stories (like *Here Come the Waves*, in which she and leading man Bing Crosby were given a delicious Harold Arlen–Johnny Mercer score, and *The Stork Club*) and costumers (like *Incendiary Blonde* and *The Perils of Pauline*). The 1945 *Stork Club* gave Hutton two additional important songs: "A Square in the Social Circle," by Jay Livingston and Ray Evans, which became a signature for her (and later the title of her first LP album collection), and "Doctor, Lawyer, Indian Chief," by Hoagy Carmichael and Paul Francis Webster, which became a number-one hit single. Many of the final notes of certain lines are written with a descending two-note phrase ("There's a doctor living in your *to-wn*"), which Hutton twists downward in an apparent suggestion of Native American intonation.

In March 1944, she made her first commercial recording since 1939, the start of roughly two dozen sessions for Capitol. The two sides were the classic ballad "It Had to Be You" (which she sings in *Incendiary Blonde*) and the zany children's song "His Rockin' Horse Ran Away" (her big number in *And the Angels Sing*, in which she and Lamour were reunited as a sister act), which she sings partly in a "mean wittle kid" voice, thereby making her a sort of female Red Skelton (in addition to being a female Danny Kaye).

The dichotomy between the two songs (issued as Capitol single 155) was carried over into *Here Come the Waves*, in which she played twin sisters, one the straight leading lady (the Dorothy Lamour–Mary Martin role) and the other the madcap, zany Hutton, the same part she'd played in every picture up to now; leading man Crosby and second lead Sonny Tufts (Sonny Tufts?) both try to make it with the normal sister while trying to avoid the wacky one. Hutton was by now a sister act all by herself, and the schizophrenia running through her life wasn't always the comic kind.

She often deploys the two personas within the same song: "Rockin' Horse" opens with a poignant description of motherhood in the verse, sounding especially serious in order to contrast with the comic raillery that's coming; she does variations on this in "That's Loyalty" (from *Red, Hot and Blue*), "Doin' It the Hard Way" (from *Duffy's Tavern*), and "Stuff Like That There," among others. As historian Randy Skretvedt has noted, the only word for Hutton's performance style is "bipolar." In *Pauline*, she's by turns insanely manic on the novelty numbers like "The Sewing Machine" and "Rumble, Rumble, Rumble," and then excessively sentimental in her weepy sob-sister love scenes.

This is not true, however, of her ballad singing, which was absolutely first-rate. It's no surprise that Crosby and Tufts (who played her romantic lead proper in *Cross My Heart*, 1946) were crazy about the "normal" Hutton, competing for her affections in *Here Come the Waves*. She could sing love songs exquisitely when she wasn't gagging them up; her "I Wish I Didn't Love You So" (from *The Perils of Pauline*) was lovely enough to help that song garner an Oscar nom, and one particular sleeper favorite of mine is "Dixie Dreams," from her quickly forgotten final big picture, *Somebody Loves Me* (1952). When she's singing a ballad this well, Hutton is almost a dead ringer, vocally, for Ella Fitzgerald.

Betty Hutton played a key role in the history of the American musical in that she was the first notable star Frank Loesser wrote for as he made the transition from being exclusively a lyricist to a writer of both words and music. In *Happy Go Lucky*, Loesser and composer Jimmy McHugh wrote both "Murder, He Says" and "The Fuddy Duddy Watchmaker" for her and they both became hits. By comparison, the superior ballad "Let's Get Lost," which was not sung by Hutton, was itself quickly lost and disappeared from sight until Chet Baker

revived it a decade later. The lyricist—and now also composer—and star were reunited for *The Perils of Pauline*, which, as mentioned, included the hit ballad "I Wish I Didn't Love You So," and was such a smash that their collaboration was extended for two more pictures, *Red, Hot and Blue* (1949) and *Let's Dance* (1950). Admittedly not the most promising title, "The Fuddy Duddy Watchmaker" is classic Loesser-Hutton double-talk; she delivers it at about a million miles an hour.

This was the first of a series of "mechanical" songs by Loesser and Hutton: *Pauline* begins with "Sewing Machine," in which she verbally imitates the "bobbin the bobbin and pedal the pedal" of that contraption, and then "Rumble, Rumble, Rumble," in which she approximates the bass and treble of a boogie-woogie piano player. *Let's Dance* also starts with a bang: She's making like an air-raid siren (now she's the female Jerry Colonna!) and goes right into "Can't Stop Talking," with Hutton rat-tat-tatting Loesser's lyrics in superduper rapid fire. Duck! *Let's Dance* enjoys the dubious distinction of being perhaps Fred Astaire's least distinguished film; on the whole, it feels as if the great dancer was merely shoe-horned into a Hutton vehicle, and he never quite gets his bearings. I'm ashamed to admit it, but I barely notice Fred in "Can't Stop Talking." Hutton not only does all the singing in her usual domineering style—it's another one of those highly repetitious blasting songs—but she actually moves well enough to keep up with him.

The most extreme song that Loesser wrote for Hutton was "Hamlet," from *Red, Hot and Blue* and also, luckily, recorded for Capitol. On the most obvious level, it's part of the then established tradition of jiving up the classics of music and literature—there was no shortage of songs that lightly spoofed classic literary characters with hipster slang (Louis Prima's "Robin Hood," to name one). However, with "Hamlet" he is not so much spoofing Shakespeare as attacking the entire idea of historical hipsterism. Lines like "He chopped down [Ophelia's] father just to teach the girl a lesson / Yes, he cut him up in slices like a pound of delicatessen" make it clear that he is a master surrealist. Yet Loesser also supplied Hutton with excellent, more traditional show tuney production numbers like "Poppa, Don't Preach to Me" (in *Perils*) and beautiful ballads like "(Where Are You) Now That I Need You" (in *Red, Hot and Blue*), a lovely follow-up to "I Wish I Didn't Love You So."

Around 1950, Hutton briefly switched from Capitol to RCA, where she at last recorded "Murder, He Says." She also enjoyed a successful collaboration with the label's top-selling star, Perry Como; the most laid-back male singer and the most decidedly unrelaxed female performer in all of music made a hit out of "A Bushel and a Peck" from *Guys and Dolls*—which must have made Frank Loesser very happy. She also recorded two songs associated with

Nat King Cole, "Orange Colored Sky" and "That's the Kind of Guy I Dream Of (You Should See the Kind I Get)." It seemed as if Nat Cole's loudest note was Betty Hutton's softest, and that Cole's most inane song was Hutton's most sophisticated. (Cole actually recorded Loesser's "Tunnel of Love," which Hutton and Astaire had sung, not especially memorably, in *Let's Dance*.) In 1956, Hutton guested on Cole's TV show; they sang together, and even in black-and-white their "Orange Colored Sky" was something to see.

Hutton's most debated film is almost certainly the 1950 MGM version of *Annie Get Your Gun*, which is far from her best. It's hard to put one's finger on why. She just never strikes the appropriate note—her manic side is far too manic, and her tender side is never entirely on target either. The soundstage-bound nature of the production doesn't help make it any more believable. Hutton was at last enjoying her revenge on Ethel Merman, who had sabotaged her in *Panama Hattie* a decade earlier. Merman had created the role of Annie Oakley on Broadway and, in a perfect world, would have done the movie. Metro's first idea, and a good one it was, was Judy Garland as Annie, Frank Morgan as Buffalo Bill, and Busby Berkeley directing. By the time the picture was released, Hutton was Annie, Louis Calhern was Buffalo Bill, and George Sidney directed. Hutton has said in interviews that the MGM staff was hostile to her because she had involuntarily replaced the beloved Garland, and most film buffs feel the same way. Hutton sings the great score wonderfully—no one can fault what she does vocally on Irving Berlin's marvelous songs—but it just isn't her movie. The sound track, released relatively recently by Rhino Records (for whatever reason, she didn't make any commercial recordings of the Berlin songs for either Capitol or RCA), is more enjoyable than the film, particularly Hutton's performance of the cut song "Let's Go West Again." *Annie Get Your Gun* was a box office success, but it isn't a fondly remembered movie.

After the disappointment of *Annie*, Hutton's career seemed anticlimactic. There was one more big, big musical at Paramount, the 1952 *Somebody Loves Me*, in which she played a historical performer for the fourth time: After doing the life story of Texas Guinan (*Incendiary Blonde*), Pearl White (*The Perils of Pauline*), and Annie Oakley, audiences were now expected to believe Hutton as twenties headliner Blossom Seeley. One of the side benefits of the project was a nice batch of recordings of standards from the period, including a lovely, sensitive ballad treatment of the jazz perennial "Rose Room." She returned to Capitol in 1953, and among her later singles for the period is a big band treatment—with Nelson Riddle's orchestra, no less—of the R&B hit "Hot Dog! That Made Him Mad," by Danny and Blue Lu Barker.

In 1952, Hutton's career was boosted by Cecil DeMille's *The Greatest Show on Earth*; this circus backstage epic was a blockbuster hit, and Hutton was the top-billed leading lady. However, she didn't get to sing (it wasn't a musical) or do her usual comic shtick, and audiences neither then nor now regard it as a classic Betty Hutton movie. Her last big vehicle was *Satins and Spurs*, a 1954 TV production—listed in some reference books as the most "spectacular" original musical produced on the small screen up to that time. *Satins and Spurs* was a sort-of variation on *Annie Get Your Gun* and predecessor of Doris Day's *Calamity Jane* (cowgirl comes east, mingles with high society). Capitol actually went to the trouble of recording and releasing a 10" LP of Hutton doing eight songs from the score by Ray Livingston and Jay Evans. As a side benefit to both her second Capitol Records contract and the *Satins and Spurs* project, Capitol exec Alan Livingston became her third husband.

Unfortunately, *Satins* was a major disaster on every level. The only song that went anywhere was "You're So Right for Me," because Livingston and Evans recycled it a mere four years later for their Broadway musical *Oh Captain!* The failure of the production pretty much put the last nails in the coffin of Hutton's career. She announced her retirement, and while no more movie offers were forthcoming, she was welcomed in nightclubs. By 1955, when she became Mrs. Livingston, Hutton's recording career was winding down, although there was an interesting date in 1956 by the two Hutton sisters (recording together for the first time).

In 1957, Hutton made her last starring film, the B-level *Spring Reunion* as well as her only original LP album, the disappointing *Betty Hutton at the Saints and Sinners Ball* for Warner Bros. Not that her career was over: Like a lot of older leading ladies (she was in her late thirties), she was transitioning from movies and recordings to TV and theater in the late fifties and early sixties. As the very entertaining Hutton fan Web site SatinsAndSpurs.com informs us, Hutton was very busy on TV in the high years of the variety show and also was seen on Broadway in *Fade Out Fade In* as a replacement for Carol Burnett, as well as starring as Mama Rose in the road company of *Gypsy* (the young Bernadette Peters was one of Baby June's Hollywood Blondes).

Alas, there would be plenty of strife and upheaval over the last forty years or so of her life; both mental and economic breakdowns, balanced by a renewed faith in Catholicism and a return to school and higher education in her sixties. She died in 2007 at age eighty-six, having lived long enough to hear "It's Oh So Quiet" recycled by HBO into an ad campaign for *Sex and the City* and re-created by Björk; Tori Amos doing "Murder, He Says"; and "Stuff Like That There" redone by both Bette Midler and Kelly Clarkson. Her reputation was safe. None of these latter-day imitators and idolaters could fly anywhere near Betty Hutton's stratospheric orbit. Bang! Zoom!

Two Inimitables: Noel Coward and Marlene Dietrich

Sir Noel Coward (1899–1973)

My basic dilemma in talking about Noel Coward is whether to place him with his fellow singing songwriters (like Hoagy Carmichael, Harold Arlen, and Johnny Mercer) or his fellow British pan-media superstars of the thirties (Gracie Fields and Hutch). But then I'm fortunate that my own focus—Coward's recording career—is specific. Anyone talking about Coward in general would have to decide whether he was primarily a playwright, a composer, a lyricist, a poet, an actor, a director, a novelist and writer of short fiction; if you told me that, in addition to writing the book, music, and lyrics for his shows, as well as directing them and acting in them, he also built the scenery and sewed the costumes with his own hands, ushered the patrons to their seats and tended bar during the intermissions, I wouldn't be surprised. When he wasn't doing all that, he somehow managed to keep a diary (to keep track of the details of his various private lives), write copious letters, and, eventually, an epic three-volume autobiography. Coward was a unique figure in twentieth-century culture. (You can only compare him to that French prodigy Sacha Guitry.)

And he was also a recording artist. Coward first made it into a recording studio in August 1925 for two sessions of songs from his early revues *London Calling* and *On with the Dance*. Those sides, in which he was accompanied by a pianist identified only with the Cowardian name of "Miss April" (quite possibly a *Playboy* centerfold), were never issued. Three years later, he returned to the HMV facility in Middlesex for eight titles from *This Year of Grace* and *Bitter Sweet*, accompanied by the American pianist and bandleader Carroll Gibbons. Here is where Coward's recording career—and his status as one of the greatest singer-songwriters—begins in earnest: The 1928–29 sessions include such Coward classics as "A Room with a View," "Dance, Little Lady," "World Weary," and "Zigeuner." He sang in a pleasantly nasal, pinched voice that exuded insouciance and even detachment, as if he was too sophisticated to be ruffled by anything. When Duke Ellington, forty years later, created a spoken routine about a finger-snapping hipster, the idea was to appear so cool that "you just don't care." That was Noel Coward, on his comedy songs in particular—much too cool to care. As Coward's famous Mrs. Wentworth-Brewster might have asked, how can anyone "afford to be so la-di-*bloody*-da!"

Which is getting ahead of our story. "Destiny's Tot," as he was nicknamed, was born on the cusp of the twentieth century on December 16, 1899, in Teddington, a suburb of London. Coward's father was a piano salesman, which partially accounts for his early exposure to the instrument, and his grandfather was a naval officer (which possibly accounts

for his long history of songs about travel and sailing away, to say nothing of his wartime naval epic, *In Which We Serve*). Nearly everybody who ever crossed paths with Coward describes him as "sophisticated," but his upbringing seems to have been resolutely middle-class; his sophistication was something that he achieved for himself, as he constructed the character of Noel Coward one element at a time.

Coward's mother, Violet, is generally depicted as an archetypal stage parent of the "sing out, Louise!" variety; she sent him to dancing and acting schools at a very early age. He took to the theater as every little fish takes to swimming, and hardly needed his mum to crack any kind of whip over his head. By his early teens, their joint efforts had paid off, and he was a much-in-demand child actor on the London stage in the late Edwardian era. (Among other things, he appeared as one of the Lost Boys in several different productions of *Peter Pan*.)

Coward began experimenting with writing lyrics and then music as a teenager, and was hired by a publishing company to pen lyrics to other people's melodies around 1917–18. Like many lyricists on both sides of the pond, he was inspired by the new African American music of the World War I era, and his 1918 song "The Story of Peter Pan" has J. M. Barrie's pirates dancing to "that wonderful rag." The 1919 "Baseball Rag" (as with the other songs listed here, the lyrics appear in the essential collection *Noël Coward: The Complete Lyrics*, compiled by Barry Day) seems like an attempt to cram as much American culture into one tune as possible: There are references galore to syncopation and jazz, not to mention baseball.

He pursued writing plays and writing songs simultaneously and with equal fervor; in 1920, he had his first theater piece, *I'll Leave It to You*, produced on the West End, and though at best a modest success, the play made it to New York. Through the twenties, Coward wrote either straight plays or revues (i.e., collections of songs and sketches without a plot). In 1928, he wrote book, music, and lyrics and starred in the successful revue *This Year of Grace*, which played in London and New York. In 1929, he wrote the full-length, full-book operetta (which he deemed an "operette") *Bitter Sweet*. He began the thirties with his most intimate (and best-known) play, the classic *Private Lives* (containing a single song, the classic waltz "Someday I'll Find You"), which he followed with his biggest spectacle, the multigenerational, sprawling saga *Cavalcade* (which included the Coward classic "20th Century Blues").

He recorded steadily for HMV for twenty-five years, the results of which were collated by EMI in time for the Great Man's centennial in a four-CD box entitled *The Master's Voice—His HMV Record-*

ings, 1928–1953. As noted elsewhere, the British recording firms were much keener than their American counterparts to record musical theater stars and original casts. In Coward's case, he not only made straight-ahead vocal recordings of his signature songs from his shows but also participated in elaborately orchestrated, extralong medleys from various scores and, further, recorded key scenes from successful plays like *Cavalcade, Shadow Play,* and *Conversation Piece;* even the classic comedy song "Has Anybody Seen Our Ship?" concludes with some extramusical bickering that makes the whole affair even funnier. On the HMV selection from *Private Lives,* Coward's dialogue with preferred leading lady Gertrude Lawrence includes the two most famous lines of Coward's dramatic career.

He (upon hearing "Someday I'll Find You" played over and over): "That orchestra has a remarkably small repertoire."

She: "Extraordinary how potent cheap music is."

Extraordinary indeed.

In the case of the *Year of Grace* selections on HMV, Coward was recording songs that he had not only written but, for the most part, introduced himself in his own shows. Yet his 78s of his own songs were so well received that the label also had him record other show and film tunes of the period, notably Robin and Rainger's "Love in Bloom," in which he was essentially competing with Bing Crosby (and, eventually, with Jack Benny). This is a rare example of Coward singing (and doing an excellent job with) an all-purpose pop song; most of the other non-Noel songs that he recorded sound exactly like what he would have written, including Sam Coslow's "Fare Thee Well." He sang four songs by Jerome Kern, the American composer with whom his music has the most in common: "We Were So Young," "Just Let Me Look at You," "The Last Time I Saw Paris," and "I'm Old-Fashioned." The two with texts by Oscar Hammerstein II, "The Last Time I Saw Paris" and especially "We Were So Young," are remarkably Cowardy, both filled with built-in nostalgia for a long departed time and place, and "Just Let Me Look at You," with a more modern lyric by Dorothy Fields, is deeply tender. You would think that the most newfangled lyricist of all—for either Coward or Kern to be involved with—is Johnny Mercer, but "I'm Old-Fashioned" is a song about being old-fashioned. Coward, in fact, makes it even more old-fashioned by retooling the lyrics: Deciding that Mercer's line "The starry song that April sings" is too recherché, he changes it to "the daffodils that April brings." And he writes a whole new second chorus—which refers to his own dialogue from *Private Lives* as well as a hit British song of the World War II era: "I'm old fashioned / I love cheap music / The feeling of Spring in the air; / Moons and Junes, / Those sentimental tunes, / Those nightingales in Berkeley Square."

After listening to as many Coward recordings as possible, I've come across only one instance when he loses his cool: In 1955, he and Mary Martin appeared on CBS in a TV special titled *Together with Music.* When Ms. Martin makes a comic show of screwing up the lyrics to Puccini's "Un Bel Di," Coward sternly reprimands her, sounding like a very, very strict headmaster from a British public school. But like his dialogue in "Has Anyone Seen Our Ship?," he's not being Noel Coward here; he's playing a character—a martinet who busts Mary Martin's chops. One of the things that makes his comic songs so funny is that he sings them with such a detached air; by downplaying the comedy he makes it funnier. In "The Stately Homes of England" he sings about the most ridiculous occurrences with a totally straight face, as if the ghosts of murdered nuns and butchered babies were the most normal thing in the world. (Interestingly, Coward did not record "I've Been to a Marvelous Party" at the time—HMV possibly ruled it out as too scandalous even for Coward, with lines like "Young Bobbie Carr / Did a stunt at the bar / With a lot of extraordinary men"— although Beatrice Lillie did wax it for the Liberty Music Shop label.)

His approach to ballads was exactly the same: He never overdoes anything, he makes a sentimental song all the more effective by singing it as subtly as possible. Rather than sounding "sophisticated" or erudite or fancy, he sings everything as directly as possible without affectation of any kind. When he's supposed to be blasé—as on "World Weary" or "Weary of It All"—he communicates maximum feeling by revealing minimal emotion; it's tremendous in its intimacy. "I Travel Alone" sounds so much more moving—he doesn't wail and gnash his teeth, even though "the dream has ended and passion has flown"; he accepts his loneliness with a detached resignation, as if to say, "So what did you expect?" His old-fashioned waltzes—like "Where Are the Songs We Sung?," which are inevitably concerned with nostalgia for one's long-lost innocent youth—benefit from the same restraint.

Noel Coward is probably the only British playwright of his generation whose work is regularly revived; likewise, he is possibly the only British songwriter whose name and songs are known to subsequent generations. At the time, he was one of many exceptional British composers of theater and pop songs in the period, like Vivian Ellis, Ivor Novello, and Noel Gay, while Ray Noble was perhaps the most important British pop composer to rise from the ranks of the dance band business (like a Brit equivalent of Victor Young or Isham Jones).

As a composer, Coward was perhaps only a notch or so below the absolute top American writers—your Jerome Kerns and Cole Porters (or even Germany's Kurt Weill). Peter Matz, who served as Coward's conductor and arranger for his American projects in the fifties, told Barry Day that Coward "was not as literate musically as he was verbally. He played the piano okay, he didn't play any wrong notes, but he was limited harmonically. Since he didn't read or write music, he had to get somebody to write down what he composed."

Coward is often paralleled with America's Cole Porter, although career-wise they have little in common, since Porter was a songwriter, possibly the greatest ever, with little ambition to act, direct, star, or even perform his own songs. Porter was almost ten years older, but his music was several generations more harmonically complex (if you want to measure music that way).

Even though Porter was born in 1891, his music belongs to the same era as his younger twentieth-century New York colleagues, the Gershwin brothers and Rodgers and Hart. Coward, on the other hand, wrote sentimental songs in the same vein as the light operettas of Victor Herbert and Sigmund Romberg, while his comedy pieces come straight out of Gilbert and Sullivan. Coward modernizes these traditions considerably, but it's like dyed hair in which you can still see the roots. And he's often amazingly effective: Kern and Hammerstein's "The Last Time I Saw Paris" sounds overdramatic and badly dated today (although less so in Coward's sprightly 1941 recording), whereas Coward's "London Pride" is every bit as moving as it ever was.

Woody Allen famously observed that intellectuals were like the Mafia, in that they only kill their own. One viewpoint that Noel and Cole shared was the realization that the most sophisticated fashion in which to appear sophisticated is to dis other sophisticated folk—the way Porter describes the lifestyles of the rich and blasé in "Well, Did You Evah" and Coward does in "I've Been to a Marvelous Party." They both come across as upper-crusty in a way that Irving Berlin's similarly minded "Slumming on Park Avenue" and "A Couple of Swells" do not. Where Coward and Porter are attacking their own kind, Berlin sounds as if he's besieging the bourgeoisie from a distinctly lower-class vantage point.

But Sir Noel (he was knighted in 1969) savages the upper classes for a reason: At the heart of a Coward lyric is a yearning for a simpler, less sophisticated lifestyle, a universe of world-weary urbanites who want to get away from it all in some dear little café. Heroes and heroines of Coward lyrics are always poor little rich girls, dense old ladies, and Parisian Pierrots who are never quite as happy as they ought to be. And why is that? Because "the limbo is calling" while their star is falling, and youth is fleeting even as the rhythm is beating. Beneath the jaded sophisticate beats the heart of a hopeless sentimentalist.

"This Is a Changing World," as Coward wrote in his 1947 show *Pacific 1860*. After the war, Coward passed into a curious phase both musically and professionally. His classic older songs, particularly "Mad About the Boy," were increasingly popular and recognized as part of the Great American Songbook—they would turn up on albums alongside those of Porter, Berlin, Gershwin, Rodgers, Burke and Van Heusen, Mercer, Loesser et al. Perhaps the greatest compliment paid to Coward in the fifties was Carmen McRae's brilliant album *Mad About the Man*—not just because she showed that his songs were as universal as those of the major American writers, but because she relied entirely on his ballads and love songs, making the case that his work could stand on its own even without those patter and comedy numbers for which he was most famous. No Uncle Harrys, Wentworth-Brewsters, Mrs. Worthingtons, mad dogs, or Englishmen here.

Yet after the war Coward seemed unable to come up with a new musical show to rival his prewar smashes. He was now competing in the brave new world of post-*Oklahoma!* musical theater rather than revue or operetta. Alas, his two most ambitious full-book shows, *Pacific 1860* and *Ace of Clubs*, were both critical and commercial disappointments—and that's despite brilliant songs like "Changing World," "Chase Me, Charlie," "Sail Away," and "Why Does Love Get in the Way?," which were Coward classics. He could compete with Rodgers and Hart, apparently, but not with Rodgers and Hammerstein.

His greatest successes in the fifties and sixties were as a performer rather than as a writer-composer. It's said that Coward first explored the idea of doing a one-man show while entertaining the troops during the Second World War: Resolutely patriotic, he belittled the idea of showing mercy to the Nazis in "Don't Let's Be Beastly to the Germans." Still, he was nothing if not balanced: Coward seemed equally opposed to British imperialism, which he ridiculed with a light though biting touch most famously in "Mad Dogs and Englishmen" and "I Wonder What Became of Him." (He continued in a sarcastically political vein by attacking red-baiting British conservatives in "Imagine the Duchess's Feelings!" and "There Are Bad Times Just Around the Corner.")

The very idea of young soldiers being inspired by Noel Coward—rather than Dorothy Lamour or Marlene Dietrich—to go do battle with the Hun somehow seems very British. Coward introduced and polished his "cabaret" act at the Café de Paris in London throughout the early fifties, and, in spite of having written "There Are Bad Times Just Around the Corner" for the 1952 *Globe Revue* (the song was also his final recording for HMV, in 1953), the big payoff was, in fact, just around that very same corner.

Tony Bennett tells the story of how the future Sir Noel took America by storm in 1955. The key player was a legendary character who was as famous in his world as Coward was in his, the infamous Joe Glaser, the veteran impresario best remembered by history as Louis Armstrong's manager. Says Bennett: "There was a time when all the Las Vegas casinos were trying to top one another with name acts, at the Desert Inn, the Flamingo, the Sands, and all that. Some guy came up with Marlene Dietrich. So another guy says, 'I want Noel Coward.' They said, 'You can't get Noel Coward.' So Joe Glaser heard about this and he said, 'Do you mind if I try to get Noel Coward for you?' So they said, 'Okay.' So Joe Glaser gets on the phone overseas. [At this point, Tony goes into an impression of Glaser's Chicago gangster accent.] 'Hello, Mr. Coward. This is Joe Glaser. I'm Louis Armstrong's manager.' 'Yes?' He said, 'The Desert Inn would like to have you for $60,000.' He said, 'I'll take it.' And they got Noel Coward in there. Columbia made a great album of that, with a wonderful cover, Noel Coward with the teacup, standing in the middle of the desert."

Coward's biographers only differ with Tony's account in the details. According to Barry Day, the figure offered was $35,000 a week, which was still a lordly sum of money in 1955, especially as the initial run was four weeks, $140,000 total, to appear at Wilbur Clark's Desert Inn. Glaser flew to London to catch Coward's act at the Café de Paris and seal the deal. As Coward recalled: "The prospect of this engagement filled me with misgivings because, although I had proved that my sophisticated songs and apparently even more sophisticated personality could go down all right with the *crème de la crème* of London Café Society, I doubted that the less urbane cross-section of Americans who frequented Las Vegas with the main objective of gambling would understand and appreciate the essential 'Englishness' of my material and my performance. My fears, however, were unfounded. From the first dinner show onwards, when I made my entrance with brisk outward assurance and inner panic, the audiences in that strange desert playground received me with the utmost generosity, attention and enthusiasm."

Coward was Americanized in one key aspect. His musical director, Norman Hackforth, was denied a work visa, and friend Marlene Dietrich steered Coward to a young arranger and conductor named Peter Matz. As Coward's companion Graham Payn related, "Pete took one look at Noel's [old] orchestrations and said, 'You're not going to use these, are you?' Noel was quick enough to say, 'No, I want you to re-orchestrate all the songs.'" When one compares the versions of the Coward classics on his HMV recordings of 1953 and earlier with those on his two 1955–56 Columbia albums, the difference, to defer to Cole Porter, is like night and day.

The best of the earlier HMV orchestrations are perfect for their time, just as the Matz orchestrations are perfect for the fifties. Matz essentially reinvented Coward and his classic songs for a new era. Payn added, "Pete modernized the material, changing tempos, making the sound fuller without drowning Noel out. By comparison, the older arrangements sounded like an English lounge trio, complete with a singer whose high notes might break at any time."

As Bennett suggests, *Noel Coward at Las Vegas* is a delight, from its iconic teacup-and-sand cover on:

Coward standing in the desert, sipping Earl Grey and looking the very picture of a mad dog of an Englishman out in the midday sun. Yet he never seems like he's slumming, he's never being a snobby Brit who condescends to bring a little class to the joint. Rather, Coward, who spent his career deflating snobs and sophisticates, was a true populist and thus was delighted to bring his comic songs ("A Bar on the Piccola Marina") as well as his sentimental ballads ("A Room with a View") to appreciative, overwrought gamblers and the dames who loved them. Thanks to Coward and Matz, everything on both the American Columbia albums strikes precisely the right note.

The *Vegas* album captured a renewed Noel Coward, still the embodiment of the charm of the best of the Old World but now also reinvigorated with the energy and audacity of the New. It did so well for Columbia that producer Goddard Lieberson decided to do a second album, this time in New York and in a studio (as opposed to live). *Noel Coward in New York* opens with "I Like America"; this ode to the Great 48 is not, however, renewed or reinvented, but actually made to work right for the first time. Graham Payn, who introduced it in *Ace of Clubs*, said that neither he nor Noel himself could make the song work for them properly, and they gave it up for dead until "Peter Matz's clever arrangement transformed it." Perhaps this, too, had something to do with the location, as here was a song that was obviously going to play better in the States than in the U.K.

It made perfect sense for Coward to include "Mad Dogs and Englishmen" in the *Vegas* album and follow it up with "I Wonder What Happened to Him" on *New York*. Both songs seemed relevant in the age of Gandhi and Nehru, after Hitler gave a bad name to the concept of world domination. More curious is the decision to include "Half-Caste Woman," a lady who fits the profile of what African American film historian Donald Bogle has identified as the "tragic mulatto" figure, which may seem out of date at a time when Eisenhower and the Supreme Court were about to integrate the public school system. That aspect of this 1931 song is indeed dated— the idea that being what they used to call "of mixed blood" automatically makes the poor girl a "strange and tragic" figure. To his credit, however, Coward avoids dwelling upon her racial background (apart from a fleeting reference to her "slanting eyes"). Rather, the Half-Caste Woman turns out to be another of Coward's Poor Little Parisian Pierrettes who face the music and dance.

Speaking of culture clash, one of the more memorable moments in the *Las Vegas* album is Coward's so-called update of the traditional Scottish air "Loch Lomond." This was a likely target for him, since it was the most famous folk song to be given the American swing treatment when, back in 1937, Maxine Sullivan subtly swung it with a gentle bounce. Coward, however, is sending up a send-up, taking a swing, so to speak, at anyone who would have the impertinence to tamper with such a classic. It works on many levels, and it's a grand example of Coward tinkering with a preexisting song and making it just as funny as one of his own patter-party pieces. Another is his update of "Let's Do It," the most famous of many readings and many updates he gave to Porter's 1928 classic, which he crammed with dozens of references—topical, political, biological, cultural, and sexual: "Liberace—we assume—does it."

Coward's last two major projects brought him back to full-scale musical theater and Broadway. *Sail Away* (1961) seemed somewhat old-fashioned, even old-hat, for the times (despite lyrics that were wittier than anything heard on Broadway in many a season), while *The Girl Who Came to Supper* (1963) wasn't even trying to be up-to-date.

Neither *Sail* nor *Girl* found an audience—even though *Sail* had particularly rich songs and Elaine Stritch besides. Yet Coward still triumphed as a performer: The composer's demo recordings of the scores to both shows were posthumously released commercially, and Coward's performances are much more enjoyable than the original cast albums and, one imagines, the actual shows themselves.

In the *Sail Away* songs in particular, the composer's demos are among his finest moments on record. When he wasn't writing about royal romance, it seemed as if world travel was his favorite theme—beginning with "World Weary" or even "Has Anybody Seen Our Ship?," a disproportionate share of his songs were about traveling somewhere, almost always on ships. (Romantic notions about railroads, as in Johnny Mercer's "On the Atchison, Topeka and Santa Fe," were primarily an American conceit.) "The Passenger's Always Right," "Useless Useful Phrases," and "Why Do the Wrong People Travel?" are among Coward's funniest patter tunes, and "Later Than Spring" shows that he could still effectively turn on the sentiment and charm in waltz time. "The Little Ones' ABC" is a tour de force written for Stritch but is even funnier when Coward sings it.

On the original Broadway cast album, "Beatnik Love Affair" comes off as incredibly square—like Gordon McRae trying to be Mark Murphy. Broadway never could and never would be able to pull off that kind of hip, not even when Cy Coleman was writing the music heard in the show. "Beatnik Love Affair" makes the point that Coward should have stuck to writing dear little waltzes in dear little cafés. But to hear the songwriter sing it, with his characteristic coolness, the song becomes über-hip, his own brilliant triple and quadruple rhymes come trippingly off the tongue, with a gloriously syncopated bongo rhythm ("upright / downright / watertight / dynamite"). Coward is instantly more hep than Jack Kerouac and Maynard G. Krebs put together, with a touch of Snoop Dogg thrown in for good measure.

He could have been billed as "the Notorious N.O.E.L."

His demo recordings for these two shows allowed him to end his career as a performer on a high note. He lived in Jamaica for his final years, having sailed away from Broadway and the West End, where he left the composing to others (famously with *High Spirits*, a 1964 musical based on his play *Blithe Spirit*, with a score by Hugh Martin and Timothy Gray); he died there in 1973. He had occasionally returned to London or New York for special occasions, as when he was made a Knight of the British Empire in 1969. One of his very last appearances on a commercial record was as a special guest with opera superstar Joan Sutherland on her 1966 LP *Songs from Noël Coward*, in which he delivered some of the essential dialogue from *Bitter Sweet* on "I'll Follow My Secret Heart."

Where contemporaries like Irving Berlin and Cole Porter thought of themselves as having outlived their own era—and surviving into an age when their songs were no longer likely to be sung by teenagers or heard on AM radio—Coward lived to enjoy a renaissance in his final decade. His plays were regularly revived, and his songs collected into new revues: *Noël Coward's Sweet Potato* opened in New York in 1968, followed by the British *Cowardy Custard* and the American *Oh, Coward!*, both from 1972. He also lived to see his work become part of the British and world cultural landscape, an influence on everyone from the Beatles to Monty Python. It's easy to imagine George Harrison's "Piggies" being sung in a Noel Coward voice; likewise, on "The Penis Song," Eric Idle saved us the trouble and recorded it in deliberately Cowardesque cadences—it was a homage, and not a parody. Suddenly, everybody wanted to throw a party where they honored Noel Coward.

After his opening at the Desert Inn, Coward noted in his diary that the Las Vegas engagement was "one of the most reverberant successes I have ever had. I am really proud and pleased that I succeeded in doing what no one suspected I could, and that is please ordinary audiences." The very fact that he acknowledged the existence of "ordinary" audiences—as opposed to the swells who came to see him at the Café de Paris—shows that there was something of an elitist about Coward (well, hel-*lo!*), but he certainly makes it clear that he would rather appeal to Joe Sixpack than to the champagne-and-caviar crowd. When he uttered his famous dictum in *Private Lives*, he was offering an obvious joke at his own expense, but also being serious. Any jackass could write so-called sophisticated songs for the upper crust, but it took a sage like Coward to fully appreciate the potency of cheap music.

Marlene Dietrich (1901–1992)

There were other major musical leading ladies besides Alice Faye; she was merely the best and the most emblematic. There were other actresses whose native habitats were islands and jungles, but none shared the humor and musicality of Dorothy Lamour. There were other funny ladies (Martha Raye, Cass Daley) who sang both ballads and swingers, but none had Betty Hutton's career—or her energy. And while we're on the subject, the overwhelming success of Shirley Temple inspired other studios to try all kinds of child performers: Bobby Breen, who starred in eight RKO features between 1936 and 1939, Deanna Durbin and then Gloria Jean at Universal, even Judy Garland at Metro. Apart from Breen, they all were teens and tweens (in the contemporary parlance), but they had one thing in common: They were presented by studios hustling for a chunk of that Temple action.

But even in an age when Hollywood copied anything that worked—there was every kind of low-rent Clark Gable and Joan Crawford—there was only one Marlene Dietrich. No one else was like her. She wasn't even an archetype. She was one of the leading dramatic actresses at the height of the Depression, making a series of erotic romances that were further charged by heavy use of music. She sustained her popularity through the war years, playing a romantic lead into her fifties, and, indeed, kept going right to the very end of the studio system. Then, when her kind of moviemaking was finished, she extended her career for several decades, taking to the road with a one-woman show that she performed all over the world. It was if she started her career like Greta Garbo and then, halfway through, became Judy Garland; the key difference is that she had a longer and more productive career in both phases than either of them.

Dietrich died in May 1992, the same month that Johnny Carson left *The Tonight Show*. The two facts are unrelated, except that in one of Carson's last shows, Bette Midler was a guest. This being the early nineties, the number-one female singer of the period was Madonna, and Midler humorously claimed credit for an "innovation" that was, at the time, associated with Madonna—namely, the idea of a female singer lounging in her lingerie. Midler, who attracted some attention at the start of her own career by describing her act as "Trash with Flash, Sleaze with Ease," had, as she claimed, performed in her drawers. Still, she was going a bit far when she told Carson, "I invented underwear!"

Midler was somehow forgetting that Marlene Dietrich sang "Falling in Love Again" resplendent in girdle and garters in the 1930 *Blue Angel*. The image of her attired thus, a man's top hat on her head and letting you see whatever you wanted, was a dominant icon of early sound cinema. In truth, it's Marlene, not Midler, not Madonna, not even Monroe, who triumphs as the seductress of the century.

Eyes gazing out into the audience, Dietrich's Lola Lola tells us in song that she's "Falling in love again / Never wanted to / Can't help it." Lola is the helpless victim of desires behind her control, a deeply complicated German concept that the American lyricist Sammy Lerner summed up succinctly with that three-beat phrase, "Can't help it." In "Hot Voodoo," Dietrich's opening number from her 1932 classic *Blonde Venus*, she sings of how the African "tom-toms" put her under a spell, powerless to stop herself from dancing, sinning, loving; it's the rhythm and the intoxicating spell of the music that renders her out of control, no longer responsible for her actions.

For years, it was believed that in real life Dietrich herself wasn't in control of her own professional destiny either: She was purely the product of the machinations of director-auteur-demigod Josef von Sternberg. The usual comparison was to Trilby and Svengali. Von Sternberg himself supported that idea when he described Dietrich as his personal "bird of paradise." But, as the smoke cleared after her death, it became more and more obvious that the Dietrich persona was strictly the supreme creation of no one but Dietrich herself.

Born in Berlin in 1901, she studied violin as a child but gave it up after injuring her wrist. However, that early musical training would serve her well. She spent the twenties in three distinct pursuits as a performer: the traditional form of acting, using her voice but not singing, in German translations of Shaw and Shakespeare and contemporary Berlin plays; acting, with her face and not her voice, in silent films; and singing in the famous Weimar era cabaret shows and theatrical revues. By 1930, Dietrich had the experience and talent to combine these three formerly separate talents into the skills necessary to succeed in the new medium of talking pictures.

The Blue Angel was all that and a bag of chips: There had been a few serious musicals in America up to then, notably Rouben Mamoulian's groundbreaking *Applause*, but generally the all-talking, all-singing, all-dancing picture was a playground for fun and frivolity. *The Blue Angel* presented Dietrich as a talking picture singer-actress the likes of whom hadn't really been seen anywhere in the world. As a top-hatted, garter-gammed siren who lures a staid professor onto the rocks, Dietrich was both an instant international sensation and an icon for the ages. Before 1930 was over, both Dietrich and von Sternberg were transplanted to Paramount in Hollywood, where they turned out a series of the most elegantly seductive pictures of the early sound era. (The third member of the collaboration was musical director Frederick Hollander, composer of the score to *Blue Angel*, who did for Dietrich musically what von Sternberg did for her visually.)

The German boxed set *Der Blonde Engel* contains, among other real rarities, an audition disc that Dietrich made for the German film company UFA in 1928. She sings "You're the Cream in My Coffee," the first of many American novelty songs she would do over the years. Apparently, she only knows eight bars of the song in English, and sings this one section over and over, interspersed with a temper tantrum in *Deutsch;* if she's acting, it's a helluva job. Between singing the same four lines over and over and the yelling and screaming, the disc has a compellingly Dadaesque quality.

Dietrich cut her first commercial recording in Berlin that same year and recorded a respectable twenty-three titles between then and 1933; even after she had established herself in Hollywood, she continued to record in Europe. (Not coincidentally, that's where most of her 78s have also been reissued on compact disc, on compilations like the recommended *Marlene Dietrich: 1928–1933.* Germany was apparently way ahead of Hollywood in terms of understanding the synergy of having film stars record the songs written for them in pictures.)

Dietrich recorded Hollander's entire score for *Blue Angel*—and very well, too, in multiple languages. But after that, film-to-disc coverage was spotty and decidedly Eurocentric: two songs from *Morocco,* "Quand l'amour meurt" and "Give Me the Man," and one, Hollander's "Jonny," from *Song of Songs.* That was about it. Considering that "Falling in Love Again" (which became her career-long signature song) and "Jonny" were megahits in Europe, one has to wonder why the domestic companies weren't more enterprising. "Jonny" is even more effective on the German recording than in the film; she positively coos this minor key song of seduction. It's one of the most erotic performances ever put on wax.

Even though Dietrich's films weren't exactly musicals—in the sense that Crosby's or Faye's were—Dietrich's singing, and her musical numbers, were a key element. In *Blonde Venus,* she sings three terrific songs (by Leo Robin, Ralph Rainger, and Sam Coslow): After her famous entrance with "Hot Voodoo," in which she becomes the gorilla of our dreams (actually, the Harpo Marx fright wig she dons after removing the monkey suit is considerably more horrifying), she also sings "You Little So-and-So" and "I Couldn't Be Annoyed." *The Devil Is a Woman* has two songs, "Then It Isn't Love" and "Three Sweethearts Have I" (recorded for American Decca but never released), and so does *Desire,* in "Awake in a Dream" and "Desire." Unfortunately, none of these was heard on commercial waxings.

In 1939, Dietrich appeared opposite James Stewart in the classic anti-Western *Destry Rides Again,* which, on the eve of World War II, put forth a pacifist (though hardly isolationist) notion that dangerous situations can be resolved without warfare. She liked to say that the only thing her audiences wanted was to see her in cowboy drag singing "The Boys in the Backroom," which she also recorded for Decca. This boisterous faux-Western song by Frank Loesser, with overtones of both Brecht and Kipling, capturing every aspect of Dietrich's seductive, fatalist personality (at once narcissistic and nihilistic), is set to a bouncy 2/4 beat. (The *Blonde Engel* box includes a German version titled "Gib Doch Den Männern Am Stammtisch Ihr Gift.")

It wasn't until long after the war that a record producer had the foresight to see the possibilities of what Dietrich could really do on disc. The much maligned (admittedly, even by me) Mitch Miller taped roughly two dozen titles with Dietrich for Columbia in the early fifties (around the same time the label was also rediscovering such intercontinental pan-sexuals as Noel Coward and Tallulah Bankhead). Columbia released some of these at the time on an early LP titled *Marlene Dietrich Overseas,* and then, forty years later, around the time of the diva's death, gathered sixteen tracks onto *The Cosmopolitan Marlene Dietrich.* During the war, Dietrich had made special propaganda broadcasts on behalf of the Allies, beamed directly at the German troops. One of Miller's best ideas was to document and preserve the special German-style arrangements that Dietrich had sung of American pop songs in German.

If you only know Dietrich's vocals from her Hollywood films, the fifties recordings will be a major surprise. Like a lot of pop singers, she tends to go flat when she's singing in a language that isn't her native tongue. (For opera and classical singers, it's a different story.) But when Dietrich sings in German, her voice becomes remarkably resonant and her intonation improves tremendously. Even in English, Dietrich could croak in dark, sultry tones, but in German—even when singing American pop songs like "Mean to Me," "I Couldn't Sleep a Wink Last Night," and especially "Time on My Hands"—she gains a sense of lightness and subtlety one never would have assumed possible from her movie singing.

Jimmy Carroll, who directed most of the accompaniment on her Columbia sessions, assists her by backing her with a traditional European chanson or musette orchestra, relying heavily on concertina and an occasional small string section. This kind of backdrop tends to bring out her latent musicality much better than an American-style dance band. She's particularly compelling on "Time on My Hands," delivered with far more subtlety and restraint than any of her imitators, rivals, or parodists could imagine, singing Vincent Youmans's melody with just enough power and passion to make it completely convincing.

Dietrich shows why the verb "interpret" has two meanings: We generally use it in this book for a singer who brings out the inner meaning of a lyric, but it also refers to the process of translating words from one language to another. In her German treatments of American songs, Dietrich does both at once. Rodgers and Hammerstein's "Surrey with the Fringe on Top" originally clip-clopped through the flat plains of *Oklahoma!,* but Dietrich makes it sound like a one-horse open sleigh traversing the

Austrian Alps. Cole Porter infused "Miss Otis Regrets" with an element of camp humor, but Dietrich makes it sound like one of Brecht and Weill's love-and-degradation numbers in the mold of "Surabaya Johnny." "Takin' a Chance on Love," like the rest of the score to *Cabin in the Sky*, took place in an unnamed town in the American South, but Dietrich relocates the action to a Berlin beer garden.

And then there are the novelty songs. Who else remembered the 1933 "Annie Doesn't Live Here Anymore" twenty years later? Dietrich transforms it into a noirlike intrigue of mystery and forbidden desires via her Rhineland rhetoric. When she reprises one of Mae West's period signatures, "A Guy What Takes His Time," she takes the time to sing it in better English than the legendary Mae, as "A Guy *Who* Takes His Time."

Dietrich also enjoyed chart success, believe it or not, with a set of extreme novelties, produced by Mitch Miller and co-starring Rosemary Clooney. Miller told me he was deliberately looking for something as offbeat and incongruous as possible for Clooney and Dietrich and came up with the idea of combining them on a country and western comedy song titled "Too Old to Cut the Mustard." Keyboardist Stan Freeman had already helped turn Clooney's "Come on-a My House" into a blockbuster hit by playing harpsichord, and Miller had him reprise his role on this tale of age and condiments. "Mustard" was such a success that Dietrich and Clooney cut a total of six songs together, which may sound like a very short album, but believe you me, six of these songs are more than you want to hear. One of the Dietrich-Clooney follow-ups, "Dot's Nice, Donna Fight," is even more of a sequel to "Come on-a My House" in that the German goddess and the Irish-American pop star cut this particular mustard in faux-Italian.

Dietrich's last regular starring role in a Hollywood feature was another off-Western—although very different in tone from *Destry:* the 1952 *Rancho Notorious*. (There would be supporting roles, cameo appearances, foreign films, and other screen shots over the next thirty years.) Dietrich was by now both the world's sexiest grandmother and the most international of all entertainers. She spent the next twenty years headlining in high-ticket nightclubs from Paris to Las Vegas and even Australia. Her subsequent recordings were mostly offshoots of her live appearances, in which she continued to balance signature songs, torch tunes, and screwy novelties (like "I Refuse to Rock and Roll," heard on the *Blonde Engel* box). For a time, she toured with Stan Freeman as her accompanist; later, Burt Bacharach temporarily abandoned his already successful career as a pop hit writer to spend a few years on the road with her.

She taught him more about life than he could ever have learned at the Brill Building.

The single most meaningful song Dietrich ever sang was, ironically, not specifically written for her, nor ever sung by her in a picture. "Lilli Marlene" (a song spelled several ways in both German and English) entered the world as a poem written by a German veteran of the First World War, with music added shortly before the Nazis marched into Poland in 1939. It was originally recorded by the German songstress Lale Andersen that year, and found a second life a few years later. As alluded to above, at the height of World War II, American stars like Glenn Miller, Bing Crosby, Dinah Shore, and, most especially, Dietrich—who was by now more resolutely American than any of them—were broadcasting American pop songs directly at the Germans as a kind of apple-pie soft propaganda. We fired "Long Ago and Far Away," "You'll Never Know," "Night and Day," and dozens of others at the Jerries, but the only song that came back in retaliation was "Lilli Marlene."

Marlene Dietrich was such a committed, lifelong anti-Nazi that she had to be coaxed into portraying an SS sweetie in Billy Wilder's *A Foreign Affair*. When "Lilli Marlene" came her way, she immediately realized that here was a way to take one of the Nazis' own morale-boosters and turn it against them. She began singing it, first as a request for American troops, in English as "Lilli Marlene," then for German POWs, and eventually as a musical weapon against her former countrymen.

She eventually recorded it in both languages for Columbia with two very differerent arrangements (both are on the *Cosmopolitan* collection), and curiously, the English version ("Lili Marlene") is more severe, with a military band intro that suggests Lili is about to face the firing squad. In contrast, the German version ("Lili Marleen") uses a soft and tasteful accordion; German may be a harsher language to most, but Dietrich's German-language "Lili" is much more tender and loving. Yet it didn't matter which language she sang it in. The Andersen original was more clearly a march, and was über-Nazi—that's the only way to describe it. Dietrich crooned it softly and sweetly, with a perfect balance of passion and restraint. Several generations later, during the Vietnam conflict, the pop market would be flooded with all kinds of antiwar songs, but in Dietrich's hands, "Lili Marleen" remains the most powerful and moving antiwar song ever written. And the saddest.

No less an authority on the subject of war—not to mention female beauty—than Ernest Hemingway once stated that Dietrich "has that beautiful body and the timeless loveliness of her face"; however, he went on, "But if she had nothing but her voice, she could still break your heart with it."

Fats's Femme Followers

Lee Morse
Ramona
Cleo Brown
Lil Hardin Armstrong
Una Mae Carlisle
Julia Lee
Nellie Lutcher
Rose Murphy
Hadda Brooks

"How would you like to submit to a blindfold test, listen to a typical Fats Waller song, then when the bandage was removed find that seated at the keyboard, instead of the 200 pounds of brown-skinned masculinity you expected, was a light, slim, smiling girl?" Those were the words of Leonard Feather, writing in 1937, describing his first experience hearing Una Mae Carlisle. At that time, Feather and his readers may have been somewhat surprised to make this discovery, but within a few years it would be obvious to everyone that Fats Waller's most important followers were female. For whatever reason, it's hard to think of a major male singer-pianist to fill the gap between Waller and Nat Cole.

In the mid- to late thirties, Waller (1904–1943) was the central figure in the jukebox-driven small combo movement, in which dozens of singing musicians made hundreds of records that were distributed to thousands of restaurants, bars, and roadhouses across the country, which collectively raked in millions of nickels. The juke records generally allotted a generous amount of solo space to instrumental soloists, and the central point of each was a vocal chorus by the singing leader, most of whom were heavily influenced by Louis Armstrong, Fats Waller, or both.

Except for Waller, hardly any of the juke singer-leaders were composers themselves; a key driving force of the movement was the pressure from publishers to feature new songs from Tin Pan Alley, Broadway, and Hollywood. In fact, these discs, in addition to documenting the playing of many key soloists from the swing era, also serve as valuable evidence of the state of the art of American songwriting at its zenith, and that's even though the songs included a few of the worst as well as many of the best.

Waller was at the center of the juke boom, yet, curiously, there were few directly Wallerian pianist-entertainers. There was Putney Dandridge on Vocalion and Bob Howard on Decca; the latter only occasionally played piano on records, although he was sometimes billed as "Fatso Howard."

But the most substantial of Fats's followers were a quartet of African American females, one of whom was actually two years older than Waller himself. All four participated in the juke jazz movement, but they also were part of other developments in African

American music, including swing, big bands, blues, and, most notably, the evolution of "race" music into rhythm and blues. Like Waller, they all were exceptional pianists, and they sang in a wide range of styles that could be traced back to Waller himself: Cleo Brown and especially Rose Murphy sang in a sweet, high voice that recalled Waller in his rare moments of straightforward ballad tenderness. Julia Lee, by contrast, had more of a guttural, blues-based style that suggests Fats at his downest and dirtiest. Like Waller, they were all consistently irreverent, and as much inclined to kid a love song, using humorous asides, as they were to sing it straight.

Lee Morse (1897–1954) and
Ramona (1909–1972)

There were at least a few notable female pianist-singers in the twenties and early thirties; two prominent (white) women who come to mind are Lee Morse and Ramona Davies, who was billed by her first name only. Ms. Morse recorded around two hundred songs between 1924 and 1932, and her wares are nicely sampled in Take Two's *Lee Morse: A Musical Portrait*. Hers was an idiosyncratic style that combined pop with twenties style hot jazz as well as what was then called "hillbilly music"; in fact, her band was billed as "Lee Morse and Her Bluegrass Boys." Morse's best music offers evidence that the stylistic boundaries between these various forms, which would become more rigid in later generations, were remarkably flexible and fluid in the pre-Depression period. It's fairly common for Morse to yodel, country-style, in the middle of a Tin Pan Alley anthem (like the 1927 "Side by Side") or stretch a note and moan like Jimmie Rodgers.

Ramona (born Estrild Raymona Myers) is principally known for her work with bandleader Paul Whiteman, not only singing with his orchestra but on a series of small band dates done under the Whiteman imprimatur with some of the big band's key players. Ramona's overall sound is more reminiscent of a theater soprano of the period than of a blues or jazz singer, even when she's singing in tempo or scatting, and her singing is sometimes slightly flat. (This is a rare complaint to level against a pianist-singer—you would think knowing her way around a keyboard would help her sing in tune.) Yet she left us with several dozen worthy period recordings of some very essential songs between 1932 and 1936. (The 1998 CD *Ramona and Her Grand Piano*, on the Old Masters label, is easily recommended.)

Cleo Brown (1909–1995) and
Lil Hardin Armstrong (1898–1971)

The prolific careers of Lee Morse and Ramona are just two examples of female pianist-singers who existed before 1934; but that year, when RCA Victor launched the Fats Waller and His Rhythm series, the genre as a whole was reinvented from the ground up. The success of Waller's Rhythm discs had a double-pronged effect: Like Louis Armstrong before him, Waller inspired many an instrumentalist—piano players in particular—to start singing. At the same time, the record labels and song publishers decided that snappy small group recordings, driven by a jocular, powerful personality, were just the thing to fill the jukeboxes that were then being installed in bars, restaurants, and roadhouses across the country. Juke discs could be sold at a profit for 35 cents, which, at five cents a play, were a solid investment for these venues. Patrons would hear the new songs in a movie or on the radio and then start dropping nickels in the slots to dance to the same songs in these informal settings. It was more of a bargain than going dancing in an actual nightspot with a live band, and also cheaper than buying the records and taking them home.

By 1935, all of Victor's competitors were releasing lively discs by small groups, which often featured many of the key soloists who were also working nightly in the big bands. The most celebrated series, after Waller's, was the Teddy Wilson and His Orchestra line on ARC, in which the young Billie Holiday did most of the singing.

In 1935, Decca launched a series by Dick Robertson, a veteran session singer, who had a knack for getting a lyric out with a clear, empathetic voice. The Robertson sessions featured many key white players; he had particular luck with trumpeters, since both Bunny Berigan and Bobby Hackett turn up on his dates. Decca also produced a string of sessions spotlighting the Wallerian singer (and occasional pianist) Bob Howard, which, in turn, featured many of the major black swing musicians; Benny Carter, Buster Bailey, Teddy Wilson, Cozy Cole, and Clarence Holiday (the guitarist who was Billie Holiday's father) all play on Howard's first Decca session, in January 1935.

But when, two months later in March, Decca recorded the first session by Cleo Brown, something new had unquestionably been added. Trumpeter-singer Scat Davis, Bob Howard, and especially Dick Robertson were all, to a degree, known commodities in the record business, but this was the first time Brown had been in a recording studio. She was somewhat known on the radio; she had, in fact, come to New York expressly to fill in for Fats Waller on CBS when the Portly One was summoned to Hollywood to make his first film.

Brown was born in Mississippi in 1909, where her father was the pastor of the Pilgrim Baptist Church, but she grew up in Chicago. As she later told Whitney Balliett, she studied piano from an early age, but her parents forbade her to play jazz and blues and other species of that Devil music. To her chagrin, her brother was already making $25 a week playing piano and consorting with such stars of the music as the legendary Pinetop Smith himself. Brown was not allowed to do as she wished until she left home at a very young age to get married and raise her son, LaVern. She worked as a solo act and in a band called the Nine Blackbirds, which took her as far afield as Canada, but she was back in Chicago when she got the call to come to New York and substitute for Fats Waller on his radio show, which apparently brought her to the attention of Decca.

Right off the bat, Brown's first date produced five amazing tracks. She was an immediate hit with a genuinely swinging version of a popular novelty called "(Lookie! Lookie! Lookie!) Here Comes Cookie" and a cheery love song called "You're a Heavenly Thing," as well as "I'll Take the South," an ode to Dixie's charms (cotton fields and Mammy's arms) by a pair of songwriters who had probably never been south of Brooklyn. Then there was one of publisher-composer Clarence Williams's many odes to getting high, "The Stuff Is Here and It's Mellow."

Although the inspiration was obviously Fats Waller, there was one immediate difference: Waller's sessions always featured two or three heavy-duty saxophone or trumpet soloists, but Brown's dates utilized rhythm sections only. The March 1935 date backed the newcomer with a highly accomplished (and, coincidentally, Caucasian) rhythm section: drummer Gene Krupa, about to be famous for his work with Benny Goodman; bassist Artie Bernstein, who would join Goodman a few years hence; and Perry Botkin (who would spend many years accompanying Bing Crosby) on guitar. Between the absence of horns and the singer's higher-pitched voice, the Brown series was, on the whole, much lighter than the Waller Rhythm discs. Everything feels faster and higher on Brown's sides, even though she uses the same kind of coloration in her singing, having developed a wide vocabulary of growls and purrs and other devices to animate her vocals.

As a kind of bonus track, Brown recorded a fifth side on the first session. After the rhythm section had packed up, she cut a solo treatment of the basic "Boogie Woogie" by Pinetop Smith, reprising the late pianist's famous narration. Brown was ahead of the curve here, as boogie-woogie wouldn't become a national trend for at least two years, and it wasn't until still later that nearly all the major black female pianists would specialize in boogie. Brown recorded another piano solo, "Pelican Stomp," at the end of a date in May, in which she appeared as the only black performer in a lineup billed as "the Decca All Star Revue." Along with Bob Crosby, Scat Davis, Ella Logan, and the Tune Twisters vocal group, she sang part of "Way Back Home," a much plugged tune of 1935 that didn't quite become a standard.

She did her own second date in June 1935, followed by only two more sessions going up to April 1936 and resulting in a total of eighteen titles (not counting the two-sided "Way Back Home"). Nearly every title is something special: "Mama Don't Want

No Peas an' Rice an' Coconut Oil," one of several pieces that combines an endearing childlike quality with an adult sensibility (i.e., a yearning to get high); "Breakin' in a Pair of Shoes" brings a distinctly feminine angle to a catchy early swing hit; "Slow Poke" is an ingenious lyric variation on Johnny Mercer's "Lazy Bones," while "Love in the First Degree" transforms courtroom language into a love song in the manner of Waller's "Where Were You on the Night of June the Third?" "My Gal Mezzanine" (yes, Mezzanine, possibly a reference to reefer peddler "Mezz" Mezzrow) is the most Walleresque of all, an infectious ode to a "red hot mama from Bahama with a red hot hootchy koo!" who happens to have a grandiosely absurd first name. "When Hollywood Goes Black and Tan" paraphrases the hi-de-ho's of Cab Calloway's (and Harold Arlen's) "Minnie the Moocher's Wedding Day" to make for a delightful period piece praising African American entertainers in cinema, from Armstrong and Calloway to Decca's own Bob Howard.

All these sides are collected on *Here Comes Cleo,* the single most essential Brown collection, on the Scottish Hep label. The Hep CD also includes four lovely tunes, very much in the Decca mold, done for a transcription service around the same time, among them "You've Got Me Under Your Thumb." The latter tune was also recorded by Waller and His Rhythm in 1937 and Brown's version by no means suffers in comparison.

Brown had already perfected a piano style that became a major inspiration to male and female players of a certain generation. As Dave Brubeck told radio journalist Sara Fishko (of WNYC), "She needed somebody to play intermissions for her, and somebody recommended me, and she was happy with me. And she gave me a note to take to Art Tatum and introduce myself. You see, I'm going from one of the greatest women pianists to the greatest man pianist! When Tatum read the note he asked me how Cleo was playing. And I said, 'She's got the fastest left hand I've ever heard!' . . . Tatum was the God of the piano, [but] when Fats Waller died, the men in that band wanted Cleo to come in and take Fats's place, that's how great she was."

Here Comes Cleo concludes with five somewhat risqué "party" records made for the under-the-counter Hollywood Hot Shots operation around 1936–37. The most memorable of these is "Who'll Chop Your Suey When I'm Gone," which Brown, with her girly style, makes into something more silly than sexual ("Who'll clam your chowder?" "Who'll tutti your frutti?"). Her treatment is also highly different—faster and zingier—from the way publisher Clarence Williams recorded it with the more traditional classic blues singer Margaret Johnson in 1925.

Which begs the question: For all the apparent success of Cleo Brown's Decca recordings, why did the label stop recording her in mid-1936? Why was she relegated to a semianonymous West Coast label that manufactured dirty records for drunks at parties? In her major published interview (with Whitney Balliett), Brown doesn't mention that her initial recording career lasted only eighteen sides and fewer than that many months. (Although, apparently, she went on broadcasting and playing major clubs.)

We'll never know why Decca abruptly discontinued its relationship with Brown, or why none of the other labels picked her up at this point (she did do a few more recordings between 1949 and 1951, about which more later). But perhaps it's not a coincidence that a few months after Brown's last session, Decca launched a new series of small group dates built around the black female pianist—and sort of singer—Lil Hardin Armstrong. Hardin had already made a place for herself in musical history as the second wife of Louis Armstrong. She had been a pivotal influence, both professional and musical, in Armstrong's early career, most importantly as the pianist with King Oliver's Creole Jazz Band and Armstrong's own Hot Five and Seven sessions.

Why Decca spotlighted Hardin, who worked under the name of Lil Armstrong even though she was long divorced from the trumpeter, as a singer is a mystery. Her best-known vocal was on the famous Hot Seven side "That's When I'll Come Back to You," where she banters agreeably in response to her husband's pleading; this disc lays the foundation for Louis Prima and Keely Smith. Mrs. Armstrong was a credible pianist in the early jazz mold, and an essential part of the greatest jazz records ever made. However, even though she recorded a couple of other vocals on various dates produced by Clarence Williams, she would never really establish her bona fides in the singing department.

The Decca series of 1936–40 is a puzzlement, especially since she primarily sings on the twenty-four titles while Billy Kyle, Frank Froeba, and others play piano; yet before, during, and after these years Hardin worked as a session pianist on many dates with various blues singers—she was a fine accompanist, yet she just doesn't seem to have played much piano on her own dates. As a singer, Hardin is a yelper, and her vocals are not the most salient feature of these sides, which have been reissued mainly because they spotlight expert black swing soloists like Charlie Shavers, Buster Bailey, Chu Berry, Joe Thomas, and company.

Hardin's most valid contribution to her own dates is as composer: Her name is on most of the songs here, and one of these, "Just for a Thrill," grew up to become a true standard. First recorded at her initial Decca date in 1936 in Chicago, "Just for a Thrill," recorded definitively by Ray Charles and which is sometimes co-credited to pianist-songwriter Don Raye, became a forerunner of the postwar R&B soul ballad. Hardin's so-so singing on her 1936–40 Decca dates is beside the point; Lil Hardin Armstrong made a major contribution to American music.

Hardin's Decca sides are much more boisterous and noisy than Brown's, given her intimate though energetic vocals and piano solos. Yet because of the timing, it's hard to escape the conclusion that Decca dropped Brown in favor of Hardin.

Brown didn't record again until thirteen years later, when she did a pleasant date of four titles for Capitol in 1949. Since Capitol was actively recording both Nellie Lutcher and Julia Lee, they were obviously cornering the market on brilliant, bluesy, Fats Waller–inspired female pianist-singers. Brown's four Capitols are a respectalde enough follow-up to the (now) classic Deccas, starting with a fast "Cleo's Boogie," a piano solo with occasional blues vocal interjections (including a paraphrase of a territory blues standard recorded as "The Duck's Yas-Yas"); then there's an amiable update of the twenties standard "I'd Climb the Highest Mountain," and two more risqué blues novelties, "Cook That Stuff" and "Don't Overdo It." The producer obviously appreciated Brown's 1935–36 sides enough to maintain what was good about them, such as the accompanying rhythm section, using two famous New Orleanians, guitarist Nappy Lamare and drummer Zutty Singleton. The Capitol session failed to make any impact; when *Billboard* reviewed it, they even dismissed Brown as a Julia Lee imitator, describing "Cook That Stuff" as a "novelty reminiscent of Julia Lee's 'Snatch and Grab It' but much bluer."

In 1950, Brown recorded two syrupy children's songs ("Two Little Twains" and the lachrymose "Coffee Colored Child," along with, frustratingly, ten unissued titles) for Albert Marx's Discovery Records, and a year later cut her two final singles, a pair of nondescript blues titles, for the independent Blue Records. It could be that her career was then in decline, but in her interview with Balliett, Brown, whose father had been a Baptist pastor, states that she got religion, felt the spirit coming on, and sensed the need to get out of showbiz altogether; in 1953 she became a Seventh Day Adventist. Now calling herself "Cleo Patra Brown," she spent roughly twenty years helping to cure people's bodies and souls, laboring as a hospital worker and praying fiercely at every opportunity.

Despite her small output, Cleo Brown's music was enormously influential: Obviously both Nellie Lutcher and Julia Lee (who was older) were heavily inspired by her work, Lutcher crediting Brown's disc of "You're a Heavenly Thing" with launching the trend for female pianists. Both Marian McPartland and Bobby Short became major fans. As Short told Balliett, "We were attracted to her sweet, sexy voice and her brilliant left hand—and her time, which was fantastic." Short also noted that a minister in his hometown, Danville, Illinois, was so moved by Brown's theme song, "The Stuff Is Here and It's Mellow," that he transformed it into a sermon. That news might have been encouraging to Brown, since she wanted to get away from those salacious songs about sex and substances and errant lovers who chop each other's suey.

It was McPartland who made it a personal mission to find Cleo Brown, and eventually tracked her down in Denver. In 1987, McPartland brought her to New York so she could appear on McPartland's *Piano Jazz*, which was a dream come true for the Queen Mum of Jazz. (The show was eventually released on CD by Audiophile Records as *Living in the Afterglow*, with McPartland guesting on four titles.) Even after the show and the album, as well as a profile in *The New Yorker* by Balliett, there was never a full-fledged Cleo Brown revival or even a real return to performing. She died in 1995, and the big event of her later life was being named as a Jazz Master by the National Endowment of the Arts. In the twenty-five-plus years that the NEA Jazz Masters Award has been in existence, Cleo Brown is quite probably its most obscure recipient, but far from its least worthy. She can chop my suey anytime.

Una Mae Carlisle (1915–1956)

After Brown (and, to an extent, Hardin), the next femme follower of Fats was Waller's lover and protégée Una Mae Carlisle. Waller first heard her in 1932, the story goes, when he was doing a radio series entitled *Fats Waller's Rhythm Club* out of station WLW in Cincinnati. She was seventeen at the time, having been born in nearby Xenia, Ohio. Waller immediately took a keen interest—both professional and personal—in the attractive and talented youngster, and persuaded her mother to let Una Mae (she pronounced it "You-na") appear regularly on his program. When he launched his big band at New York's world-famous Apollo Theater in 1935, Carlisle was on hand as his girl singer. By 1937, like several other African American female entertainers, she had found work in Europe (apparently under her own power, without Waller's help). She was working at Le Boeuf sur le Toit in Paris when she had the good fortune to be heard by the British critic-composer-producer Leonard Feather, who wrote about her enthusiastically for *Melody Maker*.

Feather was moved to produce Carlisle's premier recording date, in London for British Vocalion in May 1938, at which the first tune was the producer-songwriter's own agreeable rhythm number "Don't Try Your Jive on Me." On this well-balanced session, Feather also had her do one straight-up blues, "Hangover Blues" (for which the two shared composer credit), one jived-up standard, "Mean to Me," one relatively new song, the first-rate "Love Walked In" by the Gershwin brothers, and, appropriately, one Fats Waller favorite, "I'm Crazy 'Bout My Baby." Although Carlisle would keep working until the fifties, these five tunes are easily her overall finest: She sings and plays with an ebullience and energy that's sorely missing from most of her subsequent recordings. On "Mean to Me" she verbally encourages her British sidemen to "swing it on out there," and, among other Wallerian asides, she closes the tune with an affirmative "Yes! Yes!" If all of UMC's recordings were of this caliber, she would have had a much bigger place in music history.

Later that year, she reunited with Waller, who was then touring Europe; Carlisle was sick at the time, and he visited her at a London hospital. (In typical Fats fashion, he had such a good time hanging out with her that he missed an important performance.) She next recorded strictly as guest pianist with Danny Polo on a Feather-produced date (which included the celebrated Argentine guitarist Oscar Alemán) in Paris, in January 1939. At the end of the year, she was back in the States, and made what would probably be her most famous appearance on a record, singing a duet with Waller on "I Can't Give You Anything but Love" as part of the Waller Rhythm series on Bluebird. She made the right decision *not* to sing in the Waller style when duetting with the man himself—after all, there was no need for two Fats Wallers on the same side. She also knew that it wouldn't pay to attempt to be funny in Waller's presence, and so she sings the Fields-McHugh standard relatively straight. As a result, she comes off as something of a wet blanket, while Waller supplies all the fun here. Still, it's a classic side.

Did Waller have a hand in seeing that Carlisle began to record regularly as a featured star for Victor's subsidiary Bluebird? One never knows, do one? Her first date, perhaps not coincidentally, featured the musicians from Waller's own band (though not the Fat One himself) as her accompaniment. Her first three American dates come closest to the 1938 London session in quality and spirit, even though she only plays piano on the first two. After the date with Waller's Rhythm band, her next session featured Benny Carter (undoubtedly also a friend from Europe) playing trumpet obbligatos behind her, and then came the most reissued of UMC's recordings, a March 1941 Bluebird date in which her accompaniment was Lester Young. This session includes a famous topical blues that begins with the following couplet, designed to zing both Hitler and Stalin nine months before Pearl Harbor: "Blitzkrieg Baby, you can't bomb me / Because I'm pleading neutrality." It's a funny line, although UMC doesn't seem to be having much in the way of fun with it—or with the song in general. (All twenty-one of her first sides, including the duet with Waller, are included on the Classics release *Una Mae Carlisle, 1938–1941*, which contains all of her essential recordings.)

Perhaps by 1941 Carlisle wanted to develop an identity of her own, rather than just serve as Fats's female emissary and occasional playmate. She recorded another fifty or so sides between 1941 and 1950 (which are on two more Classics volumes, *1941–1944* and *1944–1950*), but few of these are anywhere near as interesting as her sides from 1938

to 1940 and earlier. Carlisle stopped playing piano on most of her dates, and she stopped the jivey, Wallerian asides—in general, her output became overwhelmingly tepid. Based on the bulk of her forties work, Carlisle is not nearly in a class with Cleo Brown, Julia Lee, Hadda Brooks, and especially Nellie Lutcher. It's hard to listen to a whole CD of UMC uninterrupted, despite the high caliber of her sidemen and backup bands. These included, on sixteen titles from 1941 to 1942, the entire John Kirby Sextet; even here, Carlisle does not compare with Maxine Sullivan or Mildred Bailey, who both recorded classic sides with the JK6.

One area where Carlisle, like Lil Hardin Armstrong, made an important contribution was as a composer. Her name is on two very successful songs from 1941, "Walkin' by the River" and "I See a Million People." Her gifts as a songwriter were probably what attracted the attention of publisher and producer Joe Davis, who was the primary publisher for Waller's closest composing collaborator, lyricist Andy Razaf.

After the AFM ban, Carlisle began recording for the Joe Davis label, and later there were dates for Savoy, National, and even Columbia (two sessions in which she was backed by pioneer arranger Don Redman and white bandleader Bob Chester). Most of these are fairly ho-hum affairs; she just doesn't do anything particularly interesting with her voice, and doesn't bring anything special to her interpretations.

Carlisle's final recording session, included at the end of the last Classics volume, is an out-and-out mystery: six singles tracks, apparently done for a privately released three-disc album pressed by RCA. Each track consists of three short original solo piano instrumentals, bearing titles like "A Rhythm Mood," "Escape to Nowhere," and "Jumpin' with the Stars," each lasting about a minute, introduced vocally by "You-na Mae" as she refers to herself. More than this I cannot tell you.

The health issues that plagued her back in Europe were still, unfortunately, in the picture. "Perhaps because of a lifestyle as self-indulgent as Fats's own, Una Mae never reached the plateau of fame to which her talent and beauty might have been expected to bring her," Leonard Feather wrote. "She was only thirty-seven, when, inactive and forgotten, she died in Ohio, where she was born." There's some confusion regarding these details: Feather and Ira Gitler's *Biographical Encyclopedia of Jazz* tell us she was born in 1915 and died in 1956 in New York. Assuming these latter dates are correct, Una Mae Carlisle was actually forty, just a few months older than Waller at the time of his death in 1943.

Julia Lee (1902–1958)

Thus for whatever reason, there never was a completely satisfying Femme Follower of Fats during Waller's own lifetime; the two strongest contenders, Cleo Brown and Una Mae Carlisle, were both disappointments, the first in terms of quantity, the second in terms of quality. However, after the war, Waller's two principal heiresses took the stage almost simultaneously.

Julia Lee and Nellie Lutcher were two very distinct individuals, but they were more alike than they were different. They were products of the world's two greatest jazz territories, Lee from Kansas City, Lutcher from New Orleans. They each came to fame recording for Capitol in 1946 and then 1947. Guided by producer Dave Dexter, himself a Kansas City native, between them they provided Capitol with a steady stream of hits for a few years in the late forties, and they helped establish the label's presence in the field then known as "race music."

Lee and Lutcher both worked with groups modeled loosely after Waller's Rhythm: Lee's band was billed on the Capitol labels as "Her Boy Friends"; Lutcher's group was credited as "Nellie Lutcher and Her Rhythm." They both played a key role in the evolution of black music, as small group swing and the juke-jazz style of the thirties morphed into what became known as rhythm and blues. Unfortunately, by the time that phrase was coined, both their careers had peaked. They both also sang a mixture of blues and standards and, further, there was a high sexual content to their work, which was, however, expressed in different ways. (Also, not coincidentally, they both were the subject of lavish and thoroughly deserved complete boxed sets from the German boutique label Bear Family, both with elaborate booklets and excellent biographical essays by the British scholar Bill Millar.)

Julia Lee was born in Kansas City in 1902 to a very musical family: Her father played violin and her older brother, George E. Lee, played saxophone and occasionally sang. Both father and brother led bands, and, eventually, so would she. The younger Lee was a formally trained pianist, as much as it was possible for an African American female to be early in the twentieth century; she made a serious study of theory and sight-reading at both Lincoln High School and Western University. She picked up jazz, however, somewhat less formally; in Kansas City in the immediate pre–Jazz Age, it would have been hard for her to avoid exposure to ragtime and the blues. Lee's career as a live performer divides into two distinct extended gigs. First, for fifteen years (1918–1933) she primarily played piano and occasionally sang in her brother's various bands. Then, as a solo act, she spent the next sixteen years (1934–1950) working as the regular attraction at Milton's Tap Room, one of Kaycee's top nightspots.

Lee first recorded as a pianist with George E. Lee's Novelty Singing Orchestra (then in residence at the Novelty Club) in 1929. At this time, she also recorded two exuberant performances as a solo vocalist. One was the pop song "He's Tall, Dark and Handsome," in which Lee, singing of her attraction to a "dark" man, obviously gave the song an entirely

different connotation than when it was performed by a white act, like Ted Weems and His Orchestra. The other was the older, more folk-rooted "Won't You Come over to My House?" Although the latter song was based in the blues, and this was still the era of the great classic blues singers, Lee sounds nothing like Bessie Smith—or even Ethel Waters. At this point in her development, she's an extravagant belter, more like Tess Gardella, Sophie Tucker, or any number of white singers on Broadway, but with more of a blues sensibility and a jazzy sense of time.

It was the writer and producer Dave Dexter who brought both Lee and then Lutcher to Capitol Records. He had begun his career covering music in his hometown for *Down Beat* and other publications, then made a lateral move, professionally, to producing sessions with local artists (including the formidable Big Joe Turner). He moved to Chicago and next to Los Angeles, where he went to work with Capitol, then only in business for a few months. He had grown up hearing Julia Lee around KC, and his first idea was to include her as part of a historically oriented album of Kansas City jazz he was producing for Capitol in 1944. She did two sides for the package, the first of which was a swing-styled update of "Won't You Come Over to My House?," the other the blues standard "Trouble in Mind." Back in Kansas City the following year, she made four tunes (mostly blues, all credited to her) released on the Premier label.

Lee's two sides for the Kansas City album proved popular enough for Capitol to offer her a contract of her own. Her two peak years for the label were 1946 and 1947; she was still working nightly at Milton's Tap Room in Missouri, but she made the pilgrimage to California to do a batch of sessions in August 1946 and June 1947. She returned for a third series of Capitol dates in November 1947, just in time to get some sides in before the 1948 recording ban. After the ban, in 1949, she resumed recording, but for the remainder of her association with Capitol the label allowed her to work in Kansas City, thus relieving her of having to make that killer commute to the Left Coast.

As Bill Millar notes, where most of the major labels had a "race" and a "hillbilly" division, in the mid-forties Capitol launched a series called "Americana" that catered to both the blues and country markets. The label's first big stars in the "race" area were Nat Cole, Lee, and then Lutcher. Undoubtedly, being based in KC hurt Lee's recording career—if Capitol wanted someone to cover a new song, like right now, they obviously weren't going to bring in Lee from Missouri; they'd give it to someone more conveniently located, usually Lutcher, who lived for most of her life in L.A.

With Dexter's help, Lee seems to have generated most of her own material, which, for the most part, consisted of salacious variations on the blues. Then, to prove that man (or woman) does not live by blues alone, she also occasionally recorded vintage jazz and pop standards that were already part of her Tap Room repertoire; the old Kansas City favorite "Until the Real Thing Comes Along" was a natural. Unlike Lutcher, Lee included almost no new plug songs (numbers from films or shows) in her sessions.

Dexter quickly discovered what Lee already knew: that she would get the biggest response with double entendre, risqué blues that combined sex and comedy. Her two best-remembered titles are "Snatch and Grab It" and "King Sized Papa"; the first is allegedly about opportunity ("Grab it before it gets away"), the second is supposedly about a very tall man ("There's such a lot of him, the way he grew / Enough to last till 1992"), but there was no mistaking what Lee was really singing about. Both songs, like nearly all her recordings, are animated by the impeccable sense of rhythm that's necessary both for comedy and the blues. Although just about all her songs concern themselves with Topic A, she finds infinite variety in even the thinnest of metaphors; in "I've Got a Crush on the Fuller Brush Man," she tells us of how her favorite traveling salesman "scrubs my vestibule, my back porch too." In "My Man Stands Out," she tells us, "Down at the beach when we walk by / The other girls give him the eye."

Lee was especially enamored of using food as a metaphor, as in "The Spinach Song" ("I didn't like it the first time / But oh how it grew on me!"), "All This Beef and Big Ripe Tomatoes" (no explanation necessary), and "I Was Wrong (The Diet Song)," another ode about giving in to temptation. (Too bad that she never reprised Cleo Brown's "Who'll Chop Your Suey When I'm Gone.") Still, she doesn't need sex to make food, drink, and other substances sound interesting: On "Last Call for Alcohol" it's easy to imagine her barking out to elbow-bending patrons at 6 a.m.—oven as they fall off their stools—"Drink up, drink up, then order again!" and closing with "You don't have to go home, but you can't stay here." And there are still other indulgences: "Dream Lucky" is about gambling, specifically playing the numbers, built around a phrase that fellow Kansas Cityites Count Basie and Jimmy Rushing used in "Jimmy's Blues." "Wise Guys" is addressed to ne'er-do-well characters who join the rackets to avoid honest labor. "At the end of your game / You get a number for a name," she admonishes. "Why, most of your mothers hang their heads in shame."

Lee's most overt song about unsavory habits did not, surprisingly, originate as part of the blues or "Americana" tradition, but was a number from a Hollywood musical. In 1934, the lyricist and later producer Sam Coslow wrote "Marihuana" (sometimes called "Sweet Marijuana") for the film *Murder at the Vanities*. Reefer was then still legal in many states, but it was already a taboo and risqué subject for a mainstream pop song. At some later point, Coslow changed the title, and some of the lyrics with it, to "Lotus Blossom." That it was a permanent part of Lee's repertoire is evidenced by her recording it three times, once for Premier and twice for Capitol, under both titles, although Capitol only issued the "Lotus" version at the time. (In all three labels, she received the composing credit.) Under both titles, "Marihuana" is not about getting high and having a good time; this isn't Cab Calloway extolling the joys of viperhood or Bessie Smith joyfully demanding pigfeet and beer. "Marihuana" is a song of addiction and regret. Lee's heroine wants to give up smoking dope but she just can't say no to the escape that narcotics provide her. Addressing the drug directly in the second person, Lee sings, "You alone can bring my lover back to me." She sings with the remorse of a major blues singer doing a sad blues, combining sex and drugs, euphoria and melancholy, into one especially potent cocktail.

Lee's voice is a lot darker and deeper than Cleo Brown's, Nellie Lutcher's, or Rose Murphy's—Brown and Murphy, in particular, are trilly sopranos, while Lee is a confirmed contralto; she's also much less likely to animate her lyrics with vocal effects, trills, and melismas. Her singing is direct and forthright, whether it's a raucous party blues (like "Come on Over to My House") or an old weepie (like "My Mother's Eyes"). She tempers both, making the first less one-dimensional and the second less overtly sentimental. Two titles recorded back to back in 1949 show how she could extract the same meaning from songs of widely different contexts: "You Ain't Got It No More" and "When Your Lover Has Gone."

Perhaps Lee's recording career petered out because she avoided contemporary and mainstream material and concentrated so exclusively on saucy blues and old standards; Dinah Washington, who was just launching her career at this point, would qucikly prove it was possible to sing just about anything with a blue point of view. After the 1948 ban, Capitol was recording Lee less and less frequently: twelve titles in 1949, eight in 1950, four in 1951, six in 1952, and the majority of these were not issued at the time. The 1952 date was her last for the label, though she did record a couple of later dates for smaller, Kansas City–based operations. Julia Lee died of heart disease in 1958—in Kansas City, of course—aged fifty-six. The Bear Family collection of her complete recordings (including all the unissued Capitol masters) concludes with "Rock and Bop Lullaby," which begins, "Rock me a ragtime tune, bop me some swing till noon," as if Lee was determined to take every genre she had ever worked in and combine them all into one song. Then again, she had been doing that all along.

Nellie Lutcher (1912–2007)

If Una Mae Carlisle was Waller's squeeze and Julia Lee seemed more like his older sibling, then Nellie Lutcher was his kid sister. We celebrate Lee for her directness, even in metaphor-driven, double entendre blues lyrics. Nellie Lutcher's greatest asset is her playfulness. By way of comparison, the two of them shared a signature song, or, at least, a piece of material they developed independently from a folk-blues source. Lee first recorded it in 1929 as "Won't You Come Over to My House" and then again in 1944, on her first Capitol date, as "Come on Over to My House"; Lutcher called her version "Hurry on Down," and also recorded it at her own first Capitol session, in 1947. They are similar enough to be considered variations on the same material: Lee sings, "Come on over to my house, baby / Nobody home but me," and Lutcher coos, "Hurry on down to my house, baby / Ain't nobody home but me."

With Lee, you somehow assume the song is being sung by a housewife whose kids are at school and whose husband is at work; Lutcher, in contrast, sounds like a teenaged girl whose parents have stepped out to catch a triple feature of Hopalong Cassidy. The way Lee sings it there's no doubt what she has in mind; with Lutcher, you're relatively sure, but it also sounds as if she could be looking for a play date and not necessarily in the amorous sense . . . really. Lee sings it with total deliberateness; even though it's fast and exciting, every word and every intention is crystal clear. Lutcher sings it as fast as humanly possible, without apparent regard to intelligibility, knowing that audiences wouldn't miss her larger point. Her special effects, her yelps and squeals, are more important than the actual words.

Lutcher's recording of "Hurry on Down" and her career as a recording artist in general came about after she had been working hard in dozens of joints in Los Angeles's black neighborhoods for a decade. "My life turned around in 1947," she told Whitney Balliett. "I'd been plugging along in Los Angeles for ten years when—wham!—Dave Dexter heard me on a March of Dimes radio show. I did 'The One I Love (Belongs to Somebody Else),' 'Hurry on Down,' and 'He's a Real Gone Guy,' both of which I wrote. When I woke up, I found that I had a couple of hits. A couple of weeks later, he signed me to a contract." A few sessions after that, she had her third big hit, "Fine Brown Frame"; that year, *Billboard* magazine named her second out of the four "Top Female Vocalists on Race Records" (she came in after Julia Lee and ahead of Dinah Washington and Rose Murphy).

Nellie Lutcher was born on October 15, 1912 (older sources say 1915), in Lake Charles, Louisiana, a small town under the geographical and cultural sway of New Orleans. (She would immortalize the town in her "Lake Charles Boogie" of 1947.) Her father drove a truck and played bass in the Imperial Jazz Band. She grew up equally under the influence of the local church and the nearby all-black theater, and like Lee had formal piano lessons and serious training. Her piano professor, Mrs. Reynaud (a very Creole-sounding name), was such an accomplished sight reader that "if there was a fly sitting on the sheet music, she'd play that too." By the twenties,

Nellie was serving as pianist with her dad and the Imperial Jazz Band. In 1933 she worked with the Southern Rhythm Boys, under the direction of clarinetist Paul Barnes.

In 1935, after hearing from several friends and relatives that things were easier for black people in California, Lutcher moved to Los Angeles. She landed a gig at the Dunbar Hotel, leading her own trio (rather than serving in the rhythm section of a larger group), and it was at this time that she first began to sing. She quickly integrated herself into the city's vibrant black music scene, which, though barely recorded during the swing era (Los Angeles was just another territory then), would play a key role in the development of rhythm and blues. She became friendly with the Cole brothers, bassist Eddie and pianist Nat, not long after they arrived from Chicago. Had more record companies been paying attention to the L.A. scene, Lutcher would doubtless not have had to wait until she was thirty-five to make her first disc.

Capitol was the first nationally distributed major label to profit from the local talent on Central Avenue, starting with Nat King Cole; by the time Lee and then Lutcher were signed to the label, Cole was already attracting white listeners as well as black. The label already had Julia Lee under contract, but it was plain that Lutcher could have potentially greater pop appeal; besides which, as we have seen, it was easier to get Lutcher into the studio, logistically speaking. With Lee, Dexter seems to have been more of a documentarian, letting her put down repertoire that she had already been singing for years for patrons in Kansas City. With Lutcher, Dexter took a more proactive role as a hands-on producer and A&R man. Lutcher also had the good sense to sign with Cole's manager, Carlos Gastel, who already had a track record for making stars out of black and jazz talent.

Lutcher occasionally did a Lee-style double entendre blues, like her 1947 "There's Another Mule in Your Stall," but she sings it playfully, bouncing up and down in her characteristic flea-on-a-hot-brick style. On the whole, Our Nellie is much more wholesome, more childlike than naughty Aunt Julia. In 1950–51, Lutcher recorded two additional songs about inviting company over that could function as sequels to "Hurry on Down": "Pa's Not Home—Ma's Upstairs" and "Can I Come in for a Second." The first is more about the tender trap than an erotic romp: Even though she promises her boyfriend that her parents aren't around ("The front door's locked and the back won't budge / So why are we chewing on chocolate fudge?"), it turns out that Ma and Pa are in on the fix, hoping she can ensnare him into a proposal.

"Can I Come in for a Second" reverses the equation: Here, it's the young man who is begging and pleading to be invited inside after a date. The track is done as a duet between Lutcher and her old friend

Nat Cole, and illustrates the differences between the two: The King is smooth and cool to the max, even when playing the horny young swain, and Lutcher is frisky and girly and squeally even when slamming the door in his face. When he tells her he wants her to put her heart into a kiss, she positively shrieks, "That's the only way I *kiss!*" The song is one of the few with both music and words by Sammy Cahn (although the bridge seems inspired by "Don't Sit Under the Apple Tree"), and I don't doubt that Sammy penned the dialogue between the two as well. He: "I have a lot of investments to consider . . . I brought you home in a taxi." She: "If that wasn't a bus it was the biggest taxi I ever saw!"

"Little Sally Walker" is Lutcher's own transformation of a nursery rhyme (earlier swung by Al Cooper and the Savoy Sultans) into a modern love ballad, complete with a new verse. She constantly combines the childish element with the sexual one: She had likely been singing "Princess Poo-Poo-Ly Has Plenty Papaya" since 1939, when it was recorded by Abe Lyman and his Californians. The song begins, "Princess Poo-Poo-Ly has plenty papaya / She loves to give it away," and it's possible to take this either as a sexual euphemism or just enjoy its sheer silliness—it works either way in Lutcher's delightful performance. The fun is keenly enhanced by the way she plays with words, the rhythmic repetitiveness of all those P sounds. Her timing is, as always, impeccable, especially in the coda and in the composer's vaudeville asides: "She loves to give it away—I mean papaya / She loves to give it away—got plenty of it / She loves to give it away—crazy girl!" (Once, in an after-hours session at the Café Carlyle, I was privileged to hear Bobby Short sing "Princess Poo-Poo-Ly" and share his memories of Nellie.)

"Princess Poo-Poo-Ly" is one of many examples of Lutcher combining scat singing and traditional lyrics; she favors songs that turn words into pure sonics, like the geographically motivated "Chi-Chi-Chicago" and "I Wish I Was in Walla-Walla"; then there's "Pig Latin Song," which begins "I-way ove-yay ou-yay oney-hay." "Lutcher's Leap" is a wordless scat epic, possibly inspired by Gene Krupa's "What's This" and Nat Cole's response, "That's What." In "The Dog Fight Song" she not only repeats the names of the two doggies, "Ming Toy" and "Prince," over and over in a childish-canine way, but supplies plenty of delightfully doggy sound effects, yelps and barks and bow-wows. In "Alexander's Ragtime Band" she launches into a particularly exuberant, chirpy scat episode that evolves into a series of imitations of the various instruments in the titular ensemble. This is distinctly inspired by Fats Waller, who launched a tradition of doing untraditional things with his voice (such as rapidly alternating between baritone and falsetto registers), and has little in common with Lutcher's contemporaries in early R&B like Nat Cole and Louis Jordan.

Like Waller, Lutcher has a serious side as well; she'll address the occasional standard, like "My Man," without joking it up. Lee's most incongruous recording was a boogie-woogie treatment of the traditional Italian song "Oh Marie," and Lutcher, for her part, made what is, for her, a straight version of "Cool Water." She sings the cowboy classic surprisingly convincingly, even though it's not exactly easy to imagine Miss Lutcher crossing the barren waste on a horse named Dan. Her most arresting side of a noncomic nature is "A Maid's Prayer," which has a strong undercurrent of irony. A prescient prequel to Arthur Prysock's "Working Man's Prayer," this is a semispoken, all-rubato monologue in which a working girl speculates about what existence will be like for a domestic in the hereafter. When she crosses the river Jordan, will she still have to make the beds and empty the garbage cans? Will she have to polish the stars and hang them out? She recites,

> I know I will be discouraged
> I know I will be dismayed
> If I should be a maid in Heaven
> And still be underpaid.

My favorite Nellie Lutcher track is neither one of her originals nor a blues, but a contemporary pop novelty that was more likely Capitol's idea than her own. "Kiss Me Sweet" was a 1949 hit for sweet bandleader Sammy Kaye (of "Swing and Sway" fame) written by Milton Drake, most of whose hits were of the novelty nature; I first heard it sung in a Warner Bros. cartoon by Tweety Bird (of *Tweety and Sylvester* fame). Mel Blanc, supplying the bird's voice, chirped it in a high-pitched caricature of a child's way of speaking, overflowing with infantile impediments ("Kiss me *tweet*"), but he sounds positively restrained compared to Lutcher. Her performance is by far the more compelling, first because she accentuates the correct parts of the beat and cuts off the right notes in the right places to make the piece really swing; the best the song's other interpreters can manage is to get it to bounce. (She makes it even more musically interesting by adding a key change to the bridge.)

Her recording boasts an attractive wordless episode, wherein she exchanges phrases, both from the keyboard and scatting, with guitarist John Collins (later with Nat Cole for many years). But it's what she does with the song's plain-vanilla lyric that's really remarkable. As written, "Kiss Me Sweet" (which begins "Kiss me sweet, kiss me simple / Kiss me on my little dimple") has a nursery rhyme simplicity. The song is just "Kiss me this" and "Kiss me that" over and over again, but Lutcher brilliantly animates the text by making its relentless repetition into a virtue: When she sings "Kiss me slow, kiss me dreamy / Kiss me every time you see me," she elongates the first adjective and makes the second sound wistful; on "Kiss me plain, kiss me fancy," she makes those words sound so plain and so fancy she could be singing in ancient Aramaic and you still would know what she meant.

Lutcher and Lee don't seem to have been rivals, nor did Lutcher necessarily ascend as Lee's star went the other way; the glory years for both were the immediate postwar period. Maybe there was room in the market for only one of them, and Lutcher and Lee somehow just canceled each other out (and leave us not forget that Rose Murphy was also recording by 1947). Both lost ground when the 1948 recording ban hit, at which point Capitol tried the curious move of bringing in a third Femme Follower of Fats, none other than Cleo Brown herself, for a single session. Like Lee, Lutcher was undergoing a process of diminishing returns: two sessions per year in 1949, 1950, and 1951. Still, her discs did well in England, where she made a very well received appearance in September 1950.

The bulk of Lutcher's sessions employed just a rhythm section, in contrast to the all-star horn men who guested with Julia Lee's Boyfriends. In 1951, Dexter tried stirring the mixture by backing Lutcher with Billy May's full orchestra, this being several weeks before he conducted his first date accompanying Nat Cole in a similar manner. The results were successful artistically though they made little impact commercially. Especially swell are two twenties standards, "Mean to Me" and "Birth of the Blues," which feature May's already perfected slurping saxophone sound, and make for a wonderful sonic cushion to support Lutcher on. "Let the Worry Bird Worry for You," despite an ungainly title, is a worthy new swinger by Jule Styne and Leo Robin (from *Two Tickets to Broadway*). The oddest track is "I Want to Be Near You," a vigorous march in which May makes the ensemble sound like a college football brass band, seventy-six trombones waiting for Meredith Willson, complete with a chanting choir clapping their hands on the best deep-in-the-heart-of-Texas style. Even in this most Caucasian context, a production that sounds like an idea Mitch Miller might have come up with, Lutcher makes everything swing.

Capitol followed this semisuccess with a less interesting date in which Lutcher was backed by Hal Mooney, who was then Kay Starr's regular accompanist. The model seems to have been Nat Cole's many dates with string sections, but the charts weren't nearly up to what Nelson Riddle was writing for Cole. Following this, between 1952 and 1954 Lutcher relocated to Okeh and then Decca, and made some very agreeable small group sessions that are fully on a par with her best Capitol work. She's particularly winning on a 1953 L.A. session that begins with "Whee Baby," a bluesy novelty by Peggy (not Julia) Lee, in which the musical director was Peggy's ex-husband, guitarist Dave Barbour. For a date on Okeh, Columbia's "race" subsidiary, it sounds exactly like a Capitol production.

If the Okeh date has overtones of Peggy Lee, Lutcher's two Decca dates bring to mind Louis Jordan; Jordan's producer, Milt Gabler, was probably involved, even though the first session transpired in Los Angeles. The highlights are a pair of standards by Harold Arlen and Johnny Mercer, a fine "Blues in the Night" and a marvelous recasting of "Out of This World" into a Tympany Five–style shuffle rhythm; the twenties standard "Breezin' Along with the Breeze" is also reanimated with fast-moving Latinate percussion. Her original "It's Been Said" quotes "As Time Goes By" ("Woman needs man and man must have his mate") but is otherwise exactly the kind of thing Jordan was doing all along, even though there's no mistaking Lutcher's trademarks: the trilly scatting and emphasis on repeated phrases in a fast, telegraphic tempo ("It's a fact, it's a fact, it's a natural fact"). Lutcher recorded it twice, and the second time (a date produced by Sy Oliver), the band chants behind her; the combination of the speedy tempo, the somewhat surly singing group, and the overall spirit of the piece are very similar to Jordan's 1949 "Safe, Sane, and Single."

As with Lee's, the entire Nellie Lutcher Bear Family package is well worth owning—there truly isn't a bad track among the 105 included on the five discs. You might expect her to now enter a period of artistic decline, but she doesn't. Lutcher's last major recording project was an excellent album of standards for Liberty (included on the last disc of the Bear Box), in which her still excellent vocals are framed by sympathetic arrangements by Russ Garcia, in ensembles that vary from octet to full big band. Lutcher's 1956 album, titled *Our New Nellie*, doesn't include any of her trademark novelties, blues, or rhythm songs, but she completely transforms the twelve standards into Lutcher material with her zesty rhythmic style. Garcia clearly was a fan, and he made the brass and reed orchestrations bounce right along with her. From the mambo treatment of "Ole Buttermilk Sky" to the distinctive Garcia trombones (not to mention Red Norvo's vibraphone) on "Blue Skies," this is not a fading former hit maker of the previous decade enjoying a last hurrah. Rather, this is a formidable artist, a quintessential pianist-singer at the very peak of her powers.

The last few tracks on the Bear set are, though not bad, distinctly anticlimactic: There's a session for Imperial in which she remade "Hurry on Down" and "He's a Real Gone Guy," by now singing them so fast that they move like a silent movie projected at an exaggeratedly fast speed. There's a dreary ballad called "If Your Face Was as Beautiful as Your Soul," but, in compensation, also a explosive original well-titled "I'll Never Get Tired." On songs like this, Lutcher is a veritable virtuoso of energy and rhythm. She never gets tired—she's like a double shot of espresso in swingtime—and neither does her music.

Lutcher's last session was a quartet of titles for a record label that her drummer, Lee Young, was trying to start in 1963; one is a dewaltzed retread of Irving Berlin's "Reaching for the Moon" in the teeny-bop manner of Bobby Darin's "Nature Boy." They're very professional, but Lutcher herself disavowed them. Her chart-topping days were long behind her, but she was never down and out. She continued to work, and was elected to office with the Los Angeles local of the American Federation of Musicians. She also owned and operated an apartment building on South Van Ness Avenue.

In 1973 and 1980 she played the Cookery on University Place in New York. On the latter occasion, like Cleo Brown, she was profiled by Whitney Balliett in *The New Yorker*, and made an appearance on *Piano Jazz* with Marian McPartland. She actually lived long enough to see her music enjoy a brief vogue again in England in the nineties, at which time her duet with Nat King Cole, "For You, My Love," was reissued as a CD single. She was also alive to enjoy the Bear Family box, *Nellie Lutcher and Her Rhythm*. She died in June 2007, a few months short of her ninety-fifth birthday. Even in death, Nellie Lutcher remains a real gone gal with a fine brown frame.

Rose Murphy (1913–1989)

If you had never experienced the music of Rose Murphy, you would have been completely mystified when you heard Ella Fitzgerald, at any number of concerts in the mid-fifties (the famous 1958 *Ella in Rome* set is one), go into what might seem like a very strange detour in the middle of "I Can't Give You Anything but Love." After the opening chorus, the First Lady of Song starts making mysterious noises, chirping the way a butterfly might if it could sing, twitting about on the nonsense phrase "chee chee." If Fitzgerald fans were puzzled by this in 1958, their kids must have been flabbergasted in 1962 when they heard Frankie Valli and the Four Seasons do "I Can't Give You Anything but Love." Here, too, the lead singer intones the Jimmy McHugh melody in a voice even more stratospherically high (and sexually androgynous) than usual, while he dwells on that mysterious phrase "chee chee." Even while Valli is chee-chee-ing in the foreground, the rest of the group (presumably the other three Seasons) repeats the phrase over and over, as if it were some spiritual mantra or magical incantation. Like Fitzgerald, Valli here produces high-pitched, nonverbal noises that apparently originated in the animal kingdom, like hummingbirds and purring kittens.

Fitzgerald and Valli are both, of course, affectionately imitating that famous Femme Follower of Fats, Rose Murphy, who was billed as "the Chee Chee Girl" and recorded an album called *Not Cha-Cha but Chi-Chi* (spelled slightly differently, I will admit, but Murphy was "chee chee" long before it was chi-chi). As was also true of Nellie Lutcher, however, Murphy's use of sound effects isn't as remarkable as her comic-rhythmic timing. Recorded in November

1947 at one of her first sessions, Murphy's arrangement of "I Can't Give You Anything but Love" is distinguished by her brilliant use of stop time breaks, a jazz device derived from the blues. Like Waller and Cole, she knows that the system of tension and release in music is a parallel to the comedy ideal of setup and punch line. She sets up the laugh, "I can't give you anything but love . . . ," and then, when we expect to hear her say "baby" in the lyric as Dorothy Fields wrote it twenty years earlier, she throws us off by chanting "chee chee" instead. Murphy heightens the drama (and thereby the comedy) by extending the pause before going into the last note of key lines, and throughout defies our expectations. Instead of the word we expect, she pauses and throws in a "chee chee," a hummingbird hum, a descending scatty trill, or possibly a snatch of the written lyrics to an entirely different melody.

Lee, Lutcher, and Murphy had progressively higher voices: Lee sang in a deep contralto that made her a blues-singing, Kansas City counterpart to Tallulah Bankhead, Lutcher was somewhere in the middle, but Murphy was up there in realms ornithological, higher than Cleo Brown or possibly even Blossom Dearie. She doesn't have a wide vocal range in terms of her actual chops; possibly, she developed her unique vocabulary of sound effects as a way of compensating for her comparatively narrow range.

Rose Murphy was born in Xenia, Ohio, two years before Una Mae Carlisle. Like Lee and Lutcher, she didn't begin recording until she was already in her mid-thirties. According to historian Wolfram Knauer, Murphy's first noteworthy gig was on New York's Fifty-second Street when she alternated with Count Basie at the Famous Door around 1938. Later, she was part of Bill "Bojangles" Robinson's troupe, which brought her to the West Coast during the war years. She made regular appearances on the AFRS *Jubilee*, which was the number-one program for black soldiers and black talent; at least one track from the program (an early "I Can't Give You Anything but Love") has found its way onto a commercial CD.

By 1944, Murphy was being mentioned as a possible headliner at the Blue Angel, the famed cabaret room, back in New York. In Los Angeles, however, she did something neither Brown, Lee, nor Lutcher ever did—she appeared in a major Hollywood movie musical. This was the 1945 Twentieth Century Fox *George White's Scandals*, alongside Joan Davis, Jack Haley, organ star Ethel Smith, and Gene Krupa and His Orchestra (plus, as Art Fern would say, "Scratch the Wonder Crab"). She played a maid (like virtually every other black actress in every movie ever made before 1950) but got to sing "Wishing (Will Make It So)."

In 1947, she finally began recording. As the year was drawing to a close, she laid down eighteen titles for Majestic, an independent concern that was trying to become a major label. (Many of these tracks were subsequently reissued by Mercury, a start-up label that, unlike Majestic, did graduate to conglomerate status.) Unfortunately, Murphy only seems to have commenced her contract with Majestic in November, which meant that she had only two months before the AFM curtailed all recording activity in January 1948; her entire association with the label lasted for only these eighteen songs. They were clearly made in a rush; her first recording of "Little Coquette," in fact, sounds as if she's accidentally mixed up the lyrics here and there, rather than deliberately playing with the song as she usually did. Apparently there just wasn't time for another take.

As with Lutcher's Capitol sessions, Murphy's 1947 recordings offer a congenial balance of new songs and standards. Her overall approach is to get everything going with a buoyant, danceable tempo, spicing up the tunes old and new with *chee chee*'s and other sound effects. These are the same kind of musical devices that instrumentalists use to embellish a melody; at the end of her concluding piano part on "I Can't Give You Anything but Love," she decorates the McHugh tune with a tinkling glissando, yet she's been doing the same thing all along with her voice. "Sweet Georgia Brown" is closer to a piano feature with vocal interjections: She begins with a boogie-woogie vamp intro, then launches the melody about thirty-five seconds in, singing only at the end of every A section on the words "Georgia Brown." On "Cecilia," she does the opposite, singing everything but the girl's name, substituting a few seconds of hissing sibilance instead.

Like Waller, she deflates many a sentimental old song, like the potentially sappy "A Shanty in Old Shanty Town," and even more so the archetypal torch song "Jim," making a mockery of this turgid tale of a neglectful lover who fails to bring her pretty flowers or cheer her lonely hours. Possibly the funniest is "When I Grow Too Old to Dream," which reprises the jivey update recorded earlier by the Cats and the Fiddle. When she's not using sound effects, sometimes there are distinctly Wallerian vocal interjections, as when she offers up "Oh yes they are" in the middle of "The Best Things in Life Are Free," and in Waller's own "Honeysuckle Rose" she can't help spontaneously laughing, and her chortles and giggles also become part of the music. On "Pennies from Heaven," her descending treble notes, both on voice and piano, have a distinctly penny-from-heaven quality to them.

Murphy's standards are marvelously listenable, even though they're all in the same bouncy foxtrot. On new songs, she's more likely to vary the tempo. Perhaps not coincidentally, many of the contemporary numbers she recorded allow her to accommodate her vocal shtick: On "Mm-mm Good," better known as the Campbell's Soup jingle, the humming is part of the song as written; "Midnight on the Trail," Murphy's cowboy counterpart to Lutcher's "Cool Water," has her imitating a horse's hoofbeats (at least I think so; the quality of the recording and the reissue are so murky that it's hard to say for sure). "A Little Bird Told Me" is a welcome opportunity for aviary *chee chee*'s, while "Busy Line" finds her making like a telephone busy signal. The playful lyric to the 1932 "Is I in Love? I Is" allows her to play with the words as if they were sound effects or nonsense syllables.

The latter three tunes were recorded as part of Murphy's contract with RCA Victor, which began at the conclusion of the 1948 ban (December) and lasted for seventeen tracks, recorded up through July 1949. The great boon of the RCA sessions is that the recording quality is considerably better than Majestic's, and there's also a brilliant-sounding reissue of the seventeen tracks (including several alternate takes and previously unissued items) on French RCA, titled *Rose Murphy: The Complete RCA Victor Recordings*. Other than improving the acoustics, RCA, commendably, didn't mess with the Murphy mixture. There are more standards in this batch, including a new take on "Honeysuckle Rose" and an equally ebullient "Rosetta." The new songs are also right up her alley, especially "Girls Were Meant to Take Care of Boys," which suits her kewpie-doll demeanor more than it did Billie Holiday, "You, Wonderful You" (not the song of the following year from *Summer Stock* but a goodie just the same), and "Not Tonight." The RCA sessions also include "Hey! Mama (He's Trying to Kiss Me)," which, like most of Murphy's best work, makes it impossible to imagine anyone listening to it without cracking a heavy-duty ear-to-ear smile.

Murphy next did a batch of dates for Decca in the early fifties, including a particularly zippy "Believe It Beloved" that honors Waller's memory, and more twenties tunes, like "Button Up Your Overcoat." On "I Wanna Be Loved by You" she effects a compromise between her chee chee's and the song's famous "boop-oop-a-doop" by cooing "chee-boop, chee-boop." Several of the Deccas seem deliberately aimed at children, like "Peek-a-Boo" and "The Little Red Monkey." On Vincent Youmans's "Time on My Hands" she eschews all the lyrics to simply repeat the title line, make tic-toc noises and cuckoo clock calls, and imitate a chiming timepiece on the piano. At one point, she interjects the catchphrase "Time marches on!" and follows it with an approximation of soldiers marching: "Left, right!"

In 1957, Murphy cut an album for Verve, with the witty title of *Not Cha-Cha but Chi-Chi,* and began it with her third recording of "Honeysuckle Rose." The presence of alto saxophonist Willie Smith added much to the proceedings; Murphy was an accomplished enough jazz pianist to fully complement him, and, like Nat Cole's *After Midnight* (which Smith had played on a few months earlier) *Not Cha-Cha* can be enjoyed as a swing combo album with sympathetic vocals; in fact, several tunes, including the recent show tune "Mr. Wonderful," are done entirely as instrumentals. Not every song is in the same relentless tempo; in fact, "I Ain't Got Nobody" is positively relaxed, if not exactly sad and lonely. The track labeled "By the Waters of Minnetonka" turns out to be a medley of Native American love calls, starting with "Pale Moon" and transitioning into "Minnetonka," in which Murphy uses her chirping to depict the ululations of wild Indians. There's not a lot of variety to Murphy's work overall, but this package goes down very smoothly. With the welcome contributions of Willie Smith, *Not Cha-Cha* is an adorable album all the way through.

Tom Lord's *Jazz Discography* reports that Murphy also did some "rock and roll" records for a label called Regina. There was one further album in the "classic" period, an elusive LP titled *Jazz, Joy, and Happiness*, which, apparently, was produced in New York by an outfit called Big A's and then reissued on United Artists (it features star bassist Slam Stewart, trumpeter Charlie Shavers, and multireed player Seldon Powell). Lastly, there are two elder stateswoman releases from the later part of her career, *Mighty like a Rose* (1980), in which she's accompanied by another star bassist, Major Holley, and *Live in Concert* (1982), taped in performance at the Smithsonian Institution in Washington.

The 1980 set, recorded in Nice and released on the French label Black & Blue, is a set of duos by Murphy and Holley. Murphy is up to her by now old tricks, the chee chee's and other vocal effects, but at sixty-five she's mellowed considerably, and is much less intense than on her vintage 78s. Those who thought her forties and fifties work too frantic would probably enjoy this album a lot more: She's still a fine singer and a superb pianist (particularly on a pair of instrumentals, "Caravan" and Waller's "Jitterbug Waltz"). She reprises a few old favorites, among them "Busy Line" and "Time on My Hands," which are now considerably less anxious, even though time still marches on. There's also a new "Summertime," in a very modern jazz-waltz tempo; before Murphy starts singing, you might assume the pianist was a disciple of Dave Brubeck's. Her solo after the vocal is equally contemporary; again, you couldn't tell it was Murphy except for the giggling and foot stamping.

Rose Murphy worked off and on throughout the eighties (I heard her and met her at an appearance at New York's Duke Ellington Society), before she died in 1989. Her career was comparatively small no one can say she was overrecorded—but she certainly is one of the most distinctive, not to mention delightful, performers in popular music. In fact, if delightfulness is your dish, you'd be hard pressed to name anyone who does it better. Here it is. Eat up.

Hadda Brooks (1916–2002)

It might be a stretch to call Hadda Brooks a disciple of Fats Waller's. Even though she sings with Wallerian flair for tonal color, compared to Nellie Lutcher and Rose Murphy her singing is positively straightforward, and she doesn't kid the lyrics or offer verbal encouragement to her sidemen. Chronologically, Brooks is closer to the generation of Nat King Cole, but on closer inspection, the male pianist-singer she has the most in common with is Charles Brown. Her voice is somewhat similar to his and she also shares something of his distinctive intonation, particularly on blues. Unlike Brown, however, our Miss Brooks doesn't always sound like a blues singer every time out.

She could be described as a chick chum of Charles Brown (rather than a female follower of Fats), but she also sounds like a relative of more traditional (pre-R&B) blues singers like Lil Green and Memphis Minnie. Note that we're talking the "real" country blues here, not the "classic," or more cosmopolitan, blues of Bessie Smith and the Empress's many subjects. Where Minnie played guitar, Brooks played piano, and that immediately gave her a more urban, cosmopolitan image than the guitarists, who were associated with the traditional blues. In the forties, a pianist was apparently more likely to attract a mainstream audience than a guitarist. (Times, as they say, have changed.) Unlike Charles Brown, Memphis Minnie, or Lil Green, Brooks sang at least as many standards as she did blues.

The sound of Hadda Brooks's music seems somewhat incongruous in the context of her biography. (The best I've read, incidentally, is the extensive annotation by Jim Dawson that accompanies the Virgin CD *That's My Desire,* a compilation of her Modern Records singles; both the reissue and the notes are recommended.) Like Lee, Lutcher, and Murphy, Brooks made most of her record dates in Los Angeles, but unlike those slightly older ladies, she actually was born and raised there. Born Hattie Hapgood, she was a scion of what once was called, somewhat condescendingly, the black bourgeoisie. Her grandfather owned land, her father was a deputy sheriff, her mother was a doctor. How many black female doctors could there have been in California in 1916, the year Hattie Hapgood was born? Like Lutcher, she studied music with a very formal and proper lady professor, an Italian named Mrs. Bruni, and began playing piano not because she had eyes for a career in music, but simply because it was an acceptable course of study for refined young ladies. Unlike Lutcher and Lee, who were immersed in jazz and blues from an early age, Hapgood was only allowed to listen to concert music on her radio and phonograph. "I learned the classics, that's all," she told Dawson. "I'd play popular pieces like 'Sophisticated Lady' and 'Body and Soul' but then I'd hide the sheet music when Mrs. Bruni came by on Saturdays."

Hapgood attended Northwestern University, near Chicago, and Chapman College, in Los Angeles. After graduating, instead of doing something with her piano training she married a prominent basketball player named Earl "Shug" Morrison (listed in various bios as having played with either the Broadway Clowns or the Harlem Globetrotters). They were only married for a year when, tragically, Morrison died of pneumonia. Not sure what to do next, she filled her days by working as an accompanist for dancers at the Willie Covan Dance Studio. Since her forte was classical piano, she had the bright although not altogether original idea of working up swing treatments of well-known concert pieces.

The story goes that while jamming on Franz von Suppé's *Poet and Peasant Overture*, she happened to be overheard by one Jules Bihari, a young man (of Jewish-Hungarian descent) determined to make it in the music industry, who was at that time in the jukebox business. He had money in his pocket and was trying to think of something novel that he could use to start a record company with, and thought that classically inspired boogie-woogie was precisely what he was looking for. In the forties, boogie-woogie was regarded as the bottom of the black music food chain—sort of the way rap is today—looked down on by the longhair music community and even by serious jazz pianists like Art Tatum. When the young Oscar Peterson was importuned to record a pair of boogie-woogies, he regarded it as beneath him; Fats Waller himself denounced boogie-woogie as "two handfuls of nothing."

Around 1940, a black female pianist named Hazel Scott began to build a career around the idea of jazzing up the classics—in fact, that was virtually her entire act. Scott (1920–1981) was extremely popular at the time, and she and the rather revolutionary nightclub Cafe Society essentially put each other on the map. We're not covering Scott in any detail, not only because she wasn't a singer (though she sang on a few of her recordings) but because she seems less important musically than she was culturally and politically, as the darling of Cafe Society and the celebrity wife of the most accomplished African American politician of his day, Representative Adam Clayton Powell Jr. One of her final recordings was a date for bassist (and producer) Charles Mingus's Debut label, but Hazel Scott (unlike Cleo Brown, for instance) was rarely cited as a major influence as a musician, and even less so as a singer.

Scott could be viewed, however, as a direct predecessor to Hadda Brooks, although her moment had pretty much passed at the point when Brooks and Bihari began to build her career and his new label around the idea of boogie-woogie-ing the classics. Brooks launched Bihari's label, Modern Records, with a sizable hit in the instrumental "Swingin' the Boogie," recorded in April 1945, and followed it with a series of classical boogies: "Schubert's Serenade in Boogie," "Chopin's Polonaise Boogie," and "Grieg's Concerto Boogie in A Minor." Like Charles Brown, she also recorded a two-sided treatment of Richard Addinsell's *Warsaw Concerto*. She was thoroughly

versed in the classical side of the equation, and only taught herself to play boogie by studying recordings by Pete Johnson, Albert Ammons, Meade Lux Lewis, and other masters of the form. By this time, Brooks and Bihari were a team—they successfully launched Modern Records together, and they were romantically linked as well; she later called him the love of her life, and she never would marry again.

A year and a half or so and many boogies into her recording career—by which time she was already known as the "Queen of the Boogie"—Brooks began singing, at the encouragement of bandleader Charlie Barnet. As she told her later manager Alan Eichler, the two were sharing a bill at L.A.'s Million Dollar Theatre. She did her usual set of woogies-boogie, which went over well, and so the crowd demanded an encore. Barnet suggested that rather than the "monotony of yet another boogie," she should try singing. "I can't sing!" she protested. "Fake it!" the savvy saxophonist insisted.

The Modern discography is more than a little bit muddled, to put it mildly, but Brooks's first recorded vocals include Henry Nemo's "Don't Take Your Love from Me" and "That's My Desire" by Helmy Kresa (a Hungarian songwriter best known as Irving Berlin's assistant), both of which she sang with distinctly Charles Brown–like cadences. Brooks apparently felt that to record boogie-woogies for money was one thing, but if she was forced to sing, it was going to be the music she loved, what blues historians call "supper club ballads" but what most of us call the Great American Songbook. These songs were much nearer to her heart than either Grieg or the blues.

Virtually all the popular songs Brooks recorded on Modern were older tunes that she obviously had loved for years; among them were "Bewildered" and "Trust in Me," two thirties songs revived and established as soul ballads by Billy Eckstine, "Say It with a Kiss," which she'd learned from either Maxine Sullivan or Billie Holiday, and "It All Depends on You." Her commercial instincts were justified when "That's My Desire" (backed with "Humoresque Boogie") turned out to be her biggest hit: She had actually heard this 1931 song performed by Frankie Laine (who had recorded several vocals backed by Charles Brown), but she recorded her version and released it slightly ahead of Laine's. "I've Got My Love to Keep Me Warm" was another thirties song that was successfully revived after the war, and Brooks's treatment is much slower, more intimate, and more contemplative—though not any less optimistic and winning—than the hard-swinging hit instrumental treatment by Les Brown and His Band of Renown.

Between the instrumental boogies and the vocal blues and boogies, Brooks recorded at least seventy-five to eighty titles for Modern between 1945 and 1950; in all, it's an impressive body of work. (While *That's My Desire* is an excellent compendium of highlights, it's hard to believe that there's no complete set of her Modern recordings, a perfect project for Classics or Document Records.) There also were several blues-inflected ballads in the mix, including Bill Broonzy's "Keep Your Hand on Your Heart" and "When a Woman Cries," as well as a sultry number called "Honey, Honey, Honey." According to Brooks, Bihari—as a ploy to increase sales—circulated the story that the lyrics to "Honey, Honey, Honey" were excessively suggestive. Most of the love songs she recorded were already standards, although it's hard to ascertain how old Johnny Mercer's 1944 "Dream" was when she recorded it, since the Modern sessions have not been accurately dated. She apparently liked "Don't Take Your Love from Me" so much that she did at least two other songs by Nemo, "Tough on My Heart" and "Out of the Blue." She sings all of these in an appealing, tart-edged voice that proclaims her a cousin, at least, of both Dinah Washington and Carmen McRae.

The most interesting novelty on *That's My Desire* is something called "Tootsie Timesie." Brooks told Dawson that it was written by a young female fan who came to her house and presented it to her. She described it as a variant on "Straighten Up and Fly Right," and the bridges on both songs are clearly based on "I Got Rhythm." The homage to the King Cole Trio's comedy songs is obvious, and the delicatessen-driven lyrics are similar to Cole's "Solid Potato Salad." Yet the bass clef melody, the jagged rhythmic accents, and, come to think of it, even the title sound exactly like the writing of Thelonious Monk. Go figure.

More than the other singer-pianists, Brooks had looks. When Hollywood offered her the opportunity to work in pictures, she snatched it, appearing in a couple of short subjects and then graduating to cameos in features: *Out of the Blue* (1947), with George Brent and Turhan Bey, and *The Bad and the Beautiful* (1952), with Lana Turner and Kirk Douglas (and Spike the Wonder Mule). Her most conspicuous role in her most prominent film was *In a Lonely Place* (1950), in which she played and sang a beautiful, restrained chorus of Ray Noble's "I Hadn't Anyone Till You" while Humphrey Bogart and Gloria Grahame looked on with great interest. Next time it shows up on cable, set your TiVos to "sultry."

By 1950, Brooks had helped to make Modern Records a player in the newly christened R&B market; the Bihari brothers, Joe and Jules, would eventually introduce B. B. King, Jesse Belvin, and both Elmore James and Etta James, among many others. But Brooks and Jules Bihari parted company in that year, both personally and professionally. She was by now popular enough to be upgraded from a "race"-based independent label to the black music subsidiary of a major. After a few rare sides for London Records, she began a one-year relationship with Okeh, the black music division of Columbia.

The sixteen sides Brooks cut for Okeh in 1952 (all included on the CD *Jump Back Honey: The Com-*

plete Okeh Sessions) are an interesting if mixed bag, the best known of which is the title song. This original composition by Brooks, while not a major hit for her, nonetheless became one of the signature works of the transition into rock 'n' roll in that it was widely covered by all sorts of white singers and big bands, from Vaughn Monroe to Jimmy Dorsey (not to mention Ella Mae Morse and, later, Rufus Thomas) and even the two ultra-Caucasian stars of TV's *Your Hit Parade*, Snooky Lanson and Dorothy Collins. It's one of those irresistibly bouncy, nonsensical riffs that frequently crossed over in that era, rather like "Hambone," "Tweedle-Dee-Dee," and "Sh-Boom."

The Okeh batch has a couple of oddities, like Edith Piaf's Parisian passion piece "If You Love Me" done as a mostly spoken monologue (backed by a small orchestra conducted by future arranging star Don Costa), and a very straight reading of "I Went to Your Wedding," Patti Page's lamentably lachrymose hit. Tellingly, all of the Okeh sides are vocals; the boogie instrumental series was finished before she could get around to "Bartók Boogie."

On the plus side, there's an improved remake of "Trust in Me," as well as a number of sides that were equal parts blues and torch song, while Charles Singleton's "All Night Long" likewise manages to be both romantic and erotic. In "I Don't Mind" the message is that the singer almost enjoys suffering for her man, whereas in "You Let My Love Get Cold" she retaliates with a message more like "Make *me* suffer, will you?"

The two most satisfying Okehs are a pair of standard ballads by Irving Berlin, songs I imagine Brooks learned as a little girl, seated at the Steinway, while Mrs. Bruni was looking the other way. "Remember" is, as always (and, as "Always"), a lovely, touching song, which Brooks keeps from getting sentimental by doing it slightly faster than you'd expect—and in 4/4 rather than waltz time. "When I Leave the World Behind" is a total surprise; usually done as a grandiose Jolsonesque last will and testament set to music, Brooks's interpretation is admirably restrained and underplayed—and right on the money. Overall, it's one of the most subtle—and therefore most moving—treatments ever of this rarely revived Berlin beauty.

The sixteen songs for Okeh were apparently the end of Brooks's recording career. (There were some LPs released on Crown, a bargain label, but it's hard to tell if any of these contain original material or, more likely, are strictly reissues of the Modern 78s.) For the rest of the fifties, Brooks toured Europe and worked intermittently on television; according to one account, she was the first African American woman to host her own talk show, making her the Oprah of her day. For most of the sixties, she lived and worked in Australia, then, she told Dawson, "when I came home, I retired."

For roughly fifteen years Brooks kept out of

sight, but then she came to the attention of Richard Lamparski, a journalist who made a career out of "rescuing" showbiz personalities who had been relegated to the far corners of obscurity. After Lamparski featured her in one of his *Whatever Happened To . . .* books, he put her in touch with Alan Eichler, a pop music buff and agent who likewise made a specialty of resurrecting the careers of veteran divas who had fallen through the cracks.

Eichler helped Brooks orchestrate a whole new career; starting roughly in 1986, the year she turned seventy, and continuing for roughly ten years, Brooks played major rooms all over the world, from the Fairmont in San Francisco to Michael's Pub and the Oak Room at the Hotel Algonquin in New York. She was beloved of both the lounge music movement and the swing-dance craze, not to mention being rightfully recognized as a pioneer of rhythm and blues. Her career at this point was like that of the similarly neglected Little Jimmy Scott in that she also briefly became the cause du jour of hip celebrities. Retro rockabilly star Deke Dickerson brought her in to do a duet with him on "You're My Cadillac," accompanied by his band, the Ecco-Fonics, on his album *More Million Sellers.* Johnny Depp hired her to sing in the Viper Room, a club he owned on the Sunset Strip (Depp hosted her eightieth birthday at the club, and Jack Nicholson and Uma Thurman were in attendance). Sean Penn gave her a singing and acting cameo in his 1995 film *The Crossing Guard.*

Miss Brooks had pretty much skipped over the entire LP era, but went straight from 78s in 1952 to a pair of newly recorded CDs in 1994 (*Anytime, Anyplace, Anywhere* on DRG) and in 1995 (*Time Was When* on Virgin). Both of these later albums employ a King Cole–style rhythm section with guitarist Al Viola and bassist Eugene Wright, plus, as special guests, trumpeter Jack Sheldon on the first and cellist Richard Dodd on the second. On both, she obviously sounds like a seventy-five-year-old woman whose voice has been around the block more than a few times but one who has spent all those years perfecting the craft of delivering a lyric.

There are many remakes on the two albums, including a third recording of "Trust in Me" and an update of "Don't You Think I Ought to Know?" The prize on *Time Was When* is the title song, in a slightly slower and more poignant treatment than the recording from forty-plus years earlier, as it took all the intervening years for her to fully realize exactly what time was and is; when she sang it live in a club and closed with the line "But I can remember when there was a time," nobody was about to doubt her. Her reading of the Sinatra classic "I'm a Fool to

Want You" shows that dark torch songs are her true forte, while "How Do You Speak to an Angel" bespeaks a knowledge and mastery of obscure show tunes. However, upon hearing "Need a Little Sugar in My Bowl" (associated with Bessie Smith and then Nina Simone), you would have to conclude that her true color was the basic blues.

Anytime, Anyplace, Anywhere benefits from the exuberant presence of trumpeter Jack Sheldon, particularly on the brasscentric ballad "Man with the Horn" as well as Brooks's lightly rocking "Ol' Man River." She renders the Hammerstein-Kern anthem with swing era–style jive accoutrements, including a contrapuntal riff and a fast tempo, but make no mistake: Her treatment is highly emotional, punctuated by interjections of laughter, and another very moving and personal statement about the passage of time. Sheldon also sings, deploying that marvelously scratchy voice we all know from *Schoolhouse Rock* cartoons, joining her on "All of Me."

To me, the masterpiece of the two later albums is "Don't Go to Strangers," a mainstream song long accepted into the realm of blue ballads. She sings it with just her own piano, slow and sentimental, but not too slow or too sentimental—making it highly personal but refusing to let it get maudlin. She sings with unmistakable love—romantic, maternal, whatever, it could be to a child or to a lover, it doesn't matter. She's been through it all, she's an old hand—the lyric tells us this—but the words are almost immaterial; at best they merely reinforce what we hear in the sound of Brooks's voice itself. She sings it with so much authority that from the very sound of her weather-beaten voice we realize that there's next to nothing that she doesn't know.

Hadda Brooks died in 2002, at the age of eighty-six. I saw her many times in the nineties; usually she was wonderful, and it's good to have the two later albums to back up that recollection. Once, near the end, she was clearly crocked: She sang several songs more than once, and also repeated at least one anecdote. It didn't matter.

On the *Anytime* album, she does "Heart of a Clown," a ballad she obviously learned from Nellie Lutcher, who recorded it twice. Lutcher's rendition is more than a bit artsy and heavy for her, and is hardly one of the more scintillating items in her catalogue. But Brooks puts it into more of a dance tempo, and makes it meaningful by keeping it light. She enjoyed a much bigger comeback and late-in-life career than Cleo Brown, Julia Lee, Nellie Lutcher, or Rose Murphy, and in salvaging this forgotten number from Lutcher's songbook, Hadda Brooks was closing the book on a highly worthy but woefully neglected area of American music.

Big Pop (Male)

Frankie Laine
Johnnie Ray
Guy Mitchell
Johnny Mathis
Andy Williams

Frank Sinatra was never much for giving interviews, but in 1958 he had a doozy of a conversation with the veteran music journalist Leonard Feather. Sinatra was visiting his dear friend (and, it is currently believed, occasional lover) Peggy Lee at the time, and one suspects he only agreed to the interview because Feather was a close friend of Lee's. Then, too, Sinatra was perhaps amused by the premise that Feather proposed: Imagine, the critic postulated, that you're stuck in a penthouse by yourself for a whole weekend. You can't get out, but you've been left in luxury's lap, you have hot and cold running Veuve Clicquot 1947 and a state-of-the-art hi-fi system, perhaps even one endowed with that marvel of the age, stereophonic sound. And, says Feather, you're allowed to have a total of six 12" long-playing records to listen to for three days.

Sinatra, as Feather reported in the July 1958 *Playboy,* went right along with the premise. "Now first," says Sinatra, "I'd rather concentrate mainly on the human voice because under those conditions with nobody to talk to, it would be preferable to instrumentals. So I'd like four albums: one each by Ella Fitzgerald, Peggy Lee, Nat Cole, and Perry Como." Then, Sinatra continues, he would like to have some instrumental music to listen to, and names a number of contemporary modern swing-style bandleaders. "Then I'd like to have one album specially made up, if possible, of the following: Nelson Riddle, Billy May, Les Brown, and Les Elgart. I don't want to get into the jazz field, because once I start there there'll be no stopping—I'll wind up with 60 albums." For his sixth record, he picks something that might seem a surprise to some Sinatra fans: "The other instrumental is the Vaughn Williams *Job.* I pick that because it has great variety; it's a sort of potpourri of all kinds of music. There's even syncopation, and suggestions of jazz with an alto sax. It's most interesting music."

Sinatra has now made his six choices, and so the conversation moves on. Miss Lee starts to say something, but then Sinatra, who was rarely so rude as to interrupt a lady while she was talking, bursts in with one more idea. "Hold it a minute!" says Sinatra. "I got a seventh album. The seventh album I would like made up of Elvis Presley, Johnny Mathis, Johnnie Ray, Lawrence Welk, and Sammy Kaye." Sinatra's selection of Ralph Vaughn Williams may not have raised Feather's eyebrows, but this seventh choice certainly does. "I'll tell you why I'd want that album," Frankie says, grinning. "I'd play it occasionally just to remind me how good the *other* people are."

It's fascinating to look at whom Sinatra respected and whom he had no use for among his fellow pop singers: Interestingly, he doesn't mention his three biggest influences (Bing Crosby, Billie Holiday, and Louis Armstrong), and the only one of his fellow Italian-Americans he mentions is his slightly older contemporary Como. The five artists he chose to bash also exhibit a wide, even healthy, range of dislikes: Johnny Mathis was a new pop singer, who had more in common with Cole and Sinatra than he did with Presley; Elvis Presley himself was the greatest rock 'n' roll star of all time; Johnnie Ray was, as we will see, a pop singer whose appeal spanned both the rock and the classic pop genres; Lawrence Welk was the leader of what used to be known as a sweet band who made the transition both into television and into a new musical genre known as easy listening. The same could be said of Sammy Kaye, although his orchestra remained more firmly in the traditional Mickey Mouse mold of the thirties. (Compared to Sammy Kaye, Lawrence Welk was positively avant-garde.)

The interesting thing about all the singers he trashes is that none of them specialized in the Great American Songbook. All of them sang it from time to time, but, unlike Sinatra, they didn't rely on the standards for their bread-and-butter. If you felt like listening to a great song by Rodgers and Hart, chances are you probably wouldn't put on a record by Johnny Mathis or Johnnie Ray.

Sinatra himself was the inspiration for nearly all the major singers that came after him. With Tony Bennett and Steve Lawrence and Jack Jones and Bobby Darin and Mel Tormé and Buddy Greco and Vic Damone (to name just a few post-Sinatra males), his influence was all-pervasive. Yet there was another school of male pop vocalists who dominated the charts in the fifties and sixties, who had two things in common: They all worked with Sinatra's bête noir Mitch Miller at least at some point in their careers, and, perhaps not coincidentally, they all sang as if they had absolutely never heard of Frank Sinatra.

Frankie Laine (1913–2007)

Sinatra was more or less silent on the subject of fellow Sicilian Frankie Laine, neither condemning nor condoning this iron-lunged, big-belting pop star. There was one point around 1950 when Laine was a rising star and Sinatra a falling one, and Sinatra spoofed his competition's big hit "Cry of the Wild Goose" while bounding out on the stage of the Copacabana in a coonskin hat. However, this was clearly an affectionate ribbing, delivered in the same spirit as when, years later, he referred to another fellow Italo-crooner and buddy as "Jerry *Fail*" (for Vale). Still, I can't think of any direct instance when Sinatra voiced his opinion of Laine in any of his identities—whether in the forties, when Laine billed himself as "Mr. Rhythm," or in the fifties, when he became the testosterone-driven baritone of a thousand Western movie songs, as well as the all-purpose utility singer featured in every other Mitch Miller–produced duet record.

Of all the major pop singers, with the arguable exception of Joe Williams and Carmen McRae (partly because they were essentially jazz and not pop singers), Laine took the longest to make it. Most singing stars of his generation started with a name band in their teens; Laine never landed a band berth of any import and didn't start making records until he was in his early thirties (the age when most band singers were effectively finished). He was born Francesco Paolo LoVecchio in Chicago, in 1913, the first of eight children in an immigrant family. At the age of eleven, he later said, he stumbled across blues empress Bessie Smith's "Broken Hearted Blues," and this, he later stated, inspired him, already singing in church, to want to sing professionally. A similar revelation occurred two years later when he saw Al Jolson's *The Singing Fool.* However, little happened to him over the next twenty years. He fought the Depression working in dance marathons in Chicago (where he earned the lifelong admiration of aspiring jazz babe Anita O'Day) and briefly replaced Perry Como in Freddy Carlone's Pennsylvania-based territory dance band.

Meanwhile, LoVecchio relocated to New York and then, in 1944, to Los Angeles. There he continued to scuffle, singing in any joint that would let him near the mike, and supporting himself by working in a defense plant. Laine's "discovery" story: He was sitting in at Billy Berg's and made the fortunate decision to sing Hoagy Carmichael's "Rockin' Chair"—fortunate, because Carmichael himself happened to be in the house that night, and was so taken with Laine's rendition of his 1929 classic that he insisted Berg hire him.

Laine began making records shortly thereafter, but he moved up slowly, starting with very small, minor-league labels and only gradually working his way up to the big time. He started with Atlas, which, despite the firm's ambitious name, was a tiny company based in Los Angeles. At roughly the same time, he did some of the best recording work of his career on commercial transcriptions distributed to radio stations (many of which were later issued on LP and CD by Hindsight). From the small indie Atlas, he moved to the bigger but still independent Mercury, a label that Laine and his new producer, Mitch Miller, worked hard to make into a major player. After a few promising hits, the Laine-Miller combination moved to the big time at Columbia Records, and, from then on, the world was their oyster.

As mentioned, Laine was billed as "Mr. Rhythm" in his early days, and he clearly was trying to establish himself as a singer of jazz, blues, and standards. He is even a scholar of the music: *The Return of Mr.*

Rhythm, a Hindsight collection of transcriptions from the 1945–48 period, contains Laine's vocal versions of the two most celebrated jazz solos of the twenties, Louis Armstrong's "West End Blues" and Bix Beiderbecke's "Singin' the Blues." Admittedly "jazz singing" is perhaps the most subjective term in the English language, but going by consensus, one would be hard-pressed to find any objective listener who would consider the mature Laine a jazz singer. He doesn't swing, he belts, and with the right material his belting can be tremendously effective.

It's also something of a stretch to characterize him as a traditional pop singer—at least as defined in this book—since he was one of the first big star singers who didn't depend on the Broadway-based axis of composers and what we think of as the Great American Songbook for their repertoire. He did sing standards frequently, but most of his hits and the songs he's known for are anything but. (At least one contemporary jazz musician disagrees with this assertion—the brilliant baritone saxophonist and educator Gary Smulyan feels that Laine was one of *the* great jazz singers.)

In 1955, Laine recorded *Jazz Spectacular,* a collaboration with the brilliant swing trumpeter Buck Clayton; it was clearly an effort to show what an excellent jazz singer he was, but the album achieves precisely the opposite. It reveals that even placed in a purely jazz context, he doesn't have a clue as to how to swing. He sings loud, he sings fast, he blasts and he belts and he makes a lot of noise. He's almost always exciting, but he's never swinging. He's the complete opposite of a subtle swinger like Blossom Dearie or Joe Mooney, who could sing incredible jazz without any voice at all to speak of.

But there's more to singing than jazz, or even standards. Laine's specialty is a kind of superkitsch that he makes seem like great music through sheer determination. When we listen to "High Noon" or "Blazing Saddles," we don't necessarily care about these other considerations; we only know that we're listening to an exciting singer doing an exciting song. The passion, feeling, and movement that he puts into a song are palpable, almost operatically grandiose; this approach wouldn't work for "Lush Life" or even "God Bless the Child," but it works with "Cry of the Wild Goose" and "Granada." There are good renditions of standards in his discography, and also blatantly awful ones, such as his dementedly overwrought treatment of "A Woman in Love" (from the film score of *Guys and Dolls*), which attempts to turn Loesser's love song into a torrid tango in the mold of his hit "Jealousy." (Some of Laine's treatments of contemporary show tunes are enjoyable for a variety of reasons, such as his high-camp reading of the broken-English title song from *The Most Happy Fella.*) Fittingly, some of his best standards are on his final album, *Wheels of a Dream*, in which he does considerably better singing with considerably less voice than on his youthful work.

What Laine does best are heavy-duty, angst-ridden songs about working, loving, fighting, and punching cows and people. (Not for nothing did Mitch Miller describe Laine's musical "character" as "the Blue Collar Guy.") He always sings as if he's about to bust a gut; whether he's driving mules in "Mule Train," herding cows in "Rawhide," or about to face a gunslinger who hates him in "High Noon," he delivers with the verismo and machismo of the great Neapolitan voices—more Pinza and Lanza than Sinatra or Como—bringing a touch of Italian opera to horse opera.

Laine was particularly identified with Western movie music; sometimes he actually sang over the opening titles, as on *Gunfight at the O.K. Corral*. His most famous Western song, "High Noon," was actually introduced by Tex Ritter on the movie sound track, but Laine had the hit single and the identification. Here he proved that the most authentic Western music was made by the combination of a Russian composer (Dimitri Tiomkin) and a Sicilian belter. The "High Noon" theme was later reincarnated as "Gunfight at the O.K. Corral," then the theme for the TV series *Rawhide*, and finally ingeniously self-parodied by the team of Laine and Mel Brooks in *Blazing Saddles*. The latter shows that Laine's material was often ripe for satirical purposes: "Cry of the Wild Goose," by future folk star Terry Gilkyson, was spoofed not only by Sinatra, as already mentioned, but also in a hilarious Yiddish treatment by Mickey Katz as "Geshray of the Vilde Kotchke."

Fighting and working are closely related activities in Laine's music. "Sixteen Tons" was written by Merle Travis and popularized by Tennessee Ernie Ford, bless his pea-picking heart, but no one sings it as convincingly as Laine, who truly sounds as if he wants to beat the ever-lovin' bejesus out of anyone listening. "High Noon" and "Gunfight" tell tall tales of professional law enforcers in the Old West, men whose job, in a sense, was to fight; in contrast, "Mule Train," "Sixteen Tons," "Song of the Open Road," and "Rawhide" are about men doing a dirty job and doing it so hard that they might as well be fighting.

"Cry of the Wild Goose" and "North to Alaska" and many others are, on the surface, simple paeans to the great outdoors, but if you listen a little more closely, they're really about escaping the restrictive confines of civilization—as if Laine, in his own way, was also forecasting the end of the gray flannel, button-down, suburban society of the fifties. And who could fail to get a high-camp charge out of such ersatz-religious epics as "I Believe" and "That Lucky Old Sun"? "Sun," in fact, clearly paved the way for the later and even more anthemic reading by Ray Charles.

Laine is a fighter, not a lover. He does also sing about love, but he's not particularly good at either the tender, romantic happy variety, or the torchy-bluesy sad variety of ballad. He specializes in high-dramatic songs about the extreme end of love, with extravagant tales of wicked women, evil Jezebels, and Satans-in-satin. These heartless hussies and harlots don't just send their unfortunate male victims to the nearest saloon to imbibe one for the road, as they might in a Sinatra song. Rather, the hapless guys who fall for them go straight to the inferno—do not pass "Go," do not collect $200. You could easily fill a CD with Laine's songs of Circe-like sirens who send their luckless victims crashing on the rocks: "Jezebel," "Miss Satan," "Samson," "Swamp Girl," "Hell Hath No Fury (Like a Woman Scorned)," "Satan Wears a Satin Gown," and "Cherry Red." It would be interesting to analyze these songs in light of the attitudes toward gender equality in the Eisenhower era. Let's just say that Laine has the most cynical view of man-woman relations of any singer before Nina Simone.

Some of his most memorable music was made in the company of others; both he and Miller appear to have been keen boosters of the idea of the pop duet. Laine sang with a wide range of fellow Columbia contractees, such as Jo Stafford (on an enjoyable album of New Orleans–centric material), Doris Day, and even pint-sized Jimmy Boyd; he also created effective pop gospel with the Four Lads ("Ain't It a Pity and a Shame") and fellow belter Johnnie Ray (Sister Rosetta Tharpe's rousing "Up Above My Head"). I find it hard to resist two of the most bizarrely diverse offerings of the very multiculti fifties, "Sugarbush" and "How Lovely Cooks the Meat." Both these duets with Doris Day are vaguely Slavic offerings that sound like a polka or a schottische but are actually South African songs by the folkster Josef Marais; in order to work, they need to be taken at face value, so don't make the mistake of looking for sexual innuendo here.

There are other gems in Laine's copious discography that await unearthing; fortunately, the Bear Family has undertaken a complete reissue of his output (as they have with Rosemary Clooney, Doris Day, Dean Martin, and Johnnie Ray). Laine may have made his greatest contribution to American pop as a songwriter, having written a number of pieces recorded by close friend Nat King Cole: "It Only Happens Once" and "My Magnificent Obsession." His ballad "We'll Be Together Again" is a major standard, holding a place of honor on what may well be the greatest jazz-pop album of all time, Sinatra and Riddle's *Songs for Swingin' Lovers*. The renditions of Laine's compositions by Cole and Sinatra, not surprisingly, reveal a sensitivity Laine never brought to his own singing.

Laine died in 2007, his ninety-fourth year. In 1998, he released one of the best albums in his career, *Wheels of a Dream*; in his own classic tradition he lunges into the title track, from Broadway's *Ragtime*, and creates a new Laine standard. More important, he finally got around to recording an old one, although I can't imagine why he never recorded the song that could have been his greatest, "They Call the Wind Maria" (from *Paint Your Wagon*), until he was well over eighty. But even then there was no one better at this kind of musical machismo. This I believe.

Frankie Laine and Mitch Miller were born at roughly the same time and came up in the pop music business together, and thus it wouldn't be quite right to describe Laine as a Miller "creation." The other two major male singers under Miller's control were Guy Mitchell and Johnnie Ray, who both broke through in 1950–51. Mitchell was almost exclusively a Miller creation, down to his professional name, whereas Ray protested vehemently when he was characterized as such. (I am excluding Tony Bennett— easily Miller's greatest discovery—from this discussion, since he is the only member of this group who had a substantial post-Miller recording career.)

Laine was Mitch Miller's first major collaborator, and in a sense he served as an archetype for the others. Together, Miller and Mitchell developed a kind of manufactured folk song, and Miller and Ray crafted a highly stylized take on rhythm and blues. With Laine, it was a bit of both: Some of his music is like Western and folk songs, but some of it comes out of the blues. (One of his more convincing songs in the latter mold is called "New Orleans," which turns out to be a new title for the old Louisiana blues "The House of the Rising Sun.") But the interesting thing is that all three men had an impact on the development of pop music without ever being anything like an authentic singer of jazz, blues, or standards.

Johnnie Ray (1927–1990)

Sinatra's lumping Johnnie Ray in the same category with Elvis Presley is altogether appropriate: Johnnie Ray provided one of the vital links in American pop music, linking Jolson to Elvis. Ray told one story on himself: He was riding high with a string of number-one hit singles in the early to mid-fifties (though only one blockbuster hit, as we shall see) when he did a tour of England in 1955. He returned two months later, and the reporters who greeted him at the airport back home in the U.S. asked him what he thought of Elvis Presley. He responded with a question: "What's an Elvis Presley?" As he later told Peter Grendysa, "The press got on it right away, saying it was sour grapes on my part." Being dissed by the press for inadvertently dumping on Elvis was the least of his problems, though. With the emergence of Presley, Ray's career was essentially finished: There would be another hit or two, but now the world no longer had any need for Johnnie Ray.

While others, like Bobby Darin and more recently Natalie Cole, cultivated their talents in both the youth and adult pop spheres, only Johnnie Ray was born of both worlds. His biography has traditionally been fashioned to show that this was a guy who grew up immersed in the blues. Born in Oregon, in 1927 (some sources say Hopewell, others say Dallas, Oregon), he was already a shy and withdrawn child when at the age of twelve he was playing with some bigger kids who accidentally dropped him on his head, causing him to lose much of his hearing. "The doctors didn't realize what was wrong until four years later. . . . When I couldn't understand my teachers in school, I landed at the bottom of the class. I was the dumb bunny of the crowd." Eventually he was fitted with a hearing aid (which he wore for the rest of his life) and, no less important, he "found [solace] in the melancholy message and the pure haunting beauty of the great Negro spirituals."

Ray is probably the only major white headliner who came up through the channels of black show business. Although he briefly tried Hollywood as a youngster, appearing for a time with the rising and equally young Jane Powell, he spent most of the forties "paying his dues" in black nightclubs in the Midwest. By 1950 he had made it to one of the top black clubs in the country, the Flame Bar in Detroit; he credited Maurice King, the spiritual forefather of the later Motown dynasty, with teaching him everything he knew.

Ray had written an original blues entitled "Whiskey and Gin" ("I gotta gal who drinks whiskey and gin . . .") and he caused a ruckus singing it— shouting it would be more likely. And not even just shouting, but contorting his body, jumping up and down, clenching his fingers, gnashing his teeth, and in general writhing in agony. A number of people seemed to think that "Whiskey and Gin" was a potential "race" hit, including Ray himself, who sent a demo of himself singing it to Capitol Records. Another was Danny Kessler, a talent scout for Okeh Records, which at the time was the "race" records subsidiary of the larger Columbia Records corporation. Kessler offered Ray the chance to record the song for Okeh, and he initially turned it down because he dreamed of being on Capitol.

However, Kessler soon prevailed and Ray went with Okeh. "Whiskey and Gin" earned some good notices; *Billboard* described Ray, not altogether inaccurately, as "a cross between Jimmy Scott and Kay Starr." Then he landed a megablockbuster hit, bigger than he or Kessler had dreamed of, with his third release on Okeh, "Cry," backed with "The Little White Cloud That Cried." The first was the song that launched the genre soon to be known as the "sob ballad," the work of Churchill Kohlmann, an aspiring black songwriter then working as a night watchman in a dry-cleaning plant in Cleveland. Ray himself took credit for transforming Kohlmann's original song, which, he said, was in a more gentle and sentimental vein, into, in Ray's words, "a real blood, guts, and thunder type thing." Accompanied by just a rhythm section and a backup vocal group, the Four Lads (soon to be a star attraction on their own), "Cry" became the ultimate vehicle for Ray's histrionics. By now he was sobbing, apparently uncontrollably, onstage—weeping, wailing, and gnashing even more teeth.

"Cry" was the biggest hit of 1951, instantly selling two million copies and surpassing even producer Mitch Miller's two other sensations, "Come on-a My House" by Rosemary Clooney and "Because of You" and "Cold, Cold Heart" by Tony Bennett. (Ray claimed that Miller had nothing to do with signing him to the label or the production of "Cry," but in retrospect it's clear that it was Miller who assigned him the song.) The flip side, a number-two hit in its own right, was Ray's original "The Little White Cloud That Cried." This piece also addressed the issue of tear-producing emotions, but in a more contemplative, not to say sappy, mood. (Leading to Stan Freberg's parody, "Singers do it, crowds do it / Even little white clouds do it," à la Cole Porter.)

Ray's affection for the world of black music—jazz, gospel, blues—was genuine, but some would take issue with the end product of these influences. To give him his due, he was indeed the first-ever crossover R&B star—the first white entertainer to work in the contorted, hyphenated manner (i.e., "Cah-ry-hi" instead of "cry") that characterized rhythm and blues and then doo-wop and early rock. That style of singing was already highly exaggerated and mannered, yet Ray was even more so. Was he a genuine R&B artist or merely an outrageous caricature of one? It's a matter of personal opinion. As the first white R&B headliner, he signified the first time many middle Americans had heard even a vague imitation of "race" music. As such, he was described by no less an icon of subsequent pop than Bob Dylan as "the first singer whose voice and style I totally fell in love with."

One thing Ray was proud of was that he was never a cover artist. Unlike, say, Pat Boone covering a hit by Little Richard, when Ray sang Big Joe Turner's "Flip, Flop and Fly" it was hardly a sanitized, cleaned-up treatment of that novelty blues. Instead, it was considerably more exaggerated and over-the-top than the original. His treatment of the Basie standard "Every Day I Have the Blues" seems at once like a caricature and a pale imitation of Joe Williams. Ray brought a highly stylized approach to gospel and blues material that was completely inauthentic but at times enjoyable—not unlike Guy Mitchell doing a pseudo–folk song or one of Laine's mule train epics. Whether you liked him or not, you had to admit that Ray was a man with his own style.

People came to watch him do his hits and scream and shout the blues, but along the way he also sang the occasional standard. His one major motion picture, *There's No Business Like Show Business,* had him warbling classic show tunes by Irving Berlin (not a good idea). He also made at least one jazz/standards album, *'Til Morning,* in which he was accompanied by pianist Billy Taylor and his quartet (billed as a trio on the cover for some reason), and standards figure on such live albums as *Johnnie Ray in Las Vegas,* taped at the Desert Inn. When Ray does a traditional ballad in a traditional style, such as his strings-backed treatment of "As Time Goes By," the results are, for him, tepid. When he does a standard song in his own "blood, guts, and thunder" fashion, the outcome is more interesting.

Mitch Miller occasionally selected new show tunes for him, such as "Hey There" and the tango "Hernando's Hideaway"—both from *The Pajama Game.* Someone had the idea—apparently inspired by Ray's inspiration, Kay Starr—to give the singer such forgotten Jazz Age opuses as "Here Am I Broken Hearted" and "Glad Rag Doll." Another of his big early hits, "Walkin' My Baby Back Home," seems to have been born in this fashion. This revived 1931 charmer, which Ray recorded with backing very similar to the King Cole Trio, proved a substantial hit for him, and it also seems to have inspired Nat Cole himself, in the company of Billy May, to do it on Capitol. The Cole record is obviously far superior, yet Ray got there firstest, even without necessarily the mostest, and had the bigger hit (number 4 as opposed to Cole's number 8).

In 1994, writer Jonny Whiteside published the only full-dress biography of the singer, *Cry: The Johnnie Ray Story,* which was followed by a CD retrospective from Sony of Ray's best work, the recommended *High Drama: The Real Johnnie Ray.* Mr. Whiteside writes, "Johnny Ray was the missing link between Frank Sinatra and Elvis Presley." It's very much a stretch to speak of Ray in the same breath as Sinatra and Presley, who are justly celebrated as the two greatest pop singers of all time (or two of three, with Bing). Certainly, he has nothing in common with Sinatra (who, as we have seen, was not a fan), not even material, and it's painful to compare him to Presley, who was both a superior bluesman and a superior balladeer. Both Presley and Ray recorded versions of the Clyde McPhatter–Drifters hit "Such a Night," but where Presley's is flowing, sensual, and even romantic (where Sinatra was a *swingin'* lover, Elvis was a *rockin'* lover), Ray is stilted and stiff, and next to Elvis his wailing sounds artificial and forced. Compared to Sinatra and Presley, he's extremely limited and one-dimensional, but, as I say, it's a cruel comparison.

It's also on the cruel side to suggest that Ray, who died in 1990 at sixty-three, only left behind one completely indispensable record, and his legions of fans, include those who bought the complete Johnnie Ray box series on Bear Family, would obviously disagree. I would agree that "Cry" is great pop music, or if not pop music then, at the very least, a superior piece of performance art.

Guy Mitchell (1927–1999)

What are the politics of "catchy"? If a record is "catchy," does that necessarily mean it's good? Or not good? My definition of a "catchy" song is that the rhythm and/or melody are easy to remember—whether one wants to or not. If it's easy to remember (and so hard to forget), can it still be forgettable in a larger sense? Can a song be catchy and forgettable at the same time? Are we annoyed because it's so catchy, meaning that in spite of ourselves we find ourselves going around humming "There's a pawnshop on the corner in Pittsburgh, Pennsylvania . . ." or "She wears red feathers and a hooly-hooly skirt . . ." or "I never felt more like singin' the blues . . ."? What's the difference, then, between "catchy" and "irritating"? Obviously there are melodies like commercial jingles that we can't get out of our heads no matter how hard we try. If a song is catchy, do we owe it any degree of respect, even grudgingly? Or maybe it is, in fact, great pop music.

Guy Mitchell is the most forgettable and unforgettable of major fifties pop stars. He certainly had a style and sound of his own, not only in terms of *how* he sang, but also *what* he sang. Between the how and the what, Mitchell and his producer, Mitch Miller, fixed it so that it was nearly impossible to get a Guy Mitchell record out of your head from about thirty seconds after you put the needle in the lead-in groove. Again, this is neither a good or a bad thing necessarily—but it certainly is a thing.

However, while Mitchell had something of a TV career after his run as a hit maker ended, and also had a dedicated core audience that supported him up to the time he died in 1999, the man himself fairly disappeared. Mitchell was the purest example of a complete Mitch Miller creation—the singer was so indebted to the manipulations of the producer that, born Al Cernik in 1927, he even took his professional name from Miller. Unlike Bennett, Clooney, Ray, and Laine, Mitchell seems to have brought little of his own to the table—just his good looks and a remarkable vocal instrument. (His intonation was indeed extraordinary, and he seems to have had no difficulty whatever in hitting almost any note in almost any register.) Once he met Mitch Miller, the producer could have set him up as virtually anything—a singer of big dramatic ballads like Bennett, an angst-filled quasi-blues shouter like Ray, a "blue-collar guy" like Laine, a purveyor of international novelties like Clooney, or a girl (or in his case, boy) next door like Doris Day. Everything that Mitchell ever was seemed to be entirely the creation of Miller and the songwriters who scripted his record persona, especially Bob Merrill. Mitchell was, in a sense, the first manufactured, prepackaged pop star, with a sound and a style that were completely assembled for him by others, and in that respect he was a direct forerunner of the era of producer pop and rock.

The question of who was responsible for Mitchell's sound is worth asking, not only because he was so successful but because he was so distinctive. It's unfair to say that all the Guy Mitchell hits sound alike, although they certainly do to a newcomer to his music, but in perspective he was no more or less inclined to stick as rigidly to his formula as, say, Johnny Mathis or any other grade-B pop icon (by grade-B, I mean anyone not on the level of Sinatra, Bennett, or Cole). This formula consists of certain very clearly defined stylistic points:

- Mitchell not only anticipated producer pop but the folk movement of the late fifties and early sixties as well. He didn't sing authentic folk songs, although it was claimed that some of his hits were based on traditional material; for the most part, his songs were newly written pieces that were made to sound like old songs. Think of a saloon or dance hall scene in a fifties Technicolor Western—like *Calamity Jane* or the Audie Murphy remake of *Destry Rides Again* or maybe *Rancho Notorious*. Think of a showgirl or singer doing a number onstage. This is one of the songs she would sing, something that sounds like Hollywood's approximation of a pop song from the Wild and Woolly West. Virtually everything Guy Mitchell did had a distinctly nineteenth-century feel to it, as if it could have been sung by pioneers or heard on a pirate ship.

- Producer Mitch Miller was famous—and infamous—in his day for going beyond the big band sound. He ended the domination of the brass, reeds, and rhythm—and occasional strings—format that had dominated pop since Paul Whiteman's day. With his classical background, he was attuned to all kinds of sounds not found in the dance band tradition, most famously French horns. He used French horns with Mitchell more than he did with any of his other major artists, to further enhance the feeling that here were a singer and songs out of another time, another place. Indeed, Mitchell seems as far apart from, say, the Sinatra swing or ballad albums of the period as both of them do from Elvis Presley.

- Then there's that unrelenting catchiness. Miller and his orchestrators were entirely shameless in that they would do anything to hook the listener's ear with a catchy rhythm. Among their most employed devices was a choir that repeats the hook phrases over and over—as if ramming them down your throat. And then there was the trick of casting most of Mitchell's songs in an ABAB pattern, as opposed to the AABA of most Tin Pan Alley songs, which again gives the material a distinctly nineteenth-century feeling, and also ensures more repetition of the B section, which invariably includes the hook or title phrase. But the most irritating and the most successful—not to mention the simplest—gimmick that Miller and the arrangers employed was the use of hand claps. Just throw in some clapping hands here and there and the listener is instantly hooked.

Mitchell's archetypal hit was Bob Merrill's 1951 "My Truly, Truly Fair." It opens as follows:

1) French horns pipe out a jaunty rhythm similar to a sailor's hornpipe or to an old British 6/8 one-step.

2) The choir comes in and chants "Yo-ho!," as if this were going to be some kind of sea chantey.

3) The chorus does two hand claps, then announces the song "My Truly, Truly Fair," does two more hand claps, and goes into the B section (the repeating hook section), with hand claps every couple of beats.

And that, my friends, is how pop's mixmeister supreme grabs the listener's ear even before the star singer has sung note one.

Various sources disagree as to whether Mitchell was a first-generation American child of Yugoslavian immigrants or if he was actually born in Yugoslavia; however, everyone agrees that he was born Al Cernik on February 27, 1927, and that he grew up mostly in Detroit. "My folks were used to singing while they worked. They always sang when they felt good. And when they didn't feel good, they sang to make themselves feel better." Although Mitchell himself sang at school affairs—mainly to get his teachers to think more kindly of him when they read his papers—he was more drawn to horses and the great outdoors.

Papa Cernik was a stonemason, but no matter where the family moved in search of work—St. Louis, Los Angeles, San Francisco—Al would always find the town's stables or stockyards. As a youngster, he became a leatherworker and an apprentice saddle maker. At the same time, he continued to pursue music, singing with Mission High School's resident dance band and on amateur programs on Warner Bros. radio station KFWB. At twenty, he couldn't decide which career to pursue, singing or punching cows, but Uncle Sam decided his immediate future for him and Cernik served a year and a half in the navy beginning in August 1945.

After the service he made his first move to combine both pursuits—the cowboy life and music—when he joined a hillbilly radio troupe led by a West Coast entertainer named Dude Martin. "I could at least sing like a cowboy, so I went to a radio station in San Francisco that specialized in western programs. I took along a $10 guitar with Gene Autry's picture painted on it. I had no case for the instrument, so I carried it in a pillow case," said Mitchell. "I got on, doing cowboy songs. That did it. From then on, you couldn't comb the hambo out of me."

To gain experience in a broader spectrum of pop music, his next major gig, with society sweet band leader Carmen Cavallaro, took him about as far from the hillbilly circuit as possible. "Carmen came to town with his orchestra for an engagement," remembered Mitchell, "his vocalist became ill and I was asked to take over, which I did. I later trav-

eled with Cavallaro, even got to come to New York with him when he played the Astor Hotel." Mitchell made his first records with Cavallaro's orchestra (with whom he once shared a session with Bing Crosby and the Andrews Sisters), still using his given name. Unfortunately, when the Cavallaro orchestra reached New York, Mitchell came down with an attack of ptomaine poisoning and laryngitis.

He thought he would never sing again, and told his parents to polish up his cowboy boots, as he would soon be back in the saddle again; meanwhile, Cavallaro had to hire another vocalist and move on. But as Mitchell's voice returned, he realized it might not be such a bad break at that, since he was now in New York, the music business capital of the world. He won three shots on the *Arthur Godrey Talent Scouts* radio program in November 1949 (where he would later return as guest host) and the following summer sang on a cruise ship. He worked at small nightclubs and recorded some sides for the independent King label, but though he couldn't have known it at the time, his big opportunity would come through his bread-and-butter work of the day, cutting demonstration discs of songs for composers and publishers for the princely sum of five bucks a pop. One of these demos, "My Foolish Heart," wound up in the hands of Eddie Joy, the agent and husband of Mindy Carson, a singer then under contract to Columbia Records (best remembered for her record of the immortal "I Want a Television Christmas").

Now representing Cernik as well, Joy put the young singer's disc in the hands of Mitch Miller, who had recently taken over as pop music A&R chief at Columbia. Miller signed Cernik to a contract in April 1950, and made two decisions right away concerning him. The first was to change the kid's name. "Who the hell's gonna care about listening to the romantic cowboy voice of Al Cernik?" was how Miller put it. "My name is Mitchell, and you're a nice guy, so we'll call you 'Guy Mitchell.'"

Miller also had the idea of outfitting his new signee with a different kind of material from what most other singers were using—material that was considerably less urbane than "My Foolish Heart." Thus, Guy Mitchell's first single was "Giddy-Ap" backed by "Where in the World" (by Broadway vet Harold Rome). As would turn out to be a habit with Miller, the record-buying public agreed with his conclusions a hundred and five percent. Five singles later, Miller and Mitchell would strike gold with a pairing of semitraditional songs that the producer had originally intended to record with Frank Sinatra: "The Roving Kind," inspired by an English sea chantey as recorded by the Weavers, backed by "My Heart Cries for You," Percy Faith's adaptation of a traditional French melody (said to have originated with a tune actually written by Marie Antoinette herself), marked a rare instance of both sides of a record getting on the charts and the first of nearly forty certified hits Mitchell would enjoy at Columbia over the next dozen years. The songs reached number 2 and 4 on the charts, and within a year, the disc had sold beyond the million mark and bought Mitchell his ranch in Tarzana, California.

After that first dual hit, Mitchell and Miller began their collaboration with songsmith Bob Merrill, whose early career was as a jukebox writer (his first chart-topper had been "If I Knew You Were Comin' I'd've Baked a Cake" in 1950). Miller encouraged Merrill to write some folklike airs (similar to Frankie Laine's "Cry of the Wild Goose") for Mitchell. The three Ms—Mitchell, Merrill, and Miller—were immediately successful. In 1951 alone, Guy Mitchell would land nine major chart hits, five of which had been written for him by Merrill, and they would have a total of eight hits together, which included "Sparrow in the Treetop" (which reached number 8 on the chart, and stayed on for fifteen weeks), "My Truly, Truly Fair" (number 2, nineteen weeks), "Always Room at Our House" (number 20, one week), and "Belle, Belle, My Liberty Belle" (number 9, nine weeks). The following year, Mitchell and Merrill hit their peak with their two best-remembered numbers, "Pittsburgh, Pennsylvania" (number 4, twenty-six weeks), and "Feet Up (Pat 'Em on the Po-Po)" (number 16, six weeks).

Merrill was among the most successful words-and-music men of the immediate prerock era, also writing blockbusters for Patti Page ("How Much Is That Doggie in the Window?") and Rosemary Clooney ("Mambo Italiano"). Mitchell also put over several songs by Terry Gilkyson, including the comically sardonic "Christopher Columbus" and the 1952 "The Day of Jubilo." The latter was a pop adaptation of Henry Clay Work's abolitionist anthem "The Year of Jubilo"; in Mitchell's version, the message of freedom is somewhat diluted in pop religious metaphors, but some of the song's political power still remains.

By the mid-fifties, the Mitchell-Miller-Merrill combination was beginning to run out of steam, although some of the later, less successful songs, like "The Cuff of My Shirt," are actually better musically and start to anticipate Merrill's later work on Broadway. "Perfume, Candy and Flowers" wouldn't be out of place in *Take Me Along*, an adaptation of Eugene O'Neill's *Ah, Wilderness!* that would be Merrill's most important work as a writer of both words and music. Then, too, as Mitchell's sales started decreasing, Miller seems to have tried to bolster his career with increasingly drecky material. The worst of them all may have been "(Otto Drives Me Crazy) Otto's Gotta Go." Even Perry "Hot Diggety" Como wouldn't have touched that one—it almost sounds as if someone was trying to pay back the Germans for both world wars.

Thus, in the mid-fifties, Mitchell went through a brief fall-and-rise while he adjusted his image. At the time, he attributed his lapse to the travails of his personal life. Although "Feet Up" was a song of paternal delight, kind of a bargain-basement "Soliloquy" from *Carousel*—with still more hand claps and French horns—Mitchell was still a bachelor at the time he recorded it. However, shortly thereafter he married the current Miss USA, Jackie Loughery. He was also riding high in these years with his first two movie appearances, a cameo in *Those Redheads from Seattle*, with Teresa Brewer, and a leading role in *Red Garters*, with Rosemary Clooney. "I thought there was just no stopping Guy Mitchell," he said, several years later. "The only thing was, it just wasn't true." *Red Garters* failed to establish either Mitchell or Clooney as a film star, and his marriage to Jackie Loughery ended after sixteen months in an expensive and overpublicized divorce. "All of a sudden the bottom dropped out," he told Earl Wilson. "No more records, no more movies."

Then came rock 'n' roll, which spelled disaster for many established singers at the time but offered Mitchell a second chance. "Crazy with Love" dropped the French horns in favor of a doo-woppy echo chamber, a considerably smaller backup group, reverberating electric guitars, and quivering vocal gyrations even more pronounced than he had used in the pre-Elvis era. It got on the chart—not too high, but high enough to encourage Mitchell to continue exploring this avenue.

He got married again to another world-class beauty, the Danish model Elsa Sorenson, and the couple was traveling back home from their wedding in Mississippi in 1956 when they heard a country and western record they liked, "Singin' the Blues," sung by Marty Robbins and written by Melvin Endsley, a twenty-year-old composer stricken with polio. At the time, the Mitchells were hassling with the immigration authorities to let Elsa stay in the United States, and during that period, Mitchell later said, he recorded his version of "Singin' the Blues," and channeled into it all the frustration he was feeling about his career and his wife's immigration status.

"I sang the first line of the song for the recording that day and the irony of it struck me: 'Well, I never felt more like singin' the blues.'" The song was his last blockbuster, staying on the charts for twenty-six weeks and quickly selling a million copies. Mitchell spent the remaining five years of his tenure at Columbia Records purveying a combination of country, rockabilly, and doo-wop with a bit of old-school pop sensibility thrown in—infact, many of the later hits were done with Mitch Miller's deputy Jimmy Carroll and his star arranger, Ray Conniff. Although most of his work is outside the scope of this book, his best remembered hits of the later years were 1957's "Knee Deep in the Blues" (also by Melvin Endsley) and 1959's "Heartaches by the Numbers," a vastly appealing C&W song also sung memorably by Bing Crosby.

But by this time, Mitchell had cracked the hit record charts more than thirty-five times and, as one commentator observed, "taken the lead in the ever hot disk race away from Elvis and Frankie" more than a few times. Although he had never made much of an impact in movie musicals, he went on to some success as a nonsinging actor in films—mostly Westerns—and TV. He is probably best remembered for the series *Whispering Smith,* which co-starred another nonactor, the war hero Audie Murphy. Later in the sixties, Mitchell made several country albums and another film, *The Wild Westerners.* In the seventies, he concentrated on his other love—ranching and the outdoor life—thinking that was how he would spend the rest of his days.

In 1980, however, he consented to appear in a television tribute to Mitch Miller, and the response was so favorable that it launched something of a comeback, particularly in the United Kingdom, where he had first toured in 1952 and where support for his various subgenres of quasi-Western music had always remained high. He recorded a new album in 1982, and in 1984 he toured the U.K. again. In 1986 a new single, "Heaven Knows," landed on the British charts, and in 1987 he celebrated his fortieth anniversary in show business at the London Palladium, returning successfully the following year. He went on touring the British Isles, including Ireland, for most of the decade, and by the nineties was also appearing in Australia, Spain, Holland, and Germany. In 1988 he co-starred in a BBC-TV miniseries, *Your Cheatin' Heart,* and sang on the show's sound track album—the best-selling album on the BBC label that year.

By 1986, at least eleven Guy Mitchell fan clubs (led by the Guy Mitchell Appreciation Society) proliferated just in the U.K., at least three of these being in Scotland alone, all with the cooperation of Mitchell and his third wife, Betty. Judging from reports in the British press, the 1986 tour may have been his biggest ever, with Mitchell treating his fans to the likes of "You Were Always on My Mind" and "Wind Beneath My Wings" as well as his own hits. He died in 1999 at the age of seventy-two—one of the most enigmatic figures in American pop.

Johnny Mathis (born 1935)

Even more than with almost all of the other singers considered here, it's impossible to reach a consensus on Mathis. He was one of the most popular artists of the second half of the twentieth century, and far more than is true of most of the pop vocalists covered in this book, his career never petered out: The hits kept on coming right into the seventies, and he seems to be accepted not just in what came to be known as adult contemporary and easy listening circles but in the mainstream of soul or black pop or whatever you want to call it.

As with Johnnie Ray, Mathis was not brought to Columbia by Miller. It was George Avakian, head of the corporation's jazz division, who discovered the twenty-year-old singer in San Francisco in the summer of 1955. He was born in Gilmer, Texas, in 1935, and grew up in San Francisco. His father had been in vaudeville years earlier, and taught his son the rudiments of music for both keyboards and voice. Mathis seems to be one of the few pop stars to admit to seriously studying vocal techniques (press agents of the forties and fifties just loved to write how their clients were all autodidacts). He studied singing intensely for most of his teens, garnering enough technique to handle classical music and opera as well as pop songs.

At the same time, in his teens he was an accomplished athlete—he was offered the chance to join the U.S. Olympic high jump team but turned it down to pursue music. In any case, he was still in training, and singing in a production of Leonard Bernstein's opera *Trouble in Tahiti,* when Avakian heard him singing at the Blackhawk, a Bay Area jazz club.

Avakian likes to tell the story about how he was inspired to bring in a number of arrangers to work on Mathis's first album, one of whom was the legendary Gil Evans. Unfortunately, the result—the singer's premier album, titled simply *Johnny Mathis* (1956)—was his only attempt to work in anything resembling a jazz context, and was not successful either commercially or musically.

At this point Mitch Miller stepped in, ascertaining that Mathis's was a sound for the mainstream commercial market, as distinct from jazz, and launched the singer into a string of hit singles and then to a series of albums that dominated the *Billboard* charts of the late Eisenhower era. Chief among Miller's ideas was hiring two veteran songwriters, Al Stillman and Bob Allen, to create songs specifically for Mathis's voice—the logical outgrowth of what he had done with Guy Mitchell and Bob Merrill. Before Miller, hit songs were generally a matter of hand-me-downs from film and Broadway successes, and even when, for instance, Sammy Cahn and Jule Styne (or James Van Heusen) wrote a song specifically for Sinatra's voice or persona, it was generally with a film project in mind (e.g., *Anchors Aweigh* or *The Tender Trap*). By the mid-fifties, Sinatra had a stable of songwriters working for his own publishing house who were trying to come up with hit singles for him. But no one could compete with the Mathis machine.

Mathis was an unstoppable juggernaut that continued to keep selling records almost for as long as vinyl was being pressed—and CDs and MP3s long after that. He is the only singer of his generation (or of the Mitch Miller association) with longevity to compete with Bennett's. The best and most recent double-CD Mathis compilation, titled *The Essential Johnny Mathis,* extends well into the seventies and eighties, such as his extended disco dance mix "Life Is a Song Worth Singing" (1973), and the hit duets "Too Much, Too Little, Too Late" with Deniece Williams (1977) and "Friends in Love" with Dionne Warwick (1982).

Mathis's technique and tone production are indeed impeccable but, especially with his later work, whether one finds the sound of his voice pleasing is a matter of taste. To paraphrase Sinatra, Mathis reminds me of how great Nat Cole is; Cole could also sing in a sweet high voice, but he sounds soothing where Mathis often sounds merely piercing. Cole sounds warmly human where Mathis sounds annoyingly mannered. Cole had one of the most beautiful voices in the history of recorded sound, but with him, it was never just about the sound of his voice, whereas Mathis's assets are almost exclusively sonic. Then, too, I find his approach, his backgrounds, and his material generally cloying, and his time anything but swinging— even on his alleged jazz album, *Johnny Mathis*.

There is more than a little charm in hearing Mathis sing his signature songs, particularly the two classics by Stillman and Allen, "Chances Are" and "It's Not for Me to Say." Likewise, there's a certain cachet to other early hits like "The Twelfth of Never" and "Wonderful, Wonderful." In those years, he had a close connection with the New York cabaret scene; he studied Mabel Mercer and recorded nearly a dozen songs composed by the great lady's musical director, Bart Howard. I can understand why people would want to hear him sing his chart-topping hits, but I can't for the life of me fathom why anybody would want to hear Mathis sing Cole Porter or George Gershwin.

It's hard to predict which kind of Mathis album will work and which won't. One might expect *I'll Buy You a Star* to be good because of the presence of Nelson Riddle, but in this case Riddle's excellent orchestrations only serve to point out the inescapable conclusion that Mathis is no Cole. On the other hand, Ralph Burns, who helmed the double-LP *The Rhythms and Ballads of Broadway* (1960), came up with an absolutely appropriate context for Mathis's high-pitched pipes; the Mathis-Burns "I Just Found Out About Love (And I Like It)" may come in second to the Cole-Riddle treatment of four years earlier, but it's still pretty darn exciting. Mathis also works well with exotica: "Babalu" is a highlight of *Johnny Mathis*, capturing a perfect approximation of one of the great Cuban *canciónes*, like Miguelito Valdés. "Begin the Beguine" and "Caravan" are the only songs by, respectively, Cole Porter and Duke Ellington that I want to hear him sing.

Sinatra made a point of dissing Mathis, not only in the Feather interview, but in his often rabid onstage monologues, in which he even cast aspersions upon the younger singer's lifestyle by referring to him as "the African Queen." However, Ed Walters, who worked as pit boss at the Sands during Sinatra's high-rolling heyday in Las Vegas, has an interesting take on their relationship: Sinatra may have been publicly critical of Mathis, and would put him down in front of his own friends or onstage, yet in private he actually appreciated Mathis's work. Walters quotes Sinatra as saying, at different times, "He's got a great instrument." "Listen to him sing—he's good." "It's the same stuff all the time, but he's so good at it he's gets away with it." "They like him—selling more records than I am." (The last was, in fact, true.) Once, Walters recalled, Mathis was working at the Desert Inn but was prohibited by racial discrimination from staying there. He went to Sinatra for help, and Sinatra, who owned a piece of the Sands, arranged for Mathis to stay there whenever he wished.

My favorite Mathis record, to my surprise, is *Good Night, Dear Lord*, a collection of religious songs from all the major Western faiths (alas, there's nothing for Muslims or Buddhists here). As author James Gavin has noted, while Sinatra and Peggy Lee may have an undercurrent of eroticism to their work, Mathis projects an aura of squeaky-clean, asexual romance. That purity tends to leave his treatments of, say, the lyrics of Lorenz Hart rather neutered, but serves him well in his treatment of spiritual material. His choirboy persona is made to order for religious songs both traditional ("Deep River") and secular ("May the Good Lord Keep You and Bless You"). He doubtless earned the respect of a whole other audience when he included three pieces of Jewish material—two traditional pieces, "Eli, Eli" and "Kol Nidre," and the more recent Israeli anthem, "Where Can I Go?" It was also hip, in a religious way of course, for Mathis and arranger-conductor Percy Faith to include both of the well-known settings of the "Ave Maria," by Schubert and by Bach and Gounod.

Whether this innocent approach would work for "Miss Otis Regrets" or "Sand in My Shoes" I couldn't tell you, but one thing is clear. Mathis's strengths as a pop singer are more significant than his weaknesses.

Andy Williams (born 1927)

One of the more counterproductive by-products of the perfection of the long-playing record was the industry's discovery that people didn't have to actually listen to music. Back when nearly all records were three-minute singles, you had to listen or participate actively (as by dancing) because your attention could only wander so far in three minutes. However, once it became possible to go for twenty-five minutes without having to get up and turn the disc over, it made it possible to ignore music, to put it on and forget about it. Soon a whole new genre was created, easy listening music, which should have more properly been termed "nonlistening music," or sonic wallpaper.

If there is a difference between a popular vocalist, as the term existed in, say, the age of Dick Haymes, and an easy listening artist who happens to be a vocalist (as opposed to a bandleader like Percy Faith or a choral director like Ray Conniff), then it comes to the fore in Andy Williams. He perfected the art of singing songs in such a way that you don't actually have to listen to him. It's true that Andy Williams had tons of hit singles (which were subsequently compiled into long-playing albums, since the point was never to listen to his music one 45 at a time but to put on an album and walk away). It didn't distract you the way a record by Bennett or Tormé would; it was part of the decor. By making music that no one felt obliged to pay attention to, Andy Williams became one of the most successful recording artists of his time. (It was one of the many ironies of his career that he could have been a contender—he had a beautiful, pure voice and a natural talent for phrasing—but it was not to be.)

He was born in Wall Lake, Iowa, in 1927, and like his three older brothers was encouraged and instructed in the ways of music—singing especially—by his father. In 1935, when the youngest Williams brother was eight, the foursome formed a vocal quartet that appeared on Des Moines radio. By the start of the war, the Williams Brothers were broadcasting on increasingly important stations in Cleveland and Chicago. In 1944, they provided the backup for star Bing Crosby on one of the biggest discs of the era, "Swinging on a Star" (from *Going My Way*, which won the Academy Award that year and probably would have won a Grammy, too, if they'd existed then).

According to legend, that same year Andy Williams dubbed the singing voice of new star Lauren Bacall on Hoagy Carmichael's "How Little We Know" in *To Have and Have Not* (a claim Mrs. Bogart has consistently denied). In 1947, the quartet began working with Kay Thompson, an extremely talented singer, vocal arranger, and composer. For about five years, the combination of Thompson and the Williams Brothers was one of the hottest acts on the nightclub circuit.

The act broke up in 1951, and the youngest Williams settled in New York, where, as a solo, he was astute enough and cute enough to get into television. He started as a utility singer on *The Steve Allen Show*, which led to his first record contract (with the independent Cadence Records). In 1956, he landed his first notable single, "Canadian Sunset," as well as his first album, *Andy Williams Sings Steve Allen*. By the end of the decade, he was becoming ever more popular on the small screen: He was seen on all the variety shows, including that of fellow singer Dinah Shore, and then was awarded his own summer replacement series, followed by a string of TV specials. Williams had other hits, like "Hawaiian Wedding Song" (a follow-up to "Canadian Sunset"), "I Like Your Kind of Love" (a duet with Peggy Powers), "The Village of St. Bernadette," and "Butterfly."

In 1962 and 1963, everything clicked into place, namely a big new contract with Columbia Records and then a regular weekly variety show on NBC. The timing was perfect. Perry Como—an old-fashioned singer clinging to the outdated idea that his listeners should actually listen to him—was out of weekly television by then, and there obviously was a need for an incredibly relaxed crooner to replace him. (Dean Martin would also score a major success on TV at this point, but his booze-and-babes-based program wasn't quite as family-oriented as Como's or Williams's.) The Williams-Columbia relationship was also launched just in time for the singer to cash in on the run of megahit movie theme songs by Henry Mancini, especially "Moon River," "Dear Heart," and "The Days of Wine and Roses." By the time the Beatles landed in 1964, their competition wasn't Elvis, it was Andy.

For his part, Williams had learned early on that if he couldn't lick 'em, he should join 'em. He was pop music's supreme accommodator or appeaser. His Columbia label mate Tony Bennett was determined to beat back the barbarians at the gate by sticking to his guns: the Great American Songbook and contemporary Broadway songs. The sorrow and the pity of Williams was that he had no qualms about collaborating with the enemy. Tony was the Winston Churchill of pop, while Andy was its Neville Chamberlain. Even such early hits as "Butterfly" show him operating in a stuttering, staccato style that had more in common with Elvis than Sinatra. Apart from the Mancini series, his biggest early hit on Columbia was "Can't Get Used to Losing You," by Brill Building guru Doc Pomus.

Likewise, when Columbia got a new president, the lawyer-turned-hippie-wannabe Clive Davis, Williams was all too willing to accommodate Jive Clive in his quest to sell zillions of what he termed MOR albums—the acronym meaning middle of the road. (What road? What middle?) "I urged Andy to include only the most well-known of contemporary songs in his albums," Davis writes in his memoir, *Clive: Inside the Record Business*. As Davis calculated it, each well-known song—in other words, a song that had already been a hit for someone else—increased an album's sales by 5 to 10 percent. The cover art had to be a shot of Williams smiling "in close up, with his blue eyes prominent"—that would be worth 20 percent. There had to be a strong album title and a list of those well-known contemporary songs on the cover, somewhere to the right or left of Andy's blue-eyed kisser. "It became possible, therefore," Clive concludes, "to be quite calculating about the sales of MOR albums." (Like, no kidding.)

Williams was recording everything that had even the vaguest chance of selling, whether it made sense or not, from "Never on Sunday" (sung in the original Greek) to Paul Simon's mock-Andean "El Condor Pasa." Meanwhile, Ray Conniff and Percy Faith had to be convinced to go along with the Davis-Williams formula, but eventually they, too, went for it, as did Johnny Mathis and Barbra Streisand. Only Tony Bennett was still fighting them in the fields and in the villages.

Ironically, the adult pop star who thrived most in the rock era turned out to be the least rocky of them all—a singer who made Perry Como look like Mr. Excitement by comparison. By the early seventies, when Williams's nine-year run ended with the general demise of the variety show (Ed Sullivan went off the air around the same time), the singer had already made his fortune many times over and had earned the right to be crowned "the Emperor of Easy." In 1991, he accommodated the country music market as well, by building his own $12 million theater in Branson, Missouri. In 1999, a TV commercial made a hit all over again out of one of Williams's most popular singles, the 1967 "Music to Watch Girls By." It was an appropriate coda for the career of a superstar crooner who had rarely made music worth listening to.

Hipsters and Bopsters

King Pleasure
Eddie Jefferson
Jackie Cain
Roy Kral
Irene Kral
Ann Richards
Cleo Laine

Bopsters! They're musical communists!
—Tommy Dorsey

King Pleasure (1922–1982)

"Moody's Mood for Love" (Prestige 924, as it was originally released) is one of those few superspecial records that define a moment in pop culture—even though it has a sound that can't be easily pinned down chronologically (it sounds like nothing else recorded, say, in the forties or fifties) or even by the singer, King Pleasure, who was trying to come up with something new to do with jazz singing and wound up crafting one of the most enduring of all pop records. As Jon Hendricks put it, "'Moody's Mood for Love' struck a chord in my soul."

Apart from the slightly later work of Lambert, Hendricks & Ross, it's the only indisputable masterpiece record in the entire genre that became known as vocalese, and the only really significant event in the lives of both men who were responsible for it, singer-songwriters King Pleasure and Eddie Jefferson.

When "Moody's Mood" came out in 1952 it was an instant hit, acclaimed as the "R&B Record of the Year." It was sung by Clarence Beeks, who performed under the stage name of King Pleasure, and was already the sensation of Harlem. Recently arrived in the New York area, he had entered the famous amateur show at the Apollo Theater and came out singing this strange, haunting variation on the Jimmy McHugh–Dorothy Fields standard "I'm in the Mood for Love." The idea of vocalese—taking a jazz instrumental solo and writing words to it—was not a new one: There are vocalese recordings of Bix Beiderbecke solos going back to the twenties, and others as well. Jon Hendricks was writing vocalese lyrics in the thirties and forties, and Eddie Jefferson recorded examples of the form as early as 1949.

But all these forerunners were strictly underground; when the crowd at the Apollo in 1952 heard King Pleasure singing words to a James Moody solo on "Mood for Love" (even though they probably didn't know the original record; it had been recorded in Sweden and enjoyed only limited distribution in the States), they went crazy. King Pleasure was given offers to sing professionally, and he came to the attention of Prestige, a label pretty much devoted to hardcore modern jazz produced by and for hard-core bebop buffs.

Beeks was born in Oakdale, Tennessee, on March 24, 1922, but had grown up in Cincinnati. He later said that the name "King Pleasure" came to him in a dream. According to Dizzy Gillespie, he earned it performing in live sex shows. (Or maybe Dizzy was pulling somebody's leg—who knows?)

In the wake of the success of "Moody's Mood," two other records were issued within a few months: In July 1952, a single came out on Hi-Lo Records by Eddie Jefferson, featuring "The Birdland Story" and "Honeysuckle Rose." In October, Prestige released its own follow-up to "Moody's Mood": "Twisted" and "Farmer's Market" by Annie Ross. In December, Pleasure returned to Prestige with two more titles, and before December 1953 would record a total of four sessions and ten titles for them (the last produced by Quincy Jones).

Pleasure seems to have been too much of an eccentric—perhaps "kook" is a better word—to have fully capitalized on his success. In the fifties and sixties he appears and disappears on the jazz map, like blips on a radar screen. He wrote his own liner notes to his first original 12" album, the 1960 *Golden Days* on HiFi Jazz, and rambles at considerable length about a Scientological-Theosophical-religious-technological-ass-tro-naughty concept called "Planetism," which concerned itself with "charged neutral material existence."

On the evidence of this document, Pleasure clearly was a wack job. He would have done better to expend his own charged energies on writing more material and recording more consistently. His complete output, more or less, consists of three compact discs: *King Pleasure Sings/Annie Ross Sings*, which contains the ten Prestige single tracks, plus two instrumentals from the same sessions, plus, as the title suggests, the four titles from Annie Ross's Prestige sessions. *Golden Days* is his 1960 album taped in Los Angeles, today owned by Fantasy (along with the Prestige material), and it consists of only nine tracks.

Lastly, there's *Moody's Mood for Love*, a 1962 album today owned by EMI, and combined with additional singles from Jubilee (1955) and Aladdin (1956) for a total of sixteen tracks.

Pleasure's small output seems even smaller because he sang relatively few different songs: His total discography is only about thirty-nine tracks, and he did so many songs at least twice that it makes it seem as if he was an artist of very limited imagination: There are three recordings of the same vocalese lyric on Stan Getz and Lars Gullin doing "Don't Get Scared" (the first two with Jon Hendricks singing the part of Gullin, the Swedish baritone saxophonist), two of him doing his lyric to "Parker's Mood" (a blues that Charlie Parker recorded in 1948 and which Mark Murphy later reprised effectively), two of his variations on Lester Young's earth-shattering solo on "Sometimes I'm Happy," and so on. (On the other hand, his "New Symphony Sid" is totally different from his earlier "Jumpin' with Symphony Sid.") There are no fewer than four different recordings of "Moody's Mood," with the girl's piano part sung by Blossom Dearie, Annie Ross, and a female choir. (Mysteriously, several contemporary jazz singers, including Nancy King and Kathy Kosins, have recorded a fine vocal version of the bop anthem "Dear Old Stockholm," the words to which are credited to King Pleasure—but which he seems never to have recorded himself.) The total number of pieces that Pleasure actually recorded is probably closer to twenty, most of them inspired by either Lester Young or Charlie Parker.

All of which lends credence to the claim that Pleasure did not actually write the lyrics to "Moody's Mood." Eddie Jefferson, who was apparently working as a dancer and a singer when the younger Clarence Beeks was toiling as a bartender in Cincinnati, later stated that he had written the "Moody's Mood" lyrics, was performing them around the late forties, and that Beeks had "copped" them from him. Remarkably, the jazz press believed Jefferson—in almost every story or article about him he's given credit for "Moody's Mood" even though there's not a shred of evidence to support this contention. For his part, Clarence Beeks acknowledged Jefferson, stating very specifically that "in 1946, Eddie Jefferson created the embryo of a vocal innovation in jazz." But he never gave credit to Jefferson for that song specifically. (Usually the song is listed under the original title, "I'm in the Mood for Love," with credit going to Fields and McHugh. Presumably neither Moody nor Pleasure nor Jefferson shared in any of the mechanical royalties.)

No matter who wrote the variant words, the fact remains that King Pleasure singing "Moody's Mood for Love" is an unforgettable pop record. And there are perhaps a dozen other Pleasure tracks on which the quality of the lyric writing is neither better nor worse than on "Moody's Mood," particularly among the original four 1952–53 Prestige sessions.

"Red Top" is an exuberant medium-tempo blues, with Pleasure harmonizing gloriously with the young Betty Carter; "Parker's Mood" is a moving slow blues—kind of a Kansas City version of "Blue Prelude." This is probably the most widely sung of all the lyrics known to be Pleasure's.

"Diaper Pin," based on Stan Getz's reading of "That Old Black Magic," and "Sometimes I'm Happy," based on Lester Young, are as brilliant a pair of vocal variations on standards as have ever been recorded, and for once the rerecording is justified. On the 1953 version of "Happy," Pleasure is accompanied by the Dave Lambert Singers, who sing the Vincent Youmans melody before Pleasure expertly vocalizes the Lester Young solo, after which the singers, with Lambert and Hendricks very audible, hum out the bowing-and-humming solo originated by bassist Slam Stewart before Pleasure returns, vocalizing Young's coda, and incorporating the famous "Sweetie Went Away" quotation. The 1962 remake opens with Pleasure singing, after which a big, very antiseptic studio choir and strings come in, and this time the bass solo is performed by the brasses and reeds.

Likewise, the first two versions of the fast blues "Don't Get Scared" are exhilarating—on the original (1954), Hendricks sounds more timid, like a little boy (befitting the content of his lyrics); the third (1962) has Hendricks singing out more extrovertedly, while the 1960 has Pleasure singing solo. One misses the two-voice playfulness, but there are compensating solos from tenors Harold Land and Teddy Edwards, plus pianist Gerald Wiggins.

One of his most Pleasureable performances is "No, Not Much" from *Golden Days*. It has nothing to do with vocalese or even the jazz tradition; it's just an inspired, upbeat treatment of a pop song, a Four Lads hit (based on the chords to "Pennies from Heaven"), that Pleasure sings and swings wonderfully and which has the bonus of excellent solos from Edwards, trombonist Matthew Gee, and Land. "No, Not Much" works so well one wonders why Pleasure didn't do this more often—just record either recent songs or standards with a jazzy feel and with a first-rate band. Why did he feel he had to keep doing the vocalese thing? Clearly, he was potentially better and bigger than that.

He never appears to have realized that his greatest asset was his voice: rich and thick, smooth and shiny, sweet and spicy. He had all the feeling of a blues singer, in addition to all the mellowroonie ladies' man appeal of the best crooners. His voice was as flexible as a saxophone and as mellow as a cello.

Writing about Pleasure for an LP reissue in 1972, Jon Hendricks implies that the King had already been resurrected several times, and that it was entirely possible that he would reappear yet again. Such resurrection would never take place. Clarence Beeks died in Los Angeles on March 21, 1982, three days before his fifty-ninth birthday.

Eddie Jefferson (1918–1979)

Eddie Jefferson, born in Pittsburgh in 1918, was several years older than Pleasure (1922) and Hendricks (1921), and was a working professional dancer by the mid-thirties. He was writing lyrics to solos he heard on swing band records at around the same time as the teenage Hendricks. The earliest document of his work is two songs, "Bless My Soul" (his own take on "Parker's Mood") and "Beautiful Memories" (Lester Young's "I Cover the Waterfront"), dated "circa 1949–50" in *The Jazz Discography* but only issued many years later on a British LP. In the wake of Pleasure's success, Jefferson's friend Ned Gravely recorded four songs (later sold to Savoy) of him singing numbers based on Moody solos. Within a short time, he had come into contact with Moody himself, and was working with him as a combination vocalist and road manager. Jefferson recorded frequently both with and without Moody over the next ten years, generally for Prestige, and by the mid-sixties had also done albums for Inner City (*The Jazz Singer*) and Riverside (*Letter from Home*). In the rock era, he suffered along with many other jazz instrumentalists, but by the mid-seventies his career was on the upswing. He had recorded three new albums (for Inner City and Muse) and had formed a successful working partnership with the young retro-bop alto saxophonist Richie Cole. The group was working in Detroit when Jefferson was murdered by a cab driver.

That was May 9, 1979. Carla Cook, the fine contemporary jazz singer, tells a story in her act about how she had made a reservation to come and hear Jefferson the next night, Thursday the 10th. She has said that she considers Jefferson one of the all-time greats, up there with Billie Holiday and Louis Armstrong. Later in 1979, the contemporary vocal quartet the Manhattan Transfer dedicated their album *Expansions* to him, referring to him as "the best jazz singer in the world."

This was extravagant praise, even considering that it was offered in a spirit of mourning. The consensus regarding Jefferson is hardly as high as Ms. Cook's opinion or that of the Manhattan Transfer collectively. To be fair, he had some personality and energy, as well as a dancer's sense of rhythm, but on the evidence of his records, the problem wasn't merely that he didn't have a lot of vocal chops or an attractive voice. Plenty of singers have made superb music with very small voices and a limited range (Blossom Dearie) or even with voices that are not beautiful in the traditional Western sense (Louis Armstrong and virtually every blues singer ever). It may well be that he wasn't adequately served by his many recordings, but his singing sounds consistently flat and monotonous. Jefferson's voice just wasn't appealing.

Neither could he be regarded as a particularly gifted lyricist. There is only one gold standard in the field of vocalese lyric writing, and its name is Jon Hendricks. Jefferson's writing is no worse or better than King Pleasure's, although Pleasure's sense of the bizarre and the mystic—all that "Planetism"—at least give him some kind of poetic perspective. Only Pleasure could have come up with a line like "I'm so afraid of places I'm going, and so in love with where I've been" (in "Diaper Pin"). It's cryptic and unclear, but at least it's saying something, even if we're not quite sure what. Jefferson seems never to have come up with anything as interesting.

Comparing Jefferson to Hendricks is unfair: Hendricks had the benefit of a college education and of studying the great English-language poets, from Tennyson and Keats to Hart and Porter. He had no end of narrative resources at his disposal, and he had an endless supply of stories to tell. Jefferson, by contrast, essentially wrote two kinds of texts: extravagant praise for the jazz masters whose work he was lyricizing, the kind that reads and sings like witless propaganda for the jazz cause, and love lyrics generally devoid of both the irony of the blues and the real poetry of the best Tin Pan Alley writers. His lyrics aren't only dreary, they're dreary at great length—three, four, five, or more 32-bar choruses.

It's telling that while a few contemporary singers keep some of Pleasure's songs alive—"Don't Get Scared," "Tomorrow's Another Day"—and nearly everybody sings Hendricks, it's rare to hear anyone singing the lyrics of Eddie Jefferson. Curiously, on his 1968 Prestige album *Body and Soul* he includes a new vocal interpretation of James Moody's 1949 "I'm in the Mood for Love" solo, this one called "There I Go, There I Go Again." I'm willing to give Jefferson the benefit of the doubt, but it will probably never be settled exactly who wrote the far more successful lyrics to Prestige 924.

Appropriately, memorial ballads to Jefferson and the tragedy of his murder have been played and sung by such worthy musicians as his ex-partner Richie Cole, the modern baritone saxophonist Hamiett Bluiett, West Coast tenor legend Teddy Edwards, Detroit drummer Roy Brooks, trumpeter Woody Shaw, and maverick vocalist Mark Murphy (on *Kerouac, Then and Now*). The words and music, and in Murphy's case the singing, on these performances often seem more substantial than Jefferson's own.

Jackie Cain (born 1928) and Roy Kral (1921–2002)

The last time I saw Jackie and Roy was at an all-star JVC Jazz Festival event, and I was sitting next to Gary Giddins. Halfway through their number, he turned to me and said, "I just don't *get* Jackie and Roy." I was glad he had said it first, even though I had already said the same thing in print several times.

God knows I tried to "get" Jackie and Roy. I have accumulated and listened to most of their albums, and in addition to seeing them half a dozen times at JVC concerts, I caught them every time they played Birdland in the 1990s. They are one of not even a handful of major modern jazz vocal acts I don't get—the principal others being Cleo Laine and the Four Freshmen. In the case of Eddie Jefferson, it's obvious why his music doesn't hold up well—his singing wasn't very good and his writing wasn't very good. In the case of Jackie and Roy, it's harder to say why—with them, unlike Jefferson, all the ingredients are outstanding. Jackie Cain has—as Mel Tormé and others have acknowledged—one of the finest voices, and so was potentially one of the best singers, of the modern jazz era. Her partner, both musically and maritally, Roy Kral, was a fine singer and a better pianist, and the harmonies they produced together were beautiful.

If words without thoughts will never to heaven go, then scatting without feeling, without substance, will never to anywhere else go. Jackie and Roy's long wordless episodes are not empty-headed, they're just hopelessly light—so light as to be frothy, so light as to be pointless. One never gets the sense of emotional connection prevalent in the modernist music of Mel Tormé or Betty Carter—that dynamic energy, that relentless spark of chutzpah. Everything in Jackie and Roy's music is easy-breezy; hip and swinging, certainly, but completely insubstantial. In their 1956 ABC Paramount album *The Glory of Love*, they sang a rather strained number by Fran Landesman and Tommy Wolf entitled "I Love You Real," but Jackie and Roy seemed anything but.

Artists like Tormé and Carter were willing to take chances in the name of a larger artistic possibility. Occasionally they failed—Mel got so kitschy at times (not many, I have to say) that even his hard-core fans like myself wouldn't follow him, and Carter could get so abstract she could now and then lose me. But even when J&R ventured far into the outer regions, there was never an element of danger or risk; everything about them seemed safe and predictable.

Those all-star concerts were probably the best way to see them: Jackie and Roy came off best in short doses. Whenever I attended a whole set by them, I was always very impressed with the first number or two but thoroughly bored long before the fifty minutes were up. (They also did something I've never seen any other jazz act in a club do— which is deliver the exact same set at both the 9 p.m. and 11 p.m. shows.) Their music is more interesting in perspective than up close—over their fifty years of working together they made a point of collaborating with superior musicians. They also consistently did excellent songs—including many worthies from way off the beaten path—and came up with worthwhile ideas for albums: songs associated with Humphrey Bogart; an LP in which one side was all songs from Rodgers and Hart's *By Jupiter* and the other all from the Gershwin brothers' *Girl Crazy*. They did the Beatles and bossa nova at exactly the point when it was appropriate for jazz singers to start following those trends, and they were among the first and only jazz vocal acts to do whole albums of songs by Alec Wilder and Stephen Sondheim. They did a lot of interesting things—yet they themselves just weren't very interesting.

The pair did their best work at the beginning of their career, with tenor saxophonist Charlie Ventura. Ventura was an A-level player. What he did best was function as a modern tenor equivalent of Louis Prima; where Prima's catchphrase was "Play Pretty for the People," Ventura called his band "Bop for the People." Indeed, his best ensemble—the one that featured Jackie and Roy—was animated by a healthy spirit of populism, or bopulism, as it were.

Roy Kral was born in Chicago in 1921, and Jackie Cain in Milwaukee in 1928; they began working together in 1946. By the summer of 1948, they had joined forces with Ventura to form the eight-piece Bop for the People band, a groundbreaking ensemble that aggressively blended horns and vocals, treating the two singers as if they were a section in a jazz big band, with Kral usually on piano as well. Producer Gene Norman also gave Kral credit for the band's innovative arrangements, which put the voices and horns on a level playing field.

The combination was together for less than a year, and appears to have made only four studio sessions: a very rewarding date (or, more likely, series) in Chicago for National (soon annexed by Savoy), which yielded eleven masters, and three for RCA, which brought forth only four more titles. (With and without J&R, Ventura's Savoy and BMG sessions are in dire need of a comprehensive, Mosaic-style reissue.) The Chicago titles, though valuable, are somewhat tentative, with the voices and horns feeling each other out; the recording technology, both of the time and on the LP reissue, doesn't help either—at times it's hard to distinguish the singers from the brass. Both the integration of the band and the fidelity improve considerably on the 1949 Victor titles, starting with the blues (with a bridge) "Birdland."

Perhaps Jackie and Roy were already set to leave by the spring. By May, Ventura had replaced Kral's instrumental part in the BftP band with pianist Dave McKenna. He also had worked out a vocal number that didn't involve them, "Boptura," with incidental singing by a trio of himself and two horn players. However, in May 1949 the combination produced its definitive document, a live recording from the Pasadena Civic Auditorium released (and, fortunately, available on CD) as *Charlie Ventura and His Band in Concert* (GNP Crescendo). This is the Ventura-J&R combination at its zenith, and in considerably better fidelity than any of their commercial titles. The presence of four horns—the leader alternating between tenor and baritone, altoist Boots Mussulli, trombonist Benny Green, trumpeter Conte Candoli—gives J&R a spark they never had in their own band. It's almost as if the metal voices pose a challenge, even a threat, to the flesh-and-blood instruments, and Jackie and Roy are determined to test their mettle, as it were.

They start with two titles, "Birdland" and "Flamingo," featuring the two of them singing, both done with even more animation than the recent Victor versions. The eight-minute "Birdland" (no connection to the New York club, which would open six months later, or to the George Lullaby thereof) features the singers most effectively in the ensemble passages in a hard-hitting bop blues, while "Flamingo" brings them to the fore in more of a third stream context, all very evocative and arty. Jackie Cain's most notable solo features with the band were "Deed I Do" and "Gone With the Wind" on National and "Over the Rainbow" and "Lullaby in Rhythm" in Pasadena. (Between "Flamingo" and "Rainbow," the team jumps a lot of octaves.) Particularly on "Wind" and "Rainbow"—maybe it's an elemental thing—Cain sounds a lot like Sarah Vaughan, both in the texture of her voice (even though her chops aren't nearly as big) and in what she does with it. Here, on this very dissonant treatment of "Rainbow," she displays a Vaughan-like feeling of restless embellishment and adventurousness that, again, is quite different from J&R's later work. She reharmonizes the song's ending quite radically, and at the end of the first chorus she dramatically slows down and repeats a line ("Oh why then . . . Oh why then . . ."), in order to make us think she's going to finish. But as the crowd starts to applaud she goes into a surprise out chorus, from the bridge out, and makes even more changes to the melody, adding a Billy Eckstine–inspired tag ("Why can't I fly over the rainbow, with the birds?") as the Pasadenans whistle and yell. Not everything she does works this perfectly, but just the same we're glad she took the chance.

In June, Cain and Kral became husband and wife, and four months later they recorded for the first time as Jackie and Roy, for the young producer Ahmet Ertegun's fledgling Atlantic Records. The four titles are somewhat experimental, using a two-voice front line, sounding somewhat similar to Lee Konitz and Warne Marsh in the Lennie Tristano sessions done earlier that year, with a four-piece rhythm section plus cello; at times, the cello and bass harmonize together to suggest a string quartet. It's fascinating stuff, with the twosome playing off strings and rhythm rather than horns, and a logical outgrowth of Dave Lambert and Buddy Stewart's early bop vocal duo.

Jackie and Roy didn't record again until 1953, producing the only document of a yearlong reunion with Charlie Ventura, which featured them more prominently than ever, a date with just tenor, bass, and drums plus Jackie and Roy. In the interim, the duo had taken a break while Cain gave birth to their daughter Diana Kral (not to be confused with the famous Canadian singer-pianist Diana Krall). Roy Kral worked on his own, briefly serving, among other things, as the accompanist for Anita O'Day. When Mrs. Kral returned to work, the team recorded their first LP for Brunswick, *Jackie Cain and Roy Kral*

(with Neal Hefti's Orchestra, 1954), and then for George Wein's Storyville label, *Jackie & Roy* (1954) and *Storyville Presents Jackie & Roy* (1955). (The latter was one of the rare Wein productions to be taped in Los Angeles rather than Boston, and utilized an all-star Hollywood rhythm section, with Barney Kessel, Red Mitchell, and Shelly Manne.) In the mid-fifties, Roy's younger sister, Irene, had also begun to emerge as one of the more promising jazz singers.

As James Gavin documents in his notes to *The ABC-Paramount Years*, a well-chosen anthology of their four albums for that label (1956–58), from the mid-fifties, the couple fell under the influence of the New York cabaret scene, as well as such pop song intelligentsia as Alec Wilder. They were as much a cabaret as a jazz act from that point onward—their agent Joe Glaser told them, "It's hard to book you guys, the jazz guys think you're cabaret and the cabarets think you're jazz."

The ABC-Paramount collection samples four LPs: *The Glory of Love* (1956), *Bits and Pieces* (1957), *Free and Easy* (with Bill Holman's Orchestra, 1957), and *In the Spotlight* (1958). Their biggest shot at a major label was a set of three albums for Columbia at the turn of the sixties, *Sweet and Low Down* (1960), *Double Take* (1961), and *Like Sing* (1962), followed by *By Jupiter & Girl Crazy* for Roulette (1964). Continuing without a letup, which was unusual for artists of their generation, they recorded *Changes* and *Lovesick*, both for Verve in 1966, and then moved into the seventies with *Grass* (Capitol, 1968), *Time and Love* (CTI, 1972) and *Giant Box* (CTI, 1973). In 1976, the team recorded several nights of live sets from Redondo Beach, California, which were issued on LP as *Concerts by the Sea* (Studio 7) and, thirty years later, additional material came out as *Echoes* (Jazzed Media).

They transitioned into the eighties with three well-received LPs for Concord Jazz, *Star Sounds* (1979), *East of Suez* (1980), and *High Standards* (1982). The last twenty years of Kral's life—and their partnership—were productively concluded with *A Stephen Sondheim Collection* (Finesse, 1982), *We've Got It—The Music of Cy Coleman* (Discovery, 1984), *Bogie* (Fantasy, 1986), *One More Rose* (Audiophile, 1987), *Full Circle* (Contemporary, 1988), *An Alec Wilder Collection* (Audiophile, 1990), *Forever* (Musicmasters, 1995) and *The Beautiful Sea* (DRG, 1998). As mentioned earlier, the *Bogie* collection—songs associated with Humphrey Bogart and his movies—was an especially welcome idea, and so was *The Beautiful Sea* (much of which I heard them perform at Birdland that year). The latter was not a concert by the sea but a set of songs about the sea, with sources ranging from Frank Loesser's "Slow Boat to China" to Herbie Hancock's "Dolphin Dance." (Conversely, there was no need for a whole album of Alec Wilder songs—hadn't they shoved enough of his tepid tunes down our throats already?)

When Roy Kral died at eighty-one in 2002, *The*

New York Times asked me for a quote. I felt it was inappropriate for me to give one, since I had never been a fan—in fact, the only thing that they had ever done that completely excited me was the 1949 Pasadena concert with Charlie Ventura. (Instead, I gave *The Times* Jim Gavin's number.) But present company excluded, Jackie and Roy never lacked for an audience to support them or producers who were eager to put their unique, idiosyncratic sounds down on tape—thirty albums in forty years is a very respectable showing, a lot more than Bill Henderson, Jackie Paris, Johnny Hartman, Lorez Alexandria, or dozens more I could name. (In fact, Jackie Cain, who has accepted occasional gigs over the last ten years, could probably easily find a label willing to produce a solo album by her anytime she felt like doing one—and I wish she would). Whether they were regarded as a jazz or cabaret act was strictly a moot point.

Irene Kral (1932–1978)

The late Roy Kral was surrounded for most of his life by terrific singers, most notably his wife and partner, Jackie Cain, but also Anita O'Day, whom he accompanied for a brief period in 1952, and his kid sister, Irene Kral. It's a pity that the younger Kral was not nearly so prolific or long-lived as her brother—who made it past eighty and recorded nearly thirty albums as half of Jackie and Roy. Irene Kral only made it to age forty-six before she died of cancer, and she recorded a mere eight albums. But she was potentially one of the finest singers of the modern jazz era, blessed with a beautiful voice, a strong rhythmic sense, and the capacity to be believable both on swingers and ballads. Stylistically, she belonged in the same general category as the major female singers who worked with Stan Kenton and His Orchestra—Anita O'Day and June Christy, and especially Chris Connor and Ann Richards. Obviously, part of the similarity was her Chicago background (O'Day and Christy were both from Illinois); perhaps it was a Midwestern thing to sing with a cool, dry voice and no vibrato.

The recordings that she did make are remarkably consistent, despite how virtually every one was done for a different label, in a different city, using a different arranger or accompanist. Kral grew up learning about the best in singers, musicians, and songs from big brother Roy, who was eleven years older and already playing piano around town and putting together his own bands when Irene was just discovering music. When she was sixteen, Roy carted her off to audition for local Windy City bandleader Jay Burkhardt, and she wound up singing with his orchestra for several years, and learning much of what she knew about band singing from him.

The songwriter Tommy Wolf, who served as Kral's accompanist on several occasions and wrote the notes to one of her albums, disclosed that she actually sang briefly with the Kenton band. Why she didn't stay longer is a mystery, as she would have made an ideal fit in the succession of O'Day to Christy to Connor to Ann Richards. In the mid-fifties, Kral gained a footing with two bands that existed more or less in the Kenton continuum, both of which were led by Boston-based trumpeters: Maynard Ferguson, with whom she made her first recording (four vocals on his 1957 *Boy with Lots of Brass*), and Herb Pomeroy, who accompanied her on her first album of her own, the 1958 *The Band and I*.

By the end of the decade, she had won the favor of TV megastar host Steve Allen, who was also America's busiest songwriter (most of his tunes seemed to have been written during the commercials). She appeared frequently on his show, which was good, and recorded an album of his songs (*Steverino*, 1959), which wasn't—not consistently so, at least. She settled in Los Angeles in the early sixties, with her husband, trumpeter Joe Burnett, and her daughter, Jodi, and worked occasionally with drummer-bandleader Shelly Manne and His Men, in clubs and on TV and records, too, such as his 1964 *"My Fair Lady"* with the Un-Original Cast. In the sixties, Kral worked mainly on the coast and occasionally in Las Vegas, and Wolf indicates that she was "restricting her travelling to a half-dozen or so choice solo engagements throughout the country each year."

Kral's two best albums are her first, *The Band and I*, a full orchestral project with Herb Pomeroy, and a rhythm-section-only outing, *Better Than Anything*, with the Junior Mance Trio, done in 1963 for Ava Records, run by Fred Astaire and named after his daughter. Virtually every song on both sets is an out-of-the-ordinary number prized by lovers of jazz and a good, offbeat sample of the songbook. The single strongest track I have ever heard by Kral is "Better Than Anything," a fast and witty waltz that rhythmically catalogues items that are "better than anything except being in love," ranging from characters on popular TV shows to a litany of the headliners of the jazz world. The song has gone on to become a semi-standard among jazz singers, from Sheila Jordan to the Diana Krall–Natalie Cole duo. Kral pulls off the difficult task of making the tricky jazz 3/4 work as well as the clever rhyming scheme.

She also excels on a superior reading of Bobby Troup's "The Meaning of the Blues." The other slow ballads, "No More" and "Guess I'll Hang My Tears Out to Dry," are associated with Holiday and Sinatra, respectively, but are far from the most obvious choices one would make to honor those icons. "Rock Me to Sleep" echoes and compares well to an earlier treatment of the Benny Carter bouncer by June Christy. "Passing By" is the only major jazz-pop treatment (except by Nat Cole, but only on his TV show) of the first collaboration between French singer-songwriter Charles Trenet and his major American interpreter, Jack Lawrence (the two would go on to produce "Beyond the Sea" together).

The Band and I starts off with a bang and never lets up. Three out of the first five tracks are songs that were de rigueur for jazz singers in the fifties and early sixties: "Detour Ahead," "Comes Love," and "Lazy Afternoon." Kral's treatments are textbook examples of balladeering with a strong sense of the beat, or fast and flexible swinging that does full justice to the implications of the lyric—swinging with a moral sense, you might say (both Sinatran ideals). The other two are actually underperformed by others, and Kral makes us want to hear them more often: "Everybody Knew but Me," a neglected Irving Berlin song (yes, such a thing is imaginable), and "I'd Know You Anywhere," by Mercer and McHugh (from *You'll Find Out*).

The similarities to Christy and Connor are especially pronounced on Ellington's "I Let a Song Go Out of My Heart," which isn't done by as many singers as you might think. The brassy chart sounds like something Pete Rugolo would have written for Christy, or that Connor would have made in her two-album team-up with Maynard Ferguson. Both *Better Than Anything* and *The Band and I* are full-length albums that fly by every time I spin them: It seems I'm no sooner starting off with "I'd Know You Anywhere" than I'm getting to the two marvelous songs by Tommy Wolf and Fran Landesman that come near the end, "This Little Love" and "It Isn't So Good" (the title isn't promising, but the song is a delight). She winds up *The Band* album with a surprisingly swinging "Something to Remember You By," with a hot alto solo by an unidentified Boston reedman who sounds a lot like Charlie Mariano.

Kral's career could easily rest on those two albums, but there are others: *Wonderful Life* (Mainstream, 1965) and four that she made after a hiatus from the mid-sixties to the mid-seventies, *Where Is Love?* (Choice, 1974), *Kral Space* (Catalyst, 1977), *Angel Eyes* (Trio, 1977), and *The Gentle Rain*, accompanied only by the remarkable pianist Alan Broadbent (Choice, 1977). Overall, they're not up to those first two LPs, but all of them have their moments. She died on August 15, 1978, after a bout with cancer.

Ann Richards (1935–1982)

Ann Richards also died tragically young, at forty-seven. She wasn't quite the last singer to emerge from the Stan Kenton fold, but that cycle, which begins with the great Anita O'Day and June Christy, starts to very slowly spiral down with the only slightly less great Chris Connor, and then Irene Kral (if one accepts Tommy Wolf's testimony that she sang with Kenton; there's no recorded evidence), and then further down to Richards. She is far from the end of the line where Kenton vocalists are concerned—there are also Jean Turner and the Four Freshmen—but she's the last Kenton singer we'll be dealing with here. (There's yet another obscure girl singer named Jerri Winters who worked only briefly for the band and whose few albums are highly prized by collectors.) All things considered, that five major singers passed through Kenton's ranks is amazing—only Benny Goodman, Duke Ellington, Tommy Dorsey, and a few others can rival that record.

Ann Richards, no relation to the former governor of Texas, was born in San Diego on October 1, 1935. She replaced Winters with Kenton, and her 1952 tenure was at least long enough to include a few Capitol sessions and some live airchecks. Both Winters and Richards seemed like personable gals—they both cooperated with Carol Easton on her 1973 biography of Kenton, *Straight Ahead,* one of the most compelling books ever written about a major bandleader. As a teenager in California, Richards told Easton, "He was my idol. I had his picture over my bed. I had all his albums and I would listen to them all the time when my [parents] would go out. . . . I used to think that if I had a husband like Stan Kenton, I could be happy!"

She met Kenton in Hollywood, and her head was filled with romantic imagery she had picked up from the Judy Garland–James Mason classic *A Star Is Born,* which had just been released. She had visions of the forty-year-old Kenton serving as her musical and showbiz Henry Higgins, the way Norman Maine does for Esther Blodgett, but she figured the odds were better for her since Kenton was not a drinker (or so she thought)—although for him, as she would learn, the act of keeping his orchestra going was in itself a kind of addiction. After a year on the road together, they were married in October 1955.

Fans frequently approached Richards with the observation, "Y'know, you sound just like June Christy." But Richards didn't take it as a compliment. Apparently, after hearing it too often she began to resent it, telling Easton, "That used to kill me—I didn't dig Christy's singing that much; she always sang flat and wasn't that creative a singer." Richards is speaking of Christy like a romantic rival, although Christy never had (as far as anyone knows) romantic designs on Kenton and was happily married to his former saxist Bob Cooper (in spite of her own alcohol problem). Christy was one of the gals who distinguished herself with the Kenton band, but Richards, sounding somewhat jealous, speaks of her like a trollop who wanted to bed her husband years before, they had ever met.

Surely Christy was an influence on Richards—naturally, the similarities are underlined by the consistent sound of the Kenton band—but Richards had a much more mainstream, fifties girl singer kind of a voice, whereas Christy had more character, more personality in her timbre. Richards's singing is consistently full of O'Day-Christy-Connor effects, and one wants to like her more, but she's clearly not on the level of her three predecessors, and not up to Kral either. Giving equal time, Easton quotes Mel Lewis, Kenton's drummer of that period: "Ann was the downfall of the band. . . . She wasn't classy at all. She was climbing. She just wanted to be Mrs. Stan Kenton. . . . The minute she married him, she quit singing." It should be noted that in addition to having a more mainstream vocal sound, she also had distinctly more mainstream movie starlet looks. Between the two attributes, Richards could have sung with any band she wanted or married any man she pleased. (And, according to Easton, she pleased a lot of men.)

After four years of just being Mrs. Kenton, Richards recorded her first solo album, *I'm Shooting High* (1959, Capitol), for which arranger and saxophonist Warren Barker supplied Kenton-Rugolo-style charts. She does indeed sound like a junior-league Christy, and her singing is neither as vibrant nor as textured as Connor's or Kral's. Still, she's pleasing to the ear on the exotic "Nightingale" and on the swinging "Will You Still Be Mine," which has a new set of lyrics presumably written for her by the original songwriters, Matt Dennis and Tom Adair ("When Brigitte Bardot can't get a fella / When Frank Sinatra goes to Slenderella").

She did a full-length album, *Two Much!* with the Kenton band in 1960, which seems to have been a first (he had collaborated on a whole album with Christy, *Duet*, but that was a piano-only project not involving the band). The arrangements—by three top Kenton writers, Gene Roland, Bill Holman, and Johnny Richards—were more worthy of attention than the singing.

Kenton and Richards went their separate ways in 1961, and she moved on, for a time propelling her career with the novelty of being the only jazz singer ever to appear in *Playboy* magazine—a record that, I believe, stands to this day. (I welcome any photographic evidence to the contrary.) She made two more albums, *Ann, Man!* for the Atlantic subsidiary Atco in 1961, and *Ann Richards Live . . . at the Losers* for Vee-Jay in 1962.

There are a few good moments on *Ann, Man!* She does a convincing reading of the Dinah Washington–associated "Evil Gal Blues" (undoubtedly brought to her by composer Leonard Feather, who wrote the album notes); when she sings "I've got so many guys, I don't know what to do," we certainly believe her. Although it uses a quartet setting, the Kenton connection continues to serve her well: Onetime Kenton trumpeter Jack Sheldon plays marvelous obbligatos and solos throughout. "Evil Gal Blues" is followed by two more color-coded titles, a swinging waltz by the team of Feather and Dick Hyman called "Love Is a Word for the Blues," and a good, very visual title by Gene Roland and Johnny Richards, "How Do I Look in Blue?" But the album opens with "Yes Sir, That's My Baby," in which Richards attempts to pull off the kind of starting small, ending big, bottom-to-top rhythmic tour de force that Anita O'Day had masterminded with "Honeysuckle Rose" and "Sweet Georgia Brown,"

and she just isn't up to it—the net result is to make us appreciate O'Day even more than we already do. She fairly consistently misses the mark when trying to be sexy on "An Occasional Man," or when trying to invoke the gospel spirit on Sister Rosetta Tharpe's "That's All." Still, she ends with a convincingly intimate "I Couldn't Sleep a Wink Last Night," done with just guitar.

Richards's *Live* album—her last—taped at the Losers club in Los Angeles, shows that she's considerably more seasoned at the age of twenty-nine. She's lost much of her Christy-Connor cool sound and is fitting more comfortably into the mold of a straight-ahead sixties jazz singer. "I Only Have Eyes for You" is funky and bluesy, convincingly underplayed by Richards, mainly "strolling" for the first chorus with just bass and drums. "Back Home Again in Indiana" goes beyond the O'Day school influence to a scat solo that starts out like O'Day but in the second chorus includes some very Fitzgeraldian phrases, ending on a high note that's way more Ella than Anita. "Come Rain or Come Shine" is delivered as a funky jazz waltz in the style of the period, à la Ray Brown or Vince Guaraldi.

Live at the Losers is Richards's most satisfying effort, and the only project to really suggest that she might someday have developed into an important jazz singer. On the evidence of the ironically titled *Losers*, it's a real loss that she didn't continue. By most accounts, she committed suicide in 1982.

Cleo Laine (born 1927)

Comparative logic can only get you so far: Betty Carter, Sarah Vaughan, and (especially) Mel Tormé are three of the most mannered and stylized performers I've ever heard, and I thought they all were brilliant. Dame Cleo Laine, by far the most celebrated of non-American jazz singers, is no more stylized and mannered, but I've never been able to warm up to her. Whenever I listen to her, in person or on any of her many albums, I keep thinking about the breakup line used by George Costanza on *Seinfeld*: "It's not you, it's me." There's nothing about Laine herself that I shouldn't like; it must be something wrong with me.

Mel Tormé was himself one of Ms. Laine's biggest boosters—he recorded a whole album of duets with her—and more than anything else, she could be described as a British female equivalent of the late Mel. She also is virtually the only jazz singer from England to enjoy a long and significant career on the international stage—unless you count Al Bowlly and Matt Monro. (Recently, though, she's become a role model for a rising crop of British jazz vocal stars like Ian Shaw, Claire Martin, Barb Jungr, and Tessa Souter.)

On paper, a description of Ms. Laine in action sounds a lot like Carter, Vaughan, or Tormé: Like Vaughan and Tormé, she possesses a stunningly beautiful vocal instrument, and like all three, she does a lot of scatting. I use the term as distinct from improvising, since, as with Carter and Tormé, many of these wordless passages are carefully prearranged. There's also much give-and-take between her and her musical director (and husband), the multireed player and composer John Dankworth, including some breathtaking unison passages. In general, like Carter and Tormé, she employs an abundance of intricate, not to say tricky, arrangements; there's no end of very busy business. The difference is that even though Carter and Tormé used a lot of shtick, they never let it overwhelm their very real emotions; these routines always enhanced and amplified what was in their souls. Laine, on the other hand, often seems to be using her very elaborate and rococo arrangements as a substitute for soul.

In her long and extensively documented career, there are individual moments when she puts it all together in a pleasing fashion, but most of the time she lets virtuoso technique and a relentlessly baroque sensibility get in the way of virtually everything she does.

Laine was born in Southall, London, in 1927. Her mother was English and her father was Jamaican, giving her skin a lovely color, which served her well in the famous London production of *Show Boat* (1972) that showed the world that she could act as well as sing.

Her career has been inextricably bound up with John Dankworth's. Born a month before Laine, he is best described as a sort of combination Henry Mancini and Art Pepper. According to legend, they met when she auditioned for his band—that was more than fifty years ago and they remained together until his death in 2010. In the early days, she was the vocalist with his orchestra, and though they are often equally billed, the consensus over the last few decades is that he is primarily her musical director and accompanist.

As creative musicians with distinctly Anglo sensibilities, the Dankworths have addressed all kinds of subjects from Bernstein to Shakespeare to Ellington to Schoenberg. In the early days, like Jackie Cain and Eydie Gormé (also halves of famous husband-and-wife duos, now that I think of it), she sounded a lot like the young Sarah Vaughan; by the eighties and nineties, critics were more routinely comparing her to Betty Carter. The difference—and, to state the obvious, this is all one man's highly subjective opinion—is that Carter, Vaughan, and Tormé (most of the time at least) seemed to be in touch with a higher power, serving as a channel between the audience and that divine spark of inspiration. They managed to make themselves disappear—through their stagecraft and musical smarts. Though Laine is no less musically astute, one feels one can never see past her ego when she's working. Wherever you look,

there it is, and when you look in her eyes you can never see forever.

Still, her discography is overwhelmingly capacious, and there are good moments as well as bad. In 1997, BMG America put out *The Very Best of Cleo Laine,* presumably selected by the lady herself. Everything that's wonderful seems counterbalanced by something awful: a beautiful "Dreamsville" takes on Mancini's loveliest ballad in cahoots with Gerry Mulligan on his trademark sensitive baritone sax, followed by the dreadful seventies "Gonna Get Through," full of pseudo-pop electronics, a gratuitous reference to Joni Mitchell, and gimmicky modulations. "Creole Love Call," a carefully considered treatment of the early Ellington masterpiece, with new and excellent lyrics by Lorraine Feather, is offset by "It Don't Mean a Thing," the Maestro's scat feature trivialized into a vehicle for her most vacuous showboating. Yet there are ballads—such as "What'll I Do," a duet with the late Joe Williams; "The Lies of Handsome Men," the Francesca Blumenthal song that has since become a cabaret standard; and "Bill," her big number in *Show Boat,* from Laine's Grammy-winning *Carnegie Hall Live* (1993)—where she really does manage to connect.

I had caught Laine in concert several times in the eighties and nineties before I saw her for the first time in the comparative intimacy of a nightclub. This was at her third engagement at Feinstein's at the Regency, in November 2003. She began the set with a Tormé-like medley of familiar Duke Ellington songs, including "Don't Get Around Much Anymore" and "It Don't Mean a Thing." Dankworth, however, had already satisfied the Ellingtonians in the house with his quartet treatment of "Tonight I Shall Sleep," a lesser-known item that deserves to be in the standard repertoire and which he performed with enough vibrato and glissandos to summon up Johnny Hodges and the whole Ducal reed tradition.

While Laine pushes conventional songs further than even classics can bear, I was surprised by how enjoyable her nonsong material could be. Midway through her set, she performed four settings composed by Dankworth for poems by T. S. Eliot, John Donne, W. H. Auden, and e. e. cummings. She didn't shtick these up at all but intoned them lovingly and straight-ahead—as if they really meant something to her and she wanted the audience to love them, too. And we did.

While words without music were one highlight of the Laine-Dankworth set, so, too, was the encore, in which she sang (music without words) an instrumental by Mozart. This was "Turkish Delight," Dankworth's imaginative and swinging adaptation of the famous "Blue Rondo." It was a suitably regal conclusion for the only jazz-singing Dame of the British Empire.

Lee Wiley's Boston Connection

Teddi King
Barbara Lea

In 1951, Columbia Records released one of the most important vocal jazz albums of all time, *Night in Manhattan,* by Lee Wiley, with pianist Joe Bushkin "and his swinging strings." Shortly afterward, Wiley went to work for the first time at a club called Storyville in Boston, which was owned and operated by future Newport Jazz Festival impresario George Wein. It was at this point that she was first heard by, and began to exert an influence on, a pair of local singers named Teddi King and Barbara Lea. Of the two, Lea sounds by far the closer to the older woman's burnished, smoky sound. Still, even while King reflected other influences in her sound and her overall approach, both women lived up to Wiley's ideal of cabaret jazz.

Both Lea and King were born in 1929, a short while before Wiley came to New York and hit the big time; Lea in Detroit, Michigan, on April 10, King in Revere, Massachusetts, on September 18. Both grew up singing as children, teaching themselves songs when and where they could; King studied piano as well. Lea gravitated toward jazz at an early age, especially when she later found that she could overcome her considerable stage fright (shades of Lee Wiley) when she found the safety in numbers of a band; King's first idea was to become a legit actress, and she only began to study singing seriously when she realized that this skill would give her access to a wider variety of roles. Both were singing with local bands in Boston in the late forties, where Lea had come to major in music theory at Wellesley.

Teddi King (1929–1977)

Teddi King, who died at the age of forty-eight in 1977, is something of an anomaly. In the beginning at least, she seems to have regarded herself as a "pure" jazz singer, having been raised on Billie Holiday, Mildred Bailey (and of course Wiley), and, by the time she established herself as a professional singer, she had fallen deeply under the sway of Sarah Vaughan. Her producers, as we shall see, sometimes had other ideas.

King's career began in earnest in 1949 when she won a singing contest at the Boston RKO Theatre. Shortly thereafter, she was singing with the then local pianist Nat Pierce, who was leading a "progressive" orchestra in the approximate style of Woody Herman (shortly thereafter, Pierce would become a prominent arranger for Herman himself). Through Pierce she had the opportunity to make her first record, which was done for the local Motif label. Supposedly, King was trying to reinvent herself as the white Sarah Vaughan (a singer who, perhaps not coincidentally, had also muchly impressed Lee Wiley), while the record company itself pressured her to sound as much like June Christy as she could. Whatever the

influence, the finished disc, a novelty called "Goodbye, Mr. Chops" (presumably by an area composer), became something of a local hit.

As it happens, King's early recordings, made between 1949 and 1955 in Boston and New York, are probably, overall, the best of her career. *Teddi King: In the Beginning, 1949–1954* (Baldwin Street Music) is ostensibly a collection of early rarities, but actually includes some of the very best, not to mention jazziest, singing King ever put down on records. A balance of standards and amiably dopey tunes ("Mr. Chops," surprisingly, is funnier than it sounds, and "Tea Kettle and Coffee Pot" somehow percolates nicely), the set includes five boppish numbers with Nat Pierce, and some unusual early song demos with just piano. The core of the CD, however, is the group of six numbers she made with George Shearing's classic 1952 quintet: Here she blends effortlessly with the group's famous doubled-and-tripled-note mix of piano, guitar, and vibes. She also concentrates on offbeat standards—a move that would soon be a trademark—like "Love, Your Magic Spell Is Everywhere." These are some of the nicest sides Shearing ever made with a vocalist, and considering that he's recorded with everyone from Dakota Staton to Nat Cole to Peggy Lee to Nancy Wilson to Mel Tormé to Joe Williams to John Pizzarelli to Carmen McRae to Ernestine Anderson to Michael Feinstein, that's really saying something.

In the early fifties, King made three albums produced by George Wein, for his Storyville label: two 10" LPs, *'Round Midnight* (1953), done with just Beryl Booker on piano, and *Miss Teddi King,* with a quartet featuring pianist Jimmy Jones and trumpeter Ruby Braff (1954), and one 12" album, *Now in Vogue,* which varies between the rhythm section and a more ambitious group that adds four horns. The Storyville albums, although not as well recorded as her later RCA sets, are consistently rewarding. Another concert producer, Jack Kleinsinger, later coined the useful term "cabaret jazz" for this kind of singing. King and Barbara Lea are both—like Wiley—more lyric-specific than Anita O'Day deconstructing "Tea for Two," but far looser and jazzier than, say, a Mabel Mercer waltzing over loves gone by.

The first Storyville album, *'Round Midnight,* with just piano, is the straightest of the three, but King loosens up considerably on the second thanks to the presence of Milt Hinton and Jo Jones on bass and drums, as well as pianist Jimmy Jones's Basie-like accompaniment—not to mention Ruby Braff's obligatory obbligato prodding. There are slow numbers here, too, like the haunting "Love Is a Now and Then Thing" and "It's All in Your Mind"—possibly learned from Vaughan. *Now in Vogue* is quite strong, too, if not as much so as the previous sets, in that King sounds a little uncomfortable with the cool jazz–style horn section. Still, the slower numbers (particularly "This Is Always") and the trio-only numbers are just dandy; there are also two fine tips-of-the-bonnet to Wiley, "Fools Fall in Love" and "A Ship Without a Sail," songs King could have learned from no one else.

In 1955, she was given a shot at major label success via a contract with RCA that resulted in three 12" LPs, as well as a series of singles. The RCA material in toto is not as consistently excellent as the Storyville output, even though she was given two outstanding orchestrators, Al Cohn and George Siravo, and apparently allowed to pursue her taste for eclectic material. On the Storyville projects, King seems to have perfected a sound and a style all her own, whereas she sounds more generic on some of the RCA material, which runs the gamut from moving and/or swinging to disappointingly dull. It's neither jazz nor cabaret at times but straight-down-the-middle pop singing—not of the sparkling Doris Day–Margaret Whiting variety but of the comparatively stiff Giselle MacKenzie–Gogi Grant–even Jane Morgan kind. This is especially true of the seventeen singles she cut for the corporation, but, as with the three RCA albums, there's some fine stuff there, too. Like many artists, King seems to have courted commercial success at the same time she chafed against it. In 1954, while trying to attract the attention of a major label, she took the iniative to produce her own session. The results turned out to be much more mainstream pop–oriented than anything that RCA or Coral would foist upon her: For an arranger, she hired her friend Dick Jacobs, a highly conservative hitmaker, and they picked four absolutely forgettable pop tunes (though I confess to a certain fondness for "The Dragon," a very late-in-the-game slice of faux-chinoiserie by Gladys Shelley) to sing.

The three RCA albums, *Bidin' My Time* (1955, with Cohn) and *To You* (1956, Siravo), and *A Girl and Her Songs* (1957, Siravo), have their strengths and their weaknesses. "The Way You Look Tonight," which opens *To You*, could be absolutely any voice on a jukebox or on a Sunday night TV variety show. She has a very pretty voice, but here, at least, not a distinctive one. It's highly competent and professional but lacking any spark of personality or individual style; this isn't a singer one would compare with Wiley, Christy, or Vaughan.

However, the first track on *A Girl and Her Songs*, "A Sailboat in the Moonlight," swings in a hot and lusty way I wouldn't have thought her capable of. In fact, "Sailboat" is only one tune out of a four-song session that marks the best of her RCA dates; backed by trumpeter Doc Severinson and rhythm section only, these four titles are a worthy follow-up to her earlier work with Ruby Braff. Among the other tunes here are a second item she learned from Billie Holiday, "Laughing at Life," and "My Future Just Passed" from the repertoire of both Annette Hanshaw and Kay Starr.

Although King sounds a trifle precious here and there, overall there are more than enough inspired performances throughout to keep the albums interesting: "How Come You Do Me like You Do" finds King's Wiley and traditional jazz roots showing through, and the song's bluesy edge turns out to be surprisingly compatible with her (at times) rather precious vibrato. At the same time, Jonah Jones's insistent trumpet obbligato is by itself worth the price of admission. As with the work of Barbara Lea, part of the fun is hearing songs one doesn't often encounter on fifties vocal albums: "How Come You Do Me" being one, Cole Porter's "Where Have You Been," and Eckstine's "Mister, You've Gone and Got the Blues."

King seems to have had a comparatively freer hand in choosing the songs on her albums, but RCA's A&R men most certainly picked out the contemporaneous pop songs that she recorded as singles. I can only imagine what she thought of some of these second-rate tunes, but there is some outstanding singing here as well. Surprisingly, she recorded Irving Berlin's 1932 "Say It Isn't So" as a single, and the result was a dark but swinging ballad; even more strangely, she also recorded "There's So Much More," a Rodgers and Hart obscurity (from the 1931 *America's Sweetheart*) as a 45. Particularly rewarding are the other movie and show tunes she cut as singles, such as "Traveling Down a Lonely Road," an English-language version of the theme from Fellini's *La Strada*. There's also "A Ride on a Rainbow" from Jule Styne's TV musical version of *Ruggles of Red Gap* and "Married I Can Always Get" from Gordon Jenkins's update of *Manhattan Tower*. These are some of her finest vocals, proving that she could do the mainstream pop thing whenever she wanted, and making one wonder why she was never tapped by either Broadway or Hollywood. (True, King was only four foot eleven, but she was also extraordinarily fair of face.)

On one of her first RCA dates in 1955, she recorded the title song from the forthcoming Broadway musical *Mr. Wonderful*. It became a hit for her, her only entry of note on the *Billboard* charts. For the rest of her life she was lukewarm about it. It's neither the best nor the worst of her RCA singles (admittedly, Peggy Lee's Decca version is a superior sample of pop singing). But, like Sylvia Syms and "Get Me to the Church on Time" and Felicia Sanders and "Where Is Your Heart," King's "Mr. Wonderful" is an important reminder of an age when a quality-driven but marginal artist such as King could actually have a hit record.

After leaving RCA, she made one album, *All the King's Songs*, and some miscellaneous tracks for Coral. *All the King's Songs* is no better or worse than the RCA LPs, although there are no surprises like the Doc Severinson quintet sessions to liven things up, nor are there offbeat tunes (like "I Poured My Heart into a Song" on *Bidin'*). It's a treat, though, to hear the verse to "Flamingo."

Teddi King pretty much falls off the radar in the sixties. Friend and researcher Ted Ono theorizes that the singer signed an exclusive agreement with the international circuit of Playboy Clubs, which forbade her from appearing anywhere else, including on TV or making recordings. She was also a victim of the same cultural devastation that blighted the career of every other quality singer of the era.

In the seventies King resurfaced, more marginalized than ever, and began to appear in clubs and record again just as she was diagnosed with the disease lupus. As was made clear at a 2002 tribute to her, produced by another old Boston colleague, Richard Sudhalter, for the JVC Jazz Festival, the disease ennobled her. King already was much loved by everyone in the traditional jazz community, but by devoting so much of her energy to fighting and finding a cure for lupus, she began to be spoken of as a saint. Indeed, at the 2002 tribute, King was generally described as a combination of Ella Fitzgerald and Florence Nightingale. She had made three new albums after 1973 (none of which, to my ears anyhow, is in the same league with the best of her fifties work) and was working on a fourth, a set of duets on Ira Gershwin tunes, when the lupus took her life in 1977.

At the time of her death, she was loved especially by the fraternity of lovers of jazz and the Great American Songbook who were based in the New England area. They regarded Teddi King as a genuine star, much the same way that jazz fans in New York, New Jersey, and Philadelphia regarded Etta Jones and Teri Thornton. If Ella Fitzgerald and Lee Wiley herself are remembered as first-rate jazz-pop singers, I hope it doesn't sound cruel to regard Teddi King as a very credible second-tier artist. And at her best, she was even more than that.

Barbara Lea (born 1929)

When Barbara Lea came out to do her one number at the aforementioned 2002 JVC salute to Teddi King, I remember thinking that it would be more appropriate if the Wein office would put its considerable resources behind a major effort to promote Lea herself. Here was a woman, I was thinking, who has devoted decades and decades of her life in service to jazz and the Great American Songbook. She's done nothing but the highest-quality songs in the company of the best musicians she can get. Without sounding as if she's imitating her idol, Lee Wiley, Lea has nonetheless kept the memory of Wiley alive, sharing something of the older woman's husky voice if not quite her open, earthy eroticism, as well as Wiley's tradition of teaming with the best traditional jazz and swing players. (That thought was somewhat ungrateful: It would probably be impossible for Wein and Co., who have consistently supported her in any way they could for more than fifty years, to do more for her.)

Lea inspires writers as well as musicians and singers: It's not surprising that such erudite player-scholars as Sudhalter and Loren Schoenberg would collaborate with her whenever they could, because she's just as much a historian as they are. About the

only thing Lea never achieved was an audience big enough to keep her working. In this book, I speak of both Lee Wiley and Teddi King as somewhat marginal, yet compared to Lea, despite her many excellent qualities, they're practically mainstream.

Born Barbara Ann LeCocq in Detroit in 1929, Lea came to Boston to study music theory at Wellesley College. She quickly became part of Bean Town's bustling jazz scene, and in the inner circle as it were, of Messrs. Wein and Charlie Bourgeois. When Lee Wiley played Storyville for the first time in 1951, the twenty-two-year-old Lea was collecting admissions for Wein. The cover charge was $1.25, and she never could arrange to deliver exactly the right amount of money; she told me that Wein would be more upset when the till wound up with more rather than less money than it was supposed to. "George didn't mind if we were short, but he didn't want me to clip anybody by mistake." In any case, Lea had plenty of opportunity to listen to—and study—the great Lee Wiley. Within a short while, Lea was one of the few whom Wiley considered a close friend.

Lea moved to New York for the first time in 1952, and essentially her career has been based there for the last fifty-plus years. In 1954, she made her first recording for the short-lived Cadillac label; the producers wanted her to do one "commercial" side, a pleasant piece of fluff entitled "Bet You a Kiss," while she apparently selected the flip, the Arlen-Mercer standard "Any Place I Hang My Hat Is Home." Actually, the pop side is quite appealing, if for no other reason than the naïveté of the enterprise, not on the part of Miss Lea—already an accomplished vocalist—but on the part of the producers. It's hard to imagine that they could possibly have imagined this charming number was "commercial" enough to dent the charts.

In quick succession, Lea made three fine albums: *A Woman in Love*, done for Riverside in 1955, one of producer Orrin Keepnews's first sessions and a very late entry in the 10" LP format, and two for Prestige, *Barbara Lea* (1956) and *Lea in Love* (1957), both featuring New England trumpeter Johnny Windhurst. Clearly, Lea was a later bloomer than her friend Teddi King, who was reaching the apex of her career just as Lea was starting hers. However, the Riverside and Prestige records show that her style was fully formed by her mid-twenties, and that she had already perfected her own Wiley-inspired brand of cabaret jazz—too hot for the Blue Angel and too formal for Birdland. Lea was Wiley's successor, but never her imitator.

Like King, Lea ceased recording in the late fifties, and wasn't heard from again on disc until the seventies. In the interim, she worked as an actress (in off-Broadway, summer stock, and regional theater), got married three times, moved back and forth to the West Coast, and matriculated at San Fernando Valley State College, where she received an M.A. in drama. Lea did everything, it seems, except sing professionally. She gradually eased back into making music with the encouragement of old friends like Alec Wilder and Marian McPartland.

After a twenty-year absence from the studios, Lea returned, appropriately, with the 1976 *Remembering Lee Wiley* on Audiophile. For the next thirty years or so, her output was steady and consistent. She's recorded well over a dozen albums, most for George Buck's New Orleans–based Audiophile label and producer Wendell Echols. She's participated in a diverse variety of concept projects, often songbooks—Willard Robison, Hoagy Carmichael, Noel Coward—as well as in such historical projects as the first recording of Duke Ellington's last theatrical work, *Pousse-Café.*

My favorite Lea album, however, is not a theme album at all but *You're the Cats!* This 1989 effort is a conceptless collection of great songs hardly anyone else ever bothers to do—like Rodgers and Hart's title track from *The Hot Heiress,* the Gershwins' "Do What You Do," and two infrequently heard pieces by Fats Waller, "Dixie Cinderella" and "There's a Man in My Life." The accompaniment is just as good as the material: a later edition of the Yank Lawson–Bob Haggart Jazz Band, also known as the World's Greatest Jazz Band. Whenever I listen to it, I wonder anew why more people haven't heard of Barbara Lea. She followed this with, among other things, *The Melody Lingers On,* a project co-produced by the late scholar Roy Hemming, and inspired by the title of one of his books on popular music; it contains some wonderful songs I never thought I'd hear anyone sing after the 78 era, like "A Rainy Night in Rio" and "Humpty Dumpty Heart."

It would be overdramatic to call Lea a local legend or a New York treasure; perhaps her main virtue is that she represents a high level of musicianship, an overall quality of material, presentation, and professionalism that was once taken for granted. If the three major Bostoncentric female jazz vocalists—Wiley, King, and Lea—are a family of sorts, perhaps they might be compared to a far more famous family from the same area. Lee Wiley is like Joe Kennedy, the founder of a dynasty; Teddi King is like JFK, who had a short, brilliant career and left us at an early age; Barbara Lea is the Teddy Kennedy of this bunch, who did consistently good work for decade after decade.

In her own way, she is also a pioneer—the first singing scholar and so the spiritual mother of such major cabaret singer-historians as Michael Feinstein, Mary Cleere Haran, Susannah McCorkle, Andrea Marcovicci, and more recently Maude Maggart.

As late as the excellent 2006 release *Black Butterfly* (a remarkable album done with Loren Schoenberg's big band), Barbara Lea showed she was still capable of putting a song over and singing a lyric as if she meant it. By the time of her eightieth birthday, in April 2009, she had unofficially retired from performing, due to health issues. But throughout the seventies, eighties, nineties, and into the twenty-first century, it was possible to catch her with some regularity in New York, and almost everyone who sings jazz or cabaret in this city had been to hear her at one time or another—and learned something from her.

Leading Ladies

Barbara Cook
Julie Andrews

Any discussion of the great Broadway leading ladies and what they contributed to the art of singing the American songbook surely must begin with Barbara Cook. I saw her at least a dozen times in the last decade alone, including three shows at the Café Carlyle, two at Carnegie, and at all-star events including the 2002 Richard Rodgers Centennial Celebration; I also attended the recording session for her Christmas album in fall 2003. On each occasion, I was reminded again and again what a unique treasure Barbara Cook is, and how few other Broadway performers boast her combination of amazing voice, amazing acting ability, and just plain intelligence. It isn't only that she can hit such beautiful high notes; more important, she knows just where to put the emphasis to get the maximum meaning out of every line (whether of a song or of dialogue) and the maximum drama out of every character.

There are other important Broadway divas beyond the ones I'm mentioning here, including Carol Channing, Gertrude Lawrence, Gwen Verdon, and more recently Patti LuPone, Betty Buckley, Christine Ebersole, Christine Andreas, Melissa Errico, and Kelli O'Hara. Yet eliminating those who are primarily comediennes, dancers, or actresses whose singing is secondary, I hope that the reader will agree that it's Ms. Andrews and Ms. Cook (along with Mary Martin and Ethel Merman, who are discussed elsewhere) who must be considered from a purely vocal perspective. These are the women most easily deserve to be considered major interpreters of the songbook, in the same way that Ella Fitzgerald, Judy Garland, Sarah Vaughan, and Dinah Washington are.

Barbara Cook (born 1927)

Even in that rarefied group, Barbara Cook stands out. With her, the voice always came first and foremost. She had plenty of acting talent and personality but was rarely considered a voice above all. She was never a name-above-the-title attraction—while *The*

Music Man was her biggest Broadway hit, she was billed way underneath leading man Robert Preston, even though she had more numbers than he. No composers or librettists ever got together and asked one another, "What can we do to build a show around Barbara Cook?" Yet it's doubtful that *Music Man* would have been the blockbuster hit it was without her, and she played a crucial part in making *She Loves Me* into a classic. Nor would the original albums of such less frequently seen shows as *Plain and Fancy*, *Candide*, and *The Gay Life* be so prized by lovers of the musical comedy form were it not for Cook's stunning singing.

Cook (born in Atlanta in 1927 and eight years older than Julie Andrews) and Andrews both broke through on Broadway in the 1954–55 season, Cook in *Plain and Fancy* and Andrews in *The Boy Friend*. It was immediately clear that both of them were highly gifted sopranos, of the sort that might just as easily be singing Mimi in *La Bohème*—or at least Yum Yum in *The Mikado*. Yet despite the potentially classical sound of Cook's choppers, there's something steadfastly American about her coloratura. Unlike other American opera-style divas to gain wide popularity, such as Jeanette MacDonald and Deanna Durbin (both phenomenally successful in the thirties), Cook always sounds like an American singer singing American music—even when indulging in the stratospheric operatic trills of "Glitter and Be Gay" in *Candide*. Like Andrews, Cook was singled out early on as a vocalist with abilities far beyond those of mortal Broadway men (and women); she was that rare ingenue to cut her own albums, *Songs of Perfect Propriety* (1958) and *Barbara Cook Sings from the Heart—Memorable Songs of Rodgers and Hart* (1959).

Cook was well known to Broadway devotees long before the breakthrough of *Plain and Fancy*. Indeed, in her first few years in New York she established what would become a career pattern. Even when she appeared in a flop show, such as her first Broadway vehicle, *Flahooley* (1951), it was one with a terrific score, and one that earned a place in the history of Broadway even if it wasn't immediately embraced by the big crowds. In *Flahooley*, Cook as the ingenue lead shared the stage with another vocal athlete, the multioctave South American novelty performer Yma Sumac, along with the equally surreal Bil Baird marionettes. Not surprisingly, it was she who sang "The World Is Your Balloon," virtually the only song from Yip Harburg and Sammy Fain's score ever to be heard from again.

In between that debut (her first notable appearance in New York was at the Blue Angel in 1950), and her first original hit on Broadway, Cook established another niche for herself as one of the principal performers of the canon of Richard Rodgers and especially Oscar Hammerstein. Although, unfortunately, these two leading lights of the American musical theater never created any roles or wrote any songs for her, she nonetheless became an integral part of how their work was presented. In 1953, she played the comedy lead, Ado Annie, in the City Center production (and subsequent national tour) of *Oklahoma!*, and she played both the key female roles in the City Center productions of *Carousel* (Carrie Pipperidge in 1954 and Julie Jordan in 1957, shortly before opening in *The Music Man*). In 1960, Cook played the "I" in City Center's *The King and I*, and next became the best of all postwar Magnolias in *Show Boat*, both on the 1961 Columbia Records studio cast album and in the 1966 City Center revival. She can probably claim to have played in more important productions of Oscar Hammerstein musicals than anyone else, even though she was never in any of the original Broadway casts.

The first two major roles she created in new musicals were Hilda Miller in *Plain and Fancy* and Marian the Librarian in *The Music Man*. As Marian, she played a pedagogue who advocated progressive art and culture—in short, something of a River City avant-gardist. (The description also applies to her portrayal of a proto-feminist in the 1956 TV production of *Bloomer Girl*.) In *Plain and Fancy*, she played a girl in a Pennsylvania Dutch Amish village; the story was set in the present, yet she was part of a community that advocates living in the past. The combination of past-progressive and present-retentive is key in our perception of Cook, who, unlike Ethel Merman (or even Julie Andrews in her far more limited Broadway work), would spend the lesser part of her career helping to create new roles and new shows—indeed, for various reasons, as we'll see, few would even associate her with the roles of Marian the Librarian, Cunegonde (in *Candide*), or Amalia Balash (in *She Loves Me*). Her career would be considerably less important if it were only about the roles she actually created. Carol Channing is known only as Lorelei Lee or Dolly Levi, but Barbara Cook has been or could be just about any leading lady in the history of Broadway. She is essentially the house singer for the entire postwar musical theater.

In *Plain and Fancy*, Cook was neither the comedy lead (Shirl Conway) nor the romantic ingenue (Gloria Marlowe), but merely a sort of Amish female heavy who comes between Conway and her intended. Yet when she sang the plaintive "This Is All Very New to Me" and "I'll Show Him" (a leading lady revenge song anticipating "Just You Wait, Henry Higgins"), Cook's was the voice everybody remembered. The show, with a score by Albert Hague (who went on to do *Redhead* and the marvelous songs from the original *Grinch* TV special) was successful in its day (461 performances), but is rarely if ever revived. Cook's performance is all that's remembered of the show.

In *Candide*, she was overwhelmed not by the talent onstage (her leading man was the fine tenor Robert Rounseville), but off—it seems as if every other intellectual of the midcentury worked on the thing at one time or another, including Leonard Bernstein (and later Stephen Sondheim), Lillian Hellman, John La Touche, and Dorothy Parker. (I wouldn't be surprised to learn that Norman Mailer, J. D. Salinger, and Jean-Paul Sartre all had a hack at the libretto.) Yet between the lot of them they couldn't make a workable musical out of Voltaire's classic novella. Still, Cook was the best of all possible Cunegondes, craftily claiming a space for herself amid all the baritones and tenors in Leonard Bernstein's many duets and quartets. Her "Glitter and Be Gay" is a showstopper even on the 1956 cast album, at once parodying and reveling in the tradition of coloratura exhibitionism, ascending wordlessly into the stratosphere in the manner of the "Bell Song" from *Lakmé*. With this performance, Cook established herself as Broadway's equivalent of Joan Sutherland or Sarah Vaughan.

Candide's "Quiet" quintet had Cook injecting ever increasing quantities of both character and comedy into her work, qualities that came to the fore in her next show—and greatest Broadway triumph—*The Music Man*. She was overqualified in the vocal department, which made her a perfect counterpart to Robert Preston, starring as Professor Harold Hill, about whom the opposite could be said.

Listening to the original cast album of *The Music Man*, one is struck equally by Cook's vocal versatility and the musical astuteness of composer-lyricist-librettist Meredith Willson, a man so multifaceted that he required two L's for his last name. Cook's first number, in fact, incorporates a fair amount of plot exposition and witty musical dialogue set to the ever-ascending scales and monotonous rhythms of a "Piano Lesson." A master music man himself, Willson later used an ascending solo piano passage as a transition to the first of Marian the Librarian's big solos, "Goodnight, My Someone."

She also put over "Till There Was You." Neither the Beatles, who made it virtually the only show tune they ever recorded, nor Preston, who joins her near the end of the second chorus, could wrest it from Cook. "My White Knight" also remains her song; Shirley Jones played the Librarian opposite Preston in the 1962 Warner Bros. movie version, but was deprived of the chance of singing Marian's most moving musical monologue. "White Knight" is a philosophical, as opposed to a harmonic, counterpart to Preston's number "Marian the Librarian." (Fortunately, there are some marvelous clips of Cook doing her major Marian numbers on *The Bell Telephone Hour,* which have been released on DVD by VAI home video.)

And that, unfortunately, was practically it, as far as Barbara Cook creating a new role in a major hit musical. Although Shirley Jones does a fine job with Marian onscreen, one regrets that her taking the role meant that we are denied what would have been our only chance to see Cook in a film of one of her Broadway roles—no one ever contemplated filming *Plain and Fancy, Candide, The Gay Life*, or *Something More.*

There is, however, an excellent 1956 TV version of Cook playing the lead in Harburg and Arlen's *Bloomer Girl,* a condensed production that for all the failings of early live television is considerably tauter and better put together than the 1943 Broadway version (if the 2001 City Center Encores recreation is any indication). Fortunately, the audio and video quality of the surviving kinescope, as well as the performances of Cook and Brock Peters, are good enough for some enterprising producer to consider releasing this *Bloomer Girl* on DVD. Oddly, however, though the character of Evalina is very well developed both by book writer Fred Saidy and Cook, unfortunately Evalina gets virtually none of Arlen and Harburg's best numbers, except for heckling leading man Keith Andes during "Evalina" and playing second fiddle to him during "Right as the Rain."

The early sixties brought three new shows: *The Gay Life* (1961), *She Loves Me* (1963), and *Something More!* (1964). The last turned out to be something distinctly less, based on the novel *Portofino P.T.A.* (already unsuccessfully musicalized by Sheldon Harnick as *Portofino* in 1958), with a score by Marilyn and Alan Bergman and Sammy Fain; here was a show that came and went without so much as a "World Is Your Balloon." *The Gay Life*, written by Arthur Schwartz and Howard Dietz, ran for only a few months. Everything about it was overly reminiscent of Lerner and Loewe's *Gigi*. In turn-of-the-century Europe (Vienna, not Paris), a young girl emerging into womanhood (played by the thirty-six-year-old Cook) becomes smitten with the city's most eligible bachelor and heartbreaker; the poster showed maidens typical of France parading about in Toulouse-Lautrec drag with long trains and feathery *chapeaux.*

Unlike *Something More, The Gay Life* ran long enough for Capitol to do a cast album, and here Cook shines. Judging by the album, the story and score are well integrated, although leading man Walter Chiari is even less of a polished vocalist than *Gigi*'s Louis Jourdan. Cook's big solo, "Magic Moment" (also recorded by Nat King Cole), is precisely that, a piece of buried treasure.

She Loves Me was and is a terrific show, a fact that was not recognized during its original run in 1963 but was keenly appreciated during a successful revival thirty years later. In thirties Budapest, Cook plays a firmly American Amalia opposite Daniel Massey as a British Georg and the even more American Jack Cassidy as Kodaly, the heel, nogoodnik, and hairy hound from Budapest. The writers achieved a perfect blend of songs and narrative, the leading lady achieved an equally perfect balance of singing and acting. Despite competition from everyone from Judy Garland in *In the Good Old Summertime* to Meg Ryan in *You've Got Mail* (others who have played the role in various adaptations include Gemma Craven, who was marvelous in a 1978 BBC TV production), Cook makes Amalia live and breathe like no one else excepting the sublime Margaret Sullavan in the classic 1940 Ernst Lubitsch film *The Shop Around the Corner*, on which *She Loves Me* is based.

Most of Cook's numbers are very artfully conceived scenes musicalized via rhyming dialogue ("No More Candy," "I Don't Know His Name," "Where's My Shoe?"), but there are standout fully sung solos by her as well: "Dear Friend" is the most European she ever got after *Candide*, expressing yearning and anticipation in a minor key waltz, building to a high note climax. "Ice Cream" is one of the theater's best songs of self-exploration and discovery, the kind usually given to leading men in Rodgers and Hammerstein musicals, such as the King of Siam puzzling out "A Puzzlement" and Billy Bigelow contemplating parenthood in "Soliloquy." "Ice Cream" repeatedly changes tunes, keys, tones, melodies—the works—mirroring the thought process even more ambitiously than "Adelaide's Lament" in *Guys and Dolls* in a way that seems completely random but is obviously carefully concocted.

In 1965, Cook apparently went through something of a personal meltdown after *She Loves Me* was not immediately greeted as the classic that it was, and *Something More* was, alas, recognized as an instant flop. Just as the Broadway musical form itself was starting to lose ground and work was drying up, Cook was reaching the point where she could no longer play ingenues. (It's to her credit that she was, apparently, completely convincing as the girly-girl Magnolia in Lincoln Center's 1966 revival of *Show Boat*, which led to her second recording of that role.) Worse, in 1965 she went through an unhappy divorce. According to theater historian Daniel Langan, she became erratic—not showing up for appointments, binge eating, and generally letting both her career and her figure go. It was Wally Harper, the pianist and conductor who became her musical director and professional partner for roughly thirty years, who helped her get back on her feet and reinvent herself as a solo act, switching from theaters to cabarets and concert halls. She has been by far the most successful Broadway headliner to make that transition and a role model to subsequent generations of theatrical divas.

Cook would appear in two more shows, the flop *The Grass Harp* (1971) and, much later, the epic disaster *Carrie* (she had the good sense to bail out of that loser before anyone dumped a bucket of pig's blood on her head). She also acted in several nonmusical plays, notably Jules Feiffer's *Little Murders* in 1967. Even so, in the last thirty to forty years she has spent almost all her time doing her one-woman shows and recordings.

Cook also recorded prolifically in her sixties and seventies. Typically, when someone passes the official retirement age, his or her technique is in decline. But apparently no one told Cook that the ability of her lungs, throat, and mouth to produce notes and tones was supposed to go south. Her chops have actually grown sharper, and even her interpretive skills have increased now that she's past the three-quarters-of-a-century point.

She also has enjoyed the benefit of two crucial collaborators, musical director Harper and producer Hugh Fordin. Usually credited as "arranger and conductor," Harper was foremostly Cook's "road" accompanist: Wherever Barbara goeth, there goeth Wally. Until his death in 2004, Harper played piano, arranged, and conducted whenever there was an ensemble large enough to warrant conducting—but he didn't do any or all of these religiously. Typically, Harper and Cook would work out the arrangements together, set the keys, the tempos, the general content of the chart. The actual charts were then done by a top-notch Broadway orchestrator such as Ralph Burns or Peter Matz.

Fordin's love of Cook goes back to when he saw *The Music Man* as a teenager, and he was hardly the first college boy to fall for a vivacious librarian. He has said that he was so enamored of Cook that, mischievous lad that he was, he actually stole part of the marquee from the Majestic Theatre (and, presumably, slept with it under his pillow). When Fordin and Cook formally met in 1993, the producer told the singer that it was a lifelong dream of his to produce an album with her; she then challenged him to think of a concept for such an album that she would find suitably inspirational. It didn't take him long; when he suggested a package of songs by Dorothy Fields, Cook went for it.

Cook's first solo albums, especially the 1959 Rodgers and Hart collection, set the tone for her post-Broadway recordings in that they focused on a single source for their repertoire. Since then, she has made live albums as well as thematic albums, and at least two that belong to both subsets. The concept albums from the nineties and onward have been at once unified and diverse: three collections of work by lyricists Fields (*Close as Pages in a Book*), Oscar Hammerstein (*Oscar Winners*), and Stephen Sondheim (*Mostly Sondheim*), as well as one organized around the productions of Broadway dancer-director-choreographer Gower Champion (*The Champion Season*). Here, Cook covers an amazingly wide range of shows, composers, and moods, all within the larger area of show music. (The Carnegie-Sondheim package would be even more in keeping with that general concept, however, if it included more of the lyrics that Sondheim wrote with Jule Styne, Richard Rodgers, and other composers.)

Forced to name a few favorites, I would select the two studio albums—Fields and Hammerstein—as placing with the best of Bennett and Clooney among the very few recordings of the songbook made in the nineties that would accompany me to a desert island. The Hammerstein set may have an edge, due to Cook's long relationship with the librettist and his shows, and in the way each of these songs has a strong emotional resonance with a specific character in a specific show. These texts bring out the best in her both as a vocalist and as an actress: not just as a soprano, but as Laurie and Julie Jordan and Magnolia Hawks Ravenal, not to mention Julie Laverne. She's even convincing when assuming the roles (and songs) of Curly and that infamous French planter Emile de Becque. She brings "Bill," the lovable slob, to life with greater depth than any singer since Helen Morgan, making him seem so real you can practically see his pants sagging. De Becque's lament, "This Nearly Was Mine," has long been one of the ultimate male laments of love and loss, yet Cook and Harper successfully feminize it and almost make it sound like one of the waltzes from *She Loves Me.*

Incidentally, she gets another crack at her best songs from *She Loves Me* in the studio album *All I Ask of You.* It isn't surprising that she can sing their songs better than she had thirty-five years earlier. What does give one pause is her excellent reading of the title song, "She Loves Me," not only because it's sung by the male lead in the book (she changes the pronoun to "He Loves Me") but because it's vigorously up-tempo. She was never assigned any roaringly fast numbers back in her leading-lady days, but she does a great many of them on the nineties albums. No one would mistake Cook for a swing band canary, and though she never tries to be something she's not, in her sixties and beyond she sings the up-tempo show pieces with an undeniable drive and panache. The same album contains a winning medley of her four most celebrated features from the *She Loves Me* score, as constructed by Harper; the medley is a double-whammy in that not only were listeners of the nineties more attuned to the quality of the score than they were in the sixties, but Cook is now better equipped to sing it.

Although she recorded a Christmas album in August 2003, her next release was more of a testimonial to her fifty years of exemplifying the best that Broadway music is about. This is *Mostly Sondheim*, a complete, two-hour document of a concert from Carnegie in February 2002, and it's somehow fitting that this program is not a collection of songs associated with her over the years but just the opposite, a concert built around a theater icon whom she had never worked with on Broadway.

Ms. Cook starts the concert by announcing that even though the *thème du nuit* is the music of Mr. Sondheim, she's following a precedent set by the composer himself in including not only his own songbook but songs by others that Mr. Sondheim has said publicly he wished he'd written. She starts with "I Wonder What Became of Me," and proves that the song can be utterly moving even without an Afro or blues connotation.

But it's her "Eagle and Me" that climaxes the entire concert in its first ten minutes. She prefaces the performance by announcing that a "well-meaning" fan had recently sent her a video of the 1956 TV production of *Bloomer Girl.* Back then, she sang her numbers from that score like a first-rate Broadway ingenue. Forty-five years later, she's become something far grander, and renders this typically profound E. Y. Harburg text like a designated representative of planet Earth, singing, as if from firsthand experience, of the ways of God and the universe and that day when the world was an onion.

Julie Andrews (born 1935)

As we've seen, Barbara Cook and Julie Andrews made their initial impact on Broadway within a stone's throw of each other, and in 1956 and 1957 they were both busy with the roles for which they would be best remembered, Marian (the Librarian) Paroo and Eliza Doolittle. By a strange coincidence, both gained Broadway immortality by contending with leading men (Robert Preston and Rex Harrison) who couldn't sing their way out of a paper bag yet created two of the greatest characters in musical comedy through sheer force of will. By a crazy coincidence, both men were playing pedagogues with even more coincidentally similar names: Professor Harold Hill and Professor Henry Higgins. (Makes you wonder how Henry Higgins might have fared trying to set up a boy's band in Iowa. I don't doubt Harold Hill could have taught a cockney guttersnipe how to speak the Queen's English.) The problems of both romantic situations could easily have been solved by a round of change-partners-and-dance: Marian and Prof Higgins would have hit it off immediately with their shared love for high culture, and Prof Hill would surely have found the sadder-but-wiser girl of his dreams in Eliza Doolittle.

Andrews would become one of the major film stars of the sixties, known to zillions of people across the globe who've never been in a theater or a New York cabaret. Even at the beginning of her career, she was off to an excellent start in that the character of Eliza is more inherently essential to *My Fair Lady* than Marian the Librarian is to *Music Man.* Andrews always seems to be at the center of magical transformations, from flower girl to respected lady, from Queen of all the Britons to disgraced adulteress (in *Camelot*), from a virginal (one assumes) novice in a convent to mother of an entire choir even before the end of Act One. In *Mary Poppins,* the change she inspires is not in her own character but in all those around her—the Poppins is but a carrier of transformation and personal evolution, neutral herself but altering the worldview of those she comes into contact with.

It was the combined forces of *Mary Poppins* and *The Sound of Music* that made Andrews synonymous with the kind of entertainment aimed at those no older than sixteen going on seventeen. In *My Fair*

Lady, she can't quite bring herself to say the word "hell"; instead she damns Henry Higgins to "Hartford, Heresford, and Hampshire." In the last twenty or so years of her career, she labored hard to transform her own image: She appeared topless for nanoseconds of *S.O.B* (1981) and *Duet for One* (1986), and she consorted with pansexuals (or even Peter-pan-sexuals) in the film (1982) and stage (1995) versions of *Victor/Victoria,* and still she's thought of as squeaky-clean. She's a German spy in *Darling Lili* and a raving megabitch in *Star!,* yet even after all that, Andrews is still someone you wouldn't hesitate to leave your kids with. In *My Fair Lady,* Higgins suggests that once Eliza learns to talk like a proper lady, she might get a proper job in a proper flower shop; in the light of Andrews's subsequent roles, one expects the pushy pedagogue to come up with the brainstorm that Eliza might find work as a governess. In both of her signature movie roles, Mary Poppins and Maria, Andrews plays a magical nanny who marshals the adorable little urchins in her charge into solid and upstanding albeit fun-loving citizens. It wasn't easy to think of her as remotely sexual, whether as a basic hetero temptress or some kind of deviant.

In *Victor/Victoria,* Andrews, as the title character, describes love as a "two-way street," but her character transformations are strictly one-way streets. Legend has it that when it came time to film *My Fair Lady,* executive producer Jack Warner nixed her for the role she'd immortalized on Broadway because he wanted a bigger name. Ironically, Andrews was about to appear in the two most successful musical movies of the decade—*Mary Poppins* and *The Sound of Music*—making her the last great leading lady of the Hollywood musical. By 1965, when *The Sound of Music* became the top-grossing film of all time, Warner must have been eating a steady diet of crow over not using her as Eliza Doolittle. Yet I wonder. In retrospect, it seems as if she could have played Eliza only at the beginning of her career in 1956, when she was only twenty years old. Two years later, Andrews, Rex Harrison, Robert Coote, Stanley Holloway, and virtually the same entire cast took the production to London, where it was just as successful. And that was the last time Andrews ever would—or ever could—play Eliza.

Eliza's transformation worked because Americans didn't yet know who she was—Andrews was still a wild card in 1956. Once she had gotten to the point where she was a known quantity, once she reached the Mary Poppins–Maria von Trapp level, no one would ever believe her as Eliza. The garbage-spattered, H-dropping guttersnipe was no longer consistent with her other characters. *My Fair Lady* pivoted around the idea that a street girl could transform herself into a princess; when she next returned to Broadway in 1960, as Guinevere in *Camelot,* it made far more sense for her to play a queen who gets knocked down a peg. After the original production

of *Lady,* no one watching in the audience could possibly fail to see what was coming.

Andrews's career as one of the greatest of all musical comedy voices is even more remarkable when one considers that she has appeared only four times on Broadway: *The Boyfriend* (1954), *My Fair Lady* (1956), *Camelot* (1960), and then, thirty-five years later, *Victor/Victoria* (1995). Add to these one major film production of a role created by another legendary leading lady, Maria in *The Sound of Music* (1965), and five additional very high-profile original movie musicals, *Mary Poppins* (1964), *Thoroughly Modern Millie* (1967), *Star!* (1968), *Darling Lili* (1970), and *Victor/Victoria* (1982).

That voice could always be counted on to achieve things that were extrahuman. She was born Julia Elizabeth Wells in Walton-on-Thames, Surrey, Great Britain, on October 1, 1935. In the very beginning, the later trajectory of her career was reversed: In *Poppins* and *Sound of Music,* she played an adult who consorted with children; at the start of her career she was notably a child star who could sing like an adult, an extremely gifted adult (with a four-octave range) at that. Her parents broke up when Julia was four, and her mother remarried a few years later. Her stepfather was a Canadian-born singer and guitarist named Ted Andrews, who worked in vaudeville (or variety, as it was called in Britain), and who nurtured Julia's increasingly apparent talent for singing. By World War II, the three Andrewses were working regularly, and already Julie Andrews, like Sammy Davis Jr. in the Will Mastin Trio or Judy Garland in the Gumm Sisters act on the other side of the Atlantic, was the focal point of the act.

At twelve, she made her London debut, at the Hipprodrome in a production called *Starlight Revue,* and rather than singing "Do-Re-Mi," she gave out with the aria "Je Suis Titania" from *Manon* by Jules Massenet. At thirteen, she gave a Command Performance for the royal family—the youngest performer ever to do so—at the Palladium in a bill headlined by Danny Kaye (if you don't believe me, there's a newsreel clip on YouTube). At fourteen, she did her first motion picture job, supplying the singing voice of the heroine in *La Rosa di Bagdad* (*Rose of Bagdad*); reissued in 1967 as *The Singing Princess,* this animated feature (among the first to be produced in Europe) from Italy set a precedent for Andrews as a princess. At eighteen, she made her Broadway debut in *The Boy Friend* and at twenty she achieved immortality in *My Fair Lady.* Producers relied so heavily on that magical voice of hers that in both of her most famous shows, *My Fair Lady* and *Camelot,* she was cast opposite legendary English actors who couldn't carry a note, Rex Harrison and Richard Burton, which meant that she had to be virtually the whole show, supporting the majority of the musical weight of both Lerner and Loewe scores by herself.

The *My Fair Lady* buzz also earned Andrews the

chance to work in two original television musicals by major composers, *High Tor* (actually produced before *MFL* opened on Broadway), co-starring Bing Crosby and with a score by Arthur Schwartz, and, more famously, Rodgers and Hammerstein's *Cinderella* (released on DVD in 2004). *MFL*'s success also led to a studio-cast recording of the Sigmund Romberg operetta *Rose Marie* (in which she sang opposite Italian tenor Giorgio Tozzi), and two solo albums, *The Lass with the Delicate Air* and *Julie Sings*. Oddly, none of these was on Columbia, the label that was making a fortune, no exaggeration, with the *My Fair Lady* cast album. Indeed *My Fair Lady* did so well, becoming one of the biggest-selling LPs in the history of that medium, that Columbia released it in two distinct versions, the original 1956 mono of the New York production and a 1958 stereo treatment by the London cast (which featured the same principals as the New York cast). After *Camelot* also made it onto the LP charts (though it wasn't the blockbuster *My Fair Lady* was), Columbia decided to try her with two albums, *Don't Go in the Lion's Cage Tonight,* a bizarre collection of turn-of-the-century comedy songs from both the English variety and American vaudeville stages, and *Broadway's Fair Julie,* a rather predictable idea—Andrews singing show tunes—but one that predictably delivers.

Although Andrews never quite made it as a solo album artist, the *My Fair Lady*, *Mary Poppins*, and *Sound of Music* LPs established her as a major mover of vinyl product; the combined revenue of those three blockbuster albums probably exceeds the gross national product of many countries. The solo albums could never compete with them for attention, but *Lion's Cage* and, to a degree, *Rose Marie* aside, they're quite wonderful—even more pleasurable, in retrospect, than the above-mentioned cast and sound track LPs. Here is where, even more than on Broadway or on the screen, she establishes herself as a singer of the songbook to be reckoned with.

Andrews's semiclassical style is never off-putting, and places her in the solid tradition of Brit pop leading ladies, like Gertrude Lawrence, Gracie Fields, Jessie Matthews, and, to a certain degree, Vera Lynn. These Dames (with a capital D) collectively, make the point that English pop singing is as closely related to operetta and opera style as American pop singing is to jazz and band-singing style. Even some of the band singers over there, like Anne Shelton, had a quasi-operatic sound, as well as the British jazz-slash-cabaret singer Cleo Laine, who always sounded more comfortable singing Schoenberg than the blues.

One wishes that Andrews had done full-length songbooks of the great theater composers. That even goes for Harold Arlen, the most jazzy, least Eurocentric of the Broadway big boys, although a rare Andrews misstep occurs on "A Sleepin' Bee" (on *Broadway's Fair Julie*), in which she anglicizes Truman Capote's Southern dialect from "a sleepin' bee

done tol' me" to "a sleeping bee has told me." (Well, I'm glad she never attempted a *Porgy and Bess* album.) Where Ella Fitzgerald recorded songbooks of Mercer, Berlin, Porter, Kern, and the jazzier side of Rodgers (meaning with Hart), Andrews would have been the ideal vocalist to turn out definitive albums of Coward, Novello, Romberg, Kern, and the more formal side of Rodgers (meaning with Hammerstein).

The *Lion's Cage* album, with its turn-of-the-century novelty songs rendered surprisingly humorlessly, was a waste—few of even her greatest fans can get through the whole thing (it's Andrews's equivalent to Judy Garland's *The Letter* or Sinatra's *Trilogy: The Future*). But having her sing traditional songs, particularly on *The Lass with the Delicate Air*, was a blessing. The Irish "Oh the Days of the Kerry Dancing" is more customarily heard as a dance number—in fact, twenty years earlier, Connee Boswell had proved that it works perfectly well as a swing schottische in the same mold as Maxine Sullivan's "Loch Lomond"—but Andrews turns it into a poignant air of lost innocence, as if it were as meaningful as "The Days of Wine and Roses."

While Andrews does wonderfully with a semifolk song, such as "Kerry Dancing," her real strength is helping musical theater composers like Noel Coward and Lerner and Loewe achieve authenticity when working in these idioms. Coward's "Matelot" is an Andrews masterpiece; Sir Noel wrote it for *Sigh No More* (1945), in which it was sung by the composer-playwright's future companion, Graham Payn. I had heard Coward himself singing it on his 1945 HMV disc, and thought it was suitably sentimental but not one of his greatest. Andrews shows me how wrong I was. Kostal's setting opens with a suitably Gallic concertina, telegraphing Coward's desire to simulate a traditional French folk song. Andrews is particularly effective on both of the verses, each of which opens with the hero's name, "Jean Louis Dominic Pierre Bouchon." These syllables are set to staccato 16th notes to give the melody a deliberately singsongy quality, like an old folk air that evolved into a children's song, à la "Alouette." In Andrews's hands, "Matelot"—much like another French-English hit, Charles Trenet's "La Mer" ("Beyond the Sea")—is a perfect song of postwar homecoming.

With the help of Alan Jay Lerner's thoughtful lyrics, composer Frederick Loewe was the most astute of musical mimics, and when Andrews sings "Come to Me, Bend to Me" (some time before it was on Broadway as the main theme of Lloyd Webber's *Phantom of the Opera*), she makes it sound no less authentically folkish than "The Kerry Dancing." When she sings the same team's "How Can I Wait" from *Paint Your Wagon*, a somewhat similar ingenue aria of romantic anticipation, her very proper British accent somehow doesn't prevent the song from achieving its ambition of sounding like a genuine ballad of the American frontier. Likewise, she was the perfect choice for Guinevere in *Camelot,* which L&L conspired to make reminiscent of Renaissance music. (Even though the Arthur legend dates from at least a millennium before that, from England's early post-Roman period—well, *Camelot's* score is certainly more medieval than that of *Once upon a Mattress.*)

Lerner owed both of his biggest Broadway triumphs to Andrews; none of his later shows, even the hit *On a Clear Day You Can See Forever,* came near the box office of *My Fair Lady.* The sixties ended with his landing epic movie flops with lackluster films of two of his classic shows, *Paint Your Wagon* and *Camelot* (he was credited as screenwriter on both), both of which would have benefited muchly from Andrews's participation. By the end of the sixties, her own film career was also floundering, and she, too, had her share of large-scale trainwrecks like *Star!* and *Darling Lili,* both of which had excellent scores that were excellently sung by her. There was no one better than she was at getting the most out of a minor key waltz, especially "Feed the Birds" in *Mary Poppins* and "Whistling in the Dark" in *Darling Lili.* She had an unusual number of songs in common with John Coltrane, among them "My Favorite Things" from *Sound of Music,* "Chim Chim Cher-ee" from *Poppins* (both waltzes), as well as "Little Old Lady" (which she sings on *Broadway's Fair Julie*); one wishes that the tenor sax colossus had lived long enough to do "Whistling in the Dark."

There are other outstanding documents of Andrews's singing at its finest, among them a 1992 studio cast recording of *The King and I* opposite Ben Kingsley, in which she continues following in the footsteps of Gertrude Lawrence. Most rewarding is a concert from Japan in 1977, *Live at Osaka Festival Hall,* never released, alas, on a domestic CD. It begins with a substandard song by Seals and Crofts ("I'll Play for You") and ends with an equally weak effort by Sager and Allen ("I'd Rather Leave While

I'm in Love"), but everything in between is Our Fair Julie. Particularly valuable are several songs she never recorded elsewhere: Jerome Kern and Johnny Mercer's "I'm Old Fashioned" was a natural, as was "This Is My Beloved" from *Kismet,* another product of the Broadway-opera crossover. More of a surprise was "Being Alive" from *Follies;* the arrangement is stuffed with dated, disco-style harmonies (as if it were "Stayin' Alive"), but she still sounds terrific; it makes one wish she had recorded more by later Broadway classicists like Bernstein and Sondheim.

Victor/Victoria, which she did as a semimusical film in 1982 and again as a full-dress Broadway musical in 1995, the year she turned sixty, was her swan song, and sadly, her run ended ingloriously: Andrews withdrew after a throat doctor loused up her pipes and, she said, rendered it impossible for her ever to sing again. Considering that Barbara Cook is going as strong as ever beyond eighty, it wouldn't have been surprising to think about Andrews continuing into her sixties and seventies. In the new century, she's hosted—but not sung at—several Broadwaycentric all-star concerts. (In May 2010, she attempted to give a concert without actually singing; she talked and other people sang. As the London *Evening Standard* described the affair, "Her carefully managed singing effort amounted to little more than twenty minutes over more than two hours." Neither the crowds nor the critics were remotely satisfied.)

Even though Julie Andrews no longer sings, she still acts in films. Her movie career continues to consist of stories about princesses (the two *Princess Diaries* films and another royal role in the ongoing *Shrek* series) and nannies, as she plays the caretaker of Kay Thompson and Hilary Knight's *Eloise* in two made-for-TV movies. But even given *The Rose of Bagdad, Mary Poppins,* and two *Shreks* to date, there's no animation or special effects trick out there that can compete with the magic of her singing.

Leading Men: In Defense of the Broadway Baritone

Alfred Drake
John Raitt
Gordon MacRae
Howard Keel
Robert Goulet

The most celebrated observation on the art of the leading man in musical comedy came not from a man of the theater, or even a critic, but from counterculture comedian Lenny Bruce. In a famous recorded routine, Bruce opined, "All Broadway musicals sound alike, especially the baritones." Bruce then goes into an approximation of a typical scene from a traditional Broadway show, in which two baritones—spoken by Bruce in exactly the same voice—banter back and forth, "Say, Bill, how do you

know when you're really in love?" "Why—I don't know [sings] 'I've never been in love before . . .'"

Mr. Bruce's wise-guy commentary notwithstanding, the best Broadway baritones were, in fact, superb vocal artists who made a substantial contribution to American musical and theatrical culture. And they did it with voices that, as Howard Keel, essaying the role of Wild Bill Hickcock in *Calamity Jane,* sings it, were "higher than a hawk, lower than a well."

Lenny Bruce was hardly the only one to undervalue the species known as the musical comedy leading man. For all the preponderance of baritones on Broadway, the role of men in this medium has much in common with their roles in pornography (straight pornography, that is) or those *ballerinos* whose only glory is in hoisting ballerinas. Men are necessary evils, but they're never the main focus. Was there ever a romantic male star who was the equivalent of Ethel Merman, Gertrude Lawrence, or Mary Martin? One who kept going for decade after decade, appearing in one blockbuster hit after another? Broadway was dominated by larger-than-life divas, whereas the top dogs in Hollywood were song and dance men like Crosby, Astaire, and Kelly. Hollywood grabbed the major song and dance men—most notably Astaire and Kelly. Once in a while you would see a billing like "Alfred Drake in *Kean*," but that was the exception rather than the rule—and *Kean* hardly qualifies as a hit.

The role of male singers on Broadway had undergone considerable evolution even by the time of the perfection of the modern, integrated book musical with *Oklahoma!* in 1943. Consider that when *Show Boat* was definitively filmed in 1936, the romantic lead, Gaylord Ravenal, was sung by tenor Allan Jones, probably the last notable tenor in the Broadway tradition, which, in his case, was closely intertwined with that of operetta. Jones's only notable Broadway appearance was in a revival of Noel Coward's *Bitter Sweet* in 1934, before Hollywood beckoned. Onscreen, Jones spent a lot of time playing a Zeppo Marx–like straight man to such cinematic zanies as the Marx Brothers (*A Night at the Opera, A Day at the Races*), Abbott and Costello (*One Night in the Tropics*, with a score by Jerome Kern and Dorothy Fields), and Olsen and Johnson (*Crazy House*). But along the way he appeared in a number of notable movie musicals—a surprisingly decent, underappreciated filming of Rodgers and Hart's *The Boys from Syracuse*; the Rudolf Friml operetta *The Firefly* (which yielded his theme song and only notable record hit, "The Donkey Serenade," a song he recorded on the very day his son, future pop star Jack Jones, was born); and the 1936 *Show Boat*. Jones's piercing tenor and his acting abilities were at their most effective in this, one of the great movie musicals of all time (and just about the single finest filming ever of a Broadway classic).

Jones had the rare ability to make his old-fashioned tenor seem somehow relevant. By this point, male singers in pop culture were either of the Broadway type, like Jones himself, or the crooner type, like Bing Crosby. The line was drawn stylistically, not in terms of timbre or range. Consider that Dick Powell (1904–1963) had one of the most ear-splitting tenors of all time, but was firmly on the crooning side of the fence. Kenny Baker (1912–1985) was best known for singing on *The Jack Benny Program*, and then some notable stage and screen musicals—*At the Circus* with the Marxes again, *One Touch of Venus*, *The Harvey Girls*, and as Nanki-Poo in an excellent, again underrated British film of *The Mikado*—and it was the very rare American singer who was invited to sing Gilbert and Sullivan in the comedy of veteran D'Oyly Carte players, including Martyn Green as Ko-Ko. Yet Baker always seemed a step behind the times; for all his talent and charisma, that tenor voice was just yesterday's news. Conversely, his replacement on the Benny program, Dennis Day, turned this same bug into a feature (as the tech people say). The joke was on him, but he was in on it. He was a naive young man who seemed a little dense and a little slow on the uptake in his repartee with Mr. Benny, and it was part of his personality that he didn't quite get what was going on. So it was perfectly appropriate that, in the forties, Dennis Day sang like a leading man from a full generation earlier.

When *Show Boat* opened on Broadway, there was no way Gaylord Ravenal could be sung by anyone but a tenor (one can only imagine a duet between Ravenal, the near-falsetto, and Joe, the ultra-basso, a role associated with Paul Robeson). By 1936, Bing Crosby had already transformed the art of pop singing, and raised the bar by lowering the acceptable range of the male voice. Tenors were rapidly disappearing in mainstream pop, Dick Powell being perhaps the last remaining major crooner-tenor, and the leading male singers with the big bands, like Kay Kyser's Harry Babbitt and Benny Goodman's Buddy Clark, were decidedly post-Crosby baritones. However, the Hollywood-Broadway axis wasn't too far behind the times when they kept Ravenal a tenor—especially when director James Whale employed the very appealing Allan Jones in the role. Still, it's worth noting that by the time MGM filmed *Show Boat* in 1951, there was also no question but that leading man Ravenal would now have to be a baritone—one who could seem masculine even with the first name of Gaylord.

The bullfrog calling to its mate, as lyricist Albert Hague observes in *Plain and Fancy*, "makes a noise like Vaughn Monroe." Baritones became a Broadway institution around the same time that book-style integrated musicals were perfected, and the first great Broadway baritones were the leads in the first two groundbreaking Rodgers and Hammerstein musicals: Alfred Drake, the original Curly in *Oklahoma!* (1943), and John Raitt, who created the role of Billy Bigelow in *Carousel* (1945). In terms of vocal range and sonic presence, the Broadway baritones had less in common with the first generation of baritone crooners like Crosby and his followers than with the even-deeper-voiced stars who began selling lots of records in the World War II era, such as Billy Eckstine and Vaughn Monroe, the bullfrog himself.

Alfred Drake (1914–1992)

Alfred Drake was a veteran thespian long before *Oklahoma!*, which was actually his eleventh Broadway show. He came up at the same time that Frank Sinatra and Louis Prima opened the doors for Italian-American entertainers, though it's doubtful that Drake would have ever appeared on Broadway under his given name of Alfred Capurro (his brother, a baritone at the Metropolitan, employed the equally anglicized name of Arthur Kent—you would think Italian names would be welcome in opera!).

His early career is very heavy with European imports, both of the musical and nonmusical variety: His Broadway debut was in the chorus of the 1935 revival of Gilbert and Sullivan's *Yeomen of the Guard* (he also sang in the chorus of the German operetta import *White Horse Inn* in 1936), and he played Orlando in a 1941 production of *As You Like It*. On the American side, he also sang in a series of revues, among them *One for the Money* (1939, lampooning Orson Welles and co-starring with Gene Kelly) and its follow-up, *Two for the Show* (1940, this time co-starring with Betty Hutton and Eve Arden, in which he introduced the all-time standard "How High the Moon"), and in between he appeared in *The Straw Hat Revue* (1939, with Imogene Coca, Danny Kaye, and Jerome Robbins).

In retrospect, however, Drake's most important early appearance was a small part in *Babes in Arms* (1937), in which he sang the title song along with principals Mitzi Green and Ray Heatherton and which served to bring him to the attention of Richard Rodgers. Ethan Mordden has observed, "Drake may seem an odd choice as a cowboy, since he later established himself as a debonair ham (with a flair for K-productions) in *Kiss Me, Kate*; *Kismet*; and *Kean*. But then, Curly is something of an entertainer—he's the guy telling the stories at the cookout. And Drake's opulent baritone served the part well. Remember, Curly has five big numbers and a reprise to get through, an unusual share of the singing for a musical of 1943." As the producers of the off-Broadway revue *When Pigs Fly* pointed out, the character of Curly, is, overall, suspiciously flamboyant for your average cow-puncher.

In the 1943 original cast album—which itself was a breakthrough—Drake's voice is deep and rich, a bit high compared to his own later work, but a baritone nonetheless. Though Curly is not really a star turn, Drake used his considerable star power to remarkable advantage. It was considered radical in 1943 to begin a show with just a lone singer onstage—rather than a line of chorus girls—and your typical Broadway juvenile would hardly have been equal to the task. Drake not only sets the show in motion with "Oh, What a Beautiful Mornin'," an archetypal Rodgers waltz, but he climaxes the entire evening with the Act Two finale, "Oklahoma!" It launched a Rodgers and Hammerstein tradition of gung-ho gut-busters, and from Drake's tonsils this paean to a U.S. territory is suitably rousing. Between opener and climax, Drake puts over one of the best descriptive songs ever written, "The Surrey with the Fringe on Top" (a song recorded by almost as many jazz musicians as "How High the Moon," few of whom actually ever rode in a surrey or even knew what one was) and establishes "People Will Say

We're in Love" as the model for the boy-girl love duet of the new era.

However, the more recent CD editions of the *Oklahoma!* original cast album contain the most marvelous clue about Drake's subsequent development. There's an alternate take of "Pore Jud Is Daid" that proves to be the missing link in Drake's career. This alternate is a minute longer than the issued take from the original Decca 78 album, and the extra space is mainly given to dialogue from the show in which Curly tries to sell his rival, the loathsome Jud Fry (Howard Da Silva), on the idea of committing suicide. The only way to find out how much he's loved, Curly argues, is to do himself in. Curly sucks up to Jud at the same time he puts him down ("beneath them two dirty shirts he always wore, there beat a heart as big as all outdoors. . . . He loved the birds of the forest and the beasts of the field, he loved the mice and the vermin in the barn, and he treated the rats as equals—which was right").

This is a sales job even beyond the abilities of Ali Hakim the peddler, and it shows that in Drake's hands Curly is far more than an innocent cowpoke; by contrast, Gordon MacRae doesn't do much with it in the movie version, even though he had the villainous Rod Steiger to play against. It's testimony to the developing skills of Rodgers, Hammerstein, and Drake that they were able to bring this extra dimension to Curly. The stage direction reads that Jud repeats Curly's last words "reverently, like a Negro at a revivalist meeting," indicating that there's an element of mysticism and shamanism in Drake's portrayal of Curly as a combination cowman and showman.

It's in the flimflam side of Curly that we see the beginnings of Alfred Drake the master trickster in *Kiss Me, Kate*; *Kismet*; and *Kean*. His career took a few unexpected turns in the mid-forties, which perhaps explains why he was less of a household name than his talent warranted. All three of his next Broadway appearances were a little bit too far to the left of where the political climate was going after the war: *Swing Out, Sweet Land* (1944), in which he co-starred with Burl Ives, was a revue of folk songs, and in those days such music was always at least a little subversive (in some quarters, the act of singing a folk song automatically made you a communist); the underappreciated *Beggar's Holiday* was equally noteworthy—it was both Duke Ellington's best-realized Broadway effort and the first fully racially integrated Broadway musical. There was nothing in the plot itself that was even lightly liberal, but the idea of black folks and white folks interacting as equals was new at the time. Lastly, in 1947, Drake appeared in a revival of Marc Blitzstein's unabashedly socialist offering *The Cradle Will Rock* (staged by Pore Jud himself, Howard Da Silva), which was considerably less welcome in the postwar atmosphere than it had been ten years earlier. Drake also made one film between *Oklahoma!* and *Kiss Me, Kate*, an obscure, war-era musical entitled *Tars and Spars* (1946), co-starring Janet Blair and Sid Caesar.

In 1948, Drake rejoined the theatrical and political mainstream and created his next classic role with Cole Porter's *Kiss Me, Kate,* the most successful musicalization ever of a Shakespeare comedy. Drake is the perfect singer-actor to articulate the difference between Porter's sly take on the world backstage at a Broadway musical and Porter's sly take on *The Taming of the Shrew*—not to mention, for one song, a third musical-dramatic universe, that of the Viennese operetta world they step into briefly in "Wunderbar."

The five principals of *Kiss Me, Kate*—Drake, Patricia Morison, Lisa Kirk, Harold Lang, and Lorenzo Fuller—actually recorded the Porter score twice, once in the Columbia Records original cast album of 1949, and again in a special stereo album produced by Capitol ten years later. (Coincidentally, Drake and Morison had appeared in a TV production of *Kate* a year earlier, in 1958.) But Drake doesn't really need those ten years of experience; he already sounds mature, confident, and poised in 1949. (Actually, his voice occasionally seems to sound younger and higher in the later recording.) Only thirty-four years old in 1949, Drake would clearly never play straight juvenile leads again, only wordly wise, been-around-the-block-type showmen and shamans. By slipping into falsetto as the Stupid Prince (a line of dialogue unfortunately not used in the stereo album), Drake not only shows how much preferable the baritone register is, he also makes his dual role as Petruchio and Fred Graham more believable. Even as Petruchio weds, beds, and tames Kate the cursed, Fred outfoxes both his temperamental leading lady and a gaggle of gangsters even while directing and starring in a Broadway musical. He mounts both the show and the shrew.

Drake pulls off the difficult task of being hammy and sincere at the same time, both over-the-top and right on the money. Although Petruchio-Fred doesn't get his first solo until late in Act One (long after Kirk and Morison), he is a constant presence. He gets three solo numbers (more than anyone else), all of which are showstoppers, and all of which show Petruchio in varying states of matrimonial entanglement: "I've Come to Wive It Wealthily in Padua," which is self-explanatory; "Were Thine That Special Face," in which he expresses prenuptial hesitation; and "Where Is the Life That Late I Led?" in which he expresses postnuptial hesitation, but in a highly sardonic fashion, mock-lamenting his lost bachelorhood without leading us to believe he really misses it. All three are spectacular set pieces for him. He also gets to reprise one of Porter's most effective, simplest love songs, sung earlier by Morison, the haunting, minor key "So in Love," and no man ever sounded more in love with his joy delirious. That "Wunderbar" number is nothing less than a major skirmish in the tenor versus baritone wars: By slipping into an archaic tenor voice in demonstrating an

archaic waltz from an archaic operetta (newly written by the up-to-the-minute Cole Porter), "Wunderbar" has the inadvertent (or was it?) effect of showing how much more pleasing the deeper register is by comparison. Score one more point for the baritones.

Rodgers and Hammerstein wanted Drake to play the title character in *The King and I,* the King, that is, and not the I. Drake refused, ostensibly because he wanted more money, although he served as Yul Brynner's first replacement for seven weeks in spring 1952. After *Kiss Me, Kate,* Drake made his debut as a director (*The Liar,* 1950; *Courtin' Time,* 1951) and as a director-playwright (*The Gambler,* 1952) before settling on his next major musical.

If the dual role of Petruchio and Fred Graham brought out the best in Drake, his over-the-title billing in the elaborate Arabian Nights–style fantasy *Kismet* (1953) gave him even more to do: He plays a poet who becomes a beggar (sad to say, this is considered a step up) who becomes a rich man who, by the end of Act One, becomes the Grand and All-Powerful Emir (or was it Wazir?) of all Baghdad. It was a perfect vehicle for him: Not only was he constantly modulating from one role to another in ancient Baghdad society, but everything about *Kismet* was richly multilayered. The score, by Robert Wright and George Forrest, suggested the ancient Middle East by combining Broadway with Russian opera (with melodies by Alexander Borodin, a czarist prince who worked as both a chemist and a composer).

As in *Kiss Me, Kate,* Drake—still not yet forty—plays an old stud, and there's a juvenile leading man around for contrast. In *Kate* it was Harold Lang, in *Kismet* it's Richard Kiley, who may be eight years younger but croons in a very attractive, somewhat woody voice that sounds very mature. Kiley was Drake's successor in many ways: In shows like *Redhead* (1959) and *I Had a Ball* (1964), he extends the Drakeonian concept of the baritone as con man. His best remembered role on Broadway was as Don Quixote in *Man of La Mancha* in 1966, which he pulled off with suitably Drakelike aplomb, for which he was rewarded with Joan Diener as his love interest (she had played Drake's leading lady in *Kismet*). *Kismet* might work equally well with Kiley playing the Beggar-Poet and Drake as the naive Caliph—it certainly would be worthwhile at least to hear Drake go to work on "Night of My Nights" and "Stranger in Paradise."

As the Beggar-Poet, Drake takes part in plenty of duos (his opener "Rhymes Have I" is essentially his character-establishing feature, although Doretta Morrow, as his daughter, joins in before it's done), trios, quartets, and what have you. His two major solos are quintessential Drake: "The Olive Tree" is an interior monologue set to music, using melody to illuminate the thought process. "Gesticulate" is classic Drake-style razzle-dazzle, with the Beggar-Poet as a kind of Baghdad Billy Flynn, showing off his storytelling abilities with a combination of his rich baritone voice and his miraculous articulation—making the audience feel the difference, for instance, between the words "Djinn" and "Gent." Drake also sends us on our way perfectly with a curtain call reprise of "Sands of Time." This song opens Act One as sung by tenor Richard Oneto; however, it's Drake's reprisal that makes us feel we've seen a show that is really a show, the kind we're sad to see end.

Even before *Kismet*, Drake had participated in the definitive if somewhat abbreviated recordings of two classic operettas, *Roberta* and *The Vagabond King*, both done while their composers were still alive (this wasn't much of a trick with Rudolf Friml, who died at the age of ninety-three in 1972); it must have been gratifying for Jerome Kern to hear Drake singing his score. When he recorded *Roberta* in 1944, Drake sounded considerably higher than he had the year earlier as Curly—he shoots up to tenor register on the verse to "The Touch of Your Hand" but creeps down a notch for the chorus. This studio cast album retains the triangle format of the show, with Drake singing the numbers introduced by both Ray Middleton and Bob "Huck Haines" Hope, against two leading ladies, the coloratura Kitty Carlisle and the more Broadway-styled Paula Lawrence. Drake keeps up with both of them, being operatic in "Smoke Gets in Your Eyes" and loose and almost jazzy in "Something Had to Happen." "Don't Ask Me Not to Sing" is an extended musical monologue that predates what he does with "The Life That Late I Led." ("While putting my pants on / I yodel a chanson.")

Recorded in 1952, *The Vagabond King* provided Drake with a suitable warm-up for *Kismet* a year later. The resemblance between the two roles is notable—the Vagabond King is himself a beggar-poet in medieval France, who rises to a position of great power, changes the fate of nations, alters the course of history, and sings a lot. The gut-busting Villon is a perfect part for Drake—more so than the one-named opera singer Oreste who played Villon in the 1956 Paramount film with Kathryn Grayson. With the possible exception of "The Riff Song" in *The Desert Song*, "Song of the Vagabonds" may well be the most rousing number in all of musical theater—and since he addresses the chorus as "Rabble of low degree," it's quite literally a rabble-rouser. Drake sings it as a call to arms ("Onward, onward, swords against the foe!"), and even Henry V on St. Crispin's Day didn't inspire a mob to take arms more lustily. He's more romantic on "Only a Rose"—bringing a baritone to a song associated with tenor lovers on Broadway—and "Love Me Tonight," but that "Song of the Vagabonds" is one of the great Drake moments.

Apart from *Roberta* and *The Vagabond King*, Drake participated in two further studio cast albums, *Brigadoon* and *Carousel*, the latter with Roberta Peters in the mid-sixties, but neither of these has been reissued on CD. He also recorded occasion-

ally for RCA Red Seal, including some traditional baritone stuff and light classics like "Malagueña," "The Happy Wanderer," and "The U.S. Infantry Song." The actor and singer Kenneth Kantor came into possession of Drake's private collection after his death, and it includes a series of noncommercial transcriptions of more classical material, such as arias from *Don Giovanni* and *Romeo and Juliet* (presumably the Gonoud version). It is hoped that some of this private material will be made available in the future, on a Broadway collector's specialist label.

Kean (1961) was a logical climax to Drake's career, a self-fulfilling prophecy in which he crystallized his character as musical comedy's ultimate ham actor—truly a male diva, a Norma Desmond in Petruchio drag. *Kean* was, in a sense, a follow-up to *Kismet*, with Drake in costume once again and a score by Wright and Forrest. In dramatizing episodes from the life of the great nineteenth-century matinee idol Edmund Kean, the team makes the point that the actor's own life was every bit as dramatic as the great Shakespearean parts he played. Yet Drake plays him as being as introspective—constantly pondering the nature of "Man and Shadow"—as he is extroverted and hammy, while he courts a countess and an heiress and runs afoul of the Prince of Wales. He plays Kean like a flesh-and-blood Pinocchio, a puppet who yearns to be a real boy.

The self-awareness gives Drake's Kean new depth, but at the same time it removes a lot of the potential humor from the piece. The added depth, unfortunately, ensures that Kean can never be as funny or as entertaining as Fred Graham. But *Kean* certainly delivers musically. Drake is first-rate at tavern-drinking songs of the "Get Me to the Church on Time"–"Oom-Pah-Pah" variety, "The Frog and the Grog," and there's also a comedy song, "To Look upon My Love," in which the romantic Kean tries to sing about his latest lady love while his valet continually interrupts with a countermelody trying to impress upon him how destitute they are. The show's outstanding love song is "Sweet Danger." Judy Garland was sharp enough to pick up on it for her TV show, but unfortunately Drake only sings it in a duet with Joan Weldon—one yearns to hear him reprise it in a solo in Act Two, as he did with "So in Love."

Kean was not only the fulfillment of a prophecy but it created a few new ones; even as he played an actor whose career was cresting, so, too, was his own. *Kean* would be his last major musical leading role, although he sang again on Broadway as Honoré—the Maurice Chevalier part (singing "Thank Heaven for Little Girls")—in the stage adaptation of Lerner and Loewe's *Gigi* (1973).

Drake's other notable later roles included Mr. Antrobus opposite Elizabeth Ashley in *The Skin of Our Teeth* (1975), and Claudius in *Hamlet* (1964), with Richard Burton in the title role, Hume Cronyn as Polonius, and John Cullum as Laertes, not to mention John Gielgud directing. This unique, all-star production was, fortunately, videotaped. Earlier, Drake had also starred in live TV productions of *Naughty Marietta* (1955), *Yeoman of the Guard* (1957), and *Kiss Me, Kate* (1958). All of these, Drake's major television appearances, have survived, and (with the exception of *Yeomen*) were available at one time or another on commercial DVD (and in excerpts on YouTube). The TV *Kate* is the most valuable: it co-stars the original Broadway shrew, Patricia Morison, along with cabaret star Julie Wilson (aka Lois Lane), as Bianca, and Jack Klugman (aka Oscar Madison), as one of the gangster heavies brushing up his Shakespeare. It's the only visual record that exists of Drake in one of his great roles.

In 1983, he took a supporting role in *Trading Places,* along with those other old studs Don Ameche and Ralph Bellamy; he played a regular role in the mystery soap opera *The Edge of Night* in 1982 alongside Frank Gorshin; and he supplied a voice in the Rankin-Bass puppet animation *The Life and Adventures of Santa Claus* (1985). Alfred Drake died in 1992.

John Raitt (1917–2005)

Carousel opens with a few notes played distinctly out of key. The idea is to catch our ear with a kind of hook, a bit of musical dysfunction to throw us all off balance. Rodgers then leads us into "Waltz Suite." But the intro informs us that something's going to be different about this story; it's not going to be about another clean-cut, well-meaning hero like Curly. This hero will have some dissonance about him, though Julie Jordan (hardly a queer one, no matter what the song says) is all but identical to the wholesome Laurey in *Oklahoma!* (Shirley Jones was a fine choice for the movie versions of both shows). We are thus told upfront that the relationship of that couple, Billy Bigelow and Julie Jordan, will have quite a few unresolved chords.

Where Curly was an innocent cowboy with a touch of flimflam sauce about him, Billy Bigelow was an antihero who was more hero than "anti." Contemporary audiences may find BB repellent, more because it's implied that he's smacked his wife a few times than because he gets involved in a robbery. Surely as scoundrels go, Rodgers and Hammerstein were themselves considerably more naive than Bertolt Brecht and Kurt Weill. Mack the Knife, in *The Threepenny Opera*, would consider Billy Bigelow a rank amateur in terms of both his burglary and his misogyny—unlike Mack, Bigelow only beats one wife at a time. (Recent productions of *Carousel* have taken care to up the "anti" as far as Bigelow is concerned.)

But if Bigelow was so sympathetic in the original production—perhaps even a mite too sympathetic—it was entirely due to the talents of John Raitt. Alfred Drake was a man of the theater who did more than sing—he wrote and directed and appeared in straight acting nonmusical roles—whereas Raitt was almost exclusively a musical leading man. Remarkably, he only created major roles in two classic shows, *Carousel* and *The Pajama Game*, yet he's regarded as perhaps second only to Drake as the most important of all Broadway baritones.

Carousel was actually Raitt's Broadway debut, and he came up with a corker. Before that, though, he'd played Curly in the touring company of *Oklahoma!* Born in Santa Ana, California, in 1917, Raitt as a young man sang with the Los Angeles Civic Light Opera, attracting the attention of MGM, who gave him small roles in such films as Judy Garland's *Little Nellie Kelly* and Frank Borzage's *Billy the Kid* (in which he gets a bit of a song called "Lazy Acres"). He also had bits as a soldier in *H.M. Pulham, Esq.* and as a sailor with Sinatra and Dorsey in *Ship Ahoy*, and there was a more prominent role in a costume picture of sorts, *Minstrel Man* (1944), starring old-timer Benny Fields, a rare musical from poverty row producer PRC.

But it was *Carousel* that would put John Raitt on the map—and he, it. Rodgers and Hammerstein proved that casting to type and against type was actually the same thing: Curly needs the bit of a rogue that Drake brought to him, and similarly Billy would be unappealing if he were played by less of a charmer than Raitt. In a sense, *Carousel* is an elaboration on the darkest moments in *Oklahoma!*: Bigelow is an amalgam of Curly and Jud, the light and the dark side in the same character.

Raitt pulls it off throughout. He doesn't embody the contradictions as convincingly as I like to think that Frank Sinatra would have (more about that later), but from the recorded evidence of the two cast albums Raitt made (the original production in 1945 and the Lincoln Center Revival in 1964), he brings Bigelow to life more vividly than anyone else ever has. He's selfish and egocentric, and lacks any moral center, but when he sings Bigelow's famous "Soliloquy," it's an amazing revelation of a man discovering that he cares about something beyond himself.

"If I Loved You" is full of those contradictions: Not more than a few choruses after JJ has informed BB that she never intends to marry, BB accuses her of trying to snare him in the Tender Trap, and the way Raitt plays and sings the scene, he makes the contrast perfectly believable. He excels at using the music to illustrate his moral transformation: When he's ready to repent of his sins, and asks to be sentenced by "The Highest Judge of All," he goes for the highest note of all—a positively operatic gut-buster of a note. I can't imagine what Sinatra would have done with that one.

After *Carousel*, a follow-up hit was a long time coming. Apparently, Rodgers and Hammerstein were on the right track when they transformed the Hungarian *Liliom* into the New Englander Billy

Bigelow, because audiences apparently didn't want to see Raitt playing anything but an American, as his next three shows prove: neither *Magdalena* (1948), which took place in South America, nor *Three Wishes for Jamie* (1952), in which he played an Irishman, nor *Carnival in Flanders*, which was set in Renaissance Europe, had anything like a long run. *Magdalena*, from the team of Robert Wright and George Forrest, employed the melodies of the Brazilian composer Heitor Villa-Lobos. The only recording of it was made almost forty years later in 1987, and without Raitt, so we'll never know how he sounded in it. We'll just have to take history's word that Broadway didn't want to see him playing somebody called Pedro.

On paper, *Three Wishes for Jamie* sounds a lot like *Finian's Rainbow*—an enchanted Irishman and his adventures in the American Old South. Perhaps in the wake of *Finian* and *Brigadoon*, Broadway had had enough of magical characters from the U.K. As with lots of flops, the backstage talent was formidable: music and lyrics by Ralph Blane, a book by Abe Burrows, reliable comic Bert Wheeler, and leading lady Anne Jeffreys, who'd made an impression in *Street Scene* and as a replacement in *Kiss Me, Kate*. Raitt's big ensemble number had him leading the singing and dancing chorus in "Trottin' to the Fair." "My Heart's Darlin'" was cast in the spirit of an Irish tenor air. Jamie's entrance number, "The Girl That I Court in My Mind," is an "I want" song that establishes him as dreamer and idealist. The boy-girl duet between Raitt and Jeffreys (who made her last Broadway appearance in *Jamie*) was a pretty tune with the ungainly title of "April Face."

Neither *Magdalena* nor *Three Wishes for Jamie* (for which there's at least a cast album) had much in the way of memorable songs, but even though *Carnival in Flanders* (1953) played only six performances it introduced a major standard, "Here's That Rainy Day" (which, unfortunately for Raitt, went to leading lady Dolores Gray). *Carnival* was powered by three Hollywood refugees, including the legendary Preston Sturges (book and direction), and Johnny Burke and James Van Heusen (lyrics and music), based on a much-loved 1935 French film entitled *La Kermesse Héroïque* (released in the States as *Carnival in Flanders*). This was the show that broke up Hollywood's most durable songwriting team: After it flopped, Burke insisted on trying again on Broadway while Van Heusen returned to Tinseltown, eventually forming a new partnership with lyricist Sammy Cahn. There was never so much as a whiff of a cast recording anywhere—and unfortunately Raitt never sang "Rainy Day" on either of his solo albums for Capitol—but the reliable Richard Norton lists his principal work here as being two solos ("The Sudden Thrill" and "Take the Word of a Gentleman") and two duets with Gray ("It's an Old Spanish Custom" and "A Moment of Your Love").

When I listen to the cast album of *Pajama Game*, all I can think of is Oscar Levant in the film version of *The Band Wagon*, in which, playing a thinly disguised version of screenwriter Adolph Green, he waves a script under the nose of Fred Astaire. "Smell it, boy," he barks. "Doesn't that *smell* like a hit?" Everything about *Pajama Game* smelled like a hit, starting with a book that took the Broadway musical into an area that was just different enough yet still within the comfort zone, and backstage names like Hal Prince, George Abbott, Jerome Robbins—the only comparatively untested talents were choreographer Bob Fosse and composers Richard Adler and Jerry Ross, all three of whom enjoyed their first major Broadway success with *Pajama Game*.

The character of Sid Sorokin was magnificent leading man material: He establishes his ambition with the minor key "A New Town Is a Blue Town," which turns out to be his only completely solo solo. (He had one other solo in "The World Around Us," which was cut during production, but survives from a preopening radio broadcast.) Raitt starts the proceedings in the all-company "Once a Year Day" and he makes the most of three key duets. Two of these come in rapid succession, Act One, Scenes Eight and Nine, both with leading lady Janis Paige. "Small Talk" is classic Broadway stuff, with Raitt showing his beautiful high baritone to excellent advantage, getting both belty and tender in the same number. "There Once Was a Man" has Raitt stretching his vowels over strumming guitar accompaniment while Paige hits Appalachian-style flat notes—the thing sounds like a parody of one of those pseudo–covered wagon opuses with which Frankie Laine and Guy Mitchell were both making Columbia Records rich; producer Goddard Lieberson must have chuckled when he recorded the cast album for Columbia.

Raitt's most memorable duet, "Hey There," surprisingly, is with himself, via the MacGuffin of an office Dictaphone. The song was also a number-one hit for Rosemary Clooney (which retained the overdubbed duet conceit); Raitt uses it to get about as introspective as baritones are permitted to get on Old Broadway. He offers commentary on his own vocal both in terms of spoken word ("You talkin' to me?") and musical-lyrical counterpoint ("a puppet on a string"). Raitt was also highly effective in the 1957 Warner Bros. version, co-starring Doris Day, and we should be grateful that, unlike what happened with Drake, there is a first-rate film of Raitt performing one of his classic Broadway triumphs. The sound track version of "There Once Was a Man" is even more "fierce and defiant" than the original cast recording, with Raitt and Day whooping and yelping like a couple of wild Indians. (Surprisingly, Warner Bros. left in the line "More than a dope fiend loves his dope.") Overall, Raitt is wonderful in the screen version of *The Pajama Game*—one can only assume that when Twentieth Century Fox saw it they instantly regretted not using him in their film version of *Carousel*, produced the preceding year, instead of the wooden Gordon MacRae.

Yet Raitt and R&H had other opportunities to do right by each other. The 1965 Lincoln Center revival of *Carousel* was a triumph (no Gordon MacRae here), and the new stereo cast album with Raitt was even better than the original of twenty years earlier. In addition to being the best of all possible Bigelows, he's also a Gaylord Ravenal, a Frank Butler, and a Curly for the ages in studio cast albums of *Show Boat* (1962), *Annie Get Your Gun* (1957), and *Oklahoma!* (1964). Although he gets top billing (above Barbara Cook and William Warfield) in the Columbia *Show Boat* album, unfortunately the leading man just doesn't get all that much to do in that score; the 1962 album follows the tradition of the 1953 MGM film (with Howard Keel as leading man) in making Gaylord a baritone.

However, his other two studio albums of R&H productions are major Raitt roles. In *Annie*, he turns "I'm a Bad, Bad Man" into the ultimate anthem of male chauvinism—getting in another one of his magnificent gut-buster notes on the last "bad"—and then sounds suitably humbled on "My Defenses Are Down." He never sounds stronger or more masculine than when he's admitting defeat in the romantic arena. He also does an excellent "Girl That I Marry," an Irving Berlin waltz rendered without any irony, and is aces in harmony with Mary Martin as Annie on "They Say It's Wonderful" and in competition with her in "Anything You Can Do."

In 1964 Raitt had the chance to sing *Oklahoma!* in a studio cast album with Florence Henderson and Phyllis Newman (as Ado Annie). His Curly is also aces, although one wishes that instead of using a full cast, the producers had gone the route of the Raitt–Mary Martin *Annie Get Your Gun* and many a *Porgy and Bess*, with one leading man doing all the male songs and one leading lady doing every song written for a female character—we don't need the other actor-singers here. I'd much rather hear Raitt sing "Kansas City" ("where everything's up to date") and "The Farmer and the Cowman" than Jack Elliott and Leonard Stokes, respectively. While Florence Henderson is an acceptable Laurey, I would have chosen Barbara Cook, who played Magnolia to Raitt's Ravenal in Columbia's *Show Boat*. Still, using Henderson makes more sense than the decision to use a very outlandish (even Looney-Tooney) set of orchestrations, which are decidedly not an improvement on the Robert Russell Bennett originals. Raitt is the key attraction here. He brings an enhanced sensitivity to the songs—he's especially tender and vulnerable in that song about the surrey, brings a sense of wonder to "Oh, What a Beautiful Mornin'," and is almost too convincing in "Pore Jud Is Daid."

Raitt also made two noncast albums for Capitol, *Highlights of Broadway* and *Under Open Skies*, which were reissued on a single CD by English EMI in 1992. *Highlights of Broadway* is mostly a compendium of show tunes, only a few of which Raitt would ever sing elsewhere and many of which were actually leading lady numbers, like "So in Love," "Hello, Young Lovers" (he makes it masculine in the verse by changing Tom to Anne, which is, in fact, the name of the female protagonist of *The King and I*), and "I Got the Sun in the Morning." He's especially convincing playing the role of Lieutenant Cable for three minutes in *South Pacific*'s "Younger Than Springtime" (which he sings with a level of maturity that indicates he would have made a great de Becque—pity he doesn't do "This Nearly Was Mine"), while Cole Porter's "I Love You" has him positively soaring. Two strange-ly operatic numbers, "Strange Music" (*Song of Norway*) and "Stranger in Paradise" (*Kismet*) (both by Wright and Forrest, who were hardly strangers), send him way up near the tenor register.

Under Open Skies is a concept album, as Frank Sinatra defined the term, so fully realized that it almost could have been a Broadway show, and it's a decidedly masculine collection. There are a few folk songs, like "Loch Lomond" (he doesn't do it in swing time like Maxine Sullivan, but as a jaunty Scottish dance, with authentic Scots pronounciation—"You *tack* the high road . . .") and "Sourwood Mountain," which sounds like a Broadway version of a square dance, with Raitt instructing the chorus to promenade and do-si-do, "oh-de-em-dum diddly aye day." *Open Skies* also includes a few Broadway-derived faux folk songs: *Carousel*'s sea chantey "Blow High, Blow Low," and *Paint Your Wagon*'s "They Call the Wind Maria." But the album's highlights are two very elaborate story-songs, both cast in a Western mold, that I've never heard anywhere else. "Sail Ho" is not another Long John Silver opus but a very convincing musical monologue about a prospector cracking up under the desert heat and hallucinating that he sees a boat coming to rescue him. Even more elaborate is "El Bandito," which is essentially an entire *Zorro* movie in three minutes, aided by a chorus, lots of tempo changes, a completely through-composed lyric (he never repeats any portion of it), and a board fade. Kitschy? Well, sure. (You got a problem with that?)

One wishes that, having introduced Billy Bigelow's "Soliloquy" from *Carousel* (which he reprises on *Highlights of Broadway*), Raitt would have recorded more of the major concert works, like "Ol' Man River," "Lost in the Stars," and "De Glory Road."

It's hard to believe that *Pajama Game* was his last great role—he was only thirty-seven at the time. But the traditional Broadway musical was already winding down, only a dozen or so years after it had been perfected. In 1966, *A Joyful Noise*, co-starring Raitt with Susan Watson and the excellent Karen Morrow, with songs by folkster Oscar Brand, lasted only twelve performances. In 1975, he appeared in *A Musical Jubilee*, which was exactly what the title promised, an elaborate revue co-starring a cast of Broadway biggies from decades past, among them

Tammy Grimes, Cyril Ritchard, Dick Shawn, and Larry Kert—it ran three months. From the sixties on, Raitt spent many productive decades on the "Melody Tent" circuit, doing *Carousel, La Mancha,* and *Kismet.* He also did the national tour of *Zorba,* with Vivian Blaine and Chita Rivera (believe it or not).

Raitt died in 2005 (at eighty-eight), but he did enjoy one last hurrah: In 1995 he released *Broadway Legend,* in which he reprises some of his key numbers from *Carousel* and *Annie Get Your Gun,* along with some other songs new to his discography. He's especially effective on old stud arias like "The Impossible Dream" and "Some Enchanted Evening," bringing the combination of sagacity and vocal chops that those songs require—at last we get to hear Raitt as Emile de Becque and Don Quixote. He delivers a grandfatherly melody of "Thank Heaven for Little Girls" (from *Gigi*) and "My Little Girl" (an excerpt from the *Carousel* "Soliloquy"). Even when he sings "If Ever I Would Leave You" (*Camelot*), despite the mock-medieval orchestration, he sounds more paternal than anything. His most vulnerable moment arrives on "Here's That Rainy Day" (*Carnival in Flanders*). Pushing eighty, he still sounds like Raitt, and his high notes are still everything they should be.

The sad thing about Raitt's career is that all too often today he's remembered only as the father of pop star Bonnie Raitt. Surely no one in Raitt's own family can surpass his achievements. But then again, no one in the American theater has ever done so either.

Gordon MacRae (1921–1986)

It's perhaps oversimplistic to refer to Gordon MacRae and Howard Keel as Hollywood's equivalents to Drake and Raitt; rather, MacRae and Keel were the leading men who were most frequently called upon to stand in for Drake and Raitt in recreating their most successful roles—Curly, Billy Bigelow, the Beggar-Poet, Fred Graham. When you factor in the starring roles in *The Desert Song; Annie Get Your Gun; No, No, Nanette* (aka *Tea for Two*); *Show Boat; Roberta* (aka *Lovely to Look At*); and other film adaptations of musicals, then MacRae and Keel must qualify as the most widely seen Broadway-style leading men in history.

For years I held it against Gordon MacRae that he was cast as Billy Bigelow in the film of *Carousel* (1956). It was childish of me, and reminiscent of how total strangers would walk up to Audrey Hepburn and snarl at her for shanghaiing Julie Andrews's triumph in *My Fair Lady.* The difference is that Hepburn, even though she couldn't sing, was able to make something out of her interpretation of Eliza Doolittle, whereas MacRae, who could sing beautifully, was far from able to fully embody everything that Bigelow is supposed to be. The mature Frank Sinatra couldn't sing with MacRae's operatic

grandeur (or zoom for that superhigh head tone MacRae hits in his record of "Laura"), but Sinatra could have brought an element of menace to Bigelow that MacRae sadly lacks.

Which isn't to imply that he was just a one-dimensional, cardboard cutout of a leading man. Far from it; his work had multiple textures. Of all the leading men discussed in this section, MacRae is the only one who had genuine experience with the major big bands and who had spent any time in the pop records field. Unlike most of his peers, MacRae's background was more musical than theatrical, and in addition to being fascinated with acting and singing as a child, he also learned to play various instruments, including piano, clarinet, and at least one of the saxophones. He was born in 1921 in East Orange, New Jersey, and grew up in Syracuse, New York. In 1940 he won a singing contest, and was given the opportunity to appear with the bands of Harry James and Les Brown (which couldn't have been for very long—or he would have met his future leading lady Doris Day in the Brown band). He enjoyed a more substantial tenure with another famous dance band, Horace Heidt and His Musical Knights, a somewhat less rigorously swinging outfit.

He made it to Broadway with a role in the successful nonmusical comedy *Junior Miss* but was drafted shortly thereafter. After two years in the air force, MacRae's first major civilian project helped establish him as a direct descendant of Alfred Drake. In 1940, Drake had scored a hit on Broadway in *Two for the Show,* the second of a series of revues by the team of Nancy Hamilton (lyrics and "sketches") and Morgan Lewis (music), which had begun the previous year with *One for the Money.* In 1946, they returned to the format with *Three to Make Ready,* starring veteran dancer Ray Bolger and a cast of new faces, including Carleton Carpenter and Harold Lang. It didn't yield any standards on the level of "How High the Moon," but MacRae did appear in one prophetic sketch that has been described as a "burlesque" of the Broadway smash *Oklahoma!*

Around this time, he attracted the attention of two major media outlets, Capitol Records and Warner Bros. Pictures. Warners first slotted him in a nonmusical B picture called *The Big Punch* (1948), and a few months later cast him as June Haver's leading man in their Marilyn Miller biopic, *Look for the Silver Lining* (1949); Ray Bolger was again around, billed over newcomer MacRae as Miller's mentor. MacRae co-starred with Haver once again in *The Daughter of Rosie O'Grady* (1950), another much-fictionalized account of real people, playing turn-of-the-century nightclubber (as opposed to forties bandleader) Tony Pastor. But the first few years of his career would be occupied with singing with two of the greatest women of American song, Doris Day and Jo Stafford.

Both MacRae and Day defined their screen personas in a trilogy of nostalgic musicals in the early fifties, all titled after old songs: *Tea for Two* (1950), *On Moonlight Bay* (1951), and *By the Light of the Silvery Moon* (1953). These are the films that gave Day a squeaky-clean, relentlessly perky image. Ten years later Day profitably played against that image in her sex comedies with Rock Hudson, but MacRae, alas, was never able to transcend it. He is rock solid as an old-fashioned leading man here, singing old songs and playing both comedy and love scenes with Day. *Tea for Two* is the only one of the three with a unified score, this being a retitling of the 1924 Vincent Youmans hit *No, No, Nanette*.

Gordon and Doris were the boy and girl next door. Unfortunately, conflicting label associations (Day was on Columbia, MacRae was on Capitol) prevented him from recording duets with her, but his Capitol duets with Stafford are some of the very best work of his career. They sang "Wunderbar" from *Kiss Me, Kate* without a hint of irony—unlike Drake and Patricia Morison—just as a straightahead 3/4, and on "Dearie" they have beautiful voices but not the pep and personality of Ethel Merman and Ray Bolger, who had the hit version on Decca. They're at their best when they're supposed to be completely straight, as on the traditional waltz "Neapolitan Nights" or when lightly syncopating, twenties-style, on "Say Something Sweet to Your Sweetheart," done a cappella with a large bouncy chorus (one member of which points out the absence of instruments, in case James Petrillo happens to be listening, save a ukulele). "My Darling, My Darling" calls to mind Ray Bolger yet again (it's from his hit *Where's Charlie*) as well as the rival record by Doris Day and Buddy Clark on Columbia.

Stafford and MacRae are most appealing on a series of recorded duets of traditional hymns and religious songs. They sound so straight they could be Mormons, and sing with utter conviction. They're particularly effective on such powerful anthems of devotion as "Whispering Hope," "All Through the Night" (not Cole Porter), William Henry (not Thelonious) Monk's "Abide with Me," the *Titanic* hymn "Nearer My God to Thee," and Rodgers and Hammerstein's "You'll Never Walk Alone," here doubling as show tune and spiritual. (There are two British CDs that contain most of the worthwhile Stafford-MacRae material: *Down Memory Lane* on the Memoir label contains sixteen of the secular duets, whereas *The Old Rugged Cross* on Music for Pleasure has twenty of the sacred songs.)

When he wasn't in church—and sometimes even there (as on "You'll Never Walk Alone")—MacRae served as a conduit between Broadway and the mass media. He would not appear in a show again until the 1967 *I Do, I Do!*, but he brought many a show tune onto the Hit Parade: "So in Love," "Younger Than Springtime," "How Do You Speak to an Angel" (from *Hazel Flagg*), "C'est Magnifique" (from *Can-Can*), and "Stranger in Paradise" (from *Kismet*). Onscreen, after finishing the cycle with Doris Day,

he appeared in three adaptations of Oscar Hammerstein shows, *The Desert Song* (1953), *Oklahoma!* (1955), and *Carousel* (1956). He made a convincing Curly but a disappointing Bigelow.

As it happened, MacRae really was something of a Bigelow figure in real life, and was arrested for drunk driving during the shooting of *Carousel,* even though he was never quite able to bring that sense of danger and self-destructiveness to the screen. He was a terrific leading man in *Oklahoma!*—at thirty-four he still had suitably boyish looks, and his robust baritone filled the speakers to booming. Appropriately, *Oklahoma!* made use of new technologies, such as Todd-AO (a 70 millimeter process) and stereo, and, wisely, producers Rodgers and Hammerstein filmed on location, the al fresco shooting making it all the more credible.

His last major movie took him back to the start of his film career, with *The Best Things in Life Are Free,* another biopic set in the heady days of the Roaring Twenties. Singer MacRae, dancer Dan Dailey, and heavy Ernie Borgnine play the three-man songwriting team of Buddy DeSylva, Lew Brown, and Ray Henderson. MacRae brought a lot of nuance to the role of DeSylva (he was essentially playing his boss, since DeSylva still owned a major chunk of Capitol Records) in both his singing and acting, the lyricist-turned-producer being a complex character. The picture was very nearly stolen by Norman Brooks, the most famous Al Jolson impersonator of all time, in a brief cameo, but MacRae managed to hold his own.

His singing had grown more sophisticated by the end of the fifties. Two of his later albums, *Motion Picture Soundstage* and *The Best Things in Life Are Free* (a collection of DeSylva-Brown-Henderson songs released in conjunction with the film) have been reissued on a single disc by British EMI (Capitol) and are well worth owning. The jazzy "One More Time," recorded when the song was new in 1930 by the young Bing Crosby, is MacRae's most convincing up-tempo—unlike Crosby, he doesn't quite swing, but he keeps up with the band nonetheless. When he sings "Let me do the things I used to do / Let me sit down to some tea for two," you get the feeling he's referring to his own career. His "Sonny Boy" on the album (Brooks gets to do it in the film) may be as straight as one of his earlier hymns, but MacRae has by now developed more of a humorous edge—pulling off the irony required in "Pore Jud," if not quite as convincingly as Drake.

MacRae's career was truncated both by the gradual diminishment of traditional Broadway-style music and musicals as well as his own battles with alcoholism—which he eventually conquered with the help of AA. For years he shared an act with his wife, the British-born singer Sheila MacRae (best known for her work on *The Jackie Gleason Show*). As an indicator of changing times, when they appeared together on one occasion on *The Ed Sullivan Show* in

the mid-sixties, they shared the program with the new pop band from England known as the Beatles. The husband-and-wife act ended when they broke up after twenty-six years in 1967. By the seventies, he had beaten his addiction, but work was no longer plentiful, even though he had made good on Broadway as one of the replacements in *I Do! I Do!* There were a few small roles in dramatic films (*Zero to Sixty*, 1978; *The Pilot*, 1979) but he went on playing clubs and concert halls. He suffered a stroke in 1982 and died of cancer in 1986.

Howard Keel (1919–2004)

Howard Keel—bless his beautiful hide—had a voice as big and roomy as all outdoors. His was probably the most rugged and manly of all the major Broadway-style baritones. Both his acting and singing had more of an edge to them than those of Gordon MacRae—one can't imagine MacRae as either Fred Graham in *Kiss Me, Kate* or the Beggar-Poet in *Kismet*, but Keel essayed both those roles successfully. He was a credible deputy for Alfred Drake in Hollywood—and he didn't just take over from Drake, the way a Broadway replacement would, but he brought a style to these songs and these roles that was uniquely his own.

No tenor he—there was nothing effete about this Gaylord Ravenal, and when he sang the leading role in *Show Boat* it was a sign that baritones had at last completely taken over from tenors, even in the sheltered, somewhat anachronistic realm of musical comedy. Not only were new-era composers like Rodgers and Hammerstein, Frank Loesser, Lerner and Loewe, Jule Styne, and Leonard Bernstein no longer writing roles for tenors, but now even the new films made of old operettas like *Show Boat, The Desert Song, Rose Marie*, etc. were replacing tenors with baritones.

Keel was born in Gillespie, Illinois, in 1919. His father died young and Howard grew up in California raised by his mother. As a youngster, he worked as a singing busboy for $15 a week. In his early twenties, he took a job at a defense plant, and gradually joined a troupe of Douglas Aircraft workers who sang and entertained the other employees. He eventually came to the attention of Rodgers and Hammerstein, who gave him a crack at what were already the two major roles in the Broadway baritone canon: Curly and Billy Bigelow, in various productions.

Thanks to R&H, Keel crossed the Atlantic to London in 1947. The producer-composers waited until well after the war was over before opening *Oklahoma!* in Drury Lane, and cast Keel as Curly. (According to the record books, this was the longest-running production in the history of Drury Lane, until *My Fair Lady* beat its record in 1962.) Later that year, Keel made an even greater impression as Frank Butler in the original London production of *Annie Get Your Gun*, opposite the va-va-voom Dolores

Gray as the most high-glam Annie Oakley ever. By all evidence, he made a considerably more convincing Butler than Ray Middleton, who played the role opposite Merman on Broadway. (Keel and his Laurey, Betty Jane Watson, and his Annie, Dolores Gray, were recorded in excerpts from both those London productions, which were included on the 2000 CD reissue *Americans in London* on the English Encore label.) Rodgers, Hammerstein, and Irving Berlin were all so taken with Keel—he had already made his film debut playing a bad guy in the little-known British picture called *The Small Voice* in 1949—that he was the hands-down choice to co-star with Judy Garland in the MGM version of *Annie Get Your Gun*.

If Keel's superb portrayal suffers from anything, it's that he makes Butler too lovable and admirable; he's almost too kind and compassionate, and not at all the "swell-headed stiff" Butler is usually supposed to be—perhaps because his boasting number, "I'm a Bad, Bad Man," wasn't used in the film. However, he's absolutely perfect on Butler's two waltzes, "The Girl That I Marry" and "They Say It's Wonderful," combining Broadway bombast with Sinatrian sensitivity. Though Betty Hutton was top-billed in *Annie*, released in 1950, Keel was the one who was asked to remain at MGM.

He would play Esther Williams's dry-clothed leading man in three pictures—*Pagan Love Song* (1950), *Texas Carnival* (1951), and *Jupiter's Darling* (1955)—and have a nonsinging role in the Jane Wyman comedy *Three Guys Named Mike* (1951). The next big MGM musical was *Show Boat*, the 1951 Freed unit remake, which, though not as splendiferously perfect as the 1936 James Whale version, is still a first-rate production. Kathryn Grayson, who would be Keel's most frequent co-star, is as always a bit reedy and shrill as the leading lady, Magnolia Hawks, but as noted, Keel is an excellent Ravenal. Previous Ravenals seem like foppish river dandies, but Keel is a two-fisted, deep-voiced gambling man, the kind who could survive with just his wits and his chops. It's here that his work starts to take on an edge: His Ravenal isn't always exactly what he seems. This riverboat gambler has more than a few tricks up his sleeve.

As sung by Keel, "Where's the Mate for Me (Gambler's Song)" becomes a slice of Hammersteinian musical introversion that anticipates the "Soliloquy" from *Carousel*, but he's not too jaded to miss the wide-eyed innocence of "Make Believe," the most tenory song in the score. The sonic difference between Grayson's superhigh soprano and Keel's mellow low voice is most acute here on the duets, which also include "You Are Love" and "Why Do I Love You?" However, as noted elsewhere, Ravenal doesn't have all that much to do—three duets and only one solo, "Gambler's Song" (although Kern and Hammerstein wrote another one, "I Have the Room Above Her" for Jones in the 1936 film). He does a thoughtful, solo reprise of "Make Believe" near the end, but it's very brief, and mostly talking. When *Show Boat* became one of the top-grossing hits of 1951, Keel's star status was further assured.

After a few nonmusicals, including *Callaway Went Thataway*, a witty cult favorite among fans of vintage B Westerns, he was reteamed with both Grayson and Kern in the *Roberta* remake, *Lovely to Look At* (1952). He took the Nelson Eddy role in another Hammerstein remake, the "Indian Love Call" operetta *Rose Marie* (1954), working opposite not Grayson but Ann Blyth, a fine period actress with a good classical voice, who would play his daughter (!) in *Kismet*.

Calamity Jane, for which Keel was loaned out to Warner Bros., was a virtual remake of *Annie Get Your Gun*, with a bit of *Oklahoma!* thrown in: a story of a tomboy finding love in the Old West. Doris Day is so good both here and in a later album of the *Annie* score (with Robert Goulet) that one wishes yet again that she'd starred in the 1950 Freed film of *Annie*. Keel only has one solo, "Higher Than a Hawk" and it's far from the best song in the Sammy Fain–Paul Francis Webster score, and only one major duet with Day, "I Can Do Without You," which is "Anything You Can Do" spelled sideways; strangely, they never do a love song together—there's no "They Say It's Wonderful" equivalent. Doris Day is a harder leading lady to outshine than Hutton, Williams, or Grayson, but Keel holds his own.

Keel's best vehicles are his final three major musical films, the two Drake remakes, *Kiss Me Kate* (1953) and *Kismet* (1955), and *Seven Brides for Seven Brothers* (1954). In his mid-thirties, Keel is no longer playing juvenile leads—the closest he really came was Ravenal—another tradition he inherited from Drake. As with Drake, we're supposed to believe Keel is somewhat older than he actually is in *Kate* and *Kismet*. Kathryn Grayson plays his leading lady for the last time in *Kate,* and she's considerably more believable playing the tempestuous shrew here than the sweet ingenue in her other pictures. Producer Arthur Freed wisely gives Keel rather than Grayson the chance to start "So in Love." "Wunderbar" is the single most convincing Keel-Grayson duet from all three of their films; she shows herself to be capable of using her soprano in the service of self-caricature—who would have guessed she had a sense of humor after all? Here, at last, as Petruchio, he gets a lot of solo numbers to sing: "I've Come to Wive It Wealthily in Padua," "Were Thine That Special Face," and "Where Is the Life That Late I Led?" In all the productions I've seen of *Kate*, and all the cast recordings of the score, no one sings these songs with more emotion and animation than Keel.

Kate and *Kismet* are also his two major "exotic" roles—the first having him in Elizabethan tights as Petruchio, the second in opulent ancient Eastern robes. Most of his roles—Frank Butler, Wild Bill Hickok (in *Calamity Jane*), and Adam Pontipee (in *Seven Brides*)—qualify as Americana. He shines in *Kismet*, gaining an advantage over Drake in the size and lushness of the MGM studio orchestra, given that the MGM stereo recording process is so much more vivid than Columbia's original cast album. Again there are lots of solos, and almost every one is a virtuoso showpiece for a heavy-duty singer-actor. The MGM *Kismet* does not, unfortunately, use "Rhymes Have I," the song that introduces the Beggar-Poet and his daughter, but Keel and Ann Blyth did record it, and it starts the Rhino CD of the sound track with a bang. "Fate" is a convincing contemplation of the very concept of *Kismet*, while "The Olive Tree" is another monologue set to music. As it was for Drake, "Gesticulate" is a first-rate showcase; owing to the ancient Baghdad nature of the material, Keel's voice sounds deeper than ever here, and both his singing and acting more florid and flamboyant. On "Gesticulate," in particular, his voice is a Hollywood special effects department all by itself.

Seven Brides for Seven Brothers was a personal triumph for Keel; after years of appearing in filmed versions of famous shows and operettas, this production at last gave him the chance to do what his dancing colleagues such as Gene Kelly and Fred Astaire had been doing all along—star in an original musical comedy, and create his own role rather than re-creating one. Putting him back in buckskin and coonskin, this original story combined a classical tale ("The Rape of the Sabine Women") with a Western setting and a score by Johnny Mercer and Gene DePaul that stayed true to the backwoods nature of the material while nearly matching the best of Lorenz Hart, Cole Porter, or Noel Coward for emotional depth and tricky rhyming schemes.

In Jane Powell, Keel found his best leading lady, a much more sympathetic soprano than Grayson—although unfortunately the only love duet between the two leads is a brief reprise of "When You're in Love." Keel has only three numbers to speak of, but in spite of all the fancy-pants ballet going on around him, he dominates every frame of every scene that he's in. The opener, "Bless Yore Beautiful Hide," sets the tone, establishing Adam Pontipee as a lusty pioneer. "Sobbin' Women," apart from being one of Mercer's cleverest puns, is his equivalent of "Gesticulate," a showstopper that encapsulates the whole plot in less than three minutes; Keel is particularly bracing when leading his overdubbed brood of ballet brethren gospel-style, wailing an "outlining" chorus after a key change.

Like MacRae and everyone else discussed in this section, Keel's career was even more severely amputated by changing tastes in the late fifties. Although both *Calamity Jane* and *Seven Brides* were adapted from screenplays into stage musicals, Keel never created a successful role on Broadway. He played Billy Bigelow opposite Barbara Cook in a 1959 revival of *Carousel*, and starred in two new musicals, *Saratoga* (1959) and *Ambassador* (1972), neither of which was a success.

Of all the baritones and all the cast recordings I've listened to and relistened to while working on this section, there's one track that I keep returning to. One of the few CD bonus tracks that really is a bonus, this cut is found on the recent Rhino CD of *Seven Brides for Seven Brothers*. It's described as a "rehearsal reading" of "Bless Yore Beautiful Hide," by Howard Keel, accompanied only by MGM man-about-music Saul Chaplin on piano. The way the recording is set up is either completely spontaneous or purposely designed to show off Keel learning the song, like one of those bits in a songwriter biopic wherein a singer discovering a newly written tune completely masters it within 32 bars. To the accompaniment of Chaplin's Western-style, clippety-clop pounding, Keel starts tentatively, first whistling, then half-singing the piece, half-talking it through in what one assumes is his normal speaking voice. At first he's slightly awkward, singing the song squarely on the beat, and somewhat impersonally. He also cuts off the last note of the first line, "hide," somewhat awkwardly. However, we get to hear him as he quickly perfects his interpretation, bringing it into his hearty pioneer voice. Within a minute he not only has the notes and the persona down, but is starting to add in the special effects: the growls, the grunts, the bellows, the theatrically suppressed laughter on "whoever took it would be one big fool," the not-at-all concealed leer in his voice. Toward the very end, he slips out of the interpretation, leading us to think he's run out of ideas and doesn't know what to do next. But this, too, turns out to be part of the theatrical conceit: He goes from talking the words again to a triumphant operatic ending, bringing the piece to a close with an overpowering, room-filling high note. I'd like to see some sissified tenor sing that, he seems to be telling us. Make your blood boil? Well I should say! It's as beautiful and perfect a slice of the baritone's art as I can remember hearing.

Keel, who died of cancer in 2004, kept busy till the end in dramatic roles in film and television, as well as serving as the president of the Screen Actors Guild for two years. Thanks to the soap opera *Dallas*, enough interest was generated for him to record a new album in the early eighties and to undertake a concert tour. Like any of the roles he played in his classical musical films, Howard Keel always came out on top.

Robert Goulet (1933–2007)

Exactly when did Robert Goulet become a synonym for mediocrity? It seems especially unfair, in that Goulet had always showed his willingness to poke fun at both himself and the Broadway leading man tradition. Satirizing oneself traditionally is a preemptive strike to stop others from doing it—Goulet at one point became so adept at it that he almost became better at ribbing Robert Goulet than at *being* Robert Goulet. He appeared in a late nineties TV commercial where everybody is Robert Goulet, even a female traffic cop in a dress. He turns up in *Beetlejuice* (1988), as well as a music video by Weird Al Yankovic, and on *The Simpsons,* as a Las Vegas lounge lizard rerouted into Bart Simpson's treehouse, putting everything he's got into a chorus of "Jingle Bells, Batman Smells." He supplies the singing voice of a plastic penguin in *Toy Story 2*, and the major surprise here is that he can sing in swing time better than anyone had suspected. And in the 1995 Broadway comedy *Moon Over Buffalo*, he comprehensively removes any shred of dignity that the figure of the traditional leading man may have had left. His defenses, it would seem, were permanently down.

Ironically, though Goulet was called upon to represent the Broadway-style baritone in all of these alien situations, he only created one major role: Sir Lancelot in *Camelot*. Lancelot wasn't the lead—that was King Arthur—but since Arthur was essentially a nonsinging role (rather like La Guardia in *Fiorello!*), Goulet emerged as the show's major musical male. He had two big songs, including "C'est Moi," in which he establishes the Goulet persona of the self-satirizing baritone. "C'est Moi" has Lancelot describing himself as a person of infinite virtue and excellent fancy. (Roddy McDowall sings the opposite song, "The Seven Deadly Virtues," which is all about what a rotter he is.) "If Ever I Would Leave You" left Goulet with the closest thing to a hit from the score, and it shows him at his most convincingly romantic and vulnerable, but the self-satirizing "C'est Moi" is the essence of Goulet.

After *Camelot* made Goulet into a star, the logical thing would have been for him to go into another musical, this time as the lead, without Richard Burton lording it over him. However, he seems instead to have achieved instant celebrity status and skipped directly to the point it took MacRae, Keel, and the others years to attain, having the opportunity to do concerts, nightclubs, recordings, and TV variety shows. Goulet, who was born in Lawrence, Massachusetts, had already long been a perennial on TV in Toronto, the city where he was raised, and all across Canada. After *Camelot* he supplied a voice, opposite Judy Garland, in the animated musical *Gay Purr-ee* (he also appeared on TV with the Great Garland), and essayed a self-parodying leading man in romantic comedies such as *Honeymoon Hotel* (1964) and *I'd Rather Be Rich* (1964), in which he works with the even more rigid singing nonactor Andy Williams. By this time, Goulet was sort of a singing Rock Hudson, a board-stiff, square-jawed hero. He also appeared in a trio of TV versions of classic shows—*Brigadoon* (1966), *Carousel* (1967), and *Kiss Me Kate* (1968)—that one wishes to see restored and released on DVD.

More than any of the other Broadway male voices, Goulet became an instant recording star. It was sort of odd that just when pop culture was turning away from traditional singers and traditional songs, Goulet became a major figure. After the *Camelot* original cast album on Columbia, he made fifteen albums for the label between 1961 and 1969. At one point he even induced Ralph Sharon, long-time piano partner of hit-maker supreme Tony Bennett, to leave Bennett and join him—surely proof that he was establishing himself in the big-time music stakes. By 1969, Goulet had reached the end of that particular ride, and was recording songs like "Do You Know the Way to San Jose" and "Both Sides Now."

Goulet's two best moments on record are both new productions of oft-recorded scores: *Annie Get Your Gun* (1960) and *Manhattan Tower* (1964), the 1945 song-cycle that was retooled, nineteen years later, by composer-conductor Gordon Jenkins expressly for Goulet. One wishes Jenkins had gone a little further in that direction: As in the original version, most of the songs in the 1964 *Manhattan Tower* are sung by a chorus rather than by a soloist, and Goulet serves as narrator who, curiously, gets to really sing only one song, "New York's My Home." Fortunately, Jenkins took some of the other *Tower* songs (including "Married I Can Always Get," not written as a song for a guy) and worked them into a B side, titled *The Man Who Loves Manhattan,* in which Goulet sings the whole thing straight through. By itself, *Manhattan Tower* is amazingly campy, but when you put Goulet and Jenkins together—with those strings that throb like a toothache—then time is powerless to put their kitschy philosophy out of fashion.

The *Annie* album teams Goulet with Doris Day—playing Annie Oakley at last—and he is perfect as Frank Butler. He's a big stiff, but what makes his performance brilliant is that he knows it. He's both savaging himself and being himself in a remarkable balancing act. Here's evidence that Goulet was more than a joke, even one of his own telling. His baritone is rich and mellow, deep and mellifluous, but with a sharp edge, full of character, of the sort that both Drake and Raitt would have approved. No less important, his musical acting is always dead on target. His solo on "My Defenses Are Down" has every phrase in the right place, like the high note on the opening line, "I've had my way with *so* many girls." His way of sustaining notes is particularly masterly. On "Yessss, I must confess that I like it," he sings as if he's kidding himself at the same time that he's admitting something to himself that he never cared to fess up to before. Goulet, who died in 2007 at age seventy-three, was a much better singing actor than even he was able to admit.

Dinah's Daughters: Soulful Ladies and Local Favorites

Etta Jones
Gloria Lynne
Teri Thornton
Irene Reid
Lorez Alexandria

It's pretty much agreed that a list of the major jazz divas would include Billie Holiday, Ella Fitzgerald, Dinah Washington, Sarah Vaughan, Carmen McRae, and Anita O'Day (whether Betty Carter is included is up to you). When we get to the second tier, I think that most listeners would agree that Kay Starr, Helen Humes, June Christy, Nina Simone, Della Reese, and/or Dakota Staton are surely just a notch below the Billie-Ella-Sarah echelon, if even that. But when it comes to differentiating between the second and third levels, that's when things get dicey—I'm sure that fans of Gloria Lynne and Teri Thornton, Etta Jones (and Lorez Alexandria, Helen Merrill, and a few others) would object to my positioning them this far down the food chain. But that's what makes horse races.

Like Dinah Washington, Lynne, Thornton, and Jones formulated styles that were equal parts jazz, mainstream pop, and blues (or R&B, with more than a hint of gospel). Although Lynne was and is the most polished and Thornton the most connected to the blues, one could hear the Washington and Holiday influences keenly in the work of all three.

All three had a brief crack at the big time, and unlike 99 percent of the working singers out there, managed to put their indelible stamp on a major song or two with which they'll always be associated—for Etta Jones it was "Don't Go to Strangers," for Gloria Lynne it was "I Wish You Love," and people will remember Thornton for either "Open Highway" or "Somewhere in the Night." But they never hit the big time—at least not for very long, and it's not hard to see why. While all created some memorable songs, and made some excellent tracks and whole albums, the entire output of any one of them is just less rewarding or consistent than that of a Helen Humes, say, let alone a Carmen McRae. They've all been described as "underrated," but I think that they all deserve great credit for getting as far as their talent could possibly take them.

Etta Jones (1928–2001)

Etta Jones's best-remembered performance is "Don't Go to Strangers," which she recorded for Prestige in 1960; both the album and the single were substantial hits, especially for a singer who'd been largely forgotten since her initial burst of activity as a teen star at the birth of the R&B era, fifteen years earlier, and on a label that normally recorded jazz instrumentalists and was usually delighted to sell anywhere in the five figures. She made seven more LPs for Prestige, all of which could more or less be described as follow-ups to "Strangers." One of the final entries in this series was the 1962 *Lonely and Blue*, which opens with a song called "I'll Be There," which is remarkably similar to "Strangers" in terms of lyric, melody, and philosophy. (The basic idea is also very similar to "You Belong to Me.")

"Strangers" opens with the line "Build your dreams to the stars above," while "I'll Be There" includes the phrases "Spend your dreams in wanderlust" and "build your castles in the air." Both songs are roughly inspired by Alec Wilder's "I'll Be Around," and the message in all three lyrics is as follows: I may not be the flashiest gal around, but I'm reliable, and though you may be more interested in others right now, you can count on me to always be there for you. I have no intimate knowledge of Jones's personal life, but this seems like a fairly straightforward account of her career. She wasn't as flashy or even as interesting as a lot of other singers, but she was nothing if not dependable. There may be few truly remarkable Etta Jones records, but there are no bad ones.

Etta Jones came directly out of Holiday and Washington, somewhat less sharp and biting than either one but with more consistently good intonation than Holiday (at least in Lady Day's later years) and also a somewhat less easily identifiable sound. Distinguishing Jones from Holiday or Washington is a bit like picking Chris Connor out from O'Day or Christy—the mind undergoes a process of elimination: "Hmmm, that isn't Billie, it isn't Dinah, it must be Etta."

She was supposedly born November 25, 1928, in Aiken, South Carolina, and like Helen Humes, while still prepubescent began her career recording salacious blues lyrics. In 1944, she toured as the vocalist with Buddy Johnson, the bandleader, pianist, and songwriter whose genre of music was not yet labeled "rhythm and blues."

That same year, she was singled out for stardom in the "race" market by a variety of forces, including Black & White Records, which, a few weeks after her sixteenth birthday, gave her a session in New York backed by an all-star group under the leadership of clarinetist Barney Bigard, a recent refugee from the Ellington fold. The guiding force of the date, however, was pianist Leonard Feather, whose choice of material—in addition to favoring himself as a songwriter—showed that he was intending to cast the young Jones in the same mold as Dinah Washington, who had made her shellac debut with Feather's songs and guidance only a year earlier. She recorded nine titles for "race" market independents, and then surprisingly was given a crack at the big time when RCA Victor gave her three sessions (twelve titles), with material and accompaniment again very much after the fashion of Washington ("I Sold My Heart to the Junkman," "The Richest Guy in the Graveyard"), and quickly, also like Washington, she proved herself equally adept at sentimental ballads and earthy blues.

After this early period, Jones was on the periphery for roughly a dozen years, except for a stint with Earl "Fatha" Hines (1949–1952) and a little-known album for King (*Etta Jones Sings, Sings, and Sings*, 1957), and indeed was completely out of music off and on. (It is odd that she should have fallen on hard times during the period in American pop when jazz- and blues-singing ladies were probably the most prized, but that seems to be the case.) In 1960, she submitted a demo tape to Prestige Records producer Esmond Edwards, who later wrote (in the notes to a 2001 tribute compilation), "After a few bars of music, I dropped my reading and listened attentively. Here was a female vocalist with a 'sound,' great phrasing, and warmth! Immediately I took the tape into president Bob Weinstock's office. After listening to a couple of tunes, he said 'Sign her!'"

The relationship between Jones and Edwards (and Prestige) got off to a flying start with "Don't Go to Strangers." Appropriately for a song of romantic reliability, it had been around for a while; it was by two songwriters with big band experience and deep sympathy for jazz—Dave Mann had played piano with Charlie Spivak and Jimmy Dorsey (and wrote, among other standards, "In the Wee Small Hours of the Morning") and Redd Evans had worked with a number of bands including Charlie Barnet's, and was an intimate of Anita O'Day and Nat King Cole. "Strangers" had originally hit in the mid-fifties for the bombastic bandleader Vaughn Monroe.

Though it was subsequently sung by many stars—Eydie Gormé, Sarah Vaughan, Dinah Washington, even Woody Herman—it remains Jones's property. She sings it incredibly directly, right on the beat, so straightforwardly that it doesn't seem to be as much an interpretation as a pronouncement straight from the heart. When she throws in slight blues embellishments, like stretching key words at the end of lines into two notes ("for your friends to see-*ee*"), it makes her singing seem even more heartfelt. It's a solid, reliable treatment of a song in which the underlying message is all about being reliable: She didn't just sing it, she embodied it, and it's no wonder that it became her most famous song.

She followed "Strangers" up with *Something Nice* (1960), *Hollar!* (1960), *Love Is the Thing* (1960), *So Warm* (1961), *From the Heart* (1962), *Lonely and Blue* (1962), and *Love Shout* (1962). This is a modest but meritorious body of work. The Prestige albums are all cut from the same cloth, and when you listen to them consecutively, you feel you're listening to one long mega-album. (I'm glad Fantasy has put them on CD individually rather than in a boxed set.) The Jones Prestige albums are also quite similar in ambience to the "Moodsville" series of albums that the company was producing at the same time, featuring stars like Coleman Hawkins and Oliver Nelson in laid-back, romantic-sounding settings. The atmosphere was considerably less opulent than, say, the Jackie Gleason Orchestra recordings (or any of the jazz soloists who recorded with strings), but this was a very similar sort of relaxed "make-out" sound.

At what point do virtues become failings and assets liabilities? That Jones dwelt in the midpoint between the Mississippi Delta and Tin Pan Alley wasn't always a good thing; unlike, say, Joe Williams, who sounded different when he was addressing different kinds of material, Jones—even though she might sing "Unchained Melody" one second, a genuine blues the next, and then the Gershwin brothers—made them all sound exactly the same. Likewise, the Moodsville sound of the albums gets almost oppressive after a while. Everything is in a half-slow, half-fast, relaxed and sensual tempo—it's hard enough to stay awake through a whole album, let alone listen to more than one.

She'll occasionally wake us up with a surprising piece of material, like "Hi-Lili, Hi-Lo" or her waltz time "Someday My Prince Will Come," both of which are on *Lonely and Blue*. Children's songs have traditionally provided good material for jazz singers, and these are two of Jones's most engaging performances.

She also departs from the formula in two albums with larger ensembles, *So Warm* and *From the Heart*. Both have string sections arranged and conducted by the gifted Oliver Nelson, and the string charts are lovely on *So Warm*, bringing a change of pace to the customary half-slow, half-fast, half-Broadway, half-blues mixture of all the other albums. On *From the Heart*, unfortunately, the arrangements mirror the tricked-up, gimmicky backings heard on the Dinah Washington–Belford Hendricks sessions.

Two years after the final Prestige entry, *Love Shout* (1963), Jones cut her last "classic" album; this was *Etta Jones Sings* (1965, Roulette), with a generally similar cast of characters; this set is mysteriously absent on CD. Like many singers of her generation, she then became scarce for a dozen years—from the late sixties to the mid-seventies.

From the seventies onward, she worked steadily, thanks largely to the musical and business acumen of her professional partner, the outstanding saxophonist, accompanist, and producer Houston Person. Even in periods when Jones wasn't recording, the team worked continually. Their relationship began on the short-lived Westbound Records with *Houston Person '75* and *Etta Jones '75*.

Jones's last twenty-five years would be productively documented on the Muse and HighNote labels. Unfortunately, most of the dozen or so albums she cut for Muse from 1977 to 1994, which were briefly issued on CD, are now hard to find; a worthy exception is the 1977 *My Mother's Eyes,* which was reissued by 32 Jazz. In selecting that 1928 song as her linchpin, Jones is telling us something right off the bat. For starters, she's delving into the deep tradition of African American entertainers doing traditional Yiddish songs: Ray Charles's "Where Shall I Go," Johnny Hartman's "Greena Cousina," and Billie Holiday's private recording of "My Yiddishe Momme" (not to mention Slim Gaillard doing "Matzoh Balls"). "My Mother's Eyes" isn't exactly from the Yiddish theater, but it's close enough: The famous toastmaster Georgie Jessel introduced it in what was his first and virtually only starring film role, the 1929 *Lucky Boy*. While not quite a jazz standard, it was featured by a number of African American players and singers over the decades, most notably the saxophonist Sonny Stitt, who played it on half a dozen albums. More important than the ethnic angle, with "My Mother's Eyes" Jones is once again allying herself with a reliable second-tier performer; it's a song associated with Jessel, not Jolson, and with Stitt, not Sonny Rollins or Coleman Hawkins.

By the age of forty-nine her timbre had matured to the point where she sounds both more like Billie Holiday and more like herself, and she deploys that cracked tone very carefully. *My Mother's Eyes* is a short and completely successful effort, and even though the use of electric keyboard gives it a kind of soul-jazz feeling (there's also guitar and vibes), the seven songs cover a lot of diverse moods. "Be My Love," the Mario Lanza hit, has Jones switching from virtual Yiddish to a *fugazi* Italian opera, with Jones and Person swinging it like crazy. She makes Cole Porter funky on "You Do Something to Me" and Burt Bacharach believable on "This Girl's in Love with You."

Between 1997 and her death in 2001, Jones found time to cut six more albums, nearly all with Person. (There's also an impressive live concert from Japan, at least two numbers of which are on YouTube.) Half of these were songbook concept albums and the other three were a more general sampling. The 2000 *Easy Living* is lively and nicely varied, a fine example of her later "assorted" albums, and opens winningly with a medium romper in "Did I Remember" and a ballad in medium tempo in "Easy Living," in which both Jones and Person are at their simpatico best. In "After You've Gone" and "Time After Time," she thoroughly reanimates a pair of old warhorses, and in a surprisingly flip and loosely swinging "Who Can I Turn To?" she asks the question that she had already answered in "Don't Go to Strangers" and "I'll Be There."

In her final years, Jones recorded those three tribute albums, *All the Way: Etta Jones Sings Sammy Cahn* (which, in trying to avoid the obvious, did not include "Teach Me Tonight," the Cahn lyric most performed by blues-oriented singers), and two very personal projects, *My Buddy* and *Etta Jones Sings Lady Day*, in which she celebrates two of her most important influences. *My Buddy* is, as far as I know, the only songbook album of music by Jones's first notable employer, songwriter-bandleader Buddy Johnson. Backed by Person and pianist Norman Simmons, it's a marvelous album of bluescentric songs, and is perhaps Jones's most consistently excellent later project. She's compelling on blue ballads like "I Wonder Where Our Love Has Gone" and "Save Your Love for Me" and swinging on the blue bouncers "Fine Brown Frame" and "Let's Beat Out Some Love."

In celebrating Buddy and Billie, Jones was, fittingly, coming full circle, and ending her career precisely where it began. Her main challenge with doing a Billie Holiday album must have been finding songs she hadn't already recorded; she was so steeped in Lady Day's legacy that virtually all her albums are peppered with songs from the Holiday songbook.

Jones and Person, and another first-rate pianist, Richard Wyands, recorded *Lady Day* in June 2001; it was released in October of that year, and earned Jones her sole Grammy nomination. For me, the album's highlight is its only straight-up 12-bar blues, "Fine and Mellow," which boasts especially luxurious obbligatos by Person, while Jones, for her part, stops the show (and the album) by doing a brilliant impression of Holiday herself. I've never heard any other singer so fully capture the essence of the older Lady Day in all her dying splendor. In her 1962 *Lonely and Blue*, Jones had revived the ancient Clarence Williams blues "You Don't Know My Mind," which contains the classic lines, "You see me laughin' / Laughin' just to keep from cryin'." If there ever was anyone who really understood that line, it was Etta Jones.

Gloria Lynne (born 1931)

I've been listening to Gloria Lynne for years, and she still keeps making me think of other singers—Holiday and Washington to a degree, but most often the young Carmen McRae. Which is bad only on a theoretical level: I know I should be more aesthetically pure and only praise individuality and originality, but Lynne never seems to be deliberately imitating these other ladies so much as naturally evoking them. More important, the Gloria Lynne albums on the Everest label bring to mind the freshness and purity of McRae's classic early recordings in a way that McRae herself was unwilling and unable to do after the mid-sixties. At times Lynne also sounds a lot like Abbey Lincoln, when that equally young singer was still in her pop phase. But whomever she resembles, at her best, Gloria Lynne sure sounds good, no doubt about that.

Alas, in terms of sonic quality, Lynne's best recordings have never sounded very good. She spent her glory years at the independent label Everest, which was perched somewhere between the majors and the bottom-feeding supermarket rack-job concerns. She came to the label thanks to producer Raymond Scott, who in addition to a long career as a composer, bandleader, and conductor was an inveterate audiophile, tinkerer, and inventor. He prided himself on sound quality, and Everest was an early pioneer in high-end stereo. However, they were also a budget label, so that even if their sessions were well

recorded, the discs themselves were often pressed on inferior quality material.

What's worse is that the master tapes for her albums appear to no longer exist. The major reissue package of her work is *The Best of the Everest Years*, a four-CD box on the Collectables label that contains eight of her best Everest LPs. The CDs are obviously remastered from vinyl LPs, and not necessarily clean ones—clicks and pops can occasionally be heard, and some tracks sound as if they were deliberately muffled as a way of masking the surface noise. Until the tapes are found or a better remastering job is done from the vinyl sources, this is the only way we have to evaluate Lynne's best recorded work.

Like the other soulful ladies here, Gloria Lynne, who was born in 1931 in Harlem, began singing in church—which is surprising, as she has less of a blues or soul orientation than Jones, Thornton, or Washington. With frequent exceptions, she tended to sound as though she belonged in an upscale supper club rather than a sanctified church; more at home singing "Hands Across the Table" than one of Dinah Washington's double entendre blues like "Big Long Sliding Thing" (not to mention "Take My Hand, Precious Lord"). By that standard, it's less surprising to learn that she had several years of classical training; she said that it was Ella Fitzgerald who inspired her to look beyond the church and begin exploring the dual fields of jazz and standards. At the age of twenty, like Vaughan and Fitzgerald before her, she won the amateur contest at the Apollo Theater. Then, for most of the fifties, she worked as a member of vocal groups, the Dorsey Sisters and the Bel-Tones.

In 1958, Lynne was first heard by Scott, then working as a producer/A&R man for Everest Records. Between then and 1964, she made two albums a year for Everest, a total of fifteen, starting with *Miss Gloria Lynne* (reissued in the early nineties on Evidence, a CD that itself is now hard to find). She was boosted considerably by such tastemakers as Leonard Feather, who proclaimed her the next Sarah Vaughan and the next big thing, and Ed Sullivan and Harry Belafonte, who gave her exposure on their TV shows.

The Everest albums—not one of which seems to have any direct input from Scott as composer or conductor—run pretty much the standard range of experiences for jazz-pop singers of the late fifties and early sixties: small, intimate settings (*I'm Glad There Is You*), swinging big bands (*Go! Go! Go!*), and string orchestras (*Gloria, Marty [Paich] and Strings*), studio (*After Hours*), and live sessions (*Gloria Lynne at Basin Street East, Gloria Lynne at the Las Vegas Thunderbird*), albums of romantic ballads (*Try a Little Tenderness*) and of jazzy up-tempos (*Go! Go! Go!* again).

The two strongest of the Everest releases are the slow tempo *Gloria, Marty and Strings* and the fast and swinging *Go! Go! Go!* While Lynne's performances are consistently fine throughout, these are the projects that gave her the two strongest arrangers. The first, as the title indicates, features the writing and conducting of Marty Paich, and it's interesting that at this stage of the game Paich, who had arranged for Mel Tormé, Ella Fitzgerald, Sammy Davis, and others, was as much of a name as Lynne, well known enough to be billed in the album title (à la *Rosie Solves the Swingin' Riddle* and *Bing Sings Whilst Bregman Swings*).

Go! Go! Go! is a particularly valuable recording (although the sound quality is the worst, unfortunately, of any item in the Collectables box) for the arrangements of Ernie Wilkins as well as Lynne's fine singing. Wilkins had already proved himself a first-rate jazz orchestrator in his work with Count Basie, Joe Williams, Dinah Washington, and many others.

Go! Go! Go! proves to be a very strong collaboration between Lynne and Wilkins, and two pieces based on classical sources illustrate their joint ingenuity. "I'm Always Chasing Rainbows," which started life as a parlor room kind of a song with a gentility (and a melody) derived from Chopin's *Fantasie Impromptu*, is rendered much more bluesily here, with a deep soulfulness and dramatic, blues-style repeated phrases. "And This Is My Beloved" is one of two numbers in the musical *Kismet* taken from Borodin's Second String Quartet in D-Major (the other is "Baubles, Bangles and Beads"). It was done somewhat operatically on Broadway, but it swings subtly in Lynne's and Wilkins's hands, with the emphasis on the backbeat and stop time phrases. Lynne liked the arrangement so much that she recast it for her own trio and used it to open her live album at Basin Street East.

Virtually all the Everest albums have their moments of distinction: The *Basin Street East* set, which co-stars pianist Herman Foster, consists almost entirely of show tunes, with exceptions like "Drinking Again," done roughly concurrently by the young Aretha Franklin and later claimed by Sinatra, and the blues narrative "It Just Happened to Me." "Wouldn't It Be Loverly" (which Lynne begins by singing about a "room somewhere / far away from the cold night air"), wherein the trio is expanded to quintet with the addition of Kenny Burrell (guitar) and Ray Barretto (cong) is similarly funky, in a cool, reserved sort of way, with Lynne changing tempos several times. She does that again in the album's climax, an extended, five-minute treatment of "Tall Hopes" (from *Wildcat*) that also alternates between fast (and swinging) and slow (and reverent). Lynne's other live album, done at the Las Vegas Thunderbird circa 1962, has Foster leading the trio, and also features a mixture of show tunes and blues-driven material: "Something Wonderful" is one of her most intimate and musically aware readings, while "What Kind of Fool Am I" finds more gospel cadences, and "I Believe in You" is rompingly swinging.

The slow albums are also worthwhile, among them *Try a Little Tenderness*, arranged by Leroy Holmes, and *After Hours*. *Try a Little Tenderness* is a bit much—mainly because of the gratuitous use of a choir and unneccesary Latin rhythm (on "Intermezzo"). It makes you appreciate the subtlety of Marty Paich's string charts. The big wordless choir keeps oohing and ahhing behind her, in a manner similar to Sarah Vaughan's *My Heart Sings* album and the three LPs arranged for Tony Bennett by Frank De Vol, but *Tenderness* could be worse. There's a clever, half-fast reading of Rudy Friml's "Indian Love Call." "One Step from Heaven," a pop trivialization of Leoncavallo's "Vesti la Giubba" is rendered in the overdone style of the classical albums by Della Reese and Sarah Vaughan.

After Hours is better in every way, even though the arranger-conductor is not credited. The charts and the singing are more restrained, stressing more intimate reeds with a tasteful, soft string background. From the appropriately descriptive opening track, "Blue and Sentimental," onward, both Lynne and the uncredited orchestra (at least on the Collectables CD edition) strike precisely the right note, breakup songs that leaven sentimentality with a touch of the blues, and also a touch of string section grandiosity. "'Tis Autumn," normally done somewhat whimsically (the King Cole Trio), here starts with a hint of melancholy, like such other autumn songs as "Autumn Leaves" and "Autumn Serenade." Lynne dives into composer Henry Nemo's predesignated scat episodes with gusto, and these turn out to be prophetic of the second chorus, which revs into tempo, but subtly, in a way that still seems congruent with what came before it.

After Hours is an album of ballads with a light jazzy feel, but Lynne's greatest ballad success came from the slightly less jazzy *Gloria, Marty and Strings*. Where *After Hours* contrasts big band brass and reeds with a small string section, *Gloria, Marty* is all strings. She sings, among other things, Henry Nemo's other famous song, "Don't Take Your Love from Me," and comes up with a respectable version of "The Folks Who Live on the Hill," which represents for female jazz singers (Peggy Lee, Shirley Horn) what the Kentucky Derby is for racehorses— a true test of their mettle. "Through a Long and Sleepless Night" compares favorably with Sarah Vaughan's version, thanks partly to Paich. And her reading of "The Night Is a Thousand Eyes" makes me wonder why so few major divas (Carmen, Anita) have done this one—without consulting any reference books, I can't think of a more moving interpretation.

Gloria, Marty and Strings is a superior piece of work all the way through, but Charles Trenet's "I Wish You Love" turned out to be the money track. The song had been successfully introduced in America by Keely Smith in 1958. The Lynne-Paich version was released as a single in 1964 and unexpectedly cracked the top 40; Everest quickly rushed out an *I Wish You Love* album, a mixed bag of songs from other records, but also throwing in some tacky singles-style tracks.

Gloria, Marty and Strings seems to be Lynne's last Everest release. After the success of "I Wish You Love," she switched to the more internationally centered Fontana label, for which she made a short series of albums in 1964–66, among them *Intimate Moments, Soul Serenade, Love and a Woman,* and another live album, titled simply *Gloria.* Sixteen cuts from this period are collected on the recommended anthology *Starry Nights,* issued in 1997. It starts with a jazzy Vaughan-like treatment of *Most Happy Fella*'s "Joey, Joey, Joey," and includes a bluesy, medium-up run-through of "Baby Won't You Please Come Home?" that gets faster and jazzier in the second chorus, and "Some of These Days."

"Somewhere in the Night" is a fine live reading of the *Naked City* TV show theme, and there are also two competitive treatments of numbers associated with both Washington and Cole, "Blue Gardenia" and "Nothing Ever Changes My Love for You." "I'm Gonna Laugh You Right Out of My Life," arranged by Al Cohn, is one of Lynne's most moving ballads. And the sound of the *Starry Night* collection is wondrous to hear; after suffering through the ineptly reissued Everest series, what a blessing to listen to Lynne's beautiful voice on something that sounds as if it came from a master tape.

It's easy to recommend *Starry Nights* as the single most essential compendium of Lynne's music, and as far as I can tell, it contains some of the last really fine music that she ever committed to tape. The final Fontana albums featured charts by Luchi De Jesus, who had also done tacky kiddie pop–style charts for Vaughan around this time, and Lynne doesn't seem to have recorded anything else of value. There's little to be said about *A Very Gentle Sound* (1972, Mercury), and *I Don't Know How to Love Him* (1975, ABC) is an album of mediocre pop songs from the title track on. Yet her return to recording, the 1989 *A Time for Love,* is more painfully disappointing. It contains some good songs (the title, "Trust in Me," "I'm in the Mood for Love") and was done for Muse, a firm that normally aimed its product at the jazz market and listeners with at least some kind of taste. Yet while Lynne herself sounds very good, the whole package is mired in dire, synthesizer-based orchestrations.

She made one additional album for Muse (*No Detour Ahead,* 1992) and later one for its successor, HighNote (*This One's on Me,* 1998), but the payoff finally arrived in 2007 with *From My Heart to Yours.* Assisted by the inspired arranger-pianist John di Martino (and producer Todd Barkan), Lynne delivered what everyone agreed was her best effort since the Everest years, four decades earlier. There are a couple of good bouncers, particularly "I Could Make You Care" and a very funky "Mountain Green-

ery." There are also a few excellent straightforward love songs, especially "My Funny Valentine" and "It's Magic," which are sung directly, lover-to-lover.

But where the seventy-five-year-old Lynne truly excels is not songs *of* love so much as songs *about* love, particularly James Taylor's "Secret o' Life," the Legrand-Bergman perennial "How Do You Keep the Music Playing," and, especially, Ned Washington's marvelous lyric to "Wild Is the Wind." Normally that movie theme (by Dimitri Tiomkin) belongs in the previous category, a straightforward love song sung from an "I" to a "you," but Lynne makes it into a meditation on the state of love itself. As with "Secret" and "Music," she sings to us like a maternal sage, warm and loving, offering us the benefit of seventy-five years' worth of experience on the nature of human interaction more poignantly than any singer since Rosemary Clooney. Never has Gloria Lynne's complex combination of formality and funkiness been put to better use. Some things do get better with age.

Teri Thornton (1934–2000)

It was a big deal when Teri Thornton won the Thelonious Monk Competition for jazz vocalists in 1998. This was a completely unanticipated occurrence: Like most such competitions, the Monk event was primarily an extension of the musical education system, and there was an unstated understanding that it was for student performers. That idea was not, apparently, made explicit in the rules, and there was no reason why Teri Thornton, then sixty-three, could not enter. (I don't know if the rules have been altered since.) There was no way any youngster could compete with Thornton, who had four decades of experience and three brilliant albums under her belt. Jane Monheit, the teenaged chanteuse who was the runner-up to Thornton, regarded it as an honor to come in second to her. Even if the point of the competition was somewhat skewed, the event served to bring a talented artist back onto the national scene.

When one listens to Thornton's biggest album, the 1963 *Open Highway,* one inevitably wonders what went wrong in her career—not that she was a talent on the level of a Dinah Washington, but certainly she should have been at least as prolific as Dakota Staton. Thornton had a rich, dark voice that sounds darker still on her "comeback" album, the 1999 *I'll Be Easy to Find,* and comes off as more polished than Etta Jones yet more earthy than Gloria Lynne. She was never a heavy-duty world-class artist, but her singing merited considerably more than she got.

The best account of her life is by her friend Jim Gavin in the notes to the 2001 CD issue of *Open Highway.* Thornton was born Shirley Enid Avery in 1934 (1936 in the notes to her first album); "Thornton" was the name of her first husband and the father of her two children (she was divorced before she turned twenty), and "Teri" was her own creation. She grew up in Detroit but first began working as a singer, often accompanying herself on self-taught piano, at the Ebony Club in Cleveland, and then at various spots around the Midwest and Chicago. Eventually she crossed paths with saxophonists Cannonball Adderley and Johnny Griffin, who recommended her to producer Orrin Keepnews of Riverside Records.

Recorded in late 1960 and early 1961, *Devil May Care* was a fairly imposing debut disc for a twenty-five-year-old jazz singer—even then she could easily have won the Monk competition. The voice is surprisingly low for such a youngster, and her jazzy, improvisational style is already fully formed. This is the kind of first-class production that Abbey Lincoln but not even a handful of other singers were doing with Keepnews and Riverside: well-chosen songs, well-organized, uncluttered charts, and a solid supporting cast of major musicians with considerably more of a track record than Thornton had. Keepnews and musical director Norman Simmons teamed his new discovery with a stellar backup band divided between swing era soloists (Britt Woodman, Earl Warren, Freddie Green) and more modern players (Clark Terry, Seldon Powell, Wynton Kelly). It's the kind of setting and album that every decent jazz singer should get the chance to make at least once, and Thornton rises to the occasion, sounding mournful on Billie Holiday's "Left Alone," exuberant on Bob Dorough's title track, "Devil May Care," and both on "Blue Champagne," a Glenn Miller hit unfortunately overlooked in the postwar era, which she sings wittily (and with the verse).

Devil May Care was such a strong album that it almost had a negative effect on her career, ending it rather than beginning it—Keepnews didn't work with her again, perhaps fearing that she had only one outstanding album in her and this was it. However, she attracted some attention by singing the rarely heard words to two TV themes, both crime-oriented shows with themes by major arrangers who rarely composed: "Somewhere in the Night," the theme from *Naked City,* music by Billy May, and "Open Highway," the theme from *Route 66*, music by Nelson Riddle. Apparently she recorded the *Naked City* theme on her own, and brought it to the former bassist and current publicist-manager Phil Leshin, who was suitably impressed. Leshin told Gavin that he could have done more for Thornton, but her no-account, low-down hustler of a second husband kept lousing things up through a combination of greed and stupidity. Even so, she made a second album called *Somewhere in the Night* (the only one never reissued on CD) for the Dauntless label, a full pop project with a studio orchestra and strings conducted by Larry Wilcox in 1963.

The third album, *Open Highway*, came out on Columbia that same year. For a hot minute, it looked as if Thornton might be getting somewhere—the two TV themes seemed to be attracting some attention. She was touted by talk show tastemakers like the veteran Dave Garroway and the newcomer Johnny Carson, and even sang at the openings of baseball games. *Open Highway*, also arranged by Wilcox, was a worthy follow-up to *Devil May Care,* and a suitable compromise between hard-core jazz and mainstream pop. She belts out "Baby Won't You Please Come Home" like the big showbizzy blues that it is, and delivers a tender "This Is All I Ask" (changing Gordon Jenkins's line "Beautiful girls / Walk a little slower . . ." to "Soft-spoken men / Speak a little softer . . ."). She sings worthy standards and semistandards, like "Seems Like Old Times," associated with Guy Lombardo and written by his brother Carmen; "Music, Maestro, Please," also from the big band era; the light and springy "You" (from *The Great Ziegfeld*); and Mel Tormé's "Born to Be Blue." "Maestro" is somewhat bluesier—not to mention boozier—than usual, with a big string section and an effective reading of the verse ("A table near the band . . ."), and she winds up "Blue" with a dramatic and operatic high-note closer. Thornton and Wilcox also came up with some good new songs that never made it any further: "Where Are You Running," by Woody Harris, and "Goodbye Is a Lonesome Sound," by the combination of arranger Paul Weston and the Bergmans.

Thornton also recorded seven singles tracks for Columbia, which are included on the CD edition of *Open Highway*. Markedly lesser than the album, these serve to illustrate the schizophrenia and paranoia of the era, from ersatz-soul and kiddie pop to a countrypolitan treatment of "Cold, Cold Heart." But neither the album nor any of the singles was a hit, and she didn't go on recording for Columbia.

In fact, she pretty much fell off the face of the earth for the next thirty years. Part of the problem was the changing times and tastes that were bedeviling every artist of her genre and her generation, but part of it was personal. According to various friends, Thornton was grossly mismanaged, and also suffered from substance abuse problems. As she later told Gavin, she went on singing even when she was driving a cab.

In 1985, she met the producer Suzi Reynolds, and ten years later they began slowly working toward an album. The set, which was eventually titled *I'll Be Easy to Find*, was recorded in 1997 though not released until two years later, after Thornton had won the Monk Competition. The voice sounds deeper and more weather-beaten, and for the most part she's altogether convincing. She opens with a touching, late-in-life reprise of "Somewhere in the Night," the closest thing she ever had to a hit or signature song, but the set's most moving piece is the title tune. It's a Bart Howard song that Thornton heard Johnny Mathis sing, the kind of thing that Howard would have written for Mabel Mercer. The high polish of Howard, Mercer, and Mathis makes for an effective contrast with Thornton's shopworn voice, not to mention the song's idealism ("I'll be easy to find / When love for me . . .") and her world-weary, seen-it-all, done-it-all attitude. There's an undercurrent of blues-inflected irony to it—of all the things Thornton was, easy to find was never one.

Her chops are, at times, painfully raw—there's a moment near the end of "Somewhere in the Night" where she tries to go into a head voice, but instead of impressing us with her vocal versatility, this makes her sound all the more desperate, as if her dreams really had called it a day, as the lyrics go. I'm not sure if that's the effect she intended: Sometimes her taste seems askew, as when she does a jazz treatment of "The Lord's Prayer." Instead of singing it straight, as Sarah Vaughan had the good sense to do in 1947, she throws in embellishments to both the melody and the lyrics—suffice it to say, this isn't the proper piece of material for such an approach. Yet in compensation there are two very strong, very basic blues, "Knee Deep in the Blues" (not the classic country song sung by Marty Robbins) and "Salty Mama," credited to Thornton herself, that she sings very well. "Salty Mama," the track that closes the set, is obviously a live cut from a club, although nothing in the booklet tells us exactly when and where this happened. (It could have been that there was just an audience in the studio.)

By ending with a live cut, Thornton and Reynolds would seem to be indicating that the new phase of her career was just beginning, which many thought was the case when she won the competition a few months after the sessions. However, by bringing in Norman Simmons, who played on her first album in 1960, to play on just this one cut, "Salty Mama," it seemed the producer and singer knew they were bringing her career around full circle, and that her recording career would end where it began. Not long after, Thornton discovered she had bladder cancer, and she was killed by it in 2000, when she was sixty-five.

As far as careers went, Teri Thornton started strong and ended triumphantly, but unfortunately that's pretty much all there was. It was a career that was seriously missing a middle. Don't mess, as the song says, with Mr. In-Between.

Irene Reid (1930–2008)

As we've noted, Dinah Washington was the godmother of all soulful ladies, and the woman who sounded the most like her, at least in the early part of her career, was Irene Reid. Still another winner of the Apollo Theater amateur contest, the Savannah-born Reid then made her professional debut in 1948 with Dick Vance's band at the Savoy Ballroom, a few blocks further uptown. After staying with the trumpeter for two years, she worked as a single for most of the fifties, recording for the first time for Savoy in 1955.

She got her major break, however, in 1961–62, when she toured Europe as featured vocalist with Count Basie and His Orchestra. She recorded a handful of sides with Basie for Roulette, both live and studio, and on these she sounds exactly like Washington—her version of Bessie Smith's "Backwater Blues" is almost eerily similar to Washington's, except that the arrangement Basie provided her with is superior to the one behind Washington. She has the same intense searing sound, and every time my mind drifts away for even a second, I could swear I'm listening to Washington.

Perhaps Reid's single strongest performance is "Them That's Got" with Basie. She also recorded "Unforgettable," a direct cover of a song associated with Washington (even more than Nat Cole at that point) and a deep and soulful treatment of "Alexander's Ragtime Band" that's in the spirit of Dinah's Fats Waller and Bessie Smith songbook albums. But between Reid and the Count's men, "Them That's Got" is brilliant all around; it sounds like a three-way meeting with Count Basie, Dinah Washington, and Ray Charles. She takes it slower than Charles, making it more of an aria of resignation and less of a comedy dance number. If you've ever speculated what a full-blown Washington-Basie collaboration might have sounded like (surely that was in the offing, had Washington not died at thirty-nine), then you need wonder no more. The six Roulette studio titles Reid cut with the band (and one additional song, "Almost Like Being in Love," preserved at a live concert in Stockholm) are as good as any female singer I've ever heard with the "New Testament" edition of the Basie band.

The period with Basie proved to be the launching pad for Reid's solo career. One unique idea she had to distinguish herself from the other soul sisters was to work with a traditional organ trio—the organ/guitar/drums format more often used to back up soulful tenor saxophonists than lady singers. The titles of her sixties albums offer a kind of autobiography: Reid cut her first album with a studio orchestra and strings arranged by longtime Sinatra associate George Siravo (and Dick Hyman on organ) and called it *It's Only the Beginning* (1963), then switched to Verve for a record titled *Room for One More* (1965)—presumably meaning one more daughter of Dinah, which included such classic soul-sister fare as "They All Say I'm the Biggest Fool" and "I Wonder Where Our Love Has Gone." She seemed to answer that question with *It's Too Late* (1966), and made one last Verve album in 1967, *Man Only Does (What a Woman Makes Him Do)*—ain't that the gospel truth?—another well-rounded mixture of pop and blues standards. There are a few projects scattered over the seventies and eighties, including one aptly titled *I've Been Here All the Time* (circa 1970).

Following *The Lady from Savannah* (recorded in London in 1989) and *Thanks to You* (1990) she reemerged for real in 1997. At this point she launched a whole series of strong albums for Savant Records, another independent label run by that savior of soulful ladies, Joe Fields. Surprisingly, the years 1997–2001 would be the most consistent and prolific of her career, resulting in six albums: *Million Dollar Secret* (1997), *I Ain't Doing Too Bad* (1999), *Movin' Out* (1999), *The Uptown Lowdown* (2000), *One Monkey Don't Stop No Show* (2002), and *Thanks to You* (2004).

Like Ernestine Anderson in the seventies and eighties, Reid blurs the boundaries between what we typically think of as a blues singer and a jazz singer, drawing on Washington (as well as Anderson) for inspiration but hardly stopping there. If her vocals with Basie would cause listeners taking a blindfold test to name Dinah Washington, much of her singing after 2000 suggests both Etta Jones and Etta James.

But the important thing is that the Savant albums are, overall, so good it seems foolish to spend a lot of time investigating underlying influences. The voice sounds dark but not somber, down but not out, funky but animated. Fulfilling a clever title on the *Movin' Out* album, most of what Reid sang in this period was "Blues the Whole Blues and Nothing but the Blues," yet there are a respectable number of standards on each of the five releases. *Movin' Out* features two by Harold Arlen ("A Sleepin' Bee" and "Come Rain or Come Shine") and two by Jimmy Van Heusen ("Here's That Rainy Day" and "The Second Time Around"), and Reid delivers them with the same urgency that she brings to the straight-up blues, such as "Every Day (I Have the Blues)." The last album in the series, *Thanks to You* (which is also actually the first, since it was recorded in 1990 for a private label and later more widely released on Savant in 2004), includes an especially agreeable variety of material, starting with the jukebox pop hit "Our Day Will Come" and moving on to the classic show ballad "Young and Foolish." The *You* referred to in the title may be Washington herself, since she ends with a medley of Dinah Washington signatures that she frames with "This Bitter Earth."

Reid apparently retired in her early seventies and died in 2008. She spent most of her later career in her native Savannah; surprisingly I can't recall her ever appearing in a major New York club or festival in the late nineties. Hers was a small career with an impressive final act, a rare case when a last hurrah is also a first hurrah.

Lorez Alexandria (1929–2001)

If Reid was the most derivatively and directly Washingtonian of soulful ladies, the least was probably Lorez Alexandria. She was undeniably soulful, and put the same kind of feeling into her interpretations that Washington did, and, like just about every other diva in this section, she started out singing in church and wound up working with Joe Fields. Yet apart from, at one point, her choice of an ill-advised blond wig, there's little to suggest that Alexandria knelt to pray in the Cathedral of Saint Dinah. At times she has the tone of someone from the Anita O'Day cool school, at other times her melodic playfulness suggests the canonical jazz singing of Ella Fitzgerald and Sarah Vaughan. Yet, like the heavier-voiced ladies of her generation—Della Reese, for one—Alexandria was firmly based in the gospel and blues traditions, and she could moan and wail with the best of them, although her sound was lighter and faster on its feet; in fact, the faster she sang, the lighter she sounded, like Maxine Sullivan or even Peggy Lee. In these situations she's as much one of Maxine's mentees or Peggy's posse as one of Dinah's daughters. Alexandria somehow sounded soft and gentle and sharp and biting all at the same time.

She had by far the most attractive voice of any of the ladies in this chapter, as well as the widest range and the most consistently excellent intonation—if pitch itself can be described as beautiful, that's what hers was. She was completely comfortable shouting the blues as well as Rodgers and Hart's "Little Girl Blue." The voice itself was light and sweet but capable of enormous depth; her singing was like an accordion folder that seemed small on the outside but expanded sufficiently, growing bigger and bigger, to contain whatever it needed—rapture, loneliness, exuberance, blues, humor, whimsy, and above all swing. In short, Lorez Alexandria was a major talent but with an unfortunately minor career. She never landed any of those career pegs necessary to make it to a higher level, neither a chart hit nor a signature song (like "Don't Go to Strangers"), nor a consistent series of albums with a well-distributed label, nor a regular string of appearances at major jazz festivals. Perhaps most unfortunately of all, she seems to have had few opportunities to play New York, where a review from John S. Wilson or, later, Stephen Holden would have surely been a major career boost.

Just as the fans of Etta Jones and Teri Thornton feel that those two women were unfairly overlooked by critics and audiences, others feel that way about Alexandria. However, she recorded almost two dozen albums over a thirty-five-year period, and, in the same way that Jones was a local favorite in the New York–New Jersey area, Alexandria seems to have kept continually working on the West Coast.

Having had access to roughly a dozen of her albums, I can tell you that everything I've heard has been good, at the very least, and at least two are extraordinary: These are the two Impulse! albums, appropriately titled *Alexandria the Great* and *More of the Great*, which she made in 1964 and 1965 (these were briefly combined onto one essential CD, although now the first album at least is available by itself). Her reputation could easily rest on these twenty tracks, roughly sixty-eight minutes of the finest jazz singing committed to vinyl in the mid-sixties. But though I never heard Alexandria sing in person, in a sense I had heard her long before I heard her. More than is true of almost any other singer, ideas and arrangements from her two Impulse! albums have been performed by all kinds of singers who probably don't even realize who originated them. I've heard several singers do her version of "My Little Boat" and others do her arrangement of "Over the Rainbow," which opens with "Sing a Rainbow." The fine contemporary vocalist Carolyn Leonhart has reprised Alexandria's treatment of "Show Me," which opens *Alexandria the Great,* but at least Leonhart has the class to acknowledge the inspiration.

Delorez Alexandria Turner was born in Chicago on August 14, 1929, and started by singing gospel music. She was a local favorite first in Chicago, where she sang in clubs and recorded for the first time for several local independent labels, most famously King Records and then Argo. The earliest part of her career was closely connected with that of the important Chicago pianist, composer, and bandleader Walter "King" Fleming, and her earliest known recording, as discovered by Fleming discographer Robert L. Campbell, is "Williams's Blues," on a single by Fleming's Quintette in 1953 or 1954 on Blue Lake Records. Fleming also provided the accompaniment for Alexandria's first two albums, *This Is Lorez* and *Lorez Sings Pres.* The second album boasts a marvelous concept that in itself distinguished it from other discs by other chirps, in that, as the title suggests, it's a collection of songs associated with Lester Young. Quite naturally, the *Pres* album includes a number of items from the Billie Holiday songbook, and was taped in 1957, when both Holiday and Young were still active.

Her third record, *The Band Swings—Lorez Sings,* is so strong that one forgives it that hackneyed title. Alexandria is indeed light and swinging, continually playing with the melody and the time—she sounds startlingly modern even when dropping the names of twenties movie stars in the second chorus of "My Baby Just Cares for Me." Rather than alternate between swingers and slower tunes, as most singers who weren't Sinatra generally chose to do, *The Band Swings* consists of nothing but superfast up-tempos, even on numbers traditionally done somewhat more romantically, such as "You're My Thrill" and "Don't Blame Me."

For the first time, Alexandria has the luxury of a full orchestra behind her—trombones and rhythm on some tracks ("What Is This Thing Called Love," "Dancing on the Ceiling"), trumpets and saxes joining in on others—and though the arranger-conductor is not credited, he obviously knows what he's doing (whoever he is). Alexandria makes a strong bid for jazz vocal immortality here, swinging like crazy, scatting and ingeniously paraphrasing in a way that approximates Vaughan and McRae. "Ain't Misbehavin'" has R&B overtones, including an insistent baritone in the sax section; "What Is This Thing Called Love" boasts a wild chorus in which three or four different trombonists trade fours with the drummer. The most ambitious track is easily the side-one closer, "Dancing on the Ceiling." Alexandria and her unnamed orchestrator do most of it wordlessly, with Alexandria scatting and harmonizing amid the trombone section—both this and "Misbehavin'" sound like one of the J. J. Johnson–Kai Winding all-trombone groups. Her voice swings as strongly and is as perfectly in tune as any major brass instrumentalist.

Alexandria's next album, her first for Argo, sustains this high level of creativity. *Early in the Morning* (1960) teams her with another Chicagoan, future star pianist Ramsey Lewis, who would later land many hit singles in the soul-jazz-pop crossover market; the set was also released as *Lorez Alexandria with The Ramsey Lewis Trio* on Cadet, even though Lewis is playing as part of a rhythm quartet and is not spotlighted. Like *The Band Swings*, the *Early in the Morning* album finds Alexandria successfully sustaining a single mood throughout thirty-five minutes or so. In Ralph Gleason's album notes, she cites Fitzgerald and Sinatra as her two favorite singers, a point worth mentioning in that there were and are few other singers who could sustain attention singing the same kind of song for ten tracks in a row.

Where *The Band Swings* is fast and loud, *Early in the Morning* is slow and quiet. Taking its title from Louis Jordan, the set consists of ten songs that balance balladeering with the blues, including two by Jordan's fellow early R&B pioneers Buddy Johnson ("Baby, Don't You Cry") and Ivory Joe Hunter ("I Almost Lost My Mind"), numbers from the songbooks of Billie Holiday ("Don't Explain," "Good Morning, Heartache") and Duke Ellington ("I Ain't Got Nothin' but the Blues," "I'm Just a Lucky So-and-So," and Ellington's ur-blues "Rocks in My Bed"), and also balances the earthy, traditional "So Long" (blues) with Alec Wilder's somewhat more urbane "Trouble Is a Man." We're already used to all kinds of female voices singing the blues, from the big, rough sound of Bessie Smith, the no less personal sharp and searing sounds of Holiday and Washington, and the softer sound of Peggy Lee. But we've never heard anyone like this—quiet, gentle like Lee or Maxine Sullivan, but with just enough of a bite, perhaps a little like Carmen McRae. Even when she sings a text as simple as "Baby, Don't You Cry," she already has a gift for making it unfold like a logical story, with a natural linear development, reconciling the melodic with the narrative—an obvious manifestation of Sinatra's influence.

Still in Chicago, she cut three more albums for Argo: *Sing No Sad Songs for Me* (1961), with a full string section; *Deep Roots* (1962), which featured bopper Howard McGhee on trumpet; and *For Swingers Only* (1963). The title of the final Argo album is at once accurate and misleading. Alexandria swings more than well enough to justify the title, as on "All or Nothing at All," but it also includes one of her most haunting slow ballads in "Little Girl Blue," which opens with an arresting, partly a cappella reading of the verse. The mood is at once lightly Latin and solidly swinging, thanks to Ronald Wilson's flute, which creates all kinds of musical and cultural juxtapositions. "Baltimore Oriole," Hoagy Carmichael's tale of the Tangipahoa (it's in Louisiana—I had to look it up), now has a more tropical sound, as if the oriole flew down to Key Largo. The tune I least expected to hear in this setting is "Traveling Down a Lonely Road," the English lyric to Nino Rota's theme for Fellini's *La Strada;* Alexandria and guitarist George Eskridge do it as a gracefully swinging waltz. She belts a powerful blues called "Mother Earth"—her use of restraint and low-key dynamics in a blues setting makes me think of Cassandra Wilson. Before I heard *For Swingers Only,* I would have automatically listed *Alexandria the Great* as her best album—now I'm not so sure. The only thing I can hold against *For Swingers Only* is that it's a mere eight tracks and twenty-nine minutes long.

By 1964, she had settled in Los Angeles, where she made the two Impulse! albums. They were produced by veteran orchestrator and composer Tutti (aka "Toots") Camarata, who put the singer through the paces with various combinations and arrangers. There's a memorable session with one of the famous Miles Davis rhythm sections—Wynton Kelly (piano), Paul Chambers (bass), and Jimmy Cobb (drums)—and also several sessions with larger ensembles, with West Coasters Bud Shank and Paul Horn supplying tasty flute obbligatos throughout.

I particularly like what Alexandria does with three songs from *My Fair Lady*—her opener on *Alexandria the Great,* "Show Me," then on side two, "Get Me to the Church on Time" and "I've Grown Accustomed to Her Face." All three feature big band arrangements, apparently by Bill Marx (son of Harpo), a pianist and arranger who also did excellent work with Ann Richards. "Show Me" starts with a slow bass figure from Al McKibbon over a small, tasteful string section, before Alexandria enters, taking Eliza Doolittle's aria of sexual independence and stretching it out seductively with Shank's flute behind her; for the second chorus, she and Camarata leap into tempo, with loud, dissonant brass, and the beat accentuated by a tambourine, and she concludes with a gospelesque a cappella cadenza—it's a heckuva ride for four minutes.

"Get Me to the Church on Time" starts slow and small with just rhythm, but with much anticipation: There's a touch of anxiety in her voice, which could be read as if she's looking forward to getting married, but also as if we know from the beginning that the tempo is going to pick up and the horns are going to kick in; they don't disappoint us. She keeps us on our toes with unexpected harmonic varia-

tions, as well as playing with the verb in the climactic line ("Rush me to the church . . ."). "Accustomed" is also slow and pensive, even more than the others, in that it does not resolve, in a sense, into a faster tempo or build in volume. In the notes, Alexandria correctly describes it as having a "Bill Evansish sound," with long, sustained chords. On all three, Marx's charts are mildly Kentonesque, using dissonance and slowly resolving chords to underscore Alexandria's musical and dramatic trajectory.

There are brilliant moments throughout the two *Great* albums, the second including a "Dancing on the Ceiling" done with just trio that's more literal and very different from the scatty trombone version she cut for King—it also packs a lot of pleasure into a mere minute and a half. *More of the Great* also sustains our interest with offbeat material like the Brazilian "Little Boat" and the French "Once (Ils s'aimaient)" and a very obscure show tune, "That Far Away Look," by the unique combination of Sammy Fain and the Bergmans (from the flop show *Something More*). Other tunes clearly reflect what Alexandria was listening to as a teenager in the mid-forties: Billy Eckstine's first MGM single, "The Wildest Girl in Town" (also by Sammy Fain), and Camarata's own "No More," from the Holiday canon. On side two of the second *Great* album, she lustily swings Steve Allen's "This Could Be the Start of Something Big."

Like just about everyone else in this section of this book, Alexandria, now based in L.A., virtually sat out the next ten years. There were two discs for the little known Pzazz label in 1968 and 1969, one (*Didn't We*) largely of original compositions by musical director Ronnell Bright, the other forebodingly titled *In a Different Bag* (an insulting title, considering that nothing was wrong with the bag she was in) but which also includes a few decent blues like Jay McShann's "Confessin' the Blues" and Joe Liggins's "I Got a Right to Cry," along with less appropriate material like "Hey Jude" and "My Way"—if I were to make a list of songs I never want to hear Lorez Alexandria sing, "Hey Jude" (in which she goes into a prolonged episode of gospel moaning, as if she were speaking in tongues) and "My Way" would be right at the top of it. (Thirteen tracks from these two Pzazz albums were released in the mid-nineties on a CD called *Talk About Cozy* from Hindsight. The two albums also turned up complete on a double-length disc from an outfit called Connoisseur Collections.)

In 1978 Alexandria resurfaced on Discovery Records, an independent concern based in Los Angeles, run by the veteran Albert Marx. (There also was a big band album done for a Japanese label in 1977.) The production values on these are, obviously, way below those of the Impulse! records, but her voice has held up very well in her mid-fifties, and the material is extremely attractive. Most ambitious was a series of three LPs titled *The Songs of Johnny*

Mercer, which co-star a trio of musicians with impeccable credentials: pianist Gildo Mahones (Lester Young; Lambert, Hendricks & Ross), trumpeter Al Aarons (Count Basie), and guitarist John Collins (Art Tatum, Nat Cole). There are none of the imaginative arrangements one hears on the fifties and sixties records, nothing that really surprises us and catches us off guard (though it's nice to hear her do the underperformed "Namely You" from *L'il Abner*), but the discs are workmanlike and satisfying. Overall, these are the best albums she could have made at the time.

There were other, nonsongbook projects at the time as well, most winningly the 1987 *Dear to My Heart,* accompanied by L.A. reed player Gordon Brisker, here heard effectively on clarinet. Alexandria is at her Sullivanesque, light-and-fleet-footed best on the title cut. She's also marvelous on "Zanzibar" (an up-and-swinging paraphrase of "Cara-van" and "Close Your Eyes") and on a number of ballads, including "Where Have You Been?" (not Cole Porter) and three early songs by Harold Arlen with Ted Koehler: "As Long as I Live," "When the Sun Comes Out," and "Ill Wind." She also made several sets for Japanese distribution, and in her early sixties cut her last three albums for Muse (by this point Joe Fields was running a rest home for veteran vocalists): *May I Come In* (1990), *I'll Never Stop Loving You* (1992), and *Star Eyes* (1993), the first and last benefiting from the welcome presence of tenorist Houston Person.

The 1978–93 albums were a solid conclusion to a career that had been, at times, brilliant. Lorez Alexandria retired shortly after *Star Eyes,* and died in Gardena, California, in 2001, at the age of seventy-one. As far as I'm concerned, she is one of the major, underappreciated artists in this book.

Two Soulful Gentlemen

Sam Cooke
Lou Rawls

In any discussion of African American popular music, the key word is "crossover." Apparently nobody takes you seriously in the world of black vernacular music unless at some point in your career you win the white audience over, too. But there are all kinds of crossover, and the transition of singers from band vocalists to solo acts in the mid-forties can also be described as a kind of crossover. When Frank Sinatra left Tommy Dorsey to go out on his own in 1942, he was as Moses parting the Red Sea and leading his people to the land of milk and honey. As the singer Earl Coleman (an associate of Charlie Parker and disciple of Billy Eckstine) told me, "Even the Great Mr. B, in all his glory, would have no place to go if not for Sinatra."

Eckstine was the first of a group of black male singers to have a major impact on mainstream pop music in the years leading up to the onset of what became known as "soul" music in the early sixties, the others being Nat King Cole, Sam Cooke, Arthur Prysock, Lou Rawls, Jimmy Scott, Al Hibbler, and Ray Charles. They represent the essential Stations of the Cross, as it were, in the evolution from what had existed before, namely gospel and pop, into soul.

The concept of crossover was crucial for all of them, even though they all crossed over from different places: Eckstine led his fellow black male band singers, such as Hibbler, Herb Jeffries, Hartman, and Prysock, to follow Sinatra's exit from the big bands onto the solo singer circuit (for Eckstine, there was an intermediate step in which he led his own orchestra). Cole made a complex transition from jazz pianist to pop singer, whereas Charles came out of rhythm and blues, and Cooke, like his close friend Lou Rawls, came out of gospel music.

The most consistent point in the careers of all these men was that the prize they kept their eyes on was the Great American Songbook. Eckstine's triumph was that he was able to "sing about love" as he put it, "not about work or blues or some dumb crap." For Cooke and Charles the transition was particularly important: They broke through after the emergence of Elvis, yet even though Presley had shown that there was a fortune to be made in selling singles to white teenagers in love, neither Cooke nor Charles viewed rock 'n' roll as their final destination; they wanted to play the Copacabana and sing things like "Summertime" and "Ol' Man River." Second-generation white rockers, particularly Brits, wanted to pretend they were Robert Johnson, while Charles, Rawls, and Cooke started out by trying to be Billy Eckstine and Nat King Cole; it's hardly surprising that Rawls's final album was a tribute to Sinatra.

There is no greater indication of how things changed in this era than the generation that separates Nat Cole (born 1919) from Sam Cooke (born 1931) and Lou Rawls (1934), all three of whom were sons of preachers who grew up in Chicago. When Cole was learning the piano during the Depression, he went immediately into secular music; but when Cooke and Rawls first started singing in the mid-forties, there was no question but that they would go into gospel.

By 1950, when the twenty-year-old Sam Cook (not yet "Cooke") joined the Soul Stirrers, the line between R&B and gospel was considered uncrossable. Once you sang the music of the world—or as some of the more zealous churchgoers believed, the music of the devil—your mouth was no longer clean enough to raise your voice in praise of Jesus, Joseph, and Mary. Thomas A. Dorsey had gone from blues to gospel twenty years earlier, but for a long time it looked as if he would be the only one to cross over this way.

Yet gospel and R&B had come into this world more or less together, and in retrospect, it seems inevitable that these two forms, separated at birth, would eventually reunite. It happened in the late fifties, and the new baby would be known as "soul" music. Sam Cooke arrived at soul from the gospel side and Ray Charles came to it from the R&B side, but they both wound up in the same soulful place.

As already mentioned, Cole, Cooke, and Rawls were all the sons of ministers, but unlike the protagonist played by Cole in his only starring role in a feature film (*The St. Louis Blues,* a highly fictionalized biography of blues father W. C. Handy), their preacher fathers weren't opposed to the careers of their sons in secular music. In fact, neither the Reverend Coles nor Minister Cook objected when their sons modified their names for showbiz, one dropping an "S" and the other adding an "E." Cole and Cooke were born in the Deep South (Cooke in 1931 in Clarksdale, Mississippi), and migrated with their families as children to Chicago; Rawls, who was two years younger than Cooke, was born in Chicago after the Great Migration.

Cooke and Cole, who both died tragically young, maintained strong relationships with their fathers, who outlived them; Rawls and his mother, in contrast, were deserted by his father (hardly an admirable move for a Baptist minister), and Rawls's mother left home to work in defense plants during World War II, leaving the child's grandmother to raise him. Cooke and Cole both grew up in families that were as much musical as they were religious; just as most of Cole's brothers played instruments, Cooke's brothers joined him in his first vocal group. Cooke grew up singing with his family, and Rawls grew up singing in the streets, and they were close friends from their earliest days on. Both grew up studying the entire spectrum of music, from gospel to rhythm and blues as well as the major standards singers like Cole, Eckstine, and Arthur Prysock. With his high tenor, Cooke leaned toward Cole's sweet and pretty tones, whereas Rawls from the beginning identified with the very deep baritones like Eckstine and Prysock.

Sam Cooke (1931–1964)

Daniel Wolff, in his fine biography *You Send Me: The Life and Times of Sam Cooke,* details Cooke's rise to fame very precisely: After singing with his brothers and sisters under the auspices of the Right Reverend Cook, he joined a quartet called the Highway QC's, which was roughly a junior-league version of the more famous Soul Stirrers, who had been one of the leading groups of the music since well before they first recorded in 1936. Eventually, the ambitious nineteen-year-old got the chance to graduate from the farm team to the major leagues when he joined the Soul Stirrers—and not just as a minor member

of the five-man group, but as one of the two lead singers, replacing the extremely popular and charismatic Rebert H. Harris.

The Soul Stirrers didn't land a regular recording contract until 1947, when they signed with Aladdin Records. In 1950, they switched to Art Rupe's Specialty Records, doing only one session for that Los Angeles–based label before Harris was replaced by Cooke. In 2002, Fantasy Records, owners of the Specialty catalogue, issued all the Stirrers' sessions with Cooke in a three-CD box, *Sam Cooke with the Soul Stirrers,* which is a particularly valuable set in that it includes any number of alternate takes. Even though the group honed these numbers from night to night, there are a lot of variations in the alternates—almost as many as in different takes of Charlie Parker solos. Some of the differences between takes are not necessarily the work of the group itself: One of the most engaging tracks in that first session (a marathon date that yielded thirteen complete takes of eleven different songs) is "I'm on the Firing Line," which also shows that, from the beginning, Cooke was dominating an increasing share of the numbers: "Firing Line" is primarily a Cooke vehicle all the way through. Yet on the two takes, one features the five male voices a cappella, and the other features the Soul Stirrers backed by a large female choir, obviously overdubbed sometime later.

Just as historians romance the blues before they became beloved of white people, or Nat Cole before he crossed over, so, too, it's often said that the Soul Stirrers sessions are the finest of Cooke's career. The point is valid, in that he grew up in the world of gospel and needs no adjustment in how to sing it; it could also be argued that Cooke's white pop (or rock 'n' roll, if you want to call it that) recordings are limited by the values of the watchdogs at the time, who were carefully monitoring the signals being sent to white teens. In his pop performances, Cooke was discouraged from evoking quite as orgasmic a response as he did when he sang to church audiences. Rock 'n' roll was considerably less overtly sexual than gospel.

Cooke's recordings with the Soul Stirrers illustrate the difference between gospel and earlier forms of religious music. "Must Jesus Bear This Cross Alone?" includes a long quotation from the traditional "Amazing Grace," while "Jesus, Wash Away My Troubles" does the same with "Sometimes I Feel Like a Motherless Child." Cooke's biggest hit with the group, "Nearer to Thee," is a reworking of "Nearer My God to Thee," which is an archaic Welsh hymn, earlier and later best known as the song supposedly played by the ship's band as the *Titanic* went down, but apparently the *Titanic* wasn't on anybody's mind in 1955—at least not in the black churches. (Doris Day was one of the few popular singers who recorded a straight version of the traditional "Nearer My God.") In all these examples, Cook and his fellow Stirrers are considerably more emotionally supercharged than in any previous readings of this material.

Mahalia Jackson managed to reach the mainstream not by crossing over, as Cook did, but by personally bringing her sacred music to the rest of the world. Such a phenomenon never quite occurred in the male side of the gospel world. In a sense, she was able to get the rest of the world to cross over to where she was, whereas Cooke and Rawls had to themselves cross over to where the big audiences were.

The *Soul Stirrers* boxed set illustrates the transition in dramatic terms: Cooke and the quintet finish one session with the powerful "Pilgrim of Sorrow," which is filled with religious angst, while the first tune on the next date is "Happy in Love." This is one of Cooke's only two nongospel sessions for Specialty, experimental dates in which he worked under the pseudonym of "Dale Cook." Compared to what came before and came after, they're not very good, and "Happy in Love" stands in stark contrast to the gospel session that immediately preceded it. It's mindlessly happy, almost a parody of an up-tempo pop jingle, and the lyrics mainly consist of Cook just chanting the word "happy" over and over (which would be a common trademark of his own songs). Though somewhat more soulful, "Happy in Love" has much in common with the "Happy Happy Joy Joy" jingle from the *Ren and Stimpy* cartoon show.

My favorite of the seven pop titles he recorded on those two test sessions is "Lovable," which, as becomes clear from listening to the Specialty box, is a paraphrase of "He's So Wonderful," a gospel tune Cooke had composed and cut with the Stirrers several months earlier. The two are so similar they could be alternate takes. "Lovable" isn't all that wonderful in itself, but it shows that Cooke had already arrived at a basic but profound conclusion. Without making an issue of it—like Ray Charles, who had already turned "I Got a Saviour" into "I Got a Woman"—he was operating as a reverse Thomas A. Dorsey. Just as that venerated gentleman had created gospel out of the blues, Cooke and Charles were now transmuting gospel back into pop, and Cooke's first idea was to take the essential material of religious music and refashion it for a secular audience. Indeed, Cooke's signature sound, the catchy whoa-oo-oo wail, was already a significant element of his sacred work, in which it was taken as a sign of spiritual devotion, being moved by the Spirit to speak in tongues. In pop tunes like "Forever," the trademark Cooke wail becomes a wordless cry of romantic rapture.

Even though the "Dale Cook" sessions could hardly be considered successful, Sam Cooke and his manager-producer Bumps Blackwell were convinced that this was the way to go. The song that was key was Cooke's "You Send Me," and it provoked a crisis: Art Rupe, owner of Specialty Records, completely rejected it. For some unknown reason, he just didn't like the song. Cooke and Blackwell subsequently found a home with the start-up label Keen Records, who were happy to have "You Send Me," which became Cooke's all-time biggest hit.

Both Cooke and Charles wrote much of their own material, thus positioning themselves in the succession from the old-time bluesmen, who did the same (as did Louis Jordan), and the next generation of singer-songwriters, both white and black. More important, they followed in the footsteps of Frank Sinatra as performer-producers who didn't need much in the way of outside help to get what they wanted in the studio (such as the Dixieland accompaniment behind Cooke on "Cousin of Mine"). Like Sinatra, Cooke would become something of a mini-mogul, operating several independent labels and publishing houses.

Nearly all of his hits were his own songs, and his success was predicated on "You Send Me." It wasn't the song itself that put him over, it was the way he used it as a framework for those wild, almost cantorial wails. His subsequent successes, like "Twistin' the Night Away," "Chain Gang," "Cupid," "A Change Is Gonna Come," and so on, were all mainly notable not as songs (in the sense of Cole Porter with Sinatra), but in terms of establishing a mood, be it romantic or danceable, and maintaining a groove. You can't imagine Cooke's songs without him, except in tribute. For one thing, there are so many forced and false rhymes in his lyrics—"place" and "way," "exist" and "fix"—that one sometimes wishes he'd collaborated with a professional lyricist or at least invested in a rhyming dictionary.

These songs established Cooke as one of the major hit makers of his generation, and—with Ray Charles and a few others—one of the (comparatively) elder deacons of soul. But it's worth noting that he didn't stop there, not even for a moment; even though singles now dominated the youth-driven singles market, there was still more money in reaching their parents. The album market was considerably more lucrative, just as the supper-club market was potentially more profitable than playing daytime matinees for kids in movie houses across the country. The breakthrough "You Send Me" was backed with Gershwin's "Summertime," and the next single was the ten-year-old King Cole hit "For Sentimental Reasons," which Cooke reanimates with additional yodels and whoop-whoops.

Like everyone else in the business at the time, starting with Sinatra and Cole, Cooke and Blackwell realized that singles were for new songs and albums were for standards. The transition from gospel to jukebox pop happened virtually overnight with "You Send Me," but mastering the songbook would take more time. Biographer Wolff dismisses Cooke's first standards album, *Sam Cooke*, released by Keen in 1957, as "an awful, syrupy mess." Likewise, Cooke's first appearance at the Copacabana, around the same time, was by all accounts a disaster—he just wasn't ready.

Sam Cooke was all standards except "You Send Me," and his second album, *Sam Cooke Encores*, likewise consisted of eleven older songs and one jukebox item, "Mary, Mary Lou." The second album, which is barely mentioned by either Wolff or Peter Guralnick in his more expansive bio, *Dream Boogie*, is an absolutely tremendous LP: Cooke has come a long way in a short time. There's no syrup or strings here, just twelve short, punchy renditions of generally familiar tunes, opening with "Oh, Look at Me Now," one of a number of songs on *Encores* that carry with it the baggage of the concepts of transition and crossover. It was first sung by Sinatra in 1941 as a message that Tommy Dorsey's ballad singer was adding up-tempos to his book, a message he reiterated when he rerecorded "Oh, Look at Me Now" in 1956. When Cooke took it on a year later (adding a verse of his own—at least one that I haven't heard anywhere else) and then when Bobby Darin sang it in 1962 (Darin felt so strongly that he titled his first Capitol album *Oh, Look at Me Now*), the message was that these teen idols were also transitioning, singing grown-up songs, and look at *them* now.

Then, too, similar messages were encoded in "Someday (You'll Want Me to Want You)" and "Along the Navajo Trail." The first is a song that originated in the world of country music, being a 1940 hit for cowboy Elton Britt (followed by the Mills Brothers), but which has the superior quality of a standard—I can easily imagine Crosby singing it, if not Sinatra. The second is a Tin Pan Alley song that was a hit for Crosby and the Andrews Sisters, but though it was written for a Hollywood Western, it could easily pass for an authentic C&W song. A more cynical observer might suggest that Cooke wasn't content to go after mainstream white audiences, that he wanted Nashville listeners, too; or perhaps that he wanted to convey that songs of the West mean something to him as much as they do any other young American. But the infectious joy in his voice throughout the album contradicts his having chosen any of these songs with some kind of ulterior motive: He clearly loves the material, and is having a wonderful time singing it.

Roughly half the tracks are done with a smallish big band, ostensibly conducted by Bumps Blackwell, which has the loose, unpolished quality of the bands one could find in most nightclubs at the time. It serves to give these performances an especially sincere quality. Even when he tries such a rudimentary bit of stagecraft as the modulations in "Running Wild" and "Ac-Cent-Tchu-Ate the Positive," it doesn't seem manipulative. You can also tell that he's on the level about wanting to learn the craft of singing the popular song: He knows, for instance, that experienced singers sometimes begin with a verse, a surefire way to increase the suspense. The greater the discrepancy between the tempo of the verse (normally ultraslow or rubato) and that of

the chorus, and the less familiar the audience is with a particular song's verse (he's unearthed some really rare ones), the greater the relief will be when the verse resolves into the swinging, more familiar chorus. The use of the verses here allows him to take two key songs from the repertoires of two of his favorites, Sinatra and Cole, and make them seem new to audiences who doubtless knew these songs even better than he did.

Most of the second side of the original LP doesn't use the full band but gives every impression that Cooke is improvising arrangements of standards with his rhythm section. The results are mixed, but there are enough successes in this string of tunes to justify the experiment. "When I Fall in Love" comes closer to the famous Cole recording than the single of "For Sentimental Reasons"; there are almost no whoa-whoa yodels here (although there's a bit of a "whoa-whoa" on "My Foolish Heart") as Cooke tries to sing it as directly and emotionally as he can. "I Cover the Waterfront"—recorded a few months earlier by Sinatra—is a jumping treatment of an older standard normally done as a ballad, featuring an acoustic guitar solo that's so rudimentary (and effectively so) that it makes me wonder if it might be Cooke himself playing; whoever it is, he certainly seems to be enjoying himself. "The Gypsy" was probably learned from the Ink Spots, or, I'd like to believe, Louis Armstrong, and Cooke's embellishments ("Your fears, your fears, your fears") add much to this British song. "It's the Talk of the Town" (from Billie Holiday) and "Today I Sing the Blues" (from Helen Humes) show him attempting classic torch songs, the latter with an extra-heavy touch of the blues. Even as a gospel singer, his strength was the Pearly Gates above rather than the pit below; although he's got some growing to do in the area of sad songs, it's clear that he's on his way.

The longest track on the album, "Ac-Cent-Tchu-Ate the Positive," illustrates, more than any other song, the transition Cooke was making from a preacher's son to a gospel star to a pop singer making like a Southern preacher. Significantly, Cooke, who showed himself to be very conscious of verses elsewhere, e-lim-i-nates Johnny Mercer's verse here, which sets up the scenario that this is a sundown deacon preaching to his flock ("Listen while I preach some . . ."). He just leaps into the song midpreach, and doesn't need the setup to tell his congregation to latch on to the affirmative. He also creates the illusion that a choir of the faithful is there egging him on, singing several built-in encores and, for still more excitement, throws in a false ending.

"Along the Navajo Trail," which, to my ears, is the most successful piece here, also incorporates special material. Throughout, Cooke is keen to lay on his signature whoa-whoas, which in this context suggest country-style yodeling, while both the shuffle arrangement and the irreverent attitude bring to mind Louis Prima. The piece ends with a special tag clearly designed to win approval from middle-American patrons, not just hip Harlemites, when the singer elaborates on the TV Westerns he'd like to emulate, like *Cheyenne* and *Maverick,* which leads to a sung coda ("the Indians and their bow and arrows . . ."). Here was a mixture no one had tried yet—a gospel-soul singer, a faux-Western song, and a swinging, Rat Pack–style arrangement—and Cooke makes it all hang together. His torch songs may need work, but as a swinger he's already one of the better male jazz singers around. He isn't just reveling in the groove, he's really interpreting the standard songs here; it's hard to believe that if he had done these twelve songs at the Copa just as he did them on the *Encore* album, the patrons wouldn't have loved it.

Encore is, overall, a much more satisfying project than Cooke's most ambitious album of standards, the 1959 *Tribute to the Lady,* a collection of songs associated with Billie Holiday, with Holiday's occasional collaborator Benny Carter prominently soloing on "Solitude." According to Wolff, Cooke recorded this album in January and February of 1959, when the Great Lady was still alive (in other words, he wasn't merely jumping on her posthumous bandwagon); however, Carter discographer Ed Berger feels the project was actually taped later in the year, after she had died. (RCA later reissued the set in 1975 as *Sam Cooke Interprets Billie Holiday,* informing purchasers that the album was "a collection of previously unreleased selections.") The Holiday set uses strings and horn soloists, most notably Carter, but it just doesn't hang together: Cooke was clearly not ready to take on the greatest female singer of slow ballads that ever was.

As with Ray Charles and Lou Rawls, standards remained a major part of Cooke's repertory, a fact that's easy to miss based on reissues from the compact disc era. The Billie Holiday album, for instance, is very hard to find on CD. He made at least two other standards-driven albums for RCA in 1960: *Cooke's Tour,* themed to a round-the-world motif (obviously inspired by Sinatra's *Come Fly with Me* and Crosby and Clooney's *Fancy Meeting You Here*), and *Hits of the Fifties,* which proceeds chronologically from the 1950 "Mona Lisa" to the 1959 "Venus" (stopping productively at the 1955 "Unchained Melody" along the way). Neither of these has apparently been available in any format since they were first released in 1960.

There's a standards element even in Cooke's original pop songs: "Chain Gang" was composed by Cooke but arranged for him by Abe "Glenn" Osser, an old-school orchestrator who had done "And the Angels Sing" for Benny Goodman in 1937 and *Tony Bennett Sings a String of Harold Arlen* in 1960. The amazing "Chain Gang" mixes happy and sad, triumphant and tragic; newcomers to African American music are frequently surprised about how the blues can be happy music, especially when the term "blue" itself is a synonym for melancholy, and also

that blues and gospel singers can sing about the most devastating of circumstances with smiles on their faces. "Chain Gang" is a song about convicts on a roadside labor crew, yet it's as much a party song—like "Twistin' the Night Away" or "Havin' a Party"—as it is a protest song. It takes the African American ideal of smiling in the face of catastrophe to an unbelievable extreme; it's more about optimism than despair, how "the men working on the chain gang" are motivated by the dream "of going home to see my woman, who I love so dear." It's as rhythmic as it is passionate; it's almost as if "Strange Fruit" were set to a shuffle beat. It's as rhythmic as it is compassionate—imagine "Strange Fruit" set to a shuffle beat for twistin' the night away. (In fact, in Cooke's hands, even "Twistin' the Night Away" is a message of spiritual uplift.) Ultimately, "Chain Gang," no less than "Jesus, Wash Away My Troubles" or "A Change Is Gonna Come," is a song of salvation. If there's hope even for these wretched of the earth, then Lord knows that there surely must be a Heaven for us all. All God's chillun, Cooke is telling us, got wings.

"Chain Gang" provides us with a fascinating perspective on Cooke's two classic live albums, even though, in one case, it's conspicuous by its absence. Two of his best-known albums were taped live in clubs, one in front of a predominantly black audience at the Harlem Square Club in Miami in 1963 (released in 1985), the other in front of the old-school showbiz, mostly older white patrons of the Copacabana in New York in 1964. (At the Harlem Square, Cooke is accompanied by a band led by the saxophonist and showman King Curtis, who would, like Cooke, be murdered; by a macabre coincidence, one of Curtis's own final sessions was with John Lennon, who shared a similarly violent fate.) It's important to note that "Chain Gang" is prominently featured in the "black" concert but not heard at all at the "white" show. Not only is "Chain Gang" heard in Miami, but Cooke and his backup group rough it up considerably: Abe Osser's smooth strings are gone, and the slick vocal choir is replaced by Curtis's bandsmen grunting and groaning and sounding much more like an actual chain gang.

The two live albums are cornerstones of the Cooke catalogue: Singing at the Copa, he was inclined to include more standards, not necessarily because the customers were white but because the club drew what today would be described as a mature demographic. Rock 'n' roll fans tend to downplay Cooke's standards albums, and I'm sure that they would also view the Copa album as the singer's sop to an older, whiter crowd—yet by Cooke's own measure he is obviously trying and succeeding at pleasing everybody. He gets going with "The Best Things in Life Are Free," the same kind of bright, bouncy opener than Tony Bennett might start with, while "Bill Bailey" is exactly what an old-timer like Sophie Tucker or Jimmy Durante would sing. From traditional pop, he moves to traditional blues, the Bessie Smith–associated "Nobody Knows You When You're Down and Out" and "Frankie and Johnny," the kind of well-known folk blues that a mainstream entertainer like Lena Horne would do in a nightclub. (If the clips on YouTube are any indication, we can see that Cooke was one of the few singers of the early sixties to appear regularly on TV shows for the younger set, like *American Bandstand,* as well as late-night programming for their parents, like *The Tonight Show and The Jerry Lewis Show,* doing essentially the same kind of music on both. There's a wonderful *Lewis Show* excerpt from 1962 where he comes out and sings "Twistin' the Night Away"—indeed he is—and then croons "The Riddle Song" like a more soulful Belafonte.)

Both Cooke live albums are embellished by the way he constantly spiels in and around his vocals. He never stops talking except to sing, and vice versa; he's not only his own master of ceremonies, he's a preacher, teacher, and square dance caller all at once. Cooke is so outgoing on both of these live albums that he makes Sammy Davis Jr. look like an introvert. He sings a little bit of everything, notably a medley of mostly traditional love songs—"Try a Little Tenderness," "(I Love You) For Sentimental Reasons," ending with his own "You Send Me"— before finally building up to the gospel-inflected R&B that he was known for. He climaxes the set with "Twistin' the Night Away" and the traditional hymn "This Little Light of Mine" (not Ray Charles's pop update), plus "Blowin' in the Wind"—he sings the iconic Bob Dylan composition less like a protest song and more like a rocking spiritual, or as he puts it, a "hootenanny."

"Tennessee Waltz," set to a hard-swinging shuffle beat (barely even in three), provides an unlikely closer. Cooke's energy is incredible on the Harlem Square album, but it's easy to see why he would have preferred to issue the Copa album twenty years earlier: There's something for everyone here, and he blends folk songs, blues, spirituals, pop, and soul songs with standards in a way that would profoundly influence entertainers of the sixties, from Ray Charles and Bobby Darin onward.

Cooke would record other standards over the next five years, before he was murdered in 1964. Had he not been gunned down in a sleazy motel in Los Angeles, it seems clear that the American songbook would have continued to be a big part of his music. On the day he died, Cooke told friend Al Schmitt (quoted by Wolff) that he was planning a new album of standards and traditional blues in the spirit of Billie Holiday. There's every reason to believe that he would have kept on singing both soul and standards much the way his friend Lou Rawls did for the next forty or so years—some albums of all soul, some of all standards, and quite a few that combine both very successfully.

During Cooke's lifetime, most of his producers—particularly the team of Luigi Creatore and Hugo Peretti—were keen to have him record standards and what's thought of as the Great American Songbook. Yet those who compile the posthumous reissues from Cooke's repertoire, as we've seen, apparently prefer to think that Cooke never sang anything other than gospel and soul. Even both of his biographers, Wolff and more recently Peter Guralnick (in his excellent *Dream Boogie*), give short shrift to these recordings. When standards are heard in Cooke anthologies, they almost seem to have gotten there by accident.

One CD collection, however, titled *The Rhythm and the Blues,* contains some marvelous performances of old-fashioned blues songs, like "Baby, Won't You Please Come Home" and "Trouble in Mind" (with these and "Nobody Knows You When You're Down and Out" and "Frankie and Johnny," he could have done a whole album of old-time blues). He also includes several standards that have long had a connection to black singers and blues singers, like "Out in the Cold Again," "Don't Get Around Much Anymore," and "Cry Me a River." But then he also does "But Not for Me," and even "Little Girl Blue." And then there's "Smoke Rings," the instrumental theme song of the Casa Loma Orchestra, sung by practically no one (except, famously, Harold Arlen with Leo Reisman's orchestra). To say that Cooke sings it soulfully is an understatement; he sings of smoke rings as if they were manifestations of the human soul, and their aerial ascent becomes a flight straight to heaven.

Lou Rawls (1933–2006)

Lou Rawls was raised by his grandmother until he was fourteen and, like Cooke, he started with farm-team gospel quartets such as the Teenage Kings of Harmony. He made it to the major leagues of the gospel circuit when he joined the Pilgrim Travelers, with whom he sang both before and after a two-year stint in the 82nd Airborne from 1955 to 1957. His army service indirectly saved his life: In 1958, Rawls and Cooke were sharing a ride from St. Louis to Memphis, and both were asleep when their Cadillac plowed into (and under) a soybean truck. One man instantly died, Rawls was in a coma for five and a half days; only Cooke escaped relatively uninjured. For the rest of his life, Rawls insisted that if he hadn't been taken immediately to the nearest veterans hospital he would likely not have survived.

Rawls and Cooke had already been as close as brothers; now they had very nearly died together. And like Cooke, Rawls rose to the top of the gospel quartet world before crossing over into pop. To a certain extent, their early careers paralleled each other, especially in that the Pilgrim Travelers, like the Soul Stirrers, had been a major act on Specialty Records. Rawls repeatedly acknowledged Cooke and the Soul Stirrers as major influences: In 1966, he made a fine gospel album titled *The Soul Stirring Gospel Sounds of the Pilgrim Travelers Featuring Lou Rawls.* That same year, on his album *Carryin' On!,* he sings a love song entitled "Somethin' Stirrin' in My Soul." Rawls also appeared informally on some of Cooke's records; his voice is audibly supplying part of the background on the original "Bring It on Home to Me" and "Having a Party." In 1964, he sang at Cooke's funeral, and a short while afterward recorded an album-length tribute to Cooke entitled *Bring It on Home.*

While both Rawls and Cooke were extremely soulful gentlemen, their voices couldn't be more different: As we've seen, Cooke had a sweet, high baritone that could be likened to Nat Cole's, whereas Rawls has a mellow, rich deep voice that hovered closer to the basso register, and put one more in mind of Billy Eckstine. But there's a more crucial difference in their attitude. It makes me think of a scene in Spike Lee's *Malcolm X* where the FBI is shown wiretapping Malcolm's conversations and commenting, "Compared to [Martin Luther] King, this guy is a choirboy." Where Cooke sounds pure and innocent—even when singing a song of seduction—Rawls sounds like a gigolo, a fly lothario, or some other kind of European smoothieo.

Although both graduated from the gospel circuit, a key difference between Cooke and Rawls was that when Cooke left the Soul Stirrers, he was one of the biggest stars of the gospel field and already known all over Afro-America, whereas Rawls was still a relative unknown, even in the black community. The nearly three-year difference in their ages meant that Rawls didn't have to be a pioneer in the development of soul; by the time he stepped out on his own the movement was well under way. Unlike Cooke, he was not particularly interested in anything beyond performing; he didn't write songs, produce, or publish. In a sense, this is reflected in their music: Most of Cooke's hits are about the communal experience of a group of people having a party, dancing the twist, doing the cha cha, and in general putting "trouble on the run" by boogying until daybreak (even so, Cooke could sing about "Having a Party" and break your heart with it); nearly everything Rawls sings about involves more intimate motions between two people. Cooke wants to dance the night away, Rawls just wants to love you all night long.

Rawls was out of commission for nearly a year after the accident, and elected not to return to the Travelers when he had recovered. He relocated to Los Angeles, where he got a chance to sing solo at a coffeehouse called Pandora's Box. He worked with two aspiring songwriter-producers, Lou Adler and Herb Alpert, on a scattered few singles on several very obscure labels (Shardee and Candix). But a bigger offer was looming. The producer Nick Venet (who is probably the "Nick, baby" whom Rawls asks to hand him his gin in "Rockin' Chair"), otherwise known for his work with Bobby Darin, heard Rawls and initiated the singer's long association with Capitol Records.

Rawls's first album was *Stormy Monday,* taped in February 1962, a pairing with pianist Les McCann, who was already in the forefront of the music that was becoming known as soul jazz. As with Cooke, one of Rawls's major inspirations was Billie Holiday; three songs from his first album were associated with Lady Day: "God Bless the Child," "Willow, Weep for Me," and "'Tain't Nobody's Business." It's noteworthy that both of these former gospeleers chose to sing "God Bless the Child," a song I can't imagine would be welcome in any church.

Stormy Monday joined a tradition of first-inning home runs by Capitol artists, following June Christy's *Something Cool* and Dakota Staton's *The Late, Late Show. Stormy Monday* is the culmination of what Rawls and Cooke—and Joe Williams and Billie Holiday and Dinah Washington and Arthur Prysock and Jimmy Scott—had been building toward for a while, the seamless integration of pop standards, blues standards, and jazz accompaniment. It's a record that everybody could love. Rawls and McCann refer not only to Holiday but also to Louis Jordan ("I'm Gonna Move to the Outskirts of Town"), Bessie Smith ("'Tain't Nobody's Business"), Ma Rainey ("C. C. Rider").

Over the course of his long-term evolution, Rawls's singing would grow slightly more frivolous—he would make interjections like "Baby" in the style of Sinatra and Darin, as well as gospelish embellishments—but his singing on the early albums is marvelously focused and intense. He followed *Stormy Monday* with *The Soul-Stirring Gospel Sounds* and then *Black and Blue,* a collection of big-band blues classics arranged and conducted by the brilliant but little-known Onzy Matthews. (All three albums were finished even before 1962 was over.) Drawing largely on the Count Basie and Kansas City tradition, Rawls proves himself to be a sensational successor to Big Joe Turner, Jimmy Rushing, and Joe Williams. He apparently liked the Eddie Miller blues standard "I'd Rather Drink Muddy Water" so much that, uniquely, he included it on both of his first albums, with trio on *Stormy Monday* and with full orchestra on *Black and Blue*—if anything, the second recording is even more exciting.

Here his singing is amazingly concentrated and focused. In 1966, he recorded another exceptional trio album that concentrated on the blues, *Carryin' On,* on which tracks like the blues "Mean Black Snake" are so strong that the album could have been released as *Stormy Monday, Part Two.*

Meanwhile, *Tobacco Road,* which extends the collaboration with Onzy Matthews, could have been called *Black and Blue, Part Two* (both albums were rereleased on a twofer CD together shortly after Rawls's death). From blues classics and bluescentric pop songs, Rawls and Matthews wisely branch out into popular standards associated with black entertainers, like "Georgia on My Mind" and a hard-rocking, up-tempo treatment of "Ol' Man River." He concentrates on swinging standards like "Street of Dreams," moaning the verse in the middle, Crosby-style, and there's a kick-ass version of "Rockin' Chair." There's also an homage to Armstrong (unissued until the CD era), on "When It's Sleepy Time Down South," which he opens with the bridge as verse (and eliminates the line about "Ol' Mammy" falling upon her knees—meaning to pray) and closes with a basso profundo that recalls both Armstrong and Al Hibbler.

Rawls's and Matthews's imaginations are further stimulated by "Blues for a Four-String Guitar," a very creative piece of work by film composer Elmer Bernstein with lyrics by Tin Pan Alley veteran Mack David. It's a very aggressive and imaginative jazz waltz that follows the strict rules of the blues—structually and harmonically—and also includes a bridge.

As the sixties wore on, Rawls was moving increasingly toward the mainstream—or rather what had been the mainstream a decade earlier—singing more and more out of the Great American Songbook. He never went all the way—there was never a *Lou Rawls Sings Cole Porter* album or *Lou Rawls Sings the Best of Broadway,* but his mid-sixties albums were a truly and gloriously eclectic blend of good songs from all kinds of sources.

At this point, his output was paralleling that of his fellow Capitol artist Nancy Wilson. After the death of Nat Cole, Wilson and Rawls were Capitol's leading black artists; both were equipped to go after all the demographics: black people, white people, young people, old people. They both recorded prolifically, doing mostly excellent standard songs with fine, jazzy backings. At the end of the decade, both plunged more fully into the youth market, with funk and soul hits rather than show tunes, but by then they had already recorded so much excellent music that EMI doesn't know what to do with all their good albums in the CD era.

As late as 2010, even the licensing specialist labels, like Collectors' Choice and Collectables (you see the theme here), have continued to ignore Rawls's terrific sixties LPs. Capitol has at least released two recommended CD samplers of Rawls's best work in this period (which include some duplication): *Spotlight on Lou Rawls,* which has key tracks from half a dozen albums, and *For You My Love,* a compilation of highlights from three albums: *Nobody but Lou, Your Good Thing (Is About to End),* and *The Way It Was,* the last of which teamed the singer with two outstanding arranger-saxophonists named Benny (Carter and Golson). Rawls is swingingly seductive on Carter's chart on Sammy Cahn's "If It's the Last Thing I Do," on which he both cooks and simmers, like a pot of gumbo slowly reaching a boil over a low flame. He's more agitated on "Squeeze Me," and strikes exactly the right note of curiosity on the early R&B hit "I Wonder."

But as with lots of other singers, by the end of the sixties Rawls was concentrating on jukebox material exclusively, and the marvelously multiculti feeling of his earlier albums was gone. He achieved his pop market breakthrough not only by singing, but by talking—it was as if no one had ever heard a black man speak on a record before. In 1966, he recorded *Lou Rawls Live,* which, in the spirit of Aretha Franklin's *Yeah!,* wasn't done live in a club or a concert hall but was taped in a studio with an audience of friends present. There were two monologues, one on each side of the LP, in which he talked about the Black Experience, making it sound as mean and grimy as possible, but also glamorizing it in a funny, reverse-psychology kind of a way. In the late sixties there were monologues of varying lengths on all his albums, usually leading into a song (as if on a live album) but separately banded on the vinyl so that listeners and DJs could include them or exclude them at their discretion.

Rawls's most extreme performance from this period is "Ol' Man River," from *You're Good for Me* (circa 1968), which has nothing in common with the 1962 *Black and Blue* reading. He sings it—and speaks it—every way possible for over nine minutes. It begins as a ballad, with the verse, then a funk backbeat starts and Rawls launches into a spoken monologue before he returns to singing the piece in a fast tempo that's more dramatic than swinging. He then sings it again as a soul-gospel number with a soul-gospel choir, going down to a low note—way deep in the bass-ment—in a manner that seems inspired equally by Frank Sinatra and Mahalia Jackson. In the last four minutes or so, Rawls's "River" becomes an anthem similar to Ray Charles's treatment, if even more churchified, and then becomes a funky dance number at the end—Oscar Hammerstein *au-go-go.* This "Ol' Man River" keeps on rolling for at least twice as long as it should, but one can only imagine how electrifying Rawls must have been when he performed it in person.

Rawls was now recording under the direction of producer David Axelrod, who increasingly steered him in a pop direction. "Dead End Street," which began with a full-dress monologue about wanting to leave the Windy City of Chicago, won Rawls a Grammy Award, and he also had his first major hit single with "Love Is a Hurtin' Thing." There would be others over the next twenty years or so: "A Natural Man" (1971), "Lady Love" (1978), and the best known, "You'll Never Find Another Love Like Mine" (1976).

None of these hits is particularly bad: "You'll Never Find" is a catchy and even memorable melody, introduced intriguingly by a sort of call-and-response duet between Rawls and the bass notes of a piano. The 1986 *Love All Your Blues Away,* the last of four albums he made for Epic beginning in 1982, showed that he at least could still sing. While side one consists of synthesizer soul, side two consists of four standards wonderfully arranged by Johnny Mandel and Jeremy Lubbock, and lovingly intoned by Papa Lou.

Still, in general there's little worth listening to from the seventies and eighties, which producer Billy Vera has described as Lou Rawls's "Disco-Vegas" period. It was Vera who put the singer back on the right track with three brilliant albums for the recently revived Blue Note label from 1982 to 1992: *At Last, It's Supposed to Be Fun,* and *Portrait of the Blues.* (There's also a fourth Blue Note album, *Christmas Is the Time,* a follow-up to his 1965 *Merry Christmas Ho! Ho! Ho!*). This is old-school soul at its finest, sympathetically produced by Vera and Michael Cuscuna, with both arrangements and repertory that fall in the happy spot between soul and jazz. "I'm Still in Love with You" was T-Bone Walker's best-known love song, as was "Chains of Love" (altoist Bobby Watson solos like Hank Crawford here) for Big Joe Turner, while "After the Lights Go Down Low" evokes Al Hibbler. Rawls resurrects three of bandleader Buddy Johnson's best-known hits, "Save Your Love for Me," "Fine Brown Frame," and "I Wonder Where Our Love Has Gone," his 1990 rendition being even more convincing than his 1968 recording with Benny Golson, as well as Lucky Millinder's "Sweet Slumber" and Dinah Washington's "This Bitter Earth."

One wishes that Rawls, like Dianne Reeves (who duets with him on the title track of *At Last*), had gone on to do an album for Blue Note every year or two from that point on. There were several new albums of religious music (*I'm Blessed*, 2001, and *Oh Happy Day*, 2002), but, alas, there were only two more notable recordings of jazz and standards, both with Vera producing.

Seasons 4 U (1998) returns Rawls to his early mandate of satisfying everybody: The set is an amalgam of pop vocals, soul, jazz, funk, and even classic rock. An album of seasonal songs (think Julie London's *Calendar Girl,* Eydie Gormé's *Love Is a Season,* or Bing Crosby's *Seasons*), Rawls alternates easily between "Blue Skies" (done in a playful Caribbean polyrhythm) and a highly soulful "Summertime." There are a few oldies that I didn't see coming, like "Singin' in the Rain" and Nat Cole's hit "Those Lazy, Hazy, Crazy Days of Summer." The latter is in a straight four, rather than a polka. This was a bad decision—they should have gone for "That Sunday, That Summer" instead.

Then there are a pair of latter-day pop standards that suit Rawls so well that it would have been disappointing if they weren't on there: Pete Seeger's "Turn! Turn! Turn!" and Benard Ighner's "Everything Must Change." The inclusion of two sunshine songs by the Beatles, "Here Comes the Sun" and "Good Day Sunshine," is an inspired choice: The latter is more or less in the same tempo as on the *Revolver* album, with the addition of a somewhat tacky choir. And he's at his all-time best with "Here Comes the Sun," reconfigured as a moody ballad with a trumpet solo cast in the spirit of latter-day electro–Miles Davis (as in "Time After Time").

Vera tells me that Rawls was ailing at the time they were recording *Rawls Sings Sinatra* (Savoy) in 2003; he knew he was on the way out, but refused help or even to tell anyone what was going on. He sounds considerably older than he did just five years earlier, but his heart—not to mention his rhythmic placement—is exactly where it should be. The voice has lowered considerably, but not bottomed out—he still is singing slightly higher than Prysock and Eckstine. In a career that lasted nearly fifty years, Lou Rawls hit all the right notes—and it's amazing and frustrating to think what Sam Cooke might have achieved had he been allowed to keep creating for that same span of time. Rawls recalled his old friend on *At Last.* He sings Ray Charles's hit "Two Years of Torture," and then Brother Ray himself crosses cadenzas with Rawls to pay homage to Cooke on Sam's "That's Where It's At."

Prior to this, the most important occasion when Charles and Rawls had sung on the same bill was at Sam Cooke's funeral. It seems appropriate that the three of them were united there.

Blossom's Buds and Dearie's Daughters

Barbara Carroll
Daryl Sherman
Ann Hampton Callaway

Barbara Carroll, Daryl Sherman, and Ann Hampton Callaway all have many things in common with Blossom Dearie as well as with one another. They are each equally well versed in both singing and playing the piano, and they also frequently write songs—Callaway being particularly successful in this regard. Of the three, Callaway is the one who might be described as the least traditional, and yet she, like Carroll, has spent time in the cast of a legitimate Broadway musical. And all three have, rather easily, bridged the worlds of jazz and cabaret.

Carroll can expertly talk-sing her way through almost any song, but she excels at involved, wordy texts that are essentially explained as much as sung—she talks at you friend to friend. I like Sherman best on happy, upbeat, sunny songs whereas Callaway excels at slow, sultry ballads. (I have a hard time believing Sherman has actually gone through "one whole quart of brandy" in the verse to "Bewitched" on *A Hundred Million Miracles*—likewise I am glad that Callaway, on her Ella Fitzgerald salute, did not attempt "A-Tisket, A-Tasket." I somehow doubt that AHC would be believable singing of an obsession with a little yellow basket.) Sherman has often, happily, been called upon to re-create the sound and songs of the late jazz diva Mildred Bailey (as on her 1996 CD *Celebrating Mildred Bailey and Red Norvo*), whereas, even though Callaway has recorded a tribute album to Fitzgerald (*To Ella with Love*), her Midwestern timbre actually reflects better the cool, restrained sound of Jo Stafford.

Carroll and Sherman prefer to kick it old-school, concentrating on the Great American Songbook, celebrating the virtues of swing and traditional jazz. Callaway fares best when she's allowed to bring at least a touch of the contemporary to her music and acknowledges more of the later developments in jazz and pop. All three women have long been making a vital contribution to the jazz-and-standards scene, not only in New York but all over the world, and, God willing, will continue to do so for a long time.

Barbara Carroll (born 1925)

If there's one word Barbara Carroll must be sick to death of hearing in descriptions of her music, it is "elegant." Of all the major performers of the twentieth century, only Fred Astaire and Bobby Short were more frequently described as "elegant." Here are some other words that will do equally well: classy, tasteful, and supremely melodic. By now, Carroll must be praying for just one critic to describe her as funky, soulful, and swinging, and come to think of it, those adjectives would, in fact, suit her just as perfectly as the now dreaded E word.

Sometimes she sings with a cool, restrained voice, but more often she just plays, with a keyboard style that recalls John Lewis in that it seems equally rooted in Bach and the blues. One of her earliest supporters was Leonard Feather (to his credit, a tireless champion of racial, gender, and geographic equality in jazz), who described her as the first important female pianist to absorb the influence of Bud Powell and the bebop revolution. Yet Carroll never let this pronouncement serve as a limiting factor in terms of her talent—over the decades she has played not only bebop and all varieties of jazz, but also every conceivable kind of pop—from entertaining at top cabaret rooms to appearing on the Broadway stage in the Rodgers and Hammerstein musical *Me and Juliet* (she later repaid the team by recording what must be one of the only jazz albums of the score to their hit show *Flower Drum Song*).

Born in 1925 in Worcester, Massachusetts, Carroll has spent her eighty-five years moving easily between what Dearie has described as East Side (cabaret) and West Side (jazz) nightclubs. She studied at the New England Conservatory in the early forties, and then spent the war years entertaining the troops with an "all-girl" trio for the USO. After arriving in New York, however, it took her longer than it should have to become established. Carroll has said that female pianists were still so unusual that it was, for a time, assumed that if you were a woman, you couldn't play jazz—especially of the modern variety. "When I first came to New York I couldn't get any work under using my real name. So I had friends that would send me to jobs as their sub, but they would tell the contractor to look for a 'Bobby' Carroll. By the time they realized that 'Bobby' was 'Bobbi' who was actually Barbara, it was too late." After they heard her play, Carroll was never fired, and eventually acquired a reputation under her real name and gender identity.

Carroll became a fixture on Fifty-second Street in its final years: She was the leader of her groups, whose sidemen included such stars as guitarists Chuck Wayne and Charlie Byrd and bassists Clyde Lombardi and Joe Shulman (her husband from 1954 to his death in 1957; she later married the former "sweet" bandleader Bert Block). Her trios and quartets provided accompaniment for such colossi as Paul Desmond, Stan Getz, and even Charlie Parker and Billie Holiday.

Carroll's earliest documented recording was as part of a studio band led by Ake "Stan" Hasselgard, the short-lived Swedish clarinetist who was both Benny Goodman's only protégé on his own instrument and probably the first person to play bebop on that instrument. Over the next few years she appears on many classic early modern jazz sessions, including a live recording at the Royal Roost (with J. J. Johnson, Lee Konitz, Cecil Payne, Buddy DeFranco, and Max Roach) in which she spells Bud Powell himself for one number, and a fabulous studio date (with Red Rodney, Serge Chaloff, Al Cohn, and Oscar Pettiford) that's been issued under both Chaloff's and Pettiford's names at different times.

Carroll, who in 1952 was still working exclusively as a pianist, appeared on Broadway in Rodgers and Hammerstein's flop *Me and Juliet* (1953), playing onstage, not in the pit.

In 1950, she recorded her first date as a leader, a date that included two originals, "Barbara's Carol" and "The Puppet Who Danced Bop." But she only began to sing on records when she signed to RCA Victor in 1953, a relationship that lasted approximately four years and seven albums, which were followed by an additional two for Verve in 1957 (including *Barbara* and the all-Gershwin *Funny Face*). Over the next four decades she would continue to record virtually unabated, two of her most enjoyable projects being heavily Broadway-oriented: a jazz piano version of *The King and I* (Kapp, 1960—how nice to be involved with a Rodgers and Hammerstein hit) and *Hello, Dolly!* (Warner Bros., 1964), which consists of six songs from that Jerry Herman hit and another six from Ervin Drake's well-remembered *What Makes Sammy Run*. Another Warner album called *Live* has her playing songs from *Cabaret*, *Fiddler on the Roof,* and other shows fresh in everyone's mind at that time.

There's an especially delightful moment that occurs every three or four songs in a Barbara Carroll performance, be it live or on plastic. You can hear her slow down slightly, and then play what will sound like the introduction to some famous standard, and then somehow a little birdie tells you that she's going to sing it. You hear that distinctive voice, as lean and spare as her playing is opulent but also as trim as her fingers themselves. By necessity she avoids those songs that are primarily displays of vocal virtuosity. Her Jerome Kern album, *All in Fun,* doesn't have her singing "Ol' Man River" (or playing it either, for that matter), but it does have her singing the title song, "All in Fun." Clearly she prefers the kind of story-songs that are more about the ability to convey a narrative rather than to hold a note.

That Kern album, recorded in 1996, may well be Carroll's best in terms of a special project; it's one of her only albums to use a full orchestra and strings (albeit only on some of the tracks). During the Clinton era, the political and economic conditions were apparently highly favorable in Estonia for recording large, symphony-sized string orchestras, a fact that producer Lisa Schiff took advantage of on albums with Carroll, Ann Hampton Callaway, and others; the string ensemble is especially effective behind Carroll's vocals. The second track is a medley of two songs that starts with "All in Fun" strictly as a solo—no trio, no orchestra, no strings, just piano and voice. From there, we move into "Love in Vain," in which all those elements are added. Carroll sing-speaks the lyrics (Hammerstein in the first, Leo Robin in the second) with perfect rhythmic placement and supreme credibility, ending the performance with the final 8 bars of "All in Fun."

With its string section, *All in Fun* is a Carroll rarity. Usually she works with just trio backing, and over the decades she has worked most frequently with Jay Leonhart, bass, and Joe Cocuzzo (and, more recently, Alvin Atkinson), drums. The albums *Everything I Love* (1995) and *One Morning in May* (2002) are not only a fine balance of vocals and instrumentals but of Carroll's trio with several remarkable guest horn soloists: trumpeter Randy Sandke on both, joined by clarinetist-tenorist Ken Peplowski on the latter. Her half-spoken, half-sung technique is especially winning on two songs on the latter album, in which the protagonist tries to talk the object of her affections into a state of coziness, Cahn and Chaplin's "I Could Make You Care" and Rodgers and Hart's "Can't You Do a Friend a Favor?" (from *A Connecticut Yankee*). In Carroll's dry New England accent, it's more a matter of persuasion than seduction, but having said that, I should note that the lady herself is highly persuasive.

It's possible to regard Carroll's singing as an afterthought. To this day she sings only one of every four or five numbers, whether in person or on a disc. Yet those vocals are an essential part of her appeal. If she were to renounce vocalizing and return to being a purely instrumental performer, I, and all her other fans, would surely miss it.

Her playing is, in itself, a marvelous tribute to the durability of the Great American Songbook. Carroll has the technique and skill of any great modern jazz pianist—Powell, Peterson, anyone you want to name—but she is more concerned than most with letting listeners recognize the tune. Like Ralph Sharon in his albums of various composers, she often outfits a song with new chord changes, but rather than obscuring the familiar melody, she highlights it and shows it off to best advantage. This is the opposite of standard practice for modern jazzmen, who more typically would keep the chord changes to "I Got Rhythm" but come up with their own new melody for it.

She could be said to redefine the concept of harmonic improvisation, in that she improvises with the chords while keeping the melody recognizable up front—she does the most daring things with the harmonies while letting you have all the melody you can eat. Her piano work is equal parts Bud Powell and Maurice Ravel.

For many seasons Carroll played about half the year—alternating with Peter Mintun—at Bemelmans, across the hall from where Bobby Short held forth at the Café Carlyle. A change in ownership resulted in her contract being terminated, an illegal move she contested in court. While I'm sorry she was treated so badly, I'm not distressed she's out of Bemelmans, which was a beautiful room but by the late nineties had degenerated into a horrible cigar bar where loud-voiced yuppies congregated to scream at one another and blow smoke in one another's faces. Of all the times I went to see both Mintun and Carroll in that room, I almost never actually heard them over the din of chin music or even saw them through the purple haze of nicotine.

Since her tactical retreat from the Carlyle, she's been seen and heard much more easily at Birdland (where she recorded *Live at Birdland,* 2005) and Dizzy's (setting of *Something to Live For [Live at Dizzy's],* 2008). The second album is especially rich in elegant Ellingtonia. For the last few years she's performed most Sundays at the Algonquin; all three rooms are much better listening experiences than the dreaded Bemelmans ever was.

However, wherever Barbara Carroll appears, she's definitely worth catching. She's proof that you can please everybody—from song fanciers who pooh-pooh jazz musicians for dispensing with the melody after 32 bars (or sometimes altogether) to jazz snobs who (often correctly) surmise that the musical level of most cabaret performances would have to work up to amateurish. If you want great melodies as well as great musicianship, to hear the songbook played and occasionally sung with wit and boundless imagination, Barbara Carroll offers evidence that you can have it all.

Both Daryl Sherman and Ann Hampton Callaway come from musical families (and they both have mothers named Shirley)—Sherman from the Cape Cod–Rhode Island–Boston area, and Callaway from Chicago. Daryl's father, Sammy Sherman, was a professional trombonist in the big band era, her sister is a music teacher based in New Jersey, and her Web site sports several amusing pictures of a Sherman family band, I'm guessing from the JFK era, with her brother Ben on drums and mother, Shirley Sherman, on bass.

Shirley Callaway is to this day a very respected singing teacher and vocal coach. Ann's father, Bill, is a former correspondent and television news personality for CBS-TV Chicago, and her younger sister, Liz, is herself an outstanding Broadway singer-actress. As children, Sherman and Callaway were drawn equally to singing and playing the piano, and were attracted to both jazz and show music; Sherman's father let her sit in at local Woonsocket, Rhode Island, gigs when she was twelve; Callaway's father gave her a guided tour of jazz history via his record collection.

The two eventually outgrew their hometowns, about ten years apart: Sherman in the mid-seventies, Callaway in the mid-eighties. As a newcomer in New York City, Sherman got in at the twilight of the greatest generation, working at Jilly's, where she met Sinatra himself, and singing for the last orchestra to be led in person by Artie Shaw. Callaway first recorded thanks to old-time producer Ben Bagley, a strict cabarateur you wouldn't think would have been interested in someone as cutting-edge as she is.

Sherman sings and plays almost constantly, alternating between upper-echelon hotel gigs, like the Waldorf (where she played one of Cole Porter's own pianos) and the Pierre, as well as rooms that bear a cover charge, like the Oak Room at the Algonquin and the Iridium. Much of Callaway's bread and butter comes from her mechanical royalties as a composer, having three songs sung by Barbra Streisand and the theme from the hit TV series *The Nanny*. (One of Callaway's set jokes in concert is that her accountant regards the theme to *The Nanny* as her supreme achievement.)

Daryl Sherman (born 1949)

Both Sherman and Callaway—like Carroll—have recorded for the now defunct After 9 Records, operated by Lisa Schiff, a credible producer, well fixed both culturally (being currently chairman of the board of Jazz at Lincoln Center) and politically. What is somewhat odd is that Sherman taped only one album for Schiff—but one of her finest, the 1998 *A Lady Must Live*, whereas Callaway cut four CDs on After 9: *To Ella with Love, Easy Living, Signature*, and a holiday record, *This Christmas*. This is

odd because you would think that Sherman would tend to fit the profile better than Callaway. The opening of *A Lady Must Live* is Ira Gershwin's similarly themed "One Life to Live," a song from a show about psychiatry and a denunciation of the concept of reincarnation—and with it a thumbs-down to all kinds of New Age concepts, both musical and metaphysical, and a reaffirmation of traditional values. "Give Me the Simple Life" similarly pooh-poohs the trendy and transitory; and what could exalt the glories of the past more fully than a tenor solo from the then seventy-five-year-old Frank Wess? She embraces traditions like swing and the songbook for no other reason than that they still work. As she sings in the rare second chorus of "A Lady Must Live," it's better to be an "escapist" than a "red tape–ist" (and Gershwin may well have meant that phrase to describe both a bureaucrat and a Bolshevik).

A Lady Must Live, produced by bassist Jay Leonhart, is one of Sherman's most perfect sets in other ways, too. There's a succession of songs beginning with the title track, and going through the aforementioned opener, "One Life to Live" (jaded), "I Wanna Be Bad" (naive), "When in Rome" (naughty), and "It's Love I'm After" (innocent), among others, in which Sherman mixes songs from the twenties to the fifties and maintains a careful balance between innocence and experience. Few other singers could do Helen Kane's specialty "I Wanna Be Bad" and keep their tongues out of their cheeks—that is to say, resist the temptation to camp it up. Even when Sherman sings of the downside of a love affair, she almost always seems to be coming to her material from the perspective of a true believer. In something as potentially sad as "Lover Man," she makes it plain that heartache can't exist without naïveté. Like Blossom Dearie before her, she keenly realizes that "When in Rome" would lose all its humor if she sang it at face value, from the perspective of a hip swinging chick. It's only when she makes it into a follow-up to "Always True to You in My Fashion" or "Confession"—singing about screwing around in a completely unspoiled way—that these songs really do what they are supposed to do.

Another trait that Sherman has in common with the cabaret crowd is a sense of scholarship. Her most famous gentlemen friends are two heavyweight scribes, the late trumpeter-author Richard Sudhalter and that encyclopedia who walks like a man, Dan Morgenstern. *A Lady Must Live* contains the rare second verse to "One Life to Live" as well as a lyric to Dizzy Gillespie's "Groovin' High." *Look What I Found* (1996) is titled after a long-lost Cole Porter song salvaged from Orson Welles's disastrous flop *Around the World in 80 Days*. *Jubilee* (2000) has her rescuing "Swingtime in Honolulu," which Ellington wrote for a Cotton Club production number in 1938. *Look What I Found* also contains her two most successful originals, "Simple as That" and "Something Brazilian," which has her waxing South of the

Border in the manner of Johnny Mercer's private secretary. About the highest compliment one can pay Sherman as a songwriter is that these pieces sound as if they could have been written in 1940. Thus, even when singing her own original songs, Daryl Sherman continues to seem part and parcel of the swing era.

Ann Hampton Callaway (born 1959)

I can't ever imagine Ann Hampton Callaway singing "Swingtime in Honolulu," and for more than one reason. As we've seen, the excavation and salvation of obscure songs is one of the tenets of cabaret. Even when a jazz musician rescues, say, a lesser-known work by Duke Ellington, like Branford Marsalis playing "I'm Slappin' Seventh Avenue (The Sole of My Shoe)" or even "Self-Portrait (Of the Bean)," he still never presents it like a hidden treasure—the way a cabaret singer would. One of the chief ways in which Callaway differs from Sherman, Feinstein, Marcovicci, Comstock, Haran, and company is that she expends less energy digging through dusty songbooks in dusty archives than on writing new songs.

Those two factors are why Callaway's three albums for After 9 are less successful than they might have been. On the one hand, Lisa Schiff seems not to have encouraged her to include any of her own songs, but on the other hand, neither did anyone bother to find any interesting older tunes. As a result, the three CDs are comprised of only the most obvious standards. At one point, "My Funny Valentine" became infamous as the most overdone song in history; today "You'd Be So Nice to Come Home To," "Come Rain or Come Shine," and "Skylark" are actually much more overdone, and they're all on *Signature*. I don't think I can possibly hear them again, no matter how imaginative the arrangement. Callaway is generally successful in making them sound fresh and new (even though she wasn't encouraged to take the songs as far out as, say, Cassandra Wilson), but still one yearns to hear something at least a little new or new-old, in the cabaret, or offbeat, way.

Which isn't to say that there aren't some beautiful moments in Callaway's After 9 albums. "Twisted" (on *Signature*) manages to embellish on Annie Ross's classic original by means of thoughtful electronic collage and new original lyrics, while "Pick Yourself Up" adds another level to Mel Tormé's treatment of the Kern tune, which the Velvet Fog himself sang in a tribute to Fred Astaire.

To Ella with Love is her most traditional production, utilizing a full orchestra and strings the way most of Fitzgerald's classic albums do (the difference being that these days one has to travel to the former Yugoslavia to be able to afford such amenities). The odd result of the Fitzgerald record is that it reveals Callaway's indebtedness not to the subject of the album's title, but rather, as mentioned earlier, to Jo Stafford. On tracks like "I'll Be Seeing You," Callaway

matches Stafford's timbre almost exactly; in fact, if there's any singer I'd like to hear Callaway pay tribute to, it's Stafford.

Before the After 9 series, Callaway taped two solo albums (*Ann Hampton Callaway* and *Bring Back Romance*, plus *Sibling Revelry* with Liz Callaway) for DRG Records, and it's worth noting that Hugh Fordin, hardly a slave to fast-fading trends of the moment, permitted the inclusion of some contemporary and original songs. The first album contains a remarkable original, or semioriginal—it's also another Cole Porter item, "I Gaze in Your Eyes": Callaway supplied music for a Porter song that had only survived as a lyric with no tune.

My own favorite of Callaway's albums is from the middle of her career—in between DRG and After 9—the 1994 *After Ours*, produced by Danny Weiss, one of the chief gurus of the smooth jazz movement. Callaway balances between very familiar standards, including the unavoidable "My Funny Valentine," "Teach Me Tonight," "Old Devil Moon," and other songs that are rites of passage for aspiring jazz singers. "You Are My Sunshine" is a country standard that Sheila Jordan brought into the jazz world, though there's no aural evidence that Callaway actually listened to Jordan. "The First Time Ever I Saw Your Face" is a seventies pop opus that I will probably never warm up to, but Callaway comes closer than anyone to getting me to like it. There's only one Callaway original, "The Music You Leave Inside My Mind," a convoluted title but a good song, and more surprisingly, she didn't come up with an original song to go with the evocative album title, *After Ours*. (Come on! Get with the program!)

The ghost of Miles Davis is a constant presence, from the playing of trumpeter Randy Brecker to Callaway's open, spare phrasing on songs associated with the late jazz demagogue, most notably "It Never Entered My Mind." I had previously thought that Oscar Brown's lyric to "All Blues" should never be sung by anybody other than the lyricist himself—even the old smoothie Grady Tate can't really do anything with it, and I like Grady Tate—but in this case Callaway does persuade me to change my mind. Davis's real benediction here is "Time After Time," not the Cahn-Styne/Sinatra classic, but the 1984 pop hit by that goil who just wanted to have fun, Cyndi Lauper. The song was the closest thing to a hit single that Davis enjoyed in the last few years of his life. Taking a tip from him, Callaway was the first major jazz singer to perform it, and it's become a jazz standard as of late, sung by Cassandra Wilson, among many others. Callaway and Weiss wisely open *After Ours* with "Time After Time," thereby ensuring that people will keep listening right through to the end.

I mentioned earlier that there are two reasons why Ann Hampton Callaway is unlikely to sing "Swingtime in Honolulu." It has nothing to do with a phobia about grass skirts but points to another way that Callaway has more in common with Jo

Stafford than Ella Fitzgerald. Like Stafford, Callaway keeps a firm grasp on her sense of humor, especially in the recording studio. Like Diana Krall, she has realized that humor doesn't record especially well, and the most successful of her discs are the ones where she presents herself as dark, sultry, and torchy.

Which isn't to say she doesn't *have* a sense of humor—far from it. Just as Stafford created alternate personas to express her comedic side (Darlene Edwards, Cinderella G. Stump), Callaway does most of her really funny stuff not in her music but in her intersong patter and the other extramusical aspects of her show. In fact, she's hotter than a pistol, cracking one-liners and doing impressions as well as a

longish vaudeville routine in which she composes a song on the spot based on random phrases called out by the audience. ("Shoes!" "Dick Cheney!" "British Petroleum!" "Lady Gaga!" "iPad!" "*American Idol!*" "Dame Edna!" "Health care reform!" "*Avatar!*" "Bob Gottlieb!")

As of 2010, Sherman, Callaway, and even Carroll, who turned eighty-five in January, continue to steadily record and release new albums. I have enjoyed their work so much over the decades that it seems unlikely anything new they do will top what they already have, but who knows? With luck they'll continue to surprise me, time after time.

Rock Goes Standards!

From **Connie Francis** to **Rod Stewart**

Nineteen fifty-five was the year that rock 'n' roll—an old music with a new name—announced that it was here to stay. The year began with a landmark event: On January 14, deejay and impresario Alan Freed hosted "The Rock and Roll Jubilee Ball," an all-star concert that featured headliner Fats Domino—at that time the biggest name in the music—along with Big Joe Turner, Clyde McPhatter and the Drifters, and many others. In a very literal sense, this could be considered the first rock 'n' roll concert ever: It was the first time Freed had actually used the words "rock" and/or "roll" in the title of an event. In fact, he had only recently begun using the term at all, as Domino's biographer Rick Coleman points out: He had been calling his radio show "Moondog Party," but after a lawsuit leveled against him by a performer named "Moondog" Hardin, Freed was legally prohibited from using that word. He then renamed his show "Rock and Roll Party," employing a term that went back more than twenty years, to Tampa Red's "My Daddy Rocks Me (With One Steady Roll)" and the Boswell Sisters' "Rock and Roll."

By 1960 there were two kinds of pop music—one for the World War II generation, at the time in their thirties, one for their baby boomer progeny, then in their early teens. Yet from the beginning, there were attempts to bring the two together. A few years earlier, Sinatra had slammed rock 'n' roll in a rather mean-spirited way, and Presley, courteous Southern boy that he was, got the better of the encounter with a gentlemanly, well-spoken response. Again, it was curious: Sinatra was the one with the bad attitude, Presley was the one who was respectful of his elders—it seems hard to imagine that, of the two, Presley would be perceived as a "rebel" while Sinatra was the "establishment." Yet in 1960, to commemorate Presley's being mustered out of the army, these two leaders of their respective camps performed together on television. When Sinatra sang "Love Me

Tender" and Elvis ripped into "Witchcraft" in a medley together it became clear that as enjoyable as this outing was, the two schools of pop were destined to remain in, if not open warfare, at best an uneasy détente.

But one point that's often forgotten is that the first generation of rock 'n' rollers grew up on Sinatra and Crosby and Ella Fitzgerald—how could they not, when that was virtually all that was heard on the radio when they were growing up in the forties and early fifties? (It's not like they had much of a choice in the matter.) Though many of the sixties rockers later claimed to have been inspired by Leadbelly and Muddy Waters, they surely heard more Nat King Cole and Doris Day in their homes when they were kids in postwar suburbia. A great many rock stars said they loved classic pop, even as the new sounds they were making would, in the long, long run, almost completely obliterate it. John Lennon, who famously professed his admiration for Presley and Fats Domino, later said that the Beatles' early hit "Please, Please Me" was inspired by Bing Crosby's "Please," and years later, the Fab Four included a homage to Der Bingle (and imitation thereof) in "You Know My Name (Look Up the Number)." (They also quoted "In the Mood" in the coda of "All You Need Is Love.")

Once in a while, a performer steeped in both idioms would capture both audiences. Bobby Darin was the most celebrated: He seemed to be deliberately working in different genres and gaining fans in all age brackets. Yet Ray Charles achieved the same thing more organically, integrating all the genres and races, winning white kids and black kids plus their parents—by the early sixties, he had won over their country cousins as well.

The album format had been established as the medium for the Great American Songbook, even for rock and R&B performers. There were two kinds of albums for rock and soul stars in the early days: collections of "Greatest Hits" and other previously recorded material, and albums of standards. It was Fats Domino who set the precedent for setting older standards like "My Blue Heaven" and "Blueberry Hill" to a rock 'n' roll beat.

Domino's first major follower in this area was Connie Francis (born 1938), the most successful female singer of the early rock era, who primarily marketed her music to teenaged white girls. Hers was a kinder, gentler rock 'n' roll, and she made a point of rocking up old songs in a manner inspired in equal parts by Domino ("Who's Sorry Now?") and the multiple-voice-track hits of Patti Page ("Carolina Moon"). She seems to have realized that a whole album of Brill Building pop like Neil Sedaka's "Stupid Cupid" would wear very thin, and so too would twelve old songs tricked up with triplets, in the early rock fashion. The only thing that would work was to try to sing the great songs in roughly the idiom in which they were conceived. Thus, Francis's second album is *The Exciting Connie Francis* (1959), arranged and conducted by Ray Ellis and done in roughly the same manner with which he would accompany Johnny Mathis. It seems certain that she genuinely liked songs like "Rockabye Your Baby with a Dixie Melody" and "Time After Time." In other words, this wasn't some idea she went along with for the sake of marketing.

Side one of *Exciting* is mostly up-tempo, including "The Song Is Ended" in a swinging four, and side two is mostly ballads, most interestingly a vocal version of Jackie Gleason's *Honeymooners* theme, "Melancholy Serenade." Throughout, Ellis's orchestrations are busy, busy, busy, as if he's afraid to let the singer stand or fall on her own—as if he's got to keep propping her up. There are times when her intonation and time are just right, as is her inherent understanding of what the story and the music are all about. Then, too, there are times when she loses it. This is a reminder that back in these early days, rock was still recorded like classic pop, with the singer and the band working live together in the studio; overdubbing and tape splicing were possible but rarely done. This approach gives *The Exciting Connie Francis* a natural feeling that's very welcome, and makes one more willing to accept the occasional flat note in exchange.

At times Francis can be predictable: On "Rockabye," you wait for the moment when she's going to get big; on "Time After Time" you anticipate the instant the choir will come in and Francis will go into her high head voice. It's not a harsh criticism to say that when she's still only twenty, her singing isn't quite fully mature. "Melancholy Serenade" is more whiny than melancholy, although "Time After Time" is quite winning. Some songs seem more like a series of vocal effects strung together than a heartfelt interpretation of a lyric. With work, Francis might have gone on to more fully master the adult pop idiom, although in the long run she proved content to be virtually the biggest thing in the youth pop

world rather than a second-rate singer of first-rate songs.

Apart from Bobby Darin and Ray Charles, the finest singer of standards to come from the pop-rock–doo-wop side was easily Sam Cooke (1931–1964), whose merging of gospel, jazz, soul, and pop made him a potential male answer to Dinah Washington, except that he died even younger than she did, and more tragically. We discuss Cooke's work in greater detail in another section, but for now suffice it to say that "You Send Me" (1957) is one of the more enduring records of the early rock era. Like Darin, Cooke seemed to have been loved by everybody—black, white, young, old—and there's no telling how far he might have gone had he not been murdered in 1964.

The curse of Cooke and Darin, who both died in their thirties, seemed to affect other brilliant entertainers of the era who seemed capable of making great strides in both idioms, such as Jesse Belvin and Marvin Gaye, both of whom also died violent deaths at a tragically early age. In his short life, Belvin (1933–1960) was best known as the composer of the doo-wop hit "Earth Angel," but at the time of his death in a car accident he was beginning to be recognized as a singer in his own right, and of jazz and standards as well as pop; RCA even gave him a shot at a full-fledged album, with an orchestra full of star West Coast players helmed by Marty Paich.

Marvin Gaye (1939–1984) was raised in the House of God, in which his father was a minister. This faith draws on a wide range of influences: the form is very Southern Baptist, but the content is Jewish; it's kind of the opposite of Jews for Jesus, more like goyim for Moses. Gaye's music similarly encompassed a wide range of influences and styles. As a youngster, Gaye sang in doo-wop groups like the Rainbows and the Moonglows, but when he signed to Motown in 1961, his first album, *The Soulful Moods of Marvin Gaye,* consisted almost entirely of standards. It's not quite a jazz album, though, at least not as the term is conventionally defined, as Gaye is backed up by what sounds like a standard Motown rhythm section without horns and other accoutrements; unfortunately, there's a lot of echo chamber reverb going on, so much so that the sonics actually prevent his voice from sounding natural or intimate—this is the vocal equivalent of pomaded hair.

Still, at twenty-two Gaye is remarkably polished, and projects the idea that he knows the songs (like "You Don't Know What Love Is," miscredited to two female composers, "Dawn" [Don] Raye and "Jean" [Gene] DePaul) well enough to take chances with them, personalizing them with urgent, insistent riff patterns and repeating key phrases in the gospel style. Gaye made other albums of similar material, such as *Hello Broadway* and *A Tribute to Nat King Cole.* Compared to the other short-lived pop-jazz crossovers, like Cooke, Darin, and Belvin, Gaye lived to a ripe old age, being forty-four when he was shot by his psychotic father in 1984.

Although Berry Gordy, founder and patriarch of the Motown operation, brought forth a new "sound of young America" in the sixties, he made it known that he also appreciated the sound of an older America as well. His career ambition was to bring an act into the Copacabana, the nexus of mainstream acceptance and respect. When the Four Tops first came to the label in 1964, their first album—two years before their Motown megahit "Reach Out (I'll Be There)" (which even jazz musicians like Hank Mobley covered)—was more in the tradition of the Mills Brothers than what would become the classic Motown group sound. Gordy occasionally even signed older stars like Billy Eckstine and Sammy Davis, both heroes to the black community, although their Motown albums were far from their best work. Even years later, the Four Tops were singing traditional show tunes like "Climb Every Mountain," with a lead singer sounding more like Johnny Mathis than James Brown. Even Brown, the Godfather of Soul himself, made at least one outstanding album of standards, *Gettin' Down to It*, in which his key inspiration (as the inclusion of "Strangers in the Night," "All the Way," and "Time After Time" suggests) was obviously Sinatra. This was around the same time that Sinatra himself came up with "That's Life," his own response to the defiant, blues-based attack of Ray Charles and James Brown.

Motown's most remarkable effort in the adult pop field was *The Supremes Sing Rodgers and Hart*. Whereas most of the Supremes' singles were exquisitely crafted and fine-tuned, their albums, contrastingly, were just ground out like sausages. *Rodgers and Hart*, however, was an exception. It began with a TV special called *Rodgers and Hart Today*, in which an enterprising television producer had the idea of bridging the Generation Gap by bringing together a brace of youth pop stars (Count Basie, fronting his orchestra, was the only old-timer) and putting them to work on the best show tunes of the thirties. The Mamas and the Papas were hardly the ideal interpreters of "Glad to Be Unhappy," but one of the highlights was the combination of Darin and the Supremes, backed by Basie's band, swinging "Falling in Love with Love." The results were so well received that Gordy sanctioned an entire two-LP set of the Supremes doing Rodgers and Hart, originally released as a single album, with all the tracks (and extras besides) available on a 2002 CD.

The Supremes Sing Rodgers and Hart gives us tracks like "The Lady Is a Tramp," rendered in a swingingly adult pop manner, with arrangements that seem influenced by Nelson Riddle and Billy May. In these charts, most of the focus is on lead singer Diana Ross, commanding attention with a sharp, Eartha Kitt–kind of a voice, while the other two Supremes, Florence Ballard and Mary Wilson,

are negligible, mere backup singers at best. Other tracks, like "Mountain Greenery," are rendered in much more of a sixties go-go psychedelic dance club style, but for all that, are still not bad—Rodgers and Hart have been subjected to much worse kitsch than this. (Rodgers, great sport that he was—not!—even consented to pose for a picture with Ross, Wilson, and Ballard, and the legendary song and dance man Gene Kelly wrote the notes.)

By 1970, it was less natural for "stars of young America" to address the traditional songbook. Whereas Marvin Gaye and the Supremes had grown up on Nat Cole and Ella Fitzgerald, the rock and soul stars who followed them had, in fact, grown up on Marvin Gaye and the Supremes. By this time, there were no longer two kinds of pop music, simply because the music industry was refusing to acknowledge that classic pop even existed.

Still, now and then your occasional kiddie pop idol would give it a shot: The first major star of the sixties (other than from Motown) to cut a standards album may have been Ringo Starr, whose first post-Beatles project was *Sentimental Journey*, a collection of twelve songs mostly from the World War II era recorded in the fall of 1969. Starr is hardly as polished as his countryman Matt Monro in singing "As Time Goes By" and "Whispering Grass," nor does he need to be. *Sentimental Journey* succeeds instead as an affectionate postcard from one generation to another, and it's easy to believe the oft-told tale that Ringo primarily recorded it as a special present for his mum. (On one of George Harrison's last albums, *Brainwashed*, he recorded a simple and effective treatment of Harold Arlen's "Between the Devil and the Deep Blue Sea.")

In 1973, Harry Nilsson (very much a post-Beatles singer-songwriter) released the successful *A Little Touch of Schmilsson in the Night*, a collaboration with none other than that most austere—and least rocky—of great orchestrators, Gordon Jenkins. Nilsson was gloriously untroubled by his complete lack of chops and concept as to how these songs were supposed to be sung. Though unconventional, the results of both albums are, in a kinky way, strangely enjoyable. Neither Starr nor Nilsson has any kind of technique (at least not for this material), but they bring considerable charm and they sound like they're being themselves, rather than just aping the icons of an earlier era.

In 1981, Carly Simon became the next important singer-songwriter to take the plunge with *Torch*. Considering that Simon's uncle, the critic and producer George T. Simon, undoubtedly helped expose her to pre-1960 popular music, this was a natural move on her part—certainly in 1981, almost a decade after Starr and Nilsson, she wasn't following a trend. (Unlike, say, Barbra Streisand, who would periodically release an album of standards or show tunes but only after some other diva had recently retested the waters.) *Torch* would be the first of four standards albums, so far, done over a twenty-five-year period, including *My Romance* (1990), *Film Noir* (1997), and *Moonlight Serenade* (2005).

The results of the four albums are uneven. (Some of it justifies Gary Giddins's description of *Torch* as "ersatz corn.") For some unexplained reason, *Torch* opens with an original song, "Blue of Blue." If Simon was trying to write something new in the tradition of the classic torch songs or blues of the forties and earlier, she hasn't succeeded. Some of *Torch* sounds like she's hedging her bets by doing older songs in a rock-era way, with 16th-note triplets and rock-hard drumming; the accompaniment at times sounds like the *Saturday Night Live* band. But once in a while she gets it right, and it seems that every album in the series is at least slightly better than its predecessor. *My Romance* comes closer, particularly on a thoughtful collage of "By Myself" and "I See Your Face Before Me" (the Schwartzes, composer Arthur and his son, the deejay Jonathan, were old friends of the Simons), and she's very good to Richard Rodgers here as well.

Film Noir was produced by another singer-songwriter, Jimmy Webb (he and Simon wrote the original title song together), who tries to be even more grandiose than Nilsson and Gordon Jenkins. The overall sound here takes its cue from Miklós Rósza and the other hardboiled Hollywood composers of the forties. Every number sounds like "The Love Theme from Something-or-Other," but *Film Noir* doesn't suffer because of it—the album certainly has a style and a direction. Torríe Zito's fine arrangement of "I'm a Fool to Want You" is so big and near-symphonic that Simon's vocal is followed by an additional instrumental track entitled "Fools Coda." "Spring Will Be a Little Late This Year" is a duet with Webb himself (who sounds strangely like Simon's ex-husband James Taylor here) and "Two Sleepy People" has her crossing cadenzas with John Travolta. No, he can't sing (*Grease*, anybody?), but this too is a venerable Hollywood tradition. *Moonlight Serenade* is the most thoroughly listenable and authentic album, almost too much so, opening with the Glenn Miller theme orchestrated essentially in the Miller arrangement with strings added. There's nothing incredibly original here, but she's true to the material and her voice, phrasing, and overall interpretations are well ahead of most rock-era divas who revisit the prerock past.

Simon's four standards albums are certainly well ahead, musically, of the work of the rock star who brought the standard songbook briefly back into the foreground in the mid-eighties. The most extreme case of a contempop star delving into standards was the trilogy of albums made by Linda Ronstadt, which amount to some of the stranger phenomena of the Reagan era. Thanks to Ronstadt, Johnny Burke and Cole Porter were on the charts again, and arranger Nelson Riddle, after a lifetime of what he regarded as being taken advantage of by recording

companies and star singers, was able to die a wealthy man and almost even a happy one. The benefits were considerable, until one actually took the time to listen to the music. Singing jazz and standards in any credible way takes considerable musicianship, and though Ronstadt had a pretty voice and certainly some kind of chops—she could hit high notes and hold them—the poor girl was a fish totally out of water. There's more to technique than vocal ability, and Ronstadt was sorely lacking what it took to convincingly sell a lyric or make a melody seem believable.

To personalize a lyric and make the listener feel that it's real, a singer, at least in the Sinatra-Riddle aesthetic, has to occasionally sing a note not in the written melody but taken from the chord change. And unless the singer has had schooling, whether in a conservatory or on the job, there's no way she can know what notes to hit. (Ronstadt supposedly went to Riddle's ex-lover Rosemary Clooney for help, asking her to record songs a cappella for her to study and emulate.) Although surrounded by the finest orchestrations played by the finest musicians and singing the finest pop songs ever written, Ronstadt still sounds completely clueless.

Yet the records did some good, putting standards on the map for a few years, and perhaps setting the scene for the nineties. In the years of Clinton and Bush II and beyond, the standards have been increasingly part of the contemporary music scene: The nineties began with Natalie Cole's blockbuster salute to her father and then Tony Bennett's conquest of MTV and the Grammys. Yet the best news was the mass-market success of younger singers who invariably include the songbook in their music, including Cassandra Wilson, Dianne Reeves, Michael Feinstein, Harry Connick Jr., and especially Diana Krall.

Still, the the most significant new pop star of the MTV generation turned out to be none other than Tony Bennett. One of the things that make him so beloved among Gen Xers is not his Italian crooner smoothness, out of the tradition of the young Sinatra and Damone, but that rasp in his voice, reminiscent of Louis Armstrong as well as those Italian comic geniuses of music, Louis Prima and Jimmy Durante. Bennett's Armstrong chops make him palatable to those who claim the Mississippi Delta and the South Side of Chicago, not Tin Pan Alley, as the wellsprings of pop.

The nineties would be full of raspers, but while Bennett came by his rasp honestly, Dr. John aka the Night Tripper aka Mac Rebennack cultivated his by aping the genuine rhythm and blues pioneers of old New Orleans, such as Professor Longhair. Michael Bolton (the name is apparently an Indian word meaning "wicked hair") achieved his rasp by what sounds like a direct imitation of Dr. John; we might describe this as standing on the shoulders of midgets. Steve Tyrell, a very successful producer-turned-vocalist, has sold millions of CDs in the twenty-first century singing standards in a genuine Southern accent that's also reminiscent of Dr. John.

A recent rasp belongs to the London-born rock star Rod Stewart, who turned sixty in 2005 in the middle of recording four volumes of *The Great American Songbook*. The arrangements sound like the kind of garage bands my stepfather used to horse around with in Brooklyn in the seventies, country-type bands with a heavy and unsubtle emphasis on the afterbeat; every chart Stewart sings has this guitar-driven chunka-chunka thing going all the time. The whole deal is essentially just his raspy voice and those heavy guitar chunks, dressed up with synthesized strings and occasional horns.

Stewart's four *Great American Songbook* albums make him the Ronstadt of the twenty-first century, and like her, he's a mixed blessing at best. Yes, he's introducing these songs to some new listeners, although there are a lot more singers, both young and old, doing this material now than there were twenty years ago. Unlike Ronstadt, Stewart (whose albums are frequently produced by Steve Tyrell) tries to sing the songs his own way rather than knock off Sinatra and Clooney. It's an admirable attempt, but neither the singing nor the orchestration is very good. Still, thanks largely to Stewart, Gershwin et al. are back in the marketplace. (Rod bless the child that's got his own.)

The success of Stewart and Natalie Cole obviously inspired other seventies rock-pop stars to experiment with standards: Barry Manilow and Bette Midler also belong in this group. Midler's arrangements in her tributes to Peggy Lee and Rosemary Clooney are at least well done, and her heart is obviously in the right place, but her singing, while not as embarrassingly bad as Ronstadt's, is ho-hum at best. Midler originally was known for singing contemporary songs and the occasional standard with at least a degree of camp excitement, but these later tribute albums have absolutely no energy or charm. She's neither the best nor the worst singer of this music; she is strictly a middler.

Among Friends, quite possibly the best album of jazz or standards by a rock star, was released in 2002 by Jeff Healey (1966–2008), a Canadian "blues-rocker" (as most accounts describe him), who was never as well known in the States but is regarded as a national treasure in his native land. Singing takes third place on this set, after his Djangolike virtuoso guitar solos and his rougher-hewn trumpet; his vocals were like his horn playing, longer on imagination and drive than on chops, which in a sense is what blues-based singing is supposed to be about. Working with a band of ace young traditionalists, Healey resurrects one terrific forgotten song of the thirties after another, such as Shirley Temple's "Bright Eyes" and Red Allen's melancholy "Midnight Blue." Alas, Healey died of cancer at age forty-one, making him the most recent multigenre mix master

to leave us at a tragically early age (after Darin, Cooke, and Gaye).

Tony Bennett himself figured in the transition of a contemporary pop star to go standard time, who, as it happens, is also Canadian (like Healey). Kathryn Dawn Lang (born 1961), who is billed as "k.d. lang" (in lowercase letters, like e. e. cummings and eden ahbez), is an Alberta-born chanteuse who started as a fairly traditional country and western singer. She released her first album in 1987, just around the time that Bennett was beginning his so-called comeback. In 1992, around the time of her fourth album, she came out of the closet at roughly the same moment that she transitioned from country to mainstream pop rock. In 1994 she appeared on Bennett's wildly successful *MTV Unplugged* album, and the two have been bosom buddies ever since. In October 2001, she opened for Tony at Radio City, doing a set of standards (which most of us missed because the security was so stringent in the immediate post-9/11 weeks that it took forever just to get inside the theater). She also guested with Bennett on his 2001 *Playin' with My Friends: Bennett Sings the Blues,* and their relationship was consummated, so to speak, in 2002 with *A Wonderful World,* the only full album of boy-girl duets in either career.

Lang and Bennett are simultaneously an odd and a wonderful mix. She has far greater chops than any other "outsider" to come to the standard repertory in midcareer, and what's really surprising is that she knows her harmonies. Lang can embellish a melody with the appropriate notes in a way that suggests she's been singing and studying jazz and standards her whole life, as if she had grown up a devotee of Sarah Vaughan rather than Patsy Cline. But what she doesn't have is time: She has never been able to sing with even the vaguest idea where the beat is supposed to be. When she sings a rubato ballad she sounds great, but obviously her lack of time is a detriment in addressing the music of Armstrong, the man who invented swing. Lang tends to float way over the notes, and this becomes even more noticeable when she works with Bennett, who, as he gets older, depends more than ever on his amazing sense of rhythm. Still, the charisma between them—which is more apparent in concert or on TV than in a nonvisual medium like a CD—is formidable. When she works with Bennett, he has enough swing and energy for the two of them, but she quickly becomes tiresome when singing solo. Lang is truly amazing on a tempoless tune like "Don't Smoke in Bed," even if much of the time she sings as if she's stoned.

As we've seen, almost since gospel music was perfected in the thirties, followed by rhythm and blues in the forties, many of the greatest exponents of these twin channels have expanded into pop, most famously Dinah Washington and then, a generation or two later, Aretha Franklin. Etta James is a big-voiced soul-blues singer who often addresses the standards, generally with very satisfactory results. James even took one standard, Harry Warren's "At Last," onto the charts in 1961, and is certainly more responsible for the song being known today than Glenn Miller, who introduced it. (Just to confuse everybody, the R&B-jazz singer Etta James charted with "At Last" around the same time that the blues-jazz singer Etta Jones charted with another older ballad, "Don't Go to Strangers.")

Etta James's *Mystery Lady: Songs of Billie Holiday* (1994) is typical of her work in the jazz and standards field. She just sings Holiday's songs; she doesn't try to replicate the older Lady Day's sense of high tragedy. Instead, she fluctuates between an approach that we would associate with soul and R&B and what sounds more like a jazz approach. On "Ghost of a Chance," the rollicking arrangement is a little bit too busy, but in general the charts by musical director Cedar Walton are exemplary. Tenorist Red Holloway channels Ben Webster and James's own sound is hard and uncompromising. Her first chorus on "I'll Be Seeing You" is all guts and glory, but by the time we reach the second, we've all collectively earned the right to relax with a little bossa nova.

Patti Austin is yet another soul diva who's taken the standards route. The 2002 *For Ella* is one of many posthumous tributes to Ella Fitzgerald, with arrangements by Pat Williams, best known for the Sinatra *Duets* and a string of terrific Steve & Eydie albums in the sixties (he was their finest musical director after Don Costa). The disc was recorded with the WDR Orchestra of Cologne, and there's only occasionally a sense that someone is holding something back, that this isn't a full-time jazz singer-band relationship, or that someone is a little uncomfortable with someone else.

Austin sings transcriptions of several of Fitzgerald's most famous scat features, "Mr. Paganini" and "How High the Moon," done pretty much as Fitzgerald did them, right down to "Beginning to See the Light" on the first and "Ornithology" and "Rockin' in Rhythm" on the second. Williams has devised a winning, fresh intro to "Moon," which alternates choppy, boppy trombones with sustained reeds, but no one is going to succeed in an attempt to best Fitzgerald at the game of scatting over a big band. Rather, Austin's most effective tracks are those where she pares down to the piano and stresses the basic essentials, as on "The Man I Love." The most winning cut is a song no one particularly associates with Fitzgerald (even though she sang it on *The Cole Porter Songbook*), "Miss Otis Regrets." Austin invests it with a pronounced gospel feeling, and goes all the way with it, almost as if she's singing about the ritual murder of Jesus rather than that of "Miss Otis"—or perhaps as if Miss Otis were being lynched for racial reasons rather than for homicide. It may well be the best version of the song since the ironic readings by Jimmie Lunceford and Alberta Hunter. (Her follow-up album, *Avant Gershwin*, 2007, unfortunately was all smoke and no fire, and disappointingly short on Jazz Age soul.)

When I was first listening to jazz and standard singing in the seventies and eighties, the state of the art seemed very fragile indeed, as if it might all just blow away. The aftereffect of the nineties is that, thanks largely to the efforts of Bennett, Cole, Krall, Wilson, Feinstein, and even the must-to-avoid Ronstadt and Stewart, though this music gets a relatively small piece of the pie, it's not going to go away, at least anytime soon. Like love, the songbook is here to stay.

Dynasty: Freddy Cole and Natalie Cole

The family was originally named Coles, and by the time they moved to Chicago from Montgomery, Alabama, in the early twenties, there already were two sons who were soon to achieve prominence in the musical world. The oldest, Eddie (1910–1970), had gained a measure of fame as the bassist with Noble Sissle's orchestra—a leader and a band cherished by the black community—in which the older Cole (or Coles) rubbed shoulders with such stars as reed colossus Sidney Bechet and the young Lena Horne. The second brother, Nathaniel (1919–1965), would eventually become world famous as Nat King Cole. The precocious Nat was given the chance to record for the first time at the age of seventeen; he brought his own band into Decca's Chicago studio, but the record company issued the results as by "Eddie Cole's Swingsters," simply because Eddie was better known. The third brother, Ike (more formally Isaac, born in 1927), also sang and played piano. After Nat's initial breakthrough during World

War II, both Eddie and Ike had the chance to record and perform with their own groups: Eddie cut R&B sides for the Philadelphia-based Gotham label in 1949, and Ike made an album of vocals and piano under the name of Ike "Fats" Cole; he also made a few Scopitone music videos in the sixties.

Thus the Coles founded a musical dynasty well before the last of the five siblings was even in long pants.

Freddy Cole (born 1931)

Freddy Cole was born Lionel (the name he later passed on to his own son), twelve years after his increasingly famous older brother; their relationship paralleled that of Bing Crosby and his much younger brother Bob. Each younger brother grew up with his older sibling already a star, and though their musical gifts were not the equal of their older brothers', each was able to launch a substantial career. Freddy was born and raised in Chicago, and grew up not only hearing the music of his brother but that of the entire spectrum of jazz and pop. Thanks to his family, he didn't just admire Ellington, Basie, and Hampton, he got to know them all personally. Nor was Nat the only singer who influenced him; he was particularly taken with Billy Eckstine, by then singing with the big band led by Nat's hero, Earl Hines. "He was a fantastic entertainer," the younger Cole recalls. "I learned so much from just watching and being around him."

Although Freddy seems to have had more formal musical education than any of his brothers, he was less of a jazz keyboard virtuoso than the remarkable Nat. In addition to music, Freddy also had an early career as an athlete, and was nearly good enough to go into the National Football League. In 1951 he moved to New York to study at Juilliard, and then went on the road with Earl Bostic's big band. In 1952, he recorded for the first time, landing an R&B hit for the Chicago-based Topper label, "The Joke's on Me." When this proved popular enough for Columbia Records to sign him to its R&B subsidiary, Okeh, his second hit was a revival of the Ink Spots' prewar hit "Whispering Grass."

Over the years, Freddy Cole continued to work as a pianist and singer, recording intermittently all over the world. His first album was "*Waiter, Ask the Man to Play the Blues*," done for Dot in 1959; then came sets for British Decca in 1976 and the New York–based Muse, the California LaserLight, and the French-owned Sunnyside. In 1972, he settled in Atlanta, where he recorded for Audiophile and his own imprints, First Shot and Dinky Records. One theme of his early albums, meaning those he made before he turned sixty, was a certain awkwardness with his position as the third most famous member of his immediate family; from the mid-seventies, the new star of the Coles was his niece, Natalie. Freddy recorded albums with titles like *The Cole Nobody Knows* and *I'm Not My Brother, I'm Me*. (The latter is also the title of a song that contains the lines, "My brother made a whole lot of money / But I sing the blues.")

Although Freddy and Nat Cole were cut from the same musical cloth, there are substantial differences in their musical makeup. Most important, career-wise, the older Cole was very nearly a prodigy, leading his first band and recording at seventeen and putting together the trio that would change the course of music a few years later. Freddy, on the other hand, had managed to support himself as a first-rate pianist, singer, and occasional recording artist for well over forty years before he made any sort of real impact upon the musical world. His breakthrough occurred around 1993, when he began working with the producer and impresario Todd Barkan. Together they launched a series of recordings that finally captures the magic that is uniquely Freddy Cole's (even though there are samples of his brother's repertoire on every release). It wasn't until he reached his mid-sixties that Nat's younger brother truly came into his own.

Whereas Nat was capable of all manner of moods, from high energy to intense romanticism, Freddy excels at what he refers to in his live shows as his "invitation to relaxation." Virtually everything he sings or plays is relaxed and easy, and even when he flies into a swinging up-tempo, it's more of a gentle, foot-patting rocker than an all-out, superintense screamer. (In this respect, Freddy is the polar opposite of Nat's other major living disciple, pianist-singer Buddy Greco, who injects raw, hyper energy into everything, even his love songs.) Freddy Cole is more laid back and easygoing than any figure in the jazz-pop spectrum with the possible exception of those unflappable Italo-American crooners Dean Martin and Perry Como.

As mentioned, Freddy was never the keyboard colossus his brother was. Producer Barkan wisely features his piano and trio but also supplements the singer with a well-chosen cadre of star pianists—most notably Cedar Walton, Cyrus Chestnut, and John di Martino. Yet Cole has perfected a piano sound that, if not the most technically proficient, is entirely perfect for him. No one can play for Cole better than Cole himself. My favorite example is "Something Tells Me" (a 1958 Marvin Fisher song recorded by Nat as a single), which Freddy included on his 1994 album *Live at Vartan Jazz*. Cole's playing here is precisely perfect; he lays down exactly the right chords, the right blend of rhythmic and harmonic support—his piano playing is a delight in and of itself. It's telling that on *Music Maestro Please* (2007), Cole's major collaboration with a famous pianist, even though Bill Charlap is playing throughout the album (and Charlap is my favorite pianist working today), I would still rather listen to Freddy accompany himself. There are better pianists in the world (even in Freddy's own family), but there's no one who plays better piano.

The Freddy Cole albums of the nineties and beyond have a feel that's entirely different from the classic Nat Cole recordings of the previous generation. In fact, both Diana Krall and John Pizzarelli Jr. sound much more like direct King Cole disciples than Freddy does. Freddy has a more contemporary jazz sound that saturates his entire oeuvre; his voice in his sixties and seventies is deeper than his brother's ever got to be in his thirties or forties. (Except, that is, at the very end of Nat's life, when the cigarettes he had been smoking too many of began to give his voice a basso quality.) Freddy possesses a sound that Chris Connor, in one of the testimonials offered on the cover of *A Circle of Love*, astutely described as a "deep purple mood."

Since at no point in his life did Freddy ever have the keyboard or vocal technique of Nat—that microscopically perfect intonation—he cultivated a style that doesn't require it. His music is based on a lower-key approach; it's more about mood than technique. Having lived so much longer than Nat, he's had the opportunity to perfect the craft of hiding his craft.

The Nat Cole project that Freddy's work has the most in common with is the classic 1957 vocals-and-combo set *After Midnight*. Freddy and Barkan, however, have had over a dozen albums in which to develop that sound to the highest possible degree, albums filled with the *After Midnight*–"deep purple" mood in which his very mellow voice works with a shifting cast of instrumentalists and a brilliantly selected and arranged repertory of songs.

The 1999 release, *Legrand Freddy*, collects all the Michel Legrand melodies that Cole had previously recorded and adds a few new ones to concoct a songbook album. One wishes that he would do the same with the subset of songs that he has recorded from the repertoire of his older brother. He makes a point of not doing Nat's blockbuster hits ("Mona Lisa," and so on), but he's performed many of the more obscure gems of the Cole canon, and these constitute some of his most delightful tracks: "To the Ends of the Earth," "Candy," "There, I've Said It Again," "Wild Is Love," "Never Let Me Go," and quite a few on *It's Crazy,* including the title track, plus "Meet Me at No Special Place," "That's All," "Send for Me," and "An Old Piano Plays the Blues." (Curiously, one song I've never heard Freddy sing is the one that he has told me is his all-time favorite of his brother's recordings, namely "Strange." Written by Marvin Fisher and Jack Segal, this song was done by Nat and Nelson Riddle, but *strange*-ly enough, the Nat Cole track is hard to find on an American LP or CD.)

As good as he sounds on his brother's songs, one reason I especially love Legrand *Freddy* is because none of the selections was recorded by Nat. In general, Barkan and Cole have made a commendable effort to find worthy songs not only from the golden interwar years but also from the sixties and onward; it's safe to say that no one has made the music of Michel Legrand sound Legrander: He even makes the surreal and spacey "Windmills of Your Mind" sound warm and willing. Legrand's melodies can sound minimal and repetitive, but at the same time they're lush and rhythmic, and Cole's low-key, relaxed brand of jazz complements them ideally. (Oddly, so did Jack Jones's high-energy, high-romance treatment of "Windmills" on his Legrand album of twenty-five years earlier.)

The winning streak for Cole shows no sign of running out, even after he celebrated his seventy-fifth birthday with a special engagement at Dizzy's Club in Jazz at Lincoln Center in October 2006. (He recorded a live album there, *The Dreamer in Me: Live at Dizzy's,* two years later.) In 2005, Cole, like many veteran vocalists before him, began working with High Note Records, and since then he and Barkan have released one basic and essential Freddy album (*This Love of Mine,* 2005), a tribute to a colleague (*Because of You—Freddy Cole Sings Tony Bennett,* 2006), a collaboration (*Music, Maestro Please,* with Bill Charlap, 2007), a live album (*The Dreamer in Me,* 2009), and his most recent, a salute to his origi-nal inspiration, Billy Eckstine, which is scheduled be released in the fall of 2010. Freddy Cole has not only been waving the banner high for his illustrious family name but for the entire field of jazz and standards. No singer, old or young, was more consistently excellent during the Clinton, Bush, and even the Obama years.

Natalie Cole (born 1950)

Nat Cole and his second wife, Maria Cole, had five children: Carole ("Cookie"), Natalie (nicknamed "Sweetie"), their only son, Kelly, and, lastly, the twins, Casey and Timolin. Natalie was born in 1950 and made her recording debut in the company of her father and older sister when she was not quite four, on "Ain't She Sweet" (which, surprisingly—considering that it's the only genuine nondoctored or spliced duet between Nat and Natalie—has never been reissued).

In the seventies, Natalie Cole entered that elite group of second-generation pop stars whose ranks also included Nancy Sinatra and Liza Minnelli. She had considerable success in what was then known as dance music, although I don't know enough about it to tell you whether her hits of this era should be described as R&B, soul, disco, or some combination of all three. What matters is that in the earlier part of her career the younger Cole seemed determined to sing anything but her father's music and was a highly successful exponent of the youth pop style of her day, landing such hits as "This Will Be" (1975), "I've Got Love on My Mind" (1977), and "Our Love" (1978). Doubtless she would have gone on to become an even bigger star, but she spent most of the eighties dealing with drug addiction and other problems that she relates in her highly readable memoir, *Angel on My Shoulder.*

In 1988, she landed a further hit, a cover of Bruce Springsteen's "Pink Cadillac." However, earlier in the decade she'd already taken a tentative step in the direction that would determine her later career. More or less as a lark, in the early eighties she did a concert tour in conjunction with Johnny Mathis in which she paid tribute to her late father. To be honest, most of us old-time King Cole fans were dubious: Natalie had rejected her father's music and only seemed to be turning to it as a last resort now that her career was at low ebb. Still, by the time she recorded "When I Fall in Love," a Victor Young standard associated with Nat (on her 1988 *Everlasting*), it was clear that a change of direction was in the wind.

In 1991, happily, we had occasion to change our tunes. That was the year she released *Unforgettable,* in which she took the final plunge and came up with a first-rate, fully realized tribute to her father's music. Most of Nat's classic albums—and those of Sinatra, Fitzgerald, etc.—were recorded in no more than three days (they could have been done even more quickly, were it not for union regulations).

It took Natalie months and months to see *Unforgettable* through from concept to completion, and the process involved a battery of producers and arrangers. But even though it seemed as if the production exemplified everything that was excessive about the state of pop album creation in the last decade of the century—it probably cost as much to produce as everything her father ever recorded put together—the end easily justified the means.

Unforgettable was a sensational pop album, in which Natalie Cole established herself as, so far, the only star since Bobby Darin who could switch easily between youth pop and classic pop. What made Elektra Records very happy was that the title track, an electronically crafted duet between father and daughter, became one of the biggest-selling singles of the era. (Unlike most of the tracks on Frank Sinatra's *Duets,* the record that *Unforgettable* inspired, the Nat-Natalie duet is still heard on all kinds of pop radio formats.) But if the title song was the breadwinner, the rest of the album was the real meat-and-potatoes, with the younger Cole singing generally swinging new treatments of songs associated with her father, arranged by such giants of modern jazz orchestration as Johny Mandel, Ralph Burns, Marty Paich, and Bill Holman.

With this record, Natalie Cole emerged as the only pop star of her generation who could credibly sing the Great American Songbook, in a whole other class from Linda Ronstadt, Carly Simon, Harry Nilsson, and all the others who had already tried it and would try it again in the future. Cole reinvented herself as a pop-jazz chanteuse in the great tradition—if not on the level of Fitzgerald or Vaughan, at least worthy of mention in the same breath as Gloria Lynne or even Nancy Wilson. In contrast to those sultry sisters who would come along in a few years, led by Diana Krall (who would share Cole's main producer, Tommy LiPuma), and more recently Norah Jones, Cole has a sunny upbeat sound, with highly precise diction reminiscent of both her father and her uncle, and a light tone more suggestive of the former than the latter.

That Natalie Cole is part of the contemporary pop world—even if she can credibly sing her father's music—is indicated by a line in her memoir in which she criticizes her record company for releasing the follow-up album, *Take a Look,* only two years after *Unforgettable.* It was a far cry from the days when Nat Cole and his contemporaries would release at least three LPs a year. Perhaps because her albums, done in the piecemeal style of other contemporary pop projects, are so slow in production, Cole has essentially made only a handful of noteworthy projects since *Unforgettable,* including *Take a Look* (1993) and *Stardust* (1996), and a very worthy Christmas project, *Holly and Ivy* (1994), done in the same swingingly retro (as opposed to retro swing) style.

The follow-up records are every bit as good as *Unforgettable.* Like the man she calls Uncle Freddy, Natalie alternates between songs associated with Nat and other standards, although unlike Freddy, she makes less of an effort to find doable songs written in recent decades. (In addition to celebrating her dad—most notably on an evocative "Calypso Blues"—she also becomes a one-woman Lambert, Hendricks & Ross on *Take a Look.*) In general, it seems that the greatest possible compliment you could pay the younger Cole is if you happened to randomly tune in to one of these four albums on the radio, you would in all likelihood assume you were listening to something actually recorded in the late fifties.

In 2002, Natalie Cole reunited with Tommy LiPuma for *Ask a Woman Who Knows,* in many ways the finest album of her entire standards cycle. In it, she continues to use the past in a creative way, sometimes taking older records for a model: On "Like a Lover," she is one of the few contemporary singers to tackle Dori Caymmi's samba in the original very fast dance tempo (Mark Murphy and others sing it as a superslow ballad). On "I Haven't Got Anything Better to Do" she uses the 1967 Carmen McRae arrangement as a starting point, and rather than changing anything significantly, she merely seems to be trying to outdo or at least match McRae in clarity of the lyric and emotional intensity. Whether or not she succeeds is open to discussion, but it's a laudable effort and a truly running vocal. The most entertaining track may be "Better Than Anything," the marvelous jazz waltz associated with Irene Kral, in which Natalie gets jiggy with some girl-girl action with Diana Krall. *Ask a Woman* is, overall, one of the few vocal CDs of recent years that I can listen to repeatedly from start to finish.

In 2008 she released another worthy swing-style album, which despite the title—*Still Unforgettable*—covered a wide range of standards beyond her father's. In all, Natalie Cole turned out six generally first-rate CDs in seventeen years. As I say, that's a mere fraction of what her father (who cut seven excellent albums in 1950 alone) recorded in that amount of time, and roughly half of what Freddy has done since the nineties. But, given the criteria of the current pop market, perhaps that's all we can ask for.

The obvious tragedy of Nat King Cole is that he died so young—as much as he accomplished in his short lifetime, it's a no-brainer that he could have achieved much more had he not been felled in his prime at age forty-five. The good news—or part of it anyhow—is that there have been other Coles to extend his legacy.

Contemporary Male Jazz Singers

Allan Harris
Kevin Mahogany
Kurt Elling

"There's been a resurgence in jazz singing," as Kevin Mahogany told *Jazz Times*'s Chuck Berg in 1993, "but for the most part it's the ladies who've received the attention." But one result of the recent revival of interest in vocal jazz and the popular song is the appearance of guys. The period from the mid-sixties to the mid-eighties was probably the most fallow in the history of jazz and it's hard to think of even one worthwhile new male vocalist who emerged in these years. By the late nineties, things were definitely better. In the interim, both Al Jarreau and then Bobby McFerrin had briefly entered the arena as jazz performers with jazz albums, but very quickly both of them switched over to related fields that apparently interested them more, Jarreau to pop and what some call smooth jazz, McFerrin to a very original, intriguing kind of music that contains elements of jazz (as well as classical and pop), but which neither he nor anyone else would describe as jazz.

In the nineties, however, three worthy male singers appeared: They are all stars on the jazz circuit and have made many valuable recordings. Still, none of them has become a major star, known to the world beyond the Blue Note, and of the three, one has thus far only recorded for self-produced, foreign, and independent labels and has yet to do an album for an American major.

In order of appearance: Kevin Mahogany, Allan Harris, and Kurt Elling. It's telling that they were born in different parts of the country and that each has settled in a major jazz center: Mahogany in Kansas City (and more recently Boston), Harris in Harlem, and Elling in Chicago. They come from very different backgrounds: Before making the decision to concentrate on singing, Mahogany was both a saxophone player and a music teacher, while Harris was a jock, and Elling, God help us, was a theology student.

Similarly, each has claimed a specific part of the jazz heritage as his own territory. Mahogany's is the blues; even when he's scatting or crooning a ballad, you can hear that the blues are where his roots are. Harris's strength is power and energy; he can take the most intimate Billy Strayhorn tone poem and still make it exciting. Elling's thing is restless and even reckless experimentation with the power of the sung and spoken word. I've heard detractors of all three of these gentlemen speak of these factors as if they were flaws: Mahogany is somehow enchained by the blues rather than empowered by them, Harris works too hard to make every number a loud showstopper, and Elling dwells too much in his own head. In my own listening experience with the three of them, I have been present on occasions when their individualities have been liabilities, yet most of the time they are assets, and Messrs. Mahogany, Harris, and Elling have made a substantial contribution to the art.

Allan Harris (born 1958)

Virtually every jazz singer of the last forty years has grown up with *John Coltrane and Johnny Hartman*. All three singers in this group have been profoundly influenced by it, and Mahogany and Elling have both recorded full-length tributes to Hartman. Considering that *Coltrane-Hartman* contains the single most famous modern-era performance of a Billy Strayhorn ballad, "Lush Life," and that Allan Harris has made a specialty of Strayhorn's music, it's a cinch that he knows the album well. Naturally, most singers have paid more attention to Hartman's contributions, but Harris actually seems much more influenced by Coltrane: It isn't Hartman's tenderness and vulnerability we hear in him so much as Coltrane's big sound and thunderous, rafter-shaking excitement.

Strayhorn is, to say the least, an interesting performer to apply this approach to, since his music was prized above all for its gentleness and sensitivity. And since Harris is the rare singer to have dedicated so much of his energies to Strayhorn's music—on many occasions he appeared in joint programs with the composer's biographer, David Hajdu—it makes for a fascinating dichotomy: Harris's energy with Strayhorn's tenderness. Even when doing the Strayhorn songbook, or in the comparatively exposed setting of a duo with pianist Kerem Görsev, Harris's singing is more about intensity than intimacy.

Apart from Coltrane and Hartman, Harris also shows a stylistic empathy for the music of Nat King Cole, coincidentally the first and most important interpreter of "Lush Life." In the decade following the success of Cole's posthumous blockbuster hit revival of "Unforgettable," the electronically collaged duet with his daughter Natalie, Cole enjoyed an influence on young singers unprecedented even in the peak of his fifties and early sixties fame. In addition to the seemingly millions of artists who now seemed to be doing tribute records, at least three important singers came solidly out of the Cole camp: Diana Krall, John Pizzarelli Jr., and Harris. Each of them seemed to pick up on different aspects of Cole's. Pizzarelli reconciles the apparent contradiction that a jazz musician and pop singer could be one and the same person. Harris, especially in the earlier years of his career, absorbed more of Cole's actual sound, his pure sonic texture, even if he had not yet tried to inhabit Cole's ballad territory.

When I first heard him, Harris didn't sound as if he was deliberately imitating Cole, but more as if the sound of Cole's voice was so ingrained in him, so much a part of what his definition of singing was, that he couldn't even conceive that there might be some other way to sing. He even sounded like Nat King Cole on songs that Cole never sang, or were even written after King's death, such as "The Windmills of Your Mind." Fifteen years later, the Cole influence is still present in Harris's singing, even if it's not as omnipresent as it once was.

Harris told me, around that time, that he knew he couldn't sing a ballad as well as he could swing an up-tempo—but that he was working on it. He said that male singers mature more slowly than female singers, largely because men, in general, are less in touch with their emotions than women. It was a prescient observation for Harris, who was in his early thirties at the time. I had heard only one male singer express a similar opinion previous to that, and that was Tony Bennett.

Harris was born in Brooklyn in 1956. His mother played classical piano, an aunt sang opera. He studied classical guitar from the age of twelve, by which time he was already making the long schlep uptown to the Sunday afternoon shows at Harlem's Apollo Theater. When Harris was sixteen, his family moved to Pittsburgh (Strayhorn's hometown), and he also lived in Miami for a time before resettling back in upper Manhattan. (Local papers in both Pennsylvania and Florida claim him as a hometown talent.) Harris has never been identified with a major label or a major talent agency, but, admirably, has forged a career as a headliner (with the aid of his wife of thirty years, Pat) on a grassroots level.

Harris's recordings start with his 1992 *Setting the Standard,* recorded in Miami, with (apparently) local musicians, in settings that range from strings (possibly synthesized) to Dixieland. His voice has a touch of Johnny Mathis in his own Nat Cole phase on "If I Only Had a Heart," which is neither gentle nor sentimental but riotous and rollicking, and even "It Might as Well Be Spring" is a thunderous, Ray Charles–like jazz waltz—it might as well be "Busted."

In the mid-nineties, Harris made two fine albums for the Dutch Mons label, *It's a Wonderful World* (1995), and *Here Comes Allan Harris and the Metropole Orchestra* (1996); both primarily use arrangements by the Dutch orchestrator Rob Pronk. The first was taped in New York with an all-star band (largely appearing courtesy of other labels) and the second in Pronk's more typical setting with Amsterdam's Metropole Orchestra. Harris has also recorded *Cross That River*, an original song cycle (and/or musical theater project) in which he portrays an African American cowboy in the Old West (Herb Jeffries would be proud).

Harris spent much of the late nineties working on his Billy Strayhorn project—I must have heard it at three different clubs—and recorded it at last in 2001 for his own Love Productions, as *Love Came:*

The Songs of Strayhorn. At this point, in the long wake of David Hajdu's fine biography of the composer, all of a sudden Strayhorn was the subject of what seemed like dozens of songbook and tribute albums. It has to be said that Harris's excellent album, which co-starred two simpatico sidemen in the brilliant pianist Eric Reed and tenor saxophonist Don Braden, was one of the most original, not least because of the outgoing, extroverted nature of Harris's general approach.

Fine as *Love Came* is, I actually like the way Harris sings Ellington better than his Strayhorn efforts. He joined with the outstanding cabaret singer K. T. Sullivan in October 2006 at the Oak Room, in a show that was mostly Ellington, and around the time of the Ellington Centennial he sang on two first-rate European tribute albums: *The Music of Duke Ellington* by the Rias Big Band (Germany)—mostly new arrangements of familiar Ducal chestnuts—and *Duke Ellington's Sacred Music,* an ambitious two-CD re-creation of original Ellington scores, co-starring American jazz singer Michelle Hendricks (daughter of Jon) and major trumpeter Jon Faddis.

Harris excels in both, but he's especially compelling on the *Sacred* collection: The force and the fury of his interpretations find a better outlet when they're directed at "Jesus" rather than "baby." In fact, the whole hundred-minute *Sacred* project is an Ellington delight from start to finish, with Harris taking charge on a majority of the tracks, and easily improving on some of the original singers in the actual Ellington Sacred Concerts. He really kicks it into high gear on "In the Beginning God," "Ain't but the One," and "Somethin' 'Bout Believing," to name three highlights. Even though *Duke Ellington's Sacred Music* isn't exactly an Allan Harris album, it may represent the singer's finest work on wax thus far. On "In the Beginning God," Harris precisely nails what Ellington had in mind, combining reverence with irreverence and devotion with dry wit in a way that few singers could have captured.

The first time I heard Harris, he struck me as a fine current-day subject of his majesty Nat King Cole, and finally, with *Long Live the King* (recorded live at the Kennedy Center in Washington in 2007), he brings it full circle, back to Cole. Considering that Nat Cole was his first love, one may wonder why he waited so long to do this album, but the proof is in the singing: Harris might not have felt worthy of honoring the ballad side of Cole's legacy until this point. He at last delivers consistently worthy love songs, like "The Very Thought of You," "I'll Be Seeing You" (not part of the King's royal canon, but who cares?), and especially "A Blossom Fell." The swingers, like "Straighten Up and Fly Right" and the opener "It's Only a Paper Moon," are as lively and exciting as Harris has led us to expect his work to be, but it's the love songs where he's made the most improvement.

As long as Harris keeps singing the music of

Ellington, Strayhorn, and Cole at this level, I intend to keep listening.

Kevin Mahogany (born 1958)

Even though Kevin Mahogany has lived elsewhere, he remains firmly associated with Kansas City; not only did he grow up there and use that city as his home base for most of his career, he famously appeared in the 1996 Robert Altman film of that title. He began studying music there as a very young child, concentrating on the reed family, starting with the clarinet and eventually making a specialty of the baritone saxophone. (It was only fitting that Mahogany should focus on the largest of the commonly used saxes, since he himself, in addition to having one of the biggest voices in jazz, is also an individual of imposing physical size.) By the age of fourteen, he was no longer taking saxophone lessons, he was giving them.

After college, he worked in a variety of pop bands around Kansas City, although singing—and singing jazz in particular—occupied more and more of his attention. He also reckoned, with a certain degree of calculation, that this was a particularly good time to try to make his mark. He reasoned that there hadn't been a male jazz singer of note in many a decade: Mark Murphy turned fifty in 1984, Mel Tormé was sixty the year after that. Mahogany also felt more at home as a scatting vocalist than he had as an improvising instrumentalist: "I could think of lines to play, but I couldn't connect what I was hearing in my head to what I was playing with my fingers fast enough," he told me, "but while I couldn't do that on the sax, somehow I was able to do it as a singer." In 1992, he traveled to New York with the intention of landing a record deal and wound up coming to the attention of Matthias Winckelmann of Enja Records.

In interviews, Mahogany often sounds as if singing were an afterthought, but his singing actually suggests otherwise. His voice is large and roomy; he's most comfortable as a big-voiced baritone, but he can also go both higher and lower. You can tell he loves the deep bassos like Billy Eckstine and Arthur Prysock as well as the many falsettos of doo-wop and soul.

Mahogany's first album, *Double Rainbow*, was released on Koch in June 1993. His output in his first ten years of recording (1993–2002) consists of a total of seven CDs. There were the three for Enja, *Double Rainbow, Songs and Moments* (1994), and *You Got What It Takes* (1995). As was widely predicted in the jazz press, especially after a boffo review from Whitney Balliett of *The New Yorker,* Mahogany was picked up by a major label, Warner Bros., where the singer taped three sets with producer Matt Pierson: *Kevin Mahogany* (1996), *Another Time, Another Place* (1997), and *My Romance* (1998). After a hiatus, he returned in early 2002 with *Pride and Joy,* done for the Cleveland-based Telarc label. He's also made several guest appearances, such as on *It Don't Mean a Thing* with drummer Elvin Jones and *Pussy Cat Dues*, a program of Charlie Mingus compositions done with the WDR Orchestra of Cologne and several of the great bassist's close associates.

In general, the high points of Mahogany's output are the first and last of these seven projects. His Enja releases are more purely unhyphenated jazz, and the second, *Songs and Moments,* is to me the most enjoyable because it uses a larger-ensemble format and challenging arrangements from Slide Hampton and Maria Schneider. The title track, as arranged by Fraulein Schneider, is one of my favorite recordings of the nineties, being one of the rare records from that decade which upon contact with my eardrums infuse my entire being with the pure aural pleasure usually inspired only by the best tracks of the sixties and earlier. The combination of Mahogany's deep baritone chops, offset by Schneider's lush setting, as well as three female background singers who sound like an African children's choir, is a potent and effective one. It also doesn't strike me as the least bit odd that a singer whose key strength is the blues should achieve his finest hour with a song by Brazilian master Milton Nascimento.

The overall quality of Mahogany's work did not increase with the presumably larger budgets provided by Warner Bros. The first two WEA albums sound better now than they did then, but on the whole they're a nervous mix of smooth jazz, soul, and straight-ahead jazz. Granted that the idea of mixing these genres is not inherently a bad one, and if anyone can pull it off, it's Mahogany, who has considerable experience in all of these fields. While the idea is good, the mix itself is uneasy, but there are exceptional songs—and moments—on both. Mahogany's recasting of Fats Domino's "I'm Walkin'" (on *Kevin Mahogany*) is compelling, and while his "Still Swingin'," a flagwaver for the entire jazz tradition, isn't a great song, it allows him to create an exceptional scat solo.

Mahogany sings the glories of the scat tradition more effectively on *Another Time,* particularly on "Goodbye, Pork Pie Hat," which uses a lyric by Rahsaan Roland Kirk (rather than the more familiar text by Joni Mitchell). "Parker's Mood," a duet with pianist Cyrus Chestnut, finds Mahogany touching an inner nerve; he sings King Pleasure's famous lyrics about a funeral trip to Kansas City with a considerable amount of bravura.

Upon receiving the advance copy of Mahogany's third and last Warners album, *My Romance*, I didn't know whether to expect it to be great, since it promised to be a package of love songs (all standards except for three more up-to-date items by James Taylor, Lyle Lovett, and Van Morrison). On the other hand, the presence of Bob James and Kirk Whalum, two of the smoothest jazzers around (the former as musical director), led me to worry that it might be less than marvelous. Even though I would rather Cyrus Chestnut had remained throughout the eleven tracks, James here, fortunately, is only smooth with a small "S." Mahogany had concluded *Another Time* with a growl on "Kansas City," and one expects him to open *My Romance* with similar sounds on "Teach Me Tonight"—after all, the song has long been the province of those like Dinah Washington and Joe Williams who combine blues with balladry. Instead, he teaches us tonight with some of the sweetest whispering he's ever done, and stays in that tender mood through all eleven tracks. The singer is especially compelling on two tunes associated with Billy Eckstine, "Everything I Have Is Yours" and "I Apologize"—again, instead of trying to give Mr. B a run for his money in terms of bass-baritone bombast, Mahogany keeps his chops feather-light, and to borrow a phrase one finds in the drugstore, ultrasensitive.

Artistic differences with Warners seem to have kept him from releasing any new product between 1998 and 2002—apparently, he wanted to go in more of a soul direction while Warners and producer Pierson wanted him to remain firmly in the jazz mainstream. There was one new CD in these years, *Pussy Cat Dues,* the aforementioned Mingus salute in which he sings on six out of the eight cuts, recorded in 1995 (pre-Warners) and released in 1999.

Pride and Joy (2002) shows that he's spent the intervening years productively indeed. *Mahogany Sings Motown* would have been a more descriptive title, but the material itself isn't as remarkable as the simple way he's found of blending vocal jazz and soul pop, using just enough of the rigid Motown rhythms and static pop harmony. The first thing to go is the smooth jazz element: Rather, Mahogany makes the songs of Stevie Wonder, Marvin Gaye, and Smokey Robinson (not to mention the Temptations, Gladys Knight, and others) work with a straight-ahead acoustic jazz rhythm section (some tracks also employ an a cappella vocal group) and with such jazz components as instrumental solos (by trumpeter Jon Faddis) and the star's own scat improvisations. "Never Can Say Goodbye" gives me considerably more pleasure than the original hit by the Jackson Five and "Tears of a Clown" proves that some of Smokey Robinson's songs are so good that they don't even need Smokey.

In 2004 and 2005, Mahogany independently released two albums. *To Johnny Hartman* was the official recording of a program I'd already heard him sing live many times, and, not surprisingly, provides a platform to show that his ballad work has steadily improved. *Kevin Mahogany Big Band* (also on Mahogany Music) contains no end of surprises, not least of which is the opening version of "Moonlight in Vermont," laden with heavy funk backbeats and fusiony touches that suggest the inspiration of Weather Report rather than Frank Sinatra. This was followed by "It Don't Mean a Thing (If It Ain't Got That Swing)" done more like Tito Puente than

Ellington, and not at all bad. Most of the rest of the package is more in the old-school big band style, and highly creatively so, as in Mahogany's thoughtful remakes of the Basiecentric blues numbers "In the Evenin' " and "Centerpiece." Overall, it's an excellent album, and makes it somewhat distressing that Mahogany hasn't released anything now in five years.

Mahogany's idea of blending "traditional" jazz singing—balladeering and scat—with soul and R&B is a good one, one that he could constructively spend the rest of his career refining and perfecting. In spite of occasional slight pitch issues and, for a time, a predilection for smooth jazz, Kevin Mahogany has been one of the most creative and interesting performers on the contemporary scene.

Kurt Elling (born 1967)

Is Kurt Elling, like, (a) a way-out cat who has "goofed to wig city," (b) some space cadet marooned in the outer reaches of the hiposphere, or (c) a worthy young stud who leads us, with every song, down the rabbit hole and into a musical and philosophical universe that's entirely his own? Planet Elling sounds like jazz but thinks like theology. For all his hipster irreverence, his art is ultimately about worship; however, that could mean singing the praises of some hip-swinging chicks (as in both "Tanya Jean" and "It's Just a Thing," whose heroine is even named the Swing), paying homage to cool colossi (like "A Prayer for Mr. [Miles] Davis"), and, fairly frequently, a prayer to the Creator Himself.

Elling often starts his sets, and albums, with something familiar—a standard at either medium or slow tempo—then adds something original to it. To herald the release of his 1997 album, *The Messenger* (the second of six for Blue Note), he launched what he called "The Guerilla Tour" of New York, in which he made "30 dates in 40 days," starting at Birdland on May 17 and climaxing at the Knitting Factory on June 17. Of the several shows I caught, including one at a now long departed venue called the Izzy Bar, most began with a ballad, usually "My Foolish Heart," with a poetry recitation interpolated, while *The Messenger* opened with a treatment of "Nature Boy" that launches into a wild scat.

Those who have eyes to dig Elling should start with a single, salient factoid: This guy is steeped equally in modern jazz and traditional religion. He discovered both of these institutions, in fact, in church, where he first started singing, as well as contemplating the Almighty, as a youngster in the Midwest. He played violin and French horn in his teens, and found his way into jazz (via Dave Brubeck, Dexter Gordon, Ella Fitzgerald, and Herbie Hancock) as a student at Gustavus Adolphus College in St. Peter, Minnesota, and then enrolled as a graduate student at the University of Chicago Divinity School. But before he graduated he found himself completely caught up in the city's jazz scene.

Though Elling only participated in a couple of lessons with Mark Murphy, the veteran singer and teacher was to exert a deep and profound influence on him (among many others); Elling was particularly taken with the veteran vocalist's technique of blending jazz vocals with what they used to call Beat poetry. At least two items in his early repertoire came directly from Murphy, the Landesman-Wolf "Ballad of the Sad Young Men" (on *Close Your Eyes*) and his Lord Buckley monologue.

Elling, who is thirty-four years younger than Murphy, is even more committed to the uncompromisingly eclectic, and he also delves deeper than his hipster forebear into vocalese, the trick of pinning lyrics to a well-known recorded solo. Most of his source material in this regard, at least on his earlier albums, derives from the Miles Davis–Wayne Shorter–Herbie Hancock axis, such as Hancock's "Chan's Song," Shorter's "Nightdreamer" (in which he spins an elaborate web of surrealistic imagery, recorded on his *Live in Chicago* album in 2000), "Delores" (in which he elaborates on the positives of hot chicks as well as the talents of Von Freeman), and "Gingerbread Boy" (the Jimmy Heath classic popularized by Miles Davis, done by Elling as a straight wordless scat). Appropriately, his longtime collaborator-pianist, Laurence Hobgood, is most reminiscent of Hancock back when he spoke like a child.

Like Mahogany and Harris, Elling sings in a rich, deep voice, occasionally injecting a little nasality (rather like a Brazilian singer) to give his sound a touch more color, and occasionally he will also play with the pitch of a note, but his intonation is consistently on solid ground. His signature achievement is connecting the meter of a jazz improvisation to the ebb and flow of modern poetry. Beyond employing Sinatrian long lines to get fresh takes on standards like "Polka Dots and Moonbeams" and "Prelude to a Kiss," scatting, and doing vocalese, he spontaneously improvises words and melody. He calls this latter approach "ranting," and his earliest and most primordially effective example of such a rant is "Endless" (on *The Messenger*). Here, tenorist Ed Petersen blows a phrase at him, and Elling answers back with a musical word-association test: "Trees . . . Breasts . . . Atoms . . . ICE CREAM!"

He plays with the ring of words: On a long, complicated narrative like "Tanya Jean" you're not supposed to absorb every line, but rather let the sounds and images wash over you. Other works, like "The Beauty of All Things," inspired by contemporary spiritual thought, are more hymnlike, while his harmonious duet with Cassandra Wilson on "Time of the Season," by the British Invasion band the Zombies, reminds us that a zombie is first and foremost a cocktail.

Each Elling album has at least one totally user-friendly item that newcomers, lacking a guide map to his admittedly opaque artistry, can instantly

fathom: On *Close Your Eyes*, it was his irresistible bossa nova "Never Say Goodbye." On *Messenger*, on the other hand, it's one of his most way-out works, "Just a Thing," an in-meter monologue that blends hipster slang with Jack Webb monotone ("I drew him a picture, but he couldn't hear it") and the hard-boiled parody sequence in *The Band Wagon*, in which Fred Astaire plays a Mike Hammer variation named "Rod Riley."

The 2001 *Flirting with Twilight* includes an amazingly direct "Not While I'm Around" (from *Sweeney Todd*) that's so tender and poignant it suggests that Elling and his wife, Jennifer, were already preparing for parenthood (their daughter, Louisa, arrived several years later). *Flirting with Twilight* also begins with a stunning ballad, a variation on "Moonlight Serenade" based on a bass solo by Charlie Haden. The 1999 *Live in Chicago* includes a pair of hysterical and historical duets with Jon Hendricks on "Don't Get Scared" (Hendricks sings the King Pleasure part, and Elling sings the Hendricks part) and "Goin' to Chicago" (Elling sings the instrumental parts, Hendricks sings the central Jimmy Rushing blues vocal).

The 1998 *This Time It's Love* is a whole package of love songs, including a few originals. *Man in the Air* is highlighted by a highly spiritual lyric to "Resolution," the most tuneful movement of John Coltrane's *A Love Supreme*. When I first heard these, as well as the 2007 *Nightmoves*, his seventh album and the first for Concord, I concluded that his more recent work is his most easily listenable. Yet upon relistening to the nineties albums, the earlier work sounds good, too.

The two most recent projects are most deliberately moored in canonical singers: *Dedicated to You* is his dedication (as the title suggests) to Coltrane and Hartman, and *Nightmoves* contains several extended meditations inspired by Sinatra. One track combines Jobim's "If You Never Come to Me" with Berlin's "Change Partners," so as to suggest the *Sinatra-Jobim* collaboration. Then, Elling's expanded rethinking of "In the Wee Small Hours of the Morning" introduces the FS anthem with original lyrics based on a 1994 improvisation by pianist Keith Jarrett. It can't be a coincidence that all three of the other standards were also recorded by the Chairman ("Where Are You?" "Body and Soul," and an "I Like the Sunrise" that detours into a recitation from Rumi, the thirteenth-century Persian poet). The big fun is reserved for his Bush-era update of "What a Swell Party This Is," in a duet with John Pizzarelli.

In honor of Hartman and Coltrane, *Dedicated to You* offers Elling's most accessible performances yet. This was a concert presentation, taped at the Allen Room at Jazz at Lincoln Center, that the singer is continuing to tour (as of the summer and fall of 2009), and includes a kind of spoken liner notes, a poetic contemplation of the significance of the Coltrane-Hartman collaboration, recited over a string background to the melody "It's Easy to Remember." *Dedicated* is also as romantic an offering as anybody was likely to record in 2009. Elling starts with the six classic tracks of the 1963 *Coltrane-Hartman* album and adds other ballads from Coltrane's 1962 album of that name. "Autumn Serenade" is faster than the original and "They Say It's Wonderful" utilizes swinging accents, but Elling stays true to the spirit. This live set offers proof positive that Elling can be both creative and idiosyncratic even when he's remaining well within the boundaries of familiar words and music; he doesn't have to go out on a limb or do something cuckoo to express himself. When *Dedicated to You* won the Grammy for Best Jazz Vocal Album in 2010, it was a victory for younger male jazz singers in general.

(Elling was the first dudeski to bring home the trophy since Bobby McFerrin in 1993.)

Neither does *Dedicated to You* utilize any of Elling's more radical juxtapositions, as when on *Live in Chicago,* in the middle of "My Foolish Heart," he detours through "Dark Night of the Soul" by the sixteenth-century Spanish mystic Saint John of the Cross; we've already seen how "I Like the Sunrise" (on *Nightmoves*) blends Ellington with Rumi. While Elling is definitely out beyond the cutting edge, there's something quaintly archaic about him at the same time—who else, born after 1965, addresses his musicians as "cats"? He looks back to when it was hip to look ahead. Way out and just plain goofy as he often is, at his best Elling makes hepcats of us all. Like, I'm hip.

Contemporary Cabaret

Andrea Marcovicci
Mary Cleere Haran
Michael Feinstein
Eric Comstock

Cabaret isn't easy to define except in terms of geographical imperatives. If something happens in Carnegie Hall, it's not necessarily classical music, and if an artist performs at Birdland, he's not automatically a jazz musician. The major cabaret rooms feature everyone from Broadway leading ladies and men doing one-person shows to jazz vocalists to vintage pop stars working the circuit to traditional cabaret singers and singer-pianists, yet anyone who works in any of the major cabaret rooms (the four principal joints currently in New York are the Oak Room at the Algonquin Hotel, Feinstein's at the Regency Hotel, the Café Carlyle, and the leading room for more reasonably priced talent, the Metropolitan) is unquestionably, ipso facto, a cabaret performer.

The reader will forgive my unabashed Gotham-centrism here: Like jazz and, even more so, the Broadway musical, cabaret happens primarily in New York. Other cities have their own cabaret scenes, but they're ultimately not much more than the equivalent of road companies or local bands.

Just how many kinds of cabaret are there? The classic image of the genre is a heavy-duty diva like Mabel Mercer, perched like a statue on her famous, thronelike singing stool, transforming Cole Porter into a soliloquy as serious as anything uttered by Hamlet, only with rolled "R"s. Then there's Bobby Short, who brought the traditions of African American showbiz to cabaret, with overtones of jazz and blues, of ladies like Ethel Waters and Ivie Anderson, even as he shakes the sand from his shoes. Some cabaret divas are essentially opera singers, superannuated sopranos straining for a high F. These in turn are in contrast to all those young showbiz hopefuls putting on their own shows—the topic of which is generally what it's like to be a young showbiz

hopeful—all with carefully scripted patter that gives credit to their directors and refers to their piano players as "musical directors." (Sometimes it seems that the major difference between cabaret singing and jazz singing is that jazz people never announce their light and sound guys; cabaret singers always do.) Cabaret is also notable for having its share of late starters, late bloomers, and even more late non-bloomers such as Miriam Passman, protégée of playwright Charles Busch, who waited until her kids were in college before mounting her show, *If We Only Have Love: Songs of Sondheim, Brel, and Weill,* at the Tuesday 3:45 a.m. slot at Danny's.

Cabaret also means French singers from New Jersey, the chanteurettes and chantootsies doing the music of Jacques Strappe or Charles Hasnovoice. There are evenings of music by every imaginable songwriter, encompassing, as the 2000-Year-Old Man would say, "the great and the near-great." There are tributes to legendary entertainers who are either living or dead, or perhaps dead but don't know it: Americans doing Edith Piaf or Marlene Dietrich, men who do Streisand and women who do Sinatra. (I'd like to see the various concepts combined—someone doing a whole evening of Ethel Merman singing Burt Bacharach, or maybe somebody recreating Sammy Davis Jr. doing his impression of Frankie Laine.) When someone like Bette Midler becomes a superstar (and, more recently, when big sellers like Michael Feinstein, Diana Krall, and Peter Cincotti have played the Algonquin on their way to the top), then cabaret briefly penetrates the mainstream. Conversely, when some TV actress like Cybill Shepherd or Dixie Carter turns up at Feinstein's or the Carlyle, then the mainstream penetrates cabaret.

In the Broadway musical *A Class Act*, the songwriter Ed Kleban defined musical comedy as a big theater where a lot of people have paid a lot of money to see a big show; cabaret, on the other hand, is more like a small room where a privileged few people have paid a lot of money to see a performance that's intimate. It's not a coincidence that most cabaret venues are situated in hotels—hotel rooms are traditionally where intimate things happen.

In jazz the dividing categories are more obvious—swing versus bebop, saxes versus pianos—but the concept of cabaret is such a polyglot, a mishmash of divergent styles, that it doesn't pay to look for subgenres. Cabaret is roughly half–jazz, half–musical theater, and half-pop. In fact, the whole concept of the form is dependent on a mathematical equation derived from that great economist Max Bialystock: For it to work, you have to sell at least 150 percent of it.

When we say cabaret is partially pop, we generally mean the Cole Porter–Frank Sinatra kind, but sometimes also the Leiber and Stoller–Elvis kind, or even the Barry Manilow–Bette Midler kind, and perhaps someday the N'Sync–Backstreet Boys–Teenage Mutant Ninja Turtle kind. The two living legends who could most positively be considered the leading icons of the music, the goddess-divas who do the most to inspire younger talent, could not be further apart career-wise. Margaret Whiting came out of the pop mainstream, where she enjoyed hit singles and multimedia stardom, whereas you would never find Julie Wilson on a jukebox; she was always an artist on the fringe, appealing to the cognoscenti rather than the masses. Yet both work in cabaret because they choose to.

One of the main factors that distinguish living legends from others is a serene knowledge that they themselves are the show. Among younger performers, even those in their fifties, there's a consensus that what makes cabaret different from other forms of theater and music is that it's always *about* something, there's always a show. Jazz singers can reel off one tune after another without saying anything other than "Give it up for So-and-So on bass!" (No white person should ever be allowed to utter the phrases "give it up" or "put your hands together.") Even Blossom Dearie rarely said anything unless the song she was about to sing was written either by her or one of her dearest chums. Yet generally speaking, cabaret singers have to have patter that helps fit their songs into a concept and a show. With all four of the central performers of this section, the patter is often just as entertaining—and perhaps even more central to the overall experience—as the singing itself.

In jazz, you have to be able to play or sing, and be on intimate terms with every chord progression ever devised. In cabaret, you have to know not only the words and music to a billion standard songs, but the entire history behind each one; in fact, knowing the name of the composer, lyricist, and who introduced it in whatever film or show (plus who wrote the book, designed the costumes, or sold the tickets in the box office) is far more important than knowing how to improvise on the changes. If you throw in an incorrect chord change somewhere, chances are that no one but a few musicians will notice; however if you confuse *George White's Scandals of 1926* with *Ziegfeld Follies of 1922*, a dozen geniuses in the audience will be all over you.

Which brings us to another primary difference between jazz and cabaret. When you listen to jazz, you're supposed to feel *hip*. In contrast, when you experience a cabaret show, you're supposed to feel *smart*. Andrea Marcovicci has a way of interspersing bits of knowledge in her show that are ingeniously designed to make the listener say to himself, "Aren't I smart for coming here?" And with European performers who spell "cabaret" with a "K," such as Ute Lemper, you're not only supposed to feel cultured, you're supposed to walk out of the Kafé Karlyle feeling cultured and continental. Mary Cleere Haran is the master of incorporating her songs into a larger context of narrative and comedy; no one is better than she at interweaving the songs as well as the accompanying history into a seamless dramatic narrative. She addresses her audiences as "New York Sophisticates," and, though she may be getting a laugh with the phrase, that's exactly what she makes us feel like.

Michael Feinstein has the rare gift of being able to spiel reams of factoids in such a way that you say to yourself, "Oh yes, of course I knew that," and you really think you did—he's mastered the trick of imparting information without coming off as smug or superior. By contrast, the pianist and singer Mark Nadler can make almost any piece of information seem funny; he's the incarnation of what the master Looney Tuneist Chuck Jones once distinguished as the difference between "someone who opens a funny door" and "someone who opens a door funny." KT Sullivan, who is also a superlative soprano, can get laughs on lines even when the author failed to provide any. Eric Comstock, like Feinstein and like the late, underappreciated Charles DeForest, has a knack for sharing both songs and the data concerning them like a collector friend (be it wine, songs, or stamps) talking to another, taking you on a tour of his house and pulling out rarities that will amaze and astound you—yet never coming across as an "expert," always keeping everything on a friend-to-friend level.

No matter what you sing like, cabaret is about context—the whole show rather than the individual song. (It's a rare artist like Sandy Stewart who gets through an entire show at the Algonquin without dropping one name or mentioning one fact.) There's no artist who illustrates this point better than Andrea Marcovicci, who was probably the most successful leading lady of the cabaret world in the first decade of the new millennium.

Andrea Marcovicci (born 1948)

The actor Jimmy Stewart told a story about how, early in his career, MGM pictures cast him in a Cole

Porter musical to be called *Born to Dance*. Stewart suffered no illusions about his singing ability—he knew he couldn't carry a tune across the street without breaking both legs—so he went to the composer and pleaded for a song that required more acting than singing, something with "a lot of lyrics" and not a lot of high notes. In other words, something that Stewart (not yet a Hollywood legend) could talk his way through, rather than actually have to sing.

I kept thinking about that story when I heard Andrea Marcovicci for the first time in person, after years of knowing her singing, such as it is, only from records. This was at New Year's Eve 2003–2004 at the Oak Room. I confess that I had never been to hear her in person for many years because I had only heard her on records—and it's impossible to get the point of Marcovicci from records alone. Her medium is the live show, preferably in a small room; records seem only to expose her shortcomings. No chops. No voice. No ability to hit notes, much less sustain them.

But voice is a funny thing in the cabaret world: It isn't synonymous with talent. In cabaret, you can be a great performer without a great voice or musical chops, much as you can be a great dramatic actor in the theater without a great, commanding voice. Cabaret is not like opera or baseball where you need a lot of physical ability to get the job done; cabaret is much more dependent on brainpower. If you have virtuoso pipes, like Ann Hampton Callaway, so much the better, but it's not an absolute prerequisite. (The rest of the pop music world has gone in the opposite direction, where performers in the post–*American Idol* world have determined that all there is to singing is hitting notes.)

I also knew from Marcovicci's records like *Live from London* (1998) how compelling she can be with what may be the most minimal set of pipes ever to belong to a substantial singer of the Great American Songbook. Even Mabel Mercer, minimal as her voice was, especially in her twilight years, was considerably more musical, more capable of conveying a sense of melody and rhythm. What's especially interesting is that Marcovicci doesn't fake it—she doesn't try to talk her way through a lyric.

Instead, she uses her acting ability to put the words and the stories over, while her accompanist—in this case it was the talented Shelly Markham—handles the melody. It's a theatrical illusion, comparable to the way that the trick of persistence of vision creates the illusion of moving pictures. The movies don't actually move, but when you see a sequence of slightly different still pictures flashing forward fast enough, your brain fills in the gaps, and the figures in the image appear to move. Likewise, when you hear words and music together, your ears and your mind conspire to trick you into thinking there must be some kind of singing going on.

And Marcovicci is full of tricks—she's the only singer I have ever heard who can sustain a word without sustaining a note. The word will start out on a certain pitch, and she'll give every impression of holding it, yet the note itself will often trail away while the sound of the syllable lingers on. Similarly, she'll fly into what sounds like a classical trill—she'll hit a brief scale of a couple of notes, rendered coloratura-style. These trills are completely random, having nothing to do with words or music—she seems to be throwing them in to further create the illusion that the audience is hearing a voice hitting pitches. But she more than compensates for a shortage of vocal power with a surplus of brainpower.

Marcovicci is so smart and so canny about herself that I can't help wondering if she's deliberately misleading us about one salient point: She describes herself as a "torch singer." In a sense, that's refreshing: That phrase was retired years ago, just as too many singers, following the example of Sinatra and Kay Starr, proclaimed themselves "saloon singers." It's a self-categorization that obliterates the difference between self-deprecation and self-aggrandizement. "Saloon singer" implies "My art means so much to me that I am willing to do it in a tacky dive for next to no money." Torch singing is a more positive term, mainly because it's the one that was actually used in the music industry in the prewar era.

Far be it from me to deny that Marcovicci is sufficiently torchy—she puts over her songs of "unrequited and requited love" in a way that's often quite moving. Sometimes the sad songs are a little heavy-handed, as on "Springtime" (on *Live from London*), but more often, she uses the power of suggestion, perhaps to make her sad songs seem both touching and torching. Her best ballads have the quality of restraint—a natural asset for her to employ; a refusal to indulge in oversentimentalizing.

But the real highlights for me are those songs by Cole Porter that Jimmy Stewart referred to, the list songs and the big patter comedy tours de force with, as Stewart suggests, the more lyrics, the better. When a song becomes a standout comic monologue, then the articulation, the timing, the phrasing, and the delivery of the text becomes far more important than intonation or notes. At the 2003–2004 New Year's Eve show at the Algonquin, Marcovicci achieved this over and over, most notably with Frank Loesser's "Hamlet," a showstopper he wrote for Betty Grable in the 1949 film *Red, Hot and Blue* (no connection to the Cole Porter musical) that hysterically reduces Shakespeare's tragedy to forties jive lingo. Porter's "Let's Not Talk About Love" seems to have been inspired by the agile tongues of Danny Kaye and Eve Arden; here he was moved to compete with what Ira Gershwin and Kurt Weill had wrought with Kaye in "Tchaikovsky." Porter succeeded in devising the twistiest and turniest and most complexly rhyming tongue-twister of them all, and made it somewhat spicier than Gershwin and Weill's opus in his choice of subject matter. Marcovicci convulsed us all, despite omitting the song's most

extreme line (quoted elsewhere in this book, it rhymes "Pennsylvania" with "nymphomania.")

With her rail-thin form and angular, modelesque cheekbones, Marcovicci looks the very essence of what a cabaret singer should be, using her arms and posture as much as she does notes and words to convey a narrative. Her home base is extremely upscale joints like the Oak Room and London's Pizza on the Park (where she recorded *Live from London*), and her primary audience is the well-heeled who frequent such joints. She knows the value of a song like Sondheim's "Finishing the Hat" (from *Sunday in the Park with George*), which makes us feel nothing less than righteous and justified—perhaps even noble— in our self-centered, preoccupied way. Her performances are a musical comfort food that reaches the heart by way of the brain; she makes us feel good about ourselves.

Marcovicci, who with typical cunning celebrated her sixtieth birthday six months after the fact in May 2009 in a special concert at Town Hall (her mother was on hand to celebrate her ninetieth), continually outsmarts us and makes us love her for it. She appeals to the collective cerebellum; she sings offbeat songs that only a true specialist would know; and she drops little bits of trivia—at times she's almost like Jonathan Schwartz set to piano accompaniment (with perhaps a little more of a sense of humor). Even when I think I'm a step ahead of her, she'll trot out a piece of ancient esoterica like "Umbrella Man," a screwball novelty waltz from 1939, and appeal to everybody's inner music nerd. (Admittedly, in my case it's an outer nerd.) Yet nothing that she does is truly obscure, and that's the genius of it: She knows how to light the spark of vague, distant recognition to make a listening crowd feel on top of things. She knows well that we're not as sophisticated as she makes us think we are. We file out of her shows thinking, "My, aren't I intelligent to have come here, listening to this sophisticated woman sing these sophisticated songs?" And we're right.

Mary Cleere Haran (born 1952)

Many performers resent the term "cabaret" in the same way that most traditional jazz players resent the word "Dixieland." Yet Mary Cleere Haran is fiercely proud to call herself a cabaret artist—she celebrates the medium for its intimacy, its directness, and, in her hands, its emotional honesty. Her strength is that she takes full advantage of the form's potential: A Mary Cleere Haran show is not just a bunch of songs tied together with a theme and patter, but a thoroughly written and directed one-woman production. The amount of perseverance and preparation that go into one of her productions is the same as for any off-Broadway show. The difference is not in the scope of Haran's ambitions, but that she prefers the basic conceit of cabaret: One-person shows on Broadway generally have one famous person pretending to be another. (In a fairly recent season, George Burns, Katharine Hepburn, and Golda Meir were all impersonated on the Great White Way.) In contrast, Ms. Haran always plays herself in one of her one-woman shows, addressing the audience in her dual role as scholar and interpreter of the Great American Songbook. She may play another character for a brief scene or two here and there, but she specializes in being herself. In fact, rather than subsume herself in some legendary figure, she weaves whatever topic happens to be under discussion into the context of her own life and experience. If you've seen enough of her shows, you know that sooner or later everything will wind up in a discussion of her traditional Catholic upbringing and the nuns who served as instructors and would-be role models for her childhood in San Francisco.

Haran is also an outstanding singer, with a sweetly beautiful, honey-flavored voice. You'd pay money just to hear the voice even without the rest of the package that goes with it—she can hit notes and even sustain them. Where Marcovicci sounds as if she's been listening to Mabel Mercer, the sound of Haran's voice and her approach to a song is obviously more closely informed by close contact with such superior pop singers as Doris Day, Jo Stafford, Margaret Whiting, and Rosemary Clooney. If Marcovicci had been around in the fifties, she would have been at the Blue Angel, whereas Haran would have worked at the Waldorf or the Copa. She's played almost exclusively in cabaret settings—even on her half dozen or so albums (such as *Pennies from Heaven*, 1998, and *Crazy Rhythm*, 2000)—meaning at most a trio, piano, bass, and drums. While this is hardly cause for regret, Haran has sufficient chops to make us want to hear her in other contexts as well: with a big band, maybe, or a full string orchestra, or a Dixieland band. Her voice is a major attraction unto itself; it's not merely part of a bigger picture.

Yet singing is only part of what she does. Just to hear Haran on a recording means getting only half of the experience. Watching a video of her in performance wouldn't help. It's not a question of seeing her rather than just hearing her; it's a question of being there rather than not being there: Her brand of ultra-polished, scripted, directed, and acted performance is somehow not reproducible by electronic media. Even a YouTube of Haran in action is akin to listening to an early stereo album like Sinatra's *Come Swing with Me* and only getting one of the channels. Unless you're right there in the same room with her live and in person, just as it's happening, then you're not getting the full experience.

Like Michael Feinstein, Haran grew up infatuated with old songs and old movies. Classic musical comedy shows, experienced via cast albums, have also exerted a significant influence on their work. But there's something much more vital and immediate about a classic film that Haran and Feinstein respond to which makes old Broadway productions seem academic by comparison. It's clear from CDs like Feinstein's *MGM Album* and Haran's *This Heart*

of Mine: Classic Movie Songs of the Forties that they're as interested in the films themselves as in the songs. When Haran was asked to host a concert in the *Lyrics and Lyricists* series (somewhat inaccurately named, since it often salutes composers as well as lyricists) at the 92nd Street Y, it was no surprise that she put together an evening of Harry Warren, who was, overall, Hollywood's most celebrated songwriter.

One of the main differences between Haran and Feinstein is that while he can also be funny, Haran is much more of a pundit. She can also be far more sarcastic and caustic than Marcovicci or Feinstein; she's just as likely to dwell on the mediocrity and tackiness of old Hollywood as she is to celebrate its triumphs.

Her cinemacentric outlook (she's also worked as a researcher and interviewer for numerous PBS documentaries, which are usually also movie-oriented) has led to my favorite of her albums, the aforementioned *This Heart of Mine.* She's worked with plenty of fine pianists, including Sir Richard Rodney Bennett, but Fred Hersch is probably the finest, serving also as musical director and producer here. The music nerd in me responds to the scholar in her and appreciates the chance to hear wonderful but rarely performed songs that just missed becoming standards. In several cases, these are title songs from classic films that had to play second fiddle to other numbers from the same scores. For instance, "Swinging on a Star" from *Going My Way* won the Oscar and is familiar enough to contemporary audiences that Gary Larson could build a cartoon joke around it (husband pig says to wife pig, "I never wanted to carry moonbeams home in a jar"), yet nobody remembers the even more beautiful title song from that film, in spite of marvelous performances at the time by Bing Crosby and by Johnny Desmond with Glenn Miller's Army Air Force Band. The same applies to "You Were Never Lovelier," the title of the second of the two Fred Astaire–Rita Hayworth vehicles. Everybody knows its "I'm Old Fashioned," but the title tune languished unheard for decades until an astute interpreter-scholar brought it the attention it deserved.

Feinstein and Haran are both partial to film-oriented writers—who but Feinstein would salute Livingston and Evans?—and likewise Haran leans not only toward Warren but Jimmy Van Heusen and Johnny Mercer, who's by far the best represented writer on *This Heart of Mine,* having supplied the lyrics for half the songs here. "Atchison, Topeka and the Santa Fe" is hardly obscure; it earned Mercer the first of his four Academy Awards, and is well known to anyone who owns a Judy Garland album. Haran, though, gives it a whole new face, slowing it down and accentuating unfamiliar lyrics. Her purpose is not novelty in and for itself, but to give the song new resonance. She reveals that "Atchison, Topeka" doesn't merely belong to the great tradition of train songs (or even movie train songs, like "Shuffle Off to Buffalo" and "Chattanooga Choo-Choo") but, thanks to Mercer's lyrical brilliance, uses the railroad as a metaphor for far-flung dreams. In Haran's interpretation, "Atchison, Topeka" is nothing less than a spiritual predecessor of the songwriter's more mature "Moon River."

Using Garland's classic interpretation as a point of departure—every train ride needs a starting point—Haran unveils level upon level of meaning. She shows how Mercer contrasts the glamour and the mundanity of the A, T & SF—the locals are excited by the arrival of the train, but it's just a job to those who work on it. For the song's protagonist, who travels from the comfort, but also the limitations, of home to the new frontier, the train represents a new life and a fresh start.

In the picture, "Atchison" is sung by Susan Bradley of Ohio (Garland) as she steps off the train, and Mercer's lyric has her both reflecting on her past ("Back in Ohio, where I come from . . .") and speculating about her future. Even though he wrote chorus after chorus of lyrics for the production number built around the song in *The Harvey Girls,* he was smart enough to leave a lot unsaid. The lyrics talk about dreams in the abstract, not the specific—a career, a family, a room of one's own—which makes them somehow seem more meaningful. The most arresting description of the future is that it includes a built-in reminiscence of the past: "When I'm old and gray and settled down . . ." As great as Garland is, every time I hear Haran sing "Atchison" (and it's one of her perennials) she makes me hear all kinds of things that I never heard in the song before.

Which is precisely the place where the duties of a good scholar and a good interpreter intersect. Haran finds that spot and builds all her individual songs and entire shows there. To my dismay, her career has been somewhat downsized recently. She hasn't released a new album since 2000, and there have only been a few major room appearances this decade (notably a memorable tribute to Doris Day at Feinstein's in the fall of 2007). Even so, she remains one of the very finest artists working the field of contemporary cabaret today, because she never fails to stimulate, inspire, and move us.

Michael Feinstein (born 1956)

Feinstein's singing sounds neither like a pop singer who came out of a band context, like Crosby or Sinatra, or one who emerged from a Broadway background, like John Raitt. Nor does he sound like what I would consider a classic-traditional male cabaret singer—Philip Officer, with his pleasantly nasal high notes, is a good example of the genre. Feinstein sings with a wide and rapid vibrato in a high baritone (sometimes so high it sounds like a low tenor) that draws upon all these traditions without restricting itself to any one of them. It's a beautiful voice—he does indeed have chops—but as with the other major cabareteurs, what he does with it is far more important.

Significantly, the two singers he's most often compared to are Barry Manilow and Johnny Mathis, which some might regard as an insult, but which strikes me more as confirmation that not every aspect of the music of Mathis or even Manilow is dreadful. For starters, both have sweet, genuinely pretty voices that are pleasing to listen to. This doesn't necessarily a great singer make (think of Andy Williams), but in this age of rap and grunge, to be able to start with a sound that attractive is nothing to take for granted.

It's an oversimplification to say that Feinstein sounds the way Manilow and Mathis might sound were they given a sudden infusion of class. Mathis's albums with Ralph Burns, such as *The Rhythms and Ballads of Broadway*, are certainly proto-Feinsteinian, but Feinstein's vibrato is not nearly as carnivorous as that of Mathis (who might be described as a vibrato in search of a voice), and he doesn't have the preening, self-glorifying stance of Manilow (who most often seems like a male equivalent of such ego-driven divas as Streisand, Midler, or Cher). Unlike Manilow, Feinstein sounds as if he loves the songs more than he loves the sound of his own voice.

His specialty is slow ballads; Rodgers and Hart's "Isn't It Romantic" isn't just a piece of material to him, it's a motto. When he does a tune that goes faster, it's just that—a faster love song, like "Something's Gotta Give." He's also made efforts to do out-and-out big band–style swing, and while this isn't his forte, he is, infact, very credible when singing fast-moving, Broadway-style numbers in double time or even faster—plenty of these are on *The MGM Album*. While singing fast isn't the same as swinging, Feinstein makes you feel pedantic for bothering about the difference.

The Gershwins are at the center of Feinstein's musical universe. He launched his career not as player or scholar but essentially as Ira Gershwin's assistant. Born in 1956, Feinstein first worked in local spots around his native Columbus before moving to Los Angeles in 1976. He entered the Gershwin inner circle a few months later when he met the widow of pianist-raconteur Oscar Levant, famous as a leading Gershwin interpreter, sidekick, and psychotic alter ego. From there, Feinstein met Ira Gershwin and his wife, Lenore (even people who normally never have a bad word to say about anybody, like Feinstein and Rosemary Clooney, can't think of anything positive to say about Mrs. Gershwin).

Feinstein worked as Gershwin's lieutenant until the lyricist's death six years later; he also served as Liza Minnelli's accompanist for a time. When he went for broke with his career as a singer-pianist, he already had her support, as well as Clooney's. In 1986, he officially made the big time when he opened at the Algonquin—within a few years they could no longer afford him. More remarkably, he went where no younger singer of the Great American Songbook had gone for many years when he began recording standards for a major label, the Warner Bros. conglomerate (various releases came out on Asylum and Elektra/Atlantic), beginning with *Live at the Algonquin* and *Pure Gershwin*, both from 1986. The latter was the first of several albums devoted to the songwriting team that represents the North Star in Feinstein's constellation, as well the first of his continuing series of songwriter-driven projects.

As a player-scholar, Feinstein has done a remarkable job of balancing the familiar and the obscure, carefully alternating between standards everybody knows (like "I Got Rhythm") and worthy esoterica. Apart from his Gershwin and Irving Berlin collections, he's also made a point of honoring songwriters who are both living (at least at the time) and who rarely get entire albums devoted to them, such as Burton Lane, Jule Styne, Jerry Herman, and the team of Jay Livingston and Ray Evans.

In 1996, he was in the vanguard again when he switched from the Warners conglomerate to the midsize corporation Concord Records (within a few years, every creative artist of note was recording for such midsize operations as Concord, Telarc, and Fantasy, which are now all under the same corporate umbrella), which allowed him to create Feinery, a boutique label of his own, for which he makes traditional Michael Feinstein albums and also produces historical projects, such as reissues of rare music by such icons of class pop singing as Clooney and Jo Stafford.

All in all, Feinstein has made more than two dozen albums over the last twenty years, enough to warrant *The Very Best of Michael Feinstein*, which actually came out at the time of the WEA-Concord transition, and thus covers only the first dozen years of his career. It seems somewhat premature to examine his output disc by disc when he's still so prolific—there were two albums in 2003 alone. But there are obvious highlights one can point to. In general, I prefer the more recent offerings on Concord to the earlier releases from the WEA group.

Of his more recent collections of slow, romantic treatments of classic love songs, *Michael Feinstein with the Israeli Philharmonic Orchestra* is the most successful. It was recorded in early 2001 but anticipates the kind of reaffirmation of traditional values—not to mention an outreach to America's reliable allies in the Middle East—that everybody would be doing immediately after 9/11. Whereas he often celebrates neglected tunesmiths, the *Israeli Philharmonic* set features some of the most classic of all standards: "Laura," "Stormy Weather," and "Love Is Here to Stay." The only connecting link between the twelve tunes is that they're all the work of Jewish Americans (no Harry Warren or Duke Ellington here). Along with Berlin and Gershwin, he sings Jerry Herman's "I Won't Send Roses" (from *Mack and Mabel*), and proves that, with this song, perhaps Mr. Herman's finest work, Herman does indeed deserve to be ranked alongside the canonical songwriters.

The later albums show Feinstein with an increasing confidence in singing at faster tempos. Without trying to be Ella Fitzgerald he's grown more comfortable at jazz tempos and in jazz settings, abetted by jazz solos and obbligatos—"I've Never Been in Love Before" is a strong example of this. That cut can be found on *Romance on Film, Romance on Broadway,* a very solid, workmanlike two-disc set from 2000. Feinstein employs fast tempos in the Broadway-cabaret tradition, which is normally reserved for Noel Coward–style patter songs (or Cole Porter list songs)—here, rhythm is an integral element of comedy, and makes all punch lines possible. "The Mating Season" on the *Livingston and Evans Songbook* is one of his most appealing faster numbers: He certainly knows how to be funny in tempo.

Livingston and Evans represents a model of how good these scholarly projects can be. One of the main risks of cabaret is that it takes the concept of context too far, as if it were more important to talk about the music than to sing it; as if the performers identify less with Bobby Short than with Jonathan Schwartz. But Feinstein has mastered the knack of making his scholarship accessible to the majority of people who hear him, who probably know that Ira Gershwin was not George Gershwin's "lovely wife" but in all likelihood have never heard "In the Mandarin's Orchid Garden." When Feinstein sings the verse to "Laura" or an early prototype of the lyric to "Long Ago and Far Away" no one feels left out, or that he's going over anyone's head. At the same time, he makes his point—that writers like Herman and the Livingston-Evans team are among the top songwriters, whose work deserves to be kept alive, preserved, and heard.

One obvious place for Feinstein to go has been as a presenter of other talent; Feinery Records, his imprint label at Concord Records, features other singers, such *B.J. Ward Sings Marshall Barer.* In 1999, the Regency Hotel opened a cabaret room named Feinstein's at the Regency—and it must be a source of major satisfaction to him that Feinstein's was the final club that Rosemary Clooney played in New York. He doesn't own it or manage it, but he appears there several times a year (usually in September, June, and at the beginning and end of each season, as well as a holiday show) and gives his seal of approval to everyone who performs there. In addition, he produces a series of four somewhat-scholarly songwriter-driven concerts each year at Carnegie Hall's Zankel space (mounted in conjunction with ASCAP), which features other performers, as well as a big one-man show at Carnegie's main space every year or so. As if that wasn't enough, he played in a two-person Broadway show in the spring of 2010 with Dame Edna (set to play London and Australia), and he has announced

an ongoing radio series and a three-part documentary on PBS (scheduled for the fall of 2010) on the history of the American popular song. In early 2010, it was announced that Feinstein would also be producing and starring in a series of concerts for Jazz at Lincoln Center. The project with Lincoln Center is an appropriate one, since Feinstein occupies a position analogous to the role of Wynton Marsalis in the jazz world. He has even founded the Michael Feinstein Foundation, devoted to the preservation and future of classic American popular music (and, in the interest of full disclosure, it's actually the recipient of the Herb and Will Friedwald Collection of several thousand vocal and pop LPs). In general, it seems that if the city of New York ever brings back the dreaded New York City Cabaret Identification Card law, in which singers and musicians were, in essence, licensed and approved by the government, that Feinstein would very likely be the guy issuing the cabaret cards. He has become the spokesmodel for the whole of the songbook.

Not that he takes that position for granted—he continues to find new things to do with the great songs, new angles, new approaches. His most recent album as of this writing is *The Sinatra Project,* released in late 2008. Where a lot of so-called "tribute" albums are actually rip-offs, or mere imitations, Feinstein's Sinatra set resonates as the work of one diehard Sinatra junkie for the express benefit of the rest of us diehard Sinatra junkies, a master's thesis in more tangibly enjoyable form. He looks at songs written for Sinatra that he never actually sang, like "The Same Hello, the Same Goodbye," and he considers different aspects of the Sinatra legacy. The singer and the highly creative arranger-conductor Bill Elliott also explore the lesser-traveled but no less brilliant corners of the Sinatra canon, sort of like an alternate universe in a science-fiction movie: What if, they postulate, Sinatra had done "Exactly Like You" with Billy May circa 1957, and thus they dress up that venerable standard with slurping saxophones that are very warm for May. Likewise, they come up with a treatment of "Begin the Beguine" that suggests the way Nelson Riddle would have arranged it using the "I've Got You Under My Skin" template—the resultant chart is a Cole Porter *fantasia* that could be titled either "Begin the Skin" or "I've Got You Under My Beguine," incorporating Riddle's signature baritone sax and trombone vamps and flute filigrees. Feinstein isn't afraid of the faster numbers, although that isn't his specialty; he works hard to do justice to Sinatra's effortless rhythmic style (and certainly doesn't embarrass himself). Still, obviously he's much more comfortable showcasing his trademark intimacy with his own piano on "The Same Hello, the Same Goodbye," an almost frighteningly autobiographical ballad written for the aging Blue Eyes by Alan and Marilyn Bergman.

Every time pundits advocate moving beyond the Great American Songbook, they inevitably employ the standard argument line, "How many more versions of 'My Funny Valentine' do we need?" In the light of Michael Feinstein's career, the question is immaterial. Given his brave exploration of the further recesses of the songbook, he continues to do things that no one else is doing; Michael Feinstein is as worthy an avant-gardist as American music currently has.

Eric Comstock (born 1961)

Writing about Eric Comstock poses a particular problem. While I consider myself a friend of Feinstein and Haran, Eric is the only person in the book whose wedding I attended (believe it or not, I actually played "Long Before I Knew You" on a C-melody saxophone during the reception), and he's the only person in this book who would possibly lend me money should I ever need it.

So, as I say, Eric poses a unique problem. Even though he hasn't recorded prolifically enough, he has certainly achieved enough of a career to warrant inclusion in any survey of contemporary artists who contribute to our enjoyment of the Great American Songbook. (I think enough experts on the subject, such as Gary Giddins, Rex Reed, Stephen Holden, and Jonathan Schwartz, who rarely agree with one another, would give me a consensus on that one.) But at the same time, because he's been so close a friend for twenty-five years, writing about him means risking a conflict of interest. My solution has been to quote from liner notes I wrote for Eric's first album, the 1997 *Young Man of Manhattan*. I had the same problem then, and I dealt with it by offering what I hoped was an entertaining description of Eric Comstock at work.

Incident number one: Last night we were going to hear Eric at the Supper Club (Midtown's favorite home of the five-dollar Coke), when a novice and newcomer to the group asked no one in particular just who exactly was this Eric Comstock. The woman sitting next to me pipes up, "Oh he's *mahvelous*, he's a little like Noel Coward or Bobby Short." By this she meant that Mr. Comstock was a very sophisticated entertainer indeed, you know. And he certainly is, but—buttinski that I am—I had to add my own two cents. "Coward and Short, yes but he's also like Nat Cole. Eric is much enamored of that certain kind of harmony line that's strictly from the early King Cole Trio sides, hey." "True, true," said a face for which I could not supply a name at a neighboring table, "but don't forget Fred Astaire. Not only does he know every song Astaire ever introduced, but when it's appropriate he favors those clipped, staccato lines so reminiscent of Astaire's own singing." "Ah," chimed in a stranger from across a crowded room, "leave us not neglect Melvin." "Melvin?" I stammered, sounding for all the

world like Jerry Lewis. "Yes," answered the stranger. "How can you miss it? Those Tormé-style medleys, piling up song after song in such a witty and musically sound fashion." "*Au contraire*," spoke up a decidedly jejune Kelsey Grammer look-alike ambling through the doorway, "I think that the great influence on Eric is the late Charles DeForest—he has that directness and sincerity that was Charles's exclusive *province*." "If I may just interject a notion at this juncture," interjected a thin drone with stringy hair and glasses escorting an underage Asian lass, "Eric's great strength is his sense of humor. Can't you hear it in 'A Rainy Day'? Obviously, he has carefully studied the canonical works of the legendary Shecky Greene." By now, even the wait staff wanted a piece of this action: "Bobby Darin!" shouted one waitress, while Raoul, our busboy, insistently offered, "Charles Trenet!"

Wondering how it was that everybody in the club talked like a critic, it gradually dawned on me how remarkable Eric's accomplishment is. If he had done nothing but synthesize those myriad and diverse influences into a cohesive whole, that would be accomplishment enough. But Eric has forged a piano and voice style that not only draws on the strengths of his predecessors, but is a thing of beauty unto itself. And fun. Did I forget to mention fun?

Incident number two: When I introduce someone to Eric's work, our point of reference pivots on the tastes of the inductee. If my friend is a Sinatra fan, for instance, I describe Eric as the sole pianist-singer in captivity who does "Not as a Stranger," which might be described as a substandard nonstandard by the short-lived team of Jimmy Van Heusen and lyricist Buddy Kaye. As inferior as the song is, Sinatra and Riddle elevated it into something wonderful in 1955, and Eric also made it memorable in his own way in a live performance forty years later, simply by shaking his head on the word "not."

If my friend happens to like Astaire (and who doesn't?), I describe Eric as the only person besides myself who figured out that the lyricist who wrote the most texts for Astaire (aside from Irving Berlin) was, surprisingly, Johnny Mercer. Then Eric will indulge us in a medley of Mercer-Astaire songs, and it becomes a challenge for me to anticipate what the next one will be before he gets to it. If my friend likes show tunes, then he really will be in seventh heaven, because there's no one who knows more great songs (I'm a sucker for any lyric that can rhyme "Jack the Ripper" with "Yom Kippur") from more forgotten shows, playing them with such endearing elegance and energy that it makes you question their obscurity.

Curriculum vitae: I confess I had the inside track on Eric, having first heard him in the very early eighties (he doesn't like me telling people that he's actually half a year older than I am), but it's hard to think of a major Manhattan room that Comstock hasn't played—even including a few that don't have pianos. He's been at the Algonquin Hotel's Oak Room, the Supper Club, "21," and Maxim's (not to mention Danny's Skylight Room, Five and Ten, the Townhouse, and many more that, having run out of room, we shan't mention). He's also done concerts in New York, like 1996's Tribute to Billy Strayhorn and the 2005 Harold Arlen Centennial show at Carnegie Hall, and is a regular participant in Donald Smith's Town Hall cabaret series. Comstock is also a true citizen of the world musically, basing his career in New York (logging lots of time at the Maidstone Arms and Starr Boggs in the Hamptons) and having played everywhere from Chicago (Toulouse on the Park), San Francisco (the Plush Room), and Los Angeles (the Gardenia) to Vietnam, and all points in between. He also led a full band of his own on an extended tour for the Peter Duchin Organization, a shipboard ensemble that I christened "King Comstock and His Dusky Stevedores."

And foidermore: It's easy to see that Eric is a Comstock lode of valuable scholarship on the subject of the great songs. Philip Elwood of the *San Francisco Examiner* was speaking for all of us when he described him as a "walking encyclopedia of show songs." But that's only the beginning. The same term has also been applied to know-it-all types like Jonathan Schwartz (and your humble servant). Yet all of us nerdy types, who know all the words and none of the music, would do well to eat those words in the company of Comstock. It's not enough to know every song ever written, from "Miss Otis Regrets" to "Pistol Packin' Mama" (come to think of it, they're both arias of femme fatales who come to rather violent ends). Nor is it enough to be able to sing and play them. But Eric has the apparent ability to make any tune sound good. Far from sounding scholarly, he stresses the bundle of joy that the Great American Songbook is—this isn't some kind of music museum, but an art form that's fresh and vital. And fun. Did I forget to mention fun?

Comstock is another artist who, unfortunately, got caught up in the downturn of the CD business: After twenty-five years, he's only had the chance to record a fraction of his repertoire, on *Young Man of Manhattan* (1997), *All Hart: Songs of Lorenz Hart* (2000), and *No One Knows* (2004), the last representing his jazziest effort. Yet he continues to appear in virtually every room in the city; two of his revues, *Our Sinatra* and *Made for the Movies*, were launched at the Algonquin, and a third, *Singing Astaire*, at Birdland. His is the most conversational style of the four cabareteurs listed, with the singing voice closest to his speaking voice, the one who communicates the most directly.

In addition to the upscale rooms, Comstock was a regular for over a dozen years at the late and lamented Danny's Skylight Room, which was a New York cabaret institution, presenting the ridiculous and the sublime, the good, the bad, and the ugly, from 1985 to 2006. Eric and his wife, Barbara Fasano (who wed in 2004), may be the only heterosexual married couple who met there. They gave one of their most memorable performances ever in the club's final weeks in December 2006, showing why they're one of the top teams in contemporary cabaret. (More recently, they've been fixtures at the Metropolitan Room.)

Mrs. Comstock is a charismatic stylist who effectively channels the living spirits of the divas Lena Horne and Barbra Streisand. Accordingly, her 2006 *Written in the Stars* is a collection of songs by Harold Arlen, who was closely associated with both divas. Yet her standout number at Danny's was a song recorded by neither: Kurt Weill's "It Never Was You," which she made seem urgent and important while yet at the same time keeping the pace unhurried—as if she were so sure she would find what she was looking for that she wasn't in a rush to get there.

At Danny's, Comstock's climactic song was one of his all-time perennials. "A Nightingale Sang in Berkeley Square" is one he's been doing since the earliest days of his career, though he sings it now with greater depth and understanding than a younger man could manage. Eric Maschwitz's lyric describes how time seems to stand still for lovers, so much so that a tiny country bird can be heard chirping amid a bustling metropolis. Comstock sings it slowly and tenderly, demonstrating an absolute belief in the idea that the state of being in love is the equivalent of being raised to an exalted plane, where you make yourself at once vulnerable and invincible. I know, 'cause I was there.

Closing paragraphs are generally for drawing tidy conclusions, yet it's just occurred to me that after examining a handful of artists who can be considered the crème de la crème of contemporary cabaret, we're no closer to coming up with a working definition of the genre than we were at the beginning. In their classic Broadway musical, John Kander and Fred Ebb mused that "life is a cabaret." Could be, old chum. But to the millions—well, the dozens anyway—who make cabaret a part of their daily existence, it's more like the other way around.

Harry Connick Jr. and the Retro Crooner Boychicks

Harry Connick Jr.
Michael Bublé
Jamie Cullum
Peter Cincotti

Harry Connick Jr. (born 1967)

It was Harry Connick Jr.'s *When Harry Met Sally* album that earned him both his first platinum album and his first Grammy Award. *When Harry Met Sally*—it didn't hurt that, by coincidence, the singer shared the same first name as the leading character, played by Billy Crystal—practically made him a household name overnight.

At the time, I took an instant dislike to Connick, for reasons that weren't his fault. (I have to admit that I have a perfect track record for this kind of thing: I didn't like Michael Feinstein or Diana Krall either the first few times I heard them. The singers I did like are all still out there, waiting tables.) It's said that Rob Reiner utilized Connick for the *Harry Met Sally* project because he thought the singer-pianist "sounded like a young Sinatra." In the film, "It Had to Be You" is sung by Sinatra; on the album, it's the voice of Connick you hear.

It's obvious that Mr. Reiner had lost his hearing from too much exposure to bands like Spinal Tap (who insist on playing at volume number eleven); Connick's voice couldn't be confused with Sinatra's in anyone's wildest dreams. The gatekeepers of the music and mass media industry, in that immediate pre-Internet era, began heavily pushing Connick as both substitute and successor to Sinatra. Naturally, those of us who loved the real Sinatra tended to resent how Connick, who was everywhere in that initial burst of fame, was being crammed down our throats as the *Chairman nouveau*.

Connick himself didn't much care for it either: He readily acknowledges Sinatra's place as the pre-eminent interpreter of the American songbook, but unlike other young singers attempting to do this music, he never tried to copy FS. Apart from singing some of the same songs (it would have been pointless and impossible to avoid every standard that Sinatra ever sang), Connick has carved out a unique career, and even in this early period he was already going his own way. Instead of collaborating with great arrangers, as Sinatra did, Connick made a point of writing all his own orchestrations, leading his own band, playing piano as often as possible; he's also written more than a few worthwhile original songs. (The pianist's own "A Wink and a Smile" was the big number from *Sleepless in Seattle*, Nora Ephron and Meg Ryan's unofficial follow-up to *When Harry Met Sally*.)

Apart from that, to me Connick's voice sounds nothing like Sinatra's—he doesn't have anything like the Chairman's great vocal and emotional richness, as he is the first to admit, although to this day he continues to study Sinatra's phrasing and interpretation almost obsessively. Study—not copy. Connick's voice is far hoarser and raspier—if you were to describe him as a follower of Tony Bennett you would get less of an argument from me. As a singer—his other talents aside—he does have positive attributes, such as a grounding in the blues, a capacity for swing (not the same kind as Sinatra's), and a very healthy predilection for New Orleans music in all its varieties. He also has a strong charisma that's uniquely his own.

The singer-pianist has gone from strength to strength from *Harry Met Sally* in 1989 to now, twenty years later, when, in his early forties he can look back at three Grammy awards, eleven gold or platinum albums, and accumulated sales of 20 million albums worldwide. (In addition to a movie career that includes roughly twenty feature films and many TV appearances.)

Try as I might, even I could no longer profess not to like Connick by the turn of the twenty-first century: In 2001, he was especially appealing in the ABC-TV film of Rodgers and Hammerstein's *South Pacific* (co-starring Glenn Close, and far superior to the disappointing film version of 1959); Connick vividly brought the male juvenile lead to life, with a lot more blood in his veins than I had ever suspected Lieutenant Cable had. And he was even better in the Broadway revival of *The Pajama Game* as a two-fisted, piano-playing Sid Sorokin. For a New Orleans jazz and blues piano player cum traditional pop singer, he was surprisingly solid as an old-school Broadway leading man. In the same year, 2001, he also released *Songs I Heard*, my favorite of his many albums up to that time.

Rather than compare Connick with Sinatra, it's wiser to view him essentially as a New Orleans musician (versed in jazz as well as R&B) who expanded his purview to include traditional pop as well as Broadway, and many other styles along the way. The opening track of *Songs I Heard*, in which he reimagines "Supercalifragilisticexpialidocious" (from *Mary Poppins*) as a New Orleans street parade, with band chanting and crowd noises, is a great example. Whether or not one likes his music is unimportant (and I have come to like a great deal of it); the point is that it is *his* music, not a hand-me-down version of someone else's.

By the time *When Harry Met Sally* made Connick into an "overnight" sensation, he had already been playing the piano for seventeen years. The central inspiration for all of his music is neither the Great American Songbook nor Broadway, but the city of New Orleans itself, where he was born in 1967. Both his parents were lawyers; they paid their way through law school by running a music store together. His mother (who died of cancer when Harry was thirteen) had been a judge and a State

Supreme Court justice; his father was the district attorney of New Orleans for twenty years and an avocational singer.

Connick Jr. grew up immersed in the sounds of the city with the richest musical heritage in all the Western Hemisphere, from the opera house to the brass bands of the street parades to the funk, Dixieland, zydeco, and other music heard in the French Quarter bars. The piano was always his focus: He studied jazz with master educator Ellis Marsalis (to this day he is something of an unofficial Marsalis brother) and he learned the blues from the legendary, short-lived piano wizard James Booker.

Connick also played Beethoven in concert with the New Orleans Symphony Orchestra at age nine, and made his first two albums at ten and eleven. These were *Dixieland Plus*, which was all instrumental, and *Pure Dixieland*, which was originally released under the name of trumpeter Teddy Riley but featured one vocal by Connick (possibly for that reason, it was reissued on CD by Columbia under Connick's name as *Eleven*). The youngster sings "Doctor Jazz" from the Jelly Roll Morton songbook in a wildly exuberant fashion; on a blindfold test I would have said it was a ninety-year-old bar musician trying to sound like an eleven-year-old boy.

After graduating from Jesuit High School in New Orleans, Connick arrived in New York, where he attended Hunter College and then the Manhattan School of Music. In 1987, he was heard by Dr. George Butler, head of the jazz department at Columbia Records, who was immediately interested in the charismatic young pianist. That year, the pianist released *Harry Connick Jr.*, his first Columbia album. At the time, Connick was generally assumed to be part of the new diaspora of bopcentric young lions from New Orleans, led by the Marsalis brothers.

In 1988, be released his second Columbia album, *Twenty,* and things really began to happen. *Twenty* led to the Algonquin and then to *When Harry Met Sally,* which led to an opportunity for him to put together his own big band, which he took on the road for a series of extensive national and world tours. Much of the pattern for his future career was set in 1990. In that year he released four projects:

- *We Are in Love,* which documented the debut of the Connick orchestra, and also amounted to his first major effort as an arranger and as a songwriter.

- *Lofty's Roach Soufflé,* a piano trio album, comprised of original instrumentals, heavily inspired by Thelonious Monk (although the title is more reminiscent of Charles Mingus's cryptic wordplay).

- His first home video, *Singin' & Swingin'* (okay, so the title wasn't staggeringly original).

- His first acting role, in the war epic *Memphis Belle;* there was a tint of retro here in that

Connick, who was already associated with old songs, was acting in a World War II story. However, this would not be the case for most of his subsequent films.

While 1990 was a busy year for him, for most of the last two decades he has followed a similar pattern. His "home base" is generally albums of standards (and his own original songs in the tradition of the Great American Songbook), usually sung with a big band playing his own arrangements. These releases include: *Blue Light, Red Light* (1991), the all-original *To See You* (1997), the mostly standards *Come by Me* (1999), and the somewhat more contemporary *Only You* of 2004. Connick has also released three big-selling albums of holiday music: *When My Heart Finds Christmas* (1993), *Harry for the Holidays* (2003), and *What a Night! A Christmas Album* (2008), all of which contribute to his image as a modern-day inheritor of the mantle of his fellow C-singers, Crosby, Como, and Cole.

Apart from the "mainstream vocal" albums, Connick has made a series of pianocentric and instrumental recordings, of which *25* (1992) and *30* (1997) are both notable follow-ups to *Twenty*, in that they combine piano solos with vocal-and-piano tracks. These sets are as ambitious as they are personal: Connick may rely on his own voice and keyboards (with a few guest shots) but doesn't make things easy for himself by biting off such complex compositions as John Coltrane's "Moment's Notice." On the whole, he keeps it simple, with a keyboard style that's equal parts Monk (especially on "Caravan") and James Booker; "Tangerine" has a particularly Bookerish New Orleans–style shuffle beat to it.

The three numerical albums are steeped in the diverse musical traditions of New Orleans. There's a memorable "Didn't He Ramble" on *25*, in which the old street parade theme is brought indoors and played on the piano, while *30* includes one of the national anthems of New Orleans R&B, "Junko Partner," which he commences with a rather grandiose classical introduction. Likewise "Time After Time" on *Come by Me* boasts a very third-streamy semi-classical lead-in, rather like Bartók with a beat—before going into a blues-based, Basiesque rendition of the Jule Styne melody.

The Crescent City centrism is by no means rigidly enforced: Connick's main collaboration with Wynton Marsalis is "I'll Only Miss Her (When I Think of Her)" on *30*, a sixties show tune on which both singer and trumpeter play piano at different points. Yet no matter who's at the keyboard, it's an exceptionally tender and intimate reading. When Connick recorded his two "funk" albums, *She* (1994) and *Star Turtle* (1996), it was taken as a sign that he was "deserting" jazz and the songbook; in retrospect, he was merely exploring another aspect of New Orleans music, since these two more poppish releases are primarily driven by Louisiana backbeats.

Still, his major Crescent City–inspired projects are a pair of albums from 2006, *Oh, My Nola* and *Chanson du Vieux Carré*, released simultaneously in the wake of Hurricane Katrina. *Chanson* (actually recorded in 2003) is primarily instrumental, yet the two albums, taken together, form a cohesive package. *Oh, My Nola* could be called "The New Orleans Songbook" in that it addresses a wide variety of songs associated with various strands of the city's music, from Louis Armstrong's Broadway-meets-Dixieland hit "Hello, Dolly!" to Lee Dorsey's R&B perennial "Workin' in a Coal Mine" (which is virtually the first punk rock anthem)." The two albums complement each other beautifully, as in the way Armstrong's "Someday You'll Be Sorry" on *Chanson* dovetails perfectly with Dave Bartholomew's "Someday (You'll Want Me)" on *Nola*.

Much of Connick's "mainstream" music is also animated by its proximity to the French Quarter: The 1999 *Come by Me* is highlighted by "Cry Me a River" done in the style of a funeral dirge, with mournful trumpet and trombone surrounding him, followed by a longish and very up-tempo "Love for Sale." The notion of swinging a Cole Porter ballad such as this is very much a Sinatra conceit—the Swingin' Lover ideal—but that basic concept is the only thing Connick borrows from the Chairman. His phrasing, even of the verse, is very much his own, and there's an interlude of tenor sax and piano that returns to the Monk–Charlie Rouse wellspring.

Only You (2004) has a very specific focus: standard-type songs that were popular in the early rock era. Many of these were already decades old when they became hits (usually for a second or third time) in the fifties: "The Very Thought of You," "My Blue Heaven," "My Prayer," and "I Only Have Eyes for You," among others. He renders "Prayer" with something like a salon orchestra, a potent combination of strings, solo and in ensemble, and percussion (though not notably Bartókian here). "I Only Have Eyes for You" has Connick singing legato over a staccato background, with what at first seems like an incongruous rhythm pattern, but gradually letting a Gordon Jenkinsy violin section overtake him. He finishes with "Good Night, My Love (Pleasant Dreams)," a song associated with African American baritones with very deep voices, like Earl Grant, Lou Rawls, and Barry White; Connick sings it against a saxophone quartet that gives it more of a jazz feel, and makes the song sound remarkably intimate.

Your Songs (2009), Connick's most recent album, shows that even in a time of crisis for the record industry, Connick is a dependable seller—the disc placed in the top ten of the *Billboard* 200. It's an amazingly subtle record: Producer Clive Davis gave Connick the guidelines that he wanted traditional pop songs arranged and sung in a traditional way, but Connick found ways to be creative within what might seem fairly restrictive parameters. The opener, "All the Way," is semislow, basically a ballad,

with a large orchestra and strings; in its rough outline, it sounds exactly like the way Sinatra and Riddle laid the song down for history in 1957. But when you listen closely, you realize that this is a ballad with a beat to it, a very subtle underlying kick—in fact, in attitude it sounds less like a fifties Sinatra love song than one of his later, self-empowerment anthems like "For Once in My Life" and "Maybe This Time" (in fact, Connick's arranging style is very similar to Don Costa's, and that's a compliment). Connick told me that he instructed both the Marsalis brothers (Branford solos on "All the Way," Wynton on "Can't Help Falling in Love with You") just to play the melody straight as written—and the challenge was to personalize the tunes without seriously altering them. All three were up to the task. On "Just the Way You Are" he follows Billy Joel's melody to the letter, the only difference being that he puts a subtle swing beat underneath it—now it sounds more like the fifties than the seventies. "Besame Mucho" is overtly Riddlesque—it could almost be a previously unheard Sinatra Capitol single (or even an arrangement leftover from Michael Feinstein's *The Sinatra Project*). "Who Can I Turn To" is Connick's latest homage to hero Anthony Newley. "Mona Lisa" opens with semiclassical strings—not entirely unlike Riddle's on the 1949 Nat Cole original—but almost imperceptibly settles into a slow dance groove. Connick's own singing is just as subtle—you can tell that he sweated out the orchestral arrangements for months and months, but came up with his specific phrasing more or less on the spot in the studio.

Possibly even more than the New Orleans duo (*Chanson* and *Nola*), the Connick album that would first accompany me to a desert island is *Songs I Heard*. It's a unique concept—a grown-up album of children's songs—arranged with characteristic ingenuity and sung directly *to* children, rather than *down to* them. He starts with the above mentioned street parade version of "Supercalifragilisticexpialidocious"—in which he and the band chant the title loud enough to sound more precocious than atrocious; if "Cry Me a River" represented the dirge that you would hear on the march to the graveyard, this is what the band would play on the parade back from the cemetery to the Fourth Ward. The other *Mary Poppins* song, "A Spoonful of Sugar," is treated similarly, like a brass band strutting down Bourbon Street. Apart from the two numbers from *Poppins* (the only Disney property represented), the album consists of songs from *The Wizard of Oz, Annie, The Sound of Music*, and *Willy Wonka and the Chocolate Factory*.

Connick is swinging and charismatic when treating "The Lonely Goatherd" to a vigorous two-beat and spicing it up with some biting brass in the instrumental break, not to mention a few modulations in the out chorus. Harold Arlen's *Oz* songs, particularly "Ding Dong! The Witch Is Dead" and

"The Jitterbug," are deliberately Ellingtonian; Connick is obviously mindful that Ellington and Harold Arlen got their start together at the Cotton Club. "Ding Dong!" has the melody stated on a soprano saxophone (answered by wa-wa trombones) before his vocal entrance. "Jitterbug" (famously cut from the actual film) opens with Connick and several sidemen making like the Lion, the Scarecrow, and the Tin Man (showing that Connick's movie acting career is not entirely unrelated to his record career). Throughout the yodels of the "Goatherd," the "yo-hos" of "Ding Dong!," and the childlike nonsense of "Supercalifragilistic (etc., etc.)" and "Oompa Loompa," and on virtually every track, one has to marvel at Connick's utter lack of self-consciousness; he just digs into it and sings straight-ahead, completely without fear.

You can tell *Willy Wonka* had a big impact on the young Prince Harry when it was first released in 1971 (he was four at the time); Connick's views on songs and singers are as idiosyncratic as his music is, and he tells me the late Anthony Newley is one of his heroes. Apart from the nonsense throughout *Songs I Heard*, "Pure Imagination" is one of Connick's most heartfelt performances. It may not make sense to describe it as a ballad; it's almost a spiritual, a song about the power of belief, except that the singer stops short of taking it quite that seriously. He runs "Pure Imagination" through "Candy Man," and though the medley is expertly done, he sings "Pure Imagination" so movingly I wish he'd allowed us to hear him do the whole song by itself.

The medley of "Golden Ticket" and "I Want It Now" makes more sense, the latter being a patter piece that Connick delivers like a swinging slice of hip-hop. "Golden Ticket" becomes a swinging update of "Over the Rainbow" (also heard here), a song about wishing and yearning for something better of the sort that only a child can properly express. Even more than the rest of Connick's best music, *Songs I Heard* is a golden ticket to someplace very special indeed.

Michael Bublé (born 1975)

Michael Bublé is the world's greatest wedding singer. I wish I could take credit for that line (I can't remember where I heard it, so perhaps my subconscious wants to convince me that I actually thought of it myself). Bublé has a wonderful voice and a swinging sense of time that's truly surprising for anyone born in the seventies (many decades after swing was the thing), while his personality is a combination of charisma and chutzpah that makes him like no one else. He's got everything except originality: Too much of the time he seems bent on re-creating well-known recordings, from the classic Sinatra-Riddle arrangement of "I've Got You Under My Skin" to a classic of a different sort, the 1972 Billy Paul hit "Me and Mrs. Jones." He sings them all very well, and overall he does an excellent job at every-

thing, short of interpreting these songs in a distinct and personal fashion. He's like a human jukebox, one with plenty of personality and charm, but not a style of his own. Hell, if I could hire him to sing at my wedding I would (not that I plan to have yet another one).

At times, Bublé seems to be exploiting the idea that listeners raised on post-1970 pop have no concept of interpretation: Apparently, to his fans, there's no point in singing "For Once in My Life" unless you sing the exact same arrangement that Sinatra made into a classic forty years ago. Yet I wonder: If Bublé were primarily a contemporary pop star who sang Lennon-McCartney songs almost exactly the way the Beatles recorded them or did Dylan songs exactly as they're heard on vintage Dylan albums (which Dylan himself refuses to do), he'd be relegated to working at tribute shows at brunch. Why it's acceptable to clone and cover arrangements associated with singers who didn't write their own songs is beyond me. Bublé is, in a sense, the perfect performer of the Great American Songbook for the age of karaoke and *American Idol* (there, I've said it again).

Although Bublé seems to borrow more numbers from Sinatra than from anyone else, the young singer (who was born in Burnaby, British Columbia, in 1975) was first attracted to the voice of Bing Crosby, whom he heard doing Christmas music, and then even more so to Bobby Darin. His grandfather, who was born in Italy, encouraged his singing, helping the youngster to take music lessons and, presumably, steering him to the right records to listen to. Between the ages of eighteen and twenty-five, Bublé sang and acted in a variety of miscellaneous spots (including shots on several TV shows), almost entirely in Canada.

Around 2000, he came to the attention of superstar producer David Foster; as it happened, this had come about as the result of him singing at a wedding (that of former prime minister Brian Mulroney). Foster then took the somewhat audacious step of producing and marketing him as a new-style pop idol whose gimmick was that he worked with songs and styles from the sixties and earlier. Bublé was packaged as a latter-day Rat Packer for an audience who didn't quite know what that meant, other than something to do with a cocky, "swaggering" attitude.

Bublé's recording career can be divided between his independently produced earlier work, mostly done in Canada, and more recent releases on Reprise (the label founded by Sinatra). The first group consists of three albums produced on his own dime in his twenties: *First Dance* (1995), *BaBalu* (2001), and *Dream* (2002). (There's also *Totally Bublé*, a collection of songs he recorded for the sound track of the 2001 film *Totally Blonde*.) His big-time, major label American releases include *Michael Bublé*, generally described as his debut release (2003), *It's Time* (2005), and *Call Me Irresponsible* (2007). There also are three officially released live sets, most of which have appeared both as CDs and DVDs: *Come Fly with Me* (2004), *Caught in the Act* (2005), and the latest, *Michael Bublé Meets Madison Square Garden* (2009).

Just as there are three kinds of Bublé releases—studio, live, and prehistoric—his music itself also comes in three distinct flavors. The first is those many tracks where he replicates an iconic recording almost exactly: Bobby Darin's finger-snapping treatment of "Lazy River" and boogaloo revamp of "You Must Have Been a Beautiful Baby"; Sinatra's above-mentioned "I've Got You Under My Skin" and "For Once in My Life"; Louis Prima's "Buona Sera" and his signature medley of "When You're Smiling" and "Sheik of Araby." As if to prove that Bublé owns records by non-Italians, he's also come up with virtual clones of Lou Rawls's "You'll Never Find Another Love Like Mine" and Mel Tormé's "Comin' Home, Baby." (The latter, which is one of the records Mel would probably have least liked to hear anyone re-create, is done with the vocal group Boyz II Men who have achieved the distinction of sounding exactly like a single voice overdubbed four times in as bland a way as possible.)

The second variety of Bublé music is the many cases where he sings a standard song more or less the way Sinatra (and others) did it—but not *exactly*. His "Summer Wind" doesn't employ Nelson Riddle's distinct organ countermelody, but it's cast in the same tempo, some of the same modulations, and is close enough to be considered a near-cover. Likewise, his treatment of the Sinatra-Basie "The Best Is Yet to Come" isn't quite a clone, yet it hardly has enough original DNA to stand on its own. The great majority of the arrangements that he sings fall into this category; even if they aren't total knockoffs, they might as well be. On these tracks, Bublé stands in relation to Sinatra the way a faux Gucci bag (purchased on Canal Street for whatever cash you have in your pocket) stands in relation to the thousand-dollar real thing for sale at Bloomingdale's.

But there are Bublé performances where—hello!—he actually comes close to creating something that's truly his own. "Save the Last Dance for Me," by Doc Pomus and Morty Schuman, was a signature hit for the Drifters in 1960, with something of a subtle Latin polyrhythm; in 2004, Harry Connick Jr. reconceived "Last Dance" as a romantic love song, not so much as a dance. A year later, Bublé included it on his second American album, *It's Time*, in which he sings it like the Drifters on steroids, sharpening the 4/4 swing accents and increasing the salsa content. I like the others, but am almost ashamed to admit that Bublé's is the version I play most often when I feel like listening to that song.

He has recorded at least one completely successful love song: "Wonderful Tonight" is a rock 'n' roll power ballad by Eric Clapton with something of a country feeling. Bublé sings it as a duet with Brazil-

ian singer-songwriter Ivan Lins and makes it into a credible bossa ballad. The two men sing together rather like Sinatra and Jobim on their classic collaborations, yet "Wonderful Tonight" illustrates the difference between inspiration and imitation.

Still, Bublé is best appreciated for his up-tempos, especially the ones he finds in unlikely places. Early on, he became known for a hard-swing—not to mention ass-kicking—version of "Spider-Man," in which the 1967 cartoon theme is presented as a variation on "Sing! Sing! Sing!" (This track was remixed for use on the sound track of the 2004 *Spider-Man 2*, but with the jazz elements and solos replaced by an electronic background.) There's a camp element, to be sure, but Bublé makes "Spider-Man" work as real music.

Van Morrison's "Moondance" is a rock 'n' roll anthem with roots in the swing era; the composer described it as a more "sophisticated" tune than he usually wrote (although the lyric is still considerably more awkward than if it had been written by, say, Sammy Cahn), and noted that it would be a perfectly appropriate song for Sinatra.

"Moondance" is an even more natural tune for retro swingers; Michael Feinstein also did it in 1993, and it's one of his better jazzier offerings. Bublé's "Moondance" is the most swinging of them all. Likewise, "Crazy Little Thing Called Love," by Freddie Mercury for the Britpop group Queen in the classic rockabilly style of early Elvis and Jerry Lee Lewis, needed only a minor adjustment so that Bublé could put a solid four beat to the thing. It swings gloriously, without fuss or fanfare.

Still, for every Bublé track I enjoy, there's at least another one that seems like a second-rate imitation; one doesn't have to be an idolator of the Chairman to concede that no one will ever be a better Sinatra than Sinatra. The only Bublé album I can listen to all the way through is his final independent effort, the 2002 *Dream*. At some moments you feel that he would have liked to imitate an iconic recording by Sinatra or whoever but at that point simply didn't have the economic resources for big band musicians, arrangers, and transcribers. Instead, the whole thing was done essentially with just solo guitar and muted trumpet, and the setting forces the singer to be both more original and intimate than on his later, more well-heeled productions.

The use of guitar accompaniment also affords him the opportunity to pay homage to another of his major inspirations, the Mills Brothers, and, again possibly because he's only one boy with a guitar (as opposed to four), the project comes out on the side of tribute rather than rip-off. It's a well-thought-out salute, including such Mills perennials as "Don't Be a Baby, Baby," "Maria Elena," "Daddy's Little Girl," "You Always Hurt the One You Love," "Paper Doll" (which features a second Bublé voice at one point, apparently through overdubbing), and "Till Then." Indeed, if anyone ever puts together a new, nonfamilial edition of the Mills Brothers as a touring act, Bublé's is the first number they should call.

Throughout *Dream*, Bublé sings simply and directly, like the young Chet Baker but with more expansive vocal chops, as if he's really trying to communicate a specific emotion rather than merely showing off. It's kind of frustrating to think that he made his most substantial contribution to the art of pop singing at the age of twenty-seven, long before anyone had heard of him. It's more encouraging to conclude that his best work may yet be ahead of him.

Jamie Cullum (born 1979)

If Harry Connick Jr. is somewhat cocky and Michael Bublé almost irritatingly impudent, then Jamie Cullum, who is generally categorized as Great Britain's entry in the retro boy crooner stakes, is more than downright cheeky: He's a regular wise-ass, he is. Even the titles of his albums seem to satirize the whole genre. Who else would sing "Night and Day," "Love for Sale," and "They Can't Take That Away from Me," along with seven other overly familiar standards on his first album and call the whole thing *Heard It All Before*? Indeed! And who else would begin his second album with four venerable standards in a row ("You and the Night and the Music," "I Can't Get Started," "Devil May Care," and "You're Nobody Till Somebody Loves You") and then title *that* album *Pointless Nostalgic*? With both titles, Cullum not only seemed to be making fun of himself for the very idea of singing old standards, but of us, for being pointless nostalgics square enough to keep listening again and again to songs we'd heard a million times before.

In retrospect, it turns out that Cullum is probably the best pure interpreter of the songbook in this group: Unlike Connick, he doesn't need to apply a New Orleans street beat to make a song distinctively his own, and unlike Bublé, he doesn't have to pretend that every song ever written is secretly "Sing! Sing! Sing!" in disguise. More than the others, Cullum can sing the songs more or less as written, and in the tempos and time signatures where they are most frequently played, and still sound like himself.

Most Americans first heard of Jamie Cullum when Universal Music (USA) paid a bloody million for his contract—and that's pounds, mind you, not bucks—a big gamble that he could sell like a male equivalent of their contractee Diana Krall. Indeed, the retro pop stakes are high: As already mentioned, Harry Jr. has sold a total of 25 million records. Bublé makes a more audacious claim; according to that singer's Web site, he has so far sold 20 million units—which is an awful lot in the seven-year span between 2003 and 2009. So $2 million and change for Cullum, who could potentially sell in that ballpark, was not necessarily a bad bet (particularly in the wake of Norah Jones, whose first album alone, released in 2001, has sold as many as 20 mil-

lion copies). A million pounds turned out to be a bargain; Cullum's Universal debut, *Twentysomething* (2003), established the singer-pianist as the most successful British jazz musician anyone can remember.

According to his basic biography, Cullum was born in Essex, and his family includes both Burmese and Jewish relatives. By the time he went to university, as the Brits say, he was already an experienced pianist-singer in bars, catering halls (for weddings and bar mitzvahs), and any other venues that were prepared to overlook his underage status. With albums as career milestones to mark his progress, Cullum gradually emerged: He produced *Heard It All Before* himself (and supposedly pressed a mere six hundred copies) at the age of twenty in 1999. *Pointless Nostalgic* was released by the BritJazz label Candid Records, and served to bring him to the attention of Universal, who, as noted, plunked down a huge pile of pound notes for his contract—and then got it all back almost immediately with the tremendous success of *Twentysomething* in 2003. Strangely, Cullum has only done two further studio albums since then, *Catching Tales* (2005) and *The Pursuit* (2009).

Appropriately, he has also released two DVDs, which offer a good representation of what he's like in personal appearances. If ever there was an artist to be experienced live—or at least seen as well as heard—it's Cullum. In the autumn of 2003, he made his American debut at the Oak Room and immediately established himself as one of the most dynamic, in-your-face performers ever to appear at the Gonk. Short, dark, and mop-topped, he is at once Britain's answer to Harry Connick (one of his heroes) and jazz's answer to the Monkees' Davey Jones. Cullum is wildly irreverent and renders every song with a zaniness redolent of Fats Waller on a combination of Viagra and laughing gas—as if he's unable to take anything seriously. He began the Oak Room show with "It Could Happen to You"—scatting, humming, and using his piano as percussion—pounding on the wood as if it were a conga drum.

The British press has described Cullum as "Sinatra in sneakers"; Cullum himself has encouraged the comparison with Mel Tormé by re-creating the late singer's classic treatment of "Too Close for Comfort" (on *Nostalgic*), a move that was *Pointless* indeed since it merely showed that Cullum isn't in anywhere near Tormé's ballpark in terms of vocal virtuosity. Yet it isn't sheer vocal power that makes Cullum's singing interesting, although his voice is dark and has something of a profound edge to it; rather, he relies on a combination of a restless imagination and pure cojones.

Whether singing or playing, he never hesitates to skewer melodies both old and new in the most anarchic fashion. His fellow twenty-somethings go wild when he jazzes up songs by Jimi Hendrix ("The

Wind Cries Mary," done as a gospel number with New Orleans street parade press rolls—a treatment inspired more by Connick than Hendrix) and Radiohead ("High and Dry" propelled by a hard bop beat instead of the familiar rock rhythm patterns). Likewise, the old guard of the Algonquin shrieked with surprise and delight when he rendered "I Could Have Danced All Night" as the anthem for an XTC-inspired rave-up.

Mr. Cullum confesses to having been originally inspired by Harry Connick ("I thought he invented jazz," he says), whom he salutes in "It Had to Be You," mimicking the New Orleanian's distinctive voice and idiosyncratic keyboard style. "I Get a Kick out of You," "I've Got You Under My Skin" (in which his piano solo, which starts in octaves, hews closer to the melody than his stylized vocal), and "Blame It on My Youth" use Sinatra as a starting point. "Kick" recalls Sinatra's framework, beginning, and ending (with Sinatra's famous "you give me a boot" interjection). At the Oak Room, he repeatedly pushed irreverence to a level just short of outright parody. Every time he sang "Kick," for instance, drummer Sebastiaan de Krom delivered an earthquake-level cymbal crash. In the second chorus of "Skin," when he reaches the phrase "stop before I begin," Cullum and his trio literally stopped, walked away from their instruments, adjusted their accoutrements, had a drink, and then resumed.

Cullum is entirely unafraid to go out on a limb. Yet he may be a little scared to come back in. In 2003, he was still incapable of delivering a ballad effectively. "Blame It on My Youth" came closest, but I remember thinking it would be a long time before he broke anybody's heart. (The most affecting track on *Nostalgic* was his reassessment of "In the Wee Small Hours of the Morning," which utilized "Ballad of the Sad Young Men" as an instrumental framework.) Entertaining as he was at this point, he was still a bit frantic; one twenty-something young lady sitting next to me commented, "This is why I don't date guys my age."

Twentysomething also contains his most nearly successful early ballad, "What a Diff'rence a Day Makes," which is surprisingly traditional and even reverent. "Singin' in the Rain," on the other hand, sounds more like Kraftwerk than Arthur Freed, with an electronic setting and a whole new melody that seems at odds with the familiar text. Likewise, "I Only Have Eyes for You" is a techno update of the Harry Warren classic as arranged in doo-wop style by the Flamingos—not Dick Powell. He also came up with an inspired exotica-style treatment of the 1962 pop hit "Our Day Will Come," in which a shimmering organ evokes Korla Pandit and Martin Denny playing a "Caravan"-like countermelody. (The latter two tracks come from *Catching Tales*, an album that is otherwise skewed more toward Cullum's originals and away from standards.)

In general, Cullum is not yet as compelling on record as he is in person, but that's true of a great many major performers, both classic and contemporary. In person, Mr. Cullum's knockabout, relentlessly upbeat style is exciting and vastly entertaining—an hour with him fairly flies by and leaves you exhausted in the process. There are worse things for a record company to do with a million quid.

Peter Cincotti (born 1983)

Of all the performers in this book, Peter Cincotti probably has enjoyed the shortest association with the American songbook. He debuted at the Algonquin at nineteen in 2003 (the same year as Cullum), and was almost instantly playing concert spaces and theaters, such as Carnegie Hall and Rose Hall (to name two big venues in New York alone). He had two highly successful albums on Concord, the eponymous *Peter Cincotti* (2003) and *On the Moon* (2004, both produced by pop veteran Phil Ramone), which both sold on the gold level (at least) in Europe. After another year or so of touring, Cincotti more or less retired from the standards scene. He reemerged later in the decade with a new album (*East of Angel Town*), a new label (Warner Bros.), a new producer (David Foster, although not reprising the retro-swing sound of Bublé), and a whole new direction, built on heavily layered pop originals rather than acoustic jazz standards. It's too soon to gauge how successful the transition will be.

Of the boychicks in this batch, Cincotti is by far the most prodigious as a piano player; had he applied himself on a purely instrumental level, he might have made himself into a significant force on the keyboard. In fact, the piano is overall the best reason to listen to Cincotti (in his "traditional" acoustic music at least), rather than his voice or his original songs. Where songs like "I Changed the Rules" seem like one teenager singing to his peers, his piano work (even at age nineteen) seems the work of a mature and accomplished musician, one who bespeaks a distinctly rock 'n' roll sensibility even while he's playing jazz and standards.

Cincotti is also the main retro boychick to actually come from New York, the Upper East Side of Manhattan specifically. His father, who died when Cincotti was a toddler, was a prominent New York attorney, and Cincotti attended the demanding Horace Mann School. He was already a piano wiz when he came to the attention of a pair of Jacks: jazz producer Jack Kleinsinger, who featured him in one of his *Highlights in Jazz* concerts very early on, and Jack Lewin, who employed him in the long-running off-Broadway tribute show *Our Sinatra* (where I first saw him). Cincotti played Joe's Pub at age seventeen in 2001, when he was still too young to enter a pub legally.

Apart from the piano, Cincotti's greatest asset is his personality: He's immediately likable, and not at all cheeky or impudent. That may be part of the difficulty: Perhaps the only way a twenty-one-year-old can sing the time-tested standards is by calling attention to the pointless nostalgia of it all. This kind of a disclaimer liberates one from the pressure of having to directly compete with the likes of Sinatra, Cole, and Bennett. Bublé and Cullum avoided the comparison by being wise-asses, but Cincotti, who isn't one, had no choice but to go for the gold, which put him in a further bind. Particularly in our contemporary era, in which people in general mature more slowly, Cincotti was celebrated for his youth. (Imagine! A nineteen-year-old who can sing "Ain't Misbehavin'"!) But at the same time, singing and fully understanding Rodgers and Hart or Cole Porter requires a deeper level of maturity than is possible at that age (particularly for young males).

At times, Cincotti seemed to be most successful when giving out with youthful irreverence, as on Rodgers and Hammerstein's "Bali Hai" rendered in odd-meter funk with a blues harmonica obbligato. He rewrites "I Love Paris" almost as a Latin boogie stop shuffle with a Cuban-style piano solo (he could have retitled it "I Love Havana") and reconsiders the famous minor-to-major modulation. Contrastingly, on "St. Louis Blues" (the youngest performer around seemed intent on addressing the oldest song still in the general repertoire) he extends the minor section almost indefinitely.

Like Connick and Bublé, Cincotti found an attractive middle ground in rock-era standards such as two Brill Building anthems by Carole King, "Up on the Roof" and "Some Kind of Wonderful." Goodness knows, these aren't supposed to be as deep as "Lush Life" or "Wee Small Hours," and any lyrical meaning you can bring to them seems like a bonus from God. Cincotti was also especially entertaining with his piano features: Most jazz musicians his age tend to be at the point where they're trying to drown the audience in notes in chords, but Cincotti learned early on the value of showmanship and judiciously

applied technique, which can be precisely the opposite of showing off all the way through. The obvious approach to "Cherokee" is to play it at supersonic speed, but Cincotti shows the patience to wait, almost tease us with the tune, and then, only in the climax, deluge us with notes. His homage to Erroll Garner, "Spinning Wheel" (and clever it was to pick a sixties pop hit that Garner had recorded), was an instant crowd-pleaser, too, in which he astutely captured the Imp's amazing left-handed syncopations and elbow thumps. So, too, were those tracks that added vocals to piano features, like "Ain't Misbehavin'" and "You Stepped Out of a Dream."

Entertaining as he could be, Cincotti didn't quite solve the puzzle of how one interprets the great lyrics through life experience, when, in his early twenties, he had barely even lived. He also seemed committed to a windmill-jousting-like quest of playing for audiences of his own generation; original songs like "I Changed the Rules" were aimed directly at high school kids, yet he was also determined to introduce teens and twenty-somethings to Gershwin. Even so, most of his audience (and not just at the Algonquin) seemed to be old enough to be his grandparents (the same holds true for Connick, Bublé, and Cullum).

Small wonder that Cincotti drifted to the power pop side of the fence, over to *East of Angel Town*, where a wholly different set of considerations were in play. He spent years writing and working on his pop album, and while it does seem to have done at least marginally better on the charts than the two jazz-and-standards CDs, one wonders if it was worth the considerably greater investment of funds and labor. It certainly isn't written in stone that Peter Cincotti is never going to come back to jazz and the songbook; after all, he is only (as of 2010) twenty-seven. His whole career has thus far transpired in considerably less time than it's taken me to write this book.

Extras

Folk Rock: Bob Dylan (born 1941)

Picture, if you will, two great Jewish songwriters, Sammy Cahn and Bob Dylan, sitting next to each other at an ASCAP function. You wouldn't think—at least I wouldn't—that they'd have much to say to each other, but Dylan told Sammy something that surprised him. "I just recorded one of your songs," the younger man says to the older one. Sammy then asks, "'Teach Me Tonight'?" That 1953 song was always loved by blues and rock singers ever since Dinah Washington recorded it, and Sammy always assumed that when a contemporary pop artist was doing one of his songs it would be "Teach Me Tonight." But no. Dylan says, "'All My Tomorrows.'" This takes Sammy by surprise; it's a sophisticated and somewhat obscure song, of the kind that almost no one but Frank Sinatra has been able to get right—for Dylan even to have heard of it shows he has a rather deep knowledge of the kind of American songbook that came before him.

In the mid-eighties, both Dylan and Sinatra gave interviews in which they reflect on their breakthrough moment, the tipping point, as Malcolm Gladwell would say, when they came on the scene and changed pop music forever—twenty years apart from each other. Sinatra told Sidney Zion about how, in 1941 (the year Dylan was born), he realized that he had to leave the Tommy Dorsey Orchestra and go out on his own. He could have played it safe and stayed with that band; by giving up his regular paycheck with Dorsey, he was trying something almost no one had done before. But difficult as it would be, it was a risk he had to take. He had hoped that the most that would happen would be that one single vocalist who had come up through the ranks of the swing bands could stand on his own; he didn't foresee what would happen, that dozens of singers would follow his lead, and, thanks to him, pop music would soon be transformed from an industry of bandleaders to an industry of pop singers.

Likewise, Dylan talked to Cameron Crowe, the rock journalist and filmmaker, about what might be called his own moment. "I didn't know it, but all the songs at the time"—meaning the point when Dylan arrived in New York, in 1961—"were written at Tin Pan Alley, the Brill Building. They had stables up there that provided songs for artists [performers]. I had not paid much attention. They were good songwriters but the world they knew and the world I knew were quite different. Most of the songs [then] being recorded came from there, I guess because most singers didn't write their own. Anyway, [now] Tin Pan Alley is gone. I put an end to it. People can record their own songs now—they're almost expected to do it. The funny thing is that I didn't start out as a songwriter. I just drifted into it. Those other people [Tin Pan Alley professional songwriters] had it down to a science."

The combined effect that Bob Dylan and the Beatles had on popular music was devastating; from about 1964 on, it was a whole new game, with whole new rules and a whole new value system. By the seventies, the producers were actively courting singer-songwriters like Barry Manilow, while "traditional" pop singers like Vic Damone and Steve Lawrence were all but ignored. (What goes around comes around: twenty and thirty years later, seventies icons like Manilow and Rod Stewart would be recording entire albums of traditional Tin Pan Alley–style standards.)

What hath Bob wrought? The musical revolution of the mid-sixties was the most far-reaching since Sinatra's twenty years earlier. Even the major sea change of the mid-1950s, the coming of rock 'n' roll, was only a minor disturbance by comparison. The first generation of rock had much more in common with the earlier age of pop singers and swing bands, in fact, than it did with the singer-songwriters of later decades. The years 1955 to 1964 saw a continuation of the relationship of professional singers like Elvis Presley and professional songwriters like Doc Pomus or Jerry Leiber and Mike Stoller. Despite the stylistic differences, their relationships paralleled those of Bing Crosby and Johnny Burke or Frank Sinatra and Sammy Cahn.

In a recent biography of Doc Pomus, Alex Halberstadt correctly described Dylan as "the boy genius who single-handedly demolished the Brill Building." Unlike every composer who came before him, Dylan's message to performers was not "sing my songs and earn me royalties," but rather "go forth and write your own damn songs!" I've always thought that the reference to "evening's empire" in "Mr. Tambourine Man," one of Dylan's most famous songs, could be construed as a reference to the twilight and, soon enough, the demise of the musical world that existed before him.

Not every change that occurs is a good thing; sometimes great music leads to a disastrous aftershock. I can only imagine that both Sinatra and Dylan had moments when they felt like Dr. Frankenstein: They had created a monster and couldn't control the damage it caused. I'm obviously glad that Frank Sinatra became the biggest thing in pop music in 1943, but the downside of his triumph was the eventual end of the big band era, which many of us still feel was the all-time high point of American popular music. Likewise, as great as Bob Dylan and the Beatles were, their arrival was, in many ways, a catastrophe for good music. As Dylan acknowledged, after the mid-1960s the age of professional songwriters was abruptly over. Suddenly, it just seemed old hat to sing songs written by people who weren't you. Nobody wanted to sing anybody else's songs anymore. For the last fifty years, every musical artist has been expected to be his or her own Bob Dylan; likewise, every band is expected to have its own Lennon and McCartney. Although it takes nothing away from their own work, Dylan and the

Beatles ultimately had what seems, from the vantage point of the twenty-first century, like an overall effect on the development of pop music that was hardly entirely positive.

What does Dylan mean when he says that songwriters before him "had it down to a science"? One obvious interpretation is that he's describing his own songwriting as anything but scientific. Rather than trying to appear "scientific" or professional, he deliberately cultivated a musical style that at least in the beginning seemed as casual as possible. That's obvious as soon as he opens his mouth. The first thing you notice is that he doesn't seem to have any voice whatsoever, or any kind of vocal technique or training. Gradually, it becomes clear, however, that this is only a ruse—merely what he wants you to think, it's his way of catching you off guard.

There are vocal virtuosos and there are vocal virtuosos—from Sinatra to Ezio Pinza to Big Joe Turner (as Whitney Balliett has convincingly shown) to Elvis especially—all had amazingly beautiful voices, a powerful big sound, great chops, and tons of technique all the way down. Dylan deliberately wants to avoid that: When you listen to him perform, he doesn't want you to hear chops or technique or an attractive voice. Yet he's calling attention to the voice just the same, by making it so gruff. Just the way Blossom Dearie makes us listen harder by singing softly, Dylan makes us pay more attention to the lyrics by making them harder to understand. Even when we can make out the words clearly, the business of deciphering the meaning has only just begun.

Like a lot of people, for a long time I found Dylan's songs more palatable when sung by others. I gained a grudging respect for him, however, when he appeared at a 2004 benefit (at the world-famous Apollo Theater) for Jazz at Lincoln Center. Instead of bringing his own band, Dylan appeared with trumpeter Wynton Marsalis and his sextet; he sang one of his best-known songs, "Don't Think Twice," and articulated the lyrics in such a way that I could actually follow them. For me, this was a personal revelation—it was the first time I actually found myself really liking Bob Dylan. Even then, I couldn't have predicted that, within a few years, I not only would make a point of obtaining every album he ever made, but would be listening to live recordings from 2010 concerts in Osaka.

Which goes to show how easy it is to acclimate oneself to the sound of Dylan's voice—and to grow to love it. One of the more extreme tests of how much of the Dylan voice you're willing to love arrived in the form of his 2009 release *Christmas in the Heart*. This was one of two albums he released that year, the other being the more traditional *Together Through Life*; the Christmas project was described as a "Web-only" special distributed through "alternate" retail channels to raise money for charitable causes.

Two things about *Christmas in the Heart* immediately stand out. First, this is by far the singer-songwriter's most notable homage to the pre-Dylan era of pop music, when singing and songwriting were separate professions. In other albums, Dylan has referenced all kinds of earlier styles: There are Dylan albums that are primarily country and others that are essentially bluegrass or folk. (*Good as I Been to You* [1992], for instance, is a very specific kind of folk sound; it really explores the borderline where folk music becomes the blues and vice versa.)

Prior to the release of these 2009 albums, Dylan hosted one hundred episodes of an ingenious radio series titled *Theme Time Radio Hour* (on Sirius XM Radio). Those of us who love the Dylan speaking voice were pleased to hear how good he sounded, and how natural and engaging he was when reading from a combination of a prewritten script or sometimes just talking extemporaneously. Dylan played a lot of what you'd expect him to play: 78 rpm–era folk music, blues, R&B, plus sixties soul and singer-songwriters he was fond of (he inspired in me a fondness for Van Morrison, I have to say). However, throughout the series he rarely played any "mainstream" pop from prior to 1960, and very few major vocalists like Sinatra, Crosby, or Ella Fitzgerald. Big bands (especially black ones) were somewhat better represented, but, at the same time, there were virtually no original cast albums. If *Theme Time Radio Hour* and Dylan's entire canon of thirty-three previous studio albums are any indication, the only kind of American music that he doesn't spend a lot of time listening to is traditional pop. Which explains why *Christmas in the Heart* is such a shocker: This is almost the first time that he's acknowledged that this music even exists. Prior to that, I would have been surprised to hear that Dylan even knew who Hugh Martin and Ralph Blane or Jay Livingston and Ray Evans were, let alone want to sing their songs. (I can't imagine that there's anybody out there who shares my experience of having spent forty years listening to Mel Tormé, and five years listening to Dylan. *Christmas in the Heart* seems almost like a bone he threw to me personally.)

But the main delight of the disc—to those who love his voice—is hearing those incredibly rough and scabrous tones in conspicuously bland orchestrations that sound as if they were intended for the likes of either Perry Como or Eddy Arnold, or in fact anybody *except* Bob Dylan. The voice is so chewed up and abused-sounding—almost incapable of holding a pitch—that he makes Blind Lemon Jefferson sound like Vic Damone by comparison. Dylan's voice has been famously likened to a "catarrhal death rattle," and as the man himself has accurately said, "I could sing 'How High the Moon' or 'If I Give My Heart to You' and it would come out like 'Mule Skinner Blues.'" (I applaud his choice of examples: "How High the Moon" is a song that anybody who knows the first thing about jazz or the American songbook would instantly recognize, but "I Give My Heart to You," though a hit for Doris Day and also beautifully done by Nat King Cole, has scarcely been sung by anybody since 1954.)

True to his own statement, here he makes even "Winter Wonderland" and "Little Drummer Boy" (doing the song's traditional modulation halfway through) come out like "Mule Skinner Blues." Virtually the only standard (or "show tune," as the term is generally used in this book) that Dylan had previously recorded is "Blue Moon" (on his 1970 *Self Portrait*), and he makes it clear that he learned that Rodgers and Hart classic through its rock-era interpretations: His vocal and arrangement have a lot more in common with the Marcels' big hit than with Ella Fitzgerald.

Hardcore Dylanographers, such as those who track his every move and discuss them on the Web, will probably *not* regard *Christmas in the Heart* as part of the official Dylan canon (it may well be the only album he's released without a single original song, with the arguable exception of *Good as I Been to You*). It seems, instead, that Dylan has extended a Hanukkah bonus to those of us who consider ourselves his fans who also happen to love the pre-Dylan American Songbook.

Christmas in the Heart further illustrates how Dylan's singing isn't about vocal quality or chops. It's about craft, and the way Dylan has worked out his approach to his own songs over the years. Varying his signatures from decade to decade and shifting their meaning, Dylan has shown that he has as much craft as the finest lieder singers. What he does with his voice here and elsewhere is remarkable. For starters, there's one trait he has in common with Elvis (not to mention Dean Martin, Fats Waller, and Eartha Kitt), namely, the knack of using different voices for different kinds of music.

Clearly, the idea of varying the basic quality of one's voice for different projects also comes out of folk music. Other kinds of music were about training or at least following a prescribed set of rules. If you wanted to sing opera in the thirties or forties, you went to a classical voice teacher; if you wanted to sing jazz, you got a job with a big band and tried to keep up, which amounted to the best on-the-job training. But folk music was a very specific thing—until Pete Seeger and the Weavers and then the folk boom of the late fifties, no one thought of it as being portable or teachable: Hill dwellers in the Ozarks sang mountain songs while Welshmen sang traditional Welsh songs, and there was no history of professional performers in nightclubs or in concert halls doing this kind of regional material. When young Americans started singing these songs in the Eisenhower era, the first thing they learned was that to sing Irish songs you had to sound Irish, to sing plantation songs convincingly you had to sound at least vaguely Southern. Since most of these folksingers were middle-class white kids, a whole tradition started of people trying to sound like something that they weren't, geographically or otherwise—a new idea in music.

When Dylan (né Robert Zimmerman of Duluth and then Hibbing, Minnesota) arrived in New York in 1961, folk music was the big trend, the genre that was, at the time, believed to have taken the place of what rock 'n' roll had been five years earlier. The major difference was that folk was still waiting for its Elvis, the man who would single-handedly move the music from the margins to the mainstream—roughly what Sinatra did for solo singers at the end of the big band era. Dylan, who once compared his manager, Albert Grossman, to Colonel Tom Parker, was seen by many as fulfilling that role. He also pointed out that "folk music was a strict and rigid establishment. If you sang Southern Mountain Blues, you didn't sing Southern Mountain Ballads and you didn't sing City Blues. If you sang Texas Cowboy songs, you didn't play English ballads. You just didn't. It was really pathetic."

It should be noted that in none of these subdivisions of the roots-music tradition was there a tradition of new performers writing new songs. Contemporary folksingers were expected, by and large, to treat the music like custodians in a museum; rather than create something new, the idea was to be authentic and as true to the original spirit as possible. Yet in Dylan's music, the lines between composition and interpretation are highly blurred: One of his biggest copyrights, "It Ain't Me, Babe," opens with a quote from the traditional "Go Away from My Window," while "Girl from the North Country" is taken from the same source as Simon and Garfunkel's "Scarborough Fair." At the same time, some of his acknowledged treatments of standard folk songs, as on *Good As I Been to You*, are so different from the standard sources that he could easily have collected some additional royalties by copyrighting them. Conversely, on "Frankie & Albert" (known to Tin Pan Alley and Hollywood as "Frankie and Johnny" and even "Rooty Toot Toot"), Dylan goes out of his way to show us that he learned the song from Mississippi John Hurt.

Clearly, interpretation and composition are closely related in his work, and he certainly has as much right to put his name on a folk-derived tune that he heavily adapted as does, say, W. C. Handy. Dylan also makes it clear that he doesn't regard even his own tunes as sacrosanct—like Duke Ellington and Frank Sinatra, he will vary his interpretation from year to year or decade to decade. In the eighties, for instance, he would typically do a hard rock treatment of a song he originally wrote in a folk ballad style twenty years earlier. He has done "Tambourine Man" both as a slow, soft, and monotonal folk song and as a loud and aggressive accusatory indictment, similar to "Like a Rolling Stone." "Subterranean Homesick Blues" sounds something like a hillbilly breakdown on the 1965 *Bringing It All Back Home*, but on the live bootleg *Wanted Man*, it becomes a hard rocker.

If there's any musician whom Dylan reminds me

of, it's Artie Shaw. Like Shaw, Dylan became a star in his twenties, but once he became famous for doing one specific thing, he wanted to do something else, a move that antagonized many of his fans. Shaw alienated the philistine movers and shakers of the music world, who couldn't understand that there was any artistic element to pop culture, or anything more to it than making money. Dylan, perhaps even more remarkably, managed to rebel against the rebels.

His famous break with the traditional folk music community came when he began adding electrical instruments and something like a rock 'n' roll band to his touring act in the mid-sixties. Shaw felt that the music industry wouldn't let him grow, that it wanted to turn him into a walking jukebox, endlessly regurgitating his hits, and he eventually quit making music because of it. Dylan, on the other hand, found the strength of conviction just to do whatever he wanted, even at the point where longtime fans were standing up in their seats and booing him as he sang. (No wonder one of his most bitter songs is titled "What Was It You Wanted?") Over the long haul, most of his older listeners came along for the ride even as he gained millions of new ones.

Dylan embodies another schism in American musical culture: He represents virtually all those genres where there is often no division between composer and performer—country, folk, blues—and would seem to deliberately avoid all of those where the lines are clearly drawn: big bands, Broadway shows, and what were considered "mainstream" pop singers up through the sixties. In this, he reminds me somewhat of another sixties icon, the cartoonist Robert Crumb. Born two years later (1943), Crumb was also raised in middle America (Pennsylvania rather than Minnesota), and was also drawn to music and pop culture. As with Dylan, Crumb's work is largely nonlinear, driven by surrealistic images; both were reluctant contributors to the era of psychedelic culture. Crumb once told me that when he was growing up, he came to hate all the musical genres that were omnipresent during his youth in the early to mid-fifties, and to this day, he still doesn't listen to Sinatra-era pop or the Great American Songbook. Instead, he turned to vintage jazz, blues, and country music, the stuff he could find on 78s, even as that medium was just becoming obsolete. Dylan seems to have done the same: He wanted to escape the mainstream pop material that was on radio and television, and thus was a perfect candidate to become a first-generation rock 'n' roller. In his mid-teens in Hibbing, the young Bobby Zimmerman wore a leather jacket and strutted around like a combination of Brando, Dean, and Elvis, until he discovered roots music: folk, country, and blues—and traded the motorcycle gear and pompadour for a pair of overalls.

I would have thought that neither Dylan nor Crumb could possibly listen to mass-market pop of the early fifties any more than I personally can listen with pleasure to the mass-market pop of the seventies (disco, heavy metal, glam rock, punk, or even jazz fusion)—we're all just hard-wired to hate the music that we were forced to listen to when we were growing up. (Perhaps it's also part of the impulse that pushes us to live someplace other than where we were raised: Home is a place to get away from.) Traditionally, the only mass-market pop star of the pre-Elvis era whom Dylan acknowledged as a favorite (though probably not an influence) was Johnnie Ray—hardly a traditional pop singer.

What was Dylan's singing like in his early folk period? On his earliest albums, he laid down certain ground rules with regard to his own voice. On his debut, *Bob Dylan* (recorded 1961, released 1962), the twenty-year-old artist establishes the importance of his harmonica. Like a lot of young folksingers, he's trying to sound old, weather-beaten, and "authentic," and performs the whole album solo, with voice, guitar, and harmonica. Since he can play both instruments at once (courtesy of a neck rack to hold the harmonica in place), the mouth organ makes him seem even more like a street performer. The instrument became less important in his music of the seventies and beyond, but in the early work, it almost seems even more crucial to Dylan's overall oeuvre than his voice. In fact, on a lot of the more folk-oriented recordings of 1962 to 1964 it seems like he's trying to make his voice replicate the harsh and shrill diatonic sound of the harmonica.

The first four albums (the others being *The Freewheelin' Bob Dylan*, 1963, *The Times They Are A-Changin'*, 1964, and *Another Side of Bob Dylan*, 1964) are primarily Dylan himself—guitar and harmonica. The sound of both the background and the Dylan voice itself changes wildly on *Bringing It All Back Home*, and even more so on *Highway 61 Revisited*, both from 1965. For Dylan to work with any band at all would, at this point, be a departure from what had come before, but the idea of his using rock-'n'-roll-style electric instruments would inevitably alienate some of his hard-liner folk fans at the time (who thought like Alan Lomax, and had a very narrow view of what was and wasn't authentic). *Highway 61* introduces my favorite Dylan ensemble, his pop-blues group of the mid-sixties with guitarist Mike Bloomfield and Al Kooper on Hammond organ.

Dylan's early career climaxed in 1965 and 1966 with the three albums of his folk-into-rock period, *Bringing It All Back Home*, *Highway 61 Revisited*, and *Blonde on Blonde*. During the same period, Dylan also gave the most famous—and in the eyes of many at the time, infamous—concerts of his career, notably his appearance at the Newport Folk Festival in July 1965 and his subsequent world tour (the show at Manchester's Free Trade Hall from May 1966 is the major performance to be officially released, even though, for reasons that aren't clear to me, it's titled *The Official Bootleg Series Vol. 4: The "Royal Albert Hall" Concert*). These were the performances wherein Dylan introduced his rock-influenced music and his electricity-aided band. At least one observer has pointed out that the fans who were clamoring for "The Times They Are A-Changin'" were not pleased to learn that this message now applied to them.

This particular period of Dylan's evolution ended dramatically with a motorcycle crash in the summer of 1966 that kept him largely inactive for over a year and a half (with the exception of private recordings, later partially released as *The Basement Tapes*). The three 1965–66 albums would forever after loom very large in Dylan mythology, not least for the way that each of them begins with an absolute Dylan classic: *Bringing It All Back Home* with "Subterranean Homesick Blues," *Highway 61 Revisited* with "Like a Rolling Stone," and *Blonde on Blonde* with "Rainy Day Women #12 & 35."

It's easy to see how "Subterranean Homesick Blues" would have surprised if not shocked long-standing Dylan fans, not to mention everyone else. It's an archetypal example of a Dylan song that seems to be simultaneously a political manifesto and sheer nonsense. At the time, even the parts of the songs that didn't make literal sense were taken very seriously, like the surrealism of Allen Ginsberg or Salvador Dalí, as if they were a command to disrespect authority. When, in "Subterranean Homesick Blues," he tells listeners "Don't follow leaders," you may think for half a second that he means literally that, until you get to the next line, which is "Watch the parking meters." (To make it even more whimsical, in the famous "video" of the song in the 1967 documentary *Don't Look Back*, he spells the last phrase "Pawking Metaws.") He seems to have just grabbed for any phrase that scanned and rhymed. There's an obvious connection between nonsense and political upheaval; both are calls for anarchy. (The only authority that he appears to respect is that of iambic pentameter.) The entire album *Bringing It All Back Home* contains many of his most disjointed, surreal songs, not to mention some of his most quotable lines: "He who is not busy being born is busy dying" and "Failure's no success at all." Compared to the totally bizarro "Bob Dylan's 115th Dream" (which he begins by breaking down with laughter—hopefully a sign that we aren't meant to take it too seriously) and "Subterranean," even the completely nonlinear "Mr. Tambourine Man" seems to make sense, or, if not that, to at least follow its own demented logic.

Highway 61 begins with its own strongest shot, "Like a Rolling Stone." This song seems influenced by at least two traditions in earlier American popular music, the first being the legacy of songs that bemoan "how the mighty have fallen," which are generally written in the first person. One trait that mainstream pop has in common with the blues is a long history of kiss-off songs, famously "Some of These Days" and "After You've Gone" and dozens of

other you'll-be-sorry songs; Frank Sinatra, pop culture's most famous kisser-offer, made a specialty of these, such as "You'll Get Yours" and "So Long, My Love."

"Like a Rolling Stone" encompasses both of these traditions, and a great deal more. Yet although it's one of Dylan's best-known songs, there are comparatively few really good cover versions of "Rolling Stone." (Although I do happen to be partial to recent performances of it by Barb Jungr, Paula West—which is as yet unrecorded, alas—and even Buddy Greco. No, I'm not kidding.) But unlike the case with "Blowin' in the Wind," "A Hard Rain's A-Gonna Fall," "Mr. Tambourine Man," and most of his other most famous works, generally speaking no other singer can compete with Dylan himself on "Rolling Stone." Dylan's snarls are the whole show: the finger-pointing cries of "how does it feel?" and "didn't you?" The way he just belts it out, without any inhibition or fear, puts him in the same class as Hank Williams, who likewise wasn't afraid to blurt out dramatically what he was trying to express with unrestricted emotion.

One of the many press conferences he gave during the 1966 world tour is a talk with a particularly pushy British journalist who keeps trying to get Dylan to pay lip service to Woody Guthrie, but Dylan repeatedly insists that Hank Williams is his all-time hero, and "Rolling Stone" shows why. I once asked Abbey Lincoln why she recorded "Mr. Tambourine Man" and she likened that decision to the way that Dinah Washington had sung Williams's "Cold, Cold Heart." I'm sure that Dylan would enjoy that comparison. Like Williams in virtually every song, Dylan takes everything he's feeling and just puts it right out there, unadorned and unafraid. "How does it feel?" and "didn't you?" aren't so much questions as bald-face accusations. Aren't you sorry that you did me wrong? You feel that he's totally personally involved, he's angry with this woman because she broke his heart, and the fact that she acted like a rich bitch who threw the bums a dime in her prime is only icing on her let-them-eat-cake. "Rolling Stone" is "Nobody Knows You When You're Down and Out," sung in the second person and even more powerful. Columbia Records later released a slightly longer and even more intense live version from Dylan's famous "Royal Albert Hall" (apparently actually Manchester) concert of 1966, in which the songwriter barks out the accusations in an even more confrontational fashion.

Although recorded in Nashville, the best-selling double LP *Blonde on Blonde* is widely regarded as Dylan's first major rock 'n' roll album; for a long time, it was frequently listed as the second-greatest rock album ever (right behind *Sgt. Pepper*). Yet *Blonde on Blonde* opens with a decidedly unrocky moment: "Rainy Day Women #12 & 35" is set to a bouncing oom-pah beat, and sounds heavily influenced by the early avant-gutbucket style of Charles

Mingus, as on "Better Get Hit in Your Soul." Dylan is backed by a brass band with a careering tailgate trombone, which on one level sounds like a circus band (a possible antecedent of the "circus" interlude in John Lennon's "Being for the Benefit of Mr. Kite!") or a Salvation Army band (the very effect that Mingus was after), a ragtag ensemble of musical preachers pushing street-corner salvation.

You notice the band and the beat only secondarily; the main thing is Dylan's voice, which incorporates a self-satirizing laugh—again, you're not supposed to take any of this too seriously. Most people remember the song as "Everybody must get stoned," since that's the pay-off line that Dylan repeats—as if it were the song title, in fact. As even a cursory listen immediately reveals, Dylan perhaps wanted to tantalize the listener into thinking that he meant stoned in the sense of high on drugs. He further underscores that atmosphere with the circus band and party attitude; not only Dylan, but the whole group sounds as if they were smashed at some kind of boozy Saturday night sing-along; you wonder which one of these guys is going to be the designated driver.

Yet Dylan obviously means "stoned" in the sense of defeated, messed up, sabotaged, in the sense of something that other people do to you: "They'll stone you when you're walking on the street / They'll stone you when you're trying to keep your seat." "Stone" as a verb, not "stoned" as a state of being, the result of getting high. Dylan was playing on how the most famous use of the word "stoned" in that sense is in the New Testament, when Jesus prevents a crowd from "stoning" a woman with his much-quoted line about "him who is without sin."

"Rainy Day Women #12 & 35" is not about rain, days, or women, and the numbers 12 and 35 would appear to be totally random. Yet the text itself is totally logical and progresses from point to point in a perfectly straightforward fashion. If the song were titled "Everybody Must Get Stoned," it would actually seem like one of Dylan's least surreal songs of the period. In an interview in Stockholm in April 1966 (the album was finished a month earlier), Dylan said cryptically, "'Rainy Day Women' happens to deal with a minority of cripples and Orientals and, you know, and the world in which they live. It's a sort of North Mexican kind of thing, very protesty. Very very protesty. One of the protestiest of all things I ever protested against in my protest years."

And that's just the first four minutes of *Blonde on Blonde*; elsewhere on the two-LP set, "Visions of Johanna," "I Want You," "Just Like a Woman," and "Sad Eyed Lady of the Lowlands" are all extraordinary songs that have since enjoyed long and active lives. "Stuck Inside of Mobile with the Memphis Blues Again" is a "Rolling Stone"–like epic that just goes on and on and builds and builds—in that sense, it's a psychedelic update of a Cole Porter list song like "Can-Can." (It's always seemed obvious, too, that "Stuck Inside of Mobile" was the primary inspi-

ration for John Lennon's Dylanesque "The Ballad of John and Yoko.")

Blonde on Blonde contains what may well be the songwriter's most perfect straight-up blues, "Leopard-Skin Pill-Box Hat." Dylan's relationship with the blues is as complex and rich as that of his relationship to folk, gospel, and everything else. Almost since W. C. Handy's time, there had been a clear difference between the rural blues and the urban blues (not to mention the Miles Davis kind of blues); it would be a risible mistake to contend that the Northern blues of Ethel Waters were any less authentic than the Mississippi Delta blues of Charley Patton.

When Dylan first began listening to the blues, there were two famous singers who were both named Joe Williams. The older of the two eventually came to bill himself as "Big" Joe Williams; he may have added the epithet to distinguish himself from the younger Joe Williams after the latter became a big star as a result of his association with Count Basie. Up to then, the older Williams was occasionally billed as "Po' Joe Williams"; it's not known if "Big" Joe Williams was actually bigger than Joe Williams, who was well over six feet tall. Big Joe was rough and rural, non-big Joe was urbane and sophisticated, a completely genuine but much smoother shouter of the blues. It's not surprising that Dylan would ally himself more with Big Joe than Joe; one of the earliest recordings made by the young guitarist–singer–mouth organist is of him playing harmonica behind Big Joe in March 1962 (a session produced by collector-historian Len Kunstadt, a friend of Dylan's "discoverer," John Hammond). Dylan accompanies Williams on "Sitting on Top of the World," not the Ray Henderson pop song associated with Al Jolson, but a no-less-classic blues standard introduced by the Mississippi Sheiks. (Thirty years later, Dylan sang it himself on *Good As I Been to You*.)

"Leopard-Skin Pill-Box Hat" is musically a straight-up 12-bar blues, different from most of those sung by Joe Williams in that Dylan supplies a different set of words for the second line of each chorus rather than simply repeating the first. "Pill-Box Hat" is a pure Chicago-style electric blues, the kind of thing that a sixties rocker who had grown up on Muddy Waters, Howlin' Wolf, and other Chess label icons would be moved to write, although no one else had Dylan's lyric imagination. Twenty years later, trumpeter-singer Jack Sheldon played and sang "Leopard-Skin Pill-Box Hat" as a very sophisticated bebop blues, and it worked extremely well in that format also.

Dylan's official albums of the late sixties—the period before and after the crash (and the year-and-a-half retreat that followed)—were *Blonde on Blonde* (1966), his most rockish venture yet, then *John Wesley Harding* (1967), which strikes me as a rather gritty country album, while *Nashville Skyline* (1969) is more like old-timey bluegrass. (The three could be described as Dylan's "Nashville" period, since they all were recorded there.) There's nothing like the

"Rolling Stone" snarls on either of the latter two; *John Wesley* has its tender moments, particularly the ending "I'll Be Your Baby Tonight," in which even Dylan's normally biting harmonica sounds warm and romantic. In the use of a spare rhythm section and Fender bass, it sounds more like contemporary country music; I wouldn't have a hard time imagining Merle Haggard or Waylon Jennings singing these songs with these backgrounds. *Nashville* has Dylan smiling invitingly on the cover, like a folk troubadour of the Burl Ives era (the twin-picking team of Lester Flatt and Earl Scruggs recorded a bluegrass treatment of Dylan's instrumental, "Nashville Skyline Rag"), and he sings the whole album in a warm, almost crooning voice. He's even shown tipping his hat politely, as if he only wanted to please. How does that feel? Darn good, if you ask me. But if you could somehow find an individual who had never heard of Bob Dylan, and played selections from all three albums to him or her in a blindfold test, he would probably tell you that he had just listened to three completely different singers.

The voice changed once again on the 1970 *Self Portrait*, a double album perceived as somewhat disappointing in the aftermath of the five major classics that preceded it, but which, heard today, clearly has its moments. Both the singer's voice and his songs sound relatively subdued on this effort, which doesn't include any all-time Dylan classics (other than "The Mighty Quinn," already an iconic hit for the British band Manfred Mann). Apart from his doo-wop "Blue Moon," he croons the French import "Let It Be Me" in his *Nashville Skyline* voice, and there's an homage to Paul Simon in a rather rough and rowdy treatment of "The Boxer" (from *Bridge Over Troubled Water*). Those who try to analyze Dylan's moves are confounded by *Self Portrait*, which contains fewer original songs (and is thus less of a self-portrait) than virtually any other Dylan album.

Another change had been blowin' in the wind from *Blonde on Blonde* onward. After the 1966 accident, Dylan seems to have grown progressively less interested in his early surreal-style, postpsychedelic lyrics. These texts, as we've seen, have an improvisational aesthetic to them, stringed lines of beautiful images, like a free-verse equivalent of Tourette's syndrome. There was something of a precedent in the oldest old-timey hillbilly music; most old-time breakdowns were strictly dance pieces with no lyrics needed other than square dance calls, and what words there were often turned out to be nonsense, things like "chicken in the bread-pan, kickin' out dough." Nobody was trying to be Oscar Hammerstein with old-time fiddle tunes like "Bonaparte's Retreat" (although that song had a more Tin Pan Alley–esque lyric added later, in time for Kay Starr to make a hit out of it).

Dylan apparently wanted people to believe that he just banged out his sixties songs—that he virtually improvised them, just sat down and wrote the first things that came to mind. The same way that the State Street Swingers followed "Rubbin' on the Darn Old Thing" with "New Rubbing on That Darn Old Thing" and Jimmie Rodgers kept turning out new "Blue Yodels" in numbered sequence, Dylan was moved to write "I Shall Be Free" (on *The Freewheelin' Bob Dylan*, 1963) and then come back the next year with "I Shall Be Free No. 10" (on *Another Side of Bob Dylan*, 1964). He would seem to be conveying the impression that no deliberate craft went into these lyrics. It's part of Dylan's brilliance that, in these early works, there were strong overtones of political significance even amid all the apparent randomness.

Compared to pop songwriting up to that point, Dylan's work seems at once incredibly sophisticated, with extravagant, fanciful imagery and, at the same time, completely random, as if he were just scribbling down phrases and ideas and then tossing them into a hat and letting them tumble out willy-nilly. The randomness is part of their appeal; I could believe that Lennon and McCartney tried out "I Am the Rhinoceros" or "I Am the Wombat" or even "I am the Waitress" before they settled on "Walrus," but Dylan's songs seem to have emerged from his brain fully formed. To rewrite or revise an idea would be to kill the point.

That's one of the reasons rock music in its purest form doesn't work as musical theater; that's why the songs from *Hair* seem more like theatrical music than rock or pop and *The Times They Are A-Changin'*, Twyla Tharp's 2006 attempt to cobble Dylan songs into a Broadway production, was a failure. In the world of Dylan and the Beatles and their progeny, the accepted long-form musical work is the forty-five-minute, all-original "concept album," or even a double-length album, like *Blonde on Blonde* or *The Beatles* (aka *The White Album*), not the musical comedy, with a cast of different singer-characters and a traditional narrative form. Likewise, for the most part singers accustomed to doing Cole Porter or Stephen Sondheim tend not to be able to sing Bob Dylan or the Beatles.

I don't believe that Dylan's use of surreal imagery in this period has anything to do with his fondness for marijuana. According to Beatles biographer Bob Spitz, it was Dylan who gave the Fab Four their first puffs on a reefer. Although Lennon, especially, would move on to much more potent hallucinogens, Dylan doesn't seem to have gotten involved with anything stronger than pot. His own most vehement protest seems to have been against those who tried to find literal meanings in these songs; there's a film of a press conference where he objects virulently to the suggestion that "A Hard Rain's A-Gonna Fall" is about nuclear war and fallout. (Supposedly, the overall message of "A Hard Rain" is that our culture of violence will ultimately beget more violence; the chickens will come home to roost, which is what Malcolm X tactlessly said after the assassination of President Kennedy.)

"A Hard Rain" is a brilliant example of Dylan using visual images to create what cinema theorists refer to as a hieroglyphic structure. The individual pictures don't mean much in and of themselves ("The song of a poet who died in the gutter / The sound of a clown who cried in the alley"), but the way Dylan stacks these images one on top of another in sequence gradually adds up to a cumulative meaning. In this case, the songwriter tied these apparently unrelated images together with a passive structure, a question-and-answer form inspired by the old English folk song "Lord Randall," which Dylan likely heard via Harry Belafonte.

Dylan was still using fanciful imagery, but in a much more concrete form, by the time he reached his religious period in the late seventies. As biographer David Hajdu put it, "Quite a few of the songs on the born-again Christian albums [*Slow Train Coming, Saved,* and *Shot of Love*] are fairly direct and clear. One, 'I Believe in You' [on *Slow Train Coming*] is exceptional. The changes and tune are damn good, too." Each of the three albums has at least one outstanding song: *Shot of Love* concludes with the highly moving and spiritual "Every Grain of Sand." The title song of *Saved* is traditional Southern swamp gospel at its most elemental; it sounds like what Ray Charles was listening to when he was growing up in Georgia. *Saved* also contains "In the Garden," which is not the traditional hymn, famously recorded by both Elvis Presley and Johnny Cash (not together; also by Jo Stafford and Gordon MacRae, together), but a much more grisly account of Christ's trials that might have pleased Mel Gibson.

Slow Train Coming also contains the brilliant and riveting "Gotta Serve Somebody." Like "Rainy Day Women," "Serve Somebody" could be described as a list song (though not exactly in the fashion of Cole Porter, or even Louis Jordan) with a beginning, middle, and end—in that order, no less. The most puzzling section, especially to audiences that weren't listening in 1979, is a section where Dylan delineates the various names he could be known by, which is a reference to the contemporaneous TV comic Raymond J. Johnson (aka Bill Saluga), whose sole bit was spieling out variations of his name and nickname ("You can call me Ray Jay . . ."). It's the only bit of utter nonsense in the song, yet even this would have made sense to listeners at the time.

Even long after the born-again period, Dylan continued to deliver extraordinary spiritual songs, like the amazing "Ring Them Bells" (with a "them" rather than a "dem" obviously to distinguish it from Duke Ellington) on the 1989 *Oh Mercy*. He sings it with startlingly clear articulation, so there's absolutely no ambiguity about what he says and what he means, accompanied by only solo piano (his own?); the acoustics are such to suggest an intimate hymn, a man sitting alone in a church and praying by himself.

Unlike Artie Shaw and unlike the Beatles (as a band, at least), Dylan has kept going almost without a letup far into his late sixties. Not every record is a platinum hit (although both of his most recent albums debuted at number one), but he continues to be a major force in the record industry—such as it is at the end of the first decade of the new century. The case could be made that he's more popular and relevant than ever. He continues to tour almost constantly, and fans flood the Internet with all kinds of concert recordings from all over the globe. The voice is as nasal and, often, unintelligible as ever, but he sings, either sitting at the piano (as when I heard him at New York's Beacon Theatre in 2005) or standing with a guitar, with amazing expression, emotion, and an ability to communicate that surpasses a lot of singers with more conventionally attractive pipes. Every performance I've witnessed or heard has Dylan giving everything he's got—he's almost the Judy Garland of the contemporary era.

As he gets older, Dylan seems to be growing closer to, rather than further away from, his roots. In doing so, he confounded his critics by releasing three of his best albums in his sixties: *Love and Theft* (2001), *Modern Times* (2006), and *Together Through Life* (2009). All three are heavily blues-oriented: *Love and Theft* has no shortage of Southern-style shuffle rhythms: "Tweedle Dee & Tweedle Dum" uses a New Orleans backbeat familiar to followers of Crescent City R&B or even that fans of Bo Diddley would enjoy; *Together Through Life* is primarily hard-edge blues rock. Yet Dylan is never limited by the blues: "Sugar Baby," the final track on *Love and Theft*, has a main melody and even a bridge obviously taken from the Tin Pan Alley spiritual "The Lonesome Road"; there are also allusions to "Darktown Strutters' Ball" (he sings of characters doing "the Darktown Strut") and "Ol' Man River." The second track on *Together Through Life* is "Life Is Hard," which, despite the basic-blues title, feels more like a traditional torch song, in the manner of "Maybe You'll Be There."

The album in between—Dylan's thirty-second studio project—is the most diverse and interesting. Dylan titled it *Modern Times,* but he seems to have been talking about modern in the sense of 1936 (had he meant 2006, he might have titled it *Postmodern Times*). The singer-songwriter seems to have taken a cross section of musics that were in the air at the time of Charlie Chaplin's classic 1936 film *Modern Times,* starting with the blues (then called "race music"), and spreading out into country (or "hillbilly") and even pop. There are songs inspired by Muddy Waters, Memphis Minnie, Lightnin' Hopkins, Ma Rainey, and the Stanley Brothers—which is interesting in itself.

Overall, *Modern Times* is one of Dylan's loveliest and most lyrical albums. Even in this context, it's still surprising and unprecedented in Dylan's work that two songs are based on mainstream pop tunes from the same period: "Beyond the Horizon" from the 1935 British song "Red Sails in the Sunset" (which was also the source of the 1966 pop hit "Winchester

Cathedral") and "When the Deal Goes Down," taken from Bing Crosby's signature waltz, "Where the Blue of the Night (Meets the Gold of the Day)." He knows what he's doing—he admitted in an interview that he was working on a song inspired by Crosby.

Alas, there's nothing on *Modern Times* that was based on Sammy Cahn, although *Christmas in the Heart* does include Dylan's gruff and bluesy rendition of Cahn's "The Christmas Blues." Those of us who love Dylan and Cahn in equal parts are still waiting for Bob's version of "All My Tomorrows." I bet he'd sing the hell out of it. The hell, that is.

From the beginning, Dylan's songs were performed by other artists—yet, for the most part, these performances supported rather than argued against the idea that artists should do only their own songs. When Dylan's tunes were performed by Peter, Paul, and Mary in the early sixties, or the Byrds a few years after that, or the Band (at one point his backup group), they invariably sounded like a pale imitation of the songwriter himself. That's possibly because they are keeping the songs in Dylan's backyard: folk music, folk-rock, hard rock—all musics that Dylan himself has played. (Admittedly, this can't be said of Richie Havens doing "Just Like a Woman" or Leon Russell doing "It's a Hard Rain A-Gonna Fall.")

Yet there is only a minimal tradition of Dylan's songs being *interpreted,* which is to say, being reimagined for purposes that Dylan himself might not have imagined—like Sinatra swinging a Cole Porter song originally written as a slow ballad. Sam Cooke, who was partly inspired to write his own "A Change Is Gonna Come" by Dylan's "Blowin' in the Wind" also came up with a dance version of that 1962 anthem, complete with Bobby Darin–like shuffle rhythm and modulations; Duke Ellington did a big band version with moaning trombones, while Lena Horne belted it as a swinging civil rights anthem. Johnny Cash turned in a definitive recording of "Wanted Man," a Dylan song that the writer himself generally stayed away from. Elvis Presley sang at least three Dylan songs, most notably "Tomorrow Is a Long Time," which he recorded in 1966, long before Dylan's own version (recorded in 1962) was released. Presley sings "Tomorrow" in a straight, folkish monotone rather than with the colorful effects he normally employed (some of which are heard on his later studio version of "Don't Think Twice, It's All Right"). The King also dabbled with but unfortunately didn't fully record "I Shall Be Released," which, with its religious overtones, could have been the definitive Presley-Dylan de facto collaboration.

Nina Simone also recorded at least three Dylan songs, including a churchy "I Shall Be Released," a declamatory and accusatory "The Times They Are A-Changin'," and a "Just Like a Woman" that sounds like a love song and a feminist chant at the same time. Cassandra Wilson, Simone's heiress-apparent, has also done three Dylan songs: "Shelter from the Storm" on what might be her finest album, *Belly of the Sun*, "Lay, Lady, Lay," and "Closer to You"—in fact, all three of her albums of the twenty-first century have contained one Dylan song. Wilson may well have also been influenced by Abbey Lincoln, who recorded the finest "jazz" version thus far of "Tambourine Man." I have, remarkably enough, only heard one noteworthy jazz vocal reinterpretation of "Like a Rolling Stone," by Paula West (unfortunately not yet recorded), who reimagined it as a sort of psychedelic update of Bessie Smith's "Nobody Knows You When You're Down and Out."

Of all the many new takes on Dylan, none is more essential than that of Barb Jungr, the British cabaret singer. Thus far, Jungr has recorded one whole album of his music, *Every Grain of Sand,* while two Dylan songs apiece are heard on *Love Me Tender* and *Walking in the Sun,* making a total of nineteen of his songs that she has reinterpreted. Released in 2002, *Every Grain of Sand* was the breakthrough that proved beyond a grain of sand of doubt that Bob Dylan songs can be readdressed and made vital all over again by performers in vastly different genres, just like those of Stephen Sondheim or Jerome Kern. Jungr doesn't completely rewrite the melodies, or transform them into cabaret or jazz, nor does she literalize the lyrics, which is to say, transform them into traditionally linear-style sequence; suffice it to say that she employs bits and pieces of all of these approaches in order to make the songs work for her.

Throughout the nineteen tracks, Jungr consistently elaborates on Dylan's moods, from the declamatory sermon "Ring Them Bells" to the erotic "I'll Be Your Baby Tonight," done with accordion like a musette waltz. There are also new pieces, such as "Blind Willie McTell," a basic blues elaborated with wild, biblical allusions and a tricky 5/4 time signature. At a live performance at the Metropolitan Room in 2007, Ms. Jungr also delivered an as-yet-unrecorded, stark, Sinatra-inspired saloon-song treatment of "Like a Rolling Stone." Here, she communicates the message by whispering and understating the famous tagline that everybody else shouts, "How does it feel?" Jungr deliberately swallows these payoff lines, much the way Bob Hope made a joke funnier by muttering the punch line under his breath.

In his 2004 *Chronicles,* Mr. Dylan reveals that he was profoundly influenced by Kurt Weill and Bertolt Brecht's "Pirate Jenny," yet it remained for Ms. Jungr to show that Dylan's songs can be interpreted with the same sort of sensitivity and nuance as Weill's. For all the complexity and fantastic imagery of his texts, my personal favorite remains the simplest and most direct of his works, the 1974 "Forever Young"; Ms. Jungr sings it like a toast at a Jewish wedding, a first cousin to Frank Loesser's "More I Cannot Wish You." It's so straightforward that it doesn't even sound like Bob Dylan at all—maybe it's actually by Robert Allen Zimmerman of Hibbing, Minnesota.

Gospel: Mahalia Jackson (1911–1972)

The most colorful description of Mahalia Jackson in action was provided not by a professional writer but by a member of the gospel legend's own choir. "Mahalia, she add more flowers and feathers than anybody," this chorister told scholar Marshall Stearns in the early fifties, who quoted her in *The Story of Jazz*, "and they all is exactly right." It's a vivid picture of history's greatest gospel singer in action, and for many years it was correct. By "flowers and feathers" the speaker means gospel-style embellishments, or, to use more boring terms, melismas, grace notes, trills, and other kinds of decorations—Jackson's way of personalizing a melody has a lot in common with modern gospel's two closest kinfolk, jazz and the blues.

But though she remains correct about all of Jackson's embellishments being "exactly right," the idea that Mahalia Jackson added more of these decorations to a tune than anybody else is outdated by at least thirty or forty years. Jackson's spiritual daughters, like Aretha Franklin, Della Reese, and Gladys Knight, put in more flowers and feathers than Mahalia did. In fact, they put in as many as possible without weighing down the music and losing the message.

What has happened is that since Mahalia Jackson, singers of all stripes have continued to pilfer the gospel style while ignoring its meaning. (Could there be a greater example than the music and career of Whitney Houston?) Gospel music has become the basis for much of contemporary pop, to the point where fourteen-year-old white girls, showing their itty-bitties on TV talent competitions, sound like bad caricatures of gospel singers from fifty years ago.

If, in her day, Mahalia Jackson seemed like the ultimate extreme of gospel decoration, today she seems like a model of restraint. She doesn't put anything into a song that it doesn't need. If she were to compete on *American Idol,* that show's clueless judges would tell her that she's not laying it on nearly thick enough. But that's not the kind of judgment that Jackson sang about. To Jackson, the embellishments are eternally at the service of communication: The idea isn't to show off what a wonderful voice you have, but to spread the good news of God's message, to share the glory of the Gospels. As another of her flock once observed, "Mahalia doesn't *believe* that God exists, she *knows* He does." Yet the style she created is frequently corrupted in contemporary musical culture to the point where its practitioners have become intent on glorifying themselves rather than God. In one sense, the gospel style has become the default parameter for all popular singing, if you follow the lineage that Mahalia begat Aretha who begat all those girls who screech and shriek like warmed-over, second-rate, gospel-soul singers. Yet the authentic gospel style of

Mahalia Jackson has all but vanished completely—it has retreated back to the Southern churches, and to reissues of the recordings of Jackson herself and her fellow gospel greats.

Mahalia Jackson was born in New Orleans, on October 26, 1911, and is the most famous singer to come out of that city since Louis Armstrong—including the fine blues singer Lizzie Miles, and the Boswell Sisters. It was practically preordained that she would grow up to sing the music of the church. She began singing as a little girl with a big voice, and church was the only place where she felt comfortable expressing herself. Religion was a refuge from the sorrows and hardnesses she encountered in the world beyond. Her father was a part-time preacher on Sunday and a day laborer the rest of the time, but he doesn't seem to have been particularly righteous in his treatment of his children. When Mahalia's mother died, the father remarried, and he more or less abandoned Mahalia and his other children when he went to live with his new wife.

Mahalia and her brother and sister were then raised by a wicked stepmother of an aunt. The woman seems to have delighted in giving the young Mahalia a hard time, but the more she abused her the more the girl found solace in the church. This being New Orleans, Jackson was also surrounded by jazz and the blues, and also grew to love the legendary Caruso from hearing him on records. She came to realize that all these other musics were closely related to that which she heard on Sundays.

Jazz musicians played the spiritual repertory, and there was no keeping jazz and blues out of the church—nor did Jackson intend to, not entirely. The Negro spiritual, as it used to be called, was the first African American musical form to be performed in concerts for white audiences, starting with the famous Fisk Jubilee Singers in the 1880s. By the time Mahalia Jackson was born, there were "serious" spirituals being sung in concert houses all over the world, and there was a more comedic kind of semi-religious song (along the lines of "Poor Mourner," which evolved into "Oh Mo'nah") being performed for both white and black audiences by black vaudevillians and minstrels.

In 1927, when Jackson was sixteen, she moved to Chicago and worked as a domestic and a beautician, opening her own salon and demonstrating early on her lifelong entrepreneurial spirit. At the end of the Jazz Age, black religious music was taking some interesting turns. Apart from jazz musicians playing spirituals and dirges, other kinds of performers were beginning to blur the distinction between sacred and secular forms. There was the blues singer named Blind Willie Johnson, who sang with a voice as harsh and raspy as the devil himself. His voice and style were identical to those of blues singers who sang about gin and sin, but when you could make out the words on his recordings, he was actually singing of spiritual devotion. A fire-and-brimstone preacher named Rev. J. M. Gates was a recording star, making discs that combined spirited sermons with the singing, by himself and his choir, of traditional spirituals in a decidedly down-home fashion.

At one point not long after Jackson arrived in Chicago, she was heard by pianist and bandleader Earl Hines, who made her an offer to sing with his band. Hines, however, was not the "Fatha" that Jackson wanted to sing for; throughout her entire career, she would only perform under the auspices of the church, singing religious music. The development of modern gospel music, as it came to be known, was happening in several places at once, and for all Jackson's devotion to the church and its music, none of the different varieties of black sacred music as it was heard in the church, in the theater, and in the concert hall suited her exactly. They were too formal and confining. Yet she didn't want to sing the blues, because, as she said, "when you finished, you still had the blues," even though that music was clearly influencing her developing style.

There's a good story in Chris Albertson's biography of Bessie Smith. The Empress of the Blues was invited to a party in the home of a rich white fan, and she also accepted her host's invitation to sing a couple of her trademark blues for the guests. After she finished, some stuffy dowager approached her and paid what she thought was a compliment. "My dear," she said—and the story works better if you picture Margaret Dumont peering at Bessie through a lorgnette—"how beautifully you sing spirituals." Spirituals? For most white people at the time, even as late as the Jazz Age, traditional black spirituals were the only black art music—indeed, the only indigenous American song form.

Black spirituals were having increasing impact upon both "art music" and popular music. By the twenties, there was a tradition of black classical singers like Paul Robeson, Roland Hayes, and Jules Bledsoe singing this repertoire, and some white ones as well, notably Lawrence Tibbett. Tibbett also introduced "De Glory Road" a concert "art song," written in imitation of the black folk style. *Show Boat*'s "Ol' Man River" and much of the score of *Porgy and Bess,* especially "Summertime," were heavily influenced by the traditional spirituals. (And so too were many other songs—Berlin's "Shakin' the Blues Away" and "Waiting at the End of the Road" and the Gershwins' "Clap Yo' Hands," to name a few.)

The spirituals were also played by popular bands and singers, not only in something close to their "authentic" form but in Tin Pan Alley adaptations. Noble Sissle, the pioneering African American composer, tenor, and bandleader, was one of the first to explore the possibilities of what came to be regarded as swinging spirituals, and recorded a series of these

beginning in Europe in 1928: "Great Camp Meeting Day," "You Can't Get to Heaven That Way" (a modernized "Gonna Shout All Over God's Heaven"), and later, back in the States in 1934, "The Old Ark's A-Moverin'." In those six years, the swinging spiritual had come and gone.

The swinging spiritual was one of the major musical trends of the Great Depression, and two facets were especially notable: It was essentially over by the start of the swing era in 1935, with the exception of the occasional straggler like "I Hope Gabriel Likes My Music," Mildred Bailey's 1939 treatment of "Hold On," and a more famous upgrade of "Shout All Over God's Heaven" entitled "All God's Chillun Got Rhythm." And, remarkably, after Noble Sissle, it was largely the province of white performers, the major exception being Louis Armstrong, who performed religious material with widely varying degrees of piety throughout his career. The Tin Pan Alley spirituals were, for better or worse, the white mainstream's interpretation of a black art form, and were often quite wonderful in their own way. However, it remained for black artists to reclaim this music, and that was what gospel did.

The records that most anticipate what gospel would eventually sound like come from the interaction of two unlikely bedfellows: the Tin Pan Alley spiritual and the blues. We've briefly mentioned Blind Willie Johnson, who, recording in Dallas, New Orleans, and Atlanta, left behind a legacy of more than two dozen titles that could be described as severely religious. Most of his songs, sung in his rough voice, emphasize the fear of God, and the awful things that can happen to those motherless children who fail to take heed. Then in 1930, at one of Bessie Smith's final recording sessions, she recorded a pair of popular songs written in the black spiritual style, "Moan, You Moaners" and "On Revival Day." These were her only religious recordings, and, ironically, they came from the white mainstream rather than the field of authentic black religious music. Yet this is the closest thing you will hear to Mahalia Jackson before Mahalia Jackson: someone singing of the glories of salvation with the passion and fervor of a great blues singer.

Blues and gospel represent two different approaches to the same problem. The idea behind the blues is that you confront your troubles by stooping to their level, by immersing yourself in negative energy and exorcising it. In contrast, gospel music cures you of your troubles by pointing toward the light, offering a positive role model. Keep your hand on the plow and hold on. Mahalia Jackson couldn't sing a line like "Hush little baby, don't you cry / Your mother and father bound to die." Her message is not "I have a problem," but rather "I Found the Answer" and of course that answer is Jesus. She is not a poor pilgrim of sorrow or a soul of constant misery. She is a woman of constant joy, so secure in her belief in God that she doesn't have to worry about Him providing for her in either this life or the next one. Hers is a music of major chords.

Yet when you compare Mahalia Jackson's music to earlier, more traditional performers, such as the recordings of spirituals by the great concert baritone Paul Robeson, it's immediately clear that she has much more in common with the great blues divas, especially Bessie Smith. Jackson frequently bends her notes and plays with rhythm to make a dramatic point, she'll repeat a phrase like a blues or jazz singer, and reshape a melody. The spontaneity that makes Billie Holiday or Dinah Washington great also inspires Mahalia Jackson, only Jackson has by far a greater justification. Unlike today's stars who thank "the Creator" for their Grammy Awards, as if He had nothing better to think about, Jackson would never have claimed that God was whispering in her ear telling her to rush that phrase or stretch that note; rather, her singing reflects the way she feels the Spirit, in the moment, as it's happening. Sinatra personalizes a love song to reflect his emotional truth at that instant, and likewise Jackson interprets a familiar text according to how the Spirit moves her. The religious experience is as immediate as it is unmistakable.

It seems that no sooner did Thomas A. Dorsey bring forth gospel out of blues than his immediate disciples were doing everything they could to blur whatever boundaries there were between the two forms. Singer-guitarist Sister Rosetta Tharpe had made one of the first great recordings of Dorsey's gospel standard "Peace in the Valley," and she was precisely the kind of wholly unpredictable star of African American music who could never be contained by any kind of category. Born Rosetta Nubin in Cotton Plant, Arkansas, in 1915, she grew up in the church but was paying as much attention to jazz and blues as she was to hymns and spirituals. In 1934, Nubin and her first husband, the preacher Thomas Thorpe (she later changed the spelling of the surname) moved to New York, and within a few years Sister Rosetta was touring and recording with the Harlem-based big band led by Lucky Millinder. Together, Tharpe and Millinder were one of the biggest black headlining attractions of the World War II era, and major sellers on Decca Records. The mere fact of a gospel singer appearing with a secular big band was considered scandalous by even the less conservative churchgoers, but Tharpe was happy to bounce back and forth between the world of the church and the world of the world. She not only swung up traditional sacred pieces like "Shout, Sister, Shout," "Rock, Daniel," and "The Lonesome Road," but sang completely secular blues and even sexually oriented material like "I Want a Tall Skinny Papa" and "Four or Five Times."

More recently, Document Records in Austria issued a five-CD series covering all of Tharpe's Decca titles (with and without Milliner) and the rest of her 78-era recordings. She continued to perform deep into the rock 'n' roll years: There's a brilliant series of live albums done with British "trad" trombonist Chris Barber. She's amazing on a 1957 Manchester concert issued on CD as *Lost and Found—Blues Legacy Series Vol. 1.* she is, as always, exploding with energy, and Barber's brand of New Orleans revival Dixieland (in the spirit of Bunk Johnson and George Lewis) sounds perfect behind her. It finally took a stroke to stop her, at the age of fifty-five; she died three years later, in 1973. Still, her spirit is literally everywhere in contemporary pop, in all the streams that spin out of gospel—which means practically everything.

Paradoxically, while the old-time church ladies professed to disavow Sister Rosetta, everybody else claimed her as their own: Frankie Laine and Johnnie Ray, two white pop singers who famously made a point of trying to sound black, got together on Tharpe's original "Up Above My Head"—a riotous duet in which the two headliners seem to be trying to out-Rosetta each other. Elvis Presley also named her as a favorite, and the influence is impossible to miss. Bob Dylan played her more than almost any other artist on his *Theme Time Radio Hour* series, and those who are given to deconstructing the Beatles claim that the lyrics of John Lennon's "Get Back" ("Sweet Loretta Martin") contain a coded reference to Sister Rosetta.

She was determined to save your soul but not to bore you to death in the process. Tharpe and Millinder filmed a wonderful series of "soundies" (low-budget jukebox movies) in 1941 and Tharpe is positively radiant, standing there with her guitar, feet planted firmly on the ground and wailing away, her eyes blazing with the Holy Spirit. She's so exuberant, so extravagant, so charismatic, that she doesn't make me think of even Louis Jordan, Mahalia Jackson, or almost any artist of her era—she really seems like an exact prototype for Chuck Berry or Elvis. "Shout, Sister" is an ecumenical party song, a direct forerunner of "Johnny B. Goode" and "Jailhouse Rock." If Elvis was Jesus, Sister Rosetta was John the Baptist.

And if Tharpe is a likely candidate for the title of the first and most unusual star of gospel music, Mahalia Jackson would be both the archetypical and greatest. Throughout her years in Chicago, Jackson was a member of the Greater Salem Baptist Church. She worked regularly with the Johnson Brothers, the sons of Salem Baptist's pastor, who were also instrumental in the evolution of the new gospel sound—and, business-wise, of the new gospel circuit, beginning with the Chicago-area churches. Jackson cut her first four titles at age twenty-five in 1937 at a Chicago session for Decca. She began recording in earnest nine years later for the Chicago-based label Apollo, and it was at that time she began to make an impact.

Especially considering that Apollo Records was an independent, regional label, Mahalia Jackson's singles for that concern were one of the major success stories of the postwar era. "Move on up a Little Higher" and "Silent Night" were said to have sold a million copies each internationally (apparently Apollo's Art Freeman had good distribution in Europe), and at the very least they sold something close to that. In 1954, she began an association with CBS, launching a long-running national radio series and a long-term contract with Columbia Records.

At this point in her career, mechanically reproduced performance media, such as radio and recordings (she also was appearing somewhat frequently on television), were still secondary: Her main career was focused on in-person appearances around the country in black churches and tent shows. By the end of her career, the Columbia Records connection had helped bring her to all kinds of other audiences, including the Newport Jazz Festival and international appearances, but she can't be said to have "crossed over" since she only sang the gospel repertory.

Mahalia Jackson's voice was big, deep, and rich, large enough to reach every ear in the greatest cathedrals you can imagine, yet small enough to find its way into every heart. The sound was big, and she projected it with a lot of energy, a lot of melisma, a lot of decoration, but as we've noted, in contrast to her current-day musical (and decidedly not spiritual) descendants, she never sings anything to excess. She had the chops to sing opera and the vocal and mental equipment to do heavy jazz (and scat) singing like Ella Fitzgerald or Sarah Vaughan, but that voice is so perfectly suited to the Lord's music that it's impossible to imagine Jackson doing any kind of secular song.

The two Bessie Smith ersatz-gospel titles, "Revival Day" and "Moaners," also illustrate that one of Smith's greatest bequests to Jackson was rhythm. Smith's heavy and powerful, deep-in-the-ground-beat style of singing was somewhat anachronistic even by the end of the twenties, a time when blues singers were becoming jazzier and more rhythmically lithe, so to speak. By the account of Lionel Hampton (the nephew of her final life companion), who knew a thing or two about swinging, Smith herself was starting to swing more in the final years of her career, during which she continued to work regularly. Unfortunately, we only have Hamp's word for it since she didn't make any records after 1933. Producer John Hammond liked to point out that he supervised Smith's last session immediately before Billie Holiday's first one (both involving future Swing King Benny Goodman), but to me it's just as relevant that Mahalia Jackson cut her first session a few months before Smith died in that car crash in Mississippi.

It was Jackson and her big-voiced gospel sisters who most took up the mantle of Bessie Smith's power and easy, rocking rhythmic style. When Jackson sings "Elijah Rock," "Rock of Ages," or "Rockin'

in Jerusalem" she's using the word "rock" in a musical as well as a geological sense. It was perhaps because she sang with the beat of the blues, along with the music's penchant for elaboration and highly personal interpretation and expression ("It ain't what you do, it's the way that you do it"), that she and writer Thomas A. Dorsey were initially regarded as radicals by some of the more conservative black religious institutions.

Jackson was firmly committed to her message of optimism, so much so that in her music, piety and humor were close friends. There's no better example of this than in one of her trademark songs, "Rusty Old Halo." Not a traditional spiritual, it was composed for her first Columbia session by Bob Merrill, who was writing a lot of songs for the corporation's pop singers like Rosemary Clooney and Doris Day at the time (and later would have his share of hits and flops on Broadway). The song's inspiration comes from one of the most basic tenets of Christ's teachings, and, coincidentally, one that is traditionally ignored by the religious right: that a rich man can no more enter heaven than a camel can pass through the eye of a needle.

In "Rusty Old Halo," Jackson sings of "A man, rich as a king / Still he won't give his neighbor a thing." By some miracle, and I don't use the term lightly, this character gets into heaven. However, once there, he finds that the circumstances he enjoyed in mortal life are completely reversed. Where he lived like royalty on earth, he finds that everything handed to him in the afterlife is strictly second-rate: He has to lie around on a "skinny white cloud," his wings are "secondhand" and "full of patches," and his heavenly robe is "so woolly it scratches." There's so much antic wit and irony here; Merrill and Jackson are making fun *with* religion rather than *of* religion, the way Louis Jordan did on "Deacon Jones."

Likewise, another Jackson signature is "Move on up a Little Higher," in which she sings of the passage to heaven as one in which she gets to meet the characters described in other hymns, like "Paul and Silas," two persecuted apostles who appear in many a sacred text. She even encounters "the lily of the valley." Some songs in Jackson's repertory had been there forever, like "The Saints" and "Little While to Stay Here," which were heard not only in church but also played by the brass bands of Jackson's New Orleans upbringing ("Little While to Stay" was the theme of the Eureka Brass Band).

Yet she is even more effective when singing songs that were deliberately composed for the new gospel idiom, such as "The Bible Tells Me So," by Dale Evans, Queen of the Cowboys. She is especially successful with those written by Thomas A. Dorsey himself, like his classic "Take My Hand, Precious Lord" (unfortunately, she doesn't seem to have recorded "Peace in the Valley"), "If We Never Needed the Lord Before (We Sure Do Need Him Now)," "It

Don't Cost Very Much," and "I'm Going to Live the Life I Sing About in My Song." One wishes Columbia would release a collection called "Mahalia Jackson Sings Thomas A. Dorsey" that would also include his adaptations of traditional spirituals, like "Walk Over God's Heaven."

While her records continued to sell to her traditional audiences, she was by now a star in the white secular world as well, even if she continued to perform religious material exclusively. She took full advantage of the perks of being on a major label. The bulk of the Columbia sessions have piano by Jackson's longtime accompanist Mildred Falls, often supplemented by organist Ralph Jones, and sometimes joined by crack studio jazz players, like bassist Milt Hinton and drummer Osie Johnson, as well as jazz guitarist Jimmy Raney.

Columbia recorded Jackson prolifically for roughly fifteen years, beginning, not coincidentally, at the start of the 12" LP era. One of her first projects was a collection of sacred Christmas songs, and there are albums with studio orchestras and string sections. She also collaborated with mainstream jazz-pop-Hollywood arrangers Richard Hazzard, Marty Paich, and John (then known as Johnny) Williams. There was even a whole album with Percy Faith, Columbia's "easy listening" deity; to put it mildly, this is not the kind of Faith that Jackson was usually associated with. In addition to television, she was also seen in films like *St. Louis Blues* and *Imitation of Life.*

At the start of her national celebrity, Jackson was regarded as controversial—conservative churchgoers deemed it inappropriate to use some of the vocabulary of the devil's music in singing the praises of the Lord. Now she was controversial all over again: The album with Faith, titled *The Power and the Glory,* was one of her best-selling releases. Her fee by this time was so high that she priced herself out of the market for black churches. Some of her longtime faithful bemoaned that Mahalia had gone over too deep into the secular world, even though she would never sing one note of secular music. It might well have seemed she had gone too far when, in 1963, she recorded "Guardian Awaits" accompanied by Harpo Marx, who wasn't even a Columbia contract artist. (Actually, it was a divine idea—the mute Marx Brother was a fine instrumentalist.)

Even more memorable was a collaboration between Jackson and Duke Ellington: Her vocal on his "Come Sunday" and his setting for "The 23rd Psalm" were the highlights of his 1958 Columbia album of *Black, Brown and Beige,* and by far the best thing about that otherwise disappointing revision. Her 1958 live appearance at the Newport Jazz Festival, in which she was introduced by Columbia star Frankie Laine, was another major career pinnacle. When it started to rain, the al fresco crowd didn't scatter but stayed put: "You're treating me like a star" observes Mahalia, correctly.

Jackson herself, as an African American woman

who had overcome oppression to become an international star, was a role model for a new generation, and a perfect celebrity for the era of Camelot, and her music was praised by political leaders like President Kennedy and Dr. Martin Luther King. Jackson was standing within earshot of King at the historic March on Washington in August 1963; supposedly, it was she who prompted him to give his legendary speech, the one about having a dream.

Camelot didn't last: Shortly after the assassination of Robert Kennedy, Jackson found herself singing "Precious Lord" at the funeral of Dr. King. She had reached a career and spiritual pinnacle and could go no higher. A few overly pious types lost faith in her when she went through a divorce, but more seriously, her health had begun to fail. She was too overweight and her heart was too weak. She gave a triumphal final concert in Germany in 1971, and died at the age of sixty in January 1972.

Some would argue that the glory years of gospel were already finished by the time Jackson graduated to Columbia Records in 1954. In the immediate postwar years, gospel was at least as popular as blues, country, or any other kind of pop music in Southern and especially black households—it was a profound influence on early rock 'n' rollers of all colors, especially the young Elvis Presley. Up to the mid-fifties, it was strictly a black phenomenon. When Columbia began releasing Jackson's music, more and more white people latched on to it, at the same time that black innovators like Ray Charles and Sam Cooke, working on different sides of the R&B/gospel fence, were reworking her achievements from the other way around. Instead of bringing blues devices into religious music, they were taking the feeling of gospel and merging it with R&B.

By the sixties, black pop was knee-deep in Aretha Franklin soul-sister types, who were Mahalia Jackson's daughters and granddaughters. There's irony in the way female pop singing continues to be a watered-down impersonation of Jackson and Franklin. Would Jackson be pleased that she continues to serve as a musical influence? She could hardly be happy that a style she developed to sing the praises of God has been perverted into a music in which brainless megastars assert only their own egos and sing of deluded self-love.

But ultimately it would hardly matter at all to her. Why would she have concerned herself with singers of future generations she had influenced? For Mahalia Jackson, it was always all about the souls that she had saved.

Della Reese tells my favorite story about Mahalia Jackson. In her 1997 autobiography, *Angels Along the Way,* she writes about touring as a member of Jackson's troupe in the early forties. During a performance in Richmond, Virginia, the young Reese was astonished to discover a local little girl who could apparently hit notes even higher and louder than Reese could. Reese said that she fully expected Jackson to fire her and hire this new girl in her place. Jackson had nothing like that in mind. "You're not in competition, you're in God's service," she said (tell *that* to Simon Cowell), "and neither you nor I are the only voices that He has."

And then Mahalia Jackson told her something that should be tattooed across the navel of every pop singer of the last fifty years: "It's not about how high you sing. It's about feeling the presence of God."

Rock 'n' Roll: Elvis Presley (1935–1977)

The year 2005 celebrated two major anniversaries in American popular music. It marked fifty years since 1955, when rock 'n' roll first conquered the pop singles chart, and also what would have been the seventieth birthday of Elvis Presley (who was so young when he made his initial breakthrough that his father had to co-sign his first contract with RCA Records). For Elvis, the timing was perfect. However, in terms of my own appreciation of both occurrences, the timing was completely off.

My father was born the same year as Elvis Aron Presley, and I came along a season or so after the King returned from the army. My dad was slightly too old to be part of the demographic that made Elvis a superstar, and I was too young to get it. When I was first starting to notice pop music, in the seventies, it was in a fallow period. I was caught between disco and punk, of which neither appealed to me. Rock 'n' roll was music that my parents' generation liked. It meant the Stones, the Dead, Hendrix, and other figures.

By 1977, the year both Elvis and Bing Crosby died, I had already infiltrated my father's jazz stash and begun working forward from Armstrong's Hot Fives and Bix through Duke Ellington, Charlie Parker, and John Coltrane. Along the way I also discovered Frank Sinatra, Ella Fitzgerald, and the Great American Songbook. Rock 'n' roll remained for me a bizarre thing that held some strange fascination for zillions of people but that I just couldn't get started with. One thing that I did have in common with most rock fans of my generation, which is to say everybody else, was that none of us knew what to make of Elvis Presley. By the time of his death he was a joke to high school kids born in the sixties, who listened to the Sex Pistols (whose Sid Vicious savaged both Sinatra and Presley in his parody of "My Way"), David Bowie, Kiss, or, in my case, Bing.

Elvis Presley seemed like a caricature in his last few years, but a caricature of what we didn't know, since we had never experienced him in his glory days (which had been only, in fact, a few years earlier). With those capes and jumpsuits, he appeared to belong with Liberace. His demotion from king to laughingstock was confirmed for me in the eighties and nineties, when he was increasingly spotted walking the earth, always by hayseeds: Elvis pumping gas, Elvis driving a pickup truck, Elvis ordering a bucket of chicken from the Colonel (Sanders, not Parker). But for years two people I revered, the critic

Gary Giddins and the writer and editor Robert Gottlieb, kept telling me I was wrong to dismiss Presley so offhandedly. Finally, in the summer of 2004, I decided to see what all the shaking was about. I got hold of RCA Records' four big *Essential Masters* boxes.

By the time I finished listening to them, I was completely hooked. Seventeen CDs were hardly enough. I was amazed by what I heard. After a lifetime of not getting it, I finally experienced my very own Elvis epiphany, and the mystery of why he is considered one of the great pop performers of all time was revealed to me. It was a vision straight from Graceland of a transcendental being, not in a white robe but in a white jumpsuit, with guitar rather than harp.

In his memoir *If I Can Dream*, Larry Geller, who later became Presley's hairdresser and "spiritual advisor" (somehow for one man to fulfill both of those roles in Presley's life seems perfectly appropriate), writes convincingly about being a teenager in 1956 and hearing Elvis for the first time. "I still think of 'Heartbreak Hotel' as a record that came out of nowhere. There was nothing like it before."

For a time, the early histories of rock 'n' roll (and especially film and TV documentaries) wrote off prerock popular music as a strictly white-bread confection represented by Patti Page's bland love songs and treacly novelties, that is, until Presley and the early rockers came along and left America "All Shook Up." Yet even if one ignores artists like Sinatra and Nat King Cole—whose music was considerably more exciting than "Doggie in the Window"—it's plain that both rhythm and blues (and black artists in general) and country and western had been making significant inroads into the pop mainstream long before the Presley explosion of 1956. In fact, there was a lot like "Heartbreak Hotel" before 1956, not the least of which was the dozen-plus sides Presley had recorded for Sun Records.

Geller also writes of how "Heartbreak Hotel" caught on before anyone had any idea of who Presley was, but that "not long after," Geller and his teenage pals "got the shock of our young lives when we saw a photograph of Elvis. Because of his sound and his name—what kind of a name was 'Elvis'?— we assumed that he was black." Yet that was mainly because of the single that RCA chose to promote as his first blockbuster hit: Had kids first been exposed to Presley on "Blue Moon of Kentucky," they would have assumed Presley was a veteran bluegrass singer; had they heard "My Happiness" or "That's When Your Heartaches Begin," they would have thought he was one of the many acts both black and white that imitated the Ink Spots, that enormously popular black pop vocal group.

There's a remark attributed to Sam Phillips, who owned and operated Sun Records and more than anyone deserves credit for "discovering" Elvis Presley, in which he supposedly said that he could make a fortune if he could find a white man who sang "black." In reality, there were already plenty of white singers who patterned themselves after black R&B singers. Pop music historian Arnold Shaw quotes Frankie Laine as saying that he wasn't going to make it in this business until he started "singing like a spook." Likewise, Johnnie Ray was a white singer who enjoyed a brief vogue for singing in a manner that can be described as simultaneously anticipating rock 'n' roll style and caricaturing it.

Regarding Phillips's remark, it was hardly the only time the producer-entrepreneur put all his racial cards on the table in a most undiplomatic fashion. Presley biographer Peter Guralnick quotes him as saying he was determined to find "genuine, untutored Negro music" by performers with "field mud on their boots and patches on their overalls." Even without factoring in thousands of black jazz and classical performers, nearly all of the better R&B and gospel artists were highly tutored and more likely to wear tuxedos; there was considerably more mud and other barnyard decorative material covering the boots of white country performers. But then Phillips had much in common with white ethnomusicologists in the jazz and folk fields (most famously John and Alan Lomax) who managed to backhandedly insult African American music even as they labored to preserve and record it.

Presley's innovation was neither in sounding black nor in sounding like a hillbilly, but in the brilliant way he embraced all three strains of pop music as they existed in the early fifties: rhythm and blues or black pop (and with it gospel); country music or mid-American pop; and the music of the mainstream, which, at its finest, was represented by singers who had jazz and big band experience and who sang songs from Broadway shows. The country and blues influences were probably what most attracted the teenagers of 1956, but in retrospect Presley is clearly a crooner, who comes out of a very clear-cut tradition of the finest male singers of the Great American Songbook, especially Bing Crosby, Al Jolson, Billy Eckstine, Dean Martin, and, to an extent, Frank Sinatra—and also the great crooners of the blues, like Louis Jordan, and country, like Jimmie Rodgers and Milton Brown.

It's been suggested that Presley comes most distinctly out of Martin and Crosby; Martin always sounded essentially like Crosby (although he averred on several occasions that his primary influence was Harry Mills of the Mills Brothers) tempered with occasional Italian curse words and various mannerisms designed to suggest various states of inebriation. Likewise, Presley essentially sounds like Martin with the Neapolitan trimmings replaced by what he learned from the blues and country traditions, these being the wild gyrations that thrilled teenagers, annoyed adults, and gave satirists like Stan Freberg (in his surprisingly respectful spoof of "Heartbreak Hotel") grist for the parody mill.

As Giddins has pointed out, Bing Crosby sang in a distinctly Presleyian voice in the middle of his 1950 "Sunshine Cake" (when I first heard the disc as a little kid I actually thought it was Elvis, somehow making a guest appearance on a Crosby disc); likewise, when Martin sings quasi-folkish material, the similarities to Presley are unmistakable. Dean Martin on his 1956 "Memories Are Made of This," sounds exactly like Elvis; when Presley sings "Angel" in his 1961 film *Follow That Dream,* he sounds exactly like Dino. On his 1960 single "Kiss Me Quick" by Doc Pomus (vaguely a bolero with castanets and rock 'n' roll triplets) Presley sounds even more like Dean Martin, but with a sharper sense of rhythm; his cutoffs and stops are amazing. On this disc in particular he's almost a better Dean Martin than Dean Martin. Presley also told Keely Smith that he learned a lot of his choreography and body language from Louis Prima.

Presley was, in fact, a great crooner, one of the very greatest. In spite of his way with blues and country material, it may be that his most notable strength was ballads and love songs, of both the country and the city variety. It would be foolish to deny that he was the first great rock 'n' roll star, or that he remains, to this day, the King of Rock 'n' Roll, yet from the perspective of history he has almost nothing in common vocally with subsequent rock stars. To me, he doesn't sound anything like Ozzy Osbourne, David Bowie, Neil Diamond, or even John Lennon, but he does sound a lot like the previous generation of important male pop singers.

Presley was the first rock 'n' roll superstar foremost in the sense that his music was the first to be directed at kids—and this is what separates him from all of his predecessors. It wasn't always so: The Sun records in particular offer a fascinating vision of the Elvis that might have been. He sings mainly blues ("That's All Right," "Mystery Train"), country ("Blue Moon of Kentucky," "Just Because"), and pop ("Harbor Lights") classics. It's hard to imagine another singer who would take on both Rodgers and Hart's "Blue Moon" and Bill Monroe's bluegrass classic "Blue Moon of Kentucky." It was only when RCA realized he was selling millions of records to teenagers that his material was significantly dumbed down: "Teddy Bear," "Good Luck Charm," "Wear My Ring Around Your Neck," and many others—these are perhaps the most forgettable part of his legacy.

In my head I can hear Louis Jordan or Ray

Charles doing "Blue Suede Shoes," but not "His Latest Flame" or "The Girl of My Best Friend." These last titles are particularly puerile songs of teen angst; anyone who'd gone through puberty would instantly dismiss them as juvenile above and beyond the call of duty. (Although their purely musical elements—the vocals and the instrumental work—are often ingenious.) One can't imagine any of Presley's inspirations in the country, blues, or pop fields doing them (at least not before 1950). It was part of the Presley success story that he was anointed to instigate the Generation Gap (which is depicted humorously in Broadway's 1960 *Bye Bye Birdie*). Yet it didn't have to be that way. Larry Geller remembers, "Contrary to myth, not every adult found Elvis shocking. I recall my parents watching him on *Ed Sullivan* and enjoying it quite a bit."

But that was the definition of the new music: What made rock 'n' roll different from all other earlier pop music was not that it was necessarily intended to appeal to young people—you can say the same thing about swing and about Sinatra-era pop singers—but that it was specifically designed to piss off parents. In fact, nearly every documentary on early rock or Presley devotes time to showing the reaction of the older generation. In general, this is given way too much attention—the rock bashing by church and school officials was mild compared to that directed against jazz in the twenties and swing in the thirties. The more the occasional deacon or elder condemned rock 'n' roll, the more the business and entertainment communities embraced rock 'n' roll as a new way to make lots and lots of money. It has always mystified me as to why rock is sometimes regarded as a subversive music or the sound of rebellion, when it has always been enthusiastically supported by corporate America, since even before Elvis. As for Presley himself, he would have never considered himself a rebel: Far from wanting to antagonize the older generation, he addressed all his elders as "Mister" and "Ma'am." He was a sweet-natured, levelheaded boy—before prescription medications screwed him up—and, in general, conducted himself more like Perry Como than Jim Morrison.

Somewhere along the line, someone got the idea that Presley lost his musical potency after returning from military service in Germany; the idea is articulated, though more diplomatically, by at least two of his closest friends, Joe Esposito and Larry Geller, in their autobiographies. (The field of Memphis Mafia memoirs is a growing subgenre of Elvis lit.) This idea is no more valid than the fiction that all of pop before Presley dealt with doggies in windows.

The mid-fifties—the years of Presley's breakthrough and the original first age of rock 'n' roll (conveniently demarcated by his 1958 induction)—are generally considered Presley's sweet spot: Peter Guralnick devotes roughly five hundred pages of his two-volume, 1,300-page biography to the five years leading up to his departure for Germany. RCA-BMG Records, which controls all of Presley's output, has released three five-CD box sets; while the packages devoted to the sixties and seventies are selective, and thus titled *The Essential Masters,* the box containing his fifties recordings is *The Complete Masters.* Clearly, Presley's first burst of fame and fortune is more prized than his later work. In this respect, Elvis's chroniclers risk making him into a rock 'n' roll equivalent of Louis Armstrong, whose early work (the Hot Fives and Sevens) is prized by scholars who, for many decades, derisively dismissed the rest of his brilliant career.

One preconceived notion of pop music history, however, that is largely true is that rock 'n' roll essentially faded from public consciousness after 1958; Elvis had not only left the building; he had split the entire scene, and at roughly the same time Buddy Holly, Ritchie Valens, and the Big Bopper all died in a plane crash in February 1959; Little Richard decided he'd rather sing about Jesus than "Tutti Frutti"; Chuck Berry and Jerry Lee Lewis were both virtually excommunicated for doing the wrong thing with the wrong women. The middle-class baby boomers who bought Bill Haley and Elvis records a few years earlier were now going to college and teaching themselves to pick out "Tom Dooley" on beat-up guitars. While folk was capturing the tweed-covered youth (who were causing a disturbance at the Newport jazz and folk festivals), there was also a notable resurgence in popularity of jazz-influenced pop singing in a Sinatra-influenced style. A number of the leading exponents of the traditional songbook were actually of Presley's approximate generation, like Steve Lawrence, Nancy Wilson, Jack Jones, and Bobby Darin, most of whom started out by singing triplet-heavy kiddie pop before graduating to more mature styles. Darin's 1959 "Mack the Knife" was a breakthrough blockbuster because he managed to capture both the kids who were raised on rock and their parents.

In June 1958, Presley, on leave from the army, did a session for RCA that might be considered the end of his first rock 'n' roll era. It produced a hit in "A Big Hunk o' Love." Both the song and the arrangement are rudimentary—just another 12-bar, three-chord blues; every other song Presley recorded in the fifties seemed to be one. But "Hunk o' Love" is elemental Elvis at his best; the arrangement has undeniable energy, drive, and his own brand of swing. The song charted, and remained a favorite of Presley fans long enough for the King to reference it in his 1972 hit "Burning Love."

There's nothing to suggest that either he or his audience was growing tired of such material. But there's plenty to indicate that Presley, who was twenty-five when he was mustered out of the service, was ready to grow as an artist, and fully aware that there was more to music than 12-bar, three-chord rockers. He wouldn't ever relinquish hard-core, head-banging rock 'n' roll, but he would supplement it with a wide palette of new colors. It was one of many lessons he learned from Crosby and Sinatra: never to be pinned down to a single style.

Upon returning from Germany, Presley's first move was to make his "comeback" (the first of several) on a TV special hosted by Frank Sinatra. In a much quoted statement, Sinatra had earlier blasted the entire first generation of rock 'n' rollers at the very dawn of the music's emergence. In essence, he characterized rock stars as juvenile delinquents (Sinatra's reference to "sideburns" would seem to be specifically aimed at Presley); yet long before his remark, at the time when Elvis was still singing for Sam Phillips at Sun, Sinatra had already recorded his own pseudo–rock 'n' roll single. In 1960, he paid early for the right to host Elvis's return from the service by outbidding every other TV producer. The immediate result was one of the most enjoyable duets of either man's career: Ol' Blue Eyes sings a Nelson Riddle, Swingin' Lovers–style treatment of "Love Me Tender" and the Pelvis essays "Witchcraft," complete with his trademark Elvish gyrations.

The decision of Presley's all-controlling manager, the notorious Colonel Parker, to have Elvis make his official return on Sinatra's show was strictly a matter of money and business. Yet it turned out to be a prescient decision for a number of reasons, first because Sinatra was the showbiz legend who had practically invented the concept of the comeback.

In fact, Presley's appearance on the Sinatra show signified that though he had been the original poster boy for rock 'n' roll, and had done more than anyone else to put that nascent style on the map in 1955–58, he was moving beyond it by 1960. It's wrongheaded to view this as a corruption of his more hard-rocking beginnings (there are obvious parallels to Bing Crosby's conscious decision twenty-five years earlier to move beyond his early jazz-based work, and remake himself as the Everyman of American pop). Like Crosby before him, Presley obviously realized that sticking to one style, one way of doing things, would have limited him in both the short and the long runs. There's every reason to believe he consciously took Crosby as a model; Gary Giddins has made a list of thirty-one songs that the Pelvis undoubtedly learned from Der Bingle (one of which was his only performance of a Cole Porter song, "True Love," which essentially was the final chart hit for both Crosby and Porter).

From 1955 to 1958, Presley's output was already comparatively diverse for an emerging pop star in his early twenties. Crosby, Sinatra, and Nat Cole were all much more specialized in that period of their lives (Crosby doing jazz, Sinatra doing ballads, Cole doing mostly piano). Presley, however, had the benefit of growing up with these three musical icons, among others, as guiding stars. He could switch between traditional blues and R&B, country and bluegrass, and slow love songs in a variety of genres, and do them all

convincingly even before he was twenty-four. Presley had come out of the age of covers—white singers taking the music of black and country performers and somehow both sanitizing it and mimicking it note for note (like future Elvis impersonators)—and yet when he sings material that you would think only specific performers could do, like Ray Charles's "I Got a Woman" and "What I Say," he sounds like himself and remains completely credible.

Presley's artistic growth in the postarmy years was exponential, on a Crosbyesque level. The energy of those early, three-chord and 12-bar blues rockers like "Long Tall Sally" and "Ready Teddy" is still present, but he's doing so much else as well. Even before he went into the service, in time for Christmas 1957, he taped an album of Christmas songs, climaxed by "Blue Christmas," a 1948 song that spelled instant crossover, having been done early on by Billy Eckstine and Ernest Tubb. He also had recorded several gospel classics, such as Thomas A. Dorsey's "Take My Hand, Precious Lord" and "Peace in the Valley."

Perhaps his experiences in Germany and Paris (his only significant stay in Europe) impacted upon his desire to add other elements to his music: His first notable postarmy hit was "Wooden Heart," which he had heard in Germany and sang in *G.I. Blues,* his first postarmy film and a successful attempt to cash in on the publicity surrounding his army experience. Originally titled "Muss I Den," in German, this is about as far removed from one of Presley's premilitary elemental rockers as possible, being a traditional polka composed by the future international hit maker Bert Kaempfert (who later wrote hits for both Cole, "L-O-V-E," and Sinatra, "Strangers in the Night"). He sings in a high tenor, free of gyration, and barely sounds like himself; the disc became one of his biggest European hits.

As with Crosby, the expanding diversity of Presley's music was often keyed directly to his films: That was an obvious source of inspiration for all the Hawaiian music in his career. In fact, his first big Island song, "Blue Hawaii," was a direct hand-me-down from Crosby (who introduced it in the 1937 *Waikiki Wedding*); for most of the sixties, Elvis spent much of his screen time on the sand: *Paradise, Hawaiian Style; Girls! Girls! Girls!; Clambake.* Presley did enough Hawaiian and Island songs to fill an album, and though the pictures were somewhat gimmicky—as song titles like "Rock-a-Hula Baby" indicate—you can tell he is sincere in his love for Hawaiian music, especially on "Blue Hawaii" and "Hawaiian Wedding Song." The latter is an extraordinary record: Presley sings it completely straight, with no vocal tricks or special effects, with incredible sincerity—his voice is smooth and velvety, it's one of the sexiest and most compelling vocals of his entire career. This brilliant and beautiful vocal makes it perfectly clear that Presley was the next logical step after Crosby, Eckstine, and Martin.

Presley also went Italian in these years, reinventing himself as a Neapolitan balladeer at the same moment when Dean Martin was morphing into a Gucci cowboy. He sang "O Sole Mio" as "It's Now or Never" (Tony Martin, who had a hit with the same melody titled "There's No Tomorrow," gave Presley's version his Jewish blessing). "Now or Never" opened the gates for "Surrender," based on "Come Back to Sorrento," and was also a hit for Presley, who also sang "Santa Lucia" in *Viva Las Vegas*. "Can't Help Falling in Love" (from *Blue Hawaii*) was written for Presley by the Italo-American songwriters and producers Hugo and Luigi, and was later taken up by Al Martino. "You Don't Have to Say You Love Me" was Presley's biggest hit import, and was one of the great love songs of his white jumpsuit era. Presley actually sang quite a few more Italian songs than Sinatra did.

Presley further explores a variety of polyrhythms in the sixties work, and, eventually, through Latin and clave beats. Quite a few of the fifties hits use the basic 8th- and 16th-note patterns that became an overnight cliché in early rock, but Presley was also developing his own version of the shuffle beat, which had been brought to the forefront of R&B by those two guys named Louis, Jordan and Prima, and which also served as the underlying beat of Darin's "Mack the Knife." Increasingly, various Latin, Caribbean, and Pan-American beats were finding their way into Presley's music. Even early on, there's more rhythmic variety in Presley's work than a lot of other early rock acts; the shuffle rhythm of Leiber and Stoller's "Treat Me Nice" is a lot more pleasing than most anything recorded by Presley's contemporaries. In general, Presley's sixties music is much more rhythmically interesting than the earlier work. "Kiss Me Quick," with its subtle bolero, turns out to be a mere dry run for the more ambitious "Viva Las Vegas," which brilliantly incorporates a South American samba beat into the Presley shuffle. Leiber and Stoller's "Bossa Nova Baby" (from the 1963 *Fun in Acapulco*) is admittedly a crass attempt to cash in on a contemporary trend, but Elvis's performance makes it a superior piece of work. It's not in the least Brazilian, but it gets an irresistible Latin-shuffle groove going, and as dance music is every bit as successful as "Jailhouse Rock."

One aspect of Presley's career that owed much to Sinatra was his ownership of publishing houses. As with much else in his career, it was the Colonel who pushed Elvis into the publishing business; financially it was a major boost, but artistically it could be considered a compromise of whatever artistic principles Elvis had. Joe Esposito, foreman of the Memphis Mafia and officially Presley's road manager, writes tellingly about Presley's publishing interests adversely affecting his music. Before he was in the publishing biz, Esposito writes in *Good Rockin' Tonight*, Elvis was inclined to do any song that he liked. He would hear a good country or pop tune on the radio, or he would come across a good R&B tune in one of the "race" records shops in Memphis. Yet

after 1960, Presley knew it was in his best financial interests to record as many songs as he could of which he owned at least a portion of the copyright. Thus, a lot of superior songs never got sung by the King, and a lot of crummy ones did.

Sinatra had owned several publishing houses at different points in his career (following in the footsteps of bandleaders like Tommy Dorsey); he had writers working for him, and he often came up with ideas for songs, like "Come Fly with Me," for which he would retain the publishing rights. Yet Sinatra would never have taken the idea as far as Presley and Parker did—to actually insist on owning a piece of the action of a song as a precondition for singing it. Small wonder he never sang Cole Porter after 1958.

Something that Presley had more in common with his pop-jazz predecessors than his rock descendants was that he never claimed to be a songwriter; his strength was interpreting and bringing his own personal vantage point to songs others had written. When he does do a really first-rate song, which was rare, the results are tremendous, as on his terrific 1964 treatment of Chuck Berry's fundamental rocker "Memphis, Tennessee," which is at once both touching and exuberant.

One of the easiest ways to make money where music publishing is concerned is to put one's name on something that already exists. In these years in particular, there was a major precedent for taking traditional melodies and folk songs, putting new lyrics and titles to them, and sitting back and collecting the royalties. Presley seems to have gotten stuck with more half-baked folk adaptations than anyone: The title song of the 1967 film *Stay Away, Joe* is "Jump Down, Spin Around," while "Do the Clam" comes from a folk-blues source that had already been mined for "Hey, Bo Diddley." Sometimes, the authors of these folk plagiarisms are credited for "adaptations," but the only adapting the authors of the title song of *Frankie and Johnny* did was to put the lyric into the first person and interject a few modulations into the melody.

The 1967 *Clambake* illustrates what a mixed bag Presley's movies and music had become by that time. The picture, which was also released as a twelve-track LP on RCA, is no *Gone With the Wind*, but it's not nearly as bad as the rank and file of Presley's screen efforts are supposed to be. (Presley was actually the last of the male major movie musical stars—a direct descendant of Jolson, Crosby, and Astaire—and his films are worthy of closer investigation.) The title number borrows liberally from the folk song "Shortnin' Bread," but is far from bad, and serves as the basis for a diverting dance number (with girls in shiny bikinis, how bad could it be?). Then there's "Confidence," which borrows just as liberally both musically and visually from "High Hopes," "Swingin' on a Star," and other movie numbers written (by Jimmy Van Heusen) for star singers to do with a bunch of kids.

The bulk of the other numbers in *Clambake* are just business as usual, but there are two notable exceptions: "A House That Has Everything" is a superior ballad by Presley standards, and boasts a simplicity (as well as moralizing message) that seems straight out of Hank Williams. Elvis croons it to co-star Shelley Fabares onscreen, and his performance is direct and moving, one of his most effective love songs ever; there's a plain beauty here and a lack of artifice that Nat King Cole or one of the other great male pop singers would have admired. Even better is "You Don't Know Me": Somehow Elvis put his foot down and insisted on including one of the all-time great country saloon songs. This gem is a little incongruous buried in the middle of a rather trivial film, but here it is, and Presley's performance digs considerably more deeply than co-composer Eddy Arnold's or even the iconic Ray Charles version.

It's easy to single out the inferior songs in Presley's films, but there are just as many minor classics, like "All That I Am" in *Spinout* and "Almost in Love" in *Live a Little, Love a Little,* the latter being a superior song that would have suited Tony Bennett. "A House That Has Everything" is one of the prettiest things Presley ever sang. It's worth at least a half a dozen of the three-chord rock numbers Presley cut ten years earlier, yet "A House That Has Everything" is not available in any of BMG's *Essential 60's Masters* boxes. (I had to find it on an out-of-print *Clambake* sound track disc on eBay. The *Essential 60's Masters* series deliberately avoids the movie songs, and, in fact, the time is well nigh for a big megabox of Presley's film tracks.)

There are several interviews and press conferences with Presley during which he's asked if he considers himself a country singer or a rock singer, and he answers that gospel is too much a part of what he does for him to consider himself either one.

The expected trajectory of a blues and pop singer in the mid-twentieth century was out of the church and onto the jukebox. Dinah Washington and Sarah Vaughan in the forties, Sam Cooke and Lou Rawls in the fifties, then Aretha Franklin and Gladys Knight in the sixties, to name just six, all started singing in church (and in the case of Cooke and Rawls, were stars on the gospel circuit) before they crossed over to pop. But it would be hard to think of another singer, black or white, who became a star in mainstream pop before he or she began to concentrate on spiritual music. In that aspect of his career, Presley has more in common with Duke Ellington, Leonard Bernstein, and other major American composers who began exploring their spiritual side later, rather than earlier, in their careers.

Presley's gospel recordings represent perhaps the most consistently excellent work of his entire career. He made three full albums of gospel songs, the first few tracks of which are included in the BMG *Complete 50's Masters* box. None of them are on the *Essential 60's and 70's,* although all are on the even more essential two-CD package *Amazing Grace—His Greatest Sacred Performances.* Unlike Cooke and Rawls (who were both, like Nat King Cole, the sons of preachers), Presley did not start his career by thrilling fellow parishioners; as Guralnick makes clear, he didn't really sing anywhere in public before he began recording. But nonetheless to the young Presley, singing was what you did in church, and the terms "gospel" and "music" were interchangeable. The local quartets, like the Blackwoods, were heroes to him; his highest ambition as a youngster was to land a gig singing with such a quartet. He also heard the blues, and he loved the blues; he heard country and he loved that, too. But only gospel was so real and tangible to him that he could reach out and touch it.

Presley was at his most consistently excellent when singing this music: He brings to it both a conviction and an intensity unmatched elsewhere in his catalog; he sings about God with the same power as Billie Holiday singing about her man or Jolson about his Mammy. He sang songs from both the black (blues) and white (country) traditions of religious music, songs associated with Thomas A. Dorsey, Mahalia Jackson, even the religious album by Jo Stafford and Gordon MacRae; he made the semitraditional hymn "In the Garden" into a thing of extraordinary beauty. Presley's most celebrated spiritual-oriented song was "If I Can Dream" (the climax of the 1968 so-called *Comeback Special*), which is not technically a gospel song, since it concerns itself with earthly, rather than spiritual, salvation. Even so, its lyrics allude directly to the speeches of Martin Luther King, and Presley sings it with the same inspiration and passion that he normally reserved for gospel music.

Virtually the only two Broadway show tunes that Presley sang were both transformed by him into sacred songs: "The Impossible Dream" (from *Man of La Mancha*) and "You'll Never Walk Alone" (from *Carousel*). He is just about the only performer ever to make "Impossible Dream" palatable, and he named the second as his favorite song in his famous army press conference before sailing for Germany in 1958. He didn't put "Walk Alone" on record until nearly ten years later in 1967, and even then he sang it with countrified chord substitutions that would have horrified Rodgers and Hammerstein. But it's impossible not to feel the spirit when he sings, and it isn't so much that he convinces you that he believes it, but that he makes you believe it yourself.

Presley's most famous traditional pop standard was "Are You Lonesome Tonight?," which is said to have come his way courtesy of Gene Austin via Colonel and Marie Parker. "Lonesome" was a collaboration of Lou Handman (author of one of Bessie Smith's finest nonblues songs, "My Sweetie Went Away") and Roy Turk (who wrote, among many standards, Bing Crosby's theme song, "When the

Blue of the Night [Meets the Gold of the Day]," which was also originally in 3/4). It was widely recorded in 1927, which indicates some measure of popularity, but never became an iconic hit of the era, like "My Blue Heaven" or "I Can't Give You Anything but Love."

It was then revived notably in 1950, at one of the final sessions of the World's Greatest Entertainer, Al Jolson, as well as by Blue Barron and His Orchestra. This very traditional waltz is, overall, Presley's greatest ballad, and the single most significant piece of evidence that Presley had a voice fully as beautiful as the other three guys who are generally ranked as the most successful male singers in American popular music—Bing Crosby, Frank Sinatra, and Nat King Cole. (Not to mention Billy Eckstine, Perry Como, Vic Damone, Jack Jones, and Jolson himself.) It's hard to think of anybody in the popular music sphere of the last fifty years—Broadway, country, rock, soul, or whatever—who has pipes and chops to compete.

"Are You Lonesome Tonight?" contains a feature that would be regarded as unique in any popular song: a spoken monologue, a poetry recitation of sorts. The monologue was published as part of the original sheet music, but, as far as I can tell, it was not included in any of the original twenties recordings; it doesn't seem to have been recorded until 1950. On the Blue Barron disc, the piece is recited by a local Chicago radio announcer named John McCormick (no relation to the famous Irish tenor of thirty years earlier); it was a minor chart hit that year. Jolson, not surprisingly, intones the recitation with considerably more conviction.

Tom Parker and his wife may have suggested "Lonesome" to Presley, but he had certainly heard the Jolson version. He sings it in his tenor register, high and sweet, which is reminiscent of both Gene Austin and Bill Kenny of the Ink Spots, but his confidence and sincerity recall that of the great Jolson. Then, to the surprise of the engineers at the session, he goes into the McCormick-Barron monologue. Although he had tried spoken passages in at least two earlier songs, the "Are You Lonesome Tonight?" monologue is unique. It's been suggested that Presley couldn't get through the whole thing without cracking up and the speech had to be assembled from multiple takes; the existence of a complete alternate (on the 2002 box *Today, Tomorrow and Forever*) suggests that this isn't so. It's true that Elvis, who acted on his own initiative by including the monologue, in later years frequently broke up with laughter during this song, even before he got to the spoken passage. A famous concert recording from 1969 has Presley, who could never be accused of taking himself too seriously, crooning the following couplet: "Do the lights in the parlor seem empty and bare? / Do you gaze at your bald head and wish you had hair?" The text, with its allusions to *As You Like It* ("You know, someone said that the world's a stage,

and each must play a part") is probably as close as Presley ever came to Shakespeare—at least until the 2005 Broadway musical *All Shook Up*, which expertly managed to bowdlerize both the Bard and the King.

Ervin Drake, composer of Sinatra's iconic "It Was a Very Good Year," once described a late-night conversation with Sinatra in which the subject of Presley somehow came up. Drake is one of the few songwriters whose work had been recorded by both Presley (who sang Drake's "I Believe") and Sinatra, although he certainly was much closer, personally and aesthetically, to the latter than to the former. In any event, one night a few hours after a show at the Sands, Sinatra and Drake were hanging out by the side of a pool with drinks in hand (every scene in Vegas involves pools and drinks), chatting. As Ervin told me, he said to Sinatra, "You know, I'm not exactly sure what it is that Elvis does, but whatever it is, he's the best at it—in fact, he's a real champion." At this point, Sinatra raised his glass in agreement. "Yeah, he's the best," said the Chairman of the King, "whatever it is."

Nancy Sinatra, who co-starred with Presley in the 1968 *Speedway*, once reported a conversation with her father on the subject of Elvis Presley. On this particular occasion Sinatra Senior dismissed him not on the basis of his singing talent or his taste in music, but because of his perceived inability to grow as an artist. Nancy protested that the people around Elvis wouldn't let him grow, but Sinatra pooh-poohed this excuse. As well he should have. From his perspective, we can't blame him—Sinatra wouldn't let anybody stand in his way in terms of choosing a song or polishing an arrangement or mix to perfection.

Yet this conversation represents perhaps the only time Frank Sinatra was documented as discussing Presley as even a potentially kindred spirit—which they were. They both were only children who required the company of an entourage around them after they grew up (Elvis's Memphis Mafia was his equivalent of the Rat Pack); they both were extremely attached to dominating mothers and had comparatively passive fathers. Sinatra and Presley were among the few singers who attained superstardom in Hollywood, and they both had a lot of comebacks.

More important, both Sinatra and Presley were their own tastemakers. But that may be where the similarity ends. Esposito describes how Presley would work with his recording engineers to mix his own master tapes. He would then have a one-off acetate pressed of his mix, and then compare it with the mix that RCA released. When the label tampered with his intentions, it would annoy him, but, unfortunately, not to the degree that he would actually do anything about it. The word came down from the Colonel that only Elvis himself was important: The quality of his songs or the plots of his films or anything else was irrelevant. This was precisely the opposite of Sinatra's attitude; in his music especially, Sinatra only wanted to sing the best songs. Elvis did, too, but he didn't have the attitude or temperament to stand up to the Colonel or RCA Records or Paramount Pictures. Sinatra and the equally pugnacious Ray Charles constantly made their own opportunities, and heaven help you if you got in their way. Perhaps to stick to your own standards in showbiz, you had to be something of a gangster.

One of the most repeated—and indisputable—truisms about Presley's canon is that he frequently took second-rate songs and turned them into classics—something that rarely had to be said about Sinatra or Tony Bennett, who made a point of only singing songs that were excellent to begin with. Unfortunately, Presley lacked their fortitude—otherwise, everything might have been as good as "Memphis, Tennessee" and "You Don't Know Me" or

his riveting live version of Hank Williams's "I'm So Lonesome I Could Cry." What Sinatra did for Rodgers and Hart and Cole Porter, Presley should have been for Hank Williams, Bill Monroe, Big Bill Broonzy, and Willie Dixon—he should have been the greatest interpreter of those other great American songbooks, and he should have done more traditional Tin Pan Alley songs and show tunes, too.

When the Elvis sightings of the early nineties reached a peak, I couldn't help speculating: There's so much interest in Elvis now, can you imagine what it'll be like when he actually dies? Presley's death, obviously, left a gap that no one has been able to fill. Now, in 2010, it seems more clear than ever that Elvis Presley was not the beginning of something, but an end. John Lennon famously once said, "Before Elvis, there was nothing." He had it the wrong way around: *After* Elvis, there was nothing.

Blues: Bessie Smith (1894–1937)

More than seventy years after her tragically early death (at age forty-three), it seems increasingly clear that Bessie Smith may be the most important female voice of the early twentieth century. Who else comes close? Back in the day, both Ethel Waters, who also sang the blues, and Ruth Etting, who didn't, probably sold more records, but neither is as well remembered and well reissued as Bessie Smith. (Nor, for that matter, is Kate Smith, who shared Bessie's name and her body type, but little else.) If you were to stop a hundred people on Fifth Avenue in 2010, and read them a list of singers who were stars in the acoustic era, Enrico Caruso, Al Jolson, and Bessie Smith are probably the only names anyone would recognize.

It wasn't until shortly before Smith's death in 1937 that other women's names emerged that would be familiar to passersby today: Ella Fitzgerald, Judy Garland, and Billie Holiday. There certainly wasn't a female blues singer who could challenge Smith's supremacy until the arrival of Dinah Washington, who clearly viewed Smith as the one to beat. Yet even the mighty Dinah could never eclipse Bessie in her own backyard.

Whereas the influence of most seminal artists tends to wane as the generations pass, Smith actually seems to have grown in importance; you can hear a lot more of her in Whitney Houston, Mariah Carey, or Bono than you can Jolson or Caruso (or Crosby or Sinatra, for that matter). With her big, dark, deep voice and biting attack, Smith was virtually unchallenged as blues royalty. Her power and presence were an obvious influence on such different singers as rock icon Janis Joplin in the sixties and nineties cabaret chanteuse Susannah McCorkle.

Billie Holiday is a special case. She famously said that she wanted to combine Smith's force with Louis

Armstrong's flexibility, but as Dan Morgenstern and others have pointed out, in the actual substance of Holiday's music, one can more readily detect the influence of Ethel Waters. Even so, in her tribute to Smith, Billie recorded four of Bessie's most famous numbers ("Do Your Duty," "'Tain't Nobody's Business If I Do," "Keeps on a Rainin'," and "Gimme a Pigfoot"). Apparently, Decca's Milt Gabler (although he later denied it) had planned a *Billie Sings Bessie* tribute album but only got as far as these four songs. Still, Smith would be the subject of similar tributes by singers as diverse as Dinah Washington (her heir apparent), Jimmy Rushing, and folksinger Ronnie Gilbert of the Weavers. In the summer of 2003 (when the new edition of the definitive Smith biography, Chris Albertson's *Bessie,* was published), both Bobby Short and Wynton Marsalis resurrected her 1928 masterpiece "Empty Bed Blues, Parts 1 & 2" in direct homage to the almighty Empress.

In a series of roughly 160 songs recorded between 1923 and 1933, many of her own authorship, Smith defined the blues, and left behind its most powerful catalogue of work. On the heels of Tucker and Waters, Bessie Smith was also one of the first singers in any genre to fully master the recorded medium. She may have been even more effective in person than on wax, but her discs remain amazingly potent documents of one of the greatest personalities in all of American music. A versatile musician as well as a folk hero to African American audiences of the interwar years, Smith showed and indeed continues to show generation after generation of musicians, both instrumentalists and singers, the endless variety to be mined out of the basic 12-bar blues format.

Smith, whose life and career are vividly documented in the aforementioned *Bessie,* was born in Tennessee in 1894. (The date, incidentally, is the result of Albertson's diligent research. Earlier writers, such as the usually reliable British blues scholar Paul Oliver, in his 1959 British booklet, *Bessie Smith,* give 1898. Still other sources speculate that she might have been born as early as 1892, but 1894 seems to be the consensus.) She started singing on the streets of Chattanooga and from there gradually established herself in the hierarchy of black show business, which was forming and formalizing itself in the years of her ascendance. Before she became the Empress, Smith owed her early success to two early Queens of the Blues. Gertrude "Ma" Rainey served as her blues-singing mentor, and Rainey prominently featured Smith in her touring company (the sort that Smith herself would later headline in). Then, too, both Rainey and Smith would have been mere footnotes to history had it not been for Mamie Smith (no relation); Mamie was not in Bessie's or Rainey's class as a blues singer, but she was the first important black female singer to make records, and her recordings of 1920 started a craze that revolutionized the recording industry.

In a very real sense, Bessie Smith was a product of the twenties economic boom. Both she and Ethel Waters were part of the first generation of black performers to appear before the first generation of working-class and middle-class black audiences, who themselves were a by-product of the urbanization of America and the World War I industrial expansion. Earlier black stars, most notably Bert Williams, were only granted that status because they appeared before white audiences; later, it was considered a major step forward when artists like Louis Armstrong, Cab Calloway, and Billy Eckstine "crossed over."

But in the twenties, it was an equally significant achievement for blacks to have theaters of their own. The discovery of the "race" record market was the next logical outgrowth of the Northern migration. For the first time there were now African American neighborhoods in virtually every major city in the country, even in the North and the West, and by the end of the war there had been a gradual proliferation of theaters, as well as honky-tonks and saloons, that featured music in these areas. And soon there were music shops that carried phonograph records in Harlem, Los Angeles's Central Avenue, Chicago's South Side, and other black neighborhoods. Before 1920, what records there were of black performers were primarily aimed at white buyers; no one had imagined that there was a market for black music among black people.

As the African American songwriter Perry Bradford told the story, he was trying to promote a song of his called "Crazy Blues" and took the then unheard of step of getting a female black singer, a woman named Mamie Smith, to record it for the Okeh label. (Previously he had tried to convince the established star Sophie Tucker to sing it.) "Crazy Blues" was a smash hit with black buyers: At last their music and artists of their color were being put on records. By a bizarre coincidence, four of the leading exponents of the new genre (later dubbed "classic blues" by historians) were named Smith: Mamie, Bessie, Clara, and Trixie.

Perry Bradford and Mamie Smith launched a vogue for black female singers, and African American culture received a further boost when, a year later, the Broadway show *Shuffle Along* revived mainstream interest in the black musical comedy. Then, around 1923, black jazz bands (from smaller New Orleans–style groups like King Oliver's to larger dance bands like Fletcher Henderson's) began to be regularly recorded. By the mid-twenties, a full-scale boom of African American entertainment was under way, which would keep going until Black Friday and the Great Depression.

Bessie Smith was unquestionably the most important artist of this epoch, the number-one favorite among black theatergoers and record buyers. But unlike Ethel Waters, Smith never broke through to Broadway and Hollywood, even during the post–*Shuffle Along* wave of black Broadway shows. This never seems to have concerned her, and regardless of the views of the purist historians of a generation later, or even her own later years, it seems to have worked in her favor.

On the whole, the twenties were remarkably rich years for African American vocal music (in fact, until the very late acoustic era, considerably more singers were recorded than bands), although, unfortunately, little of it is commonly available on CD or is investigated in mainstream jazz history discussions. Further, for some reason—testosterone?—male historians tend to assign too much importance to the mostly male guitarists and singers from the Mississippi Delta. Let me tell you one thing, sonny: Robert Johnson isn't nearly as crucial to American music as Bessie Smith, and the Waters who deserves the most attention is Ethel, not Muddy. It's also unfortunate that some of the singers, like the dreadful Lillie Delk Christian, who turn up on recordings with the best male instrumental soloists (like Armstrong and Sidney Bechet) do not represent the best that the era has to offer.

Jazz historians from the fifties onward spend a lot of time dissing these women, giving the impression that most of the early female blues singers were closer to Lillie Delk Christian than to Bessie Smith. In fact, Smith is presented in some histories as representing the exception to the rule. (Some of her classic twenties sides were included in the first wave of jazz reissues around 1939, and she has been represented in the Columbia catalogue almost continuously since 1923.) But the more one listens to her contemporaries—like Ma Rainey, Ida Cox, Alberta Hunter, Eva Taylor, and the other Smiths—the clearer it becomes that Bessie Smith is hardly atypical but simply the best of the best.

Even though Mamie Smith is usually (and rightfully) singled out as the woman who launched the trend, she is rarely given credit as an artist in her own right. She didn't get a major label reissue of her Okeh sides until 2003, but that collection proves she was a singer and entertainer of considerable appeal.

Bessie Smith was brought to Columbia Records in 1923 by producer, composer, and bandleader Clarence Williams, who is portrayed in Albertson's book as a not always lovable scoundrel. Still, it's hard for jazz lovers to think of him as anything other than a hero since he was directly responsible for recording much of the best music of the Jazz Age. Williams was, in many ways, the Berry Gordy of his time, equal parts hero and villain, but unlike the Motown majordomo, he was also a capable performer himself—a pianist (and, occasionally, singer). Although he was hardly a virtuoso on the same level as friend and colleague James P. Johnson, he was a thoughtful blues accompanist who could give singers the support they needed while staying out of their way.

Smith's recording career began with "Down Hearted Blues," recorded in New York circa February 16, 1923, and as with most of her earliest sessions, the accompaniment consists of just Williams on piano. Her first disc, it served notice that the most powerful female voice in the history of American vernacular music had now arrived. This basic 12-bar blues in C had been written by two other female giants of the early blues, pianist and occasional bandleader Lovie Austin and singer Alberta Hunter. The combination of their lyrics and Smith's powerful delivery establishes several metaphors and images that would become recurring icons of the blues, like the one about the three men in her life and the one about having the world in a jug ("Lord!") and the stopper in her hand. "Down Hearted Blues" established Bessie Smith as a major force in the recording industry.

"Down Hearted Blues" was an instant hit. Williams and Smith proved to Columbia, in a big way, that "race" music was an economic, as well as an artistic, boon; she was one of the label's top artists throughout the decade, black or white, male or female. Other aspects of her earliest sessions are also notable. Everything we know about acoustic era technology tells us that high voices recorded better (and were more popular) than low, although conversely male voices came off better than female. Yet Smith's low female voice comes off brilliantly in the state-of-the-art 1923 technology. (Admittedly, Columbia was using better equipment in New York than that which independents like Gennett had access to in Richmond, Indiana, or that Paramount was using on Ma Rainey in Chicago.)

With her deep voice and earthy style, Smith is considerably more convincing than any artist who had yet been documented in the classic blues era (she also beat her mentor, Ma Rainey, to the studio by several months). In fact, even on the 1923–25 acoustic sessions, the only word that can describe her is "modern." Considering that all but a handful of singers from before 1930 sound terribly dated—not just those screechy tenors already being heard on white dance band records, but even some of the black singers of the classic blues era (well beyond Ms. Delk Christian), this is a remarkable achievement. You don't need to mentally transport yourself to another time, another place, to appreciate Bessie Smith; she sounds fine right where and when she is.

One area that may, however, seem dated, is what might be called the gender politics of twenties blues, a subject that comes to the fore in "'Tain't Nobody's Business If I Do," another of her earliest recordings and one of the many songs she introduced into the permanent repertoire of the blues. Smith sounds positively defiant singing what might be considered a feminist text, asserting her right to be treated as she chooses. However, when one listens more closely, it becomes apparent that what she's actually demanding is the right to stay with her man even if he beats her: "I would rather my man would hit me / than that he would up and quit me." This blues-based song by Smith's future accompanist Porter Grainger is based on an even then ancient strain of the folk blues, which manifested itself at around the same time in a very different way as Mississippi John Hurt's "Nobody's Dirty Business."

In 1925, the coming of electrical recording meant an instant sea change for the recording industry, but the technological shift only helped Smith consolidate her gains. She sounded better than ever in the new medium. Her last excellent acoustic date occurred in January of that year, and it resulted in one of the most remarkable summit meetings in all American music: history's single greatest blues shouter and the most influential instrumentalist (and later a supreme singer himself) joining forces to take on one of the signature works of American music. Bessie Smith and Louis Armstrong doing "St. Louis Blues" was a bit like Laurence Olivier and Sarah Bernhardt teaming up in a production of *Death of a Salesman*. Regrettably, the collaboration of Bessie and Louis extended to only one recording session, but we should be grateful that it happened at all—and that W. C. Handy's already classic 1912 composition "St. Louis Blues" was the first tune on the date.

Smith is at her most powerful and Armstrong is at his most inventive; it's said that she preferred less "frisky" players than Armstrong, ones who wouldn't make her "play second fiddle" (as the title of one 1925 tune implied), yet she needn't have worried. Even if Armstrong had set about stealing her thunder—which he didn't—it's doubtful that even the greatest jazz musician of all time (which he is) could have pulled focus from Bessie Smith. The other musician on the date is keyboardist Fred Longshaw.

He played piano on other sessions with Smith, but for some reason Columbia had him accompany Smith and Armstrong on harmonium, a miniature counterpart to the traditional pipe organ heard in many small Southern houses of worship. Blues scholars have often derided his playing as well as his instrument here, but to me it gives the side a down-home churchy sound that's perfectly appropriate.

As Smith moved into the electrical era, hers was a declamatory, extroverted style, but she held her own against the more intimate singers who began emerging in both the "colored time" and the "white time" (as black entertainers used to put it). These phrases, used by Ethel Waters in her autobiography, are employed in roughly the same way as "big time" and "small time," two showbiz expressions of the era that are still in general use. Yet, in the more literal sense, time is not a major element of Smith's music, which in itself is exceptional since nearly every other singer in the jazz and blues fields tends to make a big deal out of time. Smith stays close to the beat, and tends to fill almost every space, only occasionally leaving room for a soloist to play an obbligato. With many singers, the silences can be as important as the notes; not so with Smith.

Still, even though rhythm and humor are closely related in music, Smith has perfect comic timing, evident as early as the 1923 "Sam Jones Blues." Two of her funniest sides are "Put It Right Here (Or Keep It out There)"—the phrase is the 1929 equivalent of "Show Me the Money"—and its sequel of a few months later, "Take It Right Back ('Cause I Don't Want It in Here)." As Paul Oliver has pointed out, "Put It Right Here" is a vaudeville comedy number of the sort done by such veterans of the black showbiz circuit as the team known as Butterbeans and Susie. It's also the genesis of dozens of punch line–driven blues comedy numbers done by the King Cole Trio and Louis Jordan and His Tympany Five fifteen years later, e.g., Cole's "Solid Potato Salad" ("Pick it up . . . Bring it right back!") and shows that Smith can, in fact, do a tune where rhythm is the key element.

"It" continued to serve as a key euphemism in the age of Clara Bow, as in "I've Got What It Takes, but It Breaks My Heart to Give It Away." Smith also recorded Clarence Williams's "I Want Every Bit of It." "Young Woman's Blues," an early electric side from 1926, and "Lock and Key" from the following year, represent additional examples of Smith pondering what to do with "it." "Lock and Key," for which James P. Johnson provides both the melody and Smith's accompaniment, is classic fare for Bessie Smith and the classic blues singers of her generation. It depicts a battle of the sexes that's at once earthy and urbane: She loved her man once, but he made a fool out of her. In retaliation, she's going to lock him out—and there ain't nothin' passive-aggressive about it, sugar. She even demands that her misbehaving lover return all the clothes she bought for him, right then and there, until he's literally standing in the hallway in his BVDs.

The popular belief is that the majority of the great blues lyrics begin with the cliché "Woke up this morning," and "Young Woman's Blues" is one of the few that actually does. It also includes many other familiar features of the genre: Our heroine wakes up one morning to find that her man has left her. From then on, the song refuses to follow any formula, but like Smith's singing itself, is complex and highly nuanced. On the one hand, she wants her man back, and she wants him to stop chasing other women and settle down with her. At the same time, she expresses the urge to run around; she, too, wants to go out drinking and sleeping with strangers, even though more conservative types may label her a "hobo" (and that's why the lady is a tramp). Only Smith is capable of illuminating both sides of this woman's complex personality in this surprisingly deep interpretation of one of the lesser-known songs of her career. Released as by "Bessie Smith and Her Blue Boys," this was one of many sides she cut with the accompaniment of Fletcher Henderson and various Hendersonians.

Almost everything she sings is in the classic 12-bar blues format: Her occasional pop songs, like "My Sweetie Went Away," "Alexander's Ragtime Band," and "A Hot Time in the Old Town Tonight," stand way out from the rest of her material. She generally does two types of songs: sad blues, about the man she loves who treats her awful mean; then, increasingly in the late twenties, double entendre numbers in which she sings of the boudoir prowess of her various lovermen. Customarily, she expresses this boast in what could charitably be referred to as metaphors, such as "I'm wild about that thing" and "I can't do without my kitchen man." Often erotic skill appears as a bedfellow of musical ability, as in the case of that lovin' clarinet man, "Jazzbo Brown from Memphis Town," a playin' fool who "wraps his big fat lips 'round that doggone horn."

The important thing is that, as opposed to the sadder blues pieces, the happier blues numbers show her as at least glad to get what she's getting, a little sugar in her bowl (she uses "sugar" as the same kind of code word in "What's the Matter Now?"), a little hot dog between her rolls. One can only imagine exactly what she means when she says, in recitative, at the end of "Sugar in My Bowl," "Get off your knees, I can't see what you're driving at! It's dark down there, looks like a snake. Come on there, and drop something in my bowl." Even when Nina Simone revived the song, she left that line alone. Many of Smith's numbers, like the two-part "Empty Bed Blues" of 1928, offer a mixed message. Here she sings joyfully of her man, who, we are told, is a deep-sea diver who loves to grind her coffee (let's hope he doesn't attempt these two activities simultaneously), and woefully of the loneliness that wells up inside of her when the "bed get[s] empty."

As the Jazz Age was about to implode into the

Great Depression, Smith also did a number of songs where Topic A was politics and even economics rather than sex. She spent most of her career working in what was a loose equivalent of vaudeville, touring in tent shows and theaters primarily in the South. Most of the material she presented was highly theatrical in nature, and many of her songs were written by professional composers based in the urban North. Yet that didn't stop her from occasionally recording a song that authentically reflected the trials and tribulations of her Deep South audiences, both white and black. In the 1927 "Backwater Blues," a descriptive tale of Southern rivers overflowing, she tells of having "to pack my things and go" because "my house fell down and I can't live there no mo'." Her description of the floods ravaging the country in the late twenties seems as if it could have been written anytime in the last eighty years—and it's a particularly compelling description of the devastation caused by Hurricane Katrina in 2005. A classic blues usually included in Smith tributes (like Washington's), much of the credit for it should go to accompanist James P. Johnson, who not only does the work of an entire band, but musically depicts the falling of rain and hail as well.

"Poor Man's Blues," from 1928, is about as close as Smith came to a protest song, of the kind that later folk-blues singers favored. It's hard not to be moved as she sings, "While you're living in your mansion, you don't know what hard times mean. / A working man's wife is starving, your wife is living like a Queen." Even more than usual, her delivery is direct and to the point—there's no mistaking her meaning or her message. Her rhythm style is so basic and fundamental that she rarely required what later became known as a conventional rhythm section, with bass and drums. Most of her recordings use just a piano (often played by her eloquent accompanist Porter Grainger); here there are three horns, including a moaning trombone.

Three years hence, during the depths of the Depression, she sang one of her most downhearted blues, "Long Old Road." In this exceedingly despondent D-flat dirge, Smith is "weepin' and cryin'" with her "tears fallin' on the ground." Even when she sings of meeting a friend at the end of the Long Old Road, the implication is that the only relief to be found is in death. The highly vocalized obbligatos of trumpeter Louis Metcalf and trombonist Charlie Green sound like grief-stricken mourners at a funeral. Cheerful it ain't.

Smith sounds surprisingly up-to-date even if much of her material is foreign to us. Of the roughly 160 titles she cut, fewer than a dozen are songs that have any reputation apart from her ("Baby, Won't You Please Come Home" and "Squeeze Me," to name two), and perhaps another dozen are well known to later generations from Smith herself and subsequent tribute albums, such as "Nobody Knows You When You're Down and Out." This latter song, written in 1929 by black vaudevillian Jimmy Cox, anticipates the Wall Street meltdowns of both that year and seventy-nine years later. Smith turned it into an all-time classic, which reverberates through the entire history of black music, and was heard long into the soul era, emanating from Sam Cooke, Otis Redding, Ruth Brown, Eric Clapton, and even Liza Minnelli (Liza Minnelli?). Here she puts over the image of holding on to a dollar so vividly that one can easily visualize the formidable singer squeezing it "until them eagles grin!" Among other things, "Nobody Knows You When You're Down and Out" is a direct antecedent of Bob Dylan's "Like a Rolling Stone"; when I play the Smith record, I keep expecting to hear her shout, "How does it feel?"

Still, the great bulk of songs that she sang are unfamiliar to most contemporary listeners; Ethel Waters and Ruth Etting introduced considerably more jazz and pop standards. But it's a double-edged sword: Contemporary singers can do "Dinah" or "Am I Blue" without having to acknowledge Waters, or "Love Me or Leave Me" and not associate it with Etting, yet it's nearly impossible to do anything Smith had anything to do with without her influence continuing to resonate. Every song she ever sang is a Bessie Smith song, and her identity continues to stamp those songs in a way that few other artists can claim.

Smith's material echoes back to us in funny ways: Nina Simone sang "Sugar in My Bowl" for so long that she may have come closest to making audiences forget it was associated with Smith. However, Dr. Simone didn't have the same luck with "Gimme a Pigfoot." Billie Holiday took two lines from the 1931 "Safety Mama" ("I ain't good lookin', I'm built for speed / I got everything a pigmeat needs") and made them a key part of her own "Billie's Blues." Jimmy Rushing built at least two whole blues numbers around quotes from Smith's songs. "Baby, Don't Tell on Me" begins with the line "If you catch me stealin'" from Smith's "Sorrowful Blues," whereas one of Rushing's signature phrases, "Good morning, blues (blues, how do you do?)," was sung by Smith in "Jailhouse Blues." "Hard-Lovin' Blues" by Louis Jordan and His Tympany Five, with a vocal by a female blues singer named Yack Taylor, is a pastiche of classic Smith phrases, including familiar lines from "Jailhouse Blues" and "Empty Bed Blues." Jordan also recorded "Nobody Knows You When You're Down and Out." Lester Young famously quoted "My Sweetie Went Away" (one of Smith's earliest sides, from 1923), at the close of his classic 1943 solo on "Sometimes I'm Happy"—one of the most glorious improvisations in all of jazz.

In 1930, Smith cut two Tin Pan Alley spirituals, "On Revival Day" and "Moan, You Mourners"—two pop songs with an ersatz-religious feel—which anticipate much of the gospel movement that would emerge over the next few years. However, by this time the Depression and the arrival of radio were already putting a major crimp in the "race" records market, and for a time it looked as if Smith's recording career would end with "Sugar in My Bowl" and "Safety Mama," two of her most explicitly blues numbers, rendered with the modest accompaniment of Clarence Williams's piano.

Then, in 1933, with the help of producer John Hammond, Smith was allowed to provide history with a tasty encore. She cut four numbers under his supervision, which are not typical of her earlier output but in fact illustrate that her artistry had continued to evolve over the two years she was out of the studio. All are new tunes commissioned for the occasion from the vaudeville blues team of Coot Grant and Socks Wilson, a Butterbeans and Susie–like comedy-and-blues man-and-wife duo (both teams could be described as the Burns and Allen of the blues). Hammond himself claimed to be disappointed in the songs they came up with, although his has proved to be a minority opinion. The four Grant-Wilson songs use blues elements and fit within the blues idiom, but none of them is in the standard 12-bar format. Further, while Smith had frequently employed small bands before (as opposed to piano, or piano and one-horn-only formats), she had never sung with anything like the modern, swinging group that Hammond assembled, state-of-the-art of the immediate preswing era. The four horns, for instance, were Frankie Newton, Jack Teagarden, Chu Berry, and Benny Goodman, all musicians who were more a part of the future than of the past.

This being Smith's last session, it may seem from a distance that she was, by 1933, part of the past as well. But one of the more compelling points of Albertson's biography is that he doesn't depict her as a has-been in the mid-thirties. Rather, he quotes extensively from Lionel Hampton, whose uncle Richard Morgan, a well-known Chicago-based entrepreneur (and bootlegger), was married to Smith in everything but name. Hampton and others insist that Smith's later career, though unrecorded, was actually going strong, that she was working frequently, and that she would have been a force in the swing era had she been able to stick around. As John Hammond wrote in his autobiography, "Had she lived even a few years longer she would have become a star again."

Hampton's and Hammond's testimonies are borne out by the 1933 session: Smith sounds looser and much more rhythmically motivated than even on the 1931 titles, without having lost any of the power and authority that had been her trademark from the beginning. These four final tracks, ironically, are among the most reissued and most covered of her entire canon, especially "Gimme a Pigfoot" (famously done by Billie Holiday, as we've seen, as well as Bobby Short and Nina Simone). "Do Your Duty" and "Take Me for a Buggy Ride" are her two best songs in the mode of boasting of her man's romantic accomplishments, set in the first and third person, respectively. "I'm Down in the Dumps" is a classic example of a blues-idiom song with lyrics that, when read on the page, are definitely a downer, but are imbued with that joyous aggression that is a key element of Bessie's blues. Like Sinatra swinging a torch song, confronting the blues with a smile on one's face is a way of laughing to keep from crying.

From Smith's spoken intro ("'Twenty-five cents! I wouldn't pay twenty-five cents to go in nowhere, 'cause listen here . . .'") onward, "Gimme a Pigfoot" is the archetypal document of a party atmosphere— it's the polar opposite of "Long Old Road" and "Nobody Knows You When You're Down and Out." The Grant-Wilson song paints a vivid picture of a woman in very high spirits out on a bender—it's the forerunner of "The Joint Is Jumpin'," "At the Swing Cat's Ball," "Saturday Night Fish Fry," "Louisville Lodge Meeting"—it's also "Good Rockin' Tonight," "Rock Around the Clock," "Jailhouse Rock," and practically everything ever sung by Louis Jordan and even Ray Charles and Sam Cooke (like "Having a Party" and "Twistin' the Night Away").

She is persuasive, to say the least. Far from sounding like a fading relic at her final recording, Bessie Smith is at the height of her powers on this amazing date. She was never more euphorically persuasive than on this infectious tune about going out for a good time; consuming pig feet and beer, puffing on reefer, and guzzling "a gang of gin" . . . at least "until the [police] wagon comes." Her energy and her charm are contagious: You will have a good time listening to this record because she wills you to. There's no arguing with the way she growls, "He's got rhythm—*yeah!*—when he stomps his feet!" In a very real way, "Pigfoot" is the first rhythm and blues record.

Lionel Hampton was convinced that the woman who was practically his aunt could have made the leap from the classic blues style and the Jazz Age to the swing era. "Pigfoot" shows that she could transcend her own generation and a few generations after that as well. Alas, it was not to be. Four years after producing her last record date, John Hammond would also be a key player in her death scene. Apparently he was the chief perpetrator of the widely held misconception that Smith died as a result of white racism. According to this account, Smith was injured in a car crash and died because a whites-only hospital refused to admit her.

Paul Oliver wrote in 1959 that it would be a tragedy if Smith's death were to be "exploited by racial propagandists," and that's essentially what happened. Nearly ten years after Oliver's minibook *Bessie Smith* was published, Edward Albee turned the myth into a one-act play entitled *The Death of Bessie Smith*. The story had originally come from Hammond, who heard it from the promoter Smith was working for in Mississippi. The man "was in a position to know," and thus Hammond circulated the story "in several magazines." Although he told the tale in good faith in 1937, in 1977, in his auto-biography, *John Hammond on Record*, he hinted that it might not be completely true. Albertson's account of the accident is another key strength of his book *Bessie;* he credibly debunks the tale told by Hammond and dramatized by Albee, establishing that Smith was fatally injured in the crash and beyond saving by any hospital, black or white.

As noted, Smith's recorded legacy is well pre-served, and readily available—if only the same could be said for virtually every other singer, blues and otherwise, of the years leading up to the swing era. American Sony has a ten-CD series annotated by Albertson, in sound quality that will be good enough for nearly everyone. As an added bonus, the tenth disc contains excerpts from his interviews with Ruby Walker Smith (niece of Smith's only legal husband, Jack Gee), who as a member of both her family and her touring company was in a unique position to observe Smith's inner workings—particularly her stormy marriage to Gee, a former police officer more preoccupied with breaking the law than enforcing it. However, there's an independent British label, run by and for hard-core early jazz collectors, named Frog Records that has released an eight-CD version (with alternate takes) of the entire Smith output, and the audio, as engineered by the late John R. T. Davies, is significantly more pleasing—to my ears, at least.

Both sets are titled *Complete Recordings*. Ulti-mately, everything in either edition of Smith's entire recorded output justifies the epitaph on the great diva's tombstone, unveiled in 1970: "The world's greatest blues singer will never stop singing."

Country and Western: Hank Williams (1923–1953)

Tony Bennett knows a thing or two about country music; he was actually the first mainstream pop crooner (please put quotation marks around all three of those words) to sing a Hank Williams song. Yet there had already been a lot of crossover activity between the worlds of country music and pop, most famously Bing Crosby's million-selling version of Bob Wills's "San Antonio Rose." Throughout the for-ties, big bands like Gene Krupa's played Western-oriented songs like "Along the Navajo Trail" even as Western swing groups played jazz and pop standards from Tin Pan Alley and Swing Street. Only a year before Tony's "Cold, Cold Heart," country singer Red Foley enjoyed a number-one hillbilly hit with "Chattanoogie Shoe Shine Boy," a rhythmic, quasi-novelty hit, which was covered by both Bing Crosby and Frank Sinatra—you can't get more mainstream than that.

Most country or R&B artists couldn't have been thrilled when mainstream pop singers recorded their hits; generally speaking, few performers, even in the "race" and hillbilly fields, wrote their own songs, and, unlike Elvis Presley a generation later, they didn't own any percentage of the publishing rights. Williams was a notable exception; he wrote both words and music to "Cold, Cold Heart"—and actually had a publisher who treated him fairly—and he profited immensely from the many record-ings of his songs made even in his short lifetime.

Still, we would be celebrating Hank Williams even if he had never written a single note or a single word of a song, for the same reason that we celebrate Sinatra and Bennett. Williams was a brilliant inter-preter, no matter who the original author was, on the level of the great singers of the show-music-oriented American songbook. His voice was dark and woody, with a strong Southern accent—when he announces the song "I Can't Help It (If I'm Still in Love with You)" he drops the "L" in "help," but he pronounces it properly when he sings it.

Like Sinatra, Williams knew everything that there was and is to know about bringing out the inner meaning of a song: using the right inflections to get everything that can be gotten out of a lyric, using dynamics and emphasis and a colorful range of inflections. As with Ella Fitzgerald's scat singing, even when Williams yodels (the hillbilly equivalent of scatting), there's meaning in his wordless ulula-tions. Williams is a master of extracting the meaning behind the words. Also like Sinatra, he can stretch a note and bend it to make a dramatic point, and going considerably further than that, Williams is even will-ing to sacrifice his intonation, to hit a blue note, or go out of tune entirely for additional coloration.

Listen to the way on "You're Gonna Change (Or I'm Gonna Leave)" he wails on the key word, "he's done got *peeved*"; it's a stretch of a lyric, using a word that (uniquely in his canon) sounds as if it might have come from a rhyming dictionary. ("Peeved" is not a word one imagines was used in casual conversation, even sixty years ago, in the Deep South.) But no matter, Williams hits a wild blue note right on that word, he actually stretches it into two notes. It's so extreme it's hard to make out what he's saying—but he sure does get the message across: There's absolutely no doubt as to what he means, or of the feeling behind it. By contrast, listen to the tribute versions by one of Williams's most talented disciples and successors, the C&W star George Jones, who recorded "You're Gonna Change" on his 1962 *My Favorites of Hank Williams* (actually Jones's second album-length tribute to his key inspiration). He can't help being a little self-conscious; he tries to finesse the wailing note on "peeved," but there's no way he can completely let himself go with it, the way Williams does.

Equally instructive is "Lonesome Whistle," a 1951 recording by Williams of a song co-written by him and Jimmie Davis (governor of Louisiana and a country star best known for "You Are My Sunshine"); there were any number of lonesome whistles in pop as well as in country music, and this song is mainly stitched together from stock phrases in country and blues songs. In all varieties of American pop, from blues to Broadway, whistles are somehow always lonesome—whistling is rarely a group activity, the very act of whistling conveys a state of solitude, whether it's someone on a prison train or someone whistling in the dark.

What makes Williams's song special is the way he literally transforms the word "lonesome" into a train whistle noise, turning his voice into a sound effect— another extraverbal use of the human instrument that might be compared with scat singing. "Lonesome Whistle" has been subsequently recorded by many distinctive artists in widely varying fields: the straight-ahead George Jones, the multigeneric pop crooner Bobby Darin (who did it in a big band version), and singer-songwriter Bob Dylan. They all have a different approach, but no one is as completely unselfconscious as Williams.

The only thing that matters to him is making his voice sound like a train whistle as convincingly as possible; when Hank Williams sings about trains and prisons, you can't possibly think about anything but trains and prisons. This whistle isn't just lonesome, it's violent and even ugly; he's making you confront whatever feelings you have about trains and prisons. He's one of the most expressive of all vocalists in any genre of music.

Williams is also "fortunate in his biographers" (as James L. Collier once said): Colin Escott's *Hank Williams: The Biography* (1994) is one of the major pop music bios, on a par with Guralnick (on Presley) and Giddins (on Crosby). One of the many revelatory recurring themes in Escott's book is how Williams constantly fought to keep his music as simple as possible. In the swing era, country stars like Milton Brown and, especially, Bob Wills were more than willing to import ideas from the city, and began pushing country music in the direction of urban jazz and big band music, utilizing jazzy horns (saxophones and trumpets) and more sophisticated harmonies.

Williams would have none of it. For one thing, to him, country music was just guitars and the occasional bass fiddle; there was no place for pianos and drums in his music, and to bring in a saxophone was tantamount to waving a Communist Party flag. Escott quotes many a member of Williams's bands who were directly ordered to keep those citified licks and chords out of his music and to keep everything "plain vanilla." One of the more revealing tracks on *The Unreleased Recordings* (finally released in 2008) is a version of "On Top of Old Smokey," a folk song brought to the hit parade by the Weavers. Williams introduces it by saying he's going to keep it as simple as possible, as when he first heard it as a little boy— one assumes that he means simple in comparison to the Weavers, who had full orchestral accompaniment and a complex arrangement that utilized "outlining" (having one member of the quartet speak the words first) and a Mitch Miller–style sing-along routine. Williams keeps it plaintively simple and absolutely breaks your heart with it.

As Escott suggests, the apparently conservative nature of Williams's music had cultural ramifications that the singer was probably not aware of. The early postwar era saw a major increase in the mass migration from farms to small towns, from small towns to big cities, from big cities to suburbia. Farms themselves were becoming increasingly industrialized; small, independent farms and sharecroppers grew increasingly rare as megafactory-style production was implemented. In "Settin' the Woods on Fire," perhaps the most archetypal of Williams's hell-raisin', honky-tonkin' tunes (his equivalent of Louis Jordan's "Let the Good Times Roll"), he vividly depicts a married farm couple going to town on a tear. He ends with the descriptive line "We'll do all the law's allowin' / Tomorrow I'll be right back plowin'." In truth, the audience for that song in 1952 was not only fantasizing about hitting all the honky-tonks and blowing their whole bankroll dancing until daybreak, but even the part about going back to the plow the next morning probably also held some kind of wish fulfillment for them, a nostolgic yearning to return to simpler times.

Wilfrid Sheed described Oscar Hammerstein as a "reactionary revolutionary" and the term also applies to Williams: He acts like an archconservative at the same time he's changing everything around and setting a new standard. Yet the history of American music is filled with revolutionaries who simplified rather than making things more complicated: Count Basie took the extravagant stride-piano style of the twenties and pared it down to a highly personal approach to the keyboard that relied on much less technique; Miles Davis and Ornette Coleman, in very different but related ways, reacted to the highly complex vocabulary of bebop harmony by showing how there were simpler and perhaps more satisfying ways to improvise.

Williams's innovations anticipated those of the better early rock 'n' rollers (like Fats Domino), who, a few years after his death, made their breakthroughs by paring down extraneous matter and bringing out the basic truths of the blues. Williams insisted on returning country music to its purest fundamentals. By getting down to brass tacks, he raised the bar for virtually all country music that came after him— tracks like "Your Cheatin' Heart" and "I'm So Lonesome I Could Cry" became virtual anthems for Nashville.

Williams can also be appreciated by comparing his work to that of his predecessors; the number-one country singer just before him in the mid-forties was Eddy Arnold, who continued to land top C&W hits for decade after decade. One listen shows that there's no comparison: Arnold has a pretty voice, and sings in tune, but there's none of the feeling, the passion, the inflections. He has a clean, almost immaculate sound. When he sings "Call Me Lonesome from Now On," you have to take his word for it; he doesn't sound lonesome to the very depths of his soul, to the innermost core of his being—like Williams does.

Williams can take one note of anything—even the "Ave Maria" if he wanted to—and twist it until you're so lonesome that you could cry. There's never any hint of anything happening below the surface with Arnold. To paraphrase Sinatra one more time, no one would go out and get drunk over Eddy Arnold—or Eddie Fisher or Eddy Howard or Eddy Duchin. With Williams, you feel as if everyone has gone out and drunk themselves to death before the needle has even hit the groove.

One of the key contrasts between Williams and Arnold, and, indeed, most of his other predecessors, is the blues. For the last few generations, it's been commonplace to see jazz and blues as two branches of the tree of African American music, but to Williams they were vastly different, and not to be confused. Jazz was suspicious, European chords and corruptive saxophones (he directly preaches against the evils of saxophones in "Too Many Parties"), but the blues were an essential part of his music from the beginning. It's instructive to learn that despite his passion for all things cowboy (including his colorful headgear), that he wasn't a Westerner; he was a product of the very deep South, born and raised in Alabama and spending most of his career in Louisiana and Tennessee. He rarely left Alabama at all until after he became famous, and even then, Texas and Arizona were places that he only visited when on tour. As Escott shows, Williams listened to the itinerant blues singers who traveled around the Delta and the lower South as much as he did the singing cowboys of the thirties. His mature music was equal parts Leadbelly and Gene Autry. The blues were not only a fundamental part of what he sang, they represented who he was.

Williams occasionally sang the pure 12-bar blues, but he more frequently included some sort of lyrical or melodic blues content in numbers like "The Blues Come Around"; his first big hit, the Emmett Miller–inspired "Lovesick Blues"; "Honky Tonk Blues"; and "Long Gone Lonesome Blues" to name just four. One doesn't even feel the need to qualify Williams as a white blues singer or a country blues singer. His contributions to the form are deep and profound, and on a par with blues giants both more rural (Robert Johnson and the Delta bluesmen) and more urban (Dinah Washington, Ray Charles). Small wonder that Charles sang "Move It on Over" and Washington tackled "Cold, Cold Heart."

When you listen to Hank's records in any ran- dom sequence, you never know if you'll be getting a song about a sinner who sees the light even as God comes and gathers his jewels, or about an unrepentant prodigal who is intent on honky-tonkin' until he gets the lovesick honky-tonk blues. He boldly declares "I'll Be a Bachelor Till I Die," but then, when he learns that his sweet mama will be walking down the aisle with a new sugar daddy, he laments that "Wedding Blues Will Never Ring for Me." He tells us that even though "your wedding day will be tomorrow, there'll be no teardrops tonight." He is so persuasive that he can argue both sides of any question. Two notable exceptions are "No, No, Joe" (the Cold War cowboy takes a poke at Stalin) and "Fly Trouble," in which he feels no need to offer any words in support of pests either major or minor, on either a global or decidedly local level. Joe Stalin is only slightly more annoying than your average, garden-variety household pest.

Williams is one quintessential American artist who didn't have to wait for the bootleggers to make the more obscure corners of his legacy available. The definitive collection of his work is *The Complete Hank Williams,* a ten-CD set released in 1998, fortunately annotated by Escott. Of all the comparable boxes issued by labels both general (Sony, Universal) and boutique (Mosaic, Bear Family), the Williams box has the smallest percentage of "basic" material and the largest amount of "extras." Only the first four CDs consist of legitimate commercial recordings, and even those are somewhat lessened by the presence of half a dozen or so excruciatingly off-key duets with his tone-deaf wife, Audrey Williams; God only knows the domestic politics that went into recording those. He also produced a series of spoken-word recitations recorded as "Luke the Drifter," a pseudonym that fooled no one; some of these LTD items are highly entertaining, especially "Just Waiting." (The most embarrassing is one that describes "The Funeral" of "a little colored child." I wouldn't put my name on it either.)

With the exception of Robert Johnson, Williams probably left us with a smaller official canon than any comparable icon of American music; even Charlie Christian, Bix Beiderbecke, and Clifford Brown probably recorded more. The remaining six discs of the *Complete* box are comprised of what could uncharitably be called "ephemera": broadcast recordings, song demos, and miscellania, most infamously his prerecorded "Apology" to be played at a show at Washington, D.C., that he had to miss because of surgery. (He missed dozens of performances, or showed up too drunk to go on at many others, for which he never formally apologized.) This material is mainly of interest to collectors and scholars, with the possible exception of the last disc, which is made up mostly of live appearances at the Grand Ole Opry, including some performances of Williams standards like "Cold, Cold Heart," "Lovesick Blues," and "Why Don't You Love Me" that are even more riveting than the 78 rpm versions. But overall, few will listen to discs five through ten as much as they do to one through four.

In addition to demo versions of Williams originals (which are often fascinating, even plainer versions of future standards before the arrangements were done or the songs finalized), the additional tracks contain many songs Williams never commercially recorded for either Sterling or MGM Records, the two labels to which he was contractually bound. The two discs of prerecorded radio transcriptions recorded in Shreveport, Louisiana (in 1948–49), are particularly valuable, since these are highly polished performances, made for commercial consumption (although not offered for sale until years after Williams's death), if generally not as conspicuously arranged as the Sterling and MGM sessions; many, for instance, are pure solos, with only Williams accompanying himself rather than his usual group, the Drifting Cowboys.

For me, the most remarkable of these is "Cool Water," already a classic of country music (then called "hillbilly" or, in this case, "cowboy"). It was written in 1941 by Bob Nolan, the leader of the Sons of the Pioneers. Anticipating "Cold, Cold Heart," "Cool Water" (another song of frigidity) was an early crossover from hillbilly into pop: It became a best seller for Bing Crosby and the Andrews Sisters, then later for the more bombastic belters Vaughn Monroe and Frankie Laine.

"Cool Water" is about a cowboy and his mule trying to "cross the barren waste / without a trace of water," and seeing an oasis that turns out to be a mirage. When the Sons of the Pioneers sang "Cool Water," it sounded like a highly compelling slice of genuine Americana (which is not the same as "authentic frontier gibberish," as Mel Brooks put it in *Blazing Saddles*). When Frankie Laine recorded it in 1955, it became a manly-man aria of high adventure with overtones of Kipling.

In Nolan's lyric, the cowboy protagonist is already going plum loco, talking to his mule ("Don't you listen to him, Dan") and expecting the critter to answer. Hallucinating, he thinks he sees water in the sand below and, when night falls, in the stars above. Williams's transcription, done with just his guitar, is nearly four minutes long, way too long for a 10" 78 single, and one of the lengthiest performances in his discography. When Hank Williams sings "Cool Water" it's immediately about something darker and more profound than a thirsty cowboy. It's about a man dying in the desert and seeing God as he passes away: All of a sudden, "Cool Water" becomes an epic saga of redemption and retribution, of life and death, of heaven and hell, of Mother and Jesus, even of prison and trains.

In 2008 another, even longer recording of Williams doing "Cool Water" surfaced. Between January and March 1951, Williams did a series of early morning broadcasts sponsored by Mother's Best flour; fortunately for posterity, he and his Drifting Cowboys prerecorded many of these for those frequent occasions on which he was out of town. Fifty-four of these amazing tracks were at last legally issued on a three-CD set by Time Life in 2008. Titled *The Unreleased Recordings,* these tracks are every bit as good, both sonically and musically, as Williams's concurrent commercial recordings for MGM. The shows included both "country" and "gospel" songs, and it's impossible to judge which sound better. The new performances of familiar Williams standards like "Cold, Cold Heart" and "I'm So Lonesome I Could Cry" are very welcome. So, for that matter, are the rarer songs, like Gene Autry's hit "Have I Told You Lately That I Love You," and a thoroughly passionate reading of "When the Saints Go Marching In" that could make a believer out of anybody. Here's where Williams transforms "On Top of Old Smokey" from a campfire marshmallow aria to a cautionary tale of love and loss.

"Old Smokey" and "Cool Water" are two of many performances which reveal that Williams was as expert a singer of other people's songs as of his own. As an interpreter, Williams was a spiritual peer of Bennett and Sinatra, and it's worth noting that on the only occasion when Williams and Bennett had any direct contact, the cowboy went out of his way to yank the crooner's chain. Theirs was a brief conversation that, in a sense, concerned itself with the very concept of interpretation. One day in 1951, after Bennett's version of "Cold, Cold Heart" was on the pop charts, the phone rang, and it was Hank Williams, calling him from Nashville. Bennett was surprised yet respectful, addressing him as "Mr. Williams," but Williams was direct and to the point, asking him, "What's the idea of ruining my song?"

Even at that time, Tony could tell that Mr. Williams was merely being sarcastic. (It's a Southern male thing, for one guy to introduce himself to another by insulting him.) After Williams's death, Tony appeared on the Grand Ole Opry TV show in his honor, and was told by Williams's associates that every time Hank went into a bar—which was hardly infrequently—he would drop a nickel in a jukebox to listen to Bennett's record.

What Bing Crosby once said about Louis Armstrong applies equally to Hank Williams: "When he sings a happy song, you feel happy, when he sings a sad song, you want to cry. And, when you think about it, what else is there to pop singing?"

About the Author

Will Friedwald writes about music for *The Wall Street Journal* and was the jazz (and cabaret) critic for *The New York Sun*. He is the author of eight books, including *Stardust Melodies: A Biography of Twelve of America's Most Popular Songs; Jazz Singing: America's Great Voices from Bessie Smith to Bebop and Beyond; Sinatra! The Song Is You: A Singer's Art*; and *The Good Life* (with Tony Bennett). He has written nearly five hundred liner notes for compact discs, for which he has received eight Grammy nominations. He has also written for *Vanity Fair, The Village Voice, Entertainment Weekly, American Heritage*, and *The New York Times*, among other publications.

A Note About the Type

This book was set in Minion, a typeface produced by the Adobe Corporation specifically for the Macintosh personal computer, and released in 1990. Designed by Robert Slimbach, Minion combines the classic characteristics of old style faces with the full complement of weights required for modern typesetting.

Composed by TexTech International
Printed and bound by RR Donnelley, Crawfordsville, Indiana
Designed by Virginia Tan